HOLT McDOUGAL

Literature

Grade 11

HOLT McDOUGAL

 HOUGHTON MIFFLIN HARCOURT

ART CREDITS

FRONT COVER, TITLE PAGE

(tl) The Granger Collection, New York; (tr) Alamy/Royalty Free; (cr) The Granger Collection, New York; (bc) Getty Images; (bcr) The Granger Collection, New York; (c) Dave G. Houser/Corbis; (bl) Ken Kinzie/HMH Publishers.

BACK COVER

(t) The Laughing Philosopher (1887), George C. Cox. Photograph. © Museum of the City of New York/Bridgeman Art Library; (c) David Zimmerman/Corbis; (cr) Corbis; (bl) BrandX Pictures/Alamy Images.

ISBN: 978-0-547-61848-7

4 5 6 7 8 9 10   0914   20 19 18 17 16 15 14 13 12 11

4500338804   B C D E F G

Creating the future today

HOLT MCDOUGAL LITERATURE creates the perfect environment for embracing the Common Core State Standards, making them accessible to every student. Each strand of the standards comes alive with scaffolded instruction, images, and unique technology tools to prepare students for the demands of the future.

Prepare for the future

The Common Core State Standards in Reading give equal attention to literary and informational texts. The focus on text analysis and critical thinking, including comparing and contrasting texts and mediums, prepares students to be analytical about resources and ideas.

HOLT MCDOUGAL LITERATURE is the only resource with **LINE NUMBERS** on every selection, making "citing textual evidence" a natural part of the reading process.

TEXT ANALYSIS WORKSHOPS in grades 6–10 begin each unit. Students apply newly learned skills in excerpts of quality text using Close Reading strategies. In grades 11 and 12, the workshops focus on the characteristics of genres in American and British texts.

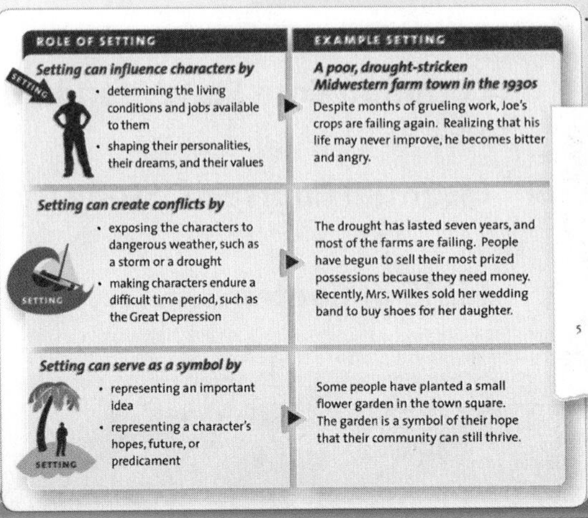

ROLE OF SETTING	EXAMPLE SETTING
Setting can influence characters by • determining the living conditions and jobs available to them • shaping their personalities, their dreams, and their values	**A poor, drought-stricken Midwestern farm town in the 1930s** Despite months of grueling work, Joe's crops are failing again. Realizing that his life may never improve, he becomes bitter and angry.
Setting can create conflicts by • exposing the characters to dangerous weather, such as a storm or a drought • making characters endure a difficult time period, such as the Great Depression	The drought has lasted seven years, and most of the farms are failing. People have begun to sell their most prized possessions because they need money. Recently, Mrs. Wilkes sold her wedding band to buy shoes for her daughter.
Setting can serve as a symbol by • representing an important idea • representing a character's hopes, future, or predicament	Some people have planted a small flower garden in the town square. The garden is a symbol of their hope that their community can still thrive.

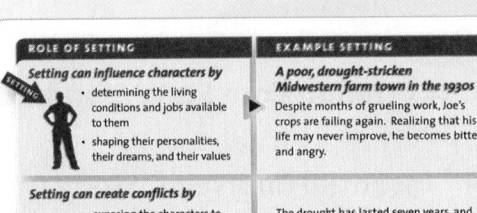

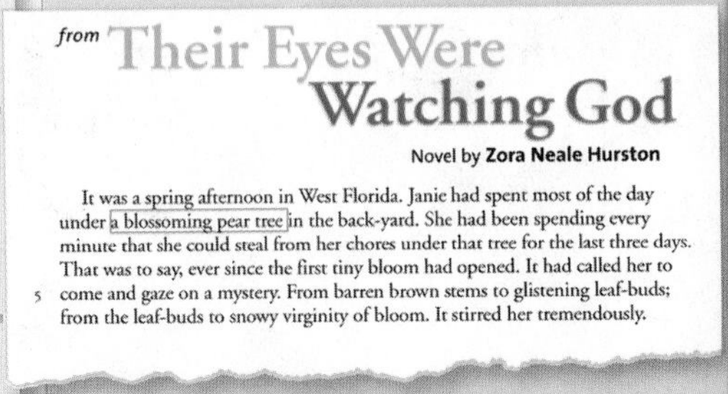

from Their Eyes Were Watching God

Novel by **Zora Neale Hurston**

It was a spring afternoon in West Florida. Janie had spent most of the day under a blossoming pear tree in the back-yard. She had been spending every minute that she could steal from her chores under that tree for the last three days. That was to say, ever since the first tiny bloom had opened. It had called her to
5 come and gaze on a mystery. From barren brown stems to glistening leaf-buds; from the leaf-buds to snowy virginity of bloom. It stirred her tremendously.

EXEMPLARY TEXTS from Common Core State Standards and hundreds of other titles, including your favorite novels, are available to explore different worlds through reading.

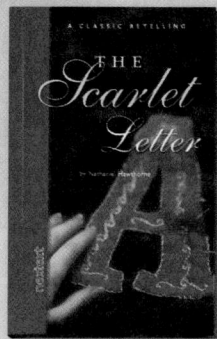

NOVELWISE offers study guides and PowerPoint® presentations that support reading and discussion of your favorite novels.

WRITING WORKSHOPS show students how to craft and support an argument and to explain their ideas.

INFORMATIONAL TEXT requires students to apply academic vocabulary in texts with different purposes and structures. Seminal works of American history are important resources for Common Core State Standards.

CONNECTIONS: NONFICTION FOR COMMON CORE CD-ROM provides additional informational texts, including seminal or foundational American works, with specific connections to selections in *Holt McDougal Literature*.

Students must think analytically and critically as they **COMPARE TEXTS** that differ in style, genre, medium, and purpose.

By learning today

The Common Core State Standards are designed for every student. Tools to scaffold learning are seamlessly integrated in *Holt McDougal Literature.*

RAYMOND'S RUN

Based on the story by
TONI CADE BAMBARA

Monitor Your Comprehension

SET A PURPOSE FOR READING
Squeaky is a young girl who loves to run races and win. Read "Raymond's Run" to find out what Squeaky learns on the day of the big race.

BACKGROUND This story is set in Harlem, a neighborhood in New York City. Since about 1910, Harlem has been one of the largest African-American communities in the United States. It is also home to people of many different backgrounds.

❶ PLOT: EXPOSITION
Look at the underlined words in lines 7–9 that describe Squeaky. On the lines below, write what you know about Squeaky so far.

Squeaky does not have to do
housework, but she looks after her
brother Raymond. Raymond needs
special care. Squeaky is protective
of him. Squeaky is short, has a
squeaky voice, and likes to run fast.

I don't have to work around the house like some girls. All I have to do is mind my brother Raymond, which is enough.

Raymond needs looking after because he's not quite right. A lot of rude people have lots to say about Raymond, but they have to say it to me. I'd much rather knock you down than talk, even though <u>I'm small</u> and <u>have a squeaky voice.</u> That's how I got my name, Squeaky. If things get rough, I run. <u>I'm the fastest thing on two feet.</u> ❷

10   There is no track meet that I don't win the first-place medal. I'm the swiftest thing in the neighborhood. That goes for Gretchen, too. She says that she is going to win the first-place medal this year. What a joke. No one can beat me.

I'm walking down Broadway practicing my breathing.

8   ELL ADAPTED INTERACTIVE READER / UNIT 1: PLOT AND CONFLICT

INTERACTIVE READERS contain selections from the Essential Course of Study with close reading support to scaffold and personalize learning.

ADAPTED INTERACTIVE READERS provide the same selections in an adapted format with additional vocabulary and comprehension support.

ENGLISH LANGUAGE LEARNER ADAPTED INTERACTIVE READERS use the same adapted selections with scaffolded instruction for English Language Learners, including academic vocabulary, language support, and a comprehensive Teacher's Guide.

AUDIO TUTOR CD provides an audio version of the adapted selections with the instructional material read in English or Spanish.

Holt McDougal Literature is a comprehensive resource addressing all of the Common Core State Standards for English Language Arts with integrated instruction in Language and Speaking and Listening.

The importance of acquiring academic vocabulary appropriate for college and career readiness is supported with every selection and reinforced with **WORDSHARP: AN INTERACTIVE VOCABULARY TUTOR CD,** which is also online to allow students to expand vocabulary independently.

GRAMMAR AND STYLE instruction at point of use within and following each selection reinforces students' command of conventions and supports their learning about language choices and style.

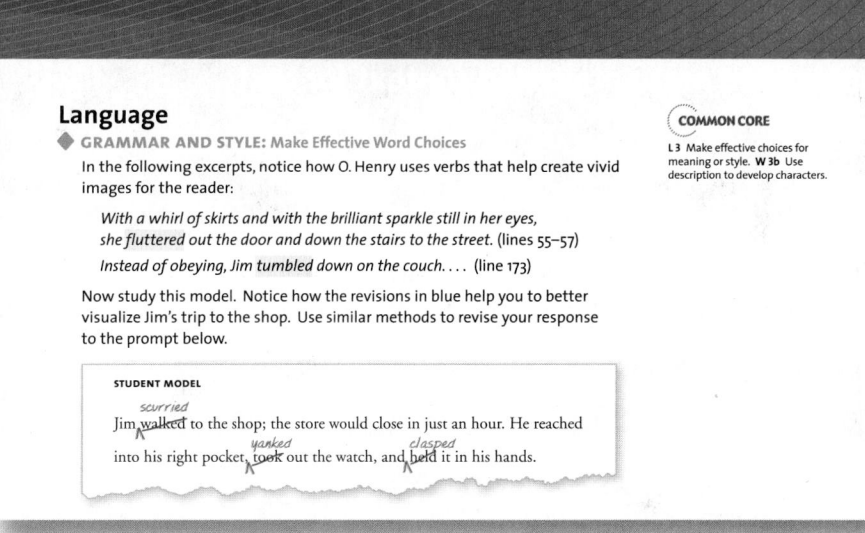

Language

◆ **GRAMMAR AND STYLE: Make Effective Word Choices**

In the following excerpts, notice how O. Henry uses verbs that help create vivid images for the reader:

> *With a whirl of skirts and with the brilliant sparkle still in her eyes, she fluttered out the door and down the stairs to the street.* (lines 55–57)
>
> *Instead of obeying, Jim tumbled down on the couch....* (line 173)

Now study this model. Notice how the revisions in blue help you to better visualize Jim's trip to the shop. Use similar methods to revise your response to the prompt below.

STUDENT MODEL

Jim walked to the shop; the store would close in just an hour. He reached into his right pocket, took out the watch, and held it in his hands.

(revisions: scurried, yanked, clasped)

COMMON CORE

L 3 Make effective choices for meaning or style. **W 3b** Use description to develop characters.

THE COMMON CORE STATE STANDARDS IN SPEAKING AND LISTENING prepare students for active participation in their future. **SPEAKING AND LISTENING WORKSHOPS** in many units teach the skills of successful group participation and the formal presentation of ideas in public settings.

With tools for tomorrow

Holt McDougal Literature's online platform provides easy access to teacher and student resources at point of use in the selection. HISTORY® film clips and full-length resources provide both motivation and context for texts.

ONLINE RESOURCES provide a wealth of instructional support material for Teacher and Student use.

MEDIASMART DVD uses movie clips, commercials, political ads, documentaries, and news reports to bring media instruction to life with critical analysis and comparisons to other mediums.

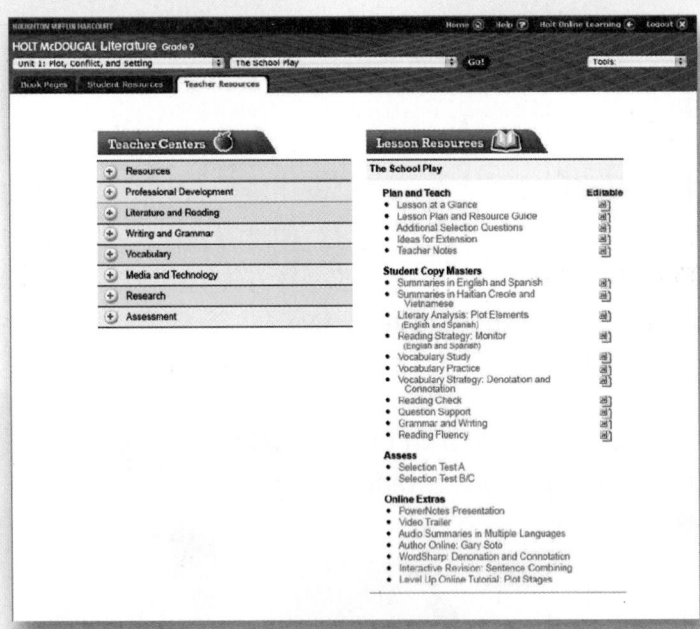

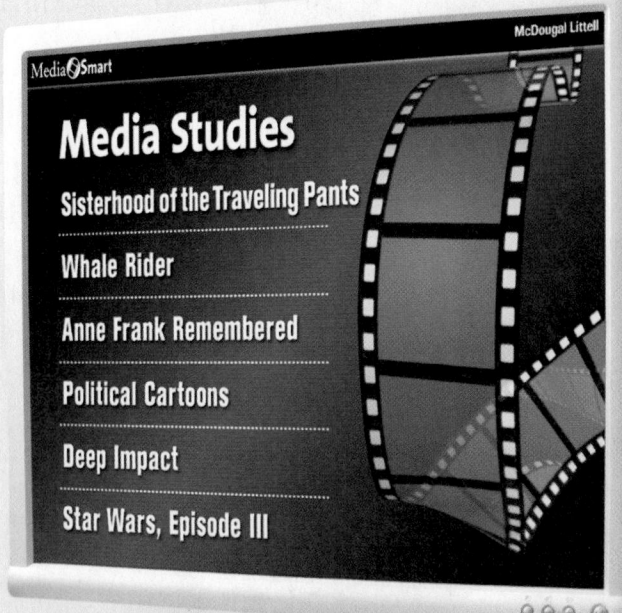

Enhance learning of rigorous standards with **HISTORY**® video streaming and resources at point of use.

HISTORY

WRITESMART CD (also online) features interactive writing instruction, from prompts to the steps of the process, including editing and revision models. An editable **RUBRIC GENERATOR** allows teachers to customize assessment.

HOLT MCDOUGAL ONLINE ESSAY SCORING provides students with the practice and immediate constructive feedback that they need to improve as writers.

WHITEBOARD-READY LESSON DEMONSTRATIONS are available for the most challenging Common Core Standards.

POWERNOTES DVD (also online) provides point-of-use images, instructional information, and background knowledge with theater-quality video trailers.

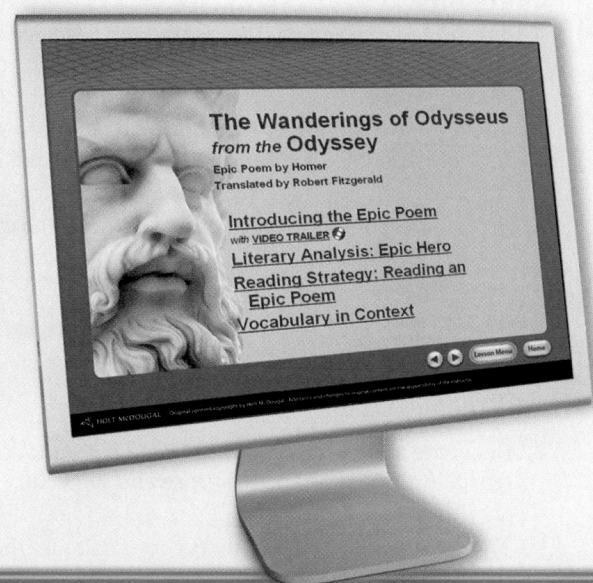

COMMON CORE

English Language Arts
Common Core State Standards

The grades 11–12 standards on the following pages define what students should understand and be able to do by the end of each grade. They correspond to the College and Career Readiness (CCR) anchor standards below by number. The CCR and grade-specific standards are necessary complements—the former providing broad standards, the latter providing additional specificity—that together define the skills and understandings that all students must demonstrate.

College and Career Readiness Anchor Standards for Reading

COMMON CORE STATE STANDARD

KEY IDEAS AND DETAILS

1. Read closely to determine what the text says explicitly and to make logical inferences from it; cite specific textual evidence when writing or speaking to support conclusions drawn from the text.

2. Determine central ideas or themes of a text and analyze their development; summarize the key supporting details and ideas.

3. Analyze how and why individuals, events, and ideas develop and interact over the course of a text.

CRAFT AND STRUCTURE

4. Interpret words and phrases as they are used in a text, including determining technical, connotative, and figurative meanings, and analyze how specific word choices shape meaning or tone.

5. Analyze the structure of texts, including how specific sentences, paragraphs, and larger portions of the text (e.g., a section, chapter, scene, or stanza) relate to each other and the whole.

6. Assess how point of view or purpose shapes the content and style of a text.

INTEGRATION OF KNOWLEDGE AND IDEAS

7. Integrate and evaluate content presented in diverse formats and media, including visually and quantitatively, as well as in words.

8. Delineate and evaluate the argument and specific claims in a text, including the validity of the reasoning as well as the relevance and sufficiency of the evidence.

9. Analyze how two or more texts address similar themes or topics in order to build knowledge or to compare the approaches the authors take.

RANGE OF READING AND LEVEL OF TEXT COMPLEXITY

10. Read and comprehend complex literary and informational texts independently and proficiently.

Reading Standards for Literature, Grades 11–12 Students

COMMON CORE STATE STANDARD	STUDENT EDITION
KEY IDEAS AND DETAILS	
1. Cite strong and thorough textual evidence to support analysis of what the text says explicitly as well as inferences drawn from the text, including determining where the text leaves matters uncertain.	4, 36–37, 45, 46–47, 53, 134–135, 163, 179, 199, 213, 318–319, 333, 348–349, 353, 354–355, 364, 435, 441, 453, 468–469, 483, 528, 530–531, 541, 546–547, 554, 556, 696–697, 709, 716–717, 727, 788, 796–797, 815, 820–821, 831, 846, 936–937, 942, 943, 950, 952–953, 958, 974, 1008–1009, 1015, 1034–1035, 1045, 1078–1079, 1090, 1130, 1166, 1168, 1300–1301, 1305
2. Determine two or more themes or central ideas of a text and analyze their development over the course of the text, including how they interact and build on one another to produce a complex account; provide an objective summary of the text.	36–37, 41, 45, 179, 213, 318–319, 326, 332, 353, 541, 546–547, 554, 598, 600, 602–603, 615, 709, 734–735, 759, 768–769, 777, 782–783, 788, 846, 968–969, 976–977, 999, 1048–1049, 1061, 1168, 1294–1295, 1299, 1306–1307, 1310, 1324
3. Analyze the impact of the author's choices regarding how to develop and relate elements of a story or drama (e.g., where a story is set, how the action is ordered, how the characters are introduced and developed).	4, 46–47, 53, 132, 134–135, 163, 179, 199, 213, 333, 410–411, 420, 432, 444–445, 448, 453, 464, 468–469, 483, 598, 602–603, 610, 615, 656, 683, 691, 696–697, 709, 712, 716–717, 727, 734–735, 759, 768–769, 777, 796–797, 815, 818, 820–821, 831, 846, 920–921, 927, 934, 943, 950, 976–977, 980, 999, 1002, 1034–1035, 1045, 1064–1065, 1069, 1075, 1130, 1162, 1164, 1166, 1178–1179, 1187, 1194–1195, 1200, 1260, R2
CRAFT AND STRUCTURE	
4. Determine the meaning of words and phrases as they are used in the text, including figurative and connotative meanings; analyze the impact of specific word choices on meaning and tone, including words with multiple meanings or language that is particularly fresh, engaging, or beautiful. (Include Shakespeare as well as other authors.)	114–115, 119, 121, 318–319, 333, 336–337, 340, 342–343, 347, 353, 354–355, 364, 410–411, 420, 432, 435, 441, 444–445, 453, 530–531, 536, 541, 542, 546–547, 556, 602–603, 611, 630, 683, 691, 703, 705, 734–735, 746, 753, 759, 768–769, 772, 820–821, 827, 846, 878–879, 884, 885, 892–893, 897, 928–929, 933, 936–937, 942, 952–953, 958, 976–977, 981, 999, 1008–1009, 1015, 1064–1065, 1074, 1075, 1130, 1170–1171, 1176, 1178–1179, 1187, 1294–1295, 1299, 1300–1301, 1305, 1306–1307, 1309, 1310, 1324
5. Analyze how an author's choices concerning how to structure specific parts of a text (e.g., the choice of where to begin or end a story, the choice to provide a comedic or tragic resolution) contribute to its overall structure and meaning as well as its aesthetic impact.	46–47, 53, 132, 134–135, 163, 179, 199, 213, 336–337, 340, 342–343, 347, 348–349, 353, 359, 435, 441, 528, 530–531, 541, 546–547, 556, 602–603, 615, 691, 782–783, 788, 878–879, 885, 886–887, 891, 928–929, 933, 934, 943, 950, 960–961, 967, 968–969, 974, 1024, 1034–1035, 1045, 1064–1065, 1069, 1075, 1194–1195, 1200, 1294–1295, 1299, R2
6. Analyze a case in which grasping point of view requires distinguishing what is directly stated in a text from what is really meant (e.g., satire, sarcasm, irony, or understatement).	199, 318–319, 333, 466, 694, 712, 714, 759, 831, 846, 920–921, 927, 936–937, 942, 1078–1079, 1090, 1130, 1164
INTEGRATION OF KNOWLEDGE AND IDEAS	
7. Analyze multiple interpretations of a story, drama, or poem (e.g., recorded or live production of a play or recorded novel or poetry), evaluating how each version interprets the source text. (Include at least one play by Shakespeare and one play by an American dramatist.)	134–135, 153, 197, 222–225, 460–463, 583, 618–619
8. (Not applicable to literature)	

Reading Standards for Literature, Grades 11–12 Students, continued

COMMON CORE STATE STANDARD	STUDENT EDITION
9. Demonstrate knowledge of eighteenth-, nineteenth- and early-twentieth-century foundational works of American literature, including how two or more texts from the same period treat similar themes or topics.	FM46–FM48, FM50–FM54, 4, 20–21, 23–31, 121, 225, 302–303, 305–313, 364, 514–515, 517–523, 541, 556, 640–641, 643–651, 768–769, 777, 780, 788, 796–797, 815, 862–863, 865–873, 886–887, 891, 892–893, 894, 897, 915, 920–921, 927, 934, 975, 1091, 1147, 1149–1157, 1260
RANGE OF READING AND LEVEL OF TEXT COMPLEXITY **10.** By the end of grade 11, read and comprehend literature, including stories, dramas, and poems, in the grades 11–CCR text complexity band proficiently, with scaffolding as needed at the high end of the range. By the end of grade 12, read and comprehend literature, including stories, dramas, and poems, at the high end of the grades 11–CCR text complexity band independently and proficiently.	299, 354–355, 364, 511, 528, 630, 637, 859, 960–961, 967, 1048–1049, 1061, 1143, 1324, 1337

Reading Standards for Informational Text, Grades 11–12 Students

COMMON CORE STATE STANDARD	STUDENT EDITION
KEY IDEAS AND DETAILS **1.** Cite strong and thorough textual evidence to support analysis of what the text says explicitly as well as inferences drawn from the text, including determining where the text leaves matters uncertain.	72–73, 79, 82–83, 89, 111, 216, 221, 245, 266-267, 276, 283, 292, 458, 590, 658–659, 671, 762, 765, 767, 815, 846, 898–899, 905, 1008-1009, 1022, 1094–1095, 1102, 1130, 1202–1203, 1215, 1250–1251, 1257, 1285, 1293
2. Determine two or more central ideas of a text and analyze their development over the course of the text, including how they interact and build on one another to provide a complex analysis; provide an objective summary of the text.	102–103, 111, 248–249, 256, 368–369, 375, 378–379, 388, 397, 400–401, 402–403, 408, 498, 570, 597, 767, 782–783, 794, 898–899, 905, 908–909, 912, 1102, 1170–1171, 1176, 1192, 1218–1219, 1228, 1262–1263, 1270, R2
3. Analyze a complex set of ideas or sequence of events and explain how specific individuals, ideas, or events interact and develop over the course of the text.	82–83, 89, 122–123, 130, 248–249, 256, 368–369, 375, 498, 572–573, 580, 1104–1105, 1110, 1178–1179, 1192, 1238–1239, 1248, 1262–1263, 1270, R2
CRAFT AND STRUCTURE **4.** Determine the meaning of words and phrases as they are used in a text, including figurative, connotative, and technical meanings; analyze how an author uses and refines the meaning of a key term or terms over the course of a text (e.g., how Madison defines *faction* in *Federalist* No. 10).	64, 92–93, 100, 131, 238–239, 245, 246, 248–249, 254, 394, 444–445, 458, 498, 558–559, 564, 568, 569, 570, 584–585, 590, 908–909, 914, 1008–1009, 1022, 1170–1171, 1176, 1202–1203, 1207, 1212, 1213, 1215, 1286–1287, 1293, 1324, R2

Reading Standards for Informational Text, Grades 11–12 Students, continued

COMMON CORE STATE STANDARD	STUDENT EDITION
5. Analyze and evaluate the effectiveness of the structure an author uses in his or her exposition or argument, including whether the structure makes points clear, convincing, and engaging.	54–55, 63, 82–83, 89, 92–93, 100, 226, 228–229, 235, 238–239, 245, 248–249, 256, 265, 266–267, 276, 397, 402–403, 406, 408, 584–585, 590, 762, 767, 782–783, 794, 898–899, 905, 1092, 1176, 1218–1219, 1227, 1228, 1230, 1233, 1272, 1277, 1278–1279, 1283, 1285, 1286–1287, 1292, 1293, R2
6. Determine an author's point of view or purpose in a text in which the rhetoric is particularly effective, analyzing how style and content contribute to the power, persuasiveness, or beauty of the text.	54–55, 58, 63, 72–73, 79, 92–93, 100, 122–123, 130, 216, 221, 226, 228–229, 235, 258–259, 265, 266–267, 276, 292, 366, 378–379, 388, 397, 402–403, 408, 558–559, 565, 570, 592, 597, 658–659, 671, 673, 682, 794, 908–909, 914, 1092, 1094–1095, 1101, 1102, 1104–1105, 1110, 1112–1113, 1115, 1116, 1130, 1178–1179, 1192, 1202–1203, 1215, 1218–1219, 1228, 1230, 1233, 1238–1239, 1242, 1248, 1250–1251, 1257, 1262–1263, 1267, 1270, 1278–1279, 1283, 1285, R2
INTEGRATION OF KNOWLEDGE AND IDEAS	
7. Integrate and evaluate multiple sources of information presented in different media or formats (e.g., visually, quantitatively) as well as in words in order to address a question or solve a problem.	32–33, 66–69, 216, 221, 314–315, 444–445, 457, 498, 524–525, 652–653, 730–733, 782–783, 793, 846, 874–875, 916–919, 1004–1007, 1008, 1021, 1026, 1033, 1130, 1158–1159, 1178–1179, 1191, 1227, 1234–1237, 1272, 1273, 1275, 1276, 1277, 1324, 1342, R2, R88
8. Delineate and evaluate the reasoning in seminal U.S. texts, including the application of constitutional principles and use of legal reasoning (e.g., in U.S. Supreme Court majority opinions and dissents) and the premises, purposes, and arguments in works of public advocacy (e.g., *The Federalist*, presidential addresses).	226, 238–239, 245, 292, 584–585, 590, 592, 597, 1202–1203, 1215
9. Analyze seventeenth-, eighteenth-, and nineteenth-century foundational U.S. documents of historical and literary significance (including The Declaration of Independence, the Preamble to the Constitution, the Bill of Rights, and Lincoln's Second Inaugural Address) for their themes, purposes, and rhetorical features.	4, 20–21, 23–31, 70–71, 72–73, 79, 102–103, 107, 111, 113, 226, 258–259, 265, 279, 302–303, 305–313, 366, 368–369, 375, 378–379, 388, 397, 514–515, 517–523, 570, 584–585, 590, 641, 643, 762, 767, 862–863, 865–873, 915, 1117, 1147, 1149–1157, 1259
RANGE OF READING AND LEVEL OF TEXT COMPLEXITY	
10. By the end of grade 11, read and comprehend literary nonfiction in the grades 11–CCR text complexity band proficiently, with scaffolding as needed at the high end of the range. By the end of grade 12, read and comprehend literary nonfiction at the high end of the grades 11–CCR text complexity band independently and proficiently.	70, 92–93, 100, 299, 366, 511, 637, 859, 898–899, 905, 1094–1095, 1102, 1143, 1324, 1337

College and Career Readiness Anchor Standards for Writing

TEXT TYPES AND PURPOSES

1. Write arguments to support claims in an analysis of substantive topics or texts, using valid reasoning and relevant and sufficient evidence.

2. Write informative/explanatory texts to examine and convey complex ideas and information clearly and accurately through the effective selection, organization, and analysis of content.

3. Write narratives to develop real or imagined experiences or events using effective technique, well-chosen details, and well-structured event sequences.

PRODUCTION AND DISTRIBUTION OF WRITING

4. Produce clear and coherent writing in which the development, organization, and style are appropriate to task, purpose, and audience.

5. Develop and strengthen writing as needed by planning, revising, editing, rewriting, or trying a new approach.

6. Use technology, including the Internet, to produce and publish writing and to interact and collaborate with others.

RESEARCH TO BUILD AND PRESENT KNOWLEDGE

7. Conduct short as well as more sustained research projects based on focused questions, demonstrating understanding of the subject under investigation.

8. Gather relevant information from multiple print and digital sources, assess the credibility and accuracy of each source, and integrate the information while avoiding plagiarism.

9. Draw evidence from literary or informational texts to support analysis, reflection, and research.

RANGE OF WRITING

10. Write routinely over extended time frames (time for research, reflection, and revision) and shorter time frames (a single sitting or a day or two) for a range of tasks, purposes, and audiences.

Writing Standards, Grades 11–12 Students

COMMON CORE STATE STANDARD	STUDENT EDITION
TEXT TYPES AND PURPOSES	
1. Write arguments to support claims in an analysis of substantive topics or texts, using valid reasoning and relevant and sufficient evidence.	215, 237, 247, 279, 280–289, 591, 597, 817, 1001, 1077, 1111, 1118–1127, 1177, 1217, 1259, 1277, R26
a. Introduce precise, knowledgeable claim(s), establish the significance of the claim(s), distinguish the claim(s) from alternate or opposing claims, and create an organization that logically sequences claim(s), counterclaims, reasons, and evidence.	280–289, 399, 817, 1118–1127, 1123, 1125, R26
b. Develop claim(s) and counterclaims fairly and thoroughly, supplying the most relevant evidence for each while pointing out the strengths and limitations of both in a manner that anticipates the audience's knowledge level, concerns, values, and possible biases.	215, 280–289, 399, 591, 817, 1118–1127, R26
c. Use words, phrases, and clauses as well as varied syntax to link the major sections of the text, create cohesion, and clarify the relationships between claim(s) and reasons, between reasons and evidence, and between claim(s) and counterclaims.	280–289, 1118–1127, 1121, R26
d. Establish and maintain a formal style and objective tone while attending to the norms and conventions of the discipline in which they are writing.	280–289, 399, 1118–1127, R26
e. Provide a concluding statement or section that follows from and supports the argument presented.	280–289, 399, 1118–1127, R26
2. Write informative/explanatory texts to examine and convey complex ideas, concepts, and information clearly and accurately through the effective selection, organization, and analysis of content.	113, 221, 341, 365, 409, 557, 617, 620–627, 729, 767, 833, 834–843, 919, 951, 1007, 1233, 1237, 1312–1321, 1358–1377, R26
a. Introduce a topic; organize complex ideas, concepts, and information so that each new element builds on that which precedes it to create a unified whole; include formatting (e.g., headings), graphics (e.g., figures, tables), and multimedia when useful to aiding comprehension.	620–627, 625, 834–843, 1271, 1312–1321, 1358–1377, R26
b. Develop the topic thoroughly by selecting the most significant and relevant facts, extended definitions, concrete details, quotations, or other information and examples appropriate to the audience's knowledge of the topic.	221, 377, 620–627, 625, 729, 834–843, 1271, 1312–1321, 1358–1377, R26

Writing Standards, Grades 11–12 Students, continued

COMMON CORE STATE STANDARD	STUDENT EDITION
c. Use appropriate and varied transitions and syntax to link the major sections of the text, create cohesion, and clarify the relationships among complex ideas and concepts.	620–627, 767, 834–843, 1358–1377, R26
d. Use precise language, domain-specific vocabulary, and techniques such as metaphor, simile, and analogy to manage the complexity of the topic.	377, 617, 620–627, 834–843, 1358–1377, R26
e. Establish and maintain a formal style and objective tone while attending to the norms and conventions of the discipline in which they are writing.	620–627, 834–843, 1017, 1319, 1358–1377, R26
f. Provide a concluding statement or section that follows from and supports the information or explanation presented (e.g., articulating implications or the significance of the topic).	620–627, 834–843, 839, 1358–1377, R26
3. Write narratives to develop real or imagined experiences or events using effective technique, well-chosen details, and well-structured event sequences.	81, 91, 434, 442, 486–495, 571, 907, 1047, 1063, 1249, R26
a. Engage and orient the reader by setting out a problem, situation, or observation and its significance, establishing one or multiple point(s) of view, and introducing a narrator and/or characters; create a smooth progression of experiences or events.	81, 91, 486–495, 491, 1063, 1103, R26
b. Use narrative techniques, such as dialogue, pacing, description, reflection, and multiple plot lines, to develop experiences, events, and/or characters.	442, 486–495, 491, 693, 711, 761, R26
c. Use a variety of techniques to sequence events so that they build on one another to create a coherent whole and build toward a particular tone and outcome (e.g., a sense of mystery, suspense, growth, or resolution).	486–495, 489, R26
d. Use precise words and phrases, telling details, and sensory language to convey a vivid picture of the experiences, events, setting, and/or characters.	81, 91, 335, 442, 486–495, 487, 489, 571, 581, 959, 1249, R26
e. Provide a conclusion that follows from and reflects on what is experienced, observed, or resolved over the course of the narrative.	486–495, 711, 1103, 1249, R26

Writing Standards, Grades 11–12 Students, continued

COMMON CORE STATE STANDARD	STUDENT EDITION
PRODUCTION AND DISTRIBUTION OF WRITING	
4. Produce clear and coherent writing in which the development, organization, and style are appropriate to task, purpose, and audience. (Grade-specific expectations for writing types are defined in standards 1–3 above.)	FM58–FM59, 14, 283, 466, 489, 623, 779, 837, 951, 1033, 1117, 1121, 1271, 1315, 1365, R26
5. Develop and strengthen writing as needed by planning, revising, editing, rewriting, or trying a new approach, focusing on addressing what is most significant for a specific purpose and audience. (Editing for conventions should demonstrate command of Language standards 1–3.)	14, 281, 285, 287, 487, 491, 493, 625, 626, 835, 839, 841, 1123, 1125, 1130, 1313, 1317, 1319, 1359, 1367, 1374, R26
6. Use technology, including the Internet, to produce, publish, and update individual or shared writing products in response to ongoing feedback, including new arguments or information.	620–627, 628–629, 844–845, 1322–1323, 1378–1379, 1342, 1378, R26
RESEARCH TO BUILD AND PRESENT KNOWLEDGE	
7. Conduct short as well as more sustained research projects to answer a question (including a self-generated question) or solve a problem; narrow or broaden the inquiry when appropriate; synthesize multiple sources on the subject, demonstrating understanding of the subject under investigation.	34–35, 281, 409, 620–627, 654–655, 767, 834–843, 876–877, 915, 1342, 1359, R44
8. Gather relevant information from multiple authoritative print and digital sources, using advanced searches effectively; assess the strengths and limitations of each source in terms of the task, purpose, and audience; integrate information into the text selectively to maintain the flow of ideas, avoiding plagiarism and overreliance on any one source and following a standard format for citation.	281, 623, 779, 834–843, 1177, 1277, 1342, 1361, 1365, 1377, R44
9. Draw evidence from literary or informational texts to support analysis, reflection, and research.	65, 225, 557, 591, 620–627, 789, 837, 1033, 1130, 1164, 1201, 1233, 1311, 1340–1341, 1342, 1358–1377, 1361, R44
a. Apply *grades 11–12 Reading standards* to literature (e.g., "Demonstrate knowledge of eighteenth-, nineteenth- and early-twentieth-century foundational works of American literature, including how two or more texts from the same period treat similar themes or topics").	779, 915, 1127, 1201, 1259, 1311

Writing Standards, Grades 11–12 Students, continued

COMMON CORE STATE STANDARD	STUDENT EDITION
b. Apply *grades 11–12 Reading standards* to literary nonfiction (e.g., "Delineate and evaluate the reasoning in seminal U.S. texts, including the application of constitutional principles and use of legal reasoning [e.g., in U.S. Supreme Court Case majority opinions and dissents] and the premises, purposes, and arguments in works of public advocacy [e.g., *The Federalist,* presidential addresses]").	283, 623, 1117, 1201, 1259, 1311
RANGE OF WRITING **10.** Write routinely over extended time frames (time for research, reflection, and revision) and shorter time frames (a single sitting or a day or two) for a range of tasks, purposes, and audiences.	FM58–FM59, 289, 316–317, 495, 654–655, 789, 843, 876–877, 1127, 1160–1161, 1168, 1321, 1340–1341

College and Career Readiness Anchor Standards for Speaking and Listening

COMMON CORE STATE STANDARD

COMPREHENSION AND COLLABORATION

1. Prepare for and participate effectively in a range of conversations and collaborations with diverse partners, building on others' ideas and expressing their own clearly and persuasively.

2. Integrate and evaluate information presented in diverse media and formats, including visually, quantitatively, and orally.

3. Evaluate a speaker's point of view, reasoning, and use of evidence and rhetoric.

PRESENTATION OF KNOWLEDGE AND IDEAS

4. Present information, findings, and supporting evidence such that listeners can follow the line of reasoning and the organization, development, and style are appropriate to task, purpose, and audience.

5. Make strategic use of digital media and visual displays of data to express information and enhance understanding of presentations.

6. Adapt speech to a variety of contexts and communicative tasks, demonstrating command of formal English when indicated or appropriate.

Speaking and Listening Standards, Grades 11–12 Students

COMMON CORE STATE STANDARD	STUDENT EDITION
COMPREHENSION AND COLLABORATION	
1. Initiate and participate effectively in a range of collaborative discussions (one-on-one, in groups, and teacher-led) with diverse partners on *grades 11–12 topics, texts, and issues,* building on others' ideas and expressing their own clearly and persuasively.	34–35, 113, 316–317, 526–527, 530–531, 658–659, 876–877, 919, 1007, 1128–1129, 1160–1161, 1162, R80
a. Come to discussions prepared, having read and researched material under study; explicitly draw on that preparation by referring to evidence from texts and other research on the topic or issue to stimulate a thoughtful, well-reasoned exchange of ideas.	65, 463, 600, 696–697, 818, 833, 1128–1129, R80
b. Work with peers to promote civil, democratic discussions and decision-making, set clear goals and deadlines, and establish individual roles as needed.	FM61–FM62, 14, 496–497, 696–697, 833, 844–845, 1128–1129, 1229, R80
c. Propel conversations by posing and responding to questions that probe reasoning and evidence; ensure a hearing for a full range of positions on a topic or issue; clarify, verify, or challenge ideas and conclusions; and promote divergent and creative perspectives.	FM63–FM64, 14, 628–629, 696–697, 1128–1129, 1229, R80
d. Respond thoughtfully to diverse perspectives; synthesize comments, claims, and evidence made on all sides of an issue; resolve contradictions when possible; and determine what additional information or research is required to deepen the investigation or complete the task.	14, 496–497, 628–629, 696–697, 1128–1129, R80
2. Integrate multiple sources of information presented in diverse formats and media (e.g., visually, quantitatively, orally) in order to make informed decisions and solve problems, evaluating the credibility and accuracy of each source and noting any discrepancies among the data.	69, 341, 463, 530–531, 654–655, 844–845, 1237, 1322–1323, 1378–1379, R2, R80, R88
3. Evaluate a speaker's point of view, reasoning, and use of evidence and rhetoric, assessing the stance, premises, links among ideas, word choice, points of emphasis, and tone used.	69, 290–291, 1128–1129, R80
PRESENTATION OF KNOWLEDGE AND IDEAS	279, 290–291, 463, 557, 600, 617, 654–655, 915, 975, 1128–1129, 1160–1161, R80
4. Present information, findings, and supporting evidence, conveying a clear and distinct perspective, such that listeners can follow the line of reasoning, alternative or opposing perspectives are addressed, and the organization, development, substance, and style are appropriate to purpose, audience, and a range of formal and informal tasks.	

Speaking and LIstening Standards, Grades 11–12 Students, continued

COMMON CORE STATE STANDARD	STUDENT EDITION
5. Make strategic use of digital media (e.g., textual, graphical, audio, visual, and interactive elements) in presentations to enhance understanding of findings, reasoning, and evidence and to add interest.	69, 625, 628–629, 733, 844–845, 919, 1007, 1322–1323, 1378–1379, R2, R80, R88
6. Adapt speech to a variety of contexts and tasks, demonstrating a command of formal English when indicated or appropriate. (See grades 11–12 Language standards 1 and 3 for specific expectations.)	225, 290–291, 365, 496–497, 557, 617, 833, 1201, R80

College and Career Readiness Anchor Standards for Language

COMMON CORE STATE STANDARD

CONVENTIONS OF STANDARD ENGLISH

1. Demonstrate command of the conventions of standard English grammar and usage when writing or speaking.

2. Demonstrate command of the conventions of standard English capitalization, punctuation, and spelling when writing.

KNOWLEDGE OF LANGUAGE

3. Apply knowledge of language to understand how language functions in different contexts, to make effective choices for meaning or style, and to comprehend more fully when reading or listening.

VOCABULARY ACQUISITION AND USE

4. Determine or clarify the meaning of unknown and multiple-meaning words and phrases by using context clues, analyzing meaningful word parts, and consulting general and specialized reference materials, as appropriate.

5. Demonstrate understanding of figurative language, word relationships, and nuances in word meanings.

6. Acquire and use accurately a range of general academic and domain-specific words and phrases sufficient for reading, writing, speaking, and listening at the college and career readiness level; demonstrate independence in gathering vocabulary knowledge when considering a word or phrase important to comprehension or expression.

Language Standards, Grades 11–12 Students

COMMON CORE STATE STANDARD	STUDENT EDITION
CONVENTIONS OF STANDARD ENGLISH	
1. Demonstrate command of the conventions of standard English grammar and usage when writing or speaking.	14, 493, 498, 694, 761, 817, 841, 846, 1117, 1118–1127, 1324, R50
a. Apply the understanding that usage is a matter of convention, can change over time, and is sometimes contested.	FM66–FM67, 14, 280–289, 486–495, 626, 834–843, 1118–1127, 1130, 1312–1321, 1358–1377
b. Resolve issues of complex or contested usage, consulting references (e.g., *Merriam-Webster's Dictionary of English Usage, Garner's Modern American Usage*) as needed.	FM66–FM67, 626, 673, 677
2. Demonstrate command of the conventions of standard English capitalization, punctuation, and spelling when writing.	14, 442, 493, 498, 623, 630, 693, 1001, 1111, 1118–1127, 1315, 1324, 1365, 1374
a. Observe hyphenation conventions.	716–717, 722, 976–977, 984, 1262–1263, 1268, R50, R54
b. Spell correctly.	82–83, 88, 287, 444–445, 452, 454, 841, 1062, 1125, R72
KNOWLEDGE OF LANGUAGE	
3. Apply knowledge of language to understand how language functions in different contexts, to make effective choices for meaning or style, and to comprehend more fully when reading or listening.	4, 14, 81, 91, 122–123, 130, 283, 318–319, 327, 335, 358, 377, 434, 498, 557, 571, 581, 591, 630, 656, 673, 682, 711, 761, 789, 796–797, 837, 959, 1063, 1077, 1103, 1177, 1271, 1319, 1324
a. Vary syntax for effect, consulting references (e.g., Tufte's *Artful Sentences*) for guidance as needed; apply an understanding of syntax to the study of complex texts when reading.	FM68–FM69, 81, 91, 92–93, 100, 114–115, 121, 215, 228–229, 235, 237, 238–239, 243, 247, 292, 335, 399, 432, 558–559, 570, 584–585, 586, 898–899, 905, 907, 951, 1001, 1017, 1047, 1125, 1217, R50
VOCABULARY ACQUISITION AND USE	
4. Determine or clarify the meaning of unknown and multiple-meaning words and phrases based on *grades 11–12 reading and content,* choosing flexibly from a range of strategies.	101, 114–115, 410–411, 429, 435, 440, 530–531, 536, 572–573, 577, 704, 707, 846, R50, R72
a. Use context (e.g., the overall meaning of a sentence, paragraph, or text; a word's position or function in a sentence) as a clue to the meaning of a word or phrase.	4, 10, 101, 131, 214, 292, 318–319, 322, 361, 453, 592, 593, 630, 846, 1130, 1258, 1268, 1324, R50, R72
b. Identify and correctly use patterns of word changes that indicate different meanings or parts of speech (e.g., *conceive, conception, conceivable*).	10, 228–229, 233, 334, 376, 398, 433, 454, 468–469, 473, 484, 616, 710, 768–769, 773, 832, 906, 1048–1049, 1052, 1229, R50, R72

Language Standards, Grades 11–12 Students, continued

COMMON CORE STATE STANDARD	STUDENT EDITION
c. Consult general and specialized reference materials (e.g., dictionaries, glossaries, thesauruses), both print and digital, to find the pronunciation of a word or determine or clarify its precise meaning, its part of speech, its etymology, or its standard usage.	4, 64, 80, 101, 112, 246, 254, 257, 334, 384, 433, 444–445, 452, 454, 468–469, 475, 692, 1046, 1076, 1278–1279, 1281, 1282, R50, R72
d. Verify the preliminary determination of the meaning of a word or phrase (e.g., by checking the inferred meaning in context or in a dictionary).	90, 101, 236, 572–573, 577, 672, 760, R50
5. Demonstrate understanding of figurative language, word relationships, and nuances in word meanings.	131, 236, 264, 541, 542, 552, 558–559, 564, 592, 595, 816, 1216, 1278–1279, 1283
a. Interpret figures of speech (e.g., hyperbole, paradox) in context and analyze their role in the text.	114–115, 121, 368–369, 372, 556, 630, 658–659, 662, 663, 673, 678, 682, 683, 686, 691, 705, 897, 1250–1251, 1257, 1258
b. Analyze nuances in the meaning of words with similar denotations.	54–55, 59, 214, 362, 568, 673, 681, 692, 703, 778, 820–821, 827, 1000, 1046, 1094–1095, 1099, 1249
6. Acquire and use accurately general academic and domain-specific words and phrases, sufficient for reading, writing, speaking, and listening at the college and career readiness level; demonstrate independence in gathering vocabulary knowledge when considering a word or phrase important to comprehension or expression.	10, 80, 236, 246, 257, 277, 334, 376, 398, 454, 484, 616, 672, 692, 710, 728, 760, 778, 816, 832, 906, 1016, 1062, 1342, R72

Essential Course of Study

The Essential Course of Study designates an efficient and effective choice of selections for mastery of the Common Core State Standards.

STRAND	Reading Literature	Reading Informational Text	Writing	Speaking and Listening	Language
UNIT 1					
Unit 1 Introduction: Early American Writing 1600–1800	Historical and Cultural Context of Early American Writing RL 9	Historical and Cultural Context of Early American Writing RI 9 Read a Timeline RI 7	Legacy of the Era W 7	Legacy of the Era SL 1	
The World on the Turtle's Back	Creation Myths RL 2 Reading Folk Literature RL 1, RL 2				
from *La Relación*		Historical Context RI 1, RI 6 Reading a Primary Source RI 1, RI 9	Explorer's Account W 3, W 3a, W 3d		Add Necessary Details L 3, L 3a Etymologies L 4c, L 6
To My Dear and Loving Husband / Upon the Burning of Our House, July 10th, 1666/ Huswifery	Figurative Language RL 4				Figurative Language L 5a Clarify Meaning in Older Poetry L 3a, L 4
from *Sinners in the Hands of an Angry God*		Persuasion RI 3, RI 6 Allusions RI 3, RI 6 Analyze Emotional Appeals RI 6 Connotation RI 4			Persuasion; Emotional Appeals L 3 Connotation L 4a, L 5
The Crucible	Conventions of Drama RL 3, RL 5 Draw Conclusions About Characters RL 1, RL 3 Behind the Curtain RL 7		Analyze Motivations W 1, W 1b		Use Realistic Dialogue L 3a Context Clues L 4a
The Crucible and McCarthyism		Understand Historical Context RI 1, RI 6, RI 7	Synthesize W 2, W 2b		
Speech in the Virginia Convention		Rhetorical Devices RI 5, RI 6 Reading a Persuasive Speech RI 5, RI 6	Compose a Persuasive Speech W 1		Vary Sentence Types L 3a Rhetorical Devices L 3a Analogies L 4d, L 5, L 6
The Declaration of Independence		Argument RI 4, RI 8 Analyze Text Structures RI 5 Political Words RI 4	Take a Stand W 1		Vary Sentence Structure L 3a Political Words L 4c, L 6
Writing Workshop: Argument: Persuasive Essay			Write a Persuasive Essay W 1a–e, W 4, W 5, W 6, W 7, W 8, W 9b (RI 1), W 10		Parallel Structure L 3

STRAND	Reading Literature	Reading Informational Text	Writing	Speaking and Listening	Language
UNIT 1 *continued*					
Speaking and Listening Workshop: Presenting and Evaluating a Persuasive Speech				Present and Evaluate a Persuasive Speech SL 3, SL 4, SL 6	
UNIT 2					
Unit 2 Introduction: American Romanticism 1800–1855	Historical and Cultural Context of American Romanticism RL 9	Historical and Cultural Context of American Romanticism RI 9 Read a Timeline RI 7	Legacy of the Era W 10	Legacy of the Era SL 1	
The Devil and Tom Walker	Satire RL 6 Analyze Imagery RL 1, RL 4		Write a Story W 3	Discuss SL 4	Recognize Parallelism L 3, L 3a Latin Roots L 4b, L 6
A Psalm of Life/ The Tide Rises, the Tide Falls	Stanza and Rhyme Scheme RL 5 Reading Traditional Poetry RL 4				
from *Self-Reliance/* from *Nature*		Transcendentalism RI 3, RI 9 Identify Theme RI 2	Update Emerson's Message W 2b, W 2d		Use Descriptive Details L 3 Affixes L 4b, L 6
from *Walden/* from *Civil Disobedience*		Essay RI 3, RI 9 Evaluate Ideas RI 2	Write a Letter to the Editor W 1a, W 1b, W 1d, W 1e		Ask Rhetorical Questions L 3a Latin Prefixes L 4b, L 6
The Raven	Sound Devices RL 4, RL 5 Make Inferences RL 1		Write a Monologue W 3, W 3b, W 3d		Craft Effective Sentences L 2
The Minister's Black Veil	Symbol RL 1 Identify Cultural Characteristics RL 3				Latin Roots L 4b, L 6
Writing Workshop: Narrative: Short Story			Write a Short Story W 3a–e, W 4, W 5, W 6, W 10		Transitional Expressions L 1 Formatting and Punctuating Dialogue L 1, L 2
Speaking and Listening Workshop: Dramatizing a Script				Dramatize a Script SL 1b, SL 1d, SL 6	
UNIT 3					
Unit 3 Introduction: From Romanticism to Realism 1855–1870	Historical and Cultural Context of the Transition from Romanticism to Realism; Dickinson and Whitman as Transitional Poets; Realism as a Literary Movement RL 9	Historical and Cultural Context of the Transition from Romanticism to Realism; Dickinson and Whitman as Transitional Poets; Realism as a Literary Movement RI 9 Read a Timeline RI 7		Legacy of the Era SL 1	

STRAND	Reading Literature	Reading Informational Text	Writing	Speaking and Listening	Language
UNIT 3 *continued*					
I Hear America Singing / from Song of Myself / A Noiseless Patient Spider / Beat! Beat! Drums!	Free Verse RL 4, RL 5 Analyze Tone RL 1, RL 4				
Because I could not stop for Death / Success is counted sweetest / Much Madness is divinest Sense / My life closed twice before its close / The Soul selects her own Society / I heard a Fly buzz—when I died / My life had stood—a Loaded Gun	Author's Style RL 4, RL 5 Reading Dickinson's Poetry RL 1, RL 4				
from Narrative of the Life of Frederick Douglass, An American Slave		Style RI 4, RI 6 Analyze Author's Purpose RI 6	Describe a Turning Point W 3, W 3d		Make Effective Word Choices L 3 Style L 3a
Text Analysis Workshop: Realism	Rise of Realism; Characteristics of Realism RL 2, RL 3				Characteristics of Realism L 1a
An Occurrence at Owl Creek Bridge	Point of View RL 3, RL 5 Analyze Structure RL 2, RL 5				Latin Roots L 4b, L 6
Writing Workshop: Informative Text: Online Feature Article			Write an Online Feature Article W 2a–f, W 4, W 5, W 6, W 7, W 8, W 9b (RI 1), W 10	Write an Online Feature Article SL 1c, SL 1d, SL 2, SL 5	Incorporating Quotations L 2 Prepositions and Usage L 2
Technology Workshop: Updating an Online Feature Article			Update an Online Feature Article W 6	Update an Online Feature Article SL 1c, SL 1d, SL 2, SL 5	
UNIT 4					
Unit 4 Introduction: Regionalism and Naturalism 1870–1910	Historical and Cultural Context of Regionalism and Naturalism RL 9	Historical and Cultural Context of Regionalism and Naturalism RI 9 Read a Timeline RI 7	Legacy of the Era W 7, W 10	Legacy of the Era SL 2, SL 4	
from The Autobiography of Mark Twain		Irony and Overstatement RI 6 Predict RI 1		Discuss SL 1	Differences in Word Meanings L 4d, L 6
The Law of Life	Theme RL 2, RL 9 Analyze Author's Perspective RL 3, RL 9				Denotation and Connotation L 5b, L 6
The Story of an Hour	Theme RL 2 Analyze Patterns of Organization RL 5		Compose a Journal Entry W 9, W 10		Use Effective Voice L 3

STRAND	Reading Literature	Reading Informational Text	Writing	Speaking and Listening	Language
UNIT 4 *continued*					
Writing Workshop: Informative Text: Analytical Essay			Write an Analytical Essay W 2a–f, W 4, W 5, W 6, W 7, W 8, W 9, W 10		Subject-Verb Agreement L 1
Technology Workshop: Creating a Class Newspaper			Create a Class Newspaper W 2a, W 6	Create a Class Newspaper SL 1b, SL 2, SL 5	
UNIT 5					
Unit 5 Introduction: The Harlem Renaissance and Modernism 1910–1940	The Harlem Renaissance and Modernism; Historical and Cultural Context RL 9	The Harlem Renaissance and Modernism; Historical and Cultural Context RI 9 Read a Timeline RI 7	Legacy of an Era W 7, W 10	Legacy of an Era SL 1	
Harlem / The Negro Speaks of Rivers / I, Too / The Weary Blues	Speaker RL 5 Analyze Rhythm and Repetition RL 5				
How It Feels to Be Colored Me		Rhetorical Techniques RI 5 Identify Main Ideas RI 1, RI 2	Write an Autobiographical Essay W 3		Vary Sentence Structure L 1a, L 3a Rhetorical Techniques L 3a Greek Roots L 4b, L 6
Text Analysis Workshop: Modernism	Modernism RL 3, RL 5, RL 9				
Acquainted with the Night / Nothing Gold Can Stay / "Out, Out—"	Frost's Style RL 4 Recognize Ambiguity RL 1, RL 6				
The Love Song of J. Alfred Prufrock	Stream of Consciousness RL 2 Summarize Stanzas RL 6				
A Rose for Emily	Point of View RL 4, RL 5 Analyze Sequence RL 3		Construct a Persuasive Argument W 1		Choose Effective Point of View L 3 Etymologies L 4c
A New Kind of War		Subjectivity in Reporting RI 6 Analyze Descriptive Details RI 1	Write a Subjective Report W 3e		Choose Effective Point of View L 3
Writing Workshop: Argument: Persuasive Essay			Write a Persuasive Essay W 1a–e, W 4, W 5, W 6, W 9, W 9a (RL 1), W 10		Parallelism and Syntax L 3a
Speaking and Listening Workshop: Participating in a Debate				Participate in a Debate SL 1a–d, SL 3, SL 4, SL 6	

STRAND	Reading Literature	Reading Informational Text	Writing	Speaking and Listening	Language
UNIT 6					
Unit 6 Introduction: Contemporary Literature 1940–Present	Historical and Cultural Context of Contemporary Literature RL 9	Historical and Cultural Context of Contemporary Literature RI 9 Read a Timeline RI 7	Legacy of the Era W 10	Legacy of the Era SL 1, SL 4	
Adam	Characterization and Tone RL 3, RL 4 Analyze Historical Context RL 3				
from *Letter from Birmingham Jail*		Allusion RI 4 Elements of an Argument RI 1, RI 6, RI 8	Write a Persuasive Argument W 2		Use Rhetorical Devices L 3a Words and Analogies L 5
Media Study: Perspectives in the News		Compare and Contrast Perspectives in a News Report and a Magazine RI 7	Create a News Feature W 2	Compare and Contrast Perspectives in a News Report and a Magazine SL 4	
Text Analysis Workshop: Voice in Contemporary Literature	Voice in Contemporary Literature RL 3, RL 9				
All Across the U.S.A.: Population Distribution and Composition, 2000		Analyze Text and Graphics RI 5, RI 7			
Straw into Gold: The Metamorphosis of the Everyday		Voice RI 4 Analyze Structure RI 5			
Writing Workshop: Informative Text: Résumé			Write a Résumé W 2a–b, W 2e, W 4, W 5, W 6, W 10		Capitalizing and Punctuating Addresses L 2 Formal Versus Informal Language L 3
Technology Workshop: Creating a Web Site			Create a Web Site W 6	Create a Web Site SL 2, SL 5	
UNIT 7					
Research Strategies Workshop		Plan and Focus Research RI 7	Plan and Focus Research W 6, W 7, W 8, W 9		Plan and Focus Research L 6
Writing Workshop: Informative Text: Research Paper			Write a Research Paper W 2a–f, W 6, W 7, W 8, W 9, W 10		Punctuating Parenthetical Citations L 2 Omitting or Adding Words in Quotations L 2
Technology Workshop: Producing a Documentary			Produce a Documentary W 6	Produce a Documentary SL 2, SL 5	

HOLT McDOUGAL

Literature

Grade 11

The GREAT GATSBY

F SCOTT FITZGERALD

COMMON CORE

EDITION

Typeset in *The Sans* from LucasFonts.

Acknowledgments appear at the back of the book, following the Index of Titles and Authors.

ART CREDITS

COVER, TITLE PAGE

Front Cover, Title Page: (tl) The Granger Collection, New York; (tr) Alamy/Royalty Free; (cr) The Granger Collection, New York; (bc) Getty Images; (bcr) The Granger Collection, New York; (c) Dave G. Houser/Corbis; (bl) Ken Kinzie/HMH Publishers.

Back Cover: (t) The Laughing Philosopher (1887), George C. Cox. Photograph. © Museum of the City of New York/Bridgeman Art Library; (c) David Zimmerman/Corbis; (cr) Corbis; (bl) BrandX Pictures/Alamy Images.

FM9: © Getty Images

FM39: © Age Fotostock America, Inc.

Art Credits are continued at the back of the book, following the Acknowledgments.

Printed in the U.S.A.

ISBN: 978-0-547-61841-8

2 3 4 5 6 7 8 9 10   868   20 19 18 17 16 15 14 13 12 11

4500000000   B C D E F G

HOLT McDOUGAL

Literature

Grade 11

Janet Allen

Arthur N. Applebee

Jim Burke

Douglas Carnine

Yvette Jackson

Carol Jago

Robert T. Jiménez

Judith A. Langer

Robert J. Marzano

Mary Lou McCloskey

Donna M. Ogle

Carol Booth Olson

Lydia Stack

Carol Ann Tomlinson

Special Contributor: Kylene Beers

HOLT McDOUGAL

HOUGHTON MIFFLIN HARCOURT

SENIOR PROGRAM CONSULTANTS

 **JANET ALLEN** Reading and Literacy Specialist; creator of the popular "It's Never Too Late"/"Reading for Life" Institutes. Dr. Allen is an internationally known consultant who specializes in literacy work with at-risk students. Her publications include *Tools for Content Literacy; It's Never Too Late: Leading Adolescents to Lifelong Learning; Yellow Brick Roads: Shared and Guided Paths to Independent Reading; Words, Words, Words: Teaching Vocabulary in Grades 4–12;* and *Testing 1, 2, 3 . . . Bridging Best Practice and High-Stakes Assessments.* Dr. Allen was a high school reading and English teacher for more than 20 years.

 **ARTHUR N. APPLEBEE** Leading Professor, School of Education at the University at Albany, State University of New York; Director of the Center on English Learning and Achievement. During his varied career, Dr. Applebee has been both a researcher and a teacher, working in institutional settings with children with severe learning problems, in public schools, as a staff member of the National Council of Teachers of English, and in professional education. He was elected to the International Reading Hall of Fame and has received, among other honors, the David H. Russell Award for Distinguished Research in the Teaching of English.

 **JIM BURKE** Lecturer and Author; Teacher of English at Burlingame High School, Burlingame, California. Mr. Burke is a popular presenter at educational conferences across the country and is the author of numerous books for teachers, including *School Smarts: The Four Cs of Academic Success; The English Teacher's Companion; Reading Reminders; Writing Reminders;* and *ACCESSing School: Teaching Struggling Readers to Achieve Academic and Personal Success.* He is the recipient of NCTE's Exemplary English Leadership Award and was inducted into the California Reading Association's Hall of Fame.

 **DOUGLAS CARNINE** Professor of Education at the University of Oregon; Director of the Western Region Reading First Technical Assistance Center. Dr. Carnine is nationally known for his focus on research-based practices in education, especially curriculum designs that prepare instructors of K–12 students. He has received the Lifetime Achievement Award from the Council for Exceptional Children and the Ersted Award for outstanding teaching at the University of Oregon. Dr. Carnine frequently consults on educational policy with government groups, businesses, communities, and teacher unions.

 **YVETTE JACKSON** Executive Director of the National Urban Alliance for Effective Education. Nationally recognized for her work in assessing the learning potential of underachieving urban students, Dr. Jackson is also a presenter for the Harvard Principal Center and is a member of the Differentiation Faculty of the Association for Supervision and Curriculum Development. Dr. Jackson's research focuses on literacy, gifted education, and cognitive mediation theory. She designed the Comprehensive Education Plan for the New York City Public Schools and has served as their Director of Gifted Programs.

 **CAROL JAGO** Teacher of English with thirty-two years of experience at Santa Monica High School in California; Author and nationally known Lecturer; and Past President of the National Council of Teachers of English. With varied experience in standards assessment and secondary education, Ms. Jago is the author of numerous books on education and is active with the California Association of Teachers of English, editing its scholarly journal *California English* since 1996. Ms. Jago also served on the planning committee for the 2009 NAEP Framework and the 2011 NAEP Writing Framework.

 **ROBERT T. JIMÉNEZ** Professor of Language, Literacy, and Culture at Vanderbilt University. Dr. Jiménez's research focuses on the language and literacy practices of Latino students. A former bilingual education teacher, he is now conducting research on how written language is thought about and used in contemporary Mexico. Dr. Jiménez has received several research and teaching honors, including two Fulbright awards from the Council for the International Exchange of Scholars and the Albert J. Harris Award from the International Reading Association.

JUDITH A. LANGER Distinguished Professor at the University at Albany, State University of New York; Director of the Center on English Learning and Achievement; Director of the Albany Institute for Research in Education. An internationally known scholar in English language arts education, Dr. Langer specializes in developing teaching approaches that can enrich and improve what gets done on a daily basis in classrooms. Her publications include *Getting to Excellent: How to Create Better Schools* and *Effective Literacy Instruction: Building Successful Reading and Writing Programs.*

ROBERT J. MARZANO Senior Scholar at Mid-Continent Research for Education and Learning (McREL); Associate Professor at Cardinal Stritch University in Milwaukee, Wisconsin; President of Marzano & Associates. An internationally known researcher, trainer, and speaker, Dr. Marzano has developed programs that translate research and theory into practical tools for K–12 teachers and administrators. He has written extensively on such topics as reading and writing instruction, thinking skills, school effectiveness, assessment, and standards implementation.

DONNA M. OGLE Professor of Reading and Language at National-Louis University in Chicago, Illinois; Past President of the International Reading Association. Creator of the well-known KWL strategy, Dr. Ogle has directed many staff development projects translating theory and research into school practice in middle and secondary schools throughout the United States and has served as a consultant on literacy projects worldwide. Her extensive international experience includes coordinating the Reading and Writing for Critical Thinking Project in Eastern Europe, developing integrated curriculum for a USAID Afghan Education Project, and speaking and consulting on projects in several Latin American countries and in Asia.

CAROL BOOTH OLSON Senior Lecturer in the Department of Education at the University of California, Irvine; Director of the UCI site of the National Writing Project. Dr. Olson writes and lectures extensively on the reading/writing connection, critical thinking through writing, interactive strategies for teaching writing, and the use of multicultural literature with students of culturally diverse backgrounds. She has received many awards, including the California Association of Teachers of English Award of Merit, the Outstanding California Education Research Award, and the UC Irvine Excellence in Teaching Award.

CAROL ANN TOMLINSON Professor of Educational Research, Foundations, and Policy at the University of Virginia; Co-Director of the University's Institutes on Academic Diversity. An internationally known expert on differentiated instruction, Dr. Tomlinson helps teachers and administrators develop effective methods of teaching academically diverse learners. She was a teacher of middle and high school English for 22 years prior to teaching at the University of Virginia. Her books on differentiated instruction have been translated into eight languages.

SPECIAL CONTRIBUTOR:
KYLENE BEERS Special Consultant; Former Middle School Teacher; nationally known Lecturer and Author on reading and literacy; and former President of the National Council of Teachers of English. Dr. Beers is the nationally known author of *When Kids Can't Read: What Teachers Can Do* and co-editor of *Adolescent Literacy: Turning Promise into Practice,* as well as articles in the *Journal of Adolescent and Adult Literacy.* Former editor of *Voices from the Middle,* she is the 2001 recipient of NCTE's Richard W. Halley Award, given for outstanding contributions to middle-school literacy.

ENGLISH LEARNER SPECIALISTS

MARY LOU McCLOSKEY Past President of Teachers of English to Speakers of Other Languages (TESOL); Director of Teacher Development and Curriculum Design for Educo in Atlanta, Georgia. Dr. McCloskey is a former teacher in multilingual and multicultural classrooms. She has worked with teachers, teacher educators, and departments of education around the world on teaching English as a second and foreign language. She is author of *On Our Way to English, Voices in Literature, Integrating English,* and *Visions: Language, Literature, Content.* Her awards include the Le Moyne College Ignatian Award for Professional Achievement and the TESOL D. Scott Enright Service Award.

LYDIA STACK International ESL consultant. Her areas of expertise are English language teaching strategies, ESL standards for students and teachers, and curriculum writing. Her teaching experience includes 25 years as an elementary and high school ESL teacher. She is a past president of TESOL. Her awards include the James E. Alatis Award for Service to TESOL (2003) and the San Francisco STAR Teacher Award (1989). Her publications include *On Our Way to English; Wordways: Games for Language Learning;* and *Visions: Language, Literature, Content.*

CURRICULUM SPECIALIST

WILLIAM L. McBRIDE Curriculum Specialist. Dr. McBride is a nationally known speaker, educator, and author who now trains teachers in instructional methodologies. A former reading specialist, English teacher, and social studies teacher, he holds a Masters in Reading and a Ph.D. in Curriculum and Instruction from the University of North Carolina at Chapel Hill. Dr. McBride has contributed to the development of textbook series in language arts, social studies, science, and vocabulary. He is also known for his novel *Entertaining an Elephant,* which tells the story of a burned-out teacher who becomes re-inspired with both his profession and his life.

MEDIA SPECIALISTS

DAVID M. CONSIDINE Professor of Instructional Technology and Media Studies at Appalachian State University in North Carolina. Dr. Considine has served as a media literacy consultant to the U.S. government and to the media industry, including Discovery Communications and Cable in the Classroom. He has also conducted media literacy workshops and training for county and state health departments across the United States. Among his many publications are *Visual Messages: Integrating Imagery into Instruction,* and *Imagine That: Developing Critical Viewing and Thinking Through Children's Literature.*

LARKIN PAULUZZI Teacher and Media Specialist; trainer for the New Jersey Writing Project. Ms. Pauluzzi puts her extensive classroom experience to use in developing teacher-friendly curriculum materials and workshops in many different areas, including media literacy. She has led media literacy training workshops in several districts throughout Texas, guiding teachers in the meaningful and practical uses of media in the classroom. Ms. Pauluzzi has taught students at all levels, from Title I Reading to AP English IV. She also spearheads a technology club at her school, working with students to produce media and technology to serve both the school and the community.

LISA K. SCHEFFLER Teacher and Media Specialist. Ms. Scheffler has designed and taught media literacy and video production curriculum, in addition to teaching language arts and speech. Using her knowledge of mass communication theory, coupled with real classroom experience, she has developed ready-to-use materials that help teachers incorporate media literacy into their curricula. She has taught film and television studies at the University of North Texas and has served as a contributing writer for the Texas Education Agency's statewide viewing and representing curriculum.

COMMON CORE

TEACHER ADVISORS

These are some of the many educators from across the country who played a crucial role in the development of the tables of contents, the lesson design, and other key components of this program:

Virginia L. Alford, MacArthur High School, San Antonio, Texas

Yvonne L. Allen, Shaker Heights High School, Shaker Heights, Ohio

Dave T. Anderson, Hinsdale South High School, Darien, Illinois

Kacy Colleen Anglim, Portland Public Schools District, Portland, Oregon

Jordana Benone, North High School, Torrance, California

Patricia Blood, Howell High School, Farmingdale, New Jersey

Marjorie Bloom, Eau Gallie High School, Melbourne, Florida

Edward J. Blotzer, Wilkinsburg Junior/Senior High School, Wilkinsburg, Pennsylvania

Stephen D. Bournes, Evanston Township High School, Evanston, Illinois

Barbara M. Bowling, Mt. Tabor High School, Winston-Salem, North Carolina

Kiala Boykin-Givehand, Duval County Public Schools, Jacksonville, Florida

Laura L. Brown, Adlai Stevenson High School, Lincolnshire, Illinois

Cynthia Burke, Yavneh Academy, Dallas, Texas

Hoppy Chandler, San Diego City Schools, San Diego, California

Gary Chmielewski, St. Benedict High School, Chicago, Illinois

Delorse Cole-Stewart, Milwaukee Public Schools, Milwaukee, Wisconsin

Kathy Dahlgren, Skokie, Illinois

Diana Dilger, Rosa Parks Middle School, Dixmoor, Illinois

L. Calvin Dillon, Gaither High School, Tampa, Florida

Dori Dolata, Rufus King High School, Milwaukee, Wisconsin

Jon Epstein, Marietta High School, Marietta, Georgia

Helen Ervin, Fort Bend Independent School District, Sugar Land, Texas

Sue Friedman, Buffalo Grove High School, Buffalo Grove, Illinois

Chris Gee, Bel Air High School, El Paso, Texas

Paula Grasel, The Horizon Center, Gainesville, Georgia

Rochelle L. Greene-Brady, Kenwood Academy, Chicago, Illinois

Christopher Guarraia, Centreville High School, Clifton, Virginia

Michele M. Hettinger, Niles West High School, Skokie, Illinois

Elizabeth Holcomb, Forest Hill High School, Jackson, Mississippi

Jim Horan, Hinsdale Central High School, Hinsdale, Illinois

James Paul Hunter, Oak Park-River Forest High School, Oak Park, Illinois

Susan P. Kelly, Director of Curriculum, Island Trees School District, Levittown, New York

Beverley A. Lanier, Varina High School, Richmond, Virginia

Pat Laws, Charlotte-Mecklenburg Schools, Charlotte, North Carolina

Diana R. Martinez, Treviño School of Communications & Fine Arts, Laredo, Texas

Natalie Martinez, Stephen F. Austin High School, Houston, Texas

Elizabeth Matarazzo, Ysleta High School, El Paso, Texas

Carol M. McDonald, J. Frank Dobie High School, Houston, Texas

Amy Millikan, Consultant, Chicago, Illinois

Eileen Murphy, Walter Payton Preparatory High School, Chicago, Illinois

Lisa Omark, New Haven Public Schools, New Haven, Connecticut

Kaine Osburn, Wheeling High School, Wheeling, Illinois

Andrea J. Phillips, Terry Sanford High School, Fayetteville, North Carolina

Cathy Reilly, Sayreville Public Schools, Sayreville, New Jersey

Mark D. Simon, Neuqua Valley High School, Naperville, Illinois

Scott Snow, Seguin High School, Arlington, Texas

Jane W. Speidel, Brevard County Schools, Viera, Florida

Cheryl E. Sullivan, Lisle Community School District, Lisle, Illinois

Anita Usmiani, Hamilton Township Public Schools, Hamilton Square, New Jersey

Linda Valdez, Oxnard Union High School District, Oxnard, California

Nancy Walker, Longview High School, Longview, Texas

Kurt Weiler, New Trier High School, Winnetka, Illinois

Elizabeth Whittaker, Larkin High School, Elgin, Illinois

Linda S. Williams, Woodlawn High School, Baltimore, Maryland

John R. Williamson, Fort Thomas Independent Schools, Fort Thomas, Kentucky

Anna N. Winters, Simeon High School, Chicago, Illinois

Tonora D. Wyckoff, North Shore Senior High School, Houston, Texas

Karen Zajac, Glenbard South High School, Glen Ellyn, Illinois

Cynthia Zimmerman, Mose Vines Preparatory High School, Chicago, Illinois

Lynda Zimmerman, El Camino High School, South San Francisco, California

Ruth E. Zurich, Brown Deer High School, Brown Deer, Wisconsin

COMMON CORE

OVERVIEW
Student Edition

LESSONS WITH EMBEDDED COMMON CORE INSTRUCTION

COMMON CORE

Look for the Common Core symbol throughout the book. It highlights targeted objectives to help you succeed in mastering the knowledge and skills you will need for college or for a career.

COMMON CORE CONTENTS

© *Getty Images*

COMMON CORE

CONTENTS IN BRIEF

FM10

Online at

Log in to learn more at thinkcentral.com, where you can access most program resources in one convenient location.

LITERATURE AND READING CENTER

- Author Biographies
- *PowerNotes* Presentations
- Professional Audio Recordings of Selections
- Graphic Organizers
- Analysis Frames
- NovelWise

WRITING AND GRAMMAR CENTER

- Interactive Student Models*
- Interactive Graphic Organizers*
- Interactive Revision Lessons*
- *GrammarNotes* Presentations and Practice

also available on WriteSmart CD-ROM

VOCABULARY CENTER

- *WordSharp* Interactive Vocabulary Tutor
- Vocabulary Practice Copy Masters

MEDIA AND TECHNOLOGY CENTER

- MediaScope: Media Literacy Instruction
- Digital Storytelling
- Speaking and Listening Support

RESEARCH CENTER

- Writing and Research in a Digital Age
- Citation Guide

Assessment Center

- Program Assessments
- Level Up Online Tutorials
- Online Essay Scoring

MORE TECHNOLOGY

Student One Stop

Access an electronic version of your textbook, complete with selection audio and worksheets.

Media⬤Smart DVD-ROM

Sharpen your critical viewing and analysis skills with these in-depth interactive media studies.

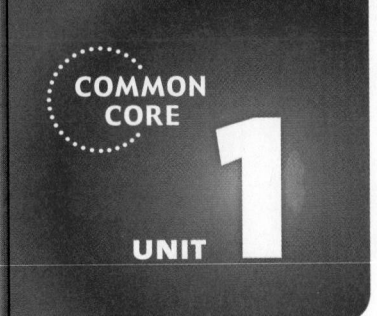

COMMON CORE
UNIT 1

An Emerging Nation
EARLY AMERICAN WRITING
1600–1800

Exploration and the Early Settlers

The Puritan Tradition

Vocabulary Strategies

Celebrating the Individual
AMERICAN ROMANTICISM

1800–1855

American Gothic

Vocabulary Strategies

Latin roots: *spec*, p. 334   Greek roots: *path*, p. 433
Words with multiple affixes, p. 376   Affixes and spelling changes, p. 454
Prefixes: *ab-* and *per-*, p. 398   Latin roots: *ambi*, p. 484

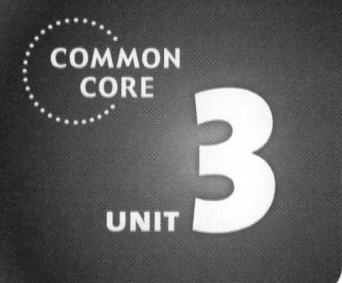

COMMON CORE

UNIT 3

An Age of Transition
FROM ROMANTICISM TO REALISM

1855–1870

STANDARDS FOCUS
Form and Meaning,
Traditional and Organic Forms,
Free Verse

Free Verse, Analyze Tone

Literature of the Civil War

> *Vocabulary Strategy*
>
> Latin roots: *lud*, p. 616

COMMON CORE
UNIT 4

Capturing the American Landscape
REGIONALISM AND NATURALISM

1870–1910

FM22

The Rise of Naturalism

A New Role for Women

Vocabulary Strategies

Differences in word meanings, *p. 672*
Thesauri and word knowledge, *p. 692*
Latin roots: *equ, p. 710*
Music terminology, *p. 728*

Greek prefixes: *epi, p. 760*
Denotation and connotation, *p. 778*
Analogies, *p. 816*
Latin roots: *rog, p. 832*

A Changing Awareness
THE HARLEM RENAISSANCE AND MODERNISM

1910–1940

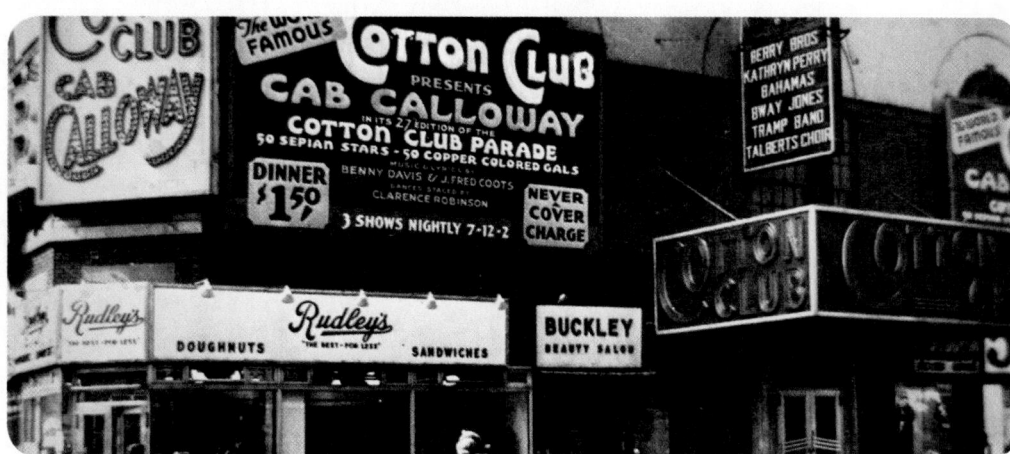

Journalism as Literature

Vocabulary Strategies

Greek roots: *cosm* or *cosmo, p. 906*   Thesauri and word choice, *p. 1046*
Context and word meanings, *p. 1000*   Spanish cognates, *p. 1062*
The origin of academic words, *p. 1016*   Word histories, or etymologies, *p. 1076*

New Perspectives
CONTEMPORARY LITERATURE

1940–PRESENT

UNIT 6 INTRODUCTION
- **QUESTIONS OF THE TIMES** • **HISTORICAL ESSAY** • **TIMELINE**
- **THE LEGACY OF THE ERA**

1144 ECOS

Modern American Drama

Responses to War

STANDARDS FOCUS
*Tone and Imagery,
Adjust Reading Strategies*

*Characterization and Tone,
Analyze Historical Context,
Analyze Visuals*

FM29

Vocabulary Strategies

Words and analogies, *p. 1216*   Context and the meaning of idioms, *p. 1258*
Greek prefixes: *syn-, p. 1229*

Investigation and Discovery
THE POWER OF RESEARCH

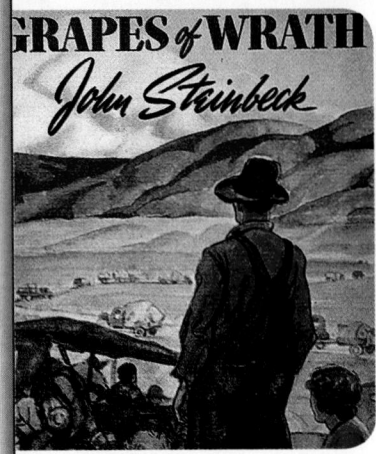

GRAPES of WRATH
John Steinbeck

FM32

Student Resource Bank

Selections by Genre

Selections by Genre

Features

WriteSmart CD-ROM

Media**Smart** DVD-ROM

STUDENT GUIDE TO ACADEMIC SUCCESS

STUDENT GUIDE

© Age Fotostock America, Inc.

FM39

The Common Core for Uncommon Achievement

Carol Jago

*"If you don't know where you are going,
any road will get you there."* — Lewis Carroll

The Common Core State Standards make clear where students are going. They describe what today's children need to know and be able to do to thrive in post-secondary education and the workplace. By focusing on results — the destination — rather than on the how — the means of transportation — the Common Core allows for a variety of teaching methods and many different classroom approaches. The challenge for teachers is to turn the daily journey towards this destination into an intellectual adventure.

One way to think about the Common Core is as a kind of GPS device to situate curriculum. While some students may choose the road less traveled, the objective is fixed. When students become lost through a wrong turn, teachers recalculate the route, providing a calm and confident voice that guides all students to academic achievement and deep literacy.

Shared Responsibility for Students' Literacy Development

The Common Core State Standards insist that the responsibility for helping students achieve literacy is not the sole responsibility of the English teacher. The introduction states clearly that, "instruction in reading, writing, speaking, listening, and language (should) be a shared responsibility within the school" (4). Citing NAEP Reading assessment test specification guidelines, the Common Core recommends that 55% of what students read in grade 8 and 70% in grade 12 should be informational text. These percentages are not meant to reflect the balance of reading materials in English class alone but rather the totality of what students should be reading across the curriculum in history/social studies, science, and technical subjects as well as in English. Given the type of reading that will be required of students in college and of graduates in the workplace, this distribution is both relevant and practical.

Understanding of Other Perspectives and Cultures

The Common Core also makes clear the importance of literature in the education of America's children. "Through reading great classic and contemporary works of literature representative of a variety of periods, cultures, and worldviews, students can vicariously inhabit worlds and have experiences much different from their own" (7). Reading literature demands that readers look inward, examine their beliefs in light of new information, consider the world through different eyes, take time for reflection. Such reading is a key to student learning.

The Purpose of Exemplar Texts

To describe the quality and complexity of the works students should read at each grade level, the Common Core offers lists of "exemplar texts." While some may choose to treat the texts on these lists as required reading, such usage would represent a misunderstanding of their purpose. "The choices should serve as useful guideposts in helping educators select texts of similar complexity, quality, and range for their own classrooms. They expressly do not represent a partial or complete reading list" (Appendix B, 2). The poems, stories, novels, and nonfiction that appear on the Common Core lists are intended as models for guiding — not dictating — text selection.

The Difference Between Persuasion and Argument

The Common Core writing standards describe the types and purposes for writing that students need to master. You will find extended definitions of argument, informative/ explanatory writing, and narrative writing in Appendix A. Of particular note is the distinction the Common Core draws between persuasion and argument. "When writing to persuade, writers employ a variety of persuasive strategies. One common strategy is an appeal to the credibility, character, or authority of the writer (or speaker). A logical argument, on the other hand, convinces the audience because of the perceived merit and reasonableness of the claims and proofs offered rather than either the emotions the writing evokes in the audience or the character or credentials of the writer" (24). Because of its importance for college and workplace readiness, argument holds a special place in the Common Core writing standards.

> *One way to think about the Common Core is as a kind of GPS device …*

Complex Literary and Informational Texts

Throughout the Common Core document you will notice the anchor standard, "Read and comprehend complex literary and informational texts independently and proficiently." It isn't enough for students to read with a teacher by their side. They need to be able, often with a little help from their friends or from the habits of mind they learned from their teachers, to read for themselves. They need to be able, like Huck Finn, to head out for the territory on their own. Such a journey requires confidence in one's ability to navigate uncharted waters and to overcome challenges their teachers can't foresee or even imagine. As we guide students on the academic adventure that is high school, let us never forget that the path we tread is the path to intellectual freedom.

WORKS CITED

Common Core State Standards for English Language Arts and History/Social Studies, Science, & Technical Subjects. 2010.

Appendix B. Common Core State Standards for English Language Arts and History/Social Studies, Science, & Technical Subjects. 2010.

Carol Jago has taught middle and high school for over 30 years and was a member of the Common Core Initiative feedback team. She serves as Past President of the National Council of Teachers of English.

Understanding the Common Core State Standards

What are the English Language Arts Common Core State Standards?

The Common Core State Standards for English Language Arts indicate what you should know and be able to do by the end of your grade level. These understandings and skills will help you be better prepared for future classes, college courses, and a career. For this reason, the standards for each strand in English Language Arts (such as reading informational text or writing) directly relate to the College and Career Readiness Anchor Standards for each strand. The Anchor Standards broadly outline the understandings and skills you should learn by the end of high school so that you are well-prepared for college or for a career.

How do I learn the English Language Arts Common Core State Standards?

Your textbook is closely aligned to the English Language Arts Common Core State Standards. Every time you learn a concept or practice a skill, you are working on mastery of one of the standards. Each unit, each selection, and each workshop in your textbook connects to one or more of the standards for English Language Arts listed on the following pages.

The English Language Arts Common Core State Standards are divided into five strands: Reading Literature, Reading Informational Text, Writing, Speaking and Listening, and Language.

Reading Literature (RL)

This strand concerns the literary texts you will read at this grade level: stories, drama, and poetry. The Common Core State Standards stress that you should read a range of texts of increasing complexity as you progress through high school.

Reading Informational Text (RI)

Informational text includes a broad range of literary nonfiction, including exposition, argument, and functional text, such as personal essays, speeches, opinion pieces, memoirs, and historical and technical accounts. The Common Core State Standards stress that you will also read a range of informational texts of increasing complexity as you progress from grade to grade.

Writing (W)

The Writing strand focuses on your generating three types of texts: arguments, informative or explanatory texts, and narratives, as well as using the writing process and technology to develop and share your writing. The Common Core State Standards also emphasize research and specify that you should write routinely for both short and extended time frames.

Speaking and Listening (SL)

The Common Core State Standards focus on comprehending information presented in a variety of media and formats, on participating in collaborative discussions, and on presenting knowledge and ideas clearly.

Language (L)

The standards in the Language strand address the conventions of Standard English grammar, usage, and mechanics; knowledge of language; and vocabulary acquisition and use.

COMMON CORE DECODER

W 1 d

Indicates that this standard is in the writing strand.

Identifies the standard number and standard subpart for the knowledge or skill.

Identifies the specific knowledge or skill for this standard.

1. Write arguments to support claims in an analysis of substantive topics or texts, using valid reasoning and relevant and sufficient evidence.

   d. Establish and maintain a formal style and objective tone while attending to the norms and conventions of the discipline in which they are writing.

English Language Arts
Common Core State Standards

Listed below are the English Language Arts Common Core State Standards that you are required to master by the end of grade 11. We have provided a summary of the concepts you will learn on your way to mastering each standard. The CCR anchor standards and high school grade-specific standards for each strand work together to define college and career readiness expectations—the former providing broad standards, the latter providing additional specificity.

College and Career Readiness Anchor Standards for Reading

COMMON CORE STATE STANDARDS

KEY IDEAS AND DETAILS

1. Read closely to determine what the text says explicitly and to make logical inferences from it; cite specific textual evidence when writing or speaking to support conclusions drawn from the text.

2. Determine central ideas or themes of a text and analyze their development; summarize the key supporting details and ideas.

3. Analyze how and why individuals, events, and ideas develop and interact over the course of a text.

CRAFT AND STRUCTURE

4. Interpret words and phrases as they are used in a text, including determining technical, connotative, and figurative meanings, and analyze how specific word choices shape meaning or tone.

5. Analyze the structure of texts, including how specific sentences, paragraphs, and larger portions of the text (e.g., a section, chapter, scene, or stanza) relate to each other and the whole.

6. Assess how point of view or purpose shapes the content and style of a text.

INTEGRATION OF KNOWLEDGE AND IDEAS

7. Integrate and evaluate content presented in diverse formats and media, including visually and quantitatively, as well as in words.

8. Delineate and evaluate the argument and specific claims in a text, including the validity of the reasoning as well as the relevance and sufficiency of the evidence.

9. Analyze how two or more texts address similar themes or topics in order to build knowledge or to compare the approaches the authors take.

RANGE OF READING AND LEVEL OF TEXT COMPLEXITY

10. Read and comprehend complex literary and informational texts independently and proficiently.

Reading Standards for Literature, Grades 11–12 Students

The College and Career Readiness Anchor Standards for Reading apply to both literature and informational text.

COMMON CORE STATE STANDARD	WHAT IT MEANS TO YOU
KEY IDEAS AND DETAILS	
1. Cite strong and thorough textual evidence to support analysis of what the text says explicitly as well as inferences drawn from the text, including determining where the text leaves matters uncertain.	You will use strong evidence from a text to support your analysis of its central ideas—both those that are stated directly and those that are suggested—and to show where the text leaves matters uncertain.
2. Determine two or more themes or central ideas of a text and analyze their development over the course of the text, including how they interact and build on one another to produce a complex account; provide an objective summary of the text.	You will analyze the development of at least two of a text's key ideas and themes by showing how they progress and interact throughout the text. You will also summarize the text as a whole without adding your own ideas or opinions.
3. Analyze the impact of the author's choices regarding how to develop and relate elements of a story or drama (e.g., where a story is set, how the action is ordered, how the characters are introduced and developed).	You will analyze the author's choices related to setting, plot structure, and characterization in a story or drama.
CRAFT AND STRUCTURE	
4. Determine the meaning of words and phrases as they are used in the text, including figurative and connotative meanings; analyze the impact of specific word choices on meaning and tone, including words with multiple meanings or language that is particularly fresh, engaging, or beautiful. (Include Shakespeare as well as other authors.)	You will analyze specific words and phrases in the text to determine both their figurative and connotative meanings, as well as how they contribute to the text's tone and meaning as a whole. You will also consider multiple-meaning words and vivid language.
5. Analyze how an author's choices concerning how to structure specific parts of a text (e.g., the choice of where to begin or end a story, the choice to provide a comedic or tragic resolution) contribute to its overall structure and meaning as well as its aesthetic impact.	You will analyze the ways in which the author has chosen to structure and order the text and determine how those choices shape the text's meaning and affect the reader.
6. Analyze a case in which grasping a point of view requires distinguishing what is directly stated in a text from what is really meant (e.g., satire, sarcasm, irony, or understatement).	You will understand a point of view in which what is really meant is different from what is said or stated.
INTEGRATION OF KNOWLEDGE AND IDEAS	
7. Analyze multiple interpretations of a story, drama, or poem (e.g., recorded or live production of a play or recorded novel or poetry), evaluating how each version interprets the source text. (Include at least one play by Shakespeare and one play by an American dramatist.)	You will compare and contrast multiple interpretations of a story, drama, or poem, and analyze how each draws from and uses the source text.
8. (Not applicable to literature)	

COMMON CORE FOCUS

RL 9 Demonstrate knowledge of eighteenth-century foundational works of American literature, including how two or more texts from the same period treat similar themes or topics.

Literature: Understanding Themes or Topics in Foundational Works

Remind students that the **topic** is the subject of a poem. A **theme** is an underlying message about this topic. Students will likely have to **infer** what the theme is, or make logical guesses about it based on

- **historical context:** the social conditions that inspired or influenced the creation of the text
- **diction:** word choice in the text that addresses the theme or topic
- **rhetorical devices:** for example, metaphors and imagery

Reading Standards for Literature, Grades 11–12 Students, continued

COMMON CORE STATE STANDARD	WHAT IT MEANS TO YOU
9. Demonstrate knowledge of eighteenth-, nineteenth- and early-twentieth-century foundational works of American literature, including how two or more texts from the same period treat similar themes or topics.	You will analyze, compare, and contrast important eighteenth-, nineteenth-, and early-twentieth-century works of American literature.
RANGE OF READING AND LEVEL OF TEXT COMPLEXITY **10.** By the end of grade 11, read and comprehend literature, including stories, dramas, and poems, in the grades 11–12 CCR text complexity band proficiently, with scaffolding as needed at the high end of the range.	You will read and understand grade-level appropriate literary texts by the end of grade 11.

Spotlight on Common Core

COMMON CORE **RL 9** Demonstrate knowledge of eighteenth-century foundational works of American literature, including how two or more texts from the same period treat similar themes or topics.

Literature: Understanding Themes or Topics in Foundational Works

Foundational works focus on major events and ideas that have shaped American culture. For example, the creation of the United States in the late eighteenth century inspired many writers to portray freedom as an essential American value.

To demonstrate how two or more foundational works from the same period treat similar themes or topics, you can follow these steps:

1. Read each text to determine the theme or topic it addresses; then, note any common, or shared, themes or topics.
2. Identify specific details within each text about the shared themes or topics.
3. Identify specific details across texts to compare and contrast how they treat the shared themes or topics.

Throughout this book, you will be asked to determine how different texts from the same time period treat similar themes or topics. Study the following example:

Phillis Wheatley (c. 1753–1784), born in Africa, was kidnapped and sold into slavery as a child, but later became a free woman. She is recognized as the first published African-American poet. Philip Freneau (1752–1832), born in New York City, was a poet and newspaper editor. A friend of James Madison and Thomas Jefferson, he wrote extensively in favor of American independence from England. Read the following excerpts from poems by Phillis Wheatley and Philip Freneau. Then answer the questions that follow the poems.

> *from* To the Right Honorable William, Earl of Dartmouth,
> His Majesty's Principal Secretary of State for North America, etc.
> by Phillis Wheatley
>
> Should you, my lord, while you peruse my song,
> Wonder from whence my love of *Freedom* sprung,
> Whence flow these wishes for the common good,
> By feeling hearts alone best understood,

I, young in life, by seeming cruel fate
Was snatch'd from *Afric's* fancy'd happy seat:
What pangs excruciating must molest,
What sorrows labor in my parent's breast?
Steel'd was that soul and by no misery mov'd
That from a father seiz'd his babe belov'd:
Such, such my case. And can I then but pray
Others may never feel tyrannic sway?

(*1773*)

from On Mr. Paine's *Rights of Man*
by Philip Freneau

Without a king, we till the smiling plain;
Without a king, we trace the unbounded sea,
And traffic round the globe, through each degree;
Each foreign clime our honored flag reveres,
Which asks no monarch, to support the STARS:
Without a *king*, the laws maintain their sway,
While honor bids each generous heart obey.
Be ours the task the ambitious to restrain,
And this great lesson teach—that kings are vain;
That warring realms to certain ruin haste,
That kings subsist by war, and wars are waste:
So shall our nation, formed on Virtue's plan,
Remain the guardian of the Rights of Man,
A vast Republic, famed through every clime,
Without a king, to see the end of time.

(*1791*)

1. How does Wheatley describe freedom? Cite specific evidence in the text.
2. How does Freneau describe freedom? Cite specific evidence in the text.
3. What are the similarities and differences in the way these poems praise freedom?

LEARN HOW Understanding Themes or Topics in Foundational Works The questions that follow
ask you to compare and contrast how two poems treat the same topic—freedom. To do this, gather
specific examples from each poem, such as the **diction**, or choice of words, and **rhetorical devices** each
writer uses to discuss this topic. Focus on one poem at a time. Notice how you must look carefully at
both poems first in order to answer the third question. Here are three examples of how to respond to
the questions.

Break students into pairs to read Wheatley's
poem, underlining words or phrases that
describe the topic of freedom or slavery.
Students should recognize Wheatley's "love of
freedom" and dislike of oppression based on
the evidence they gathered from the poem.

Follow the same steps with the excerpt
from Philip Freneau's poem. Ask students to
read Freneau's poem and underline references
to freedom or oppression. Students should
recognize that Freneau loves freedom and
dislikes oppression, but his references to it
differ from Wheatley's.

LEARN HOW Understanding Themes
or Topics in Foundational Works Remind
students that to **compare** two works is to look
for similarities between them. To **contrast** two
works is to look for differences. Have students
work in pairs to compare and contrast how the
two poets describe freedom in their poems.
Remind them to include specific references to
the poems in their comparisons.

Discuss students findings as a class. Students should recognize that Freneau is more political, focusing on the meaning of American government. Wheatley is more autobiographical, focusing on her painful personal history. However, despite their different backgrounds and writing styles, the two poets share a remarkably similar love of freedom and dislike of oppression.

1. How does Wheatley describe freedom in her poem? Cite specific evidence in the text.

> Wheatley provides an autobiographical story that explains how her "love of Freedom" sprang from her loss of freedom. Wheatley's diction emphasizes the pain she and her parents experienced when she was kidnapped into slavery. "Snatch'd from Afric's fancy'd, happy seat," she asks the reader to imagine her parents' "pangs excruciating" and "sorrows." She explicitly equates slavery with cruel oppression ("tyrannic sway"), the opposite of the freedom she loves.

— controlling idea, or thesis, for the answer

— quotations from the text to support the thesis

2. How does Freneau describe freedom in his poem? Cite specific evidence in the text.

> Using the plural pronoun "we" to address readers, Freneau outlines the nature of American freedom. He repeats the phrase "without a king" four times to introduce positive examples of the freedom Americans experience now that they are no longer ruled by a monarchy. Freneau uses negative diction, calling kings "vain" and describing how they "subsist by war, and wars are waste." In contrast, he describes America in glowing terms: "Formed on Virtue's plain," it is "the guardian of the Rights of Man."

— controlling idea, or thesis, for the answer

— quotations from the text to support the thesis

3. What are the similarities and differences in the way these poems praise freedom?

> Wheatley and Freneau both love freedom. Both poems contrast what life is like with and without it. However, Wheatley's poem is more autobiographical. Wheatley describes her personal loss of freedom as a slave as the source of her love of freedom. Freneau describes the sense of freedom America enjoys after rejecting government by a monarchy. He provides a general overview of American political life as if speaking for the entire nation.

— similarities between poems

— differences between the poets' views on freedom

As you study various eighteenth-, nineteenth-, and early twentieth-century foundational works of American literature, focus on exploring how they treat similar themes or topics. Doing so will add to your understanding of the works of that particular period, as well as of later periods.

Reading Standards for Informational Text, Grades 11–12 Students

COMMON CORE STATE STANDARD	WHAT IT MEANS TO YOU
KEY IDEAS AND DETAILS	
1. Cite strong and thorough textual evidence to support analysis of what the text says explicitly as well as inferences drawn from the text, including determining where the text leaves matters uncertain.	You will use details and information from the text to support your analysis of its central ideas—both those that are stated directly and those that are suggested—and to show where the text leaves matters uncertain.
2. Determine two or more central ideas of a text and analyze their development over the course of the text, including how they interact and build on one another to provide a complex analysis; provide an objective summary of the text.	You will analyze the development of at least two of a text's key ideas by showing how they progress and interact throughout the text. You will also summarize the text as a whole without adding your own ideas or opinions.
3. Analyze a complex set of ideas or sequence of events and explain how specific individuals, ideas, or events interact and develop over the course of the text.	You will analyze the specific interactions among a set of ideas, individuals, or a sequence of events in a text.
CRAFT AND STRUCTURE	
4. Determine the meaning of words and phrases as they are used in a text, including figurative, connotative, and technical meanings; analyze how an author uses and refines the meaning of a key term or terms over the course of a text (e.g., how Madison defines *faction* in *Federalist* No. 10).	You will analyze specific words and phrases in the text to determine their figurative, connotative, and technical meanings, as well as to uncover how an author uses them throughout a text.
5. Analyze and evaluate the effectiveness of the structure an author uses in his or her exposition or argument, including whether the structure makes points clear, convincing, and engaging.	You will examine a text's structure and evaluate whether it makes the author's claims clear, convincing, and interesting.
6. Determine an author's point of view or purpose in a text in which the rhetoric is particularly effective, analyzing how style and content contribute to the power, persuasiveness, or beauty of the text.	You will understand the author's purpose and perspective on a topic and analyze how the author uses language to affect the reader.
INTEGRATION OF KNOWLEDGE AND IDEAS	
7. Integrate and evaluate multiple sources of information presented in different media or formats (e.g., visually, quantitatively) as well as in words in order to address a question or solve a problem.	You will integrate multiple and varied sources of information to address a question or solve a problem.
8. Delineate and evaluate the reasoning in seminal U.S. texts, including the application of constitutional principles and use of legal reasoning (e.g., in U.S. Supreme Court majority opinions and dissents) and the premises, purposes, and arguments in works of public advocacy (e.g., *The Federalist*, presidential addresses).	You will analyze the reasoning and underlying principles of important historical U.S. texts for their support of the principles of democracy.

COMMON CORE FOCUS

RI 9 Analyze seventeenth-, eighteenth-, and nineteenth-century foundational U.S. documents of historical and literary significance (including The Declaration of Independence, the Preamble to the Constitution, the Bill of Rights, and Lincoln's Second Inaugural Address) for their themes, purposes, and rhetorical features.

Informational Text: Analyzing Significant U.S. Documents

Remind students that a foundational document is one that helps form the basis of U.S. history or literature. Three features that are essential to such a document are its

- **purpose:** the reason why the document was written for a specific audience
- **theme:** the message the author conveys to the reader
- **rhetorical features:** devices such as repetition of words, analogies, and word choice

LEARN HOW Analyzing Audience and Author's Purpose Make sure that students understand that when they **analyze** a document, they make connections among its different parts. Then, remind students that a document's purpose is to explain, inform, or develop an argument that supports the author's claim. Ask students to provide an example of a document that fulfills each of these purposes.

COMMON CORE STATE STANDARD	WHAT IT MEANS TO YOU
9. Analyze seventeenth-, eighteenth-, and nineteenth-century foundational U.S. documents of historical and literary significance (including The Declaration of Independence, the Preamble to the Constitution, the Bill of Rights, and Lincoln's Second Inaugural Address) for their themes, purposes, and rhetorical features.	You will read and analyze important eighteenth-, nineteenth-, and early-twentieth-century documents pertaining to American history to determine their themes, purposes, and use of language.
RANGE OF READING AND LEVEL OF TEXT COMPLEXITY 10. By the end of grade 11, read and comprehend literary nonfiction in the grades 11–CCR text complexity band proficiently, with scaffolding as needed at the high end of the range.	You will demonstrate the ability to read and understand grade-level appropriate literary nonfiction texts by the end of grade 11.

Spotlight on Common Core

COMMON CORE

RI 9 Analyze seventeenth-, eighteenth-, and nineteenth-century foundational U.S. documents of historical and literary significance (including The Declaration of Independence, the Preamble to the Constitution, the Bill of Rights, and Lincoln's Second Inaugural Address) for their themes, purposes, and rhetorical features.

Informational Text: Analyzing Significant U.S. Documents

The Common Core State Standards ask you to analyze significant literary and historical U.S. documents for their **themes, purposes, and rhetorical features, or devices**. You can do this by following these steps:

1. Identify the **purpose** of the document by determining why the document was written.
2. Identify the **theme** of the document by identifying the message its author conveys.
3. Identify **rhetorical features, or devices**, the author uses to convey the theme and to accomplish the document's purpose.

Throughout this book, you will be asked to analyze these aspects of significant U.S. historical and literary documents from various time periods. As you study the following examples, think about their purposes, themes, and use of rhetorical devices.

LEARN HOW Analyzing Audience and Author's Purpose First, you need to identify the audience for the document. Then, identify the author's purpose for writing it for this audience.

An author usually writes for one or more purposes: to inform or explain, to tell a real or imagined story, or to develop an argument that will support the author's claims about a topic or a text. For example, the purpose of a news report is to inform viewers about important events, while the purpose of a political speech is to make an argument that will persuade listeners to accept the speaker's claims. Consider the purpose for which the document is written. Then, **summarize**, or briefly restate, this purpose in your own words in no more than a few sentences. Here are two examples of how to respond to questions about audience and purpose of historical documents.

from The Declaration of Independence, 1776

> When, in the course of human events, it becomes necessary for one people to dissolve the political bands which have connected them with another, and to assume, among the powers of the earth, the separate and equal station to which the laws of nature and of nature's God entitle them, a decent respect to the opinions of mankind requires that they should declare the causes which impel them to the separation.

Preamble to the United States Constitution, 1787

> We the people of the United States, in order to form a more perfect union, establish justice, insure domestic tranquility, provide for the common defense, promote the general welfare, and secure the blessings of liberty to ourselves and our posterity, do ordain and establish this Constitution for the United States of America.

1. Who is the audience for each document?

> *The Declaration of Independence was written to George III (the British king), to the world, and to the people of the American colonies. The U.S. Constitution was written to the people of the United States.*

2. What is the purpose of each document?

> *The purpose of the Declaration of Independence was to tell the world why the colonies wanted to declare their independence by separating from England. The Preamble to the U.S. Constitution, a short introduction to the document, was written to explain the principles that would guide our nation so it would be lawful, peaceful, safe, and prosperous for years to come.*

The Common Core State Standards also ask you to consider the **themes** in significant U.S. historical documents. Read the following discussion to see how you can analyze themes in these kinds of documents.

LEARN HOW Analyzing Theme   The **theme** of a document is the message its author wishes to convey to its intended audience. You may need to **infer**, or make logical assumptions, about the theme based on a variety of elements, such as the author's choice of words. On the next page, read Amendment VI of the U.S. Constitution, the document that established the essential laws of the United States. How would you summarize the most important idea in Amendment VI? As you did with purpose and audience, state this theme briefly in your own words.

Students' answers may include
- laws: to explain a nation's rules to its people
- instruction manuals: to inform readers about how to build or operate something
- speeches: to persuade listeners to accept the speaker's claims

Have volunteers read aloud the excerpts from each document. Then, discuss the historical context surrounding each document's creation: the American colonies decision to split from England (the Declaration) and the establishment of the United States (the Preamble).

LEARN HOW Analyzing Theme   Remind students that this amendment is part of a document written in 1789. Ask students to identify the audience for this document based on its historical context. ***Possible answer: the American people or people from other nations***

Remind students that a **theme** is a message conveyed in the document. Have a volunteer read Amendment VI of the Bill of Rights aloud. Have students write a list of words from the amendment that are related. Their lists may include words such as *criminal, prosecutions, accused, trial, jury, law, accusation,* and *witnesses.*

Ask students to share examples from their lists and determine how these words are connected. ***Possible answer:*** *All the words refer to court trials in the U.S. justice system.* Discuss with students what message the amendment conveys about court trials in the U.S. ***Possible answer:*** *The amendment promises anyone accused of a crime fair treatment in the court system.*

LEARN HOW Analyzing Rhetorical **Features** Define each rhetorical devices by writing these examples on the board:

- *Repetition: I came, I saw, I conquered.*
- *Analogy: The fog comes on little cat feet.*
- *Word choice: Your money will go directly to help sick children. I am sure you don't want them to suffer.*

Point out that President Lincoln gave the speech shortly before the end of the Civil War. Ask students to imagine how people on both sides of the war might feel. Then, have them identify the audience for the speech (all Americans) and its purpose (to bring Americans together to recover after the war).

Amendment VI, ratified by Congress 1791

In all criminal prosecutions, the accused shall enjoy the right to a speedy and public trial, by an impartial jury of the State and district wherein the crime shall have been committed; which district shall have been previously ascertained by law, and to be informed of the nature and cause of the accusation; to be confronted with the witnesses against him; to have compulsory process for obtaining witnesses in his favor, and to have the assistance of counsel for his defense.

1. Who is the audience for and what is the purpose of this document?

The audience for Amendment VI is the nation as a whole and anyone else who reads the Bill of Rights. The purpose of the document is to inform the audience about how anyone charged with a crime is tried in the U.S.

2. What is the theme of Amendment VI?

The theme of Amendment VI is the right of every American to receive timely, fair, and just treatment under the law if he or she is accused of a crime. There are several phrases, such as "the accused shall enjoy the right to a speedy and public trial by an impartial jury," that highlight the legal rights of "the accused."

The authors of our important historical documents wrote masterfully and powerfully, employing a range of **rhetorical features, or devices**, to convey their messages to their audiences. The Common Core State Standards also require you to analyze the rhetorical devices incorporated into these significant documents. The following discussion will explain how you can analyze a text to determine its rhetorical features.

LEARN HOW Analyzing Rhetorical Features **Rhetorical features, or devices**, fulfill the author's purpose by vividly conveying the document's theme. Before you can understand a document's rhetorical devices, you need to identify the author's purpose and theme. Rhetorical devices may include any of the following:
- repetition of words or phrases, such as parallel grammatical structures, to create emphasis and unity
- analogies, to make a comparison to illustrate an idea
- word choice, to appeal to the audience's emotions or reason

Notice how Abraham Lincoln uses rhetorical devices in his Second Inaugural Address.

Background Abraham Lincoln gave the following speech for his inauguration as President of the U.S. for a second term in 1865. With the Civil War (1861–1865) nearing an end, the nation reeled from four years of brutal conflict and bloodshed. In the first paragraph, Lincoln recounts how the war started. In the second, he discusses what the nation should do now.

from Abraham Lincoln's *Second Inaugural Address*, 1865

On the occasion corresponding to this four years ago all thoughts were anxiously directed to an impending civil war. All dreaded it, all sought to avert it. While the inaugural address was being delivered from this place, devoted altogether to *saving* the Union without war, insurgent agents were in the city seeking to *destroy* it without war—seeking to dissolve the Union and divide effects by negotiation. Both parties deprecated war, but one of them would *make* war rather than let the nation survive, and the other would *accept* war rather than let it perish, and the war came. . . .

With malice toward none, with charity for all, with firmness in the right as God gives us to see the right, let us strive on to finish the work we are in, to bind up the nation's wounds, to care for him who shall have borne the battle and for his widow and his orphan, to do all which may achieve and cherish a just and lasting peace among ourselves and with all nations.

1. Who is the audience for Lincoln's speech? What is the purpose of the speech?

> Lincoln's audience is the people of the United States. Lincoln speaks to the entire country in order to argue that the nation must come together and heal.

2. What is the theme of Lincoln's speech?

> The theme of the speech is the need for the country to unite in order to heal and to move forward to a "just and lasting peace among ourselves and with all nations."

3. What rhetorical devices does Lincoln use in this speech?

> Lincoln uses repetition and language that appeals to the audience's emotions to achieve his purpose and convey his theme in this speech. In the first paragraph, he explains how the war began. He repeats the word "war" seven times like a drumbeat, to emphasize that the war was inevitable.
>
> In the second paragraph, Lincoln uses repetition again, but for a very different reason. First, he repeats prepositional phrases: "with charity toward all, with malice for none, with firmness in the right. . . ." Then he repeats infinitive phrases: "to finish the work we are in, to bind up the nation's wounds, to care for him who shall have borne the battle. . . ." These parallel phrases, which mirror each other, also mirror the sense of unity and purpose Lincoln hopes to inspire in the American people. Instead of reminding his audience of the inevitability of the war, Lincoln propels them toward taking positive action to preserve peace.

Break students into three groups to look for examples of each rhetorical feature. How does Lincoln use his words to convey his message to Americans and inspire them to join together to heal the country?

Ask each group to report its findings. Students' answers will vary, but they should understand how Lincoln uses each rhetorical device to convey his theme (the need for unity) and fulfill his purpose (persuading Americans to come together to heal).

In addition, Lincoln uses language that appeals to his audience's emotions, addressing them as "us" to bind them to him and to each other. He asks them to join forces to care for vulnerable Americans who have suffered in wartime: "to care for him who shall have borne the battle and for his widow and his orphan."

As you read historical documents in this book, be sure to consider their audience, purpose, theme, and rhetorical features. Focusing on these items will enrich your reading of these documents so important for our nation.

College and Career Readiness Anchor Standards for Writing

COMMON CORE STATE STANDARDS

TEXT TYPES AND PURPOSES

1. Write arguments to support claims in an analysis of substantive topics or texts, using valid reasoning and relevant and sufficient evidence.

2. Write informative/explanatory texts to examine and convey complex ideas and information clearly and accurately through the effective selection, organization, and analysis of content.

3. Write narratives to develop real or imagined experiences or events using effective technique, well-chosen details, and well-structured event sequences.

PRODUCTION AND DISTRIBUTION OF WRITING

4. Produce clear and coherent writing in which the development, organization, and style are appropriate to task, purpose, and audience.

5. Develop and strengthen writing as needed by planning, revising, editing, rewriting, or trying a new approach.

6. Use technology, including the Internet, to produce and publish writing and to interact and collaborate with others.

RESEARCH TO BUILD AND PRESENT KNOWLEDGE

7. Conduct short as well as more sustained research projects based on focused questions, demonstrating understanding of the subject under investigation.

8. Gather relevant information from multiple print and digital sources, assess the credibility and accuracy of each source, and integrate the information while avoiding plagiarism.

9. Draw evidence from literary or informational texts to support analysis, reflection, and research.

RANGE OF WRITING

10. Write routinely over extended time frames (time for research, reflection, and revision) and shorter time frames (a single sitting or a day or two) for a range of tasks, purposes, and audiences.

Writing Standards, Grades 11–12 Students

COMMON CORE STATE STANDARD	WHAT IT MEANS TO YOU
TEXT TYPES AND PURPOSES	
1. Write arguments to support claims in an analysis of substantive topics or texts, using valid reasoning and relevant and sufficient evidence.	You will write and develop arguments with strong evidence and valid reasoning that include
a. Introduce precise, knowledgeable claim(s), establish the significance of the claim(s), distinguish the claim(s) from alternate or opposing claims, and create an organization that logically sequences claim(s), counterclaims, reasons, and evidence.	**a.** a clear organization of precise claims and counterclaims
b. Develop claim(s) and counterclaims fairly and thoroughly, supplying the most relevant evidence for each while pointing out the strengths and limitations of both in a manner that anticipates the audience's knowledge level, concerns, values, and possible biases.	**b.** relevant and unbiased support for claims that incorporates audience considerations
c. Use words, phrases, and clauses as well as varied syntax to link the major sections of the text, create cohesion, and clarify the relationships between claim(s) and reasons, between reasons and evidence, and between claim(s) and counterclaims.	**c.** use of transitional words, phrases, and clauses and varied sentence structures to link information and clarify relationships
d. Establish and maintain a formal style and objective tone while attending to the norms and conventions of the discipline in which they are writing.	**d.** a tone and style that is appropriate and that adheres to the conventions, or expectations, of the discipline
e. Provide a concluding statement or section that follows from and supports the argument presented.	**e.** a strong concluding statement or section that summarizes the evidence presented
2. Write informative/explanatory texts to examine and convey complex ideas, concepts, and information clearly and accurately through the effective selection, organization, and analysis of content.	You will write clear, well-organized, and thoughtful informative and explanatory texts with
a. Introduce a topic; organize complex ideas, concepts, and information so that each new element builds on that which precedes it to create a unified whole; include formatting (e.g., headings), graphics (e.g., figures, tables), and multimedia when useful to aiding comprehension.	**a.** a clear introduction and an organization that builds on each successive idea, including formats, headings, graphic organizers (when appropriate), and multimedia
b. Develop the topic thoroughly by selecting the most significant and relevant facts, extended definitions, concrete details, quotations, or other information and examples appropriate to the audience's knowledge of the topic.	**b.** a sufficient variety of support and background information
c. Use appropriate and varied transitions and syntax to link the major sections of the text, create cohesion, and clarify the relationships among complex ideas and concepts.	**c.** appropriate and varied transitions and sentence structures

Writing Standards, Grades 11–12 Students, continued

COMMON CORE STATE STANDARD	WHAT IT MEANS TO YOU
TEXT TYPES AND PURPOSES	
d. Use precise language, domain-specific vocabulary, and techniques such as metaphor, simile, and analogy to manage the complexity of the topic.	**d.** precise language, relevant vocabulary, and the use of comparisons to express complex ideas
e. Establish and maintain a formal style and objective tone while attending to the norms and conventions of the discipline in which they are writing.	**e.** an appropriate tone and style that adheres to the conventions, or expectations, of the discipline
f. Provide a concluding statement or section that follows from and supports the information or explanation presented (e.g., articulating implications or the significance of the topic).	**f.** a strong concluding statement or section that logically relates to the information presented in the text and that restates the importance or relevance of the topic
3. Write narratives to develop real or imagined experiences or events using effective technique, well-chosen details, and well-structured event sequences.	You will write clear, well-structured, detailed narrative texts that
a. Engage and orient the reader by setting out a problem, situation, or observation and its significance, establishing one or multiple point(s) of view, and introducing a narrator and/or characters; create a smooth progression of experiences or events.	**a.** draw your readers in with a clear topic, well-developed point(s) of view, a well-developed narrator and characters, and an interesting progression of events or ideas
b. Use narrative techniques, such as dialogue, pacing, description, reflection, and multiple plot lines, to develop experiences, events, and/or characters.	**b.** use a range of literary techniques to develop and expand on events and/or characters
c. Use a variety of techniques to sequence events so that they build on one another to create a coherent whole and build toward a particular tone and outcome (e.g., a sense of mystery, suspense, growth, or resolution).	**c.** have a coherent sequence and structure that create the appropriate tone and ending for readers
d. Use precise words and phrases, telling details, and sensory language to convey a vivid picture of the experiences, events, setting, and/or characters.	**d.** use precise words, sensory details, and language in order to keep readers interested
e. Provide a conclusion that follows from and reflects on what is experienced, observed, or resolved over the course of the narrative.	**e.** have a strong and logical conclusion that reflects on the topic
PRODUCTION AND DISTRIBUTION OF WRITING	
4. Produce clear and coherent writing in which the development, organization, and style are appropriate to task, purpose, and audience.	You will produce writing that is appropriate to the task, purpose, and audience for whom you are writing.
5. Develop and strengthen writing as needed by planning, revising, editing, rewriting, or trying a new approach, focusing on addressing what is most significant for a specific purpose and audience.	You will revise and refine your writing, using a variety of strategies, to address what is most important for your purpose and audience.
6. Use technology, including the Internet, to produce, publish, and update individual or shared writing products in response to ongoing feedback, including new arguments or information.	You will use technology to share your writing, provide links to other relevant information, and to update your information as needed.

Writing Standards, Grades 11–12 Students, continued

COMMON CORE STATE STANDARD	WHAT IT MEANS TO YOU
RESEARCH TO BUILD AND PRESENT KNOWLEDGE **7.** Conduct short as well as more sustained research projects to answer a question (including a self-generated question) or solve a problem; narrow or broaden the inquiry when appropriate; synthesize multiple sources on the subject, demonstrating understanding of the subject under investigation.	You will engage in short and more complex research tasks that include answering a question or solving a problem by using multiple sources. Your understanding of the subject will be evident in the product you develop.
8. Gather relevant information from multiple authoritative print and digital sources, using advanced searches effectively; assess the strengths and limitations of each source in terms of the task, purpose, and audience; integrate information into the text selectively to maintain the flow of ideas, avoiding plagiarism and overreliance on any one source and following a standard format for citation.	You will effectively conduct searches to gather information from a variety of print and digital sources and will evaluate each source in terms of the goal of your research. You will appropriately cite your sources of information and will follow a standard format for citation, such as the MLA or APA guidelines.
9. Draw evidence from literary or informational texts to support analysis, reflection, and research. **a.** Apply *grades 11–12 Reading standards* to literature (e.g., "Demonstrate knowledge of eighteenth-, nineteenth- and early-twentieth-century foundational works of American literature, including how two or more texts from the same period treat similar themes or topics"). **b.** Apply *grades 11–12 Reading standards* to literary nonfiction (e.g., "Delineate and evaluate the reasoning in seminal U.S. texts, including the application of constitutional principles and use of legal reasoning [e.g., in U.S. Supreme Court Case majority opinions and dissents] and the premises, purposes, and arguments in works of public advocacy [e.g., *The Federalist*, presidential addresses]").	You will paraphrase, summarize, quote, and cite primary and secondary sources, using both literary and informational texts, to support your analysis, reflection, and research, for purposes including **a.** written analysis of themes, author's choices, or point of view in American literature **b.** written analysis of central ideas, text structure, word choice, point of view, or reasoning in American literary nonfiction
RANGE OF WRITING **10.** Write routinely over extended time frames (time for research, reflection, and revision) and shorter time frames (a single sitting or a day or two) for a range of tasks, purposes, and audiences.	You will write a variety of texts for different purposes and audiences over both short and extended periods of time.

COMMON CORE FOCUS

W 4 Produce clear and coherent writing in which the development, organization, and style are appropriate to task, purpose, and audience.
W 10 Write routinely over extended time frames (time for research, reflection, and revision) and shorter time frames (a single sitting or a day or two) for a range of tasks, purposes, and audiences.

Writing: Maintaining Clarity and Coherence

Remind students that **coherent writing** is writing that readers can follow—the ideas follow each other logically. Writing that is **clear** is understandable to readers. In order to create clear, coherent writing, students must first establish a framework.

LEARN HOW Planning Your Writing Process Review these important terms with students:

- Task: the type of writing, for example research paper
- Topic: what you are writing about
- Audience: who will read it
- Purpose: what you want this writing to accomplish
- Time frame: the amount of time you have to complete the task. Do you have a deadline?

Enhance students' understanding by asking them to provide their own sample answers to each question in the first chart for a typical assignment—for example, an argumentative essay in response to school budget cuts, which is due in one week. Write their responses on the board, one question at a time, providing guidance and clarifying student responses as needed. For example, are the time frames students suggest realistic? Is their purpose clear?

Spotlight on Common Core

W 4 Produce clear and coherent writing in which the development, organization, and style are appropriate to task, purpose, and audience.
W 10 Write routinely over extended time frames (time for research, reflection, and revision) and shorter time frames (a single sitting or a day or two) for a range of tasks, purposes, and audiences.

Writing: Maintaining Clarity and Coherence

The Common Core State Standards focus on your ability to communicate clearly and coherently, so your readers can follow and understand what you have written.

Before you begin writing, answer some specific questions to determine and plan your writing process. Pre-planning helps you define your project and establish a realistic timeframe for it. If your project is ill-defined or if you do not allow enough time for a smooth writing process, the clarity and coherence of your writing will inevitably suffer.

For example, what are you writing? A cover letter takes less time to write than a long essay or procedural text. However, all these documents require you to do some research. Then, you will need to allow for time to draft, revise, and proofread what you have written.

It is also wise to plan for the unexpected. Include a little more time than you think you need in case you have unpredictable scheduling conflicts, need to start over and try a new approach to your topic, or do some extra research.

LEARN HOW Planning Your Writing Process Study the chart below. It provides some additional questions that you can ask yourself before you begin writing. It will help you plan your writing process and produce your best work.

Planning Your Writing Process	
Question	**Examples**
What is my final product?	• An argumentative essay • A cover letter • A research paper
What is my topic?	• The importance of arts education • An application for an internship • Key themes in Zora Neale Hurston's *Their Eyes Were Watching God*
What is my purpose, or reason, for writing?	• To convince others to support arts education • To be hired for a summer internship • To analyze and explain a literary text
Who is my audience?	• Other students in class • A hiring manager • My English teacher
How much time do I have? Am I writing over a short or extended period of time?	• A week • A day • A month

Once you understand your task, purpose, audience, and timeframe, you can plan your writing process. For example, you can decide how much time you should spend researching your topic based on your purpose and due date. You might try drafting a schedule, using a calendar and what you already know about how much time to allow for each step in the writing process.

LEARN HOW Using Writing Strategies Having crafted a writing plan, you can concentrate on producing clear and coherent writing. The **Writing Workshops** in this book provide several strategies to help you write effectively. Study the chart below, which provides examples of some of these strategies. The highlighted text in the right column reflects the bold-faced points in the left column.

Writing Strategies

DEVELOPMENT	WHAT DOES IT LOOK LIKE?
• Include a memorable introduction and concluding statement or section. • Utilize a **controlling idea or thesis statement**. • Introduce sufficient facts, definitions, **concrete details, quotations**, and other examples that are appropriate to the audience's knowledge of the topic.	*Many schools around the nation face drastic budget cuts. One of the first areas to suffer has been arts education. John Berman, a local school board member, recently summed up many people's opinion: "What good are the arts when students need to be trained for real jobs?" This is an understandable objection, but it overlooks what we will lose if we eliminate arts education. Several students at Jefferson High School asserted that they would have dropped out of school if they had not been in music classes. Arts education is essential to our schools.*

ORGANIZATION	WHAT DOES IT LOOK LIKE?
• Establish a **logical organization** that makes sense for the purpose and audience. • Provide graphics, use formatting, or other text features to help aid comprehension, if necessary. • Use organizational patterns, such as cause-and-effect, definitions, or **compare-contrast** to help readers understand the relationship between ideas. • Include words, phrases, and clauses that link sections of text and **create cohesion**, or flow. • Organize complex ideas, concepts, and information to **make important connections and distinctions**.	*Zora Neale Hurston's Their Eyes Were Watching God includes three key themes:* • *the relationship of language and power* • *the construction of female identity* • *the use of dialect* *First, I will compare and contrast Janie Crawford's relationship to language with Jody's, and then with other characters, such as the gossiping townspeople. This comparison-contrast reveals that a character's sense of self is often mirrored in that character's complex relationship to language.*

LANGUAGE AND STYLE	WHAT DOES IT LOOK LIKE?
• Maintain an **appropriate style and tone,** such as formal and objective for academic or business writing. • Use **precise language and telling details.** • Exhibit a strong command of grammar, usage, capitalization, punctuation.	*I am applying for a summer internship as a junior photographer with The Paterson Times. I have been lead photographer on my high school newspaper for the past two years. One of my photographs won the Jimson Prize for best high school news photograph. I want to become a professional photographer, but I need to develop my skills further in a professional newspaper environment.* *The Paterson Times is famous for its award-winning photojournalism. An opportunity to work with your world-class photographers this summer would be an invaluable educational opportunity for me.*

Authors combine different strategies to maintain clarity and coherence in their writing. They apply these strategies to texts of varied lengths, purposes, and complexity. Be sure to notice these strategies as you analyze texts throughout this book, and be sure to use them to improve your own writing.

LEARN HOW **Using Writing Strategies**

Discuss each strategy with students. Challenge a student volunteer to restate each strategy in his or her own words. Challenge other students to explain how the text in the right-hand column works as an example of each strategy. If necessary, provide definitions and examples for the following terms in the left-hand column of the chart:

• **Controlling idea or thesis statement:** the main proposition that a writer attempts to support in a piece of writing. (*Arts education is essential to our schools.*)

• **Quotation:** textual evidence quoted from a source or someone's exact words enclosed in quotation marks. (*"What good are the arts when students need to be trained for real jobs?"*)

• **Cohesion:** the logical flow from one idea to the next; often created by transitional words and phrases. (*First, then*)

• **Tone:** the writer's attitude toward the subject expressed in the choice of words. (*An opportunity to work with your world-class photographers this summer would be an invaluable educational opportunity for me.*)

College and Career Readiness Anchor Standards for Speaking and Listening

COMMON CORE STATE STANDARDS

COMPREHENSION AND COLLABORATION

1. Prepare for and participate effectively in a range of conversations and collaborations with diverse partners, building on others' ideas and expressing their own clearly and persuasively.

2. Integrate and evaluate information presented in diverse media and formats, including visually, quantitatively, and orally.

3. Evaluate a speaker's point of view, reasoning, and use of evidence and rhetoric.

PRESENTATION OF KNOWLEDGE AND IDEAS

4. Present information, findings, and supporting evidence such that listeners can follow the line of reasoning and the organization, development, and style are appropriate to task, purpose, and audience.

5. Make strategic use of digital media and visual displays of data to express information and enhance understanding of presentations.

6. Adapt speech to a variety of contexts and communicative tasks, demonstrating command of formal English when indicated or appropriate.

Speaking and Listening Standards, Grades 11–12 Students

COMMON CORE STATE STANDARD	WHAT IT MEANS TO YOU
COMPREHENSION AND COLLABORATION	
1. Initiate and participate effectively in a range of collaborative discussions (one-on-one, in groups, and teacher-led) with diverse partners on grades 11–12 topics, texts, and issues, building on others' ideas and expressing their own clearly and persuasively.	You will actively participate in a variety of discussions in which you
a. Come to discussions prepared, having read and researched material under study; explicitly draw on that preparation by referring to evidence from texts and other research on the topic or issue to stimulate a thoughtful, well-reasoned exchange of ideas.	a. have read any relevant material beforehand and have come to the discussion prepared with background research
b. Work with peers to promote civil, democratic discussions and decision-making, set clear goals and deadlines, and establish individual roles as needed.	b. work with others to establish goals, processes, and roles within the group in order to have reasonable discussions
c. Propel conversations by posing and responding to questions that probe reasoning and evidence; ensure a hearing for a full range of positions on a topic or issue; clarify, verify, or challenge ideas and conclusions; and promote divergent and creative perspectives.	c. ask and respond to questions, encourage a range of positions, and relate the current topic to other relevant information and perspectives
d. Respond thoughtfully to diverse perspectives; synthesize comments, claims, and evidence made on all sides of an issue; resolve contradictions when possible; and determine what additional information or research is required to deepen the investigation or complete the task.	d. respond to different perspectives, summarize points of agreement or disagreement when needed, help to resolve unclear points, and set out a plan for additional research as needed

Speaking and Listening Standards, Grades 11–12 Students, continued

COMMON CORE STATE STANDARD	WHAT IT MEANS TO YOU
2. Integrate multiple sources of information presented in diverse formats and media (e.g., visually, quantitatively, orally) in order to make informed decisions and solve problems, evaluating the credibility and accuracy of each source and noting any discrepancies among the data.	You will integrate multiple and varied sources of information, assessing the credibility and accuracy of each source to aid the group-discussion process.
3. Evaluate a speaker's point of view, reasoning, and use of evidence and rhetoric, assessing the stance, premises, links among ideas, word choice, points of emphasis, and tone used.	You will evaluate a speaker's argument and analyze the nature of the speaker's reasoning or evidence.

PRESENTATION OF KNOWLEDGE AND IDEAS

4. Present information, findings, and supporting evidence, conveying a clear and distinct perspective, such that listeners can follow the line of reasoning, alternative or opposing perspectives are addressed, and the organization, development, substance, and style are appropriate to purpose, audience, and a range of formal and informal tasks.	You will organize and present information, evidence, and your perspective to your listeners in a logical sequence and style that are appropriate to your task, purpose, and audience.
5. Make strategic use of digital media (e.g., textual, graphical, audio, visual, and interactive elements) in presentations to enhance understanding of findings, reasoning, and evidence and to add interest.	You will use digital media to enhance understanding and to add interest to your presentations.
6. Adapt speech to a variety of contexts and tasks, demonstrating a command of formal English when indicated or appropriate.	You will adapt the formality of your speech appropriately, depending on its context and purpose.

Spotlight on Common Core

COMMON CORE

SL 1b Work with peers to promote civil, democratic discussions and decision-making, set clear goals and deadlines, and establish individual roles as needed.

Speaking and Listening: Interacting Constructively in Discussions

The Common Core State Standards emphasize the importance of working constructively with your peers in group discussions. These discussions provide an opportunity for you to learn from each other by actively sharing opinions and ideas in order to answer a question, solve a problem, or reach consensus. A productive group discussion follows a democratic model. All the participants should feel that their voices are heard, even if they have strong differences of opinion.

Before you begin your group discussion, assign roles to group members to help streamline it. You will need:

1. a **chairperson**, or facilitator, who keeps the group focused on its goal or purpose, participates in the discussion and keeps it on track, and helps resolve conflicts
2. a **recorder** who takes notes on the discussion and summarizes suggestions and decisions
3. a **timekeeper** who keeps the discussion on schedule

STUDENT GUIDE **FM61**

COMMON CORE FOCUS

SL 1b Work with peers to promote civil, democratic discussions and decision-making, set clear goals and deadlines, and establish individual roles as needed.

Speaking and Listening: Interacting Constructively in Discussions

Remind students to treat others in the group as they would wish to be treated themselves and that a constructive group discussion is a democratic one.

Offer strategies to increase positive interaction during student discussions. For example:

- Adopt a respectful attitude: listen actively; disagree diplomatically. Ask thoughtful questions. Keep an open mind so you may modify, or even change your opinion, if a classmate offers a persuasive argument.

- Even if you have a strong opinion, remain calm and flexible in response to any challenges or disagreements from other members of the group. Seek common ground, rather than being defensive or aggressive.

- To avoid misunderstandings, listen actively and carefully to all group members, summarizing what you have heard to ensure comprehension, and asking clarifying questions as needed.

After the class has had a chance to read the entire lesson, hold a group discussion with the topic "group discussions in this class." The purpose of the discussion should be to set ground rules for all future group discussions in the class. Appoint a chairperson, recorder, and timekeeper for this discussion. Afterwards, ask students to reflect on how well the discussion went. Did they successfully establish a set of ground rules for all future class discussions?

Then, answer these questions:

1. What is the goal or purpose of the discussion? In other words, what should this discussion accomplish?
2. How much time does the group have for the discussion?
3. What rules will guide the discussion?

Review the discussion's purpose and timeframe to focus the group's attention. Establish rules for the discussion to ensure that it will be productive. In order to thrive, a discussion requires a civil atmosphere that encourages the flow of ideas.

- Everyone in the group should feel they have the right to speak, but not to interrupt each other. The rest of the group needs to listen actively to what each person says until it is another person's turn to speak. If time is short, consider establishing a reasonable limit on how long each participant may speak. The timekeeper can monitor the time.
- A peer discussion should inspire a lively argument, not an angry showdown.

Nothing kills the free exchange of ideas faster than someone who stubbornly or aggressively dominates a discussion. As a result, others in the group may not have the opportunity to speak, or may even feel bullied into agreeing with the speaker. If this appears to be happening, the chairperson should quickly step in to politely remind participants to maintain a civil and respectful tone.

Active listening is the process of receiving, interpreting, evaluating, and responding to a message. It is as important as expressing your own ideas clearly and articulately.

- Fully focus your attention on what your peers say. Even if you disagree with what is being said, continue to listen respectfully. The chairperson should remind members of the group to do this if the discussion becomes too heated.
- When it's your turn, first summarize, or restate, the previous speaker's position briefly in your own words to verify that you have understood him or her. Ask the previous speaker clarifying questions if needed or refer to the recorder for further verification.
- State your own views in an articulate, thoughtful way.
- Respond to any questions about or challenges to your point of view calmly.
- Be willing to support your views, but also keep an open mind about considering new ideas.

Constructive disagreements are essential to any group discussion. Without disagreements, people are not challenged by new ideas or contrasting viewpoints and cannot grow. If there is a difference of opinion, participants should speak calmly, ask questions respectfully, and remain open-minded. Nor must all disagreements be resolved. Participants can respectfully agree to disagree. When disagreements arise:

- Participants should not aggressively interrupt or talk over one another.
- Participants must present reasons or evidence to support their positions. If you say you like or dislike an idea, you must say why you do. It is not enough to simply say you agree or disagree.
- Seek common ground. See if participants who disagree with each other can compromise or agree on part of the issue.
- Watch the time. You may not be able to come to a full agreement, but disagreements can spiral out of control. If it does not look as if agreement or compromise can be reached, participants need to agree to disagree and move on.

Spotlight on Common Core

Speaking and Listening: Encouraging Fruitful Discussion

To encourage a fruitful, wide-ranging discussion, it is important to ask questions, as well as state opinions, that expand, or build upon, that discussion.

- Ask open-ended questions that do not have a yes or no answer.
  Closed: *Did America win the Revolutionary War?*
  Open-Ended: *Why did America win the Revolutionary War?*
- Play devil's advocate by offering an opposing viewpoint.
- Ask for additional examples or other forms of evidence to support a point.
- Combine different arguments to form a new option.

LEARN HOW Encouraging Discussion In the following discussion, students are debating whether people are essentially good—that is, can we trust most people to do the right thing?

COMMON CORE

SL 1c Propel conversations by posing and responding to questions that probe reasoning and evidence; ensure a hearing for a full range of positions on a topic or issue; clarify, verify, or challenge ideas and conclusions; and promote divergent and creative perspectives.

EFFECTIVE BEHAVIOR	WHAT IT LOOKS LIKE	
Support others' contributions.	*Alejandro believes that people are essentially good: we should trust others to do the right thing. He mentions examples of courageous behavior by ordinary people during natural disasters. Genna listens attentively to Alejandro. She has just come from a discussion of slavery in America in her social studies class. She wonders how people can believe in freedom, but enslave others at the same time.*	Alejandro shares his opinion, supporting it with evidence. Genna disagrees with Alejandro but still listens carefully.
State your own views thoughtfully.	*When Alejandro finishes speaking, Genna restates his points to make sure she understands his perspective. She comments, "I understand Alejandro's position because I, too, want to believe that people are essentially good. But there are many examples from history of people treating others with cruelty by exploiting them for their own gain. Americans believed in freedom, yet some kept slaves. How is it possible to be essentially good, but then do terrible things?"*	Genna verifies that she understands Alejandro's point. Then, she offers another viewpoint, supporting it with an example.
Summarize agreements and disagreements.	*Li speaks next. He summarizes Alejandro's and Genna's opposing views, and then offers an alternative. "It may look like there is a contradiction here. Either people are essentially good or they are not. But what if there is another way of looking at this? What if people are neither one nor the other, but capable of being both?"*	By combining both arguments, Li creates an alternative view of the issue. This expands the discussion.
Justify your views or consider new ones.	*Alejandro considers what Li has said. He prepares to offer more evidence that people are essentially good, and extends his argument to respond to Genna's point as well. Perhaps outside forces may affect essential goodness and turn people toward negative thoughts or actions. He decides to mention this when his turn comes up again.* *Li's point makes Genna think, too. She makes a note to ask the group, "If what Li says is true, how do we learn how to make those choices? What makes some people choose to do good, while others choose to do terrible things? And are there times when people may not really have a choice?" Her question will also expand the discussion.*	Alejandro and Genna consider Li's point. Li's alternative offers an opportunity to delve into the original question and expand their own arguments.

COMMON CORE FOCUS

SL 1c Propel conversations by posing and responding to questions that probe reasoning and evidence, ensure a hearing for a full range of positions on a topic or issue; clarify, verify, or challenge ideas or constructions, and promote divergent and creative perspectives.

Speaking and Listening: Encouraging Fruitful Discussion

Discuss the strategies for encouraging a fruitful discussion. Then, have a class discussion about a general, fairly accessible topic, for example, "What is the price of freedom?"

LEARN HOW Encouraging Discussion

Break students into small groups to practice having a constructive, interactive discussion. Ask students a general, open-ended question that will generate a range of opinions, such as, "If you knew a friend of yours had stolen something, what would you do about it?"

Remind each group to appoint a chairperson, recorder, and timekeeper. Ask students to commit to treating each other with respect during the discussion. Have another student take notes about how group members interact. The goal of the group is to summarize the group's response to the question in a timely fashion. After the discussion, review how the group handled the practical and interpersonal aspects of the discussion.

Throughout this book you will have opportunities to contribute to a variety of group discussions. Be sure to contribute effectively by understanding and modeling appropriate attitudes and behaviors. When you learn how to contribute effectively to group discussions, your voice is more likely to be heard, and your views are more likely to be understood. And your discussion will accomplish something positive for everyone.

College and Career Readiness Anchor Standards for Language

COMMON CORE STATE STANDARDS

CONVENTIONS OF STANDARD ENGLISH

1. Demonstrate command of the conventions of standard English grammar and usage when writing or speaking.

2. Demonstrate command of the conventions of standard English capitalization, punctuation, and spelling when writing.

KNOWLEDGE OF LANGUAGE

3. Apply knowledge of language to understand how language functions in different contexts, to make effective choices for meaning or style, and to comprehend more fully when reading or listening.

VOCABULARY ACQUISITION AND USE

4. Determine or clarify the meaning of unknown and multiple-meaning words and phrases by using context clues, analyzing meaningful word parts, and consulting general and specialized reference materials, as appropriate.

5. Demonstrate understanding of word relationships and nuances in word meanings.

6. Acquire and use accurately a range of general academic and domain-specific words and phrases sufficient for reading, writing, speaking, and listening at the college and career readiness level; demonstrate independence in gathering vocabulary knowledge when considering a word or phrase important to comprehension or expression.

Language Standards, Grades 11–12 Students

COMMON CORE STATE STANDARD	WHAT IT MEANS TO YOU
CONVENTIONS OF STANDARD ENGLISH	
1. Demonstrate command of the conventions of standard English grammar and usage when writing or speaking.	You will correctly use the conventions of English grammar and usage, including
a. Apply the understanding that usage is a matter of convention, can change over time, and is sometimes contested.	**a.** demonstrating that usage follows accepted standards and can change or be contested
b. Resolve issues of complex or contested usage, consulting references (e.g., *Merriam-Webster's Dictionary of English Usage, Garner's Modern American Usage*) as needed.	**b.** using references to resolve disagreements or uncertainty about usage
2. Demonstrate command of the conventions of standard English capitalization, punctuation, and spelling when writing.	You will correctly use the conventions of standard English capitalization, punctuation, and spelling, including
a. Observe hyphenation conventions.	**a.** hyphens
b. Spell correctly.	**b.** spelling
KNOWLEDGE OF LANGUAGE	
3. Apply knowledge of language to understand how language functions in different contexts, to make effective choices for meaning or style, and to comprehend more fully when reading or listening.	You will apply your knowledge of language in different contexts to guide choices in your own writing and speaking by
a. Vary syntax for effect, consulting references (e.g., Tufte's *Artful Sentences*) for guidance as needed; apply an understanding of syntax to the study of complex texts when reading.	**a.** using appropriate references for guidance to vary your syntax and to understand syntax in complex texts
VOCABULARY ACQUISITION AND USE	
4. Determine or clarify the meaning of unknown and multiple-meaning words and phrases based on grades 11–12 reading and content, choosing flexibly from a range of strategies.	You will understand the meaning of grade-level appropriate words and phrases by
a. Use context (e.g., the overall meaning of a sentence, paragraph, or text; a word's position or function in a sentence) as a clue to the meaning of a word or phrase.	**a.** using context clues
b. Identify and correctly use patterns of word changes that indicate different meanings or parts of speech (e.g., *conceive, conception, conceivable*).	**b.** applying various forms of words according to meaning or part of speech
c. Consult general and specialized reference materials (e.g., dictionaries, glossaries, thesauruses), both print and digital, to find the pronunciation of a word or determine or clarify its precise meaning, its part of speech, its etymology, or its standard usage.	**c.** using reference materials to determine and clarify word meaning, part of speech, etymology, and standard usage
d. Verify the preliminary determination of the meaning of a word or phrase (e.g., by checking the inferred meaning in context or in a dictionary).	**d.** inferring and verifying the meanings of words in context

COMMON CORE STATE STANDARD	WHAT IT MEANS TO YOU
5. Demonstrate understanding of figurative language, word relationships, and nuances in word meanings. a. Interpret figures of speech (e.g., hyperbole, paradox) in context and analyze their role in the text. b. Analyze nuances in the meaning of words with similar denotations.	You will understand figurative language, word relationships, and slight differences in word meanings by a. interpreting figures of speech in context b. analyzing slight differences in the meanings of similar words
6. Acquire and use accurately general academic and domain-specific words and phrases, sufficient for reading, writing, speaking, and listening at the college and career readiness level; demonstrate independence in gathering vocabulary knowledge when considering a word or phrase important to comprehension or expression.	You will develop and use a range of vocabulary at the college and career readiness level and will demonstrate that you can successfully acquire new vocabulary independently.

COMMON CORE FOCUS

L 1a Apply the understanding that usage is a matter of convention, can change over time, and is sometimes contested. **L 1b** Resolve issues of complex or contested usage, consulting references (e.g., *Merriam-Webster's Dictionary of English Usage, Garner's Modern American Usage*) as needed.

Language: Understanding and Resolving Preferred Usage

Remind students that *usage* refers to the rules and conventions that govern words. Students should recognize, for example, that words that may be common in everyday, informal speech or writing may not be correct in more formal contexts. It is fine to answer a friend's request with "Okay!" It is not correct to use "okay" in a business letter or school essay.

LEARN HOW **Understanding Usage** Tell students that even professional writers have questions about correct usage, especially if two words look or sound similar.

Spotlight on Common Core

COMMON CORE

L 1a Apply the understanding that usage is a matter of convention, can change over time, and is sometimes contested. **L 1b** Resolve issues of complex or contested usage, consulting references (e.g., *Merriam-Webster's Dictionary of English Usage, Garner's Modern American Usage*) as needed.

Language: Understanding and Resolving Preferred Usage

When you understand correct usage, you recognize the accepted rules, or conventions, about words. Some words are incorrect (*ain't*) under any circumstances in academic or business contexts. Other words may be used informally, but are not acceptable for formal writing (*okay*). Still others look similar, but are actually different parts of speech (*loose* and *lose*). Even professional writers are sometimes unsure which word is the correct choice. *A lot* or *alot*? *Toward* or *towards*? *Affect* or *effect*?

Language changes over time, and inevitably, so does usage, often in response to changes in cultural beliefs. The word *mankind* has recently fallen out of favor. Writers once used this term to refer to all human beings. However, because it is a term that excludes women as human beings, it is now considered inappropriate. Writers should avoid using this term in favor of more neutral, inclusive words such as *humans, human beings,* or *people*.

LEARN HOW **Understanding Usage** *Lose* and *loose* or *fewer* and *less* are examples of words that frequently confuse writers because they look or sound alike or have similar meanings. You may consult a dictionary of English usage to learn how to use these words correctly. Here are some examples of commonly confused words. See page R79 of this book for an extended list.

Words	Definitions	Examples
lose/loose	*Lose* means "to misplace or fail to find." *Loose* means "free, not restrained."	I hope we don't **lose** any of the horses in the pasture. Who turned the horses **loose?**
less/fewer	*Less* refers to bulk quantity. *Fewer* refers to the number of separate, countable units.	We have **less** literature and **fewer** selections in this year's curriculum.

In some cases, the English language is so changeable that even experts do not fully agree about correct usage. For example, many experts believe that the words *and, also,* or *but* should never be used to begin a sentence. But a clear majority of a group of usage experts polled by *The American Heritage Dictionary* thought that it is acceptable to begin sentences with these words. Many respected publications, such as *The New York Times,* often use *and, also,* and *but* to begin sentences. The important point to remember is that what is considered acceptable usage can change, because language and our attitudes about it evolve over time.

LEARN HOW Using References to Resolve Usage You may encounter instances of usage that are complex or that you suspect may be contested. When in doubt about how to use a word, it is better to consult an authoritative reference book than make an uneducated guess. Authoritative reference books gather current findings of language experts about correct usage. Dependable reference books include *Merriam-Webster's Dictionary of English Usage, Garner's Modern American Usage,* and *The American Heritage Book of English Usage.* As in a dictionary, words are arranged alphabetically in these reference works. In some cases, even language experts may not agree on correct usage, but they usually have a preference or majority opinion about it. Make sure you read the information in the reference book carefully to determine if this is the case. Your safest bet as a writer is to go with a word's preferred usage, particularly if you are writing in a school or business context.

A common dilemma is identifying the correct form of a word. In some cases, you will find that one form is clearly correct, while the other is not. In other cases, the answer is not as clear or may even be disputed. Here are some examples.

1. Which version is correct: *alot* or *a lot?*
 • In my heart, I knew my sister cared about me *alot.*
 • In my heart, I knew my sister cared about me *a lot.*

According to *Merriam-Webster's Dictionary of English Usage, alot* is never correct. *A lot* is the only correct form. The second sentence is correct.

2. Which version is correct: *toward* or *towards?*
 • Jamie held out her hand in greeting *toward* Kaylee.
 • Jamie held out her hand in greeting *towards* Kaylee.

Experts consider the two words to be interchangeable; however, *toward* is more commonly used in American English, while *towards* is used in British English. The first sentence is the better choice for students writing in American English.

Direct students to the chart showing the correct usage of *lose* versus *loose* and *less* versus *fewer.* Ask students what dictates the correct usage of these terms. Students should notice that these words have different meanings that apply in different contexts.

Ask students to write additional sentences demonstrating the incorrect *and* correct usage of *lose* and *loose,* and *less* and *fewer* based on this information.

LEARN HOW Using References to Resolve Usage Students need to know how to research information about usage themselves. A standard dictionary may help, but authoritative reference works such as *Merriam-Webster's Dictionary of English Usage, Garner's Modern American Usage,* or *The American Heritage Book of English Usage* that focus solely on usage are the most reliable sources of information.

Copy or project a page from an authoritative reference book containing an entry for *all ready* and *already* or a similarly confusing pair of words. (See a full list of easily confused words on page R79.)

Break students into small groups. Assign each group a challenging word or word pair. Have the groups research the correct, or preferred, usage of the word or words in a usage dictionary. Students should then write sentences illustrating this correct and incorrect usage, using the four example sentences as models.

COMMON CORE FOCUS

L 3a Vary syntax for effect, consulting references (e.g., Tufte's *Artful Sentences*) for guidance as needed; apply an understanding of syntax to the study of complex texts when reading.

Language: Varying Syntax for Effect

Make sure students understand that varying syntax is not just a technical change. It may dramatically affect the impact of a writer's words on a reader.

LEARN HOW Varying Syntax Remind students of the definition of **syntax:** the arrangement of words in phrases, clauses, and sentences.

In addition, some words look so similar that it is hard to know which one to use in what context.

3. Which is the correct word to use: *affect* or *effect*?
   - Emily Dickinson's poems had a profound **affect/effect** on generations of poets.
   - Emily Dickinson's poems have profoundly **affected/effected** generations of poets.

According to usage experts, *effect* is a noun (the result of something) and *affect* is a verb (to cause something to happen). The word's role in the sentence as a noun or verb tells you which version to use. In the first sentence, *effect* is correct because it is used as a noun. In the second sentence, *affected* is correct because it is used as a verb.

4. Finally, *impact* is a word whose correct usage has changed over time. Is it correct to use it today as a noun or a verb?
   - The *impact* of the American Revolution was felt around the world. (used as a noun)
   - The health of the economy *impacts* all Americans. (used as a verb)

Experts often struggle with this question. In the past, using *impact* as a noun, not as a verb, was the sole correct usage. However, experts admit that in the past decade, *impact* appears so frequently as a verb that they no longer consider its use as such to be incorrect. However, they still prefer that *impact* be used sparingly as a verb, if at all.

As you write, be sure to employ correct usage. When in doubt, consult an authoritative reference source for information about preferred usage.

Spotlight on Common Core

COMMON CORE L 3a Vary syntax for effect, consulting references (e.g., Tufte's *Artful Sentences*) for guidance as needed; apply an understanding of syntax to the study of complex texts when reading.

Language: Varying Syntax for Effect

Syntax is the arrangement of words in phrases, clauses, and sentences. Writers want to engage their readers, but repeatedly using the same wording or sentence structure drains prose of vitality and interest. Varying syntax is the best way to create a more dynamic, engaging verbal rhythm, or flow, in your writing. Varying syntax also allows you to emphasize certain ideas or parts of a sentence to dramatic effect or to include additional information. Here are two strategies you can use to vary syntax:

1. Vary sentence structure by rearranging or adding words to individual sentences or combining multiple sentences.
2. Vary sentence lengths within paragraphs by alternating long and short sentences.

LEARN HOW Varying Syntax Varying words, phrases, and clauses in a sentence or across sentences may create a more dynamic rhythm. As you vary syntax, however, remember that your writing must remain appropriate to your task, purpose, and audience. Each sentence must be clear and coherent. For additional options about how to vary syntax, you may consult a reference (such as Virginia Tufte's *Artful Sentences: Syntax as Style*).

Here are some examples of how to revise sentence structure to vary syntax. Note how each revision changes the effect of these sentences on the reader.

The painting sold at auction. There was fierce bidding. It set a world record.

Revision to Vary Syntax	Effect
The painting sold at auction after fierce bidding that set a world record.	Improved rhythm
Setting a world record, the painting sold at auction after fierce bidding.	Improved rhythm; emphasizes world record; more dramatic
After fierce bidding, the painting sold at auction, setting a world record.	Improved rhythm; emphasizes fierce bidding; more dramatic
Against expectations, the painting sold at auction after fierce bidding, and set a world record.	Improved rhythm; more dramatic; adds information

You may also vary syntax for emphasis by varying sentence length. Read the paragraph below from "Letter from Birmingham Jail" by Martin Luther King, Jr.

. . . Let us consider a more concrete example of just and unjust laws. An unjust law is a code that a numerical or power majority group compels a minority group to obey but does not make binding on itself. This is *difference* made legal. By the same token, a just law is a code that a majority compels a minority to follow and that it is willing to follow itself. This is *sameness* made legal.

The two longest sentences in the paragraph explain unjust and just laws. King follows each long sentence with a dramatic short sentence: unjust laws do not consider people as equals ("This is *difference* made legal"), while just laws do ("This is *sameness* made legal"). These short sentences convey King's strong belief in his ideas and emphasize the contrast he makes between just and unjust laws.

In your own writing, be sure to vary syntax to affect your readers. As you analyze the texts in this book, notice how authors vary syntax to affect you as a reader.

Demonstrate how writers vary syntax. First, have a volunteer read the three sample sentences aloud so the class can hear how flat and lifeless they sound *before* revision. Then, write the first revision of the sentences from the chart on the board. Have a volunteer read it aloud. Next, ask students to identify how the writer changed the sentence to improve its rhythm. Students should point out that the writer combined all three sentences, adding *after* (to form an adverb clause) and *that* (to form an adjective clause).

Repeat this process with the other three revisions in the chart. You may break the class into small groups to identify the revisions made to each of the three sentences to vary their syntax for emphasis, greater drama, and additional information. Next, discuss how varying sentence lengths may also improve the effectiveness of the writer's message. Remind students that emphasis is a way to draw the reader's attention to a part of the text the writer considers especially important or memorable.

Exploring American Literature

INTRODUCING
THE ESSENTIALS

- **Text Analysis Workshop**
- **Academic Vocabulary Workshop**
- **Writing Process Workshop**

IN CONGRESS, JULY

A DECLARAT

BY THE REPRESENTATIVES OF

UNITED STATES OF AM

IN GENERAL CONGRESS ASSE

WHEN in the Course of human Events, it becomes necessary for one People to dissolve the Politi
with another, and to assume among the Powers of the Earth, the separate and equal Station to
Nature's God entitle them, a decent Respect to the Opinions of Mankind requires that they should
to the Separation.

We hold these Truths to be self-evident, that all Men are created equal, that they are e
unalienable Rights, that among these are Life, Liberty, and the Pursuit of Happiness—That to
instituted among Men, deriving their just Powers from the Consent of the Governed, that whenever any Form of Go
Ends, it is the Right of the People to alter or to abolish it, and to institute new Government, laying its Foundati
its Powers in such Form, as to them shall seem most likely to effect their Safety and Happiness. Prudence, indeed, w
tablished should not be changed for light and transient Causes; and accordingly all Experience hath shewn, that Mank
Evils are sufferable, than to right themselves by abolishing the Forms to which they are accustomed. But when a long T
ing invariably the same Object, evinces a Design to reduce them under absolute Despotism, it is their Right, it is their D
and to provide new Guards for their future Security. Such has been the patient Sufferance of these Colonies; and such
them to alter their former Systems of Government. The History of the present King of Great-Britain is a History of
having in direct Object the Establishment of an absolute Tyranny over these States. To prove this, let Facts be submitted t
He has refused his Assent to Laws, the most wholesome and necessary for the public Good.

About the Art The images on this spread are, clockwise from right, a photograph of civil rights activist Martin Luther King Jr. (see page 1205); a still from director Nicholas Hytner's 1996 film adaptation of Arthur Miller's *The Crucible,* with Winona Ryder and Daniel Day-Lewis (see page 153); an excerpt from the Declaration of Independence, July 4, 1776; a collage of American citizens by Jane Sterrett; poet Emily Dickinson (see page 546); *Kindred Spirits,* 1849, a painting by Asher Durand (see page 308).

For help using this Introductory Unit, see

R RESOURCE MANAGER—Introductory Unit pp. I-1–I-5

Insights and Perspectives

The introductory unit provides an overview of the major movements in American literature, essential strategies for literary criticism, and the writing process that students will study in later units.

Begin by reading aloud the introduction, **Insights and Perspectives.** Then read aloud the topics on pages 2 and 3 and the paragraphs that follow them. Use these notes to prompt exploration of the ideas.

Explore BIG IDEAS

Challenge students to give examples of "the American dream." Who seems to be achieving the American dream in today's generations? In what ways? Encourage students to cite examples of the ways in which previous generations of Americans sought out the dream.

Build CULTURAL LITERACY

Call on volunteers to answer the two questions in the paragraph. Supplement students' ideas with this information:

- Mark Twain, born Samuel Clemens in 1835, secured his place as a great American novelist with works such as *The Adventures of Tom Sawyer* and *The Adventures of Huckleberry Finn.*

- The witch trials of 1692 in Salem, Massachusetts, comprise the setting of *The Crucible,* a 1953 play by Arthur Miller. The drama can be considered a work of courage because it warns against mass hysteria and injustice, issues that Miller himself had to confront during the McCarthy era.

About the Art *The Mayflower in Plymouth Harbor* (1882), oil painting by William Formby Halsall (see page 22); photograph of author Mark Twain (see page 658).

Insights and Perspectives

America's literature comes from all of us and belongs to everyone. It began with the lore of the Native Americans, then appeared in the journals of settlers, the letters of Civil War soldiers, and the tales of Mark Twain. Fast forward another century, and it lives in the books of John Steinbeck and shines from the poems of Gwendolyn Brooks.

Why does American literature matter? Not only does it keep us connected to the past, but it also gives us insights into the events and issues that challenge the nation today. The literature in this book can help you . . .

Explore BIG IDEAS

Why do we explore new horizons? What is the American dream? Today's generations aren't the first to grapple with questions about freedom, progress, exploration, and injustice. Some ideas and issues are timeless, as you'll discover when you read the dramatic accounts of early explorers and F. Scott Fitzgerald's fiction.

Build CULTURAL LITERACY

There are some questions that all Americans should be able to answer. In the area of American literature, such questions include: Who was Mark Twain? Why was *The Crucible* a work of great courage? By reading American literature, you become aware of the pioneering authors and literary milestones that are a part of the American heritage.

Introductory Unit Resources

See resources on the **Teacher One Stop DVD-ROM** *and on* **thinkcentral.com**.

R **RESOURCE MANAGER INTRODUCTORY UNIT**
Lesson at a Glance and Note-Taking, pp. I-1– I-5

 BEST PRACTICES TOOLKIT
Read Aloud / Think Aloud p. A34
Story Map p. D14

TECHNOLOGY
- Teacher One Stop DVD-ROM
- Student One Stop DVD-ROM
- Write*Smart* CD-ROM
- GrammarNotes DVD-ROM

Connect HISTORY and Literature

Whether it's the Gettysburg Address or the poetry of the Harlem Renaissance, all works of American literature are products of the events and ideas that inspired their authors. By examining history and literature together, you can gain a deeper understanding of how the country changed over the centuries and what makes its people unique.

Appreciate a LEGACY

Trailblazers in their times, Margaret Fuller and Martin Luther King Jr. fought for equal rights—a fight that still continues. Learning about the great writers, thinkers, and ideas of the past helps you better appreciate how we all continue to build on what we learned from them.

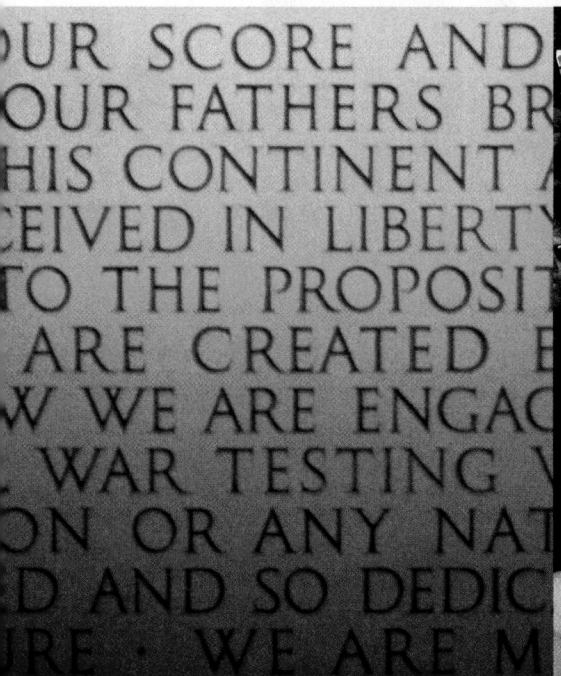

Connect HISTORY and Literature

Ask students to make connections between literature and history, using the Gettysburg Address and the poetry of the Harlem Renaissance as examples. *Possible answer:* *President Lincoln delivered his Gettysburg Address in 1863 at Gettysburg, Pennsylvania, to commemorate a Civil War battle in which both sides suffered staggering losses. Harlem, a New York City neighborhood, became the cultural center of African-American life after black farmers and sharecroppers migrated to the urban North following the Civil War. In what became known as the Harlem Renaissance, African-American artists produced new forms of expression by drawing on their own cultural resources.*

Appreciate a LEGACY

Explore with students the term *legacy:* "something, often of value, handed down from a previous generation." Open the discussion by asking students to recall the issues for which Margaret Fuller and Martin Luther King Jr. fought. *Possible answer:* *As an author, public speaker, journalist, and key figure in the transcendentalist movement, Margaret Fuller (1810–1850) fought to make women equal members of society. Until his assassination in 1968, Martin Luther King Jr. led the civil rights movement of the 1960s. What legacy followed from the struggles of Fuller and King?*

About the Art Excerpt from President Abraham Lincoln's Gettysburg Address, November 19, 1863 (see page 587); peaceful protesters in the 1960s civil rights movement (see page 316).

RL 1 Cite strong and thorough textual evidence to support analysis of what the text says explicitly as well as inferences drawn from the text, including determining where the text leaves matters uncertain. **RL 3** Analyze the impact of the author's choices regarding how to develop and relate elements of a story. **RL 9** Demonstrate knowledge of eighteenth-, nineteenth-, and early-twentieth-century works of American literature. **RI 9** Analyze foundational U.S. documents of historical and literary significance for their themes, purposes, and rhetorical features. **L 3** Apply knowledge of language to make effective choices for meaning or style. **L 4a** Use context as a clue to the meaning of a word. **L 4c** Consult reference materials to find the pronunciation of a word or determine or clarify its precise meaning, its part of speech, its etymology, or its standard usage.

Literature and Nonfiction in Context

The timeline on pages 4 and 5 provides a chronological overview of the literary movements the students will be studying this year.

Read aloud the introductory paragraph. Ask students to suggest ways in which recent or modern events have shaped contemporary literature. For example, how has the Internet influenced literary forms? Has technology been the subject of recent literary works that students have read? What major events do they think may affect the attitudes of contemporary writers?

READING SKILL

■ READ A TIMELINE

Call on volunteers to identify the three horizontal sections of the timeline:

- *Top:* Names, dates, and authors of major U.S. literary movements
- *Middle:* Picture of a representative person, place, or event in the time period
- *Bottom:* Key historical events that occurred during the same periods as the literary movements

Explain that by scanning down the vertical columns of the timeline, students can see the major authors and events of any single period.

Text Analysis Workshop

Literature and Nonfiction in Context

The growth of the Internet, the discovery of a new medical treatment, a declaration of war, a decision of the Supreme Court—consider how events like these affect your attitudes, your outlook, your politics. They shape the attitudes of writers as well, who then express their ideas in stories, poems, speeches, blogs, and public documents. In the same way, the writing of every time period reflects its unique historical context. By reading it, you can transport yourself back through time and gain perspective on people and events you could never otherwise experience.

COMMON CORE

Included in this workshop:
RL 1, RL 3, RL 9, RI 9, L 3, L 4a, L 4c

LITERARY MOVEMENTS IN CONTEXT

NATIVE AMERICAN EXPERIENCE 1200 B.C.–1600	PURITAN AGE/ COLONIAL PERIOD 1600–1700	REVOLUTIONARY PERIOD/AGE OF REASON 1750–1800	ROMANTICISM/ AMERICAN GOTHIC 1800–1855	TRANSCENDENTALISM 1840–1860
• Sioux • Okanogan • Iroquois • Kiowa	• William Bradford • Anne Bradstreet • Edward Taylor	• Ben Franklin • Thomas Jefferson • Thomas Paine	• Henry Wadsworth Longfellow • Edgar Allan Poe	• Ralph Waldo Emerson • Henry David Thoreau • Margaret Fuller

1200 B.C.–1600 Native American cultures flourish. **1492** Christopher Columbus lands in the Bahamas.	**1607** British settlers establish colony in Jamestown, Virginia. **1692** Witch trials take place in Salem, Massachussetts.	**1776** American colonies declare independence. **1788** U.S. Constitution is ratified.	**1803** Louisiana Purchase doubles the country's size. **1808** United States bans slave trade. **1812** War of 1812 spurs Industrial Revolution.	**1846** Mexican-American War begins. **1848** Gold discoveries in California lead to first gold rush. **1857** Supreme Court's Dred Scott decision denies slaves basic rights.

DIFFERENTIATED INSTRUCTION

FOR STRUGGLING READERS

Understanding a Timeline Model reading the timeline by using the column *Modernism*. Run your finger down the column while identifying the information in each row. Then provide student practice by using the third column to elicit information about the Revolutionary period or Age of Reason:

- What literary movement was occurring from 1750 to 1800? *Answer:* The Age of Reason

- What chief American authors expressed their views during this period? *Answer: Ben Franklin, Thomas Jefferson, Thomas Paine*

- What major political event happened in 1788? *Answer: The U.S. Constitution was ratified.*

Literary Movements

Think about how certain types of music reflect the times in which they were written. Some folk songs, for example, can remind listeners of an earlier time of protest. Similarly, the literature of each historical period has a unique flavor. Subject matter, style, form, and attitude all combine to create a **literary movement,** such as **realism** or **regionalism.** While not all writers fit neatly into specific categories, it is still helpful to know the major movements that have defined the nation's literature. By studying these movements in context, you can see not only the overlap between them, but also better appreciate the writers and works from particular time periods.

REALISM 1855–1900	REGIONALISM/ NATURALISM 1870–1910	MODERNISM 1910–1945	HARLEM RENAISSANCE 1920–1930	CONTEMPORARY LITERATURE 1940–PRESENT
• Stephen Crane • Ambrose Bierce	• Mark Twain • Willa Cather • Jack London	• T. S. Eliot • Ernest Hemingway • Ezra Pound	• Langston Hughes • Zora Neale Hurston • Countee Cullen	• Kurt Vonnegut Jr. • John Steinbeck • Rita Dove • Amy Tan

1861–1865 North and South fight in Civil War. **1865** 13th Amendment abolishes slavery. **1879** Thomas Edison invents the light bulb.	**1889** Oklahoma is opened for settlement, triggering a land rush. **1903** Wright brothers achieve first airplane flight.	**1917** United States enters World War I. **1920** 19th Amendment is passed, giving women the right to vote.	**1919** Race riots erupt in 25 American cities. **1929** The Wall Street stock market crashes and the Great Depression begins.	**1941** Attack on Pearl Harbor brings U.S. into World War II. **1965** U.S. enters Vietnam War. **2001** Terrorists attack U.S. cities. **2009** Barack Obama becomes first African American U.S. president.

Literary Movements

Read aloud and discuss the paragraph on page 5. Then suggest a song that was widely popular five or more years ago, and invite a volunteer to sing a few bars. Brainstorm with students what memories the song inspires. Can they recall what was happening in the nation or the world at large at that time? Was the mood of the times reflected in the music? Encourage volunteers to provide other examples of how art is influenced by political and social events of the time.

QUESTIONS

Ask students to study the literary timeline to answer these questions:

1. Who were key authors of the Harlem Renaissance? **Answer:** *Langston Hughes, Zora Neale Hurston, Countee Cullen*

2. Did major literary movements overlap one another? Give examples. **Possible answer:** *Yes. Examples of overlapping movements are romanticism (1800–1855) and transcendentalism (1840–1860), and transcendentalism and realism (1855–1900).*

3. What historical events influenced the trend of realism in literature? **Possible answer:** *The crisis of the Civil War and the turmoil of its aftermath caused authors to turn their attention to starkly realistic issues. The new Industrial Age that followed Edison's invention of the light bulb also generated a spirit of realism.*

FOR STRUGGLING READERS

Note Taking For students who need help with note-taking, hand out the copy master. After discussing **Literary Movements** with students, have them complete the copy master. Follow this procedure for the sections of the Literary Essentials Workshop beginning on pages 6 and 9.

R RESOURCE MANAGER—Copy Master
Note Taking pp. I-2, I-3

Using Critical Lenses

Determine Readiness Discuss the concepts on the page with students. Then read aloud these observations of literature and ask students to identify what critical lens the writer used to examine the subjects:

- The myth "The World on the Turtle's Back" expresses the respect that the Iroquois have for the balance of nature. (*cultural lens*)

- After reading Edgar Allan Poe's haunting tale "The Masque of the Red Death," one is not surprised to learn that Poe himself experienced a life marked by pain and loss. (*biographical lens*)

- Washington Irving's use of sensory language contributes to the images of darkness and decay in "The Devil and Tom Walker." (*literary lens*)

- The Declaration of Independence, written by Thomas Jefferson in 1776, expressed the ideals of freedom and equality for which the American Revolution was fought. (*historical lens*)

Discuss and Review Divide students into small groups and ask them to select a literary work of their choice or one of these works: a Ray Bradbury science fiction story, a short story by O. Henry, "The Raven" by Edgar Allan Poe, or *The Grapes of Wrath* by John Steinbeck. Ask students to make observations of the literature using at least two different critical lenses. Afterwards, invite each group to share their observations with the class.

Using Critical Lenses

Have you ever looked through a prism or camera lens and seen the world in an entirely new way? Critical lenses, or viewpoints from which to consider something, can affect your perception—and your reading—in a similar manner. They allow you to notice details you might otherwise have missed, and can lead you to unexpected insights about a writer and his or her work. Use the following lenses, as well as others you might develop, to see beyond your own personal perspective.

THE LENSES	QUESTIONS TO ASK	
LITERARY LENS The literary lens is the one you're used to using with literature. It focuses your attention on the author's style and on such elements as plot, setting, character, and theme.	• What is unique about this author's style? • How do the plot, characters, and setting help to communicate the author's message? • How are language and imagery used to support the themes?	
HISTORICAL AND CULTURAL LENSES Historical and cultural lenses help you consider how elements of history and culture may have influenced the author and the writing.	• What was going on in the country at the time this work was written? • What attitudes, trends, and priorities characterized the times? • How are those events and attitudes, and the author's reactions to them, reflected in the writing?	
BIOGRAPHICAL LENS The biographical lens draws you into the arena of an author's personal life. By considering a writer's heritage, experiences, and economic circumstances, you are able to "read into" a piece of literature with far more insight.	• What were some key events and people in the author's life? • What were his or her social and economic circumstances? • Did culture and heritage play a strong role in shaping the author's attitudes?	
OTHER LENSES • psychological • social • political • philosophical/moral	• What motivations might be influencing a character's behavior? (psychological) • Are the characters' choices, behavior, and actions ethical and honest? (philosophical/moral)	

DIFFERENTIATED INSTRUCTION

FOR ENGLISH LANGUAGE LEARNERS

Vocabulary Support Establish the concept of using different lenses for different reasons and outcomes by asking students how the lenses of sunglasses, binoculars, and microscopes change the view of the outside world and why these lenses are used.

MODEL: CRITICAL LENSES

The Great Gatsby is a novel set in the 1920s. World War I had just ended, and the country was embarking on a time of great self-indulgence, eager to forget what it had just experienced. In this scene, the narrator describes an outing with his friendly but mysterious neighbor, Jay Gatsby. Read the passage twice—with and without lenses.

from
The **Great** Gatsby

Novel by **F. Scott Fitzgerald**

At nine o'clock, one morning late in July, Gatsby's gorgeous car lurched up the rocky drive to my door and gave out a burst of melody from its three-noted horn. It was the first time he had called on me, though I had gone to two of his parties, mounted in his hydroplane, and, at his urgent invitation, made
5   frequent use of his beach.

"Good morning, old sport. You're having lunch with me today and I thought we'd ride up together."

He was balancing himself on the running board of his car with that resourcefulness of movement that is so peculiarly American—that comes,
10   I suppose, with the absence of lifting work or rigid sitting in youth and, even more, with the formless grace of our nervous, sporadic games. This quality was continually breaking through his punctilious manner in the shape of restlessness. He was never quite still; there was always a tapping foot somewhere or the impatient opening and closing of a hand.
15   He saw me looking with admiration at his car.

"It's pretty, isn't it, old sport!" He jumped off to give me a better view. "Haven't you ever seen it before?"

I'd seen it. Everybody had seen it. It was a rich cream color, bright with nickel, swollen here and there in its monstrous length with triumphant hat-
20   boxes and supper-boxes and tool-boxes, and terraced with a labyrinth of wind-shields that mirrored a dozen suns. Sitting down behind many layers of glass in a sort of green leather conservatory, we started to town.

I had talked with him perhaps half a dozen times in the past month and found, to my disappointment, that he had little to say. So my first impression,
25   that he was a person of some undefined consequence, had gradually faded and he had become simply the proprietor of an elaborate road-house next door.

And then came that disconcerting ride. We hadn't reached West Egg Village before Gatsby began leaving his elegant sentences unfinished and slapping himself indecisively on the knee of his caramel-colored suit.
30   "Look here, old sport," he broke out surprisingly, "what's your opinion of me, anyhow?"

Close Read

1. **Literary Lens** What do the details in lines 1–5 tell you about Gatsby and his relationship with the narrator?

2. **Cultural Lens** Reread the boxed text. What is the narrator's attitude toward Americans of this time period? What reality might this attitude be reflecting?

3. **Psychological Lens** Private cars were not common in the 1920s. Why might Gatsby not only want to own a car, but also insist on such a luxurious one?

MODEL: CRITICAL LENSES

Close Read

Possible answers:

1. *Lines 1–5 reveal that Gatsby is a wealthy man who enjoys displaying and sharing his status and privilege. The text says, "It was the first time [Gatsby] had called on me," which suggests that Gatsby and the narrator are not close friends. Some readers may infer that Gatsby, in addition to amassing material possessions, may "collect" acquaintances and followers. Perhaps the narrator is one of them.*

2. *The narrator describes Gatsby's "resourcefulness of movement" as a result of leading a carefree, charmed life. The narrator seems to be suggesting that young Americans in this time period have grown up without having had to abide by strict rules or do much hard work. Perhaps this reflects society's attitude toward privileged youth after World War I.*

3. *Gatsby probably wants to own a luxurious car to attract the admiration of friends and acquaintances. For Gatsby, the car may also serve as a status symbol of wealth and privilege. The narrator says, "I'd seen it. Everybody had seen it," which suggests just how much attention the car gets. Perhaps Gatsby is an insecure person who measures his self-worth in material possessions.*

FOR ENGLISH LANGUAGE LEARNERS
Vocabulary: Cognates Share or elicit the Spanish cognates for these words. Invite students who speak other Latin-based languages to identify the cognates in their own languages and to share them with other students.

- lens *(lente)*
- psychology *(psicología)*
- cultural *(cultural)*
- literary *(literario)*

Possible answers:

4. *Gatsby informs the narrator that he is the son of wealthy people from the Middle West, that his family is dead, and that, like his ancestors, he was educated at Oxford. These "facts" point to the cultural value placed on wealth and education, especially education in prestigious schools.*

5. *Fitzgerald uses these techniques to develop Gatsby as a character who is mysterious, friendly, insecure, impatient, materialistic, and eager to impress:*

   - *describes Gatsby's movements and clothing (lines 8–9, 13–14, 28–29)*
   - *includes Gatsby's speech and actions (lines 6–7, 34–42)*
   - *provides the narrator's reactions to and statements about Gatsby (lines 23–26, 46–47)*

Close Read

Possible answers:

1. *After Fitzgerald achieved success as a writer, he and his wife "embarked on a flamboyant, high-spending life," much like Gatsby's. Fitzgerald's own pursuit of success may have given him insight into a person who is insecure, materialistic, and eager to impress.*

2. *Like Gatsby, Fitzgerald pursued and valued a life of "wealth and privilege." Still, Fitzgerald would probably resist categorizing himself with Gatsby. Gatsby claimed that his wealth was inherited, whereas Fitzgerald earned his own wealth through work, talent, and perseverance. In parts of the excerpt, Fitzgerald takes on a gently amused, slightly mocking tone toward Gatsby's words and actions. The narrator thinks Gatsby has "little to say" and that he is not as well-educated as he claims to be.*

A little overwhelmed, I began the generalized evasions which that question deserves.

"Well, I'm going to tell you something about my life," he interrupted.
35 "I don't want you to get a wrong idea of me from all these stories you hear."

So he was aware of the bizarre accusations that flavored conversation in his halls.

"I'll tell you God's truth." His right hand suddenly ordered divine retribution to stand by. "I am the son of some wealthy people in the
40 Middle West—all dead now. I was brought up in America but educated at Oxford, because all my ancestors have been educated there for many years. It is a family tradition."

He looked at me sideways—and I knew why Jordan Baker had believed he was lying. He hurried the phrase "educated at Oxford," or swallowed it, or
45 choked on it, as though it had bothered him before. And with this doubt, his whole statement fell to pieces, and I wondered if there wasn't something a little sinister about him, after all.

"What part of the Middle West?" I inquired casually.

"San Francisco."
50 "I see."

Close Read

4. **Cultural Lens** What "facts" about himself and his background does Gatsby provide? What does this tell you about the cultural values of the time?

5. **Literary Lens** What techniques has Fitzgerald used in this excerpt to create the intriguing character of Jay Gatsby?

Now read the biographical information about F. Scott Fitzgerald and answer the questions. Refer back to the excerpt from *The Great Gatsby* as needed.

F. Scott Fitzgerald

Born in 1896 of southern and Irish heritage, Francis Scott Key Fitzgerald began writing in his early teens. Encouraged by a mentor at school, Fitzgerald pursued
5 his dream of becoming a writer, quickly neglecting his studies in the process. He served in the army during World War I, and convinced he was going to die, dashed off an autobiographical novel. A few years—and
10 several revisions—later, he sold his novel, titled *Tender Is the Night,* and became an overnight success. One week after the novel's publication, Fitzgerald married a southern belle, Zelda Sayre. He and his wife embarked on a flamboyant, high-spending life, although their extravagance and
15 Zelda's illnesses kept Fitzgerald constantly in debt. Fitzgerald died in 1940, impoverished, after spending his lifetime in pursuit of wealth and privilege.

Close Read

1. **Biographical Lens** How might Fitzgerald's own experiences have influenced his characterization of Gatsby?

2. **Biographical Lens** What similarities do you see between Fitzgerald's and Gatsby's values? What was Fitzgerald's attitude toward these values? Why do you think so?

Literature and Nonfiction Strategies

 Record your observations in your **Reader/Writer Notebook.**

❶ Understand Context

Texts of all types are shaped by different cultural and historical contexts. In addition to essays and memoirs, American nonfiction includes primary sources, such as historical accounts, letters, and journals. To understand context as you read these texts, ask yourself the following questions:

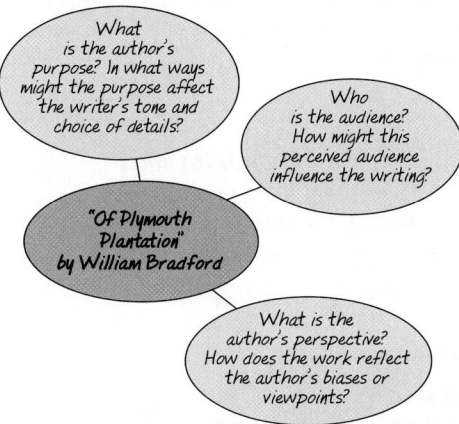

What is the author's purpose? In what ways might the purpose affect the writer's tone and choice of details?

Who is the audience? How might this perceived audience influence the writing?

"Of Plymouth Plantation" by William Bradford

What is the author's perspective? How does the work reflect the author's biases or viewpoints?

❷ Clarify Meaning

When you read American literature and nonfiction, you will encounter unfamiliar language and difficult sentence structures. Use these strategies and tips to help unlock the meaning of challenging texts.

- **Break Down Sentences** Break down complicated sentences by first locating the sentence's main subject and verb. Then, identify objects, modifiers, and phrases. Try restating the sentences more simply, rearranging word order if necessary.

- **Use Context Clues** A word's context—the words and sentences that surround it—often gives clues to the word's meaning. Dialects, for example, have their own rules of grammar and pronunciation, which you can figure out from context clues.

- **Consult References** When you encounter an unfamiliar word or allusion, check the vocabulary definitions and footnotes provided in this book or look the word up in a print or digital reference source.

❸ Ask Your Own Questions

An important part of analyzing texts is knowing what questions to ask as you read. What should you look for when you read a story, a drama, or a news article? To make your reading more meaningful, it's also important to ask the questions *you* wonder about so that you connect what you read to yourself and the world around you. The following features of your textbook will help you ask the right questions and read with your own questions in mind.

Where to Look	What You'll Find
Text Analysis Workshops (throughout every unit)	Models and **Close Read** questions
Side notes and discussion questions	Questions (throughout and following each selection) that focus on text analysis
Analysis Frames **THINK** central Go to **thinkcentral.com**. KEYWORD: HML11-9	Guided questions for analyzing different types of texts

DIFFERENTIATED INSTRUCTION

FOR STRUGGLING READERS

Basic Reading Strategies Give students these strategies to use as they read the literature and nonfiction in this book.

- **Preview** Get the gist of a selection before reading by scanning the title, headings, subheadings, captions, and illustrations.
- **Set a Purpose** Before starting a selection ask, "What is my reason for reading?"
- **Connect** While reading, continually make connections between the text and your personal knowledge and experience.

- **Use Prior Knowledge** Before reading, recall what you know; then compare it with new information as you read.
- **Predict** Make guesses about what happens next to help you understand and remember.
- **Visualize** Look for sensory details that help you "see" the characters and action.
- **Monitor** While you read, ask yourself if you're "getting it." If not, you can reread, read ahead, or ask for help.
- **Make Inferences** Use text clues to figure out things that the writer does not state.

Strategies that Work: Literature and Nonfiction Strategies

As you review the **Literature and Nonfiction Strategies,** tell students that practicing these strategies will improve the quality of their work and enhance their enjoyment of literature.

1. **Understand Context**
   Provide practice by asking students to apply the questions to one or two commonly known works, such as the Declaration of Independence or a sports article from the local newspaper.

2. **Clarify Meaning**
   Ask students to practice using the strategies to translate these difficult passages into their own words:

   - **Break Down Sentences** (page 234, "Speech in the Virginia Convention" by Patrick Henry, lines 56–60)

     "If we wish to be free—if we mean to preserve inviolate those inestimable privileges for which we have been so long contending—if we mean not basely to abandon the noble struggle in which we have been so long engaged, and which we have pledged ourselves never to abandon until the glorious object of our contest shall be obtained, we must fight!"

   - **Use Context Clues** (page 1089, "The Life You Save May Be Your Own" by Flannery O'Connor, lines 333–335)

     "My mother was a angel of Gawd," Mr. Shiftlet said in a very strained voice. "He took her from heaven and giver to me and I left her." His eyes were instantly clouded over with a mist of tears.

3. **Ask Your Own Questions**
   Point out that throughout the anthology students will be guided in asking questions that they will need to analyze in the selections. As you discuss the features listed under "Where to Look" and "What You'll Find," explain that students will find these features throughout the anthology.

 **THINK** central

Analysis Frames

The **Analysis Frames** on **thinkcentral.com** help students learn how to ask the right questions when reading, analyzing, and evaluating:

- fiction
- literary nonfiction
- drama
- informational texts
- poetry
- persuasive writing

L 4a Use context as a clue to the meaning of a word. **L 4b** Identify and correctly use patterns of word changes that indicate different meanings or parts of speech. **L 4c** Consult reference materials to find the pronunciation of a word or determine or clarify its precise meaning, its part of speech, its etymology, or its standard usage. **L 6** Acquire and use accurately general academic and domain-specific words and phrases

What Is Academic Vocabulary?

Review the Academic Vocabulary word web with students. Starting with the box labeled Language Arts, in the upper right, read the questions aloud and ask for help with answers.

- **Language Arts:** Point out to students that *illustrate* means "to clarify, or make clear, with examples." Illustrative examples are examples that clarify something, such as a novel's theme.

- **Biology:** Explain that *establish* means "to set up or cause to happen." Point out that crickets vary the loudness and rate of their chirps.

- **Physical Science:** Explain that *adequate* means "enough to meet a need; sufficient." Tell students that understanding Newtonian physics provides an understanding of the physical world.

- **Geometry:** To *construct* means to "create by systematically arranging ideas or terms." To *justify* means "to show or claim to be just or right; vindicate." When constructing a statement about the triangle, students should consider the relevant geometric ideas and make a statement that they can prove.

Academic Vocabulary Workshop

What Is Academic Vocabulary?

If you are lucky enough, or have studied hard enough, to speak two languages—English and Spanish, for example—you are bilingual. Being bilingual may mean that you use one language at home and another at school or with friends. In a sense, though, we are all bilingual: With family and friends, we use informal and conversational language, but in school, we rely on **academic vocabulary,** the language used to talk and write about school subject matter. Just as we can learn the vocabulary of everyday English, Spanish, or Cantonese, we can learn academic vocabulary.

Criteria, interpret, perspective—you may encounter academic vocabulary words such as these in all subject areas, including science, math, social studies, and language arts. Understanding and using these words correctly will help you to be successful in school and on assessments. This web shows examples of academic vocabulary words in different subject areas.

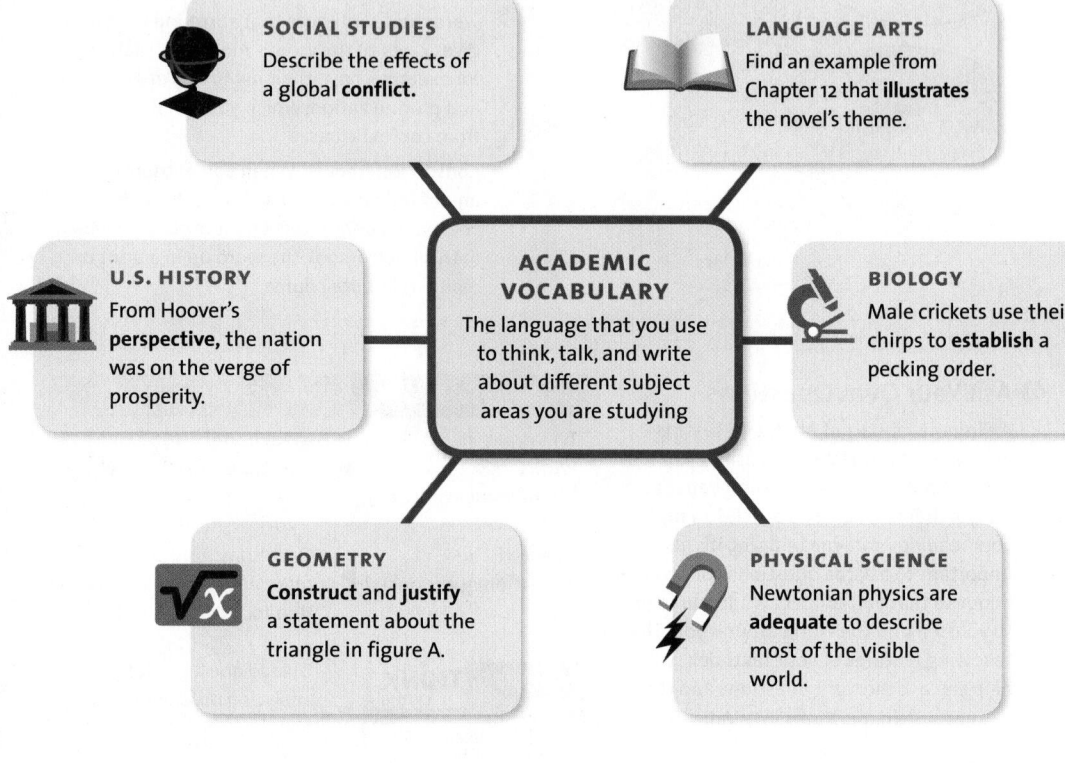

SOCIAL STUDIES
Describe the effects of a global **conflict.**

LANGUAGE ARTS
Find an example from Chapter 12 that **illustrates** the novel's theme.

U.S. HISTORY
From Hoover's **perspective,** the nation was on the verge of prosperity.

ACADEMIC VOCABULARY
The language that you use to think, talk, and write about different subject areas you are studying

BIOLOGY
Male crickets use their chirps to **establish** a pecking order.

GEOMETRY
Construct and **justify** a statement about the triangle in figure A.

PHYSICAL SCIENCE
Newtonian physics are **adequate** to describe most of the visible world.

DIFFERENTIATED INSTRUCTION

FOR ENGLISH LANGUAGE LEARNERS

Language Support Help students understand that academic vocabulary words often appear on lessons and on tests. Knowing the meaning of these academic vocabulary terms will help English language learners complete their assignments and do better on assessments. Provide students with alternate context for some of the terms listed on this page as follows:

- The popularity of music downloads *illustrates* a widespread economic trend.

- Coach wanted to *establish* his team's running game in the first quarter.

- The hikers found a cave that provided *adequate* shelter from the storm.

- Do you think hearing the refugee's story will change your *perspective*?

Use the following chart to become familiar with some of the academic vocabulary terms in this book. As you read, look for the activities labeled "Academic Vocabulary in Writing" and "Academic Vocabulary in Speaking." These activities provide opportunities to use academic language in your writing and discussions.

Word	Definition	Example
adequate	enough to meet a need; sufficient	Make sure to take detailed notes during the research phase so that you have **adequate** evidence to support your assertions.
apparent	obvious; seeming, especially without deeper examination	The dictator's **apparent** irrationality later proved a shrewd strategy of self-preservation.
confine	to keep within bounds; limit	Walt Whitman refused to **confine** his verse to strict conventions of rhyme and meter.
conflict	to be in opposition; differ; a disagreement or battle	How did the language of the U.S. Constitution **conflict** with reality for women and African Americans?
construct	to create by systematically arranging ideas or terms	**Construct** a response to your audience's potential objections.
despite	in spite of; not stopped by	**Despite** the early promises of Reconstruction, it led ultimately to a system of entrenched segregation.
establish	to set up or cause to happen	Only after her death was Emily Dickinson's reputation as one of the premier American poets **established.**
justify	to show or claim to be just or right; vindicate	In the body of your argument, **justify** your claim with evidence and logical reasoning.
illustrate	to clarify, or make clear, with examples	Which diagram correctly **illustrates** the geometric theorem above?
interpret	to explain the meaning or significance of something	Many critics **interpret** Arthur Miller's *The Crucible* as an attack on McCarthyism.
maintain	to preserve or keep up; to declare to be true	To **maintain** air pressure as temperature drops, decrease the volume of the balloon.
perspective	particular way of looking at something; point of view	The park ranger studied the hunter's observations about wolf behavior from a biological **perspective.**
qualitative	measuring the quality, or essential nature, or something	A **qualitative** analysis of the after-school program's success should include interviews with participants.
reinforce	to strengthen something by adding extra support	The images of women in fashion magazines tend to **reinforce** society's unrealistic standards of beauty.

- **U.S. History:** Point out to students that *perspective* is a "particular way of looking at something" or a "point of view." Explain to students that in 1929, at the start of Herbert Hoover's presidency, few American leaders recognized the vulnerabilities of the nation's economy.

- **Social Studies:** Explain to students that the word *global* is the adjective form of *globe*—a representation of the earth. *Global conflicts* are disagreements between nations that spread to effect more countries than were initially involved.

FOR STRUGGLING READERS

Vocabulary Support Although this workshop focuses on academic vocabulary, students may need help with other content-specific terms. Provide the following definitions.

- *segregation:* the separation of one group—such as a racial group—from the other groups in a society

- *theorem:* in math, a statement, formula, or proposition deduced from other formulas or propositions

FOR ADVANCED LEARNERS/AP

Challenge advanced learners to come up with other examples of questions and statements using some of the academic vocabulary terms on page 11.

Academic Vocabulary in Action

Review the definition of *perspective* with students. Then, have students complete the chart on their own or in pairs. See the following chart for possible responses.

Subject Area & Item or Event	Perspective 1	Perspective 2
Language Arts: the novel Moby Dick	an English teacher: The book is a classic that should be read by all.	student struggling with poor grades: The book is too long and complicated to read.
Social Studies: World War II internment of Japanese Americans	President Franklin Roosevelt signed an Executive Order in 1942 authorizing relocation of Japanese Americans to internment camps	President Ronald Reagan signed the Civil Liberties Act of 1988, acknowledging injustice of the internment and apologizing on behalf of the U.S. government

Review the definition of *economy* with students. Then have them fill out the chart, using a dictionary for help. Possible responses are provided below.

Word	Definition	Sentence
ecosystem	a community of organisms and its environment	Pollution wiped out much of the ecosystem.
economize	to practice economy; be frugal	I had to economize to stay in college.
ecologist	scientist working in the field of ecology	The ecologist studied the migration patterns of birds.

Academic Vocabulary in Action

The terms below are examples of commonly used academic vocabulary. Knowing the meaning of these terms is essential for completing the activities and lessons in this book as well as mastering test items.

perspective *(noun)*

Defining the Word

Perspective is a particular way of looking at something; it is your (or someone else's) point of view. In history class, you may read primary sources that reflect the perspectives of different parties in the same historical period. In literature class, you may read a novel narrated from the perspective of several different characters.

Using the Word

Practice using the word *perspective*.

- Using a chart like the one shown, identify items or events in two different subject areas that reflect different perspectives.
- Identify two perspectives on the same item or event. You may describe or sketch the two perspectives.

Subject Area & Item or Event	Perspective 1	Perspective 2
U.S. History: Civil War	a letter by Robert E. Lee to his son: Southerners are victims of northern aggression.	a speech by Abraham Lincoln (Gettysburg Address): The Union will continue to fight for freedom and democracy.

economic *(adjective)*

Defining the Word

Economic is the adjective form of *economy*—the system of production, distribution, and consumption and exchange of goods and services in a country, area, or period of time. It can also be used as an adjectival form of *economics*—the social science devoted to analyzing economies. Finally, *economic* can refer to the wise, sparing use of resources or language.

Using the Word

Understanding a word's root can help you understand other words with the same root. The root of *economic* and other words beginning with *eco-* is the Greek *oikos*, meaning "house." *Economy* originally referred to household management.

Word	Definition	Sentence
ecology	the connection between organisms and their environment	The ecology of the creek was damaged by fertilizer from bordering lawns.

- In a chart like the one shown, jot down all the words you can think of that begin with or contain *eco*.
- Write down your understanding of the word's meaning, and check your definition in a dictionary.
- Use the word in a sentence.

DIFFERENTIATED INSTRUCTION

FOR ENGLISH LANGUAGE LEARNERS

Language Support Have pairs of students look up and share the meanings of the examples provided, including:

- *geometry:* branch of mathematics that includes the measurement, properties, and relationships of points, lines, angles, surfaces and solids

- *distribution:* the process of dividing something among several or many

- *consumption:* the process of utilizing economic goods

- *adjectival:* adjective form of the word *adjective*

Strategies That Work: Vocabulary

Record new vocabulary words in your **Reader/Writer Notebook.**

❶ Analyze Roots in Technical Vocabulary

Some academic language is specific to particular content areas. Many of these technical words contain Greek or Latin roots. Understanding the root of a technical word can help you figure out the word's meaning. Keep a list of the roots that occur in technical words. You can remember the meaning of the root by including non-technical words in the list.

arthro (joint)	cens (opinion)	petr (rock)
arthritis	censorship	petrify
arthropod	censure	petroglyph
arthroscopy	consensus	petrochemical

You probably know that arthritis causes joint pain. This knowledge can help you remember that *arthro* comes from the Greek word for "joint," which in turn can help you understand other words containing that root.

❷ Use Context Clues

A way to recognize unfamiliar words as you read is to use context clues. When you see an unfamiliar word, look not only at its root but at the context—the words, phrases, or sentences that surround that word. Context can give you clues to the word's meaning, as in the following example:

> The President sought consensus among his advisors before taking action, although his decision sometimes ran counter to the majority opinion.

You can tell that *consensus* means "majority opinion." The clue word *although* links *consensus* to *majority opinion* by clarifying that the president did not always follow it.

❸ Use Language References

If neither roots nor context clues help you figure out an unfamiliar word, consult a print or digital language reference. A dictionary will provide most words' meanings, pronunciations, parts of speech, and origins.

Some technical or foreign expressions may be found only in specialized dictionaries, such as medical dictionaries or dictionaries of foreign terms. These may be available in your library, either in print, online, or both. Glossaries may be found at the back of technical manuals and textbooks, including this one.

Interactive Vocabulary **THINK** central
Go to **thinkcentral.com.**
KEYWORD: HML11-13

> **xenophobe** (zĕn ə-fōb, zē nə-)
> *n.*: a person unduly fearful or contemptuous of that which is foreign, especially of people from foreign countries.

For a complete list of terms in this book, see the **Glossary of Academic Vocabulary in English & Spanish** *on pages R129–R130.*

Strategies that Work: Vocabulary

Share with students that **Strategies That Work: Vocabulary** can be applied not only to Academic Vocabulary terms but also to unfamiliar words or phrases students will find in their reading. Encourage students to use these strategies in their reading both in and out of the classroom.

1. Analyze Roots in Technical Vocabulary
Have students brainstorm a list of technical words. Write some of these words on the board. Call on students to identify the roots of the technical words. Have students list and define nontechnical words that will help them remember the meaning of the roots.

2. Use Context Clues
Tell students to identify the context clues in the example given. Explain that the context of an unfamiliar word may provide clues in definitions, restatements, or examples.

3. Use Language References
Have students flip to the Glossary of Vocabulary in English and Spanish in the back of this book. Explain that this glossary provides pronunciations, parts of speech, and definitions for the vocabulary words in the selections in this book. Spanish definitions of the vocabulary words are included. Tell students that a glossary provides less information than a dictionary but may be easier to use because of its availability. The student edition also includes a Glossary of Reading and Informational Terms and a Glossary of Literary Terms.

Writing Online

THINK central

WordSharp Vocabulary Tutor provides in-depth instruction in the use of vocabulary development strategies:
- identifying context clues
- applying knowledge of word parts and word origins
- using dictionaries and other resources
- recognizing specialized vocabulary
- studying word derivations

FOR STRUGGLING READERS

Concept Support Use these activities to reinforce the teaching in the text:

1. For help identifying examples of technical vocabulary, have students think about the occupations of their parents and other adults they know. Ask students to write down terms they have heard these adults use that relate to their jobs. Have students work with a partner to decide which of the terms classify as technical vocabulary.

2. Tell students to practice using context clues when not working on school assignments. For example, context clues can help them learn unfamiliar words in magazines, novels, and other materials they read for fun.

3. Invite students to share tips about using language references. Ask students if they use glossaries in textbooks in other subjects or if they have a particular online dictionary they like to use.

COMMON CORE FOCUS

W 4 Produce clear and coherent writing in which the development, organization, and style are appropriate to task, purpose, and audience. **W 5** Develop and strenghten writing as needed by planning, revising, editing, rewriting, or trying a new approach, focusing on addressing what is most significant for a specific purpose and audience. **L 1** Demonstrate command of the conventions of standard English grammar when writing. **L 2** Demonstrate command of the conventions of standard English capitalization, punctuation, and spelling when writing. **L 3** Apply knowledge of language to understand how language functions in different contexts and to comprehend more fully when reading.

Consider Your Options

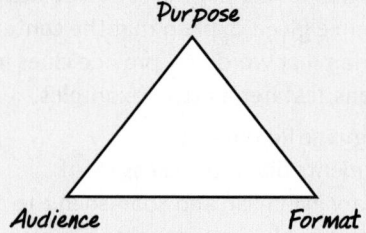

Purpose

Audience   Format

Draw a triangle on the board and label its corners Purpose, Audience, and Format.

Read the questions that appear beneath these terms in the text, as well as the answers provided. Illustrate how these writing variables affect each other. For example, an explanatory piece on penguins might be presented in these ways:

- in the format of a short story if the audience consists of children
- in the format of a research paper if the audience consists of a teacher

Expressing Ideas in Writing

Writing is a powerful tool. It can help you clarify concepts, explore opinions, and add something new to the world of ideas. That is what every writer represented in this book knew, and it's what you will discover as well. Through effective writing, you can formulate your own interpretations, challenge assumptions, and even shape others' perceptions in the process.

COMMON CORE

Included in this workshop:
W 4, W 5, L 1, L 2, L 3, SL 1b–d

Consider Your Options

Are you crafting an impassioned editorial for your school newspaper, writing a personal statement for a college application, or responding to a posting on your friend's blog? Start any writing exploration by clarifying three critical considerations—your **purpose, audience,** and **format** of your writing.

PURPOSE	AUDIENCE	FORMAT
Why am I writing?	**Who are my readers?**	**Which format will best suit my purpose and audience?**
• to entertain	• classmates	• analytical essay • summary
• to inform or explain	• teacher	• wiki
• to argue or persuade	• friends	• letter • short story
• to describe	• community members	• poem • proposal
• to reflect	• potential employer	• research paper • speech
• to inspire or motivate	• customer service department	• news article • critique
	• college admissions office	• podcast
	• Web community	• blog entry

DIFFERENTIATED INSTRUCTION

FOR STRUGGLING READERS

Note Taking Use the Writing Process Workshop to introduce students to thinking skills that contribute to effective writing, graphic organizers that facilitate this thinking, and steps in the writing process. If students need help in note taking, hand out the copy master for them to complete.

 RESOURCE MANAGER—Copy Masters
   Note Taking p. I-5

FOR ENGLISH LANGUAGE LEARNERS

Vocabulary: Word Analysis Help students grasp the stages of the writing process by discussing these prefixes and roots:

- *prewriting: Pre-* means "before," so *prewriting* refers to tasks you do before the main writing.
- *drafting:* This word comes from a Middle English word that means "to draw or pull." Drafting refers to drawing out your writing ideas.

- *revising: Re-* means "again," and *-vis-* means "to see," so revising refers to looking again at what you have written.
- *publishing:* This word comes from a Middle English word that means "to make known publicly." *Publishing* refers to taking your finished writing to the public.

Continue with the Process

As you complete the **Writing Workshops** in this book, you'll discover the process that works best for you. Use this model as a guide.

THE WRITING PROCESS

PLANNING/PREWRITING

What will you write? To begin, use one of the prewriting strategies listed on page 17. Be sure to keep your **purpose** and **audience** in mind as you refine your topic.

Depending on your **format** and your **purpose**, you also might formulate your **controlling idea** or **claim** and develop ideas to support your main points.

▶ **WHAT DOES IT LOOK LIKE?**

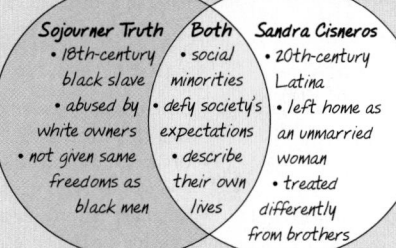

Sojourner Truth
• 18th-century black slave
• abused by white owners
• not given same freedoms as black men

Both
• social minorities
• defy society's expectations
• describe their own lives

Sandra Cisneros
• 20th-century Latina
• left home as an unmarried woman
• treated differently from brothers

DRAFTING

In a first draft, you'll move beyond your early plan to develop your ideas. An informal piece, such as a blog, allows you to start writing with no set plan—that is, to **draft to discover.** For a more formal assignment, such as an analytical essay or a research paper, you'll want to **draft from an outline.** In both cases, remember that you may need to do several drafts before you're satisfied with how you've expressed your ideas.

▶ **WHAT DOES IT LOOK LIKE?**

I. Sojourner Truth and Sandra Cisneros
  A. Different cultural heritages and time periods
  B. Similar struggles over women's social inequality
II. Sojourner Truth
  A. Suffered unequal treatment of enslaved people
  B. Summarized in her 1867 speech
III. Sandra Cisneros
  A. Experienced biased attitudes

REVISING

To strengthen your draft, evaluate its development, organization, and style. Check your draft using a **rubric**, or ask a peer for suggestions. If your draft doesn't fit your purpose or audience, you may need to rewrite some sections or try a new approach.

▶ **ASK A PEER READER**
• Have I communicated my main idea effectively?
• Where should I add more details or evidence?
• Where could I strengthen my word choice?
• Do my ideas flow smoothly? If not, where can I make improvements?

EDITING AND PUBLISHING

Edit your draft to correct any errors in the conventions of grammar, usage, and mechanics. Then **publish** your work in a way that suits your purpose, audience, and format.

▶ **WHAT DOES IT LOOK LIKE?**

Born centuries apart, Sojourner Truth and Sandra Cisneros both suffered social (tr) discrimination. Their writings, years apart, reflect society's attitude toward women and the authors' strength in defying those attitudes.

Continue with the Process

Ask volunteers to read aloud the four steps in the **Writing Process** and discuss the corresponding example for each step.

Then conduct a brief survey to determine students' familiarity with the writing process. Ask questions about their experiences at each stage.

• How do you generate ideas for a writing assignment?
• Do you write a draft from an outline form or from a graphic organizer?
• What errors do you look for in your draft?
• Do you find a peer reader helpful? Explain.
• How do you decide that your writing is ready to turn in, send out, or publish?

FOR STRUGGLING WRITERS

Concept Support Draw a flow chart on the board to help students visualize the writing process. Work with students to fill in the chart with key words, definitions, and details.

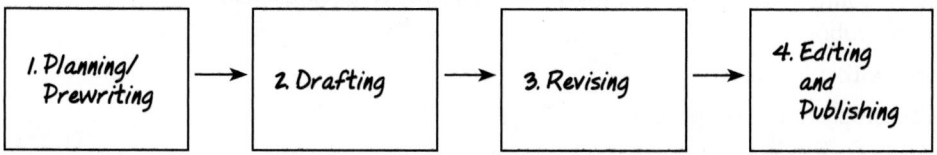

1. Planning/Prewriting → 2. Drafting → 3. Revising → 4. Editing and Publishing

Scoring Rubric

Briefly discuss the Scoring Rubric, explaining that the rubric is a means by which students can evaluate their writing. (The word rubric refers to categorizing—here, categorizing a piece of writing according to its strengths.) Tell students that the best way to understand rubrics is to use them to score an actual piece of writing. Students will have the opportunity to work with a partner to evaluate what they wrote in the Writing Workshops. Students can score each other's writing using a rubric like the one on this page. They can then write a summary evaluation using the language of the rubric to explain the reasons for the score they gave their partner.

Scoring Rubric

Score	COMMON CORE TRAITS
6	• **Development** Includes a meaningful, engaging introduction; thoroughly develops the topic with well-chosen, relevant, and sufficient evidence; ends powerfully • **Organization** Logically organizes complex ideas, concepts, and information; uses appropriate and varied transitions to create cohesion and clarify relationships among ideas • **Language** Uses precise language in imaginative ways; maintains an appropriate style and tone for the audience and purpose; shows a strong command of conventions
5	• **Development** Has an engaging introduction; develops the topic with relevant, well-chosen evidence; has an effective concluding section • **Organization** Logically organizes ideas, concepts, and information; uses appropriate transitions to create cohesion and clarify relationships • **Language** Effectively uses precise language; maintains an appropriate style and tone for the audience and purpose; has a few errors in conventions
4	• **Development** Has an introduction, but it could be more engaging; lacks sufficient support for one or two ideas; has an adequate, though routine, concluding section • **Organization** Is logically organized, with one or two exceptions; could use a few more transitions to clarify the relationships among ideas • **Language** Includes some vague word choices; has one or two lapses in style and tone; includes a few distracting errors in conventions
3	• **Development** Has both an introduction and conclusion, but they are superficial or uninteresting; includes some unsupported ideas or irrelevant evidence • **Organization** Has some flaws in organization; needs more transitions • **Language** Uses words correctly, though language is unimaginative; has frequent lapses in style and tone; has some critical errors in conventions
2	• **Development** Has an unfocused, uninteresting introduction; does not develop most ideas; ends abruptly • **Organization** Has an illogical organization; lacks transitions throughout • **Language** Uses vague language and misuses some words; lapses into an inappropriate style and tone in many places; contains many distracting errors in conventions
1	• **Development** Lacks an introduction, development, and a concluding section • **Organization** Has no discernible organization; lacks transitions or uses inappropriate ones • **Language** Uses many words incorrectly; employs an inappropriate style and tone for the audience and purpose; has major problems with conventions

DIFFERENTIATED INSTRUCTION

FOR ENGLISH LANGUAGE LEARNERS

Language Support Have pairs of students look up and share the meanings of skill words such as *coherence, composition, transitions, perspective,* and *individuality.* Also discuss the contextual meanings of these adjectives in the rubric:

• *meaningful:* with purpose

• *effective:* accomplishing a purpose

• *authentic:* not false or copied

• *original:* new, fresh

• *unique:* particular, singular

• *smooth:* easy, effortless

• *substantial:* of a considerable amount

• *discernible:* obvious, visible

Strategies That Work: Writing

 Record your writing ideas, plans, and notes in your **Reader/Writer Notebook**.

❶ Use Prewriting Strategies

Unleash your ideas using one or more of these strategies:

- **Brainstorm with others.** Generate topic ideas with a group of classmates.
- **Freewrite.** Write continuously for ten minutes, recording any ideas that pop into your head.
- **Use the news.** Stay current on scientific discoveries, controversial issues, and newsworthy events. Your next topic could be "ripped from the headlines."
- **Get visual.** Use a graphic organizer, such as a cluster diagram or a story map, to get your ideas flowing.
- **Write from a prompt.** Consult the prompts in the **Writing Workshops.**

Writing Online
Go to **thinkcentral.com**.
KEYWORD: HML11N-17

❷ Enlist a Peer Reader

Often, peer readers can identify problems that you have overlooked or can't see. Consider the following guidelines:

When You're the Writer	When You're the Reader
• Make sure your peer reader knows your purpose and audience.	• Be respectful and positive in your feedback, noting both strong and weak parts of the writing.
• Clarify the kind of feedback you want to receive. Should your reader evaluate your ideas, organization, word choice, or all of the above?	• Ask questions to clarify what the writer intends, and answer questions honestly and specifically.
• Be open to the possibility of rewriting passages that aren't working or rethinking your approach based on your reader's feedback.	• Respond thoughtfully to the writer's ideas. If you are uncertain about a change you are suggesting, help the writer determine whether to consult a reference source or gather more information.

Think About Purpose and Audience

Keep your purpose and audience in mind throughout every stage of the writing process. These two considerations should guide every decision you make, from the organization of your ideas to your choice of words. Ask yourself questions like the ones on the notebook.

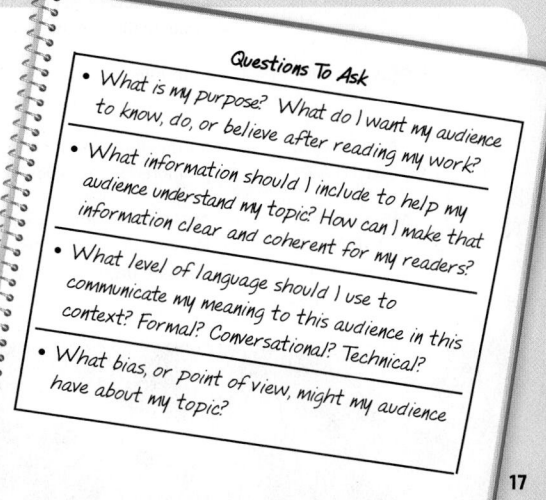

Questions To Ask

- What is my purpose? What do I want my audience to know, do, or believe after reading my work?
- What information should I include to help my audience understand my topic? How can I make that information clear and coherent for my readers?
- What level of language should I use to communicate my meaning to this audience in this context? Formal? Conversational? Technical?
- What bias, or point of view, might my audience have about my topic?

17

Strategies that Work: Writing

Share with students that **Strategies That Work: Writing** can open up exciting possibilities for them as writers. Encourage students to make constant use of the strategies to help them with their writing, both inside and outside of class.

1. Use Prewriting Strategies
Discuss the examples of prewriting strategies. Ask students if they are familiar with these strategies and, if so, which ones they have found helpful and why.

2. Enlist a Peer Reader
Discuss with students their experiences with peer readers, both positive and negative. Whatever their experiences have been, remind them that peer feedback, if done responsibly, can be invaluable in learning about themselves and each other as readers and writers. Note that whether they are the writer or the reader in a peer review, they should be as specific as possible. Point out the tips listed for peer readers and writers, emphasizing that readers and writers owe each other respect, sensitivity, and patience.

3. Think About Purpose and Audience
Review with students the information about purpose and audience listed on page 14. Then have them practice by writing two separate paragraphs with different purposes and different audiences. Have students exchange papers with a peer for feedback.

FOR STRUGGLING WRITERS

Concept Support Use these activities to reinforce the teaching in the text:

- Show students what a prompt is by looking with them at the prompt in the first Writing Workshop (page 280). Tell students that as they read various prompts, they will learn how to analyze a prompt for clues about the purpose of the writing being asked for and the audience for whom it is intended.

- Emphasize that working with peers is not limited to peer readers during the revising and editing stage; peers can help students narrow topics and clarify their plans for a piece of writing.

Writing Online

The **Writing Center** on **thinkcentral.com** includes Interactive Student Models, which show students how to read and critique others' writing. The **Writing Center** also includes
- Ideas for Writing
- Interactive Graphic Organizers
- Interactive Revision Lessons
- Writing Model Bank

UNIT GOALS

Included in this unit: RL 1, RL 2, RL 3, RL 4, RL 5, RL 7, RL 9, RL 10, RI 1, RI 2, RI 3, RI 4, RI 5, RI 6, RI 7, RI 8, RI 9, RI 10, W 1, W 2, W 3, W 7, W 9, SL 1, SL 2, SL 3, SL 4, SL 5, L 2b, L 3, L 4, L 5, L 6

Complete text of the Common Core State Standards is found in the correlation on p. T10. Standards covered in this unit are found in the standards overview (pp. 19A–19D) and on the lesson pages where they are taught.

Preview Unit Goals

This page presents an overview of the skills and strategies covered in this unit. Explain to students that they can get more from their reading by previewing. Then ask them to skim the page to preview the skills that they will learn. Note that each strand or category of skill is color-coded on this page and throughout the unit.

Model the strategy of copying the Academic Vocabulary and writing a preliminary definition for each term. Suggest that students use their **Reader/Writer Notebooks** for this purpose. Encourage them to use the terms in discussions and in writing. Also urge students to revisit each term throughout the unit and to refine its meaning.

UNIT 1

COMMON CORE

Preview Unit Goals

TEXT ANALYSIS	• Analyze historical context; analyze cultural characteristics • Identify characteristics of creation myth, trickster tale, folk tale, memoir, historical narrative, drama, and autobiography • Analyze historically important speeches, public documents, and letters • Analyze themes; analyze author's purpose; analyze characters • Analyze diction and tone; analyze imagery and figurative language • Analyze and evaluate elements of an argument • Analyze persuasive techniques and rhetorical devices • Analyze and evaluate primary sources • Analyze various structural patterns • Synthesize ideas and connect texts
READING	• Develop strategies for reading older texts • Develop comprehension monitoring skills
WRITING AND LANGUAGE	• Create a multimedia presentation • Write an argumentative essay • Use prepositional phrases and adverb clauses as modifiers • Understand and use compound and compound-complex sentences
SPEAKING AND LISTENING	• Deliver an argumentative speech • Analyze how media messages influence cultural values and stereotypes • Evaluate film techniques; evaluate multiple interpretations of a play
VOCABULARY	• Determine the meaning of multiple-meaning words • Understand and use specialized vocabulary
ACADEMIC VOCABULARY	• document • illustrate • interpret • promote • reveal
MEDIA AND VIEWING	• Analyze how words, images, graphics, and sounds impact meaning • Evaluate how media messages reflect cultural views • Evaluate the interactions of different techniques used in media

Find It Online! **THINK** central

Go to **thinkcentral.com** for the interactive version of this unit.

18

DIFFERENTIATED INSTRUCTION

FOR ENGLISH LANGUAGE LEARNERS

Academic Vocabulary Provide students with definitions of each Academic Vocabulary word.

document (dŏkyə-mənt,) *n.* something, such as a piece of writing, recording, or a photograph, that can be used to furnish evidence or information; *v.* to support (statements in a research paper, for example) with written references or citations

illustrate (ĭlə-strāt) *v.* to clarify, or make clear, with examples

interpret (ĭn-tûrprĭt) *v.* explain the meaning or significance of something

promote (prə-mōt) *v.* to help the growth of, urge the adoption of, or attempt to popularize something

reveal (rĭ-vēl) *v.* to make known; to show

Additional Academic Vocabulary Use the copy master to help students learn academic words they will use in subsequent lessons and on the Assessment Practice.

R RESOURCE MANAGER—Copy Masters
Academic Vocabulary p. 3
Additional Academic Vocabulary p. 4

Early American Writing

1600–1800

Mourning Dove

AN EMERGING NATION

- The Native American Experience
- Exploration and the Early Settlers
- The Puritan Tradition
- Writers of the Revolution

Media Smart DVD-ROM

Great Stories on Film
Examine how media stereotypes shaped society's attitudes toward Native Americans. Page 66

19

For help in planning this unit, see

R **RESOURCE MANAGER UNIT 1**
pp. 1–8

INTRODUCE THE UNIT

Call students' attention to the pictures on this page. Explain that the large picture, *Declaration of Independence,* is a painting by John Trumbull. Tell students that they will be reading the Declaration of Independence later in this unit.

Ask students if they know the writer, Mourning Dove, shown in the smaller picture on the page. Point out that Mourning Dove is the pen name of Christine Quintasket (c. 1888–1936), one of the first female Native American novelists. Explain that Mourning Dove helped to preserve traditional stories of the Okanogan and other Native American cultures. Tell students that they will read her story "Coyote and the Buffalo" in this unit. Also note that students can read more about Mourning Dove on page 46.

About the Art American artist John Trumbull (1756–1843) captured numerous prominent historical figures in his well-known oil painting *Declaration of Independence,* including Thomas Jefferson, John Adams, Benjamin Franklin, and John Hancock. The painting reflects the artist's intention to commemorate the significant historical event and to depict nearly 50 of the men involved in the creation of the Declaration. In actuality, not all of the individuals shown were present at the same time, and 15 men who did sign the Declaration do not appear in the painting.

Unit Resources

See resources on the **Teacher One Stop DVD-ROM** *and on* **thinkcentral.com**.

R **RESOURCE MANAGER UNIT 1**

UNIT AND BENCHMARK TESTS

 **BEST PRACTICES TOOLKIT**

INTERACTIVE READER

ADAPTED INTERACTIVE READER

ELL ADAPTED INTERACTIVE READER

LANGUAGE HANDBOOK

VOCABULARY PRACTICE

TECHNOLOGY

- **Teacher One Stop DVD-ROM**
- **Student One Stop DVD-ROM**
- **PowerNotes DVD-ROM**
- **Write*Smart* CD-ROM**
- **Media*Smart* DVD-ROM**
- **GrammarNotes DVD-ROM**
- **Audio Anthology CD**

Find It Online! THINK central

This unit on **thinkcentral.com** includes

- **PowerNotes** introductions to key selections
- audio support—listen or download
- **ThinkAloud** models
- **WordSharp** vocabulary tutorials
- interactive unit review and assessment

UNIT 1

COMMON CORE STRAND	Unit 1 Introduction pp. 19–35 • Questions of the Times • Historical Essay • Timeline • Legacy of the Era	Text Analysis Workshops • Historical Narratives pp. 70–71 • American Drama pp. 132–133 • Persuasive Rhetoric pp. 226–227	The World on the Turtle's Back Iroquois Creation Myth pp. 36–45 Lexile: 850 Fry: 6 Dale-Chall: 5.2	Coyote and the Buffalo Folk Tale pp. 46–53 Lexile: 710 Fry: 6/7 Dale-Chall: 5.4	Themes Across Time: from The Way to Rainy Mountain Memoir pp. 54–64 Lexile: 1000 Fry: 8 Dale-Chall: 6.4	Media Study: Changing Views of Native Americans Film Clips pp. 66–69
Reading Literature	Historical and Cultural Context of Early American Writing pp. 22–31 RL 9	Conventions of Drama pp. 132–133 RL 3, RL 5	Creation Myths pp. 37–38, 41, 44–45 RL 2 Folk Literature pp. 37, 40, 42–43, 45 RL 1, RL 2 Theme and Genre p. 44	Trickster Tales pp. 47–48, 50, 52–53 RL 3, RL 5 Predict pp. 47, 51, 53 RL 1		
Reading Informational Text	Historical and Cultural Context of Early American Writing pp. 22–31 RI 9 Read a Timeline pp. 32–33 RI 7	Characteristics of Historical Narrative pp. 70–71 RI 9, RI 10 Persuasive Techniques and Rhetorical Devices pp. 226–227 RI 5, RI 6, RI 8, RI 9			Memoir pp. 55–58, 61–63 RI 6 Analyze Structure pp. 55, 56, 60, 63 RI 5 Specialized Vocabulary p. 64 RI 4 Theme and Genre p. 62	Media Literacy pp. 67–69 RI 7
Writing	Legacy of the Era pp. 34–35 W 7			Quickwrite p. 47		
Speaking and Listening	Legacy of the Era pp. 34–35 SL 1		Discuss. p. 37 SL 1		Interview p. 55 SL 1	Produce your Own Media p. 69 SL 2, SL 3, SL 5
Language			Language Coach pp. 40, 42	Language Coach p. 50	Language Coach pp. 59–60 L 5b Specialized Vocabulary p. 64 L 4c	

ECOS				ECOS	ECOS
from **La Relación** Report pp. 72–81	*from* **The Interesting Narrative of the Life of Olaudah Equiano** Slave Narrative pp. 82–91	*from* **The General History of Virginia** Historical Narrative pp. 92–101	*from* **Of Plymouth Plantation** Chronicle pp. 102–112	**To My Dear and Loving Husband/ Upon the Burning of Our House/ Huswifery** Poetry pp. 114–121	*from* **Sinners in the Hands of an Angry God** Sermon pp. 122–131
Lexile: 1010 Fry: 10 Dale-Chall: 6.3	Lexile: 1220 Fry: College Dale-Chall: 6.9	Lexile: 1680 Fry: 8 Dale-Chall: 8.0	Lexile: 1370 Fry: 10 Dale-Chall: 6.7		Lexile: 1210 Fry: 9 Dale-Chall: 6.6
				Figurative Language pp. 115–116, 119–121 RL 4 Allusion p. 119 RL 4	
Historical Context pp. 73, 76, 78–79 RI 1, RI 6 Reading a Primary Source pp. 73–74, 77, 79 RI 1, RI 9	Slave Narrative pp. 83, 84, 87–89 RI 3, RI 5 Analyze Details pp. 83, 86–87, 89 RI 1 Theme and Genre p. 86	Narrator pp. 93, 96, 98, 100 RI 5, RI 6 Reading Older Texts pp. 93–94, 96, 99–100 RI 4 Theme and Genre p. 99	Cultural Characteristics pp. 103–104, 107, 109, 111 RI 9 Summarize pp. 103, 106, 110–111 RI 2		Persuasion pp. 123–124, 126, 130 RI 3, RI 6 Analyze Emotional Appeals pp. 123, 126, 128, 130 RI 6 Allusion p. 129 RI 3, RI 6 Connotation p. 131 RI 4
Writing Prompt p. 81 W 3, W 3a, W 3d	Writing Prompt p. 91 W 3, W 3a, W 3d			Quickwrite p. 115	
Discuss p. 73 SL 1	Test Yourself p. 83 SL 1	Discuss p. 93 SL 1	Discuss p. 103 SL 1		Role-Play p. 123 SL 1
Prepositional Phrases p. 78, 81 L 3, L 3a Etymologies p. 80 L 4c, L 6	Adverb Clauses pp. 87, 91 L 3, L 3a Language Coach p. 88 L 2b Spanish Cognates p. 90 L 4d	Reading Older Texts pp. 93–94, 96, 99–100 L 3a Language Coach p. 99 Multiple Meanings p. 101 L 4, L 4a, L 4c–d	Words from French p. 112 L 4c Language Coach pp. 108, 110	Figurative Language pp. 115–116, 119–121 L 5a Clarify Meaning in Older Poetry pp. 115–116, 118, 120–121 L 3a, L 4 Language Coach p. 118	Analyze Emotional Appeals pp. 123, 126, 130 L 3 Connotation p. 131 L 4a, L 5

ECOS

To see the complete Essential Course of Study, see pp. T23–T27.

For additional lesson planning help, see **Teacher One Stop DVD.**

COMMON CORE STRAND	ECOS *The Crucible* Drama pp. 134–215	ECOS *Linked Selections* *The Crucible and McCarthyism* Online Article, Newspaper Article, Memoir pp. 216–221	*Media Study: from The Crucible* Film Clip/ Movie Review pp. 222–224	ECOS *from Speech in the Virginia Convention* Speech pp. 228–237 Lexile: 990 Fry: 9 Dale-Chall: 7.4	ECOS *from The Declaration of Independence* Public Document pp. 238–247 Lexile: 1320 Fry: 12 Dale-Chall: 8.9
Reading Literature	Conventions of Drama pp. 135, 163, 179, 199, 213 RL 3, RL 5 Draw Conclusions pp. 135, 163, 179, 199, 213 RL 1, RL 3 Behind the Curtain pp. 153, 197 RL 7 Theme and Genre p. 138		Comparing Texts p. 223 RL 7		
Reading Informational Text		Understand Historical Context pp. 216–221 RI 1, RI 6, RI 7	Movie Review p. 224	Rhetorical Devices pp. 229–230, 232, 234–235 RI 5, RI 6 Reading a Persuasive Speech pp. 229, 232, 234–235 RI 5, RI 6	Argument pp. 239, 240, 242, 244–245 RI 4, RI 8 Analyze Text Structure pp. 239, 242, 245 RI 5 Political Words p. 246 RI 4
Writing	Writing Prompt p. 215 W 1, W 1b	Writing Prompt p. 221 W 2, W 2b		Writing Prompt p. 237 W 1	Writing Prompt p. 247 W 1
Speaking and Listening	Discuss p. 135 SL 1			Discuss p. 229 SL 1	Discuss p. 239 SL 1
Language	Use Realistic Dialogue pp. 146, 170, 186, 206, 215 L 3a Context Clues p. 214 L 4a, L 5b			Rhetorical Devices pp. 229–230, 232, 234–235 L 3a Sentence Types pp. 232, 237 L 3a Language Coach p. 233 L 4b Analogies p. 236 L 4d, L 5, L 6	Text Structure p. 243 L 3a Vary Sentence Structure pp. 244, 247 L 3a Language Coach p. 242 Political Words p. 246 L 4c, L 6

from **The Crisis** Essay pp. 248–257	**Letter to the Reverend Samson Occom/Letter to John Adams** Letters pp. 258–265	from **Benjamin Franklin's Autobiography/50 Ways to Fix Your Life** Autobiography/ Magazine Article pp. 266–278	**Wrap-Ups** • The Native American Experience p. 65 • Exploration and Early Settlers p. 113 • The Puritan Tradition p. 225 • Writers of the Revolution p. 279	**Writing Workshop: Persuasive Essay** pp. 280–289 **Speaking and Listening Workshop: Presenting and Evaluating a Persuasive Speech** pp. 290–291
Lexile: 1180 Fry: 10 Dale-Chall: 7.5	Lexile: 1230 Fry: 9 Dale-Chall: 7.9	Lexile: 1390 Fry: 8 Dale-Chall: 7.2		
			Read Foundational Works p. 225 RL 9 Read Foundational Documents p. 279 RL 9	
Persuasive Techniques pp. 249–250, 252–253, 254, 256 RI 3, RI 4, RI 5 Summarize Main Ideas pp. 249, 252, 255–256 RI 2, RI 3	Diction pp. 259, 260, 264, 265 RI 6 Reading Primary Sources pp. 259, 262, 264, 265 RI 9	Characteristics of Auto-biography pp. 267–268, 272, 274, 276 RI 5, RI 6 Make Inferences about the Author pp. 267, 270–271, 273, 276 RI 1		
Quickwrite p. 249		Quickwrite p. 267	Writing to Synthesize p. 65 W 9 Writing to Evaluate p. 113 W 2 Writing to Compare p. 225 W 9 Writing to Persuade p. 279 W 1	Writing a Persuasive Speech pp. 280–289 W 1a–e, W 4, W 5, W 7, W 8, W 9b (RI 1), W 10
	Discuss p. 259 SL 1		Discuss p. 265 SL 1, SL 1a Debate p. 113 SL 1 Extension p. 225 SL 6 Extension p. 279 SL 4	Presenting and Evaluating a Persuasive Speech pp. 290–291 SL 3, SL 4, SL 6
Language Coach p. 254 L 4c Words from Middle English p. 257 L 4c, L 6	Language Coach p. 260 Language Coach p. 264 L 5	Language Coach pp. 270, 271 Cognates p. 277 L 6		Drafting p. 283 L 3 Editing and Publishing p. 287 L 2b

ECOS

To see the complete Essential Course of Study, see pp. T23–T27.

For additional lesson planning help, see **Teacher One Stop DVD.**

Instructional Support

Resource Manager Unit 1

UNIT SUPPORT

Academic Vocabulary, p. 3

Additional Academic Vocabulary, p. 4

Grammar Focus p. 5

Text Analysis Workshop pp. 71, 266

Writing Workshop: Persuasive Essay p. 363

SELECTION SUPPORT*

Plan and Teach

Lesson planning pages

Additional leveled selection questions

Extension activities

Student Copy Masters

Selection summaries in four languages

Skills copy masters in English and Spanish

Vocabulary preteaching and support

Reading Check and Question Support

Reading Fluency

* Available for all selections

† Available on **thinkcentral.com**

Language Handbook

Vocabulary Practice

Best Practices Toolkit†

PowerNotes DVD-ROM†

Connections: Nonfiction for Common Core CD-ROM†

Teacher One Stop DVD-ROM

Student One Stop DVD-ROM

Media*Smart* DVD-ROM
Changing Views of Native Americans / from The Crucible

Write*Smart* CD-ROM†

GrammarNotes DVD-ROM†

Wordsharp CD-ROM†

Media**Smart**

Media Studies

Changing Views of Native Americans

Illustrations Inspired by Poe

American Landscapes

Advertising in the Jazz Age

Zora Neale Hurston: Jump at the Sun

Perspectives in the News

Differentiated Instruction

STRUGGLING READERS AND WRITERS	ENGLISH LANGUAGE LEARNERS	ADVANCED LEARNERS
Resource Manager Unit 1 Additional Selection Questions Question Support Reading Fluency **Interactive Reader** **Adapted Interactive Reader** **Level Up Online Tutorials** **Audio Anthology** (with Audio summaries) **Diagnostic and Selection Tests** Selection Tests A/B	**Resource Manager Unit 1** Selection Summaries in English, Spanish, Vietnamese and Haitian Creole Skills Copymasters in Spanish **English Language Learner Adapted Interactive Reader Teacher's Guide** **ELL Adapted Interactive Reader** **Guide to English for Newcomers** **Audio Anthology** **Audio Summaries in Multiple Languages** (on **thinkcentral.com**)	**Resource Manager Unit 1** Additional Selection Questions Ideas for Extension **Diagnostic and Selection Tests** Selection Tests B/C

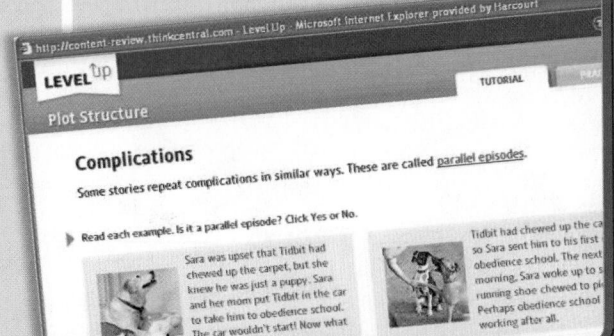

http://content-review.thinkcentral.com - Level Up : Microsoft Internet Explorer provided by Harcourt

LEVEL up

Plot Structure

TUTORIAL

Complications

Some stories repeat complications in similar ways. These are called parallel episodes.

Read each example. Is it a parallel episode? Click Yes or No.

Assessment and Reteaching

Diagnostic and Selection Tests

Unit and Benchmark Tests

ThinkCentral Online Assessment:
- All program assessments
- Level Up Online Tutorials

ExamView Test Generator on the Teacher One Stop DVD-ROM

Online Essay Scoring on **thinkcentral.com**

ThinkCentral Online Reteaching:
- Level Up Online Tutorials
- Reteaching Worksheets

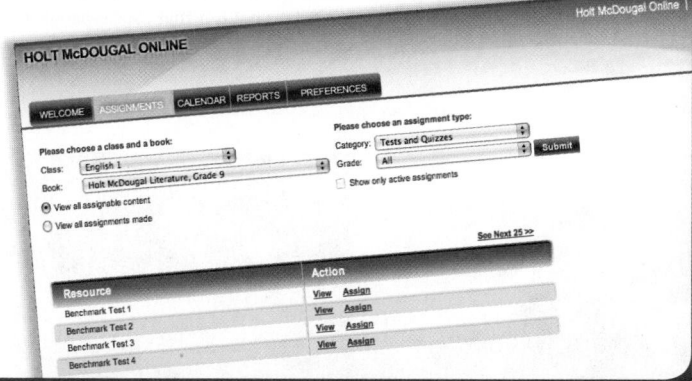

Professional Development

Video Center Based on interviews with program consultants and other educational experts, these videos feature classroom-ready teaching strategies.

Teacher Toolkit Includes a Teacher Handbook as well as a range of articles and handouts by program consultants and other educators.

Janet Allen

Kylene Beers

Jim Burke

Carol Jago

THINK central at a Glance

One Location, Endless Resources

Find Resources Browse all *Holt McDougal Literature* components for the ones that meet your students' needs and match your teaching style.

Assess Progress and Reteach Assign electronic versions of program assessments to measure your students' mastery of the Common Core State Standards. On thinkcentral.com, some tests deliver online remediation tutorials to students who have not mastered skills.

 Interactive Whiteboard Lessons

Prepare your students for college and careers by teaching relevant, real-world skills through dynamic, interactive instruction. Go to **thinkcentral.com** to browse through all whiteboard lessons, including the following:

- Citing Textual Evidence
- Historical and Cultural Context
- Evaluating Arguments

 Together Holt McDougal and HISTORY® are revolutionizing the study of English/language arts with video that helps students relive and re-imagine the people, places, and events they are discovering through reading. Look for selections with the HISTORY® icon.

COMMON CORE FOCUS

RL 9 Demonstrate knowledge of eighteenth-century foundational works of American literature, including how two or more texts from the same period treat similar themes or topics. **RI 9** Analyze documents of historical and literary significance for their themes, purposes, and rhetorical features.

Questions of the Times

Read aloud the questions on pages 20 and 21 and the paragraphs that follow them. Open the discussion of each idea by having students respond to the questions that conclude each paragraph. Use these notes to prompt further exploration of the ideas.

Who owns the LAND?

Challenge students to give reasons why one group of people should have more rights to land than another. Discuss whether the argument of "they were here first" is sufficient grounds to merit ownership forever.

What makes an EXPLORER?

Encourage students to suggest additional motivators—both internal and external—that would cause people "to seek out the unknown" despite the various risks of doing so. Extend the discussion by asking what character traits modern-day explorers are likely to share with early explorers.

Questions of the Times

DISCUSS With your whole class or in small groups, discuss these questions. Keep them in mind as you read the selections in this unit and consider how early American writers tried to answer them.

Who owns the LAND?

For thousands of years, Native Americans regarded themselves as caretakers, not owners, of the land. The Europeans who began arriving in North America, however, saw things differently. They laid claim to the land and aggressively defended it from Native Americans—and from one another. In the end, the British claim overpowered all others. Yet the question remains: What entitles people to claim land as their own?

What makes an EXPLORER?

America's early explorers traveled for many reasons: to gain glory for themselves or for their countries, to find gold or other riches, to discover new routes for travel and trade. Yet none of these motivators alone seems enough to make the uncertainties of exploration—unknown destinations, unknown rewards, unknown dangers—worth the risk. What is it that causes people to seek out the unknown?

20

○ COMMON CORE

RL 9 Demonstrate knowledge of eighteenth-century foundational works of American literature, including how two or more texts from the same period treat similar themes or topics. **RI 9** Analyze documents of historical and literary significance for their themes, purposes, and rhetorical features.

Are people basically GOOD?

Puritan settlers believed that human beings were sinful creatures doomed to a fiery eternity unless saved by the grace of God. Yet others who came to North America celebrated the powers of reason and proclaimed the goodness and intrinsic worth of humans. Are people destined always to struggle against their basest instincts? Or are they fundamentally good—and capable of becoming even better?

Who has the right to RULE?

For centuries, European kings and queens had ruled because it was believed that they had a God-given right to do so. But in the Age of Enlightenment, people began to question basic assumptions about government. In America, a popular uprising put a new kind of government to the test: democracy. With this experiment, the young American nation was asking: Who really has the right to rule?

Are people basically GOOD?

Prompt students to explain which early American group would be more likely to agree with their views—the Puritans or the settlers who celebrated the powers of reason.

Who has the right to RULE?

Have students identify the fundamental differences between a system based on "a God-given right" to rule and a system based on democracy. Challenge students to explain why one system is superior to the other in terms of reflecting the will of the people governed.

COMMON CORE FOCUS

RL 9 Demonstrate knowledge of eighteenth-century foundational works of American literature, including how two or more texts from the same period treat similar themes or topics. **RI 9** Analyze documents of historical and literary significance for their themes, purposes, and rhetorical features.

The following essay (pages 22–31) provides students with a historical context for the Unit 1 reading selections. It presents a brief overview of significant events occurring during the time period, 1600–1800, and introduces key people, places, and ideas of the times.

To get started, read and discuss the opening paragraph on page 22. Call students' attention to the various groups mentioned: explorers, settlers, colonists, revolutionaries. Ask students to review the role that each of these groups played in the creation of "an entirely new country and unique way of life." Discuss the kinds of challenges that early settlers faced, and ask why writers of the time would have wanted to record them.

READING STRATEGY

■ TAKING NOTES

Have students outline the historical essays they read. Ask volunteers to summarize what the essay is about.

About the Art *The Mayflower in Plymouth Harbor* (1882) is an oil painting by artist William Formby Halsall (1841–1919). Born in England, Halsall himself later immigrated to the United States, where he studied art at the Lowell Institute in Boston. Later, he became a sailor and went to sea for seven years. This painting shows the English ship that carried the Pilgrims to Plymouth, Massachusetts, in 1620.

Early American Writing
1600–1800

An Emerging Nation

For many people, early America was an experiment in hope. Explorers seeking adventure, settlers searching for religious freedom, colonists building communities, revolutionaries designing a new government—all embraced their challenges with a sense of faith and purpose. Writers of the day recorded and interpreted the extraordinary experiences of these ordinary people. They and their fellow colonists imagined and created an entirely new country and unique way of life.

22

DIFFERENTIATED INSTRUCTION

FOR STRUGGLING READERS

Vocabulary Support To help students understand the essay, review these words.

- *colony,* "a group of people who settle in a new country but retain ties to their home"

- *colonist,* "a person who lives in a colony"

- *chronicle,* "to write a historical account"

- *self-rule,* "government of a group by its own members"

- *subject,* "a person under the control of a sovereign power"

- *parliament,* "England's lawmaking body"

- *export,* "to send (goods) out of one's country"

- *import,* "to bring (goods) in from another country"

- *raw materials,* "materials in their natural state that can be used to manufacture products"

Early American Writing: Historical Context

Early American literature captures a nation in its infancy. From the first interactions between Native Americans and Europeans to the stirring cries of the Revolutionary War, writers chronicled the tensions and the triumphs of the day.

◯ COMMON CORE

RL 9 Demonstrate knowledge of eighteenth-century foundational works of American literature, including how two or more texts from the same period treat similar themes or topics. **RI 9** Analyze documents of historical and literary significance for their themes, purposes, and rhetorical features.

The Meeting of Two Worlds

Explorers and early settlers forged a life for themselves in America that was completely foreign to what they had known in their home countries. In fact, so extraordinary were their experiences that the earliest American writers concentrated mainly on describing and trying to make sense out of their challenging new environment and the unfamiliar people with whom they shared it. In diaries, letters, and reports back home, they recorded a historical turning point: when the world of the Europeans first intersected with that of the Native Americans.

Unknown to Europeans, people had been living in the Americas for at least tens of thousands of years, adapting to its diverse environments, forming communities, establishing trading networks, and building working cities. Millions of people lived in the Americas on the eve of the arrival of the Europeans—as many as lived in Europe at the time.

The earliest writers chronicled how the Europeans and Native Americans viewed one another and the North American land. In 1634, for example, **William Wood** of Massachusetts Bay Colony noted that the Native Americans "took the first ship they saw for a walking island, the mast to be a tree, the sail white clouds." **William Bradford,** governor of Plymouth Plantation, in turn described North America as "a hideous and desolate wilderness, full of wild beasts and wild men." The land, however, was neither desolate nor hideous, and the Native Americans were usually cooperative—at least until they began to be forced off their land by European colonists.

From Colony to Country

The first permanent colony was established at **Jamestown** in 1607. By 1733, English colonies stretched all along the Atlantic coast. Once rooted in North American soil, the colonies became increasingly self-reliant and practiced local self-rule.

LOYALTY TO ENGLAND The first colonists thought of themselves as English subjects, even though they did not have representatives in the British parliament. They supported England economically by exporting raw materials to the homeland and importing Britain's manufactured goods.

Britain, in turn, protected its territory. It sent soldiers to fight during the **French and Indian War** (1759–1763), when France allied with a

The Mayflower in Plymouth Harbor, (1882), William Formby Halsall. © Pilgrim Hall Museum, Plymouth, Massachusetts.

> ▶ **TAKING NOTES**
>
> **Outlining** As you read this introduction, use an outline to record the main ideas about the characteristics and the literature of the period. You can use article headings, boldfaced terms, and the information in these boxes as starting points. (See page R49 in the **Handbook** for more help with outlining.)
>
> *Early American Writing*
> I. *Historical Context*
> A. *The Meeting of Two Worlds*
>   I. *Early writers described land and people.*
>   2. *Native Americans had well-established communities when Europeans arrived.*
>   3. *Writers chronicled Native American and European views of one another.*
> B. *From Colony to Country*

Early American Writing: Historical Context

This section of the essay (pages 23–24) tells how the earliest American writers described the strange new environment of the Americas and the first encounters with Native Americans. The text also explains the establishment of English colonies in North America and the subsequent rebellion, resulting in the birth of the United States of America.

TIERED DISCUSSION PROMPTS

Use these prompts to help students understand the ideas in **The Meeting of Two Worlds:**

Summarize What was life like in the Americas prior to the arrival of the Europeans? *Possible answer: Native Americans enjoyed a well-established way of life.*

Analyze How do the William Wood and William Bradford quotations illustrate the clash of cultures that occurred when Europeans and Native Americans first met? *Possible answer: The quotations show how unfamiliar each group was with the other's way of life. The Native Americans had never before seen a ship, while the Europeans viewed North America as "a desolate wilderness."*

Evaluate Were Wood and Bradford fair in their assessment of the landscape and population of North America? *Possible answer: Their lack of experience with the land and people of North America made Wood and Bradford unqualified to fairly assess either. While Wood's description of the Native Americans' reaction to the ship is relatively unbiased, it is unfair of Bradford to call them "wild men." The passage also suggests that Bradford is inaccurate depiction of the American landscape as "hideous and desolate."*

FOR ENGLISH LANGUAGE LEARNERS

Cultural Connections Have students volunteer examples of colonies in their homelands, such as Spanish colonies in Latin America and French colonies in Africa.

FOR ADVANCED LEARNERS/AP*

Brainstorm Have students brainstorm a list of "the tensions and the triumphs of the day" that writers would have been most likely to chronicle. Which items on the list proved to have historical significance, and why?

* AP is a registered trademark of the College Entrance Examination Board. Use of the trademark does not constitute production, participation, sponsorship, or endorsement by the College Board.

CHECK UNDERSTANDING

Have students describe the significance of these names:

- Jamestown
- French and Indian War
- Declaration of Independence
- Constitution of the United States

About the Art The illustration of the Boston Tea Party is from an engraving (c. 1845) commemorating the dumping of tea into Boston Harbor by colonists in 1773. The skull and crossbones drawing is a cartoon inspired by the Stamp Act. It appeared in 1765 in the *Pennsylvania Journal,* a newspaper that shut down in protest of the Stamp Act.

Cultural Influences

This section of the essay (pages 24–25) explains who the Puritans were and describes their beliefs and values. The text points out positive aspects of Puritanism, such as hard work and thrift, as well as negative aspects, such as intolerance.

TIERED DISCUSSION PROMPTS

Use these prompts to discuss **Puritan Beliefs:**

Recall Why did many Puritans leave England and come to America? *Possible answer: Many Puritans left England in order to be free to worship as they pleased without fear of persecution.*

Analyze How does Winthrop's notion of the "City upon a hill" reflect the Puritan notion of the "elect"? *Possible answer: "A City upon a hill" is a fitting metaphor for the Puritan community. Puritans believed that God chose them to be above all others and to set an example of Christian piety for people to look up to and emulate.*

---

number of Native American groups to drive the British out of North America. After many defeats, England brought in new military leaders and made its own alliance with Native Americans—the powerful Iroquois. After a long and costly war, the victorious Great Britain claimed all of North America east of the Mississippi River.

A BREAK WITH ENGLAND When Great Britain tried to tax the colonists to recover some of the money spent on the war, however, it ended up losing far more than its war costs. Fired by cries of "No taxation without representation," the colonists protested British control—in both fiery words and bold actions. With each new act of British "tyranny," writers for colonial newspapers and pamphlets stirred the hearts and minds of the colonists to support independence.

The colonies declared themselves to be "free and independent" in 1776 and fought and defeated one of the greatest military powers on earth to turn their declaration into a reality. The remarkable minds of **Benjamin Franklin, Thomas Jefferson,** and other colonial thinkers put timeless words to this experiment in the form of the **Declaration of Independence** and the **Constitution of the United States.** When the Constitution was approved in 1788, the United States of America was born.

British parliament imposed the Stamp Act and the Tea Act to gain revenue from the colonies. Instead, these acts incited revolt. The Boston Tea Party was but one of many skirmishes leading to the Revolutionary War.

Cultural Influences

Religion was the most influential cultural force on writers of this period. Puritan values and beliefs directed people's everyday lives as well as the formation of an American society.

Puritan Beliefs

Many of the settlers in the 1600s were Puritans. **Puritans** were a group of English Protestants who had sought to "purify" the Church of England and return to simpler ways of worshiping. Their efforts had been most unwelcome in England, however, and many left the country for America to escape persecution.

Puritan settlers believed themselves chosen by God to create a new order in America. **John Winthrop,** for example, wrote in 1630 that "we must consider that we shall be as a City upon a hill. The eyes of all people are upon us." Puritans' values directed every aspect of their lives. They saw human struggle with sin as a daily mission and believed, above all else, that the Bible would help them through the torments of human weakness. Although they felt that humans were essentially sinful, they believed that some, the "elect," would be spared from eternal punishment by God's grace.

DIFFERENTIATED INSTRUCTION

FOR ENGLISH LANGUAGE LEARNERS

Analyze Word Connotations Ask students to look through the section on Puritan beliefs for words with positive and negative connotations. Discuss what these words reveal about the good and bad sides of Puritanism.

Positive	Negative
hard workers	inflexible
thrifty	intolerant
responsible	

FOR STRUGGLING READERS

Vocabulary Support To help students better understand the essay, review these terms.

- *alliance,* "a union or agreement between groups or nations for mutual benefit"
- *tyranny,* "unfair use of power"
- *persecution,* "mistreatment because of one's beliefs"
- *ideal,* "a perfect example of something; a goal to which people aspire"
- *democracy,* "government that is run by the people"

Hard work, thrift, and responsibility were therefore seen as morally good, a sign that God was working within. The thriving settlements and financial success that grew from these qualities were thought to be a mark of God's approval. However, Puritanism had a dark side as well. Puritans tended to be inflexible in their religious faith and intolerant of viewpoints other than their own. In one famous case, the Salem witchcraft trials, a whole community fell victim to the hysteria of the witch-hunt, ending with more than 20 people dead by execution.

Ideas of the Age

In the 1700s, both Enlightenment ideals and Puritan values contributed to the country's thirst for independence.

The Enlightenment

In the 1700s, there was a burst of intellectual energy taking place in Europe that came to be known as the **Enlightenment**. Enlightenment thinkers had begun to question previously accepted truths about who should hold the power in government. Their thinking pointed the way to a government by the people—one in which people consent to government limitations in exchange for the government's protection of their basic rights and liberties.

American colonists adapted these Enlightenment ideals to their own environment. The political writings of **Benjamin Franklin, Thomas Paine,** and **Thomas Jefferson** shaped the **American Enlightenment** and began to eclipse even the most brilliant European thought. Enlightenment ideals prompted action and gave colonists a philosophical footing for their revolution. "I know not what course others may take," **Patrick Henry** thundered to the delegates at the second Virginia Convention in 1775, "but as for me, give me liberty, or give me death!"

> **A Voice from the Times**
>
> *We hold these truths to be self-evident, that all men are created equal, that they are endowed by their Creator with certain unalienable Rights, that among these are Life, Liberty, and the pursuit of Happiness.*
>
> —Thomas Jefferson
> from the Declaration
> of Independence

The Great Awakening

At the same time, many people began to worry that Puritan values were being lost. Preachers such as **Jonathan Edwards** called for people to rededicate themselves to the original Puritan vision, and a new wave of religious enthusiasm began to rise. This movement, called the **First Great Awakening,** united colonists who were in other ways diverse. Across the colonies, people began to feel joined in the belief that a higher power was helping Americans set a new standard for an ethical life.

While the Enlightenment and the Great Awakening emphasized opposing aspects of human experience—reason and emotionalism, respectively—they had similar consequences. Both caused people to question traditional authority, eventually leading colonists to break from Britain's control and embrace democracy.

Early American Literature

This section of the essay (pages 26–31) focuses on early American writing. The text describes

- Native American oral literature
- historical narratives written by explorers, early settlers, and colonists
- sermons, histories, and poetry of Puritan writers
- political pamphlets that fueled the American Revolution
- the Declaration of Independence and the Constitution
- contributions of women writers of the time

Analyze Visuals

Possible answer: The sculpture represents the natural world playing a vital role in the world of humans. It suggests that people have a close, respectful relationship with nature.

About the Art *Raven and the First Men,* a seven-foot-tall sculpture carved by Canadian sculptor Bill Reid (1920–1998), reflects the artist's lifelong interest in Haida art and cultural tradition. The Haida are Native Americans who live on islands off the west coast of North America. Reid's mother was of Haida descent.

TIERED DISCUSSION PROMPTS

Use these prompts to help students understand the ideas in **The Native American Experience:**

Interpret From the perspective of the Native American holy woman, how is oral tradition more meaningful than the written word? *Possible answer: Oral tradition requires each person to learn and remember historical and cultural information. The written word requires only that someone read what another person has recorded.*

Evaluate Why is preservation through oral tradition more vulnerable to loss than preservation through written works? *Possible answer: Oral tradition requires people to remember and accurately communicate to others their history, legends, and myths. Written works preserve such information on the printed page, creating a lasting record.*

Early American Literature

Early American writing is as varied as early Americans themselves. Native Americans, explorers, settlers, and revolutionaries all contributed their own perspectives to our knowledge of this literary period.

The Native American Experience

When the Europeans arrived, there were more than 300 different Native American cultures in North America with strongly differing customs and about 200 different languages spoken. Yet wherever they lived—in the smoky longhouses of the Northeastern woodlands, the well-defended cliff dwellings of the desert Southwest, the cedar-scented lodges of the Pacific Northwest—one activity was common to all: storytelling.

The Native North American cultures did not have a written language. Instead, a group's history, legends, and myths were entrusted to memory and faithfully passed from generation to generation through **oral tradition.** In the words of one Native American holy woman, "When you write things down you don't have to remember them. But for us it is different. . . . [A]ll that we are, all that we have ever been, all the great names of our heroes and their songs and deeds are alive within each of us. . . living in our blood."

► *For Your Notes*

NATIVE AMERICANS

- were culturally diverse
- had an oral tradition
- had many different genres of spoken literature
- explored common themes, such as a reverence for nature and the worship of many gods

◄ **Analyze Visuals**
This modern depiction of a Haida creation story shows the Raven (a popular cultural hero in many Native American myths and legends) opening a shell to release the first humans into the world. What relationship between humans and the natural world does this sculpture suggest?

Raven and the First Men (1980), Bill Reid. Yellow cedar. University of British Columbia Museum of Anthropology, Vancouver, Canada.

DIFFERENTIATED INSTRUCTION

FOR STRUGGLING READERS

Oral Tradition Emphasize that before written language was invented, people around the world used oral tradition to preserve their literature. Today, oral tradition has been largely replaced by print and electronic media.

Vocabulary Support

- *oral tradition,* "the practice of storytelling to pass a group's memories, histories, and stories from one generation to the next"
- *legendary histories,* "stories passed down from earlier times and popularly regarded as true"

LITERARY STYLE The forms of Native American oral literature are rich and varied. Creation stories, ways to explain how the universe and humans came into being, can be found in every Native American culture. Other forms include legendary histories tracing the migration of peoples or the deeds of great leaders, fairy tales, lyrics, chants, children's songs, healing songs, and dream visions.

Tragically, much of this literature did not survive after so many Native Americans fell to European diseases. Some groups lost as many as 90 percent of their people, all of whom had a share in preserving the traditional stories. The surviving works, however, show that diverse Native American groups explored common themes in their spoken literature, including a reverence for nature and the worship of many gods.

Exploration and the Early Settlers

While Native American literature offers us a glimpse into the ways and values of America's indigenous peoples, much of our understanding of pre-colonial America comes from the first-person accounts of its early explorers, settlers, and colonists. The journals, diaries, letters, logs, and historical narratives of those first Europeans to view the American landscape describe in vivid detail its many sights and wonders, as well as its dangers and challenges.

THE EXPLORERS The first of these writings were the journals and letters of **Christopher Columbus,** which recounted his four voyages to the Americas begun in 1492. Columbus's adventures opened the door to a century of Spanish expeditions in the Americas. Incapable of visualizing the historical significance of his travels, however, he died disappointed, convinced that he had barely missed the cities of gold described by Marco Polo. His fascinating journals provide a vivid record of the most significant journeys of his time.

Just over 50 years later came *La Relación.* This report by **Álvar Núñez Cabeza de Vaca,** one of the four survivors of the 600-man Narváez expedition, chronicled his eight years of wandering through Florida, Texas, and Mexico. In it he describes the landscape and people he encountered, as well as animals that were new to Europeans. The French and Dutch also sent explorers such as **Samuel de Champlain,** the "Father of New France," who in the early 1600s wrote vivid accounts of New England and the Iroquois.

EARLY SETTLERS The early English settlers described their difficult and amazing new lives in letters, reports, and chronicles to friends and family back home. Their writings helped people in England imagine what life might be like in America. One of the most influential writings was *A Brief and True Report of the New Found Land of Virginia,* by **Thomas Harriot,** which faithfully captured the area's natural resources, the ways of life of the Native Americans, and the potential for building a successful colony. It was published in 1588 and was accompanied by illustrations that helped thousands upon thousands of English readers form their first clear picture of North America.

▶ *For Your Notes*

EXPLORERS

- Columbus's journals chronicle his four voyages to the Americas.
- Cabeza de Vaca's *La Relación* tells of his failed expedition.
- Samuel de Champlain wrote accounts of New England and the Iroquois.

EARLY SETTLERS

- Settlers described the new land for those still in Europe.
- Accounts helped English readers visualize North America.

COLONISTS

- Writers focused on the story of the new settlements and their larger purpose.
- Equiano, an enslaved African, described his unjust treatment.

Use this prompt to continue discussion of **The Native American Experience:**

Synthesize How did the arrival of the Europeans affect the preservation of Native American literature? *Possible answer: When Native Americans were exposed to European diseases, as many as 90 percent of them died. The death of so many Native Americans left fewer people to remember and, thereby, to preserve the oral tradition of their literature.*

ADDITIONAL BACKGROUND

Marco Polo (1254–1324) was an Italian traveler famous for his accounts of China. Columbus consulted Polo's writings when planning his voyage to reach Asia.

CHECK UNDERSTANDING

Ask students what accounts left by early explorers and settlers contribute to our understanding of precolonial America.

FOR STRUGGLING READERS
Vocabulary Support

- *longhouse,* "a long rectangular dwelling of some Native Americans, such as the Iroquois"
- *migration,* "movement from one region or country to another"
- *indigenous,* "originating in a region; natural"
- *expedition,* "a journey undertaken for a particular purpose, such as exploration"

FOR ADVANCED LEARNERS/AP

Explore Harriot's Work Have students locate (via the Internet or a library) and read portions of Thomas Harriot's *A Brief and True Report of the New Found Land of Virginia.* Discuss Harriot's observations and descriptions of Native Americans. If pictures accompany the text, discuss how they contribute to the students' knowledge of the time.

A modern reconstruction of the original Jamestown, Virginia, settlement

DISCUSSION PROMPT

Use this prompt to help students discuss colonial histories:

Analyze In what ways do the writings of Captain John Smith, William Bradford, John Winthrop, and Olaudah Equiano reflect their different perspectives and purposes?
Possible answer: Smith wrote vivid, "sometimes embroidered" accounts of life in the early colonies, which attracted settlers to Virginia. Bradford and Winthrop wrote more seriously, reflecting on "their role in God's plan for a better society." Equiano recounted his capture and brutal treatment, offering readers insight into the life of a slave.

COLONIAL HISTORIES As the colonies took root, writing began to focus less on pure description and more on the story of the growth of the colonies. In contrast to the carefully accurate Harriot, for example, **Captain John Smith** wrote sometimes-embroidered accounts of the history of Virginia and New England. By force of his vivid and engaging writing, he created an enduring record of life in the early colonies and an intriguing self-portrait of a man proud of his great deeds and eager to gain recognition. His accounts were also instrumental in attracting settlers to Virginia, thus ensuring the eventual success of that colony.

Other writers who documented the history of the New England settlements wrote in a plainer style and with a more serious purpose. **William Bradford,** longtime governor of Plymouth, and **John Winthrop Sr.,** who served as governor of Massachusetts, reflected upon what they saw as their role in God's plan for a better society. But not all who wrote narrative histories saw the colonists' efforts as following God's plan. **Olaudah Equiano** described his harsh capture from his African home and the brutal and "un-Christian" treatment he received as a slave in the West Indies.

> **A Voice from the Times**
>
> *So as there died sometimes two or three of a day . . . , that of one hundred and odd persons, scarce fifty remained.*
>
> —**William Bradford**
> from *Of Plymouth Plantation*

The Puritan Tradition

Puritan writers had their own purposes for recording history. They believed writing should be useful, a tool to help readers understand the Bible and guide them in their daily lives. For this reason, logic, clarity, and order were more prized in writing than beauty or adornment. One Puritan compared adorned writing to stained-glass windows. "The paint upon the glass may feed the fancy, but the room is not well lighted by it." Using a familiar, down-to-earth metaphor such as this to make a deeper point is a common feature of Puritan writing. The direct, powerful, plain language of much of American literature owes a debt to the Puritans.

> ▶ *For Your Notes*
> **PURITAN WRITERS**
> - believed writing should be useful and clear
> - wrote histories, sermons, scientific works, and essays
> - delivered sermons contrasting good and evil
> - wrote poems with religious themes

DIFFERENTIATED INSTRUCTION

FOR STRUGGLING READERS
Vocabulary Support
- *sermon,* "a public talk about religious or moral matters, usually given by a member of the clergy"
- *treatise,* "a formal piece of writing about a particular subject"
- *meditation,* "a formal speech or writing, often about sacred matters, intended to express the author's thoughts or to guide others"

FOR ADVANCED LEARNERS/AP
Joint-Stock Companies While Spanish and French rulers funded their colonies directly, British rulers granted charters for colonies to groups of investors called joint-stock companies. Have students research the joint-stock companies that financed the colonies in Virginia and New England and discuss how they may have affected the composition of the histories of those settlements.

SERMONS AND OTHER WRITINGS The works of Puritan writers, such as **Cotton Mather** and **Jonathan Edwards,** include histories of the colonies and fiery sermons on the dangers of sinful ways. Along with histories and sermons, Cotton Mather chronicled the disturbing Salem witch trials, where 20 people were condemned to death in an atmosphere of mass hysteria. He also wrote about scientific matters, including inoculation for smallpox.

Like Mather, Jonathan Edwards wrote on a variety of subjects, including the flying (or ballooning) spiders he had observed as a boy. His account of these spiders is considered the first natural history essay on that subject. A spider makes another, very different kind of appearance in Edwards's best-known work, his sermon "Sinners in the Hands of an Angry God." In that sermon he warns his listeners that God "holds you over the pit of hell, much as one holds a spider, or some loathsome insect over the fire."

Imagine the scene when Edwards first delivered this sermon: the congregation quaking in fear from Edwards's vivid descriptions of hellfire and a vengeful god. "Sinners in the Hands of an Angry God," while perhaps more fiery than most, is typical of the Puritan sermon. Melodramatic contrasts between good and evil, vivid imagery, powerful language, and strong moral lessons characterized this form of literature.

PURITAN POETRY Most Puritan writers composed "plain" sermons, histories, and treatises, but poetry was the means of expression for others. In fact, the first book issued in the North American colonies was the the *Bay Psalm Book* in 1640, in which the Bible's psalms were rewritten to fit the rhythms of familiar Puritan hymns.

Puritan poets such as **Anne Bradstreet** and **Edward Taylor** viewed poetry primarily as a means of exploring the relationship between the individual and God. Bradstreet's poems reflect her wide learning, deep faith, and love for her husband and children. They also provide insight into the position of women in the male-dominated Puritan society. Her book of poetry, *The Tenth Muse Lately Sprung Up in America* (1650), was the first work by a North American woman to be published. Minister Edward Taylor, possibly considered the best-known Puritan poet, wrote most of his poems as aids for his meditations. His poetry, like much Puritan writing, uses vivid images from nature and from everyday life as a way to help readers grasp the spiritual world beyond.

> **A Voice from the Times**
>
> *I made seeking salvation the main business of my life.*
>
> —Jonathan Edwards

Evangelical preacher George Whitefield was a key figure in the revival movement of America's "Great Awakening."

TIERED DISCUSSION PROMPTS

Use these prompts to help students understand the ideas in **The Puritan Tradition:**

Analyze The essay quotes a Puritan as saying, "The paint upon the glass may feed the fancy, but the room is not well lighted by it." Explain how this quotation represents the Puritans' approach to writing. ***Possible answer:*** *The quotation conveys this idea by noting the Puritans' preference for things that are simple and functional (plain glass) over things that are decorative and fancy (stained-glass windows).*

Synthesize On page 25 you learned that the Puritans were practical people who valued "hard work, thrift, and responsibility." How do the writings of Cotton Mather and Jonathan Edwards reflect an interest in practical as well as spiritual matters? ***Possible answer:*** *In addition to writing religious sermons, Mather and Edwards documented practical observations and historical events that help readers better understand life in the Puritan colonies. Examples include Mather's writing about the Salem witch trials and smallpox inoculation, and Edwards's writing about the spiders he remembered from childhood.*

Evaluate In what ways do the works of Puritan poets Anne Bradstreet and Edward Taylor provide insight into the Puritan way of life? ***Possible answer:*** *In addition to focusing on the Puritan ideals of faith and family, Bradstreet's poetry helps readers see the world from the perspective of a woman living in a "male-dominated Puritan society." Taylor uses familiar images "from nature and from everyday life" to explore spirituality. In this way, his poetry reflects the Puritan belief that "writing should be useful, a tool to help readers understand the Bible and guide them in their daily lives."*

FOR STRUGGLING READERS

Taking Notes Have students record the main ideas about the Puritan writing tradition (pages 28–29) in outline form. Then ask students to exchange papers and evaluate each other's work. Tell them to offer specific suggestions for possible improvement.

Sample notes:

Puritans
- Puritans believed writing should be useful.
- They prized reason, logic, clarity, and order.

Sermons and Other Writing
- Cotton Mather chronicled Salem witch trials.
- Jonathan Edwards wrote fiery sermons.

Puritan Poetry
- Puritan poetry was a means of exploring the relationship between the individual and God.
- Outstanding poets included Anne Bradstreet and Edward Taylor.

Writers of the Revolution

It is curious to consider now, but some of the most famous figures of the American Revolution lived at the same time as Puritans such as Jonathan Edwards. As products of the Enlightenment, however, revolutionary writers focused their energies on matters of government rather than religion.

PAMPHLETS AND PROPAGANDA Many of the gifted minds of this period were drawn to political writing as the effort to launch a grand experiment in government took shape in North America. The most important outlet for the spread of these political writings was the pamphlet. Between 1763 and 1783, about two thousand pamphlets were published. These inexpensive "little books" became the fuel of the revolution, reaching thousands of people quickly and stirring debate and action in response to growing discontent with British rule.

Through these pamphlets the words that would define the American cause against Great Britain became the currency of the day, and the debate about independence grew louder and louder. One such pamphlet, *Common Sense,* by **Thomas Paine,** helped propel the colonists to revolution. Though

▶ *For Your Notes*

WRITERS OF THE REVOLUTION

- expressed the ideas of the Enlightenment
- concentrated on political writing
- used pamphlets to spread ideas
- focused on natural law and human rights
- played a key role in the creation of a new nation

A Voice from the Times

These are the times that try men's souls: The summer soldier and the sunshine patriot will, in this crisis, shrink from the service of his country; but he that stands it NOW, *deserves the love and thanks of man and woman.*

—**Thomas Paine**
from *The Crisis*

Soldier of the Revolution (1876), George Willoughby Maynard. Oil on canvas, 51″ × 39″. Photo © Christie's Images Ltd.

30

---

expressing the views of the rational Enlightenment, Paine also agreed with the Puritan belief that America had a special destiny to be a model to the rest of the world. At the end of his stirring essay, he says that freedom had been hunted down around the globe and calls on America to "receive the fugitive," to give freedom a home, and to welcome people from around the world to its free society.

WRITING THAT LAUNCHED A NATION Thomas Jefferson also wrote pamphlets, but his great contribution to American government, literature, and the cause of freedom throughout the world is the **Declaration of Independence,** in which he eloquently articulated the **natural law** that would govern America. This natural law is the idea that people are born with rights and freedoms and that it is the function of government to protect those freedoms.

Eleven years later, after the Revolutionary War had ended, delegates from all but one state gathered at the Philadelphia State House—in the same room in which the Declaration of Independence had been signed—in order to discuss forming a new government. The delegates included many outstanding leaders of the time, such as **Benjamin Franklin, Alexander Hamilton,** and **George Washington.** Four months later, they emerged with perhaps the country's most important piece of writing: the **Constitution of the United States of America.** Although Washington said at the time, "I do not expect the Constitution to last for more than 20 years," it was indeed flexible enough to last through the centuries to come.

VOICES OF THE PEOPLE Statesmen were not the only ones to contribute to the discussion of the day, however. In that age of political writing, even poetry sometimes examined political and social themes. Among the finest is the work of former slave **Phillis Wheatley.** In her poems and letters, Wheatley wrote of the "natural rights" of African-Americans and pointed out the discrepancy between the colonists' "cry for freedom" and their enslavement of fellow human beings.

Another voice calling for the rights of all citizens was **Abigail Adams,** whose husband John became the nation's second president. In letters written while the couple was apart, Adams encouraged her husband to include the rights of women in the nation's founding documents.

Wheatley, Adams, and other women writers join the Native Americans, colonists, Puritans, and patriots who came before them to give us an understanding of the dreams and values that shaped our nation. All contributed their voices and ideals to building this "city upon a hill."

The "Father of American Portraiture"

Many colonial artists earned their livings with portraits, which were in high demand. Gilbert Stuart was among the best of colonial portrait painters. Because he painted the likenesses of virtually all the notable men and women of the period (including the first five American presidents), he earned himself the moniker "The Father of American Portraiture" by his contemporaries.

Painting the President One of Stuart's favorite subjects was the first president of the United States, George Washington. His 104 likenesses of Washington inform the image most of us have of our first president. In fact, one of his paintings became the basis for the one-dollar bill.

Stuart was known to chat with his subjects as they sat for his paintings. By entertaining them during the long hours of posing, he hoped to capture an unguarded, fresh expression on their faces. The serious George Washington, however, found Stuart's chat annoying. The artist says of Washington, "An apathy seemed to seize him, and a vacuity spread over his countenance, most appalling to paint." Nevertheless, in *George Washington (Vaughan portrait),* 1795, shown here, Stuart was able to capture Washington's imposing presence by placing his head high in the design and adding a crimson glow around it.

THE ARTISTS' GALLERY

American artist Gilbert Stuart (1755–1828) painted about 1000 pictures during his career, almost all of which were portraits. His numerous paintings of the first president are categorized according to their owners. Thus, the work depicted on page 31, painted in 1795, is *George Washington (Vaughan portrait).* It was bought by Samuel Vaughan, an English merchant and close friend of Washington.

Activity Ask students what qualities of George Washington they think Gilbert Stuart was trying to capture in this portrait. *Possible answer: Stuart wanted to capture Washington's dignity and self-confidence.*

DISCUSSION PROMPT

Use this prompt to help students understand the ideas in **Writers of the Revolution:**

Analyze The essay explains that in the Declaration of Independence, Jefferson argues that "people are born with rights and freedoms and that it is the function of government to protect those freedoms." How was this belief reflected in the writings of Phillis Wheatley and Abigail Adams? *Possible answer: In her poetry and letters, Wheatley wrote about the rights of African Americans and the unfairness of their enslavement. Adams's letters spoke out for the rights of women.*

CHECK UNDERSTANDING

Identify a few relevant events or figures related to each of these topics:

- The Native American Experience
- Exploration and the Early Settlers
- The Puritan Tradition
- Writers of the Revolution

FOR STRUGGLING READERS
Vocabulary Support

- *propaganda,* "ideas, opinions, or information spread to further a cause"
- *rational,* "relating to or based on reason"
- *delegate,* "a person who has the authority to act for others; representative"
- *patriot,* "a person who loves and supports his or her country"

FOR ADVANCED LEARNERS/AP

Synthesize Point out that the final sentence of the essay refers back to John Winthrop's words in the last paragraph on page 24. Ask students to review that paragraph. Then have them discuss to what extent America today still views itself as a "city upon a hill." Encourage students to support their responses with specific reasons and information.

COMMON CORE FOCUS

RI 7 Integrate and evaluate multiple sources of information presented in different media or formats as well as in words in order to address a question or solve a problem.

Connecting Literature, History, and Culture

READING SKILL — COMMON CORE RI 7

■ READ A TIMELINE

Point out that each of the three horizontal sections of the timeline—*American Literary Milestones, Historical Context,* and *World Culture and Events*—displays a sequence of events that occurred between 1600 and 1800. By looking at the vertical columns on the timeline, students can see which events were going on at approximately the same time.

Have students locate, for example, each of these events on the timeline between 1630 and 1635:

- **1630** William Bradford published *Of Plymouth Plantation.* (See *American Literary Milestones.*)

- **1632** Construction of the Taj Mahal began. (See *World Culture and Events.*)

- **1635** North America's first public school was founded. (See *Historical Context.*)

Ask students to identify events that occurred between 1787 and 1790. **Answer: *The U.S. Constitution was approved in 1787. Olaudah Equiano's narrative was published in 1789. That same year, the storming of the Bastille began the French Revolution.***

Connecting Literature, History, and Culture

Early American writing reflects the growing pains of a new nation but also reveals much about trends occurring elsewhere in the world. Use this timeline and the questions on page 33 to find connections between literature, history, and culture.

AMERICAN LITERARY MILESTONES

1600	1650
1624 John Smith publishes *The General History of Virginia.*	**1650** Anne Bradstreet's poems, collected as *The Tenth Muse Lately Sprung Up in America,* are published in London.
1630 William Bradford describes his journey across the Atlantic and pilgrims' settlement in *Of Plymouth Plantation.*	**1682** Mary Rowlandson publishes *The Sovereignty and Goodness of God,* an account of her captivity at the hands of Algonquian Indians.
1640 *Bay Psalm Book* is the first book to be printed in America. ▶	**1693** Cotton Mather publishes *The Wonders of the Invisible World* in defense of the Salem witch trials.

HISTORICAL CONTEXT

1600	1650
1607 The first permanent English settlement is founded in Jamestown, Virginia.	**1676** The Puritans' victory in King Philip's War ends Native American resistance in New England colonies.
1619 The first enslaved Africans arrive in North America at Jamestown.	**1682** William Penn founds the colony of Pennsylvania.
1620 The *Mayflower* pilgrims establish the Massachusetts Bay Colony at Plymouth. ▶	**1688** Quakers voice opposition to slavery.
1635 North America's first public school is founded in Boston.	**1692** Salem witch trials show atmosphere of mass hysteria. ▶

WORLD CULTURE AND EVENTS

1600	1650
1615 Inquisition condemns Italian scientist Galileo Galilei for supporting Copernicus's theory.	**1652** Dutch found Cape Town on the southern tip of South Africa.
1616 Shakespeare dies.	**1687** Isaac Newton publishes *Philosophiae naturalis principia mathematica,* considered to be the most important work of the Scientific Revolution.
1632 Indian emperor Shah Jahan begins construction of Taj Mahal. ▶	**1694** Japanese poet Matsuo Bashō, known for revitalizing the haiku form, dies.

DIFFERENTIATED INSTRUCTION

FOR STRUGGLING READERS

Understanding a Timeline Explain that the timeline runs chronologically (in time order) from left to right across the page. Each of the four columns represents a 50-year period between 1600 and 1800. The three parallel rows of the timeline represent events occurring simultaneously. By comparing the three rows, readers can better understand what events in literature, history, and culture were taking place at about the same time.

- Religion played a central role in America during this period. What works written at this time might support this observation?
- While American writers of this period worked mostly in nonfiction and poetry, groundbreaking novels were being written elsewhere in the world. Name one.
- The Revolutionary War was a defining event in American history. What other country held a bloody revolution during this period?

COMMON CORE

RI 7 Integrate and evaluate multiple sources of information presented in different media or formats as well as in words in order to address a question or solve a problem.

1700

1704 The *Boston Newsletter*, the first American newspaper, is established. ▶

1722 Benjamin Franklin uses humor to criticize the Puritan establishment in his first published work, *The Dogood Papers*.

1741 Jonathan Edwards delivers a sermon called "Sinners in the Hands of an Angry God." The sermon typifies the religious movement known as the Great Awakening.

1750

1774 Abigail Adams writes first entry in what is published as *Familiar Letters of John Adams and His Wife, Abigail.*

1776 Thomas Paine's widely read pamphlet *Common Sense* passionately argues the case for independence.

1776 George Washington invites Phillis Wheatley to visit after receiving from her a poem and letter.

1789 Olaudah Equiano's *The Interesting Narrative of . . . Olaudah Equiano* details harsh treatment of captive Africans. ▶

1700

1720 The colonial population reaches about a half million; Boston's population is about 12,000.

1739 The religious revival known as the Great Awakening (1739–1742) begins.

1744 The six nations of the Iroquois Confederation (whose tribe-mark is shown here) cede Ohio Valley territory north of the Ohio River to Britain. ▶

1750

1773 The Boston Tea Party marks a violent rejection of Britain's taxation policies. The Revolutionary War begins two years later. ▶

1776 July 4: Second Continental Congress adopts the Declaration of Independence.

1781 British defeat at Yorktown ends the American Revolution.

1787 U.S. Constitution is approved.

1700

1721 Johann Sebastian Bach composes the *Brandenburg Concertos.*

1725 Peter the Great, czar of Russia, dies.

1726 Jonathan Swift publishes *Gulliver's Travels.* ▶

1750

1752 Calcutta's population reaches 120,000.

1762 Catherine the Great, an "enlightened despot," becomes empress of Russia.

1784 The Indian sacred text the *Bhagavad-Gita* is translated into English for the first time.

1789 Storming of the Bastille incites the French Revolution.

1791 The classic Chinese novel *Dream of the Red Chamber* is published.

MAKING CONNECTIONS
Possible answers:

- Bay Psalm Book *(1640)*, The Sovereignty and Goodness of God *(1682)*, "Sinners in the Hands of an Angry God" *(1741)*
- Gulliver's Travels *(1726)*, Dream of the Red Chamber *(1791)*
- *France (1789)*

ADDITIONAL QUESTIONS

1. About three decades after Boston's population reached 12,000, a city in India attained a population ten times as great. Name the city. ***Answer:*** *Calcutta*

2. Fifty years after the English writer Jonathan Swift published *Gulliver's Travels,* an American writer published a pamphlet that encouraged the colonists to revolt against England. Who was the writer? What was the name of the pamphlet? ***Answers:*** *Thomas Paine;* Common Sense

FOR ADVANCED LEARNERS/AP

Making Additional Connections Ask students to choose one of the four time periods shown in the timeline and to research online, in encyclopedias, or in history texts other events that occurred during the 50-year time span. Challenge students to identify events for each category: *American Literary Milestones, Historical Context,* and *World Culture and Events.* Have students prepare and present brief oral reports, summarizing significant events and discussing their connection to events shown in the timeline or discussed in class.

The Legacy of the Era

An American Work Ethic

COMMON CORE

W 7 Conduct short research projects to answer a question; narrow the inquiry; synthesize multiple sources, demonstrating understanding of the subject. SL 1 Initiate and participate effectively in a range of collaborative discussions, building on others' ideas and expressing their own clearly and persuasively.

Shunning frivolous pleasures that would distract them from thoughts of God, Puritans instead trained their energy on hard, useful work. That hard work often led to material success, which was in turn seen as a sign of God's favor. Many Americans today also believe in the intrinsic value of hard work—as well as the idea that hard work leads to financial success.

DISCUSS With your class, discuss whether work in and of itself is something to value. What does work provide? In your opinion, does work indeed lead to success? What other factors might be involved?

34

COMMON CORE FOCUS

W 7 Conduct short research projects to answer a question; narrow the inquiry; synthesize multiple sources, demonstrating understanding of the subject. **SL 1** Initiate and participate effectively in a range of collaborative discussions, building on others' ideas and expressing their own clearly and persuasively.

An American Work Ethic

Have students read the paragraph. (You may also want to ask students to review the section on Puritan beliefs on pages 24–25 of the historical essay.) Discuss the legacy of Puritan attitudes and values. Point out that the idea of hard work leading to success is communicated to children at an early age when they are told to study hard and to get good grades.

DISCUSS Explore with students the kinds of rewards that work can provide. Elicit responses from the class, and list them on the board. ***Possible answer:*** *Work can be a source of personal satisfaction, a way to socialize with others, and a means of increasing self-esteem.* Ask the other **DISCUSS** questions. Extend the discussion by asking students how much the success of individuals can be attributed to such factors as these:

- hard work
- who you know
- luck
- perseverance
- taking risks

Encourage students to support their opinions with clear reasons.

DIFFERENTIATED INSTRUCTION

FOR STRUGGLING READERS
Vocabulary Support

- *legacy,* "something passed on from an ancestor or predecessor"
- *ethics,* "moral principles or values"
- *frivolous,* "not serious; silly"
- *intrinsic,* "essential; inherent; basic"

FOR ADVANCED LEARNERS/AP

Reflect on Working Ask students to consider how our view of work changes as we age. For example, how might a high school student's concept of hard work differ from that of a child? from that of an adult? Whose concept might be closer to the Puritan work ethic? Ask students to write an essay exploring changes in our view of work as we grow older and reflecting on the reasons for these changes. Then have students share their essays with the class.

Government by the People

Democracy is surely the most significant legacy of the early American period. Reacting against the monarchy they had left behind and embracing Enlightenment ideals, the framers of the Constitution ensured that governmental power would be shared by the people. The people would elect representatives to carry out their will, and a system of checks and balances would ensure that no one person could rule over all. More than two centuries later, the system still stands.

TAKE ACTION Contact your local representative or senator and ask for support on a current issue that affects you. For example, you may wish to discuss the condition of your local parks or the lack of an after-school center in your area. Contact information can be found at www.congress.org.

The Power of Political Writing

During the early American period, political writing served as an agent for change. Thomas Paine's *Common Sense,* for example, furthered the case for American independence. Later, when the army suffered several brutal defeats and many soldiers were deserting, Paine wrote a series of articles called *The Crisis.* These articles inspired greater public support for the war and convinced many soldiers to reenlist. Today, political writers of all stripes are working in nearly every form—hardcover, softcover, editorial, blog, newsmagazine—to influence our current political landscape.

WRITE AND DISCUSS Catalog the political writing you encounter over the course of one week. Make a list that includes the formats, the topics covered, and your response to each. Then, with a small group, discuss the issues that are motivating today's political writers. Are these writers changing the public debate, or merely recording it?

Journalist Juan Williams

FOR STRUGGLING READERS

Vocabulary Support To support instruction, clarify the meaning of these words:

- *motivate,* "encourage to act; inspire"
- *monarchy,* "a government controlled by a monarch, such as a king or queen"
- *framer,* "a person who plans or shapes something"

FOR ADVANCED LEARNERS/AP

Write to a Newspaper Have students choose an issue they feel strongly about and express their views in a letter to the editor of a local newspaper. Encourage students to take a definite position and to support their position with specific reasons and facts.

Government by the People

Have students read the paragraph. Ask volunteers to summarize the text, explaining in their own words the concept of a representative form of government.

TAKE ACTION Have students work in pairs to brainstorm local or state issues that affect them directly. Suggest they choose an issue that they can realistically address. For example, improving a local park is realistic; reducing the school week to four days is probably not. Whether students choose to contact their representative by phone, e-mail, or mail, tell them to be polite and respectful and to express their ideas clearly and specifically. Ask students to share their responses with the class.

The Power of Political Writing

Have students read the paragraph. Discuss how political writing can instigate change. Elicit or provide the various writing purposes and goals mentioned in the paragraph: *"furthered the case for . . . independence," "inspired . . . support for the war," "convinced . . . soldiers to reenlist," "influence . . . political landscape."* Ask students in what other ways political writing can affect how people think or act. *Possible answer: Political speeches influence voters.*

Point out that political writing is generally a form of persuasive writing that reflects the author's point of view. Explain that some forms of political writing are obvious, while others are more subtle. Elicit examples of both. *Possible answer: obvious—editorials, letters to the editor; more subtle—magazine articles, newspaper columns;* Then discuss how political writing is targeted to specific audiences.

WRITE AND DISCUSS Assign students the activity. Extend the discussion of their findings by exploring the similarities and differences among written pieces that address local, national, and international issues.

Focus and Motivate

COMMON CORE FOCUS

RL 1 Cite textual evidence to support analysis of what the text says explicitly as well as inferences drawn from the text, including determining where the text leaves matters uncertain. **RL 2** Determine two or more themes or central ideas of a text and analyze their development over the course of the text, including how they interact and build on one another to produce a complex account; provide an objective summary of the text.

ABOUT THE IROQUOIS

Have students read this page and summarize the key points. Students should recognize that:

- the Iroquois passed down myths such as "The World on the Turtle's Back" through oral tradition, as discussed on page 26 of the historical essay
- the term *Iroquois* refers to six separate Native American groups

NOTABLE QUOTE

"[Native American] stories . . . remind the people of who and what they are, why they are in this particular place, and how they should continue to live here."
—Larry Evers, Paul Pavich

Have students paraphrase the quotation and discuss the role of creation myths in preserving people's sense of history and tradition.

COMMON CORE

RL 1 Cite textual evidence to support analysis of what the text says explicitly as well as inferences drawn from the text, including determining where the text leaves matters uncertain.
RL 2 Determine two or more themes or central ideas of a text and analyze their development over the course of the text, including how they interact and build on one another to produce a complex account; provide an objective summary of the text.

DID YOU KNOW?

- Both the U.S. Constitution and the founding charter of the United Nations are based on ideas found in the Iroquois constitution, known as "The Great Binding Law."
- Iroquois women had many more rights than colonial American women.
- More than 50,000 Iroquois live in the United States today.

The World on the Turtle's Back

Iroquois Creation Myth

Essential Course of Study

Background

The totem, or tribal symbol, of the Iroquois

"The World on the Turtle's Back" is an Iroquois (ĭr′ə-kwoi′) creation story filled with conflict and compelling characters. The Iroquois passed down this story from one generation to the next by telling it in elaborate performances. In the 1800s, David Cusick, an Iroquois author, recorded one version of the story in print. Today, more than 25 written versions of the story exist.

The Power of Unity The term *Iroquois* refers to six separate Native American groups—the Seneca, Cayuga, Oneida, Onondaga, Mohawk, and Tuscarora. Five of these groups—all but the Tuscarora—once resided in what is now New York State. They continually waged war with one another, putting themselves at risk of attack from neighboring Algonquin tribes. Troubled by the bloodshed, a Huron named Deganawidah (də-gä′nə-wē′-də) joined forces with an Onondaga chief named Hiawatha (hī′ə-wŏth′ə) to end the fighting. Sometime between 1570 and 1600, they formed the Iroquois League, a confederacy empowered to negotiate treaties with foreign nations and to resolve conflicts among the five nations. In 1722, the Tuscarora, from North Carolina, joined the league. For the next 175 to 200 years, the Iroquois managed to dominate other Native American groups and to remain free of both British and French rule.

The Iroquois Way of Life The league's effectiveness stemmed in part from the nations' shared culture. The groups spoke similar languages, held similar beliefs, and followed similar ways of life. They lived in longhouses made of pole frames covered with elm bark, and they built fences around their villages for protection. Up to 50 people occupied each longhouse, and 300 to 600 people lived in each village. Villages were governed by a chief or chiefs, who received advice from a council of adult males. Groups of women gathered wild fruits and nuts and cultivated corn, beans, and squash. In addition to waging war, the men traded, hunted, fished, and built the longhouses.

The Iroquois Through Time During the American Revolution, the Iroquois nations disagreed about whether to support the rebelling colonists or Great Britain. This dispute severely weakened the Iroquois League. Today, the league shows renewed vigor as it fights for environmental protection and increased recognition by the U.S. government.

Author Online
Go to **thinkcentral.com**. KEYWORD: HML11-36

 THINK central

36

Selection Resources

See resources on the **Teacher One Stop DVD-ROM** *and on* **thinkcentral.com**.

 RESOURCE MANAGER UNIT 1
Plan and Teach, pp. 9–16
Summary, pp. 17–18†‡
Text Analysis and Reading Skill, pp. 19–20†, 21–22†

DIAGNOSTIC AND SELECTION TESTS
Selection Tests, pp. 25–28

 BEST PRACTICES TOOLKIT
Word Questioning, p. E9

INTERACTIVE READER

ADAPTED INTERACTIVE READER

ELL ADAPTED INTERACTIVE READER

TECHNOLOGY
- **Teacher One Stop DVD-ROM**
- **Student One Stop DVD-ROM**
- **PowerNotes DVD-ROM**
- **Audio Anthology CD**
- **GrammarNotes DVD-ROM**
- **ExamView Test Generator on the Teacher One Stop**

 **THINK** central

Find It Online!

Features on **thinkcentral.com** that support the selection include
- **PowerNotes** presentation
- **ThinkAloud** models to enhance comprehension
- **WordSharp** vocabulary tutorials
- interactive writing and grammar instruction

---

* Resources for Differentiation   † Also in Spanish   ‡ Also in Haitian Creole and Vietnamese

TEXT ANALYSIS: CREATION MYTHS

A **myth** is a traditional story, usually involving supernatural beings or events, that explains how some aspect of human nature or the natural world came to be. A **creation myth** is a specific kind of myth that typically

- describes how the universe, the earth, and life began
- explains the workings of the natural world
- supports and validates social customs and values

As you read "The World on the Turtle's Back," note the supernatural explanations it offers of the world's origin. Think about how this myth serves the functions listed here.

READING STRATEGY: READING FOLK LITERATURE

You're probably already familiar with different types of **folk literature**, which includes folk tales, myths, fables, and legends passed orally from one generation to the next. The creation myth you are about to read is another example of folk literature. Using the following strategies as you read will help you not only understand and appreciate the myth's **themes** but also glean information about the culture it comes from:

- Read the myth aloud, or imagine a storyteller's voice as you read silently.
- Note mysteries of nature and details about creation that the myth explains.
- Make inferences about the social values or customs taught through the characters and situations.
- Look for details that reveal other aspects of Iroquois culture.

As you read, use a chart like the one shown to record your notes and observations about the three kinds of information you find in this myth.

Details About Creation/Nature	Social Values or Customs	Other Cultural Details
Before the earth was created, humans and animals "of the kind that are around us now" did not exist.		

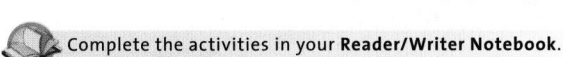 Complete the activities in your **Reader/Writer Notebook**.

How do we make SENSE of our world?

Since the beginning of time, people of all cultures have gathered to discuss one of life's biggest questions: how was the world created? The Iroquois creation myth you're about to read offers one answer to this question about the origin of the world.

DISCUSS What different accounts of creation—biblical narratives, scientific theories, or stories from other cultures, for example—have you heard or read? With a small group of classmates, summarize as many of these accounts as you know.

Teach

How do we make SENSE of our world?

Introduce the question and discuss why people are eager to understand the origin of their world. Extend the exploration by having groups complete the *DISCUSS* activity.

TEXT ANALYSIS   COMMON CORE **RL 2**

● Model the Skill: CREATION MYTHS

To model for students that different stories are used to explain the creation of the world, point out that science fiction novels and films, like *Star Trek* and *2001: A Space Odyssey,* often use supernatural and mythic elements in their narratives.

Ask students why writers at different points in history might use existing explanations of the creation of the universe to create their own myths. Point out that creation myths also reflect a culture's physical environment.

GUIDED PRACTICE Ask students what kinds of questions a creation myth is likely, or unlikely, to answer.

READING STRATEGY   COMMON CORE **RL 1 RL 2**

■ Model the Skill: READING FOLK LITERATURE

Tell students that folk literature originates in many cultures. Point out American examples, such as the Paul Bunyan folk tales, and tales from other cultures, such as ancient Greek myths, or Aesop's fables. Discuss why folk literature is popular.

R RESOURCE MANAGER—Copy Master Reading Folk Literature p. 21 (for student use while reading the selection)

DIFFERENTIATED INSTRUCTION

FOR ENGLISH LANGUAGE LEARNERS

Concept Support: Reading Folk Literature
Explain that folk literature typically teaches life lessons. For example, the story of King Midas and the golden touch presents a lesson about greed. The Greek myth of Arachne warns against boastfulness. All the fables of Aesop contain morals. By providing lessons with which listeners and readers can identify, folk literature transmits values and beliefs that are important to a culture or society.

SUMMARY

This Iroquois creation myth describes how the earth is formed. Before the earth's creation, a vast ocean lies beneath the Sky-World of the gods. When a woman falls through the floor of the Sky-World, birds set her down upon a great sea turtle. A muskrat brings her soil from the ocean bottom, which the woman uses to make the land. She gives birth to a daughter who, in turn, bears twin boys. The boys—one honest, the other devious—struggle against each other, each playing a part in creating and ruling the world.

READ WITH A PURPOSE

Help students set a purpose for reading. Tell them to read "The World on the Turtle's Back" to learn how the Iroquois believed the earth was formed.

TEXT ANALYSIS

COMMON CORE RL 2

Ⓐ CREATION MYTHS

Answers will vary. Students should cite details both from this myth and from the creation accounts they've heard or read. Some students may recognize similarities between the beginning of this myth and the biblical story of Adam and Eve, who tasted fruit of the tree of knowledge in the Garden of Eden. Eve encouraged Adam to taste the fruit against his better judgment.

The **World** on the **Turtle's Back**

Iroquois

In the beginning there was no world, no land, no creatures of the kind that are around us now, and there were no men. But there was a great ocean which occupied space as far as anyone could see. Above the ocean was a great void of air. And in the air there lived the birds of the sea; in the ocean lived the fish and the creatures of the deep. Far above this unpeopled world, there was a Sky-World. Here lived gods who were like people—like Iroquois.

In the Sky-World there was a man who had a wife, and the wife was expecting a child. The woman became hungry for all kinds of strange delicacies, as women do when they are with child. She kept her husband busy almost to distraction finding 10 delicious things for her to eat.

In the middle of the Sky-World there grew a Great Tree which was not like any of the trees that we know. It was tremendous; it had grown there forever. It had enormous roots that spread out from the floor of the Sky-World. And on its branches there were many different kinds of leaves and different kinds of fruits and flowers. The tree was not supposed to be marked or mutilated by any of the beings who dwelt in the Sky-World. It was a sacred tree that stood at the center of the universe. Ⓐ

The woman decided that she wanted some bark from one of the roots of the Great Tree—perhaps as a food or as a medicine, we don't know. She told her husband this. 20 He didn't like the idea. He knew it was wrong. But she insisted, and he gave in. So he dug a hole among the roots of this great sky tree, and he bared some of its roots. But the floor of the Sky-World wasn't very thick, and he broke a hole through it. He was terrified, for he had never expected to find empty space underneath the world.

Analyze Visuals ▶
Examine the painting on page 39. How does the artist use light and color to emphasize the division between the Sky-World and the void below it?

❶ Targeted Passage

Ⓐ CREATION MYTHS
So far, how is this myth similar to and different from other accounts of creation you've heard or read? Explain your answer, citing details.

Sky Woman (1936), Ernest Smith. Courtesy of the Rochester Museum and Science Center, Rochester, New York.

DIFFERENTIATED INSTRUCTION

FOR STRUGGLING READERS

In combination with the *Audio Anthology CD,* use one or more Targeted Passages (pp. 38, 40, 41, 42, 44) to ensure that students focus on key story events and concepts. Targeted Passages are also good for English learners.

❶ Targeted Passage [Lines 1–17]

This passage introduces the mythical setting and the woman who is a key character. It also describes the sacred Great Tree.

- What is the setting of this myth? (lines 1–6)
- Who lives in the Sky-World? (line 6)
- What two characters are introduced? (lines 7–8)
- What is special about the Great Tree? (lines 11–17)

Reading Support

This selection on **thinkcentral.com** includes embedded **ThinkAloud** models—students "thinking aloud" about the story to model the kinds of questions a good reader would ask about a selection.

Analyze Visuals

Possible answer: *The artist paints the Sky-World in bright, sunny yellow hues. In contrast, the void below the Sky-World is dark, its only light coming through the hole from the world above.*

About the Art In paintings such as *Sky Woman*, Seneca artist and craftsman Ernest Smith (1907–1975) recorded the traditions and customs of the Iroquois people. Through his clear and clean style, Smith worked to preserve the memory of cultural details that he feared might otherwise be forgotten. The painting on this page vividly depicts the events described at the beginning of "The World on the Turtle's Back."

CULTURAL CONNECTION

Myths About Twins This Iroquois creation myth centers on the rivalry between twins. In fact, twins play a central role in the legends and myths of many Native American cultures, including those of the Great Plains and the desert Southwest. The Navajo, for example, tell the story of Changing Woman and the Hero Twins, a myth of how twins rid the world of monsters, making it safe for the Navajo people. Invite students to identify stories from other cultures in which twins play an important role. Encourage them to look for common themes.

FOR ENGLISH LANGUAGE LEARNERS

Vocabulary Support Use Word Questioning to teach these words: *enormous* (line 13), *finally* (line 55), *approach* (line 86), *conflict* (line 103), *domain* (line 176).

🧰 BEST PRACTICES TOOLKIT—Transparency
Word Questioning p. E9

FOR ADVANCED LEARNERS/AP

Analyze Symbolism Have students discuss the symbolism of the Great Tree. Then ask them to recall or research the symbolism associated with trees (for example, the tree of knowledge in the Garden of Eden) and share their findings with the class. Challenge students to identify literary works that use tree symbolism, such as Shel Silverstein's *The Giving Tree*.

How do we make

SENSE

of our world?

Discuss In lines 33–67, how does the great sea turtle's role in the origin of the world explain the title of the story? *Possible answer:* *The turtle takes the falling woman on his back (lines 38–41), where she remains afloat in the ocean. The woman places dirt from the ocean bottom on the turtle's back and plants the roots from the Great Tree in the soil. In time, the "earth began to grow" and "the plants grew on the earth" (lines 65–67). Thus, the world formed on the turtle's back.*

READING STRATEGY COMMON CORE
RL 1
RL 2

B *Model the Skill:* **FOLK LITERATURE**

To model analyzing the Iroquois' attitude toward animals, read aloud lines 33–41 and lines 46–62. Discuss how the various creatures respond to the woman's situation.

Possible answer: *The animals play a significant role in the myth, helping and supporting the woman. They are depicted as wise and resourceful, suggesting that the Iroquois had a respectful, even reverential, attitude toward animals.*

IF STUDENTS NEED HELP . . . Have students review lines 33–41. Discuss how the sea creatures respond to the woman's situation.
Have students reread lines 46–62. Talk about how the animals help the woman.

Discuss how the creatures' actions and reactions reveal the Iroquois' positive feelings toward animals.

But his wife was filled with curiosity. He wouldn't get any of the roots for her, so she set out to do it herself. She bent over and she looked down, and she saw the ocean far below. She leaned down and stuck her head through the hole and looked all around. No one knows just what happened next. Some say she slipped. Some say that her husband, fed up with all the demands she had made on him, pushed her.

So she fell through the hole. As she fell, she frantically grabbed at its edges, but
30 her hands slipped. However, between her fingers there clung bits of things that were growing on the floor of the Sky-World and bits of the root tips of the Great Tree. And so she began to fall toward the great ocean far below.

The birds of the sea saw the woman falling, and they immediately consulted with each other as to what they could do to help her. Flying wingtip to wingtip they made a great feathery raft in the sky to support her, and thus they broke her fall. But of course it was not possible for them to carry the woman very long. Some of the other birds of the sky flew down to the surface of the ocean and called up the ocean creatures to see what they could do to help. The great sea turtle came and agreed to receive her on his back. The birds placed her gently
40 on the shell of the turtle, and now the turtle floated about on the huge ocean with the woman safely on his back.

The beings up in the Sky-World paid no attention to this. They knew what was happening, but they chose to ignore it.

When the woman recovered from her shock and terror, she looked around her. All that she could see were the birds and the sea creatures and the sky and the ocean.

And the woman said to herself that she would die. But the creatures of the sea came to her and said that they would try to help her and asked her what they could do. She told them that if they could find some soil, she could plant the roots stuck between her fingers, and from them plants would grow. The sea
50 animals said perhaps there was dirt at the bottom of the ocean, but no one had ever been down there so they could not be sure.

If there was dirt at the bottom of the ocean, it was far, far below the surface in the cold deeps. But the animals said they would try to get some. One by one the diving birds and animals tried and failed. They went to the limits of their endurance, but they could not get to the bottom of the ocean. Finally, the muskrat said he would try. He dived and disappeared. All the creatures waited, holding their breath, but he did not return. After a long time, his little body floated up to the surface of the ocean, a tiny crumb of earth clutched in his paw. He seemed to be dead. They pulled him up on the turtle's back and they sang and prayed
60 over him and breathed air into his mouth, and finally, he stirred. Thus it was the muskrat, the Earth-Diver, who brought from the bottom of the ocean the soil from which the earth was to grow. **B**

The woman took the tiny clod of dirt and placed it on the middle of the great sea turtle's back. Then the woman began to walk in a circle around it, moving in the direction that the sun goes. The earth began to grow. When the earth was big

---

Language Coach

Meanings of idioms. "Fed up with" in line 28 is an idiom, an expression that means something different than the literal meaning of the words. "Fed up with" means "wearied or tired of" (to the point of losing patience or control). Use this idiom to explain in your own words why the husband may have pushed his wife.

② Targeted Passage

B FOLK LITERATURE
Reread lines 46–62 and consider the role that "all the creatures" play in this myth. What does this suggest about the Iroquois' attitude toward animals?

DIFFERENTIATED INSTRUCTION

FOR STRUGGLING READERS

② Targeted Passage [Lines 29–49]

This passage explains how the first woman comes to the world and how animals help her. It also sets up the explanation for the creation of soil and plants in the world.

- How does the woman leave the Sky-World? What does she hold? (lines 29–32)

- Predict how the myth may explain the beginning of plants on the earth. (lines 48–49)

FOR ENGLISH LANGUAGE LEARNERS

Language Coach

Meanings of idioms. *Possible answer: The husband is tired of his wife's demands for new foods to eat.* Have students work in mixed-ability pairs to determine the meaning of these idioms: "to be all ears," "to be out of one's depth." Then have students write sentences demonstrating understanding of each idiom.

enough, she planted the roots she had clutched between her fingers when she fell from the Sky-World. Thus the plants grew on the earth.

To keep the earth growing, the woman walked as the sun goes, moving in the direction that the people still move in the dance rituals. She gathered roots and
70 plants to eat and built herself a little hut. After a while, the woman's time came, and she was delivered of a daughter. The woman and her daughter kept walking in a circle around the earth, so that the earth and plants would continue to grow. They lived on the plants and roots they gathered. The girl grew up with her mother, cut off forever from the Sky-World above, knowing only the birds and the creatures of the sea, seeing no other beings like herself.

❸ Targeted Passage

One day, when the girl had grown to womanhood, a man appeared. No one knows for sure who this man was. He had something to do with the gods above. Perhaps he was the West Wind. As the girl looked at him, she was filled with terror, and amazement, and warmth, and she fainted dead away. As she lay on the ground,
80 the man reached into his quiver, and he took out two arrows, one sharp and one blunt, and he laid them across the body of the girl, and quietly went away.

When the girl awoke from her faint, she and her mother continued to walk around the earth. After a while, they knew that the girl was to bear a child. They did not know it, but the girl was to bear twins.

Within the girl's body, the twins began to argue and quarrel with one another. There could be no peace between them. As the time approached for them to be born, the twins fought about their birth. The right-handed twin wanted to be born in the normal way, as all children are born. But the left-handed twin said no. He said he saw light in another direction, and said he would be born that
90 way. The right-handed twin beseeched him not to, saying that he would kill their mother. But the left-handed twin was stubborn. He went in the direction where he saw light. But he could not be born through his mother's mouth or her nose. He was born through her left armpit, and killed her. And meanwhile, the right-handed twin was born in the normal way, as all children are born. **C**

The twins met in the world outside, and the right-handed twin accused his brother of murdering their mother. But the grandmother told them to stop their quarreling. They buried their mother. And from her grave grew the plants which the people still use. From her head grew the corn, the beans, and the squash—"our supporters, the three sisters."[1] And from her heart grew the sacred tobacco, which
100 the people still use in the ceremonies and by whose upward-floating smoke they send thanks. The women call her "our mother," and they dance and sing in the rituals so that the corn, the beans, and the squash may grow to feed the people.

But the conflict of the twins did not end at the grave of their mother. And, strangely enough, the grandmother favored the left-handed twin.

The right-handed twin was angry, and he grew more angry as he thought how his brother had killed their mother. The right-handed twin was the one who did everything just as he should. He said what he meant, and he meant what he said.

---

1. **the three sisters:** Corn, beans, and squash—the Iroquois' staple food crops—were grown together. The bean vines climbed and were supported by the corn stalks; squash, which spread across the ground and kept weeds from growing, was planted around the bean plants.

THE WORLD ON THE TURTLE'S BACK **41**

COMMON CORE RL 2

C CREATION MYTHS
Mythic stories often include the miraculous birth of a child. In the *Star Wars* movies, the hero Luke Skywalker and his twin sister Leia are born when their mother dies during childbirth. The miraculous birth of the *Star Wars* twins is kept a secret from others in the story, but the Iroquois rely on this element of the text structure to show how their world was created. What else might the birth of the twins represent here?

TIERED DISCUSSION PROMPTS
In lines 85–106, use these prompts to help students understand the events leading up to the twins' birth and the effects of their birth:

Recall How is the twins' mother related to the woman who fell from the Sky-World? How are the twins related to her? *Answer: The twins' mother is the adult daughter of the woman who fell from the Sky-World. The twins are the woman's grandchildren.*

Analyze What causes the death of the twins' mother? What positive effect results from her death? What negative effect? *Possible answers: The stubborn left-handed twin wants to go toward the light he sees, so he is born through her left armpit, which kills her. A positive effect is that useful plants grow from the mother's grave. A negative effect is that the right-handed twin blames his brother for killing their mother.*

Synthesize The author writes that there "could be no peace between" the unborn twins (line 86). Symbolically, what might this conflict between the twins represent? *Possible answer: It might represent the "birth" of the struggle between good and evil in the world.*

TEXT ANALYSIS   **COMMON CORE RL 2**

C CREATION MYTHS

Possible answer: The twins' birth might represent the birth of the Iroquois people and the good and bad nature of each individual person.

FOR STRUGGLING READERS

❸ Targeted Passage [Lines 66–86]

This passage explains how plants began to grow on the earth and how the birth of the first twins brought conflict to the earth.

- From where do the roots come that the woman plants in the world? (lines 66–67)
- Who visits the girl after she has grown to womanhood? How does she respond? (lines 76–79)
- What do the twins do as they begin to grow? (line 85)

FOR ENGLISH LANGUAGE LEARNERS

Related Vocabulary Stress that the conflict between the twins takes many forms, which are signified in the author's choice of words. Teach these closely related words from page 41: *argue* (line 85), *quarrel* (line 85), *fought* (line 87), *kill* (line 90), *murdering* (line 96), *conflict* (line 103).

D Model the Skill: FOLK LITERATURE

Tell students that they can infer social values of Iroquois culture from these characters. Read aloud lines 95–112 and lead a discussion to analyze the twins' behaviors. Have students volunteer their observations about the social values illustrated in the passage.

Possible answer: The right-handed twin is characterized as admirable. He is truthful and direct, while the left-handed twin is un-truthful and devious. This characterization suggests that the Iroquois valued honesty and straightforwardness.

TIERED DISCUSSION PROMPTS

In lines 117–142, use these prompts to help students understand the role of the twins in creating a balanced world:

Connect What examples in nature can you think of that suggest "a balanced and or-derly world" (line 137)? *Possible answer: The rise and fall of the moon controls the tides.*

Analyze How do the opposing efforts of the twins create balance in the world? *Possible answer: Each twin uses his powers to counterbalance the other's creations. For example, one twin makes deer and squirrels, while the other twin creates predators who kill these animals (lines 119–125).*

Evaluate How effective is the author in showing how the twins achieved a natural balance in the newly created world? Explain. *Accept all reasonable responses.*

He always told the truth, and he always tried to accomplish what seemed to be right and reasonable. The left-handed twin never said what he meant or meant
110 what he said. He always lied, and he always did things backward. You could never tell what he was trying to do because he always made it look as if he were doing the opposite. He was the devious one. **D**

These two brothers, as they grew up, represented two ways of the world which are in all people. The Indians did not call these the right and the wrong. They called them the straight mind and the crooked mind, the upright man and the devious man, the right and the left.

The twins had creative powers. They took clay and modeled it into animals, and they gave these animals life. And in this they contended with one another. The right-handed twin made the deer, and the left-handed twin made the
120 mountain lion which kills the deer. But the right-handed twin knew there would always be more deer than mountain lions. And he made another animal. He made the ground squirrel. The left-handed twin saw that the mountain lion could not get to the ground squirrel, who digs a hole, so he made the weasel. And although the weasel can go into the ground squirrel's hole and kill him, there are lots of ground squirrels and not so many weasels. Next the right-handed twin decided he would make an animal that the weasel could not kill, so he made the porcupine. But the left-handed twin made the bear, who flips the porcupine over on his back and tears out his belly.

And the right-handed twin made berries and fruits of other kinds for his
130 creatures to live on. The left-handed twin made briars and poison ivy, and the poisonous plants like the baneberry and the dogberry, and the suicide root with which people kill themselves when they go out of their minds. And the left-handed twin made medicines, for good and for evil, for doctoring and for witchcraft.

And finally, the right-handed twin made man. The people do not know just how much the left-handed twin had to do with making man. Man was made of clay, like pottery, and baked in the fire. . . .

The world the twins made was a balanced and orderly world, and this was good. The plant-eating animals created by the right-handed twin would eat up all the vegetation if their number was not kept down by the meat-eating animals,
140 which the left-handed twin created. But if these carnivorous animals ate too many other animals, then they would starve, for they would run out of meat. So the right- and the left-handed twins built balance into the world.

As the twins became men full grown, they still contested with one another. No one had won, and no one had lost. And they knew that the conflict was becoming sharper and sharper, and one of them would have to vanquish the other.

And so they came to the duel. They started with gambling. They took a wooden bowl, and in it they put wild plum pits. One side of the pits was burned black, and by tossing the pits in the bowl and betting on how these would fall, they gambled against one another, as the people still do in the New Year's

D FOLK LITERATURE
Reread lines 95–112. Which twin is characterized as being more admirable? What does this characterization tell you about Iroquois values?

④ Targeted Passage

Language Coach

Word Definitions
Look at the word *doctoring* in line 133. Many people know the term *doctor*, but *doctoring* or *to doctor* might be unfamiliar. *Doctoring* here means "healing." What clues from the text help you guess the meaning of *doctoring*?

DIFFERENTIATED INSTRUCTION

FOR STRUGGLING READERS

④ Targeted Passage [Lines 113–142]

This passage describes the twins' role in achieving balance in the world.

- Paraphrase this sentence: "These two brothers, as they grew up, represented two ways of the world which are in all people." (lines 113–114)

- What are some of the living things that each twin created? (lines 119–128)

FOR ENGLISH LANGUAGE LEARNERS

Language Coach

Word Definitions: *Possible Answer: A clue is that the twin made medicines for doctoring.* In that same phrase, "for doctoring and for witchcraft," point out to students that the suffix *craft* means "a skill of a particular kind." Have students think of other words ending in "craft" and use them in sentences. *Possible answers: needlecraft, stagecraft*

Detail of *Sky Woman* (1936), Ernest Smith. Courtesy of the Rochester Museum and Science Center, Rochester, New York.

150 rites.[2] All through the morning they gambled at this game, and all through the afternoon, and the sun went down. And when the sun went down, the game was done, and neither one had won.

So they went on to battle one another at the lacrosse[3] game. And they contested all day, and the sun went down, and the game was done. And neither had won.

And now they battled with clubs, and they fought all day, and the sun went down, and the fight was done. But neither had won. **E**

And they went from one duel to another to see which one would succumb. Each one knew in his deepest mind that there was something, somewhere, that would vanquish the other. But what was it? Where to find it?

160 Each knew somewhere in his mind what it was that was his own weak point. They talked about this as they contested in these duels, day after day, and somehow the deep mind of each entered into the other. And the deep mind of the right-handed twin lied to his brother, and the deep mind of the left-handed twin told the truth.

On the last day of the duel, as they stood, they at last knew how the right-handed twin was to kill his brother. Each selected his weapon. The left-handed twin chose a mere stick that would do him no good. But the right-handed twin

E **FOLK LITERATURE**
Reread lines 146–156. Note in your chart the information about Iroquois customs and rituals you learn from these lines.

---

2. **New Year's rites:** various ceremonies to get ready for the New Year. They often included community confession of sins, the replenishing of hearths in the homes, and sacred dances, as well as the gambling ritual.

3. **lacrosse:** a game of Native American origin wherein participants on two teams use long-handled sticks with webbed pouches to maneuver a ball into the opposing team's goal.

Analyze Visuals

Activity Ask students what ideas this detail from the painting on page 39 emphasizes.

Possible answer: The detail emphasizes the importance of the turtle and, by extrapolation, of other animals in the creation myth of the Iroquois.

READING STRATEGY
COMMON CORE

E **FOLK LITERATURE**
RL 1
RL 2

Possible answer:

Details About Creation/ Nature	Social Values or Customs	Other Cultural Details
	The Iroquois gambled and played lacrosse. They held ceremonies to prepare for the New Year.	

FOR ADVANCED LEARNERS/AP

Analyze Tone and Style [small-group option] Have students work in small groups to discuss the author's tone and style. Have them analyze the sentence variety, diction, and author's viewpoint. Then have them consider these questions:

- Does the author reveal any personal feelings about the Iroquois' beliefs, or does the author remain totally neutral?

- Is the author's tone and style appropriate for the subject?

- In what ways might the author have changed the style and tone of the selection? How would these changes have affected the readers' response to the selection?

Encourage groups to exchange their conclusions.

TEXT ANALYSIS

**F Model the Skill:
CREATION MYTHS**

Point out to students that the left-handed twin, the grandmother's favorite, reigns over the realm of the night. Read aloud lines 177–183 and discuss how, in death, the grandmother transformed to remain near her favorite grandson.

Extend the Discussion Why do you suppose the grandmother favors the left-handed twin (see also line 104)?

THEME AND GENRE

TEXT STRUCTURE

After students have read this story, ask them to discuss films, plays, or novels that connect to other myths about creation.

SELECTION WRAP–UP

READ WITH A PURPOSE Now that students have read "The World on the Turtle's Back," ask them to consider how well the selection accomplishes the goal of telling how the world was created. ***Possible answer:*** *The myth accounts for the creation of the earth, plants, humans, and some animals. However, it does not explain the origin of animals that assist the woman from the Sky-World.*

⭐ CRITIQUE

- Have students evaluate the story. Discuss which parts were most and least interesting. Ask whether the story would have been more or less effective if told in a more conventional manner.

- After completing the After Reading questions on page 45, have students revisit their responses and tell whether they have changed their opinions.

INDEPENDENT READING

Students may also enjoy reading John Bierhorst's *Latin American Folktales: Stories from Hispanic and Indian Traditions.*

---

picked out the deer antler, and with one touch he destroyed his brother. And the left-handed twin died, but he died and he didn't die. The right-handed twin 170 picked up the body and cast it off the edge of the earth. And some place below the world, the left-handed twin still lives and reigns.

When the sun rises from the east and travels in a huge arc along the sky dome, which rests like a great upside-down cup on the saucer of the earth, the people are in the daylight realm of the right-handed twin. But when the sun slips down in the west at nightfall and the dome lifts to let it escape at the western rim, the people are again in the domain of the left-handed twin—the fearful realm of night.

Having killed his brother, the right-handed twin returned home to his grandmother. And she met him in anger. She threw the food out of the cabin onto the ground and said that he was a murderer, for he had killed his brother. He grew 180 angry and told her she had always helped his brother, who had killed their mother. In his anger, he grabbed her by the throat and cut her head off. Her body he threw into the ocean, and her head, into the sky. There, "Our Grandmother, the Moon" still keeps watch at night over the realm of her favorite grandson. **F**

The right-handed twin has many names. One of them is Sapling. It means smooth, young, green and fresh and innocent, straightforward, straight-growing, soft and pliable, teachable and trainable. These are the old ways of describing him. But since he has gone away, he has other names. He is called "He Holds Up the Skies," "Master of Life," and "Great Creator."

The left-handed twin also has many names. One of them is Flint. He is called 190 the devious one, the one covered with boils. Old Warty. He is stubborn. He is thought of as being dark in color.

> These two beings rule the world and keep an eye on the affairs of men. The right-handed twin, the Master of Life, lives in the Sky-World. He is content with the world he helped to create and with his favorite creatures, the humans. The scent of sacred tobacco rising from the earth comes gloriously to his nostrils.
>
> In the world below lives the left-handed twin. He knows the world of men, and he finds contentment in it. He hears the sounds of warfare and torture, and he finds them good.
>
> In the daytime, the people have rituals which honor the right-handed twin. 200 Through the daytime rituals, they thank the Master of Life. In the nighttime, the people dance and sing for the left-handed twin. ❧

G CREATION MYTHS
The transformation of a character is a common element of mythology, often used to explain natural phenomena. Consider the natural feature explained in lines 172–183. How does this myth explain the fact that the moon is visible mainly at night?

⑤ Targeted Passage

THEME AND GENRE
The right-handed twin is also called "the Master of Life." Many works of mythic literature are built around the idea of a good hero overcoming obstacles and eventually achieving a reward. The 2001 film *Shrek* uses some of the elements of mythic literature to illustrate the struggle of a character who must overcome the problems of an ogre to gain his reward. How would you relate the idea of a good hero who overcomes obstacles to a recent film you've seen?

DIFFERENTIATED INSTRUCTION

FOR STRUGGLING READERS

⑤ Targeted Passage [Lines 192–201]

This passage summarizes the twins' shared role in ruling the world.

- Which twin lives in the Sky-World? (lines 192–193)

- Which twin controls "the world below"? (line 196)

- How do the people show their appreciation of both twins? (lines 199–201)

FOR STRUGGLING READERS

Develop Reading Fluency Use the lyrical language in lines 184–201 to promote readers' interest. Have students work in small groups, with different individuals reading aloud one each of the five paragraphs. Remind them to be expressive and to use punctuation as a guide for pauses and other emphasis. Encourage students to share their thoughts on how a fluent reader keeps listeners interested and engaged.

Comprehension

1. **Recall** How do the animals help the woman who fell from the sky?

2. **Recall** What roles do the grandmother and her daughter play in the earth's creation?

3. **Summarize** What is the outcome of the battles between the twins?

Text Analysis

4. **Compare and Contrast** How does this myth compare with the accounts of the world's origin you summarized before you read? Use a Venn diagram to record the differences and similarities between "The World on the Turtle's Back" and one of the accounts you discussed.

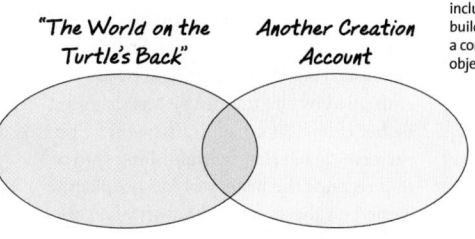

"The World on the Turtle's Back"   Another Creation Account

● 5. **Analyze a Creation Myth** Reread lines 105–112. Summarize the differences between the right-handed twin and the left-handed twin. Why do you think the Iroquois honor both twins? What elements of human nature are explained by "The World on the Turtle's Back"?

■ 6. **Draw Conclusions from Folk Literature** Folk literature often transmits central ideas about a people's culture and way of life. Review the details you noted in your chart as you read. From this myth, what did you learn about the Iroquois'

   • attitude toward nature?
   • view of their gods?
   • important food, games, and rituals?
   • beliefs about good and evil?

Text Criticism

7. **Critical Interpretations** Creation stories often serve many purposes. According to Larry Evers and Paul Pavich, scholars of Native American literature, such stories "remind the people of who and what they are, why they are in this particular place, and how they should continue to live here." Do you think that "The World on the Turtle's Back" fulfills these functions? Explain, citing evidence from the text to support your interpretation.

> *How do we make* **SENSE** *of our world?*
>
> How did the Iroquois make sense of their surroundings? Why might this story have been important to them?

COMMON CORE

RL 1 Cite textual evidence to support analysis of what the text says explicitly as well as inferences drawn from the text, including determining where the text leaves matters uncertain. **RL 2** Determine two or more themes or central ideas of a text and analyze their development over the course of the text, including how they interact and build on one another to produce a complex account; provide an objective summary of the text.

Practice and Apply

For preliminary support of post-reading questions, use these copy masters:

R RESOURCE MANAGER—Copy Masters
Reading Check p. 23
Creation Myths p. 19
Question Support p. 24

Additional selection questions are provided for teachers on page 13.

ANSWERS
COMMON CORE **RL 1, RL 2**

1. *The birds break the woman's fall; the turtle carries her on its back; the muskrat brings back soil from the ocean floor.*

2. *The woman and her daughter make the earth grow by walking around the soil. The daughter gives birth to twins, who eventually rule the earth.*

3. *The left-handed twin is defeated but reigns in the underworld, while the right-handed twin rules from the Sky-World.*

Possible answers:

4. *Answers will vary. Encourage students to be specific.*

5. ● COMMON CORE FOCUS **Analyze a Creation Myth** *The right-handed twin tells the truth and acts in a "right and reasonable" way. He creates edible berries and herbivorous animals. The left-handed twin lies, does things "backward," and acts deviously. He creates poisonous plants and carnivorous animals. The Iroquois honor both twins because they recognize "crooked" and "straight," predators and prey as necessary to a balanced world. The myth explains why humans have both virtuous and devious impulses.*

Assess and Reteach

Assess

DIAGNOSTIC AND SELECTION TESTS
Selection Test A pp. 25–26
Selection Test B/C pp. 27–28

Interactive Selection Test on **thinkcentral.com**

Reteach

Level Up Online Tutorials on **thinkcentral.com**

6. ■ COMMON CORE FOCUS **Draw Conclusions from Folk Literature** *The Iroquois respect nature. They see animals as worthy of admiration; they respect the balance of nature. The Iroquois believe the world was created by a higher power; they speak of their gods with reverence. Corn, beans, and squash are essential to the Iroquois; lacrosse is a key game and competition is important; the Iroquois perform ceremonies to get ready for the New Year. The Iroquois believe good and evil together create a balanced world.*

7. *Students may say that the myth explains where the Iroquois came from, suggests why humans feel conflicting impulses and emotions, and serves as a guide for living by teaching reverence both for the gods and for nature.*

> *How do we make* SENSE *of our world?* **Possible answer:** They used myths to explain nature; the stories provide an explanation for their creation.

Focus and Motivate

ABOUT THE AUTHOR

Have students read this page and summarize key points about Mourning Dove. Point out that, as explained in the historical essay (pages 26–27), folk tales such as "Coyote and the Buffalo" were passed down through oral tradition. By recording such stories, Mourning Dove helped to preserve them during a time when the power of oral tradition had weakened.

NOTABLE QUOTE

"Everything on the earth has a purpose, every disease an herb to cure it, and every person a mission. This is the Indian theory of existence."
—**Mourning Dove**

Ask students to summarize "the Indian theory of existence" in their own words and to compare it to "golden rules" of other cultures.

DID YOU KNOW?

Mourning Dove . . .
- was born in a canoe while her mother was crossing a river in Idaho.
- learned to read English by poring over melodramatic dime-store novels.
- was the first woman ever elected to the Colville tribal council.

The Native American Experience

Coyote and the Buffalo

Folk Tale Retold by Mourning Dove

Meet the Author

Mourning Dove c. 1885–1936

Mourning Dove is the pen name of Christine Quintasket (kwən-tăs′kət), who triumphed over adversity to become one of the first female Native American novelists. As a child, Quintasket was enthralled by the traditional stories told by her elders. As an adult, she worked to preserve these tales. By publishing stories that recount the history of her people, she carried on the work of the storytellers she so admired.

Determined to Write Quintasket grew up on the Colville Reservation in Washington State with her mother, the daughter of a Colville chief, and her father, an Okanogan. When Quintasket was 14, her mother died, leaving her to run the household and help raise her younger siblings. Despite her many responsibilities, Quintasket pushed herself to learn to write in English. She later attended secretarial school to learn how to type and business school to hone her grammar and writing skills. She drafted a novel in 1912 but put it away for several years until she met Lucullus McWhorter, a Native American–rights activist, who offered to edit it.

Battling Stereotypes Published in 1927, Mourning Dove's novel, *Cogewea, the Half-Blood,* is credited with breaking down the stereotype of Native Americans as stoic, or unfeeling. "It is all wrong, this saying that Indians do not feel as deeply as whites," the author asserted. "We do feel, and by and by some of us are going to make our feelings appreciated, and then will the true Indian character be revealed."

Chronicling Her Culture After *Cogewea* was published, Mourning Dove began to record traditional stories of the Okanogan and other Colville tribes. A migrant worker, she picked fruit ten hours a day but managed to do her writing at night. *Coyote Stories,* from which "Coyote and the Buffalo" is taken, was published in 1933. "Coyote and the Buffalo" is a folk tale once told by Okanogan storytellers in Salish, their native language. Mourning Dove's retelling includes Salish words and place names. This story and others like it help keep the Okanogan culture alive today.

Mourning Dove's Legacy In addition to preserving her people's culture, Mourning Dove worked hard to promote their welfare. She fought for their rights in court, started organizations supporting Native American crafts, and paved the way for female participation on tribal councils. Worn down by chronic illness and fatigue, the writer and activist died in 1936.

Author Online

THINK central

Go to **thinkcentral.com**. KEYWORD: HML11-46

Selection Resources

TEXT ANALYSIS: TRICKSTER TALES

You already know that a folk tale is a simple story passed orally from one generation to the next. **The trickster tale** is a type of folk tale that features an animal or human character who typically engages in deceit, violence, and magic. Often, trickster tales are mythic, explaining how some aspect of human nature or the natural world came to be. The opening lines of "Coyote and the Buffalo" announce what this trickster tale will explain.

No buffalo ever lived in the Swah-netk'-qhu *country. That was Coyote's fault.*

Tricksters are **archetypal characters**—character types that can be found in literary works from different cultures throughout the ages. As incurable practical jokers, with universal appeal, they appear frequently in American literature and film—from the coyote of Native American myths to the tricksters of 20th-century animated cartoons and beyond. As you read this tale, notice how Coyote's character is developed. He demonstrates the trickster's contradictory qualities of being foolish yet clever, greedy yet helpful, and immoral yet moral. In addition, Coyote is given the human characteristic of speech. The first words out of his mouth further clarify his character type:

"Now I will have some fun," Coyote remarked. "I will have revenge for the times Buffalo made me run."

READING STRATEGY: PREDICT

Tricksters are often schemers or scoundrels—they don't usually act as other characters do. Using your background knowledge of this character's contradictory qualities, as well as text clues, can help you **predict** upcoming story events. As you read, use a chart like the one shown to record Coyote's key traits and unusual behavior. Pause occasionally to predict what will happen next.

Coyote's Traits and Behavior	My Predictions
Coyote is "foolish and greedy"; it is his fault there are no buffalo in Swah-netk-qhu country.	This story will reveal that Coyote did something reckless or unwise to scare away the buffalo.

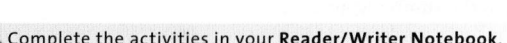 Complete the activities in your **Reader/Writer Notebook**.

Why do we root for the "BAD GUY"?

Wherever they go, they ignore the rules. They stir up trouble. And yet we admire and love them despite—or maybe because of—their bad behavior. Many societies have famous villains or trickster figures, who both infuriate and inspire the people around them.

QUICKWRITE Think about movies or books in which the villain is more compelling than the hero. What qualities does such a villain typically display? Which of these traits contribute most to his or her appeal? Record your responses in a short paragraph.

47

DIFFERENTIATED INSTRUCTION

FOR STRUGGLING READERS

Concept Support: Trickster Tales Explain that trickster tales are usually grouped in cycles. That is, they consist of a series of stories focusing on the adventures of the trickster character. Each story involves a particular incident or situation to which the trickster responds, often leading to a violent or absurd conclusion. Among the best-known trickster tales in the United States are those of the sly Brer Rabbit, a character who originated in African folk tales. Have students work in mixed-ability pairs to brainstorm some additional trickster characters. Have volunteers describe the different trickster characters to the class.

Why do we root for the "BAD GUY"?

Have students think about the different types of villains they have encountered in books, movies, and on TV. Which ones are mischievous? Which are evil? Then have students complete the *QUICKWRITE*.

TEXT ANALYSIS — COMMON CORE RL 3 RL 5

● *Model the Skill:* TRICKSTER TALES

Explain that the archetypal trickster character takes many forms. Illustrate the concept of the trickster by providing examples. Tell students that in Native American oral tradition, the trickster may be a coyote or raven. In African tales, it may be a hare or spider, while in Japan it may be a fox. The trickster usually exhibits contradictory qualities. He may be both creative and destructive, wise yet childlike. Lead students in a discussion about why trickster characters have appealed to people through the ages and in so many different cultures. Point out that the trickster embodies the contradictory qualities of human beings.

GUIDED PRACTICE Ask students to explain why a trickster character might be both likable and unlikable.

READING STRATEGY — COMMON CORE RL 1

■ *Model the Skill:* PREDICT

Tell students, "When I read, I think about the characters and plot and I draw on my knowledge of other stories. Then I predict what will happen next." Tell students that they already make predictions when they read. They predict how a character will act or how the book will end based on their understanding of character and plot and their knowledge of the real world.

GUIDED PRACTICE Elicit examples of predictions students have made in the past.

 RESOURCE MANAGER—Copy Master Predict p. 37

Practice and Apply

SUMMARY

This folk tale, retold by Mourning Dove, tells how Coyote angers Buffalo Bull, who then chases him. Coyote saves himself by offering to make Buffalo Bull new horns to replace his worn, old ones. Grateful, Buffalo Bull gives Coyote a magical cow that will always provide him with meat, so long as he does not kill it. Nevertheless, Coyote kills the cow, only to have birds eat the meat and an old woman steal the bones. Coyote tries to get another cow from Buffalo Bull but is refused, which explains why "No buffalo ever lived in the *Swah-netk'-qhu* country."

READ WITH A PURPOSE

Help students read with a purpose. Ask them to think about how a person's true nature is often revealed through his or her actions and words. Tell them to watch how the characters in the selection show their true natures through their words and actions.

TEXT ANALYSIS

COMMON CORE

RL 3
RL 5

Ⓐ TRICKSTER TALES

Possible answer: Based on lines 5–13, Coyote seems vengeful and childish.

IF STUDENTS NEED HELP . . . Have them use a Character Analysis Chart to make inferences about the trickster.

📦 BEST PRACTICES TOOLKIT—Transparency
Character Analysis Chart p. D5

COYOTE
and the
BUFFALO

Retold by Mourning Dove

BACKGROUND "Coyote and the Buffalo" is one of many traditional stories featuring the Animal People, a race of supernatural beings believed by the Okanogan to have been the first inhabitants of the world. The Animal People had magical powers and could alter their shapes. When human beings appeared on the earth, the Animal People were changed into different animal species. Coyote, one of the most important Animal People, is thought to have made the world habitable for humans by killing monsters and bringing fire and salmon.

Analyze Visuals ▶
Describe the artwork on page 49. How is the use of color significant? Does the color treatment cause this coyote to reflect the **traits** of a trickster? Explain your answer.

No buffalo ever lived in the *Swah-netk'-qhu*[1] country. That was Coyote's fault. If he had not been so foolish and greedy, the people beside the *Swah-netk'-qhu* would not have had to cross the Rockies to hunt the *quas-peet-za*[2] (curled-hairs).

This is the way it happened:

Coyote was traveling over the plains beyond the big mountains. He came to a flat. There he found an old buffalo skull. It was the skull of Buffalo Bull. Coyote always had been afraid of Buffalo Bull. He remembered the many times Bull Buffalo had scared him, and he laughed upon seeing the old skull there on the flat.

"Now I will have some fun," Coyote remarked. "I will have revenge for the
10 times Buffalo made me run."

He picked up the skull and threw it into the air; he kicked it and spat on it; he threw dust in the eye sockets. He did these things many times, until he grew tired. Then he went his way. Soon he heard a rumbling behind him. He thought it Ⓐ was thunder, and he looked at the sky. The sky was clear. Thinking he must have imagined the sound, he walked on, singing. He heard the rumbling again, only

Ⓐ Targeted Passage

Ⓐ **TRICKSTER TALES**
In the first paragraph, the Coyote is "foolish and greedy". The Joker, in Tim Burton's 1989 film *Batman,* also shares some of the traits of a trickster. Based on lines 5–13, what other **character traits** would you attribute to this trickster?

---

1. *Swah-netk'-qhu* (shwə-nĭt'kwə): the Salish name for the Columbia River and its waterfall.
2. *quas-peet-za* (kwəs-pēt'zä): a Salish word for buffalo.

Coyote Survivor, John Nieto.
Serigraph, 29″ × 22″.

DIFFERENTIATED INSTRUCTION

FOR ENGLISH LANGUAGE LEARNERS

Idioms Clarify these idioms from the story: *in the wink of an eye* (line 21) "very quickly"; *at once* (line 60) "right away"; *gave up* (line 84) "stopped"; and *set out* (line 90) "began with a certain purpose."

FOR STRUGGLING READERS

In combination with the *Audio Anthology CD,* use one or more Targeted Passages (pp. 48, 50, 51, 52) to ensure that students focus on key story events and concepts. Targeted Passages are also good for English learners.

Ⓐ **Targeted Passage** [Lines 1–13]

This passage introduces Coyote and Buffalo Bull and sets up the conflict between them. It also announces what the tale will explain.

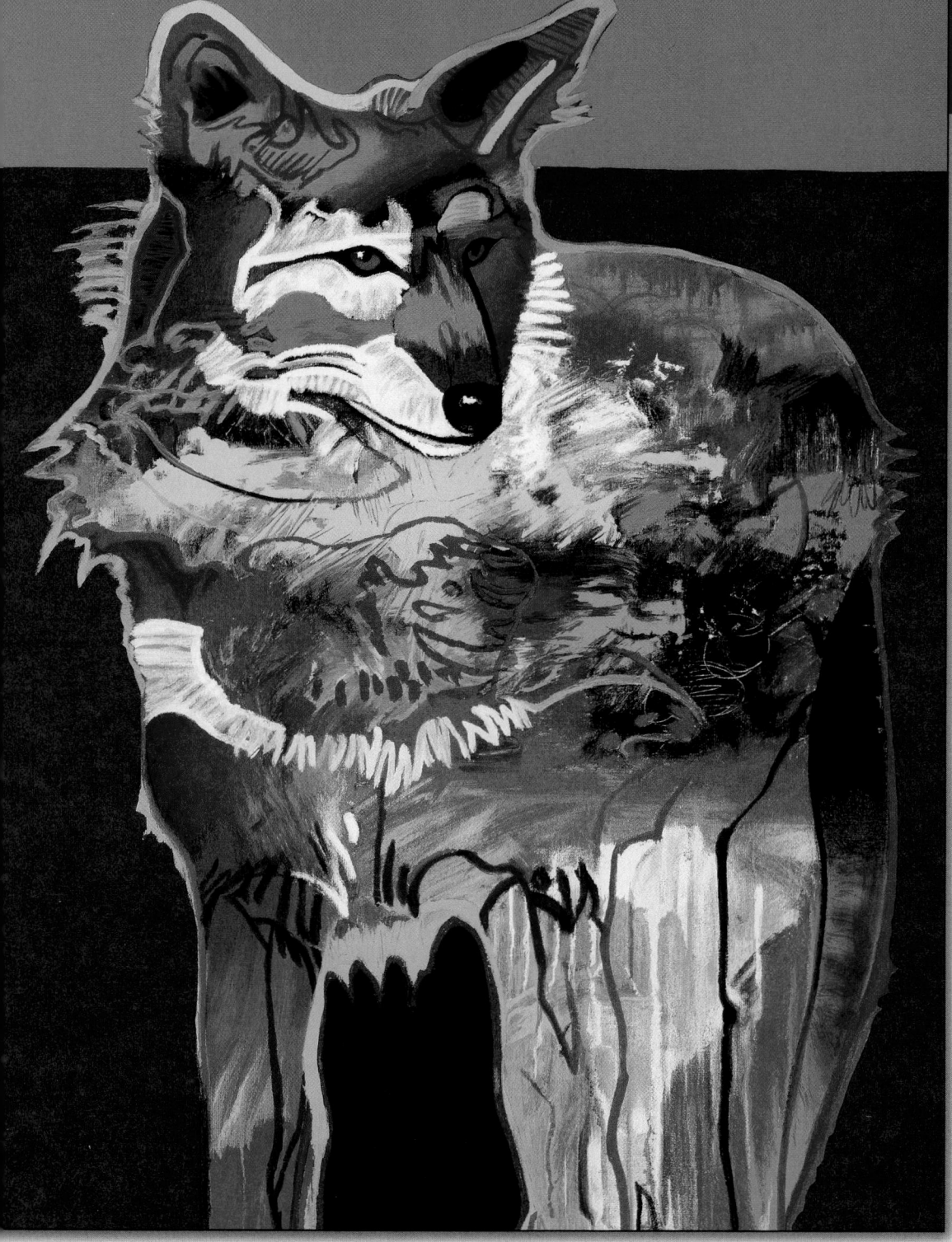

Analyze Visuals

Possible answer: *The painting uses intense primary colors to create an electric image, giving an unearthly, magical feel to the picture. This color treatment is appropriate for a trick-ster, who may be associated with supernatural powers and spirit helpers.*

About the Art In pictures such as *Coyote Survivor*, American artist John Nieto (b. 1936) uses strong colors and bold strokes to create striking images with depth and detail. He chooses common subjects but presents them in a way that gives viewers a fresh, more powerful understanding of them.

BACKGROUND

Columbia River The *Swah-netk'-qhu* (line 1) is the Columbia River in the Pacific Northwest. This river drains an extensive area that includes parts of present-day Oregon, Washington, Idaho, Montana, Nevada, Wyoming, and Utah.

- According to the opening lines of the story, what was Coyote's fault? What qualities of Coyote made this problem happen? (lines 1–3)
- What does Coyote find? How does he treat it? (lines 6–13)
- How does Coyote feel about Buffalo Bull? (lines 6–8)

FOR ADVANCED LEARNERS/AP

Native American Spirit Helpers "Coyote and the Buffalo" refers to Coyote's "power," or spirit helper, in lines 20, 34, and 43. Have students research spirit helpers in Native American literature and art. Ask students to share their findings with the class.

Use these prompts to help students understand the interaction between Coyote and Buffalo Bull as they read lines 20–40:

Connect Have you ever tried to talk your way out of a tough situation? How does that experience help you understand how Coyote feels? *Accept all reasonable responses.*

Analyze Review the trickster traits on page 47. Which of these traits are evident in these lines? Cite examples to support your answer. *Possible answer: Coyote twice resorts to magic through his link to supernatural powers. First, Squas-tenk', his spirit helper, puts trees in the path of Coyote (lines 20–21). Later, Coyote obtains a "loaded and lighted" pipe from his "medicine-power" (lines 34–35).*

REVISIT THE BIG QUESTION

Why do we root for the
"BAD GUY"?

Ask students why they might be rooting for Coyote. *Possible answers: Because Coyote is a trickster, students may not be sure of his motivations. They may be rooting for him to play a trick on the trusting Buffalo Bull.*

TEXT ANALYSIS

B *Model the Skill:*
TRICKSTER TALES

Point out that, to save his life, Coyote offers to create new, sharper horns for Buffalo Bull.

Possible answer: These lines explain why buffalo bulls have "heavy horns with sharp points."

---

much closer and louder. Turning around, he saw Buffalo Bull pounding along after him, chasing him. His old enemy had come to life!

Coyote ran, faster than he thought he could run, but Buffalo gained steadily. Soon Buffalo was right at his heels. Coyote felt his hot breath.

20 "Oh, *Squas-tenk'*,[3] help me!" Coyote begged, and his power answered by putting three trees in front of him. They were there in the wink of an eye. Coyote jumped and caught a branch of the first tree and swung out of Buffalo's way. Buffalo rammed the tree hard, and it shook as if in a strong wind. Then Buffalo chopped at the trunk with his horns, first with one horn and then the other. He chopped fast, and in a little while over went the tree, and with it went Coyote. But he was up and into the second tree before Buffalo Bull could reach him. Buffalo soon laid that tree low, but he was not quick enough to catch Coyote, who scrambled into the third and last tree.

"Buffalo, my friend, let me talk with you," said Coyote, as his enemy hacked
30 away at the tree's trunk. "Let me smoke my pipe. I like the *kinnikinnick*.[4] Let me smoke. Then I can die more content."

"You may have time for one smoke," grunted Bull Buffalo, resting from his chopping.

Coyote spoke to his medicine-power, and a pipe, loaded and lighted, was given to him. He puffed on it once and held out the pipe to Buffalo Bull.

"No, I will not smoke with you," said that one. "You made fun of my bones. I have enough enemies without you. Young Buffalo is one of them. He killed me and stole all my fine herd."

"My uncle,"[5] said Coyote, "you need new horns. Let me make new horns for
40 you. Then you can kill Young Buffalo. Those old horns are dull and worn."

Bull Buffalo was pleased with that talk. He decided he did not want to kill Coyote. He told Coyote to get down out of the tree and make the new horns. Coyote jumped down and called to his power. It scolded him for getting into trouble, but it gave him a flint knife and a stump of pitchwood.[6] From this stump Coyote carved a pair of fine heavy horns with sharp points. He gave them to Buffalo Bull. All buffalo bulls have worn the same kind of horns since. **B**

Buffalo Bull was very proud of his new horns. He liked their sharpness and weight and their pitch-black color. He tried them out on what was left of the pitchwood stump. He made one toss and the stump flew high in the air, and he
50 forgave Coyote for his mischief. They became good friends right there. Coyote said he would go along with Buffalo Bull to find Young Buffalo.

They soon came upon Young Buffalo and the big herd he had won from Buffalo Bull. Young Buffalo laughed when he saw his old enemy, and he walked out to meet him. He did not know, of course, about the new horns. It was not much of a fight,

---

3. ***Squas-tenk'*** (skwəs-tĭnk'): a Salish word referring to Coyote's spirit helper.

4. ***kinnikinnick*** (kĭn'ĭ-kĭ-nĭk'): the Salish word for the bearberry shrub. The Okanogan toasted bearberry leaves and then crumbled them and mixed them with tobacco for pipe smoking.

5. **my uncle:** Terms like *uncle, brother, sister,* and *cousin* were sometimes used as a sign of respect. Here, Coyote is using the term to flatter Buffalo Bull.

6. **pitchwood:** the sap-filled wood of a pine or fir tree.

Language Coach

Connotation The images or feelings connected to a word are its **connotation**. Why does Coyote refer to Buffalo Bull as "My uncle" in line 39 (see footnote 5)? How might the meaning differ if Coyote had used one of these terms to address Buffalo Bull: *Mister, Your Honor,* or *Worthy Opponent*?

B **TRICKSTER TALES**
This trickster tale is **mythic** in that it explains how something came to be—in this case, the lack of buffalo in a certain geographic area. What second mythic explanation is offered in lines 39–46?

DIFFERENTIATED INSTRUCTION

FOR STRUGGLING READERS

2 Targeted Passage [Lines 36–46]

This passage describes how Coyote slyly wins Buffalo Bull's approval.

• Why is Buffalo Bull angry at Coyote? (line 36)

• How does Coyote gain Buffalo Bull's friendship? (lines 39–40)

• Why does Buffalo Bull want revenge against Young Buffalo? (lines 37–38)

FOR ENGLISH LANGUAGE LEARNERS

Language Coach

Connotation Ask students to make a list of titles that convey respect in modern American culture. Explain that all cultures have titles that command respect. Ask students to explain why specific titles, such as *Doctor,* bring the person a degree of respect.

that fight between Young Buffalo and Buffalo Bull. With the fine new horns, Buffalo Bull killed the other easily, and then he took back his herd, all his former wives and their children. He gave Coyote a young cow, the youngest cow, and he said:

"Never kill her, *Sin-ka-lip'*![7] Take good care of her and she will supply you with meat forever. When you get hungry, just slice off some choice fat with a flint
60 knife. Then rub ashes on the wound and the cut will heal at once." **C**

Coyote promised to remember that, and they parted. Coyote started back to his own country, and the cow followed. For a few suns he ate only the fat when he was hungry. But after awhile he became tired of eating fat, and he began to long for the sweet marrow-bones and the other good parts of the buffalo. He smacked his lips at the thought of having some warm liver.

---

7. **Sin-ka-lip'** (sĭng'kə-lĭp'): the Salish name for Coyote; it means "imitator."

Buffalo, John Nieto. Acrylic, 30″× 40″.

C **PREDICT**
Consider what you know about the **archetypal** trickster character and think about Coyote's behavior thus far. How do you think Coyote will respond to Buffalo Bull's instructions? Give reasons for your prediction.

READING STRATEGY **COMMON CORE** RL 1

C *Model the Skill:* **PREDICT**
Remind students that predictions are based on clues in their reading and on their own knowledge of the world. Tell students, "I think that Coyote is unreliable. Tricksters I have read about rarely do what others tell them to do. I predict Coyote will get into trouble."

Possible answer: *Coyote seems to play by his own rules and is unlikely to follow anyone else's. Trickster characters are also greedy, so just slicing off some fat may not satisfy Coyote. Coyote may disregard Buffalo Bull's instructions and get into trouble.*

IF STUDENTS NEED HELP . . . Have them use the chart introduced on page 47 to list Coyote's behavior and students' predictions about it.

Coyote's Traits and Behavior	My Predictions
Coyote seems to play by his own rules and is unlikely to follow anyone else's. Trickster characters are also greedy, so just slicing off some fat may not satisfy Coyote.	Coyote will disregard Buffalo Bull's instructions and get into trouble.

Analyze Visuals

Activity Ask students how the picture helps them visualize Buffalo Bull. *Possible answer: The picture captures the buffalo's large size and sharp horns.*

FOR STRUGGLING READERS

❸ **Targeted Passage** [Lines 55–61]
This passage describes how Buffalo Bull rewards Coyote with a magical cow.

• How do the new horns help Buffalo Bull? (lines 55–57)

• How does Buffalo Bull thank Coyote? (line 57)

• What warning does Buffalo Bull give Coyote? (line 58)

FOR STRUGGLING READERS

Develop Reading Fluency Help students improve their fluency by participating in a paired oral reading. Assign each pair a paragraph from the tale. Students should take turns reading the paragraph aloud until they can read it smoothly and with expression. Then ask students to read aloud their paragraphs to the rest of the class.

Why Do We Root for the "BAD GUY"?

Discuss After students read lines 75–83, ask them the following question: Which of the two is more of a villain: the old woman or Coyote? Explain your answer. *Possible answer: The old woman is more of a villain than Coyote. She not only flatters and deceives Coyote but also steals from him. Then she taunts him by shouting, "do you want this?" (line 83)*

TEXT ANALYSIS   COMMON CORE

D TRICKSTER TALES   RL 3
                                                          RL 5

Ask volunteers to read aloud lines 77–83. Explain that the old woman's offer appeals to Coyote's vanity and while he rests she steals his soup.

Possible answer: *Students may mention trickster characters they have seen in movies, on television, or in other stories. Accept all reasonable responses.*

Extend the Discussion What additional trick is played on Coyote when he attempts to boil the bones a second time? Who do students think may have played this trick?

SELECTION WRAP–UP

READ WITH A PURPOSE Ask students to describe Coyote's character. *Possible answers: Coyote is sneaky, cowardly, and selfish.*

★ **CRITIQUE** Have students evaluate the story. Ask them which parts of the story they found most entertaining, and why.

INDEPENDENT READING

Students who enjoy reading myths and trickster tales may enjoy reading *Zoo of the Gods: World of Animals in Myth and Legend* by Anthony S. Mercatante.

"Buffalo Bull will never know," Coyote told himself, and he took his young cow down beside a creek and killed her.

As he peeled off the hide, crows and magpies came from all directions. They settled on the carcass and picked at the meat. Coyote tried to chase them away, 70 but there were too many of them. While he was chasing some, others returned and ate the meat. It was not long until they had devoured every bit of the meat.

"Well, I can get some good from the bones and marrow-fat," Coyote remarked, and he built a fire to cook the bones. Then he saw an old woman walking toward him. She came up to the fire.

"*Sin-ka-lip',*" she said, "you are a brave warrior, a great chief. Why should you do woman's work? Let me cook the bones while you rest."   **4 Targeted Passage**

Vain Coyote! He was flattered. He believed she spoke her true mind. He stretched out to rest and he fell asleep. In his sleep he had a bad dream. It awoke him, and he saw the old woman running away with the marrow-fat and the boiled 80 grease. He looked into the cooking-basket. There was not a drop of soup left in it. He chased the old woman. He would punish her! But she could run, too, and she easily kept ahead of him. Every once in awhile she stopped and held up the marrow-fat and shouted: "*Sin-ka-lip',* do you want this?" **D**

Finally Coyote gave up trying to catch her. He went back to get the bones. He thought he would boil them again. He found the bones scattered all around, so he gathered them up and put them into the cooking-basket. Needing some more water to boil them in, he went to the creek for it, and when he got back, there were no bones in the basket! In place of the bones was a little pile of tree limbs!

Coyote thought he might be able to get another cow from Buffalo Bull, so he 90 set out to find him. When he came to the herd, he was astonished to see the cow he had killed. She was there with the others! She refused to go with Coyote again, and Buffalo Bull would not give him another cow. Coyote had to return to his own country without a buffalo.

That is why there never have been any buffalo along the *Swah-netk'-qhu.* ✺

D TRICKSTER TALES
Coyote is not the only character who plays the role of trickster in this tale. Reread lines 77–83. Notice how the old woman turns the tables on Coyote, teasing him with some tricks of her own. An **archetype of mythic literature,** the trickster character appears frequently in American popular entertainment—from animated cartoons to superhero comic books and the hugely popular movies based on them. Tricks and counter-tricks have kept Wile E. Coyote in the American public eye since 1948. Where else have you seen a trickster such as Coyote in action?

DIFFERENTIATED INSTRUCTION

FOR STRUGGLING READERS

4 Targeted Passage [Lines 66–81]

In this passage, the trickster himself is tricked, losing every part of his buffalo.

- What does Coyote do that Buffalo Bull told him not to? (lines 66–67)

- What becomes of the meat and the marrow-fat? (lines 68–69)

- How does the old woman trick Coyote? (lines 73–83)

- Which of Coyote's qualities makes it possible for the old woman to trick him? (line 77)

FOR ADVANCED LEARNERS/AP

Analyze Tone Have students describe and discuss the tone of "Coyote and the Buffalo." Ask why the tone is appropriate for a folk tale and whether a more serious tone would or would not have worked equally well. Extend the discussion by asking students to compare the tone of this tale with that of other folk tales they have read.

Comprehension

1. **Recall** Why is Buffalo Bull so enraged at Coyote at the beginning of the story?

2. **Recall** How does Coyote convince Buffalo Bull to spare his life?

3. **Summarize** According to the story, why don't buffalo live in the *Swah-netk'-qhu* country?

Text Analysis

● 4. **Analyze Predictions** Review the chart you completed as you read. How accurate were your predictions? Did the fact that the trickster is a somewhat familiar **archetypal character** make it easier to predict Coyote's actions, or did his behavior surprise you? Explain your answer, referring to both your chart and the selection.

● 5. **Interpret Trickster Tales** Trickster tales endure, in part, simply because they are fun to read. But they also often serve to teach a lesson or moral. What does "Coyote and the Buffalo" teach or explain? Support your answer with specific lines from the story.

6. **Draw Conclusions** Trickster tales, like other forms of folk literature, offer readers insight into a society's way of life. What information about the following aspects of Okanogan culture did you glean from this tale?

   • traits or qualities the Okanogan admired as well as those they disapproved of

   • the traditional role of women in Okanogan society

   • Okanogan rituals and religious beliefs

7. **Make Judgments** Review the paragraph you wrote earlier about famous or compelling villains and tricksters. What character traits does Coyote share with these characters? In your opinion, is Coyote an admirable character? Explain, citing evidence from the text to support your opinion.

Text Criticism

8. **Critical Interpretations** Critic Paul Rodin has argued that a trickster "is at one and the same time creator and destroyer, giver and negator, he who dupes others and who is always duped himself.... He possesses no values, moral or social, is at the mercy of his passions and appetites." Identify the ways in which Coyote fits this definition of a trickster. Cite evidence from the selection to support your answer.

> *Why do we root for the* **"BAD GUY"?**
>
> What makes Coyote appealing, despite his character flaws? Can you think of a famous person who fits the "trickster" label?

COMMON CORE

RL 1 Cite textual evidence to support analysis of what the text says explicitly as well as inferences drawn from the text, including determining where the text leaves matters uncertain. **RL 3** Analyze the impact of the author's choices regarding how to develop and relate elements of a story. **RL 5** Analyze how an author's choices concerning how to structure specific parts of a text contribute to its overall structure and meaning as well as its aesthetic impact.

Practice and Apply

For preliminary support of post-reading questions, use these copy masters.

R RESOURCE MANAGER—Copy Masters
   Reading Check p. 39
   Trickster Tales p. 35
   Question Support p. 40

   Additional selection questions are provided for teachers on page 29.

ANSWERS COMMON CORE **RL 1, RL 3, RL 5**

1. *Buffalo Bull, who has come back to life, is enraged because Coyote had been desecrating his skull.*

2. *Coyote convinces Buffalo Bull to spare his life by offering to make Buffalo Bull new horns to use for killing Young Buffalo.*

3. *Coyote disobeyed Buffalo Bull and killed the cow Buffalo Bull had given him. Buffalo Bull refused to replace the cow. As a result, Coyote has to return to his own land without a buffalo.*

Possible answers:

4. ■ COMMON CORE FOCUS *Predict Answers will vary. Students should support their responses with evidence from their charts and details from the selection.*

5. ● COMMON CORE FOCUS *Trickster Tales This tale teaches that it pays to befriend one's enemy, that greed will be punished, and that a person can usually be tricked only once before wising up. Students should support their answers with lines from the story.*

Assess and Reteach

Assess

DIAGNOSTIC AND SELECTION TESTS
   Selection Test A, B/C pp. 29–30, 31-32

Interactive Selection Test on thinkcentral.com

Reteach

Level Up Online Tutorials on thinkcentral.com

Reteaching Worksheets on thinkcentral.com

   Literature Lesson 31, Reading Lesson 1

6. *The Okanogan admired cleverness, quick thinking, and helpfulness; they disapproved of greediness and vanity. The Okanogan followed strict gender roles— women cooked and men waged war (lines 75–76). Buffalo Bull comes back from the dead, so the Okanogan may have believed in reincarnation.*

7. *Students may note that, like many well-known villains from movies and literature, Coyote is clever, manipulative, and deceitful.*

8. *Students may say that Coyote is both*

creator (he creates Buffalo Bull's new horns) and destroyer (he kills the young cow). He is cunning (he talks Buffalo Bull out of killing him) and foolish (he is duped by the old woman).

> *Why do we root for the* **"BAD GUY"?** Students may say that Coyote is appealing because he makes us laugh and keeps us guessing.

Focus and Motivate

COMMON CORE FOCUS

RI 4 Determine the meaning of words and phrases as they are used in a text including technical meanings. **RI 5** Analyze and evaluate the effectiveness of the structure an author uses in his or her exposition, including whether the structure makes points clear, convincing, and engaging. **RI 6** Determine an author's point of view or purpose in a text in which the rhetoric is particularly effective, analyzing how style and content contribute to the power, persuasiveness, or beauty of the text. **L 4c** Consult general and specialized reference materials, both print and digital, to clarify a word's precise meaning. **L 5b** Analyze nuances in the meaning of words with similar denotations.

ABOUT THE AUTHOR

Have students summarize important points of Momaday's biography. Emphasize that the author finds "the key to self-understanding is awareness of the past." This reflects Momaday's link to his Native American heritage.

NOTABLE QUOTE

"Ask yourself how you would like to be known. Don't let yourself be determined by others." **–N. Scott Momaday**

Ask students to write a journal entry about how they think people perceive them and how they wish to be seen.

Selection Resources

*See resources on the **Teacher One Stop DVD-ROM** and on **thinkcentral.com**.*

 RESOURCE MANAGER UNIT 1

    Plan and Teach, pp. 41–48
    Summary, pp. 49–50†‡*
    Text Analysis and Reading
      Skill, pp. 51–54†*
    Vocabulary, pp. 55–57*

DIAGNOSTIC AND SELECTION
    TESTS

    Selection Tests, pp. 33–36

BEST PRACTICES TOOLKIT

TECHNOLOGY

⊘ **Teacher One Stop DVD-ROM**
⊘ **Student One Stop DVD-ROM**
⊘ **Audio Anthology CD**
⊘ **GrammarNotes DVD-ROM**
⊘ **ExamView Test Generator**
   on the **Teacher One Stop**

* Resources for Differentiation   **† Also in Spanish**   **‡ In Haitian Creole and Vietnamese**

Themes Across Time

COMMON CORE

RI 5 Analyze and evaluate the effectiveness of the structure an author uses in his or her exposition, including whether the structure makes points clear, convincing, and engaging. **RI 6** Determine an author's point of view or purpose in a text in which the rhetoric is particularly effective, analyzing how style and content contribute to the power, persuasiveness, or beauty of the text. **L 5b** Analyze nuances in the meaning of words with similar denotations.

from The Way to Rainy Mountain

Memoir by N. Scott Momaday

DID YOU KNOW?

N. Scott Momaday . . .

- rode the bus 28 miles to and from school as a teenager.
- taught both middle school and high school on the Jicarilla reservation in New Mexico before becoming a professional writer.
- won the Pulitzer Prize, the most prestigious U.S. literary award, for his very first novel.

Meet the Author

N. Scott Momaday born 1934

"The most important question one can ask is 'Who am I?'" N. Scott Momaday (mŏm'ə-dā') has asserted. "People tend to define you. As a child, you can't help that, but as you grow older, the goal is to garner enough strength to insist on your own definition of yourself." In his writing, Momaday focuses on the search for identity, and he locates the key to self-understanding in awareness of the past.

Native American Roots Momaday developed a deep sense of his own roots early on. His father, a successful artist and a member of the Kiowa (kī'ə-wô') tribe, routinely told him Kiowa folk tales. His mother, an accomplished writer of French, English, and Cherokee ancestry, instructed him in traditional ways. Momaday grew up on reservations in the Southwest and often spent his summers with his grandparents and other Kiowa relatives in Oklahoma.

The Making of a Writer Growing up on reservations, Momaday developed a reverence for the land and a strong Native American identity. "I saw people," he recalls, "who were deeply involved in their traditional life, in the memories of their blood. They had, as far as I could see, a certain strength and beauty that I find missing in the

modern world at large." The lives of these people, together with the Southwestern landscape, inspired Momaday to begin writing at an early age. With the encouragement of his parents, Momaday began composing poetry. Years of hard work and determination paid off when he was awarded a poetry fellowship by Stanford University in 1959.

Voice of the Kiowa In both his poetry and prose, Momaday pays tribute to Native American storytelling traditions and culture. His first novel, *House Made of Dawn,* tells the story of one man's struggle to recover his identity after a stint in the U.S. Army. Original in both theme and structure, the novel was awarded the Pulitzer Prize in 1969. In one of his most popular works, *The Way to Rainy Mountain,* Momaday mixes Kiowa myths, legends, and history with autobiographical details. In addition to his poetry and fiction, Momaday has published essays and articles on preserving the environment. He says, "Writing is a way of expressing your spirit. So there's much more to it than the question of material success. You are out to save your soul after all, and be the best thing that you can be."

Author Online

THINK central

Go to **thinkcentral.com**. KEYWORD: HML11-54

54

TEXT ANALYSIS: MEMOIR

A **memoir** is a form of autobiographical writing that shares personal experiences as well as observations of significant historical events or people. Memoirs often are written in a highly literary style that may include the use of rhetorical techniques such as understatement, overstatement, repetition, or parallel structure.

As you read N. Scott Momaday's memoir, note how he uses diction and tone to evoke emotion and to advance his purpose for writing. Also, try to distinguish between descriptions of personal experience and sections that comment on larger historical events.

READING SKILL: ANALYZE STRUCTURE

Writers usually arrange information using a **structure** that helps readers see how ideas are related. Momaday interweaves three distinct strands throughout his memoir: details about landscape, details about the Kiowa, and details about his grandmother. As you read, record details about each topic in a chart like the one below, and consider how the topics are related.

The Landscape	The Kiowa	Momaday's Grandmother

VOCABULARY IN CONTEXT

Momaday used the following words in this exploration of his heritage. To test your knowledge, substitute one vocabulary word for the boldfaced word or phrase in each sentence.

WORD LIST	enmity	opaque	solstice
	inherently	pillage	tenuous
	luxuriant	preeminently	
	nocturnal	profusion	

1. My mother's garden yields an **abundance** of flowers.
2. The feuding brothers eyed each other with **hostility**.
3. There is something **intrinsically** funny about seeing pictures of my father as a teenager.
4. The summer reunion is held on the **longest day of the year**.

 Complete the activities in your **Reader/Writer Notebook**.

What is your HERITAGE?

What makes you who you are? Part of the answer lies in your heritage, or the beliefs, traditions, and culture passed down to you from preceding generations. Think of the things you have gained or learned from older relatives—the recipe for your favorite meal, perhaps, or a sense of humor, or an attitude toward hardship. How have the things you've learned helped shape who you are today? In the selection that follows, N. Scott Momaday offers his own perspective on the importance of heritage.

INTERVIEW Interview one of your classmates about his or her heritage. Ask your subject about a family tradition, an important belief or value, or a story about his or her family's roots. Find out if your classmate thinks heritage has affected his or her identity.

55

What is your HERITAGE?

Discuss how heritage influences a person as a child growing up and later as an adult. Then have students do the *INTERVIEW* activity.

TEXT ANALYSIS

COMMON CORE RI 6

● *Model the Skill:* MEMOIR

Share with the class a few personal facts, such as your favorite food. Explain that a memoir provides more than just facts. Point out that in his memoir Momaday blends his knowledge of the history, myths, and legends of the Kiowa with personal thoughts and feelings.

READING SKILL

COMMON CORE RI 5

■ *Model the Skill:* ANALYZE STRUCTURE

Explain that *structure* refers to the organization that holds a work together. Provide examples, such as the use of chronological order in a historical narrative. Discuss how a clear structure aids comprehension.

GUIDED PRACTICE Ask students to describe the structure of other works they have read.

R RESOURCE MANAGER—Copy Master Analyze Structure p. 53

VOCABULARY SKILL

COMMON CORE L 4

▲ VOCABULARY IN CONTEXT

DIAGNOSE WORD KNOWLEDGE Have students complete Vocabulary in Context. Check their word choice and phrases against the following:

enmity (ĕn′mĭ-tē) *n.* hostility; hatred

inherently (ĭn-hîr′ənt-lē) *adv.* related to part of something's inmost nature

luxuriant (lŭg-zhŏŏr′ē-ənt) *adj.* characterized by abundant growth

opaque (ō-pāk′) *adj.* not allowing light to pass through

nocturnal (nŏk-tûr′nəl) *adj.* occurring at night

pillage (pĭl′ĭj) *n.* the act of looting or plundering by force

preeminently (prē-ĕm′ə-nənt-lē) *adv.* above all; most importantly

profusion (prə-fyōō′zhən) *n.* abundance; lavishness

solstice (sŏl′stĭs) *n.* either of two days of the year when the sun is farthest from the

celestial equator; the summer solstice is the longest day of the year, and the winter solstice is the shortest.

tenuous (tĕn′yōō-əs) *adj.* having little substance or strength; flimsy

PRETEACH VOCABULARY Use the copy master to help students predict the meaning of each boldfaced word in the copy master, using context clues.

 RESOURCE MANAGER—Copy Master Vocabulary Study p. 55

SUMMARY

In this memoir, an excerpt from *The Way to Rainy Mountain*, N. Scott Momaday describes his pilgrimage to visit his grandmother's grave near Rainy Mountain, an old landmark of the Kiowa in Oklahoma. The author weaves together descriptive details of his ancestral lands, historical information about his people, the Kiowa, and personal recollections of his grandmother, Aho.

READ WITH A PURPOSE

Help students read with a purpose. Tell them to read to discover how the people and places of our childhoods influence the adults we become.

READING SKILL

COMMON CORE
RI 5

A Model the Skill: ANALYZE STRUCTURE

Work with students to fill in their organizational charts from page 55 with details from the passage. On the board, draw your own chart and think aloud as you fill it in. Point out that the first paragraph focuses on physical details of the landscape and lines 15–16 focus on the author's grandmother. Help students use data from their charts to draw conclusions about the structure of this part of the selection. Tell students the selection moves from the general (the landscape) to the specific (Momaday's grandmother).

THE WAY TO
Rainy Mountain

N. Scott Momaday

BACKGROUND In the 1600s, after a bitter dispute between two chiefs, a band of Kiowa moved from what is now Montana to South Dakota's Black Hills. In around 1785, the Kiowa migrated farther south to escape attacks by neighboring tribes, settling in what is now western Kansas and Oklahoma. With their Comanche allies, the Kiowa ruled the southern Great Plains for a century. One of the last tribes to be defeated by the U.S. government, the Kiowa surrendered in 1875 and were forced onto a reservation in Oklahoma, where members of the tribe still live today.

Analyze Visuals ▶
Examine the portrait on page 57, and consider the photographer's use of high-contrast lighting. What **traits** are suggested by this emphasis of light and shadow? Do you think the subject might look stronger or more vulnerable in a different kind of light? Explain your answer.

A single knoll[1] rises out of the plain in Oklahoma, north and west of the Wichita Range. For my people, the Kiowas, it is an old landmark, and they gave it the name Rainy Mountain. The hardest weather in the world is there. Winter brings blizzards, hot tornadic winds arise in the spring, and in summer the prairie is an anvil's edge. The grass turns brittle and brown, and it cracks beneath your feet. There are green belts along the rivers and creeks, linear groves of hickory and pecan, willow and witch hazel. At a distance in July or August the steaming foliage seems almost to writhe in fire. Great green and yellow grasshoppers are everywhere in the tall grass, popping up like corn to sting the flesh, and tortoises crawl about
10 on the red earth, going nowhere in the plenty of time. Loneliness is an aspect of the land. All things in the plain are isolate; there is no confusion of objects in the eye, but one hill or one tree or one man. To look upon that landscape in the early morning, with the sun at your back, is to lose the sense of proportion. Your imagination comes to life, and this, you think, is where Creation was begun. **A**

I returned to Rainy Mountain in July. My grandmother had died in the spring, and I wanted to be at her grave. She had lived to be very old and at last infirm.

1 Targeted Passage
A ANALYZE STRUCTURE
Reread lines 1–14, and notice how the highly descriptive opening paragraph functions as both a literal and figurative "beginning," leading to the phrase "where Creation was begun." What structural relationship do you see between the first paragraph and lines 15–16?

---

1. **knoll** (nōl): a small round hill.

Edward S. Curtis Collection.
Library of Congress.

DIFFERENTIATED INSTRUCTION

FOR ENGLISH LANGUAGE LEARNERS

Vocabulary Flashcards Provide students with index cards. Tell students to write each unfamiliar word on the front of the card and its definition on the back. Have students organize their words by general topic. For example, words about plants or words about weather.

FOR STRUGGLING READERS

In combination with the *Audio Anthology CD*, use one or more Targeted Passages (pp. 56, 58, 60) to ensure that students focus on key events and concepts. Targeted Passages are also good for English learners.

1 Targeted Passage [Lines 1–16]
This passage explains what and where Rainy Mountain is, describes the region, and tells why the author is returning there.

Analyze Visuals

Possible answer: The photographer's emphasis of light and shadow suggests a reflective melancholy, especially when coupled with the subject's wide eyes and somber expression. Had the photographer used a brighter, more direct light, the subject's features would have been more sharply delineated, and she might have looked stronger. On the other hand, dimmer light would have further softened her features, making her appear more vulnerable.

BACKGROUND

The Sun Dance Ceremony The Sun Dance was important not only to the Kiowa but also to numerous other Plains Indian tribes. Have students do research to learn more about the Sun Dance. Ask students to share their findings in an oral presentation to the class.

- What is Rainy Mountain? Where is it located? (lines 1–3)
- With what group of people does the author associate himself? (line 2)
- Describe the environment of Rainy Mountain. (lines 3–10)
- Why does the author return to Rainy Mountain? (lines 15–16)

FOR ADVANCED LEARNERS/AP

Research Have students work in pairs to research the migration of the Kiowa people and create a poster-sized, annotated map that reflects the information that they discover. Review the concept of Works Cited and ask students to generate a complete list of the sources they consult.

Her only living daughter was with her when she died, and I was told that in death her face was that of a child.

I like to think of her as a child. When she was born, the Kiowas were living the last great moment of their history. For more than a hundred years they had controlled the open range from the Smoky Hill River to the Red, from the headwaters of the Canadian to the fork of the Arkansas and Cimarron. In alliance with the Comanches, they had ruled the whole of the southern Plains. War was their sacred business, and they were among the finest horsemen the world has ever known. But warfare for the Kiowas was **preeminently** a matter of disposition rather than of survival, and they never understood the grim, unrelenting advance of the U.S. Cavalry. When at last, divided and ill-provisioned, they were driven onto the Staked Plains in the cold rains of autumn, they fell into panic. In Palo Duro Canyon they abandoned their crucial stores to **pillage** and had nothing then but their lives. In order to save themselves, they surrendered to the soldiers at Fort Sill[2] and were imprisoned in the old stone corral that now stands as a military museum. My grandmother was spared the humiliation of those high gray walls by eight or ten years, but she must have known from birth the affliction of defeat, the dark brooding of old warriors. Ⓑ

Her name was Aho, and she belonged to the last culture to evolve in North America. Her forebears came down from the high country in western Montana nearly three centuries ago. They were a mountain people, a mysterious tribe of hunters whose language has never been positively classified in any major group. In the late seventeenth century they began a long migration to the south and east. It was a journey toward the dawn, and it led to a golden age. Along the way the Kiowas were befriended by the Crows,[3] who gave them the culture and religion of the Plains. They acquired horses, and their ancient nomadic spirit was suddenly free of the ground. They acquired Tai-me, the sacred Sun Dance doll, from that moment the object and symbol of their worship, and so shared in the divinity of the sun. Not least, they acquired the sense of destiny, therefore courage and pride. When they entered upon the southern Plains they had been transformed. No longer were they slaves to the simple necessity of survival; they were a lordly and dangerous society of fighters and thieves, hunters and priests of the sun. According to their origin myth, they entered the world through a hollow log. From one point of view, their migration was the fruit of an old prophecy, for indeed they emerged from a sunless world.

Although my grandmother lived out her long life in the shadow of Rainy Mountain, the immense landscape of the continental interior lay like memory in her blood. She could tell of the Crows, whom she had never seen, and of the Black Hills, where she had never been. I wanted to see in reality what she had seen more perfectly in the mind's eye, and traveled fifteen hundred miles to begin my pilgrimage.

---

2. **Fort Sill:** a U.S. army post established in 1869 in the Indian Territory (now Oklahoma).
3. **Crows:** a group of Native Americans who once inhabited the region between the Platte and Yellowstone rivers in the northern Great Plains. The Crows are now settled in Montana.

Yellowstone, it seemed to me, was the top of the world, a region of deep lakes and dark timber, canyons and waterfalls. But, beautiful as it is, one might have the
60 sense of confinement there. The skyline in all directions is close at hand, the high wall of the woods and deep cleavages of shade. There is a perfect freedom in the mountains, but it belongs to the eagle and the elk, the badger and the bear. The Kiowas reckoned their stature by the distance they could see, and they were bent and blind in the wilderness.

Descending eastward, the highland meadows are a stairway to the plain. In July the inland slope of the Rockies is **luxuriant** with flax and buckwheat, stonecrop and larkspur. The earth unfolds and the limit of the land recedes. Clusters of trees, and animals grazing far in the distance, cause the vision to reach away and wonder to build upon the mind. The sun follows a longer course in the day, and the sky is
70 immense beyond all comparison. The great billowing clouds that sail upon it are shadows that move upon the grain like water, dividing light. Farther down, in the land of the Crows and Blackfeet,[4] the plain is yellow. Sweet clover takes hold of the hills and bends upon itself to cover and seal the soil. There the Kiowas paused on their way; they had come to the place where they must change their lives. The sun is at home on the plains. Precisely there does it have the certain character of a god. When the Kiowas came to the land of the Crows, they could see the dark lees of the hills at dawn across the Bighorn River, the **profusion** of light on the grain shelves, the oldest deity ranging after the **solstices.** Not yet would they veer southward to the caldron of the land that lay below; they must wean their blood
80 from the northern winter and hold the mountains a while longer in their view. They bore Tai-me in procession to the east.

A dark mist lay over the Black Hills, and the land was like iron. At the top of a ridge I caught sight of Devil's Tower upthrust against the gray sky as if in the birth of time the core of the earth had broken through its crust and the motion of the world was begun. There are things in nature that engender an awful quiet in the heart of man; Devil's Tower is one of them. Two centuries ago, because they could not do otherwise, the Kiowas made a legend at the base of the rock. My grandmother said:

Eight children were there at play, seven sisters and their brother. Suddenly the boy
90 *was struck dumb; he trembled and began to run upon his hands and feet. His fingers became claws, and his body was covered with fur. Directly there was a bear where the boy had been. The sisters were terrified; they ran, and the bear after them. They came to the stump of a great tree, and the tree spoke to them. It bade them climb upon it, and as they did so it began to rise into the air. The bear came to kill them, but they were just beyond its reach. It reared against the tree and scored the bark all around with its claws. The seven sisters were borne into the sky, and they became the stars of the Big Dipper.*

---

4. **Blackfeet:** a group of Native Americans who once inhabited a region now occupied by parts of Montana and the Canadian provinces of Alberta and Saskatchewan.

THE WAY TO RAINY MOUNTAIN **59**

luxuriant (lŭg-zhŏŏr'ē-ənt) *adj.* characterized by abundant growth

profusion (prə-fyōō'zhən) *n.* abundance; lavishness

solstice (sŏl'stĭs) *n.* either of two days of the year when the sun is farthest from the celestial equator; the summer solstice is the longest day of the year, and the winter solstice is the shortest.

(❋) COMMON CORE L 5b

Language Coach

Formal Language Note the formal tone of lines 89–97. For example, "It bade them climb upon it" could be expressed informally as "It asked them to climb it." Why is formal language appropriate for the telling of a legend?

THE WAY TO RAINY MOUNTAIN **59**

What is your HERITAGE?

Discuss After students read lines 86–99, ask them the following question: What does Momaday's discussion of the Kiowa legend suggest about the author's feelings regarding his heritage? *Possible answer: Momaday not only recalls the Kiowa legend that his grandmother told him but also chooses to include it in detail, which suggests that his heritage means a great deal to him.*

READING SKILL

COMMON CORE **RI 5**

C *Model the Skill:* ANALYZE STRUCTURE

Tell students that the Kiowas' oral tradition has passed many legends and folk tales from one generation to another. These tales remind people of their heritage.

Possible answer: Momaday may mean that as long as the legend continues to be passed down through oral tradition, the Kiowa can take comfort in knowing that their ancestors are looking down on them from the heavens. Seeing the Big Dipper can inspire cultural pride. The inclusion of the legend adds depth to the personal elements of the memoir by drawing readers into Kiowa history and culture.

VOCABULARY

COMMON CORE **L 4**

OWN THE WORD

- **tenuous:** Remind students that *tenuous* means "having little substance or strength; flimsy." Synonyms for *tenuous* include weak, fragile, and uncertain.

- **inherently:** Tell students that the adverb *inherently* means "related to something's inmost nature; intrinsic." The sound of the Kiowa grandmother's prayers was *inherently* sad. Ask students to suggest actions or characteristics they find *inherently* joyful, or hostile. *Possible answers: a happy song, an angry stare*

From that moment, and so long as the legend lives, the Kiowas have kinsmen in the night sky. Whatever they were in the mountains, they could be no more. 100 However **tenuous** their well-being, however much they had suffered and would suffer again, they had found a way out of the wilderness. **C**

My grandmother had a reverence for the sun, a holy regard that now is all but gone out of mankind. There was a wariness in her, and an ancient awe. She was a Christian in her later years, but she had come a long way about, and she never forgot her birthright. As a child she had been to the Sun Dances; she had taken part in those annual rites, and by them she had learned the restoration of her people in the presence of Tai-me. She was about seven when the last Kiowa Sun Dance was held in 1887 on the Washita River above Rainy Mountain Creek. The buffalo were gone. In order to consummate the ancient sacrifice—to impale the 110 head of a buffalo bull upon the medicine tree—a delegation of old men journeyed into Texas, there to beg and barter for an animal from the Goodnight herd.[5] She was ten when the Kiowas came together for the last time as a living Sun Dance culture. They could find no buffalo; they had to hang an old hide from the sacred tree. Before the dance could begin, a company of soldiers rode out from Fort Sill under orders to disperse the tribe. Forbidden without cause the essential act of their faith, having seen the wild herds slaughtered and left to rot upon the ground, the Kiowas backed away forever from the medicine tree. That was July 20, 1890, at the great bend of the Washita. My grandmother was there. Without bitterness, and for as long as she lived, she bore a vision of deicide.[6]

120 Now that I can have her only in memory, I see my grandmother in the several postures that were peculiar to her: standing at the wood stove on a winter morning and turning meat in a great iron skillet; sitting at the south window, bent above her beadwork, and afterwards, when her vision failed, looking down for a long time into the fold of her hands; going out upon a cane, very slowly as she did when the weight of age came upon her; praying. I remember her most often at prayer. She made long, rambling prayers out of suffering and hope, having seen many things. I was never sure that I had the right to hear, so exclusive were they of all mere custom and company. The last time I saw her she prayed standing by the side of her bed at night, naked to the waist, the light of a kerosene lamp moving 130 upon her dark skin. Her long, black hair, always drawn and braided in the day, lay upon her shoulders and against her breasts like a shawl. I do not speak Kiowa, and I never understood her prayers, but there was something **inherently** sad in the sound, some merest hesitation upon the syllables of sorrow. She began in a high and descending pitch, exhausting her breath to silence; then again and again—and always the same intensity of effort, of something that is, and is not, like urgency in the human voice. Transported so in the dancing light among the shadows of her room, she seemed beyond the reach of time. But that was illusion; I think I knew then that I should not see her again.

---

5. **Goodnight herd:** a herd of Southern Plains bison established in the 1870s by Charles and Molly Goodnight for the purpose of preserving the animals from extinction.

6. **a vision of deicide** (dē′ə-sīd′): a picture in her mind of the killing of a god.

---

tenuous (tĕn′yōō-əs) *adj.* having little substance or strength; flimsy

C ANALYZE STRUCTURE Reread lines 98–101. What does Momaday mean when he says that "the Kiowas have kinsmen in the night sky"? How does the inclusion of this legend add depth to the personal elements of this memoir?

 Targeted Passage

Language Coach

Word Definitions *Postures* in line 121 means "the positions of the body." Grandmother's postures are peculiar to her; they distinguish her from other people the speaker knows. What postures does Momaday list? How does each add to his description of his grandmother?

inherently (ĭn-hîr′ənt-lē) *adv.* related to part of something's inmost nature

---

DIFFERENTIATED INSTRUCTION

FOR STRUGGLING READERS

Targeted Passage [Lines 102–119]

This passage describes Aho's experience with the Sun Dance ritual.

- How did Aho develop her reverence for the sun? (lines 102–119)
- What were the Sun Dances? (lines 108–114)
- What sacrifice was part of the Sun Dance? (lines 109–114)
- Why did the Kiowa stop holding the annual Sun Dance ritual? (lines 115–118)

- How did Aho react to the stopping of the Sun Dance ritual? (lines 118–119)

FOR ENGLISH LANGUAGE LEARNERS

Language Coach

Word Definitions Remind students that some words have more than one meaning or may even change parts of speech. Have students look up the word *posture* in the dictionary and discuss the different meanings. Ask volunteers to act out the meanings of the word.

Mandan Offering the Buffalo Skull, Edward S. Curtis, photographer. McCormick Library of Special Collections, Northwestern University Library.

◀ **Analyze Visuals**
In your opinion, does this photograph convey the same **mood** that Momaday evokes in his autobiography? Explain your answer, citing details from both the photograph and the text.

Houses are like sentinels in the plain, old keepers of the weather watch. There, 140 in a very little while, wood takes on the appearance of great age. All colors wear soon away in the wind and rain, and then the wood is burned gray and the grain appears and the nails turn red with rust. The windowpanes are black and **opaque**; you imagine there is nothing within, and indeed there are many ghosts, bones given up to the land. They stand here and there against the sky, and you approach them for a longer time than you expect. They belong in the distance; it is their domain. **ᴅ**

Once there was a lot of sound in my grandmother's house, a lot of coming and going, feasting and talk. The summers there were full of excitement and reunion. The Kiowas are a summer people; they abide the cold and keep to themselves, but when the season turns and the land becomes warm and vital they cannot 150 hold still; an old love of going returns upon them. The aged visitors who came to my grandmother's house when I was a child were made of lean and leather, and they bore themselves upright. They wore great black hats and bright ample shirts

opaque (ō-pāk′) *adj.* not allowing light to pass through

ᴅ **MEMOIR**
Reread lines 120–145. What words and phrases give you an indication of Momaday's **tone,** or attitude toward his subject matter?

THE WAY TO RAINY MOUNTAIN **61**

Analyze Visuals

Possible answer: The photograph does seem to convey the same mood that Momaday evokes in the text. In the picture, a lone Native American holds a buffalo skull reverentially toward the heavens, perhaps in a prayer of thanks. Momaday's memoir expresses a similar feeling of reverence—for his grandmother and for the Kiowa culture. The text makes reference to the Kiowa Sun Dance (lines 43, 105–113), a religious ceremony, and to the grandmother's "reverence for the sun" (line 102). Momaday also notes that he remembers his grandmother "most often at prayer" (lines 125–126).

TEXT ANALYSIS COMMON CORE RI 6

ᴅ **MEMOIR**

Possible answer: Phrases that suggest Momaday's somber and pensive tone include: "Now that I can have her only in memory" (line 120); "She made long, rambling prayers out of suffering and hope" (line 126); "there was something inherently sad in the sound . . . syllables of sorrow" (lines 132–133); "I think I knew then that I should not see her again" (lines 137–138); "you imagine there is nothing within, and indeed there are many ghosts" (line 143).

IF STUDENTS NEED HELP . . . Discuss the tone and the reasons behind it. Remind students that the memoir includes memories of Momaday's grandmother and recollections of the troubled times of the Kiowa.

VOCABULARY COMMON CORE L 4

OWN THE WORD

opaque: Point out to students that the root of the word *opaque* is the Latin word *opacus*, which means "shady." The meaning of *opaque* is "not admitting light," as in a shade covering a window.

What is your HERITAGE?

Discuss Lead students in a discussion of lines 146–167 by asking them the following question: How do Momaday's memories of his grandmother's house help to define his link with his heritage? *Possible answer: Momaday's remembrance of traditions and cultural details shows how meaningful these early experiences were.*

TEXT ANALYSIS

COMMON CORE
RI 6

E MEMOIR

Possible answer: The house might symbolize the old, weathered state of Kiowa strength and culture. Like the house, Kiowa culture was once vital and alive; although it is not what it once was, it continues to inspire people like Momaday.

VOCABULARY

COMMON CORE
L 4

OWN THE WORD

- **enmity:** Review the definition of *enmity*. Then have students list antonyms for *enmity*. *Possible answers: goodwill, friendliness, cordiality*

- **nocturnal:** Ask students to list events that they would categorize as *nocturnal*. *Possible answers: the prom, an owl hunting for food, a lunar eclipse*

SELECTION WRAP–UP

READ WITH A PURPOSE Ask students how the place where Momaday grew up helped shape him as a person. *Possible answer: It helped give him a great appreciation for nature and an eye for detail.*

⭐ **CRITIQUE** Have students evaluate Momaday's blend of history and personal recollection. Ask whether combining the two is effective or distracting, and why.

INDEPENDENT READING
For students interested in reading other North American Indian folktales, suggest *Folk-Lore and Legends: North American Indian* (author anonymous).

THEME AND GENRE

TEXT STRUCTURE

After students have read this story, ask them to discuss films, plays, or novels that connect to Momaday's pilgrimage.

---

that shook in the wind. They rubbed fat upon their hair and wound their braids with strips of colored cloth. Some of them painted their faces and carried the scars of old and cherished **enmities.** They were an old council of warlords, come to remind and be reminded of who they were. Their wives and daughters served them well. The women might indulge themselves; gossip was at once the mark and compensation of their servitude. They made loud and elaborate talk among themselves, full of jest and gesture, fright and false alarm. They went abroad in
160 fringed and flowered shawls, bright beadwork and German silver. They were at home in the kitchen, and they prepared meals that were banquets.

There were frequent prayer meetings, and great **nocturnal** feasts. When I was a child I played with my cousins outside, where the lamplight fell upon the ground and the singing of the old people rose up around us and carried away into the darkness. There were a lot of good things to eat, a lot of laughter and surprise. And afterwards, when the quiet returned, I lay down with my grandmother and could hear the frogs away by the river and feel the motion of the air.

Now there is a funeral silence in the rooms, the endless wake of some final word. The walls have closed in upon my grandmother's house. When I returned
170 to it in mourning, I saw for the first time in my life how small it was. It was late at night, and there was a white moon, nearly full. I sat for a long time on the stone steps by the kitchen door. From there I could see out across the land; I could see the long row of trees by the creek, the low light upon the rolling plains, and the stars of the Big Dipper. Once I looked at the moon and caught sight of a strange thing. A cricket had perched upon the handrail, only a few inches away from me. My line of vision was such that the creature filled the moon like a fossil. It had gone there, I thought, to live and die, for there, of all places, was its small definition made whole and eternal. A warm wind rose up and purled like the longing within me. **E**

180 The next morning I awoke at dawn and went out on the dirt road to Rainy Mountain. It was already hot, and the grasshoppers began to fill the air. Still, it was early in the morning, and the birds sang out of the shadows. The long yellow grass on the mountain shone in the bright light, and a scissortail hied[7] above the land. There, where it ought to be, at the end of a long and legendary way, was my grandmother's grave. Here and there on the dark stones were ancestral names. Looking back once, I saw the mountain and came away. ❧

enmity (ĕn′mĭ-tē) *n.* hostility; hatred

nocturnal (nŏk-tûr′nəl) *adj.* occurring at night

E MEMOIR
Think about how Momaday contrasts his grandmother's house as it was during his childhood visits with how it is now. What might this house **symbolize**?

THEME AND GENRE
In mythic literature, the concept of the pilgrimage carries great significance. Momaday's pilgrimage to visit his mother's grave is emblematic of a spiritual journey to uncover his ancestral roots. A contemporary version of this journey is told in Jonathan Safran Foer's 2002 novel *Everything is Illuminated*. Which recent novels you've read include or allude to the mythic idea of the pilgrimage?

---

7. **a scissortail hied:** a fork-tailed bird of the Southwest hied, or hurried.

DIFFERENTIATED INSTRUCTION

FOR STRUGGLING WRITERS
Have students read and discuss lines 168–170. Then have them write a paragraph describing a place they have revisited as teens that seemed significantly different than it seemed to them as children.

FOR RELUCTANT READERS
Tell students that Momaday looks at his heritage with clear eyes. He considers the good and the bad and is honest in his appreciation. Invite students to create a journal—written, audiotaped, videotaped, or digitally recorded—in which they discuss their feelings about an aspect of their own lives.

Comprehension

1. **Recall** Where is Rainy Mountain, and why does Momaday return there?

2. **Clarify** What two natural phenomena are explained by the Kiowa legend about the seven sisters and their brother?

3. **Summarize** What important events in Kiowa history does Momaday recount?

Text Analysis

4. **Draw Conclusions** In your opinion, what is the most important insight Momaday gains about his **heritage** during his pilgrimage from Yellowstone to his grandmother's grave at Rainy Mountain? Support your opinion with evidence from the text.

● 5. **Understand Memoirs** Reread lines 52–101. What does Momaday's account of the Kiowa's migration offer you that a description in a history book might not? Explain, citing specific lines of the selection that support your answer.

■ 6. **Analyze Structure** Review the chart you created as you read, and summarize the geographical, historical, and personal details that Momaday includes in each of the three strands. How are they related? Describe the impact of Momaday's technique of weaving the three strands together.

7. **Examine Author's Style** Although best known as a novelist, Momaday is also an accomplished poet. In what way might this selection be described as poetic? In a chart like the one shown, record examples of the poetic elements Momaday uses in his memoir. Use your completed chart to explain what you think these stylistic choices add to the selection. (Refer to the **Glossary of Literary and Nonfiction Terms** on page R104 if needed.)

Poetic Elements		
Alliteration	Consonance	Imagery
"The grass turns brittle and brown . . ."		

Text Criticism

8. **Critical Interpretations** Teacher and scholar Kenneth M. Roemer has argued that "in *The Way to Rainy Mountain*, N. Scott Momaday links the survival of his people to their ability to remember, preserve and pass on stories." Do you agree that a culture's survival rests on this ability? Explain, using evidence from this selection to support your opinion.

What is your **HERITAGE?**

How is Momaday's identity shaped by his heritage? Can you think of ways your heritage has affected your life?

COMMON CORE

RI 5 Analyze and evaluate the effectiveness of the structure an author uses in his or her exposition, including whether the structure makes points clear, convincing, and engaging. **RI 6** Determine an author's point of view or purpose in a text in which the rhetoric is particularly effective, analyzing how style and content contribute to the power, persuasiveness, or beauty of the text.

Practice and Apply

For preliminary support of post-reading questions, use these copy masters:

 **RESOURCE MANAGER**—Copy Masters
Reading Check p. 58
Memoir p. 51
Question Support p. 59
Additional selection questions are provided for teachers on page 45.

ANSWERS

COMMON CORE RI 5, RI 6

1. *Rainy Mountain is located on a plain in Oklahoma, north and west of the Wichita Range. Momaday returns to Rainy Mountain to visit his grandmother's grave.*

2. *The legend explains the creation of Devil's Tower and the stars of the Big Dipper.*

3. *Momaday recounts the Kiowa's migration from western Montana to Oklahoma, their final Sun Dance, and their surrender at Fort Sill.*

Possible answers:

4. *Students may say that Momaday learns to appreciate his grandmother's abiding influence on him. He learns the importance of place in maintaining identity, the establishment of a harmonious relationship with the natural world, and the preservation of traditions and culture.*

5. ● **COMMON CORE FOCUS** *Memoir Momaday's account offers a more emotional look at the Kiowas' migration. Supporting lines include lines 73–81 and 98–101.*

6. ■ **COMMON CORE FOCUS** *Analyze Structure Students should recognize that the three strands present an informative, yet personalized, account of the events and experiences. The impact is a memoir that serves as a moving tribute both to the Kiowa and to Momaday's grandmother.*

7. *The selection is poetic in Momaday's use of language, imagery, and rhythm (for example, lines 1–14). Examples of poetic elements include* **alliteration:** *"The grass turns brittle and brown" (line 5);* **consonance:** *"luxuriant with flax" (line 66);* **imagery:** *"the prairie is an anvil's edge" (lines 4–5), "the steaming foliage seems almost to writhe in fire" (lines 7–8).*

8. *Students may say that preserving stories enables people to maintain their cultural identity and in so doing helps the culture to survive. The Kiowa culture, for example, survives in part because its stories and myths continue to be passed on.*

What is your **HERITAGE?**
Possible answer: *Momaday's heritage helped him become a thoughtful writer and keen observer. Students should think about how their heritage affects the way they view the world.*

Vocabulary in Context

▲ VOCABULARY PRACTICE

1. *nocturnal*	6. *pillage*
2. *solstice*	7. *luxuriant*
3. *enmity*	8. *profusion*
4. *tenuous*	9. *opaque*
5. *preeminently*	10. *inherently*

 RESOURCE MANAGER—Copy Master
Vocabulary Practice p. 56

ACADEMIC VOCABULARY IN WRITING

Momaday uses historical facts to document *and vivid details to* illustrate *a lost way of life by* revealing *cultural clues to his family's way of life.*

VOCABULARY STRATEGY: SPECIALIZED VOCABULARY

COMMON CORE **RI 4, L 4c**

For words with more than one dictionary meaning, encourage students to consider all the possibilities before deciding on one.

Answers: **1.** *c,* **2.** *a,* **3.** *d,* **4.** *e,* **5.** *b; eccentric also has a non-technical meaning: "odd or unconventional"*

 RESOURCE MANAGER—Copy Master
Vocabulary Strategy p. 57

Interactive Vocabulary THINK central

Keywords direct students to a **WordSharp** tutorial on **thinkcentral.com** or to other types of vocabulary practice and review.

Assess and Reteach

Assess

DIAGNOSTIC AND SELECTION TESTS
Selection Test A, pp. 33-34
Selection Test B/C, pp. 35-36

Interactive Selection Test on thinkcentral.com

Reteach

Level Up Online Tutorials on thinkcentral.com

Vocabulary in Context

▲ VOCABULARY PRACTICE

Choose the vocabulary word that answers each riddle.

1. I refer to things that do not happen in daylight.
2. I represent extremes of time, both shortest and longest.
3. I am the opposite of friendship.
4. I describe something uncertain or insubstantial.
5. I mean the same thing as *chiefly.*
6. I am the act of looting by force.
7. I am an adjective that could describe a field filled with wildflowers.
8. I am a noun indicating an abundance of wildflowers.
9. Air filled with dense fog is one example of what I am.
10. One of my meanings is "essentially."

WORD LIST

enmity
inherently
luxuriant
nocturnal
opaque
pillage
preeminently
profusion
solstice
tenuous

ACADEMIC VOCABULARY IN WRITING

• document   • illustrate   • interpret   • promote   • reveal

Write a paragraph explaining how Momaday uses this memoir to **document** not only the end of his grandmother's life but also the "end" of a specific way of life for the Kiowa people. Use at least one Academic Vocabulary word in your response.

VOCABULARY STRATEGY: SPECIALIZED VOCABULARY

The Kiowa recognize the importance of seasonal events such as the solstices. There are a number of terms that describe other natural phenomena relating Earth to the sun and the moon. Many of them have Latin and Greek roots. Some of these terms have only technical meanings, but others are also used in more general ways.

PRACTICE Match each term with its definition. Consult a print or online dictionary if you need help. Then choose the term that also has a meaning not related to astronomy and write a definition for it.

1. apogee	a. two dates each year when day and night are of equal length
2. equinox	b. having a noncircular planetary orbits such as Earth's
3. diurnal	c. point when the moon is farthest from Earth
4. perigee	d. relating to the daily rotation of Earth
5. eccentric	e. point when the moon is closest to Earth

COMMON CORE

RI 4 Determine the meaning of words and phrases as they are used in a text including technical meanings. **L 4c** Consult general and specialized reference materials, both print and digital, to clarify a word's precise meaning.

Interactive Vocabulary THINK central

Go to thinkcentral.com.
KEYWORD: HML11-64

DIFFERENTIATED INSTRUCTION

FOR ENGLISH LANGUAGE LEARNERS

Task Support: Vocabulary Practice Help students use the riddles in conjunction with suffixes of the listed words to determine parts of speech and figure out the answers. For example, explain that *-ly* is an adverb suffix—as in *chiefly* and *essentially*—so the answers to items 5 and 10 will also be adverbs. Similarly, *-sion* is a noun suffix, which will help students determine the answer to item 8.

FOR ADVANCED LEARNERS/AP

Vocabulary in Writing Ask students to use as many vocabulary words as they can in a paragraph about the moon and the earth.

Native American Values

Native Americans have long been characterized by stereotypes in Western culture. Explorers, trappers, and settlers often had little prior knowledge of Native Americans, so early written accounts of encounters with Native Americans naturally reflect an ignorance and misunderstanding of their values. Although Europeans and Native Americans coexisted peacefully in many places for many years, hostile encounters—often prompted by government policies—encouraged later writers to indulge in blatant "cowboys and Indians" stereotyping. Reading historical and current literature by Native Americans can help you see beyond the stereotypes and gain a clearer understanding of the Native American experience.

Writing to Synthesize

When you synthesize information about a subject, you make connections between various sources, including your own prior knowledge. By combining ideas and facts from more than one source, you gain a deeper understanding of the subject and sometimes discover new insights into your own experience.

Look back through the selections in this section, and make a list of ideas and facts that connect all of the selections and your personal experience. Focus on the things that connect us all as people. Then, use your list to write one paragraph describing an early Native American value that many people still hold today. Write a second paragraph describing something normally condemned, or disapproved of, by both early Native Americans and most people today. You may want to use an outline like this one to develop your paragraphs.

Paragraph 1

Thesis statement (What value do people today hold in common with early Native Americans?)

Support for thesis (quotations or summaries from selections, areas of interest in the news, personal anecdotes)

Restatement of main idea

Paragraph 2

Thesis statement (What disagreeable actions or behaviors were similarly condemned by early Native Americans?)

Support for thesis (quotations or summaries from selections, areas of interest in the news, personal anecdotes)

Restatement of main idea

Extension Online

RESEARCH Historically, many university and professional sports teams have employed Native American mascots. In recent years, this practice has come under attack. With a partner, go online to **research** images of three such mascots and print them to share with the class. Also find out what routines or traditions each mascot has performed. Then, as a class, discuss why people might find such mascots offensive. As you discuss, be sure to consider what you learned from your reading.

The Buffalo Chase with Bow (1832), George Catlin. The Granger Collection, New York.

COMMON CORE

W 9 Draw evidence from literary texts to support analysis, reflection, and research. **SL 1** Initiate and participate effectively in a range of collaborative discussions. **SL 1a** Come to discussions prepared, having read and researched material under study.

DIFFERENTIATED INSTRUCTION

FOR STRUGGLING WRITERS

Writing Support Help students get started by directing them to relevant passages in the selections. For example, students might draw on lines 117–142 and 192–201 of "The World on the Turtle's Back" to write about how Native Americans valued "a balanced and orderly world." Or they might draw on lines 58–67 and 72–83 of "Coyote and the Buffalo" and lines 105–116 of "The World on the Turtle's Back" to write about deceitfulness and right and wrong.

FOR ENGLISH LANGUAGE LEARNERS

Writing Topic Sentences To help students create topic sentences for their paragraphs, provide sentence starters such as these:

- Like many people today, Native Americans of the past valued _____.

- One thing that Native Americans of the past found objectionable that I also find offensive is _____.

Tell students to find details in the selections to support each of their topic sentences.

COMMON CORE FOCUS

W 9 Draw evidence from literary or informational texts to support analysis, reflection, and research. **SL 1** Initiate and participate effectively in a range of collaborative discussions. **SL 1a** Come to discussions prepared, having read and researched material under study.

Wrap-Up: The Native American Experience

In this Wrap-Up, students revisit ideas about Native Americans from the literature in this section. What stereotypes of Native Americans were presented? What authentic facts and images about native cultures emerged from the writings of Native Americans? Encourage students to examine their own insights gained from the selections.

Writing to Synthesize

- Review with students that *synthesizing* means combining ideas and facts with other information and prior knowledge in order to better understand a subject or develop new ideas. Those new ideas help break down old misunderstandings and stereotypes.

- Have students think about the selections and brainstorm things that the Native Americans valued (for example, the natural world and qualities like cleverness and courage), and things that they found objectionable (for example, greediness and vanity).

Extension Online

- For online research, have students use key words such as *Native American mascots,* or *sports mascots.*

- Direct students to organize their research and thoughts by creating a Three-Column Journal, using the headings *Mascot, Routines or Traditions,* and *Possible Objections.* To help students think about possible objections, suggest that they consider their research in light of the seriousness with which Native Americans regarded totems and ceremonies.

 **BEST PRACTICES TOOLKIT—Transparency** Three-Column Journal p. B10

Focus and Motivate

⊙ COMMON CORE FOCUS

RI 7 Integrate and evaluate multiple sources of information presented in different media or formats as well as in words in order to address a question or solve a problem. **SL 2** Integrate multiple sources of information presented in diverse formats and media in order to make informed decisions and solve problems, evaluating the credibility and accuracy of each source and noting any discrepancies among the data. **SL 3** Evaluate a speaker's point of view, assessing the tone used. **SL 5** Make strategic use of digital media in presentations to enhance understanding of findings, reasoning, and evidence and to add interest.

SUMMARIES

The three clips explore the portrayal of Native Americans in film and TV.

Stagecoach A stagecoach crosses a vast, dry valley and is attacked by Native Americans.

The Lone Ranger Tonto gets a smoke signal message from his Cheyenne friends asking to see him. He leaves after he assures the Lone Ranger that he'll check in with the Indian agent on the reservation.

Smoke Signals On a train, one modern Native American gives a friend tips on how to act like a "real Indian."

How do media shape PERCEPTIONS?

To emphasize the importance of the question, take a student poll of weekly TV hours watched. Use the poll results to demonstrate the potential power of the media to reinforce stereotypes or otherwise manipulate the perceptions of its viewers. Brainstorm ideas that are shaped by media even today, such as physical appearance or materialism.

BACKGROUND

For director Chris Eyre and writer Sherman Alexie, both Native Americans, the most important mission for *Smoke Signals* was to confront the oversimplified stereotypes of Native Americans that had been built by *The Lone Ranger* and other 20th-century westerns. Their film reveals the complexity of their culture and puts Native American film on the cinematic map.

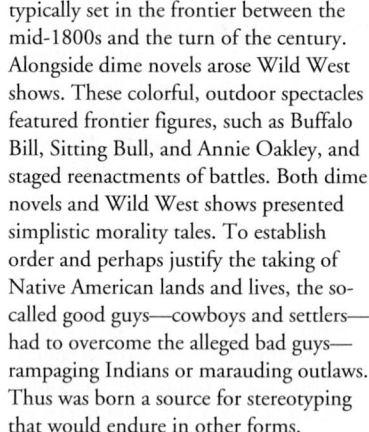

Media Study

Changing Views of Native Americans
Film Clips on Media ● Smart DVD-ROM

⊙ COMMON CORE

RI 7 Integrate and evaluate multiple sources of information presented in different media or formats as well as in words in order to address a question or solve a problem.

How do media shape PERCEPTIONS?

In this unit, Native American voices from the past and present reveal their way of life and worldview. In contrast, many 20th-century films about the Old West lacked this Native American perspective, often reinforcing inaccurate **stereotypes** and creating new ones. In this lesson, you will watch three film clips that present images of Native Americans from three different time periods.

Background

How the Western Won America's fascination with the Old West began with late 19th-century dime-novel westerns. These low-priced, fast-paced stories were typically set in the frontier between the mid-1800s and the turn of the century. Alongside dime novels arose Wild West shows. These colorful, outdoor spectacles featured frontier figures, such as Buffalo Bill, Sitting Bull, and Annie Oakley, and staged reenactments of battles. Both dime novels and Wild West shows presented simplistic morality tales. To establish order and perhaps justify the taking of Native American lands and lives, the so-called good guys—cowboys and settlers—had to overcome the alleged bad guys—rampaging Indians or marauding outlaws. Thus was born a source for stereotyping that would endure in other forms.

At the start of the 20th century, as the motion picture industry evolved, the western film genre burst onto the screen. While Hollywood filmmakers glorified the frontier by shooting in spectacular locations, they recycled the simple formulas of the earlier western forms and perpetuated some of the inaccurate images.

By the mid-1900s, as TV became commonplace, westerns dominated both big and small screens. At the peak of the western's golden age, over 20 westerns were televised each week, exposing viewers to themes and images that went unquestioned. It didn't seem to matter if an Indian's costume wasn't historically accurate or if his or her language wasn't realistic. Little was said about the effects of western expansion on Native American life and culture. The Hollywood images took hold in the minds of viewers. Aware of this, filmmakers of more recent times have made deliberate efforts to bring more authentic portrayals to the screen.

66

Media Study Resources

*See resources on the **Teacher One Stop DVD-ROM** and on **thinkcentral.com**.*

R **RESOURCE MANAGER UNIT 1**
　Plan and Teach, pp. 61–64
　Summary, pp. 65–66†‡
　Viewing Guide, p. 67
　Close Viewing, p. 68
　Media Activity, p. 69
　Produce Your Own Media, p. 70

TECHNOLOGY
　● **Teacher One Stop DVD-ROM**
　● **Student One Stop DVD-ROM**
　● **MediaSmart DVD-ROM**
　MediaScope on **thinkcentral.com**

* Resources for Differentiation　　　† Also in Spanish　　　‡ In Haitian Creole and Vietnamese

Media Literacy: Images in Mass Media

The **western** is a film and TV genre that portrays the early days of the American frontier. In many TV shows and movies, particularly classic westerns, the film and TV industry depended on **stereotypes,** oversimplified or inaccurate representations of people. Stereotypes can create misconceptions, especially when there are no alternative portrayals to displace them. Use your knowledge of characterization and film techniques to help you spot these stereotypes.

STRATEGIES FOR ANALYZING FILM AND TELEVISION STEREOTYPES

A Character's Appearance	Look for how actors are costumed and how make-up is applied. Keep in mind that most often, little historical research was done to present Native Americans accurately. Costumes and language were often a mix of different tribes.	
A Character's Dialogue	Focus on how characters speak. Which characters speak dialogue in complete sentences? Which speak in simple words or phrases? Stereotypical characters are usually depicted as being somehow outside of the mainstream culture and as holding a different set of values.	
A Character's Actions	Ask yourself: Do characters behave according to a stereotype? Are the actions more negative than positive? Notice how **lighting** and **music** reinforce these impressions. How does the director film the actions? Be aware of camera placement. • **Low-angle shots** position the camera to look up at an object or a person. Such shots convey an imposing or powerful presence. • **High-angle shots** position the camera to look down, often conveying helplessness.	
Other Characters' Responses to the Character	Notice how other characters react to the individual. Do close-up shots reveal expressions of tolerance, condescension, or superiority? In what ways do the dialogue and the acting convey how the character is regarded?	

MEDIA STUDY: TEACHING OPTIONS

Teaching Option 1: The Basics (1–2 Days)
1. Begin the Media Study using the material provided on pages 66–67.
2. Show the Introduction on Media*Smart*. Then show the First Viewing. As students watch, have them use the Viewing Guide on page 68, along with the corresponding copy master on page 67 of the Resource Manager. Discuss their responses.
3. Return to the student edition for the extension activities on page 69.

Teaching Option 2: In-Depth Study (2–3 Days)
1. Begin the Media Study using pages 66–67.
2. Show the Introduction and First Viewing from Media*Smart*. Then continue on Media*Smart* with the Media Lessons, using the teacher notes available in the Resources section.
3. Show the Guided Analysis presentation. Have students record their observations on the Student Viewing Guide available in the Resources section of Media*Smart*.
4. Return to the student edition, page 69.

Media Literacy

COMMON CORE RI 7, SL 2, SL 3, SL 5

Ask volunteers to describe the plot of a familiar film western or to invent a likely plot from their knowledge of the genre. Have them identify stereotypical characters (good guy, bad guy, beautiful woman), settings (wild west, prairie, western cow town), and typical plots. In particular, challenge students to identify ways in which Native Americans are stereotypically misrepresented in westerns. Then discuss the chart on page 67.

- **A Character's Appearance** To clarify how costuming and makeup can influence viewers' perceptions, describe two characters: one has ragged pants, a dirty headscarf, and a scarred cheek; the other has a clean white hat, a neat mustache, and shiny boots. Ask students what the appearances convey.

- **A Character's Dialogue** Read this aloud:

  Guide: See far mountain. Smoke in sky. Me help Cherokee brothers.

  Cowboy: Ride safely, my friend. Help your friends with great courage.

  Discuss how the contrast in syntax creates a stereotypical portrayal of the "white man's helper" and the cowboy. How does the limited English of the guide influence viewers' perceptions?

- **A Character's Actions** To enforce the importance of action and camera angle, have students imagine directing a scene in which Native Americans react to a threat. Ask how they would show the Native Americans as either powerful and brave or nervous and helpless. Contrast the results.

- **Other Characters' Responses to the Character** Note that a film may show positive, trustful reactions to Native American characters or hostile, suspicious reactions. Discuss how such reactions reinforce stereotypes.

  MediaSmart DVD

VIEWING GUIDE

1. To prepare students for viewing, explain that the three clips portray Native Americans differently. Encourage students to pay attention to these elements:

   - the **appearance** of the Native American characters, such as their facial expressions, costuming, and grooming

   - **dialogue** that conveys the intelligence or loyalty of Native Americans

   - **actions** and camera **shots** that suggest power or helplessness in Native American and other characters

   - **characters' reactions** that convey a positive or negative perception of Native Americans

2. Students may find stereotypical characterizations of Native Americans offensive. Ask them to identify what stereotypes are portrayed in the clips. Explain that the frightening Indian attack portrayed in *Stagecoach* was a characteristic scene in many classic westerns. *The Lone Ranger,* while portraying Native Americans as helpers, nonetheless cast them in limited roles.

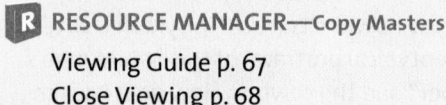 **RESOURCE MANAGER**—Copy Masters

   Viewing Guide p. 67
   Close Viewing p. 68
   Media Activity p. 69

Use this resource with the Viewing Guide:

 MediaSmart DVD-ROM

MediaScope on **thinkcentral.com**

ANSWERS

FIRST VIEWING: Comprehension

1. *The travelers begin firing their guns.*

2. *According to Victor, Native Americans should live up to the ignorant preconceived notions of outsiders by looking stoic and threatening.*

CLOSE VIEWING: Media Literacy

Possible answers:

3. *The striking musical rhythms and the low-angle camera shots underscore the stereotypically threatening presence of the Native Americans. High-angle shots make the white travelers appear vulnerable and unassuming.*

Media Smart DVD-ROM
- **Film 1:** *Stagecoach*
- **Director:** John Ford
- **Genre:** Movie Western
- **Running Time:** 2 minutes

- **Film 2:** *The Lone Ranger*
- **Genre:** TV Western
- **Running Time:** 2 minutes

- **Film 3:** *Smoke Signals*
- **Director:** Chris Eyre
- **Rating:** PG-13
- **Genre:** Drama
- **Running Time:** 2.5 minutes

Viewing Guide for

Changing Views of Native Americans

Watch the first two clips to explore how Native Americans were portrayed during the glory days of the western. The scene from *Stagecoach* (1939) brings two groups into direct contact. In the clip from *The Lone Ranger* TV series (1949–1957), the two main characters prepare to take action. Watch the third clip to see a more recent Native American portrayal—one that challenges the old Hollywood images. In *Smoke Signals* (1998), friends Victor and Thomas engage in lively conversation during a road trip.

To critically analyze the clips, view them more than once. Examine the portrayals, and answer these questions.

NOW VIEW

FIRST VIEWING: Comprehension

1. **Recall** In *Stagecoach*, what do the travelers do as soon as they spot the Native Americans?

2. **Summarize** Think about Victor in *Smoke Signals*. Summarize his view of the acceptable look and behavior for "Indian" males.

CLOSE VIEWING: Media Literacy

3. **Identify Film Techniques** Consider how the use of music and the **high-** and **low-angle** shots contribute to characterization in the beginning of the *Stagecoach* clip. How might the effect reinforce **stereotypes?**

4. **Analyze Stereotypes** In *The Lone Ranger* clip, the character Tonto might be considered an improvement over past portrayals of Native Americans. However, what might still be **stereotypical** about this character?

5. **Analyze Characters** Recall how Victor in *Smoke Signals* describes "real Indian" behavior. Might their portrayal be perceived as a step forward? Why or why not?

6. **Evaluate Characterization** *Smoke Signals* director Chris Eyre has said, "I'm interested in telling stories about Indians who are normal, everyday people." How effectively do the character portrayals in the scene from his film counter the stereotypes in *Stagecoach* and *The Lone Ranger*? Base your opinion on the modern-day setting in *Smoke Signals* and on the characterizations of Thomas and Victor.

---

4. *Tonto's style of speech is depicted as simplistic, and he displays a stoic demeanor. Viewed superficially, Tonto's actions place him in a subservient position to his counterpart, the Lone Ranger.*

5. *It is a step forward because Victor's description and the conversation of the characters involve humor as well as a consciousness of how mainstream society thinks a "real Indian" ought to behave.*

6. *The characters effectively counter stereotypes, since the young men appear in modern clothing and a modern setting. Also, Victor and Thomas act like typical teenagers, not stereotypical Native Americans.*

Produce Your Own Media

Compare Portrayals What impressions of Native Americans do you get from each clip? At the time each portrayal was first presented, how might it have affected perceptions of Native Americans? As you think about these clips, consider the following:

- the portrayals of individuals or groups
- the techniques of camera position, lighting, and music
- the fact that *Smoke Signals* was written and directed by Native Americans

Now that you have critiqued these clips, try creating a media award for a film or TV show. As a class, brainstorm about any films or TV shows that you think rise above the simplistic techniques of stereotyping. What character portrayals or story lines strike you as complex and true to life? How sensitively are different social groups portrayed? Create a name for the award, and devise criteria for judging the pieces.

Once your class has decided on the best nominees and chosen the winner, think about ways you can use multimedia to present the media award. You may want to use presentational software to display the title and attributes of each nominee. You also could use recorded music that is appropriate to each nominee, or a voice-over recording that details how one work succeeded where others failed.

Further Exploration

Hold a Native American Film Festival According to Native American filmmaker Bird Runningwater, "Filmmaking provides a new way to merge a strong oral tradition of storytelling with technology and, in the process, revitalize ourselves." Research Native American films and reviews. If possible, rent movies to view as a group, and then critique them in a panel discussion.

Conduct a Native American Film Study Savage warrior. Noble savage. Sage protector of the earth. One hundred years of moviemaking hasn't begun to cover the complexity and diversity of Native American cultural groups. Research westerns ranging from the 1950s to the present. What historical inaccuracies are evident? In contemporary works, have attempts to present more positive depictions fully succeeded?

COMMON CORE

RI 7 Integrate and evaluate multiple sources of information presented in different media or formats as well as in words in order to address a question or solve a problem. **SL 2** Integrate multiple sources of information presented in diverse formats and media in order to make informed decisions and solve problems, evaluating the credibility and accuracy of each source and noting any discrepancies among the data. **SL 3** Evaluate a speaker's point of view, assessing the tone used. **SL 5** Make strategic use of digital media in presentations to enhance understanding of findings, reasoning, and evidence and to add interest.

Media Tools THINK central

Go to thinkcentral.com.
KEYWORD: HML11-69

Assess and Reteach

Write or Discuss

COMMON CORE RI 7, SL 2, SL 3, SL 5

Compare Portrayals In their comparisons, students should include examples of characters' appearance, dialogue, and actions to support their points. For example, Tonto speaks in broken English while Victor and Thomas speak fluently. To support their analysis, have students imagine watching the clips in 1939, in the 1950s, and in 1998 as they consider the portrayal of Native Americans.

MEDIA STUDY WRAP–UP

Have students summarize what they have learned about how media can create or reinforce stereotypes. Urge students to use examples of how dialogue, appearances, actions, and reactions contribute to this process.

Further Exploration

Hold a Native American Film Festival Have students work in small groups to identify Native American films. Compile a master list and then assign a film to each group. Have the group view its assigned film, select a two-minute clip to share with the class, and prepare a discussion and critique.

Conduct a Native American Film Study To answer the questions, have students research and analyze at least one film. Have them write a short essay, using examples from the film or films to support their analysis.

Produce Your Own Media

Suggest that the class break into smaller groups to plan the multimedia presentation. Each group should work on a different aspect of the presentation, such as the soundtrack, the voice-overs, and the visuals. If students need help with the media technology, suggest that they consult the school's computer lab advisor.

Media Tools THINK central

Media study keywords point to **MediaScope**, a Web site that helps students strengthen media analysis and production skills.

Historical Narratives

If you wanted to know what life was like for someone 400 years ago, where could you get the information? History books could give you a general account, but what if you wanted to know the details of someone's daily life or what it was like to actually be at an important historical event? In American literature, there are many personal accounts that have been published and passed down through the centuries that give unique perspectives on the events of the past.

Recording the American Experience

Europeans began voyages by ship to the Americas in the late 15th century and reported news of their explorations and settlement. These historical narratives of the survivors told gripping adventure stories, written down in journals and letters, of the the first Europeans' experiences of coming to America. **Historical narratives** are accounts of real-life historical experiences, written by either a person who experienced those events or someone who studied or observed them. In many cases, the narratives became important historical documents that now exist as our principal record of events. Historical narratives can be divided into two categories:

Indian Summer, Regis François Gignoux. © Christie's Images/Corbis.

- **Primary sources** are materials written by people who were either participants in or observers of the events written about. Letters, diaries, journals, speeches, autobiographies, and interviews are all primary sources.

- **Secondary sources** are records of events written by people who were not directly involved in the events. Two typical examples of secondary sources are biographies and histories.

Bringing the Past to Life

Primary sources offer valuable insights into the thinking and culture of a given time period. Use these strategies to bring the information to life:

- Determine a document's origin.

- Try to understand the **perspective** and **motives** of the writer.

- Note **sensory details** that depict people, places, and events.

- Identify customs, values, or conditions of the **culture** or **time period.**

COMMON CORE FOCUS

RI 9 Analyze seventeenth- and eighteenth-century foundational U.S. documents of historical and literary significance for their themes, purposes, and rhetorical features. **RI 10** Read and comprehend literary nonfiction.

Recording the American Experience

Primary and Secondary Sources Discuss the key distinctions between the two kinds of sources. Then have students use a Two-Column Chart to classify these examples as primary or secondary sources, and ask volunteers to explain their answers:

- the handwritten will of a European settler in Virginia, dated 1610 *(primary)*

- an encyclopedia article entitled "Puritans" *(secondary)*

- the *Mayflower Compact,* an agreement written and signed by passengers on the Mayflower in 1620 *(primary)*

- a book entitled *Massachusetts Before the Pilgrims,* written in 1975 *(secondary)*

- a record of births and deaths kept by the residents of a village in colonial Virginia *(primary)*

 BEST PRACTICES TOOLKIT—Transparency
Two-Column Chart p. A25

Bringing the Past to Life

Reading Primary Sources Offer these additional strategies for reading historical narratives:

- Reread and paraphrase unfamiliar ideas.

- Restate the main idea in your own words.

- Visualize what the author describes.

- Predict what will happen next.

- Connect the narrative to what you know.

- Ask questions about the narrative.

- Make a timeline of the events described.

Review the excerpts on page 71, clarifying text as needed. Ask students to describe sensory images evoked by the passages. Then help them identify the main idea of each passage.

DIFFERENTIATED INSTRUCTION

FOR STRUGGLING READERS

Note Taking Explain to students that they will be learning many terms relating to historical narratives in this workshop. Discuss the boldfaced terms on this spread as students record notes.

FOR ENGLISH LANGUAGE LEARNERS

Language: Skill Words Students who speak Romance languages should know cognates for *primary, secondary, source,* and *narrative.* Ask students to say and explain cognates from their home languages. Then have volunteers say and explain the English words, repeating the pronunciations as needed. Review the definitions on page 70.

Álvar Núñez Cabeza de Vaca was one of many explorers who sailed to the New World after Christopher Columbus. The historical narrative *La Relación* (page 70) was Cabeza de Vaca's report to the king of Spain. Note the personal **perspective** he provides in this excerpt about one night in his crossing of the Atlantic Ocean.

> When night fell, only the navigator and I remained able to tend the barge. Two hours after dark he told me I must take over; he believed he was going to die that night.
>
> **—Álvar Núñez Cabeza de Vaca, *La Relación***

In 1620, the Puritans survived a journey across the Atlantic in the *Mayflower* and landed at Cape Cod. In 1630, William Bradford, Plymouth Colony's second governor, began writing *Of Plymouth Plantation* (page 104), a chronicle of his colony's experiences. Notice the use of **sensory details** in Bradford's description of the colony's first winter.

> The weather was very cold and it froze so hard as the spray of the sea lighting on their coats, they were as if they had been glazed.
>
> **—William Bradford, *Of Plymouth Plantation***

As the American colonies expanded from the 16th through the 18th centuries, the slave trade expanded as well. Olaudah Equiano was one of the millions of Africans captured and transported to the Americas. He survived this ordeal and published his autobiography in 1789. These lines from his autobiography describe the conditions below the decks of a slave ship and his first reaction to what he saw.

> When I looked round the ship too, and saw a large furnace of copper boiling, and a multitude of black people of every description chained together, every one of their countenances expressing dejection and sorrow, I no longer doubted of my fate.
>
> **—Olaudah Equiano, *The Interesting Narrative of the Life of Olaudah Equiano***

THE SLAVE NARRATIVE

The **slave narrative** is an American literary genre that portrays the daily life of slaves as written by the slaves themselves after gaining their freedom. Some 6,000 slave narratives are known to exist. The Reverend Ephraim Peabody wrote in 1849 about three recently published slave narratives:

> *We place these volumes without hesitation among the most remarkable productions of the age—remarkable as being pictures of slavery by the slave, remarkable as disclosing under a new light the mixed elements of American civilization, and not less remarkable as a vivid exhibition of the force and working of the native love of freedom in the individual mind.*
>
> **–The Reverend Ephraim Peabody**

Probably the most influential example of the genre is the autobiography of Frederick Douglass, *Narrative of the Life of Frederick Douglass, an American Slave,* published in 1845.

Close Read

Describe what you think were the writer's motives for recording the events in the first two **primary source** examples on this page.

Close Read

Point out details that are particularly vivid. Describe how you would visualize the scene.

THE SLAVE NARRATIVE

Explain that between 1760 and 1865, about 100 slave narratives were published in the United States, including that of Olaudah Equiano. Slave narratives played a crucial role in winning people over to the cause of abolitionism by informing them about the horrors of slave trade. Other slave narratives include:

- *My Bondage and My Freedom* (1855): Frederick Douglass's expanded autobiography
- *Narrative of William W. Brown, A Fugitive Slave* (1847): written by William Wells Brown, the first African American to publish a novel
- *The Narrative of Sojourner Truth* (1850): dictated by abolitionist and women's rights leader Sojourner Truth

During the 1930s, the Federal Writers' Project gathered several volumes' worth of oral histories from 2,500 former slaves. Invite students to share their feelings as to why these narratives are still important.

Close Read

Possible answer: Both writers described harrowing experiences. They probably wanted to describe to their readers what difficult hardships they had to endure.

IF STUDENTS NEED HELP . . . Ask these questions to help students infer the writers' motives:

- How would you feel if you had lived through the experience the writer is describing?
- Why would you want others to know about it?

Close Read

Possible answer: Vivid details include "large furnace of copper boiling," "multitude of black people of every description chained together," "every one of their countenances expressing dejection and sorrow." Students may visualize the scene as cramped, dark, hot, and frightening.

FOR ADVANCED LEARNERS/AP

Compare and Contrast Style [paired option]
Review that style is not what is said so much as how it is said. Components include word choice, figurative language, and sentence structure or length. Have students work in pairs to read the three narrative excerpts on page 71, and then compare and contrast the three writers' styles. Then have students write a brief passage in the style of one of these writers.

Focus and Motivate

COMMON CORE FOCUS

RI 1 Cite textual evidence to support analysis of what the text says explicitly as well as inferences drawn from the text, including determining where the text leaves matters uncertain. **RI 6** Determine an author's point of view or purpose in a text. **RI 9** Analyze foundational U.S. documents of historical and literary significance for their themes, purposes, and rhetorical features. **W 3** Write narratives to develop real or imagined experiences or events using effective technique, well-chosen details, and well-structured event sequences. **W 3a, d** Engage and orient the reader by setting out a situation and its significance, establishing one point of view, and introducing a narrator and/or characters; use precise words and phrases, telling details, and sensory language to convey a vivid picture. **L 3** Apply knowledge of language to make effective choices for meaning or style. **L 3a** Vary syntax for effect. **L 4c** Consult general and specialized reference materials, both print and digital, to determine or clarify a word's etymology. **L 6** Acquire and use accurately general and domain-specific words.

ABOUT THE AUTHOR

After students have read about Cabeza de Vaca, ask a volunteer to use a map to locate the places mentioned in the text: Tampa Bay, Mexico, the Gulf Coast, and Galveston Island. Then point out that the excerpt students are about to read recounts events described in **Disaster Strikes.**

NOTABLE QUOTE

"Better than to exaggerate, I have lessened in all things." **—Álvar Núñez Cabeza de Vaca**

Selection Resources

COMMON CORE

RI 1 Cite textual evidence to support analysis of what the text says explicitly as well as inferences drawn from the text, including determining where the text leaves matters uncertain. **RI 6** Determine an author's point of view or purpose in a text. **RI 9** Analyze foundational U.S. documents of historical and literary significance for their themes, purposes, and rhetorical features.

DID YOU KNOW?

Cabeza de Vaca . . .

- recorded the only accounts of some now-extinct Native American groups?
- was the first European to cross North and South America?
- was accompanied by an enslaved African named Esteban?

Exploration and the Early Settlers

from La Relación
Report by Álvar Núñez Cabeza de Vaca

Essential Course of Study

Meet the Author

Álvar Núñez Cabeza de Vaca c. 1490–1557

In 1536, Spanish slave hunters raiding in northern Mexico were startled by a strange sight: a Spaniard "strangely dressed and in company with Indians." Long given up for dead, Álvar Núñez Cabeza de Vaca had survived one of the most disastrous expeditions in the history of the Spanish conquest to become the first European to cross North America.

Conquering Hero Cabeza de Vaca came from a family of Spanish *conquistadors*, or conquerors. He had been a soldier for nearly 20 years when, in 1527, he joined an expedition to Spanish North America. Appointed by the king of Spain, he became treasurer and second in command, assigned the task of colonizing the territory north and east of the Gulf of Mexico.

Disaster Strikes Led by Pánfilo de Narváez, the expedition sailed with five ships and 600 men. Two ships were lost in a hurricane; 200 men drowned or deserted. After landing in Tampa Bay, Narváez sent his ships north and ordered 300 men to march to New Spain (present-day Mexico), which he guessed to be a few weeks away. Months later, the ships were gone and the desperate landing party was eating its horses to survive. Using horsehide and nails made from melted armor, they built five barges and sailed along the Gulf Coast from Florida to Texas, hoping to reach Spanish settlements in northern Mexico. Two barges and 80 men washed up on or near Galveston Island. Ultimately, only Cabeza de Vaca and three other men survived.

Cabeza de Vaca survived by adapting to his new surroundings. For six years, he lived with dozens of Native American groups in various roles—as a captive, a trader, and a well-known healer. In 1534, the four survivors escaped, setting out across the desert in search of New Spain. In 1536, they finally reached their goal. A year later, Cabeza de Vaca returned to Spain, where he wrote his account of the expedition, *La Relación* (The Account), as a report to the king.

Conqueror No More The king rewarded Cabeza de Vaca by appointing him governor of a South American colony, where his humane treatment of Native Americans may have cost him his job. By 1545, he had been ousted from his position and convicted on a corruption charge in Spain. Exiled to Africa, Cabeza de Vaca was eventually pardoned. In 1552, he returned to Spain to end his days as a judge.

Author Online
Go to **thinkcentral.com**. KEYWORD: HML11-72

72

See resources on the **Teacher One Stop DVD-ROM** and on **thinkcentral.com**.

R RESOURCE MANAGER UNIT 1

Plan and Teach, pp. 73–80
Summary, pp. 81†, 82‡
Text Analysis and Reading Skill, pp. 83–84, 85–86†
Vocabulary, pp. 87–89
Grammar and Style, p. 92

DIAGNOSTIC AND SELECTION TESTS
Selection Tests, pp. 37–40

BEST PRACTICES TOOLKIT

Jigsaw Reading, p. A1
Cluster Diagram, p. B18
Sensory Notes, p. B9

INTERACTIVE READER

ADAPTED INTERACTIVE READER

ELL ADAPTED INTERACTIVE READER

TECHNOLOGY
- **Teacher One Stop DVD-ROM**
- **Student One Stop DVD-ROM**
- **PowerNotes DVD-ROM**
- **Audio Anthology CD**
- **GrammarNotes DVD-ROM**
- **ExamView Test Generator** on the Teacher One Stop

THINK central

Find it Online!

Features on **thinkcentral.com** that support the selection include
- **PowerNotes** presentation
- **ThinkAloud** models to enhance comprehension
- **WordSharp** vocabulary tutorials
- interactive writing and grammar instruction

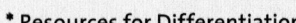

* Resources for Differentiation　　† Also in Spanish　　‡ Also in Haitian Creole and Vietnamese

● **TEXT ANALYSIS: HISTORICAL CONTEXT**

When you read historical works, you may notice statements that seem strange or even offensive. These remarks might be a reflection of the work's **historical context**—the ideas and details from the author's time that influence the written work.

It was amazing to see these wild, untaught savages howling like brutes in compassion for us.

The author's statement reflects views about Indians that most people of his time shared. While his **purpose** was to communicate the experience of a life-threatening adventure, his account was shaped by the culture that shaped him. To familiarize yourself with the historical context of *La Relación*, read the author biography on page 72 and the background information on page 74. Then, as you read the work, note details that reflect this context.

■ **READING STRATEGY: READING A PRIMARY SOURCE**

Unlike a history book, *La Relación* is an eyewitness report. Such **primary sources** give us special insight into history. When using these sources, consider the intended audience, the author's role in events, and where and when the document was written.

As you read, complete a chart like the one shown. Consult the author biography and background information as needed.

Questions	Answers
What do I know about the author and his times?	
What details tell me about life in 16th-century North America?	
What is the relationship between the author and his audience?	
What is the author's role in the events he describes?	

▲ **VOCABULARY IN CONTEXT**

The following words help bring this explorer's account to life. Choose a synonym for each word from the numbered terms.

WORD LIST	cauterize	ingratiate	locomotion
	embody	inundate	tarry

1. movement   3. burn   5. flood
2. personify   4. seek favor   6. delay

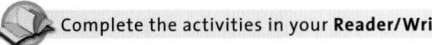 Complete the activities in your **Reader/Writer Notebook**.

What's the STORY *behind the* GLORY?

Dreams of wealth, glory, and conquest lured adventurers to the Americas, but few were prepared for the harsh reality that awaited them. For every hero who claimed a fortune, there were hundreds of others who died trying. Often, the greatest prize of all was living to tell the tale. What enabled some to survive while others failed?

DISCUSS In a small group, share stories you've read or heard that describe a person's struggle to survive in desperate circumstances, such as a shipwreck, war, or a natural disaster. Then make a list of traits that those people or characters exhibit. Decide what qualities seem essential in a survivor.

73

Teach

What's the STORY *behind the* GLORY?

After the class speculates about why some people survive an ordeal while others perish, tell students to complete the *DISCUSS* activity.

SUMMARY

This excerpt from the report *La Relación* opens with Cabeza de Vaca and his dying men adrift on a barge. They wash ashore on Galveston Island, where the Karankawa Indians welcome and feed them. When the conquistadors embark again, their barge capsizes, and the starving survivors return to shore. The Karankawas care for them again, but when disease spreads throughout the island, the Native Americans make the Spaniards serve as medicine men.

READ WITH A PURPOSE

Help students set a purpose for reading. Tell them to discover how the writer's beliefs about Native Americans change as a result of his harrowing experiences.

READING STRATEGY

COMMON CORE
RI 1
RI 9

A *Model the Skill:* **PRIMARY SOURCE**

Demonstrate the process of identifying tone by helping students find words that suggest the writer's attitude toward his subject or his audience.

Possible answer: *The author relates frightening details in a calm, objective tone. Cabeza de Vaca may have chosen this tone to present himself as a calm, clear-thinking leader to his audience: the king.*

IF STUDENTS NEED HELP . . . Work with them to answer the third question in the prereading chart introduced on page 73. Then have students use the answer to infer that Cabeza de Vaca's choice of tone reflects his desire to present himself to the king as a calm, clear-thinking leader.

Questions	Answers
What is the relationship between the author and his audience?	The author's audience is the king of Spain—the person who controls his career and future.

La Relación

Álvar Núñez Cabeza de Vaca

> **BACKGROUND** In the 1500s, Spanish conquistadors took to the seas to claim new land for Spain. Seeking gold and silver, they explored unfamiliar territory and encountered Native American cultures they did not understand. By the time Cabeza de Vaca sailed, Spaniards had conquered the Aztecs of Mexico and the Inca of Peru, two of the most advanced civilizations in the Americas. Millions of Native Americans would die in this often brutal cultural encounter. In *La Relación*, Cabeza de Vaca finds himself unexpectedly at the mercy of the people he came to conquer.

At this point in the account, Narváez's barge has abandoned the rest, and Cabeza de Vaca's barge has joined one commanded by two other officers. The next three chapters describe the shipwreck of Cabeza de Vaca's barge on Galveston Island and the crew's encounter with the Karankawa Indians who lived there.

Analyze Visuals ▶
What **details** in the image convey the desperate situation of the shipwrecked men?

A Sinking and a Landing

Our two barges continued in company for four days, each man eating a ration of half a handful of raw corn a day. Then the other barge was lost in a storm. Nothing but God's great mercy kept us from going down, too.

It was winter and bitterly cold, and we had suffered hunger and the heavy beating of the waves for many days. Next day, the men began to collapse. By sunset, all in my barge had fallen over on one another, close to death. Few were any longer conscious. Not five could stand. When night fell, only the navigator and I remained able to tend the barge. Two hours after dark he told me I must take over; he believed he was going to die that night. **A**

10 So I took the tiller. After midnight I moved over to see if he were dead. He said no, in fact was better, and would steer till daylight. In that hour I would have welcomed death rather than see so many around me in such a condition. When I had returned the helm to the navigator, I lay down to rest—but without much rest, for nothing was farther from my mind than sleep.

Near dawn I seemed to hear breakers resounding; the coast lying low, they roared louder. Surprised at this, I called to the navigator, who said he thought we

1 Targeted Passage

A PRIMARY SOURCE
Describe the **tone** of lines 4–9. In what ways might the author's choice of tone be influenced by his intended **audience?**

Illustration by Tom McNeely.

DIFFERENTIATED INSTRUCTION

FOR ENGLISH LANGUAGE LEARNERS

Options for Reading Read the selection summary aloud to give students an overview of the selection. Then, have students silently read along as they listen to the *Audio Anthology CD*. Divide students into Jigsaw groups and assign one Targeted Passage to each. Have students present their passages.

BEST PRACTICES TOOLKIT
Jigsaw Reading p. A1

FOR STRUGGLING READERS

In combination with the *Audio Anthology CD*, use one or more Targeted Passages (pp. 74, 77, 78) to ensure that students focus on key events and concepts. Targeted Passages are also good for English learners.

1 Targeted Passage [Lines 1–14]

This passage introduces students to the conflict Cabeza de Vaca and his men face in this excerpt.

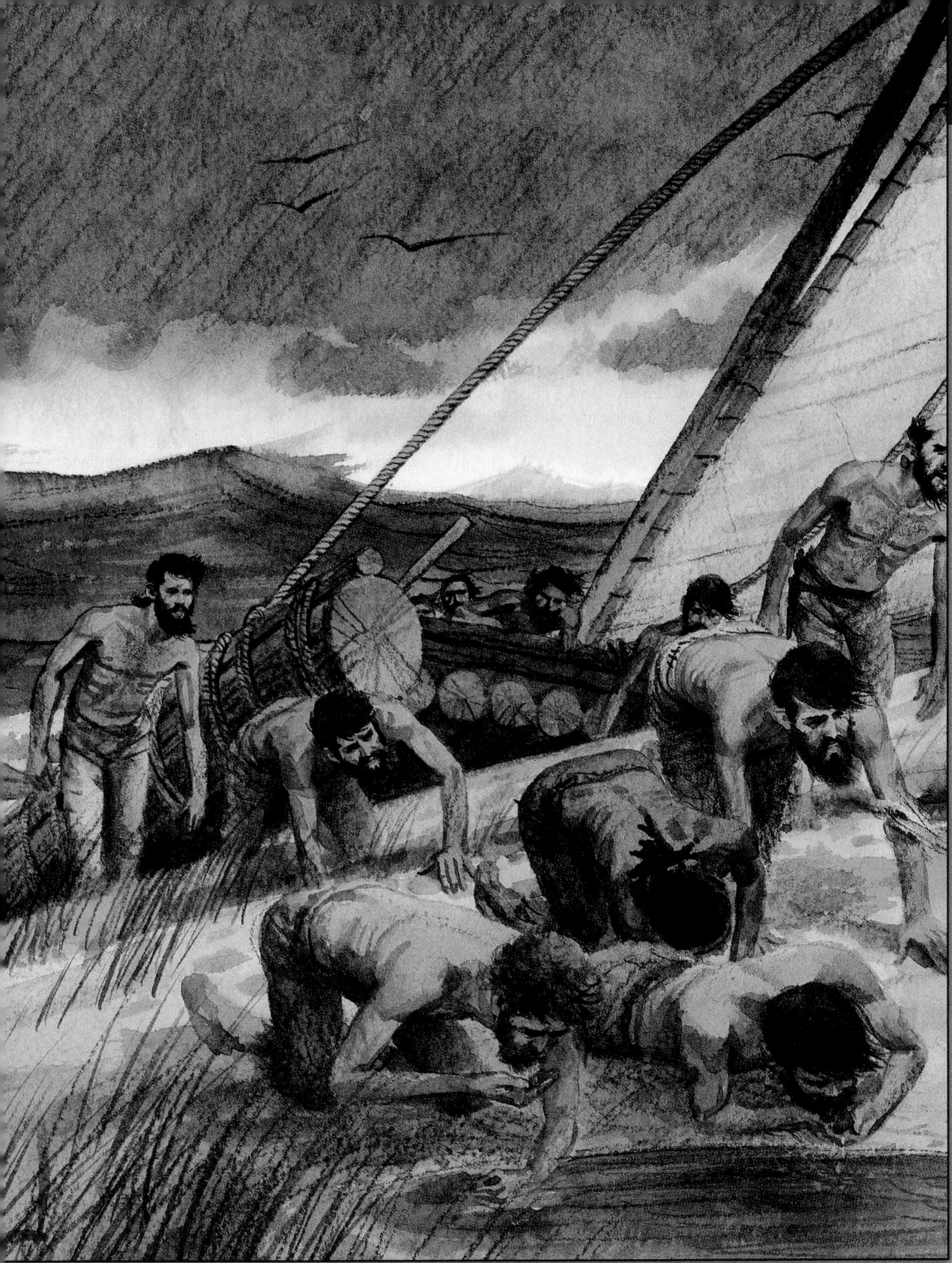

- When the excerpt begins, where are Cabeza de Vaca and his men? (lines 1–2)
- What has happened to the other barge? (line 2)
- What problems are the men facing? (lines 4–7)
- Why does Cabeza de Vaca take the tiller? (lines 8–9)
- Why does he say that he "would have welcomed death"? (lines 11–12)

FOR ADVANCED LEARNERS/AP

Research Ask students to work alone or in pairs to research the celestial navigation system that Cabeza de Vaca and his crew used to travel the seas. How did sailors in the past read the stars? What instruments did they use? Do modern navigators still use the system? Why or why not? Have students present their findings to the class or write a short essay summarizing their research.

Reading Support THINK central

This selection on **thinkcentral.com** includes embedded **ThinkAloud** models–students "thinking aloud" about the story to model the kinds of questions a good reader would ask about a selection.

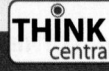

Analyze Visuals

Possible answer: *Details such as the anguished expressions on the men's faces and their need to crawl just to get water convey the men's desperate situation.*

BACKGROUND

Karankawas The now-extinct Karankawa Indians, who lived along the Gulf Coast of Texas, were a nomadic group whose movements were dictated by food supply and climate. The Karankawas lived in portable teepees, called *ba-ak,* and traveled in groups of 30 to 40 people. As new settlers began encroaching on the Karankawas' territory in Texas, confrontations became frequent. During the 1820s, Stephen F. Austin led a group of settlers to destroy the Karankawas, whose population continued to diminish due to this aggression. By 1858, about three hundred years after Cabeza de Vaca's encounter with the Karankawas, they had died out as a result of disease and American colonization.

CULTURAL CONNECTION

Conquering Cultures Spain was not the only country to attempt to conquer other cultures in the pursuit of land. Throughout history, powerful countries or cultures have tried to dominate less powerful ones for their own gain. One example of this type of conquest is the Roman Empire's use of military force to conquer England, Spain, France, Greece, the Middle East, and the North African coastal region. Invite students to share other examples of conquering cultures.

Discuss What do lines 20–24 suggest that people need to survive in desperate circumstances? **Possible answer:** *People need hope. As soon as the almost-dead men see land, they revive a bit and become more hopeful (lines 21–24). They act as if they will survive.*

TEXT ANALYSIS
COMMON CORE
RI 1
RI 6

B HISTORICAL CONTEXT

Possible answer: *Christianity was the central feature of the Spaniards' cultural identity; the Spaniards assumed that all Europeans were Christians, and that all people should be.*

VOCABULARY
COMMON CORE
L 4

OWN THE WORD

- **locomotion:** Explain that the root word *loc* is Latin for "place," and that *motion* comes from a Latin word meaning "movement."

- **ingratiate:** The word *ingratiate* suggests that the person seeking favor lacks influence. Ask students to think of reasons why they might want to ingratiate themselves to another person. **Possible answers:** *They may* ingratiate *themselves with a person who might mentor them to gain knowledge.*

---

were coming close to land. We sounded and found ourselves in seven fathoms.[1] The navigator felt we should stay clear of the shore till daylight; so I took an oar and pulled it on the shore side, wheeling the stern to seaward about a league[2] out.

20   As we drifted into shore, a wave caught us and heaved the barge a horseshoe-throw [about 42 feet] out of the water. The jolt when it hit brought the dead-looking men to. Seeing land at hand, they crawled through the surf to some rocks. Here we made a fire and parched some of our corn. We also found rain water. The men began to regain their senses, their **locomotion,** and their hope.

This day of our landing was November 6.

What Befell Oviedo with the Indians
After we ate, I ordered Lope de Oviedo, our strongest man, to climb one of the trees not far off and ascertain the lay of the land. He complied and found out from the treetop that we were on an island. [This was Galveston Island.] He also said that the ground looked as if cattle had trampled it and therefore that this
30 must be a country of Christians. **B**

I sent him back for a closer look, to see if he could find any worn trails, but warned him not to risk going too far. He went and came upon a path which he followed for half a league to some empty huts. The Indians were gone to shoal-flats[3] [to dig roots]. He took an earthen pot, a little dog, and a few mullets[4] and started back.

We had begun to worry what might have happened to him, so I detailed another two men to check. They met him shortly and saw three Indians with bows and arrows following him. The Indians were calling to him and he was gesturing them to keep coming. When he reached us, the Indians held back
40 and sat down on the shore.

Half an hour later a hundred bowmen reinforced the first three individuals. Whatever their stature, they looked like giants to us in our fright. We could not hope to defend ourselves; not half a dozen of us could even stand up.

The Inspector [Solís] and I walked out and greeted them. They advanced, and we did our best to placate and **ingratiate.** We gave them beads and bells, and each one of them gave us an arrow in pledge of friendship. They told us by signs that they would return at sunrise and bring food, having none then.

The Indians' Hospitality Before and After a New Calamity
As the sun rose next morning, the Indians appeared as they promised, bringing an abundance of fish and of certain roots which taste like nuts, some bigger than
50 walnuts, some smaller, mostly grubbed from the water with great labor.

That evening they came again with more fish and roots and brought their women and children to look at us. They thought themselves rich with the little bells and beads we gave them, and they repeated their visits on other days.

---

1. **We sounded . . . fathoms:** We measured the depth of the water and found it to be about 42 feet. (A fathom is equal to 6 feet, or 1.83 meters.)
2. **league:** a unit of distance; Cabeza de Vaca probably used the Spanish league, equal to 3.1 miles (5 kilometers).
3. **shoal-flats:** stretches of level ground under shallow water.
4. **mullets:** certain edible fish.

locomotion
(lō′kə-mō′shən) *n.* the power to move from place to place

B HISTORICAL CONTEXT
In the 1500s, "Christians" was used as a synonym for Europeans. What does this suggest about how the Spaniards saw the world? How does such a belief shape the author's purpose?

ingratiate (ĭn-grā′shē-āt′) *v.* to gain another's favor by deliberate effort

---

DIFFERENTIATED INSTRUCTION

FOR STRUGGLING READERS
Develop Reading Fluency Lead students in an echo reading activity. Read aloud a section of the text, including its heading. Then pause for the entire class to read aloud the words you just read. Tell students to mimic your cadence, intonation, and enunciation. Afterwards, ask volunteers to summarize the information in the sections they read aloud.

FOR ADVANCED LEARNERS/AP
Analyze and Research [paired option] Have student pairs find examples in the selection that show Cabeza de Vaca's Christian faith and beliefs. **Examples:** *"God's great mercy" (line 3), "The Lord willed" (line 73), "we prayed for mercy and pardon" (line 75), "Our method . . . was to . . . pray earnestly to God our Lord" (lines 122–123).* Then have students research some of the main beliefs of Christians during this time

period, recording their findings in a Cluster Diagram. For example, what did Christians believe prayer accomplished? How did they believe they should treat strangers? Did they believe in healing? After students finish the selection, have them identify actions of Cabeza de Vaca that did—or did not—reflect his Christian beliefs.

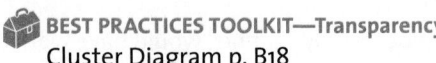 **BEST PRACTICES TOOLKIT—Transparency**
Cluster Diagram p. B18

Being provided with what we needed, we thought to embark again. It was a struggle to dig our barge out of the sand it had sunk in, and another struggle to launch her. For the work in the water while launching, we stripped and stowed our clothes in the craft.

Quickly clambering in and grabbing our oars, we had rowed two crossbow shots from shore when a wave **inundated** us. Being naked and the cold intense, 60 we let our oars go. The next big wave capsized the barge. The Inspector and two others held fast, but that only carried them more certainly underneath, where they drowned.

A single roll of the sea tossed the rest of the men into the rushing surf and back onto shore half-drowned.

We lost only those the barge took down; but the survivors escaped as naked as they were born, with the loss of everything we had. That was not much, but valuable to us in that bitter November cold, our bodies so emaciated we could easily count every bone and looked the very picture of death. I can say for myself that from the month of May I had eaten nothing but corn, and that sometimes 70 raw. I never could bring myself to eat any of the horse-meat at the time our beasts were slaughtered; and fish I did not taste ten times. On top of everything else, a cruel north wind commenced to complete our killing. **C**

The Lord willed that we should find embers while searching the remnants of our former fire. We found more wood and soon had big fires raging. Before them, with flowing tears, we prayed for mercy and pardon, each filled with pity not only for himself but for all his wretched fellows.

At sunset the Indians, not knowing we had gone, came again with food. When they saw us looking so strangely different, they turned back in alarm. I went after them calling, and they returned, though frightened. I explained to them by signs 80 that our barge had sunk and three of our number drowned. They could see at their feet two of the dead men who had washed ashore. They could also see that the rest of us were not far from joining these two.

The Indians, understanding our full plight, sat down and lamented for half an hour so loudly they could have been heard a long way off. It was amazing to see these wild, untaught savages howling like brutes in compassion for us. It intensified my own grief at our calamity and had the same effect on the other victims.

When the cries died down, I conferred with the Christians about asking the Indians to take us to their homes. Some of our number who had been to New Spain warned that the Indians would sacrifice us to their idols.[5] But death being 90 surer and nearer if we stayed where we were, I went ahead and beseeched the Indians. They were delighted. They told us to **tarry** a little while, then they would do as we wished.

Presently thirty of them gathered loads of wood and disappeared to their huts, which were a long walk away; while we waited with the remainder until near nightfall. Then, supporting us under our arms, they hurried us from one

---

inundate (ĭn'ŭn-dāt') *v.* to cover with water; to overwhelm

C **PRIMARY SOURCE**
Reread lines 68–71. What does the author's reponse to his current situation tell you about his usual diet?

② **Targeted Passage**

tarry (tăr'ē) *v.* to delay

---

5. **New Spain . . . their idols:** New Spain included what is now the southwest United States, Mexico, Central America north of Panama, and some West Indian islands. In Mexico, conquistadors had encountered Aztecs who practiced human sacrifice.

C **PRIMARY SOURCE**

Possible answer: The author does not normally eat horse meat (line 70), and he could not bring himself to do so, even though he is starving.

TIERED DISCUSSION PROMPTS

Use these prompts to help students consider the Spanish conquistadors' decision to try to leave the island as described in lines 54–86:

Connect Have you ever failed to solve a difficult problem and then confronted the same situation again? How did you respond? *Accept all reasonable responses.*

Intepret Why do you think the men decide to embark again and leave the island so soon? *Possible answer: The men feel refreshed by the food the Indians have given them. They feel a bit hopeful and think that they have enough strength to sail again. They may also feel that the Indians might not continue to be welcoming.*

Evaluate Do you think the conquistadors' decision to leave was a good one? Why or why not? *Possible answers: No; the men were obviously still weak (lines 54–56), and the Indians showed no unfriendly signs. The men had only a barge to sail on; they should have waited until they had built a more seaworthy vessel. Yes; The men needed to try to leave the island. This was the best time to leave—before any hostility developed.*

VOCABULARY   COMMON CORE
L 4

OWN THE WORD

- **inundate:** Ask students to focus on the second meaning of *inundate*. Challenge them to identify things that might *inundate* them. *Possible answer: homework*

- **tarry:** Ask students to think of synonyms for *tarry* and to discuss each word's connotation. *Possible answers: delay, postpone*

FOR STRUGGLING READERS

② **Targeted Passage** [Lines 77–92]

This passage introduces the conflict the conquistadors face after their barge capsizes.

- Why do the Indians return with food? (line 77)

- Why do the conquistadors look "so strangely different" to the Indians? (lines 78–79)

- How do the Indians respond to the conquistadors' plight? (lines 83–86)

- Why are some of the conquistadors afraid to go to the Indians' homes? (lines 87–89)

FOR ENGLISH LANGUAGE LEARNERS

Vocabulary: Idioms Help students use context clues to determine the meanings of these idioms: *brought . . . to* (lines 21–22), "brought back to consciousness"; *regain their senses* (line 24), "feel better"; *came upon* (line 32), "discovered"; *held fast* (line 61), "held on tightly"; *On top of everything else* (line 71), "Along with everything else that happened"; *as a matter of fact* (line 119), "actually."

◆ **GRAMMAR AND STYLE** COMMON CORE L 3, L 3a

Analyze Details These prepositional phrases tell readers about the setting and the men's experience. Ask students to identify other prepositional phrases that provide important details. ***Possible answers:*** *"to land," "in seven fathoms" (line 17); "of the sea," "into the rushing surf" (line 63)*

REVISIT THE BIG QUESTION

What's the STORY *behind the* GLORY?

Discuss In lines 106–109, what does the Karankawas' insistence that the Spaniards serve as medicine men tell you about their desire to survive? ***Possible answer:*** *Despite their generosity the Karankawas are willing to refuse to give the Spaniards food unless they help them overcome this lethal sickness.*

TEXT ANALYSIS COMMON CORE RI 1, RI 6

E HISTORICAL CONTEXT

Possible answer: *Both the Spanish and the Karankawas believed in a power beyond themselves that is capable of healing (lines 109–113, 122–125).*

VOCABULARY COMMON CORE L 4

OWN THE WORD

- **embody:** Have students complete this sentence: Olympic athletes embody. . . ***Possible answers:*** *strength, patriotism, integrity, and determination.*
- **cauterize:** Ask students to explain why the medicine man *cauterizes* a wound. ***Possible answers:*** *to heal it, to burn away germs.*

SELECTION WRAP-UP

READ WITH A PURPOSE Ask students to discuss the writer's attitude toward the Native Americans. ***Possible answers:*** *At the end of the selection, the author shows respect for the Native Americans despite their cultural differences. He is grateful for their kindness.*

to another of the four big fires they had built along the path. At each fire, when we regained a little warmth and strength, they took us on so swiftly our feet hardly touched ground. ◆D

Thus we made their village, where we saw they had erected a hut for us with many fires inside. An hour later they began a dance celebration that lasted all night. For us there was no joy, feasting, or sleep, as we waited the hour they should make us victims.

In the morning, when they brought us fish and roots and acted in every way hospitably, we felt reassured and somewhat lost our anxiety of the sacrificial knife.

Cabeza de Vaca learned that men from one of the other barges had also landed on the island, bringing the number of Europeans there to about 90. In a matter of weeks, all but 16 of them died of disease, which spread to the Karankawas and killed half of them as well. Some of the Karankawas wanted to put the remaining Europeans to death but were dissuaded by Cabeza de Vaca's host. Cabeza de Vaca and his men were later forced to act as healers.

How We Became Medicine-Men

The islanders wanted to make physicians of us without examination or a review of diplomas. Their method of cure is to blow on the sick, the breath and the laying-on of hands supposedly casting out the infirmity. They insisted we should do this too and be of some use to them. We scoffed at their cures and at the idea we knew how to heal. But they withheld food from us until we complied. An Indian told me I knew not whereof I spoke in saying their methods had no effect. Stones and other things growing about in the fields, he said, had a virtue whereby passing a pebble along the stomach could take away pain and heal; surely extraordinary men like us **embodied** such powers over nature. Hunger forced us to obey, but disclaiming any responsibility for our failure or success.

An Indian, falling sick, would send for a medicine-man, who would apply his cure. The patient would then give the medicine-man all he had and seek more from his relatives to give. The medicine-man makes incisions over the point of the pain, sucks the wound, and **cauterizes** it. This remedy enjoys high repute among the Indians. I have, as a matter of fact, tried it on myself with good results. The medicine-men blow on the spot they have treated, as a finishing touch, and the patient regards himself relieved.

Our method, however, was to bless the sick, breathe upon them, recite a *Pater noster* and *Ave Maria,*[6] and pray earnestly to God our Lord for their recovery. When we concluded with the sign of the cross, He willed that our patients should directly spread the news that they had been restored to health. E

In consequence, the Indians treated us kindly. They deprived themselves of food to give to us, and presented us skins and other tokens of gratitude.

Translated by Cyclone Covey

6. ***Pater noster*** (pä'tər nŏs'tər) **and *Ave Maria*** (ä'vä mə-rē'ə): the Lord's Prayer ("Our Father") and the Hail Mary, named for the prayers' opening words in Latin.

◆D **GRAMMAR AND STYLE**
Reread lines 93–98. Note how the author uses **prepositional phrases,** such as "until near nightfall" and "along the path," to add important details about where and when events are happening.

embody (ĕm-bŏd'ē) *v.* to represent in human form

(3) **Targeted Passage**

cauterize (kô'tə-rīz') *v.* to burn or sear to destroy diseased tissue

E **HISTORICAL CONTEXT**
In Cabeza de Vaca's time, no one had good knowledge of what caused disease. Reread lines 105–125. In what ways did the Spanish and the Karankawas have similiar ideas about healing?

DIFFERENTIATED INSTRUCTION

FOR STRUGGLING READERS

(3) **Targeted Passage** [Lines 115–127]

This passage shows how the Spanish and the Karankawas resolved their relationship.

- What do the Karankawa medicine men do to "heal" their patients? (lines 117–119)
- What does Cabeza de Vaca think of the Indians' remedies after he has tried them? (lines 119–121)
- When the conquistadors serve as medicine men, how do they "heal" their patients? (lines 122–123)
- How do the Karankawas respond? (lines 126–127)

FOR ADVANCED LEARNERS/AP

Analyze Have small groups discuss these questions and share their findings:

- What preconceived notions did the Spanish have about the Indians?
- Did the Karankawas' actions support the conquistadors' preconceived notions?
- How much are the preconceived notions a person holds based on historical context rather than personal experience?

Comprehension

1. **Summarize** What was life like for the Spaniards on the barges?

2. **Recall** What happened to Cabeza de Vaca's men when they tried to leave Galveston Island?

3. **Clarify** Why did the Karankawas enlist the Spaniards as healers?

Text Analysis

4. **Make Inferences** Based on the events and reactions Cabeza de Vaca describes, what appears to be the Karankawas' view of the Spaniards? Cite details to support your answer.

● 5. **Evaluate a Primary Source** Review the information you collected about *La Relación* as you read. In what ways would you consider this account a valuable and reliable source of information? What are its shortcomings? Explain your conclusions.

● 6. **Make Generalizations About Historical Context** To understand the historical context of a work, you need to consult sources outside of the work for information. Identify three passages from *La Relación* that reflect ideas, values, or events from the author's time. Then, using the footnotes to the text and the background information on page 74 as sources, explain the historical context of each example. Based on your results, what generalizations can you make about 16th-century Spanish perspectives? Create a chart to organize your notes.

Examples from Text	Information from Other Sources
•	•
•	•
•	•

Generalizations About Historical Context
•
•
•

Text Criticism

7. **Biographical Context** Later in life, Cabeza de Vaca spoke out against the enslavement of Native Americans. How might his experiences as a captive, trader, and healer among the Karankawas and other groups have influenced his position? Explain your answer, citing evidence from the text.

> *What's the* **STORY** *behind the* **GLORY?**
>
> What qualities of a hero and survivor does Cabeza de Vaca demonstrate in this selection? Support your answer with evidence from the landing on Galveston Island and from the narrator's encounters with the Karankawas.

COMMON CORE

RI 1 Cite textual evidence to support analysis of what the text says explicitly as well as inferences drawn from the text, including determining where the text leaves matters uncertain. **RI 6** Determine an author's point of view or purpose in a text. **RI 9** Analyze foundational U.S. documents of historical and literary significance for their themes, purposes, and rhetorical features.

Practice and Apply

For preliminary support of post-reading questions, use these copy masters.

R RESOURCE MANAGER—Copy Masters
Reading Check p. 90
Historical Context p. 83
Question Support p. 91

Additional selection questions are provided for teachers on page 77.

ANSWERS   COMMON CORE RI 1, RI 6, RI 9

1. *The Spaniards were lost at sea, starving to death, and freezing.*

2. *A wave capsized their barge. Three men drowned; the others washed ashore, naked and having lost all their supplies.*

3. *They believed the Spaniards to be extraordinary men with power over nature.*

Possible answers:

4. *The Karankawas are curious about the Spaniards (lines 51–52). They think the Spaniards have magical powers (lines 112–113). They are unafraid of the Spaniards and feel empathy for them (lines 83–101).*

5. ■ **COMMON CORE FOCUS** *Evaluate a Primary Source* **Reliable:** *The author uses a calm tone and gives detailed observations;* **Unreliable:** *The author has personal motives and makes cultural assumptions that can distort his interpretation of events (lines 41–43, 88–89).*

6. ● **COMMON CORE FOCUS** *Make Generalizations About Historical Context* Students should cite passages and source material that lead to valid generalizations, as shown here. *Text Example:* Spanish conquistadors were afraid that Indians would sacrifice them to their idols (lines 88–89). *Other Sources:* Footnote on page 77 supports idea; background information says conquistadors encountered Native American cultures they didn't understand. *Generalization:* In the 16th century, Spanish explorers feared and misunderstood Native Americans.

7. *He saw how compassionate and generous the Native Americans were (lines 46–47, 48–50, 77–92, 99–102). He appreciated the Indians' culture and humanity (lines 115–121). His captivity showed him that slavery was unjust (lines 105–110).*

What's the STORY *behind the* GLORY? **Possible answer:** *Cabeza de Vaca demonstrates leadership qualities by remaining calm in a crisis (lines 1–3), taking over the boat's tiller (lines 10–13), showing strength despite personal misery (lines 67–72), and consulting his crew before making a decision that may affect all their lives (lines 87–92).*

ANSWERS

Vocabulary in Context

VOCABULARY PRACTICE

1. *(d) connection*   4. *(d) weep*
2. *(c) ingratiate*   5. *(a) obtain*
3. *(c) wind*   6. *(d) construct*

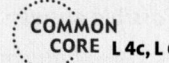 **RESOURCE MANAGER**—Copy Master
Vocabulary Practice p. 88

ACADEMIC VOCABULARY IN WRITING

Cabeza de Vaca's memoir documents *his physical hardships (hunger, pain, cold) and difficult decisions (whether to ask his men to take shelter with the Native Americans). His actions and decisions and suggest that they* reveal *him to be a true leader.*

VOCABULARY STRATEGY: ETYMOLOGIES

COMMON CORE L 4c, L 6

- Explain to students that general and specialized dictionaries are excellent sources of etymologies and can be found in print and online.

- Emphasize that etymologies can help them recognize related words and therefore figure out their meanings.

- Note that students' answers may vary slightly based on the dictionary they use.

Possible answers:

1. *Italian*

2. kunosoura, *meaning "dog's tail"; "focal point or center of attention"*

3. *The word comes from the name of a character, Mrs. Malaprop, who misuses words in Richard Brinsley Sheridan's 18th-century play* The Rivals.

4. *Latin, Old French, and Middle English*

 **RESOURCE MANAGER**—Copy Master
Vocabulary Strategy p. 89

Interactive Vocabulary   **THINK** central

Keywords direct students to a **WordSharp** tutorial on **thinkcentral.com** or to other types of vocabulary practice and review.

Vocabulary in Context

▲ VOCABULARY PRACTICE

Choose the word that is not related in meaning to the other words.

1. (a) transit, (b) locomotion, (c) movement, (d) connection
2. (a) inane, (b) incompetent, (c) ingratiate, (d) inept
3. (a) deluge, (b) inundate, (c) wind, (d) overwhelm
4. (a) cauterize, (b) sear, (c) singe, (d) weep
5. (a) obtain, (b) dawdle, (c) tarry, (d) linger
6. (a) embody, (b) personify, (c) actualize, (d) construct

WORD LIST
cauterize
embody
ingratiate
inundate
locomotion
tarry

ACADEMIC VOCABULARY IN WRITING

- document   - illustrate   - interpret   - promote   - reveal

What cultural biases about Native Americans does Cabeza de Vaca **reveal** in this selection? **Document** your answer with evidence from the text. Try to use at least three of the Academic Vocabulary words as you write.

VOCABULARY STRATEGY: ETYMOLOGIES

Many English words have intriguing histories, or **etymologies.** The etymology of a word, or its origin and history, can provide insight into the word's meaning. Standard dictionaries, as well as etymological dictionaries, are excellent sources of word histories. Information about a word's etymology will often appear near the beginning or end of a dictionary entry, as in the following example:

> **cau•ter•ize** (kô′tə-rīz′) *tr.v.* **-ized, -iz•ing, -iz•es 1.** To burn or sear with a cautery. **2.** To deaden, as to feelings or moral scruples. [Middle English *cauterizen*, from Late Latin *cauterizare*, to cauterize, brand, from Latin *cauterium*, cautery.] —**cau•ter•i•za•tion** (-tər-ĭ-zā′shən) *n.*

PRACTICE Consult a print or online dictionary to answer these questions.

1. From what language did *oratorio* enter English?
2. From which Greek word is *cynosure* derived? What is the word's current meaning?
3. What is the origin of the word *malaprop*?
4. Through which languages can the history of *querulous* be traced?

COMMON CORE

L 4c Consult general and specialized reference materials, both print and digital, to determine or clarify a word's etymology. **L 6** Acquire and use accurately general and domain-specific words.

Interactive Vocabulary **THINK** central

Go to **thinkcentral.com**.
KEYWORD: HML11-80

DIFFERENTIATED INSTRUCTION

FOR ADVANCED LEARNERS/AP

Vocabulary Strategy Have pairs select five words from Cabeza de Vaca's account and research each word's etymology. Then have them use the five words in a paragraph about some aspect of the report. Have pairs share their etymologies and paragraphs with the class.

Language

◆ **GRAMMAR AND STYLE: Add Necessary Details**

Review the **Grammar and Style** note on page 78. Cabeza de Vaca uses numerous details throughout his account to help readers visualize his amazing journey. **Prepositional phrases** include details about what happens, as well as where, when, and how. Read this example from *La Relación*:

> *A single roll of the sea tossed the rest of the men into the rushing surf and back onto shore half-drowned.* (lines 63–64)

PRACTICE Rewrite each sentence, adding prepositional phrases that modify the boldfaced words. Follow the directions in parentheses. An example has been done for you.

EXAMPLE

The barges, filled with half-starved men, **drifted** for days. (Tell where they drifted.)

The barges, filled with half-starved men, drifted on the stormy seas for days.

---

1. They told us they **would return** and bring us food. (Tell when they will return.)

2. We **traveled** through the woods to the **village**. (Add two phrases. Tell how long they traveled and where the village was located.)

3. We waited anxiously for **news**. (Tell what kind of news was expected.)

READING-WRITING CONNECTION

 YOUR TURN Expand your understanding of these excerpts from *La Relación* by responding to this prompt. Then use the **revising tips** to improve your journal entry.

WRITING PROMPT	REVISING TIPS
EXPLORER'S ACCOUNT Explorers often keep journals of their experiences. These accounts—from the writings of Lewis and Clark to the reports of a modern astronaut—describe what the explorers see and how they are changed by their experiences. Write a **two-to-four-paragraph journal entry** describing an interesting moment in an exploration. The journey can be real or fictional—a trip to a new town or galaxy, a trek across the desert, or the race to a new invention. Be sure to share your reactions to it.	• Write in the first person, using the pronouns *I* and *me*. • Clearly recount a specific event or moment in the narrator's exploration. • Concentrate on action and momentum. • Vividly describe surroundings, people, or events influencing the moment. • Show the narrator's reactions to the events.

Interactive Revision THINK central
Go to **thinkcentral.com**.
KEYWORD: HML11-81

COMMON CORE

L 3 Apply knowledge of language to make effective choices for meaning or style. **L 3a** Vary syntax for effect. **W 3** Write narratives to develop real or imagined experiences or events using effective technique, well-chosen details, and well-structured event sequences. **W 3a, d** Engage and orient the reader by setting out a situation and its significance, establishing one point of view, and introducing a narrator and/or characters; use precise words and phrases, telling details, and sensory language to convey a vivid picture.

Language 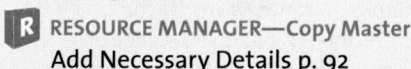 COMMON CORE L 3, L 3a, W 3, W 3a, W 3d

◆ **GRAMMAR IN CONTEXT**

Remind students that a prepositional phrase begins with a preposition (such as *of, on, in, against,* and *for*), and includes the object of the preposition and any words that modify the object. (It does not include a verb. For more on adding details with prepositional phrases, see **Grammar Handbook**, page R65.)

Possible answers:

1. *They told us they would return **in the morning** and bring us food.*

2. *We traveled **for three hours** through the woods to the village **in their territory**.*

3. *We waited anxiously for news **about the missing men**.*

 RESOURCE MANAGER—Copy Master
Add Necessary Details p. 92

READING-WRITING CONNECTION

Encourage students to use a Sensory Notes organizer to help them record vivid and meaningful descriptions that they have either experienced or imagined.

 **BEST PRACTICES TOOLKIT**—Transparency
Sensory Notes p. B9

Writing Online THINK central

The following tools are available online at **thinkcentral.com** and on **Write***Smart* **CD-ROM:**
• **Interactive Graphic Organizers**
• **Interactive Student Models**
• **Interactive Revision Lessons**
For additional grammar instruction, see **GrammarNotes** on **thinkcentral.com**.

Assess and Reteach

Assess

DIAGNOSTIC AND SELECTION TESTS
Selection Test A pp. 37–38
Selection Test B/C pp. 39–40

Interactive Selection Test on thinkcentral.com

Reteach

Level Up Online Tutorials on thinkcentral.com

FOR STRUGGLING WRITERS

Writing Support

• Help students get started by asking, When did you experience this moment? What were you exploring?

• Work with students to translate several details from their Sensory Notes organizer into sentences that describe their journey.

• Limit the length of the assignment to two paragraphs.

Focus and Motivate

COMMON CORE FOCUS

RI 1 Cite textual evidence to support analysis of what the text says explicitly. **RI 3** Analyze a complex set of ideas or sequence of events and explain how specific individuals, ideas, or events interact and develop over the course of the text. **RI 5** Analyze and evaluate the effectiveness of the structure an author uses in his or her exposition or argument, including whether the structure makes points clear, convincing, and engaging. **W 3** Write narratives to develop real or imagined experiences or events using effective technique, well-chosen details, and well-structured event sequences. **W 3a, d** Engage and orient the reader by setting out a situation and its significance, establishing one point of view; create a smooth progression of experiences or events; use precise words and phrases, telling details, and sensory language to convey a vivid picture. **L 2b** Spell correctly. **L 3** Apply knowledge of language to make effective choices for meaning and style. **L 3a** Vary syntax for effect. **L 4** Clarify the meanings of unknown words. **L 4d** Verify the preliminary determination of the meaning of a word.

ABOUT THE AUTHOR

After students have read about Equiano, have them create a timeline of his life, from his capture as a slave to his writing of his narrative. Discuss his extraordinary personal journey. Then point out that the excerpt details the events described in **Ocean Crossings.**

Selection Resources

COMMON CORE

RI 1 Cite textual evidence to support analysis of what the text says explicitly. **RI 3** Analyze a complex set of ideas or sequence of events and explain how specific individuals, ideas, or events interact and develop over the course of the text. **RI 5** Analyze and evaluate the effectiveness of the structure an author uses in his or her exposition or argument, including whether the structure makes points clear, convincing, and engaging. **L 2b** Spell correctly.

DID YOU KNOW?

Olaudah Equiano . . .

- was a best-selling author in Britain.
- owned slaves in Central America.
- married an English woman and raised two daughters.
- died a wealthy man.

(background) Diagram of the cargo hold of a fully loaded slave ship

from The Interesting Narrative of the Life of Olaudah Equiano

Slave Narrative by Olaudah Equiano

Video link at thinkcentral.com

Meet the Author

Olaudah Equiano c. 1745–1797

Soldier, sailor, North Pole explorer—Olaudah Equiano led a remarkable life by the standards of any age. Writing as a former slave in the 1700s, Equiano left powerful testimony on the brutality of enslavement that became the model for a new genre, the slave narrative.

Ocean Crossings According to his autobiography, Equiano was born a chief's son in the Ibo (or Igbo) culture of present-day Nigeria. When he was 11, he was captured and sold as a slave to a series of African masters before making the miserable journey to the Americas known as the Middle Passage. Sold in the West Indies to British navy officer Michael Pascal, Equiano returned to sea with his new owner, who renamed him Gustavus Vassa.

Equiano spent years fighting for Britain, hoping to be freed for good service. Instead, in 1762 he was sold again, to Quaker merchant Robert King, who trained him in business. In 1766, after 21 years as a slave, Equiano bought back his freedom, moved to London, and promptly launched his business career. But by 1773, he was at sea again, first on an expedition to find a northwest passage, and later traveling to Central America and Turkey.

Turning Points In the late 1770s, Equiano returned to London where he got involved in antislavery efforts and converted to Christianity. In 1789, as public debate over abolishing the slave trade began in Britain, Equiano wrote, self-published, and promoted his narrative. Equiano's life story exposed the cruelty of the slave trade and made him an important public figure. He died in 1797, just ten years before Britain abolished the slave trade.

Historians Look More Closely Equiano's narrative includes a wealth of specific details, most of which check out against other sources. But, in 1999, English professor Vincent Carretta uncovered two documents that suggested Equiano was not born in Africa: his baptismal record from England and a ship's passenger list, both of which identify Equiano's birthplace as South Carolina. Historians continue to debate the evidence and how, if at all, it changes the value of *The Interesting Narrative.* Carretta himself points out that even if the narrative is based on the oral accounts of other slaves, its descriptions still provide a valuable portrait of early African life and the Middle Passage.

Author Online
Go to thinkcentral.com. KEYWORD: HML11-82

THINK central

82

See resources on the **Teacher One Stop DVD-ROM** *and on* **thinkcentral.com.**

Video link at thinkcentral.com

 RESOURCE MANAGER UNIT 1

Plan and Teach, pp. 93–100
Summary, pp. 101†, 102‡
Text Analysis and Reading
   Skill, pp. 103–104†, 105–106†
Vocabulary, pp. 107–109
Grammar and Style, p. 112

DIAGNOSTIC AND SELECTION
   TESTS

Selection Tests, pp. 41–44

 BEST PRACTICES TOOLKIT

Word Questioning, p. E9
Observation Chart, p. C7

TECHNOLOGY

 Teacher One Stop DVD-ROM
Student One Stop DVD-ROM
Audio Anthology CD
GrammarNotes DVD-ROM
ExamView Test Generator
   on the **Teacher One Stop**

* Resources for Differentiation   † Also in Spanish   ‡ Also in Haitian Creole and Vietnamese

TEXT ANALYSIS: SLAVE NARRATIVE

Slave narratives, the life stories of people who survived slavery, help us understand the grim realities of this experience.

Olaudah Equiano wrote *The Interesting Narrative* at a time when many Africans remembered their lives before enslavement. Like other 18th-century slave narratives, his work

- portrays the culture shock of a newly captured African
- focuses criticism on slave traders, not slave owners
- includes religious and moral appeals against slavery

As you read, notice the author's purposeful use of language to both narrate and persuade .

READING SKILL: ANALYZE DETAILS

Equiano's readers had little contact with slavery. He chose powerful **descriptive details** to bring the experience to life.

The closeness of the place, and the heat of the climate, added to the number in the ship, which was so crowded that each had scarcely room to turn himself, almost suffocated us.

To reach his readers, Equiano uses

- **sensory details,** ones that appeal to the five senses
- descriptions of his own reactions
- **anecdotes,** brief stories that support his points

As you read, use a chart like the one shown to record effective examples of each kind of detail.

Sensory Details	Reactions	Anecdotes

▲ VOCABULARY IN CONTEXT

Equiano used the following words in his argument against slavery. Restate each phrase, using a different word or words for the boldfaced term.

1. **copious** amounts of rain, causing a flood
2. the **nominal** boss, but with no real authority
3. her **countenance** betraying her fear
4. cruel rulers acting without worry or **scruple**
5. to our **consternation,** revealed all our plans
6. deadly effects of **pestilential** beetles

 Complete the activities in your **Reader/Writer Notebook**.

What does it mean to be a SLAVE?

From the 1500s to the 1800s, millions of Africans were enslaved to work in the Americas. Their experiences have been documented in books and portrayed in films. What do you know about the realities of slavery?

TEST YOURSELF Decide whether each statement is true or false. Think about the facts or impressions that helped you choose your answer.

SLAVERY: *Fact or Fiction*

1. Slavery was a common practice in Africa.
   ☐ TRUE   ○ FALSE

2. No Africans participated willingly in the slave trade.
   ☐ TRUE   ○ FALSE

3. Most enslaved Africans were brought to North America.
   ☐ TRUE   ○ FALSE

4. Captured Africans were packed like cargo into slave ships.
   ☐ TRUE   ○ FALSE

5. Slave traders typically sold families as a single group.
   ☐ TRUE   ○ FALSE

83

What does it mean to be a SLAVE?

Tell students to consider the question at the end of the paragraph. Have students complete *TEST YOURSELF,* then invite them to share and explain their answers about slavery.

TEXT ANALYSIS   COMMON CORE   RI 3   RI 5

● *Model the Skill:* SLAVE NARRATIVE

Have students read **Ocean Crossings** on page 82. Ask them to describe aspects of the culture shock Equiano would have faced in his first days as a slave. ***Possible answer:** Equiano would have faced separation from his family at age 11, recognition that Africans had enslaved him, a miserable journey, and abrupt change from a chief's son to a slave.*

GUIDED PRACTICE Ask students if Equiano was always a slave. Have them discuss how his history may have influenced his slave narrative.

READING SKILL   COMMON CORE   RI 1

■ *Model the Skill:* ANALYZE DETAILS

Point out how sensory language creates imagery. Have students read the first paragraph of **Ocean Crossings.** Ask what descriptive phrases hint at details Equiano will develop in his narrative. ***Possible answer:*** *"miserable journey"* and *"sold in the West Indies"*

R RESOURCE MANAGER—Copy Master Analyze Details p. 105 (for student use while reading the selection)

VOCABULARY SKILL   COMMON CORE   L 4

▲ VOCABULARY IN CONTEXT

DIAGNOSE WORD KNOWLEDGE Have all students complete Vocabulary in Context. Check their words and phrases against the following:

consternation (kŏn′stər-nā′shən) *n.* a state of paralyzing dismay; fear

copious (kō′pē-əs) *adj.* in large amounts; abundant

countenance (koun′tə-nəns) *n.* appearance, especially the expression of the face

nominal (nŏm′ə-nəl) *adj.* in name but not in reality

pestilential (pĕs′tə-lĕn′shəl) *adj.* deadly; poisonous

scruple (skrōō′pəl) *n.* feeling of uneasiness or guilt that keeps a person from doing something

PRETEACH VOCABULARY Preteach vocabulary with this copy master.

R RESOURCE MANAGER—Copy Master Vocabulary Study p. 107

SUMMARY

This excerpt from Equiano's slave narrative details his horrendous journey on a slave ship as a captured 11-year-old boy. It opens with Equiano being forced aboard the slave ship, then recounts the inhumane conditions of the journey, including the floggings he receives for not eating. After surviving the ocean journey, Equiano and other Africans are sold as slaves. Many are cruelly separated from family members.

READ WITH A PURPOSE

Help students set a purpose for reading. Tell them to read the following excerpt from Olaudah Equiano's narrative to learn what African captives experienced on the journey across the Atlantic into slavery.

REVISIT THE BIG QUESTION

What does it mean to be a SLAVE?

Discuss In lines 4–5, what does the way in which Equiano was treated when he was carried on board the ship tell you about slavery?
Possible answer: *Slavery was dehumanizing and cruel. Equiano was "handled" and "tossed" as if he were an inanimate object and not a person.*

TEXT ANALYSIS　　COMMON CORE
RI 3
RI 5

Ⓐ *Model the Skill:* SLAVE NARRATIVE

Tell students out that Equiano is describing Europeans. Ask students how they would feel if someone described them as part of a "world of bad spirits."

Possible answer: *Equiano describes this experience from an African's point of view. Most Europeans would be startled to hear themselves and their culture described as a "world of bad spirits" (lines 5–6)—as if their culture is strange, hostile, and horrible. They would also be surprised to think that their physical attributes were perceived as abnormal (lines 6–8).*

THE INTERESTING NARRATIVE
of the Life of Olaudah Equiano

Olaudah Equiano

BACKGROUND As European colonies in the Americas expanded, so did the slave trade. Slaves were captured in Africa, then taken by ship to the West Indies—a journey called the Middle Passage. For two months, Africans lay tightly chained in storage compartments with hardly enough air to breathe. Millions died from bad food, harsh treatment, disease, and despair. Olaudah Equiano is one of the few to describe this horrific journey.

When Olaudah Equiano was 11 years old, he and his sister were kidnapped while the adults in his village were working in the fields. After being forced to travel for several days, Equiano and his sister were separated. For the next six or seven months, Equiano was sold several times to African masters in different countries. He was eventually taken to the west coast of Africa and carried aboard a slave ship bound for the West Indies.

The first object which saluted my eyes when I arrived on the coast, was the sea, and a slave ship, which was then riding at anchor, and waiting for its cargo. These filled me with astonishment, which was soon converted into terror, when I was carried on board. I was immediately handled, and tossed up to see if I were sound, by some of the crew; and I was now persuaded that I had gotten into a world of bad spirits, and that they were going to kill me. Their complexions, too, differing so much from ours, their long hair, and the language they spoke (which was very different from any I had ever heard), united to confirm me in this belief. Ⓐ
Indeed, such were the horrors of my views and fears at the moment, that, if ten
10　thousand worlds had been my own, I would have freely parted with them all to

Analyze Visuals ▶
Describe the mood of this painting. What does the image reveal about the conditions on board a slave ship?

❶ **Targeted Passage**

Ⓐ **SLAVE NARRATIVE** Note Equiano's use of **first-person point of view** in lines 1–8. In what ways might this description be startling to Equiano's mostly European audience?

Detail of *The Slave Ship* (1956), Robert Riggs. N.A. Courtesy of Les Mansfield, Cincinnati, Ohio.

DIFFERENTIATED INSTRUCTION

FOR ENGLISH LANGUAGE LEARNERS
Vocabulary Support Use Word Questioning to teach these words: *confirm* (line 8), *portion* (line 21), *element* (line 40), *likewise* (line 120).

📦 **BEST PRACTICES TOOLKIT—Transparency** Word Questioning p. E9

FOR STRUGGLING READERS
In combination with the *Audio Anthology CD*, use one or more Targeted Passages (pp. 84, 87, 88) to ensure that students focus on key events and concepts. Targeted Passages are also good for English learners.

❶ **Targeted Passage** [Lines 1–8]
This passage enables students to feel the author's fear and recognize his predicament.

Analyze visuals

Possible answer: *The mood of this painting is somber, depressing, and agonizing. The image reveals that the conditions on a slave ship were repulsive. African Americans were horribly treated. They were chained together and abused. They look unhealthy, which suggests they were fed only enough to barely survive.*

CULTURAL CONNECTION

Slavery Equiano's slave narrative explains how Africans were captured and sold as slaves in the 1700s. However, slavery has existed since the beginning of recorded history. For example, slaves of China's Shang Dynasty (18th century B.C.) were typically enslaved as a result of war or debt. The ancient Roman and Greek Empires also enslaved many of their defeated enemies. Although Equiano was not captured due to war or debt, his slave narrative reflects common aspects of how most slaves were treated. Ask students to share examples of slavery they know of from any time in history.

- What is the cargo the slave ship is waiting for? (lines 1–2)
- How does Equiano feel while on the slave ship? (lines 3–4)
- What does Equiano think is going to happen to him? (lines 5–6)

FOR ADVANCED LEARNERS/AP

Make Judgments Begin a class discussion by asking students to identify examples of injustice that exist today. Tell students to write a poem or song that exposes a specific injustice and inspires people to take action against it. Have students present their poem or song to the class. Discuss with students how music and literature can bring about social change.

 **Model the Skill: ANALYZE DETAILS**

Use the prereading chart introduced on page 83 to help students list and examine the sensory details Equiano describes and his reactions.

Possible answer: the strange appearance and unfamiliar language of the men on the ship (lines 6–8); the boiling furnace (line 12); the miserable, chained Africans (lines 13–15).

TIERED DISCUSSION PROMPTS

In lines 27–50, use these prompts to have students consider Equiano's situation:

Connect How have you reacted to a seemingly hopeless situation? *Accept all reasonable responses.*

Interpret Why might Equiano feel grief at the offer of food? *Possible answer: He longs for death at this point. (lines 35–36).*

Synthesize Based on what you know about slavery and Equiano's experiences so far, will Equiano's situation become not "so desperate" (line 50) when he reaches "the white people's country" (line 49)? Explain.
Possible answer: No; he will most likely continue to be mistreated by slave owners.

VOCABULARY

COMMON CORE
L 4

OWN THE WORD

- **countenance:** Tell students that the noun form of *countenance* also means "support or approval." Ask students to write a sentence using the noun *countenance*. *Possible answer: Abolitionists wore stern* countenances *when discussing slavery.*

- **consternation:** Ask students to list events or situations that would cause them to feel *consternation*. **Possible answer:** *taking an exam unprepared, threats or bad news*

THEME AND GENRE

After students have read the selection, ask them to discuss twentieth-century American novels, plays, or films that connect to the themes in Equiano's narrative.

---

have exchanged my condition with that of the meanest slave[1] in my own country. When I looked round the ship too, and saw a large furnace of copper boiling, and a multitude of black people of every description chained together, every one of their <u>countenances</u> expressing dejection and sorrow, I no longer doubted of my fate; and, quite overpowered with horror and anguish, I fell motionless on the deck and fainted. When I recovered a little, I found some black people about me, who I believed were some of those who had brought me on board, and had been receiving their pay; they talked to me in order to cheer me, but all in vain. I asked them if we were not to be eaten by those white men with horrible looks, red faces,
20 and long hair. They told me I was not, and one of the crew brought me a small portion of spirituous liquor in a wine glass; but, being afraid of him, I would not take it out of his hand. One of the blacks, therefore, took it from him and gave it to me, and I took a little down my palate, which, instead of reviving me, as they thought it would, threw me into the greatest <u>consternation</u> at the strange feeling it produced, having never tasted any such liquor before. Soon after this, the blacks who brought me on board went off, and left me abandoned to despair.

　I now saw myself deprived of all chance of returning to my native country, or even the least glimpse of hope of gaining the shore, which I now considered as friendly; and I even wished for my former slavery in preference to my present
30 situation, which was filled with horrors of every kind, still heightened by my ignorance of what I was to undergo. I was not long suffered to indulge my grief; I was soon put down under the decks, and there I received such a salutation in my nostrils as I had never experienced in my life; so that, with the loathsomeness of the stench, and crying together, I became so sick and low that I was not able to eat, nor had I the least desire to taste anything. I now wished for the last friend, death, to relieve me; but soon, to my grief, two of the white men offered me eatables; and, on my refusing to eat, one of them held me fast by the hands, and laid me across, I think, the windlass,[2] and tied my feet, while the other flogged[3] me severely. I had never experienced anything of this kind before, and, although not
40 being used to the water, I naturally feared that element the first time I saw it, yet, nevertheless, could I have got over the nettings,[4] I would have jumped over the side, but I could not; and besides, the crew used to watch us very closely who were not chained down to the decks, lest we should leap into the water; and I have seen some of these poor African prisoners most severely cut, for attempting to do so, and hourly whipped for not eating. This indeed was often the case with myself. In a little time after, amongst the poor chained men, I found some of my own nation, which in a small degree gave ease to my mind. I inquired of these what was to be done with us? They gave me to understand, we were to be carried to these white people's country to work for them. I then was a little revived, and thought, if
50 it were no worse than working, my situation was not so desperate; but still I feared

---

1. **the meanest slave:** the poorest or most wretched slave.
2. **windlass** (wĭnd′ləs): a device for raising and lowering a ship's anchor.
3. **flogged:** beat with a whip or rod.
4. **nettings:** networks of small ropes on the sides of a ship that were used for various purposes, such as stowing sails. On slave ships, the nettings helped keep the slaves from jumping overboard.

---

countenance
(koun′tə-nəns) *n.*
appearance, especially the expression of the face

consternation
(kŏn′stər-nā′shən) *n.*
a state of paralyzing dismay; fear

B **ANALYZE DETAILS**
Reread lines 1–26. What details reinforce Equiano's impression that he has been captured by bad spirits?

THEME AND GENRE
A common theme in literature is the struggle to overcome adversity. Autobiographical narratives like Equiano's have influenced explorations of this theme in the context of race and slavery in films like *Amistad* (1997) and in *Roots* (1976), the groundbreaking novel and TV miniseries. Why do you think this theme of triumph over adversity is so universally appealing to modern audiences?

DIFFERENTIATED INSTRUCTION

FOR STRUGGLING READERS

Develop Reading Fluency Select a passage of about 10–15 lines and read it aloud to the class. Tell students to note phrasing, rate, and intonation. Next read the first line of the passage and have students repeat it back to you as a class. Continue until students have "echoed" each line in the passage.

FOR ENGLISH LANGUAGE LEARNERS

Vocabulary: Outdated Forms Have students reread these lines and substitute these definitions for the outdated terms:

- *gave me to understand* (line 48), "explained that"
- *how comes it* (line 61), "how can it be"
- *made ready* (line 72), "got ready (to sail)"
- *they thought fit* (line 92), "they wanted"

I should be put to death, the white people looked and acted, as I thought, in so savage a manner; for I had never seen among any people such instances of brutal cruelty; and this not only shown towards us blacks, but also to some of the whites themselves. One white man in particular I saw, when we were permitted to be on deck, flogged so unmercifully with a large rope near the foremast,[5] that he died in consequence of it; and they tossed him over the side as they would have done a brute. This made me fear these people the more; and I expected nothing less than to be treated in the same manner. I could not help expressing my fears and apprehensions to some of my countrymen; I asked them if these people had no country, but lived in this hollow place (the ship)? They told me they did not, but came from a distant one. "Then," said I, "how comes it in all our country we never heard of them?" They told me because they lived so very far off. I then asked where were their women? had they any like themselves? I was told they had. "And why," said I, "do we not see them?" They answered, because they were left behind. I asked how the vessel could go? They told me they could not tell; but that there was cloth put upon the masts by the help of the ropes I saw, and then the vessel went on; and the white men had some spell or magic they put in the water when they liked, in order to stop the vessel. I was exceedingly amazed at this account, and really thought they were spirits. I therefore wished much to be from amongst them, for I expected they would sacrifice me; but my wishes were vain—for we were so quartered that it was impossible for any of us to make our escape. . . .

At last, when the ship we were in, had got in all her cargo, they made ready with many fearful noises, and we were all put under deck, so that we could not see how they managed the vessel. But this disappointment was the least of my sorrow. The stench of the hold while we were on the coast was so intolerably loathsome, that it was dangerous to remain there for any time, and some of us had been permitted to stay on the deck for the fresh air; but now that the whole ship's cargo were confined together, it became absolutely **pestilential.** The closeness of the place, and the heat of the climate, added to the number in the ship, which was so crowded that each had scarcely room to turn himself, almost suffocated us. This produced **copious** perspirations, so that the air soon became unfit for respiration, from a variety of loathsome smells, and brought on a sickness among the slaves, of which many died. . . . This wretched situation was again aggravated by the galling[6] of the chains. . . . The shrieks of the women, and the groans of the dying, rendered the whole a scene of horror almost inconceivable. Happily perhaps, for myself, I was soon reduced so low here that it was thought necessary to keep me almost always on deck; and from my extreme youth I was not put in fetters. In this situation I expected every hour to share the fate of my companions, some of whom were almost daily brought upon deck at the point of death, which I began to hope would soon put an end to my miseries. . . .

One day they had taken a number of fishes; and when they had killed and satisfied themselves with as many as they thought fit, to our astonishment who

---

5. **foremast** (fôr′məst): the mast (tall pole that supports sails and rigging) nearest the forward end of a sailing ship.

6. **galling:** rubbing or chafing, enough to produce sores.

◆ GRAMMAR AND STYLE
Reread lines 54–57. Note how Equiano uses **adverb clauses,** such as "when we were permitted to be on deck," to modify verbs and adverbs in the sentence.

◆ SLAVE NARRATIVE
Look back at lines 48–54. What does Equiano's reaction reveal about the way he regards slavery?

pestilential
(pĕs′tə-lĕn′shəl) *adj.* deadly; poisonous

copious (kō′pē-əs) *adj.* in large amounts; abundant

◆ ANALYZE DETAILS
What details in lines 75–85 does Equiano use to describe conditions below deck? What kind of image do these details create? Support your answer with evidence from these lines.

◆ GRAMMAR AND STYLE COMMON CORE L 3 L 3a

Analyze Details Equiano's use of adverb clauses allows his sentences to provide more detailed information. This phrase, for example, tells readers that the Africans are seldom allowed on deck. Tell students to identify other adverb clauses in Equiano's narrative and list the extra details these provide. Examples include "When I looked round the ship too" (line 12) and "When I recovered a little" (line 16).

TEXT ANALYSIS COMMON CORE RI 3 RI 5

◆ SLAVE NARRATIVE

Possible answer: Equiano doesn't object to being forced to work for the Europeans (slavery) nearly as much as he objects to the cruel treatment by his captors (lines 50–53).

Extend the Discussion What does Equiano's viewpoint tell you about his view of work?

READING SKILL COMMON CORE RI 1

◆ ANALYZE DETAILS

Possible answer: Descriptive details create vivid images and include "The stench of the hold" (line 75), "The closeness of the place" (lines 78–79), "the heat" (line 79), "copious perspirations" (line 81), "loathsome smells" (line 82), and "The shrieks of the women, and the groans of the dying" (lines 84–85).

VOCABULARY COMMON CORE L 4

OWN THE WORD

- **pestilential:** Have students create a semantic web. Write *pestilential* in a center circle, adding the definition given, "deadly; poisonous." Have students add synonyms to complete the web. *Possible answers: contagious, infectious, lethal*

- **copious:** Explain that the root for *copious* is *copia,* a Latin word meaning "abundance." Have students list *copious* objects in the classroom.

FOR STRUGGLING READERS

 Targeted Passage [Lines 78–90]

This passage describes the repulsive conditions below deck and how Equiano reacts.

- What nearly suffocates the slaves? (lines 78–81)

- What causes many slaves to die? (lines 81–83)

- Why is Equiano brought on deck? (lines 86–87)

FOR ADVANCED LEARNERS/AP

Research Context Refer students to the **BACKGROUND** on page 84 and note that Equiano is traveling the Middle Passage. Clarify that the selection focuses on Equiano's personal experience rather than the overall journey. Have pairs learn more about the Middle Passage, such as its exact route, its usual duration, and the origin of its name. Invite pairs to map the Middle Passage and share findings with the class.

Discuss In lines 91–98, what does this anec-dote say about how the Africans are treated under slavery? *Possible answer: The anecdote suggests that they are treated worse than ani-mals; they are not even worthy of food scraps.*

TEXT ANALYSIS COMMON CORE
RI 3
RI 5

❺ SLAVE NARRATIVE

Possible answer: Equiano's point is that it is against the men's Christian religion to treat people the way they are treating the Africans. He is appealing to the readers' personal and spiritual emotions.

VOCABULARY COMMON CORE
L 4

OWN THE WORD

- **scruple:** Have students read the para-graph beginning, "We were not many days. . ." Have volunteers list the slave auctioneer's lack of *scruples* expressed in this passage. *Possible answer: The slaves were sold without regard for keeping family members and friends together.*

- **nominal:** Tell students this adjective's meanings include, "relating to a name; existing in name only; an insignificant amount." Ask students how they believe the meaning of the term evolved. They may consider such terms as *nominal wages, nominal cost,* or *nominal increase.*

SELECTION WRAP–UP

READ WITH A PURPOSE Have students de-scribe what African captives experienced on the journey across the Atlantic into slavery. *Possible answers: confinement under the deck; floggings, forced feeding*

⭐ **CRITIQUE** Have students describe what aspects of Equiano's narrative might have had the most powerful impact on 18th-century readers. Remind students to support their answers with specific details from the text.

---

were on deck, rather than give any of them to us to eat, as we expected, they tossed the remaining fish into the sea again, although we begged and prayed for some as well as we could, but in vain; and some of my countrymen, being pressed by hunger, took an opportunity, when they thought no one saw them, of trying to get a little privately; but they were discovered, and the attempt procured them some very severe floggings. One day, when we had a smooth sea and moderate wind, two of my wearied countrymen who were chained together (I was near them at the time), preferring death to such a life of misery, somehow made through the nettings and jumped into the sea; immediately, another quite dejected fellow, who, on account of his illness, was suffered to be out of irons, also followed their example; and I believe many more would very soon have done the same, if they had not been prevented by the ship's crew, who were instantly alarmed. . . .

During the rest of his voyage to the West Indies, Equiano continued to endure hardships. After the ship anchored on the coast of Barbados, Equiano and the other slaves were brought ashore and herded together in a slave merchant's yard to be sold.

We were not many days in the merchant's custody, before we were sold after their usual manner, which is this: On a signal given (as the beat of a drum), the buyers rush at once into the yard where the slaves are confined, and make choice of that parcel[7] they like best. The noise and clamor with which this is attended, and the eagerness visible in the countenances of the buyers, serve not a little to increase the apprehension of terrified Africans, who may well be supposed to consider them as the ministers of that destruction to which they think themselves devoted. In this manner, without **scruple,** are relations and friends separated, most of them never to see each other again. I remember, in the vessel in which I was brought over, in the men's apartment, there were several brothers, who, in the sale, were sold in different lots; and it was very moving on this occasion, to see and hear their cries at parting. O, ye **nominal** Christians! might not an African ask you—Learned you this from your God, who says unto you, Do unto all men as you would men should do to you? Is it not enough that we are torn from our country and friends, to toil for your luxury and lust of gain? Must every tender feeling be likewise sacrificed to your avarice? Are the dearest friends and relations now rendered more dear by their separation from their kindred, still to be parted from each other, and thus prevented from cheering the gloom of slavery, with the small comfort of being together, and mingling their sufferings and sorrows? Why are parents to lose their children, brothers their sisters, or husbands their wives? Surely, this is a new refinement in cruelty, which . . . thus aggravates distress, and adds fresh horrors even to the wretchedness of slavery.  ❺

7. **parcel:** a group of slaves offered for sale as one "package."

COMMON CORE L 2b

Language Coach

English Spelling In *prayed* (line 94) and *wearied* (line 99), *-ed* is added to a word ending in *y* (*pray* and *weary*). *Prayed* keeps the *y,* because a vowel comes before *y.* For *weary,* the *y* is changed to an *i.* How would you spell *supply* + *-ed* or *employ* + *-ed*?

❸ Targeted Passage

scruple (skrōō´pəl) *n.* feeling of uneasiness or guilt that keeps a person from doing something

nominal (nŏm´ə-nəl) *adj.* in name but not in reality

❺ SLAVE NARRATIVE
What point is Equiano making in lines 116–118? To what emotions is he appealing?

DIFFERENTIATED INSTRUCTION

FOR STRUGGLING READERS

❸ Targeted Passage [Lines 105–116]

This passage explains what happened to the slaves once they reached shore.

- How are the slaves sold? (lines 105–108)

- How does Equiano characterize the slave buyers? (lines 109–112)

- Which of the slave buyers' actions does Equiano consider the most immoral? (lines 112–116)

FOR ENGLISH LANGUAGE LEARNERS

Language Coach COMMON CORE
L 2b

English Spelling *Answers: supplied; employed* Have students brainstorm a list of other words ending in *y* that can have *-ed* added to them.

Tell students to make a list of three such words that keep the *y* and three such words that have the *y* changed to an *i.*

Comprehension

1. **Recall** Who has brought Equiano to the slave ship?

2. **Recall** What does Equiano think will happen to him when he is brought on board ship?

3. **Clarify** What does Equiano mean when he refers to "nominal Christians"?

Text Analysis

● 4. **Analyze Descriptive Details** Review the chart you made while reading. Identify the details that had the strongest impact on you as a reader. Why were those details so effective?

5. **Compare and Contrast** Like Cabeza de Vaca, Equiano describes a journey to the Americas. In what ways does his narrative resemble *La Relación?* Identify at least two similarities and two differences.

6. **Synthesize Information** Review your answers to the quiz about **slavery** that you took before reading Equiano's narrative. What facts or details in his account most surprised you? Correct your quiz answers to reflect what you learned.

● 7. **Evaluate a Slave Narrative** Some historians have questioned whether Equiano's narrative is authentic. Read the information on this debate in the author's biography on page 82. Based on the issues raised, what you have learned about slave narratives, and your own reading, make an argument for or against the historical value of Equiano's account. Support your answer with details.

Text Criticism

8. **Biographical Context** In 1775, just 14 years before writing his life story, Equiano bought slaves to work on his Central American plantation. He explained his actions by saying he did what he could "to comfort the poor creatures, and render their condition easy." Do you find this explanation consistent with the views of slavery put forth in *The Interesting Narrative?* Cite evidence from the text to support your answer.

> *What does it mean to be a* **SLAVE?**
>
> How does this personal account add to your understanding of slavery? Cite details from the text to support your response.

COMMON CORE

RI 1 Cite textual evidence to support analysis of what the text says explicitly. **RI 3** Analyze a complex set of ideas or sequence of events and explain how specific individuals, ideas, or events interact and develop over the course of the text. **RI 5** Analyze and evaluate the effectiveness of the structure an author uses in his or her exposition or argument, including whether the structure makes points clear, convincing, and engaging.

Practice and Apply

For preliminary support of post-reading questions, use these copy masters:

R RESOURCE MANAGER—Copy Masters
Reading Check p. 110
Slave Narrative p. 103
Question Support p. 111
Additional selection questions are provided for teachers on page 97.

ANSWERS COMMON CORE **RI 1, RI 3, RI 5**

1. *The Africans who captured Equiano brought him to the slave ship.*

2. *He believes he will be killed and eaten by the white men.*

3. *Slave traffickers are Christians in name only, not in their actions.*

Possible answers:

4. ■ **COMMON CORE FOCUS** *Analyze Descriptive Details the floggings Equiano received (lines 37–39); the conditions below deck (lines 75–90); the slaves committing suicide (lines 99–104); the way the slaves were sold (lines 105–113). These details appeal to readers' senses and enable them to visualize slavery's horrors.*

5. *Similarities: Both men encounter cultures that are unfamiliar to them. Both describe how they survive great hardships and show curiosity about their new environment. Differences: Cabeza de Vaca makes his journey as a conqueror and not a captive. He does not suffer the physical cruelty that Equiano suffers.*

6. *Accept all reasonable responses. Students should refer to specific quiz answers and cite specific facts or details from the selection.*

7. ● **COMMON CORE FOCUS** *Evaluate a Slave Narrative* **For:** *The account tells how slaves were treated and proves that slavery was wrong.* **Against:** *If he did not take the journey, the details may not be correct.*

---

8. *Yes, when he said this Equiano thought slavery was acceptable, but that slaves must be treated humanely. His narrative is more about the inhumane treatment of slaves than a criticism of slavery itself.*

> *What does it mean to be a* **SLAVE?** **Possible answer:** *This account shows slaves being treated like a piece of property without rights or freedoms. Equiano's description of confinement, floggings, and the auction conveyed the physical and emotional abuse slaves endured.*

ANSWERS
Vocabulary in Context

VOCABULARY PRACTICE

1. *(a) a sad expression*
2. *(b) a serious accident*
3. *(c) a 20-inch snowfall*
4. *(a) a contagious disease*
5. *(a) an attack of conscience*
6. *(c) a leader with no real power*

 **RESOURCE MANAGER—Copy Master**
Vocabulary Practice p. 108

ACADEMIC VOCABULARY IN SPEAKING

The narrative illustrates *the harsh conditions of slavery. Equaino's descriptions of the African captives' reactions* reveal *the horrifying nature of the experience of enslavement.*

VOCABULARY STRATEGY: SPANISH COGNATES

 COMMON CORE L 4d

- For each item, help students use their knowledge of the root and context clues to determine word meaning.
- Have students consider the spellings of the Spanish cognates to give them clues about the English meaning.

Possible answers:

1. *opportunidad; opportunity*
2. *categoria; category*
3. *estudiante; student*
4. *eficiente; efficient*

 **RESOURCE MANAGER—Copy Master**
Vocabulary Strategy p. 109

Interactive Vocabulary

Keywords direct students to a **WordSharp** tutorial on **thinkcentral.com** or to other types of vocabulary practice and review.

Vocabulary in Context

▲ **VOCABULARY PRACTICE**

Choose the letter of the phrase that defines or is related to the boldfaced word.

1. **countenance:** (a) a sad expression, (b) a well-toned body, (c) a cash register
2. **consternation:** (a) a freight ship, (b) a serious accident, (c) a peace treaty
3. **copious:** (a) a nest of baby birds, (b) a xerographic machine, (c) a 20-inch snowfall
4. **pestilential:** (a) a contagious disease, (b) a cooking implement, (c) a vegetarian meal
5. **scruple:** (a) an attack of conscience, (b) a two-handed card game, (c) a ruffle on a skirt
6. **nominal:** (a) a stretch limousine, (b) a word derived from a foreign language, (c) a leader with no real power

WORD LIST
consternation
copious
countenance
nominal
pestilential
scruple

ACADEMIC VOCABULARY IN SPEAKING

- document   • illustrate   • interpret   • promote   • reveal

Olaudah Equiano's narrative serves as an eloquent **document** on the inhumanity of slavery. With a small group of your peers, discuss the details of this narrative that most forcefully **illustrate** what slavery was like. Use at least one of the Academic Vocabulary words in your contribution to the discussion.

VOCABULARY STRATEGY: SPANISH COGNATES

Many words in the English language are related to words in other languages by descent from a common language. When these words have identical or similar spellings and meanings, they are called **cognates.** For example, the English word "accident" has the same meaning as "accidente" in Spanish. You can use your knowledge of cognates to determine the meaning of unfamiliar words.

PRACTICE Choose the Spanish cognate that you think completes the meaning of each sentence. Then write the word as it is spelled in English. Verify your answers by consulting a print or online dictionary.

- categoria   • eficiente   • secreto   • estudiante   • opportunidad

1. I would like the _____ to attend college in another state.
2. The national hurricane center assigns a number to a hurricane to identify its_____ .
3. My parents want me to be a good ____.
4. It is important to be _____ in your work.

COMMON CORE

L 4d Verify the preliminary determination of the meaning of a word.

Interactive Vocabulary THINK central

Go to thinkcentral.com.
KEYWORD: HML11-90

DIFFERENTIATED INSTRUCTION

FOR STRUGGLING READERS

Vocabulary Practice Clarify that not all of the choices are definitions of the boldfaced words. Some are examples. For example, *consternation* means "fear," and "a serious accident" could cause fear. *Copious* means "a large amount," and a "twenty-inch snowfall" is an example of a large amount.

FOR ADVANCED LEARNERS/AP

Vocabulary Strategy Have students brainstorm to write five additional sentences using the five cognates listed. Then, have students look up each corresponding English word in the dictionary to determine the words' origins.

Language

◆ **GRAMMAR AND STYLE:** Add Descriptive Details

Review the **Grammar and Style** note on page 87. Equiano uses elaborate and richly detailed sentences to describe his experiences. Some of the details are contained in **adverb clauses,** as in this example:

> *These filled me with astonishment, which was soon converted into terror, when I was carried on board.* (lines 2–4)

In this sentence, the adverb clause modifies *filled*, describing when the action occurred. Adverb clauses also help answer the questions *where, why, how,* or *to what degree.* Like other **subordinate clauses,** adverb clauses include a subject and a predicate, but they cannot stand alone as independent sentences. They are often introduced with words such as *as if, because, since, so that, until, while, when,* or *where.*

PRACTICE Add adverb clauses to the following sentences to modify the boldfaced words, as instructed in parentheses. A sample answer has been done for you.

EXAMPLE

He **saw** the ship for the first time. (Tell when he saw it.)

He saw the ship for the first time when he arrived at the harbor.

---

1. The men on the ship **had been captured.** (Tell why they were captured.)

2. The prisoners **were kept** in the ship's hold. (Tell how long they were kept there.)

3. Many slaves **became** ill. (Add two details. Tell why and when the slaves became ill.)

READING-WRITING CONNECTION

Expand your understanding of these excerpts from Equiano's narrative. Then use the **revising tips** to improve your journal entry.

WRITING PROMPT	REVISING TIPS
WRITE A PERSONAL ACCOUNT Equiano uses details to provide powerful first-person testimony. Choose an experience or a scene you want to describe. Write a **one-page account** to communicate the power of the experience. Include vivid details.	• Write in the first person, using the pronouns *I* or *me.* • Rely on vivid sensory details to capture the experience. • Describe the emotional impact of the experience. • Use adverbs to relate the sequence of events.

Interactive Revision **THINK**central

Go to **thinkcentral.com.**
KEYWORD: HML11-91

COMMON CORE

L 3 Apply knowledge of language to make effective choices for meaning or style. **L 3a** Vary syntax for effect. **W 3** Write narratives to develop real or imagined experiences or events using effective technique, well-chosen details, and well-structured event sequences. **W 3a, d** Engage and orient the reader by setting out a situation and its significance, establishing one point of view; create a smooth progression of experiences or events; use precise words and phrases, telling details, and sensory language to convey a vivid picture.

Language
 COMMON CORE **L 3, L 3a, W 3, W 3a, W 3d**

◆ **GRAMMAR AND STYLE**

Possible answers:

1. *The men on the ship had been captured **so that they could be sold as slaves.***

2. *The prisoners were kept in the ship's hold **until the ship reached its destination.***

3. ***Because conditions on the ship were so poor,** many slaves became ill **as they set sail.***

R RESOURCE MANAGER—Copy Master
Add Descriptive Details p. 112

(For more on using adverb clauses to add detail, see page R67 of the **Grammar Handbook.**)

READING-WRITING CONNECTION

Remind students that Equiano's excellent use of detailed descriptions allows readers to understand his experience. Encourage students to use an Observation Chart to explore vivid details of the experience or scene they want to convey in their letters.

💼 BEST PRACTICES TOOLKIT—Transparency
Observation Chart p. C7

Writing Online **THINK**central

The following tools are available online at **thinkcentral.com** and on **Write*Smart* CD-ROM:**
• **Interactive Graphic Organizers**
• **Interactive Student Models**
• **Interactive Revision Lessons**
For additional grammar instruction, see **GrammarNotes** on **thinkcentral.com.**

Assess and Reteach

Assess

DIAGNOSTIC AND SELECTION TESTS
Selection Test A pp. 41–42
Selection Test B/C pp. 43–44

Interactive Selection Test on **thinkcentral.com**

Reteach

Level Up Online Tutorials on **thinkcentral.com**

Reteaching Worksheets on **thinkcentral.com**
Reading Lesson 4: Recognizing Main Ideas and Details

FOR STRUGGLING WRITERS

Task Support: Writing Prompt

• Work with students to complete an Observation Chart. After they describe their experience or scene, help them identify descriptive words to convey it vividly.

• Urge students to identify their audience before they begin to write. This decision can help them choose the correct tone and words for their accounts.

• Be sure that students include at least two paragraphs in their accounts. Encourage them to exchange accounts and explain how the first-person narration affected the descriptions of an experience or scene.

Focus and Motivate

COMMON CORE FOCUS

RI 4 Determine the meaning of words and phrases as they are used in a text, including technical meanings. **RI 5** Analyze and evaluate the effectiveness of the structure an author uses in his or her exposition, including whether the structure makes points clear, convincing, and engaging. **RI 6** Determine an author's point of view or purpose in a text in which the rhetoric is particularly effective. **RI 10** Read and comprehend literary nonfiction. **L 3a** Apply an understanding of syntax to the study of complex texts. **L 4** Determine or clarify the meaning of unknown and multiple-meaning words and phrases. **L 4a, c–d** Use context as a clue to the meaning of a word or phrase; consult general and specialized reference materials, both print and digital, to clarify a word's precise meaning or its standard usage; verify the preliminary determination of the meaning of a word or phrase.

ABOUT THE AUTHOR

After students have read about John Smith, have them consider whether "boastful bully" or "early American hero" is a more apt description and to keep the question in mind as they read his narrative. Point out that the first Jamestown colonists dreamed of making easy fortunes by finding gold. Many were gentlemen unused to hard labor. Their arrival also coincided with a severe drought. As a result, about half the colonists died that first year.

NOTABLE QUOTE

"He that will not work shall not eat."
—John Smith

Selection Resources

DID YOU KNOW?

John Smith . . .

- coined the name "New England."
- offered to accompany the Pilgrims—who chose Miles Standish instead.
- wrote a how-to manual on establishing colonies.
- left the Jamestown colony after two years and never went back.

Exploration and the Early Settlers

from The General History of Virginia

Historical Narrative by John Smith

 Video link at thinkcentral.com

Meet the Author

John Smith c. 1580–1631

The author of one of the earliest works of American literature continues to inspire widely varied reactions among historians. Called a boastful bully by some and an early American hero by others, John Smith created a legend around himself that lasts to this day.

Great Adventures At age 16, Smith left England to become a soldier for hire and occasional pirate. In 1605, after traveling to Austria, Turkey, and North Africa, he returned to England. Smith's military experience made him a good leader in the eyes of the Virginia Company, the group of investors hoping for huge profits from their New World venture. They hired him to help run the Jamestown colony, where he arrived in 1607.

Struggles for Control Conflicts broke out in Jamestown almost immediately. The first president died and the next two were deposed; colonists mutinied and deserted the colony, living in the nearby woods. Smith took control of the colony in 1608. As he tells it, he focused on survival—safety, shelter, and food—and led forcefully, pushing settlers of all social levels to work as hard as he did. History tells us a slightly different story: Smith was nearly executed for the deaths of two colonists on an expedition he led. It also tells us, however, that Jamestown thrived under his command and fell into greed, chaos, and starvation after his departure in 1610.

Fact or Fiction? Shortly after arriving in Virginia, John Smith was captured by the Powhatan Indians. Smith writes several times of his 1607 capture and of being brought before the tribe's leader, Powhatan. Only in the final version, the 1624 *General History of Virginia,* does Smith mention his rescue by Powhatan's daughter Pocahontas, who would have been ten years old at the time. The story may have been an attempt by Smith to cash in on Pocahontas's later fame: she had visited England in 1616 and become a celebrity.

In the meantime, Smith had fallen on hard times. After one early success, his attempts to colonize New England were dismal failures. Smith wanted to prove that hard work was the smartest way to develop a colony, but he never got his chance. He made his living from tales of his adventurous life and died unemployed in London in 1631.

Author Online
Go to **thinkcentral.com**. KEYWORD: HML11-92

THINK central

92

TEXT ANALYSIS: NARRATOR

A **narrator** is the voice that tells a story. The voice an author chooses shapes the way readers perceive the events described. Most nonfiction authors write about themselves in the **first person.** John Smith writes about himself mostly in the **third person,** using a voice that sounds like an objective observer.

As you read, notice how Smith uses the narrator to portray himself and his role in events. Consider how the third-person point of view affects your perceptions of the account.

READING STRATEGY: READING OLDER TEXTS

Reading centuries-old texts can be challenging. Use these strategies as you read this selection:

- Simplify difficult **syntax** (word order) by paraphrasing. For a difficult sentence, first establish who is doing what. Then sort out the meaning in the phrases and clauses.
- Use footnotes or side notes to translate **archaic expressions,** words, and phrases no longer in use.
- Note the many contrasts between the historical map on page 95 and the features of current maps. These differences can help you to appreciate the challenges of Smith's text.

In this case, your purpose for reading is to make sense of the conflicts among the Jamestown colonists. Use a chart like the one shown to take notes about these key individuals.

Individuals	Connection to Smith	Actions
President Wingfield		
Captain Kendall		
Robinson and Emry		
George Cassen		

▲ VOCABULARY IN CONTEXT

Choose words from the list to complete the phrases below.

WORD LIST	depose	industry	mollify
	entreaty	interim	

1. a corrupt leader whom they voted to _____
2. a peacemaker trying to _____ the unruly crowd
3. a desperate _____ for our assistance
4. admired by coworkers for her _____

 Complete the activities in your **Reader/Writer Notebook.**

What makes a LEADER?

In some societies, like 17th-century Britain, leaders were chosen on the basis of their social status. But men used to luxury and privilege didn't thrive in the Jamestown colony, where hard work and scarce supplies were facts of daily life. In this context, where leaders needed common sense and determination to succeed, a new standard of leadership emerged.

DISCUSS Working with a small group, brainstorm examples of strong leaders who demonstrate different leadership styles. Use your examples to debate the pros and cons of each style. Is any one style best in all situations?

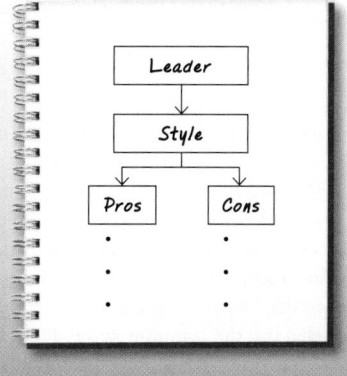

93

Teach

What makes a LEADER?

Introduce the question and discuss specific qualities that are helpful for effective leadership. Extend the *DISCUSS* activity by asking them which qualities are essential for any leader in any situation.

TEXT ANALYSIS
COMMON CORE RI 5 RI 6

● *Model the Skill:* **NARRATOR**

Point out to students how the narrator's voice shapes the story by having them identify the differences in tone in these two statements:

1. Captain Brown employed strict discipline and economy to lead his expedition through the hard winter.

2. I was forced to employ strict discipline and economy to lead this expedition through that hard winter.

Ask students which statement seems more objective and which seems more immediate. ***Possible answer:*** *Statement 1 seems more objective because the narrator speaks in the third person. Statement 2 seems more immediate because the narrator speaks in the first person.*

GUIDED PRACTICE Ask students to write a statement by a narrator describing his own experience in Brown's expedition.

READING STRATEGY
COMMON CORE RI 4 L 3a

■ *Model the Skill:* **READING OLDER TEXTS**

Assist students in using textual tools when reading older texts by previewing the text together. Point out the footnotes and side notes that translate archaic language and paraphrase difficult syntax, as well as the questions that focus on important aspects of the narrative as an "older text."

R **RESOURCE MANAGER—Copy Master**
Reading Older Texts p. 125 (for student use while reading the selection)

VOCABULARY SKILL
COMMON CORE L 4

▲ VOCABULARY IN CONTEXT

DIAGNOSE WORD KNOWLEDGE Have students complete Vocabulary in Context. Check their word choices against the following:

depose (dĭ-pōz′) *v.* to remove from rule
entreaty (ĕn-trē′tē) *n.* plea
industry (ĭn′də-strē) *n.* hard work; diligence
interim (ĭn′tər-ĭm) *n.* period in between; interval

mollify (mŏl′ə-fī′) *v.* to soothe; to reduce in intensity

PRETEACH VOCABULARY Use the copy master to help students predict meanings.

R **RESOURCE MANAGER—Copy Master**
Vocabulary Study p. 127

SUMMARY

This excerpt from John Smith's historical narrative describes Jamestown colony's struggle for survival and Smith's leadership conflicts. Smith is captured by the Powhatan Indians, but Chief Powhatan's daughter Pocahontas saves him from execution. Powhatan gives Smith control of a village in return for cannons and a millstone. In Jamestown, Smith is accused of causing two men's deaths, but his authority is strengthened.

READ WITH A PURPOSE

Have students read this historical narrative to discover how John Smith overcame conflicts to secure the success of the Virginia colony.

Analyze Visuals

Activity Have students view the geographical features and compare their accuracy to the other features of the map. *Possible answer: The sea monster and the wrecked, partially submerged ships do not seem realistic. These features represent dangers that the artist likely created to add drama to his engraving.*

READING STRATEGY

COMMON CORE
RI 4
L 3a

A *Model the Skill:*
OLDER TEXTS

Have students reread lines 8–12. Point out that Smith compares the settlers' starvation with the president's gluttony. Have students complete the first row of the prereading chart on page 93.

Possible answer: If we'd been as free from every sin as we were from gluttony and drunkenness, we could have been declared saints, but not our president, because he took oatmeal, wine, oil, brandy, eggs—everything but the common food supply—for his own use. He points out that the president's greediness is making them suffer.

THE GENERAL HISTORY OF VIRGINIA

John Smith

BACKGROUND The Jamestown colony was modeled after a military expedition, transplanting about 100 hardy men into the Virginia wilderness in May 1607. Five members of Jamestown's ruling council—Edward Wingfield, Bartholomew Gosnold, John Ratcliffe, George Kendall, and John Smith—soon found themselves wrestling for control of the colony. As Smith's account opens, the colonists' ships have returned to England for supplies, leaving the men to survive on their own.

Analyze Visuals ▶
You need no caption to know the **map** on the opposite page is very old. Notice two important ways it differs from current maps. First, it includes clearly **historical details** such as sailing ships and bows and arrows. Second, the map lacks proportion. The ships, for example, are **out of scale**. They are huge by comparison with the harbor and the islands. What additional non-standard, out-of-proportion map details can you identify?

The Struggle for Jamestown

Being thus left to our fortunes, it fortuned that within ten days, scarce ten amongst us could either go or well stand, such extreme weakness and sickness oppressed us. And thereat none need marvel if they consider the cause and reason which was this: While the ships stayed, our allowance was somewhat bettered by a daily proportion of biscuit which the sailors would pilfer to sell, give, or exchange with us for money, sassafras, furs, or love. But when they departed, there remained neither tavern, beer-house, nor place of relief but the common kettle. Had we been as free from all sins as [we were free from] gluttony and drunkenness we might have been canonized
10 for saints, but our President [Edward Wingfield] would never have been admitted for engrossing to his private, oatmeal, sack, oil, aqua vitae, beef, eggs, or what not but the kettle; that indeed he allowed equally to be distributed, and that was half a pint of wheat and as much barley boiled with water for a man a day, and this, having fried some twenty-six weeks in the ship's hold, contained as many worms as grains so that we might truly call it rather so much bran than corn; our drink was water, our lodgings castles in the air. **A**

① Targeted Passage

8 common kettle: food that was available to everyone.

11 engrossing to his private: taking for his private use; **sack:** wine; **aqua vitae:** brandy.

A OLDER TEXTS
Using the side notes, restate lines 8–12 in modern English. What joke is Smith making?

Arrival of the English in Virginia (1585–1588), Theodore de Bry. Engraving © Giraudon/Art Resource, New York.

DIFFERENTIATED INSTRUCTION

FOR ENGLISH LANGUAGE LEARNERS

Vocabulary Support Use Word Squares to teach these words: *proportion* (line 5), *sufficient* (line 20), *authority* (line 49), *conclude* (line 57), *aid* (line 87)

BEST PRACTICES TOOLKIT—Transparency Word Squares p. E10

FOR STRUGGLING READERS

In combination with the *Audio Anthology CD*, use one or more Targeted Passages (pp. 94, 96, 98, 99) to ensure that students focus on key events and concepts. Targeted Passages are also good for English learners.

① Targeted Passage [Lines 1–8]

This passage establishes the dire situation faced by the new Jamestown settlers.

Pasquenoke

Dasamonquepeuc

Roanoac

Trinety harbor

About the Art In 1590 the Flemish publisher and engraver Theodore de Bry (1528–1598) illustrated a natural history of Virginia by Thomas Hariot, a member of Sir Walter Raleigh's expedition to Roanoke, Virginia, in 1585. De Bry's engraving, *Arrival of the English in Virginia,* appears in Hariot's book, *A Briefe and True Report of the New Found Land of Virginia.*

BACKGROUND

Algonquian Neighbors The Jamestown settlers would never have survived the grim conditions John Smith describes if not for their Native American neighbors. The Powhatan Confederacy, a group of six Algonquian tribes under Powhatan's authority, traded corn and other food to the starving settlers in return for copper and iron implements. Over time, however, cultural differences led to misunderstanding and conflict.

- What is the condition of the men who stay in Jamestown after the ships return to England? (lines 1–3)

- How much time has passed since the ships left? (lines 1–3)

- Why was the men's condition better while the ships were there? (lines 4–8)

FOR ADVANCED LEARNERS/AP

Make Judgments Ask students to discuss the differences between good leaders and average ones. Have students think about what would constitute a staid, uninventive type of leadership, and how an innovative leader might act. Encourage students to compare and contrast the problems facing John Smith with those encountered by present-day leaders.

B OLDER TEXTS

Possible answer: *The pronoun* his *in line 27 refers to Smith, who heals Martin and Ratcliffe.*

IF STUDENTS NEED HELP... Point out Smith's name at the beginning of the sentence, followed by the pronoun *his*. Have students reread the sentence, substituting *Smith's* for *his*.

C *Model the Skill:* NARRATOR

Tell students that the narrator's voice shapes a story. Read aloud lines 37–41, substituting *me* for *Captain Smith* (line 37), *my* for *his* (lines 37 and 40) and *myself* for *himself* (lines 39 and 41). Discuss how the more personal tone affects the narrator's credibility.

Possible answer: *Expressed in the third person, Smith's claims sound like the observations of a neutral third party; if he had written the account in the first person, his claims would have appeared boastful.*

Extend the Discussion How reliable is John Smith's account of his own rise to power? Which details should the reader be skeptical about?

OWN THE WORD

- **depose** Point out that the Latin *deponere* means "to lay aside." Discuss how a person removed from office is "moved aside" from authority.

- **industry** *Industry* indicates hard work. Ask students to think of antonyms for *industry*. *Possible answer:* Idleness, laziness, *and* leisure *all mean the opposite of* industry.

- **interim** Ask students for examples of when they experience an *interim* or interval. *Possible answers:* Summer vacation is *an* interim *in the school year. Half-time is an* interim *in a ball game.*

With this lodging and diet, our extreme toil in bearing and planting palisades so strained and bruised us and our continual labor in the extremity 20 of the heat had so weakened us, as were cause sufficient to have made us as miserable in our native country or any other place in the world.

From May to September, those that escaped lived upon sturgeon and sea crabs. Fifty in this time we buried; the rest seeing the President's projects to escape these miseries in our pinnace by flight (who all this time had neither felt want nor sickness) so moved our dead spirits as we **deposed** him and established Ratcliffe in his place (Gosnold being dead), Kendall deposed. Smith newly recovered, Martin and Ratcliffe were by his care preserved and relieved, and the most of the soldiers recovered with the skillful diligence of Master Thomas Wotton our surgeon general. B

30 But now was all our provision spent, the sturgeon gone, all helps abandoned, each hour expecting the fury of the savages, when God, the patron of all good endeavors, in that desperate extremity so changed the hearts of the savages that they brought such plenty of their fruits and provision as no man wanted.

The new President [Ratcliffe] and Martin, being little beloved, of weak judgment in dangers, and less **industry** in peace, committed the managing of all things abroad to Captain Smith, who, by his own example, good words, and fair promises, set some to mow, others to bind thatch, some to build houses, others to thatch them, himself always bearing the greatest task 40 for his own share, so that in short time he provided most of them lodgings, neglecting any for himself. . . . C

A Surprise Attack

Smith, perceiving (notwithstanding their late misery) not any regarded but from hand to mouth, (the company being well recovered) caused the pinnace to be provided with things fitting to get provision for the year following, but in the **interim** he made three or four journeys and discovered the people of Chickahominy, yet what he carefully provided the rest carelessly spent.

Wingfield and Kendall, living in disgrace strengthened themselves with the sailors and other confederates to regain their former credit and authority, 50 or at least such means aboard the pinnace (being fitted to sail as Smith had appointed for trade), to alter her course and to go for England.

Smith, unexpectedly returning, had the plot discovered to him, much trouble he had to prevent it, till with the store of saker and musket shot he forced them [to] stay or sink in the river: which action cost the life of Captain Kendall.

These brawls are so disgustful, as some will say they are better forgotten, yet all men of good judgment will conclude it were better their baseness should be manifest to the world, than the business bear the scorn and shame of their excused disorders.

19 palisades: walls made of tall, pointed wooden stakes.

24 pinnace: a small sailing ship.

depose (dĭ-pōz') *v.* to remove from rule

B OLDER TEXTS

Reread lines 27–28. **Clarify** the pronoun referent for the word *his* in line 27. Who is responsible for healing Martin and Ratcliffe?

industry (ĭn'də-strē) *n.* hard work; diligence

37 abroad: outside the palisades.

C NARRATOR

Reread lines 35–41. Do Smith's claims sound more or less credible than they would if stated by a **first-person narrator**? Give reasons for your answer.

interim (ĭn'tər-ĭm) *n.* period in between; interval

46 Chickahominy (chĭ'kə-hä'mə-nē): a river in Virginia.

2

52 discovered: revealed.
53 saker: cannon shot.

55 Captain Kendall: Kendall was executed for mutiny in 1607.

57–59 it were ...disorders: It is better to reveal the troublemakers than to have the "business" of the colony get a bad name.

DIFFERENTIATED INSTRUCTION

FOR STRUGGLING READERS

2 Targeted Passage [Lines 42–59]

This passage describes a plot against Smith and Smith's response.

- What is Smith doing while Wingfield and Kendall are plotting against him? (lines 45–46)

- What does Smith do when he discovers the plot? (lines 53–54)

- What happens to Kendall? (lines 54–55)

FOR ENGLISH LANGUAGE LEARNERS

Vocabulary: Outdated Forms Point out examples of words that are now outdated or used differently today from the way they were used 400 years ago. Ask students to use a dictionary to find and apply current meanings for these words to the selection context: *fair* (line 38), "hopeful"; *asunder* (line 76), "into pieces"; *dolefulest* (line 119), "most terrible"; *quartered* (line 125), "stayed in"; *betimes* (line 129), "early"; *hath* (line 156), "has."

Illustration of Jamestown Fort, Virginia, about 1608. Getty Images.

60   The President and Captain Archer not long after intended also to have abandoned the country, which project also was curbed and suppressed by Smith.

   The Spaniard never more greedily desired gold than he [Smith] victual, nor his soldiers more to abandon the country than he to keep it. But [he found] plenty of corn in the river of Chickahominy, where hundreds of savages in divers places stood with baskets expecting his coming.

   And now the winter approaching, the rivers became so covered with swans, geese, ducks, and cranes that we daily feasted with good bread, Virginia peas, pumpkins, and putchamins, fish, fowl, and divers sort of wild
70 beasts as fast as we could eat them, so that none of our tuftaffety humorists desired to go for England.

   But our comedies never endured long without a tragedy, some idle exceptions being muttered against Captain Smith for not discovering the head of Chickahominy river and [he being] taxed by the Council to be too slow in so worthy an attempt. The next voyage he proceeded so far that with much labor by cutting of trees asunder he made his passage, but when his barge could pass no farther, he left her in a broad bay of danger of shot, commanding none should go ashore till his return, himself with two English and two savages went up higher in a canoe, but he was not long absent but
80 his men went ashore, whose want of government gave both occasion and opportunity to the savages to surprise one George Cassen whom they slew and much failed not to have cut off the boat and all the rest.

60 Captain Archer: Gabriel Archer had abandoned the colony and then returned. He did not support Smith.

63 victual: food.

69 putchamins: persimmons.
70 tuftaffety humorists: unreliable lace-wearers.

73 exceptions: objections.

80–82 whose want . . . the rest: the men's lack of discipline in going ashore led to the surprise attack on Cassen; only by some failure on the attackers' side did the others survive.

Analyze Visuals

Activity Ask students what this illustration of Jamestown Fort around the time of its founding shows about the conditions of the settlement. Does it support the information in John Smith's account? *Possible answer: The illustration shows that the fort was small, isolated, and primitive. It supports John Smith's account of the harsh conditions encountered by the colonists.*

TIERED DISCUSSION PROMPTS

Refer to lines 60–82 and these prompts to help students understand John Smith's ongoing challenges:

Connect How do you respond when people criticize you or oppose your ideas? *Accept all thoughtful answers.*

Interpret What seems to be John Smith's main problem in getting the settlement to run smoothly? Why are there mutterings against him? *Possible answer: Several members of the colony are vying for more power and trying to remove Smith from office; they hinder his cause through plots to undermine him or failure to obey his orders. Their mutterings are criticisms that grow out of their desire to question Smith's authority and methods (lines 60–62, 72–75).*

Evaluate How believable is Smith's suggestion that he was unfairly blamed for not finding the head of the Chickahominy and was responsible for George Cassen's death? *Some students may say that Smith's explanation is plausible. Others may argue that he showed a lack of leadership and foresight in both cases and is reacting defensively.*

FOR STRUGGLING READERS

Develop Reading Fluency To help students develop skills in reading phrases seamlessly, mark up lines 72–82, breaking each sentence into phrases. Write the marked-up lines on the board or distribute marked-up copies to the class. Then read the lines aloud for students, emphasizing appropriate phrasing. Have students read the lines aloud as a choral read.

Ⓓ NARRATOR

Possible answer: *The narrator (Smith) includes these details to exonerate himself: He has no idea that his men were attacked, as he is 20 miles away hunting for food to supply the fort (lines 83–84); Smith himself is attacked by an overwhelming force of 200 Native Americans (line 86); during this heroic struggle, he is wounded and taken prisoner (lines 87–90).*

IF STUDENTS NEED HELP . . . Clarify lines 84–85: Smith means that he assumes the two men were slain while sleeping by the canoes, not that he ordered them to be slain.

TIERED DISCUSSION PROMPTS

In lines 92–123, use these prompts to help students understand how John Smith intended the scene at Powhatan's court to affect readers:

Summarize What happens to Smith after he is taken prisoner? ***Possible answer:*** *Smith's captors take him to Powhatan, their chief (lines 91–92). They let him wash his hands and eat (lines 101–104).*

Analyze How does Smith present himself to the reader in this scene? ***Possible answer:*** *Smith presents himself as a strong leader who can calmly survive a harrowing ordeal and still effectively deal with the Powhatans.*

Evaluate Thus far, do you think Smith's account is realistic? Explain. ***Possible answer:*** *Smith's details and his survival support this account. Others may say that Smith shows himself so positively that the story is suspect.*

OWN THE WORD

- **entreaty:** Have students create a semantic map for the word *entreaty*.

Write the word in a center circle, and add the definition given. Draw spider legs from the center and have students add synonyms to complete the map. ***Possible answers:*** *request, appeal, beg*

Smith little dreaming of that accident, being got to the marshes at the river's head twenty miles in the desert, had his two men [Robinson and Emry] slain (as is supposed) sleeping by the canoe, while himself by fowling sought them victual, who finding he was beset with 200 savages, two of them he slew, still defending himself with the aid of the savage his guide, whom he bound to his arms with his garters and used him as a buckler, yet he was shot in his thigh a little, and had many arrows that stuck in his
90 clothes but no great hurt, till at last they took him prisoner. . . . Ⓓ

At Powhatan's Court

At last they brought him to Werowocomoco, where was Powhatan, their Emperor. Here more than two hundred of those grim courtiers stood wondering at him, as [if] he had been a monster, till Powhatan and his train had put themselves in their greatest braveries. Before a fire upon a seat like a bedstead, he sat covered with a great robe made of raccoon skins and all the tails hanging by. On either hand did sit a young wench of sixteen or eighteen years and along on each side [of] the house, two rows of men and behind them as many women, with all their heads and shoulders painted red, many of their heads bedecked with the white down of birds, but every
100 one with something, and a great chain of white beads around their necks.

> At his entrance before the King, all the people gave a great shout. The Queen of Appomattoc was appointed to bring him water to wash his hands, and another brought him a bunch of feathers, instead of a towel, to dry them; having feasted him after their best barbarous manner they could, a long consultation was held, but the conclusion was, two great stones were brought before Powhatan; then as many as could, laid hands on him, dragged him to them, and thereon laid his head and being ready with their clubs to beat out his brains, Pocahontas, the King's dearest daughter, when no **entreaty** could prevail, got his head in her arms and laid her own upon
> 110 his to save him from death, whereat the Emperor was contended he should live to make him hatchets, and her bells, beads, and copper, for they thought him as well of all occupations as themselves. For the King himself will make his own robes, shoes, bows, arrows, pots; plant, hunt, or do anything so well as the rest.

Two days after, Powhatan, having disguised himself in the most fearfulest manner he could, caused Captain Smith to be brought forth to a great house in the woods and there upon a mat by the fire to be left alone. Not long after, from behind a mat that divided the house, was made the most dolefulest noise he ever heard; then Powhatan more like a devil than a man,
120 with some two hundred more as black as himself, came unto him and told him now that they were friends, and presently he should go to Jamestown to send him two great guns and a grindstone for which he would give him the country of Capahowasic and forever esteem him as his son Nantaquoud.

So to Jamestown with twelve guides Powhatan sent him. That night they quartered in the woods, he still expecting (as he had done all this long time of his imprisonment) every hour to be put to one death or other, for all

84 desert: wilderness; **85–86 by fowling . . . victual:** hunted birds to find them food.

88 garters: shirtlaces; **buckler:** shield.

Ⓓ NARRATOR
Reread lines 83–90. What details does the narrator include that suggest Smith is not responsible for the deaths of the two men?

94 greatest braveries: fanciest clothes.

102 the Queen of Appomattoc (ăp′ə-măt′ək): the leader of the nearby village of Appomattoc.

❸ Targeted Passage

entreaty (ĕn-trē′tē) *n.* plea

112 as well . . . themselves: The Indians thought Smith had varied skills as they did.

122–123 the country of Capahowasic (căp′ə-hou′ə-sĭk′) . . . **Nantaquoud** (nŏn′tə-kwōōd′): Powhatan would give Smith control of a nearby village and also promised to think as highly of him as he did of his own son.

DIFFERENTIATED INSTRUCTION

FOR STRUGGLING READERS

❸ Targeted Passage [Lines 101–114]

This passage describes John Smith's imprisonment by the Powhatans and rescue by Pocahontas.

- What happens to Smith right after he is brought to see the king? (lines 101–103)

- Why do the Powhatans bring out two huge rocks? (lines 105–108)

- Who saves Smith's life? How? (lines 108–110)

FOR ENGLISH LANGUAGE LEARNERS

Vocabulary: Multiple-Meaning Words

Remind students that some words have more than one meaning in English. Ask volunteers to suggest different meanings for the word *down*. Then refer them to its use in line 99. Help students use context clues to define *down* as "the soft, fluffy under-feathers of birds." Repeat this procedure with *plenty* (line 150), "abundance or bounty"; and *crossed* (line 154), "obstructed or interfered with."

their feasting. But almighty God (by His divine providence) had **mollified** the hearts of those stern barbarians with compassion. The next morning betimes they came to the fort, where Smith having used the savages with
130 what kindness he could, he showed Rawhunt, Powhatan's trusty servant, two demi-culverins and a millstone to carry [to] Powhatan; they found them somewhat too heavy, but when they did see him discharge them, being loaded with stones, among the boughs of a great tree loaded with icicles, the ice and branches came so tumbling down that the poor savages ran away half dead with fear. But at last we regained some conference with them and gave them such toys and sent to Powhatan, his women, and children such presents as gave them in general full content. **E**

Now in Jamestown they were all combustion, the strongest preparing once more to run away with the pinnace; which, with the hazard of his life,
140 with saker falcon and musket shot, Smith forced now the third time to stay or sink.

Some, no better than they should be, had plotted with the President the next day to have him put to death by the Levitical law, for the lives of Robinson and Emry; pretending the fault was his that had led them to their ends; but he quickly took such order with such lawyers that he laid them by the heels till he sent some of them prisoners for England.

Now every once in four or five days, Pocahontas with her attendants brought him so much provision that saved many of their lives, that else for all this had starved with hunger.

150 His relation of the plenty he had seen, especially at Werowocomoco, and of the state and bounty of Powhatan (which till that time was unknown), so revived their dead spirits (especially the love of Pocahontas) as all men's fear was abandoned.

Thus you may see what difficulties still crossed any good endeavor; and the good success of the business being thus oft brought to the very period of destruction; yet you see by what strange means God hath still delivered it. ∾

THEME AND GENRE
In his historical narrative of adventure and adversity in Jamestown, Smith creates an almost mythic self-portrait of a strong and successful leader. The 2005 film *The New World* offers a different portrayal and shows Smith arriving in America as a prisoner in chains. What other 21st-century films, novels, or plays about a historical subject reexamine the facts and give a new twist to an old story?

---

mollify (mŏl′ə-fī′) *v.* to soothe; to reduce in intensity

131 **demi-culverins** (dĕm′ē-kŭl′vər-ĭnz): large cannons.

E OLDER TEXTS
Reread lines 128–137. What inferences can you make about how Europeans of the time viewed Native Americans? How does the map on page 95 reflect this view?

143 **Levitical law:** According to the Book of Leviticus in the Bible, "He that killeth any man shall surely be put to death."

Language Coach
Synonyms and Antonyms
Plenty and *bounty* (lines 150 and 151) are **synonyms,** words with similar meanings. What are their meanings? *Lack* is an **antonym** of *plenty* and *bounty:* It means the opposite of *plenty* and *bounty.* Define *lack.* What have the colonists experienced a lack of?

FOR STRUGGLING READERS

④ **Targeted Passage** [Lines 138–156]
This passage concludes the narrative by showing additional challenges Smith faces after his harrowing return to Jamestown.

- What new difficulty does Smith face upon his return to Jamestown? (lines 142–144)
- What was the result of the plot against Smith? (lines 145–146)

FOR ENGLISH LANGUAGE LEARNERS

Language Coach
Synonyms and Antonyms
Read lines 150–153 aloud. Ask students what Powhatan's people have that Smith's people do not. *Possible answers:* Plenty *and* bounty *mean that there is an abundance of goods.* Lack *means that there is not enough to go around. The colonists have lacked food.*

E OLDER TEXTS
Possible answer: *The Europeans of the time viewed Native Americans as uncultured savages. The map shows the Native Americans living in villages instead of towns or cities.*

REVISIT THE BIG QUESTION

What makes a
LEADER?

In lines 138–149, what **leadership** qualities does Smith project in this passage? ***Possible answer:*** *Smith projects presence of mind, determination, and strength by disproving the charges against him and even imprisoning some of his accusers.*

VOCABULARY   COMMON CORE   L 4

OWN THE WORD

mollify: Ask students to list additional reasons why someone might mollify a person. ***Possible answers:*** *to soothe over disappointment, to end a quarrel, to smooth hurt feelings*

THEME AND GENRE

Have students discuss examples of novels, plays, or films that explore historical events or people. Ask them whether they think new interpretations of history are of value to people today.

SELECTION WRAP–UP

READ WITH A PURPOSE Now that students have read the selection, have them analyze Smith's leadership abilities. What qualities make John Smith a successful leader? ***Possible answer:*** *Smith is able to make lasting alliances with important leaders, such as Powhatan. He maintains his authority and can make difficult decisions, such as executing those who challenge him.*

INDEPENDENT READING

Students may wish to read *The Journals of Captain Smith: A Jamestown Biography* by John Thompson, John Smith, published by National Geographic.

Practice and Apply

For preliminary support of post-reading questions, use these copy masters:

R RESOURCE MANAGER—Copy Masters
Reading Check p. 130
Narrator p. 123
Question Support p. 131
Additional selection questions are provided for teachers on page 117.

ANSWERS ·····COMMON CORE····· RI 4, RI 5, RI 6, RI 10, L 3a

1. *The Jamestown colonists have deposed the previous president.*

2. *Kendall tries to steal the colony's ship and sail for England.*

3. *Smith is attacked by Powhatan Indians while exploring the Chickahominy River.*

4. *Smith is sentenced to death but saved by Pocahontas's intervention. A ceremony confirms him as Powhatan's ally.*

Possible answers:

5. ■ **COMMON CORE FOCUS** *Interpret Older Texts Smith has a motive to portray Wingfield as corrupt and incompetent because Smith helped depose him (line 25). Smith's actions get Kendall, Cassen, Robinson, and Emry killed, actions that he justifies to clear his name (lines 52–59, 80–85).*

6. *Monarchs rule Smith's England and other European countries. He assumes that all cultures are like his own.*

7. ***Smith's Version:** He is not responsible for George Cassen's death because he told his men to stay put. They disobeyed, inviting attack. He is not responsible for Robinson's and Emry's deaths. They were slain because they fell asleep. Smith fought 200 warriors before his capture.* **Accusations Against Him:** *Smith failed to find the head of the river. He is at fault in the deaths of Cassen, Robinson, and Emry because he left them vulnerable.*

Comprehension

1. **Recall** Why does Ratcliffe become the leader of Jamestown?

2. **Recall** What leads to the killing of Captain Kendall?

3. **Clarify** How does Smith become Powhatan's captive?

4. **Summarize** What happens to Smith during his stay with Powhatan?

Text Analysis

● 5. **Interpret Older Texts** Review the character chart you made. Consider Smith's connection to each character. What motives might have influenced Smith's portrayal of his fellow colonists? Cite details to support your answer.

6. **Make Inferences About Historical Context** How does the map on page 95 lend to your understanding of John Smith and the events he narrates in this selection? Support your answer with features and details on the map that differ from features and details on current-day maps.

7. **Examine a Historical Narrative** Smith's account of his explorations along the Chickahominy River is filled with details that suggest he is a hero. But if you read closely, he reveals that he was severely criticized for the way he performed. Reread lines 72–90, and record the conflicting information in a chart like the one shown. What accusations is Smith defending himself against?

Smith's Version	Accusations Against Him

● 8. **Evaluate Narrator** Consider Smith's use of **third-person point of view** as well as the **motives** that influenced his writing. Given these factors, is Smith a credible narrator? Evaluate the reliability of Smith's narrative as a source on the following topics. Give reasons for your answers.

- daily life in Jamestown
- Native American culture
- Smith's own actions
- conflicts in Jamestown

Text Criticism

9. **Different Perspectives** If Wingfield had written a report, how might it have differed from Smith's description of these events? Cite details to support your answer.

> *What makes a* **LEADER?**
> What qualities of leadership does John Smith reveal in this selection? Cite evidence from the text to support your answer.

COMMON CORE

RI 4 Determine the meaning of words and phrases as they are used in a text, including technical meanings. **RI 5** Analyze and evaluate the effectiveness of the structure an author uses in his or her exposition, including whether the structure makes points clear, convincing, and engaging. **RI 6** Determine an author's point of view or purpose in a text in which the rhetoric is particularly effective. **RI 10** Read and comprehend literary nonfiction. **L 3a** Apply an understanding of syntax to the study of complex texts when reading.

---

8. ● **COMMON CORE FOCUS** *Evaluate Narrator The details of Jamestown life and Native American culture are probably credible, as Smith has no motive to lie. Smith's reliability as narrator is suspect when retelling his own actions or conflicts in Jamestown. His statements are self-serving: to show his merits as a leader and assert his innocence in the face of accusations.*

9. *Wingfield's report would highlight his own good efforts and diminish or criticize Smith's. He might offer a different account of the distribution of supplies (lines 11–12), his intention to flee (lines 24, 49–50), and Smith's characterization of mutiny.*

> *What makes a* LEADER? Ask students to think about how Smith's perseverance and courage show leadership. How do they feel most people would respond in the face of adversity and threatening circumstances?

Vocabulary in Context

▲ VOCABULARY PRACTICE

Decide whether the words in each pair are synonyms or antonyms.

1. depose/appoint
2. interim/gap
3. mollify/anger
4. industry/diligence
5. entreaty/plea

WORD LIST
depose
entreaty
industry
interim
mollify

ACADEMIC VOCABULARY IN WRITING

- document
- illustrate
- interpret
- promote
- reveal

Write a short paragraph to **illustrate** the conflict that sprang up among members of Smith's expedition. Use details to **document** your observations. Include at least two Academic Vocabulary words in your paragraph.

VOCABULARY STRATEGY: MULTIPLE MEANINGS

Many words have more than one meaning. To make sense of what you read, you need to make sure you understand which meaning a writer intends. This is particularly true with words that are used as more than one part of speech, or with words that occur in older texts. For example, the noun *industry* usually refers to a specific branch of manufacture or trade. Smith uses it to mean "dedication to a task." As you read authors such as Smith, be alert to the nuances of meaning in the words they use. If you encounter an unfamiliar word or a familiar word in an unfamiliar setting, examine the **context**—the surrounding words, phrases, and sentences—for clues to the writer's meaning.

PRACTICE Determine the meaning of each boldfaced word as it is used in the sentence. Consult a print or online dictionary if you need to.

1. Was John Smith a **contemporary** of Olaudah Equiano?
2. The **gravity** of the situation required the presence of several police officers.
3. What **accommodations** have the two leaders managed to reach?
4. The governor intends to **commute** several prisoners' sentences.
5. At this point we cannot **countenance** any more delays.
6. The hotel employees **agitated** for better working conditions.

COMMON CORE

L 4 Determine or clarify the meaning of unknown and multiple-meaning words and phrases. **L 4a, c–d** Use context as a clue to the meaning of a word or phrase; consult general and specialized reference materials, both print and digital, to clarify a word's precise meaning or its standard usage; verify the preliminary determination of the meaning of a word or phrase.

Interactive Vocabulary

Go to **thinkcentral.com**.
KEYWORD: HML11-101

DIFFERENTIATED INSTRUCTION

FOR ENGLISH LANGUAGE LEARNERS

Task Support: Vocabulary Practice Remind students that synonyms are words that have the same or almost the same meanings. Antonyms are words that have opposite meanings. Refer students back to the prereading vocabulary activity on page 93. Have them try to put both words in each pair into the context sentence. Explain that if both words in a pair fit the context, they are synonyms. If only one fits, the words are antonyms.

FOR STRUGGLING WRITERS

Vocabulary in Writing Have students review the selection and write a paragraph using vocabulary from the word list to describe the aspects they found most interesting.

ANSWERS

Vocabulary in Context

VOCABULARY PRACTICE

1. *antonyms*
2. *synonyms*
3. *antonyms*
4. *synonyms*
5. *synonyms*

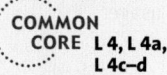 **RESOURCE MANAGER**—Copy Master
Vocabulary Practice p. 128

ACADEMIC VOCABULARY IN WRITING

The colonists' hard work and lack of food helps to *illustrate* the hard feelings between the members of the expedition.

VOCABULARY STRATEGY: MULTIPLE MEANINGS

COMMON CORE L 4, L 4a, L 4c–d

Point out to students that with multiple-meaning words, they have to use their judgment to determine which meaning is correct. Suggest that students follow these steps: Substitute the meaning you think fits. Ask whether that meaning makes sense. If not, try substituting another meaning.

Possible answers:

1. *person who lived at the same time*
2. *seriousness*
3. *reconciliation of differences; settlement*
4. *change to something less severe*
5. *approve of; tolerate*
6. *attempted to arouse public feeling*

 **RESOURCE MANAGER**—Copy Master
Vocabulary Strategy p. 129

Interactive Vocabulary THINK central

Keywords direct students to a **WordSharp** tutorial on **thinkcentral.com** or to other types of vocabulary practice and review.

Assess and Reteach

Assess

DIAGNOSTIC AND SELECTION TESTS
Selection Test A, B/C pp. 45–46, 47-48

Reteach

Level Up Online Tutorials on **thinkcentral.com**

Focus and Motivate

COMMON CORE FOCUS

RI 1 Cite textual evidence to support analysis of what the text says explicitly as well as inferences drawn from the text, including determining where the text leaves matters uncertain. **RI 2** Determine two or more central ideas of a text and analyze their development over the course of the text, including how they interact and build on one another to provide a complex analysis; provide an objective summary of the text. **RI 9** Analyze seventeenth-century foundational U.S. documents of historical and literary significance for their themes, purposes, and rhetorical features. **L 4c** Consult general and specialized reference materials, both print and digital, to determine or clarify a word's precise meaning, its etymology, or its standard usage.

ABOUT THE AUTHOR

Before students read about William Bradford, tell them that his religious devotion deeply inspired his actions and writing. During reading, help them connect this devotion and the traits Bradford showed as a young man—determination, idealism, independence, and zeal—with his ability to lead in adulthood. As students read the author biography, point out how Bradford's faith and resolve contributed to the survival of Plymouth colony.

NOTABLE QUOTE

"The difficulties were many, but not invincible." —**William Bradford**

Selection Resources

COMMON CORE

RI 2 Determine two or more central ideas of a text and analyze their development over the course of the text, including how they interact and build on one another to provide a complex analysis; provide an objective summary of the text. **RI 9** Analyze seventeenth-century foundational U.S. documents of historical and literary significance for their themes, purposes, and rhetorical features.

DID YOU KNOW?

William Bradford . . .

- lost his first wife to drowning shortly after the *Mayflower* landed.
- sold one of his farms to help pay Plymouth Colony's debts.
- was elected governor of Plymouth 30 times.

Exploration and the Early Settlers

from Of Plymouth Plantation

Chronicle by William Bradford

Meet the Author

William Bradford c. 1590–1657

Long before there were holiday legends of Pilgrims and Indians, a group of English Puritans set off to create a new, pure society in the North American wilderness. Their leader was William Bradford.

Early Rebel Born into a time of religious upheaval in England, Bradford joined the crusade for religious reform at age 12. He was inspired by the ideals of the Puritans, a Protestant religious group that wanted to purify the Church of England and create simpler, more democratic ways to worship. By 17, Bradford had joined the radical Puritans known as Separatists, who called for a total break with the official church.

Not surprisingly, the Separatists clashed with the king of England, who also headed the church. Emigration to North America offered the hope of freedom, and Bradford helped plan and finance the voyage across the Atlantic. In 1620, Bradford and his wife, Dorothy, left behind their four-year-old son to join nearly 40 other Separatists on the ship *Mayflower*. Facing the journey with typical resolve, Bradford described the group as "pilgrims," or religious wanderers, the name we use for them today.

A Natural Leader Although the Pilgrims initiated the voyage, they made up fewer than half of the ship's 102 passengers. During the long, difficult journey,

disagreements broke out among the group, and Bradford took decisive action. He helped craft the Mayflower Compact, often called the first U.S. Constitution. Signed by the 41 men on board, the compact was an agreement to work together for the good of the entire group. And they kept their promise. In April 1621, when the *Mayflower* returned to England, not one colonist left Plymouth Colony—a tribute to Bradford's sound leadership.

Bradford was also effective in forging alliances with local Native American tribes such as the Wampanoag (wäm′pə-nō′ăg), a union of tribes led by Massasoit (măs′ə-soit′). The Wampanoag, who had lost 80 percent of their people to smallpox shortly before the Pilgrims' arrival, faced their own struggle to survive. Out of mutual need, Bradford and Massasoit created a strong alliance that lasted throughout their lifetimes.

Historian in the Making With a historian's instinct, Bradford saved many documents from the trip's planning phase. During his 30 years as governor, he continued to document the challenges of the growing colony, which owed its survival to his energy, vision, and expert diplomacy. His chronicle, *Of Plymouth Plantation*, is our best history of these adventurous times.

Author Online

Go to **thinkcentral.com**. KEYWORD: HML11-102

THINK central

See resources on the **Teacher One Stop DVD-ROM** and on **thinkcentral.com**.

 RESOURCE MANAGER UNIT 1

Plan and Teach, pp. 133–140
Summary, pp. 141†–142‡
Text Analysis and Reading
　　Skill, pp. 143–146†
Vocabulary, pp. 147–149

DIAGNOSTIC AND SELECTION TESTS

Selection Tests, pp. 49–52

 BEST PRACTICES TOOLKIT

New Word Analysis, p. E8
T Chart, p. A25

TECHNOLOGY

- **Teacher One Stop DVD-ROM**
- **Student One Stop DVD-ROM**
- **Audio Anthology CD**
- **GrammarNotes DVD-ROM**
- **ExamView Test Generator on the Teacher One Stop**

***** Resources for Differentiation　　† Also in Spanish　　‡ Also in Haitian Creole and Vietnamese

● TEXT ANALYSIS: CULTURAL CHARACTERISTICS

Many texts, especially those about community life, reflect the **cultural characteristics** of the communities they describe, including their view of the human condition. *Of Plymouth Plantation* is a record of the Pilgrims' efforts to create a model Puritan society. In it, William Bradford describes the outcome of an Indian attack.

Thus it pleased God to vanquish their enemies and give them deliverance; and by His special providence so to dispose that not any one of them were either hurt or hit. . . .

Bradford's description expresses the Puritan theme that victory is a gift from God. As you read, consider what else Bradford's descriptions and sometimes subtle word choice reveal about Puritan themes and the rhetorical appeal of shared beliefs. The appeal to common beliefs can influence not only what readers think but also how they feel about a subject.

● READING STRATEGY: SUMMARIZE

When you **summarize,** you restate the **main ideas** and the most important **details** of what you read. This process will help you sift through Bradford's long, complex sentences for important clues to his beliefs and themes.

This excerpt from *Of Plymouth Plantation* has five sections. As you read each section, record the date or time of year events occur and a one- or two-sentence summary of the section.

> **Section:** *Their Safe Arrival at Cape Cod*
>
> **Time of Year:**
> **Summary:**

▲ VOCABULARY IN CONTEXT

The following boldfaced words help tell the story of the founding of Plymouth Colony. Use context clues to guess the meaning of each word; then, write a brief definition.

1. found **solace** in the peaceful woodland setting
2. her survival was an act of **providence**
3. will **tender** her resignation in a letter
4. chose a **rendezvous** convenient for everyone
5. tried to **procure** enough food for the family
6. an illness **feigned** in order to avoid work

 Complete the activities in your **Reader/Writer Notebook.**

When does HARDSHIP *unite us?*

Hard times can bring people together or tear them apart. For example, in a blackout after a serious storm, people could respond by sharing supplies or by stealing what they need from unprotected homes. When does facing hardship become a source of strength and unity rather than one of distrust and division?

DISCUSS Working with a small group, list events you know from history or from the news that imposed great hardships on a community. Compare situations that had a unifying effect with those that divided the community. Identify factors that may account for the different responses.

Teach

When does HARDSHIP *unite us?*

Introduce the question, and then use the blackout example to help students consider when facing hardship creates unity and when it creates division. Have students incorporate their responses to complete the *DISCUSS* activity.

TEXT ANALYSIS — COMMON CORE RI 9

● *Model the Skill:* CULTURAL CHARACTERISTICS

Tell students that cultural characteristics can be reflected in writing. Share this example of a diary entry:

> Dear Diary, For dinner at Jenny's house, I had veggie burgers, salad, and a fruit cup. Jenny told me she's never eaten a hamburger! When I got home, I was still hungry, so I ate a baloney sandwich. Your friend, Elisa

Tell students that Elisa's diary entry reveals information about Jenny's family's values. Point out details that show that Jenny's family members are vegetarians. Explain that for health or religious reasons, they do not believe in eating meat.

GUIDED PRACTICE Have students contrast Elisa's and Jenny's values.

READING STRATEGY — COMMON CORE RI 2

■ *Model the Skill:* SUMMARIZE

Model for students how to summarize **Early Rebel** on page 102. *Possible answer: As a youth Bradford joined the Puritan Separatists, who broke with the Church of England. In 1620, he and his wife sailed on the* Mayflower, *in search of religious freedom.*

GUIDED PRACTICE Have volunteers summarize **A Natural Leader.**

R RESOURCE MANAGER—Copy Master Summarize p. 145 (for student use while reading the selection)

VOCABULARY SKILL — COMMON CORE L 4

▲ VOCABULARY IN CONTEXT

DIAGNOSE WORD KNOWLEDGE Have all students complete Vocabulary in Context. Check their definitions against the following:

feigned (fānd) *adj.* not real; pretended **feign** *v.*
procure (prō-kyŏŏr′) *v.* to get by special effort; to obtain
providence (prŏv′ĭ-dəns) *n.* an instance of divine care

rendezvous (rän′dā-vōō) *n.* a gathering place
solace (sŏl′ĭs) *n.* comfort in sorrow or distress
tender (tĕn′dər) *v.* to offer formally
PRETEACH VOCABULARY Preteach vocabulary with this copy master. Read each item aloud.

R RESOURCE MANAGER—Copy Master Vocabulary Study p. 147

SUMMARY

This excerpt from William Bradford's chronicle opens with the Pilgrims' winter arrival in the Cape Cod wilderness. A search party explores the land and survives a surprise Indian attack. Conditions are dire, and many in the group starve or fall ill. Finally, the local Indians help them find food and ways to survive. They meet Squanto and his chief Massasoit, with whom they make a friendly pact and share a feast of thanksgiving.

READ WITH A PURPOSE

Help students set a purpose for reading. Tell them to read to discover the difficulties the Pilgrims faced and how they learned to survive in their new environment.

TEXT ANALYSIS

COMMON CORE RI 9

A CULTURAL CHARACTERISTICS

Possible answer: It reveals that the Pilgrims credited God for saving them and for watching over and protecting them; readers may feel that God was blessing their arrival.

IF STUDENTS NEED HELP . . . Direct their attention to the phrases "fell upon their knees" (lines 4–5) and "blessed the God of Heaven" (line 5). The Pilgrims gave their thanks for bringing them across the Atlantic Ocean and setting them on ground.

REVISIT THE BIG QUESTION

When does HARDSHIP unite us?

Discuss In lines 5–13, what hardships do the Pilgrims face on their voyage across the ocean? What new dangers confront them when they first arrive on Cape Cod? *Possible answer: Bradford mentions the "vast and furious ocean" (lines 5–6), referring to the dangers of a voyage across the Atlantic: storms, gales, waves, hunger, and cold weather. The Pilgrims arrive in poor condition with no shelter or friends who could help them adjust (lines 12–13).*

Of Plymouth Plantation

William Bradford

> **BACKGROUND** By the time the Pilgrims landed at Cape Cod, the local Native American tribes had had 100 years of contact and conflict with European explorers. Squanto, who became the Pilgrims' interpreter, had learned English when he was kidnapped by an English expedition in 1605. The Nauset Indians, who attacked the Pilgrims shortly after their arrival, had survived years of skirmishes with English explorers, including a 1609 battle with John Smith of Jamestown fame. Keep these events in mind as you read Bradford's account.

Their Safe Arrival at Cape Cod

But to omit other things (that I may be brief) after long beating at sea they[1] fell with that land which is called Cape Cod; the which being made and certainly known to be it, they were not a little joyful. . . .

Being thus arrived in a good harbor, and brought safe to land, they fell upon their knees and blessed the God of Heaven who had brought them over the vast and furious ocean, and delivered them from all the perils and miseries thereof, again to set their feet on the firm and stable earth, their proper element. . . .

But here I cannot but stay and make a pause, and stand half amazed at this poor people's present condition; and so I think will the reader, too, when he

10 well considers the same. Being thus passed the vast ocean, and a sea of troubles before in their preparation (as may be remembered by that which went before), they had now no friends to welcome them nor inns to entertain or refresh their weatherbeaten bodies; no houses or much less towns to repair to, to seek for

---

Analyze Visuals ▶
Describe the landscape that awaits the travellers. What emotional response might they have had to this sight?

A CULTURAL CHARACTERISTICS
Reread lines 4–7. What does this paragraph reveal about the way Puritans viewed God? How might this shared belief influence Bradford's readers?

The Landing of the Pilgrims (1803–1806), Michael Felice Corne. Tempera on canvas. Pilgrim Hall Museum. Plymouth, Massachusetts.

---

1. **they:** Bradford refers to the Pilgrims in the third person, even though he is one of them.

DIFFERENTIATED INSTRUCTION

FOR ENGLISH LANGUAGE LEARNERS
Vocabulary Support Use New Word Analysis to teach these words: *brief* (line 1), *civil* (line 29), *principal* (line 57), *couple* (line 67), *Encounter* (line 99).

BEST PRACTICES TOOLKIT—Transparency New Word Analysis p. E8

FOR ADVANCED LEARNERS/AP
Research Relations with Native Americans
The Pilgrims' relations with Native Americans were both hostile and friendly. To provide background, have students research the importance of

- the Nauset and Wampanoag tribes
- Native American allies Samoset, Squanto, Hobbamock, and Massasoit
- the Pilgrim leader Miles Standish

Encourage small groups to present oral reports of their findings.

Analyze Visuals

Possible answer: The landscape in this painting is cold, bare, and foreboding. The Pilgrims' response to such a setting would have been fearful and uncertain, because of known and unknown dangers. However, they would have also been grateful to have arrived and optimistic because of their faith.

About the Art Michael Felice Corne (1752–1815) painted this scene nearly 200 years after the Pilgrims' landing. It was based on a 1799 engraving by Samuel Hall. Corne had not read William Bradford's account of the landing, so he did not know that the Pilgrims met no Native Americans for the first four months after their arrival.

BACKGROUND

Mayflower Compact Before William Bradford and his charges ever set foot in North America, they faced challenges that threatened the success of their venture. Their ship had arrived in territory that was outside the authority of the colonial charter granted to them in England. In addition, some non-Pilgrims questioned the Pilgrim leader's command. The Mayflower Compact created a civil government and pledged loyalty to the British king. Laws approved by the majority were binding on Pilgrims and non-Pilgrims alike. The document became a landmark of American democratic government.

FOR STRUGGLING READERS

In combination with the *Audio Anthology CD,* use one or more Targeted Passages (pp. 106, 108, 109, 110) to ensure that students focus on key events and concepts. Targeted Passages are also good for English learners.

FOR ADVANCED LEARNERS/AP

Provide these independent projects to extend the lesson and and present additional challenges for students:

- Research and present findings about daily life in Europe in the 1600s.
- Write a character sketch of William Bradford.

For further details on these projects, see

> **R** RESOURCE MANAGER—Copy Master
> Ideas for Extension pp. 138–139

succor.[2] It is recorded in Scripture as a mercy to the Apostle and his shipwrecked company, that the barbarians showed them no small kindness in refreshing them,[3] but these savage barbarians, when they met with them (as after will appear) were readier to fill their sides full of arrows than otherwise. And for the season it was winter, and they that know the winters of that country know them to be sharp and violent, and subject to cruel and fierce storms, dangerous to travel to known

20 places, much more to search an unknown coast. Besides, what could they see but a hideous and desolate wilderness, full of wild beasts and wild men—and what multitudes there might be of them they knew not. Neither could they, as it were, go up to the top of Pisgah[4] to view from this wilderness a more goodly country to feed their hopes; for which way soever they turned their eyes (save upward to the heavens) they could have little **solace** or content in respect of any outward objects. For summer being done, all things stand upon them with a weatherbeaten face, and the whole country, full of woods and thickets, represented a wild and savage hue. If they looked behind them, there was the mighty ocean which they had passed and was now as a main bar and gulf to separate them from all the civil

30 parts of the world. . . . **B**

---

2. **to seek for succor:** to look for help or relief.

3. **It is . . . refreshing them:** a reference to the Biblical account of the courteous reception given to Paul ("the Apostle") and his companions by the inhabitants of Malta (Acts 27:41–28:2).

4. **Pisgah:** the mountain from whose peak Moses saw the Promised Land (Deuteronomy 34:1–4).

solace (sŏl′ĭs) *n.* comfort in sorrow or distress

B SUMMARIZE
Reread lines 16–30. What challenges confronted the colonists when they arrived at Cape Cod?

The First Winter of the Pilgrims in Massachusetts, 1620 (1800s). Colored engraving. The Granger Collection, New York.

B SUMMARIZE

Possible answer: *The colonists faced fierce weather, unsettled wilderness without comforts, and the expectation of hostile inhabitants.*

IF STUDENTS NEED HELP . . . Direct them to lines 17–18 to identify the season. Help them list nouns and descriptive words that portray the colonists' surroundings. Then work with them to complete the first section of the chart on page 103.

Analyze Visuals

Activity Ask students what the colored engraving shows about the Pilgrims' first winter. Does it accurately reflect William Bradford's account? ***Possible answer:*** *The engraving shows primitive and desperate conditions confronting the Pilgrims: freezing cold, minimal shelter, and a lack of all comforts. It accurately reflects William Bradford's account (lines 17–28).*

OWN THE WORD

solace: Have students read the paragraph beginning, "It is recorded in Scripture..." and ending with "...all the civil parts of the world..." Ask students to list sights, events, and encounters that gave Bradford little *solace* or comfort on Cape Cod. ***Possible answers:*** *inhospitable Native Americans, bitter winter weather, wild terrain and animals, distance from all he considered civilized*

DIFFERENTIATED INSTRUCTION

FOR STRUGGLING READERS

1 Targeted Passage [Lines 16–22]

This passage establishes the setting and the challenges the Pilgrims confront.

- What kind of weather do the Pilgrims face in the new land? (lines 17–20)
- How do the Pilgrims expect the Native Americans to respond to them? (lines 20–22)
- How does the land appear? (line 21)

FOR STRUGGLING READERS

Develop Reading Fluency Read aloud lines 22–30 to model reading with expression and using punctuation for guidance. Then, have students form groups. Have students read the lines to their groups as though they were narrating a personal experience to friends in England. Have students vote on the most convincing performance in their group.

The First Encounter

Being thus arrived at Cape Cod the 11th of November, and necessity calling them to look out a place for habitation (as well as the master's and mariners' importunity); they having brought a large shallop[5] with them out of England, stowed in quarters in the ship, they now got her out and set their carpenters to work to trim her up; but being much bruised and shattered in the ship with foul weather, they saw she would be long in mending. Whereupon a few of them **tendered** themselves to go by land and discover those nearest places, whilst the shallop was in mending; . . .

40 After this, the shallop being got ready, they set out again for the better discovery of this place, and the master of the ship desired to go himself. So there went some thirty men but found it to be no harbor for ships but only for boats. There was also found two of their [the Indians'] houses covered with mats, and sundry of their implements in them, but the people were run away and could not be seen. Also there was found more of their corn and of their beans of various colors; the corn and beans they [the English] brought away, purposing to give them [the Indians] full satisfaction when they should meet with any of them, as, about some six months afterward they did, to their good content.[6]

And here is to be noted a special **providence** of God, and a great mercy to this poor people, that here they got seed to plant them corn the next year, or else they 50 might have starved, for they had none nor any likelihood to get any till the season had been past, as the sequel did manifest.[7] Neither is it likely they had had this, if the first voyage had not been made, for the ground was now all covered with snow and hard frozen; but the Lord is never wanting unto His in their greatest needs; let His holy name have all the praise. **C**

The month of November being spent in these affairs, and much foul weather falling in, the 6th of December they sent out their shallop again with ten of their principal men and some seamen, upon further discovery, intending to circulate that deep bay of Cape Cod. The weather was very cold and it froze so hard as the spray of the sea lighting on their coats, they were as if they had been 60 glazed. . . . [The next night they landed and] made them a barricado[8] as usually they did every night, with logs, stakes, and thick pine boughs, the height of a man, leaving it open to leeward,[9] partly to shelter them from the cold and wind (making their fire in the middle and lying round about it) and partly to defend them from any sudden assaults of the savages, if they should surround them; so being very weary, they betook them to rest. But about midnight they heard a hideous and great cry, and their sentinel called "Arm! arm!" So they bestirred them and stood to their arms and shot off a couple of muskets, and then the noise

---

5. **shallop** (shăl′əp): an open boat usually used in shallow waters.

6. **purposing . . . content:** intending to repay the Nauset Indians for the corn and beans they took, as they in fact did, to the Indians' satisfaction, six months later.

7. **as the sequel did manifest:** as the events that followed proved to be the case.

8. **barricado** (băr′ĭ-kä′dō): a barrier for defense.

9. **to leeward:** on the side sheltered from the wind.

tender (tĕn′dər) *v.* to offer formally

providence (prŏv′ĭ-dəns) *n.* an instance of divine care

COMMON CORE RI 9

C CULTURAL CHARACTERISTICS
As you have seen from your reading so far, William Bradford believes that God played a special role in the lives of the Puritan settlers. Reread lines 48–54. In the first sentence, notice the phrase "a special providence of God." The verb form of *providence* is *provide.* This word expresses Bradford's belief that God literally provides for the Puritan settlers by giving them seed corn to plant so that they will not starve. As you read the following paragraphs (lines 55–99), look for other places where the author expresses Puritan beliefs about the role of God in their lives.

TIERED DISCUSSION PROMPTS

In lines 39–47, use these prompts to help students understand the colonists' first contact with Native American culture on Cape Cod Bay:

Interpret What do the Pilgrims learn from the Indians' abandoned homes? How does this differ from their expectations? *Possible answer: The Pilgrims learn that Native Americans are civilized (lines 41–45). They had expected and feared savage and barbarian cultures (lines 15–16).*

Synthesize What does this encounter suggest about the Pilgrims' intentions toward the Native Americans? *Possible answer: It suggests that their intentions are honest and peaceful (lines 45–47).*

TEXT ANALYSIS — **COMMON CORE RI 9**

C CULTURAL CHARACTERISTICS

Ask for volunteers to read aloud lines 55–99 emphasizing lines referring to "providence" and "thanks and praise."

Possible answer: They reached their weapons "by the good providence of God" (lines 82–83) and he proclaims God's role in the colonists' victory (lines 93–99).

Extend the Discussion How would the Pilgrims be likely to account for several men deciding to hold on to their guns?

VOCABULARY — **COMMON CORE L 4**

OWN THE WORD

- **tender:** Ask students to describe the relationship between this denotation of the verb *tender,* "to offer formally; to present for acceptance," and the noun *legal tender.*

- **providence:** Ask students to identify what Bradford saw as *providence,* or divine intervention that aided the group's survival. *Possible answers: The exploratory party found corn, giving the Pilgrims seeds to plant.*

FOR ENGLISH LANGUAGE LEARNERS

Vocabulary: Outdated Forms Help students use context to define these outdated forms: *they knew not* (line 22), "they did not know"; *more goodly* (line 23), "more promising or hopeful"; *which way soever* (line 24), "wherever"; *save* (line 24), "except"; *hue* (line 28), "appearance"; *Being thus arrived* (line 31), "Having arrived"; *whilst* (line 37), "while"; *being got ready* (line 39), "made ready for use"; *sundry* (line 42), "an assortment"; *purposing* (line 45), "planning, expecting"; *betook* (line 65), "decided to"; *Arm! arm!* (line 66), "Get your guns"; *bestirred* (line 66), "woke up"; *stood to their arms* (line 67), "stood with their guns ready."

In lines 78–99, use these prompts to help students understand the Pilgrims' first direct encounter with Native Americans:

Analyze The Pilgrims' expectations about Indian behavior were probably typical of the historical period. How would 17th-century European readers likely have responded to this passage? *Possible answer: European readers probably would have been fascinated and terrified by the attack.*

Evaluate Why do you think that Bradford wanted to create this effect? How effective is Bradford in reaching his goal? *Possible answer: He probably wanted his European readers to recognize how dangerous the Pilgrims' situation was, so that they might better appreciate God's "special providence" (lines 94–95). His description is highly effective, including vivid action and sensory details, as in lines 80–81.*

REVISIT THE BIG QUESTION

When does
HARDSHIP
unite us?

Discuss In lines 100–114, how did the Pilgrims react to hardship during the Starving Time? *Possible answer: They responded to adversity by pulling together and maintaining their optimism.*

VOCABULARY

COMMON CORE
L 4

OWN THE WORD

rendezvous: Tell students that the word *rendezvous* means "a meeting; a meeting place" and is from two Old French words, *rendre*, "to present; to return," and *vous*, "you." Ask students to list things that they might *render*. *Possible answers: assistance, thanks*

---

ceased. They concluded it was a company of wolves or such like wild beasts, for one of the seamen told them he had often heard such a noise in Newfoundland.

70   So they rested till about five of the clock in the morning; for the tide, and their purpose to go from thence, made them be stirring betimes. So after prayer they prepared for breakfast, and it being day dawning it was thought best to be carrying things down to the boat. But some said it was not best to carry the arms down, others said they would be the readier, for they had lapped them up in their coats from the dew; but some three or four would not carry theirs till they went themselves. Yet as it fell out, the water being not high enough, they laid them down on the bank side and came up to breakfast.

But presently, all on the sudden, they heard a great and strange cry, which they knew to be the same voices they heard in the night, though they varied
80   their notes; and one of their company being abroad came running in and cried, "Men, Indians! Indians!" And withal, their arrows came flying amongst them. Their men ran with all speed to recover their arms, as by the good providence of God they did. In the meantime, of those that were there ready, two muskets were discharged at them, and two more stood ready in the entrance of their **rendezvous** but were commanded not to shoot till they could take full aim at them. And the other two charged again with all speed, for there were only four had arms there, and defended the barricado, which was first assaulted. The cry of the Indians was dreadful, especially when they [the Indians] saw their men [the English] run out of the rendezvous toward the shallop to recover their arms, the Indians wheeling
90   about upon them. But some running out with coats of mail on, and cutlasses in their hands, they [the English] soon got their arms and let fly amongst them [the Indians] and quickly stopped their violence. . . .

Thus it pleased God to vanquish their enemies and give them deliverance; and by His special providence so to dispose that not any one of them were either hurt or hit, though their arrows came close by them and on every side [of] them; and sundry of their coats, which hung up in the barricado, were shot through and through. Afterwards they gave God solemn thanks and praise for their deliverance, and gathered up a bundle of their arrows and sent them into England afterward by the master of the ship, and called that place the First Encounter. . . .

The Starving Time

100 But that which was most sad and lamentable was, that in two or three months' time half of their company died, especially in January and February, being the depth of winter, and wanting houses and other comforts; being infected with the scurvy[10] and other diseases which this long voyage and their inaccommodate condition had brought upon them. So as there died some times two or three of a day in the foresaid time, that of 100 and odd persons, scarce fifty remained. And of these, in the time of most distress, there was but six or seven sound persons who to their great commendations, be it spoken, spared no pains night nor day, but with abundance of toil and hazard of their own health fetched them wood, made them fires, dressed them meat, made their beds, washed their loathsome clothes,

---

10. **scurvy** (skûr′vē): a disease caused by lack of vitamin C.

② Targeted Passage

rendezvous (rän′dā-vōō) *n.* a gathering place

Language Coach

Fixed Expressions
The phrase "depth of winter" in line 102 means "middle part of winter." Other phrases with *depth* are *in-depth* ("complete" or "thorough") and *depths of* ("the deepest point of"). Use *depths of despair* in a sentence about the colonists' situation.

DIFFERENTIATED INSTRUCTION

FOR STRUGGLING READERS

② Targeted Passage [Lines 78–95]

This passage describes the Pilgrims' violent first meeting with Native Americans.

- What happens after the Pilgrims hear the strange cry? (lines 80–81)
- What do the Pilgrims do to protect themselves? (lines 82–87)
- What weapons do the Indians have? (line 81, lines 90–91)

FOR ENGLISH LANGUAGE LEARNERS

Language Coach

Fixed Expressions Tell students that the word *depth* is used in other fixed expressions. Write these sentences on the board:

*The ship sank into the **depths of the ocean**.*

*The teacher has a **depth of knowledge**.*

Have students use each expression in a sentence of their own.

The First Thanksgiving (1914), Jennie Augusta Brownscombe. © Burstein Collection/Corbis.

110 clothed and unclothed them. . . . In a word, did all the homely and necessary offices for them which dainty and queasy stomachs cannot endure to hear named; and all this willingly and cheerfully, without any grudging in the least, showing herein their true love unto their friends and brethren; a rare example and worthy to be remembered. Two of these seven were Mr. William Brewster, their reverend Elder, and Myles Standish, their Captain and military commander, unto whom myself and many others were much beholden in our low and sick condition. And yet the Lord so upheld these persons as in this general calamity they were not at all infected either with sickness or lameness. . . . **D**

Indian Relations

All this while the Indians came skulking about them, and would sometimes show
120 themselves aloof off, but when any approached near them, they would run away; and once they [the Indians] stole away their [the colonists'] tools where they had been at work and were gone to dinner. But about the 16th of March, a certain Indian came boldly amongst them and spoke to them in broken English, which they could well understand but marveled at it. At length they understood by discourse with him, that he was not of these parts, but belonged to the eastern parts where some English ships came to fish, with whom he was acquainted and could name sundry of them by their names, amongst whom he had got his language. He became profitable to them in acquainting them with many things concerning the state of the country in the east parts where he lived, which was
130 afterwards profitable unto them; as also of the people here, of their names, number and strength, of their situation and distance from this place, and who was chief amongst them. His name was Samoset. He told them also of another Indian whose name was Squanto, a native of this place, who had been in England and could speak better English than himself.

▲ **Analyze Visuals**
Contrast the scenery in this image with the landscape on page 105. How has the view of nature changed?

D CULTURAL CHARACTERISTICS
Reread lines 106–118. Notice how Bradford holds up seven colonists as examples. What values do these seven represent? What do they mean to Bradford, and how might their example influence Bradford's readers?

3 Targeted Passage

FOR STRUGGLING READERS

3 Targeted Passage [Lines 119–134]

This passage describes the Pilgrims' evolving relationship with the local Native Americans.

- What are the Pilgrims' relations with the Indians after their illness? (lines 119–122)
- Who comes to speak with the Pilgrims? (line 132)
- What does he do for the Pilgrims? (lines 130–132)

FOR ENGLISH LEARNERS

Comprehension: Self-Monitor As students read lines 114–118, have them use context to define difficult words or phrases and restate inverted text in subject-verb sequence. Urge students to check their comprehension by paraphrasing. *Possible answer: William Brewster and Myles Standish were two of the seven men who helped the sick. We owe them a lot for their help when we were sick. The Lord protected them, so they didn't become sick.*

Analyze Visuals

Possible answer: The scenery is congenial rather than foreboding; fertile rather than bare; warm and comfortable rather than cold and miserable. Nature in this scene welcomes and nourishes the Pilgrims—as if it is a facet of divine protection.

About the Art This painting by the American artist Jennie Augusta Brownscombe presents an idyllic view of the Pilgrims' first Thanksgiving. A descendent of a *Mayflower* passenger, Brownscombe created many nostalgic scenes of colonial history, which earned her quick success during her lifetime.

TEXT ANALYSIS   COMMON CORE
                                 RI 9

D *Model the Skill:* **CULTURAL CHARACTERISTICS**

Illustrate the colonists' values by completing a concept web of actions taken by individuals on behalf of the group.

fetched wood

dressed and undressed

made fires

Self-Sacrifices

washed clothes

fixed meat

made beds

Ask yourself what specific values do these actions reveal. Start a list of values, and encourage volunteers to contribute to the list.

Possible answer: The colonists' responses to the Starving Time reflect their dedication to the welfare of the group, sacrifice, and willingness to face hardships.

Extend the Discussion How does Bradford explain the Pilgrims' survival during the Starving Time?

 **Model the Skill: SUMMARIZE**

Lead students in summarizing the events that led to the treaty. Read aloud lines 122–132 and lines 135–139. Discuss how these events strengthened the relationship between the colonists and the Indians.

Possible answer: *The Pilgrims met a Native American named Samoset who spoke English and aided them (lines 122–132); he arranged a meeting between the Pilgrims and Chief Massasoit (lines 135–139).*

Extend the Discussion How did the treaty with Massasoit contribute to the colony's survival?

VOCABULARY   COMMON CORE L 4

OWN THE WORD

- **procure:** Tell students that *procure,* "to obtain by special effort," comes from the Latin *procurare,* meaning "to care for" and *cura,* meaning "care." Have students list additional words that come from the root *cura.* **Possible answers:** *secure, insecure, manicure, curator*

- **feigned:** Have students use *feigned* in context by stating how, when, and why they have ever *feigned* anything. **Possible answers:** feigned *interest,* feigned *indifference,* feigned *illness*

SELECTION WRAP-UP

READ WITH A PURPOSE Now that students have read the selection, ask them to describe how the colonists overcame difficult times in their new environment. **Possible answer:** *Colonists worked together to survive an Indian attack and to weather illness and starvation. They made peace with the Indians, who then taught them survival skills.*

INDEPENDENT READING

Students might enjoy reading more in *Three Visitors to Early Plymouth* by John Pory, Isaak De Rasieres, and Emmanuel Altham.

Being, after some time of entertainment and gifts dismissed, a while after he came again, and five more with him, and they brought again all the tools that were stolen away before, and made way for the coming of their great Sachem,[11] called Massasoit. Who, about four or five days after, came with the chief of his friends and other attendance, with the aforesaid Squanto. With whom, after friendly
140 entertainment and some gifts given him, they made a peace with him (which hath now continued this 24 years) in these terms:

1. That neither he nor any of his should injure or do hurt to any of their people.
2. That if any of his did hurt to any of theirs, he should send the offender, that they might punish him.
3. That if anything were taken away from any of theirs, he should cause it to be restored; and they should do the like to his.
4. If any did unjustly war against him, they would aid him; if any did war against them, he should aid them.
150 5. He should send to his neighbors confederates to certify them of this, that they might not wrong them, but might be likewise comprised in the conditions of peace.[12]
6. That when their men came to them, they should leave their bows and arrows behind them.

After these things he returned to his place called Sowams,[13] some 40 miles from this place, but Squanto continued with them and was their interpreter and was a special instrument sent of God for their good beyond their expectation. He directed them how to set their corn, where to take fish, and to **procure** other commodities, and was also their pilot to bring them to unknown places for their
160 profit, and never left them till he died.

First Thanksgiving

They began now to gather in the small harvest they had, and to fit up their houses and dwellings against winter, being all well recovered in health and strength and had all things in good plenty. For as some were thus employed in affairs abroad, others were exercised in fishing, about cod and bass and other fish, of which they took good store, of which every family had their portion. All the summer there was no want; and now began to come in store of fowl, as winter approached, of which this place did abound when they came first (but afterward decreased by degrees). And besides waterfowl there was great store of wild turkeys, of which they took many, besides venison, etc. Besides they had about a peck a meal a week
170 to a person, or now since harvest, Indian corn to that proportion. Which made many afterwards write so largely of their plenty here to their friends in England, which were not **feigned** but true reports. ❧

Targeted Passage

---

11. **Sachem** (sā′chəm): chief.
12. **He should send . . . peace:** Massasoit was to send representatives to other tribes to let them know about the treaty with the Pilgrims.
13. **Sowams** (sō′əmz): near the site of present-day Barrington, Rhode Island.

 **SUMMARIZE**
Reread lines 122–141. What events led to the treaty with Massasoit?

procure (prō-kyŏŏr′) *v.* to get by special effort; to obtain

Language Coach

Homophones Words that sound alike but have different meanings and spellings are called **homophones.** *Fowl* (line 166) means "birds." Look at "foul weather" in line 55 on page 107. What does *foul* mean? How is it pronounced?

feigned (fānd) *adj.* not real; pretended **feign** *v.*

DIFFERENTIATED INSTRUCTION

FOR STRUGGLING READERS

④ **Targeted Passage** [Lines 155–172]

This passage illustrates the productive relationship between the Pilgrims and Squanto and the successful outcome of the Pilgrims' first year on Cape Cod.

- How does Squanto help the Pilgrims? (lines 156–160)

- How does the summer go for the Pilgrims? (lines 165–166)

FOR ENGLISH LANGUAGE LEARNERS

Language Coach

Homophones Tell students that *fowl* and *foul* are homophones. Read these sentences and have students identify which word is used:

A foul smell rose from the garbage can.

The cook prepared the fowl.

Have students use each word in a sentence of their own.

Comprehension

1. **Recall** What happens to the colonists during "the starving time"?

2. **Recall** Who is Squanto?

3. **Clarify** In what ways did the Wampanoag help the colonists survive?

Text Analysis

● 4. **Make Inferences About Cultural Characteristics** Bradford's **word choice** and his choice of details provide subtle clues to Puritan beliefs. Reread Bradford's account of the arrival at Cape Cod (lines 4–30). What does his description reveal about Puritan attitudes toward nature? Use a chart like the one shown to gather evidence and make inferences.

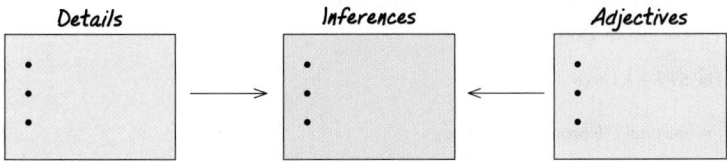

Details → *Inferences* ← *Adjectives*

● 5. **Analyze Outcomes** Using the **summary** chart you created as you read, review the events of the first year at Plymouth. How did events change the colonists'

- prospects for survival?
- impressions of Native Americans?
- attitude toward the region?
- sense of providence?

6. **Analyze Form** A **chronicle** is a chronological, objective account of historical events. What features of Bradford's narrative might have changed had he written a personal account of his experiences?

7. **Make Judgments** Review the terms of the treaty between the Plymouth colonists and the Wampanoag (lines 142–154). Notice which terms apply to both parties equally and which do not. In your opinion, is the treaty fair? Explain your answer.

Text Criticism

8. **Different Perspectives** How might a Wampanoag historian's version of events differ from Bradford's? Choose an episode from *Of Plymouth Plantation* and cite specific details that might change to reflect this different perspective.

> *When does* **HARDSHIP** *unite us?*
>
> Which beliefs most contributed to the colonists' willingness to face hardships together? And how does Bradford's appeal to common beliefs influence readers—especially Bradford's Puritan contemporaries? Support your answer with details from Bradford's account.

COMMON CORE

RI 1 Cite textual evidence to support analysis of what the text says explicitly as well as inferences drawn from the text, including determining where the text leaves matters uncertain. **RI 2** Determine two or more central ideas of a text and analyze their development over the course of the text, including how they interact and build on one another to provide a complex analysis; provide an objective summary of the text. **RI 9** Analyze seventeenth-century foundational U.S. documents of historical and literary significance for their themes, purposes, and rhetorical features.

---

8. *Students should identify a specific part of the narrative and cite appropriate details.*

> *When does* HARDSHIP *unite us?* Students should support a chosen factor with historical background and appropriate details from the text.

Practice and Apply

For preliminary support of post-reading questions, use these copy masters:

R RESOURCE MANAGER—Copy Masters
Reading Check p. 150
Cultural Characteristics p. 143
Question Support p. 151
Additional selection questions are provided for teachers on page 137.

ANSWERS  COMMON CORE RI 1, RI 2, RI 9

1. *Half of the group dies from disease, malnutrition, and lack of shelter.*

2. *Squanto is a Native American who was captured and taken to England, and so has learned to speak English. He becomes the Pilgrims' interpreter (lines 133–134, 155–157).*

3. *The Wampanoag teach the Pilgrims how to plant corn, where to fish and find resources, and how to get around the area. Their peace treaty secures the Pilgrims from Native American attack (lines 158–160).*

Possible answers:

4. ● **COMMON CORE FOCUS** *Make Inferences About Cultural Characteristics* **Details:** *calls land a hideous wilderness: no friends, no inns, no houses, no towns, wild beasts and men, terrible weather;* **Inferences:** *Nature is dangerous, people need towns, the Pilgrims face terrible weather and huge odds;* **Adjectives:** *vast and furious (sea), sharp and violent (winter); cruel and fierce storms, wild and savage (beasts and men)*

5. ■ **COMMON CORE FOCUS** *Analyze Outcomes:* *After suffering malnutrition, cold, and disease, the colony thrives and prepares for winter.* **Region:** *With Squanto's help, they learn to use the land for sustenance and profit.* **Native Americans:** *After initial fear and worry, they develop ties and view them as divine instruments.* **Providence:** *Through the worst times, they find signs of divine favor in survival and success.*

6. *He might have talked more about personal feelings and reactions, used the first-person point of view, and provided only details he witnessed.*

7. *Some students may say it is not fair because the terms aren't mutual (lines 142–145, 153–154). Others may argue that it is fair, because the weaker Pilgrims required greater protections.*

ANSWERS

Vocabulary in Context

▲ **VOCABULARY PRACTICE**

1. *go to a store*

2. *bogus*

3. *no*

4. *an unexpected victory*

5. *someone whose grandmother has just died*

6. *write a letter to the election board*

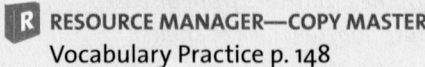 **RESOURCE MANAGER—COPY MASTER**
Vocabulary Practice p. 148

ACADEMIC VOCABULARY IN SPEAKING

Encourage students to respond to other students' ideas and responses, *promoting* a fluid discussion, rather than a disjointed one.

VOCABULARY STRATEGY: WORDS FROM FRENCH

 **COMMON CORE L 4c**

Possible answers: **1.** *to let do/letting people do as they wish;* **2.** *face to face/in relation to;* **3.** *outside the work/appetizer;* **4.** *nobility obliges/rank creates duty to those with less;* **5.** *false step/social blunder;* **6.** *stroke of mercy/finishing stroke or decisive event;* **7.** *spirit of group/group spirit;* **8.** *know how to do/ability to do the right thing*

 **RESOURCE MANAGER—Copy Master**
Vocabulary Strategy p. 149

Interactive Vocabulary — THINK central

Keywords direct students to a **WordSharp** tutorial on **thinkcentral.com** or to other types of vocabulary practice and review.

Assess and Reteach

Assess

DIAGNOSTIC AND SELECTION TESTS
Selection Test A, B/C pp. 49–52

Interactive Selection Test on thinkcentral.com

Reteach

Level Up Online Tutorials on thinkcentral.com

Vocabulary in Context

▲ **VOCABULARY PRACTICE**

Show you understand the vocabulary words by answering these questions.

1. If you wanted to **procure** something, would you go to a store or go swimming?

2. If someone's sorrow is **feigned,** is it genuine or bogus?

3. Is a **rendezvous** a good place to be alone?

4. What would be a sign of **providence**—an unexpected victory or a deadly accident?

5. Who would be in more need of **solace**—a person who has just won a race or someone whose grandmother has just died?

6. To **tender** yourself as a mayoral candidate, would you write a letter to the election board or tell a friend about your idea?

WORD LIST
feigned
procure
providence
rendezvous
solace
tender

ACADEMIC VOCABULARY IN SPEAKING

· document   · illustrate   · interpret   · promote   · reveal

With a small group of your peers, explain how William Bradford's narrative **promotes** Puritan beliefs. Include details from the selection to **document** your ideas. As you contribute, use at least one of the Academic Vocabulary words.

VOCABULARY STRATEGY: WORDS FROM FRENCH

Rendezvous is one of a number of words in English that comes directly from French. The meaning of some French words and terms may change slightly in English; *rendezvous,* for example, means "present yourself" in French. Other terms keep the same meaning. If you are not sure of the meaning of a French term when you hear or read it, consult a dictionary. Many unabridged dictionaries have short foreign-language dictionaries in the appendix where you can look up a word in a language such as French and see the English translation. Your school library may also have a French-English dictionary. Also, the Internet has many reliable resources on words and their origins. Use these kinds of references to increase your command of English words.

PRACTICE Create a three-column chart with these headings: *Term, Original Meaning,* and *Meaning in English.* Then, using a dictionary that contains etymologies, fill in the chart for each of the following terms.

1. laissez faire
2. vis-à-vis
3. hors d'oeuvre
4. noblesse oblige
5. faux pas
6. coup de grâce
7. esprit de corps
8. savoir-faire

COMMON CORE

L 4c Consult general and specialized reference materials, both print and digital, to determine or clarify a word's precise meaning, its etymology, or its standard usage.

 **Interactive Vocabulary — THINK central**

Go to **thinkcentral.com.**
KEYWORD: HML11-112

DIFFERENTIATED INSTRUCTION

FOR ENGLISH LANGUAGE LEARNERS

Task Support: Vocabulary Strategy Ask Spanish speakers to share words or phrases that are similar to the French terms that have entered English. Then have all English learners use the French terms in a sentence or describe an example of the term.

FOR ADVANCED LEARNERS/AP

Words from French Encourage students to find and define other words that have entered English from French. Students should add to the chart additional examples such as *au contraire, bonjour, cause célèbre, crêpe, fait accompli,* and *entourage.* Have students learn the correct pronunciations, then share the words and their definitions with the class.

Personal Accounts of Exploration and Settlement

The selections in this section not only provide information about life in early America but are also sources of insight into the personal challenges and moral conflicts that shaped so much of our colonial culture. Because they are all firsthand accounts, the reader's understanding of the events, places, and people described is colored by the very personal feelings of each writer. Their fears, opinions, and doubts help bring this long-past world to life, as shown here.

> *"In that hour, I would have welcomed death rather than see so many around me in such a condition."*
> **—Álvar Núñez Cabeza de Vaca**

> *"I was soon put down under the decks, and there I received a salutation in my nostrils as I had never experienced in my life; so that, with the loathsomeness of the stench, and crying together, I became so sick and low that I was not able to eat.*
> **—Olaudah Equiano**

> *"That night they quartered in the woods, he still expecting (as he had done all this long time of his imprisonment) every hour to be put to one death or other, for all their feasting."*
> **—Captain John Smith**

> *"Besides, what could they see but a hideous and desolate wilderness, full of wild beasts and wild men—and what multitudes there might be of them they knew not."*
> **—William Bradford**

Pocahontas rescues John Smith.

Extension

SPEAKING & LISTENING In a group of four students **debate** the following statement:

The narrators of the selections in this section are unreliable because of their personal and emotional involvement in the events and experiences they relate.

Writing to Evaluate

Review the selections beginning on page 72 and choose two documents that give you the most complete picture of this historical period. In a brief essay, evaluate how various features of the texts bring the ideas and events of this period to life.

Consider

- the themes of each selection
- descriptive details, images, and dialogue that enhance meaning and advance the writer's purpose
- what the writer's personal feelings and ideas add to your understanding or interest in the work

COMMON CORE

RI 9 Analyze seventeenth- and eighteenth-century foundational U.S. documents of historical and literary significance for their themes, purposes, and rhetorical features. **W 2** Write explanatory texts to examine complex ideas. **SL 1** Initiate and participate effectively in a range of collaborative discussions.

WRAP-UP **113**

COMMON CORE FOCUS

RI 9 Analyze seventeenth- and eighteenth-century foundational U.S. documents of historical and literary significance for their themes, purposes, and rhetorical features. **W 2** Write explanatory text to examine complex ideas. **SL 1** Initiate and participate effectively in a range of collaborative discussions.

Wrap-Up: Exploration and the Early Settlers

This Wrap-Up provides students with an opportunity to consider the unique views of early American life offered in the personal accounts of participants in that life. Urge students to keep in mind the prejudices and purposes of these first American writers.

Writing to Evaluate

- Review with students that *evaluating* involves forming opinions and judgments based on evidence, information, and personal insight. These critical tools allow students to make meaningful assessments of a work's value, interest, and reliability, as well as to place its historical information in the context of the writer's personal feelings and opinions.

Extension

- List the writers and selections on the board. Discuss each one, asking students whether the writer was believable or not.
- Ask students to brainstorm reasons that support or contradict the debate statement, then list these reasons in a T Chart.
- Suggest that students recall each writer's audience and purpose as they prepare to debate the statement.
- After groups complete their debate, invite them to share the results with the class.

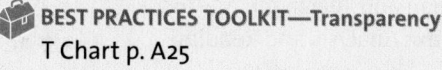 **BEST PRACTICES TOOLKIT—Transparency** T Chart p. A25

FOR STRUGGLING WRITERS

Writing Support Offer students this thesis sentence frame to begin their essays:

The firsthand account that gave me the most complete picture of _____ was "_____."

Then have students list two reasons. Tell them to develop one paragraph for each reason, using details, images, and dialogue from their chosen selection.

FOR ENGLISH LANGUAGE LEARNERS

Writing Support Review these terms from the writing assignment:

- *descriptive details,* "details that tell how a thing looks, sounds, tastes, feels, or smells"
- *images,* "mental pictures created for readers, usually with descriptive details"
- *dialogue,* "the exact words of a character"
- *visualization,* "the process of picturing a description or text in your mind"

Focus and Motivate

Essential Course of Study **ECOS**

To My Dear and Loving Husband *and* Upon the Burning of Our House, July 10th, 1666
Poetry by Anne Bradstreet

Huswifery
Poetry by Edward Taylor

COMMON CORE FOCUS

RL 4 Determine the meaning of words and phrases as they are used in the text, including figurative meanings; analyze the impact of specific word choices on meaning and tone. **RL 9** Demonstrate knowledge of how two or more works from the same time period treat similar themes or topics. **L 3a** Apply an understanding of syntax to the study of complex texts when reading. **L 4** Clarify the meaning of unknown words and phrases. **L 5a** Interpret figures of speech in context and analyze their role in the text.

COMMON CORE **RL 4** Determine the meaning of words and phrases as they are used in the text, including figurative meanings; analyze the impact of specific word choices on meaning and tone. **L 3a** Apply an understanding of syntax to the study of complex texts when reading. **L 4** Clarify the meaning of unknown words and phrases. **L 5a** Interpret figures of speech in context and analyze their role in the text.

ABOUT THE POETS

Anne Bradstreet After students have read about Bradstreet, explain that the title of her book is an allusion to the nine Muses (goddesses of the arts and sciences) in Greek mythology. Bradstreet later became famous for personal meditations such as the two poems that students are about to read.

Edward Taylor After students have read about Taylor, tell them that the discovery of his manuscripts is considered one of the most important "finds" in American literary history. Ask students to consider why Taylor, like Bradstreet, did not attempt to publish his poetry.

NOTABLE QUOTE

"Authority without wisdom is like a heavy axe without an edge, fitter to bruise than polish."
—Anne Bradstreet

Ask students what Bradstreet sees as the difference between "authority" and "wisdom."

Meet the Authors

Anne Bradstreet
c. 1612–1672

Anne Bradstreet was essentially the first notable American poet, man or woman. Considering that Puritan women were not encouraged to improve their minds—let alone express their ideas—this achievement is remarkable.

Coming to America Anne Dudley Bradstreet was born in England and raised on an estate, which her father managed for the Earl of Lincoln. With access to the earl's library, she received a good education. In 1628, 16-year-old Anne married Simon Bradstreet. Two years later, the young couple sailed for Massachusetts.

After her privileged upbringing, Anne Bradstreet was not prepared for the harsh living conditions of colonial America. Her religious faith helped her endure these hardships—as did writing poetry.

Personal Poetry Bradstreet focused primarily on the realities of her life—her husband, her eight children, and her house. In 1650, without her knowledge, Bradstreet's brother-in-law had some of her verses published in London in a volume titled *The Tenth Muse Lately Sprung Up in America.* It was the first book of poetry ever published by an American colonist.

Edward Taylor 1642?–1729

For over 200 years, the work of Edward Taylor, one of colonial America's most inventive poets, remained unread. His poetry did not come to light until the 1930s when his long-forgotten manuscripts were discovered in the Yale University Library.

Frontier Parson and Poet Born in England, Taylor came to America in 1668 to escape religious persecution in his homeland. In 1671, after graduating from Harvard University, Taylor became the minister of a church in Westfield, Massachusetts. He held that position until his death 58 years later.

The wilderness town of Westfield presented many challenges to the highly intellectual Taylor. But he undertook his roles as farmer, physician, and minister with energy. He even called his flock to worship by beating a drum.

Like Anne Bradstreet—a volume of whose work he owned—Taylor wrote his poetry to glorify God. He found his subjects in human life, nature, and everyday activities. His poems on these topics served as a form of worship.

114

Selection Resources

See resources on the **Teacher One Stop DVD-ROM** *and on* **thinkcentral.com.**

 RESOURCE MANAGER UNIT 1
Plan and Teach, pp. 153–160
Text Analysis and Reading Skill, pp. 161–164*†

DIAGNOSTIC AND SELECTION TESTS
Selection Tests, pp. 53–56

 BEST PRACTICES TOOLKIT
Two-Column Chart, p. A25

INTERACTIVE READER

ADAPTED INTERACTIVE READER

ELL ADAPTED INTERACTIVE READER

TECHNOLOGY
- Teacher One Stop DVD-ROM
- Student One Stop DVD-ROM
- PowerNotes DVD-ROM
- Audio Anthology CD
- GrammarNotes DVD-ROM
- ExamView Test Generator on the Teacher One Stop

THINK central

Video Trailer

Go to **thinkcentral.com** to preview the **Video Trailer** introducing this selection. Other features that support the selection include
- **PowerNotes** presentation
- **ThinkAloud** models to enhance comprehension
- **WordSharp** vocabulary tutorials
- interactive writing and grammar instruction

* Resources for Differentiation   † Also in Spanish

TEXT ANALYSIS: FIGURATIVE LANGUAGE

Like all poets, Puritan poets used **figurative language** to create imagery and communicate ideas beyond the literal meaning of words. Figurative language helped the Puritan poets convey ideas about their religious faith and their personal lives. As you read the poems by Anne Bradstreet and Edward Taylor, look for the types of figures of speech listed below.

- A **metaphor** is a figure of speech that directly compares two unlike things without using *like* or *as*. (*Our house is our nest.*)
- An **extended metaphor** is one that draws the comparison out and compares the two things at length and in many ways. (*Our house is our nest; we fly away only to return to its snug protection.*)
- **Personification** is a figure of speech in which an object, animal, or idea is given human characteristics. (*Our house wraps our family in a warm embrace.*)
- **Hyperbole** is a figure of speech in which the truth is exaggerated for emphasis. (*Our house means more to us than all the money in the world.*)
- Also note the effect of any biblical **allusions,** or references, and how they enhance the meaning of the poem.

READING STRATEGY: CLARIFY MEANING IN OLDER POETRY

When reading works from the Puritan era, it is important to stop and **clarify meaning** by rereading and restating difficult passages as needed in order to fully appreciate the literature. Be aware of the following as you read the Puritan poets:

- **Archaic language**—words that were once in common use but that are now considered old-fashioned or out-of-date
- **Inverted syntax**—sentence structure in which the expected order of words is reversed

As you read each poem, use a chart like the one shown to record and restate examples of archaic language and inverted syntax.

"Upon the Burning of Our House"	
Archaic Language	Inverted Syntax
"blest" (blessed)	"when rest I took" (when I took rest)

 Complete the activities in your **Reader/Writer Notebook**.

What do you VALUE most?

The things that we value in life may be actual objects or they may be less tangible. For instance, a person might prize a favorite CD or jacket. On the other hand, the gift of family may outweigh more material possessions. The Puritan poets you are about to read valued family life and their religious faith above all things. What do you prize most in your life?

QUICKWRITE Imagine that a reality show has offered you the chance to win a million dollars. The catch is that you will have to give up an object, a person, or a belief that you truly value. Assume that you are not willing to make the sacrifice. Write a brief letter to explain why you must turn down the money.

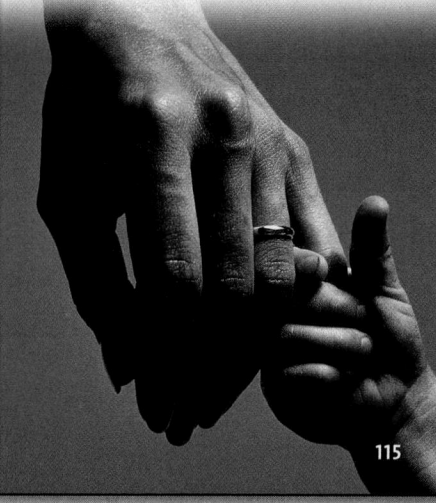

115

115

SUMMARY

The speaker in this poem describes her love for her husband and the value that she places upon his love for her. She concludes by saying that they will be rewarded in heaven for their love.

READ WITH A PURPOSE

Help students set a purpose for reading. As they read the poems, ask them to think about the religious beliefs that the speakers relay.

TEXT ANALYSIS   COMMON CORE   RL 4   L 5a

Ⓐ FIGURATIVE LANGUAGE

Possible answer: Bradstreet uses hyperbole to emphasize how she values her husband's love, which is more precious to her than "whole mines of gold" and "all the riches" of the East, and that her own love is so strong that "rivers cannot quench" it.

READING STRATEGY   COMMON CORE   L 3a   L 4

Ⓑ *Model The Skill:* CLARIFY MEANING

To clarify the meaning of lines 11–12, paraphrase these lines by restating the archaic language and untangling the inversions. Make sure students understand that "when we live no more" can be reworded as "when we aren't living anymore" and that "we may live ever" can be reworded as "we will be able to live forever."

Possible answer: Restatement: Then while we live, let's persevere in love so well that when we have died, we may live forever. These lines suggest a connection between earthly love and eternal life. By loving greatly in life, the speaker and her husband will be rewarded with everlasting life in heaven.

To My Dear and Loving Husband

Anne Bradstreet

If ever two were one, then surely we.
If ever man were loved by wife, then thee;
If ever wife was happy in a man,
Compare with me, ye women, if you can.
5   I prize thy love more than whole mines of gold
Or all the riches that the East doth hold.
My love is such that rivers cannot quench, Ⓐ
Nor ought but love from thee, give recompense.[1]
Thy love is such I can no way repay,
10   The heavens reward thee manifold, I pray.
Then while we live, in love let's so persevere[2]
That when we live no more, we may live ever. Ⓑ

Ⓐ **FIGURATIVE LANGUAGE**
Reread lines 5–7. How does the poet use **hyperbole** in these lines to emphasize her feelings for her husband?

Ⓑ **CLARIFY MEANING**
Use conventional word order to restate the **inverted syntax** in lines 11–12. What relationship do the lines suggest between earthly love and eternal life?

Analyze Visuals ▶
Many Puritan women stitched samplers like the one shown here. The samplers often depicted nature scenes or stories from the Bible. What values are suggested by the subject matter of the sampler?

1. **recompense** (rĕk'əm-pĕns'): payment in return for something, such as a service.
2. **persevere:** In Bradstreet's time, *persevere* would have been pronounced pûr-sĕv'ər, which rhymes with *ever*.

DIFFERENTIATED INSTRUCTION

FOR STRUGGLING READERS

Concept Support: Archaic Language To prepare students for some of the most common archaic language that they will encounter in the poems, write these two groups of words on the board: (1) *hast, hath, art, shalt, doth, didst* and (2) *thou, thee, thy, thine, ye.* Explain that the first group consists of older forms of the verbs *have, has, are, shall, does,* and *did.* Then explain that the second group contains older pronouns in place of which we now use *you* (*thou* and *thee*), *your* (*thy*) and *yours* (*thine*). *Ye* was originally a plural form of *you,* and was also used when addressing someone of superior rank.

Reading Support

This selection on **thinkcentral.com** includes embedded **ThinkAloud** models—students "thinking aloud" about the story to model the kinds of questions a good reader would ask about a selection.

Analyze Visuals

Possible answer: *The man and woman shown working together suggest the value of family life and the virtue of honest labor. The tree and bird convey the value of appreciating nature and its bounty. The apple tree may allude to the biblical account of Adam and Eve in the Garden of Eden and thus may suggest the value of religious faith.*

About the Art The sampler is a pillow cover made of silk and wool. The lettering reveals that it was stitched by Abigail Gould in 1796, when she was 12 years old. Like Bradstreet, Gould probably never intended her simple work to be put on display—as it is today at Boston's Museum of Fine Arts.

BACKGROUND

Puritan Belief Calvinist in their theology, Puritans believed in the absolute sovereignty of God—the idea that God is in complete control of events and ultimately works all things out for a believer's good. Anne Bradstreet reveals that belief by interpreting her personal subject matter through a religious lens. In her poems, every event, no matter how trivial, carries a divine message; each blessing or loss reveals God's will and an opportunity for spiritual growth. Bradstreet's poetry helps us understand the Puritan belief that individual events are part of God's master plan.

FOR STRUGGLING READERS

Clarify Meaning

- Explain the meaning of these archaic words from the poem: *ought* (line 8), "anything"; *manifold* (line 10), "in many ways."

- Point out that many of Bradstreet's constructions omit words that are understood. For example, in line 1 the word *are* is left out at the end: "If ever two were one, then surely we [are]." Similarly, in line 2, the words *I love*

are omitted: "If ever man were loved by wife, then [I love] thee." Work with students to add omitted words to lines 4 and 7. *Possible answers:* *Compare yourselves with me, ye women, if you can (line 4); My love is such that rivers cannot quench it (line 7).*

FOR ADVANCED LEARNERS/AP

Research Archaic Pronouns and Verbs Explain that English once had two types of second-person pronouns: the familiar singular forms *thou, thee, thy,* and *thine* plus the polite or plural forms *you/ye* and *yours.* The familiar forms were used to address friends, family members (as in Bradstreet), or God (as in Taylor). Have student pairs do research to see how the forms of *you* have changed over time. Suggest that students create a chart to summarize their research.

After her beloved home is destroyed in a fire, the poem's speaker grieves over her devastating loss but recognizes that true wealth, and her true home, are in heaven.

REVISIT THE BIG QUESTION

What do you **VALUE** *most?*

Discuss In lines 13–20, why does the speaker believe that she shouldn't value personal property? *Possible answer: She should not place too high a value on personal property because it is not really hers; it belongs to God (line 17).*

Upon the
Burning of Our House,
July 10th, 1666

Anne Bradstreet

In silent night when rest I took
For sorrow near I did not look
I wakened was with thund'ring noise
And piteous shrieks of dreadful voice.
5 That fearful sound of "Fire!" and "Fire!"
Let no man know is my desire. **C**

I, starting up, the light did spy,
And to my God my heart did cry
To strengthen me in my distress
10 And not to leave me succorless.[1]
Then, coming out, beheld a space
The flame consume my dwelling place.

And when I could no longer look,
I blest His name that gave and took,[2]
15 That laid my goods now in the dust:
Yea, so it was, and so 'twas just.
It was His own, it was not mine,
Far be it that I should repine;[3]

---

1. **succorless** (sŭk'ər-lĭs): without help or relief.
2. **I . . . took:** an allusion to Job 1:21 in the Bible—"The Lord gave, and the Lord hath taken away; blessed be the name of the Lord."
3. **repine:** to complain or fret; to long for something.

C CLARIFY MEANING
Paraphrase lines 1–6 to clarify their meaning. How does the poet use contrast to convey a sense of fear?

Language Coach

Meanings of Idioms
The phrase "Far be it" in line 18 is an **idiom**, an expression whose overall meaning is different from that of the individual words. "Far be it" means "I wouldn't dare to. . . ." How does the speaker view herself in relation to God?

FOR STRUGGLING READERS

Develop Reading Fluency Read the first stanza aloud for students. Explain to students how the line breaks and punctuation guided you in your pacing and intonation. Also, explain how you emphasized words such as "thund'ring" and "dreadful" to relay the stanza's mood. Have students form pairs and then choose a stanza to focus on. Have partners work together to examine the stanza's line breaks, punctuation marks, and important words.

FOR ENGLISH LANGUAGE LEARNERS

Language Coach

Meanings of Idioms Ask students how each of the following characters could use the idiom "far be it" in a line of dialogue:

• Cara knows that her mother just paid the bills, so she should not ask for money to go shopping.

• Rasheed would like to play hockey, but he knows that he needs to study for his exam if he wants to pass the class.

Have each student use the idiom "far be it" in a sentence that pertains to his or her own life.

He might of all justly bereft,
20 But yet sufficient for us left.
When by the ruins oft I past,
My sorrowing eyes aside did cast,
And here and there the places spy
Where oft I sat and long did lie:

25 Here stood that trunk and there that chest,
There lay that store I counted best.
My pleasant things in ashes lie,
And them behold no more shall I.
Under thy roof no guest shall sit,
30 Nor at thy table eat a bit.

No pleasant tale shall e'er be told,
Nor things recounted done of old.
No candle e'er shall shine in thee,
Nor bridegroom's voice e'er heard shall be.
35 In silence ever shalt thou lie;
Adieu, Adieu, all's vanity.[4]

Then straight I 'gin my heart to chide,[5]
And did thy wealth on earth abide?
Didst fix thy hope on mold'ring dust? **D**
40 The arm of flesh didst make thy trust?
Raise up thy thoughts above the sky
That dunghill mists away may fly.

Thou hast an house on high erect,
Framed by that mighty Architect,
45 With glory richly furnishéd,
Stands permanent though this be fled.
It's purchaséd and paid for too
By Him who hath enough to do. **E**

A price so vast as is unknown
50 Yet by His gift is made thine own;
There's wealth enough, I need no more,
Farewell, my pelf,[6] farewell my store.
The world no longer let me love,
My hope and treasure lies above.

---

4. **all's vanity:** an allusion to Ecclesiastes 1:2 in the Bible—"All is vanity," meaning that all is temporary and meaningless.

5. **chide:** to scold mildly so as to correct or improve.

6. **pelf:** wealth or riches, especially when dishonestly acquired.

COMMON CORE   RL 4

D ALLUSION
Bradstreet's Puritan readers were well acquainted with the language of the King James translation of the Bible, the authoritative English translation of their time. As daily readers of the Bible, they would have recognized numerous **biblical allusions** in the language of her poems. In the word *dust* (lines 15 and 39), they would have heard a reference to the Book of Genesis: "Dust thou art and unto dust shalt thou return." Reread lines 13–39. Then, check the footnote for the biblical allusion in line 36. How does this allusion work with the allusion in the word *dust* to express Bradstreet's theme in this poem? Explain your response.

E FIGURATIVE LANGUAGE
Reread lines 43–48. What two things does Bradstreet compare in the **metaphor** in these lines?

D ALLUSION

Tell students that an **allusion** is a reference, direct or indirect, to someone or something outside of a literary work. Allusions can refer to another work of literature or to events or persons in history, art, religion, or some other branch of culture.

Possible answer: Allusion is to the fact that the house was reduced to dust following the fire. It expresses the theme by restating the idea that material goods are not as important as spiritual goods.

E FIGURATIVE LANGUAGE

Possible answer: Bradstreet's metaphor compares a temporary earthly home with an eternal home in heaven (a home built and paid for by God and furnished with glory).

FOR STRUGGLING READERS

Comprehension Support Have students reread the poem, looking for answers to these questions:

- What vivid memories does the speaker have of the house that has been destroyed? (line 25–30)

- What events had the speaker hoped to experience in that house? (line 31–34)

- How does the speaker envision the house that will be hers after her death? (line 43–54)

FOR ADVANCED LEARNERS/AP

Write a Journal Entry Have students think about the events of the poem and draw inferences based on textual evidence. Then ask them to imagine that the speaker is a close friend of theirs. Have students write and share a journal entry about the night her house burned down and how she responded to the tragedy. Encourage them to include their feelings about the speaker and her family. Offer students the option of imagining that the speaker is the poet.

SUMMARY

In this poem, the speaker develops an extended metaphor in which he asks God to transform him so that he can become all that God wants him to be.

READING STRATEGY
COMMON CORE
L 3a
L 4

F CLARIFY MEANING

Possible answer: *These lines describe the activity of using a spinning wheel to make yarn for weaving.*

TEXT ANALYSIS
COMMON CORE
RL 4
L 5a

G *Model the Skill:* FIGURATIVE LANGUAGE

To identify the extended metaphor, point out to students phrases that illustrate the metaphor, such as "Thy spinning wheel" (line 1), "Thy holy spool" (line 4), and "weave the web Thyself" (line 9). *Possible answer:* *The extended metaphor compares the transformation of wool to cloth and clothing to the speaker's relationship with God, who transforms him.*

TIERED DISCUSSION PROMPTS

In lines 1–18, use these prompts to help students explore the poem's theme:

Interpret Why does the speaker ask God to make him a spinning wheel (line 1) and a loom (line 7)? *Possible answer:* *The speaker wants God to change him so that he will be an instrument that God controls completely.*

Synthesize How do the speaker's requests reflect Taylor's Puritan beliefs? *Possible answer:* *They reflect the Puritan belief that God controls everything.*

SELECTION WRAP–UP

READ WITH A PURPOSE Now that students have read the poems, ask them to describe a religious belief demonstrated in all three poems. *Possible answer:* *All three poems relay a reliance on God's wisdom.*

Huswifery   **Edward Taylor**

Make me, O Lord, Thy spinning wheel complete.
Thy holy word my distaff[1] make for me.
Make mine affections Thy swift flyers[2] neat,
And make my soul Thy holy spool to be.
5 My conversation make to be Thy reel,
And reel the yarn thereon spun of Thy wheel. **F**

Make me Thy loom then, knit therein this twine:
And make Thy holy spirit, Lord, wind quills:[3]
Then weave the web Thyself. The yarn is fine.
10 Thine ordinances make my fulling mills.[4]
Then dye the same in heavenly colors choice,
All pinked[5] with varnished flowers of paradise.

Then clothe therewith mine understanding, will,
Affections, judgment, conscience, memory;
15 My words and actions, that their shine may fill
My ways with glory and Thee glorify.
Then mine apparel shall display before Ye
That I am clothed in holy robes for glory. **G**

F CLARIFY MEANING
Huswifery means "housekeeping." What housekeeping activity is being described in lines 1–6?

G FIGURATIVE LANGUAGE
What **extended metaphor** does Taylor use throughout the poem to express his relationship to God?

---

1. **distaff:** staff on a spinning wheel for holding the wool or flax to be spun.
2. **flyers:** parts of spinning wheels that twist fibers into yarn.
3. **quills:** rods or spindles used to wind and hold yarn.
4. **fulling mills:** machines that beat and process woven cloth to make it denser and more compact.
5. **pinked:** decorated.

DIFFERENTIATED INSTRUCTION

FOR STRUGGLING READERS

Explore Metaphorical Details To create his extended metaphor, Taylor provides several interrelated comparisons. Work with students to complete a Two-Column Chart, such as the one begun here, that identifies the two terms in each comparison. Discuss the finished charts, making sure students understand that the details show that the speaker wants to serve God completely, in every way.

Everyday Object	Compared to …
"spinning wheel" (line 1)	"me" (the speaker)
"my distaff" (line 2)	"Thy holy word"
"flyers" (line 3)	"mine affections"
"spool" (line 4)	"my soul"
"reel" (line 5)	"My conversation"

 **BEST PRACTICES TOOLKIT—Transparency**
Two-Column Chart p. A25

Comprehension

1. **Recall** In "To My Dear and Loving Husband," what does the speaker value more than gold?

2. **Recall** When the speaker in "Upon the Burning of Our House" wakes up to find her house on fire, what is her initial reaction?

3. **Clarify** The speaker in Taylor's "Huswifery" compares himself to a loom. Who or what is compared to the weaver?

Text Analysis

● 4. **Clarify Meaning** Review the examples of **archaic language** and **inverted syntax** you recorded as you read the poems. How would you restate lines 19–20 of "Upon the Burning of Our House": "He might of all justly bereft, / But yet sufficient for us left"?

5. **Draw Conclusions** Use details from the two poems by Anne Bradstreet to explain what she reveals about her

   • marriage   • religious beliefs   • daily life

6. **Make Inferences** What did Bradstreet **value** more than her house? How did this help her accept the loss of her house by fire?

● 7. **Analyze Figurative Language** How do the "holy robes for glory" mentioned in line 18 of "Huswifery" complete the poem's **extended metaphor**?

8. **Compare Literary Works** What do the poems by Bradstreet and Taylor have in common? What distinguishes one poet's work from the other's? In a chart like the one shown, compare and contrast the poets' work, noting the religious views expressed, the formality of each poet's **style,** and the personality revealed. Use specific details from the poems to complete the chart.

	Bradstreet	Taylor
Religious Views		
Style		
Personality		

Text Criticism

9. **Examine Social Context** The Puritans strongly disapproved of women writers. A Puritan minister even wrote a letter to his sister in England saying, "Your printing of a book, beyond the custom of your sex, doth rankly smell." In spite of this disapproval, do you think the Puritan community would have considered any aspects of Anne Bradstreet's poetry praiseworthy? Explain your answer.

What do you **VALUE** most?

Consider the various things that people value in modern society. What might the Puritans think of some modern values? What do you think of modern values?

COMMON CORE

RL 4 Determine the meaning of words and phrases as they are used in the text, including figurative meanings; analyze the impact of specific word choices on meaning and tone. **RL 9** Demonstrate knowledge of how two or more works from the same period treat similar themes or topics. **L 3a** Apply an understanding of syntax to the study of complex texts when reading. **L 5a** Interpret figures of speech in context and analyze their role in the text.

Practice and Apply

For preliminary support of post-reading questions, use these copy masters:

R RESOURCE MANAGER—Copy Masters
Figurative Language p. 161
Question Support p. 165

Additional selection questions are provided for teachers on page 157.

ANSWERS **COMMON CORE RL 4, RL 9, L 3a, L 5a**

1. *Bradstreet values her husband's love more than gold.*

2. *The speaker initially prays to God for strength and help.*

3. *God is compared with the weaver.*

Possible answers:

4. ● **COMMON CORE FOCUS** *Clarify Meaning in Older Poetry* *God is entitled to take everything away but will meet our needs.*

5. *"To My Dear and Loving Husband": Lines 1–4 suggest a strong, loving marriage.* *"Upon the Burning of Our House": Lines 19–20 and 49–54 reveal a strong faith in God; lines 25–34 suggest a happy and sociable daily life*

6. *More than her house, Bradstreet valued her faith in God. This faith helped her accept her loss and recognize that material possessions are relatively unimportant.*

7. ● **COMMON CORE FOCUS** *Figurative Language* *The image of the "holy robes" completes the poem's extended metaphor by showing the garment that is the finished product of the clothing-making process the speaker has described.*

8. *Religious Views: Both poets have a deep religious faith; both look to God for help.* *Style:*

Assess and Reteach

Assess

DIAGNOSTIC AND SELECTION TESTS

Selection Test A pp. 53–54
Selection Test B/C pp. 55–56

Interactive Selection Test on thinkcentral.com

Reteach

Level Up Online Tutorials on thinkcentral.com

Reteaching Worksheets on thinkcentral.com

Literature Lessons 27, 29, 44
Study Skills Lesson 12

Bradstreet uses more accessible language; Taylor's style is more formal; both use figurative language, but Taylor's is more complex and extended; both poets also use archaic language and inverted syntax. **Personality:** *Bradstreet provides personal details and insights into her emotions, making her seem human and real; Taylor is personal but offers little insight into his life, making him seem more remote.*

9. *Yes, Puritans probably would have approved of Bradstreet's glorification of God and her reconciliation to the loss of*

material possessions. No, they might have thought it inappropriate for her poetry to focus on her personal life.

What do you **VALUE** most?

Students should use the knowledge they have obtained about Puritan values to determine what Puritans might think of modern values. Students should also relay their own thoughts about modern values.

Focus and Motivate

COMMON CORE FOCUS

RI 3 Analyze a complex set of ideas and explain how specific ideas interact and develop over the course of the text. **RI 4** Determine the meaning of words as they are used in a text, including connotative meanings. **RI 6** Determine an author's point of view or purpose in a text in which the rhetoric is particularly effective, analyzing how style and content contribute to the power, persuasiveness, or beauty of the text. **L 3** Apply knowledge of language to understand how language functions in different contexts and to comprehend more fully when reading. **L 4a** Use context as a clue to the meaning of a word. **L 5** Demonstrate understanding of nuances in word meanings.

ABOUT THE AUTHOR

After students read the biography, emphasize that Edwards's focus on emotion does not mean that he rejected careful thought. As they read the excerpt from his sermon, have students note how he structures his argument. Also, be prepared to discuss the term "born again" (a personal commitment of faith instead of reliance upon church membership or good deeds) and encourage students to see how Edwards explains the concept.

NOTABLE QUOTE

"[I wish] to lie low before God, as in the dust; that I might be nothing, and that God might be all, that I might become as a little child."
—Jonathan Edwards

Selection Resources

COMMON CORE

RI 3 Analyze a complex set of ideas and explain how specific ideas interact and develop over the course of the text. **RI 6** Determine an author's point of view or purpose in a text in which the rhetoric is particularly effective, analyzing how style and content contribute to the power, persuasiveness, or beauty of the text. **L 3** Apply knowledge of language to understand how language functions in different contexts and to comprehend more fully when reading.

DID YOU KNOW?

Jonathan Edwards . . .

- wrote a paper on spiders at age 11.
- died as a result of a smallpox inoculation.
- was the grandfather of Aaron Burr, vice-president under Thomas Jefferson.

The Puritan Tradition

from Sinners in the Hands of an Angry God

Sermon by Jonathan Edwards

VIDEO TRAILER **THINK** central KEYWORD: HML11-122A

Essential Course of Study

Meet the Author

Jonathan Edwards 1703–1758

When Jonathan Edwards delivered a sermon, with its fiery descriptions of hell and eternal damnation, people listened. Edwards believed that religion should be rooted not only in reason but also in emotion. Although 19th-century editors tried to tone down his style, Edwards is recognized today as a masterful preacher. In fact, he is considered by many to be America's greatest religious thinker.

A Spiritual Calling Born in East Windsor, Connecticut, Edwards was a child prodigy and entered what is now Yale University at the age of 12. While a graduate student there, Edwards experienced a spiritual crisis that led to what he later described as "religious joy." He came to believe that such an intense religious experience was an important step toward salvation.

In 1722, after finishing his education, Edwards followed the path of his father and grandfather and became a Puritan minister. In 1726, Edwards began assisting his grandfather, who was the minister at the parish church in Northampton, Massachusetts. When his grandfather died three years later, Edwards became the church's pastor.

Religious Revivalist Edwards soon became an effective preacher. In 1734 and 1735, he delivered a series of sermons that resulted in a great number of conversions. The converts believed they had felt God's grace and were "born again" when they accepted Jesus Christ.

Edwards's sermons helped trigger the Great Awakening, a religious revival that swept through New England from 1734 to 1750. The movement grew out of a sense among some Puritan ministers that their congregations had grown too self-satisfied. Delivered at the height of the Great Awakening, "Sinners in the Hands of an Angry God" is the most famous of Edwards's nearly 1,200 sermons.

Last Years Although Edwards inspired thousands, his church dismissed him in 1750 because he wanted to limit membership to those who had undergone conversion. A year later, Edwards went to Stockbridge, Massachusetts, where he became a missionary in a Native American settlement. In 1757, he accepted an appointment as president of what is now Princeton University.

By the time of Edwards's death the following year, the extremism of the Great Awakening had been rejected. However, his vision of humanity suspended, like a spider, over the burning pit of hell still maintains its emotional impact.

Author Online THINK central

Go to **thinkcentral.com**. KEYWORD: HML11-122B

See resources on the **Teacher One Stop DVD-ROM** *and on* **thinkcentral.com**.

** RESOURCE MANAGER UNIT 1**

Plan and Teach, pp. 167–174
Summary, pp. 175–176 † ‡*
Text Analysis and Reading Skill, pp. 177–180 †*
Vocabulary, pp. 181–183*

DIAGNOSTIC AND SELECTION TESTS

Selection Tests, pp. 57–60

** BEST PRACTICES TOOLKIT**

Open Mind, p. D9

INTERACTIVE READER

ADAPTED INTERACTIVE READER

ELL ADAPTED INTERACTIVE READER

TECHNOLOGY

- **Teacher One Stop DVD-ROM**
- **Student One Stop DVD-ROM**
- **PowerNotes DVD-ROM**
- **Audio Anthology CD**
- **GrammarNotes DVD-ROM**
- **ExamView Test Generator** on the Teacher One Stop

Video Trailer THINK central

Go to **thinkcentral.com** to preview the **Video Trailer** introducing this selection. Other features that support the selection include

- **PowerNotes** presentation
- **ThinkAloud** models to enhance comprehension
- **WordSharp** vocabulary tutorials
- interactive writing and grammar instruction

---

* Resources for Differentiation   † Also in Spanish   ‡ Also in Haitian Creole and Vietnamese

TEXT ANALYSIS: PERSUASION

Puritan theologian Jonathan Edwards delivered powerfully persuasive sermons. As in all persuasive writing, an Edwards sermon is shaped by the author's **purpose**, his **audience**, and his **context**—that is, his reason for preaching, his Puritan congregation, and the times in which the Puritans lived. One of Edwards's most prominent rhetorical or persuasive techniques is the use of biblical **allusions**—references to figures, events, or places in the Bible that he assumed his congregation would recognize.

As you read Edwards's sermon, look for passages that reveal how purpose and audience affect the tone of his sermon.

READING SKILL: ANALYZE EMOTIONAL APPEALS

Emotional appeals are messages designed to persuade an audience by creating strong feelings. They often include sensory language to create vivid imagery and loaded words to create these types of feelings:

- **fear,** which taps into a fear of losing one's safety or security
- **pity,** which draws on a sympathy or compassion for others
- **guilt,** which relies on one's sense of ethics or morality

As you read, use a chart like the one below to record examples of language that appeals to the emotions.

Examples	Emotional Appeals
"arrows of death fly unseen"	appeals to fear by creating anxiety, unease

▲ VOCABULARY IN CONTEXT

Jonathan Edwards uses the listed words to help convey his spiritual message. Choose a word from the list that is a synonym for each of the numbered words.

WORD LIST		
abhor	deliverance	mitigation
abominable	discern	whet
appease	incense	
ascribe	induce	

1. detest
2. easing
3. sharpened
4. anger greatly
5. attribute

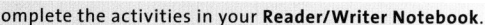 Complete the activities in your **Reader/Writer Notebook**.

What keeps you IN LINE?

A sense of morality probably keeps you from cheating on a test. In other words, you know cheating is wrong. But there are other reasons for behaving morally. Some people are anxious to please. Others fear the consequences of breaking the rules. Jonathan Edwards uses fear to get his point across in the sermon you're about to read.

ROLE-PLAY With a partner, take turns role-playing a conversation with a child who has been stealing. Your mission is to persuade him or her to stop. Before you begin, consider how best to keep the child in line. For example, you might frighten or shame the child or appeal to his or her pride.

123

What keeps you IN LINE?

Call on volunteers to name other factors that might keep people from violating standards of morality and to comment upon the idea of fear as a motivator. Suggest that students choose the most persuasive factor from the discussion as the tactic they use in the *ROLE-PLAY* activity.

TEXT ANALYSIS
COMMON CORE RI 3 RI 6

● *Model the Skill:* **PERSUASION**

Help students understand the persuasive writing used in this selection by reading this example aloud:

> You who gossip about your neighbors— your tongues will shrivel even as you speak. End your gossiping ways!

Point out that these words have a specific purpose, audience, and context. They are meant to warn people to stop gossiping, spoken to an audience of townspeople who attend a church or revival meeting.

GUIDED PRACTICE Ask students to identify the purpose, audience, and context for some advertisements they have read or seen.

READING SKILL
COMMON CORE RI 6 L 3

■ *Model the Skill:* **ANALYZE EMOTIONAL APPEALS**

Reread the example in the previous note. Examine Edwards's sensory language by pointing out that "tongues will shrivel" creates a fear of pain and physical harm.

GUIDED PRACTICE Have students reword the example to make listeners feel pity for those who gossip or guilt about having gossiped.

R RESOURCE MANAGER—Copy Master Analyze Emotional Appeals p. 179 (for student use while reading the selection)

VOCABULARY

COMMON CORE L 4

▲ VOCABULARY IN CONTEXT

DIAGNOSE WORD KNOWLEDGE Have students complete Vocabulary in Context. Check their word choices against the following:

abhor (ăb-hôr') *v.* to regard with disgust

abominable (ə-bŏm'ə-nə-bəl) *adj.* thoroughly detestable

appease (ə-pēz') *v.* to bring peace, quiet, or calm to; to soothe

ascribe (ə-skrīb') *v.* to attribute to a specified cause or source

deliverance (dĭ-lĭv'ər-əns) *n.* rescue from danger

discern (dĭ-sûrn') *v.* to perceive or recognize something

incense (ĭn-sĕns') *v.* to cause to be extremely angry

induce (ĭn-do͞os') *v.* to succeed in persuading someone to do something

mitigation (mĭt-ĭ-gā'shən) *n.* lessening of something that causes suffering

whet (hwĕt) *adj.* sharpened

R RESOURCE MANAGER—Copy Master Vocabulary Study p. 181

SUMMARY

In this sermon excerpt, Jonathan Edwards describes God's great anger toward sinners—people who may attend church and appear religious but who have not experienced a personal conversion. He warns sinners that at any moment, God may send them to hell, whose torments Edwards describes in vivid detail. He concludes, however, with an offer of hope, urging sinners to come to faith in Christ.

READ WITH A PURPOSE

Help students set a purpose for reading. Tell them to read "Sinners in the Hands of an Angry God" to learn how Jonathan Edwards used vivid, emotional language to persuade his congregation to believe deeply in a vengeful God.

TEXT ANALYSIS

COMMON CORE
RI 3
RI 6

Ⓐ Model the Skill: PERSUASION

Draw an Open Mind diagram on the board and show students how they can use it to analyze what might be going through the congregation's minds as they hear Edwards's words.

Possible answer: *The audience probably responded with curiosity about which people "now in this congregation" Edwards might have in mind and with some anxiety or dismay about what more he might say.*

> Is he saying that I'm a worm or insect?
>
> I don't want to go to hell!
>
> Could God be angry with me?

Extend the Discussion Why do you think Edwards says that God is "a great deal more angry" with some audience members than with people who have already gone to hell?

BEST PRACTICES TOOLKIT—Transparency
Open Mind p. D9

Sinners in the Hands
of an
Angry God

Jonathan Edwards

BACKGROUND Jonathan Edwards delivered his sermon "Sinners in the Hands of an Angry God" in 1741 to a congregation in Enfield, Connecticut. Edwards read the sermon, as he always did, in a composed style, with few gestures or movements. However, the sermon had a dramatic effect on his parishioners, many of whom wept and moaned.

Analyze Visuals ▶
This painting by Italian artist Giuseppe Arcimboldo presents an **allegory** of fire. What lesson or message does the painting seem to suggest about the meaning of fire?

We find it easy to tread on and crush a worm that we see crawling on the earth; so it is easy for us to cut or singe a slender thread that any thing hangs by; thus easy is it for God when he pleases to cast his enemies down to hell. . . .

They[1] are now the objects of that very same *anger* and wrath of God, that is expressed in the torments of hell. And the reason why they do not go down to hell at each moment, is not because God, in whose power they are, is not then very angry with them; as angry as he is with many miserable creatures now tormented in hell, who there feel and bear the fierceness of his wrath. Yea, God is a great deal more angry with great numbers that are now on earth; yea, doubtless, with many that are now in this congregation, who it may be are at ease, than he is with many
10 of those who are now in the flames of hell. Ⓐ

Ⓐ PERSUASION
Reread lines 8–11. Notice that Edwards directly addresses his **audience** in these lines. How do you imagine the audience responded to these words?

---

1. **they:** Earlier in the sermon, Edwards refers to all "unconverted men," whom he considers God's enemies. Unconverted men are people who have not been "born again," meaning that they have not accepted Jesus Christ.

Fire, allegory (1566), Giuseppe Arcimboldo. Painted for Emperor Maximillian II. Limewood, 66.5 cm × 51 cm. Inv. 1585. Kunsthistorisches Museum, Vienna. © Erich Lessing/Art Resource, New York.

DIFFERENTIATED INSTRUCTION

FOR ENGLISH LANGUAGE LEARNERS

Vocabulary: Word Associations Explain that Edwards compares humans to worms God can kill at any time. Have pairs of students read lines 1–3 to identify words that relate to the worms (*"tread on," "crush," "crawling on the earth,"*) and about God's power (*"cast his enemies down to hell"*).

FOR ADVANCED LEARNERS/AP

Synthesize Point out the contrast between the emotionally charged sermon text and the fact that Edwards delivered the sermon by reading it aloud in a plain way. Then challenge students to deliver a few paragraphs as they think Edwards might have done—with enough emotion to show his sincerity but not so much that the message is overpowered by theatrics.

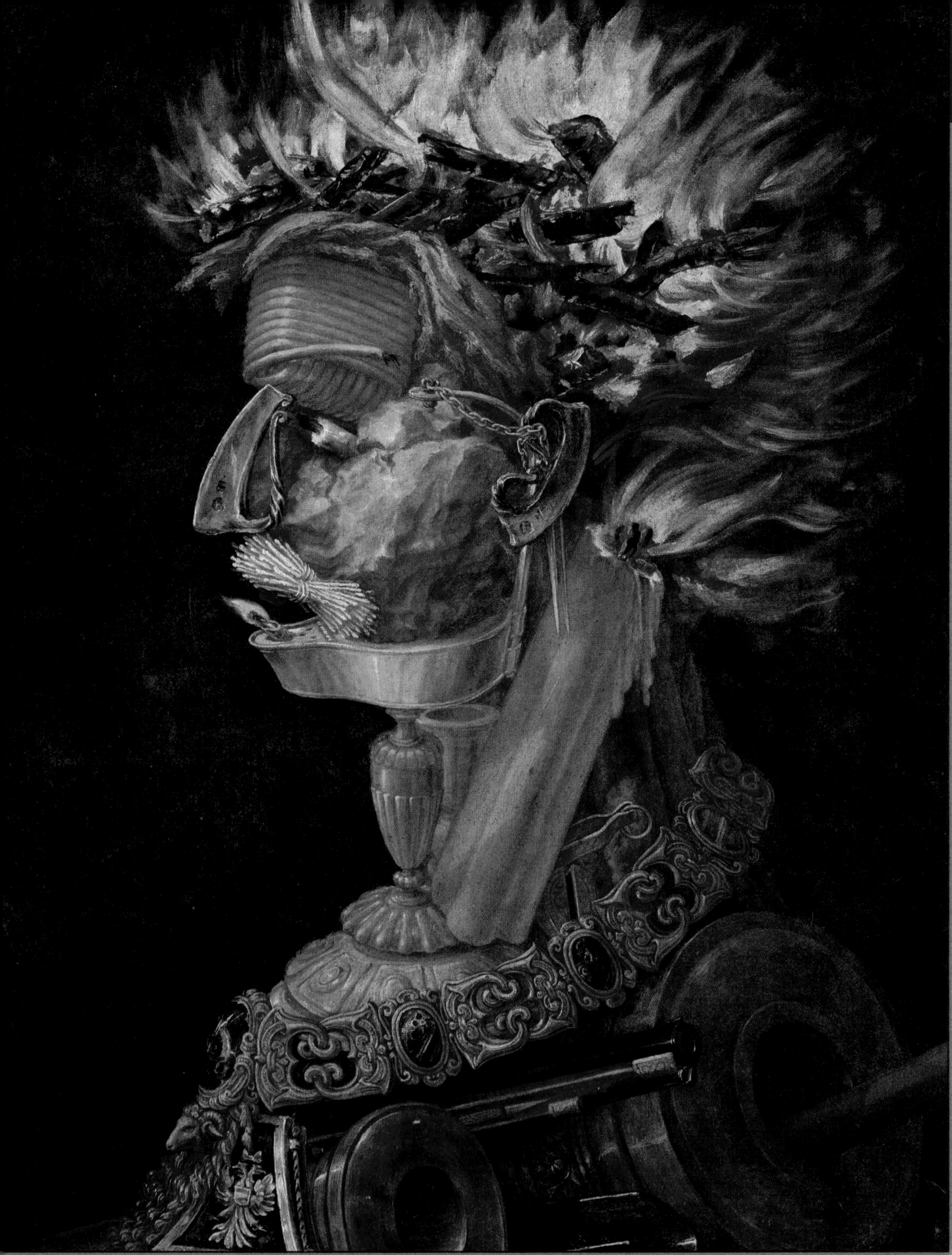

Reading Support

THINK central

This selection on **thinkcentral.com** includes embedded **ThinkAloud** models–students "thinking aloud" about the story to model the kinds of questions a good reader would ask about a selection.

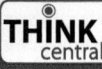

Analyze Visuals

Possible answer *The painting conveys the dehumanizing quality of fire and firepower.*

About the Art The fire is typical of the imaginative style of Giuseppe Arcimboldo (c. 1527–1593), who created portraits composed of flowers, fruit, animals, and other objects. The portraits often were mocking, satirical, or allegorical, conveying meaning about human nature rather than portraying a likeness. The image of fire is powerful in this painting—as it is in Jonathan Edwards's sermon, laced with descriptions of fiery torment in hell.

BACKGROUND

The Great Awakening The religious movement known as the Great Awakening was characterized by an enthusiasm that often evidenced itself in dynamic revival meetings—"revival" referring to the goal of renewing the spiritual passion that had marked the lives of many listeners' ancestors. Although Edwards was a major force in the movement in New England, other preachers spread the movement to all of the colonies. The movement sparked several social movements, including some early antislavery activities and missionary work among Native Americans. It also led to the founding of such prestigious colleges as Princeton, Dartmouth, and Rutgers.

FOR STRUGGLING READERS

In combination with the *Audio Anthology CD,* use one or more Targeted Passages (pp. 124, 126, 129) to ensure that students focus on key concepts in the selection. Targeted Passages are also good for English learners.

① Targeted Passage [Lines 2–6]

This introductory passage sets up the idea that God can and will judge sinners.

- According to Edwards, how hard is it for a person to crush a worm or burn the thread from which something may hang? (lines 1–3)
- Whom does God cast down to hell? Is it hard for God to take this action? (lines 2–3)
- What emotion from God do God's enemies feel most strongly? (line 4)

B ANALYZE EMOTIONAL APPEALS

Possible answer: *Edwards uses vivid images of the fires of hell, such as these: "the flames do now rage and glow" (lines 16–17); and "the pit hath opened its mouth under them" (line 18).*

C *Model the Skill:* ANALYZE EMOTIONAL APPEALS

Write *flame* and *inferno* on the board. Elicit that *inferno* is a synonym for flame but that it has negative connotations.

Possible answer: *These loaded terms have negative connotations: "the fiery pit" and "sentenced" (line 28); "dreadfully provoked" (line 29); and "suffering," "executions," and "the fierceness of his wrath in hell" (line 30).*

D PERSUASION

Possible answer: *The bow and arrow imagery may frighten the Colonialists by reminding them of Native American weapons.*

OWN THE WORD

- **whet:** Tell students that *whet* can also mean "to stimulate."

- **discern:** Have students create a semantic web for *discern*. Have students add synonyms. ***Possible answers:*** *observe, detect, notice, ascertain*

- **appease:** Tell students that antonyms for *appease* include aggravate and provoke.

- **abhor:** Ask students to complete the analogy. abhor : dislike :: idolize: ***Possible answer:*** *fancy*

So that it is not because God is unmindful of their wickedness, and does not resent it, that he does not let loose his hand and cut them off. God is not altogether such an one as themselves, though they may imagine him to be so. The wrath of God burns against them, their damnation does not slumber; the pit is prepared, the fire is made ready, the furnace is now hot, ready to receive them; the flames do now rage and glow. The glittering sword is **whet,** and held over them, and the pit hath opened its mouth under them. . . . .

20 Unconverted men walk over the pit of hell on a rotten covering, and there are innumerable places in this covering so weak that they will not bear their weight, and these places are not seen. The arrows of death fly unseen at noonday; the sharpest sight cannot **discern** them. God has so many different unsearchable ways of taking wicked men out of the world and sending them to hell, that there is nothing to make it appear, that God had need to be at the expense of a miracle, or go out of the ordinary course of his providence, to destroy any wicked man, at any moment. . . .

So that, thus it is that natural men[2] are held in the hand of God, over the pit of hell; they have deserved the fiery pit, and are already sentenced to it; and God is dreadfully provoked, his anger is as great towards them as to those that are actually 30 suffering the executions of the fierceness of his wrath in hell; and they have done nothing in the least to **appease** or abate that anger, neither is God in the least bound by any promise to hold them up one moment; the devil is waiting for them, hell is gaping for them, the flames gather and flash about them, and would fain[3] lay hold on them, and swallow them up; the fire pent up in their own hearts is struggling to break out: and they have no interest in any Mediator,[4] there are no means within reach that can be any security to them. In short, they have no refuge, nothing to take hold of. . . . **C**

The bow of God's wrath is bent, and the arrow made ready on the string, and justice bends the arrow at your heart, and strains the bow, and it is nothing but 40 the mere pleasure of God, and that of an angry God, without any promise or obligation at all, that keeps the arrow one moment from being made drunk with your blood. Thus all you that never passed under a great change of heart, by the mighty power of the Spirit of God upon your souls; all you that were never born again, and made new creatures, and raised from being dead in sin, to a state of new, and before altogether unexperienced light and life, are in the hands of an angry God. However you may have reformed your life in many things, and may have had religious affections, and may keep up a form of religion in your families and closets,[5] and in the house of God, it is nothing but his mere pleasure that keeps you from being this moment swallowed up in everlasting destruction. . . . **D**

50 The God that holds you over the pit of hell, much as one holds a spider, or some loathsome insect over the fire, **abhors** you, and is dreadfully provoked: his

---

2. **natural men:** people who have not been born again.
3. **would fain:** would rather.
4. **Mediator:** Jesus Christ, who mediates, or is the means of bringing about, salvation.
5. **closets:** private rooms for meditation.

whet (hwĕt) *adj.* sharpened

B **EMOTIONAL APPEALS** Reread lines 14–18. What **imagery** does Edwards use in these lines?

discern (dĭ-sûrn′) *v.* to perceive or recognize something

appease (ə-pēz′) *v.* to bring peace, quiet, or calm to; to soothe

C **EMOTIONAL APPEALS** **Loaded language,** or words with strong emotional associations, can be used to influence an audience's attitude. What examples of loaded language do you see in lines 27–30?

D **PERSUASION** The imagery in lines 38–42 is well suited to the serrmon's historical **context.** Why might the bow and arrow have held negative associations for Colonial Americans?

abhor (ăb-hôr′) *v.* to regard with disgust

DIFFERENTIATED INSTRUCTION

FOR STRUGGLING READERS

② **Targeted Passage** [Lines 38–49]

In this passage, Edwards declares that nothing but conversion will allow people to escape God's wrath.

- Why does God have a bow and arrows? Why hasn't he used them yet? (lines 39–41)

- Name two things that Edwards says will happen to people who are born again. (lines 44–45)

FOR ENGLISH LANGUAGE LEARNERS

Vocabulary: Prefixes As you point out the word *Unconverted* in line 19, explain that the prefix *un-,* meaning "not," gives a clue to the meaning of the word. Have students find *unsearchable* (line 22) and *unexperienced* (line 45) on the page. Point out that the prefix helps the reader determine the meaning. Ask students for additional examples of words with this prefix.

Babylon Burning. From the *Apocalypse of Saint John* (Revelations 18). Luther Bible, First Edition. 1530. Private collection. Photo © Art Resource, New York.

wrath towards you burns like fire; he looks upon you as worthy of nothing else, but to be cast into the fire; he is of purer eyes than to bear to have you in his sight; you are ten thousand times more **abominable** in his eyes, than the most hateful venomous serpent is in ours. You have offended him infinitely more than ever a stubborn rebel did his prince; and yet it is nothing but his hand that holds you from falling into the fire every moment. It is to be **ascribed** to nothing else, that you did not go to hell the last night; that you was suffered[6] to awake again in this world, after you closed your eyes to sleep. And there is no other reason to be
60 given, why you have not dropped into hell since you arose in the morning, but that God's hand has held you up. There is no other reason to be given why you have not gone to hell, since you have sat here in the house of God, provoking his pure eyes by your sinful wicked manner of attending his solemn worship.

abominable
(ə-bŏm′ə-nə-bəl) *adj.*
thoroughly detestable

ascribe (ə-skrīb′) *v.* to attribute to a specified cause or source

---

6. **you was suffered:** you were permitted.

Analyze Visuals

Activity How is the burning of Babylon relevant to Edwards's warnings to his listeners? *Possible answer: The burning of Babylon is relevant because it shows God's fiery judgment. The angels indicate that the fire was an act of God. The people in the image seem surprised. Edwards tells his listeners that they could face such a judgment at any moment.*

About the Art In Protestant thought, the city of Babylon symbolized immoral living and a disregard for the things of God. According to the New Testament book of Revelation, Babylon would find its final destruction in divine fire. This woodcut, by Lucas Cranach the Elder (1472–1553), depicts that scene; Cranach created it for the Bible that Martin Luther translated into German. Like Edwards's sermon, the image uses the motif of fire to show the severity of God's anger against sinners.

REVISIT THE BIG QUESTION

What keeps you IN LINE?

Discuss According to Edwards in lines 42–57, is morality enough to save a person from judgment? What does he indicate is needed? *Possible answer: Morality is not enough. Edwards says that even a person who has made personal reforms and who has "religious affections" is subject to "everlasting destruction." Such a fate, he says, awaits "all you that never passed under a great change of heart . . . that were never born again" (lines 42–46), indicating that a complete conversion experience is needed.*

OWN THE WORD

- **abominable:** Have students complete this sentence, The restaurant patron said the meal was *abominable* because *Possible answer: he found a fly crawling in his salad.*

- **ascribe:** Ask students to write about times they have *ascribed* a cause or origin for a specific thing or event. *Possible answer: I ascribed the bad smell to food burning on the stove.*

FOR STRUGGLING READERS

Concept Support Edwards's sermon is filled with figurative language, so pause from time to time to check students' understanding. Revisit the chart introduced on page 123, offering advice as students record and analyze examples of emotional appeals and figurative language in the sermon.

Examples	Emotional Appeals
"made drunk with your blood" (lines 41–42)	appeals to fear by creating an image of a painful death
"swallowed up in everlasting destruction" (line 49)	appeals to fear by personifying hell as a hungry beast

E ANALYZE EMOTIONAL APPEALS

Possible answer: by making the audience aware of the spider's vulnerability at the same time that it feels superior to the spider

TIERED DISCUSSION PROMPTS

Direct students to lines 66–74. Use these prompts to help students explore Edwards's use of suspense:

Analyze Who does Edwards allude to as a Mediator (line 71)? Why doesn't he explain here that the Mediator can save them? *Possible answer: Edwards refers to Jesus Christ. He does not explain here how sinners can be saved because he is building suspense.*

Evaluate Do you think that this description achieves its purpose? Why or why not? *Possible answer: Yes. The description makes the listener feel the need for an escape.*

Analyze Visuals

Activity How is the hell in the painting similar to the hell that Edwards describes? *Possible answer: Both are fiery infernos.*

About the Art Flemish painter Hendrik met de Bles (c. 1510–1550) frequently explored religious themes. This image vividly suggests hell's "exquisite horrible misery" (line 77).

OWN THE WORD

- **incense:** Point out to students that *incense* is often used in a context indicating a specific cause of extreme anger, but in the context of Edwards's sermon, *incensed* is used in a general sense, with humanity's general wickedness as the cause.

- **induce:** Tell students that *induce* comes from the Latin word *inducere*, meaning "to lead." Ask students if they have ever *induced* someone to do something. How did the situation turn out?

Yea, there is nothing else that is to be given as a reason why you do not this very moment drop down into hell. **E**

O sinner! Consider the fearful danger you are in: it is a great furnace of wrath, a wide and bottomless pit, full of the fire of wrath, that you are held over in the hand of that God, whose wrath is provoked and **incensed** as much against you, as against many of the damned in hell. You hang by a slender thread, with the
70 flames of divine wrath flashing about it, and ready every moment to singe it, and burn it asunder;[7] and you have no interest in any Mediator, and nothing to lay hold of to save yourself, nothing to keep off the flames of wrath, nothing of your own, nothing that you ever have done, nothing that you can do, to **induce** God to spare you one moment. . . .

It is *everlasting* wrath. It would be dreadful to suffer this fierceness and wrath of Almighty God one moment; but you must suffer it to all eternity. There will be no end to this exquisite[8] horrible misery. When you look forward, you shall see a long forever, a boundless duration before you, which will swallow up your

E EMOTIONAL APPEALS
Notice the use of the **simile**, or comparison, in lines 50–65. In what way does comparing the audience to a spider appeal to fear?

incense (ĭn-sĕns´) *v.* to cause to be extremely angry

induce (ĭn-dōōs´) *v.* to succeed in persuading someone to do something

---

7. **burn it asunder** (ə-sŭn´dər): burn it into separate parts or pieces.

8. **exquisite** (ĕk´skwĭ-zĭt): intensely felt.

Detail of *Hell,* Hendrik met de Bles, Kunsthistorisches Museum, Vienna. © Erich Lessing/Art Resource, New York.

DIFFERENTIATED INSTRUCTION

FOR STRUGGLING READERS

Develop Reading Fluency Read aloud lines 66–74, modeling the dramatic delivery that Edwards's sermon indicates. Tell students that the punctuation helps readers know when to pause and which words or phrases to emphasize. Then engage the class in an echo reading of the lines.

thoughts, and amaze your soul; and you will absolutely despair of ever having
80 any **deliverance,** any end, any **mitigation,** any rest at all. You will know certainly
that you must wear out long ages, millions of millions of ages, in wrestling and
conflicting with this almighty merciless vengeance; and then when you have so
done, when so many ages have actually been spent by you in this manner, you will
know that all is but a point to what remains. So that your punishment will indeed
be infinite. Oh, who can express what the state of a soul in such circumstances is!
All that we can possibly say about it, gives but a very feeble, faint representation
of it; it is inexpressible and inconceivable: For "who knows the power of God's
anger?"[9]

How dreadful is the state of those that are daily and hourly in the danger of
90 this great wrath and infinite misery! But this is the dismal case of every soul in this
congregation that has not been born again, however moral and strict, sober and
religious, they may otherwise be. . . .

And now you have an extraordinary opportunity, a day wherein Christ has
thrown the door of mercy wide open, and stands in the door calling and crying
with a loud voice to poor sinners; a day wherein many are flocking to him, and
pressing into the kingdom of God. Many are daily coming[10] from the east, west,
north, and south; many that were very lately in the same miserable condition that
you are in, are now in a happy state, with their hearts filled with love to him who
has loved them, and washed them from their sins in his own blood, and rejoicing
100 in hope of the glory of God. How awful is it to be left behind at such a day! To
see so many others feasting, while you are pining and perishing! To see so many
rejoicing and singing for joy of heart, while you have cause to mourn for sorrow
of heart, and howl for vexation of spirit! How can you rest one moment in such a
condition? . . .

Therefore, let every one that is out of Christ, now awake and fly from the wrath
to come. . . . ◈ **F**

---

9. **"who knows . . . anger?":** an allusion to Psalm 90:11 in the Bible—"Who knoweth the power
    of thine anger?"
10. **Many . . . coming:** a reference to the hundreds of people who were being converted during
    the Great Awakening.

---

deliverance (dĭ-lĭv'ər-əns)
n. rescue from danger

mitigation (mĭt-ĭ-gā'shən)
n. lessening of something
that causes suffering

⸰COMMON CORE RI 3, RI 6

F ALLUSION
Reread lines 75 to the
end, and consider how
purpose and audience
influence Edwards's
language in these lines.
As habitual readers of
the Bible, members of his
congregation would be
familiar with the biblical
contrast between a God
of wrath and a God of
mercy. In lines 87–88, they
would recognize a **biblical
allusion** or reference in
the quotation from Psalm
90. In line 99, they would
hear echoes of biblical
passages that identify
Christ as the lamb of God
and that associate Christ's
blood with the cleansing
of sin. How do allusions
such as these increase
the persuasive appeal of
Edwards's sermon? Cite
evidence from the selection
to support your response.

F ALLUSION   RI 3
                                          RI 6
Remind students that **allusions** can refer
to another work of literature or to events
or persons in history, art, religion, or some
other branch of culture. When writers
make allusions, they expect their readers
to recognize the reference.

*Possible answer: Allusions such as "flocking
to him" (line 95) helps readers relate to the
lesson that Edwards is trying to convey.*

REVISIT THE BIG QUESTION

What keeps you
IN LINE?

Discuss What does Edwards imply in lines
96–100 about morality in the kingdom of
God? *Possible answer: Edwards implies that
such morality can be practiced only by those
whose sins have been cleansed and that it is
based on love for God.*

VOCABULARY   COMMON CORE
                                          L 4

OWN THE WORD

• **deliverance:** Read aloud the sentence
  containing *deliverance.* Ask students to
  write sentences describing situations in
  which they would need *deliverance* and
  ways in which they might create their
  own *deliverance.*

• **mitigation:** Tell students that *mitigate*
  is the verb from which *mitigation* is derived. To *mitigate* is often used to mean
  "to relieve" or "to resolve." The word
  mitigation is often used in legal contexts.

FOR STRUGGLING READERS

❸ Targeted Passage [Lines 93–106]

In this passage, Edwards explains how his
listeners can avoid the fires of hell.

• What is the "extraordinary opportunity"
  that Edwards refers to in the last paragraph
  of the selection? (lines 93–96)

• What two types of people does Edwards
  describe? What creates the difference
  between them? (lines 101–104)

• What call to action does Edwards make at
  the end of his sermon? (lines 105–106)

Practice and Apply

For preliminary support of post-reading questions, use these copy masters:

 **RESOURCE MANAGER**—Copy Masters

Reading Check p. 184

Persuasion p. 177

Question Support p. 185

Additional selection questions are provided for teachers on page 171.

ANSWERS

1. *All humans suffer the threat of being snatched out of life and cast into hell at any moment.*

2. *Sinners must have "a great change of heart" and be "born again."*

3. *Edwards uses the image of fire—in particular, fire over which someone holds a fragile spider.*

Possible answers:

4. ◼ **COMMON CORE FOCUS** *Analyze Emotional Appeals* *The language helps listeners to feel God's wrath and to imagine what it might be like to suffer the torments of hell.*

5. ● **COMMON CORE FOCUS** *Persuasion* *Edwards felt that his listeners had grown complacent in their Puritan heritage. The terror in his message probably reflects his deep concern for them and his desire to grab their attention.*

6. *God: all-powerful, holy, and angry (as in lines 8–11 and 52–55); Christ: merciful, and humanity's only hope for salvation (as in lines 93–100); humanity: miserable creatures who, unconverted, are worth no more in God's eyes than loathsome spiders (as in lines 50–51)*

7. *Eternal Life: Edwards: terrifying vision of hell (lines 14–18) and welcoming vision of the kingdom of God (lines 93–100); Bradstreet: a heavenly home, provided by God ("House," lines 43–50)*

   God's Relation to People: Edwards: God is angry at sinners, who have rebelled against Him (lines 50–57), but offers salvation through Christ (lines 93–96); Bradstreet: God supplies people's needs ("House," lines 19–20 and 51–54)

   Religious Beliefs: Edwards and Bradstreet— God is all-powerful and central to human life and endeavor

---

Comprehension

1. **Recall** According to Jonathan Edwards's sermon, what is a constant threat to all human beings?

2. **Clarify** In Edwards's view, what must sinners do to be spared God's wrath?

3. **Summarize** What key image does Edwards use to persuade his audience?

Text Analysis

4. ◼ **Analyze Emotional Appeals** Review the examples of words, phrases, and images you recorded as you read. How does this language effectively appeal to the audience's emotions and get Edwards's message across?

5. ● **Analyze Persuasion** What role does the appeal to fear or terror play in Edwards's sermon? How do biblical allusions support the writer's appeal to fear? Cite evidence from the sermon to support your response.

6. **Draw Conclusions** How would you describe Jonathan Edwards's view of the following? Cite specific examples for each.

   • God   • Christ   • humanity

7. **Compare Literary Works** Use a chart like the one shown to compare some of Jonathan Edwards's and Anne Bradstreet's attitudes and beliefs. Cite specific details from their writings to support your ideas.

	Edwards	Bradstreet
Eternal Life		
God's Relation to People		
Religious Beliefs		
Human Frailty		

Text Criticism

8. **Historical Context** In the 18th century, many people died at a much younger age than they do today. How might awareness of the fragility of life have affected people's receptiveness to Edwards's sermon?

> *What keeps you* **IN LINE?**
>
> In this well-known sermon, Edwards acknowledges that his listeners may already be moral and religious. If he isn't trying to "scare" listeners into moral behavior, what is his true purpose?

Human Frailty: Edwards: Humans are at God's mercy and cannot save themselves (lines 42–49); Bradstreet: Every human possession belongs to God, who gives or takes according to divine purposes ("House," lines 13–18)

8. *Edwards's imagery of immediate danger and impending doom probably would have found fertile ground among people for whom death was a common occurrence.*

> *What keeps you* IN LINE? ***Possible answer:** Students might mention the value of encouragement from a preacher or other spiritual leader.*

Vocabulary in Context

▲ VOCABULARY PRACTICE

Decide whether the boldface words make the statements true or false.

1. If a movie is said to be **abominable**, you should expect to hate it.
2. A good way to **appease** a friend is to criticize her.
3. Feeding the hungry would result in the **mitigation** of their suffering.
4. If you **discern** a difference between two documents, you notice that they are not alike.
5. A person who **abhors** you is probably a close friend.
6. When you **ascribe** a motive to a crime, you explain why someone did it.
7. One way to **incense** someone is to say something complimentary.
8. If you have trouble cutting a steak, it might help to **whet** your knife.
9. An example of **deliverance** is the rescue of passengers from a sinking ship.
10. If I **induce** you to help me do a hard job, I have managed to persuade you.

> **WORD LIST**
> abhor
> abominable
> appease
> ascribe
> deliverance
> discern
> incense
> induce
> mitigation
> whet

ACADEMIC VOCABULARY IN WRITING

> • document • illustrate • interpret • promote • reveal

What does Edwards's sermon **reveal** about Puritan thought on the human condition? Do you think the Puritans believed that they had full control over their own lives? Write a paragraph explaining how Puritans saw themselves in relation to God, and use at least one Academic Vocabulary word in your response.

VOCABULARY STRATEGY: CONNOTATION

Though some words may have the same definition, their **connotations**, or shades of meaning, can vary. In Edwards's sermon, for example, the word *incensed* suggests a stronger feeling than *angered*. As you read large sections of text, you can use context clues to determine a word's exact shade of meaning.

PRACTICE Based on context clues, select a more intense word from the following list to replace each boldface word in the paragraph.

> • antipathy • disconsolate • contrive • momentous • negligible

Our debate team has placed second in state competition for the past three years. Next year, we have to **figure out** a way to take first place. The difference in our score and those of the teams that beat us has been **minor**, so we haven't been too **unhappy** about placing second. In fact, we have no **dislike** of the other teams. Nevertheless, bringing the trophy home next year will be a **very important** occasion.

COMMON CORE

RI 4 Determine the meaning of words as they are used in a text, including connotative meanings. **L 4a** Use context as a clue to the meaning of a word. **L 5** Demonstrate understanding of nuances in word meanings.

Interactive Vocabulary

THINK central

Go to **thinkcentral.com**.
KEYWORD: HML11-131

ANSWERS

Vocabulary in Context

▲ VOCABULARY PRACTICE

1. *true*   5. *false*   8. *true*
2. *false*   6. *true*   9. *true*
3. *true*   7. *false*   10. *true*
4. *true*

R RESOURCE MANAGER—Copy Master
Vocabulary Practice p. 182

ACADEMIC VOCABULARY IN WRITING

Answers will vary but should include an Academic Vocabulary word and discuss how Puritans viewed themselves in relation to God: they're sinners deserving of punishment, God is righteous. Discuss Puritan views on God's sovereignty—God is in control, the Puritans aren't in control.

VOCABULARY STRATEGY: CONNOTATION

COMMON CORE RI 4, L 4a, L 5

dislike: antipathy

unhappy: disconsolate

figure out: contrive

very important: momentous

minor: negligible

R RESOURCE MANAGER—Copy Master
Vocabulary Strategy p. 183

Interactive Vocabulary

THINK central

Keywords direct students to a **WordSharp** tutorial on **thinkcentral.com** or to other types of vocabulary practice and review.

Assess and Reteach

Assess

DIAGNOSTIC AND SELECTION TESTS

Selection Test A pp. 57–58
Selection Test B/C pp. 59–60

Interactive Selection Test on thinkcentral.com

Reteach

Level Up Online Tutorials on thinkcentral.com

Reteaching Worksheets on thinkcentral.com

Reading Lesson 3, Vocabulary Lesson 17

DIFFERENTIATED INSTRUCTION

FOR ENGLISH LANGUAGE LEARNERS

Task Support: Vocabulary Strategy Help students find and define the base word for these vocabulary words with suffixes: *abominable, deliverance, mitigation, momentous,* and *disconsolate*. Then have them use a dictionary to combine the base word's definition with the definition of the suffix to define the vocabulary word.

FOR ADVANCED LEARNERS/AP

Vocabulary in Writing Have students use at least four vocabulary words as they write a one-paragraph summary of "Sinners in the Hands of an Angry God."

American Drama

Have you ever gone to the theater or a movie and felt as if life were unfolding before you? Dramas that realistically portray events have a way of hitting a nerve. American playwrights, in particular, are known for writing dramas that reveal the truth of our everyday experience, and sometimes our not-so-everyday experience.

The Rise of American Drama

Though drama is one of the oldest forms of literature, it was one of the last of the literary genres to develop in the United States. The Puritans in New England regarded theatrical performances as frivolous, so few plays were staged in the 1600s. During the 18th and 19th centuries, drama gradually became an accepted form of entertainment. However, most of the plays performed in the United States were imported from Europe or were adapted from novels.

In 1920 the Broadway production of Eugene O'Neill's *Beyond the Horizon* marked a turning point in presenting true-to-life characters who were struggling to understand their lives. Building on O'Neill's achievement, American playwrights Thornton Wilder, Lillian Hellman, Tennessee Williams, and Arthur Miller created dramas in the 1930s and 1940s that met with critical and popular success. Following World War II, American dramatists Edward Albee and Lorraine Hansberry made significant contributions to the theater. Arthur Miller's 1953 *The Crucible* (page 134) is an example of a modern drama that portrays events from Puritan times.

Eugene O'Neill's *The Iceman Cometh* became an American classic.

Conventions of Drama

The two main types of drama are tragedy and comedy. A **tragedy** recounts the downfall of a main character, and a **comedy** is light and humorous in tone, usually ending happily. Many dramas combine elements of both. In addition, most dramas follow similar conventions, or rules, in how they are presented. An understanding of basic dramatic conventions can help you imagine the performance as you read.

PLOT AND STRUCTURE

The **plot** in drama, as in fiction, introduces events and character interactions that produce a **conflict,** or struggle between opposing forces. The conflict builds as the action intensifies throughout the play's **acts** and **scenes,** finally reaching a peak and then resolution. Each scene serves as a building block in the stages of the plot: **exposition, rising action, climax, falling action,** and **resolution.**

TYPES OF CHARACTERS

Drama has many of the same types of characters that are found in fiction. The **protagonist** is the central character of the play. This character is at the center of the conflict and often undergoes radical changes during the course of the play. The **antagonist** often opposes the protagonist, giving rise to the central conflict of the play. Some plays also include a **foil,** a minor character who provides a striking contrast to another character. Interplay among these characters heightens the dramatic tension as the play develops. The names of all a play's characters are listed in the **cast of characters** at the beginning of the play.

SPEECH DEVICES

In drama, the playwright develops the story line through the characters' actions and dialogue. Virtually everything of consequence—from the plot details to the character revelations—flows from **dialogue,** or conversation between characters. Other **speech devices** used by playwrights include

- **monologue:** a long speech spoken by a single character to the audience or another character

- **soliloquy:** a reflective speech in which a character speaks his or her private thoughts aloud, unheard by other characters

- **aside:** a short speech or comment that is delivered by a character to the audience but is not heard by other characters who are present

STAGE AND SETTING

Stage directions are the italicized instructions in a play. The playwright includes the stage directions in order to describe the setting, props, lighting, scenery, sound effects, and costumes. Stage directions also describe the entrances and exits of characters and how the characters look, speak, and react to events or to others. These stage directions from *The Crucible* describe the stage set at the beginning of Act Four.

(*A cell in Salem jail, that fall.*)

(*At the back is a high barred window; near it, a great, heavy door. Along the walls are two benches.*)

(*The place is in darkness but for the moonlight seeping through the bars. It appears empty. Presently footsteps are heard coming down a corridor beyond the wall, keys rattle, and the door swings open.* Marshal Herrick *enters with a lantern.*)

—**Arthur Miller,** *The Crucible*

Close Read

Why is the description of the cell important to this scene? What effect does it have on the **mood** the scene evokes?

Types of Characters Share the Greek etymology of *protagonist* and *antagonist:*

- The prefix *prot(o)-* means "first" or "leading."

- The prefix *ant(i)-* means "against."

- The root *agon* means "contest."

Elicit that a conflict is like a contest, that the protagonist is the leading character, and that the antagonist acts against him or her.

Speech Devices To distinguish the terms *monologue, soliloquy,* and *aside,* ask a student to come to the front of the room. Then follow these steps:

1. Read the definition of *monologue* aloud while looking at the student. Explain that what you have just performed is similar to a monologue because you were the only character speaking.

2. Step away from the student and read the definition of *aside* aloud while shielding your mouth from him or her but not from the class. Explain that you have just performed an aside.

3. Have the student sit down. Read the definition of *soliloquy* aloud to yourself, in a reflective manner. Explain that you have just performed a soliloquy.

Stage and Setting Ask students to describe what they visualize as they read the passage from *The Crucible.*

CLOSE READ

Possible answer: The description is important because some action (following Herrick's entrance) seems about to occur in the cell. Details such as the heavy door and moonlight cutting into the darkness create a grim but mysterious mood.

FOR ENGLISH LANGUAGE LEARNERS

Language: Skill Words Because of the large number of skill words presented on these two pages, reassure students that they will find and learn these words again as they read *The Crucible.* Ask students to explain any of the words they know from prior reading. Then focus on the remaining words. Work with students to preview the beginning of *The Crucible,* finding the stage directions, the cast of characters, and the opening dialogue.

FOR ADVANCED LEARNERS/AP

Compare and Contrast Genres Ask students to write and share responses to these questions:

- Suppose that one writer presents a story in a novel and another writer presents the same story in a play. When reading both texts, what differences would you find?

- What can drama do that fiction cannot do? What can fiction do that drama cannot do?

Focus and Motivate

COMMON CORE FOCUS

RL 1 Cite textual evidence to support analysis of what the text says explicitly as well as inferences drawn from the text, including determining where the text leaves matters uncertain. **RL 2** Determine two or more themes or central ideas of a text and analyze their development over the course of the text, including how they interact and build on one another to produce a complex account; provide an objective summary of the text. **RL 3** Analyze the impact of the author's choices regarding how to develop and relate elements of a drama. **RL 5** Analyze how an author's choices concerning how to structure specific parts of a text contribute to its overall structure and meaning, as well as its aesthetic meaning. **RL 6** Analyze a case in which grasping point of view requires distinguishing what is directly stated from what is really meant. **RL 7** Analyze multiple interpretations of a drama evaluating how each version interprets the source text. **W 1** Write arguments to support claims in an analysis of substantive topics or texts, using valid reasoning and relevant and sufficient evidence. **W 1b** Develop claim(s) fairly and thoroughly, supplying the most relevant evidence. **L 3a** Vary syntax for effect, consulting references for guidance as needed; apply an understanding of syntax to the study of complex texts when reading. **L 4a** Use context as a clue to the meaning of a word. **L 5b** Analyze nuances in the meaning of words with similar denotations.

ABOUT THE PLAYWRIGHT

After students read the biography, call on volunteers to share what they know about the Cold War era. Then discuss the connection between it and *The Crucible*.

Themes Across Time

from **The Crucible**

Video link at thinkcentral.com

Essential Course of Study

Drama by Arthur Miller

VIDEO TRAILER **THINK**central KEYWORD: HML11-134A

COMMON CORE

RL 1 Cite textual evidence to support analysis of what the text says explicitly as well as inferences drawn from the text, including determining where the text leaves matters uncertain. **RL 3** Analyze the impact of the author's choices regarding how to develop and relate elements of a drama. **RL 5** Analyze how an author's choices concerning how to structure specific parts of a text contribute to its overall structure and meaning as well as its aesthetic impact. **RL 7** Analyze multiple interpretations of a drama, evaluating how each version interprets the source text.

DID YOU KNOW?

Arthur Miller . . .

- was once rejected by the University of Michigan because of low grades.
- was once married to film star Marilyn Monroe.
- wrote *Death of a Salesman* in six weeks.

Meet the Author

Arthur Miller 1915–2005

Arthur Miller once paid playwright Edward Albee a compliment, saying that his plays were "necessary." Albee replied: "I will go one step further and say that Arthur's plays are 'essential.'" Miller's plays explore family relationships, morality, and personal responsibility. Many critics consider him the greatest American dramatist of the 20th century.

A Born Playwright Miller was born in New York City in 1915 into an upper-middle-class family. However, the family's comfortable life ended in the 1930s when Miller's businessman father was hit hard by the Great Depression. Unable to afford college, Miller worked in a warehouse to earn tuition money. He eventually attended the University of Michigan.

While in college, Miller won several awards for his plays. These successes inspired him to pursue a career in the theater. His first Broadway hit, *All My Sons* (1947), was produced when Miller was still in his early 30s. However, it was his masterpiece *Death of a Salesman* that made Miller a star. The play won a Pulitzer Prize in 1949 and earned rave reviews from both critics and the public.

Dramatic Years Miller's rise to fame occurred during a difficult period in American history. In the 1940s and 1950s, a congressional committee was conducting hearings to identify suspected Communists in American society. Miller himself was called before the congressional committee and questioned about his activities with the American Communist Party. Although Miller admitted that he had attended a few meetings years earlier, he refused to implicate others. For his refusal, he was cited for contempt of Congress—a conviction that was later overturned.

The hearings provided the inspiration for his 1953 play *The Crucible*, set during the Salem, Massachusetts, witch trials of 1692. Miller wrote the play to warn against mass hysteria and to plead for freedom and tolerance.

The Curtain Closes In the 1970s, Miller's career declined a bit. The plays he wrote did not earn the critical or popular success of his earlier work. In the 1980s and 1990s, however, he enjoyed a resurgence with revivals of *Death of a Salesman* on Broadway. He even directed a production of the play in Beijing.

To the end of his life, Miller continued to write. "It is what I do," he said in an interview. "I am better at it than I ever was. And I will do it as long as I can."

Author Online

Go to **thinkcentral.com**. KEYWORD: HML11-134B

134

Selection Resources

See resources on the **Teacher One Stop DVD-ROM** and on **thinkcentral.com**.

R **RESOURCE MANAGER UNIT 1**

Plan and Teach, pp. 187–194, 205–210, 217–222, 229–234

Summary, pp. 195–196, 211–212, 223–224, 235–236 *†‡

Text Analysis and Reading Skill, pp. 197–200, 213–215, 225–227, 237–238, 241 *†

Vocabulary, pp. 201, 239–240

Grammar and Style, p. 243

DIAGNOSTIC AND SELECTION TESTS

Selection Tests, pp. 61–76

BEST PRACTICES TOOLKIT

Sequence Chain, p. B21

INTERACTIVE READER

ADAPTED INTERACTIVE READER

ELL ADAPTED INTERACTIVE READER

Video link at thinkcentral.com

HISTORY

TECHNOLOGY

- **Teacher One Stop DVD-ROM**
- **Student One Stop DVD-ROM**
- **PowerNotes DVD-ROM**
- **Audio Anthology CD**
- **GrammarNotes DVD-ROM**
- **ExamView Test Generator** on the Teacher One Stop

Video Trailer

THINK central

Go to **thinkcentral.com** to preview the **Video Trailer** introducing this selection. Other features that support the selection include

- **PowerNotes** presentation
- **ThinkAloud** models to enhance comprehension
- **WordSharp** vocabulary tutorials
- interactive writing and grammar instruction

* Resources for Differentiation   † Also in Spanish   ‡ Also in Haitian Creole and Vietnamese

TEXT ANALYSIS: CONVENTIONS OF DRAMA

Drama is literature in play form. It is meant to be performed and seen. However, an understanding of dramatic conventions can help you picture the performance when you read a script. As you read *The Crucible*, be aware of these drama conventions:

- **Stage directions,** which Miller uses not only to describe settings and characters but also to provide historical background in the form of expository mini-essays
- **Dialogue,** the lifeblood of drama, which moves the plot forward and reveals character traits
- **Types of characters**—heroes, villains, and foils—which Miller uses to heighten the tension of his drama
- **Plot,** which is driven by **conflict** that builds throughout each act

READING SKILL: DRAW CONCLUSIONS ABOUT CHARACTERS

Characters in drama reveal their personality traits through their words and actions. The descriptions in the stage directions can also provide insight into these characters. As you read *The Crucible*, **draw conclusions** about the play's main characters. Record their important traits and the evidence that reveals these traits in a chart like the one shown. Be sure to add characters to the chart as you encounter them.

	Abigail Williams	John Proctor	Reverend John Hale
Traits	proud	assertive	
Evidence			
Motivation	resentment	pride	

▲ VOCABULARY IN CONTEXT

Arthur Miller uses the words shown here to help convey the atmosphere of the Salem witch trials. Place them in the following categories: words that describe character traits, words that describe actions, and words that are concepts.

WORD LIST		
adamant	corroborate	imperceptible
anarchy	deference	iniquity
contentious	immaculate	subservient

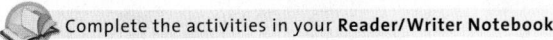 Complete the activities in your **Reader/Writer Notebook**.

What fuels a MOB?

Visualize a mob of people rampaging through the streets, whipped into a frenzy by hysteria. The fear, anger, and panic produced by hysteria can make otherwise reasonable people do irrational things. In *The Crucible*, for example, the hysteria created by the Salem witch trials makes neighbor turn against neighbor.

DISCUSS What makes people act as a mob? What are some of the results of mob action? Think about news reports or historical accounts of mobs that you've come across. In a small group, discuss what caused these mobs to form and how they behaved.

135

What fuels a MOB?

After students speculate on what fuels a mob, ask them to think about the difference between a mob and a crowd. After groups complete the *DISCUSS* activity, invite students to share their ideas about mob behavior.

TEXT ANALYSIS
COMMON CORE
RL 3
RL 5

● *Model the Skill:*
CONVENTIONS OF DRAMA

Model the skill by pointing out examples of dramatic conventions. Offer students this example:

> **Beth** *(shouting offstage where rushing water is heard).* Don't worry, Jenny! I'll save you!

Explain that the stage directions tell the actor how to perform her lines.

GUIDED PRACTICE Have students review dramatic conventions on page 132.

READING SKILL
COMMON CORE
RL 1
RL 3

■ *Model the Skill:* **DRAW CONCLUSIONS ABOUT CHARACTERS**

Refer to the dialogue in the skill box above. Say, "Based on Beth's actions and words, I conclude that her trait is to be caring."

GUIDED PRACTICE Have students add Beth to their character graphic organizer on this page and look for evidence in the play that supports their conclusions.

R RESOURCE MANAGER—Copy Master
Draw Conclusions About Characters p. 199 (for use while reading the selection)

VOCABULARY SKILL
COMMON CORE
L 4

▲ VOCABULARY IN CONTEXT

PRETEACH VOCABULARY To preteach vocabulary for *The Crucible*, use the Vocabulary Study copy master. Supply these definitions as needed for Acts One:

- Act One, line 686: **anarchy** (ăn´ər-kē) *n.* condition of lawlessness and disorder
- page 145: **corroborate** (kə-rŏb´ə-rāt´) *v.* to support with evidence
- line 156: **deference** (dĕf´ər-əns) *n.* respect and honor due to a superior or elder

- page 151: **iniquity** (ĭ-nĭk´wĭ-tē) *n.* wickedness; immorality
- line 310: **subservient** (səb-sûr´vē-ənt) *adj.* acting like a servant

R RESOURCE MANAGER—Copy Master
Vocabulary Study p. 201

Practice and Apply

SUMMARY

In this play, Arthur Miller traces the hysteria in Salem, Massachusetts, in 1692, as several girls begin to accuse their neighbors of associating with the Devil. Suspicion and ill will spread as the townspeople bring up current disputes and past grudges, implicate one another in the charge of witchcraft, and witness court proceedings against those so charged. By the time the witch trials end, Salem has been forever stained.

READ WITH A PURPOSE

Help students set a purpose for reading. Tell them to read to discover what happens to a community when rumors influence people's beliefs.

TEXT ANALYSIS   COMMON CORE

● **CONVENTIONS OF DRAMA**   RL 3
                                              RL 5

All the characters in a drama usually are presented in a list at the beginning of the play. If you were watching this play in a theater, which character would you expect to see first on the stage? ***Answer:*** *Reverend Samuel Parris would be first on the stage, because the cast is listed in the order of appearance.*

THE CRUCIBLE

Arthur Miller

136

①

CAST OF CHARACTERS
(*in order of appearance*)

Reverend Samuel Parris	Mrs. Ann Putnam	Ezekiel Cheever
Betty Parris	Thomas Putnam	Marshal Herrick
Tituba	Mercy Lewis	Judge Hathorne
Abigail Williams	Mary Warren	Martha Corey
John Proctor	Rebecca Nurse	Deputy Governor Danforth
Elizabeth Proctor	Giles Corey	
Susanna Walcott	Reverend John Hale	Girls of Salem
	Francis Nurse	Sarah Good

137

Reading Support

This selection on **thinkcentral.com** includes embedded **ThinkAloud** models—students "thinking aloud" about the story to model the kinds of questions a good reader would ask about a selection.

BACKGROUND

A Metaphorical Title Arthur Miller chose wisely when he gave this play its title. Literally, a crucible is a container that can withstand high heat. A crucible most often is associated with the melting of metal, allowing for impurities in the metal to be identified and removed. Metaphorically, crucible refers to a severe test—a test that puts great stress upon people, revealing their weaknesses and strengths. As students will see, the situation that Miller develops in *The Crucible* will put great stress upon the characters. The stress, like a fire, will burn away characters' pretenses and bring their true natures to light. Which characters will be shattered by the experience? Which will be purified? Urge students to keep these questions in mind as they read.

Analyze Visuals

Activity Ask students how this photograph suggests the atmosphere of suspicion alluded to in the **BACKGROUND** note. *Possible answer: The photograph suggests suspicion because it shows a group of men who appear ready to judge others. Visually, the men are intimidating: They stand close together, wearing stern expressions that suggest a united front in a matter of great seriousness.*

DIFFERENTIATED INSTRUCTION

- What events provide the historical basis for this play?
- What is "spectral evidence"?
- Why was no one safe in Salem during the time period covered in the play?
- Are the characters in the play purely fictional, or are they based on real people?

FOR ADVANCED LEARNERS/AP

Make Judgments Begin a class discussion by asking students to think about how important it is for a community to rely on a justice system and the law than to allow mob rule. What are the drawbacks and benefits of a justice system based on law? What are the drawbacks of mob rule? Encourage students to use specific examples when sharing opinions.

Practice and Apply

SUMMARY

Act One opens with Reverend Parris praying for his sick daughter, Betty. An essay explains the historical setting; then Parris reveals that the illness is thought to be due to bewitchment. Among the townspeople who discuss the matter is John Proctor, who had an affair with Parris's niece, Abigail. Reverend Hale comes to purge the town of witches; but in the conversations that follow, innocent people are accused of witchcraft.

THEME AND GENRE

After students have completed this play, ask them to discuss films, plays, or novels that connect to the theme of *The Crucible*.

ACT *One*

An Overture

(*A small upper bedroom in the home of* Reverend Samuel Parris, *Salem, Massachusetts, in the spring of the year 1692.*

There is a narrow window at the left. Through its leaded panes the morning sunlight streams. A candle still burns near the bed, which is at the right. A chest, a chair, and a small table are the other furnishings. At the back a door opens on the landing of the stairway to the ground floor. The room gives off an air of clean spareness. The roof rafters are exposed, and the wood colors are raw and unmellowed.

As the curtain rises, Reverend Parris *is discovered kneeling beside the bed, evidently in prayer. His daughter,* Betty Parris, *aged ten, is lying on the bed, inert.*)

THEME AND GENRE
Imagine that you thought something terrible was happening but you weren't absolutely positive. Should you act? In *The Crucible*, characters do terrible things to stop what they think are crimes. In the Pulitzer-prize winning play *Doubt* (2005), characters confront the same question: What do we do if we think something is happening but we're not sure? Can you think of other characters in recent plays, films, or novels who had to make a difficult decision about whether to act or not act on their beliefs?

At the time of these events Parris was in his middle forties. In history he cut a villainous path, and there is very little good to be said for him. He believed he was being persecuted wherever he went, despite his best efforts to win people and God to his side. In meeting, he felt insulted if someone rose to shut the door without first asking his permission. He was a widower with no interest in children, or talent with them. He regarded them as young adults, and until this strange crisis he, like the rest of Salem, never conceived that the children were anything but thankful for being permitted to walk straight, eyes slightly lowered, arms at the sides, and mouths shut until bidden to speak.

His house stood in the "town"—but we today would hardly call it a village. The meeting house[1] was nearby, and from this point outward—toward the bay or inland—there were a few small-windowed, dark houses snuggling against the raw Massachusetts winter. Salem had been established hardly forty years before. To the European world the whole province was a barbaric frontier inhabited by a sect of fanatics who, nevertheless, were shipping out products of slowly increasing quantity and value.

No one can really know what their lives were like. They had no novelists—and would not have permitted anyone to read a novel if one were handy. Their creed forbade anything resembling a theater or "vain enjoyment." They did not celebrate Christmas, and a holiday from work meant only that they must concentrate even more upon prayer.

Which is not to say that nothing broke into this strict and somber way of life. When a new farmhouse was built, friends assembled to "raise the roof," and there would be special foods cooked and probably some potent cider passed around. There was a good supply of ne'er-do-wells in Salem, who dallied at the shovelboard[2] in Bridget Bishop's tavern. Probably more than the creed, hard work kept the morals of the place from spoiling, for the people were forced

---

1. **meeting house:** the most important building in the Puritan community, used both for worship and for meetings.
2. **shovelboard:** a game in which a coin or disc is shoved across a board by hand.

Resources for Act One

See resources on the **Teacher One Stop DVD-ROM** *and on* **thinkcentral.com**.

** RESOURCE MANAGER UNIT 1**
Plan and Teach, pp. 187–194
Summary, pp. 195–196†‡*
Text Analysis and Reading Skill, pp. 197–200†*
Vocabulary, pp. 201*

DIAGNOSTIC AND SELECTION TESTS
Selection Tests, pp. 61–64

** BEST PRACTICES TOOLKIT**
Sequence Chain, p. B21
New Word Anaysis, p. E8
Two-Column Chart, p. A25
Jigsaw Reading, p. A1

INTERACTIVE READER

ADAPTED INTERACTIVE READER

ELL ADAPTED INTERACTIVE READER

TECHNOLOGY
- 💿 **Teacher One Stop DVD-ROM**
- 💿 **Student One Stop DVD-ROM**
- 💿 **PowerNotes DVD-ROM**
- 💿 **Audio Anthology CD**
- 💿 **GrammarNotes DVD-ROM**
- 💿 **ExamView Test Generator** on the Teacher One Stop

Video Trailer

Go to **thinkcentral.com** to preview the **Video Trailer** introducing this selection. Other features that support the selection include
- **PowerNotes** presentation
- **ThinkAloud** models to enhance comprehension
- **WordSharp** vocabulary tutorials
- interactive writing and grammar instruction

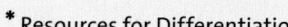

* Resources for Differentiation   **† Also in Spanish**   **‡ In Haitian Creole and Vietnamese**

Daniel Day-Lewis as John Proctor

THE CRUCIBLE: ACT ONE **139**

THE CRUCIBLE: ACT ONE **139**

TEXT ANALYSIS

COMMON CORE
RL 3
RL 5

● *Model the Skill:*
CONVENTIONS OF DRAMA

Model the skill by walking students through the opening stage directions on p. 138. Point out that the stage directions describe the set (a small, simply furnished bedroom in Parris's house) and identify the play's setting (Salem, Massachusetts, in the spring of 1692). They also identify the characters on stage (Parris and Betty, his ten-year-old daughter) and provide direction about what these characters should be doing (Parris, kneeling in prayer; Betty, lying motionless in bed).

READING SKILLS

COMMON CORE
RL 1
RL 3

■ *Model the Skill:* **DRAW CONCLUSIONS ABOUT CHARACTERS**

Model how to draw conclusions by making a list of Reverend Parris' actions, words, and traits. For example, point out that his praying suggests that he is worried about his daughter; however, in the mini-essay, Miller says that Parris is not interested in children and does not understand them. Lead students toward the conclusion that Parris's motivation for his concern is self-centered fear.

IF STUDENTS NEED HELP . . . Work with them to use the chart introduced on page 135 to draw a conclusion about Reverend Parris. Help them cite evidence to support their ideas.

DIFFERENTIATED INSTRUCTION

FOR STRUGGLING READERS

Preview Ask students to listen carefully as you read the Summary aloud. Then help them begin a Sequence Chain to organize the plot events in *The Crucible*.

> Betty Parris is ill—perhaps bewitched.

↓

>

↓

BEST PRACTICES TOOLKIT—Transparency
Sequence Chain p. B21

FOR ENGLISH LANGUAGE LEARNERS

Culture: Clarify Explain that the word *creed* in the third paragraph refers to a religious group's statement of beliefs. Invite students to respond to Miller's statement that the Puritans, a Christian sect, did not include a Christmas celebration in their culture; then explain that the Puritans felt that the ways in which most people celebrated the holiday were overindulgent and heathen. Urge students to consider these questions as they read *The Crucible:*

- Which characters in the play show the strongest support for Puritan beliefs and behavior? Which characters seem to find the Puritan way of life difficult?

- What evidence in the play suggests that there can be divisions even among people with a common culture?

- Why might having a common culture make it easier for problems to spread? for problems to be solved?

THE CRUCIBLE: ACT ONE **139**

Use these prompts to help students explore the importance of the Salem residents' interest in each other's personal lives:

Connect Have you ever encountered someone who pried into what you were doing? How did the experience affect you? *Accept all responses.*

Interpret Why does a constant interest in other people's business have the potential to make people suspicious of each other? *Possible answer: People may become suspicious because they imagine that someone is spying on them. Similarly, they may become suspicious because they think that they know the whole truth about someone they have spied on and then rush to judgment, when they probably know only a part of the story.*

Synthesize On the basis of your own experiences and what you know about the play so far, do you think that "minding other people's business" is an example of unity, which keeps a community safe, or an example of a judgmental mindset, which breeds intolerance? *Accept all thoughtful responses.*

---

to fight the land like heroes for every grain of corn, and no man had very much time for fooling around.

That there were some jokers, however, is indicated by the practice of appointing a two-man patrol whose duty was to "walk forth in the time of God's worship to take notice of such as either lye about the meeting house, without attending to the word and ordinances, or that lye at home or in the fields without giving good account thereof, and to take the names of such persons, and to present them to the magistrates, whereby they may be accordingly proceeded against." This predilection for minding other people's business was time-honored among the people of Salem, and it undoubtedly created many of the suspicions which were to feed the coming madness. It was also, in my opinion, one of the things that a John Proctor would rebel against, for the time of the armed camp had almost passed, and since the country was reasonably—although not wholly—safe, the old disciplines were beginning to rankle. But, as in all such matters, the issue was not clear-cut, for danger was still a possibility, and in unity still lay the best promise of safety.

The edge of the wilderness was close by. The American continent stretched endlessly west, and it was full of mystery for them. It stood, dark and threatening, over their shoulders night and day, for out of it Indian tribes marauded from time to time, and Reverend Parris had parishioners who had lost relatives to these heathen.

The parochial snobbery of these people was partly responsible for their failure to convert the Indians. Probably they also preferred to take land from heathens rather than from fellow Christians. At any rate, very few Indians were converted, and the Salem folk believed that the virgin forest was the Devil's last preserve, his home base and the citadel of his final stand. To the best of their knowledge the American forest was the last place on earth that was not paying homage to God.

For these reasons, among others, they carried about an air of innate resistance, even of persecution. Their fathers had, of course, been persecuted in England. So now they and their church found it necessary to deny any other sect its freedom, lest their New Jerusalem[3] be defiled and corrupted by wrong ways and deceitful ideas.

They believed, in short, that they held in their steady hands the candle that would light the world. We have inherited this belief, and it has helped and hurt us. It helped them with the discipline it gave them. They were a dedicated folk, by and large, and they had to be to survive the life they had chosen or been born into in this country.

The proof of their belief's value to them may be taken from the opposite character of the first Jamestown settlement, farther south, in Virginia. The Englishmen who landed there were motivated mainly by a hunt for profit. They had thought to pick off the wealth of the new country and then return rich to England. They were a band of individualists, and a much more ingratiating group than the Massachusetts men. But Virginia destroyed them. Massachusetts tried to kill off the Puritans, but they combined; they set up a communal society which, in the beginning, was little more than an armed camp with an autocratic and very devoted leadership. It was, however, an autocracy by consent, for they were united from top to bottom by a commonly held ideology whose perpetuation was the reason and justification for all their sufferings. So their self-denial, their purposefulness, their suspicion of all vain pursuits, their hard-handed justice, were altogether perfect instruments for the conquest of this space so antagonistic to man.

But the people of Salem in 1692 were not quite the dedicated folk that arrived on the *Mayflower.* A vast differentiation had taken place, and in their own time a revolution had unseated the royal government and substituted a junta which was at this

---

3. **New Jerusalem:** in Christianity, a heavenly city and the last resting place of the souls saved by Jesus. It was considered the ideal city, and Puritans modeled their communities after it.

DIFFERENTIATED INSTRUCTION

FOR STRUGGLING READERS
Concept Support Make sure students understand the symbolic importance of the forest. Point to details in the left column that indicate that the Puritans thought that only they had true belief in God. Help students make the connection between the forest, the Native Americans (who sometimes attacked from the forest and who generally were not Christians), and the Devil. Elicit that the forest represented things that are mysterious and evil.

FOR ENGLISH LANGUAGE LEARNERS
Related Vocabulary Make sure students understand that some charges of witchcraft originated in a desire for revenge rather than in a fear of Satan. Discuss these interrelated terms from the concluding paragraph of the mini-essay:

- *Long-held hatreds,* "Bitter resentments toward others that people refuse to resolve"
- *vengeance,* "harmful, punishing action taken against someone who has harmed you"
- *Land-lust,* "A deep desire to own a neighbor's land"
- *constant bickering,* "arguing continuously about unimportant matters"
- *cry witch,* "to accuse someone of being a witch"
- *Old scores,* "Complaints or resentment that people have had for a long time"
- *envy of the miserable,* "the jealousy that unhappy people feel toward happy people"

moment in power.[4] The times, to their eyes, must have been out of joint, and to the common folk must have seemed as insoluble and complicated as do ours today. It is not hard to see how easily many could have been led to believe that the time of confusion had been brought upon them by deep and darkling forces. No hint of such speculation appears on the court record, but social disorder in any age breeds such mystical suspicions, and when, as in Salem, wonders are brought forth from below the social surface, it is too much to expect people to hold back very long from laying on the victims with all the force of their frustrations.

The Salem tragedy, which is about to begin in these pages, developed from a paradox. It is a paradox in whose grip we still live, and there is no prospect yet that we will discover its resolution. Simply, it was this: for good purposes, even high purposes, the people of Salem developed a theocracy, a combine of state and religious power whose function was to keep the community together, and to prevent any kind of disunity that might open it to destruction by material or ideological enemies. It was forged for a necessary purpose and accomplished that purpose. But all organization is and must be grounded on the idea of exclusion and prohibition, just as two objects cannot occupy the same space. Evidently the time came in New England when the repressions of order were heavier than seemed warranted by the dangers against which the order was organized. The witch-hunt was a perverse manifestation of the panic which set in among all classes when the balance began to turn toward greater individual freedom.

When one rises above the individual villainy displayed, one can only pity them all, just as we shall be pitied someday. It is still impossible for man to organize his social life without repressions, and the balance has yet to be struck between order and freedom.

The witch-hunt was not, however, a mere repression. It was also, and as importantly, a long overdue opportunity for everyone so inclined to express publicly his guilt and sins, under the cover of accusations against the victims. It suddenly became possible—and patriotic and holy—for a man to say that Martha Corey had come into his bedroom at night, and that, while his wife was sleeping at his side, Martha laid herself down on his chest and "nearly suffocated him." Of course it was her spirit only, but his satisfaction at confessing himself was no lighter than if it had been Martha herself. One could not ordinarily speak such things in public.

Long-held hatreds of neighbors could now be openly expressed, and vengeance taken, despite the Bible's charitable injunctions. Land-lust which had been expressed before by constant bickering over boundaries and deeds, could now be elevated to the arena of morality; one could cry witch against one's neighbor and feel perfectly justified in the bargain. Old scores could be settled on a plane of heavenly combat between Lucifer and the Lord; suspicions and the envy of the miserable toward the happy could and did burst out in the general revenge.

--- ◆ ---

1 (Reverend Parris *is praying now, and, though we cannot hear his words, a sense of his confusion hangs about him. He mumbles, then seems about to weep; then he weeps, then prays again; but his daughter does not stir on the bed.*

The door opens, and his Negro slave enters. Tituba *is in her forties.* Parris *brought her with him from Barbados, where he spent some years as a merchant before entering the ministry. She enters as one does who*
10 *can no longer bear to be barred from the sight of her beloved, but she is also very frightened because her slave sense has warned her that, as always, trouble in this house eventually lands on her back.*)

Tituba (*already taking a step backward*). My Betty be hearty soon?

---

4. **a junta** (hŏŏn'tə) . . . **power:** *Junta* is a Spanish term meaning "a small, elite ruling council." The reference here is to the group that led England's Glorious Revolution of 1688–1689.

TEXT ANALYSIS   COMMON CORE   RL 3   RL 5

● CONVENTIONS OF DRAMA

In the stage directions, Miller provides concrete instructions for the characters' movements, but he also presents clues about the characters' emotions. What emotions do these stage directions suggest? *Possible answer: The stage directions refer to Parris's "confusion" (line 2). He weeps (lines 3–4), an action that suggests that he is upset. Tituba is anxious about Betty, whom she loves (lines 9–11); she also is "frightened" because she fears being treated harshly (lines 11–13).*

Extend the Discussion Reread the stage directions regarding Tituba. What do you think her life with the Parris family has been like up to this point? Explain your answer.

FOR ADVANCED LEARNERS/AP

Evaluate Author's Purpose Note that Miller's general purpose in this mini-essay is to inform. Elicit that his specific purpose is to provide background information about life in Salem. Then point out that the purpose of *The Crucible* is not primarily informative. Ask students whether they find this informative passage helpful or counterproductive; have them defend their responses. Finally, invite suggestions such as these about ways in which the information in these and other mini-essays in the play could be conveyed to an audience:

- Have an actor play the part of a narrator and present such passages (in their entirety or in summaries) to the audience.

- Print the passages in the play's program.

- Create extra dialogue that conveys the information to the audience.

● CONVENTIONS OF DRAMA

RL 3
RL 5

Lines 19–27 are a blend of stage directions and dialogue. Which words does Parris speak in these lines? *Answer: "Out of my sight! Out of my— . . . Oh, my God! God help me! . . . Betty. Child. Dear child. Will you wake, will you open up your eyes! Betty, little one . . . ."*

REVISIT THE BIG QUESTION

What fuels a
MOB?

Discuss After students read lines 57–59, ask them the following discussion question: What role do you think rumor has in the creation of hysteria in a community? *Possible answer: Rumor may be the first step in the creation of a hysterical response. Rumors often consist of falsehoods that are embellished in ways that trigger people's fears and then are taken as fact as the rumor spreads. The fear or fanaticism triggered by rumors can contribute to a community's frenzied response to an issue.*

Parris. Out of here!

Tituba (*backing to the door*). My Betty not goin' die . . .

Parris (*scrambling to his feet in a fury*). Out of my
20 sight! (*She is gone.*) Out of my—(*He is overcome with sobs. He clamps his teeth against them and closes the door and leans against it, exhausted.*) Oh, my God! God help me! (*Quaking with fear, mumbling to himself through his sobs, he goes to the bed and gently takes* Betty's *hand.*) Betty. Child. Dear child. Will you wake, will you open up your eyes! Betty, little one . . .

(*He is bending to kneel again when his niece,* Abigail Williams, *seventeen, enters—a strikingly beautiful girl,*
30 *an orphan, with an endless capacity for dissembling. Now she is all worry and apprehension and propriety.*)

Abigail. Uncle? (*He looks to her.*) Susanna Walcott's here from Doctor Griggs.

Parris. Oh? Let her come, let her come.

Abigail (*leaning out the door to call to* Susanna, *who is down the hall a few steps*). Come in, Susanna.

(Susanna Walcott, *a little younger than* Abigail, *a nervous, hurried girl, enters.*)

Parris (*eagerly*). What does the doctor say, child?

40 **Susanna** (*craning around* Parris *to get a look at* Betty). He bid me come and tell you, reverend sir, that he cannot discover no medicine for it in his books.

Parris. Then he must search on.

Susanna. Aye, sir, he have been searchin' his books since he left you, sir. But he bid me tell you, that you might look to unnatural things for the cause of it.

Parris (*his eyes going wide*). No—no. There be no unnatural cause here. Tell him I have sent for Reverend Hale of Beverly, and Mr. Hale will surely con-
50 firm that. Let him look to medicine and put out all thought of unnatural causes here. There be none.

Susanna. Aye, sir. He bid me tell you. (*She turns to go.*)

Abigail. Speak nothin' of it in the village, Susanna.

---

5. **trafficked with:** met with.

Parris. Go directly home and speak nothing of unnatural causes.

Susanna. Aye, sir. I pray for her. (*She goes out.*)

Abigail. Uncle, the rumor of witchcraft is all about; I think you'd best go down and deny it yourself. The parlor's packed with people, sir. I'll sit with her.

60 **Parris** (*pressed, turns on her*). And what shall I say to them? That my daughter and my niece I discovered dancing like heathen in the forest?

Abigail. Uncle, we did dance; let you tell them I confessed it—and I'll be whipped if I must be. But they're speakin' of witchcraft. Betty's not witched.

Parris. Abigail, I cannot go before the congregation when I know you have not opened with me. What did you do with her in the forest?

Abigail. We did dance, uncle, and when you leaped
70 out of the bush so suddenly, Betty was frightened and then she fainted. And there's the whole of it.

Parris. Child. Sit you down.

Abigail (*quavering, as she sits*). I would never hurt Betty. I love her dearly.

Parris. Now look you, child, your punishment will come in its time. But if you trafficked with[5] spirits in the forest I must know it now, for surely my enemies will, and they will ruin me with it.

Abigail. But we never conjured spirits.

80 **Parris.** Then why can she not move herself since midnight? This child is desperate! (Abigail *lowers her eyes.*) It must come out—my enemies will bring it out. Let me know what you done there. Abigail, do you understand that I have many enemies?

Abigail. I have heard of it, uncle.

Parris. There is a faction that is sworn to drive me from my pulpit. Do you understand that?

Abigail. I think so, sir.

Parris. Now then, in the midst of such disruption,
90 my own household is discovered to be the very center of some obscene practice. Abominations are done in the forest—

---

142 UNIT 1: EARLY AMERICAN WRITING

DIFFERENTIATED INSTRUCTION

FOR STRUGGLING READERS

Paraphrasing Puritan English Have students reread lines 47–51. Then model how to paraphrase lines 47–48: *No—no. Nothing supernatural is happening here.* Ask students to paraphrase lines 50–51. *Possible answer: The doctor should keep looking for the right medicine and forget the idea that there is a supernatural cause [for Betty's condition]. There is no such cause.*

FOR ENGLISH LANGUAGE LEARNERS

Vocabulary: Outdated Forms Remind students that Miller crafted authentic language for his characters that differs from modern English. Provide these terms and definitions for students. Then have them paraphrase the lines in more modern English.

- *bid me come* (line 41), "asked me to come"

- *let you tell* (line 63), "please tell"

- *witched* (line 65), "bewitched," "possessed"

- *opened with me* (line 67), "told me the truth"

Winona Ryder as Abigail Williams

READING SKILLS

COMMON CORE
RL 1
RL 3

◼ DRAW CONCLUSIONS ABOUT CHARACTERS

What do the stage directions in line 73 tell you about how Abigail is feeling? Explain. ***Possible answer:*** *The stage directions describe Abigail as "quavering," or shaking. She seems anxious about her cousin Betty's health and nervous about discussing what she and Betty did in the forest.*

READING SKILLS

COMMON CORE
RL 1
RL 3

◼ DRAW CONCLUSIONS ABOUT CHARACTER

Parris expresses concern for his daughter, but his comments to Abigail suggest that he has another motive for wanting to know what happened in the forest. What does his conversation with Abigail suggest about his personality? ***Possible answer:*** *The conversation suggests that Parris is self-interested, concerned mainly about his reputation in the village. He also may be difficult to get along with, because he is on the verge of losing his job (lines 86–87). He may be pressuring Abigail for a full, truthful report so that he can counter charges that enemies may make against him.*

FOR ENGLISH LANGUAGE LEARNERS

Vocabulary Support Ask students to work in pairs and use a dictionary for the definitions and parts of speech of the words that follow. Have students create flash cards for the words. *capacity* (line 30), *consult* (line 541), *contract* (line 594), *plus* (line 603), *definite* (line 754), *process* (line 953).

 BEST PRACTICES TOOLKIT—Transparency
New Word Analysis p. E8

FOR ADVANCED LEARNERS/AP

Analyze Dialogue and Stage Directions Have students reread Parris's conversation with Abigail in lines 57–151, envisioning Parris's movement around the stage, tone of voice, and so on. Then ask pairs of students to collaborate on a detailed set of stage directions that present their ideas in the form of instructions to an actor. Students might consider questions such as these:

- How do Parris's tone and gestures change when he talks about his enemies (beginning at line 78)?
- When Parris talks about Abigail's "name in the town" (beginning at line 127), does he move closer to her, or farther away?

After students have presented a reading that illustrates their stage directions, discuss whether Miller's limited stage directions make the actor's work more difficult or free him to interpret the role as he wishes.

DRAW CONCLUSIONS ABOUT CHARACTERS

What conclusions can you draw about Abigail's character, given Parris's remarks and her responses in lines 131–147?

Possible answer: The reader can conclude that Abigail is a proud young woman. She refuses work that she considers too lowly and is quick to defend herself against the charge of being "soiled" (lines 137–139 and 149–151). Abigail also may be a troublemaker: Since Goody Proctor fired her, no one else has wanted to hire her (lines 140–145).

REVISIT THE BIG QUESTION

What fuels a MOB?

Discuss How might comments like the ones that Mrs. Putnam makes in lines 158–166 contribute to a sense of hysteria among the townsfolk? *Possible answer: Mrs. Putnam's comments repeat a rumor, and rumors often fuel hysteria (lines 164–165). If the rumor is true, there may be cause for fear, because supernatural powers are at work. If the rumor is untrue, such comments are still dangerous because people sometimes believe the worst, even if they suspect that the information is false. Such willingness to think irrationally can lead to hysterical behavior.*

Abigail. It were sport, uncle!

Parris (*pointing at* Betty). You call this sport? (*She lowers her eyes. He pleads.*) Abigail, if you know something that may help the doctor, for God's sake tell it to me. (*She is silent.*) I saw Tituba waving her arms over the fire when I came on you. Why was she doing that? And I heard a screeching and gibberish 100 coming from her mouth. She were swaying like a dumb beast over that fire!

Abigail. She always sings her Barbados songs, and we dance.

Parris. I cannot blink what I saw, Abigail, for my enemies will not blink it. I saw a dress lying on the grass.

Abigail (*innocently*). A dress?

Parris (*It is very hard to say*). Aye, a dress. And I thought I saw—someone naked running through the trees!

110 **Abigail** (*in terror*). No one was naked! You mistake yourself, uncle!

Parris (*with anger*). I saw it! (*He moves from her. Then, resolved*) Now tell me true, Abigail. And I pray you feel the weight of truth upon you, for now my ministry's at stake, my ministry and perhaps your cousin's life. Whatever abomination you have done, give me all of it now, for I dare not be taken unaware when I go before them down there.

120 **Abigail.** There is nothin' more. I swear it, uncle.

Parris (*studies her, then nods, half convinced*). Abigail, I have fought here three long years to bend these stiff-necked people to me, and now, just now when some good respect is rising for me in the parish, you compromise my very character. I have given you a home, child, I have put clothes upon your back—now give me upright answer. Your name in the town—it is entirely white, is it not?

Abigail (*with an edge of resentment*). Why, I am sure 130 it is, sir. There be no blush about my name.[6]

Parris (*to the point*). Abigail, is there any other cause than you have told me, for your being discharged from Goody[7] Proctor's service? I have heard it said, and I tell you as I heard it, that she comes so rarely to the church this year for she will not sit so close to something soiled. What signified that remark?

Abigail. She hates me, uncle, she must, for I would not be her slave. It's a bitter woman, a lying, cold, sniveling woman, and I will not work for such a woman!

140 **Parris.** She may be. And yet it has troubled me that you are now seven month out of their house, and in all this time no other family has ever called for your service.

Abigail. They want slaves, not such as I. Let them send to Barbados for that. I will not black my face for any of them! (*with ill-concealed resentment at him*) Do you begrudge my bed, uncle?

Parris. No—no.

Abigail (*in a temper*). My name is good in the vil-150 lage! I will not have it said my name is soiled! Goody Proctor is a gossiping liar!

(*Enter Mrs. Ann Putnam. She is a twisted soul of forty-five, a death-ridden woman, haunted by dreams.*)

Parris (*as soon as the door begins to open*). No—no, I cannot have anyone. (*He sees her, and a certain **deference** springs into him, although his worry remains.*) Why, Goody Putnam, come in.

Mrs. Putnam (*full of breath, shiny-eyed*). It is a marvel. It is surely a stroke of hell upon you.

160 **Parris.** No, Goody Putnam, it is—

Mrs. Putnam (*glancing at* Betty). How high did she fly, how high?

Parris. No, no, she never flew—

Mrs. Putnam (*very pleased with it*). Why, it's sure she did. Mr. Collins saw her goin' over Ingersoll's barn, and come down light as bird, he says!

Parris. Now, look you, Goody Putnam, she never—

---

6. **There be . . . my name:** There is nothing wrong with my reputation.

7. **Goody:** short for *Goodwife*, the Puritan equivalent of *Mrs.*

DIFFERENTIATED INSTRUCTION

FOR ADVANCED LEARNERS/AP

Analyze Stage Directions Ask students to focus on the description of Mrs. Putnam that appears in the stage directions in lines 152–153. Have students write a description or draw an illustration to indicate what they think Mrs. Putnam looks like. Have students compare descriptions or drawings to see if there are any common elements. Then instruct students to write a brief character sketch about Mrs. Putnam's life and person-ality, based on Miller's stage directions. (For example, why might she have a "twisted soul"? What cause would she have to be "death-ridden" and "haunted by dreams"?) Invite students to share their ideas with the class; then urge them to keep reading to see whether their ideas are verified as the story unfolds.

(*Enter* Thomas Putnam, *a well-to-do, hard-handed landowner, near fifty.*) Oh, good morning, Mr.
170 Putnam.

Putnam. It is a providence the thing is out now! It is a providence. (*He goes directly to the bed.*)

Parris. What's out, sir, what's—?

(Mrs. Putnam *goes to the bed.*)

Putnam (*looking down at* Betty). Why, *her* eyes is closed! Look you, Ann.

Mrs. Putnam. Why, that's strange. (*to* Parris) Ours is open.

Parris (*shocked*). Your Ruth is sick?

180 **Mrs. Putnam** (*with vicious certainty*). I'd not call it sick; the Devil's touch is heavier than sick. It's death, y'know, it's death drivin' into them, forked and hoofed.

Parris. Oh, pray not! Why, how does Ruth ail?

Mrs. Putnam. She ails as she must—she never waked this morning, but her eyes open and she walks, and hears naught, sees naught, and cannot eat. Her soul is taken, surely.

(Parris *is struck.*)

190 **Putnam** (*as though for further details*). They say you've sent for Reverend Hale of Beverly?

Parris (*with dwindling conviction now*). A precaution only. He has much experience in all demonic arts, and I—

Mrs. Putnam. He has indeed; and found a witch in Beverly last year, and let you remember that.

Parris. Now, Goody Ann, they only thought that were a witch, and I am certain there be no element of witchcraft here.

200 **Putnam.** No witchcraft! Now look you, Mr. Parris—

Parris. Thomas, Thomas, I pray you, leap not to witchcraft. I know that you—you least of all, Thomas, would ever wish so disastrous a charge laid upon me. We cannot leap to witchcraft. They will howl me out of Salem for such corruption in my house.

A word about Thomas Putnam. He was a man with many grievances, at least one of which appears justified. Some time before, his wife's brother-in-law, James Bayley, had been turned down as minister of Salem. Bayley had all the qualifications, and a two-thirds vote into the bargain, but a faction stopped his acceptance, for reasons that are not clear.

Thomas Putnam was the eldest son of the richest man in the village. He had fought the Indians at Narragansett,[8] and was deeply interested in parish affairs. He undoubtedly felt it poor payment that the village should so blatantly disregard his candidate for one of its more important offices, especially since he regarded himself as the intellectual superior of most of the people around him.

His vindictive nature was demonstrated long before the witchcraft began. Another former Salem minister, George Burroughs, had had to borrow money to pay for his wife's funeral, and, since the parish was remiss in his salary, he was soon bankrupt. Thomas and his brother John had Burroughs jailed for debts the man did not owe. The incident is important only in that Burroughs succeeded in becoming minister where Bayley, Thomas Putnam's brother-in-law, had been rejected; the motif of resentment is clear here. Thomas Putnam felt that his own name and the honor of his family had been smirched by the village, and he meant to right matters however he could.

Another reason to believe him a deeply embittered man was his attempt to break his father's will, which left a disproportionate amount to a stepbrother. As with every other public cause in which he tried to force his way, he failed in this.

So it is not surprising to find that so many accusations against people are in the handwriting of Thomas Putnam, or that his name is so often found as a witness **corroborating** the supernatural testimony, or that his daughter led the crying-out at the most opportune junctures of the trials, especially when—But we'll speak of that when we come to it.

---

8. **fought the Indians at Narragansett:** The Puritans fought a series of battles against the Narragansett Indians over territory that both groups had settled on.

TIERED DISCUSSION PROMPTS

Use these prompts to help students understand the characters' growing concerns about witchcraft after they read lines 190–205:

Connect Think about a time when you or someone you know tried but failed to change someone's opinion. How might it feel to have your argument rejected—and to know that the other person continues to hold a view that you do not? *Students should note the frustration and possible suspicion that both parties might feel in such a situation.*

Analyze Why does Parris speak "with dwindling conviction now" (line 192)? *Possible answer: Parris realizes that people know that he has asked Reverend Hale to come to Salem (lines 190–191). The realization may weaken his confidence that witchcraft is not involved in the girls' condition.* Why does Parris try to change the Putnams' view about witchcraft at this point? *Possible answer: Parris wants to win the Putnams to his side before Hale arrives, to minimize the chance that he will be forced to leave Salem (lines 201–205).*

Synthesize On the basis of what you have learned about these characters so far, what do you think is the significance of Mrs. Putnam's observation that Reverend Hale "found a witch in Beverly last year" (lines 195–196)? *Possible answer: The observation is significant because it foreshadows the finding of witches in Salem.*

FOR STRUGGLING READERS

Explore Cause and Effect Help students grasp the key points of Miller's discussion of Thomas Putnam. Summarize the main idea—namely, that Putnam will be a "problem" character because he has complaints against many people of Salem. Then work with students to complete a cause-and-effect diagram that notes Putnam's chief complaints and their effect.

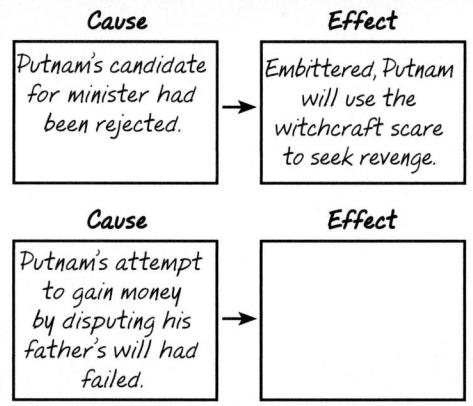

Cause	Effect
Putnam's candidate for minister had been rejected.	Embittered, Putnam will use the witchcraft scare to seek revenge.

Cause	Effect
Putnam's attempt to gain money by disputing his father's will had failed.	

FOR ENGLISH LANGUAGE LEARNERS

Vocabulary: Multiple-Meaning Words Explain that some words have more than one meaning and that students must determine the appropriate definition for a given use. Have students use a dictionary and context clues to figure out the meaning of *sport* (line 93), *dumb* (line 101), *compromise* (line 125), *white* (line 128), *discharged* (line 132), *cold* (line 138), *element* (line 198), *pray* (line 201).

● CONVENTIONS OF DRAMA

According to the stage directions in lines 206–208, why does Putnam continue to talk about witches? *Possible answer: Putnam continues to talk because he wants to cause Parris's downfall in the community. Putnam seeks revenge because his relative was not chosen to be the town's minister.*

Extend the Discussion Given this information, how might you interpret Putnam's advice to Parris in lines 249–251 and 272–276?

◆ GRAMMAR AND STYLE

COMMON
CORE L 3a

Use Realistic Dialogue Miller used examples of writing from the late 17th century as models for his writing; he wanted the characters' language and sentence structures to sound realistic for that time period. Reread lines 272–282. What repeated phrase sounds dated? *Answer: "Let you" (lines 272, 277).* What word choice adds to the realism in line 281? *Answer: the contraction "d'y'hear."* In what sense is "Now look you, sir" (line 272) an example of an inverted sentence? *Possible answer: Speakers of modern English would probably say, "Now [you] look, sir."*

Putnam (*At the moment he is intent upon getting* Parris, *for whom he has only contempt, to move toward the abyss*). Mr. Parris, I have taken your part in all contention here, and I would continue; but I cannot
210 if you hold back in this. There are hurtful, vengeful spirits layin' hands on these children.

Parris. But, Thomas, you cannot—

Putnam. Ann! Tell Mr. Parris what you have done.

Mrs. Putnam. Reverend Parris, I have laid seven babies unbaptized in the earth. Believe me, sir, you never saw more hearty babies born. And yet, each would wither in my arms the very night of their birth. I have spoke nothin', but my heart has clamored intimations.[9] And now, this year, my Ruth, my only—I see her turning
220 strange. A secret child she has become this year, and shrivels like a sucking mouth were pullin' on her life too. And so I thought to send her to your Tituba—

Parris. To Tituba! What may Tituba—?

Mrs. Putnam. Tituba knows how to speak to the dead, Mr. Parris.

Parris. Goody Ann, it is a formidable sin to conjure up the dead!

Mrs. Putnam. I take it on my soul, but who else may surely tell us what person murdered my babies?

230 **Parris** (*horrified*). Woman!

Mrs. Putnam. They were murdered, Mr. Parris! And mark this proof! Mark it! Last night my Ruth were ever so close to their little spirits; I know it, sir. For how else is she struck dumb now except some power of darkness would stop her mouth? It is a marvelous sign, Mr. Parris!

Putnam. Don't you understand it, sir? There is a murdering witch among us, bound to keep herself in the dark. (Parris *turns to* Betty, *a frantic terror rising*
240 *in him.*) Let your enemies make of it what they will, you cannot blink it more.

Parris (*to* Abigail). Then you were conjuring spirits last night.

Abigail (*whispering*). Not I, sir—Tituba and Ruth.

Parris (*turns now, with new fear, and goes to* Betty, *looks down at her, and then, gazing off*). Oh, Abigail, what proper payment for my charity! Now I am undone.

Putnam. You are not undone! Let you take hold
250 here. Wait for no one to charge you—declare it yourself. You have discovered witchcraft—

Parris. In my house? In my house, Thomas? They will topple me with this! They will make of it a— (*Enter* Mercy Lewis, *the Putnams' servant, a fat, sly, merciless girl of eighteen.*)

Mercy. Your pardons. I only thought to see how Betty is.

Putnam. Why aren't you home? Who's with Ruth?

Mercy. Her grandma come. She's improved a little,
260 I think—she give a powerful sneeze before.

Mrs. Putnam. Ah, there's a sign of life!

Mercy. I'd fear no more, Goody Putnam. It were a grand sneeze; another like it will shake her wits together, I'm sure. (*She goes to the bed to look.*)

Parris. Will you leave me now, Thomas? I would pray a while alone.

Abigail. Uncle, you've prayed since midnight. Why do you not go down and—

Parris. No—no. (*to* Putnam) I have no answer for
270 that crowd. I'll wait till Mr. Hale arrives. (*to get* Mrs. Putnam *to leave*) If you will, Goody Ann . . .

Putnam. Now look you, sir. Let you strike out against the Devil, and the village will bless you for it! Come down, speak to them—pray with them. They're thirsting for your word, Mister! Surely you'll pray with them.

Parris (*swayed*). I'll lead them in a psalm, but let you say nothing of witchcraft yet. I will not discuss it. The cause is yet unknown. I have had enough con-
280 tention since I came; I want no more.

Mrs. Putnam. Mercy, you go home to Ruth, d'y'hear?

Mercy. Aye, mum.

(Mrs. Putnam *goes out.*)

---

9. **clamored intimations** (klăm'ərd ĭn'tə-mā'shənz): nagging suspicions.

DIFFERENTIATED INSTRUCTION

FOR ENGLISH LANGUAGE LEARNERS

Language: Conversational English Patterns
Explain that some contractions in the text, especially contractions that replace the final *g* in the -*ing* ending, recreate the sound of informal, excited speech. Point out these examples: *layin'* (line 211), *nothin'* (line 218), *pullin'* (line 221), *beatin'* (line 296), *comin'* (line 299), *talkin'* (line 312), *callin'* (line 313), *hangin'* (line 317), *dancin'* (line 319).

Parris (*to* Abigail). If she starts for the window, cry for me at once.

Abigail. I will, uncle.

Parris (*to* Putnam). There is a terrible power in her arms today. (*He goes out with* Putnam.)

Abigail (*with hushed trepidation*). How is Ruth sick?

290 **Mercy.** It's weirdish, I know not—she seems to walk like a dead one since last night.

Abigail (*turns at once and goes to* Betty, *and now, with fear in her voice*). Betty? (Betty *doesn't move. She shakes her.*) Now stop this! Betty! Sit up now!

(Betty *doesn't stir.* Mercy *comes over.*)

Mercy. Have you tried beatin' her? I gave Ruth a good one and it waked her for a minute. Here, let me have her.

Abigail (*holding* Mercy *back*). No, he'll be comin' up.
300 Listen, now; if they be questioning us, tell them we danced—I told him as much already.

Mercy. Aye. And what more?

Abigail. He knows Tituba conjured Ruth's sisters to come out of the grave.

Mercy. And what more?

Abigail. He saw you naked.

Mercy (*clapping her hands together with a frightened laugh*). Oh, Jesus!

(*Enter* Mary Warren, *breathless. She is seventeen,*
310 *a* **subservient**, *naive, lonely girl.*)

Mary Warren. What'll we do? The village is out! I just come from the farm; the whole country's talkin' witchcraft! They'll be callin' us witches, Abby!

Mercy (*pointing and looking at* Mary Warren). She means to tell, I know it.

Mary Warren. Abby, we've got to tell. Witchery's a hangin' error, a hangin' like they done in Boston two year ago! We must tell the truth, Abby! You'll only be whipped for dancin', and the other things!

320 **Abigail.** Oh, *we'll* be whipped!

Mary Warren. I never done none of it, Abby. I only looked!

②

Villagers gathering to gossip

BACKGROUND

The Execution of Goody Glover Mary Warren's comment in lines 317–318 may refer to the execution of Ann "Goody" Glover, an Irish washerwoman who was hanged as a witch in Boston in 1688. Glover's case was widely publicized in an influential book published in 1689 *Memorable Providences, Relating to Witchcrafts and Possessions* by the famous Boston minister, Cotton Mather. Scholars have discovered that the "real" Samuel Parris actually kept a copy of Mather's book in his library.

Analyze Visuals

Activity Take a close look at this photograph from the 1996 film version of *The Crucible*. From what you can see of the body language and facial expressions of the people, what do you think is the mood of this crowd? Does it match the mood of the text? Explain. *Possible answer: The mood seems tense; the people seem nearly frantic. Distressed expressions appear on many faces; and some people seem to be weeping, praying, or crying out. Their bodies turn in all directions, and everyone seems to be talking at once; these details contribute to the agitated mood.*

FOR STRUGGLING READERS

② **Targeted Passage** [Lines 309–322]

This passage reveals the growing speculation and the girls' differing responses to it.

- According to Mary, who is talking about witchcraft? (lines 312–313)

- On the basis of Mercy's comment, what do you think the girls had planned to do? Why is that plan not working? (lines 316–318)

- What does Mary want the girls to do? How will that plan benefit her? (lines 318–320)

Concept Support Direct students to the departure of Mrs. Putnam (line 283) and of Reverend Parris and Mr. Putnam (line 288). Elicit that when Abigail and Mercy are left alone, they immediately start talking about Betty and the overall situation. As you discuss the scene (lines 289–372), lead students to grasp (1) the increasingly frantic tone of their comments and (2) their mutual accusations, which foreshadow even greater accusations as the play continues.

● DRAW CONCLUSIONS ABOUT CHARACTERS

What new conclusions can you draw about Abigail, given her comments in lines 353–364? **Possible answer:** *Abigail is a take-charge person, for she dominates the conversation. Her threats to harm the other girls if they do not support her story (lines 355–363) reveal that she is intimidating to the point of being cruel.*

IF STUDENTS NEED HELP . . . Work through the passage, sentence by sentence. Help students choose at least one revealing comment to add to the chart on page 135. **Extend the Discussion** How did Abigail's parents die? How might that information affect your thinking about her personality?

● CONVENTIONS OF DRAMA

On the basis of Miller's mini-essay, what role do you think John Proctor will play: hero, villain, major figure, minor figure, foil (character used as a contrast to another character)? Explain. **Possible answer:** *Proctor will be a major character, perhaps even the hero. Miller indicates that Proctor has integrity and is strong and even-tempered. These traits could be called "heroic." Furthermore, Miller says that Proctor has "a sharp and biting way with hypocrites" and that he is "not easily led." These traits could put him in conflict with major figures in the story.*

Mercy (*moving menacingly toward* Mary). Oh, you're a great one for lookin', aren't you, Mary Warren? What a grand peeping courage you have!

(Betty, *on the bed, whimpers.* Abigail *turns to her at once.*)

Abigail. Betty? (*She goes to* Betty.) Now, Betty, dear, wake up now. It's Abigail. (*She sits* Betty *up and* 330 *furiously shakes her.*) I'll beat you, Betty! (Betty *whimpers.*) My, you seem improving. I talked to your papa and I told him everything. So there's nothing to—

Betty (*darts off the bed, frightened of* Abigail, *and flattens herself against the wall*). I want my mama!

Abigail (*with alarm, as she cautiously approaches* Betty). What ails you, Betty? Your mama's dead and buried.

Betty. I'll fly to Mama. Let me fly! (*She raises her arms as though to fly, and streaks for the window, gets* 340 *one leg out.*)

Abigail (*pulling her away from the window*). I told him everything; he knows now, he knows everything we—

Betty. You drank blood, Abby! You didn't tell him that!

Abigail. Betty, you never say that again! You will never—

Betty. You did, you did! You drank a charm to kill John Proctor's wife! You drank a charm to kill Goody Proctor!

Abigail (*smashes her across the face*). Shut it! Now 350 shut it!

Betty (*collapsing on the bed*). Mama, Mama! (*She dissolves into sobs.*)

Abigail. Now look you. All of you. We danced. And Tituba conjured Ruth Putnam's dead sisters. And that is all. And mark this. Let either of you breathe a word, or the edge of a word, about the other things, and I will come to you in the black of some terrible night and I will bring a pointy reckoning that will shudder you.[10] And you know I can do it; I saw 360 Indians smash my dear parents' heads on the pillow

next to mine, and I have seen some reddish work done at night, and I can make you wish you had never seen the sun go down! (*She goes to* Betty *and roughly sits her up.*) Now, you—sit up and stop this!

(*But* Betty *collapses in her hands and lies inert on the bed.*)

Mary Warren (*with hysterical fright*). What's got her? (Abigail *stares in fright at* Betty.) Abby, she's going to die! It's a sin to conjure, and we—

370 **Abigail** (*starting for* Mary). I say shut it, Mary Warren!

(*Enter* John Proctor. *On seeing him,* Mary Warren *leaps in fright.*)

Proctor was a farmer in his middle thirties. He need not have been a partisan of any faction in the town, but there is evidence to suggest that he had a sharp and biting way with hypocrites. He was the kind of man—powerful of body, even-tempered, and not easily led—who cannot refuse support to partisans without drawing their deepest resentment. In Proctor's presence a fool felt his foolishness instantly—and a Proctor is always marked for calumny[11] therefore.

But as we shall see, the steady manner he displays does not spring from an untroubled soul. He is a sinner, a sinner not only against the moral fashion of the time, but against his own vision of decent conduct. These people had no ritual for the washing away of sins. It is another trait we inherited from them, and it has helped to discipline us as well as to breed hypocrisy among us. Proctor, respected and even feared in Salem, has come to regard himself as a kind of fraud. But no hint of this has yet appeared on the surface, and as he enters from the crowded parlor below it is a man in his prime we see, with a quiet confidence and an unexpressed, hidden force. Mary Warren, his servant, can barely speak for embarrassment and fear.

---

10. **bring . . . shudder you:** inflict a terrifying punishment on you.
11. **marked for calumny** (kăl′əm-nē): singled out to have lies told about him.

DIFFERENTIATED INSTRUCTION

FOR ADVANCED LEARNERS/AP

Synthesize "In Proctor's presence," Miller writes, "a fool felt his foolishness instantly—and a Proctor is always marked for calumny therefore." Ask students to reflect upon those comments and to consider situations that they have experienced or read about in which they think that "a Proctor" has been present. Then have students write and share a paragraph that responds to these questions:

- What is "a Proctor"?
- What traits does a person need to make a fool feel his foolishness instantly?
- Why is this kind of person "marked for calumny" (in other words, lied about in an effort to destroy his reputation)?

Mary Warren. Oh! I'm just going home, Mr. Proctor.

Proctor. Be you foolish, Mary Warren? Be you deaf? I forbid you leave the house, did I not? Why shall I pay you? I am looking for you more often than my cows!

Mary Warren. I only come to see the great doings in the world.

380 **Proctor.** I'll show you a great doin' on your arse one of these days. Now get you home; my wife is waitin' with your work! (*Trying to retain a shred of dignity, she goes slowly out.*)

Mercy Lewis (*both afraid of him and strangely titillated*). I'd best be off. I have my Ruth to watch. Good morning, Mr. Proctor.

(*Mercy sidles out. Since Proctor's entrance, Abigail has stood as though on tiptoe, absorbing his presence, wide-eyed. He glances at her, then goes to Betty on the bed.*)

Abigail. Gah! I'd almost forgot how strong you are, 390 John Proctor!

Proctor (*looking at Abigail now, the faintest suggestion of a knowing smile on his face*). What's this mischief here?

Abigail (*with a nervous laugh*). Oh, she's only gone silly somehow.

Proctor. The road past my house is a pilgrimage to Salem all morning. The town's mumbling witchcraft.

Abigail. Oh, posh! (*Winningly she comes a little closer, with a confidential, wicked air.*) We were dancin' in the woods last night, and my uncle leaped in on us. 400 She took fright, is all.

Proctor (*his smile widening*). Ah, you're wicked yet, aren't y'! (*A trill of expectant laughter escapes her, and she dares come closer, feverishly looking into his eyes.*) You'll be clapped in the stocks before you're twenty.

(*He takes a step to go, and she springs into his path.*)

Abigail. Give me a word, John. A soft word. (*Her concentrated desire destroys his smile.*)

Proctor. No, no, Abby. That's done with.

Abigail (*tauntingly*). You come five mile to see a silly 410 girl fly? I know you better.

Proctor (*setting her firmly out of his path*). I come to see what mischief your uncle's brewin' now. (*with final emphasis*) Put it out of mind, Abby.

Abigail (*grasping his hand before he can release her*). John—I am waitin' for you every night.

Proctor. Abby, I never give you hope to wait for me.

Abigail (*now beginning to anger—she can't believe it*). I have something better than hope, I think!

Proctor. Abby, you'll put it out of mind. I'll not be 420 comin' for you more.

Abigail. You're surely sportin' with me.

Proctor. You know me better.

Abigail. I know how you clutched my back behind your house and sweated like a stallion whenever I come near! Or did I dream that? It's she put me out, you cannot pretend it were you. I saw your face when she put me out, and you loved me then and you do now!

Proctor. Abby, that's a wild thing to say—

430 **Abigail.** A wild thing may say wild things. But not so wild, I think. I have seen you since she put me out; I have seen you nights.

Proctor. I have hardly stepped off my farm this sevenmonth.

Abigail. I have a sense for heat, John, and yours has drawn me to my window, and I have seen you look-ing up, burning in your loneliness. Do you tell me you've never looked up at my window?

Proctor. I may have looked up.

440 **Abigail** (*now softening*). And you must. You are no wintry man. I *know* you, John. I know you. (*She is weeping.*) I cannot sleep for dreamin'; I cannot dream but I wake and walk about the house as though I'd find you comin' through some door. (*She clutches him desperately*).

Proctor (*gently pressing her from him, with great sympathy but firmly*). Child—

Abigail (*with a flash of anger*). How do you call me child!

THE CRUCIBLE: ACT ONE **149**

READING SKILLS · COMMON CORE · RL 1 · RL 3

◼ DRAW CONCLUSIONS ABOUT CHARACTERS

Reread the stage directions in lines 391–404. What does Proctor's facial expression reveal about his attitude toward Abigail as he first addresses her? *Possible answer: Proctor's smiling (lines 391–392 and 401) reveals that he is familiar with Abigail. The nature of that familiarity becomes clear in the dialogue that develops between them.*

TIERED DISCUSSION PROMPTS

Use these prompts to help students under-stand Abigail and Proctor's relationship as they read lines 401–428:

Summarize Why does Abigail grow angry with Proctor? *Possible answer: Abigail wants physical intimacy with Proctor (begin-ning at line 402). She grows angry because he repeatedly refuses her advances (lines 408, 413, 416, 419–420, and 422).*

Analyze What caused Abigail to lose her job with the Proctors? *Possible answer: Abigail lost her job because she and Proctor had an affair. Proctor's wife ("she," line 427) learned of it, or suspected it, and sent Abigail away.*

Synthesize Why might Abigail resist Proc-tor's decision to end their affair? *Possible answer: Abigail has shown herself to be a quick-tempered young woman who tries to make others do what she wants. She has also displayed a streak of vindictiveness, so she may seek revenge against Proctor.*

FOR STRUGGLING READERS

Paraphrase Remind students that some of the characters' ways of speaking may seem awkward or out of date to speakers of modern English. Have students work in pairs to paraphrase Proctor's first words (lines 374–376). After volunteer pairs have shared their paraphrases with the class, discuss which version allows them to read more expressively.

FOR ENGLISH LANGUAGE LEARNERS

Language: Conversational English Patterns Discuss these words and phrases that Miller includes to add to the conversational feel of the dialogue on these pages: *you're a great one for lookin'* (lines 323–324); *shut it* (lines 349, 350, and 370); *Gah!* (line 389); *she's . . . gone silly* (lines 393–394); *Oh, posh!* (line 397); *aren't y'!* (line 402); *I'll not be comin' for you* (lines 419–420).

■ DRAW CONCLUSIONS ABOUT CHARACTERS

As Proctor responds to Abigail's insults about Elizabeth in lines 457–463, what do his words and the stage directions suggest about his view of his marriage? Cite evidence to explain your response. **Possible answer:** *Proctor's order that Abigail be quiet (lines 458–459) and his threat to see her punished (line 463) suggest that he wants to protect Elizabeth and their marriage. The stage directions (lines 458 and 463) verify that he indeed is angry— not only with Abigail for insulting Elizabeth, but with himself, as well (probably for having indulged in the affair in the first place).*

TEXT ANALYSIS

COMMON CORE

RL 3
RL 5

● CONVENTIONS OF DRAMA

Miller's mini-essays create two worlds: the world inhabited by the play's characters, and the world that contains him and his readers. Notice how this time Miller begins by speaking of "we," as if he and his readers are talking behind the characters' backs. Is Miller's strategy of inviting the reader into his confidence effective? Why or why not? **Possible answers:** *Yes, the strategy is effective, for it is exciting to be taken into the playwright's confidence. No, the fact that the mini-essays shift the play's focus might cause some readers to lose contact with the plot and characters.*

---

450 **Proctor.** Abby, I may think of you softly from time to time. But I will cut off my hand before I'll ever reach for you again. Wipe it out of mind. We never touched, Abby.

Abigail. Aye, but we did.

Proctor. Aye, but we did not.

Abigail (*with a bitter anger*). Oh, I marvel how such a strong man may let such a sickly wife be—

Proctor (*angered—at himself as well*). You'll speak nothin' of Elizabeth!

460 **Abigail.** She is blackening my name in the village! She is telling lies about me! She is a cold, sniveling woman, and you bend to her! Let her turn you like a—

Proctor (*shaking her*). Do you look for whippin'?

(*A psalm is heard being sung below.*)

Abigail (*in tears*). I look for John Proctor that took me from my sleep and put knowledge in my heart! I never knew what pretense Salem was, I never knew the lying lessons I was taught by all these Christian women and their covenanted[12] men! And now you

470 bid me tear the light out of my eyes? I will not, I cannot! You loved me, John Proctor, and whatever sin it is, you love me yet! (*He turns abruptly to go out. She rushes to him.*) John, pity me, pity me!

(*The words "going up to Jesus" are heard in the psalm, and* Betty *claps her ears suddenly and whines loudly.*)

Abigail. Betty? (*She hurries to Betty, who is now sitting up and screaming.* Proctor *goes to* Betty *as Abigail is trying to pull her hands down, calling* "Betty!")

Proctor (*growing unnerved*). What's she doing? Girl,

480 what ails you? Stop that wailing!

(*The singing has stopped in the midst of this, and now* Parris *rushes in.*)

Parris. What happened? What are you doing to her? Betty! (*He rushes to the bed, crying,* "Betty, Betty!" Mrs. Putnam *enters, feverish with curiosity, and with her* Thomas Putnam *and* Mercy Lewis. Parris, *at the*

bed, *keeps lightly slapping* Betty's *face, while she moans and tries to get up.*)

Abigail. She heard you singin' and suddenly she's up

490 and screamin'.

Mrs. Putnam. The psalm! The psalm! She cannot bear to hear the Lord's name!

Parris. No. God forbid. Mercy, run to the doctor! Tell him what's happened here! (Mercy Lewis *rushes out.*)

Mrs. Putnam. Mark it for a sign, mark it!

(Rebecca Nurse, *seventy-two, enters. She is white-haired, leaning upon her walking-stick.*)

Putnam (*pointing at the whimpering* Betty). That is a notorious sign of witchcraft afoot, Goody Nurse,

500 a prodigious sign!

Mrs. Putnam. My mother told me that! When they cannot bear to hear the name of—

Parris (*trembling*). Rebecca, Rebecca, go to her, we're lost. She suddenly cannot bear to hear the Lord's—

(Giles Corey, *eighty-three, enters. He is knotted with muscle, canny, inquisitive, and still powerful.*)

Rebecca. There is hard sickness here, Giles Corey, so please to keep the quiet.

Giles. I've not said a word. No one here can testify I've

510 said a word. Is she going to fly again? I hear she flies.

Putnam. Man, be quiet now!

(*Everything is quiet. Rebecca walks across the room to the bed. Gentleness exudes from her.* Betty *is quietly whimpering, eyes shut.* Rebecca *simply stands over the child, who gradually quiets.*)

A nd while they are so absorbed, we may put a word in for Rebecca. Rebecca was the wife of Francis Nurse, who, from all accounts, was one of those men for whom both sides of the argument had to have respect. He was called upon to arbitrate disputes as though he were an unofficial judge, and

---

12. **covenanted** (kŭv′ə-nən-tĭd): In Puritan religious practice, the men of a congregation would make an agreement, or covenant, to govern the community and abide by its beliefs and practices.

DIFFERENTIATED INSTRUCTION

FOR ENGLISH LANGUAGE LEARNERS

Language: Cognates Point out the English word *dispute*, meaning "quarrel," which appears as *disputes* in the final line on this page. Explain that the word derives from Latin and is similar to the Spanish *disputa*, the Italian *disputa*, and the French *dispute*. Have students who speak Latin-based languages suggest cognates for these English words that appear in the next paragraph: *suggestion, systematic, campaign, proportions*.

FOR ADVANCED LEARNERS/AP

Evaluate Plot Has Miller made it clear whether he wants the audience to believe that Betty (and, by extension, Ruth) truly is possessed by a demonic force? Have students work alone to make two lists: one stating reasons why the audience is meant to think that the girls are bewitched, and the other giving evidence that contradicts this view. Then have partners debate the question and report on the outcome.

Rebecca also enjoyed the high opinion most people had for him. By the time of the delusion,[13] they had three hundred acres, and their children were settled in separate homesteads within the same estate. However, Francis had originally rented the land, and one theory has it that, as he gradually paid for it and raised his social status, there were those who resented his rise.

Another suggestion to explain the systematic campaign against Rebecca, and inferentially against Francis, is the land war he fought with his neighbors, one of whom was a Putnam. This squabble grew to the proportions of a battle in the woods between partisans of both sides, and it is said to have lasted for two days. As for Rebecca herself, the general opinion of her character was so high that to explain how anyone dared cry her out for a witch—and more, how adults could bring themselves to lay hands on her—we must look to the fields and boundaries of that time.

As we have seen, Thomas Putnam's man for the Salem ministry was Bayley. The Nurse clan had been in the faction that prevented Bayley's taking office. In addition, certain families allied to the Nurses by blood or friendship, and whose farms were contiguous with the Nurse farm or close to it, combined to break away from the Salem town authority and set up Topsfield, a new and independent entity whose existence was resented by old Salemites.

That the guiding hand behind the outcry was Putnam's is indicated by the fact that, as soon as it began, this Topsfield-Nurse faction absented themselves from church in protest and disbelief. It was Edward and Jonathan Putnam who signed the first complaint against Rebecca; and Thomas Putnam's little daughter was the one who fell into a fit at the hearing and pointed to Rebecca as her attacker. To top it all, Mrs. Putnam—who is now staring at the bewitched child on the bed—soon accused Rebecca's spirit of "tempting her to **iniquity**," a charge that had more truth in it than Mrs. Putnam could know.

---

13. **the time of the delusion:** the era of the witchcraft accusations and trials.
14. **wardens:** officers appointed to keep order.

Mrs. Putnam (*astonished*). What have you done? (*Rebecca, in thought, now leaves the bedside and sits.*)

Parris (*wondrous and relieved*). What do you make of it, Rebecca?

520 **Putnam** (*eagerly*). Goody Nurse, will you go to my Ruth and see if you can wake her?

Rebecca (*sitting*). I think she'll wake in time. Pray calm yourselves. I have eleven children, and I am twenty-six times a grandma, and I have seen them all through their silly seasons, and when it come on them they will run the Devil bowlegged keeping up with their mischief. I think she'll wake when she tires of it. A child's spirit is like a child, you can never catch it by running after it; you must stand
530 still, and, for love, it will soon itself come back.

Proctor. Aye, that's the truth of it, Rebecca.

Mrs. Putnam. This is no silly season, Rebecca. My Ruth is bewildered, Rebecca; she cannot eat.

Rebecca. Perhaps she is not hungered yet. (*to* Parris) I hope you are not decided to go in search of loose spirits, Mr. Parris. I've heard promise of that outside.

Parris. A wide opinion's running in the parish that the Devil may be among us, and I would satisfy them that they are wrong.

540 **Proctor.** Then let you come out and call them wrong. Did you consult the wardens[14] before you called this minister to look for devils?

Parris. He is not coming to look for devils!

Proctor. Then what's he coming for?

Putnam. There be children dyin' in the village, Mister!

Proctor. I seen none dyin'. This society will not be a bag to swing around your head, Mr. Putnam. (*to* Parris) Did you call a meeting before you—?

Putnam. I am sick of meetings; cannot the man turn
550 his head without he have a meeting?

Proctor. He may turn his head, but not to Hell!

Rebecca. Pray, John, be calm. (*Pause. He defers to her.*) Mr. Parris, I think you'd best send Reverend

---

■ DRAW CONCLUSIONS ABOUT CHARACTERS

In what sense do Rebecca Nurse's words in lines 522–530 set her character apart from the others? ***Possible answer:*** *Rebecca Nurse's words show that she is calm in the presence of Betty. She uses past experience and reason, rather than hearsay and emotion, to think about the girl's illness.*

IF STUDENTS NEED HELP . . . Model the use of a Two-Column Chart to list and compare traits.

Rebecca	Other Salemites
bases reasoning on firsthand experience	base reasoning on hearsay
understanding	fearful

 BEST PRACTICES TOOLKIT—Transparency Two-Column Chart p. A25

REVISIT THE BIG QUESTION

What fuels a MOB?

Discuss After students read lines 532–552, ask them the following discussion question: What do these comments from Rebecca and Proctor suggest about the likelihood of their being caught up in a hysteria over witchcraft? ***Possible answer:*** *Their comments suggest that they are unlikely to join in the hysteria. Rebecca urges Reverend Parris not to search for "loose spirits" (lines 535–536) and advises Proctor to calm down (line 552). Proctor pushes for more open discussion of the matter (lines 540–542 and 546–548).*

FOR STRUGGLING READERS

Comprehension Support Point out that the relationship between Francis and Rebecca Nurse and Thomas Putnam is complicated and unfriendly. Using the mini-essay on this page, help students review the main reasons for the families' conflict.

LAND: Francis Nurse had a land war with a Putnam relative (past); Putnam may be among those in Salem who resent his social status (present).

MINISTRY: The Nurses successfully opposed Bayley, Putnam's choice for minister (past); Putnam may be among those in Salem who resent the Nurses' creation of Topsfield (present).

WITCHCRAFT: Rebecca Nurse is generally well respected (present), but Thomas Putnam's daughter and wife will accuse her of attacking them with witchcraft (future).

TIERED DISCUSSION PROMPTS

Use these prompts to help students explore Parris's character, as revealed in lines 594–629, in greater detail:

Recall What does Reverend Parris complain about in these lines? *Answer: Parris complains that he is not properly supplied with firewood (lines 594–597 and 600–602), that he lives in relative poverty (lines 609–611), that he has not been awarded the deed to his house (lines 618–619), and that his congregation is too quick to fire its ministers (lines 624–629).*

Analyze What do Parris's complaints suggest about how he thinks of himself? Explain. *Possible answer: The complaints suggest that Parris is a proud man. He feels that he deserves the firewood, a better salary, home ownership, and greater job security—perhaps because of his education (line 604–606) or his status as a servant of God (lines 627–629).*

Synthesize How might Parris's attitude harm his ability to deal effectively with the witchcraft scare? *Possible answer: Parris's prideful comments suggest that his attention may be divided; that is, at the same time that he is trying to deal with the witchcraft scare, he also is trying to defend himself and his ministry.*

Hale back as soon as he come. This will set us all to arguin' again in the society, and we thought to have peace this year. I think we ought rely on the doctor now, and good prayer.

Mrs. Putnam. Rebecca, the doctor's baffled!

Rebecca. If so he is, then let us go to God for the
560 cause of it. There is prodigious danger in the seeking of loose spirits. I fear it, I fear it. Let us rather blame ourselves and—

Putnam. How may we blame ourselves? I am one of nine sons; the Putnam seed have peopled this province. And yet I have but one child left of eight—and now she shrivels!

Rebecca. I cannot fathom that.

Mrs. Putnam (*with a growing edge of sarcasm*). But I must! You think it God's work you should never
570 lose a child, nor grandchild either, and I bury all but one? There are wheels within wheels in this village, and fires within fires!

Putnam (*to Parris*). When Reverend Hale comes, you will proceed to look for signs of witchcraft here.

Proctor (*to Putnam*). You cannot command Mr. Parris. We vote by name in this society, not by acreage.

Putnam. I never heard you worried so on this society, Mr. Proctor. I do not think I saw you at Sabbath meeting since snow flew.

580 **Proctor.** I have trouble enough without I come five mile to hear him preach only hellfire and bloody damnation. Take it to heart, Mr. Parris. There are many others who stay away from church these days because you hardly ever mention God any more.

Parris (*now aroused*). Why, that's a drastic charge!

Rebecca. It's somewhat true; there are many that quail to bring their children—

Parris. I do not preach for children, Rebecca. It is not the children who are unmindful of their obliga-
590 tions toward this ministry.

Rebecca. Are there really those unmindful?

Parris. I should say the better half of Salem village—

Putnam. And more than that!

Parris. Where is my wood? My contract provides I be supplied with all my firewood. I am waiting since November for a stick, and even in November I had to show my frostbitten hands like some London beggar!

Giles. You are allowed six pound a year to buy your wood, Mr. Parris.

600 **Parris.** I regard that six pound as part of my salary. I am paid little enough without I spend six pound on firewood.

Proctor. Sixty, plus six for firewood—

Parris. The salary is sixty-six pound, Mr. Proctor! I am not some preaching farmer with a book under my arm; I am a graduate of Harvard College.

Giles. Aye, and well instructed in arithmetic!

Parris. Mr. Corey, you will look far for a man of my kind at sixty pound a year! I am not used to this
610 poverty; I left a thrifty business in the Barbados to serve the Lord. I do not fathom it, why am I persecuted here? I cannot offer one proposition but there be a howling riot of argument. I have often wondered if the Devil be in it somewhere; I cannot understand you people otherwise.

Proctor. Mr. Parris, you are the first minister ever did demand the deed to this house—

Parris. Man! Don't a minister deserve a house to live in?

620 **Proctor.** To live in, yes. But to ask ownership is like you shall own the meeting house itself; the last meeting I were at you spoke so long on deeds and mortgages I thought it were an auction.

Parris. I want a mark of confidence, is all! I am your third preacher in seven years. I do not wish to be put out like the cat whenever some majority feels the whim. You people seem not to comprehend that a minister is the Lord's man in the parish; a minister is not to be so lightly crossed and contradicted—

630 **Putnam.** Aye!

Parris. There is either obedience or the church will burn like Hell is burning!

Proctor. Can you speak one minute without we land in Hell again? I am sick of Hell!

DIFFERENTIATED INSTRUCTION

FOR STRUGGLING READERS

Concept Support Miller complicates the plot by revealing conflicts between various Salemites. Have students work in pairs or small groups to summarize the conflict that exists between these characters:

- Rebecca vs. Mrs. Putnam (regarding Salem's sick children)

- Putnam vs. Proctor (regarding Proctor's spiritual condition)

- Proctor vs. Parris (regarding Parris's preaching)

- Giles vs. Parris (regarding Parris's salary and benefits)

Urge students to watch for ways in which these and other interpersonal conflicts grow and how they fuel the hysteria over possible witchcraft in Salem.

Behind the Curtain

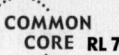

COMMON CORE RL 7

DRAMA AND FILM

These photographs show scenes from the 1996 film version of *The Crucible* that do not occur in Miller's play. One features a meeting between Proctor and Abigail; the other shows an incident that is mentioned in the play. As you study these photographs, keep in mind that on stage it is difficult and expensive to move the action from place to place by changing the set. As a result, Act I of Miller's play takes place in one bedroom. Films, however, make it possible to move a story's action rapidly from one setting to another.

- What are some advantages and disadvantages of adding these new scenes in the film version?
- What story elements is the film director trying to emphasize?

BEHIND THE CURTAIN

COMMON CORE RL 7

Scene Selection Point out that film directors often consider the text of the play a starting point and feel free to omit or add scenes, depending upon the story elements that they want to emphasize. *Adding the scene between Proctor and Abigail clarifies their relationship. Similarly, dramatizing the scene in the forest shows the audience that the girls' actions are deeply important to the story. Note that film directors also may add a scene primarily because it lends itself to visual representation.*

FOR ADVANCED LEARNERS/AP

Create an Original Scene Ask students to review the play and choose a scene that is only referred to, not dramatized on stage. Here are a few examples:

- a scene between Abigail and Elizabeth Proctor in which Abigail loses her job
- a scene showing Ruth Putnam and her mysterious illness

- a scene from the past that Miller describes in one of the informative mini-essays

Have students, either individually or in small groups, write a dramatization of the chosen scene. Remind them to include dialogue for the characters and any stage directions necessary to bring the scene to life. After volunteers perform their scenes, discuss whether each scene would contribute to or distract from the action of the play.

Use these prompts to help students understand the hostility between Parris and Proctor, which boils to the surface in lines 638–654:

Connect Have you ever been in a situation in which someone blurted out a confession or other piece of secret information? What happened as a result of the revelation? *Accept all responses.*

Analyze What can you infer about Proctor's personality and attitudes from his remark in line 646? *Possible answer: Proctor is not easily led by others. He does not like people who abuse power in an attempt to control others. He is not afraid to say what he thinks, even if his words seem rebellious.*

Synthesize What do you think Rebecca means when she says, "You are another kind, John" (line 653)? Explain. *Possible answer: Proctor seems willing to go against the group's view; he would rather live by his own code of ethics than follow a minister who he thinks is in the wrong. Rebecca probably is referring to Proctor's individualism—a trait that she views as dangerous, which is why she urges him to make peace with Parris.*

Parris. It is not for you to say what is good for you to hear!

Proctor. I may speak my heart, I think!

Parris (*in a fury*). What, are we Quakers?[15] We are not Quakers here yet, Mr. Proctor. And you may tell
640 that to your followers!

Proctor. My followers!

Parris (*Now he's out with it*). There is a party in this church. I am not blind; there is a faction and a party.

Proctor. Against you?

Putnam. Against him and all authority!

Proctor. Why, then I must find it and join it.

(*There is shock among the others.*)

Rebecca. He does not mean that.

Putnam. He confessed it now!

650 **Proctor.** I mean it solemnly, Rebecca; I like not the smell of this "authority."

Rebecca. No, you cannot break charity[16] with your minister. You are another kind, John. Clasp his hand, make your peace.

Proctor. I have a crop to sow and lumber to drag home. (*He goes angrily to the door and turns to* Corey *with a smile.*) What say you, Giles, let's find the party. He says there's a party.

Giles. I've changed my opinion of this man, John.
660 Mr. Parris, I beg your pardon. I never thought you had so much iron in you.

Parris (*surprised*). Why, thank you, Giles!

Giles. It suggests to the mind what the trouble be among us all these years. (*to all*) Think on it. Wherefore is everybody suing everybody else? Think on it now, it's a deep thing, and dark as a pit. I have been six time in court this year—

Proctor (*familiarly, with warmth, although he knows he is approaching the edge of* Giles' *tolerance with this*).
670 Is it the Devil's fault that a man cannot say you good morning without you clap him for defamation?[17] You're old, Giles, and you're not hearin' so well as you did.

Giles (*He cannot be crossed*). John Proctor, I have only last month collected four pound damages for you publicly sayin' I burned the roof off your house, and I—

Proctor (*laughing*). I never said no such thing, but I've paid you for it, so I hope I can call you deaf without charge. Now come along, Giles, and help
680 me drag my lumber home.

Putnam. A moment, Mr. Proctor. What lumber is that you're draggin', if I may ask you?

Proctor. My lumber. From out my forest by the riverside.

Putnam. Why, we are surely gone wild this year. What **anarchy** is this? That tract is in my bounds, it's in my bounds, Mr. Proctor.

Proctor. In your bounds! (*indicating* Rebecca) I bought that tract from Goody Nurse's husband five
690 months ago.

Putnam. He had no right to sell it. It stands clear in my grandfather's will that all the land between the river and—

Proctor. Your grandfather had a habit of willing land that never belonged to him, if I may say it plain.

Giles. That's God's truth; he nearly willed away my north pasture but he knew I'd break his fingers before he'd set his name to it. Let's get your lumber home, John. I feel a sudden will to work coming on.

700 **Putnam.** You load one oak of mine and you'll fight to drag it home!

Giles. Aye, and we'll win too, Putnam—this fool and I. Come on! (*He turns to* Proctor *and starts out.*)

Putnam. I'll have my men on you, Corey! I'll clap a writ on you!

(*Enter* Reverend John Hale *of Beverly.*)

---

15. **Quakers:** a radical English religious sect—much hated by the Puritans—who often "spoke their heart" during their religious meetings.

16. **break charity:** break off; end the relationship.

17. **clap ... defamation** (dĕf'ə-mā'shən): imprison him for slander.

DIFFERENTIATED INSTRUCTION

FOR STRUGGLING READERS

Vocabulary Support Have students reread the lines containing these unusual terms. After you define each one, have students paraphrase the lines.

- *a party in this church* (lines 642–643), "a group of church members who have organized to gain power (in opposition to the existing authority)"

- *iron* (line 661), "firmness (in speaking out with criticism)"

- *in my bounds* (line 687), "on my property"

- *clap a writ* (lines 704–705), "issue a warrant or court order"

FOR ADVANCED LEARNERS/AP

Research Land Ownership Have students work in pairs to research the laws and traditions of land ownership at this time in colonial America. Students should locate information about who could own land, how land was transferred from one person to another (inheritance, buying and selling, and so on), and how land disputes were settled. Ask students to prepare and share a paragraph or bulleted list that presents their main points.

Rob Campbell as Reverend Hale

Mr. Hale is nearing forty, a tight-skinned, eager-eyed intellectual. This is a beloved errand for him; on being called here to ascertain witchcraft he felt the pride of the specialist whose unique knowledge has at last been publicly called for. Like almost all men of learning, he spent a good deal of his time pondering the invisible world, especially since he had himself encountered a witch in his parish not long before. That woman, however, turned into a mere pest under his searching scrutiny, and the child she had allegedly been afflicting recovered her normal behavior after Hale had given her his kindness and a few days of rest in his own house. However, that experience never raised a doubt in his mind as to the reality of the underworld or the existence of Lucifer's many-faced lieutenants. And his belief is not to his discredit. Better minds than Hale's were—and still are—convinced that there is a society of spirits beyond our ken. One cannot help noting that one of his lines has never yet raised a laugh in any audience that has seen this play; it is his assurance that "We cannot look to superstition in this. The Devil is precise." Evidently we are not quite certain even now whether diabolism is holy and not to be scoffed at. And it is no accident that we should be so bemused.

Like Reverend Hale and the others on this stage, we conceive the Devil as a necessary part of a respectable view of cosmology.[18] Ours is a divided empire in which certain ideas and emotions and actions are of God, and their opposites are of Lucifer. It is as impossible for most men to conceive of a morality without sin as of an earth without "sky." Since 1692 a great but superficial change has wiped out God's beard and the Devil's horns, but the world is still gripped between two diametrically opposed

---

18. **cosmology** (kŏz-mŏl′ə-jē): a branch of philosophy dealing with the structure of the universe.

Use these prompts to help students grasp some of Miller's points in this mini-essay:

Restate According to the paragraph that begins this page, why is the Devil a "weapon"? *Possible answer: Miller calls the Devil a "weapon" because, in his view, churches and religious governments have repeatedly used people's fear of the Devil to force obedience to their authority.*

Analyze How is the "political inspiration of the Devil" at work in Salem? *Possible answer: Various Salemites—Reverend Parris and the Putnams, for example—are using belief in demonic activity to gain or hold power. Does Miller seem to think that this approach will work for long? How can you tell? Possible answer: Miller seems to think that the approach ultimately will not work. He says that the fact that each side in a conflict can accuse the other of "alliance with Hell" makes it hard for him to believe in the "political inspiration of the Devil."*

Evaluate Compare this mini-essay to other mini-essays in *The Crucible* so far. In your opinion, is this mini-essay as helpful as the others? Why or why not? *Possible answer: While some students may find this essay interesting and provocative, others may find it tedious. The previous mini-essays provided information about the setting and characters, but here Miller primarily discusses religious and political philosophy. Except for its beginning and end, where Miller describes Reverend Hale, the mini-essay is perhaps more distracting than helpful.*

---

absolutes. The concept of unity, in which positive and negative are attributes of the same force, in which good and evil are relative, ever-changing, and always joined to the same phenomenon—such a concept is still reserved to the physical sciences and to the few who have grasped the history of ideas. When it is recalled that until the Christian era the underworld was never regarded as a hostile area, that all gods were useful and essentially friendly to man despite occasional lapses; when we see the steady and methodical inculcation into humanity of the idea of man's worthlessness—until redeemed—the necessity of the Devil may become evident as a weapon, a weapon designed and used time and time again in every age to whip men into a surrender to a particular church or church-state.

Our difficulty in believing the—for want of a better word—political inspiration of the Devil is due in great part to the fact that he is called up and damned not only by our social antagonists but by our own side, whatever it may be. The Catholic Church, through its Inquisition,[19] is famous for cultivating Lucifer as the arch-fiend, but the Church's enemies relied no less upon the Old Boy to keep the human mind enthralled. Luther[20] was himself accused of alliance with Hell, and he in turn accused his enemies. To complicate matters further, he believed that he had had contact with the Devil and had argued theology with him. I am not surprised at this, for at my own university a professor of history—a Lutheran, by the way—used to assemble his graduate students, draw the shades, and commune in the classroom with Erasmus.[21] He was never, to my knowledge, officially scoffed at for this, the reason being that the university officials, like most of us, are the children of a history which still sucks at

the Devil's teats. At this writing, only England has held back before the temptations of contemporary diabolism. In the countries of the Communist ideology, all resistance of any import is linked to the totally malign capitalist succubi,[22] and in America any man who is not reactionary in his views is open to the charge of alliance with the Red hell. Political opposition, thereby, is given an inhumane overlay which then justifies the abrogation of all normally applied customs of civilized intercourse. A political policy is equated with moral right, and opposition to it with diabolical malevolence. Once such an equation is effectively made, society becomes a congerie of plots and counterplots, and the main role of government changes from that of the arbiter to that of the scourge of God.

The results of this process are no different now from what they ever were, except sometimes in the degree of cruelty inflicted, and not always even in that department. Normally the actions and deeds of a man were all that society felt comfortable in judging. The secret intent of an action was left to the ministers, priests, and rabbis to deal with. When diabolism rises, however, actions are the least important manifests of the true nature of a man. The Devil, as Reverend Hale said, is a wily one, and, until an hour before he fell, even God thought him beautiful in Heaven.[23]

The analogy, however, seems to falter when one considers that, while there were no witches then, there are Communists and capitalists now, and in each camp there is certain proof that spies of each side are at work undermining the other. But this is a snobbish objection and not at all warranted by the facts. I have no doubt that people *were* communing with, and even worshiping, the Devil in Salem,

---

19. **Inquisition:** a former tribunal in the Roman Catholic Church dedicated to the discovery and punishment of heresy.

20. **Luther:** Martin Luther (1483–1546), the German theologian who led the Protestant Reformation.

21. **Erasmus** (ĭ-răz′məs): Desiderius Erasmus (1466?–1536), a Dutch scholar who sought to restore Christian faith by a study of the Scriptures and classical texts.

22. **succubi** (sŭk′yə-bī): demons that assume female form. Demons that assume male form are called incubi (ĭn′kyə-bī).

23. **The Devil . . . beautiful in Heaven:** According to Christian belief, Lucifer was God's favorite angel until the angel rebelled and was cast out of Heaven.

DIFFERENTIATED INSTRUCTION

FOR STRUGGLING READERS

③ Targeted Passage [Column 2]

In this passage, Miller explains how a fear similar to the one that gripped Salem is possible in the world today.

- What political system demonizes capitalism? (lines 3–5)

- Why is it useful for governments to cast their political opponents as diabolical? (lines 11–13)

FOR ADVANCED LEARNERS/AP

Research Political Systems Have students research the basic beliefs of communism as it existed in the 1950s and capitalism as it has been practiced in the United States. Instruct them to create a chart or other graphic aid that shows why each side would equate the other with the Devil.

and if the whole truth could be known in this case, as it is in others, we should discover a regular and conventionalized propitiation of the dark spirit. One certain evidence of this is the confession of Tituba, the slave of Reverend Parris, and another is the behavior of the children who were known to have indulged in sorceries with her.

There are accounts of similar *klatches* in Europe, where the daughters of the towns would assemble at night and, sometimes with fetishes, sometimes with a selected young man, give themselves to love, with some bastardly results. The Church, sharp-eyed as it must be when gods long dead are brought to life, condemned these orgies as witchcraft and interpreted them, rightly, as a resurgence of the Dionysiac forces[24] it had crushed long before. Sex, sin, and the Devil were early linked, and so they continued to be in Salem, and are today. From all accounts there are no more puritanical mores in the world than those enforced by the Communists in Russia, where women's fashions, for instance, are as prudent and all-covering as any American Baptist would desire. The divorce laws lay a tremendous responsibility on the father for the care of his children. Even the laxity of divorce regulations in the early years of the revolution was undoubtedly a revulsion from the nineteenth-century Victorian immobility of marriage and the consequent hypocrisy that developed from it. If for no other reasons, a state so powerful, so jealous of the uniformity of its citizens, cannot long tolerate the atomization of the family. And yet, in American eyes at least, there remains the conviction that the Russian attitude toward women is lascivious. It is the Devil working again, just as he is working within the Slav[25] who is shocked at the very idea of a woman's disrobing herself in a burlesque show. Our opposites are always robed in sexual sin, and it is from this unconscious conviction that demonology gains both its attractive sensuality and its capacity to infuriate and frighten.

Coming into Salem now, Reverend Hale conceives of himself much as a young doctor on his first call. His painfully acquired armory of symptoms, catchwords, and diagnostic procedures are now to be put to use at last. The road from Beverly is unusually busy this morning, and he has passed a hundred rumors that make him smile at the ignorance of the yeomanry in this most precise science. He feels himself allied with the best minds of Europe—kings, philosophers, scientists, and ecclesiasts of all churches. His goal is light, goodness and its preservation, and he knows the exaltation of the blessed whose intelligence, sharpened by minute examinations of enormous tracts, is finally called upon to face what may be a bloody fight with the Fiend himself.

(*He appears loaded down with half a dozen heavy books.*)

Hale. Pray you, someone take these!

710 **Parris** (*delighted*). Mr. Hale! Oh! it's good to see you again! (*taking some books*) My, they're heavy!

Hale (*setting down his books*). They must be; they are weighted with authority.

Parris (*a little scared*). Well, you do come prepared!

Hale. We shall need hard study if it comes to tracking down the Old Boy. (*noticing* Rebecca) You cannot be Rebecca Nurse?

Rebecca. I am, sir. Do you know me?

Hale. It's strange how I knew you, but I suppose you 720 look as such a good soul should. We have all heard of your great charities in Beverly.

Parris. Do you know this gentleman? Mr. Thomas Putnam. And his good wife Ann.

Hale. Putnam! I had not expected such distinguished company, sir.

---

24. **Dionysiac** (dī′ə-nĭs′ē-ăk′) **forces:** forces associated with Dionysus, the Greek god of wine and ecstasy.

25. **Slav:** a generic reference to Russians and other Slavic-speaking peoples of Eastern Europe who were under the control of the Soviet Union.

■ DRAW CONCLUSIONS ABOUT CHARACTERS

Compare the concluding paragraph of this mini-essay to the opening paragraph on page 155. How would you describe Hale's view of himself and his goal in Salem?

Possible answer: *Hale views himself as a great intellect, equal to Europe's best thinkers and superior to the average villager (whom he finds rather humorous). Hale's goal is to restore Salem to a great spiritual state, and he will do anything—even fight the Devil—to succeed in that goal.*

FOR STRUGGLING READERS

Vocabulary Support As Miller waxes philosophical in his mini-essays, his diction becomes more difficult. Discuss the meanings of some or all of these terms from this page:

- *propitiation,* "an act that calms or pleases someone"
- *klatches,* "gatherings"
- *fetishes,* "objects believed to have magical power"
- *resurgence,* "return," "revival"
- *mores,* "accepted standards of behavior"
- *prudent,* "careful to avoid danger"
- *laxity,* "looseness"
- *atomization,* "breakup"
- *yeomanry,* "farmers (as a group)"
- *tracts,* "religious writings"

After students read lines 707–758, use these prompts to help students explore the initial impression of Reverend Hale:

Recall What heavy items has Reverend Hale brought with him to Salem, and why? ***Answer:*** *Hale has brought several heavy books with him; they are reference sources that he might consult as he conducts his investigation (lines 707–716).*

Analyze What evidence suggests that Hale may not be as quick to believe a charge of witchcraft as some of the Salemites seem to be? ***Possible answer:*** *Proctor calls Hale "a sensible man" (line 741), suggesting that Hale will apply reason to the situation. Furthermore, even when Hale is presented with reports of Betty Parris's bewitchment, he says that he will not proceed in the investigation unless the people promise to accept his ruling if he rules against bewitchment (lines 754–756).*

Synthesize Do you think that Hale will maintain his "sensible" attitude as the story unfolds? Why or why not? ***Possible answer:*** *Hale's "sensible" attitude may be shaken if hysteria rises in the community or if he witnesses repeated manifestations of possible demonic power.*

Putnam (*pleased*). It does not seem to help us today, Mr. Hale. We look to you to come to our house and save our child.

Hale. Your child ails too?

730 **Mrs. Putnam.** Her soul, her soul seems flown away. She sleeps and yet she walks . . .

Putnam. She cannot eat.

Hale. Cannot eat! (*Thinks on it. Then, to* Proctor *and* Giles Corey.) Do you men have afflicted children?

Parris. No, no, these are farmers. John Proctor—

Giles Corey. He don't believe in witches.

Proctor (*to* Hale). I never spoke on witches one way or the other. Will you come, Giles?

Giles. No—no, John, I think not. I have some few 740 queer questions of my own to ask this fellow.

Proctor. I've heard you to be a sensible man, Mr. Hale. I hope you'll leave some of it in Salem.

(Proctor *goes.* Hale *stands embarrassed for an instant.*)

Parris (*quickly*). Will you look at my daughter, sir? (*leads* Hale *to the bed*) She has tried to leap out the window; we discovered her this morning on the highroad, waving her arms as though she'd fly.

Hale (*narrowing his eyes*). Tries to fly.

Putnam. She cannot bear to hear the Lord's name, 750 Mr. Hale; that's a sure sign of witchcraft afloat.

Hale (*holding up his hands*). No, no. Now let me instruct you. We cannot look to superstition in this. The Devil is precise; the marks of his presence are definite as stone, and I must tell you all that I shall not proceed unless you are prepared to believe me if I should find no bruise of hell upon her.

Parris. It is agreed, sir—it is agreed—we will abide by your judgment.

Hale. Good then. (*He goes to the bed, looks down* 760 *at* Betty. *To* Parris.) Now, sir, what were your first warning of this strangeness?

Parris. Why, sir—I discovered her—(*indicating* Abigail) and my niece and ten or twelve of the other girls, dancing in the forest last night.

Hale (*surprised*). You permit dancing?

Parris. No, no, it were secret—

Mrs. Putnam (*unable to wait*). Mr. Parris's slave has knowledge of conjurin', sir.

Parris (*to* Mrs. Putnam). We cannot be sure of that, 770 Goody Ann—

Mrs. Putnam (*frightened, very softly*). I know it, sir. I sent my child—she should learn from Tituba who murdered her sisters.

Rebecca (*horrified*). Goody Ann! You sent a child to conjure up the dead?

Mrs. Putnam. Let God blame me, not you, not you, Rebecca! I'll not have you judging me any more! (*to* Hale) Is it a natural work to lose seven children before they live a day?

780 **Parris.** Sssh!

(Rebecca, *with great pain, turns her face away. There is a pause.*)

Hale. Seven dead in childbirth.

Mrs. Putnam (*softly*). Aye. (*Her voice breaks; she looks up at him. Silence.* Hale *is impressed.* Parris *looks to him. He goes to his books, opens one, turns pages, then reads. All wait, avidly.*)

Parris (*hushed*). What book is that?

Mrs. Putnam. What's there, sir?

790 **Hale** (*with a tasty love of intellectual pursuit*). Here is all the invisible world, caught, defined, and calculated. In these books the Devil stands stripped of all his brute disguises. Here are all your familiar spirits—your incubi and succubi; your witches that go by land, by air, and by sea; your wizards of the night and of the day. Have no fear now—we shall find him out if he has come among us, and I mean to crush him utterly if he has shown his face! (*He starts for the bed.*)

Rebecca. Will it hurt the child, sir?

800 **Hale.** I cannot tell. If she is truly in the Devil's grip we may have to rip and tear to get her free.

Rebecca. I think I'll go, then. I am too old for this. (*She rises.*)

Parris (*striving for conviction*). Why, Rebecca, we may open up the boil of all our troubles today!

DIFFERENTIATED INSTRUCTION

FOR ADVANCED LEARNERS/AP

Analyze Metaphor Have students reread Parris's comment in lines 804–805. Instruct them to write a brief paragraph that explains the metaphor that Parris uses and that paraphrases the line. Then ask students to create a few original metaphors that would convey the same idea. As you lead a discussion about the metaphor, call on volunteers to share their original examples of figurative language.

FOR RELUCTANT READERS

Connect to the Text Remind students to think about their own communities as they read the play. Ask them, "How do rumors or gossip affect your community? What happens when rumors spread?" Have students write short journal entries in response to the questions. Ask volunteers to share their entries. Challenge the class to compare and contrast students' experiences with those of the characters in the play.

Rebecca. Let us hope for that. I go to God for you, sir.

Parris (*with trepidation—and resentment*). I hope you do not mean we go to Satan here! (*slight pause*)

810 **Rebecca.** I wish I knew. (*She goes out; they feel resentful of her note of moral superiority.*)

Putnam (*abruptly*). Come, Mr. Hale, let's get on. Sit you here.

Giles. Mr. Hale, I have always wanted to ask a learned man—what signifies the readin' of strange books?

Hale. What books?

Giles. I cannot tell; she hides them.

Hale. Who does this?

Giles. Martha, my wife. I have waked at night many 820 a time and found her in a corner, readin' of a book. Now what do you make of that?

Hale. Why, that's not necessarily—

Giles. It discomfits me! Last night—mark this—I tried and tried and could not say my prayers. And then she close her book and walks out of the house, and suddenly—mark this—I could pray again!

Old Giles must be spoken for, if only because his fate was to be so remarkable and so different from that of all the others. He was in his early eighties at this time, and was the most comical hero in the history. No man has ever been blamed for so much. If a cow was missed, the first thought was to look for her around Corey's house; a fire blazing up at night brought suspicion of arson to his door. He didn't give a hoot for public opinion, and only in his last years—after he had married Martha—did he bother much with the church. That she stopped his prayer is very probable, but he forgot to say that he'd only recently learned any prayers and it didn't take much to make him stumble over them. He was a crank and a nuisance, but withal a deeply innocent and brave man. In court once, he was asked if it were true that he had been frightened by the strange behavior of a hog and had then said he knew it to be the Devil in an animal's shape. "What frighted you?" he was asked. He forgot everything but the word "frighted," and instantly replied, "I do not know that I ever spoke that word in my life."

* * *

Hale. Ah! The stoppage of prayer—that is strange. I'll speak further on that with you.

Giles. I'm not sayin' she's touched the Devil, now, 830 but I'd admire to know what books she reads and why she hides them. She'll not answer me, y' see.

Hale. Aye, we'll discuss it. (*to all*) Now mark me, if the Devil is in her you will witness some frightful wonders in this room, so please to keep your wits about you. Mr. Putnam, stand close in case she flies. Now, Betty, dear, will you sit up? (*Putnam comes in closer, ready-handed. Hale sits Betty up, but she hangs limp in his hands.*) Hmmm. (*He observes her carefully. The others watch breathlessly.*) Can you hear me? I am 840 John Hale, minister of Beverly. I have come to help you, dear. Do you remember my two little girls in Beverly? (*She does not stir in his hands.*)

Parris (*in fright*). How can it be the Devil? Why would he choose my house to strike? We have all manner of licentious people in the village!

Hale. What victory would the Devil have to win a soul already bad? It is the best the Devil wants, and who is better than the minister?

Giles. That's deep, Mr. Parris, deep, deep!

850 **Parris** (*with resolution now*). Betty! Answer Mr. Hale! Betty!

Hale. Does someone afflict you, child? It need not be a woman, mind you, or a man. Perhaps some bird invisible to others comes to you—perhaps a pig, a mouse, or any beast at all. Is there some figure bids you fly? (*The child remains limp in his hands. In silence he lays her back on the pillow. Now, holding out his hands toward her, he intones.*) In nomine Domini Sabaoth sui filiique ite ad infernos.[26] (*She does not stir. He turns to Abigail, his eyes narrowing.*) Abigail, what 860 sort of dancing were you doing with her in the forest?

---

26. **In nomine . . . infernos** *Latin:* "In the name of the Father and Son, get thee back to Hell."

THE CRUCIBLE: ACT ONE **159**

TEXT ANALYSIS   COMMON CORE   RL 3   RL 5

● **CONVENTIONS OF DRAMA**

Where does Miller position his mini-essay about Giles Corey? How does the placement affect the dialogue? ***Possible answer:*** *Miller places this mini-essay in the middle of Giles's comments about his wife. Miller's remarks function as an aside, and he picks up the dialogue right where he left off.*

IF STUDENTS NEED HELP . . . Ask them to imagine that this mini-essay is being presented as part of the play. Review the speech devices listed in the Text Analysis Workshop (page 133) and discuss which one best fits this situation.

Extend the Discussion Reread lines 814–831, but skip over the mini-essay this time. How might your understanding of Giles's character be different if you did not possess the information found in the mini-essay?

FOR STRUGGLING READERS

Comprehension Support Ask students to think about whether Miller intended Giles's remarks to be humorous. Have volunteers read lines 814–831 with different expressions, depending on whether they intend to emphasize humor. Discuss why Miller might add humor to this scene. (Later, when students learn Giles's fate, have them come back to this scene and discuss whether the seeming humor may also have a deeper irony.)

What fuels a
MOB?

Discuss In lines 885–919, how does Reverend Hale help create the hysteria about witches that is starting to sweep through Salem?

Possible answer: *Hale helps create hysteria by asking leading questions that plant ideas for responses in the minds of Abigail and Tituba. He also pressures them so much that they feel trapped and start looking to shift the attention onto someone else.*

Abigail. Why—common dancing is all.

Parris. I think I ought to say that I—I saw a kettle in the grass where they were dancing.

Abigail. That were only soup.

Hale. What sort of soup were in this kettle, Abigail?

Abigail. Why, it were beans—and lentils, I think, and—

Hale. Mr. Parris, you did not notice, did you, any
870 living thing in the kettle? A mouse, perhaps, a spider, a frog—?

Parris (*fearfully*). I—do believe there were some movement—in the soup.

Abigail. That jumped in, we never put it in!

Hale (*quickly*). What jumped in?

Abigail. Why, a very little frog jumped—

Parris. A frog, Abby!

Hale (*grasping Abigail*). Abigail, it may be your cousin is dying. Did you call the Devil last night?

880 **Abigail.** I never called him! Tituba, Tituba . . .

Parris (*blanched*). She called the Devil?

Hale. I should like to speak with Tituba.

Parris. Goody Ann, will you bring her up? (Mrs. Putnam *exits.*)

Hale. How did she call him?

Abigail. I know not—she spoke Barbados.

Hale. Did you feel any strangeness when she called him? A sudden cold wind, perhaps? A trembling below the ground?

890 **Abigail.** I didn't see no Devil! (*shaking* Betty) Betty, wake up. Betty! Betty!

Hale. You cannot evade me, Abigail. Did your cousin drink any of the brew in that kettle?

Abigail. She never drank it!

Hale. Did you drink it?

Abigail. No, sir!

Hale. Did Tituba ask you to drink it?

Abigail. She tried, but I refused.

Hale. Why are you concealing? Have you sold your-
900 self to Lucifer?

Abigail. I never sold myself! I'm a good girl! I'm a proper girl!

(Mrs. Putnam *enters with* Tituba, *and instantly* Abigail *points at* Tituba.)

Abigail. She made me do it! She made Betty do it!

Tituba (*shocked and angry*). Abby!

Abigail. She makes me drink blood!

Parris. Blood!!

Mrs. Putnam. My baby's blood?

910 **Tituba.** No, no, chicken blood. I give she chicken blood!

Hale. Woman, have you enlisted these children for the Devil?

Tituba. No, no, sir, I don't truck with no Devil!

Hale. Why can she not wake? Are you silencing this child?

Tituba. I love me Betty!

Hale. You have sent your spirit out upon this child, have you not? Are you gathering souls for the Devil?

920 **Abigail.** She sends her spirit on me in church; she makes me laugh at prayer!

Parris. She have often laughed at prayer!

Abigail. She comes to me every night to go and drink blood!

Tituba. You beg *me* to conjure! She beg *me* make charm—

Abigail. Don't lie! (*to* Hale) She comes to me while I sleep; she's always making me dream corruptions!

Tituba. Why you say that, Abby?

930 **Abigail.** Sometimes I wake and find myself standing in the open doorway and not a stitch on my body! I always hear her laughing in my sleep. I hear her singing her Barbados songs and tempting me with—

Tituba. Mister Reverend, I never—

Hale (*resolved now*). Tituba, I want you to wake this child.

DIFFERENTIATED INSTRUCTION

FOR STRUGGLING READERS

Explore Stage Directions Point out that except for line 878, there are no stage directions describing Hale's interrogation of Abigail. Have students work in pairs and read lines 885–908 aloud, choosing the facial expressions, vocal tones, and gestures that seem most appropriate for the dialogue. Have students make suggestions for stage directions that Miller could have included in these lines.

FOR ADVANCED LEARNERS/AP

Analyze Motive This scene is important to the plot because it sheds light on Abigail's motives. Have students reread the exchange between Abigail, Hale, and Tituba in lines 905–937. Then instruct students to write a brief character analysis that answers these questions:

• What does Abigail say Tituba made her do?

• Why does Abigail accuse Tituba of witchcraft?

• Why would Abigail single out Tituba instead of one of the other girls?

Encourage students to make a connection between Abigail's behavior and the general atmosphere in the town. Invite students to discuss their analyses with the class.

Tituba. I have no power on this child, sir.

Hale. You most certainly do, and you will free her from it now! When did you compact with the Devil?

940 **Tituba.** I don't compact with no Devil!

Parris. You will confess yourself or I will take you out and whip you to your death, Tituba!

Putnam. This woman must be hanged! She must be taken and hanged!

Tituba (*terrified, falls to her knees*). No, no, don't hang Tituba! I tell him I don't desire to work for him, sir.

Parris. The Devil?

Hale. Then you saw him! (*Tituba weeps.*) Now

950 Tituba, I know that when we bind ourselves to Hell it is very hard to break with it. We are going to help you tear yourself free—

Tituba (*frightened by the coming process*). Mister Reverend, I do believe somebody else be witchin' these children.

Hale. Who?

Tituba. I don't know, sir, but the Devil got him numerous witches.

Hale. Does he! *It is a clue.* Tituba, look into my eyes.

960 Come, look into me. (*She raises her eyes to his fearfully.*) You would be a good Christian woman, would you not, Tituba?

Tituba. Aye, sir, a good Christian woman.

Hale. And you love these little children?

Tituba. Oh, yes, sir, I don't desire to hurt little children.

Hale. And you love God, Tituba?

Tituba. I love God with all my bein'.

Hale. Now, in God's holy name—

970 **Tituba.** Bless Him. Bless Him. (*She is rocking on her knees, sobbing in terror.*)

Hale. And to His glory—

Tituba. Eternal glory. Bless Him—bless God . . .

Hale. Open yourself, Tituba—open yourself and let God's holy light shine on you.

Tituba. Oh, bless the Lord.

Hale. When the Devil comes to you does he ever come—with another person? (*She stares up into his face.*) Perhaps another person in the village? Some-

980 one you know.

Parris. Who came with him?

Putnam. Sarah Good? Did you ever see Sarah Good with him? Or Osburn?

Parris. Was it man or woman came with him?

Tituba. Man or woman. Was—was woman.

Parris. What woman? A woman, you said. What woman?

Tituba. It was black dark, and I—

Parris. You could see him, why could you not see

990 her?

Tituba. Well, they was always talking; they was always runnin' round and carryin' on—

Parris. You mean out of Salem? Salem witches?

Tituba. I believe so, yes, sir.

(*Now Hale takes her hand. She is surprised.*)

Hale. Tituba. You must have no fear to tell us who they are, do you understand? We will protect you. The Devil can never overcome a minister. You know that, do you not?

1000 **Tituba** (*kisses Hale's hand*). Aye, sir, oh, I do.

Hale. You have confessed yourself to witchcraft, and that speaks a wish to come to Heaven's side. And we will bless you, Tituba.

Tituba (*deeply relieved*). Oh, God bless you, Mr. Hale!

Hale (*with rising exaltation*). You are God's instrument put in our hands to discover the Devil's agents among us. You are selected, Tituba, you are chosen to help us cleanse our village. So speak utterly,

1010 Tituba, turn your back on him and face God—face God, Tituba, and God will protect you.

Tituba (*joining with him*). Oh, God, protect Tituba!

Hale (*kindly*). Who came to you with the Devil? Two? Three? Four? How many?

THE CRUCIBLE: ACT ONE **161**

TIERED DISCUSSION PROMPTS

Use these prompts to help students explore lines 959–997.

Connect Have you ever known someone who claimed to do or see something that he or she might not really have done or seen? How would that memory help you identify with this scene? *Students may suggest that such a memory would help them sympathize with Tituba, who is distressed at the intense questioning and who makes questionable claims out of desperation.*

Analyze What are Hale and Parris trying to get Tituba to do, and why? *Possible answer: Hale and Parris are trying to get Tituba to name the witches to whom she has referred (lines 957–958). How do the approaches of the two ministers differ? Possible answer: Although Hale is firm, he treats Tituba kindly and points her to God instead of condemning her outright. Parris, however, is curt and demanding.*

Evaluate How effective is Miller in creating suspense in this scene? Explain. *Possible answer: Miller is very effective in creative suspense in this scene. Since the questioning of Tituba is drawn out, suspense builds as readers and audience members wait to discover how far the questioning will go and what it will reveal.*

FOR ENGLISH LANGUAGE LEARNERS

Culture: Clarify Remind students that Tituba is not a native speaker of English (line 886); thus, it is not surprising to hear her speak in dialect, reflecting her upbringing in the culture of Barbados. Have students express in standard English these comments that Tituba makes: "I give she chicken blood!" (lines 910–911); "I love me Betty!" (line 917); "She beg *me* make charm—" (lines 925–926); "Why you say that, Abby?" (line 929); "No, no, don't hang Tituba! I tell him I don't desire to work for him, sir" (lines 945–947); "Mister Reverend, I do believe somebody else be witchin' these children" (lines 953–955); " . . . the Devil got him numerous witches" (lines 957–958).

REVISIT THE BIG QUESTION

What fuels a MOB?

Hysteria feeds on fear, anger, and panic. How are the seeds of hysteria sown in lines 1023–1056? *Possible answer: Hale seems to have convinced Tituba and the girls that they are doing God's will by naming others who associate with the Devil. Furthermore, the more afraid these characters become of being persecuted themselves, the more willing they are to implicate others. Thus, panic and hidden anger (such as Tituba's for Parris) cause them to act irrationally. Even if the accusations are calculated and totally false, the emotional scene in which they are made encourages the growth of hysteria.*

SELECTION WRAP-UP

READ WITH A PURPOSE Now that students have read Act One of *The Crucible*, ask them to consider the effects of rumors on a small community. *Possible answer: Rumors, even those that are highly unlikely, can sow seeds of doubt and suspicion and cause rifts in a community.*

⭐ CRITIQUE

- Ask students to think about the events that have led up to the climax of Act One and to decide whether they think that the confessions from Tituba and the girls are believable. Why or why not?

- After completing the After Reading questions on page 163, have students revisit their responses and tell whether they have changed their opinions.

(Tituba *pants, and begins rocking back and forth again, staring ahead.*)

Tituba. There was four. There was four.

Parris (*pressing in on her*). Who? Who? Their names, their names!

1020 **Tituba** (*suddenly bursting out*). Oh, how many times he bid me kill you, Mr. Parris!

Parris. Kill me!

Tituba (*in a fury*). He say Mr. Parris must be kill! Mr. Parris no goodly man, Mr. Parris mean man and no gentle man, and he bid me rise out of my bed and cut your throat! (*They gasp.*) But I tell him "No! I don't hate that man. I don't want kill that man." But he say, "You work for me, Tituba, and I make you free! I give you pretty dress to wear, and put 1030 you way high up in the air, and you gone fly back to Barbados!" And I say, "You lie, Devil, you lie!" And then he come one stormy night to me, and he say, "Look! I have *white* people belong to me." And I look—and there was Goody Good.

Parris. Sarah Good!

Tituba (*rocking and weeping*). Aye, sir, and Goody Osburn.

Mrs. Putnam. I knew it! Goody Osburn were midwife to me three times. I begged you, Thomas, did 1040 I not? I begged him not to call Osburn because I feared her. My babies always shriveled in her hands!

Hale. Take courage, you must give us all their names. How can you bear to see this child suffering? Look at her, Tituba. (*He is indicating* Betty *on the bed.*) Look at her God-given innocence; her soul is so tender; we must protect her, Tituba; the Devil is out and preying on her like a beast upon the flesh of the pure lamb. God will bless you for your help.

(Abigail *rises, staring as though inspired, and cries out.*)

1050 **Abigail.** I want to open myself! (*They turn to her, startled. She is enraptured, as though in a pearly light.*) I want the light of God, I want the sweet love of Jesus! I danced for the Devil; I saw him; I wrote in his book; I go back to Jesus; I kiss His hand. I saw Sarah Good with the Devil! I saw Goody Osburn with the Devil! I saw Bridget Bishop with the Devil!

(*As she is speaking,* Betty *is rising from the bed, a fever in her eyes, and picks up the chant.*)

Betty (*staring too*). I saw George Jacobs with the 1060 Devil! I saw Goody Howe with the Devil!

Parris. She speaks! (*He rushes to embrace* Betty.) She speaks!

Hale. Glory to God! It is broken, they are free!

Betty (*calling out hysterically and with great relief*). I saw Martha Bellows with the Devil!

Abigail. I saw Goody Sibber with the Devil! (*It is rising to a great glee.*)

Putnam. The marshal, I'll call the marshal!

(Parris *is shouting a prayer of thanksgiving.*)

1070 **Betty.** I saw Alice Barrow with the Devil!

(*The curtain begins to fall.*)

Hale (*as* Putnam *goes out*). Let the marshal bring irons!

Abigail. I saw Goody Hawkins with the Devil!

Betty. I saw Goody Bibber with the Devil!

Abigail. I saw Goody Booth with the Devil!

(*On their ecstatic cries, the curtain falls.*)

④

DIFFERENTIATED INSTRUCTION

FOR STRUGGLING READERS

④ Targeted Passage [Lines 1050–1077]

In this passage, the climax of Act One, accusations boost the plot complexity and emotional intensity of the play.

- Whose example finally compels Betty to rise and speak? What does she say? (lines 1050–1060)

- Why does Betty cry out "with great relief"? Why does Hale seem relieved? (lines 1063–1065)

- Why does Hale want the marshal to come with "irons"? Which Salemites do you think the marshal will visit? (lines 1055–1076)

Comprehension

1. **Recall** What is the cause for concern in the Parris household?

2. **Clarify** What has occurred between John Proctor and Abigail Williams before the time in which the play begins?

3. **Summarize** Why does Reverend Hale come to Salem?

Text Analysis

4. **Infer Character Motives** Reread lines 1017–1056 at the end of Act One. Why do you think Tituba and Abigail admit to having practiced witchcraft? Why do they name others?

● 5. **Draw Conclusions About Characters** Review the **traits** you recorded in your chart for the characters you have encountered so far. How would you describe the most important character traits of the following?

   • Abigail Williams   • John Proctor   • Reverend Hale

6. **Make Predictions** Based on what you have learned about Abigail in Act One, whom do you think she might accuse as the play goes on? Cite specific evidence to support your answer.

7. **Identify Beliefs** What do the characters in the play believe about witches? List their beliefs in a concept web like the one shown.

8. **Connect Setting and Mood** The setting of a literary work refers to the time and place in which the action occurs. How do you think Miller uses setting to help create mood in Act One?

Witches

● 9. **Analyze Conventions of Drama** Review the **stage directions** that take the form of mini-essays in Act One. What insights about America after the Second World War does Miller convey? Use details from the mini-essays in your answer.

Text Criticism

10. **Author's Style** The mini-essays in Act One are not usually included in a stage production of *The Crucible*. Why do you think this is so? Why do you think Miller included them in his drama?

> *What fuels a* **MOB?**
>
> What role does Abigail play in the group hysteria that develops as Act One draws to a close?

> **COMMON CORE**
>
> **RL 1** Cite textual evidence to support analysis of what the text says explicitly as well as inferences drawn from the text, including determining where the text leaves matters uncertain. **RL 3** Analyze the impact of the author's choices regarding how to develop and relate elements of a drama. **RL 5** Analyze how an author's choices concerning how to structure specific parts of a text contribute to its overall structure and meaning as well as its aesthetic impact.

Practice and Apply

For preliminary support of post-reading questions, use these copy masters:

 **RESOURCE MANAGER**—Copy Masters
   Reading Check p. 202
   Conventions of Drama p. 197
   Question Support p. 203

Additional selection questions are provided for teachers on page 191.

ANSWERS

> **COMMON CORE** RL 1, RL 3, RL 5

1. *Reverend Parris's daughter, Betty, lies in bed in a mysterious trance. Parris is concerned that witchcraft may be the cause.*

2. *Proctor and Abigail have had an illicit affair.*

3. *Hale comes to determine whether Betty's condition is the result of witchcraft. If so, he intends to fight the Devil.*

Possible answers:

4. *Tituba and Abigail admit it because the pressure is so great, but they name others in order to deflect blame from themselves.*

5. ● **COMMON CORE FOCUS** *Draw Conclusions About Characters*
   Abigail Williams: willful, self-centered, controlling, devious, and vengeful
   John Proctor: intelligent, skeptical, and courageous
   Reverend Hale: intellectual, devout, and firm yet compassionate

6. *Abigail might accuse the Proctors. Her threats (lines 353–364) reveal a vindictive nature.*

7. *(1) exist and are the Devil's agents, (2) can control people and harm children, and (3) can take the form of animals*

8. *All of Act One takes place in a small bedroom in Parris's house that Miller describes as having "an air of clean spareness." The unchanging setting creates a feeling of entrapment.*

9. ● **COMMON CORE FOCUS** *Conventions of Drama* Miller discusses the Puritan traits of discipline and hypocrisy, the relationship between America's political policy and religious beliefs, and Americans' fear of communism and mistrust of the Soviet Union.*

10. *Including the mini-essays would disrupt the action of the play. Miller probably included them to help the director, actors, and readers understand the play's characters and time period.*

> *What fuels a* **MOB?** **Possible answers:** *Abigail is the first to accuse others of witchcraft. She inspires Betty to do the same.*

Assess and Reteach

Assess

DIAGNOSTIC AND SELECTION TESTS
   Selection Test A pp. 61–62
   Selection Test B/C pp. 63–64

Interactive Selection Test on **thinkcentral.com**

Reteach

Level Up Online Tutorials on **thinkcentral.com**

Reteaching Worksheets on **thinkcentral.com**

Reading Lesson 9, Literature Lesson 1-2, 6, 23-24

Practice and Apply

SUMMARY

As Act Two begins, John and Elizabeth Proctor express concern about the growth of the witchcraft scare. Then they argue: Elizabeth urges her husband to expose Abigail as a fraud, and the two revisit his affair with her. Mary Warren brings news of further arrests and the possible implication of Elizabeth. Reverend Hale arrives and interviews the couple, and when the marshal arrests Elizabeth, Proctor condemns the desire for vengeance that is driving events, and he vows to save his wife.

Act *Two*

(*The common room of* Proctor's *house, eight days later.*

At the right is a door opening on the fields outside. A fireplace is at the left, and behind it a stairway leading upstairs. It is the low, dark, and rather long living room of the time. As the curtain rises, the room is empty. From above, Elizabeth *is heard softly singing to the children. Presently the door opens and* John Proctor *enters, carrying his gun. He glances about the room as he comes toward the fireplace, then halts for an instant as he hears her singing. He continues on to the fireplace, leans the gun against the wall as he swings a pot out of the fire and smells it. Then he lifts out the ladle and tastes. He is not quite pleased. He reaches to a cupboard, takes a pinch of salt, and drops it into the pot. As he is tasting again, her footsteps are heard on the stair. He swings the pot into the fireplace and goes to a basin and washes his hands and face.* Elizabeth *enters.*)

Elizabeth. What keeps you so late? It's almost dark.

Proctor. I were planting far out to the forest edge.

Elizabeth. Oh, you're done then.

Proctor. Aye, the farm is seeded. The boys asleep?

Elizabeth. They will be soon. (*And she goes to the fireplace, proceeds to ladle up stew in a dish.*)

Proctor. Pray now for a fair summer.

Elizabeth. Aye.

Proctor. Are you well today?

10 **Elizabeth.** I am. (*She brings the plate to the table, and, indicating the food.*) It is a rabbit.

Proctor (*going to the table*). Oh, is it! In Jonathan's trap?

Elizabeth. No, she walked into the house this afternoon; I found her sittin' in the corner like she come to visit.

Proctor. Oh, that's a good sign walkin' in.

Elizabeth. Pray God. It hurt my heart to strip her, poor rabbit. (*She sits and watches him taste it.*)

20 **Proctor.** It's well seasoned.

Elizabeth (*blushing with pleasure*). I took great care. She's tender?

Proctor. Aye. (*He eats. She watches him.*) I think we'll see green fields soon. It's warm as blood beneath the clods.

Elizabeth. That's well.

(Proctor *eats, then looks up.*)

Proctor. If the crop is good I'll buy George Jacob's heifer. How would that please you?

30 **Elizabeth.** Aye, it would.

Proctor (*with a grin*). I mean to please you, Elizabeth.

Elizabeth (*It is hard to say*). I know it, John.

(*He gets up, goes to her, kisses her. She receives it. With a certain disappointment, he returns to the table.*)

Proctor (*as gently as he can*). Cider?

Elizabeth (*with a sense of reprimanding herself for having forgot*). Aye! (*She gets up and goes and pours a glass for him. He now arches his back.*)

Joan Allen as Elizabeth Proctor

Reading Support

This selection on **thinkcentral.com** includes embedded **ThinkAloud** models—students "thinking aloud" about the story to model the kinds of questions a good reader would ask about a selection.

TIERED DISCUSSION PROMPTS

Use these prompts to help students explore the relationship between John and Elizabeth Proctor as it is revealed in lines 20–32:

Connect Think of a time when you have done something in hopes of making someone happy, only to have your effort fail. How does that experience help you understand Proctor's feelings when Elizabeth fails to respond to his attempts to make her feel better? *Accept all responses that make an effort to connect to Proctor's unsuccessful compliments and offers of gifts.*

Analyze Why does Proctor make a point of saying, "I mean to please you, Elizabeth" (line 31)? *Possible answer: Proctor probably wants Elizabeth to know that he is trying to make up for his past infidelity.* What do the stage directions in that same line suggest about Proctor's efforts? *Possible answer: The stage directions, which instruct the actor to grin, probably mean that Proctor is grinning in hopes that he can coax a smile out of Elizabeth.*

DIFFERENTIATED INSTRUCTION

FOR STRUGGLING READERS

In combination with the *Audio Anthology CD,* use one or more Targeted Passages (pp. 166, 168, 173, 174, 177, 178) to ensure that students focus on key story events. Have them use a Two-Column Chart to identify key events in Act Two.

BEST PRACTICES TOOLKIT—Transparency Two-Column Chart p. A25

FOR ENGLISH LANGUAGE LEARNERS

Vocabulary List Students may benefit from creating a glossary of unfamiliar or archaic words in the selection. Students should write down the word and the page on which it appears. Allow students time to look up the meanings in a dictionary. Explain that archaic words are no longer used regularly if it all. *Aye* (line 4) is an example of a word meaning "yes" that is rarely used.

● CONVENTIONS OF DRAMA

Miller reveals more about the Proctors' attitudes toward each other in the stage directions. Elizabeth worries that her husband was in Salem, and *"He knows what she means"* (line 65). Of what concern is John Proctor aware?

Possible answer: *Proctor is aware of Elizabeth's concern that he might have gone to Salem to see Abigail.*

IF STUDENTS NEED HELP . . . Relate the stage directions in lines 60 and 65.

- Discuss what Miller means by the comment "and yet she must" in the stage directions for line 60.

- Point out that Miller leaves part of the comment unstated but implied. Elicit that Elizabeth's description (*doesn't want friction, and yet she must,* line 60) refers to her need to express her sadness and her mistrust of her husband.

REVISIT THE BIG QUESTION

What fuels a
MOB?

Discuss In Elizabeth's mind, what is the only way to bring the rising hysteria in Salem to an end? ***Possible answer:*** *Elizabeth says that her husband must reveal what Abigail had admitted to him (lines 108–109). It is a problem because Proctor would have to reveal that they were alone together.*

Proctor. This farm's a continent when you go foot
40 by foot droppin' seeds in it.

Elizabeth (*coming with the cider*). It must be.

Proctor (*drinks a long draught, then, putting the glass down*). You ought to bring some flowers in the house.

Elizabeth. Oh! I forgot! I will tomorrow.

Proctor. It's winter in here yet. On Sunday let you come with me, and we'll walk the farm together; I never see such a load of flowers on the earth. (*With good feeling he goes and looks up at the sky through the open doorway.*) Lilacs have a purple smell. Lilac is the
50 smell of nightfall, I think. Massachusetts is a beauty in the spring!

Elizabeth. Aye, it is.

(*There is a pause. She is watching him from the table as he stands there absorbing the night. It is as though she would speak but cannot. Instead, now, she takes up his plate and glass and fork and goes with them to the basin. Her back is turned to him. He turns to her and watches her. A sense of their separation rises.*)

Proctor. I think you're sad again. Are you?

60 **Elizabeth** (*She doesn't want friction, and yet she must*). You come so late I thought you'd gone to Salem this afternoon.

Proctor. Why? I have no business in Salem.

Elizabeth. You did speak of going, earlier this week.

Proctor (*He knows what she means*). I thought better of it since.

Elizabeth. Mary Warren's there today.

Proctor. Why'd you let her? You heard me forbid her go to Salem any more!

70 **Elizabeth.** I couldn't stop her.

Proctor (*holding back a full condemnation of her*). It is a fault, it is a fault, Elizabeth—you're the mistress here, not Mary Warren.

Elizabeth. She frightened all my strength away.

Proctor. How may that mouse frighten you, Elizabeth? You—

Elizabeth. It is a mouse no more. I forbid her go, and she raises up her chin like the daughter of a

---

prince and says to me, "I must go to Salem, Goody
80 Proctor; I am an official of the court!"

Proctor. Court! What court?

Elizabeth. Aye, it is a proper court they have now. They've sent four judges out of Boston, she says, weighty magistrates of the General Court, and at the head sits the Deputy Governor of the Province.

Proctor (*astonished*). Why, she's mad.

Elizabeth. I would to God she were. There be fourteen people in the jail now, she says. (*Proctor simply looks at her, unable to grasp it.*) And they'll be tried,
90 and the court have power to hang them too, she says.

Proctor (*scoffing, but without conviction*). Ah, they'd never hang—

Elizabeth. The Deputy Governor promise hangin' if they'll not confess, John. The town's gone wild, I think. She speak of Abigail, and I thought she were a saint, to hear her. Abigail brings the other girls into the court, and where she walks the crowd will part like the sea for Israel. And folks are brought before them, and if they scream and howl and fall to the floor—the
100 person's clapped in the jail for bewitchin' them.

Proctor (*wide-eyed*). Oh, it is a black mischief.

Elizabeth. I think you must go to Salem, John. (*He turns to her.*) I think so. You must tell them it is a fraud.

Proctor (*thinking beyond this*). Aye, it is, it is surely.

Elizabeth. Let you go to Ezekiel Cheever—he knows you well. And tell him what she said to you last week in her uncle's house. She said it had naught to do with witchcraft, did she not?

110 **Proctor** (*in thought*). Aye, she did, she did. (*now, a pause*)

Elizabeth (*quietly, fearing to anger him by prodding*). God forbid you keep that from the court, John. I think they must be told.

Proctor (*quietly, struggling with his thought*). Aye, they must, they must. It is a wonder they do believe her.

Elizabeth. I would go to Salem now, John—let you go tonight.

DIFFERENTIATED INSTRUCTION

FOR STRUGGLING READERS

① Targeted Passage [Lines 82–104]

This passage reveals that the search for witches in Salem is getting out of control.

- Why has a court been set up in Salem? (lines 82–85)

- Who is the leader of the girls who claim to be bewitched? (lines 95–98)

- What system is used to determine whether the accused people are witches? (lines 98–100)

- Do Proctor and Elizabeth believe that the accused are witches? How can you tell? (lines 101–104)

FOR ENGLISH LANGUAGE LEARNERS

Vocabulary: Multiple-Meaning Words Direct students' attention to the word *court* in lines 80 and 81. Explain that *court* can be a verb, meaning "to attempt to gain someone's favor or love," or a noun, referring to "a place where accused people are judged." Elicit that *court* is a noun in these lines. Then have small groups

use a dictionary and context clues to explore these other words from this page: *fault* (line 72), *mad* (line 86), *tried* (line 89), *wild* (line 94), *clapped* (line 100), *black* (line 101), *wonder* (line 116).

Proctor. I'll think on it.

120 **Elizabeth** (*with her courage now*). You cannot keep it, John.

Proctor (*angering*). I know I cannot keep it. I say I will think on it!

Elizabeth (*hurt, and very coldly*). Good, then, let you think on it. (*She stands and starts to walk out of the room.*)

Proctor. I am only wondering how I may prove what she told me, Elizabeth. If the girl's a saint now, I think it is not easy to prove she's fraud, and

130 the town gone so silly. She told it to me in a room alone—I have no proof for it.

Elizabeth. You were alone with her?

Proctor (*stubbornly*). For a moment alone, aye.

Elizabeth. Why, then, it is not as you told me.

Proctor (*his anger rising*). For a moment, I say. The others come in soon after.

Elizabeth (*quietly—she has suddenly lost all faith in him*). Do as you wish, then. (*She starts to turn.*)

Proctor. Woman. (*She turns to him.*) I'll not have

140 your suspicion any more.

Elizabeth (*a little loftily*). I have no—

Proctor. I'll not have it!

Elizabeth. Then let you not earn it.

Proctor (*with a violent undertone*). You doubt me yet?

Elizabeth (*with a smile, to keep her dignity*). John, if it were not Abigail that you must go to hurt, would you falter now? I think not.

Proctor. Now look you—

Elizabeth. I see what I see, John.

150 **Proctor** (*with solemn warning*). You will not judge me more, Elizabeth. I have good reason to think before I charge fraud on Abigail, and I will think on it. Let you look to your own improvement before you go to judge your husband any more. I have forgot Abigail, and—

Elizabeth. And I.

Proctor. Spare me! You forget nothin' and forgive nothin'. Learn charity, woman. I have gone tiptoe in this house all seven month since she is gone. I have

160 not moved from there to there without I think to please you, and still an everlasting funeral marches round your heart. I cannot speak but I am doubted, every moment judged for lies, as though I come into a court when I come into this house!

Elizabeth. John, you are not open with me. You saw her with a crowd, you said. Now you—

Proctor. I'll plead my honesty no more, Elizabeth.

Elizabeth (*now she would justify herself*). John, I am only—

170 **Proctor.** No more! I should have roared you down when first you told me your suspicion. But I wilted, and, like a Christian, I confessed. Confessed! Some dream I had must have mistaken you for God that day. But you're not, you're not, and let you remember it! Let you look sometimes for the goodness in me, and judge me not.

Elizabeth. I do not judge you. The magistrate sits in your heart that judges you. I never thought you but a good man, John—(*with a smile*)—only somewhat

180 bewildered.

Proctor (*laughing bitterly*). Oh, Elizabeth, your justice would freeze beer![1] (*He turns suddenly toward a sound outside. He starts for the door as Mary Warren enters. As soon as he sees her, he goes directly to her and grabs her by her cloak, furious.*) How do you go to Salem when I forbid it? Do you mock me? (*shaking her*) I'll whip you if you dare leave this house again!

(*Strangely, she doesn't resist him, but hangs limply by his grip.*)

190 **Mary Warren.** I am sick, I am sick, Mr. Proctor. Pray, pray, hurt me not. (*Her strangeness throws him off, and her evident pallor and weakness. He frees her.*) My insides are all shuddery; I am in the proceedings all day, sir.

---

1. **your justice . . . beer:** Alcoholic beverages freeze at very low temperatures, so Proctor is sarcastically calling his wife cold-hearted.

READING SKILLS COMMON CORE RL 1 RL 3

■ *Model the Skill:* **DRAW CONCLUSIONS ABOUT CHARACTERS**

After students reread lines 149–164, ask them to turn to the chart introduced on p. 135. Help them draw conclusions by working with them to enter more information about Elizabeth and Proctor. Remind them to record evidence in the chart to support their information. Invite suggestions about quotations or other evidence students might glean from the passage. Then ask the following question: What character traits do Elizabeth and Proctor reveal in this dialogue?

Possible answer: *Elizabeth reveals that she is suspicious of Proctor and increasingly bold in her willingness to confront him about his affair. Proctor reveals that he is defensive about his actions and angry about Elizabeth's inability or unwillingness to forgive him.*

FOR ENGLISH LANGUAGE LEARNERS

Vocabulary Support Use New Word Analysis to teach these words: *evident* (line 192), *compensate* (line 199), *aware* (line 452), *restrain* (line 518), *image* (line 556), *define* (line 571).

 **BEST PRACTICES TOOLKIT—Transparency**
New Word Analysis p. E8

FOR ADVANCED LEARNERS/AP

Analyze Dialogue Have students discuss Proctor's outburst in lines 170–176. Encourage them to try reading it aloud a few times to get a feel for the emotions that Proctor expresses in these lines. Then ask students to write a brief essay analyzing the passage in the light of these questions:

• How did Elizabeth find out about his affair with Abigail?

• What does Proctor think about himself?

• What does he mean by the phrase "roared you down" (line 170)? How might his relationship with Elizabeth be different at this moment if he had "roared [her] down" earlier?

• What are his criticisms of Elizabeth?

As students share their essays, ask them what they think it would take for the Proctors to resolve their conflict.

◼ DRAW CONCLUSIONS ABOUT CHARACTERS

Miller provides clues about Mary Warren's character by describing her directly and by showing how other characters react to her. Reread lines 199–217. What do the stage directions suggest about how Mary feels after her day in court?

Possible answer: *The stage directions suggest that Mary feels tired, upset, anxious, and overwhelmed by what is happening.*

IF STUDENTS NEED HELP... Have them meet in small groups, using a Spider Map to consider Mary's emotions. Remind them to record both stage directions that relate to Mary's emotions and lines that describe how other characters react to her.

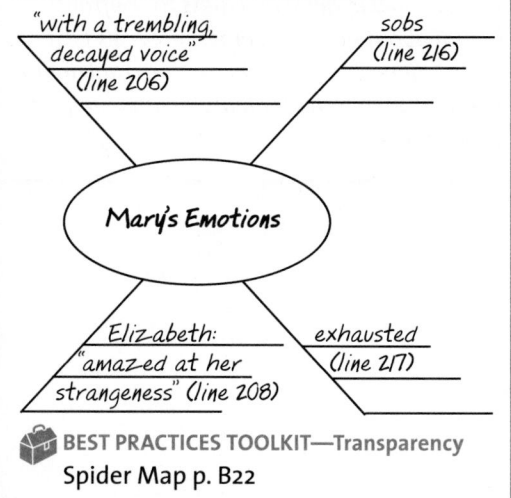

🧰 **BEST PRACTICES TOOLKIT—Transparency**
Spider Map p. B22

Proctor (*with draining anger—his curiosity is draining it*). And what of these proceedings here? When will you proceed to keep this house, as you are paid nine pound a year to do—and my wife not wholly well?

(*As though to compensate,* Mary Warren *goes to*
200 Elizabeth *with a small rag doll.*)

Mary Warren. I made a gift for you today, Goody Proctor. I had to sit long hours in a chair, and passed the time with sewing.

Elizabeth (*perplexed, looking at the doll*). Why, thank you, it's a fair poppet.[2]

Mary Warren (*with a trembling, decayed voice*). We must all love each other now, Goody Proctor.

Elizabeth (*amazed at her strangeness*). Aye, indeed we must.

210 Mary Warren (*glancing at the room*). I'll get up early in the morning and clean the house. I must sleep now. (*She turns and starts off.*)

Proctor. Mary. (*She halts.*) Is it true? There be fourteen women arrested?

Mary Warren. No, sir. There be thirty-nine now—(*She suddenly breaks off and sobs and sits down, exhausted.*)

Elizabeth. Why, she's weepin'! What ails you, child?

Mary Warren. Goody Osburn—will hang!

220 (*There is a shocked pause, while she sobs.*)

Proctor. Hang! (*He calls into her face.*) Hang, y'say?

Mary Warren (*through her weeping*). Aye.

Proctor. The Deputy Governor will permit it?

Mary Warren. He sentenced her. He must. (*to* **ameliorate** *it*) But not Sarah Good. For Sarah Good confessed, y'see.

Proctor. Confessed! To what?

Mary Warren. That she—(*in horror at the memory*)—she sometimes made a compact with Lucifer,
230 and wrote her name in his black book—with her blood—and bound herself to torment Christians till God's thrown down—and we all must worship Hell forevermore.

②

---

2. **fair poppet:** pretty doll.

168 UNIT 1: EARLY AMERICAN WRITING

(*pause*)

Proctor. But—surely you know what a jabberer she is. Did you tell them that?

Mary Warren. Mr. Proctor, in open court she near to choked us all to death.

Proctor. How, choked you?

240 Mary Warren. She sent her spirit out.

Elizabeth. Oh, Mary, Mary, surely you—

Mary Warren (*with an indignant edge*). She tried to kill me many times, Goody Proctor!

Elizabeth. Why, I never heard you mention that before.

Mary Warren. I never knew it before. I never knew anything before. When she come into the court I say to myself, I must not accuse this woman, for she sleep in ditches, and so very old and poor. But
250 then—then she sit there, denying and denying, and I feel a misty coldness climbin' up my back, and the skin on my skull begin to creep, and I feel a clamp around my neck and I cannot breathe air; and then (*entranced*) I hear a voice, a screamin' voice, and it were my voice—and all at once I remembered everything she done to me!

Proctor. Why? What did she do to you?

Mary Warren (*like one awakened to a marvelous secret insight*). So many time, Mr. Proctor, she come to
260 this very door, beggin' bread and a cup of cider—and mark this: whenever I turned her away empty, she *mumbled.*

Elizabeth. Mumbled! She may mumble if she's hungry.

Mary Warren. But *what* does she mumble? You must remember, Goody Proctor. Last month—a Monday, I think—she walked away, and I thought my guts would burst for two days after. Do you remember it?

Elizabeth. Why—I do, I think, but—

Mary Warren. And so I told that to Judge Hathorne,
270 and he asks her so. "Sarah Good," says he, "what curse do you mumble that this girl must fall sick after turning you away?" And then she replies

---

DIFFERENTIATED INSTRUCTION

FOR STRUGGLING READERS

② **Targeted Passage** [Lines 213–233]

Ask students these questions:

- How many women have been arrested? (line 215)

- What is the punishment if a person is found guilty of witchcraft? How can a person avoid that punishment? (lines 221–226)

FOR ADVANCED LEARNERS/AP

Research and Evaluate [small-group option] Ask students to reread Mary's account of what happened in court (lines 246–256) and to consider this question: What reason other than Goody Good's "witchcraft" might have caused Mary to experience the symptoms that she describes in lines 249–256? Ask students to do some research to support their answers (including some research about "false memory syndrome"). Have students share their findings and see if they can reach a consensus about the validity of Mary's experience.

(*mimicking an old crone*) "Why, your excellence, no curse at all. I only say my commandments;[3] I hope I may say my commandments," says she!

Elizabeth. And that's an upright answer.

Mary Warren. Aye, but then Judge Hathorne say, "Recite for us your commandments!" (*leaning avidly toward them*) and of all the ten she could not say a

280 single one. She never knew no commandments, and they had her in a flat lie!

Proctor. And so condemned her?

Mary Warren (*now a little strained, seeing his stubborn doubt*). Why, they must when she condemned herself.

Proctor. But the proof, the proof!

Mary Warren (*with greater impatience with him*). I told you the proof. It's hard proof, hard as rock, the judges said.

Proctor (*pauses an instant, then*). You will not go to
290 court again, Mary Warren.

Mary Warren. I must tell you, sir, I will be gone every day now. I am amazed you do not see what weighty work we do.

Proctor. What work you do! It's strange work for a Christian girl to hang old women!

Mary Warren. But, Mr. Proctor, they will not hang them if they confess. Sarah Good will only sit in jail some time (*recalling*) and here's a wonder for you; think on this. Goody Good is pregnant!

300 **Elizabeth.** Pregnant! Are they mad? The woman's near to sixty!

Mary Warren. They had Doctor Griggs examine her, and she's full to the brim. And smokin' a pipe all these years, and no husband either! But she's safe, thank God, for they'll not hurt the innocent child. But be that not a marvel? You must see it, sir, it's God's work we do. So I'll be gone every day for some time. I'm—I am an official of the court, they say, and I—(*She has been edging toward offstage.*)

310 **Proctor.** I'll official you! (*He strides to the mantel, takes down the whip hanging there.*)

Mary Warren (*terrified, but coming erect, striving for her authority*). I'll not stand whipping any more!

Elizabeth (*hurriedly, as Proctor approaches*). Mary, promise now you'll stay at home—

Mary Warren (*backing from him, but keeping her erect posture, striving, striving for her way*). The Devil's loose in Salem, Mr. Proctor; we must discover where he's hiding!

320 **Proctor.** I'll whip the Devil out of you! (*With whip raised he reaches out for her, and she streaks away and yells.*)

Mary Warren (*pointing at* Elizabeth). I saved her life today!

(*Silence. His whip comes down.*)

Elizabeth (*softly*). I am accused?

Mary Warren (*quaking*). Somewhat mentioned. But I said I never see no sign you ever sent your spirit out to hurt no one, and seeing I do live so closely with
330 you, they dismissed it.

Elizabeth. Who accused me?

Mary Warren. I am bound by law, I cannot tell it. (*to* Proctor) I only hope you'll not be so sarcastical no more. Four judges and the King's deputy sat to dinner with us but an hour ago. I—I would have you speak civilly to me, from this out.

Proctor (*in horror, muttering in disgust at her*). Go to bed.

Mary Warren (*with a stamp of her foot*). I'll not be
340 ordered to bed no more, Mr. Proctor! I am eighteen and a woman, however single!

Proctor. Do you wish to sit up? Then sit up.

Mary Warren. I wish to go to bed!

Proctor (*in anger*). Good night, then!

Mary Warren. Good night. (*Dissatisfied, uncertain of herself, she goes out. Wide-eyed, both,* Proctor *and* Elizabeth *stand staring.*)

Elizabeth (*quietly*). Oh, the noose, the noose is up!

Proctor. There'll be no noose.

---

3. **commandments:** the Ten Commandments in the Bible.

REVISIT THE BIG QUESTION

What fuels a MOB?

Discuss Point out that in lines 277–288, Mary Warren explains that Goody Good was condemned when she could not recite the Ten Commandments. How might this method of judgment indicate that Salem's hysteria over witches is growing? *Possible answer: Mary asserts that Goody Good's inability to recite the Ten Commandments is "hard proof, hard as rock" (line 287) that she's a witch, when really such a lapse is not proof at all. The leap of judgment that it takes to connect the two ideas is an indication of hysteria—that is, hysteria is causing people to make life-and-death judgments against their neighbors based on nothing more than an elderly woman's faulty memory (which might be the result of the stress of the situation).*

FOR STRUGGLING READERS

Comprehension Support Point out the word *noose* in lines 348–349. Explain that a *noose* is the loop of rope used to hang someone and that Elizabeth and Proctor use the word to refer to Elizabeth's execution, should she be convicted. Have students paraphrase these two lines, using modern English, so that it reads something like this: **Elizabeth.** *Oh, they'll hang me, they'll hang me for sure!* **Proctor.** *No one is going to hang you.*

FOR ENGLISH LANGUAGE LEARNERS

Language: Verb Tenses Explain that Mary Warren sometimes uses the present tense when describing past events, as in these examples: "she come into the court" (line 247); "I say to myself" (lines 247–248); "I never see no sign" (line 328). Elicit that *came, said,* and *saw,* respectively, are the standard verb forms in these examples. Then have pairs of students locate other uses of the present tense to relate a past event.

FOR ADVANCED LEARNERS/AP

Analyze Conflict Ask students to consider these questions as they reread lines 323–344:

- How has Mary's defense of Elizabeth in court changed the power dynamics among Mary, Elizabeth, and Proctor?

- How does that change reflect the upheaval throughout the community?

Have students summarize their analysis in a paragraph that they share with the class.

Use Realistic Dialogue Reread lines 354–356. How does Miller make this exchange realistic for the time of its setting?
Possible answer: *Miller chooses era-specific words and expressions ("cry me out") and an inverted sentence ("Sit you down") to make this exchange realistic.*

TIERED DISCUSSION PROMPTS

Use these prompts to discuss Elizabeth's thoughts in lines 378–384 about why Abigail has accused her:

Restate Retell in your words what Elizabeth says about Abigail in lines 382–384. ***Possible answer:*** *Abigail wouldn't accuse me unless she had a lot to gain. She wants to get rid of me so that she can be with you.*

Analyze How and why does Elizabeth try to show that she is different from Goody Good and Goody Osburn? ***Possible answer:*** *Elizabeth notes the flaws of the women (lines 381–382) and sets herself above them both to make her point that Abigail has a different reason for accusing her.*

Evaluate How effective is this passage in deepening our understanding of Elizabeth and Abigail? Explain. ***Possible answer:*** *The passage is very effective. It shows that Elizabeth is perceptive, realistic, and smart; it also reveals the mean-spirited, dishonest side of Abigail's personality by suggesting that to get what she wants, she would have a person executed on false charges.*

350 **Elizabeth.** She wants me dead. I knew all week it would come to this!

Proctor (*without conviction*). They dismissed it. You heard her say—

Elizabeth. And what of tomorrow? She will cry me out until they take me!

Proctor. Sit you down.

Elizabeth. She wants me dead, John, you know it!

Proctor. I say sit down! (*She sits, trembling. He speaks quietly, trying to keep his wits.*) Now we must be wise,
360 Elizabeth.

Elizabeth (*with sarcasm, and a sense of being lost*). Oh, indeed, indeed!

Proctor. Fear nothing. I'll find Ezekiel Cheever. I'll tell him she said it were all sport.

Elizabeth. John, with so many in the jail, more than Cheever's help is needed now, I think. Would you favor me with this? Go to Abigail.

Proctor (*his soul hardening as he senses . . .*). What have I to say to Abigail?

370 **Elizabeth** (*delicately*). John—grant me this. You have a faulty understanding of young girls. There is a promise made in any bed—

Proctor (*striving against his anger*). What promise!

Elizabeth. Spoke or silent, a promise is surely made. And she may dote on it now—I am sure she does— and thinks to kill me, then to take my place.

(*Proctor's anger is rising; he cannot speak.*)

Elizabeth. It is her dearest hope, John, I know it. There be a thousand names; why does she call
380 mine? There be a certain danger in calling such a name—I am no Goody Good that sleeps in ditches, nor Osburn, drunk and half-witted. She'd dare not call out such a farmer's wife but there be monstrous profit in it. She thinks to take my place, John.

Proctor. She cannot think it! (*He knows it is true.*)

Elizabeth (*"reasonably"*). John, have you ever shown her somewhat of contempt? She cannot pass you in the church but you will blush—

Proctor. I may blush for my sin.

390 **Elizabeth.** I think she sees another meaning in that blush.

Proctor. And what see you? What see you, Elizabeth?

Elizabeth (*"conceding"*). I think you be somewhat ashamed, for I am there, and she so close.

Proctor. When will you know me, woman? Were I stone I would have cracked for shame this seven month!

Elizabeth. Then go and tell her she's a whore. Whatever promise she may sense—break it, John, break it.

400 **Proctor** (*between his teeth*). Good, then. I'll go. (*He starts for his rifle.*)

Elizabeth (*trembling, fearfully*). Oh, how unwillingly!

Proctor (*turning on her, rifle in hand*). I will curse her hotter than the oldest cinder in hell. But pray, begrudge me not my anger!

Elizabeth. Your anger! I only ask you—

Proctor. Woman, am I so base? Do you truly think me base?

Elizabeth. I never called you base.

410 **Proctor.** Then how do you charge me with such a promise? The promise that a stallion gives a mare I gave that girl!

Elizabeth. Then why do you anger with me when I bid you break it?

Proctor. Because it speaks deceit, and I am honest! But I'll plead no more! I see now your spirit twists around the single error of my life, and I will never tear it free!

Elizabeth (*crying out*). You'll tear it free—when you
420 come to know that I will be your only wife, or no wife at all! She has an arrow in you yet, John Proctor, and you know it well!

(*Quite suddenly, as though from the air, a figure appears in the doorway. They start slightly. It is Mr. Hale. He is different now—drawn a little, and there is a quality of deference, even of guilt, about his manner now.*)

DIFFERENTIATED INSTRUCTION

FOR ENGLISH LANGUAGE LEARNERS
Vocabulary: Outdated Forms Discuss these examples of outdated uses of the verb *to be*:

Be for *is* and *are*: lines 379, 380, 383
Were for *was*: line 491

Make sure that students understand the meaning of each example, and encourage them to be alert to additional examples as they continue to read.

FOR STRUGGLING READERS
Develop Reading Fluency Have students work in trios to perform a readers' theater version of the scene that includes lines 181–349. Students should work together to select roles and to practice reading aloud the lines with feeling and fluency. Ask trios to take turns performing sections of the scene so that every student has a turn speaking.

Hale. Good evening.

Proctor (*still in his shock*). Why, Mr. Hale! Good
430 evening to you, sir. Come in, come in.

Hale (*to* Elizabeth). I hope I do not startle you.

Elizabeth. No, no, it's only that I heard no horse—

Hale. You are Goodwife Proctor.

Proctor. Aye; Elizabeth.

Hale (*nods, then*). I hope you're not off to bed yet.

Proctor (*setting down his gun*). No, no. (Hale *comes
further into the room. And* Proctor, *to explain his
nervousness.*) We are not used to visitors after dark,
but you're welcome here. Will you sit you down, sir?

440 **Hale.** I will. (*He sits.*) Let you sit, Goodwife Proctor.
(*She does, never letting him out of her sight. There is
a pause as* Hale *looks about the room.*)

Proctor (*to break the silence*). Will you drink cider,
Mr. Hale?

Hale. No, it rebels[4] my stomach; I have some further
traveling yet tonight. Sit you down, sir. (Proctor
sits.) I will not keep you long, but I have some
business with you.

Proctor. Business of the court?

450 **Hale.** No—no, I come of my own, without the
court's authority. Hear me. (*He wets his lips.*) I know
not if you are aware, but your wife's name is—
mentioned in the court.

Proctor. We know it, sir. Our Mary Warren told us.
We are entirely amazed.

Hale. I am a stranger here, as you know. And in my
ignorance I find it hard to draw a clear opinion of
them that come accused before the court. And so
this afternoon, and now tonight, I go from house
460 to house—I come now from Rebecca Nurse's house
and—

Elizabeth (*shocked*). Rebecca's charged!

Hale. God forbid such a one be charged. She is,
however—mentioned somewhat.

Elizabeth (*with an attempt at a laugh*). You will never
believe, I hope, that Rebecca trafficked with the Devil.

Hale. Woman, it is possible.

Proctor (*taken aback*). Surely you cannot think so.

Hale. This is a strange time, Mister. No man may
470 longer doubt the powers of the dark are gathered
in monstrous attack upon this village. There is too
much evidence now to deny it. You will agree, sir?

Proctor (*evading*). I—have no knowledge in that line.
But it's hard to think so pious a woman be secretly
a Devil's bitch after seventy year of such good prayer.

Hale. Aye. But the Devil is a wily one, you cannot
deny it. However, she is far from accused, and I
know she will not be. (*pause*) I thought, sir, to put
some questions as to the Christian character of this
480 house, if you'll permit me.

Proctor (*coldly, resentful*). Why, we—have no fear
of questions, sir.

Hale. Good, then. (*He makes himself more comfortable.*) In the book of record that Mr. Parris keeps, I
note that you are rarely in the church on Sabbath Day.

Proctor. No, sir, you are mistaken.

Hale. Twenty-six time in seventeen month, sir. I must
call that rare. Will you tell me why you are so absent?

Proctor. Mr. Hale, I never knew I must account to
490 that man for I come to church or stay at home. My
wife were sick this winter.

Hale. So I am told. But you, Mister, why could you
not come alone?

Proctor. I surely did come when I could, and when
I could not I prayed in this house.

Hale. Mr. Proctor, your house is not a church; your
theology must tell you that.

Proctor. It does, sir, it does; and it tells me that a
minister may pray to God without he have golden
500 candlesticks upon the altar.

Hale. What golden candlesticks?

---

4. **rebels:** upsets.

● **CONVENTIONS OF
DRAMA**   RL 3
                              RL 5

How do dramatic conventions in lines
436–453 show that Reverend Hale's arrival
creates a tense atmosphere in the Proctor
home?

*Possible answer: Stage directions show
the tension in the room: "to explain his
nervousness" (lines 437–438); Elizabeth sits,
"never letting [Hale] out of her sight" (line
441); Proctor offers Hale cider "to break
the silence" (line 443); Hale "wets his lips"
before speaking (line 451).*

Extend the Discussion Why do Elizabeth
and Proctor become tense and guarded
after Hale arrives? Why is Hale ill at ease
with the Proctors?

REVISIT THE BIG QUESTION

What fuels a
MOB?

Discuss After students read lines 449–472,
ask them the following question: How would
you describe Hale's view of the hysteria seen
in court? Cite evidence to support your answer. *Possible answer: Hale seems a little put
off by the hysteria in court (lines 456–458) and
tries to distance himself from it (lines 450–451);
however, he agrees with the court that there
is cause for concern about witchcraft (lines
469–472).*

FOR ADVANCED LEARNERS/AP

Analyze Action Have students meet in small
groups to discuss the scene in which Hale
interrogates Proctor (beginning in line 478).
Note that although Hale comes to visit "without the court's authority" (lines 450–451), his
conversation with Proctor feels like a court
proceeding. Also point out that Miller provides few stage directions for their exchange.
Then have students work independently to
rewrite this scene, adding stage directions
that illustrate what they consider to be the
appropriate atmosphere. Urge students to
script the body language and gestures as well
as the vocal expressions of the characters.
Invite students to test their stage directions
by having classmates enact the rewritten
scenes.

■ DRAW CONCLUSIONS ABOUT CHARACTERS

Think about Proctor's comments on this page. Why would it be reasonable to conclude that Proctor is an independent thinker?

Possible answer: Proctor is an independent thinker because he prefers to focus directly on God rather than on the rules and wishes of Reverend Parris. In particular, Proctor's decision not to have his youngest son baptized by Parris (lines 514–520) violates the rules for Puritan behavior but honors his conscience.

IF STUDENTS NEED HELP . . . Discuss the importance of Proctor's comment about not seeing any "light of God" in Reverend Parris (lines 519–520). Help students link that comment to Proctor's bitterness over the fact that Parris replaced the pewter candlesticks with golden ones (lines 502–511).

Analyze Visuals

Activity Study how the characters are positioned in the photo and what they are doing. What do their positions and activities reveal about the Proctor family? *Possible answer: The characters' positions reveal the distance between Elizabeth and Proctor by showing Elizabeth looking on from outside the group. The activity of reading, especially of Proctor reading to his sons, reveals that the household values thinking and education.*

Proctor. Since we built the church there were pewter candlesticks upon the altar; Francis Nurse made them, y'know, and a sweeter hand never touched the metal. But Parris came, and for twenty week he preach nothin' but golden candlesticks until he had them. I labor the earth from dawn of day to blink of night, and I tell you true, when I look to heaven and see my money glaring at his elbows—it hurt my
510 prayer, sir, it hurt my prayer. I think, sometimes, the man dreams cathedrals, not clapboard meetin' houses.

Hale (*thinks, then*). And yet, Mister, a Christian on Sabbath Day must be in church. (*pause*) Tell me—you have three children?

Proctor. Aye. Boys.

Hale. How comes it that only two are baptized?

Proctor (*starts to speak, then stops, then, as though unable to restrain this*). I like it not that Mr. Parris should lay his hand upon my baby. I see no light
520 of God in that man. I'll not conceal it.

Hale. I must say it, Mr. Proctor; that is not for you to decide. The man's ordained, therefore the light of God is in him.

Proctor (*flushed with resentment but trying to smile*).

What's your suspicion, Mr. Hale?

Hale. No, no, I have no—

Proctor. I nailed the roof upon the church, I hung the door—

Hale. Oh, did you! That's a good sign, then.

530 **Proctor.** It may be I have been too quick to bring the man to book,[5] but you cannot think we ever desired the destruction of religion. I think that's in your mind, is it not?

Hale (*not altogether giving way*). I—have—there is a softness in your record, sir, a softness.

Elizabeth. I think, maybe, we have been too hard with Mr. Parris. I think so. But sure we never loved the Devil here.

Hale (*nods, deliberating this. Then, with the voice of*
540 *one administering a secret test*). Do you know your Commandments, Elizabeth?

Elizabeth (*without hesitation, even eagerly*). I surely do. There be no mark of blame upon my life, Mr. Hale. I am a convenanted Christian woman.

Hale. And you, Mister?

Proctor (*a trifle unsteadily*). I—am sure I do, sir.

---

5. **bring the man to book:** judge the man.

John Proctor and his sons

DIFFERENTIATED INSTRUCTION

FOR ADVANCED LEARNERS/AP

Research: Church Membership Some scholars believe that a key aspect of the background to the Salem witch trials was the fear of certain leaders in the community that Puritan values no longer influenced citizens in the way that they once did. Challenge students to research what church membership once meant in terms of the rights and privileges it provided for Puritans in Massachusetts, and why, by the 1690s, a lapse of membership might have reminded Puritan elders that the original ideals of the "city upon a hill" had begun to fade. Ask students to summarize their findings and present them to the class.

Hale (*glances at her open face, then at* John, *then*). Let you repeat them, if you will.

Proctor. The Commandments.

550 **Hale.** Aye.

Proctor (*looking off, beginning to sweat*). Thou shalt not kill.

Hale. Aye.

Proctor (*counting on his fingers*). Thou shalt not steal. Thou shalt not covet thy neighbor's goods, nor make unto thee any graven image. Thou shalt not take the name of the Lord in vain; thou shalt have no other gods before me. (*with some hesitation*) Thou shalt remember the Sabbath Day and keep it holy. (*Pause.*

560 *Then.*) Thou shalt honor thy father and mother. Thou shalt not bear false witness. (*He is stuck. He counts back on his fingers, knowing one is missing.*) Thou shalt not make unto thee any graven image.

Hale. You have said that twice, sir.

Proctor (*lost*). Aye. (*He is flailing for it.*)

Elizabeth (*delicately*). Adultery, John.

Proctor (*as though a secret arrow had pained his heart*). Aye. (*trying to grin it away—to* Hale) You see, sir, between the two of us we do know them

570 all. (Hale *only looks at* Proctor, *deep in his attempt to define this man.* Proctor *grows more uneasy.*) I think it be a small fault.

Hale. Theology, sir, is a fortress; no crack in a fortress may be accounted small. (*He rises; he seems worried now. He paces a little, in deep thought.*)

Proctor. There be no love for Satan in this house, Mister.

Hale. I pray it, I pray it dearly. (*He looks to both of them, an attempt at a smile on his face, but his misgiv-*

580 *ings are clear.*) Well, then—I'll bid you good night.

Elizabeth (*unable to restrain herself*). Mr. Hale. (*He turns.*) I do think you are suspecting me somewhat? Are you not?

Hale (*obviously disturbed—and evasive*). Goody Proctor, I do not judge you. My duty is to add what I may to the godly wisdom of the court. I pray you

both good health and good fortune. (*to* John) Good night, sir. (*He starts out.*)

Elizabeth (*with a note of desperation*). I think you

590 must tell him, John.

Hale. What's that?

Elizabeth (*restraining a call*). Will you tell him?

(*Slight pause.* Hale *looks questioningly at* John.)

Proctor (*with difficulty*). I—I have no witness and cannot prove it, except my word be taken. But I know the children's sickness had naught to do with witchcraft.

Hale (*stopped, struck*). Naught to do—?

Proctor. Mr. Parris discovered them sportin' in the

600 woods. They were startled and took sick.

(*pause*)

Hale. Who told you this?

Proctor (*hesitates, then*). Abigail Williams.

Hale. Abigail!

Proctor. Aye.

Hale (*his eyes wide*). Abigail Williams told you it had naught to do with witchcraft!

Proctor. She told me the day you came, sir.

Hale (*suspiciously*). Why—why did you keep this?

610 **Proctor.** I never knew until tonight that the world is gone daft with this nonsense.

Hale. Nonsense! Mister, I have myself examined Tituba, Sarah Good, and numerous others that have confessed to dealing with the Devil. They have *confessed* it.

Proctor. And why not, if they must hang for denyin' it? There are them that will swear to anything before they'll hang; have you never thought of that?

Hale. I have. I—I have indeed. (*It is his own suspi-*

620 *cion, but he resists it. He glances at* Elizabeth, *then at* John.) And you—would you testify to this in court?

Proctor. I—had not reckoned with goin' into court. But if I must I will.

Hale. Do you falter here?

③

TIERED DISCUSSION PROMPTS

Use these prompts to help students explore the characterization in these critical lines, 578–595:

Summarize What does Elizabeth see in Hale's behavior that makes her desperate for Proctor to reveal what he knows about Abigail? *Possible answer: Elizabeth sees that Hale is "obviously disturbed" by the Proctors' answers to his questions and "evasive" in declaring that he supports her (line 584). She also sees that although Hale attempts to smile, "misgivings are clear" on his face (lines 579–580).*

Analyze Elizabeth nearly begs Proctor to tell Hale about Abigail. Why do you think Elizabeth doesn't reveal the information herself? *Possible answer: Elizabeth defers to her husband; she would never reveal something about him without his consent. Furthermore, it is Proctor rather than Elizabeth who would have firsthand knowledge of the conversation with Abigail.*

Evaluate Do you find Proctor's weakness in this scene believable? Why or why not? *Possible answer: Proctor's weakness—that is, his reluctance to give information that might save his wife—is believable. Readers and audience members understand and sympathize with Proctor's desire to protect himself and his wife from scandal.*

FOR STRUGGLING READERS

③ **Targeted Passage** [Lines 594–623]

In this passage, both Hale and Proctor come to a new understanding of the situation.

- What news from Proctor shocks Hale? Why is Hale suspicious? (lines 594–598, 602–604)
- How does Proctor explain his silence? (lines 610–611)
- How does Proctor explain Hale's effectiveness? (lines 612–618)
- What does Hale suspect, though he fights the suspicion? (lines 617–620)

FOR ENGLISH LANGUAGE LEARNERS

Vocabulary: Outdated Forms Discuss these terms from the dialogue that rarely appear in modern English:

- *Thou shalt* (lines 551–563), "You will"
- *pray it dearly* (line 578), "hope so very much"
- *naught* (lines 596, 598, 607), "nothing"
- *daft* (line 611), "crazy"
- *reckoned with* (line 622), "planned on"

TIERED DISCUSSION PROMPTS

Use these prompts to help students understand Elizabeth's defense before Reverend Hale in lines 648–663:

Connect Have you or someone you know ever had to put up a defense against a false accusation? How does that experience help you understand Elizabeth's risky response to Hale's concern that she does not believe in witches? *Accept all responses that attempt to connect to Elizabeth's self-defense.*

Interpret When Proctor comes to her defense during the questioning, Elizabeth cries out, "Question Abigail Williams about the Gospel, not myself!" (lines 661–662). What does she mean? *Possible answer: Elizabeth is implying that she knows the Bible and lives according to its teachings, whereas Abigail, whom everyone seems to consider above reproach, is the one who needs lessons in Christian morality (because of her lies and her illicit interest in Proctor).*

Synthesize Consider what you have learned about Elizabeth in this passage. Do you think that she will make a favorable impression in court? Why or why not? *Possible answer: Elizabeth probably will make an unfavorable impression because she is willing to speak her mind even though she voices an unpopular—and, in the mind of the court, perhaps heretical—view of witchcraft.*

Proctor. I falter nothing, but I may wonder if my story will be credited in such a court. I do wonder on it, when such a steady-minded minister as you will suspicion such a woman that never lied, and cannot, and the world knows she cannot! I may 630 falter somewhat, Mister; I am no fool.

Hale (*quietly—it has impressed him*). Proctor, let you open with me now, for I have a rumor that troubles me. It's said you hold no belief that there may even be witches in the world. Is that true, sir?

Proctor (*He knows this is critical, and is striving against his disgust with* Hale *and with himself for even answering*). I know not what I have said, I may have said it. I have wondered if there be witches in the world—although I cannot believe they come among 640 us now.

Hale. Then you do not believe—

Proctor. I have no knowledge of it; the Bible speaks of witches, and I will not deny them.

Hale. And you, woman?

Elizabeth. I—I cannot believe it.

Hale (*shocked*). You cannot!

Proctor. Elizabeth, you bewilder him!

Elizabeth (*to* Hale). I cannot think the Devil may own a woman's soul, Mr. Hale, when she keeps an 650 upright way, as I have. I am a good woman, I know it; and if you believe I may do only good work in the world, and yet be secretly bound to Satan, then I must tell you, sir, I do not believe it.

Hale. But, woman, you do believe there are witches in—

Elizabeth. If you think that I am one, then I say there are none.

Hale. You surely do not fly against the Gospel, the Gospel—

660 **Proctor.** She believe in the Gospel, every word!

Elizabeth. Question Abigail Williams about the Gospel, not myself!

(Hale *stares at her.*)

Proctor. She do not mean to doubt the Gospel, sir, you cannot think it. This be a Christian house, sir,

a Christian house.

Hale. God keep you both; let the third child be quickly baptized, and go you without fail each Sunday in to Sabbath prayer; and keep a solemn, quiet 670 way among you. I think—

(Giles Corey *appears in doorway.*)

Giles. John!

Proctor. Giles! What's the matter?

Giles. They take my wife.

(Francis Nurse *enters.*)

Giles. And his Rebecca!

Proctor (*to* Francis). Rebecca's in the *jail!*

Francis. Aye, Cheever come and take her in his wagon. We've only now come from the jail, and 680 they'll not even let us in to see them.

Elizabeth. They've surely gone wild now, Mr. Hale!

Francis (*going to* Hale). Reverend Hale! Can you not speak to the Deputy Governor? I'm sure he mistakes these people—

Hale. Pray calm yourself, Mr. Nurse.

Francis. My wife is the very brick and mortar of the church, Mr. Hale (*indicating* Giles) and Martha Corey, there cannot be a woman closer yet to God than Martha.

690 **Hale.** How is Rebecca charged, Mr. Nurse?

Francis (*with a mocking, half-hearted laugh*). For murder, she's charged! (*mockingly quoting the warrant*) "For the marvelous and supernatural murder of Goody Putnam's babies." What am I to do, Mr. Hale?

Hale (*turns from* Francis, *deeply troubled, then*). Believe me, Mr. Nurse, if Rebecca Nurse be tainted, then nothing's left to stop the whole green world from burning. Let you rest upon the justice of the court; the court will send her home, I know it.

700 **Francis.** You cannot mean she will be tried in court!

Hale (*pleading*). Nurse, though our hearts break, we cannot flinch; these are new times, sir. There is a misty plot afoot so subtle we should be criminal to cling to old respects and ancient friendships. I have seen too many frightful proofs in court—the Devil

---

DIFFERENTIATED INSTRUCTION

FOR STRUGGLING READERS

④ **Targeted Passage** [Lines 672–695]

Even the most upstanding citizens of Salem are not safe from the charge of witchcraft.

- With what crime is Rebecca Nurse charged? (lines 691–692)

- Why is it so surprising that Rebecca Nurse and Martha Corey have been accused? (lines 686–689)

- How does Elizabeth characterize the town after learning of these arrests? Why does

she direct her comment to Reverend Hale? (line 681)

Comprehension Support Hale expresses his disbelief that Rebecca Nurse could be "tainted," or guilty of association with the Devil (lines 696–698). Then read this comment aloud: "if Rebecca Nurse be tainted, then nothing's left to stop the whole green world from burning." Help students restate Hale's comment in their own words. Example: *If Rebecca Nurse is guilty of witchcraft, then no one is safe from accusation.*

is alive in Salem, and we dare not quail to follow wherever the accusing finger points!

Proctor (*angered*). How may such a woman murder children?

710 **Hale** (*in great pain*). Man, remember, until an hour before the Devil fell, God thought him beautiful in Heaven.

Giles. I never said my wife were a witch, Mr. Hale; I only said she were reading books!

Hale. Mr. Corey, exactly what complaint were made on your wife?

Giles. That bloody mongrel Walcott charge her. Y'see, he buy a pig of my wife four or five year ago, and the pig died soon after. So he come dancin' in
720 for his money back. So my Martha, she says to him, "Walcott, if you haven't the wit to feed a pig properly, you'll not live to own many," she says. Now he goes to court and claims that from that day to this he cannot keep a pig alive for more than four weeks because my Martha bewitch them with her books!

(*Enter* Ezekiel Cheever. *A shocked silence.*)

Cheever. Good evening to you, Proctor.

Proctor. Why, Mr. Cheever. Good evening.

Cheever. Good evening, all. Good evening, Mr. Hale.

730 **Proctor.** I hope you come not on business of the court.

Cheever. I do, Proctor, aye. I am clerk of the court now, y'know.

(*Enter* Marshal Herrick, *a man in his early thirties, who is somewhat shamefaced at the moment.*)

Giles. It's a pity, Ezekiel, that an honest tailor might have gone to Heaven must burn in Hell. You'll burn for this, do you know it?

Cheever. You know yourself I must do as I'm told.
740 You surely know that, Giles. And I'd as lief[6] you'd not be sending me to Hell. I like not the sound of it, I tell you; I like not the sound of it. (*He fears* Proctor, *but starts to reach inside his coat.*) Now believe me, Proctor, how heavy be the law, all its tonnage

I do carry on my back tonight. (*He takes out a warrant.*) I have a warrant for your wife.

Proctor (*to* Hale). You said she were not charged!

Hale. I know nothin' of it. (*to* Cheever) When were she charged?

750 **Cheever.** I am given sixteen warrant tonight, sir, and she is one.

Proctor. Who charged her?

Cheever. Why, Abigail Williams charge her.

Proctor. On what proof, what proof?

Cheever (*looking about the room*). Mr. Proctor, I have little time. The court bid me search your house, but I like not to search a house. So will you hand me any poppets that your wife may keep here?

Proctor. Poppets?

760 **Elizabeth.** I never kept no poppets, not since I were a girl.

Cheever (*embarrassed, glancing toward the mantel where sits* Mary Warren's *poppet*). I spy a poppet, Goody Proctor.

Elizabeth. Oh! (*going for it*) Why, this is Mary's.

Cheever (*shyly*). Would you please to give it to me?

Elizabeth (*handing it to him, asks* Hale). Has the court discovered a text in poppets now?

Cheever (*carefully holding the poppet*). Do you keep
770 any others in this house?

Proctor. No, nor this one either till tonight. What signifies a poppet?

Cheever. Why, a poppet—(*He gingerly turns the poppet over.*) a poppet may signify—Now, woman, will you please to come with me?

Proctor. She will not! (*to* Elizabeth) Fetch Mary here.

Cheever (*ineptly reaching toward* Elizabeth). No, no, I am forbid to leave her from my sight.

Proctor (*pushing his arm away*). You'll leave her out
780 of sight and out of mind, Mister. Fetch Mary, Elizabeth. (Elizabeth *goes upstairs.*)

Hale. What signifies a poppet, Mr. Cheever?

---

6. **as lief** (lēf): rather.

THE CRUCIBLE: ACT TWO **175**

COMMON CORE
RL 3
RL 5

● CONVENTIONS OF DRAMA

The characters become more agitated and the dialogue moves quickly as the plot now becomes more complicated. How does Abigail use the poppet to create further conflict between herself and Elizabeth?

Possible answer: *Abigail has sabotaged the poppet, knowing that Mary would give it to Elizabeth; then she injured herself to implicate Elizabeth falsely.*

IF STUDENTS NEED HELP . . .

- Review with them the action discussed in this scene involving Mary, Abigail, and the poppet, especially lines 799–810.
- Help students fill in a Sequence Chain to understand the steps leading to Elizabeth's being charged with the stabbing of Abigail.

Mary Warren sews a poppet in court.
↓
Abigail sticks a needle into the poppet.
↓
Mary gives the poppet to Elizabeth.
↓
Abigail falls to the ground with a needle in her belly.
↓
Abigail claims that Elizabeth's "spirit" put the needle into her.
↓
Elizabeth is arrested.

🧰 BEST PRACTICES TOOLKIT—Transparency
Sequence Chain p. B21

Cheever (*turning the poppet over in his hands*). Why, they say it may signify that she—(*He has lifted the poppet's skirt, and his eyes widen in astonished fear.*) Why, this, this—

Proctor (*reaching for the poppet*). What's there?

Cheever. Why (*He draws out a long needle from the poppet.*) it is a needle! Herrick, Herrick, it is a 790 needle!

(*Herrick comes toward him.*)

Proctor (*angrily, bewildered*). And what signifies a needle!

Cheever (*his hands shaking*). Why, this go hard with her, Proctor, this—I had my doubts, Proctor, I had my doubts, but here's calamity. (*to Hale, showing the needle*) You see it, sir, it is a needle!

Hale. Why? What meanin' has it?

Cheever (*wide-eyed, trembling*). The girl, the Wil-
800 liams girl, Abigail Williams, sir. She sat to dinner in Reverend Parris's house tonight, and without word nor warnin' she falls to the floor. Like a struck beast, he says, and screamed a scream that a bull would weep to hear. And he goes to save her, and, stuck two inches in the flesh of her belly, he draw a needle out. And demandin' of her how she come to be so stabbed, she (*to Proctor now*) testify it were your wife's familiar spirit[7] pushed it in.

Proctor. Why, she done it herself! (*to Hale*) I hope
810 you're not takin' this for proof, Mister!

(*Hale, struck by the proof, is silent.*)

Cheever. 'Tis hard proof! (*to Hale*) I find here a poppet Goody Proctor keeps. I have found it, sir. And in the belly of the poppet a needle's stuck. I tell you true, Proctor, I never warranted to see such proof of Hell, and I bid you obstruct me not, for I—

(*Enter Elizabeth with Mary Warren. Proctor, seeing Mary Warren, draws her by the arm to Hale.*)

Proctor. Here now! Mary, how did this poppet come
820 into my house?

Mary Warren (*frightened for herself, her voice very small*). What poppet's that, sir?

Proctor (*impatiently, pointing at the doll in* Cheever's *hand*). This poppet, this poppet.

Mary Warren (*evasively, looking at it*). Why, I—I think it is mine.

Proctor. It is your poppet, is it not?

Mary Warren (*not understanding the direction of this*). It—is, sir.

830 **Proctor.** And how did it come into this house?

Mary Warren (*glancing about at the avid faces*). Why—I made it in the court, sir, and—give it to Goody Proctor tonight.

Proctor (*to* Hale). Now, sir—do you have it?

Hale. Mary Warren, a needle have been found inside this poppet.

Mary Warren (*bewildered*). Why, I meant no harm by it, sir.

Proctor (*quickly*). You stuck that needle in yourself?

840 **Mary Warren.** I—I believe I did, sir, I—

Proctor (*to* Hale). What say you now?

Hale (*watching* Mary Warren *closely*). Child, you are certain this be your natural memory? May it be, perhaps, that someone conjures you even now to say this?

Mary Warren. Conjures me? Why, no, sir, I am entirely myself, I think. Let you ask Susanna Walcott—she saw me sewin' it in court. (*or better still*) Ask Abby, Abby sat beside me when I made it.

850 **Proctor** (*to* Hale, *of* Cheever). Bid him begone. Your mind is surely settled now. Bid him out, Mr. Hale.

Elizabeth. What signifies a needle?

Hale. Mary—you charge a cold and cruel murder on Abigail.

Mary Warren. Murder! I charge no—

Hale. Abigail were stabbed tonight; a needle were found stuck into her belly—

---

7. **familiar spirit:** the spirit or demon, most usually in the form of an animal such as a black cat, that was a companion and helper to a witch.

DIFFERENTIATED INSTRUCTION

FOR STRUGGLING READERS

Comprehension Support Have students reread the exchange between Hale and Mary Warren in lines 842–849. Point out that Hale's question, "May it be, perhaps, that someone conjures [bewitches] you even now to say this?" (lines 843–845) attempts to influence Mary's answer. Discuss with students whom Hale means by "someone"—the Devil? Abigail? Elizabeth?

Elizabeth. And she charges me?

Hale. Aye.

860 **Elizabeth** (*her breath knocked out*). Why—! The girl is murder! She must be ripped out of the world!

Cheever (*pointing at* Elizabeth). You've heard that, sir! Ripped out of the world! Herrick, you heard it!

Proctor (*suddenly snatching the warrant out of* Cheever's *hands*). Out with you.

Cheever. Proctor, you dare not touch the warrant.

Proctor (*ripping the warrant*). Out with you!

Cheever. You've ripped the Deputy Governor's warrant, man!

870 **Proctor.** Damn the Deputy Governor! Out of my house!

Hale. Now, Proctor, Proctor!

Proctor. Get y'gone with them! You are a broken minister.

Hale. Proctor, if she is innocent, the court—

Proctor. If *she* is innocent! Why do you never wonder if Parris be innocent, or Abigail? Is the accuser always holy now? Were they born this morning as clean as God's fingers? I'll tell you what's walking
880 Salem—vengeance is walking Salem. We are what we always were in Salem, but now the little crazy children are jangling the keys of the kingdom, and common vengeance writes the law! This warrant's vengeance! I'll not give my wife to vengeance!

⑤

Elizabeth. I'll go, John—

Proctor. You will not go!

Herrick. I have nine men outside. You cannot keep her. The law binds me, John, I cannot budge.

Proctor (*to* Hale, *ready to break him*). Will you see
890 her taken?

Hale. Proctor, the court is just—

Proctor. Pontius Pilate! God will not let you wash your hands of this![8]

Elizabeth. John—I think I must go with them. (*He cannot bear to look at her.*) Mary, there is bread

enough for the morning; you will bake, in the afternoon. Help Mr. Proctor as you were his daughter—you owe me that, and much more. (*She is fighting her weeping. To* Proctor.) When the children wake,
900 speak nothing of witchcraft—it will frighten them. (*She cannot go on.*)

Proctor. I will bring you home. I will bring you soon.

Elizabeth. Oh, John, bring me soon!

Proctor. I will fall like an ocean on that court! Fear nothing, Elizabeth.

Elizabeth (*with great fear*). I will fear nothing. (*She looks about the room, as though to fix it in her mind.*) Tell the children I have gone to visit someone sick.

(*She walks out the door,* Herrick *and* Cheever *behind*
910 *her. For a moment,* Proctor *watches from the doorway. The clank of chain is heard.*)

Proctor. Herrick! Herrick, don't chain her! (*He rushes out the door. From outside.*) Damn you, man, you will not chain her! Off with them! I'll not have it! I will not have her chained!

(*There are other men's voices against his.* Hale, *in a fever of guilt and uncertainty, turns from the door to avoid the sight;* Mary Warren *bursts into tears and sits weeping.* Giles Corey *calls to* Hale.)

920 **Giles.** And yet silent, minister? It is fraud, you know it is fraud! What keeps you, man?

(Proctor *is half braced, half pushed into the room by two deputies and* Herrick.)

Proctor. I'll pay you, Herrick, I will surely pay you!

Herrick (*panting*). In God's name, John, I cannot help myself. I must chain them all. Now let you keep inside this house till I am gone! (*He goes out with his deputies.*)

(Proctor *stands there, gulping air. Horses and a wagon*
930 *creaking are heard.*)

Hale (*in great uncertainty*). Mr. Proctor—

Proctor. Out of my sight!

Hale. Charity, Proctor, charity. What I have heard in

---

8. **Pontius** (pŏn′tē-əs) **Pilate . . . hands of this:** the Roman governor who presided over the trial and sentencing of Christ. Pilate publicly washed his hands to absolve himself of responsibility for Christ's death.

TIERED DISCUSSION PROMPTS

Use these prompts to help students explore Elizabeth's departure after they read lines 894–908:

Connect Have you ever tried to act strong in a difficult situation? Do you think that you were successful? Do you think that others noticed your attempt? *Accept all responses.*

Interpret Why is it significant that when Elizabeth realizes that she must leave her home, she immediately gives a set of ordinary household orders? *Possible answer: Elizabeth's orders are significant because they underscore her central role in her family—that of manager of the home and chief caretaker of the children. She is also trying to maintain a sense of normalcy for others as she herself faces great danger.*

Synthesize Given what you have learned about Proctor and Elizabeth, who do you think is better equipped to handle a court appearance? Explain. *Possible answer: Elizabeth seems better equipped to handle the upcoming challenge. Although she is afraid, she makes herself stand up and face the future; Proctor, however, has been reluctant to get involved because of his past relationship with Abigail.*

FOR STRUGGLING READERS

⑤ Targeted Passage [Lines 876–884]

In this passage, Proctor's outburst points to a key idea in *The Crucible.*

- According to Proctor, what does a person gain by accusing others of witchcraft? (lines 877–878)

- Why does Proctor say that the children have all the power in Salem now? What evidence might he offer to prove this claim? (lines 880–882)

FOR ADVANCED LEARNERS/AP

Analyze Character [paired option] Point out that Reverend Hale is "in a fever of guilt and uncertainty" and cannot watch as Proctor protests the chaining of Elizabeth (lines 916–918). Ask students to write a soliloquy in which Hale expresses his thoughts and feelings in this scene, drawing upon his experiences in Salem thus far and perhaps speculating about his future involvement there.

REVISIT THE BIG QUESTION

What fuels a
MOB?

After students read lines 995–1007, ask them the following question: How has hysteria created a situation that causes Proctor to say, "Now Hell and Heaven grapple on our backs, and all our old pretense is ripped away" (lines 996–998)? **Possible answer:** *Hysteria in the community has created a situation in which people's basest potential is being revealed and even encouraged. Now the Salemites must decide whether to continue along the destructive path that their hysteria has created (Hell) or to treat the accusations fairly and without fear (Heaven).*

SELECTION WRAP-UP

READ WITH A PURPOSE Now that students have finished Act Two, have them think about the impact rumors can have on a community. Based on your experiences and your reading, what happens when rumors get out of control? **Possible answers:** *Innocent people like Elizabeth Proctor can get hurt because other people like Mary Warren are trying to protect themselves.*

⭐ CRITIQUE

- Remind students that although Abigail does not appear in this act, her presence is undeniable. Have students identify and explain the moment in Act Two in which they felt Abigail's presence most strongly.

- After completing the After Reading questions on page 179, have students revisit their responses and tell whether they have changed their opinions.

---

her favor, I will not fear to testify in court. God help me, I cannot judge her guilty or innocent—I know not. Only this consider: the world goes mad, and it profit nothing you should lay the cause to the vengeance of a little girl.

Proctor. You are a coward! Though you be ordained
940 in God's own tears, you are a coward now!

Hale. Proctor, I cannot think God be provoked so grandly by such a petty cause. The jails are packed— our greatest judges sit in Salem now—and hangin's promised. Man, we must look to cause proportion- ate. Were there murder done, perhaps, and never brought to light? Abomination? Some secret blas- phemy that stinks to Heaven? Think on cause, man, and let you help me to discover it. For there's your way, believe it, there is your only way, when such
950 confusion strikes upon the world. (*He goes to* Giles *and* Francis.) Let you counsel among yourselves; think on your village and what may have drawn from heaven such thundering wrath upon you all. I shall pray God open up our eyes. ⑥

(Hale *goes out.*)

Francis (*struck by* Hale*'s mood*). I never heard no murder done in Salem.

Proctor (*He has been reached by* Hale*'s words*). Leave me, Francis, leave me.

960 **Giles** (*shaken*). John—tell me, are we lost?

Proctor. Go home now, Giles. We'll speak on it tomorrow.

Giles. Let you think on it. We'll come early, eh?

Proctor. Aye. Go now, Giles.

Giles. Good night, then.

(Giles Corey *goes out. After a moment.*)

Mary Warren (*in a fearful squeak of a voice*). Mr. Proctor, very likely they'll let her come home once they're given proper evidence.

970 **Proctor.** You're coming to the court with me, Mary. You will tell it in the court.

Mary Warren. I cannot charge murder on Abigail.

Proctor (*moving menacingly toward her*). You will tell the court how that poppet come here and who stuck the needle in.

Mary Warren. She'll kill me for sayin' that! (Proctor *continues toward her.*) Abby'll charge lechery on you, Mr. Proctor!

Proctor (*halting*). She's told you!

980 **Mary Warren.** I have known it, sir. She'll ruin you with it, I know she will.

Proctor (*hesitating, and with deep hatred of himself*). Good. Then her saintliness is done with. (Mary *backs from him.*) We will slide together into our pit; you will tell the court what you know.

Mary Warren (*in terror*). I cannot, they'll turn on me—

(Proctor *strides and catches her, and she is repeating,* "I cannot, I cannot!")

990 **Proctor.** My wife will never die for me! I will bring your guts into your mouth but that goodness will not die for me!

Mary Warren (*struggling to escape him*). I cannot do it, I cannot!

Proctor (*grasping her by the throat as though he would strangle her*). Make your peace with it! Now Hell and Heaven grapple on our backs, and all our old pre- tense is ripped away—make your peace! (*He throws her to the floor, where she sobs,* "I cannot, I cannot . . ."
1000 *And now, half to himself, staring, and turning to the open door.*) Peace. It is a providence, and no great change; we are only what we always were, but naked now. (*He walks as though toward a great horror, facing the open sky.*) Aye, naked! And the wind, God's icy wind, will blow!

(*And she is over and over again sobbing,* "I cannot, I cannot, I cannot," *as the curtain falls.*)

DIFFERENTIATED INSTRUCTION

FOR STRUGGLING READERS

⑥ **Targeted Passage** [Lines 934–954]

This passage reveals Hale's stubbornness, despite his concern about the way that Salem is handling its witchcraft scare.

- To whom does Hale refer when he says that the "the vengeance of a little girl" could not have caused the town's frenzy? (line 938)

- Why does Proctor call Hale a coward? (lines 934–940)

- Why does Hale think that such terrible events are happening in Salem? (lines 941–950) Does he think that witchcraft is the only explanation? (lines 941–950)

Comprehension Support As students reread Proctor's threat in lines 990–992, point out the word "goodness." Elicit or explain that Proctor uses the word to refer to Elizabeth; she is the "goodness" that he will not allow to be executed. Have students suggest other terms that Proctor could use to refer to his wife, based on what they have learned about Elizabeth in Act Two.

Comprehension

1. **Recall** Why does Elizabeth want John to go to Salem?

2. **Clarify** Why does Hale come to the Proctors' home?

3. **Summarize** What proof leads to Elizabeth's arrest?

Text Analysis

4. **Form Opinions** Do you think Reverend Hale believes that Elizabeth Proctor is practicing witchcraft? Support your opinion with specific details.

5. **Draw Conclusions About Characters** Review the **traits** you recorded in your chart for Elizabeth Proctor. How would you describe her character?

6. **Analyze Conventions of Drama** What does **dialogue** reveal about the complicated relationship between John and Elizabeth in the following scenes?

   • Elizabeth learns that John was alone with Abigail (lines 132–138)
   • Elizabeth asks John to break his unspoken promise to Abigail (lines 398–422)
   • John threatens Mary Warren (lines 990–1005)

7. **Analyze Dramatic Irony** Dramatic irony occurs when the readers know more about a situation than a character does. Why is John struck by Hale's declaration that "some secret blasphemy" (lines 946–947) has caused all of the confusion?

8. **Make Judgments About a Character** How would you judge John's behavior so far? Cite evidence from the play to support your judgment.

9. **Compare Characters** Compare the following characters and determine which one has the greatest faith in the court proceedings. What accounts for their differing attitudes?

   • John Proctor   • Hale   • Cheever

Text Criticism

10. **Historical Context** Miller wrote that during the anti-Communist hearings, "I saw accepted the notion that conscience was no longer a private matter but one of state administration." How does this notion apply to the witch-hunts in Salem?

What fuels a MOB?

What role does Reverend Hale play in the mob mentality that develops in Salem during Act Two?

THE CRUCIBLE: ACT TWO **179**

Practice and Apply

For preliminary support of post-reading questions, use these copy masters:

R RESOURCE MANAGER—Copy Masters
Reading Check p. 215
Conventions of Drama p. 213
Question Support p. 216

Additional selection questions are provided for teachers on page 209.

ANSWERS COMMON CORE RL 1, RL 2, RL 3, RL 5

1. *to tell the Salem court that its cases are based on Abigail's fraudulent testimony*

2. *to determine the Christian character of their household*

3. *a doll with a needle in it, linked to Abigail's claim that Elizabeth's spirit stabbed her*

Possible answers:

4. *Yes; he is "struck by the proof" of the poppet (line 811). No; he thinks she is a good woman—so much so that he turns away in "guilt and uncertainty" when she is arrested (line 917).*

5. **COMMON CORE FOCUS** *Draw Conclusions About Characters Elizabeth is virtuous, honest, and courageous, yet defensive of her position as the wronged wife and cold toward John.*

6. **COMMON CORE FOCUS** *Conventions of Drama*
   • *There still is much tension between John and Elizabeth over Abigail.*
   • *John feels that Elizabeth does not trust him, and Elizabeth feels that John is not honest about his feelings.*
   • *John truly loves Elizabeth and loathes himself for what his infidelity has produced.*

Assess and Reteach

7. *John is struck because he knows that the "secret blasphemy" might be his adultery.*

8. *So far, John appears weak and defensive. He hesitates to expose Abigail, and he is angry that Elizabeth is disappointed in him.*

9. *Proctor: He thinks the proceedings are unjust, for he knows Abigail's motives.*
   Hale: He has the greatest faith in the proceedings because he set them in motion.
   Cheever: He believes the proceedings are just because he is a court official.

10. *The notion applies to the witch-hunts because personal principles no longer seem to matter in Salem. For example, Proctor's decision not to attend church due to his moral convictions arouses suspicion.*

What fuels a MOB? *Possible answers:* *Hale's role is to find the truth, but his search only leads to more doubts and accusations.*

Assess
DIAGNOSTIC AND SELECTION TESTS
Selection Test A pp. 65–66
Selection Test B/C pp. 67–68

Interactive Selection Test on thinkcentral.com

Reteach
Level Up Online Tutorials on thinkcentral.com
Reteaching Worksheets on thinkcentral.com

Literature Lesson 1–2, 6, 23–24, Reading Lesson 9

THE CRUCIBLE: ACT TWO **179**

Practice and Apply

SUMMARY

In Act Three, Proctor brings Mary Warren to the court, where Giles Corey and Francis Nurse also are trying to defend their wives. There, Mary confesses that Abigail and the other girls are frauds. When Abigail accuses Mary of bewitching her, Mary turns from Proctor and rejoins the girls. Proctor admits his infidelity, but Elizabeth denies it to save his reputation. The girls make hysterical accusations against Proctor; when he is arrested, Reverend Hale quits in disgust.

TEXT ANALYSIS

COMMON CORE
RL 3
RL 5

● *Model the Skill:*
CONVENTIONS OF DRAMA

These stage directions describe the setting of Act Three. Call on volunteers to locate details about the set and characters in the stage directions. Then use the stage directions to help students sketch the room. Next ask the following question: Who is on stage as the act opens? Of whose presence is the audience aware? Explain.

Possible answer: *As the act opens, the stage is empty. The audience is aware of the presence of Judge Hathorne and Martha Corey, whose voices are heard offstage. They are in the meeting house, to the right of the vestry, the room that the set represents.*

Resources for Act Three

ACT *Three*

(*The vestry room of the Salem meeting house, now serving as the anteroom*[1] *of the General Court.*

As the curtain rises, the room is empty, but for sunlight pouring through two high windows in the back wall. The room is solemn, even forbidding. Heavy beams jut out, boards of random widths make up the walls. At the right are two doors leading into the meeting house proper, where the court is being held. At the left another door leads outside.

There is a plain bench at the left, and another at the right. In the center a rather long meeting table, with stools and a considerable armchair snugged up to it.

Through the partitioning wall at the right we hear a prosecutor's voice, Judge Hathorne's, *asking a question; then a woman's voice,* Martha Corey's, *replying.*)

Hathorne's Voice. Now, Martha Corey, there is abundant evidence in our hands to show that you have given yourself to the reading of fortunes. Do you deny it?

Martha Corey's Voice. I am innocent to a witch. I know not what a witch is.

Hathorne's Voice. How do you know, then, that you are not a witch?

Martha Corey's Voice. If I were, I would know it.

10 **Hathorne's Voice.** Why do you hurt these children?

Martha Corey's Voice. I do not hurt them. I scorn it!

Giles' Voice (*roaring*). I have evidence for the court!

(*Voices of townspeople rise in excitement.*)

Danforth's Voice. You will keep your seat!

Giles' Voice. Thomas Putnam is reaching out for land!

Danforth's Voice. Remove that man, Marshal!

Giles' Voice. You're hearing lies, lies!

(*A roaring goes up from the people.*)

20 **Hathorne's Voice.** Arrest him, excellency!

Giles' Voice. I have evidence. Why will you not hear my evidence?

(*The door opens and* Giles *is half carried into the vestry room by* Herrick.)

Giles. Hands off, damn you, let me go!

Herrick. Giles, Giles!

Giles. Out of my way, Herrick! I bring evidence—

Herrick. You cannot go in there, Giles; it's a court!

(*Enter* Hale *from the court.*)

30 **Hale.** Pray be calm a moment.

Giles. You, Mr. Hale, go in there and demand I speak.

---

1. **vestry room . . . anteroom:** A vestry room is a room in a church used for nonreligious meetings or church business. An anteroom is a waiting room or a room that leads into another.

---

*See resources on the **Teacher One Stop DVD-ROM** and on **thinkcentral.com**.*

 RESOURCE MANAGER UNIT 1

Plan and Teach, pp. 217–222
Summary, pp. 223–224 † ‡*
Text Analysis and Reading
Skill, pp. 225–227 †*

DIAGNOSTIC AND SELECTION TESTS

Selection Tests, pp. 69–72

 BEST PRACTICES TOOLKIT

New Word Analysis, p. E8
Jigsaw Reading, p. A1
Storyboard, p. C11

INTERACTIVE READER

ADAPTED INTERACTIVE READER

ELL ADAPTED INTERACTIVE READER

TECHNOLOGY

⊘ **Teacher One Stop DVD-ROM**
⊘ **Student One Stop DVD-ROM**
⊘ **PowerNotes DVD-ROM**
⊘ **Audio Anthology CD**
⊘ **GrammarNotes DVD-ROM**
⊘ **ExamView Test Generator** on the Teacher One Stop

Video Trailer

Go to **thinkcentral.com** to preview the **Video Trailer** introducing this selection. Other features that support the selection include

• **PowerNotes** presentation
• **ThinkAloud** models to enhance comprehension
• **WordSharp** vocabulary tutorials
• interactive writing and grammar instruction

---

* Resources for Differentiation   † Also in Spanish   ‡ Also in Haitian Creole and Vietnamese

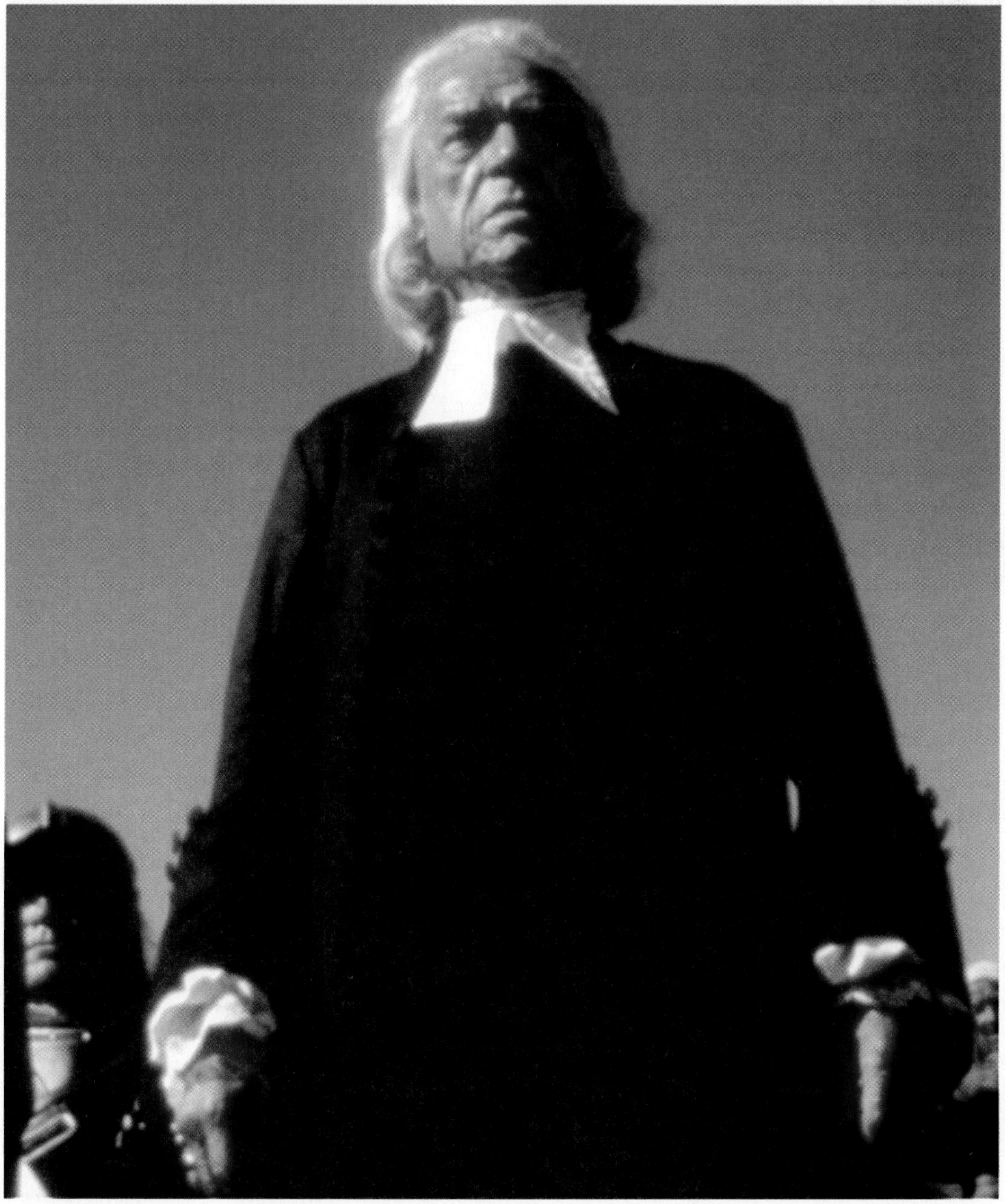

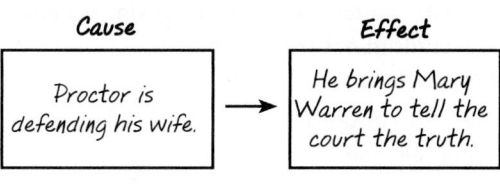

Paul Scofield as Deputy Governor Danforth

Analyze Visuals

Activity Explain that students will meet Judge Danforth on the next page (line 41). Have students use this photograph to form an initial impression of Danforth's personality. *Possible answer: The picture suggests that Judge Danforth is a serious, stern man. The character in the photograph seems powerful and intimidating and his expression is stern. The camera angle reinforces this impression.*

REVISIT THE BIG QUESTION

What fuels a MOB?

Discuss After students read lines 10–25, pose the following question: What details indicate that there is some degree of hysteria in the meeting room, which the audience cannot see? *Possible answer: The outcry of the townspeople in what should be an orderly court (lines 13 and 19) signals possible hysteria, as do the shouts of Giles Corey and Judge Hathorne's attempts to remove him and settle the room.*

DIFFERENTIATED INSTRUCTION

FOR ENGLISH LANGUAGE LEARNERS

Vocabulary Support Teach these words: *deny* (line 4), *submit* (line 79), *precise* (line 348), *legal* (line 377), *attitude* (line 799), *remove* (line 959). Allow students to work with partners to write original sentences using the new words.

🧰 BEST PRACTICES TOOLKIT—Transparency New Word Analysis p. E8

FOR STRUGGLING READERS

In combination with the *Audio Anthology CD,* use one or more Targeted Passages (pp. 182, 185, 188, 193, 196, 198) to ensure that students focus on key story events and concepts. Targeted Passages are also good for English learners.

Preview Read the Summary aloud. Have students fill in a cause-and-effect diagram:

Cause		*Effect*
Proctor is defending his wife.	→	He brings Mary Warren to tell the court the truth.

Use these prompts to help students grasp the difficulty that some Salemites have in making their voices heard, as revealed in lines 77–96:

Connect Have you or someone you know ever been unable to make a person listen to you? How did it feel to be ignored? Did you finally succeed in being heard? *Accept all reasonable responses.*

Analyze How are Hale's attempts to help Giles and Francis hindered? Why else might these men be frustrated? *Possible answers: In both of Hale's attempts (lines 77–78 and 88–89), Danforth responds by insisting that they follow legal procedure. Hathorne urges Danforth to have the men arrested (lines 93–94). They might be frustrated because this is the third day that they have tried but failed to be heard (lines 84–85); they also may fear that while they are waiting for Danforth to review a written plea (lines 95–96), their wives will be executed.*

Synthesize Do you think that the judges will be sympathetic to the husbands' efforts to save their wives? Why or why not? *Possible answers: The judges probably will not be sympathetic. In this passage, Giles receives an unsympathetic, formulaic answer: He should "submit his evidence in proper affidavit" (lines 79–80). In addition, Danforth shows a lack of sympathy when he wonders why Francis is in "such uproar" over his wife's condemnation (lines 90–91).*

Hale. A moment, sir, a moment.

Giles. They'll be hangin' my wife!

(*Judge Hathorne enters. He is in his sixties, a bitter, remorseless Salem judge.*)

Hathorne. How do you dare come roarin' into this court! Are you gone daft, Corey?

Giles. You're not a Boston judge yet, Hathorne. 40 You'll not call me daft!

(*Enter* Deputy Governor Danforth *and, behind him,* Ezekiel Cheever *and* Parris. *On his appearance, silence falls.* Danforth *is a grave man in his sixties, of some humor and sophistication that does not, however, interfere with an exact loyalty to his position and his cause. He comes down to* Giles, *who awaits his wrath.*)

Danforth (*looking directly at* Giles). Who is this man?

Parris. Giles Corey, sir, and a more **contentious**—

Giles (*to* Parris). I am asked the question, and I am 50 old enough to answer it! (*to* Danforth, *who impresses him and to whom he smiles through his strain*) My name is Corey, sir, Giles Corey. I have six hundred acres, and timber in addition. It is my wife you be condemning now. (*He indicates the courtroom.*)

Danforth. And how do you imagine to help her cause with such contemptuous riot?[2] Now be gone. Your old age alone keeps you out of jail for this.

Giles (*beginning to plead*). They be tellin' lies about my wife, sir, I—

60 **Danforth.** Do you take it upon yourself to determine what this court shall believe and what it shall set aside?

Giles. Your Excellency, we mean no disrespect for—

Danforth. Disrespect indeed! It is disruption, Mister. This is the highest court of the supreme government of this province, do you know it?

Giles (*beginning to weep*). Your Excellency, I only said she were readin' books, sir, and they come and take her out of my house for—

Danforth (*mystified*). Books! What books? ①

---

2. **contemptuous** (kən-tĕmp′chōō-əs) **riot**: disrespectful, outrageous behavior.

70 **Giles** (*through helpless sobs*). It is my third wife, sir; I never had no wife that be so taken with books, and I thought to find the cause of it, d'y'see, but it were no witch I blamed her for. (*He is openly weeping.*) I have broke charity with the woman, I have broke charity with her. (*He covers his face, ashamed.* Danforth *is respectfully silent.*)

Hale. Excellency, he claims hard evidence for his wife's defense. I think that in all justice you must—

Danforth. Then let him submit his evidence in 80 proper affidavit. You are certainly aware of our procedure here, Mr. Hale. (*to* Herrick) Clear this room.

Herrick. Come now, Giles. (*He gently pushes* Corey *out.*)

Francis. We are desperate, sir; we come here three days now and cannot be heard.

Danforth. Who is this man?

Francis. Francis Nurse, Your Excellency.

Hale. His wife's Rebecca that were condemned this morning.

90 **Danforth.** Indeed! I am amazed to find you in such uproar. I have only good report of your character, Mr. Nurse.

Hathorne. I think they must both be arrested in contempt, sir.

Danforth (*to* Francis). Let you write your plea, and in due time I will—

Francis. Excellency, we have proof for your eyes; God forbid you shut them to it. The girls, sir, the girls are frauds.

100 **Danforth.** What's that?

Francis. We have proof of it, sir. They are all deceiving you.

(Danforth *is shocked, but studying* Francis.)

Hathorne. This is contempt, sir, contempt!

Danforth. Peace, Judge Hathorne. Do you know who I am, Mr. Nurse?

FOR ENGLISH LANGUAGE LEARNERS

Preteach Vocabulary To help students understand Act Three, review the following vocabulary words in Act Three. Supply them with these definitions as needed:

- line 48: **contentious** (kən-tĕn′shəs) *adj.* quarrelsome

- line 278: **imperceptible** (ĭm′pər-sĕp′tə-bəl) *adj.* extremely slight; barely noticeable

- line 518: **immaculate** (ĭ-măk′yə-lĭt) *adj.* without stain; pure

Work with students to identify the prefixes and suffixes in the words. Review how word parts affect the meaning of a word.

FOR STRUGGLING READERS

① **Targeted Passage** [Lines 47–69]

Any comment can arouse suspicion in Salem.

- Why has Giles Corey come to court? (lines 53–56)

- Does Giles think that the court knows the truth? How can you tell? (lines 58–59)

- As he talks to Judge Danforth, what emotions rise to the surface? Explain. (line 66)

- Why does Giles feel he is responsible for his wife's situation? (lines 66–69)

Francis. I surely do, sir, and I think you must be a wise judge to be what you are.

Danforth. And do you know that near to four hun-
110 dred are in the jails from Marblehead to Lynn,[3] and upon my signature?

Francis. I—

Danforth. And seventy-two condemned to hang by that signature?

Francis. Excellency, I never thought to say it to such a weighty judge, but you are deceived.

(*Enter* Giles Corey *from left. All turn to see as he beckons in* Mary Warren *with* Proctor. Mary *is keeping her eyes to the ground;* Proctor *has her elbow as though*
120 *she were near collapse.*)

Parris (*on seeing her, in shock*). Mary Warren! (*He goes directly to bend close to her face.*) What are you about here?

Proctor (*pressing* Parris *away from her with a gentle but firm motion of protectiveness*). She would speak with the Deputy Governor.

Danforth (*shocked by this, turns to* Herrick). Did you not tell me Mary Warren were sick in bed?

Herrick. She were, Your Honor. When I go to fetch
130 her to the court last week, she said she were sick.

Giles. She has been strivin' with her soul all week, Your Honor; she comes now to tell the truth of this to you.

Danforth. Who is this?

Proctor. John Proctor, sir. Elizabeth Proctor is my wife.

Parris. Beware this man, Your Excellency, this man is mischief.

Hale (*excitedly*). I think you must hear the girl, sir,
140 she—

Danforth (*who has become very interested in* Mary Warren *and only raises a hand toward* Hale). Peace. What would you tell us, Mary Warren?

(Proctor *looks at her, but she cannot speak.*)

---
3. **Marblehead . . . Lynn:** two coastal towns in Massachusetts, near Salem.

Proctor. She never saw no spirits, sir.

Danforth (*with great alarm and surprise, to* Mary). Never saw no spirits!

Giles (*eagerly*). Never.

Proctor (*reaching into his jacket*). She has signed a
150 deposition, sir—

Danforth (*instantly*). No, no, I accept no deposi-
tions. (*He is rapidly calculating this; he turns from her to* Proctor.) Tell me, Mr. Proctor, have you given out this story in the village?

Proctor. We have not.

Parris. They've come to overthrow the court, sir! This man is—

Danforth. I pray you, Mr. Parris. Do you know, Mr. Proctor, that the entire contention of the state
160 in these trials is that the voice of Heaven is speaking through the children?

Proctor. I know that, sir.

Danforth (*thinks, staring at* Proctor, *then turns to* Mary Warren). And you, Mary Warren, how came you to cry out people for sending their spirits against you?

Mary Warren. It were pretense, sir.

Danforth. I cannot hear you.

Proctor. It were pretense, she says.

170 **Danforth.** Ah? And the other girls? Susanna Walcott, and—the others? They are also pretending?

Mary Warren. Aye, sir.

Danforth (*wide-eyed*). Indeed. (*Pause. He is baffled by this. He turns to study* Proctor's *face.*)

Parris (*in a sweat*). Excellency, you surely cannot think to let so vile a lie be spread in open court!

Danforth. Indeed not, but it strike hard upon me that she will dare come here with such a tale. Now, Mr. Proctor, before I decide whether I shall hear you
180 or not, it is my duty to tell you this. We burn a hot fire here; it melts down all concealment.

Proctor. I know that, sir.

THE CRUCIBLE: ACT THREE **183**

TEXT ANALYSIS — COMMON CORE — RL 3 / RL 5

● CONVENTIONS OF DRAMA

In lines 121–133, what does Miller's dialogue reveal about Mary Warren's participation in the court proceedings? *Possible answer: The dialogue reveals that Mary has not been at court for at least a week. Herrick says that she was sick (lines 129–130); Giles says that she has been "strivin' with her soul all week" (line 131).*

Extend the Discussion Why do you think that Mary has stayed away from court?

READING SKILL — COMMON CORE — RL 1 / RL 3

■ DRAW CONCLUSIONS ABOUT CHARACTERS

When Mary Warren confirms Proctor's claim that the girls have been lying in court, Judge Danforth is described as "wide-eyed" and "baffled" (line 173). Why would he be reluctant to believe what he has just heard? *Possible answer: Danforth would be reluctant because he, too, has found the girls to be convincing in court. If Proctor and Mary are right and the girls indeed are frauds, then Danforth and his court will look foolish for having been duped.*

FOR ENGLISH LANGUAGE LEARNERS

Language: Conversational English Patterns
Explain that a pattern of speaking, such as the use of the verb *be,* can be used to show whether a character is more or less educated. Note these examples:

- "It is my wife you be condemning now" (lines 53–54)
- "They be tellin' lies about my wife" (lines 58–59)

- "His wife's Rebecca that were condemned" (line 88)
- "Mary Warren were sick in bed" (line 128)

Have pairs of students identify other examples on these two pages and throughout the play.

FOR ADVANCED LEARNERS/AP

Analyze Dialogue Direct students' attention to this comment from Judge Danforth: "We burn a hot fire here; it melts down all concealment" (lines 180–181). Have students write and share a statement that explains (1) what the statement means in its immediate context and (2) how the statement relates to the title of the play.

TIERED DISCUSSION PROMPTS

Use these prompts to help students explore Proctor's attempts at self-defense as revealed in lines 215–241:

Recall Why does Proctor avoid church and sometimes plow on Sunday? ***Possible answer:*** *Proctor avoids church because he dislikes Reverend Parris (line 221). He sometimes plows on Sunday because he feels that he must work whenever he can to make his farm successful (lines 227–229).*

Interpret How can you give both a positive and a negative interpretation to Proctor's responses to the disclosures that he stays away from church and sometimes works on Sunday? ***Possible answer:*** *Proctor's responses can be interpreted positively if the reader considers them honest expressions of his beliefs and actions. Proctor is not a hypocrite. On the other hand, his responses can be judged negatively because they violate the rules that govern Puritan behavior.*

Evaluate How easy is it for readers to sympathize with Proctor as he answers Danforth's questions? Explain. ***Possible answer:*** *It is quite easy to sympathize with Proctor, for the reader probably shares Proctor's dislike of Parris. The reader probably also supports Proctor's desire to support his family, even if supporting his family sometimes means plowing on a Sunday.*

Danforth. Let me continue. I understand well, a husband's tenderness may drive him to extravagance in defense of a wife. Are you certain in your conscience, Mister, that your evidence is the truth?

Proctor. It is. And you will surely know it.

Danforth. And you thought to declare this revelation in the open court before the public?

190 **Proctor.** I thought I would, aye—with your permission.

Danforth (*his eyes narrowing*). Now, sir, what is your purpose in so doing?

Proctor. Why, I—I would free my wife, sir.

Danforth. There lurks nowhere in your heart, nor hidden in your spirit, any desire to undermine this court?

Proctor (*with the faintest faltering*). Why, no, sir.

Cheever (*clears his throat, awakening*). I—Your
200 Excellency.

Danforth. Mr. Cheever.

Cheever. I think it be my duty, sir—(*kindly, to* Proctor) You'll not deny it, John. (*to* Danforth) When we come to take his wife, he damned the court and ripped your warrant.

Parris. Now you have it!

Danforth. He did that, Mr. Hale?

Hale (*takes a breath*). Aye, he did.

Proctor. It were a temper, sir. I knew not what I did.

210 **Danforth** (*studying him*). Mr. Proctor.

Proctor. Aye, sir.

Danforth (*straight into his eyes*). Have you ever seen the Devil?

Proctor. No, sir.

Danforth. You are in all respects a Gospel Christian?

Proctor. I am, sir.

Parris. Such a Christian that will not come to church but once in a month!

Danforth (*restrained—he is curious*). Not come to
220 church?

Proctor. I—I have no love for Mr. Parris. It is no secret. But God I surely love.

Cheever. He plow on Sunday, sir.

Danforth. Plow on Sunday!

Cheever (*apologetically*). I think it be evidence, John. I am an official of the court, I cannot keep it.

Proctor. I—I have once or twice plowed on Sunday. I have three children, sir, and until last year my land give little.

230 **Giles.** You'll find other Christians that do plow on Sunday if the truth be known.

Hale. Your Honor, I cannot think you may judge the man on such evidence.

Danforth. I judge nothing. (*Pause. He keeps watching* Proctor, *who tries to meet his gaze.*) I tell you straight, Mister—I have seen marvels in this court. I have seen people choked before my eyes by spirits; I have seen them stuck by pins and slashed by daggers. I have until this moment not the slightest reason to
240 suspect that the children may be deceiving me. Do you understand my meaning?

Proctor. Excellency, does it not strike upon you that so many of these women have lived so long with such upright reputation, and—

Parris. Do you read the Gospel, Mr. Proctor?

Proctor. I read the Gospel.

Parris. I think not, or you should surely know that Cain were an upright man, and yet he did kill Abel.[4]

Proctor. Aye, God tells us that. (*to* Danforth) But
250 who tells us Rebecca Nurse murdered seven babies by sending out her spirit on them? It is the children only, and this one will swear she lied to you.

(Danforth *considers, then beckons* Hathorne *to him.* Hathorne *leans in, and he speaks in his ear.* Hathorne *nods.*)

---

4. **Cain...Abel:** According to the Book of Genesis in the Bible, Cain and Abel were the sons of Adam and Eve, the first humans.

DIFFERENTIATED INSTRUCTION

FOR STRUGGLING READERS

Concept Support Discuss the stage directions that describe Cheever in lines 199, 202, and 225: He is "awakening" as he addresses Danforth, and he speaks "kindly" and "apologetically" to Proctor as he gives evidence against him. Explain that it is difficult to understand Cheever's actions: He sounds sympathetic to Proctor, yet he says things that could be very damaging to Proctor. Invite students to offer their impressions of Cheever.

FOR ENGLISH LANGUAGE LEARNERS

Language: Pronoun Referents Explain that there are two different referents for the pronoun *it* in lines 225–226: "I think *it* [the fact that Proctor plowed on Sunday] be evidence, John. I am an official of the court, I cannot keep *it* [the evidence]." Then have students work in mixed-language groups to identify referents for the pronoun *it* in lines 202–209 and the pronoun *they* in lines 309–313.

Hathorne. Aye, she's the one.

Danforth. Mr. Proctor, this morning, your wife send me a claim in which she states that she is pregnant now.

260 **Proctor.** My wife pregnant!

Danforth. There be no sign of it—we have examined her body.

Proctor. But if she say she is pregnant, then she must be! That woman will never lie, Mr. Danforth.

Danforth. She will not?

Proctor. Never, sir, never.

Danforth. We have thought it too convenient to be credited. However, if I should tell you now that I will let her be kept another month; and if she begin to 270 show her natural signs, you shall have her living yet another year until she is delivered—what say you to that? (*John Proctor is struck silent.*) Come now. You say your only purpose is to save your wife. Good, then, she is saved at least this year, and a year is long. What say you, sir? It is done now. (*In conflict,* Proctor *glances at* Francis *and* Giles.) Will you drop this charge?

Proctor. I—I think I cannot.

Danforth (*now an almost imperceptible hardness in his voice*). Then your purpose is somewhat larger.

280 **Parris.** He's come to overthrow this court, Your Honor!

Proctor. These are my friends. Their wives are also accused—

Danforth (*with a sudden briskness of manner*). I judge you not, sir. I am ready to hear your evidence.

Proctor. I come not to hurt the court; I only—

Danforth (*cutting him off*). Marshal, go into the court and bid Judge Stoughton and Judge Sewall declare recess for one hour. And let them go to the tavern, if they will. All witnesses and prisoners are 290 to be kept in the building.

Herrick. Aye, sir. (*very deferentially*) If I may say it, sir, I know this man all my life. It is a good man, sir.

Danforth (*It is the reflection on himself he resents*). I am sure of it, Marshal. (Herrick *nods, then goes out.*) Now, what deposition do you have for us, Mr. Proctor? And I beg you be clear, open as the sky, and honest.

Proctor (*as he takes out several papers*). I am no lawyer, so I'll—

Danforth. The pure in heart need no lawyers. 300 Proceed as you will.

Proctor (*handing* Danforth *a paper*). Will you read this first, sir? It's a sort of testament. The people signing it declare their good opinion of Rebecca, and my wife, and Martha Corey. (Danforth *looks down at the paper.*)

Parris (*to enlist* Danforth's *sarcasm*). Their good opinion! (*But* Danforth *goes on reading, and* Proctor *is heartened.*)

Proctor. These are all landholding farmers, mem-310 bers of the church. (*delicately, trying to point out a paragraph*) If you'll notice, sir—they've known the women many years and never saw no sign they had dealings with the Devil.

(Parris *nervously moves over and reads over* Danforth's *shoulder.*)

Danforth (*glancing down a long list*). How many names are here?

Francis. Ninety-one, Your Excellency.

Parris (*sweating*). These people should be sum-320 moned. (Danforth *looks up at him questioningly.*) For questioning.

Francis (*trembling with anger*). Mr. Danforth, I gave them all my word no harm would come to them for signing this.

Parris. This is a clear attack upon the court!

Hale (*to* Parris, *trying to contain himself*). Is every defense an attack upon the court? Can no one—?

Parris. All innocent and Christian people are happy for the courts in Salem! These people are gloomy for 330 it. (*to* Danforth *directly*) And I think you will want to know, from each and every one of them, what discontents them with you!

Hathorne. I think they ought to be examined, sir.

FOR STRUGGLING READERS

② Targeted Passage [Lines 265–279]

This passage focuses on Proctor's true reasons for coming before the court.

- What offer does Danforth make to Proctor regarding Elizabeth's freedom? (lines 268–272)
- How does Proctor respond? (line 272)
- Why does Proctor choose not to drop his charges against Abigail and the other girls? (lines 276–277)

- How does his refusal affect Elizabeth? (lines 278–279)

FOR ADVANCED LEARNERS/AP

Analyze Dialogue Invite students to think about Hale's question in lines 326–327: "Is every defense an attack upon the court?" Discuss what might happen to a nation—to a government and to its citizens—when the answer to Hale's question is "yes." Have students work in groups to discuss modern cases, drawn from history or personal experience, in which criticism of power has proven dangerous.

REVISIT THE BIG QUESTION
What fuels a MOB?

Discuss After students read lines 309–333, ask the following question: How do Parris and Hathorne respond when they see the petition presented in support of Elizabeth, Martha, and Rebecca? How does their response contribute to the hysteria sweeping through Salem and nearby communities? *Possible answer: Parris and Hathorne respond by insisting that everyone who signed the petition be summoned before the court and examined (lines 319–321 and 333). Their response contributes to the hysteria because it shows that even the judges are acting upon illogical personal opinions by wanting to bring before the court everyone with an unpopular opinion. As Reverend Hale protests, "Is every defense an attack upon the court?" (lines 326–327).*

What fuels a MOB?

Discuss In lines 336–354, how does Danforth try to keep potential hysteria under control? Do you think that he will succeed? Why or why not? *Possible answer: Danforth tries to control potential hysteria by speaking calm, reassuring words to Francis (lines 336–337, 344–345, and 351–353). As long as he is dealing with Salemites on an individual basis, Danforth may succeed. In this passage, however, he also calls for 91 more people to be brought into court to testify (lines 337–339); and the more people who are added to the highly emotional proceedings, the greater the chance that hysteria will spread.*

GRAMMAR AND STYLE

COMMON CORE L 3a

Use Realistic Dialogue Reread lines 395–401. How does Miller make Danforth's words sound as though they actually might have been spoken in the late 17th century? *Possible answer: Miller chooses era-specific terms (such as "cry witchery," line 397) and an inverted sentence ("What say you to that," line 401) to make this dialogue realistic.*

Danforth. It is not necessarily an attack, I think. Yet—

Francis. These are all covenanted Christians, sir.

Danforth. Then I am sure they may have nothing to fear. (*hands* Cheever *the paper*) Mr. Cheever, have warrants drawn for all of these—arrest for examina-

340 tion. (*to* Proctor) Now, Mister, what other informa- tion do you have for us? (Francis *is still standing, horrified.*) You may sit, Mr. Nurse.

Francis. I have brought trouble on these people; I have—

Danforth. No, old man, you have not hurt these people if they are of good conscience. But you must understand, sir, that a person is either with this court or he must be counted against it, there be no road between. This is a sharp time, now, a precise time—we live no longer in the dusky afternoon

350 when evil mixed itself with good and befuddled the world. Now, by God's grace, the shining sun is up, and them that fear not light will surely praise it. I hope you will be one of those. (Mary Warren *suddenly sobs.*) She's not hearty,[5] I see.

Proctor. No, she's not, sir. (*to* Mary, *bending to her, holding her hand, quietly*) Now remember what the angel Raphael said to the boy Tobias.[6] Remember it.

Mary Warren (*hardly audible*). Aye.

Proctor. "Do that which is good, and no harm shall

360 come to thee."

Mary Warren. Aye.

Danforth. Come, man, we wait you.

(Marshal Herrick *returns, and takes his post at the door.*)

Giles. John, my deposition, give him mine.

Proctor. Aye. (*He hands* Danforth *another paper.*) This is Mr. Corey's deposition.

Danforth. Oh? (*He looks down at it. Now* Hathorne *comes behind him and reads with him.*)

Hathorne (*suspiciously*). What lawyer drew this,

370 Corey?

Giles. You know I never hired a lawyer in my life, Hathorne.

Danforth (*finishing the reading*). It is very well phrased. My compliments. Mr. Parris, if Mr. Putnam is in the court, will you bring him in? (Hathorne *takes the deposition, and walks to the window with it.* Parris *goes into the court.*) You have no legal training, Mr. Corey?

Giles (*very pleased*). I have the best, sir—I am thirty-

380 three time in court in my life. And always plaintiff, too.

Danforth. Oh, then you're much put-upon.

Giles. I am never put-upon; I know my rights, sir, and I will have them. You know, your father tried a case of mine—might be thirty-five year ago, I think.

Danforth. Indeed.

Giles. He never spoke to you of it?

Danforth. No, I cannot recall it.

Giles. That's strange, he give me nine pound dam-

390 ages. He were a fair judge, your father. Y'see, I had a white mare that time, and this fellow come to bor- row the mare—(*Enter* Parris *with* Thomas Putnam. *When he sees* Putnam, Giles' *ease goes; he is hard.*) Aye, there he is.

Danforth. Mr. Putnam, I have here an accusation by Mr. Corey against you. He states that you coldly prompted your daughter to cry witchery upon George Jacobs that is now in jail.

Putnam. It is a lie.

400 **Danforth** (*turning to* Giles). Mr. Putnam states your charge is a lie. What say you to that?

Giles (*furious, his fists clenched*). A fart on Thomas Putnam, that is what I say to that!

Danforth. What proof do you submit for your charge, sir?

Giles. My proof is there! (*pointing to the paper*) If Jacobs hangs for a witch he forfeit up his property— that's law! And there is none but Putnam with the

---

5. **hearty:** well.

6. **what the angel Raphael said ... Tobias:** In the Book of Tobit in the Apocrypha, Tobit's son Tobias cured his father's blindness with the help of the angel Raphael.

DIFFERENTIATED INSTRUCTION

FOR STRUGGLING READERS

Vocabulary Support Discuss these terms, pointing out that some words have other meanings in other contexts:

- *drew* (line 369), "prepared"
- *plaintiff* (line 380), "person who brings a case before a court of law"
- *put-upon* (line 382), "victimized"
- *tried a case* (lines 384–385), "presided over and made a judgment about a court case"
- *ease* (line 393), "relaxed attitude"

FOR ADVANCED LEARNERS/AP

Debate a Viewpoint Ask students to reread lines 344–354, especially Danforth's claim that "a person is either with this court or he must be counted against it." Divide students into two groups to debate Danforth's "all or nothing" philosophy. One side should support Danforth and the other should disagree with him, but each side should offer clear reasons to support its position.

coin to buy so great a piece. This man is killing his
410 neighbors for their land!

Danforth. But proof, sir, proof.

Giles (*pointing at his deposition*). The proof is there! I have it from an honest man who heard Putnam say it! The day his daughter cried out on Jacobs, he said she'd given him a fair gift of land.

Hathorne. And the name of this man?

Giles (*taken aback*). What name?

Hathorne. The man that give you this information.

Giles (*hesitates, then*). Why, I—I cannot give you his
420 name.

Hathorne. And why not?

Giles (*hesitates, then bursts out*). You know well why not! He'll lay in jail if I give his name!

Hathorne. This is contempt of the court, Mr. Danforth!

Danforth (*to avoid that*). You will surely tell us the name.

Giles. I will not give you no name. I mentioned my wife's name once and I'll burn in hell long enough
430 for that. I stand mute.

Danforth. In that case, I have no choice but to arrest you for contempt of this court, do you know that?

Giles. This is a hearing; you cannot clap me for contempt of a hearing.

Danforth. Oh, it is a proper lawyer![7] Do you wish me to declare the court in full session here? Or will you give me good reply?

Giles (*faltering*). I cannot give you no name, sir, I cannot.

440 **Danforth.** You are a foolish old man. Mr. Cheever, begin the record. The court is now in session. I ask you, Mr. Corey—

Proctor (*breaking in*). Your Honor—he has the story in confidence, sir, and he—

Parris. The Devil lives on such confidences! (*to Danforth*) Without confidences there could be no conspiracy, Your Honor!

Hathorne. I think it must be broken, sir.

Danforth (*to Giles*). Old man, if your informant tells
450 the truth let him come here openly like a decent man. But if he hide in anonymity I must know why. Now sir, the government and central church demand of you the name of him who reported Mr. Thomas Putnam a common murderer.

Hale. Excellency—

Danforth. Mr. Hale.

Hale. We cannot blink it more. There is a prodigious fear of this court in the country—

Danforth. Then there is a prodigious guilt in the
460 country. Are *you* afraid to be questioned here?

Hale. I may only fear the Lord, sir, but there is fear in the country nevertheless.

Danforth (*angered now*). Reproach me not with the fear in the country; there is fear in the country because there is a moving[8] plot to topple Christ in the country!

Hale. But it does not follow that everyone accused is part of it.

Danforth. No uncorrupted man may fear this court,
470 Mr. Hale! None! (*to Giles*) You are under arrest in contempt of this court. Now sit you down and take counsel with yourself, or you will be set in the jail until you decide to answer all questions.

(Giles Corey *makes a rush for* Putnam. Proctor *lunges and holds him.*)

Proctor. No, Giles!

Giles (*over* Proctor's *shoulder at* Putnam). I'll cut your throat, Putnam, I'll kill you yet!

Proctor (*forcing him into a chair*). Peace, Giles,
480 peace. (*releasing him*) We'll prove ourselves. Now we will. (*He starts to turn to* Danforth.)

---

7. **Oh . . . lawyer:** Oh, he thinks he is a real lawyer.

8. **moving:** active.

READING SKILL COMMON CORE RL 1 RL 3

■ *Model the Skill:* **DRAW CONCLUSIONS ABOUT CHARACTERS**

Read aloud lines 438–442. Then lead students in a discussion of what they already know about Giles's character and actions. Then ask: What conclusion can you draw from Giles's refusal to name the man who has implicated Putnam? *Possible answer: The reader can conclude that Giles is an honorable person who will not betray a confidence, even though he himself will suffer for his silence.*

Extend the Discussion Do you agree with Danforth's assessment that Giles is "a foolish old man" (line 440)? Why or why not?

REVISIT THE BIG QUESTION

What fuels a MOB?

Discuss In lines 463–466, Danforth's references to "fear in the country" indicate that he recognizes the spreading hysteria in the community. What does he think is the cause of that fear? *Possible answer: Danforth thinks that the fear is an emotional response to either a recognized or an instinctive fear that there is a plot to undermine Christianity in the community.* Consider what else has been said in the dialogue on this page. Do you think that Danforth is correct? Why or why not? *Possible answer: Danforth probably is not correct. It may be more likely that the cause of the hysteria is fear over the way that some people are taking advantage of the situation to ruin their neighbors' reputations and take their possessions.*

FOR STRUGGLING READERS

Explore Plot and Character Development
Have students reread lines 457–470.

- Point out that this scene is a key moment in the development of the plot. Help students summarize Hale's opinion of the court and Danforth's defense of it.

- Explain that this scene also contributes to character development. Help students identify the crucial shift in Hale's position. Also discuss what Danforth's angry words reveal about his own position.

FOR ADVANCED LEARNERS/AP

Synthesize Encourage students to reflect upon Giles's responses to Danforth in lines 411–430. Then ask them to write a brief paragraph explaining how this scene connects to the themes of *The Crucible* and to Miller's own views. Students may choose to reread the mini-essays found earlier in the play or to do brief research online for more information about Miller's views on and experiences of McCarthyism.

Giles. Say nothin' more, John. (*pointing at* Danforth) He's only playin' you! He means to hang us all!

(Mary Warren *bursts into sobs.*)

Danforth. This is a court of law, Mister. I'll have no **effrontery** here!

Proctor. Forgive him, sir, for his old age. Peace, Giles, we'll prove it all now. (*He lifts up* Mary's *chin.*) You cannot weep, Mary. Remember the angel, what he say
490 to the boy. Hold to it, now; there is your rock. (Mary *quiets. He takes out a paper, and turns to* Danforth.) This is Mary Warren's deposition. I—I would ask you remember, sir, while you read it, that until two week ago she were no different than the other children are today. (*He is speaking reasonably, restraining all his fears, his anger, his anxiety.*) You saw her scream, she howled, she swore familiar spirits choked her; she even testified that Satan, in the form of women now in jail, tried to win her soul away, and then when she refused—

500 **Danforth.** We know all this.

Proctor. Aye, sir. She swears now that she never saw Satan; nor any spirit, vague or clear, that Satan may have sent to hurt her. And she declares her friends are lying now.

(Proctor *starts to hand* Danforth *the deposition, and* Hale *comes up to* Danforth *in a trembling state.*)

Hale. Excellency, a moment. I think this goes to the heart of the matter.

Danforth (*with deep misgivings*). It surely does.

510 **Hale.** I cannot say he is an honest man; I know him little. But in all justice, sir, a claim so weighty cannot be argued by a farmer. In God's name, sir, stop here; send him home and let him come again with a lawyer—

Danforth (*patiently*). Now look you, Mr. Hale—

Hale. Excellency, I have signed seventy-two death warrants; I am a minister of the Lord, and I dare not take a life without there be a proof so **immaculate** no slightest qualm of conscience may doubt it.

---

520 **Danforth.** Mr. Hale, you surely do not doubt my justice.

Hale. I have this morning signed away the soul of Rebecca Nurse, Your Honor. I'll not conceal it, my hand shakes yet as with a wound! I pray you, sir, this argument let lawyers present to you.

Danforth. Mr. Hale, believe me; for a man of such terrible learning you are most bewildered—I hope you will forgive me. I have been thirty-two year at the bar, sir, and I should be confounded were I
530 called upon to defend these people. Let you consider, now—(*to* Proctor *and the others*) And I bid you all do likewise. In an ordinary crime, how does one defend the accused? One calls up witnesses to prove his innocence. But witchcraft is *ipso facto,*[9] on its face and by its nature, an invisible crime, is it not? Therefore, who may possibly be witness to it? The witch and the victim. None other. Now we cannot hope the witch will accuse herself; granted? Therefore, we must rely upon her victims—and they do testify, the
540 children certainly do testify. As for the witches, none will deny that we are most eager for all their confessions. Therefore, what is left for a lawyer to bring out? I think I have made my point. Have I not?

Hale. But this child claims the girls are not truthful, and if they are not—

Danforth. That is precisely what I am about to consider, sir. What more may you ask of me? Unless you doubt my probity?[10]

Hale (*defeated*). I surely do not, sir. Let you consider
550 it, then.

Danforth. And let you put your heart to rest. Her deposition, Mr. Proctor.

(Proctor *hands it to him.* Hathorne *rises, goes beside* Danforth, *and starts reading.* Parris *comes to his other side.* Danforth *looks at* John Proctor, *then proceeds to read.* Hale *gets up, finds position near the judge, reads too.* Proctor *glances at* Giles. Francis *prays silently, hands pressed together.* Cheever *waits placidly, the*

---

9. **ipso facto** *Latin:* by that very fact.
10. **doubt my probity:** question my integrity.

Use these prompts to help students explore Hale's thoughts and feelings as revealed in lines 501–525:

Connect Have you ever tried to help someone who was unknowingly heading toward danger? What was that experience like, and what challenges did you face? *Accept all thoughtful responses that apply to Hale's situation.*

Analyze What will it mean if Proctor is right about Abigail and the other girls? Why does Hale want Proctor to hire a lawyer to make his case? *Possible answer: If Proctor is right, then innocent people have been sentenced to die. Hale wants Proctor to hire a lawyer because such a charge is a matter of life or death—for the accused and perhaps even for Proctor. Hale is concerned that "a farmer" will not have the skill to present "a claim so weighty" (lines 511–512).*

Evaluate How well does Miller convey the intensity of Hale's feelings in this scene? Cite evidence. *Possible answer: Miller successfully conveys Hale's concern. Hale comes forth "in a trembling state" (line 506), and he implores Danforth to stop the proceedings "in God's name" (line 512). After signing Rebecca Nurse's death warrant, his "hand shakes yet as with a wound" (line 524) because he realizes the seriousness of the situation—and perhaps because he suspects that Proctor may be right.*

DIFFERENTIATED INSTRUCTION

FOR STRUGGLING READERS

③ Targeted Passage [Lines 526–543]

This passage presents the philosophy that allows the witch hunt to continue unchecked.

- What does Danforth think of Hale's request for more caution from the court? (lines 526–528)

- How are the accused supposed to defend themselves against charges of witchcraft? (lines 534–542)

- Why does Danforth think that there is no need for Proctor to enlist a lawyer's help? (lines 542–543)

sublime official, dutiful. Mary Warren sobs once.

560 John Proctor *touches her head reassuringly. Presently* Danforth *lifts his eyes, stands up, takes out a kerchief and blows his nose. The others stand aside as he moves in thought toward the window.*)

Parris (*hardly able to contain his anger and fear*). I should like to question—

Danforth (*his first real outburst, in which his contempt for* Parris *is clear*). Mr. Parris, I bid you be silent! (*He stands in silence, looking out the window. Now, having established that he will set the gait.*) Mr. Cheever, will 570 you go into the court and bring the children here? (Cheever *gets up and goes out upstage.* Danforth *now turns to* Mary.) Mary Warren, how came you to this turnabout? Has Mr. Proctor threatened you for this deposition?

Mary Warren. No, sir.

Danforth. Has he ever threatened you?

Mary Warren (*weaker*). No, sir.

Danforth (*sensing a weakening*). Has he threatened you?

580 **Mary Warren.** No, sir.

Danforth. Then you tell me that you sat in my court, callously lying, when you knew that people would hang by your evidence? (*She does not answer.*) Answer me!

Mary Warren (*almost inaudibly*). I did, sir.

Danforth. How were you instructed in your life? Do you not know that God damns all liars? (*She cannot speak.*) Or is it now that you lie?

Judge Danforth questioning Mary Warren

READING SKILL COMMON CORE RL 1 RL 3

■ DRAW CONCLUSIONS ABOUT CHARACTERS

As you read this page, pay attention to Danforth's dialogue and the description of his demeanor. What traits describing Danforth can you add to the prereading chart from page 135? Be sure to include evidence supporting your response.
Possible answer: Danforth is powerful and controlling. He takes charge of the situation, angrily overruling Parris (lines 567–570), and he is aggressive in his interrogation of Mary Warren (lines 576–588).

IF STUDENTS NEED HELP . . . Point out the term *set the gait* in the stage directions (line 569). Explain that the term usually refers to riding a horse. A rider who "sets the gait," or pace, at which the horse moves is controlling the movement of the animal. Discuss how the dialogue on this page illustrates what this phrase means when it is applied to Danforth.

FOR ENGLISH LANGUAGE LEARNERS

Vocabulary Support Help students use context clues to determine the meanings of these phrases:

- *Hold to* (line 490), "Remember"
- *goes to the heart of the matter* (lines 507–508), "addresses the most important point"
- *put your heart to rest* (line 551), "be calm and unworried"

- *It does not escape me* (lines 616–617), "I am not forgetting"
- *search your heart* (line 782), "think about this very carefully"
- *put her out* (line 858), "dismissed her"
- *struck me true/struck me false* (lines 969 and 975), "impressed me as being a truthful person"/"impressed me as being a liar"

FOR ADVANCED LEARNERS/AP

Synthesize a Narrative Have students examine the photograph and then write a first-person narrative from the point of view of one of the girls watching Judge Danforth and Mary Warren. Urge them to use details from the text as well as what they already have learned about Danforth and Mary. Also challenge students to write in a style that mimics Miller's representation of Puritan speech. Call on volunteers to read their finished narratives aloud to the class.

Mary Warren. No, sir—I am with God now.

590 **Danforth.** You are with God now.

Mary Warren. Aye, sir.

Danforth (*containing himself*). I will tell you this—you are either lying now, or you were lying in the court, and in either case you have committed perjury and you will go to jail for it. You cannot lightly say you lied, Mary. Do you know that?

Mary Warren. I cannot lie no more. I am with God, I am with God.

(*But she breaks into sobs at the thought of it, and the* 600 *right door opens, and enter* Susanna Walcott, Mercy Lewis, Betty Parris, *and finally* Abigail. Cheever *comes to* Danforth.)

Cheever. Ruth Putnam's not in the court, sir, nor the other children.

Danforth. These will be sufficient. Sit you down, children. (*Silently they sit.*) Your friend, Mary Warren, has given us a deposition. In which she swears that she never saw familiar spirits, apparitions, nor any manifest of the Devil. She claims as well that 610 none of you have seen these things either. (*slight pause*) Now, children, this is a court of law. The law, based upon the Bible, and the Bible, writ by Almighty God, forbid the practice of witchcraft, and describe death as the penalty thereof. But likewise, children, the law and Bible damn all bearers of false witness. (*slight pause*) Now then. It does not escape me that this deposition may be devised to blind us; it may well be that Mary Warren has been conquered by Satan, who sends her here to distract our 620 sacred purpose. If so, her neck will break for it. But if she speak true, I bid you now drop your guile and confess your pretense, for a quick confession will go easier with you. (*pause*) Abigail Williams, rise. (Abigail *slowly rises.*) Is there any truth in this?

Abigail. No, sir.

Danforth (*thinks, glances at* Mary, *then back to* Abigail). Children, a very auger bit[11] will now be

turned into your souls until your honesty is proved. Will either of you change your positions now, or do 630 you force me to hard questioning?

Abigail. I have naught to change, sir. She lies.

Danforth (*to* Mary). You would still go on with this?

Mary Warren (*faintly*). Aye, sir.

Danforth (*turning to* Abigail). A poppet were discovered in Mr. Proctor's house, stabbed by a needle. Mary Warren claims that you sat beside her in the court when she made it, and that you saw her make it and witnessed how she herself stuck her needle into it for safe-keeping. What say you to that?

640 **Abigail** (*with a slight note of indignation*). It is a lie, sir.

Danforth (*after a slight pause*). While you worked for Mr. Proctor, did you see poppets in that house?

Abigail. Goody Proctor always kept poppets.

Proctor. Your Honor, my wife never kept no poppets. Mary Warren confesses it was her poppet.

Cheever. Your Excellency.

Danforth. Mr. Cheever.

Cheever. When I spoke with Goody Proctor in that 650 house, she said she never kept no poppets. But she said she did keep poppets when she were a girl.

Proctor. She has not been a girl these fifteen years, Your Honor.

Hathorne. But a poppet will keep fifteen years, will it not?

Proctor. It will keep if it is kept, but Mary Warren swears she never saw no poppets in my house, nor anyone else.

Parris. Why could there not have been poppets hid 660 where no one ever saw them?

Proctor (*furious*). There might also be a dragon with five legs in my house, but no one has ever seen it.

Parris. We are here, Your Honor, precisely to discover what no one has ever seen.

---

11. **auger** (ô'gər) **bit:** drill.

REVISIT THE BIG QUESTION

What fuels a MOB?

Discuss As Danforth speaks to the other girls in lines 605–630, how does he try to urge them away from speaking and acting in response to hysteria? *Possible answer: Danforth warns the girls to think carefully about what they have said. He urges them not to focus upon their feelings or imagination but to remember the facts—namely, that the charge of witchcraft could result in people's deaths (lines 618–620) and that the Bible condemns liars (lines 615–616).*

TEXT ANALYSIS

COMMON CORE

● **CONVENTIONS OF DRAMA**

RL 3
RL 5

Review lines 632–662. How would you describe the atmosphere that Miller creates in this scene through his use of dialogue? Why is Proctor eventually "furious" (line 661)? *Possible answer: Miller creates an atmosphere of barely controlled chaos by having many characters speak in rapid order. (Seven characters either make accusations or give evidence.) This confusion allows logic and truth to be twisted, and Proctor becomes furious as he sees an irrational argument against Elizabeth develop.*

DIFFERENTIATED INSTRUCTION

FOR ENGLISH LANGUAGE LEARNERS
Related Vocabulary Danforth's speech to the children sets up the crucial battle that pits Mary and Proctor against Abigail and her supporters (the girls, Hathorne, and Parris). To ensure that students understand Danforth's difficult vocabulary and syntax, teach these related terms:

• *the penalty thereof* (line 614), "the punishment for that offense"

• *bearers of false witness* (lines 615–616), "liars"

• *devised to blind us* (lines 617–618), "created to fool us"

• *distract our sacred purpose* (lines 619–620), "make us forget that we are doing God's work"

• *guile* (line 621), "trickery"

• *pretense* (line 622), "deception"

Proctor. Mr. Danforth, what profit this girl to turn herself about? What may Mary Warren gain but hard questioning and worse?

Danforth. You are charging Abigail Williams with a marvelous cool plot to murder, do you understand
670 that?

Proctor. I do, sir. I believe she means to murder.

Danforth (*pointing at* Abigail, *incredulously*). This child would murder your wife?

Proctor. It is not a child. Now hear me, sir. In the sight of the congregation she were twice this year put out of this meetin' house for laughter during prayer.

Danforth (*shocked, turning to* Abigail). What's this? Laughter during—!

Parris. Excellency, she were under Tituba's power at
680 that time, but she is solemn now.

Giles. Aye, now she is solemn and goes to hang people!

Danforth. Quiet, man.

Hathorne. Surely it have no bearing on the question, sir. He charges contemplation of murder.

Danforth. Aye. (*He studies* Abigail *for a moment, then.*) Continue, Mr. Proctor.

Proctor. Mary. Now tell the Governor how you danced in the woods.

Parris (*instantly*). Excellency, since I come to Salem
690 this man is blackening my name. He—

Danforth. In a moment, sir. (*to* Mary Warren, *sternly, and surprised*) What is this dancing?

Mary Warren. I—(*She glances at* Abigail, *who is staring down at her remorselessly. Then, appealing to* Proctor.) Mr. Proctor—

Proctor (*taking it right up*). Abigail leads the girls to the woods, Your Honor, and they have danced there naked—

Parris. Your Honor, this—

700 **Proctor** (*at once*). Mr. Parris discovered them himself in the dead of night! There's the "child" she is!

Danforth (*It is growing into a nightmare, and he turns, astonished, to* Parris). Mr. Parris—

Parris. I can only say, sir, that I never found any of them naked, and this man is—

Danforth. But you discovered them dancing in the woods? (*Eyes on* Parris, *he points at* Abigail.) Abigail?

Hale. Excellency, when I first arrived from Beverly, Mr. Parris told me that.

710 **Danforth.** Do you deny it, Mr. Parris?

Parris. I do not, sir, but I never saw any of them naked.

Danforth. But she have *danced*?

Parris (*unwillingly*). Aye, sir.

(Danforth, *as though with new eyes, looks at* Abigail.)

Hathorne. Excellency, will you permit me? (*He points at* Mary Warren.)

Danforth (*with great worry*). Pray, proceed.

Hathorne. You say you never saw no spirits, Mary,
720 were never threatened or afflicted by any manifest of the Devil or the Devil's agents.

Mary Warren (*very faintly*). No, sir.

Hathorne (*with a gleam of victory*). And yet, when people accused of witchery confronted you in court, you would faint, saying their spirits came out of their bodies and choked you—

Mary Warren. That were pretense, sir.

Danforth. I cannot hear you.

Mary Warren. Pretense, sir.

730 **Parris.** But you did turn cold, did you not? I myself picked you up many times, and your skin were icy. Mr. Danforth, you—

Danforth. I saw that many times.

Proctor. She only pretended to faint, Your Excellency. They're all marvelous pretenders.

Hathorne. Then can she pretend to faint now?

Proctor. Now?

READING SKILL   COMMON CORE   RL 1   RL 3

■ DRAW CONCLUSIONS ABOUT CHARACTERS

Hathorne looks at Mary Warren "with a gleam of victory" (line 723) during his interview with her. Why does Hathorne respond to her in this way? What do his feelings of "victory" reveal about him? ***Possible answer:*** *Hathorne responds "with a gleam of victory" because he thinks that he has caught her in a lie: He reminds her that she used to faint when she pretended to see spirits. His "gleam of victory" may indicate that he enjoys manipulating people.*

Extend the Discussion Why would Hathorne be so committed to taking the side of Abigail and the other girls? What does your answer say about his ability to serve as a judge in this case?

FOR ENGLISH LANGUAGE LEARNERS

Vocabulary: Multiple-Meaning Words

Explain that some words have multiple meanings. Point out that *keep* means "to retain possession of" in line 651 but also can mean "to stay in good condition." Have Jigsaw groups of mixed language ability investigate the multiple meanings of *keep* or *kept* in lines 651, 654, and 656 and then report their findings.

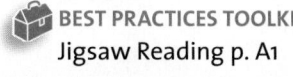 **BEST PRACTICES TOOLKIT**
Jigsaw Reading p. A1

Use these prompts to help students understand Mary Warren's dilemma in lines 738–759:

Connect Have you ever failed to do something when the need arose—something that you had done before or that you were sure you could do? How does that experience help you understand Mary Warren's position in front of the judges? *Accept all responses that relate to Mary's anxiety and confusion when she can't faint on cue.*

Analyze Why is Mary unable to faint when Parris asks her to do so? *Possible answer: She says that she has "no sense of it now" (line 750); she searches "for the emotion of it" (line 758) but cannot find it. Mary's earlier fake fainting spells were induced by the emotion of the others.*

Synthesize Consider what you have learned about Mary Warren up to this point. Why is placing great importance upon her testimony an effective way of creating suspense? *Possible answer: The method of creating suspense is effective because the reader knows that Mary is an unstable character and may not be confident enough to stand by her confession.*

Parris. Why not? Now there are no spirits attacking her, for none in this room is accused of witchcraft. 740 So let her turn herself cold now, let her pretend she is attacked now, let her faint. (*He turns to* Mary Warren.) Faint!

Mary Warren. Faint?

Parris. Aye, faint. Prove to us how you pretended in the court so many times.

Mary Warren (*looking to* Proctor). I—cannot faint now, sir.

Proctor (*alarmed, quietly*). Can you not pretend it?

Mary Warren. I—(*She looks about as though searching* 750 *for the passion to faint.*) I—have no *sense* of it now, I—

Danforth. Why? What is lacking now?

Mary Warren. I—cannot tell, sir, I—

Danforth. Might it be that here we have no afflicting spirit loose, but in the court there were some?

Mary Warren. I never saw no spirits.

Parris. Then see no spirits now, and prove to us that you can faint by your own will, as you claim.

Mary Warren (*stares, searching for the emotion of it, and then shakes her head*). I—cannot do it.

760 **Parris.** Then you will confess, will you not? It were attacking spirits made you faint!

Mary Warren. No, sir, I—

Parris. Your Excellency, this is a trick to blind the court!

Mary Warren. It's not a trick! (*She stands.*) I—I used to faint because I—I thought I saw spirits.

Danforth. *Thought* you saw them!

Mary Warren. But I did not, Your Honor.

Hathorne. How could you think you saw them 770 unless you saw them?

Mary Warren. I—I cannot tell how, but I did. I—I heard the other girls screaming, and you, Your Honor, you seemed to believe them, and I—It were only sport in the beginning, sir, but then the whole world cried spirits, spirits, and I—I promise you, Mr. Danforth, I only thought I saw them but I did not. (Danforth *peers at her.*)

Parris (*smiling, but nervous because* Danforth *seems to be struck by* Mary Warren's *story*). Surely Your Excel- 780 lency is not taken by this simple lie.

Danforth (*turning worriedly to* Abigail). Abigail. I bid you now search your heart and tell me this—and beware of it, child, to God every soul is precious and His vengeance is terrible on them that take life without cause. Is it possible, child, that the spirits you have seen are illusion only, some deception that may cross your mind when—

Abigail. Why, this—this—is a base question, sir.

Danforth. Child, I would have you consider it—

790 **Abigail.** I have been hurt, Mr. Danforth; I have seen my blood runnin' out! I have been near to murdered every day because I done my duty pointing out the Devil's people—and this is my reward? To be mistrusted, denied, questioned like a—

Danforth (*weakening*). Child, I do not mistrust you—

Abigail (*in an open threat*). Let *you* beware, Mr. Danforth. Think you to be so mighty that the power of Hell may not turn *your* wits? Beware of it! There is—(*Suddenly, from an accusatory attitude, her face* 800 *turns, looking into the air above—it is truly frightened.*)

Danforth (*apprehensively*). What is it, child?

Abigail (*looking about in the air, clasping her arms about her as though cold*). I—I know not. A wind, a cold wind, has come. (*Her eyes fall on* Mary Warren.)

Mary Warren (*terrified, pleading*). Abby!

Mercy Lewis (*shivering*). Your Honor, I freeze!

Proctor. They're pretending!

Hathorne (*touching* Abigail's *hand*). She is cold, Your Honor, touch her!

810 **Mercy Lewis** (*through chattering teeth*). Mary, do you send this shadow on me?

DIFFERENTIATED INSTRUCTION

FOR ADVANCED LEARNERS/AP

Analyze Motivation Point out that Abigail dramatically shifts attention away from herself in lines 796–805. Have students discuss these questions:

• What techniques does Abigail use to redirect the attention of the court?

• Why does she deflect interest in herself?

Have students write a brief paragraph analyzing Abigail's motives and share their responses with the class.

Mary Warren. Lord, save me!

Susanna Walcott. I freeze, I freeze!

Abigail (*shivering visibly*). It is a wind, a wind!

Mary Warren. Abby, don't do that!

Danforth (*himself engaged and entered by* Abigail). Mary Warren, do you witch her? I say to you, do you send your spirit out?

(*With a hysterical cry* Mary Warren *starts to run.*
820 Proctor *catches her.*)

Mary Warren (*almost collapsing*). Let me go, Mr. Proctor, I cannot, I cannot—

Abigail (*crying to Heaven*). Oh, Heavenly Father, take away this shadow!

(*Without warning or hesitation,* Proctor *leaps at* Abigail *and, grabbing her by the hair, pulls her to her feet. She screams in pain.* Danforth, *astonished, cries,* "What are you about?" *and* Hathorne *and* Parris *call,* "Take your hands off her!" *and out of it all comes*
830 Proctor's *roaring voice.*)

Proctor. How do you call Heaven! Whore! Whore!

(*Herrick breaks* Proctor *from her.*)

Herrick. John!

Danforth. Man! Man, what do you—

Proctor (*breathless and in agony*). It is a whore!

Danforth (*dumbfounded*). You charge—?

Abigail. Mr. Danforth, he is lying!

Proctor. Mark her! Now she'll suck a scream to stab me with, but—

840 **Danforth.** You will prove this! This will not pass!

Proctor (*trembling, his life collapsing about him*). I have known her, sir. I have known her.

Danforth. You—you are a lecher?

Francis (*horrified*). John, you cannot say such a—

Proctor. Oh, Francis, I wish you had some evil in you that you might know me! (*to* Danforth) A man will not cast away his good name. You surely know that.

---

12. **every scrap and tittle:** every tiny bit.

Danforth (*dumbfounded*). In—in what time? In what place?

850 **Proctor** (*his voice about to break, and his shame great*). In the proper place—where my beasts are bedded. On the last night of my joy, some eight months past. She used to serve me in my house, sir. (*He has to clamp his jaw to keep from weeping.*) A man may think God sleeps, but God sees everything, I know it now. I beg you, sir, I beg you—see her what she is. My wife, my dear good wife, took this girl soon after, sir, and put her out on the highroad. And being what she is, a lump of vanity, sir—(*He is being overcome.*) Excellency, forgive me, forgive
860 me. (*Angrily against himself, he turns away from the* Governor *for a moment. Then, as though to cry out is his only means of speech left.*) She thinks to dance with me on my wife's grave! And well she might, for I thought of her softly. God help me, I lusted, and there *is* a promise in such sweat. But it is a whore's vengeance, and you must see it; I set myself entirely in your hands. I know you must see it now.

Danforth (*blanched, in horror, turning to* Abigail).
870 You deny every scrap and tittle[12] of this?

Abigail. If I must answer that, I will leave and I will not come back again!

(Danforth *seems unsteady.*)

Proctor. I have made a bell of my honor! I have rung the doom of my good name—you will believe me, Mr. Danforth! My wife is innocent, except she knew a whore when she saw one!

Abigail (*stepping up to* Danforth). What look do you give me? (Danforth *cannot speak.*) I'll not have such
880 looks! (*She turns and starts for the door.*)

Danforth. You will remain where you are! (Herrick *steps into her path. She comes up short, fire in her eyes.*) Mr. Parris, go into the court and bring Goodwife Proctor out.

Parris (*objecting*). Your Honor, this is all a—

TEXT ANALYSIS

● CONVENTIONS OF DRAMA

COMMON CORE
RL 3
RL 5

Reread lines 825–842. How does the fight between Proctor and Abigail signal a turning point in the play? *Possible answer: The close physical clash between Proctor and Abigail shows that there is some terrible connection between them. It foreshadows the revelation of their affair, which will be a turning point because it dooms Proctor and also might doom Abigail.*

IF STUDENTS NEED HELP . . . Discuss Proctor's outburst, "How do you [dare you] call Heaven!" (line 831). Elicit or explain that Proctor thinks that Abigail is such a base person that she has given up her right to ask for heavenly help.

READING SKILL

■ DRAW CONCLUSIONS ABOUT CHARACTERS

COMMON CORE
RL 1
RL 3

Reread lines 841–847. What traits describing Proctor can you add to the prereading chart from page 135? What evidence reveals these traits? *Possible answer: Proctor is volatile ("Without warning or hesitation,* Proctor *leaps at* Abigail *[lines 825–826]), honest (in front of the court and his friends, he reveals his affair with Abigail [lines 835–853]), and self-critical ("Oh, Francis, I wish you had some evil in you that you might know me!" [lines 845–846]).*

FOR STRUGGLING READERS

④ **Targeted Passage** [Lines 850–868]

Proctor reveals the true reason that Abigail persists in her charges of witchcraft.

- Why is Proctor overcome with emotion? How does he show his emotion? (lines 850, 854–855, 859–863)

- What does he say motivates Abigail to lie about his wife? (line 859)

- How does Proctor hope the court will react to his revelations? (lines 866–868)

FOR ENGLISH LANGUAGE LEARNERS

Vocabulary: Cognates Point out that the Spanish word *pasión* is spelled and pronounced almost like the English word *passion* (line 750). Help students understand these words with Spanish cognates: *emotion/emoción* (line 758), *illusion/ilusión* (line 786), *deception/decepción* (line 786), *conviction/convicción* (lines 1052–1053), *denounce/denunciar* (line 1160), *proceedings/procedimientos* (line 1161).

TEXT ANALYSIS

● CONVENTIONS OF DRAMA

Skim through lines 920–958, focusing on the stage directions. Through what gestures does Elizabeth communicate her anxiety about Danforth's questions? Explain. *Possible answers: Several times, Elizabeth communicates anxiety by trying to glance at her husband, hoping to find a clue from him about how she should respond to Danforth's questions (lines 921–922, 930, and 952). She is reluctant to look at Danforth because she knows that however she answers his questions, she may hurt her husband. She also wets her lips "to stall for time" (line 927) because she is nervous about speaking.*

Extend the Discussion In what sense is Danforth's gesture in line 953 an attempt to override Elizabeth's anxiety? Why is it a powerful action?

Danforth (*sharply to* Parris). Bring her out! And tell her not one word of what's been spoken here. And let you knock before you enter. (Parris *goes out.*) Now we shall touch the bottom of this swamp. (*to*
890 Proctor) Your wife, you say, is an honest woman.

Proctor. In her life, sir, she have never lied. There are them that cannot sing, and them that cannot weep—my wife cannot lie. I have paid much to learn it, sir.

Danforth. And when she put this girl out of your house, she put her out for a harlot?[13]

Proctor. Aye, sir.

Danforth. And knew her for a harlot?

Proctor. Aye, sir, she knew her for a harlot.

900 **Danforth.** Good then. (*to* Abigail) And if she tell me, child, it were for harlotry, may God spread His mercy on you! (*There is a knock. He calls to the door.*) Hold! (*to* Abigail) Turn your back. Turn your back. (*to* Proctor) Do likewise. (*Both turn their backs—Abigail* with indignant slowness.) Now let neither of you turn to face Goody Proctor. No one in this room is to speak one word, or raise a gesture aye or nay. (*He turns toward the door, calls.*) Enter! (*The door opens. Elizabeth enters with Parris. Parris leaves her. She stands*
910 *alone, her eyes looking for* Proctor.) Mr. Cheever, report this testimony in all exactness. Are you ready?

Cheever. Ready, sir.

Danforth. Come here, woman. (Elizabeth *comes to him, glancing at* Proctor's *back.*) Look at me only, not at your husband. In my eyes only.

Elizabeth (*faintly*). Good, sir.

Danforth. We are given to understand that at one time you dismissed your servant, Abigail Williams.

Elizabeth. That is true, sir.

920 **Danforth.** For what cause did you dismiss her? (*Slight pause. Then* Elizabeth *tries to glance at* Proctor.) You will look in my eyes only and not at your husband. The answer is in your memory and

you need no help to give it to me. Why did you dismiss Abigail Williams?

Elizabeth (*not knowing what to say, sensing a situation, wetting her lips to stall for time*). She—dissatisfied me. (*pause*) And my husband.

Danforth. In what way dissatisfied you?

930 **Elizabeth.** She were—(*She glances at* Proctor *for a cue.*)

Danforth. Woman, look at me! (Elizabeth *does.*) Were she slovenly? Lazy? What disturbance did she cause?

Elizabeth. Your Honor, I—in that time I were sick. And I—My husband is a good and righteous man. He is never drunk as some are, nor wastin' his time at the shovelboard, but always at his work. But in my sickness—you see, sir, I were a long time sick after my last baby, and I thought I saw my husband somewhat turning from me. And this girl—(*She*
940 *turns to* Abigail.)

Danforth. Look at me.

Elizabeth. Aye, sir. Abigail Williams—(*She breaks off.*)

Danforth. What of Abigail Williams?

Elizabeth. I came to think he fancied her. And so one night I lost my wits, I think, and put her out on the highroad.

Danforth. Your husband—did he indeed turn from you?

Elizabeth (*in agony*). My husband—is a goodly man,
950 sir.

Danforth. Then he did not turn from you.

Elizabeth (*starting to glance at* Proctor). He—

Danforth (*reaches out and holds her face, then*). Look at me! To your own knowledge, has John Proctor ever committed the crime of lechery? (*In a crisis of indecision she cannot speak.*) Answer my question! Is your husband a lecher!

Elizabeth (*faintly*). No, sir.

Danforth. Remove her, Marshal.

---

13. **for a harlot:** as a woman of low morals.

DIFFERENTIATED INSTRUCTION

FOR STRUGGLING READERS

Comprehension Support Explain that Danforth's "Now we shall touch the bottom of this swamp" (line 889) is a metaphor. This type of figurative language makes a comparison between two things that at first do not seem comparable. Clarify students' understanding by asking these questions:

• What is being referred to as a "swamp"?

• What does Danforth mean by "touch the bottom"?

FOR ADVANCED LEARNERS/AP

Analyze Character Relationships [small-group option] Note that as Danforth has Elizabeth brought into the room, he gives equally stern instructions to Abigail and to Proctor (lines 903–907). Have students trace Danforth's dealings with Abigail throughout Act Two. Challenge students to identify the point at which the relationship changes most dramatically and to offer a reason for that change.

960 **Proctor.** Elizabeth, tell the truth!

Danforth. She has spoken. Remove her!

Proctor (*crying out*). Elizabeth, I have confessed it!

Elizabeth. Oh, God! (*The door closes behind her.*)

Proctor. She only thought to save my name!

Hale. Excellency, it is a natural lie to tell; I beg you, stop now before another is condemned! I may shut my conscience to it no more—private vengeance is working through this testimony! From the begin-
970 ning this man has struck me true. By my oath to Heaven, I believe him now, and I pray you call back his wife before we—

Danforth. She spoke nothing of lechery, and this man has lied!

Hale. I believe him! (*pointing at* Abigail) This girl has always struck me false! She has—

(Abigail, *with a weird, wild, chilling cry, screams up to the ceiling.*)

Abigail. You will not! Begone! Begone, I say!

Danforth. What is it, child? (*But* Abigail, *pointing*
980 *with fear, is now raising up her frightened eyes, her awed face, toward the ceiling—the girls are doing the same—and now* Hathorne, Hale, Putnam, Cheever, Herrick, *and* Danforth *do the same.*) What's there? (*He lowers his eyes from the ceiling, and now he is frightened; there is real tension in his voice.*) Child! (*She is transfixed—with all the girls, she is whimpering open-mouthed, agape at the ceiling.*) Girls! Why do you—?

Mercy Lewis (*pointing*). It's on the beam! Behind the rafter!

990 **Danforth** (*looking up*). Where!

Abigail. Why—? (*She gulps.*) Why do you come, yellow bird?

Proctor. Where's a bird? I see no bird!

Abigail (*to the ceiling*). My face? My face?

Proctor. Mr. Hale—

Danforth. Be quiet!

Proctor (*to* Hale). Do you see a bird?

Danforth. Be quiet!!

Abigail (*to the ceiling, in a genuine conversation with*
1000 *the "bird," as though trying to talk it out of attacking her*). But God made my face; you cannot want to tear my face. Envy is a deadly sin, Mary.

Mary Warren (*on her feet with a spring, and horrified, pleading*). Abby!

Abigail (*unperturbed, continuing to the "bird"*). Oh, Mary, this is a black art[14] to change your shape. No, I cannot, I cannot stop my mouth; it's God's work I do.

Mary Warren. Abby, I'm *here*!

Proctor (*frantically*). They're pretending, Mr.
1010 Danforth!

Abigail (*Now she takes a backward step, as though in fear the bird will swoop down momentarily*). Oh, please, Mary! Don't come down.

Susanna Walcott. Her claws, she's stretching her claws!

Proctor. Lies, lies.

Abigail (*backing further, eyes still fixed above*). Mary, please don't hurt me!

Mary Warren (*to* Danforth). I'm not hurting her!

Danforth (*to* Mary Warren). Why does she see this
1020 vision?

Mary Warren. She sees nothin'!

Abigail (*now staring full front as though hypnotized, and mimicking the exact tone of* Mary Warren's *cry*). She sees nothin'!

Mary Warren (*pleading*). Abby, you mustn't!

Abigail and All the Girls (*all transfixed*). Abby, you mustn't!

Mary Warren (*to all the girls*). I'm here, I'm here!

Girls. I'm here, I'm here!

1030 **Danforth** (*horrified*). Mary Warren! Draw back your spirit out of them!

Mary Warren. Mr. Danforth!

---

14. **a black art:** sorcery.

REVISIT THE BIG QUESTION
What fuels a MOB?

After students read lines 999–1032, ask the following question: Why does Mary Warren's desperation build toward hysteria as she suffers Abigail's persistent attacks? *Possible answer: Mary's desperation builds because she has no control over her own fate. She is powerless to stop the girls' attack on her.* Who else in this scene appears to become infected by the hysteria in the room? Explain. *Possible answer: Judge Danforth seems infected by hysteria, as evidenced by his horrified command that Mary withdraw her spirit from the girls and Mary's shock that he would say such a thing (lines 1030–1032).*

FOR STRUGGLING READERS

Comprehension: Text Structure Point out the transition that occurs immediately after Hale expresses his support of Proctor and suspicions of Abigail: Abigail screams, "You will not! Begone! Begone, I say!" (line 978) Explain that this outburst shifts attention away from the issue of Abigail's honesty. Help students use a Storyboard to trace the changing action in this scene.

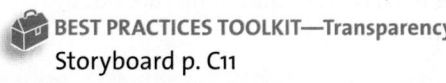
BEST PRACTICES TOOLKIT—Transparency
Storyboard p. C11

FOR ADVANCED LEARNERS/AP

Analyze Character Behavior Have students review the scene in which Elizabeth is asked to incriminate her husband. Point out that she must choose between two noble impulses: honesty and loyalty. Then have students work in small groups to discuss her choices and her decision. Invite group representatives to share with the class the negative and positive aspects of Elizabeth's honesty and loyalty.

After students read lines 1034–1054, use these prompts to help students explore the girls' roles as tormentors:

Summarize When the girls speak as a group, what do they say? Why? ***Possible answer: As a group, the girls repeat everything that Mary Warren says. They are trying to make onlookers believe that Mary is directing demonic power against them.***

Interpret How do the girls behave as Mary grows increasingly upset? ***Possible answer: As Mary grows more upset, the girls torment her more mercilessly. Mary tries to talk to them, but they continue to mock her, ignoring her pleas (lines 1048–1050).***

Synthesize What causes might explain the girls' behavior? Which cause do you think has the best textual support? ***Possible answer: The girls might be under the influence of demonic powers, but the slim evidence for that cause has become suspect by now. There is stronger evidence for the possibility that Abigail has coached them; for example, the girls do not start mimicking Mary Warren until Abigail has done so first (lines 1022–1024). The girls' behavior also might result from hysteria; in this scene, even Judge Danforth is carried away by the emotional charge in the room (lines 1038–1039 and following). Perhaps the best explanation for the girls' behavior is a combination of hysteria and coaching from Abigail.***

Girls (*cutting her off*). Mr. Danforth!

Danforth. Have you compacted with the Devil? Have you?

Mary Warren. Never, never!

Girls. Never, never!

Danforth (*growing hysterical*). Why can they only repeat you?

1040 **Proctor.** Give me a whip—I'll stop it!

Mary Warren. They're sporting.[15] They—!

Girls. They're sporting!

Mary Warren (*turning on them all hysterically and stamping her feet*). Abby, stop it!

Girls (*stamping their feet*). Abby, stop it!

Mary Warren. Stop it!

Girls. Stop it!

Mary Warren (*screaming it out at the top of her lungs, and raising her fists*). Stop it!!

1050 **Girls** (*raising their fists*). Stop it!!

(Mary Warren, *utterly confounded, and becoming overwhelmed by* Abigail's—*and the girls'—utter conviction, starts to whimper, hands half raised, powerless, and all the girls begin whimpering exactly as she does.*)

Danforth. A little while ago you were afflicted. Now it seems you afflict others; where did you find this power?

Mary Warren (*staring at* Abigail). I—have no power.

Girls. I have no power.

1060 **Proctor.** They're gulling you,[16] Mister!

Danforth. Why did you turn about this past two weeks? You have seen the Devil, have you not?

Hale (*indicating* Abigail *and the girls*). You cannot believe them! ⑤

Mary Warren. I—

Proctor (*sensing her weakening*). Mary, God damns all liars!

Danforth (*pounding it into her*). You have seen the Devil, you have made compact with Lucifer, have 1070 you not?

Proctor. God damns liars, Mary!

(Mary *utters something unintelligible, staring at* Abigail, *who keeps watching the "bird" above.*)

Danforth. I cannot hear you. What do you say? (Mary *utters again unintelligibly.*) You will confess yourself or you will hang! (*He turns her roughly to face him.*) Do you know who I am? I say you will hang if you do not open with me!

Proctor. Mary, remember the angel Raphael—do 1080 that which is good and—

Abigail (*pointing upward*). The wings! Her wings are spreading! Mary, please, don't, don't—!

Hale. I see nothing, Your Honor!

Danforth. Do you confess this power! (*He is an inch from her face.*) Speak!

Abigail. She's going to come down! She's walking the beam!

Danforth. Will you speak!

Mary Warren (*staring in horror*). I cannot!

1090 **Girls.** I cannot!

Parris. Cast the Devil out! Look him in the face! Trample him! We'll save you, Mary, only stand fast against him and—

Abigail (*looking up*). Look out! She's coming down!

(*She and all the girls run to one wall, shielding their eyes. And now, as though cornered, they let out a gigantic scream, and* Mary, *as though infected, opens her mouth and screams with them. Gradually* Abigail *and the girls leave off, until only* Mary *is left there, staring* 1100 *up at the "bird," screaming madly. All watch her, horrified by this evident fit.* Proctor *strides to her.*)

Proctor. Mary, tell the Governor what they—(*He has hardly got a word out, when, seeing him coming for her, she rushes out of his reach, screaming in horror.*)

---

15. **sporting:** playing a game.
16. **gulling you:** deceiving you.

DIFFERENTIATED INSTRUCTION

FOR STRUGGLING READERS

⑤ **Targeted Passage** [Lines 1055–1064]

- What does Danforth ask Mary Warren about power? Why does he think that she has power? (lines 1055–1057)
- How does Mary respond? Why? (line 1058)
- What do Proctor and Hale tell Danforth? (lines 1060, 1063–1064)
- Is Hale still a friend of the court? How can you tell? (lines 1063–1064)

Concept Support Point out some of the ways in which Arthur Miller creates frenzy in this critical scene:

- The din in the courtroom is palpable as the girls shout incessantly.
- Danforth grows "hysterical" (line 1038) and Mary "hysterically" stamps her feet and screams (lines 1043 and 1048–1049).
- That Mary becomes "overwhelmed" (line 1052) is proof that things are out of control.

Behind the Curtain

 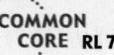
DRAMA AND FILM

The photographs here depict the scene in which Abigail and the girls claim to see Mary Warren's spirit flying overhead. The upper photograph shows a staged version of the scene; the lower one shows the same moment from a film adaptation. As you examine the stage image, notice what is visible to the audience—the entire set and all the characters present in the scene. Theater directors rely on the actors and the lighting to draw the audience's attention to part of the set or to particular characters or groups of characters. By contrast, film directors can use the camera to focus on part of the action. In the lower photograph, the camera has zoomed in to let the actors' facial expressions register on the audience. As you read the last page of Act Three, imagine that you are directing a film version of *The Crucible*. Choose one moment in which you want the camera to zoom in on John Proctor, including a close-up with just his face onscreen.

THE CRUCIBLE: ACT THREE **197**

BEHIND THE CURTAIN

Setting and Characters Remind students that although films often seem more realistic than plays presented on a stage, a theater stage puts living, breathing people in front of the audience. Spectators hear and see live action instead of action that is mediated by the camera. *Possible answer: Students may suggest the moment in lines 960–964, when Proctor commands Elizabeth to tell the truth and them watches as she is removed from the court. Students should explain that the close-up on the actor's face would reveal deep anguish.*

FOR ADVANCED LEARNERS/AP

Research and Contrast Productions Have students work in small groups to locate images from at least one stage production of *The Crucible*. Ask students to compare those representations to the text itself, as well as to photographs from the 1996 film version, which is represented in the student edition. Challenge students to contrast the strengths and weaknesses in the presentation of setting and characters in all three versions—print, stage, and film.

REVISIT THE BIG QUESTION

What fuels a MOB?

Discuss After students read lines 1108–1123, ask the following question: What part does hysteria play in Mary's decision to turn against Proctor? *Possible answer: The hysteria manufactured by Abigail and the girls has made Mary completely irrational. She also realizes that she has a better chance of staying alive if she sides with Abigail, since Abigail seems to control Danforth and the court.*

SELECTION WRAP–UP

READ WITH A PURPOSE Now that students have read Act Three, ask them how the community has changed since the beginning of the play. What role have rumors played in the change? *Possible answers: The community is torn apart by accusations based on rumors that certain people have practiced witchcraft.*

⭐ CRITIQUE

- Ask students whether Mary's decision to abandon Proctor was expected.

- After completing the After Reading questions on page 199, have students revisit their responses and tell whether they have changed their opinions.

Mary Warren. Don't touch me—don't touch me! (*At which the girls halt at the door.*)

Proctor (*astonished*). Mary!

Mary Warren (*pointing at* Proctor). You're the Devil's man! (*He is stopped in his tracks.*)

1110 **Parris.** Praise God!

Girls. Praise God!

Proctor (*numbed*). Mary, how—?

Mary Warren. I'll not hang with you! I love God, I love God.

Danforth (*to* Mary). He bid you do the Devil's work?

Mary Warren (*hysterically, indicating* Proctor). He come at me by night and every day to sign, to sign, to—

Danforth. Sign what?

Parris. The Devil's book? He come with a book?

1120 **Mary Warren** (*hysterically, pointing at* Proctor, *fearful of him*). My name, he want my name. "I'll murder you," he says, "if my wife hangs! We must go and overthrow the court," he says!

(Danforth*'s head jerks toward* Proctor, *shock and horror in his face.*)

Proctor (*turning, appealing to* Hale). Mr. Hale!

Mary Warren (*her sobs beginning*). He wake me every night, his eyes were like coals and his fingers claw my neck, and I sign, I sign . . .

1130 **Hale.** Excellency, this child's gone wild!

Proctor (*as* Danforth*'s wide eyes pour on him*). Mary, Mary!

Mary Warren (*screaming at him*). No, I love God; I go your way no more. I love God, I bless God. (*Sobbing, she rushes to* Abigail.) Abby, Abby, I'll never hurt you more! (*They all watch, as* Abigail, *out of her infinite charity, reaches out and draws the sobbing* Mary *to her, and then looks up to* Danforth.)

Danforth (*to* Proctor). What are you? (Proctor *is*
1140 *beyond speech in his anger.*) You are combined with anti-Christ,[17] are you not? I have seen your power; you will not deny it! What say you, Mister?

Hale. Excellency—

Danforth. I will have nothing from you, Mr. Hale! (*to* Proctor) Will you confess yourself befouled with Hell, or do you keep that black allegiance yet? What say you?

Proctor (*his mind wild, breathless*). I say—I say—God is dead!

1150 **Parris.** Hear it, hear it!

⑥ **Proctor** (*laughs insanely, then*). A fire, a fire is burning! I hear the boot of Lucifer, I see his filthy face! And it is my face, and yours, Danforth! For them that quail to bring men out of ignorance, as I have quailed, and as you quail now when you know in all your black hearts that this be fraud—God damns our kind especially, and we will burn, we will burn together!

Danforth. Marshal! Take him and Corey with him to the jail!

1160 **Hale** (*starting across to the door*). I denounce these proceedings!

Proctor. You are pulling Heaven down and raising up a whore!

Hale. I denounce these proceedings, I quit this court! (*He slams the door to the outside behind him.*)

Danforth (*calling to him in a fury*). Mr. Hale! Mr. Hale!

(*The curtain falls.*)

---

17. **combined with anti-Christ:** working with the Devil.

DIFFERENTIATED INSTRUCTION

FOR STRUGGLING READERS

⑥ **Targeted Passage** [Lines 1151–1157]

In this passage, Proctor passionately indicts both himself and the court.

- Whom does Proctor equate with the Devil (Lucifer) now? (lines 1151–1153)

- Why does Proctor think that God will judge him and the court harshly? (lines 1153–1156)

- What punishment does Proctor predict for himself and the judges? (lines 1156–1157)

Vocabulary Support As students reread the sentence beginning in line 1153, point out the word *quail*. Explain that although *quail* can refer to a small bird, in this context it is a verb meaning "to flinch" or "to draw back from because of fear." Help students paraphrase these lines.

After Reading

Comprehension

1. **Recall** Why does Mary Warren come to the court?

2. **Recall** What does John Proctor admit to the court?

3. **Clarify** Why is Proctor arrested at the end of the act?

Text Analysis

4. **Recognize Verbal Irony** Verbal irony occurs when someone states one thing and means another. According to the stage directions, Abigail draws the sobbing, repentant Mary to her side "out of her infinite charity" (lines 1136–1137). Why is this comment ironic?

5. **Draw Conclusions About Characters** Review the character traits you recorded in your chart for Danforth. How do these traits influence his relationship with the following?

   - John Proctor
   - Reverend Hale
   - Abigail Williams
   - Reverend Parris

6. **Make Judgments** What is your opinion of the way Danforth is conducting the court? Use details from the play to support your opinion.

7. **Analyze Character Motives** Why does Elizabeth lie to Danforth about her husband's relationship with Abigail?

8. **Analyze Conventions of Drama** Review the information on **types of characters** in the **Text Analysis Workshop** on pages 132–133. Then determine the play's central character, or **protagonist**, its major **antagonists**, and **character foils**. List these characters in a chart like the one shown and take notes on their personalities and values. What effect does the interplay among these characters have on the play?

Character-Type	Personality	Values

Text Criticism

9. **Different Perspectives** The real Abigail Williams was 11 years old in 1692 and had not had an illicit relationship with John Proctor. How would the play differ if Arthur Miller had not embellished the truth? What would be lost?

What fuels a MOB?

How does Mary Warren contribute to the mob mentality that takes over the court room in Act Three?

COMMON CORE

RL 1 Cite textual evidence to support analysis of what the text says explicitly as well as inferences drawn from the text, including determining where the text leaves matters uncertain. **RL 3** Analyze the impact of the author's choices regarding how to develop and relate elements of a drama. **RL 5** Analyze how an author's choices concerning how to structure specific parts of a text contribute to its overall structure and meaning as well as its aesthetic impact. **RL 6** Analyze a case in which grasping point of view requires distinguishing what is directly stated in a text from what is really meant.

Practice and Apply

For preliminary support of post-reading questions, use these copy masters:

R RESOURCE MANAGER—Copy Masters

Reading Check p. 227
Conventions of Drama p. 225
Question Support p. 228

Additional selection questions are provided for teachers on page 221.

ANSWERS

COMMON CORE RL 1, RL 3, RL 5, RL 6

1. *to say that the girls are lying*

2. *that he had an intimate relationship with Abigail*

3. *because Mary says he is in league with the Devil and because he says God is dead*

Possible answers:

4. *Abigail's action is insincere; she had just endangered Mary's life by lying. When Mary changes her testimony, Abigail feels victorious, not charitable.*

5. **COMMON CORE FOCUS** *Draw Conclusions About Characters* **Proctor:** *Danforth's dedication to his cause makes him suspicious of Proctor;* **Abigail:** *His dedication also makes him believe Abigail;* **Hale:** *Danforth's determination to learn the truth initially leads him to listen to Hale;* **Parris:** *Danforth's sense of honor makes him despise Parris.*

6. *Danforth is swayed by the girls and thus not conducting court well. He should know that Abigail is impious and a bully. He is acting according to the beliefs of the time. He thinks Abigail is a victim of the witches, which compels him to rely on her testimony.*

7. *Elizabeth wants to protect John's reputation and save him from being charged with adultery.*

8. **COMMON CORE FOCUS** *Conventions of Drama* **Protagonist:** *Proctor: rational, strong; truth, logic;* **Antagonist:** *Abigail: manipulative, vengeful; getting her way;* **Character Foils:** *Danforth, Hale, Mary, Elizabeth, Parris. The interplay heightens tension and further reveals their personalities and values.*

9. *A completely factual presentation might eliminate much dramatic tension. Proctor's relationships with Abigail and Elizabeth would have been different, and Proctor's personal agony and guilt would not have been central.*

What fuels a MOB? **Possible answers:** *At first, Mary is at the mercy of the mob mentality of the hysterical girls; then she joins the mob when she accuses Proctor.*

Assess and Reteach

Assess

DIAGNOSTIC AND SELECTION TESTS

Selection Test A pp. 69–70
Selection Test B/C pp. 71–72

Interactive Selection Test on thinkcentral.com

Reteach

Level Up Online Tutorials on thinkcentral.com

Reteaching Worksheets on thinkcentral.com

Literature Lessons 1–2, 6, 23–24, Reading Lesson 9

Practice and Apply

SUMMARY

Act Four takes place in the Salem jail. Several "witches" have been executed; now Proctor and Rebecca are to hang, for they refuse to confess to crimes that they say they have not committed. Hale, Parris, and Elizabeth speak with Proctor. Proctor signs a false confession, to save his life for his family's sake, but then he tears it up to save his reputation. Elizabeth watches with pride and stoic grief as he is led to the gallows.

■ *Model the Skill:* DRAW CONCLUSIONS ABOUT CHARACTERS

Review with students the conclusions chart on page 135. Remind students that dialogue and stage directions help reveal a character's traits. After students read page 200, ask them what they can conclude about Sarah Good's state of mind. Have them support their ideas with evidence.

Possible answer: *Sarah's state of mind is fragile. She seems almost delirious: she responds to the Devil as an unseen master (lines 3–4, 38) and babbles about being transformed into a bluebird and flying off to Barbados with Tituba (lines 20–22).*

Extend the Discussion To what would you attribute Sarah's attitude in this scene?

Resources for Act Four

(*A cell in Salem jail, that fall.*

At the back is a high barred window; near it, a great, heavy door. Along the walls are two benches.

The place is in darkness but for the moonlight seeping through the bars. It appears empty. Presently footsteps are heard coming down a corridor beyond the wall, keys rattle, and the door swings open. Marshal Herrick *enters with a lantern.*

He is nearly drunk, and heavy-footed. He goes to a bench and nudges a bundle of rags lying on it.)

Herrick. Sarah, wake up! Sarah Good! (*He then crosses to the other bench.*)

Sarah Good (*rising in her rags*). Oh, Majesty! Comin', comin'! Tituba, he's here, His Majesty's come!

Herrick. Go to the north cell; this place is wanted now. (*He hangs his lantern on the wall.* Tituba *sits up.*)

Tituba. That don't look to me like His Majesty; look to me like the marshal.

Herrick (*taking out a flask*). Get along with you now,
10 clear this place. (*He drinks, and* Sarah Good *comes and peers up into his face.*)

Sarah Good. Oh, is it you, Marshal! I thought sure you be the devil comin' for us. Could I have a sip of cider for me goin'-away?

Herrick (*handing her the flask*). And where are you off to, Sarah?

Tituba (*as* Sarah *drinks*). We goin' to Barbados, soon the Devil gits here with the feathers and the wings.

Herrick. Oh? A happy voyage to you.

20 **Sarah Good.** A pair of bluebirds wingin' southerly, the two of us! Oh, it be a grand transformation, Marshal! (*She raises the flask to drink again.*)

Herrick (*taking the flask from her lips*). You'd best give me that or you'll never rise off the ground. Come along now.

Tituba. I'll speak to him for you, if you desires to come along, Marshal.

Herrick. I'd not refuse it, Tituba; it's the proper morning to fly into Hell.

30 **Tituba.** Oh, it be no Hell in Barbados. Devil, him be pleasure-man in Barbados, him be singin' and dancin' in Barbados. It's you folks—you riles him up 'round here; it be too cold 'round here for that Old Boy. He freeze his soul in Massachusetts, but in Barbados he just as sweet and—(*A bellowing cow is heard, and* Tituba *leaps up and calls to the window.*) Aye, sir! That's him, Sarah!

Sarah Good. I'm here, Majesty! (*They hurriedly pick up their rags as* Hopkins, *a guard, enters.*)

See resources on the **Teacher One Stop DVD-ROM** *and on* **thinkcentral.com**.

 RESOURCE MANAGER UNIT 1

Plan and Teach, pp. 229–234
Summary, pp. 235–236 † ‡*
Text Analysis and Reading
Skill, pp. 237–240 †*

DIAGNOSTIC AND SELECTION TESTS

Selection Tests, pp. 73–76

 BEST PRACTICES TOOLKIT

Reporter's Questions, p. C9
Y Chart, p. A27
New Word Analysis, p. E8
Venn Diagram, p. A26

INTERACTIVE READER

ADAPTED INTERACTIVE READER

ELL ADAPTED INTERACTIVE READER

TECHNOLOGY

🔘 **Teacher One Stop DVD-ROM**
🔘 **Student One Stop DVD-ROM**
🔘 **PowerNotes DVD-ROM**
🔘 **Audio Anthology CD**
🔘 **GrammarNotes DVD-ROM**
🔘 **ExamView Test Generator** on the Teacher One Stop

Video Trailer

Go to **thinkcentral.com** to preview the **Video Trailer** introducing this selection. Other features that support the selection include

• **PowerNotes** presentation
• **ThinkAloud** models to enhance comprehension
• **WordSharp** vocabulary tutorials
• interactive writing and grammar instruction

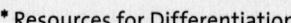
* Resources for Differentiation　　† Also in Spanish　　‡ Also in Haitian Creole and Vietnamese

John Proctor going to the gallows

Reading Support

This selection on **thinkcentral.com** includes embedded **ThinkAloud** models—students "thinking aloud" about the story to model the kinds of questions a good reader would ask about a selection.

Analyze Visuals

Activity Where are Proctor and the women probably being taken? What details in the photograph convey a sense of hopelessness?
Possible answer: Proctor and the women probably are being taken to a place of execution. In the text, Herrick comments that "it's the proper morning to fly into Hell" (lines 28–29), indicating that the day's events will be very grim. Hopelessness is conveyed through the jail-like appearance of the cart, whose pointed slats resemble prison bars. In addition, chains bind the characters, suggesting that there is no escape. The people seem hopeless, too: Proctor's vacant eyes give him the appearance of a caged animal; and the woman to his left stands with closed eyes, either trying to block out the scene or showing resignation.

DIFFERENTIATED INSTRUCTION

FOR ENGLISH LANGUAGE LEARNERS

Preteach Vocabulary Students will encounter the following vocabulary word in Act Four. Supply them with the definition as needed:

line 280: **adamant** (ăd′ə-mənt) *adj.* immovable, especially in opposing something

FOR STRUGGLING READERS

In combination with the *Audio Anthology CD*, use one or more Targeted Passages (pp. 202, 205, 206, 209, 212) to ensure that students focus on key story events and concepts. Targeted Passages are also good for English learners.

Preview Read the Summary aloud; then have students use a Reporter's Questions chart to isolate key information.

Who is featured in Act Four?	Proctor, Elizabeth, Hale, Parris
What is Proctor's dilemma?	whether to submit a false confession

🧰 BEST PRACTICES TOOLKIT—Transparency
Reporter's Questions p. C9

COMMON CORE
RL 3
RL 5

In lines 52–80, stage directions and dialogue reveal the condition of the jail cell. What is it like? Cite evidence. *Possible answer: The cell is cold, because it is "bitter cold" outside (line 58) and there is no fire for warmth (lines 76–77). The only physical comfort is "old rags and straw" (line 55), and the smell is terrible (line 80).*

Extend the Discussion What does the condition of the jail indicate about the authorities' opinion of the prisoners?

COMMON CORE
RL 1
RL 3

■ **DRAW CONCLUSIONS ABOUT CHARACTERS**

Why might Judge Danforth consider it "strange" for Parris to be praying with Hale (line 92)? *Possible answer: Meeting for prayer is "strange" because Hale and Parris have clashed over the witch trials. Parris has been ready to convict anyone charged with witchcraft, whereas Hale earlier quit the trials, decrying them as a sham.*

---

40 **Hopkins.** The Deputy Governor's arrived.

Herrick (*grabbing* Tituba). Come along, come along.

Tituba (*resisting him*). No, he comin' for me. I goin' home!

Herrick (*pulling her to the door*). That's not Satan, just a poor old cow with a hatful of milk. Come along now, out with you!

Tituba (*calling to the window*). Take me home, Devil! Take me home!

Sarah Good (*following the shouting* Tituba *out*). Tell
50 him I'm goin', Tituba! Now you tell him Sarah Good is goin' too!

(*In the corridor outside* Tituba *calls on—"Take me home, Devil; Devil take me home!" and* Hopkins' *voice orders her to move on.* Herrick *returns and begins to push old rags and straw into a corner. Hearing footsteps, he turns, and enter* Danforth *and* Judge Hathorne. *They are in greatcoats and wear hats against the bitter cold. They are followed in by* Cheever, *who carries a dispatch case[1] and a flat*
60 *wooden box containing his writing materials.*)

Herrick. Good morning, Excellency.

Danforth. Where is Mr. Parris?

Herrick. I'll fetch him. (*He starts for the door.*)

Danforth. Marshal. (Herrick *stops.*) When did Reverend Hale arrive?

Herrick. It were toward midnight, I think.

Danforth (*suspiciously*). What is he about here?

Herrick. He goes among them that will hang, sir. And he prays with them. He sits with Goody Nurse
70 now. And Mr. Parris with him.

Danforth. Indeed. That man have no authority to enter here, Marshal. Why have you let him in?

Herrick. Why, Mr. Parris command me, sir. I cannot deny him.

Danforth. Are you drunk, Marshal?

---

1. **dispatch case:** a case for carrying documents.
2. **Andover:** a town in Massachusetts northwest of Salem.

Herrick. No, sir; it is a bitter night, and I have no fire here.

Danforth (*containing his anger*). Fetch Mr. Parris.

Herrick. Aye, sir.

80 **Danforth.** There is a prodigious stench in this place.

Herrick. I have only now cleared the people out for you.

Danforth. Beware hard drink, Marshal.

Herrick. Aye, sir. (*He waits an instant for further orders. But* Danforth, *in dissatisfaction, turns his back on him, and* Herrick *goes out. There is a pause.* Danforth *stands in thought.*)

Hathorne. Let you question Hale, Excellency; I should not be surprised he have been preaching
90 in Andover[2] lately.

Danforth. We'll come to that; speak nothing of Andover. Parris prays with him. That's strange. (*He blows on his hands, moves toward the window, and looks out.*)

Hathorne. Excellency, I wonder if it be wise to let Mr. Parris so continuously with the prisoners. (Danforth *turns to him, interested.*) I think, sometimes, the man has a mad look these days.

Danforth. Mad?

100 **Hathorne.** I met him yesterday coming out of his house, and I bid him good morning—and he wept and went his way. I think it is not well the village sees him so unsteady.

Danforth. Perhaps he have some sorrow.

Cheever (*stamping his feet against the cold*). I think it be the cows, sir.

Danforth. Cows?

Cheever. There be so many cows wanderin' the highroads, now their masters are in the jails, and much
110 disagreement who they will belong to now. I know Mr. Parris be arguin' with farmers all yesterday—

FOR STRUGGLING READERS

① **Targeted Passage** [Lines 95–111]

This passage indicates that the trauma of the witchcraft scare can be seen as well as felt.

- Why is Hathorne worried about Parris? What does he think is affecting Parris? (lines 95–98)

- Why are cows roaming Salem's roads? (lines 108–109)

Explore Settings Have students reread the stage directions that begin Act Three (page 180) and Act Four (page 200). Help them note key details about each set in the two "branches" of a Y Chart. Then discuss how the sets are similar and why Miller might have wanted a similarity between them. Record students' responses in the "trunk" of the Y Chart.

 **BEST PRACTICES TOOLKIT—Transparency**
Y Chart p. A27

FOR ADVANCED LEARNERS/AP

Research Andover [small-group option] Ask students to find and present a brief introduction to the town of Andover. (See lines 88–92.) The introduction might include a map showing the relative locations of Andover and Salem and a brief explanation of Andover's early history, including information about how the community responded to the witchcraft scare that began in Salem.

there is great contention, sir, about the cows. Contention make him weep, sir; it were always a man that weep for contention. (*He turns, as do* Hathorne *and* Danforth, *hearing someone coming up the corridor.* Danforth *raises his head as* Parris *enters. He is gaunt, frightened, and sweating in his greatcoat.*)

Parris (*to* Danforth, *instantly*). Oh, good morning, sir, thank you for coming, I beg your pardon wakin'
120 you so early. Good morning, Judge Hathorne.

Danforth. Reverend Hale have no right to enter this—

Parris. Excellency, a moment. (*He hurries back and shuts the door.*)

Hathorne. Do you leave him alone with the prisoners?

Danforth. What's his business here?

Parris (*prayerfully holding up his hands*). Excellency, hear me. It is a providence. Reverend Hale has returned to bring Rebecca Nurse to God.

Danforth (*surprised*). He bids her confess?

130 **Parris** (*sitting*). Hear me. Rebecca have not given me a word this three month since she came. Now she sits with him, and her sister and Martha Corey and two or three others, and he pleads with them, confess their crimes and save their lives.

Danforth. Why—this is indeed a providence. And they soften, they soften?

Parris. Not yet, not yet. But I thought to summon you, sir, that we might think on whether it be not wise, to—(*He dares not say it.*) I had thought to put
140 a question, sir, and I hope you will not—

Danforth. Mr. Parris, be plain, what troubles you?

Parris. There is news, sir, that the court—the court must reckon with. My niece, sir, my niece—I believe she has vanished.

Danforth. Vanished!

Parris. I had thought to advise you of it earlier in the week, but—

Danforth. Why? How long is she gone?

Parris. This be the third night. You see, sir, she told
150 me she would stay a night with Mercy Lewis. And next day, when she does not return, I send to Mr. Lewis to inquire. Mercy told him she would sleep in *my* house for a night.

Danforth. They are both gone?!

Parris (*in fear of him*). They are, sir.

Danforth (*alarmed*). I will send a party for them. Where may they be?

Parris. Excellency, I think they be aboard a ship. (Danforth *stands agape.*) My daughter tells me how
160 she heard them speaking of ships last week, and tonight I discover my—my strongbox is broke into. (*He presses his fingers against his eyes to keep back tears.*)

Hathorne (*astonished*). She have robbed you?

Parris. Thirty-one pound is gone. I am penniless. (*He covers his face and sobs.*)

Danforth. Mr. Parris, you are a brainless man! (*He walks in thought, deeply worried.*)

Parris. Excellency, it profit nothing you should blame me. I cannot think they would run off
170 except they fear to keep in Salem any more. (*He is pleading.*) Mark it, sir, Abigail had close knowledge of the town, and since the news of Andover has broken here—

Danforth. Andover is remedied.[3] The court returns there on Friday, and will resume examinations.

Parris. I am sure of it, sir. But the rumor here speaks rebellion in Andover, and it—

Danforth. There is no rebellion in Andover!

Parris. I tell you what is said here, sir. Andover have
180 thrown out the court, they say, and will have no part of witchcraft. There be a faction here, feeding on that news, and I tell you true, sir, I fear there will be riot here.

Hathorne. Riot! Why at every execution I have seen naught but high satisfaction in the town.

---

3. **remedied:** no longer a problem.

TIERED DISCUSSION PROMPTS

Use these prompts to help students explore the news about Abigail and Mercy Lewis as revealed in lines 158–183:

Connect Have you ever known someone who felt so overwhelmed by a situation that he or she wanted to run away? Why does running away from stress sometimes seem like a good idea? *Accept all responses.*

Analyze Why would Abigail and Mercy Lewis "fear to keep in Salem" (line 170)? *Possible answer: Abigail and Mercy might fear a countermovement against the executions, for the people in nearby Andover have disbanded the witch trials there (lines 179–181). Because a faction in Salem is "feeding on that news" from Andover (lines 181–182), the girls who instigated the witch hunt are worried about their safety should public sentiment in Salem turn against the accusers.*

Synthesize Do you think that the girls' disappearance will affect Danforth's decision to carry out the remaining executions? Why or why not? *Possible answer: Danforth probably will not be affected by the girls' disappearance. He refuses to acknowledge any problems in Andover (lines 174–175, 178), and his stubbornness suggests that he will follow through with the planned executions. (Indeed, he later refuses to delay the executions that are about to take place [lines 246–248].)*

FOR STRUGGLING READERS

Make Inferences Point out that in lines 137–140, Parris cannot bring himself to ask Danforth a certain question. Explain that students must make an inference—a well-informed assumption—about the nature of that question. Help them review lines 126–136 and look ahead to lines 179–183 for information. Elicit or explain that Parris wants to ask Danforth to delay that day's executions. (He finally will make this request in lines 200–201.)

FOR ENGLISH LANGUAGE LEARNERS

Vocabulary: Cognates Point out that the Spanish word *materiales* is spelled and pronounced almost like the English word *materials* (line 60). Help students understand these English words with Spanish cognates: *authority/autoridad* (line 71), *continuously/continuamente* (line 96), *providence/providencia* (line 127), *confess/confesar* (line 129), *discover/descubrir* (line 161), *innocence/inocencia* (line 208), *opinion/opinión* (lines 221–222), *pardon/perdón* (line 243), *pretense/pretensión* (line 479), *agony/agonía* (line 500), *physical/físico* (line 501), *mystical/místico* (line 534), *instruction/instrucción* (line 570), *urgently/urgentemente* (line 572).

● DRAW CONCLUSIONS ABOUT CHARACTERS

Reread lines 232–236. What does Parris mean when he refers to "this sort"? Why does he oppose the hanging of "this sort"? ***Possible answer:*** *Parris is referring to condemned prisoners, such as Proctor and Rebecca, who have good reputations in Salem and who are supported by much of the town. Because Parris was instrumental in condemning them, he fears that the town will harm him if Proctor and Rebecca die.*

REVISIT THE BIG QUESTION

What fuels a
MOB?

Discuss Mob action that rises from hysteria feeds on excessive emotion from the crowd. After students read lines 203–210, ask them the following question: Why does Parris want to curb the emotion that is being generated out of sympathy for those who have died? ***Possible answer:*** *Parris wants to curb the sympathizers' emotion because he is afraid that hysteria will be created in the opposite direction; in other words, he fears that a hysterical mob could form against the court if people decide that their friends and family have died unjustly. This mob would be dangerous for Parris, because he supported the executions.*

Parris. Judge Hathorne—it were another sort that hanged till now. Rebecca Nurse is no Bridget that lived three year with Bishop before she married him. John Proctor is not Isaac Ward that drank his family
190 to ruin. (*to* Danforth) I would to God it were not so, Excellency, but these people have great weight yet in the town. Let Rebecca stand upon the gibbet[4] and send up some righteous prayer, and I fear she'll wake a vengeance on you.

Hathorne. Excellency, she is condemned a witch. The court have—

Danforth (*in deep concern, raising a hand to* Hathorne). Pray you. (*to* Parris) How do you propose, then?

200 **Parris.** Excellency, I would postpone these hangin's for a time.

Danforth. There will be no postponement.

Parris. Now Mr. Hale's returned, there is hope, I think—for if he bring even one of these to God, that confession surely damns the others in the public eye, and none may doubt more that they are all linked to Hell. This way, unconfessed and claiming innocence, doubts are multiplied, many honest people will weep for them, and our good purpose is
210 lost in their tears.

Danforth (*after thinking a moment, then going to* Cheever). Give me the list.

(Cheever *opens the dispatch case, searches.*)

Parris. It cannot be forgot, sir, that when I summoned the congregation for John Proctor's excommunication[5] there were hardly thirty people come to hear it. That speak a discontent, I think, and—

Danforth (*studying the list*). There will be no postponement.

220 **Parris.** Excellency—

Danforth. Now, sir—which of these in your opinion may be brought to God? I will myself strive with him[6] till dawn. (*He hands the list to* Parris, *who merely glances at it.*)

Parris. There is not sufficient time till dawn.

Danforth. I shall do my utmost. Which of them do you have hope for?

Parris (*not even glancing at the list now, and in a quavering voice, quietly*). Excellency—a dagger—
230 (*He chokes up.*)

Danforth. What do you say?

Parris. Tonight, when I open my door to leave my house—a dagger clattered to the ground. (*Silence.* Danforth *absorbs this. Now* Parris *cries out.*) You cannot hang this sort. There is danger for me. I dare not step outside at night!

(Reverend Hale *enters. They look at him for an instant in silence. He is steeped in sorrow, exhausted, and more direct than he ever was.*)

240 **Danforth.** Accept my congratulations, Reverend Hale; we are gladdened to see you returned to your good work.

Hale (*coming to* Danforth *now*). You must pardon them. They will not budge.

(Herrick *enters, waits.*)

Danforth (*conciliatory*). You misunderstand, sir; I cannot pardon these when twelve are already hanged for the same crime. It is not just.

Parris (*with failing heart*). Rebecca will not confess?

250 **Hale.** The sun will rise in a few minutes. Excellency, I must have more time.

Danforth. Now hear me, and beguile yourselves no more. I will not receive a single plea for pardon or postponement. Them that will not confess will hang. Twelve are already executed; the names of

---

4. **gibbet** (jĭb′ĭt): gallows.

5. **excommunication:** banishment from a church. For the Puritans in New England, this punishment resulted in the loss of church privileges.

6. **strive with him:** struggle with him through prayer.

DIFFERENTIATED INSTRUCTION

FOR STRUGGLING READERS

Comprehension Support Make sure that students understand these points:

- Parris may not like Proctor, but he does not think that Proctor is evil (lines 186–190).

- There has been a threat against Parris's life (lines 232–236).

- Danforth considers it "not just" to offer pardon—not because the convicted may not be guilty but because other convicted people already have died (lines 246–248).

FOR ADVANCED LEARNERS/AP

Research Terminology [paired option] Point out the word *gibbet* in line 192 and its definition in the footnote. Have students find how the term originated and how it became part of the language of hanging. Invite students to report their findings to the class.

these seven are given out, and the village expects to see them die this morning. Postponement now speaks a floundering on my part; reprieve or pardon must cast doubt upon the guilt of them that died till now. While I speak God's law, I will not crack
260 its voice with whimpering. If retaliation is your fear, know this—I should hang ten thousand that dared to rise against the law, and an ocean of salt tears could not melt the resolution of the statutes. Now draw yourselves up like men and help me, as you are bound by Heaven to do. Have you spoken with them all, Mr. Hale?

Hale. All but Proctor. He is in the dungeon.

Danforth (*to* Herrick). What's Proctor's way now?

270 **Herrick.** He sits like some great bird; you'd not know he lived except he will take food from time to time.

Danforth (*after thinking a moment*). His wife—his wife must be well on with child now.

Herrick. She is, sir.

Danforth. What think you, Mr. Parris? You have closer knowledge of this man; might her presence soften him?

Parris. It is possible, sir. He have not laid eyes on her these three months. I should summon her.

280 **Danforth** (*to* Herrick). Is he yet **adamant**? Has he struck at you again?

Herrick. He cannot, sir, he is chained to the wall now.

Danforth (*after thinking on it*). Fetch Goody Proctor to me. Then let you bring him up.

Herrick. Aye, sir. (Herrick *goes. There is silence.*)

Hale. Excellency, if you postpone a week and publish to the town that you are striving for their confessions, that speak mercy on your part, not faltering.

Danforth. Mr. Hale, as God have not empowered me
290 like Joshua to stop this sun from rising,[7] so I cannot withhold from them the perfection of their punishment.

Hale (*harder now*). If you think God wills you to raise rebellion, Mr. Danforth, you are mistaken!

Danforth (*instantly*). You have heard rebellion spoken in the town?

Hale. Excellency, there are orphans wandering from house to house; abandoned cattle bellow on the highroads, the stink of rotting crops hangs every-
300 where, and no man knows when the harlots' cry will end his life—and you wonder yet if rebellion's spoke? Better you should marvel how they do not burn your province!

Danforth. Mr. Hale, have you preached in Andover this month?

Hale. Thank God they have no need of me in Andover.

Danforth. You baffle me, sir. Why have you returned here?

310 **Hale.** Why, it is all simple. I come to do the Devil's work. I come to counsel Christians they should belie themselves. (*His sarcasm collapses.*) There is blood on my head! Can you not see the blood on my head!!

Parris. Hush! (*For he has heard footsteps. They all face the door.* Herrick *enters with* Elizabeth. *Her wrists are linked by heavy chain, which* Herrick *now removes. Her clothes are dirty; her face is pale and gaunt.* Herrick *goes out.*)

Danforth (*very politely*). Goody Proctor. (*She is*
320 *silent.*) I hope you are hearty?

Elizabeth (*as a warning reminder*). I am yet six month before my time.

Danforth. Pray be at your ease, we come not for your life. We—(*uncertain how to plead, for he is not accustomed to it.*) Mr. Hale, will you speak with the woman?

Hale. Goody Proctor, your husband is marked to hang this morning.

(*pause*)

330 **Elizabeth** (*quietly*). I have heard it.

---

7. **like Joshua . . . rising:** According to the Bible, Joshua became leader of the Israelites after Moses died. He led the people to the Promised Land while the sun stood still.

TIERED DISCUSSION PROMPTS

After students read lines 295–303, use these prompts to help students understand how grim things have become in Salem since the witch trials started:

Recall Why are there "orphans," "abandoned cattle," and "rotting crops" in Salem (lines 297–299)? *Possible answer: This situation has arisen because the men and women who are parents to the children and who tend to the cattle and crops have been jailed and even executed. (See also lines 108–110.)*

Interpret Why does Hale express surprise that an uprising has not yet occurred in Salem? *Possible answer: Hale expresses surprise because he thinks that the deadly miscarriage of justice is so bad and the circumstances so dire that people have legitimate reason to riot: Children whose parents have been taken have no home, cattle run loose because there is no one to care for them, and farms are in ruin because their owners are gone. People are fearful, for they know that they can lose their lives on the basis of a lie.*

Evaluate How effectively does Miller use descriptive language to provide information about conditions in Salem? Explain. *Possible answer: Miller effectively uses descriptive language by appealing to the audience's senses while providing information about Salem. For example, the orphans are "wandering" (line 297), a term that suggests a particular kind of movement. The cattle "bellow" (line 298) and the harlots "cry" (line 300). The rotting crops produce a "stink" (line 299).*

FOR STRUGGLING READERS

2 Targeted Passage [Lines 257–267]

This passage sheds light on Danforth's character and his role as a judge.

- What reasons does Danforth give for refusing to postpone the executions? (lines 257–260)

- What does he threaten to do in response to a possible rebellion from the Salemites? (lines 261–263)

- What does Danforth claim is his authority for making decisions of life and death? (lines 266–267)

Clarify Figurative Language Point out Hale's repeated "blood on my head" in lines 312–313. Explain that this is figurative, not literal, language; Miller means that Hale feels responsible for spilling the blood—that is, causing the deaths—of innocent people. Have students paraphrase lines 310–313, paying special attention to this phrase.

FOR ADVANCED LEARNERS/AP

Analyze Viewpoints By this point, several views about the fate of the convicted Salemites have been voiced. Ask students to identify the views of Danforth, Hale, and Parris. Then have students meet in three groups, each group discussing the strengths and weaknesses of one of the views. After group representatives have shared key discussion points with the class, discuss which view students think best reflects the attitude of the townspeople.

■ DRAW CONCLUSIONS ABOUT CHARACTERS

Reread lines 368–386. Why would Elizabeth show no emotion in response to Danforth's questions? Record character traits about Elizabeth in the prereading chart introduced on page 135. Include evidence. **Possible answer:** *Elizabeth would show no emotion because she is proud. She stands as silent and emotionless as a stone (line 373) because she refuses to be controlled by Danforth and his unjust court.*

Elizabeth	
Traits	*proud, defiant*
Evidence	*"I promise nothing" (line 386)*

Extend the Discussion Why would Elizabeth's silence and emotional restraint frustrate Danforth?

Ⓖ GRAMMAR AND STYLE

Use Realistic Dialogue Reread lines 344–351. Hale is speaking of serious topics—his remorse and his beliefs about God—so his language is more poetic and less colloquial; still, it is realistic for that time. What inverted sentence can you find in these lines? **Answer:** *"... the very crowns of holy law I brought ..." (lines 347–348)* What unusual word appears in the final sentence of this passage, and what does it mean? **Answer:** cleave, *which means "to cling"*

Hale. You know, do you not, that I have no connection with the court? (*She seems to doubt it.*) I come of my own, Goody Proctor. I would save your husband's life, for if he is taken I count myself his murderer. Do you understand me?

Elizabeth. What do you want of me?

Hale. Goody Proctor, I have gone this three month like our Lord into the wilderness.[8] I have sought a Christian way, for damnation's doubled on a minis-
340 ter who counsels men to lie.

Hathorne. It is no lie, you cannot speak of lies.

Hale. It is a lie! They are innocent!

Danforth. I'll hear no more of that!

Hale (*continuing to* Elizabeth). Let you not mistake your duty as I mistook my own. I came into this village like a bridegroom to his beloved, bearing gifts of high religion; the very crowns of holy law I brought, and what I touched with my bright confidence, it died; and where I turned the eye of my
350 great faith, blood flowed up. Beware, Goody Proctor—cleave to no faith when faith brings blood. It is mistaken law that leads you to sacrifice. Life, woman, life is God's most precious gift; no principle, however glorious, may justify the taking of it. I beg you, woman, prevail upon your husband to confess. Let him give his lie. Quail not before God's judgment in this, for it may well be God damns a liar less than he that throws his life away for pride. Will you plead with him? I cannot think he will
360 listen to another. ❸

Elizabeth (*quietly*). I think that be the Devil's argument.

Hale (*with a climactic desperation*). Woman, before the laws of God we are as swine! We cannot read His will!

Elizabeth. I cannot dispute with you, sir; I lack learning for it.

Danforth (*going to her*). Goody Proctor, you are not summoned here for disputation. Be there no wifely
370 tenderness within you? He will die with the sunrise. Your husband. Do you understand it? (*She only looks at him.*) What say you? Will you contend with him? (*She is silent.*) Are you stone? I tell you true, woman, had I no other proof of your unnatural life, your dry eyes now would be sufficient evidence that you delivered up your soul to Hell! A very ape would weep at such calamity! Have the devil dried up any tear of pity in you? (*She is silent.*) Take her out. It profit nothing she should speak to him!

380 **Elizabeth** (*quietly*). Let me speak with him, Excellency.

Parris (*with hope*). You'll strive with him? (*She hesitates.*)

Danforth. Will you plead for his confession or will you not?

Elizabeth. I promise nothing. Let me speak with him.

(*A sound—the sibilance of dragging feet on stone. They turn. A pause.* Herrick *enters with* John Proctor. *His wrists are chained. He is another man, bearded, filthy,*
390 *his eyes misty as though webs had overgrown them. He halts inside the doorway, his eye caught by the sight of* Elizabeth. *The emotion flowing between them prevents anyone from speaking for an instant. Now* Hale, *visibly affected, goes to* Danforth *and speaks quietly.*)

Hale. Pray, leave them, Excellency.

Danforth (*pressing* Hale *impatiently aside*). Mr. Proctor, you have been notified, have you not? (Proctor *is silent, staring at* Elizabeth.) I see light in the sky, Mister; let you counsel with your wife,
400 and may God help you turn your back on Hell. (Proctor *is silent, staring at* Elizabeth.)

Hale (*quietly*). Excellency, let—

(Danforth *brushes past* Hale *and walks out.* Hale *follows.* Cheever *stands and follows,* Hathorne *behind.* Herrick *goes.* Parris, *from a safe distance, offers.*)

---

8. **like our Lord ... wilderness:** According to the New Testament, Jesus spent 40 days wandering in the desert.

DIFFERENTIATED INSTRUCTION

FOR STRUGGLING READERS

❸ **Targeted Passage** [Lines 344–360]

In this passage, Hale admits that his initial views and zeal regarding the witch hunt were misdirected.

- What does Hale think happened as a result of his good intentions to defeat the Devil? (lines 348–350)
- According to Hale, what kind of faith should be abandoned? (lines 350–351)

- What is God's dearest gift to humanity? (lines 352–353)
- Which trait—dishonesty or pride—does Hale consider more harmful? Why? (lines 356–358)

FOR ADVANCED LEARNERS/AP

Analyze Tone [SMALL-GROUP OPTION] Have students discuss Elizabeth Proctor's tone in Act Four, covering these moments:

- her interview with Danforth, Parris, and Hale (lines 319–386)

- her private conversation with her husband (lines 410–518)
- her words when he agrees to confess (lines 541–542, 552–554)
- her comments just before he is led off to be executed (lines 781–783)

Students should identify the tone in each passage, point out shifts in tone, and offer insights into Elizabeth's character. Invite students to share their observations with the class.

Parris. If you desire a cup of cider, Mr. Proctor, I am sure I—(Proctor *turns an icy stare at him, and he breaks off.* Parris *raises his palms toward* Proctor.) God lead you now. (Parris *goes out.*)

410 (*Alone.* Proctor *walks to her, halts. It is as though they stood in a spinning world. It is beyond sorrow, above it. He reaches out his hand as though toward an embodiment not quite real, and as he touches her, a strange soft sound, half laughter, half amazement, comes from his throat. He pats her hand. She covers his hand with hers. And then, weak, he sits. Then she sits, facing him.*)

Proctor. The child?

Elizabeth. It grows.

Proctor. There is no word of the boys?

420 **Elizabeth.** They're well. Rebecca's Samuel keeps them.

Proctor. You have not seen them?

Elizabeth. I have not. (*She catches a weakening in herself and downs it.*)

Proctor. You are a—marvel, Elizabeth.

Elizabeth. You—have been tortured?

Proctor. Aye. (*Pause. She will not let herself be drowned in the sea that threatens her.*) They come for my life now.

Elizabeth. I know it.

430 (*pause*)

Proctor. None—have yet confessed?

Elizabeth. There be many confessed.

Proctor. Who are they?

Elizabeth. There be a hundred or more, they say. Goody Ballard is one; Isaiah Goodkind is one. There be many.

Proctor. Rebecca?

Elizabeth. Not Rebecca. She is one foot in Heaven now; naught may hurt her more.

440 **Proctor.** And Giles?

Elizabeth. You have not heard of it?

Proctor. I hear nothin', where I am kept.

Elizabeth. Giles is dead.

(*He looks at her incredulously.*)

Proctor. When were he hanged?

Elizabeth (*quietly, factually*). He were not hanged. He would not answer aye or nay to his indictment; for if he denied the charge they'd hang him surely, and auction out his property. So he stand mute, and 450 died Christian under the law. And so his sons will have his farm. It is the law, for he could not be condemned a wizard without he answer the indictment, aye or nay.

Proctor. Then how does he die?

Elizabeth (*gently*). They press him, John.

Proctor. Press?

Elizabeth. Great stones they lay upon his chest until he plead aye or nay. (*with a tender smile for the old man*) They say he give them but two words. "More 460 weight," he says. And died.

Proctor (*numbed—a thread to weave into his agony*). "More weight."

Elizabeth. Aye. It were a fearsome[9] man, Giles Corey. (*pause*)

Proctor (*with great force of will, but not quite looking at her*). I have been thinking I would confess to them, Elizabeth. (*She shows nothing.*) What say you? If I give them that?

Elizabeth. I cannot judge you, John.

470 (*pause*)

Proctor (*simply—a pure question*). What would you have me do?

Elizabeth. As you will, I would have it. (*slight pause*) I want you living, John. That's sure.

Proctor (*pauses, then with a flailing of hope*). Giles' wife? Have she confessed?

Elizabeth. She will not.

---

9. **fearsome:** courageous.

REVISIT THE BIG QUESTION

What fuels a MOB?

Discuss After students read lines 410–428, ask the following question: How is the Proctor family a symbol of what hysteria has done to the people in and around Salem? *Possible answer: The family is a symbol because the reader sees the real-life effects of judgments driven by hysteria:*

- *A husband and wife are torn apart.*
- *A father will die unnecessarily.*
- *Children lose their parents (for Elizabeth has not seen her sons in months, and the baby that she is carrying never will know its father).*

The hysterical search for the Devil was supposed to protect people; instead, it is destroying them.

FOR STRUGGLING READERS

Concept Support Clarify the matter of property law that is addressed in the account of Giles Corey's death (lines 446–460).

- If Giles had acknowledged that charges had been made against him but had refused to confess, he would have been declared guilty of witchcraft and hanged. His family would have lost his land because it would have been sold at auction.

- Because Giles refused to acknowledge the charges against him, he avoided being condemned for witchcraft. He was still executed, but his silence meant that his family would keep his land.

Ask students to offer opinions about Giles's decision to remain silent and then to explain the effect that the account has upon Proctor.

FOR ENGLISH LANGUAGE LEARNERS

Vocabulary Support Use New Word Analysis to teach these words: *justify* (line 354), *physical* (line 501), *release* (line 553), *issue* (line 647), *document* (line 732), *final* (line 784).

 BEST PRACTICES TOOLKIT—Transparency
New Word Analysis p. E8

DRAW CONCLUSIONS ABOUT CHARACTERS

In lines 481–487, why does Proctor say that it does not matter if he lies when confessing to acts that he did not commit? What conclusion can you draw about Proctor's opinion of himself? *Possible answer: Proctor says that it does not matter if he lies because that sin will be just one of many that he has committed; as he comments, "Nothing's spoiled . . . that were not rotten long before" (lines 483–485). Proctor seems to have a low opinion of himself, for he says, "I am no good man" (line 483).*

IF STUDENTS NEED HELP . . . Focus on Proctor's statement "My honesty is broke . . ." (lines 482–483). Ask:

- How has Proctor been dishonest in the past? *Possible answer: He has had and has tried to cover up a liaison with Abigail.*

- Why does he feel that his honesty has been broken and cannot be repaired? *Possible answer: His honesty has been irreparably broken because he has revealed his liaison to the court and because his relationship with Elizabeth has changed for the worse since then.*

Extend the Discussion How do Proctor and Elizabeth agree or disagree about Proctor's refusal to confess so far?

(*pause*)

Proctor. It is a pretense, Elizabeth.

480 **Elizabeth.** What is?

Proctor. I cannot mount the gibbet like a saint. It is a fraud. I am not that man. (*She is silent.*) My honesty is broke, Elizabeth; I am no good man. Nothing's spoiled by giving them this lie that were not rotten long before.

Elizabeth. And yet you've not confessed till now. That speak goodness in you.

Proctor. Spite only keeps me silent. It is hard to give a lie to dogs. (*Pause. For the first time he turns directly*
490 *to her.*) I would have your forgiveness, Elizabeth.

Elizabeth. It is not for me to give, John, I am—

Proctor. I'd have you see some honesty in it. Let them that never lied die now to keep their souls. It is pretense for me, a vanity that will not blind God nor keep my children out of the wind. (*pause*) What say you?

Elizabeth (*upon a heaving sob that always threatens*). John, it come to naught that I should forgive you, if you'll not forgive yourself. (*Now he turns away a little,*
500 *in great agony.*) It is not my soul, John, it is yours. (*He stands, as though in physical pain, slowly rising to his feet with a great immortal longing to find his answer. It is difficult to say, and she is on the verge of tears.*) Only be sure of this, for I know it now: Whatever you will do, it is a good man does it. (*He turns his doubting, searching gaze upon her.*) I have read my heart this three month, John. (*pause*) I have sins of my own to count. It needs a cold wife to prompt lechery.

Proctor (*in great pain*). Enough, enough—

510 **Elizabeth** (*now pouring out her heart*). Better you should know me!

Proctor. I will not hear it! I know you!

Elizabeth. You take my sins upon you, John—

Proctor (*in agony*). No, I take my own, my own!

Elizabeth. John, I counted myself so plain, so poorly made, no honest love could come to me! Suspicion kissed you when I did; I never knew how I should say my love. It were a cold house I kept! (*In fright, she swerves, as* Hathorne *enters.*)

520 **Hathorne.** What say you, Proctor? The sun is soon up.

(Proctor, *his chest heaving, stares, turns to* Elizabeth. *She comes to him as though to plead, her voice quaking.*)

Elizabeth. Do what you will. But let none be your judge. There be no higher judge under Heaven than Proctor is! Forgive me, forgive me, John—I never knew such goodness in the world! (*She covers her face, weeping.*)

(Proctor *turns from her to* Hathorne; *he is off the earth, his voice hollow.*)

530 **Proctor.** I want my life.

Hathorne (*electrified, surprised*). You'll confess yourself?

Proctor. I will have my life.

Hathorne (*with a mystical tone*). God be praised! It is a providence! (*He rushes out the door, and his voice is heard calling down the corridor.*) He will confess! Proctor will confess!

Proctor (*with a cry, as he strides to the door*). Why do you cry it? (*In great pain he turns back to her.*) It is
540 evil, is it not? It is evil.

Elizabeth (*in terror, weeping*). I cannot judge you, John, I cannot!

Proctor. Then who will judge me? (*suddenly clasping his hands*) God in Heaven, what is John Proctor, what is John Proctor? (*He moves as an animal, and a fury is riding in him, a tantalized search.*) I think it is honest, I think so; I am no saint. (*As though she had denied this he calls angrily at her.*) Let Rebecca go like a saint; for me it is fraud!

550 (*Voices are heard in the hall, speaking together in suppressed excitement.*)

DIFFERENTIATED INSTRUCTION

FOR ADVANCED LEARNERS/AP

Debate Proctor's Dilemma Have students reread lines 541–549 and think about Proctor's lament: "what is John Proctor?" (line 544) Then divide students into two groups and have them debate Proctor's dilemma: Should he submit to being hanged, or should he confess? Each group should argue for one of the options. Present these questions for students to consider:

- Would dying make Proctor a noble person, or a fraud?

- Would confessing make Proctor weak, or honest (honest about being a sinner—not honest about associating with the Devil)?

Conclude by discussing with all participants which option would better enable Arthur Miller, as the playwright, to highlight the ideas that he wanted to convey.

Elizabeth. I am not your judge, I cannot be. (*as though giving him release*) Do as you will, do as you will!

Proctor. Would you give them such a lie? Say it. Would you ever give them this? (*She cannot answer.*) You would not; if tongs of fire were singeing you you would not! It is evil. Good, then—it is evil, and I do it!

560 (*Hathorne enters with* Danforth, *and, with them,* Cheever, Parris, *and* Hale. *It is a businesslike, rapid entrance, as though the ice had been broken.*)

Targeted Passage

Danforth (*with great relief and gratitude*). Praise to God, man, praise to God; you shall be blessed in Heaven for this. (Cheever *has hurried to the bench with pen, ink, and paper.* Proctor *watches him.*) Now then, let us have it. Are you ready, Mr. Cheever?

Proctor (*with a cold, cold horror at their efficiency*). Why must it be written?

570 **Danforth.** Why, for the good instruction of the village, Mister; this we shall post upon the church door! (*to* Parris, *urgently*) Where is the marshal?

Parris (*runs to the door and calls down the corridor*). Marshal! Hurry!

John and Elizabeth Proctor before the marshal

THE CRUCIBLE: ACT FOUR **209**

Use these prompts to help students understand the chaos that results in lines 560–574 from Proctor's decision to confess:

Summarize How would a confession benefit Proctor? *Possible answer: A confession would save Proctor from execution.* How would it benefit the court? *Possible answer: It would prove the court right and represent a victory.*

Analyze Why is there such urgency in Danforth's and Parris's actions? *Possible answer: The stage directions note that Danforth speaks "with great relief and gratitude" (line 563); those positive emotions could speed up activity. In addition, both men act with haste because the hour of execution is upon them. Perhaps most important, they act with urgency because they want to record Proctor's confession as quickly as possible. They may fear that he will change his mind, thwarting their efforts.*

Synthesize Note Proctor's reaction to the chaos that follows his decision. Do you think that he will stick with his resolution to confess? Why or why not? *Possible answer: Proctor may change his mind and not confess, for he is filled with "a cold, cold horror" at seeing the court's haste. He asks suspiciously, "Why must it [the confession] be written?" (line 569)*

FOR STRUGGLING READERS

④ Targeted Passage [Lines 552–574]

In this passage, Proctor makes a decision that speeds the play's plot toward its climax.

- What advice does Elizabeth give Proctor? What does he think she would do if she were in his position? (lines 553–558)

- What announcement does Proctor make? How does Danforth respond? (lines 558–559, 563–565)

- Why does Danforth insist on a written confession? How does Proctor seem to react? (lines 568–572)

Comprehension Support Point out that the scene in the photograph and the scene in this part of the play present the same action. The filmed scene is set outside, but the scene in the play occurs inside the jail.

TEXT ANALYSIS

COMMON CORE
RL 3
RL 5

● *Model the Skill:*
CONVENTIONS OF DRAMA

How does the dialogue in lines 610–633 create suspense? *Possible answer: In this passage, Proctor is urged to testify against Rebecca as she stands in front of him. Suspense builds as Danforth asks Proctor a series of questions that are meant to push him into incriminating his neighbors. The reader or audience waits anxiously for each of Proctor's answers to discover whether he will join the long list of those who have lied about their neighbors.*

Review the mounting suspense by examining how Proctor continues to waver in his decision to lie and confess. Review the preceding exchange (lines 592–609); then elicit that Rebecca's presence weakens Proctor's resolve because (1) she challenges his decision and (2) she still refuses to confess, even though she is just minutes away from her own execution.

Danforth. Now, then, Mister, will you speak slowly, and directly to the point, for Mr. Cheever's sake. (*He is on record now, and is really dictating to* Cheever, *who writes.*) Mr. Proctor, have you seen the Devil in your life? (*Proctor's jaws lock.*) Come, man, there
580 is light in the sky; the town waits at the scaffold; I would give out this news. Did you see the Devil?

Proctor. I did.

Parris. Praise God!

Danforth. And when he come to you, what were his demand? (*Proctor is silent. Danforth helps.*) Did he bid you to do his work upon the earth?

Proctor. He did.

Danforth. And you bound yourself to his service? (*Danforth turns, as* Rebecca Nurse *enters, with*
590 Herrick *helping to support her. She is barely able to walk.*) Come in, come in, woman!

Rebecca (*brightening as she sees* Proctor). Ah, John! You are well, then, eh?

(Proctor *turns his face to the wall.*)

Danforth. Courage, man, courage—let her witness your good example that she may come to God herself. Now hear it, Goody Nurse! Say on, Mr. Proctor. Did you bind yourself to the Devil's service?

Rebecca (*astonished*). Why, John!

600 **Proctor** (*through his teeth, his face turned from* Rebecca). I did.

Danforth. Now, woman, you surely see it profit nothin' to keep this conspiracy any further. Will you confess yourself with him?

Rebecca. Oh, John—God send his mercy on you!

Danforth. I say, will you confess yourself, Goody Nurse?

Rebecca. Why, it is a lie, it is a lie; how may I damn myself? I cannot, I cannot.

610 **Danforth.** Mr. Proctor. When the Devil came to you did you see Rebecca Nurse in his company? (*Proctor is silent.*) Come, man, take courage—did you ever see her with the Devil?

Proctor (*almost inaudibly*). No.

(Danforth, *now sensing trouble, glances at* John *and goes to the table, and picks up a sheet—the list of condemned.*)

Danforth. Did you ever see her sister, Mary Easty, with the Devil?

620 **Proctor.** No, I did not.

Danforth (*his eyes narrow on* Proctor). Did you ever see Martha Corey with the Devil?

Proctor. I did not.

Danforth (*realizing, slowly putting the sheet down*). Did you ever see anyone with the Devil?

Proctor. I did not.

Danforth. Proctor, you mistake me. I am not empowered to trade your life for a lie. You have most certainly seen some person with the Devil.
630 (Proctor *is silent.*) Mr. Proctor, a score of people have already testified they saw this woman with the Devil.

Proctor. Then it is proved. Why must I say it?

Danforth. Why "must" you say it! Why, you should rejoice to say it if your soul is truly purged of any love for Hell!

Proctor. They think to go like saints. I like not to spoil their names.

Danforth (*inquiring, incredulous*). Mr. Proctor, do
640 you think they go like saints?

Proctor (*evading*). This woman never thought she done the Devil's work.

Danforth. Look you, sir. I think you mistake your duty here. It matters nothing what she thought—she is convicted of the unnatural murder of children, and you for sending your spirit out upon Mary Warren. Your soul alone is the issue here, Mister, and you will prove its whiteness or you cannot live in a Christian country. Will you tell me now what
650 persons conspired with you in the Devil's company? (*Proctor is silent.*) To your knowledge was Rebecca Nurse ever—

DIFFERENTIATED INSTRUCTION

FOR STRUGGLING READERS

Concept Support As you point out the stage directions in lines 592–602, help students interpret these terms:

- "brightening" (line 592): The sight of Proctor makes Rebecca happy.

- "turns his face to the wall" (line 594): Proctor is too ashamed of himself to look Rebecca in the face.

- "through his teeth" (line 600): Proctor forces himself to speak.

FOR ADVANCED LEARNERS/AP

Interpret Irony Have students reread lines 575–582 and then write a brief explanation of how Proctor's answer of "I did" to Danforth's question "Did you see the Devil?" can be interpreted as irony. (You might point out that in this case, irony would be the contrast between what Proctor says and what he means.) After students have shared their interpretations, have the class decide whether Proctor means to be ironic.

Proctor. I speak my own sins; I cannot judge another. (*crying out, with hatred*) I have no tongue for it.

Hale (*quickly to* Danforth). Excellency, it is enough he confess himself. Let him sign it, let him sign it.

Parris (*feverishly*). It is a great service, sir. It is a weighty name; it will strike the village that Proctor 660 confess. I beg you, let him sign it. The sun is up, Excellency!

Danforth (*considers; then with dissatisfaction*). Come, then, sign your testimony. (*to* Cheever) Give it to him. (Cheever *goes to* Proctor, *the confession and a pen in hand.* Proctor *does not look at it.*) Come, man, sign it.

Proctor (*after glancing at the confession*). You have all witnessed it—it is enough.

Danforth. You will not sign it?

670 **Proctor.** You have all witnessed it; what more is needed?

Danforth. Do you sport with me? You will sign your name or it is no confession, Mister! (*His breast heaving with agonized breathing,* Proctor *now lays the paper down and signs his name.*)

Parris. Praise be to the Lord!

(Proctor *has just finished signing when* Danforth *reaches for the paper. But* Proctor *snatches it up, and now a wild terror is rising in him, and a boundless anger.*)

680 **Danforth** (*perplexed, but politely extending his hand*). If you please, sir.

Proctor. No.

Danforth (*as though* Proctor *did not understand*). Mr. Proctor, I must have—

Proctor. No, no. I have signed it. You have seen me. It is done! You have no need for this.

Parris. Proctor, the village must have proof that—

Proctor. Damn the village! I confess to God, and God has seen my name on this! It is enough!

690 **Danforth.** No, sir, it is—

Proctor. You came to save my soul, did you not?

Here! I have confessed myself; it is enough!

Danforth. You have not con—

Proctor. I have confessed myself! Is there no good penitence but it be public? God does not need my name nailed upon the church! God sees my name; God knows how black my sins are! It is enough!

Danforth. Mr. Proctor—

Proctor. You will not use me! I am no Sarah Good or 700 Tituba, I am John Proctor! You will not use me! It is no part of salvation that you should use me!

Danforth. I do not wish to—

Proctor. I have three children—how may I teach them to walk like men in the world, and I sold my friends?

Danforth. You have not sold your friends—

Proctor. Beguile me not! I blacken all of them when this is nailed to the church the very day they hang for silence!

710 **Danforth.** Mr. Proctor, I must have good and legal proof that you—

Proctor. You are the high court, your word is good enough! Tell them I confessed myself; say Proctor broke his knees and wept like a woman; say what you will, but my name cannot—

Danforth (*with suspicion*). It is the same, is it not? If I report it or you sign to it?

Proctor (*He knows it is insane*). No, it is not the same! What others say and what I sign to is not the same!

720 **Danforth.** Why? Do you mean to deny this confession when you are free?

Proctor. I mean to deny nothing!

Danforth. Then explain to me, Mr. Proctor, why you will not let—

Proctor (*with a cry of his whole soul*). Because it is my name! Because I cannot have another in my life! Because I lie and sign myself to lies! Because I am not worth the dust on the feet of them that hang! How may I live without my name? I have given you 730 my soul; leave me my name!

TIERED DISCUSSION PROMPTS

After students read lines 716–730, use these prompts to help students understand why Proctor is so upset at the prospect of having his signed confession made public:

Restate Paraphrase Proctor's lament in lines 725–730. **Possible answer:** *Because my name is my reputation and my honor! Because I have only one chance to have a good reputation! Because I lied when I confessed and when I signed that false confession! Because I am worth so much less than the people who have died rather than confess! How may I live without my honor? I have given you my soul; leave me my good reputation!*

Interpret What does Proctor mean when he exclaims, "What others say and what I sign to is not the same" (line 719)? **Possible answer:** *Proctor means that someone else's words about him, even if the words are true, do not have the moral authority of Proctor's own signature—literally, his "name," which is synonymous with his reputation.*

Synthesize What do you think will happen after this heated exchange, and why? **Possible answer:** *Danforth, whose resolve shows no sign of weakening, will probably continue to demand that Proctor turn over the signed confession. At this point, Proctor seems equally resolved; he probably will do whatever he feels necessary to keep the confession out of Danforth's hands, even if doing so sends him to the gibbet.*

FOR ENGLISH LANGUAGE LEARNERS
Vocabulary: Prefixes and Suffixes [shared-language groups] Explain that the prefix *con-* in *confess* (line 606) means "together." *Confess* literally means "to admit together"—that is, to admit sins to someone. Direct students' attention also to *condemned* ("sentenced together," line 617). Then have shared-language groups use a dictionary and follow these steps to explore some common prefixes and suffixes:

- Find *conspired* on page 210. Discuss the use of *con-*. **Possible answer:** *Conspired* (line 650) *means "overpowered together."*

- The prefix *mis-* gives *mistake* (line 627) the literal meaning of "to take (understand) incorrectly." Think of and define two other words with the same prefix. **Possible answer:** *Misapply means "to apply incorrectly"; misfile means "to file incorrectly."*

- The suffix *-ion* identifies nouns and means "an act of" or "a state of"; it gives *confession* (line 664) the literal meaning of "an act of confessing." Find the words *dissatisfaction* and *suspicion* on page 211. Discuss the use of *-ion* in each word. **Possible answer:** *Dissatisfaction (line 662) means "a state of being dissatisfied"; suspicion (line 716) means "an act or state of being suspicious."*

REVISIT THE BIG QUESTION

What fuels a
MOB?

Discuss After students read lines 731–740, ask the following question: Why is Danforth's pronouncement of "I will not deal in lies" (line 733) ironic? *Possible answer: The pronouncement is ironic because Danforth's court and its judgments are based on lies—the lies of Abigail, the other girls, and adults who are emotionally overwrought or who use the situation to take advantage of their neighbors.* How would you describe the connection between lies and hysteria as the play now reaches its climax? *Possible answer: The connection is that hysteria has placed Proctor in this life-and-death climactic moment; ironically, the only way that he can save himself is to lie by signing a false confession.*

SELECTION WRAP-UP

READ WITH A PURPOSE After students finish reading the play, have them consider the price paid by people caught up in false rumors. Ask students how the community will recover from the effects of the hysteria inspired by the rumors. *Possible answers: The community may learn from its mistakes or it may fall apart because so many good people were punished or killed because of false rumors and hysteria.*

⭐ **CRITIQUE** Have students identify the part of *The Crucible* that had the strongest impact on them and then explain why.

Danforth (*pointing at the confession in* Proctor's *hand*). Is that document a lie? If it is a lie I will not accept it! What say you? I will not deal in lies, Mister! (Proctor *is motionless.*) You will give me your honest confession in my hand, or I cannot keep you from the rope. (Proctor *does not reply.*) Which way do you go, Mister?

(*His breast heaving, his eyes staring,* Proctor *tears the paper and crumples it, and he is weeping in fury, but* 740 *erect.*)

Danforth. Marshal!

Parris (*hysterically, as though the tearing paper were his life*). Proctor, Proctor!

Hale. Man, you will hang! You cannot!

Proctor (*his eyes full of tears*). I can. And there's your first marvel, that I can. You have made your magic now, for now I do think I see some shred of goodness in John Proctor. Not enough to weave a banner with, but white enough to keep it from such dogs. 750 (Elizabeth, *in a burst of terror, rushes to him and weeps against his hand.*) Give them no tear! Tears pleasure them! Show honor now, show a stony heart and sink them with it! (*He has lifted her, and kisses her now with great passion.*)

Rebecca. Let you fear nothing! Another judgment waits us all! ⑤

Danforth. Hang them high over the town! Who weeps for these, weeps for corruption! (*He sweeps out past them.* Herrick *starts to lead* Rebecca, *who almost* 760 *collapses, but* Proctor *catches her, and she glances up at him apologetically.*)

Rebecca. I've had no breakfast.

Herrick. Come, man.

(Herrick *escorts them out,* Hathorne *and* Cheever *behind them.* Elizabeth *stands staring at the empty doorway.*)

Parris (*in deadly fear, to* Elizabeth). Go to him, Goody Proctor! There is yet time!

(*From outside a drumroll strikes the air.* Parris *is star-* 770 *tled.* Elizabeth *jerks about toward the window.*)

Parris. Go to him! (*He rushes out the door, as though to hold back his fate.*) Proctor! Proctor!

(*again, a short burst of drums*)

Hale. Woman, plead with him! (*He starts to rush out the door, and then goes back to her.*) Woman! It is pride, it is vanity. (*She avoids his eyes, and moves to the window. He drops to his knees.*) Be his helper!— What profit him to bleed? Shall the dust praise him? Shall the worms declare his truth? Go to him, take 780 his shame away!

Elizabeth (*supporting herself against collapse, grips the bars of the window, and with a cry*). He have his goodness now. God forbid I take it from him!

(*The final drumroll crashes, then heightens violently.* Hale *weeps in frantic prayer, and the new sun is pouring in upon her face, and the drums rattle like bones in the morning air. The curtain falls.*)

DIFFERENTIATED INSTRUCTION

FOR STRUGGLING READERS

⑤ **Targeted Passage [Lines 745–756]**

This passage illustrates the idea that being true to oneself can be a source of strength.

- What is Proctor's "first marvel"? (line 746)

- What does Proctor think that he now has? How has it come to him? (lines 747–748)

- Why does Proctor urge Elizabeth not to cry? (lines 751–753)

- Why does Rebecca tell John not to fear? (lines 755–756)

FOR ENGLISH LANGUAGE LEARNERS

Related Vocabulary The climax of *The Crucible* is filled with great drama and strong passions. Make sure students are aware that Miller's word choices help create and support this mood. Then review or teach these interrelated words from the final scene:

- *heaving* (line 738), "rising and falling forcefully"

- *fury* (line 739), "intense anger"

- *hysterically* (line 742), "done in a way that suggests irrational emotionalism"

- *burst* (line 750), "sudden release"

- *terror* (line 750), "overwhelming fear"

- *collapses* (line 760), "falls down"

- *deadly* (line 767), "absolute, extreme"

- *plead* (line 774), "to make a sincere request"

- *frantic* (line 785), "marked by strong emotion and disorder"

Comprehension

1. **Recall** Why has Reverend Hale returned to Salem?

2. **Clarify** Why does Danforth summon Elizabeth Proctor?

3. **Summarize** What does John Proctor do when asked to sign a confession?

Text Analysis

4. **Infer Character Motives** Explain why each of the following characters wants John and the other prisoners to confess. Support your answer with evidence.

   • Danforth   • Parris   • Hale

5. **Examine Dialogue** Reread Elizabeth Proctor's dialogue at the end of Act Four (lines 782–783) when she says of her husband, "He have his goodness now." What do you think she means? Do you agree with her?

6. **Analyze Conventions of Drama** Much of the **plot** of *The Crucible* is built around the internal and external conflicts of John Proctor. An **internal conflict** is a struggle between opposing forces within a character. An **external conflict** pits a character against nature, society, or another character. Use a chart like the one shown to show the internal and external conflicts of John Proctor. How is each resolved?

Conflict	Internal or External?	How Resolved

7. **Draw Conclusions About Characters** Refer to the chart of character traits you have created. Which characters have changed over the course of the play? How have they changed? Cite specific details from the play.

8. **Interpret Symbol** A crucible is a severe test or trial. It is also a vessel in which materials are melted at high temperatures to produce a more refined substance. What do you think a crucible might symbolize in this drama?

9. **Synthesize Themes** A theme is a central idea the writer wishes to share with the reader. This idea may be a lesson about life or about people and their actions. What do you think are some of the themes of *The Crucible*?

Text Criticism

10. **Critical Interpretations** Many critics have observed that Miller's play goes beyond the historical events of 17th- and 20th-century America and explores universal conflicts. What universal conflicts does the play deal with?

What fuels a **MOB?**

In Act Four, what motivates several of the characters to resist the mob mentality that has swept through Salem?

COMMON CORE

RL 1 Cite textual evidence to support analysis of what the text says explicitly as well as inferences drawn from the text, including determining where the text leaves matters uncertain. **RL 2** Determine two or more themes or central ideas of a text and analyze their development over the course of the text, including how they interact and build on one another to produce a complex account; provide an objective summary of the text. **RL 3** Analyze the impact of the author's choices regarding how to develop and relate elements of a drama. **RL 5** Analyze how an author's choices concerning how to structure specific parts of a text contribute to its overall structure and meaning as well as its aesthetic impact.

THE CRUCIBLE   **213**

Practice and Apply

For preliminary support of post-reading questions, use these copy masters:

R RESOURCE MANAGER—Copy Masters
   Reading Check p. 241
   Conventions of Drama p. 237
   Question Support p. 242
   Additional selection questions are provided for teachers on page 233.

ANSWERS   COMMON CORE RL 1, RL 2, RL 3, RL 5

1. *Hale has returned to persuade the condemned to confess.*

2. *Danforth hopes that Elizabeth can persuade her husband to confess.*

3. *First, Proctor refuses to sign the confession. Then he signs it but will not give it to Danforth. Finally, he tears it up.*

Possible answers:

4. *Danforth believes that the prisoners are guilty; he wants to save their souls (lines 221–223).*

   Parris no longer believes that they are guilty; he fears that he will be held accountable for executing innocent people (lines 203–210 and 232–236).

   Hale does not believe that they are guilty; he wants to save their lives (lines 131–134).

5. *Elizabeth means that Proctor has shown true courage and character by not lying to save his life. Most students will agree.*

6. ● **COMMON CORE FOCUS** *Conventions of Drama*

   Struggle over feelings for Abigail; Internal; Comes to despise her

   Struggle over decision to confess; Internal; Recants confession to save his reputation

   Struggle with Elizabeth; External; Rediscovers his love for her

   Struggle with the court; External; Refuses to confess and so is hanged

7. ● **COMMON CORE FOCUS** *Draw Conclusions About Characters* Proctor has changed by accepting his faults and fighting for the integrity that he has left. Hale has changed by questioning himself and then taking a more compassionate stance

---

and by siding with the prisoners instead of the court.

8. *A crucible might symbolize the witch trials, which put stress upon the entire community. The trials refine some characters and destroy others.*

9. *One strong theme is that even a seemingly stable society can be shaken by irrational fear. Another is that society can imprison and persecute people, but it cannot take away their integrity.*

10. *The play addresses conflicts such as good versus evil, dissent versus authority, the individual versus society, and fear versus courage.*

What fuels a MOB? **Possible answer:** *Their sense of integrity and their belief in the truth have caused them to resist.*

ANSWERS

Vocabulary in Context

▲ VOCABULARY PRACTICE

1. *antonyms*   6. *synonyms*

2. *synonyms*   7. *synonyms*

3. *antonyms*   8. *synonyms*

4. *antonyms*   9. *synonyms*

5. *antonyms*

 **RESOURCE MANAGER—Copy Master**
Vocabulary Practice p. 239

ACADEMIC VOCABULARY IN WRITING

Students should identify and write about a specific situation that *illustrates* a loss of control. Remind them to *reveal* only details they feel comfortable sharing. Finally, they should *interpret* the lesson they learned from the experience.

VOCABULARY STRATEGY: CONTEXT CLUES

⸝COMMON CORE⸜ **L 4a, L 5b**

Tell students to look at both the words and the punctuation around the word in question to figure out its meaning, as in this example:

> The anarchy, or lawlessness, in Salem was frightening.

Explain that *anarchy* means "lawlessness." "Lawlessness," a restatement of the vocabulary word, is set off with commas.

Answers

1. *(c) lower in importance*

2. *(c) wickedness*

3. *(a) improve*

4. *(a) angry*

5. *(b) presumptuousness*

 **RESOURCE MANAGER—Copy Master**
Vocabulary Strategy p. 240

Interactive Vocabulary   **THINK** central

Keywords direct students to a **WordSharp** tutorial on **thinkcentral.com** or to other types of vocabulary practice and review.

Vocabulary in Context

▲ VOCABULARY PRACTICE

Decide whether the words in each pair are synonyms or antonyms.

1. iniquity/goodness	6. anarchy/disorder
2. contentious/argumentative	7. corroborate/substantiate
3. adamant/unsure	8. imperceptible/unnoticeable
4. immaculate/filthy	9. subservient/subordinate
5. deference/impudence	

WORD LIST

adamant
anarchy
contentious
corroborate
deference
immaculate
imperceptible
iniquity
subservient

ACADEMIC VOCABULARY IN WRITING

• document • illustrate • interpret • promote • reveal

The plot of *The Crucible* **illustrates** how rapidly a situation can spiral out of control. Write about an experience in which you lost control of a situation. What could you have done to prevent it? In your response, try to use at least one additional Academic Vocabulary word.

VOCABULARY STRATEGY: CONTEXT CLUES

⸝COMMON CORE⸜

L 4a Use context as a clue to the meaning of a word or phrase. **L 5b** Analyze nuances in the meaning of words with similar denotations.

The words, sentences, paragraphs, and even punctuation marks that surround a word make up its **context.** Often context can help you figure out the meaning of an unfamiliar word or help you better understand the various shades of meaning that words can have.

PRACTICE Locate each word below in its context in the play. Then write the letter of the correct definition for each.

1. **subservient** (page 147): (a) forceful, (b) vengeful, (c) lower in importance

2. **iniquity** (page 151): (a) forgetfulness, (b) act of not caring, (c) wickedness

3. **ameliorate** (page 168): (a) improve, (b) aggravate, (c) move farther along

4. **contentious** (page 182): (a) angry, (b) generous, (c) misguided

5. **effrontery** (page 188): (a) patience, (b) presumptuousness, (c) desire to talk a lot

Interactive Vocabulary **THINK** central

Go to **thinkcentral.com.**
KEYWORD: HML11-214

DIFFERENTIATED INSTRUCTION

FOR ENGLISH LANGUAGE LEARNERS

Task Support: Vocabulary Practice Have students work together in small mixed-language groups to find words in the Word List that have cognates in their home language or other languages they know. Help students identify these words with Spanish cognates: *anarchy, conciliatory, corroborate, deposition, immaculate, imperceptible, iniquity, subservient.*

FOR ADVANCED LEARNERS/AP

Vocabulary in Writing Have students use several vocabulary words in a paragraph that describes another character in *The Crucible* from Mary Warren's point of view. Ask students to share these paragraphs with other students who choose the same character or with the entire class. Do students agree with the character sketch as presented from Mary's perspective?

Language

◆ **GRAMMAR AND STYLE:** Use Realistic Dialogue

A play consists almost entirely of dialogue, so it is important that the characters' speech match the setting. In *The Crucible*, Arthur Miller's **word choice** and use of **inverted sentences** reflect the speech of the time, contributing to the author's realistic depiction of life in 17th-century Salem. Here are some examples:

> **Parris.** . . . *Let him look to medicine and put out all thought of unnatural causes here. There be none.* (Act One, lines 50–52)

> **Susanna.** *Aye, sir. . . .* (Act One, line 52)

> **Abigail.** *Now look you. All of you. We danced. . . .* (Act One, line 353)

Here, Miller uses *be* rather than *are*, the verb form we use in this context today. Instead of *yes*, he uses the word *aye*, a word that was commonplace in the 1600s but is rarely used today. Finally, he uses a type of inverted word order common to 17th-century speech, with the verb preceding the subject.

PRACTICE Rewrite the following sentences so that they better reflect the 17th-century speech patterns that Miller employs.

> **EXAMPLE**
> You go to the house!
> *Go you to the house!*

1. Yes, it is true I saw the devil with Rebecca Nurse.
2. Are you sure of their guilt?
3. You confess to these sins!

READING-WRITING CONNECTION

Expand your understanding of Miller's play by responding to this prompt. Then, use the **revising tips** to improve your essay.

WRITING PROMPT	**REVISING TIPS**
ANALYZE MOTIVATIONS Why does John Proctor change his mind and tear up the confession? In **four or five paragraphs,** discuss Proctor's perception of a morally righteous person and how that perception affects his decision. Think about Rebecca Nurse's reaction to his confession and Elizabeth's assertion that "there be no higher judge under Heaven than Proctor is!"	• Explain the choices Proctor must make to arrive at his decision. • Clarify how Proctor's idea of morality differs from that of the judges. • Use quotations and examples from the play to support key points.

Interactive Revision THINK central

Go to **thinkcentral.com**.
KEYWORD: HML11-215

FOR STRUGGLING WRITERS

Writing Support

- Have students reread Act Four, lines 677–749, and make some notes about the scene in question.
- Help students identify characters whose opinions Proctor would probably consider important (for example, Rebecca Nurse) or unimportant (for example, Reverend Parris).
- Use answers to some past After Reading questions to model the use of quotations and examples as support of key points.

- Suggest that students organize their analysis in this way:

Introduction: Explain what Proctor does (tears up his confession) and why he does it.
Body: Discuss his possible motivations (for example, he is worried about what others think of him, or he wants to be a moral person).
Conclusion: Review Proctor's action and make a statement about why Proctor seems to be at peace with his decision.

Language

 COMMON CORE L 3a, W 1, W 1b

◆ **GRAMMAR AND STYLE**

Tell students to pay attention to verbs as they read to recognize an inverted sentence. Explain that inverted sentences contain a subject that follows the verb or that comes in the middle of a verb phrase. (For more on inverted sentences, see page R71 in the **Grammar Handbook**.)

Possible answers:

1. *Aye, true it be that I saw the Devil with Rebecca Nurse.*
2. *Be you sure of their guilt?*
3. *Confess you to these sins!*

R **RESOURCE MANAGER**—Copy Master
Use Realistic Dialogue p. 243

READING-WRITING CONNECTION

Have students complete a Venn Diagram to compare and contrast Proctor's concept of morality to the court's (and Judge Danforth).

BEST PRACTICES TOOLKIT—Transparency
Venn Diagram p. A26

Writing Online THINK central

The following tools are available online at **thinkcentral.com** and on **WriteSmart** CD-ROM:

- **Interactive Graphic Organizers**
- **Interactive Student Models**
- **Interactive Revision Lessons**

For additional grammar instruction, see **GrammarNotes** on **thinkcentral.com**.

Assess and Reteach

Assess

DIAGNOSTIC AND SELECTION TESTS
Selection Test A pp. 73–74
Selection Test B/C pp. 75–76

Interactive Selection Test on **thinkcentral.com**

Reteach

Level Up Online Tutorials on **thinkcentral.com**

Reteaching Worksheets on **thinkcentral.com**

Literature Lesson 1–2, 6, 23–24, Reading Lesson 9, Vocabulary Lessons 11–16

COMMON CORE

L 3a Vary syntax for effect, consulting references for guidance as needed; apply an understanding of syntax to the study of complex texts when reading. **W 1** Write arguments to support claims in an analysis of substantive topics or texts, using valid reasoning and relevant and sufficient evidence. **W 1b** Develop claim(s) fairly and thoroughly, supplying the most relevant evidence.

Focus and Motivate

COMMON CORE FOCUS

RI 1 Cite textual evidence to support analysis of what the text says explicitly. **RI 6** Determine an author's point of view or purpose in a text in which the rhetoric is particularly effective, analyzing how style and content contribute to the power, persuasiveness, or beauty of the text. **RI 7** Integrate and evaluate multiple sources of information presented in different media or formats as well as in words. **W 2** Write informative/explanatory texts to examine and convey complex ideas, concepts, and information clearly and accurately through the effective selection, organization, and analysis of content. **W 2b** Develop the topic thoroughly by selecting the most significant and relevant facts, concrete details, or quotations.

SUMMARY

"*The Crucible* and McCarthyism" consists of three brief selections about Senator Joseph McCarthy's crusade against communists during the 1940s and 1950s; an online article that presents an overview of McCarthyism; a newspaper article in which Victor Navasky details Arthur Miller's comparison of Mc-Carthyism and the Salem witch trials; and an excerpt from Miller's memoir, in which he explains how he became interested in Salem's witch hunt.

Use Main Idea and Details notes to help students distinguish the three selections. Have them write the main idea of each selection in the first column of each chart. In the second column, have them write supporting details as they read, as well as any connections they see between details in the selection and details in *The Crucible*.

 BEST PRACTICES TOOLKIT—Transparency
Main Idea and Details p. B6

Teach

Standards Focus: Understand Historical Context

Emphasize that the historical context of a literary work provides clues to the characters, plot, and themes of the work.

 RESOURCE MANAGER—Copy Master
Understand Historical Context p. 253

Use with *The Crucible*,
page 136.

COMMON CORE

RI 1 Cite textual evidence to support analysis of what the text says explicitly. **RI 6** Determine an author's point of view or purpose in a text in which the rhetoric is particularly effective, analyzing how style and content contribute to the power, persuasiveness, or beauty of the text. **RI 7** Integrate and evaluate multiple sources of information presented in different media or formats as well as in words.

The Crucible and McCarthyism

- Online Article, page 217
- Newspaper Article, page 218
- Memoir, page 220

 **Essential Course of Study**

While Arthur Miller was writing *The Crucible*, Senator Joseph McCarthy was conducting a campaign to root out communists in American public life. In his memoir, *Timebends*, Miller sees a connection between the Salem witch trials and McCarthy's campaign. The following selections will help you understand that connection by providing you with information about McCarthyism and its bearing on *The Crucible*. They will also provide you with the opportunity to evaluate the objectivity of writers who have a personal stake in the subject they address. As you read, look for connections between the main idea expressed by these writers and the themes you studied as you read *The Crucible*.

Standards Focus: Understand Historical Context

To varying degrees, every literary work reflects its **historical context**—the social and political conditions that shaped the culture of its time. *The Crucible*, produced in 1953, grew out of the controversy surrounding Senator McCarthy and his anti-communism campaign. Political speeches on both sides of the issue often contained **logical fallacies**—rhetorical flaws that were intended to inflame public emotions. The most common of these are still prominent in this country's political debates.

- The **either/or fallacy** insists that only two choices exist in a complex situation, as when a politician says, "You're either with us or against us."
- **Name-calling** occurs when politicians point the finger of blame, accusing their opponents of moral failings or lack of patriotism.
- When politicians lump all the members of an opposing group into a single negative **stereotype**, they have used **overgeneralization**.
- Finally, when a politician suggests that an opponent or an opponent's policies are to blame for what's wrong with the country, **false cause** is usually at work.

To better grasp the historical context of *The Crucible*, take notes on what you learn as you read the selections and evaluate the **objectivity** of each source. An objective source provides balanced information on a subject. The first selection is about McCarthyism. As you read it, try to determine whether the article takes a position on the subject. Each of the other selections was written by someone with a personal stake in the issue at hand. As you read, look for evidence of subjectivity—a personal stake in the subject that affects the writer's stance.

SELECTION RESOURCES

See resources on the **Teacher One Stop DVD-ROM** *and on* **thinkcentral.com**.

R RESOURCE MANAGER UNIT 1
Lesson Support,* pp. 245–258

DIAGNOSTIC AND SELECTION TESTS
Selection Tests, pp. 77–80

INTERACTIVE READER

ADAPTED INTERACTIVE READER

ELL ADAPTED INTERACTIVE READER

TECHNOLOGY
- Teacher One Stop DVD-ROM
- Student One Stop DVD-ROM
- PowerNotes DVD-ROM
- Audio Anthology CD
- ExamView Test Generator on the Teacher One Stop

* Resources for Differentiation

Practice and Apply

McCARTHYISM

Throughout the 1940s and 1950s America was overwhelmed with concerns about the threat of communism growing in Eastern Europe and China. Capitalizing on those concerns, a young Senator named Joseph McCarthy made a public accusation that more than two hundred "card-carrying" communists had infiltrated the United States government. Though
10 eventually his accusations were proven to be untrue, and he was censured by the Senate for unbecoming conduct, his zealous campaigning ushered in one of the most repressive times in 20th-century American politics. **A**

Army counsel Joseph N. Welch, left, and Senator Joseph McCarthy

While the House Un-American Activities Committee (HUAC) had been formed in 1938 as an anti-Communist organ, McCarthy's accusations heightened the political tensions of the times. Known as McCarthyism, the paranoid hunt for infiltrators was notoriously difficult on writers and entertainers, many of whom were labeled
20 communist sympathizers and were unable to continue working. Some had their passports taken away, while others were jailed for refusing to give the names of other communists. The trials, which were well publicized, could often destroy a career with a single unsubstantiated accusation. Among those well-known artists accused of communist sympathies or called before the committee were Paul Robeson, Arthur Miller, Aaron Copland, Leonard Bernstein, Charlie Chaplin and Elia Kazan. In all, three hundred and twenty artists were blacklisted, and for many of them this meant the end of exceptional and promising careers. **B**

30 During this time there were few in the press willing to stand up against McCarthy and the anti-Communist machine. Among those few were comedian Mort Sahl, and journalist Edward R. Murrow, whose strong criticisms of McCarthy are often cited as playing an important role in his eventual removal from power. By 1954, the fervor had died down and many actors and writers were able to return to work. Though relatively short, these proceedings remain one of the most shameful moments in modern U.S. history.

Internet

A HISTORICAL CONTEXT
What preoccupied Americans during the 1940s and 1950s? Record your answer in your notes.

B HISTORICAL CONTEXT
Reread lines 15–29 and use the information presented to define McCarthyism. Does this paragraph explain McCarthyism objectively or does it take a position on the senator and his campaign? Support your answer with evidence from the selection.

Reading Support

This selection on **thinkcentral.com** includes embedded **ThinkAloud** models—students "thinking aloud" about the story to model the kinds of questions a good reader would ask about a selection.

INFORMATIONAL ANALYSIS   COMMON CORE   RI 1   RI 6   RI 7

A HISTORICAL CONTEXT

Possible answer: Americans were pre-occupied with the idea that communism could threaten the United States, for it had gained a foothold in Eastern Europe and China.

INFORMATIONAL ANALYSIS   COMMON CORE   RI 1   RI 6   RI 7

B Model the Skill:
HISTORICAL CONTEXT

Possible answer: The term McCarthyism refers to the "paranoid hunt for [communist] infiltrators" (line 18). Connections to The Crucible include the facts that an "unsubstantiated accusation" (line 24) could destroy a person's reputation and that many of the accused were "jailed for refusing to give the names" of possible participants (lines 21–22).

DIFFERENTIATED INSTRUCTION

FOR STRUGGLING READERS

Options for Reading Read aloud the first sentence, whose many details make comprehension difficult. Model how students might break the sentence into shorter segments:

- "Throughout the 1940s and 1950s" = The selection is about something that happened during this time.

- "America was overwhelmed with concerns" = Americans were worried.

- "about the threat of communism" = People felt that communism was dangerous.

- "growing in Eastern Europe and China" = Communism was affecting people in other parts of the world.

As students continue to read, encourage them to break apart difficult sentences in the same way to understand their meaning.

Find it Online!

Features on **thinkcentral.com** that support the selection include
- **PowerNotes** presentation
- **ThinkAloud** models to enhance comprehension

Use these prompts to help students explore Navasky's perspective as revealed in lines 1–118:

Recall According to the online article on page 217, how did Americans in the early 1950s feel about communism, and why? *Possible answer: Many Americans saw communism as a threat because it was growing in other parts of the world.*

Analyze What do "the so-called Red Menace" (line 4), "reckless charges" (lines 5–6), "'comsymps'" (line 6), and "center ring" (line 14) suggest about Navasky's view of McCarthyism? Explain. *Possible answer: The first term suggests that Navasky views McCarthyism as misguided; the second, as poorly handled; the third, as smug; and the fourth (a reference to a circus), as foolish.*

Synthesize If Navasky could have written during the McCarthy hearings, what do you think he would have urged people to do? *Possible answer: He would have urged people to require that those in charge of the investigation have a clear focus and conduct their work in an orderly, fair fashion.*

INFORMATIONAL ANALYSIS

COMMON CORE
RI 1
RI 6
RI 7

C HISTORICAL CONTEXT

Possible answer: The logical fallacy is name-calling. Refer students to page 216 and have them review the information if they have difficulty answering the question.

C HISTORICAL CONTEXT

As you read this article, keep in mind that Victor Navasky is the author of *Naming Names*, a history of McCarthyism that depicts the subject in a dramatically negative light. His goal in this article is not simply to inform readers but to support his position on McCarthyism and *The Crucible*. As evidence Navasky cites **logical fallacies** in McCarthy's political language (lines 5–6). Which logical fallacy does a speaker commit by calling his opponents spies and "comsymps"?

Reprinted from
The New York Times

SUNDAY, SEPTEMBER 8, 1996   B16

Arthur Miller prepares to testify before the House Un-American Activities Commitee, 1956.

The Demons of Salem, With Us Still
by Victor Navasky

When Arthur Miller's drama *The Crucible* first opened on Broadway in 1953, the country was in a panic about the so-called Red Menace. Senator Joseph McCarthy, with his reckless charges of spies and "comsymps,"[1] occupied the front pages, while behind the scenes J. Edgar Hoover, the director of the F.B.I., presided over and
10 manipulated a vast internal security bureaucracy, issuing periodic bulletins intended to fan the flames of the domestic cold war. **C**

In the center ring were the congressional inquisitor-investigators, asking "Are you now or have you ever been a member of the Communist Party?"

At the time, Mr. Miller and
20 Tennessee Williams were regarded as the world's two foremost playwrights. But that lofty status was an invitation rather than an obstacle to the red-hunters who wanted to talk to Mr. Miller. In fact, when he was finally summoned to appear, the committee chairman, Representative Francis Walters, let Mr. Miller know that things might go easier for him if he
30 persuaded his fiancee, Marilyn Monroe, to pose for a photograph with the chairman. Mr. Miller let that option lapse and was shortly indicted for contempt of Congress when he refused to answer the committee's questions about Communists he had known.

On the left, the hunt for subversives was routinely labeled a witch hunt, after the infamous Salem witch trials
40 of the late 17th century. And so when *The Crucible*, set in Salem in 1692 but written in the overheated atmosphere of the domestic cold war, appeared, two questions were quickly asked: Was Mr. Miller's depiction of the inhabitants and events of 1692 Salem faithful to the original? And was the original an appropriate metaphor for McCarthyism?

1. **"comsymps"**: Communist sympathizers.

DIFFERENTIATED INSTRUCTION

FOR ENGLISH LANGUAGE LEARNERS

Related Vocabulary Navasky uses a variety of terms to discuss the nation's interest in and fear of communists. Offer "Red Menace" (line 4) as an example, explaining that communism is associated with the color red and that a menace is something threatening. Then teach these related terms:

- *reckless* (line 5), "careless and unthinking"
- *inquisitor-investigators* (line 15), "questioners who are excessively harsh"
- *red-hunters* (lines 23–24), "people conducting searches for alleged communists"
- *indicted* (line 33), "formally accused of a crime"
- *subversives* (line 37), "people who want to overturn a government"

FOR ADVANCED READERS/AP

Research and Analyze Allusions [SMALL-GROUP OPTION] Have students find out more about these people mentioned on this page:

- J. Edgar Hoover
- Tennessee Williams
- Marilyn Monroe

Call on volunteers to share a few fact-filled sentences about each person and discuss the allusions.

50   On the historical front it was generally conceded when the play was written that Mr. Miller's research was accurate. His principal changes involved fusing some characters and raising the age of John Proctor's accuser, Abigail Williams, from 11 to 17 (to accommodate Mr. Miller's story of how a liaison between Abigail and John was intertwined with the accusations of

60 witchcraft against Proctor's wife).

   But even before the play was written, Mr. Miller was denounced for his metaphor. He had stopped off at the home of his friend and colleague Elia Kazan, who had directed Mr. Miller's two previous prize-winning hits, "All My Sons" and "Death of a Salesman," and who had been subpoenaed to appear before the House Committee on

70 Un-American Activities (where he ultimately named names).

   They went for a walk in the Connecticut woods and discussed Mr. Kazan's dilemma. On the one hand to be an informer was unpalatable, but on the other, as Mr. Kazan put it at the time, "Secrecy serves the Communists." **D**

   In his memoir *Timebends,* Mr. Miller

80 wrote that he was half inside his car when Molly, Kazan's wife, "came out and asked if I was staying at my house, half an hour away, and I said that I was on my way to Salem. She instantly understood what my destination meant, and her eyes widened in sudden apprehension and possible anger. 'You're not going to equate witches with this!'

   Later, Mr. Kazan reported his wife's

90 views in his own memoir, *A Life.*

   "What's going on here and now is not to be compared with the witch trials of that time," she said. "Those witches did not exist. Communists do. Here and everywhere in the world. It's a false parallel. Witch hunt! The phrase would indicate that there are no Communists

in government, none in the arts, none sending money from Hollywood to

100 12th Street." **E**

   For me, the parallel worked. The term "Communist" had been so demonized that like the word "witch" it signified something that didn't really exist in its popular meaning. Certainly the entertainment community Communists like Mr. Kazan (and for a brief period, Mr. Miller himself, although he never fully joined the party)

110 were not conscious agents of an international monolithic conspiracy to overthrow the Government by force and violence; they were, for the most part, do-gooders, who thought—misguidedly, most of them later concluded—that the Communist Party was the best agency to do something about the depression and racism at home and fascism abroad.

   As it turned out, despite mixed

120 notices for *The Crucible,* over the years it was to become Arthur Miller's most performed play, with productions in China, Poland, Britain, high schools and repertory theaters throughout the world. Now *The Crucible* is a $25 million motion picture, under the aegis of 20th Century Fox.

   Although the playwright in Mr. Miller was originally drawn to think

130 about the political and moral pressures of the domestic cold war years, when I asked him about the applicability of the play to the here and now he said:

   "I have had immense confidence in the applicability of the play to almost any time, the reason being it's dealing with a paranoid situation. But that situation doesn't depend on any particular political or sociological

140 development. I wrote it blind to the world. The enemy is within, and within stays within, and we can't get out of within. It's always on the edge of our minds that behind what we see is a nefarious plot." **F**

D HISTORICAL CONTEXT
Reread lines 61–78. In light of his comment, would you say that Elia Kazan took McCarthy's mission seriously? Explain.

E HISTORICAL CONTEXT
Given her husband's role in the McCarthy hearings, why do you think Molly Kazan might have objected to Miller's comparison between HUAC and Salem?

F HISTORICAL CONTEXT
Reread lines 79–145. Evaluate the **objectivity** of author Victor Navasky and of Molly Kazan and Arthur Miller, witnesses Navasky quotes in these paragraphs. An objective writer or witness is an observer who weighs all the evidence without being swayed by a personal stake in the subject. By contrast, a subjective writer or witness has a personal involvement and is swayed by personal beliefs on the subject. If you determine that Navasky or either of his witnesses is not objective, then carefully evaluate the evidence he or she presents. Weigh all the evidence before drawing conclusions of your own.

INFORMATIONAL ANALYSIS   COMMON CORE   RI 1   RI 6   RI 7

D HISTORICAL CONTEXT

Possible answer: Yes, Kazan seems to have taken McCarthy's mission seriously; his comment, "Secrecy serves the Communists," indicates that he understood that McCarthy's goal was to discover information that generally had been kept secret to that point.

INFORMATIONAL ANALYSIS   COMMON CORE   RI 1   RI 6   RI 7

E HISTORICAL CONTEXT

Possible answer: Molly Kazan might have objected to Miller's comparison because she feared the HUAC (lines 91–100). She might not have wanted her husband (who had directed two of Miller's earlier plays) to become involved in a play that could increase the HUAC's interest in him.

INFORMATIONAL ANALYSIS   COMMON CORE   RI 1   RI 6   RI 7

F HISTORICAL CONTEXT

Students should consider the question and the evidence carefully before drawing conclusions. You might ask students to work in mixed-ability pairs to review pages 217-219 before drawing their conclusions.

FOR ENGLISH LANGUAGE LEARNERS

Vocabulary: Cognates Point out that many Spanish cognates follow spelling patterns. For example, the Spanish word *pánico* ends in *-co* and is spelled almost exactly like the English word *panic* (line 3). Many English words that end in *-tion,* such as *invitation,* have Spanish cognates that end in *-ción* (*invitación*). Help students understand these English words with Spanish cognates:

- *domestic/doméstico* (line 13), *historical/histórico* (line 50), *monolithic/monolítico* (line 111)

- *option/opción* (line 32), *accusations/acusaciones* (line 59), *international/internacional* (line 111), *productions/producciones* (line 122), *situation/situación* (line 137).

INFORMATIONAL ANALYSIS

COMMON CORE

G HISTORICAL CONTEXT

RI 1
RI 6
RI 7

Possible answer: *Miller alludes to the significance of Starkey's book when he says that he received the book "As though it had been ordained" (lines 12–13); in other words, it was his destiny to read the book. Miller also says that eventually he felt "a living connection between [himself] and Salem" (line 21), a statement that reveals the powerful hold that the story had on him.*

INFORMATIONAL ANALYSIS

COMMON CORE

H HISTORICAL CONTEXT

RI 1
RI 6
RI 7

Tell students that to synthesize what they have learned from these selections, they should first examine their notes for similarities and differences in the main ideas of each article. Students can then use this information to draw conclusions about the common ideas running through each selection.

Possible answer: *An idea that runs through all three selections is that occasionally society will lose its bearings and develop an irrational fear of an "enemy within" and violate individuals' rights in order to identify and expel its "enemies."*

G HISTORICAL CONTEXT
Reread lines 1–17. What details indicate the significance for Miller of finding Starkey's book?

H HISTORICAL CONTEXT
As you have seen by reading these selections, politics, journalism, and literature can share ideas from a particular historical context. One article provides information on the McCarthy hearings; another addresses both the hearings and the writing of *The Crucible.* The third provides personal testimony from Miller himself. To synthesize what you have read, identify a theme or idea that runs through all three selections.

TIMEBENDS

by Arthur Miller

I had known about the Salem witchcraft phenomenon since my American history class at Michigan, but it had remained in mind as one of those inexplicable mystifications of the long-dead past when people commonly believed that the spirit could leave the body, palpably and visibly. My mother might believe it still, if only in one corner of her mind, and I 10 suspected that there were a lot of other people who, like me, were secretly open to suggestion. As though it had been ordained, a copy of Marion Starkey's book *The Devil in Massachusetts* fell into my hands, and the bizarre story came back as I had recalled it, but this time in remarkably well-organized detail. **G**

Miller at his typewriter in 1959

At first I rejected the idea of a play on the subject. My own rationality was too strong, I thought, to really allow me to capture this wildly irrational outbreak. A 20 drama cannot merely describe an emotion, it has to become that emotion. But gradually, over weeks, a living connection between myself and Salem, and between Salem and Washington, was made in my mind—for whatever else they might be, I saw that the hearings in Washington were profoundly and even avowedly ritualistic. After all, in almost every case the Committee knew in advance what they wanted the witness to give them; the names of his comrades in the Party. The FBI had long since infiltrated the Party, and informers had long ago identified the participants in various meetings. The main point of the hearings, precisely as in seventeenth-century Salem, was that the accused make public confession, damn his confederates as well as his Devil master, and guarantee his sterling new allegiance by breaking disgusting old 30 vows—whereupon he was let loose to rejoin the society of extremely decent people. In other words, the same spiritual nugget lay folded within both procedures—an act of contrition done not in solemn privacy but out in the public air. The Salem prosecution was actually on more solid legal ground since the defendant, if guilty of familiarity with the Unclean One, had broken a law against the practice of witchcraft, a civil as well as a religious offense; whereas the offender against HUAC (House Un-American Activities Committee) could not be accused of any such violation but only of a spiritual crime, subservience to a political enemy's desires and ideology. He was summoned before the Committee to be called a bad name, but one that could destroy his career. **H**

220   UNIT 1: EARLY AMERICAN WRITING

DIFFERENTIATED INSTRUCTION

FOR ENGLISH LANGUAGE LEARNERS

Language: Verb Tenses Explain that Miller uses two past tenses: The past perfect tense (*had known* [line 1]) shows what already had happened before another event, also in the past, occurred; the simple past (*rejected* [line 18]) shows what happened at a particular time. Help students identify other uses of these tenses in these paragraphs (lines 12–17, for example); then elicit that this shift in tense indicates two different but related periods of time in Miller's past.

FOR ADVANCED LEARNERS/AP

Analyze Author's Perspective Have students write and share an analysis of lines 18–23, including responses to these questions:

- What does Miller mean when he says, "My own rationality was too strong . . . to really allow me to capture this wildly irrational outbreak" (lines 18–19)?

- How does Miller finally gain insight into the thinking that informed events long ago in Salem?

Comprehension

1. **Recall** What was Senator McCarthy's mission?

2. **Recall** What kinds of professionals were targeted by McCarthy's accusations?

3. **Recall** What was the catalyst for Miller's interest in the Salem witch trials?

Text Analysis

4. **Evaluate Statements** Considering the historical context of *The Crucible* and Arthur Miller's own comments in *Timebends*, do you think Miller was really "blind to the world" when he wrote *The Crucible*? Support your opinion.

5. **Evaluate the Role of Historical Context** Is knowing *The Crucible*'s historical context necessary to understand the playwright's message? Explain.

Read for Information: Synthesize

WRITING PROMPT

Think about the social and political conditions of the time during which Arthur Miller was writing *The Crucible*. In what ways has looking through this historical lens colored your understanding of the play? In developing your new analysis, support your thesis with information from the articles you have just read and details from the play.

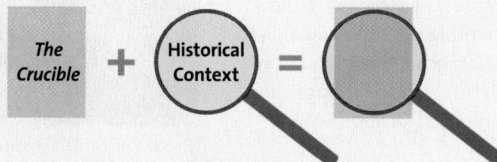

To answer this prompt, follow these steps:

1. In a sentence or two, summarize how reading these selections, evaluating their objectivity, and weighing the evidence they present has affected your understanding of the play and its historical context. Consider using this summary as your thesis statement.

2. In your notes, identify elements of the play that you now view differently. How has your sense of these elements changed? For example, are there things you now see more clearly? Does the play interest you more? Note the historical evidence that caused you to think differently.

3. Using your thesis statement and notes, write an essay in which you explain how the historical context of *The Crucible* affects your appreciation and understanding of the play.

4. Cite evidence from *The Crucible* and the selections in this Reading for Information feature.

COMMON CORE

RI 1 Cite textual evidence to support analysis of what the text says explicitly. **RI 6** Determine an author's point of view or purpose in a text in which the rhetoric is particularly effective, analyzing how style and content contribute to the power, persuasiveness, or beauty of the text. **RI 7** Integrate and evaluate multiple sources of information presented in different media or formats as well as in words. **W 2** Write informative/explanatory texts to examine and convey complex ideas, concepts, and information clearly and accurately through the effective selection, organization, and analysis of content. **W 2b** Develop the topic thoroughly by selecting the most significant and relevant facts, concrete details, or quotations.

FOR STRUGGLING READERS

Read for Information

• Direct students to write a brief summary of each of the three selections. Urge students to use these summaries as a guide for determining which historical facts made the greatest impact on their understanding of the play.

• Ask students to choose three elements of the play that have been affected by their knowledge of historical context. For each element, students should note a precise historical link that changed their thinking.

FOR ADVANCED LEARNERS/AP

Propose a New Play After students think about the message and historical context of *The Crucible*, have them write a proposal for a play that they might write, dealing with similar themes but reflecting their own political and social views.

Practice and Apply

For preliminary support of post-reading questions, use these copy masters:

R RESOURCE MANAGER—Copy Masters
    Reading Check p. 257
    Question Support p. 258
    Synthesize pp. 253, 255
    Additional selection questions are provided for teachers on page 248.

ANSWERS   COMMON CORE   RI 1, RI 6, RI 7, W 2, W 2b

1. *to identify Communists in the United States and destroy their careers*

2. *writers and entertainers*

3. *Marion Starkey's* The Devil in Massachusetts, *a book that prompted Miller to think again about the Salem witch trials*

Possible answers:

4. *Miller was not really "blind to the world" when he wrote* The Crucible; *in fact, he says that thinking about the McCarthy hearings helped him connect to and write about the Salem trials (lines 20–23 and following).*

5. *Knowing the historical context adds an extra dimension to the play's theme, but it is not necessary for understanding the play's message, which is a warning against hysteria and intolerance.*

Read for Information: Synthesize

Writing Prompt *Students should present a thesis statement that explains how McCarthyism has influenced their ideas about* The Crucible.

Assess and Reteach

Assess

DIAGNOSTIC AND SELECTION TESTS
    Selection Test A pp. 77–78
    Selection Test B/C pp. 79–80

Interactive Selection Test on **thinkcentral.com**

Reteach

Level Up Online Tutorials on **thinkcentral.com**

Reteaching Worksheets on **thinkcentral.com**

    Reading Lesson 14: Synthesizing Information

Focus and Motivate

COMMON CORE FOCUS

RL 7 Analyze multiple interpretations of a drama, evaluating how each version interprets the source text.

SUMMARY

In this film clip from *The Crucible,* John Proctor falsely confesses to witchcraft to escape hanging. He refuses, however, to accuse any fellow villagers of witchcraft. After signing, Proctor realizes he cannot let the lie be nailed to the church with his name on it. He tears up the paper, knowing that he will be hanged for his choice.

BACKGROUND

The photos that illustrate the play on pages 136–212 are stills from the movie *The Crucible.* In choosing Hog Island, Massachusetts, as the location for the film, the director and playwright were able to mirror the desperate themes of the play in the bleak, harsh, wintry landscape.

The Filmmakers' Challenge

Brainstorm ideas about how a movie is different from a play. Ask students to consider differences in dialogue, characterization, set, and scope of the story as they brainstorm.

ADDITIONAL TEACHING OPPORTUNITY

Write a Review After students watch the clip, have them write a review of the scene. Ask students to trade their reviews with their classmates, and then compare their responses to those of others. If time allows, have students find reviews of performances they have seen and books they have read to see how their responses compare with those of the reviewers.

Media Study

from The Crucible

Film Clips on Media◉Smart DVD-ROM

COMMON CORE

RL 7 Analyze multiple interpretations of a drama, evaluating how each version interprets the source text.

From Page to Screen

From the classical tragedies of Ancient Greece to the Renaissance masterpieces of Shakespeare, playwrights have examined the impact of suspicion, hysteria, and revenge, building plays around the arc of destruction these impulses unleash. So effective was *The Crucible* in depicting these timeless themes that it was declared a classic when first staged. In this lesson, view a scene from the film version to explore how a different medium changes the structure of Arthur Miller's play.

The Filmmakers' Challenge

Translating a well-known play to the big screen poses a number of challenges. Writing the screenplay, perhaps the biggest hurdle, was made a little easier in the case of *The Crucible.* Arthur Miller adapted his own work and took an active role in the film's production. Consulting with the film's director, Miller took certain liberties with the play's structure. He changed where some scenes take place and added entirely new scenes. "I did some rewriting during production to take advantage of opportunities we had with this wonderful Hog Island [Massachusetts] location," Miller recalls.

On the set, Daniel Day-Lewis with Arthur Miller

Over the past five decades, *The Crucible*'s themes have reached far beyond its place and time. As Miller points out, the play's themes "find [their] relevance in every culture. I knew a woman imprisoned for six years under the [Chinese] Mao regime.... She told me that when she saw *The Crucible* in Shanghai she couldn't believe that a non-Chinese had written it, because the interrogations in *The Crucible* had been precisely the interrogations she had endured under the Cultural Revolution."

222

Media Study Resources

See resources on the **Teacher One Stop DVD-ROM** *and on* <u>thinkcentral.com</u>.

R **RESOURCE MANAGER UNIT 1**
Plan and Teach, pp. 259–262
Summary, pp. 263†*–264‡*
Close Viewing, p. 265
Media Activity, p. 266

TECHNOLOGY
◉ **Teacher One Stop DVD-ROM**
◉ **Student One Stop DVD-ROM**
◉ **Media*Smart* DVD-ROM**
MediaScope on <u>thinkcentral.com</u>

* Resources for Differentiation † Also in Spanish ‡ In Haitian Creole and Vietnamese

Comparing Texts: Dialogue

In taking his play from the page to the screen, Arthur Miller had to make certain decisions about how much of the original dialogue he would retain. During production, actors and directors will often make changes to the dialogue to fine-tune a scene.

Compare the dialogue from the play with the dialogue that appears in the film. Notice Miller's stage direction in the text and how actor Daniel Day-Lewis, in the role of John Proctor, interprets it.

> **Danforth** (*with suspicion*). It is the same, is it not? If I report it or you sign it?
>
> **Proctor** (*he knows it is insane*). No, it is not the same! What others say and what I sign is not the same!
>
> 5 **Danforth.** Why? Do you mean to deny this confession when you are free?
>
> **Proctor.** I mean to deny nothing!
>
> **Danforth.** Then explain to me, Mr. Proctor, why you will not let—
>
> **Proctor** (*with a cry of his whole soul*). Because it is my name! Because I cannot have another in my life! Because I lie and sign myself to lies! Because I am 10 not worth the dust on the feet of them that hang! How may I live without my name? I have given you my soul; leave me my name!

Viewing Guide

Media ⬛ **Smart** DVD-ROM

- **Film:** *The Crucible*
- **Director:** Nicholas Hytner
- **Genre:** Drama
- **Running Time:** 5 minutes

In the clip from *The Crucible*, the character John Proctor has finally agreed to sign a false confession that will save him from death.

Plan on viewing the clip several times. To help you analyze the dialogue and performance, refer to the questions.

NOW VIEW

CLOSE VIEWING: Media Analysis

1. **Analyze Setting** In the play, this scene is set in jail. How does moving the setting affect (or not affect) the scene?

2. **Compare Dialogue** Compare the dialogue from the play with the dialogue in the movie. Why do you think Miller changed some of his original dialogue for the movie?

3. **Evaluate Actor's Performance** Read the stage direction the playwright included for Proctor's speech. Do you think the actor playing Proctor succeeded in portraying "a cry of his whole soul"? Cite evidence from the scene to support your opinion.

ANSWERS

CLOSE VIEWING: Media Analysis

1. *Changing the setting creates a contrast between the grim proceedings and the blue sky, beach, and woods, stressing Proctor's sacrifice in tearing up his confession.*

2. *Miller perhaps changed the dialogue to focus viewers' attention on Proctor's inner struggle. The dialogue explains Proctor's thoughts more fully. For example, the director replaces lines 3–4 with a more detailed version. Later, Proctor does not say the line "How may I live without my name?" (lines 10–11)*

3. *Possible answer: Yes. Daniel Day-Lewis gives a powerful cry to the heavens. He quakes as he yells, and by the end of his speech he seems ready to collapse.*

Comparing Texts: Dialogue

Clarify that the text on page 223 is from the play. Explain that the playwright revised the text for the screen. Then the actor interpreted the text, adding gestures, facial expressions, and vocal emphasis. Discuss possible reasons that lines 1–4 were changed from play to film. ***Possible answer:*** *Adding detail can help viewers understand Proctor's emotions and statement.*

Viewing Guide

1. Before showing the film clip explain that it includes visual cues that give information about each character.

   - Costuming and makeup give information about which characters hold power.

   - Facial expressions and body language reveal love, desperation, and pride.

2. Point out the characters that do not speak, such as the condemned women on the cart and Proctor's wife, who stands behind him. Remind students that these characters add impact and subtext to the scene.

R RESOURCE MANAGER—Copy Master

   Close Viewing p. 265

Use this resource with the Viewing Guide:

⊘ **MediaSmart DVD**

MEDIA STUDY WRAP-UP

Have students summarize what they have learned about how dialogue changes from stage to film.

RETEACH

- **Camera Shots** Have students think of facial expressions seen in close-ups. Ask students to consider how the scenes' emotional impact would be affected if shown from a distance in camera long-shots. *Characters might seem less emotionally involved.*

- **Editing** Have students consider how the scene of the condemned women would be affected if the editor had shown only the cart full of women with no shots of the watching villagers. *The women would seem more isolated, but the scene would have less dramatic impact.*

CONNECT

This selection provides additional information about the film clip that students have just viewed for the Media Study.

READING FOR INFORMATION

Point out that "The Crucible" is a movie review. Have students preview it, noting the title, photograph, and caption. Then ask

- What information does the reader learn from the title and the photograph? *Possible answer: The reader learns that subject of the review is the movie version of* The Crucible; *the director and actors are probably featured in the discussion of the film.*

- Why would a movie review focus on the actors rather than on the characters? *Possible answer: The focus reflects the reviewer's desire to talk about the way in which the characters are represented rather than about the characters themselves.*

- What is the main purpose of this review? *Possible answer: The purpose is to evaluate components of the movie, such as the film's visual style and the actors' performances.*

TIERED DISCUSSION PROMPTS

Use these prompts to help students connect the movie review to the Media Study on pages 222–223:

Connect In what ways does this review help you respond to the information presented in the Media Study? *Possible answer: The review provides more detailed information about the film and helps the reader evaluate the success of acting and scene choices discussed in the Media Study.*

Interpret Reread the second paragraph. What does the reviewer think is the film's greatest strength? *Possible answer: The reviewer praises the film's "visual energy, passionate provocation and incendiary action"—that is, the power of the film.*

Synthesize From what you know about the movie version of the play, do you think that a playwright's involvement in a film adaptation is a help or hindrance? Explain. *Possible answer: It is a help. In this case,* The Crucible *is successful as a film; and according to the Media Study, Miller's involvement was crucial in preparing the play for film production.*

MOVIE REVIEW *Rolling Stone* magazine reviewed Nicholas Hytner's film adaptation of *The Crucible* in 1996.

[REVIEW]

The Crucible

Peter Travers

Director Nicholas Hytner with cast

Arthur Miller is the first to admit that *The Crucible* must stand on its own. The playwright, now 81, sat near me at a screening of the film, unwittingly intimidating all around him. For the Pulitzer Prize–winning author of *Death of a Salesman,* attention must be paid. Miller asked for none of it. He talked with boyish zest of working with director Nicholas Hytner on re-crafting *The Crucible* as a $25 million film that would allow startling imagery to resonate with his language and burst the bounds of the stage.

Does it ever. *The Crucible,* despite some damaging cuts to the text, is a seductively exciting film that crackles with visual energy, passionate provocation and incendiary acting. . . .

The great Paul Scofield is triumphant, avoiding the easy caricature of Danforth as a fanatic. He brings the role something new: wit. We laugh with this judge, which heightens the horror later when he blinds himself to truth in the name of God and his own ambition. The scene in which he ignores Rev. Hale (Rob Campbell), who knows the girls are faking, and bullies the servant Mary Warren (Karron Graves) into delusion and madness chills the blood.

As the unforgiving wife whose "justice would freeze beer," in the words of her husband, Joan Allen is an absolute stunner in an award-caliber performance that is also a surprising source of warmth. By the seashore, where the pregnant Elizabeth has come to say goodbye to her condemned husband, she tells John, "I once counted myself so plain, so poorly made, that no honest love could come to me." Elizabeth's scene of tender reconciliation is the film's moral core. John need only sign a false confession of witchcraft to save himself from the gallows. Of course, he won't. "Because it is my name," he tells Danforth simply. "Because I cannot have another in my life."

In the film's most complex role, Daniel Day-Lewis performs with quiet power. Playing nobility can make actors insufferable, but Day-Lewis keeps John Proctor human even when saddled with smudgy makeup and fake brown teeth for his final scene. *The Crucible,* for all its timely denunciation of persecution masked as piety . . . comes down to individual resistance and how you search your heart to find it. The years haven't softened the rage against self-betrayal in *The Crucible.* This stirring film lets you feel the heat of Miller's argument and the urgent power of his kick.

ADDITIONAL TEACHING OPPORTUNITIES

Compare and Contrast Reviews Have students produce two reviews, which they will compare to other evaluations:

- Ask students to write their own review of the movie adaptation of *The Crucible,* based on the film clip that they have viewed. Students should comment on the actors' performances, as well as the visual imagery and atmosphere in the film. Then have students compare their opinions with the response presented in the review on page 224, noting similarities and differences.

- Now ask students to write a review of a movie, book, or music CD of their choice. Remind students that reviews discuss a variety of elements, such as the performers, the visual or auditory appeal, and the overall impression. Have students exchange and compare reviews.

The Puritan Legacy

In the minds of some, Puritanism is a thing of the past—an outmoded collection of beliefs from a dour and oddly-dressed group of people. Yet others insist that the spiritual, social, and cultural principles fostered by Puritanism are stubbornly present, in one way or another, in American society today. Somewhere in the middle of this debate are literary historians Richard Ruland and Malcolm Bradbury, who insist: "Puritans considered many of the literary questions we still ask today; they answered them differently."

Writing to Compare

We can all agree that the Puritan style of dress is out of fashion, but are Puritan ideas also outmoded? Consider these "literary questions" discussed in the selections you have just read:

What is true love?

Why do bad things happen to good people?

How can faith sustain us?

How can people best serve God?

Are people worthy?

Are people basically good or bad?

Choose one of the questions above, and in a brief essay explain how two of the Puritan authors in this section might have responded. (Although Arthur Miller's play was written in the twentieth century, you can include *The Crucible* since it accurately reflects the Puritan mind-set.) Give specific evidence from the texts to support your opinions and ideas.

Consider

- the themes, or central ideas, of the selections. Does the selection have a message related to one of the "literary questions" above?

- the topics, or subject that the work focuses on. The topic is what the writer describes, discusses, or talks about. A writer's choice of subject will often have an influence on the work's themes.

Extension

SPEAKING & LISTENING Imagine you are a Puritan villager in charge of welcoming new settlers. Using the selections you've just read as your resource, write and deliver an **informal speech** to your new neighbors, welcoming them and sharing a little about the values and beliefs of your community.

COMMON CORE

RL 9 Demonstrate knowledge of foundational works of American literature, including how two or more texts from the same period treat similar themes or topics. **W 9** Draw evidence from literary texts to support analysis, reflection, and research. **SL 6** Adapt speech to a variety of contexts and tasks.

The Puritan (1883–1886), Augustus Saint-Gaudens. Bronze figure. Private collection. © Art Resource, New York.

DIFFERENTIATED INSTRUCTION

FOR STRUGGLING WRITERS

Writing Support Help students get started by directing them to relevant passages in the selections. For example, students might draw on lines 488–501 in Act Two of *The Crucible* and lines 93–104 in "Sinners in the Hands of an Angry God" in response to the question "How can people best serve God?"

FOR ENGLISH LANGUAGE LEARNERS

Write Topic Sentences Help students write topic sentences for their paragraphs by discussing sentence starters like these:

- One question that was important to the Puritans but that also resonates deeply in our culture today is _____.

- Although I do not think that it is an issue today, the Puritans were very concerned with the question of _____.

COMMON CORE FOCUS

RL 9 Demonstrate knowledge of foundational works of American literature, including how two or more texts from the same period treat similar themes or topics. **W 9** Draw evidence from literary texts to support analysis, reflection, and research. **SL 6** Adapt speech to a variety of contexts and tasks.

Wrap-Up: The Puritan Tradition

This Wrap-Up provides students with the opportunity to think about Puritan beliefs as they are characterized in these selections and to reflect on similarities and differences between Puritan culture and their own. Encourage students to consider which elements of Puritan culture they admire and which they find less appealing.

Writing to Compare

- Remind students that to *compare* is to examine the essential features of two or more things and consider the similarities and differences of these features. Reflecting on how two Puritan authors might respond to the same question sheds light on what individual authors believed and how they behaved.

- To help students plan and write the essay, ask them to select two of the authors in this section that appealed to them. Then have them note a first impression for each author to each question.

Extension

- Suggest that students work in groups and review the selections that they have read. Have them list the selection titles in the first column of a Two-Column Chart.

- As they revisit each selection, direct students to record notes about its most prominent Puritan values or beliefs in the second column of the chart.

- Students should choose the Puritan principles that appear frequently in the chart as the focus for their informal speech.

 **BEST PRACTICES TOOLKIT—Transparency** Two-Column Chart p. A25

Focus and Motivate

RI 5 Analyze and evaluate the effectiveness of the structure an author uses in his or her exposition or argument, including whether the structure makes points clear, convincing, and engaging. **RI 6** Determine an author's point of view or purpose in a text in which the rhetoric is particularly effective, analyzing how style and content contribute to the power, persuasiveness, or beauty of the text. **RI 8** Delineate and evaluate the reasoning in seminal U.S. texts, including the application of constitutional principles and use of legal reasoning and the premises, purposes, and arguments in works of public advocacy. **RI 9** Analyze eighteenth-century foundational U.S. documents of historical and literary significance for their themes, purposes, and rhetorical features.

A Cause for Argument

Deductively or Inductively? To help students distinguish deductive from inductive arguments, discuss how to form the two different kinds of argument for the proposition "The school day should be longer." Have students list arguments in a Two-Column Chart.

Proposition: *The school day should be longer*	
Deductive Reasoning	**Inductive Reasoning**
Generalization: *More education is better than less.*	**Examples:** *Variety of activities possible in a longer day.*
Examples: *Variety of activities possible in a longer day.*	**Conclusion:** *A longer school day is worthwhile.*

 **BEST PRACTICES TOOLKIT—Transparency**
Two-Column Chart p. A25

Basics of an Argument Call students' attention to the sidebar on page 227. Ask whether the list gives more importance to logic or to emotion. (*logic*) Briefly discuss students' views on whether and why logic is more important to a sound argument.

Text Analysis Workshop

Persuasive Rhetoric

Persuasion is built on the power of words—words that grab your attention, keep you riveted, and influence what you think. **Persuasive rhetoric** is the art of using language to argue and convince others to adopt a position or act in a certain way.

COMMON CORE

Included in this workshop:
RI 5 Analyze and evaluate the effectiveness of the structure an author uses in his or her exposition or argument, including whether the structure makes points clear, convincing, and engaging. **RI 6** Determine an author's point of view or purpose in a text in which the rhetoric is particularly effective, analyzing how style and content contribute to the power, persuasiveness, or beauty of the text. **RI 8** Delineate and evaluate the reasoning in seminal U.S. texts, including the application of constitutional principles and use of legal reasoning and the premises, purposes, and arguments in works of public advocacy. **RI 9** Analyze eighteenth-century foundational U.S. documents of historical and literary significance for their themes, purposes, and rhetorical features.

A Cause for Argument

America's history of persuasive rhetoric began with statesmen, writers, and orators who felt strongly about the future of the colonized states. These men vigorously debated freedom—from tyranny, taxes, and censorship. Writings, such as Thomas Jefferson's Declaration of Independence (page 238), were not only official state documents but well-crafted arguments.

A 1792 British caricature of Thomas Paine, who was ridiculed in England for his appeal to overthrow the monarchy

The way ideas are organized in an **argument** can be key to the argument's persuasive power. A writer can develop an argument **deductively,** by beginning with a generalization, or premise, and proceeding to examples and supporting facts. Writers can also argue **inductively,** by beginning with examples or facts and proceeding to a conclusion.

The Power of Language

To be effective, a persuasive work must engage both the minds and the emotions of its audience. Persuasive writers use words to develop sound reasoning, to arouse emotions, and to appeal to shared values. **Persuasive techniques** fall into three basic types.

- **Logical appeals** rely on reason and facts to support a claim. For example, the Declaration of Independence cites "injuries and usurpations" committed by King George III as evidence of the need for independence (page 242).

- **Emotional appeals** present ideas that elicit strong feelings. Jefferson, for example, uses the appeal of emotionally loaded words when he associates King George with "death, desolation, and tyranny" (page 244).

- **Ethical appeals** use values or moral standards to persuade an audience. The Declaration of Independence is loaded with the language of shared values—for example, the assertion that "all men are created equal" (page 240).

DIFFERENTIATED INSTRUCTION

FOR STRUGGLING READERS

Note Taking For students who need help with note taking, hand out the note-taking copy masters before discussing this spread. Explain that students will be learning many terms relating to persuasive rhetoric in this workshop. Discuss the major terms on this spread (*deductively, inductively, logical appeals, claim, support, counterarguments, logic, conclusion, emotional appeals, ethical appeals, rhetorical question, antithesis,* *repetition, parallelism, logical fallacies, circular reasoning, hasty generalization, non sequitur*) as students record notes on the copy masters.

R RESOURCE MANAGER—Copy Master
Note Taking p. 266

In addition to persuasive techniques, writers often use **rhetorical devices** to enhance their arguments:

- A **rhetorical question** does not require a reply because the answer is obvious. In a letter to her husband (page 262), Abigail Adams asks, "Shall we not be despised by foreign powers, for hesitating so long at a word?"

- **Antithesis** occurs when contrasting ideas are expressed in a grammatically balanced statement. Notice the juxtaposition of ideas in this phrase from Thomas Paine's "The Crisis" (page 252): "I call not upon a few, but upon all."

- **Repetition** is the use of the same word or phrase more than once for emphasis. **Parallelism,** a form of repetition in which a grammatical pattern is repeated, is used effectively in this famous passage from the Declaration of Independence (page 236): "We hold these truths to be self-evident:—That all men are created equal; that they are endowed by their Creator with certain unalienable rights; that among these are life, liberty and the pursuit of happiness."

Sometimes persuasive writing includes errors in logical thinking, called **logical fallacies**. Below are some common logical fallacies.

Type of Fallacy	Definition	Example
Circular reasoning	Supporting a statement by repeating the statement using different words.	Liberty is essential to humankind. Free people must have it.
Hasty generalization	A conclusion drawn from too little evidence or from evidence that is biased.	Candidate Smith voted against my bill. He is an enemy to freedom.
Non sequitur	A conclusion that does not follow logically from the "proof" offered to support it.	The incumbent candidate is hugely popular. He must be the best qualified for office.

Rhetorical devices and persuasive techniques can be used to create arguments that are valid and sincere or artificial and insincere. It is up to the reader or listener to evaluate whether the argument is based on sound reasoning, and therefore credible and convincing, or whether the words and appeals are the sole strength of the argument.

To be effective, an argument should include

- a **claim,** or clear statement of a position on an issue
- **support** for the claim in the form of reasons and evidence
- **counterarguments,** or statements that anticipate and refute opposing views
- sound **logic** and effective language
- a **conclusion** that sums up the reasons or the call for action

The Power of Language

Persuasive Techniques Clarify these terms listed on pages 226–227:

- **Logical appeals:** Stress that in the Declaration of Independence the logical appeal consists of a list of injuries and usurpations. Ask what would be the purpose of a list of King George's unfair actions. **Possible answer:** *It would show evidence to support Jefferson's cause.*

- **Emotional appeals:** Ask students to describe likely reactions to the words "death, desolation, and tyranny." **Possible answer:** *They would create anger.*

- **Ethical appeals:** Ask students to read the quotation closely and decide how Jefferson portrayed himself. **Possible answer:** *He wanted to seem reasonable, moderate, fair, humble, and patient.*

Rhetorical Devices Discuss these different rhetorical devices:

- **Rhetorical questions:** Ask students for examples they might ask or hear in real life. **Possible answer:** *Is life always fair?*

- **Antithesis:** Write the word on the board and circle the prefix *anti-*. Ask what it means. (*"against"*) Emphasize that a sentence using antithesis contains a contrast between two opposing ideas or statements. Then read the quotation from Paine aloud and ask students to state its two opposing ideas. (*Paine speaks not to <u>a few</u>, but to <u>all</u>.*)

- **Parallelism:** Explain that parallelism can be repetition of any grammatical pattern, from an introductory word or phrase to an entire clause or sentence. Ask what the repeated pattern in the Jefferson quotation is. (*"That" followed by a clause.*)

FOR ENGLISH LANGUAGE LEARNERS
Language: Skill Words On the board, list the vocabulary shown in italics. Then share the definitions or examples and have students match them to the list.

- *logical:* appeals to reason, not emotion
- *emotional:* appeals to feelings
- *ethical:* consistent with moral values
- *rhetorical question:* "Isn't this great?"
- *antithesis:* "I'm not hungry, I'm thirsty."
- *parallelism:* "I see you, I hear you."

- *logical fallacies:* mistakes in reasoning

FOR ADVANCED LEARNERS/AP
Formulate an Argument [small-group option] Continue the argument for or against longer school days. Have students identify a logical fallacy about extending the school day, identifying whether it is circular reasoning, a hasty generalization, or a non sequitur. Then have students develop a valid position and points to support it. Then ask students whether they would choose to argue their case deductively or inductively, and why.

Focus and Motivate

COMMON CORE FOCUS

RI 5 Analyze and evaluate the effectiveness of the structure an author uses in his or her argument, including whether the structure makes points clear, convincing, and engaging. **RI 6** Determine an author's point of view or purpose in a text in which the rhetoric is particularly effective, analyzing how style and content contribute to the power, persuasiveness, or beauty of the text. **W 1** Write arguments to support claims in an analysis of substantive topic or texts, using valid reasoning and relevant and sufficient evidence. **L 3a** Vary syntax for effect, consulting references for guidance as needed; apply an understanding of syntax to the study of complex texts when reading. **L 4b** Identify and use patterns of word changes that indicate different meanings or parts of speech. **L 4d** Verify the preliminary determination of the meaning of a word or phrase. **L 5** Demonstrate understanding of word relationships. **L 6** Acquire and use accurately general academic and domain-specific words and phrases, sufficient for reading, writing, speaking.

ABOUT THE AUTHOR

To clarify Henry's "loaded analogy," explain that Brutus and other Roman senators killed the dictator Julius Caesar for fear he had too much power, and Oliver Cromwell led the effort to execute King Charles I of Britain for treason. Ask what Henry meant by "George III may profit by their example."

NOTABLE QUOTE

"If this be treason, make the most of it."
—Patrick Henry

Selection Resources

COMMON CORE

RI 5 Analyze and evaluate the effectiveness of the structure an author uses in his or her argument, including whether the structure makes points clear, convincing, and engaging. **RI 6** Determine an author's point of view or purpose in a text in which the rhetoric is particularly effective, analyzing how style and content contribute to the power, persuasiveness, or beauty of the text. **L 3a** Apply an understanding of syntax to the study of complex texts. **L 4b** Identify and correctly use patterns of word changes that indicate different meanings or parts of speech.

DID YOU KNOW?

Patrick Henry . . .

- had 16 children—6 by his first wife, who died, and then 10 by his second wife.
- owned slaves.
- advocated the right to bear arms later guaranteed by the U.S. Constitution.
- strongly supported states' rights.

(background) Virginia House of Burgesses

Writers of the Revolution

from Speech in the Virginia Convention
by Patrick Henry

 **Essential Course of Study** **ECOS**

Meet the Author

Patrick Henry 1736–1799

Known as "the Orator of Liberty," Patrick Henry made a name for himself with his speeches supporting American democracy. He was one of the earliest opponents of British rule in the American colonies. In 1765, after the British Parliament passed a tax bill called the Stamp Act, Henry was among the members of the Virginia legislature that challenged the legality of a British tax on the colonies. But he went farther than his colleagues by making a threat against the king. In his argument, so the story goes, he used a loaded analogy: "Caesar had his Brutus, Charles the First his Cromwell, and George III . . ."—at this point, shouts of "Treason!" erupted in the hall, but Henry continued—"may profit by their example." He ended his speech with the defiant words, "If this be treason, make the most of it." Henry did indeed make the most of his "treason," becoming a tireless and influential leader both before and after the Revolution.

Profitable Law Career Henry was born in Virginia to a prosperous landowner. His father, who had attended the University of Aberdeen in Scotland, gave him a classical education at home. His mother, Sarah Winston Syme, was from a wealthy family. Henry went out on his own at age 15. Although smart and industrious, he couldn't find success as a storekeeper or later as a tobacco planter. After marrying and starting a family, he decided to teach himself law, and in 1760, at the age of 24, he was admitted to the bar. Henry's eloquence, quick wit, and rhetorical gifts served him well, and his law practice grew increasingly profitable.

Popular Virginia Politician Henry is best known for his fervent "Speech in the Virginia Convention," which narrowly convinced the assembled leadership to prepare for war with Britain. In addition, he organized a Virginia militia that became part of the new Continental Army after independence was declared. He helped write the new state constitution and the Virginia Declaration of Rights, which was a major influence on the Bill of Rights added to the U.S. Constitution. He also served several terms as governor of Virginia and as a state legislator. Although President Washington offered him positions as secretary of state and Supreme Court justice, Henry declined and always remained suspicious of the federal government. In 1799, after being elected again to the state legislature, he died at his 700-acre plantation, Red Hill, before he could take office.

Author Online
Go to **thinkcentral.com**. KEYWORD: HML11-228

THINK central

228

See resources on the **Teacher One Stop DVD-ROM** and on **thinkcentral.com**.

R **RESOURCE MANAGER UNIT 1**
Plan and Teach, pp. 267–274
Summary, pp. 275–276† ‡
Text Analysis and Reading
Skill, pp. 277–280 † *
Vocabulary, pp. 281–283 *
Grammar and Style, p. 286

DIAGNOSTIC AND SELECTION TESTS
Selection Tests, pp. 81–84

BEST PRACTICES TOOLKIT
Definition Mapping, p. E6

INTERACTIVE READER

ADAPTED INTERACTIVE READER

ELL ADAPTED INTERACTIVE READER

TECHNOLOGY
- **Teacher One Stop DVD-ROM**
- **Student One Stop DVD-ROM**
- **PowerNotes DVD-ROM**
- **Audio Anthology CD**
- **GrammarNotes DVD-ROM**
- **ExamView Test Generator** on the Teacher One Stop

Video Trailer

THINK central

Go to **thinkcentral.com** to preview the **Video Trailer** introducing this selection. Other features that support the selection include
- **PowerNotes** presentation
- **ThinkAloud** models to enhance comprehension
- **WordSharp** vocabulary tutorials
- interactive writing and grammar instruction

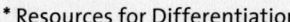

TEXT ANALYSIS: RHETORICAL DEVICES

Rhetorical devices are structures within language that appeal to readers or listeners and communicate ideas.

- A **rhetorical question** is a question to which no answer is expected. (*But when shall we be stronger?*)
- **Antithesis** expresses contrasting ideas in parallel grammatical structures. (*Give me liberty, or give me death!*)
- **Repetition** is the recurrence of words, phrases, or lines. (*Let it come! I repeat it, sir, let it come!*)
- **Parallelism** is a kind of repetition in which words or phrases in the same grammatical form connect ideas. (*Is life so dear, or peace so sweet . . .*)
- **Biblical allusions** are references to events, figures, or phrases from the Bible. In this selection, they have the rhetorical appeal of shared beliefs.

As you read Henry's speech, be on the lookout for rhetorical devices and how they might have affected his audience.

READING SKILL: READING A PERSUASIVE SPEECH

In this famous speech, Patrick Henry speaks to members of the Virginia convention, but clearly he is aware of a wider audience—even of future generations reading his words. As you read the speech, think about Henry's **audience** and how he uses language to appeal to his audience. What **tone** or attitude do you detect in his language, and how does his choice of words reveal his **purpose** as a speaker?

▲ VOCABULARY IN CONTEXT

Use context clues to write a definition of each boldfaced word.

1. **Martial** Speech Sets Stage for War
2. Never **Supinely** Accept Tyranny, Henry Says
3. **Invincible** Patriot Army Will Repel Attacks
4. **Insidious** Spies Reveal Patriots' Plans
5. Nothing Can **Extenuate** Tory Traitors
6. Citizens Told to Be **Vigilant**
7. America Must Remain **Inviolate**

 Complete the activities in your **Reader/Writer Notebook**.

When is it time to TAKE ACTION?

Whether it's the winning shot in the final seconds of the game, the right moment to ask someone out, or the decision to accept a job offer—timing is everything. In the spring of 1775, Patrick Henry had had enough of compromise with the British; it was time for armed resistance. His address to the Virginia Convention turned out to be a decisive moment not only in his own life but in the life of the United States as well.

DISCUSS With a partner, think of examples from sports, politics, or everyday life when the time was right for decisive action. Then, for one example, analyze why it was the right action at the right time.

Example of Decisive Action:

Reasons That the Time Was Right:

When is it time to TAKE ACTION?

After pairs complete the *DISCUSS* activity, invite volunteers to share their examples. Then ask students to generalize how someone might recognize a decisive moment when it occurs.

TEXT ANALYSIS
COMMON CORE
RI 5
RI 6
L 3a

● *Model the Skill:* **RHETORICAL DEVICES**

Remind students that they learned about rhetorical devices in the Text Analysis Workshop on Persuasive Rhetoric (page 226). Ask volunteers to explain how each quote from Henry's speech uses the rhetorical device it exemplifies. Point out that Henry's questions are rhetorical, and he does not expect an answer. The quote uses antithesis, presenting two opposite choices in parallel grammatical form. "Let it come!" is repeated. The grammatical form is parallel: noun + "so" + adjective.

GUIDED PRACTICE Have students write a sentence that uses one of the rhetorical devices discussed on this page.

READING STRATEGY
COMMON CORE
RI 5
RI 6

■ *Model the Skill:* **READING A PERSUASIVE SPEECH**

Tell students that in their charts, they should list speaking techniques, not rhetorical devices. In addition to the oral techniques mentioned in the instruction, suggest that students consider other performance techniques, such as gestures and facial expressions. Demonstrate how tone can affect a persuasive argument by reading a passage from Henry's speech using the appropriate tone.

R RESOURCE MANAGER—Copy Master
Reading a Persuasive Speech p. 279

VOCABULARY
COMMON CORE
L 4

▲ VOCABULARY IN CONTEXT

DIAGNOSE WORD KNOWLEDGE Have all students complete Vocabulary in Context. Check their words and phrases against the following:

extenuate (ĭk-stĕn′yōō-āt′) *v.* to lessen the seriousness of
insidious (ĭn-sĭd′ē-əs) *adj.* treacherous
invincible (ĭn-vĭn′sə-bəl) *adj.* unbeatable
inviolate (ĭn-vī′ə-lĭt) *adj.* not violated; intact

martial (mär′shəl) *adj.* warlike
supinely (sōō-pīn′lē) *adv.* in a manner with the face upward
vigilant (vĭj′ə-lənt) *adj.* alert; watchful

PRETEACH VOCABULARY Use the following copy master to help students predict meanings.

R RESOURCE MANAGER—Copy Master
Vocabulary Study p. 281

Practice and Apply

SUMMARY

Patrick Henry delivered this speech to an audience of Virginia delegates convened to decide whether to revolt against Britain. Henry begins by saying that he must speak out or consider himself guilty of treason. He argues that Britain is preparing for war against the colonies and that the colonists have tried peaceful arguments for a decade. Peace is no longer an option. If the colonists wish to be free, they must fight.

READ WITH A PURPOSE

Help students set a purpose for reading. Tell them to read to find out Patrick Henry's reasons for encouraging the colonies to fight.

REVISIT THE BIG QUESTION

When is it time to TAKE ACTION?

Discuss Based on lines 1–11, what details in this passage reveal that Henry believes he is speaking at a decisive moment? Why does he feel that free debate is essential at such a moment? *Possible answer: Henry reveals his belief that he is speaking at a decisive moment when he says, "This is no time for ceremony. The question before the House is one of awful moment to this country. For my own part I consider it as nothing less than a question of freedom or slavery . . ." (lines 6–8). He believes free debate is essential at such a moment because the stakes are so high ("freedom or slavery"). The colonists can't make the best decision if they don't hear all points of view.*

TEXT ANALYSIS

COMMON CORE
RI 5
RI 6
L 3a

A *Model the Skill:*
RHETORICAL DEVICES

Explain that writers who want to present contrasting ideas often use antithesis and set off contrasting ideas with a conjunction. Have volunteers read aloud lines 1–9, beginning with, "For my own part..." to identify examples of antithesis.

Possible answer: "same subject in different lights" (line 3), "freedom or slavery" (line 8)

SPEECH IN THE
Virginia Convention

Patrick Henry

> **BACKGROUND** In the spring of 1775, delegates from the state of Virginia could not agree whether to press for a peaceful solution with Britain or to prepare for war. Patrick Henry introduced resolutions calling for military preparedness. After politely listening to his colleagues' objections to armed rebellion, he rose to deliver this impassioned appeal.

Analyze Visuals ▶
This painting shows Patrick Henry speaking to the Virginia House of Burgesses. What different attitudes are reflected in the faces and postures of his audience members?

March 23, 1775

Mr. President:[1] No man thinks more highly than I do of the patriotism, as well as abilities, of the very worthy gentlemen who have just addressed the House. But different men often see the same subject in different lights; and, therefore, I hope that it will not be thought disrespectful to those gentlemen, if, entertaining as I do opinions of a character very opposite to theirs, I shall speak forth my sentiments freely and without reserve. This is no time for ceremony. The question before the House is one of awful moment[2] to this country. For my own part I consider it as nothing less than a question of freedom or slavery; and in proportion to the magnitude of the subject ought to be the freedom of the debate. It is only in this
10 way that we can hope to arrive at truth, and fulfill the great responsibility which we hold to God and our country. Should I keep back my opinions at such a **A**

❶ Targeted Passage

A RHETORICAL DEVICES
Reread lines 1–11. What are some examples of **antithesis,** and what kind of emphasis does it create?

---

1. **Mr. President:** the president of the Virginia Convention, Peyton Randolph.
2. **of awful moment:** of very grave importance.

Patrick Henry Before the Virginia House of Burgesses (1851), Peter F. Rothermel. Red Hill, The Patrick Henry National Memorial, Brookneal, Virginia.

DIFFERENTIATED INSTRUCTION

FOR ENGLISH LANGUAGE LEARNERS

Vocabulary Support Use Definition Mapping to teach these words: *debate* (line 9), *conduct* (line 24), *capable* (line 43), *abandon* (line 58), *acquire* (line 66).

 **BEST PRACTICES TOOLKIT**
Definition Mapping p. E6

FOR STRUGGLING READERS

In combination with the *Audio Anthology CD,* use one or more Targeted Passages (pp. 230, 232, 234) to ensure that students focus on key concepts in the selection. Targeted Passages are also good for English learners.

❶ Targeted Passage [Lines 6–11]

This passage conveys Henry's sense of urgency about the decision facing the Virginia Convention.

Reading Support

This selection on **thinkcentral.com** includes embedded **ThinkAloud** models–students "thinking aloud" about the story to model the kinds of questions a good reader would ask about a selection.

Analyze Visuals

Possible answer: *Some of the audience members look troubled or suspicious. The man with his arm outstretched seems to be pleading with Henry to stop speaking.*

About the Art This painting by Peter Frederick Rothermel (1817–1895) shows the artist's skillful use of color to dramatize historical subjects. Henry's speech before the House of Burgesses, a decade before the Virginia Convention speech, includes the **Notable Quote,** "If this be treason, make the most of it."

TIERED DISCUSSION PROMPTS

Refer to lines 1–11 and use these prompts to help students understand Henry's introduction:

Connect If you were a delegate at the Virginia Convention, how would the beginning of Henry's speech affect you? *Accept all thoughtful responses.*

Interpret What is Henry's purpose for discussing the "freedom of the debate"? **Possible answer:** *Henry wants to get the delegates to listen to him with an open mind.*

Evaluate Is this an effective opening for a speech, or as a modern reader, do you think the speech begins too slowly? Explain your response. **Possible answer:** *The beginning of the speech was effective because it showed respect to the delegates and their opinions. However, for a modern audience, Henry takes too long to make his point.*

- What does Henry mean when he says, "This is no time for ceremony"? (line 6)

- What is the "question before the House"? (line 6–7)

- What stark contrast does he present to convey the importance of this question? (line 8)

- According to Henry, why is it so important to have "freedom of the debate"? (line 9)

- Why does he mention the delegates' responsibility to "God and our country"? (line 11)

FOR ADVANCED LEARNERS/AP

Make Decisions Begin a discussion by asking students what qualities are required for making good decisions. Is wisdom more important than experience? Is decisiveness more important than analysis? Encourage students to offer specific examples when expressing their opinions.

Sidebar (left column)

Main text (center column)

time, through fear of giving offense, I should consider myself as guilty of treason towards my country, and of an act of disloyalty towards the majesty of heaven, which I revere above all earthly kings. **B**

Mr. President, it is natural to man to indulge in the illusions of hope. We are apt to shut our eyes against a painful truth, and listen to the song of that siren, till she transforms us into beasts.[3] Is this the part of wise men, engaged in a great and arduous struggle for liberty? Are we disposed to be of the number of those who, having eyes, see not, and having ears, hear not,[4] the things which so nearly concern
20 their temporal salvation? For my part, whatever anguish of spirit it may cost, I am willing to know the whole truth—to know the worst and to provide for it.

I have but one lamp by which my feet are guided; and that is the lamp of experience. I know of no way of judging of the future but by the past. And judging by the past, I wish to know what there has been in the conduct of the British ministry for the last ten years, to justify those hopes with which gentlemen have been pleased to solace themselves and the House? Is it that **insidious** smile with which our petition has been lately received? Trust it not, sir; it will prove a snare to your feet. Suffer not yourselves to be betrayed with a kiss.[5] **C**

Ask yourselves how this gracious reception of our petition comports[6] with these
30 warlike preparations which cover our waters and darken our land. Are fleets and armies necessary to a work of love and reconciliation? Have we shown ourselves so unwilling to be reconciled that force must be called in to win back our love? Let us not deceive ourselves, sir. These are the implements of war and subjugation[7]— the last arguments to which kings resort. I ask gentlemen, sir, what means this **martial** array, if its purpose be not to force us to submission? Can gentlemen assign any other possible motives for it? Has Great Britain any enemy, in this quarter of the world, to call for all this accumulation of navies and armies? No, sir, she has none. They are meant for us; they can be meant for no other. They are sent over to bind and rivet upon us those chains which the British ministry
40 have been so long forging. **D**

And what have we to oppose to them? Shall we try argument? Sir, we have been trying that for the last ten years. Have we anything new to offer on the subject? Nothing. We have held the subject up in every light of which it is capable; but it has been all in vain. Shall we resort to entreaty and humble supplication? What terms shall we find which have not been already exhausted? Let us not, I beseech you, sir, deceive ourselves longer. **E**    **Targeted Passage**

---

3. **the illusions of hope . . . into beasts:** In the *Odyssey* of Homer, the goddess Circe lures men to her island and then magically transforms them into pigs. Henry suggests that the "illusions of hope" may transform people in a similar way.

4. **having eyes . . . hear not:** an allusion to Ezekiel 12:2 in the Bible, which speaks of "who have eyes to see, but see not, who have ears to hear, but hear not."

5. **betrayed with a kiss:** an allusion to Luke 22:47–48 in the Bible, wherein Judas betrayed Jesus to the Roman soldiers by kissing him and thus identifying him.

6. **comports:** agrees or goes along with.

7. **subjugation:** control by conquering.

Sidebar (right column)

DIFFERENTIATED INSTRUCTION

FOR STRUGGLING READERS

 **Targeted Passage** [Lines 22–46]

In this passage, Henry summarizes previous failed efforts to negotiate with Britain.

- In lines 22–26, what point does Henry make about judging the future?

- What evidence does Henry cite to argue that the British are preparing for war? (lines 30–31)

- In lines 41–46, what is Henry's answer to those who favor talking to the British?

Develop Reading Fluency Model how to break down Henry's long, complicated sentences into shorter, simpler ones. For example, divide sentences that contain semicolons into separate sentences. Point out that the sentence in line 38 can be simplified like this: "They are meant for us. They can be meant for no other." Then have students work in pairs to apply this strategy to the long sentences in lines 48–53. Have students read aloud their shorter sentences.

The Bloody Massacre perpetrated in. . . Boston on March 5th, 1770 (1770), Paul Revere. Colored engraving. Private collection. /Art Resource, New York.

Sir, we have done everything that could be done to avert the storm which is now coming on. We have petitioned; we have remonstrated[8]; we have supplicated; we have prostrated ourselves before the throne, and have implored
50 its interposition[9] to arrest the tyrannical hands of the ministry and Parliament. Our petitions have been slighted; our remonstrances have produced additional violence and insult; our supplications have been disregarded; and we have been spurned, with contempt, from the foot of the throne. In vain, after these things, may we indulge the fond hope of peace and reconciliation. There is no longer any room for hope.

---

8. **remonstrated:** to object; to protest strongly.
9. **we have prostrated . . . interposition:** We have thrown ourselves at the feet of the king and have begged for intervention.

(⊙) **COMMON CORE L 4b**

Language Coach

Suffixes Read the definition for *remonstrated* (line 48). Now, note the noun *remonstrances* in line 51. What **suffix** (word part at the end of a word that forms a new word) is added to make *remonstrate* a noun? Write a definition for *remonstrances.*

Analyze Visuals

Activity Ask students what viewpoint the engraving expresses. *Possible answer: It favors the colonists, showing the British attacking civilians.*

About the Art Paul Revere was known not only for his ride on April 18, 1775, but also as a silversmith, printer, and engraver. Revere made this engraving to illustrate the Boston Massacre, which occurred on March 5, 1770, five years before Patrick Henry's speech. Like that speech, the engraving helped turn American public opinion toward revolt.

REVISIT THE BIG QUESTION

When is it time to
TAKE ACTION?

Discuss Henry lists several actions the colonies have taken to protest their treatment by the British. How do these actions show that Henry is speaking at a decisive moment in American history? *Possible answer: Henry believes the colonies have exhausted peaceful avenues for settlement with the British. Thus, the moment has come for the colonists to resort to forceful means.*

FOR STRUGGLING READERS

Reading a Persuasive Speech To help students imagine delivering lines 47–55, ask them to consider these questions:

• What words and phrases would they emphasize if they were giving the speech?

• Where would they pause for effect?

• Where would they speak loudly or softly?

FOR ENGLISH LANGUAGE LEARNERS

Language Coach   (⊙) **COMMON CORE L 4b**

Suffixes *The suffix is –ance. Remonstrance is the presenting of reasons for opposition.* Provide students with the following verbs and have them provide the noun forms: *enter, accept, disturb. (entrance, acceptance, disturbance)*

 BEST PRACTICES TOOLKIT—Transparencies
Suffixes and Base Words pp. E27, E28

⒡ RHETORICAL DEVICES

RI 5
RI 6
L 3a

Possible answer: The word *sir* literally refers to the president of the Convention, but broadly it is intended to affect all the delegates by emphasizing Henry's respect for his audience. The repetition of "let it come!" shows his determination to face the conflict and stirs an emotional response.

READING STRATEGY | COMMON CORE

⒢ PERSUASIVE SPEECH

RI 5
RI 6

Possible answer: He probably began quietly and calmly, with his words becoming increasingly loud, impassioned, and rapid. This change probably stirred the crowd to feel excitement, anger, and determination to take action.

VOCABULARY | COMMON CORE

L 4

OWN THE WORD

- **inviolate:** Have students offer examples of things that could be described as *inviolate*.

- **supinely:** Tell students that *supinely* also means "passively." Have students name fictional characters that could be described as behaving *supinely*.

- **invincible:** Have students name synonyms for *invincible*.

- **vigilant:** Have students discuss a situation in which they should be *vigilant*.

- **extenuate:** Have students create a semantic web for *extenuate*.

SELECTION WRAP-UP

READ WITH A PURPOSE Now that students have read the selection, ask them to provide reasons that, according to Henry, the colonies should battle England. *Possible answers: England is preparing for war; if the colonies do not fight, they will be enslaved; the war already has begun.*

If we wish to be free—if we mean to preserve **inviolate** those inestimable privileges for which we have been so long contending—if we mean not basely to abandon the noble struggle in which we have been so long engaged, and which we have pledged ourselves never to abandon until the glorious object of our contest

60 shall be obtained, we must fight! I repeat it, sir, we must fight! An appeal to arms and to the God of Hosts is all that is left us!

They tell us, sir, that we are weak—unable to cope with so formidable an adversary. But when shall we be stronger? Will it be the next week, or the next year? Will it be when we are totally disarmed, and when a British guard shall be stationed in every house? Shall we gather strength by irresolution and inaction? Shall we acquire the means of effectual resistance, by lying **supinely** on our backs, and hugging the delusive phantom of hope, until our enemies shall have bound us hand and foot?

Sir, we are not weak, if we make a proper use of those means which the God
70 of nature hath placed in our power. Three millions of people, armed in the holy cause of liberty, and in such a country as that which we possess, are **invincible** by any force which our enemy can send against us. Besides, sir, we shall not fight our battles alone. There is a just God who presides over the destinies of nations, and who will raise up friends to fight our battles for us. The battle, sir, is not to the strong alone;[10] it is to the **vigilant,** the active, the brave. Besides, sir, we have no election.[11] If we were base enough to desire it, it is now too late to retire from the contest. There is no retreat but in submission and slavery! Our chains are forged! Their clanking may be heard on the plains of Boston! The war is inevitable—and let it come! I repeat it, sir, let it come! ⒡

80 It is in vain, sir, to **extenuate** the matter. Gentlemen may cry, "Peace! peace!"— but there is no peace. The war is actually begun! The next gale that sweeps from the north[12] will bring to our ears the clash of resounding arms! Our brethren are already in the field! Why stand we here idle? What is it that gentlemen wish? What would they have? Is life so dear, or peace so sweet, as to be purchased at the price of chains and slavery? Forbid it, Almighty God! I know not what course others may take; but as for me, give me liberty, or give me death! ᖾ ⒢

inviolate (ĭn-vī′ə-lĭt) *adj.* not violated; intact

supinely (sōo-pīn′lē) *adv.* in a manner with the face upward

invincible (ĭn-vĭn′sə-bəl) *adj.* unbeatable

vigilant (vĭj′ə-lənt) *adj.* alert; watchful

⒡ RHETORICAL DEVICES

Why do you think Henry repeats the word *sir* so often in this paragraph? Explain the likely effect of this **repetition** as well as that of the phrase "let it come!"

extenuate (ĭk-stĕn′yōō-āt′) *v.* to lessen the seriousness of, especially by providing partial excuses

❸ Targeted Passage

⒢ PERSUASIVE SPEECH

Reread lines 80–86. Notice how the pace or momentum of the speech accelerates as Henry draws to a close. How does the change in pace affect the speaker's tone? What purpose do you detect in the pace and tone of Henry's closing lines? Cite evidence from the speech to support your answer.

---

10. **battle...strong alone:** an allusion to Ecclesiastes 9:11 in the Bible, "the race is not to the swift, nor the battle to the strong."
11. **election:** choice.
12. **the next gale...north:** Some colonists in Massachusetts had already shown open resistance to the British and were on the brink of war.

DIFFERENTIATED INSTRUCTION

FOR STRUGGLING READERS

❸ **Targeted Passage** [Lines 80–86]

This passage brings Henry's rhetoric to its height of passion as the speech closes.

- What is Henry's tone in this paragraph?

- What mood might his speech have stirred in the audience?

- What does Henry mean when he says, "give me liberty, or give me death"? (line 86)

- What does he hope to achieve by this cry?

FOR ADVANCED LEARNERS/AP

Synthesize [paired option] Have students write a news story for a colonial newspaper summarizing Henry's key points—but because colonial newspapers were often not objective, students should slant their stories for or against Henry's position.

 BEST PRACTICES TOOLKIT—Transparency
Writing Template: Eyewitness Report pp. C16, C27

Comprehension

1. **Recall** What does Patrick Henry urge the colonists to do?

2. **Paraphrase** Reread lines 22–28. What methods had the colonists already used to express their complaints against the British?

3. **Clarify** How did the British respond to those complaints?

Text Analysis

4. **Analyze a Persuasive Speech** How do beliefs shared by speaker and audience advance Henry's purpose and affect his tone in this speech? Support your answer with evidence from the speech.

5. **Interpret Allusions** Review the following allusions to the Bible that Henry uses in his speech. Explain the rhetorical appeal of each allusion.

   • lines 18–19   • lines 74–75

6. **Evaluate Appeals** How does Henry convince his audience that the **decisive moment** to fight is at hand? In a chart, summarize his reasons. Then, beside each, note whether he appeals mainly to logic or emotion. Which reasons are strongest? Explain.

Reasons to Fight	Logical or Emotional
1. If we want to be free and keep the rights and privileges we have grown accustomed to, we have to fight. (lines 56–61)	logical
2.	

7. **Make Judgments About Rhetorical Devices** Review the rhetorical devices discussed on page 229. Which devices occur most frequently in Henry's speech? Do you think that rhetorical devices are an effective way to communicate, or do you find them manipulative? Cite examples from the text to support your answer.

Text Criticism

8. **Different Perspectives** Imagine that the following people heard Henry's speech from the visitor's gallery. How might each have reacted, and why?

   • the wife of one of the delegates
   • a farmer whose parents live in England
   • a member of the Virginia militia
   • a clergyman
   • an African enslaved in the colony

When is it time to TAKE ACTION?
Patrick Henry's intense frustration compelled him to act. What circumstances in your life have triggered you to make a decision or to take action?

8. *The wife might be concerned that her husband would have to fight the British. The farmer might worry that war would cut him off from his parents in England. The militiaman might be stirred by the call to action. The clergyman might respond favorably to Henry's biblical allusions. The enslaved African might be encouraged by references to slavery to think that war would end his own bondage.*

When is it time to TAKE ACTION? Students should cite an example that challenged and frustrated them but also inspired them to take action.

Practice and Apply

For preliminary support of post-reading questions, use these copy masters:

R RESOURCE MANAGER—Copy Masters
Reading Check p. 284
Rhetorical Devices p. 277
Question Support p. 285
Additional selection questions are provided for teachers on page 271.

ANSWERS 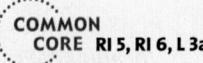 COMMON CORE RI 5, RI 6, L 3a

1. *to prepare to fight against the British*
2. *petitioning the government and asking the king to stop the tyranny*
3. *by spurning the colonists' complaints or responding violently*

Possible answers:

4. ● **COMMON CORE FOCUS Analyze a Persuasive Speech** *Henry uses biblical allusions in his speech, which allow for a connection with his audience since both he and his audience share beliefs. The tone in lines like "fulfill the great responsibility which we hold to God and our country" (lines 18-19) are therefore serious and religious.*

5. ***Odyssey, lines 15–17:** The hope for peace is a false lure. **Bible, lines 18–19:** Don't ignore clear evidence. **Bible, line 28:** Don't trust treacherous pretenses. **Bible, lines 74–75:** Our spirit can make up for our weaker force.*

6. ***Reasons: 1.** If we don't prepare now, we won't be able to resist (lines 56–60); emotional. **2.** There are three million of us willing and able to fight (lines 70–72); logical. **3.** God will help us win (lines 72–74); emotional. **4.** It's too late to back down (lines 76–77); emotional. **5.** The war has already begun (line 78); logical. **6.** Give me liberty, or give me death (lines 84–86); emotional. Accept all reasonable ranking of reasons.*

7. ● **COMMON CORE FOCUS Rhetorical Devices** *Henry uses rhetorical questions and parallelism most often. Students may say that these devices are effective ways of presenting ideas. Others may say that the devices are manipulative because they stir emotions rather than present well-reasoned arguments.*

Vocabulary in Context

▲ **VOCABULARY PRACTICE**

1. *true*	5. *true*
2. *false*	6. *false*
3. *false*	7. *false*
4. *false*	

 **RESOURCE MANAGER—Copy Master**
Vocabulary Practice p. 282

ACADEMIC VOCABULARY IN SPEAKING

Henry uses persuasive strategies, anecdotes, and emotional appeals. He also speaks with profound courtesy. Students should use several academic vocabulary terms in their discussions.

VOCABULARY STRATEGY: ANALOGIES

COMMON CORE L 4d, L 5, L 6

Point out to students that common patterns in analogies include synonyms, antonyms, examples, and variations of degree.

Possible answers:

1. **c**

2. **a**

3. **d**

4. **c**

 **RESOURCE MANAGER—Copy Master**
Vocabulary Strategy, p. 283

Interactive Vocabulary
THINK central

Keywords direct students to a **WordSharp** tutorial on **thinkcentral.com** or to other types of vocabulary practice and review.

Vocabulary in Context

▲ **VOCABULARY PRACTICE**

Decide whether these statements about the vocabulary words are true or false.

1. An **invincible** chess champion is one who has not been beaten.
2. A statue that is lying **supinely** is lying face down.
3. A **vigilant** guard usually takes naps while on duty.
4. Circumstances that **extenuate** a bad decision are those that make it worse.
5. A country that is overrun by armies from another land is experiencing **subjugation.**
6. A vase that has broken into several pieces may be described as **inviolate.**
7. A **martial** gathering is one that is organized by peace demonstrators.

WORD LIST

extenuate
insidious
invincible
inviolate
martial
supinely
vigilant

ACADEMIC VOCABULARY IN SPEAKING

• document   • illustrate   • interpret   • promote   • reveal

Patrick Henry uses several persuasive techniques to **illustrate** his points. In a small group, discuss how he presents himself to the delegates and **promotes** his argument. Use at least three Academic Vocabulary words in your discussion.

VOCABULARY STRATEGY: ANALOGIES

One way to determine word meanings is through the use of **analogies,** or comparisons between pairs of words. Here are two examples of analogies that show different kinds of relationships.

> vigilant : unobservant :: invincible : vulnerable
> (Vigilant is to unobservant as invincible is to vulnerable.)
> subjugation : prisoner :: election : governor
> (Subjugation is to prisoner as election is to governor.)

In the first example, both pairs of words are near opposites. In the second example, the relationship is one of process. Just as a prisoner has experienced subjugation, a governor has experienced election.

PRACTICE Complete each analogy by choosing the word that creates the same relationship between both pairs of words. Use a dictionary if you are uncertain about a word's meaning.

1. animal : cat :: vehicle :   (a) driving, (b) house, (c) bicycle, (d) theater
2. sad : depressed :: dry :   (a) desiccated, (b) wet, (c) arid, (d) damp
3. roof : gable :: poem :   (a) haiku, (b) prose, (c) rhyme, (d) stanza
4. vogue : anachronism :: obtuse :   (a) dull, (b) cheerful, (c) acute, (d) angle

COMMON CORE

L 4d Verify the preliminary determination of the meaning of a word or phrase. **L 5** Demonstrate understanding of word relationships. **L 6** Acquire and use accurately general academic and domain-specific words and phrases, sufficient for reading, writing, and speaking.

Interactive Vocabulary
THINK central

Go to **thinkcentral.com.**
KEYWORD: HML11-236

DIFFERENTIATED INSTRUCTION

FOR ENGLISH LANGUAGE LEARNERS

Task Support: Academic Vocabulary in Writing Help students choose three vocabulary words. Review the word meanings orally, and invite clarifying questions. To prepare for writing, have students return to the speech and study the vocabulary words in context. Suggest that students write three sentences, using one vocabulary word per sentence.

FOR ADVANCED LEARNERS/AP

Journalsim Have students write an account that might have appeared in a British paper responding to Henry's speech. Use the words on the word list.

Language

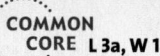 COMMON CORE

L 3a Vary syntax for effect, consulting references for guidance as needed; apply an understanding of syntax to the study of complex texts when reading. **W 1** Write arguments to support claims in an analysis of substantive topics or texts, using valid reasoning and relevant and sufficient evidence.

◆ **GRAMMAR AND STYLE:** Vary Sentence Types

Review the **Grammar and Style** note on page 232. Part of Henry's style is to vary his sentences among the four basic types:

- **Declarative,** which expresses a statement of fact, desire, intent, or feeling and ends with a period. *This is no time for ceremony.* (line 6)

- **Interrogative,** which asks a question and ends with a question mark. *Shall we try argument?* (line 41)

- **Imperative,** which gives a command and sometimes ends with an exclamation point. *Trust it not, sir.* (lines 27–28)

- **Exclamatory,** which expresses strong emotions and always ends with an exclamation point. *I repeat it, sir, we must fight!* (line 60)

Henry's skillful use of sentence variety creates an interesting melody. It also keeps the reader engaged by calling for frequent shifts in response.

PRACTICE For each sentence in this excerpt from Henry's speech, identify the type and compose your own sentence following his pattern.

> **EXAMPLE**
>
> The war is actually begun!
>
> *We won the game!*

(1) The next gale that sweeps from the north will bring to our ears the clash of resounding arms! (2) Our brethren are already in the field! (3) Why stand we here idle? (4) What is it that gentlemen wish? (5) What would they have? (6) Is life so dear, or peace so sweet, as to be purchased at the price of chains and slavery? (7) Forbid it, Almighty God!

READING-WRITING CONNECTION

 Expand your understanding of Henry's speech by responding to this prompt. Then, use the **revising tips** to improve your speech.

WRITING PROMPT	REVISING TIPS
COMPOSE A PERSUASIVE SPEECH Patrick Henry's famous speech is a classic example of effective **oratory,** the art of public speaking. Using Henry's speech as a model, write a **three-to-five paragraph persuasive speech** on a topic you feel strongly about.	• Present a clear argument. • Cite reasons and evidence. • Use rhetorical devices. • Close with a strong statement.

Interactive Revision THINK central

Go to **thinkcentral.com.**
KEYWORD: HML11-237

Language

COMMON CORE **L 3a, W 1**

◆ **GRAMMAR AND STYLE**

To familiarize students with the four types of sentences, return to lines 62–79 and ask students to find at least two examples of each type. Point out that both imperative and exclamatory sentences may end in exclamation points. (For more on sentence types, see **Grammar Handbook,** p. R64.) **Answers:** **1.** *exclamatory,* **2.** *exclamatory,* **3.** *interrogative,* **4.** *interrogative,* **5.** *interrogative,* **6.** *interrogative,* **7.** *imperative*

Students' sentences should follow the pattern of Henry's original.

 **RESOURCE MANAGER**—Copy Master
Vary Sentence Types p. 286

READING-WRITING CONNECTION

Remind students to identify the audience they hope to persuade. They should shape their argument to convince that particular audience.

Suggest that students start with a quote or a catchy opening sentence. Recommend that they begin with an introduction that flatters the audience and end with a rousing call to action. Use the Opening Lines strategy.

 BEST PRACTICES TOOLKIT—Transparency
Opening Lines p. C1

> **Writing Online** THINK central
>
> The following tools are available online at **thinkcentral.com** and on **Write*Smart* CD-ROM:**
> - **Interactive Graphic Organizers**
> - **Interactive Student Models**
> - **Interactive Revision Lessons**
> For additional grammar instruction, see **GrammarNotes** on **thinkcentral.com.**

FOR STRUGGLING WRITERS

Writing Support

- Tell students to choose a topic quickly to avoid wasting time. Suggest that they pick an issue that they feel strongly about.

- Have students write a thesis statement and then brainstorm reasons, facts, and examples to support their views, using a cluster diagram or list.

- Have students include their thesis statement in their first paragraph and follow with two substantial body paragraphs.

- Remind students that they are writing a speech, not a paper to be read silently. Urge them to imagine an audience as they write and to use conversational language, exclamatory sentences, and rhetorical questions.

- Suggest that students read their drafts aloud to themselves or partners.

Assess and Reteach

Assess

DIAGNOSTIC AND SELECTION TESTS
Selection Tests A, B/C pp. 81–84

Interactive Selection Test on thinkcentral.com

Reteach

Level Up Online Tutorials on thinkcentral.com

Reteaching Worksheets on thinkcentral.com

Focus and Motivate

COMMON CORE FOCUS

RI 1 Cite textual evidence to support inferences drawn from the text. **RI 4** Determine the meaning of words and phrases as they are used in a text, including technical meanings. **RI 5** Analyze and evaluate the effectiveness of the structure an author uses in his or her argument, including whether the structure makes points clear, convincing, and engaging. **RI 8** Delineate and evaluate the reasoning in seminal U.S. texts, including the application of constitutional principles and use of legal reasoning and the premises, purposes, and arguments in works of public advocacy. **W 1** Write arguments to support claims in an analysis of substantive topics or texts, using valid reasoning and relevant and sufficient evidence. **L 3a** Vary syntax for effect, consulting references for guidance as needed; apply an understanding of syntax to the study of complex texts when reading. **L 4c** Consult general and specialized reference materials to determine or clarify a word's etymology. **L 6** Acquire and use accurately general academic and domain-specific words and phrases.

ABOUT THE AUTHOR

Refer students to "The Enlightenment" in the Historical Essay (page 22). Explain that Jefferson helped shape the American Enlightenment, drawing on European Enlightenment ideas about the contract between people and their rulers.

NOTABLE QUOTE

"All eyes are opened, or opening, to the rights of men."—**Thomas Jefferson**

Selection Resources

COMMON CORE

RI 4 Determine the meaning of words and phrases as they are used in a text, including technical meanings. **RI 5** Analyze and evaluate the effectiveness of the structure an author uses in his or her argument, including whether the structure makes points clear, convincing, and engaging. **RI 8** Delineate and evaluate the reasoning in seminal U.S. texts, including the application of constitutional principles and use of legal reasoning and the premises, purposes, and arguments in works of public advocacy. **L 3a** Apply an understanding of syntax to the study of complex texts when reading.

DID YOU KNOW?

Thomas Jefferson . . .

- played the violin.
- was an amateur inventor.
- developed the policy of the separation of church and state.
- favored the rights of the states over the federal government.
- died on July 4, the same day as his friend and political rival, John Adams.

Jefferson's home at Monticello

Writers of the Revolution

from The Declaration of Independence

Public Document by Thomas Jefferson

Essential Course of Study

Meet the Author

Thomas Jefferson 1743–1826

Thomas Jefferson was one of the most accomplished founding fathers. Active in the cause for independence, he was governor of Virginia during the Revolutionary War and U.S. minister to France afterward. He also served the new country as the first secretary of state, the second vice-president, and the third president. As president, he acquired the vast Louisiana Territory west of the Mississippi River to the Rocky Mountains, essentially doubling the size of the country. But more important than any political office he held was the lasting impact of Jefferson's ideals of liberty and self-government so eloquently expressed in the Declaration of Independence.

Brilliant Legal Mind The son of a surveyor and gentleman farmer, Jefferson was born into a life of privilege in rural Virginia. Educated at the College of William and Mary, he was tutored in the law and practiced successfully before entering politics at age 26. As a member of the colonial Virginia legislature, he fell in with a group of radicals, among them Patrick Henry. Lacking Henry's oratorical gifts, Jefferson distinguished himself by his legal writing. Significantly, Jefferson's indelible mark on American life came largely from the many legal documents and laws he wrote promoting democracy.

Passion for Learning Jefferson had an insatiable curiosity about the world and often indulged in what he called his "canine appetite for reading." In addition to devouring works on the classics, history, law, science, and philosophy, he taught himself architecture from books. He designed his elaborate estate at Monticello and the buildings of the University of Virginia, which he also founded as the embodiment of his principles of education and individual freedom.

The Issue of Slavery Charges of hypocrisy on the issue of slavery have tarnished Jefferson's image as the "apostle of liberty." In his early writings, he denounced slavery and tried unsuccessfully to include the issue in the Declaration. Yet Jefferson always owned slaves—as many as 600 over the course of his lifetime—and in later years, he remained undecided on this issue. A defining conflict of this period in American history, the controversy over slavery is part of the historical context that shaped Jefferson's purpose as an individual and as the author of one of our most important historical documents.

Author Online

Go to **thinkcentral.com**. KEYWORD: HML11-238

238

See resources on the **Teacher One Stop DVD-ROM** and on **thinkcentral.com**.

 RESOURCE MANAGER UNIT 1

Plan and Teach, pp. 287–294
Summary, pp. 295–296 † ‡
Text Analysis and Reading
    Skill, pp. 297–300 †*
Vocabulary, pp. 301–303*
Grammar and Style, p. 306

DIAGNOSTIC AND SELECTION TESTS

Selection Tests, pp. 85–88

 BEST PRACTICES TOOLKIT

Word Questioning, p. E9
Classification Chart, p. B17
Problem and Solution Charts, p. B20

INTERACTIVE READER

ADAPTED INTERACTIVE READER

ELL ADAPTED INTERACTIVE READER

TECHNOLOGY

- **Teacher One Stop DVD-ROM**
- **Student One Stop DVD-ROM**
- **PowerNotes DVD-ROM**
- **Audio Anthology CD**
- **GrammarNotes DVD-ROM**
- **ExamView Test Generator** on the Teacher One Stop

Video Trailer

Go to **thinkcentral.com** to preview the **Video Trailer** introducing this selection. Other features that support the selection include

- **PowerNotes** presentation
- **ThinkAloud** models to enhance comprehension
- **WordSharp** vocabulary tutorials
- interactive writing and grammar instruction

---

* **Resources for Differentiation**   † **Also in Spanish**   ‡ **Also in Haitian Creole and Vietnamese**

● TEXT ANALYSIS: ARGUMENT

Jefferson's purpose in the Declaration of Independence was to make a logical argument for independence. An **argument** expresses an opinion on an issue and supports it with reasons and evidence. Beginning with a **claim,** the writer's position on the subject, an argument needs the **support** of reasons and evidence to prove its claim. A sound argument anticipates opposing views and provides **counterarguments** or **counterclaims** as evidence against them.

Jefferson's **purpose** with the Declaration was not simply to support a historically important argument. It was to inspire his **audience**—his fellow colonists, as well as future generations of Americans—to aspire to the ideals set forth in this document. As you read, look for these elements of an argument.

● READING SKILL: ANALYZE TEXT STRUCTURE

The Declaration of Independence has four main sections:

1. a **preamble,** or **foreword,** that announces the reason for the document
2. a **declaration** of people's natural rights and relationship to government
3. a long **list** of complaints against George III, the British king
4. a **conclusion** that formally states America's independence

Each section expresses abstract and complex ideas. As you read, use a chart like the one shown to identify the most important point of each section and to record some of the complex ideas put forth by the author.

Section	Main Point	Complex Ideas
1 Preamble lines 1–6	Independence requires a public statement of reasons.	The laws of nature and God support justice.

▲ VOCABULARY IN CONTEXT

Match each vocabulary word in the first column with the word or phrase in the second column that is closest in meaning.

1.	abdicate	a.	correction
2.	redress	b.	tyranny
3.	despotism	c.	treachery
4.	impel	d.	abandon
5.	mercenary	e.	drive
6.	perfidy	f.	hired soldier

When is REBELLION *justified?*

Many young people harbor a spirit of rebellion—against parents, teachers, bosses, rules, or any situation that "just isn't fair!" But how often do you attempt to explain your rebellion logically? In June of 1776, Thomas Jefferson and other colonial leaders had decided to rebel against British rule. But they needed to justify their dangerous action—to themselves, to the king, and to the world.

DISCUSS In a small group, think of several situations in which an individual or a group rebelled against a perceived injustice. The situations could be any of the following:

- local—an incident in your school or community, for example
- global—such as demonstrations against global trade policies
- historical—such as the American, French, or Russian revolutions

Then, as a group, evaluate the reasons for each rebellion and explain which ones you think are justified.

VOCABULARY SKILL

▲ VOCABULARY IN CONTEXT

DIAGNOSE WORD KNOWLEDGE Have all students complete Vocabulary in Context. Check their answers against the following:

abdicate (ăb'dĭ-kāt') *v.* to give up responsibility for

despotism (dĕs'pə-tĭz'əm) *n.* government by a ruler with unlimited power

impel (ĭm-pĕl') *v.* to drive forward; force

mercenary (mûr'sə-nĕr'ē) *n.* a professional soldier hired to fight in a foreign army

perfidy (pûr'fĭ-dē) *n.* treachery

redress (rĭ-drĕs') *n.* the correction of a wrong

PRETEACH VOCABULARY Use the following copy master to help students predict meanings.

R RESOURCE MANAGER—Copy Master
Vocabulary Study p. 301

When is REBELLION *justified?*

Note that Enlightenment thinker John Locke believed that rebellion against injustice was a basic right. Ask students whether they agree or disagree. Extend the debate during the *DISCUSS* activity.

TEXT ANALYSIS — COMMON CORE RI 4 RI 8

● *Model the Skill:* ARGUMENT

Write this example of a writer's argument on the board:

> Many people say that the loyal and friendly dog is man's (or woman's) best friend. However, I vote for the cat as our best friend. Cats are not only loyal and friendly, but also independent and undemanding. Best of all, cats make reliable foot warmers on cold nights, when dogs are snoring on the couch.

Point out to students the claim *(sentence 2),* the support *(sentences 3 and 4),* and the counterargument *(sentence 1).*

GUIDED PRACTICE Ask students to provide an opposing view and counterargument to this claim: "Nothing beats a climate with four seasons."

READING SKILL — COMMON CORE RI 5

■ *Model the Skill:* ANALYZE TEXT STRUCTURE

Point out that the four numbered parts listed on page 239 are elements included in most persuasive works, though with different labels. For example, a **declaration** and a **claim** are similar. Both present the writer's core position on an issue. Ask students to match the list of complaints to an element of argument (*support*).

GUIDED PRACTICE Ask students to suggest another common structural term for **preamble** or **foreword.**

R RESOURCE MANAGER—Copy Master
Analyze Text Structure p. 299 (for student use while reading the selection)

SUMMARY

This public document by Thomas Jefferson asserts that the people have the right and duty to form a new government when the existing government abuses their "unalienable rights." Jefferson supports his assertion with a long list of grievances against British king George III. He then concludes with a declaration that the United Colonies are free and independent, and their connection with Great Britain dissolved.

READ WITH A PURPOSE

Help students set a purpose for reading. Tell them to look for the reasons that Jefferson uses to justify the colonies' demands for independence.

TEXT ANALYSIS

COMMON CORE
RI 4
RI 8

Ⓐ Model the Skill:
ARGUMENT

Help students analyze Jefferson's claim and his support for it by referring students to the chart introduced on page 239, which provides a summary of lines 1–6. Then review this long sentence phrase by phrase, and explain the meaning of each phrase.

Part	Summary
Preamble lines 1–6	When one group of people have to form their own government, it is necessary to explain why.

Possible answer: *Jefferson claims that the colonists owe the world an explanation for their need to sever ties with Great Britain. He says he will list the reasons that force the separation.*

VOCABULARY

COMMON CORE
L 4

OWN THE WORD

impel: The root of *impel* comes from the Latin verb *pellere*, meaning "to push, drive, strike." Ask students to suggest additional words that come from this root. ***Possible answers:*** *compelling, dispel, expel, propeller, repellent.*

The Declaration of *Independence*

Thomas Jefferson

BACKGROUND In September 1774, 56 delegates met in Philadelphia at the First Continental Congress to draw up a declaration of colonial rights. They agreed to reconvene in May 1775 if their demands weren't met. At this Second Continental Congress, Thomas Jefferson joined Benjamin Franklin and John Adams on the committee to draft the Declaration of Independence. The task of writing it fell to Jefferson. Although Congress made many changes to the list of grievances, Jefferson's declaration of rights remained untouched—an abiding testament to "self-evident" truths for the nation and the world.

Analyze Visuals ▶
This is an original copy of the Declaration. What might be some of the advantages of having the whole document appear on one large sheet of paper?

In Congress, July 4, 1776

When, in the course of human events, it becomes necessary for one people to dissolve the political bands which have connected them with another, and to assume, among the powers of the earth, the separate and equal station to which the laws of nature and of nature's God entitle them, a decent respect to the opinions of mankind requires that they should declare the causes which **impel** them to the separation. Ⓐ

impel (ĭm-pĕl´) *v.* to drive forward; force

We hold these truths to be self-evident:—That all men are created equal; that they are endowed by their Creator with certain unalienable rights; that among these are life, liberty, and the pursuit of happiness. That, to secure these
10 rights, governments are instituted among men, deriving their just powers from the consent of the governed; that, whenever any form of government becomes destructive of these ends, it is the right of the people to alter or to abolish it, and to institute a new government, laying its foundation on such principles, and organizing its powers in such form, as to them shall seem most likely to effect their safety and happiness. Prudence, indeed, will dictate that governments long established should not be changed for light and transient causes; and, accordingly,

Ⓐ ARGUMENT
What **claim** does Jefferson present in the preamble of the Declaration, and what **support** does he say he will provide?

❶ **Targeted Passage**

240 UNIT 1: EARLY AMERICAN WRITING

DIFFERENTIATED INSTRUCTION

FOR ENGLISH LANGUAGE LEARNERS

Vocabulary Support Use Word Questioning to teach these words: *secure* (line 9), *consent* (line 11), *commit* (line 64), *legislate* (line 76), *publish* (line 108).

BEST PRACTICES TOOLKIT—Transparency
Word Questioning, p. E9

FOR STRUGGLING READERS

In combination with the *Audio Anthology CD*, use one or more Targeted Passages (pp. 240, 243, 244) to ensure that students focus on key concepts in the selection. Targeted Passages are also good for English learners.

❶ Targeted Passage [Lines 7–15]

This passage establishes the right of the colonists to control their government.

IN CONGRESS, JULY 4, 1776.

The unanimous Declaration of the thirteen united States of America.

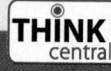

Reading Support

This selection on **thinkcentral.com** includes embedded **ThinkAloud** models–students "thinking aloud" about the story to model the kinds of questions a good reader would ask about a selection.

Analyze Visuals

Possible answer: *Having the document on one sheet meant that its parts could not be separated. Also, the document could be posted in one piece or easily held and read.*

About the Art Copies of the newly printed Declaration of Independence went out immediately to the 13 colonies by horse and by boat. Crowds gathered to hear and cheer its reading. General George Washington read it to his troops in New York. A house painter read it to a crowd near the Massachusetts State House in Boston.

BACKGROUND

An Act of Courage On July 4, 1776, the Second Continental Congress officially approved the Declaration of Independence. Americans celebrate this event each year, perhaps without understanding the courage needed to sign this document. The 56 men who did so put their lives on the line, knowing that they would be hanged for treason if Great Britain prevailed. The odds were heavily against the colonists because of Great Britain's tremendous navy, wealth, and power. Yet those first representatives were willing to risk everything, as Thomas Jefferson so eloquently explained, for the "unalienable rights" of "life, liberty, and the pursuit of happiness."

- According to the document, what rights do people have that cannot be taken away? (line 9)
- How do governments get their power? (lines 10–11)
- When do people have the right to form a new government? (lines 11–13)

FOR ADVANCED LEARNERS/AP

Evaluate Point out to students that England was one of the most powerful nations in the world. Have students evaluate the decision to abandon the ties to its economic power while simultaneously challenging its formidable military might. Encourage students to support their evaluations with specific information when possible.

Ⓑ ARGUMENT

Possible answer: *Jefferson anticipates the argument that it may be too dangerous to change a long-standing government. He claims that so many abuses have accrued that rebellion is justified (lines 19–22). He says that the British king has repeatedly injured the colonies and that he will provide facts to support his case (lines 24–27).*

IF STUDENTS NEED HELP . . . Remind them that a counterargument responds to an opponent's views. Then read lines 15–16.

Ⓒ Model the Skil: TEXT STRUCTURE

Point out that there are 18 separate complaints beginning with "He," each of which discusses an action by the king that colonists oppose. Remind students that each complaint is further support for Jefferson's argument.

Possible answer: *Jefferson wishes to show the overwhelming evidence that exists to support the case of the colonists.*

REVISIT THE BIG QUESTION

When is REBELLION *justified?*

Discuss On the basis of Jefferson's evidence in lines 30–54, were the colonies justified in their rebellion? Explain. *Most students will say that Jefferson is persuasive. Others may think rebellion is too extreme.*

OWN THE WORD

despotism: Review with students the meaning of *despotism*. Then ask students to name rulers from history who might be described as *despots*. **Possible answers:** *Tsar Ivan IV (Ivan the Terrible), Maximillien Robespierre, Joseph Stalin, Adolph Hitler, Mao Zedong*

---

all experience hath shown that mankind are more disposed to suffer, while evils are sufferable, than to right themselves by abolishing the forms to which they are accustomed. But, when a long train of abuses and usurpations, pursuing
20 invariably the same object, evinces a design to reduce them under absolute **despotism,** it is their right, it is their duty, to throw off such government, and to provide new guards for their future security. Such has been the patient sufferance of these colonies; and such is now the necessity that constrains them to alter their former systems of government. The history of the present King of Great Britain[1] is a history of repeated injuries and usurpations, all having, in direct object, the establishment of an absolute tyranny over these States. To prove this, let facts be submitted to a candid world. Ⓑ

    He has refused his assent to laws[2] the most wholesome and necessary for the public good. Ⓒ

30   He has forbidden his Governors to pass laws of immediate and pressing importance, unless suspended in their operation till his assent should be obtained; and, when so suspended, he has utterly neglected to attend to them.

    He has refused to pass other laws for the accommodation of large districts of people, unless these people would relinquish the right of representation in the legislature—a right inestimable to them, and formidable to tyrants only.

    He has called together legislative bodies at places unusual, uncomfortable, and distant from the depository of their public records, for the sole purpose of fatiguing them into compliance with his measure.

    He has dissolved representative houses repeatedly, for opposing, with manly
40 firmness, his invasions on the rights of the people.

    He has refused, for a long time after such dissolutions, to cause others to be elected; whereby the legislative powers, incapable of annihilation, have returned to the people at large for their exercise; the State remaining, in the meantime, exposed to all dangers of invasion from without, and convulsions within.

    He has endeavored to prevent the population[3] of these States; for that purpose obstructing the laws for the naturalization of foreigners; refusing to pass others to encourage their migration hither, and raising the conditions of new appropriations of lands.

    He has obstructed the administration of justice, by refusing his assent to laws
50 for establishing judiciary powers.

    He has made judges dependent on his will alone for the tenure of their offices,[4] and the amount and payment of their salaries.

    He has erected a multitude of new offices, and sent hither swarms of officers to harass our people and eat out their substance.[5]

---

1. **the present King of Great Britain:** George III, who reigned from 1760 to 1820.
2. **refused his assent to laws:** Laws passed in the colonies needed the king's approval; sometimes it took years for laws to be approved or rejected.
3. **to prevent the population:** to keep the population from growing.
4. **the tenure of their offices:** their job security.
5. **eat out their substance:** use up their resources.

---

despotism (dĕs′pə-tĭz′əm) *n.* government by a ruler with unlimited power

Ⓑ ARGUMENT
What opposing claim does Jefferson anticipate in lines 15–22? What **counterargument** does he make at the end of this paragraph, and what does he say he is about to do?

Ⓒ TEXT STRUCTURE
Why might the list of complaints make up the largest part of the four-part structure?

Language Coach

Multiple-Meaning Words
Dissolved can mean "caused to pass into solution" (such as sugar dissolved in tea). However, in line 39, *dissolved*, means "ended" or "terminated." Why would the king want to dissolve the representative houses?

DIFFERENTIATED INSTRUCTION

FOR ADVANCED LEARNERS/AP

Analyze Grievances Ask students to identify categories of grievances, such as *legislative, judicial, military,* and *trade.* Then have them place specific grievances in each category. They might adapt a Classification Chart for this purpose.

 **BEST PRACTICES TOOLKIT—Transparency**
Classification Chart p. B17

FOR ENGLISH LANGUAGE LEARNERS

Language Coach

Multiple-Meaning Words *Answer: The king would want to dissolve the houses because they opposed him.* Ask students to identify the multiple meanings of words in lines 41–44: *dissolutions (disintegrations; deaths), exercise (body movements; written problems) and convulsions (muscle spasms; fits of laughter).*

Declaration of Independence in Congress, at the Independence Hall, Philadelphia, July 4, 1776 (1819), John Trumbull. Oil on canvas. The Granger Collection, New York.

He has kept among us, in times of peace, standing armies, without the consent of our legislatures.

He has affected to render the military independent of, and superior to, the civil power.

He has combined with others to subject us to a jurisdiction foreign to our constitutions,[6] and unacknowledged by our laws; giving his assent to their acts of pretended legislation:

For quartering large bodies of armed troops among us;

For protecting them, by a mock trial, from punishment for any murders which they should commit on the inhabitants of these States;

For cutting off our trade with all parts of the world;

For imposing taxes on us without our consent;

For depriving us, in many cases, of the benefits of trial by jury;

For transporting us beyond the seas, to be tried for pretended offenses;

For abolishing the free system of English laws in a neighboring province,[7] establishing there an arbitrary government, and enlarging its boundaries, so as to render it at once an example and fit instrument for introducing the same absolute rule into these colonies;

For taking away our charters, abolishing our most valuable laws, and altering, fundamentally, the forms of our governments;

For suspending our own legislatures, and declaring themselves invested with power to legislate for us in all cases whatsoever. D

(2)

COMMON CORE L 3a

D TEXT STRUCTURE
Reread lines 59–76 and study the arrangement of paragraphs. In lines 62-76, Jefferson lists violations the English king has committed against the colonies. Jefferson emphasizes these violations by devoting a separate paragraph to each one and by using **parallel structure.** Each paragraph begins with the preposition *for,* followed by a gerund such as *quartering* or *protecting.* Read lines 59–76 aloud. How does Jefferson's use of parallelism and paragraph structure contribute to the persuasive impact of these lines?

6. **subject us . . . our constitutions:** Parliament had passed the Declaratory Act in 1766, stating that the king and Parliament could make laws for the colonies.
7. **a neighboring province:** the province of Quebec, which at the time extended south to the Ohio River and west to the Mississippi.

Analyze Visuals

Activity *Ask students to notice that by focusing the attention of all the figures on the document, the artist draws viewers' attention to it also.*

About the Art John Trumbull's oil painting measures about 30 inches wide and 20 inches high. Yet the artist fit 48 figures into this space. Jefferson stands in the middle. He is presenting the Declaration to John Hancock, president of the Second Continental Congress.

TIERED DISCUSSION PROMPTS

Refer to lines 55–76 and use these prompts to help students understand the effect of the grievances list:

Recall What are Jefferson's purposes for listing the king's despotic acts? ***Possible answer:*** *His purposes are to explain the need for a new government and gain the sympathy of undecided colonists and nations.*

Evaluate Which grievances in this passage are the most insufferable? *Students may point to the army kept on colonial soil without consent (line 55), to taxation without representation (line 66), and to the dissolution of colonial governments (lines 73–74).*

READING SKILL COMMON CORE L 3a

D TEXT STRUCTURE

Have volunteers read lines 62–76 aloud, asking them to emphasize the sentences' parallelism. Explain that this repetition gives weight to Jefferson's assertions.

Possible answer: *These devices increase the cumulative emotional impact of the wrongs that Jefferson lists.*

Extend the Discussion Ask students to consider other famous political speeches that have used this form of rhetoric.

FOR STRUGGLING READERS

(2) Targeted Passage [Lines 59–76]

This passage identifies legislation of the English Parliament that the colonies oppose.

- Why do the colonies oppose quartering the king's troops? (lines 62–64)
- Why do they oppose the king's taxes? (line 66)
- Why do they oppose Parliament making laws for them? (lines 73–76)

Develop Reading Fluency Model for students an effective way to read the list of grievances in the targeted passage. Read the first two items in the passage, pointing out its parallel structure. Point out that pausing between items adds both clarity and emphasis. Then have pairs of students practice reading the grievances aloud, choosing which words and ideas to emphasize.

THE DECLARATION OF INDEPENDENCE 243

He has **abdicated** government here, by declaring us out of his protection, and waging war against us.

He has plundered our seas, ravaged our coasts, burnt our towns,[8] and destroyed
80 the lives of our people.

He is at this time transporting large armies of foreign **mercenaries** to complete the works of death, desolation, and tyranny, already begun with circumstances of cruelty and **perfidy** scarcely paralleled in the most barbarous ages, and totally unworthy the head of a civilized nation.

He has constrained our fellow citizens, taken captive on the high seas, to bear arms against their country, to become the executioners of their friends and brethren, or to fall themselves by their hands.

He has excited domestic insurrection amongst us,[9] and has endeavored to bring on the inhabitants of our frontiers the merciless Indian savages, whose known rule
90 of warfare is an undistinguished destruction of all ages, sexes, and conditions.

In every stage of these oppressions we have petitioned for **redress,** in the most humble terms; our repeated petitions have been answered only by repeated injury. A prince whose character is thus marked by every act which may define a tyrant is unfit to be the ruler of a free people.

Nor have we been wanting in our attentions to our British brethren. We have warned them, from time to time, of attempts by their legislature to extend an unwarrantable jurisdiction over us. We have reminded them of the circumstances of our emigration and settlement here. We have appealed to their native justice and magnanimity; and we have conjured them, by the ties of our common
100 kindred, to disavow these usurpations, which would inevitably interrupt our connections and correspondence. ⓔ

They, too, have been deaf to the voice of justice and of consanguinity.[10] We must, therefore, acquiesce in the necessity which denounces our separation; and hold them, as we hold the rest of mankind, enemies in war, in peace friends. ⓕ

WE, THEREFORE, THE REPRESENTATIVES OF THE UNITED STATES OF AMERICA, in General Congress assembled, appealing to the Supreme Judge of the world for the rectitude[11] of our intentions, do, in the name and by the authority of the good people of these colonies, solemnly publish and declare, that these United Colonies are, and of right ought to be, Free and Independent States; that they are absolved
110 from all allegiance to the British crown, and that all political connection between them and the state of Great Britain is, and ought to be, totally dissolved; and that, as free and independent states, they have full power to levy war, conclude peace, contract alliances, establish commerce, and to do all other acts and things which independent states may of right do. And, for the support of this declaration, with a firm reliance on the protection of Divine Providence, we mutually pledge to each other our lives, our fortunes, and our sacred honor.

---

8. **plundered . . . our towns:** American seaports such as Norfolk, Virginia, had already been shelled.

9. **excited . . . amongst us:** George III had encouraged slaves to rise up and rebel against their masters.

10. **deaf to . . . consanguinity:** The British have ignored pleas based on their common ancestry with the colonists.

11. **rectitude:** morally correct behavior or thinking.

244 UNIT 1: EARLY AMERICAN WRITING

Comprehension

1. **Recall** Name three complaints that the colonists had against the king.

2. **Recall** What rights are specified in the Declaration?

3. **Clarify** What does Jefferson say is the purpose of government?

4. **Clarify** According to the Declaration, who gives people their rights?

Text Analysis

5. **Make Inferences** The Declaration clearly takes aim at the abuses of King George to justify the colonists' **rebellion.** But reread lines 102–104. To what extent does the document hold the British people responsible? What is the new relationship declared between Americans and their "British brethren," and how might it differ from the old?

● 6. **Analyze Elements of an Argument** How does Jefferson's awareness of his audience affect his diction—the words he chooses and the manner of their arrangement? Explain the persuasive appeal of the following words and phrases:

   • "We hold these truths to be self-evident" (line 7)
   • "endowed by their Creator" (line 8)
   • "unalienable rights" (line 8)
   • "secure these rights" (lines 9–10)

● 7. **Evaluate Text Structure** Review the chart you filled in. How effective is Jefferson's four-part structure in stating the colonists' case? Would reordering the parts make any difference? Explain your answer.

● 8. **Evaluate Elements of an Argument** Identify the major claim and the support given in the Declaration. In your opinion, is the support sufficient for the claim? Does it have to be? Explain your answer.

Text Criticism

9. **Historical Context** Jefferson's celebrated statement "All men are created equal" only applied to white men at the time. How has the meaning of Jefferson's statement changed over time? How has it stayed the same?

> *When is* **REBELLION** *justified?*
>
> Which set of reasons for breaking away from British rule strikes you as most important—the colonists' philosophical ideals, the hardships colonists suffered as a result of British policies, or the king's response to colonists' complaints? Explain your answer.

THE DECLARATION OF INDEPENDENCE **245**

─────

─────

Practice and Apply

For preliminary support of post-reading questions, use these copymasters:

R **RESOURCE MANAGER**—Copy Masters
   Reading Check p. 304
   Argument p. 297
   Question Support p. 305

Additional selection questions are provided for teachers on page 291.

ANSWERS   ○ **COMMON CORE** RI 1, RI 4, RI 5, RI 8

1. *Possible answers: kept a standing army, imposed taxes without consent, cut off trade*

2. *life, liberty, and the pursuit of happiness*

3. *to secure the rights, safety, and happiness of the people (lines 9–10)*

4. *God (line 8)*

Possible answers:

5. *The Declaration blames the British people for ignoring the colonists' appeals. It declares them no longer kin tied by blood and culture, but like any other nation: friends if at peace but enemies if at war.*

6. ● **COMMON CORE FOCUS Argument** *Jefferson's audience was intelligent and religious and so he uses both reason and God to defend his argument. Jefferson classifies human rights as a matter of reason and abiding truth; names God as the ultimate source of these sacred rights; stresses that unalienable rights are as natural as they are sacred; notes that protection of these rights is the only just purpose of government.*

7. ● **COMMON CORE FOCUS Analyze Structure** *The four-part structure is effective in establishing the colonies' cause. Reordering the parts would destroy the logic and power of Jefferson's careful argument.*

8. ● **COMMON CORE FOCUS Argument** *The major claim is that the colonies have the right and duty to separate from Great Britain and to form their own government. The long list of grievances supports this claim well. The Declaration needed strong evidence to win the support of undecided colonists and nations.*

─────

9. *Jefferson's statement has become more inclusive over the decades, expanding to apply to women and to people of color. Yet the basic concept that all people have sacred, natural rights remains a central precept of American government.*

> *When is REBELLION justified?*
> Students should select one set of reasons and defend their choice with textual evidence and logic.

ANSWERS

Vocabulary in Context

▲ **VOCABULARY PRACTICE**

1. *(c) honesty*   4. *(b) model*
2. *(d) righteousness*   5. *(c) confiscate*
3. *(c) mercenary*   6. *(d) restrain*

R RESOURCE MANAGER—Copy Master
Vocabulary Practice p. 282

ACADEMIC VOCABULARY IN WRITING

Students should write about the issues Jefferson listed in the Declaration of Independence and how these trials provoked them to fight for freedom.

VOCABULARY STRATEGY: ⟨ **COMMON CORE** RI 4, L 4c, L 6 ⟩
POLITICAL WORDS

Help students to categorize the vocabulary words under types of rulers: *regency;* types of government: *oligarchy, republic;* government philosophies: *socialism, totalitarianism.*

Possible answers:

1. *oligarchy; etymology: Greek—oligos, "few, little"*
2. *regency; etymology: Latin—regens, present participle of* regere, *"to rule"*
3. *socialism; etymology: Latin—socialis, "of companionship"*
4. *totalitarianism; etymology:* total + *(author)* itarian
5. *republic; etymology: Latin—respublica (-res, "thing" + publica, "of the people")*

R RESOURCE MANAGER—Copy Master
Vocabulary Strategy p. 303

Interactive Vocabulary   **THINK** central

Keywords direct students to a **WordSharp** tutorial on **thinkcentral.com** or to other types of vocabulary practice and review.

Vocabulary in Context

▲ **VOCABULARY PRACTICE**

Choose the word that is not related in meaning to the other words.

1. (a) disloyalty, (b) perfidy, (c) honesty, (d) treachery
2. (a) despotism, (b) dictatorship, (c) tyranny, (d) righteousness
3. (a) monarch, (b) ruler, (c) mercenary, (d) king
4. (a) redress, (b) model, (c) remedy, (d) compensation
5. (a) abandon, (b) renounce, (c) confiscate, (d) abdicate
6. (a) mobilize, (b) impel, (c) propel, (d) restrain

WORD LIST
abdicate
despotism
impel
mercenary
perfidy
redress

ACADEMIC VOCABULARY IN WRITING

• document • illustrate • interpret • promote • reveal

The Declaration of Independence **reveals** many hardships the colonists suffered at the hands of King George. Write a short paragraph discussing how these trials affected the colonists and eventually led them to **promote** the cause for freedom. Use three Academic Vocabulary words in your paragraph.

VOCABULARY STRATEGY: POLITICAL WORDS

The content areas of social studies and political science use many terms to describe systems of government. Some terms identify specific types of government; others, like the vocabulary word *despotism,* describe the practices of a government. It is useful to understand the meanings of such terms.

PRACTICE Choose the political word described by each numbered item. Then use a dictionary to trace the etymology of each word.

oligarchy regency republic socialism totalitarianism

1. a few people have the ruling power
2. a person rules in place of the regular ruler, who may be ill or too young
3. production of goods and services is under the control of government
4. one political group rules and suppresses all opposition, often with force
5. citizens elect representatives to manage the government

COMMON CORE

RI 4 Determine the meaning of words and phrases as they are used in a text, including technical meanings. **L 4c** Consult general and specialized reference materials to determine or clarify a word's etymology. **L 6** Acquire and use accurately general academic and domain-specific words and phrases.

Interactive Vocabulary   **THINK** central

Go to **thinkcentral.com**.
KEYWORD: HML11-246

DIFFERENTIATED INSTRUCTION

FOR ENGLISH LANGUAGE LEARNERS

Task Support: Vocabulary Practice In mixed-language groups, have students find cognates from their home languages for any of the answer choices in the activity. Ask each group to create a composite list, indicating the language of each cognate.

FOR ADVANCED LEARNERS/AP

Political Words Challenge students to identify additional words related to government, such as *democracy, monarchy, theocracy, monarch, president, premier, communism,* and *capitalism.* Have students create their own chart, using categories that they develop.

Language

◆ **GRAMMAR AND STYLE:** Vary Sentence Structure

Review the **Grammar and Style** note on page 244. Like most lawyers, who have to be precise as well as thorough, Jefferson uses **complex** and **compound-complex** sentences to pack in meaning.

- A **complex sentence** has one main clause (as in yellow), which can stand alone, and one or more subordinate clauses (as in green), which cannot.

  A prince whose character is thus marked by every act which may define a tyrant is unfit to be the ruler of a free people. (lines 93–94)

- A **compound-complex sentence** has two or more independent clauses (as in yellow) and one or more subordinate clauses (as in green).

  Such has been the patient sufferance of these colonies; and such is now the necessity that constrains them to alter their former systems of government. (lines 22–24)

PRACTICE Rewrite each pair of sentences as a complex or compound-complex sentence. Use the conjunction shown in parentheses.

EXAMPLE

The king exploits the people. The people move toward rebellion. (after)

After the king exploits the people, the people move toward rebellion.

1. The people declare their grievances with British rule. The British king and parliament do not listen. (when)
2. The parliament learns of the dissatisfaction of the colonists. The parliament imposes even harsher laws. (as soon as)

READING-WRITING CONNECTION

YOUR TURN

Expand your understanding of Jefferson's Declaration of Independence by responding to this prompt. Then, use the **revising tips** to improve your declaration.

WRITING PROMPT	REVISING TIPS
TAKE A STAND The Declaration of Independence has served as a model in several historical instances. Write a **declaration** for a group or individual of your choosing. Your declaration should have at least **three paragraphs** and be modeled on the Declaration of Independence.	• Include a brief declaration of rights. • List at least ten complaints. • Conclude with a resolution.

COMMON CORE

L 3a Vary syntax for effect, consulting references for guidance as needed; apply an understanding of syntax to the study of complex texts when reading. **W 1** Write arguments to support claims in an analysis of substantive topics or texts, using valid reasoning and relevant and sufficient evidence.

Interactive Revision THINK central

Go to thinkcentral.com.
KEYWORD: HML11-247

Language

COMMON CORE L 3a, W 1

◆ **GRAMMAR AND STYLE**

- Have students read the examples of complex and compound-complex sentences and explain why each clause is independent or subordinate. Then ask them to complete the ***PRACTICE.***
- For more on complex and compound-complex sentences, see **Grammar Handbook**, p. R68.

ANSWERS

1. *When the people declare their grievances with British rule, the king and parliament do not listen.*
2. *As soon as the parliament learns of the dissatisfaction of the colonists, it imposes even harsher laws.*

R RESOURCE MANAGER—Copy Master
Vary Sentence Structure p. 306

READING-WRITING CONNECTION

Remind students of the question, "When is rebellion justified?" from page 239. Ask them to recall situations they discussed as possible topics for their declaration. After choosing a situation, they might brainstorm complaints for their list.

Writing Online THINK central

The following tools are available online at thinkcentral.com and on Write*Smart* CD-ROM:

- **Interactive Graphic Organizers**
- **Interactive Student Models**
- **Interactive Revision Lessons**

For additional grammar instruction, see **GrammarNotes** on thinkcentral.com.

FOR STRUGGLING WRITERS

Writing Support

- Use the **BIG QUESTION** exploration on page 239 to help students generate three ideas for a declaration.
- Have students work in small groups to brainstorm a list of complaints.
- Give students a sentence starter for a statement of independence, such as *We, therefore, being of sound mind and body, do declare that ______.*

Assess and Reteach

Assess

DIAGNOSTIC AND SELECTION TESTS

Selection Tests A, B/C pp. 85-88

Interactive Selection Test on thinkcentral.com

Reteach

Level Up Online Tutorials on thinkcentral.com

◌ COMMON CORE

RI 2 Determine two or more central ideas of a text and analyze their development, including how they interact and build on one another to provide a complex analysis; provide an objective summary of the text. **RI 3** Analyze a complex set of ideas or sequence of events and explain how specific individuals, ideas, or events interact and develop. **RI 4** Analyze how an author uses and refines the meaning of a key term. **RI 5** Analyze and evaluate the effectiveness of the structure an author uses in his or her exposition or argument.

◌ COMMON CORE FOCUS

RI 2 Determine two or more central ideas of a text and analyze their development, including how they interact and build on one another to provide a complex analysis; provide an objective summary of the text. **RI 3** Analyze a complex set of ideas or sequence of events and explain how specific individuals, ideas, or events interact and develop. **RI 4** Analyze how an author uses and refines the meaning of a key term. **RI 5** Analyze and evaluate the effectiveness of the structure an author uses in his or her exposition or argument. **L 4c** Consult general and specialized reference materials, both print and digital, to find the pronunciation of a word or determine or clarify its precise meaning, its part of speech, its etymology, or its standard usage. **L 6** Acquire and use accurately general academic and domain-specific words and phrases.

ABOUT THE AUTHOR

After students read about Thomas Paine, clarify that the January 1776 publication of *Common Sense* formed a backdrop for publication later that year of the selection. Explain further that Paine's call for independence in *Common Sense* was an act of high treason punishable by death. The pamphlet reached more people than any other political publication of that era.

NOTABLE QUOTE

"O! Ye that love mankind! Ye that dare oppose not only tyranny, but the tyrant, stand forth!"
—Thomas Paine

Ask students to consider what the quote reveals about Paine's character and political beliefs.

Selection Resources

DID YOU KNOW?

Thomas Paine . . .

- failed out of school by age 12.
- was fired twice from a job as tax collector.
- didn't come to America until he was 37 years old.
- became involved in the French Revolution.

Meet the Author

Thomas Paine 1737–1809

Brash, bold, and fearless—and at times angry and offensive—Thomas Paine was the firebrand of the American Revolution. In the fall of 1775, few American leaders dared to advocate openly for independence. Not only did they risk being accused of treason, they were uncertain how the common people would react to such a radical notion. They turned to Tom Paine to test the waters. Paine had arrived in Philadelphia from London only the year before but was already gaining a reputation as a revolutionary writer. He eagerly took up the task and in a few months wrote *Common Sense* (1776), a 50-page pamphlet that attacked the injustices of hereditary rule and urged the colonists to form their own independent country where "the law is king." Paine's pamphlet sold 120,000 copies in the first three months. Six months later, the colonies declared their independence.

New Voice for a New Political Audience Paine's political ideas in *Common Sense* were not particularly new or original. In the Age of Enlightenment, intellectual circles were buzzing with talk of natural rights and democracy. What was new was Paine's voice—raw, direct, full of energy. Unlike most political writers of the day, such as Thomas Jefferson,

Paine addressed common men—farmers, craftsmen, and laborers—not the educated elite. His straightforward prose reinforced his democratic message that all men were capable of understanding and participating in government. People responded because Paine spoke their language. In his native England, he had worked as sailor, teacher, customs officer, grocer, and maker of ladies' corsets. He envisioned America as the place where working men like him could have political and economic power.

Limits of Success With American independence won, Paine left for Europe in 1787 to join the reform efforts brewing there. But his outspokenness got him into trouble in both conservative England and revolutionary France. His last major work, *The Age of Reason* (1794, 1795), attacked organized religion and alienated many of his supporters. By the time he returned to the United States in 1802, few politicians wanted to associate with him. He spent his last years in poverty and obscurity.

Legacy Despite Paine's later decline, his contribution to the intellectual and cultural life of Revolutionary America is indisputable. He was the radical the country needed, the spokesman for new American values and ideals.

THINK central

Author Online
Go to <u>thinkcentral.com</u>. KEYWORD: HML11-248

248

See resources on the **Teacher One Stop DVD-ROM** and on **thinkcentral.com**.

 RESOURCE MANAGER UNIT 1
Plan and Teach, pp. 307–314
Summary, pp. 315–316 † ‡*
Text Analysis and Reading
  Skill, pp. 317–320 †*
Vocabulary, pp. 321–323*

DIAGNOSTIC AND SELECTION TESTS
Selection Tests, pp. 89–92

 BEST PRACTICES TOOLKIT
Word Squares, p. E10

TECHNOLOGY
- **Teacher One Stop DVD-ROM**
- **Student One Stop DVD-ROM**
- **Audio Anthology CD**
- **GrammarNotes DVD-ROM**
- **ExamView Test Generator** on the Teacher One Stop

---

* Resources for Differentiation   † Also in Spanish   ‡ Also in Haitian Creole and Vietnamese

TEXT ANALYSIS: PERSUASIVE TECHNIQUES

Thomas Paine used a number of **persuasive techniques** in *The Crisis* to persuade Americans to join the cause. He was a master of **rhetoric,** the use of language to persuade.

- **Emotional appeals** have powerful rhetorical impact. They persuade by eliciting strong feelings, such as pity or fear.
- **Ethical appeals** influence readers by appealing to their sense of right and wrong.
- **Appeals to association** suggest that readers will gain acceptance or prestige by taking the writer's position.
- **Appeals to authority** influence readers by citing experts or others who warrant respect.

As you read, notice Paine's patriotic **purpose** and his understanding of his fellow colonists—the readers who make up his **audience**. Examine how his purpose and his audience affects his **tone** or attitude in this important historical essay.

READING STRATEGY: SUMMARIZE MAIN IDEAS

Summarizing means identifying main ideas and combining them into a brief overview of a text. As you read Paine's essay, use a chart like the one shown to identify main ideas. Afterwards, combine the main ideas into a brief paragraph.

Main Ideas	Summary
I see no real cause for fear.	

▲ VOCABULARY IN CONTEXT

Complete each phrase with the appropriate word from the list.

WORD LIST		
ardor	prudent	tyranny
celestial	relinquish	wrangling

1. _____ brothers who never seemed to get along
2. will fight _____ and other forms of oppression
3. a _____ decision in dangerous circumstances
4. would not _____ control of the property
5. music so sweet it seemed _____
6. expressed his _____ in mushy love poems

 Complete the activities in your **Reader/Writer Notebook**.

Whose SIDE are you on?

Loyalty is a value easily expressed but often difficult to uphold. Situations change, doubts creep in, and conflicts arise that can test the strongest bonds of loyalty. Paine's essay addresses the crisis of loyalty threatening the ranks of American soldiers during the dark days of the Revolutionary War.

QUICKWRITE Think about a time when your loyalty was tested and you were tempted to switch sides or give up. In a short paragraph, briefly describe the situation and explain what you decided. What was the most crucial factor in your decision?

249

Whose SIDE are you on?

Lead into the question by asking students for definitions of loyalty. Urge them to identify people and institutions that inspire loyalty, such as family, friends, or school. After students complete the *QUICKWRITE,* have them revisit their definitions. Invite students to explain any revisions they would now make.

TEXT ANALYSIS — COMMON CORE RI 3 RI 5

● *Model the Skill:*
PERSUASIVE TECHNIQUES

Help students identify the appeal in persuasive techniques by presenting this example:

Basketball star Jo Hopper says Leaping Lizards shoes make all the difference in the world to her game.

Point out that Hopper is a successful athlete and so her statement is an appeal to authority.

GUIDED PRACTICE Ask students to identify the appeal in this example: Join the parade of athletes and movie stars who wear Leaping Lizards.

GUIDED PRACTICE Ask students what emotions the example appeals to.

READING SKILL — COMMON CORE RI 2 RI 3

■ *Model the Skill:*
SUMMARIZE MAIN IDEAS

Review with students the third sentence of **New Voice for a New Political Audience**. This sentence describes and identifies what was new about Thomas Paine's writing: his raw and energetic voice.

GUIDED PRACTICE Have students identify details that support the main idea.

R RESOURCE MANAGER—Copy Master
Summarize Main Ideas p. 319

VOCABULARY SKILL — COMMON CORE L 4

▲ VOCABULARY IN CONTEXT

DIAGNOSE WORD KNOWLEDGE Have students complete Vocabulary in Context. Check their word choices against the following:

ardor (är′dər) *n.* intense enthusiasm; passion
celestial (sə-lĕs′chəl) *adj.* heavenly
prudent (prōōd′nt) *adj.* showing caution or good judgment
relinquish (rĭ-lĭng′kwĭsh) *v.* to withdraw from; to give up

tyranny (tĭr′ə-nē) *n.* cruel and oppressive government or rule
wrangling (răng′glĭng) *adj.* arguing noisily
   wrangle *v.*

PRETEACH VOCABULARY Use the following copy master to help students predict meanings.

R RESOURCE MANAGER—Copy Master
Vocabulary Study p. 321

Practice and Apply

SUMMARY

In this excerpt from his essay "The Crisis," Thomas Paine calls upon all colonists to stand firm and united despite recent military setbacks. He points out that the king's bids for peace are trickery, while independence is inevitable.

READ WITH A PURPOSE

Help students set a purpose for reading. Tell them to read "The Crisis" to learn how Thomas Paine inspired the colonists to keep fighting for independence, even though at the time of his writing, a positive outcome looked bleak.

TEXT ANALYSIS · COMMON CORE · RI 3 · RI 5

Ⓐ PERSUASIVE TECHNIQUES

Possible answer: *Loaded words include "shrink," "love," "Tyranny," "glorious," "triumph," "Heaven," "celestial," "slavery," and "God." These words have an emotional appeal and establish a fiery, emotionally heavy tone.*

VOCABULARY · COMMON CORE · L 4

OWN THE WORD

- **tyranny:** Tell students that *tyranny* and *tyrannosaurus* both use the same root, the Greek *tyrannos*, which means "absolute ruler."

- **celestial:** Point out that in this context, *celestial* means "heavenly" and is a loaded adjective. Ask students to suggest neutral replacements for *celestial*. **Possible answers:** *valuable, worthwhile, significant*

The CRISIS

Thomas Paine

Analyze Visuals ▶
A minuteman was pledged to be ready to fight on a minute's notice. What does this suggest about the preparedness of the colonists?

BACKGROUND On the blustery Christmas Eve of 1776, the situation looked bleak for the Continental Army. General Washington's ragtag troops had retreated to the western banks of the Delaware River. Tom Paine was camped with them. The British were within striking distance of Philadelphia, and Washington knew he had to advance the next day or risk losing the war. To boost the morale of his ill-equipped and outnumbered soldiers, he ordered his officers to read aloud the following essay, which Paine had written the day before.

tyranny (tĭr′ə-nē) *n.* cruel and oppressive government or rule

celestial (sə-lĕs′chəl) *adj.* heavenly

These are the times that try men's souls: The summer soldier and the sunshine patriot will, in this crisis, shrink from the service of his country; but he that stands it NOW, deserves the love and thanks of man and woman. **Tyranny,** like hell, is not easily conquered; yet we have this consolation with us, that the harder the conflict, the more glorious the triumph. What we obtain too cheap, we esteem too lightly:—' Tis dearness only that gives every thing its value. Heaven knows how to set a proper price upon its goods; and it would be strange indeed, if so **celestial** an article as FREEDOM should not be highly rated. Britain, with an army to enforce her tyranny, has declared, that she has a right (*not only to* TAX) but "to BIND us in
10 ALL CASES WHATSOEVER,"[1] and if *being bound in that manner* is not slavery, then there is not such a thing as slavery upon earth. Even the expression is impious, for so unlimited a power can only belong to God. Ⓐ **Targeted Passage** ①

Ⓐ **PERSUASIVE TECHNIQUES**
Identify the **loaded language**—words with strong connotations—in lines 1–12. What kind of emotional appeal do these words have? What tone do they establish?

---

1. **"to BIND us in ALL CASES WHATSOEVER":** a reference to wording in the Declaratory Act of 1766, in which the British parliament asserted its "power and authority" to make and enforce laws over the American colonies.

250 UNIT 1: EARLY AMERICAN WRITING

Minute Man: Liberty or Death. Private collection.
© Scala/Art Resource, New York.

DIFFERENTIATED INSTRUCTION

FOR ENGLISH LANGUAGE LEARNERS

Vocabulary Support Use Word Squares to teach these words: *enforce* (line 8), *principle* (line 42), *individual* (line 70), *link* (line 97), *credit* (line 104).

 BEST PRACTICES TOOLKIT—Transparency
Word Squares p. E10

FOR STRUGGLING READERS

In combination with the *Audio Anthology CD*, use one or more Targeted Passages (pp. 250, 252, 254) to ensure that students focus on key concepts in this selection. Targeted Passages are also good for English learners.

① Targeted Passage [Lines 1–12]
This passage defines a patriot and identifies the British as the patriots' enemy.

MINUTE MAN

LIBERTY OR DEATH

VINCE AUT MORIRE

1774 -75

Analyze Visuals

Possible answer: The name "minuteman" suggests that the colonists were ready, willing, and able to fight anytime, anyplace.

About the Art The minutemen fought the redcoats in the initial skirmishes at Lexington and Concord in April 1775. The colonists began calling for the formation of a "Grand American Army." On June 15, 1775, the Continental Congress elected George Washington as general. His job was to shape the ragtag colonial fighters, including the minutemen, into a disciplined, united Continental Army.

BACKGROUND

Surprise Attack By the late fall of 1776, British troops under General William Howe had pushed the Continental Army commanded by General George Washington across the Delaware River into Pennsylvania. Howe's troops, which included both British soldiers and paid Hessian mercenaries, settled in New Jersey and proceeded to loot, murder, and pillage. Meanwhile, the vast majority of Washington's troops had either deserted, been captured, or had expired enlistments, and fewer than 6,000 men remained under his command. On Christmas Eve of 1776, Washington prepared his men for an attack on Trenton, New Jersey, in part by having them listen to "The Crisis." The Continental Army surprised Howe's troops and won an easy victory. Washington's army took more than 900 prisoners and killed nearly 30. No colonists died, and only a few were wounded.

- Whom does Paine thank in the opening? (lines 1–2)

- What does Paine say gives freedom its value? (line 6)

- What words does Paine use to describe the actions of the British? (lines 8–10)

FOR ADVANCED LEARNERS/AP

Have students serve as speech writers for Washington. Tell them to write a speech that:

- encourages his troops as they wait on the banks of the Delaware River

- introduces Paine and his essay

- urges the soldiers to read it

As students read their speeches aloud, ask listeners to jot down examples of persuasive language.

B *Model the Skill:*
MAIN IDEAS

To help students find Paine's main idea, have them reread and summarize the paragraph.

***Possible answer:** Paine says that, with time and resolve, the colonists will recover whatever they may have lost to the British under General Howe (lines 18–21).*

IF STUDENTS NEED HELP . . . Show them how to record the main idea in a chart like the one introduced on page 249.

D **PERSUASIVE TECHNIQUES**

***Possible answer:** He says a parent should be more concerned about peace in his child's lifetime than in his own.*

OWN THE WORD

- **relinquish:** Have students name antonyms for *relinquish*. ***Possible answers:** keep, retain, hold on to*

- **prudent:** Remind students that *prudent* means "showing caution or good judgment." Ask students how they might exhibit *prudent* behavior. ***Possible answer:** by avoiding tobacco, alcohol, or other drugs*

- **wrangling:** Ask students to explain what Paine meant by "all the *wrangling* world." ***Possible answer:** In the 1770s, the people of Europe were entangled in various uprisings and wars.*

- **ardor:** Have students create a semantic web for *ardor*. Write the word in a center circle, and have students add synonyms to complete the map. ***Possible answers:** fervor, zeal, eagerness, gusto, love*

Whether the Independence of the Continent was declared too soon, or delayed too long, I will not now enter into as an argument; my own simple opinion is, that had it been eight months earlier, it would have been much better. We did not make a proper use of last winter, neither could we, while we were in a dependant state. However, the fault, if it were one, was all our own; we have none to blame but ourselves. But no great deal is lost yet; all that Howe has been doing for this month past is rather a ravage than a conquest which the spirit of the Jersies a year
20 ago would have quickly repulsed, and which time and a little resolution will soon recover. **B**

I have as little superstition in me as any man living, but my secret opinion has ever been, and still is, that God almighty will not give up a people to military destruction, or leave them unsupportedly to perish, who had so earnestly and so repeatedly sought to avoid the calamities of war, by every decent method which wisdom could invent. Neither have I so much of the infidel in me, as to suppose, that he has **relinquished** the government of the world, and given us up to the care of devils; and as I do not, I cannot see on what grounds the king of Britain can look up to heaven for help against us: A common murderer, a highwayman, or a
30 housebreaker, has as good a pretense as he. . . .

I once felt all that kind of anger, which a man ought to feel, against the mean principles that are held by the Tories:[2] A noted one, who kept a tavern at Amboy,[3] was standing at his door, with as pretty a child in his hand, about eight or nine years old, as most I ever saw, and after speaking his mind as freely as he thought was **prudent,** finished with this unfatherly expression, *"Well! give me peace in my day."* Not a man lives on the Continent but fully believes that a separation must some time or other finally take place, and a generous parent would have said, *"If there must be trouble, let it be in my day, that my child may have peace;"* and this single reflection, well applied, is sufficient to awaken every man to duty. Not a
40 place upon earth might be so happy as America. Her situation is remote from all the **wrangling** world, and she has nothing to do but trade with them. A man may easily distinguish in himself between temper and principle, and I am as confident, as I am that God governs the world, that America will never be happy until she gets clear of foreign dominion. Wars, without ceasing, will break out until that period arrives, and the Continent must in the end be conqueror; for, though the flame of liberty may sometimes cease to shine, the coal never can expire. . . . **C**

I turn with the warm **ardor** of a friend to those who have nobly stood, and are yet determined to stand the matter out: I call not upon a few, but upon all; not on this State or that State, but on every State; up and help us; lay your shoulders to
50 the wheel; better have too much force than too little, when so great an object is at stake. Let it be told to the future world, that in the depth of winter, when nothing but hope and virtue could survive, that the city and the country, alarmed at one

---

2. **the mean principles . . . Tories:** the small-minded beliefs of those colonists who remain loyal to Great Britain.

3. **Amboy:** probably Perth Amboy, a town in New Jersey.

B MAIN IDEAS
Reread lines 13–21. What is Paine's main idea in this paragraph? Support your answer with evidence from the passage.

2 **Targeted Passage**

relinquish (rĭ-lĭng′kwĭsh) *v.* to withdraw from; to give up

prudent (prood′nt) *adj.* showing caution or good judgment

wrangling (răng′glĭng) *adj.* arguing noisily **wrangle** *v.*

C **PERSUASIVE TECHNIQUES**
Notice that Paine makes an **ethical appeal** in lines 31–39. How does he say a parent should behave?

ardor (är′dər) *n.* intense enthusiasm; passion

DIFFERENTIATED INSTRUCTION

FOR STRUGGLING READERS

2 **Targeted Passage** [Lines 22–30]

In this passage, Paine asserts the justness of the patriots' cause.

- How does Paine answer those who say that the colonies should have tried harder to avoid war? (lines 24–26)

- Why does Paine think that God would be on the side of the colonies? (lines 23–27)

- To whom does he compare the king? (lines 29–30)

FOR ENGLISH LANGUAGE LEARNERS

Language: Pronoun Referents Use the context to help students identify the antecedents of these difficult pronouns: *one* (line 17), fault (line 17); *who* (line 24), people (line 23); *he* (line 30), king (line 28); *her* (line 40) and *she* (line 41), America (line 40); *that* (line 61) and *he whose* (line 62), man (line 60); *those* (line 67), people in his house; *it* (line 68), [Paine's] house (line 66).

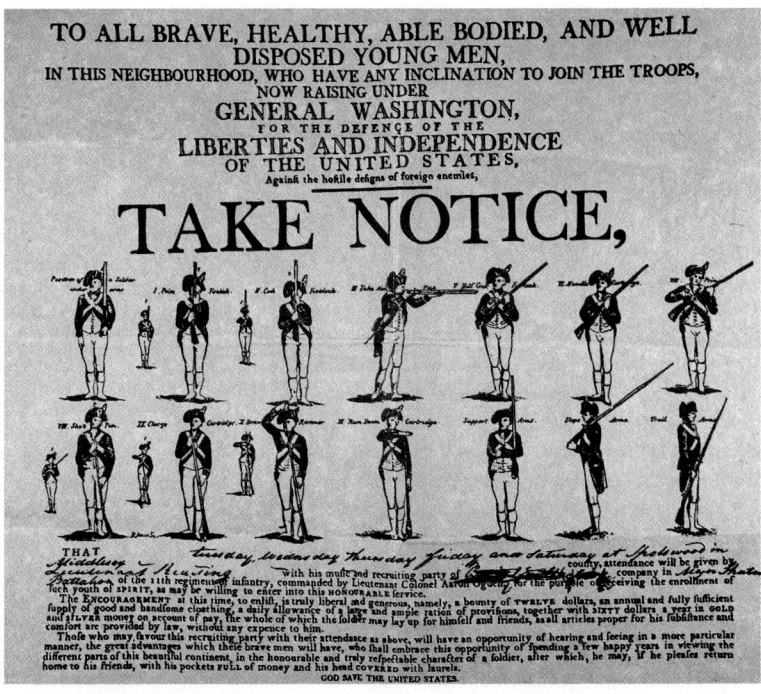

TO ALL BRAVE, HEALTHY, ABLE BODIED, AND WELL
DISPOSED YOUNG MEN,
IN THIS NEIGHBOURHOOD, WHO HAVE ANY INCLINATION TO JOIN THE TROOPS,
NOW RAISING UNDER
GENERAL WASHINGTON,
FOR THE DEFENCE OF THE
LIBERTIES AND INDEPENDENCE
OF THE UNITED STATES,
Against the hostile designs of foreign enemies,

TAKE NOTICE,

◀ **Analyze Visuals**
A broadside is a public notice printed on one side of a large sheet of paper. What feelings and emotions does this American Revolutionary War broadside appeal to?

common danger, came forth to meet and to repulse it. Say not, that thousands are gone, turn out your tens of thousands; throw not the burden of the day upon Providence, but *"shew your faith by your works,"* that God may bless you. It matters not where you live, or what rank of life you hold, the evil or the blessing will reach you all. The far and the near, the home counties and the back, the rich and the poor, shall suffer or rejoice alike. The heart that feels not now, is dead: The blood of his children shall curse his cowardice, who shrinks back at a time

60 when a little might have saved the whole, and made *them* happy. I love the man that can smile in trouble, that can gather strength from distress, and grow brave by reflection. 'Tis the business of little minds to shrink; but he whose heart is firm, and whose conscience approves his conduct, will pursue his principles unto death. My own line of reasoning is to myself as strait and clear as a ray of light. **D** Not all the treasures of the world, so far as I believe, could have induced me to support an offensive war, for I think it murder; but if a thief break into my house, burn and destroy my property, and kill or threaten to kill me, or those that are in it, and to *"bind me in all cases whatsoever,"* to his absolute will, am I to suffer it?

D PERSUASIVE TECHNIQUES
Reread lines 47–64. Notice how Paine's persuasive **purpose** and his awareness of his **audience** contribute to his attitude or **tone** of passionate conviction. He identifies with his readers by calling himself a friend. He uses emotionally loaded words to appeal to beliefs shared by the colonists who read his essays. Choose an especially persuasive sentence from this passage. What is Paine's tone in this sentence? What purpose does the sentence reveal? Explain your response.

FOR ADVANCED LEARNERS/AP

Analyze Persuasive Arguments [SMALL-GROUP OPTION] How strong is Paine's case, beyond his emotional appeals and his loaded words? Have small groups identify Paine's claims and supports and analyze their effectiveness. Ask each group to create an analysis chart of Paine's claims. Show this example for the claim made in paragraph one of the essay:

Claim: The harder the conflict, the greater the victory (lines 4–5)	Reason I: People don't value success that comes too easily.	Analysis: This is an effective argument that appeals to people's desire to master difficult challenges.

Have groups share findings with the class.

Analyze Visuals

Possible answer: *The broadside appeals to the colonists' feelings of loyalty and justice and their desire to be brave, healthy, strong, and worthy.*

TEXT ANALYSIS	COMMON CORE

D PERSUASIVE TECHNIQUES

RI 3
RI 5

Possible answer: *"The blood of his children shall curse his cowardice, who shrinks back at a time when a little might have saved the whole, and made them happy." (line 59). His tone is emotional and passionate as he tries to convince his audience to support those fighting for freedom. Paine's point is that those who do not act are cowards and are failing their children.*

IF STUDENTS NEED HELP . . . Remind students that persuasive language carries strong emotional connotations that stir people's feelings.

TIERED DISCUSSION PROMPTS

Use these prompts to help students understand Paine's appeal in lines 53–68 for unity and support:

Connect Think about situations when people in your community or family joined together for a common cause. How does that experience help you understand Paine's appeal? *Accept all thoughtful responses.*

Interpret Paine says that nothing could have made him "support an offensive war." What does he mean? ***Possible answer:*** *Paine means that the colonies did not start the war; that they are only defending their homes and property. Therefore, their fighting is justified.*

Whose SIDE

are you on?

Discuss Why in lines 69–76 does Paine say that he feels no **loyalty** to the king? *Possible answer:* He says that the king is a "sottish, stupid, stubborn, worthless, brutish man" (lines 75–76) for his actions toward the colonies, and therefore deserves no loyalty.

READING SKILL

COMMON CORE RI 4

B *Model the Skill:*
MAIN IDEAS

Possible answer: Paine says that typically the victors of war use mercy to control the vanquished, but mercy cannot exist without justice. Paine then goes on to say that responding to the "mercy" of the British by giving up arms is self-destructive and will lead to the colonists being completely dependent on the British. To avoid this end, the colonist must remember their fear of British rule, along with their love for one another.

What signifies it to me, whether he who does it, is a king or a common man; my
70 countryman or not my countryman? whether it is done by an individual villain, or an army of them? If we reason to the root of things we shall find no difference; neither can any just cause be assigned why we should punish in the one case, and pardon in the other. Let them call me rebel, and welcome, I feel no concern from it; but I should suffer the misery of devils, were I to make a whore of my soul by swearing allegiance to one, whose character is that of a sottish, stupid, stubborn, worthless, brutish man. I conceive likewise a horrid idea in receiving mercy from a being, who at the last day shall be shrieking to the rocks and mountains to cover him, and fleeing with terror from the orphan, the widow and the slain of America.

There are cases which cannot be overdone by language, and this is one. There
80 are persons too who see not the full extent of the evil that threatens them; they solace themselves with hopes that the enemy, if they succeed, will be merciful. It is the madness of folly to expect mercy from those who have refused to do justice; and even mercy, where conquest is the object, is only a trick of war: The cunning of the fox is as murderous as the violence of the wolfe; and we ought to guard equally against both. Howe's first object is partly by threats and partly by promises, to terrify or seduce the people to deliver up their arms, and receive mercy. The ministry recommended the same plan to Gage, and this is what the Tories call making their peace; *"a peace which passeth all understanding"* indeed! A peace which would be the immediate forerunner of a worse ruin than any we
90 have yet thought of. Ye men of Pennsylvania, do reason upon those things! Were the back counties to give up their arms, they would fall easy prey to the Indians, who are all armed: This perhaps is what some Tories would not be sorry for. Were the home counties to deliver up their arms, they would be exposed to the resentment of the back counties, who would then have it at their power to chastise their defection at pleasure. And were any one State to give up its arms, that State must be garrisoned by all Howe's army of Britons and Hessians to preserve it from the anger of the rest. Mutual fear is a principal link in the chain of mutual love, and woe be the State that breaks the compact. Howe is mercifully inviting you to barbarous destruction, and men must be either rogues or fools that will not see it.
100 I dwell not upon the vapours of imagination; I bring reason to your ears; and in language, as plain as A, B, C, hold up truth to your eyes. **E**

I thank God that I fear not. I see no real cause for fear. I know our situation well, and can see the way out of it. While our army was collected, Howe dared not risk a battle, and it is no credit to him that he decamped from the White Plains, and waited a mean opportunity to ravage the defenceless Jersies; but it is great credit to us, that, with an handful of men, we sustained an orderly retreat for near an hundred miles, brought off our ammunition, all our field-pieces, the greatest part of our stores, and had four rivers to pass. None can say that our retreat was

---

COMMON CORE L 4c

Language Coach

Etymology *Horrid* (line 76) comes from the Latin *horrere*, meaning "to be afraid." *Horrid* means "very bad" or "terrible." Look up these related words in a dictionary: *horrendous* and *abhor*. Use each in a sentence about Paine's beliefs.

3 **Targeted Passage**

COMMON CORE RI 4

E **MAIN IDEAS**
Reread lines 79–101, and note Paine's repetition of the word *mercy* and its related forms *merciful* and *mercifully*. *Mercy* means receiving good treatment from someone who has power over you. How does the meaning of this key term develop and change in this paragraph? How does this development support Paine's comment in lines 97–98?

DIFFERENTIATED INSTRUCTION

FOR STRUGGLING READERS

3 **Targeted Passage** [Lines 85–99]

In this passage, Paine warns that believing Howe's promises of peace is dangerous.

- What does Howe offer to get the colonists to accept his terms? (lines 85–87)

- What will happen to the back counties if they give up their arms? (lines 90–92)

- How will the other states react if one state gives up arms? (lines 95–97)

FOR ENGLISH LANGUAGE LEARNERS

Language Coach

COMMON CORE L 4c

Etymology *Horrendous* means "dreadful" and *abhor* means "to strongly dislike" or "to loathe." Have students read their sentences aloud to the class. Have the class evaluate how accurately the sentences reflect Paine's beliefs. Ask what other words students can think of that come from the same Latin root. *Possible answers:* horror, horrible, horrific

Washington Crossing the Delaware (1851), Eastman Johnson. Copy after the Emmanuel Leutze painting in the Metropolitan Museum, New York. Private collection. © Art Resource, New York.

precipitate, for we were near three weeks in performing it, and the country might
110 have time to come in. Twice we marched back to meet the enemy and remained
out till dark. The sign of fear was not seen in our camp, and had not some of the
cowardly and disaffected inhabitants spread false alarms through the country, the
Jersies had never been ravaged. Once more we are again collected and collecting;
our new army at both ends of the Continent is recruiting fast, and we shall be
able to open the next campaign with sixty thousand men, well armed and clothed.
This is our situation, and who will may know it. By perseverance and fortitude
we have the prospect of a glorious issue; by cowardice and submission, the sad
choice of a variety of evils—a ravaged country—a depopulated city—habitations
without safety, and slavery without hope—our homes turned into barracks and
120 bawdy-houses for Hessians, and a future race to provide for whose fathers we shall
doubt of. Look on this picture, and weep over it!—and if there yet remains one
thoughtless wretch who believes it not, let him suffer it unlamented.

▲ **Analyze Visuals**
What figures and objects are emphasized by the **composition,** or the arrangement of shapes? Consider what this emphasis adds to the painting's meaning.

F MAIN IDEAS
Reread this paragraph, focusing on what Paine says about fear. What is the main point he makes about fear? Support your answer with evidence from the paragraph.

THE CRISIS **255**

Practice and Apply

For preliminary support of post-reading questions, use these copy masters:

R RESOURCE MANAGER—Copy Masters
Reading Check p. 324
Persuasive Techniques p. 317
Question Support p. 325
Additional selection questions are provided for teachers on page 311.

ANSWERS

COMMON CORE **RI 2, RI 3, RI 5**

1. *perseverance and fortitude*

2. *They tried everything they could to avoid war. God would not favor the cause of a murderer such as the king.*

3. *Like fair-weather friends, they join in good times and disappear in difficult times.*

Possible answers:

4. *He means that liberty can be temporarily suppressed but cannot die. The image inspires loyalty by carrying the positive connotation of home and hearth, and by underscoring the idea that the fight is for everything the soldiers hold dear.*

5. ● **COMMON CORE FOCUS** *SUMMARIZE MAIN IDEAS The colonists will find that independence is inevitable because their people are strong and united. Though they tried to avoid war, God favors the colonists because the British are violent and immoral. Future generations of Americans will benefit from the sacrifices the colonists make. The colonists do not have a choice: they must fight. The new army will be larger and better-equipped that the previous army, and they surely will win. Answers will vary.*

6. ● **COMMON CORE FOCUS** *PERSUASIVE TECHNIQUES He favors appeals to logic, emotion, and ethics: "Not a place . . . with them" (lines 39–41), logical to location, emotional to happiness; "throw not . . . God may bless you" (lines 54–55), appeal to authority of Bible; "The blood of his children . . . made them happy" (lines 59–60), emotional appeal of children, loaded language; "It is the madness . . . trick of war" (lines 82–83), logical appeal to experience; "I dwell not . . . to your eyes" (lines 100–101), logical appeal to reason; "by cowardice . . . unlamented"*

Comprehension

1. **Recall** At the end of the essay, what two qualities does Paine say American troops need to win the war?

2. **Summarize** In the third paragraph, what reasons does Paine give for assuring the Americans that their cause is right?

3. **Clarify** What is implied by the terms "summer soldier" and "sunshine patriot" in the first paragraph?

Text Analysis

4. **Interpret Metaphor** A metaphor is a figure of speech that equates two unlike things. Explain what Paine means by the metaphor in lines 45–46. How might this metaphor serve to inspire the troops' loyalty?

5. **Summarize Main Ideas** Using the chart of main ideas you completed as you read, write a paragraph **summarizing** Paine's main ideas. Does a summary of this essay's main ideas lose the persuasive power of Paine's rhetoric? Explain your answer.

6. **Analyze Persuasive Techniques** Review the persuasive techniques on page 249. Then, find six examples of Paine's strong persuasive appeals. In a chart, record your examples and explain the types of appeals. How does Paine's use of persuasive language affect the tone of this essay? Cite evidence from your chart to support your answer.

Example from "The Crisis"	Kind of Appeal
Those soldiers who stand firm in the "service of [their] country" deserve the "love and thanks of man and woman." (lines 2–3)	ethical appeal of "service to country" plus emotional appeal of love and gratitude
"God almighty will not give up a people to military destruction . . ." (lines 23–24)	appeal to authority—in this case, the ultimate authority

Text Criticism

7. **Critical Interpretations** John Adams, second U.S. president and no fan of Paine's, nonetheless acknowledged his crucial influence: "Without the pen of Paine the sword of Washington would have been wielded in vain." Use information from Paine's essay, as well as facts from his biography on page 248, to support Adams's assessment.

> *Whose* **SIDE** *are you on?*
> Political debates often compel people to decide which side they will be loyal to. Who or what deserves your loyalty? Why?

COMMON CORE

RI 2 Determine two or more central ideas of a text and analyze their development, including how they interact and build on one another to provide a complex analysis; provide an objective summary of the text. **RI 3** Analyze a complex set of ideas or sequence of events and explain how specific individuals, ideas, or events interact and develop. **RI 5** Analyze and evaluate the effectiveness of the structure an author uses in his or her exposition or argument.

(lines 117–122), emotional appeal to fear.

7. *Paine galvanized popular support for independence among the common people who would fight the war. Without a morale boost, America's cause might have failed.*

> *Whose* SIDE *are you on? Students might mention that the side that has values similar to their own merits loyalty, or that someone who has shown commitment to a shared cause deserves loyalty.*

Vocabulary in Context

▲ **VOCABULARY PRACTICE**

Choose the letter of the phrase that defines or is related to the boldfaced word.

1. **celestial:** (a) an instrument, (b) a star in the sky, (c) a slogan
2. **tyranny:** (a) a country with no freedoms, (b) an old bicycle, (c) a relay race
3. **ardor:** (a) a grove of trees, (b) a passion for justice, (c) an accounting mistake
4. **relinquish:** (a) a building site, (b) a surrender of territory, (c) a bad argument
5. **prudent:** (a) a cautious investor, (b) a distant relative, (c) car insurance
6. **wrangling:** (a) a favor, (b) a rowing machine, (c) towns with border disputes

WORD LIST

ardor
celestial
prudent
relinquish
tyranny
wrangling

ACADEMIC VOCABULARY IN SPEAKING

• document   • illustrate   • interpret   • promote   • reveal

Paine's essay was used to inspire Washington's army to victory. Today, people sometimes use speeches, blogs, and videos to inspire others. However, even these messages started out as words on a page. In a small group, discuss the importance of the written word in **promoting** a cause or in **illustrating** important points. Use two of the Academic Vocabulary words in your discussion.

VOCABULARY STRATEGY: WORDS FROM MIDDLE ENGLISH

Many modern words from Middle English originally derive from French. Others come from Old English, the earliest recognized form of the English language. To learn the derivation of a word, you need to understand how to read a dictionary entry. The entry below begins with the word in boldface, divided into syllables, followed by the pronunciation guide in parenthesis, and then the part of speech. Two numbered definitions are provided, as well as a highlighted summary of the word's etymology—its derivation from Middle English, Old French, and Latin.

> **ar•dor** (är der) *n.* **1.** Great intensity of feeling. **2.** Strong enthusiams or devotion: zeal. [Middle English *ardour*, from Old French, from Latin *ardor*, for *ardere*, to burn.]

PRACTICE The boldface words in these sentences derive from Middle English. Use context clues to write a definition for each word. Then, consult a print or online dictionary to learn the etymology and original meaning of each word.

1. He demonstrated his athletic **prowess** by participating in the triathlon.
2. She has been a **recluse** ever since the death of her husband.
3. Her **fulsome** praise of his decision greatly embarrassed him.
4. He had the perfect **rejoinder** for every accusation of the committee.
5. The garden held a **plenitude** of rare plants and flowers.

COMMON CORE

L 4c Consult general and specialized reference materials, both print and digital, to find the pronunciation of a word or determine or clarify its precise meaning, its part of speech, its etymology, or its standard usage. **L 6** Acquire and use accurately general academic and domain-specific words and phrases.

Interactive Vocabulary **THINK** central
Go to **thinkcentral.com**.
KEYWORD: HML11-257

Vocabulary in Context

VOCABULARY PRACTICE

1. *b*	4. *b*
2. *a*	5. *a*
3. *b*	6. *c*

R RESOURCE MANAGER—Copy Master
Vocabulary Practice p. 322

ACADEMIC VOCABULARY IN SPEAKING

Have students begin by discussing how leaders, pundits, and journalists gather ideas, conduct research, and sketch outlines.

VOCABULARY STRATEGY:
WORDS FROM MIDDLE ENGLISH

COMMON CORE **L 4c, L 6**

Remind students that a word's etymology can help them remember its current meaning. Point out differences between current usage and original meaning.

Possible answers:

1. *skill (original meaning: brave)*
2. *hermit (original meaning: to close up)*
3. *flattering (original meaning: abundant)*
4. *a witty reply (original meaning: to join)*
5. *abundance (original meaning: full)*

R RESOURCE MANAGER—Copy Master
Vocabulary Strategy p. 323

Interactive Vocabulary **THINK** central

Keywords direct students to a **WordSharp** tutorial on **thinkcentral.com** or to other types of vocabulary practice and review.

DIFFERENTIATED INSTRUCTION

FOR ENGLISH LANGUAGE LEARNERS

Task Support: Vocabulary Practice Have students work in mixed-language groups. Tell groups to review the words listed as choices for the *PRACTICE* items. Students can identify cognates from their home languages for these words, then work together to create a composite list of words and home-language cognates.

FOR ADVANCED LEARNERS/AP

Vocabulary in Writing Have students write a journal entry by a colonial soldier spending Christmas Eve on the banks of the Delaware River. Challenge them to convey the writer's emotions. Students should use at least three vocabulary words in their journal entry.

Assess and Reteach

Assess

DIAGNOSTIC AND SELECTION TESTS
Selection Tests A, B/C pp. 89-92

Interactive Selection Test on **thinkcentral.com**

Reteach

Level Up Online Tutorials on **thinkcentral.com**

Focus and Motivate

COMMON CORE FOCUS

RI 5 Analyze and evaluate the effectiveness of the structure an author uses in his or her argument. **RI 6** Determine an author's point of view or purpose in a text in which the rhetoric is particularly effective, analyzing how style and content contribute to the power, persuasiveness, or beauty of the text. **RI 9** Analyze documents of historical and literary significance for their themes, purposes, and rhetorical features. **L 5** Demonstrate understanding of figurative language.

ABOUT THE AUTHORS

Phillis Wheatley Ask students to identify the details of Wheatley's life they find most surprising and notable. Explain that Wheatley's letter demonstrates her education and biblical knowledge, as well as her interest in moral and religious issues.

Abigail Adams Have students restate Adams's beliefs about women. Explain that her letter reflects Adams's acceptance of her husband's political role and her belief that men should not have "absolute power" over their wives.

NOTABLE QUOTE

*"Some view our sable race with scornful eye...
Remember, Christians, Negroes, black as Cain,
May be refin'd, and join th' angelic train."*
—Phillis Wheatley

"Remember all Men would be tyrants if they could." **—Abigail Adams**

Selection Resources

Writers of the Revolution

COMMON CORE

RI 6 Determine an author's point of view or purpose in a text in which the rhetoric is particularly effective, analyzing how style and content contribute to the power, persuasiveness, or beauty of the text. **RI 9** Analyze documents of historical and literary significance for their themes, purposes, and rhetorical features.

Letter to the Reverend Samson Occom
by Phillis Wheatley

Letter to John Adams
by Abigail Adams

Meet the Authors

Phillis Wheatley
c. 1753–1784

Phillis Wheatley was the first African-American poet to be published. Moreover, her unusual life is the stuff that movies are made of. Kidnapped at age seven in West Africa, she was sold to the prosperous Wheatley family at a Boston slave auction. Within 16 months, she had mastered English and could read the Bible. She went on to learn Latin and Greek well enough to read the classics.

Startling Success Story Encouraged by the Wheatley family, Phillis started writing poetry as a teenager; She earned fame in the colonies and England when newspapers began publishing her poems, most of them on moral and religious subjects. While in London in 1773 to publish her book of poetry, Wheatley was the toast of society, which included many nobles and dignitaries and the visiting American patriot Ben Franklin.

Life as a Free Black Woman By 1778, Wheatley had gained her freedom and married a free black man. Their life together was a losing struggle against poverty, however, for in many respects living as a free black in a colonial city was as hard as being a slave. In late 1779, Wheatley tried to get a second book of her poems published, but war-torn, financially strapped Boston had lost interest in her.

Abigail Adams
1744–1818

Abigail Adams was the wife of the second U.S. president, John Adams, and mother of the sixth, John Quincy Adams. But she is equally well-known for her outspoken opinions as expressed in thousands of personal letters.

Intelligent and Competent The daughter of a wealthy minister, young Abigail read extensively in her father's library. After marrying John Adams, she moved to a farm in Braintree, Massachusetts. As John became increasingly involved in colonial politics and the struggle for independence, Abigail managed the household and farm as well as John's business affairs.

An Early Feminist? Because of her support for women's education and her acute awareness of men's "absolute power," many have championed Abigail Adams as an early advocate of women's rights. However, although her thinking was clearly advanced for her time—she also favored the abolition of slavery—she held quite conventional views about a woman's subordinate role in society.

Author Online
THINK central
Go to **thinkcentral.com**. KEYWORD: HML11-258

258

See resources on the **Teacher One Stop DVD-ROM** and on **thinkcentral.com**.

 RESOURCE MANAGER UNIT 1
Plan and Teach, pp. 327–334
Summary, pp. 335–336 † ‡
Text Analysis and Reading
    Skill, pp. 337–340 †*

DIAGNOSTIC AND SELECTION TESTS
Selection Tests, pp. 93–96

 BEST PRACTICES TOOLKIT
New Word Analysis, p. E8

TECHNOLOGY
- **Teacher One Stop DVD-ROM**
- **Student One Stop DVD-ROM**
- **Audio Anthology CD**
- **GrammarNotes DVD-ROM**
- **ExamView Test Generator on the Teacher One Stop**

---

* Resources for Differentiation   † Also in Spanish   ‡ Also in Haitian Creole and Vietnamese

Diction is a writer's choice of words. Diction includes both vocabulary (words) and syntax (arrangement of words). Diction can be formal or informal, common or technical, abstract or concrete. Note the formal diction in this excerpt from the letter written by Abigail Adams:

How many are the solitary hours I spend, ruminating upon the past, and anticipating the future, whilst you, overwhelmed with the cares of state, have but a few moments you can devote to any individual.

Writers often communicate **tone,** or attitude toward a subject, through their diction. As you read the letters, notice words and phrases that reveal each writer's attitude toward the issues of liberty and freedom.

READING STRATEGY: READING PRIMARY SOURCES

Primary sources are materials written or made by people who took part in or witnessed the events portrayed. These sources can provide unique insights on a subject. To get the most out of a primary source, consider the following:

- Who was the writer? The age, nationality, and social class of the writer can influence the point of view.
- What is the form of the document: letter, diary, speech? How might the form have affected the content?
- When and where was it written? The time and place of a primary source's writing can provide clues to the culture and history of the period.
- Who is the intended audience? In a private letter to a loved one, a writer might voice thoughts and feelings more freely than in an open letter to a public audience.

For help analyzing the letters of Wheatley and Adams, complete a chart such as the one shown here as you read each letter.

| Writer: |
| Form: |
| When and Where Written: |
| Intended Purpose/Audience: |

 Complete the activities in your **Reader/Writer Notebook.**

Who gets to make the RULES?

Those in authority make the rules for others—whether it's in the halls of Congress or the classroom. The authors of these two letters, while agreeing wholeheartedly with the patriot cause, still felt left out of the process and the benefits of the American Revolution.

DISCUSS People today have not only more freedom than people did in colonial times but also more ways to change the laws. Think of at least three situations in which rules directly impact your life. Then for each situation, discuss ways that are available to change or modify those rules.

BALLOT BOX

259

Who gets to make the **RULES?**

As students complete the *DISCUSS* activity, have them identify the type of authority that made the rules under discussion. Encourage students to share their ideas for ways to change these rules.

TEXT ANALYSIS
COMMON CORE RI 6

● *Model the Skill:* DICTION

Tell students they can determine many things about writers and their purpose by studying diction. Write this excerpt from a letter on the board:

> I believe that you made the correct decision to acquire another company. Mr. Elvin, your decisions are always thoughtful, and I know that my project will benefit from this one.

Point out that choosing words like *believe* and *acquire* instead of *think* and *get* and syntax like "my project will benefit" give the letter formal diction.

GUIDED PRACTICE Ask students to identify the writer's attitude or tone regarding Mr. Elvin's decision.

READING STRATEGY
COMMON CORE RI 1

■ *Model the Skill:* READING PRIMARY SOURCES

Point out that that formal diction, complimentary tone, and reference to "my project" make the writer likely to be an employee, writing to his or her boss.

GUIDED PRACTICE Ask students to identify the letter's intended audience and purpose. Remind them to use a chart like the one on this page to keep track of their information.

R RESOURCE MANAGER—Copy Master
Reading Primary Sources p. 339 (for student use while reading the selections)

DIFFERENTIATED INSTRUCTION

FOR STRUGGLING READERS

Vocabulary Support To support instruction, clarify the meaning of these words:

- *abstract,* "expressing something that can only be understood intellectually"
- *concrete,* "able to be seen or touched; existing in reality, not just an idea"
- *primary,* "something that is first in order; thus, the first person to see or experience an event"

Concept Support: Reading Primary Sources To help students evaluate primary source letters, ask them to recall a letter they have written and identify its audience. Have them note information they would have omitted if the audience were different. As they read the selection letters, urge students to identify information each author might have omitted had she known the letter would be made public.

SUMMARY

Wheatley's letter applauds Occom's defense of the natural rights of African Americans and points out that people cannot claim to love freedom yet oppress others.

READ WITH A PURPOSE

Help students set a purpose for reading. As they read the two letters, ask them to find what Wheatley and Adams have in common.

TEXT ANALYSIS COMMON CORE RI 6

Ⓐ DICTION

Possible answer: Phrases such as "obliging kind epistle" (line 1) and "glorious dispensation" (line 6) give the letter a formal tone. White readers were probably surprised to encounter such writing from a black woman in a time when most black men and women were enslaved and illiterate. Wheatley's language might have caused white people to think differently about black people.

Letter to the REVEREND SAMSON OCCOM

Phillis Wheatley

> **BACKGROUND** The Reverend Samson Occom was a Mohegan Indian who became a minister after converting to Christianity. In a letter to Phillis Wheatley, he had criticized some of his fellow ministers for owning slaves. Wheatley's response to her friend, dated February 11, 1774, was later published in colonial newspapers.

Reverend and honored sir,

I have this day received your obliging kind epistle, and am greatly satisfied with your reasons respecting the negroes, and think highly reasonable what you offer in vindication of their natural rights: Those that invade them cannot be insensible that the divine light is chasing away the thick darkness which broods over the land of Africa;[1] and the chaos which has reigned so long, is converting into beautiful order, and reveals more and more clearly the glorious dispensation of civil and religious liberty, which are so inseparably united, that there is little or no enjoyment of one without the other: Otherwise, perhaps, the Israelites had been less solicitous for their freedom from Egyptian slavery;[2] I do not say they would

10 have been contented without it, by no means; for in every human breast God has implanted a principle, which we call love of freedom; it is impatient Ⓐ of oppression, and pants for deliverance; and by the leave of our modern Egyptians[3] I will assert, that the same principle lives in us. God grant deliverance in his own way and time, and get him honor upon all those whose avarice impels them to countenance and help forward the calamities of their fellow creatures. This I desire not for their hurt, but to convince them of the strange absurdity of their conduct, whose words and actions are so diametrically opposite. How well the cry for liberty, and the reverse disposition for the exercise of oppressive power over others agree—I humbly think it does not require the penetration[4] of a

20 philosopher to determine.—

---

1. **insensible . . . the land of Africa:** unaware that Christianity is spreading throughout Africa.
2. **Israelites . . . Egyptian slavery:** a biblical allusion to the Israelites who were led out of Egypt by Moses.
3. **modern Egyptians:** the owners of African slaves.
4. **penetration:** understanding; insight.

Analyze Visuals ▶
This image shows a slave auction in New Amsterdam (New York). What does this tell you about slavery in colonial America?

① Targeted Passage

Ⓐ DICTION
Describe Wheatley's **diction** in lines 1–11. How might her way of writing have struck white readers at the time?

Language Coach
Word Definitions
Absurdity (line 16) means "unreasonableness," "illogicality," or "stupidity." Wheatley is saying that slave owners are saying one thing and doing another. How do their actions conflict with their words?

First Slave Auction in New Amsterdam, 1655.
The Granger Collection, New York.

DIFFERENTIATED INSTRUCTION

FOR ENGLISH LANGUAGE LEARNERS

Language Coach

Word Definitions *Possible answer: Wheatley is saying it's absurd for colonial slaveholders to be clamoring for freedom from British rule while at the same time denying freedom to their slaves. Tell students that absurdity is a noun; absurd is the adjective that describes something as unreasonable, illogical, or stupid.*

FOR STRUGGLING READERS

In combination with the *Audio Anthology CD*, use one or more Targeted Passages (pp. 260, 262, 264) to ensure that students focus on key concepts in the selections. Targeted Passages are also good for English learners.

① Targeted Passage **[Lines 1–13]**

This passage clarifies Wheatley's view of the rights of African Americans and her acknowledgement of what they desire.

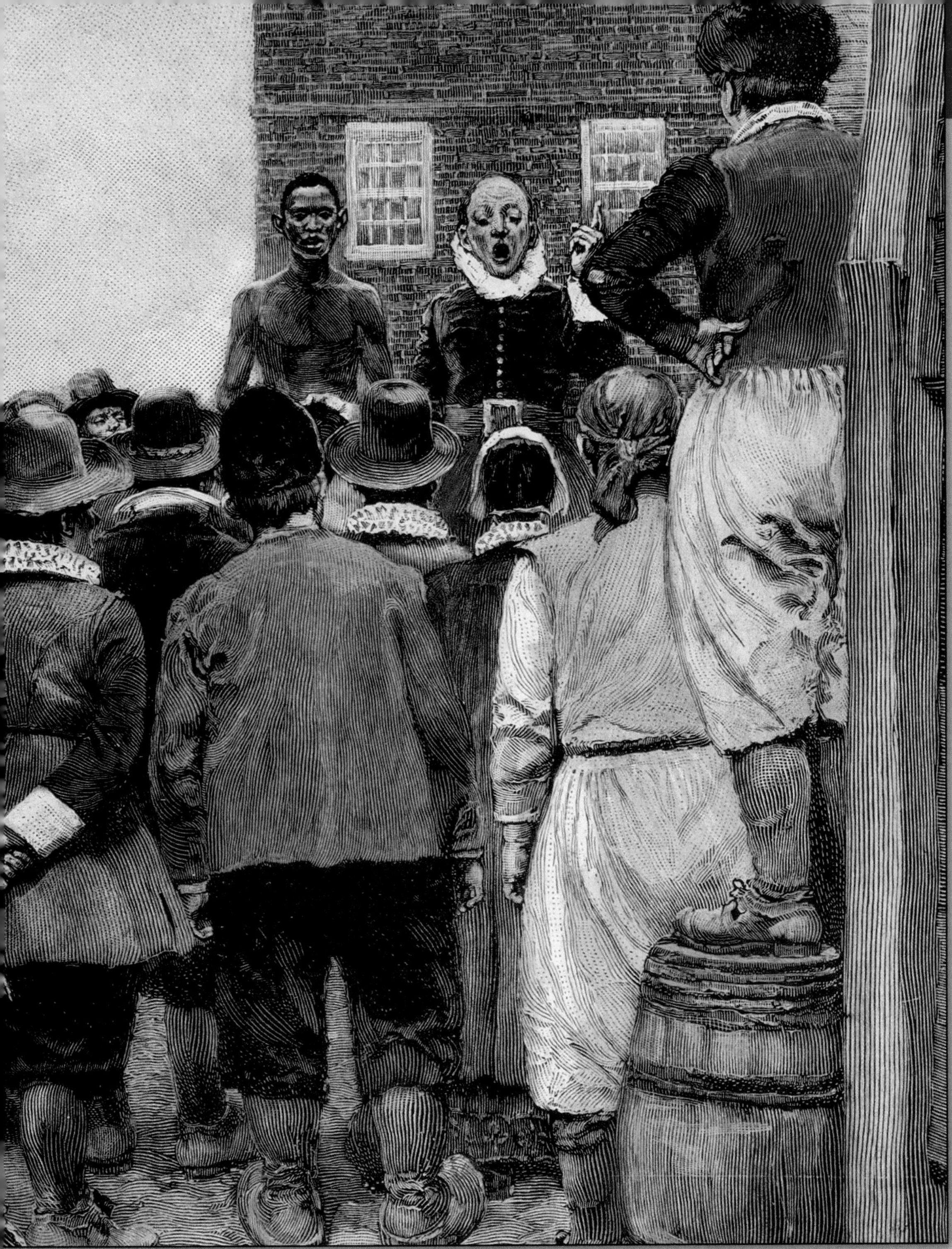

Analyze Visuals

Possible answer: *This image shows that slavery was a popular trade in colonial America. A white man is apparently attempting to sell a slave to one of the colonists. There are many colonists in the audience, which suggests that this was a common practice and that many colonists were interested in buying slaves.*

REVISIT THE BIG QUESTION

Who gets to make the
RULES?

Discuss In lines 10–19, whom does Wheatley think has the ultimate authority over people? What does she hope that authority will do?
Possible answer: *Wheatley thinks that God has the ultimate authority over people. She believes God put the desire for freedom in every human heart and will deliver that freedom when ready (lines 13–14). She hopes that God will make those who support freedom while oppressing slaves realize the error of their thinking (lines 14–15).*

- How does Wheatley feel about Reverend Occom's opinions about African Americans? (lines 1–3)
- What two rights does Wheatley believe cannot be separated? (line 7)
- Who does Wheatley compare enslaved African Americans to? Why? (lines 8–13)

FOR ENGLISH LANGUAGE LEARNERS

Vocabulary Use New Word Analysis to teach these words: *convince* (line 16), *require* (line 19); *philosophy* (line 45).

BEST PRACTICES TOOLKIT—Transparency
New Word Analysis p. E8

Abigail Adams begins her letter by expressing the value of her husband's work to found the nation over his family's needs. She then describes the chaos and lack of leadership in Boston. Adams urges the new government to declare sovereignty and points out that men's power over women contradicts their goal to liberate the nation.

READING STRATEGY

COMMON CORE
RI 9

B *Model the Skill:* PRIMARY SOURCES

Read aloud lines 1–10. Have student discuss whether they feel Adams is addressing private or public concerns. Point out that in lines 8–10, she tells her husband that she misses him. Ask students to look for remarks that are about public issues and their relationship with those that focus on personal concerns. *Possible answer: Adams says her husband's duties take precedence over their personal lives.*

REVIST THE BIG QUESTION

Who gets to make the
RULES?

Discuss In lines 13–18, does Adams characterize the people who have authority over Boston and its colonists? *Possible answer: Adams does not think the rulers are doing a good job. She believes that they are lazy and that they feel secure, when they should not (lines 13–15). She thinks they worry and focus on the wrong things (lines 15–16).*

Letter to JOHN ADAMS

Abigail Adams

> **BACKGROUND** In March of 1776, while John Adams was in Philadelphia with other delegates drafting a code of laws for the new independent country, Abigail wrote a letter asking him to "remember the ladies" in the new laws: "Be more generous and favorable to them than your ancestors. Do not put such unlimited power into the hands of husbands." John's response was to laugh and remark, "You are so saucy." The following is the next letter she sent to him.

Braintree, 7, May, 1776

How many are the solitary hours I spend, ruminating upon the past, and anticipating the future, whilst you, overwhelmed with the cares of state, have but a few moments you can devote to any individual. All domestic pleasures and enjoyments are absorbed in the great and important duty you owe your country, "for our country is, as it were, a secondary god, and the first and greatest parent. It is to be preferred to parents, wives, children, friends, and all things, the gods only excepted; for, if our country perishes, it is as impossible to save an individual, as to preserve one of the fingers of a mortified hand." Thus do I suppress every wish, and silence every murmur, acquiescing in a painful separation from the
10 companion of my youth, and the friend of my heart. B

  I believe 't is near ten days since I wrote you a line. I have not felt in a humor to entertain you if I had taken up my pen. Perhaps some unbecoming invective[1] might have fallen from it. The eyes of our rulers have been closed, and a lethargy has seized almost every member. I fear a fatal security has taken possession of them. Whilst the building is in flames, they tremble at the expense of water to quench it. In short, two months have elapsed since the evacuation of Boston,[2] and very little has been done in that time to secure it, or the harbor, from future

Analyze Visuals ▶
These pastel portraits of Abigail and John Adams were done in 1766, about two years after their marriage. How do these portraits compare with those that might be done today of a young couple?

1 Targeted Passage

B PRIMARY SOURCES
Does Adams's letter concern itself with private or public issues in lines 1–10? What does she say about the relationship between the private and the public?

---

1. **unbecoming invective:** inappropriate abusive language.
2. **two months . . . Boston:** British troops under General William Howe and more than a thousand Loyalists evacuated Boston on March 17, 1776.

262 UNIT 1: EARLY AMERICAN WRITING

DIFFERENTIATED INSTRUCTION

FOR STRUGGLING READERS

1 Targeted Passage [Lines 3–14]

This passage shows Adams's view of the newly forming country and reveals aspects of her character and relationship with John.

- To what does Adams compare the new country? Why? (line 5)

- What thoughts or feelings does Adams suppress? (lines 8–10)

- Why does Adams say that she hasn't written her husband for nearly ten days? (lines 11–13)

FOR ENGLISH LANGUAGE LEARNERS

Develop Reading Fluency Give students practice identifying fluent reading. Read the first sentence of Adams's letter aloud, emphasizing both the pauses signified by the commas that set off clauses and the word *you*. Then read the sentence aloud again, this time without pausing for commas or emphasizing *you*. Ask students which reading was clearer to understand. Then have students read the sentence chorally. Have them continue their choral reading for more practice.

Analyze Visuals

Possible answer: These portraits are more formal than the portraits that most young couples would have done today. Most contemporary portraits would be photographs and would show the couple together. They might be posed informally in a familiar home or outdoor setting. They would probably be smiling and showing affection. The dress and hairstyles would also be more natural.

TIERED DISCUSSION PROMPTS

Use these prompts to have students consider Adams's evaluation of her nation's rulers in lines 8–18:

Connect Have you or someone you know ever worried about small details at the expense of larger, more important issues? Explain. *Accept all thoughtful responses.*

Interpret Consider the time period in which Adams's letter is written, then reread lines 15–16. What does the "building in flames" represent? What does Adams mean when she writes, "they tremble . . . to quench it"? *Possible answer: The "building in flames" is the lingering fear in Boston of future invasion by the British. Though British troops evacuated the city nearly two months before, nothing since has been done to secure it, because the "rulers" or Continental Congress in Philadelphia (to which her husband is a delegate) "tremble" and won't spend the money for troops and supplies.*

Evaluate What does Adams seem to think of the response of the citizens of Boston to the crisis? *Possible answer: Adams seems impressed by the sense of personal responsibility the citizens have taken to secure their city, an action that is in sharp contrast to the "lethargy" of Congress.*

FOR STRUGGLING READERS

Concept Support: Reading Primary Sources
As students read the letter, help them fill out the reading chart introduced on page 259. Direct their attention to the boldface date and location of writing. Have them read the **BACKGROUND** for help in identifying purpose and audience.

Writer: *Abigail Adams*
Form: *personal letter*
When and Where Written: *at Adams's home in Braintree, on May 7, 1776*
Intended Purpose/Audience: *letter to her husband, John, to inform him about colonial affairs and to remind him about being fair to women with the new laws*

invasion. The people are all in a flame, and no one among us, that I have heard of, even mentions expense. They think, universally, that there has been an amazing
20 neglect somewhere. Many have turned out as volunteers to work upon Noddle's Island,[3] and many more would go upon Nantasket, if the business was once set on foot. "'T is a maxim of state, that power and liberty are like heat and moisture. Where they are well mixed, every thing prospers; where they are single, they are destructive."

A government of more stability is much wanted in this colony, and they are ready to receive it from the hands of the Congress. And since I have begun with maxims of state,[4] I will add another, namely, that a people may let a king fall, yet still remain a people; but, if a king let his people slip from him, he is no longer a king.[5] And as this is most certainly our case, why not proclaim to the world, in
30 decisive terms, your own importance?

Shall we not be despised by foreign powers, for hesitating so long at a word?

I cannot say that I think you are very generous to the ladies; for, whilst you are proclaiming peace and good-will to men, emancipating all nations, you insist upon retaining an absolute power over wives. But you must remember, that arbitrary power is like most other things which are very hard, very liable to be broken; and, notwithstanding all your wise laws and maxims, we have it in our power, not only to free ourselves, but to subdue our masters, and, without violence, throw both your natural and legal authority at our feet;—

"Charm by accepting, by submitting sway,
40 Yet have our humor most when we obey."[6]

I thank you for several letters which I have received since I wrote last; they alleviate a tedious absence, and I long earnestly for a Saturday evening, and experience a similar pleasure to that which I used to find in the return of my friend upon that day after a week's absence. The idea of a year dissolves all my philosophy.

Our little ones, whom you so often recommend to my care and instruction, shall not be deficient in virtue or probity,[7] if the precepts of a mother have their desired effect; but they would be doubly enforced, could they be indulged with the example of a father alternately before them. I often point them to their sire,
50 "engaged in a corrupted state,
Wrestling with vice and faction."[8]

A Adams

---

3. **Noddle's Island . . . Nantasket:** sites near the city of Boston. Noddle's Island is now called East Boston.

4. **maxims of state:** rules or short sayings related to government.

5. **king:** a reference to King George III, who ignored colonists' protests and put Massachusetts under military rule.

6. **"Charm . . . obey":** a couplet taken from Alexander Pope's poem *Moral Essays*.

7. **deficient . . . probity:** lacking in goodness or integrity.

8. **"engaged . . . faction":** lines taken from Joseph Addison's play *Cato*. Cato (234–149 B.C.) was a Roman politician who fought for high moral standards in the Roman Senate.

264   UNIT 1: EARLY AMERICAN WRITING

TEXT ANALYSIS

 DICTION

COMMON CORE
RI 6

Possible answer: *The words that suggest a concern with political issues include "government," "stability," and "colony" (line 25); "Congress" (line 26); "maxims of state" (line 27); and "king" and "people" (line 28). Adams's diction shows that she uses sophisticated thinking and is comfortable discussing issues of public policy.*

READING STRATEGY

 PRIMARY SOURCES

COMMON CORE
RI 9

Possible answer: *Adams points out that colonial men are interested in freeing themselves from Great Britain, but they continue to keep their wives and daughters enslaved (lines 32–34).*

TEXT ANALYSIS

 DICTION

COMMON CORE
RI 6

Possible answer: *Relationships between husbands and wives were rather formal during colonial times. Even when talking about her children to her husband, Adams uses formal language and little emotion.*

SELECTION WRAP–UP

READ WITH A PURPOSE Now that students have read the letters, they may note that both writers address the shortcomings of men who seek freedom for the colonies. Ask students what each writer wants. **Possible answers:** *Wheatley wants the men to realize that slaves, too, want and deserve freedom. Adams wants them to relinquish the power they hold over their wives, which is contradictory to their professed desire for people of all nations to be free.*

⭐ CRITIQUE

Have students evaluate whether both writers express their points clearly.

Language Coach

Similes A simile is a figure of speech that compares two similar things, using words such as *like* or *as*. What comparison does Adams mention in lines 22–24? How does the comparison express her ideas about the balance between power and liberty?

DICTION
Reread lines 25–30. How does diction contribute to Adams's tone in these lines? And how does tone help the writer to express her purpose? Cite evidence to support your answer.

PRIMARY SOURCES
What inconsistency in the attitudes of the times does Abigail Adams point out in lines 32–40?

DICTION
Reread lines 46–51. What does the formal language used to discuss both public and private matters tell you about family relations at the time?

DIFFERENTIATED INSTRUCTION

FOR STRUGGLING READERS

② Targeted Passage [Lines 32–51]

This passage reflects Adams's view of women's rights and duties.

- Why does Adams say that her husband and his colleagues aren't "very generous to the ladies"? (lines 33–34)

- Why does Adams appreciate her husband's letters? (lines 41–42)

- What qualities does Adams want to instill in her children? (line 47)

FOR ENGLISH LANGUAGE LEARNERS

Language Coach

COMMON CORE
L5

Similes *Possible answer:* Power is compared to heat, and liberty is compared to moisture. Adams uses the comparison to say that power and liberty, like heat and moisture, are best expressed together, not alone, where they can be destructive.

Comprehension

1. **Recall** What does Phillis Wheatley praise the Reverend Occom for doing?

2. **Clarify** In Wheatley's opinion, what is the cause of slavery?

3. **Recall** Why does Abigail Adams put her country before personal happiness?

4. **Clarify** What is the situation in Massachusetts that Adams complains to her husband about?

Text Analysis

5. **Compare and Contrast** In both letters, Wheatley and Adams reveal their powerlessness to change what they clearly see as wrong. How do they personally deal with this lack of **authority?** Discuss how they cope with the following situations:

   - slavery
   - lack of security due to inaction
   - absolute power of men

● 6. **Analyze Diction** For each letter, look for examples of diction that reveal the writer's **tone.** Then compare and contrast the tone of each, explaining possible reasons for any differences you find.

● 7. **Analyze Primary Sources** How are these personal letters letters useful or limited in their historical value? What insights do they provide that more formal documents, such as the Declaration of Independence, do not? How does the identity of the writer influence the content? Draw upon your chart to cite examples from the letters to prove your points.

8. **Evaluate Argument** Each woman makes an argument in her letter: Wheatley against slavery, and Adams against the "arbitrary power" of men. Who presents the stronger case? Cite evidence to support your opinion.

Text Criticism

9. **Historical Context** Personal letters, such as Wheatley's, offer a rare opportunity to hear women's voices from the past. What distinguishes Wheatley's and Adams's writing from the rhetoric of Patrick Henry, Thomas Jefferson, and Tom Paine? What do their letters reveal about how women were expected to behave in early America?

> *Who gets to make the* **RULES?**
>
> Rules are everywhere—from the laws in government down to the rules at your school or at home. Why are rules and people who are given **authority** to enforce rules important?

Adams: lines 13–24, 32–38). Disadvantages: limited perspective: Adams's view is limited by personal vulnerability and fear. She expresses views atypical of women. Each writer is influenced by her specific situation as a former slave or the wife of a statesman.

8. *Students might say that Wheatley's argument is stronger. Her facts are clear and she is unemotional. The personal details of Adams's letter can cloud her points. All answers should include support.*

9. *Henry, Jefferson, and Paine use forceful rhetoric. The women's writing is more accepting. The letters show that women were expected to accept their subordination with humility and contentment.*

> *Who gets to make the* **RULES?**
> *Students should recognize that rules help ensure an orderly society and that those responsible for enforcing them are entrusted with the responsibility to do so in a just and fair way.*

Practice and Apply

For preliminary support of post-reading questions, use these copy masters:

R **RESOURCE MANAGER**—Copy Masters
  Reading Check p. 341
  Diction p. 337
  Question Support p. 342

Additional selection questions are provided for teachers on page 331.

ANSWERS   COMMON CORE RI 5, RI 6, RI 9

1. *supporting the natural rights of African Americans*

2. *greed*

3. *because if her country perishes, then saving individuals or their happiness won't matter*

4. *The colony lacks security. Volunteers will help, but they need Congress's authority.*

Possible answers:

5. *Wheatley points out the hypocrisy of slave-holding ministers and trusts in God to stop slavery and its absolute power. Adams trusts in her husband for help with the colony's lack of security. She appears skeptical about men's absolute power changing. Both seem ultimately powerless.*

6. ● **COMMON CORE FOCUS** *Diction Lines 3–6 and 17–20 show Wheatley's formal, polite, controlled and impersonal tone. Lines 8–13, 25–30, 32–34, and 41–45 show Adams's informal, spontaneous, emotional, and personal tone. Adams's tone is more personally forceful than Wheatley's.*

7. ● **COMMON CORE FOCUS** *Reading Primary Sources Advantages: The letters give useful personal details and insights about life of the times (Wheatley: lines 13–20;*

COMMON CORE

RI 5 Analyze and evaluate the effectiveness of the structure an author uses in his or her argument. RI 6 Determine an author's point of view or purpose in a text in which the rhetoric is particularly effective, analyzing how style and content contribute to the power, persuasiveness, or beauty of the text. RI 9 Analyze documents of historical and literary significance for their themes, purposes, and rhetorical features.

Assess and Reteach

Assess

DIAGNOSTIC AND SELECTION TESTS
  Selection Tests A, B/C pp. 93–96

Interactive Selection Test on thinkcentral.com

Reteach

Level Up Online Tutorials on thinkcentral.com

Focus and Motivate

COMMON CORE FOCUS

RI 1 Cite textual evidence to support inferences drawn from the text, including determining where the text leave matters uncertain. **RI 5** Analyze and evaluate the effectiveness of the structure an author uses in his or her exposition. **RI 6** Determine an author's point of view or purpose. **L 6** Demonstrate independence in gathering vocabulary knowledge when considering a word or phrase important to comprehension or expression.

ABOUT THE AUTHOR

After students have read about Franklin's life, discuss with them why he might have decided to write an autobiography, and why people might have wanted to learn about his life. Explain to students that they are going to read an excerpt that demonstrates both his great mind and his ability to connect with people.

NOTABLE QUOTE

"If you would not be forgotten As soon as you are dead and rotten Either write things worth reading, Or do things worth the writing."—**Benjamin Franklin**

Ask students whether Franklin took his own advice, based on what they learned about his life.

Selection Resources

COMMON CORE

RI 1 Cite textual evidence to support inferences drawn from the text, including determining where the text leave matters uncertain. **RI 5** Analyze and evaluate the effectiveness of the structure an author uses in his or her exposition. **RI 6** Determine an author's point of view or purpose.

DID YOU KNOW?

Benjamin Franklin . . .

- started the first public library and fire department in America.
- founded what became the University of Pennsylvania.
- invented bifocal eyeglasses.

(background) Page from *Poor Richard's Almanack*

Writers of the Revolution

from **The Autobiography** Video link at thinkcentral.com

by Benjamin Franklin

Meet the Author

Benjamin Franklin 1706–1790

Printer, publisher, writer, scientist, inventor, businessman, philosopher, statesman—Benjamin Franklin's numerous roles only hint at the man's tremendous versatility and talent. As the oldest founding father, Franklin had already lived a full life when at the age of 70 he joined 40-year-old John Adams and 33-year-old Thomas Jefferson to draft the Declaration of Independence. Soon afterward, he loaned Congress a large sum of his own money and sailed on a leaky ship to France to arrange for more loans and a crucial alliance to fight the British. His masterly efforts abroad on behalf of the American cause earned him a reputation as one of the most successful American diplomats of all time. Only a few years before he died, his presence at the Constitutional Convention helped unify the delegates. So great was his influence that he is credited with convincing them to approve the final document by a vote of 39 to 3. A man of great integrity, intelligence, and charm, Ben Franklin embodied the best of the new nation and became its first celebrity.

Pulling Himself Up Born in Boston as the youngest of 15 children, Franklin did not want to follow in his father's footsteps to become a candle and soap maker. Instead, he joined his brother in the printing business as an apprentice. With only two years of formal education, Franklin taught himself to write by imitating the great essayists of his day. At the age of 16, he was contributing satirical pieces to his brother's newspaper. By his own account "too saucy and provoking" as a youth, he soon quarreled with his brother and struck out on his own for Philadelphia. Franklin did very well in Philadelphia, prospering in his own printing business, running the successful *Pennsylvania Gazette* newspaper, writing his popular *Poor Richard's Almanack* for 26 years, and being active in colonial politics.

Citizen of the World Franklin's writing—from humorous satires and wise sayings to serious political essays and scientific observations on electricity—as well as his diplomacy and charismatic personality made him an international celebrity. Although respected by the great minds of his age, he never lost his connection to the common people. In the words of John Adams: "His reputation is greater than that of Newton, Frederick the Great or Voltaire, his character more revered than all of them. There's scarcely a coachman or a footman or scullery maid who does not consider him a friend of all mankind."

Author Online

Go to thinkcentral.com. KEYWORD: HML11-266

THINK central

266

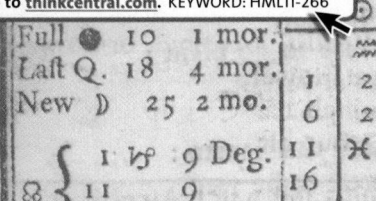

Full	10	1 mor.		
Laſt Q.	18	4 mor.	1	24
New D	25	2 mo.	6	29

See resources on the **Teacher One Stop DVD-ROM** *and on* **thinkcentral.com**.

 Video link at thinkcentral.com

HISTORY

R RESOURCE MANAGER UNIT 1
Plan and Teach, pp. 343–350
Summary, pp. 351–352 † ‡
Text Analysis and Reading Skill, pp. 353–356 †*
Vocabulary, pp. 357–359

DIAGNOSTIC AND SELECTION TESTS
Selection Tests, pp. 97–100

BEST PRACTICES TOOLKIT
Definition Mapping, p. E6
Analysis Frame: Literary Non-fiction, pp. D21, D48
Three-Column Journal, p. B10

TECHNOLOGY
- Teacher One Stop DVD-ROM
- Student One Stop DVD-ROM
- Audio Anthology CD
- GrammarNotes DVD-ROM
- ExamView Test Generator on the Teacher One Stop

***** Resources for Differentiation   † Also in Spanish   ‡ Also in Haitian Creole and Vietnamese

● TEXT ANALYSIS: CHARACTERISTICS OF AUTOBIOGRAPHY

An **autobiography** is the story of a person's life, written by that person. As you read this excerpt from Franklin's autobiography, notice the following characteristics of autobiography:

- **First person:** The author of an autobiography usually writes from the first-person point of view.
- **Dual perspective:** Often the author of an autobiography writes as an older person looking back on him- or herself as a younger person, providing opportunities for reflection.
- **Significant moments:** Autobiographies may vary from straightforward chronological accounts to impressionistic narratives. In either case, especially important events and people in the author's life are highlighted.

● READING SKILL: MAKE INFERENCES ABOUT THE AUTHOR

Making inferences means "reading between the lines"—making logical guesses based on evidence in the text to figure out what is not directly stated. As you read *The Autobiography*, make inferences about the values and motives that seem characteristic of Franklin's personality. Use a chart like the one shown to record details from the text about the 13 virtues he hopes to acquire and how he goes about doing so. What inferences can you make about him?

Details or Evidence from Text	Inference

Review: **Connect**

▲ VOCABULARY IN CONTEXT

Franklin uses the following boldfaced words in describing his efforts to improve himself. Restate each phrase, using a different word or words for the boldfaced term.

1. **unremitting** storms that went on for weeks
2. **felicity** over her great good luck
3. a mansion as one symbol of **affluence**
4. dreamed up an **artifice** to avoid doing his job
5. **incorrigible** behavior that disgraced the family
6. a **trifling** problem, easily cleared up
7. would often **contrive** to secretly meet his friends

 Complete the activities in your **Reader/Writer Notebook**.

Is PERFECTION *possible?*

As a young man, Benjamin Franklin believed that human beings could actually achieve perfection in a given area. All you needed was a reasonable plan and a lot of self-discipline. Many people today also aim for perfection, although their quest may take a different path. Bookstores have whole sections devoted to self-improvement in a variety of areas, including diet, exercise, careers, and dating.

QUICKWRITE Do you think perfection is possible or at least worth striving for? If you think so, outline a self-improvement plan that shows how you might achieve your goal. If you don't think perfection is possible, write a paragraph in which you explain why you think it is unattainable.

THE AUTOBIOGRAPHY **267**

Is PERFECTION *possible?*

Read the paragraph about Franklin's beliefs as a young man. Have students finish the *QUICKWRITE,* and then ask volunteers to share their **self-improvement** plans or to explain why perfection is impossible.

TEXT ANALYSIS
COMMON CORE
RI 5
RI 6

● *Model the Skill:* CHARACTERISTICS OF AUTOBIOGRAPHY

Help students understand characteristics of autobiography by reading aloud the first paragraph of the author biography on page 266. Identify these significant moments in Franklin's life: helping draft the Declaration of Independence, creating an alliance with France, and unifying the nation's founders. Tell students that these events will likely be described in Franklin's autobiography.

GUIDED PRACTICE Ask students to identify a significant life moment for the person featured in an autobiography they have read or viewed on film.

READING SKILL
COMMON CORE
RI 1

■ *Model the Skill:* MAKE INFERENCES ABOUT THE AUTHOR

Model how to make inferences about Franklin. Read aloud **Pulling Himself Up.** Point out that Franklin taught himself to write and he started his own printing business, details that show he must have been very intelligent and industrious.

GUIDED PRACTICE Have students read *DID YOU KNOW?* and make an inference about Franklin from these details.

R RESOURCE MANAGER—Copy Master
Make Inferences About the Author p. 355 (for student use while reading the selection)

Practice and Apply

SUMMARY

This excerpt from Benjamin Franklin's *The Autobiography* details his attempt to reach moral perfection. He creates a list of 13 virtues that he decides he must possess in order to attain perfection. Next, he creates a book that lists the 13 virtues and helps him track his attempts to acquire one virtue each week. Although Franklin cannot attain moral perfection, struggling in particular to achieve Order, he feels the experiment made him a happier, better man.

READ WITH A PURPOSE

Help students set a purpose for reading. Tell them to read "The Autobiography" to find out what Benjamin Franklin learned about himself during his experiment.

TEXT ANALYSIS

COMMON CORE

RI 5
RI 6

Ⓐ AUTOBIOGRAPHY

Possible answer: The characteristics of autobiography include Franklin's use of the pronoun I to tell about an important time in his life (lines 1–4) and his statement to the reader as to why this moment was significant (lines 9–12).

THE *Autobiography*

Benjamin Franklin

BACKGROUND Franklin was a prolific writer, producing volumes of essays, travel journals, newspaper articles, satires, speeches, almanacs, letters, and even ballads. But his great masterpiece was his *Autobiography,* which is still very popular today. The following excerpt details Franklin's plan to achieve moral perfection. He was about 20 years old when he first conceived the idea on one of his long, trans-Atlantic voyages. The plan reveals his faith in reason, order, and human perfectibility, which was typical of 18th-century thought.

It was about this time I conceived the bold and arduous project of arriving at moral perfection. I wished to live without committing any fault at any time; I would conquer all that either natural inclination, custom, or company might lead me into. As I knew, or thought I knew, what was right and wrong, I did not see why I might not always do the one and avoid the other. But I soon found I had undertaken a task of more difficulty than I had imagined. While my care was employed in guarding against one fault, I was often surprised by another; habit took the advantage of inattention; inclination was sometimes too strong for reason. I concluded, at length, that the mere speculative conviction that it was our
10 interest to be completely virtuous, was not sufficient to prevent our slipping; and that the contrary habits must be broken, and good ones acquired and established, before we can have any dependence on a steady, uniform rectitude of conduct. For this purpose I therefore contrived the following method. Ⓐ

In the various enumerations of the moral virtues I had met with in my reading, I found the catalogue more or less numerous, as different writers included more or

Analyze Visuals ▶
What do the details of this famous painting suggest about Franklin?

① Targeted Passage

Ⓐ AUTOBIOGRAPHY
What characteristics of autobiography do you find in the first paragraph of this selection?

Benjamin Franklin (1767), David Martin. Oil on canvas.
© White House Historical Association, Washington, D.C.

268 UNIT 1: EARLY AMERICAN WRITING

DIFFERENTIATED INSTRUCTION

FOR ENGLISH LANGUAGE LEARNERS

Vocabulary Support Use Definition Mapping to teach these words: *task* (line 6), *mental* (line 18), *facilitate* (line 29), *constant* (line 31), *exceed* (line 75), *scheme* (line 82).

 BEST PRACTICES TOOLKIT—Transparency
Definition Mapping p. E6

FOR STRUGGLING READERS

In combination with the *Audio Anthology CD,* use one or more Targeted Passages (pp. 268, 270, 273, 274) to ensure that students focus on key concepts in the selection. Targeted Passages are also good for English learners.

① Targeted Passage [Lines 1–13]

This passage introduces students to the purpose of this part of Franklin's autobiography.

Analyze Visuals

Possible answer: *The details of this painting suggest that Benjamin Franklin was a thoughtful and literate man. He is reading and pondering, as denoted by his look of thoughtful contemplation. He wears a wig and is elegantly dressed, which suggests that he gained some wealth and status in his life.*

REVISIT THE BIG QUESTION

Is PERFECTION *possible?*

Discuss In lines 5–9, does Franklin find self-improvement easy? **Possible answer:** *No. He realizes that when he focuses on fixing one fault, another one of his faults appears. He also finds that habit and temptation are both difficult to overcome.*

- What goal does Franklin set for himself? (lines 1–2)

- Is Franklin easily able to control his faults? Explain. (lines 5–9)

- What does Franklin say must be done in order to maintain a "uniform rectitude of conduct"? (lines 9–12)

FOR STRUGGLING READERS

Develop Reading Fluency Use the Targeted Passage on page 268 to demonstrate how to read aloud with proper attention to semicolons. Point out the four semicolons in the passage, then tell students these punctuation marks, which fall between two clauses that could stand alone as sentences, indicate a pause almost as long as a period. Ask students to listen for these pauses as you model reading the passage aloud. You may also want them to echo-read.

From line 24 through the end of the list of virtues, use these prompts to have students reflect on Franklin's list:

Connect Think about a time when you set a goal to change an aspect of your behavior. How does that experience help you understand Franklin's goals? *Answers will vary but should show an understanding of the universality of Franklin's desire to improve.*

Interpret Read virtue #4: Resolution. How would achieving this virtue lead to moral perfection? *Possible answer: If people always do what they should and do what they promise to do, then they will be reliable and trustworthy—traits that a morally perfect person must have.*

Evaluate How do you respond to Franklin's list? Would you change the virtues on it, either by adding or removing virtues? Explain. *Answers should reflect a definition of moral perfection and how adding or removing specific virtues would help achieve such perfection.*

READING SKILL
COMMON CORE RI 1

B *Model the Skill:*
MAKE INFERENCES

Tell students that they can infer that—because Franklin points out 13 areas for self-improvement—he feels his moral character is far from perfect. Have students make another inference about Franklin's list *Possible answer: Many of the areas focus on using things wisely, so Franklin must have found waste immoral.*

VOCABULARY
COMMON CORE L 4

OWN THE WORD

trifling: Have students name antonyms for *trifling*. *Possible answers: consequential, important, considerable, major, appreciable*

---

fewer ideas under the same name. Temperance, for example, was by some confined to eating and drinking, while by others it was extended to mean the moderating every other pleasure, appetite, inclination, or passion, bodily or mental, even to
20 our avarice and ambition. I proposed to myself, for the sake of clearness, to use rather more names, with fewer ideas annexed to each, than a few names with more ideas; and I included under thirteen names of virtues all that at that time occurred to me as necessary or desirable, and annexed to each a short precept, which fully expressed the extent I gave to its meaning.

These names of virtues, with their precepts were:

1. **TEMPERANCE.** Eat not to dullness; drink not to elevation.

2. **SILENCE.** Speak not but what may benefit others or yourself; avoid **trifling** conversation.

3. **ORDER.** Let all your things have their places; let each part of your business have its time.

4. **RESOLUTION.** Resolve to perform what you ought; perform without fail what you resolve.

5. **FRUGALITY.** Make no expense but to do good to others or yourself; *i.e.,* waste nothing.

6. **INDUSTRY.** Lose no time; be always employed in something useful; cut off all unnecessary actions.

7. **SINCERITY.** Use no hurtful deceit; think innocently and justly; and, if you speak, speak accordingly.

8. **JUSTICE.** Wrong none by doing injuries, or omitting the benefits that are your duty.

9. **MODERATION.** Avoid extremes; forbear resenting injuries so much as you think they deserve.

10. **CLEANLINESS.** Tolerate no uncleanliness in body, clothes, or habitation.

11. **TRANQUILLITY.** Be not disturbed at trifles, or at accidents common or unavoidable.

12. **CHASTITY.** Rarely use venery but for health or offspring, never to dulness, weakness, or the injury of your own or another's peace or reputation.

13. **HUMILITY.** Imitate Jesus and Socrates.[1] **B**

My intention being to acquire the *habitude* of all these virtues, I judged it would be well not to distract my attention by attempting the whole at once, but to fix it on one of them at a time; and, when I should be master of that, then to proceed to another, and so on, till I should have gone through the thirteen; and, as the previous acquisition of some might facilitate the acquisition of certain others, I
30 arranged them with that view, as they stand above. Temperance first, as it tends to

---

1. **Socrates** (sŏk′rə-tēz′): Greek philosopher (470?–399 B.C.) who believed that true knowledge comes through dialogue and systematic questioning of ideas; he was executed for his beliefs.

270 UNIT 1: EARLY AMERICAN WRITING

Language Coach

Conciseness in Writing Franklin's precepts (following line 24) are concise, or brief and clear. Reread lines 19–23, and explain Franklin's reasons for giving concise explanations of the virtues. Why are fewer words more effective?

trifling (trī′flĭng) *adj.* frivolous; inconsequential **trifle** *v.*

2 **Targeted Passage**

B **MAKE INFERENCES**
Based on Franklin's list of virtues, what inference can you make about his view of his own moral character? Explain.

DIFFERENTIATED INSTRUCTION

FOR STRUGGLING READERS

2 **Targeted Passage** [Lines 24–30]

This passage presents Franklin's list of virtues and explains how he intends to follow it.

- What is the first virtue on the list? What is the last one? (numbered items 1 and 13)

- Does Franklin intend to focus on all virtues at the same time? Explain. (lines 25–28)

- How will acquiring each virtue help Franklin acquire the virtues that follow? (line 29)

FOR ENGLISH LANGUAGE LEARNERS

Language Coach

Conciseness in Writing *Possible answer: Fewer words may be more effective when the writer wants to make a single point.* Ask students to rewrite this sentence making it more concise: We try to work to improve the way we act and the way we speak in order to be people who are better.

procure that coolness and clearness of head, which is so necessary where constant vigilance was to be kept up, and guard maintained against the **unremitting** attraction of ancient habits, and the force of perpetual temptations. This being acquired and established, Silence would be more easy; and my desire being to gain knowledge at the same time that I improved in virtue, and considering that in conversation it was obtained rather by the use of the ears than of the tongue, and therefore wishing to break a habit I was getting into of prattling, punning, and joking, which only made me acceptable to trifling company, I gave *Silence* the second place. This and the next, *Order,* I expected would allow me more time for

40 attending to my project and my studies. *Resolution,* once become habitual, would keep me firm in my endeavors to obtain all the subsequent virtues; *Frugality* and Industry freeing me from my remaining debt, and producing **affluence** and independence, would make more easy the practice of Sincerity and Justice, etc., etc. Conceiving then, that, agreeably to the advice of Pythagoras in his Golden Verses,[2] daily examination would be necessary, I **contrived** the following method for conducting that examination. **C**

I made a little book, in which I allotted a page for each of the virtues. I ruled each page with red ink, so as to have seven columns, one for each day of the week, marking each column with a letter for the day. I crossed these columns with

50 thirteen red lines, marking the beginning of each line with the first letter of one of the virtues, on which line, and in its proper column, I might mark, by a little black spot, every fault I found upon examination to have been committed respecting that virtue upon that day.

I determined to give a week's strict attention to each of the virtues successively. Thus, in the first week,

60 my great guard was to avoid every[3] the least offense against *Temperance,* leaving the other virtues to their ordinary chance, only marking every evening the faults of the day. Thus, if in the first week I could keep my first line, marked T, clear of spots, I supposed the habit of that virtue so much strengthened, and its opposite weakened, that I might venture

70 extending my attention to include the next, and for the following week keep both lines clear of spots. Proceeding

Form of the pages.

TEMPERANCE						
eat not to dullness; drink not to elevation.						
	S.	M.	T.	W.	T.	F.	S.
T.							
S.	•	•		•		•	
O.	••	•	•		•	•	•
R.			•			•	
F.		•			•		
I.			•	•			
S.							
J.							
M.							
C.							
T.							
C.							
H.							

2. **Pythagoras** (pĭ-thăg′ər-əs)... **Golden Verses:** Pythagoras was a Greek philosopher and mathematician (580?–500? B.C.).

3. **every:** even.

---

unremitting
(ŭn′rĭ-mĭt′ĭng) *adj.*
constant; never stopping

affluence (ăf′lōō-əns) *n.*
wealth

contrive (kən-trīv′) *v.* to plan skillfully; to design

C MAKE INFERENCES
What can you infer from lines 25–46 about Franklin's approach to problems?

Language Coach

Easily Confused Words
Although *successively* (line 59) and *successfully* sound and look similar, their meanings are different. *Successively* means "following in order, one after another." *Successfully* means "with the result of achieving a goal." Use each word in a sentence to explain Franklin's plan for perfection.

C MAKE INFERENCES

Possible answer: *Franklin is both methodical and disciplined when he attempts to solve a problem. He methodically determines a procedure for focusing on one virtue at a time (lines 25–30) and is able to explain why one virtue must be mastered before another (lines 30–44). He is disciplined enough to follow and maintain a "daily examination" of his conduct (line 45).*

IF STUDENTS NEED HELP... Refer them to lines 25–28, in which Franklin describes his methodology, and 30–44, in which he describes his reasons for that methodology. Then work with them to list details and inferences in the prereading chart introduced on page 267.

VOCABULARY   COMMON CORE L 4

OWN THE WORD

- **unremitting:** Reread the sentence containing *unremitting* and draw attention to Franklin's use of similar adjectives to reinforce his message, *"constant* vigilance," *"unremitting* attraction," and *"perpetual* temptations." Have students write a sentence that uses these three adjectives to describe a persistent situation. ***Possible answer:*** *Becoming a top athlete requires* constant *practice,* unremitting *motivation, and* perpetual *attention to diet.*

- **affluence:** Tell students that affluence comes from the Latin, *ad + fluere,* meaning "to flow toward." Ask students to name other words that come from the Latin *fluere.* ***Possible answers:*** *fluent, influence, superfluous*

- **contrive:** Tell students that the noun *contrivance* means "a device, tool, plan, or design." Have them write a pair of sentences that demonstrate understanding of the noun and the verb.

FOR STRUGGLING READERS

Summarize Reread lines 30–44 with students and ask them to explain in their own words why Franklin listed the first five virtues in the order that he did. For example, Franklin believed that temperance helped a person think clearly and avoid both old, damaging habits and temptations. This virtue, thus, would help him acquire the other 12 virtues.

FOR ENGLISH LANGUAGE LEARNERS

Language Coach

Easily Confused Words *Possible answer: Franklin felt he would* successfully *accomplish his list of virtues if he worked on them* successively. Give students more practice by having them write correct sentences for *obtain* (line 41) and *attain.*

TEXT ANALYSIS

ⓓ Model the Skill:
AUTOBIOGRAPHY

Tell students that in an autobiography an individual may analyze different phases of his or her life: Point out that Franklin wrote these words as an older man: he described his younger years in great detail.

Possible answer: *He writes about the plan he devised for achieving that goal (lines 47–74), and the analogy about the garden that he uses suggests a sense of humor about his youthful ambition to achieve perfection (lines 74–77).*

---

thus to the last, I could go through a course complete in thirteen weeks, and four courses in a year. And like him who, having a garden to weed, does not attempt to eradicate all the bad herbs at once, which would exceed his reach and his strength, but works on one of the beds at a time, and, having accomplished the first, proceeds to a second, so I should have, I hoped, the encouraging pleasure of seeing on my pages the progress I made in virtue, by clearing successively my lines of their spots, till in the end, by a number of courses, I should be happy in viewing a
80 clean book, after thirteen weeks' daily examination. . . . ⓓ

The precept of *Order* requiring that *every part of my business should have its allotted time,* one page in my little book contained the following scheme of employment for the twenty-four hours of a natural day.

ⓓ AUTOBIOGRAPHY
In what way do lines 47–80 provide an example of Franklin's **dual perspective?**

THE MORNING. *Question.* What good shall I do this day?	5 6 7	Rise, wash, and address *Powerful Goodness!* Contrive day's business, and take the resolution of the day; prosecute the present study, and breakfast.
	8 9 10 11	Work.
NOON.	12 1	Read, or overlook my accounts, and dine.
	2 3 4 5	Work.
EVENING. *Question.* What good have I done today?	6 7 8 9	Put things in their places. Supper. Music or diversion, or conversation. Conversation. Examination of the day.
NIGHT.	10 11 12 1 2 3 4	Sleep.

272   UNIT 1: EARLY AMERICAN WRITING

DIFFERENTIATED INSTRUCTION

FOR STRUGGLING READERS

Characterization Read over the page of Franklin's book regarding Order and ask students these questions to help them characterize Franklin:

- What time does Franklin arise in the morning and what does he do? (5 A.M., *wash*)
- What does he do from 9 A.M. to 5 P.M.? (*work*)

- How does he spend his evenings? **Possible answer:** *He cleans up, eats, and listens to music or converses with others.*
- What words would you use to describe Franklin based on his daily schedule and activities? **Possible answer:** *serious, organized* Help students to recognize that Franklin is disciplined, serious, and industrious.

I entered upon the execution of this plan for self-examination, and continued it with occasional intermissions for some time. I was surprised to find myself so much fuller of faults than I had imagined; but I had the satisfaction of seeing them diminish. To avoid the trouble of renewing now and then my little book, which, by scraping out the marks on the paper of old faults to make room for new ones in a new course, became full of holes, I transferred my tables and precepts to the ivory
90 leaves of a memorandum book, on which the lines were drawn with red ink, that made a durable stain, and on those lines I marked my faults with a black-lead pencil, which marks I could easily wipe out with a wet sponge. After a while I went through one course only in a year, and afterward only one in several years, till at length I omitted them entirely, being employed in voyages and business abroad, with a multiplicity of affairs that interfered; but I always carried my little book with me. **E**

My scheme of *Order* gave me the most trouble; and I found that, though it might be practicable where a man's business was such as to leave him the disposition of his time, that of a journeyman printer, for instance, it was not possible to be exactly observed by a master, who must mix with the world, and
100 often receive people of business at their own hours. *Order,* too, with regard to places for things, papers, etc., I found extremely difficult to acquire. I had not been early accustomed to it, and, having an exceeding good memory, I was not so sensible of the inconvenience attending want of method. This article, therefore, cost me so much painful attention, and my faults in it vexed me so much, and I made so little progress in amendment, and had such frequent relapses, that I was almost ready to give up the attempt, and content myself with a faulty character in that respect, like the man who, in buying an ax of a smith, my neighbor, desired to have the whole of its surface as bright as the edge. The smith consented to grind it bright for him if he would turn the wheel; he turned, while the smith pressed
110 the broad face of the ax hard and heavily on the stone, which made the turning of it very fatiguing. The man came every now and then from the wheel to see how the work went on, and at length would take his ax as it was, without farther grinding. "No," said the smith, "turn on, turn on; we shall have it bright by-and-by; as yet, it is only speckled." "Yes," says the man, *"but I think I like a speckled ax best."* And I believe this may have been the case with many, who, having, for want of some such means as I employed, found the difficulty of obtaining good and breaking bad habits in other points of vice and virtue, have given up the struggle, and concluded that *"a speckled ax was best;"* for something, that pretended to be reason, was every now and then suggesting to me that such extreme nicety as I
120 exacted of myself might be a kind of foppery in morals,[4] which, if it were known, would make me ridiculous; that a perfect character might be attended with the inconvenience of being envied and hated; and that a benevolent man should allow a few faults in himself, to keep his friends in countenance. **F**

In truth, I found myself **incorrigible** with respect to Order; and now I am grown old, and my memory bad, I feel very sensibly the want of it. But, on the whole, though I never arrived at the perfection I had been so ambitious of

---

4. **foppery in morals:** excessive regard for and concern about one's moral appearance.

THE AUTOBIOGRAPHY **273**

---

③ Targeted Passage

E MAKE INFERENCES
Reread lines 84–95. What can you infer about Franklin's persistence in pursuing his goals?

F CONNECT
What insight does Franklin come to about his quest for perfection? Consider what you have learned in your own life about perfection. Does his insight seem reasonable?

incorrigible
(ĭn-kôr′ĭ-jə-bəl) *adj.*
incapable of being reformed or corrected

READING SKILL COMMON CORE RI 1

E MAKE INFERENCES
Possible answer: Franklin is persistent in pursuing his goals. He wears out the paper of the first book he started and has to replace it (lines 87–92). He uses phrases such as "for some time" (line 85), "in a year" (line 93), and "in several years" (line 93) to show that he continued his pursuit.

TIERED DISCUSSION PROMPTS
In lines 96–108, use these prompts to help students understand Franklin's character:

Analyze What causes Franklin to have such difficulty with Order? *Possible answer: Franklin had to deal with others and meet with people for business at hours convenient to them (lines 99–100). He also had a good memory and therefore never had to order things to find them (lines 101–103).*

Synthesize Based on what you know about Franklin's character, would you expect him to give up trying to acquire Order and the other virtues? *Possible answer: No. Franklin seems clever enough to overcome his bad habits. Also, because he says he practiced his method over the years (line 93), he clearly did not stop trying.*

READING SKILL: *Review*

F CONNECT
Possible answer: Franklin decides that it might be better to accept and live with a few faults so that he won't be envied or seem too smug to his friends (lines 121–123). His insight seems reasonable, as people are imperfect and thus feel more comfortable with others who recognize this.

VOCABULARY COMMON CORE L 4

OWN THE WORD

incorrigible: Have students create a semantic web for *incorrigible.* Write the word in a center circle and add the definition given, "incapable of being reformed or corrected." Draw spider legs and have students add synonyms to complete the map. *Possible answers: irredeemable, hopeless, intractable, unruly*

FOR STRUGGLING READERS

③ Targeted Passage [Lines 84–107]

This passage shows Franklin's diligence and describes his problems in seeking perfection.

• According to Franklin, how flawed is he? How does he respond to finding faults in himself? (lines 84–92)

• Does Franklin continue to work on perfecting these virtues after his first attempt? (lines 92–95)

• What virtue does Franklin struggle with most? How does he react to this struggle? (lines 96–107)

FOR ENGLISH LANGUAGE LEARNERS

Vocabulary: Idioms Help students use context clues to determine the meanings of these idioms: *met with* (line 14), "found"; *gone through* (line 28), "completed"; *on the whole* (lines 125–126), "in summary"; *fell short of* (line 127), "failed"; *reap the benefit* (line 146), "gain or benefit."

THE AUTOBIOGRAPHY **273**

Analyze Visuals

Activity Ask students which virtue of Franklin's this picture best represents. ***Possible answer:*** *The picture suggests Franklin's success at Industry (lines 42–43, 138), as it shows him working hard at the Pennsylvania Gazette— the newspaper he ran.*

REVISIT THE BIG QUESTION
Is PERFECTION *possible?*

Discuss In lines 124–131, in what ways did Franklin succeed in his quest for self-improvement? In what ways did he fail? *Accept all thoughtful answers.*

TEXT ANALYSIS   COMMON CORE

Ⓖ AUTOBIOGRAPHY   RI 5
                            RI 6

Possible answer: *Franklin describes the significant moment when he realizes that he "fell short of" his goal of moral perfection (line 127), and yet he realizes that the attempt has still made him a better person (lines 127–128).*

VOCABULARY   COMMON CORE

OWN THE WORD   L 4

- **artifice:** Point out that *artifice* comes from the Latin *ars* "skill" + *facere* "to make."
- **felicity:** Have students write a sentence describing something that brings them *felicity* in their lives. ***Possible answer:*** *Getting together with friends gives me a great deal of* felicity.

SELECTION WRAP–UP

READ WITH A PURPOSE Ask students what Franklin learned about himself as he examined his conduct. ***Possible answer:*** *Franklin learned he had more faults than he expected, but it made him happy to watch them decline. Though he failed at mastering Order, he enjoyed trying.*

INDEPENDENT READING

For students wanting to read more about Franklin, suggest *Benjamin Franklin: An American Life* by Walter Isaacson.

obtaining, but fell short of it, yet I was, by the endeavor, a better and a happier man than I otherwise should have been if I had not attempted it; as those who aim at perfect writing by imitating the engraved copies, though they never reach
130 the wished-for excellence of those copies, their hand is mended by the endeavor, and is tolerable while it continues fair and legible. Ⓖ

It may well be my posterity should be informed that to this little **artifice,** with the blessing of God, their ancestor owed the constant **felicity** of his life, down to his 79th year, in which this is written. What reverses may attend the reminder is in the hand of Providence; but, if they arrive, the reflection on past happiness enjoyed ought to help his bearing them with more resignation. To Temperance he ascribes his long-continued health, and what is still left to him of a good constitution; to Industry and Frugality, the early easiness of his circumstances and acquisition of his fortune, with all that knowledge that enabled him to be a useful
140 citizen, and obtained for him some degree of reputation among the learned; to Sincerity and Justice, the confidence of his country, and the honorable employs it conferred upon him; and to the joint influence of the whole mass of the virtues, even in the the imperfect state he was able to acquire them, all that evenness of temper, and that cheerfulness in conversation, which makes his company still sought for, and agreeable even to his younger acquaintance. I hope, therefore, that some of my descendants may follow the example and reap the benefit. ❧

Ⓖ AUTOBIOGRAPHY
What **significant moment** or insight is described in this paragraph?

artifice (är′tə-fĭs) *n.* a clever means to an end

felicity (fĭ-lĭs′ĭ-tē) *n.* great happiness

④ Targeted Passage

DIFFERENTIATED INSTRUCTION

FOR STRUGGLING READERS

④ Targeted Passage [Lines 132–146]

This passage explains what Franklin gained from his quest for moral perfection.

- What virtues does Franklin name to show that he benefited from practicing? (lines 124–128)
- How does the imperfect practice of all of the virtues affect his life? (lines 134–145)
- What does Franklin want for his descendants? (lines 145–146)

FOR ADVANCED LEARNERS/AP

Analyze Literary Nonfiction [SMALL-GROUP OPTION] Recall with students that they learn a lot about Franklin's character through both his topic choices and writing style. Organize students into small groups. Assign groups one or two topics from the Analysis Frame: Literary Nonfiction. Have groups discuss and then summarize their thoughts for the class.

🧰 **BEST PRACTICES TOOLKIT—Transparency**
Analysis Frame: Literary Nonfiction
pp. D21, D48

from Poor Richard's Almanack

BENJAMIN FRANKLIN

He that cannot obey cannot command.

Don't count your chickens before they are hatched.

A mob's a monster; heads enough but no brains.

Well done is better than well said.

Lost time is never found again.

Early to bed, early to rise, makes a man healthy, wealthy and wise.

If you would know the worth of money, go and try to borrow some.

A friend in need is a friend indeed.

Fish and visitors smell in three days.

Love your neighbor; yet don't pull down your hedge.

God helps them that help themselves.

If you would keep your secret from an enemy, tell it not to a friend.

Be slow in choosing a friend, slower in changing.

Don't throw stones at your neighbors', if your own windows are glass.

Eat to live and not live to eat.

Love your enemies, for they tell you your faults.

Better slip with foot than tongue.

Three may keep a secret, if two of them are dead.

Never leave that till tomorrow, which you can do today.

A penny saved is a penny earned.

A rolling stone gathers no moss.

Make hay while the sun shines.

Beware of little expenses; a small leak will sink a great ship.

He that goes a borrowing goes a sorrowing.

Honesty is the best policy.

Little strokes fell big oaks.

He that lies down with dogs shall rise up with fleas.

TIERED DISCUSSION PROMPTS

Use these prompts to help students link Benjamin Franklin's sayings to the virtues he valued:

Connect What experiences do these sayings bring to mind? How do the sayings help you understand Franklin's character and search for moral perfection? *Possible answer: Accept all thoughtful answers. The sayings show that Franklin was witty, forthright, and honest, and that he valued productivity and relationships. Most of the sayings reflect at least one of his goals for moral perfection.*

Analyze Select five aphorisms. Under which of Franklin's 13 virtues would each of these aphorisms be listed? *Students' answers will vary but should reflect an understanding of the aphorism, the virtue, and a reasonable link between them. For example, the aphorism "Early to bed, early to rise, makes a man healthy, wealthy and wise" matches the virtue "Industry."*

Evaluate Focus on several aphorisms. Do you agree with the opinions Franklin expresses in them? Explain and defend your answer. *Students' answers will vary but should show an understanding of the sentiment expressed in each aphorism. For example, students may disagree with the idea of choosing friends slowly or agree with the idea of always being honest.*

Practice and Apply

For preliminary support of post-reading questions, use these copy masters:

R RESOURCE MANAGER—Copy Masters
Reading Check p. 360
Characteristics of Autobiography p. 353
Question Support p. 361

Additional selection questions are provided for teachers on page 347.

ANSWERS

COMMON CORE **RI 1, RI 5, RI 6**

1. *Jesus and Socrates*

2. *Franklin decides to attack one virtue at a time and believes that mastering some first would help him master the others later.*

3. *Franklin creates a 13-page book with pages for each virtue. He divides each page into seven columns for the days of the week and 13 rows for the virtues. Each day he marks the columns with a black spot for a lapse. Each week, he focuses on acquiring a different virtue (lines 47–72).*

Possible answers:

4. ■ **COMMON CORE FOCUS** *Make Inferences About the Author* **healthful living:** *temperance, moderation, cleanliness, tranquility;* **succeeding in the world:** *resolution, frugality, industry, order;* **getting along with others:** *silence, sincerity, justice, chastity, humility. Franklin's list of virtues reveal his belief in reason and his faith in humanity to improve and progress. He seems to value a life well lived.*

5. ● **COMMON CORE FOCUS** *Analyze Autobiography* **Young Franklin** *Character Trait: reasonable and methodical, funny, diligent;* **Evidence in Text:** *devises virtues list and orderly plan to achieve them (lines 14–30, 47–74), recognizes his habit of "prattling, punning, and joking" (lines 37–38), carries his little book with him (line 95);* **Old Franklin** *Character Trait: successful, trustworthy, cheerful, and even-tempered;* **Evidence in Text:** *acquired a fortune (line 139), gained his nation's confidence (line 141), became sought-after (lines 143–145). Students may conclude that Franklin portrays himself more favorably as an older man than as an inexperienced youth.*

Comprehension

1. **Recall** Who are Franklin's models for the virtue of humility?

2. **Clarify** Why does Franklin list the virtues in the order he does?

3. **Summarize** What is Franklin's method for acquiring the 13 virtues?

Text Analysis

● 4. **Make Inferences About the Author** Look at the details and inferences you recorded in your chart. Now assign each of Franklin's 13 virtues to one of the following categories. What can you infer about Franklin's beliefs and values in general from his list of virtues?

   • healthful living   • succeeding in the world   • getting along with others

● 5. **Analyze Autobiography** Like most autobiographies, Franklin's has a dual perspective in which he is both main character and narrator. Go back through the excerpt to find characterizations of Franklin as a young man and as an older man looking back on his life. Record your answers in two charts as shown. What differences do you find?

Young Franklin	
Character Trait	Evidence in Text
1. Ambitious	1. "I conceived the bold and arduous project of arriving at moral perfection." (lines 1–2)
2.	

Old Franklin	
Character Trait	Evidence in Text
1. Honest	1. "In truth, I found myself incorrigible with respect to Order; and now I am grown old, ... I feel very sensibly the want of it." (lines 124–125)
2.	

6. **Analyze Aphorisms** Franklin wrote many **aphorisms**—brief, clever statements that make wise observations about life. How might Franklin's aphorisms have helped him and others come closer to perfection?

Text Criticism

7. **Critical Interpretations** Some critics consider Franklin self-righteous and materialistic; others have ridiculed his plan for moral perfection as regimented and superficial. Do you find any evidence for these charges in the excerpt? Explain.

Is **PERFECTION** *possible?*

Although Franklin worked diligently, he never reached perfection in all facets of his life. In what areas have you tried to reach perfection? How would you rate your efforts at **self-improvement**?

COMMON CORE

RI 1 Cite textual evidence to support inferences drawn from the text, including determining where the text leave matters uncertain. **RI 5** Analyze and evaluate the effectiveness of the structure an author uses in his or her exposition. **RI 6** Determine an author's point of view or purpose.

---

6. *Aphorisms are easy to remember, so people seeking perfection could remind themselves about what to do and also, share the aphorisms with others.*

7. *Students may say that Franklin's virtues seem materialistic and regimented and leave no room for feelings. However, what some would see as smug or self-righteous can also appear as an honest assessment of the author's successes and failures (lines 136–146).*

Is PERFECTION *possible?*
Students may mention areas of life with which they do not yet have much experience. Remind them that, as Franklin found, it can take years to master a virtue or even make significant improvement.

Vocabulary in Context

▲ VOCABULARY PRACTICE

Show your understanding of the vocabulary words by answering these questions.

WORD LIST

WORD LIST
affluence
artifice
contrive
felicity
incorrigible
trifling
unremitting

1. Which would cause **felicity,** doing well on a test or having trouble sleeping?
2. If someone created an **artifice,** would that person be shrewd or naïve?
3. To **contrive,** would you act impulsively or by plan?
4. Who is more likely **incorrigible,** a person with five parking tickets or one with five burglary convictions?
5. Is a **trifling** problem one you should ignore or act on immediately?
6. If you wanted to hide your **affluence,** would you probably drive an inexpensive car or take a trip around the world?
7. Is a person with **unremitting** joy constantly happy or never happy?

ACADEMIC VOCABULARY IN WRITING

• document • illustrate • interpret • promote • reveal

Some people have **interpreted** Benjamin Franklin's autobiography in a negative light. Write a short paragraph discussing the kind of lifestyle Franklin **promoted.** In your paper, also discuss how close you think most people come to meeting his expectations. Use at least three Academic Vocabulary words in your writing.

VOCABULARY STRATEGY: COGNATES IN DIFFERENT LANGUAGES

The Romance languages—French, Italian, and Spanish—developed from Latin. Although English is not one of the Romance languages, many English words did originate in Latin. When words in different languages are descended from the same language and have similar or identical spellings and meanings, they are called cognates. For example, the spelling of "animal" is exactly the same in English and Spanish. The English word "rose" has a similar spelling, "rosa," in Spanish.

PRACTICE Identify the English cognate of each of the following Spanish words. Then write an English sentence using the English word.

1. tecnología
2. novela
3. diccionario
4. arrogante
5. fotographia

COMMON CORE

L 6 Demonstrate independence in gathering vocabulary knowledge when considering a word or phrase important to comprehension or expression.

Interactive Vocabulary THINK central

Go to thinkcentral.com.
KEYWORD: HML11-277

ANSWERS

Vocabulary in Context

▲ VOCABULARY PRACTICE

1. *doing well*
2. *shrewd*
3. *by plan*
4. *five convictions*
5. *ignore*
6. *drive inexpensive car*
7. *constantly happy*

R RESOURCE MANAGER—Copy Master
Vocabulary Practice p. 358

ACADEMIC VOCABULARY IN WRITING

Tell student to begin by making inferences about the lifestyle Franklin promoted and how that lifestyle translates to today's world.

VOCABULARY STRATEGY: COGNATES IN DIFFERENT LANGUAGES

COMMON CORE **L 6**

Remind students to use knowledge of roots and prefixes to determine word meaning.

Answers:

1. *technology*
2. *novel*
3. *dictionary*
4. *arrogance*
5. *photograph*

Sentences will vary.

R RESOURCE MANAGER—Copy Master
Vocabulary Strategy p. 359

Interactive Vocabulary  THINK central

Keywords direct students to a **WordSharp** tutorial on **thinkcentral.com** or to other types of vocabulary practice and review.

DIFFERENTIATED INSTRUCTION

FOR ENGLISH LANGUAGE LEARNERS

Task Support: Vocabulary Practice To help students complete the practice activity, refer to the vocabulary activity on page 267. Suggest that they insert the synonym or definition from that activity into the practice sentences on page 277. For example, if they defined *felicity* as "cheerfulness," they should easily see that this feeling would result from doing well on a test, not from having trouble sleeping.

FOR ADVANCED LEARNERS/AP

Cognates [paired option] Have pairs write a list of five sentences similar to those in the **Vocabulary Strategy.** Encourage pairs to be as creative as possible when constructing their sentences but to include enough context to clearly identify the missing word. Then have pairs switch their sentences with another pair and see if they can complete the sentences correctly.

Assess and Reteach

Assess

DIAGNOSTIC AND SELECTION TESTS
Selection Test A pp. 97–98
Selection Test B/C pp. 99–100

Interactive Selection Test on **thinkcentral.com**

Reteach

Level Up Online Tutorials on **thinkcentral.com**

Reteaching Worksheets on **thinkcentral.com**

Reading Lesson 8, Vocabulary Lesson 7

MAGAZINE ARTICLE Benjamin Franklin's drive for self-improvement may seem a little excessive, but it remains a great American ideal. This article looks at the continuing American urge to change oneself for the better.

CONNECT

This selection connects with the pursuit of self-improvement that Franklin embarks on in his autobiography. You can also use it as a mini-lesson on reading for information.

READING FOR INFORMATION

Point out that "50 Ways to Fix Your Life" is a magazine article. Then ask:

- What does the title of a magazine article tell readers? What might the writer hope to accomplish with the title? *Possible answer: The title tells readers what an article's subject will be. The writer usually hopes to engage readers' interest.*

- What is the main idea of this article? *Possible answer: It is possible to transform your life if you are ready to do so.*

TIERED DISCUSSION PROMPTS

Use these prompts to help students connect modern approaches to self-improvement with Benjamin Franklin's ideas:

Connect How did reading this article affect your response to Franklin's goal of moral perfection? *Accept all reasonable answers.*

Interpret According to this article, why are Americans so attracted to the idea of self-improvement? *Possible answer: In America, people believe that they can change themselves and their lives. They are not restricted by their current situation or by class.*

Synthesize What do this writer and Franklin both say must happen for people to improve themselves? How are the two writers' views different? *Possible answer: Both Butler and Franklin say people must want to change, that they should record their progress, and that they will gain "lasting benefits" from making the effort, even if they experience setbacks along the way. Franklin does not mention the need for social support to help people improve.*

50 Ways to Fix Your Life

by Carolyn Kleiner Butler

Americans have long been captivated by the notion of self-improvement—none more so than Benjamin Franklin. An accomplished printer, author, postmaster, scientist, inventor, and diplomat who taught himself to speak five languages, this Founding Father "conceiv'd the bold and arduous project of arriving at moral perfection."

Today, self-help is not just a way of life—it's practically a national obsession. There are 7,500 books on the topic on amazon.com alone, covering just about every imaginable bad habit or dilemma.

Such offerings "appeal to the deeply felt American idea of 'before and after,'" says Robert Thompson, professor of media and popular culture at Syracuse University in New York, who points out the underlying similarities between Franklin and, say, Dr. Phil. "If you were born a peasant in a medieval village, you knew who you were and it was very hard to change that, but here there is fluidity of class, and entire industries pop up that reflect the ultimate optimism that really anybody can be a 'swan' and completely turn [his or her] life around."

Time to change. The hard truth is that lasting change doesn't usually happen in a single TV season. In reality, of the 40 to 45 percent of people who will make New Year's resolutions come January, fewer than half will succeed within six months, according to John Norcross, professor of psychology at the University of Scranton in Pennsylvania and coauthor of *Changing for Good*. But the fact is that when someone makes a serious commitment to transform his or her life, it is possible.

How can you cross that far-off finish line? First and foremost, you really have to be ready to do it and understand that the pros outweigh the cons. Also, research shows that keeping track of your development in a visible way— charting your weight loss, for one, or graphing your heart rate and stamina— is associated with sustainable lifestyle change, as is social support, whether in the form of friends, online discussion groups, or reliable, proven, self-help books.

Lastly, and most important, don't give up if you tumble off the wagon now and then. Triumphant changers often see a setback as a reason to recommit to their goal, and they get back on the horse immediately.

In the end, simply making a concerted effort to improve your lifestyle can have lasting benefits, no matter what the final result. Indeed, Franklin recounts, "On the whole, tho' I never arrived at . . . perfection . . . I was, by the endeavour, a better and happier man than I otherwise should have been if I had not attempted it."

Revolutionary Ideas

For colonists living in the 1770s, there was one topic around which most conversation and writing revolved: the Revolution. The writing of this period was political, and it was persuasive. It had a life-and-death purpose: to win over the hearts and minds of American colonists—and the rest of the world—to the belief that rebellion was necessary.

Writing to Persuade

Reflect briefly on each of the pieces you have just read, and select two you find particularly persuasive. Then, imagine you are a colonist of the time and write a letter to your local paper in which you voice your support for the ideas of the writers chosen. Be sure to cite specific phrases or lines that you find convincing. Add your own thoughts and opinions to try to further persuade readers to support the rebellion.

Consider

- thought-provoking or incendiary sentences or passages
- your opinions on the issues discussed in the selections
- how to express your viewpoint clearly and convincingly

Give Me Liberty or Give Me Death. Patrick Henry delivering his great speech on the *Rights of the Colonies* before the Virginia Assembly, Richmond, March 23, 1775. The Granger Collection, New York.

279

Extension

SPEAKING & LISTENING
Imagine yourself on the village green, part of an impassioned gathering of colonists arguing both sides of independence from England. Recast your letter as a **speech** and deliver it to your friends, neighbors, and political opponents.

COMMON CORE

RI 9 Analyze eighteenth-century foundational U.S. documents of historical and literary significance for their themes, purposes, and rhetorical features. **W 1** Write arguments to support claims in an analysis of substantive texts, using valid reasoning and relevant and sufficient evidence. **SL 4** Present information, findings, and supporting evidence, conveying a clear and distinct perspective.

COMMON CORE FOCUS

RI 9 Analyze eighteenth-century foundational U.S. documents of historical and literary significance for their themes, purposes, and rhetorical features. **W 1** Write arguments to support claims in an analysis of substantive texts, using valid reasoning and relevant and sufficient evidence. **SL 4** Present information, findings, and supporting evidence, conveying a clear and distinct perspective.

WRAP-UP: WRITERS OF THE REVOLUTION

This Wrap-Up provides students with an opportunity to revisit ideas from the literature in this section about early America, including culture, customs, and commitment to change. Encourage students to examine their own views about early America in light of insights they gained from the selections.

Writing to Persuade

Review with students that *persuading* means using powerful words to influence others to agree with your way of thinking.

To help students write their letters, direct them to think about the selections they have read that most powerfully advanced colonial positions. Instruct them to choose a writer that they found interesting, or a position they identified with. Then, instruct them to go back to their selected piece and find excerpts that caught their attention. Have them write an outline of their letter before fleshing it out with supportive details and excerpts.

Extension

- Have students note the most passionate and persuasive comments in the selections from this section. Then ask students to consider how they might add appeals of this type to their letters. Review some of the persuasive techniques discussed in the Writing Workshop on pages 280–287.

- Direct students to organize their thoughts in a Three-Column Journal, using the headings *Author's Quotations, My Opinion,* and *Persuasive Appeals.* Remind students that their letters should include adequate support for any claims, as well as counterarguments.

 **BEST PRACTICES TOOLKIT—Transparency**
Three-Column Journal p. B10

DIFFERENTIATED INSTRUCTION

FOR STRUGGLING WRITERS

Writing Support Help students get started by directing them to relevant passages in the selections. For example, students might draw on lines 2–3 and 10–13 of "Letter to the Reverend Samson Occom" to write about natural rights and man's innate desire for freedom as arguments against slavery. Or they might draw on lines 13–31 of "Letter to John Adams" to write about what the colonists needed from their government, and why they needed to be free from England.

FOR ENGLISH LANGUAGE LEARNERS

Persuasive Techniques Ask students which selections they found most convincing and why. Help them use their responses to this question as a starting point to developing their own viewpoint.

I found Thomas Jefferson's arguments for independence very convincing. I believe that the colonies should be independent because _____.

Focus and Motivate

COMMON CORE FOCUS

W 1a–e Write arguments to support claims with valid reasoning and relevant evidence. **W 4** Produce clear and coherent writing appropriate to task, purpose, and audience. **W 5** Develop and strengthen writing as needed by planning, revising, editing, rewriting, or trying a new approach, focusing on how well purpose and audience have been addressed. **W 7** Conduct short research projects; synthesize multiple sources. **W 8** Gather relevant information from authoritative sources. **W 9b (RI 1)** Cite textual evidence. **W 10** Write routinely over shorter time frames for a range of tasks, purposes, and audiences. **L 2b** Spell correctly. **L 3** Apply knowledge of language to make effective choices for meaning and style.

WRITE WITH A PURPOSE

Have students review the Writing Task and choose an issue that interests them. Remind students that their purpose is to convince their audience to think or act in a certain way about an important issue.

COMMON CORE TRAITS

Review the *COMMON CORE TRAITS* with students, concentrating on both the development and the organization of ideas. Compare the list of traits with the rubric on page 288.

ADDITIONAL TASK

Write to Parents Write a letter to circulate to parents of students in your school, describing a way to change your school's class structure and explaining your reasons for wanting the change.

Possible subjects: college credit courses in high school, work-study programs, shortened or expanded school hours

Writing Online

The following tools are available online at **thinkcentral.com** and on **Write*Smart* CD-ROM**:
• Interactive Graphic Organizers
• Interactive Student Models
• Interactive Revision Lessons

Writing Workshop
ARGUMENT

Persuasive Essay

Essential Course of Study **ECOS**

You have seen how some of our country's founding fathers crafted arguments to support their **claims**, or positions, and to persuade readers to think a certain way. In this workshop, you will have the opportunity to assert a claim by writing a persuasive essay.

Complete the workshop activities in your **Reader/Writer Notebook**.

WRITE WITH A PURPOSE

WRITING TASK

Write a **persuasive essay** that argues a strong claim on an issue. Support your claim with reasons and evidence that will convince your audience to think or act in a certain way toward an issue that interests you.

Idea Starters
• an issue of interest to people in your school or community
• an issue involving the environment or social justice
• an issue about the freedoms and responsibilities of the media

THE ESSENTIALS

Here are some common purposes, audiences, and formats for persuasive writing.

PURPOSES	AUDIENCES	FORMATS
• to persuade people to agree with your claim • to motivate others to take action	• classmates and teacher • parents • community members • school board • customer service department • Web users	• essay for class • editorial • speech • commercial/PSA • message-board posting • business proposal • blog

COMMON CORE TRAITS

1. DEVELOPMENT OF IDEAS
• introduces a **precise, knowledgeable claim** and establishes its **significance**
• provides **valid reasons** and **relevant evidence** to support the claim
• acknowledges **opposing claims** and refutes them with **counterclaims**
• offers a **concluding section** that follows from and supports the claim

2. ORGANIZATION OF IDEAS
• **organizes** the claim, counterclaims, reasons, and evidence in a **logical sequence**
• uses varied **transitions**—words, phrases, and clauses—to create **cohesion** and **clarify relationships** among ideas

3. LANGUAGE FACILITY AND CONVENTIONS
• maintains a **formal style** and an **objective, authoritative tone**
• employs correct **grammar**, **mechanics**, and **spelling**

Writing Online **THINK** central
Go to **thinkcentral.com**.
KEYWORD: HML11N-280

Writing Workshop Resources

R RESOURCE MANAGER UNIT 1
Plan and Teach pp. 363–366
Prewriting–Editing pp. 367–371
Writing Rubric p. 372
Speaking and Listening p. 373
Writing Support p. 374*

BEST PRACTICES TOOLKIT
Writing Template: Persuasive Essay pp. C16, C31

TECHNOLOGY
 Teacher One Stop DVD-ROM
Student One Stop DVD-ROM
Write*Smart* CD-ROM
GrammarNotes DVD-ROM
Writing Center on thinkcentral.com

*See resources on the **Teacher One Stop DVD-ROM** and on **thinkcentral.com**.*

* Resources for Differentiation

Planning/Prewriting

 COMMON CORE **W 1a–e** Write arguments to support claims with valid reasoning and relevant evidence. **W 5** Develop writing by planning. **W 7** Conduct short research projects; synthesize multiple sources. **W 8** Gather relevant information from authoritative sources.

Getting Started

CHOOSE A SUBSTANTIVE ISSUE

Make a list of issues that interest you and might interest others. Select a **substantive issue**—one that you feel strongly about and can make a convincing argument for or against. The issue should be something reasonable people can disagree about—there's no point in arguing, for example, that cars should stop at school crosswalks.

THINK ABOUT AUDIENCE AND PURPOSE

Your **purpose** in writing a persuasive essay is to convince your **audience** to share your position on an issue and to take action. To convince your audience, you need to understand their background and perspective on the topic. Think about their concerns, values, and possible biases. Then you can choose the reasons and evidence that will be most convincing to them. To get your audience involved in your topic, be sure to establish the **significance** of viewpoint—why it should matter to them.

STATE YOUR CLAIM

Every issue has at least two sides—for it and against it. As a writer, you need to adopt a viewpoint on the issue and confidently state your position in a **precise claim**. Make sure your claim is a statement that you can prove and support with valid reasons and evidence. If you discover that your claim can't be supported easily, then you should rework it. Using a graphic organizer may help you clearly state your claim.

▶ **TIPS**

To find out about important issues, you could try the following:
- Talk to friends, classmates, or parents.
- Read your local newspaper.
- Attend school council meetings, school board meetings, or city or town meetings.

▶ **ASK YOURSELF:**

- Who will read my essay?
- What interest do my readers have in the issue?
- How do my readers currently feel about the issue? How do I know?
- What reasons might readers have for opposing my claim?

▶ **WHAT DOES IT LOOK LIKE?**

The Issue	Viewpoint	Claim
Cell phone use while driving	People should not be allowed to use cell phones while they drive.	Using cell phones—even hands-free models—to talk or send messages while driving must be banned now.

Planning/ Prewriting

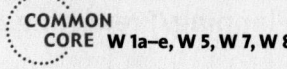 **COMMON CORE** **W 1a–e, W 5, W 7, W 8**

▶ **CHOOSE A SUBSTANTIVE ISSUE** Explain that the word *issue*, or topic of concern, implies disagreement—if everyone agrees about something, it isn't an issue. In choosing their issues, students should look for specific topics about which they have heard conflicting viewpoints.

▶ **THINK ABOUT AUDIENCE AND PURPOSE** Point out that the audience is those a persuasive essay is trying convince, so the writer must keep the audience's concerns and possible biases in mind. Remind students to ask questions from the audience's viewpoint throughout the writing process.

▶ **STATE YOUR CLAIM** To ensure that students understand the elements of a strong and successful claim, remind them that a precise claim should clearly state the writer's position on the issue. The best claims also contain a hint of a call to action, such as "We should ban cell phones."

R RESOURCE MANAGER—Copy Masters

Prewriting–Editing pp. 367–371

Writing Rubric p. 372

Writing Support p. 374

DIFFERENTIATED INSTRUCTION

FOR ENGLISH LANGUAGE LEARNERS

Language: Reinforce Persuasive Terms Write these terms on the board and review them with students:

- *credible:* worthy of being believed
- *evidence:* something that provides proof
- *relevant:* directly related to the issue or topic at hand
- *logical:* reasonable; valid

- *position:* an opinion about an issue
- *refute:* to disprove with facts or arguments
- *anecdote:* a short personal story about something to illustrate a point

Planning/Prewriting *continued*

▶ **GATHER SUPPORT FOR YOUR CLAIM**
Have students list facts, statistics, and expert opinions that support their claims and note whether their claims appeal to emotions or reason. Tell students that opposing claims can also appeal to emotions or reason. Writers should be prepared to "fight facts with facts" and to refute arguments based on emotion with logic.

Discuss the reasons for using more than one type of evidence to support a claim. To get students thinking, ask them to imagine a persuasive essay that consists of nothing but facts and statistics and to identify why such an essay might lack audience appeal. Direct attention to the quote used as evidence on the graphic organizer. Ask students to suggest other types of relevant evidence that would make the same point and thus strengthen the argument.

▶ **ANTICIPATE READER CONCERNS** Explain to students that a persuasive essay should anticipate opposing reactions and claims by the reader. Ask students to give examples of a claim, an opposing claim, and a counterclaim. Encourage students to think about what opposing claims the reader might make as they structure their essays.

 YOUR TURN Give students time to select their issues and craft their claims. Have them work independently to chart the reasons that support their opinions and then work in small groups to add counterclaims to their graphic organizers.

For interactive graphic organizers, see
💿 **Write*Smart* CD-ROM**
Writing Center on <u>thinkcentral.com</u>

Planning/Prewriting *continued*

Getting Started

GATHER SUPPORT FOR YOUR CLAIM

Strong **reasons** tell why you believe what you do. They are **logical,** or clearly and directly in support of your claim. Each reason should be supported by **evidence** that is **relevant,** or strongly tied to your issue. Types of evidence include facts and statistics, examples, anecdotes (short personal stories), expert opinions, quotations, and commonly accepted beliefs.

To support your reasons, you will use evidence from both primary and secondary sources. Because a **primary source** is a document written by someone directly involved in an issue or event, it may be stronger and more authoritative than a **secondary source,** which is created later based on primary sources.

Be sure to evaluate your sources for:
- **accuracy**—Is the information correct?
- **credibility**—Can the source be trusted as authoritative?

As you gather support, synthesize the information you find. When you **synthesize,** you make connections between a variety of sources and your prior knowledge in order to draw original conclusions about your issue.

▶ WHAT DOES IT LOOK LIKE?

Claim
"Using cell phones—even hands-free models—to talk or send messages while driving must be banned now."

Reason
When people talk or send messages on cell phones while driving, they endanger their own lives and the lives of others.

Evidence [expert opinion]
"It's absolutely clear from the research literature that talking or sending messages on a cell phone while driving does elevate the risk of a crash," said Dr. Donald Reinfurt.

ANTICIPATE READER CONCERNS

Some readers may have a claim that opposes your viewpoint. Anticipate their opposing claims and address them by providing a **counterclaim,** which is a statement that refutes their claim and explains why your viewpoint is more valid. Think of arguments you could develop to counter these claims.

▶ WHAT DOES IT LOOK LIKE?

Opposing Claim: People with limited time need to use their phones while they're driving.

Counterclaim: While their time may be limited, they would lose a lot more time if they were injured in an accident.

 PEER REVIEW Explain to a peer the claim you intend to assert and the evidence you are using to support your claim. Then ask: What other sources could I consult to provide accurate and credible information? What new approach could I take to strengthen my claim?

YOUR TURN In your *Reader/Writer Notebook,* create graphic organizers like the ones on this page to plan your claim, reasons, evidence, and counterclaims.

DIFFERENTIATED INSTRUCTION

FOR ENGLISH LANGUAGE LEARNERS
Connect Draw attention to three forms of persuasive writing from Unit 1: the sermon, the speech, and the political pamphlet. Ask students to describe similar forms of persuasive writing they have read, seen, or heard in their countries of origin.

FOR STRUGGLING WRITERS
Evidence, Audience, and Purpose Remind students that the strongest evidence in persuasive writing appeals directly to the personal concerns of the audience while advancing the writer's purpose. As they collect evidence, have students keep master lists of their strongest evidence, with notes on how it appeals to their audience.

Drafting

COMMON CORE

W 4 Produce clear and coherent writing appropriate to task, purpose, and audience. W 9b (RI 1) Cite textual evidence. L 3 Apply knowledge of language to make effective choices for meaning and style.

The following chart shows a structure for organizing an effective persuasive essay.

Organizing Your Persuasive Essay

INTRODUCTION

- Grab the audience's attention with an engaging **fact, statistic,** or **anecdote.**
- Identify the issue and state your position in a **precise, knowledgeable claim.**
- Establish the **significance of the claim.**

▼

BODY

- Present your reasons in a **logical sequence,** such as order of importance.
- Support each reason with **relevant** and **sufficient evidence.**
- Fairly address **opposing claims** and provide **well-supported counterclaims.** Acknowledge the strengths and limitations of your claim and counterclaims.
- Use transitions to create **cohesion,** or flow, and to **clarify relationships** among your ideas. **Vary your syntax** by using a mix of short and long, simple and complex sentences.
- Maintain a **formal style** by using an **objective,** or controlled, **tone.** Avoid being defensive or dismissive of other viewpoints.

▼

CONCLUDING SECTION

- Restate your **claim.**
- End with a **call to action**—tell readers to do something if they agree with your position.

GRAMMAR IN CONTEXT: PARALLEL STRUCTURE

One technique you can use to emphasize your reasons and create cohesion is **parallel structure,** stating related ideas in similar grammatical ways. Use parallel structure when you coordinate ideas, compare or contrast ideas, or link ideas with correlative conjunctions such as these:

both . . . and   either . . . or   neither . . . nor   not only . . . but also

In this example, notice how parallel structure links the variety of activities people can do while talking on a cell phone:

> People talk on the phone while watching a ballgame, while washing the dishes, and while driving to work.

YOUR TURN Use the information in the chart to draft your persuasive essay. Include at least one instance of parallel structure to enhance your argument.

FOR ENGLISH LANGUAGE LEARNERS

Parallel Structure Have students identify the grammatical pattern that is repeated in each of these parallel phrases or sentences.

"the summer soldier and the sunshine patriot"

"Give me liberty—or give me death!"

"If you are not part of the solution, you are part of the problem."

FOR ADVANCED LEARNERS/AP

Synthesize Support Material Ask students to use Analysis Frame: Persuasion to explore their topics in depth. Encourage them to conduct interviews; cite published interviews, films, and exhibits; and do other forms of creative research. Tell students to follow MLA guidelines for citing sources.

 **BEST PRACTICES TOOLKIT**
Analysis Frame: Persuasion pp. D21, D44, D45

Practice and Apply

Drafting

COMMON CORE W 4, W 9b (RI 1), L 3

▶ **INTRODUCTION** Tell students that the first sentence must grab the reader's attention and the first paragraph must tell what the writer thinks and why the reader should care. An interesting fact, statistic, or anecdote may be used to illustrate the importance of the issue.

▶ **BODY** Explain that to keep the reader interested, the body should begin with one of the strongest reasons, backed with supporting evidence. Remind students to use smooth transitions to maintain a logical flow as they anticipate opposing claims, make counterclaims, and introduce new evidence.

▶ **CONCLUDING SECTION** Explain that a concluding section should restate the original claim so that the audience will remember the writer's position. Then remind students that this section is not complete without a call to action.

GRAMMAR IN CONTEXT: PARALLEL STRUCTURE

Explain that with a pair of conjunctions, writers must make sure that the both halves of the pair follow the same grammatical pattern. The phrase *neither sun nor rain* has parallel structure. The phrase *neither sun nor raining* does not. Then ask students to find the repeated pattern in the sample sentence at the bottom of the box. Explain that the parallel structure in the sample sentence is created with adverbial phrases, each of which is introduced by the word *while.*

YOUR TURN As students draft their documents, tell them to include at least one example of parallel structure. Have students work independently to complete the **Your Turn** activity. For a persuasive essay writing template, see

WriteSmart CD-ROM

Writing Center on thinkcentral.com

Revising

COMMON CORE W 5

Model the Skill Using a draft essay on a transparency, model how to use the questions, tips, and strategies suggested in the chart to evaluate and revise writing. You might use the essay of a student from another class or from last year. Be sure to remove the student's name from the essay so that he or she is anonymous.

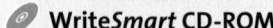

YOUR TURN Have students pair off and exchange papers with their partners for evaluation and review. Tell students to identify the strongest aspects of the essays they are reviewing and to present those aspects first as they share their ideas with the writers. Then have the student reviewers identify areas where the arguments could be strengthened, followed by specific suggestions to make those arguments more persuasive.

For interactive revision tools, see

💿 **Write*Smart* CD-ROM**

Writing Center on <u>thinkcentral.com</u>

Revising

When you revise, you evaluate the content, development, and style of your persuasive essay. Your goal is to determine if you've achieved your purpose and effectively communicated your ideas to the intended audience. The questions, tips, and strategies in the following chart can help you revise or rewrite where necessary.

PERSUASIVE ESSAY

Ask Yourself	Tips	Revision Strategies
1. Do I capture the audience's attention in my opening lines and introduce a precise, knowledgeable claim?	**Bracket** interesting statements or thought-provoking questions. **Underline** the claim.	**Add** an attention-getting statement or quotation. **Add** your claim, or **replace** the claim with a stronger one.
2. Are there at least two valid reasons that support my claim? Is there relevant evidence to support each reason?	**Highlight** the reasons that support the claim. **Circle** the evidence that supports each reason. **Draw an arrow** from the evidence to the reason.	If necessary, **add** valid reasons to support the claim. **Add** examples, anecdotes, or quotations to bolster unsupported reasons. **Elaborate** on pieces of evidence by adding more details or explanation.
3. Do I acknowledge opposing claims and present counterclaims?	**Draw a wavy** line under the opposing claims and your responses to them.	If necessary, **add** counterclaims that acknowledge the merits of your opinion and the limitations of opposing claims.
4. Are the counterclaims, reasons, and evidence in a logical sequence?	**Number** your reasons to reflect your ranking of their strength (1 = strongest, etc.).	If your strongest reason isn't last or first, **reorder** your reasons and evidence for emphasis.
5. Do I use transitions to clarify the relationships among my claim, counterclaims, reasons, and evidence?	**Draw a star** next to each transitional word or phrase.	**Check** your starred transitions and **add** variety if necessary. **Reread** the parts that lack stars. **Add** appropriate transitions to link related ideas.
6. Does the concluding section restate my claim and give the reader something to think about?	**Put a check mark** next to the restatement. **Underline** the sentence that leaves the reader with an important insight or observation.	**Add** a restatement of the claim if it is missing. **Add** a thought-provoking question or statement about human nature.

YOUR TURN **PEER REVIEW** Working with a peer, review your drafts together. Answer each question in the chart to decide how to improve your drafts and where to try a new approach. Use the strategies to help you strengthen your argument.

284 UNIT 1: EARLY AMERICAN WRITING

DIFFERENTIATED INSTRUCTION

FOR ENGLISH LANGUAGE LEARNERS

Stating a Claim Have students revise their writing to make sure that the claim is clearly stated in both the introduction and the concluding section. In addition, have students check that the reasons and pieces of evidence they have supplied actually support the claim.

FOR STRUGGLING WRITERS

Vary Sentence Structure Have students read their essays out loud to identify places where monotony is setting in. Then have them count the number of words in each sentence, noting each sentence's grammatical structure. Ask students to rewrite their sentences so that there is an interesting mix of long and short sentences; simple, compound, and complex sentences; and declarative, exclamatory, and interrogative sentences. Point out that quotations can also add variety.

Practice and Apply

ANALYZE A STUDENT DRAFT

Read this student draft, and notice the comments on its strengths as well as the suggestions for improvement.

COMMON CORE

W 5 Develop and strengthen writing as needed by revising, editing, rewriting, or trying a new approach, focusing on how well purpose and audience have been addressed.

Cell Phone Use in Cars: Hang Up—Don't Bang Up!
by Bruce Lomibao, Plainview High School

❶ Something dangerous is happening around you. Every time a motorist talks on a cellular phone, that person is endangering his or her own life and the lives of others. Using cell phones—even hands-free models—to talk or send messages while driving must be banned now.

❷ A study by the Cellular Telecommunications & Internet Association found that more than 200 million Americans use cellular telephones. People talk on the phone while watching a ballgame, washing the dishes, or driving to work. Although talking on a cell phone distracts people in each case, this distraction can have serious consequences for drivers.

❸ According to a study conducted by Dr. Donald Reinfurt of the University of North Carolina's Highway Safety Research Center, about one of every 600 driving accidents involved a cell phone. However, Reinfurt believes that "cell phones are involved in many more crashes" because most drivers won't admit they were on the phone. "Using a cell phone while driving is extremely dangerous," said Martha Kramer, whose son caused a car accident while talking on his cell phone. According to a study of drivers in Canada, "the risk of a collision when using a cellular telephone was four times higher than the risk when a cellular telephone was not being used."

> A **memorable title** identifies the issue.

> Bruce needs to revise the introduction to grab his audience's interest.

> In the introduction, Bruce clearly states his **claim** on this issue.

> Relevant and convincing **evidence**, including an expert opinion and a statistic, add **support** to Bruce's claim.

LEARN HOW Grab the Audience's Attention Bruce's first sentence may somewhat interest the audience, but it isn't descriptive enough to draw the reader fully into the essay. Bruce should add a startling fact, statistic, or anecdote to grab the audience's attention.

BRUCE'S REVISION TO PARAGRAPH ❶

Picture this: a man gets into a car, puts on a blindfold, starts the engine, puts his foot on the gas, and takes his hands off the wheel. That would never happen, you say? Maybe not, but something just as dangerous is happening around you every day. ~~Something dangerous is happening around you.~~ Every time a motorist talks on a cellular phone, that person is endangering his or her own life and the lives of others.

ANALYZE A STUDENT DRAFT

Explain that the Student Draft on this page is the first half of a persuasive essay. Model reading the draft and the annotations in blue, and explain that the yellow highlighting illustrates the student's language choices . Explain that the following *Learn How* mini-lessons hold helpful information about ways to improve this student draft as well as their own.

LEARN HOW Grab the Audience's Attention

- Analyze the revision to the first paragraph (in blue type). Have students identify the emotions aroused by the first sentence (shock and fear). Discuss why emotions grab attention.

- Ask students to think of another type of opening anecdote, such as an accident report, that might grab attention and support the writer's claim.

- Have students suggest other ideas to get readers' attention, such as unusual sights and sounds, startling facts, or witty quotes. Discuss why such methods are effective.

FOR ENGLISH LANGUAGE LEARNERS

Grab the Audience's Attention Draw attention to the rhymed slogan in the title, which helps capture the audience's attention. Explain that advertising campaigns, political speeches, and other forms of persuasive writing often use such "catchy" phrases to grab readers' attention. Ask volunteers to give examples of slogans, rhymes, and jingles they have encountered. Encourage them to turn their claims into such short, easily remembered phrases.

FOR STRUGGLING WRITERS

Grab the Audience's Attention Have students compare the first sentence in the original draft with the revised paragraph in the *Learn How* section. Point out that the writer has added details that appeal to the senses. Discuss how adding the details improves the opening by creating a vivid scene that is easy for the reader to imagine.

Explain that the Student Draft is continued and completed on this page. Read the draft and annotations aloud, and discuss them. Ask students to comment on the student writer's use of emotional and logical appeals.

LEARN HOW Include a Call to Action

- Ask students to restate the slogan in the title and the last sentence into a stronger call for action, such as, "I want you to pledge that you will never phone and drive."

- Ask for ideas on how the ending might make it easier for readers to send letters or e-mails, such as providing the e-mail addresses of lawmakers.

- Remind students that writers should tailor every part of the persuasive essay to the audience. Have students suggest other calls to action that might have greater audience appeal than letter writing, such as petition drives and community events to raise awareness.

YOUR TURN Have students work independently to complete the **Your Turn** activity. Have them incorporate feedback as they analyze their drafts to make sure the opening catches the audience's interest, the claim is strong and clear, the evidence supports the claim, and the concluding section contains a clear call to action.

For interactive revision tools, see

Write*Smart* CD-ROM

Writing Center on thinkcentral.com

---

④ Despite these statistics, some people may say their time is so valuable that they need to talk while driving. What they don't consider is how much time they'd lose if they were injured—or worse—in a car accident. Others might argue that if lawmakers ban cell-phone use, they will also have to ban distractions such as eating and listening to music. However, the Insurance Information Institute reports that "there is increasing evidence that the dangers associated with cell-phone use outweigh those of other distractions."

> Bruce gives an accurate and honest representation of **opposing claims.** He then addresses each opposing claim with a **counterclaim.**

⑤ Obviously more people are noticing this problem, but what is being done about it? Nearly 50 countries have banned or restricted the use of cell phones while driving. Here in the U.S., several states prohibit all drivers from using handheld phones for talking or texting, and over half of the states restrict the use of cell phones by inexperienced drivers. Many other states and the federal government are considering legislation related to cell phones and driving.

⑥ You could be the next victim of a driver distracted by a cell-phone conversation. So before that happens, remember: "Hang up—don't bang up!"

> Bruce restates his position in his concluding section, but he fails to include a call to action.

LEARN HOW Include a Call to Action The purposes of writing an argument are to persuade an audience to agree with a position and to motivate this audience to take action. An argument's body should persuade the audience to agree with the position, and the concluding section should include an obvious **call to action.**

> **BRUCE'S REVISION TO PARAGRAPH ⑥**
>
> You could be the next victim of a driver distracted by a cell-phone conversation. So before that happens, remember: "Hang up—don't bang up!"^
>
> *Send letters or e-mails to your local, state, and federal legislators urging them to ban the use of cell phones in cars. Do it today.*

 YOUR TURN Use the feedback from your peers and teacher, the revision strategies chart, and the two "Learn How" lessons to revise your persuasive essay. Evaluate how well your essay convinces readers to act on the issue through valid reasons, relevant and sufficient evidence, and a strong call to action.

DIFFERENTIATED INSTRUCTION

FOR ENGLISH LANGUAGE LEARNERS

Verb Forms: Commands Refer students to the **Learn How** section and explain that a call to action will almost always be in the form of a command. Point out that in a command, the verb is the same as the infinitive, but without the word *to*. *Send* is the command form of *to send*, and so forth. Ask students to identify the commands in the last three sentences of the revised paragraph: *hang up, bang up, send,* and *do.*

FOR STRUGGLING WRITERS

Include a Call to Action In the **Learn How** example, ask students to list the positive results that would happen if people did what the writer wanted. Point out that adding one or more of those positive results might strengthen the ending even more. Discuss why "You could help save lives" might be a stronger argument than "You could be the next victim." As they work on their own essays, suggest that students compose calls to action that include the actions' effects.

Editing and Publishing

COMMON CORE — **W 5** Develop and strengthen writing as needed by revising, editing, rewriting, or trying a new approach, focusing on how well purpose and audience have been addressed. **L 2b** Spell correctly.

In the editing stage, you proofread your essay to make sure that it is free of grammar, spelling, and punctuation errors. Careless spelling mistakes make you sound less authoritative to your audience. Read your essay slowly and carefully to correct any lingering misspelled words.

GRAMMAR IN CONTEXT: ESTABLISHING TONE

One of your goals in persuasive writing is to establish a **tone** of authority so that your readers take your arguments as seriously as you do. The strength of your argument can be compromised if you don't use accurate, credible sources. Whether you use a **primary source** or **secondary source,** you should always check that the information comes from a credible person or place. Use the following tips when examining primary and secondary sources to determine their suitability for citing in a convincing, authoritative essay:

- Online sources with addresses that end in *.edu* or *.gov* are generally more reliable than other sites. If you use sources with other endings, such as *.org* or *.com,* check to make sure the site was created by a trustworthy organization.
- When obtaining information from a book or magazine, be sure that the book, magazine, or newspaper was published recently.
- Always check the background of the source's author. The author should have the experience necessary to relay credible information or a valid opinion.

Notice how Bruce revised his essay to include a more credible source. This revision helps Bruce to strengthen the authoritative tone of his argument.

> ~~"Using a cell phone while driving is extremely dangerous," said Martha Kramer, whose son caused a car accident while talking on his cell phone.~~
>
> *"It's absolutely clear from the research literature that talking on a cell phone while driving does elevate the risk of a crash," said Dr. Reinfurt.*

PUBLISH YOUR WRITING

Share your persuasive essay with an audience.
- Publish your argument as an editorial for your school or local newspaper.
- Post a blog for people interested in the subject matter of the essay.
- Develop your essay into a persuasive speech to present to your class.

 YOUR TURN Correct any errors in your essay by carefully proofreading it. Check that you have included accurate, credible sources and that you have assured your audience of their validity and reliability. Then, publish your final essay.

FOR STRUGGLING WRITERS

Quoting from Sources Give students these tips for judging the credibility of a *.org* Web site.

- Check the About Us section of the site. An About Us section often contains a Mission Statement that explains the site's purpose.
- In the About Us section or elsewhere on the site, look for the organization that publishes the site. In general, Web sites of large public organizations such as museums are credible sources. Other groups should be evaluated with their Mission Statements in mind.

- In the About Us section or elsewhere on the site, look for names of people who work for the group. Their credentials should also be listed. Make sure these people are experts in their fields of study.
- As you read articles and look at pictures on the site, look for places where the writers have noted their sources. Decide if those sources are credible. (Note: Those sources can also help direct your own research.)

Practice and Apply

Editing and Publishing

COMMON CORE — W 5, L 2b

GRAMMAR IN CONTEXT: ESTABLISHING TONE

Review the definitions of *primary source* and *secondary source.* Ask students to suppose they are writing a persuasive essay about disaster relief. Ask students to determine whether the following sources are primary or secondary.

1. a letter from the survivor of a disaster
2. government statistics on disaster relief
3. interviews with officials about government disaster relief plans
4. a television news report about a disaster
5. cell phone images of a disaster happening *(Examples 1 and 5 are primary sources. Number 2 is a secondary source. Number 4 is a primary source if it is live and a secondary source if it is not.)*

PUBLISH YOUR WRITING

Brainstorm with students about additional ways to publish their persuasive essays.

YOUR TURN Allow students time to edit and revise their drafts. Encourage them to seek feedback from readers as part of this process. Suggest that students underline the items in their essays that come from outside sources and then check that there is a credible primary or secondary source for every underlined item. Also suggest that students look for arguments that might be strengthened by using more credible source material.

Scoring Rubric

Explain that students can best understand a scoring rubric by using it to score an actual piece of writing. Ask students to prepare and submit copies of their essays with their names omitted. (Number the essays as they are submitted and make a confidential list of the writers' names.) Distribute the essays to the class and have students use the rubric to evaluate each other's work. Ask students to use language from the chart to explain the scores they assign.

For Rubric Bank, see

 Write*Smart* CD-ROM

Writing Center on <u>thinkcentral.com</u>

Assess and Reteach

Assess

R RESOURCE MANAGER—Copy Master
Rubric for Evaluation, p. 372

Online Essay Scoring on <u>thinkcentral.com</u>

Reteach

Level Up Online Tutorials on <u>thinkcentral.com</u>

Reteaching Worksheets on <u>thinkcentral.com</u>
Informational Texts Lesson 15: Persuasive Techniques
Reading Lessons 14–17

Scoring Rubric

Use the rubric below to evaluate your persuasive essay from the Writing Workshop or your response to the on-demand task on the next page.

PERSUASIVE ESSAY

SCORE	COMMON CORE TRAITS
6	• **Development** Asserts a precise, knowledgeable claim; supports the claim with valid reasons and relevant, sufficient evidence; fairly and thoroughly counters opposing claims with counterclaims; ends powerfully • **Organization** Has a logical, persuasive sequence; uses transitions to create cohesion and show the relationships among the claim, reasons, and evidence • **Language** Consistently maintains a formal style and objective, authoritative tone; shows a strong command of conventions
5	• **Development** States a precise, knowledgeable claim; offers valid reasons and relevant evidence; fairly counters opposing claims with counterclaims; ends with a strong concluding section • **Organization** Is logically sequenced; uses transitions to show the relationships among the claim, reasons, and evidence • **Language** Uses a formal style and objective tone; has a few errors in conventions
4	• **Development** States a precise claim; offers mostly valid support; needs to more fairly address opposing claims; has an adequate concluding section • **Organization** Reflects a logical sequence, with one or two exceptions; could use a few more transitions • **Language** Mostly uses a formal style, but sounds defensive at times; includes a few distracting errors in conventions
3	• **Development** States a vague claim; provides some relevant support but not enough; unfairly dismisses other viewpoints; concludes somewhat weakly • **Organization** Has some flaws in organization; needs more transitions to link ideas • **Language** Often lapses into an informal style or indecisive tone; has several errors in conventions
2	• **Development** Has an uninformed claim; offers irrelevant reasons and insufficient evidence; fails to acknowledge other viewpoints; has a weak concluding section • **Organization** Has major organizational flaws; lacks transitions throughout • **Language** Uses an informal style and indecisive tone; has many errors in conventions
1	• **Development** Lacks a claim; provides no support; ignores opposing claims; ends abruptly • **Organization** Has no organization and transitions • **Language** Uses an inappropriate style and tone; has major problems with grammar, mechanics, and spelling

Preparing for Timed Writing

 **COMMON CORE** W 10 Write routinely over shorter time frames for a range of tasks, purposes, and audiences.

1. ANALYZE THE TASK   5 MIN

Read the task carefully. Then, read it again, noting on your own paper the words that tell the audience, the topic, and the purpose.

> **WRITING TASK** *Topic*
>
> Your school is debating whether to adopt a <u>school uniform policy</u> or to continue allowing students to choose what they will wear to school. Consider how each option affects the student population, the teachers, and the school environment. What is your position on the issue? In a persuasive essay, <u>convince</u> the <u>school board</u> to agree with your position.
>
> *Purpose* ↗   ↖ *Audience*

2. PLAN YOUR RESPONSE   10 MIN

- Use a chart to gather ideas. The pros are the reasons for the policy, and the cons are the reasons against the policy. Choose your viewpoint based on the number and strength of reasons. Write your claim.
- Support each reason with relevant evidence, such as facts, examples, and anecdotes. Also, address one possible opposing claim.
- Arrange your reasons and evidence in a logical sequence, such as order of importance.

School Uniforms	
Pros	
Cons	

3. RESPOND TO THE TASK   20 MIN

Begin drafting your essay. As you write, keep the following points in mind:
- In the introduction, grab your audience's interest and state a precise claim.
- In each paragraph, provide a valid reason and relevant evidence that supports it.
- Acknowledge and counter opposing claims.
- Conclude by restating your claim and proposing some action that your audience should take.

4. IMPROVE YOUR RESPONSE   5–10 MIN

Revising Review the key aspects of the essay. Do you state your claim clearly? Do you include valid reasons, relevant evidence, and a call to action?

Proofreading Proofread, or edit, your essay to correct errors in grammar, spelling, punctuation, and capitalization. Make sure edits are neat and the essay is legible.

Checking Your Final Copy Before you turn in your essay, read it one more time to catch any errors you may have missed and to make any finishing touches.

WRITING WORKSHOP   **289**

DIFFERENTIATED INSTRUCTION

FOR ENGLISH LANGUAGE LEARNERS
Writing: Persuasive Language Work with students to generate a list of verbs associated with persuasion, including *must, should,* and *ought.* Review the meaning of each word. Provide students with the following sentence frames to help them formulate a persuasive controlling idea or claim:

- We all must _____ because _____.

- I urge you to _____ because _____.

FOR STRUGGLING WRITERS
Supporting Evidence In a timed situation, students might not be able to access credible facts and statistics. Suggest that students use other forms of evidence to support their arguments, including examples, anecdotes, expert opinions, quotations, and commonly accepted beliefs.

COMMON CORE FOCUS

W 10 Write routinely over shorter time frames for a range of tasks, purposes, and audiences.

Preparing for Timed Writing

1. **Analyze the Task** Before students begin writing, encourage them to answer the following questions:
   - What is my time limit?
   - What are the core traits assessed in the scoring rubric?
   - Who is my audience?
   - What is my purpose?

2. **Plan Your Response** Draw attention to the chart and suggest that students quickly jot down pros and cons in order to decide on their viewpoints and form their claims. Tell them to use the chart to decide which claims need more support and which opposing claims should be refuted.

3. **Respond to the Task** Remind students that their claims should appear in the introduction and concluding section and be supported in the body of their essays.

4. **Improve Your Response** Ask students to check their essays against the task to make sure their claim is clear and effectively supported. Remind them to keep both the purpose and the audience in mind as they edit and revise.

Assess

Use the Scoring Rubric on page 288 to assess students' essays.

Focus and Motivate

COMMON CORE FOCUS

SL 3 Evaluate a speaker's point of view, reasoning, and use of evidence and rhetoric. **SL 4** Present information, findings, and evidence, such that listeners can follow the line of reasoning. **SL 6** Adapt speech to a variety of contexts and tasks.

SPEAK WITH A PURPOSE

Have students review the speaking task and note that they will be creating their speeches from the essays they've already written. Ask them to identify the common purpose of the essays and speeches—to persuade the audience to think and act in a certain way. Remind students that presenting a speech also gives them the opportunity to share their opinions face-to-face with their listeners.

COMMON CORE TRAITS

As students prepare to deliver their speeches, remind them to keep in mind the *COMMON CORE TRAITS* of a strong persuasive speech.

Practice and Apply

Adapt Your Essay

Model the Skill: INTRODUCTION

Model how a writer/speaker might open a speech with a mental picture or a vivid anecdote. Ask students how a spoken anecdote would differ from its written version. *(In a written essay, a writer would use words that appeal to the senses to make a story vivid, but a speaker can also use voice, facial expressions, and body language.)*

GUIDED PRACTICE Ask students to choose opening anecdotes or quotes from their essays. Working in pairs or small teams, have them read their anecdotes or quotes aloud and edit them according to the response of listeners to their spoken words.

R RESOURCE MANAGER—Copy Master
Speaking and Listening p. 373

Presenting and Evaluating a Persuasive Speech

 Essential Course of Study ECOS

If you have ever talked a friend into agreeing with your opinion, then you have spoken persuasively. Effective persuasive speeches incorporate the same techniques that are used in good persuasive essays. A speech, though, allows you to use your voice and body as well as words to make your point.

Complete the workshop activities in your **Reader/Writer Notebook.**

SPEAK WITH A PURPOSE	COMMON CORE TRAITS
TASK Adapt your **persuasive essay** into a **persuasive speech,** and present it to your class. Then, listen to and evaluate the persuasive speeches of others.	**A STRONG PERSUASIVE SPEECH . . .** • asserts a claim that reflects the speaker's distinct perspective • organizes reasons and evidence in a logical order • addresses alternative or opposing perspectives • uses persuasive **rhetoric,** or language, effectively

COMMON CORE

SL 3 Evaluate a speaker's point of view, reasoning, and use of evidence and rhetoric. **SL 4** Present information, findings, and evidence, such that listeners can follow the line of reasoning. **SL 6** Adapt speech to a variety of contexts and tasks.

Speaking & Listening Online
THINK central
Go to **thinkcentral.com.**
KEYWORD: HML11-290

Adapt Your Essay

Since your audience will be listening to your argument rather than reading it, you will need to adapt your persuasive essay so that it works as a speech. To be convincing, you will need to state your claim, or **stance,** on the topic clearly and concisely so that your audience understands your distinct perspective. You must then support that claim with evidence that is compelling, logical, and supported by reliable research.

Introduction	Body	Concluding Section
• Start with a thought-provoking quotation or tell a vivid anecdote. • State your claim clearly. • Establish the significance of your claim.	• Organize your information in order of importance. • Present valid reasons and logical, sufficient evidence. • Consider alternative perspectives and offer reasons why your claim is more valid. • Use **rhetoric,** or persuasive language, to sway your audience.	• Sum up your points and restate your claim. • Summarize your strongest evidence and the significance of your claim. • End with a statement that gives your audience something to consider.

Considering your audience will help you decide on the style, organization, and substance of your speech. Will your audience be swayed by emotional or logical appeals? Will a reference to a common experience be convincing?

290 UNIT 1: EARLY AMERICAN WRITING

DIFFERENTIATED INSTRUCTION

FOR ENGLISH LANGUAGE LEARNERS

Language: Reinforce Persuasive Terms
Explain to students that the goals of a persuasive speech and a persuasive essay are the same: to present a claim and provide convincing evidence to support that claim. Write these terms on the board and review them with students.

• *anecdote:* a short personal story

• *enunciation:* how words are pronounced or spoken aloud

• *evidence:* something that provides proof

• *techniques:* practical ways to complete a task

• *position:* an opinion about an issue

• *rhetoric:* language used to persuade

Deliver Your Speech

USE VERBAL AND NONVERBAL TECHNIQUES

Use these techniques to communicate your ideas effectively:

Verbal Techniques	Nonverbal Techniques
• Keep your **rate** of speech steady. Pause for effect when you reach key ideas. • **Enunciate** your words clearly.	• Engage your audience by making **eye contact** with individuals. • Use appropriate **gestures** to enforce key ideas.

EVALUATE PERSUASIVE SPEECHES

As you listen to your classmates' speeches, take careful notes. This will help you evaluate information and later ask pertinent questions that will stimulate a thoughtful, well-reasoned exchange of ideas. Use the following questions to focus your evaluation:

- Evaluate the speaker's **point of view.** What is the claim? On what **premises** or assumptions is the claim based? Do the premises seem logical and factual? Do they provide a strong foundation for the speaker's **stance,** or position on the issue?

- Examine the **reasoning.** Are the reasons valid and clearly linked? What reasons or ideas does the speaker emphasize? Are these **points of emphasis** effective for the audience?

- Assess the **evidence.** Is it reliable? Does it support the speaker's claim? Be on the lookout for flawed reasoning, such as overgeneralizations or exaggeration.

- Does the speaker fairly acknowledge alternate perspectives? Does he or she explain the strengths and limitations of other viewpoints?

- Analyze the speaker's language choices. Has the speaker used **rhetorical devices** such as understatement or hyperbole to influence you? Do the speaker's **tone** and **word choices** support or detract from the points made?

 YOUR TURN   **As a Speaker** Deliver your speech to a classmate, incorporating verbal and nonverbal techniques. Speak persuasively, using formal English appropriate for the topic of your speech. Have your classmate offer suggestions for improvement.

As a Listener Listen to a classmate deliver his or her speech. Take notes on the organization, substance, and style of the speech, using the questions above to help you evaluate what you're hearing.

291

FOR STRUGGLING STUDENTS

Verbal and Nonverbal Techniques Tell students to rehearse their speeches out loud while standing in front of a mirror or facing a partner who is holding a video camera. Encourage speakers to be objective as they look at themselves, to put their emotions aside, and to concentrate on improving both verbal and nonverbal delivery.

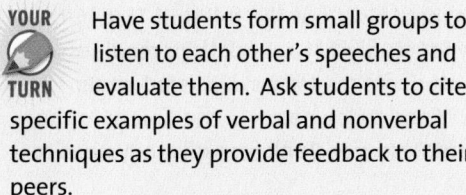

Teach

Deliver Your Speech

USE VERBAL AND NONVERBAL TECHNIQUES

Tell students that in the opening sentence, and in this section, the word *your* refers to the speaker. Draw attention to the chart. Encourage students to use both verbal and nonverbal techniques as they rehearse and deliver their speeches.

Model the Skill: EVALUATE PERSUASIVE SPEECHES

Ask students to identify the "you" in the opening paragraph *(the listener).* Draw attention to the fifth bullet point, which identifies two types of flawed reasoning.

GUIDED PRACTICE Have students name other types of flawed reasoning, such as ad hominem arguments and false analogies, and discuss why such reasoning is faulty.

YOUR TURN   Have students form small groups to listen to each other's speeches and evaluate them. Ask students to cite specific examples of verbal and nonverbal techniques as they provide feedback to their peers.

Assess and Reteach

Assess

Use the **COMMON CORE TRAITS** to assess students' persuasive speeches. A strong persuasive speech:

- asserts a claim that reflects the speaker's distinct perspective
- organizes reasons and supporting evidence in a logical order
- addresses alternative or opposing perspectives
- uses persuasive rhetoric, or language, effectively

Reteach

If students have trouble spotting flawed reasoning, have them listen to speeches again, jotting down notes about statements that seem faulty to them. At the end of the speech, have the speaker repeat those statements so that the listener can try to identify why they are faulty.

Assessment Practice

CHECK READINESS

Read aloud the paragraph under **ASSESS** and stress that this is not the full Unit Test, but a way for students to check their readiness. Have students read the skills listed under **REVIEW** and to look back in the unit or in the **Student Resource Bank** for skills they need to review.

READ THE TEXTS

Remind students to keep unit goals in mind as they read each passage and to place what they read in its historical context.

ANSWER THE QUESTIONS

Direct students to pages R96–R103 of the **Handbook** to review test-taking strategies. Remind students:

- to read directions carefully
- to read all choices in multiple-choice questions rather than choosing the first alternative that seems to fit

---

COMMON CORE

Practice Test THINK central
Take it at **thinkcentral.com**.
KEYWORD: HML11N-292

Assessment Practice

DIRECTIONS Read these selections and answer the questions that follow.

from Defense of the Constitutions of Government in Massachusetts During the Revolution *by John Adams*

1   It is become a kind of fashion among writers, to admit, as a maxim, that if you could be always sure of a wise, active, and virtuous prince, monarchy would be the best of governments. But this is so far from being admissible, that it will forever remain true, that a free government has a great advantage over a simple monarchy. The best and wisest prince, by means of a freer communication with his people, and the greater opportunities to collect the best advice from the best of his subjects, would have an immense advantage in a free state over a monarchy. A senate consisting of all that is most noble, wealthy, and able in the nation, with a right to counsel the crown at all times, is a check to ministers, and a security against abuses, such as a body of nobles who never meet, and have no such right, can never supply. Another assembly, composed of representatives chosen by the people in all parts, gives free access to the whole nation, and communicates all its wants, knowledge, projects, and wishes to government; it excites emulation among all classes, removes complaints, redresses grievances, affords opportunities of exertion to genius, though in obscurity, and gives full scope to all the faculties of man; it opens a passage for every speculation to the legislature, to administration, and to the public; it gives a universal energy to the human character, in every part of the state, such as never can be obtained in a monarchy.

2   There is a third particular which deserves attention both from governments and people. In a simple monarchy, the ministers of state can never know their friends from their enemies; secret cabals undermine their influence, and blast their reputation. This occasions a jealousy ever anxious and irritated, which never thinks the government safe without an encouragement of informers and spies, throughout every part of the state, who interrupt the tranquillity of private life, destroy the confidence of families in their own domestics and in one another, and poison freedom in its sweetest retirements. In a free government, on the contrary, the ministers can have no enemies of consequence but among the members of the great or little council, where every man is obliged to take his side, and declare his opinion, upon every question. This circumstance alone, to every manly mind, would be sufficient to decide the preference in favor of a free government.

DIFFERENTIATED INSTRUCTION

FOR ENGLISH LANGUAGE LEARNERS
Assessment Practice: Work Backward
Prepare students by having them read the questions before reading the passages. Have students work in pairs to find unfamiliar words in test directions and questions and follow these steps:

1. Write each word on an index card.
2. Look up the meaning in a dictionary and write it on the back of the card.
3. Use the cards to practice the words with their partner and to teach them to others.

Culture Remind students that Adams was a citizen of a British colony, so his model for representative government was Great Britain, which has two houses of Parliament, one for nobles and one for common people. Ask students to look for verbal clues that a similar class distinction existed in the colonies (*"all that is most noble, wealthy, and able,"* and *"the people in all parts"*).

from **Boston Tea Party**   *by George Hewes*

1   It was now evening, and I immediately dressed myself in the costume of an Indian, equipped with a small hatchet, which I and my associates denominated the tomahawk, with which, and a club, after having painted my face and hands with coal dust in the shop of a blacksmith, I repaired to Griffin's wharf, where the ships lay that contained the tea. When I first appeared in the street after being thus disguised, I fell in with many who were dressed, equipped and painted as I was, and who fell in with me and marched in order to the place of our destination. . . .

2   We then were ordered by our commander to open the hatches and take out all the chests of tea and throw them overboard, and we immediately proceeded to execute his orders, first cutting and splitting the chests with our tomahawks, so as thoroughly to expose them to the effects of the water.

3   In about three hours from the time we went on board, we had thus broken and thrown overboard every tea chest to be found in the ship, while those in the other ships were disposing of the tea in the same way, at the same time. We were surrounded by British armed ships, but no attempt was made to resist us.

4   We then quietly retired to our several places of residence, without having any conversation with each other, or taking any measures to discover who were our associates; nor do I recollect of our having had the knowledge of the name of a single individual concerned in that affair, except that of Leonard Pitt, the commander of my division, whom I have mentioned. There appeared to be an understanding that each individual should volunteer his services, keep his own secret, and risk the consequence for himself. No disorder took place during that transaction, and it was observed at that time that the stillest night ensued that Boston had enjoyed for many months. . . .

5   Another attempt was made to save a little tea from the ruins of the cargo by a tall, aged man who wore a large cocked hat and white wig, which was fashionable at that time. He had slightly slipped a little into his pocket, but being detected, they seized him and, taking his hat and wig from his head, threw them, together with the tea, of which they had emptied his pockets, into the water. In consideration of his advanced age, he was permitted to escape, with now and then a slight kick.

6   The next morning, after we had cleared the ships of the tea, it was discovered that very considerable quantities of it were floating upon the surface of the water; and to prevent the possibility of any of its being saved for use, a number of small

GO ON →

ITEM ANALYSIS

COMPREHENSION AND WRITTEN RESPONSE	ITEMS	UNIT PAGES
Elements of an Argument	1, 3, 15	227, 239
Persuasive Techniques	2, 4, 5	226, 227, 249
Historical Context	6, 7, 10, 11	73, 216
Descriptive Details	7, 12, 14	83
Primary Source	8, 13, 14	70, 71, 73

VOCABULARY	ITEMS	UNIT PAGES
Multiple-Meaning Words	4, 5, 6	101
Specialized Vocabulary	1, 2, 3	64

WRITING AND GRAMMAR	ITEMS	UNIT PAGES
Complex and Compound-Complex Sentences	2, 3	244, 247
Prepositional Phrases	4	78

Practice Test

On **thinkcentral.com** students can complete an interactive version of this practice test *and* receive remediation for the skills they have not yet mastered.

FOR STRUGGLING READERS

Assessment Support Consider these options for completing the Assessment Practice.

• Have students "work backward" to review the test questions *before* reading the passages.

• Select random questions in the Assessment, and have students demonstrate *how* and *where* to look for answers.

• Ask students to locate unfamiliar words in the Assessment. Elicit the words' meaning from the class.

• Have students record useful testing words and definitions in their journals for later reference.

• Read selections or parts of them aloud to aid in student comprehension.

Reading Comprehension

Model a thinking process for answering multiple-choice questions.

1. **C is correct.** *In paragraph 1 Adams says that a free society collects the best advice from the people. A is incorrect because Adams opposes the current monarchy. B is not a claim that Adams makes in the passage. D is not correct because Adams argues that "the best and wisest prince" can gain from such freedom.*

2. **C is correct.** *Adams uses the words to raise fears about "simple monarchy." A, B, and D are incorrect because anger, excitement, and guilt are not appropriate for the context.*

3. **D is correct.** *Adams contrasts free states with spy-riddled monarchies. A is incorrect because he asserts that in paragraph 1, not 2. B is incorrect because Adams does not mention tough-mindedness. C is incorrect because Adams does not mention the strength of opinions.*

4. **A is correct.** *Adams assumes that his readers want to be among the "manly minds." B is incorrect because the manly minds are not presented as authorities. C is incorrect because manliness is not presented as goodness. D is incorrect because "every manly mind" does not have the emotional connotations of loaded language.*

5. **D is correct.** *"Poison" is negatively loaded, and "sweetest" is positively loaded. Phrases A, B, and C use moderate language without strong emotional bias.*

6. **B is correct.** *The essay explores the idea of a free state over a monarchy. A is incorrect because Adams doesn't prefer a monarchy as a form of government. C is the opposite of the essay's message. D is incorrect because Adams's ideas are complex.*

---

boats were manned by sailors and citizens, who rowed them into those parts of the harbor wherever the tea was visible, and by beating it with oars and paddles so thoroughly drenched it as to render its entire destruction inevitable.

Reading Comprehension

> Use "Defense of the Constitutions of Government in Massachusetts During the Revolution" (p. 292) to answer questions 1–6.

1. Which position on government does Adams favor?
   A. Monarchies are the best form of government because they have wise and virtuous rulers.
   B. Writers should be consulted when a country forms its government because they are well informed.
   C. A free state is the best form of government because its ideas and opinions come from the people.
   D. Only the best and wisest prince who communicates with his subjects should rule a nation.

2. The words *enemies, informers,* and *spies* in paragraph 2 appeal to the emotion of —
   A. anger   C. fear
   B. excitement   D. guilt

3. Which claim does Adams make about a free government in paragraph 2?
   A. The best way to run a free government is with a large assembly and a small one.
   B. Members of a free government often take a tough-minded approach to governing.
   C. People who serve in a free government have similar opinions.
   D. The leaders in a free government usually have few hidden enemies.

4. "Every manly mind" in paragraph 2 is an example of which persuasive technique?
   A. An appeal by association
   B. An appeal to authority
   C. An ethical appeal
   D. Loaded language

5. Which quote is an example of loaded language?
   A. *monarchy would be the best of governments*
   B. *such as a body of nobles who never meet*
   C. *gives free access to the whole nation*
   D. *poison freedom in its sweetest retirements*

6. This excerpt reflects the view of colonists who —
   A. believed that political rivalries would destroy the British monarchy
   B. questioned British rule and tried to form a new government
   C. upheld the ideals of a monarchy
   D. had simple ideas about government

294

---

7. **A is correct.** *These items all played specific roles in the Boston Tea Party. B, C, and D could apply to other events and times.*

8. **B is correct.** *The account is written in the first person by someone who was present. A is incorrect because primary sources do not have to be political. C is incorrect because primary sources may be inaccurate. D is incorrect because many published documents are not primary sources.*

Use "Boston Tea Party" (pp. 293–294) to answer questions 7–12.

7. Which descriptive details most clearly place this account in its historical context?
   A. Tomahawk, chests of tea, coal dust
   B. Armed ships, hatches, small boats
   C. Evening, three hours, next morning
   D. Sailors, citizens, aged man

8. This narrative is a primary source because it is —
   A. a political argument
   B. a participant's report
   C. an accurate history
   D. a published document

9. This account by a colonial shoemaker calls attention to —
   A. an alliance between Native Americans and tradespeople
   B. a lack of leadership during the Revolutionary War
   C. the tension between wealthy and poor people in the colonies
   D. the role of the common people in the Revolution

10. The colonists most likely dressed as Native Americans to —
   A. honor Native American traditions
   B. forge an alliance against the British
   C. protect themselves from the British
   D. cause economic problems in the colonies

11. The descriptive anecdote in paragraph 5 suggests that —
   A. tea was a prized commodity among the colonists in Boston
   B. the elderly were treated with disrespect in colonial times
   C. many participants thought the Boston Tea Party was amusing
   D. violent attacks were characteristic of the Boston Tea Party

12. The descriptive details in this account emphasize that the Boston Tea Party was —
   A. poorly planned
   B. carried out in secret
   C. led by Native Americans
   D. authorized by the British

Use both selections to answer question 13.

13. Both primary sources give the reader insight into the —
   A. origins of the United States
   B. benefits of a constitution
   C. advantages of a monarchy
   D. fashions of the period

SHORT CONSTRUCTED RESPONSE
Write three or four sentences to answer this question.

14. Cite three details from George Hewes's account that identify it as a primary source.

Write two or three paragraphs to answer this question.

15. What argument does John Adams make in paragraph 1 in favor of an assembly of representatives? Cite three reasons he gives to support his argument.

GO ON ➡

9. **D is correct.** *The question, which names Hewes as a shoemaker, confirms that he is of the common people. A is incorrect because Native Americans are not the subject of the document. B is incorrect because the participants were well led. C is incorrect because wealth is irrelevant to Hewes's account.*

10. **C is correct.** *The story makes it clear that the "Indians" wore disguises to remain anonymous. A is incorrect because tossing tea overboard was not a Native American tradition. B is incorrect because the text never mentions alliances. D is incorrect because Native American dress did not cause economic problems.*

11. **A is correct.** *The old man wants to save some tea for his own use. B is not correct because the man got better treatment because of his age. C is incorrect because the text includes no sign of amusement. D is incorrect because the old man is not attacked violently.*

12. **B is correct.** *Paragraph 4 makes clear that the action was secret, the participants did not know each other's identities. A, C, and D contradict the text.*

13. **A is correct.** *Both sources discuss issues of the American Revolution. B and C are incorrect because Hewes's document does not discuss political theory. D is incorrect because the disguises at the tea party were not a matter of fashion.*

SHORT CONSTRUCTED RESPONSE

Possible responses:

14. *Details that identify Hewes's account as a primary source are: Hewes narrates his own role in the event (paragraph 1); Hewes relates what he saw, such as the other men's actions (paragraph 2); Hewes shows he has first-hand information, such as the commander's name (paragraph 4).*

15. *Adams argues that an assembly of representatives offers greater benefits than a monarchy. Three possible reasons are that elected representation "gives free access to the whole nation" (paragraph 1), that it "redresses grievances" (paragraph 1), and that it "gives full scope to all the faculties of man" (paragraph 1).*

Vocabulary

1. A is correct. *Adams clearly equates the words* monarchy *and* prince. *B describes a republic. C describes an oligarchy. D describes a democracy.*

2. C is correct. *The context clues are "secret," "undermine their influence," and "blast their reputation," which all hint at conspiracy. A, B, and D refer to groups of people, but lack the negative connotations.*

3. B is correct. *The words* of state *are the clue. Adams is talking about government, not religion, foreign affairs, or trade, so A, C, and D are incorrect.*

4. A is correct. *By cutting and splitting the chests, the men are carrying out orders. B is incorrect because the men were not giving orders. C is incorrect because it refers to execution in the context of killing people. D is incorrect the word does not fit this context.*

5. B is correct. *Paragraph 4 gives clues that the men did not know each other or speak to each other, thus went to different "places of residence." A is incorrect because the participants did not live in the same place. C and D refer to the numerical meaning of several.*

6. A is correct. *Substituting* actions *for* measures *in the sentence verifies the meaning. B, C, and D do not make sense in this context.*

Vocabulary

> Use context clues and your knowledge of specialized vocabulary to answer the following questions based on "Defense of the Constitutions of Government in Massachusetts During the Revolution."

1. What is the most likely meaning of the word *monarchy* as it is used in paragraph 1?
- **A.** A state headed by a leader who usually rules by hereditary right
- **B.** A body of elected officials who hold the supreme power in a nation
- **C.** A small group of persons who rule together
- **D.** A government that shares power with the people

2. What is the most likely meaning of the word *cabals* as it is used in paragraph 2?
- **A.** Social clubs
- **B.** Religious denominations
- **C.** Groups of conspirators
- **D.** Military organizations

3. What is the most likely meaning of the word *ministers* as it is used in paragraph 2?
- **A.** Church leaders
- **B.** Public officials
- **C.** Foreign diplomats
- **D.** Business tycoons

> Use context clues and your knowledge of multiple-meaning words to answer the following questions based on the excerpt from "Boston Tea Party."

4. Which meaning of the word *execute* is used in paragraph 2?
- **A.** Carry out
- **B.** Create
- **C.** Kill
- **D.** Validate

5. Which meaning of the word *several* is used in paragraph 4?
- **A.** Distant
- **B.** Separate
- **C.** Humble
- **D.** More than two or three

6. Which meaning of the word *measures* is used in paragraph 4?
- **A.** Actions
- **B.** Dimensions
- **C.** Legislative bills
- **D.** Quantities

DIFFERENTIATED INSTRUCTION

FOR ENGLISH LANGUAGE LEARNERS

Assessment Vocabulary Write these terms on the board and review them with students.

- Item 1: *position*—"an opinion about an issue"
- Item 5: *loaded language*—"words that contain unfair or unjust connotations"
- Item 6: *excerpt*—"part of a story or passage"

Revising and Editing

DIRECTIONS Read this passage and answer the questions that follow.

(1) George Washington hired engineer Pierre L'Enfant to plan a new capitol city. (2) The new city would be called Federal City and would be located in Maryland. (3) L'Enfant was later fired. (4) Surveyor Andrew Ellicott redrew the plans but upheld much of L'Enfant's vision. (5) By 1800, President John Adams had moved into the White House. (6) It was far from finished. (7) It was damp. (8) The city was later renamed. (9) Today, Washington, D.C., reflects L'Enfants vision of a city of open space.

1. What change, if any, should be made in sentence 1?
   A. Change *engineer* to **Engineer**
   B. Insert a comma after *L'Enfant*
   C. Change *capitol* to **capital**
   D. Make no change

2. What is the most effective way to combine sentences 3 and 4 to form a compound-complex sentence?
   A. L'Enfant was later fired, but when surveyor Andrew Ellicott redrew the plans, he upheld much of L'Enfant's vision.
   B. L'Enfant was later fired, and surveyor Andrew Ellicott redrew the plans but upheld much of L'Enfant's vision.
   C. When redrawing the plans, surveyor Andrew Ellicott upheld much of L'Enfant's vision, even though L'Enfant was fired.
   D. Much of L'Enfant's vision was upheld by surveyor Andrew Ellicott, who redrew the plans after L'Enfant was fired.

3. What is the most effective way to combine sentences 5 and 6 to form a complex sentence?
   A. By 1800, President John Adams had moved into the White House, even though it was far from finished.
   B. By 1800, President John Adams had moved into the White House, but it was far from finished.
   C. By 1800, President John Adams had moved into the White House; however, it was far from finished.
   D. By 1800, President John Adams had moved into the White House; it was far from finished.

4. Which prepositional phrase should be added to the end of sentence 8 to add descriptive detail?
   A. Even as it grew
   B. After Washington's death
   C. To reflect Washington's involvement
   D. Washington, D.C.

5. What change, if any, should be made in sentence 9?
   A. Spell out *D.C.*
   B. Change *L'Enfants* to **L'Enfant's**
   C. Change *reflects* to **reflected**
   D. Make no change

297

Revising and Editing

1. **C is correct.** *Capital refers to a main city, not the building for Congress. A is not capitalized because* engineer *is not part of an official title. B is incorrect because no comma is necessary. D is incorrect because the sentence has a mistake.*

2. **A is correct.** *A contains two independent clauses and a subordinate clause. B is incorrect because it is a compound sentence with two independent clauses, one that has a compound predicate. C is incorrect because it is a complex sentence. D is incorrect because it is a sentence with an adjective clause.*

3. **A is correct.** *The clause "even though it was far from finished" is a subordinate clause because it cannot stand alone as a sentence. B, C, and D are compound sentences consisting of two independent clauses.*

4. **B is correct.** *The preposition is "after." A is incorrect because it is a clause, not a phrase. C is incorrect because it is an infinitive phrase. D is incorrect because it is a proper noun.*

5. **B is correct.** *An apostrophe is needed to show the vision belonged to L'Enfant. A and C would make the text incorrect. D is incorrect because the sentence does contain a mistake.*

FOR ENGLISH LANGUAGE LEARNERS

Assessment Vocabulary Write these terms on the board and review their definitions with students.

- *complex sentence:* A sentence that has one or more dependent clauses in addition to the main clause

- *compound sentence:* a sentence that has two or more independent clauses, usually joined by conjunctions, but no dependent clause

- *compound–complex sentence:* a sentence that has two or more independent clauses, usually joined by conjunctions, as well as a dependent clause

- *context clues:* Surrounding words that help define an unfamiliar word

- *multiple-meaning words:* Words that have more than one meaning, depending on the context

Have students review the passage on page 292 and identify sentences that fit these criteria.

INTRODUCE *GREAT READS*

In Unit 1, students have discussed a number of big questions. Invite students to tell which question they found most intriguing and why, and then focus attention on the four that appear on pages 298–299. Discuss the recommended books and their summaries, pointing out how each connects to the related question. Encourage students to choose one or more of these "great reads" to read independently.

Ideas for Independent Reading

Continue exploring the Questions of the Times on pages 20–21 with these additional works.

Who owns the LAND?

The Narrative of the Captivity and Restoration of Mrs. Mary Rowlandson
by Mary Rowlandson

In February 1676, during a land dispute called King Philip's War, a minister's wife named Mary Rowlandson was taken hostage by Wampanoag warriors. Packed with violence, cruelty, piety, and anger, Rowlandson's account of her three-month captivity became one of the first bestsellers in colonial America.

The Portable North American Indian Reader
edited by Fredrick W. Turner

As an introduction to the verbal art of Native Americans, this anthology has few equals. It includes myths, tales, poetry, and speeches from the many diverse Native American cultures who thrived before, during, and after contact with European explorers and settlers. Modern selections show how traditional Indian kinship with the land continues to the present day.

Finding the Center: The Art of the Zuni Storyteller
translated by Dennis Tedlock

Thought to have descended from the Anasazi, a cliff-dwelling people of 1,000 years ago, the Zuni of present-day New Mexico enjoy a rich oral heritage handed down from long before the first Europeans arrived. The folklorist Dennis Tedlock has collected, translated, and transcribed many key Zuni stories in this volume, placing the words on the page in a manner that mimics their oral performance.

What makes an EXPLORER?

The Four Voyages
by Christopher Columbus

In these journals and eyewitness accounts, Christopher Columbus comes across as a complex, driven, yet entirely understandable person. In place of the confident adventurer of story, we see a man of mixed motives, influenced equally by greed, religious passion, and scientific curiosity. These journals shed light on the impulses that pushed Columbus to make the most significant journeys of his time.

Love and Hate in Jamestown
by David Price

In 1607, 105 Englishmen arrived in what would become the Virginia settlement of Jamestown. They came seeking gold, a route to the Orient, and survivors from the lost Roanoke Colony. What they found instead were Native American people—some friendly, some brutally hostile—and day after day of challenges, hardship, and misery.

Voyages and Discoveries
by Richard Hakluyt

Early English explorers were a fascinating breed. These sailors were willing—even eager—to face unknown dangers for the sake of their country and the glory and adventure it would bring. Using ships' records, charts, and logs, Richard Hakluyt pulls together the stories of such adventurers as Sir Francis Drake, whose yen for exploration enabled the European settlement of America.

298

COMMON CORE

RL 10 Read and comprehend literature. **RI 10** Read and comprehend literary nonfiction.

Are people basically GOOD?

The Diary and Life of Samuel Sewall
edited by Mel Yazawa

Samuel Sewall served as one of the judges in the Salem witchcraft trials, voting to hang 19 people for wholly imaginary offenses. Yet in his diary, we see another side of this forbidding figure. He wrestles with lingering guilt over his role in that public hysteria, feels remorse over the unfair treatment of the Indians, recalls the pleasures of food and marriage, and grieves bitterly over the loss of friends and family.

A Short Account of the Destruction of the Indies
by Bartolomé de Las Casas

A Spanish priest and missionary, Las Casas was appalled by the abuse and enslavement of Native Americans. He dedicated himself to their emancipation, returning to Spain to plead their case before the king, then going back to the New World to serve as their official protector.

Letters from an American Farmer
by Michel Guillaume Jean de Crèvecœur

Crèvecœur's "letters," originally written as essays, paint a mesmerizing portrait of a fertile country populated with rough-mannered yet skilled and kindhearted people. Crèvecœur addresses such difficult topics as the hardships of the frontier, the plight of women, and the evils of slavery. Yet such problems fade before his faith in the righteousness of American individualism.

Who has the right to RULE?

1776
by David McCullough

How did a ragtag group of farmers manage to defeat the world's most powerful army? That is the question historian David McCullough explores in this fascinating look at one pivotal year in our nation's history. Persistence, optimism, ingenuity, leadership, luck, and weather are the elements to which McCullough attributes the colonists' success in the Revolutionary War.

The Puritan Dilemma: The Story of John Winthrop
by Edmund S. Morgan

As the leader of Massachusetts Bay Colony for nearly 20 years, John Winthrop spent his life combining religious devotion with power politics. This biography shines a spotlight upon issues that mattered most to Winthrop: the relationship between individual liberties and community harmony, and the legitimacy of political authority.

The Adams-Jefferson Letters
edited by Lester J. Cappon

Divided by political party and regional affiliation, Thomas Jefferson of Virginia and John Adams of Massachusetts were united in their love of country and their concern for the future of democracy. This collection of letters, including contributions by Abigail Adams (John Adams's gifted wife), touches upon virtually every major issue that faced the young republic.

Get Novel Wise **THINK** central

Go to **thinkcentral.com**.
KEYWORD: HML11-299

299

THINK central

NovelWise

The keyword on this page points to **NovelWise,** a Web site that helps students choose a novel or other book-length work to read. **NovelWise** also provides

• study guides

• reading strategies and literary elements instruction

• presentations to introduce classic novels

• project ideas

COMMON CORE UNIT GOALS

Included in this unit: **RL 1, RL 2, RL 3, RL 4, RL 5, RL 6, RL 7, RL 9, RL 10, RI 1, RI 2, RI 3, RI 4, RI 5, RI 6, RI 7, RI 8, RI 9, RI 10, W 1a–e, W 2, W 2b, W 2d, W 3, W 3b, W 3d, W 4, W 5, W 7, W 10, SL 1, SL 2, SL 4, SL 6, L 1, L 1a, L 2, L 3, L 3a, L 4, L 4a–c, L 5a–b, L6**

Complete text of the Common Core State Standards is found in the correlation on p. T10. Standards covered in this unit are found in the standards overview (pp. 301A–301D) and on the lesson pages where they are taught.

Preview Unit Goals

This page presents an overview of the skills and strategies covered in this unit. Explain to students that they can get more from their reading by previewing. Then ask them to skim the page to preview the skills that they will learn. Note that each strand or category of skill is color-coded on this page and throughout the unit.

Model the strategy of copying the Academic Vocabulary and writing a preliminary definition for each term. Suggest that students use **Reader/Writer Notebooks** for this purpose. Encourage them to use the terms in discussions and in writing. Also urge students to revisit each term throughout the unit and to refine its meaning.

UNIT 2

COMMON CORE Preview Unit Goals

TEXT ANALYSIS	• Understand romanticism as a literary movement • Identify elements of transcendentalism • Identify and analyze blank verse • Identify and examine stanza, rhyme scheme, and meter • Analyze elements used to create mood; analyze theme • Identify and analyze sound devices and imagery • Interpret symbol and allegory • Identify and analyze satire and unity of effect • Analyze elements of an essay • Determine an author's point of view or purpose; analyze style and content
READING	• Paraphrase main ideas; summarize information; make inferences • Clarify meanings; examine complex sentences
WRITING AND LANGUAGE	• Write a short story • Use rhetorical questions • Identify and use parallelism and adjective clauses • Use imperative sentences and dashes
SPEAKING AND LISTENING	• Dramatize a script
VOCABULARY	• Use knowledge of word roots and affixes to determine word meaning • Research word origins
ACADEMIC VOCABULARY	• construct • expand • indicate • reinforce • role
MEDIA AND VIEWING	• Evaluate how meaning is conveyed in visual media

Find It Online!
Go to **thinkcentral.com** for the interactive version of this unit.

DIFFERENTIATED INSTRUCTION

FOR ENGLISH LANGUAGE LEARNERS

Academic Vocabulary Provide students with definition for these Academic Vocabulary words.

construct (kən-strŭkt) v. create (an argument or a sentence, for example) by systematically arranging ideas or terms; n. (kŏn strŭkt) a concept or theory

expand (ĭk-spănd) v. to enlarge; to express at length or in detail

indicate (ĭndĭ-kāt) v. to point out; to signify

reinforce (rēĭn-fôrs) v. to strengthen something by adding extra support

role (rōl) n. the character or part played by a performer; the expected behavior of an individual in society; a function or position

Additional Academic Vocabulary Use the copy master to help students learn academic words they will use in subsequent lessons and on the Assessment Practice. Follow the same procedure as for the Academic Vocabulary copy master.

 RESOURCE MANAGER—Copy Masters
Academic Vocabulary p. 3
Additional Academic Vocabulary p. 4

American Romanticism

1800–1855

Nathaniel
Hawthorne

CELEBRATING THE INDIVIDUAL

- The Early Romantics
- The Fireside Poets
- The Transcendentalists
- American Gothic

Media Smart DVD-ROM

Illustrations Inspired by Poe
Examine evocative paintings and illustrations
that take gothic into new dimensions. Page 460

301

For help in planning this unit, see

R RESOURCE MANAGER UNIT 2
pp. 1–8

INTRODUCE THE UNIT

Call students' attention to the pictures on this page. Explain that the large picture, *A View of the Mountain Pass Called the Notch of the White Mountains,* is a painting by Thomas Cole, known for his grand natural scenes. Tell students that they will read about Cole on page 307, in the historical essay.

Ask students if they know of Nathaniel Hawthorne (1804–1864), the author shown in the smaller picture on this page. Explain that in his writing, Hawthorne often examined the darker side of human nature and dealt with such themes as sin, hypocrisy, and tolerance. Tell students that in this unit they will read one of Hawthorne's short stories and an excerpt from his classic novel *The Scarlet Letter.* Also note that students can read more about Hawthorne on pages 468 and 470.

About the Art English-born American painter Thomas Cole (1801–1848), one of the best-known members of the Hudson River School, painted *A View of the Mountain Pass Called the Notch of the White Mountains* in 1839. Both the painting and the Hudson River School are discussed in **The Artists' Gallery** on page 307.

Unit Resources

See resources on the **Teacher One Stop DVD-ROM** *and on* **thinkcentral.com**.

R RESOURCE MANAGER UNIT 2

UNIT AND BENCHMARK TESTS

🧰 BEST PRACTICES TOOLKIT

INTERACTIVE READER

ADAPTED INTERACTIVE READER

ELL ADAPTED INTERACTIVE READER

LANGUAGE HANDBOOK

VOCABULARY PRACTICE

TECHNOLOGY

💿 Teacher One Stop DVD-ROM
💿 Student One Stop DVD-ROM
💿 PowerNotes DVD-ROM
💿 WriteSmart CD-ROM
💿 MediaSmart DVD-ROM
💿 GrammarNotes DVD-ROM
💿 Audio Anthology CD

Find It Online!

This unit on **thinkcentral.com**
includes
- **PowerNotes** introductions to key
  selections
- audio support—listen or download
- **ThinkAloud** models
- **WordSharp** vocabulary tutorials
- interactive unit review and
  assessment

UNIT 2

COMMON CORE STRAND	Unit 2 Introduction pp. 302–317 • Questions of the Times • Historical Essay • Timeline • Legacy of Romanticism American Masterpieces: *from* Moby Dick pp. 464–465 *from* The Scarlet Letter pp. 466–467	Text Analysis Workshops • The Art of the Essay pp. 366–367	The Devil and Tom Walker Short Story pp. 318–335 Lexile: 1120 Fry: 9 Dale-Chall: 7.3	Thanatopsis Poem pp. 336–340	A Psalm of Life/ The Tide Rises, The Tide Falls Poetry pp. 342–347
Reading Literature	American Romanticism pp. 302–313 RL 9 Text Analysis pp. 464–465 RL 3 Text Analysis pp. 466–467 RL 6		Satire pp. 319, 322, 325, 328, 329, 330, 333 RL 6 Analyze Imagery pp. 319, 320, 322, 328, 330, 332, 333 RL 1, RL 4 Theme pp. 326, 332 RL 2	Blank Verse pp. 337, 338, 339 RL 4 Understand Structure pp. 337, 338, 339 RL 5	Stanza and Rhyme Scheme pp. 343, 344, 346, 347 RL 5 Reading Traditional Poetry pp. 343, 345, 346, 347 RL 4
Reading Informational Text	American Romanticism pp. 302–313 RI 9 Read a Timeline pp. 314–315 RI 7	Characteristics of an Essay pp. 366–367 RI 6, RI 9, RI 10			
Writing	Legacy of the Era pp. 316–317 W 10 Write a Scene p. 466 W 4		Writing Prompt p. 335 W 3d		Quickwrite p. 343
Speaking and Listening	Legacy of the Era pp. 316–317 SL 1		Discuss p. 319 SL 1	Survey p. 337 SL 1	
Language			Parallelism pp. 327, 335 L 3, L 3a Language Coach pp. 322, 325, 327 L 4a, L 3 Latin Root *spec* p. 334 L 4b–c, L 6		

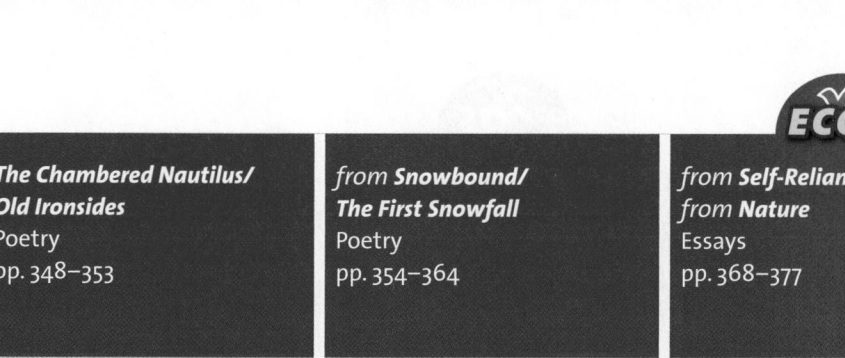

The Chambered Nautilus/ Old Ironsides Poetry pp. 348–353	from Snowbound/ The First Snowfall Poetry pp. 354–364	from Self-Reliance/ from Nature Essays pp. 368–377	from Walden/from Civil Disobedience Themes Across Cultures: On Civil Disobedience Essays/Speech pp. 378–399, 400–401
		Lexile: 1010/980 Fry: 10/7 Dale-Chall: 7.0/6.8	Lexile: 1230/880 Fry: 12/10 Dale-Chall: 6.5/6.2
Meter pp. 349, 350, 353 **RL 5** Make Inferences pp. 349, 351, 352, 353 **RL 1** Allusion p. 352	Mood pp. 355, 356, 358, 359, 361, 362, 363, 364 **RL 4** Paraphrase pp. 355, 358, 360, 362, 364 **RL 10** Text Structure p. 359 **RL 5** Figurative Language p. 364 **RL 4** Make Inferences p. 364 **RL 1**		
		Transcendentalism pp. 369, 372, 373, 375 **RI 3, RI 9** Identify Theme pp. 369, 370, 375 **RI 2**	Essay pp. 379, 380, 382, 383, 385, 386, 388, 396, 397 **RI 6** Evaluate Ideas pp. 379, 382, 383, 384, 387, 388, 390, 392, 393, 395, 397 **RI 2** Theme p. 380 Transcendentalism pp. 385, 386 **RI 3, RI 9** Language Coach p. 394 **RI 4** Read a Speech pp. 400–401 **RI 2**
	Quickwrite p. 355	Quickwrite p. 369 Writing Prompt p. 377 **W 2b, W 2d**	Writing Prompt p. 399 **W 1a–b, W 1d–e**
Discuss p. 349 **SL 1**			Discuss p. 379 **SL 1**
	Language Coach pp. 358, 361, 362 **L 3, L 4a, L 5b**	Use Descriptive Details pp. 372, 377 **L 3** Language Coach pp. 372, 374 **L 5a** Words with Multiple Affixes p. 376 **L 4b, L 6**	Rhetorical Questions pp. 393, 399 **L 3a** Language Coach pp. 384, 385, 394 **L 4c** Prefixes (ab-, per-) p. 398 **L 4b, L 6**

To see the complete Essential Course of Study, see pp. T23–T27.

For additional lesson planning help, see **Teacher One Stop DVD.**

ECOS

COMMON CORE		from **Woman in the Nineteenth Century** Nonfiction pp. 402–408	**The Fall of the House of Usher** Short Story pp. 410–434	**The Raven/ Poe Parody** Poem/Parody pp. 435–443	**Comparing Texts: American Gothic** Literary: **The Masque of the Red Death** pp. 444–454, 458 Informational: *from* **Danse Macabre** pp. 444–445, 455–456, 458 Visual: **Wait Until Dark** pp. 457, 458
STRAND		*Lexile:* 1170 *Fry:* 7 *Dale-Chall:* 7.0	*Lexile:* 1440 *Fry:* 9 *Dale-Chall:* 8.6		*Lexile:* 1240 *Fry:* 8 *Dale-Chall:* 8.0
Reading Literature			Unity of Effect pp. 411, 414, 417, 420, 423, 429, 430, 432 RL 3, RL 4 Theme p. 430	Sound Devices pp. 435, 436, 438, 439, 441 RL 4, RL 5 Make Inferences pp. 435, 436, 439, 440, 441 RL 1 Read a Parody p. 443	Suspense pp. 445, 448, 450, 452, 453, 455, 456, 458 RL 3 Clarify Meaning pp. 445, 446, 450, 451, 453, 456, 458 RL 4
Reading Informational Text		Author's Perspective pp. 403, 406, 408 RI 6 Paraphrase Main Ideas pp. 403, 404, 406, 407, 408 RI 2 Analyze Structure pp. 406, 408 RI 5			Suspense pp. 455, 456 RI 1 Theme p. 456 Clarify Meaning p. 456 RI 4 Poster p. 457 RI 7
Writing			Quickwrite p. 411 Writing Prompt p. 434 W 3	Writing Prompt p. 442 W 3, W 3b, W 3d	Writing for Assessment p. 459
Speaking and Listening		Survey p. 403 SL 1		Discuss p. 435 SL 1	What's the Connection? p. 445 SL 1
Language		Language Coach p. 407 L 1a	Complex Sentences pp. 411, 415, 417, 418, 425, 432 L 3a Add Descriptive Details pp. 415, 434 L 3 Language Coach pp. 414, 428, 429 L 1a, L 4 Greek Root *path* p. 433 L 4b–c	Craft Effective Sentences p. 442 L 2 Language Coach p. 440 L 4	Affixes and Spelling Changes p. 454 L 2b, L 4b–c, L 6 Clarify Meaning p. 456 L 4a Language Coach p. 452 L 2b, L 4c

Media Study: Illustrations Inspired by Poe Image Collection pp. 460–463	The Minister's Black Veil Short Story pp. 468–484	Wrap-Ups • The Early Romantics p. 341 • The Fireside Poets p. 365 • The Transcendentalists p. 409 • American Gothic p. 485	Writing Workshop: Short Story pp. 486–495 Speaking and Listening Workshop: Dramatizing a Script pp. 496–497
	Lexile: 1260 Fry: 10 Dale-Chall: 7.8		
Analyze Art Elements in Illustrations pp. 461–463 RL 7	Symbol pp. 469, 473, 475, 476, 477, 482, 483 RL 1 Cultural Characteristics pp. 469, 470, 474, 477, 480, 483 RL 3		
	Quickwrite p. 469	Writing to Analyze p. 341 W 2 Writing to Evaluate p. 365 W 2 Writing to Analyze p. 409 W 2, W 7 Writing to Analyze p. 485 W 2	Writing a Short Story, pp. 486–495 W 3a–e, W 4, W 5, W 10
Analyze Art Elements in Illustrations pp. 461–463 SL 1a, SL 2, SL 4 Create Gothic Artwork p. 463 SL 1a, SL 2, SL 4		Extension p. 341 SL 2 Extension p. 365 SL 6 Extension p. 485 SL 1	Dramatizing a Script pp. 496–497 SL 1b, SL 1d, SL 6
	Language Coach pp. 472, 473, 475 L 4b, L 4c Latin Root ambi p. 484 L 4b, L 6		Drafting p. 489 L 1 Editing and Publishing p. 493 L 1, L 2

ECOS

To see the complete Essential Course of Study, see pp. T23–T27.

 For additional lesson planning help, see **Teacher One Stop DVD.**

Resource Manager Unit 2

UNIT SUPPORT

Academic Vocabulary, p. 3

Additional Academic Vocabulary, p. 4

Grammar Focus p. 5

Text Analysis Workshop p. 84

Writing Workshop: Short Story, p. 229

SELECTION SUPPORT*

Plan and Teach

Lesson planning pages

Additional leveled selection questions

Extension activities

Student Copy Masters

Selection summaries in four languages

Skills copy masters in English and Spanish

Vocabulary preteaching and support

Reading Check and Question Support

Reading Fluency

* Available for all selections

† Available on **thinkcentral.com**

Language Handbook

Vocabulary Practice

Best Practices Toolkit†

PowerNotes DVD-ROM†

Connections: Nonfiction for Common Core CD-ROM†

Teacher One Stop DVD-ROM

Student One Stop DVD-ROM

Media*Smart* DVD-ROM

Illustrations Inspired by Poe

Write*Smart* CD-ROM†

GrammarNotes DVD-ROM†

Wordsharp CD-ROM†

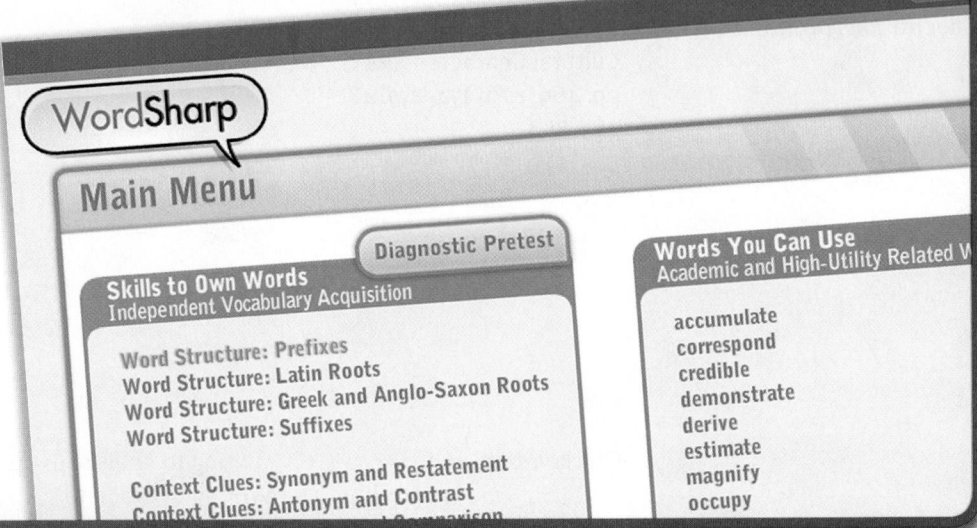

STRUGGLING READERS AND WRITERS

Resource Manager Unit 2

Additional Selection Questions

Question Support

Reading Fluency

Interactive Reader

Adapted Interactive Reader

Level Up Online Tutorials

Audio Anthology

(with Audio summaries)

Diagnostic and Selection Tests

Selection Tests A/B

ENGLISH LANGUAGE LEARNERS

Resource Manager Unit 2

Selection Summaries in English, Spanish, Vietnamese and Haitian Creole

Skills Copymasters in Spanish

English Language Learner Adapted Interactive Reader Teacher's Guide

ELL Adapted Interactive Reader

Guide to English for Newcomers

Audio Anthology

Audio summaries in Multiple Languages

(on **thinkcentral.com**)

ADVANCED LEARNERS

Resource Manager Unit 2

Additional Selection Questions

Ideas for Extension

Diagnostic and Selection Tests

Selection Tests B/C

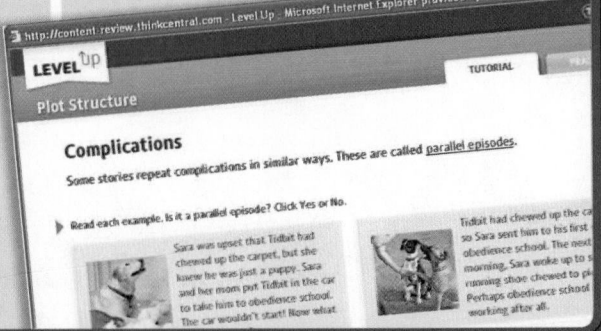

Assessment and Reteaching

Diagnostic and Selection Tests

Unit and Benchmark Tests

ThinkCentral Online Assessment:
- All program assessments
- Level Up Online Tutorials

ExamView Test Generator on the Teacher One Stop DVD-ROM

Online Essay Scoring on **thinkcentral.com**

ThinkCentral Online Reteaching:
- Level Up Online Tutorials
- Reteaching Worksheets

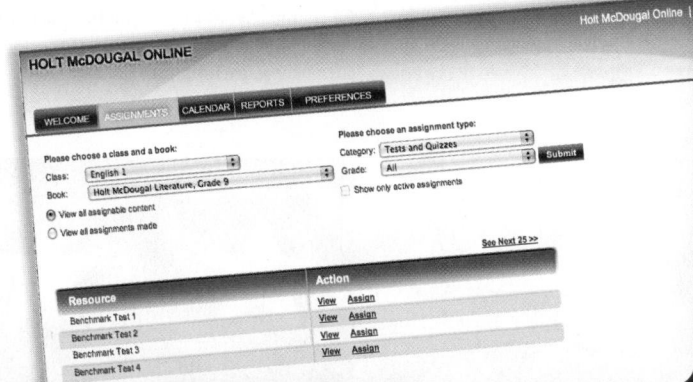

Professional Development

Video Center Based on interviews with program consultants and other educational experts, these videos feature classroom-ready teaching strategies.

Teacher Toolkit Includes a Teacher Handbook as well as a range of articles and handouts by program consultants and other educators.

Janet Allen

Jim Burke

Kylene Beers

Carol Jago

THINK central at a Glance

One Location, Endless Resources

Find Resources Browse all *Holt McDougal Literature* components for the ones that meet your students' needs and match your teaching style.

Assess Progress and Reteach Assign electronic versions of program assessments to measure your students' mastery of the Common Core State Standards. On thinkcentral.com, some tests deliver online remediation tutorials to students who have not mastered skills.

 Interactive Whiteboard Lessons

Prepare your students for college and careers by teaching relevant, real-world skills through dynamic, interactive instruction. Go to **thinkcentral.com** to browse through all whiteboard lessons, including the following:

- Poetry: Language and Form
- Figurative Language and Imagery
- Author's Purpose and Perspective
- Writing Narratives

 Together Holt McDougal and HISTORY® are revolutionizing the study of English/language arts with video that helps students relive and re-imagine the people, places, and events they are discovering through reading. Look for selections with the HISTORY® icon.

COMMON CORE FOCUS

RL 9 Demonstrate knowledge of nineteenth-century foundational works of American literature, including how two or more texts from the same period treat similar themes or topics. **RI 9** Analyze documents of historical and literary significance for their themes, purposes, and rhetorical features.

Questions of the Times

Read aloud the questions on pages 302 and 303 and the paragraphs that follow them. Open the discussion of each idea by having students respond to the questions that conclude each paragraph. Use these notes to prompt further exploration of the ideas.

Is the price of progress ever TOO HIGH?

Challenge students to give specific examples (from history or personal knowledge) of instances in which the negative consequences of progress have outweighed the benefits. Encourage students to consider both short-term and long-term effects. Extend the discussion by having students speculate about how their lives today would be different if the changes described in the paragraph had not occurred.

Is it patriotic to protest one's GOVERNMENT?

Urge students to suggest why they might want to protest the problems mentioned in the paragraph. Then challenge students to suggest specific situations in which citizens should not be allowed to protest. Encourage debate, but stress that students must support their viewpoints with well-considered reasons and examples.

UNIT 2

Questions of the Times

DISCUSS In small groups or as a class, discuss the following questions. Then read on to learn how writers—and other Americans—grappled with these issues during the American romantic period.

Is the price of progress ever TOO HIGH?

During the romantic period, America seemed limitless— new frontiers were being explored every day, and inventions advanced both farming and industry. Yet to many people, life felt frantic and soulless. Is progress always worth its price?

Is it patriotic to protest one's GOVERNMENT?

Democracy was flourishing in the early 19th century and citizens felt optimistic about their country. Yet the problems of the age—slavery, women's disenfranchisement, the mistreatment of workers—were severe, and protestors agitated for change. What role do you think activism plays in a democracy? Under what circumstances, if any, should citizens lose their right to protest?

302

COMMON CORE

RL 9 Demonstrate knowledge of nineteenth-century foundational works of American literature, including how two or more texts from the same period treat similar themes or topics. **RI 9** Analyze documents of historical and literary significance for their themes, purposes, and rhetorical features.

Does everyone have a "DARK SIDE"?

Although most romantic writers reflected the optimism of their times, some pondered the darker side of human nature. Edgar Allan Poe, for example, conjectured that in extreme situations people would reveal their true, evil natures. Do you think everyone has a dark side? What might make the dark side prevail?

Where do people look for TRUTH?

To escape the materialism and hectic pace of industrialization, many writers of the age turned to nature and to the self for simplicity, truth, and beauty. In earlier centuries, people had looked to reason or to God for answers. Where do you think people turn to make sense of their lives today?

Does everyone have a "DARK SIDE"?

Invite students to explain their concept of a "dark side" and to describe situations in which a person might have to struggle to keep his or her dark side under control. Urge students to draw upon their experiences reading and viewing TV or films as they cite examples in response to the questions.

Where do people look for TRUTH?

Discuss why some people—not just writers—might find nature a comfort and an inspiration. Challenge students to consider how people may continue to seek truth in nature, the self, or human reason—and where else they might turn to find ways to make sense of modern life. Extend the discussion by asking students how and why a person's search for truth might change as he or she grows older.

COMMON CORE FOCUS

RL 9 Demonstrate knowledge of nineteenth-century foundational works of American literature, including how two or more texts from the same period treat similar themes or topics. **RI 9** Analyze documents of historical and literary significance for their themes, purposes, and rhetorical features.

The following essay (pages 304–313) provides students with a historical context for the Unit 2 reading selections. It presents a brief overview of important events occurring during the time period 1800–1855 and discusses key people and concepts of that era.

To get started, read and discuss the opening paragraph on this page. List these contradictory pairs of words on the board: *patriotic/individualistic, urban/untamed, wealthy/enslaved.* Elicit or explain the ways in which each pair expresses a contradiction. Then briefly discuss why living in a "complex, inconsistent society" might cause people to turn inward to find truth.

READING STRATEGY

■ PREVIEW

Have students preview the historical essay by skimming the heads, boldfaced terms, and **Taking Notes** side-column features. Ask volunteers to summarize what the essay is about.

About the Art *Summer Afternoon on the Hudson* is an oil painting by Jasper Francis Cropsey (1823–1900). Such scenes on the Hudson River were a common sight for Cropsey, who was born in New York State. Cropsey was an early member of the Hudson River School (discussed on page 307). This example of his work demonstrates the romantic fascination with the majesty of the natural world.

American Romanticism
1800–1855

Celebrating
the Individual

Patriotic and individualistic, urban and untamed, wealthy and enslaved—Americans in the first half of the 19th century embodied a host of contradictions. Struggling to make sense of their complex, inconsistent society, writers of the period turned inward for a sense of truth. Their movement, known as romanticism, explored the glories of the individual spirit, the beauty of nature, and the possibilities of the imagination.

304

DIFFERENTIATED INSTRUCTION

FOR STRUGGLING READERS

Vocabulary Support To help students understand the essay, review these words.

- *individualistic,* "emphasizing the interests of the individual rather than a group or society; independent in thought or action"

- *relocate,* "to move to a new place"

- *annex,* "to add or incorporate"

- *immoral,* "not moral; contrary to what is right"

- *contiguous,* "touching; connected"

- *agrarian,* "having to do with land, farmers, or farming"

- *industrialization,* "becoming increasingly based upon mechanized production (rather than upon farming)"

- *commercialism,* "emphasis on doing business, making money, and being successful"

Use the copy master to help students take notes on the essay.

 **RESOURCE MANAGER—Copy Master** Note Taking p. 8

Romanticism: Historical Context

Historical forces clearly shaped the literature of the American romantic period. Writers responded—positively and negatively—to the country's astonishing growth and to the booming Industrial Revolution.

The Spirit of Exploration

WESTWARD EXPANSION Writers of the romantic period were witness to a period of great growth and opportunity for the young American nation. With that growth, however, came a price. In 1803, the Louisiana Purchase doubled the country's size. In the years that followed, explorers and settlers pushed farther and farther west. Settlers moved for largely practical reasons: to make money and to gain land. But each bit of land settled by white Americans was taken from Native American populations who had lived there for generations. The Indian Removal Act of 1830, for example, required Native Americans to relocate west. As whites invaded their homelands, many Native Americans saw no choice but to comply. And those who did not were simply—and often brutally—forced to leave.

Toward the middle of the century, Americans embraced the notion of **"manifest destiny"**—the idea that it was the destiny of the United States to expand to the Pacific Ocean and into Mexican territory. Mexicans disagreed, of course. When Texas was annexed from Mexico by the United States in 1845, it set off the Mexican-American War. Many Americans, including writer **Henry David Thoreau,** found the war to be immoral—a war fought mainly to expand slavery. "Can there not be a government," he wrote, "in which majorities do not virtually decide right and wrong, but conscience?" In the end, the United States defeated Mexico and, through treaties and subsequent land purchases from the Mexican government, established the current borders of the 48 contiguous United States.

Growth of Industry

The stories and essays of the romantic period reflect an enormous shift in the attitudes and working habits of many Americans. When the War of 1812 interrupted trade with the British, Americans were suddenly forced to produce many of the goods they had previously imported. The **Industrial Revolution** began, changing the country from a largely agrarian economy to an industrial powerhouse.

The factory system changed the way of life for many Americans, but not always for the better. People left their farms for the cities, working long hours for low wages in harsh conditions. In addition, Northeastern textile mills' demand for cotton played a role in the expansion of slavery in the South. Writers of this period reacted to the negative effects of industrialization—the commercialism, hectic pace, and lack of conscience—by turning to nature and to the self for simplicity, truth, and beauty.

Detail of *Summer Afternoon on the Hudson* (1852), Jasper Francis Cropsey. © Christie's Images/Corbis.

COMMON CORE

RL 9 Demonstrate knowledge of nineteenth-century foundational works of American literature, including how two or more texts from the same period treat similar themes or topics. **RI 9** Analyze documents of historical and literary significance for their themes, purposes, and rhetorical features.

▶ **TAKING NOTES**

Outlining As you read this introduction, use an outline to record the main ideas about the characteristics and the literature of the period. You can use article headings, boldfaced terms, and the information in these boxes as starting points. (See page R49 in the **Research Handbook** for more help with outlining.)

I. *Historical Context*
  A. *Spirit of Exploration*
    1. Westward Expansion
    2. Manifest Destiny
  B. *Growth of Industry*

Romanticism: Historical Context

This section of the essay (page 305) describes America's westward expansion during the first half of the 19th century and explains some negative aspects of that expansion. The text also describes the beginning of the Industrial Revolution and its impact upon Americans.

TIERED DISCUSSION PROMPTS

Use these prompts to help students understand the ideas in **The Spirit of Exploration** and **Growth of Industry:**

Interpret Reread the second sentence of **The Spirit of Exploration.** What was the "price" of the physical expansion of the United States? *Possible answer: Expansion cost Native Americans their land and often their lives. In addition, belief in the concept of "manifest destiny" led to the Mexican-American War, which cost soldiers' lives on both sides.*

Analyze What were the chief effects of the Industrial Revolution? *Possible answer: The Industrial Revolution changed the basis of the national economy from agriculture to industry and prompted the migration of people from farms to cities. It also encouraged the expansion of slavery in the South and prompted writers to seek answers to life in nature and the self.*

Synthesize Reread the final sentence of **Growth of Industry.** How does the earlier Thoreau quotation connect to that idea? *Possible answer: Thoreau's comment emphasizes the importance of conscience, an idea that reflects a belief in the ability to find "simplicity, truth, and beauty" in the self.*

FOR ENGLISH LANGUAGE LEARNERS

Set a Purpose After introducing the prime ideas on this page, ask students to look for cause-effect relationships between events as they read about westward expansion and the Industrial Revolution.

FOR ADVANCED LEARNERS/AP*

Research and Analyze [small-group option] Have small groups gather information about "manifest destiny": the origin of the term, ways in which the concept was debated, and its political impact. Have students present their findings to the class and explain why this doctrine was significant.

Cultural Influences

This section of the essay (pages 306–307) explains the growing split between North and South over the issue of slavery. The text also describes how an increasing number of Americans called for social reform, speaking out against slavery and supporting the rights of workers and women.

DISCUSSION PROMPT

Use this prompt to help students understand the ideas in **The Tragedy of Slavery:**

Synthesize Consider what you know about slavery from the account by Olaudah Equiano in Unit 1 or from any other account you have read or seen. What conclusion might you draw from this section, which describes slavery a generation after Equiano's account was published? *Possible answer: Because of increased cotton production, slavery had expanded in the American South, and its brutality affected more persons than ever. Enslaved families were broken up, and men, women, and children were subjected to cruel treatment. Southern plantation owners considered slavery essential for increasing their profits, increasing tension between pro-slavery Southerners and Northerners who considered slavery to be immoral.*

Cultural Influences

Many romantic writers were outspoken in their support for human rights. Their works created awareness of the injustice of slavery and called for reform in many other areas as well.

This antislavery medal was created to help grow support for the abolition movement.

The Tragedy of Slavery

From 1793 to 1860, cotton production rose greatly, due to the invention of the cotton gin and other farming machinery. So did the number of enslaved workers. Plantation owners were the wealthiest and most powerful people in the South, yet they were relatively few in number. Most Southern farmers held few or no slaves, but they aspired to. They felt that slavery had become necessary for increasing profits.

For slaves, life was brutal. Field workers—men, women, and children—rose before dawn and worked in the fields until bedtime. Many were beaten or otherwise abused. And worst of all, family members were sold away from one another. Often family members attempted to escape to be with one another again. Unfortunately, escapes were rarely successful.

Tension over slavery increased between the North and the South. Many in the North saw slavery as immoral and worked to have it abolished. Others worried as the balance of power between free and slave states shifted with each new state entering the Union. Romantic poets **James Russell Lowell** and **John Greenleaf Whittier** wrote abolitionist journalism and poetry, and even **Henry Wadsworth Longfellow** published a volume of antislavery poems. Perhaps the greatest social achievement of the romantics was to create awareness of slavery's cruelty.

A Voice from the Times

Men! Whose boast it is that ye
Come of fathers brave and free,
If there breathe on earth a slave,
Are ye truly free and brave?
If ye do not feel the chain,
When it works a brother's pain,
Are ye not base slaves indeed,
Slaves unworthy to be freed?

—James Russell Lowell
from "Stanzas on Freedom"

Call for Social Reform

By the mid-19th century, many Americans had joined together to fight slavery and the other social ills of the time. Many leading writers of the romantic movement were outspoken in their support for human rights. **William Cullen Bryant** and **James Russell Lowell,** for example, were prominent abolitionists who also supported workers' and women's rights.

The abolition movement began by advocating resettlement of blacks in Africa. But most enslaved African Americans had been born and raised in the United States and resented the idea of being forced to leave. Instead, white and black abolitionists (including women) began to join together to work for emancipation. They formed societies, spoke at conventions, published newspapers, and swamped Congress with petitions to end slavery.

DIFFERENTIATED INSTRUCTION

FOR STRUGGLING READERS

Taking Notes Ask students to record the main ideas relating to **Cultural Influences** (pages 306–307) in outline form. Then have students exchange papers and evaluate each other's work. Instruct students to offer specific suggestions for improvement.

Sample notes:

I. *The Tragedy of Slavery*
  A. *Demand for cotton = increase in slavery*
  B. *Brutal treatment of enslaved workers*
  C. *North-South tension over the issue*
    1. *View of South: slavery as economically necessary*
    2. *View of North: slavery as immoral*
  D. *Involvement of writers*
II. *Call for Social Reform*
  A. *Rise in opposition to social ills*
    1. *End to slavery*
    2. *Improved conditions for workers*
    3. *Opportunities for women*
  B. *Involvement of writers*

In the 1830s and 1840s, workers began to agitate as well, protesting low wages and deteriorating working conditions. Many struck, but few were successful—a large pool of immigrants was always ready to take their places. Still, workers began forming unions, and slowly conditions improved.

Women in the early 19th century found much to protest. They could neither vote nor sit on juries. Their education rarely extended beyond elementary school. When they married, their property and money became their husband's. Many even lacked guardianship rights over their children. Throughout this period, women worked for change, gathering in 1848 at Seneca Falls, New York, to continue their long fight for women's rights.

Ideas of the Age

Reflecting the optimism of their growing country, American romantic writers forged a national literature for the very first time. Yet sectionalism threatened to tear the nation apart.

Nationalism vs. Sectionalism

In the early 1800s, many Supreme Court decisions strengthened the federal government's power over the states. At the same time, Secretary of State John Quincy Adams established a foreign policy guided by **nationalism**—the belief that national interests should be placed ahead of regional concerns or the interests of other countries. Reflecting the national pride and optimism of the American people, writers of this age forged a literature entirely the nation's own. For the first time, writers were not imitating their European counterparts, but were listening to their own voices and writing with a distinctly American accent.

However, this new spirit of nationalism was challenged by the question of slavery. Up until 1818, the United States had consisted of ten free and ten slave states. As new territories tried to enter the Union, the North and South wrangled over the balance of power between free and slave states. Economic interests also challenged nationalism. Tariffs on manufactured goods from Britain forced Southerners to buy more expensive, Northern-manufactured goods. From the South's point of view, the North was getting rich at the South's expense. Sectionalism, or the placing of the interests of one's own region ahead of the nation as a whole, began to take hold.

The Hudson River School

The paintings on pages 301 and 304 are excellent examples of the works of the Hudson River School artists. This group of landscape painters flourished between 1825 and 1870. The artists knew one another and used similar techniques for portraying nature scenes.

American Style Thomas Cole painted *A View of the Mountain Pass Called the Notch of the White Mountains* (1839), shown here and on page 301. He and the other Hudson River artists created passionate wilderness scenes that appealed to the imagination and made earlier American landscapes seem weak and unobserved. Like the American romantic writers of the time, the Hudson River School artists made a conscious effort to create an American style—one based on nature and the emotions.

Real-Life Inspiration The painting shown in detail here has an interesting history. Author Nathaniel Hawthorne wrote a short story about a real-life landslide at Crawford Notch that took the lives of nine people. The story may have piqued Cole's interest in the scene. In the painting Cole highlights the insignificance and vulnerability of the human figures in the face of the coming storm. One barely notices the settlers' homes or the rider, who seems oblivious to the ominous clouds gathering at the upper left—hinting of disaster to come.

UNIT INTRODUCTION **307**

THE ARTISTS' GALLERY

The Hudson River School, whose landscape paintings captured the natural grandeur of the Hudson River Valley, Niagara Falls, the White Mountains, and other parts of New England, was influenced by European romantic ideas about nature. *A View of the Mountain Pass Called the Notch of the White Mountains* is representative of the dramatic, colorful painting of Thomas Cole, a founder and leader of the Hudson River School. Point out that Cole's placement of gnarled trees (better seen in the larger illustration on page 301) alongside the stumps of trees that have been cut down reflects the romantic opposition to the destruction of America's forests.

Activity Ask students how Cole's use of color and contrast adds drama to the painting. ***Possible answer:*** *The vivid colors and contrast of light and dark (especially in the sky) give the painting emotional depth.*

CHECK UNDERSTANDING

Ask students to explain how protest was a part of the 1830s and '40s. Then ask students why they think most of this protest took place in the North rather than in the South.

Ideas of the Age

This section of the essay (page 307) describes how sectionalism, focused largely upon the issue of slavery, threatened a rising nationalistic spirit.

CHECK UNDERSTANDING

Ask students to define *nationalism* in their own words and to explain how slavery undermined feelings of nationalism.

FOR STRUGGLING READERS
Vocabulary Support
- *abolitionist,* "person who advocated the end of slavery"
- *emancipation,* "freedom from bondage"
- *tariff,* "tax placed on imported goods"
- *free state,* "U.S. state in which slavery was prohibited before the Civil War"
- *slave state,* "U.S. state in which slavery was legal until the Civil War"

FOR ADVANCED LEARNERS/AP
Synthesize Point out that issues relating to nationalism and sectionalism are by no means limited to the nineteenth century. Have students write a brief essay explaining how conflicts over nationalism and sectionalism persist to this day. Encourage students to use their knowledge of current events and to do additional research as needed to support their ideas with specific examples.

Romantic Literature

This section of the essay (pages 308–313) focuses on the themes and writing of the American romantic movement. The text describes the work of the following groups:

- the early romantics, including William Cullen Bryant, Washington Irving, and James Fenimore Cooper

- the Fireside Poets, including Henry Wadsworth Longfellow, James Russell Lowell, Oliver Wendell Holmes, and John Greenleaf Whittier

- the transcendentalists, including Ralph Waldo Emerson and Henry David Thoreau

- the "brooding" romantics, including Edgar Allan Poe, Nathaniel Hawthorne, and Herman Melville

Analyze Visuals

Possible answer: The paintings are similar in their depiction of nature's beauty. However, Cole used a striking combination of colors in his painting, while Durand's use of color is more limited and subdued.

About the Art American artist Asher Brown Durand (1796–1886) was a successful engraver when he developed a growing interest in oil painting, especially landscapes. (Indeed, the attention to fine detail in *Kindred Spirits* reflects an engraver's skill.) Durand and Thomas Cole are considered to be the founders of the Hudson River School (see page 307), and *Kindred Spirits* often is cited as the most famous painting to come from this group. Set in the Catskill Mountains, it shows the majesty of nature; though the human beings in the scene look small by comparison to their surroundings, they fit "naturally" into the scene—an idea that early romantic writers would have embraced. Furthermore, the distance indicated in the background suggests the optimism of early romanticism.

Romantic Literature

Themes of individualism and nature unified the writing of the American romantic movement, despite dramatic differences in the writers' focus and style.

The Early Romantics

The early American romantic writers may have been influenced more by the literature of another continent than by that of their own. **Romanticism** had first emerged in Europe in the late 18th century, in reaction to the neoclassicism of the period that had preceded it. Where neoclassical writers admired and imitated classical forms, the romantics looked to nature for inspiration. Where neoclassicists valued reason, the romantics celebrated emotions and the imagination. The first American romantic writers grew

▶ *For Your Outline*
THE EARLY ROMANTICS

- were inspired by the beauty of nature
- emphasized emotions and the imagination over reason
- celebrated the individual spirit

Kindred Spirits (1849), Asher B. Durand. © Francis G. Mayer/Corbis.

◀ **Analyze Visuals**
This painting is a memorial to painter Asher B. Durand's friend and fellow Hudson River School artist Thomas Cole (here shown with romantic poet William Cullen Bryant).

Although Durand was influenced by Cole, his works express stillness and a realistic imitation of nature, in contrast to Cole's more expressive rendering. Compare this painting with Cole's on the previous page. How are they similar? How are they different?

DIFFERENTIATED INSTRUCTION

FOR STRUGGLING READERS

Vocabulary Support The "classical forms" that neoclassical writers admired and imitated were the creative works of the ancient Greeks and Romans in literature, art, and architecture. These works were characterized as simple (that is, not artificially ornate), elegant, and (as might be expected in a movement that valued reason) symmetrical.

Vocabulary Support

- *neoclassicism,* "revival of the artistic tastes and styles of ancient Greece and Rome"

- *rationality,* "reliance upon reason"

- *human nature,* "the qualities that all people share; what defines a being as human"

- *supernatural,* "that which exists or occurs beyond the natural world"

A collection of major works by early American romantics

out of this European tradition, shaping and molding it to fit their unique American identity. They too were reacting to what had come before—the rationality of the Age of Reason and the strict doctrines of Puritanism.

Indeed, much had changed since the Puritan era in America, and the writers of the early romantic period reflected the more modern sensibilities of their day. As the U.S. population exploded and the country's borders moved westward, American writers aimed to capture the energy and character of their growing country. They saw the limits of reason and instead celebrated the glories of the individual spirit, the emotions, and the imagination as basic elements of human nature. The splendors of nature inspired the romantics more than the fear of God, and some of them felt a fascination with the supernatural.

William Cullen Bryant's 1817 poem "Thanatopsis" went a long way toward establishing romanticism as the major force in the literature of mid-19th century America. Bryant followed the trend of the English romantics by celebrating nature in his work. Romanticism was not only a movement in poetry, however. **Washington Irving,** the first American writer esteemed abroad, pioneered the short story as a literary form. He put America on the literary map and also influenced other writers, particularly Nathaniel Hawthorne. **James Fenimore Cooper** is remembered for writing the first truly original American novel. He celebrated the American spirit in all his frontier novels, known as *The Leatherstocking Tales.* The early romantic writers were the pioneers of America's national literature, setting the course for those who would follow.

> **A Voice from the Times**
>
> *To him who in the love of Nature holds*
> *Communion with her visible forms, she speaks*
> *A various language; for his gayer hours*
> *She has a voice of gladness, and a smile*
> *And eloquence of beauty, and she glides*
> *Into his darker musings, with a mild*
> *And healing sympathy, that steals away*
> *Their sharpness, ere he is aware. . . .*
>
> **—William Cullen Bryant**
> *from* "Thanatopsis"

TIERED DISCUSSION PROMPTS

Use these prompts to help students understand the ideas in **The Early Romantics:**

Restate What did the romantics reject, and what did they admire? ***Possible answer:*** *The romantics rejected the neoclassical love of reason and classical forms; they admired nature, emotion, and imagination.*

Interpret What were "the more modern sensibilities" that the early romantics reflected? How did these writers respond? ***Possible answer:*** *These sensibilities were an awareness and appreciation of the country's dynamic growth. In response, the early romantics focused more upon individualism, emotion, and imagination than upon reason; they also found greater inspiration in nature than in the fear of God.*

Synthesize Given what you already know about American literature and culture, which writer of early romanticism—Bryant, Irving, or Cooper—do you think has had the greatest impact, and why? *Accept all reasonable responses.*

FOR ADVANCED LEARNERS/AP

Research Influences on Romanticism Explain that inspiration for the early American romantic writers came in part from the French writer and philosopher Jean Jacques Rousseau (1712–1778) and the German poet Johann Wolfgang von Goethe (1749–1832). Ask small groups of students to research Rousseau and Goethe. Then challenge each group to create a poster that presents this information:

- key facts about each writer's life, including major works and accomplishments
- a summary of each writer's ideas
- notes about each writer's impact upon other writers and thinkers of the time

Invite group representatives to present the posters to the class.

Use these prompts to help students understand the ideas in **The Fireside Poets:**

Restate Why were these poets called the Fireside Poets? *Possible answer: In the 19th century, a common form of family entertainment was reading poetry aloud beside the fire.*

Analyze In what sense did each member of the Fireside Poets attempt to improve the United States? *Possible answer: Lowell, Holmes, and Whittier were concerned about social issues, and they used their poetry to advocate for social reform in the United States. Longfellow may not have been as openly committed to social reform, but by frequently writing about America's past, he may have been trying to improve the United States by giving Americans a heritage of which they could be proud.*

The legendary Hiawatha, memorialized in Longfellow's poem "The Song of Hiawatha"

The Fireside Poets

Other writers influential in forging an American literature were the Fireside Poets, a group of New England poets whose work was morally uplifting and romantically engaging. The group's name came from the family custom of reading poetry aloud beside a fire, a common form of entertainment in the 19th century. With the Fireside Poets, the poetry of American writers was, for the first time, on equal footing with that of their British counterparts.

Henry Wadsworth Longfellow, the best-known member of the group, stressed individualism and an appreciation of nature in his work. His poems took for their subject matter the more colorful aspects of America's past. "Evangeline," for example, tells of lovers who are separated during the French and Indian War, while "The Song of Hiawatha" takes its themes from Native American folklore. Longfellow's fame was so great that after his death, he was honored with a plaque in Poets' Corner of Westminster Abbey in London—the only American poet ever to receive such an honor.

The other Fireside Poets, **James Russell Lowell, Oliver Wendell Holmes,** and **John Greenleaf Whittier,** were strongly committed to using poetry to bring about social reform. They were interested in such issues as abolition, women's rights, improvement of factory conditions, and temperance. They also championed the common person—perhaps as an outgrowth of the form of democracy that had been sweeping the land since President Jackson took office in 1829. Jackson had crusaded against control of the government by the wealthy and promised to look out for the interests of common people. One can see this regard for the common person in the work of Whittier, for example, who wrote of farmers, lumbermen, migrants, and the poor.

> ▶ *For Your Outline*
>
> **THE FIRESIDE POETS**
>
> - emphasized moral themes in work
> - were viewed as equals of British poets of the day
> - stressed individualism and an appreciation of nature
> - were committed to social reform

DIFFERENTIATED INSTRUCTION

FOR STRUGGLING READERS

Vocabulary Support The word *temperance* means "the practice of abstaining from alcoholic beverages." The link between drunkenness and other social problems had long been noted, but the movement to improve public life by banning alcohol gained momentum in the first half of the 19th century. By the 1830s, thousands of temperance societies around the United States and in other countries were working to reduce the consumption of alcohol.

FOR ADVANCED LEARNERS/AP

Research Quakers such as John Greenleaf Whittier played a key role in the growth of the abolitionist movement in the United States. Have students research the origins of the Society of Friends and their contributions to abolitionism, such as their foundation of numerous abolitionist societies, the "Underground Railroad," and schools for freed slaves. Have students report their findings to the class. Allow time for questions and discussion.

The Transcendentalists

By the mid-1800s, Americans were taking new pride in their emerging culture. **Ralph Waldo Emerson,** a New England writer, nurtured this pride. Emerson led a group practicing **transcendentalism**—a philosophical and literary movement that emphasized living a simple life and celebrating the truth found in nature and in personal emotion and imagination. Exalting the dignity of the individual, the transcendentalist stressed American ideas of optimism, freedom, and self-reliance.

The term transcendentalism came from Immanuel Kant, a German philosopher who wrote of "transcendent forms" of knowledge that exist beyond reason and experience. Emerson gave this philosophy a peculiarly American spin: he said that every individual is capable of discovering this higher truth on his or her own, through intuition. The transcendentalists believed that people are inherently good and should follow their own beliefs, however different these beliefs may be from the norm. Both Emerson's essay "Self-Reliance" and **Henry David Thoreau's** "Civil Disobedience" address this faith in the integrity of the individual.

Not surprisingly, a major target for the transcendentalists' criticism was their Puritan heritage, with its emphasis on material prosperity and rigid obedience to the laws of society. The transcendentalists disliked the commercial, financial side of American life and stressed instead spiritual well-being, achieved through intellectual activity and a close relationship to nature. Thoreau put his beliefs into practice by building a small cabin on Walden Pond and living there for two years, writing and studying nature.

Transcendental ideas lived on in American culture in the works of later poets such as Walt Whitman, Robert Frost, and Wallace Stevens and through the civil rights movement of the 20th century. In the short term, however, transcendentalists' optimism began to fade when confronted with the persistence of slavery and the difficulty in abolishing it.

> ▶ *For Your Outline*
>
> **THE TRANSCENDENTALISTS**
>
> - emphasized living a simple life
> - stressed a close relationship to nature
> - celebrated emotions and the imagination
> - stressed individualism and self-reliance
> - believed intuition can lead to knowledge
> - believed in the inherent goodness of people
> - encouraged spiritual well-being over financial well-being

A Voice from the Times

Go confidently in the direction of your dreams! Live the life you've imagined. As you simplify your life, the laws of the universe will be simpler.

—Henry David Thoreau

A replica of Thoreau's 10-by-15-foot cabin on the shore of Walden Pond

TIERED DISCUSSION PROMPTS

Use these prompts to help students understand the ideas in **The Transcendentalists:**

Restate What did the transcendentalists reject, and what did they admire? *Possible answer: The transcendentalists rejected commercialism and Puritan attitudes; they admired individualism, intuition, intellectualism, and a spiritual relationship with nature.*

Interpret How was Emerson's adaptation of transcendentalism "peculiarly American"? *Possible answer: Emerson stressed the individual's role in finding "higher truth" through intuition. This emphasis on individualism was very much in keeping with the American values of the era.*

Evaluate Consider what you know of American life at this time. How would you respond to someone who called transcendentalism an impractical philosophy? *Encourage answers that demonstrate an awareness of these points:*

- *the transcendentalists' unorthodoxy vs. the nation's Puritan heritage*
- *the transcendentalists' belief in reflection and personal conscience vs. the sense of national pride, unity, and drive that marked the country as a whole in the early 1800s*

FOR STRUGGLING READERS

Vocabulary Support

- *reform,* "change for the better; correction or removal of what is wrong"
- *nurture,* "to nourish and promote"
- *self-reliance,* "trust in or dependence upon one's own abilities and efforts"
- *intuition,* "insight gained through personal impression rather than logic"
- *integrity,* "personal honesty and honor"

FOR ADVANCED LEARNERS/AP

Analyze a Quotation Ask students to reflect upon Henry David Thoreau's quotation in **A Voice from the Times.** Have students discuss how the quotation relates to the ideas of the transcendentalists. Extend the discussion by asking students to write a paragraph explaining why they think Thoreau's words still are quoted today, more than a century after he wrote them. Then have them read their paragraphs aloud.

TIERED DISCUSSION PROMPTS

Use these prompts to help students understand the ideas in **American Gothic: The "Brooding" Romantics:**

Analyze How does the work of these writers compare and contrast with that of the early romantics? *Possible answer: Like the early romantics, these writers emphasized individuality, imagination, and emotion. However, these writers had a darker view of the world, humankind, and the imagination.*

Interpret Explain this statement from the essay: "For the dark romantics, the imagination led to the threshold of the unknown. . . ."
Possible answer: The "brooding" romantics cast off the restrictions of reason and followed their imagination into the darker side of human experience. Writers such as Poe, Hawthorne, and Melville explored some of the negative forces at work in human psychology and their effect on human life.

Synthesize Why would you expect a writer from this group to be reluctant about trusting personal intuition? *Possible answer: The "brooding" romantics focused on the dark mysteries of human psychology, so they probably would not trust intuition the way that optimists such as the transcendentalists did.*

American Gothic: The "Brooding" Romantics

Not all American romantics were optimistic or had faith in the innate goodness of humankind, however. Three other giants from this period, **Edgar Allan Poe, Nathaniel Hawthorne,** and **Herman Melville** are what have been called **"brooding" romantics** or **"anti-transcendentalists."** Theirs is a complex philosophy, filled with dark currents and a deep awareness of the human capacity for evil. While Irving had been satisfied if his work kept "mankind in good humor with one another," Hawthorne, Melville, and Poe were haunted by a darker vision of human existence. Their stories are characterized by a probing of the inner life of their characters, and examination of the complex and often mysterious forces that motivate human behavior. They are romantic, however, in their emphasis on emotion, nature, the individual, and the unusual.

EXPLORING THE DARKNESS Poe and Hawthorne, and to a lesser extent Melville, used **gothic** elements such as grotesque characters, bizarre situations, and violent events in their fiction. The gothic tradition had begun in Europe, perhaps inspired by the gothic architecture of the Middle Ages. European writers of the 19th century, such as Mary Shelley, author of *Frankenstein,* delighted readers with their deliciously creepy accounts of monsters, vampires, and humans with a large capacity for evil. The romantic movement itself also gave rise to gothic literature. Once the romantics freed the imagination from the restrictions of reason, they could follow it wherever it might go. For the dark romantics, the imagination led to the threshold of the unknown—that shadowy region where the fantastic, the demonic, and the insane reside.

Edgar Allan Poe, of course, was the master of the gothic form in the United States. He explored human psychology from the inside, using first-person narrators who were sometimes criminal or even insane. His plots involved extreme situations—not just murder, but live burials, physical and mental torture, and retribution from beyond the grave.

Nathaniel Hawthorne agreed with the romantic emphasis on emotion and the individual. However, he did not see these as completely positive forces. His works, such as *The Scarlet Letter* and "The Minister's Black Veil," examine the darker facets of the human soul—for example, the psychological effects sin and guilt may have on human life.

Herman Melville's early works were mostly adventure stories set in the South Pacific. *Moby Dick,* however, departed from that pattern. By concentrating on a ship's captain's obsessive quest for the whale that took his leg, Melville explores such issues as madness and the conflict of good and evil. Later, in "Bartleby the Scrivener," Melville

▶ *For Your Outline*

AMERICAN GOTHIC: THE "BROODING" ROMANTICS

- did not believe in the innate goodness of people
- explored the human capacity for evil
- probed the inner life of characters
- explored characters' motivations
- agreed with romantic emphasis on emotion, nature, and the individual
- included elements of fantasy and the supernatural in works

A Voice from the Times

I looked upon the scene before me—upon the mere house, and the simple landscape features of the domain—upon the bleak walls—upon the vacant eye-like windows—upon a few rank sedges—and upon a few white trunks of decayed trees—with an utter depression of soul which I can compare to no earthly sensation more properly than to the after-dream of the reveller upon opium—the bitter lapse into everyday life—the hideous dropping off of the veil.

—Edgar Allan Poe
from "The Fall of the House of Usher"

DIFFERENTIATED INSTRUCTION

FOR ADVANCED LEARNERS/AP

Research *Frankenstein* [small-group option] Mary Shelley's most famous book was published in 1818 (when she was only 20 years old) and has inspired a multitude of stories, novels, plays, and movies; indeed, Frankenstein's monster is a cultural icon. Have one or more small groups of students research Mary Shelley and write an essay about her life and work. Ask them also to explore the reasons for the lasting popularity of *Frankenstein* and to discuss how Shelley's novel reflects the gothic tradition. To extend the activity, encourage students to read portions of *Frankenstein* and to compare the actual text with their expectations about the story.

Like an Open-Doored Marble Tomb, George Klauba. Acrylic on panel, 18″ × 14.5″. Courtesy of Ann Nathan Gallery, Chicago, Illinois. © George Klamba.

reveals the dark side of material prosperity by exploring how the struggle for material gain affects the individual.

Perhaps the dark vision of Hawthorne, Melville, and Poe foreshadowed the tumult and tragedy that was soon to erupt in civil war in America. There is no question that these three writers profoundly affected the development of the American literary voice throughout the remainder of the 19th century.

Analyze Visuals

Activity In what sense might the image in this painting symbolize the way that the "brooding" romantics thought about life and their writing? *Possible answer: In the image, Moby Dick is mostly hidden in the ocean depths, but he is approaching the boat, his intent of destruction clear. Similarly, the "brooding" romantics explored the mysterious, hidden aspects of human psychology and often seemed haunted by the threat of impending disaster.*

DISCUSSION PROMPT

Use this prompt to help students understand the ideas in **American Gothic: The "Brooding" Romantics:**

Synthesize What aspects of early gothic literature are apparent in modern-day works? *Possible answer: Such gothic elements as "grotesque characters, bizarre situations, and violent events" remain a mainstay of modern-day horror writers, such as Stephen King.*

CHECK UNDERSTANDING

Identify a few characteristics of each of these groups of writers:

- The Early Romantics
- The Fireside Poets
- The Transcendentalists
- The "Brooding" Romantics

FOR STRUGGLING READERS
Vocabulary Support

- *brooding,* "absorbed in gloomy thoughts"
- *innate,* "inborn; natural"
- *material,* "relating to physical things, rather than to spiritual or intellectual concerns"
- *foreshadow,* "to indicate beforehand"

COMMON CORE FOCUS

RI 7 Integrate and evaluate multiple sources of information presented in different media or formats as well as in words in order to address a question or solve a problem.

Connecting: Literature, History, and Culture

COMMON CORE RI 7

■ READ A TIMELINE

Elicit or explain that each of the three horizontal sections of the timeline—*American Literary Milestones, Historical Context,* and *World Culture and Events*—displays a sequence of events that occurred between 1800 and 1855. By looking at the vertical columns on the timeline, students can see which events were taking place at about the same time.

Have students locate, for example, each of these events on the timeline in the 1820s column:

- **1823** Beethoven completes his Ninth Symphony. (See *World Culture and Events.*)
- **1824** Washington Irving's "The Devil and Tom Walker" is published. (See *American Literary Milestones.*)
- **1825** The Erie Canal is opened. (See *Historical Context.*)

Ask students to identify events that occurred between 1815 and 1817. ***Answer: Levi Coffin established the Underground Railroad in 1815; Rossini wrote* The Barber of Seville *in 1816; Bryant's "Thanatopsis" was published in 1817.***

Connecting Literature, History, and Culture

Use this timeline and the questions on the next page to gain insight about how developments during the American romantic period reflected what was happening in the world as a whole.

AMERICAN LITERARY MILESTONES

1800	1810	1820
1806 Noah Webster's first dictionary is published. It includes 5,000 words related to American customs that have never before been collected. **1809** Washington Irving publishes *A History of New York,* satirizing the young nation.	**1817** "Thanatopsis," composed by William Cullen Bryant at age 18, is published in *The North American Review.* ▼	**1824** Irving's "The Devil and Tom Walker" is published. **1826** James Fenimore Cooper writes *The Last of the Mohicans.* **1827** *Freedom's Journal,* the first African-American newspaper, is founded. ▼

FREEDOM'S JOURNAL.

HISTORICAL CONTEXT

1800	1810	1820
1803 Thomas Jefferson doubles ▲ the country's size by buying Louisiana Territory from France. **1807** Robert Fulton launches *Clermont,* the first steamboat. **1808** United States bans slave trade.	**1812** United States declares war ▲ on Great Britain. American industry booms. **1815** Quaker Levi Coffin establishes the Underground Railroad.	**1820** Missouri Compromise prohibits slavery in western territories but allows slavery in Arkansas Territory and Louisiana. **1823** The Monroe Doctrine bans European colonization in the Americas. **1825** The Erie Canal is opened, linking Lake Erie with the Hudson River. **1828** Construction begins on the first railroad in the United States.

WORLD CULTURE AND EVENTS

1800	1810	1820
1804 Napoleon is crowned emperor of France. **1806** The Holy Roman Empire reaches its last days. **1807** British slave trade is abolished.	**1813** Jane Austen publishes *Pride and Prejudice.* **1816** Rossini writes the comic opera *The Barber of Seville.* **1819** Factory work is outlawed in England for children under nine years old.	**1821** Venezuela and Mexico declare independence from Spain. ▶ **1823** Beethoven completes his Ninth Symphony. **1829** Slavery is abolished in Mexico.

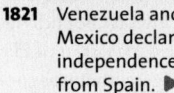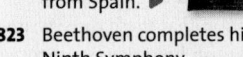

314 UNIT 2: AMERICAN ROMANTICISM

DIFFERENTIATED INSTRUCTION

FOR STRUGGLING READERS

Understanding a Timeline Explain that the timeline runs chronologically (in time order) from left to right across the page. Each of the six columns represents a ten-year period between 1800 and 1855 except for the last column, which covers only about five years. The three parallel rows of the timeline represent events occurring simultaneously. By comparing the three rows, readers can better understand what events in literature, history, and culture were taking place at about the same time.

MAKING CONNECTIONS

- Which European authors were contemporaries of American romantic writers?
- What evidence do you see that slavery was not only an American problem?
- What nations were battling for independence or dealing with its challenges?
- What inventions were moving the world into a more technological age?

COMMON CORE

RI 7 Integrate and evaluate multiple sources of information presented in different media or formats as well as in words in order to address a question or solve a problem.

1830

1835 Emerson, Thoreau, Margaret Fuller, and others form the Transcendental Club.

1838 Henry Wadsworth Longfellow's "A Psalm of Life" is published.

1839 Edgar Allan Poe's "The Fall of the House of Usher" is published.

1840

1845 Henry David Thoreau moves to Walden Pond.

1846 Herman Melville's first novel, *Typee*, is published. ▼

1850

1850 Nathaniel Hawthorne's *The Scarlet Letter* is published.

1851 Sojourner Truth delivers her "Ain't I a Woman?" speech to the Women's Rights Convention in Akron, Ohio. ▶

1852 Harriet Beecher Stowe publishes *Uncle Tom's Cabin*.

1830

1830 Indian Removal Act authorizes relocation of southeastern Native American tribes to territories west of Mississippi River.

1832 Samuel B. Morse invents the telegraph. ▼

1840

1845 Florida and Texas become the 27th and 28th states.

1848 Gold discoveries in California lead to first gold rush. ▼

1850

1850 Congress passes the Fugitive Slave Act, forcing officials in Northern states to return escaped slaves to their owners.

1851 Isaac Singer devises the sewing machine. ▼

1830

1838 Slaves mutiny aboard the ▲ Spanish ship *Amistad*.

1840

1843 Charles Dickens writes *A Christmas Carol*.

1847 Emily Brontë publishes *Wuthering Heights*.

1848 Karl Marx and Friedrich Engels publish *The Communist Manifesto*.

1850

1852 Dr. Livingston explores Zambesi.

1853 Verdi's opera *La Traviata* is first performed in Venice; Crimean War begins, involving Turkey, Russia, Britain, and France.

TIMELINE **315**

MAKING CONNECTIONS

Answers:

- *Jane Austen, Charles Dickens, Emily Brontë, Karl Marx, and Friedrich Engels were contemporaries of the American romantics.*

- *Slavery was not only an American problem, as evidenced by these facts: The British slave trade was abolished in 1807; slavery was abolished in Mexico in 1829; and slaves mutinied aboard the Spanish ship* Amistad *in 1838.*

- *Venezuela and Mexico were seeking independence; the United States was dealing with its challenges.*

- *The steamboat (1807), the telegraph (1832), and the sewing machine (1851) were technological inventions of the era.*

ADDITIONAL QUESTIONS

1. Which American author published his first novel 20 years after James Fenimore Cooper wrote *The Last of the Mohicans*? What was the title? ***Answer:*** *Herman Melville published* Typee *(1846).*

2. How many years after the United States banned the slave trade did Mexico abolish slavery? ***Answer:*** *Twenty-one years passed (1829).*

3. What innovations in transportation took place in the United States during this era? ***Answer:*** *the launching of the first steamboat (1807), the opening of the Erie Canal (1825), and the start of construction on the first railroad in the United States (1828).*

FOR ADVANCED LEARNERS/AP

Making Additional Connections Ask students to choose one of the six decades shown in the timeline and to research online, in encyclopedias, or in history texts other events that took place during that same ten-year time span. Challenge students to identify events for each category: *American Literary Milestones, Historical Context,* and *World Culture and Events.* Have students work individually, with partners, or in small groups to prepare and present brief oral reports. The students should summarize significant events and discuss their connection to events shown in the timeline or discussed in class.

COMMON CORE FOCUS

W 10 Write routinely over short time frames for a range of tasks, purposes, and audiences.
SL 1 Initiate and participate effectively in collaborative discussions, building on others' ideas and expressing their own clearly and persuasively.

Civil Rights

Have students read the paragraph. Elicit or explain that *civil disobedience* means refusing to obey the law as a nonviolent way of calling attention to injustice. People who practice civil disobedience hope to persuade the government to change or repeal unjust laws. Explain that civil disobedience usually takes the form of "passive resistance"—that is, opposition through noncooperation.

DISCUSS Work with students to explore examples of civil disobedience, discussing to what extent the actions taken were successful, and why. Connect the civil disobedience of Dr. Martin Luther King Jr. to the civil rights movement in the United States; also elicit or briefly explain the role that civil disobedience played in the work of Mohandas Gandhi in India. Then discuss Thoreau's statement, encouraging students to support their opinions with thoughtful reasons. Extend the discussion by asking students whether they think that penalties for breaking the law should be different in cases in which people are practicing civil disobedience rather than breaking the law for personal gain.

Civil Rights

COMMON CORE

W 10 Write routinely over short time frames for a range of tasks, purposes, and audiences.
SL 1 Initiate and participate effectively in collaborative discussions, building on others' ideas and expressing their own clearly and persuasively.

When faced with unjust government actions, Henry David Thoreau called for Americans to practice civil disobedience in protest. This nonviolent form of protest attained full flower in the civil rights movement of the 1960s and remains an important tactic for activists today. In strikes, marches, and candlelight vigils, protestors across the United States use nonviolent means to make their voices heard.

DISCUSS As a class, think of recent examples of citizens using civil disobedience to protest government action. Were their protests successful? Was Thoreau right when he said, "If the alternative is to keep all just men in prison, or give up . . . , the State will not hesitate which to choose"?

316

DIFFERENTIATED INSTRUCTION

FOR STRUGGLING READERS
Vocabulary Support

- *tactic,* "an action taken or method used to achieve a goal"

- *activist,* "a person who takes strong action to support or oppose a cause"

- *vigil,* "keeping watch for a particular purpose"

FOR ADVANCED LEARNERS/AP
Research Civil Disobedience Today [small-group option] Note the comment that civil disobedience "remains an important tactic for activists today." Then instruct small groups of students to find examples of civil disobedience within the past year or two. Have each group decide how to present its findings—for example, a bulletin-board display or a set of brief oral reports—always concluding with an evaluation of the effectiveness of civil disobedience.

Modern Gothic

The influence of Edgar Allan Poe is alive and well—make that undead and decaying—in the works of modern horror authors such as Stephen King and Anne Rice, and in many of the graphic novels lining today's bookstore shelves. Though their settings may be modern, these works share Poe's fascination with the dark side of humankind.

QUICKWRITE Why do you think people enjoy being frightened? Write a paragraph or two giving your reasons why so many people read gothic literature and enjoy films written in this same tradition.

The Romantic Hero

The romantic writers' focus on the individual led to the creation of a different kind of hero: unique, bold, sometimes brooding or eccentric. From the obsessed Captain Ahab, searching for his white whale in *Moby Dick,* to *The Last of the Mohicans'* noble Natty Bumppo, living on the fringes of society as both a white man and a Native American, romantic heroes were often larger than life, and always unforgettable. Their stories are still told today, and they have inspired a modern array of equally vivid characters.

CREATE With a small group, brainstorm a memorable hero for a new novel, TV show, or movie. Your hero should exemplify key aspects of the romantic spirit and must be utterly unique, a dynamic or mesmerizing individual who would capture people's imaginations.

Indiana Jones, from the movie *Raiders of the Lost Ark*, is a typical romantic hero.

Modern Gothic

After students have read the paragraph, invite comments about any of the literature mentioned with which they are familiar. Help students compile a list of elements of horror that they think most people would find frightening.

QUICKWRITE Ask volunteers to read their paragraphs to the class. Use students' responses to launch a discussion of the overall appeal of gothic literature. Expand the discussion by asking whether students think that this type of literature appeals to some groups more than others—for example, is it more popular with boys than girls, or with young people rather than older people?

The Romantic Hero

Have students read the paragraph. Ask for additional examples, drawn from novels, short stories, TV, and movies, of the "unique, bold, sometimes brooding or eccentric" romantic hero. Explore the common characteristics of the heroes that students name. Extend the discussion by asking whether students think that a romantic hero must be of a particular age or gender.

CREATE After students have finished brainstorming, challenge them to outline or summarize the plot for a story in which their hero is the main character. The plot should allow the hero to exhibit the representative characteristics of a romantic hero. Work with students to prepare a format for sharing their ideas.

FOR STRUGGLING READERS
Vocabulary Support To support instruction, clarify the meaning of these words:

- *eccentric,* "odd; unusual"
- *obsessed,* "overly and unreasonably concerned about something"
- *array,* "group"
- *dynamic,* "forceful; energetic"
- *mesmerizing,* "fascinating"

FOR ADVANCED LEARNERS/AP
Write a Short Story [paired option] Have students write a short story based on the adventures of a romantic hero. They may use the hero that their group brainstormed or create a new hero of their own. Encourage students to develop the characters in their stories and to include dialogue and descriptive details.

Focus and Motivate

COMMON CORE FOCUS

RL 1 Cite textual evidence to support analysis of inferences drawn from the text. **RL 2** Determine two themes of a text and analyze their development. **RL 3** Analyze the impact of the author's choices regarding how to develop and relate elements of a story. **RL 4** Analyze the impact of specific word choices on meaning and tone, including language that is fresh, engaging, or beautiful. **RL 6** Distinguish what is directly stated from what is really meant. **W 3d** Write narratives using precise words and phrases. **L 3** Apply knowledge of language to comprehend more fully when reading. **L 3a** Vary syntax for effect. **L 4** Determine the meanings of words and phrases as they are used in the text. **L 4a** Use context as a clue to the meaning of a word or phrase. **L 4b** Identify and use patterns of word changes that indicate different parts of speech. **L 4c** Consult reference materials to determine or clarify a word's part of speech. **L 6** Acquire and use academic words and phrases.

ABOUT THE AUTHOR

Call attention to Irving's comment that he always enjoyed "observing strange characters and manners." Point out that the selection demonstrates Irving's ability to translate his observations of human nature into fiction.

NOTABLE QUOTE

"The almighty dollar, that great object of universal devotion . . ." —**Washington Irving**

Ask students whether people's regard for "the almighty dollar" represents a particular time or place or if such "devotion" is indeed "universal."

Selection Resources

COMMON CORE

RL 1 Cite textual evidence to support analysis of inferences drawn from the text. **RL 2** Determine two themes of a text and analyze their development. **RL 4** Analyze the impact of specific word choices on meaning and tone, including language that is fresh, engaging, or beautiful. **RL 6** Distinguish what is directly stated from what is really meant. **L 3** Apply knowledge of language to comprehend more fully when reading. **L 4a** Use context as a clue to the meaning of a word or phrase.

DID YOU KNOW?

Washington Irving . . .

- was a spectator at the trial of Aaron Burr.
- served as a colonel in the War of 1812.
- inspired the name of the New York Knicks basketball team.
- lost the love of his life when she died at 17.

The Early Romantics

The Devil and Tom Walker

Short Story by Washington Irving

Essential Course of Study  **ECOS**

Meet the Author

Washington Irving 1783–1859

The Headless Horseman has thundered through readers' nightmares for nearly 200 years. Rip Van Winkle has been inspiring laughter for just as long. These characters, along with scores of others that populate his writing, helped make Washington Irving the first American writer to achieve an international reputation.

A Reluctant Lawyer Born when the nation was new and patriotism at its fiercest, Washington Irving was named for the country's first president. He began studying law at 16 but never showed much enthusiasm for it. He did, however, have a passion for writing, a playful mind, and keen powers of observation. "I was always fond of visiting new scenes and observing strange characters and manners," he once wrote. In 1807, he began publishing light satirical pieces about New York politics, culture, and theater.

Also Known As . . . In 1809, Irving penned *A History of New York from the Beginning of Time Through the End of the Dutch Dynasty,* a satire of both historical texts and the local politics they chronicled. It was considered a comic masterpiece, but for a time no one knew who had written it—the manuscript was said to have been left at an inn by an old lodger named Diedrich Knickerbocker.

Knickerbocker was one of many eccentric narrators created by Irving, who didn't sign his own name to his works until he was over 40.

American Abroad In 1815, Irving began traveling through Europe, remaining there for 17 years. With the encouragement of Sir Walter Scott—the author of *Ivanhoe* and a fan of Irving's *History*—he began writing a series of stories that blended the legends of Europe with the tales he had heard while wandering as a young man through New York's Catskill Mountains and Hudson Valley. The stories, including both "The Legend of Sleepy Hollow"and "Rip Van Winkle," appeared in 1820 as *The Sketch-Book of Geoffrey Crayon, Gent.* The collection was wildly successful. However, in 1824, Irving published *Tales of a Traveller* (which contained "The Devil and Tom Walker"), and the book was not well received. In fact, the criticism was so harsh that Irving stopped writing fiction altogether.

Irving returned to America in 1832 to live with his brother on the Sunnyside estate. He died at the age of 76 and was buried near the haunting ground of his famous horseman—in New York's Sleepy Hollow Cemetery.

318

TEXT ANALYSIS: SATIRE

Irving was a master of **satire,** a literary device in which people, customs, or institutions are ridiculed with the purpose of improving society. In this passage, Irving pokes fun at quarrelsome, complaining women:

. . . Though a female scold is generally considered to be a match for the devil, yet in this instance she appears to have had the worst of it.

Satire is often subtle, so as you read, watch for its indicators: humor, exaggeration, absurd situations, and irony.

READING SKILL: ANALYZE IMAGERY

Irving develops his characters and establishes mood through imagery—words and phrases that appeal to the five senses.

. . . There lived near this place a meager, miserly fellow, of the name of Tom Walker. He had a wife as miserly as himself. . . . They lived in a forlorn-looking house that stood alone and had an air of starvation.

As you read, use a chart like the one below to record images from the story. Also include your inferences about how the images support the story's characters and mood.

Images	Characterization	Mood
house with a look of starvation	Tom and his wife are miserly.	depressing

Review: **Make Inferences**

▲ VOCABULARY IN CONTEXT

The following words are critical to the story of a miser who would trade his soul for money. Check your understanding of each one by rewording the sentence in which it appears.

1. The **melancholy** sight of the graveyard chilled him.
2. The **persecution** of the Puritans went unchallenged.
3. The mention of gold awakened his **avarice.**
4. The corrupt **usurer** charged 20 percent interest.
5. **Speculating** in land deals held the promise of quick profits.
6. Hard economic times are **propitious** for moneylenders.
7. People who flaunt their wealth are guilty of **ostentation.**
8. He was a strict **censurer** of other people's vices.

 Complete the activities in your **Reader/Writer Notebook**.

Are you willing to PAY ANY PRICE?

People who'll stop at nothing to achieve wealth, success, or fame are often said to have "sold their soul." In other words, they have sacrificed something important—moral beliefs, privacy, family—in order to get what they want. Consider this kind of trade-off. Do you think it might ever be worth the consequences?

DISCUSS Working with a partner, list several people—real or fictional—who fit this profile. Then pick one such person and list his or her gains and their consequences. Assign a value to each item and decide whether, overall, the prize was worth the price. Share your conclusions with the rest of the class.

319

Teach

Are you willing to PAY ANY PRICE?

Explore with students the idea that negative consequences can outweigh benefits. Have students complete the *DISCUSS* activity.

TEXT ANALYSIS — COMMON CORE — RL 6

● **Model the Skill: SATIRE**

Write this passage on the board:

> Sam struggled to think of what could possibly mar his otherwise perfect self. He knew he had piercing blue eyes. He was impressed by his sculpted, golden hair. He was even amused by his own devilish laugh. "I know what's wrong," he said to himself one day. "For all of my perfect attributes, I'm just too humble!"

Ask students what the author is suggesting about people like Sam. *Possible answer: They are too vain to see their own vanity.*

GUIDED PRACTICE Ask students to give examples of satire, such as a television show.

READING SKILL — COMMON CORE — RL 1 — RL 4

■ **Model the Skill: ANALYZE IMAGERY**

Tell students that sensory language creates imagery. Ask them to identify imagery from the passage that appeals to the senses. *Possible answers: "piercing blue eyes," "sculpted, golden hair," "devilish laugh"*

R RESOURCE MANAGER—Copy Master Interpret Imagery p. 21

VOCABULARY SKILL — COMMON CORE — L 4

▲ VOCABULARY IN CONTEXT

DIAGNOSE WORD KNOWLEDGE Have all students complete Vocabulary in Context. To check their rewording, use the following:

avarice (ăv'ə-rĭs) *n.* immoderate desire for wealth; greed

censurer (sĕn'shər-ər) *n.* one who expresses strong disapproval or harsh criticism

melancholy (mĕl'ən-kŏl'ē) *adj.* gloomy; sad

ostentation (ŏs'tĕn-tā'shən) *n.* display meant to impress others; boastful showiness

persecution (pûr'sĭ-kyōō'shən) *n.* the act or practice of oppressing or harassing with ill-treatment, especially because of race, religion, gender, or beliefs

propitious (prə-pĭsh'əs) *adj.* helpful or advantageous; favorable

speculating (spĕk'yə-lā'tĭng) *n.* engaging in risky business transactions on the chance of a quick or considerable profit

usurer (yōō'zhər-ər) *n.* one who lends money, at interest, especially at an unusually or unlawfully high rate of interest

PRETEACH VOCABULARY Use the following copy master to help students predict meanings.

R RESOURCE MANAGER—Copy Master Vocabulary Study p. 23

SUMMARY

In this short story, miserly Tom Walker takes a shortcut home through a swamp. There, he meets the devil, who offers Tom buried pirates' treasure on certain conditions. When Tom tells his greedy wife, she sets off to bargain for herself and is never seen again. Tom eventually accepts the devil's offer and becomes a usurer. After a life of cold-blooded financial success, Tom regrets the deal he's made and tries to escape his fate, but to no avail. The devil claims him and obliterates his ill-gotten fortune.

READ WITH A PURPOSE

Help students set a purpose for reading. Tell them to note what Tom Walker gains and loses throughout the course of the story.

READING SKILL   COMMON CORE   **RL 1**

ANALYZE VISUALS

Ask students to take a few minutes to carefully examine this image. Remind them that art, like literature, conveys theme and mood, contains details that appeal to our senses, and elicits an emotional response.

Possible answer: *Students should discuss how the dark tones, images, and lack of color in the painting convey the story's sense of danger.*

READING SKILL   COMMON CORE   **RL 1**   **RL 4**

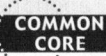 IMAGERY

Possible answer: *Details that suggest this is an ill-fated place include: "thickly wooded swamp or morass" (line 3), "the devil presided at the hiding of the money and took it under his guardianship" (lines 11–12), and "treasure . . . has been ill-gotten" (line 13).*

The DEVIL and Tom Walker

Washington Irving

BACKGROUND The story of Tom Walker is a variation on the legend of Faust, a 16th-century magician and astrologer who was said to have sold his soul to the devil for wisdom, money, and power. Washington Irving reinvented the tale, setting it in the 1720s in an area of New England settled by Quakers and Puritans. In Irving's comic retelling of the legend, the writer satirizes people who present a pious public image as they "sell their soul" for money.

A few miles from Boston in Massachusetts, there is a deep inlet, winding several miles into the interior of the country from Charles Bay, and terminating in a thickly wooded swamp or morass. On one side of this inlet is a beautiful dark grove; on the opposite side the land rises abruptly from the water's edge into a high ridge, on which grow a few scattered oaks of great age and immense size. Under one of these gigantic trees, according to old stories, there was a great amount of treasure buried by Kidd the pirate. The inlet allowed a facility to bring the money in a boat secretly and at night to the very foot of the hill; the elevation of the place permitted a good lookout to be kept that no one was at hand; while
10 the remarkable trees formed good landmarks by which the place might easily be found again. The old stories add, moreover, that the devil presided at the hiding of the money and took it under his guardianship; but this, it is well-known, he always does with buried treasure, particularly when it has been ill-gotten. Be that as it may, Kidd never returned to recover his wealth; being shortly after seized at Boston, sent out to England, and there hanged for a pirate.

Analyze Visuals ▶
Artist John Quidor is well-known for his series of fantastic paintings based on Irving's writings. In this detail, a man discovers a store of hidden gold. What clues from the painting's images, colors, and dark tones help you visualize and better understand the imagery in the story?

Ⓐ IMAGERY
Reread lines 1–15. What details in the description suggest that this is an ill-fated place?

Detail of *The Money Diggers* (1832), John Quidor.
© Brooklyn Museum of Art/Corbis.

320   UNIT 2: AMERICAN ROMANTICISM

DIFFERENTIATED INSTRUCTION

FOR ENGLISH LANGUAGE LEARNERS

Vocabulary Support Use Word Questioning to teach these words: *recover* (line 14), *detect* (line 22), *percent* (line 234), *consequent* (line 258), *rigid* (line 285).

🧰 **BEST PRACTICES TOOLKIT—Transparency**
Word Questioning p. E9

FOR STRUGGLING READERS

In combination with the *Audio Anthology CD*, use one or more Targeted Passages (pp. 322, 325, 328, 330, 332) to ensure that students focus on key story events and concepts. Targeted Passages are also good for English learners.

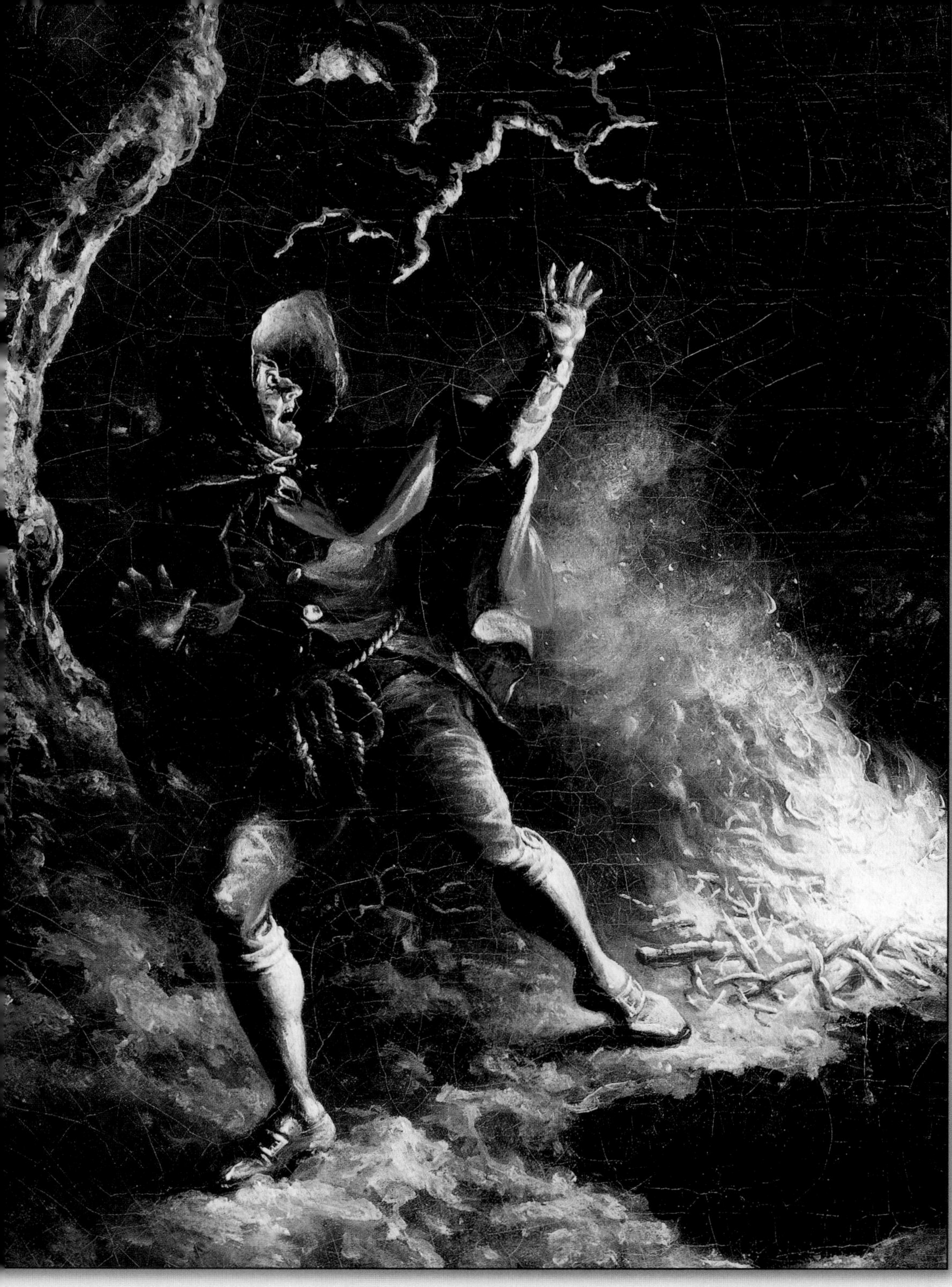

Reading Support

This selection on **thinkcentral.com** includes embedded **ThinkAloud** models–students "thinking aloud" about the story to model the kinds of questions a good reader would ask about a selection.

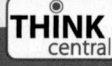

Analyze Visuals

About the Art American painter John Quidor (1801–1881) is remembered chiefly for his atmospheric and macabre scenes based on Washington Irving's stories. Like Irving, Quidor used exaggeration to achieve heightened, dramatic effects.

BACKGROUND

Captain Kidd "Kidd the pirate" (line 7) refers to William Kidd, a 17th-century Anglo-American pirate better known as Captain Kidd. Born in Scotland in 1645, William Kidd settled in New York as a successful merchant and privateer, the commander of a private ship authorized by the government to attack the enemy. Kidd pursued French and eventually pirate ships who interfered with British and American trade. In time, however, Kidd himself turned pirate. In 1699, Kidd returned to New York, hoping for a royal pardon. En route, he buried or gave away large amounts of treasure. Kidd was arrested in Boston and returned to London where he was hanged for murder and piracy in 1701. Rumors concerning the buried treasure of Captain Kidd have persisted for over three hundred years.

FOR ADVANCED LEARNERS/AP

Synthesize Instruct students to examine the paintings that appear throughout this selection. Tell them to look for common elements among the tones, colors, and images the artists used. Have students write a short paper synthesizing the commonalities of these different works of art. Discuss as a class how artwork accompanying a literary piece can enhance the reading experience.

B IMAGERY

Possible answer: Irving uses various images to help characterize Tom and his wife. He describes how they are "so miserly that they even conspired to cheat each other" (line 19). He writes that "a hen could not cackle but [the woman] was on the alert to secure the new-laid egg" (lines 20–21). Their house, where no traveler ever stops, is "forlorn-looking" with "an air of starvation" (line 24) and a gaunt horse pacing outside. Such images suggest that Tom and his wife are grasping, mean-spirited, conniving, and selfish people.

C SATIRE

Possible answer: Humorous details suggesting satire include the description of Tom's wife as a "tall termagant, fierce of temper, loud of tongue, and strong of arm" (lines 31–32); and the comment that a wayfarer would hurry by, "rejoicing, if a bachelor, in his celibacy" (line 37).

D Model the Skill: IMAGERY

Read aloud the lines and as you read identify adjectives *gloomy, dark, stagnant, half-rotting* and descriptive phrases *full of pits and quagmires, black, smothering mud.* Tell the students that these descriptive details create imagery and help establish the mood. Possible answer: *The description of the swamp establishes a dark, ominous, and gloomy mood.*

About the year 1727, just at the time that earthquakes were prevalent in New England, and shook many tall sinners down upon their knees, there lived near this place a meager, miserly fellow, of the name of Tom Walker. He had a wife as miserly as himself: they were so miserly that they even conspired to cheat each other.

20 Whatever the woman could lay hands on, she hid away; a hen could not cackle but she was on the alert to secure the new-laid egg. Her husband was continually prying about to detect her secret hoards, and many and fierce were the conflicts that took place about what ought to have been common property. They lived in a forlorn-looking house that stood alone and had an air of starvation. A few straggling savin trees, emblems of sterility, grew near it; no smoke ever curled from its chimney; no traveler stopped at its door. A miserable horse, whose ribs were as articulate as the bars of a gridiron,[1] stalked about a field, where a thin carpet of moss, scarcely covering the ragged beds of puddingstone,[2] tantalized and balked his hunger; and sometimes he would lean his head over the fence, look piteously

30 at the passerby and seem to petition deliverance from this land of famine. B

The house and its inmates had altogether a bad name. Tom's wife was a tall termagant,[3] fierce of temper, loud of tongue, and strong of arm. Her voice was often heard in wordy warfare with her husband; and his face sometimes showed signs that their conflicts were not confined to words. No one ventured, however, to interfere between them. The lonely wayfarer shrunk within himself at the horrid clamor and clapper-clawing;[4] eyed the den of discord askance;[5] and hurried on his way, rejoicing, if a bachelor, in his celibacy. C

One day that Tom Walker had been to a distant part of the neighborhood, he took what he considered a shortcut homeward, through the swamp. Like most

40 shortcuts, it was an ill-chosen route. The swamp was thickly grown with great gloomy pines and hemlocks, some of them ninety feet high, which made it dark at noonday, and a retreat for all the owls of the neighborhood. It was full of pits and quagmires, partly covered with weeds and mosses, where the green surface often betrayed the traveler into a gulf of black, smothering mud; there were also dark and stagnant pools, the abodes of the tadpole, the bullfrog, and the water snake; where the trunks of pines and hemlocks lay half-drowned, half-rotting, looking like alligators sleeping in the mire. D

Tom had long been picking his way cautiously through this treacherous forest; stepping from tuft to tuft of rushes and roots, which afforded precarious footholds

50 among deep sloughs; or pacing carefully, like a cat, along the prostrate trunks of trees; startled now and then by the sudden screaming of the bittern,[6] or the quacking of wild duck rising on the wind from some solitary pool. At length he arrived at a firm piece of ground, which ran out like a peninsula into the deep bosom of the swamp. It had been one of the strongholds of the Indians during their wars

---

1. **as articulate ... gridiron:** as clearly separated as the bars of a grill.
2. **puddingstone:** a rock consisting of pebbles and gravel cemented together.
3. **termagant** (tûr´mə-gənt): a quarrelsome, scolding woman.
4. **clapper-clawing:** scratching or clawing with the fingernails.
5. **eyed ... askance** (ə-skăns´): looked disapprovingly at the house filled with arguing.
6. **bittern:** a wading bird with mottled, brownish plumage and a deep, booming cry.

① Targeted Passage

Language Coach

Multiple-Meaning Words
Find "common property" in line 23. *Common* here means "shared." What meaning does *common* have in the expression *common thief*?

B IMAGERY
Identify the images in lines 16–30 that help to characterize Tom and his wife. What **character traits** do these images reveal?

C SATIRE
In lines 31–37, Irving satirizes scolding women and the institution of marriage. What humorous details indicate this satire?

D IMAGERY
What kind of **mood** is established by the description of the swamp in lines 40–47?

DIFFERENTIATED INSTRUCTION

FOR STRUGGLING READERS

① Targeted Passage [Lines 16–39]

This passage establishes the setting of the story and introduces two of the main characters: Tom Walker and his wife.

- When does this story take place? (line 16)
- What sort of person is Tom Walker? (line 18)
- What is Tom Walker's wife like? (lines 31–32)
- As the story begins, where is Tom going? (lines 38–39)

FOR ENGLISH LANGUAGE LEARNERS

Language Coach

Multiple-Meaning Words
Possible answer: generic *or* prevalent; Have students compile lists of five other words that have multiple meanings such as *stamp, crown, picture, field,* and *block.* Tell students to write two sentences for each word they selected showing their meanings.

with the first colonists. Here they had thrown up a kind of fort, which they had looked upon as almost impregnable, and had used as a place of refuge for their squaws and children.

Nothing remained of the old Indian fort but a few embankments, gradually sinking to the level of the surrounding earth, and already overgrown in part by
60 oaks and other forest trees, the foliage of which formed a contrast to the dark pines and hemlocks of the swamp.

It was late in the dusk of evening when Tom Walker reached the old fort, and he paused there awhile to rest himself. Anyone but he would have felt unwilling to linger in this lonely, **melancholy** place, for the common people had a bad opinion of it, from the stories handed down from the time of the Indian wars, when it was asserted that the savages held incantations[7] here, and made sacrifices to the evil spirit.

Tom Walker, however, was not a man to be troubled with any fears of the kind. He reposed himself for some time on the trunk of a fallen hemlock, listening to
70 the boding cry of the tree toad, and delving with his walking staff into a mound of black mold at his feet. As he turned up the soil unconsciously, his staff struck against something hard. He raked it out of the vegetable mold, and lo! a cloven skull, with an Indian tomahawk buried deep in it, lay before him. The rust on the weapon showed the time that had elapsed since this death-blow had been given. It was a dreary memento of the fierce struggle that had taken place in this last foothold of the Indian warriors.

"Humph!" said Tom Walker, as he gave it a kick to shake the dirt from it. **E**

"Let that skull alone!" said a gruff voice. Tom lifted up his eyes, and beheld a great black man seated directly opposite him, on the stump of a tree. He was ex-
80 ceedingly surprised, having neither heard nor seen anyone approach; and he was still more perplexed on observing, as well as the gathering gloom would permit, that the stranger was neither Negro nor Indian. It is true he was dressed in a rude half-Indian garb, and had a red belt or sash swathed round his body; but his face was neither black nor copper-color, but swarthy and dingy, and begrimed with soot, as if he had been accustomed to toil among fires and forges. He had a shock of coarse black hair, that stood out from his head in all directions, and bore an ax on his shoulder.

He scowled for a moment at Tom with a pair of great red eyes.

"What are you doing on my grounds?" said the black man, with a hoarse,
90 growling voice.

"Your grounds!" said Tom, with a sneer, "no more your grounds than mine; they belong to Deacon Peabody."

"Deacon Peabody be d—d," said the stranger, "as I flatter myself he will be, if he does not look more to his own sins and less to those of his neighbors. Look yonder, and see how Deacon Peabody is faring."

---

melancholy
(mĕl´ən-kŏl´ē) *adj.*
gloomy; sad

E MAKE INFERENCES
Look again at lines 68 and 77. What can you infer about Tom Walker from his reaction to the swamp and to his grisly discovery of the skull?

---

7. **incantations:** verbal charms or spells recited to produce a magic effect.

TIERED DISCUSSION PROMPTS
In lines 78–92, use these prompts to help students understand Irving's use of details to develop characters:

Connect When have you or someone you know unexpectedly encountered an intimidating stranger? What feelings did the encounter elicit? *Accept all reasonable responses.*

Analyze How does Washington Irving use descriptive details to create a frightening image of the man whom Tom meets in the forest? *Possible answer: Irving describes him as having a "gruff voice," "swarthy and dingy face" that was "begrimed with soot," "a shock of coarse black hair," and "great red eyes." The man, who seems to have appeared out of nowhere, is carrying an ax on his shoulder, and he scowls at Tom and challenges him in "a hoarse, growling voice."*

Evaluate Does Tom react to the stranger as one would expect? Explain your answer. *Possible answer: Some students may say that Tom should react with fear rather than defiance ("'Your grounds!' said Tom, with a sneer. . . .") Others may feel that Tom has already shown himself to be a man who is not easily intimidated.*

READING SKILL: *Review*   **COMMON CORE**

E MAKE INFERENCES   RL 1
                                                     RL 4
Possible answer: From Tom Walker's untroubled reaction to the swamp and his careless treatment of the skull, readers can infer that he is a fearless and callous person.

VOCABULARY   **COMMON CORE**

OWN THE WORD   L 4

melancholy: Tell students that *melancholy* is used as an adjective to describe a person who is affected by sadness or gloominess. Have students write sentences using *melancholy*. *Possible answers: Adria was melancholy after her beloved dog passed away. The melancholy young man seemed moved by the music.*

The Devil and Tom Walker (1856), John Quidor. Oil on canvas, 68.8 cm × 86.6 cm.
© The Cleveland Museum of Art, Mr. and Mrs. William H. Marlatt Fund, 1967.18.

▲ **Analyze Visuals**
This Quidor painting illustrates the first meeting between Tom and the devil. In your opinion, how well do the artist's choices of color and shading and his depiction of Tom's **character** match the story? Explain.

DIFFERENTIATED INSTRUCTION

FOR ENGLISH LANGUAGE LEARNERS
Vocabulary: Outdated Forms Tell students that this 19th-century text uses some word meanings that are not common today. Provide these definitions for students and then have them reread the lines, substituting the definitions for the outdated words.

- *beheld* (line 96), "saw"
- *without* (line 97), "outside"
- *sturdily* (line 119), "firmly"
- *credited* (line 123), "believed"
- *commencement* (line 127), "beginning"
- *propitiated* (line 131), "caused to gain the goodwill of"

Tom looked in the direction that the stranger pointed, and beheld one of the great trees, fair and flourishing without, but rotten at the core, and saw that it had been nearly hewn through, so that the first high wind was likely to blow it down. On the bark of the tree was scored the name of Deacon Peabody, an eminent man, who had 100 waxed wealthy by driving shrewd bargains with the Indians. He now looked around, and found most of the tall trees marked with the name of some great man of the colony, and all more or less scored by the ax. The one on which he had been seated, and which had evidently just been hewn down, bore the name of Crowninshield; and he recollected a mighty rich man of that name, who made a vulgar display of wealth, which it was whispered he had acquired by buccaneering.[8] **F**

"He's just ready for burning!" said the black man, with a growl of triumph. "You see, I am likely to have a good stock of firewood for winter."

"But what right have you," said Tom, "to cut down Deacon Peabody's timber?"

"The right of a prior claim," said the other. "This woodland belonged to me 110 long before one of your white-faced race put foot upon the soil."

"And pray, who are you, if I may be so bold?" said Tom.

"Oh, I go by various names. I am the wild huntsman in some countries; the black miner in others. In this neighborhood I am he to whom the red men consecrated this spot, and in honor of whom they now and then roasted a white man, by way of sweet-smelling sacrifice. Since the red men have been exterminated by you white savages, I amuse myself by presiding at the **persecutions** of Quakers and Anabaptists;[9] I am the great patron and prompter of slave dealers, and the grand master of the Salem witches." **G**

"The upshot of all which is that, if I mistake not," said Tom, sturdily, "you are 120 he commonly called Old Scratch."[10]

"The same, at your service!" replied the black man, with a half-civil nod.

Such was the opening of this interview, according to the old story; though it has almost too familiar an air to be credited. One would think that to meet with such a singular personage, in this wild, lonely place, would have shaken any man's nerves; but Tom was a hard-minded fellow, not easily daunted, and he had lived so long with a termagant wife that he did not even fear the devil.

It is said that after this commencement they had a long and earnest conversation together, as Tom returned homeward. The black man told him of great sums of money buried by Kidd the pirate, under the oak trees on the high ridge, not far 130 from the morass. All these were under his command, and protected by his power, so that none could find them but such as propitiated his favor. These he offered to place within Tom Walker's reach, having conceived an especial kindness for him; but they were to be had only on certain conditions. What these conditions were may be easily surmised, though Tom never disclosed them publicly. They must have been very hard, for he required time to think of them, and he was not a man

---

F MAKE INFERENCES
Reread lines 96–105. Why do you think the trees are marked with the men's names?

persecution
(pûr´sĭ-kyōo´shən) *n.* the act or practice of oppressing or harassing with ill-treatment, especially because of race, religion, gender, or beliefs

G SATIRE
Reread lines 115–118. What do they tell you about the author's attitude toward the activities of the early settlers? What led you to make that inference?

2 Targeted Passage

Language Coach
Word Definitions
Propitious means "helpful or advantageous; favorable." *Propitiated* in line 131 means "gained the good will of." On page 327, line 164, you'll see the phrase "propitiatory offering." What might *propitiatory* mean?

---

8. **buccaneering:** robbing ships at sea; piracy.

9. **presiding...Anabaptists:** exercising authority over the oppression of Christian groups that the Puritans considered heretical.

10. **Old Scratch:** a nickname for the devil.

THE DEVIL AND TOM WALKER **325**

F MAKE INFERENCES

Possible answer: The trees are marked with the names of men who have made deals with the devil, selling their souls in exchange for wealth or power.

IF STUDENTS NEED HELP . . . Ask these questions to help them connect the men's names with the devil.
- Whose ax has scored the men's names into the trees?
- What is the likely connection between these rich and powerful men and the devil?

Extend the Discussion What message about Deacon Peabody does Irving convey symbolically by noting that the tree with his name on it was "fair and flourishing without, but rotten at the core"?

TEXT ANALYSIS COMMON CORE RL 6

G SATIRE

Possible answer: By indicating that the devil is behind the activities of the early settlers, the passage suggests that Irving condemns the settlers' activities as evil.

BACKGROUND

Persecuted Groups The man in black notes several groups persecuted by New England Puritans. Quakers and Anabaptists were radical followers of the Protestant Reformation who believed in pacifism and the separation of church and state. The "Salem witches" (line 118) refers to victims of the hysteria that spread in Salem, Massachusetts, in 1692.

VOCABULARY COMMON CORE L 4

OWN THE WORD

persecution: Point out that *persecution* has a connotation of being unjust and discriminatory. Ask students to list reasons why a person might experience *persecution*. *Possible answers: race, ethnicity, religion, financial status, political views, physical appearance, athletic abilities*

FOR STRUGGLING READERS

2 Targeted Passage [Lines 111–134]

This passage reveals that the stranger is the devil and explains how he offers Tom the treasure buried by Kidd the pirate.
- Who does Tom meet in the woods? (lines 112–121)
- Why does Tom show no fear? (lines 125–126)
- What offer does the stranger make to Tom? (lines 128–132)

FOR ENGLISH LANGUAGE LEARNERS

Language Coach

Word Definitions *Possible answer:* "meant to gain goodwill" Have students write three phrases using the word *propitious* or some variation of the word. Organize the class into pairs. One of the students in each pair should read one of her phrases to her partner, who will then attempt to define its meaning.

Analyze Visuals

Activity How is Durand's depiction of the forest on this page different from *Quidor's* vision on page 324? **Possible answer:** *Durand's painting focuses on the landscape itself, emphasizing its beauty. Quidor's painting focuses on the two individuals, and depicts a dreary forest as atmospheric background.*

About the Art Like other paintings by American artist Asher Brown Durand (1796–1886), *Forest Landscape* captures the beauty and grandeur of the Hudson River Valley. For more information about Durand and the Hudson River school of painters, see page 307.

REVISIT THE BIG QUESTION

Are you willing to
PAY ANY PRICE?

Discuss In lines 144–149, what does Crowninshield's death suggest about the consequences of making a pact with the devil?
Possible answer: *Crowninshield had become a "rich buccaneer" (line 145), but in the end, the devil had cut down his tree and taken his due. Crowninshield's fate is a reminder that bargaining with the devil has inescapable consequences.*

THEME | COMMON CORE RL 2

After students read the selection, have them discuss novels, plays, or films in which the theme of greed appears.

Forest Landscape (1800s), Asher Brown Durand. Oil on canvas, 76.2 cm × 66 cm. © Brooklyn Museum of Art/Bridgeman Art Library.

to stick at trifles when money was in view. When they had reached the edge of the swamp, the stranger paused. "What proof have I that all you have been telling me is true?" said Tom. "There's my signature," said the black man, pressing his finger on Tom's forehead. So saying, he turned off among the thickets of the swamp, and
140 seemed, as Tom said, to go down, down, down, into the earth, until nothing but his head and shoulders could be seen, and so on, until he totally disappeared.

When Tom reached home, he found the black print of a finger burnt, as it were, into his forehead, which nothing could obliterate.

The first news his wife had to tell him was the sudden death of Absalom Crowninshield, the rich buccaneer. It was announced in the papers with the usual flourish that "a great man had fallen in Israel."[11]

---

11. **a great man . . . Israel:** a biblical reference—"Know ye not that there is a prince and a great man fallen this day in Israel?" (2 Samuel 3:38)—used, with unconscious irony, by the papers to mean that an important member of God's people on earth had passed away.

COMMON CORE RL 2

THEME
The theme of the danger of greed goes back to ancient Greece. When the gods give greedy King Midas the ability to turn anything he touches into gold, Midas does not realize that his touch will accidentally kill his own daughter. Tom Walker also fails to understand that his greed for wealth will require a terrible personal sacrifice. This theme continues in 20th-century fiction. In John Steinbeck's novel, *The Pearl*, a humble pearl diver and his family become unexpectedly wealthy, until the greed of their neighbors and friends for a piece of that wealth leads to tragedy. Why do you think stories about the risks of greed continue to be written?

DIFFERENTIATED INSTRUCTION

FOR ADVANCED LEARNERS/AP
Analyze and Evaluate Symbolism Have students reread lines 137–143 and discuss the symbolic significance of the two images described: the devil gradually disappearing into the earth and "the black print of a finger burnt" into Tom's forehead. Ask students whether they think these images are effective in the context of this story, and why or why not. Encourage students to give specific reasons to support their response.

Extend the discussion by asking students to recall other stories they may have read in which the devil was a character. Ask how Irving's portrayal of the devil compares to other writers' depictions.

Tom recollected the tree which his black friend had just hewn down and which was ready for burning. "Let the freebooter[12] roast," said Tom; "who cares!" He now felt convinced that all he had heard and seen was no illusion.

150   He was not prone to let his wife into his confidence; but as this was an uneasy secret, he willingly shared it with her. All her **avarice** was awakened at the mention of hidden gold, and she urged her husband to comply with the black man's terms, and secure what would make them wealthy for life. However Tom might have felt disposed to sell himself to the devil, he was determined not to do so to oblige his wife; so he flatly refused, out of the mere spirit of contradiction. Many and bitter were the quarrels they had on the subject; but the more she talked, the more resolute was Tom not to be damned to please her.

At length she determined to drive the bargain on her own account, and if she succeeded, to keep all the gain to herself. Being of the same fearless temper as her 160 husband, she set off for the old Indian fort toward the close of a summer's day. She was many hours absent. When she came back, she was reserved and sullen in her replies. She spoke something of a black man, whom she met about twilight hewing at the root of a tall tree. He was sulky, however, and would not come to terms; she was to go again with a propitiatory offering, but what it was she forbore to say.

The next evening she set off again for the swamp, with her apron heavily laden. Tom waited and waited for her, but in vain; midnight came, but she did not make her appearance; morning, noon, night returned, but still she did not come. Tom now grew uneasy for her safety, especially as he found she had carried off in her apron the silver teapot and spoons, and every portable article of value. Another night elapsed, 170 another morning came; but no wife. In a word, she was never heard of more.

What was her real fate nobody knows, in consequence of so many pretending to know. It is one of those facts which have become confounded by a variety of historians. Some asserted that she lost her way among the tangled mazes of the swamp, and sank into some pit or slough; others, more uncharitable, hinted that she had eloped with the household booty and made off to some other province; while others surmised that the tempter had decoyed her into a dismal quagmire, on the top of which her hat was found lying. In confirmation of this, it was said a great black man, with an ax on his shoulder, was seen late that very evening coming out of the swamp, carrying a bundle tied in a check apron, with an air 180 of surly triumph. **H**

The most current and probable story, however, observes that Tom Walker grew so anxious about the fate of his wife and his property that he set out at length to seek them both at the Indian fort. During a long summer's afternoon he searched about the gloomy place, but no wife was to be seen. He called her name repeatedly, but she was nowhere to be heard. The bittern alone responded to his voice, as they flew screaming by; or the bullfrog croaked dolefully from a neighboring pool. At length, it is said, just in the brown hour of twilight, when the owls began to hoot, and the bats to flit about, his attention was attracted by the clamor of carrion crows[13] hovering about a cypress tree. He looked up, and beheld a bundle tied in a

12. **freebooter:** pirate.
13. **carrion crows:** crows that feed on dead or decaying flesh.

---

avarice (ăv′ə-rĭs) *n.* immoderate desire for wealth; greed

COMMON CORE **L3**

Language Coach

Fixed Expressions Look at "confirmation of" in line 177. *Of* often follows *confirmation*, such as in the statement "I need *confirmation of* this information." Other phrases using *confirmation* include "[to] await confirmation" and "further confirmation." Use each phrase in a sentence of your own.

H GRAMMAR AND STYLE
Irving emphasizes ideas and creates lyricism through the use of **parallelism,** the repetition of grammatical structures. In lines 173–177, for example, the writer uses parallelism to present three possible fates of Tom's wife.

TIERED DISCUSSION PROMPTS

In lines 150–157, use these prompts to help students understand Tom and his wife:

Summarize What does Tom's wife want him to do? Why doesn't Tom want to do it? *Possible answer: She wants him to agree to the devil's terms so that they can be rich. He spitefully doesn't want to do this because it would please his wife.*

Analyze What does Tom's reluctance "to sell himself to the devil" suggest about his character and his relationship with his wife? *Possible answer: Tom is as spiteful as he is greedy, and his relationship with his wife is thoroughly adversarial. He may be willing to make a pact with the devil to get rich, but not if it means pleasing his wife.*

Evaluate How effective is Irving in showing how Tom and his wife feel about each other? Explain. *Possible answer: Very effective: Irving shows that Tom's wife's only concern is for wealth (certainly not for her husband's welfare), while Tom's main concern is spiting his wife.*

H GRAMMAR AND STYLE   COMMON CORE **L3 L3a**

Analyze Structure The use of parallelism in phrases or sentences adds to the rhythm and flow of words. For this reason, the use of parallel structure is common not only in written text but also in speeches and songs. Ask students to find other examples of parallelism in Irving's story, such as line 32 and lines 166–167.

VOCABULARY   COMMON CORE **L4**

OWN THE WORD

avarice: Remind students that *avarice* is based upon greed and coveting. Have students complete the following sentence "Elissa was consumed with *avarice*..." *Possible answers: when she saw her friend's new car.*

FOR ENGLISH LANGUAGE LEARNERS

Language Coach   COMMON CORE **L3**

Fixed Expressions Have students write three sentences using the word *confirmation*. The word should be used as part of a different expression in each of the three sentences. Tell students to exchange papers with a partner. Have students rewrite their partners' sentences in their own words, and without using the word *confirmation*.

FOR ADVANCED LEARNERS/AP

Analyze Technique Have students discuss how the author uses sensory imagery and descriptive words to create a particular mood in lines 183–191. Ask students to explain whether this mood heightens the satiric effect in the subsequent lines or detracts from it, and why.

check apron, and hanging in the branches of the tree, with a great vulture perched hard by, as if keeping watch upon it. He leaped with joy; for he recognized his wife's apron and supposed it to contain the household valuables. **ℹ**

"Let us get hold of the property," said he consolingly to himself, "and we will endeavor to do without the woman."

As he scrambled up the tree, the vulture spread its wide wings, and sailed off screaming into the deep shadows of the forest. Tom seized the checked apron, but, woeful sight! found nothing but a heart and liver tied up in it!

Such, according to this most authentic old story, was all that was to be found of Tom's wife. She had probably attempted to deal with the black man as she had been accustomed to deal with her husband; but though a female scold is generally considered a match for the devil, yet in this instance she appears to have had the worst of it. She must have died game, however; for it is said Tom noticed many prints of cloven feet stamped upon the tree, and found handfuls of hair that looked as if they had been plucked from the coarse black shock of the woodman. Tom knew his wife's prowess by experience. He shrugged his shoulders, as he looked at the signs of a fierce clapper-clawing. "Egad," said he to himself, "Old Scratch must have had a tough time of it!" **ℐ**

Tom consoled himself for the loss of his property with the loss of his wife, for he was a man of fortitude. He even felt something like gratitude towards the black woodman, who, he considered, had done him a kindness. He sought, therefore, to cultivate a further acquaintance with him, but for some time without success; the old blacklegs played shy, for, whatever people may think, he is not always to be had for calling for: he knows how to play his cards when pretty sure of his game.

At length, it is said, when delay had whetted Tom's eagerness to the quick, and prepared him to agree to anything rather than not gain the promised treasure, he met the black man one evening in his usual woodsman's dress, with his ax on his shoulder, sauntering along the swamp, and humming a tune. He affected to receive Tom's advances with great indifference, made brief replies, and went on humming his tune.

By degrees, however, Tom brought him to business, and they began to haggle about the terms on which the former was to have the pirate's treasure. There was one condition which need not be mentioned, being generally understood in all cases where the devil grants favors; but there were others about which, though of less importance, he was inflexibly obstinate. He insisted that the money found through his means should be employed in his service. He proposed, therefore, that Tom should employ it in the black traffic; that is to say, that he should fit out a slave ship. This, however, Tom resolutely refused: he was bad enough in all conscience; but the devil himself could not tempt him to turn slave trader.

Finding Tom so squeamish on this point, he did not insist upon it, but proposed, instead, that he should turn **usurer;** the devil being extremely anxious for the increase of usurers, looking upon them as his peculiar people.

To this no objections were made, for it was just to Tom's taste.

"You shall open a broker's shop in Boston next month," said the black man.

"I'll do it tomorrow, if you wish," said Tom Walker.

"You shall lend money at two percent a month."

"Egad, I'll charge four!" replied Tom Walker.

ℹ IMAGERY
Which images in lines 189–192 suggest that Tom's discovery won't be a pleasant one?

ℐ SATIRE
How does Irving use **humor** and **exaggeration** to satirize a "female scold" in lines 199–207?

❸ Targeted Passage

usurer (yōō′zhər-ər) *n.* one who lends money, at interest, especially at an unusually or unlawfully high rate of interest

---

READING SKILL

COMMON CORE
RL 1
RL 4

ℹ IMAGERY

Possible answer: Such images as "carrion crows hovering," "bundle tied in a check apron," and the "vulture perched . . . as if keeping watch" suggest that Tom's discovery will be unpleasant.

IF STUDENTS NEED HELP . . . Have them fill out a chart like the one introduced on page 319.

Images	Characterization	Mood
"carrion crows hovering" "bundle tied in a check apron" "vulture perched . . . as if keeping watch"		ominous

---

TEXT ANALYSIS

COMMON CORE
RL 6

ℐ SATIRE

Possible answer: Irving uses humor and exaggeration in relating details of the fight—for example, "handfuls of hair," "fierce clapper-clawing"—and explaining that "a female scold is generally considered a match for the devil" (lines 200–201). Irving also describes how Tom feels sympathy for the devil, not for his wife.

VOCABULARY

COMMON CORE
L 4

OWN THE WORD

usurer: Tell students that a *usurer* is a person who practices *usury*, the act of lending money with high interest. Historically, the *usurer* has been a loathed member of the community. This would explain why the author writes that the devil wanted Tom to become a *usurer* because he regarded them as "his peculiar people."

DIFFERENTIATED INSTRUCTION

FOR STRUGGLING READERS

❸ Targeted Passage [Lines 196–233]
This passage tells how Tom loses his wife and reaches an agreement with the devil.

- What happens to Tom's wife? (lines 196–202)

- How does Tom react to his wife's fate? (lines 205–210)

- How does Tom feel about the idea of becoming a usurer? (lines 231–233)

Concept Support: Bargains with the Devil
After students read lines 220–222, discuss the "one condition which need not be mentioned, being generally understood in all cases where the devil grants favors." Elicit or explain that, traditionally, when a character makes a pact with the devil, the character agrees to give the devil his or her soul, thereby condemning himself or herself to hell.

"You shall extort bonds, foreclose mortgages, drive the merchants to bankruptcy—"

"I'll drive them to the d——l," cried Tom Walker.

"You are the usurer for my money!" said blacklegs with delight. "When will 240 you want the rhino?"[14]

"This very night."

"Done!" said the devil.

"Done!" said Tom Walker. So they shook hands and struck a bargain. Ⓚ

A few days' time saw Tom Walker seated behind his desk in a countinghouse[15] in Boston.

His reputation for a ready-moneyed man, who would lend money out for a good consideration, soon spread abroad. Everybody remembers the time of Governor Belcher, when money was particularly scarce. It was a time of paper credit. The country had been deluged with government bills; the famous Land Bank[16] 250 had been established; there had been a rage for **speculating**; the people had run mad with schemes for new settlements; for building cities in the wilderness; land-jobbers[17] went about with maps of grants, and townships, and Eldorados[18] lying nobody knew where, but which everybody was ready to purchase. In a word, the great speculating fever, which breaks out every now and then in the country, had raged to an alarming degree, and everybody was dreaming of making sudden fortunes from nothing. As usual the fever had subsided; the dream had gone off, and the imaginary fortunes with it; the patients were left in doleful plight, and the whole country resounded with the consequent cry of "hard times."

At this **propitious** time of public distress did Tom Walker set up as usurer in 260 Boston. His door was soon thronged by customers. The needy and adventurous, the gambling speculator, the dreaming land-jobber, the thriftless tradesman, the merchant with cracked credit; in short, everyone driven to raise money by desperate means and desperate sacrifices hurried to Tom Walker.

Thus Tom was the universal friend of the needy and acted like a "friend in need"; that is to say, he always exacted good pay and good security. In proportion to the distress of the applicant was the hardness of his terms. He accumulated bonds and mortgages; gradually squeezed his customers closer and closer; and sent them at length, dry as a sponge, from his door.

In this way he made money hand over hand, became a rich and mighty man, 270 and exalted his cocked hat upon 'Change.[19] He built himself, as usual, a vast

---

14. **rhino:** a slang term for money.

15. **countinghouse:** an office in which a business firm conducts its bookkeeping, correspondence, and similar activities.

16. **Land Bank:** Boston merchants organized the Land Bank in 1739. Landowners could take out mortgages on their property and then repay the loans with cash or manufactured goods. When the Land Bank was outlawed in 1741, many colonists lost money.

17. **land-jobbers:** people who buy and sell land for profit.

18. **Eldorados:** places of fabulous wealth or great opportunity. Early Spanish explorers sought a legendary country named El Dorado, which was rumored to be rich with gold.

19. **exalted ... 'Change:** proudly raised himself to a position of importance as a trader on the stock exchange.

Ⓚ **SATIRE**
Reread lines 232–243. How does Tom compare with the devil in terms of his greed and mercilessness? Decide what comment Irving is making about usurers in general.

speculating
(spĕk′yə- lā′tĭng) n. engaging in risky business transactions on the chance of a quick or considerable profit

propitious
(prə-pĭsh′əs) adj. helpful or advantageous; favorable

BACKGROUND

The Devilish Work of Usurers A borrower pays interest to a lender in return for use of the lender's money. However, usurers charge exorbitant interest rates, often making it all but impossible for the borrower to repay the debt. When a borrower is unable to repay a loan with interest in the agreed-upon time, the lender may seize the borrower's pledged assets. For example, if a homeowner cannot repay a home mortgage loan, the lender can foreclose on, or take possession of, the home. This power of usurers to ruin people's lives helps to explain why the devil in Irving's tale views usurers as "his peculiar people" (line 230).

TEXT ANALYSIS   COMMON CORE
                                     RL 6

Ⓚ **Model the Skill: SATIRE**

Point out that the devil characterizes a usurer as someone who does his bidding. Ask students to reread lines 232–243 and look for examples of what usurers do that could be considered "the devil's work."

Possible answer: Tom is even greedier and more merciless than the devil. Irving is making clear that he considers usurers cold-blooded, ruthless creatures.

VOCABULARY   COMMON CORE
                                     L 4

OWN THE WORD

- **speculating:** Tell students that *speculate* can also mean "to meditate or reason based on inconclusive evidence." Have them write a sentence for this meaning of the word. *Possible answer:* Lianna speculated *that her accident caused her health problems.*

- **propitious:** Have students create a semantic web for *propitious.* Write the word in a center circle, adding the definition given, "advantageous or favorable." Draw spider legs out from the center circle and have students add synonyms to complete the web. *Possible answers:* *beneficial, helpful, profitable, useful, timely, fortunate*

FOR STRUGGLING READERS

Develop Reading Fluency Use the conversation in lines 232–243 to give students practice reading dialogue. Read the passage aloud, demonstrating the tone of the conversation. Next organize the class into pairs. Have students in each pair take on the role of Tom Walker and the devil, and then read the lines as if they were speaking to each other in a conversation.

FOR ADVANCED LEARNERS/AP

Analyze Tone and Language Have students reread lines 246–268 and reflect on the author's tone and choice of language as he recalls what happened during "the time of Governor Belcher." What is Irving's view of people who get caught up in "the great speculating fever"? Does he think they get what they deserve? To what extent does he feel that they are simply victims of usurers? Have students present their views in a discussion.

house, out of **ostentation**; but left the greater part of it unfinished and unfurnished, out of parsimony. He even set up a carriage in the fullness of his vainglory,[20] though he nearly starved the horses which drew it; and as the ungreased wheels groaned and screeched on the axletrees, you would have thought you heard the souls of the poor debtors he was squeezing. **L**

As Tom waxed old, however, he grew thoughtful. Having secured the good things of this world, he began to feel anxious about those of the next. He thought with regret on the bargain he had made with his black friend, and set his wits to work to cheat him out of the conditions. He became, therefore, all of a sudden,
280 a violent churchgoer. He prayed loudly and strenuously, as if heaven were to be taken by force of lungs. Indeed, one might always tell when he had sinned most during the week, by the clamor of his Sunday devotion. The quiet Christians who had been modestly and steadfastly traveling Zionward[21] were struck with self-reproach at seeing themselves so suddenly outstripped in their career by this new-made convert. Tom was as rigid in religious as in money matters; he was a stern supervisor and **censurer** of his neighbors, and seemed to think every sin entered up to their account became a credit on his own side of the page. He even talked of the expediency of reviving the persecution of Quakers and Anabaptists. In a word, Tom's zeal became as notorious as his riches. **M**
290 Still, in spite of all this strenuous attention to forms, Tom had a lurking dread that the devil, after all, would have his due.[22] That he might not be taken unawares, therefore, it is said he always carried a small Bible in his coat pocket. He had also a great folio Bible on his countinghouse desk, and would frequently be found reading it when people called on business; on such occasions he would lay his green spectacles in the book, to mark the place, while he turned round to drive some usurious bargain.

Some say that Tom grew a little crackbrained in his old days, and that fancying his end approaching, he had his horse new shod, saddled and bridled, and buried with his feet uppermost; because he supposed that at the last day the world would
300 be turned upside down; in which case he should find his horse standing ready for mounting, and he was determined at the worst to give his old friend a run for it. This, however, is probably a mere old wives' fable. If he really did take such a precaution, it was totally superfluous; at least so says the authentic old legend, which closes his story in the following manner:

One hot summer afternoon in the dog days, just as a terrible black thundergust was coming up, Tom sat in his countinghouse, in his white linen cap and India silk morning gown. He was on the point of foreclosing a mortgage, by which he would complete the ruin of an unlucky land speculator for whom he had professed the greatest friendship. The poor land-jobber begged him to grant a few
310 months' indulgence. Tom had grown testy and irritated, and refused another day.

---

20. **vainglory:** boastful, undeserved pride in one's accomplishments or qualities.

21. **Zionward:** toward heaven.

22. **the devil . . . due:** a reference to the proverb "Give the devil his due," used to mean "Give even a disagreeable person the credit he or she deserves." Here, of course, the expression is used literally rather than figuratively.

330   UNIT 2: AMERICAN ROMANTICISM

"My family will be ruined and brought upon the parish," said the land-jobber. "Charity begins at home," replied Tom; "I must take care of myself in these hard times."

"You have made so much money out of me," said the speculator.

Tom lost his patience and his piety. "The devil take me," said he, "if I have made a farthing!"[23]

Just then there were three loud knocks at the street door. He stepped out to see who was there. A black man was holding a black horse, which neighed and stamped with impatience.

320 "Tom, you're come for," said the black fellow, gruffly. Tom shrank back, but too late. He had left his little Bible at the bottom of his coat pocket, and his big Bible on the desk buried under the mortgage he was about to foreclose; never was a sinner taken more unawares. The black man whisked him like a child into the saddle,

---

23. **farthing:** a coin worth one-fourth of a penny, formerly used throughout the British Empire.

Tom Walker's Flight (about 1856), John Quidor. Oil on canvas, 26¼″ × 33¼″. The Fine Arts Museums of San Francisco, Gift of Mr. and Mrs. John D. Rockefeller 3rd, 1979.7.84.

▼ **Analyze Visuals**
What elements in this painting by Quidor emphasize the human fear of the supernatural and the consequences of greed? Explain.

THE DEVIL AND TOM WALKER **331**

Analyze Visuals

Possible answer: *The frightening figure of the devil, posed beneath the "Tom Walker Broker" sign; the dark, lightning-streaked sky; the fiery tone of the painting, and the terrified look on Tom's face as he clings to the rearing black horse all emphasize the human fear of the supernatural and the consequences of greed.*

REVISIT THE BIG QUESTION

Are you willing to
PAY ANY PRICE?

Discuss In lines 318–324, how had Tom hoped to escape the consequences of his actions?
Possible answer: Tom had hoped that by going to church and carrying around a Bible he could somehow avoid losing his soul to the devil.

FOR ENGLISH LANGUAGE LEARNERS
Vocabulary: Idioms Help students use context clues to determine the meaning of these idioms in the story:
- *In a word* (line 288), "to summarize"
- *be taken unawares* (lines 291–292), "caught by surprise"
- *crackbrained* (line 297), "crazy"
- *give (someone) a run for it* (line 301), "make into a contest"

FOR ADVANCED LEARNERS/AP
Analyze and Evaluate As students finish reading "The Devil and Tom Walker," have them reflect on its effectiveness as a story with a message. Does the story stand on its own as an exciting tale, or has the author weakened the tale by trying too hard to convey his beliefs? Have students express their views in an essay, supporting their opinions with specific ideas and details. Ask volunteers to share their essays with the class.

 IMAGERY

Possible answer: *The images suggest that wealth and material possessions are of no use to you when you are dead. People who are obsessed with acquiring riches are pursuing something that has no real meaning, but which puts them at risk of losing their souls to greed.*

THEME

COMMON CORE
RL 2

Ask students to share their own examples of Faustian literature or film. Why has this theme held such fascination for writers both before and after Irving?

SELECTION WRAP-UP

READ WITH A PURPOSE Now that students have read "The Devil and Tom Walker," have them assess what Tom gains and loses throughout the course of the story. If Tom at the end of the story could go back in time to his first meeting with the devil, do you think he would make the same deal? Why or why not? ***Possible answer:*** *No. Though he gained great wealth in his lifetime, Tom lost his soul to the devil for eternity.*

⭐ CRITIQUE

- Have students evaluate the ending of the story and explain why they think it is or is not effective. Ask students whether they feel the final paragraph (lines 346–352) is really necessary or whether it detracts from the story.

- After completing the After Reading questions on page 333, have students revisit their responses and tell whether they have changed their opinions.

Independent Reading
   Students may wish to read Washington Irving's *The Legend of Sleepy Hollow*.

332 UNIT 2: AMERICAN ROMANTICISM

---

gave the horse the lash, and away he galloped, with Tom on his back, in the midst of the thunderstorm. The clerks stuck their pens behind their ears, and stared after him from the windows. Away went Tom Walker, dashing down the streets; his white cap bobbing up and down, his morning gown fluttering in the wind, and his steed striking fire out of the pavement at every bound. When the clerks turned to look for the black man, he had disappeared.

330   Tom Walker never returned to foreclose the mortgage. A countryman, who lived on the border of the swamp, reported that in the height of the thundergust he had heard a great clattering of hoofs and a howling along the road, and running to the window caught sight of a figure, such as I have described, on a horse that galloped like mad across the fields, over the hills, and down into the black hemlock swamp toward the old Indian fort; and that shortly after a thunderbolt falling in that direction seemed to set the whole forest in a blaze.

The good people of Boston shook their heads and shrugged their shoulders, but had been so much accustomed to witches and goblins, and tricks of the devil, in all kinds of shapes, from the first settlement of the colony, that they were not 340   so much horror-struck as might have been expected. Trustees were appointed to take charge of Tom's effects. There was nothing, however, to administer upon. On searching his coffers[24] all his bonds and mortgages were found reduced to cinders. In place of gold and silver, his iron chest was filled with chips and shavings; two skeletons lay in his stable instead of his half-starved horses, and the very next day his great house took fire and burnt to the ground.

Such was the end of Tom Walker and his ill-gotten wealth. Let all griping money brokers lay this story to heart. The truth of it is not to be doubted. The very hole under the oak trees whence he dug Kidd's money is to be seen to this day; and the neighboring swamp and old Indian fort are often haunted in stormy nights 350   by a figure on horseback, in morning gown and white cap, which is doubtless the troubled spirit of the usurer. In fact the story has resolved itself into a proverb so prevalent throughout New England, of "The Devil and Tom Walker." ❧

⑤ **Targeted Passage**

N IMAGERY
Reread lines 341–345. What **message** do these images suggest about material possessions and those who seek them?

COMMON CORE RL 2

THEME
Irving's story is a satirical version of the legend of Faust, who sold his soul to the devil. The Faust theme often appears in works of literature and film. One recent example is the best-selling 2003 novel, *The Devil Wears Prada*, and its 2006 film version. In this satire of the fashion industry, a young woman begins to lose herself as she tries to please her demanding boss in order to have a successful career. What other recent stories, novels, plays, or films can you think of that relate to the Faust theme?

24. **coffers:** safes or strongboxes designed to hold money or other valuable items.

332   UNIT 2: AMERICAN ROMANTICISM

DIFFERENTIATED INSTRUCTION

FOR STRUGGLING READERS
⑤ **Targeted Passage [Lines 326–347]**
This passage describes the demise of Tom Walker and the disappearance of his riches.

- What happens to Tom Walker? (lines 326–330)

- What becomes of all the riches Tom has acquired? (lines 340–345)

- What does Washington Irving mean when he writes, "Let all griping money brokers lay this story to heart"? (lines 346–347)

FOR ENGLISH LANGUAGE LEARNERS
Vocabulary: Idioms Help students use context clues to determine the meaning of these idioms in the story:

- *caught sight of* (line 333), "saw"

- *like mad* (line 334), "at top speed"

- *take charge of* (line 341), "manage"

- *In place of* (line 343), "instead of"

Comprehension

1. **Recall** What character traits do Tom Walker and his wife share?

2. **Recall** What bargain does Tom make with the stranger in the forest?

3. **Summarize** How does Tom try to avoid fulfilling his end of the bargain?

Text Analysis

4. **Compare Character Traits** As Tom gets older, he begins to worry about his actions and becomes "a violent churchgoer." But does he really change? Support your opinion with examples from the text. Use a chart like the one shown to collect evidence.

	Before the Bargain	As He Ages
Attitude		
Statements		
Actions		

5. **Draw Conclusions** In your opinion, is there any way Tom could have escaped the consequences of his deal with the devil? Use evidence from the text and your own knowledge of human nature to support your answer.

● 6. **Analyze Imagery** What inferences can you make about how each of the following images supports characterization and mood?
   • the trees and the swamp (lines 40–47) • the hewn trees (lines 96-102)
   • Tom's new house (lines 270–272) • Tom as a churchgoer (lines 279–289)

● 7. **Analyze Satire** Through statements he makes about Tom Walker, his wife, and his community, what messages is Irving communicating about
   • women (lines 31–37)?   • the slave trade (lines 224–227)?
   • the Puritan attitude (lines 115–118)?   • moneylenders (lines 228–230)?

Text Criticism

8. **Critical Interpretations** The story of Tom Walker engaged readers both here and in Europe for many different, and sometimes conflicting, reasons. Look at the story again through the eyes of each of the following people. What reasons would you give for recommending the story to others?
   • revolutionary   • Puritan   • American politician   • banker

Are you willing to **PAY ANY PRICE?**

Tom Walker goes to extreme lengths to acquire wealth. Are there things in life that are worth paying any price for? If so, what are they, and what are the consequences of seeking them?

8. *Students may say that they would recommend the story for such reasons as these: revolutionary—might enjoy seeing people in power face the consequences of their actions; Puritan—would enjoy seeing a sinner pay for his sins; American politician—as a warning against hypocrisy; banker—as a reminder to act with compassion when dealing with people in need*

Are you willing to PAY ANY PRICE? ***Possible answers:*** Students might list things like relationships with people, saving someone's life, or staying true to a belief. Consequences might be that other areas of life, such as school, may suffer; individuals may lose friends or may become injured.

COMMON CORE

RL 1 Cite evidence to support analysis of inferences drawn from the text. **RL 3** Analyze the impact of the author's choices regarding how to develop and relate elements of a story. **RL 4** Analyze the impact of specific word choices on meaning and tone, including language that is fresh, engaging, or beautiful. **RL 6** Distinguish what is directly stated from what is really meant.

Practice and Apply

For preliminary support of post-reading questions, use these copy masters:

R RESOURCE MANAGER—Copy Masters
Reading Check p. 26
Satire p. 19
Question Support p. 27
Additional selection questions are provided for teachers on page 13.

ANSWERS   COMMON CORE RL 1, RL 3, RL 4, RL 6

1. *Tom and his wife are both miserly, grasping, mean-spirited, and without conscience.*

2. *In exchange for the pirate's treasure, Tom becomes a usurer. It is also implied that the devil will have his soul (lines 220–222).*

3. *Tom becomes zealously religious and keeps one Bible in his coat pocket and another on his desk.*

Possible answers:

4. *Tom does not really change. He goes on sinning (lines 281–282) despite his fervent church attendance, and he continues his work as a usurer, as cold-bloodedly as ever (lines 308–313).*

5. *Answers may vary, but most students are likely to say that Tom could not have escaped. His only chance for doing so might have been to repent and become a truly good person—most unlikely considering his nature.*

6. ■ **COMMON CORE FOCUS Analyze Imagery** *trees and swamp—dismal mood; hewn trees—ominous mood; new house—Tom likes to show off, but he is still miserly; Tom as churchgoer—hypocritical nature*

7. ● **COMMON CORE FOCUS Satire** *women—a scolding woman makes life miserable for everyone; Puritan attitude—the Puritans committed terrible acts in the name of God; slave trade—slavery is supremely evil; moneylenders—moneylenders do the devil's work.*

ANSWERS

Vocabulary in Context

VOCABULARY PRACTICE

1. *censurer*
2. *melancholy*
3. *propitious*
4. *ostentation*
5. *persecution*
6. *speculating*
7. *usurer*
8. *avarice*

 RESOURCE MANAGER—Copy Master
Vocabulary Practice p. 24

ACADEMIC VOCABULARY IN WRITING

Students should discuss possible positive role models that save money, do not use others cruelly, and do not sacrifice everything for wealth.

VOCABULARY STRATEGY: THE LATIN ROOT *spec*

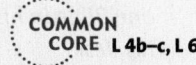 COMMON CORE **L 4b–c, L 6**

- Help students use their knowledge of the root and other word parts to match the definitions in the text.

- Explain how figuring out the part of speech from the wording of the definition can help them narrow their choices. You may want to point out that three of the words are nouns, and three are adjectives.

Answers:

1. *introspective*
2. *spectator*
3. *specter*
4. *circumspect*
5. *perspective*
6. *spectrum*

 RESOURCE MANAGER—Copy Master
Vocabulary Strategy p. 25

Interactive Vocabulary  THINK central

Keywords direct students to a **WordSharp** tutorial on **thinkcentral.com** or to other types of vocabulary practice and review.

Vocabulary in Context

▲ **VOCABULARY PRACTICE**

Choose the vocabulary word that best matches each description below.

1. someone who loves to nag, criticize, and sneer
2. your mood if you suddenly lost your job, your best friend, or your dog
3. what a hot day is to lemonade vendors
4. a pretentious display that is meant to impress others
5. what the Bill of Rights was written to prevent
6. what someone who buys stock in a struggling company is doing
7. a person you don't want to have help you out of financial difficulties
8. a feeling that can make someone drool in a department store

WORD LIST
avarice
censurer
melancholy
ostentation
persecution
propitious
speculating
usurer

ACADEMIC VOCABULARY IN WRITING

- construct • expand • indicate • reinforce • role

Irving uses several examples of wicked characters to **reinforce** the idea that greed is bad. In a short paragraph, **indicate** how Irving could have also included positive **role** models to illustrate moderation. Use three of the Academic Vocabulary words in your writing.

VOCABULARY STRATEGY: THE LATIN ROOT *spec*

When Tom Walker's neighbors speculated in land, they were hoping to spot opportunities for a quick profit. The Latin root *spec* in the word *speculating* actually means "to look at" or "to see or behold." Words containing this root, or the related forms *spect* and *spic,* usually have something to do with light, sight, or clarity.

PRACTICE Match each definition below with the appropriate word from the word web, considering what you know about the origin of the Latin root *spec* and the other word parts shown. Then, say whether the words are nouns or adjectives, checking a dictionary if necessary.

1. tending to look within, at one's own thoughts or feelings
2. an observer of an event
3. a ghostly sight or apparition
4. showing unwillingness to act rashly; prudent
5. a point of view
6. a range of colored light

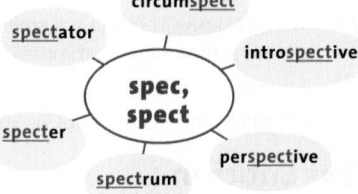

COMMON CORE

L 4b–c Identify and use patterns of word changes that indicate different parts of speech; consult reference materials to determine or clarify a word's part of speech.
L 6 Acquire and use academic words and phrases.

Interactive Vocabulary THINK central

Go to **thinkcentral.com**.
KEYWORD: HML11-334

DIFFERENTIATED INSTRUCTION

FOR ENGLISH LANGUAGE LEARNERS

Task Support: Vocabulary Strategy Help students create a home-language word web using words that contain the Latin root *spec.* For example, Spanish-speaking students may suggest such words as *espectáculo, espectador, inspector,* and *perspectiva.*

FOR ADVANCED LEARNERS/AP

Vocabulary in Writing Ask students to use as many vocabulary words as they can in a paragraph written in the first person from the point of view of someone who borrowed money from Tom Walker.

Language

COMMON CORE

L 3 Apply knowledge of language to to make effective choices for meaning or style. **L 3a** Vary syntax for effect. **W 3d** Write narratives using precise words and phrases.

◆ **GRAMMAR AND STYLE:** Recognize Parallelism

Review the **Grammar and Style** note on page 327. Irving uses parallelism—the repetition of grammatical structures—to create emphasis or to add rhythm. Look at this example:

> *Tom's wife was a tall termagant, fierce of temper, loud of tongue, and strong of arm.* (lines 31–32)

Notice that each of the highlighted phrases contains an adjective (*fierce, loud,* and *strong*) followed by a prepositional phrase (*of temper, of tongue,* and *of arm*). How does the parallelism affect the description of Tom's wife?

PRACTICE Write down each of the following sentences from the selection. Then identify the parallel elements from each sentence as shown and write your own sentence with similar parallel elements.

> **EXAMPLE**
>
> . . . No smoke ever curled from its chimney; no traveler stopped at its door.
>
> *No frown ever crossed his face; no complaint crossed his lips.*

1. "Oh, I go by various names. I am the wild huntsman in some countries; the black miner in others. . . . I am the great patron and prompter of slave dealers, and the grand master of the Salem witches."

2. . . . Midnight came, but she did not make her appearance; morning, noon, night returned, but still she did not come.

3. He built himself, as usual, a vast house, out of ostentation; but left the greater part of it unfinished and unfurnished, out of parsimony.

READING-WRITING CONNECTION

 YOUR TURN Expand your understanding of Irving's "The Devil and Tom Walker" by responding to this prompt. Then, use the **revising tips** to improve your story.

WRITING PROMPT	REVISING TIPS
WRITE A STORY An archetypal plot is a basic story line that serves as a frame for stories across time and cultures. Write a **one- to three-page story** around a situation where a character makes a "deal with the devil" in a modern setting. Be sure to show the results of the main character's actions.	• Use parallel verbs (such as *saw, went, bought*) to add rhythm and vary syntax. • Use parallel phrases to enhance your style. • Use parallel sentences to clarify meaning.

 **Interactive Revision** THINK central

Go to **thinkcentral.com**.
KEYWORD: HML11-335

Language

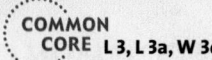 COMMON CORE **L 3, L 3a, W 3d**

◆ **GRAMMAR AND STYLE**

Explain that parallelism can make printed or spoken text dramatic. Share with students some notable examples, such as the opening paragraph of *A Tale of Two Cities* ("It was the best of times, it was the worst of times").

Possible answers:
Parallel elements: **1.** *"I am the wild . . . ," "I am the great . . .";* **2.** *"Midnight came, but she did not . . . ," "morning . . . returned, but still she did not . . .";* **3.** *"out of ostentation," "out of parsimony." Students' sentences should reflect similar parallel elements.*

 RESOURCE MANAGER—Copy Master
Recognize Parallelism p. 28

For more on parallelism, see page R68 in the **Grammar Handbook.**

READING-WRITING CONNECTION

Encourage students to be imaginative in their adaptation of the Faustian archetype. Point out that the main character may be a male or female of any age and that the story may be serious or, like "The Devil and Tom Walker," satirical. Project the short story writing template transparency and review strategies for planning and organizing a short story.

 BEST PRACTICES TOOLKIT—Transparency
Writing Template: Short Story pp. C16, C39

 THINK central

Writing Online

The following tools are available online at **thinkcentral.com** and on **WriteSmart CD-ROM:**
• **Interactive Graphic Organizers**
• **Interactive Student Models**
• **Interactive Revision Lessons**
For additional grammar instruction, see **GrammarNotes** on **thinkcentral.com**.

FOR STRUGGLING WRITERS

Writing Support

• Help students brainstorm possible scenarios that reflect the Faustian archetype.

• Encourage students to explain the choices their main character has to make and to make clear in their story how these choices affect that character as well as other characters.

• Use modeling to show students how to include dialogue between characters.

• Suggest that students create a Sequence Chain of plot events to help them in planning their story.

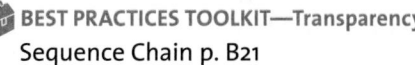 **BEST PRACTICES TOOLKIT—Transparency**
Sequence Chain p. B21

Assess and Reteach

Assess

DIAGNOSTIC AND SELECTION TESTS
Selection Test A, B/C pp. 101–102, 103–104

Interactive Selection Test on **thinkcentral.com**

Reteach

Level Up Online Tutorials on **thinkcentral.com**

Focus and Motivate

COMMON CORE FOCUS

RL 4 Analyze the impact of specific word choice on meaning and tone. **RL 5** Analyze how an author's choices concerning how to structure a text contribute to its structure and meaning, as well as its aesthetic impact.

ABOUT THE POET

Have students read this page and summarize important points of Bryant's biography. Call attention to Bryant's passion for the natural world, and point out that his love of nature is strongly reflected in "Thanatopsis."

NOTABLE QUOTE

"Truth, crushed to earth, shall rise again."
—*William Cullen Bryant*

Have students read the quotation and think about its meaning. Then ask whether students would associate the quotation with William Cullen Bryant the poet, Bryant the "committed political and social activist," or both.

The Early Romantics

Thanatopsis
Poem by William Cullen Bryant

COMMON CORE

RL 4 Analyze the impact of specific word choice on meaning and tone. **RL 5** Analyze how an author's choices concerning how to structure a text contribute to its structure and meaning, as well as its aesthetic impact.

Meet the Author

William Cullen Bryant 1794–1878

In his own day, William Cullen Bryant was a literary superstar. Schoolchildren recited his poetry. Adults pored over his newspaper editorials. And other writers praised his genius. James Fenimore Cooper even went so far as to call Bryant "the author of America" for helping to create a distinctive American literature.

All-American Poet Born in 1794 in Cummington, Massachusetts, Bryant began his writing career at an early age. At 10, he translated poems written in Latin; at 13, he published "The Embargo," a poem satirizing the policies of President Thomas Jefferson.

But the young Bryant was most inspired to write poetry about the natural world. As a boy, he spent hours exploring the forests and hills near his home. His earliest efforts reflected the influence of the English romantic poets.

In time, however, Bryant discovered his American voice. At the ripe old age of 18, he wrote "Thanatopsis," a poem inspired by his wanderings in the countryside. The American editor who published the poem was so struck by its brilliance that he asserted, "No one on this side of the Atlantic is capable of writing such a verse."

Career Moves At his father's urging, Bryant attended law school and spent ten years as a lawyer in Plainsfield, Massachusetts. But he was destined for a career in literature and writing. Leaving behind the "disagreeable drudgery" of his law practice, Bryant moved to New York City in 1825 to become a journalist.

Eventually, he became the editor-in-chief of the *New York Evening Post,* a position he held until his death. A committed political and social activist, Bryant used the newspaper to advocate for human rights and the protection of the environment.

Lifelong Naturalist Unfortunately, Bryant's journalistic work took a toll on his poetry. Nonetheless, Bryant left his mark on American literature as one of the first poets to overthrow what he called the "servile habit of copying" English poets.

Above all, Bryant is celebrated for his power to portray the wild American landscape. Walking up to 40 miles a day, he developed a deep knowledge of America's forests, streams, mountains, and valleys. "Even as an old man," noted one critic, "Bryant was never content unless he knew the name of every tree, bush, and weed in sight."

DID YOU KNOW?
William Cullen Bryant . . .
- could say the alphabet at 16 months of age.
- helped found the Republican Party.
- was an early abolitionist and staunch supporter of Abraham Lincoln.

Author Online
Go to **thinkcentral.com**. KEYWORD: HML11-336

THINK central

336

Selection Resources

See resources on the **Teacher One Stop DVD-ROM** and on **thinkcentral.com**.

 RESOURCE MANAGER UNIT 2
   Plan and Teach, pp. 29–36
   Text Analysis and Reading Skill, pp. 37–38, 39–40†*
DIAGNOSTIC AND SELECTION TESTS
   Selection Tests, pp. 105–108

TECHNOLOGY
- Teacher One Stop DVD-ROM
- Student One Stop DVD-ROM
- Audio Anthology CD
- GrammarNotes DVD-ROM
- ExamView Test Generator on the Teacher One Stop

* Resources for Differentiation   † Also in Spanish   ‡ Also in Haitian Creole and Vietnamese

TEXT ANALYSIS: BLANK VERSE

William Cullen Bryant wrote "Thanatopsis" in a verse form known as blank verse. **Blank verse** is unrhymed poetry written in **iambic pentameter.** In this meter, each line has five iambic feet, a pattern consisting of an unstressed syllable (˘) followed by a stressed syllable (´). Read the following lines from "Thanatopsis" aloud to hear the rhythm:

˘ ´ ˘ ´ ˘ ´ ˘ ´ ˘ ´
To him who in the love of Nature holds

˘ ´ ˘ ˘ ´ ˘ ´ ˘ ´ ˘ ´
Communion with her visible forms, she speaks

Notice that the lines do not have a singsong quality as some lines of rhymed poetry do. In fact, good blank verse imitates the natural rhythms of spoken English and so sounds very much like the way people talk. Bryant also achieves this effect through the use of **enjambment,** which means that one line ends without a pause and continues into the next line for its meaning. As you read "Thanatopsis," notice how the poem's rhythm imitates natural speech.

READING SKILL: UNDERSTAND STRUCTURE

In poetry, **structure** is the arrangement of words and lines to produce a desired effect. The structure of a poem usually emphasizes important aspects of content and can help a poet indicate shifts in mood. Use the following strategies to help you understand and make inferences about the structure and effects of Bryant's poem:

- Notice the indented line that indicates the beginning of each of the three verse sections in the poem.
- Summarize each section to understand the content and central ideas.
- Look for details and word choices that convey mood.

As you read "Thanatopsis," use a chart like the one shown to record the ideas and mood evoked in each section of the poem.

Section	Ideas	Mood
1st	Death comes to everyone.	bleak
2nd		
3rd		

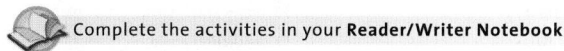 Complete the activities in your **Reader/Writer Notebook.**

What can DEATH *teach us about life?*

Some people view death as the ultimate enemy. Others, however, consider it a natural part of life. Acceptance of that fact is a theme of William Cullen Bryant's "Thanatopsis." But death—and life—have other important lessons to teach us. One is recognizing that death, since it comes to us all, makes us all equal. What are some other important life lessons?

SURVEY With a partner, conduct a survey among your classmates, friends, and family and ask them to name the five greatest lessons that life—or death—has taught them. Compile the results and share them with the rest of the class.

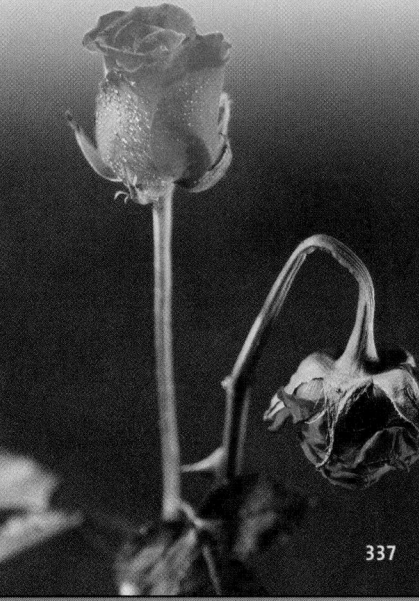

337

What can DEATH *teach us about life?*

Explore with students how life's experiences—both good and bad—can teach many different lessons if people are open to learning them. Then have students do the *SURVEY* activity.

TEXT ANALYSIS COMMON CORE **RL 4**

● *Model the Skill:*
BLANK VERSE

To help students understand blank verse, write these lines on the board:

Made strong by life and love and firm in will

To crawl, to walk, to run, and not to pause.

Ask students to explain the metric pattern of these lines. **Answer: The lines are written in iambic pentameter—five iambic feet (unstressed syllables followed by stressed syllables).**

GUIDED PRACTICE Ask students to explain how these lines exemplify enjambment.

READING SKILL COMMON CORE **RL 5**

■ *Model the Skill:*
UNDERSTAND STRUCTURE

Explain that in poetry, just as in other forms of literature, poets create a structure that helps to convey their intended meaning. For example, one stanza of a poem may present a problem while the next stanza presents a solution. Elicit other examples of structure that authors and poets use, such as chronological order or spatial order. Point out that because of the concentrated nature of poetry, poets have to narrow their focus to the arrangement of individual words and lines.

R RESOURCE MANAGER—Copy Master
Understand Structure p. 39 (for student use while reading the selection)

DIFFERENTIATED INSTRUCTION

FOR STRUGGLING READERS
Vocabulary Support

Clarify the meaning of these words:

- *meter,* "measure that refers to the pattern of stressed and unstressed syllables in a line of poetry"
- *feet,* "units of meter consisting of combinations of syllables"; for example, one iambic foot consists of an unstressed syllable followed by a stressed syllable.

Concept Support: Blank Verse Explain that unrhymed iambic pentameter, or blank verse, is one of the most common metrical patterns used for English poetry. Shakespeare used blank verse in his plays, and Milton used it in *Paradise Lost.* Point out that blank verse is *not* the same as *free verse,* which has no specific metrical pattern.

Practice and Apply

SUMMARY

William Cullen Bryant's "Thanatopsis" is a poetic reflection on death. The poem begins with a statement of the consolation and "healing sympathy" that benign and beautiful Nature provides. The poet then suggests how to accept the mortality that all humans share and to face death without fear, "sustained and soothed by unfaltering trust . . . like one who . . . lies down to pleasant dreams."

READ WITH A PURPOSE

Help students set a purpose for reading. Tell them to read "Thanatopsis" to learn the poet's beliefs about death.

TEXT ANALYSIS — COMMON CORE — RL 4

A BLANK VERSE

Possible answer: Enjambment occurs in lines 1–2 ("holds / Communion"), 2–3 ("speaks / A various language"), 3–4 ("for his gayer hours / She has"), 4–5 ("a smile / And eloquence"), 5–6 ("glides / Into"), 6–7 ("a mild / And healing sympathy"), and 7–8 ("steals away / Their sharpness"). This enjambment makes the lines flow naturally, echoing the rhythms of conversation.

READING SKILL — COMMON CORE — RL 5

B STRUCTURE

Possible answer: The central idea of the poem's first section is that all people die and their remains return to earth to become part of the whole of nature.

IF STUDENTS NEED HELP . . .

- Have them read lines 17–22. Discuss the imagery Bryant uses to describe a person who is dying.

- Have students read lines 22–30. Discuss Bryant's description of how people are "resolved to earth again . . . to mix forever with the elements."

Thanatopsis

William Cullen Bryant

To him who in the love of Nature holds
Communion with her visible forms, she speaks
A various language; for his gayer hours
She has a voice of gladness, and a smile
5 And eloquence of beauty, and she glides
Into his darker musings, with a mild
And healing sympathy, that steals away
Their sharpness, ere he is aware. When thoughts Ⓐ
Of the last bitter hour come like a blight
10 Over thy spirit, and sad images
Of the stern agony, and shroud, and pall,
And breathless darkness, and the narrow house,
Make thee to shudder, and grow sick at heart;—
Go forth, under the open sky, and list
15 To Nature's teachings, while from all around—
Earth and her waters, and the depths of air—
Comes a still voice—Yet a few days, and thee
The all-beholding sun shall see no more
In all his course; nor yet in the cold ground,
20 Where thy pale form was laid, with many tears,
Nor in the embrace of ocean, shall exist
Thy image. Earth, that nourished thee, shall claim
Thy growth, to be resolved to earth again,
And, lost each human trace, surrendering up
25 Thine individual being, shalt thou go
To mix forever with the elements,
To be a brother to the insensible rock
And to the sluggish clod, which the rude swain
Turns with his share, and treads upon. The oak
30 Shall send his roots abroad, and pierce thy mold. Ⓑ

Yet not to thine eternal resting-place
Shalt thou retire alone—nor couldst thou wish
Couch more magnificent. Thou shalt lie down
With patriarchs of the infant world—with kings,
35 The powerful of the earth—the wise, the good,
Fair forms, and hoary seers of ages past,
All in one mighty sepulcher.—The hills
Rock-ribbed and ancient as the sun,—the vales

2 communion: a close relationship.

Ⓐ **BLANK VERSE**
Reread lines 1–8 aloud. Identify the places where a phrase begins at the end of a line and continues on the next line. How does this **enjambment** affect the flow of the lines?

11–12 shroud . . . the narrow house:
A shroud is a burial garment, while a pall is a heavy garment draped over a coffin. The narrow house is the grave or coffin.

28–29 the sluggish clod . . . share:
the heavy mass of earth, which the farmer loosens with his plow.

Ⓑ **STRUCTURE**
What is the central idea of the poem's first section, lines 1–30?

33 couch: bed.

36 hoary seers: ancient wise men.

37 sepulcher: grave.

DIFFERENTIATED INSTRUCTION

FOR ENGLISH LANGUAGE LEARNERS

Vocabulary Have students skim "Thanatopsis" and make a list of any words that are unfamiliar to them. Tell students to consult a dictionary to learn the definitions of the words on their list. Have students write a sentence using each of the words on their list.

FOR STRUGGLING READERS

Develop Reading Fluency

- Have students listen to "Thanatopsis" on the *Audio Anthology CD* (also recommended for English learners) while they read along in their texts. Ask students to notice the meter and rhythm of the poem.

- Have students read a passage of the poem in the same rhythm and meter as the audio CD.

Stretching in pensive quietness between;
40 The venerable woods—rivers that move
In majesty, and the complaining brooks
That make the meadows green; and, poured round all,
Old ocean's gray and melancholy waste,—
Are but the solemn decorations all
45 Of the great tomb of man. The golden sun, **C**
The planets, all the infinite host of heaven,
Are shining on the sad abodes of death,
Through the still lapse of ages. All that tread
The globe are but a handful to the tribes
50 That slumber in its bosom.—Take the wings
Of morning—and the Barcan desert pierce,
Or lose thyself in the continuous woods
Where rolls the Oregon, and hears no sound,
Save his own dashings—yet—the dead are there;
55 And millions in those solitudes, since first
The flight of years began, have laid them down
In their last sleep—the dead reign there alone.
So shalt thou rest—and what if thou withdraw
Unheeded by the living—and no friend
60 Take note of thy departure? All that breathe
Will share thy destiny. The gay will laugh
When thou art gone, the solemn brood of care
Plod on, and each one as before will chase
His favorite phantom; yet all these shall leave
65 Their mirth and their employments, and shall come
And make their bed with thee. As the long train **D**
Of ages glide away, the sons of men,
The youth in life's green spring, and he who goes
In the full strength of years, matron and maid,
70 The speechless babe, and the gray-headed man—
Shall one by one be gathered to thy side,
By those, who in their turn shall follow them.

   So live, that when thy summons comes to join
The innumerable caravan, which moves
75 To that mysterious realm, where each shall take
His chamber in the silent halls of death,
Thou go not, like the quarry-slave at night,
Scourged to his dungeon, but, sustained and soothed
By unfaltering trust, approach thy grave,
80 Like one who wraps the drapery of his couch
About him, and lies down to pleasant dreams. **E**

40 venerable: impressive and worthy of respect because of age.

C STRUCTURE
Identify the **mood** in lines 31–45. How does it contrast with the mood in the first section?

51 Barcan desert: a desert region in northern Africa.

53 Oregon: old name for the Columbia River, which flows between the states of Washington and Oregon.

D BLANK VERSE
Tap your foot to the rhythm as you read lines 61–66. Note the motion described in these lines. How does the rhythm suggest this motion?

E STRUCTURE
Reread the last section of the poem, lines 73–81. How would you **summarize** these lines?

READING SKILL
COMMON CORE
RL 5

C *Model the Skill:* STRUCTURE

Tell students they can identify mood in poetry by studying the poet's diction and the ideas presented. Work with students to fill in the prereading chart introduced on page 337 and draw conclusions about the mood.

Section	Ideas	Mood
1st	Death comes to everyone.	bleak
2nd	When you die, you will not be alone. Nature will decorate your tomb.	hopeful, joyous, reassuring

Possible answer: The mood in these lines is hopeful and joyous, in contrast with the gloomier mood of the first section.

TEXT ANALYSIS
COMMON CORE
RL 4

D *Model the Skill:* BLANK VERSE

Tell students that, like songs, poems have built-in rhythms. Have volunteers read lines 61–66 aloud while tapping along with the rhythm of the words.

Possible answer: The insistent rhythm suggests the relentless forward movement of time and the inevitability of death.

READING SKILL
COMMON CORE
RL 5

E STRUCTURE

Possible answer: Live fully while you can, but when the time comes for you to join all those who have died before you, you can meet death serenely.

SELECTION WRAP-UP

READ WITH A PURPOSE Now that students have read "Thanatopsis," have them assess the poet's beliefs about death. Ask students what idea about death Bryant wants to convey to the reader. **Possible answer:** *It is natural and not to be feared.*

FOR STRUGGLING READERS

Comprehension Support Call students' attention to lines 48–50. Explain that when Bryant wrote "Thanatopsis," fewer people were alive on earth than the total number who had previously died. This changed in the late 1900s as the world's population grew, and the number of people living came to exceed the number who had already lived and died.

FOR ADVANCED LEARNERS/AP

Comparison Bryant composed the original draft of "Thanatopsis" in 1815. In that same year, he composed another well-known poem, "To a Waterfowl." Have students read the poem and note comparisons and contrasts with "Thanatopsis," in terms of mood and tone, setting, and theme. Ask students to write one or two paragraphs on these comparisons and contrasts and read them aloud to the class.

Practice and Apply

For preliminary support of post-reading questions, use these copy masters:

R **RESOURCE MANAGER—Copy Masters**

Blank Verse p. 37
Question Support p. 41
Additional selection questions are provided for teachers on page 33.

ANSWERS

COMMON CORE RL 4, RL 5

1. *Nature soothes and comforts people during times of sadness.*

2. *When people die, their bodies mix with the earth's elements.*

3. *People need not fear death because they will not be alone; rather, they will be joining all those who have died before.*

Possible answers:

4. *Death is viewed as a natural part of life (lines 22–30). It is not frightening or lonely (lines 31–37; 66–72), but rather welcoming and peaceful (lines 79–81).*

5. ● **COMMON CORE FOCUS** Understand Structure *Central idea—section 1: Death comes to everyone; section 2: When you die, you won't be alone; section 3: Live fully so you can meet death serenely. The three-part structure helps develop the message that death should not be feared but accepted as natural and inevitable.*

6. *Examples: "Earth, that nourished thee, shall claim / Thy growth" (lines 22–23)—thought-ful; "nor couldst thou wish / Couch more magnificent" (lines 32–33)—comforting; "So live . . . pleasant dreams" (lines 73–81)—encouraging. Tone: thoughtful, soothing, formal, gentle*

Assess and Reteach

Assess

DIAGNOSTIC AND SELECTION TESTS

Selection Test A pp. 105–106
Selection Test B/C pp. 107–108

Interactive Selection Test on thinkcentral.com

Reteach

Level Up Online Tutorials on thinkcentral.com

Comprehension

1. **Recall** According to the speaker, how does nature help people cope during times of sadness?

2. **Recall** According to lines 22–30, what happens to people when they die?

3. **Clarify** Why, according to the speaker, should people greet death without fear?

Text Analysis

4. **Analyze Title** The title of the poem combines the Greek words *thanatos* ("death") and *opsis* ("a vision"). Cite specific details from the poem to explain the vision of death presented in "Thanatopsis."

5. ● **Understand Structure** Review the notes you recorded in your chart on the ideas and mood in each section of "Thanatopsis." Identify the central idea in each section, and draw conclusions about how the poem's structure helps develop an overall message.

6. **Draw Conclusions About Tone** A writer establishes his or her tone, or attitude toward a subject, through a variety of language choices. Use a chart to jot down important examples of Bryant's word choices, details, and direct statements. Then draw conclusions about the poem's tone.

Examples	Tone

7. ● **Evaluate Blank Verse** How would the impact of Bryant's message differ if he had used a strict meter and regular pattern of rhyme in his poem? Evaluate whether his use of blank verse is an effective or pleasing way to express his ideas. Give reasons for your opinion.

8. **Recognize Characteristics of Romanticism** How does "Thanatopsis" reflect Romantic notions of nature and democratic values?

Text Criticism

9. **Different Perspectives** Bryant wrote "Thanatopsis" when he was a very young man. He was also greatly influenced by the English romantic poets. Given what you have learned about the Puritans and the romantic poets, how do you think the following people might have reacted to the poem?

   • Bryant at age 70   • a Puritan   • an English romantic poet

> *What can* **DEATH** *teach us about life?*
>
> Death is a very popular topic in literature and music. Does death as a topic teach enough lessons to warrant a large number of poems and songs? Why or why not?

COMMON CORE

RL 4 Analyze the impact of specific word choice on meaning and tone. **RL 5** Analyze how an author's choices concerning how to structure a text contribute to its structure and meaning, as well as its aesthetic impact.

---

7. ● **COMMON CORE FOCUS** Evaluate Blank Verse *Answers will vary. Students may note that blank verse is effective because it conveys the poem's message in a more natural manner that is also formal.*

8. *Images of nature serve to inspire and comfort; all people are united in death, regardless of station or status.*

9. *Bryant at age 70 might have viewed death more fearfully and less optimistically; a Puritan would likely be offended by the lack of reference to God or heaven; an English romantic poet probably would find the poem's view of nature inspirational.*

> *What can* DEATH *teach us about life?* **Possible answers:** Death is so complex and universal that it warrants many writings. Death is an overused topic in poetry and music.

Elements of Style

On the surface, it seems as if William Cullen Bryant's "Thanatopsis" and Washington Irving's "The Devil and Tom Walker" could hardly be more different. One is an elegant nature poem written in formal language.

Go forth, under the open sky, and List / To Nature's teachings
from "Thanatopsis"

The other is a short story about strange, supernatural deeds and is written in a down-to-earth, casual style.

Tom's wife was a tall termagant, fierce of temper, loud of tongue, and strong of arm.
from "The Devil and Tom Walker"

But with a more careful reading, one can find elements of romanticism in each work.

Writing to Analyze

In general, America's romantic writers shared several characteristics. They looked to nature for inspiration, they celebrated individualism, they valued emotion and the imagination, and they sometimes explored the supernatural in their work. Which of these elements can you find in the two works you've just read? Create a chart like the one here, and use it to write a brief essay explaining why these two very different writers were each good examples of the romantic movement.

Element	Selection(s)	Example(s)
nature	"Thanatopsis"	"To him who in the love of Nature holds / Communion with her visible forms, she speaks / A various language."
	"The Devil and Tom Walker"	"On one side of this inlet is a beautiful dark grove; on the opposite side the land rises abruptly from the water's edge into a high ridge, on which grow a few scattered oaks of great age and immense size."
individualism		
emotion or passion		
imagination		
supernatural		

Extension

VIEWING & REPRESENTING

Romanticism was not only a literary movement; it was a movement of the other arts as well. Romantic artists shared many of the same concerns as writers of the day. Examine the painting shown here. (If you have trouble making out the painting's details, turn to page 326, where you can view it in a larger format.) With a partner, discuss what elements you think might indicate that the work is a good example of a romantic painting.

COMMON CORE

W 2 Write an explanatory text to examine complex ideas through organization and analysis of content. **SL 2** Integrate multiple sources of information presented in diverse formats and media in order to make informed decisions.

W 2 Write an explanatory text to examine complex ideas through organization and analysis of content. **SL 2** Integrate multiple sources of information presented in diverse formats and media in order to make informed decisions.

Wrap-Up: The Early Romantics

This Wrap-Up provides students with an opportunity to review elements of romanticism and reflect on how these elements were treated in different kinds of romantic writing.

Writing to Analyze

Review with students that *analyzing* means breaking down a subject into parts and then examining each part in order to gain a fuller understanding of the subject. Analyzing the works of romantic writers helps to make clear how their literary works shared certain characteristics.

To help students create their charts, suggest that they work together in pairs or small groups to identify examples of the various elements of romanticism in "The Devil and Tom Walker" and "Thanatopsis."

Extension

- Suggest that students first study the painting individually and draw their own conclusions. Then have them compare their observations with those of their partner.

- To help students get started, encourage them to refer back to the charts they created to help them write their essay about elements of romanticism.

DIFFERENTIATED INSTRUCTION

FOR STRUGGLING WRITERS

Writing Support Help students get started by directing them to relevant passages in the selections. For example, students might examine lines 78–88 of "The Devil and Tom Walker" to write about Irving's imaginative depiction of the devil. Or, they might draw on lines 37–48 of "Thanatopsis" to write about Bryant's passionate feelings for the splendors of nature.

FOR ENGLISH LANGUAGE LEARNERS

Writing Topic Sentences To help students create topic sentences for their paragraphs, provide sentence starters such as these:

- Washington Irving's detailed and imaginative descriptions show _____.

- In "Thanatopsis," William Cullen Bryant demonstrates why _____.

Remind students to support their topic sentences with specific examples from the selections.

Focus and Motivate

COMMON CORE FOCUS

RL 4 Analyze the impact of specific word choices on meaning and tone, including language that is fresh, engaging or beautiful. **RL 5** Analyze how an author's choices concerning how to structure specific parts of a text contribute to overall structure and meaning, as well as aesthetic impact.

ABOUT THE POET

As students read the biography, note that although Longfellow came from a cultured family, was highly educated, and enjoyed early success, he suffered personal tragedies. Point out his statements about the value of nature and personal reflection in **Voice of America.** Then tell students that the poems in this lesson will show how Longfellow applied these values as he wrote about life and loss.

NOTABLE QUOTE

"We judge ourselves by what we feel capable of doing, while others judge us by what we have already done." —**Henry Wadsworth Longfellow**

After a student reads the quote aloud, invite paraphrases. Ask students how Henry Wadsworth Longfellow here expresses an aspect of the American romantic view of life that they read about in the historical essay.

Selection Resources

The Fireside Poets

A Psalm of Life
The Tide Rises, the Tide Falls
Poetry by Henry Wadsworth Longfellow

Essential Course of Study ECOS

VIDEO TRAILER **THINK**central KEYWORD: HML11-342A

COMMON CORE

RL 4 Analyze the impact of specific word choices on meaning and tone, including language that is fresh, engaging or beautiful.
RL 5 Analyze how an author's choices concerning how to structure specific parts of a text contribute to overall structure and meaning, as well as aesthetic impact.

DID YOU KNOW?

Henry Wadsworth Longfellow . . .

- was a child prodigy.
- spoke 11 languages.
- read 18 languages.
- grew a beard to hide the scars of a fire that killed his wife.

(background) Westminster Abbey

Meet the Author

Henry Wadsworth Longfellow 1807–1882

For nearly 150 years, Longfellow's "Paul Revere's Ride" has captivated readers. Its lines are as familiar as a nursery rhyme, and the image of Revere galloping into danger is imprinted on our minds. This poem, along with a number of others, made Henry Wadsworth Longfellow one of America's most popular poets.

Boy Genius Longfellow grew up in a literary household in Portland, Maine. His mother, Zilpah Wadsworth, often read aloud to him, while his father, Stephen, supplied him with numerous books. An exceptionally intelligent child, Longfellow entered school at the age of three and at six received this flattering report: "Master Henry Longfellow is one of the best boys we have in school. He spells and reads very well. He can also add and multiply numbers. His conduct is very correct and amiable."

Professor and Poet At age 13 Longfellow became a published poet, and at 15 he entered Bowdoin College in Maine where, like his classmate Nathaniel Hawthorne, he decided to devote his life to writing. While in college, he published poems in national magazines. Longfellow studied

a number of foreign languages, including French, Spanish, and Italian. He was such a gifted translator that the college offered him upon graduation the first professorship in modern languages. Longfellow taught at Bowdoin until 1834, when he transferred to Harvard. He remained there until 1854.

Voice of America Although he worked hard to introduce European literature to an American audience, Longfellow wrote about American subjects. He sought inspiration in American history and lore, as well as in the country's landscape. A poet, argued Longfellow, should take his subjects from "nature and not from books" and should try to "fathom the recesses of his own mind, and bring up rich pearls from the secret depths of thought."

Literary Fame With the publication of his books *Evangeline, A Tale of Acadie* (1847) and *The Song of Hiawatha* (1855), Longfellow became a household name. Personal tragedy, however, cast a shadow over his achievement. His first wife died following a miscarriage and his second wife was fatally burned in a fire. Longfellow coped by immersing himself in his work. In his final years, Longfellow was showered with accolades. When he died, he became the first American writer to be honored with a bust in Poets' Corner of London's Westminster Abbey.

Author Online
Go to **thinkcentral.com**. KEYWORD: HML11-342B

342

See resources on the **Teacher One Stop DVD-ROM** and on **thinkcentral.com**.

 RESOURCE MANAGER UNIT 2
Plan and Teach, pp. 43–50
Text Analysis and Reading Skill, pp. 51–52, 53–54†*

DIAGNOSTIC AND SELECTION TESTS
Selection Tests, pp. 109–112

 BEST PRACTICES TOOLKIT
Two-Column Chart, p. A25

INTERACTIVE READER

ADAPTED INTERACTIVE READER

ELL ADAPTED INTERACTIVE READER

TECHNOLOGY
- **Teacher One Stop DVD-ROM**
- **Student One Stop DVD-ROM**
- **PowerNotes DVD-ROM**
- **Audio Anthology CD**
- **GrammarNotes DVD-ROM**
- **ExamView Test Generator** on the Teacher One Stop

 **Video Trailer**

Go to **thinkcentral.com** to preview the **Video Trailer** introducing this selection. Other features that support the selection include
- **PowerNotes** presentation
- **ThinkAloud** models to enhance comprehension
- **WordSharp** vocabulary tutorials
- interactive writing and grammar instruction

* Resources for Differentiation † Also in Spanish ‡ Also in Haitian Creole and Vietnamese

TEXT ANALYSIS: STANZA AND RHYME SCHEME

Poets often organize their ideas and images in compact units known as **stanzas**—groups of lines sometimes characterized by a repeated pattern of rhyme and number of lines. Each stanza generally develops a separate idea, image, or example of figurative language; recognizing stanzas will help you trace this development.

A **rhyme scheme** is the pattern of end rhyme in a stanza or an entire poem. Rhyme helps to make the words of a poem memorable and is often used to emphasize important words in the poem.

> *Life is real! Life is earnest!*
>   *And the grave is not its goal;*
> *Dust thou art, to dust returnest,*
>   *Was not spoken of the soul.*

Here the rhyme scheme is *abab*; that is, the first and third lines (*a* and *a*) rhyme, as do the second and fourth lines (*b* and *b*).

As you read, note how Longfellow makes use of these conventions to organize his thoughts about life and express them in a form that the reader will remember.

READING STRATEGY: READING TRADITIONAL POETRY

To appreciate the musical qualities of these Longfellow poems, try the following strategies:

- Read each poem silently to interpret the basic meaning.
- Then, read them aloud, listening for the end rhyme. Notice which words are emphasized by rhyme.

In a web diagram like the one shown, note some important words that are emphasized through rhyme. You will need a separate diagram for each poem.

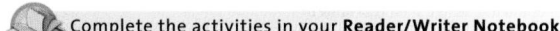
Complete the activities in your **Reader/Writer Notebook**.

What gives life PURPOSE?

People who live with purpose may be more likely to feel a sense of satisfaction or accomplishment. What is it that gives life value or meaning? Is it self-expression, creativity, following one's dream, or serving humanity? In the poems that follow, Longfellow offers his thoughts about how to lead a purposeful life.

QUICKWRITE Think of a person you know or have read about who has led a life you truly admire. How has this person made a difference in the world? Describe his or her impact on family, community, or country in a short paragraph.

343

Teach

What gives life PURPOSE?

Have students speculate about what gives life purpose. Invite comments about the purposes named or others that students suggest. Call on volunteers to share responses to the *QUICKWRITE* activity and to identify the purposes that they think these people's lives represent.

TEXT ANALYSIS   COMMON CORE **RL 5**

● *Model the Skill:* **STANZA AND RHYME SCHEME**

Examine stanza and rhyme schemes with students by writing these lines of verse on the board:

> The fiery sun, a burning blaze,
> Struck my soul into a daze
> And, with its rage of blinding light,
> Turned daytime thoughts to darkest night.

Elicit that these lines form a stanza that develops a single idea (that the blazing sun confused the speaker) and that they have a rhyme scheme of *aabb*.

GUIDED PRACTICE Have students give examples of stanzas and rhyme schemes in poems or songs they know.

READING STRATEGY   COMMON CORE **RL 4**

■ *Model the Skill:* **READING TRADITIONAL POETRY**

Explore the musical quality of traditional poetry. Refer students to the stanza from the Text Analysis activity. Discuss how rhyme emphasizes words that point to important ideas (*blaze/daze* and *light/night* emphasize the power of the sun on the speaker). Then, as students examine the web point out that the rhyming words *dream* and *seem* address the idea that things in life that *seem* real to us are only a *dream*.

 RESOURCE MANAGER—Copy Master Reading Traditional Poetry p. 53

SUMMARY

In this poem, the speaker refutes the idea that life is only "an empty dream." He declares that living a purposeful, "sublime" life, patiently but actively working toward a goal, can inspire others to do the same.

READ WITH A PURPOSE

Help students set a purpose for reading. Tell them to look for similarities between "A Psalm of Life" and "The Tide Rises, the Tide Falls" as they read these two poems.

TEXT ANALYSIS

COMMON CORE

RL 5

A *Model the Skill:* **STANZA AND RHYME SCHEME**

Show students how to analyze stanza and rhyme scheme. Have students write the rhyming words from the second stanza in the first column of a Two-Column Chart. In the second column, have them state the tone that they think the rhyming words convey.

Rhyming Words	Tone
earnest/returnest	serious, urgent
goal/soul	serious, religious

 BEST PRACTICES TOOLKIT—Transparency Two-Column Chart p. A25

Possible answer: *The rhyme scheme in the first two stanzas (abab/cdcd) helps establish a forceful, serious, earnestly moral tone.*

TIERED DISCUSSION PROMPTS

In lines 1–20, use these prompts to help students explore the poetic speaker's main ideas:

Connect What thoughts have you sometimes had about the purpose of life? How similar is your view to the speaker's view? *Accept all responses.*

Interpret What do lines 5–6 mean? *Possible answer: Life has a serious purpose; we are not here only to live out our lifespan and then die meaninglessly.*

Evaluate How convincing is the speaker's argument? How well does he support the idea that life has a serious, heroic purpose? *Accept all reasonable responses.*

A Psalm of Life

Henry Wadsworth Longfellow

*What the Heart of the Young Man
Said to the Psalmist*[1]

Tell me not, in mournful numbers,[2]
    Life is but an empty dream!—
For the soul is dead that slumbers,
    And things are not what they seem.

5 Life is real! Life is earnest!
    And the grave is not its goal;
Dust thou art, to dust returnest,
    Was not spoken of the soul. **A**

Not enjoyment, and not sorrow,
10   Is our destined end or way;
But to act, that each tomorrow
    Find us farther than today.

Art is long, and Time is fleeting,
    And our hearts, though stout[3] and brave,
15 Still, like muffled drums, are beating
    Funeral marches to the grave.

In the world's broad field of battle,
    In the bivouac[4] of Life,
Be not like dumb, driven cattle!
20   Be a hero in the strife!

A **STANZA AND RHYME SCHEME**
Review the rhyme scheme of the first two stanzas. How does the rhyme scheme contribute to the poem's **tone,** or attitude? Explain.

---

1. **Psalmist** (sä′mĭst): the author of the poems in the biblical Book of Psalms, many of which comment on the fleeting nature of life. King David of Israel is regarded as the author of most of the psalms.
2. **numbers:** metrical feet or lines; verses.
3. **stout:** strong.
4. **bivouac** (bĭv′ōō-ak′): a temporary encampment of troops.

DIFFERENTIATED INSTRUCTION

FOR ENGLISH LANGUAGE LEARNERS

Vocabulary: Outdated Forms Point out that there are many old-fashioned words in "A Psalm of Life." Have students work with English-fluent partners to identify modern equivalents for outdated words such as *thou* (line 8), *returnest* (line 8), and *forlorn* (line 31).

FOR STRUGGLING READERS

Develop Reading Fluency

- Have students listen to the two poems on the *Audio Anthology CD.* Urge students to listen for each poem's rhyme and rhythm.

- Have students compare and contrast the tone and pace that the audio reader uses in each poem.

- Have students practice reading the poems aloud in the same tone and pace as the audio reader.

The Calm After the Storm (1866), Edward Moran. Oil on canvas. Private collection. © SuperStock, Inc./SuperStock.

Trust no Future, howe'er pleasant!
    Let the dead Past bury its dead!
Act,—act in the living Present!
    Heart within, and God o'erhead!

25 Lives of great men all remind us
    We can make our lives sublime,
And, departing, leave behind us
    Footprints on the sands of time; **B**

Footprints, that perhaps another,
30   Sailing o'er life's solemn main,⁵
A forlorn and shipwrecked brother,
    Seeing, shall take heart again.

Let us, then, be up and doing,
    With a heart for any fate;
35 Still achieving, still pursuing,
    Learn to labor and to wait.

5. **main:** open ocean.

▲ **Analyze Visuals**
How might the title of this painting (*The Calm After the Storm*) connect to the **theme** of this poem?

B **TRADITIONAL POETRY**
Note the word emphasized by the end rhyme in lines 25 and 27. What might be the significance of this word?

Reading Support

This selection on **thinkcentral.com** includes embedded **ThinkAloud** models–students "thinking aloud" about the story to model the kinds of questions a good reader would ask about a selection.

Analyze Visuals

Possible answer: *The title of this painting connects with the poem's theme in that the poem urges readers to deal heroically with "storms," or difficulties (lines 17–20, and implied in lines 33–34) and thus experience calm, or a "sublime" life (lines 25–26). In addition, the content of the painting reinforces the shipwreck imagery that the speaker offers as he recommends a hopeful, heroic life (lines 29–32).*

About the Art Born in England, Edward Moran (1829–1901) moved to the United States in his teens. Like Longfellow, he took subjects from nature, and he became known as an expert painter of seascapes. This painting shows the carefully observed natural detail for which Moran was admired.

READING STRATEGY   COMMON CORE   RL 4

B **TRADITIONAL POETRY**

Possible answer: *The repetition of the word "us" in the end rhyme ("remind us/behind us") underscores the universal aspect of the ideas that the speaker is presenting. "Us" includes all his readers.*

Extend the Discussion How might the message or impact of this poem be different if the speaker had written in the first person, using *me* instead of *us* in lines 25 and 27 and *I* and *my life* instead of *We* and *our lives* in line 26?

FOR STRUGGLING READERS

Vocabulary Support: Poetic Contractions
Direct students' attention to the words *howe'er* (line 21), *o'erhead* (line 24), and *o'er* (line 30). Elicit that in all three cases, the apostrophe replaces the letter *v.* Explain that such usage is common in traditional poetry; relate it to contractions such as *I'm* and *you'll,* which students use in everyday speech. Then have students say the words with the missing *v* reinserted: *however, overhead,* and *over.*

FOR ADVANCED LEARNERS/AP

Analyze Psalms Explain that a *psalm* is a sacred song, often written in praise of God. Have students write and share a paragraph that discusses how "A Psalm of Life" reflects that genre and how a "psalm of life" may differ from some other kind of psalm. Interested students may also wish to compare and contrast the theme and tone of this poem with those of well-known biblical psalms, such as Psalm 23 or Psalm 121.

SUMMARY

The speaker of this poem describes a traveler coming to a town by way of the shore, while the tide rises and falls endlessly. The ceaselessness of the waves contrasts with the traveler's brief stay.

TEXT ANALYSIS
COMMON CORE
RL 5

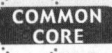 STANZA AND RHYME SCHEME

Possible answer: *Words that rhyme with* falls *occur in the first, second, and fifth lines of each stanza, emphasizing* falls. *The rhyme suggests a pattern of recurrence that imitates the rise and fall of the tide.*

READING STRATEGY
COMMON CORE
RL 4

 *Model the Skill:* TRADITIONAL POETRY

To interpret traditional poetry, have students paraphrase lines 13–14 by substituting a modern word for *nevermore* and modern word order for "returns the traveler to the shore." **Possible answer:** *The day returns, but the traveler never returns to the shore.*

Possible answer: *The difference is that daylight returns each morning but the traveler never will return.*

SELECTION WRAP–UP

READ WITH A PURPOSE Have students compare the two poems they have just read. How are they similar? **Possible answers:** *Both employ rhyme; both include the theme of a person on a journey.*

★ CRITIQUE

- Ask students what, if anything, they find too simple in Longfellow's poems, and what, if anything, they find too difficult.
- After completing the discussion questions on page 347, have students revisit their responses. Have their opinions changed?

INDEPENDENT READING

Students might enjoy Eve Merriam's *If Only I Could Tell You; Poems for Young Lovers and Dreamers.*

THE TIDE RISES,
The Tide Falls

Henry Wadsworth Longfellow

The tide rises, the tide falls,
The twilight darkens, the curlew[1] calls;
Along the sea sands damp and brown
The traveler hastens toward the town,
5   And the tide rises, the tide falls. **C**

Darkness settles on roofs and walls,
But the sea in the darkness calls and calls;
The little waves, with their soft white hands,
Efface[2] the footprints in the sands,
10   And the tide rises, the tide falls.

The morning breaks; the steeds in their stalls
Stamp and neigh, as the hostler[3] calls;
The day returns, but nevermore
Returns the traveler to the shore,
15   And the tide rises, the tide falls. **D**

---

1. **curlew:** a type of large bird often found along the shoreline.
2. **efface:** to wear away; wipe out.
3. **hostler:** person who takes care of horses.

C STANZA AND RHYME SCHEME
What rhyme occurs in three of the five lines of each stanza? What word is emphasized by this repeated rhyme? Consider the impact of this technique on the poem's meaning.

D TRADITIONAL POETRY
In terms of basic meaning, what is the difference between the day and the traveler in lines 13–14?

Singing Beach, Manchester (1863), Martin Johnson Heade. Oil on canvas, 50.8 cm × 91.4 cm. The Fine Arts Museums of San Francisco, Gift of Mr. and Mrs. John D. Rockefeller, 3rd, 1993.35.12.

DIFFERENTIATED INSTRUCTION

FOR STRUGGLING READERS

Explore Rhyme Have students use the web diagram introduced on page 343 to record the rhymes in "The Tide Rises, the Tide Falls" and to connect Longfellow's word choices to his ideas. Discuss the importance of the words *falls* and *calls;* lead students to see that, overall, the rhymes emphasize the idea that human life is short, compared to the ceaseless workings of nature.

FOR ADVANCED LEARNERS/AP

Analyze Tone Have students discuss these questions about the traveler:

- Who or what does the traveler represent?
- How does the absence of details about the traveler contribute to the tone and theme of the poem?

Then have students present their conclusions to the class.

Comprehension

1. **Recall** What record does the traveler leave behind in "The Tide Rises, the Tide Falls"? What happens to this record and to the traveler?

2. **Recall** What, according to the speaker of "A Psalm of Life," is "our destined end" or purpose?

3. **Paraphrase** What does the speaker say about the value of the lives of great people in "A Psalm of Life"?

Text Analysis

● 4. **Draw Conclusions About Traditional Poetry** Review the emphasized words you recorded in your web diagram for "A Psalm of Life." What can you conclude about the relationship between the poem's sound and its meaning?

5. **Analyze Metaphor** A metaphor compares two dissimilar things. Think about the metaphor in lines 17–18 of "A Psalm of Life." What is Longfellow saying about the world and life by comparing them to a battlefield and a bivouac?

● 6. **Examine Stanza and Rhyme Scheme** Identify the rhyme scheme used in "The Tide Rises, the Tide Falls." How does this rhyme scheme reflect the poem's central image?

7. **Interpret Repetition** Longfellow repeats the line "the tide rises, the tide falls" throughout his poem. What idea is he trying to emphasize about the difference between nature and human life through this repetition?

8. **Compare and Contrast** Reread lines 8–10 in "The Tide Rises . . ." and 25–32 in "A Psalm of Life." Consider what happens to the footprints in each poem. Based on this and other images, how would you say Longfellow's outlook on life and death in each poem is similar? In what way is it different? Use a Venn diagram like the one shown to organize your thoughts.

"A Psalm of Life"   "The Tide Rises . . ."

Text Criticism

9. **Critical Interpretations** "Longfellow," writes critic Alan Trachtenberg, "remains one of the nation's abidingly popular poets; more poems of his are probably still taken to heart and committed to memory than those of any of his more luminous 19th century peers...." Why do you think Longfellow was, and still is, popular? Use evidence to support your conclusions.

What gives life **PURPOSE?**

What, according to the speaker of "A Psalm of Life," should people do to give their lives purpose? Do you agree or disagree?

Rises, the Tide Falls" is more somber than "A Psalm of Life." In "A Psalm of Life," individuals can have an enduring impact on the world (indicated by the footprints that remain)—a view that is denied in "The Tide Rises, the Tide Falls" (indicated by the footprints that the tide erases).

9. *Longfellow's popularity may be due to the facts that his poems are accessible and that they deal with universal themes. His traditional use of rhyme and rhythm makes his poems memorable, as well.*

What gives life **PURPOSE?**
Possible answers: People should inspire others by working each day to achieve a goal. Some students may agree that labor gives life purpose. Other students may believe that purpose comes from more glamorous accomplishments.

For preliminary support of post-reading questions, use these copy masters:

R RESOURCE MANAGER—Copy Masters
  Stanza and Rhyme Scheme p. 51
  Question Support p. 55
  Additional selection questions are provided for teachers on page 47.

ANSWERS   COMMON CORE RL 4, RL 5

1. *The traveler leaves footprints in the sand. Waves efface the footprints (lines 8–9), and the traveler moves on (lines 13–14).*

2. *Our purpose is to act bravely and patiently to achieve our goals (lines 33–36).*

3. *Great people make their mark in the world and, through their example, inspire others to act (lines 25–32).*

Possible answers:

4. ■ **COMMON CORE FOCUS** Reading Traditional Poetry *The emphasized words convey life as serious and purposeful.*

5. *Like a battlefield, the world is full of strife, and that an individual's life is only a temporary "encampment," like a bivouac.*

6. ● **COMMON CORE FOCUS** Stanza and Rhyme Scheme *The rhyme scheme is aabba/aacca/aadda. This pattern evokes the image of recurring waves and underscores the cyclical, ceaseless quality of nature.*

7. *He is emphasizing the difference between the sea, which seems eternal, and a human lifetime, which is momentary by comparison.*

8. *The outlooks are similar in that both poems suggest that life is fleeting. There are several differences. For example, "The Tide*

Assess

DIAGNOSTIC AND SELECTION TESTS
  Selection Test A pp. 109–110
  Selection Test B/C pp. 111–112

Interactive Selection Test on thinkcentral.com

Reteach

Level Up Online Tutorials on thinkcentral.com

Reteaching Worksheets on thinkcentral.com

COMMON CORE

RL 1 Cite evidence to support analysis of inferences drawn from the text. **RL 5** Analyze how an author's choices concerning how to structure a text contribute to its structure and meaning, as well as its aesthetic impact.

The Chambered Nautilus
Old Ironsides

Poetry by Oliver Wendell Holmes

COMMON CORE FOCUS

RL 1 Cite evidence to support analysis of inferences drawn from the text. **RL 2** Provide an objective summary of the text. **RL 4** Determine the meanings of words and phrases as they are used in the text. **RL 5** Analyze how an author's choices concerning how to structure a text contribute to its structure and meaning, as well as its aesthetic impact.

ABOUT THE POET

As students read the biography, emphasize that Holmes had a range of interests. Point out that "The Chambered Nautilus" reflects his interest in nature and "Old Ironsides" shows his awareness and strong feelings about history and current events.

NOTABLE QUOTE

"Man's mind, once stretched by a new idea, never regains its original dimensions."
–Oliver Wendell Holmes

Read the comment aloud. Ask students to explain the figurative language that Oliver Wendell Holmes uses and then to express the literal meaning of the idea.

DID YOU KNOW?

Oliver Wendell Holmes . . .

- dropped out of law school because it bored him.
- became dean of the Harvard Medical School.
- called the subconscious mind "the underground workshop of thought" 20 years before Freud published his study of the unconscious.

Meet the Author

Oliver Wendell Holmes 1809–1894

Many people climb the ladder of success, but few make their mark in two very different fields. Oliver Wendell Holmes was both a prize-winning physician and a wildly popular poet. His discovery of the contagious nature of puerperal ("childbed") fever changed the practice of medicine. And his verse was so beloved that he was frequently called upon to write poems for public occasions.

A Cultural Elite Holmes grew up in a family steeped in history and tradition. He was descended from prominent Boston families and early Dutch settlers. His father, a Calvinist minister in Cambridge, Massachusetts, nurtured his interests in books, religion, and nature. "I am very thankful," wrote Holmes, "that the first part of my life was not passed shut in between high walls and treading the unimpressible and unsympathetic pavement."

Literary Triumph At 15, Holmes enrolled at Phillips Andover Academy, where he impressed his teachers by translating the Roman poet Virgil's *Aeneid*. After receiving a bachelor's degree and a medical degree from Harvard University, he entered private practice in Boston. Holmes achieved literary stardom at the age of 21 with the appearance of his poem "Old Ironsides." Written to protest the planned destruction of a ship that fought in the War of 1812, the poem won Holmes instant fame. Following its publication, the USS *Constitution* was returned to active duty.

Talent for Talk After his first book of poems was published in 1836, Holmes joined the lecture circuit, where he entranced audiences with his ready wit. He was equally charming in the classroom, causing his students at Harvard Medical School to greet his lectures with "a mighty shout and stamp of applause." Holmes's eloquence was also on display at the Saturday Club, a group including Ralph Waldo Emerson and Nathaniel Hawthorne. The writers met regularly to share their latest works.

Renaissance Man In addition to poetry, Holmes wrote three novels, a biography of Emerson, and numerous essays. Many of the essays appeared in *The Atlantic Monthly*, a magazine edited by Holmes's friend James Russell Lowell. Printed under the title "The Autocrat of the Breakfast Table," these essays combined prose and poetry and explored the themes of human destiny and freedom.

Author Online

Go to **thinkcentral.com**. KEYWORD: HML11-348

348

See resources on the **Teacher One Stop DVD-ROM** *and on* **thinkcentral.com**.

 RESOURCE MANAGER UNIT 2

Plan and Teach, pp. 57–64
Text Analysis and Reading
   Skill, pp. 65–66†, 67–68†*

**DIAGNOSTIC AND SELECTION
   TESTS**

Selection Tests, pp. 113–116

 BEST PRACTICES TOOLKIT

Analysis Frame: Poetic
   Language and Style,
   pp. D21, D38

TECHNOLOGY

- **Teacher One Stop DVD-ROM**
- **Student One Stop DVD-ROM**
- **Audio Anthology CD**
- **GrammarNotes DVD-ROM**
- **ExamView Test Generator on the Teacher One Stop**

* Resources for Differentiation   **† Also in Spanish**   **‡ Also in Haitian Creole and Vietnamese**

TEXT ANALYSIS: METER

Meter is one of the tools used by poets to make language memorable and pleasing to the ear. It is defined as the repetition of a regular rhythmic unit in a line of poetry. Each unit, known as a **foot,** has one stressed syllable (indicated by a ′) and either one or two unstressed syllables (indicated by a ˇ). The two basic types of metrical feet used by Holmes in these poems are the **iamb,** in which an unstressed syllable is followed by a stressed syllable (ˇ′), and the **trochee,** in which a stressed syllable is followed by an unstressed syllable (′ˇ). Two words are used to describe the meter of a line. The first word identifies the type of metrical foot—iambic, trochaic— and the second word indicates the number of feet in a line: **monometer** (one), **dimeter** (two), **trimeter** (three), **tetrameter** (four), **pentameter** (five), **hexameter** (six), and so forth. Here is a line from "Old Ironsides" with the meter marked:

Hĕr déck, ŏnce réd wĭth héroĕs' blóod

As you read these two poems by Holmes, note the meter in each and consider what it contributes to the poem's meaning and aesthetic appeal.

READING SKILL: MAKE INFERENCES

Making inferences involves "reading between the lines"— making logical guesses based on evidence in the text to figure out what is not directly stated. As you read these two poems by Holmes, you will need to make inferences to get at the author's meaning. For each poem, create a chart like the one shown.

"The Chambered Nautilus"		
Details or Evidence from Text	What I Know from Experience	Ideas Inferred
"Year after year beheld the silent toil / that spread his lustrous coil"	It takes a lot of practice to become good at a sport.	Change requires effort.

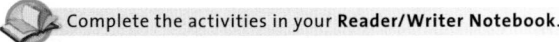 Complete the activities in your **Reader/Writer Notebook.**

When is it time to MOVE ON?

Sometimes people have to choose between cherishing the past and looking toward the future. For example, when you move out of your parents' house, will you expect them to keep your room exactly as it is or to convert it to a home office? Change can produce a renewed sense of well-being as well as a sense of loss.

DISCUSS Working with a partner, list situations or occasions in life when one must decide between holding on to the past and making a change. In each case, what are the benefits of either choice? After discussing this question with your partner, share your conclusions with others.

 349

Teach

When is it time to MOVE ON?

Briefly discuss why people might be reluctant to make a change in their lives; urge students to keep that discussion in mind as they complete the **DISCUSS** activity.

TEXT ANALYSIS　　COMMON CORE　RL 5

● *Model the Skill:* **METER**

Tell students that they can explore meter in poetry by tapping out the rhythm of the lines. Tap the beat to help students distinguish an iamb from a trochee; also present the adjective forms *iambic* and *trochaic*. Note the prefixes in the names of the metrical feet and share a few other words that use the same prefixes (such as *triangular* and *pentagon*). Have students tap out the iambic tetrameter in the line from "Old Ironsides."

GUIDED PRACTICE Have students tap out examples of various meters, such as iambic pentameter (ˇ′ ˇ′ ˇ′ ˇ′ ˇ′) and trochaic trimeter (′ˇ ′ˇ ′ˇ).

READING SKILL　　COMMON CORE　RL 1

■ *Model the Skill:* **MAKE INFERENCES**

To help students see how personal experience can aid understanding of a text, give this example: "Never did I expect the day / we all would sing his praise." Ask what students think the author means. *Point out that the person praised in the line may be someone who no one had thought praiseworthy.*

GUIDED PRACTICE Call on volunteers to discuss using the chart to correlate personal experience to the detail from the poem.

R RESOURCE MANAGER—Copy Master
Make Inferences p. 67 (for student use while reading the selections)

DIFFERENTIATED INSTRUCTION

FOR STRUGGLING READERS

Concept Support: Make Inferences Students should find it easier to make inferences if they first "translate" figurative lines of verse into literal statements. Have them work in pairs or small groups to paraphrase passages. Suggest that they expand the first column of the chart presented on this page to show not only the detail or evidence from the text but also a modern paraphrase, as in this example:

"The Chambered Nautilus"		
Details or Evidence from Text	What I Know from Experience	Ideas Inferred
"Year after year beheld the silent toil / That spread his lustrous coil" → *As time passed, the nautilus quietly worked to expand its shiny shell.*	It takes a lot of practice to become good at a sport.	Change requires effort.

SUMMARY

The speaker describes the process by which the chambered nautilus expands its spiral shell as it grows. He sees in that process a message about the importance of the soul's personal growth.

READ WITH A PURPOSE

Help students set a purpose for reading. Tell them to note how the chambered nautilus and Old Ironsides change throughout the poems.

TEXT ANALYSIS   COMMON CORE   **RL 5**

Ⓐ Model the Skill: METER

Have students read lines 1, 2, and 9 aloud, listening to the accented first syllable of each line. For further examples of words that the beginning trochaic foot emphasizes, refer them to these lines: 15, 17, 19, 21, 22, 23, 24, 29, 31, 33, 35.

Possible answer: *Many of the lines begin with a trochaic foot. This variation puts an emphasis on important words (such as the word "Wrecked" in line 9) and thus helps convey the speaker's intellectual urgency.*

TIERED DISCUSSION PROMPTS

In lines 15–21, use these prompts to help students grasp the process that this stanza describes:

Connect Have you or someone you know ever relocated to another school or place to live? How might that experience help someone identify with the chambered nautilus? *Accept all responses.*

Analyze What details suggest that the growth pattern of the chambered nautilus is a beautiful but natural phenomenon? **Possible answer:** *Details such as "lustrous coil" and "shining archway" suggest beauty; "as the spiral grew," "Built up" suggest natural phenomenon.*

Synthesize On the basis of this stanza, predict what the speaker may say about the nature of change. **Possible answer:** *The speaker may say that change is a natural, and not a fearsome, phenomenon.*

The Chambered Nautilus

Oliver Wendell Holmes

This is the ship of pearl, which, poets feign,[1]
   Sails the unshadowed main,—
   The venturous bark that flings
On the sweet summer wind its purpled wings
5 In gulfs enchanted, where the Siren[2] sings,
   And coral reefs lie bare,
Where the cold sea-maids rise to sun their streaming hair.

Its webs of living gauze no more unfurl;
   Wrecked is the ship of pearl!
10   And every chambered cell,
Where its dim dreaming life was wont to dwell,
As the frail tenant shaped his growing shell,
   Before thee lies revealed,—
Its irised ceiling rent,[3] its sunless crypt unsealed! Ⓐ

15 Year after year beheld the silent toil
   That spread his lustrous coil;
   Still, as the spiral grew,
He left the past year's dwelling for the new,
Stole with soft step its shining archway through,
20   Built up its idle door,
Stretched in his last-found home, and knew the old no more.

Thanks for the heavenly message brought by thee,
   Child of the wandering sea,
   Cast from her lap, forlorn!
25 From thy dead lips a clearer note is born

Ⓐ **METER**
Although the basic meter of this poem is **iambic**, what kind of **foot** is substituted for the iamb at the beginning of many of the lines? How does this variation affect the feel of these lines?

---

1. **feign:** imagine.
2. **Siren:** a partly human female creature in Greek mythology that lured sailors to destruction with sweet, magical songs.
3. **its irised ceiling rent:** its rainbow-colored ceiling ripped apart.

DIFFERENTIATED INSTRUCTION

FOR ENGLISH LANGUAGE LEARNERS

Vocabulary: Outdated Forms Point out that there are many words in "The Chambered Nautilus" that are not commonly used today. Have students consult a dictionary to identify modern equivalents for outdated words such as *thee* (line 13), *lustrous* (line 16), and *thine* (line 35).

FOR STRUGGLING READERS

Develop Reading Fluency

- Have students listen to the poems on the *Audio Anthology CD* (also recommended for English learners) while they read along in their texts. Encourage students to listen for the meter in each poem.

- Urge students to compare and contrast how each audio reader presents the poem. Then have them practice reading aloud.

Than ever Triton blew from wreathèd horn![4]
    While on mine ear it rings,
Through the deep caves of thought I hear a voice that sings:—

Build thee more stately mansions, O my soul,
30   As the swift seasons roll!
    Leave thy low-vaulted past!
Let each new temple, nobler than the last,
Shut thee from heaven with a dome more vast,
    Till thou at length art free,
35 Leaving thine outgrown shell by life's unresting sea! **B**

◄ **Analyze Visuals**
As the nautilus grows, it adds a new chamber to its spiral shell, abandoning the old chamber for the new one. What might this process of growth suggest about the role of change in life?

B **MAKE INFERENCES**
Reread lines 29–35. What inference can you make about what it might mean for the soul to escape its shell?

---

4. **Triton . . . wreathèd horn:** Triton, a sea god in Greek mythology, is usually pictured blowing a wreathed, or coiled, conch-shell horn.

Analyze Visuals

Possible answer: *This process of growth might suggest that change has a necessary role in life and that people should strive to achieve changes that enlarge them instead of just accepting the changes that come.*

Activity Use the photograph to help students visualize the process that Holmes describes in the poem. Have students follow the spiral, beginning with its smallest, innermost segment and proceeding to the open end. Discuss the effectiveness of the nautilus as a metaphor for human life.

READING SKILL   COMMON CORE RL 1

B **MAKE INFERENCES**

Possible answer: *The reader can infer that the "shell" is the human body and that when the body dies, the soul will "escape" to a happy afterlife (for the speaker says that the soul then will be "free," no longer "Shut . . . from heaven" [lines 33–34]).*

REVISIT THE BIG QUESTION

When is it time to MOVE ON?

Discuss In lines 29–31, what kind of change is the speaker referring to when he talks of building "more stately mansions" (line 29)? How could people put that idea into practice? ***Possible answer:*** *The speaker is referring to a change to greater or nobler thoughts or endeavors. People could put that idea into practice by committing to improving themselves, experiencing new challenges, and becoming better human beings.*

FOR STRUGGLING READERS

Comprehension Support Have students work in pairs or small groups to solve problems of literal comprehension, using a dictionary if possible. Offer this advice:

- Look up difficult or old-fashioned words such as *wont* (line 11).
- Figure out which meaning is used in multiple-meaning words such as *bark* (line 3).

FOR ADVANCED LEARNERS/AP

Analyze Poetic Language [paired option] Have students write an analysis of Holmes's language. Urge them to use an Analysis Frame as they plan, noting Holmes's word choice and imagery and the effect that both have on readers of his time and ours.

  BEST PRACTICES TOOLKIT—Transparency
Analysis Frame: Poetic Language and Style pp. D21, D38

The ironic speaker first urges that the USS *Constitution*, which played a heroic role in American history, be destroyed as planned. He then recounts the ship's history and declares that it would be better for the ship to sink in a storm than to meet such a humiliating end.

TEXT ANALYSIS

● ALLUSION

Ask students to name allusions they remember from other poems they have read in this text. Ask them to explain how allusions contribute to the poem's meaning and effect upon the reader.

Possible answer: Allusion to "Sirens" and "harpies" provide insight into nature's beauty and danger.

READING SKILL

COMMON CORE
RL 1

● *Model the Skill:* MAKE INFERENCES

To help students identify irony, read aloud the first two stanzas. Tell students to identify details that suggest how the author really feels about Old Ironsides.

Possible answer: The speaker is being ironic. He says that it would be better for the ship to be sunk than demolished, but he really wants it to be preserved as part of the nation's heritage.

SELECTION WRAP—UP

READ WITH A PURPOSE Now that students have read these selections, have them assess how the chambered nautilus and Old Ironsides changed throughout the course of the poems. How were their transformations different? *Possible answer:* The chambered nautilus grew larger and more impressive, whereas Old Ironsides deteriorated with age.

INDEPENDENT READING

Students interested in reading more about life changes might enjoy *Step Lightly: Poems for the Journey* by Nancy Willard.

OLD IRONSIDES
Oliver Wendell Holmes

Ay, tear her tattered ensign[1] down!
　　Long has it waved on high,
And many an eye has danced to see
　　That banner in the sky;
5 Beneath it rung the battle shout,
　　And burst the cannon's roar;—
The meteor of the ocean air
　　Shall sweep the clouds no more.

Her deck, once red with heroes' blood,
10　　Where knelt the vanquished foe,
When winds were hurrying o'er the flood,
　　And waves were white below,
No more shall feel the victor's tread,
　　Or know the conquered knee;—
15 The harpies[2] of the shore shall pluck
　　The eagle of the sea!

Oh, better that her shattered hulk
　　Should sink beneath the wave;
Her thunders shook the mighty deep,
20　　And there should be her grave;
Nail to the mast her holy flag,
　　Set every threadbare sail,
And give her to the god of storms,
　　The lightning and the gale! ●

---

1. **ensign:** flag.
2. **harpies:** evil monsters from Greek mythology that are half woman and half bird.

● ALLUSION
Oliver Wendell Holmes assumed that his readers would be familiar with the basics of Greek mythology, so it is not surprising that his poems include classical **allusions**—references to characters, locations, or events in classical myths that enrich the reader's experience of Holmes's poems. Read foonote 2 on page 350 and footnote 2 at the bottom of this page. How do the allusions explained here contribute to your understanding of the poems? Explain your response.

● MAKE INFERENCES
Reread the third stanza. Based on what has been said in previous stanzas about the ship's gloried past, do you think the speaker is being sincere or **ironic** about the fate of Old Ironsides? Explain.

DIFFERENTIATED INSTRUCTION

FOR STRUGGLING READERS
Explore Allusion Point out the footnote that explains the allusion to "harpies" (line 15). Add to the explanation by telling students that harpies were terrible creatures that flew off with food, objects, and even people (thus, Holmes's "shall pluck / The eagle of the sea"). Elicit that the "harpies" to whom Holmes refers are those who might plan to have the USS *Constitution* destroyed.

FOR ADVANCED LEARNERS/AP
Compare and Contrast Poems Challenge students to compare and contrast Holmes's understanding of change in the two poems. Pose such questions as: What kind of change does Holmes view as natural and desirable? Why? What kind of change is unnatural and undesirable? Why? Have them write two paragraphs on their conclusions and share them with the class.

Comprehension

1. **Recall** What event involving Old Ironsides took place during the war?

2. **Recall** According to the speaker, what should be the ship's fate?

3. **Summarize** In lines 1–14 of "The Chambered Nautilus," what does the speaker imagine and notice about the nautilus?

Text Analysis

4. **Analyze Symbol** What do you think the chambered nautilus **symbolizes,** or represents, for the speaker of the poem? Use evidence to support your answer.

● 5. **Make Inferences** Look back at the inferences and evidence you recorded as you read. What ideas about change does Holmes convey in "The Chambered Nautilus"? How does Holmes use each of the following images to express his thoughts about change?

   • the shell's appearance in the speaker's hands (lines 8–14)
   • the growth of the shell (lines 15–21)
   • the message the shell conveys (lines 29–35)

6. **Identify Tone** The attitude that a writer takes toward a particular subject is called **tone.** How would you describe the tone of each poem? What words and figures of speech help establish this tone? Use a chart like the one shown to record your answers.

> "Old Ironsides"
>
> **Tone:** sardonic
>
> **Words:** "Oh, better that her shattered hulk / Should sink beneath the wave" (lines 17–18)
>
> "The Chambered Nautilus"
>
> **Tone:**
>
> **Words:**

● 7. **Interpret Meter** Review the metric pattern you identified in "Old Ironsides." Then read the poem aloud. How does this meter reflect the poem's subject matter? Explain.

Text Criticism

8. **Author's Style** Recall from Holmes's biography on page 348 that the poem "Old Ironsides" was instrumental in saving the USS *Constitution.* What techniques and details used in the poem might have motivated readers to act? Cite evidence to support your answer.

When is it time to **MOVE ON?**

Consider the "heavenly message" presented in "The Chambered Nautilus." In what ways might you leave your "low-vaulted past" and "build more stately mansions" throughout your life?

COMMON CORE

RL 1 Cite evidence to support analysis of inferences drawn from the text. RL 2 Provide an objective summary of the text. RL 4 Analyze the impact of specific words on meaning and tone. RL 5 Analyze how an author's choices concerning how to structure a text contribute to its structure and meaning, as well as its aesthetic impact.

Practice and Apply

For preliminary support of post-reading questions, use these copy masters:

R **RESOURCE MANAGER**—Copy Masters
Meter p. 65
Question Support p. 69
Additional selection questions are provided for teachers on page 61.

ANSWERS   COMMON CORE RL 1, RL 2, RL 4, RL 5

1. *The ship was victorious in battle.*

2. *The speaker says that it would be better for the ship to sink in a storm rather than be demolished.*

3. *The speaker imagines that the nautilus has sailed through the ocean realms where "Sirens" and mermaids live. He notices that the shell is now so damaged that he can see its chambers.*

Possible answers:

4. *It represents personal, spiritual growth, as Holmes explains in the final stanza.*

5. ■ **COMMON CORE FOCUS Make Inferences** *Holmes indicates that change enables people to mature.*

   • *Lines 8–14 convey that in life the nautilus saw many changes and that death also has changed it.*

   • *Lines 15–21 convey the process of change that the nautilus experienced as it grew.*

   • *Lines 29–35 convey the message that the speaker draws from the nautilus: namely, it is important for people to undergo a change in which they embrace greater, nobler thoughts.*

Assess and Reteach

6. *The tone of "Old Ironsides" is sardonic, angry, serious, and ironic; an example would be "Ay, tear her tattered ensign down!" (line 1). The tone of "The Chambered Nautilus" is romantic, as evidenced by such phrases as "ship of pearl" (line 1), and "Child of the wandering sea" (line 23).*

7. ● **COMMON CORE FOCUS Meter** *The odd-numbered lines of each stanza are in iambic tetrameter and the even-numbered lines in iambic trimeter, with variations when lines begin with a trochaic foot. The briskness of the meter reflects the speaker's urgency.*

8. *The poem's images, such as the tattered flag waving high and the deck red with heroes' blood, probably evoked readers' patriotism. The rhymes and meter create a stirringly oratorical rhythm.*

When is it time to **MOVE ON?**
Students should describe some type of intellectual, moral, or spiritual growth, such as going to college.

Assess

DIAGNOSTIC AND SELECTION TESTS
   Selection Test A pp. 113–114
   Selection Test B/C pp. 115–116

Interactive Selection Test on thinkcentral.com

Reteach

Level Up Online Tutorials on thinkcentral.com

Reteaching Worksheets on thinkcentral.com

   Literature Lesson 20

Focus and Motivate

COMMON CORE FOCUS

RL 1 Cite evidence to support analysis of inferences drawn from the text. **RL 4** Analyze the impact of specific word choices on meaning and tone, including language that is fresh, engaging, or beautiful. **RL 5** Analyze how an author's choices concerning how to structure a text contribute to its structure and meaning, as well as its aesthetic impact. **RL 9** Demonstrate knowledge of how two or more texts from the same period treat similar themes or topics. **RL 10** Read and comprehend poetry. **L 3** Apply knowledge of language to comprehend more fully when reading. **L 4a** Use context as a clue to the meaning of a word or phrase. **L 5b** Analyze nuances in the meaning of words with similar denotations.

MEET THE AUTHORS

John Greenleaf Whittier Explain that the adjective *idyllic* refers to an idealized rural scene. (Students will see the noun *idyll* in "Snowbound.") Ask students what Whittier might say in an idyllic poem about being snowbound.

James Russell Lowell Point out the final sentence of the biography. Briefly discuss why someone's lasting fame might come from writing instead of from other achievements.

COMMON CORE

RL 1 Cite evidence to support analysis of inferences drawn from the text. **RL 4** Analyze the impact of specific word choices on meaning and tone, including language that is fresh, engaging, or beautiful. **RL 10** Read and comprehend literature.

The Fireside Poets

from Snowbound
Poem by John Greenleaf Whittier

The First Snowfall
Poem by James Russell Lowell

Meet the Authors

John Greenleaf Whittier
1807–1892

John Greenleaf Whittier embodied the idealism of his age, which combined social activism and literary activity. He devoted most of his waking hours to the abolition of slavery, even risking his own life for the cause. Yet he also managed to write hundreds of poems. Many express an idyllic view of rural life and a profound moral aversion to slavery.

Rural Childhood Whittier's social consciousness derived from his modest background. Born to devout Quakers, Whittier was taught to believe in the equality of all people, the immorality of war, and the importance of thrift. Working long days on his family's farm in Haverhill, Massachusetts, Whittier also learned about nature.

Poet and Politician Unlike most of his literary contemporaries, Whittier received little formal schooling. He was, however, an avid reader, devouring the poetry of John Milton, Robert Burns, and other poets. When Whittier was 19, his poetry was discovered by the abolitionist and editor William Lloyd Garrison. In later years, Whittier contributed poems to various newspapers.

James Russell Lowell
1819–1891

To his contemporaries, James Russell Lowell was the quintessential New England man of letters. He wrote poetry that stirred the emotions, newspaper editorials that influenced public opinion, and literary criticism.

Rebel with a Cause Lowell was born into a prominent New England family. In 1834, he entered Harvard, where he exasperated his teachers with his spoiled, immature behavior. His flouting of school rules and his disregard for his studies eventually led to his suspension. In 1844, Lowell married Maria White, who set her husband on the path to more mature behavior. In later years, Lowell published several volumes of verse and numerous articles in support of the abolitionist movement. He opposed slavery, the Mexican War, and corruption in politics.

Poet and Diplomat Lowell's talents were not limited to writing. He served as editor of *The Atlantic Monthly*, as an American diplomat in Spain, and as ambassador to Great Britain. While he enjoyed much public success in these roles, Lowell is today best remembered for his poetry.

Author Online
Go to **thinkcentral.com**. KEYWORD: HML11-354

THINK central

354

Selection Resources

See resources on the **Teacher One Stop DVD-ROM** and on **thinkcentral.com**.

 RESOURCE MANAGER UNIT 2
  Plan and Teach, pp. 71–78
  Text Analysis and Reading
    Skill, pp. 79–80, 81–82†*

DIAGNOSTIC AND SELECTION TESTS
  Selection Tests, pp. 117–120

 BEST PRACTICES TOOLKIT
  Cluster Diagram, p. B18
  What's Most Important, p. D4
  Showing, Not Telling, With Literature, p. D1
  Analysis Frame: Poetic Content, pp. D21, D36
  Jigsaw Reading, p. A1
  Evaluating a Poem, p. D17

TECHNOLOGY
  ⊘ **Teacher One Stop DVD-ROM**
  ⊘ **Student One Stop DVD-ROM**
  ⊘ **Audio Anthology CD**
  ⊘ **GrammarNotes DVD-ROM**
  ⊘ **ExamView Test Generator**
    on the **Teacher One Stop**

---

* Resources for Differentiation   **† Also in Spanish**   **‡ Also in Haitian Creole and Vietnamese**

TEXT ANALYSIS: MOOD

Mood is the feeling or atmosphere that a writer creates for the reader. Although it may seem that mood is simply inherent in a piece, it is actually achieved through the use of various devices, such as the following:

- **figurative language:** language that communicates ideas beyond the literal meaning of words
- **imagery:** descriptive words and phrases a writer uses to re-create sensory experiences
- **meter:** repetition of a regular rhythmic unit in a line of poetry
- **rhyme:** similarity of sound between two words

Notice, for example, how Lowell uses all four devices in the following stanza from "The First Snowfall":

I stood and watched by the window
  The noiseless work of the sky,
And the sudden flurries of snowbirds,
  Like brown leaves whirling by.

As you read the poems by Lowell and Whittier, look for the devices that help to create a different mood in each poem.

READING STRATEGY: PARAPHRASE

Sometimes, the surest way to get through a difficult passage is to **paraphrase** it, or restate the ideas in simpler words. To paraphrase a line or stanza in a poem, determine its main idea and replace difficult words with easier ones. In some cases, footnotes will help you clarify meaning. Consider the following lines from Lowell's poem "The First Snowfall":

And the poorest twig on the elm-tree
  Was ridged inch deep with pearl.

Here is a paraphrase of the lines above in simpler language:

An inch of snow covered the slender twig on the elm tree.

As you read, use a chart like the one shown to record difficult words or phrases and how you might paraphrase them.

Original Word(s)	My Paraphrase

Review: Make Inferences

 Complete the activities in your **Reader/Writer Notebook**.

What can NATURE teach us?

What lessons about life have you learned from nature? Perhaps waiting out a thunderstorm taught you something about patience. Or maybe watching monkeys at the zoo helped you to understand group behavior. The selections that follow describe kernels of wisdom two poets gleaned from the natural world.

QUICKWRITE In your notebook, list some insights you have gained from nature. How could you apply these insights to your own life? Write down your thoughts and ideas in a short paragraph.

Scene or Event	Insights
thunderstorm	Nature puts things in perspective.

355

What can NATURE teach us?

Call on volunteers to suggest other lessons that might come from observing nature (for example, lessons about cleverness or cooperation). As students begin the *QUICKWRITE* activity, urge them to consider how the insights that they gained from nature challenged their thinking. Allow students to share their finished paragraphs in small groups.

TEXT ANALYSIS — COMMON CORE RL 4

Model the Skill: MOOD

To demonstrate the use of literary devices in setting mood, identify the four devices in the sample stanza: figurative language in the comparison of snowbirds to brown leaves; imagery in the "sudden flurries of snowbirds"; the meter, which mixes iambic and anapestic feet in a predictable pattern; and the *abcb* rhyme scheme. Elicit that the mood of the stanza is rather reflective and possibly sad.

GUIDED PRACTICE Have students brainstorm a variety of possible moods that a poem could express.

READING STRATEGY — COMMON CORE RL 10

Model the Skill: PARAPHRASE

Remind students that paraphrasing is restating ideas using simpler words. Have students paraphrase the stanza from "The First Snowfall" in the Text Analysis discussion. Tell them that one way to phrase the same idea would be, "*I stood by the window and watched the busy but silent sky. The groups of snowbirds that flew by reminded me of swirls of brown leaves.*"

 RESOURCE MANAGER—Copy Master
Paraphrase p. 81 (for student use while reading the selection)

DIFFERENTIATED INSTRUCTION

FOR STRUGGLING READERS

Concept Support: Paraphrase [small-group option] Give small groups of students the same passage, five to eight sentences in length, from a piece of modern prose that is somewhat difficult but not as challenging as the poems in this lesson. A passage from a textbook on history or science might be a good choice. Instruct each group to make a chart similar to the one presented on this page and then to work together to para- phrase sentences, one by one. (Depending on the material, some sentences may not need much paraphrasing.) When the group arrives at a satisfactory paraphrase for a sentence, have a group secretary write the paraphrase on the chart. Post the original passage and the groups' paraphrase charts in the classroom for students to compare and contrast.

SUMMARY

The speaker recalls a childhood memory of the coming and aftermath of a snowstorm. He remembers wondering at the snow-transformed scene, digging a path through the snow to the barn, and spending a tranquil evening with his family by a blazing hearth fire.

READ WITH A PURPOSE

Help students set a purpose for reading. Tell them to read "Snowbound" and "The First Snowfall" to learn about each speaker's state of mind.

TEXT ANALYSIS

COMMON CORE
RL 4

A MOOD

Read aloud lines 1–8, stressing the rhyme word pairs. Then have students cite familiar jingles and identifying rhyming words, and the moods these rhymes create.

Possible answer: four pairs: day, gray; noon, moon; sky, prophecy; threat, set; mood is gloomy, uncertain, depressing

---

TIERED DISCUSSION PROMPTS

In lines 9–25, use these prompts to help students explore the description of the gathering storm:

Connect How do you feel when a storm is approaching? Do your feelings vary according to the kind of storm? *Students may suggest excitement, worry, fear, and so on, especially if the approaching storm has potential for harm.*

Analyze In what way are some details like a weather report? *Possible answer: References to the bitter cold and the direction of the wind are similar to a weather report.* How does the speaker convey a sense of normalcy despite the gathering storm? *Possible answer: The speaker conveys normalcy by describing how he participated in the usual evening chores.*

SNOWBOUND
A Winter Idyll

John Greenleaf Whittier

The sun that brief December day
Rose cheerless over hills of gray,
And, darkly circled, gave at noon
A sadder light than waning[1] moon.
5 Slow tracing down the thickening sky
Its mute and ominous prophecy,
A portent[2] seeming less than threat,
It sank from sight before it set. **A**
A chill no coat, however stout,
10 Of homespun stuff could quite shut out,
A hard, dull bitterness of cold,
That checked, mid-vein, the circling race
Of lifeblood in the sharpened face,
The coming of the snowstorm told.
15 The wind blew east; we heard the roar
Of Ocean on his wintry shore,
And felt the strong pulse throbbing there
Beat with low rhythm our inland air.

Meanwhile we did our nightly chores,—
20 Brought in the wood from out of doors,
Littered the stalls, and from the mows
Raked down the herd's grass for the cows:
Heard the horse whinnying for his corn;
And, sharply clashing horn on horn,
25 Impatient down the stanchion rows[3]

---

1. **waning:** lessening in intensity.
2. **portent:** omen.
3. **stanchion** (stăn′chən) **rows:** lines of devices that fit loosely around the necks of animals such as cows in order to limit their motion.

A MOOD

Poets often use structural elements, such as meter and rhyme scheme, to help create a particular **mood. Meter** is simply the repetition of a rhythmic unit, and **rhyme** is the use of words (most often at the end of lines) that share a similar sound. Reread the first eight lines of the poem, and write down the words that rhyme. How many pairs of rhyme words do you see? What mood do these words help create?

Analyze Visuals ►
To what senses does this photograph appeal, in addition to sight?

DIFFERENTIATED INSTRUCTION

FOR ENGLISH LANGUAGE LEARNERS

Vocabulary: Outdated Forms Point out that much of the descriptive vocabulary of "Snowbound" is old-fashioned or poetic. Have students work with English-fluent partners to paraphrase outdated words such as *homespun* (line 10), *hoary* (line 33), *firmament* (line 51), and *sage* (line 91) and poetic words such as *whirl-dance* (line 34), *wingëd* (line 36), and *ere* (line 37).

FOR STRUGGLING READERS

Develop Reading Fluency

- Have students listen to the two poems on the *Audio Anthology CD*. Encourage students to listen for ways in which the reader's voice sets a mood for each poem.

- After students have listened to the CD, tell them to read the poems out loud to practice using their voice to set a mood.

Analyze Visuals

Possible answer: *The lack of human activity suggests silence, which appeals to the sense of hearing. The photograph also appeals to the sense of touch by suggesting the feel of tree bark, snowflakes, and coldness.*

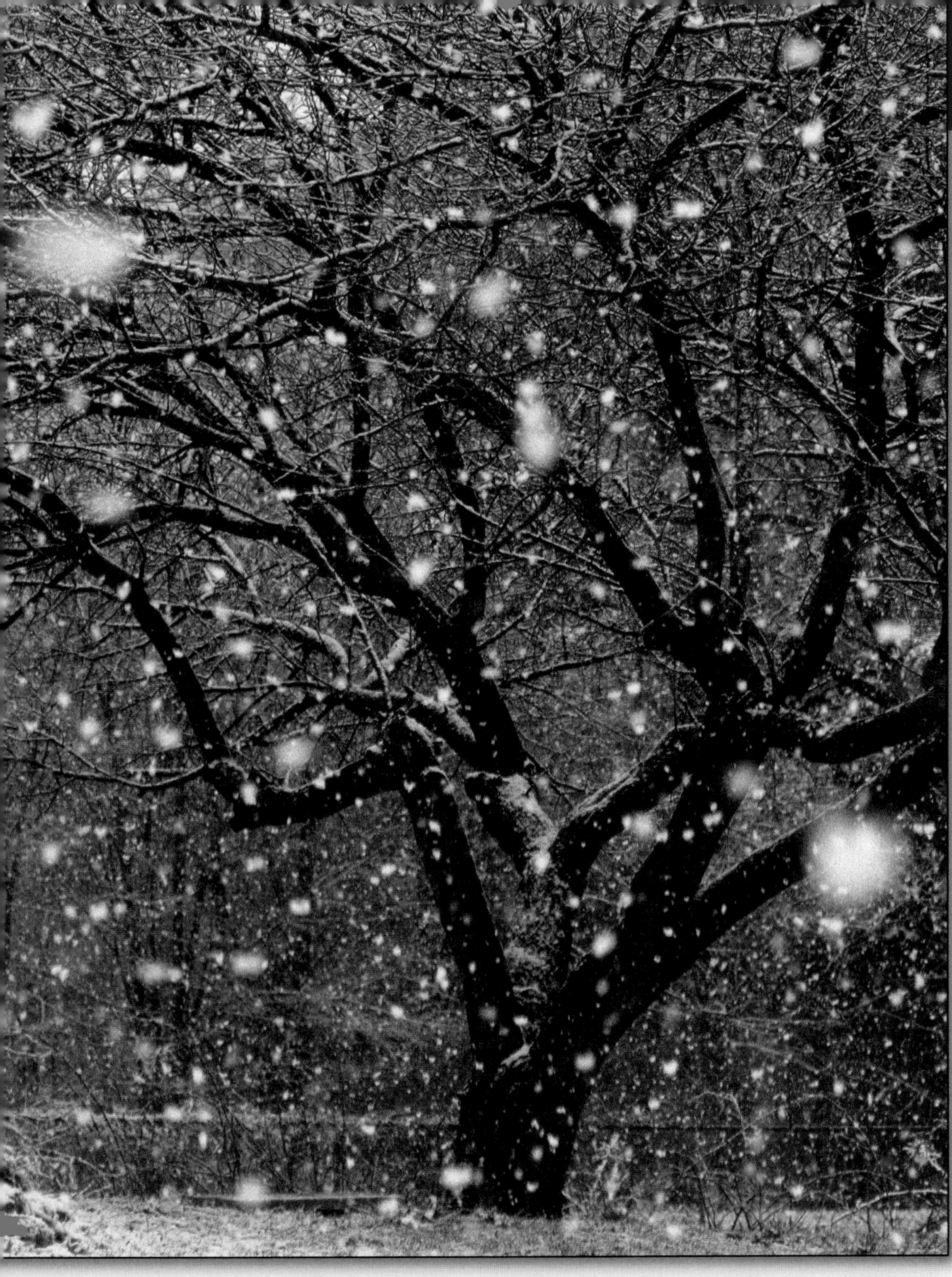

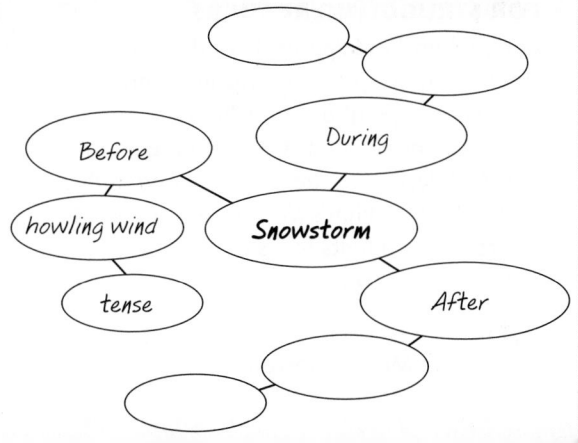

REVISIT THE BIG QUESTION

What can NATURE *teach us?*

Discuss In lines 1–18, what attitude toward nature does Whittier present in this first stanza—mainly positive, mainly negative, or a mix of both? ***Possible answer:*** *The view is mainly negative because the sky is an "ominous . . . portent" of the storm (lines 6–7), and images of cold and darkness prevail. However, there is also something exciting in feeling the "strong pulse" of the wind-stirred ocean (lines 15–18) and perhaps in seeing the fulfillment of the "prophecy" (line 6) of an approaching storm.*

CULTURAL CONNECTION

Storms Around the World Snowstorms are frequent in New England, where "Snowbound" is set. Other kinds of storms take place elsewhere in the United States and the world—tornadoes in the Midwest and Central Plains; hurricanes in the Atlantic Ocean, eastern Pacific Ocean, and the Caribbean; sandstorms in the Middle East and parts of Africa and China; and typhoons in Southeast Asia. Invite students to share information about and personal experiences with storms.

FOR STRUGGLING READERS

Explore Mood To help students sense the mood of the poem, have them imagine that they are members of the family portrayed. Have them work in pairs or small groups to fill out a Cluster Diagram, recording words and phrases that express what they might see, hear, and feel before, during, and after a snowstorm.

BEST PRACTICES TOOLKIT—Transparency
Cluster Diagram p. B18

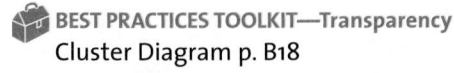

REVISIT THE BIG QUESTION

What can NATURE *teach us?*

Discuss In lines 31–54, identify some details of nature that Whittier presents. What do you think the speaker, as a young boy, learned from this experience with nature? *Possible answer: Natural details include the gray sky, night, whirling snowflakes, a blinding storm, snowdrifts, a sunless morning, geometric traces of snow, and a clear blue sky. The speaker might have learned that one's perception of the world can change suddenly and that nature can provide beauty and wonder in the midst of ordinary human life.*

TEXT ANALYSIS   COMMON CORE   RL 4

B MOOD

Possible answer: By comparing the clothesline posts to ghosts, the poet presents a simile that creates a mood of eerie wonder.

READING STRATEGY   COMMON CORE   RL 10

C PARAPHRASE

Possible answer: Familiar landmarks have been covered by snow, and the whole landscape seems to consist of nothing but snow and sky.

IF STUDENTS NEED HELP . . . Remind them to use the chart introduced on page 355. Suggest that as students paraphrase, they should try to not be distracted by line breaks, for the meaning of a thought can run for several lines.

Original Word(s)	My Paraphrase
No cloud above, no earth below— / A universe of sky and snow!	All familiar features were erased. The landscape was made only of snow and sky.

The cattle shake their walnut bows;
While, peering from his early perch
Upon the scaffold's pole of birch,
The cock his crested helmet bent
30 And down his querulous[4] challenge sent.

Unwarmed by any sunset light
The gray day darkened into night,
A night made hoary with the swarm
And whirl-dance of the blinding storm,
35 As zigzag, wavering to and fro,
Crossed and recrossed the wingëd snow:
And ere the early bedtime came
The white drift piled the window frame,
And through the glass the clothesline posts
40 Looked in like tall and sheeted ghosts.

So all night long the storm roared on:
The morning broke without a sun;
In tiny spherule[5] traced with lines
Of Nature's geometric signs,
45 In starry flake, and pellicle,[6]
All day the hoary meteor fell;
And, when the second morning shone,
We looked upon a world unknown,
On nothing we could call our own.
50 Around the glistening wonder bent
The blue walls of the firmament,
No cloud above, no earth below—
A universe of sky and snow! C
The old familiar sights of ours
55 Took marvelous shapes; strange domes and towers
Rose up where sty or corncrib stood,
Or garden wall, or belt of wood;
A smooth white mound the brush pile showed,
A fenceless drift what once was road;
60 The bridle post an old man sat
With loose-flung coat and high cocked hat;
The well curb[7] had a Chinese roof;

---

4. **querulous** (kwĕr′ə-ləs): complaining.
5. **spherule** (sfîr′ōōl): a little sphere.
6. **pellicle:** a thin film or skin.
7. **well curb:** framing around the neck of a well.

COMMON CORE L3

Language Coach

Oral Fluency The two dots over the e in *wingëd* (line 36) indicate that the *e* should be pronounced. *Winged* is normally pronounced in one syllable as /weengd/, but here it is pronounced in two syllables as /weeng ehd/. Read lines 35–36, pronouncing *winged* in one syllable, then in two syllables. How does the sound of the lines change?

B MOOD

A **simile** is a figure of speech comparing two things using the words *like* or *as*. What mood does the poet create with the simile in lines 39–40?

C PARAPHRASE

How has the world been transformed by snow in lines 50–53?

DIFFERENTIATED INSTRUCTION

FOR STRUGGLING READERS

Comprehension Support If students have trouble following the descriptions and events of the poem, point out that "Snowbound" is a narrative poem—that is, despite the abundance of descriptive details, the poem tells a story. Use the What's Most Important strategy to help students focus on the key events of the poetic narrative.

BEST PRACTICES TOOLKIT
What's Most Important p. D4

FOR ENGLISH LANGUAGE LEARNERS

Language Coach   COMMON CORE L3

Oral Fluency *Possible answer: Pronouncing the word as one syllable disrupts the rhythm of the lines.* Have students work with a partner to identify other words ending in *ed* that can be pronounced in one or two syllables. *Learned* is one possible example. Call on pairs to share an item from their list with the class.

And even the long sweep,[8] high aloof,
In its slant splendor, seemed to tell
65 Of Pisa's leaning miracle.[9]

A prompt, decisive man, no breath
Our father wasted: "Boys, a path!"
Well pleased, (for when did farmer boy
Count such a summons less than joy?)
70 Our buskins[10] on our feet we drew;
With mittened hands, and caps drawn low,
To guard our necks and ears from snow,
We cut the solid whiteness through.
And, where the drift was deepest, made
75 A tunnel walled and overlaid
With dazzling crystal: we had read
Of rare Aladdin's wondrous cave,[11]
And to our own his name we gave,
With many a wish the luck were ours
80 To test his lamp's supernal[12] powers.
We reached the barn with merry din,
And roused the prisoned brutes within.
The old horse thrust his long head out,
And grave with wonder gazed about;
85 The cock his lusty greeting said,
And forth his speckled harem led;
The oxen lashed their tails, and hooked,
And mild reproach of hunger looked;
The hornëd patriarch of the sheep,
90 Like Egypt's Amun[13] roused from sleep,
Shook his sage head with gesture mute,
And emphasized with stamp of foot. **D**

All day the gusty north wind bore
The loosening drift its breath before;
95 Low circling round its southern zone,
The sun through dazzling snow-mist shone.
No church bell lent its Christian tone

---

8. **sweep:** a long pole connected to a bucket, used for raising water from a well.

9. **Pisa's leaning miracle:** the Leaning Tower of Pisa, Italy.

10. **buskins:** high leather boots.

11. **Aladdin's wondrous cave:** In *The Thousand and One Nights*, the boy Aladdin used a magic lamp to discover a treasure in a cave.

12. **supernal:** heavenly; supernatural.

13. **Amun** (ä'mən): the supreme god of the ancient Egyptians, often represented as having a ram's head.

TIERED DISCUSSION PROMPTS

In lines 66–92, use these prompts to help students explore a practical aspect of the storm's aftermath:

Recall What do the tasks performed before the storm (lines 19–30) tell you about the family's daily life? *Possible answer: The tasks show that family members have daily chores, including taking care of the farm's animals.*

Interpret What is the main subject of this stanza? *Possible answer: The main subject is that the speaker and his family, while awe-struck by the scene, go to work to dig a path to the barn so that they can take care of their animals.* What does it add to the poem? *Possible answer: The stanza adds action to the narrative, brightens the tone, and widens the reader's view of the speaker's family.*

Evaluate Does Whittier succeed at making the chore that this stanza presents seem wondrous? Explain your answer.
Possible answer: Whittier succeeds because he describes the chore in exotic terms. For example, a tunnel through the snow is like Aladdin's cave (line 77). He also presents the animals in exotic, humorous terms—the grave old horse, the rooster and his harem of hens, the regal ram, and so on (lines 83–92).

THEME COMMON CORE RL 5

TEXT STRUCTURE

After students have read the entire poem, ask them to discuss films, plays, or novels that relate to the theme of nature's beauty. Ask them especially to focus on how the text or narrative structures of each work affects how this theme is expressed.

TEXT ANALYSIS COMMON CORE RL 4

D MOOD

Possible answer: Examples of figurative language include "his speckled harem" (line 86) and "Like Egypt's Amun roused from sleep" (line 90). Examples of imagery include "We cut the solid whiteness through" (line 73) and "A tunnel walled and overlaid / With dazzling crystal" (lines 75–76). The mood is one of enchantment, good humor, and youthful zeal.

FOR STRUGGLING READERS

Vocabulary Support Write these challenging terms on the board and have students find definitions. Urge students to substitute the definition for the term as they read the lines from the poem.

- *slant* (line 64), "slanting"
- *summons* (line 69), "a call to do something"
- *overlaid* (line 75), "covered"
- *din* (line 81), "loud noise"
- *prisoned* (line 82), "imprisoned," "trapped"

- *grave* (line 84), "very serious"
- *lusty* (line 85), "hearty"
- *forth* (line 86), "forward"
- *reproach* (line 88), "disapproval"
- *patriarch* (line 89), "male head of a family"
- *roused* (line 90), "awakened"
- *mute* (line 91), "silent"

What can
NATURE *teach us?*

Discuss In lines 93–115, what overall impression of nature does the poet convey? What mood results from this description? Cite specific details that contribute to this effect.

Possible answer: *The overall impression is one of solitude, and the mood is rather melancholy. Details that create this effect include the lack of neighboring chimney smoke (lines 98–99), the shrieking and moaning of the wind in the trees (lines 102–103), the beating of sleet on glass windows (lines 104–105), and the absence of welcome sounds such as the brooklet (lines 110–111).*

READING STRATEGY

E *Model the Skill:*
PARAPHRASE

Use the Showing, Not Telling, with Literature strategy to guide students as they analyze the psychological effect that Whittier creates in the passage.

Possible answer: *The snowstorm makes the family feel isolated and enclosed within its home while the elements rage outside.*

 BEST PRACTICES TOOLKIT
Showing, Not Telling, with Literature
p. D1

To the savage air, no social smoke
Curled over woods of snow-hung oak.
100 A solitude made more intense
By dreary-voicëd elements,
The shrieking of the mindless wind,
The moaning tree boughs swaying blind,
And on the glass the unmeaning beat
105 Of ghostly fingertips of sleet.
Beyond the circle of our hearth
No welcome sound of toil or mirth
Unbound the spell, and testified
Of human life and thought outside. **E**
110 We minded that the sharpest ear
The buried brooklet could not hear,
The music of whose liquid lip
Had been to us companionship,
And, in our lonely life, had grown
115 To have an almost human tone.

As night drew on, and, from the crest
Of wooded knolls that ridged the west,
The sun, a snow-blown traveler, sank
From sight beneath the smothering bank,
120 We piled, with care, our nightly stack
Of wood against the chimney back,—
The oaken log, green, huge, and thick,
And on its top the stout backstick;
The knotty forestick laid apart,
125 And filled between with curious art
The ragged brush; then, hovering near,
We watched the first red blaze appear,
Heard the sharp crackle, caught the gleam
On whitewashed wall and sagging beam,
130 Until the old, rude-furnished room
Burst, flowerlike, into rosy bloom;
While radiant with a mimic flame
Outside the sparkling drift became,
And through the bare-boughed lilac tree
135 Our own warm hearth seemed blazing free.
The crane and pendent trammels showed,
The Turks' heads on the andirons[14] glowed;

E PARAPHRASE
Reread lines 106–109. What effect does the snowstorm have on the family's sense of itself and the world outside?

---

14. **The crane . . . the andirons:** The crane was the movable arm on which the trammels, or adjustable pothooks, hung. The andirons, or metal supports holding the fireplace wood, were topped with turbanlike knots.

DIFFERENTIATED INSTRUCTION

FOR STRUGGLING READERS
Vocabulary Support

- *mirth* (line 107), "merriness"
- *testified* (line 108), "gave evidence"
- *minded* (line 110), "noticed"
- *knolls* (line 117), "small, rounded hills"
- *fancy* (line 138), "imagination"
- *prompt* (line 138), "quick"
- *Transfigured* (line 145), "Changed"
- *Dead* (line 147), "Completely"
- *save* (line 147), "except"

- *unwarming* (line 152), "not providing warmth"
- *baffled* (line 158), "frustrated"
- *rafter* (line 162), "beam that supports the roof"
- *draught* (line 163), "draft of air"
- *silhouette* (line 167), "shadow"
- *meet* (line 169), "fitting," "appropriate"

While childish fancy, prompt to tell
The meaning of the miracle,
140 Whispered the old rhyme: *"Under the tree,*
When fire outdoors burns merrily,
There the witches are making tea." ❶

The moon above the eastern wood
Shone at its full; the hill range stood
145 Transfigured in the silver flood,
Its blown snows flashing cold and keen,
Dead white, save where some sharp ravine
Took shadow, or the somber green
Of hemlocks turned to pitchy black
150 Against the whiteness at their back.
For such a world and such a night
Most fitting that unwarming light,
Which only seemed where'er it fell
To make the coldness visible.

155 Shut in from all the world without,
We sat the clean-winged hearth[15] about,
Content to let the north wind roar
In baffled rage at pane and door,
While the red logs before us beat
160 The frost line back with tropic heat; ❷
And ever, when a louder blast
Shook beam and rafter as it passed,
The merrier up its roaring draught
The great throat of the chimney laughed;
165 The house dog on his paws outspread
Laid to the fire his drowsy head,
The cat's dark silhouette on the wall
A couchant[16] tiger's seemed to fall;
And, for the winter fireside meet,
170 Between the andirons' straddling feet,
The mug of cider simmered slow,
The apples sputtered in a row,
And, close at hand, the basket stood
With nuts from brown October's wood.

---

15. **clean-winged hearth:** Hearths were commonly swept with a turkey wing.
16. **couchant** (kou'chənt): lying down, but with head raised.

SNOWBOUND   **361**

---

❶ MOOD
In lines 116–142, what techniques does the poet use to create a mood of security and warmth in the midst of nature's cold and snow?

Word Definitions At the end of line 155, you might read the word *without* and think "without what?" Here, *without* means "outside." In lines 155–160, how does the world *within* differ from the world *without*?

❷ MAKE INFERENCES
Reread lines 155–160. Why is the north wind baffled?

---

❶ *Model the Skill:* MOOD

To involve students in analyzing mood, read aloud lines 116–142. Lead a discussion about how the poet used imagery, figurative language, allusion, and the connotations of carefully chosen words in the passage.

Possible answer: *The poet uses imagery, figurative language, allusion, and the connotations of carefully chosen words to create a mood of security and warmth. The imagery of firewood and a warm hearth runs throughout the passage, in descriptions such as "We watched the first red blaze appear, / Heard the sharp crackle, caught the gleam / On whitewashed wall . . . " (lines 127–129). Figurative language, such as "Burst, flowerlike, into rosy bloom" (line 131), enriches the scene. The allusion to an "old rhyme" (lines 140–142) creates a feeling of comfort in tradition. Words chosen for their positive connotation include* radiant *(line 132),* sparkling *(line 133),* warm hearth *(line 135),* glowed *(line 137), and* miracle *(line 139).*

---

❷ MAKE INFERENCES

Possible answer: *The north wind is baffled because it is blocked by the door and windowpane and by the heat of the fireplace.*

If students need help . . . Work with them to paraphrase these lines and to contrast the cold, windy outdoor scene with the interior scene by the cozy hearth.

FOR ADVANCED LEARNERS/AP

Analyze the Complete Text [small-group option] Explain that this excerpt of "Snowbound" is part of a longer poem. The rest of the poem consists of character sketches and a description of the community reestablishing contact with the outside world—it reveals that the speaker and his brother are the only family members still alive. Have students read the complete poem and write an essay that answers these questions:

Whom does the speaker describe? Why are these people important to him?

FOR ENGLISH LANGUAGE LEARNERS

Word Definitions *Possible answer: The world "within" is warm and peaceful; the world "without" is raging and cold.* Have students write two sentences for each word conveying its meaning.

Prereading for this poem is found on page 355.

SUMMARY

As the speaker watches the first snowfall of the year, he envisions the snow that is falling upon his dead daughter's grave. His living daughter enters and asks, "Father, who makes it snow?" He kisses her and tells her about God, but he does not tell her that his kiss is intended for her dead sister.

TEXT ANALYSIS

COMMON CORE RL 4

ⓗ Model the Skill: MOOD

Tell students that to experience the mood created by rhyme and meter, it is most effective to read the lines aloud. Have volunteers read aloud lines 1–16 and discuss with students their reactions to the effect of meter and rhyme.

Possible answer: *The mood is quiet and dignified but observant. The simple rhymes, the abcb rhyme scheme, and the variances in meter keep the verse from being sing-songy and thus the mood from seeming contrived.*

READING STRATEGY

COMMON CORE RL 10

ⓘ PARAPHRASE

Possible answer: *Paraphrase: "I thought of a grave with a small headstone at Mount Auburn Cemetery; I imagined snow falling on it, gently protecting it, as a mother robin protects her young." The introduction of this image saddens the mood.*

IF STUDENTS NEED HELP . . . Ask:

- What other place does the speaker think of as he watches the falling snow?
- What special detail comes to his mind?
- Why does he compare snowflakes to robins?
- How much of a change is this scene from the scene in lines 1–16?

THE FIRST SNOWFALL

James Russell Lowell

The snow had begun in the gloaming,[1]
    And busily all the night
Had been heaping field and highway
    With a silence deep and white.

5 Every pine and fir and hemlock
    Wore ermine[2] too dear for an earl,
And the poorest twig on the elmtree
    Was ridged inch deep with pearl.

From sheds new-roofed with Carrara[3]
10   Came Chanticleer's[4] muffled crow,
The stiff rails softened to swan's-down,
    And still fluttered down the snow.

I stood and watched by the window
    The noiseless work of the sky,
15 And the sudden flurries of snowbirds,
    Like brown leaves whirling by. ⓗ

I thought of a mound in sweet Auburn[5]
    Where a little headstone stood;
How the flakes were folding it gently,
20   As did robins the babes in the wood. ⓘ

Up spoke our own little Mabel,
    Saying, "Father, who makes it snow?"
And I told of the good All-father
    Who cares for us here below.

---

1. **gloaming:** twilight.
2. **ermine:** the expensive white fur of a type of weasel.
3. **Carrara:** Carrara marble, a white marble named after the Italian city where it is mined.
4. **Chanticleer's:** a rooster's.
5. **Auburn:** Mount Auburn Cemetery, located in Cambridge, Massachusetts.

COMMON CORE L 5b

Language Coach

Synonyms Often the word *dear* (line 6) is used as a term of affection. However, *dear* can also mean "high-priced." Other words with similar meanings, or **synonyms**, of *dear* include *costly*, *valuable*, and *precious*. Read lines 5–8, and write down the words related to wealth or luxury. How are the descriptions in the poem enhanced by these words?

ⓗ **MOOD**
Reread lines 1–16. How would you describe the mood created by the poet's use of **rhyme** and **meter**? Explain your answer.

ⓘ **PARAPHRASE**
Paraphrase lines 17–20. How does the mood shift in these lines?

DIFFERENTIATED INSTRUCTION

FOR STRUGGLING READERS

Comprehension Support Have groups of students read through "The First Snowfall" together, using the Analysis Frame: Poetic Content to grasp the core of the poem's subject, its speaker and other characters, its events, and its themes.

 **BEST PRACTICES TOOLKIT—Transparency**
Analysis Frame: Poetic Content
pp. D21, D36

FOR ENGLISH LANGUAGE LEARNERS

Language Coach
COMMON CORE L 5b

Synonyms *Answer:*
ermine, dear, pearl

Have students read "The First Snowfall" and select three words not already discussed in this Language Coach. Tell students to identify at least two synonyms for each of the words they selected.

◀ **Analyze Visuals**
This photograph shows Mount Auburn Cemetery, which is mentioned in the poem. What **mood** is suggested by the photograph, what details support the mood, and how does the mood of the picture match that of the poem?

25 Again I looked at the snowfall,
        And thought of the leaden sky
    That arched o'er our first great sorrow,
        When that mound was heaped so high. **J**

    I remembered the gradual patience
30   That fell from that cloud like snow,
    Flake by flake, healing and hiding
        The scar that renewed our woe.

    And again to the child I whispered,
        "The snow that husheth all,
35 Darling, the merciful Father
        Alone can make it fall!" **K**

    Then, with eyes that saw not, I kissed her;
        And she, kissing back, could not know
    That *my* kiss was given to her sister,
40   Folded close under deepening snow.

J **MAKE INFERENCES**
In line 17, "mound" refers to the daughter's grave. What else does "mound" refer to in line 28?

K **MOOD**
What mood does the speaker create at the end of the poem by invoking the "merciful Father"?

THE FIRST SNOWFALL **363**

Analyze Visuals

Possible answer: *The photograph suggests a reflective and somber or grieving mood. The details of the old gravestones, the snow, the bare tree, and the neutral color scheme support the mood. The mood of the photograph matches the mood of the poem in that both suggest sadness.*

READING STRATEGY: *Review*   COMMON CORE   RL 10

J *Model the Skill:* **MAKE INFERENCES**

Explain that while the word *mound* in line 17 refers to the the small hill of earth that marked his daughter's newly dug grave, the word *mound* can be a figurative reference to a large amount of something.

Possible answer: *"Mound" also refers to a great sorrow that the speaker has felt.*

TEXT ANALYSIS   COMMON CORE   RL 4

K **MOOD**

Possible answer: *The reference to the "merciful Father" creates a spiritual mood—a sense of religious faith providing a means to deal with grief.*

SELECTION WRAP—UP

READ WITH A PURPOSE Now that students have read the poems, have students assess the state of mind of each speaker. How is the state of mind of the speaker in "Snowbound" different from that of the speaker in "The First Snowfall"? ***Possible answer:*** *The speaker in "Snowbound" has a nostalgic state of mind, whereas the speaker in "The First Snowfall" has a somber state of mind.*

⭐ **CRITIQUE**

- Ask students which poem presents the speaker's feelings more effectively.

- After completing the discussion questions on page 364, have students revisit their responses and tell whether they have changed their opinions.

FOR STRUGGLING READERS

Concept Support: Paraphrase The final four stanzas (lines 25–40) are crucial for understanding the speaker's grief and the family's history. Have students work in small groups to paraphrase these stanzas. You might use a Jigsaw strategy to have pairs or individual students specialize in paraphrasing different stanzas and then regroup to share their paraphrases.

 **BEST PRACTICES TOOLKIT**
Jigsaw Reading p. A1

FOR ADVANCED LEARNERS/AP

Compare Poetic Views [paired option] Ask students to present a brief comparison of William Cullen Bryant's "Thanatopsis," which appears earlier in this unit, with "The First Snowfall." Urge them to focus on these questions:

- How does each poem convey the idea that nature can soften thoughts of death?

- Are thoughts of nature sufficient comfort for each poem's speaker? How can you tell?

Practice and Apply

For preliminary support of post-reading questions, use these copy masters:

R RESOURCE MANAGER—Copy Masters
Mood p. 79
Question Support p. 83
Additional selection questions are provided for teachers on page 75.

ANSWERS

COMMON CORE RL 1, RL 4, RL 9, RL 10

1. *The family brings in wood from outside and feeds the animals. The family stays indoors until the storm is over, makes a path through the snow when the sun appears, and gathers around a fire when its windy.*

2. *The family seems to enjoy the adventure.*

3. *The snowfall transforms the landscape into something that is silent yet majestic.*

4. *The family has suffered the death of a daughter.*

Possible answers:

5. *At first they find the storm threatening, then dreary, and then pleasing. Their responses suggest that they love each other.*

6. *The simile of "gradual patience" falling "from that cloud like snow" suggests that the pain of sorrow eventually softens; the family may find some solace in nature.*

7. ● **COMMON CORE FOCUS Para-phrase** *Lowell believes in a God who controls the universe and loves humankind (lines 23–24 and 35). Believing that God ultimately is good helps the poet cope with his pain.*

Assess and Reteach

Assess

DIAGNOSTIC AND SELECTION TESTS
Selection Test A pp. 117–118
Selection Test B/C pp. 119–120

Interactive Selection Test on **thinkcentral.com**

Reteach

Level Up Online Tutorials on **thinkcentral.com**

Reteaching Worksheets on **thinkcentral.com**

Literature Lesson 44; Reading Lessons 8

Comprehension

1. **Recall** In what ways does the family in "Snowbound" prepare for and cope with the storm?

2. **Clarify** How does the family in "Snowbound" feel about being snowed in?

3. **Summarize** How does the snowfall transform the landscape in lines 1–14 of "The First Snowfall"?

4. **Clarify** In "The First Snowfall," what has happened to the family?

Text Analysis

5. **Make Inferences** How do the people in "Snowbound" react to the storm? What do their responses say about their relationship to one another?

6. **Interpret Figurative Language** Reread lines 29–32 of "The First Snowfall." What does the figurative language in this stanza suggest about the family's grief and the relation of their sorrow to the natural world?

● 7. **Paraphrase to Draw Conclusions** Review the paraphrases you made in your chart as you read Lowell's poem. Describe the speaker's religious beliefs. How do they help him cope with his pain?

● 8. **Analyze Mood** Poets can use a variety of devices to establish mood, including **figurative language, imagery, rhyme,** and **meter.** In each of the poems, identify two devices used to create mood, giving examples. For each poem, which device would you say is the more important? Explain.

9. **Associate Ideas** In these poems and elsewhere, snow is often referred to as having a quieting effect. What are some common metaphors or images used to express our associations with other kinds of weather, such as downpours, torrid heat, windstorms, and Indian summers?

Text Criticism

10. **Historical Context** Whittier and Lowell were two of a group known as the Fireside Poets. (See page 310.) This name refers to a popular family pastime of the period: reading poetry aloud in front of the fireplace after dinner. The poems of the group were very popular and read as entertainment not only in homes but also in schools. Why might the poetry of this group have played such an important role in people's lives? Support your opinion.

> *What can* **NATURE** *teach us?*
>
> In "The First Snowfall," the speaker draws a parallel between a natural weather event and the healing of a great grief. How does nature speak to you? Can you think of a natural object or event that has held special meaning for you?

COMMON CORE

RL 1 Cite evidence to support analysis of inferences drawn from the text. RL 4 Analyze the impact of specific word choices on meaning and tone, including language that is fresh, engaging, or beautiful. RL 9 Demonstrate knowledge of how two or more texts from the same period treat similar themes or topics. RL 10 Read and comprehend poetry.

---

8. ● **COMMON CORE FOCUS Mood** *Each poem provides examples of all four techniques. In "The First Snowfall," Lowell's personification of "The snow that husheth all" (line 34) helps establish a mood of quiet acceptance. In lines 66–92 of "Snowbound," Whittier's iambic tetrameter couplets convey an exuberant, cheerful mood. Answers will vary as to which technique is the most important.*

9. *Accept all reasonable answers.*

10. *Relatively little public entertainment was available during the time that the Fireside Poets wrote. Reading aloud made poetry a social rather than solitary pastime.*

> *What can* NATURE *teach us?* Students should describe a natural object (for example, a mountain or tree) or event (for example, sunrise or a thunderstorm) that has held special meaning for them.

Fireside Poets in Perspective

The Fireside Poets were extremely popular in their day. Indeed, they were so beloved that many families read their works aloud by the fire as a form of nightly entertainment. They were respected as well, becoming the first poets to be considered on equal footing with their British counterparts. Over the years, however, the group's works fell out of favor with critics, who began to look upon them with more affection than respect. Only in recent years have critics again begun to appreciate the craft of the Fireside Poets.

Writing to Evaluate

With a group of classmates, come up with several criteria for evaluating the poems on pages 344–363. Then use your criteria to write a brief evaluation of the work of the Fireside Poets as a whole.

Consider

- what elements (vivid imagery, precise word choice, or thought-provoking themes) you think distinguish "good" poetry from "bad"
- whether the poems contain those elements
- whether your opinion of the poems changed upon rereading

Extension

SPEAKING & LISTENING Perform an **oral interpretation** of one poem from this group of Fireside Poets' work. Let your opinion of the Fireside Poets in general and of this work in particular inform your reading. For example, if you admire a particular poem, you may wish to read it in a lively and engaging voice. If, on the other hand, you found a poem too sentimental, let your reading reflect this judgment.

COMMON CORE

W 2 Write explanatory texts to examine complex ideas, concepts, and information through the analysis of content. **SL 6** Adapt speech to a variety of contexts and tasks.

365

 COMMON CORE FOCUS

W 2 Write explanatory texts to examine complex ideas, concepts, and information through the analysis of content. **SL 6** Adapt speech to a variety of contexts and tasks.

Wrap-Up: The Fireside Poets

This Wrap-Up provides students with the opportunity to consider the Fireside Poets' craft in light of changing literary tastes. Encourage students to think about their positive and negative responses to the poems of Longfellow, Holmes, Whittier, and Lowell and to give evaluations that express their views honestly while demonstrating an understanding of the tastes of the past.

Writing to Evaluate

- Review with students that *evaluating* means forming a reasoned judgment about value. Evaluating literature means expressing an opinion, but it is not a mere personal like or dislike; an effective evaluation must provide support for the opinion (in particular, citations from within the work).
- To help students write their evaluations, have groups begin by discussing criteria for poetry in general. Have them use an Evaluating a Poem form as they look for evidence for those criteria (or a lack thereof) in the work of the Fireside Poets. Point out that opinions of poetry are an individual matter, having much to do with how powerfully the poetry speaks to the reader.

BEST PRACTICES TOOLKIT—Transparency
Evaluating a Poem p. D17

Extension

- A poem's mood will shape its oral interpretation, so have students review their notes from reading or class discussion about the mood of the chosen poem.
- Oral interpretations might include group or choral readings. Students who choose this option should spend time discussing the poem and should come to a consensus of opinion about it.

RI 6 Determine an author's point of view or purpose in a text in which the rhetoric is effective, analyzing how style and content contribute to the power, persuasiveness, or beauty of the text.
RI 9 Analyze documents of literary significance for their themes, purposes, and rhetorical features.
RI 10 Read and comprehend literary nonfiction.

First Attempts

Essay Activate students' prior knowledge to compare and contrast the essay form with other short nonfiction forms, such as the news story, the feature article, the editorial, and the newspaper column. Display examples of these forms from a recent newspaper. Discuss whether some or all of these forms could be considered types of essays. ***Possible answer:*** *The essay form is encompassing enough to include the column and the editorial; the news story and the feature article usually do not express the author's opinion and therefore are not essays.* Provide examples of essays from various sources. Have volunteers read aloud the opening paragraphs of various essays to preview the form's diversity. Post the essays as a classroom library exhibit that students can examine to gain familiarity with this form.

Text Analysis Workshop

The Art of the Essay

When you write an essay for class, you are taking part in a literary tradition that goes back hundreds of years. In classroom writing, the essay may have many rules governing its structure and topic, but in the literary world, essays come in all shapes and sizes, accommodate any topic, and can be found in books, magazines, and daily newspapers.

First Attempts

COMMON CORE

Included in this workshop:
RI 6 Determine an author's point of view or purpose in a text in which the rhetoric is effective, analyzing how style and content contribute to the power, persuasiveness, or beauty of the text. **RI 9** Analyze documents of literary significance for their themes, purposes, and rhetorical features. **RI 10** Read and comprehend literary nonfiction.

An **essay** is a short work of nonfiction that offers a writer's opinion on a particular subject. The length can vary greatly. Some are personal, while others are coldly factual. The essay originated with the 16th-century French philosopher Michel de Montaigne, who first introduced the form when he published a collection of writings entitled *Essais,* a French word meaning "attempts." English writers began using the form, and eventually it became commonplace.

Two masters of the American essay in the 19th century were Ralph Waldo Emerson and Henry David Thoreau. These writers used the form to express their philosophies and personal views on a variety of topics, from the ideal lifestyle to the beauty of nature. Using notes he recorded in his journals, Emerson created essays that gave his ideas structure and refined his concepts. In turn they became the cornerstone of **transcendentalism,**

Thoreau's Walden Pond today, located just outside Concord, Massachusetts.

a literary and philosophical movement that emphasized individualism and intuition as a means to understanding reality. Among Thoreau's works is a series of essays, entitled *Walden,* in which he describes his experience of living out the ideals of individualism at Walden Pond (see page 380).

Emerson and Thoreau laid the groundwork for the American essay. Since then, numerous writers have gained reputations as respected authors of the form, including H. L. Mencken, Ernest Hemingway, E. B. White, Joan Didion, and Amy Tan.

The Craft of Expressing Ideas

Essays generally fall into one of two traditions. **Formal essays** explore topics in a serious and organized manner. **Informal essays** adopt a more casual tone and may include humor and unconventional topics. These essays are often more personal in nature. Emerson's "Self-Reliance" (see page 370) is a formal essay, whereas Thoreau's *Walden* essays are more informal.

DIFFERENTIATED INSTRUCTION

FOR STRUGGLING READERS

Note Taking For students who need help with note taking, hand out the note-taking copy master before discussing these pages.

Explain that students will be learning many terms relating to essays in this workshop. Discuss the major terms on this spread

(formal essay, informal essay, persuasive, expository, descriptive, narrative, organization, supporting details, diction, tone) as students record notes on their copy masters.

 RESOURCE MANAGER—Copy Master
Note Taking p. 84

Whether the essay's purpose is to be **persuasive, expository, descriptive,** or **narrative,** essayists typically rely on these elements to express their ideas:

- **Organization** is the arrangement of the main ideas and supporting details. Some essays may be narratives that read like a story, while others may follow a strict pattern of organization, such as **cause-and-effect** or **compare-and-contrast.**

- **Supporting details** include facts, opinions, reasons, sensory details, anecdotes, and examples that support the **main idea,** the most important idea about a topic.

- **Diction** is the way a writer uses and arranges language. Some writers use simple and casual words and sentences that may create a personal voice. Others are more formal, using elevated language and complex sentence structures.

- **Tone** is the expression of a writer's attitude toward a subject and may be described as serious, humorous, sarcastic, and so on. The writer's diction and details will provide clues to his or her tone.

"Self-Reliance" is a carefully constructed argument in the form of an essay. Emerson organizes his ideas step by step, leading the reader to the conclusion he wants them to reach—an understanding of his philosophy of individualism. Note Emerson's **opinions,** abstract **language,** and formal **tone** in this passage from "Self-Reliance":

> There is a time in every man's education when he arrives at the conviction that envy is ignorance; that imitation is suicide; that he must take himself for better for worse as his portion . . . .
>
> —**Ralph Waldo Emerson, "Self-Reliance"**

Close Read

What ideas does Emerson introduce in this sentence? Paraphrase his ideas in your own words.

Thoreau, on the other hand, takes a more personal and informal approach in *Walden.* Even though his **sentence structure** is complicated and lengthy, the **language** is simple, and the **details** are concrete.

> When first I took up my abode in the woods, that is, began to spend my nights as well as days there, which, by accident, was on Independence day, or the fourth of July 1845, my house was not finished for winter, but was merely a defense against the rain, without plastering or chimney, the walls being of rough weather-stained boards, with wide chinks, which made it cool at night.
>
> —**Henry David Thoreau, *Walden***

Close Read

Note the **diction** and **details** in this passage. What do they reveal about Thoreau's **tone?**

FOR ENGLISH LANGUAGE LEARNERS

Language: Skill Words To help students understand *tone,* suggest that they try to hear the author saying the words in their minds. As an example, say, "That's a nice haircut," first seriously and then sarcastically. To clarify *diction,* first say, "That's a nice haircut," and then, "That's a cool haircut." Ask which wording is more casual. *(the second wording)*

FOR ADVANCED LEARNERS/AP

Compare and Contrast Essays Have students find essays by writers such as Michel de Montaigne, Joseph Addison, Richard Steele, Charles Lamb, Robert Louis Stevenson, Virginia Woolf, George Orwell, Jorge Luis Borges, Natalia Ginzburg, Annie Dillard, and Lewis Thomas. Have students choose two writers, then compare and contrast their styles, tones, and topics. Invite students to share their thoughts orally.

The Craft of Expressing Ideas

Formal and Informal Essays Tell students that modern essays tend to be personal and informal. Discuss each of the bulleted essay elements and invite students to suggest how these might appear in either a formal or an informal essay.

Possible answers:

- *Formal essays usually have clearly defined structures with few digressions, while informal essays may have loose and meandering structures.*

- *Supporting details in formal essays may emphasize facts, statistics, and expert opinions, while those in informal essays may emphasize anecdotes, examples, and sensory details.*

- *Diction in informal essays is likely to be conversational and may include colloquialisms, while formal essays will not contain colloquialisms.*

- *A humorous or sarcastic tone would usually not be found in formal essays, which typically have a more serious tone.*

Close Read

Possible answer: Emerson introduces the idea *that people should accept themselves rather than envy or imitate others. Paraphrase: There comes a time in everyone's life when he or she realizes that envying others is pointless; that imitating others is self-destructive; that you have to accept yourself as you are.*

Close Read

Possible answer: The diction and details reveal *that Thoreau's tone is conversational.*

IF STUDENTS NEED HELP . . . Direct their attention to the phrases "that is," "by accident," and "made it cool at night," which seem conversational within their historical context. Also point out the use of the first-person pronouns *I* and *my,* which suggest the writer is speaking to the reader, as if in a conversation.

Focus and Motivate

COMMON CORE FOCUS

RI 2 Determine two or more central ideas of a text and analyze their development over the course of the text. **RI 3** Analyze a complex set of ideas and explain how specific ideas interact and develop over the course of the text. **RI 9** Analyze documents of literary significance for their themes, purposes, and rhetorical features. **W 2b** Develop the topic by selecting the most significant and relevant facts, extended definitions, concrete details, quotations, or other information and examples. **W 2d** Use precise language to manage the complexity of a topic. **L 3** Apply knowledge of language to make effective choices for meaning and style. **L 4b** Identify and correctly use patterns of word changes that indicate different meanings or parts of speech. **L 5a** Interpret figures of speech in context and analyze their role in the text. **L 6** Acquire and use accurately general academic words and phrases.

ABOUT THE AUTHOR

Point out that after Emerson resigned as minister and before he settled in Concord, he traveled to Europe. There he met the English romantic writers William Wordsworth, Samuel Taylor Coleridge, and Thomas Carlyle, and German philosophers and writers whose ideas were a key influence on transcendentalism.

COMMON CORE

RI 2 Determine two or more central ideas of a text and analyze their development over the course of a text. **RI 3** Analyze a complex set of ideas and explain how specific ideas interact and develop over the course of the text. **RI 9** Analyze documents of literary significance for their themes, purposes, and rhetorical features. **L 5a** Interpret figures of speech in context and analyze their role in the text.

DID YOU KNOW?

Ralph Waldo Emerson . . .

- entered Harvard when he was only 14.
- was named class poet at Harvard—but only after seven other students had refused the honor.
- published *Nature*, one of his most famous works, anonymously.

Old North Bridge, Concord, Massachusetts

The Transcendentalists

from **Self-Reliance**
from **Nature**

Essential Course of Study ECOS

Essays by Ralph Waldo Emerson

VIDEO TRAILER **THINK** central   KEYWORD: HML11-368A

Meet the Author

Ralph Waldo Emerson 1803–1882

As the acknowledged leader of the transcendentalists, Ralph Waldo Emerson, poet, essayist, and lecturer, was a towering figure in the 19th-century literary world. He helped shape a new, uniquely American body of literature and is often cited as one of the most significant writers in American history. "All life is an experiment," the radical thinker and writer once said. "The more experiments you make, the better."

An Average Student Emerson was born in Boston, Massachusetts. His father, a prominent Unitarian minister, died when Emerson was eight, plunging the family into financial trouble. Although money was tight, funds were found to enroll Emerson at Harvard. When he graduated in 1821, ranked 30th out of a class of 59, there was little indication that Emerson would soon become one of the most celebrated literary figures of all time.

Spiritual Crisis In 1825, Emerson returned to Harvard to study for the Unitarian ministry and was ordained in 1829. Just over a year later, his beloved wife, Ellen, died of tuberculosis. Ellen's death threw Emerson into a state of spiritual crisis, causing him to question many aspects of the Christian tradition and his duties as a minister. In 1832, after much consideration, Emerson resigned his post.

The Voice of Transcendentalism Following his wife's death, Emerson settled in Concord, Massachusetts, and devoted himself to the study of philosophy, religion, and literature. In 1836 Emerson published *Nature*, in which he eloquently articulated his transcendental philosophy, an outgrowth of European romanticism. That same year, Emerson formed the Transcendental Club with a group of like-minded friends, including Henry David Thoreau and Margaret Fuller. *Nature*, with its emphasis on self-reliance and individuality, became the group's unofficial manifesto.

The Sage of Concord Those who met Emerson in person often thought him a rather stiff and formal person, dressed always in black. He reserved his passion for the page and the podium, where he elaborated upon his ideas in essays and a series of popular lectures. By the 1840s the Sage of Concord, as he was known, had become a major literary force whose influence is still evident in American culture today.

Author Online **THINK** central
Go to **thinkcentral.com**. KEYWORD: HML11-368B

368

Selection Resources

See resources on the **Teacher One Stop DVD-ROM** and on **thinkcentral.com**.

R **RESOURCE MANAGER UNIT 2**

Plan and Teach, pp. 85–92
Summary, pp. 93–94†‡*
Text Analysis and Reading Skill, pp. 95–96†, 97–98†*
Vocabulary, pp. 99–101
Grammar and Style, p. 104

DIAGNOSTIC AND SELECTION TESTS

Selection Tests, pp. 121–124

BEST PRACTICES TOOLKIT

New Word Analysis, p. E8
Spider Map, p. B22

INTERACTIVE READER

ADAPTED INTERACTIVE READER

ELL ADAPTED INTERACTIVE READER

TECHNOLOGY

- **Teacher One Stop DVD-ROM**
- **Student One Stop DVD-ROM**
- **PowerNotes DVD-ROM**
- **Audio Anthology CD**
- **GrammarNotes DVD-ROM**
- **ExamView Test Generator** on the **Teacher One Stop**

Video Trailer  **THINK** central

Go to **thinkcentral.com** to preview the **Video Trailer** introducing this selection. Other features that support the selection include

- **PowerNotes** presentation
- **ThinkAloud** models to enhance comprehension
- **WordSharp** vocabulary tutorials
- interactive writing and grammar instruction

---

* Resources for Differentiation   † Also in Spanish   ‡ Also in Haitian Creole and Vietnamese

TEXT ANALYSIS: TRANSCENDENTALISM

Ralph Waldo Emerson's motto was "Trust thyself." This principle lies at the heart of **transcendentalism,** an intellectual movement that emphasized the dignity of the individual and advocated a simple, mindful life. The transcendentalists, led by Emerson himself, wanted to transcend—or go beyond—the limitations of the senses and everyday experience. Key tenets of transcendentalism include

- a theory that "transcendent forms" of truth exist beyond reason and experience; every individual is capable of discovering this truth on his or her own, through intuition
- a conviction that people are inherently good and should follow their own beliefs, however controversial they may be
- a belief that humankind, nature, and God are all interconnected

As you read, consider how Emerson's writing articulates his belief in the importance of the individual as well as his ideas about humankind's relationship to the natural world.

READING SKILL: IDENTIFY THEME

Theme is the underlying message or the central idea of a work, which can be stated in one sentence. Usually, writers do not state the theme directly; instead, readers must make inferences based on clues in the text. As you read "Self-Reliance" and *Nature*, record your inferences about each work's theme in a chart like the one below.

Theme of "Self-Reliance"	Theme of *Nature*

▲ VOCABULARY IN CONTEXT

Emerson uses these words to state his convictions. Test your knowledge by deciding which word is suggested by each phrase.

WORD LIST	aversion	exhilaration	nonconformist
	decorum	importune	occult

1. a food you do not like
2. a race you have just won
3. a well-behaved crowd
4. a nagging younger sibling

 Complete the activities in your **Reader/Writer Notebook.**

What is your MOTTO?

The ancient Roman poet Horace gravely advised, "Never despair." Modern comedian Woody Allen quipped that the secret to success in life is simple: "Eighty percent of success is showing up." Each of these mottos captures an individual's attitude toward life in one pithy phrase. Ralph Waldo Emerson's motto, "Trust thyself," distills the essence of the ideals he expressed in his essays and lectures.

QUICKWRITE Create your own personal motto. To get started, consider the traits or resources that helped you solve a difficult problem, or the best advice you have ever given a friend. Use your answers to develop a personal motto that is short and to the point.

369

Teach

What is your MOTTO?

Write the United States' motto, *E Pluribus Unum* ("From Many, One"), on the board. Discuss why it is an appropriate motto to express our national ideals. Then suggest that students consider their own ideals and attitudes as they complete the *QUICKWRITE.*

TEXT ANALYSIS — COMMON CORE — RI 3 RI 9

● *Model the Skill:* **TRANSCENDENTALISM**

To examine transcendentalism, ask students how the transcendentalists might have reacted to these statements:

1. Some people are just bad apples.
2. Go with your gut.

Possible answers: They would have disagreed with statement 1 because they believed that people are inherently good. They would have agreed with statement 2 because they believed that people should trust their intuition, or "gut."

GUIDED PRACTICE Ask students to come up with a statement that the transcendentalists would probably have agreed with, and to explain why.

READING SKILL — COMMON CORE — RI 2

■ *Model the Skill:* **IDENTIFY THEME**

Tell students that all literary works have a central idea, or theme. For example, the theme of *The Grapes of Wrath* addresses the plight of the dispossessed. Have students recall favorite books they have read and discuss their themes.

VOCABULARY SKILL — COMMON CORE — L 4

▲ VOCABULARY IN CONTEXT

DIAGNOSE WORD KNOWLEDGE Have all students complete Vocabulary in Context. Check their phrases against the following:

aversion (ə-vûr′zhən) *n.* a strong dislike

decorum (dǐ-kôr′əm) *n.* good taste in conduct or appearance

exhilaration (ǐg-zǐl′ə-rā′shən) *n.* a feeling of high spirits or lively joy

importune (ǐm′pôr-tōon′) *v.* to ask urgently or repeatedly; to annoy or trouble

nonconformist (nŏn′kən-fôr′mǐst) *n.* one who does not follow generally accepted beliefs, customs, or practices

occult (ə-kŭlt′) *adj.* secret or hidden from view

PRETEACH VOCABULARY Use the following copy master to help students predict meanings.

R RESOURCE MANAGER—Copy Master
Vocabulary Study p. 99

Practice and Apply

SUMMARY

In this excerpt from his essay, Emerson argues that people should trust their own judgment about what is right and wrong, rather than conform to other people's opinions. He insists that we should feel free to change our beliefs and concludes by offering historical examples to support his view that "[t]o be great is to be misunderstood."

READ WITH A PURPOSE

Help students set a purpose for reading. Have them read the following two selections to discover Emerson's beliefs about the human condition.

READING SKILL — COMMON CORE RI 2

A Model the Skill: THEME

To help students identify the theme of a passage, work through lines 1–11 with them, helping them paraphrase difficult phrases or clauses, such as "imitation is suicide." **Possible answer:** *The theme addresses self-reliance, or Emerson's belief that people should rely upon their own capabilities and instincts.*

VOCABULARY — COMMON CORE L 4

OWN THE WORD

nonconformist: Remind students that the word *nonconformist* refers to "one who does not follow accepted beliefs or practices." Ask students to explain why they think Emerson used this word in the sentence, "Whoso would be a man, must be a *nonconformist*." **Possible answer:** Conforming *may hinder a person. Sometimes walking a different path is necessary to make new discoveries, new theories, new greatness for humanity.*

Self-Reliance

RALPH WALDO EMERSON

There is a time in every man's education when he arrives at the conviction that envy is ignorance; that imitation is suicide; that he must take himself for better for worse as his portion; that though the wide universe is full of good, no kernel of nourishing corn can come to him but through his toil bestowed on that plot of ground which is given to him to till. . . .

Trust thyself: every heart vibrates to that iron string. Accept the place the divine providence has found for you, the society of your contemporaries, the connection of events. Great men have always done so, and confided themselves childlike to the genius of their age, betraying their perception that the absolutely trustworthy[1]
10 was seated at their heart, working through their hands, predominating[2] in all their being. . . . **A**

Whoso would be a man, must be a **nonconformist.** He who would gather immortal palms[3] must not be hindered by the name of goodness, but must explore if it be goodness. Nothing is at last sacred but the integrity of your own mind. Absolve you to yourself, and you shall have the suffrage[4] of the world. I remember an answer which when quite young I was prompted to make to a valued adviser

Analyze Visuals ▶

What elements of **transcendentalism** are reflected in the painting on the opposite page?

1 Targeted Passage

A THEME
Re-read the ideas in lines 1–11. Based on these lines, what inferences can you make about the theme of this selection?

nonconformist
(nŏn′kən-fôr′mĭst) *n.*
one who does not follow generally accepted beliefs, customs, or practices

---

1. **the absolutely trustworthy:** God.
2. **predominating:** being predominant, or having controlling influence.
3. **immortal palms:** everlasting triumph and honor. In ancient times, people carried palm leaves as a symbol of victory, success, or joy.
4. **suffrage:** approval; support.

Wanderer Above the Sea of Fog (1818), Caspar David Friedrich. Oil on canvas, 94.8 cm × 74.8 cm.

DIFFERENTIATED INSTRUCTION

FOR ENGLISH LANGUAGE LEARNERS

Vocabulary Support Use New Word Analysis to teach these words: from "Self-Reliance": *integrity* (line 14), *estimate* (line 32); from *Nature: period* (line 6), *reside* (line 26).

 BEST PRACTICES TOOLKIT—Transparency
New Word Analysis p. E8

FOR STRUGGLING READERS

In combination with the *Audio Anthology CD*, use one or more Targeted Passages (pp. 370, 372, 374) to ensure that students focus on key concepts in these selections. Targeted passages are also good for English learners.

1 Targeted Passage [Lines 1–11]

This passage introduces Emerson's crucial belief in the importance of relying on oneself.

This selection on **thinkcentral.com** includes embedded **ThinkAloud** models—students "thinking aloud" about the story to model the kinds of questions a good reader would ask about a selection.

Analyze Visuals

Possible answers: The solitary figure reflects the transcendentalist ideal of individualism. His contemplation of an awe-inspiring natural setting reflects the transcendentalist view that nature and humankind are interconnected.

About the Art The landscapes of the German painter Caspar David Friedrich (1774–1840) capture romanticism's emphasis on the grandeur of nature. *Wanderer Above the Sea of Fog* shows a solitary figure with his back to the viewer, in a pose that recalls Emerson's famous description of himself in the presence of nature: "I become a transparent eye-ball; I am nothing; I see all" (page 373, lines 12–13).

BACKGROUND

Immanuel Kant The German philosopher Immanuel Kant (1724–1804) strongly influenced the transcendentalists. Kant argued that we impose certain structures (such as space, time, and causality) on what we perceive, and we can understand our perceptions only when they conform to this mental system. Kant also believed that there are some "unknowable" concepts (God, freedom, immortality) that exist independently of our mental rules and, therefore, can't be proved or disproved by reason. The transcendentalists reinterpreted Kant's philosophy of "transcendental idealism" to mean that there is knowledge that transcends reason that we can know only by intuition.

- How does Emerson feel about envy and imitation? (lines 1–2)
- What does Emerson believe that people must do to receive their share of the world's goodness—their "nourishing corn"? (lines 2–5)
- According to Emerson, why should people trust themselves? (lines 6–11)

FOR ADVANCED LEARNERS/AP

Make Judgments Have students write a short speech addressing the question: how much should a person trust in herself and how much a person should rely on others? Tell students to include examples from their own lives in their speeches. After students have finished writing, organize the class into pairs and have students read their speeches to their partners.

importune (ĭm′pôr-tōōn′)
v. to ask urgently or
repeatedly; to annoy
or trouble

TEXT ANALYSIS

COMMON CORE RI 3 RI 9

Ⓑ TRANSCENDENTALISM

Possible answer: By using the word
"*sacred*", Emerson implies that people
should follow their own impulses because
these impulses come from God.

Ⓒ GRAMMAR AND STYLE

COMMON CORE L 3

Analyze Adjective Clauses Explain that
adjective clauses may provide specific
information about a noun or pronoun by
telling *which one, what kind,* or *how many.*
Ask students to find two adjective clauses
in lines 37–48.

REVISIT THE BIG QUESTION

What is your MOTTO?

Discuss According to Emerson in lines 24–31,
why is it so hard to follow his ideal of nonconformity? *Possible answer:* It's hard because
"*the world whips you with its displeasure*"
(*line 31*) when you ignore popular opinion.

VOCABULARY

COMMON CORE L 4

OWN THE WORD

- **importune:** Have students look up
  synonyms for *importune* and write a
  sentence that shows an understanding
  of the word. *Possible answer: I love my
  grandmother, but she* importunes *me
  about my college applications.*

- **aversion:** Remind students that *aversion*
  means "a strong dislike" or "an avoidance." Have students list things to which
  they may have an *aversion.* **Possible
  answers:** *certain types of foods, people,
  or activities*

---

saying, "What have I to do with the sacredness of traditions, if I live wholly from
within?" my friend suggested—"But these impulses may be from below, not from
20 above." I replied, "They do not seem to me to be such; but if I am the Devil's child,
I will live then from the Devil." No law can be sacred to me but that of my nature.
Good and bad are but names very readily transferable to that or this; the only right
is what is after my constitution;[5] the only wrong what is against it. . . . Ⓑ

What I must do is all that concerns me, not what the people think. This
rule, equally arduous in actual and in intellectual life, may serve for the whole
distinction between greatness and meanness.[6] It is the harder because you will
always find those who think they know what is your duty better than you know it.
It is easy in the world to live after the world's opinion; it is easy in solitude to live
after our own; but the great man is he who in the midst of the crowd keeps with
30 perfect sweetness the independence of solitude. . . . Ⓒ

For nonconformity the world whips you with its displeasure. And therefore
a man must know how to estimate a sour face. The by-standers look askance on
him in the public street or in the friend's parlor. If this **aversion** had its origin
in contempt and resistance like his own he might well go home with a sad
countenance; but the sour faces of the multitude, like their sweet faces, have no
deep cause, but are put on and off as the wind blows and a newspaper directs. . . .

The other terror that scares us from self-trust is our consistency; a reverence for
our past act or word because the eyes of others have no other data for computing
our orbit than our past acts, and we are loth to disappoint them. . . .

40 A foolish consistency is the hobgoblin[7] of little minds, adored by little
statesmen and philosophers and divines.[8] With consistency a great soul has simply
nothing to do. He may as well concern himself with his shadow on the wall. Speak
what you think now in hard words and tomorrow speak what tomorrow thinks
in hard words again, though it contradict everything you said today.—"Ah, so
you shall be sure to be misunderstood."— Is it so bad then to be misunderstood?
Pythagoras was misunderstood, and Socrates, and Jesus, and Luther, and
Copernicus, and Galileo, and Newton,[9] and every pure and wise spirit that ever
took flesh. To be great is to be misunderstood. ∾ ② **Targeted Passage**

Ⓑ TRANSCENDENTALISM
Transcendentalists
believed in disregarding
external authority in favor
of one's own experience
and intuition. What is
implied by the word
sacred in line 21?

Ⓒ GRAMMAR AND STYLE
Emerson adds detail and
precision to his writing by
using **adjective clauses,**
which modify nouns
and pronouns. In line
27 and lines 29–30, he
uses adjective clauses
beginning with *who*
to describe specific types
of people.

aversion (ə-vûr′zhən) *n.* a
strong dislike

COMMON CORE L 5a

Language Coach
Figurative Language In
lines 37–39, "computing
our orbit" is an
example of figurative
language, language that
communicates ideas
beyond the literal meaning
of words. "Computing our
orbit" can be understood
as "deciding what we'll do
next." State lines 37–39 in
your own words.

---

5. **after my constitution:** consistent with my nature.
6. **meanness:** the state of being inferior in quality, character, or value.
7. **hobgoblin:** a source of fear or dread.
8. **divines:** religious leaders.
9. **Pythagoras** (pĭ-thăg′ər-əs) . . . **Newton:** great thinkers whose radical theories and viewpoints caused
   controversy.

DIFFERENTIATED INSTRUCTION

FOR STRUGGLING READERS

② **Targeted Passage [Lines 37–48]**

In this passage, Emerson explains his belief
that consistency is unimportant.

- According to Emerson, why are people
  afraid of being inconsistent? (lines 37–39)

- What kinds of people think that consistency
  is important? (lines 40–41)

- What kinds of people are not afraid to be inconsistent and misunderstood? (lines 45–48)

FOR ENGLISH LANGUAGE LEARNERS

Language Coach
COMMON CORE L 5a

Figurative Language Students'
answers will vary. Have students reread
this page and identify another example of
figurative language, such as "hobgoblin of
little minds." Tell students to rewrite the
phrase they selected in their own words.

Nature

RALPH WALDO EMERSON

Nature is a setting that fits equally well a comic or a mourning piece. In good health, the air is a cordial of incredible virtue. Crossing a bare common, in snow puddles, at twilight, under a clouded sky, without having in my thoughts any occurrence of special good fortune, I have enjoyed a perfect **exhilaration.** I am glad to the brink of fear. In the woods too, a man casts off his years, as the snake his slough,[1] and at what period soever of life, is always a child. In the woods, is perpetual youth. Within these plantations of God, a **decorum** and sanctity reign, a perennial festival is dressed, and the guest sees not how he should tire of them in a thousand years. In the woods, we return to reason and faith. There I feel that
10 nothing can befall me in life,—no disgrace, no calamity, (leaving me my eyes,) which nature cannot repair. Standing on the bare ground,—my head bathed by the blithe air, and uplifted into infinite space,—all mean egotism vanishes. I become a transparent eye-ball; I am nothing; I see all; the currents of the Universal Being circulate through me; I am part or particle of God. The name of the nearest friend sounds then foreign and accidental: to be brothers, to be acquaintances,— master or servant, is then a trifle and a disturbance. I am the lover of uncontained and immortal beauty. In the wilderness, I find something more dear and connate[2] than in streets or villages. In the tranquil landscape, and especially in the distant line of the horizon, man beholds somewhat as beautiful as his own nature. **D**

---

1. **slough** (slŭf): the cast-off skin of a snake.
2. **connate:** agreeable; able to be related to.

exhilaration
(ĭg-zĭl′ə-rā′shən) *n.* a feeling of high spirits or lively joy

decorum (dĭ-kôr′əm) *n.* good taste in conduct or appearance

D TRANSCENDENTALISM
Review the elements of transcendentalism listed on page 369. Which aspect of transcendentalist thought is reflected in lines 12–19? Explain your answer.

SUMMARY

In this book excerpt, Emerson explores his powerful connection to nature. He says that in the presence of nature, he feels exhilarated, restored, and part of God. We delight in nature, he claims, because we behold in it something as beautiful as our own spiritual nature.

TEXT ANALYSIS

COMMON CORE
RI 3
RI 9

D *Model the skill:*
TRANSCENDENTALISM

Explain that transcendentalism is a belief that all living things are connected. Read aloud lines 12–19. Help students paraphrase difficult phrases in the passage. ***Possible answer:*** *Lines 12–19 reflect the transcendentalist belief that humankind, nature, and God are all interconnected.*

TIERED DISCUSSION PROMPTS

In lines 1–14, use these prompts to help students understand Emerson's intense connection to nature:

Connect Have you ever felt "perfect exhilaration" or any other strong emotion in a natural setting? Describe your experience. *Accept all thoughtful responses.*

Interpret What does Emerson mean when he says, "I become a transparent eye-ball" (lines 12–13)? ***Possible answer:*** *In the presence of nature, he feels so connected to nature that he loses the awareness of his own self; he becomes part of what he is seeing.*

VOCABULARY

COMMON CORE
L 4

OWN THE WORD

• **exhilaration:** Tell students that the connotation of *exhilaration* is extreme happiness. For example, "Being on the debate team makes me happy, but being chosen as the captain fills me with *exhilaration*." Have students create two related statements to show that *exhilaration* is stronger than *happiness*.

• **decorum:** Ask students to list situations when they should exhibit *decorum*. ***Possible answer:*** *during class, at a wedding or religious service, during a job interview*

FOR STRUGGLING READERS

Develop Reading Fluency Emerson's long, complicated sentences often contain a series of phrases and clauses. Model how to fluently read these sentences by selecting a passage and reading it aloud to the class. Tell students to pay attention to the pauses in your speech. Have student pairs practice reading the passage aloud to each other.

FOR ADVANCED LEARNERS/AP

Analyze Figures of Speech Emerson uses figures of speech to create vivid images and express complex ideas. For example, in line 7 he uses a metaphor when he describes the woods as "plantations of God." Have students analyze the figures of speech in *Nature* and "Self-Reliance." Tell them to pay close attention to implied metaphors—those that suggest a comparison without directly stating it. Have students present their analyses to the class, inviting questions and feedback.

Analyze Visuals

Possible answer: The painting conveys a tranquil mood. Elements such as the glowing sky and water, the fluffy clouds, and the feathery trees help establish this mood.

About the Art Thomas Doughty (1793–1856) was an early member of the Hudson River School of landscape painters (see page 307). Like the transcendentalists of the same period, these artists wanted to depict the power and beauty of nature. Doughty is best known for his serene, pastoral landscapes of river valleys.

OWN THE WORD

occult: Remind students that one meaning of the adjective, *occult*, is "secret or hidden from view." Ask students why Emerson may have found "... an *occult* relation between man and the vegetable" to be delightful. *Possible answer: It appears that Emerson greatly enjoyed being "one with nature" and found peace and delight at being alone outdoors.*

SELECTION WRAP–UP

READ WITH A PURPOSE Now that students have read the selections, have them describe Emerson's beliefs about the human condition in relation to others and nature. *Possible answer: Emerson believes that, although interconnected with each other, humans should not be reliant upon others. He also holds that people have an innate spiritual inclination to delight in nature.*

⭐ **CRITIQUE** Ask students whether they find Emerson's transcendentalist ideas persuasive, and why or why not.

---

20   The greatest delight which the fields and woods minister, is the suggestion of an **occult** relation between man and the vegetable. I am not alone and unacknowledged. They nod to me, and I to them. The waving of the boughs in the storm, is new to me and old. It takes me by surprise, and yet is not unknown. Its effect is like that of a higher thought or a better emotion coming over me, when I deemed I was thinking justly or doing right.

Yet it is certain that the power to produce this delight, does not reside in nature, but in man, or in a harmony of both. It is necessary to use these pleasures with great temperance. For, nature is not always tricked[3] in holiday attire, but the same scene which yesterday breathed perfume and glittered as for the frolic of the

30   nymphs, is overspread with melancholy today. Nature always wears the colors of the spirit. To a man laboring under calamity, the heat of his own fire hath sadness in it. Then, there is a kind of contempt of the landscape felt by him who has just lost by death a dear friend. The sky is less grand as it shuts down over less worth in the population. ∽

---

3. **tricked:** dressed.

occult (ə-kŭlt′) *adj.* secret or hidden from view
❸ **Targeted Passage**

Language Coach

Word Definitions In line 26, *reside* means "live" or "exist." (Think of related words: *residence* and *resident*.) Where does Emerson say the power to appreciate nature exists? Now, read lines 30–34. What is Emerson saying about our perception of the natural world?

▼ **Analyze Visuals**
Emerson says that "nature always wears the colors of the spirit." What **mood** does this painting convey? Describe the elements of the painting that establish this mood.

Ben Lomond (1829–1830), Thomas Doughty. Oil on canvas. © Christie's Images/SuperStock.

374   UNIT 2: AMERICAN ROMANTICISM

DIFFERENTIATED INSTRUCTION

FOR STRUGGLING READERS

❸ Targeted Passage [Lines 20–27]

In this passage, Emerson states his view of the connection between people and nature.
- According to Emerson, what is the "greatest delight" that nature provides? (lines 21–22)
- What does Emerson mean when he says that the fields and woods "nod" to him? (lines 22–23)
- What effect does nature have on Emerson? (lines 23–25)
- What causes our delight in nature? (lines 26–27)

FOR ENGLISH LANGUAGE LEARNERS

Language Coach

Word Definitions *Possible answers: It rests in humankind. People's appreciation of natural surroundings is influenced by their emotions.* Have students rewrite the sentence in lines 26–27 three times. Tell students to use a different word for *reside* in each rewritten sentence.

Comprehension

1. **Recall** According to "Self-Reliance," what is the only law that Emerson can hold sacred?

2. **Summarize** What are three ways the woods can transform a man, according to Emerson in *Nature*?

3. **Clarify** In *Nature*, Emerson discusses the "delight" the natural world often inspires. What does Emerson think this power to delight comes from?

Text Analysis

4. **Draw Conclusions** Reread lines 37–48 of "Self-Reliance." What is Emerson speaking of when he mentions consistency, and why does he berate it as "the hobgoblin of little minds"? Consider the following examples of Emerson's statements as you formulate your response:

   • "Good and bad are but names very readily transferable to that or this...."
   • "...The sour faces of the multitude ... have no deep cause, but are put on and off as the wind blows...."

5. **Identify Elements of Transcendentalism** Review the elements of transcendentalism listed on page 369. Then reexamine "Self-Reliance" and *Nature*, identifying key ideas that reflect each tenet of transcendentalism. Record your answer in a chart like the one shown.

Element of Transcendentalism	Example from the Text
Every individual is capable of discovering higher truths on his or her own, through intuition.	"Nothing is at last sacred but the integrity of your own mind." ("Self-Reliance," line 14)

6. **Analyze Theme** Look at the themes you recorded for each of Emerson's writings. How does each theme relate to the ideals of transcendentalism?

Text Criticism

7. **Critical Interpretation** Writer Henry James argued that Emerson had no concept of the evil that exists in the world. In James's words, it was "a side of life as to which Emerson's eyes were thickly bandaged.... He had no great sense of wrong ... no sense of the dark, the foul, the base." In your opinion, is this a valid criticism of Emerson? Citing evidence, explain why or why not.

> *What is your* **MOTTO?**
> What are some of the ideals, or beliefs, that you adhere to? How are your ideals different from those of the people you know best?

SELF-RELIANCE / NATURE **375**

7. *Students may say that Emerson himself would describe the term "evil" as just a name society ascribes to our actions rather than a definable concept. However, some students may support James's criticism by arguing that Emerson does not explain how his ideal of self-reliance applies to people who have committed terrible crimes.*

> *What is your* **MOTTO?** Students should describe their ideals and explain how they are different from those of their friends or relatives.

Practice and Apply

For preliminary support of post-reading questions, use these copy masters:

R RESOURCE MANAGER—Copy Masters
Reading Check p. 102
Transcendentalism p. 95
Question Support p. 103
Additional selection questions are provided for teachers on page 89.

ANSWERS COMMON CORE RI 2, RI 3, RI 9

1. *Emerson holds sacred the law of his own intuition.*

2. *The woods can make a man feel young again, restore his faith and reason, and create a sense of calm and tranquility.*

3. *The power to delight comes from man or from a harmony between man and nature.*

Possible answers:

4. *By "consistency," Emerson means not changing your beliefs. He berates it by arguing that consistency for its own sake can stifle personal discovery and growth.*

5. ● **COMMON CORE FOCUS** **Transcendentalism** *Element: Every individual is capable of discovering higher truths on his or her own, through intuition. Examples: "Nothing is at last sacred ... own mind" ("Self-Reliance," line 14); "No law can be sacred ... the only wrong what is against it" ("Self-Reliance," lines 21–23); "In the woods, we return to reason and faith" (Nature, line 9); Element: People are inherently good and should follow their own beliefs, however controversial these may be. Examples: "Whoso would be a man, must be a nonconformist" ("Self-Reliance," line 12); "What I must do ... the people think" ("Self-Reliance," line 24); Element: Humankind, nature, and God are all interconnected. Examples: "I become a transparent eye-ball ... I am part or particle of God" (Nature, lines 12–14); "The greatest delight ... not alone and unacknowledged" (Nature, lines 20–22); "Nature always ... the spirit" (Nature, lines 30–31)*

6. ■ **COMMON CORE FOCUS** **Identify Theme** *Students should match the themes they recorded with transcendentalist ideals such as "people should follow their own beliefs" and "humankind, nature, and God are all interconnected."*

SELF—RELIANCE / NATURE **375**

ANSWERS
Vocabulary in Context

 VOCABULARY PRACTICE

1. *exhilaration*   4. *occult*
2. *importune*   5. *nonconformist*
3. *decorum*   6. *aversion*

 RESOURCE MANAGER—Copy Master
Vocabulary Practice p. 100

ACADEMIC VOCABULARY IN SPEAKING

Guide students to explain their views to a partner before they share them with their small group. Have partners identify statements that might lend themselves to a vocabulary word. Tell students that they can incorporate additional vocabulary words into their discussion.

VOCABULARY STRATEGY: WORDS WITH MULTIPLE AFFIXES

COMMON CORE
L 4b, L 6

- Model the practice using these examples: *unmentionable* and *irreplaceable*. Show students how to find the root by removing the prefix and suffix.

- Review spelling rules that apply to added suffixes: Keep the silent *e* if the base word ends in *-ge* or *-ce* and the suffix begins with *a* or *o*, as in *interchangeable* and *unnoticeable*. Keep the final silent *e* before adding a suffix that begins with a consonant, as in *hopefully*.

Possible answers:

1. *fabricate*   4. *page*
2. *diverse*   5. *fatigue*
3. *repute*   6. *negate*

 **RESOURCE MANAGER—Copy Master**
Vocabulary Strategy p. 101

Interactive Vocabulary   THINK central

Keywords direct students to a **WordSharp** tutorial on **thinkcentral.com** or to other types of vocabulary practice and review.

Vocabulary in Context

▲ **VOCABULARY PRACTICE**

Choose the vocabulary word that best completes each sentence.

1. An unexpected tragedy can quickly turn _____ into grief.
2. To constantly _____ a friend for favors can destroy the friendship.
3. One should act with _____ on serious or formal occasions.
4. It is not wise to pry into the _____ intrigues of others.
5. Certain values are held by every person, whether a traditionalist or a(n) _____.
6. It makes sense to avoid anything to which one has a(n) _____.

WORD LIST
aversion
decorum
exhilaration
importune
nonconformist
occult

ACADEMIC VOCABULARY IN SPEAKING

- construct   - expand   - indicate   - reinforce   - role

Although Emerson believed that nature played an important **role** in life, he also saw it as inferior to the power found in humans. In fact, Emerson believed that nature **reinforces** what is already present in humankind. In a small group, discuss how people view nature and self-sufficiency today. In your discussion, use at least three of the Academic Vocabulary words.

VOCABULARY STRATEGY: WORDS WITH MULTIPLE AFFIXES

You can decipher many long words if you are able to locate a recognizable base word within them. Removing the prefix and the suffix from the vocabulary word *nonconformist*, for example, reveals the base word *conform*. What meanings do the affixes add to the base word? Analyze similar words by separating them into a base word and affixes. Remember that many base words drop the final *e* before suffixes are added.

COMMON CORE

L 4b Identify and correctly use patterns of word changes that indicate different meanings or parts of speech. **L 6** Acquire and use accurately general academic words and phrases.

PRACTICE Write the base word and the affixes that make up each word listed. Then write a sentence that demonstrates the meaning of the longer word.

1. prefabricated
2. undiversified
3. disreputable
4. repagination
5. indefatigable
6. abnegation

Interactive Vocabulary   THINK central
Go to **thinkcentral.com**.
KEYWORD: HML11-376

DIFFERENTIATED INSTRUCTION

FOR ENGLISH LANGUAGE LEARNERS

Task Support: Vocabulary Practice Point out that the French cognate *conformer* is similar to the English word *conform*, which forms the base word in *nonconformist*. Encourage students who speak Latin-based languages to search for and explain vocabulary words similar to those in their home languages. Have students compare the similarities in their languages.

FOR ADVANCED LEARNERS/AP

Words with Multiple Affixes Use the word *transcendentalism* as the first entry on a list of words with multiple affixes. Have students add to the list by locating other multiple-affix words in the two Emerson pieces. Then challenge students to exchange word lists with a partner and try to create new forms for each of their partner's words by adding, removing, or replacing affixes.

Language

◆ **GRAMMAR AND STYLE:** Use Descriptive Details

Review the **Grammar and Style** note on page 372. The precision of Emerson's prose owes much to his skillful use of **adjective clauses**—subordinate clauses that add important details about nouns and pronouns. An adjective clause usually follows the word it modifies and is introduced by words such as *when, who, whom, whose, that,* and *which.* Here is an example from "Self-Reliance":

> *There is a time in every man's education when he arrives at the conviction that envy is ignorance; that imitation is suicide; that he must take himself for better for worse as his portion....* (lines 1–3)

Notice that each of the highlighted clauses offers information about the noun it modifies. The first clause tells you about the "time in every man's education" Emerson is discussing. The second, third, and fourth clauses explain what kind of conviction he embraces at this time.

PRACTICE Identify the adjective clause in each sentence from Emerson's work. Then write your own sentences, using adjective clauses as Emerson does.

> **EXAMPLE**
>
> He who would gather immortal palms must not be hindered by the name of goodness, but must explore if it be goodness.
>
> *Those who wish to make a true difference cannot worry what others might say behind their backs.*

1. There is a kind of contempt of the landscape felt by him who has just lost by death a dear friend.

2. Nature is a setting that fits equally well a comic or a mourning piece.

READING-WRITING CONNECTION

YOUR TURN

Expand your understanding of Emerson's writing by responding to this prompt. Then, use the **revising tips** to improve your speech.

WRITING PROMPT	**REVISING TIPS**
UPDATE EMERSON'S MESSAGE Emerson's ideas about nonconformity are still relevant today. Write a **short speech** presenting an updated version of Emerson's message for an audience of contemporary high school students. Use at least one adjective clause in your speech.	• Direct your speech to your peers. • Check your examples to make sure they are current and that they support Emerson's ideas.

Interactive Revision THINK central
Go to **thinkcentral.com**.
KEYWORD: HML11-377

COMMON CORE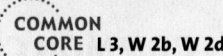

L 3 Apply knowledge of language to make effective choices for meaning and style. **W 2b** Develop the topic by selecting the most significant and relevant facts, extended definitions, concrete details, quotations, or other information and examples. **W 2d** Use precise language to manage the complexity of a topic.

Language

COMMON CORE **L 3, W 2b, W 2d**

GRAMMAR AND STYLE

Have students reread their speeches, looking for ways to add adjective clauses. (For more on adjective clauses, see **Grammar Handbook,** page R67.)

Possible answers:

1. *Clause:* "who has just lost by death a dear friend." There is a kind of happiness felt by those who have just aced a test.

2. *Clause:* "that fits equally well a comic or a mourning piece." A library is a place that houses a wealth of knowledge.

R RESOURCE MANAGER—Copy Master
Use Descriptive Details p. 104

READING-WRITING CONNECTION

Convincing, up-to-date examples of non-conformity would show how an individual's nontraditional thinking yielded a positive outcome. Have students use a Spider Map to help plan their work.

 BEST PRACTICES TOOLKIT—Transparency
Spider Map p. B22

Writing Online THINK central

The following tools are available online at **thinkcentral.com** and on **Write*Smart* CD-ROM:**
• **Interactive Graphic Organizers**
• **Interactive Student Models**
• **Interactive Revision Lessons**
For additional grammar instruction, see **GrammarNotes** on **thinkcentral.com**.

Assess and Reteach

Assess

DIAGNOSTIC AND SELECTION TESTS
Selection Tests A, B/C pp. 121–124

Interactive Selection Test on **thinkcentral.com**

Reteach

Level Up Online Tutorials on **thinkcentral.com**

Reteaching Worksheets on **thinkcentral.com**

Vocabulary Lesson 1

FOR STRUGGLING WRITERS

Writing Support

• Limit the length of the speech to two or three paragraphs.

• Provide a sentence starter for students to use as they draft their thesis statements (such as *Emerson's ideas about self-reliance are still relevant today because _____*).

• Have students read their speeches aloud to a partner.

Focus and Motivate

COMMON CORE FOCUS

RI 2 Determine two or more central ideas of a text and analyze their development; provide an objective summary of the text. **RI 4** Determine the connotative meanings of words as they are used in a text. **RI 5** Analyze and evaluate the effectiveness of the structure an author uses. **RI 6** Determine an author's point of view or purpose in a text in which the rhetoric is effective, analyzing how style and content contribute to the power, persuasiveness, or beauty of the text. **RI 9** Analyze documents of literary significance for their themes, purposes, and rhetorical features. **W 1a–b** Introduce precise, knowledgeable claims, develop claims and counterclaims, supplying the most relevant evidence for each. **W 1d–e** Establish and maintain a formal style and objective tone; provide a concluding statement that follows from the argument presented. **L 3a** Apply an understanding of syntax to the study of complex texts when reading. **L 4b** Identify and use patterns of word changes that indicate different meanings or parts of speech. **L 4c** Consult reference materials, both print and digital, to find the pronunciation of a word. **L 6** Acquire and use academic words and phrases.

ABOUT THE AUTHOR

Emphasize the importance of Thoreau's friendship with Emerson. Emerson urged Thoreau to keep a journal, and he published Thoreau's work in the transcendentalist magazine *The Dial*. Emerson also owned the land on which Thoreau built his cabin.

Selection Resources

The Transcendentalists

from Walden
from Civil Disobedience
Essays by Henry David Thoreau

 Video link at thinkcentral.com

Essential Course of Study ECOS

VIDEO TRAILER THINKcentral KEYWORD: HML11-378A

COMMON CORE

RI 2 Determine two or more central ideas of a text and analyze their development; provide an objective summary of the text. **RI 6** Determine an author's point of view or purpose in a text in which the rhetoric is effective, analyzing how style and content contribute to the power, persuasiveness, or beauty of the text. **RI 9** Analyze documents of literary significance for their themes, purposes, and rhetorical features.

Meet the Author

Henry David Thoreau 1817–1862

Henry David Thoreau (thə-rō′) advocated simple, mindful living and rejected a lifestyle dedicated to the pursuit of wealth. Thoreau spent much of his life writing and observing nature, devoting only a minimum of time to earning a wage. He published just two books, both of which sold very poorly in his own lifetime. Few of his contemporaries would have judged him much of a success. In the years since his death, however, his reputation has grown tremendously. Today, he is regarded as a writer of uncommon vision and remembered as one of the first environmentalists.

Independent Spirit Thoreau was born and raised in Concord, Massachusetts, and attended Harvard University. After graduating, he returned to Concord to teach school. Though some of Thoreau's neighbors viewed him as eccentric, he was a careful observer and a deep thinker. Taking to heart the ideas of his friend Ralph Waldo Emerson, Thoreau tried to live by his own values, often doing odd jobs that would earn him just enough money to meet his own modest needs.

Defiant Nonconformist Thoreau's life was full of examples of his nonconformity to society's norms. As a Harvard student, he was required to wear a black coat but sported a green one instead. In his first year of teaching, he refused to punish his students physically, a harsh but common practice of the time, and resigned his post. In 1845, he conducted his famous experiment, living simply and frugally in a small cabin on the shores of Walden Pond. In 1846, he was arrested and spent a night in jail for refusing to pay a poll tax, an act of protest against the U.S. government's war with Mexico and its support of slavery. This exercise of conscience over law later became known as civil disobedience.

Influential Thinker At the time of Thoreau's death from tuberculosis at age 44, he was viewed as an unsuccessful nature writer. Today, however, he is known as the father of American nature writing and an important political thinker. His observations about the natural world and the value of the simple life, as well as his promotion of nonviolent protest, have helped bring about great societal change. He has provided inspiration to many, including conservationist John Muir and civil rights leader Martin Luther King Jr.

DID YOU KNOW?

Henry David Thoreau . . .

• worked off and on as a pencil maker in his family's pencil factory.

• kept a journal that when published filled 20 volumes.

• pared down his expenses to 27 cents a week, which he earned by working only six weeks a year.

SITE OF THOREAU'S CABIN

Author Online
Go to **thinkcentral.com**. KEYWORD: HML11-378B

378

See resources on the **Teacher One Stop DVD-ROM** and on **thinkcentral.com**.

 RESOURCE MANAGER UNIT 2
Plan and Teach, pp. 105–112
Summary, pp. 113–116†‡*
Text Analysis and Reading
   Skill, pp. 117–118, 119–120†*
Vocabulary, pp. 121–123
Grammar and Style, p. 127

DIAGNOSTIC AND SELECTION TESTS
Selection Tests, pp. 125–128

 BEST PRACTICES TOOLKIT
Venn Diagram, p. A26
INTERACTIVE READER
ADAPTED INTERACTIVE READER
ELL ADAPTED INTERACTIVE READER

HISTORY. Video link at thinkcentral.com

TECHNOLOGY
⊘ **Teacher One Stop DVD-ROM**
⊘ **Student One Stop DVD-ROM**
⊘ **PowerNotes DVD-ROM**
⊘ **Audio Anthology CD**
⊘ **GrammarNotes DVD-ROM**
⊘ **ExamView Test Generator**
   on the **Teacher One Stop**

Video Trailer THINKcentral

Go to **thinkcentral.com** to preview the **Video Trailer** introducing this selection. Other features that support the selection include
• **PowerNotes** presentation
• **ThinkAloud** models to enhance comprehension
• **WordSharp** vocabulary tutorials
• interactive writing and grammar instruction

* Resources for Differentiation   † Also in Spanish   ‡ Also in Haitian Creole and Vietnamese

TEXT ANALYSIS: ESSAY

An **essay** is a work of nonfiction, often loosely structured, expressing the writer's personal views on a single subject. To analyze an essay, pay careful attention to the rhetorical or persuasive power of the following elements:

- the writer's **tone**, or attitude toward his or her subject
- **figurative language** that makes abstract ideas more appealing and easier to grasp
- **anecdotes,** or short accounts of personal incidents
- **imagery** that creates vivid impressions for the reader

As you read, consider how these rhetorical elements illuminate Thoreau's ideas and contribute to the power and persuasiveness of the text.

Review: **Transcendentalism**

READING SKILL: EVALUATE IDEAS

To **evaluate** a writer's ideas, you must examine them carefully and then make judgments about their value. **Summarizing** can help. As you read the selections from *Walden* and "Civil Disobedience," use a chart like the one shown to briefly restate Thoreau's main ideas. After you summarize each idea, note your reaction to it.

	Thoreau's Ideas and Beliefs	My Reactions
Walden		
"Civil Disobedience"		

▲ VOCABULARY IN CONTEXT

Thoreau uses the following words to present his theories about simple, principled living. To see how many you know, choose the word that is closest in meaning to each numbered term.

WORD LIST	abject	impetuous	pervade
	congenial	misgiving	transgress
	deliberately	perturbation	

1. err
2. disturbance
3. doubt
4. wretched
5. friendly
6. permeate
7. impulsive
8. thoughtfully

Complete the activities in your **Reader/Writer Notebook**.

Do you chart your own COURSE?

"Cranks," "crackpots," "oddballs"—society has been quick to apply a negative label to people outside the mainstream. Although Thoreau was probably never called an "oddball," he was certainly regarded as an eccentric. Nonconformity has never been an easy choice, as people often condemn nonconformists without bothering to find out why they embrace a different set of values. Nevertheless, history has shown that many nonconformists, like Thoreau, are often simply ahead of their time.

DISCUSS With a small group of classmates, create a list of famous nonconformists. How did the individuals you listed depart from the norms of their time? Were they punished for their actions? Were they able to win others to their point of view? Discuss these questions with your group.

WALDEN / CIVIL DISOBEDIENCE **379**

Teach

Do you chart your own COURSE?

Ask the question, making sure that students understand the figure of speech. Call on volunteers to suggest examples of nonconformity in tastes, opinions, and so on. Use responses to prompt the *DISCUSS* activity, and invite groups to share the lists that they create.

TEXT ANALYSIS
COMMON CORE RI 6

● *Model the Skill:* ESSAY

To model how to understand figurative language, share this example with students:

> The silvery pond was a mirror, reflecting the trees that leaned over the water, as if dipping their boughs into the sky.

Discuss the ideas that the figurative language in this image might evoke, such as the beauty of the natural scene and a respect for nature.

GUIDED PRACTICE Ask students how the imagery might change if the author wanted to convey an angry tone.

READING SKILL
COMMON CORE RI 2

■ *Model the Skill:* EVALUATE IDEAS

Tell students that Thoreau's philosophical ideas led him to live by his own rules. Have students summarize **Defiant Nonconformist** in the Thoreau biography and then express a reaction to it.

R RESOURCE MANAGER—Copy Master
Evaluate Ideas p. 119 (for student use while reading the selections)

VOCABULARY SKILL
COMMON CORE L 4

▲ VOCABULARY IN CONTEXT

DIAGNOSE WORD KNOWLEDGE Have students complete Vocabulary in Context.

abject (ăb′jĕkt′) *adj.* low; contemptible; wretched

congenial (kən-jēn′yəl) *adj.* suited to one's needs or nature; agreeable

deliberately (dĭ-lĭb′ər-ĭt-lē) *adv.* in an unhurried and thoughtful manner

impetuous (ĭm-pĕch′o͞o-əs) *adj.* acting with sudden or rash energy; hasty

misgiving (mĭs-gĭv′ĭng) *n.* a feeling of doubt, mistrust, or uncertainty

perturbation (pûr′tər-bā′shən) *n.* disturbance of the emotions; agitation; uneasiness

pervade (pər-vād′) *v.* to spread through every part of

transgress (trăns-grĕs′) *v.* to violate a command or law

R RESOURCE MANAGER—Copy Master
Vocabulary Study p. 121

Practice and Apply

SUMMARY

In these essay excerpts, Thoreau explains that he went to Walden Pond to experience the essentials of life. He describes feeling in tune with nature and being transformed by following his personal vision. Anecdotes such as the tale of a bug that hatches after a 60-year dormancy convey Thoreau's hope for human revival and transcendence.

READ WITH A PURPOSE

Help students set a purpose for reading. Have them read the following selections to learn Thoreau's views about human society.

THEME

After students have completed this selection, ask them to discuss films, plays, or novels that connect to the theme of *Walden*.

TEXT ANALYSIS

COMMON CORE
RI 6

Ⓐ *Model the Skill:* ESSAY

Possible answer: Thoreau's tone is admiring (lines 6–9). The reader gets the sense that the essay will show the writer as someone who enjoys a simpler life and wants to share the benefits of simple, purposeful living.

IF STUDENTS NEED HELP . . . Point out words and phrases with positive connotations, such as *abode, freshly planed, clean and airy,* and *saturated with dew,* to help students identify the tone as admiring.

Extend the Discussion On what day does Thoreau move into the house, full-time? What does that fact suggest about his views or personality, even though he calls the date an accident (line 2)?

WALDEN

Henry David Thoreau

BACKGROUND Like Ralph Waldo Emerson and other transcendentalists, Thoreau felt a need to affirm his unity with nature. On July 4, 1845, he began an experiment in what he thought of as "essential living"—living simply, studying the natural world, and seeking truth within himself. On land owned by Emerson near Concord, Massachusetts, Thoreau built a small cabin by Walden Pond and lived there for more than two years, writing and studying nature. *Walden* is the record of his experiences.

from WHERE I LIVED, AND WHAT I LIVED FOR

When first I took up my abode in the woods, that is, began to spend my nights as well as days there, which, by accident, was on Independence day, or the fourth of July, 1845, my house was not finished for winter, but was merely a defense against the rain, without plastering or chimney, the walls being of rough weather-stained boards, with wide chinks, which made it cool at night. The upright white hewn studs and freshly planed door and window casings gave it a clean and airy look, especially in the morning, when its timbers were saturated with dew, so that I fancied that by noon some sweet gum would exude from them. . . . Ⓐ

10   I was seated by the shore of a small pond, about a mile and a half south of the village of Concord and somewhat higher than it, in the midst of an extensive wood between that town and Lincoln, and about two miles south of that our only field known to fame, Concord Battle Ground; but I was so low in the woods that the opposite shore, half a mile off, like the rest, covered with wood, was my most distant horizon. For the first week, whenever I looked out on the pond it impressed me like a tarn high up

Analyze Visuals ▶
Consider the tranquil scene depicted in the photograph on the opposite page. What aspect of the photograph is most responsible for conveying this sense of tranquility, and why?

❶ Targeted Passage

Ⓐ ESSAY
Think about Thoreau's **tone** as he describes his crude, unfinished house. What sense of the writer's views or personality do you get from these opening lines?

16 tarn: a small mountain lake or pool.

DIFFERENTIATED INSTRUCTION

FOR ENGLISH LANGUAGE LEARNERS

Vocabulary: Read lines 1–24 to the class. Invite students to write down as they listen any words that are unfamiliar to them. Have students turn in their lists without their names. Select words from the students' lists to read aloud. Discuss as a class their meanings.

FOR STRUGGLING READERS

In combination with the *Audio Anthology CD*, use one or more Targeted Passages (pp. 380, 384, 387) to ensure that students focus on key concepts in these selections. Targeted passages are also good for English language learners.

❶ Targeted Passage [Lines 1–15]

This passage introduces the setting outisde Concord, Massachusetts, where Thoreau's personal exploration will take place.

Reading Support

This selection on **thinkcentral.com** includes embedded **ThinkAloud** models—students "thinking aloud" about the story to model the kinds of questions a good reader would ask about a selection.

Analyze Visuals

Possible answer: *The sense of tranquility is conveyed mainly by the stillness of the pond. The gentle light on the pond and the leafy trees also add to the sense of peace. All of these features suggest a welcoming place where a visitor might rest and contemplate the scene.*

BACKGROUND

The Walden Pond Cabin Thoreau's house was only 10 feet wide and 15 feet long—just large enough for a bed, a table, a desk, and three chairs. To save money on construction, Thoreau bought used windows, boards, and bricks from people whose houses were being torn down. His careful journal shows that the entire cabin cost him $28.12, an extremely low cost even by 1845 standards. The minimal price of construction, the small size of the cabin, and its setting in the woods allowed Thoreau to live up to his ideals of simplicity and appreciation of nature.

- At what time of year does Thoreau begin living in the house? (lines 1–3)
- How does Thoreau describe his house? (lines 3–9)
- What natural features surround Thoreau in his new home? (lines 10–15)

FOR ADVANCED LEARNERS/AP
Hypothesize Have students suppose that they will be spending the next two years living in a log cabin out in the wilderness. Tell them to write a journal entry describing what they believe a typical day would be like in their new home. Have students read their entries to the class.

B EVALUATE IDEAS

Possible answer: *Summary: Thoreau moved to the woods to live simply and deliberately and to experience the essence of life. Accept all thoughtful opinions.*

Extend the Discussion In lines 34–37, Thoreau refers to the first item in the *Westminster Larger Catechism,* a collection of questions and answers relating to the doctrine held by Puritans and some other Protestant groups. How does Thoreau—as an individual or as a transcendentalist—feel about that particular teaching? What would he say is "the chief end of man"?

C ESSAY

Possible answer: *The "clouds and storms and quicksands" might be the troubles that accompany a full, civilized life, such as problems with jobs, family, and finances. These demands might cause a person to "founder"—that is, to be so busy that he or she becomes incapable of discovering the real essence of life, which exists beyond everyday experience.*

IF STUDENTS NEED HELP . . . Explain that Thoreau uses the word *civilized* to refer to life in groups or communities. He is suggesting not that his life at Walden Pond is uncivilized, but that it is simple and uncomplicated.

OWN THE WORD

deliberately Point out that *deliberately* is the adverbial form of *deliberate,* which can be used both as a verb or an adjective. All forms refer to thinking "carefully, in an unhurried and thoughtful manner." Ask students what types of changes they might see in their lives if they were to live more *deliberately.* *Possible answer:* *might choose to spend more time with family and friends; might feel less stressed; might have time for special activities*

on the side of a mountain, its bottom far above the surface of other lakes, and, as the sun arose, I saw it throwing off its nightly clothing of mist, and here and there, by degrees, its soft ripples or its smooth reflecting surface
20 was revealed, while the mists, like ghosts, were stealthily withdrawing in every direction into the woods, as at the breaking up of some nocturnal conventicle. The very dew seemed to hang upon the trees later into the day than usual, as on the sides of mountains. . . .

I went to the woods because I wished to live **deliberately,** to front only the essential facts of life, and see if I could not learn what it had to teach, and not, when I came to die, discover that I had not lived. I did not wish to live what was not life, living is so dear; nor did I wish to practice resignation, unless it was quite necessary. I wanted to live deep and suck out all the marrow of life, to live so sturdily and Spartan-like as to put to rout all that
30 was not life, to cut a broad swath and shave close, to drive life into a corner, and reduce it to its lowest terms, and, if it proved to be mean, why then to get the whole and genuine meanness of it, and publish its meanness to the world; or if it were sublime, to know it by experience, and be able to give a true account of it in my next excursion. For most men, it appears to me, are in a strange uncertainty about it, whether it is of the devil or of God, and have *somewhat hastily* concluded that it is the chief end of man here to "glorify God and enjoy him forever." **B**

Still we live meanly, like ants; though the fable tells us that we were long ago changed into men; like pygmies we fight with cranes; it is error
40 upon error, and clout upon clout, and our best virtue has for its occasion a superfluous and evitable wretchedness. Our life is frittered away by detail. An honest man has hardly need to count more than his ten fingers, or in extreme cases he may add his ten toes, and lump the rest. Simplicity, simplicity, simplicity! I say, let your affairs be as two or three, and not a hundred or a thousand; instead of a million count half a dozen, and keep your accounts on your thumbnail. In the midst of this chopping sea of civilized life, such are the clouds and storms and quicksands and thousand-and-one items to be allowed for, that a man has to live, if he would not founder and go to the bottom and not make his port at all, by dead
50 reckoning, and he must be a great calculator indeed who succeeds. Simplify, simplify. Instead of three meals a day, if it be necessary eat but one; instead of a hundred dishes, five; and reduce other things in proportion. . . . **C**

Why should we live with such hurry and waste of life? We are determined to be starved before we are hungry. Men say that a stitch in time saves nine, and so they take a thousand stitches today to save nine to-morrow. As for *work,* we haven't any of any consequence. We have the Saint Vitus' dance, and cannot possibly keep our heads still. If I should only give a few pulls at the parish bell-rope, as for a fire, that is, without setting the bell, there is hardly a man on his farm in the outskirts of Concord, notwithstanding that
60 press of engagements which was his excuse so many times this morning,

22 **conventicle:** a secret religious meeting.

deliberately (dĭ-lĭb′ər-ĭt-lē) *adv.* in an unhurried and thoughtful manner

29 **Spartan-like:** in a simple and disciplined way, like the inhabitants of the ancient city-state of Sparta.

B EVALUATE IDEAS
Reread lines 24–37. **Summarize** Thoreau's reasons for moving to the woods. What do you think of these reasons?

41 **evitable:** avoidable.

C ESSAY
In this essay, Thoreau often uses **figurative language** to present his observations. In lines 46–50, he likens civilized life to a rough sea. What might "the clouds and storms and quicksands" of life be? How might one "founder," or sink, in civilized life?

56 **Saint Vitus' dance:** a disorder of the nervous system, characterized by rapid, jerky, involuntary movements.

DIFFERENTIATED INSTRUCTION

FOR ADVANCED LEARNERS/AP

Make Judgments [small-group option] Ask students to reread and reflect upon lines 41–52, in which Thoreau criticizes overly complex lives. Then have students write an essay in which they respond to these questions:.

• What does Thoreau mean when he says, "Our life is frittered away by detail" (line 41)?

• What are the advantages and disadvantages of living simply?

• What would it mean to simplify life to the barest necessities? Give examples.

• Do you agree with Thoreau's views on this topic? Why or why not?

Invite students to meet in small groups to compare their responses.

nor a boy, nor a woman, I might almost say, but would forsake all and follow that sound, not mainly to save property from the flames, but, if we will confess the truth, much more to see it burn, since burn it must, and we, be it known, did not set it on fire,—or to see it put out, and have a hand in it, if that is done as handsomely; yes, even if it were the parish church itself. Hardly a man takes a half hour's nap after dinner, but when he wakes he holds up his head and asks, "What's the news?" as if the rest of mankind had stood his sentinels. Some give directions to be waked every half hour, doubtless for no other purpose; and then, to pay for it, they tell
70 what they have dreamed. After a night's sleep the news is as indispensable as the breakfast. "Pray tell me any thing new that has happened to a man any where on this globe,"—and he reads it over his coffee and rolls, that a man has had his eyes gouged out this morning on the Wachito River; never dreaming the while that he lives in the dark unfathomed mammoth cave of this world, and has but the rudiment of an eye himself. **D**

For my part, I could easily do without the post-office. I think that there are very few important communications made through it. To speak critically, I never received more than one or two letters in my life—I wrote this some years ago—that were worth the postage. The penny-post is, commonly,
80 an institution through which you seriously offer a man that penny for his thoughts which is so often safely offered in jest. And I am sure that I never read any memorable news in a newspaper. If we read of one man robbed, or murdered, or killed by accident, or one house burned, or one vessel wrecked, or one steamboat blown up, or one cow run over on the Western Railroad, or one mad dog killed, or one lot of grasshoppers in the winter,—we never need read of another. One is enough. . . .

Let us spend one day as deliberately as Nature, and not be thrown off the track by every nutshell and mosquito's wing that falls on the rails. Let us rise early and fast, or break fast, gently and without **perturbation**; let
90 company come and let company go, let the bells ring and the children cry,— determined to make a day of it. . . .

Time is but the stream I go a-fishing in. I drink at it; but while I drink I see the sandy bottom and detect how shallow it is. Its thin current slides away, but eternity remains. I would drink deeper; fish in the sky, whose bottom is pebbly with stars. I cannot count one. I know not the first letter of the alphabet. I have always been regretting that I was not as wise as the day I was born. The intellect is a cleaver; it discerns and rifts its way into the secret of things. I do not wish to be any more busy with my hands than is necessary. My head is hands and feet. I feel all my best faculties concentrated
100 in it. My instinct tells me that my head is an organ for burrowing, as some creatures use their snout and fore-paws, and with it I would mine and burrow my way through these hills. I think that the richest vein is somewhere hereabouts; so by the divining rod and thin rising vapors I judge; and here I will begin to mine. **E**

D **ESSAY**
What situation does Thoreau exaggerate in lines 66–75, and what is the rhetorical effect of his exaggeration? Would you respond differently to Thoreau's point if he stated his view here without exaggeration? Explain your answer.

79–81 penny-post . . . jest: Thoreau jokingly connects the postage rate at the time (a penny per letter) with the phrase "a penny for your thoughts."

perturbation (pûr′tər-bā′shən) *n.* disturbance of the emotions; agitation; uneasiness

E **EVALUATE IDEAS**
Summarize lines 87–104. What does Thoreau want to spend his time trying to understand, and how does he plan to achieve this understanding? Decide what you think about this desire.

D **ESSAY**

Possible answer: Thoreau exaggerates the importance that the average person gives to the daily news. Presenting the caricature of a person who demands to be awakened with the latest news is a more memorable way of expressing his views than merely saying, "People care too much about the news."

REVISIT THE BIG QUESTION

Do you chart your own
COURSE?

Discuss In lines 66–86, what do Thoreau's ideas about the news and about letters reveal about his nonconformity? *Possible answer: The rejection of outside information reveals the extent of Thoreau's desire to live independently.*

READING SKILL COMMON CORE RI 2

E **EVALUATE IDEAS**

Possible answer: Summary: Spend your life deliberately. Time passes quickly, so try to open yourself to simple tasks and ideas. Look to the spaces around you for meaning and significance. Thoreau wants to spend his time figuring out "the secret of things" (lines 97–98). He plans to achieve this understanding by delving intellectually and deeply into every situation in search of the answers he seeks. Accept all thoughtful evaluations.

VOCABULARY COMMON CORE L 4

OWN THE WORD

perturbation: Tell students that *perturbation* is related to the verb *perturb*, and its root is a Latin term meaning "to throw into disorder." Ask students why Thoreau used the word in "Let us rise early and fast, or break fast, gently and without *perturbation*." *Possible answer: Thoreau is encouraging the reader to "get up on the bright side" of the day, to have a peaceful morning when loved ones meet without the "disturbance of emotions and agitation."*

FOR ENGLISH LANGUAGE LEARNERS

Comprehension: Text Structure Have students scan this selection and take note of the subheadings. Explain that these are Thoreau's titles for different entries in his record of life at Walden. Clarify that each has been further excerpted here. Then focus on the structure of the first excerpt, "Where I Lived, and What I Lived For." Point out the main sections of this excerpt.

- Lines 1–23 contain Thoreau's description of the cabin, the woods, and the pond.
- Lines 24–37 contain Thoreau's reasons for living at Walden Pond.
- Lines 38–86 contain Thoreau's conclusions about modern life.
- Lines 87–104 contain Thoreau's call to action, in which he makes suggestions for how to live a simple and solitary life.

 Model the Skill:
EVALUATE IDEAS

Tell students one way to evaluate ideas is to use tools such as the chart introduced on page 379.

Essay	Thoreau's Ideas and Beliefs	My Reactions
Walden	Loneliness is a result of spiritual separation, not physical distance.	I feel distant from people if we don't understand each other, even if we are physically close.

Possible answer: *Summary: Loneliness is a result of spiritual distance between us, not physical distance. This is true because people can be physically close to others but feel lonely because they are spiritually disconnected. Students may say that they or others have felt lonely in a crowd because people don't always stop to understand an individual's emotions.*

OWN THE WORD

- **congenial:** Tell students that the definition of "suited to one's needs or nature; agreeable" fits Thoreau's sentiments. *Congenial* also refers to "having the same tastes or temperament," or "being friendly and sociable." Ask students to write a sentence that shows an understanding of *congenial*. **Possible answer:** *Reading under a shady tree is a most congenial activity for me; Michelle and I enjoy a congenial friendship; Matthew is a congenial, generous host.*

- **pervade:** Point out that *pervade* has the connotation of invading, saturating, or filling fully. Have students list things that might *pervade* a situation or environment. **Possible answers:** *music filling a room; laughter; feeling of well being; sense of evil; pollution; disease; flood waters*

---

from SOLITUDE

This is a delicious evening, when the whole body is one sense, and imbibes delight through every pore. I go and come with a strange liberty in Nature, a part of herself. As I walk along the stony shore of the pond in my shirt sleeves, though it is cool as well as cloudy and windy, and I see nothing special to attract me, all the elements are unusually **congenial** to me. The
110 bullfrogs trump to usher in the night, and the note of the whippoorwill is borne on the rippling wind from over the water. Sympathy with the fluttering alder and poplar leaves almost takes away my breath; yet, like the lake, my serenity is rippled but not ruffled. These small waves raised by the evening wind are as remote from storm as the smooth reflecting surface. Though it is now dark, the wind still blows and roars in the wood, the waves still dash, and some creatures lull the rest with their notes. The repose is never complete. The wildest animals do not repose, but seek their prey now; the fox, and skunk, and rabbit, now roam the fields and woods without fear. They are Nature's watchmen,—links which connect the days
120 of animated life. . . .

> Men frequently say to me, "I should think you would feel lonesome down there, and want to be nearer to folks, rainy and snowy days and nights especially." I am tempted to reply to such,—This whole earth which we inhabit is but a point in space. How far apart, think you, dwell the two most distant inhabitants of yonder star, the breadth of whose disk cannot be appreciated by our instruments? Why should I feel lonely? Is not our planet in the Milky Way? This which you put seems to me not to be the most important question. What sort of space is that which separates a man from his fellows and makes him solitary? I have found that no exertion of the legs
130 can bring two minds much nearer to one another. . . . **F**

---

from THE POND IN WINTER

Every winter the liquid and trembling surface of the pond, which was so sensitive to every breath, and reflected every light and shadow, becomes solid to the depth of a foot or a foot and a half, so that it will support the heaviest teams, and perchance the snow covers it to an equal depth, and it is not to be distinguished from any level field. Like the marmots in the surrounding hills, it closes its eye-lids and becomes dormant for three months or more. Standing on the snow-covered plain, as if in a pasture amid the hills, I cut my way first through a foot of snow, and then a foot of ice, and open a window under my feet, where, kneeling to drink, I look down into the quiet
140 parlor of the fishes, **pervaded** by a softened light as through a window of

---

congenial (kən-jēn′yəl) *adj.* suited to one's needs or nature; agreeable

Language Coach

Synonyms *Rippled* and *ruffled* (line 113) are synonyms, words with similar meanings. Thoreau contrasts their meanings, though. With a partner, look up each word in a dictionary; then, decide what difference in meaning Thoreau intended for them to have.

 Targeted Passage

F **EVALUATE IDEAS**
Reread lines 121–130. **Summarize** Thoreau's ideas about loneliness. Do you agree with his assessment of this condition? Explain your answer.

135 marmots: burrowing rodents that hibernate in winter; also known as groundhogs or woodchucks.

pervade (pər-vād′) *v.* to spread through every part of

 DIFFERENTIATED INSTRUCTION

FOR STRUGGLING READERS

 Targeted Passage [Lines 121–130]
This passage illustrates Thoreau's views on solitude and loneliness.

- What does Thoreau frequently hear from other people? (lines 121–123)

- How does he respond to these comments? (lines 123–127)

- According to Thoreau, what truly makes people lonely? (lines 127–130)

FOR ENGLISH LANGUAGE LEARNERS

Language Coach

Synonyms *Accept all reasonable responses.* Have students reread the text on this page and make a list of five words they find interesting. Tell students to exchange their lists with a partner. Each student should then identify one synonym for every word on his or her partner's list.

ground glass, with its bright sanded floor the same as in summer; there a
perennial waveless serenity reigns as in the amber twilight sky, corresponding
to the cool and even temperament of the inhabitants. Heaven is under our
feet as well as over our heads. . . . **G**

from SPRING

One attraction in coming to the woods to live was that I should have leisure
and opportunity to see the spring come in. The ice in the pond at length
begins to be honey-combed, and I can set my heel in it as I walk. Fogs and
rains and warmer suns are gradually melting the snow; the days have grown
sensibly longer; and I see how I shall get through the winter without adding
150 to my woodpile, for large fires are no longer necessary. I am on the alert for
the first signs of spring, to hear the chance note of some arriving bird, or the
striped squirrel's chirp, for his stores must be now nearly exhausted, or see
the woodchuck venture out of his winter quarters. . . .

The change from storm and winter to serene and mild weather, from dark
and sluggish hours to bright and elastic ones, is a memorable crisis which
all things proclaim. It is seemingly instantaneous at last. Suddenly an influx
of light filled my house, though the evening was at hand, and the clouds
of winter still overhung it, and the eaves were dripping with sleety rain. I
looked out the window, and lo! where yesterday was cold gray ice there lay
160 the transparent pond already calm and full of hope as in a summer evening,
reflecting a summer evening sky in its bosom, though none was visible
overhead, as if it had intelligence with some remote horizon. . . . **H**

from CONCLUSION

I left the woods for as good a reason as I went there. Perhaps it seemed to me
that I had several more lives to live, and could not spare any more time for
that one. It is remarkable how easily and insensibly we fall into a particular
route, and make a beaten track for ourselves. I had not lived there a week
before my feet wore a path from my door to the pond-side; and though it
is five or six years since I trod it, it is still quite distinct. It is true, I fear that
others may have fallen into it, and so helped to keep it open. The surface of
170 the earth is soft and impressible by the feet of men; and so with the paths
which the mind travels. How worn and dusty, then, must be the highways
of the world, how deep the ruts of tradition and conformity! I did not wish
to take a cabin passage, but rather to go before the mast and on the deck of

---

G TRANSCENDENTALISM
What transcendentalist ideal
is reflected in lines 143–144?

149 **sensibly:** noticeably.

H ESSAY
Even when an essay does not
argue a particular point, the
writer uses **rhetorical
techniques,** or methods that
have persuasive appeal. For
example, in lines 143–144, when
Thoreau says "Heaven is under
our feet," his use of figurative
language has strong emotional
appeal. Re-read lines 145–162.
What effect does Thoreau's use of
imagery have in this description?

Language Coach

Figurative Language "Beaten
track" (line 166) and "ruts" (line
172) can be used as figurative
language, language that
communicates ideas beyond
the literal meaning of the
words. How can "beaten track"
and "ruts" be understood both
literally and figuratively?

172–175 On a sailing ship, passengers
stayed in private compartments, or
cabins, near the middle of the ship,
while the crew shared living quarters
at the front, where more was visible.

WALDEN **385**

TEXT ANALYSIS: *Review*   COMMON CORE   RI 9

G TRANSCENDENTALISM

Possible answer: *These lines reflect the
ideal that humankind, nature, and God are
interconnected and that the divine spirit is
therefore reflected in the natural world.*

IF STUDENTS NEED HELP . . . Refer them
to the list of transcendentalist ideals on
page 369.

TEXT ANALYSIS   COMMON CORE   RI 6

H ESSAY

Read lines 145–162 aloud, asking students
to visualize the changes Thoreau describes.
How does his imagery effect the seasonal
change for readers? *Possible answer:* *His
use of imagery creates a vivid picture
of spring emerging from winter, as the
weather warms, the animals venture out,
and his house floods with light.*

Extend the Discussion What picture does
Thoreau paint of his experience of living in
the woods?

TIERED DISCUSSION PROMPTS

Refer to lines 163–172 and use these prompts
to discuss why Thoreau leaves Walden Pond:

Connect Have you ever felt stuck in a
routine? How did you respond? *Accept all
reasonable responses.*

Interpret What does Thoreau mean by
"make a beaten track for ourselves" (line
166)? How has he made a beaten track for
himself? *Possible answer:* *Thoreau means
that people fall into a routine. He suggests
that by living in the same place for two years,
he, too, has fallen into a routine.*

Synthesize How are Thoreau's reasons
for leaving Walden Pond the same as his
reasons for going there? *Possible answer:*
*Thoreau went to Walden Pond to get away
from everyday routines that interfere with
essential thought. He leaves Walden Pond,
in part, because he has fallen into everyday
routines there, too.*

FOR STRUGGLING READERS

Develop Reading Fluency Read the "from
Spring" section of the Thoreau's essay to your
class. Have students work in pairs with each
student reading aloud one of the paragraphs.
Remind them to use your example as well as
the text punctuation to guide the rate and
intonation of their speech.

FOR ENGLISH LANGUAGE LEARNERS

Language Coach

Figurative Language *Possible answer:*
"Beaten track" *is literally a path carved
into a woods.* "Ruts" *are tracks worn into a
road from wheels passing over its surface.
Figuratively, the terms can mean a staid or
stale way of doing things.* Have students
identify examples of language that can be
used literally and figuratively.

Direct students to lines 176–187. Use these prompts to explore what Thoreau has learned from his time at Walden Pond:

Recall What was the goal of Thoreau's experiment? *Possible answer: Thoreau wanted to see what he could learn by living simply and deliberately (lines 24–52).*

Synthesize In what ways has Thoreau achieved his goals at Walden Pond? *Possible answer: Thoreau has learned to live life deliberately and simply. He has also realized that pursuing dreams is very important for personal growth.*

TEXT ANALYSIS	COMMON CORE
	RI 6

❶ ESSAY

Possible answer: Thoreau compares life to highways, which are "worn and dusty" with deep "ruts of tradition and conformity." He avoids this "rut" by leaving Walden.

TEXT ANALYSIS: *Review*	COMMON CORE
	RI 9

❷ *Model the Skill:* TRANSCENDENTALISM

Tell students that Thoreau wants people to trust their own ideas. Discuss the "different drummer" analogy. Elicit that Thoreau wants people to follow their own beats, even if they fall out of step with others.

Possible answer: He embraces the transcendentalist value of following one's own beliefs—living according to one's intuition rather than to society's expectations.

VOCABULARY	COMMON CORE
	L 4

OWN THE WORD

- **misgiving:** Ask students if they have ever had *misgivings* about someone or something. Ask them to explain the situation.
- **abject:** Explain to students that *abject* describes severe conditions that are "contemptible or wretched," and, per the Latin root *abicere*, need to be "cast away." An example is *abject* poverty.

---

the world, for there I could best see the moonlight amid the mountains. I do not wish to go below now. ❶

    I learned this, at least, by my experiment; that if one advances confidently in the direction of his dreams, and endeavors to live the life which he has imagined, he will meet with a success unexpected in common hours. He will put some things behind, will pass an invisible boundary; new, universal, 180 and more liberal laws will begin to establish themselves around and within him; or the old laws be expanded, and interpreted in his favor in a more liberal sense, and he will live with the license of a higher order of beings. In proportion as he simplifies his life, the laws of the universe will appear less complex, and solitude will not be solitude, nor poverty poverty, nor weakness weakness. If you have built castles in the air, your work need not be lost; that is where they should be. Now put the foundations under them. . . .

    Why should we be in such desperate haste to succeed, and in such desperate enterprises? If a man does not keep pace with his companions, 190 perhaps it is because he hears a different drummer. Let him step to the music which he hears, however measured or far away. It is not important that he should mature as soon as an appletree or an oak. Shall he turn his spring into summer? If the condition of things which we were made for is not yet, what were any reality which we can substitute? We will not be shipwrecked on a vain reality. Shall we with pains erect a heaven of blue glass over ourselves, though when it is done we shall be sure to gaze still at the true ethereal heaven far above, as if the former were not? . . . ❶

    However mean your life is, meet it and live it; do not shun it and call it hard names. It is not so bad as you are. It looks poorest when you are richest. 200 The fault-finder will find faults even in paradise. Love your life, poor as it is. You may perhaps have some pleasant, thrilling, glorious hours, even in a poorhouse. The setting sun is reflected from the windows of the almshouse as brightly as from the rich man's abode; the snow melts before its door as early in the spring. I do not see but a quiet mind may live as contentedly there, and have as cheering thoughts, as in a palace. The town's poor seem to me often to live the most independent lives of any. May be they are simply great enough to receive without **misgiving.** Most think that they are above being supported by the town; but it oftener happens that they are not above supporting themselves by dishonest means, which should be 210 more disreputable. Cultivate poverty like a garden herb, like sage. Do not trouble yourself much to get new things, whether clothes or friends. Turn the old; return to them. Things do not change; we change. Sell your clothes and keep your thoughts. God will see that you do not want society. If I were confined to a corner of a garret all my days, like a spider, the world would be just as large to me while I had my thoughts about me. The philosopher said: "From an army of three divisions one can take away its general, and put it in disorder; from the man the most **abject** and vulgar one cannot take away his thought." Do not seek so anxiously to be developed, to subject

---

189–191 If a man . . . away: This is one of Thoreau's most famous passages. The "different drummer" evolved from a journal entry describing how he fell asleep to the sound of someone beating a drum "alone in the silence and the dark." The phrase "marching to the beat of a different drummer" became popular during the 1960s and 1970s.

❶ **TRANSCENDENTALISM**
What key feature of transcendentalism does Thoreau embrace in lines 189–191?

misgiving (mĭs-gĭv′ĭng) *n.* a feeling of doubt, mistrust, or uncertainty

215 the philosopher: Confucius (551–479 B.C.), Chinese teacher of moral living, who had an influence on Thoreau's ideas.

abject (ăb′jĕkt′) *adj.* low; contemptible; wretched

DIFFERENTIATED INSTRUCTION

FOR ENGLISH LANGUAGE LEARNERS

Comprehension: Text Structure Help students identify examples of the three main strands in "Conclusion": (1) why Thoreau left the woods, (2) life observations, and (3) aphorisms or life lessons. Read lines 198–199 aloud and paraphrase them to clarify: "If your life is difficult, make the best of it. Don't complain or avoid living fully." Urge students to paraphrase to better understand Thoreau's three idea strands.

FOR ADVANCED LEARNERS/AP

Research While Thoreau describes many of his experiences at Walden in minute detail, he omits other experiences entirely. Have students research what Thoreau's life was actually like during his *Walden* years and write one or two paragraphs on how experiences he does not recount in *Walden* might have influenced the personal growth he recounts in his book.

yourself to many influences to be played on; it is all dissipation. Humility
220 like darkness reveals the heavenly lights. The shadows of poverty and
meanness gather around us, "and lo! creation widens to our view." We are
often reminded that if there were bestowed on us the wealth of Croesus, our
aims must still be the same, and our means essentially the same. Moreover,
if you are restricted in your range by poverty, if you cannot buy books
and newspapers, for instance, you are but confined to the most significant
and vital experiences; you are compelled to deal with the material which
yields the most sugar and the most starch. It is life near the bone where it is
sweetest. You are defended from being a trifler. No man loses ever on a lower
level by magnanimity on a higher. Superfluous wealth can buy superfluities
230 only. Money is not required to buy one necessary of the soul. . . . **K**

The life in us is like the water in the river. It may rise this year higher than
man has ever known it, and flood the parched uplands; even this may be the
eventful year, which will drown out all our muskrats. It was not always dry
land where we dwell. I see far inland the banks which the stream anciently
washed, before science began to record its freshets. Every one has heard the
story which has gone the rounds of New England, of a strong and beautiful
bug which came out of the dry leaf of an old table of apple-tree wood,
which had stood in a farmer's kitchen for sixty years, first in Connecticut,
and afterward in Massachusetts,—from an egg deposited in the living tree
240 many years earlier still, as appeared by counting the annual layers beyond it;
which was heard gnawing out for several weeks, hatched perchance by the
heat of an urn. Who does not feel his faith in a resurrection and immortality
strengthened by hearing of this? Who knows what beautiful and winged
life, whose egg has been buried for ages under many concentric layers of
woodenness in the dead dry life of society, deposited at first in the alburnum
of the green and living tree, which has been gradually converted into the
semblance of its well-seasoned tomb,—heard perchance gnawing out now
for years by the astonished family of man, as they sat round the festive
board,—may unexpectedly come forth from amidst society's most trivial
250 and handselled furniture, to enjoy its perfect summer life at last!

I do not say that John or Jonathan will realize all this; but such is the
character of that morrow which mere lapse of time can never make to
dawn. The light which puts out our eyes is darkness to us. Only that day
dawns to which we are awake. There is more day to dawn. The sun is but a
morning star. ❧

222 Croesus (krē'səs): an ancient king legendary for his great wealth.

K EVALUATE IDEAS
Summarize Thoreau's ideas about poverty. Do you think his view of the poor and the lives they lead is realistic? Record your thoughts in your chart.

235 freshets: overflowings of a stream caused by heavy rain or melting snow.

❸ Targeted Passage

245 alburnum (ăl-bûr'nəm): the part of a tree's trunk through which sap flows.

251 John or Jonathan: the common man (as in the more current expression "Tom, Dick, and Harry").

WALDEN **387**

READING SKILL

COMMON CORE
RI 2

K EVALUATE IDEAS

Possible answer: _Thoreau believes that the poor and the rich can receive the same benefits from nature. He thinks that poverty gives people a certain independence, and he urges readers to "cultivate poverty" rather than be trapped in materialism (lines 210–213). Accept all thoughtful responses to Thoreau's ideas._

IF STUDENTS NEED HELP . . . Ask these questions to help students evaluate Thoreau's ideas about poverty:

- According to lines 223–227, what advantage is there in not having enough money to buy books and newspapers?

- What does _superfluities_ (line 229) mean?

- How would you explain the image "life near the bone" (line 227)?

REVISIT THE BIG QUESTION

Do you chart your own
COURSE?

Discuss In lines 251–255, how does Thoreau's reference to "John or Jonathan" suggest that he recognizes his own nonconformity?
Possible answer: _Thoreau knows that most people, represented by the common names John and Jonathan, will not appreciate his values. In this statement, he acknowledges that he is different from other people._

FOR STRUGGLING READERS

❸ Targeted Passage [Lines 235–250]

In this concluding passage, Thoreau explains how he draws inspiration from a frequently told anecdote.

- Where is the bug? What happens to it? What is unusual about its situation? (lines 235–242)

- How does this story restore faith? (lines 242–243)

- How does the story make Thoreau feel about life? about the future? (lines 243–250)

FOR ADVANCED LEARNERS/AP

Hypothesize Point out that many people's response to spending two years alone in the woods would have been much different from Thoreau's response. Challenge students to use Thoreau's "Conclusion" as a model for a journal entry in which someone with different values discusses leaving the woods and offers some observations and life lessons based on the experience. Invite volunteers to read their journal entries aloud for the class to compare and enjoy.

Practice and Apply

For preliminary support of post-reading questions, use these copy masters:

R RESOURCE MANAGER—Copy Masters
Reading Check p. 124
Essay p. 117
Question Support pp. 125, 126
Additional selection questions are provided for teachers on page 109.

ANSWERS

COMMON CORE
RI 2, RI 6, RI 9

1. *to live simply and purposefully and to learn from nature*

2. *to simplify, live deliberately, and ignore material gain*

3. *Most correspondence is worthless, the daily news contains no memorable or important information, and we place too much importance on both forms of communication.*

Possible answers:

4. *The pond (lines 15–23), living deliberately (lines 24–34), living simply (lines 43–52), nature and solitude (lines 105–120), following one's own "drumbeat" (lines 189–191), and personal integrity (lines 207–210) were important to Thoreau.*

5. ● **COMMON CORE FOCUS Analyze the Essay Metaphor:** *"The intellect is a cleaver" (line 97);* **Simile:** *"Still we live meanly, like ants" (line 38);* **Personification:** *"I look down into the quiet parlor of the fishes" (lines 139–140). The figurative language gives readers a vivid picture of Walden Pond and a deeper understanding of Thoreau's experiences.*

6. ● **COMMON CORE FOCUS Evaluate Ideas** *Answers should demonstrate a thorough understanding of Thoreau's ideas.*

7. *It would be more challenging for a modern American to live as Thoreau did because, as La Ferle suggests, we are used to more comfortable standards than were the norm in Thoreau's time. On the other hand, it would be as challenging today as it was then to live deliberately and to consider every choice, avoiding blind conformity and mindless tradition, as Thoreau suggests.*

8. *Yes, the comment applies. Thoreau often shows his amazement at his natural surroundings, as in " . . . there a perennial waveless serenity reigns" (lines 141–142) and "I looked out the window, and lo! where yesterday was cold gray ice there lay the transparent pond . . . as if it had intelligence" (lines 158–162).*

After Reading

Comprehension

1. **Recall** What were Thoreau's reasons for moving to the woods?

2. **Recall** What does Thoreau advise people to do to ensure their lives are not "frittered away by detail"?

3. **Summarize** What are Thoreau's views on correspondence and the daily news?

Text Analysis

4. **Make Inferences** Thoreau rejects many things as inessential or unimportant. List at least three things that *were* important to him, citing specific lines from the text to support your answer.

● 5. **Analyze the Essay** Thoreau was a poet as well as an essayist, and in *Walden*, he uses **figurative language** to express abstract concepts. Complete the chart by finding examples of such language. Use your completed chart to describe what you think Thoreau's use of figurative language adds to this essay.

Type of Figurative Language	Examples from Walden
metaphor	"Time is but the stream I go a-fishing in."
simile	
personification	

● 6. **Evaluate Ideas** Review the philosophical ideas you summarized as you read. Choose two ideas—Thoreau's view of the poor, for example, or the way he feels about civilized life. Explain whether or not you think the ideas you chose have merit, citing reasons for your opinions.

7. **Compare Texts** In "Thoreau Still Beckons, *if* I Can Take My Laptop" on page 389, Cynthia G. La Ferle argues that "making choices is so much more difficult in a culture fueled by sheer busyness and commercialism. There are few places . . . where one can escape." Do you agree that it would be more challenging for a modern American to live as Thoreau did? Explain why or why not, using details from both texts to support your opinion.

Text Criticism

8. **Critical Interpretations** According to Frank Stewart, author of *A Natural History of Nature Writing*, nature writers are "moved by the joyous, wild, and dazzling beauty in the world." Do you think this comment applies to Thoreau? Cite examples from *Walden* to support your opinion.

> *Do you chart your own* **COURSE?**
>
> In his day, Thoreau's living habits were probably considered unusual and even eccentric. In what place and in what manner might a nonconformist today live?

388 UNIT 2: AMERICAN ROMANTICISM

COMMON CORE

RI 2 Determine two or more central ideas of a text and analyze their development; provide an objective summary of the text. **RI 6** Determine an author's point of view or purpose in a text in which the rhetoric is effective, analyzing how style and content contribute to the power, persuasiveness, or beauty of the text. **RI 9** Analyze documents of literary significance for their themes, purposes, and rhetorical features.

Do you chart your own **COURSE?**
Students might mention people who live in total isolation or those who live in communes.

388 UNIT 2: AMERICAN ROMANTICISM

MAGAZINE ARTICLE Thoreau's call for a simpler life continues to resonate with Americans. Those struggling with a hectic lifestyle may recall his words with a particular sense of longing. Read on to hear one busy woman's reflection on the topic.

THOREAU STILL BECKONS,
if I Can Take My Laptop

By Cynthia G. La Ferle

Thanks to the wonders of modern technology, I now have a mind-boggling array of options.

I can shop for birthday gifts on the Internet, watch a funeral in Britain on "live" television, and order a complete wardrobe from a computer catalog. . . .

Every day I have more choices than I can reasonably consider. And so, like other tired Americans, I carry the burden of complexity—a burden so overwhelming, in fact, that there are times when I imagine trading places with Henry David Thoreau.

It's only fitting that I rediscovered Thoreau the week I purged my home office with a dust rag and a vacuum cleaner. The autumn mornings felt ripe for pitching and sorting. "Walden," Thoreau's famous treatise on simple living, was jammed behind a pile of unread paperbacks. . . .

It occurred to me that things were vastly different for Thoreau. The "comforts of life" in the 1840s were not exactly cushy by today's standards. His concept of luxury might have been taking tea in his mother's bone china saucers. So what had he given up to commune with nature?

Even before he moved to Walden Pond, Thoreau hadn't accumulated three television sets or a closetful of designer clothes. He didn't own several pairs of expensive athletic shoes for all those philosophical walks he took. His cot in the cabin couldn't have been more lumpy than the straw-filled mattresses in most mid-19th-century homes. And Thoreau never had to trade a personal computer for a pencil.

With all due respect, I wonder, how tough was Thoreau's two-year sabbatical with simplicity? Is it true that he occasionally walked from Walden Pond back to Concord, where Emerson's wife had a home-cooked supper waiting for him? . . .

And yet, just as Thoreau did, I'd like to weed out, pare down, live deliberately, be a resident philosopher. . . .

Visiting the "real" Walden Pond this fall, I was amazed and disappointed to find the place overrun. Locals were strewn on its small beach. You couldn't walk the path around the pond without rubbing shoulders with other sightseers; there wasn't a spot left for solitary reflection.

If nothing else, my rendezvous with Thoreau got me thinking. What—and how much—do I really need? What price have I paid for modern technology and "convenience"? In which landfill will all my stuff end up? . . .

Could I survive in a one-room cabin with barely more than a chair, a wooden table, a bowlful of raw vegetables, and my laptop? Honestly, I wish I could.

CONNECT

This selection offers a modern reaction to the ideas in Thoreau's *Walden*. You can also use it as a mini lesson on reading for information.

READING FOR INFORMATION

Point out that "Thoreau Still Beckons, *if* I Can Take My Laptop" is a magazine article. Have students preview the article by reading the introductory note. Then ask

- How do the words and the design of the title help prepare you for what La Ferle may say in the article? *Possible answer: The title makes the reader aware that La Ferle will say something about Thoreau's ideas. The words and the styling of the title—presenting the main statement in bold capital letters but then drawing attention to the italicized* if *and the more meek-looking qualifying statement that follows—also prepare the reader for a humorous take on the topic.*

- How is the tone of La Ferle's article different from the tone of Thoreau's essay? *Possible answer: La Ferle's informal language and exaggerations create a humorously self-critical tone, whereas Thoreau's tone is serious and contemplative.*

TIERED DISCUSSION PROMPTS

Use these prompts to help students connect the magazine article to the excerpts from *Walden* on pages 380–387:

Connect How does this article help you apply Thoreau's ideas to your life? *Accept all reasonable responses.*

Interpret Why does the writer consider it "fitting" that she found *Walden* while cleaning her office? *Possible answer: It is fitting because one of Thoreau's directives is to simplify life by getting rid of unnecessary goods.*

Synthesize What passages in *Walden* suggest Thoreau's possible reaction to La Ferle's ideas? *Possible answer: Thoreau would probably scold La Ferle for clinging to material possessions. He would use his thoughts about news and communication (lines 66–86) to scold her for her attachment to television sets and laptops. He would commiserate with her disappointment over the crowded condition of Walden Pond because he has clear ideas about the value of solitude.*

SUMMARY

In these excerpts from "Civil Disobedience," Thoreau argues that citizens must follow their conscience and fight government injustice in a peaceful manner. For example, he refuses to pay taxes that fund causes that he opposes—an action that lands him in jail but frees him spiritually.

READ WITH A PURPOSE

Help students set a purpose for reading. Have them read the following selection to learn how Thoreau protested the policies of his government.

READING SKILL

COMMON
CORE
RI 2

A *Model the Skill:* EVALUATE IDEAS

To help students understand and evaluate these lines, paraphrase for students the two mottos:

• "The best government is the one that does the least," and

• "The best government is the one that does nothing."

Now ask them to evaluate whether the second statement is a natural outgrowth of the first.

Possible answer: Some students will agree that if "least" is good, then "nothing" must be better. Others may feel that this is an exaggeration or distortion of the first principle; that some government is always still necessary.

Extend the Discussion Why might modern readers be less surprised by these comments than readers of Thoreau's time might have been?

Civil D I S O B E D I E N C E
Henry David Thoreau

Analyze Visuals ▶
The photographer who created the image on the opposite page chose to focus not on the people in the crowd, but on their shadows. Why might she have made this choice?

BACKGROUND Thoreau put into practice the ideas expressed in Ralph Waldo Emerson's "Self-Reliance." In 1846, he spent a night in jail for refusing to pay a poll tax—a tax one had to pay in order to vote—as an act of protest against the U.S. government. Thoreau was enraged by the government's support of slavery and its war against Mexico, which he viewed as a case of a stronger country overpowering a weaker one simply to expand its own borders. Inspired by his experience in jail, Thoreau wrote this essay to add his voice to the ongoing debate about a citizen's responsibility to pay for a war he did not support.

A EVALUATE IDEAS
Sometimes writers may make false or misleading statements, known as **logical fallacies,** to bolster their arguments. Examine Thoreau's progression of ideas in lines 1–10, when he says that if you accept the motto, "That government is best which governs least" then it naturally follows that "That government is best which governs not at all." Some might say that the second statement is a **non sequitur,** or a conclusion that does not follow from the evidence. What do you think? Explain why you think Thoreau's statement is or is not valid.

I heartily accept the motto, "That government is best which governs least;" and I should like to see it acted up to more rapidly and systematically. Carried out, it finally amounts to this, which also I believe,—"That government is best which governs not at all;" and when men are prepared for it, that will be the kind of government which they will have. Government is at best but an expedient; but most governments are usually, and all governments are sometimes, inexpedient. The objections which have  been brought against a standing army, and they are many and weighty, and deserve to prevail, may also at last be brought against a standing
10 government. The standing army is only an arm of the standing government. The government itself, which is only the mode which the people have chosen to execute their will, is equally liable to be abused and perverted before the people can act through it. Witness the present Mexican war, the work of comparatively a few individuals using the standing government as their tool; for, in the outset, the people would not have consented to this measure. . . .

But, to speak practically and as a citizen, unlike those who call themselves no-government men, I ask for, not at once no government, but *at once* a

① Targeted Passage
13 the present Mexican war: the 1846–1848 war between Mexico and the United States.

DIFFERENTIATED INSTRUCTION

FOR STRUGGLING READERS

① Targeted Passage [Lines 5–16]

In this passage, Thoreau explains that he responding to perceived government abuse.

• To what does Thoreau compare a government? Why? (lines 7–10)

• What problems can government face? (lines 11–13)

• How does Thoreau believe most people feel about the war? (lines 14–16)

Analyze Visuals

Possible answer: By showing just the shadows, the photographer equalizes the people in this crowd. They are no longer individuals, distinguished by wealth, race, age, or gender; instead, they are human presences in a unified force that works together to convey its ideas or take action.

BACKGROUND

The Mexican War As part of his 1844 reelection bid, President John Tyler pushed for the annexation of Texas, then an independent nation. Although Tyler lost the election, the issue consolidated opposing views: southerners favored annexing Texas as a slave state, whereas northerners feared that doing so would give slave states too much power in Congress. The annexation succeeded under Tyler's successor, James K. Polk, who inherited a boundary dispute with Mexico. Polk offered to buy the disputed area from Mexico, along with what is now New Mexico and California. When Mexico refused, war broke out. The hostilities lasted much longer than the quick series of battles that Polk had hoped for, but it finally ended with the Treaty of Guadalupe Hidalgo in 1848, in which the Rio Grande border was finalized and Mexico ceded New Mexico and California to the United States for $15 million.

FOR ADVANCED LEARNERS/AP

Synthesize After students have read the first paragraph of Thoreau's essay and listened to the **BACKGROUND** information on the war with Mexico, pose these questions:

- How might Tyler and Polk have responded to Thoreau's ideas in the first paragraph?

- How might a proslavery southerner have responded to Thoreau's views?

- How might a settler in the disputed area have responded to Thoreau's statements about the people's role in government?

Have students write a brief paragraph in response to one of these questions. Then invite students to share their paragraphs with the class. Allow time for questions and discussion.

B EVALUATE IDEAS

Possible answer: *Summary: Individual conscience should win out over majority rule. Doing what is right is more important than obeying the law. Accept all thoughtful reactions.*

Extend the Discussion How would a nation's government be affected if its leaders held Thoreau's position?

TIERED DISCUSSION PROMPTS

In lines 38–46, use these prompts to help students explore Thoreau's challenging views about the military:

Restate What does Thoreau mean by an "undue respect for law"? *Possible answer: Thoreau refers to an unquestioning acceptance of a law, just because it is a law.*

Interpret How does Thoreau think that soldiers feel about going to war? *Possible answer: He thinks that soldiers go to war because they respect the law but that they usually don't wish to fight and often don't support the cause for which they fight.*

Synthesize How does Thoreau's view relate to his transcendentalist ideals? *Possible answer: Thoreau says that soldiers march "against their common sense and consciences" (line 41) and that they become "small movable forts and magazines" (lines 44–45). This view reflects the transcendentalist ideal of being an individual and following one's conscience, regardless of the majority view.*

---

better government. Let every man make known what kind of government
20 would command his respect, and that will be one step toward obtaining it.
   After all, the practical reason why, when the power is once in the hands
of the people, a majority are permitted, and for a long period continue,
to rule is not because they are most likely to be in the right, nor because
this seems fairest to the minority, but because they are physically the
strongest. But a government in which the majority rule in all cases cannot
be based on justice, even as far as men understand it. Can there not be a
government in which majorities do not virtually decide right and wrong,
but conscience?—in which majorities decide only those questions to which
the rule of expediency is applicable? Must the citizen ever for a moment,
30 or in the least degree, resign his conscience to the legislator? Why has every
man a conscience, then? I think that we should be men first, and subjects
afterward. It is not desirable to cultivate a respect for the law, so much as for
the right. The only obligation which I have a right to assume is to do at any
time what I think right. It is truly enough said, that a corporation has no
conscience; but a corporation of conscientious men is a corporation *with* a
conscience. Law never made men a whit more just; and, by means of their
respect for it, even the well-disposed are daily made the agents of injustice. **B**
A common and natural result of an undue respect for law is, that you may
see a file of soldiers, colonel, captain, corporal, privates, powder-monkeys,
40 and all, marching in admirable order over hill and dale to the wars, against
their wills, ay, against their common sense and consciences, which makes it
very steep marching indeed, and produces a palpitation of the heart. They
have no doubt that it is a damnable business in which they are concerned;
they are all peaceably inclined. Now, what are they? Men at all? or small
movable forts and magazines, at the service of some unscrupulous man
in power? Visit the Navy-Yard, and behold a marine, such a man as an
American government can make, or such as it can make a man with its black
arts—a mere shadow and reminiscence of humanity, a man laid out alive
and standing, and already, as one may say, buried under arms with funeral
50 accompaniments, though it may be,—

> "Not a drum was heard, not a funeral note,
> As his corse to the rampart we hurried;
> Not a soldier discharged his farewell shot
> O'er the grave where our hero we buried."

   The mass of men serve the state thus, not as men mainly, but as
machines, with their bodies. They are the standing army, and the militia,
jailers, constables, *posse comitatus,* etc. In most cases there is no free exercise
whatever of the judgment or of the moral sense; but they put themselves
on a level with wood and earth and stones; and wooden men can perhaps
60 be manufactured that will serve the purpose as well. Such command no
more respect than men of straw or a lump of dirt. They have the same sort
of worth only as horses and dogs. Yet such as these even are commonly

---

B EVALUATE IDEAS
Reread lines 21–37. What position does Thoreau take in the conflict between majority rule and individual conscience? On your chart, **summarize** and react to his position.

39 powder-monkeys: boys with the job of carrying gunpowder to artillery crews.

45 magazines: places where ammunition is stored.

47–48 black arts: witchcraft.

51–54 "Not a drum ... we buried": opening lines of "The Burial of Sir John Moore After Corunna" by the Irish poet Charles Wolfe (1791–1823).

57 posse comitatus (pŏs'ē kōm-ə-tā'-təs): group of people that can be called on by the sheriff to help enforce the law [*Latin*, literally, the power of the county].

DIFFERENTIATED INSTRUCTION

FOR ADVANCED LEARNERS/AP

Compare and Contrast Views [paired option] Pair students to study Thoreau's description of soldiers (lines 38–62). Have students use a Venn Diagram to compare Thoreau's interpretation of the soldiers' internal views with the government's view of them. Ask students to share their ideas.

BEST PRACTICES TOOLKIT—Transparency
Venn Diagram p. A26

Internal Views — Don't want to fight but feel obligated.

Both — Recognize the obligation of soldiers.

Government Views — Men are machines for fighting.

esteemed good citizens. Others—as most legislators, politicians, lawyers, ministers, and office-holders—serve the state chiefly with their heads; and, as they rarely make any moral distinctions, they are as likely to serve the Devil, without *intending* it, as God. A very few—as heroes, patriots, martyrs, reformers in the great sense, and *men*—serve the state with their consciences also, and so necessarily resist it for the most part; and they are commonly treated as enemies by it. . . . **C**

70 Unjust laws exist: shall we be content to obey them, or shall we endeavor to amend them, and obey them until we have succeeded or shall we **transgress** them at once? Men generally, under such a government as this, think that they ought to wait until they have persuaded the majority to alter them. They think that, if they should resist, the remedy would be worse than the evil. But it is the fault of the government itself that the remedy *is* worse than the evil. *It* makes it worse. Why is it not more apt to anticipate and provide for reform? Why does it not cherish its wise minority? Why does it cry and resist before it is hurt? Why does it not encourage its citizens to be on the alert to point out its faults, and *do* better than it would have them? Why
80 does it always crucify Christ, and excommunicate Copernicus and Luther, and pronounce Washington and Franklin rebels? . . . **D**

If the injustice is part of the necessary friction of the machine of government, let it go, let it go: perchance it will wear smooth, certainly the machine will wear out. If the injustice has a spring, or a pulley, or a rope, or a crank, exclusively for itself, then perhaps you may consider whether the remedy will not be worse than the evil; but if it is of such a nature that it requires you to be the agent of injustice to another, then, I say, break the law. Let your life be a counter-friction to stop the machine. What I have to do is to see, at any rate, that I do not lend myself to the wrong which
90 I condemn. . . .

I meet this American government, or its representative, the state government, directly, and face to face, once a year—no more—in the person of its tax-gatherer; this is the only mode in which a man situated as I am necessarily meets it; and it then says distinctly, Recognize me; and the simplest, most effectual, and, in the present posture of affairs, the indispensablest mode of treating with it on this head, of expressing your little satisfaction with and love for it, is to deny it then. My civil neighbor, the tax-gatherer, is the very man I have to deal with,—for it is, after all, with men and not with parchment that I quarrel,—and he has voluntarily
100 chosen to be an agent of the government. How shall he ever know well what he is and does as an officer of the government, or as a man, until he is obliged to consider whether he shall treat me, his neighbor, for whom he has respect, as a neighbor and well-disposed man, or as a maniac and disturber of the peace, and see if he can get over this obstruction to his neighborliness without a ruder and more **impetuous** thought or speech corresponding with his action. I know this well, that if one thousand, if one hundred, if ten men

C EVALUATE IDEAS
Reread lines 55–69. Which way of serving the state does Thoreau approve of? Which ways does he condemn? Decide whether you agree with his assessment of soldiers and others who serve.

transgress (trăns-grĕs′) *v.* to violate a command or law

80 **Copernicus** (kō-pûr′nə-kəs) **and Luther:** Radicals in their time, Polish astronomer Nicolaus Copernicus theorized that the sun rather than the earth was the center of our planetary system; German theologian Martin Luther was a leader in the Protestant Reformation.

D GRAMMAR AND STYLE
In lines 70–81, Thoreau adds emphasis and emotion to his writing by asking **rhetorical questions**—questions that do not require a reply because the writer assumes the answers are obvious.

95 **posture of affairs:** situation.

impetuous (ĭm-pĕch′ōō-əs) *adj.* acting with sudden or rash energy; hasty

READING SKILL · COMMON CORE RI 2

C EVALUATE IDEAS

Possible answer: Thoreau approves of those who serve the state as "heroes, patriots, martyrs, [and] reformers" (lines 66–67) because they serve with their consciences. He condemns those who serve with only their bodies (such as the militia) or only their heads (politicians, for example). Accept all thoughtful opinions.

D GRAMMAR AND STYLE · COMMON CORE L 3a

Ask Rhetorical Questions Point out that the tone of a question differs from that of a declarative sentence. Explain that **rhetorical questions** draw readers into the essay by seeming to require an opinion. Ask students to rewrite the paragraph, changing the rhetorical questions to declarative or exclamatory statements.

REVISIT THE BIG QUESTION

Do you chart your own
COURSE?

Discuss In lines 91–106, in what way is Thoreau's nonconformity made more difficult because it must involve his neighbor, the tax-gatherer? *Possible answer:* Thoreau likes his neighbor and feels respected by him. He does not want to destroy their relationship.

FOR STRUGGLING READERS

Comprehension Support Write these names from lines 80–81 on the board: Christ, Copernicus, Luther, Washington, Franklin. Explain that each of these people was judged harshly by his community but was exonerated later by history. Explain that by linking these people to his own unpopular resistance, Thoreau is suggesting that his behavior, too, will be validated eventually.

FOR ADVANCED LEARNERS/AP

Research and Analyze Have students research to determine why each figure named in lines 80–81 faced condemnation. Ask students to compare and contrast Thoreau with the figures that he cites. Invite volunteers to form a panel discussion in which they share their observations and relate them to this comment in Emerson's "Self-Reliance" : "For nonconformity the world whips you with its displeasure" (page 372, line 31).

VOCABULARY · COMMON CORE L 4

OWN THE WORD

• **transgress:** Have students reread the sentence that contains *transgress* using the context of the sentence to determine the meaning of the word.

• **impetuous:** Have students create a semantic web for the word *impetuous*. Write the word in the center circle along with the definition. Have students add synonyms to complete the map. *Possible answer:* brash, foolhardy, impulsive

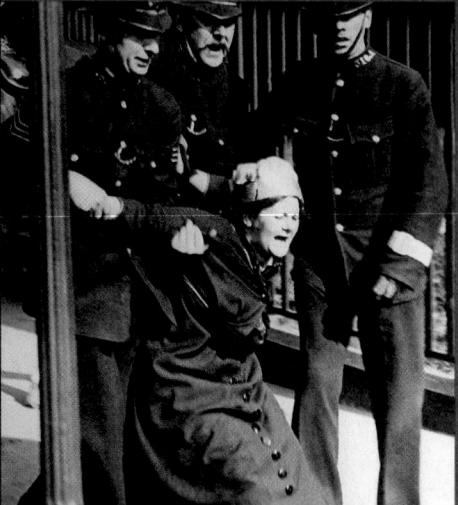

Left: London police arresting a suffragist, 1914; *center:* Gandhi marching to the sea, in defiance of the British salt monopoly

Analyze Visuals

Activity Invite comments about these historical images; then focus on the image of Mohandas K. Gandhi, whose writing students will sample on pages 400–401. Explain that in 1930, Indians were forbidden to take salt from the sea because of Britain's colonial monopoly on salt production. In protest, Gandhi led a 240-mile march to gather salt from the sea. He and his followers were arrested, but their act drew worldwide attention and condemnation of the British. Ask students which of Thoreau's ideas Gandhi would have agreed with. *Possible answer: Gandhi would have agreed with Thoreau's idea of a "peaceable revolution" (line 135).*

TIERED DISCUSSION PROMPTS

In lines 106–113, use these prompts to help students grasp Thoreau's position on the use of civil disobedience to protest slavery:

Restate What is Thoreau's position on the value of being jailed for disobeying a law? *Possible answer: He believes that this method of protest is valuable.*

Interpret What does Thoreau mean by saying that the jailing of "one honest man" would bring "the abolition of slavery in America"? *Possible answer: Thoreau means that one man's action would inspire others to protest, beginning the process of change.*

Evaluate Do you agree with Thoreau's statement that "Reform keeps many scores of newspapers in its service, but not one man" (lines 112–113)? Why or why not? *Possible answers: Yes, because many people will read about problems but not do anything about them. No, because he himself has been arrested for his beliefs and thus disproves his point.*

whom I could name,—if ten *honest* men only,—ay, if *one* honest man, in this State of Massachusetts, *ceasing to hold slaves,* were actually to withdraw from this copartnership, and be locked up in the county jail therefor, it
110 would be the abolition of slavery in America. For it matters not how small the beginning may seem to be: what is once well done is done forever. But we love better to talk about it: that we say is our mission. Reform keeps many scores of newspapers in its service, but not one man. . . .

Under a government which imprisons any unjustly, the true place for a just man is also a prison. The proper place today, the only place which Massachusetts has provided for her freer and less desponding spirits, is in her prisons, to be put out and locked out of the State by her own act, as they have already put themselves out by their principles. It is there that the fugitive slave, and the Mexican prisoner on parole, and the Indian come to
120 plead the wrongs of his race should find them; on that separate, but more free and honorable ground, where the State places those who are not *with* her, but *against* her,—the only house in a slave State in which a free man can abide with honor. If any think that their influence would be lost there, and their voices no longer afflict the ear of the State, that they would not be as an enemy within its walls, they do not know by how much truth is stronger than error, nor how much more eloquently and effectively he can combat injustice who has experienced a little in his own person. Cast your whole vote, not a strip of paper merely, but your whole influence. A minority is powerless while it conforms to the majority; it is not even a minority then;
130 but it is irresistible when it clogs by its whole weight. If the alternative is to keep all just men in prison, or give up war and slavery, the State will not hesitate which to choose. If a thousand men were not to pay their tax bills

394 UNIT 2: AMERICAN ROMANTICISM

DIFFERENTIATED INSTRUCTION

FOR ENGLISH LANGUAGE LEARNERS

Language: Pronoun Referents Explain that pronoun referents are the nouns or pronouns to which pronouns refer. Point out that sometimes a pronoun referent is unstated, making it difficult to tell what the author means. In addition, unusual pronouns may be used to replace nouns, such as *her* for the name of a state or ship. Help students identify the antecedent of these pronouns:

• *her* (line 116), "the state of Massachusetts"

• *any* (line 123), "protesters"

• *one* (line 136), "a tax-gatherer"

FOR ENGLISH LANGUAGE LEARNERS

Language Coach COMMON CORE RI 4

Connotation *Possible answer: Abiding with honor would allow an individual to endure unpleasant conditions.* Lead the class in a discussion about other possible phrases, for which the listed connotations of *abide* would be appropriate.

Left: Dr. Martin Luther King Jr., jailed for civil disobedience; *center:* Vietnam war protester burns his military draft card; *right:* Beijing man stands in front of tanks during the 1989 Tiananmen Square uprising.

this year, that would not be a violent and bloody measure, as it would be to pay them, and enable the State to commit violence and shed innocent blood. This is, in fact, the definition of a peaceable revolution, if any such is possible. If the tax-gatherer, or any other public officer, asks me, as one has done, "But what shall I do?" my answer is, "If you really wish to do anything, resign your office." When the subject has refused allegiance, and the officer has resigned his office, then the revolution is accomplished. But
140 even suppose blood should flow. Is there not a sort of blood shed when the conscience is wounded? Through this wound a man's real manhood and immortality flow out, and he bleeds to an everlasting death. I see this blood flowing now. . . . **E**

I have paid no poll-tax for six years. I was put into a jail once on this account, for one night; and, as I stood considering the walls of solid stone, two or three feet thick, the door of wood and iron, a foot thick, and the iron grating which strained the light, I could not help being struck with the foolishness of that institution which treated me as if I were mere flesh and blood and bones, to be locked up. I wondered that it should have concluded
150 at length that this was the best use it could put me to, and had never thought to avail itself of my services in some way. I saw that, if there was a wall of stone between me and my townsmen, there was a still more difficult one to climb or break through before they could get to be as free as I was.
I did not for a moment feel confined, and the walls seemed a great waste of stone and mortar. I felt as if I alone of all my townsmen had paid my tax. They plainly did not know how to treat me, but behaved like persons who are underbred. In every threat and in every compliment there was a blunder; for they thought that my chief desire was to stand the other side of

E EVALUATE IDEAS
Thoreau holds an **assumption**—an opinion or belief that is taken for granted—that civil disobedience is the only sensible and moral course to take. Reread lines 114–143. How convincing are the reasons Thoreau gives in support of his belief?

② **Targeted Passage**

157 **underbred:** ill-mannered.

CIVIL DISOBEDIENCE **395**

BACKGROUND

Poll Taxes The poll tax that Thoreau discusses was imposed upon every adult, usually as a requirement for voting. As a result, adults who could not afford to pay the tax—in Thoreau's time, poor white males—were unable to vote. Using the poll tax as a voting requirement was abolished nationwide by the 24th Amendment (1964) and by a Supreme Court ruling (1966), thus granting the vote to millions of Americans living in poverty.

READING SKILL | COMMON CORE RI 2

E **EVALUATE IDEAS**

Possible answer: *Thoreau is convincing when he argues that truth holds power and that people should not fear to withhold support from an unjust government. He is less convincing when he argues that a thousand people should go to prison to protest the government, for this action is not practical for many.*

REVISIT THE BIG QUESTION

Do you chart your own **COURSE?**

Discuss Direct students to lines 144–156. Although Thoreau demonstrated his nonconformity by not paying his poll tax for six years, why does the night in jail make him feel as if he has been the only one to pay the tax? *Possible answer:* *By spending a night in jail, Thoreau feels that he has paid his tax by putting his ideas into practice. He has given the government what he has to give: his conviction to his ideals. Others have given their money but nothing of themselves.*

FOR STRUGGLING READERS

② **Targeted Passage** [Lines 144–153]

In this passage, Thoreau explains the result of his protest of the poll tax.

- For how long has Thoreau not paid his poll tax, and how long did he stay in jail? (lines 144–145)
- During that imprisonment, whom did he think was more free: himself, or the townspeople outside the jail? (lines 151–153)

- How did he feel about being confined? (lines 147–151)

FOR ADVANCED LEARNERS/AP

Research and Evaluate [small-group option] Remind students that the ideas in "Civil Disobedience" have inspired protests for more than 100 years. Draw attention to the photographs on these two pages. Have students choose two photographs, besides that of Gandhi, to research, using these search terms: *suffrage movement, Martin Luther King, Jr,.* or

civil rights movement, Vietnam draft resistance, and *Tiananmen Square uprising.* Instruct students to focus their research on answering this question: How is the protester using Thoreau's model to demonstrate his or her beliefs? Invite students to share their findings and conclusions with the class.

F ESSAY

Possible answer: Thoreau's anecdote illustrates how a jailed person with a clear conscience is freer than someone who blindly serves an unjust system (lines 151–156).

G *Model the Skill:* ESSAY

Possible answer: Thoreau's example of the acorn and the chestnut conveys the message that he will not give in to the government's demands. Instead, he will live and die according to his own laws and his own nature.

Help students understand Thoreau's use of personification in these lines by asking them why an acorn and a chestnut respond differently to their surroundings. Explain that Thoreau believes that each person is as different from the next as an acorn is from a chestnut.

SELECTION WRAP–UP

READ WITH A PURPOSE Now that students have read the selections, ask them to describe Thoreau's views of human society. What advice does Thoreau offer people? *Possible answers: People are too concerned with conformity and living up to society's expectations. They should instead seek truth within themselves, pursue their dreams, live life simply and deliberately, and oppose government injustice.*

⭐ **CRITIQUE** What would society be like if everyone followed Thoreau's advice? Give examples.

INDEPENDENT READING

Students interested in individuals standing up to governmental injustice may wish to read Thomas Paine's *Common Sense*.

---

that stone wall. I could not but smile to see how industriously they locked
160 the door on my meditations, which followed them out again without let or
hindrance, and *they* were really all that was dangerous. As they could not
reach me, they had resolved to punish my body; just as boys, if they cannot
come at some person against whom they have a spite, will abuse his dog. I
saw that the State was half-witted, that it was timid as a lone woman with
her silver spoons, and that it did not know its friends from its foes, and
I lost all my remaining respect for it, and pitied it. **F**

Thus the State never intentionally confronts a man's sense, intellectual
or moral, but only his body, his senses. It is not armed with superior wit or
honesty, but with superior physical strength. I was not born to be forced.
170 I will breathe after my own fashion. Let us see who is the strongest. What
force has a multitude? They only can force me who obey a higher law than I.
They force me to become like themselves. I do not hear of *men* being *forced*
to live this way or that by masses of men. What sort of life were that to live?
When I meet a government which says to me, "Your money or your life,"
why should I be in haste to give it my money? It may be in a great strait, and
not know what to do: I cannot help that. It must help itself; do as I do. It is
not worth the while to snivel about it. I am not responsible for the successful
working of the machinery of society. I am not the son of the engineer. I
perceive that, when an acorn and a chestnut fall side by side, the one does
180 not remain inert to make way for the other, but both obey their own laws,
and spring and grow and flourish as best they can, till one, perchance,
overshadows and destroys the other. If a plant cannot live according to its
nature, it dies; and so a man. ❧ **G**

160–161 without let or hindrance: without encountering obstacles.

 **Targeted Passage**

F ESSAY
Why do you think Thoreau includes this personal **anecdote** about his night in jail? Consider why he feels free as he stands in his cell, contemplating his own imprisonment.

G ESSAY
What **message** does Thoreau convey through his example of the acorn and the chestnut?

DIFFERENTIATED INSTRUCTION

FOR STRUGGLING READERS

Targeted Passage [Lines 159–166]

In this passage, Thoreau explains his attitude as a prisoner of conscience.

- What part of Thoreau did the locked doors of the jail confine? (lines 161–162)
- To whom does Thoreau compare the State? (lines 163–165)
- By the end of his stay, what is Thoreau's opinion of the State? Why? (lines 165–166)

FOR ENGLISH LANGUAGE LEARNERS

Vocabulary Support Explain that Thoreau contrasts his body and his mind to emphasize his sense of intellectual freedom in jail. To help students grasp Thoreau's point, clarify these contrasting elements:

- "me" vs. "my body" (line 162)
- "intellectual" vs. "body" (lines 167–168)
- "wit or honesty" vs. "physical strength" (lines 168–169)

Comprehension

1. **Recall** According to Thoreau, what should be respected more than the law?

2. **Summarize** What should a citizen do about an unjust law?

3. **Clarify** List the three ways Thoreau says a citizen may serve the state. With which did Thoreau agree?

Text Analysis

4. **Make Judgments** Consider the **historical context** of Thoreau's essays. Would it be easier to practice nonconformity today? Consider the contemporary consequences of refusing to pay a tax ("Civil Disobedience," lines 144–166) or of celebrating or "cultivating" poverty (*Walden*, lines 198–230).

● 5. **Analyze Essays** Even when they discuss serious or even lofty ideas, essays are often loosely structured and highly personal. **Skim** *Walden* and "Civil Disobedience," noting passages in which Thoreau refers to himself. Identify his personal feelings and instances when he shares his own experiences, such as the night he spent in jail. How do these passages influence your acceptance of his arguments? Explain, citing specific lines from both essays.

6. **Interpret Paradox** A **paradox** seems to contradict itself but suggests an important truth. Reexamine both selections and record in a chart the examples of paradox you find. Then explain what truth or idea each paradox illustrates.

Paradox	Explanation
"I did not wish to live what was not life...." (*Walden*, lines 26–27)	

● 7. **Evaluate Ideas** Ralph Waldo Emerson said of Thoreau, "No truer American ever lived." Review the political ideas you summarized as you read "Civil Disobedience." Do you consider Thoreau's arguments to be those of a patriot or those of a traitor? In your response, consider Thoreau's points on the necessity of government, how unjust laws may be changed, and majority rule.

Text Criticism

8. **Critical Interpretations** Critic Andrew Delbanco asserts that Thoreau is, "despite all the barricades he erected around himself, an irresistible writer; to read him is to feel wrenched away from the customary world and delivered into a place we fear as much as we need." What does it mean when we say we both need and fear the world Thoreau creates? Explain your response.

Do you chart your own **COURSE?**

The result of Thoreau's civil disobedience was a night spent in jail. In what ways do people today react to nonconformity? How do you act towards those who refuse to conform?

life than to be confused by too much information.

7. ■ **COMMON CORE FOCUS** **Evaluate Ideas** Students' answers should demonstrate an understanding of Thoreau's positions: (1) that government should be smaller and less invasive; (2) that unjust laws will be changed if enough people protest them; and (3) that the majority is not always correct.

8. Delbanco means that we need Thoreau to remind us that a simple, unmaterialistic life is possible, as is a life dedicated to

fighting for one's convictions; but that we fear Thoreau because we do not want to give up our possessions or go to jail. Accept all thoughtful responses.

Do you chart your own **COURSE?**
Students might cite examples of ridicule, shunning, arrests, and lawsuits. Student reactions will vary.

For preliminary support of post-reading questions, use these copy masters:

R **RESOURCE MANAGER**—Copy Masters
Reading Check p. 124
Essay p. 117
Question Support pp. 125–126

Additional selection questions are provided for teachers on page 109.

ANSWERS COMMON CORE RI 2, RI 5, RI 6, RI 9

1. *one's conscience or sense of right and wrong*

2. *disobey it*

3. *Citizens can serve with their bodies, as soldiers, jailers, and constables do; with their heads, as legislators and politicians do; or with their consciences, as heroes, patriots, and reformers do. Thoreau preferred serving with the conscience.*

Possible answers:

4. *Students' responses should consider each example and explain how they think Thoreau's actions would be received today.*

5. ● **COMMON CORE FOCUS** **Analyze Essay** *The excerpts from* Walden *are full of references to the author's life, such as when Thoreau gives his views of correspondence and the news (lines 76–86). Such references in "Civil Disobedience" include lines 91–106, where Thoreau describes his conflict between his respect for his tax-gatherer neighbor and his disrespect for the state; and lines 144–166, in which he describes how acting on his principles by protesting the poll tax landed him in jail. These personal experiences lend credibility to Thoreau's argument by revealing that he lives according to the philosophy that he preaches. However, the fact that he spent only one night in jail weakens his sacrifice and suggests a superior attitude.*

6. *Paradox: "'That government is best which governs least.'" ("Civil Disobedience," line 1) Explanation: A government that stays out of its citizens' personal actions is the strongest. Paradox: "We are determined to be starved before we are hungry." (Walden, lines 53–54) Explanation: People worry too much, even though they have plenty. Paradox: "I have always been regretting that I was not as wise as the day I was born." (Walden, lines 96–97) Explanation: Sometimes it is better to know less about*

ANSWERS

Vocabulary in Context

▲ VOCABULARY PRACTICE

1. *false*	5. *true*
2. *false*	6. *false*
3. *true*	7. *false*
4. *true*	8. *true*

R RESOURCE MANAGER—Copy Master
Vocabulary Practice p. 122

ACADEMIC VOCABULARY IN WRITING

Students should provide specific details about how they have lived out a particular belief. Their paragraphs should include at least three academic vocabulary words.

VOCABULARY STRATEGY: THE PREFIXES *ab-* AND *per-*

COMMON CORE **L 4b, L 6**

- Model the strategy, using these examples: *aboriginal, abnormal, abstain, peroxide, permissive, persistent.* Point out that the root word may not stand on its own, as a base word does.

- Encourage students to use a dictionary to define the Latin roots.

Possible answers:

1. *causing harm*
2. *to refrain from*
3. *decisive, absolute*
4. *careful, restrictive*
5. *indifferent, without concern; hidden (oneself) away*

R RESOURCE MANAGER—Copy Master
Vocabulary Strategy p. 123

Interactive Vocabulary

THINKcentral

Keywords direct students to a **WordSharp** tutorial on **thinkcentral.com** or to other types of vocabulary practice and review.

Vocabulary in Context

▲ VOCABULARY PRACTICE

Decide whether each statement is true or false.

1. If an odor were to **pervade** a room, it would be escaping through a chimney.
2. A person who is experiencing **perturbation** usually feels relaxed and confident.
3. An **impetuous** act is one that you do on the spur of the moment.
4. If you have some **misgiving** about attending a party, you should consider not going.
5. A **congenial** person usually gets along with others.
6. If you act **deliberately,** you act with haste and lack of concern.
7. **Abject** sorrow is sadness that will pass quickly.
8. If you **transgress** a law, you break it.

WORD LIST

abject
congenial
deliberately
impetuous
misgiving
perturbation
pervade
transgress

ACADEMIC VOCABULARY IN WRITING

• construct	• expand	• indicate	• reinforce	• role

Thoreau **expanded** on Emerson's ideas by living them out—even to the point of being jailed for civil disobedience. In a short paragraph, discuss how you have **reinforced** a belief in your life. Use at least three Academic Vocabulary words in your writing.

VOCABULARY STRATEGY: THE PREFIXES *ab-* AND *per-*

Though the prefixes *ab-* and *per-* are sometimes combined with recognizable base words, often they are attached to Latin roots, as in the vocabulary words *abject* and *pervade.* When you think you recognize the prefix *ab-* or *per-* in a word, look for context clues that support your guess. Then use the meaning of the prefix—and of the root, if you know it—to decipher the word's definition.

PRACTICE The prefix *ab-* or *per-* occurs in each boldfaced word below. Use context clues and root and prefix meanings—or a dictionary, if necessary—to define each word.

1. That man's **pernicious** lies have totally destroyed his son's reputation.
2. To get out of debt, I have decided to **abjure** going to the mall for three months.
3. The recruits immediately obeyed the officer's **peremptory** command.
4. **Abstemious** eating habits can help a person lose weight.
5. His **perfunctory** effort to learn who had **absconded** with the money was unsuccessful.

COMMON CORE

L 4b Identify and use patterns of word changes that indicate different meanings or parts of speech. **L 6** Acquire and use academic words and phrases.

Prefix	Meaning
ab-	"away"; "away from"
per-	"through"; "thoroughly, very"

Interactive Vocabulary
THINKcentral
Go to **thinkcentral.com.**
KEYWORD: HML11-398

DIFFERENTIATED INSTRUCTION

FOR ENGLISH LANGUAGE LEARNERS

Task Support: Vocabulary Practice To increase understanding of the *Word List,* work through the **Vocabulary Practice** with students, pointing out context clues that suggest the actual meaning of each boldfaced word. Have students rewrite each false statement so that it uses the vocabulary word correctly.

FOR ADVANCED LEARNERS/AP

Vocabulary in Context To increase students' vocabulary and knowledge of affixes and word families, ask students to think of one additional form of each word in the **Word List,** such as *impetuosity* or *transgression.* Using the **Vocabulary Practice** as a model, have students write sentences for the new words. Ask pairs to exchange their sentences and decide if each new statement is true or false.

Language

◆ **GRAMMAR AND STYLE:** Ask Rhetorical Questions

Review the **Grammar and Style** note on page 393. Thoreau asks a number of thought-provoking questions in "Civil Disobedience." But he's not expecting any answers. The questions he asks are **rhetorical questions;** they don't require a reply. Writers often use these types of **interrogative sentences** to drive home a point or evoke an emotional response. Here is an example from the text:

> But even suppose blood should flow. *Is there not a sort of blood shed when the conscience is wounded?* (lines 139–141)

Read this passage aloud. Consider how it would sound if it lacked a rhetorical question—if the second sentence read, "A sort of blood flows when the conscience is wounded." Do you think the rhetorical question makes Thoreau's argument more compelling?

PRACTICE Rewrite the following paragraph, changing some sentences to rhetorical questions.

> Thoreau suggests that if citizens disagree with their government's actions, they should stop paying taxes. However, if a large number of Americans refused to pay their taxes this year, the results would be disastrous. Public schools would collapse, salaries for police officers and firefighters would go unpaid, and services from public transportation to public hospitals would crumble. I do not see how a good citizen could allow this to happen. I do not see the honor in such an act.

READING-WRITING CONNECTION

Expand your understanding of Thoreau's writing by responding to this prompt. Then, use the **revising tips** to improve your letter.

WRITING PROMPT	**REVISING TIPS**
WRITE A LETTER TO THE EDITOR Thoreau proposed radical ideas in "Civil Disobedience." Some people found them thrilling; others found them threatening. Choose one of the ideas proposed in "Civil Disobedience." Write a **three-paragraph letter** to the editor of a local newspaper in which you explain the idea and argue for or against implementing it. Include at least two rhetorical questions in your letter.	• Check to make sure your letter includes a strong argument. • Include at least three reasons that support your argument. • Keep the tone of your letter polite. • End the letter with a request for action.

Interactive Revision — THINK central
Go to **thinkcentral.com.**
KEYWORD: HML11-399

COMMON CORE

L 3a Apply an understanding of syntax to the study of complex texts when reading. **W 1a–b** Introduce precise, knowledgeable claims; develop claims and counterclaims, supplying the most relevant evidence for each. **W 1d–e** Establish and maintain a formal style and objective tone; provide a concluding statement that follows from the argument presented.

Language

 COMMON CORE **L 3a, W 1a–b, W 1d–e**

◆ **GRAMMAR AND STYLE**

Writers often use **rhetorical questions** to ask readers to consider an issue in depth. In lines 30–31 of "Civil Disobedience," Thoreau asks, "Why has every man a conscience, then?" Thoreau expects readers to answer it mentally. Urge students to use this technique in their letters. ***Possible answer:*** *Thoreau suggests that if citizens disagree with their government's actions, they should stop paying taxes. However, if Americans refused to pay their taxes this year, what would the results be? Public schools would collapse, salaries for police officers and firefighters would go unpaid, and services would crumble. What good citizen would allow this to happen? Where is the honor in such an act?*

R **RESOURCE MANAGER—Copy Master**
Ask Rhetorical Questions p. 127

READING-WRITING CONNECTION
Letters to the editor are written in formal language. Convincing letters present a clear opinion, support it with a well-reasoned argument, and maintain a respectful tone.

Writing Online THINK central

The following tools are available online at **thinkcentral.com** and on **WriteSmart CD-ROM:**
• **Interactive Graphic Organizers**
• **Interactive Student Models**
• **Interactive Revision Lessons**
For additional grammar instruction, see **GrammarNotes** on **thinkcentral.com.**

Assess and Reteach

Assess

DIAGNOSTIC AND SELECTION TESTS

Selection Tests A, B/C pp. 125–128

Interactive Selection Test on thinkcentral.com

Reteach

Level Up Online Tutorials on thinkcentral.com

FOR STRUGGLING WRITERS

Task Support Remind students that a letter to the editor is persuasive writing. Discuss these techniques, which can strengthen this type of persuasive appeal:

• Use direct, strong language—that is, language that is clear and vivid but that usually does not have over-emotional connotations.

• Consider omitting expressions such as "I think," "It seems to me," or "In my opinion";

readers assume that you are presenting and defending a viewpoint.

• Explain each point of your argument in a single paragraph. Carefully choose your support for each point; do not burden readers with unrelated details.

• Write a strong conclusion that restates your view and includes a call to action or other specific response from readers.

BACKGROUND

Britain's Colonial Rule of India Britain began its direct rule of India in 1858, developing the nation's resources for its own economic benefit. The British colonial leaders were a minority in India but they held the nation's ruling positions. As upper-class Indians became educated in Britain, they began a nationalist movement that sought to unify India's many diverse ethnicities in opposing colonial power. Their efforts toward self-rule found a leader in Mohandas Gandhi and his ideas about peaceful resistance.

On *Civil Disobedience*

Mohandas K. Gandhi

BACKGROUND Mohandas K. Gandhi (1869–1948), called Mahatma ("Great Soul"), helped free India of British rule. As a student, he greatly admired Thoreau's essay "Civil Disobedience." Thoreau's ideas helped shape Gandhi's key principle—*satyagraha* (sə-tyä′grə-hə), or "truth-force." In the following excerpt from a 1916 speech, Gandhi describes this powerful weapon for fighting oppression.

July 27, 1916

There are two ways of countering injustice. One way is to smash the head of the man who perpetrates injustice and to get your own head smashed in the process. All strong people in the world adopt this course. Everywhere wars are fought and millions of people are killed. The consequence is not the progress of a nation but its decline. . . . No country has ever become, or will ever become, happy through victory in war. A nation does not rise that way, it only falls further. In fact, what comes to it is defeat, not victory. And if, perchance, either our act or our purpose was ill-conceived, it brings disaster to both belligerents.[1]

10 But through the other method of combating injustice, we alone suffer the consequences of our mistakes, and the other side is wholly spared. This other method is *satyagraha*.[2] One who resorts to it does not have to break another's head; he may merely have his own head broken. He has to be prepared to die himself, suffering all the pain. In opposing the atrocious laws of the Government of South Africa,[3] it was this method that we adopted. We made it clear to the said Government that we would never bow to its outrageous laws. No clapping is possible without two hands to do it, and no quarrel without two persons to make it. Similarly, no State is possible without two entities, the rulers and the ruled. You are our sovereign, our Government, only so long as we consider ourselves your subjects. When we are not subjects, you are not the 20 sovereign either. So long as it is your endeavour to control us with justice and love, we will let you to do so. But if you wish to strike at us from behind, we cannot permit it. Whatever you do in other matters, you will have to ask our opinion about the laws that concern us. If you make laws to keep us suppressed in a wrongful manner and without taking us into confidence, these laws will merely adorn the statute-books. We will never obey them. Award us for it what punishment you like, we will put up with it. Send us to prison and we will live there as in a paradise. Ask us to mount the

---

1. **belligerents:** participants in a war.
2. **satyagraha** (sə-tyä′grə-hə) *Sanskrit:* insistence on truth. Gandhi used this term to describe his policy of seeking reform by means of nonviolent resistance.
3. **atrocious laws . . . South Africa:** Gandhi led the Indian community in opposition to racial discrimination in South Africa, where he lived for several years.

Gandhi in 1948, after ending a six-day hunger strike for peace

scaffold[4] and we will do so laughing. Shower what sufferings you like upon us, we will
calmly endure all and not hurt a hair of your body. We will gladly die and will not so
30 much as touch you. But so long as there is yet life in these our bones, we will never
comply with your arbitrary laws. ॐ

---

4. **mount the scaffold:** ascend the platform on which one is executed by hanging.

Text Analysis

1. **Summarize** What two ways of countering injustice does Gandhi describe?
Explain which approach Gandhi adopted.

2. **Interpret** Reread lines 16–20. What point is Gandhi making about the
relationship between a government and its citizens?

3. **Compare Texts** Henry David Thoreau's ideas influenced many 20th-century
reformers, including Gandhi. What connections do you see between the
views Thoreau presents in *Walden* and "Civil Disobedience" and Gandhi's
beliefs? Cite evidence from both texts to support your answer.

THEMES ACROSS CULTURES   **401**

About the Art

About the Art Even after British colonial rule
ended, India's troubles were not over. Religious and cultural differences divided India's
people and weakened the newly independent
nation's young government. To protest the
riots in Delhi, and to force opposing factions to
cooperate, Gandhi began a hunger strike that
lasted 122 hours. This picture was taken after
he decided to end the fast with the pledge of
cooperation among the leaders of the Muslim,
Hindu, and Sikh communities. This method
was typical of his peaceful means of protest.

ANSWERS   COMMON CORE RI 2

Possible answers:

1. *Gandhi describes countering injustice by
smashing the heads of the men who perpetrate injustice or through satyagraha—
what Ghandi called nonviolent resistance.
Gandhi adopted satyagraha.*

2. *By the image of two hands clapping,
Gandhi shows how a state is not possible
if its two parts—the rulers and the ruled—
do not exist in harmony. He further makes
the point that a government in fact does
not exist without people to govern.*

3. *Both Gandhi and Thoreau say that they are
willing to suffer the consequences of their
protest. In "Civil Disobedience," Thoreau
says, "Let your life be a counter-friction to
stop the machine" (line 88). Gandhi says,
"He has to be prepared to die himself, suffering all the pain" (lines 13–14). Both argue
that the government cannot rule without
the consent of the governed. Thoreau
writes, "When the subject has refused allegiance, and the officer has resigned his
office, then the revolution is accomplished"
("Civil Disobedience," lines 138–139). Gandhi
writes, "no State is possible without two entities, the rulers and the ruled" (lines 17–18).*

FOR ADVANCED LEARNERS/AP

Evaluate Ideas Tell students that Gandhi was
educated as a lawyer and that he had spent
many years in peaceful resistance of South
Africa's government before returning to his
homeland of India. He used hunger strikes,
protest marches, and boycotts as methods of
peaceful resistance.

Organize students into small groups to read
the speech aloud and identify its elements
of persuasive writing. Encourage students
to consider the structure of Gandhi's speech,
looking for such features as his use of facts,
personal experience, explanation of theory,
and call to action. Urge discussion of the
speech's persuasiveness.

Focus and Motivate

 COMMON CORE FOCUS

RI 2 Determine two or more central ideas of a text and analyze their development, including how they interact and build on one another. **RI 5** Analyze the effectiveness of the structure. **RI 6** Determine an author's point of view, analyzing how style and content contribute to the persuasiveness of the text. **RI 8** Evaluate purposes and arguments in works of public advocacy. **L 1a** Apply the understanding that usage can change over time.

ABOUT THE AUTHOR

Margaret Fuller After students have read about Fuller, explain that although she had the privilege of a good education, her life was not without its problems. By the age of 20, she was plagued by migraine headaches nearly every day. Those who met her complimented her intelligence but not always her personality or behavior. In one account, Emerson expressed his annoyance at her nasal voice and habit of constantly blinking her eyes. Others complained that she was conceited, having too high an opinion of herself.

COMMON CORE

RI 2 Determine two or more central ideas of a text and analyze their development, including how they interact and build on one another. **RI 5** Analyze the effectiveness of the structure. **RI 6** Determine an author's point of view, analyzing how style and content contribute to the persuasiveness of the text. **RI 8** Evaluate purposes and arguments in works of public advocacy. **L 1a** Apply the understanding that usage can change over time.

DID YOU KNOW?

Margaret Fuller . . .

- learned to read when she was 3 years old.
- suffered from nightmares in which she dreamed horses were galloping across her head.
- inspired Edgar Allan Poe to quip, "There are three species: men, women, and Margaret Fuller."

The Transcendentalists

from Woman in the Nineteenth Century

Nonfiction by Margaret Fuller

Meet the Author

Margaret Fuller 1810–1850

Margaret Fuller spent much of her life fighting to make women equal members of society. At a time when a woman's only place was thought to be the small sphere of the home, Fuller became a respected author, a commanding public speaker, a popular journalist, and a key figure in the transcendentalist movement. One literary historian observed that Fuller "transcended virtually every stereotype American women had to endure in the first half of the 19th century."

A Demanding Childhood Sarah Margaret Fuller was born in Cambridgeport, Massachusetts. Her father, a stern and formidable man, had high expectations for her. When she was only 10 years old, he counseled that excelling "in all things should be your constant aim." As a teenager, Fuller typically started her studies at five in the morning and sometimes did not finish until eleven at night.

Coming into Her Own Fuller's father died suddenly when she was 25, and she became a teacher to help support her family. Through a mutual acquaintance, she met Ralph Waldo Emerson, who was much impressed by her intelligence and wit. She began attending meetings of the Transcendental Club. In 1840, Fuller became the editor of *The Dial,* a short-lived but highly influential literary magazine. Fuller solicited poems, essays, and fiction from leading transcendentalists and wrote much of the content herself.

An Influential Voice In 1844, Fuller started writing the literary column for the *New York Tribune,* perhaps the most widely read newspaper of its day. In addition to reviewing literary works, she addressed social issues such as poverty and slavery. In 1845, Fuller published *Woman in the Nineteenth Century,* a revolutionary feminist work that paid tribute to women's intellectual and creative abilities and declared that women must be accepted as equal to men. The first edition sold out in two weeks.

Romance and Tragedy In 1846, the *New York Tribune* sent Fuller to cover civil unrest in Europe. She settled in Rome, where she fell in love with and married Italian aristocrat Giovanni Angelo Ossoli. When revolution broke out in Rome in 1848, Fuller supported the cause by volunteering at a hospital while her husband fought for the republic. The revolution failed, and Fuller, Ossoli, and their young son sailed to the United States in 1850. With New York City almost in sight, their ship hit a sandbar and sank. Fuller, Ossoli, and their son drowned.

Author Online

THINK central

Go to **thinkcentral.com**. KEYWORD: HML11-402

402

Selection Resources

See resources on the **Teacher One Stop DVD-ROM** and on **thinkcentral.com**.

R RESOURCE MANAGER UNIT 2
Plan and Teach, pp. 129–136
Summary, pp. 137–138 †‡*
Text Analysis and Reading
   Skill, pp. 139–140, 141–142†*

DIAGNOSTIC AND SELECTION TESTS
Selection Tests, pp. 129–132

BEST PRACTICES TOOLKIT
New Word Analysis, p. E8

TECHNOLOGY
- Teacher One Stop DVD-ROM
- Student One Stop DVD-ROM
- Audio Anthology CD
- GrammarNotes DVD-ROM
- ExamView Test Generator on the Teacher One Stop

* Resources for Differentiation   † Also in Spanish   ‡ Also in Haitian Creole and Vietnamese

TEXT ANALYSIS: AUTHOR'S PERSPECTIVE

Differences of opinion in politics, art, or any subject are often debated formally and informally in speech and writing. When people engage in a **debate,** they exchange their opinions on an issue, often approaching the discussion with a unique set of ideas and experiences. **Author's perspective** refers to the distinct combination of opinions, values, and beliefs that influence the way a writer looks at a topic. Margaret Fuller takes a unique approach to advocating her views in a debate with a fictional character. As you read, pay close attention to **rhetorical techniques**—the methods an author employs to influence readers and convey ideas. These techniques vary from writer to writer, but they always provide clues to a writer's view. To identify Margaret Fuller's perspective, examine the following rhetorical elements:

- the writer's **tone,** or attitude toward the subject
- **details** the writer chooses to include or emphasize
- rhetorical devices and logical fallacies
- how the writer portrays specific individuals

As you read this excerpt, use these elements to help you analyze the author's perspective.

READING STRATEGY: PARAPHRASE MAIN IDEAS

When you read challenging texts such as this one, it is important to pay careful attention to the author's **main ideas.** One way to make sure that you are understanding these key points is to **paraphrase** them, or restate the information in your own words. A good paraphrase is about the same length as the original text but is written in simpler language. As you read, paraphrase the annotated passages to achieve a better understanding of Fuller's main ideas. Record your work in a chart like the one shown.

Fuller's Main Ideas	My Paraphrases
"I was talking on this subject with Miranda, a woman, who, if any in the world could, might speak without heat or bitterness of the position of her sex."	I spoke about this with Miranda. If any woman can talk about gender issues calmly and rationally, Miranda can.

 Complete the activities in your **Reader/Writer Notebook**.

What does society EXPECT *of us?*

In the 19th century, society expected women to be loving wives, adoring mothers, and expert housekeepers. Women were not expected to be great thinkers; they were to leave the thinking to men. Some women, including Margaret Fuller, rejected these limiting expectations.

SURVEY Does society still have different expectations for men and women? Complete the following survey, marking which jobs you think would most likely be held by men, which would mostly likely be held by women, and which would have roughly equal numbers of each. Then write a paragraph discussing what your results might indicate about how gender influences societal expectations.

Survey: Gender and Jobs

Occupation	Mostly Male	Mostly Female	Equal
1. Kindergarten teacher			
2. Carpenter			
3. Hairstylist			
4. Surgeon			
5. Firefighter			
6. College professor			
7. Personal shopper			
8. Architect			

Teach

What does society EXPECT *of us?*

Point out that during Fuller's time there was an active **debate** on what a woman's role in society should be. And even today we still **debate** this important issue. To help students explore this idea have them complete the *SURVEY* activity.

TEXT ANALYSIS

● Model the Skill: AUTHOR'S PERSPECTIVE

To introduce students to the writer's perspective, write these lines on the board:

> The surgeon was kind in her relations with patients, expert in her understanding of illness, and intolerant of those who doubted her skill.

Point out that these lines reveal the author's perspective. By portraying the individual with positive descriptions, the author shows belief in the woman's abilities.

GUIDED PRACTICE Ask students how the passage would change if the author disapproved of the surgeon.

READING STRATEGY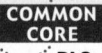

■ Model the Skill: PARAPHRASE MAIN IDEAS

To help students understand the author's main ideas have them paraphrase the first paragraph of the author biography on page 402. Tell students that Margaret Fuller fought for equal rights for women. Though women's occupations were restricted, Fuller had a successful career as a speaker and writer. She did not fit the stereotypes of the early 19th century.

R RESOURCE MANAGER—Copy Master Paraphrase Main Ideas p. 141 (for student use while reading the selection)

DIFFERENTIATED INSTRUCTION

FOR STRUGGLING READERS

Vocabulary Support To support instruction, clarify the meaning of these words:

- *perspective,* "a point of view"
- *annotated,* "marked with explanatory notes"
- *indicate,* "to signify or be a sign of"
- *societal,* "of or relating to society"

Concept Support: Paraphrase Main Ideas

Unlike a paraphrase, a summary restates only main ideas and thus will be shorter than the original. Explain that students may need to use dictionaries to find the meaning of new or unfamiliar words and thesauruses to find simpler alternative words. Urge students to list new words, meanings, and alternatives to reference when they paraphrase.

Practice and Apply

SUMMARY

This excerpt from Fuller's nonfiction writings begins with the fictional Miranda's childhood. An adoring father supports Miranda's education and quick mind. In time, Miranda's confidence impresses her friends and gains her the respect of both men and women. She explains, however, that many men see a smart woman as one with a "manly mind" and says that she wishes minds were not judged by their gender.

READ WITH A PURPOSE

Help students set a purpose for reading. Tell them to read to find out what other people think of Miranda.

READING STRATEGY

COMMON CORE
RI 2

A Model the Skill: PARAPHRASE MAIN IDEAS

Remind students that paraphrasing main ideas is an effective comprehension tool. Work with them to organize their thoughts in the prereading chart introduced on page 403. To prompt students' thinking, discuss the main ideas that must be included in their paraphrase.

Fuller's Main Ideas	My Paraphrases
"Her father was a man who cherished no sentimental reverence for woman, but a firm belief in the equality of the sexes."	Miranda's father believed in the equality of men and women.

Possible answer: *Miranda's father did not have idealized notions about women in general. He believed strongly in gender equality.*

Woman
in the Nineteenth Century
Margaret Fuller

> **BACKGROUND** From 1839 to 1844 in the context of the great debate about the equality of men and women, Fuller led a series of seminars for women called "Conversations." She lectured on topics ranging from ethics to art and then asked her listeners to discuss each topic, thus helping the women to recognize their own intellectual abilities. The sessions led Fuller to write *Woman in the Nineteenth Century*, in which she insists society accept women and men as equals. Here, Fuller presents her views as a debate between herself and the fictional "Miranda," a woman who, like Fuller, had from childhood been encouraged to exercise her mind.

I was talking on this subject with Miranda, a woman, who, if any in the world could, might speak without heat and bitterness of the position of her sex. Her father was a man who cherished no sentimental reverence for woman, but a firm belief in the equality of the sexes. She was his eldest child, and came to him at an age when he needed a companion. From the time she could speak and go alone, he addressed her not as a plaything, but as a living mind. Among the few verses he ever wrote was a copy addressed to this child, when the first locks were cut from her head, and the reverence expressed on this occasion for that cherished head, he never belied. It was to him the temple of immortal intellect. He respected his child, however, too much
10 to be an indulgent parent. He called on her for clear judgment, for courage, for honor and fidelity; in short, for such virtues as he knew. In so far as he possessed the keys to the wonders of this universe, he allowed free use of them to her, and by the incentive of a high expectation, he forbade, as far as possible, that she should let the privilege lie idle.

Thus this child was early led to feel herself a child of the spirit. She took her place easily, not only in the world of organized being, but in the world of mind. A dignified sense of self-dependence was given as all her portion,[1] and she found it a

---
1. **all her portion:** something that she had a right to expect.

Analyze Visuals ▶
In your opinion, what **traits** does the subject of this portrait project? After you've read the selection, revisit your answer. Tell whether you think the woman in the portrait might share any of Miranda's qualities.

A PARAPHRASE MAIN IDEAS
Paraphrase lines 2–4. What were Miranda's father's views on gender equality?

① Targeted Passage

Portrait of Ann Cochrells (1848), David Parr. Oil on canvas, 9″ × 11″. © Christie's Images Ltd.

DIFFERENTIATED INSTRUCTION

FOR ENGLISH LANGUAGE LEARNERS
Vocabulary Support Use New Word Analysis to teach these words: *sex* (line 2), *incentive* (line 13), *bias* (line 37), *attain* (line 40), *energy* (line 98).

 BEST PRACTICES TOOLKIT—Transparency
New Word Analysis p. E8

FOR STRUGGLING READERS
In combination with the *Audio Anthology CD*, use one or more Targeted Passages (pp. 404, 407) to ensure that students focus on key events and concepts. Targeted passages are also good for English learners.

① Targeted Passage [Lines 9–14]

This passage shows that Miranda's father educated her and valued her mind.

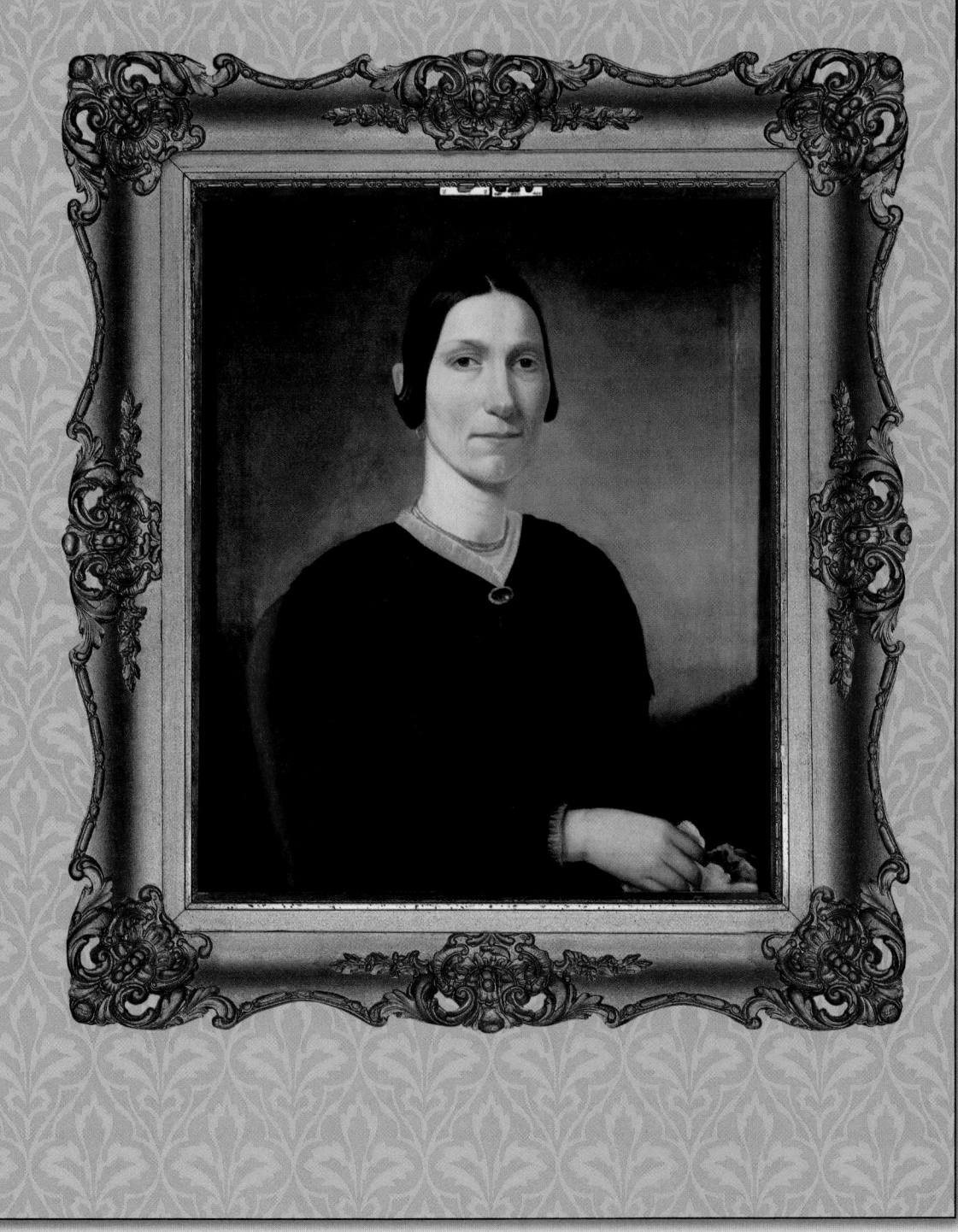

Analyze Visuals

Possible answer: The portrait's subject projects sensibility and modesty with her plain clothing and simple hairstyle. She seems to share Miranda's serious, no-nonsense approach to life.

BACKGROUND

Higher Education for Women In the early 19th century, women had few educational options after elementary school. However, opportunities were beginning to take shape. In 1837, Mount Holyoke College was established in South Hadley, Massachusetts. It was the first of what would be called the Seven Sisters: seven liberal arts colleges that admitted women only. The other six are Vassar (1861), Wellesley (1870), Smith (1871), Bryn Mawr (1885), Barnard (1889), and Radcliffe (1893).

TIERED DISCUSSION PROMPTS

In lines 1–14, use these prompts to address Fuller's ideas about a parent's involvement in a child's education:

Connect How do you feel about Miranda's father? Explain. *Accept all thoughtful responses.*

Analyze What does the anecdote about Miranda's first haircut reveal? **Possible answer:** *The poem shows the father's great love for his daughter.*

Synthesize How does Miranda's childhood reflect what you know about Fuller? **Possible answer:** *Like Fuller, Miranda's father encouraged her studies and did not limit her because of her gender.*

- How did Miranda's father treat his daughter? (lines 9–10)
- What qualities did Miranda's father expect from her? (lines 10–11)
- How did Miranda's father help her learn about the world? (lines 11–14)

FOR ADVANCED LEARNERS/AP

Hypothesize Have students imagine that they could not receive an education after elementary school. Tell them to write a short paper describing what they think their lives would be like. After they finish writing, have students share their ideas in a class discussion.

TEXT ANALYSIS — COMMON CORE RI 6

B AUTHOR'S PERSPECTIVE

Possible answer: Fuller values Miranda's independence, self-sufficiency, originality, relationships with others, and self-respect.

READING STRATEGY — COMMON CORE RI 2

C PARAPHRASE MAIN IDEAS

Possible answer: Paraphrase: Only those people who think it is hopeless and those who try too hard are unable to overcome the restrictions placed on women. Fuller sees Miranda as an example of a woman capable of transcending society's limited view of women.

READING STRATEGY — COMMON CORE RI 5

D ANALYZE STRUCTURE

Possible answer: Fuller is making a hasty generalization. Not all men believed that women should be denied equal opportunity. In fact, Miranda's own father proves that there were men on the other side of this important debate.

TEXT ANALYSIS — COMMON CORE RI 6

E *Model the skill:* AUTHOR'S PERSPECTIVE

Explain that Fuller expects the reader to make inferences about how women should be educated.

Possible answer: Details about being "overloaded with precepts by guardians" (line 50) and how women's minds can be "impeded by doubts" (line 52) contrast Miranda's upbringing with other women's. This contrast helps Fuller advocate an upbringing that encourages self-confidence and intellectual independence.

Extend the Discussion How did most parents raise their daughters in Fuller's era? What were the effects of such upbringing?

sure anchor. Herself securely anchored, her relations with others were established with equal security. She was fortunate in a total absence of those charms which might have drawn to her bewildering flatteries, and in a strong electric nature, which repelled those who did not belong to her; and attracted those who did. With men and women her relations were noble,—affectionate without passion, intellectual without coldness. The world was free to her, and she lived freely in it. Outward adversity came, and inward conflict, but that faith and self-respect had early been awakened which must always lead at last, to an outward serenity and an inward peace.

Of Miranda I had always thought as an example, that the restraints upon the sex were insuperable[2] only to those who think them so, or who noisily strive to break them. She had taken a course of her own, and no man stood in her way. Many of her acts had been unusual, but excited no uproar. Few helped, but none checked her, and the many men, who knew her mind and her life, showed to her confidence, as to a brother, gentleness as to a sister. And not only refined, but very coarse men approved and aided one in whom they saw resolution and clearness of design. Her mind was often the leading one, always effective.

When I talked with her upon these matters, and had said very much what I have written, she smilingly replied: "and yet we must admit that I have been fortunate, and this should not be. My good father's early trust gave the first bias, and the rest followed of course. It is true that I have had less outward aid, in after years, than most women, but that is of little consequence. Religion was early awakened in my soul, a sense that what the soul is capable to ask it must attain, and that, though I might be aided and instructed by others, I must depend on myself as the only constant friend. This self dependence, which was honored in me, is deprecated as a fault in most women. They are taught to learn their rule from without, not to unfold it from within.

"This is the fault of man, who is still vain, and wishes to be more important to woman than, by right, he should be."

"Men have not shown this disposition toward you," I said.

"No! because the position I early was enabled to take was one of self-reliance. And were all women as sure of their wants as I was, the result would be the same. But they are so overloaded with precepts by guardians, who think that nothing is so much to be dreaded for a woman as originality of thought or character, that their minds are impeded by doubts till they lose their chance of fair free proportions. The difficulty is to get them to the point from which they shall naturally develop self-respect, and learn self-help. E

"Once I thought that men would help to forward this state of things more than I do now. I saw so many of them wretched in the connections they had formed in weakness and vanity. They seemed so glad to esteem women whenever they could.

"'The soft arms of affection,' said one of the most discerning spirits, 'will not suffice for me, unless on them I see the steel bracelets of strength.'"

---

2. **insuperable:** incapable of being overcome.

B AUTHOR'S PERSPECTIVE

Consider Fuller's **tone** in lines 15–26. What can you **infer** about the traits Fuller found admirable?

C PARAPHRASE MAIN IDEAS

Paraphrase the main idea Fuller states in lines 27–29. Of what does Fuller see Miranda as an "example"?

COMMON CORE RI 5

D ANALYZE STRUCTURE

Fuller begins her argument about women's equality with a portrayal of Miranda, a self-reliant and well-educated fictional friend. In a well-reasoned explanation, Miranda credits her father with raising her to be an intellectual equal of men. Reread Fuller's response in lines 45–46. Is this statement logical? Do you think Fuller has introduced a **logical fallacy** (an error in thinking), such as an **oversimplification** or a **hasty generalization?** Explain your answer.

E AUTHOR'S PERSPECTIVE

Consider the **details** Fuller chooses to focus on. By contrasting Miranda's upbringing with that of most 19th-century women, what type of upbringing is Fuller advocating?

DIFFERENTIATED INSTRUCTION

FOR STRUGGLING READERS

Develop Reading Fluency Point out the long sentences in lines 35–44, and help students use the punctuation cues as a guide for pauses and other emphasis. Organize the class into groups of three. Have each student take turns reading aloud the passage. Encourage students to note their partners' speech patterns and apply what they learn to their own reading of the passage.

FOR ADVANCED LEARNERS/AP

Analyze [small-group option] Like Miranda, Fuller was blessed with a "total absence of those charms which might have drawn to her bewildering flatteries" (lines 19–20). Have small student groups analyze Fuller's suggestion that beauty or charm is a disadvantage for women who wish to be taken seriously. Does physical attractiveness have the same impact for men as it does for women? Invite groups to share their analysis with the class.

60　But early I perceived that men never, in any extreme of despair, wished to be women. On the contrary they were ever ready to taunt one another at any sign of weakness, with,

> *Art thou not like the women, who—*

The passage ends various ways, according to the occasion and rhetoric of the speaker. When they admired any woman they were inclined to speak of her as "above her sex." Silently I observed this, and feared it argued a rooted scepticism, which for ages had been fastening on the heart, and which only an age of miracles could eradicate. Ever I have been treated with great sincerity; and I look upon it as a signal instance of this, that an intimate friend of the other sex said, in a fervent
70　moment, that I "deserved in some star to be a man." He was much surprised when I disclosed my view of my position and hopes, when I declared my faith that the feminine side, the side of love, of beauty, of holiness, was now to have its full chance, and that, if either were better, it was better now to be a woman, for even the slightest achievement of good was furthering an especial work of our time. He smiled incredulously. "She makes the best she can of it," thought he. "Let Jews believe the pride of Jewry, but I am of the better sort, and know better."[3] **F**

Another used as highest praise, in speaking of a character in literature, the words "a manly woman."

> "So in the noble passage of Ben Jonson:
>
> 80　*'I meant the day-star should not brighter ride,*
> *　　Nor shed like influence from its lucent seat;*
> *I meant she should be courteous, facile, sweet,*
> *　　Free from that solemn vice of greatness, pride;*
> *I meant each softest virtue there should meet,*
> *　　Fit in that softer bosom to abide,*
> *Only a learned and a manly soul,*
> *　　I purposed her, that should with even powers,*
> *The rock, the spindle, and the shears control*
> *　　Of destiny, and spin her own free hours.'"[4]*
>
> 90　"Methinks," said I, "you are too fastidious in objecting to this. Jonson in using the word 'manly' only meant to heighten the picture of this, the true, the intelligent fate, with one of the deeper colors."
>
> "And yet," said she, "so invariable is the use of this word where a heroic quality is to be described, and I feel so sure that persistence and courage are the most womanly no less than the most manly qualities, that I would exchange these words for others of a larger sense at the risk of marring the fine tissue of the verse. Read 'A heavenward and instructed soul,' and I should be satisfied. Let it not be said, wherever there is energy or creative genius, 'She has a masculine mind.'" ◈

---

3. **'She makes … know better':** Miranda's male friend uses a religious slur to discount women.
4. **'I meant … free hours':** These lines are taken from the poem "On Lucy, Countess of Bedford." Their author, Ben Jonson (1573?–1637), was an English playwright and poet.

F PARAPHRASE MAIN IDEAS
Paraphrase lines 65–68 in your chart. What way of thinking does Miranda describe, and how easy does she think it will be to reverse?

2 Targeted Passage

COMMON CORE L 1a
Language Coach

Archaic Expressions
Words and phrases no longer in use are **archaic expressions.** *Methinks* is meaning "it seems to me" or "in my opinion." Write the sentence in lines 90–93 in your own—modern—words.

REVISIT THE BIG QUESTION
What does society **EXPECT** *of us?*

Discuss Direct students to lines 68–76. What expectations about men and women are revealed in the remark that Miranda "'deserved in some star to be a man'" (line 70)? What does Miranda's response convey about those expectations? *Possible answer: The remark suggests that women are not expected to think and act independently as men do. Miranda's response suggests that she rejects those expectations.*

READING STRATEGY　COMMON CORE RI 2

F PARAPHRASE MAIN IDEAS

Possible answer: Paraphrase: Men thought an admirable woman was not really a woman but was like a man. I worried that their view of women as by nature inferior to men could never be changed. Miranda suggests that this shows a deeply held belief about the inferiority of women, one that will be very hard to reverse.

SELECTION WRAP–UP

READ WITH A PURPOSE Now that students have read the excerpt, ask them to consider other people's opinions of Miranda. What bothers Miranda about the opinions that others hold of her? *Possible answer: Though other people tend to admire her, they still view her in terms of her gender.*

FOR STRUGGLING READERS

2 Targeted Passage [Lines 79–98]

In this passage, Miranda explains her dislike of *manly* as a synonym for *heroic.*

- Which word in Jonson's poem does Miranda dislike? (lines 87, 93–95)
- How does the speaker interpret Jonson's use of the word in his poem? (lines 90–92)
- How does Miranda think Jonson's poem should be worded? (lines 95–97)

FOR ENGLISH LANGUAGE LEARNERS

Language Coach　COMMON CORE L 1a

Archaic Expressions *Answer: Answers will vary, but should show an understanding of the sentence's meaning.* Have students review the selection and identify another example of archaic language. Tell them to rewrite in their own words the sentence in which the archaic language appears.

Practice and Apply

For preliminary support of post-reading questions, use these copy masters:

R **RESOURCE MANAGER**—Copy Masters

Reading Check p. 143
Author's Perspective p. 139
Question Support p. 144
Additional selection questions are provided for teachers on page 133.

ANSWERS

1. *Miranda's father believed that men and women were equal.*

2. *The men mean that Miranda possesses admirable qualities. They see the qualities of courage, confidence, and intelligence as male traits, and they view men as inherently better than women.*

Possible answers:

3. ■ **COMMON CORE FOCUS Paraphrase Main Ideas** *Fuller's main point is that persistence, courage, and other heroic qualities are not male qualities, but universal ones. She says they "are the most womanly no less than the most manly qualities" (lines 94–95). She no longer wants them to be labeled as male traits.*

4. ● **COMMON CORE FOCUS Author's Perspective** *Fuller believes that self-reliance is crucial if a woman is to transcend society's expectations. She must have her own resources to overcome inward conflict and outward adversity.*

Assess and Reteach

Assess

DIAGNOSTIC AND SELECTION TESTS
Selection Test A pp. 129–130
Selection Test B/C pp. 131–132

Interactive Selection Test on thinkcentral.com

Reteach

Level Up Online Tutorials on thinkcentral.com

Reteaching Worksheets on thinkcentral.com

Literature Lesson 45

Comprehension

1. **Recall** What did Miranda's father believe in regard to the equality of the sexes?

2. **Clarify** What do the men Miranda describes mean when they comment that a woman they admire is "above her sex"?

Text Analysis

■ 3. **Analyze Main Ideas** Examine the main ideas you **paraphrased** as you read. Then reread the selection's last two paragraphs. What is Fuller's main point about "heroic" qualities such as persistence, confidence, and creativity? Use your paraphrases and specific lines from the text to support your answer.

● 4. **Examine Author's Perspective** Recall that Fuller was in the Transcendental Club, and think about the ideals that this group embraced. Through her description of Miranda, what was Fuller saying about the traits a woman needed to transcend society's expectations? Restate Fuller's perspective in one or two sentences. Consider the following in your answer:

   • Miranda's statement that women "are taught to learn their rule from without, not to unfold it from within." (lines 43–44)

   • The contrast between Miranda's upbringing and that of women "so overloaded with precepts by guardians ... that their minds are impeded by doubts." (lines 50–52)

● 5. **Draw Conclusions About Author's Perspective** Why might Fuller have chosen to present her views as a dialogue between herself and the fictional Miranda, instead of simply stating her beliefs and advocating her position outright? Explain the rhetorical impact of the dialogue—how it influences readers and conveys ideas. Cite at least one example from the text to support your analysis.

6. **Compare Texts** Compare Fuller's main ideas with the beliefs Ralph Waldo Emerson sets forth in "Self-Reliance" (page 370). What common elements do the two texts share? In what ways does their focus differ? Cite examples.

Text Criticism

7. **Historical Context** A friend of Fuller's once described her as possessing "what in woman is generally called a masculine mind; that is, its action was determined by ideas rather than sentiments." Do contemporary Americans still believe that men are governed by reason while women are driven by emotion? Explain your answer.

> *What does society* **EXPECT** *of us?*
>
> Margaret Fuller felt that society expected too little of women. What expectations do people, such as parents, teachers, mentors, and society, have of you?

COMMON CORE

RI 2 Determine two or more central ideas of a text and analyze their development, including how they interact and build on one another. **RI 5** Analyze the effectiveness of the structure. **RI 6** Determine an author's point of view, analyzing how style and content contribute to the persuasiveness of the text. **RI 8** Evaluate purposes and arguments in works of public advocacy.

---

5. ● **COMMON CORE FOCUS Author's Perspective** *This format allows Fuller to address and refute arguments more easily, as when she suggests Miranda's objections are too particular (lines 90–92).*

6. *Fuller's and Emerson's texts are similar because both present self-reliance as a crucial trait. They differ in focus because Fuller is concerned with how women gain or are prevented from gaining self-reliance and self-determination, whereas Emerson discusses nonconformity and consistency.*

7. *Answers will vary, but students should express and support opinions about emotional reactions as a womanly trait.*

> *What does society* **EXPECT** *of us?* Student answers will vary. Their responses may include taking responsibility for actions, developing mature thinking skills, acting wisely, and obeying the rules.

The Transcendental Spirit

In the 19th century, transcendentalism emerged as a fresh intellectual framework for addressing social, economic, political, and cultural changes in America's increasingly complex society. Many of the issues writers of the day struggled with continue to be relevant today. Get into a "transcendental" frame of mind by taking the following quiz.

How TRANSCENDENTAL Are You?

* Do you ever take a walk with no destination in mind? ☐ yes ☐ no

* Do you express your opinions even when they aren't popular? ☐ yes ☐ no

* Would you accept very low pay for a job that you loved? ☐ yes ☐ no

* Do you think there are too many gadgets and gizmos in modern life and that we should all aim to simplify? ☐ yes ☐ no

* Would you go to jail rather than conform to a law that goes against your conscience? ☐ yes ☐ no

Writing to Analyze

Select one of the questions above and respond to it in a focused, well-developed paragraph. Give at least one example from your life to support your answer. Then write one more paragraph analyzing how one of the transcendental writers whose work you've just read might have responded to the same question.

Consider

• which question resonated with you the most

• what example(s) from your life might best reveal your beliefs to your audience

• how particular sentences or passages in the readings relate to the question you chose

Extension Online

INQUIRY & RESEARCH Search the Internet for evidence of Henry David Thoreau's legacy. Use the key words *Thoreau* and *Walden* to find several different types of memorials for one of transcendentalism's greatest thinkers. You will find many nonprofit organizations, projects, schools, and centers dedicated to promoting or remembering Thoreau's ideas. Of his various beliefs, which ones resonate most with modern day audiences? Report your findings to your class.

COMMON CORE

W 2 Write informative/explanatory texts to examine and convey complex ideas, concepts, and information clearly and accurately through the effective selection, organization, and analysis of content. **W 7** Conduct short research projects to answer a question or solve a problem.

COMMON CORE FOCUS

W 2 Write informative/explanatory texts to examine and convey complex ideas, concepts, and information clearly and accurately through the effective selection, organization, and analysis of content. **W 7** Conduct short research projects to answer a question or solve a problem.

Wrap-Up: The Transcendentalists

This Wrap-Up provides students with an opportunity to revisit the basic tenets of transcendentalism introduced in the literature of this section. How do students' personal beliefs coincide with these ideas? Encourage students to notice how the ideas of transcendentalism remain applicable today.

Writing to Analyze

• Remind students that to *reflect* is to think about an event or issue, then explore its meaning or importance. Reflecting helps readers internalize information they've read, such as about transcendentalism, and apply it to their own lives. In this way, they recall ideas longer and more vividly.

• To find material for the second paragraph, have students decide which author—Emerson, Thoreau, or Fuller—they think spoke most eloquently on transcendentalism. Suggest that students reread selections by that author looking for quotations or supporting ideas.

Extension Online

• As students research online, suggest that they open new windows for each new link. They might also save the URLs of each promising page to preserve them for ongoing reference.

• Instruct students to give a short presentation of their research findings. Presentations could include printed materials from the sites, quotations about the missions of the organizations, or other relevant artifacts that make the memorials interesting.

DIFFERENTIATED INSTRUCTION

FOR ENGLISH LANGUAGE LEARNERS

Writing Topic Sentences To help students create a topic sentence, have them restate their chosen question as a sentence. Offer these suggestions:

• I often take a walk with no destination in mind.

• Sometimes I express my opinions even when they aren't popular.

• For a job I loved, I would accept very low pay.

• In modern life, there are too many gadgets and gizmos, and we should all aim to simplify.

• I would go to jail rather than follow a law that goes against my beliefs.

Focus and Motivate

ABOUT THE AUTHOR

After students read this page, discuss how Poe's "unstable life" resembled a Gothic horror story, full of melodramatic gloom, psychological storms, and picturesque suffering.

Selection Resources

DID YOU KNOW?

Edgar Allan Poe . . .

- invented the modern detective story.
- inspired the name of the Baltimore Ravens football team.
- briefly wrote a literary gossip column.
- publicly denounced the work of Henry Wadsworth Longfellow.

(background) Baltimore, Maryland, scene of Poe's mysterious death

---

American Gothic

The Fall of the House of Usher

 Video link at thinkcentral.com

Short Story by Edgar Allan Poe

Meet the Author

Edgar Allan Poe c. 1809–1849

"The Raven" has been called the best-known poem in American literature; "The Fall of the House of Usher" is a masterpiece of Gothic horror. Both of these works were the creation of one feverish imagination, that of poet, critic, and fiction innovator Edgar Allan Poe.

Haunted by Death Once called one of literature's "most brilliant, but erratic, stars," Poe is as well-known for his unstable life as for his formidable talent. Abandoned by his father as an infant, Poe lost his mother to tuberculosis by the age of 3. He was taken in by John Allan, a wealthy Virginia businessman, but the two had a stormy relationship. At age 18, Poe got himself thrown out of college for gambling debts, beginning a lifelong pattern of self-sabotage. Estranged from Allan as a young man, Poe formed a new family with his aunt and his young cousin, Virginia Clemm. In 1836, he and Virginia married publicly, although they had probably married in secret the year before, when she was only 13. She died 11 years later, and the devastated Poe died 2 years after. Theories about the cause of his death range from alcohol poisoning to brain lesions to rabies.

Making Ends Meet For much of his adult life, Poe struggled to support his family. He landed promising positions at a series of literary magazines, spoiling one opportunity after another with his erratic behavior. At the same time, his scathing reviews made him a feared and respected critic, and his inventive short stories brought him acclaim. Although his life matched the Romantic ideal of the starving artist who suffered for the purity of his art, Poe's stories were designed to reach a wide audience. His successes with horror, science fiction, and detective stories proved his mastery of popular genres.

Tortured Soul Poe's distinctive themes included madness, untimely death, and obsession. Given his troubled life, many critics have interpreted Poe's deranged narrators as reflections of the author's own state of mind. But Poe was a brilliant and controlled stylist, whose theories of art championed rigorous structure, careful use of language, and the masterful creation of a single, calculated effect. His fascination with the macabre was equaled by his interest in logic; his supremely rational detective C. Auguste Dupin inspired Sir Arthur Conan Doyle's scientific sleuth Sherlock Holmes. Poe's life and work exemplify the deepest divisions of the self: the conflict of beautiful ideals and dark impulses.

Author Online
Go to thinkcentral.com. KEYWORD: HML11-410

THiNK central

410

● TEXT ANALYSIS: UNITY OF EFFECT

Some writers insist that plot or character drives a story. Edgar Allan Poe wanted his stories to achieve a **unity of effect,** where every element—plot, character, setting, and imagery—helped create a single effect, or **mood,** as in this opening sentence from the selection:

During the whole of a dull, dark, and soundless day in the autumn of the year, when the clouds hung oppressively low . . .

The ominous details set a scene of instant gloom. As you read, note the choices Poe makes to achieve his intended effect.

● READING SKILL: UNDERSTAND COMPLEX SENTENCES

Poe's sentences have a nervous, excited quality: they pile on details and jump from one subject to another. Use these strategies to help you understand Poe's complex sentences:

- Focus on the main idea. Finding the main subject and verb of a sentence can help you identify its main idea.
- Break long sentences into shorter ones that focus on one idea. Group modifiers with the words they describe.
- Keep reading. Poe often restates ideas, and a confusing sentence might be followed by one easier to understand.

Apply these strategies as you read. Using a chart like the one shown, paraphrase five especially complex sentences.

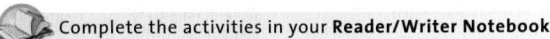

Line Numbers for Poe's Sentence	My Paraphrase

▲ VOCABULARY IN CONTEXT

Poe was fascinated with unusual language. Review the vocabulary words, noting any familiar roots, prefixes, or suffixes that might help you unlock the meaning of the words.

WORD LIST	affinity	demeanor	insipid
	alleviation	equivocal	pertinacity
	anomaly	inordinate	vagary
	apathy		

Complete the activities in your **Reader/Writer Notebook.**

Where does TERROR *begin?*

Fear can be a reasonable response to an immediate danger, like the instant alarm you would feel upon seeing a car racing toward you. But some of the things we find most terrifying don't present any real threat. A strange noise in the night, a creepy phone call, a creaking door slowly opening—what makes us afraid of things that can't really hurt us?

QUICKWRITE Recall times when you were frightened for no good reason: a walk in a familiar place that seemed strangely spooky or a sudden paranoia about being home alone. Describe what triggered your fear and why. How much of your terror was the result of your own imagination?

411

Where does TERROR *begin?*

Ask whether a terrifying feeling can sometimes be enjoyable, and if so, why. Have students complete the QUICKWRITE. Invite students who wish to read their quickwrites aloud to do so.

TEXT ANALYSIS
COMMON CORE
RL 3
RL 4

● *Model the Skill:* UNITY OF EFFECT

To show students how story elements work together to achieve unity of effect, share this example:

> The lone rider pulled his coat tightly around him to ward off the cold wind. Dark, threatening clouds rushed to fill the sky. He urged his nervous horse forward into the valley, where shadows obscured the path and unseen creatures screeched.

Point out that details such as "lone rider," "cold wind," "dark, threatening clouds," "nervous horse," "shadows," and "unseen creatures" contribute to the ominous effect of the passage.

GUIDED PRACTICE Have students write sentences that add to the unity of effect of the passage.

READING SKILL
COMMON CORE
L 3a

■ *Model the Skill:* UNDERSTAND COMPLEX SENTENCES

To help students understand Poe's complex sentence structures, point out the three bulleted strategies for understanding Poe's sentences. Guide students in applying these suggestions to the first sentence of "The Fall of the House of Usher" (p. 412, lines 1–5).

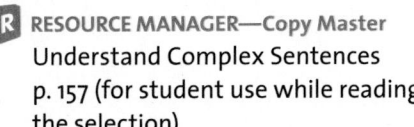 RESOURCE MANAGER—Copy Master
Understand Complex Sentences p. 157 (for student use while reading the selection)

VOCABULARY
COMMON CORE
L 4

▲ VOCABULARY IN CONTEXT

DIAGNOSE WORD KNOWLEDGE Have all students complete Vocabulary in Context.

affinity (ə-fĭn′ĭ-tē) *n.* a kinship or likeness

alleviation (ə-lē′vē-ā′shən) *n.* relief

anomaly (ə-nŏm′ə-lē) *n.* departure from the normal rules

apathy (ăp′ə-thē) *n.* lack of feeling or interest

demeanor (dĭ-mē′nər) *n.* behavior

equivocal (ĭ-kwĭv′ə-kəl) *adj.* ambiguous

inordinate (ĭn-ôr′dn-ĭt) *adj.* exceeding reasonable limits; excessive

insipid (ĭn-sĭp′ĭd) *adj.* lacking in flavor; bland

pertinacity (pûr′tn-ăs′ĭ-tē) *n.* stubbornness; persistence

vagary (vā′gə-rē) *n.* strange idea

PRETEACH VOCABULARY Use the copy master to help students predict meanings.

R RESOURCE MANAGER—Copy Master
Vocabulary Study p. 159

SUMMARY

This short story begins as the narrator arrives at the home of his boyhood friend, Roderick Usher. The narrator finds Usher greatly changed and depressed, and his home in decay. The narrator tries to raise his friend's spirits, but during his visit, Usher's ailing sister, Madeline, dies. After her burial, Usher and the narrator hear strange sounds. Then Madeline appears, dressed in her burial garments. Falling into each other's arms, brother and sister die together. As the narrator flees, the mansion splits apart and falls into the lake.

READ WITH A PURPOSE

Help students set a purpose for reading. Tell them to read to discover why Poe named this story the "The Fall of the House of Usher."

THE FALL OF THE
House of Usher

Edgar Allan Poe

Son coeur est un luth suspendu;
Sitôt qu'on le touche il résonne.
—De Béranger

"His heart is a hanging lute; / As soon as one touches it, it sounds" (lines from a poem by the 19th-century French poet Pierre Jean de Béranger).

During the whole of a dull, dark, and soundless day in the autumn of the year, when the clouds hung oppressively low in the heavens, I had been passing alone, on horseback, through a singularly dreary tract of country, and at length found myself, as the shades of the evening drew on, within view of the melancholy House of Usher. I know not how it was—but, with the first glimpse of the building, a sense of insufferable gloom pervaded my spirit. I say insufferable; for the feeling was unrelieved by any of that half-pleasurable, because poetic, sentiment with which the mind usually receives even the sternest natural images of the desolate or terrible. I looked
10 upon the scene before me—upon the mere house, and the simple landscape features of the domain—upon the bleak walls—upon the vacant, eye-like windows—upon a few rank sedges—and upon a few white trunks of decayed trees—with an utter depression of soul which I can compare to no earthly sensation more properly than to the after-dream of the reveller

Analyze Visuals ▶

What mood does this image convey? Identify specific elements, such as color, texture, and composition, that contribute to this mood.

① Targeted Passage

12 rank sedges: overgrown grassy plants.

Illustrations by Shane Rebenscheid.

DIFFERENTIATED INSTRUCTION

FOR ENGLISH LANGUAGE LEARNERS

Related Vocabulary Teach these related words that help build mood: *dull, dark* (line 1); *oppressively* (line 2); *dreary* (line 3); *melancholy* (line 5); *gloom* (line 6); *desolate* (line 9); *bleak, vacant* (line 11); *decayed, depression* (line 13).

FOR STRUGGLING READERS

In combination with the *Audio Anthology CD*, use one or more Targeted Passages (pp. 412, 415, 417, 418, 423, 425, 428, 430) to ensure that students focus on key story events and concepts. Targeted Passages are also good for English learners.

① Targeted Passage [Lines 1–13]

This passage describes the narrator's journey to the House of Usher and establishes a unified effect of gloom.

Analyze Visuals

Possible answer: *The image conveys a mood of gloom, decay, melancholy, and foreboding. Specific elements that contribute to this mood include the dark colors, the bareness of the sky and earth, the bare branches in the foreground, the chilly white light on some of the branches, and the pattern of cracks that gives the effect of an old painting.*

BACKGROUND

Poe and the Gothic Tale Emphasize to students that, as they read in the Unit 2 historical essay, Poe was a leading master of American gothic literature. As such, he sought to examine the emotional side of the human experience. When he describes the setting and characters of "The House of Usher" in minute detail, it is not for the primary purpose of creating a mental image for the reader, but rather to show the psychology of horror and madness through the perceptions of the narrator. This narrator not only witnesses madness and horror in the House of Usher, but participates in it as well.

- What is the narrator doing in this passage? (lines 1–5)
- What mood is the narrator in? (lines 5–9)
- What do the landscape and the house look like? (lines 9–13)

FOR ADVANCED LEARNERS/AP

Analyze Have students analyze the opening lines to "The Fall of the House of Usher." Tell them to write an opening to their own story that matches the mood set by Poe. Have students read their story openings aloud to the class.

Ⓐ *Model the Skill:* UNITY OF EFFECT

Point out some of the narrator's physical reactions, and have students paraphrase them in order to describe the mood. Have them use the chart on page 411 to paraphrase mood-creating details of the scene.

Line Numbers for Poe's Sentence	My Paraphrase
16–18	I felt a sinking, heartsick feeling, and I couldn't snap myself out of it.

Possible answer: *The mood is one of gloom and dread. Details include the narrator's unnerved feeling and "shadowy fancies" (lines 19–21); the "precipitous brink of a black and lurid tarn" (lines 28–29); and the narrator's "shudder" at the lake's "ghastly" reflections of the house (lines 30–31).*

TIERED DISCUSSION PROMPTS

In lines 33–46, use these prompts to help students understand the characters:

Recall What has been the narrator's relationship with Roderick Usher in the past? Why did Usher write to him? ***Possible answer:*** *Usher was one of the narrator's "boon companions in boyhood" (line 35), but the two have not seen each other in many years. Usher wrote to ask that the narrator visit him to alleviate a mysterious illness.*

Synthesize How do these lines contribute to the story's unity of effect? ***Possible answer:*** *The description of Usher complements the setting's gloominess.*

OWN THE WORD

alleviation: Tell students that *alleviation* is the noun form of the verb *alleviate.* The modern use refers to "relief" or "freedom, especially from pain." Have students complete the following sentence: "Alyssa needs *alleviation . . .*" ***Possible answers:*** *from the pain of her toothache; from the boredom of her dull afternoon.*

---

upon opium—the bitter lapse into everyday life—the hideous dropping off of the veil. There was an iciness, a sinking, a sickening of the heart—an unredeemed dreariness of thought which no goading of the imagination could torture into *aught* of the sublime. What was it—I paused to think—what was it that so unnerved me in the contemplation of the House of
20 Usher? It was a mystery all insoluble; nor could I grapple with the shadowy fancies that crowded upon me as I pondered. I was forced to fall back upon the unsatisfactory conclusion, that while, beyond doubt, there *are* combinations of very simple natural objects which have the power of thus affecting us, still the analysis of this power lies among considerations beyond our depth. It was possible, I reflected, that a mere different arrangement of the particulars of the scene, of the details of the picture, would be sufficient to modify, or perhaps to annihilate its capacity for sorrowful impression; and, acting upon this idea, I reined my horse to the precipitous brink of a black and lurid tarn that lay in unruffled lustre by the dwelling, and gazed
30 down—but with a shudder even more thrilling than before—upon the remodelled and inverted images of the grey sedge, and the ghastly tree-stems, and the vacant and eye-like windows. Ⓐ

　　Nevertheless, in this mansion of gloom I now proposed to myself a sojourn of some weeks. Its proprietor, Roderick Usher, had been one of my boon companions in boyhood; but many years had elapsed since our last meeting. A letter, however, had lately reached me in a distant part of the country—a letter from him—which, in its wildly importunate nature, had admitted of no other than a personal reply. The MS. gave evidence of nervous agitation. The writer spoke of acute bodily illness—of a mental
40 disorder which oppressed him—and of an earnest desire to see me, as his best, and indeed his only personal friend, with a view of attempting, by the cheerfulness of my society, some **alleviation** of his malady. It was the manner in which all this, and much more, was said—it was the apparent *heart* that went with his request—which allowed me no room for hesitation; and I accordingly obeyed forthwith what I still considered a very singular summons.

　　Although, as boys, we had been even intimate associates, yet I really knew little of my friend. His reserve had been always excessive and habitual. I was aware, however, that his very ancient family had been noted, time
50 out of mind, for a peculiar sensibility of temperament, displaying itself, through long ages, in many works of exalted art, and manifested, of late, in repeated deeds of munificent yet unobtrusive charity, as well as in a passionate devotion to the intricacies, perhaps even more than to the orthodox and easily recognizable beauties, of musical science. I had learned, too, the very remarkable fact, that the stem of the Usher race, all time-honored as it was, had put forth, at no period, any enduring branch; in other words, that the entire family lay in the direct line of descent, and had always, with very trifling and very temporary variation, so lain. It was this

---

Language Coach

Homophones Words that sound alike but have different meanings and spellings are homophones. *Aught* (line 18) and *ought* are both pronounced /awt/. *Aught,* though, means "anything" or "all" and *ought* is similar to "should." What might "aught of the sublime" mean here?

28–29 precipitous . . . tarn: steep bank of a small black, repulsive-looking mountain lake.

Ⓐ UNITY OF EFFECT

Reread lines 16–32. Describe the **mood** of the scene. What details of the narrator's reactions contribute to this effect?

38 had admitted of no other than: had required; **MS.:** an abbreviation of *manuscript.*

alleviation (ə-lē′vē-ā′shən) *n.* relief

52 munificent yet unobtrusive: generous yet inconspicuous.

DIFFERENTIATED INSTRUCTION

FOR ENGLISH LANGUAGE LEARNERS

Vocabulary Support Use Definition Mapping to teach these words: *temporary* (line 58), *estate* (line 65), *sole* (line 69), *volume* (line 354), *region* (line 389), *resolve* (line 414).

 BEST PRACTICES TOOLKIT—Transparency Definition Mapping p. E6

FOR ENGLISH LANGUAGE LEARNERS

Language Coach

Homophones *Answer:* "Aught of the sublime" can mean "anything good or noble at all." Have students identify two other sets of homophones. Tell them to write sentences using the words in their homophone sets, demonstrating their different meanings.

deficiency, I considered, while running over in thought the perfect keeping
of the character of the premises with the accredited character of the people,
and while speculating upon the possible influence which the one, in the
long lapse of centuries, might have exercised upon the other—it was this
deficiency, perhaps, of collateral issue, and the consequent undeviating
transmission, from sire to son, of the patrimony with the name, which had, at
length, so identified the two as to merge the original title of the estate in the
quaint and **equivocal** appellation of the "House of Usher"—an appellation
which seemed to include, in the minds of the peasantry who used it, both
the family and the family mansion. **B**

I have said that the sole effect of my somewhat childish experiment—that
of looking down within the tarn—had been to deepen the first singular
impression. There can be no doubt that the consciousness of the rapid increase
of my superstition—for why should I not so term it?—served mainly to
accelerate the increase itself. Such, I have long known, is the paradoxical law of
all sentiments having terror as a basis. And it might have been for this reason
only, that, when I again uplifted my eyes to the house itself, from its image
in the pool, there grew in my mind a strange fancy—a fancy so ridiculous,
indeed, that I but mention it to show the vivid force of the sensations which
oppressed me. I had so worked upon my imagination as really to believe that
about the whole mansion and domain there hung an atmosphere peculiar
to themselves and their immediate vicinity—an atmosphere which had no
affinity with the air of heaven, but which had reeked up from the decayed
trees, and the gray wall, and the silent tarn—a pestilent and mystic vapor, dull,
sluggish, faintly discernible, and leaden-hued.

Shaking off from my spirit what *must* have been a dream, I scanned
more narrowly the real aspect of the building. Its principal feature seemed
to be that of an excessive antiquity. The discoloration of ages had been
great. Minute fungi overspread the whole exterior, hanging in a fine tangled
web-work from the eaves. Yet all this was apart from any extraordinary
dilapidation. No portion of the masonry had fallen; and there appeared to
be a wild inconsistency between its still perfect adaptation of parts, and the
crumbling condition of the individual stones. In this there was much that
reminded me of the specious totality of old wood-work which has rotted
for long years in some neglected vault, with no disturbance from the breath
of the external air. Beyond this indication of extensive decay, however,
the fabric gave little token of instability. Perhaps the eye of a scrutinizing
observer might have discovered a barely perceptible fissure, which, extending
from the roof of the building in front, made its way down the wall in a
zigzag direction, until it became lost in the sullen waters of the tarn. **C**

Noticing these things, I rode over a short causeway to the house. A
servant in waiting took my horse, and I entered the Gothic archway of the
hall. A valet, of stealthy step, thence conducted me, in silence, through
many dark and intricate passages in my progress to the *studio* of his master.

62–63 this deficiency . . . issue: for some reason, the Ushers have few descendants.

equivocal (ĭ-kwĭv′ə-kəl) *adj.* ambiguous

B COMPLEX SENTENCES
Identify the main idea of lines 62–68. What are the two meanings of the phrase "the House of Usher"?

affinity (ə-fĭn′ĭ-tē) *n.* a kinship or likeness

 **Targeted Passage**

92 specious totality: false appearance of soundness.

96 fissure: long narrow crack.

C GRAMMAR AND STYLE
Reread lines 95–98. Note how Poe uses the **participle** "scrutinizing" and the **participial phrase** "extending from the roof of the building in front" as modifiers.

THE FALL OF THE HOUSE OF USHER **415**

READING SKILL COMMON CORE L 3a

B COMPLEX SENTENCES

Possible answer: For some reason, the Ushers produce few descendants, so the only living members of the family are those who live in the mansion. The phrase "House of Usher" refers to the family members and to the house itself.

IF STUDENTS NEED HELP . . .
- Have them look up difficult words such as *deficiency, collateral, consequent,* and *undeviating* (line 63).
- Point out that *collateral* and *issue* (line 63) are multiple-meaning words. Remind students to find the right meanings for the context.

 **GRAMMAR AND STYLE** COMMON CORE L3

Participles and Participial Phrases Remind students that a participle is a verb form used as an adjective. Participles ending in *-ing* are present participles; participles ending in *-ed* are past participles. A participial phrase is one that contains a participle and words that modify it. In lines 95–98, "scrutinizing" modifies "observer." The phrase "extending from the roof of the building in front" modifies "fissure." Have students find more examples of participles and participial phrases.

VOCABULARY COMMON CORE L 4

OWN THE WORD
- **equivocal:** Tell students that *equivocal* means "ambiguous," or "open to two or more interpretations." Ask students to recall situations where their actions may have been *equivocal*. ***Possible answer: answering "nothing" when asked if something was wrong***
- **affinity:** Remind students that *affinity* means "a kinship or likeness." Other meanings include "a natural attraction or liking" as in *I have an affinity for computers.* Have students list things for which they have an *affinity*. ***Possible answer: science, sports***

FOR STRUGGLING READERS

2 Targeted Passage [Lines 84–98]

This passage describes the house lived in by the Ushers.

- What is the main feature the narrator observes? (lines 84–86)
- In what condition is the house? (lines 86–91)
- What evidence of decay does the narrator describe? (lines 91–95)
- What is the "fissure"? (lines 95–98)

FOR ENGLISH LANGUAGE LEARNERS

Comprehension: Text Structure Remind students that Poe often uses long, complex sentences with difficult constructions. Give the examples "It was possible . . . eye-like windows" (25–32) and "It was this deficiency . . . the family mansion" (58–68). Guide students in using one or more of the strategies for understanding complex sentences, outlined on page 411, to decipher these sentences.

In lines 126–146, use these prompts to help students understand Roderick Usher:

Summarize What are the principal qualities that mark Roderick Usher's appearance? *Possible answer: He has a striking, handsome face with a pale complexion, soft, fine hair, and a lack of energy. His complexion has become "ghastly."*

Analyze What inner changes can you infer from the outer changes in Usher? *Possible answer: He is suffering from emotional distress.*

Evaluate Do you think Poe overwrites in his description of Usher, or do you think the abundance of complex detail makes his description more effective? *Some students may say that Poe's style is antiquated and too ornate to convey a vivid picture; others will say that his rich descriptions draw the reader in.*

VOCABULARY

COMMON CORE
L 4

OWN THE WORD

inordinate: Point out that *inordinate* means "exceeding reasonable limits." Ask students what picture is evoked with the use of this word in the phrase "... hair of a more than web-like softness ... with an *inordinate* expansion above the regions of the temple ..." *Possible answer: a balding man*

Much that I encountered on the way contributed, I know not how, to heighten the vague sentiments of which I have already spoken. While the objects around me—while the carvings of the ceilings, the sombre tapestries of the walls, the ebon blackness of the floors, and the phantasmagoric armorial trophies which rattled as I strode, were but matters to which, or to such as which, I had been accustomed from my infancy—while I hesitated not to acknowledge how familiar was all this—I still wondered to find how
110 unfamiliar were the fancies which ordinary images were stirring up. On one of the staircases, I met the physician of the family. His countenance, I thought, wore a mingled expression of low cunning and perplexity. He accosted me with trepidation and passed on. The valet now threw open a door and ushered me through into the presence of his master.

The room in which I found myself was very large and lofty. The windows were long, narrow, and pointed, and at so vast a distance from the black oaken floor as to be altogether inaccessible from within. Feeble gleams of encrimsoned light made their way through the trellissed panes, and served to render sufficiently distinct the more prominent objects around; the eye,
120 however, struggled in vain to reach the remoter angles of the chamber, or the recesses of the vaulted and fretted ceiling. Dark draperies hung upon the walls. The general furniture was profuse, comfortless, antique, and tattered. Many books and musical instruments lay scattered about, but failed to give any vitality to the scene. I felt that I breathed an atmosphere of sorrow. An air of stern, deep, and irredeemable gloom hung over and pervaded all.

Upon my entrance, Usher arose from a sofa on which he had been lying at full length, and greeted me with a vivacious warmth which had much in it, I at first thought, of an overdone cordiality—of the constrained effort of the *ennuyé* man of the world. A glance, however, at his countenance
130 convinced me of his perfect sincerity. We sat down; and for some moments, while he spoke not, I gazed upon him with a feeling of half pity, half of awe. Surely, man had never before so terribly altered, in so brief a period, as had Roderick Usher! It was with difficulty that I could bring myself to admit the identity of the wan being before me with the companion of my early boyhood. Yet the character of his face had been at all times remarkable. A cadaverousness of complexion; an eye large, liquid, and luminous beyond comparison; lips somewhat thin and very pallid, but of a surpassingly beautiful curve; a nose of a delicate Hebrew model, but with a breadth of nostril unusual in similar formations; a finely moulded chin, speaking, in its
140 want of prominence, of a want of moral energy; hair of a more than web-like softness and tenuity; these features, with an **inordinate** expansion above the regions of the temple, made up altogether a countenance not easily to be forgotten. And now in the mere exaggeration of the prevailing character of these features, and of the expression they were wont to convey, lay so much of change that I doubted to whom I spoke. The now ghastly pallor of the skin, and the now miraculous lustre of the eye, above all things startled and

106–107 phantasmagoric (făn-tăz′mə-gôr′ĭk) **armorial trophies:** fantastic wall decorations bearing coats of arms.

121 vaulted and fretted: arched and decorated with interlaced designs.

129 *ennuyé* (äN-nwē-yā′) *French:* bored.

136 cadaverousness of complexion: a corpselike appearance.

inordinate (ĭn-ôr′dn-ĭt) *adj.* exceeding reasonable limits; excessive

---

DIFFERENTIATED INSTRUCTION

FOR ADVANCED LEARNERS/AP
Critical Interpretation Scholars point out similarities between the instability of Usher's house and the mental instability of Usher. At the beginning of the story, we see the house in a state of decay, one that affects the narrator with "insufferable gloom" (line 6). When the narrator enters the house, he finds his friend in the same decaying condition. Ask students to identify and discuss other parallels between Usher and the house and to provide an interpretation of the meaning of these connections.

FOR ENGLISH LANGUAGE LEARNERS
Language: Punctuation and Print Cues Poe frequently uses dashes, as in lines 105, 108, 109, 128, 151, 153, 159, 160, 168, 182, 183, and 189. What effects do these print cues create? *Possible answer: They produce a spontaneous look and flow, as though the narrator is quickly jotting down his uncensored impressions.*

even awed me. The silken hair, too, had been suffered to grow all unheeded, and as, in its wild gossamer texture, it floated rather than fell about the face, I could not, even with effort, connect its Arabesque expression with any idea
150 of simple humanity. **D**

In the manner of my friend I was at once struck with an incoherence— an inconsistency; and I soon found this to arise from a series of feeble and futile struggles to overcome an habitual trepidancy—an excessive nervous agitation. For something of this nature I had indeed been prepared, no less by his letter, than by reminiscences of certain boyish traits, and by conclusions deduced from his peculiar physical conformation and temperament. His action was alternately vivacious and sullen. His voice varied rapidly from a tremulous indecision (when the animal spirits seemed utterly in abeyance) to that species of energetic concision—that abrupt,
160 weighty, unhurried, and hollow-sounding enunciation—that leaden, self-balanced, and perfectly modulated guttural utterance, which may be observed in the lost drunkard, or the irreclaimable eater of opium, during the periods of his most intense excitement.

It was thus that he spoke of the object of my visit, of his earnest desire to see me, and of the solace he expected me to afford him. He entered, at some length, into what he conceived to be the nature of his malady. It was, he said, a constitutional and a family evil, and one for which he despaired to find a remedy—a mere nervous affection, he immediately added, which would undoubtedly soon pass off. It displayed itself in a host of unnatural
170 sensations. Some of these, as he detailed them, interested and bewildered me; although, perhaps, the terms and the general manner of their narration had their weight. He suffered much from a morbid acuteness of the senses; the most **insipid** food was alone endurable; he could wear only garments of certain texture; the odors of all flowers were oppressive; his eyes were tortured by even a faint light; and there were but peculiar sounds, and these from stringed instruments, which did not inspire him with horror.

To an anomalous species of terror I found him a bounden slave. "I shall perish," said he, "I *must* perish in this deplorable folly. Thus, thus, and not otherwise, shall I be lost. I dread the events of the future, not in themselves,
180 but in their results. I shudder at the thought of any, even the most trivial, incident, which may operate upon this intolerable agitation of soul. I have, indeed, no abhorrence of danger, except in its absolute effect—in terror. In this unnerved—in this pitiable, condition—I feel that the period will sooner or later arrive when I must abandon life and reason together, in some struggle with the grim phantasm, FEAR." **E**

I learned, moreover, at intervals, and through broken and equivocal hints, another singular feature of his mental condition. He was enchained by certain superstitious impressions in regard to the dwelling which he tenanted, and whence, for many years, he had never ventured forth—in
190 regard to an influence whose supposititious force was conveyed in terms too

149 Arabesque (ăr′a-běsk′): intricately interwoven, like the design of an Oriental rug.

D UNITY OF EFFECT
Reread lines 132–150. Poe often uses **exaggeration** to add drama to his descriptions. Which details of Roderick's appearance show this technique at work?

159 concision: terseness; brevity in use of words.

3 Targeted Passage

insipid (ĭn-sĭp′ĭd) *adj.* lacking in flavor; bland

175 but peculiar: only certain.

E COMPLEX SENTENCES
Reread the description of Roderick's state of mind in lines 177–185, and identify the idea that is repeatedly emphasized. What does Roderick seem to be afraid of?

190 supposititious: supposed.

D UNITY OF EFFECT

Possible answer: Details of Roderick's appearance that use exaggeration to add drama include his cadaverous complexion; his "eye large, liquid, and luminous beyond comparison" (lines 136–137); his thin and pale but beautiful lips; his unusual nostrils; the "inordinate expansion" above his temples (lines 141–142); the "ghastly pallor of the skin" (lines 145–146); his wild, floating hair; and the lack of connection between these features and "any idea of simple humanity" (lines 149–150).

READING SKILL | COMMON CORE | L 3a

E COMPLEX SENTENCES

Possible answer: Roderick believes his fear itself will kill him. He is as afraid of his own fear as he is of death.

VOCABULARY | COMMON CORE | L 4

OWN THE WORD

insipid: Tell students that *insipid* is an adjective that means lacking in flavor; bland" or "lacking exciting qualities; dull." Have students write a sentence for each definition. *Possible answers: My breakfast was the same old thing: an insipid bowl of oatmeal and a piece of toast. The insipid accountant failed again to get the promotion he so desperately wanted.*

FOR STRUGGLING READERS

3 Targeted Passage [Lines 164–185]

This passage describes Roderick's view of his own psychological state.

- What things has Roderick become sensitive to? (lines 172–176)
- What explanations does Roderick give for his current condition? (lines 166–169)
- What is Roderick afraid will happen to him? (lines 183–185)

FOR ADVANCED LEARNERS/AP

Epigraph Have students reread the epigraph at the beginning of the story on page 412. Ask them to discuss how this epigraph can be applied to the description of Roderick Usher on page 417. How do the description and the epigraph enhance each other's meaning?

shadowy here to be re-stated—an influence which some peculiarities in the mere form and substance of his family mansion had, by dint of long sufferance, he said, obtained over his spirit—an effect which the *physique* of the gray walls and turrets, and of the dim tarn into which they all looked down, had, at length, brought about upon the *morale* of his existence.

He admitted, however, although with hesitation, that much of the peculiar gloom which thus afflicted him could be traced to a more natural and far more palpable origin—to the severe and long-continued illness—indeed to the evidently approaching dissolution—of a tenderly beloved
200 sister—his sole companion for long years—his last and only relative on earth. "Her decease," he said, with a bitterness which I can never forget, "would leave him (him, the hopeless and the frail) the last of the ancient race of the Ushers." While he spoke, the lady Madeline (for so she was called) passed through a remote portion of the apartment, and, without having noticed my presence, disappeared. I regarded her with an utter astonishment not unmingled with dread—and yet I found it impossible to account for such feelings. A sensation of stupor oppressed me as my eyes followed her retreating steps. When a door, at length, closed upon her, my glance sought instinctively and eagerly the countenance of the brother—but he had buried
210 his face in his hands, and I could only perceive that a far more than ordinary wanness had overspread the emaciated fingers through which trickled many passionate tears.

The disease of the lady Madeline had long baffled the skill of her physicians. A settled **apathy**, a gradual wasting away of the person, and frequent although transient affections of a partially cataleptical character were the unusual diagnosis. Hitherto she had steadily borne up against the pressure of her malady, and had not betaken herself finally to bed; but on the closing in of the evening of my arrival at the house, she succumbed (as her brother told me at night with inexpressible agitation) to the prostrating
220 power of the destroyer; and I learned that the glimpse I had obtained of her person would thus probably be the last I should obtain—that the lady, at least while living, would be seen by me no more.

For several days ensuing, her name was unmentioned by either Usher or myself; and during this period I was busied in earnest endeavors to alleviate the melancholy of my friend. We painted and read together, or I listened, as if in a dream, to the wild improvisations of his speaking guitar. And thus, as a closer and still closer intimacy admitted me more unreservedly into the recesses of his spirit, the more bitterly did I perceive the futility of all attempt at cheering a mind from which darkness, as if an inherent positive
230 quality, poured forth upon all the objects of the moral and physical universe in one unceasing radiation of gloom.

I shall ever bear about me a memory of the many solemn hours I thus spent alone with the master of the House of Usher. Yet I should fail in any attempt to convey an idea of the exact character of the studies, or of the

Analyze Visuals ▶
What techniques has the artist used to create contrast between Madeline and the two men?

④ **Targeted Passage**

apathy (ăp′ə-thē) *n.* lack of feeling or interest

215 transient . . . cataleptical (kăt′l-ĕp′tĭ-kəl) **character:** temporary episodes of a trancelike condition.

Ⓕ **COMPLEX SENTENCES**
Reread lines 226–231. **Paraphrase** this sentence by breaking it into two shorter sentences, each beginning with the word *I*. What has changed in the narrator's relationship with Roderick?

Ⓕ **COMPLEX SENTENCES**

Possible answer: *Paraphrase: I became closer to Roderick. I saw that it was useless to try to cheer him up. The narrator has learned more about Roderick but despairs of helping him in any way.*

IF STUDENTS NEED HELP . . . Have students add to the chart introduced on page 411 by producing a written paraphrase.

Line Numbers for Poe's Sentence	My Paraphrase
226–231	I became closer to Roderick. I saw that it was useless to try to cheer him up.

OWN THE WORD

apathy: Tell students that *apathy* is a noun used to describe a "lack of feeling or interest." An *apathetic* person lacks interest in particular things. Have students list antonyms that relate to *apathy*. **Possible answers:** *compassion, passion, interest, empathy, responsiveness*

DIFFERENTIATED INSTRUCTION

FOR STRUGGLING READERS

④ **Targeted Passage** [Lines 196–207]

This passage describes the appearance of Madeline Usher, Roderick's twin sister.

• What important event is described in this passage? (lines 203–205)

• What would happen if Madeline died? (lines 201–203)

• How does the narrator react to Madeline's appearance? (lines 205–207)

FOR ENGLISH LANGUAGE LEARNERS

Vocabulary: Outdated Forms Point out that Poe often uses words and phrases that are not used today. Provide the definitions and have students insert them in place of the older terms.

• *by dint of long sufferance* (lines 192–193), "over a long time"

• *not unmingled* (line 206), "mixed"

• *overspread* (line 211), "spread across"

• *borne up against* (line 216), "withstood"

Possible answer: *The two men are seen only partially. One of them is in silhouette and mostly in shadow; the head of the other is outside the frame of the picture. Madeline, in contrast, is seen in detail and framed in a doorway to focus the viewer's eye. On the other hand, the men are in the foreground and Madeline in the background. This may imply that while Madeline is an intriguing figure, she is less important to the story than Roderick.*

Activity Have students decide which of the male figures in the foreground is Roderick and which is the narrator. Have them explain their opinions.

FOR STRUGGLING READERS

Comprehension Support: Using the Illustration Have students compare the picture of Madeline on page 419 with the verbal portrait of her in lines 196–207 and 213–220. Have them find details in the illustration that convey traits described in the passage. ***Possible answer:*** *Her pallor and her frail, forlorn appearance confirm what the passages state about her illness.*

FOR ADVANCED LEARNERS/AP

Write: Interior Monologue Have students write brief interior monologues for Madeline, Roderick, and the narrator, expressing those characters' thoughts and feelings as Madeline walks through the house. Have students share their writings with the class. Discuss insights and interpretations that the writings provide.

Where does TERROR *begin?*

Discuss Find words and phrases in lines 239–275 that convey a mood of dread or that foreshadow terrifying things to come.

Possible answer: "*I shuddered knowing not why*" *(lines 241–242), "an intensity of intolerable awe" (line 249), "phantasmagoric conceptions" (line 251), "ghastly" (line 259), "the tottering of his lofty reason" (line 275).*

TIERED DISCUSSION PROMPTS

In lines 261–275, use these prompts to help students understand how Roderick's music signaled a collapse of his reason:

Recall What type of music is Roderick restricted to? Why? *Possible answer: Because of his nervous disorder, Roderick is restricted to music created by stringed instruments.*

Analyze Why does the narrator conclude from Roderick's music that his friend is losing control of his "lofty reason" (line 275)? *Possible answer: The narrator observes the "fervid" facility (line 265) of his playing, his intense concentration, his artificial excitement, and the "mystic current of its meaning" (line 273). He concludes from these qualities that his friend is losing his reason.*

Evaluate Do you agree with the narrator that artistic creations can give insight into a person's mental and emotional makeup? Explain. *Possible answer: Art is an expression of what its creator thinks and feels, and gives clues about the person's mind.*

TEXT ANALYSIS   COMMON CORE   RL 3   RL 4

G UNITY OF EFFECT

Read lines 251–260 aloud. Then lead a discussion about the image presented in this passage. How does Poe project a sense of gloom in his character's painting?

Possible answer: The painting described here shows Roderick's morbid delusion and preoccupation with terror. It sounds like an underground vault, or tomb, and illustrates his obsession with death.

Extend the Discussion How does the sheer simplicity of Usher's paintings induce shudders in the viewer?

---

occupations, in which he involved me, or led me the way. An excited and highly distempered ideality threw a sulphureous lustre over all. His long improvised dirges will ring forever in my ears. Among other things, I hold painfully in mind a certain singular perversion and amplification of the wild air of the last waltz of Von Weber. From the paintings over which his

240 elaborate fancy brooded, and which grew, touch by touch, into vagueness at which I shuddered the more thrillingly, because I shuddered knowing not why,—from these paintings (vivid as their images now are before me) I would in vain endeavor to educe more than a small portion which should lie within the compass of merely written words. By the utter simplicity, by the nakedness of his designs, he arrested and over-awed attention. If ever mortal painted an ideal, that mortal was Roderick Usher. For me at least—in the circumstances then surrounding me—there arose out of the pure abstractions which the hypochondriac contrived to throw upon his canvas, an intensity of intolerable awe, no shadow of which felt I ever yet in the

250 contemplation of the certainly glowing yet too concrete reveries of Fuseli.

One of the phantasmagoric conceptions of my friend, partaking not so rigidly of the spirit of abstraction, may be shadowed forth, although feebly, in words. A small picture presented the interior of an immensely long and rectangular vault or tunnel, with low walls, smooth, white, and without interruption or device. Certain accessory points of the design served well to convey the idea that this excavation lay at an exceeding depth below the surface of the earth. No outlet was observed in any portion of its vast extent, and no torch or other artificial source of light was discernable; yet a flood of intense rays rolled throughout, and bathed the whole in a ghastly and

260 inappropriate splendor. **G**

I have just spoken of that morbid condition of the auditory nerve which rendered all music intolerable to the sufferer, with the exception of certain effects of stringed instruments. It was, perhaps, the narrow limits to which he thus confined himself upon the guitar which gave birth, in great measure, to the fantastic character of his performances. But the fervid *facility* of his *impromptus* could not be so accounted for. They must have been, and were, in the notes, as well as in the words of his wild fantasias (for he not unfrequently accompanied himself with rhymed verbal improvisations), the result of that intense mental collectedness and concentration to which

270 I have previously alluded as observable only in particular moments of the highest artificial excitement. The words of one of these rhapsodies I have easily remembered. I was, perhaps, the more forcibly impressed with it as he gave it, because, in the under or mystic current of its meaning, I fancied that I perceived, and for the first time, a full consciousness on the part of Usher of the tottering of his lofty reason upon her throne. The verses, which were entitled "The Haunted Palace," ran very near, if not accurately, thus:—

236 distempered . . . sulphureous (sŭl-fər′ē-əs) **lustre:** diseased creativity gave a nightmarish quality.

239 Von Weber (vŏn vā′bər): the German romantic composer Karl Maria von Weber (1786–1826).

250 Fuseli (fyōō′zə-lē′): the Swiss-born British painter Henry Fuseli (1741–1825), many of whose works feature fantastic or gruesome elements.

COMMON CORE RL 3, RL 4

G UNITY OF EFFECT
Details of **setting** play a major role in this story's **mood**, or atmosphere, of unrelenting gloom. Reread lines 251–260, a description of one of Roderick Usher's paintings. Notice how **details** work together with **diction**, or choice of words, to create an imaginary setting every bit as disturbing as the story's actual setting. What do you see in Usher's painting? How does the painting reflect the artist's character?

266 impromptus (ăn-prôŋp-tü′) *French:* musical pieces made up as they are played.

DIFFERENTIATED INSTRUCTION

FOR STRUGGLING READERS

Concept Support: Unity of Effect Remind students of Poe's belief that every detail in a story should contribute to building a single unified effect. Ask students to describe in one word the single effect, or mood, in "The Fall of the House of Usher." *Possible answer: terror.* Ask how the descriptions on this page help build that effect. *Possible answer: The descriptions of Roderick's paintings and music show him on the verge of a frightening mental breakdown.*

FOR ENGLISH LANGUAGE LEARNERS

Vocabulary: Prefixes Help students identify the prefixes and clarify the meanings for these words: *distempered* (line 236), *improvised* (line 237), *endeavor* (line 243), *surrounding* (line 247), *hypochondriac* (line 248), *intolerable* and *exception* (line 262), *previously* (line 270), *impressed* (line 272), and *entitled* (line 276).

I

In the greenest of our valleys,
  By good angels tenanted,
Once a fair and stately palace—
  Radiant palace—reared its head.

280

In the monarch Thought's dominion—
  It stood there!
Never seraph spread a pinion
  Over fabric half so fair.

283–284 **Never seraph** (sĕr'əf) . . .
half so fair: No angel ever spread
its wing over half so beautiful a
structure.

II

Banners yellow, glorious, golden,
  On its roof did float and flow;
(This—all this—was in the olden
  Time long ago)

290

And every gentle air that dallied,
  In that sweet day,
Along the ramparts plumed and pallid,
  A winged odor went away.

III

Wanderers in that happy valley
  Through two luminous windows saw
Spirits moving musically
  To a lute's well-tunèd law,
Round about a throne, where sitting
  (Porphyrogene!)

298 **Porphyrogene** (pôr-fîr'ə-jēn'):
a son born to a ruling king.

In state his glory well befitting,
  The ruler of the realm was seen.

300

IV

And all with pearl and ruby glowing
  Was the fair palace door,
Through which came flowing, flowing, flowing
  And sparkling evermore,
A troop of Echoes whose sweet duty
  Was but to sing,
In voices of surpassing beauty,
  The wit and wisdom of their king.

REVISIT THE BIG QUESTION

Where does TERROR *begin?*

Discuss Reread the first four stanzas of the poem (lines 277–308). How does the palace in the poem underscore the terrifying nature of the House of Usher? *Possible answer: The palace is described as a "radiant" place, where banners fly and beautiful voices sing of "The wit and wisdom of their king" (line 308). The beauty of the palace starkly contrasts the dark, melancholy house of Usher.*

FOR STRUGGLING READERS

Develop Reading Fluency Read aloud "The Haunted Palace" to the class. Tell students to note the intonation and rate of your speech. Next, read the first stanza of the poem and have students repeat it back to you as a class. Continue until students have "echoed" the entire poem.

FOR ADVANCED LEARNERS/AP

Discuss Have students compare and contrast the poem "The Haunted Palace" and the story in which it is inserted. Categories to discuss include style, imagery, theme, setting, plot, and characters. Have students discuss whether they find the poem effective in itself, and why or why not.

In lines 277–324, use these prompts to help students comprehend and interpret the poem:

Recall What is the poem about? *Possible answer: It is about a palace "in the olden / Time long ago" (lines 287–288) that fell on hard times.*

Interpret What do the haunted palace and the House of Usher have in common? *Possible answer: They are both grand homes that are haunted by the past and fall into ruin.*

Evaluate Does the poem contribute to the story's unity of effect, or detract from it? *Possible answers: It adds to the unity of effect by providing a comparison that parallels the main story; it detracts from the unity of effect by creating a digression that may puzzle the reader.*

VOCABULARY

COMMON CORE
L 4

OWN THE WORD

pertinacity: *Pertinacity* is related to *tenacious*, which means "holding persistently to something." The prefix *per-* means "through," giving *pertinacity* the connotation of meaning "extremely or perversely persistent." Synonyms that further define *pertinacity* include: bullheadedness, doggedness, obstinacy, pigheadedness, and willfulness.

V

310   But evil things, in robes of sorrow,
            Assailed the monarch's high estate;
    (Ah, let us mourn, for never morrow
            Shall dawn upon him, desolate!)
    And, round about his home, the glory
            That blushed and bloomed
    Is but a dim-remembered story
            Of the old time entombed.

VI

    And travellers now within that valley,
            Through the red-litten windows see
    Vast forms that move fantastically
320   To a discordant melody;
    While, like a rapid ghastly river,
            Through the pale door,
    A hideous throng rush out forever,
            And laugh—but smile no more.

   I well remember that suggestions arising from this ballad led us into a train of thought wherein there became manifest an opinion of Usher's which I mention not so much on account of its novelty (for other men have thought thus), as on account of the **pertinacity** with which he maintained it. This opinion, in its general form, was that of the sentience of all vegetable 330 things. But, in his disordered fancy, the idea had assumed a more daring character, and trespassed, under certain conditions, upon the kingdom of inorganization. I lack words to express the full extent, of the earnest *abandon* of his persuasion. The belief, however, was connected (as I have previously hinted) with the gray stones of the home of his forefathers. The conditions of the sentience had been here, he imagined, fulfilled in the method of collocation of these stones—in the order of their arrangement, as well as in that of the many *fungi* which overspread them, and of the decayed trees which stood around—above all, in the long undisturbed endurance of this arrangement, and in its reduplication in the still waters of the tarn. Its 340 evidence—the evidence of the sentience—was to be seen, he said (and I here stared as he spoke), in the gradual yet certain condensation of an atmosphere of their own about the waters and the walls. The result was discoverable, he added, in that silent yet importunate and terrible influence which for centuries had moulded the destinies of his family, and which made *him* what I now saw him—what he was. Such opinions need no comment, and I will make none.

   Our books—the books which, for years, had formed no small portion of the mental existence of the invalid—were, as might be supposed, in strict keeping with this character of phantasm. We pored together over such works

pertinacity (pûr′tn-ăs′ĭ-tē) *n.* stubbornness; persistence

329–330 sentience (sĕn′shəns) **of all vegetable things:** consciousness of all growing things.

DIFFERENTIATED INSTRUCTION

FOR STRUGGLING READERS
Vocabulary Support Work with students to use context clues to understand words and phrases important to the passage.

• *manifest* (line 326), "visible; understandable; clear"

• *abandon* (line 332), "wild freedom"

• *collocation* (line 336), "arrangement"

• *condensation* (line 341), "change of a gas into a liquid"

• *importunate* (line 343), "urgent"

• *invalid* (line 348), "someone inactive because of long illness"

• *phantasm* (line 349), "ghost; supernatural spirit"

350 as the Ververt et Chartreuse of Gresset; the Belphegor of Machiavelli; the
Heaven and Hell of Swedenborg; the Subterranean Voyage of Nicholas
Klimm by Holberg; the Chiromancy of Robert Flud, of Jean D'Indaginé,
and of De la Chambre; the Journey into the Blue Distance of Tieck; and
the City of the Sun of Campanella. Our favorite volume was a small octavo
edition of the *Directorium Inquisitorium,* by the Dominican Eymeric de
Gironne; and there were passages in Pomponius Mela, about the old African
Satyrs and Aegipans, over which Usher would sit dreaming for hours. His
chief delight, however, was found in the perusal of an exceedingly rare and
curious book in quarto Gothic—the manual of a forgotten church—the
360 *Vigiliae Mortuorum secundum Chorum Ecclesiae Maguntinae.*

I could not help thinking of the wild ritual of this work, and of its
probable influence upon the hypochondriac, when, one evening, having
informed me abruptly that the lady Madeline was no more, he stated his
intention of preserving her corpse for a fortnight (previously to its final
interment), in one of the numerous vaults within the main walls of the
building. The worldly reason, however, assigned for this singular proceeding,
was one which I did not feel at liberty to dispute. The brother had been led
to his resolution (so he told me) by consideration of the unusual character
of the malady of the deceased, of certain obtrusive and eager inquiries on
370 the part of her medical men, and of the remote and exposed situation of the
burial-ground of the family. I will not deny that when I called to mind the
sinister countenance of the person whom I met upon the staircase, on the
day of my arrival at the house, I had no desire to oppose what I regarded
as at best but a harmless, and by no means an unnatural, precaution.

At the request of Usher, I personally aided him in the arrangements for
the temporary entombment. The body having been encoffined, we two
alone bore it to its rest. The vault in which we placed it (and which had
been so long unopened that our torches, half smothered in its oppressive
atmosphere, gave us little opportunity for investigation) was small, damp,
380 and entirely without means of admission for light; lying, at great depth,
immediately beneath that portion of the building in which was my own
sleeping apartment. It had been used, apparently, in remote feudal times, for
the worst purposes of a donjonkeep, and, in later days, as a place of deposit
for powder, or some other highly combustible substance, as a portion of its
floor, and the whole interior of a long archway through which we reached
it, were carefully sheathed with copper. The door, of massive iron, had been,
also, similarly protected. Its immense weight caused an unusually sharp,
grating sound, as it moved upon its hinges. **ⓗ**

Having deposited our mournful burden upon tressels within this region
390 of horror, we partially turned aside the yet unscrewed lid of the coffin,
and looked upon the face of the tenant. A striking similitude between the
brother and sister now first arrested my attention; and Usher, divining,
perhaps, my thoughts, murmured out some few words from which I learned

**350–356 Ververt et Chartreuse
. . . Pomponius Mela:** extravagantly
imaginative works of fiction,
theology, philosophy, and geography.

**360 *Vigiliae Mortuorum secundum
Chorum Ecclesiae Maguntinae*** Latin:
Wakes for the Dead, in the Manner
of the Choir of the Church of Mainz.

**364–365 for a fortnight . . .
interment:** for two weeks prior to its
final burial.

⑤ Targeted Passage

383 donjonkeep (dŏn′jən-kēp):
dungeon.

ⓗ UNITY OF EFFECT
Reread lines 377–388. Why might
Poe have provided so much **detail**
about the structure of the vault?

TEXT ANALYSIS COMMON CORE

ⓗ UNITY OF EFFECT RL 3 / RL 4

Possible answer: *Poe might have provided
so much detail in order to heighten the
reader's feeling of dread.*

IF STUDENTS NEED HELP . . . Ask these
questions:

- What words and phrases make the
  description of Madeline's burial vault
  especially vivid?

- What effect or mood do those details
  create?

FOR STRUGGLING READERS

⑤ Targeted Passage [Lines 375–388]

This passage describes the burial of Madeline
Usher after her death.

- Where do Usher and the narrator bury
  Madeline? (lines 376–378)

- What was the vault once used for? (lines
  382–384)

- What is the atmosphere like in the vault?
  (lines 377–380)

FOR ENGLISH LANGUAGE LEARNERS

Related Vocabulary [small-group option]
Several words on page 423 are related to the
subject of death: *interment* (line 365), *deceased*
(line 369), *entombment* (line 376), *vault* (line
377), *mournful* (line 389), and *coffin* (line 390).
Have students, working in groups, use a
dictionary or thesaurus to find the meanings
of the words. Tell students that some of the
words, such as *deceased, interment,* and *coffin,* are commonly used, whereas other words
are less commonly used today.

Analyze Visuals

Activity What aspects of the picture might be considered terrifying? *Possible answers: Aspects of the picture that might be considered terrifying include the open coffin and the lifelike pink flush and faint smile on the dead woman's face.*

424 UNIT 2: AMERICAN ROMANTICISM

DIFFERENTIATED INSTRUCTION

FOR STRUGGLING READERS

Comprehension Support Have students find details in lines 395–403 that match the details of the illustration. *Possible answers: Madeline's "mockery of a faint blush upon . . . the face" and the "lingering smile upon the lip."*

FOR ENGLISH LANGUAGE LEARNERS

Vocabulary: Idioms Have students work in Jigsaw groups and use context clues to figure out the meaning of these idioms on page 425:

- *gone out* (line 409), "disappeared"
- *to and fro* (lines 427–428), "one way and then the other way"
- *Shaking . . . off* (line 431), "Overcoming the feeling"

BEST PRACTICES TOOLKIT
Jigsaw Reading p. A1

424 UNIT 2: AMERICAN ROMANTICISM

that the deceased and himself had been twins, and that sympathies of a scarcely intelligible nature had always existed between them. Our glances, however, rested not long upon the dead—for we could not regard her unawed. The disease which had thus entombed the lady in the maturity of her youth, had left, as usual in all maladies of a strictly cataleptical character, the mockery of a faint blush upon the bosom and the face, and 400 that suspiciously lingering smile upon the lip which is so terrible in death. We replaced and screwed down the lid, and, having secured the door of iron, made our way, with toil, into the scarcely less gloomy apartments of the upper portion of the house.

And now, some days of bitter grief having elapsed, an observable change came over the features of the mental disorder of my friend. His ordinary manner had vanished. His ordinary occupations were neglected or forgotten. He roamed from chamber to chamber with hurried, unequal, and objectless step. The pallor of his countenance had assumed, if possible, a more ghastly hue—but the luminousness of his eye had utterly gone out. The 410 once occasional huskiness of his tone was heard no more; and a tremulous quaver, as if of extreme terror, habitually characterized his utterance. There were times, indeed, when I thought his unceasingly agitated mind was laboring with some oppressive secret, to divulge which he struggled for the necessary courage. At times, again, I was obliged to resolve all into the mere inexplicable **vagaries** of madness, for I beheld him gazing upon vacancy for long hours, in an attitude of the profoundest attention, as if listening to some imaginary sound. It was no wonder that his condition terrified—that it infected me. I felt creeping upon me, by slow yet certain degrees, the wild influences of his own fantastic yet impressive superstitions.

420 It was, especially, upon retiring to bed late in the night of the seventh or eighth day after the placing of the lady Madeline within the donjon, that I experienced the full power of such feelings. Sleep came not near my couch—while the hours waned and waned away. I struggled to reason off the nervousness which had dominion over me. I endeavored to believe that much, if not all of what I felt, was due to the bewildering influence of the gloomy furniture of the room—of the dark and tattered draperies, which, tortured into motion by the breath of a rising tempest, swayed fitfully to and fro upon the walls, and rustled uneasily about the decorations of the bed. But my efforts were fruitless. An irrepressible tremor gradually pervaded 430 my frame; and, at length, there sat upon my very heart an incubus of utterly causeless alarm. Shaking this off with a gasp and a struggle, I uplifted myself upon the pillows, and, peering earnestly within the intense darkness of the chamber, hearkened—I know not why, except that an instinctive spirit prompted me—to certain low and indefinite sounds which came, through the pauses of the storm, at long intervals, I knew not whence. Overpowered by an intense sentiment of horror, unaccountable yet unendurable, I threw on my clothes with haste (for I felt that I should sleep no more during the night), and endeavored to arouse myself from the pitiable condition into which I had fallen, by pacing rapidly to and fro through the apartment. **I**

⑥ Targeted Passage

vagary (vā′gə-rē) *n.* strange idea

423 **couch:** bed.

430 **incubus:** something that burdens like a nightmare.

I COMPLEX SENTENCES
Reread lines 431–435. Identify the main subject and verb of the sentence. Which participial phrases modify this subject?

TIERED DISCUSSION PROMPTS

In lines 420–439, use these prompts to help students comprehend and interpret the developing plot:

Connect What is the narrator feeling? Why? *Possible answer: He is feeling a sense of growing terror, due in part to his surroundings, but also due to his own inability to control his emotions.*

Analyze What evidence can you find that hints at the narrator's state of mind? *Possible answers: He cannot sleep; he becomes tremulous and stares intently into the darkness; he leaps out of bed and paces about the apartment to shake off his nervousness.*

Synthesize What kind of effect does Poe achieve in this passage? How? *Possible answer: Poe achieves a mood of building torment and terror by balancing the narrator's description of his surroundings with the description of his inner struggles.*

READING SKILL COMMON CORE L 3a

I Model the Skill:
COMPLEX SENTENCES

The main subject is *I.* There are two main verbs, since the sentence has a compound predicate: *uplifted* and *hearkened*. Participial phrases modifying the subject are *Shaking this off* and *peering earnestly*.

Present this model to help students understand participial phrases.

Gazing out the window, she looked at the rain.

Ask students to identify the subject, verb, and participial phrase. **Answer: Subject: she; verb: looked; participial phrase: Gazing out the window.**

VOCABULARY COMMON CORE L 4

OWN THE WORD

vagary: The Latin word *vagus* means "wandering" and *vagary* means "strange idea," or "erratic notion or action." Have students describe a person motivated by *vagaries*. **Possible answer: People with vagaries are not easily dissuaded; they may seem restless until they take action.**

FOR STRUGGLING READERS

⑥ Targeted Passage [Lines 404–419]

This passage describes Roderick Usher's advancing decline and the narrator's increasing terror.

• What changes come over Roderick after his sister's burial? (lines 404–414)

• How does the narrator change as he watches the alterations in Usher's looks and behavior? (lines 417–419)

FOR RELUCTANT READERS

Connect to the Text "The Fall of the House of Usher" places three characters in an intensely dramatic setting. As they read, have students consider which current movie actors would be best suited to portray the characters in a film adaptation of this story. Call on students to share the actors they chose and the reasons for their selections.

Where does TERROR *begin?*

In lines 452–465, how does the weather contribute to the terrifying atmosphere of this scene? *Possible answer: The whirlwind threatens to destroy the house. In addition, this weather is terrifying because of the unnatural—or supernatural—luminous gas that surrounds the mansion.*

VOCABULARY

COMMON CORE
L 4

OWN THE WORD

- **demeanor:** *Demeanor* refers to behavior that reveals one's personality. Ask students to list words of similar meaning that could replace *demeanor* in the phrase "...restrained hysteria in his whole *demeanor.*" *Possible answer: bearing, carriage, conduct, manner*

- **anomaly:** Explain that an *anomaly* is something that "departs from the normal rules" or is "abnormal." Have students write a sentence demonstrating their understanding of the word.
Possible answers: Snow in July is an anomaly, *even here in Colorado. A goose living with swans is an* anomaly *to the flock.*

---

440   I had taken but a few turns in this manner, when a light step on an adjoining staircase arrested my attention. I presently recognized it as that of Usher. In an instant afterward he rapped, with a gentle touch, at my door, and entered, bearing a lamp. His countenance was, as usual, cadaverously wan—but, moreover, there was a species of mad hilarity in his eyes—an evidently restrained *hysteria* in his whole **demeanor.** His air appalled me— but any thing was preferable to the solitude which I had so long endured, and I even welcomed his presence as a relief.

     "And you have not seen it?" he said abruptly, after having stared about him for some moments in silence—"you have not then seen it?—but, stay!
450 you shall." Thus speaking, and having carefully shaded his lamp, he hurried to one of the casements, and threw it freely open to the storm.

     The impetuous fury of the entering gust nearly lifted us from our feet. It was, indeed, a tempestuous yet sternly beautiful night, and one wildly singular in its terror and its beauty. A whirlwind had apparently collected its force in our vicinity; for there were frequent and violent alterations in the direction of the wind; and the exceeding density of the clouds (which hung so low as to press upon the turrets of the house) did not prevent our perceiving the lifelike velocity with which they flew careering from all points against each other, without passing away into the distance. I say that even
460 their exceeding density did not prevent our perceiving this—yet we had no glimpse of the moon or stars, nor was there any flashing forth of lightning. But the under surfaces of the huge masses of agitated vapor, as well as the terrestrial objects immediately around us, were glowing in the unnatural light of a faintly luminous and distinctly visible gaseous exhalation which hung about and enshrouded the mansion.

     "You must not—you shall not behold this!" said I, shuddering, to Usher, as I led him, with a gentle violence, from the window to a seat. "These appearances, which bewilder you, are merely electrical phenomena not uncommon—or it may be that they have their ghastly origin in the rank
470 miasma of the tarn. Let us close this casement;—the air is chilling and dangerous to your frame. Here is one of your favorite romances. I will read, and you shall listen;—and so we will pass away this terrible night together."

     The antique volume which I had taken up was the "Mad Trist" of Sir Launcelot Canning; but I had called it a favorite of Usher's more in sad jest than in earnest; for, in truth, there is little in its uncouth and unimaginative prolixity which could have had interest for the lofty and spiritual ideality of my friend. It was, however, the only book immediately at hand; and I indulged a vague hope that the excitement which now agitated the hypochondriac, might find relief (for the history of mental disorder is full of
480 similar **anomalies**) even in the extremeness of the folly which I should read. Could I have judged, indeed, by the wild overstrained air of vivacity with which he hearkened, or apparently hearkened, to the words of the tale, I might well have congratulated myself upon the success of my design.

demeanor (dĭ-mē′nər) *n.* behavior

458 careering: going at top speed.

462–463 huge masses ... terrestrial objects: the huge, fast-moving clouds, as well as the objects on the ground.

470 miasma (mī-ăz′mə): poisonous vapors.

475–476 uncouth ... prolixity (prō-lĭk′sĭ-tē): clumsy and unimaginative wordiness.

anomaly (ə-nŏm′ə-lē) *n.* departure from the normal rules

DIFFERENTIATED INSTRUCTION

FOR STRUGGLING READERS

Vocabulary Support Poe uses vivid but ornate vocabulary to describe the whirlwind and its effects. Help students find synonyms for the difficult words.

- *casements* (line 451), "windows"
- *impetuous* (line 452), "violent"
- *alterations* (line 455), "changes"
- *density* (line 456), "thickness"
- *velocity* (line 458), "speed"

- *careering* (line 458), "rushing"
- *perceiving* (lines 458, 460), "seeing"
- *terrestrial* (line 463), "earthly"
- *luminous* (line 464), "glowing"
- *enshrouded* (line 465), "covered"

Analyze Visuals

Activity How does this image capture the narrator's description in lines 453–465 of the tempestuous night sky? ***Possible answers:*** *The image captures the eerie beauty of the night sky, one in which the "exceeding density of the clouds" (line 456) is broken by a "faintly luminous and distinctly visible gaseous exhalation" (line 464). The lone figure staring out from the half-open window could be either Roderick or the narrator.*

FOR ADVANCED LEARNERS/AP

Analyze Tone Have students analyze the tone of the passage in which the narrator helps Roderick confront the whirlwind (lines 440–472). Ask students to examine the diction of the descriptive passages and the two characters' dialogue in making their analyses. Point out that tone changes in the course of this passage; have them pinpoint places where the tone becomes more, or less, excited. Then invite students to rewrite passages to change the tone. They may wish to heighten the emotional intensity of the quieter passages such as lines 440–443, or they may wish to reduce the emotional intensity of the more frantic passages. Have students read their versions aloud. Discuss what impact these changes have on the effect of the tale.

In lines 497–527, use these prompts to help students understand the story within the story and the connections between these two tales:

Recall What causes the narrator to pause in his reading of the story of the "Mad Trist"? *Possible answer: During his first pause, the narrator hears the sound of cracking and ripping similar to that described in the story. The second time he pauses, he hears a "harsh, protracted . . . screaming or grating sound" (lines 524–525), also like that in the story.*

Analyze How do events in the "Mad Trist" help build suspense? *Possible answer: The first sound described in the "Mad Trist" is replicated in the House of Usher. As a result, readers suspect that additional events described in the tale will also be echoed in events in the house. The reader anticipates these events and the anticipation builds suspense.*

Synthesize Based on events that have already occurred and on inferences you make from this description of events during the reading of the "Mad Trist," what do you predict will happen next? Explain. *Accept all thoughtful responses. Students should cite evidence and reasons for their predictions.*

I had arrived at that well-known portion of the story where Ethelred, the hero of the Trist, having sought in vain for peaceable admission into the dwelling of the hermit, proceeds to make good an entrance by force. Here, it will be remembered, the words of the narrative run thus:

"And Ethelred, who was by nature of a doughty heart, and who was now mighty withal, on account of the powerfulness of the wine which he
490 had drunken, waited no longer to hold parley with the hermit, who, in sooth, was of an obstinate and maliceful turn, but, feeling the rain upon his shoulders, and fearing the rising of the tempest, uplifted his mace outright, and, with blows, made quickly room in the plankings of the door for his gauntleted hand; and now pulling therewith sturdily, he so cracked, and ripped, and tore all asunder, that the noise of the dry and hollow-sounding wood alarumed and reverberated throughout the forest."

At the termination of this sentence I started and, for a moment, paused; for it appeared to me (although I at once concluded that my excited fancy had deceived me)—it appeared to me that, from some very remote portion
500 of the mansion, there came, indistinctly, to my ears, what might have been, in its exact similarity of character, the echo (but a stifled and dull one certainly) of the very cracking and ripping sound which Sir Launcelot had so particularly described. It was, beyond doubt, the coincidence alone which had arrested my attention; for, amid the rattling of the sashes of the casements, and the ordinary commingled noises of the still increasing storm, the sound, in itself, had nothing, surely, which should have interested or disturbed me. I continued the story:

"But the good champion Ethelred, now entering within the door, was sore enraged and amazed to perceive no signal of the maliceful hermit;
510 but, in the stead thereof, a dragon of scaly and prodigious demeanor, and of a fiery tongue, which sate in guard before a palace of gold, with a floor of silver; and upon the wall there hung a shield of shining brass with this legend enwritten—

Who entereth herein, a conqueror hath bin;
Who slayeth the dragon, the shield he shall win;

And Ethelred uplifted his mace, and struck upon the head of the dragon, which fell before him, and gave up his pesty breath, with a shriek so horrid and harsh, and withal so piercing, that Ethelred had fain to close his ears with his hands against the dreadful noise of it, the like whereof was never
520 before heard."

Here again I paused abruptly, and now with a feeling of wild amazement—for there could be no doubt whatever that, in this instance, I did actually hear (although from what direction it proceeded I found it impossible to say) a low and apparently distant, but harsh, protracted, and most unusual screaming or grating sound—the exact counterpart of what

492–494 uplifted his mace . . . gauntleted hand: raised his spiked club and cut a space in the door for his armored, gloved hand.

COMMON CORE L 1a
Language Coach
Formal Language *Termination* (line 497) means "end" or "conclusion." *Termination* usually has a formal tone, and is often used these days in legal or official language. How is Poe using *termination* here, though?

⑦

517 pesty: poisonous.

DIFFERENTIATED INSTRUCTION

FOR STRUGGLING READERS

⑦ Targeted Passage [Lines 497–507]

In this passage, the narrator reads from the "Mad Trist," a story that parallels events in the narrative.

- Why does the narrator pause in his reading? (lines 497–503)

- What does the narrator hear? (lines 500–506)

- How does he react? (lines 503–507)

FOR ENGLISH LANGUAGE LEARNERS

Language Coach **COMMON CORE L 1a**
Formal Language *Answer:*
Poe is using the word simply to mean "end." He doesn't mean it in a legal or official sense. Have students scan the story for another example of formal language. Instruct students to then explain how Poe uses the word(s) they identified.

my fancy had conjured up for the dragon's unnatural shriek as described by the romancer. **J**

Oppressed, as I certainly was, upon the occurrence of this second and most extraordinary coincidence, by a thousand conflicting sensations,
530 in which wonder and extreme terror were predominant, I still retained sufficient presence of mind to avoid exciting, by any observation, the sensitive nervousness of my companion. I was by no means certain that he had noticed the sounds in question; although, assuredly, a strange alteration had, during the last few minutes, taken place in his demeanor. From a position fronting my own, he had gradually brought round his chair, so as to sit with his face to the door of the chamber; and thus I could but partially perceive his features, although I saw that his lips trembled as if he were murmuring inaudibly. His head had dropped upon his breast—yet I knew that he was not asleep, from the wide and rigid opening of the eye as I
540 caught a glance of it in profile. The motion of his body, too, was at variance with this idea—for he rocked from side to side with a gentle yet constant and uniform sway. Having rapidly taken notice of all this, I resumed the narrative of Sir Launcelot, which thus proceeded:

"And now, the champion, having escaped from the terrible fury of the dragon, bethinking himself of the brazen shield, and of the breaking up of the enchantment which was upon it, removed the carcass from out of the way before him, and approached valorously over the silver pavement of the castle to where the shield was upon the wall; which in sooth tarried not for his full coming, but fell down at his feet upon the silver floor, with a mighty
550 great and terrible ringing sound."

No sooner had these syllables passed my lips, than—as if a shield of brass had indeed, at the moment, fallen heavily upon a floor of silver—I became aware of a distinct, hollow, metallic, and clangorous, yet apparently muffled, reverberation. Completely unnerved, I leaped to my feet; but the measured rocking movement of Usher was undisturbed. I rushed to the chair in which he sat. His eyes were bent fixedly before him, and throughout his whole countenance there reigned a stony rigidity. But, as I placed my hand upon his shoulder, there came a strong shudder over his whole person; a sickly smile quivered about his lips; and I saw that he spoke in a low, hurried, and
560 gibbering murmur, as if unconscious of my presence. Bending closely over him, I at length drank in the hideous import of his words.

"Not hear it?—yes, I hear it, and *have* heard it. Long—long—long—many minutes, many hours, many days, have I heard it—yet I dared not—oh, pity me, miserable wretch that I am!—I dared not—I *dared* not speak! *We have put her living in the tomb!* Said I not that my senses were acute? I *now* tell you that I heard her first feeble movements in the hollow coffin. I heard them—many, many days ago—yet I dared not—*I dared not speak!* And now—to-night—Ethelred—ha ha!—the breaking of the hermit's door, and the death-cry of the dragon, and the clangor of the shield!—say, rather, the

J UNITY OF EFFECT
Reread lines 521–527. What coincidence is repeated?

COMMON CORE L 4

Language Coach

Fixed Expressions The term *fixed expression* refers to the normal combination of words— the ways they are often used. Note "by no means certain" (line 532). *By no means* is often used before *certain*. Create a sentence with one of these fixed expressions: *almost certain, [to] grow certain.*

TEXT ANALYSIS

COMMON CORE

J UNITY OF EFFECT

RL 3
RL 4

Possible answer: The repeated coincidence is that after reading about an eerie sound, the narrator hears such a sound in the house.

Extend the Discussion Repetition is one way Poe achieves unity of effect in this story. What are some other ways?

FOR ADVANCED LEARNERS/AP

Synthesize The theme of burial alive was a favorite of Poe's. He used it in several stories, including "The Cask of Amontillado" and "The Premature Burial." Why do you think an author would turn to this same macabre topic again and again? *Possible answers: The topic is frightening, and so it helped Poe achieve his intended effect on the reader; the topic may have reflected an obsessive fear in Poe.*

FOR ENGLISH LANGUAGE LEARNERS

Language Coach

COMMON CORE L 4

Fixed Expressions *Answer:*
Answers will vary. Lead a class discussion in which students brainstorm other examples of fixed expressions. Have a volunteer write the examples on the board. Randomly call on students to use a fixed expression on the board in a sentence.

430   UNIT 2: AMERICAN ROMANTICISM

K UNITY OF EFFECT

Possible answer: *The earlier description of the vault (lines 375–388) alerts the reader that there is something odd about the circumstances of the burial. The vault is "half smothered," which subtly foreshadows Madeline's condition. The "immense weight" of the door makes Madeline's later escape seem all the more horrible.*

Analyze Visuals

Possible answers: *Yes; the artist's interpretation is effective, because the blood on Madeline's dress and the shadows on her face are frightening and ominous. No; the artist's interpretation is not as effective as the description, because it does not reproduce the sound and movement or capture the narrator's horror.*

THEME

TEXT STRUCTURE

After students have completed this short story, ask them to discuss films, plays, or novels that relate to the theme of decay or decline. Ask them especially to focus on the text or narrative structures that hide the true decay or decline of a place or person.

---

570 rending of her coffin, and the grating of the iron hinges of her prison, and her struggles within the coppered archway of the vault! Oh! whither shall I fly? Will she not be here anon? Is she not hurrying to upbraid me for my haste? Have I not heard her footstep on the stair? Do I not distinguish that heavy and horrible beating of her heart? MADMAN!"—here he sprang furiously to his feet, and shrieked out his syllables, as if in the effort he were giving up his soul—"MADMAN! I TELL YOU THAT SHE NOW STANDS WITHOUT THE DOOR!" K

As if in the superhuman energy of his utterance there had been found the potency of a spell, the huge antique panels to which the speaker pointed threw slowly back, upon the instant, their ponderous and ebony jaws. It 580 was the work of the rushing gust—but then without those doors there did stand the lofty and enshrouded figure of the lady Madeline of Usher. There was blood upon her white robes, and the evidence of some bitter struggle upon every portion of her emaciated frame. For a moment she remained trembling and reeling to and fro upon the threshold—then, with a low moaning cry, fell heavily inward upon the person of her brother, and in her violent and now final death-agonies, bore him to the floor a corpse, and a victim to the terrors he had anticipated.

From the chamber, and from that mansion, I fled aghast. The storm was still abroad in all its wrath as I found myself crossing the old causeway. 590 Suddenly there shot along the path a wild light, and I turned to see whence a gleam so unusual could have issued; for the vast house and its shadows were alone behind me. The radiance was that of the full, setting, and blood-red moon, which now shone vividly through that once barely discernible fissure, of which I have before spoken as extending from the roof of the building, in a zigzag direction, to the base. While I gazed, the fissure rapidly widened—there came a fierce breath of the whirlwind—the entire orb of the satellite burst at once upon my sight—my brain reeled as I saw the mighty walls rushing asunder—there was a long tumultuous shouting sound like the voice of a thousand waters—and the deep and dank tarn at my feet closed 600 sullenly and silently over the fragments of the "HOUSE OF USHER." ❧

K UNITY OF EFFECT
Reread lines 568–571. Recall the description of the vault you read earlier. In what way does that description help set up the situation of the story's **climax**?

⑧ **Targeted Passage**

Analyze Visuals ▶
Compare the image on the opposite page with the description in lines 581–587. Is the artist's interpretation of the scene effective? Support your answer with details from the selection.

THEME
Many works of literature touch on the theme of decay or decline. In "The Fall of the House of Usher," Poe explores this theme though his description of the Usher family and their decaying mansion. Stories that center on this theme tend to follow the same text structure: on the outside things seem to be stable or alive, but in fact they are decaying and rotting from the inside, leading to a dramatic collapse. For example, in the novels of William Faulkner, such as *The Sound and the Fury* (1929), Faulkner writes about the decline of a southern community. What other novels, plays, or films touch on the theme of decay and decline?

DIFFERENTIATED INSTRUCTION

FOR STRUGGLING READERS

⑧ **Targeted Passage** [Lines 573–587]

This passage highlights the story's height of horror.

• What does Roderick hear on the stair? (lines 573–574)

• Who stands outside the door? (lines 580–581)

• How does Roderick meet his end? (lines 584–587)

FOR ADVANCED LEARNERS/AP

Plot Devices [paired option] Have students work in pairs to use the Analysis Frame: Plot to analyze the plot devices Poe uses in "The Fall of the House of Usher" and to evaluate the effectiveness of those devices in the story.

 BEST PRACTICES TOOLKIT—Transparency Analysis Frame: Plot pp. D21, D28

REVISIT THE BIG QUESTION

Where does TERROR *begin?*

In lines 577–600, how does the terrifying mood reach its most intense point in the story's concluding scene? ***Possible answer:*** *Madeline's appearance, along with her death and the death of her brother bring all of the mysterious happenings to a culmination. Roderick's and the narrator's fears reach a breaking point that ends the story.*

SELECTION WRAP-UP

READ WITH A PURPOSE Now that students have read the selection, tell them to consider the story's title. How does the title relate to the events of the story? ***Possible answer:*** *"The Fall of the House of Usher" describes the literal collapse of the mansion as well as the end of the Usher family line.*

⭐ CRITIQUE

- Ask students to compare "The Fall of the House of Usher" to other terrifying stories or films. Have them explain their answers.

- After completing the After Reading questions on page 432, have students revisit their responses and tell whether they have changed their opinions.

INDEPENDENT READING

Students can read about another eerie house in *The House of Seven Gables* by Nathaniel Hawthorne.

FOR ADVANCED LEARNERS/AP

Critical Interpretation [small-group option] The story includes some interesting mirror images, including the image of the House of Usher mirrored in the tarn, the decay of the house mirrored in the decay of Roderick, and the twins, Roderick and Madeline, who mirror each other. Critics have offered many interpretations of the meaning of these double images. Invite students to work in groups to examine them further.

How many instances of mirror images can they find and how elaborate are they? Roderick and Madeline, for example, are twins and share a "striking similitude" (line 391), they share a family illness, and they die together. Have students develop their own interpretations of the purpose of these mirror images. How do they contribute to the theme and plot of the story? Ask groups to share their ideas with the class.

Practice and Apply

For preliminary support of post-reading questions, use these copy masters:

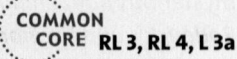 **RESOURCE MANAGER—Copy Masters**
Reading Check p. 162
Unity of Effect p. 155
Question Support p. 163
Additional selection questions are provided for teachers on page 149.

ANSWERS

COMMON CORE **RL 3, RL 4, L 3a**

1. *He has come to help his childhood friend Roderick Usher, who invited him to visit.*

2. *She takes to her bed and is expected to die soon.*

3. *He fears that her body may be stolen.*

Possible answers:

4. ● COMMON CORE FOCUS **Understand Complex Sentences** *The mood is less terrifying when conveyed in simple, everyday language.*

5. *The title describes the decline and fall of both a family and a mansion, and it anticipates both kinds of collapse.*

6. ● COMMON CORE FOCUS **Analyze Unity of Effect** *Setting: old, decaying house; windows inaccessible; feeble light; dark draperies, old furniture; gloomy atmosphere;* ***Character traits:*** *Roderick is distressed, distracted, and hypersensitive to light and sound;* ***Plot developments:*** *Madeline's illness, death, burial, and re-emergence parallel the intensity of Roderick's emotions and changes in the narrator;* ***Imagery:*** *images of darkness, dreariness, and decay throughout*

7. *Students may say yes because the mood is compelling and the elements of the story work together. Others may say that the mood overwhelms other aspects of the story.*

8. *Students may disagree by challenging the idea that a story must have deep meaning, or by saying that this story vividly portrays a sick mind. They may agree by citing story elements that seem chosen solely for sensationalistic effect.*

After Reading

Comprehension

1. **Recall** Why does the narrator come to the House of Usher?

2. **Recall** What change in Madeline's condition occurs shortly after the narrator's arrival?

3. **Clarify** What are Roderick's reasons for placing Madeline in the vault below the house?

Text Analysis

● 4. **Examine Complex Sentences** Review the chart you created as you read. Compare your paraphrases with Poe's original sentences. Without Poe's elaborate language, does the story have the same **mood?** Explain.

5. **Interpret Title** Reread lines 58–68. Based on this passage, explain two possible meanings of the story's title. In what ways does the title help you anticipate the ending of the story?

● 6. **Analyze Unity of Effect** In what way does each of the following demonstrate Poe's principle of the single effect? Cite key details that show Poe's use of the specified story element to build **mood.**

   - setting (lines 115–125)
   - character traits (lines 172–176)
   - plot developments (lines 216–222)
   - imagery (lines 452–465)

7. **Evaluate Author's Technique** In your opinion, does Poe's technique of the unified effect accomplish its intended purpose? What, if any, are the disadvantages of his approach? Explain.

Text Criticism

8. **Critical Interpretations** The literary critic Cleanth Brooks dismissed "The Fall of the House of Usher" as an "essentially meaningless" exercise in horror for its own sake. Considering your own reading of the story, do you agree or disagree with this opinion? Cite details to support your answer.

> *Where does* **TERROR** *begin?*
>
> How does Poe's use of the first-person point of view help communicate the experience of terror?

COMMON CORE

RL 3 Analyze the impact of the author's choices regarding how to develop and relate elements of a story. **RL 4** Analyze the impact of specific word choices on meaning and tone. **L 3a** Apply an understanding of syntax to the study of complex texts when reading.

Where does TERROR *begin?*
Possible answer: The reader follows in the narrator's footsteps, experiencing the terror firsthand.

Vocabulary in Context

▲ **VOCABULARY PRACTICE**

Choose the word that is not related in meaning to the other words.

1. (a) dull, (b) uninteresting, (c) insipid, (d) insecure
2. (a) demeanor, (b) antique, (c) manner, (d) interaction
3. (a) conception, (b) delusion, (c) vagary, (d) tome
4. (a) connection, (b) disturbance, (c) affinity, (d) relationship
5. (a) deviation, (b) oddity, (c) representative, (d) anomaly
6. (a) bureaucratic, (b) extravagant, (c) extreme, (d) inordinate
7. (a) apathy, (b) ecstasy, (c) indifference, (d) unconcern
8. (a) agony, (b) torment, (c) alleviation, (d) anguish
9. (a) persistence, (b) perseverance, (c) pretense, (d) pertinacity
10. (a) hazy, (b) ambiguous, (c) contentious, (d) equivocal

WORD LIST

affinity
alleviation
anomaly
apathy
demeanor
equivocal
inordinate
insipid
pertinacity
vagary

ACADEMIC VOCABULARY IN WRITING

• construct • expand • indicate • reinforce • role

Poe uses a creepy setting, a disturbed character, and mounting suspense to **reinforce** horror in his story. Think about which of these elements had the most success in creating a sense of horror for you. Then, in a paragraph discuss why that particular element played such an important **role** in the story. Use at least three of the Academic Vocabulary words in your paragraph.

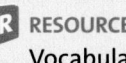

⦙ **COMMON CORE**

L 4b–c Identify and use patterns of word changes that indicate different meanings or parts of speech; consult general reference materials.

VOCABULARY STRATEGY: THE GREEK ROOT *path*

The vocabulary word *apathy* contains the Greek root *path*, which means "feel" or "suffer." This root is found in a number of English words. To understand words with *path*, use context clues as well as your knowledge of the root's meaning.

PRACTICE Choose the word from the word web that best completes each sentence. Consider what you know about the Greek root and the other word parts shown. If necessary, consult a dictionary.

apathy   pathos
antipathy   **path**   psychopathic
empathize   telepathy

1. Her brother's cruel actions caused her to feel a strong _____ for him.
2. The characters' tearful farewell evoked a sense of _____ in the audience.
3. Their thoughts were so aligned that it seemed they could communicate by _____.
4. Many criminals' behavior tends to be _____.
5. Parents are often able to _____ with their children's problems and frustrations.

Interactive Vocabulary **THINK** central

Go to **thinkcentral.com**.
KEYWORD: HML11-433

THE FALL OF THE HOUSE OF USHER **433**

ANSWERS

Vocabulary in Context

VOCABULARY PRACTICE

1. *(d) insecure*   6. *(a) bureaucratic*
2. *(b) antique*   7. *(b) ecstasy*
3. *(d) tome*   8. *(c) alleviation*
4. *(b) disturbance*   9. *(c) pretense*
5. *(c) representative*   10. *(c) contentious*

R RESOURCE MANAGER—Copy Master
Vocabulary Practice p. 160

ACADEMIC VOCABULARY IN WRITING

Answers will vary, but should demonstrate an understanding of the word's meanings.

VOCABULARY STRATEGY:
THE GREEK ROOT *path*

⦙ **COMMON CORE L 4b–c**

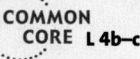

In addition to context clues, tell students to use the other word parts in a *path* word in order to figure out its meaning. For example, *antipathy* contains the prefix *anti-* and the suffix *-y*. *Telepathy* has the prefix *tele-* and the suffix *-y*. *Apathy* has the prefix *a-* and the suffix *-y*. *Empathize* has the suffix *-ize*. The suffixes give clues to the words' parts of speech: *-y* for state-of-being nouns, and *-ize* for verbs.

Answers: 1. *antipathy* **2.** *pathos* **3.** *telepathy*, **4.** *psychopathic* **5.** *empathize*

R RESOURCE MANAGER—Copy Master
Vocabulary Strategy p. 161

Interactive Vocabulary **THINK** central

Keywords direct students to a **WordSharp** tutorial on **thinkcentral.com** or to other types of vocabulary practice and review.

Language

GRAMMAR AND STYLE

Focus students' attention on the difference between participles ending in *-ed* or *-ing* and verbs with the same endings. Remind them that a participle modifies a noun or pronoun. An example is "the cooked food." In contrast, the word *cooked* could be a verb when it indicates an action, as in, "I cooked the food." (For more on participles and participial phrases, see page R66 in the **Grammar Handbook.**)

Possible answers: 1. *The firefighters ran toward the burning building.* **2.** *Researching my report, I discovered many new facts.* **3.** *Snow fell thickly over the woods, creating an enchanted scene.*

 RESOURCE MANAGER—Copy Master
Add Descriptive Details p. 164

READING-WRITING CONNECTION

Have students use the Observation Chart to select details for their descriptions. Have them select an everyday location and write details on the chart as they visualize it. Tell them to refer to the chart as they write, adding modifiers to the details to make the description more eerie and terrifying.

 BEST PRACTICES TOOLKIT—Transparency
Observation Chart p. C7

Writing Online  THINK central

The following tools are available online at **thinkcentral.com** and on **Write*Smart* CD-ROM:**
- **Interactive Graphic Organizers**
- **Interactive Student Models**
- **Interactive Revision Lessons**
  For additional grammar instruction, see **GrammarNotes** on **thinkcentral.com.**

Assess and Reteach

Assess

DIAGNOSTIC AND SELECTION TESTS
Selection Test A, B/C pp. 133–134, 135–136

Interactive Selection Test on **thinkcentral.com**

Reteach

Level Up Tutorials on **thinkcentral.com**

Language

◆ **GRAMMAR AND STYLE:** Add Descriptive Details

Review the **Grammar and Style** note on page 415. Poe is a master of elaborate, ornate descriptions that are packed with details. Some of his descriptive words are **participles,** verb forms that function as adjectives, as in this example:

His long improvised dirges will ring forever in my ears. (lines 236–237)

Participles usually end in *-ing* or *-ed* and can be combined with modifiers and complements to make **participial phrases.**

PRACTICE Read each of the following sentences from Poe's story, noting the boldfaced participle or participial phrase. Then, write your own sentence, using a participle as instructed in parentheses. An example has been done for you.

> **EXAMPLE**
>
> His countenance, I thought, wore a **mingled** expression of low cunning and perplexity. (Use a past participle, one that ends with *-ed.*)
>
> *The cat, I noticed, carried a mangled mouse in her jaws.*

1. A sensation of stupor oppressed me as my eyes followed her **retreating** steps. (Use a present participle, one that ends with *-ing.*)

2. **Shaking off from my spirit what *must* have been a dream,** I scanned more narrowly the real aspect of the building. (Use a participial phrase to begin your sentence. Make sure your phrase modifies the subject.)

3. Minute fungi overspread the whole exterior, **hanging in a fine tangled web-work from the eaves.** (Use a participial phrase at the end of your sentence. Make sure the phrase modifies the subject.)

READING-WRITING CONNECTION

 YOUR TURN Expand your understanding of Poe's writing by responding to this prompt. Then, use the **revising tips** to improve your description.

WRITING PROMPT	REVISING TIPS
WRITE A DESCRIPTION You don't need far-off locales and crumbling castles to inspire **terror.** Using a few well-chosen details, you can turn a familiar scene into an unsettling backdrop for eerie events. Write a **two- to four-paragraph description** that makes an everyday location seem terrifying. Choose descriptive details that suggest something strange or unsettling is at work.	• Use descriptive details that appeal to the five senses. • Arrange your description in spatial order so readers can better understand what you are describing. • Include recognizable elements of terror that are subtle, yet alarming.

 COMMON CORE

L 3 Apply knowledge of language to understand how language functions in different contexts, to make effective choices for meaning or style, and to comprehend more fully when reading. **W 3** Write narratives that use telling details and sensory language to convey a vivid picture of the experiences, events, setting and/or characters.

Interactive Vocabulary THINK central
Go to **thinkcentral.com**.
KEYWORD: HML11-434

DIFFERENTIATED INSTRUCTION

FOR STRUGGLING WRITERS
Writing Support

- Have students work in a group to brainstorm possible topics.
- Allow more than one student to use the same topic.
- Limit the description to two paragraphs.

- Have students' peers read the first drafts and provide feedback, especially concerning places where the writers could add more details and use more vivid words.
- If possible, allow students time for revision.
- Recommend that students use a thesaurus and a dictionary to find descriptive words.

The Raven

Essential Course of Study ✓ **ECOS**

Poem by Edgar Allan Poe

COMMON CORE

RL 1, RL 4, RL 5, L 4

VIDEO TRAILER **THINK** central KEYWORD: HML11-435A

TEXT ANALYSIS: SOUND DEVICES

First published in 1845, "The Raven" became an instant hit. Part of the poem's popularity was due to Poe's clever use of **sound devices**, patterns of word sounds used to create musical effects.

- **Rhyme,** the repetition of similar sounds, is one of the easiest sound devices to spot. Poe adds variety by using **internal rhyme,** rhyming words that fall inside a line.

  Ah, distinctly I remember it was in the bleak December;

- **Repetition,** of rhymes and of words and phrases, helps give "The Raven" its distinctive rhythm.

  As of someone gently rapping, rapping at my chamber door.

- **Alliteration,** the repetition of initial consonant sounds, is used to create rhythm or to stress key words.

  While I nodded, nearly napping . . .

- **Onomatopoeia** is the use of words that sound like their meaning, such as the word *rustling* in this example:

  And the silken, sad, uncertain rustling of each purple curtain

As you read, note how Poe combines these sound devices to form complex rhythmic patterns.

Review: **Stanza and Rhyme Scheme**

READING SKILL: MAKE INFERENCES

"The Raven" tells a story without directly stating all of the important details. You'll need to use clues in the poem to **make inferences** about the speaker's situation. As you read, use a chart like the one shown to record your inferences and the clues that helped you. By the end of the poem, you'll be able to **draw conclusions** about what the speaker experiences.

	Inferences About the Speaker	Clues
State of Mind		
Recent Experiences		

 Complete the activities in your **Reader/Writer Notebook.**

How do people handle LOSS?

At some point in our lives, we all face loss—of someone we love, our favorite pet, or even a cherished dream. But even though the experience of loss is universal, people can choose many different ways to cope with the sadness and grief they feel. What do people need to do to face their grief and move on?

DISCUSS Working in small groups, think about some ways people respond to a serious loss. Discuss how they express their own feelings and what they do to adjust to the changes that the loss creates. What patterns can you identify?

Authors Online **THINK** central

Go to thinkcentral.com.
KEYWORD: HML11-435

435

DIFFERENTIATED INSTRUCTION

FOR STRUGGLING READERS

Concept Support: Make Inferences Remind students that the purpose of the chart on this page is to make inferences that are specifically about the speaker of the poem, not about other aspects of the poem. With the help of the chart, students should formulate an impression of the speaker. They should make guesses about what has happened in his life and how he has responded to it. They should seek clues to whether he is sane or mad, and whether he is believable or not.

FOR ENGLISH LANGUAGE LEARNERS

Concept Support: Sound Devices To expose students to the rhythmic patterns Poe creates, read aloud lines 1–12, emphasizing the rhyme and cadence of the lines. Point out the rhyme, repetition, and alliteration Poe uses in this passage. Then have mixed-ability pairs take turns in reading the lines. Discuss how well they create rhythmic patterns in their reading.

Teach

COMMON CORE FOCUS

RL 1 Cite evidence to support analysis of inferences drawn from the text. **RL 4** Analyze the impact of specific word choices on meaning and tone. **RL 5** Analyze how an author's choices concerning how to structure a text contribute to its overall structure and meaning, as well as its aesthetic impact. **W 3** Write narratives using effective technique, well-chosen details, and well-structured event sequences. **W 3b** Use narrative technique such as dialogue to develop a character. **W 3d** Use precise words and phrases to convey a vivid picture of the character. **L 2** Demonstrate command of the conventions of standard English capitalization and punctuation when writing. **L 4** Determine the meanings of words and phrases as they are used in the text.

How do people handle LOSS?

Read aloud the paragraph. As students suggest ways in which people cope with grief, list their answers on the board. Encourage them to refer to the list as they complete the *DISCUSS* activity.

TEXT ANALYSIS

COMMON CORE
RL 4
RL 5

● *Model the Skill:* SOUND DEVICES

Have students read these lines of verse:

> The clank of armor, the clank of steel
> Echoed all that dismal day.
> We in the crowd could keenly feel
> The gallant knight's strength slip away.

Point out these examples of rhyme, repetition, alliteration, and onomatopoeia in the lines *rhyme: steel/feel, day/away; repetition: clank; alliteration: dismal/day, crowd/could/keenly, strength/slip; onomatopoeia: clank.*

GUIDED PRACTICE Ask students to find sound devices in other poems.

READING SKILL

COMMON CORE
RL 1

■ *Model the Skill:* MAKE INFERENCES

Have students fill out inferences for the four-line verse in the Text Analysis box. Have them begin a chart for "The Raven" and complete it as they read.

R **RESOURCE MANAGER**—Copy Master
Make Inferences p. 175

Practice and Apply

SUMMARY

In this poem, the speaker is sitting at home grieving over the loss of his love, Lenore, when a raven enters through the window. The speaker asks the raven's name and the bird replies, "Nevermore." As the speaker asks the bird for relief from suffering, for assurance that he and Lenore will be reunited, and finally for the bird to leave, the bird repeats, "Nevermore."

READ WITH A PURPOSE

Help students set a purpose for reading. Tell them to read the poem to learn if the raven provides the speaker relief from his grief.

TEXT ANALYSIS　　　COMMON CORE　RL 4　RL 5

A Model the Skill: SOUND DEVICES

Point out that the sound device of internal rhyme consists of a rhyme that occurs within a single line of a poem, not at the ends of two different lines.

Answer: *There is a rhyming pair in the first line (dreary/weary) and one in the third line (napping/tapping), that repeats in the fourth and fifth lines (rapping, tapping). The pattern varies in subsequent stanzas.*

READING SKILL　　　COMMON CORE　RL 1

B Model the Skill: MAKE INFERENCES

To assist students in making inferences, have them begin filling out the chart that was introduced on page 435.

	Inferences About the Speaker	Clues
State of Mind	grief	repetition of "sorrow"
Recent Experiences	lost his love, Lenore	"sorrow for the lost Lenore," "nameless <u>here</u> forevermore"

Possible answer: *Lenore is a woman the speaker loved, who has died. Details: "sorrow for the lost Lenore," "angels"*

The

Raven

Edgar Allan Poe

Once upon a midnight dreary, while I pondered, weak and weary,
Over many a quaint and curious volume of forgotten lore—
While I nodded, nearly napping, suddenly there came a tapping,
As of someone gently rapping, rapping at my chamber door.
5　"'Tis some visitor," I muttered, "tapping at my chamber door—
　　Only this and nothing more." **A**

Ah, distinctly I remember it was in the bleak December;
And each separate dying ember wrought its ghost upon the floor.
Eagerly I wished the morrow;—vainly I had sought to borrow
10　From my books surcease[1] of sorrow—sorrow for the lost Lenore—
For the rare and radiant maiden whom the angels name Lenore—
　　Nameless *here* forevermore. **B**

And the silken, sad, uncertain rustling of each purple curtain
Thrilled me—filled me with fantastic terrors never felt before;
15　So that now, to still the beating of my heart, I stood repeating
"'Tis some visitor entreating entrance at my chamber door;—
Some late visitor entreating entrance at my chamber door;—
　　That it is and nothing more."

---

1. **surcease:** an end.

Analyze Visuals ▶
What techniques has the photographer used that make the raven on page 437 seem mysterious?

A SOUND DEVICES
Reread lines 1–6. What pattern of **internal rhyme** does Poe establish in the first stanza?

B MAKE INFERENCES
Reread lines 9–12. What does this passage imply about Lenore's connection to the speaker and the reason for her absence? Give details to support your answer.

DIFFERENTIATED INSTRUCTION

FOR ENGLISH LANGUAGE LEARNERS

Language: Punctuation and Print Cues
Students may be confused by Poe's frequent use of dashes. Point out that the dashes often introduce repetitions of word patterns or ideas, as in "perched above my chamber door— / Perched . . . just above my chamber door" (lines 40–41). These repetitions indicate the speaker's excited, distressed state of mind. Invite relatively fluent students to read such passages aloud in an appropriate dramatic tone.

FOR STRUGGLING READERS

Develop Reading Fluency
- Have students listen to "The Raven" on the *Audio Anthology CD*. Encourage them to listen for how inflections in the reader's voice establish mood.

- Have students practice establishing mood by reading the poem aloud with the same inflections as the audio reader.

Reading Support

This selection on <u>thinkcentral.com</u> includes embedded **ThinkAloud** models—students "thinking aloud" about the story to model the kinds of questions a good reader would ask about a selection.

Analyze Visuals

Possible answer: The photographer uses black and white with high contrast and blurred details, making the raven jump out at viewers while appearing slightly indistinct. The effect is one of uncertainty or mystery.

TIERED DISCUSSION PROMPTS

In lines 1–18, use these prompts to help students understand the poem's emotions:

Connect Have you or anyone you know ever been startled by an unexpected visitor? How did it feel? *Accept all reasonable responses.*

Interpret What does the speaker's frequent repetition tell you about his emotional state? *Possible answer: He is agitated and obsessed.*

Evaluate Does Poe's use of repetition in the first three stanzas achieve its purpose? *Possible answer: It achieves its purpose by emphasizing the speaker's disturbed state.*

BACKGROUND

Ravens Ravens are large, loud, aggressive birds; they are keen-sighted, wary, and usually solitary. They are long-lived and, as pets, may learn to mimic several words. Ravens were a symbol of prophecy to many cultures who associated them with mystery, evil omens, death, and disease. Ravens' fearlessness and cleverness have earned them admiration. Poe's raven alights on a bust of the Greek goddess of wisdom, Pallas Athena, whose symbol was the owl. Poe first considered using an owl or parrot as his bird, but chose a raven because of its symbolic associations.

FOR STRUGGLING READERS

Comprehension Ask three volunteers to read each of the first three stanzas aloud. After all three stanzas have been read, ask students to predict who is tapping at the speaker's door and why.

FOR ADVANCED LEARNERS/AP

Evaluate Have students suppose that Poe wrote about an owl, parrot, or some other bird in this poem. Tell students to rewrite two stanzas, substituting another bird for "raven" whenever it appears in the text. Students should make any other changes to the text in their stanzas that would better suit the different bird choice. Afterwards, have students evaluate Poe's choice of raven for his poem.

C STANZA AND RHYME SCHEME

Answer: abcbbb. *The fourth and fifth lines repeat the same rhyming word, which is not true end rhyme.*

TEXT ANALYSIS

COMMON CORE
RL 4
RL 5

D SOUND DEVICES

Remind students that onomatopoeia means words that sound like their meaning. **Answer:** *An example of onomatopoeia is "flutter."*

TEXT ANALYSIS

COMMON CORE
RL 4
RL 5

E SOUND DEVICES

Possible answer: *Examples of alliteration include "horn, shaven, sure, shore; ghastly, grim". Alliterated words are emphasized.*

Extend the Discussion What mood or emotion is emphasized by the alliteration of these specific words?

Presently my soul grew stronger; hesitating then no longer,
20   "Sir," said I, "or Madam, truly your forgiveness I implore;
But the fact is I was napping, and so gently you came rapping,
And so faintly you came tapping, tapping at my chamber door,
That I scarce was sure I heard you"—here I opened wide the door;—
     Darkness there and nothing more. **C**

25 Deep into that darkness peering, long I stood there wondering, fearing,
Doubting, dreaming dreams no mortal ever dared to dream before;
But the silence was unbroken, and the stillness gave no token,
And the only word there spoken was the whispered word, "Lenore!"
This I whispered, and an echo murmured back the word "Lenore!"
30   Merely this and nothing more.

Back into the chamber turning, all my soul within me burning,
Soon again I heard a tapping somewhat louder than before.
"Surely," said I, "surely that is something at my window lattice;
Let me see, then, what thereat is, and this mystery explore—
35 Let my heart be still a moment and this mystery explore;—
     'Tis the wind and nothing more!"

Open here I flung the shutter, when, with many a flirt and flutter,
In there stepped a stately Raven of the saintly days of yore.[2]
Not the least obeisance[3] made he; not a minute stopped or stayed he;
40 But, with mien[4] of lord or lady, perched above my chamber door—
Perched upon a bust of Pallas[5] just above my chamber door—
     Perched, and sat, and nothing more. **D**

Then this ebony bird beguiling my sad fancy into smiling,
By the grave and stern decorum of the countenance it wore,
45 "Though thy crest be shorn and shaven, thou," I said, "art sure no craven,[6]
Ghastly grim and ancient Raven wandering from the Nightly shore—
Tell me what thy lordly name is on the Night's Plutonian[7] shore!"
     Quoth the Raven, "Nevermore." **E**

Much I marveled this ungainly fowl to hear discourse so plainly,
50 Though its answer little meaning—little relevancy bore;
For we cannot help agreeing that no living human being

---

2. **days of yore:** days of long ago.
3. **obeisance** (ō-bā′səns): a gesture of respect.
4. **mien** (mēn): appearance.
5. **bust of Pallas:** statue of the head and shoulders of Pallas Athena, Greek goddess of wisdom.
6. **craven:** coward.
7. **Plutonian:** having to do with Pluto, Roman god of the dead and ruler of the underworld.

438   UNIT 2: AMERICAN ROMANTICISM

C STANZA AND RHYME SCHEME
Recall that a poem's rhyme scheme is its pattern of **end rhyme**. Describe the rhyme scheme of this poem. How does Poe use **repetition** as part of the rhyme scheme?

D SOUND DEVICES
Reread lines 37–38. What example of **onomatopoeia** can you find?

E SOUND DEVICES
Identify the **alliteration** in lines 45–46. What words are emphasized by using this technique?

DIFFERENTIATED INSTRUCTION

FOR STRUGGLING READERS
Vocabulary Support

- *implore* (line 20), "beg"
- *token* (line 27), "sign"
- *lattice* (line 33), "window frame"
- *beguiling* (line 43), "tricking"
- *decorum* (line 44), "formal behavior"
- *countenance* (line 44), "facial expression"
- *discourse* (line 49), "speech"

Ever yet was blessed with seeing bird above his chamber door—
Bird or beast upon the sculptured bust above his chamber door,
 With such name as "Nevermore."

55 But the Raven, sitting lonely on the placid bust, spoke only
That one word, as if his soul in that one word he did outpour.
Nothing farther then he uttered—not a feather then he fluttered—
Till I scarcely more than muttered "Other friends have flown before—
On the morrow *he* will leave me, as my hopes have flown before."
60 Then the bird said, "Nevermore." **F**

Startled at the stillness broken by reply so aptly spoken,
"Doubtless," said I, "what it utters is its only stock and store
Caught from some unhappy master whom unmerciful Disaster
Followed fast and followed faster till his songs one burden[8] bore—
65 Till the dirges[9] of his Hope that melancholy burden bore
 Of 'Never—nevermore.'"

But the Raven still beguiling all my fancy into smiling,
Straight I wheeled a cushioned seat in front of bird, and bust and door;
Then, upon the velvet sinking, I betook myself to linking
70 Fancy unto fancy, thinking what this ominous bird of yore—
What this grim, ungainly, ghastly, gaunt, and ominous bird of yore
 Meant in croaking, "Nevermore." **G**

This I sat engaged in guessing, but no syllable expressing
To the fowl whose fiery eyes now burned into my bosom's core;
75 This and more I sat divining,[10] with my head at ease reclining
On the cushion's velvet lining that the lamp-light gloated o'er,
But whose velvet violet lining with the lamp-light gloating o'er,
 She shall press, ah, nevermore!

Then, methought, the air grew denser, perfumed from an unseen censer
80 Swung by Seraphim[11] whose foot-falls tinkled on the tufted floor.
"Wretch," I cried, "thy God hath lent thee—by these angels he hath sent thee
Respite—respite and nepenthe[12] from thy memories of Lenore;
Quaff,[13] oh quaff this kind nepenthe and forget this lost Lenore!"
 Quoth the Raven, "Nevermore."

---

8. **burden:** the chorus or refrain of a song.
9. **dirges:** songs of mourning.
10. **divining:** guessing from incomplete evidence.
11. **censer / Swung by Seraphim** (sĕr'ə-fĭm): container of sweet burning incense swung by angels of the highest rank.
12. **respite . . . and nepenthe** (nĭ-pĕn'thē): temporary relief and a forgetfulness that eases grief.
13. **quaff:** drink deeply.

F MAKE INFERENCES
Reread lines 58–59. What does this comment suggest about the speaker's past experiences and his current mood? Explain.

G SOUND DEVICES
Identify the sound device used in lines 71–72. What qualities of the raven are emphasized by the use of this device?

How do people handle LOSS?

Discuss In lines 89–96, what what words does the speaker express his hope for relief from grief? **Possible answer:** "'Is there balm in Gilead?'" (line 89) is a request for relief from grief. "'Tell this soul with sorrow laden if . . . / It shall clasp a sainted maiden whom the angels name Lenore'" (lines 93–94) expresses the wish that he be united with Lenore in heaven.

READING SKILL

COMMON CORE RL 1

🄷 MAKE INFERENCES

Possible answer: The speaker is so desperate and grief-stricken that he clings to an irrational hope that the bird will say something comforting.

ADDITIONAL TEACHING OPPORTUNITY

Interpret Remind students that a work of literature may support more than one interpretation. In the case of a Poe poem or story, the question often arises, "How much of this is really happening, and how much takes place in the character's mind?" Ask students whether, in their opinion, the raven is a figment of the speaker's imagination. Have them find details in the text of the poem to support their view.

SELECTION WRAP–UP

READ WITH A PURPOSE Now that students have read the selection, ask them to describe how the raven influences the speaker's state of mind. **Possible answer:** The raven frustrates and upsets the speaker and leaves him even more grieved than before.

⭐ CRITIQUE

- Ask students how convincing Poe makes this narrative.

- After completing the After Reading questions on page 441, have students revisit their responses and tell whether they have changed their opinions.

---

85 "Prophet!" said I, "thing of evil!—prophet still, if bird or devil!—
    Whether Tempter[14] sent, or whether tempest tossed thee here ashore,
    Desolate yet all undaunted, on this desert land enchanted—
    On this home by Horror haunted—tell me truly, I implore—
    Is there—*is* there balm in Gilead?[15]—tell me—tell me, I implore!"
90   Quoth the Raven, "Nevermore."

    "Prophet!" said I, "thing of evil!—prophet still, if bird or devil!
    By that Heaven that bends above us—by that God we both adore—
    Tell this soul with sorrow laden if, within the distant Aidenn,[16]
    It shall clasp a sainted maiden whom the angels name Lenore—
95 Clasp a rare and radiant maiden whom the angels name Lenore."
        Quoth the Raven, "Nevermore." 🄷

    "Be that word our sign of parting, bird or fiend!" I shrieked, upstarting—
    "Get thee back into the tempest and the Night's Plutonian shore!
    Leave no black plume as a token of that lie thy soul hath spoken!
100 Leave my loneliness unbroken!—quit the bust above my door!
    Take thy beak from out my heart, and take thy form from off my door!"
        Quoth the Raven, "Nevermore."

    And the Raven, never flitting, still is sitting, *still* is sitting
    On the pallid bust of Pallas just above my chamber door;
105 And his eyes have all the seeming of a demon's that is dreaming,
    And the lamp-light o'er him streaming throws his shadow on the floor;
    And my soul from out that shadow that lies floating on the floor
        Shall be lifted—nevermore!

---

14. **Tempter:** the devil.
15. **balm** (bäm) **in Gilead** (gĭl′ē-əd): relief from suffering.
16. **Aidenn** (ād′n): heaven (from the Arabic form of the word *Eden*).

COMMON CORE L 4

Language Coach

Words Easily Confused *Tempter* and *tempest* (both in line 86) are pronounced and spelled similarly, but have different meanings. *Tempter*, here, means "the Devil" and *tempest* means "violent storm." What effect does Poe's use of these similar sounding words have?

🄷 **MAKE INFERENCES** Given the bird's repeated response, what does the speaker's persistent questioning of the raven suggest about his state of mind? Explain your answer.

DIFFERENTIATED INSTRUCTION

FOR ADVANCED LEARNERS/AP

Evaluate Writing in 1893, naturalist and writer John Burroughs criticized Poe as a poet whose only skill was verbal acrobatics. He went on to say that Poe's writing showed a lack of literary thought and an absence of sympathy or love for anything. Ask students to write one or two paragraphs stating whether they agree with Burroughs and why. Remind them to use evidence from Poe's writings.

FOR ENGLISH LANGUAGE LEARNERS

Language Coach

COMMON CORE L 4

Words Easily Confused *Possible answer: The use of these similar words in this line is meant to show that the speaker is confused.* Has the raven been sent by the Devil (Tempter), or just blown in by a passing storm (tempest)? Have students reread "The Raven" and identify a different word that is pronounced and spelled similarly to another word in the poem.

Comprehension

1. **Recall** Where and when do the events of the poem take place?

2. **Recall** What is the raven's response to all of the speaker's questions?

3. **Clarify** What is the speaker's explanation of the raven's one response?

Text Analysis

4. **Make Inferences** Review the **inferences** you made as you read. What conclusions did you draw about the speaker and his emotional state?

5. **Examine Tone** For each of the following passages, describe the speaker's tone, or attitude, toward the raven. What explains the speaker's changing responses to his mysterious visitor?

   - the raven's first appearance (lines 43–44)
   - the thoughts the raven inspires (lines 71–74)
   - the purpose the speaker attributes to the raven (lines 81–84)
   - the speaker's command to the raven (lines 97–98)

6. **Compare and Contrast Imagery** Poe uses imagery to create a stark contrast between Lenore and the raven. Using a chart like the one shown, list images that describe each character. What do these images communicate about each character? Cite evidence.

Lenore	Raven

7. **Evaluate Sound Devices** Reread lines 79–84. Identify the rhymes and other sound devices used in this stanza, and give examples of each technique. Which of these devices do you find most compelling or effective? Explain your answer.

Text Criticism

8. **Author's Style** In an essay about "The Raven," Poe claimed that he started with the word *nevermore* (he liked its vowel sounds), then added the death of a beautiful woman ("the most poetical topic in the world"). Only later did he invent the story and characters that readers have found so moving and memorable. Poe seems to have been more interested in form than content. Which do you find more important in this poem? Cite details in your answer.

> *How do people handle* **LOSS**?
>
> Consider the speaker's changing responses to the raven throughout the poem. What does the speaker's conflict with the raven suggest about the behavior of people who are struggling with grief?

COMMON CORE

RL 1 Cite evidence to support analysis of inferences drawn from the text. **RL 4** Analyze the impact of specific word choices on meaning and tone. **RL 5** Analyze how an author's choices concerning how to structure a text contribute to its overall structure and meaning, as well as its aesthetic impact.

Practice and Apply

For preliminary support of post-reading questions, use these copy masters:

 **RESOURCE MANAGER—Copy Masters**
Sound Devices p. 173
Question Support p. 177
Additional selection questions are provided for teachers on page 169.

ANSWERS COMMON CORE RL 1, RL 4, RL 5

1. *The events take place at midnight on a stormy night in December in the speaker's chamber.*

2. *The raven's response is "Nevermore."*

3. *The speaker explains that the raven picked up the word from its master, who must have had exceptionally bad luck to have repeated the word often enough for the bird to learn it.*

Possible answers:

4. **COMMON CORE FOCUS Make Inferences** *Some students may say the speaker is mad with grief; others may say he is emotionally unstable, dreaming, or both.*

5. *Lines 43–44: amused; lines 71–74: thoughtful, fascinated; lines 81–84: anguished; lines 97–98: enraged. The raven's unchanging response irritates and exasperates the speaker to madness.*

6. *Lenore: angels, radiant, sainted maiden; raven: black, stern, hellish, deathlike (Plutonian), ancient, grim, tempter. Based on these images, Lenore represents happiness, love, innocence; the raven represents torment and despair.*

7. **COMMON CORE FOCUS Sound Devices** *Onomatopoeia: tinkled; alliteration: censer, swung, Seraphim, foot-falls, floor, tinkled, tufted; end-rhyme: floor, Lenore, Nevermore; internal rhyme: denser, censer, lent thee, sent thee, Nepenthe; repetition: words such as respite, quaff, and Lenore. Students' opinions of the devices will vary.*

---

8. *Accept all reasonable answers.*

> *How do people handle* LOSS?
> **Possible answer:** The volatile emotions of people struggling with grief can cause them to engage in irrational behavior.

Language

◆ **GRAMMAR AND STYLE**

To further model the activity, ask volunteers to make up imperative sentences and say them aloud. Then have students add dashes to those sentences to give urgency. Since Poe often inserts dashes when adding repetitions of phrases or clauses, suggest that students use this technique in their sample sentences. (For more on imperative sentences, see **Grammar Handbook, page R64.**)

 RESOURCE MANAGER—Copy Master
Craft Effective Sentences p. 178

READING-WRITING CONNECTION

Have students use the Freewriting strategy to set their or their speaker's thoughts down spontaneously.

 BEST PRACTICES TOOLKIT
Freewriting p. C1

> ## Writing Online
> **THINK** central
>
> The following tools are available online at **thinkcentral.com** and on **Write*Smart* CD-ROM:**
> - **Interactive Graphic Organizers**
> - **Interactive Student Models**
> - **Interactive Revision Lessons**
> For additional grammar instruction, see **GrammarNotes** on **thinkcentral.com**.

Assess and Reteach

Assess

DIAGNOSTIC AND SELECTION TESTS
Selection Test A pp. 137–138
Selection Test B/C pp. 139–140

Interactive Selection Test on **thinkcentral.com**

Reteach

Level Up Online Tutorials on **thinkcentral.com**

Reteaching Worksheets on **thinkcentral.com**

Literature Lesson 19, Literature Lesson 21, Literature Lesson 22, Reading Lesson 8

Language

◆ **GRAMMAR AND STYLE:** Craft Effective Sentences

Poe uses **imperative sentences**—sentences that give orders or make requests—and **dashes** to convey his character's excitable state. The use of dashes and a tone of breathless urgency are distinctive features of Poe's style.

> *"Be that word our sign of parting, bird or fiend!" I shrieked, upstarting—*
> *"Get thee back into the tempest and the Night's Plutonian shore!"* (lines 97–98)

PRACTICE Using the following verse from "The Raven" as a model, compose your own stanza in the style of Poe, incorporating dashes and imperative sentences. Feel free to choose a different subject, but make sure to follow Poe's rhyme scheme and to echo his tone. A sample beginning is provided for you.

> **EXAMPLE**
>
> "Prophet!" said I, "thing of evil!—prophet still, if bird or devil!—
> *"You pest, begone!" I cried—near choking. "Take from me your wretched joking!"*

> "Prophet!" said I, "thing of evil!—prophet still, if bird or devil!—
> Whether Tempter sent, or whether tempest tossed thee here ashore,
> Desolate yet all undaunted, on this desert land enchanted—
> On this home by Horror haunted—tell me truly, I implore—
> Is there—*is* there balm in Gilead?—tell me—tell me, I implore!"
>   Quoth the Raven, "Nevermore."

READING-WRITING CONNECTION

 Expand your understanding of Poe's "The Raven" by responding to this prompt. Then, use the **revising tips** to improve your monologue.

WRITING PROMPT	REVISING TIPS
WRITE A MONOLOGUE A monologue is a lengthy passage or speech in which a single character expresses thoughts in an uninterrupted flow, with no other character's words intervening. Monologues in literature often explore a character's feelings. Write a **one-page prose monologue,** in your own voice or that of a fictional character, that explores an emotion, such as grief or joy. In your monologue reveal details about your speaker's personality and the reasons for his or her emotional response.	• Include your speaker's thoughts, emotions, and spoken words. • Use first-person pronouns, such as *I, me,* and *my.* • Include at least one sentence that gives an order or makes a request. • Use dashes to show pauses, urgency, or strong emotions.

COMMON CORE

L 2 Demonstrate command of the conventions of standard English capitalization and punctuation when writing. **W 3** Write narratives using effective technique, well-chosen details, and well-structured event sequences. **W 3b** Use narrative technique such as dialogue, to develop a character. **W 3d** Use precise words and phrases to convey a vivid picture of the character.

 Interactive Vocabulary THINK central

Go to **thinkcentral.com**.
KEYWORD: HML11-442

DIFFERENTIATED INSTRUCTION

FOR STRUGGLING WRITERS
Writing Support

- Point out that a monologue may contain sentence fragments and run-on sentences in order to capture the feeling of real thought.

- Although students' freewriting may produce good first drafts by capturing a spontaneous flow of thought, urge students to revise their monologues carefully to express the feelings and thoughts they want in exact language.

- Suggest that students choose a specific emotion first as a way of focusing their monologues.

- Remind students to include specific facts and details about the speaker's situation rather than merely expressions of feeling.

PARODY Like other well-known and well-loved works of literature, "The Raven" has inspired many a **parody**—a comic imitation of another work or type of literature. As you read the following parody, note the points of imitation in form or content. In what ways does the parodist turn Poe's ideas to comic effect?

What Troubled Poe's Raven

John Bennett

Could Poe walk again to-morrow, heavy with
   dyspeptic sorrow,
While the darkness seemed to borrow darkness
   from the night before,
From the hollow gloom abysmal, floating
   downward, grimly dismal,
Like a pagan curse baptismal from the bust above
   the door,
5 He would hear the Raven croaking from the dusk
   above the door,
     "Never, never, nevermore!"

And, too angry to be civil, "Raven," Poe would
   cry "or devil,
Tell me why you will persist in haunting Death's
   Plutonian shore?"
Then would croak the Raven gladly, "I will tell
   you why so sadly,
10 I so mournfully and madly, haunt you, taunt you,
   o'er and o'er,
Why eternally I haunt you, daunt you, taunt you,
   o'er and o'er —
     Only this, and nothing more.

"Forty-eight long years I've pondered, forty-eight
   long years I've wondered,
How a poet ever blundered into a mistake so sore.
15 How could lamp-light from your table ever in the
   world be able,
From *below*, to throw my sable shadow 'streaming
   on the floor,'
When I perched up here on Pallas, high above
   your chamber-door?
     Tell me that — if nothing more!"

Then, like some wan, weeping willow, Poe
   would bend above his pillow,
20 Seeking surcease in the billow where mad
   recollections drown,
And in tearful tones replying, he would groan
   "There's no denying
Either I was blindly lying, or the world was
   upside down—
Say, by Joe!—it was just midnight—so the
   world *was* upside down—
     Aye, the world was upside down!"

COMMON CORE FOCUS

RL 1 Cite evidence to support analysis of inferences drawn from the text regarding how to develop. **RL 3** Analyze the impact of the author's choices regarding how to develop and relate elements of a story. **RL 4** Determine the meanings of words and phrases as they are used in the text, including figurative and connotative meanings; analyze the impact of specific word choices on meaning and tone. **RI 1** Cite evidence to support analysis of inferences drawn from the text. **RI 4** Determine the meaning of words and phrases as they are used in a text, including figurative, connotative and technical meanings. **RI 7** Evaluate multiple sources of information presented in different media or formats as well as in words to address a question. **L 2b** Spell correctly. **L 4a** Use context as a clue to the meaning of a word or phrase. **L 4b** Identify and use patterns of word changes that indicate different meanings or parts of speech. **L 4c** Consult reference materials to find the pronunciation of a word. **L 6** Acquire and use academic words and phrases.

ABOUT THE AUTHORS

Edgar Allan Poe Ask students why Poe's stories have had such timeless appeal. *Students should note that many of Poe's stories function as psychological thrillers as well as allegories that teach moral lessons.*

Stephen King Ask students to identify a key factor in the launching of King's literary career. *Students should note that the encouragement of King's wife played a key role in his early writing career.*

The Masque of the Red Death
Short Story by Edgar Allan Poe

from Danse Macabre
Essay by Stephen King

Wait Until Dark
Movie Poster

COMMON CORE **RL 3** Analyze the impact of the author's choices regarding how to develop and relate elements of a story. **RL 4** Determine the meanings of words and phrases as they are used in the text, including figurative and connotative meanings; analyze the impact of specific word choices on meaning and tone. **RI 4** Determine

the meaning of words and phrases as they are used in a text, including figurative, connotative and technical meanings. **RI 7** Evaluate multiple sources of information presented in different media or formats as well as in words to address a question. **L 2b** Spell correctly. **L 4c** Consult reference materials to find the pronunciation of a word.

Meet the Authors

Edgar Allan Poe c. 1809–1849

Edgar Allan Poe was a master of the psychological thriller. His tales of the ghastly and the grotesque are peopled with distraught narrators, deranged heroes, and doomed heroines. They move beyond the sunlit, rational world to explore the dark, irrational depths of the human mind. (For more about Poe, see page 410.)

A Gothic Allegory "The Masque of the Red Death," first published in 1842, is timeless in its appeal. We can enjoy it for its thrills or as an **allegory**. In an allegory, characters and objects stand for abstract ideas such as good and evil. Often meant to teach moral lessons, allegories typically feature simple characters and unnamed settings, somewhat like fairy tales.

Poe's Enduring Legacy Generations of mystery and suspense writers have been influenced by the brooding atmosphere and eerie tension of Poe's stories. In fact, two of the most highly regarded American short stories written since Poe's death owe a debt to the Gothic master. "An Occurrence at Owl Creek Bridge" (page 604) has the ghostly mood of Poe's fiction. The creepy tension that pervades "A Rose for Emily" (page 1066) can be traced to Poe's haunted settings. In the twentieth century, with the advent of movies, Poe found a wider audience in films adapted from his stories. In 1964, for example, "The Masque of the Red Death" was made into a movie starring Vincent Price, a well-known horror-movie actor of the time.

Stephen King born 1947

Stephen King's phenomenal success began in 1974, with the publication of *Carrie.* Discouraged, King had thrown an unfinished manuscript of the novel in the trash. His wife retrieved it and urged him to finish it; the rest is history. King went on to become one of the bestselling writers of all time. His novels have contributed to a revival of horror fiction and horror movies. In fact, he's been called a "one-man entertainment industry."

Terror and Suspense No living American author has achieved the success we

associate with King's Gothic page-turners and the movies that have been adapted from them. *Carrie* was a huge commercial success. Turned into a classic horror movie, also titled *Carrie*, it has inspired a movie sequel, a Broadway musical, a made-for-television movie, and a non-musical stage parody. His novels have sold in the millions, and the movies made from them have found a worldwide audience. They testify to the enduring appeal of the elements in fiction that both excite and frighten us.

THINKcentral

Author Online
Go to **thinkcentral.com**. KEYWORD: HMD11-444

See resources on the **Teacher One Stop DVD-ROM** and on **thinkcentral.com**.

R **RESOURCE MANAGER UNIT 2**
Lesson Support, pp. 179–186

DIAGNOSTIC AND SELECTION TESTS
Selection Tests, pp. 141–144

BEST PRACTICES TOOLKIT
Making Inferences, p. A13
Jigsaw Reading, p. A1
Word Questioning, p. E9

TECHNOLOGY
- Teacher One Stop DVD-ROM
- Student One Stop DVD-ROM
- Audio Anthology CD
- GrammarNotes DVD-ROM
- ExamView Generator on the Teacher One Stop

* Resources for Differentiation

● TEXT ANALYSIS: SUSPENSE

One of the most important elements of a Gothic story is **suspense**—the combination of excitement and anxiety that readers feel about coming events in a plot. In "The Masque of the Red Death," readers feel excited about an extravagant masquerade party, but they begin to feel anxious when Poe describes a clock that makes the guests nervous each time it strikes the hour. As you read the story, notice the elements in the party that make you eager for more or that make you feel a sense of dread about the outcome. Then, when you read Stephen King's essay, notice how he explains the element of fear and terror in suspense. How does this nonfiction excerpt add to your appreciation of writers such as Poe?

● READING STRATEGY: CLARIFY MEANING

Poe's unusual, archaic vocabulary reinforces this story's feeling of antiquity. To help you clarify the meaning of difficult words and phrases, consult the side notes for helpful information. In addition, use **context clues** in surrounding phrases to figure out unfamiliar words. Finally, **paraphrase** difficult passages, using simpler language. By contrast with the Poe story, Stephen King's nonfiction excerpt is written in contemporary, accessible language. As you read King, pay special attention to his comments about a closed door and the role it plays in suspense. Remember that the best way to understand any suspense story is to become engaged in the author's mixture of excitement and dread.

▲ VOCABULARY IN CONTEXT

Poe used the following words in his eerie tale. Complete each phrase with an appropriate word from the list.

WORD LIST	blasphemous	disapprobation	propriety
	cessation	impede	reverie

1. wandered the halls lost in a _____
2. a peace treaty following the _____ of hostilities
3. her friends' _____ after her unwise decision
4. tried not to _____ the flow of traffic
5. deeply offended by his _____ arguments
6. acted with decorum and _____

 Complete the activities in your **Reader/Writer Notebook**.

445

Is SAFETY an illusion?

We like to feel that there are steps we can take to keep ourselves safe. To protect ourselves from theft, we can install an alarm or add high-security locks. To protect our health, we can exercise and eat healthy food. But do our precautions really keep danger away, or do they just give us an illusion of safety?

What's the Connection?

As you study these texts, think about the elements that make a story, a movie, or even a movie poster suspenseful. With Edgar Allan Poe's story "The Masque of the Red Death," you will experience actual suspense in the hands of a master. Afterwards, as you read Stephen King's explanation of suspense, think about how it applies to your experience as a reader. Finally, when you examine the poster for *Wait Until Dark,* think about how images create suspense.

Teach

Is SAFETY an illusion?

Read the first paragraph. Ask students to suggest present-day situations when safety might be an illusion.

WHAT'S THE CONNECTION?

Ask students to identify examples from modern society in which people try to isolate themselves from situations or people they perceive to be dangerous. How successful have they been in these efforts?

TEXT ANALYSIS — COMMON CORE RL 3

● *Model the Skill:* SUSPENSE

To help students identify the story elements that create suspense, direct them to Poe's elaborate description of the imperial suite. Have students take notes on suspense-building story elements as they read "The Masque of the Red Death." Point out that King's essay explains how difficult it is for writers to scare audiences, thus making Poe's achievement in "The Masque of the Red Death" even more impressive.

GUIDED PRACTICE Ask students why King would be interested in analyzing Poe's works.

READING STRATEGY — COMMON CORE RL 4

■ *Model the Skill:* CLARIFY MEANING

Choose a word in Poe's story that may be unfamiliar to students. Demonstrate how using context clues can help them figure out the word's meaning. Discuss why the language in Poe's story is so different than that of King's excerpt. Point out that Poe wrote his fictional story in the mid-1800s and used a style that was popular in his day, whereas King, writing a nonfiction piece in modern times, wrote in a contemporary style.

VOCABULARY

COMMON CORE L 4

▲ VOCABULARY IN CONTEXT

DIAGNOSE WORD KNOWLEDGE Have all students complete Vocabulary in Context. Check their phrases against the following:

blasphemous (blăs′fə-məs) *adj.* disrespectful or offensive

cessation (sĕ-sā′shən) *n.* a coming to an end; a stopping

disapprobation (dĭs-ăp′rə-bā′shən) *n.* disapproval

impede (ĭm-pēd′) *v.* to interfere with or slow the progress of

propriety (prə-prī′ĭ-tē) *n.* the quality of being proper; appropriateness

reverie (rĕv′ə-rē) *n.* daydream

PRETEACH VOCABULARY Use the following copy master to help students predict meanings.

 RESOURCE MANAGER—Copy Master Vocabulary Study p. 193

Practice and Apply

SUMMARY

This short story tells the tale of Prince Prospero, whose country is plagued by a horrible epidemic of the Red Death. To escape the disease, the prince and his friends lock themselves away in the prince's abbey. Thinking themselves safe, the prince and his friends amuse themselves while the Red Death ravages the countryside. They hold a masked ball, where they discover an uninvited guest dressed as the Red Death. The guest turns out to be the plague itself, which brings death to all.

READ WITH A PURPOSE

Help students set a purpose for reading. Tell them to read the selection to learn if the prince meets a fate he deserves.

WHAT'S THE CONNECTION?

Both Poe and King are effective writers of suspenseful fiction. "The Masque of the Red Death" portrays this genre in action, while the King essay analyzes the literary tools used to create such work.

THE *Masque* OF THE RED DEATH

Edgar Allan Poe

> **BACKGROUND** Around 1350, Europe was struck by an epidemic of bubonic plague (Black Death) that killed more than a quarter of its population. The plague killed its victims quickly—within three to five days—and there was no cure. Artwork from that time is full of haunting symbols like the Dance of Death, where Death, personified as a skeleton, whirls anonymous figures to their graves. These grisly allegorical images spoke to the deepest fears of their audience, for whom death was a nearby presence. Note how Poe borrows from this history in his own tale of death.

The "Red Death" had long devastated the country. No pestilence had ever been so fatal, or so hideous. Blood was its Avatar and its seal—the redness and horror of blood. There were sharp pains, and sudden dizziness, and then profuse bleeding at the pores, with dissolution. The scarlet stains upon the body, and especially upon the face of the victim, were the pest ban which shut him out from the aid and from the sympathy of his fellow men. And the whole seizure, progress, and termination of the disease were the incidents of half an hour. **A**

But the Prince Prospero was happy and dauntless and sagacious. When his
10 dominions were half depopulated, he summoned to his presence a thousand hale and lighthearted friends from among the knights and dames of his court,

① Targeted Passage

2 Avatar (ăv'ə-tär'): the physical form of an unseen force.

5 pest ban: announcement of infection with the plague.

A CLARIFY MEANING
Use the **side notes** to help you restate lines 1–8. What can you **infer** about the mood of the country from this description?

DIFFERENTIATED INSTRUCTION

FOR ENGLISH LANGUAGE LEARNERS
Vocabulary: Outdated Forms Provide these definitions for outdated terms. Have students reread the lines, substituting the definitions for the outdated words.

- *massy* (line 15), "heavy, bulky"
- *might bid defiance to contagion* (lines 18–19), "might disregard disease"
- *depended (from the roof)* (line 50), "hung"
- *hearken* (line 68), "listen carefully"

FOR STRUGGLING READERS
In combination with the *Audio Anthology CD*, use one or more Targeted Passages (pp. 446, 451, 452) to ensure that students focus on key story events and concepts. Targeted Passages are also good for English learners.

① Targeted Passage [Lines 1–11]

This passage describes the Red Death and tells of Prince Prospero's response to it.

BACKGROUND

Black Death Poe's vision of the Red Death may have been influenced by the Black Death, which reached Europe from Asia in 1347. After fading in 1351, it recurred five more times in the 14th century. Towns had a higher death rate than the countryside, and monasteries had one of the highest rates. As in "The Masque of the Red Death," royalty did not escape the plague: Eleanor of Aragon and King Alfonso XI of Castile died, and Princess Joan of England died on the way to her wedding. Two successive Archbishops of Canterbury and one quarter of the papal court at Avignon, France, died. Social effects were many. Temporarily, wars ceased and trade slumped. More lastingly, a shortage of farm labor and of artisans enabled workers to demand higher wages, a change that resulted in greater spending power for those classes, and thus the rise of a new middle class and a weakening of the old feudal class distinctions.

Poe's vision of a plague may also have been affected by the frequent outbreaks of yellow fever and cholera that afflicted American cities in the early 1800s. In 1832, while Poe was living in Baltimore, a cholera epidemic killed 853 residents of that city.

- What is the Red Death? (lines 1–8)
- How does Prince Prospero feel? Is he concerned about it? (line 9)
- When does he take action? (lines 9–10)
- Whom does he summon? (lines 10–11)

FOR ADVANCED LEARNERS/AP

Hypothesize Tell students to suppose that a plague wiped out half of the population in their country. Have students write a short paper describing how they think the outbreak would affect the economy, government, and daily life in their nation and hometown. Afterwards, lead a discussion in which students share their ideas.

Ⓑ SUSPENSE

Ask for volunteers to read lines 44–60 aloud. Have students note the eerie details of the chamber's decor, particularly the bright, blood-red light that flames cast through the scarlet windows. *Possible answer: The windows are "a deep blood color." The mention of blood heightens the mood of suspense. The firelight shines through "the blood-tinted panes," casting horrible shadows. The red tints it splashes on the faces of those who enter the room reminds them of the plague. This frightens guests away and spreads unease through the group.*

Extend the Discussion Why do the visual effects of the firelight shining through the red windows startle or upset the guests?

TIERED DISCUSSION PROMPTS

In lines 13–26, use these prompts to help students understand how the prince and his friends reacted to the threat of the Red Death:

Connect Have you or someone you know ever tried to escape something that seemed unavoidable? How does that experience help you understand what Prospero was trying to do? *Accept all reasonable responses.*

Analyze Why did Prospero choose to hold the ball just as the "pestilence raged most furiously"? *Possible answer: After many months of living in confinement, the people probably needed a diversion to maintain their spirits and endure boredom. Also, Prospero refused to consider the threat outside the abbey.*

Predict Do you think the prince's precautions will protect those inside the abbey? Explain. *Possible answer: They didn't know how the Red Death spread. Closing doors might not keep it out.*

OWN THE WORD

impede: Tell students that synonyms for *impede* include *hinder, hold back, obstruct.* Ask students to list things that might *impede* them from pursuing a hobby. *Possible answer: lack of time, equipment, or supplies; a part-time job, school activities*

---

and with these retired to the deep seclusion of one of his castellated abbeys. This was an extensive and magnificent structure, the creation of the prince's own eccentric yet august taste. A strong and lofty wall girdled it in. This wall had gates of iron. The courtiers, having entered, brought furnaces and massy hammers and welded the bolts. They resolved to leave means neither of ingress or egress to the sudden impulses of despair or of frenzy from within. The abbey was amply provisioned. With such precautions the courtiers might bid defiance to contagion. The external world could take care of itself. In the meantime
20 it was folly to grieve, or to think. The prince had provided all the appliances of pleasure. There were buffoons, there were improvisatori, there were ballet-dancers, there were musicians, there was Beauty, there was wine. All these and security were within. Without was the "Red Death."

It was toward the close of the fifth or sixth month of his seclusion, and while the pestilence raged most furiously abroad, that the Prince Prospero entertained his thousand friends at a masked ball of the most unusual magnificence.

It was a voluptuous scene, that masquerade. But first let me tell of the rooms in which it was held. There were seven—an imperial suite. In many palaces, however, such suites form a long and straight vista, while the folding
30 doors slide back nearly to the walls on either hand, so that the view of the whole extent is scarcely **impeded.** Here the case was very different; as might have been expected from the duke's love of the *bizarre.* The apartments were so irregularly disposed that the vision embraced but little more than one at a time. There was a sharp turn at every twenty or thirty yards, and at each turn a novel effect. To the right and left, in the middle of each wall, a tall and narrow Gothic window looked out upon a closed corridor which pursued the windings of the suite. These windows were of stained glass whose color varied in accordance with the prevailing hue of the decorations of the chamber into which it opened. That at the eastern extremity was
40 hung, for example, in blue—and vividly blue were its windows. The second chamber was purple in its ornaments and tapestries, and here the panes were purple. The third was green throughout, and so were the casements. The fourth was furnished and lighted with orange—the fifth with white—the sixth with violet. The seventh apartment was closely shrouded in black velvet tapestries that hung all over the ceiling and down the walls, falling in heavy folds upon a carpet of the same material and hue. But in this chamber only, the color of the windows failed to correspond with the decorations. The panes here were scarlet—a deep blood color. Now in no one of the seven apartments were there any lamp or candelabrum amid the profusion
50 of golden ornaments that lay scattered to and fro or depended from the roof. There was no light of any kind emanating from lamp or candle within the suite of chambers. But in the corridors that followed the suite, there stood, opposite to each window, a heavy tripod, bearing a brazier of fire that projected its rays through the tinted glass and so glaringly illumined the room. And thus were produced a multitude of gaudy and fantastic appearances. But in the western or black chamber the effect of the firelight that streamed upon the dark hangings through the blood-tinted panes, was

12 castellated abbeys (kăs′tə-lā′tĭd ăb′ēz): castle-like buildings once used as monasteries ("abbeys").

16–17 ingress (ĭn′grĕs′) **or egress** (ē′grĕs′): entry or exit.

18 provisioned: stocked with supplies.

21 improvisatori (ĭm-prŏv′ĭ-zə-tôr′ē): poets who compose verses aloud.

impede (ĭm-pēd′) *v.* to interfere with or slow the progress of

Ⓑ SUSPENSE
Reread Poe's description of the seventh room used by guests of the masquerade party (lines 44–60). Notice that the details establish an eerie **mood**—an important part of Gothic **suspense.** Nothing frightening happens in these lines, but the **setting** itself gives the reader an unsettling sense that terror awaits. How does the narrator's description of the windows (lines 46-48) contribute to the story's suspenseful atmosphere? What effect does firelight in the room have on Prince Prospero's guests? Finally, how does their reaction add to the suspense?

53 brazier (brā′zhər): metal pan for holding a fire.

DIFFERENTIATED INSTRUCTION

FOR STRUGGLING READERS
Concept Support To help students clarify the long description that covers all of page 448, use Jigsaw Reading so that students are responsible for smaller chunks of text and share their clarifications with others.

 **BEST PRACTICES TOOLKIT**
Jigsaw Reading p. A1

FOR ENGLISH LANGUAGE LEARNERS
Vocabulary Support Use Word Questioning to teach these words: *structure* (line 13), *external* (line 19), *correspond* (line 47), *emphasis* (line 66), *similar* (line 76), *role* (line 145).

 **BEST PRACTICES TOOLKIT—Transparency**
Word Questioning p. E9

Analyze Visuals

Activity Ask students how the image on this page differs from, yet captures, the description of the setting and mood of Prince Prospero's apartment. ***Possible answer:*** *The clock in the image on this page does not match the description of the clock in the story, which is made of ebony (line 62). Moreover, the panes look out onto open scenery, while the "castellated" abbey in which the Prince and his courtiers have taken refuge is surrounded by a wall. However, like the masquerade, the image is fantastical and surreal. The clock dominates the image, superimposed upon blood red windows, making the barren landscape outside seem blighted and threatening.*

ghastly in the extreme, and produced so wild a look upon the countenances of those who entered, that there were few of the company bold enough to
60 set foot within its precincts at all. **B**

It was in this apartment, also, that there stood against the western wall a gigantic clock of ebony. Its pendulum swung to and fro with a dull, heavy, monotonous clang; and when the minute hand made the circuit of the face, and the hour was to be stricken, there came from the brazen lungs of the clock a sound which was clear and loud and deep and exceedingly musical, but of so peculiar a note and emphasis that, at each lapse of an hour, the musicians of the orchestra were constrained to pause, momentarily, in their performance, to hearken to the sound; and thus the waltzers perforce ceased their evolutions; and there was a brief disconcert of the whole gay company;
70 and, while the chimes of the clock yet rang, it was observed that the giddiest turned pale, and the more aged and sedate passed their hands over their

58 countenances (koun'tə-nəns-əz): faces.

62 ebony (ĕb'ə-nē): a hard, very dark wood.

64 brazen: brass.

69 evolutions: intricate patterns of movement; **disconcert:** state of confusion.

FOR ADVANCED LEARNERS/AP

Compare and Contrast [small-group option]
In his essay *Nature* (pages 373–374), Ralph Waldo Emerson praises contact with nature as a source of "perfect exhilaration." Have students work in groups to compare and contrast Emerson's view of nature with Poe's. Elicit an awareness that in "The Masque of the Red Death," nature is a source of disease. In "The Fall of the House of Usher," nature is a source of decay and destruction, represented by unhealthy vegetation and a bleak tarn.

Then point out that the contrast may not be as simple as that seems, for Emerson also sees a melancholy side of nature in lines 1 and 28–33 of his essay. To help students explore this viewpoint, have them consider these questions:

• What might Emerson say about Poe's view of nature?

• Would he necessarily disagree with it?

• If he did, with whom would you agree?

fully ceased, a light laughter at once pervaded the assembly; the musicians
looked at each other and smiled as if at their own nervousness and folly,
and made whispering vows, each to the other, that the next chiming of the
clock should produce in them no similar emotion; and then, after the lapse
of sixty minutes (which embrace three thousand and six hundred seconds of
the Time that flies), there came yet another chiming of the clock, and then
were the same disconcert and tremulousness and meditation as before. **C**

80   But, in spite of these things, it was a gay and magnificent revel. The
tastes of the duke were peculiar. He had a fine eye for colors and effects. He
disregarded the *decora* of mere fashion. His plans were bold and fiery, and
his conceptions glowed with barbaric lustre. There are some who would have
thought him mad. His followers felt that he was not. It was necessary to hear
and see and touch him to be *sure* that he was not.

    He had directed, in great part, the movable embellishments of the seven
chambers, upon occasion of this great *fête;* and it was his own guiding taste
which had given character to the masqueraders. Be sure they were grotesque.
There were much glare and glitter and piquancy and phantasm—much of
90 what has been seen since in *Hernani.* There were arabesque figures with
unsuited limbs and appointments. There were delirious fancies such as the
madman fashions. There was much of the beautiful, much of the wanton,
much of the *bizarre,* something of the terrible, and not a little of that
which might have excited disgust. To and fro in the seven chambers there
stalked, in fact, a multitude of dreams. And these—the dreams—writhed
in and about, taking hue from the rooms, and causing the wild music of
the orchestra to seem as the echo of their steps. And, anon, there strikes the
ebony clock which stands in the hall of velvet. And then, for a moment,
all is still, and all is silent save the voice of the clock. The dreams are stiff-
100 frozen as they stand. But the echoes of the chime die away—they have
endured but an instant—and a light, half-subdued laughter floats after them
as they depart. And now again the music swells, and the dreams live, and
writhe to and fro more merrily than ever, taking hue from the many-tinted
windows through which stream the rays of the tripods. But to the chamber
which lies most westwardly of the seven, there are now none of the maskers
who venture; for the night is waning away; and there flows a ruddier light
through the blood-colored panes; and the blackness of the sable drapery
appalls; and to him whose foot falls upon the sable carpet, there comes
from the near clock of ebony a muffled peal more solemnly emphatic than
110 any which reaches *their* ears who indulge in the more remote gaieties of the
other apartments. **D**

    But these other apartments were densely crowded, and in them beat
feverishly the heart of life. And the revel went whirlingly on, until at length
there commenced the sounding of midnight upon the clock. And then
the music ceased, as I have told; and the evolutions of the waltzes were
quieted; and there was an uneasy <u>cessation</u> of all things as before. But now
there were twelve strokes to be sounded by the bell of the clock; and thus

450   UNIT 2: AMERICAN ROMANTICISM

---

reverie (rĕv'ə-rē) *n.* daydream

C   SUSPENSE
How does the clock described
in lines 71–79 contribute to the
story's developing suspense?

82 *decora:* fine things.

90 *Hernani* (ĕr'nä-nē): a play by
French writer Victor Hugo, first
staged in 1830 and notable for its
use of color and spectacle; **arabesque**
(ăr'ə-bĕsk'): intricately designed.

D   CLARIFY MEANING
Paraphrase lines 104–111. Why
do none of the guests venture
into the seventh room?

cessation (sĕ-sā'shən) *n.* a
coming to an end; a stopping

TEXT ANALYSIS   COMMON CORE RL 3

C SUSPENSE

*Possible answer: The chiming clock reminds
readers that time is moving toward something frightening. The clock thus adds to the
air of doom and suspense.*

ADDITIONAL TEACHING OPPORTUNITY

Personification Tell students that allegories
often personify abstract qualities, such as
good or evil, as human characters. Personification can also be used to endow animals and
objects with human traits.

REVISIT THE BIG QUESTION

Is SAFETY an illusion?

Discuss What details in lines 80–111 suggest
that the partygoers feel an illusion of safety?
What detail suggests that they may feel less
safe than before? *Possible answer: Illusion of
safety: Prospero's followers do not think him
mad; the laughter when the peal of the clock
fades. Less safe than before: the fact that no
one goes into the seventh apartment.*

READING STRATEGY   COMMON CORE RL 4

D CLARIFY MEANING

*Possible answer: The light in that room
becomes redder as the night wanes; the
black decorations are unsettling; the clock is
heard more loudly there than elsewhere.*

VOCABULARY   COMMON CORE L 4

OWN THE WORD

- **reverie:** Remind students that *reverie*
refers to daydreaming. Have students
explain when they might spend time in
reverie. *Possible answer: listening to music, relaxing in the yard*

- **cessation:** Point out that *cessation* is the
noun form of the verb *cease* and both
refer to "a stopping." Have students write
a sentence using the word correctly.
*Possible answer: After the cessation of the
protests, we could finally hear the speaker.*

DIFFERENTIATED INSTRUCTION

FOR ADVANCED LEARNERS/AP

Analyze Ask students to recall the three
major types of irony: verbal, situational, and
dramatic. Have them find examples of irony
in the descriptions of the ball and identify the
type of irony each example represents. Have
students discuss the reasons for their choices.
Students may find that some examples belong to more than one type.

FOR STRUGGLING READERS

Develop Reading Fluency Select a long paragraph from the selection and read it aloud to
the class. Instruct students to pay attention
to the intonation, phrasing, and rate of your
speech. After you have read the paragraph,
read the first sentence and have students
repeat it back to you. Continue until students
have "echoed" the entire paragraph. Conclude
by having the class read aloud the entire
paragraph in unison.

it happened, perhaps, that more of thought crept, with more of time, into the meditations of the thoughtful among those who reveled. And thus,
120 too, it happened, perhaps, that before the last echoes of the last chime had utterly sunk into silence, there were many individuals in the crowd who had found leisure to become aware of the presence of a masked figure which had arrested the attention of no single individual before. And the rumor of this new presence having spread itself whisperingly around, there arose at length from the whole company a buzz, or murmur, expressive of **disapprobation** and surprise—then, finally of terror, of horror, and of disgust.

In an assembly of phantasms such as I have painted, it may well be supposed that no ordinary appearance could have excited such sensation. In truth the masquerade license of the night was nearly unlimited; but the
130 figure in question had out-Heroded Herod, and gone beyond the bounds of even the prince's indefinite decorum. There are chords in the hearts of the most reckless which cannot be touched without emotion. Even with the utterly lost, to whom life and death are equally jests, there are matters of which no jest can be made. The whole company, indeed, seemed now deeply to feel that in the costume and bearing of the stranger neither wit nor **propriety** existed. The figure was tall and gaunt, and shrouded from head to foot in the habiliments of the grave. The mask which concealed the visage was made so nearly to resemble the countenance of a stiffened corpse that the closest scrutiny must have had difficulty in detecting the cheat. And
140 yet all this might have been endured, if not approved, by the mad revellers around. But the mummer had gone so far as to assume the type of the Red Death. His vesture was dabbled in *blood*—and his broad brow, with all the features of the face, was besprinkled with the scarlet horror. **E**

When the eyes of Prince Prospero fell upon this spectral image (which with a slow and solemn movement, as if more fully to sustain its *role*, stalked to and fro among the waltzers), he was seen to be convulsed, in the first moment with a strong shudder either of terror or distaste; but, in the next, his brow reddened with rage.

"Who dares?" he demanded hoarsely of the courtiers who stood near
150 him—"who dares insult us with this **blasphemous** mockery? Seize him and unmask him—that we may know whom we have to hang at sunrise, from the battlements!"

It was in the eastern or blue chamber in which stood the Prince Prospero as he uttered these words. They rang throughout the seven rooms loudly and clearly—for the prince was a bold and robust man, and the music had become hushed at the waving of his hand.

It was in the blue room where stood the prince, with a group of pale courtiers by his side. At first, as he spoke, there was a slight rushing movement of this group in the direction of the intruder, who at the moment
160 was also near at hand, and now, with deliberate and stately step, made closer approach to the speaker. But from a certain nameless awe with which the mad assumptions of the mummer had inspired the whole party, there

disapprobation
(dĭs-ăp′rə-bā′shən)
n. disapproval

130 out-Heroded Herod: been more extreme than the biblical King Herod, who ordered the deaths of all male babies in order to kill the infant Jesus. This expression is also used in Shakespeare's *Hamlet.*

propriety (prə-prī′ĭ-tē) *n.* the quality of being proper; appropriateness

137 habiliments (hə-bĭl′ə-mənts): clothing.

② **Targeted Passage**

E **CLARIFY MEANING**
Reread lines 127–143. Use **context clues** to determine the meaning of the words *decorum, visage,* and *vesture.* What details help explain why the figure's appearance is so shocking?

blasphemous (blăs′fə-məs) *adj.* disrespectful or offensive

162 mummer: a person dressed for a masquerade.

Lines 134–152
TIERED DISCUSSION PROMPTS
Use these prompts to help students consider the significance of the unknown masked figure who appears at the ball:

Recall How do guests respond to the stranger dressed as the Red Death? *Possible answer: They are frightened and disturbed.*

Interpret Why does Prince Prospero respond to the stranger's costume with "terror or distaste" and "rage"? *Possible answer: He is frightened of the plague and does not feel as secure in his abbey as he pretends to be.*

READING STRATEGY   COMMON CORE
E **CLARIFY MEANING**   RL 4

Possible answer: Decorum *means "polite behavior"; clues are "beyond the bounds" and "propriety."* Visage *means "face"; a clue is "mask which concealed."* Vesture *means "clothing"; a clue is "costume." The figure is shocking in costume and bearing: "neither wit nor propriety existed" (lines 135–136).*

VOCABULARY   COMMON CORE
                                               L 4
OWN THE WORD

- **disapprobation:** Tell students that *disapprobation* means "disapproval" with the connotation of moral condemnation. Ask students for situations in which they may feel *disapprobation. Possible answer: cheating, lying*

- **propriety:** Remind students that *propriety* means "proper and appropriate." Ask students to explain this phrase in context to the story, ". . . in the costume and bearing of the stranger neither wit nor *propriety* existed." *Possible answer: The guests felt the stranger acted without* propriety *by dressing as a grisly corpse.*

- **blasphemous:** Ask students to use *blasphemous* in a sentence. *Possible answer: The woman's* blasphemous *remarks irritated the police officer.*

FOR STRUGGLING READERS
② **Targeted Passage** [Lines 134–152]

This passage describes the appearance of a masked figure dressed as the Red Death.

- What does the uninvited guest's costume look like? (lines 134–143)

- How does the prince respond to the guest? (lines 144–148)

- What does the prince order to be done to this masked figure? (lines 150–152)

FOR ENGLISH LANGUAGE LEARNERS
Vocabulary Support Poe frequently uses words in close proximity that are opposites or show contrasts. Discuss the meanings and connotations of these examples:

- *beautiful, wanton* (line 92)

- *wild music* (line 96); *light, half-subdued laughter floats* (line 101); *again the music swells* (line 102); *music ceased* (line 115)

- *surprise, terror, horror, disgust* (line 126)

TEXT ANALYSIS

F SUSPENSE

Read aloud lines 157–190 and have students take note of the plot's quickening pace, which adds to the suspense and instills a feeling of inevitability.

Possible answer: *Fearful events come faster and faster in the closing scene, adding to the intensity of the suspense.*

REVISIT THE BIG QUESTION

Is SAFETY *an illusion?*

Discuss In lines 185–190, what happens to the prince's and the revelers' illusions of safety? What meaning does this outcome have for life beyond the abbey walls? ***Possible answer:*** *Their illusions of safety are shattered. The larger meaning may be that all illusions of escaping death are foolish.*

SELECTION WRAP–UP

READ WITH A PURPOSE Now that students have read the selection, ask them to consider the prince's actions. Did he deserve his fate? ***Possible answer:*** Yes; he held a party for himself and his friends, while his people died from the plague, so it is fitting that the prince succumbed to the disease.

★ CRITIQUE

- Ask students how well they feel the story holds up after more than 150 years. Have them explain their opinions.

- After completing the After Reading questions on page 453, have students revisit their responses and tell whether they have changed their opinions.

INDEPENDENT READING

For students who want to read more about the plague, suggest Mary Shelley's *The Last Man*.

---

were found none who put forth hand to seize him; so that, unimpeded, he passed within a yard of the prince's person; and, while the vast assembly, as if with one impulse, shrank from the centers of the rooms to the walls, he made his way uninterrupted, but with the same solemn and measured step which had distinguished him from the first, through the blue chamber to the purple—through the purple to the green—through the green to the orange—through this again to the white—and even thence to the violet,
170 ere a decided movement had been made to arrest him. It was then, however, that the Prince Prospero, maddening with rage and the shame of his own momentary cowardice, rushed hurriedly through the six chambers while none followed him on account of a deadly terror that had seized upon all. He bore aloft a drawn dagger, and had approached, in rapid impetuosity, to within three or four feet of the retreating figure, when the latter, having attained the extremity of the velvet apartment, turned suddenly and confronted his pursuer. There was a sharp cry—and the dagger dropped gleaming upon the sable carpet, upon which, instantly afterwards, fell prostrate in death the Prince Prospero. Then, summoning the wild courage
180 of despair, a throng of the revellers at once threw themselves into the black apartment, and seizing the mummer, whose tall figure stood erect and motionless within the shadow of the ebony clock, gasped in unutterable horror at finding the grave-cerements and corpselike mask, which they handled with so violent a rudeness, untenanted by any tangible form. **F**

And now was acknowledged the presence of the Red Death. He had come like a thief in the night. And one by one dropped the revellers in the blood-bedewed halls of their revel, and died each in the despairing posture of his fall. And the life of the ebony clock went out with that of the last of the gay. And the flames of the tripods expired. And Darkness and Decay and the Red
190 Death held illimitable dominion over all.

Language Coach

English Spelling Usually you write *ie* when the sound is long *e*, except after *c*. *Seize* (line 163), which has a long *e* sound, is an exception. Pronounce the following words aloud: *either, neighbor, protein, height.* Check your pronunciations in a dictionary.

3 Targeted Passage

183–184 finding the . . . form: ripping off the figure's burial garments and mask to find nothing underneath.

F SUSPENSE

How does the quickening pace of the plot's closing moments contribute to this story's suspense?

190 illimitable dominion (ĭ-lĭm′ĭ-tə-bəl də-mĭn′yən): unlimited power.

DIFFERENTIATED INSTRUCTION

FOR STRUGGLING READERS

3 Targeted Passage [Lines 170–190]

This passage concludes the story by showing how fate catches up to the characters.

- What does Prince Prospero try to do, and what happens as a result? (lines 170–179)

- What do the guests find when they seize the stranger? (lines 180–185)

- What happens to the guests in the end? (lines 186–188)

FOR ENGLISH LANGUAGE LEARNERS

Language Coach

English Spelling Have each student compile a list of five words that contain an *ie* combination. Next have students make a list of five words that contain an *ei* combination. Tell students to take turns pronouncing the words on their lists with a partner.

Comprehension

1. **Recall** Why does Prince Prospero seal himself and his guests in the abbey?

2. **Recall** What effect does the striking of the clock have on the revellers?

3. **Summarize** What happens after the mysterious figure is unmasked?

Text Analysis

4. **Make Inferences** What does each of the following reveal about Prince Prospero?

   - his response to the crisis in his country (lines 1–12)
   - his plans for the masquerade (lines 86–94)
   - his response to the masked figure (lines 144–152)

5. **Clarify Meaning** Explain how context clues and the author's use of suspense help you to understand the narrator's description of firelight (lines 51-60).

6. **Analyze Descriptive Details** For each of the following examples, identify the contrast drawn between the seventh room and the rest of Prince Prospero's suite. Based on these contrasts, what might the seventh room represent?

   - its decorations (lines 44–48) • its location (lines 104–105)
   - its atmosphere (lines 56–60) • what occurs there (lines 174–179)

7. **Evaluate Suspense** For you as a reader, what is the most suspenseful moment in Poe's story and how does the narrator create suspense at this point? Support your answer with evidence from the story.

8. **Analyze Mood** As you learned reading "The Fall of the House of Usher" (page 412), the mood or atmosphere of Poe's stories contributes to an overall unity of effect. What kind of mood does Poe establish in "The Masque of the Red Death"? How does the mood of the story contribute to the suspense? Support your response with evidence from the selection.

Text Criticism

9. **Critical Interpretations** Some critics have argued that "The Masque of the Red Death" takes place in Prospero's mind. Cite details from the story that support this interpretation. How does this view change the story's meaning?

> *Is* SAFETY *an illusion*?
>
> Consider the desperate measures the characters take to achieve safety. In what ways, if any, do their behaviors reflect real-world responses to a deadly threat?

COMMON CORE

RL 1 Cite evidence to support analysis of inferences drawn from the text. **RL 3** Analyze the impact of the author's choices regarding how to develop and relate elements of a story. **RL 4** Determine the meanings of words and phrases as they are used in the text, including figurative and connotative meanings; analyze the impact of specific word choices on meaning and tone. **L 4a** Use context as a clue to the meaning of a word or phrase.

Practice and Apply

For preliminary support of post-reading questions, use these copy masters:

R **RESOURCE MANAGER**—Copy Masters
Reading Check p. 196
Suspense p. 189
Question Support p. 197

Additional selection questions are provided for teachers on page 183.

ANSWERS    **COMMON CORE** RL 1, RL 3, RL 4, L 4a

1. *to escape the Red Death*

2. *It makes them pause fearfully.*

3. *The prince and all the guests die, the clock stops working, and the braziers go out.*

Possible answers:

4. *He doesn't care about his countrymen, only that he and his friends remain safe (lines 1–12); he is a little odd, possibly insane, and enjoys garish spectacle (lines 86–94); he is arrogant and does not accept challenges to his authority (lines 144–152).*

5. ● **COMMON CORE FOCUS** **Clarify Meaning** *Context clues signal to readers that images of firelight are not just details of setting, but are symbols of an unnamed and frightening force. Suspense, playing on the reader's fear of the unknown, supports context clues by suggesting that something worse than firelight awaits as the story progresses.*

6. *The room is black with blood-red windows and is the only room in which the windows don't match the décor. It is the only room the guests are fearful of entering. It lies farthest west. Prospero is killed there. The room may represent death.*

7. ● **COMMON CORE FOCUS** **Suspense** *Accept reasonable answers that students can support with evidence from the story.*

---

8. *The mood created is one of dread and terror. The mood contributes to the suspense as characters become increasingly afraid. Guests were hesitant to enter the seventh chamber because of the blood-red lights cast on their faces. They shrank back in fear and disgust from the mysteriously costumed stranger.*

9. *Details that support the interpretation include words like dreams, fancies, delirious, and phantasms; the comment that some thought Prospero mad; the unrealistic nature of the story; and the fact that* Prospero *is the only distinct character. In this interpretation the story might be less an allegory of life and death and more an illustration of madness.*

> *Is* SAFETY *an illusion?* **Possible answers:** *The behavior of trying to isolate themselves is a common human response to a deadly threat.*

ANSWERS

Vocabulary in Context

▲ VOCABULARY PRACTICE

1. *slow down the process*
2. *controversial*
3. *detention*
4. *distracted*
5. *being polite*
6. *one participant walking away*

 **RESOURCE MANAGER—Copy Master**
Vocabulary Practice p. 194

ACADEMIC VOCABULARY IN SPEAKING

Students should discuss what inspires them as well as what inspires writers. Answers will vary.

VOCABULARY STRATEGY: AFFIXES AND SPELLING CHANGES

COMMON CORE **L 2b, L 4b–c, L 6**

Point out that for some words, such as *cessation,* the word's etymology (Latin *cessare,* to stop) is helpful in determining the base word. *Students' sample sentences will vary.*

1. *deride; yes*
2. *contend; yes*
3. *permeate; yes*
4. *pomp; yes*
5. *acclaim; no*
6. *revoke; yes*
7. *despise; yes*
8. *cease; yes*
9. *sober; no*
10. *measure; no*

 **RESOURCE MANAGER—Copy Master**
Vocabulary Strategy p. 195

Interactive Vocabulary THINK central

Vocabulary keywords direct students to a **WordSharp** tutorial on **thinkcentral.com** or to other types of vocabulary practice and review.

Assess and Reteach

Assess

DIAGNOSTIC AND SELECTION TESTS
Selection Test A, B/C pp. 141–142, 143–144

Interactive Selection Test on **thinkcentral.com**

Reteach

Level Up Online Tutorials on **thinkcentral.com**

Vocabulary in Context

▲ VOCABULARY PRACTICE

Show you understand the vocabulary words by answering these questions.

1. Will an attempt to **impede** the passage of a law speed up the process or slow it down?
2. Would a **blasphemous** comment be considered controversial or appeasing?
3. Which would more likely result in a parent's **disapprobation**—a detention or a school award?
4. Would someone's **reverie** make them attentive or distracted?
5. If I act with **propriety,** am I being polite or asking uncomfortable questions?
6. Which would cause the **cessation** of a conversation—one participant nodding in agreement or one participant walking away?

WORD LIST
blasphemous
cessation
disapprobation
impede
propriety
reverie

ACADEMIC VOCABULARY IN SPEAKING

• construct   • expand   • indicate   • reinforce   • role

Poe, who was a master of horror stories, sometimes **constructed** his stories around true accounts. In a small group, discuss what inspires you to write creatively. Then, **expand** this idea by brainstorming where professional writers get their inspiration. Use at least three of the Academic Vocabulary words in your discussion.

VOCABULARY STRATEGY: AFFIXES AND SPELLING CHANGES

Some base words are hard to recognize because they are spelled differently when affixes are added. For example, the vocabulary word *cessation* includes the base word *cease* and the suffix *-ation.* Note how the spelling of the base word changes in the new word. These spelling changes may reflect the word's etymology (its history and origins), or they may simply reflect new pronunciation that made the word easier to say. To decipher words of this type, look for related base words and use context clues to unlock meaning.

PRACTICE Identify the appropriate base word for each of the following numbered words. Then write a sentence that demonstrates the meaning of each numbered word. Finally, use a dictionary to research the word's origins. Did the spelling change as a result of the word's history?

1. derisive
2. contentious
3. impermeable
4. pomposity
5. acclamation
6. irrevocable
7. despicable
8. incessant
9. sobriety
10. commensurate

COMMON CORE

L 2b Spell correctly.
L 4b–c Identify and use patterns of word changes that indicate different meanings or parts of speech; consult reference materials. **L 6** Acquire and use academic words and phrases.

Interactive Vocabulary THINK central
Go to **thinkcentral.com.**
KEYWORD: HML11-454

DIFFERENTIATED INSTRUCTION

FOR ENGLISH LANGUAGE LEARNERS

Task Support: Vocabulary Practice Point out that several of the vocabulary words have suffixes that show their function as a part of speech. The *-ous* in *blasphemous* shows that the word is an adjective. The *-tion* in *cessation* and *disapprobation* and the *-ty* in *propriety* show that they are nouns. Have students say other words that have those endings. Remind students to consider the part of speech when figuring out meanings of vocabulary words.

FOR ADVANCED LEARNERS/AP

Connotations Have students explore the connotations of the vocabulary words by using each word in a paragraph about a subject of their choice. Then have them revise the paragraph, using more common synonyms for the vocabulary words. Have students assess the differences, in tone and meaning, between the two versions. Students should find that the vocabulary words are more formal and old-fashioned than their synonyms.

Essay

In "The Masque of the Red Death," you experienced suspense. Now, in an excerpt from Stephen King's *Danse Macabre*, you'll read about what creates suspense in a work of art.

from
Danse Macabre

Essay by Stephen King

BACKGROUND Stephen King may well be the best-known writer of horror fiction since Edgar Allan Poe. In 1981, after writing a number of best-selling novels, King wrote *Stephen King's Danse Macabre*, a nonfiction work in which he discussed horror in literature and film and examined the psychology of terror. The book's title is a reference to the "Dance of Death," a symbolic representation of death, in the form of a skeleton, leading people to their graves. This dance was commonly depicted on cemetery walls and in the European art of the Middle Ages and the Renaissance.

I want to say something about imagination purely as a tool in the art and science of scaring people. The idea isn't original with me; I heard it expressed by William F. Nolan at the 1979 World Fantasy Convention. Nothing is so frightening as what's behind the closed door, Nolan said. You approach the door in the old, deserted house, and you hear something scratching at it. The audience holds its breath along with the protagonist as she or he (more often she) approaches that door. The protagonist throws it open, and there is a ten-foot-tall bug. The audience screams, but this particular scream has an oddly relieved sound to it. "A bug ten feet tall is pretty horrible," the audience thinks, "but I can deal with
10 a ten-foot-tall bug. I was afraid it might be a *hundred* feet tall.". . . **A**

Bill Nolan was speaking as a screenwriter when he offered the example of the big bug behind the door, but the point applies to all media. What's behind the door or lurking at the top of the stairs is never as frightening as the door or the staircase itself. And because of this, comes the paradox: the artistic work of horror is almost always a disappointment. It is the classic no-win situation. You can scare people with the unknown for a long, long time (the classic example, as Bill Nolan also pointed out, is the Jacques Tourneur film with Dana Andrews, *Curse of the Demon*), but sooner or later, as in poker, you have to turn your down cards up. You have to open the door and show the audience what's behind it. And if what happens to be behind it is a bug,
20 not ten but a hundred feet tall, the audience heaves a sigh of relief (or utters a scream

A **SUSPENSE**
In lines 4–10, how does the image of a door, with a giant bug behind it, contribute to your understanding of suspense? Explain.

SUMMARY

In this excerpt, Stephen King discusses how terror and suspense are treated in literature and film.

Essay

Both "The Masque of the Red Death" and the excerpt from King's "Danse Macabre" deal with terror and suspense. After students read King's selection, guide them in a class discussion about how each selection relates to the other.

TEXT ANALYSIS	COMMON CORE
	RI 1

A SUSPENSE

Possible answer: Suspense comes from not knowing what's behind the door. When the door opens to reveal a giant bug, we are momentarily frightened, but the suspense is gone. Suspense works by suggesting danger but not revealing the source of the danger.

DIFFERENTIATED INSTRUCTION

FOR ENGLISH LANGUAGE LEARNERS
Explore Allusions

- Point out to students that King's reference to Bluebeard (lines 33–35) comes from the fairy tale "Barbe Bleue," recorded by Charles Perrault more than 300 years ago. In that tale, Bluebeard warns his wife not to enter a certain room; still, she opens the door— and discovers the skeletons of Bluebeard's previous wives. (When Bluebeard learns what she has done, she escapes death only because her brothers arrive and rescue her.)

- Most students will recognize the name *Dracula*, the title character of Bram Stoker's 1897 novel. Explain that in lines 36–38, King alludes to Harker's encounter with three female vampires (an encounter from which Dracula rescues Harker).

- Invite students to comment about both stories and about King's possible reasons for not being specific about either outcome.

of relief) and thinks, "A bug a hundred feet tall is pretty horrible, but I can deal with that. I was afraid it might be a *thousand* feet tall." . . . **B**

The danse macabre is a waltz with death. This is a truth we cannot afford to shy away from.

Like the rides in the amusement park which mimic violent death, the tale of horror is a chance to examine what's going on behind doors which we usually keep double-locked. Yet the human imagination is not content with locked doors. Somewhere there is another dancing partner, the imagination whispers in the night—a partner in a rotting ball gown, a partner with empty eyesockets, green 30 mold growing on her elbow-length gloves, maggots squirming in the thin remains of her hair. To hold such a creature in our arms? Who, you ask me, would be so mad? Well . . . ?

"You will not want to open this door," Bluebeard tells his wife in that most horrible of all horror stories, "because your husband has forbidden it." But this, of course, only makes her all the more curious . . . and at last, her curiosity is satisfied. **C**

"You may go anywhere you wish in the castle," Count Dracula tells Jonathan Harker, "except where the doors are locked, where of course you will not wish to go." But Harker goes soon enough.

And so do we all. Perhaps we go to the forbidden door or window willingly 40 because we understand that a time comes when we must go whether we want to or not . . . and not just to look, but to be pushed through. Forever. ❧

456 UNIT 2: AMERICAN ROMANTICISM

Movie Poster

The movie poster shown on this page advertised *Wait Until Dark,* a very successful movie from 1967. Based on a stage play, the film tells the story of a recently blind woman threatened by thugs in her basement apartment. The poster's split image shows a match flame in the dark and the dimly lit face of a woman opening her mouth to scream. Think about how the image works with the words in the poster to create suspense. Respond to the questions below, citing evidence from the poster to support your answers.

COMMON CORE

RI 7 Evaluate multiple sources of information presented in different media or formats as well as in words to address a question.

1. **ANALYZE**
   Study the split image in the poster. Examine the woman's facial expression and the contrast between darkness and the match flame. What kind of atmosphere do these elements create? If you had only the images to analyze, what kind of story would you expect them to represent?

2. **INTERPRET**
   Examine the language to the right of the split image. How do the words themselves and the diminishing type size contribute to the impact of the poster? What purpose do they help the poster to achieve?

Practice and Apply

COMMON CORE FOCUS

RI 7 Evaluate multiple sources of information presented in different media or formats as well as in words to address a question.

Movie Poster

The flame illuminates the woman so the viewer can see her. Since we know the woman is blind, we know that she is reacting to the sounds of the blinds, the squeaking shoes, the smell of the match, and to the fact that no one is talking. The diminishing type increases tension, as the blind woman struggles to hear.

ANALYZE VISUALS   COMMON CORE RI 7

1. ANALYZE

Possible answer: The woman's terrified expression and the contrast between light and dark create a suspenseful, frightening atmosphere. I would expect them to represent a story with psychological or horrific aspects.

ANALYZE VISUALS   COMMON CORE RI 7

2. INTERPRET

Possible answer: The words indicate that the person in the room is quietly evaluating the woman and purposely intimidating her. The diminishing type size contributes a sense of mounting suspense and fear, as if the woman is frightened almost to the point of fainting.

ANSWERS

1. *We don't know what's behind it.*

2. *Some amusement park rides frighten riders by making it look as if something terrible is about to happen to them. Horror stories do the same thing using words.*

Possible answers:

3. ● **COMMON CORE FOCUS** Suspense *Being afraid of something you can't see is frightening. In the absence of information, the mind enlarges the source of the fear. Once you see the source of the fear—what's behind the door—your mind will stop making it worse.*

4. ■ **COMMON CORE FOCUS** Clarify Meaning *In poker, suspense comes from not knowing what cards an opponent has. It's like not knowing what's behind a closed door. Once you see an opponent's hand, the suspense is over.*

5. *Suspense means getting very close to something you fear. Suspense is like a waltz in that it involves stepping close to a source of fear, such as death, over and over again.*

6. ■ **COMMON CORE FOCUS** Clarify Meaning *Accept answers that students support with evidence from the selection. Students may respond that we open the door because we know that eventually we must face that which we fear.*

7. *Answers will vary; accept reasonable responses that students can support with examples from literature or film.*

8. *The plague is outside the walls of the prince's abbey, lurking as an unseen danger. The seventh room in the abbey is like King's closed door. It is black with blood-red windows and a ghastly firelight. It suggests that horror awaits, but like a closed door, it doesn't reveal the nature of the horror. The uninvited guest is also like a closed door. He is a source of fear in disguise. In the climactic scene, when the prince and his guests confront the uninvited guest, the scene is like opening King's door. The source of fear and suspense is revealed.*

After Reading

Comprehension

1. **Summarize** According to Stephen King, what makes a closed door so frightening?

2. **Clarify** In this discussion of suspense, what do some amusement park rides have in common with tales of horror?

Text Analysis

● 3. **Analyze Suspense** Why, according to King, is a closed door more frightening than what is actually behind the door (lines 12-13)? Explain.

■ 4. **Clarify Meaning** What does the author mean, in lines 17-18, when he compares creating suspense to playing poker? Explain.

5. **Interpret Metaphor** What does King mean when he compares the experience of suspense to a waltz with death (line 23)?

■ 6. **Clarify Meaning** In the concluding paragraph, why does King think we willingly open the forbidden door of suspense? Support your answer with evidence from the text.

7. **Make Inferences** How does King's essay help to explain the success of suspenseful books and movies of the twentieth and twenty-first centuries? Support your response with examples from your own reading or film viewing.

Comparing Themes Across Genres

8. What elements in "The Masque of the Red Death" (page 446) illustrate what King means with his metaphor of a closed, forbidden door? Explain your answer, citing evidence from Poe's story.

> *Is* **SAFETY** *an illusion?*
>
> A locked door can make us feel safe from threats. But is a locked door merely an illusion of safety? Using evidence from Stephen King's essay, explain how he would answer this question. How would you answer the question? Explain your answer.

COMMON CORE

RI 1 Cite evidence to support analysis of inferences draw from the text. **RI 4** Determine the meaning of words and phrases as they are used in a text, including figurative, connotative and technical meanings.

> *Is SAFETY an illusion?*
>
> **Possible answer:** King would say it is an illusion, because something dangerous could be lurking behind the door.

Assessment Practice: Short Constructed Response

LITERARY TEXT: "THE MASQUE OF THE RED DEATH"

On assessments you are expected to read carefully and answer questions that focus on particular passages from a text. To strengthen your close-reading skills, read the **short constructed response question** at left below and practice the strategies suggested at right.

> Examine Poe's description of the effect a masked figure has on guests at the masked ball. How does this description contribute to the story's developing suspense?

◀ **STRATEGIES IN ACTION**

1. List words or phrases that have a foreboding tone.
2. Identify elements of the action that cause anxiety for the guests and the reader.
3. Use evidence you circled or underlined to support your answer.

NONFICTION TEXT: from *DANSE MACABRE*

On assessments you are expected to identify key ideas in a piece of text. Practice this skill as you respond to the **short constructed response question** below. Be sure to follow the steps outlined to the right of the question.

> In the opening paragraph, King introduces a metaphor that expresses the central idea of the text. What is the metaphor and what idea does it express about suspense?

◀ **STRATEGIES IN ACTION**

1. Reread the opening paragraph and identify a metaphor/idea that plays a key role in the rest of the essay.
2. Briefly explain the idea conveyed by the metaphor and identify why it is so important to King.

COMPARING LITERARY AND NONFICTION TEXTS

To succeed on assessments, you will need to identify thematic connections between literary and nonfiction texts. Practice this valuable skill by responding to the following **short constructed response question** about "The Masque of the Red Death" and the excerpt from *Danse Macabre*.

> As a nonfiction text, *Danse Macabre* has an explicit main idea. Poe's short story, by contrast, has an implied theme. What is King's explicit main idea and how is it reflected in "The Masque of the Red Death"?

◀ **STRATEGIES IN ACTION**

1. Reread King's opening paragraph and identify the essay's main idea.
2. From Poe's story, select two or three details or scenes that illustrate King's main idea.

Assessment Practice: Short Constructed Response

LITERARY TEXT: "THE MASQUE OF THE RED DEATH" **Possible answer:** *The lines add to the suspense by introducing a character whose identity is disguised. Information about him is sparingly revealed by the guests' reactions of disapproval, terror, horror, and disgust. With each revelation, the suspense mounts. Phrases such as "blood-tinted panes," "ghastly in the extreme," and "the countenance of a stiffened corpse" create a foreboding tone.*

NONFICTION TEXT: "from DANSE MACABRE" **Possible answer:** *The metaphor is the closed door. It expresses the idea that suspense comes from the unknown—not knowing what is behind the door. King and other writers create suspense by suggesting danger without revealing its source.*

COMPARING LITERARY AND NONFICTION TEXTS **Possible answer:** *King's thesis is that nothing is scarier than what's behind a closed door (an unknown source of danger). This idea is expressed in "The Masque of the Red Death" through Poe's description of the seventh room, the chiming clock, and the masked figure, all of which suggest danger without revealing what exactly it is (what's behind the door).*

DIFFERENTIATED INSTRUCTION

FOR STRUGGLING WRITERS

Analyze the Prompt Remind students that they should fully understand what is asked of them before they begin to write. Point out that each of the questions contains key words that are to be the focus of the students' answers. Instruct students to identify these key words: *developing suspense, meta-phor,* and *explicit thesis*. Tell students to focus on the key words they identified as they review the text before writing their answers.

COMMON CORE FOCUS

RL 7 Analyze multiple interpretations of a story, evaluating how each version interprets the source text. **SL 1a** Research material under study and refer to evidence from the texts and other research to stimulate an exchange of ideas. **SL 2** Integrate information presented in diverse formats and media. **SL 4** Present findings, conveying a clear perspective, such that listeners can follow the line of reasoning, and the organization, development and style are appropriate to the purpose and audience.

SUMMARY

In this image collection, students view illustrations by Clive Barker, Gris Grimly, Edmund Dulac, Charles Addams, and others. They focus on two works by Arthur Rackham. In "The Fall of the House of Usher," a rider views a spooky, melancholy house that rises from a swampy lake and is framed by jagged, craggy trees. In the image "The Pit and the Pendulum," burning iron walls drive the prisoner to the edge of the deadly pit at the center of his cell.

What does GOTHIC *look like?*

Help students brainstorm elements that characterize the gothic spirit, such as frantic facial expressions, dramatic color schemes, and dark, foreboding scenes. Ask students why such a style is appropriate to Poe's work.

BACKGROUND

Arthur Rackham (1867–1939) is one of the foremost British children's illustrators of the early twentieth century. His work is characterized by magical fairies, fantastical gnomes, and ugly ogres. His illustrations of Poe's stories are less fantastical than most of his art, and reveal his understanding of human nature and its psychological depth.

Media Study

Illustrations Inspired by Poe
Image Collection on Media **Smart** DVD-ROM

COMMON CORE

RL 7 Analyze multiple interpretations of a story, evaluating how each version interprets the source text.

What does GOTHIC *look like?*

Shadows and gargoyles and pervading gloom all evoke the **gothic spirit** that Edgar Allan Poe depicted so well in his stories and poems. Countless artists have been inspired by Poe's works—writers, musicians, architects, and certainly visual artists. British illustrator Arthur Rackham had a particular affinity for Poe's writing. In examining Rackham's illustrations in this lesson, you'll see how an artist influenced by Poe's gothic style expresses his own personal interpretation.

Background

American Gothic It's not simply the plots and characters Poe created that have mesmerized readers and artists over time. It's what his writing revealed of our dark side, of our capacity for decadence and even insanity, that has given him such lasting influence. Though the term *gothic* has been applied to other art forms such as architecture and music, it is in Poe's writing that the psychological elements of gothic are most sharply defined.

At the time Poe's work was first published, illustrators were regularly hired to create images to accompany his text. As Poe's reputation grew and more people read his often disturbing stories, painters and artists found great imaginative fodder in Poe's phantasmagorical tales. You can see his influence in the work of countless illustrators over the past 150 years, including Poe contemporary Gustave Doré, Arthur Rackham, Edward Gorey, Charles Addams (creator of "The Addams Family" cartoon), and even popular children's book illustrator Stephen Gammell. Many of today's graphic novelists are heavily influenced by Poe's sense of gothic.

Media Study Resources

See resources on the **Teacher One Stop DVD-ROM** *and on* <u>thinkcentral.com</u>.

R **RESOURCE MANAGER UNIT 2**

Plan and Teach pp. 199–202
Summary pp. 203†*, 204‡*
Viewing Guide p. 205
Close Viewing p. 206
Media Activity p. 207
Produce Your Own Media p. 208

TECHNOLOGY

📀 **Teacher One Stop DVD-ROM**
📀 **Student One Stop DVD-ROM**
📀 **Media*Smart* DVD-ROM**

* Resources for Differentiation   † Also in Spanish   ‡ Also in Haitian Creole and Vietnamese

Media Literacy: Art Elements in Illustrations

In Edgar Allan Poe's writing, he often expresses his style through imagery that re-creates certain sensory experiences. In "The Fall of the House of Usher," Poe's description of the house is one of decay and desolation. In order to translate such descriptions into a visual image, an illustrator relies on the art elements of **color, line, shape,** and **texture** to evoke similar feelings. Another aspect of visual art is **dominance,** which is created when one or more parts of an image are given more importance than the others.

Consider these elements when analyzing this 1935 Arthur Rackham illustration for "The Fall of the House of Usher." Think about the deliberate stylistic choices made by the illustrator to match the mood and tone of Poe's writing.

STRATEGIES FOR ANALYZING ILLUSTRATIONS

1 **Color** is used to highlight important aspects and create mood in an image. To analyze an illustrator's use of color, think about the overall mood of the image. Are the colors warm (red and orange) or cool (blue and green)? Do the muted colors in this image seem to reflect Poe's descriptions?

2 **Line** is a stroke or a mark. Vertical, horizontal, jagged, curved—lines have expressive qualities. Look at the style of lines an artist uses. Here, for example, the vertical lines are strong and varied and suggest the dreary atmosphere of Poe's setting.

3 **Shape** is the outline of an object in an image. Notice the tension created by the strong yet warped lines of the dead trees against the severe lines of the house.

4 **Texture** is the surface quality of an image. Examine how this artist manipulates visual elements to create different textures. Ask yourself: If I could touch this image, how would it feel?

5 Be aware of the primary object that draws your eye. Here the house of Usher is the dominant image.

Media Literacy

Ask a volunteer to remind the class of the plot of "The Fall of the House of Usher." Review with students the mood and tone of Poe's writing. List descriptive words that students suggest, such as *ominous, eerie, psychological,* and *desolate.* Then discuss the illustration by Arthur Rackham and how it creates a similar mood.

- **Color** Point out that the image is drawn in a monochromatic color scheme. Ask students to describe the mood created by the gray, white, and black colors.

- **Line** Note that the line weights are stronger on the trees than on the house. The black lines of the trees further emphasize the emptiness inside them. Ask students how the lines help define the elements of the drawing that are most important.

- **Shape** Clarify that the illustrator emphasized the house's stiff, upright shape by framing it with twisted, curving trees.

- **Texture** Draw attention to the smudged, watercolor effect of the sky as it contrasts with the sharper pen-and-ink appearance of the road. Ask students what is different about these textures.

- **Dominance** Explain that dominance in a painting is created by color, size, line, and position. In this image, the house is the lightest part of the drawing, as well as the largest part. It is also framed by the lines of the trees on both sides and positioned close to the center of the illustration, making it the dominant image.

⊘ **Media*Smart* DVD-ROM**

MEDIA STUDY: TEACHING OPTIONS

Teaching Option 1: The Basics (1–2 Days)
1. Begin the Media Study using the material provided on pages 460–461.
2. Show the Introduction on Media*Smart.* Have students use the Viewing Guide on page 462, along with the corresponding copy master on page 205 of the Resource Manager. Discuss their responses.
3. Return to the pupil book for the extension activities on page 463.

Teaching Option 2: In-Depth Study (2–3 Days)
1. Begin the Media Study using pages 460–461.
2. Show the Introduction from Media*Smart.*
3. Continue on Media*Smart* with the Media Lessons, using the teacher notes available in the Resources section.
4. Show the Guided Analysis presentation. Have students record their observations on the Student Viewing Guide available in the Resources section of Media*Smart.*
5. Return to the pupil book, page 463.

Practice and Apply

VIEWING GUIDE

1. As students prepare to view the images, tell them they will be asked to identify and analyze aspects of color, line, and dominance. Display each image one at a time, and then repeat the process. Encourage students to study all the images before answering the questions. Suggest that they pay attention to these points:

   - background details that convey information and set the mood of the illustration through **color, line,** and **shape**

   - the perspective from which the image is drawn and the position of the viewer in relation to the scene of the illustration

   - how ordinary items such as a staircase or a house are made to look frightening

   - how position and **dominance** of elements in the illustration support its mood

2. Encourage students to consider how each illustration reflects Poe's fascination with the macabre and creates a sense of terror. As they view the collection, help them make connections to related scenes from the Poe literature.

R RESOURCE MANAGER—Copy Masters
> Viewing Guide p. 205
> Close Viewing p. 206
> Media Activity p. 207

Use this resource with the Viewing Guide:

◉ Media*Smart* DVD-ROM
Media*Scope* on thinkcentral.com

ANSWERS

FIRST VIEWING: Comprehension

1. *The narrator appears in the foreground across the moat from the house.*

2. *The man is standing at the edge of the pit.*

CLOSE VIEWING: Media Literacy

Possible answers:

3. *The colors are monochromatic, in shades of gray. They create a foreboding and frightening mood.*

4. *In "The Pit and the Pendulum," lines define the stone floor and suggest physical distress in the figure's legs and tunic. The shadowy vertical lines in the background hint at something evil or frightening. In "The Fall of the House of Usher," the primarily vertical lines define the twisted, craggy tree and the*

Media◉Smart DVD-ROM
- **Selection 1:** "The Fall of The House of Usher"
- **Selection 2:** "The Pit and the Pendulum"
- **Type:** Illustration
- **Illustrator:** Arthur Rackham

Viewing Guide for
Illustrations Inspired by Poe

Access the full-sized images on the DVD. Examine each image carefully, jotting down your initial impressions. Look for common elements, themes, and subjects in the images. To help you analyze each image in terms of color, shape, line, texture, and dominance, use the viewing strategies detailed on page 461. You can also refer to the Elements of Design section of the Media Handbook (pages R94–R95). Answer the questions to help you analyze the images.

NOW VIEW

FIRST VIEWING: Comprehension

1. **Describe** Where does the narrator of "The Fall of the House of Usher" appear in Rackham's illustration?

2. **Identify** Where is the man standing in "The Pit and the Pendulum" illustration?

CLOSE VIEWING: Media Literacy

3. **Analyze Color** What colors does Rackham use in the "House of Usher" illustration, and what mood do these create? Explain your answer.

4. **Compare Line** Look carefully at the way line is used in both illustrations. In which image is line used most effectively? Explain.

5. **Compare Dominance** Consider the images for "The Fall of the House of Usher" and "The Pit and the Pendulum." One part of each image is dominant. How does the illustrator achieve this effect? Think about

   - the use of shape in the images
   - how color is used to create dominance

stoic, imposing house. Rackham uses lines most effectively in "The Fall of the House of Usher" because they are more severe and create a unified effect.

5. In "The Fall of the House of Usher," the house is dominant. It is framed by the craggy trees, the glassy moat, and the dark grey sky. In "The Pit and the Pendulum," the man at the edge of the pit is dominant because of his central location and lighter color. The darker shapes behind him and at his feet help accent his dominance.

Write or Discuss

Describe Unity of Effect Poe believed in writing to achieve "unity of effect," in which every detail of a work contributes to a single overall feeling. This idea guided his word choices, sentence structures, and subject matter. Look at the two Rackham illustrations in this Media Study. How do you think Rackham's decisions as an artist create unity of effect? Describe to your classmates what Rackham achieves with these gothic images. Consider these elements:

- Rackham's use of color, line, shape, and texture in the images
- the parts of Poe's stories that each work depicts
- the overall mood of each illustration

Produce Your Own Media

Create Gothic Artwork How would you visually represent something in the gothic style? Use your understanding of the term to create a gothic piece of **artwork.** It can be a photograph, a painting, a computer-generated image, a drawing, even a collage of magazine clippings.

HERE'S HOW Here are a few suggestions for creating gothic visual art:

- No matter what type of gothic piece you will create, make notes on your intentions and how you plan to achieve them.
- Decide on the psychological mood you want to express.
- Keep in mind the visual art elements.
- Consider what colors you'll need to use. If creating a gothic photograph, consider the lighting effects you might employ, or whether to use color or black-and-white film.
- Try to establish a dominant element in your piece, something that the viewer will quickly focus on.

Further Exploration

Contrasting Styles Revisit the variety of additional Poe-inspired images on the DVD, or look for other examples on your own. Explore how these works are all influenced by Poe's writing in some way. What Poe-inspired similarities can you find between the images? Cite specific elements from the images. Think about

- line, shape, color, and texture
- how the images reflect a gothic sensibility
- how the images express the psychological

Find the Gothic in Your Life Think about other art forms—movies, music, live theater—where you find gothic elements. Describe a movie, song, or play in which you can identify these elements.

COMMON CORE

RL 7 Analyze multiple interpretations of a story, evaluating how each version interprets the source text. **SL 1a** Research material under study and refer to evidence from the texts and other research to stimulate an exchange of ideas. **SL 2** Integrate information presented in diverse formats and media. **SL 4** Present findings, conveying a clear perspective, such that listeners can follow the line of reasoning, and the organization, development and style are appropriate to the purpose and audience.

Media Tools — **THINK** central

Go to **thinkcentral.com**.
KEYWORD: HML11-463

Tech Tip
If available, use a design program to turn a photograph of a happy occasion into a gothic representation.

Produce Your Own Media

Rubric: Create Gothic Artwork Strong artwork should have:

- a unified mood that conveys gothic themes, such as psychological distress and deep emotion
- visual elements such as color, shape, and texture that support the mood
- effective lighting that creates a gothic effect
- a dominant figure or image created by color, line, and shape

R RESOURCE MANAGER—Copy Master
Produce Your Own Media p. 208

Further Exploration

Contrasting Styles Point out the bulleted text. Have students record these features for each work.

Find the Gothic in Your Life Recall the artists named in **Background** on page 460. Then, help students brainstorm additional examples of gothic work, such as Mary Shelley's *Frankenstein* or the film *Psycho*.

Write or Discuss

COMMON CORE RL 7, SL 1a, SL 2, SL 4

Describe Unity of Effect Students should address the techniques used to create the feeling of foreboding in the illustrations, such as *line, color, shape,* and *texture.* For example, the textures in "The Pit and the Pendulum" image help unify it. Have students discuss the moods in the Poe literature and illustrations, supporting their ideas with examples.

MEDIA STUDY WRAP-UP

Have students summarize what they have learned about how illustrators convey mood through line, shape, color, and dominance. Encourage students to use their understanding as they evaluate illustrations throughout their reading.

RETEACH

For students who are unable to apply the Media Study skills, select from these reteaching options:

- **Psychological Aspects of Dominance** Use a design program to alter the illustration from "The Pit and the Pendulum" so that the central figure is much smaller than the surrounding images. Ask students whether the new illustration is more or less threatening than the original. Discuss whether they feel the central figure is in greater or less danger.
- **Color and Mood** If available, use a design program to alter the color palette in the illustration from "The House of Usher," changing its tones to brighter colors. Show students the illustration and ask whether they feel the mood has changed and, if so, how? (If it is not feasible to alter the illustration, ask students how brighter colors affect the mood.)

Media Tools — **THINK** central

Media study keywords point to **MediaScope,** a Web site that helps students strengthen media analysis and production skills.

RL 3 Analyze the impact of the author's choices regarding how to develop and relate elements of a story.

BACKGROUND In 1850, Melville and his wife bought a Massachusetts farm, called Arrowhead, near the home of Nathaniel Hawthorne. Melville and Hawthorne became friends, and Hawthorne proved to be a major influence upon Melville's decision to infuse *Moby Dick* with spiritual and allegorical elements. Ironically, those very elements contributed to the lack of critical praise for *Moby Dick* and to the book's poor sales (only 3,000 copies in Melville's lifetime). Today, however, *Moby Dick* is considered Melville's greatest achievement.

TEXT ANALYSIS Before students read the passage, explain these points:

- Moby Dick is a rare white sperm whale (a "parmacetty," Daggoo says). Hunted in the past, he has turned on his attackers and now is thought to be very dangerous.

- In a previous hunt, Ahab lost a leg to Moby Dick. He now has a peg leg made of whalebone—and an obsession with revenge.

- Tashtego, Daggoo, and Queequeg are harpooners aboard the *Pequod*. Starbuck, Stubb, and Flask are ship's officers.

UNDERSTAND DIALOGUE Remind students to pay attention to punctuation marks when they assess dialogue.

American Masterpiece

from Moby Dick

Novel by Herman Melville

Herman Melville

BACKGROUND "Call me Ishmael," says the narrator of *Moby Dick* in the novel's famous opening words. Ishmael, the sole survivor of the lost whaling ship the *Pequod*, tells the story of Captain Ahab and his relentless pursuit of the great white whale, Moby Dick. A tale of harrowing adventure, *Moby Dick* is also a complex examination of obsession, of the conflict between fate and free will. A critical and financial failure during Herman Melville's lifetime (1819–1891), the novel is recognized today as one of the greatest works of American fiction.

TEXT ANALYSIS In the scene you are about to read, Captain Ahab speaks with several of his crewmen about Moby Dick. Melville uses **dialogue** to provide explicit information about the white whale, but in the way each of the characters speaks, the author also **characterizes** Captain Ahab and the crewmen present in this scene. As you read the scene, pay special attention to Captain Ahab as the main speaker. What do you learn from him about Moby Dick? What is his attitude toward the whale? What do you learn about Captain Ahab's personal history that can help you to understand his motivation for hunting the white whale?

UNDERSTAND DIALOGUE After you have read the scene, complete a chart like the one below, providing details for each category.

Dialogue	
News about Moby Dick:	Speaker's attitude:
News about Ahab:	Ahab's motivation:

Whenever you read dialogue, concentrate on two things—the information provided by speaking characters and the way their words convey what kind of characters they are.

"Whosoever of ye raises me a white-headed whale with a wrinkled brow and a crooked jaw; whosoever of ye raises me that white-headed whale, with three holes punctured in his starboard fluke—look ye, whosoever of ye raises me that same white whale, he shall have this gold ounce, my boys!"

"Huzza! huzza!" cried the seamen, as with swinging tarpaulins they hailed the act of nailing the gold to the mast.

"It's a white whale, I say," resumed Ahab, as he threw down the top-maul; "a white

464

DIFFERENTIATED INSTRUCTION

FOR STRUGGLING READERS

Character Remind students of the title of this novel and explain that the whale is much more than the object of a hunt: it is a character. As students read the passage, have them complete a Character Traits Web with details that describe the whale. Afterward, ask them what those details suggest about the whale. **Possible answer:** *The whale has battled with many hunters and is tough and dangerous.*

BEST PRACTICES TOOLKIT—Transparency
Character Traits Web p. D7

"three holes punctured in his starboard fluke"

THE WHITE WHALE

"that accursed white whale that razed me"

"harpoons lie all twisted and wrenched in him"

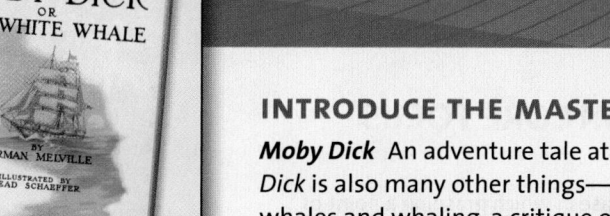

whale. Skin your eyes for him, men; look sharp for white water; if ye see but a bubble, sing out."

10   All this while Tashtego, Daggoo, and Queequeg had looked on with even more intense interest and surprise than the rest, and at the mention of the wrinkled brow and crooked jaw they had started as if each was separately touched by some specific recollection.

   "Captain Ahab," said Tashtego, "that white whale must be the same that some call Moby Dick."

   "Moby Dick?" shouted Ahab. "Do ye know the white whale then, Tash?"

   "Does he fan-tail a little curious, sir, before he goes down?" said the Gay-Header deliberately.

   "And has he a curious spout, too," said Daggoo, "very bushy, even for a
20 parmacetty, and mighty quick, Captain Ahab?"

   "And he have one, two, tree-oh! good many iron in him hide, too, Captain," cried Queequeg disjointedly, "all twisketee be-twisk, like him—him—" faltering hard for a word, and screwing his hand round and round as though uncorking a bottle—"like him—him—"

   "Corkscrew!" cried Ahab, "aye, Queequeg, the harpoons lie all twisted and wrenched in him; aye, Daggoo, his spout is a big one, like a whole shock of wheat, and white as a pile of our Nantucket wool after the great annual sheep-shearing; aye, Tashtego, and he fan-tails like a split jib in a squall. Death and devils! men, it is Moby Dick ye have seen—Moby Dick—Moby Dick!"

30   "Captain Ahab," said Starbuck, who with Stubb and Flask, had thus far been eyeing his superior with increasing surprise, but at last seemed struck with a thought which somewhat explained all the wonder. "Captain Ahab, I have heard of Moby Dick—but it was not Moby Dick that took off thy leg?"

   "Who told thee that?" cried Ahab; then pausing, "Aye, Starbuck, aye, my hearties all round; it was Moby Dick that dismasted me; Moby Dick that brought me to this dead stump I stand on now. Aye, aye," he shouted with a terrific, loud, animal sob, like that of a heart-stricken moose; "Aye, aye! it was that accursed white whale that razed me; made a poor pegging lubber of me forever and a day!" Then tossing both arms, with measureless imprecations he shouted out: "Aye, aye! and I'll chase him
40 round Good Hope, and round the Horn, and round the Norway Maelstrom, and round perdition's flames before I give him up. And this is what ye have shipped for, men! to chase that white whale on both sides of land, and over all sides of earth, till he spouts black blood and rolls fin out. What say ye, men, will ye splice hands on it, now? I think ye do look brave."

   "Aye, aye!" shouted the harpooneers and seamen, running closer to the excited old man: "A sharp eye for the White Whale; a sharp lance for Moby Dick!"

465

INTRODUCE THE MASTERPIECE

Moby Dick An adventure tale at its core, *Moby Dick* is also many other things—a discourse on whales and whaling, a critique of commercial expansion at sea, an obsessive tragedy, and an examination of the conflicts between the individual and society, and society and nature. Novelist D. H. Lawrence once said of *Moby Dick*: "[It is] one of the strangest and most wonderful books in the world."

TIERED DISCUSSION PROMPTS

Use these prompts to help students consider Ahab's mindset:

Connect How have you or someone you know reacted when wronged or hurt in some way? How natural is a desire for revenge? *Accept all reasonable responses.*

Interpret How does Ahab introduce the true purpose of this voyage? *Possible answer: Ahab introduces the true purpose of the voyage—to find and kill Moby Dick—by offering an ounce of gold as a reward to the first person to see the white whale. As he speaks excitedly about Moby Dick, Starbuck makes the connection that Moby Dick is the whale responsible for Ahab's missing leg; and when he asks the question, Ahab confirms that this is to be a voyage of revenge.* What does Ahab want the crew to believe and to do? *Possible answer: Ahab wants the crew to believe that Moby Dick is evil and deserves to die. He wants the crew's help in hunting and killing the whale.*

Synthesize What evidence in this passage suggests that *Moby Dick* is "a tragedy of human obsession"? *Possible answer: Ahab's final speech in the passage clearly declares his obsession; for example, Ahab declares that he will chase the whale "round Good Hope, and round the Horn, and round the Norway Maelstrom, and round perdition's flames."*

from **The Scarlet Letter**

Novel by Nathaniel Hawthorne

COMMON CORE FOCUS

RL 6 Analyze a case in which grasping a point of view requires distinguishing what is directly stated in a text from what is really meant.
W 4 Produce clear and coherent writing in which the development, organization, and style are appropriated to task, purpose, and audience.

BACKGROUND Intense guilt over an ancestor's role in the Salem witch trials caused Nathaniel Hawthorne to change the spelling of his last name from "Hathorne" to "Hawthorne." His comment about removing "any curse incurred by them" is (at least, in part) a reference to the story that Sarah Good, one of Salem's convicted witches, had cursed Judge Hathorne before she died. In *The Scarlet Letter*, Hawthorne translates his personal experience with guilt into a literary theme that drives much of the story. It can be said that the novel exists because of Hawthorne's wife, Sophia. In 1848, Hawthorne lost his job at the Boston Custom House; Sophia, however, had saved enough money to support the family for a time, and she encouraged him to write the novel that became *The Scarlet Letter*.

TEXT ANALYSIS Point out the universal themes that are mentioned; then explain that the novel also focuses on people's capacity for cruelty, as students will see in the upcoming passage. Elicit that the "punishing" letter *A* stands for *adultery* and that its scarlet color is meant to be noticed and to suggest the immorality of the act.

WRITE Tell students if they base their scenes on an actual event, they should change the crime that was allegedly committed and the names of the people involved.

Nathaniel Hawthorne

COMMON CORE

RL 6 Analyze a case in which grasping a point of view requires distinguishing what is directly stated in a text from what is really meant. **W 4** Produce clear and coherent writing in which the development, organization, and style are appropriated to task, purpose, and audience.

BACKGROUND Published in 1850, *The Scarlet Letter* is a short historical novel set in Salem in the earliest days of the Massachusetts Bay colony. Vividly re-creating the world of Puritan New England, Nathaniel Hawthorne's novel explores universal themes of sin, retribution, and forgiveness. It traces the story of Hester Prynne, who commits the sin of adultery and is publicly punished for it, and the two men in her life—her one-time lover and her vengeful husband—who keep their own sins hidden from public view. Part of Hester's punishment is to wear, for all her life, a scarlet letter *A* sewn onto the bodice of her gown. "The publication of *The Scarlet Letter* was in the United States a literary event of the first importance," wrote author and critic Henry James. The carefully crafted novel, with its serious themes and complex symbolism, showed that writers in the young nation could produce literature equal to that of Britain and could draw on America's history and heritage in producing it.

TEXT ANALYSIS In the following scene from the novel's opening, Hester Prynne is about to appear in public for the first time with the scarlet letter on her gown. Waiting for her appearance outside the jail door, members of the community talk about her and her crime. As the focus shifts from one speaker to another, readers get slightly different perspectives on Hester. All of the women condemn her, but they each have their own point of view. Some are harsher than others, and some hint at Hester's strong and defiant personality, which will emerge as a major force in the novel. Read the passage carefully, and note how the shifts in point of view slowly reveal a subtle range of attitudes in the community.

WRITE We have all stood in a group of people and discussed (or heard discussed) another person's behavior or situation. In some cases, the tone might have been respectful and generous; in others, it may have been gossipy and judgmental. Imagine that you have just witnessed such a discussion about someone who is accused of committing a crime. Imagine what that crime was, what the speakers might say, and how their views and perspectives might be subtly or completely different. Then write the scene out, using the excerpt on the right as a model for formatting and punctuation.

466

DIFFERENTIATED INSTRUCTION

FOR STRUGGLING READERS

Comprehension Support Work with students to complete a Two-Column Chart that contrasts the women's descriptions of themselves with their descriptions of Hester Prynne. Discuss what these descriptions suggest about the women's attitudes and whether such descriptions are fair.

Words Used to Describe Themselves	Words Used to Describe Hester Prynne
church members	hussy
good repute	naughty baggage

 BEST PRACTICES TOOLKIT—Transparency
Two-Column Chart p. A25

"Goodwives," said a hard-featured dame of fifty, "I'll tell ye a piece of my mind. It would be greatly for the public behoof, if we women, being of mature age and church-members in good repute, should have the handling of such malefactresses as this Hester Prynne. What think ye, gossips? If the hussy stood up for judgment before us five, that are now here in a knot together, would she come off with such a sentence as the worshipful magistrates have awarded? Marry, I trow not!"

"People say," said another, "that the Reverend Master Dimmesdale, her godly pastor, takes it very grievously to heart that such a scandal should have come upon 10 his congregation."

"The magistrates are God-fearing gentlemen, but merciful overmuch, — that is a truth," added a third autumnal matron. "At the very least, they should have put the brand of a hot iron on Hester Prynne's forehead. Madam Hester would have winced at that, I warrant me. But she, — the naughty baggage, — little will she care what they put upon the bodice of her gown! Why, look you, she may cover it with a brooch, or such like heathenish adornment, and so walk the streets as brave as ever!"

"Ah, but," interposed, more softly, a young wife, holding a child by the hand, "let her cover the mark as she will, the pang of it will be always in her heart."

"What do we talk of marks and brands, whether on the bodice of her gown, 20 or the flesh of her forehead?" cried another female, the ugliest as well as the most pitiless of these self-constituted judges. "This woman has brought shame upon us all, and ought to die. Is there not law for it? Truly there is, both in the Scripture and the statute-book. Then let the magistrates, who have made it of no effect, thank themselves if their own wives and daughters go astray!"

"Mercy on us, goodwife," exclaimed a man in the crowd, "is there no virtue in woman, save what springs from a wholesome fear of the gallows? That is the hardest word yet! Hush, now, gossips; for the lock is turning in the prison-door, and here comes Mistress Prynne herself."

FOR STRUGGLING READERS
Vocabulary Support
- *behoof* (line 2), "benefit"
- *malefactresses* (line 4), "female criminals"
- *hussy* (line 5), "an immoral woman"
- *Marry* (line 7), "Well" (for emphasis)
- *trow* (line 7), "believe; think"
- *magistrates* (line 11), "officials who administer laws"
- *heathenish* (line 16), "irreligious; uncivilized"

FOR ADVANCED LEARNERS/AP
Evaluate [small-group option] Have small groups discuss these questions and then share their views:

- Do you agree with the woman who says, ". . . the pang of it will be always in her heart"? As you defend your answer, consider what a person must feel in order to experience "the pang of it."

- Would public shame be effective retribution today? Why or why not?

INTRODUCE THE MASTERPIECE
Before students read the passage, point out that its dialogue (except for the final paragraph) occurs among the women of Salem. Explain that *goodwife* is a term of courtesy that generally was used before the name of a married woman. As students read, ask them to analyze the tone of the passage and to determine the consensus among the women regarding Hester Prynne.

TIERED DISCUSSION PROMPTS
Use these prompts to help students consider the themes in this passage:

Recall Why has Hester Prynne been jailed? *Answer: Hester Prynne has been jailed for having committed adultery.*

Interpret Reread the next-to-last paragraph. What does this woman think should happen to Hester Prynne? Why? *Possible answer: This woman thinks that Prynne should be executed for her adultery and that both the law and the Bible support her view. She believes that Prynne has given a bad name to women in general and that if she is not made an example of, then other women may stray.* Which characters come the closest to speaking up for Hester Prynne, and what do they say? What is the response to their words? *Possible answer: The young wife in the fourth paragraph expresses sympathy, and in the last paragraph, a man chastises the last woman to speak for the harshness of her words. The young wife is ignored; the excerpt does not reveal the reaction to the man's words.*

Synthesize What themes are discussed in this passage? *Possible answer: The passage addresses sin in the form of Hester Prynne's transgression and various responses to it; retribution, in the women's discussion of possible forms of punishment for that sin; and forgiveness, in the women's eagerness to talk about the sin and its punishment, without a thought of forgiveness.*

Focus and Motivate

COMMON CORE FOCUS

RL 1 Cite evidence to support analysis of what the text says explicitly as well as inferences drawn from the text, including determining where the text leaves matters uncertain. **RL 3** Analyze the impact of the author's choices regarding how to develop and relate elements of a story. **L 4b–c** Identify and use patterns of word changes that indicate different meanings or parts of speech; consult reference materials. **L 6** Acquire and use academic words and phrases.

ABOUT THE AUTHOR

After students have read about Hawthorne's life, discuss why sin, hypocrisy, and guilt would be considered hidden character motivations—and why those themes might have appealed to a writer with Hawthorne's family history. As students read "The Minister's Black Veil," encourage them to watch for the appearance of these themes and to think about how they are connected to the "black veil" of the title.

COMMON CORE

RL 1 Cite evidence to support analysis of what the text says explicitly as well as inferences drawn from the text, including determining where the text leaves matters uncertain. **RL 3** Analyze the impact of the author's choices regarding how to develop and relate elements of a story. **L 4b–c** Identify and use patterns of word changes that indicate different meanings or parts of speech; consult reference materials.

DID YOU KNOW?

Nathaniel Hawthorne . . .

- achieved his first literary success writing stories for children.

- was a mentor to Herman Melville, who dedicated *Moby Dick* to him.

- wrote a campaign biography for his college friend Franklin Pierce, who became the 14th U.S. president.

American Gothic

The Minister's Black Veil

Short Story by Nathaniel Hawthorne

Essential Course of Study

VIDEO TRAILER THINKcentral KEYWORD: HML11-468A

Meet the Author

Nathaniel Hawthorne c. 1804–1864

An intensely private man who allowed few to know him well, Nathaniel Hawthorne was fascinated by the dark secrets of human nature. In his greatest novels and short stories, including his masterpieces *The Scarlet Letter* and *The House of the Seven Gables,* he explored such themes as sin, hypocrisy, and guilt. One of the first American writers to explore his characters' hidden motivations, Hawthorne broke new ground in American literature with his morally complex characters.

Legacy of Guilt Born in Salem, Hawthorne was a descendant of the Puritan settlers of Massachusetts. His great-great-grandfather was a judge at the infamous Salem witch trials—the only one who refused to apologize for his role in sentencing innocent people to death. Though he tried to distance himself from his family's dark legacy, Hawthorne shared the Puritan belief that people are basically sinful. But where Puritans believed that society could be purified by the actions of a righteous few, Hawthorne was more pessimistic: he believed that perfection was impossible and remained skeptical of all attempts to reform or improve society.

Difficult Compromises Throughout his life,

Hawthorne was torn between his literary calling and his desire for a stable, respectable profession. By the time he left for Bowdoin College in 1821, Hawthorne knew he wanted to write. After graduation, he lived alone for 12 years, dedicated to building his literary career. By 1842, he had achieved some success and had married his great love, Sophia Peabody. Their otherwise happy marriage was constantly shadowed by financial woes. When times were tough, Hawthorne had well-connected friends set him up with government jobs, whose dull routines choked his imagination and limited his time to write. Although he never stopped writing, work, illness, and family duties dominated Hawthorne's later years. He died in 1864 of a sudden illness.

Challenging Questions One of Hawthorne's great talents was his mastery of symbolism. He often chose symbols whose meaning was ambiguous, forcing readers to think deeply about his characters and their conflicts. Despite his pessimism, he found hope in the redeeming power of love, a theme he developed in his mature works. Hawthorne's efforts to come to terms with his own past inspired profound reflections on American identity that still resonate today.

Author Online
Go to thinkcentral.com. KEYWORD: HML11-468B

THINKcentral

468

Selection Resources

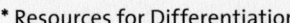

TEXT ANALYSIS: SYMBOL

A **symbol** is something concrete—a person, a place, an object, or an action—used to stand for an abstract idea or feeling. In some works, symbols may be subtle and hard to identify. In this story, Hawthorne identifies his main symbol outright:

Know, then, this veil is a type and a symbol . . .

Stories of veiled or masked figures can be traced back to myth. Such stories continue to fascinate audiences today. The challenge for readers is to interpret the symbolism of the veil. A rich symbol has many possible meanings. To interpret the veil or mask story, pay close attention to the veil's context in the work, including ideas and feelings associated with it and how it affects the **plot**, or the structure of the story.

As you read, use a concept map to note details about the minister's black veil, the main symbol in this story.

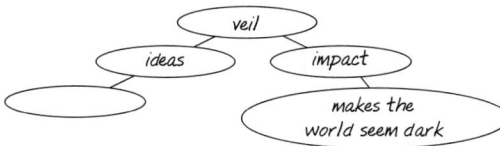

READING SKILL: IDENTIFY CULTURAL CHARACTERISTICS

As you read, keep in mind that the story is set in an 18th-century Puritan town. The parishioners' responses to their minister are meant to illustrate the traits that, in Hawthorne's eyes, define Puritan culture. As the story unfolds, think about the values, beliefs, and social constraints that are revealed by the parishioners' behavior.

▲ VOCABULARY IN CONTEXT

The boldfaced words helped Hawthorne tell his tale of Puritan life. Use context clues to write a definition of each.

1. messages filled with confusion and **ambiguity**
2. a **zealous** speaker whose eyes blazed intensely
3. a tale of sin and **iniquity**
4. an event so unusual that it seemed **preternatural**
5. an **ostentatious** costume that made people stare
6. **imbued** with great hopes for the future
7. her **tremulous** voice that revealed her nervousness
8. a sign that might **portend** trouble ahead

 Complete the activities in your **Reader/Writer Notebook**.

How does someone become a STRANGER?

Your best friend suddenly doesn't like the things she's always liked. Your brother comes home from college with a new haircut, listening to strange new music. What happens when someone you thought you knew changes? Can you still recognize the person you knew, or do his or her new behaviors lead to estrangement?

QUICKWRITE Recall a time when someone close to you changed in a way that made him or her seem like a different person. Write a paragraph to describe the change. Explain why it made you see the person so differently.

469

How does someone become a STRANGER?

Ask the question. Explain that estrangement is the feeling of being alienated from others. After students have finished the *QUICK-WRITE*, point out that this activity should help them understand how people could become estranged.

TEXT ANALYSIS   **COMMON CORE RL 1**

● *Model the Skill:* SYMBOL

To help students identify symbols, read aloud this example:

> Heidi's new hairstyle changed more than her appearance; everything about her now seemed different. Lisa no longer knew who Heidi was.

Point out that to Lisa, the hairstyle symbolized an entirely different individual, one that Lisa no longer felt she knew.

R RESOURCE MANAGER—Copy Master
Symbol p. 219 (for student use while reading the selection)

READING SKILL   **COMMON CORE RL 3**

■ *Model the Skill:* IDENTIFY CULTURAL CHARACTERISTICS

To tie characters' behavior to their beliefs, have students reread **Legacy of Guilt** in the Hawthorne biography and identify some cultural characteristics of Puritans. *Point out the Puritans' concern about sinfulness. They believed that people were essentially sinful, but they also believed that people who lived morally could improve society by their example.*

GUIDED PRACTICE Ask students to identify some cultural characteristics in another story that they have read or have seen on film or television.

VOCABULARY   **COMMON CORE L 4**

▲ VOCABULARY IN CONTEXT

DIAGNOSE WORD KNOWLEDGE Have all students complete Vocabulary in Context.

ambiguity (ăm′bĭ-gyōō′ĭ-tē) *n.* unclearness; uncertainty

imbued (ĭm-byōō′d) *adj.* deeply influenced by **imbue** *v.*

iniquity (ĭ-nĭk′wĭ-tē) *n.* wickedness

ostentatious (ŏs′tĕn-tā′shəs) *adj.* loud; overdone

portend (pôr-tĕnd′) *v.* to serve as an omen of; to signify

preternatural (prē′tər-năch′ər-əl) *adj.* supernatural

tremulous (trĕm′yə-ləs) *adj.* trembling; quivering

zealous (zĕl′əs) *adj.* eager and enthusiastic

PRETEACH VOCABULARY Use the copy master

R RESOURCE MANAGER—Copy Master
Vocabulary Study p. 223

SUMMARY

As Hawthorne's short story begins, the people of Milford are shocked to see that the Reverend Mr. Hooper has covered his face with a black veil. The veil makes people uncomfortable and alienates his fiancée, but Mr. Hooper will not clarify its meaning. Ironically, however, it makes him a more effective pastor, earning him the name "Father Hooper." He wears the veil for the rest of his life, even on his deathbed.

READ WITH A PURPOSE

Help students set a purpose for reading. Tell them to read this story to discover if Reverend Hooper ever removes the veil from his face.

READING SKILL

COMMON CORE

RL 3

Ⓐ CULTURAL CHARACTERISTICS

Possible answer: The importance of Sunday worship is revealed by the fact that it is attended by a "throng" (line 6) of people of all ages. Furthermore, children are dressed in and understand the importance of "Sunday clothes" (lines 2–4), and bachelors feel that "Sabbath sunshine" (line 5) makes the young women more lovely.

THE MINISTER'S BLACK VEIL

Nathaniel Hawthorne

> **BACKGROUND** In the Puritan town of 18th-century Massachusetts, the meetinghouse was the center of the community life. Used for both religious and civil gatherings, meetinghouses were simple and plain, with no obviously religious decorations. Families did not sit together during religious services, which lasted most of the day on Sundays. Men and women sat on opposite sides, and worshipers were seated according to their age and social standing. The oldest and most distinguished citizens were rewarded with seats closest to the pulpit, the raised platform from which the pastor delivered his sermons. As services began, all eyes turned expectantly toward the pulpit, awaiting the pastor's entrance.

Analyze Visuals ▶
Simplicity was a central value of Puritan life. What elements of this painting help create its simple style? Consider the use of color, line, and texture, as well as the composition of the image, in your answer.

The sexton[1] stood in the porch of Milford meetinghouse, pulling lustily at the bell rope. The old people of the village came stooping along the street. Children, with bright faces, tripped merrily beside their parents, or mimicked a graver gait,[2] in the conscious dignity of their Sunday clothes. Spruce bachelors looked sidelong at the pretty maidens, and fancied that the Sabbath sunshine made them prettier than on weekdays. When the throng had mostly streamed into the porch, the sexton began to toll the bell, keeping his eye on the Reverend Mr. Hooper's door. The first glimpse of the clergyman's figure was the signal for the bell to cease its summons. Ⓐ

Ⓐ CULTURAL CHARACTERISTICS
Reread lines 1–9. What details reveal the importance of Sunday worship for the people of Milford?

---

1. **sexton:** church employee who takes care of church property and performs various other duties.
2. **mimicked a graver gait:** followed their parents' example and walked in a more dignified way.

Church at Head Tide #2 (1938–1940), Marsden Hartley. Oil on academy board, 37 ¹/₄″ × 31 ¹/₄″ × 2 ¹/₄″. Gift of Mr. and Mrs. John Cowles. The Minneapolis Institute of Arts.

DIFFERENTIATED INSTRUCTION

FOR ENGLISH LANGUAGE LEARNERS

Vocabulary: Multiple-Meaning Words Point out that certain words have more than one meaning and that students must determine the appropriate definition in a given use. As students begin reading this story, help them use context clues to figure out the meaning of *lustily* (line 1), *bright* (line 3), *Spruce* (line 4), *toll* (line 7), and *figure* (line 8).

FOR STRUGGLING READERS

In combination with the *Audio Anthology CD*, use one or more Targeted Passages (pp. 472, 473, 479, 481, 482) to ensure that students focus on key story events and concepts. Targeted Passages are also good for English learners.

Reading Support

This selection on <u>thinkcentral.com</u> includes embedded **ThinkAloud** models—students "thinking aloud" about the story to model the kinds of questions a good reader would ask about a selection.

Analyze Visuals

Possible answer: *The simple style is achieved though the neutral colors of the painting, the plain lines of the church, and the relative lack of detail in both the church and the background. In addition, the texture of the painting is simple because the scene does not have much depth; the church almost blends into the background.*

About the Art Marsden Hartley (1877–1943), an American modernist painter, was born in Lewiston, Maine. Although they were not contemporaries, both Hartley and Hawthorne used their work to explore their New England roots. Furthermore, Hawthorne and Hartley were interested in religion: Hawthorne explored Puritan ideas in his writings, and many of Hartley's paintings present religious images. *Church at Head Tide #2* suggests the dominance of the Church, much as the meetinghouse is the focus of Puritan culture at the beginning of Hawthorne's story.

FOR ADVANCED LEARNERS/AP

Evaluate Begin a class discussion by having students consider the "masks" that people wear in today's society. Have students suppose that they had to wear an actual mask for one day that reflected something about their true identity. Tell students to draw a picture of what this mask might look like. Afterwards, have students present and describe their masks to the class.

TIERED DISCUSSION PROMPTS

In lines 10–33, use these prompts to help students explore Mr. Hooper's action and Hawthorne's purpose:

Connect Has someone ever done something out of the ordinary that caught your attention? How did you react? *Accept all appropriate responses.*

Interpret On first sight of the veil, how might the villagers interpret Mr. Hooper's appearance? Explain. *Possible answer: The villagers may think that Mr. Hooper has something to hide or be ashamed of. They may also think that he has gone insane.*

Synthesize Consider what you learned about Hawthorne on page 468. What might Hawthorne want readers to think about by presenting this odd event? *Possible answer: Hawthorne was interested in the "dark secrets" that people hide. He might want readers to think about what secrets they may be keeping—and how obvious their secrecy may be to others.*

REVISIT THE BIG QUESTION

How does someone become a
STRANGER?

Discuss In lines 34–39, how do the comments in this passage show that people already feel some estrangement from their minister?
Possible answer: All three comments suggest alienation: The sexton cannot think of the person he sees as Mr. Hooper; the old woman says that the minister has become "something awful"; and Goodman Gray calls him "mad."

---

10   "But what has good Parson Hooper got upon his face?" cried the sexton in astonishment.

All within hearing immediately turned about, and beheld the semblance of Mr. Hooper, pacing slowly his meditative way towards the meetinghouse. With one accord they started, expressing more wonder than if some strange minister were coming to dust the cushions of Mr. Hooper's pulpit.

"Are you sure it is our parson?" inquired Goodman³ Gray of the sexton.

"Of a certainty it is good Mr. Hooper," replied the sexton. "He was to have exchanged pulpits with Parson Shute of Westbury; but Parson Shute sent to excuse himself yesterday, being to preach a funeral sermon."

20   The cause of so much amazement may appear sufficiently slight. Mr. Hooper, a gentlemanly person about thirty, though still a bachelor, was dressed with due clerical neatness, as if a careful wife had starched his band, and brushed the weekly dust from his Sunday's garb. There was but one thing remarkable in his appearance. Swathed about his forehead, and hanging down over his face, so low as to be shaken by his breath, Mr. Hooper had on a black veil. On a nearer view, it seemed to consist of two folds of crape,⁴ which entirely concealed his features, except the mouth and chin, but probably did not intercept his sight, farther than to give a darkened aspect to all living and inanimate things. With this gloomy shade before him, good Mr. Hooper walked onward, at a slow and quiet pace,

30   stooping somewhat and looking on the ground, as is customary with abstracted⁵ men, yet nodding kindly to those of his parishioners who still waited on the meetinghouse steps. But so wonder-struck were they that his greeting hardly met with a return.

"I can't really feel as if good Mr. Hooper's face was behind that piece of crape," said the sexton.

"I don't like it," muttered an old woman, as she hobbled into the meetinghouse. "He has changed himself into something awful, only by hiding his face."

"Our parson has gone mad!" cried Goodman Gray, following him across the threshold.

40   A rumor of some unaccountable phenomenon had preceded Mr. Hooper into the meetinghouse, and set all the congregation astir. Few could refrain from twisting their heads towards the door; many stood upright, and turned directly about; while several little boys clambered upon the seats, and came down again with a terrible racket. There was a general bustle, a rustling of the women's gowns and shuffling of the men's feet, greatly at variance with that hushed repose which should attend the entrance of the minister. But Mr. Hooper appeared not to notice the perturbation of his people. He entered with an almost noiseless step, bent his head mildly to the pews on each side, and bowed as he passed his oldest parishioner, a white-haired great-grandsire, who occupied an armchair in the

50   centre of the aisle. It was strange to observe how slowly this venerable man became conscious of something singular in the appearance of his pastor. He seemed not

---

3. **Goodman:** the Puritan equivalent of Mr.
4. **crape** (krāp): a piece of dark material worn as a sign of mourning. Also called *crepe.*
5. **abstracted:** preoccupied, or lost in thought.

Language Coach

Word Definitions
Accord (line 14) means "agreement." *With one accord* means "all in agreement." What reaction are the churchgoers feeling with one accord?

① **Targeted Passage**

DIFFERENTIATED INSTRUCTION

FOR STRUGGLING READERS

① **Targeted Passage** [Lines 10–33]

This passage introduces Mr. Hooper's veil and the first reactions to it.

- Why are people unsure if the man walking toward them is Mr. Hooper? (lines 20–25)

- How does the veil affect the view of Mr. Hooper's face? (lines 25–27)

- Do the people of Milford quickly get used to the veil? How can you tell? (lines 32–33)

FOR ENGLISH LANGUAGE LEARNERS

Language Coach

Word Definitions *Possible answer: They were in accord in feeling shock and curiosity at Parson Hooper wearing a black veil.* Have students think of other phrases that mean "agreement." Tell students to rewrite the sentence in lines 13–15 using one of the phrases they identified in place of "With one accord."

fully to partake of the prevailing wonder till Mr. Hooper had ascended the stairs, and showed himself in the pulpit, face-to-face with his congregation, except for the black veil. That mysterious emblem was never once withdrawn. It shook with his measured breath as he gave out the psalm; it threw its obscurity between him and the holy page, as he read the Scriptures; and while he prayed, the veil lay heavily on his uplifted countenance. Did he seek to hide from the dread Being[6] whom he was addressing?

Such was the effect of this simple piece of crape, that more than one woman of 60 delicate nerves was forced to leave the meetinghouse. Yet perhaps the pale-faced congregation was almost as fearful a sight to the minister as his black veil to them.

Mr. Hooper had the reputation of a good preacher, but not an energetic one: he strove to win his people heavenward by mild persuasive influences, rather than to drive them thither by the thunders of the Word. The sermon which he now delivered was marked by the same characteristics of style and manner as the general series of his pulpit oratory. But there was something, either in the sentiment of the discourse itself, or in the imagination of the auditors, which made it greatly the most powerful effort that they had ever heard from their pastor's lips. It was tinged, rather more darkly than usual, with the gentle gloom 70 of Mr. Hooper's temperament. The subject had reference to secret sin, and those sad mysteries which we hide from our nearest and dearest, and would fain conceal from our own consciousness, even forgetting that the Omniscient[7] can detect them. A subtle power was breathed into his words. Each member of the congregation, the most innocent girl, and the man of hardened breast, felt as if the preacher had crept upon them, behind his awful veil, and discovered their hoarded **iniquity** of deed or thought. Many spread their clasped hands on their bosoms. There was nothing terrible in what Mr. Hooper said; at least, no violence; and yet, with every tremor of his melancholy voice, the hearers quaked. An unsought pathos came hand in hand with awe. So sensible were the audience of some 80 unwonted attribute in their minister, that they longed for a breath of wind to blow aside the veil, almost believing that a stranger's visage would be discovered, though the form, gesture and voice were those of Mr. Hooper. **B**

At the close of the services, the people hurried out with indecorous confusion, eager to communicate their pent-up amazement, and conscious of lighter spirits the moment they lost sight of the black veil. Some gathered in little circles, huddled closely together, with their mouths all whispering in the centre; some went homeward alone, wrapped in silent meditation; some talked loudly, and profaned the Sabbath day with **ostentatious** laughter. A few shook their sagacious heads, intimating that they could penetrate the mystery; while one or two affirmed that 90 there was no mystery at all, but only that Mr. Hooper's eyes were so weakened by the midnight lamp as to require a shade. After a brief interval, forth came good Mr. Hooper also, in the rear of his flock. Turning his veiled face from one group to another, he paid due reverence to the hoary heads, saluted the middle-aged with kind dignity, as their friend and spiritual guide, greeted the young with mingled

---

6. **the dread Being:** the awe-inspiring God.

7. **the Omniscient:** a title for God, signifying that he is all-knowing.

COMMON CORE L 4b

Language Coach

Suffixes A **suffix** is a word part that appears at the end of a root or base word to form a new word. The suffix *–ward* means "in the direction of." What do *heavenward* (line 63) and *homeward* (line 87) mean?

②ᵇ Targeted Passage

iniquity (ĭ-nĭk′wĭ-tē) *n.* wickedness

B SYMBOL
Reread lines 62–82. Describe the change that occurs in Mr. Hooper's preaching. What seems to cause the listeners' unusual response?

ostentatious
(ŏs′tĕn-tā′shəs) *adj.* loud; overdone

TEXT ANALYSIS

COMMON CORE
RL 1

B Model the Skill: SYMBOL

Remind students that a symbol is something that stands for something other than itself. To understand the change in Mr. Hooper's preaching, work with students to review these lines and to record some thoughts on the concept map introduced on page 469.

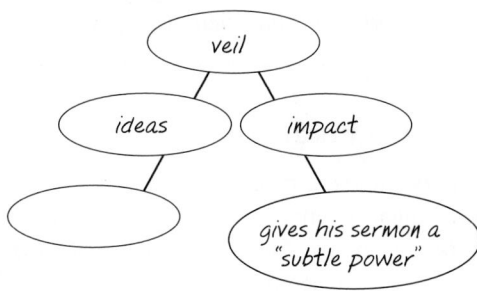

Possible answer: *It seems as if the veil has given him a "subtle power" (line 73) to reach his audience and know their secrets (lines 74–78). The listeners' unusual response seems to rise from their imagination, the sermon's topic (lines 66–67) and the minister's strange appearance.*

Extend the Discussion How might a modern audience react to the veil?

VOCABULARY

COMMON CORE
L 4

OWN THE WORD

- **iniquity:** *Iniquity* refers to "wickedness" or "gross injustice." Have students complete the following sentence: "Nadine hid her *iniquity* from her family, but . . ." **Possible answer:** *her remorse caused her to confess her misdeed.*

- **ostentatious:** Tell students that *ostentatious* is the adjective form of the noun *ostentation*, and both refer to being pretentious. Ask students why they think someone would be *ostentatious*. **Possible answer:** *Students may say an ostentatious person boasts to gain attention.*

FOR STRUGGLING READERS

②ᵇ Targeted Passage [Lines 62–82]

This passage shows how the veil actually enhances Mr. Hooper's abilities.

- What type of preacher has Mr. Hooper been in the past? (lines 62–64)

- What is the topic of Mr. Hooper's sermon this day? How is the sermon similar to and different from his previous sermons? (lines 64–73)

- How do members of the congregation react to the sermon? (lines 73–82)

FOR ENGLISH LANGUAGE LEARNERS

Language Coach

COMMON CORE
L 4b

Suffixes *Answer: Heavenward means "in the direction of heaven;" homeward means "in the direction of home."* Tell students to reread the text on this page and identify at least three other suffixes. Have students then define each suffix and write sentences using the three suffixes as parts of other words.

READING SKILL

COMMON CORE
RL 3

C CULTURAL CHARACTERISTICS

Possible answer: Mr. Hooper has an established relationship with all age groups and has been treated as a respected friend and mentor (lines 93–95). People usually "aspired to the honor of walking by their pastor's side" (lines 97–98), but on this day, they do not. In addition, no one invites Mr. Hooper to dinner. The change suggests that the villagers value associating with people in authority but that their loyalty is weak.

Analyze Visuals

Activity How do the people in this scene look similar to what you would expect of the characters in "The Minister's Black Veil"? How does the crowd seem to be responding to the person addressing them? *Possible answer: The people look very proper in their Puritan clothing, as seems to be true of the Puritans in the story. The crowd seems to be unsure of the speaker. They are attentive, but do not show emotion or express agreement or disagreement with the speaker.*

About the Art Alton Tobey (1912–2005) is best known for his realistic and historical art portraits and murals. This scene, a detail from one of his murals, shows Tobey's ability to capture details, including the precise Puritan attire. Notice that the speaker's face is hidden from viewers of the painting, as Mr. Hooper's is hidden from the villagers.

---

authority and love, and laid his hands on the little children's heads to bless them. Such was always his custom on the Sabbath day. Strange and bewildered looks repaid him for his courtesy. None, as on former occasions, aspired to the honor of walking by their pastor's side. Old Squire Saunders, doubtless by an accidental lapse of memory, neglected to invite Mr. Hooper to his table, where the good clergyman

100 had been wont to bless the food almost every Sunday since his settlement. He returned, therefore, to the parsonage, and at the moment of closing the door, was observed to look back upon the people, all of whom had their eyes fixed upon the minister. A sad smile gleamed faintly from beneath the black veil, and flickered about his mouth, glimmering as he disappeared. **C**

   "How strange," said a lady, "that a simple black veil, such as any woman might wear on her bonnet, should become such a terrible thing on Mr. Hooper's face!"

   "Something must surely be amiss with Mr. Hooper's intellects," observed her husband, the physician of the village. "But the strangest part of the affair is the effect of this vagary, even on a sober-minded man like myself. The black veil,

The Last Halt: Stop of Hooker's Band in East Hartford before Crossing River (1939), Alton S. Tobey. Study for East Hartford, Connecticut Postal Office. Oil on fiberboard, 26" x 44 1/8". Transfer from General Services Administration. Smithsonian American Art Museum, Washington, D.C. Photo © Smithsonian American Art Museum, Washington, D.C./Art Resource, New York. © Alton Tobey Collection/www.altontobey.org

C CULTURAL CHARACTERISTICS
Reread lines 92–100. Identify details that convey Mr. Hooper's social status in Milford. What does the change in the villagers' behavior toward the minister suggest about their values?

DIFFERENTIATED INSTRUCTION

FOR ADVANCED LEARNERS/AP

Analyze a Conversation [small-group option] Ask students to reread the exchange between the physician and his wife in lines 105–114. Then have them write and share an analysis in which they respond to these questions:

• How could the same black veil be fine on a woman's bonnet but "terrible" when covering the minister's face?

• Is it the veil itself that is the real problem, or is it the way that it makes the Puritan villagers feel? Explain your answer.

• What does the physician mean by saying that people sometimes are afraid to be alone? What does it mean, then, to know that Mr. Hooper has chosen to do something that may result in solitude?

• What is Hawthorne's purpose in including this brief conversation?

110 though it covers only our pastor's face, throws its influence over his whole person, and makes him ghost-like from head to foot. Do you not feel it so?"

"Truly do I," replied the lady; "and I would not be alone with him for the world. I wonder he is not afraid to be alone with himself!"

"Men sometimes are so," said her husband.

The afternoon service was attended with similar circumstances. At its conclusion, the bell tolled for the funeral of a young lady. The relatives and friends were assembled in the house, and the more distant acquaintances stood about the door, speaking of the good qualities of the deceased, when their talk was interrupted by the appearance of Mr. Hooper, still covered with his black veil. It was now an
120 appropriate emblem. The clergyman stepped into the room where the corpse was laid, and bent over the coffin, to take a last farewell of his deceased parishioner. As he stooped, the veil hung straight down from his forehead so that, if her eyelids had not been closed forever, the dead maiden might have seen his face. Could Mr. Hooper be fearful of her glance, that he so hastily caught back the black veil? A person, who watched the interview between the dead and the living, scrupled not to affirm that, at the instant when the clergyman's features were disclosed, the corpse had slightly shuddered, rustling the shroud[8] and muslin cap, though the countenance retained the composure of death. A superstitious old woman was the only witness of this prodigy. From the coffin, Mr. Hooper passed into the chamber
130 of the mourners, and thence to the head of the staircase, to make the funeral prayer. It was a tender and heart-dissolving prayer, full of sorrow, yet so **imbued** with celestial hopes, that the music of the heavenly harp, swept by the fingers of the dead, seemed faintly to be heard among the saddest accents of the minister. The people trembled, though they but darkly understood him, when he prayed that they, and himself, and all of mortal race might be ready, as he trusted this young maiden had been, for the dreadful hour that should snatch the veil from their faces. The bearers went heavily forth, and the mourners followed, saddening all the street, with the dead before them, and Mr. Hooper in his black veil behind. **D**

"Why do you look back?" said one in the procession to his partner.
140 "I had a fancy," replied she, "that the minister and the maiden's spirit were walking hand in hand."

"And so had I, at the same moment," said the other.

That night, the handsomest couple in Milford village were to be joined in wedlock. Though reckoned a melancholy man, Mr. Hooper had a placid cheerfulness for such occasions, which often excited a sympathetic smile, where livelier merriment would have been thrown away. There was no quality of his disposition which made him more beloved than this. The company at the wedding awaited his arrival with impatience, trusting that the strange awe, which had gathered over him throughout the day, would now be dispelled. But such was
150 not the result. When Mr. Hooper came, the first thing that their eyes rested on was the same horrible black veil, which had added deeper gloom to the funeral, and could **portend** nothing but evil to the wedding. Such was its immediate effect on the guests, that a cloud seemed to have rolled duskily from beneath the

---

8. **shroud:** burial garment.

COMMON CORE L 4c

Language Coach

Topically Related Words
Lines 115–141 describe a scene from a funeral. Look up the following words in a dictionary: *deceased, corpse, coffin, farewell, shroud, mourner, bearer, procession.* Using the words listed, explain what is occurring at the funeral.

imbued (ĭm-byōo′d) *adj.* deeply influenced by **imbue** *v.*

D SYMBOL
Paraphrase lines 133–138. In this context, what could Mr. Hooper mean when he refers to "the dreadful hour that should snatch the veil from their faces"?

portend (pôr-tĕnd′) *v.* to serve as an omen of; to signify

REVISIT THE BIG QUESTION

How does someone become a
STRANGER?

Discuss In lines 105–114, how does the conversation between husband and wife reveal about the villagers' estrangement from their pastor? *Possible answer: The villagers now fear Mr. Hooper and feel that he has brought his estrangement on himself.*

TEXT ANALYSIS   COMMON CORE   RL 1

D SYMBOL

Possible answer: Paraphrase: "The people shook, even though they barely understood him, when Mr. Hooper prayed that everyone might be ready for the moment of death, as he hoped this young woman had been ready. Her body was carried out, and the grieving people followed, with Mr. Hooper following." Mr. Hooper's reference could mean death or Judgment Day, when all human secrets will be revealed.

VOCABULARY   COMMON CORE   L 4

OWN THE WORD

- **imbued:** Inform students that *imbued* refers to something that is "deeply influenced or inspired by" a concept. The word derives from the Latin *imbuere*, "to moisten or stain," which gives a deeper meaning of something being saturated or permeated with inspiration.

- **portend:** Remind students that *portend* means "to serve as an omen of; to signify." Synonyms include *bode, forecast, foreshadow,* and *foretell,* all of which indicate something happening in advance. Have students write a sentence to show their understanding of the word. *Possible answers: The heavy, dark clouds portend that our picnic will be rained out. The debate team's positive spirit portends a victory at the competition.*

FOR ADVANCED LEARNERS/AP

Analyze Tone Invite students to respond to one or both of these prompts:

- Notice the narrator's comments in lines 98–100 and 128–129. How sympathetic is the narrator to Mr. Hooper?

- Review the funeral scene and the wedding scene. What words establish the tone of each scene? Are the tones identical, related, or sharply different?

FOR ENGLISH LANGUAGE LEARNERS

Language Coach   COMMON CORE   L 4c

Topically Related Words *Possible answer: The mourners, who were sad their friend had died, approached her coffin, where they saw her corpse lying wrapped in its shroud. After the prayer, the bearers carried the coffin in a procession.* Instruct students to reread lines 115–141 and identify three words associated with a funeral.

E SYMBOL

Have students name movie characters who have worn masks and explain what these masks symbolized. What clues in the mask itself revealed character traits? *Possible answer: In this story the veil generates dread and fear in the observers and in the wearer, as well. Catching sight of himself, Hooper becomes overwhelmed with horror.*

Extend the Discussion Discuss with students the roles that masks or veils play in today's society, such as on Halloween, in weddings or other religious ceremonies.

TIERED DISCUSSION PROMPTS

In lines 175–199, use these prompts to help students grasp the changed relationship between Mr. Hooper and the people of Milford:

Summarize Thus far, what has been the general reaction to Mr. Hooper's altered appearance? *Possible answer: People seem confused by it and somewhat fearful of it.*

Analyze Why is it significant that "the busybodies and impertinent people in the parish" (lines 175–176) do not ask Mr. Hooper why he wears the veil? *Possible answer: The fact is significant because these are the people who have not hesitated to raise questions in the past (lines 177–179). Their silence now reflects their fear.*

OWN THE WORD

COMMON
CORE
L 4

tremulous: Have students rewrite the sentence with *tremulous*, replacing it with a synonym.

---

black crape, and dimmed the light of the candles. The bridal pair stood up before the minister. But the bride's cold fingers quivered in the **tremulous** hand of the bridegroom, and her death-like paleness caused a whisper that the maiden who had been buried a few hours before was come from her grave to be married. If ever another wedding were so dismal, it was that famous one where they tolled the wedding knell.[9] After performing the ceremony, Mr. Hooper raised a glass
160 of wine to his lips, wishing happiness to the new-married couple, in a strain of mild pleasantry that ought to have brightened the features of the guests, like a cheerful gleam from the hearth. At that instant, catching a glimpse of his figure in the looking glass, the black veil involved his own spirit in the horror with which it overwhelmed all others. His frame shuddered—his lips grew white—he spilt the untasted wine upon the carpet—and rushed forth into the darkness. For the Earth, too, had on her Black Veil. **E**

The next day, the whole village of Milford talked of little else than Parson Hooper's black veil. That, and the mystery concealed behind it, supplied a topic for discussion between acquaintances meeting in the street, and good women
170 gossiping at their open windows. It was the first item of news that the tavern keeper told to his guests. The children babbled of it on their way to school. One imitative little imp covered his face with an old black handkerchief, thereby so affrighting his playmates that the panic seized himself, and he well-nigh lost his wits by his own waggery.[10]

It was remarkable that, of all the busybodies and impertinent people in the parish, not one ventured to put the plain question to Mr. Hooper, wherefore he did this thing. Hitherto, whenever there appeared the slightest call for such interference, he had never lacked advisers, nor shown himself averse to be guided by their judgment. If he erred at all, it was by so painful a degree of self-distrust
180 that even the mildest censure would lead him to consider an indifferent action as a crime. Yet, though so well acquainted with this amiable weakness, no individual among his parishioners chose to make the black veil a subject of friendly remonstrance. There was a feeling of dread, neither plainly confessed nor carefully concealed, which caused each to shift the responsibility upon another, till at length it was found expedient to send a deputation to the church, in order to deal with Mr. Hooper about the mystery, before it should grow into a scandal. Never did an embassy so ill discharge its duties. The minister received them with friendly courtesy, but became silent, after they were seated, leaving to his visitors the whole burden of introducing their important business. The topic, it might be supposed,
190 was obvious enough. There was the black veil, swathed round Mr. Hooper's forehead, and concealing every feature above his placid mouth, on which, at times, they could perceive the glimmering of a melancholy smile. But that piece of crape, to their imagination, seemed to hang down before his heart, the symbol of a fearful secret between him and them. Were the veil but cast aside, they might speak freely of it, but not till then. Thus they sat a considerable time, speechless,

tremulous (trĕm′yə-ləs) *adj.* trembling; quivering

E SYMBOL
At this point in the story, note how the minister's veil has changed the way others react to him. Reactions to a veil or mask have been a part of mythic stories in every age and culture. The characters in ancient Greek plays were represented on stage by actors wearing different masks. This allowed male actors to also play female roles. Masks in African myths like the *Epic of Sundiata* were believed to be the place where spirits were created. What reaction or belief does the veil or mask generate here? Cite details from lines 159–166 to support your response.

---

9. **If . . . the wedding knell:** a reference to "The Wedding Knell," a story by Hawthorne in which a bell-tolling appropriate for a funeral is sounded at a wedding.

10. **waggery:** mischievous merriment.

DIFFERENTIATED INSTRUCTION

FOR STRUGGLING READERS

Characterization Have students reread lines 177–183; then discuss these questions to help them characterize Mr. Hooper:

• Does Mr. Hooper have a reputation for being unwilling to take advice?

• Does he take making mistakes lightly?

• Therefore, do you see him as the kind of person who would make a decision (such as wearing a black veil) easily or carelessly?

FOR ENGLISH LANGUAGE LEARNERS

Vocabulary: Outdated Forms Ask students to record these outdated terms and their meanings in a Two-Column Chart. Then have them reread the lines, substituting the definitions for these terms.

• *affrighting* (line 173), "frightening"

• *ill* (line 187), "poorly"

• *suffer* (line 220), "allow"

• *do away* (line 232), "stop; end"

• *abroad* (line 234), "circulating"

confused, and shrinking uneasily from Mr. Hooper's eye, which they felt to be fixed upon them with an invisible glance. Finally, the deputies returned abashed to their constituents, pronouncing the matter too weighty to be handled, except by a council of the churches, if, indeed, it might not require a general synod.[11]

200 But there was one person in the village unappalled by the awe with which the black veil had impressed all beside herself. When the deputies returned without an explanation, or even venturing to demand one, she, with the calm energy of her character, determined to chase away the strange cloud that appeared to be settling round Mr. Hooper, every moment more darkly than before. As his plighted wife,[12] it should be her privilege to know what the black veil concealed. At the minister's first visit, therefore, she entered upon the subject, with a direct simplicity, which made the task easier both for him and her. After he had seated himself, she fixed her eyes steadfastly upon the veil, but could discern nothing of the dreadful gloom that had so overawed the multitude: it was but a double fold of crape, hanging
210 down from his forehead to his mouth, and slightly stirring with his breath. **G**

"No," said she aloud, and smiling, "there is nothing terrible in this piece of crape except that it hides a face which I am always glad to look upon. Come, good sir, let the sun shine from behind the cloud. First lay aside your black veil: then tell me why you put it on."

Mr. Hooper's smile glimmered faintly.

"There is an hour to come," said he, "when all of us shall cast aside our veils. Take it not amiss, beloved friend, if I wear this piece of crape till then."

"Your words are a mystery too," returned the young lady. "Take away the veil from them, at least."

220 "Elizabeth, I will," said he, "so far as my vow may suffer me. Know, then, this veil is a type and a symbol, and I am bound to wear it ever, both in light and darkness, in solitude and before the gaze of multitudes, and as with strangers, so with my familiar friends. No mortal eye will see it withdrawn. This dismal shade must separate me from the world: even you, Elizabeth, can never come behind it!"

"What grievous affliction hath befallen you," she earnestly inquired, "that you should thus darken your eyes forever?"

"If it be a sign of mourning," replied Mr. Hooper, "I, perhaps, like most other mortals, have sorrows dark enough to be typified by a black veil."

"But what if the world will not believe that it is the type of an innocent
230 sorrow?" urged Elizabeth. "Beloved and respected as you are, there may be whispers that you hide your face under the consciousness of secret sin. For the sake of your holy office, do away this scandal!"

The color rose into her cheeks, as she intimated the nature of the rumors that were already abroad in the village. But Mr. Hooper's mildness did not forsake him. He even smiled again—that same sad smile, which always appeared like a faint glimmering of light proceeding from the obscurity beneath the veil.

"If I hide my face for sorrow, there is cause enough," he merely replied; "and if I cover it for secret sin, what mortal might not do the same?"

---

11. **a general synod:** a meeting of the governing body of the churches.
12. **plighted wife:** fiancée.

F CULTURAL CHARACTERISTICS
Paraphrase lines 175–199. Explain what motivates the parishioners to confront Mr. Hooper. What do their fears reveal about Puritan culture?

G SYMBOL
Reread lines 200–210. Contrast the response of the minister's fiancée to the veil with the responses of the other villagers. What might explain the difference in her response?

F CULTURAL CHARACTERISTICS

Possible answer: *Paraphrase: With all of these gossips around, it was surprising that no one bothered to ask Mr. Hooper why he wore the veil. People had never been shy about offering him advice before. He was so given to feelings of guilt that the slightest criticism could make him feel as if he'd done something terrible. Although everyone knew this about him, no one said anything. Finally, they sent a group to visit Mr. Hooper, lest his behavior grow into a scandal. Their fears suggest that features of Puritan culture include a discomfort about things that are different, a worry about scandal, and a superstitious nature.*

TEXT ANALYSIS — COMMON CORE RL 1

G SYMBOL

Possible answer: *Elizabeth does not share the other villagers' fear of the veil (lines 208–209); she confronts Mr. Hooper directly about it (lines 206–207), unlike the parishioners, who never ask him. Elizabeth probably reacts differently because she loves him and because, as his fiancée, she knows him better than others do.*

FOR STRUGGLING READERS

Develop Reading Fluency Read aloud the conversation between Mr. Hooper and Elizabeth in lines 211–238. Next have students reread the passage. Remind them that quotation marks indicate when a character is speaking. Have students take turns reading the passage aloud to a partner. Conclude by calling on students to read the conversation to the class.

FOR ADVANCED LEARNERS/AP

Analyze Character Mr. Hooper's conversation with Elizabeth is the first time that readers learn about Mr. Hooper from his own words instead of from the narrator's comments or the parishioners' dialogue. Readers also learn about Elizabeth in this conversation. Instruct students to reread the interaction between Elizabeth and Mr. Hooper (lines 200–259) and to fill out a Character Traits and Textual Evidence chart for each character. Then have them use their notes to write a brief essay that addresses these questions:

- What insight into Mr. Hooper's character does his explanation of the veil provide?
- Does Hawthorne expect readers to agree with Elizabeth's final response to Mr. Hooper? Explain.

 BEST PRACTICES TOOLKIT—Transparency Character Traits and Textual Evidence p. D6

Portrait of Alice Irene Harvey (1912), Mark Gertler. Oil on canvas, 60.9 cm × 50.8 cm. © Leeds Museums and Galleries, Leeds, United Kingdom/Bridgeman Art Library.

DIFFERENTIATED INSTRUCTION

FOR ADVANCED LEARNERS/AP

Critical Interpretations [small-group option]
Critics disagree about the meaning of the black veil. Edgar Allan Poe once argued that the minister wears the veil out of remorse for a secret sin involving the young woman whose funeral he attends (lines 115–142). Other critics have interpreted the veil as a device that the minister uses to dramatize the universal idea that everyone has a secret sin and, therefore, we should not judge others. A third interpretation is that the wearing of the veil is itself the minister's sin—Hooper's prideful obsession with an idea has warped his life and hurt others. Yet another interpretation is that Hawthorne does not intend readers to uncover the meaning of the veil. His story is about concealment, and the meaning of the veil is part of what is concealed. Have groups debate these interpretations, citing textual evidence for and against each view.

And with this gentle but unconquerable obstinacy did he resist all her
240 entreaties. At length Elizabeth sat silent. For a few moments she appeared lost in
thought, considering, probably, what new methods might be tried to withdraw
her lover from so dark a fantasy, which, if it had no other meaning, was perhaps a
symptom of mental disease. Though of a firmer character than his own, the tears
rolled down her cheeks. But, in an instant, as it were, a new feeling took the place
of sorrow: her eyes were fixed insensibly on the black veil, when, like a sudden
twilight in the air, its terrors fell around her. She arose, and stood trembling
before him.

"And do you feel it then at last?" said he mournfully.

She made no reply, but covered her eyes with her hand, and turned to leave
250 the room. He rushed forward and caught her arm.

"Have patience with me, Elizabeth!" cried he passionately. "Do not desert
me, though this veil must be between us here on earth. Be mine, and hereafter
there shall be no veil over my face, no darkness between our souls! It is but a
mortal veil—it is not for eternity! Oh! you know not how lonely I am, and how
frightened to be alone behind my black veil. Do not leave me in this miserable
obscurity forever!"

"Lift the veil but once, and look me in the face," said she.

"Never! It cannot be!" replied Mr. Hooper.

"Then, farewell!" said Elizabeth.

260 She withdrew her arm from his grasp and slowly departed, pausing at the door
to give one long, shuddering gaze that seemed almost to penetrate the mystery of
the black veil. But even amid his grief, Mr. Hooper smiled to think that only a
material emblem had separated him from happiness, though the horrors which
it shadowed forth must be drawn darkly between the fondest of lovers.

From that time no attempts were made to remove Mr. Hooper's black veil or,
by a direct appeal, to discover the secret which it was supposed to hide. By persons
who claimed a superiority to popular prejudice, it was reckoned merely an eccentric
whim, such as often mingles with the sober actions of men otherwise rational, and
tinges them all with its own semblance of insanity. But with the multitude, good
270 Mr. Hooper was irreparably a bugbear.[13] He could not walk the streets with any
peace of mind, so conscious was he that the gentle and timid would turn aside to
avoid him, and that others would make it a point of hardihood to throw themselves
in his way. The impertinence of the latter class compelled him to give up his
customary walk, at sunset, to the burial ground, for when he leaned pensively over
the gate, there would always be faces behind the gravestones, peeping at his black
veil. A fable went the rounds that the stare of the dead people drove him thence.
It grieved him to the very depth of his kind heart to observe how the children
fled from his approach, breaking up their merriest sports, while his melancholy
figure was yet afar off. Their instinctive dread caused him to feel, more strongly
280 than aught else, that a **preternatural** horror was interwoven with the threads of

---

13. **bugbear:** a source of dread or fear.

◀ **Analyze Visuals**
In what ways does the
woman depicted in the
painting on the opposite
page reflect the character
of Elizabeth as described
in lines 240–244? What
could the woman's white
dress **symbolize?**

③ **Targeted Passage**

preternatural
(prē'tər-năch'ər-əl) *adj.*
supernatural

Analyze Visuals

Possible answer: *The woman in the painting
reflects the sadness and inner reflection that
Elizabeth experiences in the scene. Her white
dress could symbolize innocence or purity of
thought and action.*

REVIST THE BIG QUESTION
How does someone become a STRANGER?

Discuss In lines 248–258, what do Mr. Hooper's
comments to Elizabeth suggest about his willingness to experience estrangement? Explain
your answer. ***Possible answer:*** *His comments
suggest that his estrangement is a reluctant
one. He is not happy about how the veil makes
him feel (line 248), and he begs Elizabeth
not to abandon him (lines 251–252). It is as if
Mr. Hooper sincerely regrets the estrangement
that the veil causes, yet he feels compelled to
wear it, regardless of the professional or personal cost.*

VOCABULARY
COMMON
CORE
L 4

OWN THE WORD

preternatural: Tell students that preternatural stems from the Latin word meaning
"beyond nature" and is defined as being
"supernatural." Ask students to explain why
they think the author used this word in the
phrase, "...that a preternatural horror was
interwoven with the threads of the black
crepe." ***Possible answer:*** *Wearing the black
veil was frightening and confusing to the
people around the minister, and since he did
not explain why he wore it nor removed it, or
seemed to not be able to take it off, people
felt that an evil or supernatural force was at
work.*

FOR STRUGGLING READERS
③ Targeted Passage [Lines 243–266]

This passage, a narrative turning point,
magnifies story conflicts.

- When does Mr. Hooper realize that Elizabeth now fears him, too? (line 248)?

- What does Mr. Hooper ask of Elizabeth?
What does she ask of him? (lines 251–257)

- Why does Elizabeth leave? According to the
narrator, why is her departure important?
(lines 260–266)

Summarize Have students reread lines
266–270 and then summarize the two ways
in which the villagers now explain Mr. Hooper
and his black veil. Ask students to identify
the opinion that they agree with and to
defend their view.

How does someone become a STRANGER?

Discuss In lines 294–311, how does Mr. Hooper's estrangement, caused by the veil, actually help others? Explain the irony in this situation. *Possible answer: The veil and the estrangement it causes make him a better minister; in particular, they seem to give him a power over people who are "in agony for sin" (line 297). The situation is ironic because the very estrangement that causes Mr. Hooper to suffer personally also enables him to help people, even people who are fearful of him (lines 301–304). The irony suggests that if Mr. Hooper had not experienced estrangement due to the black veil, he probably would not have become as effective a minister as he has.*

READING SKILL   COMMON CORE   RL 3

Ⓗ *Model the Skill:* CULTURAL CHARACTERISTICS

Help students evaluate cultural characteristics by asking them the following questions: Why do you think that dying sinners want Mr. Hooper to come to them? What might they think that he can do for them?

Possible answer: Readers can conclude that Puritan worshipers are very concerned with recognizing and dealing with sin.

VOCABULARY   COMMON CORE   RL 1

OWN THE WORD

ambiguity: Remind students that *ambiguity* refers to a meaning or understanding that is "unclear or uncertain" and that could have more than one interpretation. The adjective form of the word is *ambiguous.* Synonyms include obscure, vague, and cryptic.

---

the black crape. In truth, his own antipathy to the veil was known to be so great that he never willingly passed before a mirror, nor stooped to drink at a still fountain, lest, in its peaceful bosom, he should be affrighted by himself. This was what gave plausibility to the whispers that Mr. Hooper's conscience tortured him for some great crime too horrible to be entirely concealed, or otherwise than so obscurely intimated. Thus, from beneath the black veil there rolled a cloud into the sunshine, an **ambiguity** of sin or sorrow, which enveloped the poor minister, so that love or sympathy could never reach him. It was said that ghost and fiend consorted with him there. With self-shudderings and outward terrors, he walked
290 continually in its shadow, groping darkly within his own soul, or gazing through a medium that saddened the whole world. Even the lawless wind, it was believed, respected his dreadful secret, and never blew aside the veil. But still good Mr. Hooper sadly smiled at the pale visages of the worldly throng as he passed by.

Among all its bad influences, the black veil had the one desirable effect, of making its wearer a very efficient clergyman. By the aid of his mysterious emblem—for there was no other apparent cause—he became a man of awful power, over souls that were in agony for sin. His converts always regarded him with a dread peculiar to themselves, affirming, though but figuratively, that before he brought them to celestial light, they had been with him behind the
300 black veil. Its gloom, indeed, enabled him to sympathize with all dark affections. Dying sinners cried aloud for Mr. Hooper, and would not yield their breath till he appeared; though ever, as he stooped to whisper consolation, they shuddered at the veiled face so near their own. Such were the terrors of the black veil, even when Death had bared his visage! Strangers came long distances to attend service at his church, with the mere idle purpose of gazing at his figure, because it was forbidden them to behold his face. But many were made to quake ere they departed! Once, during Governor Belcher's[14] administration, Mr. Hooper was appointed to preach the election sermon. Covered with his black veil, he stood before the chief magistrate, the council, and the representatives, and wrought so
310 deep an impression that the legislative measures of that year were characterized by all the gloom and piety of our earliest ancestral sway. [15] Ⓗ

In this manner Mr. Hooper spent a long life, irreproachable in outward act, yet shrouded in dismal suspicions; kind and loving, though unloved, and dimly feared; a man apart from men, shunned in their health and joy, but ever summoned to their aid in mortal anguish. As years wore on, shedding their snows above his sable veil, he acquired a name throughout the New England churches, and they called him Father Hooper. Nearly all his parishioners, who were of a mature age when he was settled, had been borne away by many a funeral: he had one congregation in the church, and a more crowded one in the churchyard; and
320 having wrought so late into the evening, and done his work so well, it was now good Father Hooper's turn to rest.

---

14. **Governor Belcher's:** referring to Governor Jonathan Belcher (1682–1757), colonial governor of the Massachusetts Bay Colony from 1730 to 1741, and later of New Jersey.

15. **earliest ancestral sway:** the Puritans who held power in 17th-century America.

480   UNIT 2: AMERICAN ROMANTICISM

---

ambiguity
(ăm′bĭ-gyōō′ĭ-tē) *n.*
unclearness; uncertainty

Ⓗ CULTURAL CHARACTERISTICS
Once Mr. Hooper is perceived to have intimate knowledge of sin, he becomes a famous and respected clergyman. Based on this fact, what would you conclude is the main concern of Puritan worshipers?

DIFFERENTIATED INSTRUCTION

FOR STRUGGLING READERS
Paraphrase As students move into the final phase of the story, make sure they understand that Mr. Hooper continues to wear the veil in spite of his personal discomfort. Read aloud lines 281–283; then help students paraphrase it. *Possible answer: Truthfully, he disliked the veil so much that he never intentionally passed by a mirror or stopped to drink at a fountain, because he did not want to scare himself.*

FOR ADVANCED LEARNERS/AP
Hypothesize [small-group option] Point out the change from "Mr. Hooper" to "Father Hooper" (lines 315–317). Have students write a response to these questions and then compare their responses in small groups:

• When the story opens, Mr. Hooper already has the respect of his congregation. Why do you think that he does not receive the title of "Father" until late in his life?

• What might the change in title represent?

Several persons were visible by the shaded candlelight in the death chamber of the old clergyman. Natural connections[16] he had none. But there was the decorously grave, though unmoved physician, seeking only to mitigate the last pangs of the patient whom he could not save. There were the deacons, and other eminently pious members of his church. There, also, was the Reverend Mr. Clark, of Westbury, a young and **zealous** divine, who had ridden in haste to pray by the bedside of the expiring minister. There was the nurse, no hired handmaiden of death, but one whose calm affection had endured thus long, in secrecy, in solitude,
330 amid the chill of age, and would not perish, even at the dying hour. Who, but Elizabeth! And there lay the hoary head of good Father Hooper upon the death pillow, with the black veil still swathed about his brow and reaching down over his face, so that each more difficult gasp of his faint breath caused it to stir. All through life that piece of crape had hung between him and the world: it had separated him from cheerful brotherhood and woman's love, and kept him in that saddest of all prisons, his own heart; and still it lay upon his face, as if to deepen the gloom of his darksome chamber, and shade him from the sunshine of eternity.

For some time previous, his mind had been confused, wavering doubtfully between the past and the present, and hovering forward, as it were, at intervals,
340 into the indistinctness of the world to come. There had been feverish turns, which tossed him from side to side and wore away what little strength he had. But in the most convulsive struggles, and in the wildest vagaries of his intellect, when no other thought retained its sober influence, he still showed an awful solicitude lest the black veil should slip aside. Even if his bewildered soul could have forgotten, there was a faithful woman at his pillow, who, with averted eyes, would have covered that aged face, which she had last beheld in the comeliness of manhood. At length the death-stricken old man lay quietly in the torpor of mental and bodily exhaustion, with an imperceptible pulse, and breath that grew fainter and fainter, except when a long, deep, and irregular inspiration seemed to prelude the flight of his spirit.

350 The minister of Westbury approached the bedside.

"Venerable Father Hooper," said he, "the moment of your release is at hand. Are you ready for the lifting of the veil, that shuts in time from eternity?"

Father Hooper at first replied merely by a feeble motion of his head; then, apprehensive, perhaps, that his meaning might be doubtful, he exerted himself to speak.

"Yea," said he, in faint accents, "my soul hath a patient weariness until that veil be lifted."

"And is it fitting," resumed the Reverend Mr. Clark, "that a man so given to prayer, of such a blameless example, holy in deed and thought, so far as mortal
360 judgment may pronounce; is it fitting that a father in the church should leave a shadow on his memory that may seem to blacken a life so pure? I pray you, my venerable brother, let not this thing be! Suffer us to be gladdened by your

④ **Targeted Passage**

zealous (zĕl′əs) *adj.* eager and enthusiastic

---

16. **natural connections:** relatives.

THE MINISTER'S BLACK VEIL   **481**

TIERED DISCUSSION PROMPTS

In lines 333–357, use these prompts to introduce students to the story's concluding deathbed scene:

Restate According to the narrator, what has wearing the black veil done to Mr. Hooper? *Possible answer: Wearing the veil has kept him from having friends and from being married; in short, it has made him lonely.*

Interpret What do you learn about Elizabeth from this passage? *Possible answer: Elizabeth is willing to let Mr. Hooper die as he wishes instead of lifting the veil for a last look at the man she once hoped to marry. In fact, she would cover his face if the veil slipped, because she knows that it is what he would want (lines 344–346).*

Evaluate How well does the narrator strike a balance in showing both Mr. Hooper's feebleness and his determination? Explain. *Possible answer: The narrator effectively strikes a balance. He tells readers that Mr. Hooper is suffering from confusion and from debilitating bouts with fever (lines 338–341); but he also makes it clear that the one thought that Mr. Hooper retains, despite his weakness and discomfort, is that his veil not be removed (lines 341–344).*

VOCABULARY

COMMON CORE
L 4

OWN THE WORD

zealous: Tell students that *zealous* is the adjective form of the noun *zeal*, which means "eager and enthusiastic devotion to a cause, ideal, or goal." Ask students to list things for which they might show *zeal*. *Possible answer: political activity, people they love, sporting event or team, environmental cause*

FOR STRUGGLING READERS

④ **Targeted Passage** [Lines 350–362]

- Who speaks with the dying Mr. Hooper in these lines? What do we know about this person? (lines 350–352)

- What does Mr. Hooper tell him? To what "veil" is he referring? (lines 356–357)

- What reasons does Mr. Clark give Mr. Hooper for lifting the veil off his face? (lines 358–362)

Paraphrase Make sure students understand the loyalty and love that Elizabeth shows to Mr. Hooper in his last moments. Read aloud the full sentence that begins in line 344 and invite students to paraphrase it. *Possible answer: Even if he was too confused to know to keep the veil on, Elizabeth would have looked away and covered his lined and wrinkled face, the face that she had last seen when he was a handsome young man.*

How does someone become a
STRANGER?

Discuss In lines 371–372, what does Mr. Clark's comment imply about the cause for Mr. Hooper's estrangement? What do you think is the cause? *Possible answer: Mr. Clark's comment suggests that Mr. Hooper wears the black veil to signify some terrible and secret sin—the implied cause for his estrangement. The real cause seems to be that the parishioners have judged him and have refused to examine themselves honestly.*

TEXT ANALYSIS

COMMON CORE
RL 1

❶ SYMBOL

Possible answer: Father Hooper reproaches the villagers for making him an object of fear (lines 379–383), when the true cause of their fear has been their unwillingness to be honest about themselves with one another and with God (lines 383–387). His comment that everyone wears a Black Veil (lines 386–387) suggests that the veil represents the part of a person's life that he or she tries to keep secret from others.

SELECTION WRAP–UP

READ WITH A PURPOSE Now that students have read the selection, ask them who finally convinces Father Hooper to remove the veil. Is Father Hooper's final decision about the veil good or bad? *Possible answer: No one; he is buried with the veil still covering his face. Accept any answers that students can justify.*

★ CRITIQUE

- Ask students whether or not the black veil is an effective symbol. Have them back up their answer with textual evidence.

- After completing the After Reading questions on page 483, have students revisit their responses and tell whether they have changed their opinions.

---

triumphant aspect, as you go to your reward. Before the veil of eternity be lifted, let me cast aside this black veil from your face!"

And thus speaking, the Reverend Mr. Clark bent forward to reveal the mystery of so many years. But, exerting a sudden energy that made all the beholders stand aghast, Father Hooper snatched both his hands from beneath the bedclothes and pressed them strongly on the black veil, resolute to struggle, if the minister of Westbury would contend with a dying man.

370 "Never!" cried the veiled clergyman. "On earth, never!"

"Dark old man!" exclaimed the affrighted minister, "with what horrible crime upon your soul are you now passing to the judgment?"

Father Hooper's breath heaved; it rattled in his throat; but with a mighty effort, grasping forward with his hands, he caught hold of life, and held it back till he should speak. He even raised himself in bed; and there he sat shivering, with the arms of death around him, while the black veil hung down, awful, at that last moment, in the gathered terrors of a lifetime. And yet the faint, sad smile, so often there, now seemed to glimmer from its obscurity, and linger on Father Hooper's lips.

"Why do you tremble at me alone?" cried he, turning his veiled face round 380 the circle of pale spectators. "Tremble also at each other! Have men avoided me, and women shown no pity, and children screamed and fled, only for my black veil? What, but the mystery which it obscurely typifies, has made this piece of crape so awful? When the friend shows his inmost heart to his friend; the lover to his best beloved; when man does not vainly shrink from the eye of his Creator, loathsomely treasuring up the secret of his sin; then deem me a monster, for the symbol beneath which I have lived, and die! I look around me, and, lo! On every visage a Black Veil!"

While his auditors shrank from one another, in mutual affright, Father Hooper fell back upon his pillow, a veiled corpse, with a faint smile lingering on his lips. 390 Still veiled, they laid him in his coffin, and a veiled corpse they bore him to the grave. The grass of many years has sprung up and withered on that grave, the burial stone is moss-grown, and good Mr. Hooper's face is dust; but awful is still the thought, that it mouldered beneath the Black Veil! ❧

⑤ **Targeted Passage**

❶ **SYMBOL**
Explain Father Hooper's reproach in lines 380–387. What do his comments suggest about the meaning of the veil?

DIFFERENTIATED INSTRUCTION

FOR STRUGGLING READERS

⑤ **Targeted Passage** [Lines 382–393]

This concluding passage suggests a meaning for the veil and presents the narrator's final commentary about it.

- What does Mr. Hooper say that people must do before they can call him a "monster"? (lines 382–385)

- What does he say that they hide? What does he say that they wear? (lines 385–387)

- What final image does the narrator pres-

ent? How does he feel about that image? (lines 390–393)

FOR ENGLISH LANGUAGE LEARNERS

Language: Punctuation and Print Cues
Point out the exclamation point in line 364 and explain that it indicates that Mr. Clark feels strongly about what he is asking Mr. Hooper to do. Have students discuss the use of exclamation points in lines 370, 371, 380, 386, and 387, and then in line 393. Discuss why exclamation points might be so prominent at the end of the story.

Comprehension

1. **Recall** What is the topic of the first sermon Mr. Hooper gives while wearing the veil?

2. **Recall** What reason does Mr. Hooper give Elizabeth for wearing the veil?

3. **Summarize** As time goes by, how do Mr. Hooper's relationships change?

Text Analysis

● 4. **Identify Cultural Characteristics** What does the story reveal about Puritan religious beliefs, rules of behavior, and values and ideals?

● 5. **Interpret Symbol** Review the concept map you created as you read. Based on this information, what does the black veil represent? Explain your answer.

6. **Examine Character Ambiguity** The minister is an ambiguous character: he can be seen as an innocent victim of others' fears or as a man driven to isolate himself, convinced of his own moral superiority. Identify at least two details that support each perspective. Which interpretation do you find more compelling? Give reasons for your answer.

7. **Make Judgments About Character Motivations** Mr. Hooper's wearing of the black veil leads to his isolation from his congregation. Based on the following passages, what argument would you make about the real causes of the villagers' discomfort in the minister's presence?

   • the first sighting of the minister (lines 34–39)
   • parishioners' comments after services (lines 105–113)
   • his arrival at the wedding (lines 147–152)
   • the attempt to confront him (lines 190–197)

Text Criticism

8. **Biographical Context** Reread the biography of Hawthorne on page 468. Explain the personal motives that inspired Hawthorne's critical portrayal of Puritan culture. In what ways might Mr. Hooper represent Hawthorne's struggle with his own guilt?

> *How does someone become a* **STRANGER?**
>
> In line 336, the narrator calls the human heart the "saddest of all prisons." What does this mean? What does it suggest about our relationships with others?

COMMON CORE

RL 1 Cite evidence to support analysis of what the text says explicitly as well as inferences drawn from the text, including determining where the text leaves matters uncertain. **RL 3** Analyze the impact of the author's choices regarding how to develop and relate elements of a story.

Practice and Apply

For preliminary support of post-reading questions, use these copy masters:

R RESOURCE MANAGER—Copy Masters
Reading Check p. 226
Identify Cultural Characteristics p. 221
Question Support p. 227
Additional selection questions are provided for teachers on page 213.

ANSWERS

COMMON CORE **RL 1, RL 3**

1. *The sermon topic is secret sin.*

2. *Mr. Hooper never gives a straight answer, but says that the veil is a symbol that he must always wear.*

3. *The first change is that Mr. Hooper goes from being respected and loved to being feared and avoided. Over time, however, people seek him out. They think that he is intimate with sin and therefore can help them deal with their own sins.*

Possible answers:

4. ■ **COMMON CORE FOCUS Identify Cultural Characteristics** *The story reveals the importance of Sunday worship (lines 1–9); the importance of rank (lines 92–98); the prevalence of gossip (lines 85–91 and 105–114) and superstition (lines 125–129 and 150–152); an obsession with sin (lines 73–78 and 230–232); and hypocrisy (lines 379–387). Students may suggest that some of these traits are not limited to Puritan culture.*

5. ● **COMMON CORE FOCUS Symbol** *The veil may be a symbol of sin. Mr. Hooper makes people feel that their wicked thoughts are known (lines 73–76 and 192–194). He implies such an interpretation in lines 227–228, 237–238, and 384–387.*

6. *Innocent victim: He remains a good, kind person; he begs Elizabeth not to leave him (lines 251–256). Arrogant isolationist: He chooses to wear the veil (lines 220–224); he refuses to offer a clear explanation of it (lines 220–240).*

7. *The villagers' discomfort is caused by their own fears, which lead them to be intolerant of differences and to see sin and evil everywhere.*

8. *Hawthorne was critical because he felt guilty about having a Puritan ancestor who was an intolerant persecutor. Mr. Hooper might represent Hawthorne's struggle in that both are aware of flaws in Puritan culture but are unable to escape them.*

> *How does someone become a* STRANGER? **Possible answer:** Loneliness is a prison. People have a tendency to isolate themselves from others.

ANSWERS

Vocabulary in Context

▲ VOCABULARY PRACTICE

1. *antonyms*
2. *antonyms*
3. *synonyms*
4. *synonyms*
5. *antonyms*
6. *synonyms*
7. *antonyms*
8. *synonyms*

R RESOURCE MANAGER—Copy Master
Vocabulary Practice p. 224

ACADEMIC VOCABULARY IN SPEAKING

Answers will vary. Students should support their opinions with specific examples, and include at least one academic vocabulary word in their discussions.

VOCABULARY STRATEGY: THE LATIN ROOT *ambi*

COMMON CORE L 4b, L 6

For each item, help students use their knowledge of the root, suffixes (which identify the part of speech needed), and context clues to choose the correct word.

Answers:

1. *ambidextrous*
2. *ambiance*
3. *ambivalent*
4. *ambit*
5. *ambient*

R RESOURCE MANAGER—Copy Master
Vocabulary Strategy p. 225

Interactive Vocabulary

THINK central

Keywords direct students to a **WordSharp** tutorial on **thinkcentral.com** or to other types of vocabulary practice and review.

Assess and Reteach

Assess

DIAGNOSTIC AND SELECTION TESTS
Selection Test A pp. 145–146
Selection Test B/C pp. 147–184

Interactive Selection Test on thinkcentral.com

Reteach

Level Up Online Tutorials on thinkcentral.com

Vocabulary in Context

▲ VOCABULARY PRACTICE

Decide whether the words in each pair are synonyms or antonyms.

1. ostentatious/discreet
2. ambiguity/clarity
3. portend/predict
4. iniquity/vice
5. zealous/halfhearted
6. imbued/infused
7. preternatural/ordinary
8. tremulous/quaking

WORD LIST

ambiguity
imbued
iniquity
ostentatious
portend
preternatural
tremulous
zealous

ACADEMIC VOCABULARY IN SPEAKING

• construct   • expand   • indicate   • reinforce   • role

Appearance plays a powerful **role** in our society. With a partner, discuss whether you think someone's appearance reveals his or her identity or conceals it, or both. Support your opinion with specific examples and try to use at least one Academic Vocabulary word in your discussion.

VOCABULARY STRATEGY: THE LATIN ROOT *ambi*

The vocabulary word *ambiguity* contains the Latin root *ambi*. This root, which can mean either "both" or "around," can be found in many English words in all content areas, from science to philosophy. When you encounter the root *ambi* in a word, you can often use context clues to determine which meaning of the root is involved.

COMMON CORE

L 4b Identify and use patterns of word changes that indicate different meanings or parts of speech. **L 6** Acquire and use academic words and phrases.

PRACTICE Choose the word from the word web that best completes each sentence. Consider what you know about the Latin root and the other word parts shown. If necessary, consult a dictionary.

1. Because Peter was _____, he could write with either hand.
2. Their home had a pleasant and gracious _____.
3. Beth was_____ about joining the group and could not make up her mind.
4. The _____ of their property extends to that line of trees.
5. The _____ temperature in the room was too warm to preserve the specimens.

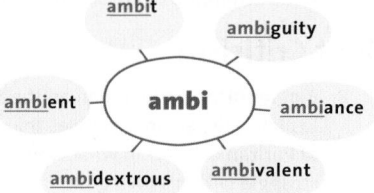

Interactive Vocabulary
THINK central

Go to **thinkcentral.com**.
KEYWORD: HML11-484

DIFFERENTIATED INSTRUCTION

FOR ENGLISH LANGUAGE LEARNERS

Task Support: Vocabulary Strategy [small-group option] Have small groups work with a dictionary to locate the etymology of each word in the word web. Help them create a very literal definition for each word, based on the meaning of *ambi*. (For example, students might define *ambidextrous* as "both right-handed" and *ambiance* as "aroundness.")

FOR ADVANCED LEARNERS/AP

Vocabulary in Writing Ask students to assume the role of Mr. Hooper and write a journal entry that describes how he feels about his break-up with Elizabeth. Ask them to use at least four of the vocabulary words in their entry. Encourage students to share their journal entries and to compare them to the entries written from Elizabeth's perspective.

The Gothic Perspective

Although the romantic period was mostly characterized by a feeling of optimism, American gothic literature showed a fascination with the dark side of human nature. Sin, deception, hedonism, guilt, death—all are subjects upon which gothic writers based their dark tales, as illustrated beautifully in this excerpt from Edgar Allan Poe's "The Masque of the Red Death."

> *"The 'Red Death' had long devastated the country. No pestilence had ever been so fatal, or so hideous. Blood was its Avatar and its seal—the redness and horror of blood. There were sharp pains, and sudden dizziness, and then profuse bleeding at the pores, with dissolution. . . .*
>
> *But the Prince Prospero was happy and dauntless and sagacious. When his dominions were half depopulated, he summoned to his presence a thousand hale and lighthearted friends from among the knights and dames of his court, and with these retired to the deep seclusion of one of his castellated abbeys."*

Literary critic Paul Zweig has a few words to say about the importance of Poe's dark perspective.

> *"Poe's achievement . . . was to give literary expression to the dread that haunted America's dream of success in the 19th century. If anything was possible in this land of wealth and change, then personal failure, even simple unhappiness, was obscene, a skeleton in the cellar of democracy."*

Writing to Analyze

Nathaniel Hawthorne is also a master of the gothic genre. Do you think Zweig's comments about Poe can apply to Hawthorne's work as well? Write a brief response, citing evidence from "The Minister's Black Veil" to support your opinion.

Consider

- characters' personal failings
- characters' unhappiness or fears
- the message you take away from the story

Extension

SPEAKING & LISTENING

Although Poe and Hawthorne both wrote gothic literature, the nature of their work differs quite a bit. While Poe was the master of supernatural horror, Hawthorne focused on more everyday, realistic fears. With your classmates, **discuss** what frightens you more—the fantastic or the realistic?

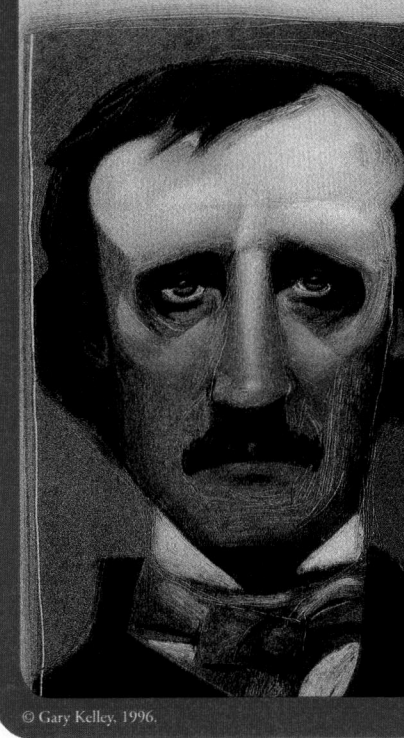

© Gary Kelley, 1996.

··· COMMON CORE

W 2 Write informative/ explanatory texts to examine and convey complex ideas, concepts and information through the selection, organization, and analysis of content. **SL 1** Participate in a range of collaborative discussions.

··· COMMON CORE FOCUS

W 2 Write informative/explanatory texts to examine and convey complex ideas, concepts and information through the selection, organization, and analysis of content. **SL 1** Participate in a range of collaborative discussions.

Wrap-Up: American Gothic

This Wrap-Up provides students with the opportunity to revisit the major ideas of gothic literature and to compare two gothic writers. Encourage students to examine their own views about the subjects that gothic writers frequently explored.

Writing to Analyze

- Remind students that *analyzing* involves examining complex things. In analytical writing, students discuss elements of a complex idea (noted in this feature by the bulleted list under **Consider**) as they support a general determination (a main idea) about the topic.

- To help students plan and write the essay, have them first paraphrase and discuss Zweig's statement. Then suggest that they focus on the words *dread* and *failure* in the statement and think about how both words reflect the "dark side" in gothic writing. Have students jot down their thoughts about each word in the context of "The Minister's Black Veil" and then relate each note to one of the three bulleted considerations in the prompt.

Extension

- Before students enter into discussion, have them summarize what they consider to be the most frightening but realistic parts of "The Minister's Black Veil" and the most frightening and supernatural elements of the Poe selections that they read.

- Ask students to discuss which selection frightened them the most and why. Then have them answer the discussion question.

FOR STRUGGLING WRITERS

Writing Support Help students paraphrase Zweig's comments, making sure that they understand these words and phrases:

- *to give literary expression to,* "to write about"
- *dread,* "intense fear"
- *obscene,* "offensive; disgusting"
- *a skeleton in the cellar,* "something that is terrible and that should be kept hidden"

Elicit that Zweig is saying that Americans felt that their personal failures and unhappiness should be hidden as potential sources of shame in a society that valued success above all else. Also help students write a thesis statement, such as "Zweig's comments apply not only to Poe but also to Hawthorne. In 'The Minister's Black Veil,' the characters. . . ."

Focus and Motivate

COMMON CORE FOCUS

W 3a–e Write narratives to develop real or imagined experiences or events using effective technique, well-chosen details, and well-structured event sequences. **W 4** Produce clear and coherent writing appropriate to task, purpose, and audience. **W 5** Develop and strengthen writing as needed by planning, revising, editing, rewriting, or trying a new approach, focusing on addressing what is most significant for a specific purpose and audience. **W 10** Write routinely over shorter time frames for a range of tasks, purposes, and audiences. **L 1** Demonstrate command of grammar and usage. **L 2** Demonstrate a command of capitalization, punctuation, and spelling.

WRITE WITH A PURPOSE

Tell students to select a conflict that they find interesting. Remind them that their purpose is to create a short story that expresses their ideas and engages readers—such as teachers, class-mates, or other students—through the actions of fully realized characters in a realistic setting.

COMMON CORE TRAITS

Review the *COMMON CORE TRAITS* with students. Have them focus on the develop-ment of ideas and organization of ideas as they write. Compare the list of traits with the rubric on page 494.

ADDITIONAL TASK

Write Historical Fiction Write a short story that is set in a specific historical time period. Conduct research to provide accurate details and to prompt ideas for your story.

Possible subjects: the Black Plague, the Revolu-tionary War, the Montgomery Bus Boycott

---

Writing Workshop
NARRATIVE

Short Story

Essential Course of Study **ECOS**

You have seen how writers in past centuries wrote short stories to entertain readers and to provide insight into the way people think and feel. In this workshop, you will learn how to craft a short story that entertains and engages readers.

 Complete the workshop activities in your **Reader/Writer Notebook**.

WRITE WITH A PURPOSE

WRITING TASK

Write a **short story** that engages readers with a strong plot, complex characters, and a vivid setting. Build your story around a central conflict.

Idea Starters
- a real-life situation
- an interesting-looking person
- a news story
- a dream
- an inexplicable sound, smell, sight, or event

THE ESSENTIALS

Here are some common purposes, audiences, and formats for writing a short story.

PURPOSES	AUDIENCES	FORMATS
• to entertain your readers • to express yourself creatively	• classmates and teacher • other students in your school • Web users • contest judges	• story for class • school's literary magazine • school's Web site • short story contest

COMMON CORE TRAITS

1. DEVELOPMENT OF IDEAS
- focuses on a **central conflict**
- introduces and develops a **narrator** and **characters**
- uses techniques such as **dialogue, description, reflection,** and **multiple plot lines** to develop the plot and characters
- offers a **conclusion** that follows from the events in the story
- conveys the **significance** of the events in the story

2. ORGANIZATION OF IDEAS
- presents a smooth **progression of events** to create a coherent story
- uses effective **pacing** to advance the plot

3. LANGUAGE FACILITY AND CONVENTIONS
- maintains a consistent **point of view**
- uses **precise words, telling details,** and **sensory language**
- **formats** and **punctuates dialogue** correctly
- employs correct **grammar, mechanics,** and **spelling**

Writing Online **THINK central**

Go to **thinkcentral.com**.
KEYWORD: HML11N-486

Writing Workshop Resources

 **RESOURCE MANAGER UNIT 2**

Plan and Teach pp. 229–232
Prewriting–Editing pp. 233–237
Writing Rubric p. 238
Speaking and Listening p. 239
Writing Support p. 240*

BEST PRACTICES TOOLKIT
Writing Template: Short Story p. C39

TECHNOLOGY

- **Teacher One Stop DVD-ROM**
- **Student One Stop DVD-ROM**
- **WriteSmart CD-ROM**
- **GrammarNotes DVD-ROM**

Writing Center on **thinkcentral.com**

*See resources on the **Teacher One Stop DVD-ROM** and on **thinkcentral.com**.*

* **Resources for Differentiation**

Planning/Prewriting

 COMMON CORE W 3a–e Write narratives to develop real or imagined experiences or events using effective technique, well-chosen details, and well-structured event sequences. W 5 Develop and strengthen writing as needed by planning.

Getting Started

EXPLORE STORY IDEAS

Using your imagination to explore "What if?" scenarios is a good way to brainstorm story ideas. Since your purpose is to entertain readers, try to think of "What if?" questions that have intriguing answers. The situation you decide on is the starting point for developing the rest of your story.

▶ **ASK YOURSELF:**

- How would a person with a certain kind of temperament and background react to an unexpected, extraordinary event?
- What would happen if a historical or a current event had played out differently?
- How would life change if something that is now impossible became possible?

THINK ABOUT AUDIENCE AND PURPOSE

As you plan your short story, keep your audience and purpose in mind. Your **purpose** is to entertain readers and to express yourself creatively. Your **audience** will be your teacher and classmates but may also include a wider audience of teens and young adult readers.

▶ **ASK YOURSELF:**

- What effect do I want my story to have on my audience?
- What do I want my audience to know about each scene?
- What do I want my audience to know that the characters in my story do not know?

IMAGINE CHARACTERS

Short stories usually focus on one or two **main characters** and sometimes include **minor characters** as well. Use these techniques to bring your characters to life:

- Reveal key character traits by providing **relevant, descriptive details** about the characters' appearance, behavior, and actions.
- Include **telling details,** or pieces of description or dialogue, that reveal important or interesting information about the characters.
- Use **dialogue** (the characters' actual words) and **interior monologue** (the characters' unspoken thoughts, feelings, and reflections) to reveal personality and **perspective,** or **point of view.**

▶ **ASK YOURSELF:**

- How do the characters look and move?
- What do the characters' actions reveal?
- What distinctive gestures or expressions are typical of the characters?
- What causes conflicts for the characters?
- What personality traits come to light as the characters face their conflicts?
- How do the characters grow or change because of their conflicts?
- How do the characters speak and think?
- Is there any disconnect between what the characters say to others, what they think to themselves, and how they act?

IMAGINE SETTING

Imagine a **setting,** or time and place, for your story. **Sensory language** helps to paint a vivid picture of the setting.

▶ **ASK YOURSELF:**

- What time period or place do I find interesting?
- If I were to visit an imaginary place, what would it look, sound, smell, and feel like?

WRITING WORKSHOP **487**

DIFFERENTIATED INSTRUCTION

FOR ENGLISH LANGUAGE LEARNERS

Language: Reinforce Narrative Terms Review these terms with students:

- *point of view:* the vantage point from which events in a story or novel are told
- *characterization:* the techniques a writer uses to develop, or help readers understand, characters
- *chronological order:* the arrangement of events in the order in which they would have actually happened

- *flashback:* a scene that interrupts the action of a narrative to describe events that took place at an earlier time
- *flash-forward:* a scene that interrupts the action of a narrative to describe events that take place at a later time
- *climax:* the moment in the story's plot when a reader's interest and emotional intensity reach a peak
- *suspense:* the excitement or tension that readers feel as they become involved in a story and eagerly await the outcome

---

Planning/ Prewriting

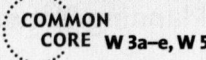 **COMMON CORE** W 3a–e, W 5

▶ **EXPLORE STORY IDEAS** Tell students that their "What if?" scenarios may evolve during the process of writing their short stories. Advise students to sharpen their focus before they begin writing. For example, instead of writing about the general idea that the South won the Civil War, have them concentrate on how one pivotal incident during the Battle of Gettysburg changed the outcome of the war.

▶ **THINK ABOUT AUDIENCE AND PURPOSE** Remind students that they can entertain their audience by creating an intriguing conflict or including imaginative sensory language that will engage the reader. Whatever they choose to write about, students should keep their purpose and audience in mind.

▶ **IMAGINE CHARACTERS** Ask students to write a psychological profile of their main character before beginning their stories. Explain to students that the profile should relay aspects of the character's background that contribute to his or her personality and behavior. Give students the following example: *My main character, Celina, is a seventeen-year-old honor-roll student. She is a very responsible teenager who always takes control of the situations around her. Growing up with a single mother and two younger sisters, Celina often had to take care of her younger sisters while her mother worked or slept during her shifts. Celina is accustomed to being responsible and in control. However, friends and classmates often feel that she is bossy.*

▶ **IMAGINE SETTING** Ask students to create a sense of time and place using sensory language for each scene in their stories. Tell students to include specific details, such as sights, sounds, smells, and sensations.

 RESOURCE MANAGER—Copy Masters

    Prewriting–Editing, pp. 233–237
    Writing Rubric, p. 238
    Writing Support, p. 240

WRITING WORKSHOP **487**

Planning/Prewriting *continued*

▶ **PLOT YOUR STORY** Ask students to discuss the plots of stories you have read in class. What happened in those stories? What did the characters want? What problems did they face? How did they resolve them?

Explain that the plot plan on this page illustrates one student's plan for her story. Point out how the plot's sequence of events creates suspense and keeps readers engaged. Ask students to compare the plan to the actual student draft that appears on pages 491–492 of this workshop. Tell them to use the plot plan to begin crafting their stories.

YOUR TURN Give students time to develop a plot plan independently. Have students organize their ideas from brainstorming, but encourage them to add or alter ideas if necessary to create a story that will engage the reader. As students work, monitor their progress by making sure students' plots establish a clear conflict, build to a climax, and provide a resolution that follows from the sequence of events.

For interactive graphic organizers, see

💿 **WriteSmart CD-ROM**

Writing Center on thinkcentral.com

Planning/Prewriting *continued*

Getting Started

PLOT YOUR STORY

To keep your readers interested in your story, something has to happen. The **sequence of events** in a short story is called the **plot**. Most plots begin with an **exposition**, which introduces the characters, their setting, and their **conflict**—a problem or situation to be solved. Next is the **rising action**, in which **complications** arise as the characters attempt to resolve their conflict. The conflict escalates until it reaches a turning point, or **climax**. During the **falling action** and the **resolution**, the conflict is resolved and the story ends.

As you plan your story, keep **pacing** in mind. You can create intensity or excitement by keeping the action moving from one event to the next and not focusing on unimportant details. You can build **suspense**, a feeling of uncertainty and curiosity about what will happen next, by lingering over details that describe characters or setting. You can create **tension** by speeding up the narrative.

If you plan to write a longer short story, experiment with **multiple plot lines,** or subplots, that relate to the main plot or central conflict.

▶ **WHAT DOES IT LOOK LIKE?**

> *Plot Plan*
>
> **Characters:** *David and Nadine*
>
> **Setting:** *kitchen at David's house*
>
> **Exposition:** *A college letter has arrived; David hesitates to open it. His conflict is internal. He fights his nervousness and uncertainty about his future.*
>
> **Rising Action:** *Nadine comes in, gets a drink of water, and reads the letter silently.*
>
> **Climax:** *Nadine tells David that he is accepted to college in Boston.*
>
> **Falling Action:** *Nadine and David celebrate together and then catch their breath.*
>
> **Resolution:** *Nadine and David watch a movie together, knowing everything has changed.*

PEER REVIEW Describe your story's sequence of events to a peer. Then ask: Is the sequence clear and compelling? What kinds of details can I include to create suspense?

YOUR TURN In your *Reader/Writer Notebook,* develop your plot plan. Ask yourself the following questions as you develop your plot:

- Do the main characters have a conflict with one another or with some other external or internal force?
- How do the main characters' actions or decisions further complicate the problem?
- What happens to make the conflict reach a climax, or turning point?
- How is the conflict resolved?
- How have the characters changed by the end of the story?
- What is the significance of what has happened?

488 UNIT 2: AMERICAN ROMANTICISM

DIFFERENTIATED INSTRUCTION

FOR ENGLISH LANGUAGE LEARNERS

Writing: Plot Draw a diagram of a hill on the board. Tell students that the hill represents the "shape" of the story. Work with students to determine where on the hill the exposition, rising action, climax, falling action, and resolution should go. After students have developed their plot plans, have them create a diagram for their own story. Then, ask students whether the "shape" of their story makes sense, or whether they have placed events on the wrong part of the hill.

FOR STRUGGLING WRITERS

Plot Plan Work with students to fill in a plot plan using the events of a story you have recently read in class. Then have students work in pairs to fill one in on their own using the events of a movie they have both seen. Have each pair write their plot plan on the board and explain why they categorized each event as a part of the rising action, climax, falling action, or resolution.

Drafting

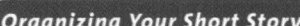 **COMMON CORE** **W 3c** Use a variety of techniques to sequence events. **W 4** Produce clear and coherent writing appropriate to task, purpose, and audience. **L1** Demonstrate command of grammar and usage.

The following chart shows a structure for organizing an effective short story.

Organizing Your Short Story

EXPOSITION

- Engage and orient your readers by introducing the **characters, setting,** and **central conflict.**
- Choose the point of view you will use throughout the story. The **point of view** is the **vantage point,** or **perspective,** from which a writer tells a story. If you are writing a longer short story, using **multiple points of view** gives readers more than one perspective on the characters, setting, and plot. Choose from the following points of view: first person, third-person limited, or third-person omniscient.
  - **First person:** The narrator is a character in the story. He or she tells only what he or she knows and experiences. The narrator uses first-person pronouns: *I, me, my, we, us.*
  - **Third-person limited:** The narrator is not a character. The narrator focuses on one character's knowledge and experiences. The narrator uses third-person pronouns: *he, she, they, his, her, their, them.*
  - **Third-person omniscient:** An all-knowing narrator tells the story, using third-person pronouns. The narrator knows what all characters are thinking and feeling.

▼

RISING ACTION AND CLIMAX

- Develop the characters with such techniques as **dialogue** and **reflection.**
- Introduce plot complications.
- Although you'll present most plot points in **chronological order,** you may sometimes skip forward **(flash-forward)** or backward in time **(flashback).**
- Include **precise words** and **phrases, telling details,** and **sensory language** to describe the characters and settings and to create a mood.
- Use **pacing** that helps keep the action moving and creates a smooth progression from one event to the next.
- Bring the plot to a **climax.**

▼

FALLING ACTION AND RESOLUTION

- **Resolve** the conflict and reveal the final outcome. Convey the **significance** of the events.

GRAMMAR IN CONTEXT: TRANSITIONAL EXPRESSIONS

Transitional expressions create **coherence,** or a strong connection between ideas. In short stories, they help the reader follow the progression of the plot. Transitional expressions may be prepositions or adverbs. Notice how an adverb is used as a transitional expression:

> They laughed at the situation. **After** their laughter faded, Nadine congratulated David.

 YOUR TURN Following the plot plan you created earlier and the chart on this page, write a draft of your short story. Be sure to use a consistent point of view, pacing that moves the story along, descriptive and sensory language, and transitional expressions.

FOR STRUGGLING WRITERS

Transitional Expressions Tell students that in short stories transitional expressions will often show the sequence of events. Provide students with the following common transitional expressions that show time sequence: *after a while, at that time, before, earlier, eventually, meanwhile, next, soon, then.*

Ask students whether they can think of other transitional expressions that show time sequence. Encourage students to make a list of these transitional expressions and to refer to the list as they write.

FOR ADVANCED LEARNERS/AP

Acceleration Have students choose an alternate form in which to write a story. They may want to write it in the form of a letter, a play, or an epic poem. Remind them that no matter what form they use, they must consider characters, setting, and plot. After students have finished their work, have them exchange projects with another student. Have each student write a short critique of the other student's work, examining its strengths and making some positive suggestions for improvement.

Practice and Apply

Drafting

 **COMMON CORE W 3c, W 4, L1**

▶ **EXPOSITION** Tell students that they should introduce the plot and grab their readers' attention in the exposition. Discuss point of view, and give students examples of short stories they have recently read that are told from each point of view.

▶ **RISING ACTION AND CLIMAX** Point out that although most of their plot events will progress in chronological order, they can also "flash back" to earlier events. "Flashing back" can help grab readers' attention.

Remind students to incorporate sensory language and telling details to enhance both plot and characters.

▶ **FALLING ACTION AND RESOLUTION** Remind students that as they resolve their stories' conflicts in the climax, they should reveal details of the final outcome. Tell students that resolving their conflict should cause the characters to change in some way. Emphasize that their readers should be left with something to think about.

GRAMMAR IN CONTEXT: TRANSITIONAL EXPRESSIONS

For practice, have students add a transitional word or phrase to each sentence or pair of sentences.

- Mario had a quick snack. _____, he did his homework. *[After he ate]*

- The nurse had the patient sit down _____ took his blood pressure. *[and then]*

- First, boil the water. _____, add the noodles. *[Next]*

 YOUR TURN Ask students to complete the **Your Turn** activity independently. Remind students to use a consistent point of view and to connect ideas using transitional expressions. Suggest that students write their drafts double-spaced so they can make revisions more easily later.

For a short story writing template, see

📦 **BEST PRACTICES TOOLKIT—Transparency**
Writing Template: Short Story, p. C39

Revising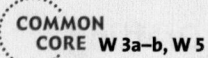

Model the Skill Using a draft short story on a transparency, model how to use the questions, tips, and revision strategies suggested in the chart to evaluate and revise, edit, or rewrite. You might use a story written by a student from another class or from last year. Before you evaluate and revise, edit, or rewrite the draft, be sure to remove the student's name from the document so that he or she is anonymous.

YOUR TURN Remind students that in peer review they should offer positive, constructive responses to each other's writing. Tell students that peer reviewers should let their partners know when they come to story passages that they find confusing. They do not have to solve the problem for the writers, but they should call their partners' attention to it and offer clear suggestions for revising, editing, rewriting, or trying a new approach. When they have worked their way through one partner's story, they should switch roles and review the second student's draft.

For more interactive revision tools, see

Write*Smart* CD-ROM

Writing Center on thinkcentral.com

Revising

When revising, consider your story's characters, setting, plot, pacing, and resolution. Your goal is to determine whether you've achieved your purpose and effectively expressed your story idea to your audience. The questions, tips, and strategies in the following chart can help you revise and improve your draft.

SHORT STORY

Ask Yourself	Tips	Revision Strategies
1. Does the story's exposition introduce the main characters and establish the setting? Does it initiate the central conflict?	**Highlight** details about the main characters and setting. **Draw a wavy line** under the event or situation that initiates the central conflict.	**Add** details about the main characters and setting. **Add** a sentence that initiates the central conflict.
2. Does the story have a clear point of view? Is the point of view developed consistently?	**Underline** phrases that indicate the point of view. **Label** the point of view in the margin.	**Delete** information that the narrator would not know. **Reword** sentences to make the point of view consistent.
3. Is the plot developed with actions and decisions that complicate the problem? Does the conflict build toward a climax?	**Draw a star** by each plot complication. **Draw two stars** by the story's climax. Make sure that there is a smooth progression of events building toward the climax.	**Add** actions or decisions that create complications. **Add** an event, an action, a decision, or a realization to bring about the climax.
4. Does the story use precise words and phrases, telling details, and sensory language to develop the plot and characters?	**Draw a dotted line** under the characters' spoken words or unspoken thoughts and feelings. **Put parentheses** around descriptive details about characters.	**Add** dialogue and interior monologue. **Elaborate** on characters with descriptions of physical appearance, behavior, and actions.
5. Is pacing used effectively to advance the plot?	**Draw a box** around any details that are unrelated to the central conflict.	**Delete** any unnecessary details to tighten the pace and move the action forward.
6. Does the story's conclusion resolve the conflict and show the significance of the events?	**Circle** the sentences that resolve the conflict. **Bracket** the sentences that show the significance of events.	**Add** sentences that resolve the conflict. **Add** a sentence or two to show the significance of events.

YOUR TURN **PEER REVIEW** Working with a peer, review your draft. Answer each question in the chart to evaluate how to make improvements. Then, revise your draft, using the tips and revision techniques. If your story is not flowing smoothly, try a new approach to make it more cohesive.

DIFFERENTIATED INSTRUCTION

FOR STRUGGLING WRITERS

Advance Plot with Dialogue Write the following unrelated lines of dialogue on the board. Ask students whether each line might advance the plot of a story, and if so, how.

- "You'll never believe what I just heard." [*advances plot by creating suspense*]

- "Pass the salt." [*does not advance plot*]

- "It's great to see you again—it seems like forever, doesn't it?" [*advances plot by establishing a relationship between characters*]

FOR ADVANCED LEARNERS/AP

Acceleration Have pairs of students choose a passage from any work of fiction that gives information without using dialogue. Pairs should prepare and perform a scene that uses dialogue to convey the information in the passage. Then, have the audience read the original passage and rate how well the students' scene relayed the information in the passage.

ANALYZE A STUDENT DRAFT

Read this student draft; note the comments on its strengths as well as suggestions for improvement.

COMMON CORE

W 3a–b Set out a problem and its significance; use dialogue to develop events and characters. **W 5** Develop and strengthen writing as needed by revising, editing, rewriting, or trying a new approach, focusing on addressing what is most significant for a specific purpose and audience.

The Discovery
by Maile Cortese, Weddington High School

❶ As David drove into the driveway, he became oddly calm. He turned down the radio so that he could hear his heart beating. Easing the door open, he stepped out of the car, walked down to the mailbox, and looked inside. "There it is." Hands shaking, he reached in for the letter.

> Maile presents the **main character** and uses telling details to characterize him as nervous.

❷ David gently carried the envelope into the house as if it were made of glass. As he sat down at his kitchen table, he became numb. The envelope was addressed to him, but he didn't really feel like it was for him. He read the address line. "David Kalinger," he announced to no one in particular. "Yep, it's for me."

> Here, Maile introduces the **central conflict.**

❸ Fingers trembling, he slowly raised his hand to open it. He slid his thumb under the flap and tore the paper. The letter was sitting in the envelope so peacefully, waiting for someone to read its secret. Just as he was pulling the letter out of the envelope, his sister Nadine strolled in through the side door. David sighed.

> This paragraph slows down the pacing to build **suspense**— Nadine's arrival postpones the opening of the letter.

❹ Nadine explained that she rushed home to find out about the acceptance letter. Then, she reached into the cabinet to get a glass for water.

> Maile should use **dialogue** to show the reader what happens, rather than simply telling the reader what happens. An exchange of dialogue would help develop the characters and plot.

LEARN HOW Develop Plot and Characters with Dialogue Maile can develop the plot more effectively by inserting dialogue. Dialogue can be used to extend the moment and develop the characters and their relationship. It can also reveal information that is important to the plot. Maile decides to revise the fourth paragraph, replacing it with dialogue that creates suspense and provides information about the relationship between the two characters.

MAILE'S REVISION TO PARAGRAPH ❹

~~Nadine explained that she rushed home to find out about the acceptance letter. Then, she reached into the cabinet to get a glass for water.~~

"Nadine! What are you doing here?" he asked.

"I heard you were getting your acceptance letter today, so I just ran over here. Man, I'm so out of breath! Can I get a glass of water?" she panted as she reached into the cabinet.

"Sure, go ahead," David muttered, knowing she already had. As Nadine sat down, David just stared at the envelope and held his breath.

ANALYZE A STUDENT DRAFT

Explain that the Student Draft on this page is the first half of a short story. Model reading the draft and the annotations in blue, and explain that the yellow highlighting illustrates the student's language choices. Explain that the following *Learn How* mini-lessons provide helpful information about ways to improve this student draft as well as their own.

LEARN HOW Develop Plot and Characters with Dialogue

- Explain to students that adding dialogue develops the plot by showing readers what is happening, rather than just telling them about it. This helps build the suspense that the writer has already established.

- Point out to students that in paragraph 4 the original text indicates that the character Nadine is speaking, but does not convey her actual words. Tell students that including dialogue between the two characters helps readers feel more in touch with what is happening in the scene.

- Remind students to use dialogue to reveal their characters' emotions and motivations as well as important plot information.

- Have students highlight at least two places in their drafts where they can develop the plot with dialogue. Tell students to look for sentences that discuss what a character says but does not state the character's actual words.

Explain that the Student Draft is continued and completed on this page. Read the draft and annotations aloud, and discuss them. Refer students to the plot plan on page 488. Have them comment on how well the student writer followed the plot plan.

LEARN HOW Show Significance in the Conclusion

- Explain that a common mistake student writers make in writing story conclusions is not fully indicating the significance of the event to the story's characters.

- Point out that the student writer has revised her conclusion to explain how the coming change in David's life will affect David and Nadine's relationship. Read the student's first draft and compare it with her revised version. Ask students to determine whether the revision effectively concludes the story. If students think that the revision is ineffective, ask them how they would revise the story's ending.

- Ask students to make notes on their drafts of revisions that would strengthen the significance of their stories' conclusions. Inform them that story conflicts do not need to be completely resolved, but some closure or change must occur. Explain to students that a satisfying ending can raise questions about what happened next. Many good stories leave readers wanting more.

YOUR TURN Ask students to work individually to complete the **Your Turn** activity. Remind them to find places in their stories to insert dialogue and to ensure that their ending shows the significance of their stories' events.

For interactive revision tools, see

WriteSmart CD-ROM

Writing Center on thinkcentral.com

ANALYZE A STUDENT DRAFT *continued*

⑤   "So have you even looked at it yet?" Nadine asked.

⑥   David shook his head miserably. "Would you do it for me?" he pleaded.

⑦   Nadine gave him an inquisitive look but then quickly snatched the envelope, opened the letter, and started to read it silently.

⑧   "What? What? Read it aloud! What are you doing?" he shouted in misery.

⑨   "Oh no, David. I was afraid of this," she said in a sorrowful voice, her face grim. David put his head in his hands, moaning softly.

⑩   "David, I'm not going to have you around here to keep me company any more. You've been accepted! You're going to Boston!" she shouted triumphantly.

⑪   David jumped to his feet, knocking over the chair, and gave Nadine a playful shove. "You'll be sorry!" he shouted as he reached for Nadine.

⑫   They fell to the floor, laughing hysterically.

> Maile uses **dialogue** to heighten the **suspense**.

> The story reaches its **climax** when Nadine tells David the contents of the letter.

> This conclusion needs to be revised to show the significance of the event.

LEARN HOW Show Significance in the Conclusion   Maile shows how David's central conflict has been resolved, but she does not show why the event is significant. Maile decides to add a few sentences to the resolution to reflect on why the event is significant to David and Nadine's relationship.

MAILE'S REVISION TO PARAGRAPH ⑫

They fell to the floor, laughing hysterically.

Soon, their howls ended and they stood up and hugged each other. After catching their breath, David set up the movie while Nadine made the popcorn, just like every other Friday night since they were young. However, they both knew that David's move to Boston would be a big change for them both.

YOUR TURN Use the feedback from your peers and teacher, the revision strategies chart, and the two "Learn How" lessons to revise or rework your story. Evaluate whether your audience will find your story entertaining and whether you have expressed your story idea in a creative, unique way.

DIFFERENTIATED INSTRUCTION

FOR ENGLISH LANGUAGE LEARNERS

Writing: Conclusion To help students understand how to develop a conclusion, introduce the following vocabulary related to the **Learn How** activity:

- conclude—*to bring to an end*
- conflict—*a disagreement or problem*
- resolution—*a solution to a problem*
- unresolved—*not solved or ended*

To provide English language learners with additional writing support, see

R RESOURCE MANAGER—Copy Masters

Writing Support, p. 240

FOR ADVANCED LEARNERS/AP

Acceleration Challenge students to write three variations of the ending to their story. Have students present their alternate endings to the class. Their peers can discuss which ending is best and why.

Editing and Publishing

 **COMMON CORE** W 5 Develop and strengthen writing as needed by revising, editing, rewriting, or trying a new approach. L 1 Demonstrate a command of grammar and usage. L 2 Demonstrate a command of capitalization, punctuation, and spelling.

In the editing stage, you proofread your short story to make sure that it is free of grammar, usage, and punctuation errors. Pay close attention to your grammar and word usage, such as verb tenses and parts of speech. Make sure that you have chosen your words carefully. Also, read carefully to catch any spelling errors, even after doing a word-processing spell-check. These kinds of mistakes keep your audience from fully enjoying your story.

> **GRAMMAR IN CONTEXT: FORMATTING AND PUNCTUATING DIALOGUE**
>
> Since your short story will include a good amount of dialogue, you will need to make sure that it is formatted and punctuated correctly. Every time you have dialogue that comes from a new speaker, you should start a new paragraph.
>
> When used with quotation marks, **commas** and **periods** are placed within the closing quotation marks.
>
> > *"Oh no, David. I was afraid of this," she said in a sorrowful voice, her face grim.*
>
> **Question marks** and **exclamation points** are placed inside the closing quotation marks if the quotation itself is a question or an exclamation. Otherwise, they are placed outside the quotation marks.
>
> > *"So have you even looked at it yet?" Nadine asked.*

PUBLISH YOUR WRITING

Share your short story with an audience.
- Submit your story to your school's literary magazine or Web site.
- Submit your story to a short story contest. Ask your school librarian or media specialist to help you identify several contests.
- Adapt your short story into a script. Then, collaborate with classmates to perform your script for the class.

 YOUR TURN Proofread your final draft. As you proofread, check your dialogue to see that you have formatted and punctuated it correctly. Correct any errors you find in your story. Then, publish your completed work.

FOR ENGLISH LANGUAGE LEARNERS

Writing: Dialogue Tell students that when writing dialogue they should use conversational language rather than stiff, formal language. Remind them that conversational language should reflect the way people really speak to one another rather than grammatical rules. Therefore, when writing dialogue, it is acceptable to break grammatical rules if the dialogue reflects the way a character would really speak. Give students the following example:

Unrealistic Dialogue: "How are you going to acquire the necessary tools to fix the automobile?"

Realistic Dialogue: "How're ya gonna get the tools to fix the car?"

Have partners work together to write a dialogue exchange between two students who are discussing an upcoming event at their school, such as a dance or play. Remind students to start new paragraphs for new speakers, to put punctuation marks in the correct places, and to reflect realistic ways of speaking.

Editing and Publishing

 **COMMON CORE** W 5, L 1, L 2

GRAMMAR IN CONTEXT: FORMATTING AND PUNCTUATING DIALOGUE

Tell students that making sure their stories are free of errors in grammar, usage, and punctuation will enhance their readers' understanding and pleasure. Remind them that dialogue requires care in formatting and punctuation.

- For practice formatting and punctuating dialogue, have students identify the dialogue errors in the following paragraph:

  "Trevor, stop holding your nose when you jump in the water"! Maria exclaimed, pacing at the side of the pool. Trevor peeled off his goggles and gazed up at his big sister. "Then, how do I keep water from going up my nose"? he asked.

- Tell students to circle all the punctuation marks at the ends of quotations in their short stories. Then, have students edit their stories to make sure that all periods, commas, question marks, and exclamation points that are part of quotations are placed inside the end quotes.

PUBLISH YOUR WRITING

Brainstorm with students additional ways to publish their short stories.

 YOUR TURN Allow students time to proofread their drafts. Remind them to review every line of dialogue to check for formatting or punctuation errors. Also remind students to be sure that they have included transitional expressions so that readers can follow the progression of the plot.

Scoring Rubric

Tell students that the best way to understand a scoring rubric is to use it to score actual writing. Have students work with partners and evaluate each other's short stories using the rubric. After they talk with their partners, ask students to score their own short stories and then write a brief paragraph using the language of the rubric to explain the score.

For Rubric Bank, see

WriteSmart CD-ROM

Writing Center on thinkcentral.com

Assess and Reteach

Assess

R RESOURCE MANAGER—Copy Master
Rubric for Evaluation, p. 238

Online Essay Scoring on thinkcentral.com

Reteach

Level Up Online Tutorial on thinkcentral.com

Reteaching Worksheets on thinkcentral.com

Literature Lesson 5: Elements of Plot

Writing Lesson 3: Thinking About Purpose, Audience, and Form

Scoring Rubric

Use the rubric below to evaluate your short story from the Writing Workshop or your response to the on-demand task on the next page.

SHORT STORY

SCORE	COMMON CORE TRAITS
6	• **Development** Skillfully introduces, develops, and resolves a conflict; develops compelling, believable characters; effectively uses dialogue, description, reflection, and one or more plot lines • **Organization** Has a smooth, coherent event sequence that builds to a strong conclusion; uses effective pacing • **Language** Consistently maintains one or more points of view; weaves in precise words, telling details, and sensory language; shows a strong command of conventions
5	• **Development** Effectively introduces, develops, and resolves a conflict; develops interesting, believable characters; ably uses dialogue, description, reflection, and one or more plot lines • **Organization** Has a coherent event sequence that builds to a conclusion; uses mostly effective pacing • **Language** Maintains one or more points of view; includes precise words, telling details, and sensory language; has a few errors in conventions
4	• **Development** Introduces, develops, and resolves a conflict; has interesting characters with some believable traits; could use some more dialogue, description, and reflection • **Organization** Includes some extraneous events, resulting in ineffective pacing • **Language** Mostly maintains a point of view; needs more precise words, telling details, and sensory language; has a few distracting errors in conventions
3	• **Development** Introduces and resolves a conflict, but it needs more development; has some underdeveloped characters; needs more dialogue, description, and reflection • **Organization** Has a confusing sequence caused by some extraneous events; has a lagging pace at times • **Language** Has a few lapses in point of view; lacks enough precise words, telling details, and sensory language; has some significant errors in conventions
2	• **Development** Introduces a conflict but does not develop or resolve it; inadequately develops characters; lacks sufficient dialogue, description, and reflection • **Organization** Includes too many events that distract from the plot; has choppy pacing • **Language** Uses an inconsistent point of view; mostly lacks precise words, telling details, and sensory language; has many distracting errors in conventions
1	• **Development** Has no identifiable conflict; includes underdeveloped characters; lacks any dialogue, description, and reflection • **Organization** Has no apparent organization • **Language** Never establishes a clear point of view; lacks precise words, telling details, and sensory language; has major problems with conventions

Preparing for Timed Writing

COMMON CORE

W 10 Write routinely over shorter time frames for a range of tasks, purposes, and audiences.

1. ANALYZE THE TASK 5 MIN

Read the task carefully. Then, read it again, noting on your own paper the words that tell the topic, the purpose, and the audience.

WRITING TASK

Topic

Write a short story in which <u>characters react to an unexpected event</u> in their own neighborhood. In your story, try <u>to entertain</u> <u>peers and adults</u> by presenting a lively description of how the main character and others handle the unexpected event, and what happens as a result.

Purpose   *Audience*

2. PLAN YOUR RESPONSE 10 MIN

Use a graphic organizer to brainstorm details for your story. Answer the questions below to fill in information for each part of the graphic organizer.

1. **Exposition:** What is the unexpected event? What does the main character say, think, feel, and do as a result of the event? What conflict does the event create?
2. **Rising Action:** What complications arise as the characters try to resolve the central conflict?
3. **Climax:** What is the most exciting or suspenseful part of the story? Who is involved?
4. **Falling Action:** What events or actions occur that indicate the conflict is close to being resolved?
5. **Resolution:** How is the conflict resolved? Do the neighborhood and characters change because of the unexpected event? If so, how?

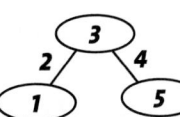

3. RESPOND TO THE TASK 20 MIN

Begin drafting your short story. A quick way to begin is to write a short dialogue that introduces the characters and establishes the setting and central conflict. As you write the rest of your draft, be sure to maintain a consistent point of view.

4. IMPROVE YOUR RESPONSE 5–10 MIN

Revising Go back to the key aspects of the task. Does your story have a vivid setting and an interesting main character? Have you developed a plot that begins with an unexpected event and then tells what happens? Is your point of view consistent? If not, add these elements.

Proofreading Correct errors in grammar, spelling, punctuation, and capitalization. Make sure that your edits are neat and that the paper is legible.

Checking Your Final Copy Before you turn in your paper, read it one more time to catch any errors you may have missed.

WRITING WORKSHOP **495**

DIFFERENTIATED INSTRUCTION

FOR ENGLISH LANGUAGE LEARNERS

Writing: Key Story Elements Review these terms with students: *exposition:* the beginning of the story, which introduces characters, setting, and conflict; *rising action:* the point in which complications arise as the characters try to resolve the conflict; *climax:* the moment when a reader's interest and emotional intensity reach a peak; *falling action:* the point when it appears the conflict is close to being resolved; *resolution:* the point in which the final

outcome is revealed and loose ends are tied up. After students have written their first draft, have them underline their story elements.

FOR STRUGGLING WRITERS

Ask students to review their work and pay attention to all the details. Is it easy to understand who the characters are and why they are in the situation? What would make the story clearer? Are there any details that do not add anything to the story? Are there any details that may confuse readers?

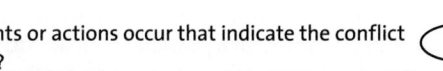
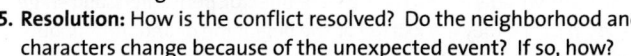

COMMON CORE FOCUS

W 10 Write routinely over shorter time frames for a range of tasks, purposes, and audiences.

Preparing for Timed Writing

1. **Analyze the Task** Before students begin writing, encourage them to answer the following questions:
   - What is my time limit?
   - What are the core traits assessed in the scoring rubric?
   - Who is my audience?
   - What is my purpose?

2. **Plan Your Response** Point out to students that the scoring rubric emphasizes that writers should focus on creating a clear and compelling central conflict around which to build their stories. Remind students that their characters will express themselves in dialogue that will advance the plot of the story and will work to resolve the conflict. Remind students that their stories will start out with exposition that states the unexpected event that creates the conflict, as well as introducing their main character and his or her reactions to the conflict-causing event.

3. **Respond to the Task** Tell students to begin drafting their stories by writing their exposition, including an exchange of dialogue between their main character and another individual. Tell them this allows them to introduce the topic of their conflict as well as their characters. Tell them to choose the point of view from which they will tell their stories and to maintain that same point of view in their drafts.

4. **Improve Your Response** Tell students that as they revise their drafts they should pay particular attention to the elements of conflict, main character, setting, and point of view. Remind them that their point of view must be consistent and that if the other elements seem weak, they should clarify and enrich them through revision.

Assess

Use the Scoring Rubric on p. 494 to assess students' essays.

COMMON CORE FOCUS

SL 1b, d Work with peers to promote civil discussions and decision-making, set clear goals and deadlines, and establish roles; respond thoughtfully to diverse perspectives. **SL 6** Adapt speech to a variety of contexts and tasks.

SPEAK WITH A PURPOSE

Advise students to think about how their performance will affect the audience.

COMMON CORE TRAITS

Tell students that scriptwriters describe each character's traits and relationships, and provide stage directions for the cast and crew. Remind them to keep in mind the *COMMON CORE TRAITS* of a strong script.

Practice and Apply

Adapt Your Short Story

Model the Skill: MAKE THE SIGNIFICANCE OF THE EVENTS CLEAR

Have students review the following excerpt:

> "After catching their breath, David set up the movie while Nadine made the pop-corn.... David's move to Boston would be a big change for them both."

In a script, the dialogue and stage directions will relay the significance of the events. Provide students with the following adaptation:

> *[They sit and catch their breath for a moment. Nadine gives a serious look.]*
>
> **NADINE:** Well, we better enjoy our Friday night movies while they last.
>
> *[Nadine and David give each other a warm smile. David starts the DVD, while Nadine grabs a pack of popcorn from the kitchen.]*

GUIDED PRACTICE Have students adapt short stories into dialogue and stage directions.

R RESOURCE MANAGER—Copy Master
Speaking and Listening Workshop, p. 239

Speaking & Listening Workshop

Dramatizing a Script

You have probably seen actors perform in a play at school or in a local theater. Before these actors could perform, they needed a script to tell them what to say and how to act.

Complete the workshop activities in your **Reader/Writer Notebook**.

SPEAK WITH A PURPOSE	COMMON CORE TRAITS
TASK Adapt your short story into a **script**. Play the main character, and select classmates to play the other roles. Practice your script, and then present it to your class.	**A STRONG SCRIPT . . .** • develops and resolves a central conflict • uses dialogue to further the plot, reveal character traits and relationships, and develop and resolve conflicts • presents a smooth progression of events to create a coherent story • has stage directions that give guidance to the director, performers, and stage crew • conveys the significance of the events in the story

COMMON CORE

SL 1b, d Work with peers to promote civil discussions and decision-making, set clear goals and deadlines, and establish roles; respond thoughtfully to diverse perspectives. **SL 6** Adapt speech to a variety of contexts and tasks.

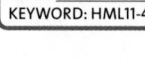

THINK central

Speaking & Listening Online

Go to **thinkcentral.com**.
KEYWORD: HML11-496

Adapt Your Short Story

Short stories and scripts are crafted differently, but they have the same goal—to tell a story. A script is the text of a play, film, or broadcast. It consists of dialogue and stage directions—the writer's instructions for the director, performers, and stage crew. Usually set in italics, they are located at the beginning of and throughout a script. Scripts are also divided into scenes. Each scene portrays a new setting.

Use the following tips and techniques to adapt your short story into a script:

• **Examine and Revise Dialogue** During a play, film, or broadcast, the only thing the audience hears is dialogue. Dialogue must further the plot, reveal character traits and relationships, develop and resolve conflicts, and convey the significance of the events. Make sure your dialogue accomplishes all of these things.

• **Add Stage Directions** Go through your short story and highlight precise words and phrases, telling details, and sensory language that convey the setting, plot details, character traits, and character relationships. Turn these details into stage directions that tell the actors how the characters should be portrayed and tell the director or stage crew how the scene should look.

• **Make the Significance of the Events Clear** Read your dialogue and stage directions. Does your script convey the significance of the events clearly? You can do this explicitly—in a direct manner—or implicitly—indirectly—through clues. These clues could include characterization, mood, symbolism, foreshadowing, and irony. Be sure to include several kinds of clues to help your audience understand the significance of your story.

DIFFERENTIATED INSTRUCTION

FOR ENGLISH LANGUAGE LEARNERS
Language: Reinforce Literary and Dramatic Terms Tell students that a short story and a script contain many of the same elements, such as plot, character, setting, and conflict. However, emphasize that because scripts are meant for a performance, other terms relate solely to scripts. Review these terms, some of which relate to both short stories and scripts, while others relate only to scripts:

• *director:* a person who directs the performance of the script

• *role:* the character that an actor or actress plays during a performance

• *stage directions:* the playwright's instructions for the director, performers, and stage crew, usually set in italics and located at the beginning of and throughout a script

• *mood:* the feeling or state of mind that the writer creates for the reader

• *symbolism:* the use of a person, place, or object to stand for something else, such as an idea or a feeling

• *foreshadowing:* a writer's use of hints or clues about events that will occur in a story

• *irony:* a contrast between what is expected and what happens, or what is said and what is meant

Present Your Script

CHOOSE TECHNIQUES FOR YOUR PERFORMANCE

As author of the story, you are the director of the performance. You should also portray the main character. Choose classmates to help you present your script and portray other characters. Read through the script with these classmates. As a group, discuss the different verbal and nonverbal techniques you should use to portray your characters. You and your classmates may disagree about the techniques. Respond respectfully to their viewpoints and try to resolve any differences. But if disagreement persists, you as the director may choose the techniques for the performance of your script.

Tips

VERBAL TECHNIQUES	NONVERBAL TECHNIQUES
• Decide what your **speaking rate** should be in various parts of the story. Base your speaking rate on the character's personality and situation. For instance, if your character is nervous, you might want to increase the rate of your speech. • **Enunciate** your words clearly and speak loudly. Even if the script instructs a character to whisper, you should whisper loudly enough so the audience can hear you.	• Remember that your character's **body language** can convey important information. For instance, if a character is hunched over and always hovering in corners, the audience may conclude that this character is shy. • Use **facial expressions** to convey your character's thoughts and emotions. For instance, an angry character may exhibit a prominent scowl.

PREPARE FOR YOUR PERFORMANCE

Review the criteria for adapting your short story into a script and the effective use of verbal and nonverbal techniques in the performance. Set clear goals for you and your classmates to work toward as you prepare for your performance. To do this, create a rubric or checklist using agreed upon criteria for evaluation. Set a deadline for when you will be ready for your performance. Rehearse your performance several times before presenting it to the class.

 YOUR TURN

As a Speaker Use the rubric as you practice. Perform your script for the class. After your performance, promote discussion with your audience by asking for their feedback about the script and the performance. Use their feedback to revise your script and adjust your performance.

As a Listener Watch another group perform a script. Use the rubric that your group developed to evaluate the performance. After the performance, offer the writer feedback on the effectiveness of the script. Also, respond respectfully when you critique the actors' performances.

497

Teach

Present Your Script

Model the Skill: **CHOOSE TECHNIQUES FOR YOUR PERFORMANCE**

Perform the following for students, using verbal and nonverbal techniques:

> *[Laura flips through the papers in her folder and then throws herself back in her chair, defeated.]*

LAURA: *Oh, no! I left my homework at home.* Point out that the stage directions add detail on how to deliver the dialogue.

GUIDED PRACTICE Have students work with a partner to create and share an original model of a verbal and nonverbal scenario.

 YOUR TURN After each performance, give the audience at least five minutes to relay feedback based on the rubric.

Assess and Reteach

Assess

Use the **Common Core Traits** to assess students' scripts and performances. A strong script:

- develops and resolves a central conflict
- uses dialogue to further the plot, reveal character traits and relationships, and develop and resolve conflicts
- presents a smooth progression of events to create a coherent story
- has stage directions that give guidance to the director, performers, and stage crew
- conveys the significance of the events in the story

Reteach

Have partners read each other's short stories and scripts to determine whether key details, such as character traits or stage directions, were left out. Then have partners work together to incorporate details into the script.

Speaking and Listening Online  THINK central

- Public speaking tips
- Strategies for effective listening

Assessment Practice

RI 1 Cite evidence to support analysis of what the text says explicitly as well as inferences drawn from the text. **RI 2** Determine two central ideas of a text and analyze their development over the course of the text. **RI 3** Analyze a sequence of events and explain how specific individuals interact and develop over the course of the text. **RI 4** Determine the meaning of words and phrases as they are used in a text, including figurative, connotative, and technical meanings. **RI 5** Analyze the effectiveness of the structure. **RI 7** Evaluate information presented in different media or formats. **W 4** Produce clear and coherent writing in which the development, organization, and style are appropriate to task, purpose, and audience. **W 5** Strengthen writing by revising and editing. **L 1** Demonstrate command of the conventions of standard English grammar and usage when writing or speaking. **L 2** Demonstrate command of the conventions of standard English capitalization, punctuation, and spelling when writing. **L 3** Apply knowledge of language to make effective choices for meaning or style.

CHECK READINESS

Read aloud the paragraph under **ASSESS,** and stress to students that this is not the full Unit Test, but a way for them to check their readiness for it. Then have students examine the skills listed under **REVIEW** and look back in the unit or in the **Student Resource Bank** for any skills they need to review.

READ THE TEXTS

Remind students to keep unit goals in mind as they read each passage, paying particular attention to these literary and reading skills:

- theme
- making inferences
- drawing conclusions
- making connections between texts

ANSWER THE QUESTIONS

Direct students to pages R96–R103 of the **Handbook** to review test-taking strategies. Remind students to:

- read directions carefully
- read all choices in multiple-choice questions rather than choosing the first alternative that seems to fit

---

COMMON CORE

Assessment Practice

ASSESS
Taking this practice test will help you assess your knowledge of these skills and determine your readiness for the Unit Test.

REVIEW
After you take the practice test, your teacher can help you identify any standards you need to review.

COMMON CORE

RI 2 Determine two central ideas of a text and analyze their development over the course of the text. **RI 3** Analyze a sequence of events and explain how specific individuals interact and develop over the course of the text. **RI 4** Determine the meaning of words and phrases as they are used in the text, including figurative and connotative meanings. **RI 7** Evaluate information presented in different media or formats. **L 1** Demonstrate command of the conventions of standard English grammar and usage when writing. **L 2** Demonstrate command of the conventions of standard English capitalization, punctuation, and spelling. **L 3** Apply knowledge of language to make effective choices for meaning or style.

Practice Test
THINK central
Take it at **thinkcentral.com**.
KEYWORD: HML11N-498

DIRECTIONS Read the two selections and the viewing and representing piece. Then answer the questions that follow.

The Daydreamer   *by Magdalena Gómez*

1   "I'm going to Spain," I announced to my Puerto Rican mother and Spanish gypsy father the night before my fourteenth birthday.

2   Looking over the top of the *Daily News*, my father, Virgilio Segarra-Fernandez, asked: "Huh?" Only one of his eardrums worked properly.

3   "To Spain. I'm going to Spain. I want to learn to dance like my grandmother. I want to see the castles in Valledolid. I want to go—"

4   "How? Your poor father doesn't even have a box to drop dead in," interrupted my mother, Lydia Segarra, as she pressed pleats into my birthday dress.

5   "I'm getting a job. Monday I can apply for working papers."

6   "No daughter of Virgilio Segarra-Fernandez is going to work. You go to school. You learn and go to college, then you can work anywhere you want," said my father, his attention going back to the *Daily News*.

7   "Your papí is right. And besides that, an educated woman doesn't have to get married if she doesn't want to."

8   Papí gave Mamí one of those serious looks of his when she said that. The air was getting thick and I thought maybe Papí's neck veins might start getting wiggly, so I just shut up.

9   That night, I hated my Castro Convertible bed in the living room more than ever. I would be fourteen years old in a matter of hours and didn't even have my own room. The radiator pipes played poor-people music all night long. Clink, clank, clunk, pssssst . . . clunk, clink, pssst, clank; Doña Rosa's French poodle tap-danced on the linoleum upstairs, and mice held their nightly festivals inside the walls. That was it! I'd had it! I was going to school *and* getting a job, and not just any job either. I was going to be a cashier in a supermarket. I would start by packing groceries and work my way up.

10 I took my notebook and a flashlight into bed and wrote down everything I had to do to get ready. The first thing was to talk my father into it; next, polish my dress shoes; next, practice my cursive for the job application; next, straighten my hair with big rollers so it wouldn't look frizzy—nobody who worked in the supermarket had frizzy hair, except the cleaning guy, Don Luis, and he was really old. He had fake teeth and would put them in his mouth weird to make us kids laugh. I secretly wished he was my grandfather, since I never had one. Anyway, I filled two pages in my notebook, no skipping lines, and fell asleep like I was dead.

11 In the morning, my mother sang "Happy Birthday" in Spanish and told me to take a good bath, brush my teeth, and braid my hair because all the family from

---

DIFFERENTIATED INSTRUCTION

FOR ENGLISH LANGUAGE LEARNERS
Assessment Practice: Work Backward
Prepare students by having them read the questions *before* reading the passages. Have pairs find unfamiliar words in test directions and questions and follow these steps:

1. Write each word on an index card.
2. Look up the meaning in a dictionary and write it on the back of the card.
3. Use the cards to practice the words with your partner and to teach them to others.

Culture: Clarify Tell students that both the fiction and the nonfiction piece are set in New York City. Point out to students that in a large city, many different cultures may coexist. People of the same culture often form their own ethnically rich communities, which helps people maintain their cultural identity but can also foster intolerance between people of different cultures. Notice that the narrator and her family members are comfortable using both English and Spanish (lines 7–8, 20, and 28).

her side was coming for my birthday. My father didn't have a family in the Bronx. They all lived in Spain and didn't believe in taking airplanes. They were just scared of them, like my father was, but I pretended that I didn't know so that he wouldn't be embarrassed.

12   None of my friends from school were coming, except Amparo, because my mother thought they were all a bunch of good-for-nothings. Amparo lived with her strict grandmother and had to stay home all the time, just like me. I liked Amparo, but she was so pretty I always felt fat and ugly around her. All the boys liked her, but she had to act like she didn't care or her grandmother would have an attack of nerves. I *really* didn't care, because all I could think about was being a cashier in a pink uniform with my name embroidered on the pocket. I would do the embroidery myself. No plastic name tags for me. Sometimes you just have to be different or you feel boring.

13   I did all my birthday stuff, put on my dress, and waited in the kitchen for everybody to show up. The first one to arrive was Tía Consuelo. I saw the soft package under her flabby arm and I knew she had knitted me another hat with *lentejuelas* on it, those big tacky sequins. The kind of hat I wouldn't wear if my hair looked like Brillo and it was minus 100 degrees. God knows, I would never get a job wearing *that*. I thought to myself that when I did get that job, and I knew that I would, I would buy my own birthday presents, and a real fine hat made of velvet, the kind that is so soft it makes me want to cry.

14   A whole gang of cousins showed up, all of them too young or too old to play with. I got all kinds of presents: toys I had outgrown or clothes I'd have to grow into, but nothing that would help me get a job. One nice dress from my mother, a little too pink, good for a party, not for a job. I drank soda and ate cake, ice cream, candy—all the stuff my mom won't let me eat until I finish all my vegetables and what she calls "real food." No vegetables on my birthday; that was the best part. There was lots of real food, but with so many people to entertain, my mother didn't notice if I ate it or not.

15   Some neighbors showed up and told jokes that I didn't think were funny, but I laughed anyway. I didn't want to hurt their feelings. Grownups get hurt really easily and then they get mad. So everybody laughed, played music, and had a good time. Nobody seemed to really care if I was there or not, or if I was really happy. I was just the excuse for them to have a party.

16   It didn't matter. All I could think about was my new job that I didn't have yet.

17   When I got to school on Monday, I went to the guidance counselor, Mrs. Mason, to see about working papers. Mrs. Mason said my parents would have to sign them. I told her about my supermarket idea, and she said I should try babysitting

GO ON →

ITEM ANALYSIS

COMPREHENSION AND WRITTEN RESPONSE	ITEMS	UNIT PAGES
Theme	1, 10	369, 379, 382–384
Imagery	4, 12, 14	319, 320
Author's Perspective	12, 13, 15, 16, 18	403
Inferences	16–18	323, 349, 351, 363

VOCABULARY	ITEMS	UNIT PAGES
Context Clues	17	369, 379

WRITING AND GRAMMAR	ITEMS	UNIT PAGES
Adjective Clauses	3	372, 377

Practice Test

On **thinkcentral.com** students can complete an interactive version of this practice test *and* receive remediation for the skills they have not yet mastered.

FOR STRUGGLING READERS

Assessment Support Consider these options for completing the Assessment Practice:

- Have students "work backward" to review the test questions *before* reading the passages.
- Select random questions in the Assessment, and have students demonstrate *how* and *where* to look for the answers.
- Ask students to locate unfamiliar vocabulary words in the Assessment. Elicit the words' meanings from the class.
- Have students record useful testing words and definitions in their journals for later reference.
- Read the selections or parts of them aloud to aid in student comprehension.

first because she didn't think I was old enough to handle money. I told her I was an "A" student in math, and she just cleared her throat and adjusted her glasses. I said, "Thank you very much" and put my working papers in my sock, since I had left my book bag in class.

18   I went back to class and got in trouble during Social Studies. The teacher, Mr. Moss, said I was daydreaming and that I could do that on my own time. He said daydreamers don't get into college. I told him, "Yes, you're right. They become Albert Einstein." He turned beet red and sent me to the principal's office.

19   Outside Mr. No-Neck's office (his real name was Mr. Nobeck) the walls were the color of *café con leche* that's a little too strong, and there was one of those "Do Your Best" kind of posters on the wall with phony smiling kids on it.

20   I have to admit, I was sweating. If my parents ever found out I was kicked out of class, there's no way I'd get either of them to sign my working papers, not to mention the scolding I'd get. My mother would scream and my father would give me the silent treatment, then they'd scream at each other. "She's *your* daughter," my mother would yell. My father would sit there, his neck veins getting wiggly, thinking of something to say, and once he said it, World War Three would break out, and all the neighbors would know everything I'd done wrong since the day I was born.

21   Mr. No-Neck came out of his office and called me in. "Miss Segarra, I hear you have a very smart mouth. Mr. Moss is very upset. His note also says you were daydreaming in class," No-Neck said, trying hard to sound like he doesn't come from the Bronx.

22   "I didn't mean to be smart, and I was just thinking," I mumbled, my eyes looking down at my scuffed shoes.

23   "Thinking? And about exactly *what* were you thinking?" he asked, poking holes in the air with his finger.

24   "My job. The one I'm going to get, I mean, at the supermarket; I'm going to be a cashier and save money so I can go to Spain," I said, looking at his veiny nose.

25   "Spain? Why Spain?" He seemed really interested.

26   "Because that's where my father's from. I want to see the castles and learn to dance like my grandmother." I forgot I was nervous.

27   "You want to dance the flamingo?"

28   "No, I want to dance *flamenco*. No offense, Mr. Nobeck, but flamingo is a bird."

29   I couldn't help myself. I was tired of people getting away with that *flamingo* thing. It's like calling Puerto Rico Porto Reek-o. I bit my lip and waited for No-Neck to blow his top.

30   "Well, Miss Segarra, it seems you do indeed have a smart mouth, and I'm not so sure that's such a bad thing." He said it very softly. I got sweaty-suspicious. "How do you say it, fla-mink-ko?" he asked sincerely.

31   "No. *Fla-men-co*," I said slowly. "Fla-maine-co. Fla-man-co. Flamenco." He kept trying until he got it. Then he got quiet for a really long time. I got nervous

500

DIFFERENTIATED INSTRUCTION

FOR STRUGGLING READERS

Test Preparation Explain to students that if they develop a system for test preparation, they will not need to spend an excessive amount of time cramming for a test. Present students with the following strategies for test preparation:

- Read over the syllabus to determine when your exams will be. Mark these dates on a calendar.

- Take thorough notes during class and review on a weekly basis. Make sure to do this as a few short review sessions, rather than one long review session.

- Invite other students to join you in your review sessions.

- Make flashcards as you learn new information. Reviewing these flashcards for a few minutes a day will keep the information fresh in your mind and prepare you for the test, without forcing you to commit huge blocks of time to studying.

again. "It's too bad you have your heart set on that supermarket job." As he spoke, his right pointer finger was bouncing off his lips.

32 "How come?" I asked.

33 "Well, some of the seniors could use a Spanish tutor after school."

34 "Seniors?" I gulped.

35 "Yes. They need a tutor so that *they* don't go around saying *flamingo* when they mean *flamenco*. But I don't suppose you'd be interested." Nobeck looked out his window.

36 "Maybe. What does the job pay?" I asked in my best business voice.

37 "Two dollars an hour," he said in a very flat voice, looking me dead in the eyes now.

38 My mind raced between Don Luis and his funny teeth and my name embroidered on the pink smock, and all the work I had done to prepare for my big interview.

39 "I would be happy to speak with your parents. We must have their permission," he said.

40 I figured he had a better chance talking my parents into it than I would, since grownups listen to each other more often than they listen to kids. "Okay, Mr. Nobeck, I'll try it." The thought of tutoring seniors made my stomach quake. "How many hours a week?" I asked, trying hard to act cool.

41 "An hour and a half, three times a week."

42 "That's only nine dollars a week." I felt limp.

43 "That's right."

44 "How many weeks?"

45 "Thirty. It's for the whole rest of the school year."

46 "That's two hundred seventy dollars." I was showing off how good my math was.

47 "Correct. Well?" He was standing up now.

48 "It's a deal."

49 I shook his hand. There was no turning back now. My parents had taught me that a handshake is your word of honor. They would have to sign the papers now, they would never, ever want me to go back on my word. I liked that about my parents. I didn't always like what they said, and I still hated vegetables and hats with lentejuelas, and my father's wiggly veins, and my mother's screaming, but they weren't so bad. They always kept their word. They just didn't remember how hard it was to be fourteen. Getting the rent paid was hard enough.

50 Nobeck said goodbye and added, "Einstein said that imagination is better than knowledge. I'm sure you'll get to Spain, Miss Segarra. And stay out of trouble. Don't stop daydreaming, just don't do it in class. And I expect you to apologize to Mr. Moss." His hands were in his pockets now.

51 "Yes, Mr. Nobeck. Thank you."

52 I left thinking about going to Puerto Rico next. Maybe I would invite Amparo. In my mind, I embroidered my name in the sky.

GO ON ▶

501

The Secret Latina

by Veronica Chambers
from Essence, July 2000

1   She's a platanos-frying, malta Dukesa-drinking, salsa-dancing Mamacita—my dark-skinned Panamanian mother. She came to this country when she was 21, her sense of culture intact, her Spanish flawless. Even today, more than 20 years since she left her home country to become an American citizen, my mother still considers herself Panamanian and checks 'Hispanic' on census forms.

2   As a Black woman in America, my Latin identity is murkier than my mother's, despite the fact that I, too, was born in Panama, and call that country 'home.' My father's parents came from Costa Rica and Jamaica, my mother's from Martinique. I left Panama when I was 2 years old. My family lived in England for three years then came to the States when I was 5. Having dark skin and growing up in Brooklyn in the 1970's meant I was Black, period. You could meet me and not know I was of Latin heritage. Without a Spanish last name or my mother's fluent Spanish at my disposal, I often felt isolated from the Latin community.

3   I found it almost impossible to explain to my elementary-school friends why my mother would speak Spanish at home. They would ask if I was Puerto Rican and look bewildered when I told them I was not. To them, Panama was a kind of nowhere. There weren't enough Panamanians in Brooklyn to be a force. Everybody knew where Jamaicans were from because of famous singers like Bob Marley. Panamanians had Ruben Blades, but most of my friends thought he was Puerto Rican, too.

4   In my neighborhood, where the smell of somebody's grandmother's cooking could transform a New York corner into Santo Domingo, Kingston or Port-au-Prince, a Panamanian was a sort of fish with feathers—assumed to be a Jamaican who spoke Spanish. The analogy was not without historical basis: A century ago, Panama's Black community was largely drawn to the country from all over the Caribbean as cheap labor to build the Panama Canal.

5   My father didn't mind that we considered ourselves Black rather than Latino. He named my brother Malcolm X, and if my mother hadn't put her foot down, I would have been called Angela Davis Chambers. It's not that my mother didn't admire Angela Davis, but you have only to hear how 'Veronica Victoria' flows off her Spanish lips to know that she was homesick for Panama and for those names that sang like timbales on carnival day. So between my father and my mother was a Black-Latin divide. Because of my father, we read and discussed books about Black history and civil rights. Because of my mother, we ate Panamanian food, listened to salsa and heard Spanish at home.

502

DIFFERENTIATED INSTRUCTION

FOR STRUGGLING READERS

Strategies for Timed Tests Remind students that they will often be given only a certain amount of time to take a test. Give students the following strategies for timed test situations:

- Bring a watch with you, in case a clock is not available or in clear view.

- Preview the test before you begin. Allot a certain amount of time for each section. Note any sections that have high point values so that you can devote an adequate amount of time to these sections. Look for sections that you think will be easier for you to complete, and begin with those sections.

- Avoid spending too much time on one item. If you have difficulty answering an item, skip it and come back to it after you have answered the other items.

- If you complete the test before the time has expired, look back through your answers to check for mistakes.

6   Still, it wasn't until my parents divorced when I was 10 that my mother tried to teach Malcolm and me Spanish. She was a terrible language teacher. She had no sense of how to explain structure, and her answer to every question was "That's just the way it is." A few short weeks after our Spanish lessons began, my mother gave up and we were all relieved. But I remained intent on learning my mother's language. When she spoke Spanish, her words were a fast current, a stream of language that was colorful, passionate, fiery. I wanted to speak Spanish because I wanted to swim in the river of her words, her history, my history, too.

7   At school I dove into the language, matching what little I knew from home with all that I learned. One day, when I was in the ninth grade, I finally felt confident enough to start speaking Spanish with my mother. I soon realized that by speaking Spanish with her, I was forging an important bond. When I'd spoken only English, I was the daughter, the little girl. But when I began speaking Spanish, I became something more—a hermanita, a sisterfriend, a Panamanian homegirl who could hang with the rest of them. Eventually this bond would lead me home.

8   Two years ago, at age 27, I decided it was finally time. I couldn't wait any longer to see Panama, the place my mother and my aunts had told me stories about. I enlisted my cousin Digna as a traveling companion and we made arrangements to stay with my godparents, whom I had never met. We planned our trip for the last week in February—carnival time.

9   Panama, in Central America, is a narrow sliver of a country: You can swim in the Caribbean Sea in the morning and backstroke across the Pacific in the afternoon. As our plane touched down, bringing me home for the first time since I was 2, I felt curiously comfortable and secure. In the days that followed, there was none of the culture shock that I'd expected—I had my mother and aunts to thank for that. My godmother Olga reminded me of them. The first thing she did was book appointments for Digna and me to get our eyebrows plucked and our nails and feet done with Panamanian-style manicures and pedicures. "It's carnival," Aunt Olga said, "and you girls have to look your best." We just laughed.

10   In Panama, I went from being a lone Black girl with a curious Latin heritage to being part of the Latinegro tribe or the Afro-Antillianos, as we were officially called. I was thrilled to learn there was actually a society for people like me. Everyone was Black, everyone spoke Spanish and everyone danced the way they danced at fiesta time back in Brooklyn, stopping only to chow down on a smorgasbord of souse, rice with black-eyed peas, beef patties, empanadas and codfish fritters. The carnival itself was an all-night bacchanal with elaborate floats, brilliantly colored costumes and live musicians. In the midst of all this, my godmother took my cousin and me to a photo studio to have our pictures taken in polleras, the traditional dress. After spending an hour on makeup and hair and donning a rented costume, I looked like Scarlett in Gone With the Wind.

GO ON ➡

503

FOR STRUGGLING READERS

Justify Responses After students have answered the questions, go through the test, asking students for their response to each item. For items in which students have varying responses, have students form groups with other students who gave the same response. Have each group write a rationale for the answer, similar to the rationales given in answers on pages 506–509. Encourage groups to consider changing their response and writing a different rationale if they find that their original choice was incorrect.

11   Back in New York, I gave the photo to my mother. She almost cried. She says she was so moved to see me in a pollera because it was "such a patriotic thing to do." Her appreciation made me ridiculously happy; ever since I was a little girl, I'd wanted to be like my mother. In one of my most vivid memories, I am 7 or 8 and my parents are having a party. Salsa music is blaring and my mother is dancing and laughing. She sees me standing off in a corner, so she pulls me into the circle of grown-ups and tries to teach me how to dance to the music. Her hips are electric. She puts her hands on my sides and says, "Move these," and I start shaking my hip bones as if my life depends on it.

12   Now I am a grown woman, with hips to spare. I can salsa. My Spanish isn't shabby. You may look at me and not know that I am Panamanian, that I am an immigrant, that I am both Black and Latin. But I am my mother's daughter, a secret Latina, and that's enough for me.

DIFFERENTIATED INSTRUCTION

FOR STRUGGLING READERS

Cultural Terms To help students understand the selections and the Reading Comprehension questions, teach the following cultural terms to students:

- *cultural heritage:* the traditions and beliefs of a group of people, passed down through generations

- *cultural identity:* a person's view of him- or herself, based on the traditions and beliefs of the person's homeland or ancestral homeland

- *culture shock:* a discomfort that occurs when a person thrusts him- or herself into an unfamiliar place that has a different culture than he or she is accustomed to

Master all the **Hottest Dances!**

Salsa, Tango, Rumba, Mambo, Merengue, and more

Classes taught
by Salsa Champion

Victoria Marquez Salinas

at the Latin Dance Studio in
downtown Springville

Learn Latin Dance
for *FUN* and
EXERCISE

Sign up now!
Call **555-6759**

¡El baile latino es muy caliente!

505

Reading Comprehension

1. B is correct. In paragraph 3, the narrator describes her desire to go to her father's home country and "learn to dance like [her] grandmother." Then, in paragraph 5, she states that she will pay for it by getting a job. A and C are incorrect because the narrator never expresses a desire to do either. D is incorrect because it is not her main reason for wanting a job.

2. B is correct. In paragraph 9, the narrator complains about her circumstances and then says, "That was it! I'd had it!" Then, she brainstorms steps she must take to get a job that will change her circumstances. A is incorrect because the narrator doesn't show any excitement for her birthday in paragraphs 9 and 10. C is incorrect because the way that narrator falls asleep is only briefly mentioned. D is incorrect because the problems in the house are not the main focus.

3. D is correct. In paragraph 14, the narrator lists the junk food she eats on her birthday and says that not eating vegetables on her birthday was "the best part." A is not an event that the narrator mentions in the story. B and C are incorrect because the narrator does not enjoy the neighbors' jokes nor her cousins' presents.

4. A is correct. Firm is the opposite of flabby. B and C are incorrect because neither word is a direct opposite of flabby. D is incorrect because loose is a synonym of flabby.

5. C is correct. The extra space represents the passage of time from her birthday to going to school. A is incorrect because the author does not need to include extra space to introduce a new character. B is incorrect because a different theme is not introduced in either paragraph. D is incorrect because the narrator does not tell a story about her father in either paragraph.

6. D is correct. In paragraph 17, Mrs. Mason shares a concern about the narrator being too young "to handle money." A is incorrect because Mrs. Mason never states a concern about the narrator's intelligence. B and C are incorrect because the events stated do not occur in the story.

7. B is correct. The narrator believes the kids on the poster are acting and giving

fake smiles. A is incorrect because it is an antonym of phony. C is incorrect because phony does not relate to distance or physical location. D is incorrect because phony does not relate to sound or volume.

8. B is correct. The narrator's retort makes the teacher's face turn "beet red," and then he sends her to the principal's office (paragraph 18). A is incorrect because the teacher does not ask the narrator a question. C is incorrect because the principal does not ask to meet with the narrator. D is incorrect

because the teacher does not send her to the office for daydreaming.

9. D is correct. Mr. Nobeck shows an interest in the narrator's knowledge of the pronunciation. A is incorrect because even after the narrator says "flamenco," it takes him several tries to pronounce it correctly. B is incorrect because Mr. Nobeck was not offended by the correction; he wanted to learn how to say it. C is incorrect because Mr. Nobeck acknowledges her response to his mispronunciation.

Reading Comprehension

> Use "The Daydreamer" (pp. 498–501) to answer questions 1–11.

1. The main reason the narrator wants to get a job is —
   A. to help her family survive
   B. to travel and learn about her heritage
   C. to pay for college
   D. to buy herself a birthday present

2. Paragraphs 9 and 10 are mainly about —
   A. how excited the narrator is for her birthday
   B. the narrator's desire to change her circumstances
   C. how the narrator falls asleep
   D. the problems in the narrator's house

3. For the girl, the highlight of her birthday party is —
   A. her friends singing Happy Birthday in Spanish
   B. laughing at her neighbors' jokes
   C. receiving presents from her cousins
   D. eating only what she wants

4. An antonym for *flabby* in paragraph 13 is —
   A. firm
   B. healthy
   C. loose
   D. strong

5. The author inserts an extra space between paragraphs 16 and 17 to —
   A. introduce a new character
   B. write about a different theme
   C. indicate a passage of time
   D. tell a story about the father

6. In paragraph 17, the narrator tells the guidance counselor that she is an A student in math because —
   A. the counselor doesn't think she is smart enough to get a job
   B. the narrator is sharing part of her resume with the counselor
   C. the counselor is trying to convince the parents to let the narrator get a job
   D. the narrator is showing she can be responsible with money

7. In paragraph 19, *phony* means —
   A. authentic
   B. false
   C. distant
   D. loud

8. The narrator is sent out of class because —
   A. she will not answer the teacher's question
   B. she has embarrassed the teacher
   C. the principal wants to talk to her about a job
   D. she is not paying attention

9. Mr. Nobeck, the principal, doesn't get angry with the narrator when she corrects his pronunciation because —
   A. he was just testing her
   B. she said "No offense."
   C. he didn't hear her clearly
   D. she knew what she was talking about

10. Which of the following sentences from the selection best expresses a theme of the story?
    A. You learn and go to college, then you can work anywhere you want.
    B. It's too bad you have your heart set on that supermarket job.
    C. Einstein said that imagination is better than knowledge.
    D. My parents had taught me that a handshake is your word of honor.

11. The narrator ends the story talking about Puerto Rico because —
    A. she has already made it to Spain in her mind
    B. it is cheaper to go to Puerto Rico than to Spain
    C. her friend Amparo is from Puerto Rico
    D. she is bored in class

> Use "The Secret Latina" (pp. 502–504) to answer questions 12–17.

12. Paragraph 1 is mainly about —
    A. the eating and drinking habits of Panamanians
    B. the mother's cultural identity
    C. the requirements to be "Hispanic" on the census form
    D. how long it takes to become an American citizen

13. In paragraph 2, the author says she considered herself Black because —
    A. there weren't many Panamanians living in Brooklyn
    B. she didn't have a Latin last name
    C. other Latinos disliked Panamanians
    D. she was a Latina with dark skin

14. The expression "a sort of fish with feathers" in paragraph 4 means —
    A. a person new to a neighborhood
    B. an unfamiliar combination of two familiar qualities
    C. an everyday sight
    D. a name for Jamaicans who speak Spanish

15. The father teaches his children about Black history and civil rights because —
    A. he wants to teach them about his new identity
    B. the mother wants the children to know about both cultures
    C. he knows the mother can't teach them Spanish
    D. the children consider themselves Black

16. In paragraph 9, the reader can conclude that the author didn't experience culture shock because —
    A. she had been taught about the culture and language
    B. she wasn't in Panama very long
    C. her relatives planned everything for her
    D. she went with her cousin

17. In paragraph 10, the word *smorgasbord* means —
    A. one plate with lots of food
    B. a buffet of hot and cold dishes
    C. a party where food is served
    D. a type of Panamanian food

GO ON ➡

10. **C is correct.** *In paragraph 50, Mr. Nobeck encourages the narrator to pursue her dreams. A is incorrect because a college education is not the main focus of the story. B is incorrect because, although the narrator's desire for the job is a catalyst for the theme, the theme does not center around the job. D is incorrect because the significance of a handshake is a minor point in the story.*

11. **A is correct.** *Now that the narrator has a job to pay for her trip to Spain, she begins planning her next trip. B, C, and D are not supported by information in the selection.*

12. **B is correct.** *Paragraph 1 focuses on aspects of the mother's cultural identity, such as her salsa dancing. A is incorrect because the focus is on the narrator's mother, rather than all Panamanians. C and D are incorrect because census forms and citizenship are not the main focus of the paragraph.*

13. **D is correct.** *In paragraph 2, the narrator states that she was considered Black in her community because of her dark skin. A and B are true, but they are not the reasons that the narrator considered herself Black. C is not supported by information in the selection.*

14. **B is correct.** *In paragraph 4, the narrator states that because Panamanians were dark skinned, people thought they were Jamaicans who spoke Spanish—an unfamiliar combination of two familiar qualities. A is incorrect because the narrator was not new to the neighborhood. C is incorrect because a "fish with feathers" is not an everyday sight. D is incorrect because the term refers to Panamanians, not Jamaicans.*

15. **D is correct.** *In paragraph 5, the narrator says that their father "didn't mind that [they] considered [themselves] Black" and that he taught them about Black history. A, B, and C are not supported by information in the selection.*

16. **A is correct.** *The narrator heard Spanish growing up and learned to speak the language with her mother as a teen, and her mother and aunts told her stories about Panama. B and D are true, but not the reasons why the narrator did not experience culture shock. C is incorrect because the narrator does not indicate that her relatives' plans for her prevented culture shock.*

DIFFERENTIATED INSTRUCTION

FOR ENGLISH LANGUAGE LEARNERS
Assessment Vocabulary To help students understand the Comprehension questions, teach or review these vocabulary words:

- Item 3: *highlight*—the most important or best part
- Item 6: *résumé*—a written compilation of a person's work experience, education, and applicable skills, presented to prospective employers in hopes of a job offer
- Item 9: *pronunciation*—the manner of pronouncing, or saying, a word
- Item 17: *buffet*—a meal composed of various kinds of food, set out for guests to serve themselves
- Item 21: *impact*—significance of an effect

ASSESSMENT PRACTICE **507**

ANSWERS

17. B is correct. *A variety of different kinds of food were available for everyone at the carnival. A is incorrect because there was more than just one plate of food. C is incorrect because* smorgasbord *does not refer to the type of party. D is incorrect because the narrator refers to more than one type of food.*

18. C is correct. *Both narrators hope that they will learn more about their cultural heritage by visiting the country of their ancestors. A is incorrect because the narrators were able to learn the language. B is incorrect because parents in "The Secret Latina" help the narrator understand her identity. D is incorrect because neither narrator focuses on school being necessary for travel.*

19. C is correct. *The advertisement offers different types of dance lessons for fun and exercise. A is incorrect because there are other Latin dances taught besides the tango. B and D are incorrect because the advertisement is not about lighting or costumes.*

20. D is correct. *Stating that the teacher is a salsa dancing champion shows that she really knows what she is doing. A, B, and C are incorrect because other dance studios can offer these opportunities.*

SHORT CONSTRUCTED RESPONSE

Possible responses:

21. *Mr. Nobeck takes the time to listen to her dreams and provide her with a way to achieve them. Her family dismisses her dream because of a lack of money. The guidance counselor suggests an easier job without knowing why she wants a job. The teacher assumes that college will help her achieve her goals.*

22. *Although the narrator looks Black, she is Latina. However, for many years she didn't know what that meant. After she visits Panama, she puts the pieces of her cultural identity together. Learning about her Latina identity changes her relationship with her mother. She is no longer only a daughter—she is "a hermanita, a sisterfriend," and her mother's appreciation makes her "ridiculously happy."*

---

18. The narrators of both selections would probably agree that —
  - **A.** Spanish is a difficult language to learn
  - **B.** parents don't understand their children
  - **C.** culture is an important part of identity
  - **D.** school is necessary for travel

19. The purpose of the photograph on the poster is most likely to —
  - **A.** teach how to dance the tango
  - **B.** emphasize the importance of dramatic lighting
  - **C.** inspire viewers to take a dance class
  - **D.** model proper dance costuming

20. Which of these elements of the poster supports the dance studio's credibility?
  - **A.** *Come Learn All the Hottest Dances*
  - **B.** *Salsa, Tango, Rumba, Mambo, Merengue, and more*
  - **C.** *Learn to Dance for Fun, for Exercise*
  - **D.** *Classes taught by Salsa Champion Victoria Marquez Salinas*

SHORT CONSTRUCTED RESPONSE
Write a short constructed response to each question, using text evidence to support your response.

21. Who do you think has the greatest impact on the narrator of "The Daydreamer"? Support your response with evidence from the selection.

22. In what ways is "The Secret Latina" about discovering one's cultural heritage? In what ways is it about the changing relationship between a parent and child? Support your response with evidence from the selection.

Write a short constructed response to the following question, using text evidence from both selections to support your response.

23. What is one characteristic shared by both narrators? Support your response with evidence from **both** selections.

---

23. *Both narrators believe that visiting a country from which their family came will help them connect with a piece of their family's culture. In "The Daydreamer" the narrator wants to go to Spain to see and do things her grandmother did. She doesn't know much about her father's side of the family because they don't like traveling by plane.*

In "The Secret Latina" the narrator admires her mother and the way she uses language. However, she feels isolated from the local Latin community because of her non-Spanish last name and her lack of Spanish language skills. Learning Spanish and visiting Panama enhance her Latin heritage.

Revising and Editing

DIRECTIONS Read this passage and answer the questions that follow.

---

(1) The honeybee is well known for its production of honey and beeswax. (2) It is also renowned, however, for its exceptional memory and its language system, which is complex. (3) The honeybee has an excellent short-term memory. (4) It remembers where the best food sources are and knows when their quality is best. (5) The honeybee locates these food sources by remembering the color and scent of the flowers. (6) The honeybee forms a short-term memory of the flower's color. (7) It converts this initial memory to a long-term memory through a biological process. (8) Even after winter hibernation, these foragers go right to the flowers they visited the summer before. (9) One group of honeybees was even able to fly through a maze!

---

1. What change, if any, should be made in sentence 1?

A. Change *its* to **it's**

B. Change *beeswax* to **beezwax**

C. Insert a comma after *honey*

D. Make no change

2. What is the most effective way to revise sentence 2?

A. It is also renowned, however, for its exceptional memory and complex language system.

B. It is also renowned, however, for its exceptional memory; also, its language system is complex.

C. It is also renowned, however, for its exceptional memory and has a language system that is complex.

D. It is also renowned, however, for its memory, which is exceptional, and it has a complex language system.

3. What is the most effective way to add details to sentence 5 using an adjective clause?

A. The honeybee dutifully locates these food sources by remembering the color and scent of the flowers.

B. The honeybee locates these food sources by remembering the rich color and aromatic scent of the flowers.

C. The honeybee locates these food sources by remembering the color and scent of the flowers that provide the best pollen and nectar.

D. The honeybee locates these food sources by remembering the best pollen and nectar food sources and the color and scent of the flowers.

4. What is the most effective way to improve the organization of the paragraph?

A. Move sentence 1 to the end of the paragraph

B. Switch sentences 8 and 9

C. Delete sentence 9

D. Switch sentences 6 and 7

 STOP

509

DIFFERENTIATED INSTRUCTION

FOR STRUGGLING READERS

Assessment Support: Participles and Parallelism

- Review with students that a participle is a verb form that is used as an adjective and ends with *–ed* or *–ing*. A participle modifies a noun or pronoun.

- Ask students to identify participles in the first sentence of "The Secret Latina." *(platanos-frying, malta Dukesa-drinking, salsa-dancing)*

- Review that parallelism is the repetition of words or phrases in the same grammatical form to link ideas; for example, "I wasn't sure when they left, where they went, or why they disappeared."

- Have students find an example of parallelism in the last paragraph of "The Secret Latina." *("...and not know that I am Panamanian, that I am an immigrant, that I am both Black and Latin. But I am my mother's daughter, a secret Latina, and that's enough for me.")*

INTRODUCE *GREAT READS*

In Unit 2, students have discussed a number of big questions. Invite students to tell which question they found most intriguing and why, and then focus attention on the four that appear on pages 510–511. Discuss the recommended books and their summaries, pointing out how each connects to the related question. Encourage students to choose one or more of these "great reads" to read independently.

UNIT 2
Great Reads

Ideas for Independent Reading

Continue exploring the Questions of the Times on pages 302–303 with these additional works.

Is the price of progress ever TOO HIGH?

Rip Van Winkle and Other Stories
by Washington Irving

Behind the high jinks and folklore of the stories in this collection, there lurks a mingled sense of wonder and worry at the rapid changes taking place in America in the early 19th century. In the title tale, for example, Rip Van Winkle falls asleep in a British colony and wakes 20 years later in a new nation, his village's statue of King George replaced with one of George Washington. With insight and humor, Irving makes a profound social comment on the changes taking place in his time.

The Last of the Mohicans
by James Fenimore Cooper

The hero of this story, Natty Bumppo, lives on the borderline between two cultures—admired by both Indians and whites, but truly at home with neither. Here, Natty and his Indian friend Chingachgook escort two British maidens through hostile territory during the French and Indian War. Breathtaking chases and gun battles ensue. Yet through the course of the story a deeper theme emerges: that the United States, in its desire for wealth, may have forsaken the rewards of living in harmony with nature.

Is it patriotic to protest one's GOVERNMENT?

Uncle Tom's Cabin
by Harriet Beecher Stowe

Written toward the end of the romantic period, Stowe's novel changed history. Appalled by the institution of slavery, Stowe set out to make whites see slaves as human beings—mothers, fathers, children, *people* with hearts and souls like any other. Her work became immensely popular and did in fact influence opinions and garner support for the abolitionist movement. Indeed, the novel had so great an impact that it has often been cited as one of the causes of the Civil War.

The Night Thoreau Spent in Jail
by Jerome Lawrence and Robert E. Lee

Issues of moral and civic responsibility take center stage in this play dramatizing the risks Thoreau took to follow his conscience. As the curtain rises, Thoreau is behind bars—his punishment for committing an act of civil disobedience. When Ralph Waldo Emerson visits, Thoreau challenges him to defy a government that fosters injustice.

The Poetry of John Greenleaf Whittier: A Readers' Edition
by John Greenleaf Whittier

John Greenleaf Whittier was committed to using poetry to bring about social reform. This anthology includes several poems that explore the evils of slavery. One such poem, "Ichabod," savaged real-life senator Daniel Webster for his support of the Missouri Compromise and the Fugitive Slave Act.

510

COMMON CORE

RL 10 Read and comprehend literature. **RI 10** Read and comprehend literary nonfiction.

Does everyone have a
"DARK SIDE"?

The Fall of the House of Usher and Other Writings
by Edgar Allan Poe

Does everyone have a "dark side"? Over and over again, Poe answered that question with a resounding yes. In so doing, he helped establish the modes of horror and fantasy, which to this day dominate much of American culture. For an overview of the best of Poe's writing, this edition is the book to read. Murderous delusions, decadent appetites, and unspeakable cruelty pepper the stories and poems found here.

The House of the Seven Gables
by Nathaniel Hawthorne

This gothic romance tells of the Pyncheon family (owners of "the house of the seven gables"), whose ancestor Colonel Pyncheon has cursed them with his wicked deeds. In the book's preface, Hawthorne conveys its theme: "The wrong-doing of one generation lives into the successive ones, and . . . becomes a pure and uncontrollable mischief."

American Gothic Tales
edited by Joyce Carol Oates

Oates's anthology of haunting tales shows the far reaches of the gothic imagination in American literature. The collection includes short stories from over 40 of the best American horror writers of the past 200 years, ranging from Washington Irving to Stephen King.

Where do people look for
TRUTH?

The Portable Thoreau
by Henry David Thoreau

An icon of individualism, Henry David Thoreau looked for the truth in two main places: nature and himself. Generations of readers have concluded not only that those are good places to search for the truth, but also that Thoreau—for all his peculiarities—did a fine job of finding it. This edition contains the full text of *Walden*, as well as poems, notebooks, journal entries, and essays such as "Civil Disobedience." These works allow readers to see past the confident sage of Walden to the prickly, affectionate, politically motivated man beneath.

The Essential Transcendentalists
edited by Richard G. Geldard

America's best transcendentalist thinkers and writers grappled with many questions of their day: What is woman's role in society? When and how should a person protest the government? How can we live ethical lives? Where can one find the truth? The works in this collection explore these and many other ideas as relevant today as they were nearly 200 years ago.

Get Novel Wise

THINK central

Go to **thinkcentral.com**.
KEYWORD: HML11-511

NovelWise

The keyword on this page points to **NovelWise**, a Web site that helps students choose a novel or other book-length work to read. **NovelWise** also provides

- study guides
- reading strategies and literary elements instruction
- presentations to introduce classic novels
- project ideas

COMMON CORE — UNIT GOALS

Included in this unit: **RL 1, RL 2, RL 3, RL 4, RL 5, RL 7, RL 8, RL 9, RL 10, RI 1, RI 2, RI 3, RI 4, RI 5, RI 6, RI 8, RI, 9, RI 10, W 1, W 1b, W 2a–f, W 3, W 3d, W 4, W 5, W 6, W 7, W 8, W 9, W 9b, W 10, SL 1, SL 1a, SL 1c, SL 1d, SL 2, SL 4, SL 5, SL 6, L 1, L 1a, L 1b, L 2, L 2b, L 3, L 3a, L 4, L 4a, L 4b, L 4d, L 5, L 5a, L 6**

Complete text of the Common Core State Standards is found in the correlation on p. T10. Standards covered in this unit are found in the standards overview (pp. 513A -513D) and on the lesson pages where they are taught..

Preview Unit Goals

This page presents an overview of the skills and strategies covered in this unit. Explain to students that they can get more from their reading by previewing. Then ask them to skim the page to preview the skills that they will learn. Note that each strand or category of skill is color-coded on this page and throughout the unit.

Model the strategy of copying the Academic Vocabulary and writing a preliminary definition for each term. Suggest that students use their **Reader/Writer Notebooks** for this purpose. Encourage them to use the terms in discussions and in writing. Also urge students to revisit each term throughout the unit and to refine its meaning.

UNIT 3

COMMON CORE — Preview Unit Goals

TEXT ANALYSIS	• Understand the historical and cultural contexts of romanticism and realism; understand realism as a literary movement • Analyze tone • Analyze and evaluate free verse • Analyze elements of style, including tone, sentence structure, figurative language, and dialogue • Analyze the styles of Whitman and Dickinson • Analyze narrative elements, including theme, structure, conflict, and characterization • Analyze primary sources • Analyze author's purpose • Evaluate the structure and reasoning used in a work
READING	• Take notes; synthesize information
WRITING AND LANGUAGE	• Make effective word choices; use vivid verbs • Use language that conveys tone • Write an informative article
VOCABULARY	• Use knowledge of Latin roots to understand word meaning
ACADEMIC VOCABULARY	• element • emphasis • conflict • create • perspective
MEDIA AND VIEWING	• Compare and contrast print and film versions of a work • Maintain an online feature article

Find It Online!
Go to **thinkcentral.com** for the interactive version of this unit.

DIFFERENTIATED INSTRUCTION

FOR ENGLISH LANGUAGE LEARNERS

Academic Vocabulary Provide students with definitions for these Academic Vocabulary words.

conflict (kŏnflĭkt) *n.* a struggle or clash between people, ideas, or interests. *v.* (kən-flĭkt) to be in opposition; differ

create (krē-āt) *v.* to make or cause; to produce through artistic effort

element (ĕlə-mənt) *n.* a basic or essential part of something

emphasis (ĕmfə-sĭs) *n.* special attention or effort directed toward something; stress on a syllable, word, or words

perspective (pər-spĕktĭv) *n.* particular way of looking at something; point of view

Additional Academic Vocabulary Use the copy master to help students learn academic words they will use in subsequent lessons and on the Assessment Practice.

R RESOURCE MANAGER—Copy Masters
Academic Vocabulary p. 3
Additional Academic Vocabulary p. 4

Frederick Douglass

From Romanticism to Realism 1855–1870

AN AGE OF TRANSITION
- **Brilliant Mavericks: Whitman and Dickinson**
- **Literature of the Civil War**

Media Smart DVD-ROM

From Page to Screen
View a film version of "An Occurrence at Owl Creek Bridge" that evokes the dark-hued themes of Ambrose Bierce. Page 618

For help in planning this unit, see

R RESOURCE MANAGER UNIT 3
pp. 1–10

INTRODUCE THE UNIT
Call students' attention to the pictures on this page. Explain that the large picture, *Union Soldiers Fighting in the Field,* is a painting by Albert Bierstadt. Point out that it depicts the Civil War, a turning point in American life, and that students will be reading literature of the Civil War later in this unit.

Ask students if they know of Frederick Douglass (c. 1817–1895), the author shown in the smaller picture. Explain that Douglass was born into slavery but escaped to freedom as a young man. He became active in the antislavery cause as a writer, editor, and speaker. Tell students that they will read an excerpt from his autobiography later in this unit. Also note that students can read more about Douglass on page 558.

About the Art Artist Albert Bierstadt (1830–1902) was born in Germany but came to the United States with his family at the age of two. As an artist, he gained fame for his large, inspiring landscapes of the American West as well as for his Civil War scenes. *Union Soldiers Fighting in the Field* realistically portrays Union soldiers taking aim at Confederate cavalrymen on the far side of the field. The anonymity of the soldiers and the setting makes the viewer feel that these soldiers could be anyone, in any place. The landscape is idyllic and the cottage appears peaceful; in reality, however, the scene is one of destruction.

Unit Resources

See resources on the **Teacher One Stop DVD-ROM** and on **thinkcentral.com**.

R RESOURCE MANAGER UNIT 3

UNIT AND BENCHMARK TEST

BEST PRACTICES TOOLKIT

INTERACTIVE READER

ADAPTED INTERACTIVE READER

ELL ADAPTED INTERACTIVE READER

LANGUAGE HANDBOOK

VOCABULARY PRACTICE

TECHNOLOGY
- **Teacher One Stop DVD-ROM**
- **Student One Stop DVD-ROM**
- **PowerNotes DVD-ROM**
- **WriteSmart CD-ROM**
- **MediaSmart DVD-ROM**
- **GrammarNotes DVD-ROM**
- **Audio Anthology CD**

Find It Online!
This unit on **thinkcentral.com** includes
- **PowerNotes** introductions to key selections
- audio support—listen or download
- **ThinkAloud** models
- **WordSharp** vocabulary tutorials
- interactive unit review and assessment

513

UNIT 3

ECOS

Unit 3 Introduction
pp. 512–527
• Questions of the Times
• Historical Essay
• Timeline
• Legacy of the Civil War Era
American Masterpieces: *from* **The Red Badge of Courage**
Novel
pp. 600–601

ECOS

Text Analysis Workshops
• Form and Content in Poetry
pp. 528–529
• Realism pp. 598–599

ECOS

Selected Poetry
by Walt Whitman
Themes Across Cultures: Ode to Walt Whitman
Poetry
pp. 530–545

STRAND			
Reading Literature	Historical and Cultural Context of the Transition from Romanticism to Realism pp. 514–523 **RL 9** Text Analysis pp. 600–601 **RI 2** Theme p. 601	Traditional and Organic Poetic Forms pp. 528–529 **RL 1, RL 5, RL 10** Realism pp. 598–599 **RL 2, RL 3**	Free Verse pp. 531–532, 534–536, 538–539, 541 **RL 4, RL 5** Analyze Tone pp. 531–532, 534–539, 541 **RL 1, RL 4** Language Coach p. 536 **RL 4** Figurative Language pp. 542–545 **RL 4**
Reading Informational Text	Historical and Cultural Context of the Transition from Romanticism to Realism pp. 514–523 **RI 9** Read a Timeline pp. 524–525 **RI 7**		Read an Essay p. 540
Writing	Legacy of the Era pp. 526–527		
Speaking and Listening	Legacy of the Era pp. 526–527 **SL 1** Discuss p. 600 **SL 1a, SL 4**		Discuss p. 531 **SL 1, SL 2**
Language		Realism pp. 598–599 **L 3a**	Figurative Language pp. 542–545 **L 5** Language Coach p. 536 **L 4**

Selected Poetry by Emily Dickinson
Poetry
pp. 546–556

from **Narrative of the Life of Frederick Douglass, an American Slave**
Slave Narrative
pp. 558–571

from **Incidents in the Life of a Slave Girl**
Slave Narrative
pp. 572–581

	Lexile: 970 *Fry: 7* *Dale-Chall: 6.1*	*Lexile: 810* *Fry: 6* *Dale-Chall: 5.9*

Author's Style pp. 547–548, 551–553, 556 **RL 4, RL 5**
Reading Dickinson's Poetry pp. 547–548, 550–553, 556 **RL 1, RL 4**
Allusion p. 554 **RL 1, RL 2**

Compare Interpretations
pp. 582–583 **RL 7**

Read a Letter p. 555

Style pp. 559–560, 563–564, 566, 570 **RI 4, RI 6**
Analyze Author's Purpose pp. 559, 563, 565, 569–570 **RI 6**
Language Coach pp. 564, 568, 569 **RI 4**

Narrative Elements pp. 573, 574, 576, 578, 579, 580 **RI 3**
Reading a Narrative pp. 573, 576, 579–580 **RI 3**

Quickwrite p. 547

Quickwrite p. 559
Writing Prompt p. 571 **W 3, W 3d**

Writing Prompt p. 581 **W 3d**

Discuss p. 573 **SL 1**

Author's Style p. 552 **L 5**

Style pp. 559, 566, 570 **L 3a**
Make Effective Word Choices pp. 563, 571 **L 3**
Language Coach pp. 563, 564, 568 **L 5, L 5b**

Establish Tone pp. 576, 581 **L 3**
Language Coach pp. 577, 579 **L 4, L 4d**

To see the complete Essential Course of Study, see pp. T23–T27.

 For additional lesson planning help, see **Teacher One Stop DVD.**

	Linked Selections		An Occurrence at Owl Creek Bridge
COMMON CORE **STRAND**	**The Gettysburg Address/The Emancipation Proclamation** Speech/Proclamation pp. 584–591 *Lexile: 1170/1990* *Fry: 8/11* *Dale-Chall: 7.0/9.4*	**Voices from the Civil War** Letters, Diary Entry, Speech pp. 592–597	Short Story pp. 602–616 *Lexile: 1000* *Fry: 9* *Dale-Chall: 6.9*
Reading Literature			Point of View pp. 603–604, 607–608, 615 RL 3, RL 5 Analyze Structure pp. 603, 607–608, 612, 614, 615 RL 2, RL 5 Characterization p. 610 RL 3 Language Coach p. 611 RL 4 Primary Source Documents p. 614
Reading Informational Text	Audience and Form pp. 585, 588, 590 RI 8, RI 9 Analyze an Author's Beliefs pp. 585, 589, 590 RI 4, RI 8	Analyze Primary Sources pp. 593, 595–597 RI 2, RI 6, RI 8	
Writing	Writing Prompt p. 591 W 1, W 1b, W 9	Writing Prompt p. 597 W 1	
Speaking and Listening	Test Yourself p. 585		Discuss p. 603 SL 1
Language	Audience and Form p. 586 L 3a Use Language Effectively pp. 586, 591 L 3 Language Coach p. 589	Language Coach pp. 593, 595 L 4a, L 5	Latin Root *lud* p. 616 L 4b, L 6 Language Coach pp. 606, 612

Media Study: *from **An Occurrence at Owl Creek Bridge*** Film Clips pp. 618–619	**Wrap-Ups** • Brilliant Mavericks p. 557 • Literature of the Civil War p. 617	**Writing Workshop: Online Feature Article** pp. 620–627 **Technology Workshop: Updating an Online Article** pp. 628–629
Comparing Texts: Point of View pp. 618–619 **RL 7**		
	Writing to Compare p. 557 **W 2, W 9** Writing to Synthesize p. 617 **W 2, W 2d**	Writing an Online Feature Article pp. 620–627 **W 2 a–f, W 4, W 5, W 6, W 7, W 8, W 9b (RI 1), W 10** Updating an Online Article pp. 628–629 **W 6**
	Extension p. 557 **SL 4** Extension p. 617 **SL 4, SL 6**	Writing an Online Feature Article pp. 602–627 **SL 5** Updating an Online Article pp. 628–629 **SL 1c, SL 1d, SL 5**
	Extension p. 557 **L 3**	Drafting p. 623 **L 2** Editing and Publishing p. 626 **L 1a–b, L 2**

To see the complete Essential Course of Study, see pp. T23–T27.

For additional lesson planning help, see **Teacher One Stop DVD.**

Instructional Support

Resource Manager Unit 3

UNIT SUPPORT

Academic Vocabulary, p. 3

Additional Academic Vocabulary, p. 4

Grammar Focus p. 5

Text Analysis Workshop pp. 9, 107

Writing Workshop: Online Feature
Article p. 137

SELECTION SUPPORT*

Plan and Teach

Lesson planning pages

Additional leveled selection questions

Extension activities

Student Copy Masters

Selection summaries in four languages

Skills copy masters in English and Spanish

Vocabulary preteaching and support

Reading Check and Question Support

Reading Fluency

* Available for all selections

† Available on **thinkcentral.com**

Language Handbook

Vocabulary Practice

Best Practices Toolkit

PowerNotes DVD-ROM†

**Connections: Nonfiction for
Common Core** CD-ROM†

Teacher One Stop DVD-ROM

Student One Stop DVD-ROM

Media*Smart* DVD-ROM
from Page to Screen: Occurrence

Write*Smart* CD-ROM†

GrammarNotes DVD-ROM†

Wordsharp CD-ROM†

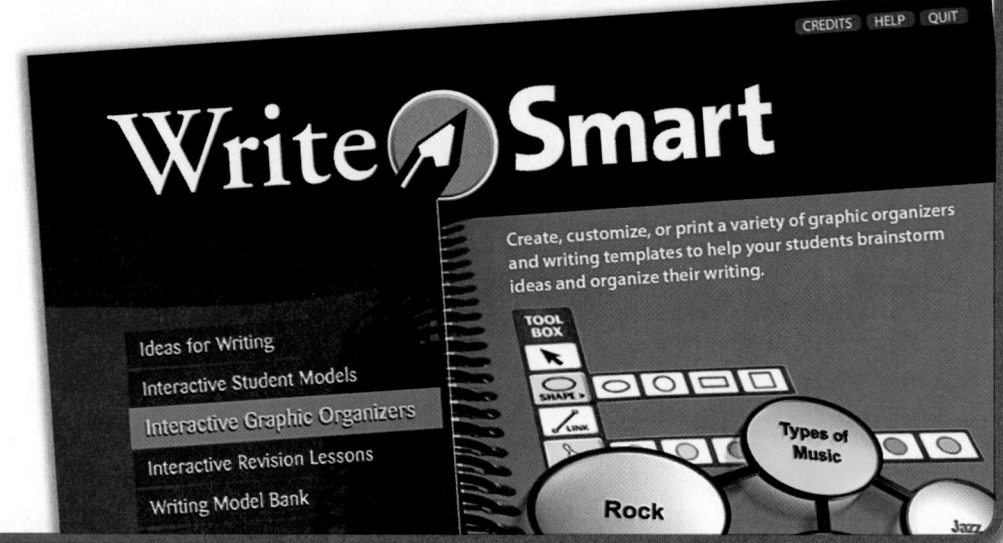

Write Smart

CREDITS HELP QUIT

Create, customize, or print a variety of graphic organizers and writing templates to help your students brainstorm ideas and organize their writing.

Ideas for Writing
Interactive Student Models
Interactive Graphic Organizers
Interactive Revision Lessons
Writing Model Bank

TOOL BOX

Types of Music

Rock

Jazz

Differentiated Instruction

STRUGGLING READERS AND WRITERS

Resource Manager Unit 3

Additional Selection Questions

Question Support

Reading Fluency

Interactive Reader

Adapted Interactive Reader

Level Up Online Tutorials

Audio Anthology

(with Audio summaries)

Diagnostic and Selection Tests

Selection Tests A/B

ENGLISH LANGUAGE LEARNERS

Resource Manager Unit 3

Selection Summaries in English, Spanish, Vietnamese and Haitian Creole

Skills Copymasters in Spanish

English Language Learner Adapted Interactive Reader Teacher's Guide

ELL Adapted Interactive Reader

Guide to English for Newcomers

Audio Anthology

Audio Summaries in Multiple Languages
(on **thinkcentral.com**)

ADVANCED LEARNERS

Resource Manager Unit 3

Additional Selection Questions

Ideas for Extension

Diagnostic and Selection Tests

Selection Tests B/C

http://content.review.thinkcentral.com - Level Up - Microsoft Internet Explorer provided by Harcourt

LEVEL up

TUTORIAL

Plot Structure

Complications

Some stories repeat complications in similar ways. These are called parallel episodes.

Read each example. Is it a parallel episode? Click Yes or No.

Sara was upset that Tidbit had chewed up the carpet, but she knew he was just a puppy. Sara and her mom put Tidbit in the car to take him to obedience school. The car wouldn't start! Now what

Tidbit had chewed up the ca so Sara sent him to his first obedience school. The next morning, Sara woke up to running shoe chewed to p Perhaps obedience school working after all.

Assessment and Reteaching

Diagostic and Selection Tests

Unit and Benchmark Tests

ThinkCentral Online Assessment:

- All program assessments
- Level Up Online Tutorials

ExamView Test Generator on the Teacher One Stop DVD-ROM

Online Essay Scoring on **thinkcentral.com**

ThinkCentral Online Reteaching:

- Level Up Online Tutorials
- Reteaching Worksheets

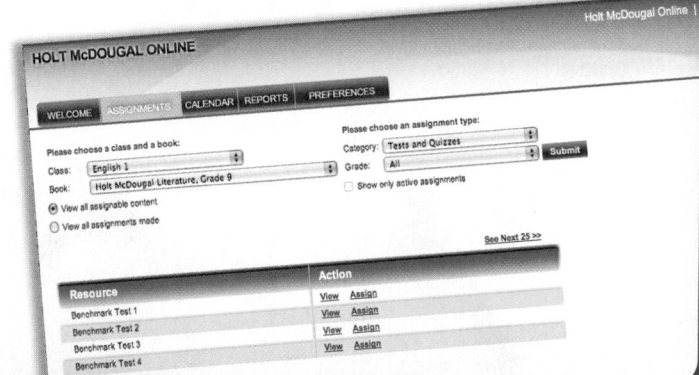

Professional Development

Video Center Based on interviews with program consultants and other educational experts, these videos feature classroom-ready teaching strategies.

Teacher Toolkit Includes a Teacher Handbook as well as a range of articles and handouts by program consultants and other educators.

Janet Allen

Jim Burke

Kylene Beers

Carol Jago

THINK central **at a Glance**

One Location, Endless Resources

Find Resources Browse all *Holt McDougal Literature* components for the ones that meet your students' needs and match your teaching style.

Assess Progress and Reteach Assign electronic versions of program assessments to measure your students' mastery of the Common Core State Standards. On thinkcentral.com, some tests deliver online remediation tutorials to students who have not mastered skills.

 Interactive Whiteboard Lessons

Prepare your students for college and careers by teaching relevant, real-world skills through dynamic, interactive instruction. Go to **thinkcentral.com** to browse through all white-board lessons, including the following:

- Poetry: Language and Form
- Word Choice and Tone
- Synthesizing Information

Together Holt McDougal and HISTORY® are revolutionizing the study of English/language arts with video that helps students relive and re-imagine the people, places, and events they are discovering through reading. Look for selections with the HISTORY® icon.

COMMON CORE FOCUS

RL 9 Demonstrate knowledge of nineteenth-century foundational works of American literature, including how two or more texts from the same period treat similar themes or topics. **RI 9** Analyze nineteenth-century foundational U.S. documents of historical and literary significance for their themes, purposes, and rhetorical features.

Questions of the Times

Read aloud the questions on pages 514 and 515 and the paragraphs that follow them. Open the discussion of each idea by having students respond to the questions that conclude each paragraph. Use these notes to prompt further discussion of the ideas.

What DIVIDES *a nation?*

Explain that students will learn more about the issues leading up to the Civil War when they read the Historical Essay (pages 516–523). For now, have students brainstorm a list of issues that divide Americans today and then rank their importance. Extend the discussion by asking

- What issues unite Americans today?
- Which are more powerful, the divisive issues or the uniting issues?

Is anything worth DYING FOR?

Invite students to identify causes for which they might risk their lives; have them explain their reasons. Challenge the class to create a master list of characteristics that make a cause great and a sacrifice worthwhile.

UNIT 3

Questions of the Times

DISCUSS After reading these questions and talking about them with a partner, share your views with the class as a whole. Then read on to explore the ways in which writers of the Civil War era dealt with the same issues.

What DIVIDES *a nation?*

In the years leading up to the Civil War, the agrarian South, whose economy depended upon slave labor, and the industrialized North, which became increasingly opposed to slavery, began to see each other as enemies. Slavery was one of many issues that divided Americans of the day. What issues or beliefs typically cause conflict between citizens? What divides Americans today?

Is anything worth DYING FOR?

During the Civil War, boys and young men on both sides of the conflict marched off to war with visions of becoming heroes in the service of a great cause. Hundreds of thousands never returned home. Was their sacrifice worthwhile? Would you ever be willing to risk your life for a flag, a group, or an idea?

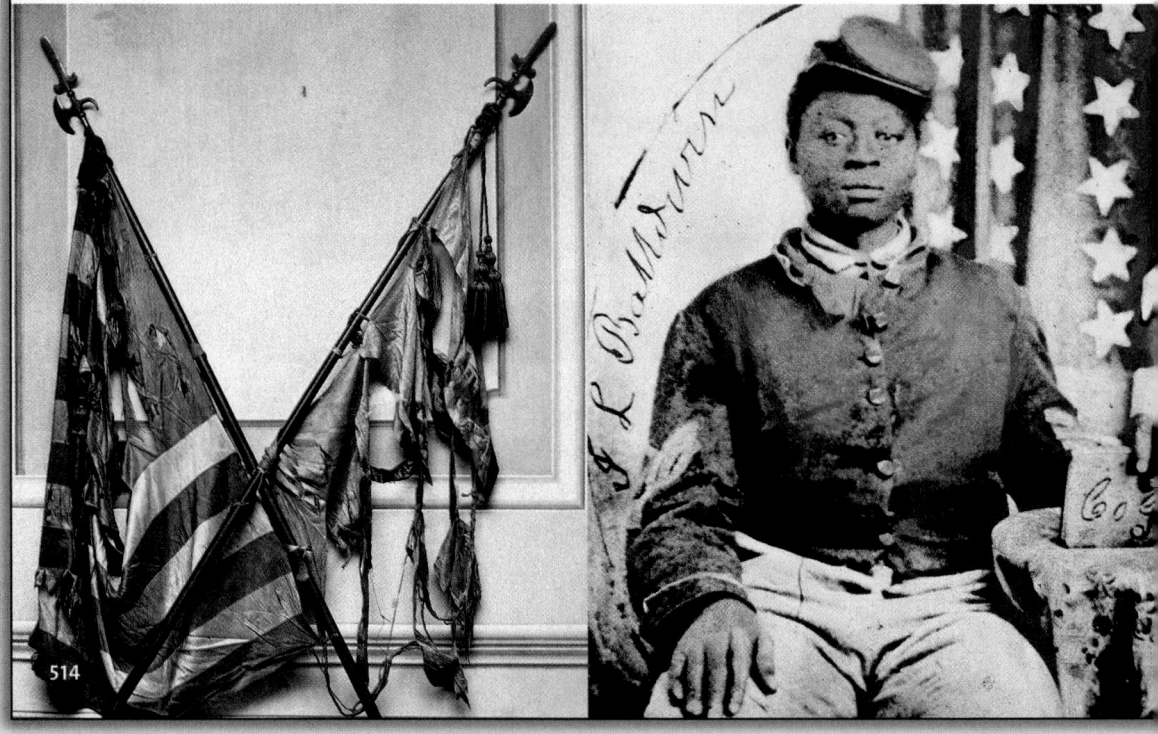

514

Why do people BREAK RULES?

Poets Walt Whitman and Emily Dickinson broke well-established conventions of poetic form and content, and today they are celebrated for their ingenuity. Yet, during their lives few readers recognized their genius because their work was radically different from the popular poetry of the day. Why do you think people break the rules if they will not be rewarded for it? Do artists, especially, tend to break the rules?

COMMON CORE

RL 9 Demonstrate knowledge of nineteenth-century foundational works of American literature, including how two or more texts from the same period treat similar themes or topics. **RI 9** Analyze nineteenth-century foundational U.S. documents of historical and literary significance for their themes, purposes, and rhetorical features.

Is it important to FACE REALITY?

After the horrors of the Civil War, romantic attitudes no longer captured the spirit of America. Instead, artists and writers turned to a new movement known as realism, which reflected a different view of life—unsentimental, honest, and often harsh or even ugly. Do you think writers and artists should deal with life's realities or take us away from them?

Why do people BREAK RULES?

Ask students to give examples that distinguish between breaking rules for a constructive purpose and breaking rules for a destructive purpose. Then challenge students to cite cases in which people who are not artists—perhaps including the students themselves—break rules. Discuss positive and negative effects of such rule-breaking. Elicit that rewards are not always material things (such as money or trophies), nor is genius always recognized in a person's lifetime.

Is it important to FACE REALITY?

Review key characteristics of romanticism, challenging students to name writers and works that they associate with that movement. Then ask students to define *face reality* in their own words. Focus on the question in the text by asking students to cite examples of realistic art and escapist art and to defend their preferences—realism versus escapism—in art and entertainment.

515

COMMON CORE FOCUS

RL 9 Demonstrate knowledge of nineteenth-century foundational works of American literature, including how two or more texts from the same period treat similar themes or topics. **RI 9** Analyze nineteenth-century foundational U.S. documents of historical and literary significance for their themes, purposes, and rhetorical features.

The following essay (pages 516–523) provides students with a historical context for the Unit 3 reading selections. It presents a brief overview of significant events occurring during the time period of 1855–1870 and introduces key people, places, and ideas of the times.

To get started, read and discuss the opening paragraph on page 516. Ask students how they would have answered the questions that appear early in the paragraph if they had been Northerners at that time and then if they had been Southerners.

READING STRATEGY

◼ PREVIEW

Have students preview the historical essay by skimming the heads, boldfaced terms, and **Taking Notes** side-column features. Ask volunteers to summarize what the essay is about.

About the Art This image is a detail from Mort Künstler's painting *Battle for the Shenandoah* (1982), which captures an 1864 campaign known for combat among soldiers on horseback.

From Romanticism to Realism
1855–1870

An Age of Transition

The Civil War was a violent clash, not just of armies, but of ideas. Who was right, and who was wrong? What did it mean to be an American? Was any price too high to pay to keep the nation whole? There was nothing theoretical about the conflict—real people died, hundreds of thousands of them: fathers, sons, and brothers. But the war began before a single shot was ever fired. Writers served as its first soldiers, and the battle lines were drawn in ink.

DIFFERENTIATED INSTRUCTION

FOR STRUGGLING READERS
Vocabulary Support

- *regional*, "having to do with a particular part of the earth's surface"
- *financial*, "having to do with how money is managed"
- *economy*, "the production of goods and services in a nation or other group"
- *agricultural*, "having to do with farming"
- *export*, "the practice of sending things to be sold in a place where they are not made"

- *sidestep*, "to attempt to avoid"
- *confrontation*, "a clash or conflict"
- *ballots*, "votes"
- *abolitionist*, "one who works to bring an end to slavery"
- *sacking*, "the destructive stealing of things from a town"

Use this copy master to help students take notes on the essay, pages 516–523:

 **RESOURCE MANAGER—Copy Master**
Note Taking p. 8

Emerging Realism: Historical Context

The central influence on literature of this period was the conflict between North and South that ended in the Civil War. Although romantic attitudes helped push the nation into war, four years of bitter fighting led to a new realism.

A Cultural Divide

"A house divided against itself cannot stand," wrote **Abraham Lincoln** in 1858, referring to the bitterly divided United States. Since colonial times, the South and the North had shown strong regional differences. Most of the manufacturing and financial services of the nation were located in the North, whose economy was based primarily on trade and industry. In contrast, the South had developed an agricultural way of life—growing cotton, tobacco, and sugar cane for export to the North and Europe—that relied on the labor of nearly four million slaves. Most Southerners opposed any interference with slavery by the federal government because of the region's economic dependence on it, the widespread fear of slave unrest, and the belief that states should control their own affairs.

SLAVERY DIVIDES THE NATION Although national political leaders tried to sidestep the slavery issue, growing Northern opposition to slavery and its expansion into the West made confrontation inevitable. In the 1850s, several events moved the country to its breaking point. In Kansas, the vote over whether to join the Union as a free state or a slave state turned deadly when gun-toting mobs swarmed over the border from Missouri to cast illegal ballots in favor of slavery. Continuing violence between proslavery and antislavery settlers led people to begin calling the territory **Bleeding Kansas.** Abolitionist **John Brown** played a role in Bleeding Kansas in 1856, killing five proslavery men as revenge for the sacking of the antislavery town of Lawrence. Three years later, Brown again shocked the nation when he led a bloody raid on the federal arsenal at Harpers Ferry, hoping to spark a slave uprising. Writer **Henry David Thoreau** called Brown "an angel of light"; but fellow writer **Nathaniel Hawthorne** retorted, "No man was ever more justly hanged."

CONFLICT REACHES THE GOVERNMENT Even the floor of the U.S. Senate became a battleground. In 1856, Massachusetts senator Charles Sumner gave an impassioned speech against slavery, berating his colleagues for two days for their support of slavery. A few days later, Carolina congressman Preston S. Brooks retaliated by attacking Sumner with his cane, beating the Massachusetts senator unconscious. When writer **William Cullen Bryant** heard about the caning, he was outraged. "Has it come to this," he asked in the *New York Evening Post,* "that we must speak with bated breath in the presence of our Southern masters? . . . Are we, too, slaves, slaves for life, a

Battle for the Shenandoah © Mort Künstler, Inc.

COMMON CORE

RL 9 Demonstrate knowledge of nineteenth-century foundational works of American literature, including how two or more texts from the same period treat similar themes or topics. **RI 9** Analyze nineteenth-century foundational U.S. documents of historical and literary significance for their themes, purposes, and rhetorical features.

▶ **TAKING NOTES**

Outlining As you read this introduction, use an outline to record main ideas about the historical characteristics and literature of this period. You can use headings, boldfaced terms, and the information in boxes like this one as starting points. (See page R49 in the **Research Handbook** for more help with outlining.)

I. *Historical Context*
  A. *Cultural Divide*
   1. *Northern economy based on trade and industry; Southern based on agriculture and slavery*
   2. *slavery's expansion west provoked confrontation*

Emerging Realism: Historical Context

This section of the essay (pages 517–519) summarizes the important events and political issues—chiefly, slavery and regional economic differences—that led to the Civil War. This section also describes the beginning of the war, whose early battles created a shocking reality for the nation's previously romantic mindset.

TIERED DISCUSSION PROMPTS

Use these prompts to help students understand the ideas in **A Cultural Divide:**

Interpret In what sense was the United States in 1858 "a house divided against itself"? *Possible answer: The United States was like a house because it was a large dwelling for many people and should have been unified; it was divided against itself because many people in that "house" upheld slavery at the same time that many other people wanted to see slavery end.*

Synthesize Compare and contrast the divisions in the United States during the pre–Civil War era with divisions that have occurred in later periods. *Possible answer: Political divisions in later periods sometimes have been sharp, but they have remained relatively peaceful in comparison to the divisions of the Civil War era.*

FOR ENGLISH LANGUAGE LEARNERS

Set a Purpose Have students use the boldfaced terms to help locate important people and events that played roles in the conflict between North and South—that is, in the prelude to the Civil War. Encourage students to read the details to fully understand the boldfaced terms.

FOR ADVANCED LEARNERS/AP

Research and Analyze Present students with this question: "Given the state of the nation in the 1850s, was the Civil War inevitable?" Encourage students not only to reflect upon what they have read but also to do further research to form and support a view. Urge them, as well, to think beyond the simplistic "The South wanted slavery but the North did not," considering the economy of each part of the country and the importance of the

states' rights issue. Have students share their responses and reasoning in a class discussion. If you have students on both sides of the issue, work with them to present a brief debate.

Have students explain the **Dred Scott** case, focusing on (1) why it was harmful to African Americans and (2) how it reflected issues in the United States at that time.

TIERED DISCUSSION PROMPTS

Use these prompts to help students understand the ideas in **The Civil War:**

Restate Why did Lincoln's election cause the southern states to secede? *Possible answer: The states seceded because of Lincoln's pledge to stop the spread of slavery into the West.*

Analyze How was the Civil War an expression of romanticism at first? How and why did that romantic attitude change? *Possible answer: At first, people expected a quick, painless war. They had a romantic view of warfare and the people who fought it, and they welcomed the chance to earn glory in (or to be entertained by) battle. Later, when horrific battles such as Bull Run revealed the brutal reality of war, people began to abandon their romantic idealism.*

Synthesize Why would people idealize or romanticize a war in its early stages? *Possible answer: At the beginning, a war would not have as many casualties as would mount up over time. If many years had passed since the previous war, the current generation would have little experience with war's horrors and therefore might idealize or romanticize what they had read or heard about war.*

---

target for their brutal blows, when we do not comport ourselves to please them?" Meanwhile, newspapers across the South applauded the attack, describing abolitionists as unruly dogs to be collared and disciplined. Such angry name-calling and accusations reflected—and added to—the growing sense on both sides that Northerners and Southerners were no longer simply Americans from different regions, but foreigners and enemies.

In 1857, the Supreme Court entered the fray by hearing the case of **Dred Scott,** a slave whose owner had taken him to spend several years in a free state. Scott argued that living in a free state made him free; the Supreme Court ruled against him. Worse, it went on to say that even free blacks "had no rights which a white man was bound to respect." The *Dred Scott* decision sent shock waves through the already divided nation. Northerners were outraged and alarmed. Was the South's "peculiar institution" of slavery to become the law of the whole land?

An 1856 cartoon of Congressman Preston S. Brooks attacking Senator Charles Sumner on the Senate floor.

The Civil War

Ironically, none of these acts led to the final break. Instead, the lawful election in 1860 of a politically moderate U.S. president, Abraham Lincoln, ignited war. Enraged at Lincoln's pledge to stop the western spread of slavery, the Southern states seceded to form the **Confederate States of America.**

For a generation that had grown up on the literary ideal of the brave, dashing **Romantic hero,** the booming of Confederate cannons firing on Fort Sumter in the spring of 1861 was a call to glory. Boys and young men rushed off to join the Union or Confederate army. Southerners boasted that a single one of them could lick ten Yankees; Northerners were sure that "Johnny Reb" would turn and run at the first shot. For many, the biggest fear was that the war would end too soon and they would miss their chance to become heroes.

The mood was nearly festive on the sunny July day when fresh Union forces marched south into Virginia to confront the rebels at Bull Run. Soldiers wandered from their lines to pick blackberries and drink cool water from the creek, and the cream of Washington society drove down in carriages with bottles of champagne and picnic baskets to enjoy the spectacle.

REALITY STRIKES By late afternoon, thousands of dead and wounded soldiers lay near the banks of Bull Run. On the losing side, panic-stricken Union soldiers stumbled away from the battlefield, their feet tangling in shawls and parasols that had been dropped by terrified civilians as they fled. The party was over.

> ### A Voice from the Times
>
> *Future years will never know the seething hell and the black infernal background of countless minor scenes and interiors, (not the official surface courteousness of the Generals, not the few great battles) . . . the real war will never get in the books.*
>
> —Walt Whitman

DIFFERENTIATED INSTRUCTION

FOR STRUGGLING READERS

Main Ideas and Supporting Details [paired option] Ask pairs of students to summarize the main idea of the section **The Civil War** in one sentence. *Possible answer: At the beginning of the Civil War, some people did not take it seriously enough, but their view changed as the realities of battle became evident.* Then have the student pairs write details from the section that support the main idea. *Answers will vary but should address the idealization of the war at first, the way in which that view changed, and the great losses that the war ultimately produced.* Ask students to read their main idea sentences aloud; discuss differences among them. Remind students to use their main idea sentence in their outlines.

The blood-soaked **Battle of Bull Run** gave everyone (especially the losing Union side) a taste of the reality of war, but it was only the beginning. Four long years of fighting followed. Names of battle sites became synonymous with death: Shiloh, Antietam, Fredericksburg, Gettysburg, Vicksburg. When the war ended at last, in April 1865, with **General Robert E. Lee's** surrender to **General Ulysses S. Grant** at Appomattox Courthouse, approximately 618,000 men had died—nearly as many Americans as have died in all other wars that the United States has ever fought. Much of the South lay in ruins, scarred by gutted plantation houses, burned bridges, and uprooted railroad lines.

Ideas of the Age

Americans in the postwar period embraced notions of freedom and unity. At the same time, they lost their taste for romanticism, having been confronted with the harsh realities of war.

Freedom and Unity

The United States was changed by the Civil War. It had suffered bitterly and was now a wiser, more somber nation. Yet the ideals of America's founders had survived the devastation of war. For the first time, the Declaration of Independence's notions of equality and liberty for all were brought closer to fruition. Slavery was dead— outlawed by Lincoln's bold **Emancipation Proclamation** and the **Thirteenth Amendment** to the Constitution. "We shout for joy that we live to record this righteous decree," said **Frederick Douglass.** "Free Forever!"

The Civil War had divided the country; its end brought the country back together. This time the country was united in a new way. Before the war, people were used to saying "The United States *are* . . . ," with the emphasis on the individual states more than on the united interests of all. After the war, people began saying "The United States *is* . . . ." A group of independent states had become one nation, indivisible, with the goal of liberty for all.

The Civil War changed not only American society but its literary culture as well. In the years following the war, American readers and writers found they had lost their taste for romanticism. Many had witnessed war's grim nature firsthand, and it shaped their view of life. Gallant heroism and adventure no longer suited America's tastes; nor did meditations on the beauty of nature or the worth of the individual. Writing became more honest, unsentimental, and ironic. A new style, **realism,** would predominate in the years to come.

> **A Voice from the Times**
>
> [W]e here highly resolve that these dead shall not have fought in vain—that this nation, under God, shall have a new birth of freedom— and that government of the people, by the people, for the people, shall not perish from the earth.
>
> —Abraham Lincoln

Abraham Lincoln Reading the Emancipation Proclamation Before His Cabinet Members, undated color illustration after painting by Francis Bicknell Carpenter. © Bettmann/Corbis.

Ideas of the Age

This section of the essay (page 519) explores the country's postwar focus on freedom, unity, and realism. The text also notes how the Civil War changed literary culture as well as societal tastes.

TIERED DISCUSSION PROMPTS

Use these prompts to help students understand the ideas in **Freedom and Unity:**

Analyze In what sense was the United States "a wiser, more somber nation" after the Civil War? *Possible answer: The United States was "wiser" and "more somber" after the war because Americans then understood more clearly the importance of being a unified nation. In addition, romantic idealizations of nature, adventure, and heroism no longer seemed as believable, and a more realistic view of life took hold.*

Synthesize How might one challenge the idea that the United States was wiser after the Civil War? *Possible answer: Refuters might point out that Reconstruction, the national process of reunification, generally is considered not to have been wisely conducted; in particular, it did not result in equality for African Americans, nor did it heal the bitterness of Southerners.*

About the Art This illustration, after a painting by Francis Bicknell Carpenter (1830–1900), shows a meeting of Lincoln and his cabinet in September 1862. At that meeting they read the Emancipation Proclamation, which became effective on January 1, 1863.

FOR STRUGGLING READERS
Vocabulary Support
- *comport,* "to behave in a certain way"
- *moderate,* "not taking extreme political positions"
- *seceded,* "broke away from membership [in the United States]"
- *festive,* "merry and partylike"
- *cream,* "the most refined people"
- *decree,* "a legal order"

- *independent,* "separate from each other"
- *indivisible,* "unable to be divided"
- *unsentimental,* "having little or no appeal to the emotions"
- *ironic,* "focusing on differences between what is expected and what actually happens"
- *predominate,* "to take and hold control"

FOR ADVANCED LEARNERS/AP
Analyze a Quotation Ask students to think about the quotation from Abraham Lincoln in **A Voice from the Times**. Have them discuss the tone of the comment and its connection to the Civil War. (You might explain that it comes from the Gettysburg Address, which students will read on page 586.) Extend the discussion by asking students why Americans consider Lincoln's words inspiring and relevant even today.

Literature of the Times

This section of the essay (pages 520–523) introduces the great American poets Walt Whitman and Emily Dickinson and their literary innovations. The section also surveys the literature of the Civil War, including these genres:

- slave narratives
- diaries and letters
- speeches

The section concludes by introducing the realism of the postwar period, exemplified by Stephen Crane and Ambrose Bierce.

TIERED DISCUSSION PROMPTS

Use these prompts to help students understand the ideas in **Brilliant Mavericks: Whitman and Dickinson:**

Interpret Reread the comment from Ralph Waldo Emerson. What did he want poetry to do? **Possible answer:** *Emerson wanted poetry to take life as its subject and to be deep without being ornate.*

Analyze How were Whitman and Dickinson alike? How were they unalike? **Possible answer:** *Whitman and Dickinson were alike in being individualists who broke with previous ideas about poetry. They both were ambitious, as well: Whitman wanted to cover the whole American experience, and Dickinson dealt with the deepest poetic themes. They were unalike in their lifestyles and their poetic styles. Whitman was an outgoing traveler; Dickinson, a shy recluse. Whitman wrote free verse in long lines; Dickinson wrote rhymed verse in short lines.*

Literature of the Times

The Civil War was a transitional period for writers of the day. Groundbreaking poets, former slaves, famous public figures and everyday people all contributed their ideas as the country and its literature moved from romanticism to realism.

Brilliant Mavericks: Whitman and Dickinson

In 1842, when the conflicts leading to the Civil War were just beginning to brew and the romantic movement was going strong, writer **Ralph Waldo Emerson** issued a challenge to America. The nation needed a poet worthy of itself—a truly fresh voice with limitless passion and originality. "I look in vain," lamented Emerson, "for the poet whom I describe. We do not with sufficient plainness, or sufficient profoundness, address ourselves to life. . . ." In the coming decades, two poets would answer Emerson's bold call: **Walt Whitman** and **Emily Dickinson.**

Outwardly, Whitman and Dickinson had little in common. Whitman, big, bearded, and outspoken, was always in the thick of things and wrote many poems about current issues and events, from the sad plight of the slave to the shocking assassination of President Lincoln. Dickinson, on the other hand, was shy and reclusive, living her whole life in her native New England, and finding inspiration for her poetry in her own thoughts.

RULE-BREAKERS The two, however, were not entirely unalike. Both felt hemmed in by conventional ideas of how poems ought to look and what poems ought to say. Both wrote poetry so radical in form and content that it took many years for readers to appreciate it. (In Dickinson's case, appreciation didn't come until after her death.) Together, they broke poetry wide open, creating the most remarkable work of the Civil War era.

In 1855, Whitman published at his own expense a book of poetry called *Leaves of Grass.* The book was small, but it contained a huge ambition. Whitman saw America as a great poem, the greatest in the world, and his job was to capture it on paper. A sprawling, rowdy, vigorous young nation, he believed, could not be squeezed into traditional poetic forms. Instead, he wrote in **free verse,** unconfined by formal patterns of rhyme and meter. His lines were loose and rambling, his language colorful and vigorous, and he refused to limit himself to "poetic" subjects. If it was a part of American life, it was his to write about, even if it was a topic others might consider common or vulgar.

Emily Dickinson also found traditional poetic forms inadequate. Yet, where Whitman's poems were expansive, hers were terse and compressed—a few brief lines packed with complex, original images. Her subject matter was intensely personal, and her themes

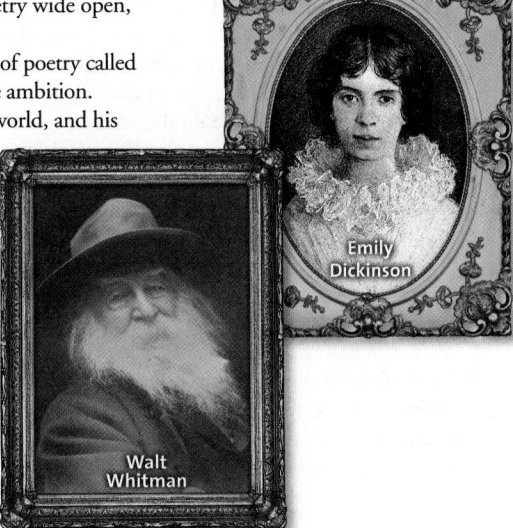

Emily Dickinson

Walt Whitman

DIFFERENTIATED INSTRUCTION

FOR ENGLISH LANGUAGE LEARNERS

Set a Purpose Ask students to look for information in this essay about each writer named. Encourage students to use a Character Traits Web to record key facts, as in this example:

 BEST PRACTICES TOOLKIT—Transparency
Character Traits Web p. D7

shy, reclusive

almost unknown during her lifetime

Emily Dickinson

used short, compressed poetic lines and original imagery

wrote about cosmic themes

FOR ADVANCED LEARNERS/AP

Synthesize Why would a poet find the forms of his or her time inadequate? Why would a poet rebel against those forms and deliberately write in a way that readers would find unfamiliar? Have students discuss these questions and speculate about how poets today might innovate new forms. If time permits, have students write and share brief "manifestoes" that proclaim ideas for new poetic forms.

EMILY DICKINSON

© Tom Gauld/Heart USA Inc.

◄ **Analyze Visuals**

This cartoon is one artist's representation of Emily Dickinson's reclusive nature. What other personality traits does the artist suggest about Dickinson in these panels?

were the great themes of life: love, death, immortality, and nature. Although she wrote nearly 1,800 poems, only a handful appeared in print during her lifetime. In fact, she was virtually unknown in her time, living a reclusive life that belied the intense creative fervor of her inner world.

Neither Dickinson nor Whitman can be easily categorized. Although Whitman can be considered a romantic poet because of his emphasis on individualism, emotion, and nature, his exploration of topics others found vulgar was certainly not romantic. Dickinson, too, could be aggressively unromantic, with her images of ordinary household items and her abrupt, unemotional tone. Perhaps both poets can be seen as transitional, moving with Americans of the day from romanticism to realism.

Analyze Visuals

Possible answer: *The cartoon gives the impression that Dickinson was a quiet, shy person who may have been snobbish or fearful of the world—but who also may not have been entirely comfortable with her isolation.*

TIERED DISCUSSION PROMPTS

Use these prompts to help students understand the ideas in **Brilliant Mavericks: Whitman and Dickinson:**

Analyze Reread Emerson's comment at the beginning of this section. How did Whitman and Dickinson fulfill Emerson's vision?
Possible answer: *Emerson envisioned "plainness" in poetry, and both Whitman and Dickinson are very readable. Emerson also wanted "profoundness," and both poets presented original, important ideas. Finally, Emerson wanted poetry to address life; Whitman addressed the vital life of America, and Dickinson addressed her interior life.*

Interpret What does the essay mean by calling these two writers "transitional" poets?
Possible answer: *The essay means that Whitman and Dickinson do not fit easily into a category; rather, they create a link between one era (romanticism) and another (realism).*

FOR STRUGGLING READERS

Vocabulary Support

- *mavericks,* "people who do things their own way, not like everyone else"
- *conventional,* "accepted; traditional"
- *radical,* "extremely different"
- *rowdy,* "disorderly and rough"
- *expansive,* "covering a wide range of things"
- *terse,* "using few words"
- *compressed,* "short"

Concept Support Some students may not grasp how poetic form changes. Read aloud lines from a traditional poem that they have read, such as Holmes's "The Chambered Nautilus" (page 350). Then help students revise the lines experimentally, keeping the line breaks and imagery but removing meter and rhyme. Ask students to imagine what readers would think of the revision if the only poetry that they knew was the traditional kind; elicit that many readers would not even recognize

the new style as poetry. (You might compare the situation with people today who hear a new musical style and respond, "That's not music, it's noise!") Lead students to conclude that the first free-verse poets faced a challenge in persuading readers to accept a new kind of poetry.

TIERED DISCUSSION PROMPTS

Use these prompts to help students understand the ideas in **Literature of the Civil War:**

Restate What would typical readers of the Civil War era learn from a slave narrative?

Possible answer: *Readers would learn that slaves experienced degradation; that slaves were people just like them and therefore deserved equal justice; and that, after obtaining freedom, former slaves made important contributions to American society.*

Synthesize Why are slave narratives important, both in their own time and today?

Possible answer: *For their own time, these narratives described the reality of enslavement, contradicting pro-slavery propaganda. For our time, they provide a lasting document of a piece of history that people ought to remember and learn from, as well as a source of inspiration about enduring and overcoming hardship.*

About the Art This wood engraving, made by an anonymous American artist in 1864, shows a Civil War scene. The fugitive slaves are trying to reach the Union army lines.

Literature of the Civil War

Of all human actions, none speaks so dramatically nor so violently as war. Of all wars, civil war by its very nature divides a nation's voice into factions. Among the diverse literary voices heard during the Civil War, some of the most powerful were African American.

Often at the urging of abolitionists, former slaves who escaped to the North published **slave narratives** detailing their experiences. These tales of suffering were immensely important to the cause of antislavery. Not simply autobiography, they were testimony, giving lie to Southern claims that slaves were happy and well-treated, that slavery was a "positive good" for both master and slave, and that people of African descent were inferior to whites. More than that, the narratives made readers *care* by showing that slaves were real human beings who suffered and wept and longed for freedom.

▶ *For Your Outline*

LITERATURE OF THE CIVIL WAR

- Slave narratives revealed the true nature of slavery and made readers care.
- Diaries and letters gave personal responses to historical events.
- Public documents influenced a large audience.
- Later fiction moved toward realism.

Fugitive slaves flee a Southern plantation at night in an attempt to reach the North.

522

DIFFERENTIATED INSTRUCTION

FOR STRUGGLING READERS

Vocabulary Support

- *factions,* "groups that oppose each other"
- *slave narratives,* "stories of slavery, written or told by slaves in their own words"
- *realism,* "writing that shows life as it really is"
- *fugitive,* "someone who is trying to escape from the law"
- *plantation,* "a large Southern farm with a grand house in which the owners lived"

- *typhoid fever,* "an easily spread, deadly disease common in the 19th century, marked by high body temperature, coughing, internal bleeding, and red blotches on the skin"
- *front,* "the part of a battlefield at which the opposing armies face each other"

Personal experience was central to the literature of the time, because everyday life now had great historical significance. Writers—male and female, white and black, from the highest-ranking general down to the common foot soldier—shared "their" Civil War in **diaries** and **letters**.

> ### Voices from the Times
>
> *Many times I sat down in the mud determined to go no further, and willing to die to end my misery. But soon a friend would pass and urge me to make another effort, and I would stagger a mile further.*
>
> —Union soldier Elisha Rhodes
>
> *I daily part with my raiment for food. We find no one who will exchange eatables for Confederate money. So we are devouring our clothes.*
>
> —Southern diarist Mary Chesnut

While these writers addressed their words to friends and family (or even to themselves), others, such as President **Abraham Lincoln,** wrote for a larger audience. Still, Lincoln underestimated the reach of his words. "The world will little note, nor long remember, what we say here," he proclaimed in his **Gettysburg Address,** which in fact proved to be one of the most enduring works of the Civil War era.

Lincoln's speech, with its inspiring message and elevated language, represents the highest ideals of the period. The fiction created after the war by realistic writers such as **Ambrose Bierce** and **Stephen Crane,** however, shows the period in a harsher light. Their stories focus on the human tragedy of a war that destroyed hundreds of thousands of American lives, even as it freed many more.

In the years to come, **realism** would grow and refine itself to include the work of writers countrywide, from the frozen arctic north of Jack London to the plains of Willa Cather's frontier. It would develop to include the work of naturalist writers who viewed human beings as passive victims of their environment. Brought on by the brutalities of the Civil War, realism would become the form that to some extent still dominates American literature today.

THE ARTISTS' GALLERY

Prisoners from the Front (1866), Winslow Homer. Oil on canvas, 24″ × 38″. The Metropolitan Museum of Art, Gift of Mrs. Frank B. Porter, 1922 (22.207). Photo © 1995 The Metropolitan Museum of Art, New York.

Winslow Homer

Known for his bold technique and unsentimental style, **Winslow Homer** was one of the most admired artists of the 19th century. He first rose to acclaim during the Civil War.

Behind Union Lines When war broke out, *Harper's Weekly* sent Homer south, to draw illustrations for the magazine. The young artist camped out with the Union army and shared the soldiers' hardships, from meager rations to the deadly threat of typhoid fever.

Homer rarely drew a battle scene, spurning the romantic elements of high drama and heroism. Instead, he recorded the reality of everyday life in camp—the boredom and sadness of men far from home. In 1863, a critic praised him as "the first of our artists who has endeavored to tell us any truth about the war."

Civil War Masterpiece At first glance, the painting shown here might seem like nothing special, just soldiers standing in an empty field. Yet *Prisoners from the Front,* painted just after the war ended, won acclaim as the most powerful painting of the war. Why?

For Americans, this work had a deep symbolic meaning. In the soldiers, Homer conveys two opposing worldviews: the romantic, long-haired Southern officer confronts his Northern counterpart, who eyes him coolly. Behind them, the devastated landscape of the South tells the story of how the Civil War ends.

UNIT INTRODUCTION **523**

THE ARTISTS' GALLERY

American artist Winslow Homer (1836–1910) painted *Prisoners from the Front* in 1866. After the war, Homer turned his attention to more peaceful scenes, especially everyday life, the countryside, and the sea. His depictions of those subjects are considered today to be among his finest work. An artist who worked in both watercolor and oil, Homer is known for his **realism** and his brilliant use of color. Tell students that they will see more of Homer's paintings accompanying the poems of Walt Whitman (pages 533 and 535).

Activity Ask students to interpret the thoughts and feelings of the characters in the painting. *Possible answer: The Union officer, on the right, looks smugly triumphant; the long-haired Confederate officer, in the center of the painting, seems to show a defiant sense of honor and pride at a time of loss; the Confederate enlisted man, with beard and folded hands, appears to be humbled.*

CHECK UNDERSTANDING

Have students identify a few names and characteristics for each of these literary groups:

- "mavericks" (Whitman, Dickinson)
- writers during the Civil War
- the early postwar realists

UNIT INTRODUCTION **523**

COMMON CORE FOCUS

RI 7 Integrate and evaluate multiple sources of information presented in different media or formats as well as in words in order to address a question or solve a problem.

READING SKILL

COMMON CORE
RI 7

■ READ A TIMELINE

Elicit or explain that each of the three horizontal sections of the timeline—*American Literary Milestones, Historical Context,* and *World Culture and Events*—displays a sequence of events that occurred between 1855 and 1870. By looking at the vertical columns on the timeline, students can see which events were taking place at about the same time. For example, have students locate these events, which occurred between 1863 and 1866:

- In 1863, Abraham Lincoln delivered the Gettysburg Address. (See *American Literary Milestones*.)
- In 1864, Louis Pasteur invented pasteurization. (See *World Culture and Events*.)
- In 1865, the Civil War ended. (See *Historical Context*.)

Ask students what events occurred in 1855.
Answer: *Frederick Douglass published his autobiographical narrative,* My Bondage and My Freedom; *Walt Whitman published the first edition of* Leaves of Grass; *Florence Nightingale introduced hygienic standards into military hospitals.*

Connecting Literature, History, and Culture

As you read this timeline and answer the questions on the next page, think about the ways in which American literature was influenced by—and itself influenced—national and world events.

AMERICAN LITERARY MILESTONES

1855

1855 Frederick Douglass's autobiographical slave narrative, *My Bondage and My Freedom,* is published; Walt Whitman publishes the first edition of *Leaves of Grass* at his own expense.

1857 The *Atlantic Monthly,* a journal of literature and opinion, is founded. Over the years, Emerson, Longfellow, and other writers and editors will contribute to the magazine.

1859

1859 Henry David Thoreau writes "A Plea for Captain John Brown," in which he refers to the condemned abolitionist as "an angel of light."

1861 The first autobiography by a formerly enslaved woman, Harriet Jacobs's *Incidents in the Life of a Slave Girl,* is published. ▶

1862 Emily Dickinson writes 366 poems within the year.

HISTORICAL CONTEXT

1855

1856 Preston S. Brooks beats Massachusetts senator Charles Sumner with a cane on the floor of the Senate in retaliation for Sumner's antislavery speech.

1857 Supreme Court's *Dred Scott* decision declares that slaves and former slaves are not U.S. citizens and thus not entitled to basic rights. ▶

1859

1859 Abolitionist John Brown is hanged for treason after leading a raid on the federal arsenal at Harpers Ferry.

1860 Abraham Lincoln is elected president; in response, South Carolina secedes from the Union, followed eventually by ten other Southern states.

1861 Confederate guns fire on Fort Sumter, launching the Civil War. ▶

WORLD CULTURE AND EVENTS

1855

1855 British nurse Florence Nightingale introduces hygienic standards into military hospitals during the Crimean War. ▶

1856 Two states of Australia introduce the voting procedure known as the Australian, or secret, ballot.

1857 Indians rebel against British occupation of the subcontinent.

1859

1859 British naturalist Charles Darwin publishes *Origin of Species,* giving his theory of evolution.

1861 Czar Alexander II of Russia frees serfs; in England, Charles Dickens publishes *Great Expectations.*

1862 French physicist Jean Foucault calculates the speed of light; Victor Hugo publishes *Les Misérables.*

DIFFERENTIATED INSTRUCTION

FOR STRUGGLING READERS

Understanding a Timeline Explain that the timeline runs chronologically (in time order) from left to right across the page. Each of the four columns represents a four-year period between 1855 and 1870. The three parallel rows of the timeline represent events occurring simultaneously. By comparing the three rows, readers can better understand what events in literature, history, and culture were taking place at about the same time.

MAKING CONNECTIONS

- What examples do you see of American writers being influenced by political events?
- What evidence shows that the nation was sharply divided before the Civil War?
- How did African Americans contribute to the literary culture of America during this period?
- What important scientific theories and discoveries arose during this period?

COMMON CORE

RI 7 Integrate and evaluate multiple sources of information presented in different media or formats as well as in words in order to address a question or solve a problem.

1863

1863 Abraham Lincoln delivers Gettysburg Address. ▶

1864 The *New Orleans Tribune*, one of the first daily newspapers produced by African Americans, begins publication.

1865 Walt Whitman pens his classic ode to Abraham Lincoln, "When Lilacs Last in the Dooryard Bloom'd."

1867

1867 Mark Twain publishes *The Celebrated Jumping Frog of Calaveras County and Other Sketches*.

1868 Part 1 of *Little Women*, Louisa May Alcott's classic novel about four sisters, is published. ▶

1870 Bret Harte publishes story collection *The Luck of Roaring Camp and Other Sketches*.

1863

1863 Lincoln signs Emancipation Proclamation; the 54th Massachusetts Volunteer Infantry, one of the first African-American regiments, is founded. ▶

1864 Union general William Tecumseh Sherman marches from Atlanta to the Atlantic Ocean.

1865 Civil War ends; Lincoln is assassinated; 13th Amendment abolishes slavery.

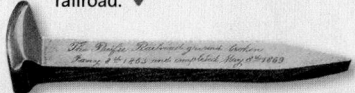

1867

1867 United States buys Alaska from Russia.

1868 Congress passes 14th Amendment, prohibiting discrimination against African Americans.

1869 The hammering of a golden spike at Promontory Point, Utah, marks completion of the transcontinental railroad. ▼

1870 The first African-American senator, Hiram R. Revels, takes his seat.

1863

1863 Leo Tolstoy publishes *War and Peace*.

1864 Louis Pasteur invents pasteurization.

1865 Telegraph cable is laid across the Atlantic Ocean. ▶

1866 Fyodor Dostoyevsky publishes *Crime and Punishment*.

1867

1868 Remains of Cro-Magnon man discovered in Europe; Meiji era in Japan begins period of modernization.

1869 Suez Canal is completed in Egypt.

1870 After a troubled reign, Queen Isabella II of Spain abdicates throne in favor of her son, Alfonso XII.

MAKING CONNECTIONS

Possible answers:

- *American writers who were influenced by political events include Frederick Douglass and Harriet Jacobs, who wrote about their experiences with slavery; Emerson and Longfellow, who contributed to a journal of opinion; Thoreau, who wrote an abolitionist essay; Lincoln, who wrote statesmanly rhetoric about major issues; and Whitman, who wrote an ode to Lincoln.*

- *Division is seen in these events: Preston Brooks beat Senator Charles Sumner with a cane on the floor of the Senate; the Dred Scott decision set back the cause of African-American freedom; John Brown was hanged for leading an anti-slavery raid; South Carolina seceded after Lincoln's election.*

- *African Americans contributed to literary culture by writing slave narratives and producing newspapers such as the* New Orleans Tribune.

- *Scientific theories and discoveries included the development of the theory of evolution; the calculation of the speed of light; the invention of pasteurization; and the discovery of prehistoric human remains.*

ADDITIONAL QUESTIONS

1. What advance in human rights occurred in Russia during the first year of the American Civil War? ***Answer:*** *Czar Alexander II advanced human rights by freeing the serfs (1861).*

2. What was significant about the railroad that was completed in 1869? ***Answer:*** *That railroad was significant because it spanned the North American continent.*

3. How many years passed between Whitman's publication of *Leaves of Grass* and his writing of "When Lilacs Last in the Dooryard Bloom'd"? ***Answer:*** *Ten years passed (from 1855 to 1865).*

FOR ADVANCED LEARNERS/AP

Making Additional Connections Ask students to choose one of the four time periods shown in the timeline and to do research online or in encyclopedias or history texts to learn about other events that took place during that same interval. Challenge students to identify events for each category: *American Literary Milestones, Historical Context,* and *World Culture and Events.* Have students work individually, with partners, or in small groups to prepare and present brief oral reports, summarizing significant events and discussing their connection to events shown in the timeline or discussed in class.

COMMON CORE FOCUS

SL1 Initiate and participate in a range of collaborative discussions, building on other's ideas and expressing their own clearly and persuasively.

War Stories

Have students read the paragraph. Discuss some aspects of the Civil War that led people to adopt a more realistic attitude toward war—for example, the war's high casualty rate (far higher than the total for all other American conflicts up to that time), the destruction of civilian property, and the way that the issues of the war split families. Also invite suggestions about why people sometimes romanticize war, even today.

DISCUSS Point out that Stephen Crane's Civil War novel *The Red Badge of Courage* (which students will read more about in the American Masterpieces feature on pages 600–601) began a tradition of realistic war fiction that later would include Ernest Hemingway's World War I novel *A Farewell to Arms,* World War II novels by Norman Mailer and James Jones, and Vietnam fiction by Tim O'Brien. Also note that movies such as Steven Spielberg's *Saving Private Ryan,* as well as television news reporting broadcasts right from the battlefields have greatly enhanced people's ability to visualize war. As students share their insights, challenge them to name factors that influence people's impressions of war.

War Stories

COMMON CORE

SL1 Initiate and participate in a range of collaborative discussions, building on others' ideas and expressing their own clearly and persuasively.

Steven Spielberg's 1998 movie *Saving Private Ryan* was noted for its realistic portrayal of battle.

Before the Civil War, most American writers depicted war romantically, focusing on the glory of a battle, the justness of a cause, or the heroism of a leader. Later, writers such as Stephen Crane began to depict war in all its grim reality, uncovering the daily discomforts of military life, the horrors of the battlefield, and the lasting and unexpected consequences of war. Americans today are still drawn to war stories of all kinds.

DISCUSS As a class, discuss which elements in current war stories (novels, movies, TV shows, news reports) are realistic and which are romantic in nature. Give specific examples.

DIFFERENTIATED INSTRUCTION

FOR ADVANCED LEARNERS/AP

Write a War Story Invite students to write brief stories set during a war that interests them. Urge students to strive for physical realism in their portrayal of war and for psychological realism in their depiction of characters' responses to the main event featured in each story's plot. In addition, encourage students to do enough research to keep their stories historically accurate, considering questions such as these:

- Why was the war being fought?
- What were the climate and terrain like?
- How did the characters dress? What arms were available to them?
- What kind of medical care did they have?

Have students who wish to do so present their work in an oral storytelling session. Afterward, invite the class to discuss aspects of the stories that they thought were especially realistic or otherwise powerful.

Artistic Innovators

Who are the blue men in this picture, and what do they have to do with Walt Whitman and Emily Dickinson? The Blue Man Group is just one example of many current artistic innovators who can tip their hats to the mavericks of an earlier era: Whitman and Dickinson. Since Whitman and Dickinson's bold experiments with poetic form and content in the 19th century, writers, musicians, and artists have increasingly pushed the limits of what is considered art, broadening Americans' tastes and imaginations in the process.

QUICKWRITE With your classmates, list as many artistic innovators as you can think of from the Civil War period to today. What do they have in common? What value do they bring to our society?

African-American Influence

One lasting legacy of the Civil War period has been the rise of African Americans to leadership positions and levels of prominence. Beginning with abolitionists such as Sojourner Truth and Frederick Douglass, African Americans have made their way into all spheres of American public life, from politics, education, and the sciences to the arts and entertainment.

CREATE With a partner, create a poster or collage highlighting the achievements of three African American leaders today. Include photographs of three leaders who are working in different fields, and list their accomplishments. Consult a dictionary of quotations or other sources for quotations by or about each person.

From top, Scientist George Washington Carver, activist Rosa Parks, President Barack Obama, writer Maya Angelou, activist Martin Luther King Jr., media mogul Oprah Winfrey

Artistic Innovators

As students read the paragraph, explain that Blue Man Group combines music, comedy, and multimedia to create distinctive theatrical presentations. The group's name refers to the blue makeup that the performers wear. The group's unique instruments include the cimbalon and the Chapman Stick, which are stringed instruments; a two-story Drum Wall; airpoles, which are fiberglass tubes that make a swooshing sound in the air; and PVC tubes that are struck with paddles or sticks.

QUICKWRITE You might have students make their lists independently and then read them aloud to classmates; alternatively, have small groups work together on a list. Work with students to create master lists of common traits and values.

African-American Influence

Before students read the paragraph, review the meaning of *abolitionist* and the fact that the Civil War ultimately ensured freedom for African Americans. Invite students to share what they know of the people pictured and to name other African-American leaders.

CREATE Encourage students to use print and online resources including a dictionary of quotations for their research and to make the lists of accomplishments as up-to-date as possible. Have students organize and present a display of the finished posters or collages for the class.

FOR STRUGGLING READERS

Vocabulary Support

- *justness,* "moral rightness"
- *consequences,* "results; outcomes"
- *innovators,* "people who do new things"
- *slew,* "large number"
- *prominence,* "importance; distinction"
- *spheres,* "areas"

FOR ADVANCED LEARNERS/AP

Research and Analyze [mixed-interest groups] Invite small groups of students to research one of the artistic innovators named in the *QUICKWRITE* activity on this page. Have each group create and give a multimedia presentation, teaching the class about the kind of art that the innovator created, why the art was innovative, and what influence it has had on other artists.

COMMON CORE FOCUS

RL 1 Cite strong and thorough textual evidence to support analysis of what the text says explicitly. **RL 5** Analyze how an author's choices concerning how to structure specific parts of a text contribute to its overall structure and meaning as well as its aesthetic impact. **RL 10** Read and comprehend literature, including poems.

Form and Function

Provide these brief explanations of the traditional fixed forms:

- A **sonnet** has 14 lines and a specific rhyme scheme and meter.
- A **ballad** tells a story and usually has meter, rhyme, and repeated passages.
- An **epic** is a long narrative about the adventures of a hero.
- An **elegy** is a long, thoughtful poem about a serious subject (especially death).
- An **ode** is a complex lyric poem (that is, a poem that expresses personal thoughts and feelings) on a serious, dignified theme.
- A **villanelle** has 19 lines arranged in a strict order, including repeated lines.
- **Blank verse** is unrhymed iambic pentameter.

Use a Two-Column Chart to discuss the differences between fixed and organic forms. Invite students to share thoughts about poems of either type that they have read or have written in the past.

Fixed Form	Organic Form
The form was invented before the poem was written.	Each poem has its own form, chosen by the poet.
Has regular rhythm; may have rhyme.	May or may not have regular rhythm and rhyme.

 **BEST PRACTICES TOOLKIT—Transparency**
Two-Column Chart p. A25

Form and Content in Poetry

Do you think everything has already been said? Throughout American history, poets have prided themselves on finding new ways to say things, as well as inventing new poetic forms in which to say them.

COMMON CORE

Included in this workshop:
RL 1 Cite strong and thorough textual evidence to support analysis of what the text says explicity. **RL 5** Analyze how an author's choices concerning how to structure specific parts of a text contribute to its overall structure and meaning as well as its aesthetic impact. **RL 10** Read and comprehend literature, including poems.

Form and Function

All works of art have **form,** a particular organization of parts that makes a whole. In poetry, form is referred to as **poetic structure:** the way words are arranged in lines, lines are arranged in stanzas, and units of sound are organized to achieve rhythm and rhyme. In general, poetic forms fall into two categories, traditional and organic. Poems in **traditional form** follow certain fixed conventions. For example, they can have a limited number of lines, a specified meter and rhyme scheme, and a definite structure. Such poems are also called **fixed form** poems and include the **sonnet,** the **ballad,** the **epic,** the **elegy,** the **ode,** the **villanelle,** and **blank verse.** Often, poets choose a form that fits the subject matter. For example, a sonnet was originally intended only for the

Engraving of Walt Whitman by Max Beerbohm, 1904

subject of love. The great English poets, such as William Shakespeare and John Milton, used traditional poetic forms, as did many early American poets.

The **organic form** of poetry, also known as **irregular form,** developed in the early 19th century. The English romantic poets wanted more flexible verse forms to fit the new content of their poetry. Unlike traditional forms, which provide an ideal pattern for poems to follow, organic form takes its shape and pattern from the content of the poem itself. That is, the form of a poem "grows" naturally out of what the poem says. A poem in organic form may have meter and rhyme, but the poet may vary the rhythm and rhyme scheme in irregular and unexpected ways. In searching for ways to find new expression, several American poets, such as Walt Whitman and Emily Dickinson, began experimenting with organic form.

Poetic Form in Action

One way to understand the difference between traditional and organic forms is to compare the poetry of Henry Wadsworth Longfellow and Emily Dickinson. Longfellow was somewhat conventional in most of his poems, using a predictable alternating rhyme scheme and punctuation. The excerpted lines shown here from Longfellow's "Psalm of Life" have a regular meter.

DIFFERENTIATED INSTRUCTION

FOR STRUGGLING READERS

Note Taking For students who are unfamiliar with poetry or need help with note taking, hand out the copy master before discussing this page. Explain that they will be learning many terms relating to poetic form in this workshop. Discuss the major terms on this spread (*form/structure, traditional/fixed form, organic/irregular form, free verse*) as students record notes on their copy masters.

R RESOURCE MANAGER—Copy Master
Note Taking p. 8

> Tell me not, in mournful numbers,   *a*
>
> Life is but an empty dream!—   *b*
>
> For the soul is dead that slumbers,   *a*
>
> And things are not what they seem.   *b*
>
> **—Henry Wadsworth Longfellow, "A Psalm of Life"**

Close Read

Study the pattern of rhythm in the first two lines, and then sound out and note the stressed and unstressed syllables in lines 3 and 4.

Now look at the first stanza of a poem by Dickinson. She also used meter and rhyme, but she added rhythmical variations, which characterize it as organic. The first line has four accents, while the next three lines each have three accented syllables and are **enjambed,** or **run-on,** ending without a grammatical or normal speech pause.

> My life closed twice before its close—   *a*
>
> It yet remains to see   *b*
>
> If Immortality unveil   *c*
>
> A third event to me   *b*
>
> **—Emily Dickinson, "My life closed twice before its close"**

Close Read

Notice the difference in rhythm between line 1 and lines 2–4. What effect does this shift have on the way the poem sounds? How might the change in rhythm emphasize the writer's meaning?

Free verse is an organic form that lacks regular meter and rhyme. Although free verse still has rhythm and may include an occasional rhyme within a line, it does not follow any strict rules. Like all forms of poetry, however, it may include a variety of sound devices, such as repetition and alliteration, to achieve a musical quality.

The great master of free verse in American poetry was Walt Whitman. At a time when American poetry followed traditional forms, Whitman went his own way and created a form that grew purely out of the ideas expressed. In this passage from "I Hear America Singing," notice the language and sound devices that create a poetic effect in sentences that are almost like those in prose.

> I hear America singing, the varied carols I hear,
> Those of mechanics, each one singing his as it should be blithe and strong,
> The carpenter singing his as he measures his plank or beam,
> **—Walt Whitman, "I Hear America Singing"**

Close Read

Examine and compare the three examples on this page. How do they vary in content?

TEXT ANALYSIS WORKSHOP   **529**

POETIC FORM IN ACTION

To help students understand enjambment, call their attention to the ends of lines in the Longfellow and Dickinson excerpts. Have students decide whether each line is meant to end with a normal speech pause. ***Answer:*** *All Longfellow's lines and the first line of Dickinson's poem end with a normal speech pause, but Dickinson's last three lines are enjambed.* Ask the same question after students have read the Whitman excerpt. ***Answer:*** *There is a normal speech pause after each of Whitman's lines, but his lines are much longer and have internal pauses as well.*

Close Read

Answer: *Lines 3 and 4 repeat the pattern of rhythm found in the first two lines.*

Close Read

Possible answer: *The shift makes the shorter lines seem quicker than the longer ones—more like a writer's spontaneous thought.*

IF STUDENTS NEED HELP ... Point out that line 1 is a complete statement but that the next complete statement takes three lines to express. Discuss the link between breaking up the statement and changing the rhythm.

Close Read

Possible answer: *The Longfellow excerpt is energetic in rejecting the philosophy of life that some listeners may hold. The Dickinson excerpt also considers issues of life and death but expresses more uncertainty. Whitman's poem expresses exuberant optimism about life, with no mention of uncertainty or concerns about death.*

FOR ENGLISH LANGUAGE LEARNERS

Language: Skill Words Help students understand the words *form* and *structure* by suggesting objects in the world that have a structure or form, such as a ball game or a building. Then discuss the difference between *fixed (traditional) form* and *organic (irregular) form:*

- Explain that if a form is *fixed,* the form doesn't change. Point out the other meaning of *fixed* and show the similarity; for example, if something broken is *fixed,* it becomes the same as before.

- Ask students if they have ever seen or eaten organic foods. Elicit or explain that organic foods are grown naturally. Similarly, *organic form* in poetry means that the form of a poem grows naturally from the poet's mind and that it is not based on a rule.

Focus and Motivate

COMMON CORE FOCUS

RL 1 Cite textual evidence to support analysis of what the text says explicitly as well as inferences drawn from the text. **RL 2** Determine themes or central ideas of a text; provide an objective summary of the text. **RL 4** Analyze the impact of specific word choices on meaning and tone, including words with multiple meanings or language that is particularly fresh, engaging, or beautiful. **RL 5** Analyze how an author's choices concerning how to structure specific parts of a text contribute to its overall structure and meaning as well as its aesthetic impact. **RL 9** Demonstrate knowledge of how two or more texts from the same period treat similar themes or topics. **SL 1** Participate in collaborative discussions. **SL 2** Integrate multiple sources of information presented in diverse formats and media. **L 4** Determine or clarify the meaning of multiple-meaning words. **L 5** Demonstrate understanding of figurative language.

ABOUT THE POET

After students have read the biography, point out these aspects of Whitman's life that give clues to the nature of his poetry:

- He grew up in a crowded American city, and he often described scenes of city life.

- He held many jobs, and he wrote about many occupations.

- He found inspiration in Emerson; like Emerson, he wrote in celebration of nature.

- He was independent, freewheeling, and optimistic—traits that appear in his poetry.

Selection Resources

COMMON CORE

RL 1 Cite textual evidence to support analysis of what the text says explicitly as well as inferences drawn from the text. **RL 4** Analyze the impact of specific word choices on meaning and tone, including words with multiple meanings or language that is particularly fresh, engaging, or beautiful. **RL 5** Analyze how an author's choices concerning how to structure specific parts of a text contribute to its overall structure and meaning as well as its aesthetic impact. **SL 1** Participate in collaborative discussions. **SL 2** Integrate multiple sources of information presented in diverse formats and media. **L 4** Determine or clarify the meaning of multiple-meaning words.

DID YOU KNOW?

Walt Whitman . . .

- dropped out of school at age 11.

- sent a copy of *Leaves of Grass* to poet John Greenleaf Whittier, who threw it into the fire.

- had Thomas Edison record him reading one of his poems.

Brilliant Mavericks: Whitman and Dickinson

Selected Poetry
by Walt Whitman

VIDEO TRAILER  KEYWORD: HML11-530A

Essential Course of Study **ECOS**

Meet the Author

Walt Whitman 1819–1892

When Walt Whitman's book of poems *Leaves of Grass* first appeared, many people were shocked by its controversial content and revolutionary form. Of the 800 copies printed, most were eventually thrown away. However, a few readers recognized the poet's genius. In a letter to Whitman, Ralph Waldo Emerson called *Leaves of Grass* "the most extraordinary piece of wit and wisdom that America has yet contributed."

The Making of a Poet Nothing Whitman wrote before *Leaves of Grass* contained any hint of what was to come. He burst onto the literary scene full-bodied and brash, like one of his poems.

His early years offered little in the way of preparation. Born in 1819, Whitman grew up in rural Long Island and crowded Brooklyn. He held a series of jobs including office boy, typesetter, printer, newspaper editor, school teacher, carpenter, and journalist.

In the 1840s, Whitman published a number of poems and short stories—and even a fairly successful novel—but these were conventional efforts.

Apparently, however, Whitman was just waiting for the proper inspiration. Upon reading Emerson, he realized that he could celebrate all aspects of nature and humanity by using spiritual language. "I was simmering, simmering, simmering," he once declared. "Emerson brought me to a boil."

An American Bard In the early 1850s, Whitman quit his job as a journalist and worked on *Leaves of Grass*. Declaring a kind of literary Independence Day, he printed his 12-poem book on July 4, 1855, at his own expense; he even set some of the type himself. Throughout his lifetime, Whitman would continue to rewrite, revise, and expand *Leaves of Grass*. The ninth and final edition, published in 1892, contained nearly 400 poems.

Unfettered by traditional poetic conventions and grammatical structures, Whitman captured the vitality, optimism, and voice of his native land. He celebrated all aspects of American life—the unique and the commonplace, the beautiful and the ugly.

Whitman once claimed that "the proof of a poet is that his country absorbs him as affectionately as he has absorbed it." By that measure and any other, Whitman is one of the most successful poets in history. Today *Leaves of Grass* is widely regarded as the most influential book of poetry in American literature.

Author Online
Go to **thinkcentral.com**. KEYWORD: HML11-530B

530

See resources on the **Teacher One Stop DVD-ROM** and on **thinkcentral.com**.

 RESOURCE MANAGER UNIT 3
Plan and Teach, pp. 11–18
Text Analysis and Reading Skill, pp. 19–22†*

DIAGNOSTIC AND SELECTION TESTS
Selection Tests, pp. 149–152

 BEST PRACTICES TOOLKIT
Jigsaw Reading, p. A1
Venn Diagram, p. A26

INTERACTIVE READER

ADAPTED INTERACTIVE READER

ELL ADAPTED INTERACTIVE READER

TECHNOLOGY
- **Teacher One Stop DVD-ROM**
- **Student One Stop DVD-ROM**
- **PowerNotes DVD-ROM**
- **Audio Anthology CD**
- **GrammarNotes DVD-ROM**
- **ExamView Test Generator** on the Teacher One Stop

Video Trailer

Go to **thinkcentral.com** to preview the **Video Trailer** introducing this selection. Other features that support the selection include

- **PowerNotes** presentation
- **ThinkAloud** models to enhance comprehension
- **WordSharp** vocabulary tutorials
- interactive writing and grammar instruction

---

* Resources for Differentiation   † Also in Spanish   ‡ Also in Haitian Creole and Vietnamese

TEXT ANALYSIS: FREE VERSE

Walt Whitman is the great master of free verse in American poetry. **Free verse** is poetry that does not contain regular patterns of rhyme and meter. The lines in free verse often flow more naturally than do rhymed, metrical lines and so sound more like everyday speech. Note, however, that Whitman does use the following poetic devices to create rhythm:

- **cataloging:** frequent lists of people, things, and attributes

  The shoemaker singing as he sits on his bench, the hatter singing as he stands

- **repetition:** repeated words or phrases at the beginning of two or more lines

  Beat! beat! drums!—blow! bugles! blow!

- **parallelism:** related ideas phrased in similar ways

  Born here of parents born here from parents the same, and their parents the same

As you read the poems, notice how Whitman uses these devices to achieve rhythm, musical effects, and a style all his own.

READING SKILL: ANALYZE TONE

To help you understand Whitman's poems, pay attention to their tone. **Tone** is an expression of a writer's attitude toward his or her subject. For example, a writer's tone might be respectful, angry, or amused. Tone can be communicated through choice of words and details. Notice the triumphant tone in these lines from "Song of Myself":

I celebrate myself, and sing myself,
And what I assume you shall assume,
For every atom belonging to me as good belongs to you.

As you read Whitman's poems, jot down examples of words and details that communicate tone in a chart like the one shown.

	Examples	Tone
"I Hear America Singing"	"blithe and strong"	happy, confident
"Song of Myself"		
"A Noiseless Patient Spider"		
"Beat! Beat! Drums!"		

 Complete the activities in your **Reader/Writer Notebook**.

What does AMERICA look like?

What images come to mind when you think about America? Maybe you see big cities or rolling farmland. Maybe you picture the mountains or the coasts. Or maybe you focus on the people rather than the land. Many of Walt Whitman's poems contain vivid images of America in the mid-1800s. What— and who—captures America's spirit and reality today?

DISCUSS Imagine that you have been asked to design a poster that will help introduce tourists and newcomers to America. Get together in a small group and discuss the images that represent the people and places of America. Be sure to include images that symbolize all aspects of the country.

What does AMERICA look like?

Ask the question. As students read the paragraph that follows the question, suggest that they visualize the scenes of America that it describes and add visualizations of other American scenes. Have them use their visualizations as a starting point for the *DISCUSS* activity; afterward, invite students to follow through and create a classroom display of posters.

TEXT ANALYSIS   COMMON CORE
RL 4
RL 5

● *Model the Skill:* FREE VERSE

Help students identify the poetic elements that can be used in free verse by writing these lines on the board:

> Going to school, I dress quickly, eat in a rush, run for the bus.

> Going to school, I read closely, listen, speak, write, rush to the next class.

Point out to students that the list of actions is an example of cataloging, the repeated phrase "Going to school" displays repetition, and the repetition of the grammatical structure "I + [verb] + [adverb]" relays parallelism.

GUIDED PRACTICE Have students write and share two lines of free verse on a topic of their choice.

READING SKILL   COMMON CORE
RL 1
RL 4

■ *Model the Skill:* ANALYZE TONE

To help students identify tone in poetry, suggest words that describe the tone of the example of free verse in the previous activity. Then have students reread the free verse that they wrote for **GUIDED PRACTICE** and describe its tone. Offer students guidance, if needed.

 RESOURCE MANAGER—Copy Master
Analyze Tone p. 21 (for student use while reading the selections)

DIFFERENTIATED INSTRUCTION

FOR ENGLISH LANGUAGE LEARNERS

Cultural Context Explain to students that Walt Whitman is revered as one of the great American poets. Ask students what poets from their own country are highly regarded. Have students work in mixed-ability pairs to research a poet from their own country. Have students answer the following questions:

- Does the poet often write in free verse or in a more traditional form?

- What are some common topics or themes the poet addresses?

- What is a common tone of his or her poems?

FOR ADVANCED LEARNERS/AP

Contrast Free Verse and Prose [paired option] Ask pairs of students to discuss the differences between free verse and prose. Have them consider (1) whether some free verse is little more than prose broken into lines and (2) why that idea is not true of Whitman, whose free verse is clearly poetry. Invite students to share their insights with the class.

SUMMARY

The speaker catalogs the kinds of singing that he hears in the daily life and work of average Americans.

READ WITH A PURPOSE

Help students set a purpose for reading. Tell them to read to discover how Whitman viewed the world around him. Encourage students to think about how they would describe Whitman, based upon his writing.

TEXT ANALYSIS	COMMON CORE
	RL 4
	RL 5

Ⓐ FREE VERSE

Possible answer: The cataloging creates a rhythm that suggests movement and vitality.

READING SKILL	COMMON CORE
	RL 1
	RL 4

Ⓑ ANALYZE TONE

Possible answer: Whitman expresses an admiring, grateful, fraternal attitude. Words and details that help convey this attitude include "robust," "friendly," "Singing with open mouths," "strong," and "melodious."

ANSWERS

Possible answers:

1. *Whitman celebrates men and women who work with their hands and keep the country going.*

2. *The singing represents the sound of people working in harmony and enjoying life, the hum of progress and the development of America.*

3. *Whitman may have omitted these Americans because he believes they are not the backbone of the country; they are in charge of others and don't perform the actual work themselves.*

I Hear America Singing

Walt Whitman

I hear America singing, the varied carols I hear,
Those of mechanics, each one singing his as it should be blithe and strong,
The carpenter singing his as he measures his plank or beam, Ⓐ
The mason singing his as he makes ready for work, or leaves off work,
5 The boatman singing what belongs to him in his boat, the deckhand singing on the steamboat deck,
The shoemaker singing as he sits on his bench, the hatter singing as he stands,
The wood-cutter's song, the ploughboy's on his way in the morning, or at noon intermission or at sundown,
The delicious singing of the mother, or of the young wife at work, or of the girl sewing or washing,
Each singing what belongs to him or her and to none else,
10 The day what belongs to the day—at night the party of young fellows, robust, friendly,
Singing with open mouths their strong melodious songs. Ⓑ

Ⓐ FREE VERSE
Notice the use of **cataloging** throughout the poem. What rhythmic effect does the poet create with his list of the men and women at work in America?

Ⓑ ANALYZE TONE
Reread lines 10–11. What attitude does the speaker express toward the young men? Note the words and details that help convey that attitude.

Text Analysis

1. **Summarize** What types of workers does Whitman celebrate in this poem?

2. **Clarify** What do you think singing represents in the poem?

3. **Make Inferences** Why do you think Whitman does not mention wealthy entrepreneurs, prominent leaders, or powerful politicians?

The Reaper (1878), Winslow Homer. Watercolor. Private collection. Photo © Art Resource, New York.

DIFFERENTIATED INSTRUCTION

FOR STRUGGLING READERS

Develop Reading Fluency

- Have students listen to the poems on the *Audio Anthology CD* (also recommended for English language learners) while they read along in their texts. Ask students to listen for and then describe the speaker's tone in each poem.

- Have groups prepare and perform choral readings of "I Hear America Singing."

Remind them to review Whitman's intent and to discuss tone, intonation, expression, and pacing as they plan and rehearse their performances. Emphasize to students that punctuation marks and line breaks will help them determine proper pacing and intonation. Follow up by inviting participants to share any insights into the poem that they gained through the activity.

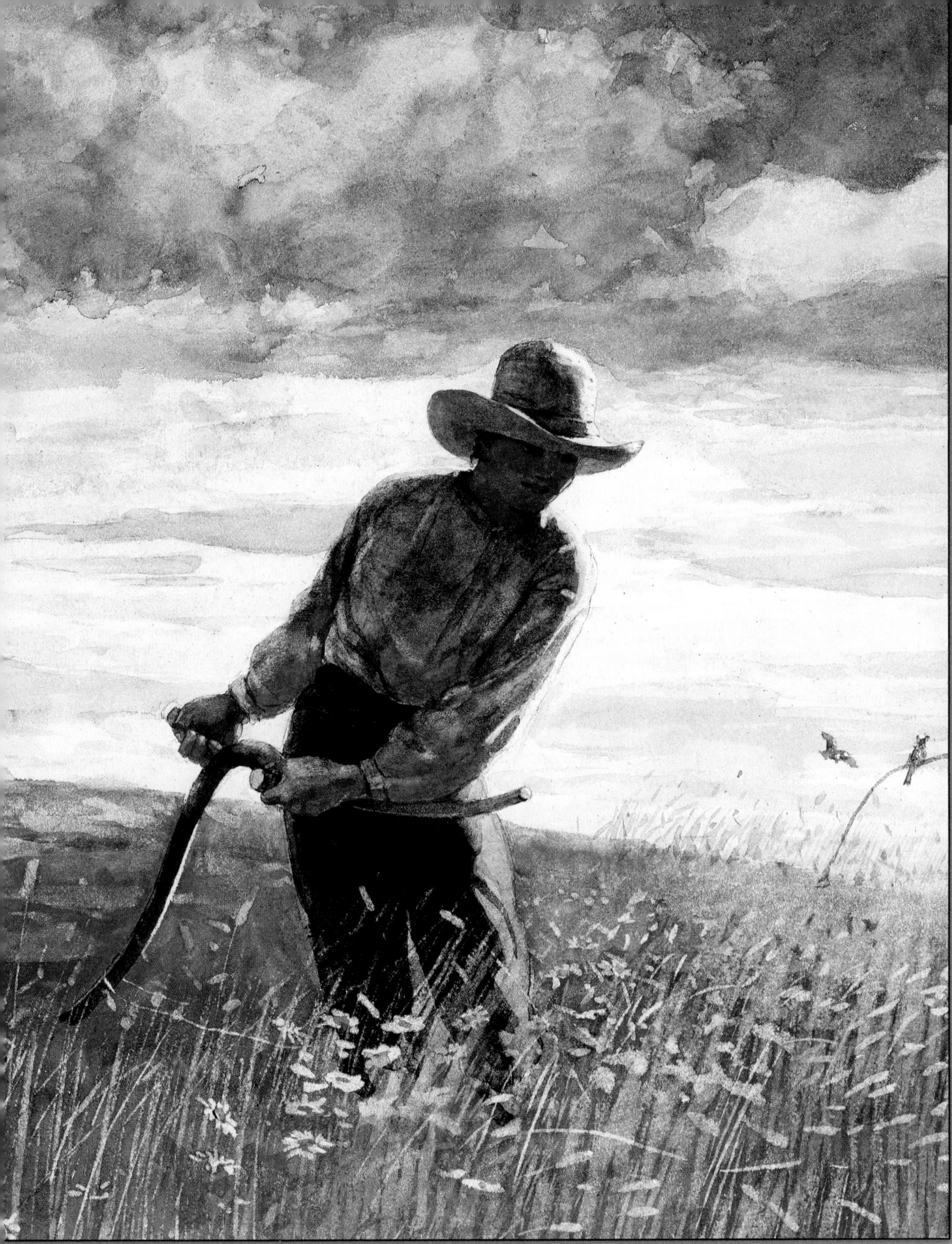

Reading Support THINK central

This selection on **thinkcentral.com** includes embedded **ThinkAloud** models–students "thinking aloud" about the story to model the kinds of questions a good reader would ask about a selection.

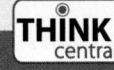

BACKGROUND

Agriculture and Industry in Whitman's America The United States was a much more agrarian nation in Whitman's time than it is today. In 1862, 90 percent of Americans were engaged in farming; today, the figure is less than 2 percent.

Cultural Connection In many nations today, agriculture still occupies most people. In Haiti, for example, two-thirds of the people work in small-scale farming and related occupations. Invite students to share what they know about the importance of agriculture and industries in their home cultures.

About the Art This watercolor by American painter Winslow Homer (1836–1910) shows a farmer reaping—cutting grain—with a scythe. He would fit easily into Whitman's catalog of energetic workers in "I Hear America Singing." The painting shows Homer's ability to create a sense of action in watercolor, a medium that he helped make important in American art. The farmer's leaning, angular figure is caught in motion against three horizontal bars: earth, sky, and cloud.

REVISIT THE BIG QUESTION

What does AMERICA *look like?*

Discuss In lines 9–11, what is Walt Whitman's view of America? ***Possible answer:*** *He sees America as energetic, hardworking, and joyously facing the future, one day at a time.*

FOR ENGLISH LANGUAGE LEARNERS

Vocabulary Support

- *carols* (line 1), "songs of joy or praise"
- *blithe* (line 2), "carefree"
- *mason* (line 4), "a worker who builds with stone or brick"
- *ploughboy* (line 7), "a young male farm worker"
- *intermission* (line 7), "a break from work"
- *robust* (line 10), "energetic and healthy"

SUMMARY

The speaker rejoices in nature and in his own energetic, expansive spirit.

TIERED DISCUSSION PROMPTS

In lines 1–13, use these prompts to help students understand the poem's ideas and tone:

Connect Do you identify with what the speaker says about himself? Why or why not? *Possible answers: Yes, because I like myself. No, because I think he is bragging.*

Interpret What impression of the speaker do these lines give you? *Possible answer: The speaker is confident, observant, at times reflective, at other times more enthusiastic.*

Synthesize Consider what you know about traditional poetic forms. How is the tone in this free-verse expression different from what it would be if the same ideas were expressed in a traditional poetic form? *Possible answer: Here the tone is freer, more expansive, more joyous.*

TEXT ANALYSIS

COMMON CORE
RL 4
RL 5

C *Model the Skill:* FREE VERSE

To analyze the effects of parallelism, focus students' attention on the details cited in lines 1-3. Discuss how each detail reflects the belief that the speaker and the reader are intertwined.

Possible answer: The parallelism in "what I assume you shall assume" and in "belonging to me as good belongs to you" creates a bond between the speaker and the reader.

READING SKILL

COMMON CORE
RL 1
RL 4

D ANALYZE TONE

Possible answer: The tone in lines 4–5 is quiet and contemplative; the tone in lines 12–13 is dynamic and energetic. The tone in both pairs of lines is self-affirming.

Song of Myself

Walt Whitman

1

I celebrate myself, and sing myself,
And what I assume you shall assume,
For every atom belonging to me as good belongs to you. **C**

I loaf and invite my soul,
5 I lean and loaf at my ease observing a spear of summer grass.

My tongue, every atom of my blood, form'd from this soil, this air,
Born here of parents born here from parents the same, and their parents the same,
I, now thirty-seven years old in perfect health begin,
Hoping to cease not till death.

10 Creeds and schools in abeyance,
Retiring back a while sufficed at[1] what they are, but never forgotten,
I harbor for good or bad, I permit to speak at every hazard,
Nature without check with original energy. **D**

6

A child said *What is the grass?* fetching it to me with full hands,
15 How could I answer the child? I do not know what it is any more than he.
I guess it must be the flag of my disposition, out of hopeful green stuff woven.

Or I guess it is the handkerchief of the Lord,
A scented gift and remembrancer designedly dropt,[2]

---

1. **sufficed at:** satisfied with.
2. **remembrancer designedly dropt:** a purposely dropped token of affection.

C FREE VERSE
Read lines 1–3 aloud and listen to the rhythm created by **parallelism.** In what ways does the use of this technique reflect the relationship between the speaker and the reader?

D ANALYZE TONE
Compare the tone in lines 4–5 with that in lines 12–13. How does the tone change? How is the tone in both pairs of lines similar?

DIFFERENTIATED INSTRUCTION

FOR STRUGGLING READERS

Concept Support: Paraphrase To help students with lines 10–13, have them use the Jigsaw Reading strategy, with each student or group paraphrasing one of the four lines. Point out words with multiple meanings: *schools, retiring, harbor, permit, hazard, check,* and *original.* Have students continue this process as they read, with each student or group specializing in a stanza.

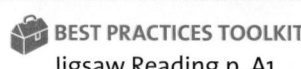 **BEST PRACTICES TOOLKIT**
Jigsaw Reading p. A1

Boys in Pasture, Winslow Homer. © Burstein Collection/Corbis.

Bearing the owner's name someway in the corners, that we may see
and remark, and say *Whose?*

20 Or I guess the grass is itself a child, the produced babe of the
vegetation.

Or I guess it is a uniform hieroglyphic,[3] **⑤**
And it means, Sprouting alike in broad zones and narrow zones,
Growing among black folks as among white,
Kanuck, Tuckahoe, Congressman, Cuff,[4] I give them the same, I
receive them the same.

25 And now it seems to me the beautiful uncut hair of graves.

Tenderly will I use you curling grass,
It may be you transpire[5] from the breasts of young men,
It may be if I had known them I would have loved them,
It may be you are from old people, or from offspring taken soon
out of their mothers' laps,
30 And here you are the mothers' laps. **⑥**

⑤ FREE VERSE
Be aware of the **repetition**
in lines 16–21. What is the
relationship between the
repeated elements?

⑥ ANALYZE TONE
What attitude does the
speaker express toward
the dead in lines 25–30?

---

3. **hieroglyphic:** a system of symbols that represent meanings or speech sounds.

4. **Kanuck, Tuckahoe, . . . Cuff:** slang terms for various groups of people. A Kanuck (now
spelled Canuck) is a Canadian, especially a French Canadian; a Tuckahoe is someone
from the coast of Virginia; a Cuff is an African American.

5. **transpire:** emerge; ooze out.

Analyze Visuals

Activity Note that *Boys in Pasture* was painted
by Winslow Homer, the same artist who
painted *The Reaper* on page 533. Have students
examine both paintings and find resem-
blances that define Homer's subject matter
and style. Then have them complete a
Venn Diagram like this one to explore why
Homer's paintings make good illustrations
for Whitman's poems.

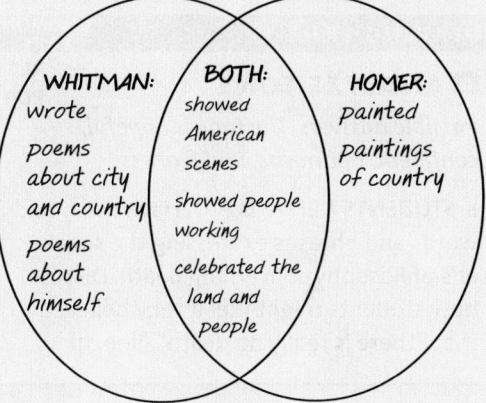

WHITMAN:
wrote
poems
about city
and country
poems
about
himself

BOTH:
showed
American
scenes
showed people
working
celebrated the
land and
people

HOMER:
painted
paintings
of country

BEST PRACTICES TOOLKIT—Transparency
Venn Diagram p. A26

TEXT ANALYSIS   COMMON CORE

⑤ FREE VERSE   RL 4
                                      RL 5

Possible answer: *The repeated element is*
"I guess," which refers to possible meta-
phorical meanings of the grass.

READING SKILL   COMMON CORE
                                      RL 1
⑥ *Model the Skill:*   RL 4
ANALYZE TONE

To identify the speaker's attitude, point
out words and phrases that relay this attitude, such as *beautiful, Tenderly, loved,* and
mothers' laps.

Possible answer: *The speaker expresses a*
tender, loving attitude toward the dead.

FOR ADVANCED LEARNERS/AP

Analyze Challenge students to extend their
analysis of these excerpts from "Song of
Myself" by responding briefly to one or more
of these writing prompts:

• Why does the speaker emphasize that his
American heritage goes back for many
generations (lines 6–7)?

• What does the speaker think of traditional
institutions? What does he think is more

important? Cite evidence from Section 1 to
support your answers.

• What might the "child" (line 14) symbolize?

• In Section 6, how does Whitman keep his
description of gravesites from becoming
grotesque?

• How do the speaker's comments in Section
52 recall Section 1? Do they bring the poem
to a satisfying conclusion?

CULTURAL CONNECTION

Afterlife In lines 38–45, the speaker presents a view of death and the afterlife. Many cultures have beliefs about the afterlife; for example, Hindus believe in reincarnation, based upon the good and bad actions of a person in earlier lives. Have students compare and contrast the view presented in these lines with beliefs in their culture and other beliefs with which they may be familiar.

READING SKILL   COMMON CORE
          RL 1
G ANALYZE TONE   RL 4

Possible answer: *The tone is hopeful, confident, optimistic, and fearless.*

IF STUDENTS NEED HELP . . . Have them find words and phrases expressing the speaker's philosophy concerning death. Discuss how students might feel if they believed that "there is really no death" (line 41).

TEXT ANALYSIS   COMMON CORE
          RL 4
H FREE VERSE   RL 5

Possible answers: *The parallel structure of the defiant line 47, the repetition of "I" at the beginnings of lines, and the lines' strident rhythm emphasize an untamed nature.*

Extend the Discussion What does the speaker mean by calling his poetry "my barbaric yawp" (line 48)? Do you like the idea of a poem being a "barbaric yawp"? Why, or why not?

This grass is very dark to be from the white heads of old mothers,
Darker than the colorless beards of old men,
Dark to come from under the faint red roofs of mouths.

O I perceive after all so many uttering tongues,
35 And I perceive they do not come from the roofs of mouths for
     nothing.

I wish I could translate the hints about the dead young men and
     women,
And the hints about old men and mothers, and the offspring taken
     soon out of their laps.

What do you think has become of the young and old men?
And what do you think has become of the women and children?

40 They are alive and well somewhere,
The smallest sprout shows there is really no death,
And if ever there was it led forward life, and does not wait at the
     end to arrest it,
And ceas'd the moment life appear'd.

All goes onward and outward, nothing collapses,
45 And to die is different from what any one supposed, and luckier. **G**

52

The spotted hawk swoops by and accuses me, he complains of my
     gab and my loitering.

I too am not a bit tamed, I too am untranslatable,
I sound my barbaric yawp[6] over the roofs of the world. **H**

The last scud[7] of day holds back for me,
50 It flings my likeness after the rest and true as any on the shadow'd
     wilds,
It coaxes me to the vapor and the dusk.

I depart as air, I shake my white locks at the runaway sun,
I effuse my flesh in eddies,[8] and drift it in lacy jags.

---

6. **yawp:** loud, rough speech.
7. **scud:** wind-blown cloud.
8. **effuse . . . eddies:** scatter my flesh in swirling currents.

COMMON CORE RL 4, L 4

Language Coach

Multiple-Meaning Words
You may be familiar with the meaning of *arrest* (line 42) in a law-enforcement context ("being taken into custody by law enforcement"). *Arrest* also means "to stop." Reread line 42–43. What does *arrest* mean here? What is Whitman saying about death?

G ANALYZE TONE
What words would you use to describe the tone in lines 38–45, where the speaker discusses life and death?

H FREE VERSE
Reread lines 47–48. What **poetic devices** in these lines emphasize the speaker's untamed nature?

DIFFERENTIATED INSTRUCTION

FOR STRUGGLING READERS

Concept Support: Analyze Tone Have students continue working with the prereading chart on page 531. Because this excerpt from "Song of Myself" contains three distinct sections, instruct students to fill out at least one line for each section, analyzing the section's tone.

Examples	Tone
"Nature without check" (Section 1, line 13)	defiant
"mothers' laps" (Section 6, line 30)	nostalgic
"not a bit tamed" (Section 52, line 47)	proud

FOR ENGLISH LANGUAGE LEARNERS

Language Coach   COMMON CORE RL 4, L 4
Multiple-Meaning Words *Possible answer: stop; Whitman says there really is no death.* Explain that when a word has more than one meaning, students must examine context to determine which meaning a writer has used.

I bequeath[9] myself to the dirt to grow from the grass I love,
55 If you want me again look for me under your boot-soles. ▪

You will hardly know who I am or what I mean,
But I shall be good health to you nevertheless,
And filter and fibre your blood.

Failing to fetch me at first keep encouraged,
60 Missing me one place search another,
I stop somewhere waiting for you.

_____

9. **bequeath:** hand over, as if in a will.

Text Analysis

1. **Clarify** According to the speaker, in lines 40–43, why is there "really no death"?

2. **Summarize** To what does the speaker compare himself in section 52?

3. **Analyze Symbols** What do you think grass symbolizes in this poem?

Return from the Farm (1915–1920), Elliott Daingerfield. Smithsonian American Art Museum, Washington, D.C. Photo © Smithsonian American Art Museum/Art Resource, New York.

▪ **ANALYZE TONE**
What words and details does the poet use in lines 49–55 to create a defiant tone?

▼ **Analyze Visuals**
This painting by American artist Elliott Daingerfield shows a man returning home after working on his farm. What **images** in the painting are similar to those described in the poem?

Prereading for this poem is found on page 530.

SUMMARY

The speaker compares his soul's progress to a spider's web-building process.

About the Art Victor Hugo (1802–1885) was perhaps the greatest French romantic poet; he also wrote the classic novel *Les Misérables*, which inspired a hit musical that has played around the world. Hugo, however, also was a fine artist. He frequently drew and painted to explore ideas for his writing, much as Whitman here finds that observing the artistry of a spider has led him to a writing idea.

TEXT ANALYSIS

COMMON CORE
RL 4
RL 5

○ FREE VERSE

Possible answer: The parallelism suggests a connection between spider and speaker: Both are alone and must launch themselves into the void in order to find an anchor.

IF STUDENTS NEED HELP . . . Ask:
- Whom is the speaker describing in line 5? in line 8?
- How are the two descriptions similar?

READING SKILL

COMMON CORE
RL 1
RL 4

○ ANALYZE TONE

Possible answers: Overall, the tone is musing and thoughtful, suggesting a sense of aloneness. Details such as "isolated" (line 2), "vacant vast surrounding" (line 3), "detached" (line 7), and "measureless oceans of space" (line 7) communicate that tone.

Extend the Discussion How does the tone of this poem differ from the tone of the previous Whitman poems in this lesson?

Crossing the Spider Web, Victor Hugo. Watercolor. Maison Victor Hugo. Musée de la Ville de Paris. Photo © Giraudon/Art Resource, New York.

A Noiseless **Patient Spider**

Walt Whitman

A noiseless patient spider,
I mark'd where on a little promontory[1] it stood isolated,
Mark'd how to explore the vacant vast surrounding,
It launch'd forth filament, filament, filament, out of itself,
5 Ever unreeling them, ever tirelessly speeding them.

And you O my soul where you stand,
Surrounded, detached, in measureless oceans of space,
Ceaselessly musing, venturing, throwing, seeking the spheres to
    connect them, ○
Till the bridge you will need be form'd, till the ductile[2] anchor
    hold,
10 Till the gossamer[3] thread you fling catch somewhere, O my soul. ○

---

1. **promontory:** a high ridge of land or rock jutting out over water or land.
2. **ductile:** capable of being drawn or stretched out.
3. **gossamer:** extremely light or fine.

○ **FREE VERSE**
Compare the use of **parallelism** in lines 5 and 8. What do these parallel elements suggest about the relationship between the spider and speaker?

○ **ANALYZE TONE**
What is the overall tone of the poem? What details communicate that tone?

DIFFERENTIATED INSTRUCTION

FOR ENGLISH LANGUAGE LEARNERS
Vocabulary Support
- *mark'd* (line 2), "noticed"
- *vast* (line 3), "vastness; huge space"
- *filament* (line 4), "a slender thread"
- *detached* (line 7), "not connected"
- *measureless* (line 7), "too big to measure"
- *musing* (line 8), "thinking"

FOR ADVANCED LEARNERS/AP
Compare and Contrast Poems Walt Whitman's musings about a spider (1868) are reminiscent of the musings that Oliver Wendell Holmes recorded (1858) in "The Chambered Nautilus" (page 350). Have students reread and reflect upon both poems. Then have them write an essay that compares the poems. Work with students to create a format for sharing their insights.

Beat! Beat! Drums!

Walt Whitman

Beat! beat! drums!—blow! bugles! blow!
Through the windows—through doors—burst like a ruthless force,
Into the solemn church, and scatter the congregation,
Into the school where the scholar is studying;
5 Leave not the bridegroom quiet—no happiness must he have now
    with his bride,
Nor the peaceful farmer any peace, ploughing his field or
    gathering his grain,
So fierce you whirr and pound you drums—so shrill you bugles
    blow. **L**

Beat! beat! drums!—blow! bugles! blow!
Over the traffic of cities—over the rumble of wheels in the streets;
10 Are beds prepared for sleepers at night in the houses? no sleepers
    must sleep in those beds,
No bargainers' bargains by day—no brokers or speculators—
    would they continue?
Would the talkers be talking? would the singer attempt to sing?
Would the lawyer rise in the court to state his case before the
    judge?
Then rattle quicker, heavier drums—you bugles wilder blow.

15 Beat! beat! drums!—blow! bugles! blow!
Make no parley—stop for no expostulation,[1]
Mind not the timid—mind not the weeper or prayer,
Mind not the old man beseeching the young man,
Let not the child's voice be heard, nor the mother's entreaties,
20 Make even the trestles[2] to shake the dead where they lie awaiting
    the hearses,
So strong you thump O terrible drums—so loud you bugles blow. **M**

L ANALYZE TONE
Describe the tone in lines 1–7. Why is this tone appropriate for the subject matter?

M FREE VERSE
Notice the **parallel structure** in the last line of each stanza. What impact does this device have on the poem's message?

---

1. **parley:** a discussion or conference; **expostulation:** argument.

2. **trestles:** tables, in this case, upon which coffins sit until the undertaker comes to take them away.

Prereading for this poem is found on page 530.

SUMMARY
The speaker addresses the drums and bugles of war, urging them to call people to action.

BACKGROUND
Drummer Boys In the Civil War, drummers and buglers accompanied army troops. Many of the musicians were mere boys. The most famous Civil War drummer boy, Johnny Clem, who enlisted at age 11, lived to be 85 and may have been the subject of the song "When Johnny Comes Marching Home."

READING SKILL	COMMON CORE
L ANALYZE TONE	RL 1 RL 4

Possible answers: The tone is loud, forceful, and urgent. This tone is appropriate because war can be characterized in all those ways.

TEXT ANALYSIS	COMMON CORE
M FREE VERSE	RL 4 RL 5

Possible answer: The parallel structure makes the sounds of the drums and bugles seem more insistent and loud, thus making the poem's message more forceful.

SELECTION WRAP–UP

READ WITH A PURPOSE Now that students have read the poems, ask them to describe how Whitman viewed the world around him and the type of person he probably was. *Possible answer:* Whitman viewed the world with wonder and passion. He was probably a free-spirited, optimistic person.

INDEPENDENT READING
Students who have enjoyed Whitman may want to read *Ode to Common Things* by Pablo Neruda who, crediting Whitman as inspiration, writes poems celebrating life.

FOR STRUGGLING READERS
Concept Support: Analyze Tone Have groups of students share their completed versions of the prereading chart from page 531. Ask them to offer feedback on their peers' perceptions of tone in the poems. Also invite students to discuss whether they think that there is a "typical" tone found throughout these poems or whether each poem has its own unique tone.

FOR ADVANCED LEARNERS/AP
Evaluate Remind students that Whitman was considered a disturbing, revolutionary poet when *Leaves of Grass* first appeared: He was considered revolutionary in his style and form; he was seen as disturbing for his voice, his ideas, his subject matter, and his personal image. Have students discuss whether there is still something disturbing or unconventional about Whitman or whether time has completely tamed him.

CONNECT

This selection provides additional information on Whitman's sense of Americanism. You can also use it as a minilesson on reading for information.

READING FOR INFORMATION

Point out that the Preface to *Leaves of Grass* is a brief prose introduction to a book of poems. In this case, the Preface was written by the poet himself. Then ask:

- What help does this Preface provide for previewing the book that it introduces?
  Possible answer: It gives the reader an idea of the subject matter of the book and the poet's attitude toward that subject.

- What is the main idea of this Preface?
  Possible answer: The main idea is that the United States is a vast and diverse nation, comparable to a free-verse poem.

TIERED DISCUSSION PROMPTS

Use these prompts to help students relate Whitman's personal statement to the poems that they have just read:

Connect As you read this Preface, did you find it inspiring? informative? vivid? Provide other adjectives of your own to describe your response. *Accept all reasonable answers.*

Interpret In Whitman's view, what is great about the United States? *Possible answer: The United States is great because of the multitude and variety of its common people.*

Synthesize Suppose that you were a reader in Whitman's era, reading *Leaves of Grass* for the first time. How good a preparation for the poems do you think this Preface would be, and why? *Possible answer: The Preface would be an excellent preparation because (1) it reflects the tone and subject matter of the poems and (2) the styles of Whitman's prose and verse are similar.*

ESSAY Among the most important themes of Walt Whitman's poetry is the magnificence of America as seen in the nation's common people. In his preface to *Leaves of Grass*, his great life work, he introduces this idea quite emphatically.

from the Preface to

Leaves of GRASS

Walt Whitman

The Americans of all nations at any time upon the earth have probably the fullest poetical nature. The United States themselves are essentially the greatest poem. In the history of the earth hitherto the largest and most stirring appear tame and orderly to their ampler largeness and stir. Here at last is something in the doings of man that corresponds with the broadcast doings of the day and night. Here is not merely a nation but a teeming nation of nations. Here is action untied from strings necessarily blind to particulars and details magnificently moving in vast masses. Here is the hospitality which forever indicates heroes. . . . Here are the roughs and beards and space and ruggedness and nonchalance that the soul loves. Here the performance disdaining the trivial unapproached in the tremendous audacity of its crowds and groupings and the push of its perspective spreads with crampless and flowing breadth and showers its prolific and splendid extravagance. One sees it must indeed own the riches of the summer and winter, and need never be bankrupt while corn grows from the ground or the orchards drop apples or the bays contain fish or men beget children upon women.

Other states indicate themselves in their deputies . . . but the genius of the United States is not best or most in its executives or legislatures, nor in its ambassadors or authors or colleges or churches or parlors, nor even in its newspapers or inventors . . . but always most in the common people. Their manners speech dress friendships—the freshness and candor of their physiognomy—the picturesque looseness of their carriage . . . their deathless attachment to freedom—their aversion to anything indecorous or soft or mean—the practical acknowledgment of the citizens of one state by the citizens of all other states—the fierceness of their roused resentment—their curiosity and welcome of novelty—their self-esteem and wonderful sympathy—their susceptibility to a slight—the air they have of persons who never knew how it felt to stand in the presence of superiors—the fluency of their speech—their delight in music, the sure symptom of manly tenderness and native elegance of soul . . . their good temper and openhandedness—the terrible significance of their elections—the President's taking off his hat to them not they to him—these too are unrhymed poetry. It awaits the gigantic and generous treatment worthy of it.

540   UNIT 3: FROM ROMANTICISM TO REALISM

Comprehension

1. **Recall** What two things does Whitman compare in "A Noiseless Patient Spider"?

2. **Summarize** In "Beat! Beat! Drums!" whom do the drums and bugles call to action?

3. **Paraphrase** How would you paraphrase lines 16–19 of "Beat! Beat! Drums!"?

Text Analysis

4. **Examine Imagery** Think about the images of mid-19th-century America that Whitman conveys in his poems. How do these images compare with what America looks like today? Cite specific details from the poems to support your comparisons.

5. **Analyze Tone** Review the examples of tone that you recorded as you read the poems. What can you conclude about Whitman's attitude toward the following?

   • manual labor   • the soul   • himself   • war

6. **Analyze Metaphor** Reread lines 16–25 of "Song of Myself." What metaphors does the speaker use to describe what grass means to him? What ideas does each metaphor suggest?

7. **Compare Poems** Use a chart like the one shown to compare the **images** and **mood** of "A Noiseless Patient Spider" and "Beat! Beat! Drums!" Based on your notes, what is the overall impact of each poem?

	Images	Mood
"A Noiseless Patient Spider"		
"Beat! Beat! Drums!"		

8. **Compare Texts** In what ways are the pronouncements made in Whitman's preface (page 540) reflected in his poems? Consider the content of what he says as well as the manner in which he states it. Provide details to support your ideas.

9. **Evaluate Free Verse** Why is free verse an appropriate form for Whitman's poems? Support your opinion.

Text Criticism

10. **Author's Style** In another section of "Song of Myself," Whitman writes: "He most honors my style who learns under it to destroy the teacher." What does he mean? Do you think Whitman encourages this position in the poems you have read? Use evidence from the poems to support your opinion.

What does AMERICA look like?

In his poems, Walt Whitman explored many different aspects of Americans and their lives. Think about your classmates and the people in your community. Do you think they are a good representation of the many different kinds of people in America? Explain your answer.

COMMON CORE

RL 1 Cite textual evidence to support analysis of what the text says explicitly as well as inferences drawn from the text. **RL 2** Determine themes or central ideas of a text; provide an objective summary of the text. **RL 4** Analyze the impact of specific word choices on meaning and tone, including words with multiple meanings or language that is particularly fresh, engaging, or beautiful. **RL 5** Analyze how an author's choices concerning how to structure specific parts of a text contribute to its overall structure and meaning as well as its aesthetic impact. **RL 9** Demonstrate knowledge of how two or more texts from the same period treat similar themes or topics. **L 5** Demonstrate understanding of figurative language.

Practice and Apply

For preliminary support of post-reading questions, use these copy masters:

R RESOURCE MANAGER—Copy Masters
Free Verse p. 19
Question Support p. 23
Additional selection questions are provided for teachers on page 15.

ANSWERS COMMON CORE RL 1, RL 2, RL 4, RL 5, RL 9, L 5

1. *Whitman compares the speaker's soul to a spider that is building a web.*

2. *The drums and bugles call churchgoers, scholars, bridegrooms, farmers, city dwellers, singers, and lawyers to action.*

3. *Possible answer: Don't listen to antiwar or timid voices.*

Possible answers:

4. *In "Song of Myself," America is mainly agricultural; today, cities and suburbs dominate the country. In "Beat! Beat! Drums!" Whitman assumes that war will rally the nation; today, war often divides the nation.*

5. **COMMON CORE FOCUS** *Analyze Tone Manual labor is honorable, necessary, and valuable; the soul is individualistic but united with the cosmos; he is expansive and energetic; war is a noble common cause.*

6. *The metaphor "the flag of my disposition" (line 16) suggests a display of life and hope; "the handkerchief of the Lord" (line 17) suggests a gift of God's love; "a child" (line 20) suggests possibility, promise, and innocence; "a uniform hieroglyphic" (line 21) suggests equality and fraternity among all people; and "the beautiful uncut hair of graves" (line 25) suggests the cycle of life and death.*

7. *"A Noiseless Patient Spider": images: isolation, detachment, and striving; mood: somber. The overall impact is of quiet*

Assess and Reteach

Assess

DIAGNOSTIC AND SELECTION TESTS
Selection Tests A, B/C pp. 149–150, 151–152
Interactive Selection Test on thinkcentral.com

Reteach

Level Up Online Tutorials on thinkcentral.com

---

contemplation. *"Beat! Beat! Drums!":* **images:** *drums, bugles, people leaving civilian life; mood: martial enthusiasm. The overall impact is of noise and activity.*

8. *The democratic ideals in Whitman's Preface reflect "I Hear America Singing." His reference to grass and earth reflects "Song of Myself." His use of cataloging and parallelism, his reference to unrhymed poetry, and his equation of people with poetry reflect his poems in general.*

9. **COMMON CORE FOCUS** *Free Verse Free verse really has no rules, so it is*

an appropriate form to capture Whitman's individualistic views on America and life.

10. *He urges an individualistic approach to life. He encourages the position in "I Hear America Singing," where he values working people over wealthy people; in "Song of Myself" he expects the reader to answer questions independently.*

What does AMERICA look like?
Answers will vary.

COMMON CORE FOCUS

RL 4 Determine the meaning of words and phrases as they are used in the text, including figurative meanings; analyze the impact of specific word choices on meaning and tone, including words with multiple meanings or language that is particularly fresh, engaging, or beautiful. **L 5** Demonstrate understanding of figurative language.

BACKGROUND

Neruda: Latin-American Classic Pablo Neruda is considered perhaps the greatest Latin-American poet of the 20th century. His birth name was Neftalí Ricardo Reyes Basoalto. Because his family disapproved of poetry as a profession, he took the name Pablo Neruda when he published his first book of poems at the age of 19. One year later, his volume *Twenty Love Poems and a Song of Despair* made Neruda famous.

Neruda in Government Appointing poets to diplomatic posts is something of a tradition. (Students have seen this tradition at work in the biography of James Russell Lowell, in Unit 2. Other Latin-American poet/diplomats have included Octavio Paz of Mexico and Miguel Asturias of Guatemala.) In 1927 Neruda began his diplomatic career in Burma (today Myanmar); he later served as Chilean consul in Argentina, Spain, and Mexico. In 1945 he was elected to the Chilean Senate; however, when a new government took power, Neruda was expelled from the Senate and fled the country. He returned in 1952 when the government lifted the ban. Later, he was named Chilean ambassador to France. Neruda continued to write poetry prolifically throughout his public career. In 1971 he received the Nobel Prize for Literature. He died of leukemia on September 23, 1973.

READ WITH A PURPOSE

Help students set a purpose for reading. Tell them to note how Neruda feels Whitman inspired him to write poetry.

COMMON CORE

RL 4 Determine the meaning of words and phrases as they are used in the text, including figurative meanings; analyze the impact of specific word choices on meaning and tone, including words with multiple meanings or language that is particularly fresh, engaging, or beautiful.
L 5 Demonstrate understanding of figurative language.

Ode to Walt Whitman

Pablo Neruda

BACKGROUND Pablo Neruda (1904–1973), a Nobel Prize–winning poet from Chile, was greatly inspired by Walt Whitman's poetry. In a speech delivered in 1972, he said, "I was barely 15 when I discovered Walt Whitman, my primary creditor. I stand among you today still owing this marvelous debt that has helped me live." In the following poem, Neruda echoes Whitman's joyful exuberance and describes Whitman by using a variety of metaphors—a comparison of two things without using words such as *like* or *as*.

I do not remember
at what age
nor where:
in the great damp South
5 or on the fearsome
coast, beneath the brief
cry of the seagulls,
I touched a hand and it was
the hand of Walt Whitman.
10 I trod the ground
with bare feet,
I walked on the grass,
on the firm dew
of Walt Whitman.

15 During
my entire
youth
I had the company of that hand,
that dew,
20 its firmness of patriarchal pine, its
prairie-like expanse,
and its mission of circulatory peace.

DIFFERENTIATED INSTRUCTION

FOR STRUGGLING READERS
Vocabulary Support

- *creditor* (background), "a person to whom one owes something"
- *exuberance* (background), "enthusiasm"
- *patriarchal* (line 20), "like a father"
- *disdaining* (line 23), "looking down on; thinking ill of"
- *copious* (line 26), "plentiful"

- *capital* (line 27), "the top part of a column"
- *tutelary* (line 44), "teaching; acting as a tutor"
- *subterranean* (line 45), "underground"
- *humiliated* (line 66), "made to feel worthless"
- *stature* (line 68), "height; level of importance"
- *stoke-hole* (line 73), "the opening in a furnace through which fuel is inserted"
- *acacia* (line 85), "a kind of tree"

Not
disdaining
the gifts
25 of the earth,
nor the copious
curving of the column's capital,
nor the purple
initial
30 of wisdom,
you taught me
to be an American,
you raised
my eyes
35 to books,
towards
the treasure
of the grains:
broad,
40 in the clarity
of the plains,
you made me see
the high
tutelary
45 mountain. From subterranean
echoes,
you gathered
for me
everything;
50 everything that came forth
was harvested by you,
galloping in the alfalfa,
picking poppies for me,
visiting
55 the rivers,
coming into the kitchens
in the afternoon.

But not only
soil
60 was brought to light
by your spade:
you unearthed
man,
and the
65 slave
who was humiliated
with you, balancing
the black dignity of his stature,
walked on, conquering
70 happiness.

To the fireman
below,
in the stoke-hole,
you sent
75 a little basket
of strawberries.
To every corner of your town
a verse
of yours arrived for a visit,
80 and it was like a piece
of clean body,
the verse that arrived,
like
your own fisherman beard
85 or the solemn tread of your acacia
legs.

ODE TO WALT WHITMAN **543**

TIERED DISCUSSION PROMPTS
For lines 22–70, use these prompts to help students explore the first section of Neruda's ode:

Summarize According to the speaker, what did Whitman teach him? *Possible answer: Whitman taught him to be an American (lines 31–32); to love books and the land (lines 33–57); and to love humankind (lines 62–70).*

Interpret Explain the meaning of this metaphor: "you made me see / the high / tutelary / mountain" (lines 42–45). *Possible answer: The speaker means that Whitman's poetry made him aware of the beauty and importance of the earth, which taught the speaker much.*

Evaluate Why might Neruda have chosen to write such short lines in this poem? Are the short lines an effective device, or would the poem have worked better if Neruda had joined some lines to make them longer? *Possible answer: The short lines highlight key words and cause the reader to slow down and consider the poem's meanings; the short lines are an affectation that tries to make the poem seem longer and thus more important.*

FOR ADVANCED LEARNERS/AP

Explore and Interpret Neruda Ask students to explore the poetry of Neruda in more depth. Suggest that students browse through collections such as *Twenty Love Poems and a Song of Despair* or *The Essential Neruda* and find two poems that strike them as intellectually or emotionally powerful. In addition, ask students to locate interpretations of Neruda's work (and of their chosen poems, if possible) in critical studies or biographies.

Instruct students to use their findings to write brief essays in which they convey critics' interpretations and add their own. Have students read their chosen poems aloud and comment about the interpretations. Gather students' essays and make the collection available to the class.

TIERED DISCUSSION PROMPTS

In lines 97–133, use these prompts to help students explore the final section of Neruda's ode:

Interpret What does "Elder first cousin / of my roots" (lines 98–99) mean? Why might Neruda use the word *cousin* rather than *father* or *brother*? **Possible answer:** *In these lines, the speaker views Whitman as a model, an inspiration, and an older poet who has shown him the way. The use of* cousin *may refer to the fact that because Whitman and Neruda lived at different times and in different lands and wrote in different languages, Neruda knew Whitman only at a distance and so could not claim a closer relationship.*

Evaluate In lines 111–133, the speaker brings public issues such as Lincoln's assassination into the poem. He might also be alluding to the outcome of the Spanish Civil War, in which the side that Neruda had supported lost. Does the poem gain from the allusion? Why or why not? *Accept all reasonable opinions, such as that the poem gains because Whitman wrote about Lincoln and cared about justice for all people; or, that the allusion represents Neruda's personal political views and should not intrude into a poem that celebrates life and art.*

Your silhouette
passed among the soldiers:
the poet, the wound-dresser,
the night attendant
90 who knows
the sound
of breathing in mortal agony
and awaits with the dawn
the silent
95 return
of life.

Good baker!
Elder first cousin
of my roots,
100 araucaria's
cupola,
it is
now
a hundred
105 years
that over your grass
and its germinations,
the wind
passes
110 without wearing out your eyes

New
and cruel years in your Fatherland:
persecutions,
tears,
115 prisons,
poisoned weapons
and wrathful wars
have not crushed
the grass of your book;
120 the vital fountainhead
of its freshness.
And, alas!
those
who murdered
125 Lincoln
now
lie in his bed.
They felled
his seat of honor
130 made of fragrant wood,
and raised a throne
spattered
with misfortune and blood.

View from Neruda's house on Isla Negra, Chile, with antique sailboat figureheads hanging in the window

DIFFERENTIATED INSTRUCTION

FOR STRUGGLING READERS
Vocabulary Support
- *araucaria* (line 100), "a Chilean cone-bearing tree"
- *cupola* (line 101), "small dome on a roof"
- *germinations* (line 107), "[cycles of] growth from seed"
- *fountainhead* (line 120), "source, as of a stream"

- *felled* (line 128), "cut down, as a tree is brought down"
- *vespertine* (line 141), "happening in the evening"
- *congregate* (line 158), "to gather"
- *magnitude* (line 160), "large size; broadness"

FOR ENGLISH LANGUAGE LEARNERS
Culture: Connect [mixed-readiness groups] Have students find a copy of this ode in Spanish, or do so yourself. Then ask Spanish-speaking students, and native English speakers studying Spanish, to read the poem in its original language. Encourage students to try to make their own translations of passages from the poem. Have students read their translations aloud and comment upon differences from the translation in the text.

But
135 your voice
sings
in the suburban
stations,
in
140 the
vespertine
wharfs,
your word
splashes
145 like
dark water.
Your people,
white
and black,
150 poor
people,
simple people
like
all

155 people
do not forget
your bell:
They congregate singing
beneath
160 the magnitude
of your spacious life.
They walk among the peoples with your
love
caressing
the pure development
165 of brotherhood on earth.

Text Analysis

1. **Analyze Metaphor** Neruda uses various metaphors to characterize Whitman's poems. What does each of these metaphors suggest about Whitman's verse?

   - Whitman's hand (lines 8–9)
   - Whitman as harvester (lines 47–70)
   - a basket of strawberries (lines 71–76)
   - a bell (lines 147–157)

2. **Compare Texts** Neruda has acknowledged Whitman's influence on his own verse. What elements of "Ode to Walt Whitman" reveal this influence? Be specific, citing evidence from this poem as well as from the Whitman poems you read on pages 532–539.

ANSWERS
Possible answers:

1. ***Whitman's hand:*** *Whitman's verse is welcoming, friendly, loving.* **Whitman as harvester:** *Whitman unearthed everything that he saw and experienced, from many parts of America, and he made the fruits of his "harvest" useful to the world.* **A basket of strawberries:** *Whitman's poetry was a gift of goodness and beauty in the midst of hard times.* **A bell:** *Whitman's voice called to the people of the world.*

2. *Accept all reasonable answers, such as the fact that both poets wrote free verse; that both cataloged occupations and landscapes; and that both displayed democratic attitudes, seeking universal brotherhood and celebrating ordinary working people of all ethnicities.*

FOR ADVANCED LEARNERS/AP
Emulate Poets Challenge students to write poems that emulate the style, subject matter, and themes of a poet whose work they enjoy. The poems may be serious or parodic. Form, word count, and line length are up to the student. After volunteers have read their poems aloud, invite discussion about how each poem resembles (1) Neruda's ode and (2) the work of the poet who inspired it. Assemble the poems into a chapbook and display it, perhaps alongside the collection that resulted from the **Explore and Interpret Neruda** activity at the bottom of page 543. Students who wish to do so may illustrate their poems or their peers' poems, as well.

Focus and Motivate

COMMON CORE FOCUS

RL 1 Cite textual evidence to support analysis of what the text says explicitly as well as inferences drawn from the text. **RL 2** Determine two or more themes or central ideas of a text. **RL 4** Determine the meaning of words and phrases used in the text, including figurative meanings; analyze the impact of specific word choices on meaning and tone, including language that is particularly fresh, engaging, or beautiful. **RL 5** Analyze how an author's choices concerning how to structure specific parts of a text contribute to its overall structure and meaning as well as its aesthetic impact. **RL 9** Demonstrate knowledge of how two or more texts from the same period treat similar themes or topics. **L 5** Demonstrate understanding of figurative language. **L 5a** Interpret figures of speech in context and analyze their role in text.

ABOUT THE AUTHOR

As students read the biography, invite them to imagine Dickinson's way of life. Point out that she wrote her poems in secret, making them known only to a handful of trusted people, and that she published very few during her lifetime. Dickinson's poetry was also private, concerned with events on a small scale. However, while she remained in one house almost all her life, her thoughts and imagination ranged widely. Urge students to look for both traits—the small scale and the wide range—when they read these selections.

Selection Resources

Selected Poetry
by Emily Dickinson

Essential Course of Study ECOS

VIDEO TRAILER THINK central KEYWORD: HML11-546A

COMMON CORE

RL 1 Cite evidence to support analysis of what the text says explicitly as well as inferences drawn from the text. **RL 2** Determine two or more themes or central ideas of a text. **RL 4** Determine the meaning of words and phrases used in the text, including figurative meanings; analyze the impact of specific word choices on meaning and tone, including language that is particularly fresh, engaging, or beautiful. **RL 5** Analyze how an author's choices concerning how to structure specific parts of a text contribute to its overall structure and meaning as well as its aesthetic impact.

DID YOU KNOW?

Emily Dickinson . . .

- sometimes signed her letters "Uncle Emily."
- dressed only in white in the last 16 years of her life.
- had eye problems and feared that she might go blind.

Meet the Author

Emily Dickinson 1830–1886

Emily Dickinson rarely ventured beyond the confines of her family home in Amherst, Massachusetts, but her restless mind and creativity knew no such boundaries. In her bedroom overlooking the village graveyard, Dickinson meditated on life and death and wrote about these subjects with startling originality. Today she and Walt Whitman are considered the greatest American poets of the 19th century.

Family Ties Dickinson was born in 1830 into a well-to-do family, which would become the center of her existence. She stood in awe of her father, a stern, imposing man committed to Puritan ideals, and felt estranged from her mother, who "did not," Dickinson once commented in a letter, "care for thought." However, she had a close relationship with her older brother, Austin, and her younger sister, Vinnie.

In 1847, Dickinson left home to attend Mount Holyoke Female Seminary in nearby South Hadley, but she left after just one year. She missed her family, but she also resented the intense pressure she felt there to join the church. All her life, Dickinson felt torn between her own convictions and the religious beliefs of those around her. This conflict is reflected in many of her poems.

A Writer's Life In the 1850s, Dickinson began to devote herself to poetry. Late at night, she wrote by candlelight. During the day, she jotted down her thoughts between household chores. Inspired by her own observations and experiences, Dickinson composed a remarkable number of profound, gemlike poems.

Perhaps because of this newfound focus on her writing, Dickinson gradually withdrew from the world. However, she did not become a total recluse. She entertained occasional visitors in her home and maintained contact with friends and family by means of a lively correspondence.

Poetic Legacy Early in 1886, Dickinson wrote a letter to her cousins that simply read "Called back." She seemed to have realized that she was dying. Following her death, her sister Vinnie discovered a box full of Dickinson's poems bound into neat booklets. As a result of Vinnie's perseverance, the first volume of Dickinson's poetry appeared four years after the poet's death. Her poems—1,775 in all—finally revealed to the world the passionate, witty woman who never flinched from the truth.

Author Online THINK central

Go to **thinkcentral.com**. KEYWORD: HML11-546B

546

See resources on the **Teacher One Stop DVD-ROM** and on **thinkcentral.com**.

R **RESOURCE MANAGER UNIT 3**
Plan and Teach, pp. 25–32
Text Analysis and Reading
  Skill, pp. 33–36†*

DIAGNOSTIC AND SELECTION TESTS
Selection Tests, pp. 153–156

BEST PRACTICES TOOLKIT
Two-Column Chart, p. A25
Visualizing, p. A11

INTERACTIVE READER

ADAPTED INTERACTIVE READER

ELL ADAPTED INTERACTIVE READER

TECHNOLOGY
- **Teacher One Stop DVD-ROM**
- **Student One Stop DVD-ROM**
- **PowerNotes DVD-ROM**
- **Audio Anthology CD**
- **GrammarNotes DVD-ROM**
- **ExamView Test Generator** on the **Teacher One Stop**

Video Trailer THINK central

Go to **thinkcentral.com** to preview the **Video Trailer** introducing this selection. Other features that support the selection include
- **PowerNotes** presentation
- **ThinkAloud** models to enhance comprehension
- **WordSharp** vocabulary tutorials
- interactive writing and grammar instruction

TEXT ANALYSIS: AUTHOR'S STYLE

Emily Dickinson's style is as unique and personal as her observations about the world. Here are some of the distinctive stylistic elements you will find in Dickinson's poetry:

- dense **quatrains,** or four-line stanzas, that echo the simple rhythms of church hymns
- **slant rhymes,** or words that do not exactly rhyme ("chill"/"Tulle")
- inventive punctuation and sentence structure, including the use of dashes to highlight important words and break up the rhythm of her poems
- irregular capitalization and inverted syntax to emphasize words
- surprisingly unconventional **figurative language,** including similes, metaphors, and personification

As you read, think about the effect of these style elements in Dickinson's poems.

READING STRATEGY: READING DICKINSON'S POETRY

To get the most out of Dickinson's poetry, try reading each poem three times.

- The first time, read for an overall impression. Pause when you encounter dashes, and be aware of the poem's **rhythm.**
- The second time, note the use of **imagery** and **figurative language.** Pay attention to the words capitalized for emphasis.
- The third time, read the poem aloud. Think about what the imagery and figurative language convey about meaning.

Use a chart like the one shown for each poem. Jot down your thoughts and ideas after each reading.

"Because I could not stop for Death"		
1st Reading	2nd Reading	3rd Reading
Poem has a calm, reflective mood.	Images of death are not frightening.	Poem suggests that death and dying are not frightening.

 Complete the activities in your **Reader/Writer Notebook.**

What are life's ESSENTIAL TRUTHS?

Love, loss. Joy, death. When you focus on life's real meaning, you explore its essential truths. These truths, of course, are the natural focus of poets. For instance, in the poems that follow, Emily Dickinson has a great deal to say about death and dying. But does she—or any other poet—speak for you? What do you think about such weighty matters as death, success, and solitude? What is your truth?

QUICKWRITE Create your own top-five list of life's essential truths. Begin with number five and work your way up to number one. Feel free to express your truths in statements, phrases, questions, or any form you want.

 547

What are life's ESSENTIAL TRUTHS?

Ask the question and have students read and discuss the paragraph that follows. Emphasize that some essential truths may apply to a large number of people, whereas others may be highly individualistic. Have students complete the *QUICKWRITE*, then compare volunteers' lists in a brief, respectful discussion.

TEXT ANALYSIS
COMMON CORE
RL 4
RL 5

● *Model the Skill:* **AUTHOR'S STYLE**

To examine Emily Dickinson's style, write the first quatrain from Dickinson's poem "My Life had stood—a Loaded Gun—" page 554 the board. Point out examples of the distinctive elements of Dickinson's style, such as dashes, inventive sentence structure, irregular capitalization, and figurative language (metaphor).

GUIDED PRACTICE Write the next quatrain from "My Life had stood—a Loaded Gun—" on the board, and have students identify elements of Dickinson's style.

READING STRATEGY
COMMON CORE
RL 1
RL 4

■ *Model the Skill:* **READING DICKINSON'S POETRY**

To help students understand Emily Dickinson's poetry, read the quatrain in the previous activity three times according to the directions in the text.

GUIDED PRACTICE Have students chorally read the next quatrain in "My Life had stood—a Loaded Gun—" three times. Discuss what students learned with each read.

R RESOURCE MANAGER—Copy Master Reading Dickinson's Poetry p. 35 (for student use while reading the selections)

DIFFERENTIATED INSTRUCTION

FOR ENGLISH LANGUAGE LEARNERS

Language: Punctuation and Print Clues [mixed-readiness pairs] Early editions of Dickinson's poems regularized the poet's punctuation and capitalization. English learners will find reading Dickinson easier if they work with partners who are more fluent, turning the uppercase letters within lines to lowercase and substituting commas or periods for dashes. (If you use this activity, have students recall it when they answer Question 9 on page 556.)

FOR STRUGGLING READERS

Concept Support: Style Ask students what the word *style* means to them. It might mean the way that someone wears his or her hair, or the kind of music the person likes. Elicit or explain that *style* in writing is similar: Just as each student has a personal way of wearing his or her hair or choosing music, each writer has a personal way of using words. Ask students to describe what they like in the styles of various writers.

Practice and Apply

SUMMARY

The speaker describes a ride in Death's carriage.

READ WITH A PURPOSE

Help students set a purpose for reading. Tell them to read to discover how Emily Dickinson viewed the world around her.

TEXT ANALYSIS   COMMON CORE

Ⓐ *Model the Skill:*
AUTHOR'S STYLE   RL 4   RL 5

Point out specific details that relay how Death is personified, such as "kindly stopped" and "The Carriage held."

Possible answer: *Death is personified as a kind gentleman who drives a carriage.*

READING STRATEGY   COMMON CORE

Ⓑ **DICKINSON'S POETRY**   RL 1   RL 4

Possible answer: *The house probably represents the speaker's grave.*

IF STUDENTS NEED HELP . . . Urge them to visualize the quatrain. Ask:

- What is the purpose of a house?

- If the top of the house is "scarcely visible" and "in the Ground," where is the house?

- Why does this house resemble "A Swelling of the Ground"?

TIERED DISCUSSION PROMPTS

Use these prompts to help students explore the poem's ideas:

Analyze Which details indicate that the speaker is leaving her life behind? ***Possible answer:*** *She speaks of putting away both labor and leisure in lines 6–7; in lines 9–12 she passes schoolchildren at play, fields of grain, and even the setting sun.*

Synthesize How does the final quatrain change the reader's interpretation of the poem? ***Possible answer:*** *Up to the final quatrain, the reader assumes that the speaker has just died; in the final quatrain, the reader realizes that her "recent" memories are, in fact, centuries old.*

Because I could not stop for Death—

Emily Dickinson

Because I could not stop for Death—
He kindly stopped for me—
The Carriage held but just Ourselves—
And Immortality. **Ⓐ**

5   We slowly drove—He knew no haste
And I had put away
My labor and my leisure too,
For His Civility[1]—

We passed the School, where Children strove
10   At Recess—in the Ring—
We passed the Fields of Gazing Grain[2]—
We passed the Setting Sun—

Or rather—He passed Us—
The Dews drew quivering and chill—
15   For only Gossamer,[3] my Gown—
My Tippet—only Tulle[4]—

We paused before a House that seemed
A Swelling of the Ground—
The Roof was scarcely visible—
20   The Cornice[5]—in the Ground— **Ⓑ**

Since then—'tis Centuries—and yet
Feels shorter than the Day
I first surmised the Horses' Heads
Were toward Eternity—

Ⓐ AUTHOR'S STYLE
Reread lines 1–4 and notice the use of **personification**, a figure of speech in which an object, animal, or idea is given human characteristics. How is Death personified?

Ⓑ DICKINSON'S POETRY
Note the **imagery** used to describe the house in lines 17–20. What do you think the house represents?

Analyze Visuals ▶
Why might the artist have chosen to keep this photograph out of focus?

---

1. **Civility:** politeness.
2. **Gazing Grain:** grain leaning toward the sun.
3. **Gossamer:** a thin, light cloth.
4. **My Tippet—only Tulle** (to͞ol): My shawl was only a fine net cloth.
5. **Cornice** (kôr'nĭs): the molding around the top of a building.

DIFFERENTIATED INSTRUCTION

FOR STRUGGLING READERS
Develop Reading Fluency

- Have students listen to the poems on the *Audio Anthology CD* (also recommended for English language learners) while they read along in their texts. Ask students to consider what makes each poem unusual.

- Invite fluent readers to read the poems aloud. Encourage readers to strive for a tone that matches the meaning of the poem and to consider how they will convey Dickinson's unusual punctuation and capitalization. After each reading, discuss how the reader's oral interpretation affects the listeners' responses to the poem presented.

Reading Support

This selection on **thinkcentral.com** includes embedded **ThinkAloud** models—students "thinking aloud" about the story to model the kinds of questions a good reader would ask about a selection.

Analyze Visuals

Possible answer: *The artist might have kept the photograph out of focus to evoke a mood of mystery. The effect encourages the reader to speculate about what the carriage is, who is in it, and where it is going.*

BACKGROUND

Dickinson's Amherst The town of Amherst, in west-central Massachusetts, was founded in 1703 and was a farming community in Dickinson's day. Today it is the home of two well-known institutions of higher learning: Amherst College and the University of Massachusetts. At various times, lexicographer Noah Webster (1758–1843) and poet Robert Frost (1874–1963) lived in Amherst. Dickinson's grandfather, Samuel Fowler Dickinson, helped establish Amherst College, which was founded to train Christian ministers and strove to reinforce the Puritan values of the early leaders of Massachusetts. Dickinson's father, Edward Dickinson, a strict Calvinist, served as the college's treasurer in addition to serving in the Massachusetts legislature and in Congress. Her brother, William Austin Dickinson, was a prominent attorney in town and lived next door to his parents and two sisters. The house in Amherst in which Emily Dickinson spent most of her life has been designated a National Historic Landmark.

FOR STRUGGLING READERS

Concept Support: Reading Dickinson's Poetry Have students reread the notes about this poem in the chart introduced on page 547. Work with students to find passages in the poem that might have prompted the notes. *Possible answer: Lines 5–8 might have prompted the first note; lines 9–12, the second note; and lines 1–4 and 21–24, in conjunction with the previous references, the third note.*

FOR ADVANCED LEARNERS/AP

Analyze Authors' Styles Challenge students to think about the writing style of two or three authors whose work they have read in this text. Then ask students to write a description of each author's style, including a statement about what they like or dislike about that style. Invite students to share and compare their analyses.

SUMMARY

The speaker notes that people who fail appreciate success the most.

ANSWERS

Possible answers:

1. *The "purple Host" is the army that has achieved victory (symbolized by capturing the opponent's flag).*

2. *The dying soldier on the losing side, hearing the far-off sound of the winners' celebration, knows the meaning of victory better than the victors do.*

3. *Accept all reasonable responses.*

Success is counted sweetest

Emily Dickinson

Success is counted sweetest
By those who ne'er succeed.
To comprehend a nectar[1]
Requires sorest need.

5   Not one of all the purple Host[2]
Who took the Flag[3] today
Can tell the definition
So clear of Victory

As he defeated—dying—
10 On whose forbidden ear
The distant strains of triumph
Burst agonized and clear! **C**

C DICKINSON'S POETRY
Read lines 9–12 aloud. What elements create the **rhythm** in these lines?

---

1. **To comprehend a nectar:** to fully appreciate a delicious beverage.
2. **Host:** army.
3. **took the Flag:** captured the enemy's flag as a token of victory.

550

Text Analysis

1. **Clarify** Who is the "purple Host" in line 5?

2. **Paraphrase** Reread lines 9–12. How would you paraphrase these lines?

3. **Form Opinions** Do you agree that those who fail are better able to appreciate success than those who win? Explain your answer.

Much Madness is divinest Sense—

Emily Dickinson

Much Madness is divinest Sense—
To a discerning Eye—
Much Sense—the starkest Madness— **D**
'Tis the Majority
5 In this, as All, prevail—
Assent—and you are sane—
Demur[1]—you're straightway dangerous—
And handled with a Chain[2]—

---

1. **demur** (dĭ-mûr'): voice opposition; object.
2. **handled with a Chain:** In the 19th century, those who were considered insane were often kept chained in asylums.

D AUTHOR'S STYLE
Pay attention to the use of capitalization in lines 1–3. Which two words are twice capitalized? Why do you think Dickinson chose to capitalize those words?

My life closed twice before its close—

Emily Dickinson

My life closed twice before its close—
It yet remains to see
If Immortality unveil
A third event to me

5 So huge, so hopeless to conceive
As these that twice befell.
Parting is all we know of heaven,
And all we need of hell. **E**

E DICKINSON'S POETRY
After your first reading of the poem, what is your overall impression of its subject?

SUMMARIES

"Much Madness is divinest Sense—" The speaker notes that standards of "madness" and "sense" are determined by the majority.

"My life closed twice before its close—" The speaker reflects upon the pain of parting.

TEXT ANALYSIS
COMMON CORE
RL 4
RL 5

D AUTHOR'S STYLE

Possible answer: The words "Madness" and "Sense" are repeatedly capitalized, perhaps to emphasize their importance.

REVISIT THE BIG QUESTION

What are life's
ESSENTIAL TRUTHS?

Discuss What essential truths about one's place in society does Dickinson convey in "Much Madness is divinest Sense—"? *Possible answer: As Dickinson sees it, whatever group forms the majority in society determines what is "madness" and what is "sense." She also comments that a person who doesn't want to be considered "dangerous" needs to express agreement with the majority view.*

READING STRATEGY
COMMON CORE
RL 1
RL 4

E DICKINSON'S POETRY

Possible answer: The overall impression is that the poem's subject is loss, especially the pain of losing human relationships.

FOR STRUGGLING READERS

Comprehension Support Use a Two-Column Chart to help students distinguish the views in "Much Madness is divinest Sense—," as in this example:

Majority View	Speaker's View
Madness = "dangerous"	Madness = "divinest sense"
Sense = "assent" (agreement)	Sense = "starkest madness"

 BEST PRACTICES TOOLKIT—Transparency
Two-Column Chart p. A25

FOR ADVANCED LEARNERS/AP

Analyze a Critical Interpretation [small-group option] Explain that Dickinson admired and reportedly was in love with a married minister, the Reverend Charles Wadsworth, who moved to California in 1862. That year, Dickinson wrote 366 poems. Dickinson's sister-in-law felt that Dickinson's separation from Wadsworth was partly responsible for her seclusion, but many scholars see that as an incomplete explanation. Ask small groups of students to reread "My life closed twice before its close—" in light of that theory, paying particular attention to lines 7–8. Instruct each group to research biographies and critical works. Then have groups decide (1) whether the poem is about a lost romance and (2) what role Wadsworth might have played in Dickinson's development as a poet. Have each group present its decisions.

552   UNIT 3: FROM ROMANTICISM TO REALISM

SUMMARY

The speaker conveys the experience of choosing a friend.

READING STRATEGY   **COMMON CORE** RL 1 RL 4

F DICKINSON'S POETRY

Possible answer: *The dashes and the abbreviated use of words break up the rhythm; emphasize important words; and create an unusual rhythmic, musical effect.*

Extend the Discussion How do these stylistic techniques affect readers?

TEXT ANALYSIS   **COMMON CORE** L 5

G AUTHOR'S STYLE

Ask for volunteers to read lines 1–12. Discuss with students how Dickinson personifies the Soul as an individual not easily influenced by others. With that in mind, what image does the simile suggest?

Possible answer: *The comparison suggests the emotional stoniness of the soul's decision to close off attention to all but one chosen person.*

Extend the Discussion What does it mean for a person to be like stone?

ANSWERS

Possible answers:

1. *According to the second quatrain, the Soul is not impressed by society's standards of greatness.*

2. *The Soul sometimes chooses to associate with one person out of all others.*

3. *"Society" means those with whom the Soul wishes to associate.*

The Soul
selects her own
Society—

Emily Dickinson

The Soul selects her own Society—
Then—shuts the Door—
To her divine Majority[1]—
Present no more—

5 Unmoved—she notes the Chariots[2]—pausing—
At her low Gate—
Unmoved—an Emperor be kneeling
Upon her Mat— F

I've known her—from an ample nation—
10 Choose One—
Then—close the Valves of her attention—
Like Stone— G

---

1. **divine Majority:** other souls.
2. **the Chariots:** the Emperor's chariots.

Text Analysis

1. **Summarize** How would you summarize the second quatrain?

2. **Paraphrase** Reread lines 9–10. How would you paraphrase these lines?

3. **Draw Conclusions** What do you think the speaker means by "Society"?

F DICKINSON'S POETRY
Reread lines 5–8. What are some of the effects of the dashes and the poet's abbreviated use of words?

COMMON CORE L 5

G AUTHOR'S STYLE
A poet's **style** can be recognized by the distinctive way he or she writes. In addition to Dickinson's unusual capitalization and use of dashes, she also uses creative similes. A **simile** is a figure of speech that compares two things that have something in common, using *like* or *as*. What image does the comparison in the last quatrain suggest?

DIFFERENTIATED INSTRUCTION

FOR ENGLISH LANGUAGE LEARNERS
Vocabulary Support

- *Unmoved* (line 5), "not affected; remaining emotionally cold"

- *ample* (line 9), "large; having many people"

- *Valves* (line 11), "gates; devices that control by opening and shutting"

FOR ADVANCED LEARNERS/AP

Hypothesize Invite students to discuss how the theme of "The Soul selects her own Society—" may be an expression of Dickinson's decision to shut herself off from society. Extend the discussion by asking to what extent readers can infer elements of a poet's life from the poet's work; have students support their responses by referring to poets or other writers whose works they have read in this text.

I heard a *Fly buzz—* when I died—

Emily Dickinson

I heard a Fly buzz—when I died—
The Stillness in the Room
Was like the Stillness in the Air—
Between the Heaves[1] of Storm— **H**

5 The Eyes around—had wrung them dry—
And Breaths were gathering firm
For that last Onset—when the King[2]
Be witnessed—in the Room—

I willed my Keepsakes—Signed away
10 What portion of me be
Assignable—and then it was
There interposed[3] a Fly—

With Blue—uncertain stumbling Buzz—
Between the light—and me—
15 And then the Windows failed—and then
I could not see to see— **I**

---

1. **Heaves:** risings and fallings.
2. **the King:** God.
3. **interposed:** came between.

H AUTHOR'S STYLE
Notice the **simile** in the first quatrain. What is being compared? Why is this comparison appropriate?

I DICKINSON'S POETRY
Reread lines 13–16. What final images does the speaker describe? What is ironic about this **imagery?**

SUMMARY
The speaker describes her final moments in life, the climax of which is interrupted by a buzzing fly.

TEXT ANALYSIS · COMMON CORE

H AUTHOR'S STYLE RL 4 / RL 5

Possible answer: The stillness in the room is being compared to the calm between storms. The comparison is appropriate because it describes the quiet before a death.

READING STRATEGY · COMMON CORE

I DICKINSON'S POETRY RL 1 / RL 4

Possible answer: The speaker describes a fly that buzzes into her line of sight, blocking the dimming light from the windows as her eyes fail. The imagery is ironic because instead of describing something cosmic at a moment of supreme transition, the speaker describes something seemingly insignificant: a fly.

IF STUDENTS NEED HELP . . . Use these questions to focus on the poem's irony:

- Why were people quiet around the speaker? What were they expecting to happen?
- In what sense does the buzzing fly take the place of the Angel of Death?
- What does this irony suggest about the speaker's view of life and death?

FOR STRUGGLING READERS
Comprehension Support Use a Visualizing diagram to help students imagine and thus better understand the scene that the speaker of this poem describes.

 BEST PRACTICES TOOLKIT—Transparency
Visualizing p. A11

FOR ADVANCED LEARNERS/AP
Compare and Contrast Texts "I heard a Fly buzz—when I died—" like "Because I could not stop for Death—" (found on page 548) describes the moment of death as an arrival of a visitor. Have students write a brief essay comparing and contrasting the two poems, focusing on how each visitor represents a different understanding of death.

As students prepare their essays, have them consider

- the language used to describe each visitor's arrival
- the speaker's experience after each arrival

Have students find opportunities to share their essays with the class.

SUMMARY

The speaker compares her life to a loaded gun.

J ALLUSION
RL 1
RL 2

Guide students in a brief discussion about allusions they might use in their own writing.

Possible answer: *The speaker's allusion is powerful because an erupting volcano provides a dramatic image and contributes to the powerful imagery of a loaded gun.*

REVISIT THE BIG QUESTION

What are life's ESSENTIAL TRUTHS?

Discuss What essential truths about life does this poem express? **Possible answer:** *Every life needs a purpose; being aware of one's personal power is key to having a full life.*

SELECTION WRAP–UP

READ WITH A PURPOSE Now that students have read Dickinson's poems, ask them to describe what Dickinson's writing says about how she viewed the world around her. **Possible answer:** *Dickinson viewed the world with a curious, but critical viewpoint, often questioning common perceptions and ideas.*

INDEPENDENT READING

Students may also enjoy reading *The Complete Poems of Emily Dickinson* by Thomas H. Johnson [ed.].

My Life had stood— a Loaded Gun— Emily Dickinson

My Life had stood—a Loaded Gun—
In Corners—till a Day
The Owner passed—identified—
And carried Me away—

5 And now We roam in Sovereign Woods[1]—
And now We hunt the Doe—
And every time I speak for Him—
The Mountains straight reply—

And do I smile, such cordial light
10 Upon the Valley glow—
It is as a Vesuvian face
Had let its pleasure through— **J**

And when at Night—Our good Day done—
I guard My Master's Head—
15 'Tis better than the Eider-Duck's
Deep Pillow—to have shared—

To foe of His—I'm deadly foe—
None stir the second time—
On whom I lay a Yellow Eye—
20 Or an emphatic Thumb—

Though I than He—may longer live
He longer must—than I—
For I have but the power to kill,
Without—the power to die—

---

1. **Sovereign** (sŏv′ər-ĭn) **Woods:** God's woods.

COMMON CORE RL 1, RL 2

J ALLUSION
Reread lines 1–12. Notice that the narrator imagines herself to have the destructive power of a gun carried by its owner into the woods to hunt deer. In line 9, the narrator equates the firing of a gun with a smile—an image that she develops with a classical **allusion,** a reference to Mount Vesuvius that she assumes her readers will recognize. A volcanic mountain, Vesuvius erupted in A.D. 79 and buried the Roman city of Pompeii under hot ash. How does this allusion contribute to the poem's imagery and themes? Cite evidence from the poem to support your response.

DIFFERENTIATED INSTRUCTION

FOR STRUGGLING READERS
Concept Support: Reading Dickinson's Poetry Continue working with the chart introduced on page 547. Alternatively, model the use of Interactive Notes with the first quatrain of this poem; then have students continue on their own and draw upon their responses as you discuss the poem in class.

 BEST PRACTICES TOOLKIT—Transparency
Interactive Notes p. B4

FOR ADVANCED LEARNERS/AP
Create a Learning Diagram Have analytical and visual learners work together to create a diagram that teaches this rather challenging poem. Suggest that students use an Analysis Frame: Poetic Content or create an original diagram to present the poem's themes and the techniques that Dickinson uses to convey the themes.

 BEST PRACTICES TOOLKIT—Transparency
Analysis Frame: Poetic Content
pp. D21, D36

LETTER In April 1862, Thomas Wentworth Higginson wrote an essay offering advice to beginning writers, urging them, "Charge your style with life." Emily Dickinson, 32 years old at the time, responded to his essay, submitting four poems along with the following unsigned letter. In place of a signature, she enclosed a signed calling card.

Letter to Mr. T. W. Higginson

April 15, 1862

Mr Higginson,

Are you too deeply occupied to say if my Verse is alive?

The Mind is so near itself—it cannot see, distinctly—and I have none to ask—

Should you think it breathed—and had you the leisure to tell me, I should feel quick gratitude—

If I make the mistake—that you dared to tell me— would give me sincerer honor—toward you—

I enclose my name—asking you, if you please— Sir—to tell me what is true?

That you will not betray me—it is needless to ask— since Honor is it's own pawn—

Miss Emily E. Dickinson

READING FOR INFORMATION **555**

CONNECT

This selection provides additional information on Dickinson's sense of herself as a poet. You can also use it as a minilesson on reading for information.

READING FOR INFORMATION

Point out that this selection is a letter written by Emily Dickinson to someone whom she had not met but whose essay of advice she had read. Then ask:

- What does the date on the letter indicate about the letter's historical context? *Possible answer: The date indicates that Dickinson wrote the letter during the Civil War.*

- Paraphrase the question that begins the letter. *Possible answer: If you are not too busy, could you tell me whether my poetry is any good?*

- What element of the typical letter is missing from this letter? *Possible answer: A signature is missing.*

TIERED DISCUSSION PROMPTS

Use these prompts to help students relate Dickinson's sense of herself to the poems that they have just read:

Connect Have you ever asked someone to evaluate your efforts? How did you feel about asking? *Accept all reasonable answers.*

Interpret What is the meaning of these lines: " . . . tell me what is true? That you will not betray me—it is needless to ask—since Honor is its own pawn—"? *Possible answer: Dickinson asks Higginson to be honest in evaluating her poems. She adds that she knows he will not tell others about her poems because he is an honorable person.*

Synthesize What inference might Higginson make about the writer of the letter? *Possible answer: Higginson might infer that she was shy, unworldly, and unsure of herself—or that she was secretly proud of her poetry while being outwardly modest.*

Practice and Apply

For preliminary support of post-reading questions, use these copy masters:

R RESOURCE MANAGER—Copy Masters
Author's Style p. 33
Question Support p. 37
Additional selection questions are
provided for teachers on page 29.

ANSWERS

COMMON
CORE RL 1, RL 4, RL 5, RL 9, L 5a

1. *The speaker has died.*

2. *The speaker is disdainful of the Majority
   and wary of its misconceptions.*

3. *In these lines, the people in the room are
   preparing themselves for the moment of
   the speaker's death.*

Possible answers:

4. *"My life...": Parting from loved ones is a
   hellish experience; "I heard...": Dying is
   mundane but also a prelude to something
   greater.*

5. ● **COMMON CORE FOCUS** *Author's Style
   "Much Madness...": Capitalization emphasizes the dichotomy between madness and
   sense; "The Soul...": Capitalization emphasizes the isolation of the soul.*

6. ■ **COMMON CORE FOCUS** *Analyze Dickinson's Poetry The tone of Dickinson's poems
   is thoughtful, quirky, and often deceptively
   cheerful.*

7. *"Success...": **paradox**—"Success is counted
   sweetest / By those who ne'er succeed";
   truth—Failures value success more than successful people do. "Much Madness...":
   paradox—"Much Madness is divinest Sense";*

Assess and Reteach

Assess

DIAGNOSTIC AND SELECTION TESTS

Selection Test A pp. 153–154
Selection Test B/C pp. 155–156

Interactive Selection Test on **thinkcentral.com**

Reteach

Level Up Online Tutorials on **thinkcentral.com**

Reteaching Worksheets on **thinkcentral.com**

Literature Lesson 44: Style and
   Syntax
Literature Lesson 45: Author's
   Perspective

Comprehension

1. **Recall** What has happened to the speaker in "Because I could not stop
   for Death—"?

2. **Clarify** What do you think is the speaker's attitude toward the Majority
   in "Much Madness is divinest Sense"?

3. **Summarize** How would you summarize lines 5–8 of "I heard a Fly buzz—
   when I died—"?

Text Analysis

4. **Make Inferences** What essential truths about death and dying does
   Dickinson convey in the following poems? Cite specific details.

   • "My life closed twice before its close—"
   • "I heard a Fly buzz—when I died—"

● 5. **Analyze Author's Style** What ideas are emphasized by the unusual use
   of capitalization in the following poems? Be specific.

   • "Much Madness is divinest Sense"
   • "The Soul selects her own Society—"

■ 6. **Analyze Dickinson's Poetry** Review the thoughts and ideas you recorded as
   you read and reread the poems. Based on Dickinson's **imagery** and **figurative
   language,** how would you characterize the overall **tone** of her poems?

7. **Evaluate Paradox** A **paradox** is a statement that seems to contradict
   itself but may nevertheless suggest an important truth. Use a diagram
   like the one shown to identify the paradoxes in "Success is counted
   sweetest," "Much Madness is divinest Sense," and "My Life had
   stood—a Loaded Gun—." What truth does each paradox convey?

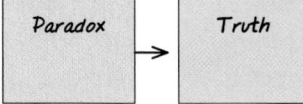

8. **Compare Texts** What style elements of the poet do you recognize in Emily
   Dickinson's letter to Thomas Wentworth Higginson (page 555)?

Text Criticism

9. **Different Perspectives** Until 1955, editors published "corrected" versions of
   Dickinson's poems with dashes removed, rhyme and meter made regular, and
   metaphors replaced with more conventional figures of speech. By eliminating
   these things, what was lost? Use details from the poems to support your ideas.

> *What are life's* **ESSENTIAL TRUTHS?**
>
> Dickinson, like many other poets, spent time focusing on important truths
> about life. Do you believe people today think often enough about the
> essential truths in life? Explain your answer.

COMMON CORE

RL 1 Cite evidence to support
analysis of what the text says
explicitly as well as inferences drawn
from the text. **RL 4** Determine
the meaning of words and phrases
used in the text, including figurative
meanings; analyze the impact of
specific word choices on meaning
and tone, including language that
is particularly fresh, engaging, or
beautiful. **RL 5** Analyze how an
author's choices concerning how
to structure specific parts of a text
contribute to its overall structure
and meaning as well as its aesthetic
impact. **RL 9** Demonstrate
knowledge of how two or more texts
from the same period treat similar
themes or topics. **L 5a** Interpret
figures of speech in context and
analyze their role in text.

---

*truth—It is hard to tell the difference
between sanity and insanity. "My Life...":
paradox—"For I have but the power to kill,
/ Without—the power to die"; **truth**—
Human beings, because they are mortal, have
a sanctity that inanimate objects do not.*

8. *Common elements include the use of dashes,
   personification, metaphor, condensed words
   and syntax, unusual expressions, ambiguous
   meaning, and a primary focus upon impressions and feelings.*

9. *The "corrections" might have caused the
   poems to lose their power to surprise and
   disconcert; omitting dashes and regularizing
   rhyme and meter would have caused the
   poems to lose their unusual musicality.
   Details will vary.*

> *What are life's* ESSENTIAL
> TRUTHS? **Answers will vary. Some
> students may believe that most people
> think about essential truths often. Others
> may think that people don't consider life
> truths enough. All answers should include
> explanations.**

The Innovations of Whitman and Dickinson

Although Emily Dickinson and Walt Whitman were both revolutionary in their approach to poetic form and content, their poems look quite different. Dickinson wrote short and concise lines; Whitman, long and sprawling ones.

> *Success is counted sweetest*
> *By those who ne'er succeed.*
>
> **—Emily Dickinson**
>
> *I wish I could translate the hints about the dead young men*
> *   and women,*
> *And the hints about old men and mothers, and the offspring taken*
> *   soon out of their laps.*
>
> **—Walt Whitman**

Dickinson concentrated on private and personal experiences; Whitman, on representative experiences of the American people.

> *I heard a Fly buzz—when I died—*
>
> **—Emily Dickinson**
>
> *I hear America singing, the varied carols I hear,*
>
> **—Walt Whitman**

Writing to Compare

Write an essay to further compare the work of Dickinson and Whitman. Cite specific lines from the poems on page 532 through 554 to support your comparison and thoroughly develop your ideas.

Consider

- each poet's style and form (that is, word choice, imagery, line length, stanzas, rhythm, rhyme), using precise terms to discuss poetic features
- the poems' subject matter and general themes
- which words, lines, or stanzas will provide you with effective evidence and details

© Mike Caplanis/Luminarygraphics.com.

Extension

SPEAKING & LISTENING

With a partner, create a dialogue between Whitman and Dickinson in which they discuss their topics, themes, and techniques. Then, **perform** your conversation for the class. Use speaking styles that you think are appropriate for the two poets, based on your understanding of their content and style.

COMMON CORE

W 2 Write explanatory texts to examine and convey complex ideas, concepts, and information. **W 9** Draw evidence from literary texts to support analysis. **SL 4** Present information such that substance and style are appropriate to purpose and task. **SL 6** Adapt speech to context and task. **L 3** Make effective choices for meaning or style.

WRAP-UP   **557**

COMMON CORE FOCUS

W 2 Write explanatory texts to examine and convey complex ideas, concepts, and information. **W 9** Draw evidence from literary texts to support analysis. **SL 4** Present information such that substance and style are appropriate to purpose and task. **SL 6** Adapt speech to context and task. **L 3** Make effective choices for meaning and style.

Wrap-Up: Brilliant Mavericks

This Wrap-Up provides students with an opportunity to compare and contrast the poetry of Walt Whitman and Emily Dickinson. After students have read the first pair of examples, briefly discuss how they can recognize the author of each example through the appearance of the lines. Then have students read the second pair of examples and describe the subject matter in a way that compares and contrasts.

Writing to Compare

- Remind students to consider similarities and differences in their essays, for the term *compare* can include both comparison and contrast. Students need not cite lines from every poem that they have read in this cluster, but urge them to cover at least two poems from each poet.
- Advise students not to choose poems at random. One way to choose is to select a quality or device, such as imagery, and then search for interesting examples in each poet's work. Another method is to choose poems that seem either especially different or especially alike.

Extension

- Suggest that students clarify their images of the two poets by recalling the poems and reading over any notes that they have taken.
- Suggest that partners review both poets and use Questioning the Author as they formulate questions and answers.
- Urge students to rehearse, refining their questions and answers as they do so.

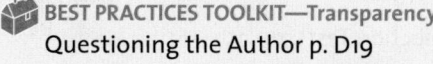 **BEST PRACTICES TOOLKIT—Transparency**
Questioning the Author p. D19

FOR ENGLISH LANGUAGE LEARNERS

Creating Dialogue For students who need practice with conversational English, use this dialogue to practice questions and answers. Start by modeling an exchange with an English-fluent volunteer. Pitch the conversation to the level that your English learners require. It may be as simple as "How are you, Walt?" / "I am fine, Emily." On the other hand, it may involve simple statements of poetic technique. Then have students try an exchange, using starter sentences such as these:

- "What kinds of poems do you write?"
- "Do you write free verse?"
- "I like using short lines in my poems. What kinds of lines do you write?"
- "I use rhyme and meter. Do you?"
- "I write about America. What do you write about?"

Focus and Motivate

COMMON CORE FOCUS

RI 2 Determine two or more central ideas of a text.
RI 4 Determine the meaning of words and phrases as they are used in a text, including figurative and connotative meanings. **RI 6** Determine an author's point of view or purpose in a text in which the rhetoric is particularly effective, analyzing how style and content contribute to the power, persuasiveness, or beauty of a text. **RI 9** Analyze nineteenth-century foundational U.S. documents of literary significance for their themes, purposes, and rhetorical features.
W 3 Write narratives to develop real or imagined experiences or events using effective technique, well-chosen details, and well-structured event sequences. **W 3d** Use precise words and phrases, telling details, and sensory language to convey a vivid picture of the experiences, events, setting, and/or characters. **L 3** Apply knowledge of language to make effective choices for meaning or style. **L 3a** Apply an understanding of syntax to the study of complex texts when reading. **L 5** Demonstrate understanding of figurative language and nuances in word meanings. **L 5b** Analyze nuances in the meanings of words with similar denotations.

ABOUT THE AUTHOR

After students have read about Frederick Douglass, explain that the excerpt they are about to read takes place after he had left the Aulds' home (**Forbidden Education**) and before he had escaped to freedom (**From Slave to Abolitionist**). Also point out that in 1855, Douglass published an expanded version of his autobiography entitled *My Bondage and My Freedom,* which includes an account of his work as an abolitionist.

Selection Resources

COMMON CORE

RI 4 Determine the meaning of words and phrases as they are used in a text, including figurative and connotative meanings. **RI 6** Determine an author's point of view or purpose in a text in which the rhetoric is particularly effective, analyzing how style and content contribute to the power, persuasiveness, or beauty of a text. **L 3a** Apply an understanding of syntax to the study of complex texts when reading. **L 5** Demonstrate understanding of figurative language and nuances in word meanings.

DID YOU KNOW?

Frederick Douglass . . .

- escaped to the North by disguising himself as a sailor.
- made his home a stop on the Underground Railroad.
- was an early defender of women's rights.

Literature of the Civil War

from **Narrative of the Life of Frederick Douglass, an American Slave**

 Video link at thinkcentral.com

Essential Course of Study

Slave Narrative by Frederick Douglass

VIDEO TRAILER **THINK** central | KEYWORD: HML11-558A

Meet the Author

Frederick Douglass c. 1817–1895

Frederick Douglass endured 21 years of slavery before he escaped to freedom in the North, where he became an outspoken and influential abolitionist. In the years leading up to the Civil War, his powerful speeches spurred the nation to move against slavery and to extend equal rights to all its citizens.

Forbidden Education As a boy, Douglass worked as a slave in the home of Hugh and Sophia Auld of Baltimore, Maryland. Although it was against the law, Mrs. Auld taught Douglass how to read. After Mr. Auld commanded his wife to stop her lessons, Douglass educated himself in secret, studying from a textbook on public speaking titled *The Columbian Orator.*

From Slave to Abolitionist Douglass escaped and in 1838 settled in New Bedford, Massachusetts. Three years later, he spoke so eloquently to the Massachusetts Anti-Slavery Society that they hired him to lecture about his experiences. Proslavery hecklers frequently attacked him, hurling insults and even rotten eggs and vegetables, but Douglass continued, undeterred.

In 1845, with the publication of his autobiography,

Narrative of the Life of Frederick Douglass, an American Slave, Douglass rose to international fame—dangerous attention for a runaway slave. To avoid being recaptured, Douglass left for a two-year speaking tour of Great Britain. During the trip, two friends raised the money to purchase his freedom.

Tireless Reformer Returning to the United States as a free man, Douglass settled in Rochester, New York, and founded an antislavery newspaper, the *North Star.* During the Civil War, he advised President Abraham Lincoln and helped recruit the first African-American soldiers for the Union army. For Douglass, the end of slavery was only a first step to achieving a greater goal: full and equal civil rights for African Americans.

In the years after the Civil War, Douglass was appointed to several government posts, including U.S. marshal for the District of Columbia and minister to Haiti. To the end of his life, he continued his fight for full citizenship for African Americans and his support for other causes, including women's rights, land reform, and public education.

Author Online

Go to **thinkcentral.com**. KEYWORD: HML11-558B

558

See resources on the **Teacher One Stop DVD-ROM** and on **thinkcentral.com**.

 Video link at thinkcentral.com

 RESOURCE MANAGER UNIT 3

Plan and Teach, pp. 39–46
Summary, pp. 47–48†‡*
Text Analysis and Reading
   Skill, pp. 49–52†*
Grammar and Style, p. 55

DIAGNOSTIC AND SELECTION TESTS

Selection Tests, pp. 157–160

 BEST PRACTICES TOOLKIT

Word Questioning, p. E9
Cluster Diagram, p. B18
Timeline, p. B23

INTERACTIVE READER

ADAPTED INTERACTIVE READER

ELL ADAPTED INTERACTIVE READER

TECHNOLOGY

- **Teacher One Stop DVD-ROM**
- **Student One Stop DVD-ROM**
- **PowerNotes DVD-ROM**
- **Audio Anthology CD**
- **GrammarNotes DVD-ROM**
- **ExamView Test Generator** on the Teacher One Stop

Video Trailer

Go to **thinkcentral.com** to preview the **Video Trailer** introducing this selection. Other features that support the selection include

- **PowerNotes** presentation
- **ThinkAloud** models to enhance comprehension
- **WordSharp** vocabulary tutorials
- interactive writing and grammar instruction

---

* Resources for Differentiation   † Also in Spanish   ‡ In Haitian Creole and Vietnamese

TEXT ANALYSIS: STYLE

Style is a writer's distinctive way of expressing ideas—not what is said, but how it is said. Douglass uses a formal, elegant style that demonstrates his masterful command of language.

After running thus for a considerable distance, they finally upset the cart, dashing it with great force against a tree, and threw themselves into a dense thicket.

Elements that characterize style include

- **tone,** conveyed by choice of words and details
- **sentence patterns and structures**
- use of **figurative language**
- use of **dialogue**

Douglass combines crisp, factual narration with bursts of poetic language. As you read, note the choices Douglass makes that contribute to his sophisticated style. Examine how the author's style and tone contribute to his viewpoint or perspective on the institution of slavery.

READING SKILL: ANALYZE AUTHOR'S PURPOSE

An author creates a work to achieve a specific **purpose,** or goal. In general, an author writes to inform, to express thoughts or feelings, to persuade, or to entertain. However, a complex work will often have more than one purpose.

Frederick Douglass wrote his autobiography mainly to persuade readers that slavery should be abolished. To achieve his purpose, he described the physical realities that slaves endured and his responses to his life as a slave.

We were often in the field from the first approach of day till its last lingering ray had left us . . .

As you read, use a chart like the one shown to take notes on Douglass's experiences. Notice when he provides factual details about the general conditions of slave life and when he describes his personal responses to his situation.

Physical Realities	Responses to Situation

 Complete the activities in your **Reader/Writer Notebook**.

Can you set yourself FREE?

Separated from his parents, denied the right to an education, and moved from place to place at the convenience of his owners, Frederick Douglass learned that nothing in his life was under his control. Rejecting the injustice of slavery, he risked his life to escape. With his decision to set himself free, he claimed the right to self-determination: he would be a man and not a slave.

QUICKWRITE Without mentioning any names, contrast two people you know of—one who has self-determination and one who does not. Would you attribute the differences beween them more to circumstances or to attitude?

A	M
stands up to defend the rights of others	afraid to disagree with her boyfriend

559

Can you set yourself FREE?

Ask the question, and then invite students to suggest definitions for self-determination, such as "the freedom to make your own decisions" or "standing up for your beliefs." After students complete the *QUICKWRITE,* have them reevaluate their definitions. Invite volunteers to explain whether their definitions have changed.

TEXT ANALYSIS — COMMON CORE RI 4 · RI 6 · L 3a

Model the Skill: STYLE

Describe to students the style of the author biography on page 558. Point out that its style is straightforward and factual. The sentences are not extremely complex. The vocabulary is formal, not colloquial, but it is not poetic. There is no figurative language or dialogue.

GUIDED PRACTICE Ask students to describe the style of an article in a newspaper or a popular magazine.

READING SKILL — COMMON CORE RI 6

Model the Skill: ANALYZE AUTHOR'S PURPOSE

Identify the purpose of the biography about Frederick Douglass on page 558. Explain to students that the purpose of the biography is to inform students about Frederick Douglass's life so that they are prepared to read the excerpt from his autobiography.

GUIDED PRACTICE Have students identify the author's purpose or purposes in a newspaper editorial, a mystery novel, and a movie review.

R RESOURCE MANAGER—Copy Master Analyze Author's Purpose p. 51 (for student use while reading the selection)

DIFFERENTIATED INSTRUCTION

FOR ENGLISH LANGUAGE LEARNERS

Cultural Context Tell students that Frederick Douglass was one of many people who risked their lives to promote freedom for African Americans. These people forced the United States to improve as a nation. Ask students to think of a person from their home country who sacrificed to improve his or her nation. Have students research this person, using the following questions for guidance:

- What was this person trying to accomplish?
- What did he or she have to sacrifice and/or risk to pursue his or her goal?
- What changes occurred because of his or her hard work and sacrifices?
- How has this person's work affected the citizens that live in your home country today?
- Why is your home country a better place because of this person's work?

Practice and Apply

SUMMARY

In this excerpt from his slave narrative, Frederick Douglass describes a turning point in his life. When he is a teenager, his owner, Master Thomas, hires him out for a year to Mr. Covey to work as a field hand. Covey beats him mercilessly, but when Douglass turns to Master Thomas for protection, his owner orders him back to serve out his year. Determined never to take another beating, Douglass fights Covey, restoring his own self-respect and determination to be free.

READ WITH A PURPOSE

Help students set a purpose for reading. Tell them to read to discover how Frederick Douglass triumphed over the bonds of slavery.

REVISIT THE BIG QUESTION

Can you set yourself FREE?

Discuss In lines 1–11, how much self-determination, or control over his own life, does Douglass appear to have? Explain. ***Possible answer:** Douglass appears to have no control over his own life. He cannot prevent his owner from hiring him out to a brutal man.*

TEXT ANALYSIS   COMMON CORE

Ⓐ STYLE   RI 4
                                RI 6

Possible answer: *"This affair" refers to his brutal whipping. The word choice is surprising because Douglass describes this act of violence in an offhand, neutral way.*

IF STUDENTS NEED HELP . . . Reread lines 4–6, and then ask students what noun they would use to label the event Douglass describes. Contrast students' choices with the word *affair*.

Narrative *of the Life* of Frederick Douglass

Frederick Douglass

BACKGROUND Douglass wrote his autobiography to convince skeptics that such an eloquent speaker had indeed once been a slave. His book became one of the most famous slave narratives ever published and played an enormous role in rallying support for the abolition of slavery. This excerpt recounts a period in Douglass's life during which his owner, Hugh Auld's brother, Thomas, had hired him out to a man with a reputation as a "slave breaker."

I left Master Thomas's house, and went to live with Mr. Covey, on the 1st of January, 1833. I was now, for the first time in my life, a field hand. In my new employment, I found myself even more awkward than a country boy appeared to be in a large city. I had been at my new home but one week before Mr. Covey gave me a very severe whipping, cutting my back, causing the blood to run, and raising ridges on my flesh as large as my little finger. The details of this affair are Ⓐ as follows: Mr. Covey sent me, very early in the morning of one of our coldest days in the month of January, to the woods, to get a load of wood. He gave me a team of unbroken oxen. He told me which was the in-hand ox, and which the off-
10 hand[1] one. He then tied the end of a large rope around the horns of the in-hand ox, and gave me the other end of it, and told me, if the oxen started to run, that

> **Ⓘ Targeted Passage**
> **Analyze Visuals ▶**
> Describe the **style** of this painting. What impression of its subject does the painting convey?
>
> **Ⓐ STYLE**
> Explain what Douglass means by "this affair" in line 6. What is surprising about his **word choice**?

---

1. **in-hand . . . off-hand:** In a team of animals trained to pull loads, the in-hand animal is the one on the left; the animal on the right is the off-hand one.

Panel 30 from *The Frederick Douglass Series* (1938–1939), Jacob Lawrence. Hampton University Museum. © 2007 The Jacob and Gwendolyn Lawrence Foundation, Seattle/Artists Rights Society (ARS), New York.

DIFFERENTIATED INSTRUCTION

FOR ADVANCED LEARNERS/AP

Expert Groups Have students research one of these topics:

- slave resistance and Nat Turner's rebellion
- fugitive slave laws
- Douglass's work as an abolitionist
- Douglass's work in the women's rights movement

Have students prepare an oral report or a multimedia presentation to share with the class.

FOR STRUGGLING READERS

In combination with the *Audio Anthology CD*, use one or more Targeted Passages (pp. 560, 563, 565, 566, 568, 569) to ensure that students focus on key events and concepts. Targeted Passages are also good for English learners.

Ⓘ Targeted Passage [Lines 1–10]

This passage introduces the setting and the conflict that Douglass faces in this excerpt from his narrative.

THINK
central

Reading Support

This selection on **thinkcentral.com** includes embedded **ThinkAloud** models—students "thinking aloud" about the story to model the kinds of questions a good reader would ask about a selection.

Analyze Visuals

Possible answer: The style is expressionistic; the painting uses exaggerated colors and flat, oversimplified shapes. It portrays Douglass as serious and dignified.

About the Art One of the most important American artists of the 20th century, Jacob Lawrence (1917–2000) created several series of paintings depicting important events and leaders in African-American history, such as Frederick Douglass and Harriet Tubman (see page 562). *The Frederick Douglass Series* comprises 32 paintings that present key moments in the abolitionist leader's life. This painting celebrates his 1877 appointment as United States Marshal of the District of Columbia.

BACKGROUND

The Brutality of Slavery In 1830 there were 2.3 million African Americans in the United States. The vast majority were American-born slaves, like Frederick Douglass. White Southerners defended the institution of slavery. Slave owners wielded absolute authority over their "property." Slaves had no legal rights, and in addition to enduring grueling labor and appalling living conditions, many were regularly whipped. They also endured the emotional brutality of forced separation from their loved ones.

- What kind of work does Douglass begin to do when he goes to live with Covey? (line 2)
- Why is Douglass awkward in this work? (line 2)
- What does Covey do to Douglass? (lines 4–6)
- Where does Covey send Douglass, and why is the trip so difficult? (lines 7–9)

FOR ENGLISH LANGUAGE LEARNERS

Vocabulary Support Use Word Questioning to teach these words: *team* (line 9), *considerable* (line 17), *pursue* (line 188), *stable* (line 210), *persist* (line 226).

BEST PRACTICES TOOLKIT—Transparency
Word Questioning p. E9

FOR STRUGGLING READERS

Develop Reading Fluency Read aloud the background note, pointing out punctuation marks that help determine pacing and intonation. Point out the quotation marks around "property," and show students how to stress this word when speaking. Emphasize a somber tone, so that students recognize that their speaking tone should match the somber tone of the text. Have students practice reading the background note aloud with a partner.

The Life of Harriet Tubman, #9 (1940), Jacob Lawrence. Casein tempera on hardboard, 12″ × 17 7/8″. Hampton University Museum. Photo courtesy of Gwendolyn Knight Lawrence/Art Resource, New York. © 2007 The Jacob and Gwendolyn Lawrence Foundation, Seattle/Artists Rights Society (ARS), New York.

I must hold on upon the rope. I had never driven oxen before, and of course I was very awkward. I, however, succeeded in getting to the edge of the woods with little difficulty; but I had got a very few rods[2] into the woods, when the oxen took fright, and started full tilt, carrying the cart against trees, and over stumps, in the most frightful manner. I expected every moment that my brains would be dashed out against the trees. After running thus for a considerable distance, they finally upset the cart, dashing it with great force against a tree, and threw themselves into a dense thicket.

20   How I escaped death, I do not know. There I was, entirely alone, in a thick wood, in a place new to me. My cart was upset and shattered, my oxen were entangled among the young trees, and there was none to help me. After a long spell of effort, I succeeded in getting my cart righted, my oxen disentangled, and again yoked to the cart. I now proceeded with my team to the place where I had, the day before, been chopping wood, and loaded my cart pretty heavily, thinking in this way to tame my oxen. I then proceeded on my way home. I had now

▲ **Analyze Visuals**
Identify details in this painting that are used to represent the experience of slavery. What effects are achieved by centering the image of the figures' feet?

---

2. **rods:** units of length equal to 5 1/2 yards.

consumed one half of the day. I got out of the woods safely, and now felt out of danger. I stopped my oxen to open the woods gate; and just as I did so, before I could get hold of my ox rope, the oxen again started, rushed through the gate,

30 catching it between the wheel and the body of the cart, tearing it to pieces, and coming within a few inches of crushing me against the gate-post. Thus twice, in one short day, I escaped death by the merest chance. On my return, I told Mr. Covey what had happened, and how it happened. He ordered me to return to the woods again immediately. I did so, and he followed on after me. Just as I got into the woods, he came up and told me to stop my cart, and that he would teach me how to trifle away my time, and break gates. He then went to a large gum-tree, and with his axe cut three large switches, and, after trimming them up neatly with his pocket-knife, he ordered me to take off my clothes. I made him no answer, but stood with my clothes on. He repeated his order. I still made him no answer,

40 nor did I move to strip myself. Upon this he rushed at me with the fierceness of a tiger, tore off my clothes, and lashed me till he had worn out his switches, cutting me so savagely as to leave the marks visible for a long time after. This whipping was the first of a number just like it, and for similar offenses. **B**

I lived with Mr. Covey one year. During the first six months, of that year, scarce a week passed without his whipping me. I was seldom free from a sore back. My awkwardness was almost always his excuse for whipping me. We were worked fully up to the point of endurance. Long before day we were up, our horses fed, and by the first approach of day we were off to the field with our hoes and ploughing teams. Mr. Covey gave us enough to eat, but scarce time to eat it. We were often

50 less than five minutes taking our meals. We were often in the field from the first approach of day till its last lingering ray had left us; and at saving-fodder time, midnight often caught us in the field binding blades.[3] **C**

Covey would be out with us. The way he used to stand it, was this. He would spend the most of his afternoons in bed. He would then come out fresh in the evening, ready to urge us on with his words, example, and frequently with the whip. Mr. Covey was one of the few slaveholders who could and did work with his hands. He was a hard-working man. He knew by himself just what a man or a boy could do. There was no deceiving him. His work went on in his absence almost as well as in his presence; and he had the faculty of making us feel that he was ever

60 present with us. This he did by surprising us. He seldom approached the spot where we were at work openly, if he could do it secretly. He always aimed at taking us by surprise. Such was his cunning, that we used to call him, among ourselves, "the snake." When we were at work in the cornfield, he would sometimes crawl on his hands and knees to avoid detection, and all at once he would rise nearly in our midst, and scream out, "Ha, ha! Come, come! Dash on, dash on!" This being **D** his mode of attack, it was never safe to stop a single minute. His comings were like a thief in the night. He appeared to us as being ever at hand. He was under every

---

3. **saving- fodder ... binding blades:** They are gathering and bundling ("binding") corn-plant leaves ("blades") to use for livestock ("fodder").

Language Coach

Fixed Expressions The term *fixed expression* refers to the normal combination of words—the ways they are often used. "Merest chance" (line 32) means "only by chance." Other fixed expressions with *chance* are "strong chance" and "reasonable chance." Use each expression in a sentence.

B STYLE
Reread lines 31–43. What is the effect of Douglass's choice to use little imagery or figurative language in his narration?

C AUTHOR'S PURPOSE
Reread lines 46–52. What details does Douglass use to inform his readers about the working conditions of slaves?

D GRAMMAR AND STYLE
Reread lines 63–65. Note how Douglass uses the **vivid verbs** *crawl* and *scream* to characterize Covey's menacing behavior.

TEXT ANALYSIS

B STYLE

COMMON CORE
RI 4
RI 6

Possible answer: By using minimal imagery and figurative language, Douglass creates a factual, understated tone. By offering a straightforward recitation of what happened, he lets the facts speak for themselves without embellishment.

READING SKILL

COMMON CORE
RI 6

C *Model the Skill:* **AUTHOR'S PURPOSE**

To highlight Douglass's use of vivid detail, read lines 46–52 aloud, emphasizing the descriptions with which he paints the slaves' working day.

Possible answer: Douglass includes these details to inform readers about the slaves' working conditions: They worked "to the point of endurance" (line 47), were in the fields by daybreak (lines 47–49), had "less than five minutes" for meals (line 50), and worked from sunrise to well into the night (lines 50–52).

Extend the Discussion How does this catalog of information about working conditions serve Douglass's main purpose: to persuade readers that slavery should be abolished?

D GRAMMAR AND STYLE
COMMON CORE L 3

Analyze Word Choice Ask students how the description of Covey would be different if Douglass had used the verbs *go* and *call* instead of *crawl* and *scream*. *Possible answer: The words* crawl *and* scream *have much stronger negative connotations.* Crawl *suggests that Covey behaved like a snake, while* scream *conveys brutal or savage anger.* Have students find other examples of vivid verbs in the excerpt.

FOR STRUGGLING READERS

2 Targeted Passage [Lines 27–43]

This passage reveals Covey's character and the brutality of slavery.

- How do the oxen damage Covey's gate? (lines 28–30)
- Where does Covey send Douglass after he learns about the accident? (lines 33–34)
- What does Covey do to Douglass? (lines 40–42)

FOR ENGLISH LANGUAGE LEARNERS

Language Coach

Fixed Expressions *Answers will vary.* Tell students that fixed expressions are commonly used in everyday conversations. Present students with commonly used fixed expressions: *by the time, in general, on purpose.* Use each expression in a sentence, then have students create their own sentences using the expressions.

E STYLE

RI 4
RI 6

Possible answer: Metaphors: "bitterest dregs" (lines 78–79), "cheerful spark" (line 87), "dark night of slavery" (lines 87–88). Repetition: "worked/work" (lines 80–82), "breaking/broken" (line 85). Parallelism: "never too hot . . . never rain . . . too hard" (lines 80–81), "longest days . . . too short . . . shortest nights too long" (lines 82–83), "elasticity . . . crushed . . . intellect languished . . . disposition . . . departed . . . spark . . . died . . . dark night . . . closed" (lines 86–88). These poetic devices create an emotional, despairing tone that stresses the unending misery of Douglass's life.

TIERED DISCUSSION PROMPTS

For lines 78–95, use these prompts to help students understand how Douglass uses his own experience to convey the effects of slavery:

Summarize How does Douglass change during his first six months with Covey? *Possible answer: He is completely "broken in body, soul, and spirit" (line 85). He loses his intellectual interest and sense of hope (lines 86 and 92). He feels that he has been "transformed into a brute" (line 88).*

Analyze Why is it significant that Douglass's transformation occurs in only six months? *Possible answer: Douglass is suggesting that slavery can dehumanize a person in a relatively short period of time.*

Synthesize Douglass is strong, intelligent, and resourceful. Consider how just six months of abuse affect him. What is Douglass suggesting about slavery's effects? *Possible answer: The brutality and degradation of slavery dehumanize a strong, lively, intelligent young man in just six months. Douglass is implying that slavery will destroy anyone, weak or strong.*

---

tree, behind every stump, in every bush, and at every window, on the plantation. He would sometimes mount his horse, as if bound to St. Michael's,[4] a distance of
70 seven miles, and in half an hour afterwards you would see him coiled up in the corner of the wood-fence, watching every motion of the slaves. He would, for this purpose, leave his horse tied up in the woods. Again, he would sometimes walk up to us, and give us orders as though he was upon the point of starting on a long journey, turn his back upon us, and make as though he was going to the house to get ready; and, before he would get half way thither, he would turn short and crawl into a fence-corner, or behind some tree, and there watch us till the going down of the sun. . . .

If at any one time of my life more than another, I was made to drink the bitterest dregs of slavery, that time was during the first six months of my stay with Mr.
80 Covey. We were worked in all weathers. It was never too hot or too cold; it could never rain, blow, hail, or snow, too hard for us to work in the field. Work, work, work, was scarcely more the order of the day than of the night. The longest days were too short for him, and the shortest nights too long for him. I was somewhat unmanageable when I first went there, but a few months of this discipline tamed me. Mr. Covey succeeded in breaking me. I was broken in body, soul, and spirit. My natural elasticity was crushed, my intellect languished, the disposition to read departed, the cheerful spark that lingered about my eye died; the dark night of slavery closed in upon me; and behold a man transformed into a brute! **E**
    Sunday was my only leisure time. I spent this in a sort of beast-like stupor,
90 between sleep and wake, under some large tree. At times I would rise up, a flash of energetic freedom would dart through my soul, accompanied with a faint beam of hope, that flickered for a moment, and then vanished. I sank down again, mourning over my wretched condition. I was sometimes prompted to take my life, and that of Covey, but was prevented by a combination of hope and fear. My sufferings on this plantation seem now like a dream rather than a stern reality. . . .
    I have already intimated that my condition was much worse, during the first six months of my stay at Mr. Covey's, than in the last six. The circumstances leading to the change in Mr. Covey's course toward me form an epoch in my humble history. You have seen how a man was made a slave; you shall see how a
100 slave was made a man. On one of the hottest days of the month of August, 1833, Bill Smith, William Hughes,[5] a slave named Eli, and myself, were engaged in fanning wheat.[6] Hughes was clearing the fanned wheat from before the fan. Eli was turning, Smith was feeding, and I was carrying wheat to the fan. The work was simple, requiring strength rather than intellect; yet, to one entirely unused to such work, it came very hard. About three o'clock of that day, I broke down; my strength failed me; I was seized with a violent aching of the head, attended with

---

4. **St. Michael's:** a town southeast of Baltimore, on the east side of the Chesapeake Bay.
5. **Bill Smith, William Hughes:** Bill Smith was a hired man, and William Hughes was Mr. Covey's cousin.
6. **fanning wheat:** using a machine that blows air to separate grains of wheat from the unusable husks.

COMMON CORE   RI 4, L 5

Language Coach

Figurative Language
"Bitterest dregs of slavery" is **figurative language,** language that communicates meaning beyond the literal meaning of the words. Read lines 78–80. (*Dregs* means "residue settled at the bottom of a liquid.") What does "bitterest dregs of slavery" mean?

E STYLE
Reread lines 78–88. Identify examples of metaphor, repetition, and parallelism. What **tone** is created by this use of language? What kind of perspective on slavery does it help the writer to achieve?

DIFFERENTIATED INSTRUCTION

FOR ENGLISH LANGUAGE LEARNERS

Language Coach

COMMON CORE
RI 4, L 5

Figurative Language *Answer: Douglass is referring to the absolute worst time of his experience as a slave.* Tell students that figurative language allows writers to describe situations, thoughts, ideas, or feelings in an original, creative way. Encourage students to use figurative language in their own writing.

FOR ADVANCED LEARNERS/AP

Christianity and Slavery Point out line 89: "Sunday was my only leisure time." Clarify that slaves didn't work on Sunday because their Christian masters observed the Sabbath. Have students research and then discuss the role of Christianity in the lives of slaves, focusing on these questions: Why did slave owners initially resist efforts to convert slaves to Christianity? Why did they change their minds?

extreme dizziness; I trembled in every limb. Finding what was coming, I nerved myself up, feeling it would never do to stop work. I stood as long as I could stagger to the hopper[7] with grain. When I could stand no longer, I fell, and felt as if held down by an immense weight. The fan of course stopped; every one had his own work to do; and no one could do the work of the other, and have his own go on at the same time.

Mr. Covey was at the house, about one hundred yards from the treading-yard where we were fanning. On hearing the fan stop, he left immediately, and came to the spot where we were. He hastily inquired what the matter was. Bill answered that I was sick, and there was no one to bring wheat to the fan. I had by this time crawled away under the side of the post and rail-fence by which the yard was enclosed, hoping to find relief by getting out of the sun. He then asked where I was. He was told by one of the hands. He came to the spot, and, after looking at me awhile, asked me what was the matter. I told him as well as I could, for I scarce had strength to speak. He then gave me a savage kick in the side, and told me to get up. I tried to do so, but fell back in the attempt. He gave me another kick, and again told me to rise. I again tried, and succeeded in gaining my feet; but, stooping to get the tub with which I was feeding the fan, I again staggered and fell. While down in this situation, Mr. Covey took up the hickory slat with which Hughes had been striking off the half-bushel measure, and with it gave me a heavy blow upon the head, making a large wound, and the blood ran freely; and with this again told me to get up. I made no effort to comply, having now made up my mind to let him do his worst. In a short time after receiving this blow, my head grew better. Mr. Covey had now left me to my fate. At this moment I resolved, for the first time, to go to my master, enter a complaint, and ask his protection. In order to do this, I must that afternoon walk seven miles; and this, under the circumstances, was truly a severe undertaking. I was exceedingly feeble; made so as much by the kicks and blows which I received, as by the severe fit of sickness to which I had been subjected. I, however, watched my chance, while Covey was looking in an opposite direction, and started for St. Michael's. I succeeded in getting a considerable distance on my way to the woods, when Covey discovered me, and called after me to come back, threatening what he would do if I did not come. I disregarded both his calls and his threats, and made my way to the woods as fast as my feeble state would allow; and thinking I might be overhauled by him if I kept the road,[8] I walked through the woods, keeping far enough from the road to avoid detection, and near enough to prevent losing my way. I had not gone far before my little strength again failed me. I could go no farther. I fell down, and lay for a considerable time. The blood was yet oozing from the wound on my head. For a time I thought I should bleed to death; and think now that I should have done so, but that the blood so matted my hair as to stop the wound. After lying there about three quarters of an hour, I nerved myself up again, and started on my

③ Targeted Passage

7. **hopper:** a funnel-shaped container for storing grain.
8. **kept the road:** stayed on the road.

COMMON CORE RI 6

F AUTHOR'S PURPOSE
Reread lines 113–128. Notice the description of Mr. Covey's violence and the author's reaction to it. Without making judgments about Covey's behavior, Douglass advances a persuasive purpose—to expose slavery's unacceptable brutality. Now read lines 129–144, paying special attention to Douglass's tone and to what he reports about himself and Mr. Covey. How does Douglass advance his purpose in these lines?

F AUTHOR'S PURPOSE

Have volunteers read aloud first lines 113–128 and then lines 129–144. Point out that in the first segment Douglass relays how he physically feels during the event, but he does not recount his emotions about the ordeal or any judgment of Covey. Tell students that this approach allows readers to focus on the horrific factual details of the event. Ask for students' analysis of Douglass's tone and actions in the second segment. *Possible answer: Douglass's tone is not sentimental or judgmental. Instead, he states what happened in a casual way. This type of objective reporting allows Covey's brutality to speak for itself, enabling readers to be persuaded to sympathize with Douglass, based upon the facts of the events alone.* Read aloud lines 97–100, beginning with, "The circumstances..." and ending with, "how a slave was made a man." Ask students how Douglass's actions in lines 113–114 illustrate this emotional transformation.

Extend the Discussion How does Douglass's resolve to speak with Master Thomas enable him to endure the seven-mile trek?

REVISIT THE BIG QUESTION

Can you set yourself FREE?

Discuss In lines 130–150, after Covey beats him, what step does Douglass take toward self-determination? Why do you think he decides to take this step? *Possible answer: Douglass decides to run away to Master Thomas to complain about Covey and ask for protection. He realizes that Covey will continue to attack him and that he may not survive another beating. Perhaps he thinks that Master Thomas will take pity on him or at least decide to protect his "property."*

FOR STRGGLING READERS

③ Targeted Passage [Lines 113–131]

This passage describes a dramatic moment in Douglass's conflict with Covey.

- Why is Douglass lying down? (lines 115–116)
- How does Covey react to the news that Douglass is sick? (lines 121–128)
- What does Douglass then decide to do? (lines 130–131)

FOR ADVANCED LEARNERS/AP

Synthesize [small-group option] Have students review the Text Analysis Workshop on historical narratives (pages 70–71). Then ask them to identify sensory details and other pieces of information in Douglass's narrative that provide insight into its culture and time period. Tell students to consider how this historical insight contributes to the impact of the narrative as a primary source. Have students discuss their ideas in a small group.

In lines 150–171, use these prompts to help students understand slavery's dehumanizing effect:

Connect Have you ever asked for help but been rejected? How did the experience make you feel? *Accept all thoughtful responses.*

Analyze Why does Master Thomas refuse to help Douglass? *Possible answer: He has hired Douglass out to Covey for a year, so if he allowed Douglass to leave Covey, he would have to compensate Covey for his financial loss. Master Thomas's financial interest makes him unable to react humanely to Douglass's situation. He is also probably afraid of defying Covey—of supporting a slave's complaint against a slave owner.*

Synthesize What do readers learn about slavery from this scene? *Possible answer: Treating a human being as property dehumanizes everyone, even those who might otherwise have felt compassion for another human being.*

TEXT ANALYSIS

COMMON CORE
RI 4
RI 6
L 3a

G *Model the Skill:* **STYLE**

Illustrate the effects of the author's style by rereading the lines aloud, emphasizing the word *that*. Then point out how the repetition of the word *that* creates an insistent rhythm that reflects the manner in which Thomas relayed his list of excuses to Douglass.

Possible answer: The repetition of the word that *adds emphasis to each clause and creates an insistent rhythm unlike the conversational flow of quoted dialogue. This repetition makes Thomas's responses sound like a catalog of excuses and lies.*

---

way, through bogs and briers, barefooted and bareheaded, tearing my feet sometimes at nearly every step; and after a journey of about seven miles, occupying some five hours to perform it, I arrived at master's store. I then presented an appearance enough to affect any but a heart of iron. From the crown of my head to my feet, I was covered with blood. My hair was all clotted with dust and blood; my shirt was stiff with blood. My legs and feet were torn in sundry places with briers and thorns, and were also covered with blood. I suppose I looked like a man who had escaped a den of wild beasts, and barely escaped them. In this state I appeared before my master, humbly entreating him to interpose his authority for my protection. I told him all the circumstances as well as I could, and it seemed, as I spoke, at times to affect him. He would then walk the floor, and seek to justify Covey by saying he expected I deserved it. He asked me what I wanted. I told him, to let me get a new home; that as sure as I lived with Mr. Covey again, I should live with but to die with him; that Covey would surely kill me; he was in a fair way for it. Master Thomas ridiculed the idea that there was any danger of Mr. Covey's killing me, and said that he knew Mr. Covey; that he was a good man, and that he could not think of taking me from him; that, should he do so, he would lose the whole year's wages; that I belonged to Mr. Covey for one year, and that I must go back to him, come what might; and that I must not trouble him with any more stories, or that he would himself *get hold of me.* After **G** threatening me thus, he gave me a very large dose of salts,[9] telling me that I might remain in St. Michael's that night, (it being quite late,) but that I must be off back to Mr. Covey's early in the morning; and that if I did not, he would get *hold of me*, which meant that he would whip me. I remained all night, and, according to his orders, I started off to Covey's in the morning, (Saturday morning,) wearied in body and broken in spirit. I got no supper that night, or breakfast that morning. I reached Covey's about nine o'clock; and just as I was getting over the fence that divided Mrs. Kemp's fields from ours, out ran Covey with his cowskin, to give me another whipping. Before he could reach me, I succeeded in getting to the cornfield; and as the corn was very high, it afforded me the means of hiding. He seemed very angry, and searched for me a long time. My behavior was altogether unaccountable. He finally gave up the chase, thinking, I suppose, that I must come home for something to eat; he would give himself no further trouble in looking for me. I spent that day mostly in the woods, having the alternative before me,—to go home and be whipped to death, or stay in the woods and be starved to death. That night, I fell in with Sandy Jenkins, a slave with whom I was somewhat acquainted. Sandy had a free wife who lived about four miles from Mr. Covey's; and it being Saturday, he was on his way to see her. I told him my circumstances, and he very kindly invited me to go home with him. I went home with him, and talked this whole matter over, and got his advice as to what course it was best for me to pursue. I found Sandy an old adviser. He told me, with great solemnity, I

4 Targeted Passage

G **STYLE**
Reread lines 159–167. Note that Douglass chooses to convey this dialogue without the use of quotations. What effect does he achieve instead by repeating the word *that*?

---

9. **salts:** mineral salts used to relieve faintness and headache or to reduce swelling.

DIFFERENTIATED INSTRUCTION

FOR STRUGGLING READERS

4 Targeted Passage [Lines 150–173]

This passage describes Douglass's encounter with Master Thomas, his owner.

- How does Douglass look when he arrives at Master Thomas's store? (lines 150–155)
- What does he tell Master Thomas about why he is there? (lines 156–162)
- What threat is made? (lines 166–167)

FOR ADVANCED LEARNERS/AP

Free African Americans Point out line 184: "Sandy had a free wife…" Have students research the topic of free African Americans in the South, focusing on: How had most free African Americans achieved their freedom? Where did they live? How did they support themselves? What discrimination and restrictions did they face? What churches and organizations did they form? Have students present their research in an oral report.

Panel #10 from *The Frederick Douglass Series of 1938-1940*, Jacob Lawrence. © 2007 The Jacob and Gwendolyn Lawrence Foundation, Seattle/Artists Rights Society (ARS), New York.

Analyze Visuals

About the Art Jacob Lawrence (1917–2000) was a highly acclaimed figurative painter renowned for visual dramatizations of the African-American experience. He often devoted series of paintings to single historical figures who symbolized the struggle for emancipation and equality. This painting is the 10th in a series of 32 panels chronicling the life of Frederick Douglass.

Lawrence's work is in the permanent collections of the nation's leading museums, including the Museum of Modern Art and the Metropolitan Museum of Art in New York. He held honorary doctorates from numerous institutions, including Yale and Harvard.

FOR STRUGGLING READERS

Comprehension Support Discuss why Master Thomas "would lose the whole year's wages" (line 165) if he allowed Douglass to return to him. Clarify that Master Thomas owns Douglass but has hired him out to Covey for a year, receiving payment in exchange for the value of Douglass's labor. If Douglass stopped working for Covey, Master Thomas would have to pay Covey the equivalent of Douglass's lost labor.

FOR ENGLISH LANGUAGE LEARNERS

Language: Pronoun Referents Help students understand the long, complicated sentence in lines 162–167 by clarifying the different referents for the pronouns *he* and *him*. Explain that sometimes these pronouns refer to Master Thomas, while other times they refer to Mr. Covey. Write the first part of the sentence on the board, underlining the pronouns that refer to Master Thomas and double underlining those that refer to Mr. Covey: "Master Thomas

ridiculed the idea that there was any danger of Mr. Covey's killing me, and said that he knew Mr. Covey; that he was a good man, and that he could not think of taking me from him; that, should he do so, he would lose the whole year's wages...." Have students work in mixed-language groups to identify the referents for the pronouns *he* and *him* in the rest of the sentence, beginning with "that I belonged to Mr. Covey...."

For lines 183–218, use these prompts to help students understand how this encounter with Sandy affects Douglass:

Connect In your experience, how does kindness affect people who are experiencing problems in their lives? *Students will probably recognize that kindness can have a powerful, restorative effect on people, especially during desperate times.*

Analyze What does Sandy give Douglass, both literally and symbolically? *Possible answer: Literally, Sandy gives Douglass a root as a talisman that will supposedly protect him from being whipped. Symbolically, Sandy gives Douglass the gifts of self-confidence, courage, and hope. By showing Douglass kindness and providing him with a safe haven, Sandy empowers Douglass to move forward and face his problems.*

Synthesize In what ways might the root protect Douglass, even if it doesn't literally protect him against being whipped? *Possible answer: Douglass's belief in the power of the root might protect him against the worst degradation of slavery: losing his humanity. His restored self-confidence, the result of both his belief in the root and Sandy's kindness, might empower him to stand up for himself against Covey and thus turn him from a slave into a man (lines 99–100).*

must go back to Covey; but that before I went, I must go with him into another
190 part of the woods, where there was a certain *root,* which, if I would take some of it with me, carrying it *always on my right side,* would render it impossible for Mr. Covey, or any other white man, to whip me. He said he had carried it for years; and since he had done so, he had never received a blow, and never expected to while he carried it. I at first rejected the idea, that the simple carrying of a root in my pocket would have any such effect as he had said, and was not disposed to take it; but Sandy impressed the necessity with much earnestness, telling me it could do no harm, if it did no good. To please him, I at length took the root, and, according to his direction, carried it upon my right side. This was Sunday morning. I immediately started for home; and upon entering the yard gate, out
200 came Mr. Covey on his way to meeting.[10] He spoke to me very kindly, made me drive the pigs from a lot near by, and passed on towards the church. Now, this singular conduct of Mr. Covey really made me begin to think that there was something in the *root* which Sandy had given me; and had it been on any other day than Sunday, I could have attributed the conduct to no other cause than the influence of that root; and as it was, I was half inclined to think the *root* to be something more than I at first had taken it to be. All went well till Monday morning. On this morning, the virtue of the *root* was fully tested. Long before daylight, I was called to go and rub, curry, and feed, the horses. I obeyed, and was glad to obey. But whilst thus engaged, whilst in the act of throwing down some
210 blades from the loft, Mr. Covey entered the stable with a long rope; and just as I was half out of the loft, he caught hold of my legs, and was about tying me. As soon as I found what he was up to, I gave a sudden spring, and as I did so, he holding to my legs, I was brought sprawling on the stable floor. Mr. Covey seemed now to think he had me, and could do what he pleased; but at this moment— from whence came the spirit I don't know—I resolved to fight; and, suiting my action to the resolution, I seized Covey hard by the throat; and as I did so, I rose. He held on to me, and I to him. My resistance was so entirely unexpected, that Covey seemed taken all aback. He trembled like a leaf. This gave me assurance, and I held him uneasy, causing the blood to run where I touched him with the
220 ends of my fingers. Mr. Covey soon called out to Hughes for help. Hughes came, and, while Covey held me, attempted to tie my right hand. While he was in the act of doing so, I watched my chance, and gave him a heavy kick close under the ribs. This kick fairly sickened Hughes, so that he left me in the hands of Mr. Covey. This kick had the effect of not only weakening Hughes, but Covey also. When he saw Hughes bending over with pain, his courage quailed. He asked me if I meant to persist in my resistance. I told him I did, come what might; that he had used me like a brute for six months, and that I was determined to be used so no longer. With that, he strove to drag me to a stick that was lying just out of the stable door. He meant to knock me down. But just as he was leaning over to get

⑤ Targeted Passage

COMMON CORE RI 4, L 5b

Language Coach

Connotation A word's **connotations** are the images and feelings associated with the word. *Brute* (line 227) is very similar in meaning to *animal,* but its connotations are negative ("unable to reason," "cruel," "stupid"). Why is *brute* appropriate here?

---

10. **meeting:** church service.

DIFFERENTIATED INSTRUCTION

FOR STRUGGLING READERS

⑤ Targeted Passage [Lines 209–228]

This passage describes the climax of Douglass's conflict with Covey.

- What happens in the stable? (lines 210–211)
- What is Douglass's response? (lines 211–216)
- What does Douglass do to Hughes when he tries to interfere? (lines 221–225)
- Why won't Douglass stop resisting? (lines 226–228)

FOR ENGLISH LANGUAGE LEARNERS

Language Coach

COMMON CORE RI 4, L 5b

Connotation *Possible answer: Douglass is emphasizing how cruelly Covey has treated him, as if he were unworthy of respect.* Tell students that they should always consider a word's connotations when using it in a sentence. Write the following on the board and discuss the meanings: *Zoe looked at me. Zoe glared at me.*

230 the stick, I seized him with both hands by his collar, and brought him by a
sudden snatch to the ground. By this time, Bill came. Covey called upon him
for assistance. Bill wanted to know what he could do. Covey said, "Take hold of
him, take hold of him!" Bill said his master hired him out to work, and not to
help to whip me; so he left Covey and myself to fight our own battle out. We
were at it for nearly two hours. Covey at length let me go, puffing and blowing
at a great rate, saying that if I had not resisted, he would not have whipped me
half so much. The truth was, that he had not whipped me at all. I considered
him as getting entirely the worst end of the bargain; for he had drawn no blood
from me, but I had from him. The whole six months afterwards, that I spent
240 with Mr. Covey, he never laid the weight of his finger upon me in anger. He
would occasionally say, he didn't want to get hold of me again. "No," thought I,
"you need not; for you will come off worse than you did before."

This battle with Mr. Covey was the turning-point in my career as a slave. It
rekindled the few expiring embers of freedom, and revived within me a sense
of my own manhood. It recalled the departed self-confidence, and inspired me
again with a determination to be free. The gratification afforded by the triumph
was a full compensation[11] for whatever else might follow, even death itself. He
only can understand the deep satisfaction which I experienced, who has himself
repelled by force the bloody arm of slavery. I felt as I never felt before. It was
250 a glorious resurrection, from the tomb of slavery, to the heaven of freedom.
My long-crushed spirit rose, cowardice departed, bold defiance took its place;
and I now resolved that, however long I might remain a slave in form, the day
had passed forever when I could be a slave in fact. I did not hesitate to let it be
known of me, that the white man who expected to succeed in whipping, must
also succeed in killing me. **H**

From this time I was never again what might be called fairly whipped,
though I remained a slave four years afterwards. I had several fights, but was
never whipped. ✎

G Targeted Passage

COMMON CORE RI 4

Language Coach

Figurative Language "Getting … the worst end of the bargain" (line 238) means "having the loss while the other person has the gain"; it is **figurative language,** language that communicates meaning beyond the literal meaning of the words. Why does Douglass have the better position?

H AUTHOR'S PURPOSE Reread lines 243–253. How might this description have helped Douglass achieve his purpose?

---

11. **compensation:** payment; something of equivalent value.

REVISIT THE BIG QUESTION

Can you set yourself FREE?

Discuss In lines 243–250, how does Douglass's fight with Covey help him move toward self-determination? *Possible answer: His decision to fight back revives his sense of manhood and his "determination to be free" (line 246). It is the "turning-point" (line 243) that allows him to renounce the shackles of mental slavery, so that he is no longer "a slave in fact" (line 253).*

READING SKILL   COMMON CORE RI 6

H AUTHOR'S PURPOSE

Possible answer: Most readers would have been moved by his account of triumph over brutality and degradation.

IF STUDENTS NEED HELP… Work with them to use the chart introduced on page 559 to analyze Douglass's responses to his fight with Covey. Then ask students to consider why Douglass might have chosen to express his feelings here, while elsewhere he lets the facts speak for themselves.

Physical Realities	Responses to Situation
"I resolved to fight …" (line 215)	revived his sense of manhood and desire to be free (lines 243–246)

SELECTION WRAP–UP

READ WITH A PURPOSE Now that students have read the selection, ask them how Douglass is triumphant after the events, despite the fact that he remained a slave for four more years. *Possible answer: Douglass is triumphant because he reclaimed his sense of worth and desire to be free.*

Practice and Apply

For preliminary support of post-reading
questions, use these copy masters:

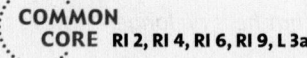 **RESOURCE MANAGER—Copy Masters**
Reading Check p. 53
Style p. 49
Question Support p. 54
Additional selection questions are
provided for teachers on page 43.

ANSWERS   **COMMON CORE** RI 2, RI 4, RI 6, RI 9, L 3a

1. *Douglass had broken the gate and the oxcart (lines 29–30).*

2. *Master Thomas ridiculed Douglass's claim that Covey might kill him. He told Douglass that he had to return to Covey. Master Thomas said that he would whip Douglass if he kept complaining (lines 162–167).*

3. *Douglass realized that he could defend himself and take control of his own life.*

Possible answers:

4. ● **COMMON CORE FOCUS** *Analyze Author's Purpose* *Factual details inform readers about how brutally slaves were treated. Emotional details give readers insight into Douglass's personal experience. By using both kinds of details, Douglass can inform and persuade readers who respond to facts as well as those who respond to emotions.*

5. ● **COMMON CORE FOCUS** *Style* *Tone: either detached and factual or emotional and poetic;* *Diction: complex sentences, strong verbs;* *Figurative language: occasional metaphor;* *Dialogue: indirect dialogue. Some students may link Douglass's credibility as a narrator to his objective style. Others may argue that his more emotional passages establish his credibility because he speaks from personal experience.*

6. *Inverted parallelism: "You have seen how a man was made a slave; you shall see how a slave was made a man." Douglass has described how his physical experiences crushed his spirit. Then he shows how, by standing up to Covey, he reasserts his humanity and regains his self-worth.*

After Reading

Comprehension

1. **Recall** What was Covey's first reason for beating Douglass?

2. **Summarize** How did Master Thomas respond when Douglass asked for protection from Covey?

3. **Clarify** How was the battle with Covey a turning point in Douglass's life as a slave?

Text Analysis

● 4. **Analyze Author's Purpose** Review the chart you created as you read. Given his main purpose, why might Douglass have chosen to include both kinds of detail in his narrative? Explain your answer.

● 5. **Analyze Style** Describe the main elements of Douglass's style. Which elements, if any, help Douglass establish himself as a credible **narrator**? Support your answer with details.

6. **Examine Rhetorical Devices** Douglass was a great orator, and his style was influenced by his mastery of rhetorical devices. One of his signature techniques was his use of **inverted parallelism,** a reversal of ideas expressed in parallel phrases or clauses: "The longest days were too short for him, and the shortest nights too long for him." Identify the inverted parallelism in lines 99–100. In what ways does this reversal of ideas summarize Douglass's emotional experiences in this selection?

7. **Make Generalizations from Conflicts** What do the conflicts between Douglass and Covey reveal about slavery's effects on both slaves and masters? Use charts like the ones shown to make generalizations about slavery based on Douglass's experiences.

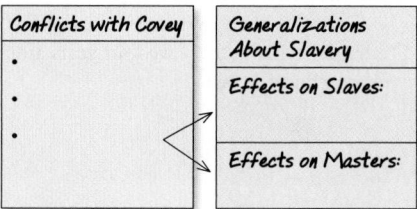

8. **Draw Conclusions** Consider how Douglass portrays his triumphant moment of self-determination. In what ways does his experience illustrate each of the following classic American ideas? Support your answers with details.

• individual rights   • self-reliance   • resistance to tyranny

Text Criticism

9. **Different Perspectives** In what ways might a slave narrative written by an enslaved woman differ from Douglass's account? Explain your answer.

> *Can you set yourself* **FREE?**
>
> When Frederick Douglass eventually realized his dream of freedom, he declared his right to self-determination. In what areas do you think a free person is able to control his or her own life? What aspects of your life are you unable to control?

570   UNIT 3: FROM ROMANTICISM TO REALISM

COMMON CORE

RI 2 Determine two or more central ideas of a text. **RI 4** Determine the meaning of words and phrases as they are used in a text, including figurative and connotative meanings. **RI 6** Determine an author's point of view or purpose in a text in which the rhetoric is particularly effective, analyzing how style and content contribute to the power, persuasiveness, or beauty of a text. **RI 9** Analyze nineteenth-century U.S. documents of literary significance for their themes, purposes, and rhetorical features. **L 3a** Apply an understanding of syntax to the study of complex texts when reading.

---

7. *Effects on Slaves: The abuse that masters like Covey inflicted on slaves robbed them of their humanity.* *Effects on Masters: Slavery also turned masters into animals, whose brutality and insensitivity to suffering robbed them of their own humanity.*

8. *Individual rights: Douglass sees himself as a man who deserves full human rights.* *Self-reliance: Douglass decides to trust his own beliefs and take control of his own destiny.* *Resistance: Douglass asserts himself against injustice and brutality.*

9. *A woman's slave narrative would not identify freedom with manhood, as Douglass does. A woman's narrative might describe different types of threats to her humanity and dignity.*

> *Can you set yourself* FREE? Answers will vary. Students may say that they are free to make their own choices in life; they also may point to laws, rules, and governing authorities that prevent them from having control in some areas.

Language

♦ **GRAMMAR AND STYLE: Make Effective Word Choices**

Review the **Grammar and Style** note on page 563. To convey the brutal conditions he endured as a slave, Douglass used **vivid verbs,** ones that convey precise actions or emotions and draw readers into the reality of his experiences.

> *I was seized with a violent aching of the head, attended with extreme dizziness; I trembled in every limb. Finding what was coming, I nerved myself up, feeling it would never do to stop work. I stood as long as I could stagger to the hopper with grain.* (lines 106–109)

The verbs *seized, trembled, nerved,* and *stagger* help communicate the urgency of Douglass's situation.

PRACTICE Rewrite each sentence, replacing the boldface words with vivid verbs. An example has been done for you.

> **EXAMPLE**
>
> I **walked** into the room where the baby was **crying** and **helped** her back to sleep.
>
> *I crept into the room where the baby was whimpering and coaxed her back to sleep.*

1. The wind **blew** as he **walked** through the dark forest.

2. A sudden wave of illness made me **hold** my stomach.

3. The waves **moved** the ship back and forth as the storm **continued.**

READING-WRITING CONNECTION

Expand your understanding of Frederick Douglass by responding to this prompt. Then, use the **revising tips** to improve your description.

WRITING PROMPT	REVISING TIPS
DESCRIBE A TURNING POINT Douglass viewed his fight with the cowardly overseer Covey as a turning point in his life. Think of an episode from your own life that you would describe as a turning point. Write a **three-paragraph description** of the episode. Make effective word choices to convey the significance of the event to your readers.	• Include all the necessary background information to help readers understand the significance of the event. • Tell your story using chronological order. • Use precise verbs and sensory details that vividly describe your experience.

Interactive Revision

Go to **thinkcentral.com**.
KEYWORD: HML11-571

◦ COMMON CORE

L 3 Apply knowledge of language to make effective choices for meaning or style. **W 3** Write narratives to develop real or imagined experiences or events using effective technique, well-chosen details, and well-structured event sequences. **W 3d** Use precise words and phrases, telling details, and sensory language to convey a vivid picture of the experiences, events, setting, and/or characters.

Language

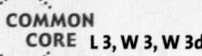
COMMON CORE **L 3, W 3, W 3d**

♦ **GRAMMAR AND STYLE**

Suggest that students use a print or online thesaurus to find vivid verbs that they can substitute for weak ones. Remind students that vivid verbs are specific, rather than vague. (For more on using language effectively, see **Writing Handbook,** pp. R26–R38. For more on verbs, see **Grammar Handbook,** pp. R59–R61.)

Possible answers:

1. *blew:* raged; *walked:* staggered

2. *hold:* clutch, grasp

3. *moved:* pitched; *continued:* persisted

 RESOURCE MANAGER—Copy Master
Make Effective Word Choices p. 55

READING-WRITING CONNECTION

Give examples of possible turning points, such as confronting a strong-willed friend or older sibling, standing up for somebody else, or speaking out for a cause. Have students use a Cluster Diagram to brainstorm ideas and list elements of significance for each idea.

 BEST PRACTICES TOOLKIT—Transparency
Cluster Diagram p. B18

Writing Online

The following tools are available online at **thinkcentral.com** and on **Write*Smart* CD-ROM:**
• **Interactive Graphic Organizers**
• **Interactive Student Models**
• **Interactive Revision Lessons**
For additional grammar instruction, see **GrammarNotes** on **thinkcentral.com**.

Assess and Reteach

Assess

DIAGNOSTIC AND SELECTION TESTS
    Selection Tests A, B/C pp. 157–160

Interactive Selection Test on thinkcentral.com

Reteach

Level Up Online Tutorials on thinkcentral.com

Reteaching Worksheets on thinkcentral.com

    Literature Lesson 44, Reading Lesson 3

DIFFERENTIATED INSTRUCTION

FOR STRUGGLING WRITERS
Writing Support

• Limit the length of the assignment to two paragraphs.

• Provide a sentence starter for students to use as they draft their descriptions (such as *An event that had a great impact on me was* _____).

• Have students use a timeline to map out the sequence of events that occurred in the episode.

• As students draft their paragraphs, have them flesh out each event by adding descriptive details.

• Ask students to write a summary sentence that states what they learned from the episode.

 BEST PRACTICES TOOLKIT—Transparency
Timeline p. B23

Focus and Motivate

COMMON CORE FOCUS

RI 3 Analyze a complex sequence of events and explain how specific individuals interact and develop over the course of the text. **W 3d** Use precise words to convey a vivid picture of the characters. **L 3** Apply knowledge of language to make effective choices for meaning and style. **L 4** Determine or clarify the meaning of multiple-meaning words. **L 4d** Verify the preliminary determination of the meaning of a word.

ABOUT THE AUTHOR

After students have read about Jacobs's life, ask them to point out several details that show her strong character. Explain that this excerpt from *Incidents in the Life of a Slave Girl* reveals Jacobs's character, explores her decision to leave her children, and describes some of her time in hiding.

NOTABLE QUOTE

"Slavery is terrible for men; but it is far more terrible for women." —**Harriet Jacobs**

Ask students to discuss how the meaning of Harriet Jacobs's quote might be demonstrated in her narrative and also applicable to all female slaves.

COMMON CORE

RI 3 Analyze a sequence of events and explain how specific individuals interact and develop over the course of the text. **L 4** Determine or clarify the meaning of multiple-meaning words. **L 4d** Verify the preliminary determination of the meaning of a word.

DID YOU KNOW?

Harriet Jacobs . . .

- was described in a runaway slave notice as having run away "without any known cause or provocation."
- used fictitious names in her autobiography because she "deemed it kind and considerate toward others."
- was asked by the son of her former owner for help in getting a job after the Civil War.

Literature of the Civil War

from Incidents in the Life of a Slave Girl

Slave Narrative by Harriet Jacobs

Meet the Author

Harriet Jacobs 1813–1897

Harriet Jacobs's *Incidents in the Life of a Slave Girl* is one of the few slave narratives to recount the anguish of slavery from a female point of view. The book ranks as one of the most powerful and important examples of the slave narrative genre.

Defying Her Owner Jacobs was born into slavery in Edenton, North Carolina. Her first owner was a relatively kind woman who taught her to read and sew. When Jacobs was 12, the woman died, and Jacobs was willed to the 3-year-old daughter of Dr. James Norcom—the man she calls "Dr. Flint" in her autobiography. Norcom began making sexual advances toward Jacobs when she was in her teens. Jacobs resisted him and instead started a relationship with Norcom's neighbor, a white lawyer named Samuel Sawyer ("Mr. Sands" in the narrative), hoping the relationship would put a stop to Norcom's unwanted attentions. Jacobs had two children with Sawyer, but Norcom continued harassing her. Infuriated by her refusals, he punished Jacobs by sending her and her young children to work for his son ("Mr. Flint"), who he hoped would be able to break her resistance.

Seven Years in Hiding Shortly after arriving at the son's plantation, Jacobs made the painful decision to run away and leave her children behind. She hoped that her leaving would make the Norcoms sell the children to their father, Sawyer. Unlike many runaways, Jacobs did not immediately flee north. She hid in a tiny attic space in her grandmother's house. She remained there for seven years, but was able to take comfort in the knowledge that her children had been bought by Sawyer and saved from plantation life. In 1842, friends arranged for Jacobs to escape to New York. Once there, she found work as a nanny for a white family. Even so, Jacobs was always in danger of losing her freedom. Fugitive slave laws allowed for slave catchers to capture slaves who had escaped to the North and return them to slavery in the South. Fortunately, in 1852, Jacobs's employer purchased Jacobs's freedom and that of her two children.

Abolitionist and Author In the North, Jacobs became involved in the abolitionist movement. Abolitionist friends encouraged her to write *Incidents in the Life of a Slave Girl,* which she published in 1861 under the pseudonym Linda Brent, the name she uses to refer to herself in the narrative.

Author Online
Go to **thinkcentral.com**. KEYWORD: HML11-572

572

Selection Resources

See resources on the **Teacher One Stop DVD-ROM** and on **thinkcentral.com**.

 RESOURCE MANAGER UNIT 3
Plan and Teach, pp. 57–64
Summary, pp. 65–66†‡*
Text Analysis and Reading
   Skill, pp. 67–70†
Grammar and Style, p. 73

DIAGNOSTIC AND SELECTION TESTS
Selection Tests, pp. 161–164

 BEST PRACTICES TOOLKIT
Analysis Frame: Theme, pp.
   D21, D32
Character Traits Web, p. D7
Making Inferences, p. A13

TECHNOLOGY
- **Teacher One Stop DVD-ROM**
- **Student One Stop DVD-ROM**
- **Audio Anthology CD**
- **GrammarNotes DVD-ROM**
- **ExamView Test Generator** on the Teacher One Stop

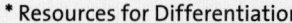

* Resources for Differentiation   **†** Also in Spanish   **‡** In Haitian Creole and Vietnamese

TEXT ANALYSIS: NARRATIVE ELEMENTS

The events in Jacobs's autobiography are true, not fictional, yet Jacobs selects and arranges them to tell a compelling story. Critics have noted, not always admiringly, how much her book resembles a novel. As you read, notice the following narrative characteristics:

- Linda, the main character, experiences internal and external **conflicts** resulting from slavery. An **internal conflict** is a struggle within a character; an **external conflict** is a struggle between a character and an outside force.
- These conflicts result in **suspense,** or excitement and tension, as readers wonder about the outcome of the complex sequence of events.
- Direct comments and telling details develop the strong **characterizations** of Linda and the slave owners, making their personalities clear yet complex.

READING STRATEGY: READING A NARRATIVE

Numerous characters are mentioned in this selection, and because the excerpt is from the middle of the book, it is not always clear who they are. Some are never given names. Study Jacobs's biography on page 572, and then match characters in the narrative to the actual figures in Jacobs's life. Pay attention to the background paragraphs that precede each part of the selection. As you read, use a graphic organizer to keep track of the characters and their relation to the narrator. Note whether they support or oppose her.

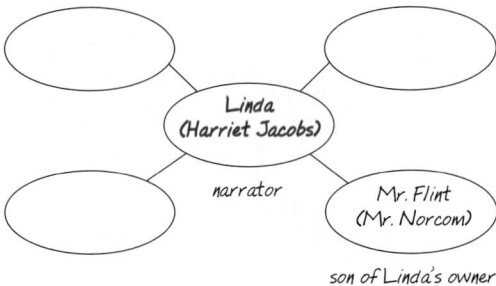

Linda
(Harriet Jacobs)

narrator

Mr. Flint
(Mr. Norcom)

son of Linda's owner

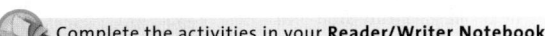

Complete the activities in your **Reader/Writer Notebook.**

What is the PRICE of freedom?

Parents often put their children's welfare before their own. In Harriet Jacobs's case, the sacrifice she made for her children was tremendous. Running away put her at risk of being caught and severely beaten, jailed, or sold. In addition, she deprived herself of the opportunity to play a role in the raising of her own children.

DISCUSS Think about sacrifices people have made for their own or their children's freedom. Discuss examples from the past or the present with a group of classmates. Can the price of freedom ever be too high?

The Ride for Freedom, The Fugitive Slaves (1862), Eastman Johnson. Oil. The Granger Collection, New York.

573

Teach

What is the PRICE of freedom?

Explain that *price* in this context does not refer to the monetary expense of freedom. Instead, it means the personal cost or sacrifice required to gain freedom. Read the question and the paragraph that follows, and have students generate examples for the *DISCUSS* activity. Then discuss the last question as a class.

TEXT ANALYSIS   COMMON CORE
                                 RI 3

● Model the Skill: NARRATIVE ELEMENTS

To identify conflict within a narrative, read aloud this example:

> Mrs. Bell wondered if her son would be happier at a different school. Mr. Evans said Stephen was the best football player on his team and hoped he would stay, but Mrs. Bell was not sure this was a good enough reason to keep Stephen at a school where he was unhappy.

Point out to students that Mrs. Bell's struggle is within herself, so she is having an internal conflict. She has to decide whether to keep Stephen at his current school or move him to a different school.

GUIDED PRACTICE: Ask students to identify the suspense in this passage.

READING STRATEGY   COMMON CORE
                                 RI 3

■ Model the Skill: READING A NARRATIVE

Read aloud the narrative example again. Identify for students how Mr. Evans is connected to Stephen and why he is important. Point out that Mr. Evans is Stephen's football coach and probably cares about Stephen's happiness.

GUIDED PRACTICE Have students read the text on page 574. Help them describe Jacobs's relationship with her grandmother.

R RESOURCE MANAGER—Copy Master
Reading a Narrative p. 69 (for student use while reading the selection)

DIFFERENTIATED INSTRUCTION

FOR ENGLISH LANGUAGE LEARNERS

Background Have students read the background note on page 575. Elaborate on the note by presenting students with the following information:

- In 1839, Mississippi became the first state in which a married woman could own property in her own name. However, she had to have her husband's permission to do so.
- In the early 1800s, career opportunities for American women were very limited.

Although women could become teachers or writers, many other professions were closed to them.

- In the United States, women were not granted the right to vote until 1920.

Discuss with students whether white women in America may have sympathized with the slaves' plights partly because of their own history of less dire oppression.

SUMMARY

This excerpt from the slave narrative *Incidents in the Life of a Slave Girl* begins with Linda's realization that the Flints will take control of her children to subdue her. To save her children, Linda decides to flee, hoping their father, a white man, will buy them. She hides at a friend's house while Mr. Flint searches for her and offers a reward for her capture. Linda's children, aunt, and brother are thrown in jail to pressure them for information about her.

READ WITH A PURPOSE

Help students set a purpose for reading. Tell them to read to discover how various people react to Linda's escape.

TEXT ANALYSIS

COMMON CORE
RI 3

Ⓐ Model the Skill:
NARRATIVE ELEMENTS

To point out how details details build characters, read aloud lines 1–8 and list the details that flesh out the characters of Mr. and Mrs. Flint. For instance, point out that Mrs. Flint was more concerned about her carpet than she was about Linda's need for a bed.

Possible answer: *The Flints are selfish and unfeeling people. Details that build this characterization include their lack of concern for the comfort or feelings of their servants (lines 6–8) and their singular focus on how their servants can serve them (lines 1–2).*

REVISIT THE BIG QUESTION

What is the PRICE *of freedom?*

Discuss In lines 9–13, what decision does Linda make that reflects her willingness to sacrifice for her children? Is this an easy decision for her? Explain. ***Possible answer:*** *She decides to leave her children so that they will not fall into the Flints' hands (lines 9–10). She sacrifices her safety and time with her children so that they will be safe. It is not an easy decision for her. She knows it will cause her grandmother worry and grief.*

Incidents in the Life of a Slave Girl

Harriet Jacobs

BACKGROUND At this point in the narrative, Linda has spent six weeks at the plantation of old Dr. Flint's son, Mr. Flint, making the house ready for his new bride, who is now at the house. Mr. Flint has said openly that he plans to break Linda's willful spirit, as his father had not been able to do. In addition, Linda has learned that the next day, her children are to be brought from their grandmother's house, where they are loved, to the plantation, where they will be put to work and used to keep Linda in line. Be warned that this selection contains a racial slur.

The Flight

MR. FLINT was hard pushed for house servants, and rather than lose me he had restrained his malice. I did my work faithfully, though not, of course, with a willing mind. They were evidently afraid I should leave them. Mr. Flint wished that I should sleep in the great house instead of the servants' quarters. His wife agreed to the proposition, but said I mustn't bring my bed into the house, because it would scatter feathers on her carpet. I knew when I went there that they would never think of such a thing as furnishing a bed of any kind for me and my little one. I therefore carried my own bed, and now I was forbidden to use it. I did as I Ⓐ was ordered. But now that I was certain my children were to be put in their power, 10 in order to give them a stronger hold on me, I resolved to leave them that night. I remembered the grief this step would bring upon my dear old grandmother; and nothing less than the freedom of my children would have induced me to disregard her advice. I went about my evening work with trembling steps. Mr. Flint twice called from his chamber door to inquire why the house was not locked up. I replied that I had not done my work. "You have had time enough to do it," said he. "Take care how you answer me!"

Analyze Visuals ▶
What can you **infer** about the enslaved family pictured in this photograph from South Carolina?

① Targeted Passage

Ⓐ **NARRATIVE ELEMENTS** Notice how the details in lines 1–8 build the **characterization** of the Flints. What kind of people are they?

DIFFERENTIATED INSTRUCTION

FOR ADVANCED LEARNERS/AP

Expert Groups Have students research one of these topics:

- slave literacy laws
- other slave narratives
- female African-American abolitionists, such as Harriet Tubman and Sojourner Truth
- procedures for buying a slave's freedom

Have students prepare an oral report or a multimedia presentation to share with the class.

FOR STRUGGLING READERS

In combination with the *Audio Anthology CD*, use one or more Targeted Passages (pp. 574, 576, 579) to ensure that students focus on key events and concepts. Targeted Passages are also good for english language learners.

① Targeted Passage [Lines 2–13]

This passage introduces Linda's plight with the Flints, her reason for leaving her children, and the resulting conflicts.

BACKGROUND

Female Slave Narrative The female slave narrative was intended to influence white northern middle-class women. Many of the trials that Jacobs endures, such as separation from her children, resonated with white women who cared for their own children and saw themselves as the protectors of morality. This slave narrative's purpose was to make white women empathize with slave women and recognize that slavery was immoral.

TIERED DISCUSSION PROMPTS

In lines 1–16, use these prompts to help students consider Linda's situation and agonizing decision:

Connect Have you or someone you know ever had to make a difficult decision? What made the situation difficult? *Accept all thoughtful responses.*

Interpret Why does Linda decide she must leave her children? *Possible answer: She believes that the Flints will take her children in order to subdue her (lines 9–10).*

Evaluate Does Linda's description of her circumstances justify her decision? Why or why not? *Possible answer: Yes; she explains how uncaring and thoughtless the Flints are (lines 4–9, 14–16). Her characterizations prove that leaving would save her children.*

Analyze Visuals

Possible answer: The family members value one another. The women clasp the children, and the family has members of many ages. Everyone in the photo looks sad, as if perhaps they are fearful or unsure about whether they will be separated.

- Why do the Flints want Linda to stay in their house? (line 3)
- How do the Flints treat Linda? (lines 6–8)
- What do the Flints intend to do with Linda's children? How does that influence Linda's decision to leave her children? (lines 9–10)
- How does Linda hope her decision will help her children? (lines 12–13)
- What worry does she have about leaving? (lines 10–11)

FOR STRUGGLING READERS

Develop Reading Fluency Show students the difference between a poor reading and an effective reading. Read aloud the text on page 574, without pausing for punctuation marks and without using proper intonation and expression. Then, reread the passage, using proper pausing, intonation, and expression. Discuss the difference between your two readings. Then, have students practice reading this passage aloud with a partner.

B NARRATIVE ELEMENTS

Possible answer: Linda has a conflict with the Flints, who plan to take her children (lines 9–10). She also has an internal conflict of worrying that running away will grieve her grandmother (line 11) or that she will fail and endanger her children (lines 19–21). Lines 17–21 build suspense as Linda waits to escape and fears being caught.

C *Model the Skill:* READING A NARRATIVE

Model use of the graphic organizer introduced on page 573. Focus on lines 31–32 and the author's biography, and clarify that Jacobs used the name Linda to protect herself from discovery and capture.

Sally (friend of Linda's grandmother)

Mr. Sands (Samuel Sawyer)

Linda (Harriot Jacobs)

Possible answer: Sally is a friend who lives with Linda's grandmother. Mr. Sands is the father of Linda's children. Jacobs made up the name Mr. Sands to refer to Mr. Sawyer, who was the father of her real children.

D GRAMMAR AND STYLE   COMMON CORE   L 3

Establish Tone Jacobs's emotional writing style helps readers empathize with her horrid circumstances. Ask students to find charged adjectives in lines 50–54 and describe the resulting tone. ***Possible answer: Adjectives include "fatherless and motherless" and "innocent little." The tone is desperate.***

I shut all the windows, locked all the doors, and went up to the third story, to wait till midnight. How long those hours seemed, and how fervently I prayed that God would not forsake me in this hour of utmost need! I was about to risk
20 everything on the throw of a die; and if I failed, O what would become of me and my poor children? They would be made to suffer for my fault. **B**

     At half past twelve I stole softly down stairs. I stopped on the second floor, thinking I heard a noise. I felt my way down into the parlor, and looked out of the window. The night was so intensely dark that I could see nothing. I raised the window very softly and jumped out. Large drops of rain were falling, and the darkness bewildered me. I dropped on my knees, and breathed a short prayer to God for guidance and protection. I groped my way to the road, and rushed towards the town with almost lightning speed. I arrived at my grandmother's house, but dared not see her. She would say, "Linda, you are killing me;" and I
30 knew that would unnerve me. I tapped softly at the window of a room, occupied by a woman, who had lived in the house several years. I knew she was a faithful friend, and could be trusted with my secret. I tapped several times before she heard me. At last she raised the window, and I whispered, "Sally, I have run away. Let me in, quick." She opened the door softly, and said in low tones, "For God's sake, don't. Your grandmother is trying to buy you and de chillern. Mr. Sands was here last week. He tole her he was going away on business, but he wanted her to go ahead about buying you and de chillern, and he would help her all he could. Don't run away, Linda. Your grandmother is all bowed down wid trouble now." **C**

     I replied, "Sally, they are going to carry my children to the plantation to-
40 morrow; and they will never sell them to any body so long as they have me in their power. Now, would you advise me to go back?"

     "No, chile, no," answered she. "When dey finds you is gone, dey won't want de plague[1] ob de chillern; but where is you going to hide? Dey knows ebery inch ob dis house."

     I told her I had a hiding-place, and that was all it was best for her to know. I asked her to go into my room as soon as it was light, and take all my clothes out of my trunk, and pack them in hers; for I knew Mr. Flint and the constable would be there early to search my room. I feared the sight of my children would be too much for my full heart; but I could not go out into the uncertain future without
50 one last look. I bent over the bed where lay my little Benny and baby Ellen. Poor little ones! fatherless and motherless! Memories of their father came over me. He wanted to be kind to them; but they were not all to him, as they were to my womanly heart. I knelt and prayed for the innocent little sleepers. I kissed them lightly, and turned away. **D**

     As I was about to open the street door, Sally laid her hand on my shoulder, and said, "Linda, is you gwine all alone? Let me call your uncle."

     "No, Sally," I replied, "I want no one to be brought into trouble on my account."

---

1. **plague:** nuisance.

B NARRATIVE ELEMENTS
Describe the **conflicts** presented in lines 9–21. Which lines build **suspense?**

2 Targeted Passage

C READING A NARRATIVE
Reread lines 28–38. Who are Sally and Mr. Sands? How does Linda interact with them? Refer to Jacobs's biography on page 572 if necessary.

D GRAMMAR AND STYLE
Examine lines 50–54. Notice how the writer uses emotionally charged **adjectives** to express the depth of her despair.

DIFFERENTIATED INSTRUCTION

FOR STRUGGLING READERS

Targeted Passage [Lines 22–45]

- How does Linda escape? (lines 22–25)
- Where does Linda first go when she escapes? Where does she go next? (lines 27–32)
- Does Sally agree with Linda's decision? What does Linda ask Sally to do? (lines 34–38)
- What does Mr. Sands plan to do? (lines 35–37)

FOR ENGLISH LANGUAGE LEARNERS

Language: Conversational English Patterns Explain that Sally's dialect reflects the typical speech of many slaves. Read lines 42–44 aloud and help students decipher them. ***Possible answer:*** *"No, child, no. When they find that you are gone, they won't want the nuisance of the children; but where are you going to hide? They know every inch of this house."* Help pairs decipher Sally's other dialogue.

I went forth into the darkness and rain. I ran on till I came to the house of the friend who was to conceal me.

60 Early the next morning Mr. Flint was at my grandmother's inquiring for me. She told him she had not seen me, and supposed I was at the plantation. He watched her face narrowly, and said, "Don't you know any thing about her running off?" She assured him that she did not. He went on to say, "Last night she ran off without the least provocation. We had treated her very kindly. My wife liked her. She will soon be found and brought back. Are her children with you?" When told that they were, he said, "I am very glad to hear that. If they are here, she cannot be far off. If I find out that any of my niggers have had any thing to do with this damned business, I'll give 'em five hundred lashes." As he started to go to his father's, he turned round and added, persuasively, "Let her be brought back,
70 and she shall have her children to live with her."

The tidings made the old doctor rave and storm at a furious rate. It was a busy day for them. My grandmother's house was searched from top to bottom. As my trunk was empty, they concluded I had taken my clothes with me. Before

INCIDENTS IN THE LIFE OF A SLAVE GIRL **577**

(COMMON CORE L 4, L 4d)

Language Coach

Multiple-Meaning Words
Narrowly (line 62) is a
multiple-meaning word,
a word with more than
one meaning. Look up
narrow in a dictionary,
and select the meaning
that fits the context of
the sentence.

TIERED DISCUSSION PROMPTS

In ines 60–70, use these prompts to help understand the tension and conflict between Mr. Flint and Linda's grandmother:

Connect Think about a time when someone has asked you for answers you could not supply. How did you feel? How did that person respond? *Accept all thoughtful responses.*

Interpret What does Mr. Flint's remark that Linda ran off "without the least provocation" tell you about him? How does he view Linda? *Possible answer: He can't imagine that the threat of putting her children to work would upset and provoke Linda. He doesn't view Linda as having a mother's normal feelings, but rather sees her as a disobedient possession.*

Synthesize On the basis of the selection and your own experiences, do you believe Mr. Flint's promise that Linda's children can live with her if she returns? Explain. *Possible answer: No; based on his character, he is probably lying to trick Linda's grandmother into giving up Linda.*

FOR ENGLISH LANGUAGE LEARNERS

Language Coach
(COMMON CORE L 4, L 4d)

Multiple-Meaning Words Answer:
Here, narrow *means "close" or "careful."*
Mr. Flint is looking for any hints to Linda's
whereabouts. Explain to students that when they encounter a multiple-meaning word, they should examine the surrounding words to determine which meaning the

writer used. To give students an example, point out the multiple-meaning word *die* in line 20. Write possible meanings of *die* on the board. Tell students that the words *throw of a* are clues to the correct meaning of *die.* Ask students which meaning is used in this sentence

FOR ADVANCED LEARNERS/AP

Analyze Theme [small-group option] Have students make inferences using textual evidence to determine some of the narrative's themes. Have students discuss the questions in the Analysis Frame: Theme and decide whether the themes they identified are universal and still relevant today.

BEST PRACTICES TOOLKIT—Transparency
Analysis Frame: Theme pp. D21, D32

What is the PRICE *of freedom?*

Discuss In lines 76–79, who makes a sacrifice for Linda? What does that sacrifice suggest about slave families? *Possible answer: Linda's grandmother makes a sacrifice for Linda by agreeing to take Linda's children. This shows that slave families were quite close and trusted and depended on one another. They banded together to help one another fight their oppressors.*

TEXT ANALYSIS

COMMON CORE

RI 3

❻ NARRATIVE ELEMENTS

Possible answer: Linda portrays herself as a "weak and oppressed" (line 97) victim who cunningly outwits a tyrant (lines 95–98). Readers are likely to feel sympathy for her and rejoice in her triumph.

IF STUDENTS NEED HELP . . . Urge them to visualize the scene Linda describes and identify how they feel about her. Then remind them that characterization is built from descriptions of a character's words, actions, and attitudes, and help them complete a Character Traits Web to identify information about Linda that created their response.

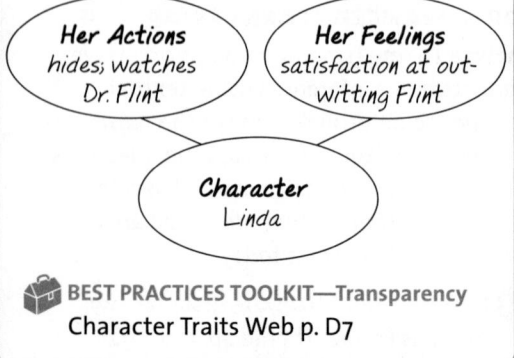

Her Actions hides; watches Dr. Flint

Her Feelings satisfaction at out-witting Flint

Character Linda

📂 **BEST PRACTICES TOOLKIT—Transparency**
Character Traits Web p. D7

---

ten o'clock every vessel northward bound was thoroughly examined, and the law against harboring[2] fugitives was read to all on board. At night a watch was set over the town. Knowing how distressed my grandmother would be, I wanted to send her a message; but it could not be done. Every one who went in or out of her house was closely watched. The doctor said he would take my children, unless she became responsible for them; which of course she willingly did. The next day was 80 spent in searching. Before night, the following advertisement was posted at every corner, and in every public place for miles round:—

> *$300 REWARD! Ran away from the subscriber,[3] an intelligent, bright, mulatto[4] girl, named Linda, 21 years of age. Five feet four inches high. Dark eyes, and black hair inclined to curl; but it can be made straight. Has a decayed spot on a front tooth. She can read and write, and in all probability will try to get to the Free States. All persons are forbidden, under penalty of the law, to harbor or employ said slave. $150 will be given to whoever takes her in the state, and $300 if taken out of the state and delivered to me, or lodged in jail. DR. FLINT.*

> For a week, Linda hides in the house of an unnamed friend. Her pursuers come so close to finding her that she rushes from the house into the bushes, where she is bitten by a poisonous snake or lizard. She suffers greatly until an old woman treats her with a folk remedy. Vowing "give me liberty or death," she refuses to return to the Flints. Then a sympathetic white woman, an old friend of her grandmother's, offers to conceal Linda in a small storage room in her house. The woman makes them promise never to tell, as she is the wife of a prominent slaveholder. The woman sends her cook, Linda's friend Betty, to meet Linda and take her to the house.

Months of Peril

90 I went to sleep that night with the feeling that I was for the present the most fortunate slave in town. Morning came and filled my little cell with light. I thanked the heavenly Father for this safe retreat. Opposite my window was a pile of feather beds. On the top of these I could lie perfectly concealed, and command a view of the street through which Dr. Flint passed to his office. Anxious as I was, I felt a gleam of satisfaction when I saw him. Thus far I had outwitted him, and I triumphed over it. Who can blame slaves for being cunning? They are constantly compelled to resort to it. It is the only weapon of the weak and oppressed against the strength of their tyrants. ❻

❻ **NARRATIVE ELEMENTS**
Consider how Jacobs develops the **characterization** of Linda in this paragraph. How are readers likely to feel toward her?

---

2. **harboring:** sheltering or protecting.
3. **the subscriber:** the person placing the notice, Dr. Flint.
4. **mulatto:** of mixed black and white ancestry.

DIFFERENTIATED INSTRUCTION

FOR ENGLISH LANGUAGE LEARNERS

Language: Conversational English Patterns
Reread lines 128–130 and remind students that they reflect typical slave dialect. Clarify that *chile* means "child," and rephrase the lines for students. Explain that *chick'n hearted* means "weak and fearful like a chicken." Betty is telling Linda that she needs to be tougher if she is going to survive life's challenges.

FOR ADVANCED LEARNERS/AP

Synthesize Remind students that the law against harboring fugitives was read to every northbound ship (lines 74–75). Have students research to learn about fugitive slave laws. Ask students to write a short paragraph that might have been read aboard these ships. Encourage pairs to share their paragraphs with the class. Ask them to explain what would probably have happened to Linda had she been found.

I was daily hoping to hear that my master had sold my children; for I knew
100 who was on the watch to buy them. But Dr. Flint cared even more for revenge
than he did for money. My brother William, and the good aunt who had served
in his family twenty years, and my little Benny, and Ellen, who was a little over
two years old, were thrust into jail, as a means of compelling my relatives to give
some information about me. He swore my grandmother should never see one of
them again till I was brought back. They kept these facts from me for several days.
When I heard that my little ones were in a loathsome jail, my first impulse was to
go to them. I was encountering dangers for the sake of freeing them, and must I
be the cause of their death? The thought was agonizing. My benefactress[5] tried to
soothe me by telling me that my aunt would take good care of the children while
110 they remained in jail. But it added to my pain to think that the good old aunt,
who had always been so kind to her sister's orphan children, should be shut up in
prison for no other crime than loving them. I suppose my friends feared a reckless
movement on my part, knowing, as they did, that my life was bound up in my
children. I received a note from my brother William. It was scarcely legible, and
ran thus: "Wherever you are, dear sister, I beg of you not to come here. We are all
much better off than you are. If you come, you will ruin us all. They would force
you to tell where you had been, or they would kill you. Take the advice of your
friends; if not for the sake of me and your children, at least for the sake of those
you would ruin." **F**
120   Poor William! He also must suffer for being my brother. I took his advice and
kept quiet. My aunt was taken out of jail at the end of a month, because Mrs.
Flint could not spare her any longer. She was tired of being her own housekeeper.
It was quite too fatiguing to order her dinner and eat it too. My children remained
in jail, where brother William did all he could for their comfort. Betty went to see
them sometimes, and brought me tidings. She was not permitted to enter the jail;
but William would hold them up to the grated window while she chatted with
them. When she repeated their prattle, and told me how they wanted to see their
ma, my tears would flow. Old Betty would exclaim, "Lors, chile! what's you crying
'bout? Dem young uns vil kill you dead. Don't be so chick'n hearted! If you does,
130 you vil nebber git thro' dis world." **G**

---

5. **benefactress:** a woman who gives aid.

INCIDENTS IN THE LIFE OF A SLAVE GIRL   **579**

---

③ Targeted Passage

Language Coach

Antonyms An **antonym** is a word with a meaning opposite that of another word. *Reckless* (line 112) and *careful* are antonyms. Read lines 112–121. What reckless action might Linda take? What advice is Linda given?

F NARRATIVE ELEMENTS
What new **conflict** is presented in this paragraph?

G READING A NARRATIVE
Review the paragraph that begins "For a week…" on page 578. Who is Betty, mentioned in lines 124–130?

REVISIT THE BIG QUESTION

What is the PRICE of freedom?

Discuss Linda has given up her children to protect them. In lines 99–108, how does her family sacrifice to help her meet that goal? *Possible answer: Her children, her brother, and her aunt go to jail, sacrificing their freedom in order to protect Linda from discovery. They know that her absence offers the best chance that Dr. Flint will agree to sell the children to their father, Mr. Sands.*

TEXT ANALYSIS   COMMON CORE   RI 3

F NARRATIVE ELEMENTS

Possible answer: Linda has an internal conflict with herself. Her brother, aunt, and children are placed in jail, and she wants to "go to them" (line 107). However, Linda cannot risk going to them.

READING STRATEGY   COMMON CORE   RI 3

G READING A NARRATIVE

Possible answer: Betty is Linda's friend, who works for the white woman who is hiding Linda.

SELECTION WRAP-UP

READ WITH A PURPOSE Now that students have read the selection, ask them what Linda learns about the Flints and her own family members after her escape. *Possible answer: Linda learns that the Flints will go to great lengths to keep her oppressed and that her family will go to great lengths to protect her.*

FOR STRUGGLING READERS

③ Targeted Passage [Lines 101–121]

- What happens to Linda's children, her aunt, and her brother? (lines 101–104)
- How does Linda feel about what happens? (lines 106–112)
- What does William ask Linda to do? Why does he ask this of her? (lines 115–119)
- Does Linda honor her brother's request? (lines 120–121)

FOR ENGLISH LANGUAGE LEARNERS

Language Coach

Antonyms *Answer: Linda might be reckless and turn herself in. She is advised to be cautious and wait.* Ask students to name a television or movie character who can be described as reckless and a character who can be described as careful. Have students explain their responses.

INCIDENTS IN THE LIFE OF A SLAVE GIRL   **579**

Practice and Apply

For preliminary support of post-reading questions, use these copy masters:

R RESOURCE MANAGER—Copy Masters
Reading Check p. 71
Narrative Elements p. 67
Question Support p. 72
Additional selection questions are provided for teachers on page 61.

ANSWERS

COMMON
CORE **RI 3**

1. *She learns the Flints are going to take her children in order to control her.*

2. *They search her grandmother's house and northbound ships, offer a reward for her capture, and jail her relatives.*

3. *She wants Mr. Sands to buy them so they can be with their father and escape mistreatment by the Flints.*

Possible answers:

4. ■ **COMMON CORE FOCUS** *Reading a Narrative Opposing characters:* The Flints and Linda's grandmother oppose her flight; **Supportive characters:** Linda's grandmother, Sally, Mr. Sands, William, Aunt Betty, and the white woman who hides her support her.

5. ● **COMMON CORE FOCUS** *Narrative Elements* **External conflicts:** with Dr. Flint about sexual advances, with Mr. Flint about her children (lines 9–10), with her grandmother over running away (lines 10–13) **Internal conflicts:** love for children versus love for her grandmother (lines 11–13, 35–38), love for her children versus her safety (lines 19–21), wanting to convey her safety to her grandmother versus danger to herself and her grandmother (lines 76–78), wanting to rescue her children in jail versus dire consequence of this action (lines 106–119). The conflicts prove the injustice of slavery and highlight the painful sacrifices it required of slaves.

6. ● **COMMON CORE FOCUS** *Analyze Characterization* She is hardworking (line 2). She loves her children deeply. She is considerate of others and takes responsibility for her own actions.

7. *She characterizes the Flints as blind to their own cruelty, unfeeling, and selfish, and herself as a loving mother and oppressed victim.*

After Reading

Comprehension

1. **Recall** What prompts Linda to make the decision to escape?

2. **Summarize** What actions do the Flints take after they find out Linda has left?

3. **Clarify** Why does Linda want the Flints to sell her children?

Text Analysis

4. **Reading a Narrative** Review the web you made as you read, considering how each person listed interacts with the narrator. Which characters support Linda and which oppose her? Share questions you have about them.

5. **Examine Narrative Elements** Describe different **conflicts**—internal and external—that develop through the events in this excerpt. What do these conflicts reveal about the institution of slavery and the sacrifices forced by it?

6. **Analyze Characterization** How does the writer present herself? Discuss what you learn about her character and values from
   - her attitude toward her work (lines 2–3)
   - her thoughts as she visits her children (lines 48–54)
   - her insistence upon escaping alone (line 57)

7. **Contrast Characterizations** Contrast the writer's portrayal of herself with her portrayal of the Flints. What does she reveal about the Flints' character and values?

8. **Draw Conclusions** How might the writer's political purpose and the knowledge that she was writing for an audience of Northern white women have influenced her characterizations?

9. **Compare Texts** Read "Free Labor" and "Go Down, Moses" on pages 582 and 583. How do they compare with Harriet Jacobs's narrative in their **tone** and their messages about slavery?

Text Criticism

10. **Author's Style** Jacobs's style was influenced by the literature popular in her time. Nineteenth-century women's novels were melodramatic, arousing readers' emotions with suspenseful plots that usually involved virtuous characters pitted against evil villains. *Uncle Tom's Cabin*, an immensely popular antislavery novel, included such elements as well. It also rendered the speech of slave characters in heavy dialect, a convention of the time. How do you, as a modern reader, respond to Jacobs's style? Evaluate the effects of her style on the power of her narrative.

> *What is the* **PRICE** *of freedom?*
>
> A person who makes a sacrifice always gives up something. What did Harriet Jacobs give up in order to be free? Do you think the end result (freedom) was worth what she had to give up? Why or why not?

COMMON CORE

RI 3 Analyze a complex sequence of events and explain how specific individuals or events interact and develop over the course of the text.

---

8. *To convince Northern white women to act against slavery, she shows how her values are similar to those of her audience. She wants to show Northern women how slavery subverts moral values in slaveholders and also how it victimizes women.*

9. *Both the poems and Jacobs's narrative speak of slavery in a somber tone. Both express the message of slavery's inhumanity.*

10. *Students may say that Jacobs's emotional style contributes to the power of her work and enables readers to feel anger. Others may argue that the use of slave dialect robs these characters of dignity.*

> *What is the* PRICE *of freedom?* **Possible answer:** For a while, Jacobs sacrifices freedom to move around as she pleases—she is isolated from almost everyone. Until she goes north, she gives up a normal life to avoid capture. Answers will vary. Students should provide support for their answers.

Language

◆ **GRAMMAR AND STYLE:** Establish Tone

Review the **Grammar and Style** note on page 576. **Tone** is a writer's attitude toward a subject. In Jacobs's compelling narrative, she uses emotionally charged language to establish a tone of melancholy and desperation. In the following example, the **adjectives** *loathsome* and *agonizing* succinctly convey the turmoil and conflict the narrator is experiencing and help elicit empathy from her readers.

> *When I heard my little ones were in a loathsome jail, my first impulse was to go to them. I was encountering dangers for the sake of freeing them, and must I be the cause of their death? The thought was agonizing.* (lines 106–108)

PRACTICE Copy the numbered sentences below. Then rewrite them, using adjectives, verbs, and additional phrases to effectively convey a tone of fear or sorrow. A sample answer has been done for you.

EXAMPLE

I fainted when I heard Linda had run off, leaving her children behind.

I collapsed to the floor when I heard poor Linda had run off, tearing herself away from the dear babies she cherished.

---

1. I'm an old woman, but I tried to be strong as Mr. Flint asked me questions about Linda.

2. The children cried when they heard their mother had left them behind.

3. It made me sad to see them feeling so bad. It is very hard for the little children.

READING-WRITING CONNECTION

 Expand your understanding of Harriet Jacobs's writing by responding to this prompt. Then, use the **revising tips** to improve your response.

WRITING PROMPT	**REVISING TIPS**
EXPLORE POINT OF VIEW *Incidents in the Life of a Slave Girl* is told from the first-person point of view and thus focuses on the thoughts, words, and actions of the narrator, Linda (Harriet Jacobs). Choose one of the other people mentioned in the narrative—Sally, or Linda's grandmother, aunt, or brother. Write a **three-paragraph response,** told from that character's point of view, reacting to the news that Linda has run away. As a starting point, reread Linda's descriptions of how any of these characters did or would react.	• Use precise language to relate your character's thoughts, feelings, spoken words, and actions. • Use the first-person point of view in your response. ▶ • Choose a tone that you think is appropriate for your character.

Interactive Revision
Go to **thinkcentral.com**.
KEYWORD: HML11-581

COMMON CORE

L 3 Apply knowledge of language to make effective choices for meaning or style. **W 3d** Use precise words to convey a vivid picture of the characters.

DIFFERENTIATED INSTRUCTION

FOR STRUGGLING WRITERS
Writing Support
- Help students to locate dialogue spoken by their character or comments by Linda about their character. Then help them make inferences and identify the character's point of view about Linda's flight.

- Ask students to describe the mood they think fits their character's feelings about Linda's flight. Encourage them to brainstorm a list of adjectives that will convey the character's emotions or the mood.

- Remind students that their response should be written in the first person and should include the pronoun *I*.

- Aid students in writing a point-of-view thesis statement in which they reveal their character's opinion of Linda's escape and set the mood for the response.

Language

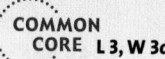

◆ **GRAMMAR AND STYLE**

Encourage students to use a thesaurus to choose words.

Possible answers:

1. *I'm just a feeble old woman, but I willed myself to be strong as Mr. Flint fired questions at me about Linda.*

2. *The children wept inconsolably on hearing their mother had abandoned them.*

3. *It broke my heart to see them so forlorn. What a burden for the innocent little ones to bear!*

R RESOURCE MANAGER—Copy Master
Establish Tone p. 73

READING-WRITING CONNECTION

Explain to students that they may have to make inferences about how their chosen character would react to Linda's escape. Urge students to use a Making Inferences chart.

BEST PRACTICES TOOLKIT—Transparency
Making Inferences p. A13

 **Writing Online**

The following tools are available online at **thinkcentral.com** and on **Write***Smart* CD-ROM:
- **Interactive Graphic Organizers**
- **Interactive Student Models**
- **Interactive Revision Lessons**

For additional grammar instruction, see **GrammarNotes** on **thinkcentral.com**.

Assess and Reteach

Assess

DIAGNOSTIC AND SELECTION TESTS
Selection Test A pp. 161–162
Selection Test B/C pp. 163–164

Interactive Selection Test on **thinkcentral.com**

Reteach

Level Up Online on **thinkcentral.com**
Reteaching Worksheets on **thinkcentral.com**

Literature Lesson 3, Literature Lesson 6, Reading Lesson 2, Informational Text Lesson 2

COMMON CORE FOCUS

RL 7 Analyze multiple interpretations of a poem (e.g., recorded or live production of a play or recorded novel or poetry), evaluating how each version interprets the source text.

TIERED DISCUSSION PROMPTS

Use these prompts to help students compare how this poem's speaker and Linda view slavery:

Connect What response have you had when you or someone you know was unfairly treated? *Accept all thoughtful answers.*

Interpret What does the speaker mean in lines 1–8? How do these lines work with the poem's title to convey the speaker's feelings about slave labor? *Possible answer: The speaker means that she is wearing clothing that was not created by a slave. These lines, along with the poem's title, suggest that the speaker feels slave labor is unfair. Slaves are forced to work while they cry in "hopeless anguish" (line 3). The speaker does not want to support slave labor, and wants clothing made from paid, or freely given, labor.*

Synthesize What feelings does the poem's speaker share with Linda? Would Linda agree with the speaker's view of slave labor? *Possible answer: The speaker mentions the heart of a poor woman whose household is torn apart (lines 17–20), just as Linda's is. The speaker calls on God to recognize slavery's oppression (lines 25–28) as Linda cries to God for help (lines 18–19). Linda would agree with the speaker's view of slave labor, saying that it is unfair, and that the oppressors are wrong and guilty.*

Free Labor

Frances Ellen Watkins Harper

I wear an easy garment,
  O'er it no toiling slave
Wept tears of hopeless anguish,
  In his passage to the grave.

5 And from its ample folds
  Shall rise no cry to God,
Upon its warp and woof shall be
  No stain of tears and blood.

Oh, lightly shall it press my form,
10 Unladened with a sigh,
I shall not 'mid its rustling hear,
  Some sad despairing cry.

This fabric is too light to bear
  The weight of bondsmen's tears,
15 I shall not in its texture trace
  The agony of years.

Too light to bear a smother'd sigh,
  From some lorn woman's heart,
Whose only wreath of household love
20 Is rudely torn apart.

Then lightly shall it press my form,
  Unburden'd by a sigh;
And from its seams and folds shall rise,
  No voice to pierce the sky,

25 And witness at the throne of God,
  In language deep and strong,
That I have nerv'd Oppression's hand,
  For deeds of guilt and wrong.

Go Down, Moses

Traditional Spiritual

When Israel was in Egypt's land,
Let my people go!
Oppressed so hard they could not stand,
Let my people go!

5 Go down, Moses,
'Way down in Egypt's land,
Tell old Pharoah, "Let my people go!"

"Thus saith the Lord" bold Moses said,
Let my people go!
10 "If not I'll smite your first-born dead,"
Let my people go!

Go down, Moses,
'Way down in Egypt's land,
Tell old Pharoah, "Let my people go!"

15 No more in bondage shall they toil,
Let my people go!
Let them come out with Egypt's spoil,
Let my people go!

Go down, Moses,
20 'Way down in Egypt's land,
Tell old Pharoah, "Let my people go!"

COMMON CORE RL 7

COMPARE INTERPRETATIONS
As with any song, different singers of "Go Down, Moses" emphasize different phrases, affecting tone and meaning. Compare the recording of "Go Down, Moses" found on the *Literature* Audio Anthology with a version sung by civil-rights activist Paul Robeson (available online or at a library). Which interpretation do you find more powerful? Why?

Focus and Motivate

COMMON CORE FOCUS

RI 1 Cite evidence to support inferences drawn from the text. **RI 4** Analyze how an author uses and refines the meaning of a key term or terms over the course of a text. **RI 5** Analyze and evaluate the effectiveness of the structure an author uses in his or her exposition or argument, including whether the structure makes points clear, convincing, and engaging. **RI 8** Delineate and evaluate the reasoning in seminal U.S. texts, including the application of constitutional principles and the use of legal reasoning. **RI 9** Analyze foundational U.S. documents of historical and literary significance for their themes, purposes, and rhetorical features. **W 1** Write arguments to support claims in an analysis of substantive topics or texts, using valid reasoning and relevant and sufficient evidence. **W 1b** Develop claim thoroughly in a manner that anticipates the audience's knowledge level, concerns, values, and possible biases. **W 9** Draw evidence from literary or informational texts to support reflection. **L 3** Apply knowledge of language to make effective choices for meaning and style. **L 3a** Apply an understanding of syntax to the study of complex texts when reading.

ABOUT THE AUTHOR

After students read about Lincoln, stress that his key political goal was to preserve the Union, not to abolish slavery. Then ask how Lincoln's political goals affected his decision to fight a civil war and to issue the Emancipation Proclamation. *Students should grasp that Lincoln fought the war to preserve the Union and supported emancipation to help the North win it.*

Selection Resources

COMMON CORE

RI 4 Analyze how an author uses and refines the meaning of a key term or terms over the course of a text. **RI 5** Analyze and evaluate the effectiveness of the structure an author uses in his or her exposition or argument, including whether the structure makes points clear, convincing, and engaging. **RI 8** Delineate and evaluate the reasoning in seminal U.S. texts, including the application of constitutional principles and use of legal reasoning. **RI 9** Analyze foundational U.S. documents of historical and literary significance for their themes, purposes, and rhetorical features. **L 3a** Apply an understanding of syntax to the study of complex texts when reading.

DID YOU KNOW?

Abraham Lincoln . . .

- loved the works of Edgar Allan Poe.
- was a talented mimic who enjoyed playing practical jokes.
- made Thanksgiving Day a national holiday.
- suffered from bouts of depression.

Literature of the Civil War

The Gettysburg Address
Speech by Abraham Lincoln

The Emancipation Proclamation
Proclamation by Abraham Lincoln

 Video link at thinkcentral.com

Meet the Author

Abraham Lincoln 1809–1865

Abraham Lincoln led the United States during its greatest crisis—the Civil War. Dedicated to keeping the nation together, Lincoln guided the country toward a new national identity, that of a nation committed to the principle of union, in which slavery no longer had a place.

Humble Origins Born on the Kentucky frontier to illiterate parents, Lincoln rarely went to school and was largely self-educated. As a young man, he moved with his family to Illinois, where he worked as a shopkeeper, rail-splitter, and surveyor and studied law. He served in the state legislature from 1834 to 1841, becoming a lawyer in 1836.

Evolving Views Although Lincoln opposed slavery as "injustice and bad policy," he was not an abolitionist; he preferred to free slaves gradually. In 1854, he began a vigorous public campaign to block the expansion of slavery to the western territories. His eloquent speeches and famous debates with Senator Stephen A. Douglas raised his political profile and strengthened his opposition to slavery.

A House Divided In 1860, Lincoln was elected president on his antislavery platform, prompting seven Southern states to secede from the Union before he even took office. In 1861, two months after his inauguration, the Civil War began.

As the fighting wore on, Lincoln faced increasing pressure to move against slavery while he struggled to keep the loyalty of the Union states that permitted slavery within their borders. After nearly two years of fighting, Lincoln issued the Emancipation Proclamation, which freed slaves in the rebelling states.

Tragic Ending Throughout the war, Lincoln faced opposition and ridicule from the public, his generals, and his own cabinet. The prospect of a Union victory, however, earned him reelection, and the Confederate armies surrendered weeks into his second term. Just five days later, Lincoln was assassinated, the first such occurrence in American history. His shocking murder and the end of war made him an instant hero. Today, he is one of the country's most widely respected presidents.

Author Online
Go to thinkcentral.com. KEYWORD: HML11-584

THINK central

584

---

*See resources on the **Teacher One Stop DVD-ROM** and on **thinkcentral.com**.*

 Video link at thinkcentral.com

R **RESOURCE MANAGER UNIT 3**
Plan and Teach, pp. 75–82
Summary, pp. 83–84†‡*
Text Analysis and Reading
Skill, pp. 85–88†
Grammar and Style, p. 91

DIAGNOSTIC AND SELECTION TESTS
Selection Tests, pp. 165–168

BEST PRACTICES TOOLKIT
Definition Mapping, p. E6

TECHNOLOGY
- **Teacher One Stop DVD-ROM**
- **Student One Stop DVD-ROM**
- **Audio Anthology CD**
- **GrammarNotes DVD-ROM**
- **ExamView Test Generator** on the **Teacher One Stop**

---

* Resources for Differentiation   † Also in Spanish   ‡ In Haitian Creole and Vietnamese

TEXT ANALYSIS: AUDIENCE AND FORM

Lincoln was a master orator and an expert lawyer. He was keenly aware that the **form** of a piece of writing affects what the writer can say to his or her **audience.**

- A **speech,** such as the Gettysburg Address, is often prepared for a specific audience. The speaker chooses rhetorical techniques that influence the audience and evoke emotion. Note Lincoln's effective use of parallel structure.

  The world will little note nor long remember what we say here, but it can never forget what they did here.

- A **proclamation,** such as the Emancipation Proclamation, is a legal document that announces official state business. As with any legal document, the writer is a person of authority and addresses the general public using clear reasoning and precise, technical language that can be clearly interpreted in a court of law.

  I, Abraham Lincoln, President of the United States, by virtue of the power in me vested as Commander-in-Chief . . .

As you read these texts, note how the structures conventional to each form shape the way Lincoln expresses his message or argument.

READING SKILL: ANALYZE AN AUTHOR'S BELIEFS

A thoughtful, principled man, Lincoln tried to act in accordance with his beliefs. To identify those beliefs in his writing, consider the ideals he invokes, the actions he takes, and the reasons he gives for his actions, as well as how he expresses the meaning of key terms such as *nation, consecrate,* and *freedom.* As you read, note details that reveal

- the reason he felt the war was necessary
- his views on the responsibilities of the president
- the reasons he opposed slavery

Use a chart like the one shown to record your notes.

Beliefs About . . .	Gettysburg Address	Emancipation Proclamation
the necessity of war		
the duties of the president		
slavery		

 Complete the activities in your **Reader/Writer Notebook**.

What makes a great LEGACY?

Washington, Jefferson, Lincoln—these legendary figures top most lists of greatest American presidents. In each case, the legacy is more complicated than the heroic myths suggest. What are the real reasons some leaders hold such a prominent place in history?

TEST YOURSELF What ideas come to mind when you think of Abraham Lincoln and the times in which he lived? Decide whether each statement is fact or myth.

Myth or History?

1. Hard-working Abe Lincoln was a poor country boy who rose to become president.
   ☐ TRUE ◯ FALSE

2. Lincoln led the fight to abolish slavery.
   ☐ TRUE ◯ FALSE

3. The Civil War was fought to free the slaves.
   ☐ TRUE ◯ FALSE

4. The Emancipation Proclamation ended slavery in the United States.
   ☐ TRUE ◯ FALSE

5. All of the Union states opposed slavery.
   ☐ TRUE ◯ FALSE

Teach

What makes a great LEGACY?

Read the question and the paragraph that follows. Clarify that a legacy is how a figure from the past affects the present. After students suggest why some leaders have memorable legacies, have them consider their answers as they complete the *TEST YOURSELF* activity.

● *Model the Skill:* **AUDIENCE AND FORM**

Identify for students the form and audience of the author biography on page 584. Point out that it is a biographical sketch written as background for students.

GUIDED PRACTICE Ask how the convention of subheads serves the feature's form and helps its audience.

■ *Model the Skill:* **ANALYZE AN AUTHOR'S BELIEFS**

Read this speech to students:

  My fellow students, Lisa Jones spoke out earlier today in favor of a school uniform. People booed and hissed so loudly, she couldn't finish. I'm speaking today because this behavior is wrong. Though I personally hate the idea of uniforms, we must hear each other out regardless of our personal beliefs.

Write the speech on the board and underline details that relay the speaker's beliefs, such as "we must hear each other out."

GUIDED PRACTICE Ask students to explain what this entry reveals about the speaker's beliefs about free speech.

R RESOURCE MANAGER—Copy Master
Analyze an Author's Beliefs p. 87
(for student use while reading)

DIFFERENTIATED INSTRUCTION

FOR ENGLISH LANGUAGE LEARNERS

Options for Reading: Questioning Encourage students to ask themselves questions as they read the Gettysburg Address. Provide students with the following questions, but encourage them to create their own questions during the course of their reading.

- Who is Lincoln speaking to? What does Lincoln ask of these people?
- Who does the speech honor?

- What does Lincoln accomplish with his speech?
- How does the location and event add to the message of the speech?

After students have read the speech, have a class discussion in which students relay the answers to these questions. Also, have students share any questions they created, along with their answers.

Practice and Apply

SUMMARY

In this speech, Lincoln recalls the principles upon which the Union was founded. He says that the purpose of the gathering is to consecrate a battlefield, but that the soldiers who fought and died have already sanctified it through their sacrifices. He exhorts the living to honor the fallen soldiers by continuing their struggle for freedom.

READ WITH A PURPOSE

Help students set a purpose for reading. Tell them to read to discover what Abraham Lincoln accomplishes with these two documents.

TEXT ANALYSIS
COMMON CORE L 3a

Ⓐ AUDIENCE AND FORM

Read the speech aloud and then conduct a choral reading with students. Point out the rhythm or cadence that develops from the lines' parallelism. **Possible answer:** *The parallelism creates a deliberate type of rhythm that emphasizes the importance of each phrase.*

Extend the Discussion Discuss how this type of evocative language and rhythm can be used today to describe current news events.

Ⓑ GRAMMAR AND STYLE
COMMON CORE L 3

Use Language Effectively Ask students why Lincoln emphasizes the words *dedicate* and *consecrate*. **Possible answer:** *He is linking America's past with her present and future, connecting the founding fathers' dedication to the soldiers' dedication and, he hopes, his listeners' dedication to the principles of freedom. He is also linking the soldiers' honor in fighting for freedom with the goal of honoring them with equal dedication to the cause of freedom.*

THE GETTYSBURG ADDRESS

Abraham Lincoln

> **BACKGROUND** The Battle of Gettysburg was fought July 1–3, 1863. The victory for Union forces marked a turning point in the Civil War, but the losses on both sides were staggering: 28,000 Confederate soldiers and 23,000 Union soldiers were killed or wounded. Lincoln delivered his Gettysburg Address on November 19, 1863, at a ceremony dedicating a national cemetery on the battle site.

Four score and seven years ago[1] our fathers brought forth on this continent a new nation, conceived in liberty, and dedicated to the proposition that all men are created equal.

Now we are engaged in a great civil war, testing whether that nation, or any nation so conceived and so dedicated, can long endure. We are met on a great battlefield of that war. We have come to dedicate a portion of that field as a final resting place for those who here gave their lives that that nation might live. It is altogether fitting and proper that we should do this. Ⓐ

But, in a larger sense, we cannot dedicate—we cannot consecrate—we cannot
10 hallow[2]—this ground. The brave men, living and dead, who struggled here have consecrated it far above our poor power to add or detract. The world will little note nor long remember what we say here, but it can never forget what they did Ⓑ here. It is for us, the living, rather, to be dedicated here to the unfinished work which they who fought here have thus far so nobly advanced. It is rather for us to be here dedicated to the great task remaining before us—that from these honored dead we take increased devotion to that cause for which they gave the last full measure of devotion; that we here highly resolve that these dead shall not have died in vain; that this nation, under God, shall have a new birth of freedom; and that government of the people, by the people, for the people, shall not perish from
20 the earth. ❧

---

1. **four score . . . ago:** 87 years ago—that is, in 1776. (*Score* means "a group of 20.")
2. **hallow:** set apart as holy.

COMMON CORE L 3a

Ⓐ **AUDIENCE AND FORM**
The Gettysburg Address is perhaps the most famous speech in the history of this country. In under 300 words, Lincoln crafted a masterpiece of oratory, using **parallel structure** and evocative language to inspire a nation. In the second paragraph, notice the rhythm Lincoln achieves with parallel clauses and phrases: *we are engaged, we are met, we have come; so conceived and so dedicated.* There is powerful emotional appeal here. After reading the speech silently, read it aloud. What effect does Lincoln's use of parallelism have on your delivery?

Ⓑ **GRAMMAR AND STYLE**
Reread lines 9–13. Note how **repetition** emphasizes the verbs *dedicate* and *consecrate* and refines their meaning.

DIFFERENTIATED INSTRUCTION

FOR ENGLISH LANGUAGE LEARNERS
Point out to students Lincoln's use of the term "resting place." Ask students why they think he chose this term.

FOR STRUGGLING READERS
In combination with the *Audio Anthology CD*, use one or more Targeted Passages (pp. 586, 588) to ensure that students focus on key concepts in the selections. Targeted Passages are also good for English learners.

① Targeted Passage [Lines 6–14]
This passage explains the significance of the soldiers' sacrifices.

Analyze Visuals

Created by sculptor Daniel Chester French, the statue of Abraham Lincoln is the center-piece of the Lincoln Memorial in Washington, D.C. The walls of the main chamber contain inscriptions of the Gettysburg Address and of Lincoln's second inaugural address. Ask students whether the Gettysburg Address is a fitting inscription for the Lincoln Memorial. Why or why not? Students should recognize that the Gettysburg Address aptly honors Lincoln—his humanity, his devotion to the nation's ideals, and his recognition of the Civil War's importance to the nation.

BACKGROUND

The Turning Tide In the summer of 1863, Confederate General Robert E. Lee led his troops into Pennsylvania. There, the Battle of Gettysburg began almost by chance. Out scouting for a supply of shoes, Southern soldiers ran into Union forces. The battle raged for three days and was a disaster for the Confederacy. It ended Lee's plans for attacking the North and left him entirely on the defensive. Vicksburg also fell, splitting the Confederacy in two and leaving the core of the South open to attack. The war's tide turned for the North.

REVISIT THE BIG QUESTION

What makes a great LEGACY?

Discuss In lines 10–14, what legacy does Lincoln say the fallen soldiers have "so nobly advanced"? *Possible answer: They have advanced the nation's legacies of liberty and equality.*

- According to Lincoln, why are he and others gathered at this battlefield? (lines 6–8)
- What were the soldiers fighting for? (line 7)
- How can the living honor the dead? (lines 13–20)

FOR STRUGGLING READERS

Develop Reading Fluency Emphasize that a significant, solemn speech should be read slowly and with a serious tone. Tell students to use commas, periods, and semicolons as signals to pause and dashes as signals to emphasize phrases or statements. However, stress that students should look for natural pausing points when a longer sentence does not contain commas. To demonstrate, read aloud the first two paragraphs. Point out natural pausing points in sentences.

Practice and Apply

SUMMARY

In his proclamation, Lincoln declares that slaves residing in secessionist states are free.

BACKGROUND

A Moral Cause Although the Emancipation Proclamation applied only to slaves in areas outside Union control, it served important moral and political purposes. It heartened abolitionists and African Americans. For many Northerners, it highlighted abolition as the war's high moral cause. Confederate President Jefferson Davis understood that the proclamation would settle the issue of slavery, ruining the Confederacy's chances for support from pro-abolition European nations.

TEXT ANALYSIS · COMMON CORE · RI 8 · RI 9

C *Model the Skill:*
AUDIENCE AND FORM

Tell students that the diction in a document or speech should match its purpose. While a text to friends is naturally informal, a governmental document requires a more academic level of speech.

Possible answer: *The word choice is formal and legalistic; the sentence structure is phrase-heavy and complex. Lincoln uses the diction of a legal document.*

TEXT ANALYSIS · COMMON CORE · RI 8 · RI 9

D AUDIENCE AND FORM

Possible answer: *Paraphrase: On January 1, 1863, the president will determine which states or parts of states are rebelling. Those in Congress will usually be seen as not rebelling. Lincoln's purpose is to establish clear, legal grounds for his actions.*

REVISIT THE BIG QUESTION

What makes a great LEGACY?

Discuss The Emancipation Proclamation is considered a significant part of Lincoln's legacy, despite its limitations. After reading lines 1–11, why do you think this is the case? ***Possible answer:*** *The document advanced the legacy of the founding fathers.*

THE EMANCIPATION PROCLAMATION
January 1, 1863

Abraham Lincoln

> **BACKGROUND** The Emancipation Proclamation was more of a symbolic gesture than an enforceable law. The document applied only to territory the Union did not control; it did not free slaves held by states that were loyal to the Union. Though the proclamation had little immediate legal impact, its promises inspired nearly 200,000 African Americans to join the Union army. Their efforts helped the North win the war.

A Transcription By the President of the United States of America:
A Proclamation.

Whereas, on the twenty-second day of September, in the year of our Lord one thousand eight hundred and sixty-two, a proclamation was issued by the President of the United States, containing, among other things, the following, to wit: **C**

"That on the first day of January, in the year of our Lord one thousand eight hundred and sixty-three, all persons held as slaves within any State or designated part of a State, the people whereof shall then be in rebellion against the United States, shall be then, thenceforward, and forever free; and the Executive Government of the United States, including the military and naval authority thereof, will recognize and maintain the freedom of such persons, and will do no

10 act or acts to repress such persons, or any of them, in any efforts they may make for their actual freedom. **1**

"That the Executive will, on the first day of January aforesaid,[1] by proclamation, designate the States and parts of States, if any, in which the people thereof, respectively, shall then be in rebellion against the United States; and the fact that any State, or the people thereof, shall on that day be, in good faith, represented in the Congress of the United States by members chosen thereto at elections wherein a majority of the qualified voters of such State shall have participated, shall, in the absence of strong countervailing[2] testimony, be deemed conclusive evidence that such State, and the people thereof, are not then in

20 rebellion against the United States." **D**

Now, therefore I, Abraham Lincoln, President of the United States, by virtue of the power in me vested as Commander-in-Chief, of the Army and Navy of

---

1. **aforesaid:** mentioned earlier.
2. **countervailing:** contradicting.

C AUDIENCE AND FORM
Describe the word choice and sentence structure of lines 1–3. In what ways does the form of the writing—namely, a presidential proclamation—affect Lincoln's **diction?** What technical terms does Lincoln use?

Targeted Passage

D AUDIENCE AND FORM
Paraphrase lines 12–20. What is Lincoln's legal reasoning for this proclamation? What is the **purpose** of the complicated and careful definitions in this paragraph?

DIFFERENTIATED INSTRUCTION

FOR STRUGGLING READERS

1 Targeted Passage [Lines 4–11]

In this passage, the president declares the freedom of slaves in rebellious states.

- When does the Emancipation Proclamation become law? (line 4)
- Which states does it refer to? (lines 5–6)
- Which slaves does it free? (lines 5–6)
- What will the government do to help freed slaves? (lines 7–11)

FOR ENGLISH LANGUAGE LEARNERS

Vocabulary Support Use Definition Mapping to teach these words: *whereas* (line 1), *maintain* (line 9), *invoke* (line 52).

 BEST PRACTICES TOOLKIT—Transparencies
Definition Mapping p. E6

the United States in time of actual armed rebellion against the authority and government of the United States, and as a fit and necessary war measure for suppressing said rebellion, do, on this first day of January, in the year of our Lord one thousand eight hundred and sixty-three, and in accordance with my purpose so to do publicly proclaimed for the full period of one hundred days, from the day first above mentioned, order and designate as the States and parts of States wherein the people thereof respectively, are this day in rebellion against the United

30 States, the following, to wit:

Arkansas, Texas, Louisiana, (except the Parishes of St. Bernard, Plaquemines, Jefferson, St. John, St. Charles, St. James Ascension, Assumption, Terrebonne, Lafourche, St. Mary, St. Martin, and Orleans, including the City of New Orleans)[3] Mississippi, Alabama, Florida, Georgia, South Carolina, North Carolina, and Virginia, (except the forty-eight counties designated as West Virginia,[4] and also the counties of Berkley, Accomac, Northampton, Elizabeth City, York, Princess Ann, and Norfolk, including the cities of Norfolk and Portsmouth), and which excepted parts, are for the present, left precisely as if this proclamation were not issued.

40 And by virtue of the power, and for the purpose aforesaid, I do order and declare that all persons held as slaves within said designated States, and parts of States, are, and henceforward shall be free; and that the Executive government of the United States, including the military and naval authorities thereof, will recognize and maintain the freedom of said persons.

And I hereby enjoin upon[5] the people so declared to be free to abstain from all violence, unless in necessary self-defence; and I recommend to them that, in all cases when allowed, they labor faithfully for reasonable wages.

And I further declare and make known, that such persons of suitable condition, will be received into the armed service of the United States to garrison[6] forts,

50 positions, stations, and other places, and to man vessels of all sorts in said service.

And upon this act, sincerely believed to be an act of justice, warranted by the Constitution, upon military necessity, I invoke the considerate judgment of mankind, and the gracious favor of Almighty God. **E**

In witness whereof, I have hereunto set my hand and caused the seal of the United States to be affixed.

Done at the City of Washington, this first day of January, in the year of our Lord one thousand eight hundred and sixty three, and of the Independence of the United States of America the eighty-seventh.

By the President: ABRAHAM LINCOLN
WILLIAM H. SEWARD, Secretary of State.

---

3. **except the Parishes . . . New Orleans:** Parishes, or counties, occupied by Union forces.

4. **the forty-eight . . . Virginia:** the western counties of Virginia broke from the Confederacy to form a new state. West Virginia joined the Union as a slave state in 1863.

5. **enjoin upon:** to direct.

6. **garrison:** to occupy as troops.

THE EMANCIPATION PROCLAMATION **589**

Language Coach

Word Definitions In line 41, *said* means "mentioned earlier." What purpose might the phrase "said designated States" serve here?

E AUTHOR'S BELIEFS Reread lines 51–53. What constitutional principles does Lincoln cite for freeing the slaves?

TIERED DISCUSSION PROMPTS

In lines 40–53, use these prompts to help students appreciate the many ramifications of the Emancipation Proclamation:

Analyze Why might some abolitionists and African Americans have felt betrayed by the proclamation? *Possible answer: The Emancipation Proclamation did not free all slaves. Its purpose was more political than ethical, and it left uncertainty around the issue of slavery.*

Synthesize The Emancipation Proclamation took effect six months before the Battle of Gettysburg. What effects of this document are apparent in the Gettysburg Address? *Possible answer: In the Gettysburg Address Lincoln focuses on freedom and equality as the causes for which his soldiers are fighting. His references to these causes are an allusion to emancipation.*

READING SKILL

COMMON CORE
RI 4
RI 8

E Model the Skill: AUTHOR'S BELIEFS

Help students identify Lincoln's several reasons by reading lines 51–53 aloud.

Possible answer: Lincoln believes that emancipation is just, supported by the Constitution, and a military necessity.

Extend the Discussion Lincoln personally believed in the rightness of the Proclamation. What, according to these lines, did he believe would be the reaction of most other people?

SELECTION WRAP–UP

READ WITH A PURPOSE Now that students have read the selections, ask them how Lincoln's two writings advance freedom. *Possible answer: Lincoln's writings advance freedom by asking citizens to continue fighting for freedom and by freeing slaves.*

FOR ENGLISH LANGUAGE LEARNERS

Language Coach

Word Definitions
Possible answer: Using "said designated states" keeps Lincoln from having to repeat the lengthy list of the previous paragraph. Tell students that this definition of *said* is not normally used in conversational language; it is often used in legal documents, such as contracts or wills.

FOR ADVANCED LEARNERS/AP

Analyze Repetition Point out that the document declares the freedom of slaves in two places, lines 4–11 and lines 40–44. Invite students to analyze this repetition, considering its function in both locations. Challenge students to compare and contrast the two declarations and then to consider the legal, military, political, and ethical underpinnings of these two declarations.

Practice and Apply

For preliminary support of post-reading questions, use these copy masters:

R RESOURCE MANAGER—Copy Masters
Reading Check p. 89
Audience and Form p. 85
Question Support p. 90
Additional selection questions are provided for teachers on page 79.

ANSWERS

COMMON CORE RI 1, RI 4, RI 5, RI 8, RI 9

1. *the dedication of a cemetery on the site of a major Civil War battle (lines 5–7)*

2. *The battle was fought to keep the nation alive and to defend its founding principles of freedom and democracy (lines 14–20).*

3. *He is the commander-in-chief in wartime (lines 51–53).*

4. *The proclamation applies only to areas in rebellion against the Union (lines 5–7).*

Possible answers:

5. *Historical context, Address: two years of war, a bloody battle leading to Union victory, after the Emancipation Proclamation; Historical context, Proclamation: Union needed soldiers, a way to weaken the South, a way to take the moral high ground. Political pressures: Some wanted more aggressive moves to end slavery, which would have further antagonized the South. Lincoln needed to inspire military victories to motivate and unite the public behind him.*

6. ● **COMMON CORE FOCUS Audience and Form Address: Form:** *speech;* **Audience:** *mourners, union supporters;* **Diction:** *clear, rhetorical, poetic, straightforward* **Tone:** *solemn, reverent;* **Proclamation: Form:** *legal document;* **Audience:** *entire nation, southern slaves;* **Diction:** *legalistic, convoluted, complex, detailed* **Tone:** *official, serious; The form supports each message. In the address, simplicity, brevity, and straightforwardness underscore the point that the soldiers died for the freedom all Americans hold dear. The proclamation's complexity supports its legal and military message that slaves in rebellious states are free.*

Comprehension

1. **Recall** For what occasion did Lincoln deliver the Gettysburg Address?

2. **Clarify** According to Lincoln, for what cause or idea was the Battle of Gettysburg fought?

3. **Recall** What authority does Lincoln claim for issuing the Emancipation Proclamation?

4. **Summarize** What exceptions limit the effect of Lincoln's proclamation?

Text Analysis

5. **Examine Historical Context** Using details from the author's biography on page 584 and from the background paragraphs on pages 586 and 588, describe the historical context of each document. What political pressures influenced Lincoln's public statements? What legal reasoning did he use?

● 6. **Compare Audience and Form** Use a chart like the one shown to compare and contrast Lincoln's two works. In what ways does the form or structure used influence Lincoln's message or argument?

● 7. **Draw Conclusions About Author's Beliefs** Review the chart you created as you read. Based on your answers, what would you consider to be Lincoln's fundamental values? Cite evidence to support your answer.

	Gettysburg Address	Emancipation Proclamation
Form		
Audience		
Diction		
Tone		

● 8. **Evaluate Form** Which of the two works better conveys each of the following ideas? Support your answers with details.

- a sense of presidential authority
- the urgency of the national crisis
- the value of freedom
- Lincoln's personal voice

Text Criticism

9. **Critical Interpretations** Often critical of Lincoln's policies, Frederick Douglass also spoke warmly of his honesty and moral conviction. He stated, "The image of the man went out with his words, and those who read them knew him." Based on your own reading, what impressions do you have of Lincoln's character? Explain your answer.

> *What makes a great* **LEGACY?**
>
> Abraham Lincoln is remembered for his leadership during the Civil War and for helping to end slavery. What kind of legacy would you like to leave? Explain your answer.

COMMON CORE

RI 1 Cite evidence to support inferences drawn from the text. **RI 4** Analyze how an author uses and refines the meaning of a key term or terms over the course of a text. **RI 5** Analyze and evaluate the effectiveness of the structure an author uses in his or her exposition or argument, including whether the structure makes points clear, convincing, and engaging. **RI 8** Delineate and evaluate the reasoning in seminal U.S. texts, including the application of constitutional principles and use of legal reasoning. **RI 9** Analyze foundational U.S. documents of historical and literary significance for their themes, purposes, and rhetorical features.

---

7. ● **COMMON CORE FOCUS Analyze an Author's Beliefs** *Lincoln shows a fundamental belief in democracy, fairness, clear thinking, and responsibility.*

8. ● **COMMON CORE FOCUS Audience and Form** *Answers will vary, but should be supported with details from the relevant work.*

9. *Students' responses should recognize that Lincoln was an honest man devoted to his country and its founding principles while also practical in pursuing his political aims.*

> *What makes a great*
> **LEGACY?** Answers will vary.

Language

COMMON CORE

L 3 Apply knowledge of language to make effective choices for meaning or style. **W 1** Write arguments to support claims in an analysis of substantive topics or texts, using valid reasoning and relevant and sufficient evidence. **W 1b** Develop claim thoroughly in a manner that anticipates the audience's knowledge level, concerns, values, and possible biases. **W 9** Draw evidence from literary or informational texts to support reflection.

◆ **GRAMMAR AND STYLE: Use Language Effectively**

Review the **Grammar and Style** note on page 586. In the Gettysburg Address, Lincoln makes effective use of the rhetorical device of **repetition.** Here is an example:

> *It is for us, the living, rather, to be dedicated here to the unfinished work which they who fought here have thus far so nobly advanced. It is rather for us to be here dedicated to the great task remaining before us . . .* (lines 13–15)

To emphasize the purpose of the solemn occasion, Lincoln repeats the word *dedicate,* as well as other verbs and abstract nouns, throughout his address. As he repeats words, he sometimes introduces subtle shifts in their meaning, encouraging reflection among the mourners.

PRACTICE Rewrite the following paragraph, incorporating repetition to emphasize key points.

> I was among the mourners who heard your eloquent and inspiring speech at Gettysburg. It made me want to write to you, and it caused me to think about what we are fighting for. My son was 19 years old when he enlisted. He was 20 when he was killed. My family and I can hardly bear the loss, but we have no other choice. We can only hope that his death—and the loss of thousands of others—will not have been in vain. As a parent, it is my sincere hope this is true. Speaking as a citizen of the United States, I can only pray the soldiers have not died for nothing.

READING-WRITING CONNECTION

YOUR TURN Expand your understanding of Abraham Lincoln's writing by responding to this prompt. Then, use the **revising tips** to improve your persuasive letter.

WRITING PROMPT	**REVISING TIPS**
WRITE A PERSUASIVE LETTER Knowing he would be speaking to an audience of people mourning the tremendous losses of the Civil War, Lincoln chose his words carefully. To show his respect for their heavy sacrifices, he used elevated language that conveyed a sense of their importance in history. Imagine that you had just heard Abraham Lincoln give his speech. Write a **three-paragraph persuasive letter** to your relatives supporting Lincoln's argument for the Civil War.	• Include a strong statement expressing your opinion. • Support your opinion by developing at least three examples that suit your audience. • Use evidence such as facts, statistics, expert opinions, and personal examples in your letter. • Conclude your letter by asking your relatives to take action in some way.

Interactive Revision THINK central

Go to **thinkcentral.com.**
KEYWORD: HML11-591

Language

COMMON CORE L 3, W 1, W 1b, W 9

◆ **GRAMMAR AND STYLE**

Point out to students other repeated words from the Gettysburg Address.

Possible rewrite (first four sentences): *I was among the mourners who heard your eloquent and inspiring speech at Gettysburg. It inspired me to write to you, and it inspired me to think about what we are fighting for. My son was 19 years old when he enlisted. My son was 20 years old when he was killed.*

R RESOURCE MANAGER
Use Language Effectively p. 91

READING-WRITING CONNECTION

Provide students with the following sentence model to help them organize their ideas:

I support/oppose the Civil War because _____, _____ and _____

Tell students to brainstorm specific examples, facts, or anecdotes to support the reasons they stated in the sentence model. Give students the following example of support:

Reason: *Slaves should be free.*

Support for Reason: *Families should not be torn apart.*

Writing Online

 THINK central

The following tools are available online at **thinkcentral.com** and on **WriteSmart CD-ROM:**
• **Interactive Graphic Organizers**
• **Interactive Student Models**
• **Interactive Revision Lessons**
For additional grammar instruction, see **GrammarNotes** on **thinkcentral.com.**

Assess and Reteach

Assess

DIAGNOSTIC AND SELECTION TESTS
Selection Tests A, B/C pp. 165–166, 167–168

Interactive Selection Test on thinkcentral.com

Reteach

Level Up Online Tutorials on thinkcentral.com

DIFFERENTIATED INSTRUCTION

FOR STRUGGLING WRITERS

Provide students with the following guidance for each paragraph of their persuasive letter:

• **First Paragraph:** Have students begin with an informal greeting, such as "I hope all is well with you and your family." Stress that this informal beginning is possible because the letter is directed to a relative. After the greeting, students should relay their intentions and their position concerning the Civil War.

• **Second Paragraph:** Have students state their reasons and support in this paragraph. Tell students that this paragraph will most likely be the lengthiest paragraph in their letter.

• **Third Paragraph:** Tell students to sum up their ideas and restate their position in the last paragraph. Then, have students end with a friendly closing. For instance, students could write, "I hope to see you soon."

Focus and Motivate

COMMON CORE FOCUS

RI 2 Provide an objective summary of the text.
RI 6 Determine an author's point of view or purpose in a text in which the rhetoric is particularly effective, analyzing how style and content contribute to the power, persuasiveness, or beauty of the text. **RI 8** Delineate and evaluate the reasoning in seminal U.S. texts, including the premises, purposes, and arguments in works of public advocacy. **W 1** Write arguments to support claims in an analysis of texts. **L 4a** Use context as a clue to the meaning of a word. **L 5** Demonstrate understanding of figurative language.

SUMMARY

"Voices from the Civil War" consists of four primary sources: a letter from Robert E. Lee to his son, clarifying allegiance to Virginia; a letter from Union officer Sullivan Ballou to his wife, expressing devotion to family and country; Mary Chesnut's wartime diary; Sojourner Truth's speech on women's civil rights.

Use the Directed Reading-Thinking Activity (DRTA) to prepare students. Have them quickly preview and make a prediction about each source. During reading, have them check each prediction and summarize main ideas.

 BEST PRACTICES TOOLKIT—Transparencies
Directed Reading-Thinking Activity (DRTA) p. A20

Teach

Standards Focus: Analyze Primary Sources

- Remind students of other primary source selections they have read in Units 1 and 3. Encourage them to list the genre of each and then brainstorm additional kinds of primary sources, such as newspaper articles, letters, and photographs. Discuss what the examples have in common, and how they differ.

- For instructional support, have students use the chart on this page to analyze one of the primary sources they have read. *Answers will vary but should reflect understanding of the genre, selection, and the author.*

R RESOURCE MANAGER—Copy Master
Analyze Primary Sources p. 101

Reading for Information

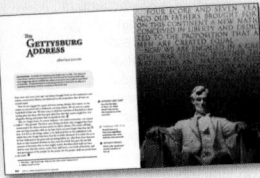

Use with the Gettysburg Address, page 586.

COMMON CORE

RI 6 Determine an author's point of view or purpose in a text in which the rhetoric is particularly effective, analyzing how style and content contribute to the power, persuasiveness, or beauty of the text. **RI 8** Delineate and evaluate the reasoning in seminal U.S. texts, including the premises, purposes, and arguments in works of public advocacy. **L 4a** Use context as a clue to the meaning of a word. **L 5** Demonstrate understanding of figurative language.

Voices from the Civil War

- Letter, page 593
- Letter, page 594
- Diary Entry, page 595
- Speech, page 596

Abraham Lincoln delivered the Gettysburg Address to an audience gathered in honor of fallen Union soldiers. How do you think they reacted to it? Might the same speech have been received differently by a Southern audience? The following documents can give you some insight into differing perspectives on the Civil War. After reading each text, take a moment to imagine how each author might have responded to Lincoln's message; later, you'll be asked to write such a response.

Standards Focus: Analyze Primary Sources

Primary sources are documents written by people who participated in or witnessed the events described in the document. Consequently, primary sources can describe personal experiences that are usually lacking in a more removed account. Later in this unit, when reading "An Occurrence at Owl Creek Bridge" (page 604), you will have the opportunity to relate the main ideas in a literary work to these primary source documents.

The letters, diary entry, and speech you are about to read are all primary sources of information on the Civil War. Read the background paragraph before each document as well as its title and date, noting

- the form of the document (letter, diary entry, or speech)
- when and where it was written or delivered
- whether it was intended for a public or private audience
- some of the details that shaped the author's perspective

Record what you learn on a chart such as the one shown here. Then, as you read the texts, consider how these factors relate to the author's purpose for writing.

Author	Form of Writing	Time & Place Created	Intended Audience	Relevant Details About the Author
Robert E. Lee				
Sullivan Ballou				
Mary Chesnut				
Sojourner Truth				

Selection Resources

See resources on the **Teacher One Stop DVD-ROM** *and on* **thinkcentral.com**.

 RESOURCE MANAGER UNIT 3
Lesson Support,* pp. 93–106

DIAGNOSTIC AND SELECTION TESTS
Selection Tests, pp. 169–172

 BEST PRACTICES TOOLKIT
Directed Reading-Thinking Activity (DRTA) p. A20

TECHNOLOGY
- Teacher One Stop DVD-ROM
- Student One Stop DVD-ROM
- Audio Anthology CD
- ExamView Test Generator on the Teacher One Stop

* Resources for Differentiation   † Also in Spanish   ‡ In Haitian Creole and Vietnamese

Robert E. Lee had a distinguished career in the U.S. Army until his home state of Virginia seceded from the Union. At that point, his loyalty to Virginia compelled him to join the Confederate army, where he became a general and one of the Confederacy's greatest heroes.

Letter to His Son

January 23, 1861

... The South, in my opinion, has been aggrieved by the acts of the North, as you say. I feel the aggression, and am willing to take every proper step for redress. It is the principle I contend for, not individual or private gain. As an American citizen, I take pride in my country, her prosperity and institutions, and would defend any State if her rights were invaded. But I can anticipate no greater calamity for the country than a dissolution of the Union. It would be an accumulation of all the evils we complain of, and I am willing to sacrifice everything but honor for its preservation. **A** I hope, therefore, that all constitutional means will be exhausted before there is a recourse to force. Secession is nothing but revolution. The framers
10 of our Constitution never exhausted so much labor, wisdom and forbearance in its formation, and surrounded it with so many guards and securities, if it was intended to be broken by every member of the Confederacy at will. It was intended for 'perpetual union' so expressed in the preamble, and for the establishment of a government, not a compact, which can only be dissolved by revolution, or the consent of all the people in convention assembled. It is idle to talk of secession. Anarchy would have been established, and not a government by Washington, Hamilton, Jefferson, Madison, and the other patriots of the Revolution. . . . Still, a Union that can only be maintained by swords and bayonets, and in which strife and civil war are to take the place of brotherly love
20 and kindness, has no charm for me. I shall mourn for my country and for the welfare and progress of mankind. If the Union is dissolved, and the Government disrupted, I shall return to my native State and share the miseries of my people, and save in defence will draw my sword on none. **B**

COMMON CORE L 4a

Language Coach

Antonyms An **antonym** is a word with a meaning opposite that of another word. *Dissolution* (line 6) and *preservation* (line 8) are antonyms. Based on the context of the words, what does each word mean?

A PRIMARY SOURCES
Reread lines 5–8. What does Lee want to preserve at any cost but his honor? What is his point of view concerning secession?

B PRIMARY SOURCES
Based on lines 18–21, how does Lee feel about maintaining the Union "by swords and bayonets"? Why?

593

Practice and Apply

INFORMATIONAL ANALYSIS COMMON CORE
RI 2
RI 6
RI 8

A Model the Skill: PRIMARY SOURCES

To help students examine this example of a primary source document, write lines 5–8 on the board. Use an arrow to clarify that the possessive pronoun "its" in line 7 refers back to the words "the Union" in line 6. Then read line 9 aloud, emphasizing the sentence "Secession is nothing but revolution."

Possible answer: Lee wants to preserve the Union at all costs "but honor" (lines 5–8). He views secession as "revolution" (line 9).

INFORMATIONAL ANALYSIS COMMON CORE
RI 2
RI 6
RI 8

B PRIMARY SOURCES

Possible answer: Lee says that maintaining the Union with "swords and bayonets" (lines 18–19) holds no charm for him, because it would make the Union a place where "strife and civil war" would "take the place of brotherly love and kindness" (lines 19–20).

DIFFERENTIATED INSTRUCTION

FOR ENGLISH LANGUAGE LEARNERS

Language Coach COMMON CORE
L 4a

Antonyms *Possible answer:* Dissolution *here means "destruction" or "breaking up of."* Preservation *means "state of being intact or whole."* Have students reread Lee's letter and choose three words for which they can think of antonyms.

FOR STRUGGLING READERS

Comprehension Support Clarify that Robert E. Lee's career in the U.S. Army was so distinguished that Lincoln tried to enlist Lee as commander of the Union forces. Lee opposed secession but would not attack his own state of Virginia. Lee's letter was written a few weeks before seven Southern states formed the Confederate States of America on February 4, 1861. Virginia joined them on April 17, 1861.

C PRIMARY SOURCES

Have volunteers take turns reading aloud lines 14–25. Discuss with students the specific sentiments the writer expresses, including his hopes for the future. Have students make notes of the writer's thoughts and hopes. Have them refer to their notes when they are reading "An Occurrence at Owl Creek Bridge" to glean the main idea and relate it to this primary source document.

TIERED DISCUSSION PROMPTS

In lines 14–31, use these prompts to help students analyze the effect of Ballou's raw emotions:

Connect How do you feel about Ballou and the sentiments he expresses here? *Accept all thoughtful responses.*

Analyze Does your knowledge of Ballou's fate affect your reaction to this letter? Explain. *Possible answer: Knowing that Ballou did not survive to see his family again makes his letter all the more poignant.*

Synthesize How do Ballou's feelings about his cause compare with Abraham Lincoln's in the Gettysburg Address? *Possible answer: Ballou and Lincoln express similar sentiments about their devotion to the cause of the Founding Fathers and about their debt to the first Americans who fought the Revolutionary War.*

Major Sullivan Ballou of the Second Rhode Island Regiment wrote the following letter to his wife on July 14, 1861. He was killed about a week later, at the first battle of Bull Run.

Letter to Sarah Ballou

My very dear Sarah:

The indications are very strong that we shall move in a few days—perhaps tomorrow. Lest I should not be able to write again, I feel impelled to write a few lines that may fall under your eye when I shall be no more. . . .

I have no misgivings about, or lack of confidence in the cause in which I am engaged, and my courage does not halt or falter. I know how strongly American Civilization now leans on the triumph of the Government, and how great a debt we owe to those who went before us through the blood and sufferings of the Revolution. And I am willing—perfectly willing—to lay down all my joys in this life, to help maintain this Government, and to pay that debt. . . .

10 Sarah my love for you is deathless, it seems to bind me with mighty cables that nothing but Omnipotence could break; and yet my love of Country comes over me like a strong wind and bears me unresistibly on with all these chains to the battlefield.

The memories of the blissful moments I have spent with you come creeping over me, and I feel most gratified to God and to you that I have enjoyed them so long. And hard it is for me to give them up and burn to ashes the hopes of future years, when, God willing, we might still have lived and loved together, and seen our sons grown up to honorable manhood, around us. I have, I know, but few and small claims upon Divine Providence, but something whispers to me—

20 perhaps it is the wafted prayer of my little Edgar, that I shall return to my loved ones unharmed. If I do not my dear Sarah, never forget how much I love you, and when my last breath escapes me on the battlefield, it will whisper your name. Forgive my many faults, and the many pains I have caused you. How thoughtless and foolish I have often times been! How gladly would I wash out with my tears every little spot upon your happiness. . . . C

But, O Sarah! If the dead can come back to this earth and flit unseen around those they loved, I shall always be near you; in the gladdest days and in the darkest nights . . . always, always, and if there be a soft breeze upon your cheek, it shall be my breath, as the cool air fans your throbbing temple, it shall be my spirit

30 passing by. Sarah do not mourn me dead; think I am gone and wait for thee, for we shall meet again. . . .

C PRIMARY SOURCES

This letter from Sullivan Ballou is a **primary source** document of the Civil War. Because Major Ballou was a participant in the war, his reflections on its necessity and on his personal expectations provide valuable insight into the cultural and historical setting. Pay special attention to the sentiments expressed in lines 14–25. Then, as you read "An Occurrence at Owl Creek Bridge" later in this unit (page 604), consider how a main idea in that literary work relates to this primary source document.

DIFFERENTIATED INSTRUCTION

FOR STRUGGLING READERS

Comprehension Support Work with students to enter details about Sullivan Ballou's letter in the prereading chart introduced on page 592.

FOR ENGLISH LANGUAGE LEARNERS

Vocabulary: Idioms Help students use context clues to define these idioms:

- *lay down* (line 8), "give up"
- *comes over me* (lines 11–12), "influences me, inspires me"
- *bears me . . . on* (line 12), "carries me along"
- *give them up* (line 16), "sacrifice them, lose them"

Wife of a former South Carolina senator, James Chesnut, and a member of the Southern gentility, Mary Chesnut socialized with many prominent Confederates. In her extensive diaries, she kept notes on the social and political conditions in the wartime South.

A Diary from Dixie

1864

September 1st — The battle is raging at Atlanta, our fate hanging in the balance.

September 2nd — Atlanta is gone. Well that agony is over. Like David, when the child was dead, I will get up from my knees, will wash my face and comb my hair. There is no hope, but we will try to have no fear. . . .

September 21st — The President has gone West. He sent for Mr. Chesnut.

I went with Mrs. Rhett to hear Dr. Palmer. I did not know before how utterly hopeless was our situation. This man is so eloquent; it was hard to listen and not give way. Despair was his word, and martyrdom. He offered us nothing more in this world than the martyr's crown. He is not for slavery, he says; he is for freedom,
10 the freedom to govern our own country as we see fit. He is against foreign interference in our state matters. That is what Mr. Palmer went to war for, it appears. Every day shows that slavery is doomed the world over. For that he thanked God. He spoke of this time of our agony; and then came the cry: "Help us, Oh God! Vain is the help of man." So we came away shaken to the depths. . . .

The end has come, no doubt of the fact. Our Army has so moved as to uncover Macon and Augusta. We are going to be wiped off the face of the earth. Now what is there to prevent Sherman taking General Lee in the rear. We have but two armies, and Sherman is between them now. **D**

September 29th — These stories of our defeats in the Valley fall like blows upon a
20 dead body. Since Atlanta, I have felt as if all were dead within me, forever. Captain Ogden of General Chesnut's staff dined here today. Had ever a Brigadier with little or no brigade so magnificent a staff? The reserves, as somebody said, are gathered by robbing the cradle and the grave of men too old and boys too young. . . .

General Chesnut was away in Camden, but I could not wait. I gave the beautiful bride, Mrs. Darby, a dinner which was simply perfect. I was satisfied for once in my life with my own table, and I know pleasanter guests were never seated around any table whatsoever in the world. My house is always crowded. After all, what a number of pleasant people are thrown by war's catastrophes into Columbia. I call such society glorious. It is the wind-up, the Cassandra in me says; and the
30 old life means to die royally.

595

Speech to the American Equal Rights Association

May 9, 1867

My friends, I am rejoiced that you are glad, but I don't know how you will feel when I get through. I come from another field—the country of the slave. They have got their liberty—so much good luck to have slavery partly destroyed; not entirely. I want it root and branch destroyed. Then we will all be free indeed. I feel that if I have to answer for the deeds done in my body just as much as a man, I have a right to have just as much as a man. There is a great stir about colored men getting their rights, but not a word about the colored women; and if colored men get their rights, and not colored women theirs, you see the colored men will be masters over the women, and it will be just as bad as it was before. So I am for keeping the thing going while things are stirring; because if we
10 wait till it is still, it will take a great while to get it going again. . . . I want women to have their rights. In the courts women have no right, no voice; nobody speaks for them. I wish woman to have her voice there among the pettifoggers. If it is not a fit place for women, it is unfit for men to be there. **E**

    I am above eighty years old; it is about time for me to be going. I have been forty years a slave and forty years free, and would be here forty years more to have equal rights for all. I suppose I am kept here because something remains for me to do; I suppose I am yet to help to break the chain. I have done a great deal of work; as much as a man, but did not get so much pay. I used to work in the field and bind grain, keeping up with the cradler; but men doing no more, got twice as much pay; so with
20 the German women. They work in the field and do as much work, but do not get the pay. We do as much, we eat as much, we want as much. I suppose I am about the only colored woman that goes about to speak for the rights of the colored women. I want to keep the thing stirring, now that the ice is cracked. What we want is a little money. You men know that you get as much again as women when you write, or for what you do. When we get our rights we shall not have to come to you for money, for then we shall have money enough in our own pockets; and may be you will ask us for money. But help us now until we get it. It is a good consolation to know that when we have got this battle fought we shall not be coming to you any more. You have been having our rights so long, that you think, like a slaveholder, that you own us. I know that it is hard for
30 one who has held the reins for so long to give up; it cuts like a knife. It will feel all the better when it closes up again. I have been in Washington about three years, seeing about these colored people. Now colored men have the right to vote. There ought to be equal rights now more than ever, since colored people have got their freedom. **F**

E PRIMARY SOURCES
Is Sojourner Truth rejoicing over the outcome of the war? Why or why not?

F PRIMARY SOURCES
What is Sojourner Truth advocating, or arguing for? What are two reasons she gives to support her claim?

Teacher Notes (left column)

INFORMATIONAL ANALYSIS   COMMON CORE   RI 2   RI 6   RI 8

E PRIMARY SOURCES

Possible answer: No; she is rejoicing at the gladness of others who are pleased with the war's outcome (line 1), but she herself is still seriously focused on doing more work to destroy slavery "root and branch" (lines 3–4). She is also concerned that, until women get their rights, the Union will not be a fit place for anyone (lines 10–13).

INFORMATIONAL ANALYSIS   COMMON CORE   RI 2   RI 6   RI 8

F PRIMARY SOURCES

Possible answer: She is arguing for full civil rights for women. Students should note at least two of these supporting reasons: 1) "If colored men get their rights . . . it will be just as bad as it was before" (lines 7–9). 2) "In the courts women have no right, no voice; nobody speaks for them" (lines 11–12). 3) "We [women] do as much [as men], we eat as much, we want as much" (line 21). Therefore, she argues, women should get paid as much. 4) If women get equal pay, then they won't have to come to men for money (lines 25–26). 5) "There ought to be equal rights now more than ever, since colored people have got their freedom" (lines 32–33).

DIFFERENTIATED INSTRUCTION

FOR STRUGGLING READERS

Check Predictions Have students complete the Directed Reading-Thinking Activity. Ask them to check their prereading predictions about the content of this letter, then summarize the letter's main points.

  BEST PRACTICES TOOLKIT—Transparency
Directed Reading-Thinking Activity
p. A20

FOR ADVANCED LEARNERS/AP

Analyze Figurative Language Have students identify Sojourner Truth's use of figurative language. Ask students to classify each example as imagery, metaphor, or simile, and then to explain how each example serves Truth's writing goal: to advocate for the rights of African Americans and women. Invite students to create and share a chart showing their examples and explanations.

Comprehension

1. **Recall** How did Robert E. Lee plan to respond if the Union was dissolved?

2. **Recall** What did Sullivan Ballou think would be his fate in battle?

3. **Recall** How did Mary Chesnut spend her time during the month of September 1864?

4. **Summarize** In the primary sources you just read, Union and Confederate soldiers and civilians reveal some of the motives they had for engaging in the Civil War. Summarize these motives.

Text Analysis

5. **Analyze Author's Purpose** Think about what Ballou shares with his wife, Sarah. For what purpose—or purposes—would you say he is writing to her? How do the style and content of the letter help him achieve this purpose?

6. **Evaluate Reasoning** Think about the context in which Sojourner Truth gave her speech. How effective do you think her audience would have found her reasoning in advocating for women's rights? Explain.

7. **Analyze Author's Perspective** An author's perspective is the combination of life experiences, culture, values, and beliefs that influences his or her view on a topic. Drawing upon the information you recorded on your chart, describe each author's perspective on the Civil War.

Read for Information: Synthesize

WRITING PROMPT

Choose one of the four writers whose documents you just read, and imagine how this person might have responded to Lincoln's Gettysburg Address. Then summarize the imagined response, and support your ideas with evidence from the text.

To answer this prompt, choose a writer whose perspective on the war you think you understand well. Then follow these steps:

1. Reread the Gettysburg Address to remind yourself of Lincoln's message.

2. Bearing in mind the personal experiences and loyalties of your chosen writer and the thoughts and feelings he or she expresses about the war, imagine how he or she might have reacted to Lincoln's speech. Summarize this imaginary response.

3. Support your notion of that person's response with evidence from your chart and from the primary source written by that individual.

⊙ **COMMON CORE**

RI 2 Provide an objective summary of the text.
RI 6 Determine an author's point of view or purpose in a text in which the rhetoric is particularly effective, analyzing how style and content contribute to the power, persuasiveness, or beauty of the text. **RI 8** Delineate and evaluate the reasoning in seminal U.S. texts, including the premises, purposes, and arguments in works of public advocacy. **W 1** Write arguments to support claims in an analysis of texts.

Practice and Apply

For preliminary support of post-reading questions, use these copy masters:

R RESOURCE MANAGER—Copy Masters
Reading Check p. 105
Question Support p. 106
Synthesize p. 101
Additional selection questions are provided for teachers on page 96.

ANSWERS ⊙ COMMON CORE RI 2, RI 6, RI 8, W 1

1. *He planned to return to Virginia to share the miseries of his people and, if necessary, to fight in defense.*

2. *Ballou hoped that he would return to his loved ones unharmed, but he knew that he might not.*

3. *She followed the news, attended a lecture by Dr. Palmer, had Captain Ogden to dinner, planned and threw a perfect dinner party for Mrs. Darby, and maintained an active social life and busy household.*

4. *Lee fought in self-defense, out of loyalty to families and neighbors. Sullivan Ballou fought to preserve the Union and from duty to the Founding Fathers. Dr. Palmer fought to preserve the right to self-government, while Sojourner Truth fought to gain rights for slaves and women.*

Possible answers:

5. *He is writing to explain his commitment to fighting, to express his love, to ask for forgiveness of his faults and of pain he may have caused, and to offer hope that he will return and consolation if he does not.*

6. *The audience for Sojourner Truth's speech was progressive, already supporting of rights for enslaved men. She challenged them to extend their views to include women and women's rights.*

7. *Students should recognize Ballou's belief in America's founding principles, Lee's and Chesnut's commitment to state rights, and Truth's devotion to civil rights for all.*

Read for Information: Synthesize

Writing Prompt *Student responses should reflect an understanding of Lincoln's desire to preserve the Union and his belief in the principles of equality and freedom, and a response appropriate to the chosen writer's perspective as presented in the selection.*

Assess and Reteach

Assess

DIAGNOSTIC AND SELECTION TESTS
Selection Tests A, B/C pp. 169–170, 171–172

Interactive Selection Test on thinkcentral.com

Reteach

Level Up Online Tutorials on thinkcentral.com
Reteaching Worksheets on thinkcentral.com

Reading Lesson 14: Synthesizing Information

Study Skills Lesson 5: Using Primary and Secondary Sources

COMMON CORE FOCUS

RL 2 Determine two or more themes or central ideas of a text and analyze their development over the course of the text. **RL 3** Analyze the impact of the author's choices regarding how to develop and relate elements of a story. **L 1a** Apply the understanding that usage is a matter of convention and can change over time.

The Rise of Realism

To help students understand the qualities of realism, draw attention to the photograph on this page, and ask what makes the photograph realistic. ***Possible answer:*** *It is a photograph of real people in a real place. It shows ordinary people at their jobs. It does not glorify its subject.* Then show a copy of a recent issue of a major news or literary magazine such as *Time* or *The New Yorker,* and let students study both its editorial and advertising images. Ask students to classify photographs as either realistic or romantic, and to explain why.

Characteristics of Realism

COMPLEX CHARACTERS IN ORDINARY PLACES

Have students read the instructional passage and the three bulleted items under this heading. Then ask students to identify examples of realistic works of fiction, including films or television shows. *Students may suggest television crime or hospital dramas as examples of realism. They might also cite situation comedies as realistic if the settings, characters, and plots resemble reality.* Ask students to identify the specific ingredients that make each example realistic, listing these in a Three-Column Journal. For example, a show about detectives might present the detectives as hard-working ordinary people with personal problems, rather than as Sherlock-Holmes-type deductive geniuses. Such shows often portray urban settings realistically.

 **BEST PRACTICES TOOLKIT—Transparency**
Three-Column Journal p. B10

Realism

Most modern readers expect stories to be like real life. In the mid-19th century, however, a "realistic" story was considered radical and was even criticized. Despite this outcry, several famous American writers persevered, and in doing so, they initiated one of the most enduring movements in literary history.

COMMON CORE

Included in this workshop:
RL 2 Determine two or more themes or central ideas of a text and analyze their development over the course of the text.
RL 3 Analyze the impact of the author's choices regarding how to develop and relate elements of a story. **L 1a** Apply the understanding that usage is a matter of convention and can change over time.

The Rise of Realism

Realism in literature refers to writing that offers an accurate and detailed portrayal of actual life. It also refers to a literary movement that first developed in France in the mid-19th century and then spread to England, Russia, and the United States. Realism was born as a reaction to **romanticism,** an artistic and literary movement that glorified the individual and celebrated the emotions and imagination; it dominated literature during the early 19th century. Unlike the romantics, realists did not want to glorify anything. They simply wanted to depict reality, no matter how ordinary the characters or their circumstances. In basing their literature on careful observations of commonplace events and people, the realists believed they could shed light on greater social issues and concerns.

New York City sweatshop, circa 1912

In the United States, realism was also the product of a rapidly changing society. By the end of the Civil War in 1865, America was changing from a predominantly rural society to an urban one and was experiencing the effects of the Industrial Revolution. Many writers were inspired to depict the effects of these dramatic social changes on the average citizen. The first American writers to experiment with realism—in the 1870s and 1880s—were Mark Twain, William Dean Howells, and Henry James. In the following decades, the realist movement spawned several related movements, such as **naturalism, regionalism,** and **local color** (see pages 656–657).

Characteristics of Realism

COMPLEX CHARACTERS IN ORDINARY PLACES

In realist fiction, character exploration and development became more important than plot. Often the characters were laborers, businessmen, or housewives from the lower and middle classes. Exploring details of a personality or a relationship could reveal important complexities, contradictions, and ironies, especially those related to social or economic issues.

DIFFERENTIATED INSTRUCTION

FOR STRUGGLING READERS

Note Taking For students who are unfamiliar with realism or need help with note taking, hand out the copy master before discussing this page. Explain that they will be learning terms and concepts relating to realism in this workshop. Discuss the difference between realism and romanticism as students record notes on the copy master.

 RESOURCE MANAGER—Copy Master
Note Taking p. 107

The realist writer might write long, involved descriptions of a character's inner thoughts, usually focused on personal concerns or the mundane events of his or her everyday life. Realist fiction would typically

- focus on **complex characters** who are ordinary people, not heroes or villains

- portray ordinary **settings,** especially those that allow for accurate depictions of society and culture

- depict true-to-life **dialogue** that captures the dialects and idioms of conversation, reflecting the usage conventions of a particular time, place, and social group

DETACHED NARRATION

Realist writers adopted the scientific method of detached observation. This allows the narrator of a story to sound unbiased and distant, as if simply recording the complete facts of the story. The reader is then allowed to draw his or her own conclusions. Notice the detached perspective of the narrator and the detailed **description** in this passage.

> A man stood upon a railroad bridge in northern Alabama, looking down into the swift water twenty feet below. The man's hands were behind his back, the wrists bound with a cord. A rope closely encircled his neck.
>
> —**Ambrose Bierce, "An Occurrence at Owl Creek Bridge"**

SOCIAL THEMES

The literature of realism sought to explore the key issues of the time: What are the implications of modern technology? What are the effects of urbanization? Realist **themes** are typically concerned with class conflicts, urbanization, marriage, and family life. In his novel *The Rise of Silas Lapham*, author William Dean Howells tells the story of a family coming to terms with new wealth, acquisition, and corruption. In the following passage, Howells relates the family's initial responses to their newfound wealth.

> Their first years there were given to careful getting on Lapham's part, and careful saving on his wife's. Suddenly the money began to come so abundantly that she need not save; and then they did not know what to do with it. A certain amount could be spent on horses, and Lapham spent it; his wife spent on rich and rather ugly clothes and a luxury of household appointments. Lapham had not yet reached the picture-buying stage of the rich man's development, but they decorated their house with the costliest and most abominable frescoes. . . .
>
> —**William Dean Howells, *The Rise of Silas Lapham***

To understand the different perspectives and subject matter of romanticism and realism, consider these two prose examples:

Romanticism
In that moment of the afternoon, the sun fell upon the snow drifts in an ethereal light, and all the heavens seemed to shine down upon the frozen fields, as if promising, one day, the ascent of spring.

Realism
At 4:00 each afternoon, the sunlight cast long shadows along the frozen landscape. The whistle of the clothing factory would blow, and the workers would stream out from the opened doors and squint into the last light of the day.

Close Read

What effect does the detached perspective in Bierce's passage have on the reader? From these few lines, what is your reaction to this character?

Close Read

What do you think might happen to the Laphams, given what you know about the typical **themes** in realism?

ROMANTICISM VS. REALISM

Have students read the examples and find words and phrases that exemplify romanticism and realism. ***Possible answers:*** *Romanticism: "ethereal light," "all the heavens seemed to shine"; Realism: "whistle of the clothing factory"*

DETACHED NARRATION

To reinforce comprehension, have students read the opening paragraphs of one or more news stories from a current issue of a newspaper. Make sure the articles are "hard news" rather than feature stories. Have students find similarities between the perspective of the articles and that of the Bierce paragraph.

Close Read

Possible Answer: *Some students will say the detached perspective makes them feel distant from the character. Others will say that objective details, such as the wrists bound with cord, make them see the scene more vividly. Students' reactions to the character may include sympathy for his fate, curiosity about why he is there and what has happened to him, and suspicion because he is apparently a criminal.*

SOCIAL THEMES

Have students read the Howells paragraph. Discuss the social themes present in it (*money, upward mobility, marriage*). Brainstorm social themes that fiction today might deal with.

Close Read

Possible Answer: *Students may say that the Laphams will encounter marital conflict because of differences over money and spending, or that they will fall from wealth into poverty.*

FOR ENGLISH LANGUAGE LEARNERS

Language: Skill Words Clarify the word *detached* through contrast with the familiar word *attached.* Show and identify items, such as a decorative pin, as attached, then as detached. Explain that *perspective* describes how a person views objects, such as close up or far away, and contrast objects at each distance. In writing, a close perspective might show a character's thoughts, while a distant one would show only outward actions.

FOR ADVANCED LEARNERS/AP

Research Realism To broaden students' introduction to realism, suggest that they briefly research these 19th-century realists: Leo Tolstoy, Fyodor Dostoyevsky, Anton Chekhov, Gustave Flaubert, Honoré de Balzac, George Eliot, Henry James. Urge students to scan one work by any two authors and note similarities they find in character, setting, or dialogue.

COMMON CORE FOCUS

RL 2 Determine two or more themes or central ideas of a text. **SL 1a** Refer to evidence from texts to stimulate a thoughtful, well-reasoned exchange of ideas. **SL 4** Present information, findings, and supporting evidence.

BACKGROUND The 14th child of a Methodist minister, Stephen Crane began writing stories when he was just 8 years old. By the time he was 16, Crane was writing articles for the *New York Tribune*. Years later, after publication of *The Red Badge of Courage*, Crane became a war correspondent, covering the Greco-Turkish War and the Spanish-American War. Finally, he observed battle himself. However, Crane nearly drowned when his ship capsized on the way to Cuba to report on the insurrection there. That incident inspired his famous story "The Open Boat" (page 736); it also contributed to the poor health that claimed his life at the age of 28.

TEXT ANALYSIS Clarify that this excerpt opens just before members of the Confederate army face Henry and his fellow Union soldiers. The passage describes the Union soldiers' reactions to the coming battle and actions during it. Point out that Crane uses the soldiers' actions and dialogue—including those of higher military officials—to display realism. Tell students to notice how Crane did not glorify higher military officials.

DISCUSS Encourage students to make a reference list of the characteristics of realism as they reread the Text Analysis Workshop. Also, provide students with photocopies of the excerpt from *The Red Badge of Courage*. Encourage students to mark the copies, indicating text details that illustrate the characteristics of realism.

American Masterpiece

from The Red Badge of Courage

Novel by Stephen Crane

Stephen Crane
1871–1900

COMMON CORE

RL 2 Determine two or more themes or central ideas of a text. **SL 1a** Refer to evidence from texts to stimulate a thoughtful, well-reasoned exchange of ideas. **SL 4** Present information, findings, and supporting evidence.

BACKGROUND Imagination, not experience, explains Stephen Crane's achievements in realism. His first novel, *Maggie: A Girl of the Streets*, exposed the brutal realities of New York slum life, but Crane wrote a first draft of the narrative while still in college, before moving to the slums himself in search of work as a journalist. Crane's talent for realism also explains *The Red Badge of Courage*, a Civil War novel acclaimed by soldiers and veterans for presenting combat realistically, despite the fact that the author had not served as a soldier or observed the battlefield firsthand. Crane's masterpiece focuses on a single, unnamed Civil War battle. The protagonist Henry Fleming, a young private in the Union army, is anything but heroic. Through Henry's eyes, readers experience the long and tedious waiting for battle, the utter chaos once the fighting begins, and the ironic twists of fate that determine who will survive and who will perish. Much of the action takes place in Henry's mind as he struggles to adapt to his environment, tries to comprehend his new experiences, and worries about whether he will prove courageous or cowardly.

TEXT ANALYSIS "There was no real literature of our Civil War," Ernest Hemingway once observed, "until Stephen Crane wrote *The Red Badge of Courage*." Crane's great novel is considered a pioneering work of **realism**, breaking with tradition in a number of ways. First, it focuses not on kings or generals but on a lowly private caught up in the action. Second, it ignores the great sweep of history and deals instead with one character's impressions. Finally, the novel is almost completely devoid of heroics. "The idea of falling like heroes on ceremonial battlefields," remarked novelist and critic Ford Madox Ford, "was gone forever."

DISCUSS After you read the excerpt, review the Text Analysis Workshop on Realism (pages 598–599). Then, with a small group of your peers, make a list of the characteristics of realism you see in the Crane excerpt. For each item on your list, include at least one quotation from the excerpt that illustrates the realist trait. When your group has finished, share your observations with the class as a whole. **Note:** Consider saving your notes from this activity so that you can refer to them when you read Stephen Crane's short story "The Open Boat" (page 736), a masterpiece of realist fiction.

600

DIFFERENTIATED INSTRUCTION

FOR STRUGGLING READERS

Identify Characteristics of Realism Help students identify the passage's characteristics of realism by asking them to fill out a Two-Column Chart that lists each characteristic and the text details that display the characteristics. To help students understand their task, fill in the first one or two rows of the chart for them.

Characteristics of Realism	Text Details
true-to-life dialogue	"A-all r-right, General" (line 12)
detached narration	"the youth was momentarily startled" (line 5)

BEST PRACTICES TOOLKIT—Transparency
Two-Column Chart p. A25

"Here they come! Here they come!" Gun locks clicked.

Across the smoke-infested fields came a brown swarm of running men who were giving shrill yells. They came on, stooping and swinging their rifles at all angles. A flag, tilted forward, sped near the front.

As he caught sight of them the youth was momentarily startled by a thought that perhaps his gun was not loaded. He stood trying to rally his faltering intellect so that he might recollect the moment when he had loaded, but he could not.

10 A hatless general pulled his dripping horse to a stand near the colonel of the 304th. He shook his fist in the other's face. "You've got to hold 'em back!" he shouted, savagely; "you've got to hold 'em back!"

In his agitation the colonel began to stammer. "A-all r-right, General, all right, by Gawd! We-we'll do our—we-we'll d-d-do—do our best, General." The general made a passionate gesture and galloped away. The colonel, perchance to relieve his feelings, began to scold like a wet parrot. The youth, turning swiftly to make sure that the rear was unmolested, saw the commander regarding his men in a highly resentful manner, as if he regretted above everything his association with them.

The man at the youth's elbow was mumbling, as if to himself: "Oh, we're in for it now! oh, we're in for it now!"

20 The captain of the company had been pacing excitedly to and fro in the rear. He coaxed in schoolmistress fashion, as to a congregation of boys with primers. His talk was an endless repetition. "Reserve your fire, boys—don't shoot till I tell you—save your fire—wait till they get close up—don't be damned fools—"

Perspiration streamed down the youth's face, which was soiled like that of a weeping urchin. He frequently, with a nervous movement, wiped his eyes with his coat sleeve. His mouth was still a little way open.

He got the one glance at the foe-swarming field in front of him, and instantly ceased to debate the question of his piece being loaded. Before he was ready to begin—before he had announced to himself that he was about to fight—he threw 30 the obedient, well-balanced rifle into position and fired a first wild shot. Directly he was working at his weapon like an automatic affair.

He suddenly lost concern for himself, and forgot to look at a menacing fate. He became not a man, but a member. He felt that something of which he was a part—a regiment, an army, a cause, or a country—was in a crisis. He was welded into a common personality which was dominated by a single desire. For some moments he could not flee, no more than a little finger can commit a revolution from a hand.

THEME
The narrative structure of Crane's novel reflects the themes of conflict, fear, and courage often found in stories of war. Recent films about World War II such as *Letters from Iwo Jima* and *Flags of Our Fathers* also develop a strong narrative to relate the horror and courage that shaped the war in the Pacific.

INTRODUCE THE MASTERPIECE

The Red Badge of Courage As students begin to read, ask them to look for evidence of emotion in the soldiers' words and behavior. Urge them to note descriptive language, dialogue, and Henry's thoughts. Then, ask students to discuss and describe the mood this passage creates. **Possible answer:** *The mood of this passage is frantic and terrifying.*

TIERED DISCUSSION PROMPTS

Use these prompts to help students consider what Henry sees and feels:

Connect How have you or someone you know reacted when you were in a tense or dangerous situation? *Accept all thoughtful responses.*

Interpret Why do you think that Henry is "momentarily startled by a thought that perhaps his gun was not loaded"? Read the second to last paragraph. Why does he no longer question whether his gun is loaded at this point? **Possible answer:** *In the beginning of the passage, Henry sees the enemy approaching and is most likely nervous and scared, so he begins to doubt everything, including whether his gun is loaded. It is as if his brain is paralyzed by fear. By the end of the passage, Henry has overcome his fear and paralysis and is as ready as he can be for battle.*

Synthesize Does Henry "adapt to his environment"? In this passage, does he prove "courageous" or "cowardly"? **Possible answer:** *Henry has adapted to his environment. He matures from being horribly nervous to being an effective fighter. He becomes courageous, as he no longer considers his "menacing fate" but instead thinks of himself as a member of a team who is helping his country.*

THEME

Point out to students that the narrative structure used in these two films is used in many of the short stories and novels they have read. Ask students to cite additional 21st-century films that reflect the narrative structure found in Crane's classic story of war.

FOR ENGLISH LANGUAGE LEARNERS

Vocabulary: Multiple-Meaning Words Point out that certain words have more than one meaning. Students must determine the appropriate definition for a given use. Help students use context clues to figure out the meaning of *rear* (line 16), *unmolested* (line 16), *regarding* (line 16), *fire* (line 22), *piece* (line 28), *directly* (line 30), *working at* (line 31), *automatic* (line 31), and *affair* (line 31).

FOR ADVANCED LEARNERS/AP

Analyze Similes [paired option] Have students identify several similes in the passage that Crane uses to enhance the feelings of the characters as well as to create the mood of the passage. Challenge pairs to write five similes that describe the feelings of the characters or that adequately portray the mood of the passage. Encourage pairs to share their similes.

Focus and Motivate

COMMON CORE FOCUS

RL 2 Provide an objective summary of the text.
RL 3 Analyze the impact of the author's choices regarding how to develop and relate the elements of a story. **RL 4** Analyze the impact of specific word choices on meaning and tone, including words with multiple meanings. **RL 5** Analyze how an author's choices concerning how to structure specific parts of a text contribute to its overall structure and meaning as well as its aesthetic impact.
L 4b Identify and correctly use patterns of word changes that indicate different meanings or parts of speech. **L 6** Acquire and use accurately general academic words.

ABOUT THE AUTHOR

After students have read about Bierce's life, have them discuss how his experiences in the Civil War may have changed his idealistic viewpoint. Explain that "An Occurrence at Owl Creek Bridge" describes the kind of "strange and horrible death" that fascinated Bierce, and it includes both idealistic and dark views of war and death.

NOTABLE QUOTE

"Nothing is so improbable as that which is true." —**Ambrose Bierce**

Ask students how Ambrose Bierce's life experiences have contributed to his belief in this statement.

Selection Resources

COMMON CORE

RL 2 Provide an objective summary of the text.
RL 3 Analyze the impact of the author's choices regarding how to develop and relate the elements of a story. **RL 4** Analyze the impact of specific word choices on meaning and tone, including words with multiple meanings. **RL 5** Analyze how an author's choices concerning how to structure specific parts of a text contribute to its overall structure and meaning as well as its aesthetic impact.

DID YOU KNOW?

Ambrose Bierce . . .

- was one of 13 children, whose names all began with the letter *A*.
- was awarded 15 commendations for bravery under fire.
- was nicknamed Bitter Bierce for his cynical humor and cruel wit.
- also wrote under the names Mrs. J. Milton Bowers and Dod Grile.

Literature of the Civil War

An Occurrence at Owl Creek Bridge
Short Story by Ambrose Bierce

Essential Course of Study

VIDEO TRAILER **THINK**central KEYWORD: HML11-602A

Meet the Author

Ambrose Bierce 1842–c. 1914

As a Civil War soldier, Ambrose Bierce was an eyewitness to the harsh realities of war. The brutal contrast between soldiers' dreams of glory and the senselessness of warfare became a recurring theme in Bierce's postwar short stories, including his suspenseful tale "An Occurrence at Owl Creek Bridge."

In the Line of Fire Born into a poor, intensely religious family, Bierce spent his early years on an Indiana farm. At age 15, he left home for a job at a newspaper, where he set type. Three years later, the Civil War broke out, and the idealistic Bierce immediately volunteered for the Union army. Fighting in some of the war's bloodiest battles, Bierce watched many of his comrades die and nearly died himself from a head wound.

When the war was over, Bierce moved to San Francisco, which was then the literary center of the West. Determined to become a writer, Bierce took a job as a night watchman, which allowed him ample time for reading and for polishing his writing skills. He started writing a regular newspaper column and became famous for exposing bigotry, hypocrisy, and corruption with razor-sharp satire. His cutting wit earned him the title "the Wickedest Man in San Francisco." Such a reputation delighted Bierce, who kept on his desk a human skull that he claimed belonged to one of his critics.

A Morbid Imagination Bierce began publishing short stories in the 1870s, when realism was becoming the dominant literary style in American fiction. Although Bierce's true-to-life war stories inspired realist writers like Stephen Crane, his fiction often included surreal or ghostly events. Like Edgar Allan Poe, to whom he was often compared, Bierce was fascinated with strange and horrible deaths, and he described them with his characteristic dark humor and a sense of irony. Bierce also went beyond realism in his experiments with narration, pioneering the use of multiple points of view in a single story.

Vanished At 71, Bierce revisited Civil War battle sites where he had fought and then went to Mexico to report on the Mexican Revolution as an observer with Pancho Villa's rebel army. He never returned to the United States, and no trace of him was found. Before he left, he wrote to a niece, "If you hear of my being stood up against a Mexican stone wall and shot to rags, please know that I think that a pretty good way to depart this life. It beats old age, disease or falling down the cellar stairs."

Author Online

Go to **thinkcentral.com**. KEYWORD: HML11-602B

602

See resources on the **Teacher One Stop DVD-ROM** and on **thinkcentral.com**.

 RESOURCE MANAGER UNIT 3

Plan and Teach, pp. 109–116
Summary, pp. 117–118† ‡*
Text Analysis and Reading Skill, pp. 119–122†*
Vocabulary, pp. 123–125*

DIAGNOSTIC AND SELECTION TESTS

Selection Tests, pp. 173–176

 BEST PRACTICES TOOLKIT

Definition Mapping, p. E6
Sequence Chain, p. B21
Analysis Frame: Plot, pp. D21, D28
Three-Column Journal, p. B10

INTERACTIVE READER

ADAPTED INTERACTIVE READER

ELL ADAPTED INTERACTIVE READER

TECHNOLOGY

- **Teacher One Stop DVD-ROM**
- **Student One Stop DVD-ROM**
- **PowerNotes DVD-ROM**
- **Audio Anthology CD**
- **GrammarNotes DVD-ROM**
- **ExamView Test Generator** on the Teacher One Stop

Video Trailer

Go to **thinkcentral.com** to preview the **Video Trailer** introducing this selection. Other features that support the selection include

- **PowerNotes** presentation
- **ThinkAloud** models to enhance comprehension
- **WordSharp** vocabulary tutorials
- interactive writing and grammar instruction

---

* Resources for Differentiation   † Also in Spanish   ‡ In Haitian Creole and Vietnamese

● **TEXT ANALYSIS: POINT OF VIEW**

Because the narrator is the voice that tells a story, the reader knows only what the narrator is able to tell. Therefore, the narrator's point of view greatly affects the story's events as well as the internal and external development of characters. Types of **point of view** include

- **first person:** told by a character in the work whose knowledge is limited to his or her own experiences
- **third-person omniscient:** told by a voice outside the story who reveals the thoughts and feelings of all the characters
- **third-person limited:** told by a voice outside the story who focuses on one character's thoughts and feelings

As you read, look for clues in the narration that help identify the point of view in Ambrose Bierce's story, and consider the impact of that choice.

● **READING SKILL: ANALYZE STRUCTURE**

To analyze the **structure** of a literary work, you examine the relationship between its parts and its content. This story is divided into three numbered sections, each of which occurs at a different point in time. After you read each section, summarize the events that occur and note when they take place. Use a chart like the one shown to record your notes.

	What Happens	*When*
Section 1		

▲ **VOCABULARY IN CONTEXT**

Bierce used the words in Column A in his tale of a man facing death. Test your knowledge by matching each vocabulary word with its synonym in Column B.

Column A	**Column B**
1. interminable	**a.** swaying
2. poignant	**b.** painful
3. ineffable	**c.** predicting
4. summarily	**d.** unending
5. oscillation	**e.** indescribable
6. ludicrous	**f.** immediately
7. presaging	**g.** laughable

 Complete the activities in your **Reader/Writer Notebook**.

Can we escape the
INEVITABLE?

"An Occurrence at Owl Creek Bridge" opens with an execution about to take place. Standing on an isolated, heavily guarded bridge, with a noose around his neck, the protagonist is doomed. There is no escape. Or is there?

DISCUSS In a small group, list ways people respond when faced with a bad situation they cannot change. Classify each response as useful or destructive. When does it make sense to look for a way out, and when is it time to accept the inevitable?

603

Can we escape the
INEVITABLE?

Ask the question, and then have students read the paragraph that follows it. After the class speculates on the meaning of the question "Or is there?" have them complete the *DISCUSS* activity. Then, invite volunteers to explain when it is sensible to escape and when it is time to accept that there is no escape.

TEXT ANALYSIS   COMMON CORE
RL 3
RL 5

● *Model the Skill:* **POINT OF VIEW**

To help students identify point of view, write this passage on the board:

> Harry knew that if the fire continued to spread, he would never escape. His fear paralyzed him. Then, he heard the stairs collapse.

Circle words that relay the passage's point of view, such as *he* and *His*. Then, point out that the passage's point of view is third-person limited.

GUIDED PRACTICE Ask students to identify the point of view in a favorite story or novel.

READING SKILL   COMMON CORE
RL 2
RL 5

■ *Model the Skill:* **ANALYZE STRUCTURE**

Explain to students that when a story's structure includes different time periods, readers must use textual evidence and context clues to put the parts together. Point out that the story begins with a character in crisis, so readers need clues explaining how the crisis arose. Also, emphasize that structuring the story out of sequence creates suspense.

GUIDED PRACTICE Ask students to identify another literary work in which the author generated suspense by structuring the story out of sequence.

R RESOURCE MANAGER—Copy Master
Analyze Structure page 121 (for student use while reading the selection)

VOCABULARY SKILL   COMMON CORE
L 4

▲ **VOCABULARY IN CONTEXT**

DIAGNOSE WORD KNOWLEDGE Have all students complete Vocabulary in Context. Check their answers against the following:

ineffable (ĭn-ĕf′ə-bəl) *adj.* beyond description; inexpressible
interminable (ĭn-tûr′mə-nə-bol) *adj.* endless
ludicrous (loo′dĭ-krəs) *adj.* laughably absurd; ridiculous
oscillation (ŏs′ə-lā′shən) *n.* the action of swinging back and forth

poignant (poin′yənt) *adj.* physically or mentally painful
presaging (prĕs′ĭj-ĭng) *adj.* predicting
summarily (sə-mĕr′ə-lē) *adv.* quickly and without ceremony

PRETEACH VOCABULARY Use the following copy master to help students predict meanings.

R RESOURCE MANAGER—Copy Master
Vocabulary Study p. 123

Practice and Apply

SUMMARY

Bierce's short story begins with Peyton Farquhar, a Southern planter, standing on a bridge in Alabama, about to be hanged by Union soldiers for attempting to set fire to Owl Creek Bridge. He falls through the bridge and hangs for a moment before the rope breaks and falls into the water. He unties his hands, dodges bullets, and swims ashore. He runs through the forest to his home, where he sees his wife. Then he feels a pain on his neck and hangs, dead. His escape was a fantasy.

READ WITH A PURPOSE

Help students set a purpose for reading. Tell them to read to discover how the main character found himself in such a dire situation.

TEXT ANALYSIS

COMMON CORE
RL 3
RL 5

Ⓐ *Model the Skill:*
POINT OF VIEW

To help students identify the story's point of view, point out the absence of the pronoun *I* which would indicate first-person point of view.

Possible answer: *The point of view is third-person omniscient. The narrator describes a man who is about to be hung (lines 2–4) and the soldiers (lines 6–12) in a calm tone that suggests the narrator is detached and objective, able to report all aspects of the event factually.*

An Occurrence at Owl Creek Bridge

Ambrose Bierce

I

A man stood upon a railroad bridge in northern Alabama, looking down into the swift water twenty feet below. The man's hands were behind his back, the wrists bound with a cord. A rope closely encircled his neck. It was attached to a stout cross-timber above his head and the slack fell to the level of his knees. Some loose boards laid upon the sleepers[1] supporting the metals of the railway supplied a footing for him and his executioners—two private soldiers of the Federal army, directed by a sergeant who in civil life may have been a deputy sheriff. At a short remove upon the same temporary platform was an officer in the uniform of his rank, armed. He was a captain. A sentinel at each end of the bridge stood with his
10 rifle in the position known as "support," that is to say, vertical in front of the left shoulder, the hammer resting on the forearm thrown straight across the chest—a formal and unnatural position, enforcing an erect carriage of the body. It did not appear to be the duty of these two men to know what was occurring at the center of the bridge; they merely blockaded the two ends of the foot planking that traversed it. **Ⓐ**

Beyond one of the sentinels nobody was in sight; the railroad ran straight away into a forest for a hundred yards, then, curving, was lost to view. Doubtless there was an outpost farther along. The other bank of the stream was open ground—a gentle acclivity[2] topped with a stockade of vertical tree trunks, loopholed for rifles,
20 with a single embrasure[3] through which protruded the muzzle of a brass cannon commanding the bridge. Midway of the slope between bridge and fort were the spectators—a single company of infantry in line, at "parade rest," the butts of the rifles on the ground, the barrels inclining slightly backward against the right

---

1. **sleepers:** railroad ties.
2. **acclivity:** an upward slope.
3. **embrasure:** a flared opening in a wall for a gun, with sides angled so that the inside opening is larger than that on the outside.

604 UNIT 3: FROM ROMANTICISM TO REALISM

Analyze Visuals ▶
Based on this image, what do you predict will happen in the story?

① Targeted Passage

Ⓐ POINT OF VIEW
Identify the point of view used in lines 1–15. What does the **tone** of the description tell you about the narrator's perspective?

DIFFERENTIATED INSTRUCTION

FOR ENGLISH LANGUAGE LEARNERS
Vocabulary Support Use Definition Mapping to teach these words: *Federal* (line 6), *code* (line 32), *undertake* (line 89), *reluctance* (line 140), *perspective* (line 255).

BEST PRACTICES TOOLKIT—Transparency Definition Mapping p. E6

FOR STRUGGLING READERS

In combination with the *Audio Anthology CD*, use one or more Targeted Passages (pp. 604, 608, 610, 612, 614) to ensure that students focus on key story events and concepts. Targeted Passages are also good for English language learners.

① Targeted Passage [Lines 1–15]

This passage introduces students to the story setting at Owl Creek Bridge as well as to the main character and his pending execution.

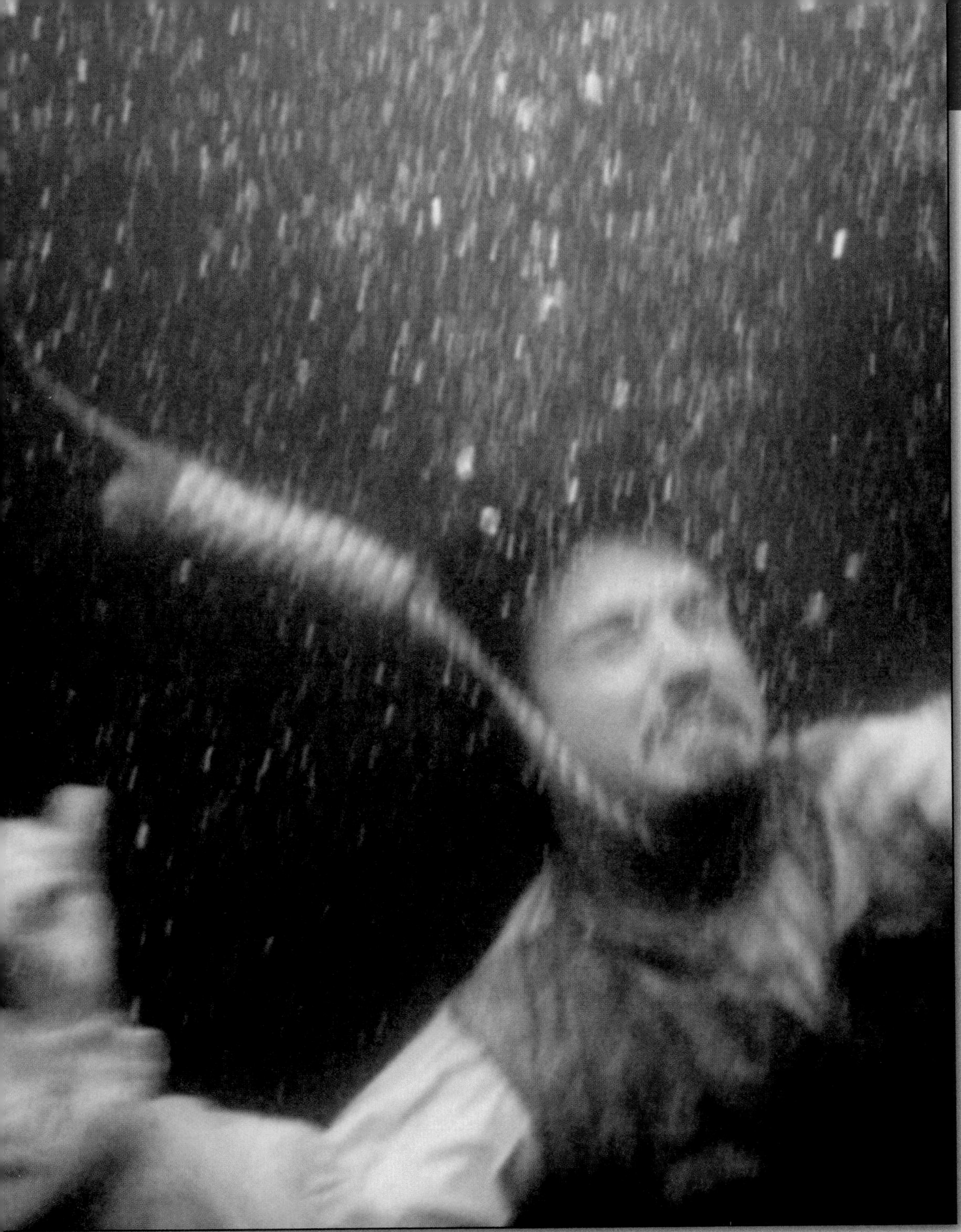

Reading Support

This selection on **thinkcentral.com** includes embedded **ThinkAloud** models–students "thinking aloud" about the story to model the kinds of questions a good reader would ask about a selection.

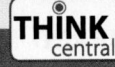

Analyze Visuals

Possible answer: *This image suggests that a man is going to hang from somewhere that drops him into water.*

REVISIT THE BIG QUESTION

Can we escape the INEVITABLE?

Discuss Given what you discovered about the man's situation in lines 1–15, does he have a chance of escape? Explain. ***Possible answer:*** *It does not seem that he has any chance at all of escape. He already is tied with a rope around his neck (lines 2–3). His executioners are already on the bridge (line 6), and soldiers guard both ends of the bridge (line 9).*

- Where and when does the story take place? (lines 1–6)
- What other people are with the man? What are they doing? (lines 6–15)
- What is happening to the man? (lines 2–4)

FOR ADVANCED LEARNERS/AP

Provide these projects to extend the lesson:

- Create a portrait of Farquhar.
- Write a letter from Farquhar to his wife.
- Evaluate an ideological statement from the story.

Have students present their projects to the class with an explanation of their ideas.

RESOURCE MANAGER—*Copy Masters*
Ideas for Extension pp. 114–115

FOR STRUGGLING READERS

Develop Reading Fluency Tell students that when they read the beginning of a story aloud, they should read slowly enough for listeners to catch all of the important details that introduce them to the story's situation. Read aloud the story's first paragraph. After reading, discuss your pacing, pointing out places you chose to pause in the longer sentences. Then, have students practice reading this paragraph with a partner.

In lines 57–70, use these prompts to help students envision the main character's situation:

Connect In your experience, how do people's senses change in an alarming situation? *Accept all thoughtful responses.*

Interpret Why does the man's ticking of his watch bother him so much? ***Possible answer:*** *The man appears to be in a state of heightened consciousness, perhaps from fear. He relates the regular ticking to "the tolling of a death knell" (line 65). The sounds of his watch do not really increase "in strength and sharpness" (line 68), but seem to as his fear increases. This fear also makes him experience the watch sounds more intensely, "like the thrust of a knife" (line 69).*

Evaluate Is it believable that a watch could become so loud? ***Possible answer:*** *Yes; for example, when a person gets really nervous, he may hear his heartbeat as if it is in his ear. Sounds and sensations become more pronounced in fearful situations, just as they have for the main character.*

shoulder, the hands crossed upon the stock.[4] A lieutenant stood at the right of the line, the point of his sword upon the ground, his left hand resting upon his right. Excepting the group of four at the center of the bridge, not a man moved. The company faced the bridge, staring stonily, motionless. The sentinels, facing the banks of the stream, might have been statues to adorn the bridge. The captain stood with folded arms, silent, observing the work of his subordinates, but making no sign. Death is a dignitary who when he comes announced is to be received with formal manifestations of respect, even by those most familiar with him. In the code of military etiquette silence and fixity are forms of deference.

The man who was engaged in being hanged was apparently about thirty-five years of age. He was a civilian, if one might judge from his habit, which was that of a planter. His features were good—a straight nose, firm mouth, broad forehead, from which his long, dark hair was combed straight back, falling behind his ears to the collar of his well-fitting frock-coat. He wore a mustache and pointed beard, but no whiskers; his eyes were large and dark gray, and had a kindly expression which one would hardly have expected in one whose neck was in the hemp. Evidently this was no vulgar assassin. The liberal military code makes provision for hanging many kinds of persons, and gentlemen are not excluded.

The preparations being complete, the two private soldiers stepped aside and each drew away the plank upon which he had been standing. The sergeant turned to the captain, saluted and placed himself immediately behind that officer, who in

Language Coach

Topically Related Words
Read lines 30–32. Look up *dignitary, etiquette,* and *deference* in a dictionary. How is each word related to the ideas of formality or respect?

---

4. **stock:** the wooden part of the rifle that serves as a handle.

DIFFERENTIATED INSTRUCTION

FOR ENGLISH LANGUAGE LEARNERS

Language Coach

Topically Related Words *Answer:* Dignitary: *a high position that is worthy of respect;* etiquette: *actions showing formality or respect;* deference: *courteous respect.* Have students use each word in a sentence. Then, have students trade papers with a partner and decide whether their partner used each word correctly.

FOR ADVANCED LEARNERS/AP

Analyze Personification and Tone [paired option] Have students identify the figure of speech being used in lines 30–32 (*personification*) and paraphrase them for the class. Then have pairs write and exchange five sentences that personify fear and death. Finally, have small groups discuss these questions:

- How do these sentences explain the way soldiers are meant to react to death? How might that differ from civilian reactions?

- What do you think the "code of military etiquette" (line 32) means? What evidence have you seen so far in the story that displays military etiquette?

- What is the narrator's tone in lines 40–41? What is he suggesting in those lines about the military code?

turn moved apart one pace. These movements left the condemned man and the sergeant standing on the two ends of the same plank, which spanned three of the cross-ties of the bridge. The end upon which the civilian stood almost, but not quite, reached a fourth. This plank had been held in place by the weight of the captain; it was now held by that of the sergeant. At a signal from the former the

50 latter would step aside, the plank would tilt and the condemned man go down between two ties. The arrangement commended itself to his judgment as simple and effective. His face had not been covered nor his eyes bandaged. He looked a moment at his "unsteadfast footing," then let his gaze wander to the swirling water of the stream racing madly beneath his feet. A piece of dancing driftwood caught his attention and his eyes followed it down the current. How slowly it appeared to move! What a sluggish stream! **B**

He closed his eyes in order to fix his last thoughts upon his wife and children. The water, touched to gold by the early sun, the brooding mists under the banks at some distance down the stream, the fort, the soldiers, the piece of drift—all

60 had distracted him. And now he became conscious of a new disturbance. Striking through the thought of his dear ones was a sound which he could neither ignore nor understand, a sharp, distinct, metallic percussion like the stroke of a blacksmith's hammer upon the anvil; it had the same ringing quality. He wondered what it was, and whether immeasurably distant or near by—it seemed both. Its recurrence was regular, but as slow as the tolling of a death knell.[5] He awaited each stroke with impatience and—he knew not why—apprehension. The intervals of silence grew progressively longer; the delays became maddening. With their greater infrequency the sounds increased in strength and sharpness. They hurt his ear like the thrust of a knife; he feared he would shriek. What he heard

70 was the ticking of his watch.

He unclosed his eyes and saw again the water below him. "If I could free my hands," he thought, "I might throw off the noose and spring into the stream. By diving I could evade the bullets and, swimming vigorously, reach the bank, take to the woods and get away home. My home, thank God, is as yet outside their lines; my wife and little ones are still beyond the invader's farthest advance."

As these thoughts, which have here to be set down in words, were flashed into the doomed man's brain rather than evolved from it the captain nodded to the sergeant. The sergeant stepped aside. **C**

II

Peyton Farquhar was a well-to-do planter, of an old and highly respected Alabama

80 family. Being a slave owner and like other slave owners a politician he was naturally an original secessionist and ardently devoted to the Southern cause. Circumstances of an imperious nature, which it is unnecessary to relate here, had prevented him from taking service with the gallant army that had fought the disastrous campaigns ending with the fall of Corinth,[6] and he chafed under the

---

5. **the tolling of a death knell:** the slow, steady ringing of a bell at a funeral or to indicate death.

6. **Corinth:** a town in Mississippi that was the site of a Civil War battle in 1862.

B POINT OF VIEW
Note that the third-person point of view narrows from omniscient to limited. What **sensory details** alert you to this change in perspective?

C ANALYZE STRUCTURE
If the story were told in chronological order, what would you expect to happen next?

TEXT ANALYSIS | COMMON CORE RL 3 RL 5

B POINT OF VIEW

Possible answer: The sensory details that signify the change in point of view include the main character seeing the "swirling water of the stream" (lines 53–54) and the "piece of dancing driftwood" (line 54) that he thinks moves slowly. At this point, the narrator describes only the main character's sights and thoughts.

REVISIT THE BIG QUESTION

Can we escape the
INEVITABLE?

Discuss In lines 71–75, how does the main character think he can escape? What does this suggest about human nature in general?
Possible answer: He thinks that he can untie his hands, take off his noose, swim in the water, and get to his home. This shows that even in the most desperate and hopeless situations, human beings continue to hope.

READING SKILL | COMMON CORE RL 2 RL 5

C Model the Skill:
ANALYZE STRUCTURE

Help students analyze the story's structure by referring to lines 47–51 and explaining that when the sergeant steps aside, the "plank would tilt," and the man would fall and thus hang. Also, note that in line 78, the sergeant steps aside.

Possible answer: At this point in the story, you would expect that the man would be hanged.

FOR STRUGGLING READERS

Concept Support: Analyze Structure After students complete Section I, help them add to the prereading chart introduced on page 603. Have students use their charts to generate questions about Section I. Tell students to pause again after each remaining section to add to the chart and list more questions. Urge them to read on to answer their questions.

Clarify that in the prereading chart, the heading *When* refers to an event's place in the story sequence, not to its historical period.

What Happens	When
on a railroad bridge in northern Alabama, a man is about to be hanged	action takes place at beginning of story

FOR ENGLISH LANGUAGE LEARNERS

Culture: Clarify Explain that the story is set during the American Civil War. Point out clues that explain Farquhar's allegiance to the Southern cause and therefore hint that he may be the man about to be hanged by Federal (Union) soldiers. Explain that he lives in the Southern state of Alabama and is a slave owner. He is a secessionist (line 81), which means that he supports the South's separating from the Union.

D ANALYZE STRUCTURE

Possible answer: **The details that connect these two sections of the story include the mention of the railroad bridge (lines 1 and 100–101), a hanging (lines 2–4 and 101), and the stockade (lines 19 and 99).**

E POINT OF VIEW

Possible answer: **The reader knows that the soldier who gives Farquhar the information about Owl Creek Bridge is actually a Federal spy (line 116). The third-person omniscient point of view gives readers details that the characters are unaware of.**

IF STUDENTS NEED HELP . . . Clarify that a scout is a spy.

OWN THE WORD

- **summarily:** Ask students why they think any civilian caught interfering with the railroad will be *summarily* hanged. *Possible answer:* **The army hopes to deter people by relaying that they would have no trial or chance of escape.**

- **poignant:** Point out that the Latin root word for *poignant* is *pungere,* which means "to prick." When a feeling is *poignant,* it "pricks" at you emotionally or physically. Have students make a list of emotions they would consider *poignant.* *Possible answers:* **melancholy, nostalgia**

---

inglorious restraint, longing for the release of his energies, the larger life of the soldier, the opportunity for distinction. That opportunity, he felt, would come, as it comes to all in war time. Meanwhile he did what he could. No service was too humble for him to perform in aid of the South, no adventure too perilous for him to undertake if consistent with the character of a civilian who was at heart a

90 soldier, and who in good faith and without too much qualification assented to at least a part of the frankly villainous dictum that all is fair in love and war.

One evening while Farquhar and his wife were sitting on a rustic bench near the entrance to his grounds, a gray-clad soldier rode up to the gate and asked for a drink of water. Mrs. Farquhar was only too happy to serve him with her own white hands. While she was fetching the water her husband approached the dusty horseman and inquired eagerly for news from the front.

"The Yanks are repairing the railroads," said the man, "and are getting ready for another advance. They have reached the Owl Creek bridge, put it in order and built a stockade on the north bank. The commandant has issued an order, which is

100 posted everywhere, declaring that any civilian caught interfering with the railroad, its bridges, tunnels or trains will be **summarily** hanged. I saw the order." **D**

"How far is it to the Owl Creek bridge?" Farquhar asked.

"About thirty miles."

"Is there no force on this side the creek?"

"Only a picket post[7] half a mile out, on the railroad, and a single sentinel at this end of the bridge."

"Suppose a man—a civilian and student of hanging—should elude the picket post and perhaps get the better of the sentinel," said Farquhar, smiling, "what could he accomplish?"

110 The soldier reflected. "I was there a month ago," he replied. "I observed that the flood of last winter had lodged a great quantity of driftwood against the wooden pier at this end of the bridge. It is now dry and would burn like tow."[8]

The lady had now brought the water, which the soldier drank. He thanked her ceremoniously, bowed to her husband and rode away. An hour later, after nightfall, he repassed the plantation, going northward in the direction from which he had come. He was a Federal scout. **E**

III

As Peyton Farquhar fell straight downward through the bridge he lost consciousness and was as one already dead. From this state he was awakened— ages later, it seemed to him—by the pain of a sharp pressure upon his throat,

120 followed by a sense of suffocation. Keen, **poignant** agonies seemed to shoot from his neck downward through every fiber of his body and limbs. These pains appeared to flash along well-defined lines of ramification[9] and to beat with an inconceivably rapid periodicity. They seemed like streams of pulsating fire heating

---

② Targeted Passage

summarily (sə-mĕr′ə-lē) *adv.* quickly and without ceremony

D ANALYZE STRUCTURE Compare lines 97–101 with the description in lines 1–21. What details connect these two sections of the story?

E POINT OF VIEW Reread lines 113–116. Explain what the reader knows that Peyton Farquhar does not. Which type of third-person point of view allows the author to give the reader details that are hidden from the characters?

poignant (poin′yənt) *adj.* physically or mentally painful

---

7. **picket post:** the camp of soldiers who are assigned to guard against a surprise attack.

8. **tow** (tō): coarse, dry fiber.

9. **flash . . . ramification:** spread out rapidly along branches from a central point.

608 UNIT 3: FROM ROMANTICISM TO REALISM

DIFFERENTIATED INSTRUCTION

FOR STRUGGLING READERS

Comprehension Support Point out that Bierce's long sentences can be difficult to understand. Help students use punctuation to break them into manageable chunks. Have students practice on lines 82–91. *Possible answer:* **Farquhar regrets that he did not fight in the war. He wants to find a way to help the Southern cause. He is willing to do anything he can, even if it is dangerous or dishonest.**

② Targeted Passage [Lines 92–116]

This passage sets up the actions that may later get Peyton Farquhar hanged.

- How do the Farquhars greet the visiting soldier? (lines 94–96)

- What does the soldier say about the Yanks? What order have they posted? (lines 97–101)

- What does Farquhar ask the soldier? (lines 107–109)

- What army is the soldier from? (line 116)

FOR ENGLISH LANGUAGE LEARNERS

Culture: Clarify Explain that "Yanks" (line 97) are Yankees or Northerners—those fighting against the South. Clarify that the soldier who approaches Farquhar is dressed in the gray uniform of the Southern army and appears as a comrade to him. In fact, line 116 reveals that he is a Federal, or Northern, scout in disguise. Farquhar takes information from a man he would consider an enemy.

him to an intolerable temperature. As to his head, he was conscious of nothing but a feeling of fullness—of congestion. These sensations were unaccompanied by thought. The intellectual part of his nature was already effaced; he had power only to feel, and feeling was torment. He was conscious of motion. Encompassed in a luminous cloud, of which he was now merely the fiery heart, without material substance, he swung through unthinkable arcs of **oscillation,** like a vast
130 pendulum. Then all at once, with terrible suddenness, the light about him shot upward with the noise of a loud plash; a frightful roaring was in his ears, and all was cold and dark. The power of thought was restored; he knew that the rope had broken and he had fallen into the stream. There was no additional strangulation; the noose about his neck was already suffocating him and kept the water from his lungs. To die of hanging at the bottom of a river!—the idea seemed to him **ludicrous.** He opened his eyes in the darkness and saw above him a gleam

oscillation (ŏs′ə-lā′shən) *n.* the action of swinging back and forth

ludicrous (lōō′dĭ-krəs) *adj.* laughably absurd; ridiculous

◀ **Analyze Visuals**
Whose point of view does the image reflect? What details can you not see when limited to this point of view?

AN OCCURRENCE AT OWL CREEK BRIDGE **609**

TIERED DISCUSSION PROMPTS

In lines 85–112, use these prompts to get students thinking about Farquhar's motivation:

Interpret What is Farquhar suggesting he might do? What are his motives? *Possible answer: Farquhar is suggesting that he will destroy the bridge. His motives are to help the Southern cause and become a hero.*

Synthesize Based on what you read about the Civil War in the historical essay (page 518), is it convincing that Farquhar would take such a risk with his life? Explain. *Possible answer: Yes; Farquhar likely grew up with the ideal of the romantic hero. He longs for glory and imagines himself an unrecognized hero (lines 85–91). He also does not know that he has been tricked by a Federal scout and so does not realize the danger.*

Analyze Visuals

Possible answer: This image reflects Farquhar's point of view, as he stands on the plank and looks downward. This point of view does not allow one to see the face of the person standing on the plank, where the rope is actually tied, or who else is standing nearby.

VOCABULARY

COMMON CORE L 4

OWN THE WORD

- **oscillation:** Point out that *oscillation* may have come from the Latin *oscillum*, which was used by Virgil in the Georgics in reference to Bacchus mask swinging back and forth in trees.

- **ludicrous:** Ask students to list synonyms for *ludicrous*. **Possible answers:** *foolish, absurd*

FOR STRUGGLING READERS
Concept Support: Analyze Structure Point out to students that Section III appears to continue where Section I left off. After students add Section II information to their prereading chart, suggest that they also plot the important story events on a Sequence Chain. Help students begin with the details from Section II.

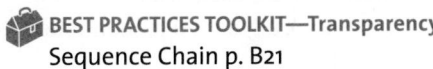 **BEST PRACTICES TOOLKIT—Transparency**
Sequence Chain p. B21

FOR ENGLISH LANGUAGE LEARNERS
Vocabulary Support Explain that Bierce uses opposites in his descriptive language to stress the intensity of Farquhar's experiences. Point out contrasts between light and dark, heat and cold: "pulsating fire . . . intolerable temperature" (lines 123–124), "fiery heart" (line 128), and "light . . . shot upward" (lines 130–131) versus "cold and dark" (line 132) and "in the darkness" (line 136).

FOR ADVANCED LEARNERS/AP
Analyze Realism Remind students that Bierce's writings frequently include surreal elements. As students read Section III, challenge them to determine whether this section is realistic or surreal and why. Have them identify important details of both types, then use these details to discuss why Bierce uses both realistic and surreal details in his short story.

F CHARACTERIZATION

Read aloud lines 143–160, emphasizing the lines where the point of view shifts from third-person limited to first-person.

Possible answer: The sudden wrenching pains vividly show Farquhar's panic. This makes the character extremely real, as his fear grips the reader.

Extend the Discussion What changes in Farquhar's perceptions accompany this shift to first-person point of view?

REVISIT THE BIG QUESTION

Can we escape the
INEVITABLE?

Discuss Do you think Farquhar has been able to escape? Use details from lines 143–160 to explain. *Possible answer: It is difficult to tell. Many of the details suggest that he hasn't really escaped but rather may be dreaming or having a near-death experience. For example, words such as "not conscious" (line 143) and "superhuman strength" (line 146), as well as Farquhar watching his "disobedient hands" (line 156) make the account seem dreamlike or like a near-death experience. However, there are also some details that describe a realistic escape, such as when he emerges from the water, finds the sunlight very bright, gulps air, and yells aloud (lines 158–160).*

---

of light, but how distant, how inaccessible! He was still sinking, for the light became fainter and fainter until it was a mere glimmer. Then it began to grow and brighten, and he knew that he was rising toward the surface—knew it with

140 reluctance, for he was now very comfortable. "To be hanged and drowned," he thought, "that is not so bad; but I do not wish to be shot. No; I will not be shot; that is not fair."

He was not conscious of an effort, but a sharp pain in his wrist apprised him that he was trying to free his hands. He gave the struggle his attention, as an idler might observe the feat of a juggler, without interest in the outcome. What splendid effort!—what magnificent, what superhuman strength! Ah, that was a fine endeavor! Bravo! The cord fell away; his arms parted and floated upward, the hands dimly seen on each side in the growing light. He watched them with a new interest as first one and then the other pounced upon the noose at his neck.

150 They tore it away and thrust it fiercely aside, its undulations resembling those of a water-snake. "Put it back, put it back!" He thought he shouted these words to his hands, for the undoing of the noose had been succeeded by the direst pang that he had yet experienced. His neck ached horribly; his brain was on fire; his heart, which had been fluttering faintly, gave a great leap, trying to force itself out at his mouth. His whole body was racked and wrenched with an insupportable anguish![10] But his disobedient hands gave no heed to the command. They beat the water vigorously with quick, downward strokes, forcing him to the surface. He felt his head emerge; his eyes were blinded by the sunlight; his chest expanded convulsively, and with a supreme and crowning agony his lungs engulfed a great

160 draught of air, which instantly he expelled in a shriek! **F**

He was now in full possession of his physical senses. They were, indeed, preternaturally keen and alert. Something in the awful disturbance of his organic system had so exalted and refined them that they made record of things never before perceived. He felt the ripples upon his face and heard their separate sounds as they struck. He looked at the forest on the bank of the stream, saw the individual trees, the leaves and the veining of each leaf—saw the very insects upon them: the locusts, the brilliant-bodied flies, the gray spiders stretching their webs from twig to twig. He noted the prismatic colors in all the dewdrops upon a million blades of grass. The humming of the gnats that danced above the eddies of

170 the stream, the beating of the dragon-flies' wings, the strokes of the water-spiders' legs, like oars which had lifted their boat—all these made audible music. A fish slid along beneath his eyes and he heard the rush of its body parting the water.

He had come to the surface facing down the stream; in a moment the visible world seemed to wheel slowly round, himself the pivotal point, and he saw the bridge, the fort, the soldiers upon the bridge, the captain, the sergeant, the two privates, his executioners. They were in silhouette against the blue sky. They shouted and gesticulated, pointing at him. The captain had drawn his pistol, but did not fire; the others were unarmed. Their movements were grotesque and horrible, their forms gigantic.

---

10. **racked . . . anguish:** stretched and twisted with unendurable physical pain.

S Targeted Passage

F CHARACTERIZATION
Characterization refers to the techniques a writer uses to develop characters. With third-person limited point of view, Bierce can observe his main character from a distance, as he does in the first two parts of this story, conveying character externally through details of action and dialogue. In Part III, however, the point of view shifts to record the sensations and emotions of Peyton Farquhar's inner life. Reread lines 143–160. What details does the author use to capture the panic of a man in danger of drowning? How do these details contribute to character development? Cite evidence from the paragraph to support your response.

DIFFERENTIATED INSTRUCTION

FOR STRUGGLING READERS

S Targeted Passage [Lines 147–164]

This passage explains that Farquhar escapes and shows his heightened senses.

- How does Farquhar get rid of the noose? (lines 147–151)
- How does Farquhar feel while in the water? (lines 153–160)
- What clues suggest that something strange is happening? (lines 161–164)

FOR ENGLISH LANGUAGE LEARNERS

Related Vocabulary Explain to students that the narrator uses vivid sensory language to describe Farquhar's pain as he is under the water and swims to the surface. Help students to understand these physical descriptions of pain:

- *brain was on fire* (line 153), "head ached"
- *his heart . . . gave a great leap* (lines 153–154), "his heart was beating hard"

- *body was racked and wrenched* (line 155), "body was twisted by the pain"
- *insupportable anguish* (lines 155–156), "unbearable pain"
- *his chest expanded convulsively* (lines 158–159), "he had difficulty catching his breath"
- *his lungs engulfed a great draught of air, which instantly he expelled in a shriek* (lines 159–160), "he took a great gulp, then yelled"

180 Suddenly he heard a sharp report and something struck the water smartly within a few inches of his head, spattering his face with spray. He heard a second report, and saw one of the sentinels with his rifle at his shoulder, a light cloud of blue smoke rising from the muzzle. The man in the water saw the eye of the man on the bridge gazing into his own through the sights of the rifle. He observed that it was a gray eye and remembered having read that gray eyes were keenest, and that all famous marksmen had them. Nevertheless, this one had missed.

A counter-swirl had caught Farquhar and turned him half round; he was again looking into the forest on the bank opposite the fort. The sound of a clear, high voice in a monotonous singsong now rang out behind him and came across the
190 water with a distinctness that pierced and subdued all other sounds, even the beating of the ripples in his ears. Although no soldier, he had frequented camps enough to know the dread significance of that deliberate, drawling, aspirated chant; the lieutenant on shore was taking a part in the morning's work. How coldly and pitilessly—with what an even, calm intonation, **presaging,** and enforcing tranquillity in the men—with what accurately measured intervals fell those cruel words:

"Attention, company! . . . Shoulder arms! . . . Ready! . . . Aim! . . . Fire!"

COMMON CORE RL 4

Language Coach

Multiple-Meaning Words *Report* (line 180) is a **multiple-meaning word,** a word with more than one meaning. In this context, *report* means "loud, explosive noise." With a partner, identify the words in the paragraph that point to the appropriate meaning of this word.

presaging (prĕs′ĭj-ĭng) *adj.* predicting **presage** *v.*

TIERED DISCUSSION PROMPTS

In lines 173–186, use these prompts to help students decide if details in this passage are real or fantastic:

Restate In lines 176–179, how does Farquhar describe the soldiers' reaction to his escape? *Possible answer:* *Farquhar describes the soldiers as shouting and gesturing, but not shooting. He says all but the captain were unarmed.*

Analyze Would you expect soldiers to respond this way to a prisoner's escape? Why or why not? *Possible answer:* *No, they would typically be armed, not unarmed (line 178), and they would shoot immediately at him, not wait (lines 177–178).*

Synthesize Use what you know about Farquhar's situation to decide if his descriptions here are realistic or fantastic. *Possible answer:* *The men seem to behave as Farquhar would want them to, which suggests that the descriptions are a fantasy. In addition, the words "grotesque and horrible, their forms gigantic" (lines 178–179) suggest fantastic images. Finally, Farquhar says that he could see the "gray eye" (line 185) of the shooter, which is unlikely, especially as the shooter misses Farquhar. All of these details suggest a scene that Farquhar hopes for or dreams.*

VOCABULARY   COMMON CORE L 4

OWN THE WORD

presaging: Ask students why they think the author chose to use *presaging* in this context. *Possible answer:* Presaging *indicates a knowledge of some degree of future events. Using it here indicates the lieutenant is trying to "enforce tranquility" on his men.*

FOR RELUCTANT READERS

Connect to the Text Point out to students that "An Occurrence at Owl Creek Bridge" contains a description of a suspenseful action scene. Have students think of a suspenseful action scene from one of their favorite movies or television shows. For example, they could think of a high-speed chase or a narrow escape from death. Remind students that these movie or television scenes always begin in a writer's hands. Have students write a short paragraph describing their television or movie scene.

FOR ENGLISH LANGUAGE LEARNERS

Language Coach   COMMON CORE RL 4

Multiple-Meaning Words *Answer:* "sharp report," "heard a report," "rifle" Write the following sentences on the board, and have students determine which sentence uses the same meaning of *report* as is used in line 180. *Our English* report *is due today. We heard the loud* report *of the fireworks.*

Niagara Falls The "voice of Niagara" (line 199) refers to Niagara Falls, which is a massive waterfall on the border between New York State and Ontario, Canada. This reference means that the water was very loud in Farquhar's ears.

REVISIT THE BIG QUESTION

Can we escape the
INEVITABLE?

Discuss In lines 204–211, read about and then evaluate Farquhar's escape. Do you think he will succeed? Why, or why not? *Possible answer: On the one hand, he seems to have made important progress toward escape. He is downstream away from the shooters (line 205), and feels energized by adrenaline (lines 209–210). On the other hand, his ability to think at lightning speed (line 211), and to swim while dodging bullets (lines 208–209) seems impossible. The escape seems less and less likely to succeed because it seems less and less believable. Instead, it seems more like a fantasy of events Farquhar wishes for.*

ANALYZE STRUCTURE

After students read the selection, have them discuss novels, plays, or films in which the narrative structure is non-linear. What is the impact on the reader?

Farquhar dived—dived as deeply as he could. The water roared in his ears like the voice of Niagara, yet he heard the dulled thunder of the volley and, rising 200 again toward the surface, met shining bits of metal, singularly flattened, oscillating slowly downward. Some of them touched him on the face and hands, then fell away, continuing their descent. One lodged between his collar and neck; it was uncomfortably warm and he snatched it out.

As he rose to the surface, gasping for breath, he saw that he had been a long time under water; he was perceptibly farther down stream—nearer to safety. The soldiers had almost finished reloading; the metal ramrods flashed all at once in the sunshine as they were drawn from the barrels, turned in the air, and thrust into their sockets. The two sentinels fired again, independently and ineffectually.

The hunted man saw all this over his shoulder; he was now swimming 210 vigorously with the current. His brain was as energetic as his arms and legs; he thought with the rapidity of lightning.

"The officer," he reasoned, "will not make that martinet's[11] error a second time. It is as easy to dodge a volley as a single shot. He has probably already given the command to fire at will. God help me, I cannot dodge them all!"

An appalling plash within two yards of him was followed by a loud, rushing sound, *diminuendo*,[12] which seemed to travel back through the air to the fort and died in an explosion which stirred the very river to its deeps! A rising sheet of water curved over him, fell down upon him, blinded him, strangled him! The cannon had taken a hand in the game. As he shook his head free from the 220 commotion of the smitten water he heard the deflected shot humming through the air ahead, and in an instant it was cracking and smashing the branches in the forest beyond.

"They will not do that again," he thought; "the next time they will use a charge of grape.[13] I must keep my eye upon the gun; the smoke will apprise me—the report arrives too late; it lags behind the missile. That is a good gun."

Suddenly he felt himself whirled round and round—spinning like a top. The water, the banks, the forests, the now distant bridge, fort and men—all were commingled and blurred. Objects were represented by their colors only; circular horizontal streaks of color—that was all he saw. He had been caught in a vortex 230 and was being whirled on with a velocity of advance and gyration that made him giddy and sick. In a few moments he was flung upon the gravel at the foot of the left bank of the stream—the southern bank—and behind a projecting point which concealed him from his enemies. The sudden arrest of his motion, the abrasion of one of his hands on the gravel, restored him, and he wept with delight. He dug his fingers into the sand, threw it over himself in handfuls and audibly blessed it. It looked like diamonds, rubies, emeralds; he could think of nothing beautiful which it did not resemble. The trees upon the bank were giant garden plants; he

---

11. **martinet's:** alluding to a strict disciplinarian or person who demands that regulations be followed exactly.
12. ***diminuendo*** (dĭ-mĭn'yōō-ĕn'dō) *Italian:* gradually decreasing in loudness.
13. **grape:** short for grapeshot, a cluster of several small iron balls fired in one shot from a cannon.

Language Coach

Formal Language Read lines 210–211. Note the words "with the rapidity of lightning." Now, compare those words with these: "with lightning-fast speed." Which phrase do you find more formal? Consider both word order and word choice.

ANALYZE STRUCTURE

The structure of Bierce's story, in which events are not told in chronological order, is similar to the narrative technique employed by Charles Frazier in his 1997 Civil War novel, *Cold Mountain*, which was made into a film in 2003. The novel alternates between the stories of the two main characters, lovers who are separated by war. What are other examples of twentieth-century novels, plays, or films that use this non-sequential method of storytelling?

DIFFERENTIATED INSTRUCTION

FOR STRUGGLING READERS

④ Targeted Passage [Lines 226–235]

This passage shows readers that Farquhar is spinning in the water.

- How is Farquhar moving? (line 229)
- What does he see as he moves? (lines 226–229)
- How does he feel while he is moving? How does he feel when he stops moving? (lines 230–234)

FOR ENGLISH LANGUAGE LEARNERS

Language Coach

Formal Language *Answer:* Students will probably choose "with the rapidity of lightning" as the more formal language. Reasons why might include the word choice of *rapidity* instead of *fast*, and the use of *lightning* as part of a prepositional phrase instead of a modifier. Write the following sentences on the board, and work with

students to revise them to include more formal language: *This guy has loads of problems. I doubt he'll be able to get himself out of this mess.* **Possible answer:** *The main character is in a dire situation. A safe escape seems increasingly unlikely.*

Analyze Visuals

Possible answer: Like the place Farquhar describes, this image has trees that appear to be in a definite order (lines 237–238) and a light that shines through them (line 239). Both scenes remind readers of a new awakening, a hopeful dream, or even a glimpse of heaven.

VOCABULARY COMMON CORE L 4

OWN THE WORD

interminable: Ask students to explain why the forest seemed *interminable.* ***Possible answer:*** *The forest seemed* interminable *because it is difficult to see where it ends.*

noted a definite order in their arrangement, inhaled the fragrance of their blooms. A strange, roseate light shone through the spaces among their trunks and the wind 240 made in their branches the music of æolian harps.[14] He had no wish to perfect his escape—was content to remain in that enchanting spot until retaken.

A whiz and rattle of grapeshot among the branches high above his head roused him from his dream. The baffled cannoneer had fired him a random farewell. He sprang to his feet, rushed up the sloping bank, and plunged into the forest.

All that day he traveled, laying his course by the rounding sun. The forest seemed **interminable;** nowhere did he discover a break in it, not even a woodman's road. He had not known that he lived in so wild a region. There was something uncanny in the revelation.

▲ **Analyze Visuals**
Compare this image with the description given in lines 237–240. What associations does each scene call to mind?

interminable
(ĭn-tûr′mə-nə-bol)
adj. endless

---

14. **music of æolian** (ē-ō′lē-ən) **harps:** heavenly, or unearthly, music.

FOR STRUGGLING READERS

Foreshadowing Point out these references and help students recognize what these clues might foreshadow:

- *strange, roseate light shone through the spaces* (line 239)
- *æolian harps* (line 240)
- *enchanting spot* (line 241)
- *something uncanny in the revelation* (line 248)

Possible answer: The light suggests a near-death experience and the heavenly harps reinforce this suggestion. These clues foreshadow Farquhar's death.

FOR ADVANCED LEARNERS/AP

Analyze Character Behavior Challenge students to find textual evidence on pages 612–613 that Farquhar is actually aware that he is hanging *(lines 219–222; 226–233).* Ask them to write a brief essay outlining their findings and explaining why Farquhar might still be thinking positively instead of negatively at this point. Invite students to share their essays.

Can we escape the
INEVITABLE?

Discuss In lines 249–266, how is Farquhar really going to escape his situation? What clues suggest his likely escape? ***Possible answer:*** *Farquhar is going to escape his present situation by dying. The pain he feels is actually the noose strangling him (lines 261–264).*

TEXT ANALYSIS

G PRIMARY SOURCE DOCUMENTS

Ask students what is revealed by this change of point of view. How does this revelation relate Farquhar's experience to Sullivan Ballou's experience?
Possible answer: *Each man thinks about his wife and family before dying.*

Extend the Discussion How can relating a primary source to a fictional work legitimize themes and ideas in the fictional work?

TEXT ANALYSIS

H ANALYZE STRUCTURE

Point out to students that the surprise ending has become a commonly used plot device in short stories and novels as well as in films and television. As student cite examples of surprise endings, have them recall in each case how the storyteller may have structured the plot in order to achieve the maximum dramatic effect at the end.
Possible response: *The Sixth Sense*

VOCABULARY

OWN THE WORD

ineffable: Ask students to explain how an emotion like joy is *ineffable*. ***Possible answer:*** *Joy is ineffable when it brings happiness beyond description.*

SELECTION WRAP-UP

READ WITH A PURPOSE Ask students whether Farquhar's actions merit this punishment.
Answers will vary, but students will likely think that the punishment is unfair.

By night fall he was fatigued, footsore, famishing. The thought of his wife
250 and children urged him on. At last he found a road which led him in what he knew to be the right direction. It was as wide and straight as a city street, yet it seemed untraveled. No fields bordered it, no dwelling anywhere. Not so much as the barking of a dog suggested human habitation. The black bodies of the trees formed a straight wall on both sides, terminating on the horizon in a point, like a diagram in a lesson in perspective. Overhead, as he looked up through this rift in the wood, shone great golden stars looking unfamiliar and grouped in strange constellations. He was sure they were arranged in some order which had a secret and malign significance. The wood on either side was full of singular noises, among which—once, twice, and again, he distinctly heard whispers in an
260 unknown tongue.

His neck was in pain and lifting his hand to it he found it horribly swollen. He knew that it had a circle of black where the rope had bruised it. His eyes felt congested; he could no longer close them. His tongue was swollen with thirst; he relieved its fever by thrusting it forward from between his teeth into the cold air. How softly the turf had carpeted the untraveled avenue—he could no longer feel the roadway beneath his feet!

Doubtless, despite his suffering, he had fallen asleep while walking, for now he sees another scene—perhaps he has merely recovered from a delirium. He stands at the gate of his own home. All is as he left it, and all bright and beautiful in the
270 morning sunshine. He must have traveled the entire night. As he pushes open the gate and passes up the wide white walk, he sees a flutter of female garments; his wife, looking fresh and cool and sweet, steps down from the veranda to meet him. At the bottom of the steps she stands waiting, with a smile of **ineffable** joy, an attitude of matchless grace and dignity. Ah, how beautiful she is! He springs forward with extended arms. As he is about to clasp her he feels a stunning blow upon the back of the neck; a blinding white light blazes all about him with a sound like the shock of a cannon—then all is darkness and silence! **G**

Peyton Farquhar was dead; his body, with a broken neck, swung gently from side to side beneath the timbers of the Owl Creek bridge. ∾ **H**

ineffable (ĭn-ĕf′ə-bəl)
adj. beyond description; inexpressible

G PRIMARY SOURCE DOCUMENTS
Reread lines 270–279, and think about the main idea that is revealed by the changing point of view at the end. How do Peyton Farquhar's thoughts relate to those expressed in the **primary source** "Letter to Sarah Ballou," which you read earlier in this unit (page 594)? Remember that Sullivan Ballou was killed in battle about a week after writing the letter to his wife.

H ANALYZE STRUCTURE
"An Occurrence at Owl Creek Bridge" is a classic example of a story whose plot is structured to deliver a surprise ending. Such endings have the power to overturn all previous notions about the story. What surprise endings or intriguing plot twists can you cite from other works?

DIFFERENTIATED INSTRUCTION

FOR STRUGGLING READERS

S Targeted Passage [Lines 261–279]
This passage gives the final details of Farquhar strangling and lets readers know that he has been dying all along.

- What physical condition is Farquhar in? (lines 261–266)
- What is really happening to Farquhar now? What is he visualizing or thinking about? (lines 268–279)
- How does Farquhar die? (lines 278–279)

FOR ADVANCED LEARNERS/AP

Analyze Plot Remind students that this story has an atypical plot in many ways, largely because of its unconventional sequence. Organize students into small groups, and have each group discuss the questions in the Analysis Frame: Plot. Encourage groups to share their answers with one another.

 BEST PRACTICES TOOLKIT—Transparency
Analysis Frame: Plot pp. D21, D28

After Reading

Comprehension

1. **Summarize** What is Peyton Farquhar's background?

2. **Recall** How does Farquhar die?

3. **Clarify** Why did the soldier who visited Farquhar give him such detailed information about the bridge?

Text Analysis

4. **Make Inferences** What is the Union soldiers' reason for hanging Farquhar? Cite evidence to support your inference.

● 5. **Analyze Structure** Review the chart you created as you read. How would the story be different if it were told in chronological order?

● 6. **Examine Point of View** Citing at least two examples from the story, explain how the shifts in point of view affect the level of **suspense**. What would be different about the story if it were told entirely from the **third-person omniscient** point of view?

7. **Make Inferences about Character Development** Bierce uses sensory details to suggest Farquhar's state of mind. In each of the following episodes, what sensory details suggest that Farquhar's perceptions may be unreliable?

   • on the bridge (lines 60–70)
   • in the river (lines 161–172)
   • reaching land (lines 231–240)
   • in the woods (lines 255–260)

8. **Interpret Themes** Reread lines 80–91. Based on Farquhar's dreams of glory and his ultimate fate, what point might Bierce be making about

   • heroism   • the realities of war   • the dangers of fantasy

9. **Evaluate Narrative Devices** In your opinion, did Bierce intend Farquhar's **escape** to seem believable? Cite textual evidence to support your view.

Text Criticism

10. **Author's Style** Compare Bierce's use of realistic and fantastic elements in this story. Which label—realistic or fantastic—best describes Bierce's style? Support your answer with details.

Can we escape the INEVITABLE?

As Peyton Farquhar awaited his fate on the bridge, his mind began to wander toward the possibility of escape. Was he giving rational consideration to escape, or was his mind merely "killing time"? Do you think his thoughts were useful or destructive? Why?

AN OCCURRENCE AT OWL CREEK BRIDGE   **615**

COMMON CORE

RL 2 Determine two or more themes or central ideas of a text and analyze their development over the course of the text. **RL 3** Analyze the impact of the author's choices regarding how to develop and relate the elements of a story. **RL 5** Analyze how an author's choices concerning how to structure specific parts of a text contribute to its overall structure and meaning as well as its aesthetic impact.

Practice and Apply

For preliminary support of post-reading questions, use these copy masters:

R RESOURCE MANAGER—Copy Masters
   Reading Check p. 126
   Point of View p. 119
   Question Support p. 127
   Additional selection questions are provided for teachers on page 113.

ANSWERS   COMMON CORE RL 2, RL 3, RL 5

1. *He is a wealthy Southern planter, slave owner, and Confederate sympathizer.*

2. *He is hanged at Owl Creek Bridge.*

3. *He was a Union spy. He was trying to trick Farquhar into committing a crime.*

Possible answers:

4. *They hang Farquhar because he was caught attempting to sabotage Owl Creek Bridge. Evidence includes the suggestive conversation between Farquhar and the Federal scout (lines 102–112), the fact that he wants to be a war hero (lines 85–87), and the opening scene of the hanging (lines 1–15).*

5. ● **COMMON CORE FOCUS** *Analyze Structure Students may say there would be no suspense or surprise ending if readers knew why Farquhar is being hanged and that he does not escape.*

6. ● **COMMON CORE FOCUS** *Point of View The shifts in point of view increase the suspense in the story. When the point of view shifts from omniscient to limited in lines 42–56, readers know only how Farquhar feels. This draws them into Farquhar's experience. In Section III, the point of view again shifts from omniscient to limited. This allows readers to experience Farquhar's emotions and thoughts, creates suspense about his fate, and supports the fantasy. Without the departures into omniscient point of view, readers would not recognize the fantasy.*

7. *Farquhar's state of mind is suggested by his distorted perception of sounds and time while on the bridge, his absurdly acute senses while in the river, his odd perceptions of the surroundings and of heavenly harps when he reaches land, and the voices he hears and sinister perceptions he feels while in the woods.*

8. *Bierce suggests that heroism is a foolish dream; that war is treacherous and dangerous, not glorious or ideal; and that dreams can lead you into danger.*

9. *Answers may vary. Bierce uses many realistic details in Section I. The details get increasingly fantastic, which suggests by Section III that the escape is unlikely to be real.*

10. *Answers may vary.* **Realistic:** *military actions, conversation with Federal scout, description of scenes;* **Fantastic:** *hallucinatory imagery, escape details*

Can we escape the INEVITABLE?

Possible answer: Farquhar was merely concentrating on pleasant thoughts before being hanged. Some students may say his thoughts were useful because they took his mind off his imminent death, while others may suggest that he could have used that time to consider a real attempt at escape.

AN OCCURRENCE AT OWL CREEK BRIDGE   **615**

ANSWERS

Vocabulary in Context

VOCABULARY PRACTICE

1. *false*   5. *false*
2. *false*   6. *true*
3. *true*   7. *true*
4. *false*

R RESOURCE MANAGER—Copy Master
Vocabulary Practice p. 124

ACADEMIC VOCABULARY IN WRITING

Before students begin writing, have them make a list of the reasons why the scout might feel justified in his actions.

VOCABULARY STRATEGY: THE LATIN ROOT *lud*

COMMON CORE L 4b, L 6

For each item, help students use their knowledge of the root and context clues to determine word meaning.

Answers:

1. *interlude*
2. *delusion*
3. *illusory*
4. *prelude*
5. *collusion*

R RESOURCE MANAGER—Copy Master
Vocabulary Strategy p. 125

Interactive Vocabulary THINK central

Keywords direct students to a **WordSharp** tutorial on **thinkcentral.com** or to other types of vocabulary practice and review.

Assess and Reteach

Assess

DIAGNOSTIC AND SELECTION TESTS
Selection Tests A, BC pp. 173–176

Interactive Selection Test on thinkcentral.com

Reteach

Level Up Online Tutorials on thinkcentral.com
Reteaching Worksheets on thinkcentral.com

Literature Lesson 10: Types of Point of View
Reading Lesson 6: Recognizing Sequence and Chronological Order
Vocabulary Lesson 7: Latin Roots: Active Verbs

Vocabulary in Context

▲ **VOCABULARY PRACTICE**

Decide whether these statements using the vocabulary words are true or false.

1. A **ludicrous** TV show would probably make you cry.
2. A job that is performed **summarily** tends to take a long time.
3. An **ineffable** pleasure is likely to leave you speechless with joy.
4. Climbing a very steep ladder is an example of **oscillation.**
5. You would typically describe a standup comic's performance as **poignant.**
6. Messages **presaging** happiness tend to make a fortuneteller popular.
7. If a school day seems **interminable,** it feels like it will never be over.

WORD LIST
ineffable
interminable
ludicrous
oscillation
poignant
presaging
summarily

ACADEMIC VOCABULARY IN WRITING

• conflict • create • element • emphasis • perspective

An easily overlooked **element** of this story is the fact that Peyton Farquhar, a civilian, was "set up" by a Federal scout posing as a Confederate soldier. Write a paragraph from the **perspective** of the scout, justifying the deceit that resulted in Farquhar's death. Use at least one Academic Vocabulary word in your response.

VOCABULARY STRATEGY: THE LATIN ROOT *lud*

The vocabulary word *ludicrous* contains the root *lud*, meaning "play." This root, which may also be spelled *lus*, has its origin in Latin, the language of ancient Rome. *Lud* or *lus* is found in a number of English words from a variety of content areas. To understand words with *lud* or *lus*, use your knowledge of the root meaning and the meanings of affixes, as well as context clues.

COMMON CORE

L 4b Identify and correctly use patterns of word changes that indicate different meanings or parts of speech. **L 6** Acquire and use accurately general academic words.

PRACTICE Choose the word from the word web that best completes each sentence. Consider what you know about the Latin root and the context of each sentence. If necessary, consult a dictionary.

1. In the _____ between the scenes, a violinist performed for the audience.
2. He suffers from the _____ that he is a good golfer.
3. Though she dresses expensively, her wealth is more _____ than real.
4. As a _____ to the main act, a young, inexperienced band played.
5. As a result of the two guards' _____, a prisoner escaped.

illusory   ludicrous
interlude   **lud, lus**   prelude
delusion   collusion

Interactive Vocabulary THINK central

Go to **thinkcentral.com**.
KEYWORD: HML11-616

DIFFERENTIATED INSTRUCTION

FOR ENGLISH LANGUAGE LEARNERS

Task Support: Vocabulary Practice Have home-language group students create word webs with cognates for four of the English words in the **WORD LIST.** If their home language has no cognates for these words, ask students to identify the common suffixes in the **WORD LIST** and provide a general meaning for each one.

FOR ADVANCED LEARNERS/AP

Vocabulary in Writing Have students use at least five of the words in the **WORD LIST** to write a short paragraph that summarizes the ending of the story. As an extension, students might write from the point of view of an observer to the hanging.

Voices of the Civil War

Near the outbreak of the Civil War, writer Ralph Waldo Emerson remarked, "All arts disappear in the one art of war." In other words, the necessities of warfare—military, political, economic, and social—act somehow to discourage or diminish the creation of what might be termed "serious literature." Nevertheless, fine nonfiction writing about pressing national issues emerged in the years prior to, during, and immediately following the Civil War.

The selections beginning on page 558 include many forms of nonfiction: autobiographies, speeches, documents, letters, and diaries. Perhaps these forms served as better vehicles than poems or short stories might have for the people of the day who wanted to explore their personal responses to the war. In any case, the nonfiction here is valuable for several reasons:

- It gives readers a glimpse into the events and culture of the writers' troubled time.
- It provides each writer's personal response to what was happening all around.
- It presents a good overview of the many different factions that made up the country at the time.

Writing to Synthesize

Write an essay describing both the historical and personal insights you gained from reading the nonfiction in this unit.

Consider

- the historical facts you learned from the selections (important figures, dates, battles, and so forth)
- the personal concerns of the writers
- what you can infer about the country as a whole from the many voices of its writers

Conclude by making a comparison or analogy to our current events, concerns, and national mood.

Lincoln at Gettysburg II (1939–1942), William H. Johnson. Gouache and pen and ink on paper, 19 ³/₄" × 17 ¹/₁₆".

Extension

SPEAKING & LISTENING

Examine the image of Lincoln shown here. Based on your reading and your prior knowledge of President Lincoln, give a brief **oral critique** of how he is portrayed in this painting. Discuss the style of the work as a whole, Lincoln's placement in relation to other figures in the painting, the colors used, and any other aspects you consider important. Be sure to use precise, formal language in your speech.

 COMMON CORE

W 2 Write explanatory texts. **W 2d** Use techniques such as analogy to manage the complexity of the topic. **SL 4** Present information, findings, and supporting evidence, such that the development and substance are appropriate to purpose. **SL 6** Demonstrate a command of formal English when indicated.

COMMON CORE FOCUS

W 2 Write explanatory texts. **W 2d** Use techniques such as analogy to manage the complexity of the topic. **SL 4** Present information, findings, and supporting evidence, such that the development and substance are appropriate to purpose. **SL 6** Demonstrate a command of formal English when indicated.

Wrap-Up: Literature of the Civil War

This Wrap-Up provides students with an opportunity to revisit ideas from the nonfiction literature in this section about the Civil War and to reflect on how writers of that era responded to the major issues of their time. Urge students to reexamine their own views about the Civil War in light of insights gained from the selections.

Writing to Synthesize

Review with students that *synthesizing* means putting different parts together to make a whole. Students must combine their historical knowledge and the inferences they have made about this time period when writing their essays.

To help students write their essays, ask them to complete a Three-Column Journal with heads that correspond to the three bulleted items. Remind students that they should record as much as possible in their journals, but should plan to focus on only the best examples in their essays.

🛠 BEST PRACTICES TOOLKIT—Transparency
Three-Column Journal p. B10

Extension

- Suggest that students first write a list of facts they know about Lincoln. Then have them consider these notes as they analyze the painting.
- Remind students to consider their knowledge of the time period as well as the title of the painting during their analysis. Explain that the critique should persuade listeners with a well-supported interpretation. Encourage students to write brief notes before giving their oral critiques.

FOR STRUGGLING WRITERS

Writing Support Have students circle some of the examples in their journals to write about and find textual evidence to support their statements and inferences. For example, in response to Harriet Jacobs's slave narrative, students might identify and support her personal concern that slavery was immoral and should be abolished. From this, they can infer that slavery was a "hot topic" during this time period.

FOR ENGLISH LANGUAGE LEARNERS

Writing Topic Sentences Provide these topic sentence starters for essay support:

- One of the most important people during the Civil War period was _____.
- One popular opinion expressed by writers during the Civil War was _____.
- These writers' voices prove that the country was _____ during the Civil War.

Focus and Motivate

COMMON CORE FOCUS

RL 7 Analyze multiple interpretations of a story, evaluating how each version interprets the source text.

SUMMARY

In the first film clip from *An Occurrence at Owl Creek Bridge*, Peyton Farquhar is hanged by soldiers. When the rope breaks, he falls into the river, swims to shore, and charges off into the woods. The second clip shows his night walk and the visions he sees of his family. The third clip shows Farquhar reuniting with his wife; however, viewers are pulled back at the last moment by the sharp tightening of the noose. Farquhar's life has flashed before his eyes as he dies. The entire journey has taken place in his mind.

BACKGROUND

The actors cast as the soldiers in the film are not routine movie extras. Nearly 40 roles were cast from a pool of Civil War living history impressionists. Each actor had years of experience working to educate the public on Civil War history. They each gave careful attention to the accuracy of their appearance and deportment, giving the film an authentic feeling.

The Filmmakers' Challenge

Before students read the feature, ask them whether it is easier to express feelings, emotions, and thoughts in print than it is on film. Help students brainstorm devices that can be used to express thoughts or emotions in each genre. *Possible answers: In print, writers use point of view, internal monologue, dialogue, and description to express characters' thoughts and feelings. Filmmakers may use voice-overs, acting, shot selection, and dialogue.*

Comparing Texts: Point of View

Replay the film clips several times. Have students point out when the filmmaker uses an objective point of view (*showing soldiers loading their guns*) and when he uses a subjective point of view.

Media Study

from An Occurrence at Owl Creek Bridge
Film Clips on Media ● Smart DVD-ROM

COMMON CORE

RL 7 Analyze multiple interpretations of a story, evaluating how each version interprets the source text.

From Page to Screen

Since 1932, the short story "An Occurrence at Owl Creek Bridge" has been adapted for the screen at least four times. Its Civil War setting, heart-pounding suspense, and surprise ending make it an ideal story to adapt to film. One of the most famous versions appeared on the television series *The Twilight Zone*. In this lesson, you'll view three clips from the 2005 version to explore one of the ways Ambrose Bierce's tale has been adapted for the big screen.

The Filmmaker's Challenge

The fact that the main action of the story takes place in the mind of the character Peyton Farquhar creates a challenge for a filmmaker. To reveal a character's thoughts, a filmmaker must rely on such devices as **voice-over narration**, in which the character speaks his or her thoughts, and **flashbacks**, which present a scene from the character's memory.

In his film, director Brian James Egen provided only subtle clues that what the audience sees is not what is actually happening. "I had to create a feeling," Egen says, "from the time the rope breaks to the end, as if it was real. I wanted the audience to be taken completely by surprise, so we created the scenes as realistically as possible."

Brian James Egen directs an actor on location.

Comparing Texts: Point of View

Point of view in film can be either objective or subjective. In the **objective point of view,** the camera acts as a neutral recorder of action. It is used to show scenes as they would occur in reality. In the **subjective point of view,** the camera becomes a participant in the scene and seems to get inside a character's head by showing the viewer exactly what the character sees.

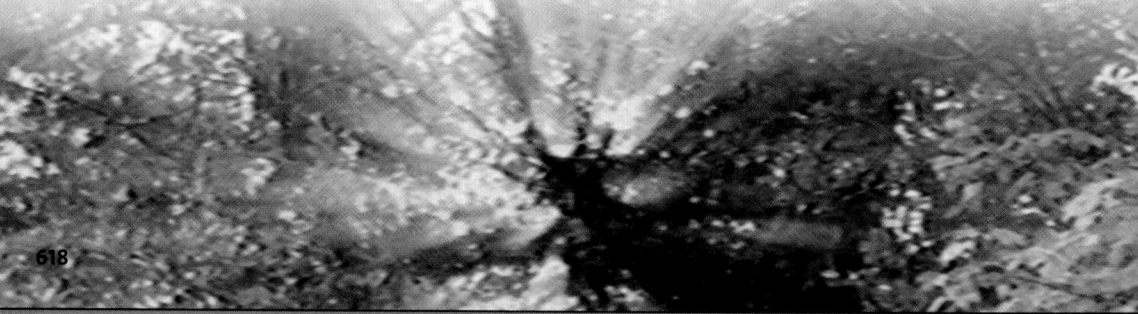

618

Media Study Resources

See resources on the **Teacher One Stop DVD-ROM** *and on* **thinkcentral.com**.

 RESOURCE MANAGER UNIT 3
Plan and Teach pp. 129–132
Summary pp. 133 †*-134 ‡*
Close Viewing p. 135

TECHNOLOGY
- Teacher One Stop DVD-ROM
- Student One Stop DVD-ROM
- Media*Smart* DVD-ROM

MediaScope on **thinkcentral.com**

* Resources for Differentiation   † Also in Spanish   ‡ In Haitian Creole and Vietnamese

Read the following passage from the story and visualize the events. When you view the clips, pay special attention to this moment in the film. How close does the film come to the scene as you imagined it? Compare Bierce's use of the **third-person limited point of view** with the point of view used by the filmmaker. Notice the ways in which both the story and the film emphasize this moment.

Media Tools
THINK central
Go to **thinkcentral.com**.
KEYWORD: HML11-619

> He felt his head emerge; his eyes were blinded by the sunlight; his chest expanded convulsively, and with a supreme and crowning agony his lungs engulfed a great draught of air, which instantly he expelled in a shriek!
>
> He was now in full possession of his physical senses. They were, indeed, preternaturally keen and alert. Something in the awful disturbance of his organic system had so exalted and refined them that they made record of things never before perceived. He felt the ripples upon his face and heard their separate sounds as they struck. He looked at the forest on the bank of the stream, saw the individual trees, the leaves and the veining of each leaf—saw the very insects upon them: the locusts, the brilliant-bodied flies, the gray spiders stretching their webs from twig to twig. He noted the prismatic colors in all the dewdrops upon a million blades of grass.

Viewing Guide

Media Smart DVD-ROM

- **Film:** *An Occurrence at Owl Creek Bridge*
- **Director:** Brian James Egen
- **Genre:** Historical thriller
- **Running Time:** 14 minutes

The three clips you'll view from *An Occurrence at Owl Creek Bridge* include Farquhar's hanging and escape, his long walk through the night to reach his wife, and, of course, the sudden ending. You may want to watch the clips more than once in order to analyze them.

NOW VIEW

CLOSE VIEWING: Media Analysis

1. **Compare Point of View** Think about the scene in the film that corresponds to the passage shown from the story. Did the filmmaker use the **objective** or **subjective point of view?** What is the effect of this point of view in comparison with Bierce's use of the **third-person limited?**

2. **Analyze Montage** A **montage** is a succession of shots, often short and without dialogue, intended to create a particular effect or suggest meaning. What do you think the filmmaker wanted to convey with the montage of Farquhar's family and home in the third clip?

3. **Evaluate the Adaptation** How effective do you think the filmmaker was in adapting Bierce's story to the big screen? Think about the following:
   - the rising suspense in the hanging scene
   - the voice-over narration
   - moments in the film that do not appear in the story

For example: "I walked into the room and sat down" becomes "Taylor slouched through the door, sank into a chair, and glared at everyone."

ANSWERS

CLOSE VIEWING: Media Analysis

Possible answers:

1. *Subjective: viewers see and hear Farquhar's experience as he escapes. In contrast, Bierce's use of the third-person keeps the reader more distant.*

2. *The montage shows what goes through Farquhar's mind in the moment before he dies. He sees the things he cares most about—his wife, children, and home.*

3. *The adaptation is mainly effective. Suspense is high in the moments before the hanging. The filmmaker uses voice-over narration of Farquhar's thoughts, but the elements of the film that do not appear in the story detract from the effectiveness of the adaptation.*

Teach

Viewing Guide

1. Tell students that they will be asked to compare the points of view in the film and the story. Urge them to pay attention to the lack of dialogue. The only words are the voice-over narration of Peyton Farquhar.

2. Explain that the story takes place during the American Civil War and that Farquhar is being hanged for attempting to burn Owl Creek Bridge.

R RESOURCE MANAGER—Copy Master
Close Viewing p. 135

Use this resource with the Viewing Guide:

🔘 **Media*Smart* DVD-ROM**

MEDIA STUDY WRAP–UP

Have students summarize what they have learned about how point of view differs in film and short story.

RETEACH

For students who are unable to apply the Media Study skills, select from these reteaching options:

- **Experiencing Events From First-Person Point of View** Give students a short news item from the newspaper and ask how they might rewrite it as a journal entry from the first-person point of view. *(They would change pronouns to* I *and* we *and give vivid descriptions of sights, sounds, and feelings as though the event were happening to them.)*

- **Writing a Film Script** Make a two-column chart on the board, labeling one column "Real Life" and one column "Film Script." Have students select an episode from a typical day in their lives, e.g., taking a science test, getting together with friends. Have students describe their actions in the episode from the first-person point of view. Write their responses in the "Real Life" column. When you have several responses, ask students to change each one into a dramatic third-person limited action point of view.

Media Tools
THINK central

Media study keywords point to **MediaScope**, a Web site that helps students strengthen media analysis and production skills.

Focus and Motivate

COMMON CORE FOCUS

W 2a–f Write informative/explanatory texts to examine and convey complex information; include formatting, graphics, and multimedia; develop topic thoroughly by extended definitions or other information. **W 4** Produce clear and coherent writing. **W 5** Develop and strengthen writing by revising, editing, rewriting, or trying a new approach. **W 6** Use technology to produce and publish individual writing products. **W 7** Conduct short research projects to answer a question. **W 8** Gather information from multiple sources and follow a standard format for citation. **W 9b (RI 1)** Draw evidence from informational texts to support analysis. **L 1a–b** Apply the understanding that usage is sometimes contested; resolve issues of contested usage. **L 2** Demonstrate command of the conventions of standard English capitalization, punctuation, and spelling. **SL 5** Make strategic use of digital media.

WRITE WITH A PURPOSE

Help students to choose a topic by identifying issues or people that are frequently in the news. Subjects that surface repeatedly in conversations with friends or at home may also point them toward a topic for an article.

COMMON CORE TRAITS

Review the *COMMON CORE TRAITS* with students, focusing on the development and organization of ideas. Compare the list of traits with the rubric on page 627.

ADDITIONAL TASKS

Write About the Environment Write an online feature article about how people interact with the natural world.
Possible topics: parks and other green spaces; best places to swim or hike in your community

Write About Education Write an online feature article on learning outside of the classroom. Try focusing on a certain age group, such as teens.
Possible topics: mentoring, field trips, apprenticeships; internships; learning traditional crafts, outdoor survival skills

Writing Online

THINK central

The following tools are available online at **thinkcentral.com** and on **WriteSmart CD-ROM**:
- Interactive Graphic Organizers
- Interactive Student Models
- Interactive Revision Lessons

Writing Workshop
INFORMATIVE TEXT

Online Feature Article

Essential Course of Study ECOS

In this unit, you discovered the events, figures, and literature of the Civil War. The World Wide Web is home to discussions about this era and about the significant issues of today. Now, you will write about one legacy of your era in an **online feature article**—an informative piece of writing on a topic or trend.

 Complete the workshop activities in your **Reader/Writer Notebook**.

WRITE WITH A PURPOSE

WRITING TASK

Inform your audience by writing an **online feature article** that answers this research question: What is one topic, trend, person, or phenomenon that has defined *your* time? Choose a topic that people will still read and talk about 100 years from now.

Idea Starters
- a ground-breaking technology
- an important figure, such as an inventor or human-rights crusader
- an event, such as a presidential election, a war, or a terrorist attack
- a social or environmental issue

THE ESSENTIALS

Here are some common purposes, audiences, and formats for online feature articles and other informative/explanatory writings.

PURPOSES	AUDIENCES	FORMATS
• to inform readers about a topic	• classmates and teacher	• magazine article
• to help readers gain a unique perspective on the topic	• friends and family on a social networking site	• wiki article
		• news report
		• blog posting
	• Web users with similar interests	• podcast
• to develop and maintain an online readership	• community members	• video blog

COMMON CORE TRAITS

1. DEVELOPMENT OF IDEAS
- provides an engaging **introduction** with a clear **controlling idea**
- develops the topic and supports it with **evidence**, such as **facts, extended definitions, concrete details,** and **quotations**
- provides a **concluding section** that supports the information

2. ORGANIZATION OF IDEAS
- logically **organizes** complex ideas, concepts, and information to **create a unified whole**
- uses appropriate and varied **transitions** and **syntax** to create cohesion and connect ideas
- includes **formatting, links, graphics,** and **multimedia**

3. LANGUAGE FACILITY AND CONVENTIONS
- uses **precise language, domain-specific vocabulary,** and **literary techniques**
- establishes and maintains a **formal style** and **objective tone**
- employs correct **grammar, mechanics,** and **spelling**

Writing Online

Go to **thinkcentral.com**.
KEYWORD: HML11N-620

Writing Workshop Resources

 RESOURCE MANAGER UNIT 3
Plan and Teach pp. 137–140
Prewriting–Editing pp. 141–145
Writing Support p. 148*

TECHNOLOGY
- **Teacher One Stop DVD-ROM**
- **Student One Stop DVD-ROM**
- **WriteSmart CD-ROM**
- **GrammarNotes DVD-ROM**
- **Writing Center on thinkcentral.com**

*See resources on the **Teacher One Stop DVD-ROM** and on **thinkcentral.com**.*

---

* Resources for Differentiation

Planning/Prewriting

 COMMON CORE **W 2a–f** Write informative/explanatory texts to examine and convey complex information. **W 6** Use technology to produce and publish individual writing products. **W 7** Conduct short research projects to answer a question.

Getting Started

CHOOSE A TOPIC

Use the Idea Starters on the previous page to brainstorm several topics that interest you and will likely interest your audience. Come up with at least three ideas for a topic, and then do a preliminary search online for each one. Choose a topic that has ample available information, but isn't so broad that you can't write a short article on it. Be sure to frame your topic in the form of a specific, tightly focused **research question** to help guide your research and writing.

THINK ABOUT AUDIENCE AND PURPOSE

As you prepare to write your article, consider your **audience** and **purpose**. Understanding your audience will help you know what information to include and what **voice** and **style** to use while writing. Knowing your audience and purpose will also help you decide where to publish your online article.

FIND MULTIPLE AUTHORITATIVE SOURCES

Look for reputable sources in your school and local libraries and on the Web. Determine the strengths and limitations of each source by considering whether it is appropriate for your **audience** and **purpose**.

Choose authoritative online sources by looking for sites that are developed by experts in their field and that include information that can be verified by other sources. Find articles from official news sources, such as magazines and newspapers, or educational publications. Make sure you don't rely too heavily on just one source.

Record the title, author, and page number or Web address for each source. Remember, it's your responsibility to avoid plagiarism.

See pages 1344–1351 for more information on locating and evaluating potential sources.

▶ **TIPS FOR GENERATING TOPIC IDEAS:**
- Review national and international news sources for interesting current events.
- Visit community Web sites for popular topics of conversation.
- Read blogs or wikis that your teachers or classmates recommend, especially ones that your peers contribute to.
- Consider major events that have affected your life.

▶ **ASK YOURSELF:**
- What **background information** do I need to include? For example, are there **domain-specific vocabulary terms** that I should explain or define?
- What aspects of this topic might my audience wish to learn more about?
- Where will I publish, or post, my article?

▶ **WHAT DOES IT LOOK LIKE?**

Sources	Notes
www.cnn.com/ELECTION/2008/results/president/	results of 2008 election for U.S. president
Book: _Narrative of the Life of Frederick Douglass_	Frederick Douglass's autobiography
www.biography.com/articles/Barack-Obama-12782369	comprehensive biography of Barack Obama

---

DIFFERENTIATED INSTRUCTION

FOR ENGLISH LANGUAGE LEARNERS

Language: Reinforce Terms Write these terms on the board and review them with students:

- _research:_ careful study and investigation in a topic to find information
- _sources:_ works that supply information, such as books and Web sites
- _link:_ highlighted or underlined words or phrases on a Web page that connect to a new Web page or different Web site
- _post:_ to send items to a Web site for viewing

- _storyboard:_ a drawing that shows how text features, words, and images will be organized in an online feature article
- _navigate:_ to move from one section of an online feature article to another
- _multimedia:_ different forms of media, such as video, photographs, and music, used together to communicate information
- _citation:_ a text note or footnote naming the sources used in an article

---

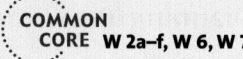

Planning/ Prewriting

COMMON CORE **W 2a–f, W 6, W 7**

▶ **CHOOSE A TOPIC** It may be difficult for students to identify subjects that define their era. Ask: "What topic, trend, or person made the news just one year ago, or five years ago? Is that still being talked about today? What does it mean to you?" Here is one way to do the research online:

- Type "best of 2011" or any other fairly recent year into your browser window.
- Scan the results for year-end "best of" features reported on in magazines, newspapers, blogs, and other venues. Depending on the media outlet, any number of people, inventions, and topics will be presented.
- Ask: "Is this subject still important today? Will it matter five years from now? How will it affect my community and myself ten years from now?" Tell students they should choose a subject that had an impact on people's lives both then and now.

▶ **THINK ABOUT AUDIENCE AND PURPOSE** Give students examples of different voices and styles they can write in, such as chatty and informal or matter-of-fact and formal. Remind them that whatever voice or style they use, it should be appropriate for their audience and purpose.

▶ **FIND MULTIPLE AUTHORITATIVE SOURCES** Remind students of the pitfalls of relying on just one or two sources, such as developing a perspective that is too narrow. Broadly-based research ensures students hear multiple viewpoints. Let them know that good research leads to a better article. You may want to set a minimum on the number of sources students use for their articles. Depending on the subject, it may be appropriate to ask for a certain number of primary and secondary sources as well.

R RESOURCE MANAGER—Copy Masters
Plan and Teach pp. 137–140
Prewriting–Editing pp. 141–145
Writing Support p. 148*

Planning/Prewriting *continued*

▶ **COLLECT AND SYNTHESIZE INFORMATION** To help in synthesizing research, encourage students to read for a purpose. Have students look for recurring themes or ideas among their sources. Once identified, they can use the information to make connections to what they already know. Point out to students that they synthesize information every day, either in their studies or when learning a new skill. For example, they may know the basics of how to steer a vehicle from riding a bike, pushing a grocery cart, or operating a video game. They will collect and synthesize all of their steering skills in a certain way when they learn to drive a car.

▶ **DRAFT A CONTROLLING IDEA** Tell students to keep their research questions in mind as they learn more about their topics. While reading, students should ask themselves: How does this address my research question? Their answers will help in shaping a controlling idea. Remind students that they may want to revise or rework their controlling ideas several times as they research their online article.

▶ **GENERATE A STORYBOARD** Have students think about elements that they like to see on a Web page. During their research, students should choose the pages they found easiest or most pleasurable to read. Ask: "Which elements contributed to a good user experience?" Guide students in incorporating headings, links, and other text features into their storyboards.

YOUR TURN Direct students to work in pairs to critique their storyboards. Encourage them to emphasize readability, ease-of-use, and attention-grabbing elements of their Web pages.

💿 **Write*Smart* CD-ROM**

Writing Center on thinkcentral.com

Planning/Prewriting *continued*

Getting Started

COLLECT AND SYNTHESIZE INFORMATION

While researching your topic, keep a record of **relevant quotations, facts, details, examples,** and **multimedia** that you come across. As you take notes, look for opportunities to **synthesize** information—to make connections and combine facts in a way that provides a broader understanding of the subject. Use a variety of reputable sources and your own previous knowledge to draw original conclusions about your topic.

▶ **WHAT DOES IT LOOK LIKE?**

> "From the first I saw no chance of bettering the condition of the freedman until he should ... become a citizen."
> —Frederick Douglass, 1892

> "One hundred years later, the life of the Negro is still sadly crippled by the manacles of segregation and the chains of discrimination."
> —Martin Luther King Jr., 1963

> For over a century, influential African Americans fought for equality under the law in addition to freedom from slavery.

DRAFT A CONTROLLING IDEA

Craft a **controlling idea**, or thesis statement. Your research question can serve as the basis for your controlling idea, which should precisely identify what you want your audience to learn about your topic. Modify or refine your controlling idea as you draft.

▶ **WHAT DOES IT LOOK LIKE?**

> The years of struggle by past African-American leaders created the foundation for the historic election of the first African-American president of the United States.

GENERATE A STORYBOARD

Use a storyboard to outline how your information will appear on Web pages. Keep in mind that Web users are less likely to notice elements on the right side and bottom of the page, or on pages that appear cluttered. Use **text features,** such as headings and links, to organize your Web pages and to make them easy to read and navigate. Plan how you will use multimedia and where you will locate it on the page or via a link.

▶ **WHAT DOES IT LOOK LIKE?**

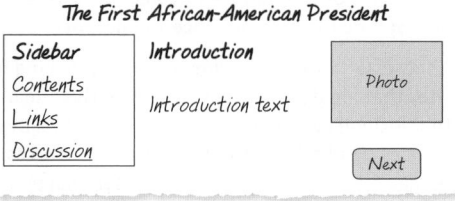

PEER REVIEW Show your **controlling idea** to another student and explain your **audience** and **purpose.** Discuss your evidence and how well it supports your controlling idea.

YOUR TURN List possible topics in your *Reader/Writer Notebook.* Choose a specific topic that interests you and draft a research question. Gather your sources, synthesize the information, and draft a controlling idea. Generate a storyboard to plan your article.

DIFFERENTIATED INSTRUCTION

FOR ENGLISH LANGUAGE LEARNERS
Writing: Collecting Information Provide students with sentence frames such as these to help them collect information from each source:

- The source I am reading is _____.
- The source article talks mostly about _____.
- The source article uses evidence such as _____ and _____ to support its claims.

FOR STRUGGLING WRITERS
Audience and Purpose Bring in printed copies of online feature articles. Have students work with partners to study the style and voice of each article. Ask them to answer the following questions:

- What is the article's style and voice?
- For whom is the article written?
- How do style and voice make it a successful or unsuccessful article?

Drafting

COMMON CORE

W 4 Produce clear and coherent writing. **W 8** Gather information from multiple sources and follow a standard format for citation. **W 9b (RI 1)** Draw evidence from informational texts to support analysis. **L 2** Demonstrate command of conventions.

The following chart shows a structure for outlining a **clear** and **coherent** online feature article.

Organizing Your Online Feature Article

INTRODUCTION

- Grab your audience's attention with a **compelling quotation, question,** or **anecdote.**
- Supply your audience with the **background information** they need to grasp the topic.
- Use **precise language** to introduce a clear **controlling idea,** or thesis statement.
- Establish a **formal style** and an **objective tone,** or attitude.

BODY

- Organize information in a logical way, so that each new idea builds upon previous ideas. Include the most **significant** and **relevant facts, quotations, definitions,** and **multimedia.**
- Use appropriate **transitions** to link ideas, create cohesion, and clarify relationships.
- **Vary your syntax** instead of relying on the same words, phrases, and clauses.
- Use literary techniques, such as **metaphors, similes,** and **analogies,** to help your audience understand complex or abstract ideas and to add interest.
- Document the **source** of each idea. See pages 1344–1351 for information on citations.

CONCLUDING SECTION

- Restate your **controlling idea** and explain the significance of your topic.

GRAMMAR IN CONTEXT: INCORPORATING QUOTATIONS

Quoting primary sources and experts increases your credibility and gives readers a broader understanding of your topic. When quoting someone else's work, cite your source both in the running text of your article and in the Works Cited section. Follow these guidelines:

- Use quotation marks at both the beginning and the end of someone else's direct words.
- Integrate short quotations into your own sentences.
- Use ellipses to indicate where you've omitted any words from the quotation.
- Enclose the author's last name and the page number of the quote in parentheses at the end of the sentence. If you've already referenced the author, include only the page number.
- Hyperlink your in-text citation to your Works Cited section.

> American historian Steven Lawson said of Obama's historic victory, "In becoming commander in chief, Obama has inherited the legacy of countless civil rights warriors who risked their lives ... to gain the right to vote, not as an empty symbol, but as a genuine tool for freedom and equality" (2).

See pages 1376–1377 for Modern Language Association guidelines for creating a Works Cited list.

YOUR TURN

Develop a first draft of your online feature article. Make sure to integrate quotations. Add multimedia and links to aid understanding and navigation.

FOR ENGLISH LANGUAGE LEARNERS

Writing: Quotations Students may benefit from reading interviews and articles with many quotations. Have students pair off and read such articles to one another aloud. Point out how the syntax, or structure, of spoken—or quoted—speech differs from that of purely written speech. Help students to notice that quotations add variety and interest to their online articles.

FOR STRUGGLING WRITERS

Partial Quotations Provide students with printed copies of a variety of long quotations from published online articles. Have students independently practice shortening the quotations by turning them into partial quotations with ellipses as needed. Students may then work in pairs to check one another's work for sense and appropriate punctuation.

Practice and Apply

Drafting

COMMON CORE W 4, W 8, W 9b (RI 1), L 2

▶ **INTRODUCTION** Tell students that the introduction is their opportunity to pull readers into their article. Encourage students to spend some time, free from distractions, to think about their introduction. Ask students if any facts, ideas, or quotations grabbed their attention while doing the research. Have them consider creative ways to use that information when writing their introduction.

▶ **BODY** Remind students that the most relevant ideas will go into the body of their article. Tell students to keep the article's controlling idea in mind as they write. Have them pay particular attention to their use of transitions. Remind students that effective transitions connect ideas together and help readers make sense of any difficult concepts.

▶ **CONCLUDING SECTION** Tell students that by restating the controlling idea, they signal readers that the article is coming to a close. Their restated controlling idea now helps their readers to synthesize all that they have read up to this point. Remind students that their concluding section must include a *Works Cited* list for all of the sources, print and nonprint, that they credit in their articles.

GRAMMAR IN CONTEXT: INCORPORATING QUOTATIONS

Give students these additional guidelines for incorporating quotations:

- Use only interesting, relevant quotations.
- If you can find a better way to express what someone else has said, then do so, but be sure to still attribute the idea to the source.
- Do not feel compelled to use full quotations. Partial quotations are fine, as long as they are kept in the context of their original intent.

YOUR TURN

Ask students to complete the **Your Turn** activity independently. Have students go back and highlight all quotations used in their drafts. Ask students to make sure they have included citations for all quotations. Suggest that students write their drafts double-spaced so that they can make revisions easily later.

For interactive revision tools, see

 Write*Smart* CD-ROM

Writing Center on thinkcentral.com

Revising

 COMMON CORE W 2a–b, W 5, SL 5

Model the Skill Using a draft feature article on a transparency or electronic whiteboard, model how to use the questions, tips, and strategies suggested in the chart to evaluate and revise. Consider using a feature article written by a student from a different class or from a previous year. Be sure to remove the writer's name from the article so that the writer remains anonymous.

YOUR TURN Encourage peer reviewers to begin by saying something positive about their partner's work. Tell students to use a colored pen—any color but red—to mark where their partner's article needs revision. Remind them to mark the article to show where use of multimedia is distracting. Have students offer their partners kindly worded suggestions on how to make their articles easier to navigate.

For interactive revision tools, see

💿 **WriteSmart CD-ROM**

Writing Center on thinkcentral.com

Revising

Best-selling author Michael Crichton once said, "Books aren't written—they're rewritten." Revising, rewriting, and, if necessary, trying a new approach are essential to the writing process. The following chart will help you revise and rewrite where necessary.

ONLINE FEATURE ARTICLE

Ask Yourself	Tips	Revision Strategies
1. Does my introduction grab the audience's attention?	▶ **Highlight** attention-grabbing quotes, anecdotes, or facts.	▶ **Add** a compelling question, quotation, or anecdote to engage your audience.
2. Is my controlling idea clear and appropriate for my task, purpose, and audience?	▶ **Underline** your controlling idea, or thesis statement.	▶ **Add** a controlling idea if one is missing. **Rework** your existing one if it is unclear or doesn't fit your task, purpose, or audience.
3. Is my organization logical, effective, and easy to navigate?	▶ **Circle** headings, links, and menu options.	▶ **Group** related paragraphs under boldfaced headings. **Add** more links to your menu to allow users to easily move to each section of your article.
4. Did I use significant and relevant evidence and multimedia to support my controlling idea?	▶ **Place a check mark** next to relevant evidence and multimedia that supports your controlling idea.	▶ **Delete** information that isn't relevant to your controlling idea. **Add** additional details for any ideas that are not sufficiently supported.
5. Does my concluding section restate my controlling idea and explain my topic's significance?	▶ **Underline** your restated controlling idea and explanation of the topic's significance.	▶ **Insert** sentences that restate your controlling idea and explain your topic's significance.
6. Are all of my sources correctly cited? Have I included a Works Cited section?	▶ **Highlight** evidence. **Place a check mark** next to each citation and Works Cited entry.	▶ **Add** in-text citations and/or Works Cited entries for any evidence that hasn't been properly cited.

YOUR TURN **PEER REVIEW** Working with a partner, review your draft. Answer each question in the chart to decide how your draft can be improved. Ask: Is my use of multimedia distracting?

DIFFERENTIATED INSTRUCTION

FOR ENGLISH LANGUAGE LEARNERS

Writing: Supporting the Controlling Idea Provide students with sentence frames such as these to help them decide if they have provided evidence to support the controlling idea:

- My controlling idea states _____.
- This fact (quote, detail, example) states _____. It supports my controlling idea by _____.

FOR ADVANCED LEARNERS/PRE-AP

Analyze the Evidence Have students choose an article with a clear controlling idea from among their sources. Ask students to create a chart with headings that organize the types of evidence used, such as facts, extended definitions, concrete details, quotations, and multimedia. Students should note if each piece of evidence supported the controlling idea. Next have them create a similar chart for their articles.

ANALYZE A STUDENT DRAFT

Read this draft; notice the comments on its strengths as well as suggestions for improvement.

COMMON CORE

W 2a–b Include formatting, graphics, and multimedia; develop topic thoroughly by extended definitions or other information. **W 5** Develop and strengthen writing by revising, rewriting, or trying a new approach. **SL 5** Make strategic use of digital media.

The First African-American President
by Damien F.

▼ Contents
Introduction
History of the Civil
Rights Movement
Barack Obama's Early
Political Career
The 2008 Campaign
Conclusion

▼ Additional Resources
Photos
Speeches
Discussion Board
Feedback

Introduction

In 1863, Abraham Lincoln declared in his Gettysburg Address that all men are created equal. At the time, the Civil War raged between the South and the North. Many African Americans were enslaved, and even those who were free were denied many rights—including the right to vote. No one attending Lincoln's address could have imagined that 145 years later, an African American would be elected president of the United States.

Barack Obama started his political career as a little known politician in Illinois, the same state that Lincoln hailed from. Before Obama won election to the U.S. Senate, only two previous African Americans had been elected as senators since Reconstruction. Four years later, he ran for president and won with 53 percent of the vote.

President Obama

The work of many influential African Americans built toward this historic election. Frederick Douglass's autobiography and speeches made many Americans reevaluate their views of enslaved and free African Americans. One hundred years later, Martin Luther King, Jr., and Malcolm X worked for equality under the law for African Americans. Though they all had different philosophies and methods, their efforts and those of many other Civil Rights leaders led to monumental changes in the law and throughout society.

Next: History of the Civil Rights Movement

Damien grabs the attention of his audience with a **compelling introduction**.

Damien could add more depth to his article by providing **additional details** and links to external sources.

Damien uses **transitions** to create cohesion and connect ideas.

 LEARN HOW Link to External Sources Damien can provide his readers with links to **authoritative** Web sites for more background information, biographies, and extended definitions. He provides sufficient links in the bottom paragraph, but not in his second paragraph. He decided to add a link to the election results.

DAMIEN'S REVISION TO *INTRODUCTION*

Four years later, he ran for president and <u>won with 53 percent of the vote</u>.
Link to official 2008 presidential election results ∧

 YOUR TURN Use feedback from your peers and teacher as well as the "Learn How" lesson to revise or rewrite parts of your online feature article. Make sure that any links you provide are only to reliable Web sites.

FOR ENGLISH LANGUAGE LEARNERS

Link to External Sources To make sure students understand the importance of external source links, have students view live online feature articles. Explain that writers sometimes link to other pages or sections within the article. At other times they may link to outside or external, Web sites. Remind students that for this task, they will want to focus on providing links to external sources for their online articles.

Read through an online article with students, pausing to click on external links as you encounter them. Lead them in a discussion of what each link adds to that particular point in the article. Ask: "Why did the writer place a link here? How does the link enrich the article?" Finally, have students work with a partner to determine the best places to link to external sources within their own articles.

ANALYZE A STUDENT DRAFT

Explain that the Student Draft on this page is the first screen of an online feature article. Model reading the draft and the annotations in blue that explain the student's language choices. Explain that the *Learn How* mini-lesson has helpful information about a way to improve the student draft as well as their own.

LEARN HOW Link to External Sources

- Tell students that their online readers will expect to see links to external sources sprinkled throughout their article. When done properly, links can add richness to their articles by providing additional information and interactivity.

- Have students read through their drafts, looking for places that could benefit from links to external Web sites.

- Remind students to link only to reliable and relevant Web sites. Suggest they look through their source material and *Works Cited* lists for possible links.

 YOUR TURN Have students complete the **Your Turn** independently. Tell students to review their drafts to make sure they have provided enough background information, biographical data, or extended definitions about their topic. Tell students to place asterisks in the margins next to places that could be improved by a link to an external source.

For interactive revision tools, see

Write*Smart* CD-ROM

Writing Center on <u>thinkcentral.com</u>

Editing and Publishing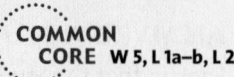

COMMON CORE W 5, L 1a–b, L 2

GRAMMAR IN CONTEXT: PREPOSITIONS AND USAGE

For practice, have students identify all of the prepositions in the introduction to their articles. Next, tell students to revise the sentences below by removing the prepositions from the end of the sentence. Challenge students to tighten up the wording of the sentences while keeping the same meaning as the originals.

1. The skating rink is where they came out <u>of</u>. (*They came out of the skating rink.*)

2. Abby moved the plant that the teacher's desk was <u>by</u>. (*Abby moved the plant that was by the teacher's desk.*)

3. Desi and Jake toured the factory that their grandmother worked <u>at</u>. (*Desi and Jake toured the factory where their grandmother worked.*)

PUBLISH YOUR WRITING

Brainstorm with students about additional ways to publish their online feature articles.

 YOUR TURN Allow time for students to proofread their articles. Remind them to check their drafts to see how they used prepositions and how they could improve their writing by using prepositions more effectively.

Editing and Publishing

 COMMON CORE

W 5 Strengthen writing by editing. **L 1a–b** Apply the understanding that usage is sometimes contested; resolve issues of contested usage. **L 2** Demonstrate command of the conventions of standard English capitalization, punctuation, and spelling.

In the editing stage, you proofread your article to eliminate errors. You also need to ensure that all of your links and multimedia elements are functioning properly. Lastly, do a final check to make sure that your pages are formatted consistently and are easy to read and navigate.

GRAMMAR IN CONTEXT: PREPOSITIONS AND USAGE

A **preposition** is a word that relates one word to another word. Common prepositions are *at, by, for, from, in, of, on, to,* and *with.* Many people believe that a sentence should never end with a preposition. In some cases, it is now acceptable to end a sentence with a preposition, especially if rewording the sentence would make it awkward. However, a sentence should not end with a preposition if you could tighten up the wording and keep the same meaning.

Discuss with a partner the following example from Damien's introduction and decide which version you both think is more appropriate. If your teacher requires you to follow a particular style manual, such as *The Chicago Manual of Style,* you may use that as a reference.

> **Damien's original sentence:**
> Barack Obama started his political career as a little known politician in Illinois, the same state that Lincoln hailed from.
>
> **Damien's revised sentence:**
> Like Lincoln, Barack Obama started his political career as a little known politician from Illinois.

PUBLISH YOUR WRITING

When you are finished proofreading your article, you are ready to post it online.

- Send an e-mail or text message to friends and family to notify them that your article is available for viewing.
- Post a link to your article in related forums or online communities.
- Update your status on any social media networks that you participate in to include a link to your article.
- Exchange links with classmates who have written articles on similar topics.

YOUR TURN Carefully proofread your article and correct any errors in conventions. Be sure to check that you have used prepositions effectively. After you've completed these final touches, publish your online feature article.

DIFFERENTIATED INSTRUCTION

FOR ENGLISH LANGUAGE LEARNERS

Language: Prepositions First, ask for students' help in listing prepositions on the board, such as *above, across, at, before, during, for, in, of, out, over, to, up,* and *with.* Ask students to suggest phrases using the prepositions, for example, *the light above the piano, bread with water, in the bottle, out of the house.* As examples are called out or written on the board, make sure that the prepositions have been used correctly.

FOR STRUGGLING WRITERS

Identifying Prepositions Use a draft of an online feature article on a transparency or interactive whiteboard. Begin by underscoring several prepositions in the article. Then point to random words or phrases within the article and ask: "Is this a preposition?" If the word or phrase is a preposition, underscore it. If the word or phrase is not a preposition, circle it and move on to the next example. Finally, have students work in pairs to mark copies of their own drafts for prepositions.

Scoring Rubric

Use the rubric below to evaluate your online feature article.

ONLINE FEATURE ARTICLE

SCORE	COMMON CORE TRAITS
6	• **Development** Effectively introduces a topic; states an insightful controlling idea; is well-developed with significant, relevant evidence; ends powerfully • **Organization** Organizes complex ideas to create a unified whole; uses appropriate transitions and varied syntax; effectively uses formatting and multimedia; correctly cites sources • **Language** Uses precise wording effectively; maintains formal style and objective tone; shows strong command of conventions
5	• **Development** Competently introduces a topic; states a clear controlling idea; is well-developed with relevant evidence; ends capably • **Organization** Logically organizes ideas; uses transitions and varied syntax; uses formatting and multimedia; correctly cites sources • **Language** Uses precise language; generally maintains formal style and objective tone; makes a few errors in conventions
4	• **Development** Adequately introduces a topic; states a controlling idea; includes some relevant evidence; ends adequately • **Organization** Is mostly well-organized; uses adequate transitions, syntax, formatting, and multimedia; cites most sources • **Language** Needs more precise words; mostly maintains formal style and objective tone; has some errors in conventions
3	• **Development** States a controlling idea, but lacks a compelling introduction and sufficient evidence; ends with a weak concluding section • **Organization** Has weaknesses in organization; uses some transitions and variety of syntax; has inconsistent formatting, multimedia, and source citations • **Language** Sometimes uses vague language; has inconsistent style and tone; has many errors in conventions
2	• **Development** Has a weak controlling idea and introduction; does not support most ideas; ends abruptly • **Organization** Has serious organizational flaws; often lacks transitions; lacks formatting and multimedia; rarely cites sources • **Language** Uses vague language; uses informal style and tone; has major errors in conventions
1	• **Development** Lacks a controlling idea, supporting evidence, and a concluding section • **Organization** Has no organization, formatting, multimedia, or citations • **Language** Often uses vague language; has an inappropriate style and tone; shows no command of conventions

Scoring Rubric

Tell students that the best way to understand a scoring rubric is to use it to evaluate an actual piece of writing. Have students work with partners to evaluate each other's online feature article. Then have them write a brief paragraph using the language of the rubric to explain the reasons for their score.

For Rubric Bank, see

💿 Write*Smart* CD-ROM

Writing Center on **thinkcentral.com**

Assess and Reteach

Assess
Online Essay Scoring on **thinkcentral.com**

Reteach
Level Up Online Tutorial at **thinkcentral.com**

Focus and Motivate

COMMON CORE FOCUS

W 6 Use technology to update individual writing products in response to ongoing feedback.
SL 1c, d Pose and respond to questions; synthesize comments; determine what additional information is required. **SL 5** Make strategic use of digital media.

PRODUCE WITH A PURPOSE

Encourage students to review their online feature articles regularly in order to keep them fresh and updated. Remind students that on-line articles are a work-in-progress. Poor links and navigation errors can affect the credibility of their work. Have students test all the links in their articles to ensure their relevancy.

COMMON CORE TRAITS

As students update their online feature articles, have them keep in mind the *COMMON CORE TRAITS* of a successful online article.

Practice and Apply

Maintaining Your Article

Model the Skill: RESPOND TO FEEDBACK

Students may struggle to maintain objectivity when reading comments posted to their online feature articles. Tell students that spoken criticisms are sometimes easier to take because speakers use vocal nuance and facial expressions to relay messages. Written criticisms lack spoken nuance, and so may be harder to digest. Help students distinguish between strong criticisms and inappropriate comments. Advise students to make prompt and respectful replies to feedback as needed. Replies to some questions or comments may require research. If so, direct students to let the reader know they have read the comment and will make a complete reply as soon as possible.

Technology Workshop

Essential Course of Study ECOS

Updating an Online Feature Article

Unlike an article published in a print periodical, an online feature article is always a work in progress. That's because the World Wide Web is never static; content is continually being added, updated, reorganized, or deleted to accommodate new information, new multimedia, and new ideas. As the author of an online feature article, you must regularly maintain your published work. If you want readers to consider your article a reliable source, you need to keep it updated. In this workshop, you will learn how to effectively update, improve, and enhance your online article.

Complete the workshop activities in your **Reader/Writer Notebook**.

PRODUCE WITH A PURPOSE	COMMON CORE TRAITS
TASK **Update your online feature article** to replace dead links, improve design and navigation, and provide updated information on your topic.	**A SUCCESSFUL UPDATE . . .** • replaces outdated information with new content from current and reliable sources • repairs broken links • responds promptly and respectfully to readers' questions, comments, and feedback • modifies design or navigation features for greater ease in viewing and navigation • promotes growth in readership by seeking new audiences and encouraging visitors to return

COMMON CORE

W 6 Use technology to update individual writing products in response to ongoing feedback. **SL 1c, d** Pose and respond to questions; synthesize comments; determine what additional information is required. **SL 5** Make strategic use of digital media.

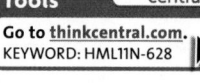

Media Tools **THINK central**
Go to **thinkcentral.com**.
KEYWORD: HML11N-628

Maintaining Your Article

Frequently visit your online feature article and spend a few minutes maintaining it. Use these guidelines to help you:

- **Keep Your Links Current** Web sites often move or remove pages. For this reason, it's essential that you regularly check all of your links and make sure that the Web address, or URL, is still functional and connects to the correct information. When you locate dead or incorrect links, update them to reflect the new URL, find suitable replacement links, or delete the links from your article.

- **Respond to Feedback** Promptly read all questions and comments posted to your article. Politely reply when appropriate; delete inappropriate comments right away. Replying thoughtfully to feedback can stimulate discussion, which encourages more reader participation and return visitors.

- **Include a *Last Updated* Date** Provide a line of text that states the date when you last updated your article. This note shows readers how current your information is and how committed you are to keeping it up-to-date.

DIFFERENTIATED INSTRUCTION

FOR ENGLISH LANGUAGE LEARNERS

Language: Reinforce Online Publication Terms As students update their online feature articles, review online publication terms to clarify the process. Write the following terms on the board and review them with students:

- *feedback*: any comments, questions, or criticisms of someone's work

- *functional*: working properly, such as a functional Web page or link

- *modifications*: changes made to a piece of work, such as to an online article

- *dynamic*: full of energy; a *dynamic* Web page is appealing both to look at and to use

- *readership*: a group or body of readers, such as all those who have viewed a writer's work

Modifying and Improving Your Article

Part of updating an online article is modifying and improving it as you receive feedback and learn more about your topic. You might modify your article for a variety of reasons, including:

- **To Improve Content** As new information about your topic becomes available, delete out-of-date information and revise your article to include the updated content, such as new links and multimedia. Make sure that any information you consider adding comes from a reliable source. If you have chosen a topic about something that changes frequently, consider adding an Updates section. Subscribing to a Web feed is a good way to stay current on your topic.

- **To Address User Feedback** Readers may offer feedback on the accuracy of your facts, your site design, or your navigational features. Before making significant changes, synthesize feedback you've received and decide what additional information or research is required. Be willing to revise your work, or even try a new approach, to address valid reader feedback.

- **To Redesign Your Web Pages** Trying a new design can give your article a more contemporary look and keep it visually appealing. You could reorganize the navigational features, add new multimedia, or try a new font. Make sure that navigation remains simple and easy for your readers.

- **To Grow Your Readership** Anytime you update or redesign your article, consider posting a status update on social media networks. Send email updates to your readers and post a link to your article on forums that your audience frequents. This way you can encourage new readers to visit and old readers to return.

> **Bethany1** (reader) said . . .
>
> Great article, but I think you need information on Rosa Parks. BTW, do you know any events planned for Black History Month?
>
> January 15, 7:45 AM
>
> ---
>
> **Allan2** (reader) said . . .
>
> I'm not sure information on Rosa Parks would fit well with Damien's topic. It might be distracting.
>
> January 15, 1:18 PM
>
> ---
>
> **DamienF** (Site Administrator) said . . .
>
> Thanks for your feedback, Bethany and Allan! I'll do a little research and think about it. But can you tell me more about why you think Parks should/should not be included? Does anyone else have any thoughts?
>
> January 15, 6:25 PM

NEWS FEED

DamienF Check out my updated feature article! I've added a new section on Civil Rights leaders and additional information on Obama's presidency. And look for a schedule of Black History Month events, coming soon!

YOUR TURN Regularly visit your online feature article. Check if your links are still functional and update, replace, or delete dead links. Politely and thoughtfully respond to questions, comments, and feedback. Keep your content up-to-date to engage your current readers and attract new ones.

FOR STRUGGLING STUDENTS

Responding to Feedback Direct students to work in small groups to come up with suitable responses to reader feedback. Provide them with a list of questions to ask for each item of feedback:

- What kind of feedback is this: comment, question, or critique?
- Is this comment appropriate?
- Does this comment require a response?
- What kind of response, if any, is required?

Encourage students to help one another in forming responses to valid reader feedback. Have them suggest updates to articles that might address reader feedback.

Teach

Modifying and Improving Your Article

Model the Skill: UPDATE INFORMATION

Show various Web articles and point out the information on the pages that can be used to determine if the article is current, such as a last updated note or an Updates section. Let them know that it is their job to sift through Web feeds and other sources that might contain new information. As they read, suggest to students that they copy and paste a list of links or a list of headlines to help them determine what additional information is required to ensure that their article remains current.

GUIDED PRACTICE Have pairs work together to verify the currency of Web articles for which you provide the links or URLs.

YOUR TURN Direct students to work in pairs to assess one another's Web pages before and after updates have been made. Have students post critiques on changes to content and text features directly to their partner's Web page. Remind them to begin by telling their partners what they liked about the changes.

Assess and Reteach

Assess

Use the *COMMON CORE TRAITS* to assess updates to students' online feature articles.

A successful update

- replaces outdated information with new content from current and reliable sources
- repairs broken links
- responds promptly and respectfully to readers' questions, comments, and feedback
- modifies design or navigation

Reteach

Some students may have difficulty modifying the design or navigation of their online articles. Ask volunteers to give the class tips on ways to improve their Web pages.

Media Tools

Media study keywords point to **MediaScope**, a Web site that helps students strengthen media analysis and production skills.

Assessment Practice

CHECK READINESS

Read aloud the paragraph under **ASSESS** and stress that this is not the full Unit Test, but a way for students to check their readiness. Have students read the skills listed under **REVIEW** and to look back in the unit or in the **Student Resource Bank** for skills they need to review.

READ THE TEXTS

Remind students to keep the unit goals in mind as they read the selections and to focus on the structure and elements of poetry.

ANSWER THE QUESTIONS

Direct students to pages R96–R103 of the **Handbook** to review test-taking strategies. Remind students:

• to read directions carefully

• to read all choices in multiple-choice questions rather than choosing the first alternative that seems to fit

---

COMMON CORE

ASSESS
Taking this practice test will help you assess your knowledge of these skills and determine your readiness for the Unit Test.

REVIEW
After you take the practice test, your teacher can help you identify any standards you need to review.

Practice Test
THINK central
Take it at **thinkcentral.com**.
KEYWORD: HML11N-630

Assessment Practice

DIRECTIONS Read these poems and answer the questions that follow.

The Wind begun to knead the Grass—
by Emily Dickinson

The Wind begun to knead the Grass—
As Women do a Dough—
He flung a Hand full at the Plain—
A Hand full at the Sky—
5 The Leaves unhooked themselves from Trees—
And started all abroad—
The Dust did scoop itself like Hands—
And throw away the Road—

The Wagons quickened on the Street—
10 The Thunders gossiped low—
The Lightning showed a Yellow Head—
And then a livid Toe—
The Birds put up the Bars to Nests—
The Cattle flung to Barns—
15 Then came one drop of Giant Rain—
And then, as if the Hands
That held the Dams—had parted hold—
The Waters Wrecked the Sky—
But overlooked my Father's House—
20 Just Quartering a Tree—

630 UNIT 3: FROM ROMANTICISM TO REALISM

DIFFERENTIATED INSTRUCTION

FOR ENGLISH LANGUAGE LEARNERS
Assessment Practice: Work Backward
Prepare students by having them read the questions before reading the passages. Have students work in pairs to find unfamiliar words in test directions and questions and follow these steps:

1. Write each word on an index card.

2. Look up the meaning in a dictionary and write it on the back of the card.

3. Use the cards to practice the words with their partner and to teach them to others.

Culture: Clarify Remind students that Dickinson wrote this poem in the 19th century, when nearly everyone baked their own bread (*"The Wind begun to knead the Grass—As Women do a Dough—" lines 1–2*). Ask students to look for additional clues that the poem describes an earlier era. (*"The Dust did scoop itself like Hands—And throw away the Road—" lines 7–8, and "The Wagons quickened on the Street—" line 9*).

Patroling Barnegat *by Walt Whitman*

Wild, wild the storm, and the sea high running,
Steady the roar of the gale, with incessant undertone muttering,
Shouts of demoniac laughter fitfully piercing and pealing,
Waves, air, midnight, their savagest trinity lashing,
5 Out in the shadows there milk-white combs careering,
On beachy slush and sand spirts of snow fierce slanting,
Where through the murk the easterly death-wind breasting,
Through cutting swirl and spray watchful and firm advancing,
(That in the distance! is that a wreck? is the red signal flaring?)
10 Slush and sand of the beach tireless till daylight wending,
Steadily, slowly, through hoarse roar never remitting,
Along the midnight edge by those milk-white combs careering,
A group of dim, weird forms, struggling, the night confronting,
That savage trinity warily watching.

ITEM ANALYSIS

COMPREHENSION AND WRITTEN RESPONSE	ITEMS	UNIT PAGES
Tone	6, 14, 15	531, 532, 535
Free Verse	11	529, 531, 532, 535
Elements of Style	1–9	547, 548, 551–553
Figurative Language	2–4, 8	547, 548, 552–554
Punctuation and Sentence Structure	1, 7, 9	547, 550–552

VOCABULARY	ITEMS	UNIT PAGES
Latin Roots	1–3	616

WRITING AND GRAMMAR	ITEMS	UNIT PAGES
Tone	1	531, 532, 535
Effective Word Choice	5, 6	560, 563, 568, 586

Practice Test

On **thinkcentral.com** students can complete an interactive version of this practice test *and* receive remediation for the skills they have not yet mastered.

FOR STRUGGLING READERS

Assessment Support Consider these options for completing the Assessment Practice.

- Have students "work backward" to review the test questions *before* reading the passages.

- Select random questions in the Assessment, and have students demonstrate *how* and *where* to look for answers.

- Ask students to locate unfamiliar words in the Assessment. Elicit the words' meaning from the class.

- Have students record useful testing words and definitions in their journals for later reference.

- Read selections or parts of them aloud to aid in student comprehension.

Reading Comprehension

Model a thinking process for answering multiple-choice questions.

1. **C is correct.** *The dashes create pauses, which in turn affect the poem's rhythm. A is incorrect because the dashes set apart lines, not words. B is not correct because there are similes and metaphors in almost every line. D is not an accurate description of where the dashes are.*

2. **D is correct.** *Kneading dough requires strength. In A, the words* gently ruffling *do not express the meaning of* knead. *B is incorrect because the image is a metaphor and has nothing to do with actual baking. C is incorrect because the poem says nothing about the wind's direction.*

3. **B is correct.** *All the comparisons are intended to help describe the storm. A, C, and D are all incorrect because they are part of the comparisons, not the subjects of description.*

4. **C is correct.** *Powerful actions include* flung *(line 3),* unhooked *(line 5), and* scoop *(line 7). A is incorrect because natural order is not addressed in the poem. B and D connote gentleness and thus are inappropriate for a storm.*

5. **B is correct.** *The wind is the subject of the image in lines 6 to 8. A and C are incorrect because the wagons and travelers are figurative, not literal. D is incorrect because the leaves and dust imply similar images.*

6. **C is correct.** *The sense of exhilaration is the dominant tone of the poem because the speaker enjoys the storm. A and B are incorrect by implications as opposites of C. D is incorrect because optimism and confidence do not suggest the excitement of the storm.*

7. **A is correct.** *Capitalization makes a word seem important. B is incorrect because rain doesn't arrive until the end of the poem. C and D are incorrect because the capitalized words, mostly nouns, do not show emotions or opinions.*

Reading Comprehension

> **Use "The Wind begun to knead the Grass—" (p. 630) to answer questions 1–8.**

1. What effect do the dashes have on your reading and understanding of the poem?
   - **A.** They tell you to read some words without emphasis because they are less important to the poem's meaning.
   - **B.** They show where similes and metaphors occur and help convey their meaning.
   - **C.** They help establish the poem's rhythm and indicate a pause after each description.
   - **D.** They call attention to rhyming words and mark the end of sentences within the poem.

2. What does the simile in lines 1–2 suggest about the wind?
   - **A.** The wind is gently ruffling the grass.
   - **B.** A windy day is a good day for baking.
   - **C.** The direction of the wind is inconsistent.
   - **D.** The wind is strong as it pushes against the grass.

3. Dickinson uses similes and personification to describe different aspects of —
   - **A.** someone's personality
   - **B.** a thunderstorm
   - **C.** a dam breaking
   - **D.** small-town life

4. The personification of the wind, the leaves, and the dust conveys a sense of —
   - **A.** natural order
   - **B.** gentle guidance
   - **C.** unpredictable power
   - **D.** domestic happiness

5. The slant rhyme of *abroad* and *road* in lines 6 and 8 draws attention to the —
   - **A.** wagons hurrying on the road
   - **B.** chaotic unruliness of the wind
   - **C.** travelers caught by the weather
   - **D.** contrast of the leaves against the dust

6. The speaker's tone in lines 1–18 is best described as —
   - **A.** fearful and serious
   - **B.** gloomy and somber
   - **C.** exhilarated and playful
   - **D.** optimistic and confident

7. Dickinson most likely uses irregularly capitalized words in this poem to emphasize —
   - **A.** key words that tell the story
   - **B.** the rhythm of the rain
   - **C.** her opinion of the events
   - **D.** emotions conveyed in the poem

8. Dickinson personifies the "Thunders" in line 10 as people who gossip to call attention to thunder's —
   - **A.** dramatic display
   - **B.** sinister rumbling
   - **C.** meaningless noise
   - **D.** frightening power

632

---

8. **B is correct.** *The adjective* sinister *aligns most closely with the word* gossip. *A is incorrect because gossip is not usually openly displayed. C and D are incorrect because gossip is usually meaningful and not frightening.*

9. **C is correct.** *Whitman repeats the first two words, and the second clause is inverted word order. Line 1 does not use the poetic techniques described in A, B, and D.*

Use "Patroling Barnegat" (p. 631) to answer questions 9–14.

9. Which poetic devices does Whitman use in line 1 to make a dramatic exclamation?

   A. Cataloging and parallelism
   B. Simile and personification
   C. Repetition and inverted word order
   D. Slant rhymes and inventive punctuation

10. By ending each line with a participle, Whitman is using —

   A. imagery to convey an idea
   B. parallelism to create rhythm
   C. details to communicate tone
   D. personification to describe an object

11. Whitman uses the irregular meter of free verse to —

   A. convey the wildness of the storm
   B. present a contrast with the subject
   C. suggest daily life near the sea
   D. establish movement in the poem

12. The effect of Whitman's catalog of sights and sounds on the beach is to —

   A. build tension
   B. emphasize ideas
   C. honor people
   D. celebrate everyday diction

13. What effect does Whitman achieve by repeating the word *through* in lines 7–11?

   A. He interrupts the chronological order of events.
   B. He mimics the sound of the wind blowing across the beach.
   C. He emphasizes the relentlessness of the darkness, the waves, and the wind.
   D. He focuses attention on how a storm damages the surrounding area.

14. Whitman's tone in lines 1–8 is —

   A. hysterical
   B. suspenseful
   C. tragic
   D. triumphant

Use both poems to answer question 15.

15. Which statement best contrasts the tone at the end of the two poems?

   A. The Dickinson poem is factual; the Whitman poem is reflective.
   B. The Dickinson poem is sad; the Whitman poem is exuberant.
   C. The Dickinson poem is peaceful; the Whitman poem is frantic.
   D. The Dickinson poem is menacing; the Whitman poem is distant.

SHORT CONSTRUCTED RESPONSE
Write three or four sentences to answer this question.

16. Whitman often repeats words and phrases in his poetry. What effect does he achieve in "Patroling Barnegat" by writing the phrases "savagest trinity" in line 4, "savage trinity" in line 14, and "milk-white combs careering" in lines 5 and 12?

Write two or three paragraphs to answer this question.

17. Compare Whitman's and Dickinson's writing styles. Which poetic devices does Dickinson use to describe a storm? Which poetic devices does Whitman use?

GO ON ➡

633

10. **B is correct.** The participles ensure that the lines end with the same verb form, which links them rhythmically. Whitman's imagery (A) tone (C) and personification (D) do not depend on having lines that end alike.

11. **A is correct.** The poet's words surge with the storm's energy. A fixed, or regular, meter would have worked just as well for B, C, or D.

12. **A is correct.** Cataloging is intended to create suspense. B is incorrect because the images do not imply ideas. C is incorrect because the images are not about people. D is incorrect because diction is not always everyday.

13. **C is correct.** Repeating through implies the storm's powerful force by showing what it can move through. A is incorrect because the lines do not address chronology. B is incorrect because while the sound of through may mimic wind, the repetition also addresses darkness and waves. D is incorrect because through does not describe damage.

14. **B is correct.** Whitman builds suspense and the possibility of imminent danger. A is incorrect because Whitman does not show the storm as out of control. C is incorrect because no specific loss is shown. D is incorrect because the lines do not show triumph.

15. **C is correct.** Dickinson's poem ends after the storm, while Whitman's ends with struggle. In A, B, and D, none of the descriptions of tone are valid for both poems.

SHORT CONSTRUCTED RESPONSE
Possible responses:

16. Through repetitions Whitman achieves an effect of emphasizing the power and turbulence of the storm. Repeating the phrases also keeps the images of whitecaps in the reader's mind.

17. The poets' styles contrast in many ways. Dickinson uses regular meter, slant rhyme, irregular capitalization, figurative language, concise diction, and inventive punctuation to describe the storm. Whitman creates drama with cataloging and repetition, and conveys images and meaning with sophisticated language.

DIFFERENTIATED INSTRUCTION

FOR ENGLISH LANGUAGE LEARNERS
Assessment Vocabulary Write these terms on the board and review them with students.

- *context clues:* surrounding words that help define an unfamiliar word
- *prefix:* a syllable placed before a noun or another prefix, altering the meaning
- *root definitions:* definitions derived from knowing parts of the words in their original languages

Vocabulary

1. **B is correct.** A streak of lightning is a pale, bluish white color. A and C are incorrect because the lightning does not display emotional reactions. D is incorrect because lightning is not leaden, or grey, in color.

2. **A is correct.** It is the logical combination of *not* and *to stop*. B and C are incorrect because they negate the meaning of the prefix. D is incorrect because the context describes sound that has not stopped.

3. **A is correct.** It is the logical interpretation of *to send back* and best describes an abating storm. B is incorrect because once a storm begins, it does not wait. C and D are incorrect because they describe human actions, not meteorological ones.

4. **D is correct.** In the context, the storm has split a tree. The other choices are incorrect because storms do not locate, make trees visible, or measure.

5. **B is correct.** Shouts of piercing laughter could be described as fiendish. A, C, and D are not synonyms for *demoniac*, nor do they make sense in context.

6. **D is correct.** The waves move quickly; they rush. A is incorrect because the waves are not described as falling. B is incorrect because growth is not relevant to the description of waves. C is incorrect because the description emphasizes rapid motion, not sound.

Vocabulary

Use context clues and the Latin word and root definitions to answer the following questions.

1. The Latin word *livere* means "to be bluish." The most likely meaning of the word *livid* as it is used in line 12 of "The Wind begun to knead the Grass—" is —
   A. extremely calm
   B. very pale
   C. in a state of shock
   D. leaden colored

2. The Latin prefix *in-* means "not" and the Latin word *cessare* means "to stop." The most likely meaning of the word *incessant* as it is used in line 2 of "Patroling Barnegat" is —
   A. continuing without interruption
   B. concluding a recent action
   C. pausing periodically
   D. resuming activity

3. The word *remit* comes from the Latin prefix *re-*, which means "backward," and the Latin word *mittere*, which means "to send." The most likely meaning of the word *remitting* as it is used in line 11 of "Patroling Barnegat" is —
   A. letting up
   B. waiting
   C. forgiving
   D. restoring

Use context clues to answer the following questions.

4. What is the most likely meaning of the word *quartering* as it is used in line 20 of "The Wind begun to knead the Grass—"?
   A. Locating
   B. Making visible
   C. Measuring
   D. Splitting into parts

5. The most likely meaning of *demoniac* as it is used in line 3 of "Patroling Barnegat" is —
   A. comical
   B. fiendish
   C. sincere
   D. thunderous

6. The most likely meaning of the word *careering* as it is used in lines 5 and 12 of "Patroling Barnegat" is —
   A. falling
   B. growing
   C. pounding
   D. rushing

Revising and Editing

DIRECTIONS Read this passage and answer the questions that follow.

> (1) With a weight of 13,632 tons and a length of 729 feet, the *Edmund Fitzgerald* was the largest carrier on the Great Lakes when it first sailed in 1958. (2) Seventeen years later, the ship would sink in Lake Superior. (3) At 2:20 p.m. on November 9th, 1975, the *Fitzgerald* departed, Superior, Wisconsin, destined for Detroit. (4) The National Weather Service issued gale warnings for the area. (5) The next day, winds gusting up to 70 knots and waves cresting as high as 30 feet shook the ship. (6) Water came onto the deck. (7) At approximately 7:15 that evening, the ship vanished from radar observation, and <u>all 29 crew members were lost</u>. (8) That fateful day of November 10, 1975, will always be remembered. (9) It was later discovered that the ship had dropped about 530 feet to the bottom of Lake Superior.

1. What change, if any, should be made in sentence 1?
   A. Change *tons* to **ton's**
   B. Insert a comma after *Lakes*
   C. Change *sailed* to **sailing**
   D. Make no change

2. What is the most effective way to revise sentence 2 to convey a more somber tone?
   A. Seventeen years later, the hefty ship would sink in Lake Superior.
   B. Seventeen short years later, the ship would sink in Lake Superior.
   C. Seventeen productive years later, the ship would sink in Lake Superior.
   D. Seventeen years later, the doomed ship would sink in Lake Superior.

3. What change, if any, should be made in sentence 3?
   A. Delete the comma after *departed*
   B. Change *9th* to **Ninth**
   C. Delete the comma after *Wisconsin*
   D. Make no change

4. Which transition word or phrase should be added to the beginning of sentence 4?
   A. As a result,   C. Shortly afterwards,
   B. In short,   D. Therefore,

5. Which vivid verb should replace the verb in sentence 6?
   A. Crashed   C. Squirted
   B. Seeped   D. Washed

6. What is the most effective way to revise the underlined portion of sentence 7 to convey a more somber tone?
   A. all 29 crew members were tragically lost
   B. all 29 crew members were unfortunately lost
   C. all 29 crew members were suddenly lost
   D. all 29 crew members were definitely lost

7. What is the most effective way to improve the organization of the paragraph?
   A. Delete sentence 5
   B. Switch sentences 5 and 6
   C. Delete sentence 7
   D. Move sentence 8 to the end of the paragraph

 STOP

635

COMMON CORE FOCUS

RL 10 Read and comprehend literature. **RI 10** Read and comprehend literary nonfiction.

INTRODUCE *GREAT READS*

In Unit 3, students have discussed a number of big questions. Invite students to tell which question they found most intriguing and why, and then focus attention on the four that appear on pages 636–637. Discuss the recommended books and their summaries, pointing out how each connects to the related question. Encourage students to choose one or more of these "great reads" to read independently.

Ideas for Independent Reading

Continue exploring the Questions of the Times on pages 514–515 with these additional works.

What DIVIDES *a nation?*

Classic Slave Narratives
edited by Henry Louis Gates Jr.

This collection of classic slave narratives provides testimony to the horrors of bondage and sheds light on the American slave experience. The volume contains two of the best-known examples of "literature of escape"—the stories of Frederick Douglass and Olaudah Equiano—as well as two narratives by women—Harriet Jacobs and Mary Prince.

Battle Cry of Freedom
by James M. McPherson

This history of the Civil War brings all aspects of the conflict to vivid life, from the momentous episodes that preceded the war, to the battles, politics, and personalities of the war itself. James McPherson provides readers with the framework they need to understand the complex economic, political, and social forces that divided the nation and led the country to war.

Journal of a Residence on a Georgian Plantation in 1838–1839
by Frances Anne Kemble

After her marriage, Fanny Kemble discovered the source of her wealthy husband's income: rice plantations that depended upon the labor of more than 600 slaves. This journal, published after her divorce, describes the appalling conditions Fanny found on one of the plantations and her attempts to improve life for the slaves there.

Is anything worth DYING FOR?

The Personal Memoirs of Ulysses S. Grant
by Ulysses S. Grant

Dying of throat cancer, Ulysses S. Grant spent his last days looking back upon the most important years of his life—the years he spent as the commander of the Union army in the Civil War. Here, in what Mark Twain called "the best [memoirs] of any general's since Caesar," Grant recalls how he managed to defeat Robert E. Lee and the Confederate army.

Co. Aytch: A Confederate Memoir of the Civil War
by Sam R. Watkins

Sam Watkins was 21 years old when the Civil War broke out. A native of Columbia, Tennessee, he didn't want to miss out on the "big show." Volunteering as a private, he served in Company H of the Maury Grays, First Tennessee Regiment. From that lowly position, Watkins fought in almost every major clash, from the battle of Shiloh to the battle of Nashville.

Lincoln
by David Herbert Donald

Pulitzer Prize–winning author David Donald tells the story of Abraham Lincoln, the man who managed to hold together a nation of vastly differing regional interests during the turmoil and tragedy of the Civil War. Donald's Lincoln emerges as ambitious yet fallible, with a remarkable capacity for growth— a man who spent his whole life learning and growing to eventually become one of our nation's greatest presidents.

636

COMMON CORE

RL 10 Read and comprehend literature. **RI 10** Read and comprehend literary nonfiction.

Why do people BREAK RULES?

Leaves of Grass
by Walt Whitman

Walt Whitman created a daring new kind of poetry that would become a major force in the world of literature. Whitman first published this volume himself, in 1855, with only 12 poems. He expanded and revised the book over the course of his life as his experiences and the nation's history changed and grew.

Letters of Emily Dickinson
by Emily Dickinson

Emily Dickinson's ingenuity, sensitivity, and wit course through her letters as well as her poetry. Compiled by a close friend, Dickinson's letters were first published in 1894, eight years after her death. Although she became increasingly reclusive and rarely saw her friends in her later years, this volume of letters shows that she thought of them often and affectionately.

Daisy Miller
by Henry James

In this short novel, a wealthy young woman named Daisy Miller takes the grand tour of Europe. In the 19th century, such a long trip was a rite of passage for well-to-do young Americans. In Rome, Daisy's friendship with an Italian man, though innocent, causes her to be shunned by her peers. Yet she refuses to change her carefree ways. By disregarding the social rules of her community, Daisy sets herself up for tragedy.

Is it important to FACE REALITY?

Shiloh: A Novel
by Shelby Foote

This modern novel gives readers an up-close impression of the battle of Shiloh from the perspectives of many different soldiers who fought in it. Each chapter consists of the first-person accounts of various narrators, Union and Confederate, telling of what transpires in their own little corner of the battle.

Ambrose Bierce's Civil War
by Ambrose Bierce, edited by William McCann

Ambrose Bierce is one of the few writers of his day who actually fought in the Civil War. As a result, his gritty depictions of battle and close observation of soldiers' daily lives have the ring of authenticity. This collection includes both personal memoirs and fictional accounts of the war.

Life in the Iron Mills
by Rebecca Harding Davis

Decades before most Americans took notice, Rebecca Harding Davis unveiled the human costs of industrialism in *Life in the Iron Mills*. She concentrated on the stunted lives of factory workers, showing the dirty hovels where they lived, their unwholesome food, their constant labor, and their lack of education. Her story was one of the first works of American fiction to acknowledge such realities. Yet Davis also looked beyond social conditions to explore her characters' hidden yearnings for artistic expression and lasting love.

Get Novel Wise **THINK** central

Go to **thinkcentral.com**.
KEYWORD: HML11-637

637

NovelWise **THINK** central

The keyword on this page points to **NovelWise,** a Web site that helps students choose a novel or other book-length work to read. **NovelWise** also provides
- study guides
- reading strategies and literary elements instruction
- presentations to introduce classic novels
- project ideas

UNIT GOALS

Included in this unit: RL 1, RL 2, RL 3, RL 4, RL 5, RL 6, RL 9, RL 10, RI 1, RI 2, RI 5, RI 6, RI 7, RI 9, RI 10, W 1, W 1a–b, W 2, W 2a–f, W 3b, W 3e, W 4, W 5, W 6, W 7, W 8, W 9, W 9a (RL 2), W 10, SL 1, SL 1a–d, SL 2, SL 4, SL 5, SL 6, L 1, L 1a, L 1b, L 2, L 2a–b, L 3, L 4, L 4a–b, L 4c, L 4d, L 5, L 5a–b, L 6

Complete text of the Common Core State Standards is found in the correlation on p. T10. Standards covered in this unit are found in the standards overview (pp. 639A–639D) and on the lesson pages where they are taught.

Preview Unit Goals

This page presents an overview of the skills and strategies covered in this unit. Explain to students that they can get more from their reading by previewing. Then ask them to skim the page to preview the skills that they will learn. Note that each strand or category of skill is color-coded on this page and throughout the unit.

Model the strategy of copying the Academic Vocabulary and writing a preliminary definition for each term. Suggest that students use **Reader/Writer Notebooks** for this purpose. Encourage them to use the terms in discussions and in writing. Also urge students to revisit each term throughout the unit and to refine its meaning.

UNIT 4

COMMON CORE

Preview Unit Goals

TEXT ANALYSIS	• Analyze descriptive language, including imagery, figurative language, repetition, and diction • Analyze regionalism and naturalism as literary movements • Analyze rhetorical techniques in literature • Identify and analyze literary elements, including setting, plot, conflict, theme, tone, and character development • Analyze irony, hyperbole, and understatement • Analyze author's perspective • Analyze primary sources • Analyze how an author's choice of genre or text structure affects the expression of a theme or topic
READING	• Make inferences and draw conclusions about characters
WRITING AND LANGUAGE	• Write an analytical essay • Use gerunds and gerund phrases • Use passive and active voice effectively
VOCABULARY	• Use knowledge of Latin and Greek roots to understand word meanings • Discriminate between connotative and denotative meanings of words • Use context clues to detemine shades of meanings • Read and understand analogies
ACADEMIC VOCABULARY	• apparent • confine • expose • focus • perceive
MEDIA AND VIEWING	• Create a class newspaper • Interpret and evaluate messages in photography and fine art • Create a visual representation

Find It Online!

Go to **thinkcentral.com** for the interactive version of this unit.

638

DIFFERENTIATED INSTRUCTION

FOR ENGLISH LANGUAGE LEARNERS

Academic Vocabulary Provide students with the definition of each Academic Vocabulary word.

apparent (ə-păr ə nt) *adj.* obvious; seeming, especially without deeper examination

confine (kən-fīn) *v.* to keep within bounds; limit

expose (ĭk-spōz) *v.* to subject to an action, influence, or condition; to make visible; to make known, especially something negative

focus (fōkəs) *n.* a center of interest; close attention, concentration; *v.* to direct toward a particular point or purpose

perceive (pər-sēv) *v.* to become aware of through the senses, especially sight or hearing; to notice; to grasp an understanding

Additional Academic Vocabulary Use the copy master to help students learn academic words they will use in subsequent lessons and on the Assessment Practice.

R RESOURCE MANAGER—Copy Masters
Academic Vocabulary p. 3
Additional Academic Vocabulary p. 4

Regionalism and Naturalism

1870–1910

Willa Cather

CAPTURING THE AMERICAN LANDSCAPE

- Regionalism and Local Color Writing
- The Rise of Naturalism
- A New Role for Women

Media Smart DVD-ROM

American Landscapes

Discover the techniques used to create stirring images of America. Page 730

639

For help in planning this unit, see

R RESOURCE MANAGER UNIT 4
pp. 1–10

INTRODUCE THE UNIT

Call students' attention to the pictures on this page. Explain that the large picture, *The Jolly Flatboatmen,* is an oil painting by American artist George Caleb Bingham. Point out that it captures a distinctive way of life in one part of America—much as many of the writers in this unit have attempted to do in their writing.

Ask students if they have heard of Willa Cather (1873–1947), the author shown in the smaller picture. Explain that Cather was a novelist and short-story writer whose work was greatly influenced by her childhood on the Nebraska prairie. Tell students that they will read one of Cather's short stories in this unit. Also note that students can read more about Cather on page 716.

About the Art American artist George Caleb Bingham (1811–1879) painted *The Jolly Flatboatmen* in 1877–1878. Bingham's views of everyday life in the West often included scenes of the Missouri River. Explain to students that a *flatboat* is a boat with a flat bottom and square ends, used to transport freight. Ironically, by the time Bingham painted this work, steamboats and America's ever-growing railroad system had largely replaced flatboats, and the colorful flatboatmen quickly were becoming a memory.

Unit Resources

See resources on the **Teacher One Stop DVD-ROM** and on **thinkcentral.com**.

R RESOURCE MANAGER UNIT 4

UNIT AND BENCHMARK TESTS

BEST PRACTICES TOOLKIT

INTERACTIVE READER

ADAPTED INTERACTIVE READER

ELL ADAPTED INTERACTIVE READER

LANGUAGE HANDBOOK

VOCABULARY PRACTICE

TECHNOLOGY

- Teacher One Stop DVD-ROM
- Student One Stop DVD-ROM
- PowerNotes DVD-ROM
- WriteSmart CD-ROM
- MediaSmart DVD-ROM
- GrammarNotes DVD-ROM
- Audio Anthology CD

Find It Online!

This unit on **thinkcentral.com** includes

- **PowerNotes** introductions to key selections
- audio support—listen or download
- **ThinkAloud** models
- **WordSharp** vocabulary tutorials
- interactive unit review and assessment

COMMON CORE STRAND

	Unit 4 Introduction pp. 640–655 • Questions of the Times • Historical Essay • Timeline • Legacy of Romanticism and Naturalism American Masterpieces: from The Adventures of Huckleberry Finn pp. 694–695 from Ethan Frome pp. 818–819	Text Analysis Workshops • Setting in Regional Literature pp. 656–657 • Social Themes in Fiction pp. 780–781	from The Autobiography of Mark Twain Autobiography pp. 658–672 Lexile: 1120 Fry: College Dale-Chall: 7.1	from Life on the Mississippi Memoir pp. 673–682 Lexile: 1120 Fry: 9 Dale-Chall: 6.5
Reading Literature	Regionalism and Naturalism pp. 642–651 RL 9 Text Analysis pp. 694–695 RL 6 Text Analysis pp. 818–819 RL 3	Regionalism pp. 656–657 RL 3 Social Themes pp. 780–781 RL 9		
Reading Informational Text	Regionalism and Naturalism pp. 642–651 RI 9 Read a Timeline pp. 652–653 RI 7		Irony and Overstatement pp. 659, 665–666, 669, 671 RI 6 Predict pp. 659–660, 664, 666, 668, 671 RI 1 Read Epigrams p. 760	Voice pp. 673, 676, 678, 680, 682 RI 6
Writing	Legacy of the Era pp. 654–655 W 7, W 10			
Speaking and Listening	Legacy of the Era pp. 654–655 SL 2, SL 4 Discuss p. 694 Discuss p. 818 SL 1a		Discuss p. 659 SL 1	
Language	Text Analysis pp. 694–695 L 1, L 1a	Regional Writing pp. 656–657 L 1a, L 3	Overstatement p. 662 L 5a Language Coach pp. 662, 663, 666 L 5a Homographs p. 672 L 4d, L 6	Paraphrase pp. 673, 676–677, 681–682 L 3 Language Coach pp. 677, 678, 681 L 1b, L 5a–b

The Notorious Jumping Frog of Calaveras County Short Story pp. 683–693	The Outcasts of Poker Flat/ from Lake Wobegon Days Short Story/Novel pp. 696–711, 712–715	A Wagner Matinee Short Story pp. 716–728	Media Study: American Landscapes Image Collection pp. 730–733
Lexile: 1620 Fry: College Dale-Chall: 7.5	Lexile: 1170 Fry: 11 Dale-Chall: 7.8	Lexile: 1470 Fry: College Dale-Chall: 7.6	
Tall Tale pp. 683, 688–689, 691 RL 3	Regionalism pp. 697, 700–701, 704, 709, 714 RL 3, RL 6 Clarify Meaning pp. 697–698, 700, 703, 704, 707–709 RL 1 Character Types p. 714 RL 6 Language Coach pp. 703, 705 RL 4	Setting pp. 717–718, 721, 723, 726–727 RL 3 Draw Conclusions about Character pp. 717, 721–722, 724–725, 727 RL 1 Theme p. 718	
			Compare Photographs and Paintings pp. 731–733 RI 7
Writing Prompt p. 693 W 3b	Writing Prompt p. 711 W 3b, W 3e		
Discuss p. 683 SL 1	Debate p. 697 SL 1	Discuss p. 717 SL 1	Compare Photographs and Paintings pp. 731–733 SL 5
Tall Tale pp. 683, 686, 688–689, 691 L 5a Understand Dialect pp. 683, 687–688, 691 L 1a Create Realistic Characters pp. 690, 693 L 1a, L 2 Thesauri and Word Knowledge p. 692 L 4c, L 5b, L 6 Language Coach pp. 686, 687 L 1a	Add Descriptive Details pp. 703, 711 L 3 Latin Roots (equ) p. 710 L 4b, L 6 Language Coach pp. 703–705, 707 L 4, L 5a–b	Music Terminology p. 728 L 6 Language Coach pp. 720, 722, 724 L 2a	

ECOS

To see the complete Essential Course of Study, see pp. T23–T27.

For additional lesson planning help, see **Teacher One Stop DVD.**

COMMON CORE

STRAND

	Linked Selections		The Law of Life	Comparing Texts: A New Role for Women
	The Open Boat Short Story pp. 734–761	**The Wreck of the Commodore** Newspaper Articles pp. 762–767	(ECOS) **The Law of Life** Short Story pp. 768–778	(ECOS) **Comparing Texts: A New Role for Women** Literary: **The Story of an Hour** pp. 782–789, 794 Informational: **Joyas Voladoras** pp. 790–792, 794 Visual: **Calvin and Hobbes** pp. 793–794
	Lexile: 980 Fry: 7 Dale-Chall: 6.3		Lexile: 910 Fry: 9 Dale-Chall: 6.5	Lexile: 970/1170 Fry: 10/8 Dale-Chall: 6.2/7–8
Reading Literature	Naturalism pp. 735, 738, 740–741, 743, 745, 749, 751–752, 754, 756–757, 759 RL 2, RL 3 Analyze Descriptive Language pp. 735–736, 738, 744, 749, 753–754, 759 RL 4 Examine Dramatic Irony p. 759 RL 6 Language Coach pp. 746, 753 RL 4		Theme pp. 769–770, 772, 774–777 RL 2, RL 9 Analyze Author's Perspective pp. 769, 772, 776–777 RL 3, RL 9 Language Coach p. 772 RL 4	Theme pp. 783, 786–788, 790, 792, 794 RL 2 Analyze Patterns of Organization pp. 783, 786–788, 791–792, 794 RL 5
Reading Informational Text	Primary Sources p. 739	Analyze Primary Sources p. 765 RI 1, RI 2, RI 5, RI 9		Theme pp. 783, 786–788, 790, 792, 794 RI 2 Organization pp. 783, 786–788, 791–792, 794 RI 5 Cartoon p. 793 RI 7
Writing	Writing Prompt p. 761 W 3b	Writing Prompt p. 767 W 2, W 2c, W 7	Quickwrite p. 769	Writing Prompt p. 789 W 9, W 10 Writing for Assessment p. 795
Speaking and Listening	Discuss p. 735 SL 1			What's the Connection? p. 783 SL 1
Language	Use Effective Description pp. 751, 761 L 1, L 3 Greek Prefixes (epi-) p. 760 L 4d, L 6 Language Coach pp. 738, 739	Language Coach pp. 763, 764	Denotation and Connotation p. 778 L 5b, L 6 Language Coach p. 773 L 4b	Use Effective Voice pp. 786, 789 L 3

The Yellow Wallpaper
Short Story
pp. 796–817
	April Showers
	Short Story
	pp. 820–832
		Wrap–Ups
		• Regionalism & Local Color
		  p. 729
		• The Rise of Naturalism
		  p. 779
		• A New Role for Women
		  p. 833
			Writing Workshop:
			Analytical Essay
			pp. 834–843
			
			Technology Workshop:
			Creating a Class Newspaper
			pp. 844–845

Lexile: 930 *Fry: 7* *Dale-Chall: 5.8*	*Lexile: 1010* *Fry: 9* *Dale-Chall: 6.8*		
First-Person Narrator pp. 797, 800, 803, 805, 808–813, 815 **RL 1, RL 3** Understand Social Context pp. 797–798, 803–804, 815 **RL 3, RL 9**	Character Development pp. 821–822, 824, 826, 830–831 **RL 3** Make Inferences about Characters pp. 821, 824–825, 831 **RL 1** Language Coach p. 827 **RL 4**		
Read a Journal Article p. 814			
Quickwrite p. 797 Writing Prompt p. 817 **W 1,** **W 1a–b**	Quickwrite p. 797	Writing to Synthesize p. 729 **W 2, W 2b** Writing to Evaluate p. 779 **W 4, W 9a (RL 2)** Writing to Compare p. 833 **W 1**	Writing an Analytical Essay pp. 834–843 **W 2a–f, W 4,** **W 5, W 7, W 9, W 10** Creating a Class Newspaper pp. 844–845 **W 6**
		Extension p. 833 **SL 1a–b,** **SL 6**	Creating a Class Newspaper pp. 844–845 **SL 1b, SL 2, SL 5**
Verb Tenses pp. 801, 817 **L 1** Word Analogies p. 816 **L 5,** **L 6** Language Coach pp. 800, 808, 809	Latin Roots (*rog*) p. 832 **L 4b, L 6** Language Coach pp. 826, 827, 829 **L 5b**		Drafting p. 837 **L 3** Editing and Publishing p. 841 **L 1, L 2b**

ECOS

To see the complete
Essential Course
of Study, see
pp. T23–T27.

For additional
lesson planning
help, see **Teacher**
One Stop DVD.

Instructional Support

Resource Manager Unit 4

UNIT SUPPORT
Academic Vocabulary, p. 3
Additional Academic Vocabulary, p. 4
Grammar Focus p. 5
Text Analysis Workshop pp. 9, 170
Writing Workshop: Analytical Essay, p. 229

SELECTION SUPPORT*

Plan and Teach
Lesson planning pages
Additional leveled selection questions
Extension activities

Student Copy Masters
Selection summaries in four languages
Skills copy masters in English and Spanish
Vocabulary preteaching and support
Reading Check and Question Support
Reading Fluency

*Available for all selections

† Available on **thinkcentral.com**.

Language Handbook
Vocabulary Practice
Best Practices Toolkit†
PowerNotes DVD-ROM†
Connections: Nonfiction for Common Core CD-ROM†

Teacher One Stop DVD-ROM
Student One Stop DVD-ROM
Media*Smart* DVD-ROM
American Landscapes
Write*Smart* CD-ROM†
GrammarNotes DVD-ROM†
WordSharp CD-ROM†

Media**Smart**
Media Studies
Changing Views of Native Americans

Illustrations Inspired by Poe

American Landscapes

Advertising in the Jazz Age

Zora Neale Hurston: Jump at the Sun

Perspectives in the News

Differentiated Instruction

STRUGGLING READERS AND WRITERS	ENGLISH LANGUAGE LEARNERS	ADVANCED LEARNERS
Resource Manager Unit 4 Additional Selection Questions Question Support Reading Fluency **Interactive Reader** **Adapted Interactive Reader** **Level Up Online Tutorials** **Audio Anthology** (with Audio summaries) **Diagnostic and Selection Tests** Selection Tests A/B	**Resource Manager Unit 4** Selection Summaries in English, Spanish, Vietnamese and Haitian Creole Skills Copymasters in Spanish **English Language Learner Adapted Interactive Reader Teacher's Guide** **ELL Adapted Interactive Reader** **Audio Tutor** **Guide to English for Newcomers** **Audio Anthology** **Audio Summaries in Multiple Languages** (on **thinkcentral.com**)	**Resource Manager Unit 4** Additional Selection Questions Ideas for Extension **Diagnostic and Selection Tests** Selection Tests B/C

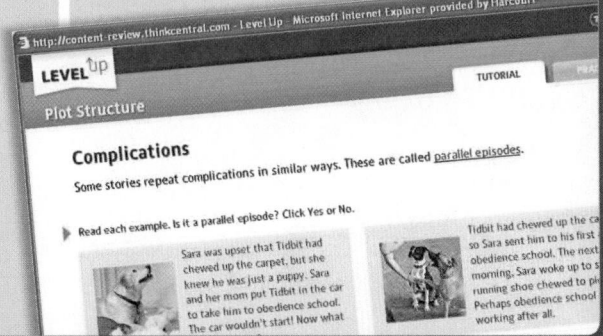

Assessment and Reteaching

Diagnostic and Selection Tests

Unit and Benchmark Tests

ThinkCentral Online Assessment:
- All program assessments
- Level Up Online Tutorials

ExamView Test Generator on the Teacher One Stop DVD-ROM

Online Essay Scoring on **thinkcentral.com**

ThinkCentral Online Reteaching:
- Level Up Online Tutorials
- Reteaching Worksheets

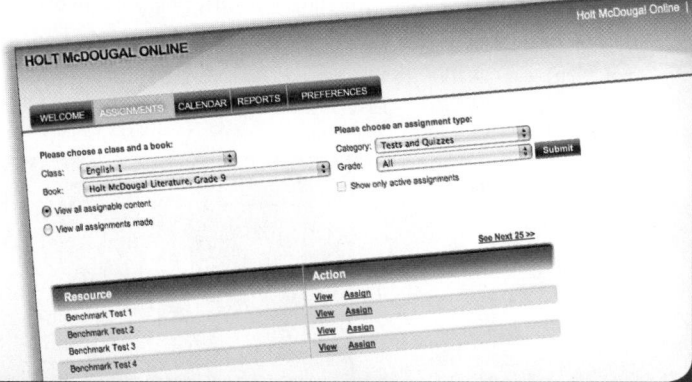

Professional Development

Video Center Based on interviews with program consultants and other educational experts, these videos feature classroom-ready teaching strategies.

Teacher Toolkit Includes a Teacher Handbook as well as a range of articles and handouts by program consultants and other educators.

Janet Allen

Kylene Beers

Carol Jago

Jim Burke

THINKcentral at a Glance

One Location, Endless Resources

Find Resources Browse all *Holt McDougal Literature* components for the ones that meet your students' needs and match your teaching style.

Assess Progress and Reteach Assign electronic versions of program assessments to measure your students' mastery of the Common Core State Standards. On thinkcentral.com, some tests deliver online remediation tutorials to students who have not mastered skills.

 Interactive Whiteboard Lessons

Prepare your students for college and careers by teaching relevant, real-world skills through dynamic, interactive instruction. Go to **thinkcentral.com** to browse through all whiteboard lessons, including the following:

- Irony and Satire
- Role of Setting
- Character Development and Motivation
- Theme/Central Idea

Together Holt McDougal and HISTORY® are revolutionizing the study of English/language arts with video that helps students relive and re-imagine the people, places, and events they are discovering through reading. Look for selections with the HISTORY® icon.

COMMON CORE FOCUS

RL 9 Demonstrate knowledge of nineteenth- and early-twentieth-century foundational works of American literature, including how two or more texts from the same period treat similar themes or topics. **RI 9** Analyze documents of historical and literary significance for their themes, purposes, and rhetorical features.

Questions of the Times

Read aloud the questions on pages 640 and 641 and the paragraphs that follow them. Open the discussion of each idea by having students respond to the questions that conclude each paragraph. Use these notes to prompt further exploration of the ideas.

What makes a place UNIQUE?

Invite students to identify parts of the United States with regional identities today and to name characteristics of the region to which they feel the greatest connection. Urge students to be specific in their responses to the question, considering the concept of uniqueness in terms of geography, history, culture, and other regional characteristics.

Does the universe CARE?

Challenge students to name some hardships that people faced during the post–Civil War era. Encourage opinions on both sides of the question, but urge students to support their views with thoughtful reasons and examples. Extend the discussion by asking students whether they consider this a universal, timeless question—and, if so, why.

Questions of the Times

DISCUSS Consider the following questions with your classmates. Then read on to learn how these issues affected people living during this period and how the questions were reflected in the writing of the time.

What makes a place UNIQUE?

In the post–Civil War years, the United States was growing and changing at such a rapid pace that many Americans felt they were losing their regional identities. People were proud of the things they felt made them unique, and writers responded to this impulse by attempting to record the character of the country's distinct regions. What is it exactly that makes a place unique?

Does the universe CARE?

Life was quite difficult for many Americans during this period. Native Americans, African Americans, immigrants, factory workers, laborers, and farmers struggled daily against poverty and oppression. To many, it seemed that life was unfair—that despite their efforts, they could not escape their fate. Do you think people can control their destiny, or are they simply victims of circumstance?

640

⊙ COMMON CORE

RL 9 Demonstrate knowledge of nineteenth- and early-twentieth-century foundational works of American literature, including how two or more texts from the same period treat similar themes or topics. **RI 9** Analyze documents of historical and literary significance for their themes, purposes, and rhetorical features.

How are women's ROLES CHANGING?

Women of this era were becoming more educated, politically aware, and ambitious. Yet they were not allowed to vote, and those who stepped outside their homes to become artists, writers, and reformers faced strong disapproval and warnings that such activities were "unnatural" for women. How have women's roles evolved over the years?

Why are there "haves" and "HAVE-NOTS"?

This period was a time of harsh extremes. Industry was controlled by a handful of businesses owned by a few people who became very wealthy. These businesses were supported by countless laborers who worked long hours for low wages in dangerous conditions. Why do some people reap huge benefits while others are locked into hardship? Should the government ensure opportunity for all?

641

How are women's ROLES CHANGING?

Have students explain the importance of being able to vote and comment on the fact that women of this era faced condemnation when they "stepped outside" traditional roles. Urge students to draw upon their knowledge of history and current events as they respond to the questions. Extend the discussion by asking how women's lives have become easier—and harder—since that time, and whether the term *women's roles* is relevant today.

Why are there "haves" and "HAVE-NOTS"?

Prompt students to explain the words *haves* and *have-nots,* both in terms of the discussion in the paragraph and in terms of society today. Encourage reasonable, well-supported comments as students debate the government's role in ensuring "opportunity for all."

⋯⋯ COMMON CORE FOCUS

RL 9 Demonstrate knowledge of nineteenth- and early-twentieth-century foundational works of American literature, including how two or more texts from the same period treat similar themes or topics. **RI 9** Analyze documents of historical and literary significance for their themes, purposes, and rhetorical features.

The following essay (pages 642–651) provides students with a historical context for the Unit 4 reading selections. It presents a brief overview of important events occurring during the time period, 1870–1910, and introduces key people, places, and ideas of the times.

To get started, read and discuss the opening paragraph on page 642. Ask students to recall how the Civil War (1861–1865) affected the nation and its people. Discuss reasons why the postwar years were "filled with seemingly limitless possibility" but also were characterized by "hardship and even despair."

About the Art Massachusetts-born artist Childe Hassam (1859–1935), a relative of Nathaniel Hawthorne, captured the essence of a regional celebration in 1890 with *Country Fair, New England.* Adapting the style of French Impressionism, Hassam created vivid oil paintings, pastels, and watercolors of typically American scenes. He painted a variety of city scenes, rural landscapes, seascapes, and portraits, many of them noted for their use of color and light.

Regionalism and Naturalism
1870–1910
Capturing the American Landscape

Vast, varied, filled with seemingly limitless possibility—that was the United States in the years following the Civil War. Yet, all around them in this land of hope and opportunity, writers saw fellow Americans living lives of hardship and even despair. Regionalism tried to capture the reality of ordinary people's lives; naturalism searched for explanations.

DIFFERENTIATED INSTRUCTION

FOR STRUGGLING READERS
Vocabulary Support

- *primary,* "basic or most important"
- *transcontinental,* "extending across a continent"
- *diversity,* "variety, as of people and places"
- *local color,* "having to do with the atmosphere and features of a particular place and its people, as described in writing"
- *hub,* "center of activity; central point"
- *exponentially,* "rapidly and to a great degree"
- *prosperity,* "economic success or well-being"

Use this copy master to help students take notes on the essay, pages 642–651:

R RESOURCE MANAGER—Copy Masters
Note Taking p. 8

Regionalism and Naturalism: Historical Context

The post–Civil War period saw the nation reunited and transformed. Writers responded by attempting to preserve in their writing the distinct character of America's regions and to come to terms with some of its harsh new realities.

Reconstruction's Failures and Successes

The Civil War left the South in ruins. Its primary labor system, slavery, had been abolished. Freed African Americans lacked money, property, education, and opportunity. Farms, factories, and plantations had been destroyed, and rail lines were unusable. The federal government had to come up with a plan to solve these problems and to readmit the Southern states to the union. That plan was **Reconstruction.**

Reconstruction did not go smoothly. The president and Congress clashed over how to best carry it out. Southern states resisted many of the protections granted to newly freed blacks, while blacks felt that too little was being done to ensure their civil rights and economic independence. However, Reconstruction did succeed in a few significant ways. African Americans gained citizenship and equal protection under the law as well as the right to vote, and all of the Confederate states returned to the Union.

Although Americans were glad to move past the divisiveness of the war years, they regretted losing their regional identities and were unsettled by the many changes taking place in the country. These circumstances influenced writers of the time to begin trying to capture the customs, character, and landscapes of the nation's distinct regions—a type of writing that would come to be called **regionalism.**

A Nation Transformed

In the decades following the Civil War, the country as a whole changed radically. In 1869, the first **transcontinental railroad** was completed. It was an event of huge importance. The railroad brought a flood of new settlers west—so many, in fact, that in 1890 the government announced the closing of the frontier. This westward expansion was yet another influence on writers of the time. It created an appreciation for America's diversity, which was celebrated by **local color writers** such as **Mark Twain** and **Bret Harte.**

The railroad also expanded industry. By 1885, four transcontinental lines had been completed, creating manufacturing hubs in Pittsburgh, Cleveland, Detroit, and Chicago. In turn, cities grew exponentially as more and more people came looking for work. In 1850, Chicago was a small town of 20,000; by 1910, the population was more than 2 million. Yet although new technologies and industrial modernization ensured the nation's prosperity, much of its wealth lay in the hands of only a few.

Country Fair, New England (1890), Childe Hassam. 24 ¼″ × 20 ⅛″.
© Manoogian Collection, Taylor, Michigan.

◯ **COMMON CORE**

RL 9 Demonstrate knowledge of nineteenth- and early-twentieth-century foundational works of American literature, including how two or more texts from the same period treat similar themes. **RI 9** Analyze documents of historical and literary significance for their themes, purposes, and rhetorical features.

▶ **TAKING NOTES**

Outlining As you read this introduction, use an outline to record the main ideas about the characteristics and literature of the period. You can use headings, boldfaced terms, and the information in these boxes as starting points. (See page R49 in the **Research Handbook** for more help with outlining.)

I. *Historical Context*
   A. *Reconstruction*
      1. *Failures*
      2. *Successes*
      3. *Effect on writers*
   B. *Transformed Nation*

Regionalism and Naturalism: Historical Context

This section of the essay (page 643) summarizes the aftermath of the Civil War, focusing on the stress of Reconstruction and the loss of some regional identity. The text also describes the close of the American frontier and the growth of American cities, explaining how both led to new kinds of writing.

TIERED DISCUSSION PROMPTS

Use these prompts to help students understand the ideas in **Reconstruction's Failures and Successes** and **A Nation Transformed:**

Summarize In what ways was Reconstruction successful? *Possible answer: African Americans gained citizenship, legal protection, and voting rights; in addition, all of the Confederate states rejoined the Union.*

Analyze How did the transcontinental railroad transform the United States? *Possible answer: The railroad transformed the United States by bringing many settlers to the West and by encouraging the expansion of industry. The expansion of industry caused cities to grow, as people came from rural areas in search of work.*

Synthesize Reread the final sentence of **A Nation Transformed.** Do you think the same might be said about America today? Why, or why not? *Accept all answers that students can support.*

FOR ENGLISH LANGUAGE LEARNERS

Set a Purpose Ask students to look for information in this essay about changes in American life. Encourage students to use a Two-Column Chart to make the relationships clear, as in this example:

Before the Civil War	*After the Civil War*
enslaved blacks throughout South	*citizenship for African Americans*
Population concentrated in the East and South	*flood of new settlers in the West*

 **BEST PRACTICES TOOLKIT—Transparency**
Two-Column Chart p. A25

FOR ADVANCED LEARNERS/AP

Analyze Historical Facts Ask students to use their prior knowledge of the era (from the end of the Civil War to the eve of World War I) to brainstorm a list of "harsh new realities" that Americans writing at the time might have wanted to address. Have students discuss which items on their list proved to be the most historically significant, and why.

Cultural Influences

This section of the essay (pages 644–646) emphasizes inequities of "the Gilded Age." At one end of the spectrum, a few men enjoyed wealth and power. At the other end, Native Americans were being forced off their land, African Americans were restricted by Jim Crow laws, immigrants labored in sweatshops, and farmers were losing their farms. The text also explains how naturalism reflected the helplessness that some Americans were feeling.

DISCUSSION PROMPT

Use this prompt to help students understand the ideas in **The Gilded Age:**

Analyze According to the text, why was this period called **The Gilded Age?** *Possible answer: The term captures the idea that the period was known for its "sparkle and glitter, luxury and excess," as evidenced by the mansions and jewels that industrial tycoons like the Rockefellers and Vanderbilts displayed. More money, innovations that encouraged spending, and more leisure time allowed many average Americans to enjoy a wealthier lifestyle than they once had known, as well.*

Analyze Visuals

Possible answer: The purpose of the painting on page 644 is to portray the wealth, order, and stability of a prominent family. The purpose of the photograph on page 645 is to document a prominent Native American leader, Chief Joseph of the Nez Perce, at the time that the settlement of the West was forcing the Nez Perce and other Native American tribes onto reservations.

About the Art Eastman Johnson (1824–1906) painted scenes from everyday life as well as portraits of the wealthy and famous. The Hatch Family shows three generations of the family of Wall Street broker Alfrederick Hatch in the library of his mansion on Park Avenue in New York City.

The Hatch Family (1871), Eastman Johnson. Oil on canvas, 48″ × 73 ⅜″. The Metropolitan Museum of Art, Gift of Frederic H. Hatch, 1926 (26.97). Photo © 1999 The Metropolitan Museum of Art.

◀ **Analyze Visuals**
What might have been the artist's purpose in rendering the scene in this painting? What conclusions can you draw about these people based on their clothing and surroundings?

Cultural Influences

Industry's success created a better life for many Americans. For a few, it brought great wealth, but others suffered poverty and hardship. Both regional and naturalist writers were influenced by these developments.

The Gilded Age

As the 1800s drew to an end, a very small group of men controlled the vast majority of industry, including the enormously profitable steel, railroad, oil, and meatpacking sectors. Captains of industry such as John D. Rockefeller, the oil tycoon, and Cornelius Vanderbilt, the railroad magnate, enjoyed showing off the vast fortunes they had made. They built palatial mansions, draped their wives and daughters in diamonds, and threw extravagant parties (at one, guests were handed silver shovels and invited to dig in a sandbox filled with jewels)—in short, they did everything but actually coat themselves in gold. When writers **Mark Twain** and **Charles Dudley Warner** dubbed this period "the Gilded Age," they did not exaggerate. It was a time of sparkle and glitter, luxury and excess.

Many ordinary people had more money too and all sorts of new things to spend it on. They could take the train to an amusement park and ride the Ferris wheel, then snack on soda and a candy bar. City dwellers could shop in the new department stores, while country folks pored over the mail-order catalog from Sears, Roebuck (known as "the wish book," it offered everything from skin lotion to bicycles, and even an entire house—assembly required).

A Voice from the Times
The only way not to think about money is to have a great deal of it.

—Edith Wharton

DIFFERENTIATED INSTRUCTION

FOR STRUGGLING READERS
Vocabulary Support
- *captain of industry,* "an important or powerful person in a particular type of manufacturing"
- *tycoon,* "a wealthy, powerful businessperson"
- *magnate,* "a person of great power, importance, or wealth in business or industry"
- *segregationist,* "relating to a policy of separating people of different races as a form of discrimination"
- *sharecropper,* "a farmer who works land owned by another person in return for a share of the value of the crops"
- *tenement,* "an apartment building that is poorly built or cared for"
- *sweatshop,* "a business that requires employees to work for long hours, at low wages, and under poor conditions"

There were telephones now, thanks to Alexander Graham Bell. In 1908 Henry Ford brought out the first Model T, a "horseless carriage" cheap enough for his own factory workers to buy. Thomas Edison alone patented more than 1,000 inventions, from the phonograph to the electric light bulb.

The Have-Nots

Unfortunately, the Gilded Age was not so shiny for many other Americans. The settling of the West forced Native Americans off their land and onto reservations. Although Native Americans fought back—among them **Chief Joseph** of the Nez Perce and the legendary Sioux warriors Crazy Horse and Sitting Bull—there was no stopping the tide.

Life was hard for freed African Americans as well. The failures of Reconstruction in the South left many poor and powerless, held down by segregationist Jim Crow laws and forced to work as sharecroppers under conditions much like slavery.

Others who found themselves facing hard times during this period were many immigrants who had come to America in search of freedom and opportunity. Russian, Italian, Scandinavian, German, Dutch, and Japanese immigrants—all were seeking a better life. Some joined the settlers heading west; others stayed in the cities, where they lived in crowded tenements and found work in factories. Unfortunately, many of these new city-dwelling Americans found themselves working 16-hour days in airless sweatshops for subsistence wages.

A Voice from the Times
I Will Fight No More Forever

Tell General Howard I know his heart. What he told me before, I have in my heart. I am tired of fighting. Our chiefs are killed. Looking Glass is dead. Toohoolhoolzote is dead. The old men are all dead. It is the young men who say yes or no. He who led on the young men is dead. It is cold and we have no blankets. The little children are freezing to death. My people, some of them, have run away to the hills, and have no blankets, no food; no one knows where they are—perhaps freezing to death. I want to have time to look for my children and see how many of them I can find. Maybe I shall find them among the dead. Hear me, my chiefs! I am tired; my heart is sick and sad. From where the sun now stands I will fight no more forever.

—**Chief Joseph of the Nez Perce,**
from his 1877 surrender speech

Use these prompts to help students understand the ideas in **The Have-Nots:**

Analyze Generally speaking, which groups of people did not benefit from the advantages of the Gilded Age? Explain. *Possible answer: Groups that did not benefit included Native Americans, who were being driven from their land; African Americans, who were oppressed by Jim Crow laws; and recent immigrants, who were working long hours in sweatshops.*

Synthesize Think about the immigrants who had come to North America some 250 years earlier. How does their situation compare with that of the immigrants described here? *Possible answer: Both groups of immigrants were motivated by a desire for freedom and opportunity in a new land. The earlier immigrants had to build a new society, but they prospered; these later immigrants found a society ready to exploit them, and they struggled under unfair conditions.*

FOR STRUGGLING READERS

Taking Notes Help students use a Main Idea and Details organizer to identify important ideas and supporting facts in **Cultural Influences** (pages 644–646).

 BEST PRACTICES TOOLKIT—Transparency
Main Idea and Details p. B6

Vocabulary Support Explain that Jim Crow laws were discriminatory laws, passed in Southern states after Reconstruction, that segregated African Americans and restricted their rights. For example, African Americans might be allowed to sit only in certain seats on railroad cars or to enter public establishments only through certain doors (if at all). The name "Jim Crow" came from an 1830s minstrel-show character and reflected negative stereotyping of African Americans.

CHECK UNDERSTANDING

Ask students to recall in what ways **The Gilded Age** was an era of both Haves and Have-Nots. *Possible answer: While the upper classes were enjoying a more luxurious lifestyle, many groups such as Native Americans, African Americans, and immigrants were fighting oppression, discrimination, and poverty.*

Ideas of the Age

This section of the essay (page 646) summarizes major scientific, political, and economic ideas of the era, including Darwin's theory of natural selection, laissez-faire economics, and the progressive movement.

DISCUSSION PROMPT

Use this prompt to help students understand the ideas in **Laissez Faire vs. Progressivism:**

Analyze Explain the connection between Darwin's theory of natural selection, the beliefs of the Social Darwinists, and progressivism. *Possible answer: Herbert Spencer called Darwin's theory of natural selection "survival of the fittest," and he applied the idea to people's success or lack of success in society. The Social Darwinists used Spencer's ideas to justify the gap between rich and poor people and to support a laissez-faire economic policy. Progressivism took issue with Social Darwinism, asserting that the government needed to protect people.*

Even independent farmers faced hard times. They borrowed money from the banks for new machinery that made them more productive than ever before; but high yields meant low prices, and when they couldn't pay back their loans they lost their farms.

People knew that they were missing out on the prosperity that others were enjoying, and it made them angry. Workers began to form **labor unions;** many farmers, white and black, joined the **Populist Party,** hoping to make the government more responsive to workers' needs. However, the opposition had money and power, and these early efforts often ended in bitter defeat.

More and more, the individual seemed helpless, at the mercy of forces beyond his or her understanding or control. Life became a constant struggle, and the world appeared to be a harsh, uncaring place. These feelings found their voice in a literary movement called **naturalism.** Naturalist writers, such as **Stephen Crane,** were concerned with the impact of social and natural forces on the individual. These writers tended to portray characters victimized by brutal forces and unable to control their lives.

Ideas of the Age

During this period, some Americans believed in "survival of the fittest," while others worked for social justice.

Laissez Faire vs. Progressivism

Many of the naturalists' ideas corresponded to new scientific, political, and economic theories emerging at the time. Various thinkers of the day felt that Charles Darwin's theory of natural selection could be applied to human society. An English philosopher named Herbert Spencer called this idea **survival of the fittest,** claiming that those who rose to the top of society were "fit," while those who suffered at the bottom were best left to die out. **Social Darwinists** used these ideas to justify the huge gap between rich and poor and to push a governmental policy of **laissez faire** (French for "allow to do"), meaning that business should not be regulated, because the law of nature would ensure success for the "fittest" and inevitable failure for everyone else.

This self-serving philosophy infuriated many Americans. A **progressive movement** emerged, which aimed to restore economic opportunities and correct injustices in American life. The progressives did not see inequality as the way of the world. They believed that social change was possible and necessary and that it was the job of the government to make laws to protect people.

Industrialist John D. Rockefeller is portrayed as a wealthy king, with the oil and railroad industries as the "jewels" in his crown.

A Voice from the Times

Let no one underestimate the need of pity. We live in a stony universe whose hard, brilliant forces rage fiercely.

—Theodore Dreiser

DIFFERENTIATED INSTRUCTION

FOR STRUGGLING READERS

Concept Support Charles Darwin's principle of *natural selection* described an evolutionary process in which those individuals or groups having traits best adapted to their environment tend to survive and pass those traits on to their offspring. Herbert Spencer's term *survival of the fittest* referred to a social order based on Darwin's theory.

FOR ADVANCED LEARNERS/AP

Research and Evaluate Challenge students to extend their knowledge by responding to one of these writing prompts:

- Gather information about the founding, goals, and achievements of the progressives. As you write, identify some modern social causes that you think effectively carry on the progressive vision.

Regional and Naturalist Literature

The country's rapid growth and change was reflected in new literary movements and voices, including regionalism, naturalism, and women's writing.

Regionalism and Local Color Writing

The end of the Civil War, the country's rapid expansion, and the growth of industry all led to the birth of local color writing, a form of regionalism. Aware of the speed with which the nation was changing, regional writers sought to record for the future the unique character of their areas.

Prominent among the early local colorists were **Bret Harte** and **Mark Twain.** Their versions of life on the frontier captured the imagination of readers in the more settled communities of the East, Midwest, and South. For those who could not hop aboard the new transcontinental train and see the country for themselves, reading all about it was the next best thing. Americans were endlessly fascinated by tales of life in the mining camps, on the cattle ranches, and in the frontier towns. The new regionalist literature satisfied this curiosity with its honest portrayals of the people and their way of life in different areas of the country, especially the West. Writers carefully recorded how ordinary people spoke, dressed, acted, thought, and looked, from the knobby, roughened hands of a Nebraska farm woman to the dust-covered boots of a California gambler.

AN OUTGROWTH OF REALISM Regionalism, with its emphasis on everyday experience and accuracy, grew out of **realism.** Many regionalist writers, such as **Willa Cather,** shared the realist goal of showing ordinary lives as they

▶ *For Your Outline*

REGIONALISM AND LOCAL COLOR

- Writing was influenced by end of Civil War, country's expansion, and industry's growth.
- Regionalists sought to record for the future the unique character of a region.
- Regionalists captured life on the frontier and in other regions.
- Regionalism was an outgrowth of realism.
- Native American oral literature was a form of regionalism.
- *Huckleberry Finn* is a masterpiece of regionalism.

Deadwood in 1876.

647

Regional and Naturalist Literature

This section of the essay (pages 647–648) focuses on the writing of the regionalist and naturalist movements. The text describes the work of these groups:

- regionalist writers, including Bret Harte, Mark Twain, and Willa Cather
- naturalist writers, including Theodore Dreiser, Frank Norris, Jack London, and Stephen Crane
- women writers, including Charlotte Perkins Gilman, Kate Chopin, Edith Wharton, and Mary Wilkins Freeman

DISCUSSION PROMPT

Use this discussion prompt to help students understand the ideas in **Regionalism and Local Color Writing:**

Summarize How did regionalist writing satisfy the curiosity of people who did not live on the frontier? *Possible answer: By sharing tales of life in mining camps, cattle ranches, and frontier towns, regionalist writing entertained distant readers and helped them learn about the West.*

FOR STRUGGLING READERS

Vocabulary Support

- *labor union,* "an organization of workers formed to advance its members' interests, especially regarding wages and working conditions"
- *realism,* "a literary style that stresses a true and objective representation of life"

FOR ADVANCED LEARNERS/AP

Map a Movement [small-group option] Have one or more small groups of students create a map of the United States, c. 1880, showing states and territories. Use the finished map or maps as a springboard for a discussion in which students identify (1) some of the regions that probably were written about in the regionalist and local color movements and (2) a few likely distinct characteristics of each region.

Use these prompts to help students understand the ideas in **Native American Literature** and An **"American" Novel:**

Analyze How did the settlement of the West threaten the survival of Native American oral literature? *Possible answer: The settlement of the West caused Native American tribes to scatter, making it much more difficult to pass on oral literature. Children were separated from their parents and made to attend "Indian schools," where they were forced to disassociate themselves from their Native American heritage and to assimilate into the mainstream American society.*

Interpret In what sense did *The Adventures of Huckleberry Finn* mark a whole new level in regionalism and local color? *Possible answer: The Adventures of Huckleberry Finn was a landmark because it did more than just present regional characters and customs—it had a unique but consistent "American" voice, and it dealt with a widespread American issue in its handling of racism.*

were, without romance or sentimentality. Cather's story, "A Wagner Matinee," for example, gives a very unromantic view of life on the plains. Other writers tended to exaggerate a bit, either for comic effect—as in Twain's "The Notorious Jumping Frog of Calaveras County"—or to make their stories livelier. Our national legend of the Wild West, with its gunslingers, saloons, and sheriffs, had its origins in the picturesque settings and characters of writers like **Bret Harte.**

NATIVE AMERICAN LITERATURE While this kind of regional literature thrived, another was under siege. For generations, Native American tribes had passed down from one generation to the next folk tales, legends, and other **oral literature,** relying on the memories of traditional storytellers and their audiences. Now, the tribes found themselves scattered. Children were forcibly taken from their elders and sent away to "Indian schools," where teachers demanded they forget their language and heritage and assimilate into American society. Entire cultures were rapidly disappearing. However, through the efforts of Native Americans and sympathetic outsiders who helped them write their stories down, some of the literature was saved, thus giving another view of life in the West.

AN "AMERICAN" NOVEL With the publication in 1884 of Mark Twain's *The Adventures of Huckleberry Finn,* regionalism and local color writing reached a zenith. *Huckleberry Finn* was the first novel written entirely in "American"—that is, it was told in the colorful, colloquial, and often ungrammatical voice of its young narrator, Huck. Twain was known for using his gift of humor to make a serious point, and in this novel he used biting satire to tackle the issue of racism in America. Despite Twain's immense popularity with readers worldwide, critics of the time dismissed *Huckleberry Finn,* calling it vulgar and immoral, and libraries banned the book from their shelves as "the veriest trash." Today, many consider it not only Twain's finest work but possibly the best book ever written by an American author. The novel had a huge influence on later writers, among them Ernest Hemingway, who said, "All modern American literature comes from one book by Mark Twain called *Huckleberry Finn.* There was nothing before. There has been nothing as good since."

The Rise of Naturalism

As the 19th century came to a close, several factors led to the rise of a literary movement called **naturalism.** The final decades of the century were a time of rapid change and sharp contrasts—a time when "captains of industry" amassed vast fortunes by exploiting the cheap labor of immigrants and other workers who flooded the cities in search of work. By 1916, the majority of American workers were industrial laborers in factories.

A Voice from the Times

Authorship is not a trade, it is an inspiration; authorship does not keep an office, its habitation is all out under the sky, and everywhere the winds are blowing and the sun is shining and the creatures of God are free.

—Mark Twain

DIFFERENTIATED INSTRUCTION

FOR STRUGGLING READERS
Vocabulary Support

- *gunslinger,* "a person known for skill and speed in using a gun"

- *picturesque,* "memorably vivid"

- *oral literature,* "literature passed from one generation to the next through oral storytelling rather than writing"

- *assimilate,* "to absorb into the culture of a group of people"

- *veriest,* "most extreme"

FOR ADVANCED LEARNERS/AP

Research Critical Views This essay notes Ernest Hemingway's admiration for *The Adventures of Huckleberry Finn,* but he is not alone in that view. Ask students to locate another critical comment that summarizes the importance of Twain's novel. Have students share the comments in class, either now or when they read the American Masterpiece feature about *The Adventures of Huckleberry Finn* on pages 694–695.

WRITING REFLECTS REALITY The work of naturalist writers, such as Theodore Dreiser, reflected this harsh new reality. In the first pages of his novel *The Financier*, for example, a boy named Frank stares through the window of a fish shop at a lobster and a squid that have been placed together in a tank. Day after day, the two creatures battle it out, the sharp-clawed lobster attacking, the squid fighting for its life. At last, the lobster devours the squid. That's the way of the world, Frank thinks—one creature lives off another. When Frank grows up and becomes a banker, he applies this lesson to the ruthless world of business.

Why do people do the things they do? Are humans capable of choice, or do they act on instinct, like other animals? Is life a losing battle? Looking to the theories of Darwin and other scientists, naturalists such as **Dreiser, Frank Norris, Jack London,** and **Stephen Crane** saw human beings as helpless creatures moved by forces beyond their understanding or control.

Despite this grim attitude, many naturalist writers were quite popular. Some, like Frank Norris, gave a voice to ordinary people and portrayed the rich and influential in an unflattering light, as in his famous 1901 novel *The Octopus*, which attacked the railroad interests in his home state of California. Jack London, on the other hand, captured readers with his tales of an arctic world entirely outside their everyday experience. Riveted by the exotic setting and thrilling action of novels such as *White Fang* and *The Call of the Wild*, readers were willing to accept less-than-happy endings.

> ### A Voice from the Times
>
> *A man said to the universe:*
> *"Sir, I exist!"*
> *"However," replied the universe,*
> *"The fact has not created in me*
> *A sense of obligation."*
>
> **—Stephen Crane**

▶ *For Your Outline*

THE RISE OF NATURALISM

- Naturalism reflected time of rapid changes and sharp contrasts, when wealth was concentrated in few hands.
- Naturalists saw humans as helpless from forces beyond their control.

649

Use these prompts to help students understand the ideas in **A New Role for Women:**

Interpret Reread the first paragraph. What does the quotation suggest about women's place in society in the late 1800s? *Possible answer: According to the quotation, it is women who keep society decent, and they do so by being refined, gentle, and elegant. The quotation suggests that women were expected to take a generally passive role, not to display active leadership.*

Evaluate Does the quotation have any relevance today? Why or why not? *Possible answer: The quotation has a limited relevance. There is still a value in "refinement, gentleness, and etiquette," and there are appropriate times to exercise those traits; furthermore, women and men alike have a responsibility to preserve order and decency in society. However, women today generally act with greater empowerment than the quotation suggests.*

Summarize How did Charlotte Perkins Gilman, Kate Chopin, and Edith Wharton contribute to the women's movement? *Possible answer: Gilman was a leading advocate for women; she wrote and spoke out to promote women's rights. Chopin depicted some of women's troubles and expressed their frustrations in her stories. In her novels, Wharton criticized small-minded upper-class society.*

A New Role for Women

Women writing in this period in the United States tended to be realists. Some were regionalists and others embraced naturalist themes, but all were breaking barriers as women's roles slowly shifted. "The power of a woman is in her refinement, gentleness, and elegance; it is she who makes etiquette, and it is she who preserves the order and decency of society." So said a popular book of etiquette in 1880, voicing a widely held notion about women's place in society.

At the same time, however, the movement to give women the **right to vote** was reemerging after a period of inactivity in the years immediately following the Civil War, when male reformers argued that black and white women should wait until black men gained their rights. Women were growing impatient, not just for the vote, but to have a larger voice in every aspect of public life, from politics to literature.

▶ *For Your Outline*
A NEW ROLE FOR WOMEN

- Women writers tended to be realists, whether working as regionalists or naturalists.
- They broke barriers as women's roles shifted.
- The women's suffrage movement reemerged.
- University education became more available to women.
- Women's writing reflected society's limitations.

DIFFERENTIATED INSTRUCTION

FOR ENGLISH LANGUAGE LEARNERS
Vocabulary Support
- *etiquette,* "forms of proper conduct in society"
- *reformer,* "a person who works to improve conditions or correct injustice"
- *advocate,* "someone who supports or promotes the interests of a person or group"
- *domination,* "control or influence"
- *modernism,* "a movement to break with the past and find new forms of expression"

FOR ADVANCED LEARNERS/AP
Research and Synthesize Review this comment from the first paragraph of page 651: "[women] found that the limited roles assigned them did not make full use of their abilities and knowledge." Invite students to gather information about some women of this era who refused to be bound by expectation. These are a few of the women that students might research:

One important factor in the growth of the women's movement was the spread of **university education** among women of the era. Newspapers of the day trumpeted the dangers of this development. An 1896 *New York Journal* headline proclaimed: "Are We Destroying Woman's Beauty? The Startling Warning of a Great English Physician Against Higher Education of Women. How Intellectual Work Destroys Beauty." Despite such dire warnings, women continued to seek education. Then they found that the limited roles assigned them did not make full use of their abilities and knowledge.

BREAKTHROUGH WRITERS Charlotte Perkins Gilman—related on her father's side to a noted family of writers and social reformers that included Harriet Beecher Stowe, the author of *Uncle Tom's Cabin*—became one of the most well-known advocates for women. Fleeing a repressive marriage, **Gilman** moved from the East Coast to California, where she wrote and spoke out on behalf of women's rights and against male domination. One of her most famous stories is "The Yellow Wallpaper," about a woman writer who, as treatment for her "nervous condition," is forbidden to write.

Kate Chopin wrote fiction that articulates the frustrations of generations of women confined to a sort of extended childhood by the men in their lives. Her gentle stories depicting some of the most obvious of women's troubles were extremely popular in the 1890s. Her 1899 novel *The Awakening,* however, stepped over the line in its portrayal of a woman's hidden passion, arousing a public protest so vigorous that Chopin ceased writing completely.

Works by women of this period often end tragically, in madness, ruin, scandal, and death. In part, this was a reflection of their **naturalist** leanings; at the same time, though, it grew out of their own experiences in a culture that did not encourage women's artistic goals. **Edith Wharton,** who in novels such as *The Age of Innocence* and *The House of Mirth* decried the stifling small-mindedness of upper-class society, made her own escape by running off to Paris, only to have her marriage fall apart. Facing overwhelming obstacles, women writers fought with, in the words of New England's local color writer **Mary Wilkins Freeman,** "little female weapons." When the weapon was a pen, the impact could be revolutionary.

As the country moved farther into the 20th century, writers would begin to turn from regionalism and naturalism to the more experimental works that characterize modernism. Thankfully Twain, London, Chopin, and the other writers of their time captured for future generations the unique spirit of late 19th- and early 20th-century America.

THE ARTISTS' GALLERY

American Impressionism

During this period, the revolutionary style pioneered by French painters such as Claude Monet and Auguste Renoir made its mark in the United States. American artists took the basic goal of **impressionism**—to capture reality as we actually see it in the moment, not as formal rules of art say we should see it—and adapted it to their own situation.

Style and Subject Like their European counterparts, American impressionists focused on the effects of light and color and liked to paint outdoors. Often they painted what a new American leisure class wanted to buy: idyllic landscapes that let them "get away" and portraits of themselves relaxing in their homes or picnicking at the seaside. Paintings like these were not only a pleasure to look at but a status symbol too—proof that the owner (perhaps the son or grandson of a penniless immigrant) had acquired taste and culture.

Progressive Woman One of the few women who exhibited with the impressionists in Paris was an American artist named **Mary Cassatt,** whose work *In the Garden* (1904) is shown here. At a time when no respectable woman traveled alone, lived alone, or pursued a career in art, Cassatt did all three. Known as "a painter of mothers and children," her works reflect a surprisingly modern sensibility. Though her paintings show women in conventional settings, she gives them a new sense of purpose. Cassatt's women do not exist just to be looked at; they are the heroes of their own lives.

THE ARTISTS' GALLERY

Freedom with the brush and the use of bright color are two characteristics of American impressionist art; they appear in Mary Cassatt's painting on this page and in Childe Hassam's painting on page 642. Information about Hassam appears on page 642 as well. American artist Mary Cassatt (1844–1926) was born in Pennsylvania but moved to Paris in 1874; she lived and worked in France for the rest of her life. Rather than paint commissioned portraits, Cassatt used family members as the subjects of her paintings. Her paintings reflect some influence of the French artist Edgar Degas, with whom she often worked. It was Degas, in fact, who introduced Cassatt to the French impressionists.

Activity Ask students to explain what Cassatt's painting may suggest about the artist's feelings about family. *Possible answer: The pleasant, upbeat feeling in this scene, which depicts a quietly shared mother-daughter moment, suggests that Cassatt placed high value on family closeness.*

CHECK UNDERSTANDING

Have students identify a few names and characteristics related to each of these topics:

- Regionalism and Local Color Writing
- The Rise of Naturalism
- A New Role for Women

- reformer Jane Addams
- journalist Nellie Bly
- attorney Belva Lockwood
- suffragist Elizabeth Cady Stanton

Have students present their findings in brief oral reports. To extend the activity, ask students whether or not this expectation persists to this day. Encourage them to support their responses with facts and examples drawn from their knowledge of modern society and current events.

Create an Impressionist Display [small-group option] Have a group of students collect and review a variety of impressionist paintings and share them with the class. Some paintings may come from the late 19th and early 20th centuries; others may be contemporary works that use impressionist techniques. Discuss why impressionism was so revolutionary and why it pleases many art lovers even today.

RI 7 Integrate and evaluate multiple sources of information presented in different formats as well as in words in order to address a question or solve a problem.

Connecting Literature, History, and Culture

READING SKILL

COMMON CORE
RI 7

■ READ A TIMELINE

Elicit or explain that each of the three horizontal sections of the timeline—*American Literary Milestones, Historical Context,* and *World Culture and Events*—displays a sequence of events that occurred between 1870 and 1910. By looking at the vertical columns on the timeline, students can see which events were occurring at about the same time. For example, have students locate these events, which occurred between 1901 and 1906:

- In 1901, Britain's Queen Victoria died. (See *World Culture and Events.*)

- In 1903, Jack London published *The Call of the Wild.* (See *American Literary Milestones.*)

- In 1906, an earthquake devastated San Francisco. (See *Historical Context.*)

Ask students what events occurred in 1899 and 1900. ***Answer:*** *In 1899, Kate Chopin published* The Awakening; *in 1900, Theodore Dreiser published* Sister Carrie, *and the Boxer Rebellion took place in China.*

Connecting Literature, History, and Culture

Use the timeline and the questions on the next page to gain insight about how developments in the United States during this period reflected those in the world as a whole.

AMERICAN LITERARY MILESTONES

1870	1880
1870 Bret Harte publishes his story collection *The Luck of Roaring Camp and Other Sketches.* ▶ **1876** Mark Twain completes *The Adventures of Tom Sawyer* and begins writing *The Adventures of Huckleberry Finn.*	**1881** Henry James publishes *The Portrait of a Lady.* **1883** Mark Twain's *Life on the Mississippi* is published. ▶ **1885** Libraries across America ban Mark Twain's *The Adventures of Huckleberry Finn,* published the previous year; William Dean Howells publishes *The Rise of Silas Lapham.* **1887** Diary of Chief Seattle is published.

HISTORICAL CONTEXT

1870	1880
1872 Susan B. Anthony is arrested and fined for leading a group of women to test their right to vote. ▶ **1876** Alexander Graham Bell patents first telephone; at Battle of Little Bighorn, 1,500 Sioux and Cheyenne warriors defeat and kill about 200 U.S. Army troops, commanded by George A. Custer. **1877** Chief Joseph of the Nez Perce tribe surrenders to U.S. Army; Thomas Edison invents the phonograph.	**1880** John D. Rockefeller's Standard Oil Company of Ohio controls U.S. refining; George Eastman patents his rolled camera film. **1883** The first metal-framed skyscraper, ten stories high, is built in Chicago. **1886** The Statue of Liberty, a gift from France to the United States, is dedicated in New York Harbor. ▶

WORLD CULTURE AND EVENTS

1870	1880
1871 Franco-Prussian War ends and Germany is unified; French naturalist writer Émile Zola publishes the first book in his 20-novel series *Les Rougon-Macquart.* **1872** Critics coin the term *impressionism* after viewing Claude Monet's painting *Impression: Sunrise.* **1879** The British defeat the Zulus in South Africa.	**1883** The Orient Express makes its first rail run from Paris to Istanbul. **1887** Fictional detective Sherlock Holmes makes his first appearance in *A Study in Scarlet,* by Sir Arthur Conan Doyle. ▶ **1889** The Eiffel Tower is completed in Paris.

DIFFERENTIATED INSTRUCTION

FOR STRUGGLING READERS

Understanding a Timeline Explain that the timeline runs chronologically (in time order) from left to right across the page. Each of the four columns represents a ten-year period between 1870 and 1910. The three parallel rows of the timeline represent events occurring simultaneously. By comparing the three rows, readers can better understand what events in literature, history, and culture were taking place at about the same time.

MAKING CONNECTIONS

- Who were some inventors at work in Europe and the United States?
- How did American women fare in gaining the right to vote as compared with New Zealand women?
- What evidence do you see that the United States was becoming an imperial power?
- Name two works of American literature from this period that describe real people or events.

◌ **COMMON CORE**

RI 7 Integrate and evaluate multiple sources of information presented in different formats as well as in words in order to address a question or solve a problem.

1890

1890 Charlotte Perkins Gilman describes the emotional and intellectual decline of a young wife and mother in "The Yellow Wallpaper."

1893 Stephen Crane publishes *Maggie: A Girl of the Streets*; Paul Laurence Dunbar publishes his first volume of poetry, *Oak and Ivy*, while working as an elevator operator.

1899 Kate Chopin publishes her novel *The Awakening*.

1900

1900 Theodore Dreiser publishes *Sister Carrie*.

1901 Booker T. Washington publishes *Up From Slavery: An Autobiography*.

1903 Jack London publishes *The Call of the Wild*; W. E. B. Du Bois publishes *The Souls of Black Folk*.

1905 Edith Wharton publishes *The House of Mirth*.

1906 Upton Sinclair's *The Jungle* ▶ exposes dangerous conditions in meatpacking factories.

1890

1892 New York's Ellis Island becomes entry point for European immigrants.

1896 Supreme Court upholds "separate but equal" doctrine of Jim Crow laws, widely used to discriminate against African Americans; the Klondike gold rush begins in Alaska and Canada.

1898 The Spanish-American War results in United States gaining control of Guam, Puerto Rico, and the Philippines; U.S. also annexes Hawaii.

1900

1901 William McKinley is assassinated; Theodore Roosevelt becomes president of the United States.

1903 Near Kitty Hawk, North Carolina, Orville and Wilbur Wright make first flight in engine-powered airplane.

1906 Earthquake and fire destroy much of San Francisco.

1908 Ford Motor Company brings out the first Model T automobile.

1890

1893 New Zealand becomes first country to grant women suffrage.

1894 Rudyard Kipling publishes *The Jungle Book*.

1896 Italian physicist Guglielmo Marconi invents first radio; first modern Olympic games are held in Athens.

1897 Edmond Rostand publishes *Cyrano de Bergerac*.

1900

1900 The Boxer Rebellion protests foreign influence in China.

1901 After 64 years as ruler of Great Britain, Queen Victoria dies. ▶

1902 Joseph Conrad publishes *Heart of Darkness*.

1904 James Joyce begins *Dubliners*.

1905 Albert Einstein formulates his theory of relativity.

TIMELINE **653**

MAKING CONNECTIONS

Possible answers:

- *Inventors Alexander Graham Bell, Thomas Edison, George Eastman, Orville and Wilbur Wright, and Guglielmo Marconi were at work during this time.*

- *Women in New Zealand gained the right to vote in 1893. At that time, American women were still fighting for that right.*

- *American imperialism is seen in two events from 1898: (1) the annexation of Hawaii and (2) the acquisition of Guam, Puerto Rico, and the Philippines as a result of the Spanish-American War.*

- *Answers will vary but may include any two:* Life on the Mississippi; *diary of Chief Seattle;* Up from Slavery: An Autobiography; The Souls of Black Folk; The Jungle.

ADDITIONAL QUESTIONS

1. Which English author published *The Jungle Book* 21 years after Mark Twain published *Life on the Mississippi*? **Answer:** *Rudyard Kipling published* The Jungle Book *in 1894.*

2. How long after the Orient Express made its first run from Paris to Istanbul did the Wright brothers make their first airplane flight? **Answer:** *The Wright Brothers made their flight 20 years later (in 1903).*

FOR ADVANCED LEARNERS/AP

Making Additional Connections Ask students to choose one of the four decades shown in the timeline and to do research online or in encyclopedias or history texts to learn about other events that took place during that ten-year time span. Challenge students to identify events for each category: *American Literary Milestones, Historical Context, and World Culture and Events.* Have students work individually, with partners, or in small groups to prepare and present brief oral reports, summarizing significant events and discussing their connection to events shown in the timeline or discussed in class.

W 7 Conduct short research projects to answer a question. **W 10** Write over shorter time frames for a range of tasks and purposes. **SL 2** Integrate multiple sources of information. **SL 4** Present information, findings, and supporting evidence.

The Wild, Wild West

Have students read the paragraph. Explain that Western books, movies, and TV shows were especially popular from the 1940s through the 1960s. Ask students to name Western books, movies, TV shows, characters, and scenes (such as the depicted duel at high noon) with which they are familiar. Point out that some Western characters were fictional (for example, the Lone Ranger and Tonto) but that others were real people. Students may recall such Western characters—some heroes, some villains—as Wyatt Earp, Doc Holliday, Jesse James, Calamity Jane, and Annie Oakley, all of whom were real people in addition to being characters in books and on screen.

QUICKWRITE As students plan and write their paragraphs, encourage them to consider (1) why people generally enjoy reading about life in the past, and (2) why the Wild West seems appealing despite the real-life difficulties of living in such a time and place. After volunteers have shared their explanations, have the class reach a consensus opinion that completes this sentence: *The Wild West is an appealing image because* _____. Extend the discussion by asking whether students think that any other American setting—any region, at any time— holds the same kind of appeal.

The Legacy of the Era

The Wild, Wild West

COMMON CORE

W 7 Conduct short research projects to answer a question. **W 10** Write over shorter time frames for a range of tasks and purposes. **SL 2** Integrate multiple sources of information. **SL 4** Present information, findings, and supporting evidence.

It's high noon and two cowboys face off on a deserted street, spurs jingling, fingers twitching. Sound familiar? Although the real Wild West lasted just a few decades, it lives on today in Westerns—a genre of novels, television shows, and movies inspired originally by the stories of Bret Harte and other regionalist writers such as Zane Grey and Owen Wister.

QUICKWRITE What is it about the Wild West that makes it so appealing to Americans? Write a paragraph or two explaining why, in your opinion, the legend lives on.

654

DIFFERENTIATED INSTRUCTION

FOR STRUGGLING READERS
Vocabulary Support

- *spur,* "a pointed device attached to the heel of a rider's boot, used to urge the horse forward"

- *genre,* "a particular kind of literary or artistic work"

FOR ADVANCED LEARNERS/AP

Research Real Heroes [paired option] Have students do Internet research to identify popular TV Westerns of the 1950s and 1960s that were based on the lives of real people. Ask them to determine which people were truly heroes and which were simply glorified by Hollywood. As students share their findings, discuss how TV writers' portrayal of these characters influenced Americans' view of life in the Old West.

The Labor Movement

In the post–Civil War period, many laborers, unhappy with the appalling working conditions of their day, began to join unions and strike for better wages and conditions. Business leaders feared the growth of unions and tried to break their power with lockouts, firings, and even violence. Slowly, however, unions increased their membership and their power, eventually changing the way many Americans worked.

ONLINE RESEARCH Today, workers consider 8 hours a full day. Contrast that with the 10 to 12 hours typically worked in the 19th century, and you will see one benefit won by early unions. What issues are today's unions focusing on? Visit the Web site of a modern labor union, and report to the class on its top concerns.

Regionalism Today

Local color writing is still very popular in America. Writers such as Garrison Keillor, Larry McMurtry, and Fannie Flagg capture regions as we know them today, from small-town Minnesota to the great spaces of Texas to sleepy towns of the South.

REPORT Do some research to find out if there are any writers working today who are capturing the flavor of the region in which you live. Report to the class on the writer or writers you discover. What have they written? Is their work well-known? Do they write in dialect, describe landscapes or towns, work in fiction or nonfiction? Explore these and any other questions that arise as you research.

Garrison Keillor

655

The Labor Movement

Review with students the definition of *labor union:* "an organization of workers formed to advance its members' interests." Then have students read and discuss the paragraph. In particular, discuss how the expression *There is strength in numbers* pertains to unions and why business leaders might be opposed to the formation of unions.

ONLINE RESEARCH Have students combine their findings by creating a chart of the largest labor unions in the United States. Charts should include such information as each union's total membership, its year of formation, and the union's goals and accomplishments.

Regionalism Today

Before students read the paragraph, review the fact that *local color* refers to writing that captures the atmosphere and features of a particular place, time, and people. As you discuss the paragraph, ask students whether they think that local color writing generally appeals only to people who live in the region described or whether it has a broad appeal.

REPORT Suggest that students begin by looking for writers who regularly contribute to local or regional newspapers and magazines. After students have done their research, invite volunteers to share passages that capture the flavor of your region. Discuss what makes each writer's approach to the material unique.

FOR STRUGGLING READERS
Vocabulary Support

- *appalling,* "awful; shocking"
- *lockout,* "an employer's closing of a workplace in order to prevent employees from working during a labor dispute"
- *dialect,* "a regional variety of a shared language"

FOR ADVANCED LEARNERS/AP
Write with Local Color Challenge students to try their hand at local color writing by writing a short story, essay, or article that captures the flavor of the region in which they live. Encourage students to consider such details as regional landmarks and events; also urge them to think about how people talk and the things about which they talk. Have volunteers share their finished work with the class.

RL 3 Analyze the impact of the author's choices regarding how to develop and relate elements of a story. **L 1a** Apply the understanding that usage is a matter of convention. **L 3** Apply knowledge of language to make effective choices for meaning or style.

The Growth of Regional Literature

Regional Writing Explain that regional differences became increasingly evident as the United States grew in geographic size and in population. People's curiosity about these differences encouraged writers to capture the atmosphere and features of small-town and rural life, in particular, in the South, the West, New England, and other parts of the country. Such magazines as Boston's *Atlantic Monthly* and New York City's *Harper's New Monthly Magazine* brought local color to urban readers.

Ask students how today's readers satisfy their curiosity about various regions of the country, urban as well as rural. Elicit a range of local color sources, including regional and local newspapers and magazines, television and radio, the Internet, and movies.

The Importance of Setting

Setting Point out that setting is a key element in almost all literature but that it is especially important in regional literature. In regional literature, the setting is viewed not just as a contributing element; it is a subject that is interesting in itself. Furthermore, regional writers look to their settings for inspiration in creating characters, situations, and imagery. Point out, too, that even though regional writers might focus on a particular setting, their writing frequently deals with concerns that people everywhere find relevant.

Text Analysis Workshop

Setting in Regional Literature

Many places in the world are fascinating, but some of the most ordinary places can be interesting, too, if you notice what is unique about them. In the last half of the 19th century, regional writers in the United States strove to depict in their stories the unique aspects of a specific place and of its people. These enduring tales give readers a glimpse into the past and inspire a tradition that continues to this day.

The Growth of Regional Literature

COMMON CORE

Included in this workshop:
RL 3 Analyze the impact of the author's choices regarding how to develop and relate elements of a story. **L 1a** Apply the understanding that usage is a matter of convention. **L 3** Apply knowledge of language to make effective choices for meaning or style.

Regional literature arose from an effort to accurately represent the speech, manners, habits, history, folklore, and beliefs of people in specific geographical areas. Although regionalism is considered an offshoot of realism, it has been part of American literature from the beginning. Washington Irving's tales of Dutch New York and Nathaniel Hawthorne's stories of Puritan New England are just two examples. After the Civil War, however, when realism became the dominant literary movement, writers began to focus on the lives of ordinary people and to avoid the supernaturalism and sentimentality found in much of the work of Irving, Hawthorne, and Edgar Allan Poe.

Mark Twain relaxes on a ship's deck.

A factor that contributed to the growth of regional writing was the boom in publishing in the late 1800s. Popular magazines sprang up all over the United States to meet the demand for information about the rest of the country. Mark Twain's "The Notorious Jumping Frog of Calaveras County," for example, was first published in a New York magazine and became an immediate sensation.

The Importance of Setting

The effectiveness of regional writing depends to a large extent on the depiction of **setting,** the time and place in which a story's events occur. Key elements of setting in regional literature include the following:

- geographical location and physical features, such as a river, a camp, a house, or a mode of transportation

- the time in which the events take place—a season of the year or a historical period

- the jobs and daily activities of the characters

- the culture of the characters, including their religious and moral beliefs and the social and economic conditions in which they live

---

DIFFERENTIATED INSTRUCTION

FOR STRUGGLING READERS

Note Taking For students who are unfamiliar with setting in regional literature or need help with note taking, hand out the copy master before discussing these pages.

Explain to students that they will encounter several terms relating to setting in regional literature in this workshop. Discuss the major terms on this spread (*regional literature, setting, dialect, detailed description, local color writing*) as students record notes on the copy master.

 RESOURCE MANAGER—Copy Master
Note Taking p. 8

Two means of conveying setting that are commonly found in regional literature are the use of **dialects**—distinctive forms of language spoken in particular areas or by particular groups of people—and **detailed descriptions** of location. Read this example from Twain's "The Notorious Jumping Frog of Calaveras County" (page 684).

> "Rev. Leonidas W. H'm, Reverend Le— Well, there was a feller here once by the name of Jim Smiley, in the winter of '49—or maybe it was the spring of '50—I don't recollect exactly, somehow, though what makes me think it was one or the other is because I remember the big flume warn't finished when he first come to the camp. . . ."
>
> **—Mark Twain, "The Notorious Jumping Frog of Calaveras County"**

The pronunciations indicated by the spellings *feller* and *warn't*, the expression "I don't recollect," and the use of *come* rather than *came* all contribute to the regional flavor of the piece. Although this dialect is not standard English, its conventions are established by its speakers.

Now look at this description from Willa Cather's "A Wagner Matinee" (page 718), in which the narrator recalls the Nebraska farm where he grew up. Notice the harshness and the lack of color in the setting described; both the landscape and the evidence of human habitation are black, pitted, and bare.

> I saw again the tall, naked house on the prairie, black and grim as a wooden fortress; the black pond where I had learned to swim, its margin pitted with sun-dried cattle tracks; the rain gullied clay banks about the naked house, the four dwarf ash seedlings where the dish-cloths were always hung to dry before the kitchen door.
>
> **—Willa Cather, "A Wagner Matinee"**

In regional literature, setting, characters, and plot are usually inseparable. As you read regional writing, notice the relationship between the characters and the setting. Ask yourself how the characters react to the setting. Then decide how this relationship is significant to the story's plot.

LOCAL COLOR REALISM

Prospectors pan for gold during the gold rush, 1889.

In 1868, a popular story about the California gold rush—Bret Harte's "The Luck of Roaring Camp"—launched a specific form of regional writing called **local color writing.** Mark Twain, with his memorable characters, was a master of this form. Other local color realists of the time include Joel Chandler Harris in the South and Sarah Orne Jewett and Mary Wilkins Freeman in New England. Later regional writers, such as Willa Cather, William Faulkner, and Flannery O'Connor, developed sophisticated ways of making universal statements about the human condition while focusing on the local and the particular.

Close Read

What feeling about life on the frontier do you get from the description? How could you rewrite the passage to change that feeling?

Dialects Explain that through well-written dialect, writers convey realism not only in setting but also in characterization. In addition to geographical origins, a particular dialect may suggest a character's educational background or social status. For example, an ungrammatical dialect may suggest that a character has had limited formal education. (Note that as the story unfolds, however, such a character may prove to be quite clever and may even be the story's hero.)

Detailed Descriptions Explain that writers convey setting through the use of sensory details—showing how things look, taste, smell, sound, and feel. Through such details, writers can give readers a clear impression of the setting and also create a mood or atmosphere, as Willa Cather does in the example on page 657.

LOCAL COLOR REALISM

Explain that local color realists tried to convey a realistic sense of specific towns or regions throughout the United States, such as villages in New England, the plains and cities of the Midwest and the towns, deserts, and mountains of the West.

Close Read

Possible answer: *The feeling is that life on the frontier was bleak, empty, and lonely. To change that feeling, a writer might add color to the description and use more upbeat and varied adjectives than* black *(used twice),* grim, *and* naked *(also used twice).*

FOR ENGLISH LANGUAGE LEARNERS
Language: Skill Words

- *setting:* place and time in which the action of a literary work occurs—for example, San Francisco in 1889
- *dialect:* form of language of a particular region or group of people—for example, the New England and Coastal Southern dialects
- *description:* account that gives a vivid impression of an experience—for example, enjoying a home-cooked meal or seeing a new invention for the first time

FOR ADVANCED LEARNERS/AP
Consider Regional Differences Ask students to respond to these questions:

- What differences in perspective would you expect to find between a regional writer from the West and one from the East? What differences might there be between a writer who is a city dweller and a writer who lives in a rural town?
- How can reading the work of writers from various regions benefit a person?

COMMON CORE FOCUS

RL 3 Analyze the impact of the author's choices regarding how to develop and relate elements of a story. **RL 4** Analyze the impact of specific word choices on meaning and tone. **RL 5** Analyze how an author's choices concerning how to structure specific parts of a text contribute to its overall structure and meaning as well as its aesthetic impact. **RI 1** Cite evidence to support inferences drawn from the text. **RI 6** Determine an author's point of view or purpose in a text in which the rhetoric is effective. **W 3b** Use narrative techniques, such as dialogue and pacing, to develop characters. **SL 1** Participate effectively in collaborative discussions, building on others' ideas and expressing their own. **L 1a** Apply the understanding that usage is a matter of convention. **L 1b** Resolve issues of complex or contested usuage, consulting references as needed. **L 2** Demonstrate command of the conventions of standard English punctuation and spelling when writing. **L 3** Apply knowledge of language to comprehend more fully when reading. **L 4c** Consult general and specialized reference materials to determine or clarify a word's precise meaning. **L 4d** Verify the preliminary determination of the meaning of a word or phrase. **L 5a** Interpret figures of speech in context and analyze their role in the text. **L 5b** Analyze nuances in the meaning of words with similar denotations. **L 6** Acquire and use accurately general academic words.

ABOUT THE AUTHOR

Point out that Twain's autobiography is a loose collection of character sketches, essays, diary entries, and letters.

COMMON CORE

RI 1 Cite evidence to support inferences drawn from the text.
RI 6 Determine an author's point of view or purpose in a text in which the rhetoric is effective.
SL 1 Participate effectively in collaborative discussions, building on others' ideas and expressing their own. **L 5a** Interpret figures of speech in context and analyze their role in the text.

DID YOU KNOW?

Mark Twain . . .

- used multiple pen names, including S. L. C., Josh, and Thomas Jefferson Snodgrass.
- served briefly in the Confederate Army.
- took his name from a nautical term for water depth meaning "two fathoms deep."

Regionalism and Local Color

from The Autobiography of Mark Twain
by Mark Twain

Video link at thinkcentral.com

VIDEO TRAILER THINK central   KEYWORD: HML11-658A

Essential Course of Study ECOS

Meet the Author

Mark Twain 1835–1910

Readers of all ages have followed the youthful adventures of Huck Finn and Tom Sawyer for more than 100 years. Many have also enjoyed the witty and sharp social commentary in Mark Twain's lectures and journalism. A man who found humor in a life filled with tragedy, Mark Twain remains one of America's greatest literary voices.

Life on the River Samuel Langhorne Clemens—as Twain was named at birth—grew up in the Mississippi River town of Hannibal, Missouri. The river and the town shaped young Clemens's early years. After his father's death, he began working at an early age to help support his family. Work for a printer and a newspaper began a lifelong connection to journalism and led to his first published writing—a humorous sketch. Planning to write travel sketches, Clemens signed on with a river pilot. He spent four years on the river, where he met many different kinds of people. After the Civil War, river travel was largely replaced by railroad travel, but Clemens remembered the river's lessons as he took the pen name by which his readers came to know him.

On the Move Twain kept traveling, first to the American West, where he panned for gold. He gained literary recognition with his tall tale "The Notorious Jumping Frog of Calaveras County," set in California. Twain also traveled the world, sharing his experiences in sketches, letters, and lectures. Travel writings such as *The Innocents Abroad* artfully combined wit and serious information and were vastly popular.

Twain's Great Legacy After his 1870 marriage, Twain based his growing family in Hartford, Connecticut, where he produced his most lasting works, *The Adventures of Tom Sawyer* and *The Adventures of Huckleberry Finn.* These books secured Twain's place as a great American novelist.

Tragedy Haunts the Later Years Despite literary success, Twain found himself in debt from unsuccessful business ventures. Facing bankruptcy in 1893, he traveled once again, delivering humorous lectures amidst the great personal sorrow of two daughters' deaths and his wife's fading health. Twain's last works reflect the sorrow and anger of this period, which lasted until his death.

Author Online
Go to thinkcentral.com. KEYWORD: HML11-658B

See resources on the **Teacher One Stop DVD-ROM** *and on* **thinkcentral.com.**

Video link at thinkcentral.com

R RESOURCE MANAGER UNIT 4

Plan and Teach, pp. 11–18, 31–38, 47–54
Summary, pp. 19–20, 39–40, 55–56 †‡*
Text Analysis and Reading Skill, pp. 21–24†*, 41–44†*, 57–60†*
Vocabulary, pp. 25–27, 61–63
Grammar and Style, p. 66

DIAGNOSTIC AND SELECTION TESTS

Selection Tests, pp. 177–180, 181–184, 185–188

INTERACTIVE READER

ADAPTED INTERACTIVE READER

ELL ADAPTED INTERACTIVE READER

TECHNOLOGY

- 🔘 **Teacher One Stop DVD-ROM**
- 🔘 **Student One Stop DVD-ROM**
- 🔘 **PowerNotes DVD-ROM**
- 🔘 **Audio Anthology CD**
- 🔘 **GrammarNotes DVD-ROM**
- 🔘 **ExamView Test Generator** on the **Teacher One Stop**

Video Trailer THINK central

Go to **thinkcentral.com** to preview the **Video Trailer** introducing this selection. Other features that support the selection include

- **PowerNotes** presentation
- **ThinkAloud** models to enhance comprehension
- **WordSharp** vocabulary tutorials
- interactive writing and grammar instruction

---

* Resources for Differentiation   † Also in Spanish   ‡ In Haitian Creole and Vietnamese

● TEXT ANALYSIS: IRONY AND OVERSTATEMENT

In Mark Twain's true-life adventure stories, Twain often used life's absurdities to evoke emotions and influence readers. To help create meaning and generate humor, Twain used the following literary techniques:

- **situational irony**—a contrast between what is expected and what actually happens
- **dramatic irony**—when readers know more about a situation or character than the characters do
- **verbal irony**—a contrast between what is stated and what is meant
- **overstatement**—an exaggeration for emphasis or for humorous effect (also called *hyperbole*)

Watch for examples of irony and overstatement as you read.

● READING STRATEGY: PREDICT

When you **predict,** you use text clues to make a reasonable guess about what will happen in a story. Sometimes a story will surprise you with a plot twist; sometimes your predictions will hit the mark. Either way, watching for text clues can help you find the situational irony in Twain's story. As you read, use a chart like the one shown to record your predictions and the clues from the text that led you to make your educated guess.

Predictions	Text Clues
I predict he'll find a way to get involved.	Narrator says he can't resist the temptation to be a subject.

▲ VOCABULARY IN CONTEXT

Match each vocabulary word in the first column with the word in the second column that is closest in meaning.

1.	unassailable	a.	trust
2.	multifariously	b.	peeved
3.	minutest	c.	spellbound
4.	implacable	d.	overtrusting
5.	credulity	e.	tiniest
6.	rapt	f.	unquestionable
7.	nettled	g.	unyielding
8.	gullible	h.	variously

 Complete the activities in your **Reader/Writer Notebook**.

Have you ever put on an ACT?

Occasionally we are tempted to try to fool others into thinking we are smarter, cooler, richer, or more popular than we really are. Sometimes it's as simple as putting on a new pair of sunglasses or pretending to know more about something than we really do. In his autobiography, Mark Twain recalls from his youth a more extreme version of this kind of deception.

DISCUSS With your classmates, come up with a list of ways in which people pretend to be something they're not. Examples can range from simple social posing to more outrageous, even criminal, forms of falsified identity. Then review these examples, considering people's motives for such deception.

659

Have you ever put on an ACT?
Introduce the activity by asking students to explore the consequences of deception. Can fooling others ever lead to a positive outcome—and if so, for whom?

TEXT ANALYSIS
COMMON CORE
RI 6

● *Model the Skill:* IRONY AND OVERSTATEMENT

To begin a discussion of irony and overstatement, point out that both techniques restate facts to achieve an effect. Then have students identify these examples of overstatement and of irony as situational, dramatic, or verbal:

1. Emily opens her lunch bag, pulls out a squashed baloney sandwich, and exclaims, "Another gourmet meal!" (*verbal irony*)

2. Jaime stays up until 2:00 a.m. studying for a math exam, only to fall asleep during the test. (*situational irony*)

3. Alex, a character in a movie, is worried that his girlfriend is spending a lot of time with his best friend, but the audience knows that they are planning Alex's surprise party. (*dramatic irony*)

4. After the marathon, Jorge drank enough water to float a battleship. (*overstatement*)

VOCABULARY SKILL
COMMON CORE
L 4

▲ VOCABULARY IN CONTEXT

DIAGNOSE WORD KNOWLEDGE Have students complete Vocabulary in Context. Check their word choices against the following:

credulity (krĭ-dōō'lĭ-tē) *n.* an inclination to believe too readily

gullible (gŭl'ə-bəl) *adj.* easily deceived or tricked

implacable (ĭm-plăk'ə-bəl) *adj.* impossible to satisfy

minutest (mī-nōō'tĭst) *adj.* smallest; most precise

multifariously (mŭl'tə-f,r'ē-əs-lē) *adv.* in many and various ways

nettled (nĕt'əld) *adj.* irritated; annoyed **nettle** *v.*

rapt (răpt) *adj.* deeply moved, delighted, or absorbed

unassailable (ŭn'ə-sā'lə-bəl) *adj.* impossible to dispute or disprove

---

READING STRATEGY
COMMON CORE
RI 1

■ *Model the Skill:* PREDICT

Point out that even a story featuring situational irony includes text clues that help readers make predictions. The clues sometimes turn out to be false leads, tempting us to expect things that don't occur.

 RESOURCE MANAGER—Copy Master
Predict p. 23 (for student use while reading the selection)

SUMMARY

In this excerpt from his autobiography, Twain tells of a mesmerizer's visit to his hometown. Jealous of audience members who serve as the mesmerizer's subjects, the teenaged Twain fakes being hypnotized. He soon becomes the star of the show; in fact, he is so convincing that by the time the mesmerizer leaves town, Twain is the only person who doesn't believe in hypnotism. Years later, when he confesses the deception to his mother, she refuses to believe him. Twain concludes that a well-told lie has a long life.

READ WITH A PURPOSE

Help students set a purpose for reading. Tell them to note instances in which Twain uses forms of irony to make his point.

READING STRATEGY

COMMON CORE
RI 1

Ⓐ Model the Skill: PREDICT

Explain how to predict events based on contextual clues. Have students reread lines 1–9 and identify the person who arrives in the village. Review the definition of *mesmerizer*. Suggest that misunderstandings might arise when people are hypnotized, and have them predict what types of misunderstanding might occur between a mesmerizer and the townspeople.

Possible answer: Readers can predict that the young Twain might interact with the mesmerizer who has come to his village.

Extend the Discussion What clues lead you to that prediction?

The Autobiography of Mark Twain

Mark Twain

BACKGROUND This excerpt from Mark Twain's autobiography focuses on a traveling show that visited Twain's small town around 1850. These entertainment shows were popular in a time before radio, television, or computers. They featured magic acts, ventriloquists, and mesmerizers (or hypnotists). Hypnotists placed people in suggestible, trancelike states and then ordered them to perform various antics.

An exciting event in our village was the arrival of the mesmerizer.[1] I think the year was 1850. As to that I am not sure but I know the month—it was May; that detail has survived the wear of fifty years. A pair of connected little incidents of that month have served to keep the memory of it green for me all this time; incidents of no consequence and not worth embalming,[2] yet my memory has preserved them carefully and flung away things of real value to give them space and make them comfortable. The truth is, a person's memory has no more sense than his conscience and no appreciation whatever of values and proportions. However, never mind those trifling incidents; my subject is the mesmerizer now. **Ⓐ**

10 He advertised his show and promised marvels. Admission as usual: 25 cents, children half price. The village had heard of mesmerism in a general way but had not encountered it yet. Not many people attended the first night but next day they had so many wonders to tell that everybody's curiosity was fired and after

---

1. **mesmerizer:** hypnotist; from the name of an Austrian physician, Franz Anton Mesmer, who popularized hypnotism in the 1770s.
2. **embalming:** preserving.

Analyze Visuals ▶
Look at the poster on page 661, especially at the image in the top circle. What can you **infer** about the mesmerizer depicted?

Ⓐ PREDICT
Based on the clues presented in this first paragraph, what can you predict about what might happen in the story?

DIFFERENTIATED INSTRUCTION

FOR ENGLISH LANGUAGE LEARNERS

Textual Context Point out to students that Twain frequently gives words unusual nuances in his writing. Read aloud lines 3–4, beginning with, "A pair of . . ." and ending with, ". . . not worth embalming,". Have students look up the definitions of *green* and *embalming*. Ask volunteers to explain what is unusual about Twain's use of these words in the passage. *Possible answer: Green* usually refers to the color or to new plant growth, not to freshness. *Embalming* refers primarily to preserving a dead body from decay.

FOR STRUGGLING READERS

In combination with the *Audio Anthology CD*, use one or more Targeted Passages (pp. 662, 664, 666, and 668) to ensure that students focus on key events and concepts. Targeted passages are also good for English language learners.

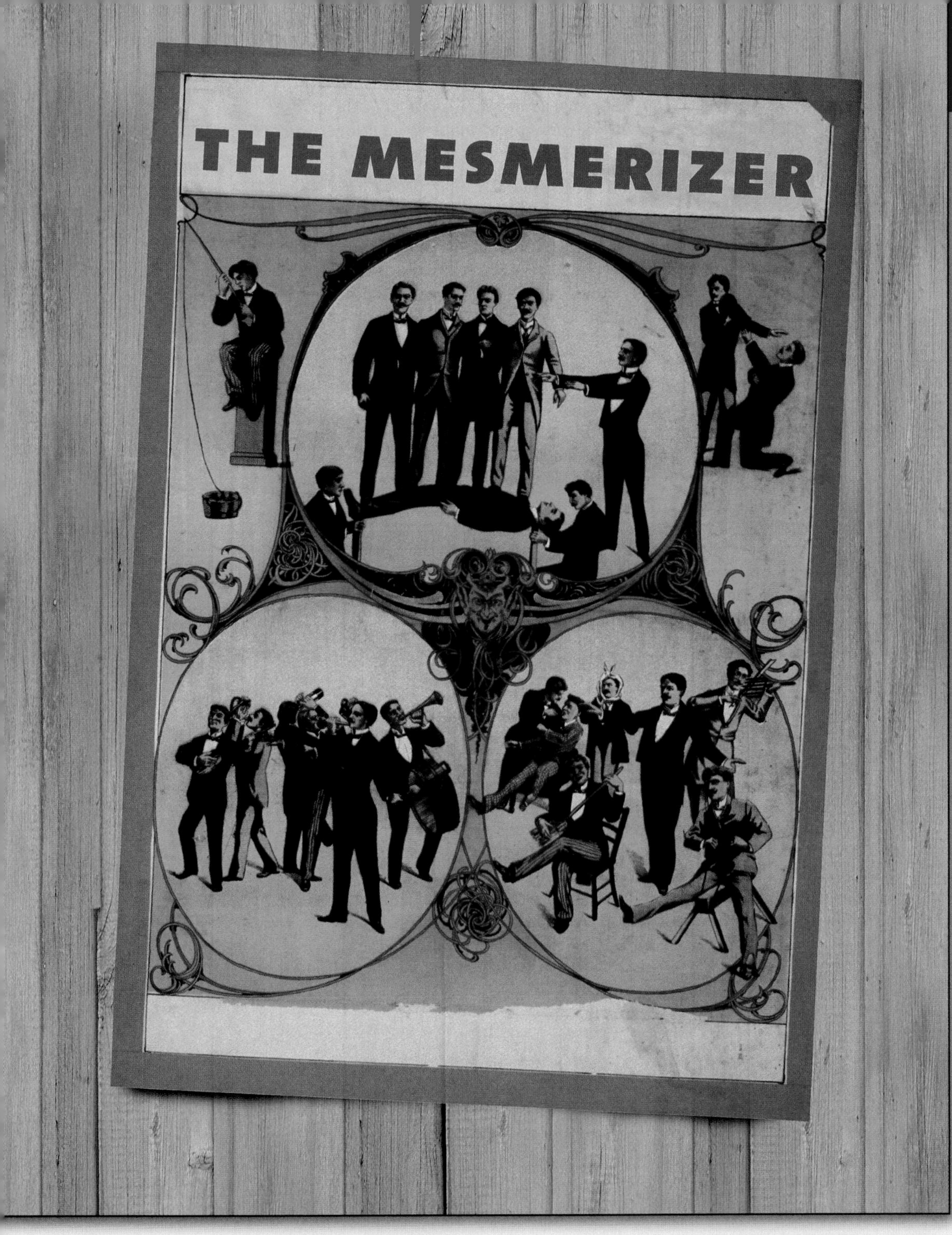

Reading Support

This selection on **thinkcentral.com** includes embedded **ThinkAloud** models—students "thinking aloud" about the story to model the kinds of questions a good reader would ask about a selection.

Analyze Visuals

Possible answer: The viewer can infer that the mesmerizer can control the behavior of other people—and can even defy the law of gravity—simply by using his hands.

BACKGROUND

Mesmerism Franz Anton Mesmer (1734–1815) was an Austrian doctor who gave his name to what he considered a system for curing illness. Mesmer believed that every part of the universe was connected by magnetic fluid and that illness occurred when the balance of fluid in a person's body was disturbed. According to Mesmer, magnetic passes of a doctor's hands over the patient's body could cure sickness by redirecting that fluid. After frenzied convulsions or hypnotic trances, Mesmer's patients reported themselves restored to health.

Mesmer experienced considerable success when he introduced his system of "animal magnetism" to Paris in 1778. King Louis XVI was skeptical, however, and he appointed a scientific commission to investigate Mesmer's claims. Benjamin Franklin and other commission members declared Mesmer a fraud, concluding that his cures were simply the product of people's imaginations.

Although Mesmer's theory of magnetism as a therapeutic technique was discredited, interest in the hypnotic trance state flourished during the 19th century. In the United States, mesmerism became a form of entertainment—the kind of traveling performance that young Mark Twain encounters in this account.

FOR ADVANCED LEARNERS/AP

Science and History Ask students to analyze the illustrations on page 661. Which images appear to be scientific, and which seem to be mere showmanship? What about the concept of mesmerism may have appealed to the people of the 1800s?

Direct students to lines 20–47. Use these prompts to help students explore young Twain's motivation and character:

Recall Why does Twain pretend to be mesmerized? *Possible answer: Twain is jealous of the attention that Hicks is getting (lines 28–32) and wants to outdo him (lines 46–47). Since Twain seems resistant to mesmerism (lines 20–23), he decides to pretend.*

Analyze What does this passage reveal about young Twain's character? Cite evidence. *Possible answer: This passage shows that Twain cannot resist temptation. He is observant, able to imitate the other subjects by watching their actions. Twain is competitive, determined to replace Hicks; and he is dishonest, willing to deceive people to gain attention.*

TEXT ANALYSIS

COMMON CORE L 5a

B OVERSTATEMENT

Discuss how exaggeration can add humor. For example, mice do not roar, and cookies are not as big as the moon. Then read aloud lines 14–19. Point out the exaggeration in the phrase "suffer all things short of death by fire." Tell students that the author uses overstatement in this phrase to emphasize his eagerness and anticipation. *Possible answer: The overstatement shows how much Twain wanted the crowd's attention. Overstatement makes the lines humorous and make readers hope he gets his chance to be mesmerized.*

Extend the Discussion In what ways do the media commonly use overstatement?

---

that for a fortnight[3] the magician had prosperous times. I was fourteen or fifteen years old, the age at which a boy is willing to endure all things, suffer all things short of death by fire, if thereby he may be conspicuous and show off before the public; and so, when I saw the "subjects" perform their foolish antics on the platform and make the people laugh and shout and admire I had a burning desire to be a subject myself. **B**

20   Every night for three nights I sat in the row of candidates on the platform and held the magic disk[4] in the palm of my hand and gazed at it and tried to get sleepy, but it was a failure; I remained wide awake and had to retire defeated, like the majority. Also, I had to sit there and be gnawed with envy of Hicks, our journeyman;[5] I had to sit there and see him scamper and jump when Simmons the enchanter exclaimed, "See the snake! See the snake!" and hear him say, "My, how beautiful!" in response to the suggestion that he was observing a splendid sunset; and so on—the whole insane business. I couldn't laugh, I couldn't applaud; it filled me with bitterness to have others do it and to have people make a hero of Hicks and crowd around him when the show was over and ask him for more and

30 more particulars of the wonders he had seen in his visions and manifest in many ways that they were proud to be acquainted with him. Hicks—the idea! I couldn't stand it; I was getting boiled to death in my own bile.

    On the fourth night temptation came and I was not strong enough to resist. When I had gazed at the disk a while I pretended to be sleepy and began to nod. Straightway came the professor and made passes over my head and down my body and legs and arms, finishing each pass with a snap of his fingers in the air to discharge the surplus electricity;[6] then he began to "draw" me with the disk, holding it in his fingers and telling me I could not take my eyes off it, try as I might; so I rose slowly, bent and gazing, and followed that disk all over the place,

40 just as I had seen the others do. Then I was put through the other paces. Upon suggestion I fled from snakes, passed buckets at a fire, became excited over hot steamboat-races, made love to imaginary girls and kissed them, fished from the platform and landed mud cats that outweighed me—and so on, all the customary marvels. But not in the customary way. I was cautious at first and watchful, being afraid the professor would discover that I was an impostor and drive me from the platform in disgrace; but as soon as I realized that I was not in danger, I set myself the task of terminating Hicks's usefulness as a subject and of usurping his place.

    It was a sufficiently easy task. Hicks was born honest, I without that incumbrance[7]—so some people said. Hicks saw what he saw and reported

50 accordingly, I saw more than was visible and added to it such details as could help. Hicks had no imagination; I had a double supply. He was born calm, I was

---

3. **fortnight:** 14 days.

4. **magic disk:** the object used by the mesmerizer to focus a subject's attention, helping him or her to achieve a hypnotic state.

5. **journeyman:** a competent and experienced, but not brilliant, craftsman.

6. **discharge...electricity:** It was once erroneously believed that hypnosis was linked to electricity and magnetism.

7. **incumbrance:** earlier spelling of *encumbrance,* here meaning "burden; obligation."

COMMON CORE L 5a

B OVERSTATEMENT
Remember that **overstatement**, or hyperbole, is an exaggeration used to emphasize a point or create humor. Reread lines 14–19, looking for instances of Twain's use of this rhetorical technique. Why do you think Twain uses overstatement here? How might his use of overstatement in a work of nonfiction affect readers?

1 Targeted Passage

Language Coach

Etymology *Usurping* (line 47) means "taking control by force." *Usurp* comes from the Latin word *usurpare,* meaning "to seize for use." Read lines 44–47. Why does Twain want to usurp Hicks's place? Explain your answer, using the word *usurp.*

FOR STRUGGLING READERS

1 Targeted Passage [Lines 20–40]

This passage describes Twain's inner conflict as he watches the mesmerizer's show.

- How does Twain participate in the magician's attempts to hypnotize his subjects? What is the outcome? (lines 20–23)

- How does Twain feel as he watches Hicks? (lines 27–32)

- How does Twain give in to temptation and resolve his frustration? (lines 39–40)

Comprehension Support Help students break down long, complicated sentences like the one in lines 14–19 by reducing them to one set or more of basic components: subject, verb, and object. Ask:

- Who or what is the sentence (clause) about?

- What action does the subject do?

- Who or what receives the action of the verb(s)?

FOR ENGLISH LANGUAGE LEARNERS

Language Coach

Etymology *Answer: Twain is jealous of the attention Hicks receives during his "mesmerism." Twain wants to* usurp *Hicks and receive the attention himself.*

In public life, when is the media likely to discuss something being *usurped*?

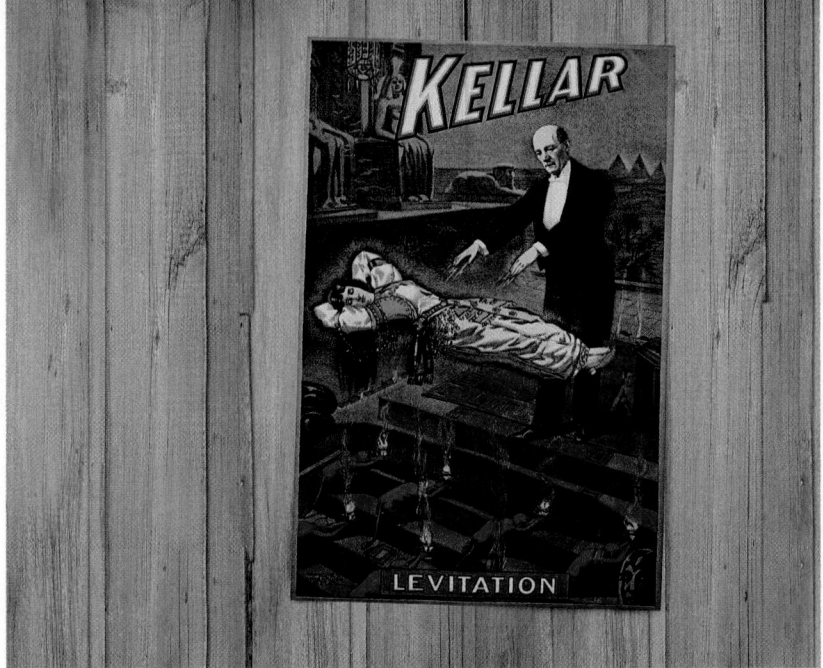

KELLAR

LEVITATION

born excited. No vision could start a rapture in him and he was constipated as to language, anyway; but if I saw a vision I emptied the dictionary onto it and lost the remnant of my mind into the bargain.

At the end of my first half-hour Hicks was a thing of the past, a fallen hero, a broken idol, and I knew it and was glad and said in my heart, "Success to crime!" Hicks could never have been mesmerized to the point where he could kiss an imaginary girl in public or a real one either, but I was competent. Whatever Hicks had failed in, I made it a point to succeed in, let the cost be what it might,
60 physically or morally. He had shown several bad defects and I had made a note of them. For instance, if the magician asked, "What do you see?" and left him to invent a vision for himself, Hicks was dumb and blind, he couldn't see a thing nor say a word, whereas the magician soon found out that when it came to seeing visions of a stunning and marketable sort I could get along better without his help than with it.

Then there was another thing: Hicks wasn't worth a tallow dip[8] on mute mental suggestion. Whenever Simmons stood behind him and gazed at the back of his skull and tried to drive a mental suggestion into it, Hicks sat with vacant face and never suspected. If he had been noticing he could have seen by
70 the **rapt** faces of the audience that something was going on behind his back that required a response. Inasmuch as I was an impostor I dreaded to have this test put upon me, for I knew the professor would be "willing" me to do something, and as

---

8. **wasn't worth a tallow dip:** wasn't any good. A tallow dip was an inexpensive candle.

COMMON CORE L 5a

Language Coach

Metaphors A **metaphor** is a figure of speech that compares two things that have something in common. In lines 55–56, Twain directly compares Hicks to a fallen hero and a broken idol. What does Twain mean by this comparison?

rapt (răpt) *adj.* deeply moved, delighted, or absorbed

Have you ever put on an
ACT?

Discuss Based on lines 55–65, how effective is young Twain's deception? How can you tell?
Possible answer: Twain's deception is very effective: Within a half hour he replaces Hicks in the crowd's affections, and Simmons himself soon realizes that Twain is a better "subject" than Hicks.

About the Art Harry Kellar (1849–1922), an entertainer who combined magic tricks with elaborate presentations, was known as the "Dean of American Magicians." His illusions, or misleading versions of reality, were accomplished by clever mechanical arrangements. This poster shows one of his most famous illusions: the levitation of a girl who rose from a couch and then disappeared into thin air.

VOCABULARY COMMON CORE L 4

OWN THE WORD

rapt: The Latin word for *rapt* means "to seize" and is related to the word *enrapture*. Both words are descriptive of being "deeply moved or delighted; engrossed." Ask students to describe a situation that kept their *rapt* attention.

Possible answer: Answers could include a theatrical performance, magic trick, ball game, a documentary, or a lecture.

FOR ENGLISH LANGUAGE LEARNERS

Language Coach COMMON CORE L 5a

Metaphors *Possible Answer: Twain means that he is the crowd's new hero and Hicks has lost, or fallen from, their attention.* If a hero who has fallen out of favor is described as "a broken idol," what type of character might the metaphor "a bad apple" describe?

FOR ADVANCED LEARNERS/AP

Research Hypnotism Have small groups of students find out more about these hypnotism-related topics:

• the roots of hypnotism in rites practiced by ancient Hindus and other early cultures and its use in place of surgical anesthesia

• reasons that the practice has been dismissed as a parlor trick practiced by charlatans

Have groups present their findings to the class.

C PREDICT

Possible answer: Given the character traits that Twain has exhibited and the statements that he has made about himself, readers can predict that he will rise to the challenge and invent a scenario that will both fool and entertain the audience.

REVISIT THE BIG QUESTION

Have you ever put on an ACT?

Discuss Based on lines 74–98, how does this part of Twain's account indicate that Twain isn't the only character with some skill at deception? In what sense is this turn of events an example of situational irony? *Possible answer: Twain is worried about being disgraced when his deception is revealed (lines 77–78), but he is not "exposed and denounced," because Simmons himself is an impostor who is happy to take advantage of Twain's deception (lines 93–98). Ironically, Twain is not punished for his deception, because an even greater deception is going on—the mesmerizer's.*

VOCABULARY

COMMON CORE
L 4

OWN THE WORD

minutest: Tell students that *minutest* and *minute* are both adjectives that describe the "smallest; most precise" things. Have students use either word to create a sentence that shows an understanding of the word. *Possible answer: Trent needed a microscope to view the* minute *species of plankton.*

I couldn't know what it was, I should be exposed and denounced. However, when my time came, I took my chance. I perceived by the tense and expectant faces of the people that Simmons was behind me willing me with all his might. I tried my best to imagine what he wanted but nothing suggested itself. I felt ashamed and miserable then. I believed that the hour of my disgrace was come and that in another moment I should go out of that place disgraced. I ought to be ashamed to confess it but my next thought was not how I could win the compassion of kindly 80 hearts by going out humbly and in sorrow for my misdoings, but how I could go out most sensationally and spectacularly. **C**

There was a rusty and empty old revolver lying on the table among the "properties" employed in the performances. On May Day two or three weeks before there had been a celebration by the schools and I had had a quarrel with a big boy who was the school bully and I had not come out of it with credit.[9] That boy was now seated in the middle of the house, halfway down the main aisle. I crept stealthily and impressively toward the table, with a dark and murderous scowl on my face, copied from a popular romance, seized the revolver suddenly, flourished it, shouted the bully's name, jumped off the platform and made a 90 rush for him and chased him out of the house before the paralyzed people could interfere to save him. There was a storm of applause, and the magician, addressing the house, said, most impressively—

"That you may know how really remarkable this is and how wonderfully developed a subject we have in this boy, I assure you that without a single spoken word to guide him he has carried out what I mentally commanded him to do, to the **minutest** detail. I could have stopped him at a moment in his vengeful career by a mere exertion of my will, therefore the poor fellow who has escaped was at no time in danger."

So I was not in disgrace. I returned to the platform a hero and happier than 100 I have ever been in this world since. As regards mental suggestion, my fears of it were gone. I judged that in case I failed to guess what the professor might be willing me to do, I could count on putting up something that would answer just as well. I was right, and exhibitions of unspoken suggestion became a favorite with the public. Whenever I perceived that I was being willed to do something I got up and did something—anything that occurred to me—and the magician, not being a fool, always ratified it. When people asked me, "How *can* you tell what he is willing you to do?" I said, "It's just as easy," and they always said admiringly, "Well, it beats *me* how you can do it."

Hicks was weak in another detail. When the professor made passes over him 110 and said "his whole body is without sensation now—come forward and test him, ladies and gentlemen," the ladies and gentlemen always complied eagerly and stuck pins into Hicks, and if they went deep Hicks was sure to wince, then that poor professor would have to explain that Hicks "wasn't sufficiently under the influence." But I didn't wince; I only suffered and shed tears on the inside. The miseries that a conceited boy will endure to keep up his "reputation"! And so

---

9. **credit:** honor or distinction.

C PREDICT
Reread lines 66–81. How do you predict Twain will respond to the challenge of "mute mental suggestion" from Simmons?

2 Targeted Passage

minutest (mī-nōō′tĭst) *adj.* smallest; most precise

DIFFERENTIATED INSTRUCTION

FOR STRUGGLING READERS

2 Targeted Passage [Lines 82–98]

In this passage, Twain continues his deception through an inventive response to the mesmerizer's mental suggestion.

- How does Twain make use of his experience with the school bully? (lines 86–90)
- How does the audience react? (lines 90–91)
- Why does the mesmerizer take credit for Twain's actions? How do his words keep Twain's secret safe? (lines 93–98)

FOR ENGLISH LANGUAGE LEARNERS

Vocabulary: Idioms Share or elicit the meanings of these expressions; then help students use them in original sentences:

- *count on* (line 102), "to be confident about"
- *putting up* (line 102), "creating"
- *it beats me* (line 108), "I don't understand"
- *was sure to* (line 112), "definitely would"
- *shed tears* (line 114), "cried"
- *air it* (line 134), "to speak about it in public"

will a conceited man; I know it in my own person and have seen it in a hundred thousand others. That professor ought to have protected me and I often hoped he would, when the tests were unusually severe, but he didn't. It may be that he was deceived as well as the others, though I did not believe it nor think it possible.

120 Those were dear good people but they must have carried simplicity and **credulity** to the limit. They would stick a pin in my arm and bear on it until they drove it a third of its length in, and then be lost in wonder that by a mere exercise of will power the professor could turn my arm to iron and make it insensible to pain. Whereas it was not insensible at all; I was suffering agonies of pain.

After that fourth night, that proud night, that triumphant night, I was the only subject. Simmons invited no more candidates to the platform. I performed alone every night the rest of the fortnight. Up to that time a dozen wise old heads, the intellectual aristocracy of the town, had held out as **implacable** unbelievers. I was as hurt by this as if I were engaged in some honest occupation. There is 130 nothing surprising about this. Human beings feel dishonor the most, sometimes, when they most deserve it. That handful of overwise old gentlemen kept on shaking their heads all the first week and saying they had seen no marvels there that could not have been produced by collusion; and they were pretty vain of their unbelief too and liked to show it and air it and be superior to the ignorant and the **gullible.** Particularly old Dr. Peake, who was the ringleader of the irreconcilables and very formidable; for he was an F.F.V.,[10] he was learned, white-haired and venerable, nobly and richly clad in the fashions of an earlier and a courtlier day, he was large and stately, and he not only seemed wise but was what he seemed in that regard. He had great influence and his opinion upon any matter was worth much 140 more than that of any other person in the community. When I conquered him at last, I knew I was undisputed master of the field; and now after more than fifty years I acknowledge with a few dry old tears that I rejoiced without shame. **D**

In 1847 we were living in a large white house on the corner of Hill and Main Streets—a house that still stands but isn't large now although it hasn't lost a plank; I saw it a year ago and noticed that shrinkage. My father died in it in March of the year mentioned but our family did not move out of it until some months afterward. Ours was not the only family in the house; there was another, Dr. Grant's. One day Dr. Grant and Dr. Reyburn argued a matter on the street with sword canes and Grant was brought home **multifariously** punctured. Old Dr. 150 Peake caulked the leaks and came every day for a while to look after him.

The Grants were Virginians, like Peake, and one day when Grant was getting well enough to be on his feet and sit around in the parlor and talk, the conversation fell upon Virginia and old times. I was present but the group were probably unconscious of me, I being only a lad and a negligible quantity. Two of

---

10. **F.F.V.:** First Family of Virginia. Dr. Peake has high social status because his ancestors were among the first settlers of Virginia.

credulity (krĭ-dōō'lĭ-tē) *n.* an inclination to believe too readily

implacable (ĭm-plăk'ə-bəl) *adj.* impossible to satisfy

gullible (gŭl'ə-bəl) *adj.* easily deceived or tricked

D IRONY
Reread lines 125–142. Identify the **situational irony** in Twain's reaction to the skeptical wise old men in the crowd. What does this suggest about him?

multifariously
(mŭl'tə-fâr'ē-əs-lē) *adv.* in many and various ways

FOR STRUGGLING READERS

Draw Conclusions Call students' attention to lines 117–119. Ask students why they think that the mesmerizer does not try to protect Twain if, as Twain suspects, he is not fooled by Twain's performance. *Possible answers: The mesmerizer remains silent because he does not care about Twain's comfort; he is willing to let Twain suffer to gain more popularity for his show and, ultimately, more money for himself.*

FOR ADVANCED LEARNERS/AP

Analyze Figurative Language Twain uses metaphors to enliven ordinary language, encourage interpretation, and provide maximum meaning with a minimum of words. In lines 149–150, for example, he uses a plumbing metaphor to describe the nature of Dr. Grant's injuries and Dr. Peake's treatment. Challenge students to locate and explain other examples of Twain's use of metaphor, such as in lines 53, 189–191, and 278–279.

TIERED DISCUSSION PROMPTS

Refer to lines 124–142 and use these prompts to help students understand that yet another conflict lies ahead for Twain:

Summarize So far, whom has Twain convinced of his ability to be mesmerized? *Possible answer: Twain seems to have convinced just about everyone in town.*

Evaluate Does Twain sharing his thoughts about the outcome of the story before actually telling the story ruin the outcome for readers? Why or why not? *Accept all reasonable answers.*

TEXT ANALYSIS  COMMON CORE **RI 6**

D IRONY AND OVERSTATEMENT

Possible answer: The situational irony is that Twain's reaction to the old men's skepticism is the opposite of what readers would expect. Twain says that he was as hurt as if he were telling the truth (line 129). This ironic reaction suggests that he is fully engaged in the role that he has created.

VOCABULARY COMMON CORE **L 4**

OWN THE WORD

- **credulity:** *Credulity* refers to someone's "inclination to believe too readily." Have students provide synonyms. *Possible answers: easy, naive*

- **implacable:** Tell students that an idiom is a phrase that represents a concept or thought. An idiom for *implacable* is "stubborn as a mule."

- **gullible:** Remind students that gullible means "easily deceived." Antonyms include: *cynical, suspicious.* Ask students to write a sentence using *gullible* correctly. *Possible answer: Ramon thought his sister gullible to believe in ghosts.*

- **multifariously:** Have students create a semantic web for the word *multifariously.* Write the word and definition in the center circle. Draw spider legs from the center and have students use a thesaurus to find synonyms. *Possible answers: diversified, miscellaneous*

Possible answer: *Twain probably will succeed by thinking up some imaginative trick to convince the wise old men. He may describe a vision based on one or both of the accounts that he heard these men tell a few years earlier: the Richmond theater fire (lines 154–162) and the Peakes' colonial mansion (lines 164–171).*

TEXT ANALYSIS — COMMON CORE RI 6

F *Model the Skill:* **IRONY AND OVERSTATEMENT**

Remind students that in lines 151–163, Twain had been present when Dr. Peake and Mrs. Crawford vividly described the Richmond fire.

Possible answer: *Readers know that Twain is retelling an overheard eyewitness account of the Richmond fire. The effect of this irony—the fact that Dr. Peake is taken in by Twain's deception—is to reinforce Twain's cunning (for Twain remembers the details that he heard) and to suggest that the wise old men of the town may not be as wise as they seem.*

VOCABULARY — COMMON CORE L 4

OWN THE WORD

unassailable: Explain that *unassailable* is an adjective made from the verb *assail* which means "to attack or trouble; to ridicule or disprove."

---

the group—Dr. Peake and Mrs. Crawford, Mrs. Grant's mother—had been of the audience when the Richmond theater burned down thirty-six years before, and they talked over the frightful details of that memorable tragedy. These were eyewitnesses, and with their eyes I saw it all with an intolerable vividness: I saw 160 the black smoke rolling and tumbling toward the sky, I saw the flames burst through it and turn red, I heard the shrieks of the despairing, I glimpsed their faces at the windows, caught fitfully through the veiling smoke, I saw them jump to their death or to mutilation worse than death. The picture is before me yet and can never fade.

In due course they talked of the colonial mansion of the Peakes, with its stately columns and its spacious grounds, and by odds and ends I picked up a clearly defined idea of the place. I was strongly interested, for I had not before heard of such palatial things from the lips of people who had seen them with their own eyes. One detail, casually dropped, hit my imagination hard. In the wall by the great front door there was a round hole as big as a saucer—a British cannon ball 170 had made it in the war of the Revolution. It was breathtaking; it made history real; history had never been real to me before.

Very well, three or four years later, as already mentioned, I was king bee and sole "subject" in the mesmeric show; it was the beginning of the second week; the performance was half over; just then the majestic Dr. Peake with his ruffled bosom and wrist-bands and his gold-headed cane entered, and a deferential citizen vacated his seat beside the Grants and made the great chief take it. This happened while I was trying to invent something fresh in the way of vision, in response to the professor's remark—

"Concentrate your powers. Look—look attentively. There—don't you see 180 something? Concentrate—concentrate! Now then—describe it." **E**

Without suspecting it, Dr. Peake, by entering the place, had reminded me of the talk of three years before. He had also furnished me capital and was become my confederate, an accomplice in my frauds. I began on a vision, a vague and dim one (that was part of the game at the beginning of a vision; it isn't best to see it too clearly at first, it might look as if you had come loaded with it). The vision developed by degrees and gathered swing, momentum, energy. It was the Richmond fire. Dr. Peake was cold at first and his fine face had a trace of polite scorn in it; but when he began to recognize that fire, that expression changed and his eyes began to light up. As soon as I saw that, I threw the valves wide open and 190 turned on all the steam and gave those people a supper of fire and horrors that was calculated to last them one while! They couldn't gasp when I got through—they were petrified. Dr. Peake had risen and was standing—and breathing hard. He said, in a great voice:

"My doubts are ended. No collusion could produce that miracle. It was totally impossible for him to know those details, yet he has described them with the clarity of an eyewitness —and with what **unassailable** truthfulness God knows I know!" **F**

I saved the colonial mansion for the last night and solidified and perpetuated

---

Language Coach

Word Definitions
Eyewitnesses (line 158) means "people who have seen something personally and can report on it." What had Dr. Peake and Mrs. Crawford personally seen? Answer the question using the phrases *give eyewitness accounts of* or *eyewitnesses to.*

E PREDICT
Predict how Twain will win over the wise old men of the town.

3 Targeted Passage

unassailable
(ŭn′ə-sā′lə-bəl) *adj.*
impossible to dispute or disprove

F IRONY
What do you know that Dr. Peake doesn't? Explain how this **dramatic irony** affects your impression of the characters involved, including young Twain.

DIFFERENTIATED INSTRUCTION

FOR STRUGGLING READERS

 **Targeted Passage** [Lines 181–197]

In this passage, Twain converts his most notable skeptic to belief in mesmerism.

- What does Twain remember when Dr. Peake enters? (lines 181–182)
- Why does Dr. Peake's facial expression change as Twain describes his vision? (lines 187–188)

- Why does Twain refer to Dr. Peake as a "confederate" and an "accomplice"? (line 183)
- Why is Dr. Peake convinced that he has experienced a miracle? (lines 194–196)

FOR ENGLISH LANGUAGE LEARNERS

Language: Punctuation and Print Cues Have students reread lines 157–162. Note that each item in the series begins with "I saw," "I heard," or "I glimpsed," and the items are separated by commas. Note that Twain uses another comma within one of these items. Modern punctuation style usually mandates semicolons to separate items in a series if any of the items includes an internal comma.

Language Coach

Word Definitions *Possible answer: Dr. Peake and Mrs. Crawford gave eyewitness accounts of a fire they had seen in a Richmond theater.* Point out that *eyewitnesses* is a compound word. Ask students how the separate words "eye" and "witnesses" help them figure out the word's definition.

Dr. Peake's conversion with the cannon-ball hole. He explained to the house that
200 I could never have heard of that small detail, which differentiated this mansion
from all other Virginian mansions and perfectly identified it, therefore the fact
stood proven that I had *seen* it in my vision. Lawks![11]

It is curious. When the magician's engagement closed there was but one person
in the village who did not believe in mesmerism and I was the one. All the others
were converted but I was to remain an implacable and unpersuadable disbeliever
in mesmerism and hypnotism for close upon fifty years. This was because I never
would examine them, in after life. I couldn't. The subject revolted me. Perhaps it
brought back to me a passage in my life which for pride's sake I wished to forget;

---

11. **Lawks!:** an expression of wonder or amusement, shortened from "Lord, have mercy!"

THE AUTOBIOGRAPHY OF MARK TWAIN **667**

TIERED DISCUSSION PROMPTS

In lines 203–210, use these prompts to help students explore Twain's reflection upon his experiences with the mesmerizer:

Restate How does Twain feel about his experience with the mesmerizer? *Possible answer: Twain is torn between feeling triumph for his achievement and regret for his deception.*

Analyze Why is it ironic that Twain became the "one person in the village who did not believe in mesmerism"? *Possible answer: It is ironic that Twain is the only doubter because it is his performance as a subject that has persuaded everyone else to believe in mesmerism.*

Evaluate Is Twain's cynical response to his experience believable? Defend your opinion. *Most students will find Twain's response believable, citing examples of cheaters who assume that the rest of the world is dishonest.*

FOR ADVANCED LEARNERS/AP

Analyze Tone Have students write an essay contrasting Twain's tone in lines 203–208 with the tone used earlier, such as in lines 99–100 and 172–173. Ask students to address these questions:

- How does the tone change during the excerpt? What might cause the change?
- How does the tone influence your understanding of Twain's account?

FOR STRUGGLING READERS

Develop Reading Fluency Use the anecdote in the targeted passage on page 666 to give students practice in pacing. Point out how Dr. Peake's response changes as Twain's "vision" unfolds. Then have students practice reading aloud in small groups to illustrate Dr. Peake's gradual recognition of Twain's story. Remind students that they can use volume, speed, and emphasis to highlight Dr. Peake's response.

Have you ever put on an ACT?

Discuss In lines 211–226, what is Twain saying in this passage about the consequences of deception, at least for him? *Possible answer: Twain is saying that he was unable to enjoy the consequences of his deception because he became quite uncomfortable over repeated compliments about his fraudulent triumphs.* Is his experience typical, or do most liars and cheaters manage to enjoy the fruits of their deception—and even the glory of undeserved praise? Explain. *Accept all thoughtful responses.*

READING STRATEGY

 **PREDICT**

COMMON CORE **RI 1**

Possible answer: Twain's mother may not believe him at first; he begins the paragraph by saying that it is hard to undo a lie (lines 227–228).

VOCABULARY

COMMON CORE **L 4**

OWN THE WORD

nettled: Tell students that a *nettle* is a prickly plant. When used as a verb, *nettled* refers to being "irritated or annoyed." Have students list things that *nettle* them. *Possible answers: nagging, boorish behavior; not being taken seriously; pesky siblings*

---

210 though I thought, or persuaded myself I thought, I should never come across a "proof" which wasn't thin and cheap and probably had a fraud like me behind it.

The truth is I did not have to wait long to get tired of my triumphs. Not thirty days, I think. The glory which is built upon a lie soon becomes a most unpleasant incumbrance. No doubt for a while I enjoyed having my exploits told and retold and told again in my presence and wondered over and exclaimed about, but I quite distinctly remember that there presently came a time when the subject was wearisome and odious to me and I could not endure the disgusting discomfort of it. I am well aware that the world-glorified doer of a deed of great and real splendor has just my experience; I know that he deliciously enjoys hearing about it for three or four weeks and that pretty soon after that he begins to dread the 220 mention of it and by and by wishes he had been with the damned before he ever thought of doing that deed. I remember how General Sherman[12] used to rage and swear over "While we were marching through Georgia," which was played at him and sung at him everywhere he went; still, I think I suffered a shade more than the legitimate hero does, he being privileged to soften his misery with the reflection that his glory was at any rate golden and reproachless in its origin, whereas I had no such privilege, there being no possible way to make mine respectable.

How easy it is to make people believe a lie and how hard it is to undo that work again! Thirty-five years after those evil exploits of mine I visited my old mother, whom I had not seen for ten years; and being moved by what seemed 230 to me a rather noble and perhaps heroic impulse, I thought I would humble myself and confess my ancient fault. It cost me a great effort to make up my mind; I dreaded the sorrow that would rise in her face and the shame that would look out of her eyes; but after long and troubled reflection, the sacrifice seemed due and right and I gathered my resolution together and made the confession. **G**

To my astonishment there were no sentimentalities, no dramatics, no George Washington effects; she was not moved in the least degree; she simply did not believe me and said so! I was not merely disappointed, I was **nettled** to have my costly truthfulness flung out of the market in this placid and confident way when I was expecting to get a profit out of it. I asserted and reasserted, with rising heat, 240 my statement that every single thing I had done on those long-vanished nights was a lie and a swindle; and when she shook her head tranquilly and said she knew better, I put up my hand and *swore* to it—adding a triumphant, "*Now* what do you say?"

It did not affect her at all; it did not budge her the fraction of an inch from her position. If this was hard for me to endure, it did not begin with the blister she put upon the raw[13] when she began to put my sworn oath out of court with *arguments* to prove that I was under a delusion and did not know what I was talking about. Arguments! Arguments to show that a person on a man's outside can know better what is on his inside than he does himself. I had cherished some

---

G PREDICT
Reread lines 227–234. How do you think Twain's mother will respond to his confession? Explain why you think this.

nettled (nĕt´əld) *adj.* irritated; annoyed **nettle** v.

④ Targeted Passage

---

12. **General Sherman:** William Tecumseh Sherman, Union commander who led a destructive march in 1864 from Atlanta, Georgia, to the Atlantic, cutting the Confederacy in two.

13. **the blister . . . raw:** a bad thing made even worse.

DIFFERENTIATED INSTRUCTION

FOR STRUGGLING READERS

④ **Targeted Passage** [Lines 228–249]

This passage explains what happens 35 years later, when Twain confesses the truth about his deception to his mother.

- How does Twain expect his mother to react to his confession? How does she actually react? (lines 232–237)

- How does Twain try to change his mother's mind, and what is her response? (lines 239–243)

- Why is he so bothered by her arguments? (lines 237–239)

FOR ENGLISH LANGUAGE LEARNERS

Culture: Clarify Tell the story of George Washington and the cherry tree. Emphasize that Washington was praised for his honesty rather than reprimanded for his action. Then ask students to explain what Twain meant by his reference to "George Washington effects" (lines 235–236). *Possible answer: Twain was expecting praise for his honesty in confessing his deception, even 35 years after the event.*

250 contempt for arguments before, I have not enlarged my respect for them since. She refused to believe that I had invented my visions myself; she said it was folly: that I was only a child at the time and could not have done it. She cited the Richmond fire and the colonial mansion and said they were quite beyond my capacities. Then I saw my chance! I said she was right—I didn't invent those, I got them from Dr. Peake. Even this great shot did not damage. She said Dr. Peake's evidence was better than mine, and he had said in plain words that it was impossible for me to have heard about those things. Dear, dear, what a grotesque and unthinkable situation: a confessed swindler convicted of honesty and condemned to acquittal by circumstantial evidence furnished by the swindled! Ⓗ

260 I realized with shame and with impotent vexation that I was defeated all along the line. I had but one card left but it was a formidable one. I played it and stood from under. It seemed ignoble to demolish her fortress after she had defended it so valiantly but the defeated know not mercy. I played that master card. It was the pin-sticking. I said solemnly—

"I give you my honor, a pin was never stuck into me without causing me cruel pain."

She only said—

"It is thirty-five years. I believe you do think that now but I was there and I know better. You never winced."

270 She was so calm! and I was so far from it, so nearly frantic.

"Oh, my goodness!" I said, "let me *show* you that I am speaking the truth. Here is my arm; drive a pin into it—drive it to the head—I shall not wince."

She only shook her gray head and said with simplicity and conviction—

"You are a man now and could dissemble the hurt; but you were only a child then and could not have done it."

And so the lie which I played upon her in my youth remained with her as an unchallengeable truth to the day of her death. Carlyle[14] said "a lie cannot live." It shows that he did not know how to tell them. If I had taken out a life policy on this one the premiums would have bankrupted me ages ago. ❧

Ⓗ **IRONY**
Reread lines 244–259. Identify the **situational irony** that underlies Twain's confession to his mother. What statement is Twain making about honesty and deception?

14. **Carlyle:** Thomas Carlyle, a British historian and essayist.

FOR ADVANCED LEARNERS/AP

Analyze Point of View Ask students to analyze how Twain's first-person point of view contributes to the excerpt's dramatic and situational irony. Elicit that the first-person point of view creates dramatic irony because readers know the truth about Twain's actions but other characters do not. The first-person point of view also allows readers to appreciate the excerpt's situational irony (and humor) by highlighting the contrast between what Twain expects to happen and what really does happen.

To test this analysis, have students rewrite a brief section of the excerpt from the point of view of a minor character—for example, Hicks or Dr. Peake. Then ask students to consider this question: Is there a narrator whose first-person point of view might create a completely different type of dramatic irony? If so, what would this narrator and dramatic irony be like?

TEXT ANALYSIS

COMMON CORE
RI 6

Ⓗ **IRONY AND OVERSTATEMENT**

Possible answer: *The situational irony is that when Twain finally tells his mother the truth about his deception, she thinks that he is lying (or, at least, failing to remember the truth). Moreover, she offers as proof of his past honesty the very proof that he used to carry out his deception. Twain is making the point that honesty and deception can be hard to prove and that a lie can be difficult to undo.*

SELECTION WRAP–UP

READ WITH A PURPOSE Now that students have read the selection, ask them to describe incidents in which Twain's humor made his story more memorable or striking. *Possible answer:* *Twain's description of his mother's disbelief of his confession is ironic and clever. Its humor highlights an important truth about unreliable memories and the endurance of lies.*

⭐ **CRITIQUE**

• Ask students how true to life they find Twain's autobiographical account.

• After completing the After Reading questions on page 671, have students revisit their responses and tell whether they have changed their opinions.

INDEPENDENT READING

Students may also enjoy *American Satire: An Anthology of Writings from Colonial Times to the Present* by Nicholas Bakalar and Stephen Kock.

TIERED DISCUSSION PROMPTS

Use these prompts to help students appreciate Twain's wit and wisdom:

Restate Express one of Twain's epigrams in your own words. What twist does Twain add to an otherwise straightforward observation or piece of advice? ***Possible answer: Restatements will vary. In general, Twain adds a skepticism to his observations and advice about life, especially when it comes to personal virtue and human interactions.***

Analyze Which epigram best fits the theme or message of the excerpt from Twain's *Autobiography*? Explain the connection. *Accept all well-reasoned responses; for example, students may choose the epigram about a lie's having more lives than a cat, because young Twain's experience with the mesmerizer was built on a lie.*

Evaluate Which epigram do you find the most relevant to your life or the lives of people you know? Explain why you consider this epigram particularly insightful or personally meaningful. *Accept all thoughtful responses.*

A popular writer and a sought-after public speaker, Mark Twain was full of witty remarks. What do these **epigrams**—short, clever, and sometimes paradoxical statements—reveal about Twain's view of human nature?

Epigrams
Mark Twain

Don't, like the cat, try to get more out of an experience than there is in it. The cat, having sat upon a hot stove lid, will not sit upon a hot stove lid again. Nor upon a cold stove lid.

· · · · · · · · ·

It is by the goodness of God that in our country we have those three unspeakably precious things: freedom of speech, freedom of conscience, and the prudence never to practice either of them.

· · · · · · · · ·

Man is the only animal that blushes. Or needs to.

· · · · · · · · ·

I am an old man and have known a great many troubles, but most of them have never happened.

· · · · · · · · ·

Nothing so needs reforming as other people's habits.

· · · · · · · · ·

When I was a boy of fourteen, my father was so ignorant I could hardly stand to have the old man around. But when I got to be twenty-one, I was astonished at how much the old man had learned in seven years.

· · · · · · · · ·

Put all your eggs in one basket, and—watch the basket.

There are several good protections against temptations, but the surest is cowardice.

· · · · · · · · ·

If you pick up a starving dog and make him prosperous, he will not bite you. This is the principal difference between a dog and a man.

· · · · · · · · ·

Good breeding consists in concealing how much we think of ourselves and how little we think of the other person.

· · · · · · · · ·

To promise not to do a thing is the surest way in the world to make a body want to go and do that very thing.

· · · · · · · · ·

Habit is habit, and not to be flung out of the window by any man, but coaxed downstairs a step at a time.

· · · · · · · · ·

One of the most striking differences between a cat and a lie is that a cat only has nine lives.

· · · · · · · · ·

Each person is born to one possession which outvalues all the others—his last breath.

· · · · · · · · ·

Everyone is a moon, and has a dark side which he never shows to anybody.

Comprehension

1. **Recall** What position or role does young Twain want to have? Why?

2. **Summarize** What weaknesses made Hicks a bad subject?

3. **Clarify** What does Twain do to get the mesmerizer to choose him?

COMMON CORE

RI 1 Cite evidence to support inferences drawn from the text.
RI 6 Determine an author's point of view or purpose in a text in which the rhetoric is effective.

Text Analysis

4. **Examine Predictions** Review your list of predictions and clues. Were you able to correctly predict everything that happened? Or were you surprised by how some aspects of the story developed? Cite details from the story in your answer.

5. **Contrast Characters** To become the mesmerizer's subject, Twain must displace Hicks. Twain presents himself as very different from Hicks. Based on this contrast, what does Twain seem to value and admire in a person? Use a chart like the one shown to collect evidence.

Hicks	Twain

6. **Analyze Irony** By its very nature, irony presents a degree of tension wherever it appears—the tension between expectations and reality. In many cases, it also adds humor. Review Twain's use of irony in the following passages. What's funny about them?

   • "Hicks was born honest, I without that incumbrance [burden]—so some people said." (lines 48–49)
   • Young Twain is genuinely hurt by those who do not believe his performances. (lines 127–129)
   • Twain identifies with great heroes who tire of hearing their praises sung. (lines 213–223)

7. **Draw Conclusions About Changing Perspective** In writing this piece, the adult Twain had a different view of himself, his boyhood deception, and the people of his hometown than he had as a young boy. What does this dual perspective show you about his growth from boyhood to adulthood?

Text Criticism

8. **Author's Perspective** Reread Twain's epigrams on page 670. What view of human nature do they reflect? Explain how this view is played out in the *Autobiography*, giving evidence from both texts to support your answer.

Have you ever put on an **ACT**?

Mark Twain indicates in his autobiography that as a young person, he was not very honest. Based on Twain's views later in life and those expressed in his epigrams, what effect do you think deception had on Twain?

THE AUTOBIOGRAPHY OF MARK TWAIN **671**

---

7. *As a boy, Twain is impressed with his ability to fool people. He thinks that the people of his hometown are gullible and foolish, and he feels superior to them. As an adult, he is ashamed of his deception and his need for attention and glory; he also realizes that a lie has a long life, even if the liar wants to confess the truth. His dual perspective suggests that people are gullible and perhaps foolish—but that he is able to recognize his own foolishness, as well.*

8. *Students should point to the cynical, critical view of human nature that Twain expresses in his epigrams; then they should cite specific text details to show how this cynicism appears throughout the excerpt from the* Autobiography.

Have you ever put on an **ACT**?
Possible answer: *The deception made Twain question people's motives and the "truth" of any situation.*

Practice and Apply

For preliminary support of post-reading questions, use these copy masters:

R RESOURCE MANAGER—Copy Masters
Reading Check p. 28
Irony p. 21
Question Support p. 29

Additional selection questions are provided for teachers on page 15.

ANSWERS

COMMON CORE RI 1, RI 6

1. *Twain wants to be the star subject in the mesmerizer's show because he wants to be the center of attention.*

2. *According to Twain, Hicks is a bad subject because he has no imagination, is too calm, can't use inventive language, and can describe only what he sees.*

3. *Twain gets the mesmerizer to choose him by pretending to be hypnotized.*

Possible answers:

4. ● **COMMON CORE FOCUS** **Predict** *Students should cite specific events from the excerpt and explain why they were or were not able to predict these events based on text clues.*

5. *Young Twain values imagination, enthusiasm, verbal dexterity, craftiness, self-control, and the abilities to read people and think on one's feet.* **Hicks:** *Honest (line 48), unimaginative (lines 51 and 61–63); calm (line 51); describing only what he sees (lines 49–50); not good with words (lines 52–53); unable to take "mental suggestions" (lines 66–67); unable to ignore pain (lines 109–114).* **Twain:** *Dishonest (lines 48–49); embellishes everything (lines 50–51); imaginative (line 51); able to use language well (lines 53–54); able to figure out what is expected and fake it (lines 63–65 and 82–91); able to ignore pain (line 114).*

6. ● **COMMON CORE FOCUS** **Analyze Irony** *Lines 48–49: Honesty usually is regarded as a positive trait, but Twain regards it as a burden that he has been spared. Lines 127–129: Instead of being satisfied by the number of people whom he has deceived, Twain is hurt that "a dozen wise old heads" have not fallen for his tricks. Lines 213–223: Twain is far from being a great hero.*

ANSWERS

Vocabulary in Context

▲ **VOCABULARY PRACTICE**

1. *true*   5. *false*
2. *true*   6. *true*
3. *false*   7. *false*
4. *true*   8. *true*

 RESOURCE MANAGER—COPY MASTER
Vocabulary Practice p. 26

ACADEMIC VOCABULARY IN SPEAKING

Student's should give examples of how Twain *exposes* people's ridiculous behaviors and lies.

VOCABULARY STRATEGY: DIFFERENCES IN WORD MEANINGS

 COMMON CORE L 4d, L 6

Point out that students will not know how to pronounce a homograph until they see it in the context of a sentence.

Possible answers:

a. *garbage; We refuse to settle for less. P*

b. *musical instrument with low tones; I caught a five-pound* bass. *P*

c. *extinct elephant; He made a* mammoth *birthday cake.*

d. *strike against forcefully; We filled our plates at the* buffet. *P*

e. *a model or idea; The children will* construct *a sand castle. P*

 RESOURCE MANAGER—Copy Master
Vocabulary Strategy p. 27

Interactive Vocabulary   THINK central

> Keywords direct students to a **WordSharp** tutorial on **thinkcentral.com** or to other types of vocabulary practice and review.

Assess and Reteach

Assess
DIAGNOSTIC AND SELECTION TESTS

Selection Tests A, B/C pp. 177–180

Interactive Selection Test on **thinkcentral.com**

Reteach

Level Up Online Tutorials on **thinkcentral.com**

Vocabulary in Context

▲ **VOCABULARY PRACTICE**

Decide whether these statements about the vocabulary words are true or false.

1. Someone with many career changes can be said to have worked **multifariously.**
2. Believing everything a fortuneteller tells you is an example of **credulity.**
3. A person who pays **rapt** attention to a performance is probably bored with it.
4. You might feel **nettled** if it rains on your picnic.
5. If you are **gullible,** you have an enormous appetite for sweet foods.
6. A defendant with an **unassailable** alibi should feel confident testifying in court.
7. If you record the **minutest** facts about an event, you are noting only how long it took.
8. A person with **implacable** demands is not likely to be easily satisfied.

WORD LIST

credulity
gullible
implacable
minutest
multifariously
nettled
rapt
unassailable

ACADEMIC VOCABULARY IN SPEAKING

• apparent   • confine   • expose   • focus   • perceive

Mark Twain used his autobiography to **expose** some of the humorous and interesting things that happened in his life. In a small group, discuss some of the pros and cons of using an autobiographical format to tell a story. Use at least two of the Academic Vocabulary words in your discussion.

VOCABULARY STRATEGY: DIFFERENCES IN WORD MEANINGS

Homographs are words that are spelled the same but differ in meaning, derivation, or pronunciation. Sometimes these words have totally different meanings, and sometimes the shifts in meaning are more nuanced, or subtle. An example of a word with totally different meanings is *minute* (mī-nōot'), meaning "small," and *minute* (mĭn'ĭt), meaning "60 seconds." An example of a word with a slight, or subtle, shift in meaning is *relative*, which may mean "kinship or relationship by blood" or may mean "relevant or pertinent." To determine the meaning of such a word, analyze the context of the sentence or paragraph and check the meanings in a dictionary.

PRACTICE Write the definition of each boldfaced word in the sentence below. After each definition, write a new sentence using a different meaning of the word. If the pronunciation is different, write P.

a. Take the household **refuse** to the dump.
b. The band has a new upright **bass** player.
c. They found the tusk of a **mammoth** in our state.
d. The wind from the storm began to **buffet** the boat.
e. The scientist proposed a theoretical **construct.**

COMMON CORE

L 4d Verify the preliminary determination of the meaning of a word or phrase. **L 6** Acquire and use accurately general academic words.

Interactive **THINK** central
Vocabulary
Go to **thinkcentral.com**.
KEYWORD: HML11-672

DIFFERENTIATED INSTRUCTION

FOR ENGLISH LANGUAGE LEARNERS

Task Support: Academic Vocabulary in Speaking Suggest that students use a Main Idea and Details organizer as they discuss the pros and cons of the autobiographical format. For each pro and con, have them choose a vocabulary word that makes sense.

 BEST PRACTICES TOOLKIT—Transparency
Main Idea and Details p. B6

FOR ADVANCED LEARNERS/AP

Write with Homographs Challenge pairs of students to compose and share sentences that use the feature's homograph pairs correctly. *Example: As partygoers lined up at the buffet, heavy winds began to buffet the tables.* To extend the activity, have partners brainstorm a list of additional homographs and then create and share similar sentences using them.

Regionalism and Local Color

from Life on the Mississippi
Memoir by Mark Twain

COMMON CORE

RI 6, L 1b, L 3, L 5a–b

● **TEXT ANALYSIS: VOICE**

Voice is a writer's unique use of language. It allows a reader to "hear" the writer's personality in his or her writing. Mark Twain's distinctive voice is full of dry wit.

Here was something fresh—this thing of getting up in the middle of the night.... It was a detail ... that had never occurred to me at all. I knew that boats ran all night, but somehow I had never happened to reflect that somebody had to get up out of a warm bed to run them.

A writer's voice is established through **diction**, or word choice and order, and **tone**, or attitude toward the subject. As you read, look for Twain's ironic or humorous tone.

● **READING STRATEGY: PARAPHRASE**

Twain often uses deadpan humor. However, it can take some digging to figure out just what he's saying. **Paraphrasing** can help; if you slow down and restate hard sentences in simpler language, you'll find it easier to follow them. By recognizing his use of **understatement** (downplaying the importance of things) or his use of **overstatement** (exaggeration, or hyperbole) and other figures of speech, you can paraphrase better.

Within ten seconds more I was set aside in disgrace, and Mr. Bixby was ... flaying me alive with abuse of my cowardice.

With a dictionary, you can paraphrase this sentence.

1. **Paraphrase it literally:** "I was promptly disgraced, and Mr. Bixby was skinning me alive and calling me a coward."
2. **Notice where Twain is stretching the truth:** Bixby is not really skinning him alive, but abusing him verbally.

Your final paraphrase can read, "Soon I had gotten into trouble and Mr. Bixby was shouting at me, calling me a coward." Record your paraphrases in a chart like the one shown.

Difficult Passage	Literal Paraphrase	Final Paraphrase (when appropriate)

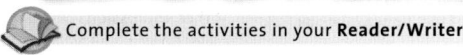 Complete the activities in your **Reader/Writer Notebook**.

Is IGNORANCE *really bliss?*

People who don't pay attention to the news or world affairs are sometimes described as burying their heads in the sand. This is not a compliment. However, it's also acknowledged that these people are sometimes happier or less worried than those who experience more. Mark Twain discovers that his experiences on the Mississippi River come at a price.

PRESENT Consider people you know who seek varied experiences and others who prefer to remain sheltered. Then list the advantages and disadvantages of each approach. Decide which approach makes the most sense to you, and identify two reasons for your choice. Share your conclusions with the class.

673

DIFFERENTIATED INSTRUCTION

FOR ENGLISH LANGUAGE LEARNERS

Reading: Preview Before students read, preview some of the old-fashioned or unfamiliar terms they will encounter in the selection: *flaying* (whipping); *dunderhead* (idiot); *trifle* (small amount); and *rapture* (joy). Discuss the words' definitions and help students find more familiar synonyms. Tell students that replacing unfamiliar words with more familiar terms is one way to *paraphrase*, or restate a passage in their own words.

Is IGNORANCE *really bliss?*

Introduce the question and discuss the quotation from a poem by Thomas Gray: "... where ignorance is bliss, / 'Tis folly to be wise." As students complete the **PRESENT** activity, have them think about ways in which the things that people experience bring happiness or unhappiness.

TEXT ANALYSIS COMMON CORE RI 6

● ***Model the Skill:* VOICE**

To help students recognize an author's voice, discuss these questions to demonstrate the humor and irony that mark Twain's tone:

- Twain refers to having to work in the middle of the night as "something fresh." Point out that the humor lies in the fact that the expression suggests something welcome, but Twain finds the call to get up unwelcome.
- Irony arises when the expected and unexpected clash. Tell students that Twain's expectation that the boat will run through the night clashes with the unexpected reality that he and others must work to make it run.

READING STRATEGY COMMON CORE L 3

■ ***Model the Skill:* PARAPHRASE**

Write this sentence on the board:

While the crisp night air proved salubrious, I'd have willingly traded it for a lengthier period of recuperation in my bunk.

Demonstrate that paraphrasing can make text more understandable by showing students this rewrite: *The cool night air turned out to be good for my health, but I would rather have had a little more sleep.*

R **RESOURCE MANAGER—Copy Master** Paraphrase p. 43 (for student use while reading the selection)

SUMMARY

In this excerpt from his memoir *Life on the Mississippi,* Twain recalls his first lessons as an apprentice riverboat pilot. Naïve and inexperienced, he is shocked at first by the realities of the work. As Twain learns to read the river and pilot the boat, he laments that he has lost his appreciation for the beauty and romance of the Mississippi River.

READ WITH A PURPOSE

Help students set a purpose for reading. Tell them to note details that explain what Twain learned about the river and about himself while on the Mississippi.

REVISIT THE BIG QUESTION

Is IGNORANCE
really bliss?

Discuss In lines 1–10, what can you infer about Twain's desire to experience life? *Possible answer: Twain's resolve to follow through on his fascination with "river life" and his plan to explore the Amazon imply that he desires to experience the adventures that life has to offer.*

Life on the Mississippi

Mark Twain

> **BACKGROUND** In this excerpt from his memoir, Mark Twain describes his first days as an apprentice riverboat pilot. Piloting a paddle steamboat was dangerous and tricky, because the Mississippi was constantly changing. The powerful current moved from one side to the other, especially in the windy parts of the river. Along this twisting course lurked hidden sandbars and submerged wrecks. Riverboat pilots gathered—and exchanged—precious information about the river's changing current.

A Cub-Pilot's Experience

What with lying on the rocks four days at Louisville, and some other delays, the poor old *Paul Jones* fooled away about two weeks in making the voyage from Cincinnati to New Orleans. This gave me a chance to get acquainted with one of the pilots, and he taught me how to steer the boat, and thus made the fascination of river life more potent than ever for me. . . .

I soon discovered two things. One was that a vessel would not be likely to sail for the mouth of the Amazon under ten or twelve years; and the other was that the nine or ten dollars still left in my pocket would not suffice for so impossible an exploration[1] as I had planned, even if I could afford to wait for a ship. Therefore
10 it followed that I must contrive a new career. The *Paul Jones* was now bound for

① Targeted Passage

Analyze Visuals ▶
What does this illustrated map tell you about the size of the Mississippi River compared with the town on its banks? What other impressions of the river do you glean?

---

1. **mouth of the Amazon . . . exploration:** Twain, having read that an American expedition had been unable to finish its exploration of the Amazon River, went to New Orleans with the idea that he would be able to travel to South America and complete the job.

674 UNIT 4: REGIONALISM AND NATURALISM

FOR ENGLISH LANGUAGE LEARNERS

Vocabulary Support Use Word Questioning to teach these words and phrases: *fooled away* (line 2), *potent* (line 5), *vessel* (line 6), *suffice* (line 8), *contrive* (line 10)

 BEST PRACTICES TOOLKIT—Transparency Word Questioning p. E9

FOR STRUGGLING READERS

In combination with the *Audio Anthology CD,* use one or more Targeted Passages (pp. 674, 676, 678, and 681) to ensure that students focus on key events and concepts. Targeted Passages are also good for English language learners.

① Targeted Passage [Lines 1–10]

This introductory passage sets the scene and explains how Twain became interested in learning to pilot a steamboat.

A VOICE

Possible answer: Twain's tone suggests that his younger self is overconfident—that is, he believes that the pilot's job is easy to do and easily learned. The tone also suggests that Twain is highly confident about his intelligence and his ability to learn.

B PARAPHRASE

Possible answer: When Mr. Bixby had calmed down, he explained that the waters are calm closer to the shore of the river and that the current is strong in the center. Therefore, a pilot should stay close to the shore when going upstream, to take advantage of the calm water, and should stay farther out when going downstream, to take advantage of the stronger current. Twain learns how the two currents are different and why that information is important to a pilot. He decides that in the future, he will pilot ships that are going downstream only because then he will not need to steer so dangerously close to other boats when he encounters them.

IF STUDENTS NEED HELP . . . Have them use the chart introduced on page 673 to paraphrase the passage, one sentence at a time.

Difficult Passage	Literal Paraphrase	Final Paraphrase
Mr. Bixby "trimmed the ships so closely that disaster seemed ceaselessly imminent."	Mr. Bixby was so close to the other steamboats that it seemed at any moment he would cause disaster.	Mr. Bixby steered so close to the other steamboats that it seemed he would wreck the boat.

St. Louis. I planned a siege against my pilot, and at the end of three hard days he surrendered. He agreed to teach me the Mississippi River from New Orleans to St. Louis for five hundred dollars, payable out of the first wages I should receive after graduating. I entered upon the small enterprise of "learning" twelve or thirteen hundred miles of the great Mississippi River with the easy confidence of my time of life. If I had really known what I was about to require of my faculties, I should not have had the courage to begin. I supposed that all a pilot had to do was to keep his boat in the river, and I did not consider that that could be much of a trick, since it was so wide. **A**

20   The boat backed out from New Orleans at four in the afternoon, and it was "our watch" until eight. Mr. Bixby, my chief, "straightened her up," plowed her along past the sterns of the other boats that lay at the Levee,[2] and then said, "Here, take her; shave those steamships as close as you'd peel an apple." I took the wheel, and my heartbeat fluttered up into the hundreds; for it seemed to me that we were about to scrape the side off every ship in the line, we were so close. I held my breath and began to claw the boat away from the danger; and I had my own opinion of the pilot who had known no better than to get us into such peril, but I was too wise to express it. In half a minute I had a wide margin of safety intervening between the *Paul Jones* and the ships; and within ten seconds more I

30   was set aside in disgrace, and Mr. Bixby was going into danger again and flaying me alive with abuse of my cowardice. I was stung, but I was obliged to admire the easy confidence with which my chief loafed from side to side of his wheel, and trimmed the ships so closely that disaster seemed ceaselessly imminent. When he had cooled a little he told me that the easy water was close ashore and the current outside, and therefore we must hug the bank, upstream, to get the benefit of the former, and stay well out, downstream, to take advantage of the latter. In my own mind I resolved to be a downstream pilot and leave the upstreaming to people dead to prudence.[3] **B**

Now and then Mr. Bixby called my attention to certain things. Said he, "This

40   is Six-Mile Point." I assented. It was pleasant enough information, but I could not see the bearing of it. I was not conscious that it was a matter of any interest to me. Another time he said, "This is Nine-Mile Point." Later he said, "This is Twelve-Mile Point." They were all about level with the water's edge; they all looked about alike to me; they were monotonously unpicturesque. I hoped Mr. Bixby would change the subject. But no; he would crowd up around a point, hugging the shore with affection, and then say: "The slack water ends here, abreast this bunch of China trees; now we cross over." So he crossed over. He gave me the wheel once or twice, but I had no luck. I either came near chipping off the edge of a sugar plantation, or I yawed[4] too far from shore, and so dropped back into disgrace

50   again and got abused.

The watch was ended at last, and we took supper and went to bed. At midnight the glare of a lantern shone in my eyes, and the night watchman said, "Come!

---

2. **Levee** (lĕv'ē): a landing place for boats on a river.

3. **dead to prudence:** lacking good judgment.

4. **yawed:** swerved.

② Targeted Passage

A VOICE
Reread lines 6–19. What does Twain's **tone** suggest about his youthful confidence?

B PARAPHRASE
Reread and paraphrase lines 33–38. What does Twain learn about the upstream and downstream currents? What decision does he make about the future?

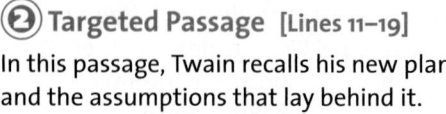

DIFFERENTIATED INSTRUCTION

FOR STRUGGLING READERS

② Targeted Passage [Lines 11–19]

In this passage, Twain recalls his new plan and the assumptions that lay behind it.

- What does young Twain pester the pilot to do for him? What terms does the pilot set when he agrees? (lines 11–13)

- What does Twain expect his training to be like? What does he not expect? (lines 17–19)

- Looking back, what does the older Twain think of his youthful decision? (lines 16–17)

FOR ENGLISH LANGUAGE LEARNERS

Vocabulary: Idioms Help students to use context clues to determine meaning of these words:

- *Now and then* (line 39), "At various times"

- *came near* (line 48), "almost succeeded in"

- *Turn out* (line 53), "Get out of bed"

- *as like as not* (line 57), "probably"

- *turning in* (line 59), "going to bed"

- *made for* (line 72), "went toward"

- *this beats anything* (line 84), "this is amazing"

Turn out!" And then he left. I could not understand this extraordinary procedure; so I presently gave up trying to, and dozed off to sleep. Pretty soon the watchman was back again, and this time he was gruff. I was annoyed. I said,

"What do you want to come bothering around here in the middle of the night for? Now, as like as not, I'll not get to sleep again to-night."

The watchman said, "Well, if this ain't good, I'm blessed."

The "offwatch"[5] was just turning in, and I heard some brutal laughter from
60 them, and such remarks as "Hello, watchman! ain't the new cub turned out yet? He's delicate, likely. Give him some sugar in a rag, and send for the chambermaid to sing 'Rock-a-by Baby' to him."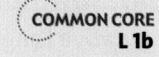

About this time Mr. Bixby appeared on the scene. Something like a minute later I was climbing the pilothouse steps with some of my clothes on and the rest in my arms. Mr. Bixby was close behind, commenting. Here was something fresh—this thing of getting up in the middle of the night to go to work. It was a detail in piloting that had never occurred to me at all. I knew that boats ran all night, but somehow I had never happened to reflect that somebody had to get up out of a warm bed to run them. I began to fear that piloting was not quite so
70 romantic as I had imagined it was; there was something very real and worklike about this new phase of it. . . .

M r. Bixby made for the shore and soon was scraping it, just the same as if it had been daylight. And not only that, but singing:

Father in heaven, the day is declining, etc.

It seemed to me that I had put my life in the keeping of a peculiarly reckless outcast. Presently he turned on me and said, "What's the name of the first point above New Orleans?"

I was gratified to be able to answer promptly, and I did. I said I didn't know. "Don't *know?*"
80 This manner jolted me. I was down at the foot[6] again, in a moment. But I had to say just what I had said before.

"Well, you're a smart one!" said Mr. Bixby. "What's the name of the *next* point?" Once more I didn't know.

"Well, this beats anything. Tell me the name of *any* point or place I told you." I studied awhile and decided that I couldn't.

"Look here! What do you start out from, above Twelve-Mile Point, to cross over?"
"I—I—don't know."
"You—you—don't know?" mimicking my drawling manner of speech. "What *do* you know?"
90 "I—I—nothing, for certain."
"By the great Caesar's ghost, I believe you! You're the stupidest dunderhead I ever saw or ever heard of, so help me Moses! The idea of *you* being a pilot—*you!* Why, you don't know enough to pilot a cow down a lane."

---

5. "**offwatch**": those sailors who had just completed their watch.
6. **down at the foot:** at the bottom of the class.

C **PARAPHRASE**
Twain's frequent use of **dialogue** and **dialect,** or regional speech, is one of the challenging qualities about his writing. Paraphrase the dialogue in lines 51–62. What are the other crew members saying about him?

COMMON CORE L 1b

Language Coach

Word Definitions *Made for* in line 72 means "went toward." Look up *make* in a dictionary, and note the different prepositions that can be combined with *made* to create new meanings. What do *make up,* *make off with*, and *make over* mean?

FOR ENGLISH LANGUAGE LEARNERS

Language Coach **COMMON CORE L 1b**
Word Definitions

Possible answer: make up: *forgive;* make off with: *steal;* make over: *revise.* Provide students with other examples of words that create new meanings with prepositions: *came across* and *came to;* or *looked through* and *looked for.*

FOR ADVANCED LEARNERS/AP

Analyze Dialogue In lines 75–93, Twain often describes his replies rather than quoting them, yet he always uses dialogue to report Mr. Bixby's comments. Ask students to rewrite this scene, first by using dialogue for both speakers and then by describing their words without using dialogue. Have students read both versions aloud to a partner and then discuss how the decision to report or describe dialogue affects the scene's pace and focus.

C *Model the Skill:* **PARAPHRASE**
Tell students that paraphrasing can help them understand this passage. Read lines 51–61 aloud, emphasizing the emotion expressed by each character. Have volunteers restate the exchange in their own words, acting out the parts of Twain, the watchman, and other crew members.

Possible answer: Paraphrase: "Come on, get out of bed!" / "Why do you keep interrupting my sleep? Now I'll probably never get back to sleep!" / "Well, I can't believe this!" / "Hey, watchman! Isn't the new pilot out of bed yet? Maybe he's spoiled. Feed him something sweet, and call his nurse to sing him a lullaby." The other crew members are saying that Twain is too immature to become a pilot.

TIERED DISCUSSION PROMPTS

In lines 72–93, use these prompts to help students explore the relationship between Twain and Bixby:

Connect Have you ever learned a skill from a master? Describe the experience. *Accept all thoughtful responses.*

Analyze How does Twain reveal the tension between master and apprentice as the scene progresses? Cite examples. *Possible answer: Twain reveals the tension through Mr. Bixby's dialogue. He first questions Twain in a casual way (lines 76–77). When Twain cannot answer, the italics in Mr. Bixby's reply (line 79) suggest irritation. Tension grows with the sarcastic "Well, you're a smart one!" (line 82) and the frustrated "Well, this beats anything" (line 84). Finally, Mr. Bixby angrily mocks Twain's halting speech (line 88) and insults him (lines 91–93).*

Evaluate Is Mr. Bixby an effective teacher? Why or why not? *Possible answers: No; Mr. Bixby has failed to explain to his pupil the nature of their lessons. Yes; He has reinforced for Twain just how much he has to learn.*

TEXT ANALYSIS

D Model the Skill: VOICE

Show students how diction provides information about the author. Say: *Mr. Bixby exhausted his anger.* Ask students what that statement tells them about the speaker. Then compare it to the sentence beginning, "You could have drawn a . . . ." Point out that the second example provides information about the speaker's river background and his wit.

Possible answer: *Twain's choice of language makes the descriptions of Mr. Bixby much more lively and vivid. Most of the paragraph is a description of Mr. Bixby's frenetic energy; the humor lies in the change of pace when he settles down to speak gently to young Twain.*

TEXT ANALYSIS

E VOICE

Possible answer: *Twain's tone becomes more factual ("the information was to be found only in my notebook—none of it was in my head") but also a bit sad and nostalgic ("It made my heart ache to think I had only got half of the river set down. . . .").*

REVISIT THE BIG QUESTION

Is IGNORANCE *really bliss?*

Discuss Based on lines 117–125, what life lessons does young Twain learn as he experiences the river on the way to St. Louis? *Possible answer: Humbled by his experience, Twain learns to respect a profession that he had underestimated and to be a more realistic judge of his abilities.*

Oh, but his wrath was up! He was a nervous man, and he shuffled from one side of his wheel to the other as if the floor was hot. He would boil awhile to himself, and then overflow and scald me again.

"Look here! What do you suppose I told you the names of those points for?"

I tremblingly considered a moment, and then the devil of temptation provoked me to say, "Well to—to—be entertaining, I thought."

100   This was a red rag to the bull.[7] He raged and stormed so (he was crossing the river at the time) that I judged it made him blind, because he ran over the steering oar of a trading scow.[8] Of course the traders sent up a volley of red-hot profanity. Never was a man so grateful as Mr. Bixby was, because he was brimful, and here were subjects who could *talk back*. He threw open a window, thrust his head out, and such an irruption followed as I never had heard before. The fainter and farther away the scowmen's curses drifted, the higher Mr. Bixby lifted his voice and the weightier his adjectives grew. When he closed the window he was empty. You could have drawn a seine[9] through his system and not caught curses enough to disturb your mother with. Presently he said to me in the gentlest way, "My boy,

110 you must get a little memorandum book; and every time I tell you a thing, put it down right away. There's only one way to be a pilot, and that is to get this entire river by heart. You have to know it just like A B C." **D**

   That was a dismal revelation to me, for my memory was never loaded with anything but blank cartridges. However, I did not feel discouraged long. I judged that it was best to make some allowances, for doubtless Mr. Bixby was "stretching." . . .[10]

   By the time we had gone seven or eight hundred miles up the river, I had learned to be a tolerably plucky upstream steersman, in daylight; and before we reached St. Louis I had made a trifle of progress in night work, but only a trifle.

120 I had a notebook that fairly bristled with the names of towns, "points," bars, islands, bends, reaches, etc.; but the information was to be found only in the notebook—none of it was in my head. It made my heart ache to think I had only got half of the river set down; for as our watch was four hours off and four hours on, day and night, there was a long four-hour gap in my book for every time I had slept since the voyage began. . . . **E**

   The face of the water, in time, became a wonderful book—a book that was a dead language to the uneducated passenger, but which told its mind to me without reserve, delivering its most cherished secrets as clearly as if it uttered them with a voice. And it was not a book to be read once and thrown aside, for

130 it had a new story to tell every day. Throughout the long twelve hundred miles there was never a page that was void of interest, never one that you could leave unread without loss, never one that you would want to skip, thinking you could find higher enjoyment in some other thing. There never was so wonderful a book

---

7. **a red rag to the bull:** Bullfighters wave capes to both provoke and distract the bull.

8. **scow:** a flat-bottomed boat used chiefly to transport freight.

9. **seine** (sān): large fishing net.

10. **"stretching":** exaggerating.

Language Coach

Figurative Language
"He would boil . . . and scald me again" (lines 95–96) is an example of **figurative language,** language that communicates meaning beyond the literal meaning of the words. How do words about boiling water express Mr. Bixby's anger?

③ Targeted Passage

D VOICE
Reread this paragraph, focusing on lines 104–112. Notice the elaborate **diction** Twain uses to describe Mr. Bixby's behavior, especially as Mr. Bixby finally quiets down. How does this choice of language affect the pacing and humor of this paragraph?

E VOICE
Reread lines 117–125. What **tone** does Twain take here in describing his own progress? Give details from the text to support your answer.

DIFFERENTIATED INSTRUCTION

FOR STRUGGLING READERS

③ Targeted Passage [Lines 109–125]

In this passage, Twain finally realizes the full extent of what he must learn before he can pilot the boat safely.

- What "homework" does Mr. Bixby assign Twain? (lines 109–111)

- Why is Twain worried about completing this assignment? (lines 113–114)

- Why isn't he discouraged for long? (lines 114–116)

FOR ENGLISH LANGUAGE LEARNERS

Comprehension: Text Structure Point out that in lines 126–145, Twain develops an extended metaphor comparing the river with a book. To help students understand the comparison, have them complete a Two-Column Chart.

🧰 BEST PRACTICES TOOLKIT—Transparency
Two-Column Chart p. A25

Language Coach

Figurative Language
Answer: *The comparison to boiling water indicates that Mr. Bixby's emotions are boiling over and "scalding" or injuring those around him.* Review with students the phrase "in hot water" and discuss the meaning of that figurative language.

Activity In this selection, Twain stresses the mental work of learning to be a pilot. Have students examine the image closely and then describe what it suggests about the physical work of piloting. *Possible answer: The image shows that the pilot is hard at work, straining his back as he grasps the wheel to steer. The pilot seems to be in good physical shape; he undoubtedly needs strength to do the job. Wind blows the pilot's shirt and neckerchief, indicating that exposure to the elements was part of the physical aspect of the job.*

written by man; never one whose interest was so absorbing, so unflagging, so sparklingly renewed with every reperusal.[11] The passenger who could not read it was charmed with a peculiar sort of faint dimple on its surface (on the rare occasions when he did not overlook it altogether); but to the pilot that was an *italicized* passage; indeed, it was more than that, it was a legend of the largest capitals,[12] with a string of shouting exclamation points at the end of it, for it
140 meant that a wreck or a rock was buried there that could tear the life out of the strongest vessel that ever floated. It is the faintest and simplest expression the water ever makes, and the most hideous to a pilot's eye. In truth, the passenger who could not read this book saw nothing but all manner of pretty pictures in it,

11. **reperusal** (rē′pə-rōō′zal): rereading.
12. **a legend of the largest capitals:** an inscription in large capital letters.

FOR ADVANCED LEARNERS/AP

Analyze Style Challenge students to identify three types of repetition in lines 126–141 and to explain how they strengthen the meaning of the passage:

- the repetition of the word *book*, which strengthens the extended metaphor
- the repetition of the word *never* in lines 131–134, which strengthens Twain's main point about the allure of the river
- the repetition of the word *so* plus an adjective in lines 133–135, which intensifies meaning

Encourage students to discuss how the focus of the passage might change if Twain had not used repetition.

FOR STRUGGLING READERS

Develop Reading Fluency Use the narrator's language of disappointment and frustration in lines 109–125 to promote readers' interest. Have students work in small groups, with different individuals reading aloud from each of the three paragraphs. Remind students to be expressive in explaining Mr. Bixby's "gentle" guidance and the speaker's "dismal" response. Encourage students to use punctuation as a guide to break up long sentences.

Ⓕ VOICE

Possible answer: Twain's descriptions change to become more vivid and more detailed, revealing close observation. Twain also uses figurative language, whereas before he presented simple, rather plain descriptions. His diction is more serious than before, reflecting his new maturity.

IF STUDENTS NEED HELP . . . Have them contrast the tone and diction in these lines with that in lines 39–50.

TIERED DISCUSSION PROMPTS

Direct student to lines 146–164. Use these prompts to help students appreciate Twain's imagery:

Connect Have you ever witnessed a sunset or other scene of natural beauty? How did it affect you? *Accept all thoughtful responses.*

Evaluate Does Twain's description convince readers of "the grace, the beauty, the poetry" of the river (lines 149–150)? Explain. *Students may suggest that Twain's respectful tone and vivid poetic language capture these aspects of the river.*

About the Art The firm of Nathaniel Currier (1813–1888) and James Merritt Ives (1824–1895) became famous for its popular lithographs, producing more than 7,000 images that chronicled scenes and events of the 19th century.

---

painted by the sun and shaded by the clouds, whereas to the trained eye these were not pictures at all, but the grimmest and most dead earnest of reading matter.

Now when I had mastered the language of this water, and had come to know every trifling feature that bordered the great river as familiarly as I knew the letters of the alphabet, I had made a valuable acquisition. But I had lost something, too. I had lost something which could never be restored to me while I lived. All the
150 grace, the beauty, the poetry, had gone out of the majestic river! I still keep in mind a certain wonderful sunset which I witnessed when steamboating was new to me. A broad expanse of the river was turned to blood; in the middle distance the red hue brightened into gold, through which a solitary log came floating, black and conspicuous; in one place a long, slanting mark lay sparkling upon the water; in another the surface was broken by boiling, tumbling rings, that were as many-tinted as an opal; where the ruddy flush was faintest, was a smooth spot that was covered with graceful circles and radiating lines, ever so delicately traced; the shore on our left was densely wooded, and the somber shadow that fell from this forest was broken in one place by a long, ruffled trail that shone like silver; and high
160 above the forest wall a clean-stemmed dead tree waved a single leafy bough that glowed like a flame in the unobstructed splendor that was flowing from the sun. There were graceful curves, reflected images, woody heights, soft distances; and over the whole scene, far and near, the dissolving lights drifted steadily, enriching it every passing moment with new marvels of coloring. Ⓕ

> Ⓕ **VOICE**
> Consider Twain's **tone** and **diction** earlier in the selection, as he was first learning his way around the ship. Then reread lines 126–164. How does Twain's voice change as he explains his increased knowledge of the river? Give details.

Champions of the Mississippi, Currier and Ives. Lithograph. Museum of the City of New York, New York. © Scala/Art Resource, New York.

DIFFERENTIATED INSTRUCTION

FOR ADVANCED LEARNERS/AP

Synthesize In both the excerpt from *The Autobiography of Mark Twain* and the excerpt from *Life on the Mississippi,* a mature author reflects on his younger self. The episode from the *Autobiography* comes from Twain's adolescence; the period of apprenticeship to Mr. Bixby dates to Twain's early 20s. Have students develop and share profiles of the three versions of Twain they encounter in these selections, drawing evidence from both texts. Urge students to respond to these questions:

- What matters most to Twain at each time of his life?

- What mistakes are the boy and young man prone to make?

- How has Twain matured between his participation in the mesmerizer's act and his apprenticeship to Mr. Bixby?

- What characteristics have stayed with Twain from boyhood through maturity?

I stood like one bewitched. I drank it in, in a speechless rapture. The world was new to me, and I had never seen anything like this at home. But as I have said, a day came when I began to cease from noting the glories and the charms which the moon and the sun and the twilight wrought upon the river's face; another day came when I ceased altogether to note them. Then, if that sunset scene had been repeated, I should have looked upon it without rapture, and should have commented upon it, inwardly, after this fashion: "This sun means that we are going to have wind tomorrow; that floating log means that the river is rising, small thanks to it; that slanting mark on the water refers to a bluff reef[13] which is going to kill somebody's steamboat one of these nights, if it keeps on stretching out like that; those tumbling 'boils' show a dissolving bar and a changing channel there; the lines and circles in the slick water over yonder are a warning that that troublesome place is shoaling up[14] dangerously; that silver streak in the shadow of the forest is the 'break' from a new snag, and he has located himself in the very best place he could have found to fish for steamboats; that tall dead tree, with a single living branch, is not going to last long, and then how is a body ever going to get through this blind place at night without the friendly old landmark?"

No, the romance and beauty were all gone from the river. All the value any feature of it had for me now was the amount of usefulness it could furnish toward compassing the safe piloting of a steamboat. Since those days, I have pitied doctors from my heart. What does the lovely flush in a beauty's cheek mean to a doctor but a "break" that ripples above some deadly disease? Are not all her visible charms sown thick with what are to him the signs and symbols of hidden decay? Does he ever see her beauty at all, or doesn't he simply view her professionally, and comment upon her unwholesome condition all to himself? And doesn't he sometimes wonder whether he has gained most or lost most by learning his trade?

---

13. **bluff reef:** an underwater ridge of rock.
14. **shoaling up:** becoming too shallow for safe navigation because of a buildup of sand or silt in the riverbed.

LIFE ON THE MISSISSIPPI **681**

COMMON CORE L 5b

Language Coach

Synonyms A **synonym** is a word with a meaning similar to that of another word. *Bewitched* (line 165) means "placed under a spell" or "enthralled." Synonyms of *bewitched* are *charmed* and *enchanted*. What common theme do these words have?

4 Targeted Passage

G PARAPHRASE
Reread lines 184–190 and paraphrase the comments about what a doctor sees. What parallel is Twain drawing between the doctor's plight and his own?

REVISIT THE BIG QUESTION

Is IGNORANCE really bliss?

Discuss In lines 165–169, how do the young Twain's experiences change his thoughts about the river? *Possible answer: As he gains piloting experience, Twain thinks less about the river's "charms," until he finally loses all sense of wonder.*

  COMMON CORE L 3

G PARAPHRASE

Possible answer: Paraphrase: Since then, I have sincerely pitied doctors. To a doctor, might not a beautiful woman have pink cheeks because she is deathly ill? Are not her lovely physical traits overshadowed by possible symptoms of illness? Can the doctor ever recognize her beauty, or does he see her only as a patient, and speak of her to himself as such? And doesn't he sometimes wonder whether learning his profession has been worth that cost? Twain's parallel makes the point that professional knowledge stifles one's sensitivity to beauty.

SELECTION WRAP–UP

READ WITH A PURPOSE Now that students have finished reading the selection, have them review what Twain has learned from his experience. What has Twain learned about the river and himself? *Possible answer: Twain has learned how to "read" the river in order to navigate it. He found that learning the river's secrets took away his appreciation of its beauty.*

⭐ **CRITIQUE** Ask students whether they are convinced of the young Twain's rapid maturation from careless cub pilot to confident veteran pilot.

---

4 Targeted Passage [Lines 166–184]

In this passage, the mature Twain reflects on what he lost by gaining the experience needed to pilot a steamboat.

- According to Twain, what happened on a certain day? (lines 167–169)
- Before Twain became a pilot, the Mississippi River seemed enchanting and peaceful. How does it seem to him now? (lines 182–184)

- Does Twain regret having learned to pilot? Explain your answer. (line 182)

FOR ENGLISH LANGUAGE LEARNERS

Language Coach
COMMON CORE L 5b

Synonyms *Answer: The words' common theme is magic, a kind of spell that makes people lose their senses.* Review with students what conditions lead the speaker to become "bewitched."

LIFE ON THE MISSISSIPPI **681**

Practice and Apply

For preliminary support of post-reading questions, use these copy masters:

 **RESOURCE MANAGER—Copy Masters**

Reading Check p. 45

Voice p. 41

Question Support p. 46

Additional selection questions are provided for teachers on page 35.

1. *Twain begins the job of apprentice to a riverboat pilot.*

2. *Twain reacts by ignoring the instruction.*

3. *Twain learns to read and respect the river.*

Possible answers:

4. ● **COMMON CORE FOCUS Examine Paraphrases** *Students may mention regional dialect or technical terminology as difficult aspects.*

5. *Lines 23–38: Twain's attitude is fear—he is afraid to steer the boat to open but less calm waters. Lines 51–71: Twain's attitude is amazement—he is ignorant about work obligations. Lines 75–112: Twain's attitude is frustration—he seems unable to learn the river. In each case, the humor relates to young Twain's overconfidence.*

6. ● **COMMON CORE FOCUS Analyze Voice** *To that point, readers hear the voice of an overconfident cub who thinks he knows it all. As Twain learns more about the river and what it takes to be a pilot, his diction becomes more sophisticated and his tone more respectful.*

Assess and Reteach

Assess

DIAGNOSTIC AND SELECTION TESTS

Selection Test A, B/C pp. 181–182, 183–184

Interactive Selection Test on **thinkcentral.com**

Reteach

Level Up Online Tutorials on **thinkcentral.com**

After Reading

Comprehension

1. **Recall** What new job does Mark Twain begin?

2. **Recall** How does Twain react to Mr. Bixby's initial instruction?

3. **Summarize** As Twain's training continues, what does he learn?

Text Analysis

4. **Examine Paraphrases** Review the paraphrases you recorded as you read. In the end, what were the most difficult aspects of Twain's writing? Explain.

5. **Analyze Humor** In any piece of humorous writing, the humor usually springs from a general underlying attitude toward the subject. Review the following humorous passages from the selection and in each case identify the attitude expressed. What do the passages have in common?
   - Twain tries to steer the boat for the first time (lines 23–38)
   - Twain fails to show up for his first night watch (lines 51–71)
   - Twain learns that he has to learn the entire river by heart (lines 75–112)

6. **Analyze Voice** Twain's voice undergoes a distinct change at line 126. Describe his voice both up to and after this point in terms of its **diction** and **tone**. What change in attitude is reflected by this change in voice?

7. **Draw Conclusions** In this selection, Twain develops an **extended metaphor** comparing the river with a book. In a chart like this one, identify the points of this comparison. Through this metaphor, what is he saying about the river and his experience as a student pilot?

Line Numbers	Passage	What It Says About the River
126–127	"The face of the water ... became a wonderful book—a book that was a dead language to the uneducated passenger"	It's "wonderful" but cannot be understood by the uneducated.

Text Criticism

8. **Author's Style** *Life on the Mississippi* first appeared serially in the *Atlantic Monthly* magazine in 1875. In 1874, Twain wrote the magazine's editor that he liked writing for the audience of the *Atlantic* "for the simple reason that it don't require a 'humorist' to paint himself stripèd and stand on his head every fifteen minutes." In other words, he liked an audience that appreciated subtle humor. Do you find this sensibility reflected in the selection you have just read? Explain.

> *Is* **IGNORANCE** *really bliss?*
>
> Twain states that after he learned his trade, he was never able to see the Mississippi the same way again. What has experience caused you to see differently? What kinds of revelations can be negative? Explain.

---

7. *Lines 126–127: The river is like a book.* *Lines 130–135: Like a great book, the ever-changing river is endlessly fascinating.* *Lines 135–142: Passengers can see only the river's beauty, while the pilot sees each detail as important in "reading" the river.* *Lines 142–145: Passengers see "pictures," but pilots see the significance of every nuance. Twain's metaphor says that the river is complex and that he has learned to understand it as the layman cannot.*

8. *Most students will find that the selection reflects the sensibility: Its humor is subtle, based on voice rather than on situation.*

> *Is* IGNORANCE *really bliss?*
> Students may see their revelations as positive because they gained in knowledge or maturity. Their revelations may be negative if described uncomfortable truths.

The Notorious Jumping Frog of Calaveras County

Short Story by Mark Twain

COMMON CORE

RL 3, RL 4, L 1a, L 5a

● **TEXT ANALYSIS: TALL TALE**

The **tall tale** is a distinctively American form of storytelling featuring outlandish characters and events, often with a comic effect. Based on oral tradition, the tall tale generally aims to fool or impress the listener or reader, using various devices. Look for these techniques and consider their impact:

- **Hyperbole**—a figure of speech exaggerating or overstating a claim or point
- **Understatement**—the technique of downplaying the significance of the outlandish, often to ironic or humorous effect
- **Local color**—writing that brings a region alive by portraying its dress, mannerisms, customs, character types, and speech

● **READING SKILL: UNDERSTAND DIALECT**

Dialect is the distinct form of a language spoken in one geographic area or by a particular group. Writers use dialect to establish setting, provide local color, and develop characters. In this story, Twain uses a frontier dialect. Because of its unfamiliar usage, idioms, and strange spellings, dialect can be challenging to read. These strategies will help:

- **Read slowly**—Try reading aloud to help you recognize words you may have heard but don't normally see in print.
- **Use context clues**—When Twain writes, "You'd see that frog whirling in the air like a doughnut—see him turn one summerset," context tells you that *summerset* must mean the same as *somersault.*

As you read, jot down unfamiliar words and what you think they mean.

▲ **VOCABULARY IN CONTEXT**

Which of the following words do you know? Write definitions for the words and then check the definitions as you read.

WORD LIST	cavorting	enterprising	infamous
	conjecture	garrulous	tranquil
	dilapidated	indifferent	

 Complete the activities in your **Reader/Writer Notebook**.

Can you spot a TALL TALE?

You listen to a friend recount the events of the weekend and you're pretty sure the story is way too wild to be true. You hear a politician describe great accomplishments and you just know it's a stretch. These situations inspire the skepticism you need to read about a frog that turns somersaults.

DISCUSS Work with a small group to play the game "Two Truths and a Lie." Take a few minutes for each of you to come up with two truths and one lie. The statements can be about anything from personal experience to oddball facts. Take turns sharing statements. Can you guess which are the lies and which are the truths? Compare your answers and explain what made you believe or disbelieve each statement.

Teach

Can you spot a TALL TALE?

Introduce the question and explain that skepticism means "doubt" or "disbelief." Invite students to tell about a time when they felt skeptical about a situation; then urge them to draw upon their experiences as they complete the activity.

TEXT ANALYSIS **COMMON CORE**

RL 3
L 5a

● *Model the Skill:* **TALL TALE**

Illustrate characteristics of tall tales by writing this passage on the board:

> Sally Britches was taller than a redwood. Why, when she was born, her ma was sorter surprised-like to see that her baby gal was too big fer young'un clothes. "Oh, well," sighed her ma. "I guess you kin jist wear yer pa's ole britches."

Point out that the tall-tale devices in these lines include: *hyperbole: "taller than a redwood"; understatement: "sorter surprised-like"; local color: regional speech (dialect)*

GUIDED PRACTICE Have students cite tall tales, such as stories about John Henry or Paul Bunyan.

READING SKILL **COMMON CORE**

L 1a

■ *Model the Skill:*
UNDERSTAND DIALECT

Tell students that dialect features slang, non-standard grammar, and unconventional spellings. Have students read the passage aloud and determine the meaning of these examples of dialect: *young'un, kin, jist,* and *britches.* **Answers:** *"children's," "can," "just," "pants"*

R **RESOURCE MANAGER—Copy Master**
Understand Dialect p. 59 (for student use while reading the selection)

VOCABULARY SKILL **COMMON CORE**

L 4

▲ **VOCABULARY IN CONTEXT**

DIAGNOSE WORD KNOWLEDGE Have students complete Vocabulary in Context. Check their word choices with the following:

cavorting (kə-vôr′tĭng) *adj.* prancing about in a playful manner **cavort** *v.*

conjecture (kən-jĕk′chər) *v.* to guess

dilapidated (dĭ-lăp′ĭ-dā′tĭd) *adj.* in a state of disrepair; rundown **dilapidate** *v.*

enterprising (ĕn′tər-prī′zĭng) *adj.* possessing imagination and initiative

garrulous (găr′ə-ləs) *adj.* extremely talkative

indifferent (ĭn-dĭf′ər-ənt) *adj.* having no particular interest

infamous (ĭn′fə-məs) *adj.* having a very bad reputation; disgraceful

tranquil (trăng′kwəl) *adj.* peaceful

PRETEACH VOCABULARY Use this copy master to help students predict meanings.

R **RESOURCE MANAGER—Copy Master**
Vocabulary Study p. 61

Practice and Apply

SUMMARY

The narrator of this tall tale locates Simon Wheeler in a mining camp and asks if he knows Leonidas W. Smiley. Wheeler does not, but launches into a reminiscence about *Jim* Smiley, who would bet on anything. Wheeler tells how Smiley once engaged a stranger in a frog jumping contest. The stranger tricked Smiley by making Smiley's frog swallow quail shot so that it was too heavy to jump. The narrator makes his escape just as Wheeler launches into another story.

READ WITH A PURPOSE

Help students set a purpose for reading. Tell them to note examples of the narrator exaggerating events to make a good story.

TIERED DISCUSSION PROMPTS

Direct students to lines 1–9. Use these prompts to help students understand Twain's narrative technique:

Connect Have you ever had to listen to a long, boring story? Describe the experience. *Accept all responses.*

Evaluate Is this introduction effective, or does the narrator undermine Wheeler's tale by describing it as boring? Explain. *Students may consider the opening effective because it makes readers realize that they can't accept the narrator's opinion as truth.*

The Notorious JUMPING FROG of Calaveras County

Mark Twain

BACKGROUND Twain got the idea for this story during his days panning for gold in California. Local storytellers told this tale without cracking a smile, teaching Twain two important lessons about humor: one, that the manner in which a person tells a story is what makes it funny, and two, that a humorist should always pretend to be dead serious.

Analyze Visuals ▶
What techniques in this illustration can be compared with the storytelling techniques of a tall tale? Explain.

In compliance with the request of a friend of mine who wrote me from the East, I called on good-natured, **garrulous** old Simon Wheeler and inquired after my friend's friend, Leonidas W. Smiley, as requested to do, and I hereunto append[1] the result. I have a lurking suspicion that *Leonidas W.* Smiley is a myth, that my friend never knew such a personage, and that he only **conjectured** that if I asked old Wheeler about him, it would remind him of his **infamous** *Jim* Smiley and he would go to work and bore me to death with some exasperating reminiscence of him as long and as tedious as it should be useless to me. If that was the design, it succeeded.

garrulous (găr′ə-ləs) *adj.* extremely talkative

conjecture (kən-jĕk′chər) *v.* to guess

infamous (ĭn′fə-məs) *adj.* having a very bad reputation; disgraceful

 Targeted Passage

---

1. **hereunto append:** add to this document.

684 UNIT 4: REGIONALISM AND NATURALISM

DIFFERENTIATED INSTRUCTION

FOR ENGLISH LANGUAGE LEARNERS

Vocabulary Support Use New Word Analysis to teach these words: *append* (line 3), *design* (line 8), *paragraph* (line 21), *initial* (line 22).

BEST PRACTICES TOOLKIT—Transparency
New Word Analysis p. E8

FOR STRUGGLING READERS

In combination with the *Audio Anthology CD*, use one or more Targeted Passages (pp. 684, 688, 689, 690) to ensure that students focus on key story events and concepts. Targeted Passages are also good for English language learners.

1 Targeted Passage [Lines 1–9]

This passage sets up the narrative structure of the frame story, or story within a story,

Possible answer: *The illustration includes the tall tale techniques of exaggeration and understatement. The rider's head is exaggerated; the understatement is that the rider acts as if there is nothing unusual about riding a frog.*

About the Art This caricature is a copy of a portrait of Twain on his celebrated jumping frog, done by English caricaturist Frederick Waddy in 1872.

BACKGROUND

More About Tall Tales A tall tale is a type of folk tale—a story that originally was passed down orally from generation to generation and that expresses the values and beliefs of its culture. Other types of folk tales include myths, legends, fairy tales, and fables. What distinguishes a tall tale from other types of folk tales is its use of hyperbole for comic effect. Many American tall tales are linked to the frontier. Most tall tales focus on the superhuman feats of a larger-than-life hero, such as Davy Crockett, Paul Bunyan, or John Henry. Many tall tales feature two characters: a confident braggart, like Jim Smiley, and a stranger who tricks him, like the man who wins the frog-jumping competition.

by introducing the narrator of the outer story and preparing readers to meet Simon Wheeler, the narrator of the inner story.

- Why does the narrator seek out Simon Wheeler? What is the narrator's attitude toward this task? (lines 3–5)
- Why does Wheeler mention Jim Smiley? (lines 6–8)
- What story is the narrator preparing readers to read, and who will tell it? (lines 3–4)

FOR ADVANCED LEARNERS/AP

Compare Tone Review some commonly known tall tales such as Paul Bunyan and John Henry. Have students read a few paragraphs of each and compare the tone of those tales with Twain's "Jumping Frog." Have students discuss how Twain's purpose differs from that of the other tales, and how his tone helps him achieve that purpose.

TALL TALE

Remind students that many older tall tales are exaggerated versions of stories about real people. For example, the tales about Johnny Appleseed were based on the life of American pioneer John Chapman. Other tales such as those about Paul Bunyan were based on mythical heroes. Ask students to discuss recent examples of tall tales they are familiar with from books, movies, plays, or television. What do their examples have in common with this tall tale by Twain?

VOCABULARY

OWN THE WORD

- **dilapidated:** Ask students to describe the "*dilapidated* tavern." ***Possible answer:*** *broken windows and doors; peeling paint; shabby curtains*
- **tranquil:** *Tranquil* refers to being "undisturbed or peaceful" and "free from anxiety." Ask students to write sentences using both definitions.

---

10   I found Simon Wheeler dozing comfortably by the barroom stove of the **dilapidated** tavern in the decayed mining camp of Angel's, and I noticed that he was fat and baldheaded and had an expression of winning gentleness and simplicity upon his **tranquil** countenance. He roused up and gave me good day. I told him that a friend of mine had commissioned me to make some inquiries about a cherished companion of his boyhood named *Leonidas W.* Smiley—*Rev. Leonidas W.* Smiley, a young minister of the Gospel, who he had heard was at one time a resident of Angel's Camp. I added that if Mr. Wheeler could tell me anything about this Rev. Leonidas W. Smiley, I would feel under many obligations to him.

   Simon Wheeler backed me into a corner and blockaded me there with his chair, 20 and then sat down and reeled off the monotonous narrative which follows this paragraph. He never smiled, he never frowned, he never changed his voice from the gentle-flowing key to which he tuned his initial sentence, he never betrayed the slightest suspicion of enthusiasm, but all through the interminable narrative there ran a vein of impressive earnestness and sincerity which showed me plainly that, so far from his imagining that there was anything ridiculous or funny about his story, he regarded it as a really important matter and admired its two heroes as men of transcendent genius in *finesse.*[2] I let him go on in his own way and never interrupted him once.

   "Rev. Leonidas W. H'm, Reverend Le—Well, there was a feller here once by 30 the name of *Jim* Smiley, in the winter of '49—or maybe it was the spring of '50—I don't recollect exactly, somehow, though what makes me think it was one or the other is because I remember the big flume[3] warn't finished when he first come to the camp; but anyway, he was the curiousest man about always betting on anything that turned up you ever see, if he could get anybody to bet on the other side, and if he couldn't he'd change sides. Any way that suited the other man would suit *him*—any way just so's he got a bet, *he* was satisfied. But still he was lucky, uncommon lucky; he most always come out winner. He was always ready and laying for a chance; there couldn't be no solit'ry thing mentioned but that feller'd offer to bet on it and take ary side you please, as I was just telling you. If 40 there was a horse race, you'd find him flush or you'd find him busted at the end of it; if there was a dogfight, he'd bet on it; if there was a cat fight, he'd bet on it; if there was a chicken fight, he'd bet on it; why, if there was two birds setting on a fence, he would bet you which one would fly first; or if there was a camp meeting, he would be there reg'lar to bet on Parson Walker, which he judged to be the best exhorter about here, and so he was too, and a good man. If he even see a straddlebug[4] start to go anywheres, he would bet you how long it would take him to get to—to wherever he was going to, and if you took him up, he would foller that straddlebug to Mexico but what he would find out where he was bound for and how long he was on the road. Lots of the boys here has seen that Smiley and 50 can tell you about him. Why, it never made no difference to *him*—he'd bet on

---

2. **men of . . . *finesse*:** exceptionally brilliant men.
3. **flume:** a wooden trough built as a channel for running water—used in gold mining for separating particles of gold.
4. **straddlebug:** a long-legged beetle.

---

686   UNIT 4: REGIONALISM AND NATURALISM

---

dilapidated
(dĭ-lăp´ĭ-dā´tĭd) *adj.*
in a state of disrepair; rundown **dilapidate** *v.*

tranquil (trăng´kwəl) *adj.*
undisturbed; peaceful

Language Coach

Word Definitions
Monotonous (line 20) means "having little variety in tone or pitch." Reread lines 21–23. What surrounding words and phrases hint at the meaning of *monotonous*?

TALL TALE

In his tall tales, Twain perfected a mixture of humor and exaggeration that calls on readers to go along with wildly unbelievable events. The characteristics of the tall tale that we see in Twain's story can also be found in comic-book superhero films. What are some examples of tall tales that you have enjoyed recently in novels, plays, or movies?

DIFFERENTIATED INSTRUCTION

FOR STRUGGLING READERS

Explore Narrators Make sure students understand that there are two narrators in Twain's story. The story begins with an unnamed narrator who provides the context for the tall tale told by Simon Wheeler, the second narrator. Explain that the first narrator is telling the outer story of a frame story, whereas Simon Wheeler is telling the inner story about Jim Smiley. Have students distinguish the narrators by recording details in this graphic organizer:

Narrator: formal language; irritated, skeptical, bored

Simon Wheeler: dialect; earnest, sincere, humorless, rambling, exaggerating

FOR ENGLISH LANGUAGE LEARNERS

Language Coach

Word Definitions

Answer: *"never smiled," "never frowned," "never changed his voice" indicate that* monotonous *means "the same."* Ask students to look for clues indicating that a *monotonous* story may also be boring.

any thing—the dangdest feller. Parson Walker's wife laid very sick once for a good while, and it seemed as if they warn't going to save her; but one morning he come in and Smiley up and asked him how she was, and he said she was considerable better—thank the Lord for his inf'nite mercy—and coming on so smart that with the blessing of Prov'dence she'd get well yet; and Smiley, before he thought, says, 'Well, I'll resk two-and-a-half she don't anyway.' **B**

"Thish-yer Smiley had a mare—the boys called her the fifteen-minute nag but that was only in fun, you know, because of course she was faster than that—and he used to win money on that horse, for all she was so slow and always had the
60 asthma, or the distemper, or the consumption,[5] or something of that kind. They used to give her two or three hundred yards' start and then pass her under way, but always at the fag end[6] of the race she'd get excited and desperatelike, and come **cavorting** and straddling up and scattering her legs around limber, sometimes in the air and sometimes out to one side among the fences, and kicking up m-o-r-e dust and raising m-o-r-e racket with her coughing and sneezing and blowing her nose—and always fetch up at the stand just about a neck ahead, as near as you could cipher it down.[7]

"And he had a little small bull-pup, that to look at him you'd think he warn't worth a cent but to set around and look ornery and lay for a chance to steal
70 something. But as soon as money was up on him he was a different dog; his underjaw'd begin to stick out like the fo'castle[8] of a steamboat and his teeth would uncover and shine like the furnaces. And a dog might tackle him and bullyrag[9] him, and bite him and throw him over his shoulder two or three times, and Andrew Jackson—which was the name of the pup—Andrew Jackson would never let on but what *he* was satisfied and hadn't expected nothing else—and the bets being doubled and doubled on the other side all the time, till the money was all up; and then all of a sudden he would grab that other dog jest by the j'int of his hind leg and freeze to it—not chaw, you understand, but only just grip and hang on till they throwed up the sponge,[10] if it was a year. Smiley always come out winner on that pup till he
80 harnessed a dog once that didn't have no hind legs, because they'd been sawed off in a circular saw, and when the thing had gone along far enough and the money was all up and he come to make a snatch for his pet holt,[11] he see in a minute how he'd been imposed on and how the other dog had him in the door, so to speak, and he 'peared surprised, and then he looked sorter discouragedlike and didn't try no more to win the fight, and so he got shucked out bad. He give Smiley a look, as much as to say his heart was broke, and it was *his* fault for putting up a dog that hadn't no hind legs for him to take holt of, which was his main dependence in a fight, and

---

5. **distemper . . . consumption:** Distemper is a viral disease caught by dogs and other four-legged mammals. Consumption is an old-fashioned name for tuberculosis.

6. **fag end:** final part.

7. **cipher** (sīˈfər) **it down:** calculate it; figure it.

8. **fo'castle** (fōkˈsəl): forecastle—here, the protruding front deck of a steamboat.

9. **bullyrag:** harass.

10. **throwed up the sponge:** gave up.

11. **pet holt:** favorite grip.

B DIALECT
Paraphrase the passage written in dialect in lines 29–56. What point is Simon Wheeler making about Smiley?

cavorting (kə-vôrˈtĭng) *adj.* prancing about in a playful manner **cavort** *v.*

COMMON CORE L 1a

Language Coach

Regional Dialects Reread lines 57–67, paying special attention to the dialect. As noted on page 683, Twain uses frontier dialect in this story to reflect the usage and pronunciations conventional to a certain group of people. Using the Internet or a history of the English language—a historical reference book that discusses the origins and uses of English—make a list of regional dialects in the United States.

READING SKILL   **COMMON CORE L 1a**

B DIALECT

Possible answer: Paraphrase: Why, he didn't care—he would bet on anything—he was the most annoying fellow! Parson Walker's wife once was quite ill for some time, and it seemed that she was going to die. Then, one morning, the parson came in, and Smiley asked how his wife was feeling; and the parson said that she was much better—thank God for His unending mercy—and that she was doing so well that with God's help, she would recover, after all! Smiley, without thinking, said, "Well, I'll bet two-and-a-half that she dies anyway." Wheeler is making the point that Smiley bets without thinking, regardless of the nature of the wager, people's feelings, or the consequences of the bet.

BACKGROUND

Andrew Jackson Smiley named his dog after Andrew Jackson (1767–1845), who served as the seventh president of the United States (1829–1837). Known as "Old Hickory," Jackson was perceived as tough; in this story, so is his canine namesake.

VOCABULARY   **COMMON CORE L 4**

OWN THE WORD

cavorting: Remind students that *cavorting* is related to the root verb *cavort* and refers to "prancing about in a playful manner." Have students list things that could be seen as *cavorting*. **Possible answers:** *playful children, puppies, dancers, butterflies, gazelles*

FOR ENGLISH LANGUAGE LEARNERS

Language Coach   **COMMON CORE L 1a**
Regional Dialects

Examples of regional dialects might include: New York, New England, Great Lakes, Pennsylvania Dutch, Midwest, and so forth. You might want to encourage students to discuss the different regional dialects they have heard and the clues they used to identify each of them.

FOR ADVANCED LEARNERS/AP
Analyze Characterization Review methods of characterization:

- With **direct characterization,** the writer tells readers about a character.

- With **indirect characterization,** the writer suggests a character's traits by showing the character's thoughts, words, and actions, as well as the character's effect on other characters.

Have students use a Character Traits and Textual Evidence chart to record examples of characterization in the story. Then discuss why the narrator includes Wheeler's anecdotes about the parson's wife, Andrew Jackson, and Daniel Webster. By the end of the story, elicit that these anecdotes reveal Smiley's character—in particular, his passion for betting—so that readers can better appreciate the stranger's triumph.

 BEST PRACTICES TOOLKIT—Transparency
Character Traits and Textual Evidence p. D6

then he limped off a piece and laid down and died. It was a good pup, was that Andrew Jackson, and would have made a name for hisself if he'd lived, for the stuff
90 was in him and he had genius—I know it, because he hadn't no opportunities to speak of, and it don't stand to reason that a dog could make such a fight as he could under them circumstances if he hadn't no talent. It always makes me feel sorry when I think of that last fight of his'n and the way it turned out. **C**

"Well, thish-yer Smiley had rat terriers, and chicken cocks, and tomcats and all them kind of things till you couldn't rest, and you couldn't fetch nothing for him to bet on but he'd match you. He ketched a frog one day and took him home, and said he cal'lated[12] to educate him; and so he never done nothing for three months but set in his back yard and learn that frog to jump. And you bet you he *did* learn him, too. He'd give him a little punch behind, and the next minute you'd see that
100 frog whirling in the air like a doughnut—see him turn one summerset, or maybe a couple if he got a good start, and come down flatfooted and all right, like a cat. He got him up so in the matter of ketching flies, and kep' him in practice so constant, that he'd nail a fly every time as fur as he could see him. Smiley said all a frog wanted was education and he could do 'most anything—and I believe him. Why, I've seen him set Dan'l Webster down here on this floor—Dan'l Webster was the name of the frog—and sing out, 'Flies, Dan'l, flies!' and quicker'n you could wink he'd spring straight up and snake a fly off'n the counter there, and flop down on the floor ag'in as solid as a gob of mud, and fall to scratching the side of his head with his hind foot as **indifferent** as if he hadn't no idea he'd been doin' any more'n
110 any frog might do. You never see a frog so modest and straight-for'ard as he was, for all he was so gifted. And when it come to fair and square jumping on a dead level, he could get over more ground at one straddle than any animal of his breed you ever see. Jumping on a dead level was his strong suit, you understand; and when it come to that, Smiley would ante up money on him as long as he had a red.[13] Smiley was monstrous proud of his frog, and well he might be for fellers that had traveled and been everywheres all said he laid over any frog that ever *they* see. **D**

"Well, Smiley kep' the beast in a little lattice box, and he used to fetch him downtown sometimes and lay for a bet. One day a feller—a stranger in the camp, he was—come acrost him with his box and says:
120 "'What might it be that you've got in the box?'

"And Smiley says, sorter indifferent-like, 'It might be a parrot, or it might be a canary, maybe, but it ain't—it's only just a frog.'

"And the feller took it and looked at it careful, and turned it round this way and that, and says, 'H'm—so 'tis. Well, what's *he* good for?'

"'Well,' Smiley says, easy and careless, 'he's good enough for *one* thing, I should judge—he can outjump any frog in Calaveras County.'

"The feller took the box again and took another long, particular look, and give it back to Smiley and says, very deliberate, 'Well,' he says, 'I don't see no p'ints[14] about that frog that's any better'n any other frog.'

---

12. **cal'lated:** calculated; intended.

13. **a red:** a red cent (slang for a penny).

14. **p'ints:** points.

688 UNIT 4: REGIONALISM AND NATURALISM

TEXT ANALYSIS

COMMON CORE

RL 3
L 5a

C TALL TALE

Possible answer: The main characteristic is hyperbole: Wheeler's assertion that Andrew Jackson wouldn't fight back until bets were doubled (lines 74–79), that the dog died of a broken heart after losing and feeling betrayed by Jim Smiley (lines 85–88), and that the dog was a "genius" (line 90).

READING SKILL

COMMON CORE

L 1a

D *Model the Skill:* DIALECT

To illustrate Twain's characterization of the frog, read aloud lines 104–111, beginning with, "Why, I've seen him . . ." and ending with, ". . . he was so gifted." Discuss how phrases such as ". . . he'd been doin' any more'n any frog might do" add drama to the activities of an ordinary frog.

Possible answer: The use of dialect in the characterization adds to the humor and makes the frog seem like the kind of colorful character that belongs in the frontier setting of the story. The frog is characterized as "modest," "straight-for'ard," and "gifted," human character traits that usually are not attributed to an animal.

VOCABULARY

COMMON CORE

L 4

OWN THE WORD

indifferent: Ask students to describe how they might act if they were acting *indifferently* in class. *Possible answer:* not paying attention; making little or no effort

C TALL TALE
Reread lines 68–93. What device characteristic of the tall tale is on display in this paragraph?

2 Targeted Passage

indifferent (ĭn-dĭf'ər-ənt) *adj.* having no particular interest

D DIALECT
Reread lines 110–111. How does the dialect in this sentence, and throughout the paragraph, help to characterize the frog?

DIFFERENTIATED INSTRUCTION

FOR STRUGGLING READERS

2 Targeted Passage [Lines 94–116]

This passage introduces the jumping frog of the story's title.

• What name did Smiley give to the frog? (lines 105–106)

• What kind of education did Smiley give the frog? (lines 97–98)

• How did Smiley plan to use the frog? (line 114)

FOR ADVANCED LEARNERS/AP

Research and Analyze Tell students that Twain was so annoyed by the first French translation of this story that he "retranslated" it from French into English to point out its stupidity. He gave the tongue-in-cheek retranslation this subtitle: "In English, then in French, then clawed back into a civilized language once more by patient, unremunerated toil." Ask a small group of students to read Twain's retranslation. Have them prepare a group essay answering these questions:

• In addition to the comic plot of the story, what makes the retranslation humorous?

• What techniques does Twain use to show—directly or indirectly—that the French translation was a poor one? Give some examples.

• What humorous elements in the retranslation are similar to humorous elements in the original?

Frog of Calaveras County. The Granger Collection, New York.

130   '"Maybe you don't,' Smiley says. 'Maybe you understand frogs and maybe you don't understand 'em; maybe you've had experience and maybe you ain't only a amature, as it were. Anyways, I've got *my* opinion, and I'll resk forty dollars that he can outjump any frog in Calaveras County.'

    "And the feller studied a minute and then says, kinder sad-like, 'Well, I'm only a stranger here and I ain't got no frog; but if I had a frog, I'd bet you.'

    "And then Smiley says, 'That's all right—that's all right—if you'll hold my box a minute, I'll go and get you a frog.' And so the feller took the box and put up his forty dollars along with Smiley's, and set down to wait. **E**

    "So he set there a good while thinking and thinking to himself, and then he got

140 the frog out and prized his mouth open and took a teaspoon and filled him full of quail shot[15]—filled him pretty near up to his chin—and set him on the floor. Smiley he went to the swamp and slopped around in the mud for a long time, and finally he ketched a frog and fetched him in and give him to this feller, and says:

    "'Now, if you're ready, set him alongside of Dan'l, with his forepaws just even with Dan'l's, and I'll give the word.' Then he says, 'One—two—three—*git!*' and him and the feller touched up the frogs from behind, and the new frog hopped off

❸ Targeted Passage

E **TALL TALE**
Reread the dialogue in lines 120–138. What does the straightfaced understatement reveal about the two characters?

15. **quail shot:** small lead pellets for firing from a shotgun.

THE NOTORIOUS JUMPING FROG OF CALAVERAS COUNTY   **689**

Analyze Dialogue Grammar and word choice are tools that authors use to convey how dialogue should be read. Remind students that coordinating conjunctions such as *and, but, or, nor, for,* and *yet* are used to join clauses that hold equal importance. Dashes are used to show sudden breaks or changes in speech. As Wheeler reaches the end of his tale, the coordinating conjunctions and dashes show that he is so excited that he cannot pause for breath and that he is hardly able to include all the details. Have students find other places in the story where Twain uses coordinating conjunctions or dashes in dialogue.

enterprising: Ask students to give examples of times when they may have been *enterprising*.

SELECTION WRAP-UP

READ WITH A PURPOSE Ask students to consider how the narrator's exaggeration created a good story. *Possible answer: Exaggerating the "education" of a frog and the tricks played during the jumping contest enhances the humor of the story.*

INDEPENDENT READING

Students may also enjoy *Tall Tale America: A Legendary History of our Humourous Heroes* by Walter Blair.

---

lively, but Dan'l give a heave and hysted up his shoulders—so—like a Frenchman, but it warn't no use—he couldn't budge; he was planted as solid as a church, and he couldn't no more stir than if he was anchored out. Smiley was a good deal
150 surprised, and he was disgusted too, but he didn't have no idea what the matter was, of course. **F**

"The feller took the money and started away, and when he was going out at the door, he sorter jerked his thumb over his shoulder—so—at Dan'l and says again, very deliberate, 'Well,' he says, '*I* don't see no p'ints about that frog that's any better'n any other frog.'

"Smiley he stood scratching his head and looking down at Dan'l a long time, and at last he says, 'I do wonder what in the nation that frog throw'd off for—I wonder if there ain't something the matter with him—he 'pears to look mighty baggy, somehow.' And he ketched Dan'l by the nap of the neck and hefted him,
160 and says, 'Why, blame my cats if he don't weigh five pound!' and turned him upside down and he belched out a double handful of shot. And then he see how it was, and he was the maddest man—he set the frog down and took out after that feller, but he never ketched him. And—"

[Here Simon Wheeler heard his name called from the front yard and got up to see what was wanted.] And turning to me as he moved away, he said: "Just set where you are, stranger, and rest easy—I ain't going to be gone a second."

But, by your leave, I did not think that a continuation of the history of the **enterprising** vagabond *Jim* Smiley would be likely to afford me much information concerning the Rev. *Leonidas W.* Smiley and so I started away.
170 At the door I met the sociable Wheeler returning, and he buttonholed me and recommenced:[16]

"Well, thish-yer Smiley had a yaller one-eyed cow that didn't have no tail, only just a short stump like a bannanner, and—"

However, lacking both time and inclination, I did not wait to hear about the afflicted cow but took my leave.

F GRAMMAR AND STYLE
Reread lines 144–151.
Notice how Twain uses **coordinating conjunctions** and **dashes** to convey Simon's breathless retelling of the story.

④ Targeted Passage

enterprising
(ĕn′tər-prī′zĭng) *adj.*
possessing imagination and initiative

---

16. **buttonholed . . . recommenced:** detained me for conversation and began talking again.

DIFFERENTIATED INSTRUCTION

FOR ADVANCED LEARNERS/AP

Analyze Archetypal Characters Point out that the humorous characters in this story represent universal types: the outsider, the deadpan storyteller, the trickster, and the stranger (who may be a trickster, too). Have students identify these archetypal characters in the story and then brainstorm other examples of these character types from folk tales, fiction, movies, television, or cartoons.

FOR STRUGGLING READERS

④ **Targeted Passage** [Lines 149–163]

In this passage, Smiley solves the mystery of his loss, and Wheeler's tale ends.

- How does the stranger react to winning the contest? How does Smiley react to losing? (lines 149–155)

- How does Smiley react after he realizes that he has been tricked? (lines 162–163)

FOR ADVANCED LEARNERS/AP

Analyze Style Twain uses dialect and idioms, humorous subject matter, irony, offbeat similes and metaphors, rambling, and indirect narrative. Have students use an Analysis Frame: Author's Craft to identify and analyze these elements in Twain's writing.

🧰 BEST PRACTICES TOOLKIT—Transparency
Analysis Frame: Author's Craft
pp. D21, D24

Comprehension

1. **Recall** How does the narrator hear the story of the jumping frog?

2. **Recall** What is Smiley always willing to do?

3. **Summarize** What happens to Smiley's frog?

Text Analysis

4. **Make Inferences About Characters** What can you infer about Jim Smiley based on each of the following examples?

   • Smiley betting on the health of the parson's wife

   • Smiley spending three months teaching a frog to jump

   • Smiley studying why the frog couldn't jump

5. **Understand Dialect** Review the dialect and translations you recorded as you read. In general, what does the use of dialect contribute to **characterization** and **setting** in this story? Cite specific examples.

6. **Analyze Overstatement** Simon Wheeler makes liberal use of overstatement, or hyperbole, in describing Jim Smiley; some of what he says is totally improbable, and some is simply a bit of a stretch. List several examples of overstatement and rate each on a scale of one to five, with five being the most outrageous. At any point, did your doubts prevent you from enjoying the story? Explain.

7. **Make Judgments About the Tall Tale** Twain sets this story in a **frame**—a story within a story—in which the first-person narrator asks about a man named Leonidas Smiley but gets a story about Jim Smiley instead. In the end, the narrator makes a show of going away disappointed. How does this device contribute to the impact of the tall tale? Explain how the story would have been different if the original first-person narrator had simply told the story in his own voice, or if Wheeler himself had been the first-person narrator. Do you think this frame is an effective technique? Why or why not?

Text Criticism

8. **Critical Interpretations** According to one critic, Twain's organization of this tale "seems wholly directionless," yet "actually it is carefully molded for climax." Do you agree? Look back at the story and explain how the elaborate setup affects the impact of the story's punchline. Use examples from the story to support your ideas.

> *Can you spot a* **TALL TALE?**
>
> A tall tale, like this one by Twain, usually makes people laugh because they know it's not true. What stories and ideas in real life cause people to be skeptical? Do you think any of those stories have a basis in fact? Why or why not?

THE NOTORIOUS JUMPING FROG OF CALAVERAS COUNTY **691**

COMMON CORE

RL 3 Analyze the impact of the author's choices regarding how to develop and relate elements of a story. **RL 4** Analyze the impact of specific word choices on meaning and tone. **RL 5** Analyze how an author's choices concerning how to structure specific parts of a text contribute to its overall structure and meaning as well as its aesthetic impact. **L 1a** Apply the understanding that usage is a matter of convention. **L 5a** Interpret figures of speech in context and analyze their role in the text.

Practice and Apply

For preliminary support of post-reading questions, use these copy masters:

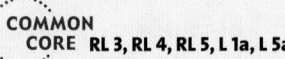 **RESOURCE MANAGER**—Copy Masters

Reading Check p. 64
Tall Tale p. 57
Question Support p. 65
Additional selection questions are provided for teachers on page 51.

ANSWERS **COMMON CORE** RL 3, RL 4, RL 5, L 1a, L 5a

1. *The narrator visits Simon Wheeler to ask about a man named Leonidas W. Smiley. Wheeler's response is to tell the narrator stories about Jim Smiley instead.*

2. *Smiley is always willing to place a bet.*

3. *The frog wins many bets for Smiley but loses when a crafty stranger weighs the frog down with quail shot.*

4. *Possible answers: The parson's wife: Smiley values gambling over sensitivity or kindness. Teaching the frog: Smiley is determined and patient. Studying the frog: Smiley is intelligent, thorough, and good at solving problems.*

5. ■ **COMMON CORE FOCUS Understand Dialect** *The dialect contributes to characterization by capturing Wheeler's talkative, colorful, folksy, and naïve personality and Smiley's shrewd frontier attitude. The dialect helps depict the setting by conveying the language spoken in the California mining camp, showing who is part of that community and who is an outsider. Examples of character-revealing dialect include the beginning of Simon Wheeler's story and the dialogue that he quotes between Smiley and the stranger.*

6. ● **COMMON CORE FOCUS Analyze Overstatement** *Examples of overstatement include "If he even see a straddlebug . . ." (lines 45–49); "But as soon as money was up on him he was a different dog" (line 70); "He gave Smiley . . . laid down and died" (lines 85–88); "he never done . . . jump" (lines 97–98); and "And when . . . you ever see" (lines 111–113). Most students will feel that their skepticism added to their enjoyment of the story.*

7. ● **COMMON CORE FOCUS Tall Tale** *The frame story structure allows readers to understand the techniques of the tall tale. Wheeler's tale would not be as outrageous if it were not set in contrast to the narrator's dry voice and bored response. If the*

---

narrator had told the story himself, the tale would lack overstatement, dialect, and local color. If Wheeler had narrated the story alone, readers would not understand the condescending perspective of the narrator.

8. *Despite the appearance of Wheeler's wandering narrative, every detail in the tale demonstrates both the character of Jim Smiley and his community. Wheeler appears to ramble, so readers may be lulled*

into distraction, allowing the story's twist to come as a surprise.

> *Can you spot a* **TALL TALE?**
> Students might say that people are skeptical when stories sound too good. They might say that the story appears to be an elaboration on a real-life storyteller.

ANSWERS

Vocabulary in Context

▲ **VOCABULARY PRACTICE**

1. *(d) lonesome*   5. *(d) conjecture*

2. *(b) argumentative* 6. *(b) expensive*

3. *(c) unhappy*   7. *(d) unnoticeable*

4. *(a) unusual*   8. *(a) cavorting*

R RESOURCE MANAGER—Copy Master
Vocabulary Practice p. 62

ACADEMIC VOCABULARY IN WRITING

Possible answer: A tall tale could focus on a famous basketball player by exaggerating his or her *apparent* qualities and talents. For example, a player could be *perceived* as twenty feet tall who could sink a basket from a mile away.

VOCABULARY STRATEGY: THESAURI AND WORD KNOWLEDGE

 **COMMON CORE** L 4c, L 5b, L 6

- Encourage students to see the differences between words with similar meanings. For example, the word *rich* has different associations than *wealthy*.

- Point out that some synonyms may have positive and negative connotations. For example, a person might want to be called *casual*, but would not want to be called *lazy*.

Possible answers:

1. *money, possessions, riches*

2. *praise, please*

3. *center, central, amidst*

4. *chilly, icy, frigid*

5. *assist, suggest*

R RESOURCE MANAGER—Copy Master
Vocabulary Strategy p. 63

Interactive Vocabulary THINK central

Keywords direct students to a **WordSharp** tutorial on **thinkcentral.com** or to other types of vocabulary practice and review.

Vocabulary in Context

▲ **VOCABULARY PRACTICE**

Choose the word that is not related in meaning to the other words.

1. (a) dilapidated, (b) decaying, (c) neglected, (d) lonesome
2. (a) chatty, (b) argumentative, (c) garrulous, (d) verbose
3. (a) serene, (b) tranquil, (c) unhappy, (d) placid
4. (a) unusual, (b) infamous, (c) disreputable, (d) notorious
5. (a) comfort, (b) condolence, (c) consolation, (d) conjecture
6. (a) imaginative, (b) expensive, (c) enterprising, (d) resourceful
7. (a) unconcerned, (b) detached, (c) indifferent, (d) unnoticeable
8. (a) cavorting, (b) trembling, (c) shaking, (d) jarring

WORD LIST
cavorting
conjecture
dilapidated
enterprising
garrulous
indifferent
infamous
tranquil

ACADEMIC VOCABULARY IN WRITING

• apparent • confine • expose • focus • perceive

Tall tales often **focus** on larger-than-life heroes and amazing exploits. In a short paragraph, discuss some modern-day people and events that could be made into tall tales. Be sure to include why you think the people and events are worthy of a tall tale. Use at least one Academic Vocabulary word in your paragraph.

VOCABULARY STRATEGY: THESAURI AND WORD KNOWLEDGE

A thesaurus is a reference book that helps you find specific, or precise, words for more general terms. In a thesaurus, words are arranged by their meanings and by their parts of speech rather than by alphabetical order, as in a dictionary. You can use a thesaurus to choose a specific word to show a subtle difference in meaning or to avoid monotony in your writing. For example, to replace the vocabulary word *infamous*, you could find *wrong*, *disreputable*, and *dishonorable*.

PRACTICE Use a thesaurus to identify the following words.

1. Three nouns you might use when talking about "wealth"
2. Two or three verbs related to the noun "flattery"
3. Words that could replace "middle" in referring to distance or space
4. Three adjectives to describe the feeling of being "cold"
5. Words to suggest what you might do rather than "advise"

COMMON CORE

L 4c Consult general and specialized reference materials to determine or clarify a word's precise meaning. **L 5b** Analyze nuances in the meaning of words with similar denotations. **L 6** Acquire and use accurately general academic words and phrases.

 **Interactive Vocabulary** THINK central

Go to **thinkcentral.com**.
KEYWORD: HML11-692

DIFFERENTIATED INSTRUCTION

FOR ENGLISH LANGUAGE LEARNERS

Task Support: Vocabulary Practice Point out that the Spanish cognate *tranquilo* and the French cognate *tranquille* are similar to the English word *tranquil*. Encourage students who speak Latin-based languages to find home-language cognates for at least two other vocabulary words.

FOR ADVANCED LEARNERS/AP

Academic Vocabulary in Writing Challenge students to use as many vocabulary words as they can to write two paragraphs—one from the point of view of a casual onlooker (who may find the contest foolish) and one from the point of view of someone who knows about Smiley's love of wagering (and who may find the contest humorous). Invite students to compare their responses in small groups to see how they used the words and to discuss how the narrator's attitude determines word choice.

Language

◆ **GRAMMAR AND STYLE: Create Realistic Characters**

Review the **Grammar and Style** note on page 690. Mark Twain creates convincing dialogue to help establish the character of Simon Wheeler. Look at this example from the story:

> *And a dog might tackle him and <u>bullyrag</u> him, and bite him and throw him over his shoulder two or three times, and Andrew Jackson—which was the name of the pup—Andrew Jackson would never let on but what he was satisfied and hadn't expected nothing else. . . .* (lines 72–75)

Notice how Twain uses the highlighted **coordinating conjunctions** to reflect Simon's long, rambling sentences. He also uses **dashes** to show how Simon interrupts himself. Finally, the underlined word is **dialect**, showing that Simon is rooted in his local culture.

PRACTICE After you respond to the prompt below, rewrite the conversation in dialect. You may use either the same Western dialect that Twain uses or a dialect from a different place and time that is familiar to you. Make use of coordinating conjunctions, dashes, and regional vocabulary, as well as any special spellings or contractions that will help your reader "hear" the dialect as it would be spoken.

> **EXAMPLE**
>
> "My goodness! If I had known you felt that way about it, I never would have said anything in the first place."
>
> *"Well, shut my mouth! If I'da known you felt that way 'bout it, I never woulda said nothin' in th' first place."*

READING-WRITING CONNECTION

YOUR TURN Expand your understanding of Twain's writing by responding to this prompt. Then use the **revising tips** to improve your dialogue.

WRITING PROMPT	**REVISING TIPS**
WRITE A DIALOGUE A **conversation** can reveal a great deal about its participants. Characters' words and gestures as well as the pace and flow of their speech all make a story's characters believable. Write a **one-page conversation** between two real people or fictional characters. Like Twain, have them share amazing—and possibly exaggerated—experiences.	• Start a new paragraph to indicate a change in speakers and to reflect the pacing of the conversation. • Be sure to set punctuation, such as commas and periods, inside closing quotation marks. • Use exaggeration and irony to make your experiences humorous.

Interactive Revision THINK central Go to **thinkcentral.com**. KEYWORD: HML11-693

FOR STRUGGLING WRITERS

Writing Support As students review the draft of their dialogues, help them focus on the effectiveness of each comment in the conversation.

- Explain that dialogue serves two functions: characterization and plot advancement.

- Using their draft or a copy of it (on which students might reduce the text to provide a wide margin), have students highlight each line of dialogue with a colored marker, using a different color for each character.

- Provide these notations: **1.** Shows character trait: _____; **2.** Reveals attitude: _____; **3.** Reveals background information: _____.

- In the margins, have students write the correct notation for each line of dialogue by filling in the trait, attitude, or background information that they intend to convey.

- Then have students share their annotated dialogues with a partner. Ask partners to comment on whether each line conveys the writer's intent. If not, have partners offer specific suggestions for revising the dialogue.

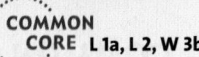

Language

◆ **GRAMMAR AND STYLE**

Encourage students to use the grammar and usage aspects of the dialect that they choose rather than simply producing random phonetic misspellings. Caution students against using dialect to ridicule particular social or ethnic groups.

R RESOURCE MANAGER—Copy Master
Create Realistic Characters p. 66

READING-WRITING CONNECTION

• Remind students that dialect can be used to reveal a number of things about a character, including their location, their education, and their age. Point out that the dialect they choose will reveal the personality and background of their character.

As part of the prewriting process, encourage students to watch a conversation on a television program that they enjoy. Suggest that students use an Observation Chart to record key points in the conversation as well as the characters' facial expressions, gestures, and body language. Students can use these notes as a starting point for their dialogues.

BEST PRACTICES TOOLKIT—Transparency
Observation Chart p. C7

Assess and Reteach

Assess

DIAGNOSTIC AND SELECTION TESTS

Selection Test A pp. 185–186
Selection Test B/C pp. 187–188

Interactive Selection Test on thinkcentral.com

Reteach

Level Up Online Tutorials on thinkcentral.com

Reteaching Worksheets on thinkcentral.com

Literature Lesson 41: Dialogue and Dialect
Literature Lesson 44: Style and Syntax
Writing Lesson 32: Writing Dialogue
Vocabulary Lesson 1: Base Words, Suffixes, and Roots
Vocabulary Lesson 2: Prefixes
Vocabulary Lesson 3: Prefixes with Multiple Meanings

COMMON CORE FOCUS

RL 6 Analyze a case in which grasping point of view requires distinguishing what is directly stated in a text from what is really meant. **L 1** Demonstrate command of the conventions of English grammar and usage when writing. **L 1a** Apply the understanding that usage is a matter of convention and can change over time.

BACKGROUND Huck's story begins when he runs away to Jackson's Island to escape his abusive father. On the island, he meets Jim, a runaway slave. Together they flee down the Mississippi River on a raft in an attempt to reach Ohio and freedom. During their journey, they form a close friendship.

TEXT ANALYSIS Explain that *The Adventures of Huckleberry Finn* is a coming-of-age novel about a Missouri boy. A pioneering work of American regionalism, it brilliantly capture the flavor of a particular time and place. Its critique of slavery and small-town prejudices makes *The Adventures of Huckleberry Finn* a scathing satire of 19th century social institutions.

DISCUSS As students find examples if irony, point out how Twain uses the technique to make social commentary. Draw their attention to Huck's declaration, "All right, then, I'll go to hell," and have them explain the passage's irony and significance.

American Masterpiece

from The Adventures of Huckleberry Finn

Novel by Mark Twain

COMMON CORE

RL 6 Analyze a case in which grasping point of view requires distinguishing what is directly stated in a text from what is really meant. **L 1** Demonstrate command of the conventions of English grammar and usage when writing. **L 1a** Apply the understanding that usage is a matter of convention and can change over time.

BACKGROUND Although Mark Twain first won fame as a Western humorist writing about life in the California gold-mining camps, he drew on his Missouri childhood for many of his best-known works, including *The Adventures of Huckleberry Finn*, widely regarded as one of the greatest American novels. Set in the years before the Civil War, when slavery was still legal in Missouri, the novel follows its protagonist Huck and a runaway slave named Jim on an adventure by raft down the Mississippi River. With the novel's hero, Twain depicts the conflict between what society expects and what conscience demands of individuals. In the excerpt on the following page, for example, Huck has just done what his society has taught him is the right thing to do: he has written a note to Miss Watson, reporting the whereabouts of her runaway slave, Jim. However, Huck has deep misgivings about this action.

TEXT ANALYSIS Twain narrates Huck's tale in first person point of view, taking the voice of Huck himself—an uneducated Missouri boy of the mid-nineteenth century. Huck's story is sprinkled with **colloquial language**—words and phrases taken from informal English. The result is a book that sounds not like Mark Twain writing but like Huck Finn speaking. His language includes slang, as well as incorrect grammar conventional to the place and time of the story.

Twain achieves much more, however, in writing *Huck Finn* from the point of view of an uneducated, somewhat naïve, young man. The author uses **irony** to comment on the values of Huck's society. **Dramatic irony** occurs when readers know more than a character knows. Early in the story, for example, Huck tells about his chance to join a gang led by his friend Tom Sawyer: "…he hunted me up and said he was going to start a band of robbers, and I might join if I would go back to the widow and be respectable." Readers know that joining a group of thieves is the opposite of "respectable," but Huck does not. This is also an example of **verbal irony.** Twain is clearly being ironic when he has Huck use the word "respectable." The author is saying one thing but meaning its opposite.

DISCUSS Read the passage with a small group of your peers. Make a list of colloquial words and phrases that make the writing sound as if Huck is speaking to you. Then, read the passage a second time and identify at least one instance of irony—a place in the writing where both readers and author know more than Huck knows. Afterward, share your findings with your class as a whole.

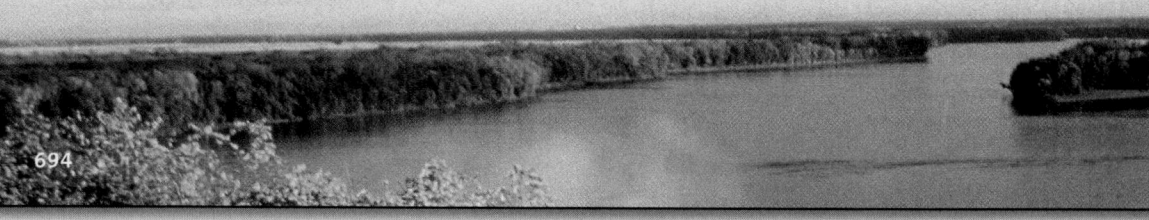

694

DIFFERENTIATED INSTRUCTION

FOR STRUGGLING READERS

Taking Notes Ask students to record the main ideas of each section on page 694 in outline form. Then have students exchange papers, evaluate each other's work, and offer suggestions for possible improvement.

Possible beginning of outline:

I. About the author
   A. Before becoming a writer
      1. Sam Clemens's youth in Hannibal, Missouri
      2. His work as a riverboat pilot
      3. "Mark Twain" = Mississippi riverboat workers' shout
   B. As a writer
      1. Famous humorist
      2. Best-known works: The Adventures of Tom Sawyer (1876); Life on the Mississippi (1883); The Adventures of Huckleberry Finn (1884)

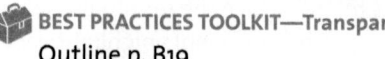 BEST PRACTICES TOOLKIT—Transparency
Outline p. B19

I felt good and all washed clean of sin for the first time I had ever felt so in my life, and I knowed I could pray now. But I didn't do it straight off, but laid the paper down and set there thinking—thinking how good it was all this happened so, and how near I come to being lost and going to hell. And went on thinking. And got to thinking over our trip down the river; and I see Jim before me, all the time, in the day, and in the nighttime, sometimes moonlight, sometimes storms, and we a floating along, talking, and singing, and laughing. But somehow I couldn't seem to strike no places to harden me against him, but only
10 the other kind. I'd see him standing my watch on top of his'n, stead of calling me, so I could go on sleeping; and see him how glad he was when I come back out of the fog; and when I come to him again in the swamp, up there where the feud was; and such-like times; and would always call me honey, and pet me, and do everything he could think of for me, and how good he always was; and at last I struck the time I saved him by telling the men we had small-pox aboard, and he was so grateful, and said I was the best friend old Jim ever had in the world, and the only one he's got now; and then I happened to look around, and see that paper.

It was a close place. I took it up, and held it in my hand. I was a trembling, because I'd got to decide, forever, betwixt two things, and I knowed it. I studied
20 a minute, sort of holding my breath, and then says to myself:

"All right, then, I'll *go* to hell"—and tore it up.

It was awful thoughts, and awful words, but they was said. And I let them stay said; and never thought no more about reforming. I shoved the whole thing out of my head; and said I would take up wickedness again, which was in my line, being brung up to it, and the other warn't. And for a starter, I would go to work and steal Jim out of slavery again; and if I could think up anything worse, I would do that, too; because as long as I was in, and in for good, I might as well go the whole hog.

Then I set to thinking over how to get at it, and turned over considerable many ways in my mind; and at last fixed up a plan that suited me. So then I took the
30 bearings of a woody island that was down the river a piece, and as soon as it was fairly dark I crept out with my raft and went for it, and hid it there, and then turned in. I slept the night through, and got up before it was light, and had my breakfast, and put on my store clothes, and tied up some others and one thing or another in a bundle, and took the canoe and cleared for shore. I landed below where I judged was Phelps's place, and hid my bundle in the woods, and then filled up the canoe with water, and loaded rocks into her and sunk her where I could find her again when I wanted her, about a quarter mile below a little steam sawmill that was on the bank.

695

INTRODUCE THE MASTERPIECE

As students prepare to read the excerpt, point out that because Huck Finn is the narrator, readers see everything from his perspective. Afterward, discuss how Huck's thoughts and actions reveal his character.

TIERED DISCUSSION PROMPTS

Use these prompts to help students explore the characterization of Envy:

Connect Have you or someone you know ever had to choose between doing what someone else said was right and doing what you felt was right? How did you or the other person make the choice? *Accept all thoughtful responses.*

Analyze Explain the internal conflict that Huck is experiencing. Why does he feel this conflict? *Possible answer: Huck considers turning Jim in, for he knows that his society believes it right for him to do so. Huck feels the conflict because he cannot find "places to harden [him] against [Jim]." Instead, he remembers how Jim has called Huck his best—and only—friend in the world. Ultimately, Huck cannot bring himself to turn his friend in.*

Synthesize In what ways are Huck and Jim alike? *Possible answer: Huck and Jim are both trying to escape from abusive situations and find freedom. Huck is fleeing from the "drunken lout" who is his father; Jim is fleeing slavery. Both characters also value each other as friends, despite differences in race and situation.*

FOR ENGLISH LANGUAGE LEARNERS

Vocabulary Support Explain that Twain's use of informal, regional dialect helps make Huck realistic and his narrative authentic. Call students' attention to these elements of dialect; then help them "translate" the examples into standard English:

- *ungrammatical expressions:* "I knowed" (line 2), "how near I come" (line 4), "I couldn't seem to strike no places" (line 9), "see him how glad he was" (line 11), "says to myself"

(line 20), "never thought no more" (line 23), "being brung up to it" (lines 24–25)

- *regional language:* "straight off" (line 3), "we a floating along" (line 8), "such-like times" (line 13), "take up wickedness" (line 24), "for a starter" (line 25), "go the whole hog" (line 27), "considerable many ways" (lines 28–29), "down the river a piece" (line 30)

- *regional pronunciations:* "his'n" (line 10), "warn't" (line 25)

FOR ADVANCED LEARNERS/AP

Research and Evaluate Explain that *The Adventures of Huckleberry Finn* is one of the best-known—and most controversial—works in American literature. Ask students to research the basic arguments that opponents of the novel offer. Have them write and share a brief essay in which they outline those arguments, cite objections that the passage on this page might raise, and offer a supporting or countering argument.

Focus and Motivate

COMMON CORE FOCUS

RL 1 Cite evidence to support analysis of what the text says explicitly. **RL 2** Determine two or more themes or central ideas of a text. **RL 3** Analyze the impact of the author's choices regarding how to develop and relate elements of a story. **RL 4** Analyze the specific impact of word choices on meaning and tone. **W 3b, e** Use narrative techniques, such as description; provide a conclusion that follows from and reflects on what is observed. **SL 1a–d** Draw on preparation to stimulate a thoughtful, well-reasoned exchange of ideas; work with peers to promote civil, democratic discussions; pose and respond to questions that probe reasoning and evidence; ensure a hearing for a full range of positions on a topic or issue; clarify, verify, or challenge ideas and conclusions; promote divergent and creative perspectives; respond thoughtfully to diverse perspectives; synthesize comments, claims, and evidence on an issue. **L 3** Apply knowledge of language to make effective choices for style. **L 4b** Identify and correctly use patterns of word changes that indicate different meanings or parts of speech. **L 5a** Interpret figures of speech in context and analyze their role in the text. **L 5b** Analyze nuances in the meaning of words with similar denotations. **L 6** Acquire and use accurately general academic words and phrases.

ABOUT THE AUTHOR

After students read Bret Harte's biography, explain that in "The Outcasts of Poker Flat" they will encounter several of the familiar Western characters mentioned in the first sentence.

Selection Resources

The Outcasts of Poker Flat

HISTORY Video link at **thinkcentral.com**

Short Story by Bret Harte

COMMON CORE

RL 1 Cite evidence to support analysis of what the text says explicitly. **RL 3** Analyze the impact of the author's choices regarding how to develop and relate elements of a story.
SL 1a–d Draw on preparation to stimulate a thoughtful, well-reasoned exchange of ideas; work with peers to promote civil, democratic discussions; pose and respond to questions that probe reasoning and evidence; ensure a hearing for a full range of positions on a topic or issue; clarify, verify, or challenge ideas and conclusions; promote divergent and creative perspectives; respond thoughtfully to diverse perspectives; synthesize comments, claims, and evidence on an issue.

DID YOU KNOW?

Bret Harte . . .

- was called "Dickens among the pines" for the vivid and recognizable characters he created.
- worked as a shotgun rider on a California stagecoach.
- worked as an abolitionist during the Civil War, often speaking out against the harsh treatment of minorities.

Meet the Author

Bret Harte 1836–1902

Many of the familiar characters in Western stories and films—saloon keepers, fallen ladies, hard-bitten gamblers, mining prospectors, and dewy-eyed youngsters—can be found in the stories of Bret Harte. Harte's colorful writing helped shape the Western genre. It also inspired emigration to the developing region of the American west. Harte's writing made him—for a short while—one of America's most popular and highly paid literary figures.

A Man of Many Hats Born into an educated but financially struggling family, Bret Harte moved often during his childhood. Although the frequent moves and his poor health kept him from formal schooling, he read widely on his own and published his first writing at age 11. After his father died, Harte began working—first for a pharmacist, then a lawyer, and later as a tutor, a miner, and finally a journalist for a newspaper in California, where the family had moved after his mother's remarriage. It was at this newspaper that Harte began to publish his stories and articles.

Good Times In the early 1860s, Harte moved to San Francisco and began to hone his literary craft. He wrote and edited stories, articles, humor, and literary criticism for two newspapers, the *Golden Era* and then the *Californian.* At the *Californian,* Harte helped along the career of a young, unknown Mark Twain. Becoming founding editor of the *Overland Monthly,* Harte soon wrote and published "The Luck of Roaring Camp" and "The Outcasts of Poker Flat," stories of outcasts with hearts of gold. These stories put him on the literary map. Suddenly, he was the talk of the town with his work much discussed, often imitated, and highly sought after. When the *Atlantic Monthly* in Boston offered Harte an annual contract with a big salary, he moved his family back east.

. . . And Bad Times Harte was careless about fulfilling his *Atlantic Monthly* contract, and it was not renewed. He tried lecturing, novel writing (*Gabriel Conroy*), and playwriting with Mark Twain (*Ah Sin*), but was left with a failing literary career. His marriage had also deteriorated. Finally, in 1877, friends helped Harte get an appointment as U.S. consul in Germany. By 1885 he had landed in London. Bret Harte, who played a key role in creating the popular portrait of the Old West, lived in London for the rest of his life, dying there in 1902.

Author Online
Go to **thinkcentral.com**. KEYWORD: HML11-696

THINK central

See resources on the **Teacher One Stop DVD-ROM** *and on* **thinkcentral.com**.

HISTORY Video link at **thinkcentral.com**

 RESOURCE MANAGER UNIT 4
Plan and Teach, pp. 67–74
Summary, pp. 75–76†‡*
Text Analysis and Reading
  Skill, pp. 77–78†*, 79–80†*
Vocabulary, pp. 81–83*
Grammar and Style, p. 86

DIAGNOSTIC AND SELECTION TESTS
Selection Tests, pp. 189–192

 BEST PRACTICES TOOLKIT
Definition Mapping, p. E6
Jigsaw Reading, p. A1
Cluster Diagram, p. B18

TECHNOLOGY
- **Teacher One Stop DVD-ROM**
- **Student One Stop DVD-ROM**
- **Audio Anthology CD**
- **GrammarNotes DVD-ROM**
- **ExamView Test Generator on the Teacher One Stop**

---

* Resources for Differentiation   † Also in Spanish   ‡ In Haitian Creole and Vietnamese

TEXT ANALYSIS: REGIONALISM

A natural outgrowth of realism, **regionalism** was a literary movement of the 19th century that focused on the speech, habits, history, and beliefs of people in a specific geographic area. In "The Outcasts of Poker Flat," the **setting**—the physical features of a particular landscape and its time period—plays a prominent role in the plot. Harte has assembled a representative group of characters from the rapidly-expanding American West. Readers meet a gambler, two women with bad reputations, and a town drunk. Regionalist writers like Harte were so successful with these **character types,** or characters with a similar set of traits, that their creations continue to show up in literature, in movies, and in television shows today. As you read, pay careful attention to how Harte creates and develops these traditional characters in this specific time and place.

READING SKILL: CLARIFY MEANING

As you read this story, make sure to **clarify** any portions of the story that seem unclear on first reading. Stop and ask yourself questions such as these:

- What just happened?
- What do the characters' words and actions reveal about them?
- What meaning can be extracted from the narrator's comments and expressions?

▲ VOCABULARY IN CONTEXT

Harte uses a rich and challenging vocabulary in this story of the Old West. Choose the word from the list that you would associate with or use to describe an individual who

1. can see into the future
2. is constantly joking
3. criticizes others
4. complains all the time
5. utters a curse
6. is friendly to everyone
7. is an exile
8. has a steady outlook
9. weeps in sad movies
10. is avoided by others

WORD LIST	amicable	jocular	prescience
	anathema	maudlin	querulous
	equanimity	pariah	vituperative
	expatriated		

 Complete the activities in your **Reader/Writer Notebook.**

What does it mean to be an OUTCAST?

In ancient times, people were sent into exile as a form of punishment. They were cast out of society and set adrift, often in harsh and dangerous wilderness. In this story, the characters are exiled into the California mountains, where they face both psychological and physical challenges.

DEBATE In a small group, prepare arguments for or against the statement "We need society to live." In developing your argument, consider the consequences of living outside of society. Conduct a debate, providing evidence for your position and asking questions that probe the reasoning of the opposing position. Respond thoughtfully to a range of ideas different from your own. After the debate, discuss whether you would support exile as a form of modern punishment.

697

What does it mean to be an OUTCAST?

Introduce the question and after students share their ideas about why exile is both an effective and an extreme punishment, tell them to recall these ideas as they carry out the *DEBATE* activity.

TEXT ANALYSIS
COMMON CORE
RL 3

● *Model the Skill:* **REGIONALISM**

To illustrate characteristics of regionalism, write this passage on the board:

> The town of Bickforth in 1853 was as bleak, barren, and gray a place as any in the world. Dust and dirt seemed to cover the stores and people alike. Jethro Rank had lived in Bickforth for all 16 years of his life, and he was fed up.
>
> "Gonna get me a new horse and ride outta this-here town," Jethro told his friend Tully.
>
> Tully snickered. "You all a time talkin' like that, but you ain't never really gonna do it."

Point out regional literature characteristics such as description of setting and use of dialect.

GUIDED PRACTICE Ask students to find a passage in present-day literature that similarly captures the flavor of time and place.

READING SKILL
COMMON CORE
RL 1

■ *Model the Skill:* **CLARIFY MEANING**

Have students reread the passage on the board. Discuss what the characters' words reveal, such as that they have known each other for some time and that Tully doesn't take Jethro's statements seriously.

 RESOURCE MANAGER—Copy Master
Clarify Meaning p. 79 (for student use while reading the selection)

VOCABULARY SKILL
COMMON CORE
L 4

▲ VOCABULARY IN CONTEXT

DIAGNOSE WORD KNOWLEDGE Have all students complete Vocabulary in Context. Check their word choices against the following:

amicable (ăm′ĭ-kə-bəl) *adj.* characterized by friendly goodwill

anathema (ə-năth′ə-mə) *n.* a strong denunciation; a curse

equanimity (ē′kwə-nĭm′ĭ-tē) *n.* evenness of temper, especially under stress

expatriated (ĕk-spā′trē-ā′tĭd) *adj.* sent out of a country or area; banished **expatriate** v.

jocular (jŏk′yə-lər) *adj.* humorous

maudlin (mô-d′lĭn) *adj.* excessively sentimental

pariah (pə-r′īə) *n.* an outcast

prescience (prĕsh′əns) *n.* knowledge of events before they occur, especially under stress

querulous (kwĕr′ə-ləs) *adj.* complaining

vituperative (vī-tōo′pər-ə-tĭv) *adj.* abusively critical

Practice and Apply

SUMMARY

The citizens of Poker Flat cast out of their town certain undesirable persons: the gambler John Oakhurst, "The Duchess," "Mother Shipton," and "Uncle Billy." While traveling to a neighboring town, the outcasts meet young Tom Simson and his fiancée Piney Woods. The group is snowed in as they cross the mountains, and Billy sneaks off with their mules. As the days pass, supplies dwindle and the outcasts remain trapped. They draw comfort from one another, but eventually perish. Oakhurst, "at once the strongest and yet the weakest," commits suicide.

READ WITH A PURPOSE

Help student set a purpose for reading. Tell students to note details that describe why the characters in the story should or should not be "outcasts."

READING SKILL

A Model the Skill: CLARIFY MEANING

To help students clarify details that might be unclear on first reading, read aloud lines 3–6. Tell students to take note of the statement that the men "exchanged significant glances" and that the settlement was "unused to Sabbath influences." Have students restate the phrases in their own words to explain what John Oakhurst notices that morning in Poker Flat.

Possible answer: *The first paragraph suggests that Mr. John Oakhurst, a gambler, has violated the moral standards of Poker Flat (lines 2–3; lines 5–6) and earned the disapproval of its citizens (line 4).*

The Outcasts of Poker Flat

Bret Harte

> **BACKGROUND** Many of Bret Harte's stories highlighted both the lure of gold in California and the challenge of battling a harsh landscape of huge spaces and towering mountains. During the California Gold Rush, which began in 1848, thousands of people poured into the state, creating towns such as the one in this story. These towns, which developed from miners' camps, were often rough and featured the homemade style of justice that sets this story's events in motion.

As Mr. John Oakhurst, gambler, stepped into the main street of Poker Flat on the morning of the twenty-third of November, 1850, he was conscious of a change in its moral atmosphere since the preceding night. Two or three men, conversing earnestly together, ceased as he approached, and exchanged significant glances. There was a Sabbath lull in the air, which, in a settlement unused to Sabbath influences, looked ominous. **A**

Mr. Oakhurst's calm, handsome face betrayed small concern in these indications. Whether he was conscious of any predisposing cause, was another question. "I reckon they're after somebody," he reflected; "likely it's me." He
10 returned to his pocket the handkerchief with which he had been whipping away the red dust of Poker Flat from his neat boots, and quietly discharged his mind of any further conjecture.

In point of fact, Poker Flat was "after somebody." It had lately suffered the loss of several thousand dollars, two valuable horses, and a prominent citizen. It was experiencing a spasm of virtuous reaction, quite as lawless and ungovernable as any of the acts that had provoked it. A secret committee had determined to rid the town of all improper persons. This was done permanently in regard of two

Analyze Visuals ▶
Describe the sense of time and place conveyed in this image. What details give you this sense?

A CLARIFY MEANING
Reread the first paragraph. What has happened thus far?

 **Targeted Passage**

Deadwood, South Dakota, 1877. The Granger Collection, New York.

DIFFERENTIATED INSTRUCTION

FOR ENGLISH LANGUAGE LEARNERS
Vocabulary Support Use Definition Mapping to teach these words: *significant* (line 4), *professional* (line 21), *shift* (line 118), *prospect* (line 171), *theory* (line 230).

🧰 BEST PRACTICES TOOLKIT—Transparency
Definition Mapping p. E6

FOR STRUGGLING READERS

In combination with the *Audio Anthology CD,* use one or more Targeted Passages (pp. 698, 700, 703, 708) to ensure that students focus on key story events and concepts. Targeted Passages are also good for English language learners.

1 Targeted Passage [Lines 1–12]

This passage establishes the setting of the story and introduces the main character, John Oakhurst.

BACKGROUND

The American Frontier The concept of the frontier—a region at the edge of or just beyond settled land—has played a key role in American identity and popular culture. Because of its distance from Eastern political institutions, the frontier was a free-spirited place that beckoned many like the outcasts of Poker Flat. Frontier towns, much like those in the story, maintained their own standards of justice and means of law enforcement. By 1890, the frontier line had disappeared, but the frontier remained as a fabled time and place. In his famous if somewhat idealized essay of 1893, "The Significance of the Frontier in American History," the historian Frederick Jackson Turner memorialized those who braved the frontier when he declared "this expansion westward with its new opportunities, its continuous touch with the simplicity of primitive society, furnish the forces dominating American character."

- What character is introduced as the story begins? (line 1)
- What does this character do for a living? (line 1)
- What is the character's state of mind? (line 7)
- When does this story take place? (line 2)
- Where does the story take place? (line 1)

FOR ADVANCED LEARNERS/AP

Analyze Setting Have students work in small groups to discuss the importance of setting in the selection. Have them review the analysis of the American Frontier on page 699. Then have them consider these questions:

- Could these actions have taken place in a more "civilized" environment?
- How would the outcasts have been treated in a large city?

- Does a frontier location give the characters more freedom, or does it limit their actions and behaviors?

Encourage groups to share their conclusions.

READING SKILL

B CLARIFY MEANING

Possible answer: The narrator is critical of the "virtuous reaction" because it is "quite as lawless and ungovernable as any of the acts that had provoked it" (lines 15–16).

TEXT ANALYSIS

C Model the Skill:
REGIONALISM

Read aloud lines 13–29, asking students to note the crimes and punishments named in this passage, along with any indications of the motivation for these judgments.
Possible answer: Life in Poker Flat is rough and governed less by law than by the narrow-mindedness and greed of its citizens.

REVISIT THE BIG QUESTION

What does it mean to be an
OUTCAST?

Discuss In lines 23–50, on what information do the citizens of Poker Flat base their decision to send these four people into exile? *Possible answer: The "spasm of virtuous reaction" (line 15) and secret committee suggest the decision was based on questionable information, hearsay, and rumors.*

READING SKILL

D CLARIFY MEANING

Possible answer: Oakhurst is calm and philosophical in his acceptance of events; other characters are more emotional.

VOCABULARY

OWN THE WORD

- **expatriated:** Tell students that a person who is "sent out of a country or banished" is known as an *expatriate.* Have students list reasons why people might be *expatriated.* **Possible answers:** *sent overseas for a job; exiled due to political reasons*

- **anathema:** Ask students to create a pair of related statements that show how an *anathema* is stronger than mere dislike.

700 UNIT 4: REGIONALISM AND NATURALISM

---

men who were then hanging from the boughs of a sycamore in the gulch, and temporarily in the banishment of certain other objectionable characters. I regret
20 to say that some of these were ladies. It is but due to the sex, however, to state that their impropriety was professional, and it was only in such easily established standards of evil that Poker Flat ventured to sit in judgment. **B**

Mr. Oakhurst was right in supposing that he was included in this category. A few of the committee had urged hanging him as a possible example, and a sure method of reimbursing themselves from his pockets of the sums he had won from them. "It's agin justice," said Jim Wheeler, "to let this yer young man from Roaring Camp[1]—an entire stranger—carry away our money." But a crude sentiment of equity residing in the breasts of those who had been fortunate enough to win from Mr. Oakhurst overruled this narrower local prejudice. **C**
30 Mr. Oakhurst received his sentence with philosophic calmness, none the less coolly that he was aware of the hesitation of his judges. He was too much of a gambler not to accept Fate. With him life was at best an uncertain game, and he recognized the usual percentage in favor of the dealer.

A body of armed men accompanied the deported wickedness of Poker Flat to the outskirts of the settlement. Besides Mr. Oakhurst, who was known to be a coolly desperate man, and for whose intimidation the armed escort was intended, the **expatriated** party consisted of a young woman familiarly known as "The Duchess," another who had won the title of "Mother Shipton,"[2] and "Uncle Billy," a suspected sluice-robber[3] and confirmed drunkard. The cavalcade
40 provoked no comments from the spectators, nor was any word uttered by the escort. Only, when the gulch which marked the uttermost limit of Poker Flat was reached, the leader spoke briefly and to the point. The exiles were forbidden to return at the peril of their lives.

As the escort disappeared, their pent-up feelings found vent in a few hysterical tears from the Duchess, some bad language from Mother Shipton, and a Parthian volley of expletives[4] from Uncle Billy. The philosophic Oakhurst alone remained silent. He listened calmly to Mother Shipton's desire to cut somebody's heart out, to the repeated statements of the Duchess that she would die in the road, and to the alarming oaths that seemed to be bumped out of Uncle Billy as he
50 rode forward. With the easy good-humor characteristic of his class, he insisted upon exchanging his own riding-horse, "Five Spot," for the sorry mule which the Duchess rode. But even this act did not draw the party into any closer sympathy. The young woman readjusted her somewhat draggled plumes with a feeble, faded coquetry; Mother Shipton eyed the possessor of "Five Spot" with malevolence, and Uncle Billy included the whole party in one sweeping **anathema**. **D**

---

1. **Roaring Camp:** name applied to a wild California settlement that was established in the 1830s by Isaac Graham. Harte used the name in his story "The Luck of Roaring Camp."
2. **"Mother Shipton":** originally, a 16th-century English woman who was accused of being a witch.
3. **sluice-robber** (slōos′rŏb-ər): a person who steals gold from sluices, or the water troughs used by miners to sift gold.
4. **Parthian volley of expletives:** crude or hostile remarks made when leaving. Soldiers from the ancient Asian land of Parthia typically shot at their enemies while pretending to retreat on horseback.

700 UNIT 4: REGIONALISM AND NATURALISM

B CLARIFY MEANING
Reread lines 13–22. What is the narrator's attitude toward the "virtuous reaction" of Poker Flat?

C REGIONALISM
What can you **infer** about life in Poker Flat?

expatriated
(ĕk-spā′trē-ā′tĭd) *adj.* sent out of a country or area; banished **expatriate** *v.*

 Targeted Passage

anathema (ə-năth′ə-mə) *n.* a strong denunciation; a curse

D CLARIFY MEANING
Reread lines 44–55. What is your impression of Oakhurst at this point in the story? Compare him with the other outcasts.

DIFFERENTIATED INSTRUCTION

FOR STRUGGLING READERS

② Targeted Passage [Lines 34–50]

This passage introduces "The Duchess," "Mother Shipton," and "Uncle Billy." It also explains the outcasts' situation and describes their reactions.

- Which characters are described here? (lines 35–39)

- Why have these characters been escorted out of town? (lines 34–35)

- How does each character react to the situation? (lines 34–37)

FOR ADVANCED LEARNERS/AP

Analyze Tone As students read the story, have them reflect on the author's tone. What are Bret Harte's apparent feelings toward each of the characters? What does he think about their situation? Are their circumstances simply a matter of luck? Ask students to write a few paragraphs summarizing their observations and supporting their conclusions. Then have them share their paragraphs with the class.

The road to Sandy Bar—a camp that, not having as yet experienced the regenerating influences of Poker Flat, consequently seemed to offer some invitation to the emigrants—lay over a steep mountain range. It was distant a day's severe travel. In that advanced season, the party soon passed out of the moist, temperate regions of the foot-hills into the dry, cold, bracing air of the Sierras.[5] The trail was narrow and difficult. At noon the Duchess, rolling out of her saddle upon the ground, declared her intention of going no farther, and the party halted.

The spot was singularly wild and impressive. A wooded amphitheatre, surrounded on three sides by precipitous cliffs of naked granite, sloped gently toward the crest of another precipice that overlooked the valley. It was, undoubtedly, the most suitable spot for a camp, had camping been advisable. But Mr. Oakhurst knew that scarcely half the journey to Sandy Bar was accomplished, and the party were not equipped or provisioned for delay. This fact he pointed out to his companions curtly, with a philosophic commentary on the folly of "throwing up their hand before the game was played out." But they were furnished with liquor, which in this emergency stood them in place of food, fuel, rest, and **prescience.** In spite of his remonstrances, it was not long before they were more or less under its influence. Uncle Billy passed rapidly from a bellicose state into one of stupor, the Duchess became **maudlin,** and Mother Shipton snored. Mr. Oakhurst alone remained erect, leaning against a rock, calmly surveying them.

Mr. Oakhurst did not drink. It interfered with a profession which required coolness, impassiveness, and presence of mind, and, in his own language, he "couldn't afford it." As he gazed at his recumbent fellow-exiles, the loneliness begotten of his **pariah**-trade, his habits of life, his very vices, for the first time seriously oppressed him. He bestirred himself in dusting his black clothes, washing his hands and face, and other acts characteristic of his studiously neat habits, and for a moment forgot his annoyance. The thought of deserting his weaker and more pitiable companions never perhaps occurred to him. Yet he could not help feeling the want of that excitement which, singularly enough, was most conducive to that calm **equanimity** for which he was notorious. He looked at the gloomy walls that rose a thousand feet sheer above the circling pines around him; at the sky, ominously clouded; at the valley below, already deepening into shadow. And, doing so, suddenly he heard his own name called.

A horseman slowly ascended the trail. In the fresh, open face of the new-comer Mr. Oakhurst recognized Tom Simson, otherwise known as "The Innocent" of Sandy Bar. He had met him some months before over a "little game," and had, with perfect equanimity, won the entire fortune—amounting to some forty dollars—of that guileless youth. After the game was finished, Mr. Oakhurst drew the youthful speculator behind the door and thus addressed him: "Tommy, you're a good little man, but you can't gamble worth a cent. Don't try it over again." He then handed him his money back, pushed him gently from the room, and so made a devoted slave of Tom Simson.

---

5. **Sierras:** the Sierra Nevada range of mountains, in eastern California.

E REGIONALISM
Setting, the place and time in which a story is set, is an essential element of Regionalism. Reread lines 56–65, and note Harte's **diction,** or word choice, as he describes the characters' physical surrounding: "steep mountain range"; "bracing air"; "singularly wild"; "precipitous cliffs"; "naked granite." Do you see words in the passage that indicate the time in history or time of season in which the story is set?

prescience (prĕsh′əns) *n.* knowledge of events before they occur

maudlin (môd′lĭn) *adj.* excessively sentimental

pariah (pə-rī′ə) *n.* an outcast, someone or something looked down on by others

equanimity (ē′kwə-nĭm′ĭ-tē) *n.* evenness of temper, especially under stress

---

E REGIONALISM

Ask for volunteers to read lines 56–65 aloud. Tell students to note the stark wildness of the setting, such as the "wooded amphitheatre" and "naked granite" cliffs. Explain that these details help ground the story in a particular place. Have them look for clues that suggest a time period, such as the "severe day's travel" by horseback necessary to get from one camp to another.

Possible answer: The characters ride horses for travel, indicating that the story is set in an earlier time. The "advanced season" indicates that winter is approaching.

Extend the Discussion Why is Oakhurst concerned about stopping for the night?

OWN THE WORD

- **prescience:** Have students look at the context of the story where *prescience* is used. Ask them to explain the author's meaning. *Possible answer: The traveling party was more interested in drinking than in understanding what lies ahead in their journey.*

- **maudlin:** Tell students that *maudlin* means "extremely sentimental." Have students describe when they may have felt *maudlin*. *Possible answers: meeting with a new boyfriend or girlfriend*

- **pariah:** Tell students that *pariah* originates from the caste system of southern India, in which social outcasts are called *pariahs* or "untouchables." Ask students to explain why Mr. Oakhurst and his fellow travelers are considered *pariahs*. *Possible answer: They are undesirable because of their criminal activities.*

- **equanimity:** Remind students that *equanimity* means "evenness of temper, especially under stress." Have students list professions that require *equanimity*. *Possible answers: police, firefighters, air traffic controllers*

FOR ADVANCED LEARNERS/AP
Recognizing Stock Characters Explain that Bret Harte's stories include characters who may seem somehow familiar. This is in part because they are *stock characters*—characters in fiction or drama who represent types of characters rather than unique individuals. Examples of stock characters in literature include the rakish hero, the fool, the scheming villain, the innocent youth, the wicked witch, and the fallen woman with a heart of gold. When reading fiction, it is useful to be familiar with stock characters in order to recognize the roles they are intended to play in a story. As students read about Mr. Oakhurst, the Duchess, Mother Shipton, Uncle Billy, Tom Simson, and Piney Woods, have them identify stock traits in each character and share their findings with the class.

TIERED DISCUSSION PROMPTS

In lines 89–114, use these prompts to help students better understand the character of John Oakhurst:

Connect Have you ever felt the need to stand up for, or protect, someone younger than you? Why did you feel that way? *Accept all thoughtful responses.*

Analyze How does Harte use the relationship between Oakhurst and Tom Simson to further develop Oakhurst's character? *Possible answer: Oakhurst's attitude toward "The Innocent" is protective almost to the point of being paternal. Not only does Oakhurst return Tom's poker money, but he also tries to dissuade him from gambling again (lines 94–96). Oakhurst kicks Uncle Billy to keep him quiet (lines 110–111), and he tries to talk Tom out of remaining with their group (lines 112–114).*

Evaluate Is it believable that a professional gambler like Oakhurst would be concerned about someone like Tom? Why or why not? *Possible answers: Yes, because Oakhurst recognizes young Tom's youthful innocence and perhaps recalls when he himself was Tom's age. No, because Oakhurst does not trouble himself with sentiment, and may really think of "Innocent" Tom only as a potential liability.*

There was a remembrance of this in his boyish and enthusiastic greeting of Mr. Oakhurst. He had started, he said, to go to Poker Flat to seek his fortune. "Alone?"

100 No, not exactly alone; in fact (a giggle), he had run away with Piney Woods. Didn't Mr. Oakhurst remember Piney? She that used to wait on the table at the Temperance House?[6] They had been engaged a long time, but old Jake Woods had objected, and so they had run away, and were going to Poker Flat to be married, and here they were. And they were tired out, and how lucky it was they had found a place to camp and company. All this the Innocent delivered rapidly, while Piney, a stout, comely damsel of fifteen, emerged from behind the pine tree, where she had been blushing unseen, and rode to the side of her lover.

Mr. Oakhurst seldom troubled himself with sentiment, still less with propriety; but he had a vague idea that the situation was not fortunate. He retained,

110 however, his presence of mind sufficiently to kick Uncle Billy, who was about to say something, and Uncle Billy was sober enough to recognize in Mr. Oakhurst's kick a superior power that would not bear trifling. He then endeavored to dissuade Tom Simson from delaying further, but in vain. He even pointed out the fact that there was no provision, nor means of making a camp. But, unluckily, the Innocent met this objection by assuring the party that he was provided with an extra mule loaded with provisions, and by the discovery of a rude attempt at a log house near the trail. "Piney can stay with Mrs. Oakhurst," said the Innocent, pointing to the Duchess, "and I can shift for myself."

---

6. **Temperance House:** a place where customers could not drink.

DIFFERENTIATED INSTRUCTION

FOR ENGLISH LANGUAGE LEARNERS
Vocabulary: Multiple-Meaning Words Explain that *hanging* (line 24) means "executing (someone) by suspending by the neck until dead." However, *hanging* can also mean "attaching without support from below," as in "hanging a picture." Discuss how context clues can help students determine the appropriate meaning of multiple-meaning words. Then have mixed-language-ability Jigsaw groups investigate these other multiple-meaning words and report their findings: *body* (line 34), *bracing* (line 60), *coolness* (line 77), *habits* (line 81), *want* (line 84), *wait* (line 101), *provision* (line 114).

BEST PRACTICES TOOLKIT
Jigsaw Reading p. A1

FOR STRUGGLING READERS
Develop Reading Fluency Use the dramatic situation unfolding in lines 142–160 to promote students' interest in the plot complication. Conduct an echo reading with the class, reading aloud a paragraph and having students read it back aloud. As students read, visually monitor their enunciation and reading. Stop and ask questions at intervals to make sure that students understand the gravity of the situation facing the characters.

Nothing but Mr. Oakhurst's admonishing foot saved Uncle Billy from bursting
120 into a roar of laughter. As it was, he felt compelled to retire up the canyon until
he could recover his gravity. There he confided the joke to the tall pine trees, with
many slaps of his leg, contortions of his face, and the usual profanity. But when
he returned to the party, he found them seated by a fire—for the air had grown
strangely chill and the sky overcast—in apparently **amicable** conversation. Piney
was actually talking in an impulsive, girlish fashion to the Duchess, who was
listening with an interest and animation she had not shown for many days. The
Innocent was holding forth, apparently with equal effect, to Mr. Oakhurst and
Mother Shipton, who was actually relaxing into amiability. "Is this yer a d—d
picnic?" said Uncle Billy, with inward scorn, as he surveyed the sylvan group, the
130 glancing firelight, and the tethered animals in the foreground. Suddenly an idea
mingled with the alcoholic fumes that disturbed his brain. It was apparently of
a **jocular** nature, for he felt impelled to slap his leg again and cram his fist into
his mouth. **F**

As the shadows crept slowly up the mountain, a slight breeze rocked the tops
of the pine trees, and moaned through their long and gloomy aisles. The ruined
cabin, patched and covered with pine boughs, was set apart for the ladies. As
the lovers parted, they unaffectedly exchanged a kiss, so honest and sincere
that it might have been heard above the swaying pines. The frail Duchess and
the malevolent Mother Shipton were probably too stunned to remark upon this
140 last evidence of simplicity, and so turned without a word to the hut. The fire was
replenished, the men lay down before the door, and in a few minutes were asleep. **G**

Mr. Oakhurst was a light sleeper. Toward morning he awoke benumbed and
cold. As he stirred the dying fire, the wind, which was now blowing strongly,
brought to his cheek that which caused the blood to leave it—snow!

He started to his feet with the intention of awakening the sleepers, for there
was no time to lose. But turning to where Uncle Billy had been lying, he found
him gone. A suspicion leaped to his brain and a curse to his lips. He ran to the
spot where the mules had been tethered; they were no longer there. The tracks
were already rapidly disappearing in the snow.

150 The momentary excitement brought Mr. Oakhurst back to the fire with his
usual calm. He did not waken the sleepers. The Innocent slumbered peacefully,
with a smile on his good-humored, freckled face; the virgin Piney slept beside her
frailer sisters as sweetly as though attended by celestial guardians, and Mr. Oakhurst,
drawing his blanket over his shoulders, stroked his mustaches and waited for the
dawn. It came slowly in a whirling mist of snowflakes, that dazzled and confused the
eye. What could be seen of the landscape appeared magically changed. He looked
over the valley, and summed up the present and future in two words—"snowed in!"

A careful inventory of the provisions, which, fortunately for the party, had
been stored within the hut, and so escaped the felonious fingers of Uncle Billy,
160 disclosed the fact that with care and prudence they might last ten days longer.

amicable (ăm′ĭ-kə-bəl)
adj. characterized by
friendly goodwill

jocular (jŏk′yə-lər) *adj.*
humorous

F **CLARIFY MEANING**
Reread lines 117–133.
What effect has the
arrival of Tom and Piney
had on the outcasts?

G **GRAMMAR AND STYLE**
Reread lines 134–135.
Note that the **verbs** *crept*
and *moaned* are used to
personify the shadows
and the breeze.

3 **Targeted Passage**

COMMON CORE RL 4, L 5b

Language Coach

Word Choice *Felonious*
(line 159) means
"criminal" and is related
to the word *felony* (a
term for a serious crime).
Read lines 158–160. Why
do you think Harte might
have chosen to use the
word *felonious* instead of
criminal?

THE OUTCASTS OF POKER FLAT **703**

FOR STRUGGLING READERS

3 Targeted Passage [Lines 142–160]

This passage describes how the outcasts get
snowed in and tells how Uncle Billy has taken
the mules and abandoned the group.

• What event occurred overnight? (line 144)

• What is the result of this event? (line 157)

• What did Uncle Billy do? (lines 146–149)

• How long can the outcasts' provisions last?
(line 160)

Language Coach COMMON CORE RL 4, L 5b

Word Choice *Possible answer:*
Harte might have chosen felonious *because
the outcasts are themselves criminals. Discuss other words related to* felonious *such
as* guilty, convicted, *or* lawbreaker.

READING SKILL COMMON CORE RL 1

F CLARIFY MEANING

Possible answer: *The arrival of Tom and
Piney has had a positive, calming effect
on the outcasts. The group as a whole has
become friendlier and more relaxed. Uncle
Billy is amused by Tom's mistaking the
Duchess for "Mrs. Oakhurst" (line 117). Piney
and the Duchess are happily chatting
(lines 124–126) together, as are Tom, Mother
Shipton, and Oakhurst (lines 126–128).*

G GRAMMAR AND STYLE COMMON CORE L 3

Analyze Personification Elicit or explain
that personification is the attribution of
human qualities to objects, events, ideas,
or animals. Personification is common in
poetry and often appears in other types of
writing as well, helping to bring description to life. Ask students to find other examples of personification in Harte's story,
such as those in lines 232, 247, and 290.

VOCABULARY COMMON CORE L 4

OWN THE WORD

• **amicable:** Have students reread the
sentence "But when he returned to the
party, he found them seated by a fire. . .in
apparently *amicable* conversation." Ask
students to describe the characterization of this scene as presented. ***Possible
answer:*** *Uncle Billy came back to the camp
to find everyone sitting around the fire
enjoying warm, friendly conversation.*

• **jocular:** Remind students that *jocular*
means "humorous, comedic, or given to
joking." Have students complete the following sentence: "The circus clowns had
a *jocular* air about them as. . ." ***Possible
answer:*** *they tried to pile into the tiny car.*

THE OUTCASTS OF POKER FLAT **703**

"That is," said Mr. Oakhurst, *sotto voce*[7] to the Innocent, "if you're willing to board us." If you ain't—and perhaps you'd better not—you can wait till Uncle Billy gets back with provisions." For some occult reason, Mr. Oakhurst could not bring himself to disclose Uncle Billy's rascality, and so offered the hypothesis that he had wandered from the camp and had accidentally stampeded the animals. He dropped a warning to the Duchess and Mother Shipton, who of course knew the facts of their associate's defection. "They'll find out the truth about us *all* when they find out anything," he added, significantly, "and there's no good frightening them now."

170　　Tom Simson not only put all his worldly store at the disposal of Mr. Oakhurst, but seemed to enjoy the prospect of their enforced seclusion. "We'll have a good camp for a week, and then the snow'll melt, and we'll all go back together." The cheerful gaiety of the young man and Mr. Oakhurst's calm infected the others. The Innocent, with the aid of pine boughs, extemporized a thatch for the roofless cabin, and the Duchess directed Piney in the rearrangement of the interior with a taste and tact that opened the blue eyes of that provincial maiden to their fullest extent. "I reckon now you're used to fine things at Poker Flat," said Piney. The Duchess turned away sharply to conceal something that reddened her cheeks through its professional tint, and Mother Shipton requested Piney not to "chatter." But when Mr. Oakhurst returned

180　　from a weary search for the trail, he heard the sound of happy laughter echoed from the rocks. He stopped in some alarm, and his thoughts first naturally reverted to the whiskey, which he had prudently cached.[8] "And yet it don't somehow sound like whiskey," said the gambler. It was not until he caught sight of the blazing fire through the still-blinding storm and the group around it that he settled to the conviction that it was "square fun."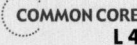

　　Whether Mr. Oakhurst had cached his cards with the whiskey as something debarred the free access of the community, I cannot say. It was certain that, in Mother Shipton's words, he "didn't say cards once" during the evening. Haply the time was beguiled by an accordion, produced somewhat ostentatiously by

190　　Tom Simson from his pack. Notwithstanding some difficulties attending the manipulation of this instrument, Piney Woods managed to pluck several reluctant melodies from its keys, to an accompaniment by the Innocent on a pair of bone castanets. But the crowning festivity of the evening was reached in a rude camp-meeting hymn, which the lovers, joining hands, sang with great earnestness and vociferation. I fear that a certain defiant tone and Covenanter's swing[9] to its chorus, rather than any devotional quality, caused it speedily to infect the others, who at last joined the refrain:

> "I'm proud to live in the service of the Lord,
> And I'm bound to die in His army."[10] ●

---

7. **sotto voce** (sŏt'ō vō'chē) *Italian*: in a low voice.

8. **prudently cached** (kăshd): wisely hidden away.

9. **Covenanter's swing:** the strong rhythms of songs sung by Scottish Presbyterians, who made covenants or agreements to oppose the Church of England.

10. **"I'm proud...army":** lines from the early American spiritual "Service of the Lord."

704　UNIT 4: REGIONALISM AND NATURALISM

---

200   The pines rocked, the storm eddied and whirled above the miserable group, and the flames of their altar leaped heavenward, as if in token of the vow.

    At midnight the storm abated, the rolling clouds parted, and the stars glittered keenly above the sleeping camp. Mr. Oakhurst, whose professional habits had enabled him to live on the smallest possible amount of sleep, in dividing the watch with Tom Simson, somehow managed to take upon himself the greater part of that duty. He excused himself to the Innocent, by saying that he had "often been a week without sleep." "Doing what?" asked Tom. "Poker!" replied Oakhurst, sententiously; "when a man gets a streak of luck, he don't get tired. The luck gives in first. Luck," continued the gambler, reflectively, "is a mighty queer thing. All

210 you know about it for certain is that it's bound to change. And it's finding out when it's going to change that makes you. We've had a streak of bad luck since we left Poker Flat—you come along, and slap you get into it, too. If you can hold your cards right along you're all right. For," added the gambler, with cheerful irrelevance,

    "I'm proud to live in the service of the Lord,
    And I'm bound to die in His army."

    The third day came, and the sun, looking through the white-curtained valley, saw the outcasts divide their slowly decreasing store of provisions for the morning meal. It was one of the peculiarities of that mountain climate that its rays diffused

220 a kindly warmth over the wintry landscape, as if in regretful commiseration of the past. But it revealed drift on drift of snow piled high around the hut—a hopeless, uncharted, trackless sea of white lying below the rocky shores to which the castaways still clung. Through the marvelously clear air the smoke of the pastoral village of Poker Flat rose miles away. Mother Shipton saw it, and from a remote pinnacle of her rocky fastness, hurled in that direction a final malediction.[11] It was her last **vituperative** attempt, and perhaps for that reason was invested with a certain degree of sublimity. It did her good, she privately informed the Duchess. "Just you go out there and cuss, and see." She then set herself to the task of amusing "the child," as she and the Duchess were pleased to call Piney. Piney was

230 no chicken, but it was a soothing and original theory of the pair thus to account for the fact that she didn't swear and wasn't improper.

    When night crept up again through the gorges, the reedy notes of the accordion rose and fell in fitful spasms and long-drawn gasps by the flickering campfire. But music failed to fill entirely the aching void left by insufficient food, and a new diversion was proposed by Piney—storytelling. Neither Mr. Oakhurst nor his female companions caring to relate their personal experiences, this plan would have failed, too, but for the Innocent. Some months before he had chanced upon a stray copy of Mr. Pope's ingenious translation of the *Iliad*.[12] He now proposed

---

11. **malediction:** curse.
12. **Mr. Pope's...Iliad:** British poet Alexander Pope published his translation of Homer's *Iliad* in 1720.

---

vituperative
(vĭ-tōō′pər-ə-tĭv) *adj.*
abusively critical

COMMON CORE RL 4, L 5a

Language Coach

Figurative Language
Read lines 232–233. Knowing that *spasms* are involuntary muscle movements and *gasps* are labored or difficult breaths, can you tell what Harte is saying through his description of Piney's accordion playing?

TIERED DISCUSSION PROMPTS

Direct students to lines 217–224. Use these prompts to help students understand the role that nature plays in the story:

Summarize What is the situation that threatens the outcasts? ***Possible answer:*** *Heavy snows have trapped them in the mountains, and Uncle Billy has run off with their mules. The outcasts have already consumed more than two days' worth of their provisions.*

Analyze Oakhurst, the Duchess, and Mother Shipton all seem to have both a rough side to their character and a gentler side. How does Harte reflect a similar contrast in his depiction of nature? ***Possible answer:*** *Harte describes how the sun's rays "diffused a kindly warmth over the wintry landscape, as if in regretful commiseration of the past." He also mentions "the marvelously clear air." However, at the same time, Harte also tells how the snow drifts have created "a hopeless, uncharted, trackless sea of white."*

VOCABULARY   COMMON CORE   L 4

OWN THE WORD

vituperative: Read aloud the definition of *vituperative* and ask students to explain why the author wrote "It was her last *vituperative* attempt . . ." ***Possible answer:*** *The sweetness of the budding friendships between these rough people seems destined for tragedy, and Mother Shipton appears moved to curse and swear no more after her parting shots toward the town that exiled them.*

FOR STRUGGLING READERS

Comprehension Support Call attention to the challenging style and language of lines 224–227. Elicit or provide the meaning of *pinnacle* ("peak"), *fastness* ("a secure place"), and *sublimity* ("grandness"). Point out the imagery of Mother Shipton hurling a curse "from a remote pinnacle of her rocky fastness." Then help students paraphrase the sentences.
Possible answer: *Mother Shipton saw the smoke rise from Poker Flat and directed a curse toward the village. Her words took on a certain grandness.*

FOR ENGLISH LANGUAGE LEARNERS

Language Coach   COMMON CORE RL 4, L 5a

Figurative Language *Answer:*
Harte says that Piney's accordion playing is so uneven that it sounds like someone gasping for breath. If the accordion playing resembles someone unable to breathe satisfactorily, what is Harte saying about its entertainment value?

to narrate the principal incidents of that poem—having thoroughly mastered the
240 argument and fairly forgotten the words—in the current vernacular of Sandy Bar.
And so for the rest of that night the Homeric demigods again walked the earth.
Trojan bully and wily Greek wrestled in the winds, and the great pines in the
canyon seemed to bow to the wrath of the son of Peleus.[13] Mr. Oakhurst listened
with quiet satisfaction. Most especially was he interested in the fate of "Ash-heels,"
as the Innocent persisted in denominating the "swift-footed Achilles." ❶

   So with small food and much of Homer and the accordion, a week passed over
the heads of the outcasts. The sun again forsook them, and again from leaden skies
the snowflakes were sifted over the land. Day by day closer around them drew
the snowy circle, until at last they looked from their prison over drifted walls of
250 dazzling white, that towered twenty feet above their heads. It became more and
more difficult to replenish their fires, even from the fallen trees beside them, now
half hidden in the drifts. And yet no one complained. The lovers turned from the
dreary prospect and looked into each other's eyes, and were happy. Mr. Oakhurst
settled himself coolly to the losing game before him. The Duchess, more cheerful
than she had been, assumed the care of Piney. Only Mother Shipton—once the
strongest of the party—seemed to sicken and fade. At midnight on the tenth day
she called Oakhurst to her side. "I'm going," she said, in a voice of **querulous**
weakness, "but don't say anything about it. Don't waken the kids. Take the bundle
from under my head and open it." Mr. Oakhurst did so. It contained Mother
260 Shipton's rations for the last week, untouched. "Give 'em to the child," she said,
pointing to the sleeping Piney. "You've starved yourself," said the gambler. "That's

---

13. **son of Peleus** (pē′lē-əs): Achilles (ə-kĭl′ēz), the Greek hero in the *Iliad*. Tom Simson mispronounces his name as "Ash-heels."

what they call it," said the woman, querulously, as she lay down again, and, turning her face to the wall, passed quietly away. **K**

The accordion and the bones were put aside that day, and Homer was forgotten. When the body of Mother Shipton had been committed to the snow, Mr. Oakhurst took the Innocent aside, and showed him a pair of snowshoes, which he had fashioned from the old pack saddle. "There's one chance in a hundred to save her yet," he said, pointing to Piney; "but it's there," he added, pointing toward Poker Flat. "If you can reach there in two days she's safe." "And
270 you?" asked Tom Simson. "I'll stay here," was the curt reply.

The lovers parted with a long embrace. "You are not going, too?" said the Duchess, as she saw Mr. Oakhurst apparently waiting to accompany him. "As far as the canyon," he replied. He turned suddenly, and kissed the Duchess, leaving her pallid face aflame, and her trembling limbs rigid with amazement.

Night came, but not Mr. Oakhurst. It brought the storm again and the whirling snow. Then the Duchess, feeding the fire, found that someone had quietly piled beside the hut enough fuel to last a few days longer. The tears rose to her eyes, but she hid them from Piney.

The women slept but little. In the morning, looking into each other's faces,
280 they read their fate. Neither spoke; but Piney, accepting the position of the stronger, drew near and placed her arm around the Duchess's waist. They kept this attitude for the rest of the day. That night the storm reached its greatest fury, and, rendering asunder[14] the protecting pines, invaded the very hut.

Toward morning they found themselves unable to feed the fire, which gradually died away. As the embers slowly blackened, the Duchess crept closer to Piney, and broke the silence of many hours: "Piney, can you pray?" "No, dear," said Piney,

---

14. **rending asunder:** forcefully ripping apart.

K CLARIFY MEANING
What happens to Mother Shipton? Explain whether or not you were surprised by this development, and why or why not.

COMMON CORE L4

Language Coach

Multiple-Meaning Words *Attitude* (line 282) is most often associated with a mental or emotional state. *Attitude* can also mean "posture" or "position." Why are Piney and the Duchess keeping this attitude?

K CLARIFY MEANING

Possible answer: Mother Shipton starves herself in order to save her food for Piney, so that the girl might survive. This is a surprising development, since Mother Shipton has been severe up until this point.

Extend the Discussion Why did Mother Shipton do what she did?

TIERED DISCUSSION PROMPTS

Direct students to lines 265–277. Use these prompts to help students understand the worsening circumstances:

Recall Why has the outcasts' situation now become dire? *Possible answer: They are out of food, nearly out of firewood, and still trapped by the snow with no sign of a break in the storm.*

Interpret What last-ditch efforts does Oakhurst make to save the outcasts? *Possible answer: He makes snowshoes for Tom, in hopes that Tom can reach Poker Flat and get help. Readers can also infer that it was Oakhurst who piled firewood beside the hut (lines 276–277).*

Synthesize How will the story end for Oakhurst, the Duchess, and Piney? Cite evidence for the prediction. *Accept all reasonable responses.*

FOR ENGLISH LANGUAGE LEARNERS

Language Coach COMMON CORE L4

Multiple-Meaning Words *Possible answer: The characters keep this physical attitude to show affection and to keep warm.* Read lines 281–282. Ask students to describe the mental attitude of Piney and the Duchess at this point in the story.

FOR ADVANCED LEARNERS/AP

Evaluate Direct students' attention to lines 271–274. Ask why Oakhurst kisses the Duchess at this point. Have students write a paragraph explaining whether this action is or is not consistent with Oakhurst's character, and why. After students finish reading the story, have them review their paragraphs and decide whether they maintain their original answers.

READING SKILL

COMMON CORE RL 1

L CLARIFY MEANING

Possible answer: *The Duchess and Piney froze to death, "locked in each other's arms" (line 299). The narrator seems to be making the point that black-and-white judgments of innocence and guilt are irrelevant in the face of death and perhaps were unfair to begin with.*

READING SKILL

COMMON CORE RL 1

M CLARIFY MEANING

Possible answer: *Perhaps Oakhurst, thinking as a gambler, coolly assessed the odds of his desperate situation, realized that he had no chance of surviving, and took his own life.*

SELECTION WRAP-UP

READ WITH A PURPOSE Now that students have finished reading the selection, have them review the characters' position as "outcasts." In what ways are the characters truly outcasts of society, and in what ways are they models of behavior? ***Possible answer:*** *The characters are deemed social outcasts because they are morally "impure." However, their behavior toward one another shows their character and compassion.*

⭐ CRITIQUE

- Have students rate the story on a scale of 1 to 5. Ask students whether they would have rated the story higher if it had ended differently. Why, or why not?

- After completing the After Reading questions on page 709, have students revisit their responses and tell whether they have changed their opinions.

INDEPENDENT READING

For students interested in reading other works by Harte, suggest *Selected Stories of Bret Harte,* which contains more stories about the California Gold Rush.

---

simply. The Duchess, without knowing exactly why, felt relieved, and, putting her head upon Piney's shoulder, spoke no more. And so reclining, the younger and purer pillowing the head of her soiled sister upon her virgin breast, they fell asleep.

290   The wind lulled as if it feared to waken them. Feathery drifts of snow, shaken from the long pine boughs, flew like white-winged birds, and settled about them as they slept. The moon through the rifted clouds looked down upon what had been the camp. But all human stain, all trace of earthly travail, was hidden beneath the spotless mantle mercifully flung from above.

They slept all that day and the next, nor did they waken when voices and footsteps broke the silence of the camp. And when pitying fingers brushed the snow from their wan faces, you could scarcely have told from the equal peace that dwelt upon them, which was she that had sinned. Even the law of Poker Flat recognized this, and turned away, leaving them still locked in each other's arms. **L**

300   But at the head of the gulch, on one of the largest pine trees, they found the deuce of clubs[15] pinned to the bark with a bowie-knife. It bore the following, written in pencil, in a firm hand:

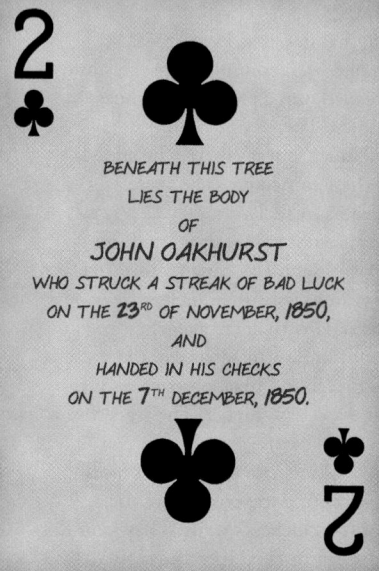

BENEATH THIS TREE
LIES THE BODY
OF
JOHN OAKHURST
WHO STRUCK A STREAK OF BAD LUCK
ON THE 23RD OF NOVEMBER, 1850,
AND
HANDED IN HIS CHECKS
ON THE 7TH DECEMBER, 1850.

And pulseless and cold, with a Derringer[16] by his side and a bullet in his heart, though still calm as in life, beneath the snow lay he who was at once the strongest and yet the weakest of the outcasts of Poker Flat. ✍ **M**

_____

15. **deuce of clubs:** the lowest card in a deck of playing cards—thus a loser's card.

16. **Derringer:** a short-barreled pistol invented by American gunsmith Henry Derringer.

L CLARIFY MEANING
Summarize what has happened to the Duchess and Piney. What point does the narrator seem to be making in lines 279–299?

4 Targeted Passage

M CLARIFY MEANING
Why has Oakhurst committed this final act?

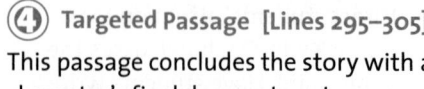

DIFFERENTIATED INSTRUCTION

FOR STRUGGLING READERS

4 Targeted Passage [Lines 295–305]

This passage concludes the story with a character's final desperate act.

- What happens to the Duchess and Piney Woods at the end of the story? (lines 295–298)

- What happens to Oakhurst? (lines 303–305)

FOR ENGLISH LANGUAGE LEARNERS

Vocabulary Support Discuss the meaning of these opposites:

- *purer, virgin/soiled* (line 289): Innocent Piney and the "soiled" Duchess die together.

- *human stain/spotless mantle* (lines 293–294): The "human stain" of the outcasts is covered by the "spotless mantle" of snow.

- *strongest/weakest* (lines 304–305): Oakhurst showed strength as a leader but weakness in committing suicide.

Comprehension

1. **Recall** Why do Mr. Oakhurst and the others leave Poker Flat?

2. **Recall** Who joins the traveling group at their camp?

3. **Summarize** What happens to the travelers at the camp?

Text Analysis

● 4. **Clarify Meaning** Review the following quotations within the context of the story and paraphrase what they mean:

   • "There was a Sabbath lull in the air, which, in a settlement unused to Sabbath influences, looked ominous." (lines 5–6)

   • "Mr. Oakhurst seldom troubled himself with sentiment, still less with propriety; but he had a vague idea that the situation was not fortunate." (lines 108–109)

● 5. **Examine the Main Character** Bret Harte was known for portraying the character type of an outcast with a heart of gold. How does John Oakhurst fit this formula of the character with contradictory traits? Use a chart to explore this question.

Outcast Traits	Virtuous Traits

6. **Interpret Author's Perspective** Personal experience and historical context influence the characters and conflicts that a writer chooses to depict. Based on events in this story and their outcome, how would you describe Harte's opinion of the following?

   • John Oakhurst   • society in the Old West   • human nature

● 7. **Evaluate Use of Regionalism** The goal of regionalists was to capture life at a particular time in history. In your opinion, how well did Harte convey the region, the people, and the times in "The Outcasts of Poker Flat"? Cite evidence to support your view.

Text Criticism

8. **Critical Interpretations** Mark Twain said that it was Bret Harte who "trimmed and schooled me patiently until he changed me from an awkward utterer of coarse grotesqueness to a writer of paragraphs and chapters." Harte also influenced Ambrose Bierce and Rudyard Kipling. Why do you think Harte might have had a strong impact on so many writers?

> *What does it mean to be an* **OUTCAST?**
> Besides being literally "cast out" of Poker Flat, in what way are Oakhurst, the Duchess, Mother Shipton, and Uncle Billy exiles from society? What moral statement does the author make about their fellow townspeople?

8. *Harte created interesting and complex characters who have both positive and negative traits—just as real people do.*

> *What does it mean to be an* OUTCAST? Ask students to think about legal statutes that the characters may have violated. Then ask them to consider the morality of the townspeople who cast out the characters. Suggest that Harte indicates the townspeople are blind to their own hypocrisy.

Practice and Apply

For preliminary support of post-reading questions, use these copy masters:

R RESOURCE MANAGER—Copy Masters
   Reading Check p. 84
   Regionalism p. 77
   Question Support p. 85

Additional selection questions are provided for teachers on page 71.

ANSWERS   COMMON CORE RL 1, RL 2, RL 3

1. *Oakhurst and the others are forced to leave when the town deems them to be undesirable influences.*

2. *Two innocent young people—Tom Simson and his fiancée, Piney Woods—join the group at the camp.*

3. *The travelers get snowed in and eventually perish.*

Possible answers:

4. ■ **COMMON CORE FOCUS Clarify Meaning** *"There was . . . ": The silence suggested that something significant or worrisome was taking place; "Mr. Oakhurst . . . ": Although Oakhurst is generally unconcerned with social conventions, he has a bad feeling about the Innocents joining their group.*

5. ● **COMMON CORE FOCUS Examine the Main Character** *Outcast Traits: gambler, loner, no emotional attachments; Virtuous Traits: kind, caring*

6. *Oakhurst: heroic, yet vulnerable, and not as strong as everyone thinks; society: perhaps too narrowly restrictive in its moral code; human nature: surprisingly good, for the most part, though positive traits may be hidden beneath rough exteriors.*

7. ● **COMMON CORE FOCUS Evaluate Use of Regionalism** *Harte effectively captures the different types of people living in the rough settlement, contending with the moral code of the times and the merciless power of nature.*

COMMON CORE

RL 1 Cite evidence to support analysis of what the text says explicitly. **RL 2** Determine two or more themes or central ideas of a text. **RL 3** Analyze the impact of the author's choices regarding how to develop and relate elements of a story.

ANSWERS
Vocabulary in Context
▲ VOCABULARY PRACTICE

1. *calm*	6. *shunned*
2. *a mushy love story*	7. *anger*
3. *find fault*	8. *a comedian*
4. *in exile*	9. *predict future events*
5. *a party host*	10. *scold them*

 **RESOURCE MANAGER—Copy Master**
Vocabulary Practice p. 82

ACADEMIC VOCABULARY IN WRITING

It becomes apparent that Oakhurst is admirable when his leadership skills and his kindness become evident. The characters have obvious flaws, but their humanity and strength are exposed as they face difficulties.

VOCABULARY STRATEGY:
THE LATIN ROOT *equ*

COMMON CORE **L 4b, L 6**

- Point out that students will recognize the prefix form of the root from such words as *equal, equator, equation,* and *equinox.*

- Explain how figuring out the part of speech from the sentence context can help students narrow their choices. You may want to point out that three of the words are nouns, two are adjectives, and one is a verb.

Answers:

1. *equivocate*

2. *equidistant*

3. *equilibrium*

4. *equivalency*

 RESOURCE MANAGER—Copy Master
Vocabulary Strategy p. 83

Interactive Vocabulary  THINK central

Keywords direct students to a **WordSharp** tutorial on **thinkcentral.com** or to other types of vocabulary practice and review.

Vocabulary in Context

▲ VOCABULARY PRACTICE

Show you understand the vocabulary words by answering these questions.

1. If I handled a situation with **equanimity,** would I be upset about it or calm?
2. Which could be considered **maudlin,** a stern lecture or a mushy love story?
3. Would a **querulous** person be more likely to enjoy a party or find fault with it?
4. If I am **expatriated,** am I living in exile or returning to my own country?
5. Is a party host or a prosecuting lawyer more likely to be **amicable?**
6. Is a **pariah** shunned or welcomed into gatherings?
7. If a person utters an **anathema,** is he or she expressing anger or compassion?
8. Who is more likely to be **jocular,** a runner or a comedian?
9. Does someone with **prescience** predict future events or excel in chemistry?
10. Would a **vituperative** tutor encourage her students or scold them?

WORD LIST

amicable
anathema
equanimity
expatriated
jocular
maudlin
pariah
prescience
querulous
vituperative

ACADEMIC VOCABULARY IN WRITING

> • apparent • confine • expose • focus • perceive

Which character, in your opinion, proves to be the most admirable? After you select a character, write a paragraph describing when it becomes **apparent** that the character is admirable. **Focus** your description on some specific action of the character, and use at least one Academic Vocabulary word in your response.

COMMON CORE

L 4b Identify and correctly use patterns of word changes that indicate different meanings or parts of speech. **L 6** Acquire and use accurately general academic words and phrases.

VOCABULARY STRATEGY: THE LATIN ROOT *equ*

The origin of the root *equ,* which means "even," "just," or "equal," is the Latin language. The vocabulary word *equanimity* contains this root. Occasionally spelled *iqu,* this root is found in a number of English words. In its prefix form *equi,* it is sometimes combined with existing words to form new words, as in *equiprobable.* To understand words with *equ,* use context clues and your knowledge of root and affix meanings.

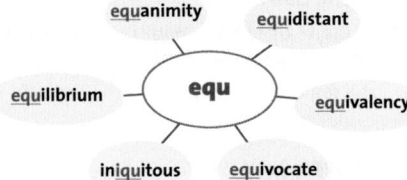

PRACTICE Apply what you know about *equ, equi,* and other word parts to help you understand the words in the web. Then choose the word that best completes each sentence. If necessary, consult a dictionary.

1. If you _____, it may be said that you are talking out of both sides of your mouth.
2. What town is _____ between Chicago and Milwaukee?
3. The accident affected her _____, and she often felt dizzy.
4. Passing a high school _____ test can take the place of actually graduating.

Interactive Vocabulary THINK central

Go to **thinkcentral.com.**
KEYWORD: HML11-710

DIFFERENTIATED INSTRUCTION

FOR ENGLISH LANGUAGE LEARNERS

Task Support: Vocabulary Strategy Discuss words in home languages with the Latin root *equ/iqu* or the Latin prefix *equi-.* There are other forms of some of the words in the organizer on page 686 that may occur in home languages as well. For example, *equi,* meaning "wrong" or "incorrect," appears in Spanish *equívoco.*

FOR ADVANCED LEARNERS/AP

Academic Vocabulary in Writing Ask students to use as many vocabulary words as they can in a brief dialogue between two of the characters from the story.

Language

COMMON CORE

L 3 Apply knowledge of language to make effective choices for style. W 3b, e Use narrative techniques, such as description; provide a conclusion that follows from and reflects on what is observed.

◆ **GRAMMAR AND STYLE: Add Descriptive Details**

Review the **Grammar and Style** note on page 703. Harte uses **personification**—the attribution of human qualities to objects or ideas—to enliven his descriptions of inanimate objects. Here is an example from the story:

> The third day came, and the sun, *looking through the white-curtained valley, saw* the outcasts divide their slowly decreasing store of provisions for the morning meal. (lines 217–219)

Harte's use of the highlighted **participial phrase** and **verb** creates an ethereal image of the sun "watching" the outcasts.

PRACTICE Rewrite each of the following sentences to include personification.

> **EXAMPLE**
>
> We could see the town at the top of the mountain but couldn't see most of its buildings.
>
> *The town seemed to turn its back on us, hiding its buildings from our view down in the valley.*

1. The mountain was solid rock, very steep, and very tall.

2. Lights were shining in some of the windows.

3. Snow began to fall, making it harder to see the town way above us.

READING-WRITING CONNECTION

Expand your understanding of "The Outcasts of Poker Flat" by responding to this prompt. Then, use the **revising tips** to improve your description.

WRITING PROMPT	REVISING TIPS
WRITE A DESCRIPTION Think of a real or fictional society that you might like to write about in a short story. Then, write a three- or four-paragraph description of that society from the perspective of a person who has been sent into exile and must live just on the outskirts of the city or town. Your character should conclude by reflecting on the good and bad points about the place.	• Add precise words and sensory details to make your description vivid and realistic. • Write from a first-person point of view, using the personal pronoun I. • Include a description of setting, the time and place in which your society exists.

Interactive Revision **THINK**central

Go to **thinkcentral.com**.
KEYWORD: HML11-711

Language

◆ **GRAMMAR AND STYLE**

Point out that personification may be based in a metaphor or simile. Help students compare these examples: *The clock radio told me to wake up* (metaphor); *The cat stood like an angry parent ready to scold us for forgetting to feed her* (simile).

Possible answers:

1. *The mountain stood before us like a muscular athlete challenging his opponents.*

2. *Lights greeted us happily from the windows.*

3. *The falling snow covered our eyes with wintry fingers.*

R RESOURCE MANAGER—Copy Master
Personification p. 86

READING-WRITING CONNECTION

Suggest that students use a Cluster Diagram to help them brainstorm their real or fictional society's institutions, buildings, and holidays. Encourage students to reflect on the interactions between people of various social and economic groups and people of different ages and genders.

BEST PRACTICES TOOLKIT—Transparency
Cluster Diagram p. B18

Writing Online  **THINK**central

The following tools are available online at **thinkcentral.com** and on **WriteSmart** CD-ROM:

• Interactive Graphic Organizers
• Interactive Student Models
• Interactive Revision Lessons

For additional grammar instruction, see **GrammarNotes** on **thinkcentral.com**.

Assess and Reteach

Assess

DIAGNOSTIC AND SELECTION TESTS
Selection Test A, B/C pp. 189–190, 191–192

Interactive Selection Test on thinkcentral.com

Reteach

Level Up Online Tutorials on thinkcentral.com

FOR STRUGGLING WRITERS

Writing Support

• Help students brainstorm institutions, buildings, holidays, and other aspects of their society.

• Help students project themselves into their society and imagine how their fellow citizens from various socioeconomic backgrounds interact with one another.

• Offer students suggestions for beginning their description. For example, they might start with a broad overview and then focus on specific places or people. Or, they might first discuss people, then places, then customs and beliefs.

• Remind students to include specific details—especially sensory details that make their descriptions come alive.

ABOUT THE AUTHOR

Born in 1942 in Anoka, a town about 20 miles northwest of Minneapolis, Keillor began demonstrating his skills while involved with his college literary magazine and radio station. Those experiences eventually led to *A Prairie Home Companion,* the radio program that blends storytelling, music, and comedy. *Lake Wobegon Days,* published in 1985, is one of numerous books by Keillor.

TIERED DISCUSSION PROMPTS

In lines 1–7, these prompts to help students explore Keillor's description of Lake Wobegon:

Connect Have you ever visited a place like Lake Wobegon? If so, what was it like? *Accept all thoughtful responses.*

Analyze In this opening paragraph, how does Keillor establish the location and spirit of Lake Wobegon? ***Possible answer:*** *Keillor describes Lake Wobegon as an out-of-the-way place (lines 1–2) with a folksy charm (as seen in events such as Toast 'n Jelly Days) and perhaps a greater affection for its own people than for outsiders (lines 1–2). Keillor's conversational style makes Lake Wobegon seem like a place that readers would want to visit.*

---

from Lake Wobegon Days

Garrison Keillor

BACKGROUND Garrison Keillor follows in the tradition of such great regional storytellers as Mark Twain and Will Rogers. Like his predecessors, Keillor draws on childhood experiences to paint whimsical pictures of the characters and local color of small-town life. *Lake Wobegon Days* is a novel set in Wobegon, Minnesota, a fictionalized version of his hometown. Keillor, a Minnesota native, originally wrote many of the Wobegon stories for a weekly variety show on public radio called *A Prairie Home Companion.* The show first aired in 1974 and, with one six-year hiatus, continued into the 21st century. Keillor's stories of life in rural Minnesota share an especially close kinship with Twain's stories of life along the Mississippi River in Missouri.

People who visit Lake Wobegon come to see somebody, otherwise they missed the turn on the highway and are lost. *Ausländers,* the Germans call them. They don't come for Toast 'n Jelly Days, or the Germans' quadrennial Gesuffa Days, or Krazy Daze, or the Feast Day of St. Francis, or the three-day Mist County Fair with its exciting Death Leap from the top of the grandstand to the arms of the haystack for only ten cents. What's special about here isn't special enough to draw a major crowd, though Flag Day—you could drive a long way on June 14 to find another like it.

Flag Day, as we know it, was the idea of Herman Hochstetter, Rollie's dad, who ran the dry goods store and ran Armistice Day, the Fourth of July, and Flag Day. For the
10 Fourth, he organized a double-loop parade around the block which allowed people to take turns marching and watching. On Armistice Day, everyone stepped outside at 11 A.M and stood in silence for two minutes as Our Lady's bell tolled eleven times.

BACKGROUND
The Lake Wobegon Effect Tell students that according to Garrison Keillor, all of the children of Lake Wobegon are above average. So popular has that description become that it has inspired "the Lake Wobegon effect," a term referring to the overestimation of one's own or someone else's abilities. (The term appears often in educational and business circles.) As students read this selection, invite them to comment about how "the Lake Wobegon effect" might apply to Herman Hochstetter's view of himself and his fellow townspeople in creating the Living Flag.

FOR ENGLISH LANGUAGE LEARNERS
Culture: Clarify Explain the meaning of these observances:

- *Armistice Day* (line 9), the former name for Veterans Day (November 11), which honors people who have served in the armed forces of the United States and which is celebrated on the anniversary of the signing of the document that ended World War I

- *Flag Day* (line 9), a day that commemorates the adoption (June 14, 1777) of the United States flag

FOR ADVANCED LEARNERS/AP
Research a Holiday Have a group of students do research to learn about the history and significance of Flag Day and to share their findings with the class in a format of their choice. Ask the group to include the origins of the holiday and examples of ways in which it is celebrated in the United States. Follow up with a brief discussion about why the holiday might be important to the people of Lake Wobegon.

In lines 48–75, use these prompts to help students understand how Keillor creates an entertaining narrative:

Recall What problem does Herman encounter in creating the Living Flag? *Possible answer: The people forming the flag want to break out of their positions to see what the flag looks like from overhead.*

Analyze How does Keillor integrate humor into his account of Herman Hochstetter's efforts? Be specific. *Possible answer: Keillor creates lively visual images that are amusing to picture. For example, he creates the image of the flag participants racing up to the roof in order see what their Living Flag looks like (lines 55–56). When too many participants leave, Keillor describes how the flag looked as though it had been "shot through by cannon fire" (lines 73–74). Finally, he creates the image of participants looking up into the mirror on the roof—which, of course, only causes the flag to disappear (lines 77–79).*

TEXT ANALYSIS

COMMON CORE RL 6

Ⓐ CHARACTER TYPES

Remind students that because of many factors, today regionalism is not as noticeable as it was even fifty years ago. Still, regional character types, and stereotypes, exist. Read aloud lines 40–49. Ask students to notice that although Herman is frustrated and sincere in his directions, his instructions can be seen as quite humorous.

Possible answer: Keillor uses irony in having the townspeople question the nature of what Herman is doing; i.e., a director is supposed to tell people what to do. Another irony is that of people wanting to be part of the presentation, yet not being able to view and appreciate the presentation's effect.

Extend the Discussion How does the crowd's pride get in the way of what they and Herman are trying to accomplish?

Flag Day was his favorite. For a modest price, he would install a bracket on your house to hold a pole to hang your flag on, or he would drill a hole in the sidewalk in the front of your store with his drill gun powered by a .22 shell. *Bam!* And in went the flag. On patriotic days, flags flew all over; there were flags on the tall poles, flags on the short, flags in the brackets on the pillars and the porches, and if you were flagless you could expect to hear from Herman. His hairy arm around
20 your shoulder, his poochlike face close to yours, he would say how proud he was that so many people were proud of their country, leaving you to see the obvious, that you were a gap in the ranks.

In June 1944, the day after D-Day, a salesman from Fisher Hat called on Herman and offered a good deal on red and blue baseball caps. "Do you have white also?" Herman asked. The salesman thought that white caps could be had for the same wonderful price. Herman ordered two hundred red, two hundred white, and one hundred blue. By the end of the year, he still had four hundred and eighty-six caps. The inspiration of the Living Flag was born from that overstock.

On June 14, 1945, a month after V-E Day, a good crowd assembled in front of the Central Building in response to Herman's ad in the paper:

30   Honor "AMERICA" June 14 AT 4 P.M. Be proud
        of "Our Land & People". Be part of the "LIVING
        FLAG". Don't let it be said that Lake Wobegon was
        "Too Busy". Be on time. 4 P.M. "Sharp".

His wife Louise handed out the caps, and Herman stood on a stepladder and told people where to stand. He lined up the reds and whites into stripes, then got the blues into their square. Mr. Hanson climbed up on the roof of the Central Building and took a photograph, they sang the national anthem, and then the Living Flag dispersed. The photograph appeared in the paper the next week. Herman kept the caps.
40   In the flush of victory, people were happy to do as told and stand in place, but in 1946 and 1947, dissension cropped up in the ranks: people complained about the heat and about Herman—what gave *him* the idea he could order *them* around? "People! Please! I need your attention! You blue people, keep your hats on! Please! Stripe No. 4, you're sagging! You reds, you're up here! We got too many white people, we need more red ones! Let's do this without talking, people! I can't get you straight if you keep moving around! Some of you are not paying attention! Everybody shut up! Please!"

One cause of resentment was the fact that none of them got to see the Flag they were in; the picture in the paper was black and white. Only Herman and Mr. Hanson
50 got to see the real Flag, and some boys too short to be needed down below. People wanted a chance to go up to the roof and witness the spectacle for themselves. Ⓐ

"How can you go up there if you're supposed to be down here?" Herman said. "You go up there to look, you got nothing to look at. Isn't it enough that you're doing your part?"

On Flag Day, 1949, just as Herman said, "That's it! Hold it now!" one of the reds made a break for it—dashed up four flights of stairs to the roof and leaned over and had a long look. Even with the hole he left behind, it was a magnificent sight. The

COMMON CORE RL 6

Ⓐ **CHARACTER TYPES**
As an offshoot of Realism, **Regionalism** sought to accurately portray the speech, manners, and habits of people from a particular geographic region. Like Mark Twain a century before him, Keillor favors common characters whose sincerity and humility are often in stark contrast to the absurdity of their words and actions. Twain was exceptionally skilled at creating humor through irony. Reread lines 40–51, and look for ways in which Keillor uses irony to reveal the humor of his characters' words and actions.

DIFFERENTIATED INSTRUCTION

FOR ENGLISH LANGUAGE LEARNERS

Culture: Clarify Explain the meaning of these terms:

- *D-Day* (line 22), June 6, 1944, the day on which Allied forces began invading France during World War II

- *V-E Day* (line 28), "Victory in Europe" Day: May 8, 1945, the day on which the surrender of Germany to the Allies was declared during World War II

FOR ADVANCED LEARNERS/AP

Rewrite a Scene Keillor's simple, breezy style makes his narrative come to life. Have students describe the same scene that Keillor does in lines 34–74, but in their own style. Encourage students to draw upon details from the text but also to use their imagination to expand and develop those details as needed. Have volunteers share their work with the class; invite insights and constructive criticism.

Living Flag filled the street below. A perfect Flag! The reds so brilliant! He couldn't
take his eyes off it. "Get down here! We need a picture!" Herman yelled up to him.
60 "How does it look?" people yelled up to him. "Unbelievable! I can't describe it!"
he said.

So then everyone had to have a look. "No!" Herman said, but they took a vote and
it was unanimous. One by one, members of the Living Flag went up to the roof and
admired it. It *was* marvelous! It brought tears to the eyes, it made one reflect on this
great country and on Lake Wobegon's place in it. One wanted to stand up there all
afternoon and just drink it in. So, as the first hour passed, and only forty of the five
hundred had been to the top, the others got more and more restless. "Hurry up! Quit
dawdling! *You've* seen it! Get down here and give someone else a chance!" Herman
sent people up in groups of four, and then ten, but after two hours, the Living Flag
70 became the Sitting Flag and then began to erode, as the members who had had a look
thought about heading home to supper, which infuriated the ones who hadn't. "Ten
more minutes!" Herman cried, but ten minutes became twenty and thirty, and people
snuck off and the Flag that remained for the last viewer was a Flag shot through by
cannon fire.

In 1950, the Sons of Knute took over Flag Day. Herman gave them the boxes of
caps. Since then, the Knutes have achieved several good Flags, though most years
the attendance was poor. You need at least four hundred to make a good one. Some
years the Knutes made a "no-look" rule, other years they held a lottery. One year they
experimented with a large mirror held by two men over the edge of the roof, but
80 when people leaned back and looked up, the Flag disappeared, of course. ❧

Text Analysis

1. **Analyze Local Color** One of the primary characteristics of regional writing
   is **local color,** or writing that portrays the customs, character types,
   mannerisms, and speech of a region. What elements of local color do you
   find in this excerpt? Citing evidence from the text, characterize the residents
   of small-town Minnesota as portrayed by Keillor.

2. **Compare Texts** As Twain does in the excerpt from his *Autobiography*
   and in "The Notorious Jumping Frog of Calaveras County," Keillor depicts
   a community event in a small town. Which author uses dialect or local
   conventions of language usage more effectively to portray setting?
   Explain, citing evidence from the texts.

THEMES ACROSS TIME **715**

Focus and Motivate

ABOUT THE AUTHOR

After students have read about Willa Cather, ask them to summarize key points of her biography. Point out that students will see Cather's application of her early experiences on the Nebraska prairie in the characters and settings of "A Wagner Matinee."

NOTABLE QUOTE

"The only reason I write is because it interests me more than any other activity I've ever found." **— Willa Cather**

Ask students how the quotation expresses the path that Willa Cather chose for her life. Discuss how living the kind of life that made a writing career possible underscores Cather's devotion to that path.

Regionalism and Local Color

A Wagner Matinee

Short Story by Willa Cather

Meet the Author

Willa Cather 1873–1947

Willa Cather believed that "the most basic material a writer works with is acquired before the age of 15." Indeed, it was the American West of Cather's early years that inspired the majority of her literary successes.

The Power of Place At age nine, Virginia-born Willa Cather moved to Nebraska with her family. The prairie challenged Cather—and almost all other settlers—with its "erasure of personality" and made her feel that she "would go under." But after a difficult transition, Cather grew to love the harsh prairie and to admire the immigrants—especially women—who struggled daily against an unforgiving climate. Though they lived by hard physical labor, many of these immigrants were educated people. They introduced Cather to French and German literature, also teaching her Latin and Greek. Nebraska and Cather's childhood neighbors—whose stories "went round and round in [her] head"— dramatically influenced her writing.

Seeing the World After college, where she did some writing, Cather went back east and worked as a journalist, teacher, and magazine editor. During this time, she met her best friend, Isabelle McClung, who sparked in her a lifelong interest in music, which can be seen in "A Wagner Matinee." She also formed lifelong relationships with her companion Edith Lewis and writer Sarah Orne Jewett. Cather also saw something of the world on several trips to France and then to the American Southwest.

Developing a Voice Around 1906, Cather moved to New York City and began a full-time writing career. Though she never lived in Nebraska again, the prairie was never far from her work. Many of her 12 novels and 58 stories had prairie settings or immigrant characters, showing Cather's respect for the grit needed to endure everyday life. Some of these characters were directly drawn from real people Cather had known, such as childhood friend Annie (Anna) who formed the basis of the main character in her novel *My Ántonia*.

Choices Willa Cather chose an artist's life rather than the everyday family life she so closely observed in her Nebraska neighbors. She once said to a friend that "nothing mattered to her but writing books, and living the kind of life that makes it possible to write them." Willa Cather lived that life until her death in 1947.

DID YOU KNOW?

Willa Cather . . .

- had such a sharp memory for mannerisms and turns of speech that she never took notes.
- wrote six novels about her home town of Red Cloud, Nebraska, while living in New York's Greenwich Village.
- received the Pulitzer Prize in 1923.

Author Online

THINK central

Go to **thinkcentral.com**. KEYWORD: HML11-716

716

Selection Resources

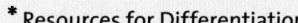

● TEXT ANALYSIS: SETTING

In Willa Cather's fiction, the development of the plot and characters is heavily influenced by the **setting,** or the time and place in which the story occurs. In "A Wagner Matinee," the narrator's aunt has moved from Boston to the Nebraska frontier; these places determine the kind of person she becomes. Setting can also serve as a **symbol.** As you read, note the details of each location and what they seem to represent.

● READING SKILL: DRAW CONCLUSIONS ABOUT CHARACTER

Understanding a character in a story is like getting to know a real person. You **draw conclusions,** or make reasonable judgments, about the person by combining the impressions you have already formed with new facts you discover. To become better acquainted with Aunt Georgiana, the main character in "A Wagner Matinee," look closely at the details as you read the story. Create a chart like the one shown, using it to record details and **make inferences** about Aunt Georgiana. At the end of the story, you will use these specific inferences to draw larger conclusions about her character.

Observations About...	What They Reveal
physical appearance: • •	
major decision: • •	
actions and reactions: • •	

▲ VOCABULARY IN CONTEXT

Cather uses the listed words to develop setting and character. Choose a word from the list to complete each phrase.

WORD LIST	callow	overture	tentatively
	excruciatingly	somnambulant	veritable
	myriad	sordid	

1. _____ employees with more bravado than experience
2. _____ tasks to complete—almost too many to count
3. living in _____, disgusting conditions
4. agreed _____ to take on the additional work

 Complete the activities in your **Reader/Writer Notebook.**

Does it matter where we LIVE?

Imagine life on an island with only a few dozen other people. How would it shape your social life? your work habits? your relationship to nature? Now think about life in a big city. How would these things be different? The places we live really shape our personality and values.

DISCUSS As a class, choose two very different places and discuss the lifestyles of the people who live there. Then consider how life in each place would shape the personalities of its inhabitants.

Teach

Does it matter where we LIVE?

As students address the *DISCUSS* activity, urge them to draw upon memories of places where they have actually lived rather than possibilities that they imagine or have seen portrayed on TV and in films.

● *Model the Skill:* SETTING

Write this passage on the board:

> Jason wiped the sweat from his sun-burned brow, surveyed the half-plowed field, and groaned. As a boy, he'd planned to be living in a big city by June 14, 1891, his 18th birthday. But here he was, 22 years old and still breaking his back in tiny, dusty Greenville. He'd give anything to be gone, but he couldn't do that to his folks. Without his help, they'd never survive.

Point out the details that show physical setting and time period. *a family farm in "tiny, dusty Greenville" in 1895 or 1896*

GUIDED PRACTICE Ask students to share a passage in another work that effectively conveys the setting.

■ *Model the Skill:* DRAW CONCLUSIONS ABOUT CHARACTER

Have students reread the passage on the board. Ask them to draw conclusion about Jason.

GUIDED PRACTICE Ask students to describe the structure of other works they have read, such as articles, essays, and stories.

Ⓡ **RESOURCE MANAGER—Copy Master** Draw Conclusions About Character p. 99

▲ VOCABULARY IN CONTEXT

DIAGNOSE WORD KNOWLEDGE Have students complete Vocabulary in Context. Check their choices against the following:

callow (kăl′ō) *adj.* lacking adult experience
excruciatingly (ĭk-skrōō′shē-ā′tĭng-lē) *adv.* in a way that causes great pain or distress
myriad (mĭr′ē-əd) *adj.* exceedingly numerous
overture (ō′vər-chōŏr′) *n.* the orchestral introduction to a musical dramatic work

somnambulant (sŏm-năm′byə-lənt′) *adj.* sleepwalking
sordid (sôr′dĭd) *adj.* dirty; morally degraded
tentatively (tĕn′tə-tĭv-lē) *adv.* in a hesitant or uncertain manner
veritable (vĕr′ĭ-tə-bəl) *adj.* true; not imaginary

Ⓡ **RESOURCE MANAGER—Copy Master** Vocabulary Study p. 101

SUMMARY

A visit from Aunt Georgiana causes Clark, the narrator of this story, to recall her caring for him when he was a boy on the Nebraska prairie. Aunt Georgiana had been a music teacher in Boston before eloping to Nebraska, where she and her husband have been homesteading for thirty years under harsh conditions. Clark, now living in Boston, takes his aunt to a concert. Though she has seemed distracted and aloof, she is profoundly affected by Wagner's music: When the concert ends, she cries out that she does not want to leave.

READ WITH A PURPOSE

Help students set a purpose for reading. Tell them to read to discover what Aunt Georgiana misses most about life in the city.

TEXT ANALYSIS

COMMON CORE
RL 3

A *Model the Skill:* SETTING

Call attention to the description details in lines 3–4. Help students recognize that the letter comes from a place where transporting mail seems not to be a high priority. Then ask students what they infer from the narrator's reaction. Is he surprised to see letters in such condition?

Possible answer: *The description shows that the letter probably comes from a place where such conveniences as post offices are not easily accessible. The narrator's observations show that he lives in a place where people are unaccustomed to seeing letters in such condition.*

THEME

After students have completed this selection, ask them to discuss films, plays, or novels that relate to the theme of *A Wagner Matinee.*

A Wagner Matinee

Willa Cather

Analyze Visuals ▶
Look at the painting on page 719. What might souvenirs like these signify to a settler who left the city for life on the prairie? Explain.

THEME
When you grow old, will you be satisfied with the life you've lived? That's a question people have been asking for ages. Several modern writers and filmmakers have created characters who have regrets about their lives. Can you think of any 21st-century works that share this focus?

BACKGROUND "A Wagner Matinee" takes place in Nebraska and Boston around 1900. At the time, Bostonians could attend concerts of works by European composers such as Richard Wagner (väg'nər). Americans who moved west, such as Willa Cather's family and Aunt Georgiana in this story, left such worldly pleasures behind. Instead, the settlers endured long hours of strenuous labor, and natural disasters such as drought, flood, and prairie fires.

I received one morning a letter, written in pale ink on glassy, blue-lined note-paper, and bearing the postmark of a little Nebraska village. This communication, worn and rubbed, looking as though it had been carried for some days in a coat pocket that was none too clean, was from my Uncle Howard and informed me that his wife had been left a small legacy by a bachelor relative who had recently died, and that it would be necessary for her to go to Boston to attend to the settling of the estate. He requested me to meet her at the station and render her whatever services might be necessary. On examining the date indicated as that of her arrival, I found it no later than tomorrow. He had characteristically delayed
10 writing until, had I been away from home for a day, I must have missed the good woman altogether. **A**

The name of my Aunt Georgiana called up not alone her own figure, at once pathetic and grotesque, but opened before my feet a gulf of recollection so wide and deep, that, as the letter dropped from my hand, I felt suddenly a stranger to all the present conditions of my existence, wholly ill at ease and out of place amid the familiar surroundings of my study. I became, in short, the gangling farmer-boy

① Targeted Passage

A SETTING
What does the **description** of the letter tell you about the place the letter was sent from? What does the description suggest about the place the letter was sent to? Give details to support your answer.

718   UNIT 4: REGIONALISM AND NATURALISM

Old Souvenirs (about 1881–1901), John F. Peto. Bequest of Oliver Burr Jennings, 1968 (68.205.3). Metropolitan Museum of Art, New York.

DIFFERENTIATED INSTRUCTION

FOR ENGLISH LANGUAGE LEARNERS

Vocabulary Support Use Word Questioning to teach these words: *section* (line 45), *flexible* (line 62), *text-book* (line 70), *passive* (line 111), *theme* (line 151), *relax* (line 231).

🧰 **BEST PRACTICES TOOLKIT—Transparency**
Word Questioning p. E9

FOR STRUGGLING READERS

In combination with the *Audio Anthology CD*, use one or more Targeted Passages (pp. 718, 721, 723, 726) to ensure that students focus on key story events and concepts. Targeted Passages are also good for English language learners.

① Targeted Passage [Lines 1–11]

This passage establishes the first-person narrator and the reason for his aunt's journey to Boston.

Analyze Visuals

Possible answer: *Souvenirs such as the news-paper would remind the prairie settler what life in the city had been like; other souvenirs, such as the photograph, would help the settler remember people and places that he or she had left behind.*

About the Art American still-life painter John F. Peto (1854–1907) is known for his colorful and inventive *trompe l'oeil*, or "fool-the-eye," works. This style of painting, made popular by 17th-century Dutch artists, creates the illusion that the painting is an arrangement of actual objects.

- From whom does the narrator receive a letter? Where does the letter come from? (lines 2–4)

- Why is the narrator's aunt coming to Boston? (lines 5–6)

- What does the letter ask? (lines 7–8)

- How does the narrator feel about the person who wrote the letter? How can you tell? (lines 10–11)

FOR ADVANCED LEARNERS/AP

Compare Setting Use a Comparison Matrix to discuss and compare the two settings described in the selection. Then discuss the significance of the differences:

- Georgiana's work in Boston and in Nebraska

- music and art in Boston and Nebraska

- family life in Boston and Nebraska

BEST PRACTICES TOOLKIT —Transparency
Comparison Matrix, p. A24

Direct students to lines 12–21. Use these prompts to help students grasp the narrator's reaction to the letter:

Connect Have someone's words ever made you recall experiences from your childhood? Explain. *Accept all thoughtful responses.*

Evaluate How effective is Cather's use of detail in describing the narrator's memories? Explain. *Possible answer: The use of detail is quite effective, for the description is vivid and appeals to the senses.*

REVIST THE BIG QUESTION

Does it matter where we LIVE?

Discuss Based on lines 30–33, how does the narrator's comparison in these lines show that he is aware of the effect that places have upon people? *Possible answer: The comparison of haggard Aunt Georgiana to explorers who have faced the rigors of the Arctic and Africa shows that the narrator understands that a place can take a physical toll upon a person.*

VOCABULARY

COMMON CORE
L 4

OWN THE WORD

tentatively: Remind students that tentatively refers to having "a hesitant or uncertain manner" or "not fully worked out." Have students write sentences for both definitions. *Possible answer: Julia entered the room* tentatively *since she knew few people at the party. I have* tentatively *scheduled my doctor's appointment for Monday.*

---

my aunt had known, scourged with chilblains[1] and bashfulness, my hands cracked and sore from the corn husking. I felt the knuckles of my thumb **tentatively,** as though they were raw again. I sat again before her parlor organ, fumbling the scales with my stiff, red hands, while she, beside me, made canvas mittens for the huskers.[2]

The next morning, after preparing my landlady somewhat, I set out for the station. When the train arrived I had some difficulty in finding my aunt. She was the last of the passengers to alight, and it was not until I got her into the carriage that she seemed really to recognize me. She had come all the way in a day coach; her linen duster[3] had become black with soot and her black bonnet grey with dust during the journey. When we arrived at my boarding-house the landlady put her to bed at once and I did not see her again until the next morning.

Whatever shock Mrs. Springer experienced at my aunt's appearance, she considerately concealed. As for myself, I saw my aunt's misshapen figure with that feeling of awe and respect with which we behold explorers who have left their ears and fingers north of Franz-Josef-Land, or their health somewhere along the Upper Congo.[4] My Aunt Georgiana had been a music teacher at the Boston Conservatory, somewhere back in the latter sixties. One summer, while visiting in the little village among the Green Mountains[5] where her ancestors had dwelt

---

1. **scourged with chilblains:** tormented with painful swelling or sores on the hands or feet caused by exposure to the cold.
2. **huskers:** farm workers who remove cornhusks by hand.
3. **duster:** a long, lightweight overgarment to protect clothing from dust.
4. **Franz-Josef-Land . . . Upper Congo:** Franz-Josef-Land is a group of small, mostly ice-covered islands in the Arctic Ocean, north of Russia. The Upper Congo is part of a major river in central Africa.
5. **Green Mountains:** a mountain range in Vermont.

Family and Their Dugout (1870s), Anonymous. Photo 11″ × 14″. Near McCook, Nebraska. © Nebraska State Historical Society, Lincoln, Nebraska.

---

tentatively
(tĕn′tə-tĭv-lē) *adv.* in a hesitant or uncertain manner

Language Coach

Prefixes *Misshapen* (line 30) means "badly shaped" or "deformed." The prefix *mis-* means "wrong," "badly," or "not." Using this information, give the meanings of the following words: *misadvise, misdeed, misunderstood.*

DIFFERENTIATED INSTRUCTION

FOR ENGLISH LANGUAGE LEARNERS

Language Coach

Prefixes
Answers: misadvise: *to advise badly;* misdeed: *a wrong action;* misunderstood: *wrongly interpreted.*

Challenge students to use their knowledge of the *mis-* prefix to define *misbehave, misinform,* and *misprint.*

FOR ENGLISH LANGUAGE LEARNERS

Related Vocabulary Discuss these descriptive phrases, clarifying individual words as needed:

Aunt Georgiana's physical appearance:

• *linen duster . . . black with soot; black bonnet grey with dust* (line 26)

• *sunken chest* (lines 58–59)

• *ill-fitting false teeth* (line 60)

for generations, she had kindled the **callow** fancy of the most idle and shiftless of all the village lads, and had conceived for this Howard Carpenter one of those extravagant passions which a handsome country boy of twenty-one sometimes inspires in an angular, spectacled woman of thirty. When she returned to her
40 duties in Boston, Howard followed her, and the upshot of this inexplicable infatuation was that she eloped with him, eluding the reproaches of her family and the criticisms of her friends by going with him to the Nebraska frontier. Carpenter, who, of course, had no money, had taken a homestead in Red Willow County,[6] fifty miles from the railroad. There they had measured off their quarter section themselves by driving across the prairie in a wagon, to the wheel of which they had tied a red cotton handkerchief, and counting off its revolutions. They built a dugout in the red hillside, one of those cave dwellings whose inmates so often reverted to primitive conditions. Their water they got from the lagoons where the buffalo drank, and their slender stock of provisions was always at the
50 mercy of bands of roving Indians. For thirty years my aunt had not been further than fifty miles from the homestead. **B**

But Mrs. Springer knew nothing of all this, and must have been considerably shocked at what was left of my kinswoman. Beneath the soiled linen duster which, on her arrival, was the most conspicuous feature of her costume, she wore a black stuff[7] dress, whose ornamentation showed that she had surrendered herself unquestioningly into the hands of a country dressmaker. My poor aunt's figure, however, would have presented astonishing difficulties to any dressmaker. Originally stooped, her shoulders were now almost bent together over her sunken chest. She wore no stays, and her gown, which trailed unevenly behind, rose in a sort
60 of peak over her abdomen. She wore ill-fitting false teeth, and her skin was as yellow as a Mongolian's from constant exposure to a pitiless wind and to the alkaline water which hardens the most transparent cuticle into a sort of flexible leather. **C**

I owed to this woman most of the good that ever came my way in my boyhood, and had a reverential affection for her. During the years when I was riding herd for my uncle, my aunt, after cooking the three meals—the first of which was ready at six o'clock in the morning—and putting the six children to bed, would often stand until midnight at her ironing-board, with me at the kitchen table beside her, hearing me recite Latin declensions and conjugations,[8] gently shaking me when my drowsy head sank down over a page of irregular verbs. It was to her, at her ironing
70 or mending, that I read my first Shakespeare, and her old text-book on mythology was the first that ever came into my empty hands. She taught me my scales and exercises, too—on the little parlor organ, which her husband had bought her after fifteen years, during which she had not so much as seen any instrument, but an accordion that belonged to one of the Norwegian farmhands. She would sit beside me by the hour, darning and counting while I struggled with the "Joyous Farmer,"[9] but she seldom talked to me about music, and I understood why. She was a pious

---

6. **Red Willow County:** county in southwestern Nebraska, bordering on Kansas.

7. **stuff:** a woolen material.

8. **Latin declensions and conjugations:** forms of Latin nouns and verbs representing different cases and tenses.

9. **"Joyous Farmer":** one of a series of musical pieces for children by German composer Robert Schumann.

A WAGNER MATINEE   **721**

callow (kăl'ō) *adj.* lacking adult experience; immature

2 Targeted Passage

B SETTING
Consider the **description** of the homestead in lines 43–51. How do you think life in such a place might affect a woman with Aunt Georgiana's background?

C DRAW CONCLUSIONS
Reread lines 52–62. What can you **infer** about Aunt Georgiana based on Cather's vivid description of her physical appearance?

READING SKILL — COMMON CORE RL 1

D Model the Skill: DRAW CONCLUSIONS

To improve students' understanding of Aunt Georgiana read aloud lines 76–82. Then have students identify details that describe how Georgiana teaches Clark his lessons. Ask students what Georgiana's careful attention to education, literature, and music reveals about her own values and interests.

Possible answer: *Aunt Georgiana's treatment of her nephew suggests that she is a kind, loving person and a tireless worker. She regrets some of the sacrifices that she has made, but she takes comfort in religion.*

TIERED DISCUSSION PROMPTS

Direct students to lines 94–105. Use these prompts to help students explore Aunt Georgiana's state of mind:

Interpret How has Aunt Georgiana's attitude toward city life changed over the past 30 years? Explain. ***Possible answer:*** *When she used to live and work in Boston, Aunt Georgiana was at ease in and seemed to enjoy life in the city. Now, however, she seems timid, out of place, distracted, and disoriented. She appears to be preoccupied with farm chores rather than focused on the city around her (lines 100–105).*

Synthesize Will Aunt Georgiana enjoy attending the concert? Why or why not? *Accept all thoughtful responses.*

VOCABULARY — COMMON CORE L 4

OWN THE WORD

- **sordid:** Tell students that *sordid* can mean "morally degraded" or "wretched; dirty." Have students use the context of the story to determine which definition is used. ***Possible answer:*** Sordid *describes Aunt Georgiana's life—wretched in its poverty and hard work.*
- **somnambulant:** Tell students that *somnambulant* refers to sleepwalking and connotes a sense of sluggishness and dazed appearance.

woman; she had the consolations of religion and, to her at least, her martyrdom was not wholly **sordid.** Once when I had been doggedly beating out some easy passages from an old score of *Euryanthe*[10] I had found among her music books, she came up to me and, putting her hands over my eyes, gently drew my head back upon her shoulder, saying tremulously, "Don't love it so well, Clark, or it may be taken from you. Oh! dear boy, pray that whatever your sacrifice may be, it be not that." **D**

When my aunt appeared on the morning after her arrival, she was still in a semi-**somnambulant** state. She seemed not to realize that she was in the city where she had spent her youth, the place longed for hungrily half a lifetime. She had been so wretchedly train-sick throughout the journey that she had no recollection of anything but her discomfort, and, to all intents and purposes, there were but a few hours of nightmare between the farm in Red Willow County and my study on Newbury Street. I had planned a little pleasure for her that afternoon, to repay her for some of the glorious moments she had given me when we used to milk together in the straw-thatched cowshed and she, because I was more than usually tired, or because her husband had spoken sharply to me, would tell me of the splendid performance of the *Huguenots*[11] she had seen in Paris, in her youth. At two o'clock the Symphony Orchestra was to give a Wagner program, and I intended to take my aunt; though, as I conversed with her, I grew doubtful about her enjoyment of it. Indeed, for her own sake, I could only wish her taste for such things quite dead, and the long struggle mercifully ended at last. I suggested our visiting the Conservatory and the Common[12] before lunch, but she seemed altogether too timid to wish to venture out. She questioned me absently about various changes in the city, but she was chiefly concerned that she had forgotten to leave instructions about feeding half-skimmed milk to a certain weakling calf, "old Maggie's calf, you know, Clark," she explained, evidently having forgotten how long I had been away. She was further troubled because she had neglected to tell her daughter about the freshly-opened kit of mackerel in the cellar, which would spoil if it were not used directly.

I asked her whether she had ever heard any of the Wagnerian operas,[13] and found that she had not, though she was perfectly familiar with their respective situations, and had once possessed the piano score of *The Flying Dutchman.* I began to think it would have been best to get her back to Red Willow County without waking her, and regretted having suggested the concert.

From the time we entered the concert hall, however, she was a trifle less passive and inert, and for the first time seemed to perceive her surroundings. I had felt some trepidation lest she might become aware of the absurdities of her attire, or might experience some painful embarrassment at stepping suddenly into the world to which she had been dead for a quarter of a century. But, again, I found how superficially I

sordid (sôr'dĭd) *adj.* wretched; dirty; morally degraded

D DRAW CONCLUSIONS
Reread lines 63–82. What does Aunt Georgiana's treatment of her nephew reveal about her?

somnambulant (sŏm-năm'byə-lənt') *adj.* sleepwalking

COMMON CORE L 2a

Language Coach

Compound Adjectives *Freshly-opened* (line 104) is an example of a **compound adjective.** This phrase modifies the noun *kit.* To avoid confusion, the words in a compound adjective are normally separated by a hyphen (-) when they appear immediately before the word they modify. If they follow the word they modify, no hyphen is needed: *The kit of mackerel was freshly opened.* What are some other common compound adjectives?

10. ***Euryanthe*** (yŏŏr'ē-ăn'thē): an opera by German composer Carl Maria von Weber.
11. ***Huguenots*** (hyōō'gə-nŏts'): an opera by German composer Giacomo Meyerbeer.
12. **the Common:** Boston Common, a public park.
13. **Wagnerian operas:** The orchestra will play selections from several operas composed by Wagner, including *The Flying Dutchman, Tannhäuser, Tristan and Isolde,* and a cycle of four operas called *The Ring of the Nibelung.*

DIFFERENTIATED INSTRUCTION

FOR ADVANCED LEARNERS/AP

Analyze Tone and Characterization Encourage students to reflect upon Willa Cather's tone and characterization. What can students infer about her feelings toward Aunt Georgiana? Does Cather respect her? admire her? feel sorry for her?

Ask students to write two paragraphs summarizing and supporting their conclusions. Then have students meet in small groups to compare their observations.

FOR ENGLISH LANGUAGE LEARNERS

Language Coach — COMMON CORE L 2a

Compound Adjectives ***Possible answer:*** *Examples of some other compound adjectives include* part-time worker, well-kept secret, middle-aged man.

had judged her. She sat looking about her with eyes as impersonal, almost as stony, as those with which the granite Rameses[14] in a museum watches the froth and fret that ebbs and flows[15] about his pedestal—separated from it by the lonely stretch of centuries. I have seen this same aloofness in old miners who drift into the Brown
120 hotel at Denver, their pockets full of bullion,[16] their linen soiled, their haggard faces unshaven; standing in the thronged corridors as solitary as though they were still in a frozen camp on the Yukon, conscious that certain experiences have isolated them from their fellows by a gulf no haberdasher[17] could bridge.

❸ **Targeted Passage**

We sat at the extreme left of the first balcony, facing the arc of our own and the balcony above us, <u>veritable</u> hanging gardens, brilliant as tulip beds. The matinée audience was made up chiefly of women. One lost the contour of faces and figures, indeed any effect of line whatever, and there was only the color of bodices past counting, the shimmer of fabrics soft and firm, silky and sheer; red, mauve, pink, blue, lilac, purple, ecru, rose, yellow, cream, and white, all the colors that an
130 impressionist[18] finds in a sunlit landscape, with here and there the dead shadow of a frock coat. My Aunt Georgiana regarded them as though they had been so many daubs of tube-paint on a palette.

veritable (vĕr′ĭ-tə-bəl) *adj.* true; not unreal or imaginary

When the musicians came out and took their places, she gave a little stir of anticipation and looked with quickening interest down over the rail at that invariable grouping, perhaps the first wholly familiar thing that had greeted her eye since she had left old Maggie and her weakling calf. I could feel how all those details sank into her soul, for I had not forgotten how they had sunk into mine when I came fresh from ploughing forever and forever between green aisles of corn, where, as in a treadmill, one might walk from daybreak to dusk without
140 perceiving a shadow of change. The clean profiles of the musicians, the gloss of their linen, the dull black of their coats, the beloved shapes of the instruments, the patches of yellow light thrown by the green shaded lamps on the smooth, varnished bellies of the 'cellos and the bass viols in the rear, the restless, wind-tossed forest of fiddle necks and bows—I recalled how, in the first orchestra I had ever heard, those long bow strokes seemed to draw the heart out of me, as a conjurer's stick reels out yards of paper ribbon from a hat. ⓔ

ⓔ SETTING
Reread lines 133–146. How does Aunt Georgiana respond to the setting of the Boston concert hall?

The first number was the *Tannhauser* <u>overture.</u> When the horns drew out the first strain of the Pilgrim's chorus, my Aunt Georgiana clutched my coat sleeve. Then it was I first realized that for her this broke a silence of thirty years; the
150 inconceivable silence of the plains. With the battle between the two motives, with the frenzy of the Venusberg theme and its ripping of strings, there came to me an overwhelming sense of the waste and wear we are so powerless to combat;

overture (ō′vər-chŏŏr′) *n.* the orchestral introduction to a musical dramatic work

---

14. **Rameses** (răm′ĭ-sēz′): one of the ancient kings of Egypt of that name.
15. **froth ... flows:** happiness and sadness that come and go.
16. **bullion:** gold.
17. **haberdasher:** a dealer in men's clothing and accessories.
18. **impressionist:** a follower of a movement in French painting that emphasized the play of light and color.

A WAGNER MATINEE **723**

FOR STRUGGLING READERS

❸ **Targeted Passage** [Lines 116–132]

This passage contrasts the concert hall setting with Aunt Georgiana's attitude.

- Describe the appearance of the audience. (lines 126–131)
- What does the narrator mean when he says that his aunt regarded the audience members "as though they had been so many daubs of tube-paint on a palette"? (lines 131–132)

FOR ENGLISH LANGUAGE LEARNERS

Comprehension: Text Structure Help students identify the particular qualities that Cather is calling attention to by establishing these comparisons:

- Aunt Georgiana compared first to "the granite Rameses" (lines 116–119) and then to "old miners" (lines 119–123)
- the concert hall and audience compared first to flowers (lines 124–125) and then to impressionistic painting (lines 126–132)

REVISIT THE BIG QUESTION

Does it matter where we LIVE?

Discuss Cather compares Aunt Georgiana's initial reaction to the concert hall to the "aloofness in old miners" who visit a Denver hotel. Based on lines 111–123, how are Aunt Georgiana and the miners alike? *Possible answer: They are alike in that both have been strongly affected by the places in which they have lived—harsh places, away from the mainstream of society—and the length of time that they have lived there. The miners, who have lived "in a frozen camp on the Yukon," now feel isolated from the people around them in the hotel. Aunt Georgiana, who has lived on the Nebraska frontier for thirty years, acts as though she feels similarly isolated in Boston.*

TEXT ANALYSIS
COMMON CORE
RL 3

ⓔ SETTING

Possible answer: At first, Aunt Georgiana seems rather detached and passive. When the musicians enter, however, she becomes increasingly interested.

Extend the Discussion What does Clark mean when he says that he "could feel how all those details sank into her soul, for I had not forgotten how they had sunk into mine ..." (lines 136–137)? What inferences can you make about the ways in which Clark's life has changed since he left Nebraska?

VOCABULARY
COMMON CORE
L 4

OWN THE WORD

- **veritable:** *Veritable* stems from noun *verity,* "being true or real." Have students complete this sentence: *The campaign headquarters was a* veritable *hothouse of ... Possible answer: excitement as the voting results indicated victory.*

- **overture:** Tell students that *overture* derives from the Latin term meaning "to open." In music, an *overture* is an "orchestral introduction or prelude." It can also refer to a "proposal that indicates readiness" to take the next step in an action.

A WAGNER MATINEE **723**

Direct students to lines 149–159. Use these prompts to help students understand the barrenness of prairie life:

Summarize What impression does Clark give of the prairie? **Possible answer:** *Clark gives the impression that the prairie is a primitive, grim place that seems to go on forever.*

Evaluate How well does Cather's description capture the atmosphere of the narrator's early life on the prairie? Explain. *Accept all answers that students can support.*

READING SKILL

COMMON CORE
RL 1

F DRAW CONCLUSIONS

Possible answer: The reader can infer that Aunt Georgiana has retained her love of music and that she acutely feels the low priority that it has had in her life as a Nebraska homesteader.

VOCABULARY

COMMON CORE
L 4

OWN THE WORD

excruciatingly: Tell students that *excruciatingly* is an adverb that refers to "ways that cause great pain or distress; agonizingly; intensely, extremely." Ask students to list situations they may find *excruciatingly* difficult to endure. **Possible answer:** *loss of a friend; severe illness or disease; car accident*

---

and I saw again the tall, naked house on the prairie, black and grim as a wooden fortress; the black pond where I had learned to swim, its margin pitted with sun-dried cattle tracks; the rain-gullied clay banks about the naked house, the four dwarf ash seedlings where the dish-cloths were always hung to dry before the kitchen door. The world there was the flat world of the ancients; to the east, a cornfield that stretched to daybreak; to the west, a corral that reached to sunset; between, the conquests of peace, dearer bought than those of war.

160   The overture closed, my aunt released my coat sleeve, but she said nothing. She sat staring at the orchestra through a dullness of thirty years, through the films made little by little by each of the three hundred and sixty-five days in every one of them. What, I wondered, did she get from it? She had been a good pianist in her day I knew, and her musical education had been broader than that of most music teachers of a quarter of a century ago. She had often told me of Mozart's operas and Meyerbeer's, and I could remember hearing her sing, years ago, certain melodies of Verdi's. When I had fallen ill with a fever in her house she used to sit by my cot in the evening—when the cool, night wind blew in through the faded mosquito netting tacked over the window and I lay watching a certain bright

170   star that burned red above the cornfield—and sing "Home to our mountains, O, let us return!" in a way fit to break the heart of a Vermont boy near dead of homesickness already.

I watched her closely through the prelude to *Tristan and Isolde,* trying vainly to conjecture what that seething turmoil of strings and winds might mean to her, but she sat mutely staring at the violin bows that drove obliquely downward, like the pelting streaks of rain in a summer shower. Had this music any message for her? Had she enough left to at all comprehend this power which had kindled the world since she had left it? I was in a fever of curiosity, but Aunt Georgiana sat silent upon her peak in Darien.[19] She preserved this utter immobility throughout

180   the number from *The Flying Dutchman,* though her fingers worked mechanically upon her black dress, as though, of themselves, they were recalling the piano score they had once played. Poor old hands! They had been stretched and twisted into mere tentacles to hold and lift and knead with; the palms unduly swollen, the fingers bent and knotted—on one of them a thin, worn band that had once been a wedding ring. As I pressed and gently quieted one of those groping hands, I remembered with quivering eyelids their services for me in other days.

Soon after the tenor began the "Prize Song," I heard a quick drawn breath and turned to my aunt. Her eyes were closed, but the tears were glistening on her cheeks, and I think, in a moment more, they were in my eyes as well. It never

190   really died, then—the soul that can suffer so **excruciatingly** and so interminably; it withers to the outward eye only; like that strange moss which can lie on a dusty shelf half a century and yet, if placed in water, grows green again. She wept so throughout the development and elaboration of the melody. **F**

---

19. **peak in Darien:** a mountain in what is now Panama, referred to in English poet John Keats's "On First Looking into Chapman's Homer" as a place where the Pacific was contemplated with silence and awe by Spanish explorers.

Language Coach

Fixed Expressions A **fixed expression** is a group of words that are usually combined in the same way to express a specific meaning. The fixed expression "fallen ill" (line 167) has to do with illness. Explain these fixed expressions about illness: *come down with, [have] a bout of.*

excruciatingly
(ĭk-skrōō′shē-ā′tĭng-lē)
adv. in a way that causes great pain or distress

F DRAW CONCLUSIONS
Reread lines 187–193. What **inferences** can you make about Aunt Georgiana's feeling for music, based upon her reaction to it?

DIFFERENTIATED INSTRUCTION

FOR ENGLISH LANGUAGE LEARNERS
Vocabulary: Multiple-Meaning Words Explain that *bows* (line 175) refers here to the rod that a violinist draws across the strings of the instrument. However, *bow* also has several other meanings, such "a weapon used to shoot arrows." Discuss how students can use context clues to figure out the appropriate meaning of multiple-meaning words. Then have mixed-readiness Jigsaw groups investigate these other multiple-meaning words (all of which

have at least one meaning that relates to music) and share their findings: *strings, winds* (line 174); *number* (line 180); *band* (line 184); *drawn* (line 187); *concert* (line 194).

📦 **BEST PRACTICES TOOLKIT**
Jigsaw Reading p. A1

FOR ENGLISH LANGUAGE LEARNERS

Language Coach

Fixed Expressions *Answer:* Come down with *and* have a bout of *both mean to become sick with a specific illness, as in "to come down with a cold," or "to have a bout of the flu."* Point out other examples of set language relating to illness or good health, for example: *the fever broke* (the patient's temperature fell) or the person was *fit as a fiddle* (in excellent health).

During the intermission before the second half of the concert, I questioned my aunt and found that the "Prize Song" was not new to her. Some years before there had drifted to the farm in Red Willow County a young German, a tramp cow puncher, who had sung the chorus at Bayreuth,[20] when he was a boy, along with the other peasant boys and girls. Of a Sunday morning he used to sit on his gingham-sheeted bed in the hands' bedroom which opened off the kitchen, cleaning the leather of his boots and saddle, singing the "Prize Song," while my aunt went about her work in the kitchen. She had hovered about him until she had prevailed upon him to join the country church, though his sole fitness for this step, in so far as I could gather, lay in his boyish face and his possession of this divine melody. Shortly afterward he had gone to town on the Fourth of July, been drunk for several days, lost his money at a faro table, ridden a saddled Texas steer on a bet, and disappeared with a fractured collar-bone. All this my aunt told me huskily, wanderingly, as though she were talking in the weak lapses of illness. **G**

200

G DRAW CONCLUSIONS
Reread lines 194–207. How does Cather use a plot event to further the internal development of the narrator and the external development of Aunt Georgiana?

20. **Bayreuth** (bī-roit'): a town in the Bavarian region of Germany where annual Wagner music festivals are held.

Two on the Aisle (1927), Edward Hopper © Francis G. Mayer/Corbis. © Heirs of Josephine N. Hopper, licensed by the Whitney Museum of American Art.

READING SKILL COMMON CORE RL 1

G DRAW CONCLUSIONS

Possible answer: By inserting the performance of "Prize Song" in the plot, the narrator adds further depth to the characters of Aunt Georgiana and Clark. "Prize Song" shows the aunt's sensitivity to music and remembrance of seemingly insignificant events on the prairie. It also shows the narrator's keen powers of observation, as he listens carefully to her tale and understands the importance of details.

Analyze Visuals

Activity How does the scene in Hopper's painting compare with Cather's description of the concert hall? *Possible answer: Hopper's painting has a subdued, detached feeling; its colors are limited, and only three people appear in the scene. In contrast, Cather's description (lines 124–131, for example) is warmer and more colorful and suggests the presence of many more people.*

About the Art American realist Edward Hopper (1882–1967) liked to paint places where people gathered, such as theaters, restaurants, and offices. His scenes often had a bleak or lonely atmosphere, however, showing just a few people in an otherwise empty setting. *Two on the Aisle*, painted in 1927, is typical of Hopper's simple, spare style.

FOR STRUGGLING READERS
Clarify Sequence This critical scene is built upon elements of the concert and Aunt Georgiana's reaction to each one. To make the connection clear, work with students to complete a Timeline that shows the progression of events and responses.

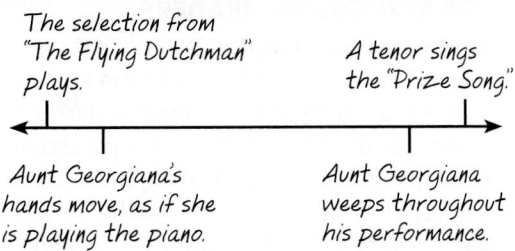

The selection from "The Flying Dutchman" plays.

A tenor sings the "Prize Song."

Aunt Georgiana's hands move, as if she is playing the piano.

Aunt Georgiana weeps throughout his performance.

BEST PRACTICES TOOLKIT—Transparency
Timeline p. B23

FOR ADVANCED LEARNERS/AP
Analyze Structure Cather uses flashbacks to provide background information. For example, lines 63–82 recall one of Clark's boyhood memories of his aunt, and lines 153–159 describe the house on the prairie. Ask students to reread lines 194–207. Then, have them write a paragraph or two in which they discuss (1) why Cather may have included this flashback and (2) whether it is important—or even necessary—to the story.

 SETTING

Possible answer: *The metaphor suggests that years of strenuous daily labor on the prairie, with the only musical outlet being the singing of hymns, might wear down a person's ability to comprehend or appreciate a wider "world" of music.*

REVISIT THE BIG QUESTION

Does it matter where we LIVE?

Discuss In lines 223–229, how do the places that Aunt Georgiana visits—in her imagination—as the music plays compare to the place from which she has come? ***Possible answer:*** *The imagined places may be happy, even though they are compared to graveyards; at least, they are places of hope and rest.*

OWN THE WORD

myriad: Share with students that *myriad* comes from the Greek *murias* that means "ten thousand," and *murios* meaning "countless." English use of the word began as a noun (a *myriad* of stars), but later developed into use as a noun or an adjective (*myriad* stars). The Greeks used *myriad* as a noun in prose and mathematics, and as an adjective in poetry.

SELECTION WRAP–UP

READ WITH A PURPOSE Now that students have read the selection, have them evaluate what Georgiana misses about city life. Ask: What has been the hardest thing for Georgiana to give up about city living? ***Possible answer:*** *Giving up music is the most difficult, since loss of music represents all the other deprivations.*

"Well, we have come to better things than the old *Trovatore*[21] at any rate, Aunt Georgie?" I queried, with a well meant effort at jocularity.

210 Her lip quivered and she hastily put her handkerchief up to her mouth. From behind it she murmured, "And you have been hearing this ever since you left me, Clark?" Her question was the gentlest and saddest of reproaches.

The second half of the program consisted of four numbers from the *Ring*, and closed with Siegfried's funeral march. My aunt wept quietly, but almost continuously, as a shallow vessel overflows in a rainstorm. From time to time her dim eyes looked up at the lights which studded the ceiling, burning softly under their dull glass globes; doubtless they were stars in truth to her. I was still perplexed as to what measure of musical comprehension was left to her, she who had heard nothing but the singing of Gospel Hymns at Methodist services in the

220 square frame school-house on Section Thirteen for so many years. I was wholly unable to gauge how much of it had been dissolved in soapsuds, or worked into bread, or milked into the bottom of a pail.

The deluge of sound poured on and on; I never knew what she found in the shining current of it; I never knew how far it bore her, or past what happy islands. From the trembling of her face I could well believe that before the last numbers she had been carried out where the **myriad** graves are, into the grey, nameless burying grounds of the sea; or into some world of death vaster yet, where, from the beginning of the world, hope has lain down with hope and dream with dream and, renouncing, slept.

230 The concert was over; the people filed out of the hall chattering and laughing, glad to relax and find the living level again, but my kinswoman made no effort to rise. The harpist slipped its green felt cover over his instrument; the flute-players shook the water from their mouthpieces; the men of the orchestra went out one by one, leaving the stage to the chairs and music stands, empty as a winter cornfield.

I spoke to my aunt. She burst into tears and sobbed pleadingly. "I don't want to go, Clark, I don't want to go!"

I understood. For her, just outside the door of the concert hall, lay the black pond with the cattle-tracked bluffs; the tall, unpainted house, with weather-curled boards;

240 naked as a tower, the crook-backed ash seedlings where the dish-cloths hung to dry; the gaunt, molting turkeys picking up refuse about the kitchen door. ✑

⑪ SETTING
Reread lines 220–222. What does this **metaphor** suggest about how a place might affect one's appreciation of music?

myriad (mîr′ē-əd) *adj.* exceedingly numerous

④ Targeted Passage

---

21. ***Trovatore*** (trō′vä-tôr′ě): *Il Trovatore* is an opera by the Italian composer Giuseppe Verdi.

DIFFERENTIATED INSTRUCTION

FOR STRUGGLING READERS

Develop Reading Fluency Explain that the drama in this passage takes place in Aunt Georgiana's mind. Help students understand the conclusion by conducting a choral reading with the group. As the group reads aloud, pause for comprehension checks at passages such as "I don't want to go!" and "just outside the door of the concert hall."

④ Targeted Passage [Lines 230–241]

Here, Aunt Georgiana voices her thoughts about returning to her homestead.

- What does Aunt Georgiana do while everyone else is leaving the concert hall? (lines 231–232)

- How does she react when Clark speaks to her? (lines 236–237)

- What place is Clark describing in the final paragraph? (lines 238–241)

Comprehension

1. **Recall** Why does Aunt Georgiana travel to Boston?

2. **Recall** Why does Clark take his aunt to the concert?

3. **Summarize** How do Clark and his aunt respond to the concert?

COMMON CORE

RL 1 Cite evidence to support inferences drawn from the text.
RL 3 Analyze the impact of the author's choices regarding how to develop and relate elements of a story.

Text Analysis

4. **Predict Events** In your opinion, will Aunt Georgiana return to Nebraska, or will she stay in Boston? Give evidence to support your answer.

5. **Make Inferences** Aunt Georgiana warns Clark, "Don't love it so well, Clark, or it may be taken from you." What does this suggest about the role of music in her own life?

6. **Draw Conclusions About Character** Look back at the **inferences** you recorded in your chart as you read. Judging from the choices that Aunt Georgiana has made in her life, what conclusions can you draw about her character? What emotions does she seem to experience, and how does she handle them?

7. **Contrast Settings** The two settings in this story—the Nebraska prairie and the Boston concert hall—are both significant for Aunt Georgiana. What do they **symbolize?** Support your answer with details from the story.

8. **Make Judgments** How might Aunt Georgiana be different if she had stayed in Boston? Use examples from the story and your views about the importance of place to support your answer.

Text Criticism

9. **Biographical Context** "A Wagner Matinee" created a stir when it appeared in 1904. Cather's family objected to the fictional portrait of her real-life aunt Franc. One of her friends remarked: "The stranger to this state will associate Nebraska with the aunt's wretched figure, her ill-fitting false teeth, her skin yellowed by the weather." Do you agree? Examine the **imagery** and **figurative language** used to describe the people and scenes of Nebraska. Do you think Cather's Nebraska relatives were justified in taking offense? Cite evidence from the story to support your answer.

> *Does it matter where we* **LIVE?**
>
> What effect has frontier life in Nebraska had on Aunt Georgiana? In what way has place had no effect at all on Aunt Georgiana? In your opinion, how does the place we live affect our true character, if at all?

8. *If Aunt Georgiana had stayed, she probably would have continued her career as a music teacher while partaking in the musical and other cultural offerings of Boston. Her elopement seemed an act of desperation; had she stayed in Boston, she might never have married. City life probably would not have taken such a physical and emotional toll on her as frontier life has done, and certainly her appearance would be not only healthier but also more stylish.*

9. *Students' answers and evidence will vary, but students may agree that Cather's portrayal of Aunt Georgiana and her life on the Nebraska prairie is harsh and unflattering.*

> *Does it matter where we* LIVE?
> Students may say that frontier life weathered Georgiana, but her kindness, talents, and love of music remained the same. The place we live may or may not be a spot that allows our true character to flourish.

Practice and Apply

For preliminary support of post reading questions, use these copy masters:

R RESOURCE MANAGER—Copy Masters
Reading Check p. 104
Setting p. 97
Question Support p. 105
Additional selection questions are provided for teachers on page 91.

ANSWERS

COMMON CORE RL 1, RL 3

1. *Aunt Georgiana travels to Boston to claim a small legacy left by a bachelor relative.*

2. *Clark takes his aunt to the concert because he knows that she loves music and because he wants to give something back to her for all that she did for him as a child.*

3. *Clark at first wonders whether his aunt can still appreciate music, but he then sees that she does retain deep feelings for it. Aunt Georgiana is emotionally overwhelmed by the music and doesn't want to leave.*

Possible answers:

4. *Aunt Georgiana's reaction at the end of the concert suggests that she may be tempted to remain in Boston. However, she has lived in Nebraska for thirty years, and her roots there are likely to draw her back.*

5. ■ **COMMON CORE FOCUS Make Inferences** *The warning suggests that Aunt Georgiana loves music and has deep regrets about having sacrificed it in exchange for a harsh life on the prairie.*

6. ■ **COMMON CORE FOCUS Draw Conclusions About Character** *The reader can conclude that once Aunt Georgiana makes a commitment, she has the courage to stick with it, as evidenced by her thirty years on the frontier with her husband. Although she may feel loneliness, sadness, and regret, she does not let these feelings rule her life.*

7. ● **COMMON CORE FOCUS Setting** *The elegant, vibrant opera house represents culture and sophistication; the Nebraska prairie represents hard work and practicality. The main support comes from vivid description, which contrasts the lavishness of the opera house with the bleakness of the homestead.*

ANSWERS

Vocabulary in Context

▲ VOCABULARY PRACTICE

1. *tentatively*
2. *somnambulant*
3. *sordid*
4. *myriad*
5. *callow*
6. *veritable*
7. *overture*
8. *excruciatingly*

 **RESOURCE MANAGER—Copy Master**
Vocabulary Practice p. 102

ACADEMIC VOCABULARY IN WRITING

Possible answer: Georgiana's feelings are *exposed* when she hears beautiful music. Hearing the music, she *perceives* the loss of art and culture that she has tried to ignore as she toiled on the prairie.

VOCABULARY STRATEGY: MUSIC TERMINOLOGY

 COMMON CORE **L 6**

- Point out that many words related to opera come from Italian. The word *opera* itself comes from the Latin word meaning "work."
- Model how to research word origin using the etymology of *concert,* which comes from the Italian *concerto.*

Answers:

1. *f,* Italian
2. *d,* Italian
3. *a,* Italian
4. *e,* Italian
5. *b,* Italian
6. *c,* French

 **RESOURCE MANAGER—Copy Master**
Vocabulary Strategy p. 103

Interactive Vocabulary THINK central

Keywords direct students to a **WordSharp** tutorial on **thinkcentral.com** or to other types of vocabulary practice and review.

Assess and Reteach

Assess

DIAGNOSTIC AND SELECTION TESTS
Selection Test A, B/C pp. 193–194, 195–196
Interactive Selection Test on thinkcentral.com

Reteach

LevelUp Online Tutorials on thinkcentral.com

Vocabulary in Context

▲ VOCABULARY PRACTICE

Choose the word from the list that best completes each sentence.

1. Though uncertain whether Aunt Georgiana would enjoy the concert, Clark _____ made plans to go.
2. Earlier, his aunt had seemed dazed, walking around in an almost _____ state.
3. Her life on the farm, while not _____, was certainly harsh and difficult.
4. She was worn down from the _____ jobs she performed from dawn to dusk.
5. But Aunt Georgiana was not a(n) _____ young girl with no experience or culture.
6. She was a(n) _____ treasure chest of musical knowledge.
7. When the _____ was played, she became a new woman.
8. Yet she found it _____ difficult to listen to the beautiful music.

WORD LIST
callow
excruciatingly
myriad
overture
somnambulant
sordid
tentatively
veritable

ACADEMIC VOCABULARY IN WRITING

• apparent • confine • expose • focus • perceive

Assume the role of Aunt Georgiana, and write several paragraphs describing your return to Boston. **Expose** Aunt Georgiana's innermost feelings during the concert, when she **perceives** what she has missed by living on the frontier. Use at least one Academic Vocabulary word in your response.

VOCABULARY STRATEGY: MUSIC TERMINOLOGY

Knowledge of the academic vocabulary used in specific content areas is important to your success in school. Many academic vocabulary words have their origins in other languages. For example, *sociology* comes from the French *sociologie*, *history* from the Latin word *historia*. Many of the academic words associated with music come from Italian or French. For example, the vocabulary word *overture*, which refers to the introductory piece in an opera or other musical drama, is derived from a French word.

PRACTICE Match each term in the lefthand column with its definition in the righthand column. Research the origin of each word to determine whether it is Italian, French, or some other language.

1. concerto
2. contralto
3. aria
4. diva
5. andante
6. tenor

a. an elaborate melody in an opera, sung by one person
b. a moderately slow tempo, or pace
c. a man who sings with a higher voice
d. a woman who sings with a lower voice
e. a leading woman soloist in an opera company
f. a piece in which a soloist performs with an orchestra

COMMON CORE

L 6 Acquire and use accurately general academic and domain-specific words and phrases.

 **Interactive Vocabulary** THINK central

Go to **thinkcentral.com**.
KEYWORD: HML11-728

DIFFERENTIATED INSTRUCTION

FOR ENGLISH LANGUAGE LEARNERS

Task Support: Vocabulary Strategy Some students may find that many musical terms in English are similar or even identical to the terms in their home language. For example, such words as *tenor, soprano,* and *andante* have the same spellings and meanings in both English and Spanish. Ask pairs of students who speak the same home language to identify other such cognates and then share their findings with the class.

FOR ADVANCED LEARNERS/AP

Academic Vocabulary in Writing Challenge students to use as many vocabulary words as they can in a paragraph written in the first person from Clark's point of view but set after Aunt Georgiana's return to Nebraska (or her decision to remain in Boston). Invite volunteer to read the results to the class.

America's Literary Regions

Indiana author Edward Eggleston made this claim in 1892.

> *"It used to be a matter of no little jealousy to us, I remember, that the manners, customs, thoughts and feelings of New England country people filled so large a place in books, while our life, not less interesting, not less romantic, and certainly not less filled with humorous and grotesque material, had no place in literature. It was as though we were shut out of good society."*

By the end of the 19th century, however, virtually every region of the country—from the cities of the Northeast, to the mining camps of California, to the Southern bayou, to the northern plains—had its own local colorist capturing the region's distinctive features in writing. These local color writers portrayed the dialects, dress, mannerisms, customs, character types, and landscapes of their regions with an eye for accurate detail.

Writing to Synthesize

Make a chart like the one shown, listing each of the selections you've read in this section (pages 658–728). On your chart, note what you've learned about the way the people in each region speak, the way they dress, their customs, and their landscapes. Then use your chart to write a one-paragraph description of each region you've encountered in your reading. Based on all of your descriptions, write a concluding sentence or two in which you sum up what the regions have in common.

	How People Speak	How People Dress	Local Customs	Local Landscape
The Autobiography of Mark Twain				

Extension

VIEWING & REPRESENTING

Create a **single-frame cartoon** to represent the region you live in. You may want to focus on the way people speak and dress, or you may prefer to characterize the landscape.

COMMON CORE

W 2 Write informative/explanatory texts to examine and convey complex ideas, concepts, and information clearly and accurately.
W 2b Develop the topic thoroughly by selecting the most significant and relevant facts, concrete details, or other information and examples.

A homesteader's dugout house in Pie Town, New Mexico

729

COMMON CORE FOCUS

W 2 Write informative/explanatory texts to examine and convey complex ideas, concepts, and information clearly and accurately. **W 2b** Develop the topic thoroughly by selecting the most significant and relevant facts, concrete details, or other information and examples.

Wrap-Up: Regionalism & Local Color Writing

This Wrap-Up provides students with an opportunity to review elements of regionalism and local color writing and to reflect on how these elements capture the flavor of different parts of the United States. Have students read and comment on the statement from Edward Eggleston; elicit that he probably would want to read or write about life in the Midwest.

Writing to Synthesize

- Review with students the concept of *synthesizing*—combining ideas and facts with other information and prior knowledge in order to understand a subject better or to develop new ideas. In this activity, synthesizing will help students draw conclusions about various regions of the United States and the people who live there.

- As students create their charts, suggest that they work in pairs to list specific details relating to speech, dress, customs, and landscape for each selection. Urge students to note specific passages that they can refer to when writing their paragraphs. Students also should refer to their charts when writing their one- or two-sentence conclusions that sum up what the regions have in common.

Extension

- Point out that a cartoon, like a written work, has a purpose and a tone. For example, a cartoon might entertain through gentle humor and an affectionate tone. Encourage students to identify a tone and a purpose before sketching their cartoons.

- Invite students to be imaginative in combining text and visual images. Suggest that they look at single-frame cartoons in newspapers or magazines for ideas.

DIFFERENTIATED INSTRUCTION

FOR STRUGGLING WRITERS

Writing Support Help students get started by directing them to relevant passages in a few selections. For example, students might review lines 1–29 of "The Outcasts of Poker Flat" or lines 1–12 of *Lake Wobegon Days* to get a sense of people and customs; they might review lines 39–62 of "A Wagner Matinee" for information about landscape and dress.

FOR ENGLISH LANGUAGE LEARNERS

Writing Topic Sentences To help students create topic sentences for their paragraphs, provide sentence starters such as these:

- Garrison Keillor's account of the people and events of Lake Wobegon suggests that _____.

- In "A Wagner Matinee," Willa Cather makes clear that life on the frontier _____.

Remind students to support their topic sentences with specific details from the selections.

Focus and Motivate

SUMMARY

The four images in this collection present a contrast between photography and painted landscapes. The first pair of images depicts a canyon in Yellowstone National Park. Thomas Moran's painting reveals the grandeur of the waterfall and rock formations. William Henry Jackson's photograph captures the same scene in black and white. The second pair of images focuses on the Park's Castle Geyser. Both artists make artistic choices, Jackson to make the pool dominate and Moran to blend land and sky more fluidly.

Can pictures DEVELOP *new frontiers?*

Read the question aloud. Remind students that 19th-century **Western expansion** occurred in response to many economic and social factors, and point out examples of these on page 643 of the historical essay. Ask students to consider how photography would have been useful to anyone wishing to encourage the expansion.

BACKGROUND

Moran and Jackson traveled on the newly completed transcontinental railroad to Yellowstone, then by horse and into the wilderness. Moran created rough watercolor sketches as the basis for his finished art. Jackson's photography equipment was fragile and heavy. Each photograph had to be prepared and developed on site, taking up to an hour to complete.

American Landscapes

Image Collection on Media  Smart DVD-ROM

Can pictures DEVELOP *new frontiers?*

Paintings and photographs can have a profound effect on us. They can enlighten us, frighten us, elicit our sympathies, even inspire us. In this lesson, you'll examine the landscape work of two 19th-century artists and discover how paintings and photographs helped to spur **Western expansion.**

Background

Framing New Views In the late 1800s, at a time when writer Mark Twain portrayed a romanticized view of the West, the new medium of photography gained popularity for revealing American life as it really was. For many painters of the day, photography posed a new challenge. While some saw it as displacing traditional forms of representation, others embraced it as a liberating artistic force.

Photography was also having an impact on the mass media. Because people were increasingly interested in facts and in realistic portrayals of events, they turned to the burgeoning newspaper industry and the day's more "realistic" writers. With the portability of cameras, photographers could supply newspapers, magazines, and advertisers with images in a short period of time, exposing viewers to faraway locations.

At the same time, Western expansion was being promoted by the federal government and by land developers from the East and Midwest. Photographic images of the new frontier were frequently used by advertisers and marketers to entice Americans to go West and settle the sparsely populated territory. In 1871, painter Thomas Moran joined forces with photographer William Henry Jackson and embarked on a geological expedition to document Western lands. These two artists found inspiration in surroundings of astounding natural beauty. Examples of their work appear in this lesson.

730

Media Study Resources

See resources on the **Teacher One Stop DVD-ROM** *and on* <u>thinkcentral.com</u>.

R **RESOURCE MANAGER UNIT 4**
Plan and Teach, pp. 107–110
Summary, pp. 111†*, 112‡*
Viewing Guide, p. 113
Close Viewing, p. 114
Media Activity, p. 115
Produce Your Own Media, p. 116

TECHNOLOGY
 Teacher One Stop DVD-ROM
Student One Stop DVD-ROM
Media*Smart* DVD-ROM

MediaScope on <u>thinkcentral.com</u>

* Resources for Differentiation   † Also in Spanish   ‡ In Haitian Creole and Vietnamese

Media Literacy: Photographs and Paintings

The paintings of Thomas Moran and the photographs of William Henry Jackson were instrumental in convincing Congress to declare Yellowstone, in 1872, the country's first national park. Shown here are a painting by Moran and a photograph by Jackson of a canyon scene. Analyze these images by considering how each artist used certain elements to achieve compelling landscape art.

STRATEGIES FOR ANALYZING PHOTOGRAPHS AND PAINTINGS

Composition is the arrangement of subject elements within an image. Scan each image from top to bottom, side to side, and corner to corner, noting how each artist has arranged the elements in the frame. Ask yourself: Where is the **focal point,** or main focus, of the painting and of the photograph? What section of the image first catches my eye? In both of these images, the focal point is the waterfall.

For painters, **perspective** is a technique that creates the illusion of depth, making objects look three-dimensional. To determine the perspective of an image, try to identify the **horizon line,** the horizontal section that appears to your eye to be at the farthest distance in a landscape. In both of these images, the horizon line appears near the top, where the sky meets the uppermost part of the valley.

Depth of field is the area in front of and behind a focused subject in which the image appears sharp. Photographers achieved this effect by adjusting camera lenses. Notice in the photograph how depth of field creates an impression of distance.

Texture is the surface quality of an image—what the image would feel like if we could touch it. Ask yourself:
• What materials or techniques did the photographer use to create a sense of texture?
• With paintings, where does the paint seem to rise slightly from the canvas?
  In these canyon images, your own knowledge of what is being depicted adds to your interpretation and appreciation of the textures conveyed.

MEDIA STUDY   **731**

Media Literacy

Help students analyze the images on page 731 by listing their similarities and differences on a Two-Column Chart. Discuss these points to help guide students' comparisons:

• **Composition** Point out that Moran's painting uses dark shadows to frame the light waterfall. Note that the waterfall appears in the center of both images, making a simple and striking composition.

• **Focal Point** Explain that although the focal point of the painting is the waterfall, Moran has included several figures in the foreground. Point out that these figures help show the great size of the canyon. They also invite viewers into the scene to visualize themselves in the setting.

• **Perspective** Offer an example of perspective in Jackson's photograph by pointing out the relative size of the trees. Those in the foreground are larger than those in the distance.

• **Horizon Line** Challenge students to imagine how the composition of Jackson's photograph would change if the horizon line did not appear in the photograph. How does the horizon line help the composition?

• **Depth of Field** Point out that the farthest hills in the photograph appear shrouded in haze. Explain that this adds depth to the image.

• **Texture** Encourage students to notice that in both the photograph and the painting, there are smooth and rough areas. The intricate textures add interest to the scene.

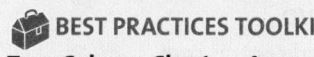 **BEST PRACTICES TOOLKIT**
Two-Column Chart, p. A25

MEDIA STUDY: TEACHING OPTIONS

Teaching Option 1: The Basics (1–2 Days)
1. Begin the Media Study using the material provided on pages 730–731.
2. Show the Introduction from Media*Smart*. Have students use the Viewing Guide on page 732, along with the corresponding copy master on page 113 of the Resource Manager. Discuss their responses.
3. Return to the pupil book for the extension activities on page 733.

Teaching Option 2: In-Depth Study (2–3 Days)
1. Begin the Media Study using pages 730–731.
2. Show the Introduction from Media*Smart*. Then continue on Media*Smart* with the Media Lessons, using the teacher notes available in the Resources section.
3. Show the Guided Analysis presentation. Have students record their observations on the Student Viewing Guide available in the Resources section of Media*Smart*.
4. Return to the pupil book, page 733.

Practice and Apply

VIEWING GUIDE

1. To prepare students for viewing the image collection, explain that the purpose of the exercise is not to determine which form of art is better or more effective, but rather to find the strengths of each form. Encourage them to consider these elements:

   - Point out that while all early photography was in black and white, both Jackson and Moran use color as elements of **composition.**

   - Jackson and Moran use **depth of field** to orient viewers in an image, a **focal point** to draw viewers' eyes to specific elements, and **perspective** to create realistic images. Together, these techniques convey the artists' reactions to Yellowstone's natural features.

   - The **textures** in the photographs and paintings show how the unfamiliar Yellowstone landscape would feel if viewers could touch it. This works with the visual images to help place viewers in the scene.

2. Remind students that one purpose of the art was to share the beauties of the natural setting with Americans who had never traveled west. For this reason, the artists were likely careful not to distort the scene.

R RESOURCE MANAGER—Copy Masters

    Viewing Guide p. 113
    Close Viewing p. 114
    Media Activity p. 115

Use this resource with the Viewing Guide:

MediaSmart DVD

MediaScope on **thinkcentral.com**

ANSWERS

FIRST VIEWING: Comprehension

1. *The elements of nature in the images include the waterfall, trees, the canyon, the horizon, steep cliffs, and shadowy hills.*

2. *Moran's painting has people in it.*

CLOSE VIEWING: Media Literacy

Possible answers:

3. *The artists' composition sought to show the canyon's enormity, the great distance of the land, and the waterfall's power.*

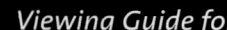

Media Smart DVD-ROM

Paintings by Thomas Moran
- **Selection 2:** "Grand Canyon of the Yellowstone"
- **Selection 4:** "Castle Geyser"

Photographs by William Henry Jackson
- **Selection 1:** "Grand Canyon of the Yellowstone"
- **Selection 3:** "Castle Geyser"

732

---

4. *Moran's painting of the Grand Canyon has more texture than "Castle Geyser." The geysers appear smooth with a hazy sky and calm waters, whereas the canyon has ragged trees, jagged cliffs and solid rocky outcroppings that give textural contrast to the smooth plateau in the foreground.*

5. *Two geysers, a rainbow, steam, and several trees rise from the horizon in Moran's "Castle Geyser."*

Viewing Guide for
American Landscape Artists

Look at the full-sized images on the DVD. Examine each image carefully, jotting down your initial impressions. To help you analyze the paintings of Thomas Moran and the photographs of William Henry Jackson in terms of certain design elements, refer to the details on page 731. You can also refer to the Elements of Design section of the Media Handbook (pages R94–R95) to review the visual art elements of color, shape, line, and texture. Then consider these questions to help you analyze the images.

NOW VIEW

FIRST VIEWING: Comprehension

1. **Identify** In both Grand Canyon images, what elements of nature do you see?

2. **Clarify** Which Grand Canyon image has people in it?

CLOSE VIEWING: Media Literacy

3. **Analyze Composition** In each of the Grand Canyon images, the artist chose to depict the widest possible view. Through this composition, what effect do you think each artist was trying to achieve?

4. **Compare Texture** Consider both Moran paintings. Which appears to have more texture? Explain your choice.

5. **Analyze Perspective** In the color painting "Castle Geyser" by Thomas Moran, find the horizon line. Name whatever objects you can that rise up from this line.

6. **Compare Images** Both the painting and the photograph of the geyser on this page have an otherworldly look and feel. Which image looks more alien to you? Support your response in terms of your view of

   - in the painting, the stark color contrast between the deep blue of the pool and the lighter tone of the sky

   - in the photograph, the placement of the camera and the lens to make the pool seem as large as possible

---

6. *In the painting, the stark color contrast between the dark pool and the light sky and earth show a formation that looks unnatural and invented. The wide pool in the photograph looks more realistic, since it includes such details such as trees, rocks, and steam—familiar, worldly features that can be seen in other places.*

Write or Discuss

Judge an Image The landscape paintings and photographs of this lesson not only inspired thousands to journey to the West but also inspired the protection of one of America's most striking natural regions. Among these four images, pick one that you think is the most interesting. In a short oral or written evaluation, describe what elements it has that make it a fine example of landscape art. If possible, include the image in your presentation. Base your criteria on these considerations:

- the **composition** and **perspective** in the paintings or the effect of the **depth of field** in the photographs
- the aim of Thomas Moran and William Henry Jackson to capture stunning scenes of natural beauty
- the aspects of the painting or photograph that especially appeal to you (for example, the specific subject matter, use or absence of color, overall mood or feeling)

COMMON CORE

RI 7 Integrate and evaluate multiple sources of information presented in different media or formats. **SL 5** Make strategic use of digital media in presentations to enhance understanding of findings, reasoning, and evidence and to add interest.

Produce Your Own Media

Create Your Personal Landscape Think of a favorite place. How would you represent it visually? Create a landscape image of your choice. It can be a photograph, a painting, a computer-generated image, or a drawing.

HERE'S HOW Decide what landscape you want to capture and which medium you want to use. Here are some things to keep in mind:

- Be aware of composition. What you show and don't show in an image defines your vision of the landscape. Is there a dominant element you want to focus on?
- Try to provide some texture to your image regardless of the medium you've chosen.
- Give your work a horizontal landscape orientation. Experiment with giving your image an illusion of depth. For a drawing or painting, determine where to position the lines that will establish the perspective. For a photograph, determine the depth of field by adjusting lenses or camera position.
- No matter what type of image you create, make notes on what your intentions were and how you planned to create it.

Media Tools THINK central

Go to **thinkcentral.com**. KEYWORD: HML11-733

Tech Tip

Use a software program to experiment with various effects.

Further Exploration

View More Photographs The equipment the early photographers used was quite unwieldy. Photographers had to carry their big box cameras and heavy film plates to their subjects, so you can imagine the rigors of filming a vast and remote landscape like the Grand Canyon.

Look at the early photographs on the DVD or research your own examples of early photography, and choose an image that most interests you.

MEDIA STUDY **733**

Produce Your Own Media

Rubric: Create Your Personal Landscape
A strong landscape should have

- a clear, dominant image shown by color, composition, or texture
- textural interest within the composition
- depth in the landscape created by lines or camera angle
- a clear, written explanation of the intention of the artwork and the methods that were used to create it

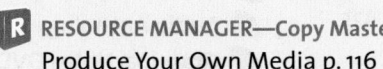 **RESOURCE MANAGER—Copy Master**
Produce Your Own Media p. 116

Assess and Reteach

Write or Discuss
COMMON CORE RI 7, SL 5

Judge an Image In their judgments, students should note the similarities between the works in terms of *composition, perspective, depth of field,* and *texture.* Students should also express an opinion about the piece of art, explaining why it is most interesting to them. For example, they may comment that the photography conveys less emotion but more visual accuracy, or that color intensifies the mood and feeling of the paintings in comparison to the photographs.

MEDIA STUDY WRAP–UP

Have students summarize what they have learned about analyzing photographs and paintings for techniques and message. Encourage students to use terms such as *composition, perspective, depth of field,* and *texture* in their summaries.

RETEACH

For students who are unable to apply the MediaStudy skills, select from these reteaching options:

- **Camera Shots** Provide students with photographs that show the textures of an image, such a smooth lake or a pebbly beach. Ask, How did photographers capture the texture of an image? *(They might use close-up photography or special lighting.)*
- **Editing** Provide students with a landscape picture or photograph. Have them analyze the image and select a smaller section to focus on. Have students explain how their "new" image changes the focal point or composition of the original.
- **Drawing** Ask students to draw simple stick pictures of a character in a landscape. In their simple drawings, have them draw and label a horizon line and a focal point.

Media Tools THINK central

Media study keywords point to **MediaScope**, a Web site that helps students strengthen media analysis and production skills.

Focus and Motivate

COMMON CORE FOCUS

RL 2 Determine two or more themes or central ideas of a text and analyze how they interact to produce a complex account. **RL 3** Analyze the impact of the author's choices regarding how to develop and relate elements of a story. **RL 4** Determine the meaning of words and phrases as they are used in the text, including figurative meanings; analyze the impact of specific word choices on meaning and tone, including words with multiple meanings. **RL 6** Analyze a case in which grasping point of view requires distinguishing what is directly stated in a text from what is really meant. **W 3b** Use narrative techniques, such as description and reflection, to develop characters. **L 1** Demonstrate command of the conventions of standard English grammar when writing. **L 3** Apply knowledge of language to make effective choices for meaning or style. **L 4d** Verify the preliminary determination of the meaning of a word. **L 6** Acquire and use accurately general academic words and phrases.

ABOUT THE AUTHOR

Point out that "The Open Boat" resulted from one of Crane's journeys as a war correspondent. Despite his status as a journalist, Crane also did the work of a crew member on the *Commodore*. His experiences on the journey contributed to his failing health.

COMMON CORE

RL 2 Determine two or more themes or central ideas of a text and analyze how they interact to produce a complex account. **RL 3** Analyze the impact of the author's choices regarding how to develop and relate elements of a story. **RL 4** Determine the meaning of words and phrases as they are used in the text, including figurative meanings; analyze the impact of specific word choices on meaning and tone, including words with multiple meanings.

DID YOU KNOW?

Stephen Crane . . .

- spent most of his two semesters in college playing baseball.
- claimed that his understanding of combat in *The Red Badge of Courage* came from watching football games.
- wrote powerful poetry, including "Do Not Weep, Maiden, for War Is Kind."

The Open Boat

Short Story by Stephen Crane

Meet the Author

Stephen Crane 1871–1900

When Crane's novel *The Red Badge of Courage* was published in 1895, it caused a literary sensation. Critics hailed its unromanticized portrayal of a young soldier's struggles during one battle of the Civil War. As one reviewer exclaimed, "The style is as rough as it is direct. . . . But the original power of the book is great enough to set a new fashion in literature." War veterans, unimpressed by literary fashion, were struck by the graphic depiction of combat. So vivid was the battlefield experience in the novel that they assumed the story was a factual eyewitness account. But the author was only 23 years old at the time and had not yet seen war. Such was the power of Crane's imagination that he was able in his short life to create works of great integrity as well as artistic force.

Living on the Edge Born in Newark, New Jersey, the youngest of 14 children, Stephen Crane came from a family of writers. His father, a Methodist minister, and his mother both wrote religious articles, and two of his brothers were journalists. A stint in military school nourished the teenage Crane's interest in the Civil War, but college life bored him. "Not that I disliked books," he insisted, but that "humanity was a much more interesting study." And study it he did—first as a freelance journalist living in the slums of New York City's Bowery, then as a reporter traveling in Mexico and the American Wild West, and finally as a war correspondent shipping out to hot spots in Cuba and Greece. Twelve years of living on the edge gave Crane material not only for numerous news articles but also for three novels, several volumes of poetry, and some of the best-known short stories in American literature, including "The Open Boat," "The Blue Hotel," and "The Bride Comes to Yellow Sky."

The Cost of Adventure Adventure often comes at a price. Biographers cite the deprivations of Crane's years in the New York slums, the dangers of traveling to far-off places, and his own neglect of his health as contributing to his death from tuberculosis at age 28. But Crane had matured far beyond his years. True to his early intentions, he was a great student of humanity, and he developed a philosophy described by one critic as a "bold and robust humanism." As a naturalist writer, Crane believed that nature was a powerful force that shaped our lives. But as a humanist, he also had faith in his fellow humans' ability to act responsibly and honestly.

Author Online

THINK central

Go to **thinkcentral.com**. KEYWORD: HML11-734

734

Selection Resources

See resources on the **Teacher One Stop DVD-ROM** and on **thinkcentral.com**.

 RESOURCE MANAGER UNIT 4

Plan and Teach, pp. 117–124
Summary, pp. 125–126†‡*
Text Analysis and Reading
  Skill, pp. 127–130†*
Vocabulary, pp. 131–133*
Grammar and Style, p. 136

DIAGNOSTIC AND SELECTION TESTS

Selection Tests, pp. 197–200

 BEST PRACTICES TOOLKIT

Word Squares, p. E10
Making Inferences, p. A13
Two-Column Chart, p. A25
Freewriting, p. C1
Three-Column Journal, p. B10
Sequence Chain, p. B21
Character Traits and Textual
  Evidence, p. D6

TECHNOLOGY

- Teacher One Stop DVD-ROM
- Student One Stop DVD-ROM
- Audio Anthology CD
- GrammarNotes DVD-ROM
- ExamView Test Generator
  on the **Teacher One Stop**

---

* Resources for Differentiation   † Also in Spanish   ‡ In Haitian dCreole and Vietnamese

TEXT ANALYSIS: NATURALISM

Naturalism is an offshoot of **realism,** the 19th-century literary movement that examines the effect of natural and social forces on the individual. While naturalism aims to depict people accurately, it tends toward pessimism by showing human beings at the mercy of the environment and their own instincts. With an emphasis on setting, theme, conflict, and irony, naturalism paints human destiny as beyond individual control.

Naturalist writers often chose **mythic situations,** retelling ancient stories from a naturalist perspective. For example, stories about individuals at the mercy of the ocean are included in the myths of many ancient cultures. "The Open Boat" is a naturalistic version of such a story. As you read, look for characteristics of naturalism in the story, and compare Crane's story with other tales about individuals lost at sea.

READING SKILL: ANALYZE DESCRIPTIVE LANGUAGE

Naturalist writers use vivid and detailed **descriptive language** in their study of human behavior. Effective description relies on various literary elements.

- **imagery**—descriptive words that create sensory experiences
- **figurative language**—language that goes beyond the literal to make a vivid comparison
- **tone**—a writer's attitude toward the subject
- **mood**—the feeling the writer creates for the reader

As you read, record examples of Crane's use of these elements.

▲ VOCABULARY IN CONTEXT

Match each vocabulary word in the first column with the word or phrase in the second column that is closest in meaning.

1. dearth		a. comply	
2. ingenuously		b. abnormality	
3. aberration		c. raucous	
4. acquiesce		d. compel	
5. motley		e. shortage	
6. epithet		f. relief	
7. respite		g. insulting name	
8. obstreperous		h. naively	
9. coerce		i. assorted	

 Complete the activities in your **Reader/Writer Notebook**.

Does NATURE play fair?

A lioness kills an antelope. An earthquake destroys one small town and leaves other nearby towns untouched. Diseases kill millions worldwide. Does this seem fair? Does nature stack the deck against certain creatures? As one of the leading writers in the naturalist movement, Stephen Crane addresses this issue in "The Open Boat."

DISCUSS With a small group, discuss how you explain the inequities found in nature. First, list some specific natural disasters or dangers that you know of. Then, discuss the reasons why each one may have happened the way it did.

735

Does NATURE play fair?

Ask the question and challenge students to consider the ways in which people have learned to control, adapt to, or use nature, and the ways in which nature continues to be beyond human control. Ask students to keep this balance in mind as they complete the *DISCUSS* activity.

TEXT ANALYSIS
COMMON CORE
RL 2
RL 3

● *Model the Skill:* NATURALISM

Read the following statements aloud and discuss how naturalists might react to them.

1. Some people are kind to the core.
2. You can be whatever you want to be.

Point out that naturalists would have agreed with the first statement but doubted the second because they believed that heredity determines behavior and potential.

READING SKILL
COMMON CORE
RL 4

■ *Model the Skill:* ANALYZE DESCRIPTIVE LANGUAGE

Illustrate the use of descriptive language by reading aloud this example:

> The sluggish sun slouched over the glassy lake, its rays rippling across the ice like a spider flinging out strands of web.

Point out imagery such as "sluggish" and "glassy," and figurative language including the simile comparing the sun to a spider. Tell students that the tone is negative, casting nature as lazy and threatening.

R RESOURCE MANAGER—Copy Master
Analyze Descriptive Language p. 129 (for student use while reading the selection)

VOCABULARY SKILL
COMMON CORE
L 4

▲ VOCABULARY IN CONTEXT

DIAGNOSE WORD KNOWLEDGE Have students complete Vocabulary in Context. Check their choices against the following:

aberration (ăb′ə-rā′shən) *n.* a disorder of the mind

acquiesce (ăk′wē-ĕs′) *v.* to comply or give in

coerce (kō-ûrs′) *v.* to force

dearth (dûrth) *n.* lack

epithet (ĕp′ə-thĕt′) *n.* an abusive word or phrase

ingenuously (ĭn-jĕn′yōō-əs-lē) *adv.* in a manner showing childlike innocence or simplicity

motley (mŏt′lē) *adj.* composed of diverse, often mismatched elements

obstreperous (ŏb-strĕp′ər-əs) *adj.* very noisy and unruly

opprobrious (ə-prō′brē-əs) *adj.* scornful; derogatory

respite (rĕs′pĭt) *n.* a period of rest or relief

PRETEACH VOCABULARY Use the following copy master to help students predict meanings.

R RESOURCE MANAGER—Copy Master
Vocabulary Study p. 131

Practice and Apply

SUMMARY

In this short story, Crane describes four men's experience escaping a shipwreck in a small boat. The ship's captain directs the men, who take turns rowing toward shore through a long day. Their troubles go unrecognized by those on land, and the men struggle to get to shore. After a long night contemplating eternity, they finally decide that they must chance it or die. They plunge shoreward, jumping from their capsizing boat to swim the final yards toward safety.

READ WITH A PURPOSE

Help students set a purpose for reading. Tell them to read for details about how the men help one another survive in the open boat.

Ⓐ *Model the Skill:*

DESCRIPTIVE LANGUAGE

Read the first paragraph aloud, emphasizing Crane's imagery of the "jagged" sea with waves pointed "like rocks" rushing constantly toward the boat.

Possible answer: Crane emphasizes the aspect of nature that endangers the men. The men are so focused on the threatening waves that they have no time to look at the sky (lines 3–4). The details that describe the waves—their color, size, shape, and motion—make it clear that the waves can kill the men, while the sky cannot (lines 4–8).

THE OPEN BOAT

STEPHEN CRANE

BACKGROUND On New Year's Eve, 1896, Stephen Crane was traveling on the ship *Commodore* to Cuba to report on an impending revolution. Loaded with ammunition and Cuban rebels, the ship was damaged by a sandbar outside of Jacksonville, Florida, and two days later sank in the open sea. Most survivors filled the lifeboats, but Crane and four others ended up in a much smaller boat. This is the story he wrote about his harrowing ordeal. It has been called one of the world's great short stories.

A tale intended to be after the fact. Being the experience of four men from the sunk steamer *Commodore*.

I

None of them knew the color of the sky. Their eyes glanced level, and were fastened upon the waves that swept toward them. These waves were the hue of slate, save for the tops, which were of foaming white, and all of the men knew the colors of the sea. The horizon narrowed and widened, and dipped and rose, and at all times its edge was jagged with waves that seemed thrust up in points like rocks. **Ⓐ**

Many a man ought to have a bathtub larger than the boat which here rode
10 upon the sea. These waves were most wrongfully and barbarously abrupt and tall, and each froth top was a problem in small boat navigation.

Analyze Visuals ▶
Look at the art on page 737. Apart from the men's appearance, what do the colors of the water and the sky suggest about their situation? Explain.

❶ Targeted Passage

Ⓐ DESCRIPTIVE LANGUAGE
The first paragraph is not really about the color of the sky. What does Crane emphasize by beginning the story this way?

German Shipwreck Survivors (image manipulated), Achille Beltrame. Engraving in Italian newspaper *La Domenica del Corriere*, February 1941. © Dagli Orti/The Art Archive.

DIFFERENTIATED INSTRUCTION

FOR ENGLISH LANGUAGE LEARNERS

Vocabulary Support Use Word Squares to teach these words: *decade* (line 26), *incline* (line 41), *occupy* (line 57), *occur* (line 190), *series* (line 286), *area* (line 307), *despite* (line 442).

📚 BEST PRACTICES TOOLKIT—Transparency
Word Squares p. E10

FOR STRUGGLING READERS

In combination with the *Audio Anthology CD*, use one or more Targeted Passages (pp. 736, 738, 741, 745, 749, 754, 758) to ensure that students focus on key story events and concepts. Targeted Passages are also good for English language learners.

❶ Targeted Passage [Lines 3–11]

This passage introduces the conflict of men against nature and sets the scene at sea.

- Where are the men? (lines 9–10)
- What dangers does nature present to the men? (lines 6–8)
- What problem do they have? (lines 10–11)

BACKGROUND

Cuban Rebellion Throughout the latter part of the 19th century, many Cubans sought to free themselves from the Spanish empire. Armed rebellion broke out between 1868 and 1878, and again in 1895. Some rebels were even based in the United States, and ships like the *Commodore* were used to run arms, ammunition, and expatriated Cuban soldiers to Cuba in support of the rebellion against Spain. Many Americans who had financial interests in Cuba read journalists' reports of events occurring there with interest. The United States finally intervened militarily in 1898 with the outbreak of the Spanish American War.

B NATURALISM

Possible answer: *Readers can infer that the "seven turned faces" were men who looked at the captain as the ship sank. The "stump of a topmast" was the captain's last view of the ship before it sank. These details tell readers that the captain watched his ship sink, and finds the memory traumatic.*

IF STUDENTS NEED HELP . . . Discuss a captain's responsibility to his ship and crew. Then help students complete a Making Inferences chart to explore how a captain might react to failing at that responsibility:

Story Details	I Know	I Infer
captain sees ship sink	captains take care of ships	captain upset that ship sank

 BEST PRACTICES TOOLKIT—Transparency Making Inferences p. A13

READING SKILL · COMMON CORE · RL 4

C DESCRIPTIVE LANGUAGE

Possible answer: *The bronco metaphor emphasizes that the boat is hard to ride and moves unpredictably. The men may easily be unseated and tossed into the sea.*

REVISIT THE BIG QUESTION

Does NATURE *play fair?*

Discuss Based on lines 43–52, how does nature, in the form of the waves, have an unfair advantage over the men? *Possible answer: The waves have no end and never tire, offering always "another . . . just as important" (lines 44–45). The men, by contrast, will tire soon.*

The cook squatted in the bottom and looked with both eyes at the six inches of gunwale[1] which separated him from the ocean. His sleeves were rolled over his fat forearms, and the two flaps of his unbuttoned vest dangled as he bent to bail out the boat. Often he said: "Gawd! That was a narrow clip." As he remarked it he invariably gazed eastward over the broken sea.

The oiler,[2] steering with one of the two oars in the boat, sometimes raised himself suddenly to keep clear of water that swirled in over the stern. It was a thin little oar and it seemed often ready to snap.

20 The correspondent, pulling at the other oar, watched the waves and wondered why he was there.

The injured captain, lying in the bow, was at this time buried in that profound dejection and indifference which comes, temporarily at least, to even the bravest and most enduring when, willy nilly, the firm fails, the army loses, the ship goes down. The mind of the master of a vessel is rooted deep in the timbers of her, though he command for a day or a decade, and this captain had on him the stern impression of a scene in the grays of dawn of seven turned faces, and later a stump of a topmast with a white ball on it that slashed to and fro at the waves, went low and lower, and down. Thereafter there was something strange in his voice.

30 Although steady, it was deep with mourning, and of a quality beyond oration or tears. **B**

"Keep 'er a little more south, Billie," said he.

"'A little more south,' sir," said the oiler in the stern.

A seat in this boat was not unlike a seat upon a bucking bronco, and, by the same token, a bronco is not much smaller. The craft pranced and reared, and plunged like an animal. As each wave came, and she rose for it, she seemed like a horse making at a fence outrageously high. The manner of her scramble over these walls of water is a mystic thing, and, moreover, at the top of them were ordinarily these problems in white water, the foam racing down from the summit

40 of each wave, requiring a new leap, and a leap from the air. Then, after scornfully bumping a crest, she would slide, and race, and splash down a long incline and arrive bobbing and nodding in front of the next menace. **C**

A singular disadvantage of the sea lies in the fact that after successfully surmounting one wave you discover that there is another behind it just as important and just as nervously anxious to do something effective in the way of swamping boats. In a ten-foot dinghy[3] one can get an idea of the resources of the sea in the line of waves that is not probable to the average experience, which is never at sea in a dinghy. As each slaty wall of water approached, it shut all else from the view of the men in the boat, and it was not difficult to imagine that

50 this particular wave was the final outburst of the ocean, the last effort of the grim water. There was a terrible grace in the move of the waves, and they came in silence, save for the snarling of the crests.

---

1. **gunwale** (gŭn'əl): the upper edge of a boat.
2. **oiler:** a worker who cares for the machinery in the engine room of a ship.
3. **dinghy** (dĭng'ē): a small open boat.

② Targeted Passage

Language Coach

Word Definitions *Willy nilly* (line 24) means "spontaneously" or "without regard to choice." How do you think the captain, the person ultimately responsible for the ship, would feel when his ship goes down?

B NATURALISM

Reread lines 22–31. What can you **infer** about the "seven turned faces" and the "stump of a topmast"? Consider what these things tell you about the captain's recent experience.

C DESCRIPTIVE LANGUAGE

Notice the descriptive language in lines 34–42. What quality of the boat does the bronco **metaphor** emphasize? Explain your answer.

DIFFERENTIATED INSTRUCTION

FOR STRUGGLING READERS

② Targeted Passage [Lines 12–31]

This passage introduces the protagonists.

- Who are the stranded men? (lines 12–22)
- What was the relationship of these men while they were on the ship? (lines 12–22)
- How has that relationship changed now? (lines 12–22)
- Where is the captain? What has happened to him? (lines 22–25)

FOR ENGLISH LANGUAGE LEARNERS

Language Coach

Word Definitions

Answer: Having something go so utterly wrong would be hard for the captain. He would be crushed—or feel numb—that it was not in his power to keep his crew and ship safe. Point out that *willy nilly* has the connotation of randomness. The captain's ship has sunk *willy nilly,* or without apparent cause or reason.

In the wan light, the faces of the men must have been gray. Their eyes must have glinted in strange ways as they gazed steadily astern. Viewed from a balcony, the whole thing would doubtlessly have been weirdly picturesque. But the men in the boat had no time to see it, and if they had had leisure there were other things to occupy their minds. The sun swung steadily up the sky, and they knew it was broad day because the color of the sea changed from slate to emerald green, streaked with amber lights, and the foam was like tumbling snow. The process of
60 the breaking day was unknown to them. They were aware only of this effect upon the color of the waves that rolled toward them.

In disjointed sentences the cook and the correspondent argued as to the difference between a lifesaving station and a house of refuge. The cook had said: "There's a house of refuge just north of the Mosquito Inlet Light, and as soon as they see us, they'll come off in their boat and pick us up."

"As soon as who see us?" said the correspondent.

"The crew," said the cook.

"Houses of refuge don't have crews," said the correspondent. "As I understand them, they are only places where clothes and grub are stored for the benefit of
70 shipwrecked people. They don't carry crews."

"Oh, yes, they do," said the cook.

"No, they don't," said the correspondent.

"Well, we're not there yet, anyhow," said the oiler, in the stern.

"Well," said the cook, "perhaps it's not a house of refuge that I'm thinking of as being near Mosquito Inlet Light. Perhaps it's a lifesaving station."

"We're not there yet," said the oiler, in the stern. **D**

II

As the boat bounced from the top of each wave, the wind tore through the hair of the hatless men, and as the craft plopped her stern down again the spray slashed past them. The crest of each of these waves was a hill, from the top of which the
80 men surveyed, for a moment, a broad tumultuous expanse, shining and wind-riven. It was probably splendid. It was probably glorious, this play of the free sea, wild with lights of emerald and white and amber.

"Bully good thing it's an on-shore wind,"[4] said the cook. "If not, where would we be? Wouldn't have a show."

"That's right," said the correspondent.

The busy oiler nodded his assent.

Then the captain, in the bow, chuckled in a way that expressed humor, contempt, tragedy, all in one. "Do you think we've got much of a show, now, boys?" said he.
90 Whereupon the three were silent, save for a trifle of hemming and hawing. To express any particular optimism at this time they felt to be childish and stupid, but they all doubtless possessed this sense of the situation in their mind. A young man thinks doggedly at such times. On the other hand, the ethics of their condition was decidedly against any open suggestion of hopelessness. So they were silent.

---

4. **on-shore wind:** wind that blows toward the shore.

THE OPEN BOAT   **739**

D **PRIMARY SOURCES**
Following this short story, you will find several newspaper accounts of the 1897 sinking of the *Commodore*. The article written by Stephen Crane, "Stephen Crane's Own Story" (page 765), is an excellent example of a **primary source**—an account of the disaster written by a participant in the event. Reread lines 62–76. Then, read Crane's newspaper article, and note the similarities you find between this literary work and the primary source document.

Language Coach

Formal Language
Whereupon is a formal word meaning "following afterward and as a result of." Read lines 87–94. Why are the men silent, and what are they responding to?

READING SKILL

D **PRIMARY SOURCES**
Discuss with students the differences between primary and secondary sources. Then lead a discussion about differences between factual and fictional accounts of the same, or similar, event. Read aloud lines 62–76, emphasizing the cook's need to believe in a rescue crew, and the oiler's pessimism. Then have a volunteer read aloud lines 103–142 from the article, "Stephen Crane's Own Story" on page 766. Discuss with students the similar details found in each account of the event.

Possible answer: Students should note that Crane's fictional story uses characters (the cook and correspondent) and place names (Mosquito Inlet) from the actual event reported in the primary source.

Extend the Discussion What effect does Crane's participation in the actual event have on the dramatic impact of his fictional account?

TIERED DISCUSSION PROMPTS

In lines 62–72, use these prompts to help students understand how the men's hopes and fears affect their conversation:

Connect Think about how hope and fear battle inside people during times of crisis. How does this help you understand the men's emotions? *Answers will vary but should show an understanding of the men's volatile emotions.*

Analyze Which dialogue indicates the men's hope that they will be saved? Which dialogue reveals their fears that they will drown? *Possible answers: The cook's claims of nearby help indicate hope (lines 64–65). The correspondent's doubt about houses of refuge is less hopeful (lines 68–70), and the oiler's repeated insistence that "we're not there yet" (lines 73, 76) hints at the fear that they won't get to shore at all.*

FOR ENGLISH LANGUAGE LEARNERS

Language Coach

Formal Language *Answer: It seems as if the men are not sure how to react to the captain's joke. They do not want to appear too optimistic or too pessimistic.* Offer students other examples of formal compound words such as *herewith, thereupon,* and *whereas,* and ask them where they think they would find such language today.

FOR STRUGGLING READERS

Comprehension Support Clarify Crane's meaning in lines 90–94. Explain that the men feel it would jeopardize their chances of rescue to speak their hopes aloud and also that as men they should not show such hope. They also feel that as men and sailors they should not speak their fear of dying aloud. Left unable to express either their hope or fear, they say nothing.

E Model the Skill:
NATURALISM

Remind students that naturalists considered nature to be indifferent to humans. Read aloud lines 101–103 to highlight the contrast between the men and the birds. Point out the descriptive details in line 105 that suggest a sinister aspect to the birds and nature.

Possible answer: *The author suggests nature's indifference by contrasting the gulls, so at home on the sea, and the men, so threatened by the waves (lines 99–103). The author suggests hostility, too, when the gull pesters the captain; and to shoo it away might capsize the boat (lines 108–114).*

REVISIT THE BIG QUESTION
Does NATURE
play fair?

Discuss Sometimes nature is kind, not hostile. How does nature help the men in lines 129–132? Does this make nature fair? Explain.
Possible answer: *The presence of seaweed mats assures the men that they are rowing toward the shore, where rescuers may spot them. Nature is random, rather than fair or unfair.*

"Oh, well," said the captain, soothing his children, "we'll get ashore all right."

But there was that in his tone which made them think, so the oiler quoth: "Yes! If this wind holds!"

The cook was bailing. "Yes! If we don't catch hell in the surf."

100 Canton flannel gulls[5] flew near and far. Sometimes they sat down on the sea, near patches of brown seaweed that rolled over the waves with a movement like carpets on a line in a gale. The birds sat comfortably in groups, and they were envied by some in the dinghy, for the wrath of the sea was no more to them than it was to a covey of prairie chickens a thousand miles inland. Often they came very close and stared at the men with black bead-like eyes. At these times they were uncanny and sinister in their unblinking scrutiny, and the men hooted angrily at them, telling them to be gone. One came, and evidently decided to alight on the top of the captain's head. The bird flew parallel to the boat and did not circle, but made short sidelong jumps in the air in chicken fashion. His black eyes were wistfully fixed upon the captain's head. "Ugly brute," said the oiler to the bird.

110 "You look as if you were made with a jackknife." The cook and the correspondent swore darkly at the creature. The captain naturally wished to knock it away with the end of the heavy painter,[6] but he did not dare do it, because anything resembling an emphatic gesture would have capsized this freighted boat, and so with his open hand, the captain gently and carefully waved the gull away. After it had been discouraged from the pursuit the captain breathed easier on account of his hair, and others breathed easier because the bird struck their minds at this time as being somehow gruesome and ominous. **E**

In the meantime the oiler and the correspondent rowed. And also they rowed.

They sat together in the same seat, and each rowed an oar. Then the oiler

120 took both oars; then the correspondent took both oars; then the oiler; then the correspondent. They rowed and they rowed. The very ticklish part of the business was when the time came for the reclining one in the stern to take his turn at the oars. By the very last star of truth, it is easier to steal eggs from under a hen than it was to change seats in the dinghy. First the man in the stern slid his hand along the thwart[7] and moved with care, as if he were of Sèvres.[8] Then the man in the rowing seat slid his hand along the other thwart. It was all done with the most extraordinary care. As the two sidled past each other, the whole party kept watchful eyes on the coming wave, and the captain cried: "Look out now! Steady there!"

The brown mats of seaweed that appeared from time to time were like islands,

130 bits of earth. They were traveling, apparently, neither one way nor the other. They were, to all intents, stationary. They informed the men in the boat that it was making progress slowly toward the land.

The captain, rearing cautiously in the bow, after the dinghy soared on a great swell, said that he had seen the lighthouse at Mosquito Inlet. Presently the cook

---

5. **canton flannel gulls:** gulls looking as if they were made of canton flannel, a heavy type of cotton that is soft on one side and ribbed on the other.

6. **painter:** a line used for towing or securing a boat.

7. **thwart:** a seat that extends across a boat.

8. **Sèvres:** a type of fine china made in Sèvres, France.

E NATURALISM
Reread lines 99–117. How does the author suggest the indifference or even hostility of nature in these lines?

DIFFERENTIATED INSTRUCTION

FOR STRUGGLING READERS

Make Inferences Clarify that the men's survival depends on many unknowns. Help students analyze these challenges by identifying the three if-then statements on pages 740–741. Point out that in two of the statements, readers must infer the "then" statement. Have students complete a Two-Column Chart to organize their ideas.

If . . .	Then . . .
"If this wind holds!" (line 97)	The men will get near shore and be rescued.
"If we don't catch hell in the surf." (line 98)	The boat will stay afloat so the men can be rescued.

BEST PRACTICES TOOLKIT—Transparency
Two-Column Chart p. A25

FOR ENGLISH LANGUAGE LEARNERS

Related Vocabulary In lines 99–117 Crane groups difficult words to create a mood of dread and fear: *uncanny, sinister, unblinking, ugly, brute, gruesome, ominous.* Share or elicit the meanings of these words; then have students arrange the words in a word web and discuss how they work together to create the mood.

remarked that he had seen it. The correspondent was at the oars, then, and for some reason he too wished to look at the lighthouse, but his back was toward the far shore and the waves were important, and for some time he could not seize an opportunity to turn his head. But at last there came a wave more gentle than the others, and when at the crest of it he swiftly scoured the western horizon.

140 "See it?" said the captain.

"No," said the correspondent, slowly, "I didn't see anything."

"Look again," said the captain. He pointed. "It's exactly in that direction."

At the top of another wave, the correspondent did as he was bid, and this time his eyes chanced on a small still thing on the edge of the swaying horizon. It was precisely like the point of a pin. It took an anxious eye to find a lighthouse so tiny.

"Think we'll make it, Captain?"

"If this wind holds and the boat don't swamp, we can't do much else," said the captain.

The little boat, lifted by each towering sea, and splashed viciously by the crests,
150 made progress that in the absence of seaweed was not apparent to those in her. She seemed just a wee thing wallowing, miraculously, top up, at the mercy of five oceans. Occasionally, a great spread of water, like white flames, swarmed into her. **Ⓕ**

"Bail her, cook," said the captain, serenely.

"All right, Captain," said the cheerful cook.

III

It would be difficult to describe the subtle brotherhood of men that was here established on the seas. No one said that it was so. No one mentioned it. But it dwelt in the boat, and each man felt it warm him. They were a captain, an oiler, a cook, and a correspondent, and they were friends, friends in a more curiously ironbound degree than may be common. The hurt captain, lying against the
160 water jar in the bow, spoke always in a low voice and calmly, but he could never command a more ready and swiftly obedient crew than the **motley** three of the dinghy. It was more than a mere recognition of what was best for the common safety. There was surely in it a quality that was personal and heartfelt. And after this devotion to the commander of the boat there was this comradeship that the correspondent, for instance, who had been taught to be cynical of men, knew even at the time was the best experience of his life. But no one said that it was so. No one mentioned it.

"I wish we had a sail," remarked the captain. "We might try my overcoat on the end of an oar and give you two boys a chance to rest." So the cook and the
170 correspondent held the mast and spread wide the overcoat. The oiler steered, and the little boat made good way with her new rig. Sometimes the oiler had to scull⁹ sharply to keep a sea from breaking into the boat, but otherwise sailing was a success.

Meanwhile the lighthouse had been growing slowly larger. It had now almost assumed color, and appeared like a little gray shadow on the sky. The man at the

---

9. **scull:** to propel a boat by rowing from side to side, reversing the oar at each turn.

---

③ Targeted Passage

Ⓕ NATURALISM
In lines 149–152, what images, words, and phrases suggest the overwhelming power of nature and the smallness of humanity?

motley (mŏt'lē) *adj.* composed of diverse, often mismatched elements

---

Ⓕ NATURALISM

Possible answer: The power of nature is suggested by the words "towering," "viciously," and "swarmed" and by the phrases "at the mercy of five oceans" and "a great spread of water, like white flames." The smallness of humanity is represented by the boat, which is "little" and "wee" and survives the sea "miraculously."

Extend the Discussion How are lines 153–154, which include the modifiers *serenely* and *cheerful*, a reaction to the description of the sea and the boat?

VOCABULARY   COMMON CORE
L 4

OWN THE WORD

motley: *Motley* has its origins from the Middle English use for "variegated cloth" as in the many colored costume of a court jester. The word refers to "composed of diverse, often mismatched elements." Ask students to write a sentence that shows an understanding of the meaning and use of the word. *Possible answers: The* motley *band of dogs roamed freely through the neighborhood. During the clothing drive, we gathered a* motley *assortment of garments.*

FOR STRUGGLING READERS

③ Targeted Passage [Lines 135–154]

This passage describes a key turning point in the men's efforts to survive.

- What is the correspondent looking for? What does he see? (line 136)
- What does the captain predict will happen to the men? (line 147)
- What is the men's mood now? (lines 153–154)

FOR ADVANCED LEARNERS/AP

Analyze Theme Lines 155–167 interrupt the plot to discuss the developing bonds among the men. Have students examine the key idea in the passage: ". . . there was this comradeship that the correspondent, for instance, who had been taught to be cynical of men, knew even at the time was the best experience of his life" (lines 164–166).

Ask students to consider these questions:

- What circumstances led to the developing bonds?
- How can an ordeal at sea be "the best experience" of a life?

Have students explore their responses with the Freewriting strategy, then write and share a brief analysis of the passage's theme.

 **BEST PRACTICES TOOLKIT**
Freewriting p. C1

Does NATURE *play fair?*

Discuss In lines 185–188, the wind dies down. How does this change in nature work against the men? How does it help them? *Possible answer: When the wind dies down, it no longer pushes the rigged sail, so the oiler and the correspondent must begin to row again (line 188). On the other hand, when the wind dies down, the cook and the correspondent are no longer "obliged to slave in order to hold high the oar" (line 186).*

Analyze Visuals

Activity Ask students how the viewpoint of the painting and the meeting of sky and sea at the horizon help readers understand what the men see "at the top of each wave." *Possible answer: The viewpoint of the painting is from atop a wave. This gives viewers a better view of the horizon. Because the land in the story is so far away and so thinly spread on the horizon, the men can only see it from atop a wave.*

About the Art The son of immigrants, Thomas Moran (1837–1926) traveled the nation and frontier to sketch and paint wonders such as the Grand Canyon, Yellowstone, and the Rockies. Later, Moran became fascinated by seascapes as well as landscapes. He moved to Long Island, built a studio, and observed the moods of the sea. The location gave him many opportunities to observe and paint the shipwrecks along the coast, capturing the power of the sea.

The Much Resounding Sea (1884), Thomas Moran. 25″ × 62″.

oars could not be prevented from turning his head rather often to try for a glimpse of this little gray shadow.

At last, from the top of each wave the men in the tossing boat could see land. Even as the lighthouse was an upright shadow on the sky, this land seemed but a
180 long black shadow on the sea. It certainly was thinner than paper. "We must be about opposite New Smyrna,"[10] said the cook, who had coasted this shore often in schooners. "Captain, by the way, I believe they abandoned that lifesaving station there about a year ago."

"Did they?" said the captain.

The wind slowly died away. The cook and the correspondent were not now obliged to slave in order to hold high the oar. But the waves continued their old

---

10. **New Smyrna:** New Smyrna Beach, a city on the eastern coast of Florida, about 15 miles south of Daytona Beach.

DIFFERENTIATED INSTRUCTION

FOR STRUGGLING READERS

Concept Support: Tone After students read lines 180–184, discuss how tone can reveal meaning beyond a person's literal words. For example, here the men speak in a flat, emotionless tone that belies the damaging impact of their words. Help students understand that the men are probably trying to downplay their worry, both to each other and themselves.

FOR ENGLISH LANGUAGE LEARNERS

Vocabulary: Outdated Forms Tell students that *woundily* (line 188) is not in use today. Students can build meaning, however, by linking the word to other familiar words. Have students make a cluster diagram, placing *woundily* in the center and more familiar words such as *wound* or *wounded* on the outside. Point out that *wound* can be both verb and noun.

impetuous swooping at the dinghy, and the little craft, no longer under way, struggled woundily over them. The oiler or the correspondent took the oars again.

Shipwrecks are *apropos* of nothing. If men could only train for them
190 and have them occur when the men had reached pink condition, there would be less drowning at sea. Of the four in the dinghy none had slept any time worth mentioning for two days and two nights previous to embarking in the dinghy, and in the excitement of clambering about the deck of a foundering[11] ship they had also forgotten to eat heartily. **G**

For these reasons, and for others, neither the oiler nor the correspondent was fond of rowing at this time. The correspondent wondered **ingenuously** how in the name of all that was sane could there be people who thought it amusing to row a boat. It was not an amusement; it was a diabolical punishment, and even

G NATURALISM
In lines 189–194, the author uses **verbal irony**, suggesting something different from what is literally meant. In this paragraph, what is Crane suggesting about the timing of shipwrecks? Explain.

ingenuously
(ĭn-jĕn′yo͞o-əs-lē) *adv.* in a manner showing childlike innocence or simplicity

---

11. **foundering:** sinking.

THE OPEN BOAT **743**

TIERED DISCUSSION PROMPTS
In lines 178–196, use these prompts to help students understand the men's worsening situation:

Summarize What weather change has happened? *Possible answer: The wind that had been pushing the boat dies away.*

Synthesize How does the need for team-work apply to the men as well as to other life-threatening situations? *Possible answer: Teamwork requires that individuals work together for the common good. The men must take turns rowing and must help each other stay focused and hopeful in order to survive. This is true in most life-threatening situations involving groups; all members must work together to achieve survival.*

TEXT ANALYSIS — COMMON CORE — RL 2 RL 3

G NATURALISM

Possible answer: Crane is suggesting that the timing of shipwrecks is unpredictable and random. Here the wreck has happened at the worst possible time, when the men are already exhausted and weak. If people knew they would shortly be shipwrecked, Crane implies, they would eat well, get a good night's sleep, and be ready.

Extend the Discussion What grim humor does the verbal irony in lines 193–194 contain?

VOCABULARY — COMMON CORE — L 4

OWN THE WORD

ingenuously: Have students create a semantic web for the word *ingenuously.* Write the word in the center circle along with the given definition, "manner showing childlike innocence." Draw spider legs out from the center circle and have students use a thesaurus to find appropriate synonyms to complete the web. *Possible answers: genuinely, honestly, openheartedly, naturally, directly, frankly*

FOR RELUCTANT READERS
Connect to the Text "The Open Boat" describes men who are thrown together by fate, yet grow to respect their different abilities. Ask students to consider how team-work can bring out the best in people. Have students brainstorm a list of qualities that arise from teamwork. Then have a discussion about the pros and cons of working as a team, as compared to working as individuals.

REVIST THE BIG QUESTION

Does NATURE *play fair?*

Discuss Compare the descriptions of land in lines 207–208 and line 216. What do the two descriptions have in common? How do they convey the ways nature can support people?
Possible answer: *The land appears "Slowly" (line 207) and "Slowly and beautifully" (line 216), almost like a plant growing out of the sea. Details that stand for the men's survival—trees and sand—become visible. The land conveys nature's support by offering the men hope and a chance for survival.*

READING SKILL   **COMMON CORE**   **RL 4**

 DESCRIPTIVE LANGUAGE

Possible answer: *The author calls the men "waifs" (line 232), implying that they are like small, helpless children, and says that they "rode impudently in their little boat" (line 232), as if they are boldly disregarding nature's power. They smoke their cigars as if celebrating an "impending rescue" (line 233) and "judged well and ill of all men"(line 234), as if they are in a position to do so. This language suggests that the men may have relaxed too soon.*

VOCABULARY   **COMMON CORE**   **L 4**

OWN THE WORD

aberration: Tell students that *aberration* has various definitions that refer to something being "abnormal or unexpected." The story uses the word to describe "a disorder of the mind." Synonyms include *irregularity, rambling, lapsing, craziness, dementia, delusion, derangement.*

---

a genius of mental **aberrations** could never conclude that it was anything but a
200 horror to the muscles and a crime against the back. He mentioned to the boat in general how the amusement of rowing struck him, and the weary-faced oiler smiled in full sympathy. Previously to the foundering, by the way, the oiler had worked double watch in the engine room of the ship.

"Take her easy, now, boys," said the captain. "Don't spend yourselves. If we have to run a surf[12] you'll need all your strength, because we'll sure have to swim for it. Take your time."

Slowly the land arose from the sea. From a black line it became a line of black and a line of white—trees and sand. Finally, the captain said that he could make out a house on the shore. "That's the house of refuge, sure," said the cook.
210 "They'll see us before long, and come out after us."

The distant lighthouse reared high. "The keeper ought to be able to make us out now, if he's looking through a glass," said the captain. "He'll notify the lifesaving people."

"None of those other boats could have got ashore to give word of the wreck," said the oiler, in a low voice. "Else the lifeboat would be out hunting us."

Slowly and beautifully the land loomed out of the sea. The wind came again. It had veered from the northeast to the southeast. Finally, a new sound struck the ears of the men in the boat. It was the low thunder of the surf on the shore. "We'll never be able to make the lighthouse now," said the captain. "Swing her head a
220 little more north, Billie."

"'A little more north' sir," said the oiler.

Whereupon the little boat turned her nose once more down the wind, and all but the oarsman watched the shore grow. Under the influence of this expansion doubt and direful apprehension was leaving the minds of the men. The management of the boat was still most absorbing, but it could not prevent a quiet cheerfulness. In an hour, perhaps, they would be ashore.

Their backbones had become thoroughly used to balancing in the boat and they now rode this wild colt of a dinghy like circus men. The correspondent thought that he had been drenched to the skin, but happening to feel in the top
230 pocket of his coat, he found therein eight cigars. Four of them were soaked with seawater; four were perfectly scatheless. After a search, somebody produced three dry matches, and thereupon the four waifs rode impudently in their little boat, and with an assurance of an impending rescue shining in their eyes, puffed at the big cigars and judged well and ill of all men. Everybody took a drink of water.

IV

"Cook," remarked the captain, "there don't seem to be any signs of life about your house of refuge."

"No," replied the cook. "Funny they don't see us!"

A broad stretch of lowly coast lay before the eyes of the men. It was of dunes topped with dark vegetation. The roar of the surf was plain, and sometimes they

---

12. **run a surf:** row through the surf to get to shore.

aberration (ăb′ə-rā′shən)
n. a disorder of the mind

H DESCRIPTIVE LANGUAGE
Reread lines 227–234. Cite examples of the author's language that suggests the assurance of the men might be premature.

DIFFERENTIATED INSTRUCTION

FOR STRUGGLING READERS

Comprehension Support Crane's sentences are complex and sometimes include archaic words. Model these strategies for paraphrasing difficult passages:

- Use a dictionary and thesaurus to define unfamiliar words and replace them with more familiar synonyms.

- Using punctuation such as semicolons or commas as a guide, break long, complicated sentences into shorter, simpler sentences that can be more easily paraphrased.

- Identify the main idea and supporting details and list these in outline form.

- Build a paraphrase by organizing the short paraphrase sentence to fit the outline's arrangement of ideas.

240 could see the white lip of a wave as it spun up the beach. A tiny house was blocked out black upon the sky. Southward, the slim lighthouse lifted its little gray length.

Tide, wind, and waves were swinging the dinghy northward. "Funny they don't see us," said the men.

The surf's roar here dulled, but its tone was, nevertheless, thunderous and mighty. As the boat swam over the great rollers, the men sat listening to this roar. "We'll swamp sure," said everybody.

> It is fair to say here that there was not a lifesaving station within twenty miles in either direction, but the men did not know this fact and in consequence they made dark and **opprobrious** remarks concerning the eyesight of the nation's
> 250 lifesavers. Four scowling men sat in the dinghy and surpassed records in the invention of **epithets.**
>
> "Funny they don't see us."
>
> The lightheartedness of a former time had completely faded. To their sharpened minds it was easy to conjure pictures of all kinds of incompetency and blindness and, indeed, cowardice. There was the shore of the populous land, and it was bitter and bitter to them that from it came no sign. ❶
>
> "Well," said the captain, ultimately, "I suppose we'll have to make a try for ourselves. If we stay out here too long, we'll none of us have strength left to swim after the boat swamps."
>
> 260 And so the oiler, who was at the oars, turned the boat straight for the shore. There was a sudden tightening of muscles. There was some thinking.

"If we don't all get ashore—" said the captain. "If we don't all get ashore, I suppose you fellows know where to send news of my finish?"

They then briefly exchanged some addresses and admonitions. As for the reflections of the men, there was a great deal of rage in them. Perchance they might be formulated thus: "If I am going to be drowned—if I am going to be drowned—if I am going to be drowned, why, in the name of the seven mad gods who rule the sea,[13] was I allowed to come thus far and contemplate sand and trees? Was I brought here merely to have my nose dragged away as I was about to nibble
270 the sacred cheese of life? It is preposterous. If this old ninny-woman, Fate, cannot do better than this, she should be deprived of the management of men's fortunes. She is an old hen who knows not her intention. If she has decided to drown me, why did she not do it in the beginning and save me all this trouble. The whole affair is absurd. . . . But, no, she cannot mean to drown me. She dare not drown me. She cannot drown me. Not after all this work." Afterward the man might have had an impulse to shake his fist at the clouds. "Just you drown me, now, and then hear what I call you!" ❸

The billows that came at this time were more formidable. They seemed always just about to break and roll over the little boat in a turmoil of foam. There was
280 a preparatory and long growl in the speech of them. No mind unused to the sea would have concluded that the dinghy could ascend these sheer heights in time.

---

13. **seven mad . . . the sea:** possibly a reference to the gods of the seven major seas of the world.

THE OPEN BOAT **745**

---

opprobrious (ə-prō′brē-əs) *adj.* scornful; derogatory

epithet (ĕp′ə-thĕt′) *n.* an abusive word or phrase

④ **Targeted Passage**

❶ **NATURALISM**
Dramatic irony is the technique of allowing the reader to know more than the characters do about their own situation. What does the author emphasize with his use of dramatic irony in lines 247–256?

❸ **NATURALISM**
Reread lines 264–277. What techniques does the author use here to suggest the indifference or hostility of nature?

In lines 304–308, use these prompts to help students relate to the physical struggles of the oarsmen:

Connect Have you or someone you know ever been so exhausted that you could sleep anywhere, no matter how uncomfortable the setting? *Accept all thoughtful responses.*

Evaluate Is it believable that the men could sleep through their pain, the uncomfortable and moving boat, and the cold seawater drenching them? Explain. *Possible answer: Yes. The men are so exhausted and have worked so hard to overcome their pain that they can sleep through anything.*

obstreperous: Remind students that *obstreperous* is an adjective used to describe something that is "very noisy and unruly." Have students reread the sentence containing this word and describe the scene portrayed. *Possible answer: An exhausted man lies in a boat with his head on a seat, just inches from the edge. The sea is rough and noisy, and occasionally, a wave sweeps over him with a roar, drenching him as it fills the boat.*

The shore was still afar. The oiler was a wily surfman. "Boys," he said, swiftly, "she won't live there minutes more and we're too far out to swim. Shall I take her to sea again, Captain?"

"Yes! Go ahead!" said the captain.

This oiler, by a series of quick miracles, and fast and steady oarsmanship, turned the boat in the middle of the surf and took her safely to sea again.

There was a considerable silence as the boat bumped over the furrowed sea to deeper water. Then somebody in gloom spoke. "Well, anyhow, they must have
290 seen us from the shore by now."

The gulls went in slanting flight up the wind toward the gray desolate east. A squall, marked by dingy clouds, and clouds brick-red, like smoke from a burning building, appeared from the southeast.

"What do you think of those lifesaving people? Ain't they peaches?"

"Funny they haven't seen us."

"Maybe they think we're out here for sport! Maybe they think we're fishin'. Maybe they think we're damned fools."

It was a long afternoon. A changed tide tried to force them southward, but wind and wave said northward. Far ahead, where coastline, sea, and sky formed
300 their mighty angle, there were little dots which seemed to indicate a city on the shore.

"St. Augustine?"[14]

The captain shook his head. "Too near Mosquito Inlet."

And the oiler rowed, and then the correspondent rowed. Then the oiler rowed. It was a weary business. The human back can become the seat of more aches and pains than are registered in books for the composite anatomy of a regiment. It is a limited area, but it can become the theatre of innumerable muscular conflicts, tangles, wrenches, knots, and other comforts.

"Did you ever like to row, Billie?" asked the correspondent.
310 "No," said the oiler. "Hang it."

When one exchanged the rowing seat for a place in the bottom of the boat, he suffered a bodily depression that caused him to be careless of everything save an obligation to wiggle one finger. There was cold seawater swashing to and fro in the boat, and he lay in it. His head, pillowed on a thwart, was within an inch of the swirl of a wave crest, and sometimes a particularly **obstreperous** sea came inboard and drenched him once more. But these matters did not annoy him. It is almost certain that if the boat had capsized he would have tumbled comfortably out upon the ocean as if he felt sure that it was a great soft mattress.

"Look! There's a man on the shore!"
320 "Where?"

"There! See 'im? See 'im?"

"Yes, sure! He's walking along."

"Now he's stopped. Look! He's facing us!"

"He's waving at us!"

---

14. **St. Augustine:** a city about 65 miles north of New Smyrna Beach, along the northeastern coast of Florida.

Figurative Language
Peaches (line 294) is an example of figurative language, language that communicates meaning beyond the literal meaning of the words. Here, *peaches* means "people who have peachlike qualities —sweet, wonderful." Read lines 294–297. What do the men think of the people?

obstreperous
(ŏb-strĕp′ər-əs) *adj.* very noisy and unruly

FOR STRUGGLING READERS

Read Dialogue Students sometimes read short lines of dialogue so quickly that they lose track of the events described. Organize students in groups of four to read the dialogue in lines 319–351 aloud. Allow students to choose which lines each will speak, since no dialogue tags identify the speakers, and then provide these instructions to guide students:

- Omit lines 329–333, which are not dialogue.
- Imagine the situation. Is rescue at hand or not? How would the men say each line under these terrible circumstances?
- Decide as a group where pauses and breaks in the dialogue would occur as the men watched the people on shore.

After groups finalize and practice their readings, have them present to the class.

FOR ENGLISH LANGUAGE LEARNERS

Figurative Language

The men use the word "peaches" ironically, since they are angry that the people on shore are not helping them. Provide students with other examples of figurative language relating to food and have students determine their meaning: "bowl of cherries," "apple of her eye," "a cupcake," "a lemon."

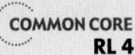

"So he is! By thunder!"

"Ah, now, we're all right! Now we're all right! There'll be a boat out here for us in half an hour."

"He's going on. He's running. He's going up to that house there."

330 The remote beach seemed lower than the sea, and it required a searching glance to discern the little black figure. The captain saw a floating stick and they rowed to it. A bath towel was by some weird chance in the boat, and, tying this on the stick, the captain waved it. The oarsman did not dare turn his head, so he was obliged to ask questions.

"What's he doing now?"

"He's standing still again. He's looking, I think. . . . There he goes again. Toward the house. . . . Now he's stopped again."

"Is he waving at us?"

"No, not now! He was, though."

"Look! There comes another man!"

340 "He's running."

"Look at him go, would you."

"Why, he's on a bicycle. Now he's met the other man. They're both waving at us. Look!"

"There comes something up the beach."

"What the devil is that thing?"

"Why, it looks like a boat."

"Why, certainly it's a boat."

"No, it's on wheels."

"Yes, so it is. Well, that must be the lifeboat. They drag them along shore on 350 a wagon."

"That's the lifeboat, sure."

"No, by——it's—it's an omnibus."[15]

"I tell you it's a lifeboat."

"It is not! It's an omnibus. I can see it plain. See? One of those big hotel omnibuses."

"By thunder, you're right. It's an omnibus, sure as fate. What do you suppose they are doing with an omnibus? Maybe they are going around collecting the lifecrew, hey?"

"That's it, likely. Look! There's a fellow waving a little black flag. He's standing 360 on the steps of the omnibus. There come those two other fellows. Now they're all talking together. Look at the fellow with the flag. Maybe he ain't waving it!"

"That ain't a flag, is it? That's his coat. Why, certainly, that's his coat."

"So it is. It's his coat. He's taken it off and is waving it around his head. But would you look at him swing it!"

"Oh, say, there isn't any lifesaving station there. That's just a winter resort hotel omnibus that has brought over some of the boarders to see us drown."

"What's that idiot with the coat mean? What's he signaling, anyhow?"

"It looks as if he were trying to tell us to go north. There must be a lifesaving

---

15. **omnibus:** bus. At this time, a bus would have been pulled by horses.

REVISIT THE BIG QUESTION
Does NATURE
play fair?

Discuss In lines 329–369, how does nature make it hard for the men in the boat to see or hear the shore, and thus create obstacles that keep them from communicating with the people on the shore? How does nature help the men communicate? *Possible answer: Nature presents two main obstacles to communication. First, the beach is "remote" (line 329) because the men have been kept from the shore by the surf. Second, the sound of the sea is loud, so shouting across the distance is not possible. But nature helps the men by providing a stick they can tie the towel to.*

FOR ADVANCED LEARNERS/AP

Analyze Dialogue Have students list examples of punctuation and style in lines 319–367 in a Three-Column Journal. Then, ask pairs to discuss:

- the frequent use of exclamation points
- the difference between dashes and ellipses and how each affects spoken language
- the increasing informality of the language

Exclamation Points	Dashes/ Ellipses	Informality
"Look!" "There!" "Yes, sure!"	Ellipses: Lines 335–336 Dashes: Line 352	"ain't" (line 361) mild oath "idiot" (line 367)

Have students also consider how the lack of dialogue tags affects readers' understanding. Invite pairs to share their charts and analysis with the class.

 **BEST PRACTICES TOOLKIT—Transparency**
Three-Column Journal p. B10

Analyze Visuals

Activity Ask students to try, as the men in the boat repeatedly had to do, to discern what is on the horizon at the top of the painting. Have pairs compare their descriptions. Then discuss why it is difficult to determine what is on the horizon and ask students what skills they must use to guess what the brown form in the center top is. *Possible answers: There appears to be a boat on the horizon. It is difficult to discern the image because it is small and blends in to the horizon. Viewers must refer to mental images of what a boat looks like and contrast the brown image with the colors of the surrounding sky and water in forming a guess about the brown object.*

About the Art Like the men in the boat, impressionist painter Edouard Manet (1832–1883) was fascinated by the endless motion of the sea and attempted to capture it in the short, broken brushstrokes of the impressionist style. Impressionists tried to capture the way light illuminated and re-flected off objects, and the naturally reflective surface of the water gave them opportunities to perfect this technique.

The Escape of Henri de Rochefort, March 20, 1874 (1880–1881), Edouard Manet. Oil on canvas, 80 cm × 73 cm. Musée d'Orsay, Paris. © Bridgeman Art Library.

station up there."

370   "No! He thinks we're fishing. Just giving us a merry hand. See? Ah, there, Willie."

"Well, I wish I could make something out of those signals. What do you suppose he means?"

"He don't mean anything. He's just playing."

"Well, if he'd just signal us to try the surf again, or to go to sea and wait, or go north, or go south, or go to hell—there would be some reason in it. But look at him. He just stands there and keeps his coat revolving like a wheel. The ass!"

"There come more people."

"Now there's quite a mob. Look! Isn't that a boat?"

748   UNIT 4: REGIONALISM AND NATURALISM

DIFFERENTIATED INSTRUCTION

FOR STRUGGLING READERS

Comprehension Support Use these questions to help students understand the men's confusion as they try to interpret the waving from shore:

- What do the men hope the waving means?
- What possible meanings for the waving do some of the men suggest?
- How do the men respond to the waving man's ineffective communication?

FOR ENGLISH LANGUAGE LEARNERS

Comprehension: Self–Monitor Note and clarify difficult elements in lines 396–397: *Holy smoke,* an idiom; *impious,* a challenging word; *monkeying,* animal metaphor; *flounder,* animal metaphor. Remind students to use fellow English learners as resources for understanding. Then have groups paraphrase the lines.

380 "Where? Oh, I see where you mean. No, that's no boat."

"That fellow is still waving his coat."

"He must think we like to see him do that. Why don't he quit it. It don't mean anything."

"I don't know. I think he is trying to make us go north. It must be that there's a lifesaving station there somewhere."

"Say, he ain't tired yet. Look at 'im wave."

"Wonder how long he can keep that up. He's been revolving his coat ever since he caught sight of us. He's an idiot. Why aren't they getting men to bring a boat out. A fishing boat—one of those big yawls[16]—could come out here all right.
390 Why don't he do something?"

"Oh, it's all right, now."

"They'll have a boat out here for us in less than no time, now that they've seen us."

A faint yellow tone came into the sky over the low land. The shadows on the sea slowly deepened. The wind bore coldness with it, and the men began to shiver.

"Holy smoke!" said one, allowing his voice to express his impious mood, "if we keep on monkeying out here! If we've got to flounder out here all night!"

"Oh, we'll never have to stay here all night! Don't you worry. They've seen us now, and it won't be long before they'll come chasing out after us."

400 The shore grew dusky. The man waving a coat blended gradually into this gloom, and it swallowed in the same manner the omnibus and the group of people. The spray, when it dashed uproariously over the side, made the voyagers shrink and swear like men who were being branded. **K**

"I'd like to catch the chump who waved the coat. I feel like soaking him one, just for luck."

"Why? What did he do?"

"Oh, nothing, but then he seemed so damn cheerful."

In the meantime the oiler rowed, and then the correspondent rowed, and then the oiler rowed. Gray-faced and bowed forward, they mechanically, turn by turn,
410 plied the leaden oars. The form of the lighthouse had vanished from the southern horizon, but finally a pale star appeared, just lifting from the sea. The streaked saffron in the west passed before the all-merging darkness, and the sea to the east was black. The land had vanished, and was expressed only by the low and drear thunder of the surf.

"If I am going to be drowned—if I am going to be drowned—if I am going to be drowned, why, in the name of the seven mad gods who rule the sea, was I allowed to come thus far and contemplate sand and trees? Was I brought here merely to have my nose dragged away as I was about to nibble the sacred cheese of life?" **L**
420 The patient captain, drooped over the water jar, was sometimes obliged to speak to the oarsman.

---

16. **yawls:** sailboats with two masts.

---

⑤ Targeted Passage

K DESCRIPTIVE LANGUAGE
What mood is established by the **description** in lines 394–403?

L NATURALISM
Reread lines 415–419. There is something almost comical about the repeated image of a man "about to nibble the sacred cheese of life." Why do you think Crane might have chosen to strike such a **tone** in reference to such a serious topic? Explain.

REVISIT THE BIG QUESTION

Does NATURE play fair?

Discuss In lines 394–414, the men complete their first day in the boat. What new threats will nature pose as night arrives? **Possible answer:** Night brings colder temperatures to the soaked, exhausted men (line 395). Their already limited vision will be cut even further as the shore and waving man disappear (lines 400–402). The darkness means that the men cannot see the waves to prepare for them (lines 402–403).

READING SKILL

COMMON CORE
RL 4

K DESCRIPTIVE LANGUAGE

Possible answer: The description of the man on shore establishes a mood of growing frustration as what seems like a good sign— the men in the boat have been sighted— turns out to be nothing but a man waving to a passing boat. The men cannot at first believe that the man on shore does not react to their plight, and as they wonder what the man is up to, they become aware that the sun is setting (lines 400–402).

TEXT ANALYSIS

COMMON CORE
RL 2
RL 3

L NATURALISM

Possible answer: The humorous tone is ironic, highlighting the indifference of nature to the fate of the individual by suggesting that people are no more important to nature than a mouse.

FOR STRUGGLING READERS

⑤ Targeted Passage [Lines 400–414]

In this passage, the men grow weary and realize that help is not coming soon.

- Does the waving man get help for the stranded men? (lines 400–402)
- Why is it getting cold and dark? (lines 410–414)
- What are the conditions on the boat as night falls? (lines 407–410)

Develop Reading Fluency Explain that conditions in this passage gradually change from positive to negative. Have students conduct a Partner Reading, starting with line 398. Ask students to practicing reading with the appropriate vocal inflection, beginning with the hopeful quotation at the beginning and ending with "low and drear" thunder of line 414. Tell partners to make a clear transition in tone from the beginning to the end of the passage.

In lines 439–456, use these prompts to help students understand the conditions in the little boat:

Restate What are the men doing? *Answer: They are huddled in the bottom of the boat, sleeping in uncomfortable positions. Only the person rowing is awake.*

Analyze What details suggest that the men's physical condition is deteriorating? In contrast, what does the passage reveal about their mental state? *Possible answer: The men are now so tired that they can no longer fight off sleep. They are hardly roused even by large waves crashing into the boat (lines 442–445) and the oiler actually falls asleep while rowing (lines 450–451). Mentally, however, the men have maintained a sense of dignity and compassion for each other. They speak politely and even "meekly" to each other (line 453).*

Synthesize Identify the repeated references to sleep that mark this passage. Has sleep become a friend or a foe to the men? What will happen if the men all fall asleep? *Possible answer: The author refers to sleep in lines 445, 448, 450–451, and 455–456. Sleep has become both friend and foe to the men. They desperately need rest, but any time the oarsman falls asleep, they are in greater danger than ever. If the men all fall asleep, the boat may drift out to sea and the men will likely die.*

"Keep her head up! Keep her head up!"

"'Keep her head up,' sir." The voices were weary and low.

This was surely a quiet evening. All save the oarsman lay heavily and listlessly in the boat's bottom. As for him, his eyes were just capable of noting the tall black waves that swept forward in a most sinister silence, save for an occasional subdued growl of a crest.

The cook's head was on a thwart, and he looked without interest at the water under his nose. He was deep in other scenes. Finally he spoke. "Billie," he 430 murmured, dreamfully, "what kind of pie do you like best?"

V

"Pie," said the oiler and the correspondent, agitatedly. "Don't talk about those things, blast you!"

"Well," said the cook, "I was just thinking about ham sandwiches, and—"

A night on the sea in an open boat is a long night. As darkness settled finally, the shine of the light, lifting from the sea in the south, changed to full gold. On the northern horizon a new light appeared, a small bluish gleam on the edge of the waters. These two lights were the furniture of the world. Otherwise there was nothing but waves.

Two men huddled in the stern, and distances were so magnificent in the dinghy 440 that the rower was enabled to keep his feet partly warmed by thrusting them under his companions. Their legs indeed extended far under the rowing seat until they touched the feet of the captain forward. Sometimes, despite the efforts of the tired oarsman, a wave came piling into the boat, an icy wave of the night, and the chilling water waked them anew. They would twist their bodies for a moment and groan, and sleep the dead sleep once more, while the water in the boat gurgled about them as the craft rocked.

The plan of the oiler and the correspondent was for one to row until he lost the ability, and then arouse the other from his seawater couch in the bottom of the boat.

450 The oiler plied the oars until his head drooped forward, and the overpowering sleep blinded him. And he rowed yet afterward. Then he touched a man in the bottom of the boat, and called his name. "Will you spell me for a little while?" he said, meekly.

"Sure, Billie," said the correspondent, awakening and dragging himself to a sitting position. They exchanged places carefully, and the oiler, cuddling down in the seawater at the cook's side, seemed to go to sleep instantly.

The particular violence of the sea had ceased. The waves came without snarling. The obligation of the man at the oars was to keep the boat headed so that the tilt of the rollers would not capsize her, and to preserve her from filling when the 460 crests rushed past. The black waves were silent and hard to be seen in the darkness. Often one was almost upon the boat before the oarsman was aware.

In a low voice the correspondent addressed the captain. He was not sure

---

DIFFERENTIATED INSTRUCTION

FOR ENGLISH LANGUAGE LEARNERS

Related Vocabulary Lines 484–501 use many words and phrases that describe light and how it reflects on the shark's movement through the water. Help students locate these words and phrases, define them, and organize them in a word web. Point out that some of the words, such as *blue* and *bluish*, describe the color of the light, while others, such as *gleaming* and *crystalline*, describe the quality of the light. Students should locate these words and phrases:

- *gleaming trail of phosphorescence* (lines 484–485)
- *blue flame* (line 485)
- *long flash of bluish light* (line 489)
- *crystalline spray* (line 492)
- *long glowing trail* (line 492)
- *long sparkling streak* (line 498)

movement words: flame, spray, trail, streak

light

color words: blue, bluish

quality words: gleaming, flash, glowing, sparkling

that the captain was awake, although this iron man seemed to be always awake. "Captain, shall I keep her making for that light north, sir?"

The same steady voice answered him. "Yes. Keep it about two points off the port bow."[17]

The cook had tied a life belt around himself in order to get even the warmth which this clumsy cork contrivance could donate, and he seemed almost stovelike when a rower, whose teeth invariably chattered wildly as soon as he ceased his
470 labor, dropped down to sleep.

The correspondent, as he rowed, looked down at the two men sleeping under foot. The cook's arm was around the oiler's shoulders, and, with their fragmentary clothing and haggard faces, they were the babes of the sea, a grotesque rendering of the old babes in the wood.[18]

Later he must have grown stupid at his work, for suddenly there was a growling of water, and a crest came with a roar and a swash into the boat, and it was a wonder that it did not set the cook afloat in his life belt. The cook continued to sleep, but the oiler sat up, blinking his eyes and shaking with the new cold.

"Oh, I'm awfully sorry, Billie," said the correspondent, contritely.
480 "That's all right, old boy," said the oiler, and lay down again and was asleep.

Presently it seemed that even the captain dozed, and the correspondent thought that he was the one man afloat on all the oceans. The wind had a voice as it came over the waves, and it was sadder than the end.

There was a long, loud swishing astern of the boat, and a gleaming trail of phosphorescence, like blue flame, was furrowed on the black waters. It might have been made by a monstrous knife.

Then there came a stillness, while the correspondent breathed with the open mouth and looked at the sea.

Suddenly there was another swish and another long flash of bluish light, and
490 this time it was alongside the boat, and might almost have been reached with an oar. The correspondent saw an enormous fin speed like a shadow through the water, hurling the crystalline spray and leaving the long glowing trail.

The correspondent looked over his shoulder at the captain. His face was hidden, and he seemed to be asleep. He looked at the babes of the sea. They certainly were asleep. So, being bereft of sympathy, he leaned a little way to one side and swore softly into the sea.

But the thing did not then leave the vicinity of the boat. Ahead or astern, on one side or the other, at intervals long or short, fled the long sparkling streak, and there was to be heard the whiroo of the dark fin. The speed and power of
500 the thing was greatly to be admired. It cut the water like a gigantic and keen projectile.

The presence of this biding thing did not affect the man with the same horror that it would if he had been a picnicker. He simply looked at the sea dully and swore in an undertone.

---

17. **two points off the port bow:** two compass points, or a total of 45 degrees, to the left.

18. **babes in the wood:** a reference to an old nursery rhyme in which two children are abandoned in the woods and die there in the night.

752 UNIT 4: REGIONALISM AND NATURALISM

Nevertheless, it is true that he did not wish to be alone with the thing. He wished one of his companions to awaken by chance and keep him company with it. But the captain hung motionless over the water jar and the oiler and the cook in the bottom of the boat were plunged in slumber.

VI

510 "If I am going to be drowned—if I am going to be drowned—if I am going to be drowned, why, in the name of the seven mad gods who rule the sea, was I allowed to come thus far and contemplate sand and trees?" **O**

During this dismal night, it may be remarked that a man would conclude that it was really the intention of the seven mad gods to drown him, despite the abominable injustice of it. For it was certainly an abominable injustice to drown a man who had worked so hard, so hard. The man felt it would be a crime most unnatural. Other people had drowned at sea since galleys[19] swarmed with painted sails, but still—

When it occurs to a man that nature does not regard him as important, and that she feels she would not maim the universe by disposing of him, he at first 520 wishes to throw bricks at the temple, and he hates deeply the fact that there are no bricks and no temples. Any visible expression of nature would surely be pelleted with his jeers. **P**

Then, if there be no tangible thing to hoot he feels, perhaps, the desire to confront a personification and indulge in pleas, bowed to one knee, and with hands supplicant, saying: "Yes, but I love myself."

A high cold star on a winter's night is the word he feels that she says to him. Thereafter he knows the pathos of his situation.

The men in the dinghy had not discussed these matters, but each had, no doubt, reflected upon them in silence and according to his mind. There was 530 seldom any expression upon their faces save the general one of complete weariness. Speech was devoted to the business of the boat.

To chime the notes of his emotion, a verse mysteriously entered the correspondent's head. He had even forgotten that he had forgotten this verse, but it suddenly was in his mind.

> *A soldier of the Legion lay dying in Algiers,*
> *There was lack of woman's nursing, there was **dearth** of woman's tears;*
> *But a comrade stood beside him, and he took that comrade's hand,*
> *And he said: "I never more shall see my own, my native land."*[20]

In his childhood, the correspondent had been made acquainted with the fact 540 that a soldier of the Legion lay dying in Algiers, but he had never regarded it as important. Myriads of his schoolfellows had informed him of the soldier's plight, but the dinning had naturally ended by making him perfectly indifferent. He had never considered it his affair that a soldier of the Legion lay dying in Algiers, nor

---

19. **galleys:** large medieval ships propelled by sails and oars.

20. ***A soldier ... native land:*** condensed first stanza of Caroline E. S. Norton's poem "Bingen on the Rhine." The Legion is the French Foreign Legion; Algiers is the capital city of the African nation Algeria.

Sidebar (left column)

O NATURALISM

***Possible answer:** The tone of the third repetition is more desperate than the earlier repetitions. It is shorter, with no hint of humor and no personification of Fate. The tone has shifted from philosophical and reflective to bitter and angry.*

IF STUDENTS NEED HELP . . . Refer them to the first two repetitions in lines 264–277 and 415–419. Point out the difference in the passage lengths. Then ask students what is missing from the third repetition and what this absence suggests about the outcry.

P NATURALISM

***Possible answer:** Crane says that "despite the abominable injustice of it," it is nature's intent to drown him. He describes it as a "crime most unnatural."*

OWN THE WORD

dearth: Tell students that *dearth* refers to "a lack or scarce supply." Have students write a sentence that shows an understanding of the word. ***Possible answer:** During the severe drought, there was a dearth of food, and people began to suffer.*

Margin notes (right column)

O NATURALISM
What is the tone of this third repetition of the men's outcry against fate?

P NATURALISM
What does the author say about nature's regard for the individual in lines 518–522?

dearth (dûrth) *n.* lack

DIFFERENTIATED INSTRUCTION

FOR STRUGGLING READERS

Clarify Meanings Point out the word *pathos* in line 527. Explain that *pathos* is an emotion of sympathetic pity. In this situation, nature makes the man feel alone and unimportant because it does not acknowledge his existence. He feels great pity, or pathos, for himself. Then focus on the poem the correspondent recalls in lines 535–538, clarifying it to ensure that students will recognize the parallels between it and the correspondent's situation. Make sure students understand that the soldier misses the comfort that women bring to the injured, that the soldier is not alone as he dies, and that the pronoun "he" in line 538 refers to the soldier, not to his comrade.

FOR ENGLISH LANGUAGE LEARNERS

Conversational English Patterns Point out these two elliptical speeches: *Pretty long night* (lines 567–568); *Wish I had known you were awake* (line 572). Explain that people sometimes converse in incomplete thoughts, leaving out words that make sentences clear. Readers must then infer the missing words to get the sentences' meanings. Help students complete the lines.

had it appeared to him as a matter for sorrow. It was less to him than the breaking of a pencil's point.

Now, however, it quaintly came to him as a human, living thing. It was no longer merely a picture of a few throes in the breast of a poet, meanwhile drinking tea and warming his feet at the grate; it was actuality—stern, mournful, and fine.

The correspondent plainly saw the soldier. He lay on the sand with his feet out
550 straight and still. While his pale left hand was upon his chest in an attempt to thwart the going of his life, the blood came between his fingers. In the far Algerian distance, a city of low square forms was set against a sky that was faint with the last sunset hues. The correspondent, plying the oars and dreaming of the slow and slower movements of the lips of the soldier, was moved by a profound and perfectly impersonal comprehension. He was sorry for the soldier of the Legion who lay dying in Algiers. **Q**

The thing which had followed the boat and waited had evidently grown bored at the delay. There was no longer to be heard the slash of the cutwater,[21] and there was no longer the flame of the long trail. The light in the north still glimmered,
560 but it was apparently no nearer to the boat. Sometimes the boom of the surf rang in the correspondent's ears, and he turned the craft seaward then and rowed harder. Southward, some one had evidently built a watch fire on the beach. It was too low and too far to be seen, but it made a shimmering, roseate reflection upon the bluff back of it, and this could be discerned from the boat. The wind came stronger, and sometimes a wave suddenly raged out like a mountain-cat and there was to be seen the sheen and sparkle of a broken crest.

The captain, in the bow, moved on his water jar and sat erect. "Pretty long night," he observed to the correspondent. He looked at the shore. "Those lifesaving people take their time."
570 "Did you see that shark playing around?"

"Yes, I saw him. He was a big fellow, all right."

"Wish I had known you were awake."

Later the correspondent spoke into the bottom of the boat.

"Billie!" There was a slow and gradual disentanglement. "Billie, will you spell me?"

"Sure," said the oiler.

As soon as the correspondent touched the cold comfortable seawater in the bottom of the boat, and had huddled close to the cook's life belt he was deep in sleep, despite the fact that his teeth played all the popular airs. This sleep was so
580 good to him that it was but a moment before he heard a voice call his name in a tone that demonstrated the last stages of exhaustion. "Will you spell me?"

"Sure, Billie."

The light in the north had mysteriously vanished, but the correspondent took his course from the wide-awake captain.

Later in the night they took the boat farther out to sea, and the captain directed the cook to take one oar at the stern and keep the boat facing the seas. He was to

---

21. **cutwater:** the front part of a ship.

Q DESCRIPTIVE LANGUAGE
The description in lines 549–556 paints the correspondent's mental picture of the soldier in the poem. What does this **imagery** suggest about the correspondent's own plight?

COMMON CORE RL 4

Language Coach
Multiple-Meaning Words
Airs (line 579) is a multiple-meaning word, a word with more than one meaning. Here, *airs* means "melodies." What does Crane mean by teeth playing melodies?

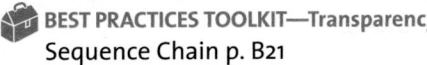

call out if he should hear the thunder of the surf. This plan enabled the oiler and the correspondent to get **respite** together. "We'll give those boys a chance to get into shape again," said the captain. They curled down and, after a few preliminary
590 chatterings and trembles, slept once more the dead sleep. Neither knew they had bequeathed to the cook the company of another shark, or perhaps the same shark.

As the boat caroused on the waves, spray occasionally bumped over the side and gave them a fresh soaking, but this had no power to break their repose. The ominous slash of the wind and the water affected them as it would have affected mummies.

"Boys," said the cook, with the notes of every reluctance in his voice, "she's drifted in pretty close. I guess one of you had better take her to sea again." The correspondent, aroused, heard the crash of the toppled crests.

As he was rowing, the captain gave him some whiskey and water, and this
600 steadied the chills out of him. "If I ever get ashore and anybody shows me even a photograph of an oar—"

At last there was a short conversation.

"Billie. . . . Billie, will you spell me?"

"Sure," said the oiler.

VII

When the correspondent again opened his eyes, the sea and the sky were each of the gray hue of the dawning. Later, carmine and gold was painted upon the waters. The morning appeared finally, in its splendor, with a sky of pure blue, and the sunlight flamed on the tips of the waves. **R**

On the distant dunes were set many little black cottages, and a tall white
610 windmill reared above them. No man, nor dog, nor bicycle appeared on the beach. The cottages might have formed a deserted village.

The voyagers scanned the shore. A conference was held in the boat. "Well," said the captain, "if no help is coming, we might better try a run through the surf right away. If we stay out here much longer we will be too weak to do anything for ourselves at all." The others silently **acquiesced** in this reasoning. The boat was headed for the beach. The correspondent wondered if none ever ascended the tall wind tower, and if then they never looked seaward. This tower was a giant, standing with its back to the plight of the ants. It represented in a degree, to the correspondent, the serenity of nature amid the struggles of the individual—nature
620 in the wind, and nature in the vision of men. She did not seem cruel to him then, nor beneficent, nor treacherous, nor wise. But she was indifferent, flatly indifferent. It is, perhaps, plausible that a man in this situation, impressed with the unconcern of the universe, should see the innumerable flaws of his life and have them taste wickedly in his mind and wish for another chance. A distinction between right and wrong seems absurdly clear to him, then, in this new ignorance of the grave edge, and he understands that if he were given another opportunity he would mend his conduct and his words, and be better and brighter during an introduction, or at a tea. **S**

R DESCRIPTIVE LANGUAGE
Note the change in mood. What descriptive language has been used to achieve this?

acquiesce (ăk′wē-ĕs′) v. to comply or give in

6 Targeted Passage

S NATURALISM
Reread lines 612–628. Which sentence in this paragraph do you think most effectively expresses the indifference of nature to the struggles of the individual? Explain.

respite (rĕs′pĭt) n. a period of rest or relief

READING SKILL | **COMMON CORE** RL 4

R DESCRIPTIVE LANGUAGE

Possible answer: The mood shifts to one of greater hope. The author uses color imagery to achieve this change in mood, for example, describing the sky as "pure blue" and the waters as golden (lines 606–608). Also, the time of day is symbolically significant as dawn often symbolizes the hope that a new day offers. Because this is a dawn of "splendor," that hope is greater.

TEXT ANALYSIS | **COMMON CORE** RL 2 RL 3

S NATURALISM

Accept all reasonable answers. Some students may cite the sentence in which the lighthouse tower is compared to a giant and humans to ants as best expressing nature's indifference (lines 617–618). Others may cite the sentence following, in which the correspondent links the tower to nature amidst individual struggles (lines 618–620).

VOCABULARY | **COMMON CORE** L 4

OWN THE WORD

- **respite:** Tell students that *respite* derives from the Latin *respectus* meaning "refuge; looking back." Ask students to list activities from which they would like a *respite*. **Possible answers:** *homework and household chores; stresses of life*
- **acquiesce:** Tell students that *acquiesce* means "to comply or give in." Have students list antonyms for this word. **Possible answers:** *resist, fight, refuse, protest*

DIFFERENTIATED INSTRUCTION

FOR STRUGGLING READERS

6 Targeted Passage [Lines 612–628]
This passage explores the men's choices and regrets as they face the prospect of death.
- **What have the men decided they must do? Why?** (lines 612–615)
- **To what does the correspondent compare nature? What does he think of nature?** (lines 619–622)
- **What regrets does the correspondent have about his life?** (lines 624–628)

Moonlit Shipwreck at Sea (1901), Thomas Moran. 30″ × 40 ¼″. © Christie's Images Limited.

"Now, boys," said the captain, "she is going to swamp sure. All we can do is to
630 work her in as far as possible, and then when she swamps, pile out and scramble
for the beach. Keep cool now, and don't jump until she swamps sure."

The oiler took the oars. Over his shoulders he scanned the surf. "Captain,"
he said, "I think I'd better bring her about, and keep her head-on to the seas and
back her in."

"All right, Billie," said the captain. "Back her in." The oiler swung the boat then
and, seated in the stern, the cook and the correspondent were obliged to look over
their shoulders to contemplate the lonely and indifferent shore.

The monstrous inshore rollers[22] heaved the boat high until the men were
again enabled to see the white sheets of water scudding up the slanted beach.
640 "We won't get in very close," said the captain. Each time a man could wrest his

---

22. **inshore rollers:** long waves swelling close to the shore.

> ▲ **Analyze Visuals**
> In your opinion, how well
> does this painting reflect
> the men's situation?
> Reread the description of
> the waves on this page
> and compare them to the
> waves as portrayed by
> the artist.

---

❶ NATURALISM

Point out to students that as they will see in the article, "Stephen Crane's Own Story," the media bring us real-life accounts of human struggles against the elements. Ask students to compare this passage to other fictional accounts with which they are familiar. If any have not viewed or read other storm-oriented stories, have them compare the passage with media accounts of such events.

Possible answer: *Students' responses will vary; accept all thoughtful answers.*

Extend the Discussion How do the men attempt to deal with their worsening situation and meager chances for survival?

TIERED DISCUSSION PROMPTS

In lines 669–683, use these prompts to help students comprehend the men's dire situation:

Connect Have you heard the phrase "Out of the frying pan, into the fire"? What does it mean? *Accept all thoughtful responses.*

Synthesize How might the advantages and disadvantages of seizing control be reflected in an attempt to face a challenge? *Possible answer: Many situations offer the advantage of gaining control over difficulty, but with control may come risk. For example, to take control and escape a fire, one might need to climb out a window.*

OWN THE WORD

coerce: Remind students that *coerce* means "to force; dominate." Ask students why the author used *coerce* in the sentence, "He tried to *coerce* his mind into thinking of it . . ." *Possible answer: It illustrates that the captain was so overwhelmed that he had to try to force himself to think.*

---

attention from the rollers, he turned his glance toward the shore, and in the expression of the eyes during this contemplation there was a singular quality. The correspondent, observing the others, knew that they were not afraid, but the full meaning of their glances was shrouded.

As for himself, he was too tired to grapple fundamentally with the fact. He tried to **coerce** his mind into thinking of it, but the mind was dominated at this time by the muscles, and the muscles said they did not care. It merely occurred to him that if he should drown it would be a shame.

There were no hurried words, no pallor, no plain agitation. The men simply
650 looked at the shore. "Now, remember to get well clear of the boat when you jump," said the captain.

Seaward the crest of a roller suddenly fell with a thunderous crash, and the long white comber²³ came roaring down upon the boat.

"Steady now," said the captain. The men were silent. They turned their eyes from the shore to the comber and waited. The boat slid up the incline, leaped at the furious top, bounced over it, and swung down the long back of the wave. Some water had been shipped and the cook bailed it out.

But the next crest crashed also. The tumbling boiling flood of white water caught the boat and whirled it almost perpendicular. Water swarmed in from all
660 sides. The correspondent had his hands on the gunwale at this time, and when the water entered at that place he swiftly withdrew his fingers, as if he objected to wetting them.

The little boat, drunken with this weight of water, reeled and snuggled deeper into the sea. ❶

"Bail her out, cook! Bail her out," said the captain.

"All right, Captain," said the cook.

"Now, boys, the next one will do for us, sure," said the oiler. "Mind to jump clear of the boat."

The third wave moved forward, huge, furious, implacable. It fairly swallowed
670 the dinghy, and almost simultaneously the men tumbled into the sea. A piece of life belt had lain in the bottom of the boat, and as the correspondent went overboard he held this to his chest with his left hand.

The January water was icy, and he reflected immediately that it was colder than he had expected to find it off the coast of Florida. This appeared to his dazed mind as a fact important enough to be noted at the time. The coldness of the water was sad; it was tragic. This fact was somehow so mixed and confused with his opinion of his own situation that it seemed almost a proper reason for tears. The water was cold.

When he came to the surface he was conscious of little but the noisy water.
680 Afterward he saw his companions in the sea. The oiler was ahead in the race. He was swimming strongly and rapidly. Off to the correspondent's left, the cook's great white and corked back bulged out of the water, and in the rear the captain was hanging with his one good hand to the keel of the overturned dinghy.

---

23. **comber:** a large wave that breaks on a beach.

coerce (kō-ûrs′) *v.* to force

❶ NATURALISM

Ancient literature in every culture includes stories of people at the mercy of natural forces. From the epic flood in the Babylonian story *Gilgamesh* to Odysseus' dangerous sea voyage, there are many stories about humans cast loose on unstill waters. These stories are as old as human history and as recent as the hugely successful television series *Lost.* They include Ernest Hemingway's powerful novel *The Old Man and the Sea* as well as the 2000 film *The Perfect Storm.* Reread lines 645–664. How does this passage compare with stories you've read or seen in which humans struggle against storms or other violent natural forces?

DIFFERENTIATED INSTRUCTION

FOR ENGLISH LANGUAGE LEARNERS
Vocabulary: Prefixes Have students work in small groups to define these words:

- *overboard* (line 672), over—across, board—side of a boat
- *overturned* (line 683), over—across, turned—flipped
- *immovable* (line 684), im—not, movable—able to be moved

- *extraordinary* (line 699), extra—beyond, ordinary—the usual
- *undressing* (line 720), un—to remove, dress—clothing

For each word listed, groups should identify and define the prefix and root, then check the definition of the word in context.

There is a certain immovable quality to a shore, and the correspondent wondered at it amid the confusion of the sea.

It seemed also very attractive, but the correspondent knew that it was a long journey, and he paddled leisurely. The piece of life preserver lay under him, and sometimes he whirled down the incline of a wave as if he were on a hand sled.

But finally he arrived at a place in the sea where travel was beset with difficulty.
690 He did not pause swimming to inquire what manner of current had caught him, but there his progress ceased. The shore was set before him like a bit of scenery on a stage, and he looked at it and understood with his eyes each detail of it.

As the cook passed, much farther to the left, the captain was calling to him, "Turn over on your back, cook! Turn over on your back and use the oar."

"All right, sir." The cook turned on his back, and, paddling with an oar, went ahead as if he were a canoe.

Presently the boat also passed to the left of the correspondent with the captain clinging with one hand to the keel. He would have appeared like a man raising himself to look over a board fence, if it were not for the extraordinary gymnastics
700 of the boat. The correspondent marveled that the captain could still hold to it.

They passed on, nearer to shore—the oiler, the cook, the captain—and following them went the water jar, bouncing gaily over the seas.

The correspondent remained in the grip of this strange new enemy—a current. The shore, with its white slope of sand and its green bluff, topped with little silent cottages, was spread like a picture before him. It was very near to him then, but he was impressed as one who in a gallery looks at a scene from Brittany[24] or Holland.

He thought: "I am going to drown? Can it be possible? Can it be possible? Can it be possible?" Perhaps an individual must consider his own death to be the final phenomenon of nature. ⓤ
710 But later a wave perhaps whirled him out of this small deadly current, for he found suddenly that he could again make progress toward the shore. Later still, he was aware that the captain, clinging with one hand to the keel of the dinghy, had his face turned away from the shore and toward him, and was calling his name. "Come to the boat! Come to the boat!"

In his struggle to reach the captain and the boat, he reflected that when one gets properly wearied, drowning must really be a comfortable arrangement, a cessation of hostilities accompanied by a large degree of relief, and he was glad of it, for the main thing in his mind for some moments had been horror of the temporary agony. He did not wish to be hurt.
720 Presently he saw a man running along the shore. He was undressing with most remarkable speed. Coat, trousers, shirt, everything flew magically off him.

"Come to the boat," called the captain.

"All right, Captain." As the correspondent paddled, he saw the captain let himself down to bottom and leave the boat. Then the correspondent performed his one little marvel of the voyage. A large wave caught him and flung him with

---

24. **Brittany:** a region in northwestern France.

ⓤ **NATURALISM**
Reread lines 707–709. How does the correspondent come to view death as he is faced with the prospect of drowning?

TEXT ANALYSIS   COMMON CORE

ⓤ **NATURALISM**   RL 2
                                     RL 3

Some students may say that the correspondent becomes somewhat detached from the prospect of drowning, as if it is just another natural event to observe. Others may say that he comes to think death represents the final reconciliation of the individual and nature.

IF STUDENTS NEED HELP . . . Remind them that naturalists believed human destiny was beyond the individual's control.
Extend the Discussion Why might people feel resignation at the edge of death? How does death's approach affect the human desire for life?

FOR ADVANCED LEARNERS/AP

Synthesize Refer students to the *Notable Quote* on page 734. Ask students to decide if the correspondent in the story shares the views expressed in the quote. Have them discuss the quote in light of the selection's final pages, focusing on these questions:

- In what new ways has the correspondent's experience with nature changed his vision of the world, as he describes in lines 689–692 and 703–706?

- How does the correspondent's vision of the world fit with the personal qualities that led him to be a reporter or storyteller? How does it fit the "eyes he was born with"?

- How do lines 707–709 reveal the quality of the correspondent's personal honesty?

- How does the correspondent's realization of nature's indifference, expressed in lines 612–628, prepare him for this final crisis?

Does
NATURE *play fair?*

Discuss After deciding the sea is indifferent to his fate in lines 725–728, why does the correspondent now consider the wave "a true miracle of the sea"? How might this experience affect his views about nature? *Possible answer: He considers the wave a miracle because after nearly killing him, the sea has saved him. He may reconsider his assessment of nature as indifferent or he may see this as further evidence of nature's randomness.*

SELECTION WRAP–UP

READ WITH A PURPOSE Now that students have finished reading the selection, have them review details about how the men worked together to survive in the open boat. How did the men help one another in the face of danger? *Possible answer: They kept up one another's spirits and drew on their knowledge of the sea; they shared duties, such as rowing.*

⭐ **CRITIQUE** Ask students to evaluate the story's ending and tell if they think it is a fitting end to the saga. Ask students how they would feel if the captain or the correspondent had not survived.

---

ease and supreme speed completely over the boat and far beyond it. It struck him even then as an event in gymnastics, and a true miracle of the sea. An overturned boat in the surf is not a plaything to a swimming man.

730   The correspondent arrived in water that reached only to his waist, but his condition did not enable him to stand for more than a moment. Each wave knocked him into a heap, and the undertow pulled at him.

    Then he saw the man who had been running and undressing, and undressing and running, come bounding into the water. He dragged ashore the cook, and then waded toward the captain, but the captain waved him away, and sent him to the correspondent. He was naked, naked as a tree in winter, but a halo was about his head, and he shone like a saint. He gave a strong pull, and a long drag, and a bully heave at the correspondent's hand. The correspondent, schooled in the minor formulæ, said: "Thanks, old man." But suddenly the man cried: "What's that?" He pointed a swift finger. The correspondent said: "Go."

740   In the shallows, face downward, lay the oiler. His forehead touched sand that was periodically, between each wave, clear of the sea.

⑦ **Targeted Passage**

    The correspondent did not know all that transpired afterward. When he achieved safe ground he fell, striking the sand with each particular part of his body. It was as if he had dropped from a roof, but the thud was grateful to him.

    It seems that instantly the beach was populated with men with blankets, clothes, and flasks, and women with coffeepots and all the remedies sacred to their minds. The welcome of the land to the men from the sea was warm and generous, but a still and dripping shape was carried slowly up the beach, and the land's welcome for it could only be the different and sinister hospitality of the grave.

750   When it came night, the white waves paced to and fro in the moonlight, and the wind brought the sound of the great sea's voice to the men on shore, and they felt that they could then be interpreters. ◐

DIFFERENTIATED INSTRUCTION

FOR STRUGGLING READERS

⑦ **Targeted Passage** [Lines 729–741]

This passage resolves the plot by explaining what becomes of the men.

- Why is reaching the shore not enough to save the correspondent? (lines 730–731)
- How is the correspondent saved? (lines 736–737)
- What happens to the oiler? (lines 740–741)

FOR ENGLISH LANGUAGE LEARNERS

Language: Pronoun Referents Clarify the nouns or pronouns referenced by each of these pronouns:

- *It* (line 726), the wave tossing him to safety
- *he* (line 732), the correspondent
- *He* (line 733), the man from the shore
- *It* (line 745), the correspondent's experience
- *it* (line 749), the oiler's dead body
- *they* (line 752), the men on shore

FOR ADVANCED LEARNERS/AP

Make Inferences Ask students to discuss why the only named character is also the only character that dies. Have them use these questions to make inferences: Why might the author have withheld the other characters' names? How does the correspondent's pity for the death of the fictional Legion soldier of Algiers prepare readers for the oiler's death?

💼 BEST PRACTICES TOOLKIT—Transparency
Making Inferences p. A13

Comprehension

1. **Recall** Which character in the story doesn't survive?

2. **Clarify** Why don't the men row the boat directly onto the beach?

3. **Clarify** Why don't the people on shore rescue the men?

Text Analysis

4. **Make Inferences About Conflict** The sea is the great **antagonist** in Crane's story. Are the men saved primarily by their own efforts or by chance? How does their struggle compare to stories you've read or movies you've seen in which water plays the role of antagonist?

● 5. **Examine Naturalism** Reread lines 509–522 at the beginning of section VI, where the correspondent rails against the "abominable injustice" of **nature**. Is nature really unjust in the story? What characteristics of nature are suggested in these lines and in other places in the story?

6. **Examine Dramatic Irony** Naturalistic writers often use irony to express their worldview. Find two instances in "The Open Boat" in which the characters' perceptions don't match the reality of the situation. Then, explain how the two examples of irony interact to build toward Crane's naturalistic theme.

7. **Analyze Tone** The narrative voice of this story is quite detached, relating highly dramatic events with a mild and even slightly humorous tone. Find examples of this detachment. How does this tone affect the story's message or overall impact? Explain.

● 8. **Evaluate Descriptive Language** Identify the section of the story (a page or more) that you find most compelling. Now review the examples of descriptive elements that you recorded as you read. What role does descriptive writing play in this passage? How do you think the description affects your feelings about it? Cite details from the text to support your answer.

Text Criticism

9. **Author's Style** One writer described Stephen Crane's stories as "intensely realistic." He attributed this realism to Crane's training as a reporter, saying "his English flow[s] simple and pure." Do you agree? Explain why or why not, citing evidence from the story to support your answer.

> *Does* **NATURE** *play fair?*
>
> In "The Open Boat," do you think Crane portrays "nature" as evil, kind, or indifferent to humans? Why might he have chosen "nature," "Fate," and "the seven mad gods who rule the sea" as the ambiguous objects of his questions?

COMMON CORE

RL 2 Determine two or more themes or central ideas of a text and analyze how they interact to produce a complex account. **RL 3** Analyze the impact of the author's choices regarding how to develop and relate elements of a story. **RL 4** Analyze the impact of specific word choices on meaning and tone, including language that is particularly fresh, engaging, or beautiful. **RL 6** Analyze a case in which grasping point of view requires distinguishing what is directly stated in a text from what is really meant.

THE OPEN BOAT **759**

Practice and Apply

For preliminary support of post-reading questions, use these copy masters:

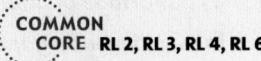 **R** RESOURCE MANAGER—Copy Masters

Reading Check p. 134

Naturalism p. 127

Question Support p. 135

Additional selection questions are provided for teachers on page 121.

ANSWERS COMMON CORE RL 2, RL 3, RL 4, RL 6

1. *The oiler, Billie, does not survive.*

2. *The strong surf will capsize the boat.*

3. *These people are not trained lifesavers, or they do not realize the men are in danger.*

Possible answers:

4. *The men's efforts to keep the boat afloat and their sense of brotherhood save them. Chance also plays a role: the shipwreck happens close to shore, weather is fair, and a wave pulls one man out of a deadly current. Past events also matter: the oiler may have drowned because he was exhausted from working a double shift.*

5. ● **COMMON CORE FOCUS Examine Naturalism** *Nature is not unjust, "cruel . . . nor wise" (lines 620–621). Instead, the sea is as unfeeling as a "high cold star on a winter's night" (line 526). The story shows nature to be ultimately "indifferent" (line 622).*

6. *Ironic misperception occurs when those in the boat and on shore misunderstand each other. The men think a lifesaving station is near and wonder why the people do not organize a rescue. An ironic reversal is the strong, calm oiler's death. These ironies show that nature's unpredictability limits human ability to shape fate.*

7. *Examples of detachment include: "A singular . . . swamping boats" (lines 43–46); "Shipwrecks . . . eat heartily" (lines 189–194); "But the thing . . . projectile" (lines 497–501). The detached, mildly humorous tone stresses the naturalist theme that humans' fate rests with forces beyond our control.*

---

8. ■ **COMMON CORE FOCUS Analyze Descriptive Language** *Accept all well-analyzed section choices. In lines 34–42, Crane describes the boat's motion by comparing it to riding a bronco. He also uses vivid language to describe that motion, from "a leap from the air" to "slide, and race, and splash." This description stresses nature's unpredictability and creates a vivid image.*

9. *Students who agree that Crane's realism derives from his journalistic training may cite Crane's strictly chronological text structure as realistic. Students who*

disagree may cite Crane's use of figurative language, such as his description of the shark as "a monstrous knife" (line 486).

> *Does* **NATURE** *play fair?* Students will probably conclude that Crane portrays nature as indifferent or malevolent. Some students may suggest that Crane questioned "nature," "Fate," and "the seven mad gods" to avoid a more direct philosophical question about the existence of God and evil.

THE OPEN BOAT **759**

ANSWERS

Vocabulary in Context

▲ **VOCABULARY PRACTICE**

1. *(a) someone being robbed*
2. *(c) a show of anger*
3. *(a) polka dots with plaid*
4. *(b) a noisy argument*
5. *(c) a shortage of good ideas*
6. *(a) halftime at a game*
7. *(c) the habits of an eccentric*
8. *(b) a believer in fairy tales*
9. *(b) a scornful laugh*
10. *(a) an army's surrender*

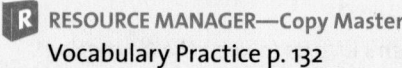 **RESOURCE MANAGER—Copy Master**
Vocabulary Practice p. 132

ACADEMIC VOCABULARY IN WRITING

Possible answer: *The correspondent initially* perceives *his situation as dangerous, but he gains hope when the group sights the lighthouse and land. Traveling the final short distance to shore is a danger that the correspondent had not expected.*

VOCABULARY STRATEGY: THE GREEK PREFIX *epi-*

COMMON CORE L 4d, L 6

- Help students use their knowledge of the root words and context clues to determine word meaning.
- For Item 2, point out other words that tell about skin, such as *dermatologist,* as an aid to comprehension.

Answers:

1. *epicenter*
2. *epidermis*
3. *epidemic*

 **RESOURCE MANAGER—Copy Master**
Vocabulary Strategy p. 133

Interactive Vocabulary **THINK central**

Keywords direct students to a **WordSharp** tutorial on **thinkcentral.com** or to other types of vocabulary practice and review.

Vocabulary in Context

▲ **VOCABULARY PRACTICE**

Choose the letter of the phrase that defines or is related to the boldfaced word.

1. **coerce:** (a) someone being robbed, (b) someone singing, (c) someone writing
2. **epithet:** (a) a sincere apology, (b) a two-handed card game, (c) a show of anger
3. **motley:** (a) polka dots with plaid, (b) a portrait of twins, (c) a thunderstorm
4. **obstreperous:** (a) a severe cold, (b) a noisy argument, (c) a lazy summer day
5. **dearth:** (a) a large fireplace, (b) a song played at funerals, (c) a shortage of good ideas
6. **respite:** (a) halftime at a game, (b) jealous anger, (c) paying back a debt
7. **aberration:** (a) a pilot in training, (b) a small city park, (c) the habits of an eccentric
8. **ingenuously:** (a) a sudden change in weather, (b) a believer in fairy tales, (c) a clever invention
9. **opprobrious:** (a) a clever comedian, (b) a scornful laugh, (c) a wildlife refuge
10. **acquiesce:** (a) an army's surrender, (b) a child's naptime, (c) a bird's piercing call

WORD LIST

aberration
acquiesce
coerce
dearth
epithet
ingenuously
motley
obstreperous
opprobrious
respite

ACADEMIC VOCABULARY IN WRITING

- apparent • confine • expose • focus • perceive

How does the correspondent initially **perceive** his situation in "The Open Boat"? Write a paragraph explaining how his attitude changes by the end of the story, and use at least one Academic Vocabulary word in your response.

VOCABULARY STRATEGY: THE GREEK PREFIX *epi-*

The prefix *epi-*, which has its origin in the Greek language, means "upon," "among," or "in addition." *Epi-* is found in a number of English words, including the vocabulary word *epithet.* You can use your knowledge of the origin of this prefix, in addition to the context of a word, to help determine the word's meaning.

PRACTICE Choose the word from the word web that best completes each sentence. Consider what you know about the Greek prefix and the other word parts shown. If necessary, consult a dictionary.

1. The _____ of the earthquake was 200 miles from the city.
2. The top layer of skin in humans is called the _____.
3. The _____ spread illness and disease throughout the region.

COMMON CORE

L 4d Verify the preliminary determination of the meaning of a word. **L 6** Acquire and use accurately general academic words and phrases.

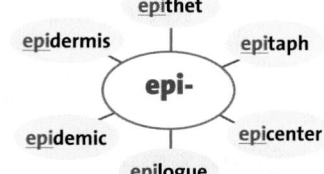

Interactive Vocabulary **THINK central**

Go to **thinkcentral.com**.
KEYWORD: HML11-760

DIFFERENTIATED INSTRUCTION

FOR ENGLISH LANGUAGE LEARNERS

Task Support: Vocabulary Practice Point out that although *epi-* is a Greek prefix, it was borrowed into Latin and appears in Romance languages such as Spanish. Students may know cognates for words beginning with *epi-* in their home languages, for example, *epithet/epíteto* and *epidemic/epidemia.*

FOR ADVANCED LEARNERS/AP

Academic Vocabulary in Writing Have students write a definition of *naturalism* using appropriate vocabulary words. Suggest that they use their description of the correspondent's changing attitude toward his situation as a starting point.

Language

◆ **GRAMMAR AND STYLE: Use Effective Description**

Review the **Grammar and Style** note on page 751. Crane uses gerunds and gerund phrases in some unusual ways, creating energetic phrases and sentences. A **gerund** is a verb form that ends in *-ing* and functions as a noun. A **gerund phrase** includes a gerund and its modifiers and complements. In this example from "The Open Boat," notice how "snarling of the crests" functions as a noun in the sentence:

> *There was a terrible grace in the move of the waves, and they came in silence, save for the* snarling of the crests. (lines 51–52)

The gerund emphasizes the action of the waves more than the simple noun *snarl* would. It's a subtle difference that, when used strategically in your writing, can have a cumulative impact.

PRACTICE Rewrite each of the following sentences so that it contains a gerund phrase. You may want to change an existing verb into a gerund or add an entirely new idea. (Remember that a participial phrase, which also uses the *-ing* form of a verb, is used as an adjective, whereas a gerund phrase is used as a noun.)

> **EXAMPLE**
>
> The sun sank gradually, and their hearts sank soon after.
>
> *The gradual sinking of the sun was followed by the sinking of their hearts.*

1. The surf roared, announcing the nearness of the shore.

2. The gulls cried and gave voice to their own despair.

3. The men looked warily at the shark fin as it coolly sliced the water.

READING-WRITING CONNECTION

Expand your understanding of "The Open Boat" by responding to this prompt. Then, use the **revising tips** to improve your character sketch.

WRITING PROMPT	**REVISING TIPS**
WRITE A CHARACTER SKETCH The most compelling character in "The Open Boat" is the sea. To describe the sea, Crane frequently uses **personification**, a figure of speech in which an object is given human features. Write a **short character sketch** about a non-human character such as the sea in "The Open Boat." Use Crane's story as a model for your character sketch.	• Use personification to make your non-human character come to life. • Include descriptive details as well as a reflection on the importance or effect of the subject. • Use precise words and phrases that will convey a vivid mood.

Interactive Revision **THINK** central

Go to **thinkcentral.com**.
KEYWORD: HML11-761

FOR DEVELOPING WRITERS

Writing Support

• Limit the length of the sketch to one or two paragraphs.

• Provide sentences that model how to incorporate textual support with correct punctuation and citation format. Review the rules for quoting, paraphrasing, and summarizing text.

• Provide a starter sentence: In Stephen Crane's short story "The Open Boat," the sea is a _____ character and interacts with the human characters.

Language

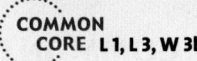

◆ **GRAMMAR AND STYLE**

Help students distinguish *-ing* forms by asking them to write a pair of sentences for reference. Provide these sentences as models:

• *I enjoy playing guitar.* Here, *playing* is a gerund that is the object of the verb *enjoy*.

• *The playing puppy collapsed.* Here, *playing* is a participle that modifies *puppy*.

(For more on gerunds and gerund phrases, see **Grammar Handbook,** page R66.)

Possible answers:

1. *The roaring of the surf announced the nearness of the shore.*

2. *The gulls' crying gave voice to their own despair.*

3. *The men looked warily at the cool slicing of the shark's fin through the water.*

 RESOURCE MANAGER—Copy Master
    Use Effective Description p. 136

READING-WRITING CONNECTION

Guide students to gather and organize information for their paragraphs by using a Character Traits and Textual Evidence chart. Students may skim the story for material or refer to their notes and to the marginal annotations to focus on likely passages.

 **BEST PRACTICES TOOLKIT**—Transparency
    Character Traits and Textual Evidence p. D6

> **Writing Online**   **THINK** central
>
> The following tools are available online at **thinkcentral.com** and on **Write*Smart* CD-ROM:**
>
> • **Interactive Graphic Organizers**
> • **Interactive Student Models**
> • **Interactive Revision Lessons**
>   For additional grammar instruction, see **GrammarNotes** on **thinkcentral.com**.

Assess

Assess

DIAGNOSTIC AND SELECTION TESTS
    Selection Test A, B/C pp. 197–198, 199–200

Interactive Selection Test on **thinkcentral.com**

COMMON CORE

L1 Demonstrate command of the conventions of standard English grammar when writing.
L3 Apply knowledge of language to make effective choices for meaning or style. **W 3b** Use narrative techniques, such as description and reflection, to develop characters.

Focus and Motivate

COMMON CORE FOCUS

RI 1 Cite textual evidence to support inferences drawn from the text, including determining where the text leaves matters uncertain. **RI 2** Provide an objective summary of the text. **RI 5** Analyze and evaluate the effectiveness of the structure an author uses in his or her exposition, including whether the structure makes points clear and engaging. **RI 9** Analyze nineteenth-century documents of historical significance. **W 2** Write explanatory texts to examine and convey complex ideas clearly and accurately through the effective selection, organization, and analysis of content. **W 2c** Use appropriate transitions to clarify the relationships among complex ideas and concepts. **W 7** Synthesize multiple sources on a subject.

SUMMARY

In these newspaper articles, reporters and survivors of the wreck of the *Commodore* inform the public of the details and losses of the accident and praise its heroes. The articles appear over a period of five days, during which more facts and stories come to light. The final article, by Crane himself, gives the fullest account of the accident.

 **BEST PRACTICES TOOLKIT—Transparency**
KWL p. A21

Teach

Standards Focus: Analyze Primary Sources

- Remind students that primary sources are materials created by people who were present at events, either as participants or observers. Such sources provide direct, first-hand knowledge about an event or person, which can help readers understand an event and its participants as close observers did.

- Remind them that sometimes eyewitnesses to and even participants in the event may not remember or report details accurately.

R RESOURCE MANAGER—Copy Master
Analyze Primary Sources p. 145

Reading for Information

Use with "The Open Boat," page 736.

COMMON CORE

RI 1 Cite textual evidence to support inferences drawn from the text, including determining where the text leaves matters uncertain. **RI 5** Analyze and evaluate the effectiveness of the structure an author uses in his or her exposition, including whether the structure makes points clear and engaging. **RI 9** Analyze nineteenth-century documents of historical significance.

The Wreck of the *Commodore*
Newspaper Articles

"The Open Boat" was based on Stephen Crane's experience with the wreck of the *Commodore,* a ship on a private mission to arm rebels fighting in the Cuban civil war. Crane had joined these filibusters, as these men were known, in search of adventure and a good story. When the ship went down, however, he acted as far more than a journalist. You'll now read news stories about this sensational event, including an account by Crane himself.

Standards Focus: Analyze Primary Sources

The 1897 articles about the wreck of the *Commodore* are **primary sources** of information on that event. You can also look to them as evidence of the kind of writing that appeared in newspapers of the day. As you read the articles, make connections between the three texts and synthesize, or bring together, your ideas about the event. Keep the following questions in mind:

- Who is the intended **audience**?
- What techniques are used to capture the readers' interest?
- What is the **tone** of the piece?
- What is its **scope** and **focus**? In other words, how much is covered, and what in the piece is most important?
- What **structure** is used to organize the information in the piece?
- How much **imagery** or other colorful language does it contain?
- How does the piece differ from something you might find in a newspaper today?

Note your observations and textual evidence in a chart such as this one.

"The Commodore Sinks at Sea"	"More of the Filibusters Safe"	"Stephen Crane and His Work"	"Stephen Crane's Own Story"
lots of stacked headlines			

Selection Resources

See resources on the **Teacher One Stop DVD-ROM** and on **thinkcentral.com**.

R **RESOURCE MANAGER UNIT 4**
Lesson Support,* pp. 137–150

DIAGNOSTIC AND SELECTION TESTS
Selection Tests, pp. 201–204

 BEST PRACTICES TOOLKIT
KWL: Know, Want to Know, Learned
p. A21

TECHNOLOGY

- **Teacher One Stop DVD-ROM**
- **Student One Stop DVD-ROM**
- **ExamView Test Generator** on the **Teacher One Stop**

* Resources for Differentiation

THE FLORIDA TIMES-UNION

SUNDAY, JANUARY 3, 1897   PRICE 5 CENTS.

THE COMMODORE SINKS AT SEA

The Little Vessel Lost with Her Cargo of Arms and Ammunition

HER NUMEROUS COMPANY REACH LAND IN SAFETY

They are Compelled to Take to the Boats and Abandon the Sinking Vessel

An Overload of Coal the Probable Cause Ⓐ

THE STEAMER COMMODORE, which left here Thursday night with an expedition for the Cuban insurgents, is now resting on the bottom of the sea, twenty fathoms below the surface, about eighteen miles northeast of Mosquito Inlet.

All of the men on the vessel, twenty-eight in number, reached the
10 shore in safety, and twelve of them arrived in Jacksonville last night over the Florida East Coast railway. The other sixteen are still down the coast, but are expected to arrive here on a special train this morning. . . .

DETAILS OF THE ACCIDENT

About 12 o'clock Friday night it was discovered that the boat was leaking badly. The swash of the water in the hold as the vessel rolled from side to side
20 soon alarmed everyone on board. A panic ensued, but Captain Murphy, Stephen Crane, R. A. Delgado and one or two others soon quieted the excitement and put everybody to work

on the pumps and with buckets. The steam pump was started and for two hours the water was poured over the sides in streams.

At 2:30 A.M., it was seen that the water was steadily gaining, and it was
30 decided to abandon the vessel.

IN THE BOATS

Paul Rojo, R. A. Delgado, Franco Blanco, the old Cuban pilot, and nine other men took one of the boats and left the steamer. Captain Murphy, the first and second mate, the engineer and assistant, Stephen Crane and ten men took the large yawl boat, and at 3 o'clock they left the Commodore to her fate. The night was dark and they
40 could not see what became of her, but as she was rapidly filling with water, they are all confident that she is now resting on the bottom, and old Neptune has been supplied with enough arms and ammunition to blow up the island of Cuba. . . . Ⓑ

READING FOR INFORMATION   **763**

Ⓐ **PRIMARY SOURCES**
Compare these headlines with those in papers today. Why do you think there are so many?

Language Coach

Fixed Expressions "Panic ensued" in line 21 means "panic followed." Other **fixed expressions**—normal combinations of words—are *panic broke out* and *panic spread through.* Explain the cause of the panic, using one of these fixed expressions.

Ⓑ **PRIMARY SOURCES**
Reread lines 43–47. What does the writer mean by this comment?

INFORMATIONAL ANALYSIS   COMMON CORE · RI 1 · RI 2 · RI 5 · RI 9

Ⓐ *Model the Skill:* **PRIMARY SOURCES**

Bring in several current newspapers and review the headlines from the first page with the class. Write them on the board and discuss.

Possible answer: Today's papers have at most a headline and a subhead. This article has a headline, three small subheads, and a subhead in capital letters. These heads serve as an outline of the most important details about the accident. Students may say that there were many headlines because the event was hugely interesting or because this was one way to sell newspapers.

INFORMATIONAL ANALYSIS   COMMON CORE · RI 1 · RI 2 · RI 5 · RI 9

Ⓑ **PRIMARY SOURCES**

Possible answer: The writer means that the arms and ammunition meant for rebels in Cuba are now on the sea floor.

Extend the Discussion What is the effect of alluding to Neptune in these lines?

DIFFERENTIATED INSTRUCTION

FOR ENGLISH LANGUAGE LEARNERS

Language Coach

Fixed Expressions *Possible answer: When the passengers felt the boat rolling from side to side,* panic *broke in the group.* Point out that in the expressions, *panic* is personified and takes on the characteristics of an animal; it roams and spreads fear as it goes. Ask students for other fixed expressions in which something takes action.

FOR STRUGGLING READERS

Vocabulary Support

- *fathoms* (line 5), "a unit of length used to measure depth of water"

- *swash* (line 18), "the motion of water splashing and the sound this makes"

- *hold* (line 19), "the area below the deck of a ship where cargo is carried"

- *ensued* (line 21), "happened next or as a result of"

BACKGROUND

Neptune According to Roman mythology, Neptune was the god of the sea. Greek myths give the name Poseidon to the same figure. Neptune was the son of Saturn, and brother to Jupiter and Pluto.

INFORMATIONAL ANALYSIS

C Model the Skill: PRIMARY SOURCES

Point out that primary sources often contain direct quotes from sources other than the author. Quotations can bring exciting events to life and introduce other viewpoints, as well.

Possible answer: *The writer of this article chose to quote the cook at length as a way of assuring readers that he has not told any "awful woppers."*

Extend the Discussion Were you surprised to find the cook so talkative, given how many lines of dialogue he has in the story? Explain.

INFORMATIONAL ANALYSIS

D PRIMARY SOURCES

Possible answer: *The editors chose to emphasize Crane's publishing credits and foreign correspondence work because they are thrilled to be able to claim a fellow writer as a hero.*

IF STUDENTS NEED HELP . . .
Help them identify the article's tone as more speculative and boastful than straightforward and factual.

Language Coach

Word Definitions *Nervy* (line 2) means "bold" or "strong." Reread the first paragraph. What details does the cook give to back up his assessment of Crane?

C PRIMARY SOURCES
Note that this article consists entirely of a quotation by the cook. Why do you think the writer of this article chose to quote him at such length?

D PRIMARY SOURCES
This paper portrays Crane as quite a hero, citing his bravery and pluck. In this article, why do you think the editors have chosen to make so much of his "Cuban letters," or his work as a foreign correspondent?

The New York Press

MONDAY, JANUARY 4, 1897   SECTION 1

MORE OF THE FILIBUSTERS SAFE

STEPHEN CRANE, NOVELIST, SWIMS ASHORE

DAYTONA, Fla., Jan. 3.—"That newspaper feller was a nervy man," said the cook of the ill-fated Commodore to-night in reference to Stephen Crane, the novelist, who is after material for stories. "He didn't seem to know what fear was. When we started out he insisted upon doing a seaman's work, and he did it well, too.

10 "When the boats were launched he was the last one, except Captain Murphy, to get in, and his nerve greatly encouraged all hands. In the small dingy he rowed as well as the others, notwithstanding he was so worn out that he could hardly hold his oar straight in the terrific seas.

SAVES A DROWNING MAN

"Both he and Captain Murphy were thrown out on the same side. Crane was 20 partially thrown under the overturned boat and but for Captain Murphy's readiness in catching him by the collar he would have gone under. We all battled there in the water for hours, it seemed to us. Crane was a good swimmer, and he really saved one of the sailors, as the man could not swim a stroke, and Crane had to keep him up by the aid of an oar. These newspaper 30 fellers have got spunk, if they do tell such awful woppers at times," concluded the cook, as he took another big swig of the "life preservative" provided by the good people here. . . . **C**

STEPHEN CRANE AND HIS WORK

How He Came to Be on the Unlucky Commodore

TO WRITE FOR THE PRESS

Brilliant Author Not of the Sort to Give Up His Cuban Letters Because of Shipwreck

STEPHEN CRANE, the writer, is safe and readers of The Press may expect in a short time a treat from his versatile pen. . . .

Mr. Crane was on the way to Cuba to write about the war there. He will get to Cuba as soon as he can. He is not of the sort who are frightened by an experience in a lifeboat. His letters will 10 appear in The Press as soon as they arrive.

Mr. Crane has not intimated just what he is going to write; probably he does not know himself. But that his letters will be intensely interesting and true to life readers of his stories, "The Red Badge of Courage," "The Third Violet," "George's Mother" and "Maggie, a Girl of the Streets," feel 20 assured. **D**

DIFFERENTIATED INSTRUCTION

FOR STRUGGLING READERS

Concept Support: Analyze Primary Sources [small-group option] Have students add to the chart introduced on page 762, listing details of the wreck as the cook recalls them and answering the other bulleted questions on page 762.

"More of the Filibusters Safe"	"Stephen Crane and His Work"
Audience: readers of New York Press	**Audience:** readers of New York Press
Techniques: long quotation	**Techniques:** details about Crane's talent and fame
Imagery: Crane thrown overboard	**Imagery:** little

FOR ENGLISH LANGUAGE LEARNERS

Language Coach

Word Definitions

Possible answer: *The cook says that Crane was fearless and not afraid of hard work.* Point out how the cook also uses the word *nerve* in line 13. Here the word means "strength, control, or endurance." Ask students for situations in which a person might exhibit *nerve* or act in a *nervy* way.

The New York Press

THURSDAY, JANUARY 7, 1897   **SECTION 1**

STEPHEN CRANE'S OWN STORY

JACKSONVILLE, FLA., Jan. 6.—It was the afternoon of New Year's. The Commodore lay at her dock in Jacksonville and negro stevedores processioned steadily toward her with box after box of ammunition and bundle after bundle of rifles. Her hatch, like the mouth of a monster, engulfed them. It might have been the feeding
10 time of some legendary creature of the sea. It was in broad daylight and the crowd of gleeful Cubans on the pier did not forbear to sing the strange patriotic ballads of their island. . . . The revenue cutter Boutwell, the old isosceles triangle that protects United States interests in the St. John's, lay at anchor, with no sign of excitement aboard her.

SLEEP IMPOSSIBLE

As darkness came upon the waters,
20 the Commodore was a broad, flaming path of blue and silver phosphorescence, and as her stout bow lunged at the great black waves she threw flashing, roaring cascades to either side. And all that was to be heard was the rhythmical and mighty pounding of the engines.

THE COOK IS HOPEFUL

The cook was asleep on a bench in the galley. He woke as I entered the galley and delivered himself of some
30 dolorous sentiments: "I don't feel right about this ship, somehow. It strikes me that something is going to happen to us. I don't know what it is, but the old ship is going to get it in the neck, I think."

Author Stephen Crane

"Well, how about the men on board of her?" said I. "Are any of us going to get out, prophet?"

"Yes," said the cook. "Sometimes I have these damned feelings come over
40 me, and they are always right, and it seems to me, somehow, that you and I will both get [out] and meet again somewhere, down at Coney Island, perhaps, or some place like that."

Here I first came to know a certain young oiler named Billy Higgins. He was sloshing around this inferno filling buckets with water and passing them to a chain of men that extended up the
50 ship's side. **E**

A WHISTLE OF DESPAIR

Now the whistle of the Commodore had been turned loose, and if there ever was a voice of despair and death, it was in the voice of this whistle. It had gained a new tone. It was as if its throat was already choked by the water, and this cry on the sea at night, with a wind blowing

continued

continued

COMMON CORE RI 1

E **PRIMARY SOURCES**
The very title "Stephen Crane's Own Story" tells you that the article is a primary-source document. It is Crane's first-person narrative of his experience during the Commodore disaster. Reread lines 45–50. Then compare the datelines of the three articles, and consider why Crane provides so little information about why the men are passing buckets of water. What other connections can you make between the articles? Based on these accounts, what conclusion can you draw about Stephen Crane himself?

TIERED DISCUSSION PROMPTS

Use these prompts to help students consider the language Crane uses in lines 1–26 to describe the *Commodore*:

Summarize What activities are described in these lines? *The Commodore is loaded with its cargo and departs on its trip.*

Evaluate How well does Crane succeed in casting the ship as a heroic character in this adventure? *Possible answer: Although the image of the ship as a hungry monster is not attractive, the description of the ship in lines 19–26 is exciting and heroic.*

INFORMATIONAL ANALYSIS   COMMON CORE RI 1

E **PRIMARY SOURCES**

Remind students that primary sources are eyewitness accounts. They reflect personal views and may be biased. Have a volunteer read lines 45–50 aloud. Note with students this is Crane's first mention of the ship's leak. Ask students whether they think Crane felt the bucket brigade was important in context of the ship's eventual fate.

Possible answer: According to the datelines of the stories, Crane's was the last published. He may have said little about the passing of the buckets because this early attempt to stop the ship's sinking was abandoned when the situation grew worse. All the articles mention Crane's involvement in the event. The first identifies him as a participant. In "More Filibusters Save," Crane is described as a determined reporter who will not let a shipwreck keep him from reporting on a war. In Crane's own account, he focuses on the heroism of others. Readers may conclude that Crane is strong, modest, and not easily panicked.

FOR ADVANCED LEARNERS/AP

Employ Figurative Language Have students reread the article, noting the descriptive techniques Crane uses to help readers visualize the ship. Have them write an essay employing sensory details to create mood and establish tone in describing a voyage they have undertaken by ship, plane, train, or other vehicle.

F PRIMARY SOURCES

Possible answer: *In lines 19–26, Crane uses imagery of the boat as a moving light and a powerful force that carves through water. In lines 51–63, Crane uses the image of the boat as a living thing crying out in loss. The mood in the early lines is one of power and hope, while in the later lines the mood has shifted to loss and grief.*

G PRIMARY SOURCES

Possible answer: *According to lines 89–102, the men still aboard the ship drowned. The captain could not get the boat close enough to let the stranded men board without endangering the three men with him, and the extra weight probably would have swamped the boat as well had he tried to.*

IF STUDENTS NEED HELP . . . Students may be confused because the first article claims that all hands were rescued (lines 8–10). Clarify that the first article was written four days earlier, before all the information about the accident was available.

H PRIMARY SOURCES

Possible answer: *Crane adopts a tone of admiration for Kitchell, while entirely omitting his own bravery. Crane's tone likely makes readers believe his accounting as accurate because it does not flatter him.*

F PRIMARY SOURCES
Reread lines 51–63. Identify the **imagery** used to describe the *Commodore*. What **mood** does Crane achieve with this language?

G PRIMARY SOURCES
Reread lines 81–102. What happened to the men still aboard the ship?

H PRIMARY SOURCES
What **tone** does Crane adopt in the last paragraph? Explain how this tone affects your perception of these events.

JANUARY 7, 1897   THE NEW YORK PRESS   SECTION 1

the spray over the ship, and the waves roaring over the bow, and swirling white
60 along the decks, was to each of us probably a song of man's end. The boat moved at last and swung down toward the water. **F**

IN THE TEN-FOOT DINGY

The captain was just about to swing over the rail when a dark form came forward and a voice said: "Captain, I go with you."

The captain answered: "Yes, Billy; get in."

HIGGINS LAST TO LEAVE SHIP

70 It was Billy Higgins, the oiler. Billy dropped into the boat and a moment later the captain followed, bringing with him an end of about forty yards of lead line. The other end was attached to the rail of the ship.

As we swung back to leeward the captain said: "Boys, we will stay right near the ship till she goes down."

This cheerful information, of course,
80 filled us all with glee.

When came the gray shade of dawn, the form of the Commodore grew slowly clear to us as our little ten-foot boat rose over each swell. She was floating with such an air of buoyancy that we laughed when we had time, and said "What a gag it would be on those other fellows if she didn't sink at all."

But later we saw men aboard of her,
90 and later still they began to hail us.

We rowed back to the ship, but did not approach too near, because we were four men in a ten-foot boat, and we knew that the touch of a hand on our gunwale would assuredly swamp us. . . .

THE COMMODORE SINKS

The cook let go of the line. We rowed around to see if we could not get a line from the chief engineer, and

all this time, mind, there were no
100 shrieks, no groans, but silence, silence and silence, and then the Commodore sank. **G**

She lurched to windward, then swung afar back, righted and dove into the sea, and rafts were suddenly swallowed by this frightful maw of the ocean. And then by the men of the ten-foot dingy were words said that were still not words—something far beyond
110 words.

The lighthouse of Mosquito Inlet stuck up above the horizon like the point of a pin. We turned our dingy toward the shore.

The history of life in an open boat for thirty hours would no doubt be instructive for the young, but none is to be told here and now. For my part I would prefer to tell the story at once,
120 because from it would shine the splendid manhood of Captain Edward Murphy and of William Higgins, the oiler, but let it suffice at this time to say that when we were swamped in the surf and making the best of our way toward the shore the captain gave orders amid the wildness of the breakers as clearly as if he had been on the quarter deck of a battleship.

130 John Kitchell of Daytona came running down the beach, and as he ran the air was filled with clothes. If he had pulled a single lever and undressed, even as the fire horses harness, he could not seem to me to have stripped with more speed. He dashed into the water and dragged the cook. Then he went after the captain, but the captain sent him to me, and then it was that he saw Billy
140 Higgins lying with his forehead on sand that was clear of the water, and he was dead. **H**

STEPHEN CRANE

DIFFERENTIATED INSTRUCTION

FOR STRUGGLING READERS

Clarify Meaning Point out and clarify the ironic statements that occasionally surface in Crane's narrative. In lines 79–80, for example, the men in the boat receive the "cheerful information" with anything but glee. In lines 107–110, the men speak words that are not words because there are no words sufficient to describe what they feel about the disaster.

FOR ENGLISH LANGUAGE LEARNERS

Vocabulary: Multiple-Meaning Words Share or elicit the usual meanings of these words. Then help students use context to build appropriate meaning:

- *lead* (line 73), "a rope used to control something, like a leash"
- *shade* (line 81), "color"
- *air* (line 85), "spirit or mood"
- *gag* (line 87), "joke or trick"
- *dove* (line 104), "past tense of *dive*"

Comprehension

1. **Summarize** What happened to the *Commodore* and her crew?

Text Analysis

2. **Examine Text Features** Review the headlines of these articles. Consider their content and number. What logical connections can you make between them, in terms of **tone?** Explain. How do they support the structure of the articles?

● 3. **Analyze Primary Sources** Consider the headlines, contents, and tone of the articles. Based on these examples, how would you synthesize your ideas into a general statement about 19th-century journalism? Cite evidence to support your generalization.

COMMON CORE

RI 1 Cite textual evidence to support inferences drawn from the text. **RI 2** Provide an objective summary of the text. **RI 5** Analyze and evaluate the effectiveness of the structure an author uses in his or her exposition. **RI 9** Analyze nineteenth-century documents of historical significance. **W 2** Write explanatory texts to examine and convey complex ideas clearly and accurately through the effective selection, organization, and analysis of content. **W 2c** Use appropriate transitions to clarify the relationships among complex ideas and concepts. **W 7** Synthesize multiple sources on a subject.

Read for Information: Compare Forms

WRITING PROMPT

In Stephen Crane's article about the wreck of the *Commodore*, he wrote:

The history of life in an open boat for thirty hours would no doubt be instructive for the young, but none is to be told here and now. . . . I would prefer to tell the story at once, because from it would shine the splendid manhood of Captain Edward Murphy and of William Higgins, the oiler.

Based on your reading of "The Open Boat" and "Stephen Crane's Own Story," why might Crane have reserved the tale of the open boat for a short story? What does he do with the short story that he can't or doesn't do in the article?

The following steps will help you answer the prompt:

1. Compare the short story and the article, considering the following elements:

	Article	Short Story
Audience and Purpose	to describe shipwreck for newspaper readers	
Character Development		
Coverage of Events		
Imagery and Figurative Language		
Theme and Main Idea		

2. Based on this comparison, consider why Crane may have made the choices he did in writing each piece.

3. Finally, try to explain Crane's decision to write "The Open Boat" by evaluating the strengths of the short story over the article. Support your ideas with details from each text, and use appropriate transitions to show the connections between your ideas.

FOR STRUGGLING WRITERS

Read for Information

• Direct students to complete the chart first for just the article, and then for just the short story alone, addressing one piece at a time.

• Urge them to consider the process in Step 2 piece by piece as well. This process will allow them to gain mastery of each piece before proceeding to the more complex task of comparing the two pieces.

FOR ADVANCED LEARNERS/AP

Analyze Author's Purpose After students have completed the writing exercise, challenge them to debate whether "The Open Boat" is in fact "instructive for the young," as Crane says it "would no doubt" be (last article, lines 115–117). After the debate, invite students to present the consensus of the group to the whole class.

Practice and Apply

For preliminary support of post-reading questions, use these copy masters:

R RESOURCE MANAGER—Copy Master
    Reading Check p. 149
    Question Support p. 150
    Additional selection questions are provided for teachers on page 140.

ANSWERS

COMMON CORE **RI 1, RI 2, RI 5, RI 9, W 2, W 2c, W 7**

1. *The* Commodore *sank and many of her crew drowned. Crane and three other men escaped in a small dinghy. After 30 hours, they reached shore but one man died.*

Possible answers:

2. *There are many headlines because these allow readers to get the gist quickly and also pique readers' curiosity. They all convey a tone of objectivity.*

3. ● **COMMON CORE FOCUS** Analyze **Primary Sources** *General statements: 19th-century journalism was sensational (using zingy headlines), subjective (giving writers' feelings on topics), and colorful (calling liquor a "life preservative"). It used narrative elements such as foreshadowing, imagery, and mood.*

Read for Information: Compare Forms

Writing Prompt *Responses will vary, but students should explain Crane's writing choices and contrast the strengths of the two works, supporting their ideas with details.*

Assess and Reteach

Assess

DIAGNOSTIC AND SELECTION TESTS
    Selection Test A pp. 201–202
    Selection Test B/C pp. 203–204

Interactive Selection Test on **thinkcentral.com**

Reteach

Level Up Online Tutorials on **thinkcentral.com**

Reteaching Worksheets on **thinkcentral.com**

    Research and Study Skills Lesson 5: Using Primary and Secondary Sources

Focus and Motivate

COMMON CORE FOCUS

RL 2 Determine two or more themes or central ideas of a text and analyze their development over the course of the text. **RL 3** Analyze the impact of the author's choices regarding how to develop and relate elements of a story. **RL 4** Analyze the impact of specific word choices on meaning and tone, including words with multiple meanings. **RL 9** Demonstrate knowledge of early-twentieth-century works of American literature **L 4b** Identify and correctly use patterns of word changes that indicate different meanings or parts of speech. **L 5b** Analyze nuances in the meaning of words with similar denotations. **L 6** Acquire and use accurately general academic words and phrases.

ABOUT THE AUTHOR

Jack London pursued writing as he did everything else, with enthusiasm and relentless energy. He studied magazine content, analyzed readers' desires, and composed at least 1,000 words a day on his way to fame and financial success.

NOTABLE QUOTE

"The proper function of man is to live, not to exist.
I shall not waste my days in trying to prolong them.
I shall use my time." **—Jack London**

Lead students in a discussion of the distinction London makes between existing and living. Challenge students to paraphrase London's quotation in their own words.

Selection Resources

COMMON CORE

RL 2 Determine two or more themes or central ideas of a text and analyze their development over the course of the text. **RL 3** Analyze the impact of the author's choices regarding how to develop and relate elements of a story. **RL 4** Analyze the impact of specific word choices on meaning and tone, including words with multiple meanings. **RL 9** Demonstrate knowledge of early-twentieth-century works of American literature. **L 4b** Identify and correctly use patterns of word changes that indicate different meanings or parts of speech.

DID YOU KNOW?

Jack London . . .

- was the first American author to become a millionaire from his writing.
- pioneered the field of sports writing.
- covered the Russo-Japanese War and the Mexican Revolution as a correspondent.

The Rise of Naturalism

The Law of Life

Short Story by Jack London

Essential Course of Study ECOS

Meet the Author

Jack London 1876–1916

According to critic Alfred Kazin, "The greatest story Jack London ever wrote was the story he lived." Before London had turned 21 he had had more adventures than a Hollywood action hero. Once he began publishing stories about his experiences, he became an international celebrity. His works, many set in the wilds of Alaska and the American West, brought before the reading public a fresh style and subject matter that proved popular and profitable.

The Call of Adventure Born in San Francisco, Jack London grew up in Oakland, California. Disowned by his biological father, he took the name of his stepfather, John London. Although a decent man, the stepfather couldn't make much of a living, so London spent much of his youth working. Periods of backbreaking manual labor—in factories, canneries, a power plant, and a laundry—alternated with high adventure. The 16-year-old Jack became an oyster pirate in San Francisco Bay before switching sides to join the shore police. At age 17, he boarded a ship for a seal-hunting expedition to the Bering Sea. At 18, he quit work altogether to travel the country as a hobo. These escapades came to an abrupt halt when he was arrested for vagrancy in New York

State and jailed for 30 days. Moved by the hard-luck stories of the men he had met on the road and in prison, London could see where his life was heading and decided to turn it around. I ran back to California and opened the books," he explained. By the time he was 20, he had enrolled at the University of California at Berkeley and become a writer.

From Rags to Riches Although writing steadily, London could get nothing published. News of the Klondike Gold Rush in 1897 inspired him to head to Alaska in hopes of striking it rich. Instead of finding gold, however, he got a bad case of scurvy and returned home after less than a year. Still, London admitted, "It was in the Klondike that I found myself." Equally important, he found a wealth of material and formulated the naturalistic philosophy that would make him a blockbuster writer. He shot to international fame with *The Call of the Wild* (1903), and within six years had produced most of his greatest works—*The Sea Wolf* (1904), *White Fang* (1906), *The Road* (1907), the autobiographical *Martin Eden* (1909), and several collections of short stories. London inspired many in the next generation of writers, including Ernest Hemingway, Jack Kerouac, and Norman Mailer.

Author Online

Go to **thinkcentral.com**. KEYWORD: HML11-768

768

See resources on the **Teacher One Stop DVD-ROM** and on **thinkcentral.com**.

R RESOURCE MANAGER UNIT 4
Plan and Teach, pp. 151–158
Summary, pp. 159–160†‡*
Text Analysis and Reading Skill, pp. 161–164†*
Vocabulary, pp. 165–167*

DIAGNOSTIC AND SELECTION TESTS
Selection Tests, pp. 205–208

BEST PRACTICES TOOLKIT
Jigsaw Reading, p. A1
Making Inferences, p. A13
Personal Word List, p. E2
Story Map, p. D14

INTERACTIVE READER

ADAPTED INTERACTIVE READER

ELL ADAPTED INTERACTIVE READER

TECHNOLOGY
- **Teacher One Stop DVD-ROM**
- **Student One Stop DVD-ROM**
- **PowerNotes DVD-ROM**
- **Audio Anthology CD**
- **ExamView Test Generator** on the Teacher One Stop

Find it Online!

Features on **thinkcentral.com** that support the selection include
- **PowerNotes** presentation
- **ThinkAloud** models to enhance comprehension
- **WordSharp** vocabulary tutorials

---

* Resources for Differentiation   † Also in Spanish   ‡ In Haitian Creole and Vietnamese

TEXT ANALYSIS: THEME

Theme is the central message communicated by a literary work. It may be stated directly, but it usually emerges through literary elements as a comment on the human condition. The answers to certain questions can help you identify a story's theme or themes.

- What is the resolution of the primary **conflict?**
- What traits do the main **characters** display?
- What about the physical or cultural **setting** is significant?
- What **point of view** is used to describe the experiences of the main character?
- What meaning does the **title** convey?

Ask yourself these questions as you read "The Law of Life," recording the answers and other details in a chart.

Details Revealing Theme					
Conflict	Character	Setting	Point of View	Symbol	Title

Review: **Naturalism**

● READING SKILL: ANALYZE AUTHOR'S PERSPECTIVE

An **author's perspective** is the unique combination of background, experiences, beliefs, and values that influences the way a writer looks at a topic and the choices he or she makes in writing about it. This story reflects London's experiences in Alaska and the Klondike, where he had gone in hopes of striking it rich in the goldfields. Reread London's biography on page 768. As you read the story, draw on what you know of London's life to help you understand his perspective on such subjects as youth and old age, strength and weakness, survival and death.

▲ VOCABULARY IN CONTEXT

Restate each phrase, using a different word or words for the boldfaced term.

1. need to **replenish** the water supply
2. a **slovenly** fellow, with dirty hair and unshined shoes
3. the **inexorable** passage of time
4. willing to **attest** to his honesty
5. a cat attempting to **harry** the mouse it caught

 Complete the activities in your **Reader/Writer Notebook**.

How do people face DEATH?

Death comes to all of us, but different cultures approach the inevitable end in various ways. The death described in London's story may seem cruel to you, but consider the cultural context of the community described in the story.

QUICKWRITE Think about how your own culture treats people who are dying. Are they treated with indifference or respect? In a more hostile environment, such as a natural disaster, do you think society could maintain the same customs? In your notebook, jot down your thoughts about these issues.

769

Teach

How do people face DEATH?

Introduce the question and invite students to share traditions their culture has for preparing for death. As students complete the *QUICKWRITE*, suggest that they consider how such traditions serve individuals, families, and friends who must face death.

SUMMARY

This short story opens with the blind, aged former leader of an Alaskan tribe listening to the sounds of his tribe departing for new hunting grounds. The old man knows he will be left behind and bids his son a ritual but loving farewell. As he awaits death in the snow, he recalls moments from his youth and considers the inevitable end of all living things. Finally, his fire goes out and a ring of wolves prepares to attack.

READ WITH A PURPOSE

Help students set a purpose for reading. Tell them to read "The Law of Life" to discover different attitudes toward death.

REVISIT THE BIG QUESTION

How do people face DEATH?

Discuss After students read lines 1–12, ask the following question: What details in the text alert readers that Koskoosh is nearing death? Why will he be left behind when the tribe leaves? *Possible answer: He is blind and wrinkled, and his hand is palsied. He will be left behind when the tribe leaves because he can no longer contribute and will slow the tribe's travel down.*

TEXT ANALYSIS   COMMON CORE
                          RL 2
                          RL 9

Ⓐ Model the Skill: THEME

Discuss the details of the setting with students. Ask them how a dark, cold winter day may affect the way they feel. Challenge them to see the connection between setting and mood.

Possible answer: The setting is that of a camp in the snow being broken as the characters prepare for a long day's journey (lines 5–9). The mood created is wintry and bleak, which reflects the grandfather's forlorn and helpless state.

IF STUDENTS NEED HELP . . . Have them reread lines 5–9 and note setting and action words.

THE LAW OF LIFE

JACK LONDON

BACKGROUND Written when London was about 25 years old, this story was included in his second collection of short stories about Alaska, *Children of the Frost* (1902). The characters are members of a nomadic native tribe whose customs are shaped by the harsh conditions of the Arctic. The law they live by expresses London's naturalistic vision at its most brutal.

Analyze Visuals ▶
Look at the image on page 771. What elements of the man's clothing and facial expression give clues to the photo's **setting?** Explain.

Old Koskoosh listened greedily. Though his sight had long since faded, his hearing was still acute, and the slightest sound penetrated to the glimmering intelligence which yet abode behind his withered forehead, but which no longer gazed forth upon the things of the world. Ah! that was Sit-cum-to-ha, shrilly anathematizing the dogs as she cuffed and beat them into the harness. Sit-cum-to-ha was his daughter's daughter, but she was too busy to waste a thought upon her broken grandfather, sitting alone there in the snow, forlorn and helpless. Camp must be broken. The long trail waited while the short day refused to linger. Life called her, and the duties of life, not death. And he was very close to death now. Ⓐ

① **Targeted Passage**

10   The thought made the old man panicky for the moment, and he stretched forth a palsied hand which wandered tremblingly over the small heap of dry wood beside him. Reassured that it was indeed there, his hand returned to the shelter of his mangy furs, and he again fell to listening. The sulky crackling of half-frozen hides told him that the chief's moose-skin lodge had been struck, and

Ⓐ THEME
What is significant about the **setting** described in the first paragraph, and what **mood** does it create?

DIFFERENTIATED INSTRUCTION

FOR ENGLISH LANGUAGE LEARNERS

Options for Reading Read the selection summary aloud so that students have an overview of events before they read on their own. Then have students read silently as they listen to the *Audio Anthology CD*. Finally, divide students into Jigsaw groups and assign one Targeted Passage to each. Have students present their passages to the other groups.

R RESOURCE MANAGER
Jigsaw Reading p. A1

FOR STRUGGLING READERS

In combination with the *Audio Anthology CD*, use one or more Targeted Passages (pp. 770, 772, 776) to ensure that students focus on key story events and concepts. Targeted Passages are also good for English language learners.

① **Targeted Passage** [Lines 1–9]

This passage introduces the main character, Koskoosh; the Arctic setting; and the presence of death in the story.

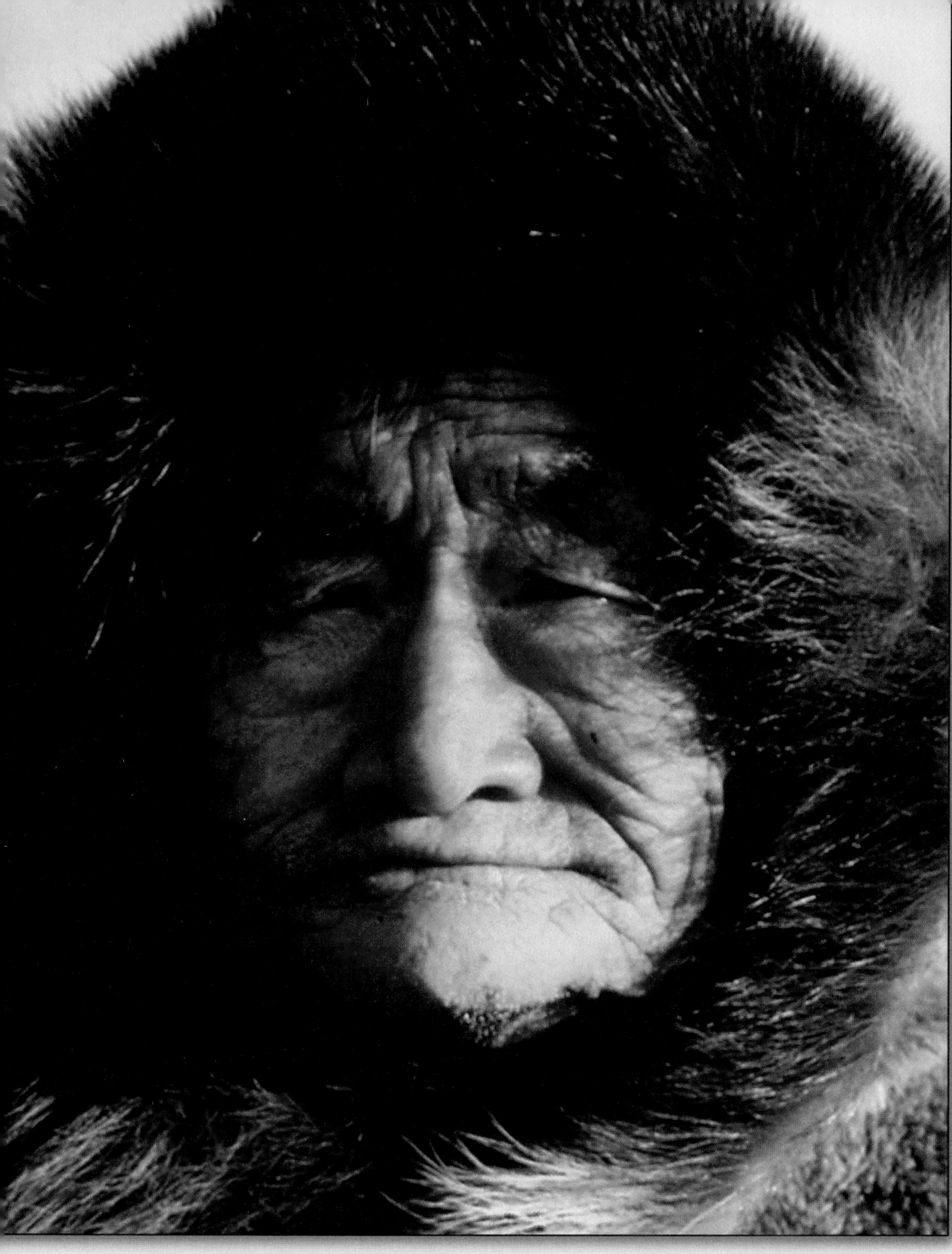

Analyze Visuals

Possible answer: *The man's fur hat suggests that he lives in a very cold setting. His facial expression suggests that he is bracing himself against something difficult, such as cold weather or a difficult physical task.*

BACKGROUND

Nomadic Life Tribes living in Koskoosh's area of Alaska were part of a larger group of Native Americans called Athabascans. Some Athabascans fished for salmon for food, while others hunted large animals, especially caribou. Their way of life was to follow migrating herds in winter, setting up and then quickly striking camps as necessary to keep up with the herds. In summer many Athabascan peoples set up fishing camps on rivers and lakes and briefly lived a more settled life.

- Who is Koskoosh? (lines 5–7)
- What are the conditions like where he is? (lines 7–9)
- What activity is he listening to? (lines 4–5)
- Why doesn't he participate in the activity? (lines 1–4, 9)

FOR ADVANCED LEARNERS/AP

Research and Compare Cultures Have students research and compare different cultures' approach to death. Students should begin by writing in a journal about their own experiences and observations and then do some research into at least one other culture. (Students may be interested in exploring the Athabascan culture to see if London depicts it fairly or if he embellishes for dramatic effect.) Ask students to share their findings with the class.

even then was being rammed and jammed into portable compass. The chief was his son, stalwart and strong, head man of the tribesmen, and a mighty hunter. As the women toiled with the camp luggage, his voice rose, chiding them for their slowness. Old Koskoosh strained his ears. It was the last time he would hear that voice. There went Geehow's lodge! And Tusken's! Seven, eight, nine; only the shaman's[1] could be still standing. There! They were at work upon it now. He could hear the shaman grunt as he piled it on the sled. A child whimpered, and a woman soothed it with soft, crooning gutturals.[2] Little Koo-tee, the old man thought, a fretful child, and not overstrong. It would die soon, perhaps, and they would burn a hole through the frozen tundra and pile rocks above to keep the wolverines away. Well, what did it matter? A few years at best, and as many an empty belly as a full one. And in the end, Death waited, ever-hungry and hungriest of them all. **B**

What was that? Oh, the men lashing the sleds and drawing tight the thongs. He listened, who would listen no more. The whip-lashes snarled and bit among the dogs. Hear them whine! How they hated the work and the trail! They were off! Sled after sled churned slowly away into the silence. They were gone. They had passed out of his life, and he faced the last bitter hour alone. No. The snow crunched beneath a moccasin; a man stood beside him; upon his head a hand rested gently. His son was good to do this thing. He remembered other old men whose sons had not waited after the tribe. But his son had. He wandered away into the past, till the young man's voice brought him back.

"Is it well with you?" he asked.

And the old man answered, "It is well."

"There be wood beside you," the younger man continued, "and the fire burns bright. The morning is gray, and the cold has broken. It will snow presently. Even now it is snowing."

"Ay, even now it is snowing."

"The tribesmen hurry. Their bales are heavy, and their bellies flat with lack of feasting. The trail is long and they travel fast. I go now. It is well?"

"It is well. I am as a last year's leaf, clinging lightly to the stem. The first breath that blows, and I fall. My voice is become like an old woman's. My eyes no longer show me the way of my feet, and my feet are heavy, and I am tired. It is well."

He bowed his head in content till the last noise of the complaining snow had died away, and he knew his son was beyond recall. Then his hand crept out in haste to the wood. It alone stood between him and the eternity that yawned in upon him. At last the measure of his life was a handful of fagots.[3] One by one they would go to feed the fire, and just so, step by step, death would creep upon him. When the last stick had surrendered up its heat, the frost would begin to gather strength. First his feet would yield, then his hands; and the numbness would travel, slowly, from the extremities to the body. His head would fall forward upon his knees, and he would rest. It was easy. All men must die. **C**

---

1. **shaman's:** belonging to a priest who uses magic to cure the sick or predict events.
2. **gutturals:** sounds that are made in the throat.
3. **fagots:** sticks of wood.

He did not complain. It was the way of life, and it was just. He had been born close to the earth, close to the earth had he lived, and the law thereof was not new to him. It was the law of all flesh. Nature was not kindly to the flesh. She had
60 no concern for that concrete thing called the individual. Her interest lay in the species, the race. This was the deepest abstraction old Koskoosh's barbaric mind was capable of, but he grasped it firmly. He saw it exemplified in all life. The rise of the sap, the bursting greenness of the willow bud, the fall of the yellow leaf—in this alone was told the whole history. But one task did Nature set the individual. Did he not perform it, he died. Did he perform it, it was all the same, he died. Nature did not care; there were plenty who were obedient, and it was only the obedience in this matter, not the obedient, which lived and lived always. The tribe of Koskoosh was very old. The old men he had known when a boy, had known old men before them. Therefore it was true that the tribe lived, that it stood for
70 the obedience of all its members, way down into the forgotten past, whose very resting-places were unremembered. They did not count; they were episodes. They had passed away like clouds from a summer sky. He also was an episode, and would pass away. Nature did not care. To life she set one task, gave one law. To perpetuate was the task of life, its law was death. A maiden was a good creature to look upon, full-breasted and strong, with spring to her step and light in her eyes. But her task was yet before her. The light in her eyes brightened, her step quickened, she was now bold with the young men, now timid, and she gave them of her own unrest. And ever she grew fairer and yet fairer to look upon, till some hunter, able no longer to withhold himself, took her to his lodge to cook and toil
80 for him and to become the mother of his children. And with the coming of her offspring her looks left her. Her limbs dragged and shuffled, her eyes dimmed and bleared, and only the little children found joy against the withered cheek of the old squaw by the fire. Her task was done. But a little while, on the first pinch of famine or the first long trail, and she would be left, even as he had been left, in the snow, with a little pile of wood. Such was the law. **D**

He placed a stick carefully upon the fire and resumed his meditations. It was the same everywhere, with all things. The mosquitoes vanished with the first frost. The little tree-squirrel crawled away to die. When age settled upon the rabbit it became slow and heavy, and could no longer outfoot its enemies. Even the
90 big bald-face grew clumsy and blind and quarrelsome, in the end to be dragged down by a handful of yelping huskies. He remembered how he had abandoned his own father on an upper reach of the Klondike one winter, the winter before the missionary came with his talk-books and his box of medicines. Many a time had Koskoosh smacked his lips over the recollection of that box, though now his mouth refused to moisten. The "painkiller" had been especially good. But the missionary was a bother after all, for he brought no meat into the camp, and he ate heartily, and the hunters grumbled. But he chilled his lungs on the divide by the Mayo,[4] and the dogs afterwards nosed the stones away and fought over his bones.

---

4. **the Mayo:** a small river in the Yukon Territory in northwestern Canada.

THE LAW OF LIFE **773**

COMMON CORE L 4b

Language Coach

Related Words
Exemplified (line 62) means "shown by example." How can you tell that the words *example* and *exemplified* are related? When might you use *example*, and when might you use *exemplify*?

D **THEME**
Reread lines 57–85. In one or two sentences, summarize the theme expressed here about the relationship between nature and the individual. What kind of comment on the human condition does this naturalist theme express? Explain your response.

TIERED DISCUSSION PROMPTS
Use these prompts to help students understand how Koskoosh and his people view Nature as revealed in lines 57–74:

Connect Have you ever felt that Nature was indifferent to people's wishes and needs? Explain. *Accept all thoughtful responses.*

Evaluate Have Koskoosh and his people done well according to Nature's goals? Explain. ***Possible answer:*** *Yes; the tribe has succeeded in meeting Nature's goals. It is healthy, with a long history behind it (lines 68–69) and a promising future ahead. Koskoosh himself has a son, now chief, and at least one grandchild. The tribe is a success, even if he dies.*

TEXT ANALYSIS: *Review*

COMMON CORE
RL 2
RL 9

D **THEME**

Possible answer: *Nature does not care about the individual, only about making sure that the species continues. The naturalist theme states that the individual is valued only in terms of his or her usefulness. When individuals can no longer contribute or care for themselves, they will be abandoned by the group.*

FOR ADVANCED LEARNERS/AP
Analyze Figures of Speech [small–group option] London personifies Nature in lines 57–74. Have students write a journal entry exploring the effect of this personification on Koskoosh's understanding of "the law." To prepare, have student groups discuss this question:

• Why does London personify Nature as a woman rather than as a man?

FOR ENGLISH LANGUAGE LEARNERS

Language Coach   **COMMON CORE** L 4b

Related Words Example *is the noun form and* exemplify *is the verb.* Tell students that example derives from Latin words meaning "to take out." Point out that in both example and exemplify, the prefix *ex-* means "out." Challenge students to think of other words that use the prefix *ex-. (exact, exasperate, exchange, exercise)*

Use these prompts to help students understand the connection Koskoosh makes between plenty and warfare:

Connect Are you more agreeable or more argumentative when things are going your way? *Accept all thoughtful responses.*

Interpret What can readers infer about why the tribe is more warlike when it is well-fed? *Possible answer: When the people are hungry, they are weaker and must spend their energy on finding food. They can't bother with war. But when they have food surpluses, they have time to do something other than hunt, fish, and gather. Then "ancient quarrels" (line 117) come to mind, and they decide to finish the conflict begun by men older than they.*

TEXT ANALYSIS — COMMON CORE

© THEME — RL 2 / RL 9

Possible answer: Koskoosh's memory is ironic because at the time, the old man watched the death of the moose with excitement. Now, his situation is similar as he faces his own death.

IF STUDENTS NEED HELP . . . Clarify the meaning of *ironic* in this context.

VOCABULARY — COMMON CORE

OWN THE WORD — L 4

- **replenish:** Remind students that *replenish* means "to fill up again." Have students write a sentence using the word correctly. *Possible answer: Mom went to the grocery store to replenish our snack supply before the big game.*

- **harry:** Tell students that *harry* refers to being tormented, "often by constant attack." Ask students to share reasons why a person might feel *harried*. *Possible answers: stress from work, running late, not enough sleep, too many daily tasks*

---

100 Koskoosh placed another stick on the fire and harked back deeper into the past. There was the time of the Great Famine, when the old men crouched empty-bellied to the fire, and let fall from their lips dim traditions of the ancient day when the Yukon ran wide open for three winters, and then lay frozen for three summers. He had lost his mother in that famine. In the summer the salmon run had failed, and the tribe looked forward to the winter and the coming of the caribou. Then the winter came, but with it there were no caribou. Never had the like been known, not even in the lives of the old men. But the caribou did not come, and it was the seventh year, and the rabbits had not **replenished,** and the dogs were naught but bundles of bones. And through the long darkness the
110 children wailed and died, and the women, and the old men; and not one in ten of the tribe lived to meet the sun when it came back in the spring. That *was* a famine!

But he had seen times of plenty, too, when the meat spoiled on their hands, and the dogs were fat and worthless with overeating—times when they let the game go unkilled, and the women were fertile, and the lodges were cluttered with sprawling men-children and women-children. Then it was the men became high-stomached, and revived ancient quarrels, and crossed the divides to the south to kill the Pellys, and to the west that they might sit by the dead fires of the Tananas.[5] He remembered, when a boy, during a time of plenty, when he saw a moose pulled
120 down by the wolves. Zing-ha lay with him in the snow and watched—Zing-ha, who later became the craftiest of hunters, and who, in the end, fell through an air-hole on the Yukon. They found him, a month afterward, just as he had crawled halfway out and frozen stiff to the ice.

But the moose. Zing-ha and he had gone out that day to play at hunting after the manner of their fathers. On the bed of the creek they struck the fresh track of a moose, and with it the tracks of many wolves. "An old one," Zing-ha, who was quicker at reading the sign, said—"an old one who cannot keep up with the herd. The wolves have cut him out from his brothers, and they will never leave him." And it was so. It was their way. By day and by night, never resting, snarling on his
130 heels, snapping at his nose, they would stay by him to the end. How Zing-ha and he felt the blood-lust quicken! The finish would be a sight to see! **©**

Eager-footed, they took the trail, and even he, Koskoosh, slow of sight and an unversed tracker, could have followed it blind, it was so wide. Hot were they on the heels of the chase, reading the grim tragedy, fresh-written, at every step. Now they came to where the moose had made a stand. Thrice the length of a grown man's body, in every direction, had the snow been stamped about and uptossed. In the midst were the deep impressions of the splay-hoofed game, and all about, everywhere, were the lighter footmarks of the wolves. Some, while their brothers **harried** the kill, had lain to one side and rested. The full-stretched impress of their
140 bodies in the snow was as perfect as though made the moment before. One wolf had been caught in a wild lunge of the maddened victim and trampled to death. A few bones, well picked, bore witness.

---

5. **Pellys . . . Tananas:** *Pellys* probably refers to native peoples who lived near the Pelly River. The Tananas are native people who traditionally lived in areas of Alaska and the Yukon.

774   UNIT 4: REGIONALISM AND NATURALISM

---

replenish (rĭ-plĕn′ĭsh) *v.* to fill up again

© THEME
In lines 124–131, the third-person-limited point of view reveals Koskoosh's memory of the old moose and his own reaction at the time. What is **ironic** about this recollection?

harry (hăr′ē) *v.* to torment, often by constant attack

DIFFERENTIATED INSTRUCTION

FOR STRUGGLING READERS

Make Inferences London often implies information rather than stating it directly. Readers must make inferences to dig out the implied information. Model for students the use of a Making Inferences chart.

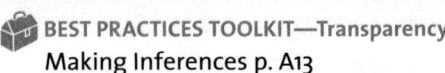
BEST PRACTICES TOOLKIT—Transparency
Making Inferences p. A13

Story Details +	What I Know =	Inference
The boys played at hunting in the "manner of their fathers" (lines 124–125).	Young people often play at grown-up jobs such as teaching or firefighting.	Zing-ha and Koskoosh were young men when they followed the moose.

Analyze Visuals

Activity Have students describe how the composition of the photograph on page 775 particularly defines the wolf as a predator. **Possible answer:** *The focal point of the photograph is the wolf's open mouth and sharp teeth.*

TEXT ANALYSIS	COMMON CORE
	RL 2
F THEME	RL 9

Possible answer: *The surprising element of the moose's struggle is that it actually manages to briefly get away from its stronger predators (lines 147–148). The moose's struggle represents the determination of living things to survive.*

Again, they ceased the uplift of their snowshoes at a second stand. Here the great animal had fought desperately. Twice had he been dragged down, as the snow **attested,** and twice had he shaken his assailants clear and gained footing once more. He had done his task long since, but none the less was life dear to him. Zing-ha said it was a strange thing, a moose once down to get free again; but this one certainly had. The shaman would see signs and wonders in this when they told him. **F**

150   And yet again, they came to where the moose had made to mount the bank and gain the timber. But his foes had laid on from behind, till he reared and fell back upon them, crushing two deep into the snow. It was plain the kill was at hand, for their brothers had left them untouched. Two more stands were hurried past, brief in time-length and very close together. The trail was red now, and the clean stride of the great beast had grown short and **slovenly.** Then they heard the first sounds of the battle—not the full-throated chorus of the chase, but the short, snappy bark which spoke of close quarters and teeth to flesh. Crawling up the wind, Zing-ha bellied it through the snow, and with him crept he, Koskoosh, who was to be chief of the tribesmen in the years to come. Together they shoved aside the under

160   branches of a young spruce and peered forth. It was the end they saw.

The picture, like all of youth's impressions, was still strong with him, and his dim eyes watched the end played out as vividly as in that far-off time. Koskoosh

attest (ə-tĕst′) *v.* to affirm to be true; to be proof of

F THEME
Reread lines 143–149. What is surprising about the moose's struggle with the wolves? Consider the significance of this **conflict.**

slovenly (slŭv′ən-lē) *adj.* untidy in personal appearance

VOCABULARY	COMMON CORE
OWN THE WORD	L 4

- **attest:** Explain to students that *attest* means "to be true; to be proof of" and is derived from the Latin, meaning "to be witness." Synonyms include "testify, confirm, corroborate, indicate." Ask students to explain why the author used *attest* in the sentence, "Twice had he been dragged down, as the snow *attested...*" **Possible answer:** *Footprints, drag marks, and blood in the snow* attest *to, or "are proof of," the wolves' attack.*

- **slovenly:** Tell students that *slovenly* can mean either "untidy in personal appearance," or "marked by negligence." Have students write a sentence for each of the definitions. **Possible answers:** *Rick's mother said that his* slovenly *outfit was not appropriate for work. Troy says he can't be bothered to change the* slovenly *appearance of his bedroom.*

READING SKILL — COMMON CORE RL 3, RL 9

G AUTHOR'S PERSPECTIVE

Possible answer: *This passage demonstrates a harsh means of settling differences (lines 164–166) and shows that people are accustomed to violence. London's travels among hard, tough people convey this image.*

REVISIT THE BIG QUESTION

How do people face DEATH?

Discuss After students read lines 179–187, ask the following question: How does Koskoosh's vision of his death change in these lines? ***Possible answer:*** *He realizes that it will not be an easy death after all (line 179), but a painful, violent death by "slavered fangs" (line 184).*

TEXT ANALYSIS — COMMON CORE RL 2, RL 9

H THEME

Possible answer: *The old bull moose stands for the aged chief, cut off from his herd and vulnerable. This symbol suggests a thematic message that we face death alone.*

VOCABULARY — COMMON CORE L 4

OWN THE WORD

inexorable: Explain to students that someone who is *inexorable* is "relentless and not capable of being persuaded; stubborn or uncompromising." Ask students to use a thesaurus to develop a list of antonyms for *inexorable.* ***Possible answers:*** *sympathetic, tender, compassionate, indulgent*

SELECTION WRAP-UP

READ WITH A PURPOSE Now that students have read "The Law of Life," ask them to consider the attitudes toward death illustrated by the story. ***Possible answers:*** *The moose resists death and so does Koskoosh until he realizes that he must respect the law of life.*

marvelled at this, for in the days which followed, when he was a leader of men and a head of councillors, he had done great deeds and made his name a curse in the mouths of the Pellys, to say naught of the strange white man he had killed, knife to knife, in open fight. G

For long he pondered on the days of his youth, till the fire died down and the frost bit deeper. He replenished it with two sticks this time, and gauged his grip on life by what remained. If Sit-cum-to-ha had only remembered her grandfather, and gathered a larger armful, his hours would have been longer. It would have been easy. But she was ever a careless child, and honored not her ancestors from the time the Beaver, son of the son of Zing-ha, first cast eyes upon her. Well, what mattered it? Had he not done likewise in his own quick youth? For a while he listened to the silence. Perhaps the heart of his son might soften, and he would come back with the dogs to take his old father on with the tribe to where the caribou ran thick and the fat hung heavy upon them.

He strained his ears, his restless brain for the moment stilled. Not a stir, nothing. He alone took breath in the midst of the great silence. It was very lonely. Hark! What was that? A chill passed over his body. The familiar, long-drawn howl broke the void, and it was close at hand. Then on his darkened eyes was projected the vision of the moose—the old bull moose—the torn flanks and bloody sides, the riddled mane, and the great branching horns, down low and tossing to the last. He saw the flashing forms of gray, the gleaming eyes, the lolling tongues, the slavered fangs. And he saw the **inexorable** circle close in till it became a dark point in the midst of the stamped snow. H

A cold muzzle thrust against his cheek, and at its touch his soul leaped back to the present. His hand shot into the fire and dragged out a burning fagot. Overcome for the nonce[6] by his hereditary fear of man, the brute retreated, raising a prolonged call to his brothers; and greedily they answered, till a ring of crouching, jaw-slobbered gray was stretched round about. The old man listened to the drawing in of this circle. He waved his brand wildly, and sniffs turned to snarls; but the panting brutes refused to scatter. Now one wormed his chest forward, dragging his haunches after, now a second, now a third; but never a one drew back. Why should he cling to life? he asked, and dropped the blazing stick into the snow. It sizzled and went out. The circle grunted uneasily, but held its own. Again he saw the last stand of the old bull moose, and Koskoosh dropped his head wearily upon his knees. What did it matter after all? Was it not the law of life? ∾

G AUTHOR'S PERSPECTIVE
Reread lines 162–166. What sensibility about human relationships is revealed in the struggle described here? Consider how this sensibility might be rooted in London's life experiences.

(3) Targeted Passage

inexorable
(ĭn-ĕk′sər-ə-bəl) *adj.* relentless

H THEME
Reread lines 177–185. What does the old bull moose represent? Consider the thematic message suggested by this **symbol.**

6. **for the nonce:** for the time being.

DIFFERENTIATED INSTRUCTION

FOR STRUGGLING READERS

(3) Targeted Passage [Lines 177–197]

This passage concludes the story with Koskoosh's surprising final moments: He will die by wolf attack, not from cold.

- What emotions does Koskoosh feel? (lines 178–179)
- What does Koskoosh do to stop the wolves? Why does he stop doing it? (lines 187, 197)

FOR ENGLISH LANGUAGE LEARNERS

Related Vocabulary Violence is central to the story's final scene. Teach these interrelated words and have students group them in a Personal Word List: *torn flanks, bloody sides* (line 181); *gleaming eyes, slavered fangs* (lines 183–184); *ring of crouching, jaw-slobbered gray* (lines 189–190); *panting brutes* (line 192).

BEST PRACTICES TOOLKIT
Personal Word List p. E2

Comprehension

1. **Recall** How does Koskoosh die?

2. **Clarify** How has he expected to die?

3. **Summarize** Describe the conditions of life for the tribe.

Text Analysis

4. **Interpret Theme** Look back at the details about narrative elements you recorded in your chart as you read. Taken together, what do these details suggest about the fate of Koskoosh and all humans?

5. **Analyze Cultural Context** Explain how each of the following factors might contribute to the tribe's attitude about death:

   • the tribe's connection "to the earth" (lines 57–67)
   • what the tribe sees as "the task of life" (lines 73–85)
   • the Arctic environment (lines 101–123)

6. **Analyze Point of View** Imagine that this story had been written without any insight into Koskoosh's thoughts. What information or ideas would be missing? With this in mind, explain whether or not you think the point of view plays a crucial role in expressing the story's **theme.** Cite evidence from the story to support your view.

7. **Examine Author's Perspective** In your opinion, has London created a credible portrayal of the Native Americans and their values? How do you think this portrayal reflects London's own life experiences? In developing your answer, give details from the story as well as from the biography on page 768.

8. **Compare Expressions of Naturalism** Compare and contrast London's portrayal of nature in this story with Crane's in "The Open Boat." Consider in particular the characters' fates and any differences in tone. Record your answers with evidence from the stories in a Venn diagram. In which version of nature would you prefer to live? Explain.

Text Criticism

9. **Critical Interpretation** The writer E. L. Doctorow said, "It was Jack London's capacity for really living in the world, for taking it on in self-conscious and often reckless acts of courage, that made him our first writer-hero." Given what you have read in London's biography and your reading of "The Law of Life," do you agree with the notion of London as a hero? Explain.

> *How do people face* **DEATH?**
>
> What comment on the human condition does London make through Koskoosh's last thoughts? Do you think this attitude toward death is ultimately hopeful or hopeless? Explain.

COMMON CORE

RL 2 Determine two or more themes or central ideas of a text and analyze their development over the course of the text. **RL 3** Analyze the impact of the author's choices regarding how to develop and relate elements of a story. **RL 9** Demonstrate knowledge of nineteenth- and early-twentieth-century works of American literature, including how two or more texts from the same period treat similar themes or topics.

Practice and Apply

For preliminary support of post-reading questions, use these copy masters:

R **RESOURCE MANAGER**—Copy Masters
Reading Check p. 168
Analyze Author's Perspective p. 163
Question Support p. 169
Additional selection questions are provided for teachers on page 155.

ANSWERS   COMMON CORE **RL 2, RL 3, RL 9**

1. *Wolves kill him.*

2. *He expected to freeze to death.*

3. *The tribe follows game that can be scarce.*

Possible answers:

4. ● **COMMON CORE FOCUS** **Interpret Theme** *The details suggest that death is the inevitable end of human life, and that nature does not wait for or care about individuals.*

5. *Tribe members are tied "to the earth" because they depend on nature for food and shelter and face death without rain and caribou. They see "the task of life" as having offspring to continue the tribe. The harsh Arctic environment means that death is an ever-present threat.*

6. *Students may say that point of view is crucial to the story's theme because Koskoosh's memories are symbolic and move the narrative along. Other students may say that the story of an aged man left to die alone is powerful no matter who tells it.*

7. ■ **COMMON CORE FOCUS** **Examine Author's Perspective** *Students may say that London has romanticized the tribe and its values. Others may say that the portrayal is realistic. All students should cite London's hardscrabble experiences.*

---

8. *Difference:* Crane's characters achieve brotherhood and stick together while London's main character is abandoned. *Similarity:* In both stories, nature is indifferent to human suffering.

9. *Students may say that London lived heroically, seeking adventure from a young age and packing experience into every day.*

> *How do people face* DEATH?
> *Possible answers:* London is suggesting a realistic if hard fact of life—that we all die, and death is never what we expect. Students may suggest that acceptance of death is a hopeful stance.

Vocabulary in Context

VOCABULARY PRACTICE

1. *harry*
2. *inexorable*
3. *replenish*
4. *slovenly*
5. *attest*

 RESOURCE MANAGER—Copy Master
Vocabulary Practice p. 166

ACADEMIC VOCABULARY IN WRITING

Students writing should address the prompt and include the Academic Vocabulary terms.

VOCABULARY STRATEGY: DENOTATION AND CONNOTATION

COMMON CORE L 5b, L 6

- Preview the listed words by asking students if they have positive or negative associations with each.
- Model how to find a synonym that fits the connotation required by sentence context and match this to a list word.

1. *discriminating*
2. *charlatan*
3. *resolute*
4. *subservient*
5. *ostentatious*
6. *traditional*

 **RESOURCE MANAGER—Copy Master**
Vocabulary Strategy p. 167

Interactive Vocabulary **THINK** central

Keywords direct students to a **WordSharp** tutorial on **thinkcentral.com** or to other types of vocabulary practice and review.

Assess and Reteach

Assess

DIAGNOSTIC AND SELECTION TESTS
Selection Test A, B/C pp. 205–206
Selection Test B/C pp. 207–208

Interactive Selection Test on thinkcentral.com

Reteach

LevelUp Online Tutorials on thinkcentral.com

Vocabulary in Context

▲ VOCABULARY PRACTICE

Determine the relationship between the first pair of words in each analogy. Then choose the vocabulary word that best completes the second pair.

1. *Nurse* is to *care* as *pest* is to _____.
2. *Impressive* is to *splendid* as _____ is to *unyielding*.
3. *Agree* is to *contradict* as _____ is to *deplete*.
4. *Well-groomed* is to *dandy* as _____ is to *slob*.
5. *Refuse* is to *decline* as _____ is to *declare*.

WORD LIST
attest
harry
inexorable
replenish
slovenly

ACADEMIC VOCABULARY IN WRITING

• apparent • confine • expose • focus • perceive

In a few paragraphs, make a case for or against leaving elderly people to die in a society such as the one in this story. You may **confine** your argument to practical aspects of the practice, or you may choose to **focus** on the relative value of life that it implies. Use at least one Academic Vocabulary word in your response.

VOCABULARY STRATEGY: DENOTATION AND CONNOTATION

Every word has a **denotation,** or basic dictionary meaning. Some words have additional nuances, or shades of meaning. We call such a subtle distinction of meaning a **connotation.** For example, the word *slovenly* means "untidy," but it has a more strongly negative connotation. When you encounter a new word, analyze its context to draw a conclusion about any connotation it might have.

COMMON CORE

L 5b Analyze nuances in the meaning of words with similar denotations. **L 6** Acquire and use accurately general academic words and phrases.

PRACTICE The connotation of each boldfaced word makes it inappropriate in the context. Write the word from the list provided that would be more suitable in each case. Explain why the word you chose is a better match for the context.

charlatan   discriminating   ostentatious   resolute   subservient   traditional

1. His **picky** taste was evident in his beautiful suits and well-chosen ties.
2. That **beguiler!** She convinced the children that she was their long-lost aunt.
3. I admire **inflexible** leaders who make hard decisions and then stick with them.
4. Her **humble** attitude impressed her employers, but behind their backs she belittled them constantly.
5. The **elegant** ballroom had more than its share of gold chandeliers, gaudy silk couches, and overly elaborate draperies.
6. The mayor espouses **reactionary** values such as hard work and love of family.

Interactive Vocabulary **THINK** central

Go to **thinkcentral.com**.
KEYWORD: HML11-778

DIFFERENTIATED INSTRUCTION

FOR ENGLISH LANGUAGE LEARNERS

Task Support: Vocabulary Strategy Tell students that all the listed words except one are adjectives. Review what adjectives are; then have students check each word to determine which is not an adjective (*charlatan*) and identify its part of speech (*noun*).

FOR ADVANCED LEARNERS/AP

Vocabulary in Writing Have students write a narrative describing the death of Zing-ha, alluded to in lines 120–123, using the five vocabulary words. Students may choose from what perspective they want to narrate the story.

Naturalistic Perspectives

As illustrated in the short stories by Stephen Crane and Jack London you have just read, the central assumption of naturalism is that human beings have very little control over their own lives, but instead are at the mercy of the natural world and the impersonal force of fate. The following quotations all explore a similarly naturalistic attitude.

"Nature, to be commanded, must be obeyed."

—Sir Francis Bacon

"It clearly matters very little to nature whether man has a mind or not."

—Eugène Delacroix

"At no time and in no place, will nature ever ask your permission."

—Fyodor Dostoyevsky

"Man and nature have such different views about the good of the world."

—George Gissing

"In nature there are neither rewards nor punishments—there are consequences."

—R. G. Ingersoll

Writing to Evaluate

Choose the quotation on this page that you think best represents a key theme of "The Open Boat" or "The Law of Life." Write an essay defending your choice, using details from the story as support.

Consider
- the main message of each story
- the subtle and sometimes not-so-subtle differences between the quotations
- which details from the story support your choice of quotation

Extension Online

INQUIRY & RESEARCH A tornado demolishes a house yet skips its neighbor; a marathon runner dies of a heart attack; a woman loses her retirement fund after working loyally for a company for 25 years. Every day it seems there is another story in the newspaper about the randomness of nature or the inability of humans to control their own lives. **Search** three online newspapers for stories that seem to support the naturalistic viewpoint. Print out one story to share with your classmates.

779

Wrap-Up: The Rise of Naturalism

This wrap-up provides students with an opportunity to reconsider naturalism after having seen its tenets explored in stories. Encourage students to think carefully about the idea that humans lack control of their destinies, and remind them to use their own insights about human decision-making as they read the quotes.

Writing to Evaluate

Review with students that *evaluating* means making a judgment about something. Analysis often precedes evaluation because readers must understand thoroughly in order to evaluate effectively.

To help students write their essays, break down the process into these steps:

1. Choose a story and determine its main message.
2. Decide which quote best represents the story's main message.
3. Skim the story for details that support the quotation's ideas.
4. Outline and draft the essay.

Extension Online

- As students are researching online, suggest that they visit sites maintained by their local newspaper and by other well-known, reliable newspapers.
- Encourage students to complete a Story Map for the article they select in order to identify key story points for discussion.

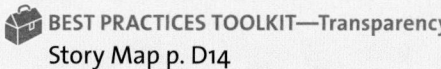 **BEST PRACTICES TOOLKIT—Transparency** Story Map p. D14

DIFFERENTIATED INSTRUCTION

FOR STRUGGLING WRITERS

Writing Support Urge students to write about "The Law of Life" because it is the shorter of the two stories. Success in analyzing a shorter piece will build confidence for future analysis of longer pieces. To make the tasks more manageable, encourage students to discuss main story ideas with a partner and skim for supporting details one page at a time.

FOR ENGLISH LANGUAGE LEARNERS

Review Theme Remind students that the main message of a story is its theme. Then discuss these questions with them:

- What is the theme of the chosen story?
- What events, dialogue, or setting details from the story support this theme?
- How does the theme statement connect to the chosen quote?

COMMON CORE FOCUS

RL 9 Demonstrate knowledge of early-twentieth-century foundational works of American literature, including how two or more texts from the same period treat similar themes or topics.

Dramatizing Social Issues

Social Themes Clarify that in the context of this workshop, the terms *theme* and *issue* are used interchangeably. Then, focus on the category of social issues and give students practice recognizing these themes. Have students identify the social issues among these examples and record them on a concept web:

- family connections
- racial prejudice *(social)*
- bonds of friendship
- religious intolerance *(social)*
- economic hardship *(social)*
- unfair working conditions *(social)*
- honesty
- homelessness *(social)*
- the power of the ocean

Explain that a theme typically requires a complete sentence to fully convey it. Urge students to write a theme statement about each social issue on their web. For example, for *racial prejudice,* they might write "Racial prejudice undermines hopes and dreams," while for *economic hardship,* they might write "Economic hardship wears down individuals."

Text Analysis Workshop

Social Themes in Fiction

People often talk about social issues—such as poverty, racism, or crime—in a general sense, but how do these issues affect individuals' lives in reality? In 19th-century America, writers began to explore these issues in fiction.

COMMON CORE

Included in this workshop:
RL 9 Demonstrate knowledge of early-twentieth-century foundational works of American literature, including how two or more texts from the same period treat similar themes or topics.

Dramatizing Social Issues

Typical themes in literature deal with issues that are common to most people, such as the loss of innocence, difficult family relationships, or a new love. **Social themes,** however, deal with issues that concern a particular group of people, such as those in a certain neighborhood, geographical region, or religious community. These issues are usually specific to a time and place, but they may echo in other cultures and times as well. For example, the dynamics of Puritan society inspired a number of great literary works with social themes, from Nathaniel Hawthorne's *The Scarlet Letter* (1850) to Arthur Miller's *The Crucible* (1953). While Hawthorne explored the effects of Puritan morality on individual lives, Miller chose to expose the wrongs committed in the name of righteousness during the Salem witch trials as a way to explore parallel events of his own time.

Two suffragettes, circa 1905, stand on an American city street, promoting women's rights.

In the late 19th and early 20th centuries, novels and short stories with a contemporary social theme typically dealt with issues that generated strong public reaction and debate for that era. These issues included industrialism, urbanization, and the displacement of Native Americans. In this way, literature became a powerful tool for social change.

Identifying Social Themes

Novels and short stories of the period often portray characters struggling against poverty, prejudice, and other social obstacles. One social issue in particular that emerged in the second half of the 19th century was the role of women in society. This issue preoccupied writers of many nationalities during this time and inspired feminist writers in the 20th century. All of the stories in this part of Unit 4 address this issue in one way or another. To help you identify the social themes in these and other stories, consider the following:

- Look for **characters** who have little control over their fate, and ask yourself what **social factors** contribute to their situation.

DIFFERENTIATED INSTRUCTION

FOR STRUGGLING READERS

Note Taking For students who are unfamiliar with social themes in fiction or need help with note taking, hand out the copy master at the start of the workshop. Explain to students that they will be learning many terms in this workshop related to social themes in fiction. Discuss the major terms on this spread (*themes, social themes, issues, characters, social factors, conflicts, character's or narrator's opinions*) as students record notes on the copy master.

 RESOURCE MANAGER—Copy Master
Note Taking p. 170

- Clarify the **conflicts** in the story and determine to what extent they are caused by forces beyond a character's control.

- Examine direct statements of a **character's or narrator's opinions** to see whether these provide clues to a theme.

- Think about the **author's reason** for writing the story. What was he or she trying to achieve?

Works that address social issues often focus on people who have few, if any, rights and privileges in society. The first-person narrator of "The Yellow Wallpaper" (page 798), although comfortably middle-class, has no control over her life. Early in the story, she explains her complete submission to her doctor and her husband.

> So I take phosphates . . . and tonics, and journeys, and air, and exercise, and am absolutely forbidden to "work" until I am well again.
>
> Personally, I disagree with their ideas.
>
> Personally, I believe that congenial work, with excitement and change, would do me good.
>
> But what is one to do?
>
> **—Charlotte Perkins Gilman, "The Yellow Wallpaper"**

Close Read

Based on the narrator's statements in this passage, how would you describe her relationship with the doctor and her husband?

In "The Story of an Hour" (page 784), the main character, after hearing that her husband is dead, reflects on the control he has exercised over her. Notice how her thoughts are a statement on the relationships between men and women in general.

> There would be no one to live for her during those coming years; she would live for herself. There would be no powerful will bending hers in that blind persistence with which men and women believe they have a right to impose a private will upon a fellow creature.
>
> **—Kate Chopin, "The Story of an Hour"**

Close Read

How is this character's attitude different from that expressed in "The Yellow Wallpaper"?

Identifying Social Themes

Suggest that students ask these questions to help them identify social themes:

- What do characters' comments—even those beyond directly stated opinions— suggest about a social message?

- What lessons do characters learn that reflect a social message?

- How do the time and place affect the characters?

- What part do social factors play in the story's conflict and resolution?

- Is the character struggling against poverty, prejudice, or injustice?

Review the excerpts on page 781 with students, clarifying the text as needed. Ask students to paraphrase each one.

Close Read

Possible answer: The narrator has strong opinions, but appears to fear conflict with others and also feels powerless to voice her opinions or to act on them.

IF STUDENTS NEED HELP . . . Ask these questions:

- How does the narrator feel about following the suggested regimens and giving up work?

- What does she believe would do her good?

Then read the final statement "But what is one to do?" and ask students what that statement suggests about the narrator's actions and feelings.

Close Read

Possible answer: Chopin's character seems more self-assured and able to act on her own views.

IF STUDENTS NEED HELP . . . Reread the first part of the second sentence: *There would be no powerful will bending hers.*

FOR ENGLISH LANGUAGE LEARNERS

Language: Skill Words Help students use context to determine the meanings of the boldface words: *theme,* "big idea or message of a story"; *social themes,* "big ideas or messages that have to do with society or the general public"; *social factor,* "causes or reason having to do with society"; *conflicts,* "struggles, battles, disagreements."

FOR ADVANCED LEARNERS/AP

Analyze Social Themes Encourage students to identify social issues and themes in works they have read, such as *The Crucible,* "Common Sense," and Frederick Douglass's slave narrative. Encourage them to share their findings with the class.

Focus and Motivate

Comparing Texts

A New Role for Women

COMMON CORE FOCUS

RL 1 Cite evidence to support inferences drawn from the text. **RL 2** Determine themes or central ideas of a text. **RL 5** Analyze how an author's choices concerning how to structure specific parts of a text contribute to its overall structure and meaning as well as its aesthetic impact. **RL 9** Demonstrate knowledge of how two or more texts from the same period treat similar themes or topics. **RI 2** Determine two or more central ideas of a text and analyze their development over the course of the text. **RI 5** Analyze and evaluate the effectiveness of the structure an author uses in his or her exposition or argument, including whether the structure makes points clear, convincing, and engaging. **RI 6** Analyze how style and content contribute to the power, persuasiveness, or beauty of the text. **RI 7** Integrate and evaluate multiple sources of information presented in different media or formats as well as in words in order to address a question. **W 9** Draw evidence from literary texts to support reflection. **W 10** Write over shorter time frames for a range of tasks. **L 3** Apply knowledge of language to make effective choices for meaning or style.

ABOUT THE AUTHOR

Remind students of the era in which Chopin lived: Women who asserted and expressed themselves were told that their behavior was unnatural. After students read, discuss what the intense criticism of her novel suggests about this period in history. ***Possible answer:** The turn-of-the-century public wasn't ready for Chopin's risqué subject matter.*

Selection Resources

COMMON CORE

RL 2 Determine themes or central ideas of a text. **RL 5** Analyze how an author's choices concerning how to structure specific parts of a text contribute to its overall structure and meaning as well as its aesthetic impact. **RI 2** Determine two or more central ideas of a text and analyze their development over the course of the text. **RI 5** Analyze and evaluate the effectiveness of the structure an author uses in his or her exposition or argument, including whether the structure makes points clear, convincing, and engaging. **RI 7** Integrate and evaluate multiple sources of information presented in different media or formats as well as in words in order to address a question.

The Story of an Hour
Short Story by Kate Chopin

VIDEO TRAILER  KEYWORD: HML11-782A

Joyas Voladoras
Essay by Brian Doyle

Essential Course of Study **ECOS**

Calvin and Hobbes
Cartoon Strip by Bill Watterson

Meet the Author

Kate Chopin 1850–1904

When her second volume of short stories was published in 1897, Kate Chopin's literary career was already thriving. Critics had praised her first collection, *Bayou Folk,* for its local-color realism, calling her tales "charming" and "quaint." Two years later came the bombshell: Chopin published *The Awakening,* a novel about a housewife's sexual and artistic awakening, complete with an adulterous affair and suicide as a last, desperate act of freedom. A chorus of outraged reviewers reviled the novel as immoral, drowning out the few brave enough to praise it. No publisher would touch her next collection, *A Vocation and a Voice,* which included "The Story of an Hour." Chopin died soon after, and *The Awakening* languished out of print for 50 years.

Faithful Wife and Mother Born into a socially prominent family, and esteemed for her beauty, intelligence, and wit, Kate Chopin married when she was 19. She and her husband settled in New Orleans, where their six children were born. Chopin had no difficulty reconciling the demands of her family with her strong independent streak. With the support of her husband, she smoked cigarettes and explored the city unescorted—scandalous behavior for an upper-class woman at the time.

A Budding Writer Chopin started writing at the age of 32. After her husband died, she returned to St. Louis, where her doctor suggested she write stories to work through her grief. Encouraged that her very first story was published, Chopin studied the work of French short story master Guy de Maupassant and honed her craft. She gradually developed an interest in complex issues such as the longing for freedom and self-fulfillment among women.

A Late-Blooming Classic Though *The Awakening* ended its author's career, it went on, after her death, to become a classic. Critics in the 1950s rediscovered the novel and, proclaiming Chopin "ahead of her time," sparked renewed interest in her modern sensibilities. Of *The Awakening's* heroine, Edna Pontellier, Chopin once said, "I never dreamed of Mrs. Pontellier making such a mess of things. . . . If I had the slightest intimation of such a thing I would have excluded her from the company." The controversial heroine made Chopin a legend. Today, *The Awakening* is among the five most-read American novels in colleges and universities.

Author Online
Go to **thinkcentral.com.** KEYWORD: HML11-782B
THINK central

See resources on the **Teacher One Stop DVD-ROM** and on **thinkcentral.com**.

 RESOURCE MANAGER UNIT 4
Plan and Teach, pp. 171–178
Summary, pp. 179–180†‡*
Text Analysis and Reading Skill, pp. 181–184†*
Grammar and Style, p. 187

DIAGNOSTIC AND SELECTION TESTS
Selection Tests, pp. 209–212

 BEST PRACTICES TOOLKIT
Three-Column Journal, p. B10

INTERACTIVE READER

ADAPTED INTERACTIVE READER

ELL ADAPTED INTERACTIVE READER

TECHNOLOGY
- **Teacher One Stop DVD-ROM**
- **Student One Stop DVD-ROM**
- **PowerNotes DVD-ROM**
- **Audio Anthology CD**
- **GrammarNotes DVD-ROM**
- **ExamView Test Generator** on the **Teacher One Stop**

Video Trailer  **THINK** central

Go to **thinkcentral.com** to preview the **Video Trailer** introducing this selection. Other features that support the selection include
- **PowerNotes** presentation
- **ThinkAloud** models to enhance comprehension
- **WordSharp** vocabulary tutorials
- interactive writing and grammar instruction

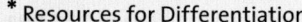 * Resources for Differentiation   † Also in Spanish   ‡ In Haitian Creole and Vietnamese

● **TEXT ANALYSIS: THEME**

At the heart of every effective piece of writing is a **theme**—a message the writer wants readers to understand or a perception about life the writer wants to share. A good short story writer doesn't express his or her theme explicitly but rather expects readers to draw their own conclusions about the story's central meaning. A rich story may have more than one theme. In "The Story of an Hour," Kate Chopin focuses on the internal life of a woman in the immediate aftermath of traumatic news. As you read the story, pay attention to Mrs. Mallard's reactions to the story's opening event. Use a chart like the one below to record clues to the story's theme or themes.

Mrs. Mallard's feelings	Mrs. Mallard's thoughts	Mrs. Mallard's actions
"wept with sudden wild abandonment"		

By contrast with a short story, an essay usually has an explicit theme—often expressed in an easily identified **thesis statement**. "Joyas Voladoras," however, is an essay without an explicit message. Instead of supporting a thesis statement, Brian Doyle reflects on the hummingbird, its heart, and the hearts of other animals. As you read the essay, pay special attention to the writer's attitude. Doyle's clearly emotional response to his subject provides clues to his themes.

● **READING SKILL: ANALYZE PATTERNS OF ORGANIZATION**

Short story and essay writers organize their material in very different ways. Short stories follow a **plot**—from exposition and rising action to **climax**, falling action, and **resolution**. Kate Chopin organizes "The Story of an Hour" by tracing the rising action to a climax. She starts with a shocking event and follows its aftermath chronologically. As you read, trace the rising action by noting Mrs. Mallard's emotional state. In Brian Doyle's essay, look for a pattern that takes the place of plot. Notice that Doyle begins with the hummingbird and its heart. Then, each paragraph takes up a related subject. Following this essay is like following a writer's train of thought.

 Complete the activities in your **Reader/Writer Notebook**.

Do all CAGES have bars?

Prisons and detention centers, animal cages, even children's playpens—all have bars to keep their inhabitants from escaping. But are these the only kinds of constraints that restrict freedom? In "The Story of an Hour," Kate Chopin explores just how restrictive invisible bars can be.

What's the Connection?

As you study the texts in this section, look for thematic connections among them. In "The Story of an Hour," a woman with a heart condition reacts to two shocking events in a short period of time. In "Joyas Voladoras," Brian Doyle reflects with awe on the hummingbird heart and on related subjects. In the *Calvin and Hobbes* cartoon strip, a young boy muses on how short life is. What kind of attitude toward life do you find in each of these selections?

783

Teach

Do all CAGES have bars?

Read the question aloud. Make sure students understand that a constraint is something that holds a person back. Ask them what effect invisible constraints have on people.

What's the Connection?

Ask students to share examples from history, literature, or personal experience in which people express their views about life. What aspect of life do they focus on—its brevity, its sweetness, or its hardships?

TEXT ANALYSIS — COMMON CORE — RL 2 / RI 2

● **Model the Skill: THEME**

Remind students that a theme is an idea expressed in a complete sentence. Give an example theme, such as "Life is too short." Point out that the graphic organizer illustrates how a character's thoughts, feelings, and reactions reveal the theme.

GUIDED PRACTICE Elicit from students themes from other stories they have read. Ask how students identified the themes.

READING SKILL — COMMON CORE — RL 5 / RI 5

■ **Model the Skill: ANALYZE PATTERNS OF ORGANIZATION**

Tell students that the plot of a story usually tells events in chronological order, but an expository essay may use order of importance, cause-and-effect, or comparison-and-contrast to present information. To help students visualize the pattern, draw a flow chart on the board. As students read "The Story of an Hour," ask them to identify events to go in the boxes.

GUIDED PRACTICE Ask students for examples of selections they have already read that use the chronological order of organization.

R RESOURCE MANAGER—Copy Master
Analyze Patterns of Organization
p. 183

DIFFERENTIATED INSTRUCTION

FOR ENGLISH LANGUAGE LEARNERS

Theme Make sure that students understand what *theme* means in this context. Explain that theme is a multiple-meaning word. Its definitions include "the message of a literary work," "the topic of a lecture or talk," "a written composition," "a musical phrase that recurs in a piece of music," and "a unifying idea." Challenge students to use the word in a sentences that express its different meanings.

SUMMARY

This short story opens with a sensitive group of characters gathered around Mrs. Mallard. Because Mrs. Mallard suffers from heart trouble, her sister gently tells her the news of her husband's death. Mrs. Mallard weeps and then retreats to her room, where she gives in to joy over her new, free life. Coaxed from her room, she dies upon seeing her husband, who is not dead after all, as he enters their home.

READ WITH A PURPOSE

Help students set a purpose for reading. As they read "The Story of an Hour," ask them to consider how Mrs. Mallard felt about being married.

BACKGROUND

Marriage at the Turn of the Century In 1900, around the time that Kate Chopin wrote "The Story of an Hour," most married women were homemakers. Nearly half of college-educated women chose not to marry at all. Only about five percent of college-educated women held jobs. However, the situation of women in the United States was changing. Divorce was rising: one of 12 marriages ended in divorce. Women who stayed at home to raise a family suddenly had more opportunities for self-fulfillment. Time-consuming tasks in the home were gradually being replaced by new technology (sewing and washing machines, vacuum cleaners)—allowing women to direct their attention to other endeavors. Professions in law, medicine, and journalism began to open up. The women's rights movement also led women to expect more about what roles they would play at home and in society.

The Story of an Hour

KATE CHOPIN

BACKGROUND This story takes place around 1900, when the status of women was radically different than it is today. Because women could not vote, they had almost no political or legal power; because they could not own property and had few chances to gain education or employment, they had little or no financial independence. Few careers were open to middle- and upper-class women, who were expected to be supported by their husbands. In most American marriages of the time, the husband was the undisputed head of the household.

Analyze Visuals ▶
In the era in which this story is set, women were deemed fragile, sensitive, and submissive. What artistic elements help to convey these attributes in the painting on page 785?

Knowing that Mrs. Mallard was afflicted with a heart trouble, great care was taken to break to her as gently as possible the news of her husband's death.

It was her sister Josephine who told her, in broken sentences; veiled hints that revealed in half concealing. Her husband's friend Richards was there, too, near her. It was he who had been in the newspaper office when intelligence of the railroad disaster was received, with Brently Mallard's name leading the list of "killed." He had only taken the time to assure himself of its truth by a second telegram, and had hastened to forestall any less careful, less tender friend in bearing the sad message.

① Targeted Passage

A Sketch of a Faraway Look, Herman Jean Joseph Richir. Bonhams, London. © Bridgeman Art Library/SuperStock.

DIFFERENTIATED INSTRUCTION

FOR ENGLISH LANGUAGE LEARNERS

Research and Describe Have students work in mixed-ability pairs to research and write a description of what women's lives were like in the 19th century. Guide them toward exploring women's rights, particularly voting and owning property. Have students read aloud their descriptions to the class.

FOR STRUGGLING READERS

In combination with the *Audio Anthology CD,* use one or more Targeted Passages (pp. 784, 786, 787) to ensure that students focus on key story events and concepts. Targeted Passages are also good for English language learners.

① Targeted Passage **[Lines 1–6]**

The opening passage establishes the main characters, the setting, and the major conflict.

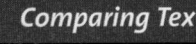

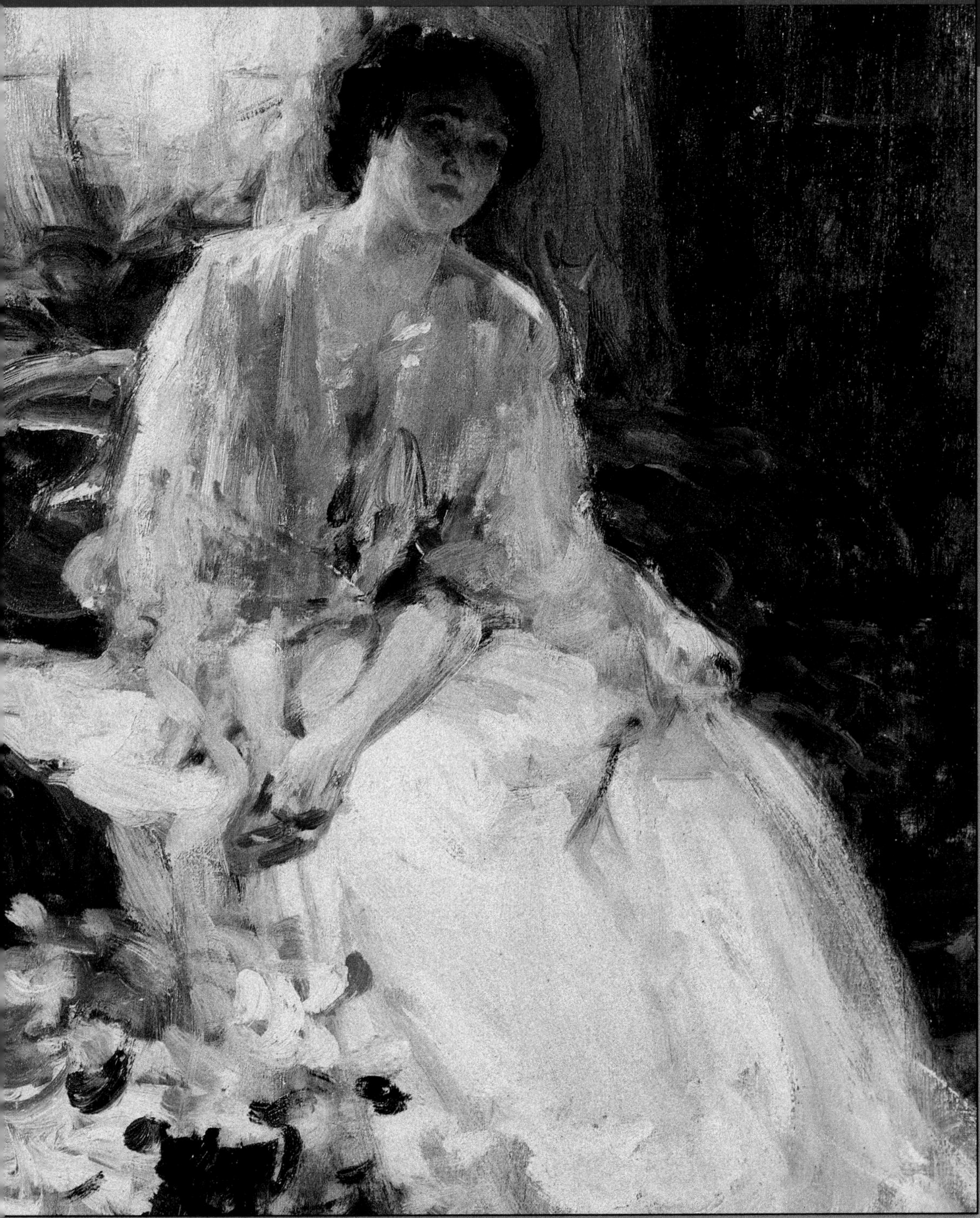

Reading Support

THINK central

This selection on **thinkcentral.com** includes embedded **ThinkAloud** models–students "thinking aloud" about the story to model the kinds of questions a good reader would ask about a selection.

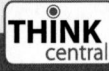

Analyze Visuals

Possible answer: *The muted colors, stooped posture, and pale, chalky complexion suggest those attributes. The images of the flowers and the woman blend together, suggesting that she is as fragile, sensitive, and beautiful as those flowers.*

About the Art The subject of Herman Richir's painting is attired in the typical Victorian fashion of the well-to-do: a long gown, perhaps beribboned and hand-embroidered, with yards of fabric and petticoats. Such fashion was a statement of the Victorian woman's purity, femininity, and modesty.

- When does the story take place? (Background, sentence 1)
- What is wrong with Mrs. Mallard? (line 1)
- What news is she about to hear? (line 2)
- Why is Mrs. Mallard's sister so worried about breaking this news? (line 1)

FOR ADVANCED LEARNERS/AP

Express Opinions Begin a class discussion by asking students to think about why marriage is important to society. Why do people marry today? What are the benefits and drawbacks of marriage? Encourage students to use specific language when expressing their opinions.

FOR STRUGGLING READERS

Develop Reading Fluency Have students participate in an echo reading. Because much of the story takes place in Mrs. Mallard's head, you can help convey the character's feelings through your tone and expressiveness. Read a section aloud for the class, evoking the character's emotional state. Then have students read the same section, mirroring your tone and expressiveness.

A GRAMMAR AND STYLE

COMMON CORE L 3

Possible answer: The active voice suggests the power of her feelings and emotions, in contrast to the delicacy and fragility implied with the use of the passive voice in the first sentence.

READING STRATEGY

COMMON CORE RL 5

B Model the Skill:
PATTERNS OF ORGANIZATION

Talk with students about the story's organizational pattern. Say: "At first Mrs. Mallard seems to despair, but then she grows calm. I think I see a pattern. The story follows the ups and downs of the character's feelings." *Possible answer: Her emotions swing from despair to calm as she moves from grief to realization that she is free, setting a pattern of moving from one extreme emotion to another.*

TEXT ANALYSIS

COMMON CORE RL 2

C Model the Skill: THEME

Remind students that writers use a character's thoughts, words, and actions to reveal the theme. Point out how Mrs. Mallard rejoices as she says the words. *Possible answer: She is free of her husband and her marriage. She must have felt trapped in her marriage and now is glad to be free.*

REVISIT THE BIG QUESTION
Do all CAGES *have bars?*

Discuss After students read lines 44–48, ask them this question: What are these constraints? What is her reaction to this change? *Possible answer: She believes that she will no longer be restrained by the wishes, needs, and demands of her husband and that the years ahead will "belong to her absolutely" (line 47). She joyously welcomes this change.*

786 UNIT 4: REGIONALISM AND NATURALISM

She did not hear the story as many women have heard the same, with a
10 paralyzed inability to accept its significance. She wept at once, with sudden, wild abandonment, in her sister's arms. When the storm of grief had spent itself she went away to her room alone. She would have no one follow her.

There stood, facing the open window, a comfortable, roomy armchair. Into this she sank, pressed down by a physical exhaustion that haunted her body and seemed to reach into her soul.

She could see in the open square before her house the tops of trees that were all aquiver with the new spring life. The delicious breath of rain was in the air. In the street below a peddler was crying his wares. The notes of a distant song which someone was singing reached her faintly, and countless sparrows were twittering
20 in the eaves.

There were patches of blue sky showing here and there through the clouds that had met and piled one above the other in the west facing her window.

She sat with her head thrown back upon the cushion of the chair, quite motionless, except when a sob came up into her throat and shook her, as a child who has cried itself to sleep continues to sob in its dreams.

She was young, with a fair, calm face, whose lines bespoke repression and even a certain strength. But now there was a dull stare in her eyes, whose gaze was fixed away off yonder on one of those patches of blue sky. It was not a glance of reflection, but rather indicated a suspension of intelligent thought.
30 There was something coming to her and she was waiting for it, fearfully. What was it? She did not know; it was too subtle and elusive to name. But she felt it, creeping out of the sky, reaching toward her through the sounds, the scents, the color that filled the air. A

Now her bosom rose and fell tumultuously. She was beginning to recognize this thing that was approaching to possess her, and she was striving to beat it back with her will—as powerless as her two white slender hands would have been. B

When she abandoned herself a little whispered word escaped her slightly parted lips. She said it over and over under her breath: "free, free, free!" The vacant stare and the look of terror that had followed it went from her eyes. They stayed keen
40 and bright. Her pulses beat fast, and the coursing blood warmed and relaxed every inch of her body. C

She did not stop to ask if it were or were not a monstrous joy that held her. A clear and exalted perception enabled her to dismiss the suggestion as trivial.

She knew that she would weep again when she saw the kind, tender hands folded in death; the face that had never looked save with love upon her, fixed and gray and dead. But she saw beyond that bitter moment a long procession of years to come that would belong to her absolutely. And she opened and spread her arms out to them in welcome.

 **Targeted Passage**

A GRAMMAR AND STYLE
Reread lines 30–33. Notice how Chopin uses the **active voice**, with the subjects performing the action in the sentences. Contrast this with her use of the **passive voice** in the first sentence of the story.

B PATTERNS OF ORGANIZATION
Reread lines 13–36. What kind of pattern do you see in Mrs. Mallard's emotions and how does this pattern lend organization to the story?

C THEME
What does Mrs. Mallard mean when she says, "free, free, free"? What kind of idea or message do you think these words convey? Explain.

786 UNIT 4: REGIONALISM AND NATURALISM

DIFFERENTIATED INSTRUCTION

FOR STRUGGLING READERS

 **Targeted Passage** [Lines 10–38]

In this passage, the rising action, climax, and resolution of the story occur.

- How does Mrs. Mallard react when her sister first breaks the news of her husband's death? (lines 10–12)

- In her room, what is she afraid of? (lines 30–36)

- Why does she say "free, free, free" over and over? (lines 37–38)

FOR ENGLISH LANGUAGE LEARNERS

Vocabulary Support Have students list words related to life outside the house in lines 16–22. Provide an example, and then have partners identify additional examples: *open square, tops of trees* (line 16); *new spring life, rain* (line 17); *peddler, distant song* (line 18); *countless sparrows* (line 19); *patches of blue sky, clouds* (line 21).

There would be no one to live for her during those coming years; she would
50 live for herself. There would be no powerful will bending hers in that blind
persistence with which men and women believe they have a right to impose a
private will upon a fellow creature. A kind intention or a cruel intention made
the act seem no less a crime as she looked upon it in that brief moment of
illumination.

And yet she had loved him—sometimes. Often she had not. What did it matter!
What could love, the unsolved mystery, count for in face of this possession of self-
assertion which she suddenly recognized as the strongest impulse of her being!

"Free! Body and soul free!" she kept whispering.

Josephine was kneeling before the closed door with her lips to the keyhole,
60 imploring for admission. "Louise, open the door! I beg; open the door—you will
make yourself ill. What are you doing, Louise? For heaven's sake open the door."

"Go away. I am not making myself ill." No; she was drinking in a very elixir
of life[1] through that open window.

> Her fancy was running riot along those days ahead of her. Spring days, and
> summer days, and all sorts of days that would be her own. She breathed a quick
> prayer that life might be long. It was only yesterday she had thought with a
> shudder that life might be long. **D**
>
> She arose at length and opened the door to her sister's importunities. There was
> a feverish triumph in her eyes, and she carried herself unwittingly like a goddess
> 70 of Victory. She clasped her sister's waist, and together they descended the stairs.
> Richards stood waiting for them at the bottom.
>
> Someone was opening the front door with a latchkey. It was Brently Mallard
> who entered, a little travel-stained, composedly carrying his grip-sack[2] and
> umbrella. He had been far from the scene of accident, and did not even know
> there had been one. He stood amazed at Josephine's piercing cry; at Richards'
> quick motion to screen him from the view of his wife.
>
> But Richards was too late.
>
> When the doctors came they said she had died of heart disease—of joy that
> kills. **E**

D **PATTERNS OF ORGANIZATION**
Reread lines 49–67, with close attention to Mrs. Mallard and her emotional state. What kind of order do you detect in this part of the story? Explain.

❸ Targeted Passage

E **THEME**
In the story's closing line, are the doctors correct in saying that Mrs. Mallard died "of joy that kills"? And how does the closing line add to the message or idea you have found in Mrs. Mallard's thoughts and feelings as the story developed? Explain your answer, citing evidence from the story.

---

1. **elixir of life:** a medicine that restores vigor or the essence of life.
2. **grip-sack:** a small traveling bag or satchel.

FOR STRUGGLING READERS

❸ Targeted Passage [Lines 64–79]

This passage contains the story's surprise ending.

- How is Mrs. Mallard feeling when she leaves her room with her sister? (lines 68–70)
- Who comes through the front door? (lines 72–74)
- What happens to Louise when she sees that her husband is still alive? (lines 78–79)

FOR ADVANCED LEARNERS/AP

Oxymoron Remind students that an oxymoron is a figure of speech in which contradictory terms are connected. Have students discuss the final words of the story: "joy that kills." What is the literal and figurative meaning of this phrase? Compare this example with "monstrous joy" in line 42. How does each example contribute to the story's irony? Ask students to write two paragraphs about the use of oxymoron in the selection and share their findings with the class.

TIERED DISCUSSION PROMPTS
Use these prompts to help students understand the levels of irony in lines 55–79:

Summarize What news has Louise just received? How does she react, publicly and privately? *Possible answer: Louise has just received news that her husband was killed. Publicly, she appears distraught; privately, she is elated.*

Analyze What does the reader know that Josephine does not? How does this dramatic irony work during the scene when Louise is alone in her room? *Possible answer: Josephine does not know that Louise is overjoyed with her anticipated freedom rather than devastated by her husband's death. It heightens the irony that Josephine is so worried about her sister's well-being.*

READING STRATEGY   COMMON CORE · RL 5

D **PATTERNS OF ORGANIZATION**

Possible answer: The story continues to follow the rising action of Mrs. Mallard's escalating emotional state as she realizes the freedom that lies ahead of her.

TEXT ANALYSIS   COMMON CORE · RL 2

E **THEME**

Possible answer: The doctors are wrong; Mrs. Mallard dies not of joy but the shock of realizing that she is not free after all. The line highlights what Mrs. Mallard is supposed to feel but does not (lines 42–48). Instead of feeling despair at her husband's death, she feels "like a goddess of Victory." (lines 68–70) Instead of feeling relief at her husband's return, she dies of a heart attack (lines 78–79).

SELECTION WRAP-UP

READ WITH A PURPOSE Now that students have read the selection, ask them to make a list of words that describe Mrs. Mallard's feelings about her marriage. *Possible answers: conflicted, unhappy, sad, oppressed*

Practice and Apply

For preliminary support of post-reading questions, use these copy masters:

R RESOURCE MANAGER—Copy Masters
Reading Check p. 185
Analyze Patterns of Organization p. 183
Question Support p. 186
Additional selection questions are provided for teachers on page 175.

ANSWERS

COMMON CORE RL 1, RL 2, RL 5, RL 9

1. *She learns that her husband had died in a train accident; she feels more joy over her new freedom than grief over her loss.*

2. *Mrs. Mallard dies of a heart attack after her husband, who is very much alive, walks through the door.*

Possible answers:

3. ● **COMMON CORE FOCUS** **Analyze Theme** *Although Mrs. Mallard was afflicted with heart trouble and "wept with wild abandonment," she began to realize a sense of relief and a desire for freedom. Mrs. Mallard had conflicting feelings about her marriage.*

4. ■ **COMMON CORE FOCUS** **Analyze Patterns of Organization** *The news of Mr. Mallard's death begins the rising action, spurring Mrs. Mallard's reactions and thoughts. The climax, or moment of greatest suspense, is the moment that Mr. Mallard returns home.*

5. *The sights and sounds from her window are images of life, hope, promise, and freedom; they support her yearning for freedom, which makes her a sympathetic character.*

6. *Mrs. Mallard: free only outside marriage; resents male power; not in control of own destiny until widowed; begins to dream of self-fulfillment. Aunt Georgiana: works within constraints of marriage; revolts only when opportunity arises and she's sure she's right; accepts husband's power; takes pride in her role as wife and mother. Both: repress their desires; taste freedom and don't want to let it go*

7. *Students may say that with greater equality women are more likely to be happy in marriage. Others may say that women's freedom creates more conflict.*

Comprehension

1. **Summarize** Describe the news Mrs. Mallard receives at the beginning of the story and explain how she reacts.

2. **Clarify** What happens at the end of the story?

Text Analysis

● 3. **Analyze Theme** Examine your chart on Mrs. Mallard's feelings, her thoughts, and her actions. What messages or key ideas can you infer from the interactions of the items on your chart? Explain.

■ 4. **Analyze Patterns of Organization** Chopin uses a traditional plot to structure this story. What starts the rising action and where does the story reach its climax? Support your answer with evidence from the story.

5. **Interpret Imagery** Reread lines 16–22. How does Chopin's use of imagery contribute to your understanding of Mrs. Mallard's character and situation? Did the imagery make you more or less sympathetic toward her? Explain, citing specific lines from the story that influenced your response.

6. **Compare Characters** Both Mrs. Mallard and Aunt Georgiana in "A Wagner Matinee" by Willa Cather (page 718) face **constraints** that confine them to a specific way of life. In a Venn diagram like the one shown, compare and contrast these two characters' situations. Use your completed diagram to explain what message each author might be trying to convey through her main character.

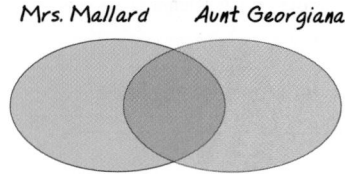

Mrs. Mallard   Aunt Georgiana

Text Criticism

7. **Social Context** Women's roles have certainly changed since Chopin wrote this story, but has the institution of marriage? Reread lines 49–54 of "The Story of an Hour." Is the imposition of will by both men and women that Chopin describes still an issue in contemporary marriages? Explain your opinion.

> *Do all* **CAGES** *have bars?*
>
> Before the beginning of "The Story of an Hour," what made Mrs. Mallard feel confined? Why, during the story, does she feel as if she has been released from a cage? Cite evidence from the story to support your answer.

COMMON CORE

RL 1 Cite evidence to support inferences drawn from the text. **RL 2** Determine two or more themes or central ideas of a text, including how they interact and build on one another to produce a complex account; provide an objective summary of the text. **RL 5** Analyze how an author's choices concerning how to structure specific parts of a text contribute to its overall structure and meaning as well as its aesthetic impact. **RL 9** Demonstrate knowledge of how two or more texts from the same period treat similar themes or topics.

Do all CAGES have bars? **Possible answers:** *At first, Mrs. Mallard is confined by a heart condition and a feeling of exhaustion; then, she begins to notice the wider world outside her window and realize that she would not have to deal with her husband's "powerful will." Finally, she can breathe, walk like "a goddess of Victory," and begin to enjoy life and asserting herself.*

Language

◆ **GRAMMAR AND STYLE:** Use Effective Voice

Review the **Grammar and Style** note on page 786. The **active voice** indicates that the subject of a sentence is *performing* the action. The **passive voice** indicates that the subject of a sentence is *receiving* the action. A writer may use the passive voice to create a particular effect or to indicate that the performer of an action is indefinite or unknown. Here are examples of each type of voice:

> **Active:** *Someone was opening the front door with a latchkey.* (line 72)

> **Passive:** *It was he who had been in the newspaper office when intelligence of the railroad disaster was received. . . .* (lines 5–6)

Kate Chopin effectively uses the active and passive voices to mirror her character's emotional transition from repression to liberation. She begins the story in the passive voice, when Mrs. Mallard is still under constraint, but later switches to the active voice as Mrs. Mallard begins to acknowledge her own identity.

PRACTICE Change the voice of the following sentences as indicated in parentheses.

> **EXAMPLE**
>
> He gave me my freedom. (Change to the passive voice.)
>
> *Freedom was given to me.*

1. A life of adventure is desired by everyone. (Change to the active voice.)
2. I will spend my days as I wish. (Change to the passive voice.)
3. No one will be consulted about my plans. (Change to the active voice.)

READING-WRITING CONNECTION

Expand your understanding of "The Story of an Hour" by responding to this prompt. Then, use the **revising tips** to improve your journal entry.

WRITING PROMPT	**REVISING TIPS**
COMPOSE A JOURNAL ENTRY "The Story of an Hour" focuses on Mrs. Mallard's feelings about her husband's reported death. Think about the moment her feelings suddenly shift from sorrow to joy. Imagine you are Mrs. Mallard. Write a **three-paragraph journal entry** in which you detail some of the thoughts that might have gone through her mind as she pondered her future.	• Make sure your entry reflects Mrs. Mallard's struggle with her feelings, showing a clear progression from grief to joy. • Give concrete examples of how she believes her life might change. • Use language and sentence types that capture her emotions.

Interactive Revision THINK central
Go to thinkcentral.com.
KEYWORD: HML11-789

THE STORY OF AN HOUR **789**

COMMON CORE

L 3 Apply knowledge of language to make effective choices for meaning or style. **W 9** Draw evidence from literary texts to support reflection. **W 10** Write over shorter time frames for a range of tasks.

Language

COMMON CORE **L 3 W 9, W 10**

◆ **GRAMMAR AND STYLE**

Ask students to identify the subject and verb in each example. (For more on active and passive voice, see page R60 in the **Grammar Handbook**.)

Answers:
1. *Everyone desires a life of adventure.*
2. *My days will be spent according to my wishes.*
3. *I will consult no one about my plans.*

R RESOURCE MANAGER—Copy Master
Use Effective Voice p. 187

READING-WRITING CONNECTION

Have students use a Three-Column Journal to write their ideas about how Mrs. Mallard felt about each part of her life before and after she learned of her husband's death.

Feelings About	Before the news	After the news
child care	overburdened	will get more help
finances	dependent	independent
education; artistic pursuits	unfulfilled	will go to college; will write

 BEST PRACTICES TOOLKIT—Transparency
Three-Column Journal p. B10

Writing Online THINK central

The following tools are available online at **thinkcentral.com** and on Write*Smart* CD-ROM:
• **Interactive Graphic Organizers**
• **Interactive Student Models**
• **Interactive Revision Lessons**
For additional grammar instruction, see **GrammarNotes** on **thinkcentral.com**.

Assess and Reteach

Assess

DIAGNOSTIC AND SELECTION TESTS
Selection Test A pp. 209–210
Selection Test B/C pp. 211–212

Interactive Selection Test on **thinkcentral.com**

Reteach

Level Up Online Tutorials on **thinkcentral.com**

THE STORY OF AN HOUR **789**

DIFFERENTIATED INSTRUCTION

FOR STRUGGLING WRITERS

Writing Support
• Offer students a starter for their journal entry: My first reaction upon hearing the news of my husband's death was profound grief. My second reaction was _____.
• Suggest that they use their Three-Column Journal as a basis for writing two paragraphs. Encourage them to add details to each paragraph.

Practice and Apply

SUMMARY

The writer considers the hearts of hummingbirds and other creatures, including whales, fish, reptiles, and worms. He discusses the speed, size, and mechanics of the creatures' hearts before concluding with some thoughts on the vulnerability of the human heart.

Essay

Both "The Story of an Hour" and "Joyas Voladoras" suggest that the human heart is fragile and easily broken. Use a Two-Column Chart to help students compare the ideas about the heart's ability to absorb pain suggested in each piece.

 BEST PRACTICES TOOLKIT—TRANSPARENCY
Two-Column Chart, p. A25

TEXT ANALYSIS
COMMON CORE
RI 2

Ⓐ THEME

Remind students that tone is the writer's attitude toward his or her subject or audience. Writers reveal their attitude by the words they use. Model the skill by thinking aloud. Say: "In the first paragraph, the writer uses the expression 'flying jewels' to describe the birds. He also uses fun, energetic words such as *whirring* and *zooming* to describe them." *Possible answers: The writer's tone is playful and admiring. His message may be that hummingbirds have amazing hearts.*

Essay

In Kate Chopin's short story, you saw how a lifetime can fit into the space of an hour. In "Joyas Voladoras," you'll read about the short life of the hummingbird and the remarkable heart that keeps the bird alive.

Joyas Voladoras

Brian Doyle

> **BACKGROUND** We are often fascinated with extremes in nature: minute, complex organisms that function at a high level of efficiency, as well as enormous animals that make us feel insignificant by comparison. In the following essay, Brian Doyle reflects on the tiny hummingbird and its incredibly fast heart. From the hummingbird, Doyle moves on to consider the blue whale and its absurdly large heart. Finally, he expands his subject to the properties of the heart that cannot be weighed or counted. Brian Doyle is the author of several books of essays, including *The Wet Engine*, a meditation on the heart.

Consider the hummingbird for a long moment. A hummingbird's heart beats ten times a second. A hummingbird's heart is the size of a pencil eraser. A hummingbird's heart is a lot of the hummingbird. *Joyas voladoras*, flying jewels, the first white explorers in the Americas called them, and the white men had never seen such creatures, for hummingbirds came into the world only in the Americas, nowhere else in the universe, more than three hundred species of them whirring and zooming and nectaring in hummer time zones nine times removed from ours, their hearts hammering faster than we could clearly hear if we pressed our elephantine ears to their infinitesimal chests.

Each one visits a thousand flowers a day. They can dive at sixty miles an hour.
10 They can fly backward. They can fly more than five hundred miles without pausing to rest. But when they rest they come close to death: on frigid nights, or when they are starving, they retreat into torpor, their metabolic rate slowing to a fifteenth of their normal sleep rate, their hearts sludging nearly to a halt, barely beating, and if they are not soon warmed, if they do not soon find that which is sweet, their hearts grow cold, and they cease to be. Consider for a moment those hummingbirds who did not open their eyes again today, this very day, in the Americas: bearded helmetcrests and booted racket-tails, violet-tailed sylphs and violet-capped woodnymphs, crimson topazes and purple-crowned fairies, red-tailed comets and amethyst woodstars, rainbow-bearded thornbills and glittering-bellied emeralds, velvet-purple coronets and golden-bellied
20 star-frontlets, fiery-tailed awlbills and Andean hillstars, spatuletails and pufflegs, each the most amazing thing you have never seen, each thunderous wild heart the size of an infant's fingernail, each mad heart silent, a brilliant music stilled. Ⓐ

Ⓐ THEME
In lines 9–22, the writer's **tone**—his attitude toward hummingbirds—provides clues to the theme of this message. How would you describe the writer's tone in these lines? What message do you infer from this tone? Explain.

B PATTERNS OF ORGANIZATION

Possible answer: *The repetition of heart is the clue to the writer's theme—the power of the heart.*

IF STUDENTS NEED HELP . . . Point out that by the end of the third paragraph, the writer begins to make connections to the hearts of other creatures. Suggest that students write down all the creatures whose hearts the writer discusses. Work with them to identify an overarching idea. Example: All hearts beat and contain "interior liquid motion"; hearts are the source of life and are vulnerable to pain.

Hummingbirds, like all flying birds but more so, have incredible enormous immense ferocious metabolisms. To drive those metabolisms they have race car hearts that eat oxygen at an eye-popping rate. Their hearts are built of thinner, leaner fibers than ours. Their arteries are stiffer and more taut. They have more mitochondria in their heart muscles—anything to gulp more oxygen. Their hearts are stripped to the skin for the war against gravity and inertia, the mad search for food, the insane idea of flight. The price of their ambition is a life closer to death; they suffer more heart
30 attacks and aneurysms and ruptures than any other living creature. It's expensive to fly. You burn out. You fry the machine. You melt the engine. Every creature on earth has approximately two billion heartbeats to spend in a lifetime. You can spend them slowly, like a tortoise, and live to be two hundred years old, or you can spend them fast, like a hummingbird, and live to be two years old. **B**

The biggest heart in the world is inside the blue whale. It weighs more than seven tons. It's as big as a room. It *is* a room, with four chambers. A child could walk around in it, head high, bending only to step through the valves. The valves are as big

B PATTERNS OF ORGANIZATION
In the first three paragraphs, this essay addresses a wide range of subjects related to the hummingbird—all of them organized around the writer's repetition of the word *heart*. Why do you think the author chose this word as the organizing focus for his essay? Explain.

JOYAS VOLADORAS   **791**

DIFFERENTIATED INSTRUCTION

FOR ENGLISH LANGUAGE LEARNERS
Vocabulary: Word Associations Write the word *heart* on the board. Then ask students to call out words or ideas they associate with the heart. Write students' answers on the board. Afterwards, ask students to classify the associations as positive or negative.

FOR STRUGGLING READERS
Develop Reading Fluency Read aloud lines 23–30 on page 791, emphasizing the natural pauses indicated by punctuation. Then read the lines a second time, with students joining you in an echo reading. Ask them to duplicate your intonation and pauses.

Use these prompts to help students understand and appreciate the author's use of the metaphorical heart in lines 57–72:

Connect The author suggests that young people have a different perspective on matters of the heart than older people do. What are your thoughts about love and hearts? Do you think they will change? *Possible answers: Some students may say that they are hopeful about love because they are young and because their culture stresses the importance of finding true love. Others may suggest that romantic love is unrealistic.*

Analyze What image does the author use to suggest that the heart can never be completely protected from pain? How does the image prove his point? *Possible answers: He uses the image of a brick wall to suggest that people may try to protect their hearts from pain, but the walls easily crumble. He gives several examples of moments or events that make the wall fall down (lines 67–72).*

Evaluate How effectively does the author use language to paint a vivid picture in this passage? Explain. *Accept all thoughtful responses.*

READING SKILL | **COMMON CORE** **RI 5**

C PATTERNS OF ORGANIZATION

Possible answer: The paragraph about the blue whale fits because it changes the focus from one of the smallest hearts in the animal kingdom to the largest.

TEXT ANALYSIS | **COMMON CORE** **RI 2**

D THEME

Possible answer: The author is suggesting that the heart is not just an organ that pumps blood and keeps us alive; it is also the seat of our emotions, and it can be broken.

---

as the swinging doors in a saloon. This house of a heart drives a creature a hundred feet long. When this creature is born it is twenty feet long and weighs four tons. It is

40 waaaaay bigger than your car. It drinks a hundred gallons of milk from its mama every day and gains two hundred pounds a day, and when it is seven or eight years old it endures an unimaginable puberty and then it essentially disappears from human ken, for next to nothing is known of the mating habits, travel patterns, diet, social life, language, social structure, diseases, spirituality, wars, stories, despairs, and arts of the blue whale. There are perhaps ten thousand blue whales in the world, living in every ocean on earth, and of the largest mammal who ever lived we know nearly nothing. But we know this: the animals with the largest hearts in the world generally travel in pairs, and their penetrating moaning cries, their piercing yearning tongue, can be heard underwater for miles and miles. **C**

50 Mammals and birds have hearts with four chambers. Reptiles and turtles have hearts with three chambers. Fish have hearts with two chambers. Insects and mollusks have hearts with one chamber. Worms have hearts with one chamber, although they may have as many as eleven single-chambered hearts. Unicellular bacteria have no hearts at all; but even they have fluid eternally in motion, washing from one side of the cell to the other, swirling and whirling. No living being is without interior liquid motion. We all churn inside.

So much held in a heart in a lifetime. So much held in a heart in a day, an hour, a moment. We are utterly open with no one, in the end—not mother and father, not wife or husband, not lover, not child, not friend. We open windows to each but we

60 live alone in the house of the heart. Perhaps we must. Perhaps we could not bear to be so naked for fear of a constantly harrowed heart. When young we think there will come one person who will savor and sustain us always; when we are older we know this is the dream of a child, that all hearts finally are bruised and scarred, scored and torn, repaired by time and will, patched by force of character, yet fragile and rickety forevermore, no matter how ferocious the defense and how many bricks you bring to the wall. You can brick up your heart as stout and tight and hard and cold and impregnable as you possibly can and down it comes in an instant, felled by a woman's second glance, a child's apple breath, the shatter of glass in the road, the words "I have something to tell you", a cat with a broken spine dragging itself into the forest

70 to die, the brush of your mother's papery ancient hand in the thicket of your hair, the memory of your father's voice early in the morning echoing from the kitchen where he is making pancakes for his children. **∿ D**

C PATTERNS OF ORGANIZATION
After three paragraphs about the hummingbird, in line 35 Brian Doyle changes the subject and writes about the blue whale. Reread lines 35–49. Then explain why you think Doyle included this paragraph in the essay.

D THEME
The first two sentences of Doyle's last paragraph have the same beginning: "So much held in a heart." What message do you think the author wants to convey to you in this statement? Explain.

DIFFERENTIATED INSTRUCTION

FOR RELUCTANT READERS

Analyze Theme Encourage students to show their understanding of the text by connecting lines 57–72 to critical thinking questions. Read lines 57–72 aloud then tell students you are going to extend the discussion. On the board, write the following: *The writer says that in our lives we are not totally open emotionally with anyone. Why does the writer say this? How does he say people attempt to protect and repair their hearts? What is the* end result of such attempts? *Possible answers: Accept all thoughtful responses.*

FOR ADVANCED LEARNERS/AP

Research Literature Suggest that students look at poetry for examples of the image of the heart. Students should be able to compare the image of the heart as it is used by poets with the way Brian Doyle uses it in the final paragraph of "Joyas Voladoras." Ask students to share their findings with the class.

Cartoon

You have studied a short story about sudden news and sudden death, as well as an essay about the hearts of hummingbirds and other creatures. Now you will examine *Calvin and Hobbes,* a popular cartoon strip by Bill Watterson. As you study each frame and read the dialogue, think about how the images and words work together to convey meaning. Then, respond to the questions alongside the cartoon, citing evidence to support your answers.

 COMMON CORE

RI 7 Integrate and evaluate multiple sources of information presented in different media or formats as well as in words in order to address a question.

1. **ANALYZE**
   Examine the first two frames of the cartoon. How do the words and the cartoonist's drawings work together to convey a theme?

2. **INTERPRET**
   Examine the last frame in this cartoon strip, paying special attention to facial expressions and the night sky behind Calvin and Hobbes. What purpose does the cartoonist achieve with this image? Why do you think he closes the strip without words?

Practice and Apply

Cartoon

 COMMON CORE RI 7

"The Story of an Hour," "Joyas Voladoras," and the Calvin and Hobbes cartoon focus on the quest for making the most of one's brief life-time. Tell students to imagine a conversation in which the authors Kate Chopin and Brian Doyle talk with Calvin, the boy in the cartoon strip. Have students meet in small groups to share their ideas. Suggest that each group member "stand in" for an author or the cartoon character. Ask groups to share their ideas.

ANALYZE VISUALS  COMMON CORE RI 7

1. ANALYZE

Possible answer: *The first two frames show the two characters examining the sidewalk. In the dialogue, Calvin speaks about the sidewalk as a metaphor for life. Together the words and images suggest that ordinary life can be filled with deep moments.*

ANALYZE VISUALS COMMON CORE RI 7

2. INTERPRET

Possible answer: *The image and the lack of dialogue shows readers that the characters have been standing and pondering Calvin's idea about the meaning of life for several hours.*

Practice and Apply

ANSWERS

1. *Their hearts slow down and nearly stop beating. They grow cold.*

2. *Their hearts wear out quickly because they beat so fast.*

Possible answers:

3. ● **COMMON CORE FOCUS** **Analyze Theme** *The tone is tender and vulnerable. The tone supports the theme that the heart is an organ that makes biological life (for every creature) and emotional life (for humans) possible. Students should point to the details in the essay about how the heart works physically and notice that in the final paragraph, the writer emphasizes the heart's vulnerability.*

4. ■ **COMMON CORE FOCUS** **Analyze Patterns of Organization** *Each paragraph of the essay focuses on some aspect or function of the heart. He begins by focusing on the physical aspects of hummingbirds and then moves to other animals, including the blue whale. The final paragraph transitions neatly from focusing on the physical characteristics of mammals' hearts to the emotional aspects of the human heart.*

5. *The writer using "the house of the heart" as a symbol for humans' emotional centers and says that people do not fully open themselves up emotionally to others, although "we open windows to [others] (line 59). However, attempts to lock our hearts behind brick walls are foiled by "a child's apple breath" and other human interactions (lines 67–72).*

6. *The writer achieves a poetic effect, especially in the final paragraph where he evokes images of love and heartbreak.*

7. *The writer relies on imagery that appeals to the sense of sight in order to help read-*

Assess and Reteach

Assess

DIAGNOSTIC AND SELECTION TESTS
Selection Test A, B/C pp. 209–212

Interactive Selection Test on **thinkcentral.com**

Reteach

Level Up Online Tutorials on **thinkcentral.com**

After Reading

Comprehension

1. **Recall** What happens to hummingbirds when they are cold or starving?

2. **Explain** Why do hummingbirds have such a short life cycle?

Text Analysis

● 3. **Analyze Theme** Describe the writer's tone in the last paragraph of the essay and explain how the tone conveys a theme. Support your answer with evidence from the essay.

■ 4. **Analyze Patterns of Organization** How does the writer keep this essay focused and organized, even when he changes the subject? Explain your answer.

5. **Analyze Metaphor** What do you think Doyle means by the line, "we live alone in the house of the heart" (lines 59–60)? Cite evidence from the essay to support your answer.

6. **Analyze Diction** What effect does the writer achieve by using ornate, elaborate language?

7. **Evaluate Imagery** How does Doyle's use of **imagery,** or language that appeals to the senses, enhance the effectiveness of this essay? Cite examples in your response.

Comparing Themes Across Genres

8. **Analyze Theme** What messages about life does Brian Doyle's essay share with Kate Chopin's "The Story of an Hour"? Cite evidence from both the essay and the story to support your answer.

> *Do all* **CAGES** *have bars?*
>
> In "Joyas Voladoras," Brian Doyle celebrates the heart as an organ and the heart as a metaphor for much, much more. How are human beings both restricted and made free by the heart? Support your response with evidence from Doyle's essay.

COMMON CORE

RI 2 Determine two or more central ideas of a text. **RI 5** Analyze and evaluate the effectiveness of the structure an author uses in his or her exposition or argument, including whether the structure makes the points clear, convincing, and engaging. **RI 6** Analyze how style and content contribute to the power, persuasiveness, or beauty of the text.

---

ers understand the physical attributes of hearts. For example, he compares hummingbird hearts to pencil erasers and machines and whale hearts to rooms.

8. *Both authors understand that the life of the heart is short and can end at any moment. Mrs. Mallard realizes that she has never been free. She has only begun to appreciate her freedom when the shock of her husband's arrival gives her a heart attack, and she dies. Similarly, a hummingbird must forage for food and stay warm or its heart will slow down and stop.*

> *Do all* **CAGES** *have bars?* **Possible answer:** *Humans can live only as long as their hearts work, but their hearts allow them to love and feel deeply and freely. Students should point to Doyle's comparison of the hummingbird and the tortoise; each has two billion heartbeats, but one lives centuries and one lives just two years.*

Assessment Practice: Short Constructed Response

LITERARY TEXT: "THE STORY OF AN HOUR"

On assessments you are expected to make inferences as you read. Practice this skill as you answer the **short constructed response question** below. Be sure to follow the steps outlined to the right of the question.

> This story closes with an instance of dramatic irony. Irony always involves a contrast between appearance and reality. Dramatic irony occurs when readers know more about something in a story than the characters know. What is the dramatic irony that closes this story and how does it express the author's theme?

◀ **STRATEGIES IN ACTION**

1. Make a list of words that describe Mrs. Mallard's state of mind during the time she spends alone after hearing that her husband has died in a train accident.

2. In light of your list, why do you think Mrs. Mallard cries out when she discovers that her husband is alive?

3. Identify the mistake the doctors make when they explain why Mrs. Mallard dies. The dramatic irony that lies in their misunderstanding is a clue to the theme.

NONFICTION TEXT: "JOYAS VOLADORAS"

On assessments you are expected to read carefully and answer questions that focus on particular passages from a text. To strengthen your close-reading skills, read the **short constructed response question** at left below and practice the strategies suggested at right.

> In the second-to-last paragraph of this essay, what purpose does the writer achieve by describing the hearts of numerous kinds of animals?

◀ **STRATEGIES IN ACTION**

1. Closely reread the paragraph, looking for clues to Doyle's purpose in the descriptions themselves.

2. Look for a message from the writer in the paragraph's opening or closing sentence.

COMPARING LITERARY AND NONFICTION TEXTS

On assessments you will need to identify thematic connections between literary and nonfiction texts. Practice this valuable skill by responding to the **short constructed response question** at left below and using the strategies provided at right.

> How do the authors of both "The Story of an Hour" and "Joyas Voladoras" use the heart as a metaphor?

◀ **STRATEGIES IN ACTION**

1. Doyle explicitly discusses the heart throughout. Briefly write what "heart" means to him.

2. Identify something in Mrs. Mallard's heart and life that resembles your answer to number 1.

Assessment Practice: Short Constructed Response

LITERARY TEXT: "THE STORY OF AN HOUR"
Possible answer: *The irony of the story's closing line is that joy at seeing her husband, who was thought to be dead, did not kill Mrs. Mallard. In fact, Mrs. Mallard was feeling joy at the freedom she would enjoy after his death. Instead, it was the shock of realizing that she was not free that killed her.*

NONFICTION TEXT: "JOYAS VOLADORAS"
Possible answer: *The writer helps readers understand the many similarities among the hearts of different animals. He suggests that every living creature shares the quality of an "interior liquid motion." The writer considers that internal movement a universal trait among living creatures.*

COMPARING LITERARY AND NONFICTION TEXTS
Possible answers: *In both selections, the heart is the seat of one's emotions and a machine that eventually fails. Both Mrs. Mallard and Brian Doyle, the author of "Joyas Voladoras," understand that the heart is not a fortress; it can't withstand great emotional damage. When Mrs. Mallard realizes that she may never be free from her marriage, her heart gives out. Doyle suggests that a heart may be broken—literally by burning out—or figuratively by a painful memory or experience.*

DIFFERENTIATED INSTRUCTION

FOR STRUGGLING WRITERS

Analyze the Prompt Help prepare students for writing by reading aloud the prompts and by defining any literary terms they need to address. For example, make sure that students understand the definition of *irony* before they begin their response to the prompt for "The Story of an Hour" and the definition of *metaphor* before they address the short constructed response question.

In addition, make sure that students understand their purpose for writing for each prompt. Ask students the following question: *What do you need to do in order to answer the question?* For example, in answering the Expository Selection prompt, students need to do two things. First they must analyze the writer's use of description and then they must identify the purpose it serves.

Focus and Motivate

COMMON CORE FOCUS

RL 1 Cite evidence to support analysis of what the text says explicitly as well as inferences drawn from the text, including determining where the text leaves matters uncertain. **RL 3** Analyze the impact of the author's choices regarding how to develop and relate elements of a story. **RL 9** Demonstrate knowledge of nineteenth-century foundational works of American literature. **RI 1** Cite evidence to support analysis of what the text says explicitly as well as inferences drawn from the text. **W 1** Write arguments to support claims in an analysis of texts, using valid reasoning and relevant and sufficient evidence. **W 1a–b** Introduce a precise claim; develop claim and counterclaims fairly and thoroughly, supplying the most relevant evidence for each in a manner that anticipates the audience's possible biases. **L 1** Demonstrate command of the conventions of standard English grammar and usage when writing. **L 3** Apply knowledge of language to comprehend more fully when reading. **L 5** Demonstrate understanding of word relationships. **L 6** Acquire and use accurately general academic words and phrases.

ABOUT THE AUTHOR

After students read Gilman's biography, ask how the Beechers might have affected her. *Possible answer: They fostered her interest in women's rights and social change.* Have students predict what might cause the narrator in "The Yellow Wallpaper" to go mad. *Students may suggest that unhappiness with inequality leads to the narrator's madness.*

Selection Resources

A New Role for Women

COMMON CORE

RL 1 Cite evidence to support analysis of what the text says explicitly as well as inferences drawn from the text, including determining where the text leaves matters uncertain. **RL 3** Analyze the impact of the author's choices regarding how to develop and relate elements of a story. **RL 9** Demonstrate knowledge of nineteenth-century foundational works of American literature. **L 3** Apply knowledge of language to comprehend more fully when reading.

The Yellow Wallpaper

Short Story by Charlotte Perkins Gilman

Meet the Author

Charlotte Perkins Gilman 1860–1935

As a feminist writer, social activist, public lecturer, editor, and publisher, Charlotte Perkins Gilman rode the wave of reform that washed over the United States in the late 19th and early 20th centuries. Her 1898 landmark study, *Women and Economics*—called "the Bible of the woman's movement" at the time—argued persuasively that women's economic dependence on men made them veritable slaves in U.S. society. To rectify the inequities, she advocated child-care centers and communal kitchens so that women could earn money outside the home. In addition, her startlingly original story "The Yellow Wallpaper," published in 1892, discredited a popular treatment for women's so-called "nervous disorders." Looking beyond suffrage, Gilman sought to free women from domestic servitude and foster their intellectual and emotional growth.

Formative Early Years Gilman got a rather shaky start in life. Her father abandoned the family shortly after her birth in Hartford, Connecticut. Her mother, possibly in reaction to her dire circumstances, adopted the odd child-rearing habits of withholding affection and forbidding her daughter to read fiction or form close friendships. Fortunately, financial hardship forced the family to live with relatives, the most prominent among them being Harriet Beecher Stowe, the abolitionist author of *Uncle Tom's Cabin,* and the feminists Catherine Beecher and Isabella Beecher Hooker. Guided by her strong, successful aunts, young Charlotte grew into a well-adjusted, independent woman.

Sweetening Reform with Humor Gilman's first published work was a volume of poetry, *In This Our World,* which attracted attention for the humorous way she ridiculed social injustice and inequality. *Women and Economics* garnered similar praise despite its frontal assault on conventional marriage. One reviewer praised the "wit and sarcasm" that made Gilman's "profound social philosophy" such an entertaining read. After publishing several more sociological studies, Gilman returned to writing fiction. *Herland* (1915) is a science-fiction satire about the comic misadventures of three men who stumble upon an all-female society. Still, Gilman's most popular work continues to be "The Yellow Wallpaper," the grim but fascinating portrait of a woman's descent into madness. The one-of-a-kind story has never gone out of print.

DID YOU KNOW?

Charlotte Perkins Gilman ...

- moved 19 times in her first 18 years.
- produced eight novels, six nonfiction books, almost 200 short stories, hundreds of poems, and thousands of essays.
- founded and ran her own feminist magazine, the *Forerunner.*

Author Online

THINKcentral

Go to **thinkcentral.com.** KEYWORD: HML11-796

796

See resources on the **Teacher One Stop DVD-ROM** and on **thinkcentral.com**.

 RESOURCE MANAGER UNIT 4

Plan and Teach, pp. 189–196
Summary, pp. 197–198
Text Analysis and Reading
  Skill, pp. 199–202
Vocabulary, pp. 203–205
Grammar and Style, p. 208

DIAGNOSTIC AND SELECTION TESTS

Selection Tests, pp. 213–216

 BEST PRACTICES TOOLKIT

Jigsaw Reading, p. A1
Comparison Matrix, p. A24
Three-Column Journal, p. B10
Two-Column Chart, p. A25
Open Mind, p. D9
Classification Chart, p. B17

TECHNOLOGY

- **Teacher One Stop DVD-ROM**
- **Student One Stop DVD-ROM**
- **Audio Anthology CD**
- **GrammarNotes DVD-ROM**
- **ExamView Test Generator** on the **Teacher One Stop**

---

* Resources for Differentiation   † Also in Spanish   ‡ In Haitian Creole and Vietnamese

TEXT ANALYSIS: FIRST-PERSON NARRATOR

A story's **narrator**—the character or voice that relates events to the reader—can have a marked effect on how you perceive the events of the story. A **first-person narrator** is a character in the story. This story is narrated by a woman diagnosed with a "nervous condition." From reading her journal entries, you learn what she is experiencing mentally and emotionally. As you read, ask yourself how she changes and what causes her to change. Consider whether she is a reliable source of information and what might be left out of her narration.

● READING SKILL: UNDERSTAND SOCIAL CONTEXT

Social context, or the social conditions that inspired or influenced the author, is key to this story's **setting**. In 1892, when the story was written, women held a very different place in society than they do today. Use your own knowledge, as well as the background on page 796, to analyze the social context of this story. Note what the annotated passages reveal about how women were treated and how they were expected to behave. Consider what Gilman may have thought about these conditions and how they influence the way she chooses to present her narrator in "The Yellow Wallpaper."

Story Passages	Notes on Social Context
"John laughs at me, of course, but one expects that in marriage."	The narrator does not expect that a husband would take his wife's ideas seriously. At this time, men wielded the power in most American households.

▲ VOCABULARY IN CONTEXT

Gilman uses these words in her harrowing story of stress and power. Determine the meaning of each word from its context.

1. doctor's orders **misconstrued** because of their complexity
2. a **recurrent** ailment, returning every few months
3. a delicate **temperament**, prone to worrying
4. disturbed by intense, **lurid** dreams
5. flashy, **flamboyant** drawings representing her state of mind
6. **undulating** patterns that made her feel seasick
7. a twisted **convolution** of nightmarish thoughts
8. ignorant remarks that demonstrated her **fatuity**

 Complete the activities in your **Reader/Writer Notebook**.

What if no one took you SERIOUSLY?

A friend rolls his or her eyes in disbelief as you tell a story. Your parents don't believe that you really are sick, not just feigning illness to get out of a test. A teacher or coach refuses to listen to your perspective before launching into a lecture. On at least one occasion, you've probably felt the sting of someone dismissing your feelings or refusing to listen to you. An isolated instance is bad enough, but if everyone around you refused to take you seriously, you might feel utterly powerless.

QUICKWRITE Try to imagine a whole day during which, no matter what happened, no one took you seriously. Envision yourself in the middle of such a day; then write a journal entry describing your reaction.

797

Teach

What if no one took you SERIOUSLY?

After posing the question to students, ask them to offer definitions of powerless. After they complete the *QUICKWRITE,* have them revisit their definitions and suggest possible revisions.

TEXT ANALYSIS   COMMON CORE   RL 1   RL 3

● Model the Skill: FIRST-PERSON NARRATOR

Share this example with students:

> If only my son Jesse's math teacher saw his brilliance. Jesse's memory of baseball statistics is amazing for a high school student. The teacher should not worry that Jesse is failing math. One day Jesse will find a job he loves—then, look out!

Point out the narrator's attitude toward Jesse. He puts a positive spin on Jesse's failure, and perhaps overestimates his strengths.

GUIDED PRACTICE Ask students how Jesse's math teacher might respond to the narrator's attitude.

READING SKILL   COMMON CORE   RL 3   RL 9

■ Model the Skill: UNDERSTAND SOCIAL CONTEXT

Remind students that besides drawing on their prior knowledge, they can also research a story's historical context to better understand the social context of the work. Suggest that students fill out the Understand Social Context chart with any passage they think might relate to social context. They can discuss any passage they are uncertain of.

GUIDED PRACTICE Ask students for words that describe their own social context.

R RESOURCE MANAGER—Copy Master
Understand Social Context p. 201 (for student use while reading the selection)

VOCABULARY SKILL   COMMON CORE   L 4

▲ VOCABULARY IN CONTEXT

DIAGNOSE WORD KNOWLEDGE Have all students complete Vocabulary in Context. Check their definitions against the following:

convolution (kŏn′və-lōō′shən) *n.* a form or shape that is folded into curved, complicated windings

fatuity (fə-tōō′ĭ-tē) *n.* something foolish or stupid

flamboyant (flăm-boi′ənt) *adj.* marked by strikingly elaborate or colorful display

lurid (lŏor′ĭd) *adj.* shocking; gruesome

misconstrued (mĭs′kən-strōōd′) *adj.* misunderstood; misinterpreted **misconstrue** *v.*

recurrent (rĭ-kûr′ənt) *adj.* occurring time after time

temperament (tĕm′prə-mənt) *n.* a person's characteristic mode of emotional response

undulating (ŭn′jə-lā′tĭng) *adj.* appearing to move in waves **undulate** *v.*

R RESOURCE MANAGER—Copy Master
Vocabulary Study p. 203

SUMMARY

In this short story, the narrator, whose doctor-husband has prescribed a "rest cure" for her depression, keeps a secret diary of a summer spent mostly in bed at a rented country home. She grows increasingly obsessed with the room's yellow wallpaper, imagining a woman trapped in it and wanting to free her by peeling off the paper. Finally, her husband finds her creeping around the room, certain she has freed *herself* from the torn-off wallpaper.

READ WITH A PURPOSE

Help students read with a purpose. Tell them to notice how the main character changes over the course of the story.

READING SKILL

COMMON CORE
RL 3
RL 9

A SOCIAL CONTEXT

Possible answer: Gilman conveys the belief about women's instability through John. He dismisses his wife's feelings and intuitions as unscientific and superstitious, and he laughs and scoffs at her (lines 7–10). He does not believe she is ill (line 14).

IF STUDENTS NEED HELP . . . Review the chart introduced on page 797 and help students list additional examples.

Story Passages	Notes on Social Context
"John is practical . . . in figures." (lines 8–10)	Doctors at this time discounted emotional issues as unimportant.
"He does not believe I am sick!" (line 14)	Emotional illness was not taken seriously

---

REVISIT THE BIG QUESTION

What if no one took you SERIOUSLY?

Discuss After students read lines 11–15, ask: How does the narrator's passivity reinforce her sense that she is powerless? *Possible answer: She says, "And what can one do?" (line 15), which suggests that she feels she must acquiesce to her husband's and others' opinions.*

The Yellow WALLPAPER

CHARLOTTE PERKINS GILMAN

BACKGROUND If a woman sought medical treatment for a disorder such as depression or anxiety in 1892, her ills were often diagnosed as trivial "nervous conditions," curable through isolation and prolonged rest. Today it is believed that some of these disorders were caused in part by the stress of living within the rigid social roles to which women were confined. Doctors of the time, however, typically felt that their patients' gender lay at the root of the problem. Many saw women as weak and emotionally unstable, and thus predisposed to illness.

Analyze Visuals ▶
Examine this painting. Describe the woman's size, position, and coloring relative to the flowers in the foreground. How does she look next to the flowers? Explain.

It is very seldom that mere ordinary people like John and myself secure ancestral halls for the summer.

A colonial mansion, a hereditary estate, I would say a haunted house, and reach the height of romantic felicity—but that would be asking too much of fate!

Still I will proudly declare that there is something queer about it.

Else, why should it be let so cheaply? And why have stood so long untenanted?

John laughs at me, of course, but one expects that in marriage.

John is practical in the extreme. He has no patience with faith, an intense horror of superstition, and he scoffs openly at any talk of things not to be felt and
10 seen and put down in figures.

John is a physician, and *perhaps*—(I would not say it to a living soul, of course, but this is dead paper and a great relief to my mind)—*perhaps* that is one reason I do not get well faster.

You see he does not believe I am sick!

And what can one do? **A**

① Targeted Passage

A SOCIAL CONTEXT
Consider what you learned from the background paragraph at the top of this page. How does Gilman convey the belief prevalent in her time that women were emotionally unstable and prone to illness?

Geraniums (1888), Childe Hassam. 18 ¹/₄″ × 12 ⁷/₈″. The Hyde Collection, Glens Falls, New York. Photo © Michael Fredericks.

DIFFERENTIATED INSTRUCTION

FOR ENGLISH LANGUAGE LEARNERS

Options for Reading Read aloud the summary for students to provide them with an overview of the selection. Then ask students to listen to the *Audio Anthology CD* as they read the story silently. Finally, divide students into Jigsaw groups, and assign one Targeted Passage to each. Have students present their passages to the other groups.

BEST PRACTICES TOOLKIT
Jigsaw Reading p. A1

FOR STRUGGLING READERS

In combination with the *Audio Anthology CD*, use one or more Targeted Passages (pp. 798, 801, 803, 806, 808, 810, 811, 813) to ensure that students focus on key story events and concepts. Targeted Passages are also good for English language learners.

Analyze Visuals

Possible answer: *The woman, sitting in the corner, perhaps doing needlework, seems small in relation to the flowers in the foreground. In coloring, her white dress contrasts with the colored flowers, while her dark hair and white dress blend into the background.*

About the Art Childe Hassam (1859–1935), America's leading impressionist, painted country life in America as it was once lived in houses like the one the narrator and her husband have rented, using light and color to convey nostalgia for that lifestyle gone by.

TIERED DISCUSSION PROMPTS

Use these prompts to help students explore the conflict between the two main characters as revealed in lines 8–13:

Connect What does the expression "opposites attract" mean? How does it help you understand the narrator's relationship with her husband? *Accept all thoughtful answers.*

Analyze In what way does the narrator imply that she and John are opposites? *Possible answer:* *She suggests that John is practical and rational, while she is emotional and intuitive.*

Synthesize How would you expect their differences to prove problematic for the narrator? *Possible answer:* *The narrator believes that she is sick. John's doubt of this and his dismissal of her instincts could cause problems if her condition persists or worsens.*

---

① Targeted Passage [Lines 1–15]

This passage introduces the main characters of the narrator and her husband, the rented home setting, and the main conflict over the narrator's health.

- Where does the story take place? (lines 1–3)
- What does the narrator's husband do? (line 11)
- About what do the narrator and her husband disagree? (lines 3–7)

FOR STRUGGLING READERS

Develop Reading Fluency Students may have trouble with the story's nineteenth-century syntax and diction. To help, have them read along silently while listening to the *Audio Anthology CD*. After students listen and read a section, such as a paragraph or a page, stop and ask volunteers to summarize what they have read or to ask questions.

What if no one took you SERIOUSLY?

Discuss After students read lines 16–32, pose the following question: How does the narrator's husband contribute to her sense of being powerless? *Possible answer: The narrator's husband insists that her only problem is a nervous depression (lines 17–18). He prescribes a cure that does not allow her to work (line 22), despite her belief that it would do her good (lines 24–25). The fact that he ignores her feelings, wishes, and needs makes her feel helpless and contributes to her illness.*

TEXT ANALYSIS · COMMON CORE · RL 1 · RL 3

**B Model the Skill:
FIRST-PERSON NARRATOR**

Point out that using the first-person point of view introduces the reader to the narrator's thought processes and feelings.

Possible answer: The narrator takes pride in the house but also has a growing sense of uneasiness about it (lines 33–44). She feels there is something strange about the house and, since her husband chastises her for a lack of "proper self-control," she begins to hide her feelings (lines 44–50).

If a physician of high standing, and one's own husband, assures friends and relatives that there is really nothing the matter with one but temporary nervous depression—a slight hysterical[1] tendency—what is one to do?

My brother is also a physician, and also of high standing, and he says the same
20 thing.

So I take phosphates or phosphites—whichever it is, and tonics, and journeys, and air, and exercise, and am absolutely forbidden to "work" until I am well again.

Personally, I disagree with their ideas.

Personally, I believe that congenial work, with excitement and change, would do me good.

But what is one to do?

I did write for a while in spite of them; but it *does* exhaust me a good deal—having to be so sly about it, or else meet with heavy opposition.

I sometimes fancy that in my condition if I had less opposition and more
30 society and stimulus—but John says the very worst thing I can do is to think about my condition, and I confess it always makes me feel bad.

So I will let it alone and talk about the house.

The most beautiful place! It is quite alone, standing well back from the road, quite three miles from the village. It makes me think of English places that you read about, for there are hedges and walls and gates that lock, and lots of separate little houses for the gardeners and people.

There is a *delicious* garden! I never saw such a garden—large and shady, full of box-bordered paths, and lined with long grape-covered arbors with seats under them.
40 There were greenhouses, too, but they are all broken now.

There was some legal trouble, I believe, something about the heirs and coheirs; anyhow, the place has been empty for years.

That spoils my ghostliness, I am afraid, but I don't care—there is something strange about the house—I can feel it.

I even said so to John one moonlight evening, but he said what I felt was a *draft,* and shut the window.

I get unreasonably angry with John sometimes. I'm sure I never used to be so sensitive. I think it is due to this nervous condition.

But John says if I feel so, I shall neglect proper self-control; so I take pains to
50 control myself—before him, at least, and that makes me very tired. **B**

I don't like our room a bit. I wanted one downstairs that opened on the piazza and had roses all over the window, and such pretty old-fashioned chintz hangings![2] but John would not hear of it.

He said there was only one window and not room for two beds, and no near room for him if he took another.

He is very careful and loving, and hardly lets me stir without special direction.

---

1. **hysterical:** Hysteria is the presence of a physical ailment with no underlying physical cause.

2. **chintz hangings:** curtains made out of chintz, a printed cotton fabric.

Language Coach

Antonyms An **antonym** is a word with a meaning opposite that of another word. Gilman is contrasting the words *opposition* and *society* in lines 29–31. Knowing that *opposition* means "action working against something or someone," what must *society* mean here?

B FIRST-PERSON NARRATOR
Reread lines 32–50. Notice how the narrator combines details of the house with her personal feelings about it. How does the author's use of first-person point of view lend to the internal development of the narrator? Support your answer with evidence from the selection.

DIFFERENTIATED INSTRUCTION

FOR STRUGGLING READERS

Visualize Gilman uses strong visual images to create the story's setting. Ask students to try to picture these descriptions as you read aloud: the grounds (lines 33–40), the top-floor room (lines 63–70), and the wallpaper (lines 71–80). Challenge students to recall details after each description. As they read on, urge them to notice how the narrator's perception of each element changes as her mental health deteriorates.

FOR ENGLISH LANGUAGE LEARNERS

Language Coach

Antonyms *Possible answer: "friendly cooperation"* Point out to students that Gilman also contrasts *stimulus* and *opposition.* Explain that stimulus means "something that excites a person or cause him or her to take action." Ask students to explain how *opposition* is an antonym of *stimulus.* *Possible answer:* Opposition prevents a person from taking action.

FOR ADVANCED LEARNERS/AP

Synthesize Author's Views [small-group option] Have students reread the author biography on page 796, then relate Gilman's thesis in *Women and Economics* to the views on self-control expressed in lines 49–50 of the story. Small groups might consider these questions: What does John mean by "self-control"? How does enslavement relate to control and self-control? Have students share their discussion results.

I have a schedule prescription for each hour in the day; he takes all care from me, and so I feel basely ungrateful not to value it more.

He said we came here solely on my account, that I was to have perfect rest and
60 all the air I could get. "Your exercise depends on your strength, my dear," said he, "and your food somewhat on your appetite; but air you can absorb all the time." So we took the nursery at the top of the house.

It is a big, airy room, the whole floor nearly, with windows that look all ways, and air and sunshine galore. It was nursery first and then playroom and gymnasium, I should judge; for the windows are barred for little children, and there are rings and things in the walls.

The paint and paper look as if a boys' school had used it. It is stripped off—the paper—in great patches all around the head of my bed, about as far as I can reach, and in a great place on the other side of the room low down. I never saw a worse
70 paper in my life.

One of those sprawling **flamboyant** patterns committing every artistic sin.

It is dull enough to confuse the eye in following, pronounced enough to constantly irritate and provoke study, and when you follow the lame uncertain curves for a little distance they suddenly commit suicide—plunge off at outrageous angles, destroy themselves in unheard of contradictions.

The color is repellent, almost revolting; a smouldering unclean yellow, strangely faded by the slow-turning sunlight.

It is a dull yet **lurid** orange in some places, a sickly sulphur tint in others.

No wonder the children hated it! I should hate it myself if I had to live in this
80 room long.

There comes John, and I must put this away,—he hates to have me write a word.

We have been here two weeks, and I haven't felt like writing before, since that first day.

I am sitting by the window now, up in this atrocious nursery, and there is nothing to hinder my writing as much as I please, save lack of strength. ◆

John is away all day, and even some nights when his cases are serious.

I am glad my case is not serious!

But these nervous troubles are dreadfully depressing.

John does not know how much I really suffer. He knows there is no *reason* to
90 suffer, and that satisfies him.

Of course it is only nervousness. It does weigh on me so not to do my duty in any way!

I meant to be such a help to John, such a real rest and comfort, and here I am a comparative burden already!

Nobody would believe what an effort it is to do what little I am able,—to dress and entertain, and order things.

flamboyant (flăm-boi′ənt) *adj.* marked by strikingly elaborate or colorful display

lurid (lŏŏr′ĭd) *adj.* shocking; gruesome

② **Targeted Passage**

◆ **GRAMMAR AND STYLE**
Notice that Gilman chose to tell this story in the **present tense.** This lends the narrative a sense of immediacy and allows readers to feel as though they're witnessing new developments in the narrator's condition as they unfold.

It is fortunate Mary is so good with the baby. Such a dear baby!

And yet I *cannot* be with him, it makes me so nervous.

I suppose John never was nervous in his life. He laughs at me so about this
100 wallpaper!

At first he meant to repaper the room, but afterwards he said that I was letting
it get the better of me, and that nothing was worse for a nervous patient than to
give way to such fancies.

He said that after the wallpaper was changed it would be the heavy bedstead, and
then the barred windows, and then that gate at the head of the stairs, and so on.

"You know the place is doing you good," he said, "and really, dear, I don't care
to renovate the house just for a three months' rental."

"Then do let us go downstairs," I said, "there are such pretty rooms there."

Then he took me in his arms and called me a blessed little goose, and said he

A Woman Seated at a Table by a Window, Carl Holsoe. Oil on canvas. © SuperStock.

◄ **Analyze Visuals**
How would you describe
the **mood** of this painting?
In your opinion, is it
similar to or different from
the mood of the story?
Explain, citing specific
details from each that
influenced your answer.

Analyze Visuals

Possible answer: *The painting, unlike the story,
has a serene and calm mood. The woman sits
meditatively gazing out the window. It is open,
not barred. The room is simple but attractive,
not decaying as in the story. The yellow light
reinforces the calm, open feeling, while in the
story it suggests decay. The woman's pose beside the door suggests that she may be waiting
for someone's arrival, expectantly but without
the desperation of the story narrator.*

About the Art Carl Holsoe (1863–1935), a
Danish contemporary of Gilman's, reproduced
everyday objects and spaces in his paintings.
Many of his paintings, like this one, focus on
domestic interiors and celebrate the beautiful
light of his country.

DIFFERENTIATED INSTRUCTION

FOR ADVANCED LEARNERS/AP

Compare and Contrast [small-group option]
Point out the narrator's comment that "John
never was nervous in his life" (line 99). Have
small groups discuss similarities and differences between the narrator and her husband.
Urge them to explore these questions:

• How do their differences drive the action of
  the story?

• What effect do their differences have on
  the narrator's illness?

• What do they have in common?

• What feelings do they seem to have for
  each other?

Ask students to create a graphic organizer,
such as a Comparison Matrix, to illustrate
their findings. Invite students to share their
work.

 BEST PRACTICES TOOLKIT—Transparency
Comparison Matrix p. A24

110 would go down to the cellar, if I wished, and have it whitewashed into the bargain. **D**

But he is right enough about the beds and windows and things.

It is an airy and comfortable room as anyone need wish, and, of course, I would not be so silly as to make him uncomfortable just for a whim.

I'm really getting quite fond of the big room, all but that horrid paper.

Out of one window I can see the garden, those mysterious deepshaded arbors, the riotous old-fashioned flowers, and bushes and gnarly trees.

Out of another I get a lovely view of the bay and a little private wharf belonging to the estate. There is a beautiful shaded lane that runs down there from the house. I always fancy I see people walking in these numerous paths and arbors,
120 but John has cautioned me not to give way to fancy in the least. He says that with my imaginative power and habit of story-making, a nervous weakness like mine is sure to lead to all manner of excited fancies, and that I ought to use my will and good sense to check the tendency. So I try.

I think sometimes that if I were only well enough to write a little it would relieve the press of ideas and rest me.

But I find I get pretty tired when I try.

It is so discouraging not to have any advice and companionship about my work. When I get really well, John says we will ask Cousin Henry and Julia down for a long visit; but he says he would as soon put fireworks in my pillowcase as to
130 let me have those stimulating people about now.

I wish I could get well faster.

But I must not think about that. This paper looks to me as if it *knew* what a vicious influence it had!

There is a **recurrent** spot where the pattern lolls like a broken neck and two bulbous eyes stare at you upside down.

I get positively angry with the impertinence of it and the everlastingness. **E** Up and down and sideways they crawl, and those absurd, unblinking eyes are everywhere. There is one place where two breadths didn't match, and the eyes go all up and down the line, one a little higher than the other.
140 I never saw so much expression in an inanimate thing before, and we all know how much expression they have! I used to lie awake as a child and get more entertainment and terror out of blank walls and plain furniture than most children could find in a toy store.

I remember what a kindly wink the knobs of our big, old bureau used to have, and there was one chair that always seemed like a strong friend.

I used to feel that if any of the other things looked too fierce I could always hop into that chair and be safe.

The furniture in this room is no worse than inharmonious, however, for we had to bring it all from downstairs. I suppose when this was used as a playroom they
150 had to take the nursery things out, and no wonder! I never saw such ravages as the children have made here.

(3) Targeted Passage

D SOCIAL CONTEXT
Reread lines 99–110 and describe the relationship between the narrator and her husband. What might Gilman be saying about how women were viewed in the late 1800s?

recurrent (rĭ-kûr′ənt) *adj.* occurring time after time

E FIRST-PERSON NARRATOR
How are the narrator's feelings about the wallpaper changing? Explain whether or not her response to the room's décor seems rational to you.

READING SKILL COMMON CORE
RL 3
RL 9

D *Model the Skill:* **SOCIAL CONTEXT**

Help students by asking them how John responds to the narrator's wishes to change the wallpaper or live downstairs. Point out that the endearment "blessed little goose" (line 109) is more suited to addressing a young child than a wife.

Possible answer: The narrator is subservient to her husband. He treats her dismissively, like a child who is not capable of making serious decisions or thinking wisely for herself (lines 101–105). With this portrait of the marriage, Gilman illustrates how much husbands controlled and infantilized their wives in the late 1800s.

TEXT ANALYSIS COMMON CORE

E **FIRST–PERSON NARRATOR** RL 1
RL 3

Possible answer: The wallpaper is capturing more and more of the narrator's attention. It seems, in her mind, to be coming to life, as she attributes to it human qualities such as "impertinence" (line 136) and says that it seems to know what a "vicious influence" (line 133) it has.

Extend the Discussion How does the narrator connect her feelings about the wallpaper to those about her health?

VOCABULARY COMMON CORE
L 4

OWN THE WORD

recurrent: Ask students to write a sentence demonstrating the meaning of the adjective as "occurring time after time." *Possible answer: Tyrell's recurrent headaches have forced him to miss school.*

FOR STRUGGLING READERS

(3) Targeted Passage [Lines 134–143]

This passage shows the narrator's changing perception of the wallpaper.

• What does the narrator now see in the wallpaper? (lines 134–135)

• How does she feel about what she sees? (line 136)

• What childhood "entertainment" does the narrator recall? (lines 141–143)

FOR ENGLISH LANGUAGE LEARNERS

Related Vocabulary Provide the Three-Column Journal and have students find examples of the following categories from lines 115-133: garden (*mysterious, deep shaded*), narrator's temperament (*imaginative, power*), wallpaper (*vicious, influence*).

BEST PRACTICES TOOLKIT—Transparency
Three-Column Journal p. B10

The wallpaper, as I said before, is torn off in spots, and it sticketh closer than a brother—they must have had perseverance as well as hatred.

Then the floor is scratched and gouged and splintered, the plaster itself is dug out here and there, and this great heavy bed which is all we found in the room, looks as if it had been through the wars.

But I don't mind it a bit—only the paper.

There comes John's sister. Such a dear girl as she is, and so careful of me! I must not let her find me writing.

160 She is a perfect and enthusiastic housekeeper, and hopes for no better profession. I verily believe she thinks it is the writing which made me sick!

But I can write when she is out, and see her a long way off from these windows. **F**

There is one that commands the road, a lovely shaded winding road, and one that just looks off over the country. A lovely country, too, full of great elms and velvet meadows.

This wallpaper has a kind of sub-pattern in a different shade, a particularly irritating one, for you can only see it in certain lights, and not clearly then.

But in the places where it isn't faded and where the sun is just so—I can see a strange, provoking, formless sort of figure, that seems to skulk about behind that
170 silly and conspicuous front design.

There's sister on the stairs!

Well, the Fourth of July is over! The people are all gone and I am tired out. John thought it might do me good to see a little company, so we just had mother and Nellie and the children down for a week.

Of course I didn't do a thing. Jennie sees to everything now.

But it tired me all the same.

John says if I don't pick up faster he shall send me to Weir Mitchell[3] in the fall.

But I don't want to go there at all. I had a friend who was in his hands once, and she says he is just like John and my brother, only more so! **G**

180 Besides, it is such an undertaking to go so far.

I don't feel as if it was worth while to turn my hand over for anything, and I'm getting dreadfully fretful and querulous.

I cry at nothing, and cry most of the time.

Of course I don't when John is here, or anybody else, but when I am alone.

And I am alone a good deal just now. John is kept in town very often by serious cases, and Jennie is good and lets me alone when I want her to.

So I walk a little in the garden or down that lovely lane, sit on the porch under the roses, and lie down up here a good deal.

I'm getting really fond of the room in spite of the wallpaper. Perhaps *because*
190 of the wallpaper.

It dwells in my mind so!

I lie here on this great immovable bed—it is nailed down, I believe—and

---

3. **Weir Mitchell:** Dr. Silas Weir Mitchell, a physician famous for his "rest cure" for nervous diseases, which is no longer considered effective.

F SOCIAL CONTEXT

Possible answer: The narrator's description of John's sister suggests that in this setting women are expected to be "perfect and enthusiastic housekeeper[s]" (line 160), and to find happiness and fulfillment in domestic life. It also shows that the narrator's desire for a more intellectual or introspective life through her writing is thought odd or abnormal.

Extend the Discussion What does the narrator's comment that John's sister "hopes for no better" (line 160) suggest about the narrator herself?

G SOCIAL CONTEXT

Possible answer: The fact that all male characters in the story share these traits suggests that the traits are widely found among men of the time period and underscores how the social context created stifling conditions for women. The male doctors believe they know what ails the narrator, but don't listen to her (lines 16–20); her husband dismisses her suffering (lines 89–90) and disapproves of her writing (line 81).

F SOCIAL CONTEXT
Examine the narrator's description of John's sister in lines 158–162. How do these lines add to your understanding of the story's setting and how it affects the narrator?

G SOCIAL CONTEXT
Reread lines 177–179. What is suggested or highlighted by the fact that all the male characters in the story share common **traits**? What role does the social context play in shaping the story's setting? Cite evidence to support your answer.

DIFFERENTIATED INSTRUCTION

FOR STRUGGLING READERS

Concept Support Clarify the allusion in lines 152–153. It refers to the words "and it sticketh closer than a brother," which appear in the Book of Proverbs in the Hebrew Bible, or Old Testament. Ask students what the narrator means. *Possible answer: The narrator means that the wallpaper is glued tightly to the wall, and therefore, the children who tore it off must have been very determined to do so.*

FOR ADVANCED LEARNERS/AP

Analyze Character Foil [paired option] Remind students that a foil is a minor character that presents a striking contrast with a main character. This contrast sheds light on the traits and motivations of the main character. Ask students what purpose the contrast between John's sister and the narrator serves. What do readers learn about the narrator because of the sister's presence in the story? Have partners brainstorm responses to this question, then

write character descriptions of the narrator with and without the information provided by the foil of John's sister. Invite students to share their descriptions to prompt a class discussion of how the sister adds to the story.

follow that pattern about by the hour. It is as good as gymnastics, I assure you. I
start, we'll say, at the bottom, down in the corner over there where it has not been
touched, and I determine for the thousandth time that I *will* follow that pointless
pattern to some sort of a conclusion.

I know a little of the principle of design, and I know this thing was not
arranged on any laws of radiation, or alternation, or repetition, or symmetry, or
anything else that I ever heard of.

200 It is repeated, of course, by the breadths, but not otherwise.

Looked at in one way each breadth stands alone, the bloated curves and
flourishes—a kind of "debased Romanesque" with *delirium tremens*[4]—go waddling
up and down in isolated columns of **fatuity**.

But, on the other hand, they connect diagonally, and the sprawling outlines run
off in great slanting waves of optic horror, like a lot of wallowing seaweeds in full
chase.

The whole thing goes horizontally, too, at least it seems so, and I exhaust myself
in trying to distinguish the order of its going in that direction.

They have used a horizontal breadth for a frieze, and that adds wonderfully to
210 the confusion.

There is one end of the room where it is almost intact, and there, when the
crosslights fade and the low sun shines directly upon it, I can almost fancy
radiation after all,—the interminable grotesques seem to form around a common
center and rush off in headlong plunges of equal distraction.

It makes me tired to follow it. I will take a nap I guess.

I don't know why I should write this.

I don't want to.

I don't feel able.

And I know John would think it absurd. But I *must* say what I feel and think
220 in some way—it is such a relief!

But the effort is getting to be greater than the relief.

Half the time now I am awfully lazy, and lie down ever so much.

John says I mustn't lose my strength, and has me take cod liver oil and lots of
tonics and things, to say nothing of ale and wine and rare meat.

Dear John! He loves me very dearly, and hates to have me sick. I tried to have
a real earnest reasonable talk with him the other day, and tell him how I wish he
would let me go and make a visit to Cousin Henry and Julia.

But he said I wasn't able to go, nor able to stand it after I got there; and I did
not make out a very good case for myself, for I was crying before I had finished. Ⓗ

230 It is getting to be a great effort for me to think straight. Just this nervous
weakness I suppose.

And dear John gathered me up in his arms, and just carried me upstairs and
laid me on the bed, and sat by me and read to me till it tired my head.

---

4. **"debased Romanesque" with *delirium tremens*:** Romanesque is an artistic style characterized by simple
ornamentation. *Delirium tremens* refers to violent trembling and hallucinations caused by excessive
drinking.

fatuity (fə-tōō′ĭ-tē) *n.*
something foolish or
stupid

Ⓗ **FIRST-PERSON
NARRATOR**
Reread lines 223–229.
Imagine the "real earnest
reasonable talk" the
narrator describes. How
might the account of this
scene be different if John
were the narrator? How
do you think the change
in point of view would
affect your perception
of the main character?
Explain your answer.

TIERED DISCUSSION PROMPTS

Use these prompts to help students link the
narrator's deteriorating state of mind to her
obsession with the wallpaper as revealed in
lines 152–171:

Connect How would you respond if a friend
said that he or she had seen a "formless
figure" in the wallpaper? *Most students will
express worry for the friend's mental state.*

Analyze Why doesn't the narrator mention
the "formless figure" to her sister-in-law?
*Possible answer: The narrator doesn't trust
her and also may fear that she would be dismissive or would relate the narrator's report
to John.*

Synthesize How would you characterize
the narrator's changing perception of the
wallpaper? *Possible answer: The narrator's
perception has grown increasingly distorted.
Her hallucinations are becoming more
distinct and animated as her mental health
deteriorates.*

TEXT ANALYSIS
COMMON CORE
RL 1
RL 3

Ⓗ FIRST-PERSON NARRATOR

*Possible answer: Readers may doubt that
the narrator is capable of a "real earnest
reasonable talk," especially since she tells
us that she started crying before she could
finish. John would have focused on her
emotional outburst and on his own view
of her condition. He might have given
a rational account of the situation, but
ignored her feelings.*

VOCABULARY
COMMON CORE
L 4

OWN THE WORD

fatuity: Remind students that the connotation of the noun *fatuity* is extreme stupidity.
The adjective form is *fatuous*. You could say,
"I often find slapstick humor in movies to
be stupid, but that actor's movies are characterized by *fatuity*." Ask students to create
a pair of related statements that show how
fatuity is stronger than stupidity.

FOR ENGLISH LANGUAGE LEARNERS

Vocabulary Support Point out and help
students use context to define these
expressions:

- *it had been through the wars* (line 156),
"it had been used a lot"

- *tired out* (line 172), "exhausted"

- *had [people] down* (lines 173–174), "had
[people] visit"

- *sees to everything* (line 175), "takes care of
everything"

- *all the same* (line 176), "even so"

- *pick up* (line 177), "improve"

- *in his hands* (line 178), "under his care"

- *a good deal* (line 188), "often"

- *on the other hand* (line 204), "in contrast"

- *to say nothing of* (lines 224), "and also"

- *to think straight* (line 230), "concentrate"

Analyze Visuals

Possible answer: The subject's expression conveys worry, concern, and even helplessness. Some students may say that the image of a concerned doctor makes them feel more sympathy, as it stresses John's good intentions. Others may say that John's good intentions do not compensate for his inability to empathize with his wife or to really listen to what she is telling him.

REVIST THE BIG QUESTION

What if no one took you SERIOUSLY?

Discuss In lines 236–237, John tells the narrator that she is not powerless over her situation. What power does he suggest she has? How useful or realistic is that power, especially in the situation John has placed the narrator? *Possible answer: John suggests that the narrator can affect her situation by using the power of her will and self-control to restrain her imagination. This power is not very useful or realistic because her imagination is central to her identity. Also, he has placed her in a situation where she has little to do but imagine.*

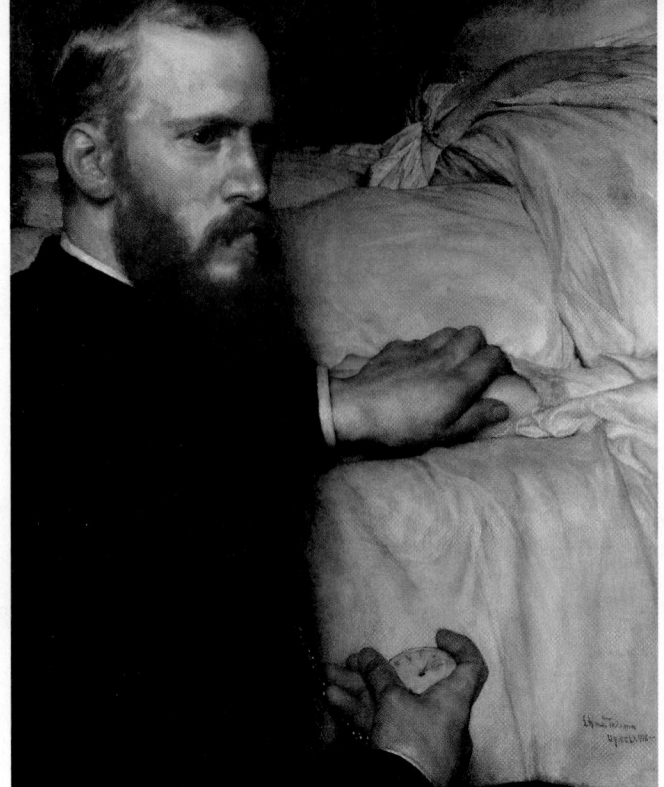

Portrait of Dr. Washington Epps, My Doctor (1885), Sir Lawrence Alma-Tadema. Oil on canvas, 64.2 cm × 51 cm. Private collection. © Bridgeman Art Library.

He said I was his darling and his comfort and all he had, and that I must take care of myself for his sake, and keep well.

He says no one but myself can help me out of it, that I must use my will and self-control and not let any silly fancies run away with me.

There's one comfort, the baby is well and happy, and does not have to occupy this nursery with the horrid wallpaper.

240 If we had not used it, that blessed child would have! What a fortunate escape! Why, I wouldn't have a child of mine, an impressionable little thing, live in such a room for worlds.

I never thought of it before, but it is lucky that John kept me here after all, I can stand it so much easier than a baby, you see.

Of course I never mention it to them any more—I am too wise,—but I keep watch of it all the same.

There are things in that paper that nobody knows but me, or ever will.

Behind that outside pattern the dim shapes get clearer every day.

It is always the same shape, only very numerous.

4 Targeted Passage

DIFFERENTIATED INSTRUCTION

FOR STRUGGLING READERS

4 Targeted Passage [Lines 236–249]

This passage shows the narrator's battle for sanity and her husband's misguided approach to helping her.

- How does John say that the narrator can get well? (lines 236–237)
- Why doesn't the narrator mention what she sees in the wallpaper? (line 245)

- How has the wallpaper changed? (lines 247–249)

FOR ENGLISH LANGUAGE LEARNERS

Vocabulary Support Clarify that Gilman is contrasting self-control with imagination. Work with students to complete a Two-Column Chart to list and define the vocabulary that establishes this contrast.

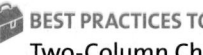 BEST PRACTICES TOOLKIT—Transparency
Two-Column Chart p. A25

Self-Control	Imagination
• *will* (line 236), "determination, strength of character"	• *silly fancies* (line 237), "foolish daydreams or fantasies"
• *self-control* (line 237), "discipline, restraint"	• *run away with* (line 237) "take control of"
• *stern* (line 285), "strict, harsh"	• *fancy* (line 289), "unwise impulse"

250 And it is like a woman stooping down and creeping about behind that pattern. I don't like it a bit. I wonder—I begin to think—I wish John would take me away from here!

It is so hard to talk with John about my case, because he is so wise, and because he loves me so.

But I tried it last night.

It was moonlight. The moon shines in all around just as the sun does.

I hate to see it sometimes, it creeps so slowly, and always comes in by one window or another.

John was asleep and I hated to waken him, so I kept still and watched the
260 moonlight on that **undulating** wallpaper till I felt creepy.

The faint figure behind seemed to shake the pattern, just as if she wanted to get out.

I got up softly and went to feel and see if the paper *did* move, and when I came back John was awake.

"What is it, little girl?" he said. "Don't go walking about like that—you'll get cold."

I thought it was a good time to talk, so I told him that I really was not gaining here, and that I wished he would take me away.

"Why darling!" said he, "our lease will be up in three weeks, and I can't see how
270 to leave before.

"The repairs are not done at home, and I cannot possibly leave town just now. Of course if you were in any danger, I could and would, but you really are better, dear, whether you can see it or not. I am a doctor, dear, and I know. You are gaining flesh and color, your appetite is better, I feel really much easier about you."

"I don't weigh a bit more," said I, "nor as much; and my appetite may be better in the evening when you are here, but it is worse in the morning when you are away!"

"Bless her little heart!" said he with a big hug, "she shall be as sick as she pleases! But now let's improve the shining hours[5] by going to sleep, and talk about it in the morning!"
280 "And you won't go away?" I asked gloomily.

"Why, how can I, dear? It is only three weeks more and then we will take a nice little trip of a few days while Jennie is getting the house ready. Really dear you are better!"

"Better in body perhaps—" I began, and stopped short, for he sat up straight and looked at me with such a stern, reproachful look that I could not say another word.

"My darling," said he, "I beg of you, for my sake and for our child's sake, as well as for your own, that you will never for one instant let that idea enter your mind! There is nothing so dangerous, so fascinating, to a **temperament** like yours. It is a false and foolish fancy. Can you not trust me as a physician when I tell you so?"

---

5. **improve the shining hours:** make good use of time—an allusion to the poem "Against Idleness and Mischief" by Isaac Watts.

---

undulating (ŭn′jə-lā′tĭng) *adj.* appearing to move in waves **undulate** *v.*

temperament (tĕm′prə-mənt) *n.* a person's characteristic mode of emotional response

---

TIERED DISCUSSION PROMPTS

Use these prompts to help students relate the narrator's frustration with her husband to her deteriorating mental health described in lines 267–289:

Connect In your experience, how hard is it to change somebody's mind when the person is convinced of an idea? *Students should recognize that it can be very difficult to overcome strong convictions.*

Analyze Why is John so convinced about the causes of and appropriate treatment for his wife's illness? Consider his training as a doctor and his expectations as a husband. *Possible answer: As a doctor, John has been trained to treat his wife's symptoms in a prescribed way. As a husband, he has been conditioned to value his views over his wife's. This training prevents him from seeing that the treatment isn't working.*

VOCABULARY  COMMON CORE L4

OWN THE WORD

- **undulating:** Tell students that *undulating* comes from the verb *undulate,* which means "to move in waves or wavelike." Have students list things that make *undulating* movements. *Possible answers: ocean, seas, rivers, prairie grasses, leaves, snakes, swimming fish*

- **temperament:** Point out that *temperament* is a person's manner of emotional response. Often the term is used to refer to someone's tendency toward irritability or sensitivity and carries a negative connotation. It implies that the person makes demands and does not work well with others.

FOR ADVANCED LEARNERS/AP

Contrast Character Types [small-group option] Have students work in groups to explore whether John is a flat or round character. Ask groups to poll members and tally the results. Then, urge groups to discuss these questions:

- What character traits define John?
- What emotions does he display?
- How, if at all, is he stereotypical?

- How, if at all, does John change in the course of the story?
- How does his character development reflect his role in the story?

After the discussion, challenge groups to revisit the question of whether John is a round or flat character. Have them take a new poll and tally. Invite groups to share both tallies and explain any changes in their response.

❶ FIRST-PERSON NARRATOR

Possible answer: Her mind is beginning to seem anything but normal. She now sees a figure shaking the wallpaper, as if trying to escape.

IF STUDENTS NEED HELP . . . Reread lines 257–262 and 291–293 with them.

REVISIT THE BIG QUESTION

What if no one took you
SERIOUSLY?

Discuss In lines 319–329, the narrator explains how she follows John's orders to rest after every meal, despite her belief that this is a bad habit. How does this suggest that she feels powerless? How do the narrator's feelings toward John seem to be changing as a result? *Possible answer: She is beginning to fear John (line 323) and to suspect that the paper is influencing him (lines 325–326).*

OWN THE WORD

- **convolution:** Point out that, although "intricacy" and "involvedness" are synonyms, neither produces the sense of malice or malevolence that *convolution* produces in this context. Have students write a sentence in which *convolution* produces a sense of brightness or benevolence.

---

290   So of course I said no more on that score, and we went to sleep before long. He thought I was asleep first, but I wasn't, and lay there for hours trying to decide whether that front pattern and the back pattern really did move together or separately.

On a pattern like this, by daylight, there is a lack of sequence, a defiance of law, that is a constant irritant to a normal mind. ❶

    The color is hideous enough, and unreliable enough, and infuriating enough, but the pattern is torturing.

    You think you have mastered it, but just as you get well underway in following, it turns a back-somersault and there you are. It slaps you in the face, knocks you 300 down, and tramples upon you. It is like a bad dream.

    The outside pattern is a florid arabesque,[6] reminding one of a fungus. If you can imagine a toadstool in joints, an interminable string of toadstools, budding and sprouting in endless **convolutions**—why, that is something like it.

    That is, sometimes!

    There is one marked peculiarity about this paper, a thing nobody seems to notice but myself, and that is that it changes as the light changes.

    When the sun shoots in through the east window—I always watch for that first long, straight ray—it changes so quickly that I never can quite believe it.

    That is why I watch it always.

310   By moonlight—the moon shines in all night when there is a moon—I wouldn't know it was the same paper.

    At night in any kind of light, in twilight, candle light, lamplight, and worst of all by moonlight, it becomes bars! The outside pattern I mean, and the woman behind it is as plain as can be.

    I didn't realize for a long time what the thing was that showed behind, that dim sub-pattern, but now I am quite sure it is a woman.

    By daylight she is subdued, quiet. I fancy it is the pattern that keeps her so still. It is so puzzling. It keeps me quiet by the hour.

    I lie down ever so much now. John says it is good for me, and to sleep all I can.

320   Indeed he started the habit by making me lie down for an hour after each meal.

    It is a very bad habit I am convinced, for you see I don't sleep.

    And that cultivates deceit, for I don't tell them I'm awake—O no!

    The fact is I am getting a little afraid of John.

    He seems very queer sometimes, and even Jennie has an inexplicable look.

    It strikes me occasionally, just as a scientific hypothesis,—that perhaps it is the paper!

    I have watched John when he did not know I was looking, and come into the room suddenly on the most innocent excuses, and I've caught him several times *looking at the paper!* And Jennie too. I caught Jennie with her hand on it once.

330   She didn't know I was in the room, and when I asked her in a quiet, a very quiet voice, with the most restrained manner possible, what she was doing with

---

6. **florid arabesque:** an elaborate interwoven pattern.

❶ FIRST-PERSON NARRATOR
Consider the narrator's statement in lines 294–295. Based on her description of the wallpaper, would you say she has "a normal mind"? Explain your answer.

convolution
(kŏn′və-lōō′shən) *n.* a form or shape that is folded into curved, complicated windings

❺ Targeted Passage

Language Coach

Prefixes A **prefix** is a word part attached to the beginning of a word root. The prefix *sub-* means "under" or "beneath." What does *sub-pattern* (line 316) mean, and what clues to its meaning can you find in lines 315–316?

DIFFERENTIATED INSTRUCTION

FOR STRUGGLING READERS

❺ Targeted Passage [Lines 305–318]

This passage reveals the narrator's hallucinations about the wallpaper.

- What does the narrator say happens to the wallpaper as the light changes? Why does she watch it? (lines 307–309)

- What does she see behind the wallpaper? (lines 313–314)

- Why does the narrator think the woman remains still? (line 317)

FOR ENGLISH LANGUAGE LEARNERS

Language Coach

Prefixes

Possible answers: Sub-pattern *means "secondary pattern." A clue in the sentence is "what the thing was that showed behind." Ask students to apply their knowledge of the prefix* sub- *and context to guess the meaning of the word* subdued *in line 317. Students should suggest that the word means "quiet or withdrawn."*

the paper—she turned around as if she had been caught stealing, and looked quite angry—asked me why I should frighten her so!

Then she said that the paper stained everything it touched, that she had found yellow smooches[7] on all my clothes and John's, and she wished we would be more careful!

Did not that sound innocent? But I know she was studying that pattern, and I am determined that nobody shall find it out but myself! **J**

Life is very much more exciting now than it used to be. You see I have something
340 more to expect, to look forward to, to watch. I really do eat better, and am more quiet than I was.

John is so pleased to see me improve! He laughed a little the other day, and said I seemed to be flourishing in spite of my wallpaper.

I turned it off with a laugh. I had no intention of telling him it was *because* of the wallpaper—he would make fun of me. He might even want to take me away.

I don't want to leave now until I have found it out. There is a week more, and I think that will be enough.

I'm feeling ever so much better! I don't sleep much at night, for it is so interesting to watch developments; but I sleep a good deal in the daytime.
350 In the daytime it is tiresome and perplexing.

There are always new shoots on the fungus, and new shades of yellow all over it. I cannot keep count of them, though I have tried conscientiously.

It is the strangest yellow, that wallpaper! It makes me think of all the yellow things I ever saw—not beautiful ones like buttercups, but old foul, bad yellow things.

But there is something else about that paper—the smell! I noticed it the moment we came into the room, but with so much air and sun it was not bad. Now we have had a week of fog and rain, and whether the windows are open or not, the smell is here.

It creeps all over the house.
360 I find it hovering in the dining room, skulking in the parlor, hiding in the hall, lying in wait for me on the stairs.

It gets into my hair.

Even when I go to ride, if I turn my head suddenly and surprise it—there is that smell!

Such a peculiar odor, too! I have spent hours in trying to analyze it, to find what it smelled like.

It is not bad—at first, and very gentle, but quite the subtlest, most enduring odor I ever met.

In this damp weather it is awful, I wake up in the night and find it hanging
370 over me.

It used to disturb me at first. I thought seriously of burning the house—to reach the smell.

---

7. **smooches:** smudges.

J FIRST-PERSON NARRATOR
Reread lines 323–338. How has the narrator's attitude toward John and Jennie changed? What do you think they might say about her feelings if they were aware of them?

Language Coach
Word Definitions
Skulking (line 360) means "moving in a secretive manner" or "hiding with a bad intent." What human qualities is the narrator giving to the smell?

J FIRST-PERSON NARRATOR

Possible answer: *The narrator fears that the wallpaper has made John and Jennie "queer" and "inexplicable" (line 324). She doesn't trust them, but rather sees them as adversaries and sneaky intruders (lines 327–329). If they knew this, they would probably dismiss her fears and suggest that she try to exert more self-control over her foolish fantasies.*

IF STUDENTS NEED HELP... Work with them to complete an Open Mind diagram about the narrator. Urge students to list the narrator's views about John and Jennie as they appear chronologically throughout the story.

- John does not believe she is sick, but he is careful and loving (lines 14, 56).
- John hates when she writes (line 81).
- It is hard to talk to John about her feelings (line 253).
- John's sister thinks that writing makes the narrator sick (line 161).
- Jennie is good and leaves the narrator alone (line 186).
- Jennie has "an inexplicable look" (line 324).

 BEST PRACTICES TOOLKIT—Transparency
Open Mind p. D9

FOR ENGLISH LANGUAGE LEARNERS

Language Coach
Word Definitions
Possible answer: *The smell is creepy, sly, and wants to do harm.* Have students reread lines 360–371 and make a list of the words that describe the wallpaper's smell. Have them consult a dictionary to find the words' exact meanings.

FOR ADVANCED LEARNERS/AP

Synthesize [paired option] Ask students how the narrator's sensory perceptions have changed since she first observed the wallpaper. Invite partners to track the narrator's visual, aural, and kinesthetic responses as her mental state deteriorates. Then, ask how her heightened awareness relates to her imaginativeness. What does Gilman suggest about the link between art and madness? Have students share their findings with the class.

Activity Ask students to imagine they are viewing this painting at a museum. Ask students what response they would have to the subject of the painting and to the wallpaper within it. Challenge them to consider how their response differs from viewing the painting in the context of this story. *Possible answer: Viewed in a museum, the painting seems to show a peacefully idle and sensuous woman surrounded by merely decorative wallpaper. In the context of the story, the painting reflects some of the disturbed qualities of the narrator and her perception of the wallpaper, making the woman seem distressed and the wallpaper seem overdone.*

In Bed (1878), Federico Zandomeneghi. Oil on canvas, 60.5 cm × 73.5 cm. Galleria d'Arte Moderna, Florence. © Alinari/Art Resource, New York.

TEXT ANALYSIS	COMMON CORE
	RL 1
	RL 3

Ⓚ FIRST-PERSON NARRATOR

Possible answer: While in her own mind, the narrator sees her obsession as a belief in real events, a switch to an impartial, omniscient narrator would reveal that the woman's mind is becoming unhinged. She seriously considers burning her own house down "to reach the smell" (lines 371–372), and she has become obsessed with the wallpaper. She sees it as a living entity and spends hours analyzing it (lines 365–366). She is increasingly agitated, secretive, desperate, and irrational as her mental illness deepens.

IF STUDENTS NEED HELP... Urge them to reread lines 348–374.

But now I am used to it. The only thing I can think of that it is like is the *color* of the paper! A yellow smell. Ⓚ

There is a very funny mark on this wall, low down, near the mopboard. A streak that runs round the room. It goes behind every piece of furniture, except the bed, a long, straight, even *smooch*, as if it had been rubbed over and over.

I wonder how it was done and who did it, and what they did it for. Round and round and round—round and round and round—it makes me dizzy!

380 I really have discovered something at last.

Through watching so much at night, when it changes so, I have finally found out. The front pattern *does* move—and no wonder! The woman behind shakes it!

Sometimes I think there are a great many women behind, and sometimes only one, and she crawls around fast, and her crawling shakes it all over.

Ⓚ FIRST-PERSON NARRATOR

How would an impartial, omniscient narrator describe the woman's mind at this point? How would this change in the story's point of view affect Gilman's depiction of her main character? Explain your answer.

Ⓖ **Targeted Passage**

DIFFERENTIATED INSTRUCTION

FOR STRUGGLING READERS

Ⓖ **Targeted Passage [Lines 380–388]**

This passage shows the narrator's changing perception of the "woman" in the wallpaper.

- Why does the narrator think the front pattern moves? (line 381)
- Whom does the narrator see behind the front pattern? (lines 382–383)
- What is the woman behind the pattern trying to do? (line 384)

FOR ENGLISH LANGUAGE LEARNERS

Vocabulary: Idioms and Phrasal Verbs Use context to clarify these idioms from pages 810–811:

- *used to it* (line 373), "accustomed to it"
- *found out* (line 381), "discovered"
- *keeps still* (line 385), "doesn't move"
- *takes hold* (line 386), "grabs"
- *half so bad* (line 391), "terrible"

- *away off* (line 409), "far away"
- *open country* (line 409), "distance"
- *It does not do* (lines 413–414), "It is not advisable"
- *a good deal* (line 419), "a lot"
- *see through him* (line 423), "see his deception"

Then in the very bright spots she keeps still, and in the very shady spots she just takes hold of the bars and shakes them hard.

And she is all the time trying to climb through. But nobody could climb through that pattern—it strangles so; I think that is why it has so many heads.

⑥ **Targeted Passage**
continued

They get through, and then the pattern strangles them off and turns them
390 upside down, and makes their eyes white!

If those heads were covered or taken off it would not be half so bad.

I think that woman gets out in the daytime!

And I'll tell you why—privately—I've seen her!

I can see her out of every one of my windows!

It is the same woman, I know, for she is always creeping, and most women do not creep by daylight.

I see her on that long road under the trees, creeping along, and when a carriage comes she hides under the blackberry vines.

I don't blame her a bit. It must be very humiliating to be caught creeping by
400 daylight!

I always lock the door when I creep by daylight. I can't do it at night, for I know John would suspect something at once.

And John is so queer now, that I don't want to irritate him. I wish he would take another room! Besides, I don't want anybody to get that woman out at night but myself.

I often wonder if I could see her out of all the windows at once.

But, turn as fast as I can, I can only see out of one at one time.

And though I always see her, she *may* be able to creep faster than I can turn!

I have watched her sometimes away off in the open country, creeping as fast
410 as a cloud shadow in a high wind.

I f only that top pattern could be gotten off from the under one! I mean to try it, little by little.

I have found out another funny thing, but I shan't tell it this time! It does not do to trust people too much.

There are only two more days to get this paper off, and I believe John is beginning to notice. I don't like the look in his eyes.

And I heard him ask Jennie a lot of professional questions about me. She had a very good report to give.

She said I slept a good deal in the daytime.
420 John knows I don't sleep very well at night, for all I'm so quiet!

He asked me all sorts of questions, too, and pretended to be very loving and kind.

As if I couldn't see through him! ⬤

🄛 FIRST-PERSON NARRATOR
Consider the narrator's statements in lines 403–404 and line 423. Why is she turning against her husband? Explain what John's real concerns might be.

THE YELLOW WALLPAPER **811**

TIERED DISCUSSION PROMPTS
Use these prompts to help students understand the narrator's confusion and bizarre behavior in lines 392–410:

Connect Have you ever known a small child who imagines people or animals or monsters? How does that experience help you understand the narrator's mental state? *Students should recognize that, like a small child, the narrator has lost the ability to differentiate fantasy and reality.*

Analyze Why does the narrator lock the door when she creeps by daylight? ***Possible answer:** The narrator does not wish to be seen by Jennie or John. She is now fearful and paranoid about their intentions. On some level she may also be aware that her behavior is odd.*

Evaluate How would you assess the effects of the "rest cure" on the narrator? *Most students will recognize that the rest cure is an abysmal failure that has contributed to the narrator's mental deterioration.*

TEXT ANALYSIS

COMMON CORE
RL 1
RL 3

🄛 FIRST-PERSON NARRATOR

***Possible answer:** The narrator is turning against her husband because she believes that John is not motivated by love, but by malevolent intentions (lines 413–414). She thinks that he wants to remove the woman from the wallpaper (lines 404–405). Students should recognize that the narrator's perceptions are paranoid and distorted. However, they should also appreciate that John's real concerns—his desire to help his wife and keep her safe—have backfired and harmed her.*

Extend the Discussion In what ways does John deserve the narrator's antagonism? Explain.

FOR ADVANCED LEARNERS/AP
Symbolism Have students speculate on the meaning of the woman in the wallpaper. Who does she represent? Is she an aspect of the narrator's mind or a symbol of women in general? Does her situation reflect the narrator's plight or the plight of all women of Gilman's time? Encourage students to write a persuasive paragraph in response to these questions. Have the class consider the paragraphs and voice opinions.

FOR RELUCTANT READERS
Connect with the Text Ask students as they read the story if they feel more sympathy for the narrator or for her husband. Do they believe that the narrator sees a woman in the wallpaper? How would they respond if someone they knew claimed to see things that were not real? Lead a class discussion in which students talk about strategies for responding to someone who may be confused but strongly believes that he or she is right.

THE YELLOW WALLPAPER **811**

Ⓜ FIRST-PERSON NARRATOR

Review with students the differences that result from first-person and omniscient narration. Then have students read lines 426–442, making notes of details they find compelling or disturbing. Discuss why first-person narration is critical to this story. **Possible answer:** *The narrator feels she is in partnership with the woman she sees in the wallpaper (lines 430–433); the narrator hears the wallpaper pattern laughing at her (lines 435–436).*

Extend the Discussion How has the narrator's assessment of Jennie's character and motivations changed?

TIERED DISCUSSION PROMPTS

Use these prompts to help students trace the narrator's mental collapse detailed in lines 443–467:

Connect How do you feel about the narrator at this point in the story? What are your concerns for her? *Accept all thoughtful responses.*

Analyze How would you characterize the narrator's behavior? Give examples to support your characterization. ***Possible answer:*** *The narrator is behaving bizarrely. She has torn down the wallpaper (lines 443, 465), gnawed and chewed on the bedstead (lines 453, 463–464), locked the door and thrown the key out the window (line 455), brought up a rope to tie up the woman (lines 459–460), and tried pushing the nailed bed until she was lame (line 463).*

Synthesize How will John respond to the narrator's turn for the worse? *Some students will say that John will finally recognize that his treatment has failed. Others will say that he, like Jennie, will try in vain to pacify the narrator.*

Still, I don't wonder he acts so, sleeping under this paper for three months.

It only interests me, but I feel sure John and Jennie are secretly affected by it.

Hurrah! This is the last day, but it is enough. John to stay in town overnight, and won't be out until this evening.

Jennie wanted to sleep with me—the sly thing! but I told her I should undoubtedly rest better for a night all alone.

430 That was clever, for really I wasn't alone a bit! As soon as it was moonlight and that poor thing began to crawl and shake the pattern, I got up and ran to help her.

I pulled and she shook, I shook and she pulled, and before morning we had peeled off yards of that paper.

A strip about as high as my head and half around the room.

And then when the sun came and that awful pattern began to laugh at me, I declared I would finish it today!

We go away tomorrow, and they are moving all my furniture down again to leave things as they were before.

440 Jennie looked at the wall in amazement, but I told her merrily that I did it out of pure spite at the vicious thing.

She laughed and said she wouldn't mind doing it herself, but I must not get tired. How she betrayed herself that time! Ⓜ

But I am here, and no person touches this paper but me,—not *alive!*

She tried to get me out of the room—it was too patent! But I said it was so quiet and empty and clean now that I believed I would lie down again and sleep all I could; and not to wake me even for dinner—I would call when I woke.

So now she is gone, and the servants are gone, and the things are gone, and there is nothing left but that great bedstead nailed down, with the canvas mattress we found on it.

450 We shall sleep downstairs tonight, and take the boat home tomorrow.

I quite enjoy the room, now it is bare again.

How those children did tear about here!

This bedstead is fairly gnawed!

But I must get to work.

I have locked the door and thrown the key down into the front path.

I don't want to go out, and I don't want to have anybody come in, till John comes.

I want to astonish him.

I've got a rope up here that even Jennie did not find. If that woman does get

460 out, and tries to get away, I can tie her!

But I forgot I could not reach far without anything to stand on!

This bed will *not* move!

I tried to lift and push it until I was lame, and then I got so angry I bit off a little piece at one corner—but it hurt my teeth.

Then I peeled off all the paper I could reach standing on the floor. It sticks horribly and the pattern just enjoys it! All those strangled heads and bulbous eyes and waddling fungus growths just shriek with derision!

Ⓜ FIRST-PERSON NARRATOR

The anonymous narrator of this story influenced the development of a character type in American literature and film—the emotionally disturbed wife. Sue Kaufman's 1967 novel *Diary of a Mad Housewife,* which was later made into a film, owes much to Gilman's disturbing experiment in first-person narration. Laura Brown, a character in the novel and film *The Hours,* is a more recent example of the "mad housewife." Reread lines 426–442. Which details in this section of the narrative do you find compelling? Explain your answer.

DIFFERENTIATED INSTRUCTION

FOR ADVANCED LEARNERS/AP

Analyze Word Choice Encourage students to study the dictionary definitions for the word *creep.* Have them work in pairs to discuss the word's various meanings and connotations, then to consider these questions: How does the word connect with the narrator's feelings about the colonial mansion, her husband, and her general predicament? Is Gilman's use of this word ironic? How does the word accumulate new meaning and connotation during the course of the narrative? How would the final scenes of the story be different if Gilman had used a different word, such as *sneak, slink,* or *skulk?* Invite partners to share their thoughts with the class.

I am getting angry enough to do something desperate. To jump out of the window would be admirable exercise, but the bars are too strong even to try.

470 Besides I wouldn't do it. Of course not. I know well enough that a step like that is improper and might be **misconstrued.**

I don't like to *look* out of the windows even—there are so many of those creeping women, and they creep so fast.

I wonder if they all come out of that wallpaper as I did? **N**

But I am securely fastened now by my well-hidden rope—you don't get *me* out in the road there!

I suppose I shall have to get back behind the pattern when it comes night, and that is hard!

It is so pleasant to be out in this great room and creep around as I please!

480 I don't want to go outside. I won't, even if Jennie asks me to.

For outside you have to creep on the ground, and everything is green instead of yellow.

But here I can creep smoothly on the floor, and my shoulder just fits in that long smooch around the wall, so I cannot lose my way.

Why there's John at the door!

It is no use, young man, you can't open it!

How he does call and pound!

Now he's crying for an axe.

It would be a shame to break down that beautiful door!

490 "John dear!" said I in the gentlest voice, "the key is down by the front steps, under a plantain leaf!"

That silenced him for a few moments.

Then he said—very quietly indeed, "Open the door, my darling!"

"I can't," said I. "The key is down by the front door under a plantain leaf!"

And then I said it again, several times, very gently and slowly, and said it so often that he had to go and see, and he got it of course, and came in. He stopped short by the door.

"What is the matter?" he cried. "What are you doing!"

I kept on creeping just the same, but I looked at him over my shoulder.

500 "I've got out at last," said I, "in spite of you and Jane.[8] And I've pulled off most of the paper, so you can't put me back!"

Now why should that man have fainted? But he did, and right across my path by the wall, so that I had to creep over him every time! ❧

---

8. **in spite of you and Jane:** As Jane is previously unmentioned, the name may be a typographical error by the original printer of the story in place of the name of the housekeeper, Jennie, or Cousin Julia; or it may denote the narrator herself, freed from her commonplace, wifely, "Jane" persona.

---

misconstrued
(mĭs′kən-strōōd′)
adj. misunderstood; misinterpreted
misconstrue *v.*

N FIRST-PERSON NARRATOR
What does the narrator now believe about the wallpaper?

7 Targeted Passage

N FIRST-PERSON NARRATOR

RL 1
RL 3

Possible answer: *The narrator now believes that she has freed all the women in the wallpaper and that she herself has escaped from it.*

IF STUDENTS NEED HELP... Reread lines 392–394 and 472–474.

REVISIT THE BIG QUESTION

What if no one took you **SERIOUSLY?**

Discuss In your opinion, does the narrator feel powerless in lines 477–484? Why or why not? *Possible answer:* *The narrator says that it is "pleasant" to be out and creeping about the room "as I please" (line 479). Her comments suggest that, ironically, she is contented. She has achieved a kind of freedom from her concerns about pleasing John and meeting the expectations of other people. Now she is doing what she chooses, however crazy it may be, and so feels less powerless.*

VOCABULARY   COMMON CORE   L 4

OWN THE WORD

misconstrued: Tell students that *misconstrued* is synonymous with misunderstanding or misinterpreting. Ask students if they have ever *misconstrued* someone's comments or actions and, so, how they dealt with the situation. *Possible answer: Students should give examples of misunderstandings and how they resolved them.*

SELECTION WRAP-UP

READ WITH A PURPOSE Now that students have read the story, ask them to compare the narrator's state of mind at the beginning and end of the story. *Possible answer: In the beginning, the narrator is nervous and restless, but by the end, she has lost her reason.*

INDEPENDENT READING

Students might enjoy Henry James' *The Portrait of a Lady,* a novel of psychological realism concerning a woman trapped by social conventions.

FOR STRUGGLING READERS

7 Targeted Passage [Lines 485–503]

This passage shows the narrator's final descent into madness.

- How does John get into the room? (lines 494–497)
- What is the narrator doing? (lines 500–501)
- What is John's reaction? (line 502)

FOR ENGLISH LANGUAGE LEARNERS

Vocabulary Support Point out and teach these expressions on page 813, using context to help students build meaning:

- *well enough* (line 470), "of course"
- *as I please* (line 479), "as much as I want to"
- *lose my way* (line 484), "get lost, wander"
- *stopped short* (lines 496–497), "stopped suddenly"
- *just the same* (line 499), "as I was before"

CONNECT

This selection provides insight into Gilman's approach to writing "The Yellow Wallpaper." You can also use it as a minilesson on reading for information.

READING FOR INFORMATION

Point out that "Why I Wrote 'The Yellow Wallpaper'" is an article that Charlotte Perkins Gilman wrote for her feminist magazine. Discuss the article's likely audience. Then ask

• Who is the likely audience of *Forerunner*?

• How might awareness of her audience affect Gilman's writing?

TIERED DISCUSSION PROMPTS

Use these prompts to help students link Gilman's personal experience with mental illness to her writing of "The Yellow Wallpaper":

Connect In what ways can it be helpful during a difficult time to hear how someone else survived a difficult experience? *Accept all thoughtful responses.*

Analyze Gilman's mental breakdown followed an unhappy and stifling marriage. Use this information and her article to explain why she wrote "The Yellow Wallpaper." *Possible answer: She wrote it to illustrate the dangers of "rest cures" for depression, to help others suffering from similar conditions, and perhaps to share the devastating effects of an unhappy marriage.*

Synthesize What traits and experiences do you think Gilman and the narrator of "The Yellow Wallpaper" have in common? *Possible answer: Both Gilman and the narrator have imaginative power and a habit of story-making, a tendency toward melancholia, and a strong desire to write and to work. Both felt powerless in their marriages and both wished to be more than just enthusiastic housekeepers.*

Reading for Information

JOURNAL ARTICLE Charlotte Perkins Gilman herself suffered a profound depression and was prescribed a "rest cure" by a noted neurologist of the day. In this 1913 article from her feminist journal *Forerunner*, she says she wrote "The Yellow Wallpaper" to bear witness to the horrors of this "cure" and to attest to her recovery.

THE FORERUNNER

A MONTHLY MAGAZINE

CHARLOTTE PERKINS GILMAN

WHY I WROTE "THE YELLOW WALLPAPER"

Many and many a reader has asked that. When the story first came out, in the *New England Magazine* about 1891, a Boston physician made protest in *The Transcript.* Such a story ought not to be written, he said; it was enough to drive anyone mad to read it.

Another physician, in Kansas I think, wrote to say that it was the best description of incipient insanity he had ever seen, and—begging my pardon—had I been there?

Now the story of the story is this:

For many years I suffered from a severe and continuous nervous breakdown tending to melancholia—and beyond. During about the third year of this trouble I went, in devout faith and some faint stir of hope, to a noted specialist in nervous diseases, the best known in the country. This wise man put me to bed and applied the rest cure, to which a still good physique responded so promptly that he concluded there was nothing much the matter with me, and sent me home with solemn advice to "live as domestic a life as far as possible," to "have but two hours' intellectual life a day," and "never to touch pen, brush or pencil again as long as I lived." This was in 1887.

I went home and obeyed those directions for some three months, and came so near the border line of utter mental ruin that I could see over.

Then, using the remnants of intelligence that remained, and helped by a wise friend, I cast the noted specialist's advice to the winds and went to work again—work, the normal life of every human being; work, in which is joy and growth and service, without which one is a pauper and a parasite; ultimately recovering some measure of power.

Being naturally moved to rejoicing by this narrow escape, I wrote *The Yellow Wallpaper,* with its embellishments and additions to carry out the ideal (I never had hallucinations or objections to my mural decorations) and sent a copy to the physician who so nearly drove me mad. He never acknowledged it.

The little book is valued by alienists and as a good specimen of one kind of literature. It has to my knowledge saved one woman from a similar fate—so terrifying her family that they let her out into normal activity and she recovered.

But the best result is this. Many years later I was told that the great specialist had admitted to friends of his that he had altered his treatment of neurasthenia since reading *The Yellow Wallpaper.*

It was not intended to drive people crazy, but to save people from being driven crazy, and it worked.

Comprehension

1. **Summarize** Describe the "rest cure" treatment and explain why it is prescribed for the narrator.

2. **Recall** Why does the narrator hate the wallpaper at first?

3. **Clarify** Who does the narrator think she is at the end of the story?

Text Analysis

● 4. **Analyze First-Person Narrator** The narrator of this story is **unreliable**—you can't always trust that what she says is accurate or complete. How does her highly subjective account contribute to your perception of her character's internal development? Cite evidence from the story to support your answer.

5. **Interpret Symbolism** Reread lines 380–391 and consider the narrator's **powerlessness**. What might the yellow wallpaper symbolize in the story? Consider the following as you formulate your answer:

   • the narrator's attitude toward both her "condition" and her marriage
   • what she sees in the "strangling" pattern of the paper
   • her exhilaration when she rips the wallpaper off the wall

● 6. **Understand Social Context** Examine the chart you filled in as you read. What conclusions can you draw about the social context of this story? Citing evidence from both the short story and the article on page 814, explain

   • how wives were expected to behave in the 1890s
   • how women seem to have been treated by the men—husbands, brothers, doctors—who cared for them
   • what Gilman thought about women's being denied meaningful work and personal power, and how she addresses these issues in this story

Text Criticism

7. **Different Perspectives** At the time "The Yellow Wallpaper" was published, most critics read it as a horror tale about madness or, after Gilman's explanation appeared in 1913, as an exposé of women's medical treatment. Only a few saw what feminists in the 1970s would interpret as Gilman's **political assumptions.** Feminists read the story as a criticism of marriage and the oppression of women. Explain which of these interpretations you favor, citing evidence from the text.

What if no one took you **SERIOUSLY?**

In "The Yellow Wallpaper," the narrator is doubted by the doctor and her own husband, with devastating consequences. Is it possible to believe in yourself if no one else seems to? Explain your answer.

THE YELLOW WALLPAPER **815**

7. **Gothic Horror Tale:** the setting; the "living" wallpaper; the trapped woman that drives the narrator insane; **Exposé:** treatment harmed both the narrator and Gilman; **Feminist Critique:** women's social and economic oppression leads to madness; "cure" makes them worse.

What if no one took you **SERIOUSLY?**

Answers will vary, but students may say that it is possible to believe in yourself without the support of others, although it is more difficult in that situation.

COMMON CORE

RL 1 Cite evidence to support inferences drawn from the text, including determining where the text leaves matters uncertain. **RL 3** Analyze the impact of the author's choices regarding how to develop and relate elements of a story. **RL 9** Demonstrate knowledge of nineteenth-century foundational works of American literature. **RI 1** Cite evidence to support analysis of what the text says explicitly as well as inferences drawn from the text.

Practice and Apply

For preliminary support of post-reading questions, use these copy masters:

R RESOURCE MANAGER—Copy Masters
Reading Check p. 206
First-Person Narrator p. 199
Question Support p. 207
Additional selection questions are provided for teachers on page 193.

ANSWERS

COMMON CORE RL 1, RL 3, RL 9, RI 1

1. *The rest cure calls for little activity or stimulation and long hours of sleep. It is prescribed for the narrator's depression.*

2. *Its sickly yellow color and gaudy, chaotic pattern offend her artistic sensibility.*

3. *She thinks she is one of the women released from the wallpaper.*

Possible answers:

4. ● **COMMON CORE FOCUS Analyze First-Person Narrator** *Readers experience a compelling account of madness in which it is unclear whether the narrator is sane. The narrator is unreliable, so readers struggle to separate reality from hallucination and may find the end of the story unclear.*

5. *The wallpaper, with its elaborately changing patterns and trapped women, could represent the narrator's madness. It could also symbolize her marriage, which imprisons, then enrages, and finally drives her mad. Or it might represent society that imprisons women with expectations.*

6. ■ **COMMON CORE FOCUS Understand Social Context** *Women should avoid artistic pursuits, control emotions and imagination, limit intellectual activity, and find happiness in domesticity (lines 49–50, 81, 109, 121–123, 219, 236–237; article paragraph 4). Women were dismissed, infantilized, controlled, scoffed at, told not to question (lines 7, 9, 14, 219, 267–279, 345; article paragraphs 4–5). Gilman thought that work generates meaning, power, and self-confidence (lines 24–25; article paragraph 6). Gilman wrote her story in response to experiencing this treatment of women in her own life.*

ANSWERS

Vocabulary in Context

▲ VOCABULARY PRACTICE

1. *(d) lowly*   5. *(b) favor*
2. *(a) undulating*   6. *(b) misconstrued*
3. *(a) consideration* 7. *(d) vapid*
4. *(c) refused*   8. *(a) humidity*

 RESOURCE MANAGER—Copy Master
Vocabulary Practice p. 204

ACADEMIC VOCABULARY IN WRITING

Answers will vary, but should identify a social issue and use at least one academic vocabulary word.

VOCABULARY STRATEGY: WORD ANALOGIES

 **COMMON CORE** L5, L6

Answers:

1. *(c) drought : famine*
2. *(d) retribution : punishment*
3. *(a) accept : forbid*
4. *(d) garden : tomato*

 **RESOURCE MANAGER**—Copy Master
Vocabulary Strategy p. 205

Interactive Vocabulary **THINK** central

Keywords direct students to a **WordSharp** tutorial on **thinkcentral.com** or to other types of vocabulary practice and review.

Vocabulary in Context

▲ VOCABULARY PRACTICE

Choose the word that is not related in meaning to the other words.

1. (a) extravagant, (b) showy, (c) flamboyant, (d) lowly
2. (a) undulating, (b) flying, (c) soaring, (d) gliding
3. (a) consideration, (b) convolution, (c) intricacy, (d) complexity
4. (a) periodic, (b) repeated, (c) refused, (d) recurrent
5. (a) fatuity, (b) favor, (c) silliness, (d) folly
6. (a) miscellaneous, (b) misconstrued, (c) various, (d) diversified
7. (a) vivid, (b) lurid, (c) sensational, (d) vapid
8. (a) humidity, (b) personality, (c) disposition, (d) temperament

WORD LIST
convolution
fatuity
flamboyant
lurid
misconstrued
recurrent
temperament
undulating

ACADEMIC VOCABULARY IN WRITING

• apparent   • confine   • focus   • expose   • perceive

"The Yellow Wallpaper" **exposes** social issues from the late 1800s. If you were writing a short story, which issues would you **focus** on? Explain your answer in a short paragraph, using at least two of the Academic Vocabulary words.

VOCABULARY STRATEGY: WORD ANALOGIES

A **word analogy** is a statement that compares, or shows the relationships, between pairs of words. Relationships frequently expressed include synonyms, antonyms, cause and effect, part and whole, and location. Analogies are normally written like the following example.

FLAMBOYANT : PLAIN :: textured : smooth

Studying the word relationships in analogies can increase your vocabulary.

PRACTICE For each item, choose the word pair that expresses a relationship most similar to that of the capitalized words. Then identify the relationship type.

1. HURRICANE : FLOOD ::
   a. plumber : pipes   **b.** calm : agitated   **c.** drought : famine   **d.** lawyer : court
2. SAGACIOUS : SHREWD ::
   a. messy : tidy   **b.** shy : careless   **c.** joy : gloom   **d.** retribution : punishment
3. EXTRAVAGANT : FRUGAL ::
   a. accept : forbid   **b.** crime : robbery   **c.** merry : cheerful   **d.** courage : bravery
4. CHOIR : TENOR ::
   a. key : lock   **b.** rider : horse   **c.** shallow : deep   **d.** garden : tomato

COMMON CORE

L 5 Demonstrate understanding of word relationships. **L 6** Acquire and use accurately general academic words and phrases.

Interactive Vocabulary **THINK** central
Go to **thinkcentral.com**.
KEYWORD: HML11-816

DIFFERENTIATED INSTRUCTION

FOR ENGLISH LANGUAGE LEARNERS

Task Support: Vocabulary Practice Ask students which words in the box are cognates from their home languages. Discuss whether students have heard or read the words in those languages. Urge them to use their knowledge of the cognate meanings to help construct meaning for the English word.

FOR ADVANCED LEARNERS/AP

Temperament Words Ask partners to brainstorm additional temperament words, then classify the words by the four categories in the **Practice** or other categories of their choosing. Urge students to use a Classification Chart or other appropriate graphic organizer to organize and analyze the frequency of words in the different categories. Which category has the most words? What range of words is available, from mild to extreme, in each category? Invite students to speculate about the reasons for variations in frequency and range.

📦 BEST PRACTICES TOOLKIT—Transparency
Classification Chart p. B17

Language

◆ **GRAMMAR AND STYLE:** *Choose Effective Verb Tense*

Review the **Grammar and Style** note on page 801. The immediacy and power of "The Yellow Wallpaper" come in part from Gilman's choice to have the narrator tell the story mostly in the **present tense** as though writing in a diary. In this way, the reader plunges directly into the narrator's mind and follows its dark descent. Notice the use of **present-tense verbs** in this chilling example from the end of the story:

> But I *am* securely fastened now by my well-hidden rope—you *don't get* me out in the road there! (lines 475–476)

PRACTICE The following paragraph is a sample from another short story. Notice how the past-tense verbs create a certain distance between the reader and the events. Revise the paragraph, writing it in the present tense to achieve a different effect.

I threw another log on the fire, waiting for Ahmer to come home. Dinner sat on the table, growing cold. Ahmer had been gone for hours and I was sure he had left with hurt feelings. Why did we always argue this way on special occasions? It was as though we didn't really want to celebrate, or didn't know how.

READING-WRITING CONNECTION

Expand your understanding of "The Yellow Wallpaper" by responding to this prompt. Then, use the **revising tips** to improve your analysis.

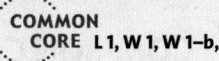
COMMON CORE

L1 Demonstrate command of the conventions of standard English grammar and usage when writing. **W1** Write arguments to support claims in an analysis of texts, using valid reasoning and relevant and sufficient evidence. **W1a–b** Introduce a precise claim; develop claim and counterclaims fairly and thoroughly, supplying the most relevant evidence for each in a manner that anticipates the audience's possible biases.

WRITING PROMPT	REVISING TIPS
WRITE AN ANALYSIS Although most contemporary readers respond positively to "The Yellow Wallpaper," the editor of the *Atlantic Monthly* in 1892 rejected it for publication. By way of explanation, he offered this candid reaction: "I could not forgive myself if I made others as miserable as I have made myself." How did the story affect you? Write a **three-to-five-paragraph analysis** explaining your own thoughts and feelings about the story. In your analysis, discuss the effect Gilman's present-tense narration had on you.	• In your first paragraph, include a thesis statement that brings out the controlling idea of your analysis. • Cite examples and quotations from the story to support your conclusions. • Include your personal thoughts and comments about the examples you used from the story. • Respond to any opposing claims that you expect readers might make.

Interactive Revision
Go to **thinkcentral.com**.
KEYWORD: HML11-817

FOR STRUGGLING WRITERS

Writing Support
• Offer this thesis sentence starter for students' personal response: My overall response to "The Yellow Wallpaper" was _____.

• Suggest that students use two literary features from the Two-Column Chart as a basis for writing two paragraphs after their thesis statement.

• Encourage students to add details that support their opinions.

Language

COMMON CORE L1, W1, W1–b,

◆ **GRAMMAR AND STYLE**

Help students rewrite the first example in the past tense for comparison. ***Possible answer:*** *But I was securely fastened by my well-hidden rope—you could not have gotten me out in the road!* (For more on verb tenses, see pages R59–R60 of the **Grammar Handbook**.)

Possible answer: *I throw another log on the fire. Then I wait for Ahmer to come home. Dinner sits on the table. It grows cold. Ahmer has been gone for hours, and I am sure that his feelings are hurt. Why do we always argue this way on special occasions? It is as though we don't really want to celebrate, or don't know how.*

R **RESOURCE MANAGER**—Copy Master
Choose Effective Verb Tense p. 208

READING-WRITING CONNECTION
Have students begin by listing their response to story features—topic, character, setting, plot, and theme—in a Two-Column Chart.

BEST PRACTICES TOOLKIT—Transparency
Two-Column Chart p. A25

Writing Online

The following tools are available online at **thinkcentral.com** and on **Write*Smart*** CD-ROM:
• Interactive Graphic Organizers
• Interactive Student Models
• Interactive Revision Lessons
For additional grammar instruction, see **GrammarNotes** on **thinkcentral.com**.

Assess and Reteach

Assess
DIAGNOSTIC AND SELECTION TESTS
Selection Test A pp. 213–214
Selection Test B/C pp. 215–216

Interactive Selection Test on **thinkcentral.com**

Reteach

Level Up Online Tutorials on **thinkcentral.com**

Reteaching Worksheets on **thinkcentral.com**

Literature Lesson 10, Grammar Lesson 16

COMMON CORE FOCUS

RL 3 Analyze the impact of the author's choices regarding how to develop and relate elements of a story. **SL 1a** Come to discussions prepared, having read and researched material under study; draw on that preparation by referring to evidence from texts to stimulate a thoughtful, well-reasoned exchange of ideas.

BACKGROUND Tell students that Edith Wharton was a prolific writer. Her writings include 25 novels and novellas, more than 80 short stories, an autobiography, a book on the theory of fiction, several collections of poetry and nonfiction, plus numerous translations, reviews, and articles, including accounts of her visits to the front line during World War I. Wharton received the Pulitzer Prize for her novel *The Age of Innocence* (1920).

TEXT ANALYSIS Remind students that writers develop characterization directly—by telling readers what a character is like—and indirectly—through a character's own words, thoughts, feelings and actions. As students read this feature, have them focus on the two characters' thoughts, feelings, and actions. Also, tell them that Ethan Frome, like other Wharton protagonists, resists social expectations and taboos with tragic consequences.

DISCUSS Draw a two-column chart on the board, labeling one column *Ethan* and the other *Mattie*. Ask students to provide details about each character found in the text. Students should suggest that Wharton's characterization reveals that Ethan is really sensitive and kind but worn down by his circumstances. Her characterization of Mattie shows that the character has not yet been dragged down or altered by her changed circumstances. Write students' predictions on the board.

from Ethan Frome

Novel by Edith Wharton

Edith Wharton
1862-1937

COMMON CORE

RL 3 Analyze the impact of the author's choices regarding how to develop and relate elements of a story. **SL 1a** Come to discussions prepared, having read and researched material under study; draw on that preparation by referring to evidence from texts to stimulate a thoughtful, well-reasoned exchange of ideas.

BACKGROUND Edith Wharton grew up in the rarefied atmosphere of New York wealth and wrote about it in most of her novels. Yet *Ethan Frome*, one of her best-known works, was set not in upper-crust New York society, but rather in a poor New England village. A novella, *Ethan Frome* takes place in a Massachusetts village called Starkfield, the name clearly evoking the bleak lifestyle that Wharton wished to portray. The story is told by an engineer who visits Starkfield and grows interested in a "ruin of a man" he sees there named Ethan Frome. Frome himself, we learn, had always wanted to be an engineer and to live in cities, "where there were lectures and big libraries." Instead, poverty and tradition have restricted him to a barren farm and an equally barren marriage. A visit from his sickly wife Zeena's young cousin, Mattie Silver, brings a spark of joy into Frome's grim life. His tragic attempt to grasp that joy forms the central conflict of the tale.

TEXT ANALYSIS Told in prose as spare and lean as the New England farm on which it is set, *Ethan Frome* contrasts sharply with Wharton's urban novels—lushly detailed portraits of Gilded Age Manhattan. *Ethan Frome* is similar to Wharton's other books, however, in that its characters seem to have very little influence over their own lives. In this respect, Wharton was a **naturalist** writer, exploring how human beings are shaped by forces beyond their control.

The excerpt on the opposite page describes Ethan Frome's changing relationship with Mattie Silver and the strong emotions that she has awakened in him. As you read the text, notice Wharton's subtle **characterization** of both her protagonist and the young woman who has come to spend time on his farm. The novelist gives readers access to the entire range of Frome's character—**internal** and **external.** We observe the lonely farmer's thoughts and feelings, as well as how his environment and his visitor shape his character. By contrast, readers see Mattie Silver exclusively from the outside. The author shares with us only what her protagonist sees of this new influence in Frome's life.

DISCUSS After you have read the excerpt from *Ethan Frome*, join a small group of your peers and review the characteristics of naturalism, which are described on pages 648–649. Then, discuss Wharton's characterization of Ethan Frome and Mattie Silver. How does her characterization, especially of Frome, reflect the way naturalist writers viewed the world? Finally, discuss your predictions for Ethan Frome. What kind of impact will Mattie's presence have on him in the end? If time allows, share your group's perceptions with the rest of the class.

DIFFERENTIATED INSTRUCTION

FOR STRUGGLING READERS

Note-Taking Ask students to identify the main ideas and important details of each section on page 818. Remind them that the main idea is what the section is mostly about. Details are facts and information that support the main idea. Use this example to model:

Background

Main Idea: Although Wharton usually wrote about New York's high society, *Ethan Frome* is set in a poor, rural village.

Detail 1: Ethan Frome is a man whose dreams of living in the city are ruined.

Detail 2: Frome lives a life of poverty and loneliness until his wife's cousin visits and causes conflict.

Frome was in the habit of walking into Starkfield to fetch home his wife's cousin, Mattie Silver, on the rare evenings when some chance of amusement drew her to the village. It was his wife who had suggested, when the girl came to live with them, that such opportunities should be put in her way. Mattie Silver came from Stamford, and when she entered the Fromes' household to act as her cousin Zeena's aid it was thought best, as she came without pay, not to let her feel too sharp a contrast between the life she had left and the isolation of a Starkfield farm. But for this—as Frome sardonically reflected—it would hardly have occurred
10 to Zeena to take any thought for the girl's amusement.

When his wife first proposed that they should give Mattie an occasional evening out he had inwardly demurred at having to do the extra two miles to the village and back after his hard day on the farm; but not long afterward he had reached the point of wishing that Starkfield might give all its nights to revelry.

Mattie Silver had lived under his roof for a year, and from early morning till they met at supper he had frequent chances of seeing her; but no moments in her company were comparable to those when, her arm in his, and her light step flying to keep time with his long stride, they walked back through the night to the farm. He had taken to the girl from the first day, when he had driven over to the Flats to
20 meet her, and she had smiled and waved to him from the train, crying out, "You must be Ethan!" as she jumped down with her bundles, while he reflected, looking over her slight person: "She don't look much on housework, but she ain't a fretter, anyhow." But it was not only that the coming to his house of a bit of hopeful young life was like the lighting of a fire on a cold hearth. The girl was more than the bright serviceable creature he had thought her. She had an eye to see and an ear to hear: he could show her things and tell her things, and taste the bliss of feeling that all he imparted left long reverberations and echoes he could wake at will.

It was during their night walks back to the farm that he felt most intensely the sweetness of this communion. He had always been more sensitive than the people
30 about him to the appeal of natural beauty. His unfinished studies had given form to this sensibility and even in his unhappiest moments field and sky spoke to him with a deep and powerful persuasion. But hitherto the emotion had remained in him as a silent ache, veiling with sadness the beauty that evoked it. He did not even know whether any one else in the world felt as he did, or whether he was the sole victim of this mournful privilege. Then he learned that one other spirit had trembled with the same touch of wonder: that at his side, living under his roof and eating his bread, was a creature to whom he could say: "That's Orion down yonder; the big fellow to the right is Aldebaran, and the bunch of little ones—like bees swarming—they're the Pleiades . . . ."

INTRODUCE THE MASTERPIECE

Ethan Frome Remind students that Edith Wharton was part of the literary movement called naturalism. Naturalists believed that people were helpless in the wake of certain forces that determined the outcome of their lives. As they read, have students notice the kinds of economic, social, and natural/physical forces that play a role in the life of Ethan Frome.

TIERED DISCUSSION PROMPTS

Use these prompts to help students understand the dynamic between Ethan Frome and Mattie Silver:

Connect Did you ever meet a new friend just when you were feeling terribly bored or miserable? How does that experience help you to understand Ethan Frome's reaction to Mattie? *Students should recognize that Mattie Silver provided Ethan Frome relief from his grim existence.*

Analyze What feelings does Mattie evoke in Ethan Frome? *Possible answer: She evokes feelings of happiness and connection to others. She makes him feel more effective, more alive, and less lonely than he had felt before her arrival.*

Synthesize What contrast does Wharton suggest between Ethan Frome's old life on a "barren farm" and in a "barren marriage" and his new relationship with Mattie? How do these contrasts affect readers? *Possible answer: Wharton shows that Ethan's relationship with Mattie contains wonder, excitement, and an interest in nature and beauty, all qualities that have been deadened by Ethan's barren marriage and barren farm life. These contrasts make the reader feel for and sympathize with Ethan Frome's budding hopes and desires.*

FOR STRUGGLING READERS

Characterization Help students create two Character Traits Webs, one for Ethan Frome and one for Mattie Silver. After they finish, have students circle any traits that the two characters have in common.

 **BEST PRACTICES TOOLKIT—Transparency** Character Traits Web p. D7

FOR ADVANCED LEARNERS/AP

Hypothesize Ask students to suggest the forces at work on Ethan Frome and Mattie. Have them consider how these forces drive the characters together and keep them apart. Then challenge students to hypothesize on the remaining plot events in the novel. Urge them to read the novel to check their hypotheses, or if they know the novel, to explain whether they were surprised by its outcome.

Focus and Motivate

COMMON CORE FOCUS

RL 1 Cite evidence to support inferences drawn from the text. **RL 3** Analyze the impact of the author's choices regarding how to develop and relate elements of a story. **RL 4** Determine the meaning of words and phrases as they are used in the text, including connotative meanings. **RL 6** Analyze a case in which grasping point of view requires distinguishing what is directly stated in a text from what is really meant. **L 4b** Identify and correctly use patterns of word changes that indicate different meanings or parts of speech. **L 5b** Analyze nuances in the meaning of words with similar denotations. **L 6** Acquire and use accurately general academic words and phrases.

ABOUT THE AUTHOR

Point out that although Wharton had an interest in women's roles in society, she was not specifically a feminist writer. Rather, she was interested in the way society's roles trap people, by gender or by other features. In "April Showers," Wharton uses light social satire to gently attack the roles confining a young woman with artistic aspirations.

April Showers

Short Story by Edith Wharton

COMMON CORE

RL 1 Cite evidence to support inferences drawn from the text.
RL 3 Analyze the impact of the author's choices regarding how to develop and relate elements of a story. **RL 4** Determine the meaning of words and phrases as they are used in the text, including connotative meanings. **L 5b** Analyze nuances in the meaning of words with similar denotations.

DID YOU KNOW?

Edith Wharton . . .

- privately published her first book of poetry at age 16.
- published a book each year from 1902 until her death in 1937.
- entertained President Theodore Roosevelt at her home in France.
- had such a forceful personality that her friends pretended to cower in fear when they saw her coming.

Meet the Author

Edith Wharton 1862–1937

To understand Edith Wharton is to know something about the insular upper-class society that produced her. Rich and fashionable "old New York" consisted of established families, like Wharton's own, descended from English and Dutch colonists and having inherited "old money" made in banking, shipping, and real estate. For Wharton, it was a restrictive world of narrow minds and rigid, arbitrary rules, where "'bad manners' were the supreme offense." It was a world already starting to disintegrate in the late 19th and early 20th century as new immigrants poured into New York and "new money" was being made in industry and manufacturing. But it was the world Wharton struggled with and wrote about with the satiric wit of an insider who had found a way to be free.

The Compensations of Wealth Wharton was educated at home by governesses and spent her youth as expected, traveling with her parents to Europe and dutifully attending the lavish balls and dinners during New York's social season. Her happiest times, however, were spent in her father's large library, reading and writing. Her cold, domineering mother thwarted the young Edith's literary ambitions by limiting her supply of paper and forcing her to marry a rich banker 12 years her senior. Depressed by her empty marriage and frivolous social life, Wharton used her characteristic moral strength and imaginative powers to break out. She had her own country estate built in Lenox, Massachusetts, where she could associate with people who shared her interests in art and literature. She also escaped to Europe each winter, where she cultivated friendships with famous artists and writers, such as her mentor, rival, and long-time friend, Henry James. Ultimately, she divorced her husband and moved permanently to France, living alternately outside Paris and on the Riviera.

Fame and Fulfillment? The novel that brought Wharton her first great success was *The House of Mirth* (1905), the story of a young woman crushed by the ranks of old New York when she tries to live by her own moral standards. Many of Wharton's other novels and stories sympathetically portray individuals who try but fail to find happiness in unconventional ways. *Ethan Frome* (1911), perhaps her best-known novel, depicts a doomed pair of lovers in a poor farming community. Wharton was the most celebrated American woman writer of her time but had a rather skeptical view of personal fulfillment. "If only we'd stop trying to be happy," she once said, "we could have a pretty good time."

Author Online
Go to **thinkcentral.com.** KEYWORD: HML11-820

THiNK central

Selection Resources

See resources on the **Teacher One Stop DVD-ROM** *and on* **thinkcentral.com**.

R RESOURCE MANAGER UNIT 4

Plan and Teach, pp. 209–216
Summary, pp. 217–218†‡*
Text Analysis and Reading
   Skill, pp. 219–222†*
Vocabulary, pp. 223–225*

DIAGNOSTIC AND SELECTION TESTS

Selection Tests, pp. 217–220

 BEST PRACTICES TOOLKIT

Word Questioning, p. E9
Character Traits and Textual
   Evidence, p. D6
Comparison Matrix, p. A24
Two-Column Chart, p. A25

TECHNOLOGY

- **Teacher One Stop DVD-ROM**
- **Student One Stop DVD-ROM**
- **Audio Anthology CD**
- **ExamView Test Generator**
   on the Teacher One Stop

---

* Resources for Differentiation   **† Also in Spanish**   **‡ In Haitian Creole and Vietnamese**

● TEXT ANALYSIS: CHARACTER DEVELOPMENT

Sometimes writers develop characters by revealing directly what characters think or feel. At other times, writers tell you indirectly about the character's thoughts and feelings by describing how the character acts, speaks, and reacts. Often, though, writers use both methods to develop their characters.

In "April Showers," the writer describes some of Theodora's thoughts and feelings, but much of her character is revealed through her actions. As you read, analyze Theodora's actions and ask yourself what they say about her.

■ READING SKILL: MAKE INFERENCES ABOUT CHARACTERS

Writers don't reveal everything about their characters directly. Instead, they expect readers to **make inferences,** or logical assumptions, about characters based on how those characters think and behave. Inferences must be supported by evidence from the text. As you read, jot down revealing actions and dialogue, as well as the inferences you draw from them.

Evidence from the Text	My Inferences
"Lingeringly, tenderly she gathered up the pages of her novel … and tied them with the blue satin ribbon…. She had meant to wear the ribbon with her new dotted muslin on Sundays, but this was putting it to a nobler use. She bound it round her manuscript, tying the ends in a pretty bow."	Theodora cares more abut her novel than she does about her clothes. But she's also dressing up the novel like a doll, not just sending it out, as a serious, more experienced writer would do.

▲ VOCABULARY IN CONTEXT

Wharton uses these words in her story about a writer waiting for a lucky break. Choose the word that completes each phrase.

WORD LIST		
admonitory	harassing	predecessor
commiseration	impending	retrospective
dastardly	interrogation	

1. wrote stories of evil villains and their _____ deeds
2. ignored _____ advice that success doesn't come overnight
3. modeled herself after her famous _____
4. sent impatient letters _____ those reviewing her work
5. feared _____ failure when no one responded

Complete the activities in your **Reader/Writer Notebook.**

What is your DREAM JOB?

You've probably answered the question "What do you want to be when you grow up?" more than a few times. But take a minute to think about your ultimate ambition. What is it about your dream job that's so appealing? Money? Fame? The thrill of doing something you love? The main character in this story dreams of becoming a writer, but does she have what it takes?

QUICKWRITE Imagine that you're filling out an application for your dream job (even if your chosen job—be it rock star or international soccer sensation—isn't one you'd typically fill out an application to get). What skills or traits make you the perfect candidate for the job? Why do you want it? What are you willing to do to get it?

821

What is your DREAM JOB?

Pose the Big Question and then ask students whether ambition is a good motivator. What negative impact can ambition have? After students identify appealing aspects of their dream job, have them complete the *QUICKWRITE*. Discuss trade-offs students are willing to make.

TEXT ANALYSIS COMMON CORE RL 3

● *Model the Skill:* **CHARACTER DEVELOPMENT**

Read aloud lines 1–6 on page 822 and point out the way the author uses third-person limited point of view to reveal Theodora's character through her actions (reading aloud, sighing, signing her pen name) and thoughts (her memory of girls crying over sad writing).

GUIDED PRACTICE Ask students to make a short list of Theodora's characteristics.

READING SKILL COMMON CORE RL 1

■ *Model the Skill:* **MAKE INFERENCES ABOUT CHARACTERS**

Point out that readers can make logical assumptions about characters by how they think and behave. Wharton lived an unconventional life for her era and professed an interest in characters "who try but fail to find happiness in unconventional ways." Readers can infer that the author enjoyed creating characters who live life on their own terms.

ℝ RESOURCE MANAGER—Copy Master Make Inferences About Characters p. 239 (for student use while reading the selection)

VOCABULARY SKILL

COMMON CORE L 4

▲ VOCABULARY IN CONTEXT

DIAGNOSE WORD KNOWLEDGE Have students complete Vocabulary in Context. Check their word choices against the following:

admonitory (ăd-mŏn′ĭ-tôr′ē) *adj.* warning

commiseration (kə-mĭz′ə-rā′shən) *n.* a feeling of sympathy or pity

dastardly (dăs′tərd-lē) *adj.* characterized by underhandedness or treachery

harassing (hə-răs′ĭng) *adj.* persistently annoying **harass** *v.*

impending (ĭm-pĕn′dĭng) *adj.* about to occur **impend** *v.*

interrogation (ĭn-tĕr′ə-gā′shən) *n.* a questioning

predecessor (prĕd′ĭ-sĕs′ər) *n.* a person who precedes or comes before

retrospective (rĕt′rə-spĕk′tĭv) *adj.* looking back into the past

---

SUMMARY

Theodora sends her first novel to *Home Circle*, dreaming that it will bring her fame and fortune. An acceptance letter offers fleeting glory, until she discovers that the magazine had meant the letter for another writer. Her father's sympathy softens the blow.

READ WITH A PURPOSE

Help students set a purpose for reading. Tell them to read in order to discover Wharton's attitude toward artists and their craft.

TEXT ANALYSIS COMMON CORE RL 3

A *Model the Skill:* **CHARACTER DEVELOPMENT**

Point out that Theodora reveals her evaluation of her novel in her thoughts and actions, and that both also paint a picture of her character.

Possible answer: Theodora has a high opinion of her novel. She believes its sad ending will appeal to young female readers. Her thoughts reveal that she is young, has high self-esteem, and is rather naive.

IF STUDENTS NEED HELP . . . Point out the sentimental and flowery ending Theodora has written, which is a way of saying that Guy never got over Muriel's death.

REVISIT THE BIG QUESTION

What is your DREAM JOB?

Discuss On the basis of lines 1–18, what is Theodora's ambition? How is she working to achieve it? *Possible answer: Theodora hopes to become a famous writer. She is working late into the night to finish her novel.*

VOCABULARY COMMON CORE L 4

OWN THE WORD

admonitory: Tell students that *admonitory* is the adjective form of *admonition*, which means "mild or cautionary warning." Ask students to use *admonitory* in a sentence. *Possible answer: The teacher shook an admonitory finger at us.*

April Showers
EDITH WHARTON

BACKGROUND By the turn of the 20th century, popular magazines—*Scribner's, Harper's, Century,* the *Atlantic Monthly,* and *Ladies' Home Journal*—paid good money to publish short stories, essays, and also longer works in serial form as, say, several chapters per issue. Edith Wharton first published her stories in magazines and serialized her Pulitzer Prize–winning novel, *The Age of Innocence,* as well as her autobiography. Such a publishing bonanza was great encouragement for writers of varying degrees of talent.

Analyze Visuals ▶
Describe the **mood** suggested in this painting. Which is more responsible for conveying the mood, the subject's pose and expression or the artist's use of light and shadow? Explain your choice.

"But Guy's heart slept under the violets on Muriel's grave."

It was a beautiful ending; Theodora had seen girls cry over last chapters that weren't half as pathetic. She laid her pen aside and read the words over, letting her voice linger on the fall of the sentence; then, drawing a deep breath, she wrote across the foot of the page the name by which she had decided to become known in literature—Gladys Glyn.

Downstairs the library clock struck two. Its muffled thump sounded like an **admonitory** knock against her bedroom floor. Two o' clock! and she had promised her mother to be up early enough to see that the buttons were sewn
10 on Johnny's reefer, and that Kate had her cod-liver oil[1] before starting for school!

Lingeringly, tenderly she gathered up the pages of her novel—there were five hundred of them—and tied them with the blue satin ribbon that her Aunt Julia had given her. She had meant to wear the ribbon with her new dotted muslin on Sundays, but this was putting it to a nobler use. She bound it round her manuscript, tying the ends in a pretty bow. Theodora was clever at making bows, and could have trimmed hats beautifully, had not all her spare moments been given to literature. Then, with a last look at the precious pages, she sealed and addressed the package. She meant to send it off next morning to the *Home Circle*.[2] She knew it would be hard to obtain access to a paper which numbered so many popular authors among
20 its contributors, but she had been encouraged to make the venture by something her Uncle James had said the last time he had come down from Boston.

A CHARACTER DEVELOPMENT
Wharton uses **third-person limited point of view** for this story, focusing on Theodora and her thoughts and feelings. In lines 1–6, what does Theodora think of the novel she has finished, and what do her thoughts reveal about her character?

admonitory
(ăd-mŏn′ĭ-tôr′ē) *adj.* warning

① Targeted Passage

---

1. **cod-liver oil:** a foul-tasting liquid once commonly taken as a source of vitamins A and D.
2. ***Home Circle:*** a magazine popular in the late 19th and early 20th centuries.

Girl Reading (1909), Edmund Charles Tarbell. Oil on canvas, 32 ¼″ × 28 ½″. The Hayden Collection, Charles Henry Hayden Fund 09.209. © Museum of Fine Arts, Boston.

DIFFERENTIATED INSTRUCTION

FOR ENGLISH LANGUAGE LEARNERS

Vocabulary Support Teach these words: *obtain* (line 19), *contribute* (line 48), *publication* (line 158), *invest* (line 190).

 **BEST PRACTICES TOOLKIT—Transparency**
Word Questioning p. E9

FOR STRUGGLING READERS

In combination with the *Audio Anthology CD,* use one or more Targeted Passages (pp. 822, 825, 827, 828–829, 830) to ensure that students focus on key story events and concepts. Targeted Passages are also good for English language learners.

① Targeted Passage [Lines 7–18]

The opening passage establishes the setting; the main character, Theodora; and the story's central conflict.

ⓑ CHARACTER DEVELOPMENT

Possible answer: Uncle James likes to live well and to boast about it to his brother. (lines 22–27) He seems to pity his brother having children to take care of (lines 27–28). He also like to name drop, as when he mentions his famous neighbor, novelist Kathleen Kyd (lines 30–32). This point of view allows readers to "hear" this conversation through Theodora's ears. Theodora believes Kyd is talented, whereas her father and uncle do not.

ⓒ Model the Skill: MAKE INFERENCES

Tell students to make inferences about the character by using the chart on page 821. Make the connection between the evidence of Uncle James's behavior and the inference regarding his character.

Possible answer: Uncle James distinguishes between "pleasant, social women" and "female writers" because he disapproves of the latter (line 40). He calls Kyd's writing "sentimental trash" and sternly warns that Theodora should not read it lest it "infect" her "system" (line 50). Uncle James seems both judgmental and sexist.

OWN THE WORD

- **predecessor:** Remind students that *predecessor* refers to "a person who comes before."

- **retrospective:** Tell students that *retrospective* is a look into the past that relates past experiences to the present. Ask students to explain the phrase, ". . . and she remembered, with a touch of *retrospective* compassion. . ." *Possible answer: When contemplating her future success as a writer, Theodora remembered that her success might not come until later in life.*

He had been telling his brother, Doctor Dace, about his new house out at Brookline.[3] Uncle James was prosperous, and was always moving into new houses with more "modern improvements." Hygiene was his passion, and he migrated in the wake of sanitary plumbing.

"The bathrooms alone are worth the money," he was saying, cheerfully, "although it *is* a big rent. But then, when a man's got no children to save up for—" he glanced compassionately round Doctor Dace's crowded table "—and it *is* something to be in a neighborhood where the drainage is A-one. That's what
30 I was telling our neighbor. Who do you suppose she is, by the way?" He smiled at Theodora. "I rather think that young lady knows all about her. Ever heard of Kathleen Kyd?"

Kathleen Kyd! The famous "society novelist," the creator of more "favorite heroines" than all her **predecessors** put together had ever turned out, the author of *Fashion and Passion, An American Duchess, Rhona's Revolt.* Was there any intelligent girl from Maine to California whose heart would not have beat faster at the mention of that name? ⓑ

"Why, yes," Uncle James was saying, "Kathleen Kyd lives next door. Frances G. Wollop is her real name, and her husband's a dentist. She's a very pleasant, sociable
40 kind of woman; you'd never think she was a writer. Ever hear how she began to write? She told me the whole story. It seems she was a saleswoman in a store, working on starvation wages, with a mother and a consumptive[4] sister to support. Well, she wrote a story one day, just for fun, and sent it to the *Home Circle.* They'd never heard of her, of course, and she never expected to hear from them. She did, though. They took the story and passed their plate for more. She became a regular contributor and eventually was known all over the country. Now she tells me her books bring her in about ten thousand a year. Rather more than you and I can boast of, eh, John? Well, I hope *this* household doesn't contribute to her support." He glanced sharply at Theodora. "I don't believe in feeding youngsters
50 on sentimental trash; it's like sewer gas—doesn't smell bad, and infects the system without your knowing it." ⓒ

Theodora listened breathlessly. Kathleen Kyd's first story had been accepted by the *Home Circle,* and they had asked for more! Why should Gladys Glyn be less fortunate? Theodora had done a great deal of novel reading—far more than her parents were aware of—and felt herself competent to pronounce upon the quality of her own work. She was almost sure that "April Showers" was a remarkable book. If it lacked Kathleen Kyd's lightness of touch, it had an emotional intensity never achieved by that brilliant writer. Theodora did not care to amuse her readers; she left that to more frivolous talents. Her aim was to stir the depths of human nature,
60 and she felt she had succeeded. It was a great thing for a girl to be able to feel that about her first novel. Theodora was only seventeen; and she remembered, with a touch of **retrospective** compassion, that George Eliot[5] had not become famous till she was nearly forty.

---

3. **Brookline:** a town in Massachusetts, just west of Boston.
4. **consumptive:** having consumption, or tuberculosis.
5. **George Eliot:** the pseudonym of the great 19th-century English novelist Mary Ann Evans.

predecessor (prĕd′ĭ-sĕs′ər) *n.* a person who precedes or comes before

ⓑ **CHARACTER DEVELOPMENT**
Reread lines 22–37. What does the dialogue reveal about Dr. Dace and Uncle James? What does third-person limited point of view reveal about Theodora? How does she differ from her father and uncle? Support your answer with evidence from these lines.

ⓒ **MAKE INFERENCES**
Why does Uncle James distinguish between "pleasant, sociable" women and female writers? Explain what you can infer about his character from these lines.

retrospective (rĕt′rə-spĕk′tĭv) *adj.* looking back into the past

---

DIFFERENTIATED INSTRUCTION

FOR ENGLISH LANGUAGE LEARNERS

Idioms and Phrasal Verbs [mixed-readiness groups] Share or elicit meanings for these expressions, and help students use them in original sentences:

- *for fun* (line 43), "for entertainment"
- *passed their plate for more* (line 45), "asked for more"
- *bring her in* (line 47), "earn for her"
- *write the book down* (lines 67–68), "make the book easier to understand"

FOR STRUGGLING READERS

Develop Reading Fluency Use Uncle James' monologue in lines 38–51 as an opportunity to study his character. Remind students that authors reveal much about their characters through dialogue. Model an effective reading aloud of lines 38–51, using your voice to convey the character's meaning and tone. Then have the class read the same passage aloud, reproducing your intonation, pacing, and volume.

No, there was no doubt about the merit of "April Showers." But would not an inferior work have had a better chance of success? Theodora recalled the early struggles of famous authors, the notorious antagonism of publishers and editors to any new writer of exceptional promise. Would it not be wiser to write the book down to the average reader's level, reserving for some later work the great "effects" into which she had thrown all the fever of her imagination? The
70 thought was sacrilege! Never would she lay hands on the sacred structure she had reared; never would she resort to the inartistic expedient of modifying her work to suit the popular taste. Better obscure failure than a vulgar triumph. The great authors never stooped to such concessions, and Theodora felt herself included in their ranks by the firmness with which she rejected all thought of conciliating an unappreciative public. The manuscript should be sent as it was. **D**

She woke with a start and a heavy sense of apprehension. The *Home Circle* had refused "April Showers"! No, that couldn't be it; there lay the precious manuscript, waiting to be posted. What was it, then? Ah, that ominous thump below stairs— nine o'clock striking! It was Johnny's buttons!
80 She sprang out of bed in dismay. She had been so determined not to disappoint her mother about Johnny's buttons! Mrs. Dace, helpless from chronic rheumatism, had to entrust the care of the household to her eldest daughter; and Theodora honestly meant to see that Johnny had his full complement of buttons, and that Kate and Bertha went to school tidy. Unfortunately, the writing of a great novel leaves little time or memory for the lesser obligations of life, and Theodora usually found that her good intentions matured too late for practical results.

Her contrition was softened by the thought that literary success would enable her to make up for all the little negligences of which she was guilty. She meant to spend all her money on her family; and already she had visions of a wheeled
90 chair for her mother, a fresh wallpaper for the doctor's shabby office, bicycles for the girls, and Johnny's establishment at a boarding school where sewing on his buttons would be included in the curriculum. If her parents could have guessed her intentions, they would not have found fault with her as they did; and Doctor Dace, on this particular morning, would not have looked up to say, with his fagged, ironical air:

"I suppose you didn't get home from the ball till morning?"

Theodora's sense of being in the right enabled her to take the thrust with a dignity that would have awed the unfeeling parent of fiction.

"I'm sorry to be late, father," she said.
100 Doctor Dace, who could never be counted on to behave like a father in a book, shrugged his shoulders impatiently.

"Your sentiments do you credit, but they haven't kept your mother's breakfast warm." **E**

"Hasn't mother's tray gone up yet?"

"Who was to take it, I should like to know? The girls came down so late that

D MAKE INFERENCES
Consider Theodora's sympathy for George Eliot in lines 61–63 and her opinion of the "average reader." What inferences can you make about Theodora's character based on her thoughts about her own work?

② **Targeted Passage**

E MAKE INFERENCES
Theodora muses repeatedly that Dr. Dace does not act as a father in a work of fiction would. What does she mean by this?

FOR STRUGGLING READERS

② **Targeted Passage** [Lines 76–86]

This passage shows the difficulty of Theodora's role in the family.

- Why does Theodora's mother need help? (lines 81–82)

- What was Theodora supposed to do for Mrs. Dace? (lines 80–84)

- On what does Theodora blame her forgetfulness? (lines 84–86)

FOR ADVANCED LEARNERS/AP

Analyze Satire Have students discuss the satire in Wharton's descriptions of Kathleen Kyd and her writing (lines 33–51) and of Theodora's literary aspirations (lines 52–75). What is Wharton's opinion of writers like Kyd? What is her opinion of Theodora's writing? Have students decide whom Wharton satirizes more sharply, Kyd or Theodora, and share their views with the class.

READING SKILL   COMMON CORE RL 1

D MAKE INFERENCES

Possible answer: Theodora's sympathy for the great George Eliot is humorous and ironic. Readers can infer from her reaction that she can be pretentious and condescending, but also that she is naive. She is, after all, still a teenager, who has lived a relatively sheltered life, and who views herself as very special.

IF STUDENTS NEED HELP . . . Clarify that George Eliot is a famous and well-regarded novelist, while Theodora is a teenager trying to sell a mediocre first novel.

BACKGROUND

Rheumatism Much like arthritis, Mrs. Dace's chronic rheumatism would produce painful joints and muscles and make everyday chores such as sewing on a button very difficult.

REVISIT THE BIG QUESTION

What is your
DREAM JOB?

Discuss What do lines 87–96 suggest about Theodora's ambitions? *Possible answer: Theodora dreams of fame for herself and fortune to help her family, which is struggling financially.* How do Theodora's dreams of helping her family soften readers' appraisal of her? *Possible answer: Her desire to help her family makes readers forgive her pretensions about her accomplishments and instead wish her well.*

READING SKILL   COMMON CORE RL 1

E MAKE INFERENCES

Possible answer: Theodora means that he doesn't act like the type of idealized, romanticized father that might be found in her book or in Kyd's book. Such a father would quickly understand, forgive, and forget Theodora's shortcomings. Dr. Dace doesn't act as Theodora wishes he would. Instead, he is reproachful and sarcastic.

Use these prompts to help students understand Theodora's state of mind, as she waits to hear from *Home Circle* magazine in lines 115–133:

Connect Have you ever felt excited and nervous as you anticipated important news? How does that experience help you understand Theodora's reaction waiting for news from *Home Circle*? Explain. *Accept all reasonable responses.*

Analyze What effect is Theodora's nervous anticipation having on her family? ***Possible answer: Theodora forgets to help her mother with the children and to do the mending.***

Synthesize Why is it so important for Theodora to sell her book? What will happen to her if she does not? ***Possible answer: Theodora probably feels unhappy about her limited choices in life and the family responsibilities that she is expected to shoulder. If she does not sell her book, she will face "an obscure existence of mending and combing" (line 121).***

TEXT ANALYSIS

COMMON CORE
RL 3

F CHARACTER DEVELOPMENT

Possible answer: Miss Brill is the neighborhood busybody, a gossipy vulture whose visits make others feel terrible. Wharton develops this character by noting her behavior, citing that "It was very kind of her to come, for she was the busiest woman in Norton" (lines 134–135) and comments that the town has the "benefit" of Miss Brill's "supervision" (lines 136–137).

IF STUDENTS NEED HELP... Work with them to complete a Character Traits and Textual Evidence chart like this one. Model how to use this evidence both to determine what kind of woman Miss Brill is and to identify the details Wharton uses to develop the character.

Quote (p. 826): "It was very kind of her to come, for she was the busiest woman in Norton."	Explanation: Miss Brill is busy bothering people.

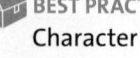 BEST PRACTICES TOOLKIT—Transparency
Character Traits and Textual Evidence p. D6

I had to hustle them off before they'd finished breakfast, and Johnny's hands were so dirty that I sent him back to his room to make himself decent. It's a pretty thing for the doctor's children to be the dirtiest little savages in Norton!"

110 Theodora had hastily prepared her mother's tray, leaving her own breakfast untouched. As she entered the room upstairs, Mrs. Dace's patient face turned to her with a smile much harder to bear than her father's reproaches.

"Mother, I'm *so* sorry—"

"No matter, dear. I suppose Johnny's buttons kept you. I can't think what that boy does to his clothes!"

Theodora sat the tray down without speaking. It was impossible to own to having forgotten Johnny's buttons without revealing the cause of her forgetfulness. For a few weeks longer she must bear to be misunderstood; then—ah, then if her novel were accepted, how gladly would she forget and forgive! But what if it were refused? She turned aside to hide the dismay that flushed her face. Well, then

120 she would admit the truth—she would ask her parents' pardon, and settle down without a murmur to an obscure existence of mending and combing.

She had said to herself that after the manuscript had been sent, she would have time to look after the children and catch up with the mending; but she had reckoned without the postman. He came three times a day; for an hour before each ring she was too excited to do anything but wonder if he would bring an answer this time, and for an hour afterward she moved about in a leaden stupor of disappointment. The children had never been so trying. They seemed to be always coming to pieces, like cheap furniture; one would have supposed they had been put together with bad glue. Mrs. Dace worried herself ill over Johnny's tatters,

130 Bertha's bad marks at school, and Kate's open abstention from cod-liver oil; and Doctor Dace, coming back late from a long round of visits to a fireless office with a smoky lamp, called out furiously to know if Theodora would kindly come down and remove the "East, West, home's best" that hung above the empty grate.

In the midst of it all, Miss Sophy Brill called. It was very kind of her to come, for she was the busiest woman in Norton. She made it her duty to look after other people's affairs, and there was not a house in town but had the benefit of her personal supervision. She generally came when things were going wrong, and the sight of her bonnet on the doorstep was a surer sign of calamity than a crepe bow on the bell.[6] After she left, Mrs. Dace looked very sad, and the doctor punished

140 Johnny for warbling down the entry:

"Miss Sophy Brill
Is a bitter pill!"

while Theodora, locking herself in her room, resolved with tears that she would never write another novel. **F**

The week was a long nightmare. Theodora could neither eat nor sleep. She was up early enough, but instead of looking after the children and seeing that breakfast

---

Language Coach

Word Definitions
"Reckoned without" (line 124) means "hadn't taken into consideration." Read lines 122–127. How has Theodora's plan for the day been disrupted by the postman?

F CHARACTER DEVELOPMENT
What kind of person is Miss Brill? Why does her visit have such a dramatic effect on Theodora? Cite evidence from the story to support your response.

---

6. **crepe bow on the bell:** a signal that someone had died. Clothing made from black crepe (a silk material) used to be worn by those in mourning.

DIFFERENTIATED INSTRUCTION

FOR STRUGGLING READERS

Concept Support Review with students that tone reflects the author's attitude toward the characters. One effective way to recognize tone is to read a work aloud in character. Often readers will naturally choose the correct tone of voice for the context. Work with students to read lines 134–150 aloud. As students find the correct tone, pause and ask them to describe the tone. Is it sarcastic, annoyed, amused, and so on?

FOR ENGLISH LANGUAGE LEARNERS

Language Coach
Word Definitions

Answer: Theodora cannot concentrate on her chores: She is distracted before the postman comes and by disappointment after he leaves. Explain that *reckon* is now considered an old-fashioned word. Tell students that the word comes from an Old English word meaning "to count."

was ready, she wandered down the road to meet the postman, and came back wan and empty-handed, oblivious of her morning duties. She had no idea how long the suspense would last; but she didn't see how authors could live if they were kept
150 waiting more than a week.

Then suddenly, one afternoon—she never quite knew how or when it happened—she found herself with a *Home Circle* envelope in her hands, and her dazzled eyes flashing over a wild dance of words that wouldn't settle down and make sense.

"Dear Madam:" (They called her *Madam!* And then; yes, the words were beginning to fall into line now.) "Your novel, 'April Showers,' has been received, and we are glad to accept it on the usual terms. A serial on which we were counting for immediate publication has been delayed by the author's illness, and the first chapters of 'April Showers' will therefore appear in our midsummer number. Thanking you
160 for favoring us with your manuscript, we remain," and so forth.

Theodora found herself in the wood beyond the schoolhouse. She was kneeling on the ground, brushing aside the dead leaves and pressing her lips to the little bursting green things that pushed up eager tips through last year's decay. It was spring—spring! Everything was crowding toward the light and in her own heart hundreds of germinating hopes had burst into sudden leaf. She wondered if the thrust of those little green fingers hurt the surface of the earth as her springing raptures hurt—yes, actually hurt!—her hot, constricted breast! She looked up through interlacing boughs at a tender, opaque blue sky full of the coming of a milky moon. She seemed enveloped in an atmosphere of loving comprehension.
170 The brown earth throbbed with her joy, the treetops trembled with it, and a sudden star broke through the branches like an audible "I know!"

Theodora, on the whole, behaved very well. Her mother cried, her father whistled and said he supposed he must put up with grounds in his coffee now, and be thankful if he ever got a hot meal again; while the children took the most deafening and **harassing** advantage of what seemed a sudden suspension of the laws of nature.

Within a week everybody in Norton knew that Theodora had written a novel, and that it was coming out in the *Home Circle*. On Sundays, when she walked up the aisle, her friends dropped their prayer books and the soprano sang false in
180 her excitement. Girls with more pin money than Theodora had ever dreamed of copied her hats and imitated her way of speaking. The local paper asked her for a poem; her old school teachers stopped to shake hands and grew shy over their congratulations; and Miss Sophy Brill came to call. She had put on her Sunday bonnet and her manner was almost abject. She ventured, very timidly, to ask her young friend how she wrote, whether it "just came to her," and if she had found that the kind of pen she used made any difference; and wound up by begging Theodora to write a sentiment in her album.

③ Targeted Passage

harassing (hə-răs'ĭng) *adj.* persistently annoying **harass** *v.*

Activity Ask students to compare and contrast *In the Station Waiting Room, Boston* with *Girl Reading* on page 823, also painted by Edmund Charles Tarbell. Have them compare the use of light and shadow to convey mood and contrast the portrayal of women in each painting. *Possible answer: Both paintings create a pensive and serious mood and direct viewers' focus through the use of shadow and light. Both portray women at the turn of the 20th century. However,* In the Station Waiting Room, Boston, *which is a later work, shows women out in the world, while* Girl Reading *shows a woman at home involved in domestic activity. The difference perhaps reflects the changing role of women, whose influence and spheres of activity were expanding. In addition, both works were painted in oil.*

Even Uncle James came down from Boston to talk the wonder over. He called Theodora a "sly baggage," and proposed that she should give him her earnings to
190 invest in a new patent grease-trap company. From what Kathleen Kyd had told him, he thought Theodora would probably get a thousand dollars for her story. He concluded by suggesting that she should base her next romance on the subject of sanitation, making the heroine nearly die of sewer gas poisoning because her parents won't listen to the handsome young doctor next door, when he warns them that their plumbing is out of order. That was a subject that would interest everybody, and do a lot more good than the sentimental trash most women wrote.

At last the great day came. Theodora had left an order with the bookseller for the midsummer number of the *Home Circle* and before the shop was open she was waiting on the sidewalk. She clutched the precious paper and ran home without
200 opening it. Her excitement was almost more than she could bear. Not heeding her father's call to breakfast, she rushed upstairs and locked herself in her room. Her hands trembled so that she could hardly turn the pages. At last—yes, there it was: "April Showers."

The paper dropped from her hands. What name had she read beneath the title? Had her emotion blinded her?

"April Showers, by *Kathleen Kyd*."

Kathleen Kyd! Oh, cruel misprint! Oh, **dastardly** typographer! Through tears of rage and disappointment Theodora looked again; yes, there was no mistaking the hateful name. Her glance ran on. She found herself reading a first paragraph

④ Targeted Passage

dastardly (dăs′tərd-lē) *adj.* characterized by underhandedness or treachery

In the Station Waiting Room, Boston (1915), Edmund Charles Tarbell. Oil on canvas, 24 ³/₈″ × 32″. Gift of Dr. Joseph R. Fazzano. © Crocker Art Museum, Sacramento, California.

DIFFERENTIATED INSTRUCTION

FOR STRUGGLING READERS

④ Targeted Passage [Lines 197–211]

This passage describes a surprising turn of events for Theodora's literary hopes.

- What does Theodora pick up at the bookseller's shop? (lines 197–199)
- What does she discover when she sees "April Showers"? (lines 206–207)
- What does she realize when she reads the first paragraph? (lines 209–211)

FOR ENGLISH LANGUAGE LEARNERS

Related Vocabulary [mixed-readiness groups] The mistake that *Home Circle* makes and Theodora's reaction to it convey important plot information. Make sure students understand that Theodora is disappointed and the magazine is regretful and embarrassed. Then teach these related words on pages 828–829:

- *cruel; dastardly* (line 207)
- *rage and disappointment* (line 208)
- *hateful* (line 209)
- *strange; horrible* (line 210)
- *bland apology; unfortunate accident* (line 235)
- *by mistake* (line 237)
- *should . . . have been; regrettable oversight* (line 238)
- *accidents . . . happen* (lines 238–239)
- *sure she understood* (line 239)

210 that she had never seen before. She read farther. All was strange. The horrible
truth burst upon her: *It was not her story!*

④ Targeted Passage *continued*

She never knew how she got back to the station. She struggled through the crowd
on the platform, and a gold-banded arm pushed her into the train just starting
for Norton. It would be dark when she reached home; but that didn't matter—
nothing mattered now. She sank into her seat, closing her eyes in the vain attempt
to shut out the vision of the last few hours; but minute by minute memory forced
her to relive it; she felt like a rebellious school child dragged forth to repeat the
same detested "piece."

Although she did not know Boston well, she had made her way easily enough
220 to the *Home Circle* building; at least, she supposed she had, since she remembered
nothing till she found herself ascending the editorial stairs as easily as one does
incredible things in dreams. She must have walked very fast, for her heart was
beating furiously, and she had barely breath to whisper the editor's name to a
young man who looked out at her from a glass case, like a zoological specimen.
The young man led her past other glass cases containing similar specimens to
an inner enclosure which seemed filled by an enormous presence. Theodora felt
herself enveloped in the presence, submerged by it, gasping for air as she sank
under its rising surges.

Gradually fragments of speech floated to the surface. "'April Showers?' Mrs.
230 Kyd's new serial? *Your* manuscript, you say? You have a letter from me? The name,
please? Evidently some unfortunate misunderstanding. One moment." And then
a bell ringing, a zoological specimen ordered to unlock a safe, her name asked for
again, the manuscript, her own precious manuscript, tied with Aunt Julia's ribbon,
laid on the table before her, and her outcries, her protests, her **interrogations,**
drowned in a flood of bland apology: "An unfortunate accident—Mrs. Kyd's
manuscript received the same day—extraordinary coincidence in the choice of a
title—duplicate answers sent by mistake—Miss Dace's novel hardly suited to their
purpose—should of course have been returned—regrettable oversight—accidents
would happen—sure she understood."

240 The voice went on, like the steady pressure of a surgeon's hand on a shrieking
nerve. When it stopped she was in the street. A cab nearly ran her down, and a car
bell jangled furiously in her ears. She clutched her manuscript, carrying it tenderly
through the crowd, like a live thing that had been hurt. She could not bear to look
at its soiled edges and the ink stain on Aunt Julia's ribbon.

The train stopped with a jerk and she opened her eyes. It was dark, and by the
windy flare of gas on the platform she saw the Norton passengers getting out. She
stood up stiffly and followed them. A warm wind blew into her face the fragrance
of the summer woods, and she remembered how, two months earlier, she had
knelt among the dead leaves, pressing her lips to the first shoots of green. Then
250 for the first time she thought of home. She had fled away in the morning without a
word, and her heart sank at the thought of her mother's fears. And her father—how
angry he would be! She bent her head under the coming storm of his derision.

APRIL SHOWERS **829**

Language Coach

Fixed Expressions The term *fixed expression* refers to the normal combination of words—the ways they are often used. "Vain attempt" (line 215) means an "unsuccessful effort." ("Futile attempt" and "botched attempt" are similar expressions.) Use one of these expressions in a sentence.

interrogation
(ĭn-tĕr′ə-gā′shən) *n.* a questioning

TIERED DISCUSSION PROMPTS

Use these prompts to help students understand Theodora's presence of mind as she deals with her great disappointment in lines 212–244:

Connect How do many people react to terrible disappointment? *Responses should reflect an understanding that many people feel depressed and sad, and possibly angry.*

Analyze How would you characterize the way Theodora faces her disappointing situation? *Possible answer: She faces the situation bravely, taking a train into Boston and demanding to know what has happened.*

FOR ADVANCED LEARNERS/AP

Analyze Realism Remind students that realism emphasizes everyday experience, depicting ordinary lives without romance or sentimentality. Encourage students to analyze Wharton's use of realism in this story in a brief essay. They might consider this question:

• How does Wharton use realistic elements to ironic and satiric purposes?

FOR ENGLISH LANGUAGE LEARNERS

Language Coach

Fixed Expressions *Possible answer: After neglecting to rehearse, Kristin made a* futile attempt *at the drama audition.* Explain that students use fixed expressions all the time without thinking about them. Ask students for examples and write them on the board. *Possible answers: what in the world, put in a good word, I don't get it, hold on a second*

VOCABULARY

COMMON CORE
L 4

OWN THE WORD

interrogation: Remind students that *interrogation* refers to questioning and connotes a strong investigation. Have students complete the following sentence to demonstrate their understanding of the word. "The detectives brought the suspect in for *interrogation* because..." *Possible answer: they wanted to ask her questions in order to find out who committed the crime.*

APRIL SHOWERS **829**

What is your DREAM JOB?

Discuss After students read lines 283–284, pose the following discussion question: How were Dr. Dace's ambitions like Theodora's? *Possible answer: Both wanted to be novelists and to be viewed as special.*

CHARACTER DEVELOPMENT

Possible answer: Theodora's father reveals that he had wanted to be a novelist, but that publishers had rejected his manuscript. He also shows himself to be empathetic to his daughter's disappointment. Theodora learns not to take her father's reactions for granted.

OWN THE WORD

- **impending:** *Impending* describes something that is about to occur. What did Theodora fear when she "shrank back involuntarily from [her father's] *impending* mirth?" *Possible answer: Theodora feared that her father was trying not to laugh at her.*

- **commiseration:** Tell students that *commiseration* refers to sharing a feeling of sympathy or pity. Ask students if they have ever felt *commiseration* with someone. Have them explain who, when, and why they *commiserated* with this person.

SELECTION WRAP-UP

READ WITH A PURPOSE Now that students have read "April Showers," ask them to articulate Wharton's attitude toward Theodora and her writing. *Possible answer: Although Wharton seems to make light of Theodora's sense of writerly genius, she does understand the effort writers make and their ability to experience rejection.*

The night was cloudy, and as she stepped into the darkness beyond the station a hand was slipped in hers. She stood still, too weary to feel frightened, and a voice said, quietly:

"Don't walk so fast, child. You look tired."

"Father!" Her hand dropped from his, but he recaptured it and drew it through his arm. When she found voice, it was to whisper, "You were at the station?"

"It's such a good night I thought I'd stroll down and meet you."

260 Her arm trembled against his. She could not see his face in the dimness, but the light of his cigar looked down on her like a friendly eye, and she took courage to falter out: "Then you knew—"

"That you'd gone to Boston? Well, I rather thought you had."

They walked on slowly, and presently he added, "You see, you left the *Home Circle* lying in your room."

How she blessed the darkness and the muffled sky! She could not have borne the scrutiny of the tiniest star.

"Then mother wasn't very much frightened?"

"Why, no, she didn't appear to be. She's been busy all day over some toggery
270 of Bertha's."

Theodora choked. "Father, I'll—" She groped for words, but they eluded her. "I'll do things—differently; I haven't meant—" Suddenly she heard herself bursting out: "It was all a mistake, you know—about my story. They didn't want it; they won't have it!" and she shrank back involuntarily from his **impending** mirth.

She felt the pressure of his arm, but he didn't speak, and she figured his mute hilarity. They moved on in silence. Presently he said:

"It hurts a bit just at first, doesn't it?"

"O father!"

He stood still, and the gleam of his cigar showed a face of unexpected
280 participation.

"You see I've been through it myself."

"You, father? You?"

"Why, yes. Didn't I ever tell you? I wrote a novel once. I was just out of college, and didn't want to be a doctor. No; I wanted to be a genius, so I wrote a novel."

The doctor paused, and Theodora clung to him in a mute passion of **commiseration.** It was as if a drowning creature caught a live hand through the murderous fury of the waves.

"Father—O father!"

"It took me a year—a whole year's hard work; and when I'd finished it the
290 public wouldn't have it, either; not at any price and that's why I came down to meet you, because I remembered my walk home."

impending (ĭm-pĕn'dĭng) *adj.* to be about to occur
impend *v.*

⑤ Targeted Passage

commiseration (kə-mĭz'ə-rā'shən) *n.* a feeling of sympathy or pity

⑥ CHARACTER DEVELOPMENT
Reread lines 281–291. What does the dialogue reveal about Theodora's father? What kind of lesson does Theodora learn here? Explain your answer.

DIFFERENTIATED INSTRUCTION

FOR STRUGGLING READERS

⑤ Targeted Passage [Lines 271–291]

This passage resolves the plot: Dr. Dace helps Theodora cope with disappointment.

- How does Theodora expect her father to react to her news? How does he react? (line 274)

- What surprising information does Theodora learn about her father? (lines 281–284)

- How does Theodora feel about her father by the end of the story? (lines 285–288)

FOR RELUCTANT READERS

Connect to the Text Ask students if they identify with Theodora and why (or why not). Ask students to write a journal entry or draw an image or cartoon strip about their own dreams for success and what they might entail. Invite volunteers to share their work and then lead the class in a discussion of what obstacles or challenges young people face in trying to fulfill their ambitions.

Comprehension

1. **Summarize** Describe Theodora's family situation and responsibilities.

2. **Recall** What does Theodora plan to do with the money she expects to earn?

3. **Clarify** How does the *Home Circle* editor explain the mix-up?

4. **Clarify** What does Theodora's father reveal to her at the end of the story?

Text Analysis

● 5. **Analyze Character Development** Reread lines 52–75. What clues does Wharton provide in these lines to indicate that Theodora might not be the "great author" she thinks herself to be? Cite specific evidence from these lines to support your answer.

■ 6. **Make Inferences About Characters** Review the inferences you recorded as you read, and recall Theodora's disappointment that her father does not act the way she thinks the parent in a novel would. How might their relationship change as a result of the disastrous "April Showers" incident?

7. **Interpret Satire** A satire ridicules ideas and behavior to expose human faults or weakness. Satire is sometimes hard to detect, but a writer's tone is often an indication— reading a satire can feel as

Character	Satirized for ...	Evidence in Story
Uncle James	being crude and materialistic	• talks obsessively about indoor plumbing and "sewer gas" at the dinner table (lines 24–51) • brags about his money and even asks Theodora to invest the money from her novel in one of his schemes (lines 26–29, 188–196)

though the author were winking at you while telling the story. Explain what characters and behavior Wharton satirizes in this story by filling out a chart like the one shown.

Text Criticism

8. **Historical Context** A contemporary critic commented, "When we look beneath the high surface gloss of Wharton's world, we see a marketplace, pure and simple. Hers is an almost purely economic conception of life." What insights does this story give you into the economic position of women at the turn of the 20th century? What kinds of work were available to them, and at what kinds of wages? Is it surprising that an educated young woman would try to make money by writing? Support your answer with evidence.

> *What is your* **DREAM JOB?**
>
> In "April Showers," Theodora's ambition is to write a novel. Do you think there are positive as well as negative motivations for choosing a career? Explain your answer.

> *What is your* **DREAM JOB?**
> Students may suggest that positive motivations include personal satisfaction, money, and independence. Negative motivations may include wanting to avoid debt or needing to get out of a bad situation.

COMMON CORE

RL 1 Cite evidence to support inferences drawn from the text. **RL 3** Analyze the impact of the author's choices regarding how to develop and relate elements of a story. **RL 6** Analyze a case in which grasping point of view requires distinguishing what is directly stated in a text from what is really meant.

Practice and Apply

For preliminary support of post-reading questions, use these copy masters:

R RESOURCE MANAGER—Copy Masters
Reading Check p. 226
Character Development p. 219
Question Support p. 227
Additional selection questions are provided for teachers on page 213.

ANSWERS   COMMON CORE **RL 1, RL 3, RL 6**

1. *Theodora's mother is ill, leaving Theodora the household chores and care of her three siblings.*

2. *Theodora plans to spend the money on her family.*

3. *Another author sent the magazine a manuscript with the same title. In error, the magazine sent two acceptance letters.*

4. *Dr. Dace reveals that he once wrote a novel and received a painful rejection.*

Possible answers:

5. ● **COMMON CORE FOCUS** **Analyze Character Development** *Theodora seems to have delusions of grandeur. Young Theodora is certain she has written a "remarkable book" (line 56), comparing herself favorably to George Eliot (lines 62–63) and insisting that she will never "dumb down" her work (lines 70–72).*

6. ■ **COMMON CORE FOCUS** **Make Inferences About Characters** *Students may say that Theodora and her father will achieve new closeness and respect. Others may say that demands on Theodora will still fray their relationship. Students should cite text evidence and life experience to support their views.*

7. *Character: Miss Brill, Satirized for: being a busybody, Evidence: lines 134–137, 184–187; Character: Theodora, Satirized for: literary pretensions, Evidence: lines 11–18, 52–75, 161–171; Character: Uncle James, Satirized for: small-mindedness and materialism, Evidence: lines 22–51, 188–196*

8. *Women in the story are stuck in lowly unpaid domestic work, like Theodora. They are ill, like Mrs. Dace and Kathleen Kyd's sister. They have low-paying, dull jobs, such as saleswomen, or hat trimmers (line 16). It makes sense that Theodora would want to be a writer, as this is the only attractive occupation for women in the story.*

Vocabulary in Context

▲ **VOCABULARY PRACTICE**

1. *betraying a friend*
2. *about to happen*
3. *late*
4. *to irritate*
5. *take it seriously*
6. *get information*
7. *sending flowers*
8. *my grandmother*

 RESOURCE MANAGER—Copy Master
Vocabulary Practice p. 224

ACADEMIC VOCABULARY IN SPEAKING

Answers will vary. Some students may say that Theodora has a valid reason for her forgetfulness and neglect. Others will see her excuses as a poor reflection on her character.

VOCABULARY STRATEGY:
THE LATIN ROOT *rog*

 COMMON CORE L 4b, L 6

Point out to students that knowing prefixes such as *ab-*, *pre-*, and *inter-* can help them use a word's root to build meaning. Roots often do not provide an exact meaning, so students must also use context clues.

Answers:

1. *prerogative*
2. *surrogate*
3. *arrogate*
4. *derogatory*
5. *abrogate*

 RESOURCE MANAGER—Copy Master
Vocabulary Strategy p. 225

Interactive Vocabulary  THINK central

Keywords direct students to a **WordSharp** tutorial on **thinkcentral.com** or to other types of vocabulary practice and review.

Assess and Reteach

Assess

DIAGNOSTIC AND SELECTION TESTS

Selection Test A pp. 217–218
Selection Test B/C pp. 219–220

Interactive Selection Test on thinkcentral.com

Reteach

Level Up Online Tutorials on thinkcentral.com

Vocabulary in Context

▲ **VOCABULARY PRACTICE**

Show that you understand the vocabulary words by answering these questions.

1. Which is a **dastardly** deed, betraying a friend or voting in an election?
2. If an investigation is **impending**, is it over or about to happen?
3. Would an artist have a **retrospective** exhibit early or late in his or her career?
4. What is the intent of a **harassing** letter, to schedule an appointment or to irritate the recipient into action?
5. If I make an **admonitory** statement, do I expect you to laugh or take it seriously?
6. Is an **interrogation** intended to get information or rehearse a performance?
7. Which would be a gesture of **commiseration,** sending flowers or watching a lengthy movie?
8. Who would be your mother's **predecessor** in life, you or your grandmother?

WORD LIST
admonitory
commiseration
dastardly
harassing
impending
interrogation
predecessor
retrospective

ACADEMIC VOCABULARY IN SPEAKING

• apparent • confine • expose • focus • perceive

The reason for Theodora's lack of interest in daily affairs becomes **apparent** when her family realizes that she has written a novel and sent it off to be published. In a small group, discuss your thoughts about Theodora's actions and whether you agree or disagree with her excuses. Use at least three Academic Vocabulary words in your discussion.

VOCABULARY STRATEGY: THE LATIN ROOT *rog*

The word root *rog*, which has its origin in Latin, means "ask," "ask for," or "propose." *Rog* is found in a number of English words, including the vocabulary word *interrogation*. To understand words built around *rog*, use your knowledge of the Latin origin and meaning of the root and affixes as well as context clues.

COMMON CORE

L 4b Identify and correctly use patterns of word changes that indicate different meanings or parts of speech. **L 6** Acquire and use accurately general academic words and phrases.

PRACTICE Apply what you know about the Latin root *rog* and the other word parts to help you understand the words in the web. Then choose the word that best completes each sentence. If necessary, consult a dictionary.

1. It is the race winner's _____ to wear the yellow jersey.
2. The official could not attend the ceremony, so he sent a(n) _____.
3. They feared that the new judge would _____ to herself powers that belonged to the legislature.
4. Jake tends to make _____ remarks about people he does not like.
5. People _____ their responsibility when they do not care for their pets.

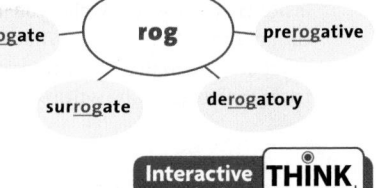

Interactive Vocabulary THINK central

Go to **thinkcentral.com**.
KEYWORD: HML11-832

DIFFERENTIATED INSTRUCTION

FOR ENGLISH LANGUAGE LEARNERS

Task Support: Vocabulary Practice To help students remember the words on the Word List, define these prefixes:

- *ad-*, "to, toward"
- *com-*, "together, with"
- *im-*, "against"
- *inter-*, "between"
- *pre-*, "before"
- *retro-*, "back"

FOR ADVANCED LEARNERS/AP

The Latin Root *rog* Ask partners to do a word search for synonyms of each word containing the root *rog*. Have them create a graphic organizer for each *rog* word and its synonyms, illustrating differences in meaning. Students might focus on differences of degree, connotation, or another criterion of their choosing.

Women's Changing Roles

A woman's role in American society was rigidly defined in the late 19th and early 20th centuries. Women of this period could not vote, few owned businesses, and few gained a higher education. Yet women were increasingly agitating for change in both big and small ways. The writers in this section (pages 782–832) gave voice to the struggles of women attempting to fashion a new role for themselves and break free from restricting social expectations. As critic Richard Gray noted, "Humanity, if it is repressed, will always have its revenge."

Writing to Compare

Think about how women's roles have changed since the times of Kate Chopin and Edith Wharton. Using the stories you have just read and your knowledge of American society today, write a comparison of women's roles then and now.

Consider

- what each text tells you about society's expectations for women at that time
- how things have or have not changed since the days these writers were working
- what details from the texts best illustrate women's roles in the past
- what examples from today best illustrate women's roles now

833

Extension

SPEAKING & LISTENING

With a partner, **role-play** a conversation between two of the main characters from this section of the book. You will need to prepare by working together to select characters, review the stories, and draft your character's words before your first rehearsal. Discuss your family life, your work, your frustrations, and so on. Alternatively, role-play two of the main characters' husbands or fathers discussing the women in their lives. Adapt your speech to suit the characters' language conventions.

COMMON CORE

W 2 Write informative/explanatory texts to examine and convey complex ideas, concepts, and information clearly and accurately through the effective selection and analysis of content. **SL 1a–b** Draw on preparation by referring to evidence from texts; work with peers to set clear goals and deadlines and establish individual roles as needed. **SL 6** Adapt speech to a variety of contexts and tasks.

DIFFERENTIATED INSTRUCTION

FOR STRUGGLING WRITERS

Writing Support Offer students these steps to structure their writing of each paragraph:

1. Write a sentence about women's roles in Chopin's age.

2. Give an example from one or more of the selections.

3. Tell how that situation is the same or different today.

4. Give one or more examples from their own experience or reading.

Ask students to write four paragraphs. Of these, two should show similarities; two should show differences.

COMMON CORE FOCUS

W 2 Write informative/explanatory texts to examine and convey complex ideas, concepts, and information clearly and accurately through the effective selection and analysis of content. **SL 1a–b** Draw on preparation by referring to evidence from texts; work with peers to set clear goals and deadlines and establish individual roles as needed. **SL 6** Adapt speech to a variety of contexts and tasks.

Wrap-Up: A New Role for Women

This Wrap-Up provides students with an opportunity to consider how the roles of women have changed since Chopin, Gilman, and Wharton wrote their stories. Encourage students to keep in mind that the end of the 19th century was a time of transition and change for women.

Writing to Compare

Review with students that *comparing* involves identifying both similarities and differences. The process of comparing offers the reader a more complete understanding of both subjects of comparison.

Suggest that students enter each selection on a Comparison Matrix with the headings *Historical Roles, Details, Current Roles,* and *Examples*. As they consider each bulleted item on page 833, students can list their responses in the appropriate column. Encourage students to complete the first and third columns of the chart first, and then retrace to add details and examples in the second and fourth columns.

Extension

- Ask volunteers to list the selections, their main characters, and the husbands or fathers of the main characters on the board.

- Ask partners to select two characters and brainstorm ideas related to women's roles, family life, work, frustrations, restrictions, responsibilities, hopes, and dreams.

- Suggest that partners outline a rough script for their dramatizations.

- When they have practiced, invite students to present their dramatizations to the class.

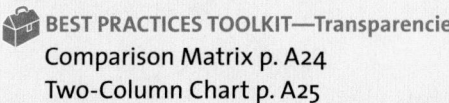 **BEST PRACTICES TOOLKIT—Transparencies**
Comparison Matrix p. A24
Two-Column Chart p. A25

Focus and Motivate

COMMON CORE FOCUS

W 2a–f Write informative texts to convey complex ideas clearly and accurately. **W 4** Produce clear and coherent writing appropriate to task, purpose, and audience. **W 5** Develop and strengthen writing as needed by planning, revising, editing, or trying a new approach, addressing a specific purpose. **W 7** Conduct short research projects; synthesize multiple sources. **W 8** Gather information from multiple sources. **W 9** Draw evidence from texts to support analysis. **W 10** Write routinely over shorter time frames for a range of tasks, purposes, and audiences. **L 1** Demonstrate command of standard English grammar and usage. **L 2b** Spell correctly. **L 3** Apply knowledge of language to make effective choices for meaning.

WRITE WITH A PURPOSE

Tell students to choose one or more authors whose works particularly interest them. Remind them that their purpose is to examine how the author's works reflect broader cultural ideas or literary movements.

COMMON CORE TRAITS

Review the *COMMON CORE TRAITS* with students, focusing on organization and development of ideas. Compare the list of traits with the rubric on page 842.

ADDITIONAL TASK

Write a Review Write a review of one or more texts by a favorite author, explaining why you think this author deserves literary honors.

Writing Online

The following tools are available online at **thinkcentral.com** and on **Write*Smart* CD-ROM:**
- Interactive Graphic Organizers
- Interactive Student Models
- Interactive Revision Lessons

Writing Workshop
INFORMATIVE TEXT

Analytical Essay

Essential Course of Study **ECOS**

As you have seen in this unit, literature often reveals more than just a series of events. It can mirror the beliefs and ideas of a specific region, convey thoughts about cultural or societal change, or explore philosophical questions. In this workshop, you will write an analytical essay to examine how an author's works reflect broader ideas and movements.

Complete the workshop activities in your **Reader/Writer Notebook.**

WRITE WITH A PURPOSE

WRITING TASK

Write an **analytical essay** that examines a literary movement or the broader ideas reflected in an author's various works. Keep your audience in mind as you gather evidence and details to support your controlling idea.

Idea Starters
- a literary movement associated with a specific author
- beliefs of a specific culture or historical period
- social change as presented in an author's works

THE ESSENTIALS

Here are some common purposes, audiences, and formats for writing an analytical essay.

PURPOSES	AUDIENCES	FORMATS
• to analyze how an author's works reflect literary movements or cultural ideas • to convey your understanding of an author's works	• classmates and teacher • other students • Web users	• essay for class • Web site • classroom bulletin board display • class newspaper

COMMON CORE TRAITS

1. DEVELOPMENT OF IDEAS
- includes an **introduction** that clearly identifies the **topic** and **controlling idea**
- uses **significant and relevant evidence**—facts, extended definitions, concrete details, and quotations—to develop the topic
- offers a **concluding section** that supports the information

2. ORGANIZATION OF IDEAS
- **organizes** ideas and evidence in a **logical way**
- uses **transitions** to create **cohesion** and **clarify relationships** among ideas

3. LANGUAGE FACILITY AND CONVENTIONS
- maintains a **formal style** and **objective tone**
- uses **precise language, domain-specific vocabulary,** and **literary techniques**
- aligns **subject-verb agreement**
- employs correct **grammar, mechanics,** and **spelling**

Writing Online **THiNK central**

Go to **thinkcentral.com.**
KEYWORD: HML11N-834

Writing Workshop Resources

R RESOURCE MANAGER UNIT 4
Plan and Teach pp. 229–232
Prewriting–Editing pp. 233–237
Writing Rubric p. 238
Speaking and Listening p. 239
Writing Support p. 240*

TECHNOLOGY
- **Teacher One Stop DVD-ROM**
- **Student One Stop DVD-ROM**
- **Write*Smart* CD-ROM**
- **GrammarNotes DVD-ROM**

Writing Center on thinkcentral.com

See resources on the **Teacher One Stop DVD-ROM** *and on* **thinkcentral.com.**

* Resources for Differentiation

Planning/Prewriting

COMMON CORE **W 2a–f** Write informative texts to convey complex ideas clearly and accurately. **W 5** Develop writing by planning. **W 7** Conduct short research projects; synthesize multiple sources. **W 8** Gather information from multiple sources.

Getting Started

CHOOSE A TOPIC

Choose an author whose works reflect an important idea. You might want to explore an author whose work you already know. Conduct a short research project to determine whether the author's writing reflects a particular literary movement or broader idea and to get general information about the author's historical and geographical background. You will need to read several of the author's texts, so choose an author who wrote shorter texts, such as short stories or poems.

Once you have a sense of the author's overall work and impact, narrow your **topic** to a specific idea or movement. Make sure that your focus is broad enough for a full-length essay.

THINK ABOUT AUDIENCE AND PURPOSE

When planning an analytical essay, consider your **purpose** for writing—to analyze a topic and convey your insights. Also, consider your **audience,** in this case your teacher and classmates. When referring to literary texts in your essay, assume that your audience has not read them. Be sure to provide readers with adequate **context** and background information about literary texts and historical time periods.

Consider **domain-specific vocabulary,** such as literary terms, that may not be understood by your audience. You might explain unfamiliar topics by using a comparison. For example, you could use a **metaphor, simile,** or **analogy** to compare the ideas of a literary movement to a subject that is more familiar to the audience.

▶ **WHAT DOES IT LOOK LIKE?**

Questions and answers

What short story or poem from this book or elsewhere left a lasting impression on me? **Jack London's "The Law of Life"**

Is it possible that the author's works might reflect a literary movement or a cultural idea? **Yes, it is possible. "The Law of Life" reflects the literary movement called naturalism, so maybe London's other works reflect this movement as well.**

Has the author written other short stories or poems that I can read and analyze for my essay? **Yes, Jack London has written other short stories that I can read and analyze for my essay.**

Will I be able to find a variety of sources about this author? **Yes, Jack London is a famous writer.**

▶ **ASK YOURSELF:**

- What background information will my audience need in order to understand my analysis?
- What story or poem details would a reader need in order to understand my reference to a particular literary text?
- Have I equipped an uninformed reader with everything he or she needs to understand my analysis?

Teach

Planning/ Prewriting

COMMON CORE **W 2a–f, W 5, W 7, W 8**

▶ **CHOOSE A TOPIC** Explain that students will get better results if they write about literary texts that have already made them think—that's a sign that the texts have rich content that will reward analysis. Encourage students to select an author or authors whose work deals with themes that are of special interest to them. Direct attention to the "What Does It Look Like?" column and suggest that students enter these and similar questions in their *Reader/Writer Notebooks* to help them select the authors about whose work they will write.

▶ **THINK ABOUT AUDIENCE AND PURPOSE** Point out that "convey your understanding," one of the purposes in the chart on page 834, applies especially to essays that are to be read or published for the class. Suggest that students ask themselves how their essays can further their classmates' understanding. Discuss the domain-specific vocabulary students might use in their essays. What are some ways that they can make literary terms understandable to their audience? If they use an analogy to explain perspective, for example, they can explain that perspective in a literary text is much like perspective in a painting. Both an artist and an author provide a specific point of view for the audience. Remind students to ask questions from the readers' viewpoint throughout the writing process.

R RESOURCE MANAGER—Copy Masters

Prewriting–Editing p. 233–237
Writing Rubric p. 238
Writing Support p. 240

DIFFERENTIATED INSTRUCTION

FOR ENGLISH LANGUAGE LEARNERS

Language: Reinforce Analytical Terms Write these terms on the board and review them with students.

- *analogy:* comparison of similar features in two different things
- *controlling idea:* a statement that sums up the author's position on an issue or topic
- *evidence:* something that provides proof
- *logical:* reasonable; valid
- *metaphor:* comparison of two things that are considered different

- *perspectives:* ways of looking at the world, including topics, events, places, and people
- *simile:* comparison of two things that are considered different; uses the words *as* or *like*
- *social themes:* big ideas or messages that have to do with society or the general public
- *source:* material used for research
- *theme:* the big idea or message of a work of literature
- *tone:* a writer's style of writing

Planning/Prewriting *continued*

▶ **GATHER AND REVIEW SOURCES** Explain that in writing their literary analysis essays students must provide ideas, not just opinions. They must also back up their ideas with evidence from multiple sources that they have evaluated for reliability, relevance, and authority. Point out that evidence for academic ideas can include

- details from the text that clearly support the controlling idea. Such details should be directly quoted in the analytical essay.
- viewpoints (also supported by the text) of reputable scholars.

Remind students to accurately cite their sources.

▶ **DRAFT AND SUPPORT YOUR CONTROLLING IDEA** Remind students that a controlling idea, or thesis statement, is a summary of an essay's topic and points written in one or two sentences. Share these tips for determining a controlling idea:

- Stay focused on the text of the literature. All outside material, such as facts about the author or about social movements, should be supporting details for main ideas in the text.
- Rewrite the controlling idea to make it as short as possible. For example, the statement in the "What does it look like?" column could read, *"London champions the naturalistic philosophy, showing how both natural and societal forces can defeat a person's will."*

YOUR TURN Give students time to select their topics and craft controlling ideas. Have them work individually to list the evidence that supports their main points and to compile lists of sources where more evidence might be found.

For interactive graphic organizers, see

Write*Smart* CD-ROM

Writing Center on thinkcentral.com

Planning/Prewriting *continued*

Getting Started

GATHER AND REVIEW SOURCES ▶

As you gather information from multiple sources, evaluate their reliability, relevance, and authority. Sources should contain accurate information and credible ideas and should come from reputable publishers. Evaluate Internet sources carefully to see who created the site and where the author found the information. Use sources that convey a variety of perspectives on the topic.

For this essay, begin by collecting sources about the author's historical time period and the literary movements that were prevalent during that time period. Then, collect several of the author's literary texts. As you read, take notes about relevant facts or concrete details that reflect a literary movement or broader idea. You will use the notes to **synthesize**, or make connections between, the information you gather from these authoritative sources.

TIPS

- For online sources offering authoritative literary scholarship, start with addresses that end in *.edu*, which indicates that the site is affiliated with a college or university. If you use sources with other endings, such as *.org* or *.com*, confirm that the site was created by a reliable organization.
- When using information from the Web sites of educational institutions (*.edu* Web addresses), be sure that the information comes from a source that is an authority on the author or literary movement, rather than from a student paper.
- When researching information about current issues, look for the most current sources. For some topics, such as those involving historical time periods, older sources—especially primary sources—may be more relevant.

DRAFT AND SUPPORT YOUR CONTROLLING IDEA ▶

Review your notes, and write a sentence or two summarizing the topic of your essay. This is your **controlling idea,** or thesis statement. Next, use your notes to develop main points that support your controlling idea. Use the **evidence** that you have drawn from the literary and informative texts to support your main points.

WHAT DOES IT LOOK LIKE?

Controlling Idea: London's works promote the naturalistic view in two distinct ways, showing how both harsh natural forces and human society can defeat human will.

First Main Point: In "The Law of Life," he expresses a naturalistic view by showing how a man who resigns himself to death by brutal cold is defeated by nature's unexpected cruelty.

PEER REVIEW Share your controlling idea, main points, and evidence with a partner. Ask whether the evidence sufficiently supports the main points and controlling idea. If the evidence is not sufficient, revise or rework your plan to provide more support for your main points.

YOUR TURN After you have gathered and reviewed sources, draft a controlling idea in your *Reader/Writer Notebook.* Then, develop main points and decide which evidence you should use to support your main points and controlling idea.

DIFFERENTIATED INSTRUCTION

FOR STRUGGLING WRITERS

Create a Controlling Idea Share these further tips with students who are having trouble forming a controlling idea.

- Ask yourself, "If the audience remembers only one idea from my essay, which one should it be?"
- Select a single quote from your author that clearly supports your controlling idea. Explain your choice to yourself.

- Try restating the controlling idea as the title of the essay, as in *Forces against Human Will: Jack London's Naturalist Philosophy*
- If you cannot find enough evidence to support your controlling idea, consider taking a new approach for your analysis.

R RESOURCE MANAGER—Copy Masters
 Writing Support p. 240

Drafting

COMMON CORE — W 4 Produce clear and coherent writing appropriate to task, purpose, and audience. W 9 Draw evidence from texts to support analysis. L 3 Apply knowledge of language to make effective choices for meaning.

The following chart shows how to organize your draft to create an effective analytical essay.

Organizing Your Analytical Essay

INTRODUCTION
- Draw the reader into your analysis by including a **memorable quotation** or **interesting detail.**
- Introduce your **topic**, state your **controlling idea**, and identify the author(s) on whom you will focus.

▼

BODY
- Organize the information in your essay so that each idea builds on the one that precedes it. You may choose **comparison-contrast** (similarities and differences between two ideas), **logical order** (related ideas grouped together), **order of importance** (most to least important ideas or vice versa), or a combination of these.
- Include your main points and **relevant textual evidence** that supports your main points and controlling idea. If necessary, include **parenthetical citations**—sources enclosed in parentheses.
- Establish and maintain a **formal style** and **objective tone**.
- Provide **context** so that your audience can fully understand your points.
- Use **precise language**, define any **domain-specific vocabulary,** and weave in **metaphors, similes,** or **analogies** to help your audience understand complex ideas.
- Use **varied transitions** to create cohesion and clarify relationships among the main points and textual evidence.

▼

CONCLUDING SECTION
- Restate your controlling idea and main points, noting the **implications**, or significance, of the topic.
- Include a Works Cited list. (See example on page 840.)

GRAMMAR IN CONTEXT: TEXTUAL EVIDENCE

You must include **sufficient textual evidence**, such as relevant facts, concrete details, extended definitions, quotations, paraphrases, and summaries, from your sources to support your main points. A quotation is the actual text from the source. A paraphrase is a restatement of information in one's own words. A summary is a brief retelling of the main ideas of a piece of writing.

Include a citation if you are paraphrasing, stating the author's original ideas, or if you are providing specific, little-known facts. Keep in mind that you do not need to include a citation for general, well-known information. The example below shows one way of directly quoting text.

> *Naturalism blends realism's practical focus with an emerging philosophy known as determinism, which can be described as the belief "that humans have little ability to impose will upon their own destinies" ("The American Novel").*

 YOUR TURN Using your notes and the information in the chart, write a draft of your essay. Be sure to support your main points with textual evidence.

FOR ENGLISH LANGUAGE LEARNERS

Textual Evidence: Punctuate Citations
Review the conventions of punctuation for citing the following types of textual evidence.

- a direct quote included within a sentence or paragraph
- an indirect quote or paraphrase within a sentence or paragraph
- a source cited in parentheses

FOR STRUGGLING WRITERS

Incorporate Textual Evidence For additional practice with the writing conventions of using textual evidence, have students follow these steps.

- Select an arresting quote from the author's work. Write a correctly punctuated paragraph that includes that *direct quote*.
- *Paraphrase* the paragraph, stating the same ideas, but without the quote.
- Write a one-sentence *summary* of the paragraph.

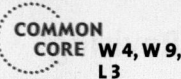 # Practice and Apply

Drafting

COMMON CORE — W 4, W 9, L 3

▶ **INTRODUCTION** Point out that to engage readers' interest in their essays students must create attention-grabbing introductions. Discuss ways to draw readers into a subject, such as using quotes that appeal to readers' deepest feelings.

▶ **BODY** Point out that this section deals with the essay's content and style. Before they begin writing, encourage students to outline their essays, focusing on both ideas and organization.

▶ **CONCLUDING SECTION** Explain that students should restate the controlling idea so their audience will remember it.

GRAMMAR IN CONTEXT: TEXTUAL EVIDENCE

Define *textual evidence* as supporting details that come directly from the literature that is being analyzed. Textual evidence is the strongest form of evidence in an essay about literature. Review the definitions of *quotation, paraphrase,* and *summary* and remind students that these are three ways to present relevant textual evidence in their writing.

 YOUR TURN Ask students to work independently to complete the **Your Turn** activity. Have students use the Organizing Your Analytical Essay chart a checklist as they draft their essays. Remind them to include sufficient textual evidence to support each main point. Suggest that they write their drafts double-spaced to make revision easier.

 Write*Smart* CD-ROM

Writing Center on <u>thinkcentral.com</u>

Revising

Model the Skill Using a draft essay on a transparency, model how to use the questions, tips, and strategies suggested in the chart to evaluate and revise writing. You might use the essay of a student from another class or from last year. Be sure to remove the student's name from the essay so that he or she is anonymous.

YOUR TURN Have students pair off and exchange papers with their partners for evaluation and review. After students read their partner's drafts, have them take one minute to freewrite a response explaining whether they find the essay compelling and understandable. Then allow students a few minutes to share their responses with one another. Students should begin by making a positive comment about the draft and then provide supportive suggestions on how their partners can clarify any confusing passages, reorganize the information so it is more coherent, or revise the tone so it is more appropriate for the purpose or audience.

For interactive revision tools, see

WriteSmart CD-ROM

Writing Center on thinkcentral.com

Revising

When you revise, your goal is to determine whether you have effectively presented your topic to your audience and supported it with relevant evidence. The questions, tips, and strategies in the following chart can help you revise or rewrite where necessary.

ANALYTICAL ESSAY

Ask Yourself	Tips	Revision Strategies
1. Does the introduction draw the audience into the analysis? Does it introduce the topic and the author and state a clear controlling idea?	▶ **Circle** text that draws the audience into the analysis. **Underline** the topic and the name of the author. **Double underline** the controlling idea.	▶ **Add** a memorable quotation or interesting detail. **Add** a sentence introducing the topic. **Add** the author's name. **Add** a clearer controlling idea.
2. Do main points support the controlling idea and build on one another? Does evidence support each main point?	▶ **Bracket** each main point. **Highlight** evidence that supports each main point.	▶ **Replace** paragraphs or sentences that don't support the controlling idea. **Add** relevant textual evidence to support the main points.
3. Is the essay's organization logical and effective? Are transitions used to clarify relationships among the main points and textual evidence?	▶ **Put a plus sign** next to sentences that help the organization. **Put a minus sign** next to sentences that stray from the organization. **Circle** transitional words and phrases.	▶ **Rearrange** the order of ideas to reflect the desired organization. **Add** appropriate transitions to link related ideas.
4. Do context, precise language, and definitions help the audience understand information?	▶ **Place a box** around context, language, and definitions that help the reader understand information from sources.	▶ **Add** relevant facts, details, precise language, and definitions of domain-specific vocabulary.
5. Do I maintain a formal style and objective tone throughout the analysis?	▶ **Draw a wavy line** under any contractions, casual slang, or informal language.	▶ **Reword** text to avoid slang. **Replace** instances of informal language with precise, formal words.
6. Does the concluding section restate the controlling idea and explain its significance?	▶ **Underline** the sentence or sentences that restate the controlling idea.	▶ **Restate** the controlling idea. **Elaborate** on why it is significant.

YOUR TURN **PEER REVIEW** Working with a classmate, review each other's drafts. Ask about confusing sections and give each other specific, constructive suggestions about how to revise or try a new approach with the essays.

DIFFERENTIATED INSTRUCTION

FOR ENGLISH LANGUAGE LEARNERS

Writing: Concluding Section Provide students with sentence frames such as these to help them develop their concluding sections.

• To paraphrase my controlling idea, I _____.

• My chosen author's texts reflect _____.

• I would like my readers to understand _____.

FOR STRUGGLING WRITERS

Check Structure and Order Have students use these tips to edit and revise their essays:

• Check the draft essay against the outline to make sure all outline points are covered.

• Check each paragraph to make sure appropriate transitions connect ideas logically.

For interactive graphic organizers, see

WriteSmart CD-ROM

Writing Center on thinkcentral.com

ANALYZE A STUDENT DRAFT

Read these excerpts from a student draft, and note the comments on its strengths as well as suggestions for improvement.

COMMON CORE W 2f Provide a concluding section that follows from and supports the information. W 5 Develop and strengthen writing as needed by revising, editing, rewriting, or trying a new approach, addressing a specific purpose.

London's Naturalistic Expressions
by Omar Bradford, Randall High School

1 Throughout American history, societal beliefs and philosophies have had a strong influence on literary movements. The naturalistic literary movement of the late 19th century and early 20th century was no exception. Commonly recognized as an offshoot of realism, naturalism blends realism's practical focus with an emerging philosophy known as determinism, which can be described as the belief "that humans have little ability to impose will upon their own destinies" ("The American Novel"). One author whose name is synonymous with this naturalistic movement is Jack London. London's works promote the naturalistic view in two distinct ways, showing how both harsh natural forces and human society can defeat human will.

> Omar defines **domain-specific vocabulary** to help his audience understand this concept.

> The **controlling idea** summarizes Omar's analysis.

2 The power of nature is a theme that runs rampant through London's writing. London's short story "The Law of Life" displays the naturalistic belief in the inability of human will to triumph over natural forces. The main character contemplates his life and death, eventually relinquishing his will to live with the knowledge that the harsh severity of death is the natural way of things and that he should simply succumb to it.

> Although Omar explains how the story relates to the controlling idea, he does not provide enough context for the reader.

LEARN HOW Provide Context   In his second paragraph, Omar discusses how the short story "The Law of Life" expresses naturalism. Omar successfully explains the story's connection with naturalism, but he does not provide enough context for the audience to understand the events of the story. Omar revised the paragraph to provide more context.

OMAR'S REVISION TO PARAGRAPH 2

The story details an older tribesman's last hours. After his people leave him alone in the snow, he ~~The main character~~ contemplates his life and death, eventually relinquishing his will to live with the knowledge that the harsh severity of death is the natural way of things and that he should simply succumb to it.

ANALYZE A STUDENT DRAFT

Explain that the Student Draft on this page is the first half of an analytical essay. Model reading the draft and the annotations in blue, and explain that the yellow highlighting illustrates the student's language choices. Explain that the following *Learn How* mini-lessons hold helpful information about ways to improve this student draft as well as their own.

LEARN HOW Provide Context

- Direct attention to the text that has been added to the sample paragraph (blue type). Ask students to identify why the change improves the paragraph. *(It provides a supporting detail that explains the story.)*

- Encourage students to look back over their essays, underline every controlling idea or restatement, and make sure there is enough context to make the meaning clear to the reader.

- Remind students that they mustn't lose sight of the purpose of the essay and their audience's knowledge of the subject. To make context significant, students must select relevant details that clarify the ideas in the essay and add to the reader's understanding.

FOR ENGLISH LANGUAGE LEARNERS

Provide Context   Explain that *context* has multiple meanings. In the context of this *Learn How* mini-lesson, *context* means "the set of circumstances or facts that surround a particular event, situation, or idea."

FOR STRUGGLING WRITERS

Provide Context   Share these tips for providing additional context for a general statement:

- Look for cause and effect. Decide if your writing explains *why* an event or situation is relevant.

- Choose memorable examples that have strong emotional appeal.

- Avoid including too much information.

ANALYZE A STUDENT DRAFT *continued*

Explain that the Student Draft is continued and completed on this page. Read the draft and annotations aloud and discuss why the changes were made. Ask students to comment on the student writer's use of transitional words and phrases.

LEARN HOW Strengthen Your Concluding Section

- Direct attention to the revision of the last paragraph (blue type). Discuss why the revision is an improvement. *(The new ending tells why the controlling idea should matter to the reader.)*
- Have students suggest other endings that would appeal to your classroom audience, such as references to themes your class has been discussing.
- Encourage students to examine the endings of their essays to make sure they restate the controlling idea and explain why the audience should care about it.

YOUR TURN Ask students to work independently to complete the **Your Turn** activity. Have them analyze and revise their drafts to make sure the opening catches the audience's interest, the controlling idea is strong and clear, the evidence supports the controlling idea, and the concluding section logically follows from the information that was presented.

WriteSmart CD-ROM

Writing Center on thinkcentral.com

ANALYZE A STUDENT DRAFT *continued*

③ In contrast, London uses manmade, societal forces to express naturalism in the short story "Li-Wan the Fair." The main character, Li-Wan, is a tribeswoman whose will has been smothered by the people around her. As a child, she dreams of her past. Her tribe discount her dreams, insisting that they are crazy imaginings. Eventually, Li-Wan's beliefs fall in line with the beliefs of the societal forces that surround her. She concurs that the dreams were "'ill dreams of childhood, shadows of things not real'" (London 461). Then, after she has been taken from her tribe and forced to marry a brutal renegade named Canim, she finally realizes the truth about her dreams. She gains the will to escape her situation, but once again the force of the people around her thwarts her will. Canim, along with two unsympathetic women and a language barrier, force her to remain in her desperate situation. Despite her strong will to escape, societal forces mar Li-Wan's efforts— revealing the story's naturalistic framework.

> Omar uses the **transitional phrase** "In contrast" to link ideas between main points and to show that he is using comparison-contrast organization.

④ Whether London expresses naturalism through the power of natural or societal forces, he successfully explores one of the philosophies that was on the minds of many during that time in history.

> Omar restates his controlling idea in his concluding section, but he does not discuss the implications, or significance, of the information.

Works Cited

"The American Novel." pbs.org. March 2007. 10 March 2009. <http://www.pbs.org/wnet/americannovel/timeline/naturalism.html>

London, Jack. Jack London: The Call of the Wild, White Fang, The Sea-Wolf, 40 Short Stories. Ed. Paul Horowitz. New York: Chatham River Press, 1983.

LEARN HOW Strengthen Your Concluding Section In his last paragraph, Omar restates his controlling idea effectively, but he does not leave the audience with something to think about. Omar revised the paragraph to explain the significance of his analysis.

OMAR'S REVISION TO PARAGRAPH ④

. . . he successfully explores one of the philosophies that was on the minds of many during that time in history.
Through his work and the work of his contemporaries, we can better understand the ideas of those who lived before us and the ways they helped shape modern thought.

YOUR TURN Use the feedback from your peers and teacher, the revision strategies chart, and the two "Learn How" lessons to revise or rework your essay. Evaluate how well you have presented your analysis and supported your controlling idea.

DIFFERENTIATED INSTRUCTION

FOR ENGLISH LANGUAGE LEARNERS

Vocabulary: Context Clues Have students work in mixed-ability pairs to determine the meaning of the following phrases.

Paragraph 3: "whose will has been smothered" (*whose self-determination and desires have been broken down*); "Li-Wan's beliefs fall in line with" (*come into agreement with*); "thwarts her will" (*defeats her*)

FOR STRUGGLING WRITERS

Strengthen Your Concluding Section
In the *Learn How* example, ask students why the writer included the plural pronouns *we* and *us* in the new ending. Discuss how this revision appeals to the audience and draws them into the writer's mental orbit.

Editing and Publishing

 COMMON CORE **W 5** Develop and strengthen writing by editing. **L 1** Demonstrate command of standard English grammar and usage. **L 2b** Spell correctly.

In the editing stage, you proofread your analytical essay to make sure that it is free of grammar, spelling, and punctuation errors. Read your essay slowly and carefully to correct any remaining misspelled words. Careless spelling mistakes make you sound less authoritative to your audience.

GRAMMAR IN CONTEXT: SUBJECT-VERB AGREEMENT

When you edit, check for errors in **subject-verb agreement** throughout your writing. Keep the following guidelines in mind:

- If a compound subject is combined with *and*, it usually requires a plural verb. If a compound subject is combined with *or, nor, neither . . . nor,* or *either . . . or,* the verb agrees with the subject that is closest to it.

Incorrect	Correct
Societal beliefs and philosophies **has** had a strong influence on literary movements.	Societal beliefs and philosophies **have** had a strong influence on literary movements.

- If a prepositional phrase comes between the subject and the verb, be careful not to mistake the object of the preposition for the subject.

Incorrect	Correct
The naturalistic literary movement of the late 19th century and early 20th century **were** no exception.	The naturalistic literary movement of the late 19th century and early 20th century **was** no exception.

As Omar edited his essay, he realized he had used a plural verb with a collective noun that refers to a single group. He changed the verb to give the collective noun a singular sense.

Incorrect	Correct
Her tribe **discount** her dreams . . .	Her tribe **discounts** her dreams . . .

PUBLISH YOUR WRITING

Share your analytical essay with an audience.
- Create a display of your essay and a photo of the author you wrote about.
- Include your essay in a class newspaper that you create with classmates.
- Publish your essay on your school Web site.
- Find a Web site about the author you focused on in your essay. Send an e-mail to the creators of the site, asking if they will publish your analytical essay online.

 YOUR TURN Proofread your essay to correct any errors. Make sure that you have achieved subject-verb agreement. Then, publish your completed essay for your audience.

FOR ENGLISH LANGUAGE LEARNERS

Subject-Verb Agreement Make a chalkboard list of singular and plural pronouns (see the Differentiated Instruction for struggling writers on page 840). Add grid lines to create a two-column chart, with columns labeled "Present Tense" and "Past Tense." Ask students to suggest a common verb. Have students help fill in the chart with verbs that are in agreement with their pronouns.

FOR STRUGGLING WRITERS

Subject-Verb Agreement Based on the Grammar in Context section, have students define *compound subject*. Ask students to suggest examples of compound subjects, listing their suggestions on the board. Add grid lines to create a two-column chart, with columns labeled "Present Tense" and "Past Tense." Have students help fill in the chart with verbs that are in agreement with their subjects. Repeat the process for collective nouns.

Editing and Publishing

 **COMMON CORE** **W 5, L 1, L 2b**

GRAMMAR IN CONTEXT: SUBJECT-VERB AGREEMENT

Review the grammatical rule for subject-verb agreement: the subject and verb of a sentence must have the same number—a singular subject goes with the singular verb form, while a plural subject goes with the plural verb form. Then direct attention to the three white boxes, which contain charts showing corrections. For each box, have students explain the reason for the change.

- For the top box, ask students to identify the form of the correct verb (*plural*).
- For the middle box, ask students to identify the form of the correct verb (*singular*).
- For the bottom box, ask students to identify the number of the subject (*singular*).

PUBLISH YOUR WRITING

Brainstorm with students about additional ways to publish their analytical essays.

 YOUR TURN Allow students time to edit and revise their drafts. Encourage them to seek feedback from readers as part of this process.

- Emphasize the importance of correcting spelling, punctuation, and grammar mistakes.
- Suggest that students underline the subjects and verbs throughout their essays to make sure every sentence has correct subject-verb agreement.
- Have students look for general statements that can be strengthened by using more direct material from the literary texts.
- Encourage students to work with computers to publish a single-issue literary journal that is a collection of analytical essays.

Scoring Rubric

Explain that the best way to understand a scoring rubric is to use it to score an actual piece of writing. Ask students to prepare and submit copies of their essays with their names removed. (Number the essays as they are submitted and make a confidential list of the writers' names.) Distribute the essays to the class and have students use the rubric to evaluate each other's work. Ask students to use language from the chart to explain the scores they assign.

For Rubric Bank, see

WriteSmart CD-ROM

Writing Center on thinkcentral.com

Assess and Reteach

Assess

R RESOURCE MANAGER—Copy Master
Rubric for Evaluation, p. 238

Online Essay Scoring on thinkcentral.com

Reteach

Level Up Online Tutorials on thinkcentral.com

RETEACHING WORKSHEETS
   Writing Lesson 14: Writing a Controlling Idea

Scoring Rubric

Use the rubric below to evaluate your analytical essay from the Writing Workshop or your response to the on-demand task on the next page.

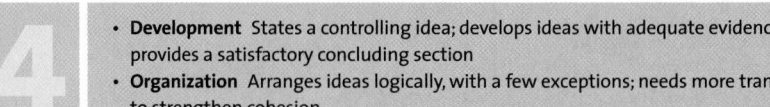

ANALYTICAL ESSAY

SCORE	COMMON CORE TRAITS
6	• **Development** Has an engaging introduction that clearly identifies the controlling idea; is developed thoroughly with significant and relevant evidence; ends powerfully • **Organization** Arranges ideas in an effective, logical order, creating a unified whole; uses varied transitions to create cohesion and link ideas • **Language** Consistently maintains a formal style and objective tone; uses precise language; shows a strong command of conventions
5	• **Development** States a clear controlling idea; develops ideas with relevant evidence; has a strong concluding section • **Organization** Arranges ideas logically; uses transitions to create cohesion and link ideas • **Language** Uses a formal style and objective tone; has few errors in conventions
4	• **Development** States a controlling idea; develops ideas with adequate evidence; provides a satisfactory concluding section • **Organization** Arranges ideas logically, with a few exceptions; needs more transitions to strengthen cohesion • **Language** Mostly uses a formal style; includes some vague language and a few distracting errors in conventions
3	• **Development** States a controlling idea that could be more precise; provides some evidence; has a weak concluding section • **Organization** Has flaws in organization; needs more transitions to link ideas • **Language** Often lapses into an informal style or subjective tone; has several errors
2	• **Development** Has a vague controlling idea; offers mostly irrelevant and insufficient evidence; has a weak concluding section • **Organization** Has major organizational flaws; lacks transitions throughout, with little cohesion • **Language** Uses an inappropriate style and subjective tone; has many errors
1	• **Development** Lacks a controlling idea; fails to use evidence; ends abruptly • **Organization** Has no organization, no transitions, and no sense of cohesion • **Language** Uses an inappropriate style and tone; has major problems with grammar, mechanics, and spelling

Preparing for Timed Writing

COMMON CORE

W 10 Write routinely over shorter time frames for a range of tasks, purposes, and audiences.

1. ANALYZE THE TASK   5 MIN

Read the task carefully. Then, read it again, underlining words that tell the topic, the audience, and the purpose.

> **WRITING TASK**   *Topic*
>
> Write a comparison-contrast essay about <u>two of your favorite literary texts.</u> Your essay should concentrate on key aspects of the texts, such as characters, theme, setting, plot, and conflict. Your essay should give your audience, such as <u>your teacher and classmates,</u> <u>new insights into the literary texts.</u> ← *Purpose*   ↖ *Audience*

2. PLAN YOUR RESPONSE   10 MIN

Begin by choosing two literary texts that you know well. Then, use a Venn diagram to compare and contrast several aspects of the two texts. Be sure to include aspects that are listed in the task.

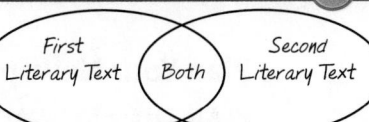

First Literary Text | Both | Second Literary Text

3. RESPOND TO THE TASK   20 MIN

Begin drafting your essay. Write a controlling idea that summarizes your essay's main points. Keep the following guidelines in mind as you write:

- In the introduction, catch your audience's attention with a question, quotation, or interesting detail.
- Choose either a point-by-point (compares and contrasts both texts, one point at a time), or subject-by-subject (discusses the first literary text, then moves on to the second) organization. Support each point with relevant textual evidence.
- Use transitions such as *both, like, similarly,* and *also* to show similarities, and *in contrast, instead, on the other hand,* and *however* to show differences.
- Give your audience something to think about in your concluding section. Consider adding a summary of your comparison or a new but related idea.

4. IMPROVE YOUR RESPONSE   5–10 MIN

Revising Check your draft against the task. Have you focused on key aspects of the texts? Have you offered additional insights into the texts?

Proofreading Correct errors in grammar, usage, spelling, punctuation, and capitalization. Make sure that your paper and any edits are neatly written and legible.

Checking Your Final Copy Before you turn in your paper, read it one more time to catch any errors you may have missed.

WRITING WORKSHOP   **843**

COMMON CORE FOCUS

W 10 Write routinely over shorter time frames for a range of tasks, purposes, and audiences.

Preparing for Timed Writing

1. **Analyze the Task** Before students begin writing, encourage them to answer the following questions:
   - What is my time limit?
   - What are the core traits assessed in the scoring rubric?
   - Who is my audience?
   - What is my purpose?

2. **Plan Your Response** Draw attention to the chart and have students fill in the Venn diagram to focus on their comparisons and contrasts.

3. **Respond to the Task** Encourage students to create an attention-grabbing introduction and to choose a logical organization. Remind students that their controlling ideas should appear in the introduction and concluding section and be supported by the body of their essays.

4. **Improve Your Response** Ask students to check their essays against the task to make sure all the key elements are included. Remind them to keep both the purpose and the audience in mind as they edit and revise.

Assess

Use the Scoring Rubric on page 842 to assess students' essays.

DIFFERENTIATED INSTRUCTION

FOR ENGLISH LANGUAGE LEARNERS

Writing: Comparison Words Review the definition of *transitional phrase* and have students identify the examples provided under Step 3. Encourage them to look for places in their work where such phrases would improve the flow of ideas.

FOR STRUGGLING WRITERS

Writing: Comparisons Review the examples provided under Step 3 of transitional phrases that are used as comparisons. Ask students which phrases they would use to describe material in each section of the Venn diagram. Encourage them to look for places in their work where correct use of such phrases would improve the flow of ideas.

Focus and Motivate

COMMON CORE FOCUS

W 6 Use technology to produce and publish writing products. **SL 1b** Work with peers to promote decision-making, set clear goals and deadlines, and establish individual roles. **SL 2** Integrate multiple sources of information. **SL 5** Make strategic use of digital media in presentations.

PRODUCE WITH A PURPOSE

Read aloud the *COMMON CORE TRAITS* description of a strong class newspaper. Tell students that their paper should present in-depth coverage of school events and thought-provoking examinations of local and broader issues, accompanied by supporting visuals.

COMMON CORE TRAITS

As students prepare their newspapers, remind them to keep in mind the *COMMON CORE TRAITS* of a strong class newspaper.

Practice and Apply

Plan Your Newspaper

Plan the Newspaper's Sections Model the steps of planning a newspaper's sections.

- Review the parts of a newspaper, including the banner, headlines, features, graphics, and special sections, such as the sports section and the editorial pages.

- Have students work in teams to choose the sections of the newspaper and the editors for each.

Plan the Staff and Contents Encourage students to select groups whose members have complementary skills, such as writing, computer skills, and graphics ability.

- Have the section groups meet to plan content and design.

- Give groups a deadline for submitting their final plans to the class and ask them to create a schedule with deadlines for each part of the project.

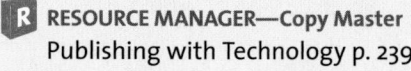 **RESOURCE MANAGER—Copy Master**
Publishing with Technology p. 239

Technology Workshop

Creating a Class Newspaper

Essential Course of Study **ECOS**

Think of a newspaper that you have read before. What types of articles did you like reading? What types of articles did you dislike? In this workshop, you and your classmates will create a newspaper using publishing technology such as layout and design software.

Complete the workshop activities in your **Reader/Writer Notebook.**

PRODUCE WITH A PURPOSE	*COMMON CORE TRAITS*
TASK Work with classmates to gather and develop content for a **class newspaper.** Then, use computer software to create your newspaper.	**A STRONG CLASS NEWSPAPER . . .** • contains clearly written, thoroughly researched, and informative articles • contains relevant graphics and images

COMMON CORE

W 6 Use technology to produce and publish writing products. **SL 1b** Work with peers to promote decision-making, set clear goals and deadlines, and establish individual roles. **SL 2** Integrate multiple sources of information. **SL 5** Make strategic use of digital media in presentations.

Plan Your Newspaper

PLAN THE NEWSPAPER'S SECTIONS

With classmates, decide on the newspaper's name and sections. You may want to include sections that cover issues and events in your school, your community, and the world beyond. As you discuss options, recognize that in order to be productive, you will need to listen to a range of ideas. Here are some additional ideas:

- a section that highlights upcoming school or community events
- a section that details students' recent achievements in academics, sports, or music
- a section that shares students' opinions about current issues

PLAN THE STAFF AND CONTENTS

Work with your classmates to establish an editorial team for each section. Teams should meet to brainstorm ideas for articles, graphics, and images and decide who will write each article and who will create or obtain each graphic and image. After teams have established their roles and plans, have the entire staff regroup. Create a chart like the one below to summarize your plan for the newspaper. As a group, set a deadline for the publication of your newspaper. Discuss and set any intermediate deadlines that each team should meet.

Section	Articles/Writers	Graphics and Images/Artists and Researchers

 **Media Tools** **THINK** central

Go to **thinkcentral.com.**
KEYWORD: HML11-844

DIFFERENTIATED INSTRUCTION

FOR ENGLISH LANGUAGE LEARNERS

Language: Reinforce Newspaper Terms Write these terms on the board and review them with students.

- *editorial team:* a group of workers who write, revise, and edit the contents of a publication

- *graphics:* maps, diagrams, and charts that present information in visual form

- *layout:* a sketch or drawing that shows where the various elements of a newspaper appear on the printed page

- *software:* programs that enable computers to perform specific functions, such as word processing or graphics creation

- *template:* in electronic publishing, a page that has a built-in design for elements such as sections, column width, and type size

Create the Newspaper

Before your editorial team begins to create content using publishing software, take time to plan the layout of your section. Consider how pages will be formatted, including how many columns of text will appear on a page and where headlines and graphics will go. While planning articles, each member of your team should keep in mind any space limitations needed to fit your planned format.

GATHER INFORMATION AND CREATE CONTENT

When creating and gathering content for the newspaper, keep the following guidelines in mind:

- When gathering information for an article, interview knowledgeable people. Take notes or use an audio recorder during the interview. Refer to your notes or recording to find interesting quotations to put into your article.

- When researching information for an article, look at multiple sources of information. Be sure to evaluate the credibility and accuracy of each source before using the information in your article. If you find any discrepancies in the information, do additional research to determine which source is correct.

- When writing articles, answer the 5 W's *(Who? What? Where? When?* and *Why?)*. Think of a title that tells your reader the basic focus of your article. Begin your article with a **lead,** an interest-grabbing sentence that states the main idea of the article.

- Edit one another's articles to be sure they are free of grammar, usage, and spelling errors.

- When gathering graphics or images, respect copyright laws by using only materials that don't require permission.

CREATE AND DISTRIBUTE THE FINAL PRODUCT

- Work with your classmates to insert the articles, graphics, and images into the publishing program your team is using. If necessary, cut, add, or revise material to meet space requirements.

- Print several copies of your newspaper and distribute them throughout your school. If your newspaper covers community issues, distribute it to members of the community as well.

 YOUR TURN As a class, discuss and make decisions on criteria for evaluating your class newspaper. Distribute your newspaper and ask for volunteers to use the rubric to provide feedback.

TECHNOLOGY WORKSHOP **845**

Assessment Practice

COMMON CORE FOCUS

RL 1 Cite evidence to support analysis of what the text says explicitly as well as inferences drawn from the text. **RL 2** Determine themes or central ideas of a text. **RL 3** Analyze the impact of the author's choices regarding how to develop and relate elements of a story. **RL 4** Determine the meaning of words and phrases as they are used in the text, including figurative meanings. **RL 6** Distinguish what is directly stated in a text from what is really meant. **RI 1** Cite evidence to support analysis of what the text says explicitly. **RI 7** Evaluate sources of information presented in different media or formats as well as in words. **L 1** Demonstrate command of the conventions of standard English grammar. **L 4** Determine the meaning of multiple-meaning words. **L 4a** Use context as a clue to the meaning of a word.

CHECK READINESS

Read aloud the paragraph under **ASSESS,** and stress that this is not the full Unit Test but a way for students to check their readiness. Have students read the skills listed under **REVIEW** and to look back in the unit or in the **Student Resource Bank** for skills they need to review.

READ THE TEXTS

Remind students to keep the unit goals in mind as they read the selections and to focus on analyzing and writing about an author's work.

ANSWER THE QUESTIONS

Direct students to pages R96–R103 of the Handbook to review test-taking strategies. Remind students:

- to read directions carefully
- to read all choices in multiple-choice questions rather than choosing the first alternative that seems to fit

---

Assessment Practice

ASSESS
Taking this practice test will help you assess your knowledge of these skills and determine your readiness for the Unit Test.

REVIEW
After you take the practice test, your teacher can help you identify any standards you need to review.

COMMON CORE

RL 1 Cite evidence to support analysis of what the text says explicitly as well as inferences drawn from the text. **RL 2** Determine themes or central ideas of a text. **RL 3** Analyze the impact of the author's choices regarding how to develop and relate elements of a story. **RL 4** Determine the meaning of words and phrases as they are used in the text, including figurative meanings. **RL 6** Distinguish what is directly stated in a text from what is really meant. **RI 1** Cite evidence to support analysis of what the text says explicitly. **RI 7** Evaluate sources of information presented in different media or formats as well as in words. **L 1** Demonstrate command of the conventions of standard English grammar. **L 4** Determine the meaning of multiple-meaning words. **L 4a** Use context as a clue to the meaning of a word.

Practice Test THINK central

Take it at thinkcentral.com.
KEYWORD: HML11N-846

DIRECTIONS Read the two selections and the viewing and representing piece. Then answer the questions that follow.

A Call Loan *by O. Henry*

1   In those days the cattlemen were the anointed. They were the grandees of the grass, kings of the kine, lords of the lea, barons of beef and bone. They might have ridden in golden chariots had their tastes so inclined. The cattleman was caught in a stampede of dollars. It seemed to him that he had more money than was decent. But when he had bought a watch with precious stones set in the case so large that they hurt his ribs, and a California saddle with silver nails and Angora skin *suaderos,* and ordered everybody up to the bar for whisky—what else was there for him to spend money for?

2   Not so circumscribed in expedient for the reduction of surplus wealth were those lairds of the lariat who had womenfolk to their name. In the breast of the rib-sprung sex the genius of purse lightening may slumber through years of inopportunity, but never, my brothers, does it become extinct.

3   So, out of the chaparral came Long Bill Longley from the Bar Circle Branch on the Frio—a wife-driven man—to taste the urban joys of success. Something like half a million dollars he had, with an income steadily increasing.

4   Long Bill was a graduate of the camp and trail. Luck and thrift, a cool head, and a telescopic eye for mavericks had raised him from cowboy to be a cowman. Then came the boom in cattle, and Fortune, stepping gingerly among the cactus thorns, came and emptied her cornucopia at the doorstep of the ranch.

5   In the little frontier city of Chaparosa, Longley built a costly residence. Here he became a captive, bound to the chariot of social existence. He was doomed to become a leading citizen. He struggled for a time like a mustang in his first corral, and then he hung up his quirt and spurs. Time hung heavily on his hands. He organised the First National Bank of Chaparosa, and was elected its president.

6   One day a dyspeptic man, wearing double-magnifying glasses, inserted an official-looking card between the bars of the cashier's window of the First National Bank. Five minutes later the bank force was dancing at the beck and call of a national bank examiner.

7   This examiner, Mr. J. Edgar Todd, proved to be a thorough one.

8   At the end of it all the examiner put on his hat, and called the president, Mr. William R. Longley, into the private office.

9   "Well, how do you find things?" asked Longley, in his slow, deep tones. "Any brands in the round-up you didn't like the looks of?"

10   "The bank checks up all right, Mr. Longley," said Todd; "and I find your loans in very good shape—with one exception. You are carrying one very bad

---

DIFFERENTIATED INSTRUCTION

FOR ENGLISH LANGUAGE LEARNERS

Assessment Practice: Work Backward
Prepare students by having them read the questions before reading the passages. Have students work in pairs to find unfamiliar words in test directions and questions, and instruct them to follow these steps:

1. Write each word on an index card.
2. Look up the meaning in a dictionary and write it on the back of the card.
3. Use the cards to practice the words with their partner and to teach them to others.

FOR STRUGGLING READERS

Assessment Support: Allusion Read aloud paragraph 4, and point out that the author makes a direct allusion to the Roman goddess Fortuna (Fortune) in connection with Long Bill Longley. Ask students how the author uses the allusion to illustrate a development in the selection. (*Fortuna, the Roman goddess of luck and fate, empties her cornucopia—or horn of plenty—at the doorstep of Longley's ranch. Longley becomes wealthy during the boom in cattle.*)

bit of paper—one that is so bad that I have been thinking that you surely do not realise the serious position it places you in. I refer to a call loan of $10,000 made to Thomas Merwin. Not only is the amount in excess of the maximum sum the bank can loan any individual legally, but it is absolutely without endorsement or security. Thus you have doubly violated the national banking laws, and have laid yourself open to criminal prosecution by the Government. A report of the matter to the Comptroller of the Currency—which I am bound to make—would, I am sure, result in the matter being turned over to the Department of Justice for action. You see what a serious thing it is."

11   Bill Longley was leaning his lengthy, slowly moving frame back in his swivel chair. His hands were clasped behind his head, and he turned a little to look the examiner in the face. The examiner was surprised to see a smile creep about the rugged mouth of the banker, and a kindly twinkle in his light-blue eyes. If he saw the seriousness of the affair, it did not show in his countenance.

12   "Of course, you don't know Tom Merwin," said Longley, almost genially. "Yes, I know about that loan. It hasn't any security except Tom Merwin's word. Somehow, I've always found that when a man's word is good it's the best security there is. Oh, yes, I know the Government doesn't think so. I guess I'll see Tom about that note."

13   Mr. Todd's dyspepsia seemed to grow suddenly worse. He looked at the chaparral banker through his double-magnifying glasses in amazement.

14   "You see," said Longley, easily explaining the thing away, "Tom heard of 2000 head of two-year-olds down near Rocky Ford on the Rio Grande that could be had for $8 a head. I reckon 'twas one of old Leandro Garcia's outfits that he had smuggled over, and he wanted to make a quick turn on 'em. Those cattle are worth $15 on the hoof in Kansas City. Tom knew it and I knew it. He had $6,000, and I let him have the $10,000 to make the deal with. His brother Ed took 'em on to market three weeks ago. He ought to be back 'most any day now with the money. When he comes Tom'll pay that note."

15   The bank examiner was shocked. It was, perhaps, his duty to step out to the telegraph office and wire the situation to the Comptroller. But he did not. He talked pointedly and effectively to Longley for three minutes. He succeeded in making the banker understand that he stood upon the border of a catastrophe. And then he offered a tiny loophole of escape.

16   "I am going to Hilldale's to-night," he told Longley, "to examine a bank there. I will pass through Chaparosa on my way back. At twelve o'clock to-morrow I shall call at this bank. If this loan has been cleared out of the way by that time it will not be mentioned in my report. If not—I will have to do my duty."

17   With that the examiner bowed and departed.

GO ON ▶

ITEM ANALYSIS

COMPREHENSION AND WRITTEN RESPONSE	ITEMS	UNIT PAGES
Analyze Descriptive Language	6	735, 736, 738
Analyze Literary Elements		
Plot	10	783, 786, 788
Conflict	7	783, 786, 788
Tone	8	821, 822, 824, 826, 829, 830
Analyze Irony	13	659, 662, 665, 666, 669
Make Inferences and Draw Conclusions	3, 4, 11	717, 721, 722, 724, 725

VOCABULARY	ITEMS	UNIT PAGES
Context Clues	5, 9	

WRITING AND GRAMMAR	ITEMS	UNIT PAGES
Passive and Active Voice	1	786, 789
Verb Tenses	2	801

Practice Test

On **thinkcentral.com** students can complete an interactive version of this practice tests *and* receive remediation for the skills they have not yet mastered.

FOR STRUGGLING READERS

Assessment Support: Conflict Have students review paragraphs 6–16. Then ask them to describe the conflict facing Longley. *Possible answer: Longley loaned his friend a large sum without security, and Todd will report this if Longley doesn't get the money back.* Discuss how the two characters view the situation.

FOR STRUGGLING READERS

Assessment Support: Analyze Setting Review the importance of setting. Have students discuss details that capture a way of life in a particular place and time.

- What details indicate location and time-frame?
  Possible answer: cattle ranches, cowboys, "on the Frio," cactus (paragraphs 1–4); "In those days," telegraph office (paragraphs 1–15)

18　The President of the First National lounged in his chair half an hour longer, and then he lit a mild cigar, and went over to Tom Merwin's house. Merwin, a ranchman in brown duck, with a contemplative eye, sat with his feet upon a table, plaiting a rawhide quirt.

19　"Tom," said Longley, leaning against the table, "you heard anything from Ed yet?"

20　"Not yet," said Merwin, continuing his plaiting. "I guess Ed'll be along back now in a few days."

21　"There was a bank examiner," said Longley, "nosing around our place to-day, and he bucked a sight about that note of yours. You know I know it's all right, but the thing *is* against the banking laws. I was pretty sure you'd have paid it off before the bank was examined again, but the son-of-a-gun slipped in on us, Tom. Now, I'm short of cash myself just now, or I'd let you have the money to take it up with. I've got till twelve o'clock to-morrow, and then I've got to show the cash in place of that note or—"

22　"Or what, Bill?" asked Merwin, as Longley hesitated.

23　"Well, I suppose it means be jumped on with both of Uncle Sam's feet."

24　"I'll try to raise the money for you on time," said Merwin, interested in his plaiting.

25　"All right, Tom," concluded Longley, as he turned toward the door; "I knew you would if you could."

26　Merwin threw down his whip and went to the only other bank in town, a private one, run by Cooper & Craig.

27　"Cooper," he said, to the partner by that name, "I've got to have $10,000 to-day or to-morrow. I've got a house and lot there that's worth about $6,000 and that's all the actual collateral. But I've got a cattle deal on that's sure to bring me in more than that much profit within a few days."

28　Cooper began to cough.

29　"Now, for God's sake don't say no," said Merwin. "I owe that much money on a call loan. It's been called, and the man that called it is a man I've laid on the same blanket with in cow-camps and ranger-camps for ten years. He can call anything I've got. He can call the blood out of my veins and it'll come. He's got to have the money. He's in a devil of a—Well, he needs the money, and I've got to get it for him. You know my word's good, Cooper."

30　"No doubt of it," assented Cooper, urbanely, "but I've a partner, you know. I'm not free in making loans. And even if you had the best security in your hands, Merwin, we couldn't accommodate you in less than a week. We're just making a shipment of $15,000 to Myer Brothers in Rockdell, to buy cotton with. It goes down on the narrow-gauge to-night. That leaves our cash quite short at present. Sorry we can't arrange it for you."

848

---

31   Merwin went back to his little bare office and plaited at his quirt again. About four o'clock in the afternoon he went to the First National Bank and leaned over the railing of Longley's desk.

32   "I'll try to get that money for you to-night—I mean to-morrow, Bill."

33   "All right, Tom," said Longley quietly.

34   At nine o'clock that night Tom Merwin stepped cautiously out of the small frame house in which he lived. It was near the edge of the little town, and few citizens were in the neighbourhood at that hour. Merwin wore two six-shooters in a belt, and a slouch hat. He moved swiftly down a lonely street, and then followed the sandy road that ran parallel to the narrow-gauge track until he reached the water-tank, two miles below the town. There Tom Merwin stopped, tied a black silk handkerchief about the lower part of his face, and pulled his hat down low.

35   In ten minutes the night train for Rockdell pulled up at the tank, having come from Chaparosa.

36   With a gun in each hand Merwin raised himself from behind a clump of chaparral and started for the engine. But before he had taken three steps, two long, strong arms clasped him from behind, and he was lifted from his feet and thrown, face downward upon the grass. There was a heavy knee pressing against his back, and an iron hand grasping each of his wrists. He was held thus, like a child, until the engine had taken water, and until the train had moved, with accelerating speed, out of sight. Then he was released, and rose to his feet to face Bill Longley.

37   "The case never needed to be fixed up this way, Tom," said Longley. "I saw Cooper this evening, and he told me what you and him talked about. Then I went down to your house to-night and saw you come out with your guns on, and I followed you. Let's go back, Tom."

38   They walked away together, side by side.

39   "'Twas the only chance I saw," said Merwin presently. "You called your loan, and I tried to answer you. Now, what'll you do, Bill, if they sock it to you?"

40   "What would you have done if they'd socked it to you?" was the answer Longley made.

41   "I never thought I'd lay in a bush to stick up a train," remarked Merwin; "but a call loan's different. A call's a call with me. We've got twelve hours yet, Bill, before this spy jumps onto you. We've got to raise them spondulicks somehow. Maybe we can—Great Sam Houston! do you hear that?"

42   Merwin broke into a run, and Longley kept with him, hearing only a rather pleasing whistle somewhere in the night rendering the lugubrious air of "The Cowboy's Lament."

43   "It's the only tune he knows," shouted Merwin, as he ran. "I'll bet—"

44   They were at the door of Merwin's house. He kicked it open and fell over an old valise lying in the middle of the floor. A sunburned, firm-jawed youth, stained by travel, lay upon the bed puffing at a brown cigarette.

GO ON ➡️

849

---

45   "What's the word, Ed?" gasped Merwin.

46   "So, so," drawled that capable youngster. "Just got in on the 9:30. Sold the bunch for fifteen, straight. Now, buddy, you want to quit kickin' a valise around that's got $29,000 in greenbacks in its in'ards."

The Next Frontier

by S. C. Gwynne
from **Texas Monthly**

1   It is a fine, sunny, mid-April morning in South Texas. The weather has been unusually cool and rainy, and the spacious, pool-table-flat wedge of land between the Nueces River and the Mexican border—which the Spanish once called El Desierto de los Muertos[1]—today looks as green as Ireland. I am in a pickup, bouncing through a pasture on the 237,348-acre Norias division of the King Ranch, one of four massive chunks of land that make up the 825,000-acre (1,300-square-mile) spread. The truck belongs to Dave DeLaney, a rangy 51-year-old who runs the ranch's cattle operation. With roughly 43,500 head, it is the nation's largest. DeLaney is giving me the grand tour, which will ultimately take the better part of two days. . . .

2   What is most striking about the place, not surprisingly, is its tremendous scale—nearly unimaginable for those of us who live in places where real estate is calibrated in fractions of city blocks. The pasture we are in, for example, encompasses 30,000 acres—or 47 square miles. The live oak grove (or motte, as they call it here) we just drove through comprises 60,000 acres. And the land is not only vast. It is also beautiful. Though beauty is not a quality generally associated with South Texas, Norias is one of the loveliest pieces of coastal real estate I've ever seen, a place of swaying bluestem grasses; lush, wide-open coastal plain; rolling bone-white sand dunes; and rain-detonated explosions of daisies, coreopsis, and dayflowers. Animals are everywhere we look: scores of wild turkeys, some of them in mating dances; white-tailed deer and bobwhite quail in almost every meadow; ducks; javelinas; feral hogs; brilliantly colored scissor-tailed flycatchers; and red-winged blackbirds.

---

1. **El Desierto de los Muertos:** Spanish for The Desert of the Dead.

850

3   Beyond the size and beauty of the physical environment, there is the weight of history. The King Ranch was the first ranch in Texas, the cornerstone of the cattle business in the West, one of the originators of the great cattle drives to the Kansas railheads and later of the fenced pastures that killed the drives off. At the time of his death, in 1885, founder Richard King owned half a million acres and was the wealthiest man in Texas. His grandson Robert J. Kleberg Jr. built the business into a 15-million-acre global empire, with ranches spread from Argentina to Australia. Kleberg invented the Santa Gertrudis, the first American cattle breed and the first new breed anywhere in one hundred years; he bred the first registered American quarter horse and the Thoroughbred stallion Assault, which won the Triple Crown in 1946. If that wasn't enough, Kleberg also invented the root plow and the cattle prod, eradicated Texas tick fever, and arranged the largest oil lease ever on private land.

4   All this history lives on, pervasive as the mesquite and huisache trees. I can feel it in the vast muscular land and see it in the glorious Main House, with its battlements, multichromatic terra-cotta tiles, Tiffany-designed furniture and art glass, Italian marble stairs, and teak floors. Drifting along the ranch's two thousand miles of asphalt, caliche, and dirt roads, I can't help feeling a certain sense of timelessness, as though nothing on this splendid Rhode Island–size ranch has really changed since the days when Captain King's *vaqueros* rounded up tens of thousands of cattle for the northern trail drives.

5   But those are appearances only, mirages of the South Texas heat. The truth is that the King Ranch is not at all what it once was. As a business, it is profoundly and irreversibly changed from the time when Kleberg would receive potentates[2] and movie stars on the Main House porch and sit like a Middle Eastern pasha[3] in his reviewing stand, gazing at million-dollar horses. Fifty-six years of enlightened despotism had left the ranch singularly dependent on him, and when he died, in 1974, the machinery of empire immediately began to creak and then to fail. Battles of succession led to wars of secession. Family members forced the ranch to buy them out, causing it to incur massive debt; lawsuits followed, then the remaining heirs grabbed most of the oil royalties that had been floating the operation for forty years. Drained of most of its oil money, the business staggered forward under the burden of its archaic, nearly feudal cradle-to-grave welfare system for the hundreds of workers and their families who resided on the King Ranch. Had things gone only slightly differently, these forces might have easily led to the breakup of the King Ranch, as they have for thousands of other family-owned outfits.

---

2. **potentates** (pō-tən-tāts): people who have great power or sway.

3. **pasha** (pə-'shä): a man of high rank or office.

GO ON

FOR STRUGGLING READERS

Build Comprehension Tell students that the article explains the King Ranch's historical influence. Have students note events in paragraph 3 that illustrate the phrase "the weight of history."

Examples: *first ranch in Texas; an originator of cattle drives; an originator of fenced pastures that killed off cattle drives; development of a new cattle breed; invention of cattle prod; largest oil lease on private land*

FOR STRUGGLING READERS

Assessment Practice: Draw Conclusions In paragraph 5 the writer refers to the "enlightened despotism" of Robert Kleberg Jr. Have students reread paragraphs 3–5 and draw a conclusion as to what the writer feels was despotic about Kleberg's management of the King Ranch. (*"ranch singularly dependent on him"; "nearly feudal cradle-to-grave welfare system for the hundreds of workers and their families"*)

6　　But this did not happen. Instead came sweeping change, driven by an entirely new concept of the ranch. What Captain King founded was a simple cattle operation. Then it became a cattle and oil business. As the King Ranch struggled to survive, it came to be seen as a business, to be sure, but also as a *legacy*, something to be shielded, protected, and preserved. The result is that over the past quarter century its owners have, laboriously and at considerable risk, built an elaborate financial carapace[4] around the 825,000 acres of the home ranches in South Texas. Ironically, in order to protect the four divisions of this acreage (Santa Gertrudis, Laureles, Norias, and Encino), the King Ranch has been forced to branch out into new enterprises that are antithetical to everything the ranch once held holy. The business is now built around commercial hunting leases, which let thousands of outsiders into the private kingdom, and farming, long considered by ranch folk as a pedestrian, second-class business and pointedly banned by Kleberg. With 36,000 acres of Florida citrus groves, the King Ranch is the leading citrus grower in America. It is also one of the nation's ten-biggest sugarcane producers. It owns huge sod, cotton, and milo farms in Texas and Florida. Buffered from the cruel volatility of the markets, the ranch lives on, working cattle and sustaining its old romance. But today the King Ranch exists in the form of a large and diversified agribusiness conglomerate, carefully designed to prevent the sacred acres from ever being sold.

7　　Along the way it has become something the previous generations could never have foreseen or imagined. "If Captain King sat down with us today, he'd say, 'Well, how are things going?'" said Helen Kleberg Groves, known as Helenita, Kleberg's only child and one of the matriarchs of the family. "And we'd say, 'They are going fine. We don't have that many cattle or horses anymore. It is hard to make any money at ranching. We've got hunting leases and citrus groves and sod and cane farms.' He would think we had lost our minds."

---

4. **carapace** (ker-ə-pās): a protective shell.

852

DIFFERENTIATED INSTRUCTION

FOR ALL READERS
Assessment Practice: Analyze Irony Ask students to write at least two sentences identifying what the writer sees as ironic in the preservation of King Ranch.

FOR ALL READERS
Assessment Practice: Making Inferences Have students reread paragraphs 6 and 7. Ask them what they can infer about how Richard King and Robert Kleberg, Jr., might react to current conditions on the King Ranch?

Teen Money

The Magazine for Teens Managing Money

TOP 10 SUMMER JOBS

Get More than a Tan This Year

TEEN ENTREPRENEURS
Got a Great Idea? Make It Pay!

YOUR ALLOWANCE
Spend It Now . . . or Later?

SAVE MONEY FOR COLLEGE
Live Below Your Means

853

FOR ALL READERS

Assessment Practice: Analyzing Visuals Ask students which of the articles in this issue of *Teen Money* they think this magazine cover illustrates and why they think so. Tell them to explain their answers. Have them also indicate why they think this is or is not an appropriate illustration for that article.

(Article: Teen Entrepreneurs; it's a good illustration because most teens can identify with walking dogs and would feel this is a job they could also perform)

FOR ENGLISH LANGUAGE LEARNERS

Assessment Practice: Analyzing Visuals Ask students to suggest photographs or other illustrations they believe would make the best magazine cover for the article "Top 10 Summer Jobs." Ask them to explain why specific images would best convey the main idea for this article.

Reading Comprehension

Model a thinking process for answering multiple-choice questions.

1. **C is correct.** *Cattlemen could not spend all their money regardless of how much they bought. A and B are not correct because the text mentions only the profits, not the expenses or difficulties, of raising cattle. D is incorrect because although there are examples of spending, the paragraphs focus on the fact that they keep earning more money.*

2. **B is correct.** *The employees do everything the bank examiner asks because he is unpleasant. A is incorrect because it is an antonym. C and D are incorrect because the description does not fit these choices.*

3. **D is correct.** *In paragraph 12, Longley said he accepted Merwin's word as security for the loan. A is incorrect because he provides the bank examiner access to everything. B is incorrect because the bank examiner is ready to report the bad loan to the Comptroller of the Currency. C is not correct because Cooper & Craig is a rival bank.*

4. **A is correct.** *There is nothing positive about the bank examiner in the story. B is incorrect because it's clear that Longley is the main character. There is not enough evidence to support either C or D.*

5. **D is correct.** *In paragraph 26, Merwin throws down his whip, which was referred to as a quirt in paragraph 18. A, B, and C do not make sense in context.*

6. **A is correct.** *Tom and Bill have been through a lot together. B is incorrect because Tom does not die. C and D are incorrect because although Tom wants to repay the loan, he still doesn't have the money.*

7. **C is correct.** *Tom needs to figure out how to pay his debt to his friend. A, B, and D are incorrect because they are external conflicts.*

8. **G is correct.** *The dash marks the shift in emotion. The tone of the passage does not match A, C, or D.*

9. **B is correct.** *The men need money to repay the loan. A, B, and D are incorrect because they do not make sense in context.*

Reading Comprehension

Use "A Call Loan" (pp. 846–850) to answer questions 1–12.

1. The author chooses to begin the story by relating —
   A. how expensive cattle ranching is
   B. how hard it is to make a living raising cattle
   C. how much money could be made in cattle ranching
   D. how cattlemen spend their money

2. In paragraph 6, the word *dyspeptic* means —
   A. content
   B. disgruntled
   C. lean
   D. satisfied

3. One of the reasons the bank president doesn't want to call Tom Merwin's loan is that —
   A. he doesn't like government interference
   B. the bank examiner is corrupt
   C. Cooper & Craig will get more business
   D. he knows Tom keeps his word

4. Based on the description and behavior of the national bank examiner, the reader can conclude that —
   A. the author probably didn't like bank examiners
   B. the examiner is the main character in the story
   C. the bank president enjoyed his visits
   D. the examiner didn't like the bank president

5. Which word from paragraphs 18–27 help the reader understand the meaning of the word *quirt*?
   A. Collateral
   B. Note
   C. Table
   D. Whip

6. In paragraph 29, Tom Merwin says that Bill Longley "can call the blood out of my veins." The author uses this statement to —
   A. show how much respect Tom has for Bill
   B. foreshadow that Tom will die trying to repay the loan
   C. imply that Tom doesn't want to repay the loan
   D. establish security for Tom to repay the loan

7. A source of internal conflict for Tom Merwin is —
   A. his rivalry with Bill Longley
   B. his disagreement with Cooper
   C. his desire to make things right
   D. his disgust for the bank examiner

8. The tone of paragraph 41 changes from —
   A. serious to humorous
   B. despair to hope
   C. tolerable to bitter
   D. sympathetic to thoughtless

9. In paragraph 41, the word *spondulicks* means —
   A. beef
   B. cash
   C. cows
   D. trains

10. When Ed says things are "So, so" in response to Tom's breathless question, it is an example of —
   A. connotation
   B. sarcasm
   C. satire
   D. understatement

11. Based on paragraph 46, the reader can infer that —
   A. the bank examiner reports First National Bank of Chaparosa to the Department of Justice
   B. Long Bill Longley leaves town
   C. Tom Merwin pays the call loan
   D. Ed, Tom's brother, keeps all the money

12. Which of the following best expresses a theme of the selection?
   A. A friend should do whatever it takes to pay back a friend.
   B. Keeping one's word is important, especially to a friend.
   C. Banks should not be trusted to loan money.
   D. Mixing business and friendship is never good.

> **Use "The Next Frontier" (pp. 850–852) to answer questions 13–18.**

13. In paragraph 1, the fact that the land was called *El Desierto de los Muertos* ("The Desert of the Dead") is ironic now because the land —
   A. receives plenty of rain
   B. is filled with graves
   C. is green and lush
   D. is empty and unusable

14. Read the following dictionary entry.

   scale \'skāl\ *n* **1.** a series of musical notes **2.** a series of marks or points at known intervals used to measure distances **3.** a distinctive relative size, extent, or degree **4.** a graded series of tests to rate individual achievement or intelligence

   Which definition best matches the meaning of the word *scale* as it is used in paragraph 2?
   A. Definition 1
   B. Definition 2
   C. Definition 3
   D. Definition 4

15. The author includes background information on the ranch to —
   A. show how the King Ranch is like other places in South Texas
   B. reveal how the King Ranch failed
   C. highlight the importance and the achievements of the King Ranch
   D. explain the author's connection to the King Ranch

16. Problems for the King Ranch began when —
   A. members of the family wanted to get out of the business
   B. Robert J. Kleberg Jr. didn't have any children
   C. the farm equipment began to fail
   D. Richard King died in 1885

17. In paragraph 6, the word *antithetical* means —
   A. analogous
   B. contradictory
   C. hypothetical
   D. similar

GO ON ➡

DIFFERENTIATED INSTRUCTION

FOR ENGLISH LANGUAGE LEARNERS

Assessment Vocabulary Review with students the definitions of the following terms from the practice test.

Item 7: *internal conflict* "struggle within a character"
Item 8: *tone* "the writer's attitude toward a subject"
Item 10: *climax* "the turning point in a plot"

FOR STRUGGLING READERS

Assessment Support: Reading Items Remind students to read test items carefully, underlining or circling key words, phrases, or details. Tell students that they cannot respond accurately if they are not certain how they are being asked to respond. For example, point out that the word *best* is critical in items 12 and 14. A given answer may offer a plausible response. However, if the answer is not the most effective—that is, best—solution, it is not correct.

---

10. **D** *is correct.* *When Ed responds to Tom's frantic question in a casual manner, he is deliberately down-playing the importance of his accomplishment. A is incorrect because it does not fit the context of the event. B is incorrect because Ed is not being bitter or caustic. C is incorrect because Ed is not ridiculing or belittling Tom.*

11. **C** *is correct.* *Tom has enough cash to repay the loan. A is incorrect because with the loan repaid, the examiner would not report the bank. B and D are incorrect because they are not supported by the text.*

12. **B** *is correct.* *Tom keeps his word to repay Bill. A is incorrect because Bill doesn't want Tom to rob the train in order to repay him. C is incorrect because banks make money by loaning it. D is incorrect because in this case, there is a happy ending.*

13. **C** *is correct.* *The author compares the land to Ireland. A is incorrect because the author says "unusually cool and rainy." B is incorrect because there is no mention of cemeteries. D is incorrect because the area is a working ranch.*

14. **C** *is correct.* *The passage describes the size and extent of the ranch. A, B, and D do not fit the context of the article.*

15. **C** *is correct.* *The ranch was the first in the state and has long list of accomplishments and successes. A is incorrect because the author does not compare the King Ranch to other places. B is incorrect because the King Ranch has not failed. D is incorrect because the author interviews the family and gets a tour of the ranch.*

16. **A** *is correct.* *The ranch went into debt when it bought out the shares from family members. B is incorrect because Helen is his daughter. D is incorrect because the article doesn't refer to farm equipment. D is incorrect because the ranch flourished after 1885.*

17. **B** *is correct.* *The ranch is going against what it used to stand for. A and D are incorrect because they mean the opposite of antithetical. C has a different prefix and a different meaning.*

ANSWERS

18. D is correct. *At the end of the article, Helen mentions that there isn't much money in ranching. Now the King Ranch's income is mainly from hunting leases and farming. A, B, and C describe earlier stages of the business.*

19. A is correct. *Bill Longley and Captain King made their money in cattle ranching, but today, there isn't a lot of money in ranching. There is not enough evidence to support B, C, or D.*

20. C is correct. *An entrepreneur goes into business for him- or herself. A is incorrect because the title does not deal with electronics or affording purchases. B and D are incorrect because they both refer to the topics of other articles.*

21. A is correct. *Dog walkers typically are self-employed entrepreneurs. B is incorrect because the image does not indicate that the teen owns all the dogs. C is incorrect because the teen's appearance is neutral. D is incorrect. Although the image appears urban, it doesn't indicate that this job is unique to the city.*

SHORT CONSTRUCTED RESPONSE

Possible responses:

22. The author uses dialogue to reveal his characters. Although Bill Longley has made lots of money and is the bank president, he still talks like he is riding the trails. His language is filled with references to horses and cattle. However, the bank examiner speaks in a more educated, refined way.

23. Richard King, also known as Captain King, established the ranch in Texas with cattle. As the cattle business slowed down, his grandson expanded the ranch into an empire by getting into the oil business. Along the way, he invented tools and bred new animals as well. When internal family issues threatened to ruin the ranch, again the ranch reached into new areas such as hunting leases and farming.

24. From "A Call Loan" I'd like to be friends with Bill Longley. He is willing to help his friends through any tough situation. He trusts his friend, Tom Merwin, and cares about him enough to stop him from potentially ruining his life by robbing a train.

---

18. According to the article, the King Ranch operates largely through —

- **A.** tourism
- **B.** cattle and horses
- **C.** oil
- **D.** farming and hunting leases

> Use "A Call Loan" and "The Next Frontier" to answer question 19.

19. The authors of both selections would agree that —

- **A.** cattle ranching used to be a lucrative business
- **B.** money trouble follows a family for many generations
- **C.** it is important to stay with one career
- **D.** bankers do not trust farmers

> Use the visual representation on page 853 to answer questions 20–21.

20. A reader turning to the article "Teen Entrepreneurs: Got a Great Idea? Make it Pay!" will find tips on —

- **A.** affording the latest electronics
- **B.** saving for college
- **C.** creating a successful business
- **D.** finding a summer job

21. The designer most likely chose the photograph to —

- **A.** illustrate a teen entrepreneur at work
- **B.** persuade teens to buy more dogs
- **C.** convince teens to take their jobs seriously
- **D.** show that urban teens have unique job opportunities

SHORT CONSTRUCTED RESPONSE

Write a short constructed response to each question, using text evidence to support your response.

22. Why does O. Henry use dialogue? Support your response with evidence from the selection.

23. How does the King Ranch change from the beginning of the article to the end? Support your response with evidence from the selection.

Write a short constructed response to the following question, using text evidence from both selections to support your response.

24. Which rancher from "A Call Loan" and "The Next Frontier" would you like to have as a friend? Support your response with evidence from **both** selections.

From "The Next Frontier" I'd like to be friends with Robert J. Kleberg Jr. He was a brilliant businessman and inventor. Plus, he was friends with powerful people and movie stars.

Revising and Editing

DIRECTIONS Read this passage and answer the questions that follow.

(1) In the 1770s, the first permanent settlement in Chicago was established by a Haitian trader named Jean Baptiste Point du Sable. (2) The community developed slowly at first. (3) The growth of Chicago was spur by the construction of railroads in the mid-1800s. (4) Its progress came to a halt when the city was destroyed by a fire in 1871. (5) Organizations immediately offered aid, however. (6) Triumphantly, the city bounced back. (7) In 1893, Chicago hosted the World's Fair.

1. What is the most effective way to revise sentence 1?

  A. In the 1770s, a Haitian trader named Jean Baptiste du Sable established the first permanent settlement in Chicago.

  B. The first permanent settlement in Chicago was established in the 1770s by a Haitian trader named Jean Baptiste Point du Sable.

  C. In Chicago in the 1770s, the first permanent settlement was established by a Haitian trader named Jean Baptiste Point du Sable.

  D. The first permanent settlement in Chicago was established by a Haitian trader named Jean Baptiste Point du Sable in the 1770s.

2. What change, if any, should be made in sentence 3?

  A. Change *growth* to **grow**

  B. Insert a comma after *spur*

  C. Change *spur* to **spurred**

  D. Make no change

3. Which transition could best be added to the beginning of sentence 4?

  A. In addition,

  B. Finally,

  C. Therefore,

  D. Unfortunately,

4. What is the most effective way to revise sentence 5?

  A. Organizations immediately started to arrange clean-up crews to assist the city, however.

  B. Organizations immediately started forming relief and clean-up crews, however.

  C. Organizations immediately helped, however.

  D. Assisting organizations immediately helped, however.

5. What is the most effective way to combine sentences 6 and 7?

  A. Triumphantly, the city bounced back; however, in 1893, Chicago hosted the World's Fair.

  B. Triumphantly, the city bounced back and hosted the World's Fair in 1893.

  C. In 1893, Chicago hosted the World's Fair, but triumphantly, the city bounced back.

  D. In 1893, Chicago hosted the World's Fair; otherwise, the city triumphantly bounced back.

STOP

ANSWERS

Revising and Editing

1. A is correct. A changes the sentence from passive voice to active voice. B, C, and D are all in the passive voice.

2. C is correct. The sentence describes past growth. A is incorrect because the subject must be a noun. B is incorrect because a comma is not necessary before the by-phrase. D is incorrect because there is an error in the sentence.

3. D is correct. There is a contrast from the previous sentence. A is incorrect because sentence 4 is not part of a list with sentence 3. B is incorrect because it is the middle of the paragraph. C is incorrect because sentence 4 does not have a cause and effect relationship with sentence 3.

4. B is correct. The word forming is the clue. A, C, and D do not contain gerund phrases.

5. B is correct. Chicago is the subject of both sentences and doesn't have to be repeated. A, C, and D are illogical and contain internal contradictions.

DIFFERENTIATED INSTRUCTION

FOR STRUGGLING READERS

Assessment Support: Sentence Structure
Provide students with additional practice creating complex sentences. Ask students to combine the sentence pairs below into complex sentences.

- Clearing airport security can take a long time. My family is driving to the airport two hours before our flight. (*My family is driving to the airport two hours before our flight because clearing airport security can take a long time.*)

- I intend to apply to the state university next year. I have to work on improving my grades. (*I have to work on improving my grades, as I intend to apply to the state university next year.*)

- In 2008 Senator Barack Obama ran for president. The United States elected its first African American president. (*The United States elected its first African American president in 2008 when Senator Barack Obama ran for the office.*)

INTRODUCE *GREAT READS*

In Unit 4, students have discussed a number of big questions. Invite students to tell which question they found most intriguing and why, and then focus attention on the four questions that appear on pages 858–859. Discuss the recommended books and their summaries, pointing out how each connects to the related question. Encourage students to choose one or more of these "great reads" to study independently.

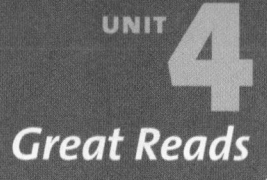

Ideas for Independent Reading

Continue exploring the Questions of the Times on pages 640–641 with these additional works.

What makes a place UNIQUE?

My Ántonia
by Willa Cather

This novel, recognized as Willa Cather's finest, depicts through the voice of the immigrant Ántonia Shimerda the hardships and rewards of pioneer life and the strength of America's frontier women. As Ántonia grows into womanhood, she overcomes poverty, disappointment, and family tragedy to become a mother and a successful farmer—a woman who "had not lost the fire of life."

American Indian Stories, Legends, and Other Writings
by Zitkala-Sa

This collection of works by Sioux writer and activist Zitkala-Sa (1876–1938) contains retellings of traditional Native American legends as well as stories, poems, essays, and speeches focused on the Native American experience.

The Virginian: A Horseman of the Plains
by Owen Wister

The strong-but-silent cowboy, the saintly schoolmarm, the climactic shootout—all have become standards of American Westerns but were brand-new ideas when Owen Wister penned *The Virginian* in 1902. His story of "the Virginian," a man torn between his love for a woman and his quest for justice, was the first true American Western.

Does the universe CARE?

Sister Carrie
by Theodore Dreiser

Carrie Meeber arrives in Chicago filled with vague hopes of fun and comfort. Meanwhile, across town, George Hurstwood, a well-to-do restaurant manager, is living the life of his dreams, respected by his peers and hobnobbing with famous actors. In *Sister Carrie,* Dreiser brings these two people together and lets us watch, amazed and appalled, as Carrie is taken to heights of glory while Hurstwood falls to the depths of despair.

The Best Short Stories of Jack London
by Jack London

No issue engaged writer Jack London more consistently than the clash between a seemingly uncaring natural world and the striving creatures who inhabit it. Intense, thrilling, and thought-provoking, the ten short stories in this collection show why London was so popular in his day and remains one of the most widely read of all American authors.

McTeague: A Story of San Francisco
by Frank Norris

Frank Norris set the literary establishment on its ear when he published *McTeague,* a naturalistic story of a San Francisco dentist. The title character, spurred by a strange force of self-destruction, makes one bad decision after another. Finally, he commits a murder and winds up fighting for his life in the harsh alkali deserts of California.

COMMON CORE

RL 10 Read and comprehend literature. **RI 10** Read and comprehend literary nonfiction.

How are women's ROLES CHANGING?

The Awakening
by Kate Chopin

Causing a storm of controversy when published in 1899, *The Awakening* follows the daily life of an attractive, well-to-do New Orleans matron named Edna Pontellier. Married into a prominent family, Edna leads a very comfortable existence, with good friends, a fine house, and nothing very pressing to do. Yet Edna is assailed by a nameless discontent. Although she cannot articulate exactly what she wants, she knows that the options open to women in her society are slowly making her die inside.

The House of Mirth
by Edith Wharton

The daughter of a failed New York businessman, Lily Bart is pretty, independent-minded, and cultivated. She is also penniless. Living with her rich yet miserly aunt, she spends her time socializing with New York's aristocrats. In such a situation, Lily's course of action is obvious to everyone. If she wants to maintain her lifestyle, she must find a rich man and marry him. Yet selling her beauty to the highest bidder strikes Lily as savage. Unable to find a path that would bring her both self-respect and material comfort, Lily drifts from party to party, trying not to think about what is going to happen to her. Lily's ultimately tragic fate is clearly the blame of a society that values wealth and convention above all.

Why are there "haves" and "HAVE-NOTS"?

The Jungle
by Upton Sinclair

No other novel in American literature has had a more direct impact upon daily life than *The Jungle*. Based upon extensive research conducted in Chicago's slaughterhouses, Sinclair's novel was intended to turn a blinding light on unfair labor practices and rally readers to the cause of socialism. Instead, its descriptions of unclean meatpacking practices caused a steep decline in the sales of beef and pork and brought about federal laws to keep food healthy. "I aimed at the public's heart, and by accident hit it in the stomach," Sinclair ruefully remarked. Nevertheless, *The Jungle* remains jarring in its description of the appalling conditions laborers were forced to endure.

A Hazard of New Fortunes
by William Dean Howells

In this novel of class conflict, a mild-mannered editor moves to New York from Boston, looking to enhance his career. He takes charge of a magazine sponsored by a ruthless financier and comes into contact with his old German tutor, who has become a political radical. Torn between his sympathy for the working poor and his need to stay on good terms with his rich patron, the editor does not know what to do. When a violent streetcar strike breaks out, he can no longer remain a bystander. He has to decide whether to support what he knows is right or to play it safe and keep his job.

Get Novel Wise

THINK central

Go to **thinkcentral.com**.
KEYWORD: HML11-859

859

THINK central

NovelWise

The keyword on this page points to **NovelWise**, a Web site that helps students choose a novel or other book-length work to read. **NovelWise** also provides

• study guides
• reading strategies and literary elements instruction
• presentations to introduce classic novels
• project ideas

UNIT GOALS

Included in this unit: **RL 1, RL 2, RL 3, RL 4, RL 5, RL 6, RL 9, RL 10, RI 1, RI 2, RI 3, RI 4, RI 5, RI 6, RI 7, RI 9, RI 10, W 1, W 2, W 2e, W 3, W 3a, W 3d–e, W 4, W 5, W 7, W 9, W 10, SL 1, SL 4, SL 5, L 1, L 1a, L 2, L 2a, L 3, L3a, L 4a, L 4b, L 4c, L 5b, L 6**

Complete text of the Common Core State Standards is found in the correlation on p. T10. Standards covered in this unit are found in the standards overview (pp. 861A–861D) and on the lesson pages where they are taught.

Preview Unit Goals

This page presents an overview of the skills and strategies covered in this unit. Explain to students that they can get more from their reading by previewing. Then ask them to skim the page to preview the skills that they will learn. Note that each strand or category of skill is color-coded on this page and throughout the unit.

Model the strategy of copying the Academic Vocabulary and writing a preliminary definition for each term. Suggest that students use their **Reader/Writer Notebooks** for this purpose. Encourage them to use the terms in discussions and in writing. Also urge students to revisit each term throughout the unit and to refine its meaning.

UNIT 5

COMMON CORE

Preview Unit Goals

TEXT ANALYSIS	• Understand Harlem Renaissance and modernism as literary movements • Identify and analyze literary elements, including tone, theme, diction, voice, mood, irony, imagery, setting, and character development • Identify and analyze rhyme scheme in poetry • Identify and analyze individual styles, including Frost's and Hemingway's • Analyze and interpret modern, narrative, and imagist poetry • Identify and analyze author's purpose and viewpoint • Distinguish literal from figurative meaning
READING	• Make inferences and draw conclusions • Identify explicit and implicit main ideas
WRITING AND LANGUAGE	• Write a persuasive essay • Craft effective sentences by using vivid language, phrases, and coordinating conjunctions
SPEAKING AND LISTENING	• Participate in a debate
VOCABULARY	• Use knowledge of Latin and Greek word roots to understand word meaning • Use a thesaurus to find precise words and understand nuances of words
ACADEMIC VOCABULARY	• conclude • criteria • despite • justify • maintain
MEDIA AND VIEWING	• Interpret and evaluate information presented in media and illustrations • Analyze and evaluate persuasive techniques in print advertising

Find It Online!

Go to **thinkcentral.com** for the interactive version of this unit.

THINK central

DIFFERENTIATED INSTRUCTION

FOR ENGLISH LANGUAGE LEARNERS

Academic Vocabulary Provide students with the definition of these Academic Vocabulary words.

conclude (kən-klood) *v.* to arrive at a belief based on evidence, experience, or reasoning; to end

criteria (krī-tîrē-ə) *n. pl.* set of standard or rules by which something can be evaluated

despite (dĭ-spīt) *prep.* in spite of; not stopped by

justify (jŭstə-fī) *v.* to show or claim to be just or right; vindicate

maintain (mān-tān) *v.* to preserve or keep up; to declare to be true

Additional Academic Vocabulary Use the copy master to help students learn academic words they will use in subsequent lessons and on the Assessment Practice.

R RESOURCE MANAGER—Copy Masters
    Academic Vocabulary p. 3
    Additional Academic Vocabulary p. 4

The Harlem Renaissance & Modernism

1910–1940

Langston Hughes

A CHANGING AWARENESS

- **The Harlem Renaissance**
- **The New Poetry**
- **The Modern Short Story**
- **Journalism as Literature**

Media Smart DVD-ROM

Zora Neale Hurston's Biography

Explore how documentary filmmakers bring a writer and her world to vivid life. Page 916

861

For help in planning this unit, see

R RESOURCE MANAGER UNIT 5 pp. 1–8

INTRODUCE THE UNIT

Call students' attention to the pictures on this page. Explain that the large picture, *The Bicycle Race* (1912), is a painting by Lyonel Feininger. Tell students that Feininger's work is influenced by such modern artistic movements as Cubism and Futurism. Students will read modern poetry and short stories later in this unit.

Ask students whether they know the writer, Langston Hughes, shown in the smaller picture on the page. Point out that Langston Hughes is recognized as a central figure of the Harlem Renaissance, a period of artistic flowering in the African-American community. Explain that Hughes was a writer of the people. He wrote works about ordinary people that were intended for ordinary people to read. Tell students that they will read some of his works in this unit. Also note that students can read more about Langston Hughes on page 878.

About the Art Although American artist Lyonel Feininger (1871–1956) was born in New York City, he lived and worked in Europe for most of his professional career. Dividing his time between Germany and France, Feininger began his career as a cartoonist, working for a number of magazines and newspapers both in America and abroad. While living in Paris in the early 1900s, Feininger fell under the artistic influence of Cubism and Futurism, which inspired his later work as a painter. Feininger's work attracted the scrutiny of the Nazi Party and was labeled as "degenerate art" in 1937, causing Feininger to flee Germany for the United States.

Unit Resources

See resources on the **Teacher One Stop DVD-ROM** *and on* **thinkcentral.com**.

R RESOURCE MANAGER UNIT 5

UNIT AND BENCHMARK TESTS

 BEST PRACTICES TOOLKIT

INTERACTIVE READER

ADAPTED INTERACTIVE READER

ELL ADAPTED INTERACTIVE READER

LANGUAGE HANDBOOK

VOCABULARY PRACTICE

TECHNOLOGY

- Teacher One Stop DVD-ROM
- Student One Stop DVD-ROM
- PowerNotes DVD-ROM
- WriteSmart CD-ROM
- MediaSmart DVD-ROM
- GrammarNotes DVD-ROM
- Audio Anthology CD

THINK central

Find It Online!

This unit on **thinkcentral.com** includes

- **PowerNotes** introductions to key selections
- audio support—listen or download
- **ThinkAloud** models
- **WordSharp** vocabulary tutorials
- interactive unit review and assessment

UNIT 5

STRAND	✓ECOS Unit 5 Introduction pp. 860–877 • Questions of the Times • Historical Essay • Timeline • Legacy *Masterpieces: from* The Great Gatsby pp. 1002–1003 *from* The Grapes of Wrath pp. 1024–1025	✓ECOS Text Analysis Workshops • Modernism pp. 934–935 • Journalism as Literature pp. 1092–1093	✓ECOS Selected Poetry by Langston Hughes Poetry pp. 878–885	My City/If We Must Die Poetry pp. 886–891	Any Human to Another/Storm Ending/A Black Man Talks of Reaping Poetry pp. 892–897	✓ECOS How It Feels to Be Colored Me Essay pp. 898–907 Lexile: 920 Fry: 11 Dale-Chall: 6.4	Thoughts on the African-American Novel Literary Criticism pp. 908–914 Lexile: 1130 Fry: College Dale-Chall: 7.0
Reading Literature	The Harlem Renaissance and Modernism pp. 862–873 RL 9 Text Analysis p. 1002 RL 3 Text Analysis p. 1024 RL 5	Modernism pp. 934–935 RL 3, RL 5, RL 9	Speaker pp. 879, 882–883, 885 RL 5 Rhythm and Repetition pp. 879–880, 882, 884–885 RL 5 Language Coach p. 884 RL 4	Sonnet pp. 887–888, 890–891 RL 5 Form and Meaning pp. 887–888, 890–891 RL 5, RL 9	Theme pp. 893–894, 896–897 RL 9 Figurative and Literal Meaning pp. 893–897 RL 4	Rhetorical Techniques pp. 899–900, 902, 905 RI 5 Main Ideas pp. 899, 902, 904–905 RI 1, RI 2	
Reading Informational Text	The Harlem Renaissance and Modernism pp. 862–873 RI 9 Read a Timeline pp. 874–875 RI 7	Journalism pp. 1092–1093 RI 5, RI 6					Rhetorical Techniques pp. 909, 913–914 RI 4, RI 6 Author's Viewpoint pp. 909, 913–914 RI 6 Analyze p. 912 RI 2
Writing	Legacy of the Era pp. 876–877 W 7, W 10				Quickwrite p. 893	Writing Prompt p. 907 W 3	Quickwrite p. 909
Speaking and Listening	Legacy of the Era pp. 876–877 SL 1		Discuss p. 879 SL 1	Present p. 887 SL 1			
Language						Vary Sentence Structure pp. 904, 907 L 1a, L 3a Greek Roots (*cosm* or *cosmo*) p. 906 L 4b, L 6	Language Coach p. 912

Media Study: Jump at the Sun Documentary pp. 916–919	Richard Cory/ Miniver Cheevy/Lucinda Matlock Poetry pp. 920–927	Chicago/Grass Poetry pp. 928–933	Selected Poetry by Robert Frost Poetry pp. 936–942	The Death of the Hired Man Narrative Poem pp. 943–951	In a Station of the Metro/ Helen/Spring and All/This Is Just to Say Poetry pp. 952–959	anyone lived in a pretty how town/Poetry/ Recuerdo Poetry pp. 960–967
	Characterization pp. 921–922, 924, 926–927 **RL 3** Speaker's Attitude pp. 921–922, 925–927 **RL 6, RL 9**	Tone and Diction pp. 929–930, 932–933 **RL 4, RL 5** Synthesize Details pp. 929–930, 933 **RL 4, RL 5**	Frost's Style pp. 937–938, 940–942 **RL 4** Recognize Ambiguity pp. 937–938, 941–942 **RL 1, RL 6** Theme p. 938	Narrative Poetry pp. 943–944, 946, 947–950 **RL 3, RL 5** Understand Form in Poetry pp. 943–944, 946, 948, 950 **RL 1, RL 5**	Imagism pp. 953–954, 956–958 **RL 4** Inferences pp. 953–954, 958 **RL 1**	Form in Modern Poetry pp. 961–962, 964, 966–967 **RL 5** Reading Modern Poetry pp. 961–962, 964–967 **RL 10**
Analyze and Plan a Documentary pp. 917–919 **RI 7**						
Documentary p. 919 **W 2**		Quickwrite p. 929	Quickwrite p. 937	Writing Prompt p. 951 **W 2, W 4**	Writing Prompt p. 959 **W 3d**	
Documentary p. 919 **SL 1, SL 5**	Discuss p. 921 **SL 1**					Discuss p. 961 **SL 1**
	Language Coach p. 925			Infinitive Phrases p. 951 **L 3a** Language Coach pp. 947, 948	Create Imagery p. 959 **L 3**	

ECOS

To see the complete Essential Course of Study, see pp. T23–T27.

For additional lesson planning help, see **Teacher One Stop DVD.**

STRAND	The Love Song of J. Alfred Prufrock Poem pp. 968–974	Winter Dreams Short Story pp. 976–1001	Media Study: Advertising... Jazz Age Print Advertisements pp. 1004–1007	Comparing Text Selections Literary: In Another Country pp. 1008–1022 Informational: Healing War's Wounds pp. 1009, 1018–1020, 1022 Visual: Moving a Nation pp. 1021–1022	Photo Essay: The Grapes of Wrath Photo Essay pp. 1026–1033	The Jilting of Granny Weatherall Short Story pp. 1034–1047	A Worn Path Short Story pp. 1048–1063
		Lexile: 1100 Fry: College Dale-Chall: 6.6		Lexile: 1050 Fry: 6 Dale-Chall: 5.4	Lexile: 1200 Fry: College Dale-Chall: 7.6	Lexile: 820 Fry: 6 Dale-Chall: 5.4	Lexile: 770 Fry: 12 Dale-Chall: 5.1
Reading Literature	Stream of Consciousness pp. 969, 971–974 RL 2 Summarize Stanzas pp. 969, 971, 974 RL 5	Motivation and Traits pp. 977–978, 982, 985–987, 989–990, 997, 999 RL 3 Predict Story Development pp. 977, 980, 992, 995, 999 RL 3		Tone pp. 1009–1010, 1014–1015 RL 4 Make Inferences pp. 1009, 1012–1013, 1015 RL 1		Stream of Consciousness pp. 1035–1036, 1038–1039, 1041–1042, 1044–1045 RL 1, RL 3, RL 5 Clarify Sequence pp. 1035, 1039–1040, 1045 RL 3, RL 5	Universal Theme pp. 1049–1050, 1052–1053, 1054, 1056, 1059, 1061 RL 2 Monitor Comprehension pp. 1049, 1053, 1055–1056, 1061 RL 2
Reading Informational Text			Persuasion in 1920s Ads pp. 1005–1007 RI 7	Tone pp. 1009, 1019–1020, 1022 RI 4 Make Inferences pp. 1009, 1018, 1020, 1022 RI 1 Book Cover p. 1021 RI 7	Analyze Photographs pp. 1026–1033 RI 7		Memoir p. 1060
Writing	Quickwrite p. 969	Quickwrite p. 977 Writing Prompt p. 1001 W 1	Produce Your Own Media p. 1007 W 2	Writing Prompt p. 1017 W 2e Writing Assessment p. 1023	Writing Prompt p. 1033 W 4, W 9	Quickwrite p. 1035 Writing Prompt p. 1047 W 3	Writing Prompt p. 1063 W 3, W 3a
Speaking and Listening			Ad Techniques pp. 1005–1006 Ad Poster p. 1007 SL 1, SL 5	What's the Connection? p. 1009 SL 1			Discuss p. 1049 SL 1
Language	Language Coach pp. 971, 972	Words from the Jazz Age p. 1000 L 1a, L 5b Craft Effective Sentences pp. 991, 1001 L 2, L 3a		Establish Tone pp. 1014, 1017 L 3a Academic Words p. 1016 L 6		Effective Sentences pp. 1040, 1047 L 3a Thesauri and Word Choice p. 1046 L 4c, L 5b	Details pp. 1053, 1063 L 3 Language Coach p. 1052 L 4b Cognates p. 1062 L 2b, L 6

A Rose for Emily Short Story pp. 1064–1077	**The Life You Save May Be Your Own** Short Story pp. 1078–1090	**A New Kind of War** News Dispatch pp. 1094–1103	**A Book of Great Short Stories** Book Review pp. 1104–1111	**The Duty of Writers** Essay pp. 1112–1116	**Wrap-Ups** • The Harlem Renaissance p. 915 • Modernist Style p. 975 • The Modern Short Story p. 1091 • Journalism as Literature p. 1117	**Writing Workshop: Persuasive Essay** pp. 1118-1127 **Speaking & Listening Workshop: Participating in a Debate** pp. 1128-1129
Lexile: 1120 *Fry: 11* *Dale-Chall: 6.4*	*Lexile: 1000* *Fry: 7* *Dale-Chall: 5.6*	*Lexile: 990* *Fry: 9* *Dale-Chall: 5.7*	*Lexile: 1030* *Fry: 9* *Dale-Chall: 7.0*	*Lexile: 1210* *Fry: College* *Dale-Chall: 7.7*		
Point of View pp. 1065, 1066, 1069–1070, 1073, 1075 **RL 3, RL 5** Analyze Sequence pp. 1065, 1068, 1072, 1075 **RL 3** Mood pp. 1068, 1074, 1075 **RL 4**	Irony pp. 1079, 1083–1085, 1088–1090 **RL 6** Descriptive Details pp. 1079–1080, 1083, 1085, 1087, 1090 **RL 1**				Analyze p. 915 **RL 9** Synthesize p. 975 **RL 9** Evaluate p. 1091 **RL 9**	
		Subjectivity pp. 1095–1096, 1098, 1100–1102 **RI 6** Descriptive Details pp. 1095, 1098–1099, 1102 **RI 1**	Style pp. 1105, 1106, 1108, 1110 **RI 3** Reading a Book Review pp. 1105, 1109–1110 **RI 6**	Style and Diction pp. 1113, 1115–1116 **RI 6** Author's Message pp. 1113, 1115–1116 **RI 6**	Analyze p. 915 **RI 9** Evaluate p. 1117 **RI 9**	
Writing Prompt p. 1077 **W 1**	Quickwrite p. 1079	Writing Prompt p. 1103 **W 3a, W 3e**	Quickwrite p. 1105 Writing Prompt p. 1111 **W 1**		Analyze p. 915 **W 7, W 9a** Evaluate p. 1117 **W 4**	Persuasive Essay pp. 1118–1127 **W 1a–e, W 4, W 5, W 9, W 9, W 10**
Discuss p. 1065 **SL 1**		Discuss p. 1095 **SL 1**		Discuss p. 1113 **SL 1**	Extension pp. 915, 975, 1117 **SL 4**	Participating in a Debate pp. 1128–1129 **SL 1a–d, SL 3, SL 4**
Point of View pp. 1070, 1077 **L 3** Etymologies p. 1076 **L 4c**	Language Coach pp. 1082, 1089	Point of View pp. 1098, 1103 **L 3** Language Coach p. 1099 **L 5b**	Voice pp. 1109, 1111 **L 2** Language Coach p. 1108		Extension p. 1117 **L 1**	Editing and Publishing p. 1125 **L 2b, L 3a**

✓ ECOS

To see the complete Essential Course of Study, see pp. T23–T27.

For additional lesson planning help, see **Teacher One Stop DVD.**

Instructional Support

Resource Manager Unit 5

UNIT SUPPORT

Academic Vocabulary p. 3

Additional Academic Vocabulary p. 4

Grammar Focus p. 5

Text Analysis Workshop pp. 124, 339

Writing Workshop: Persuasive
Essay, p. 393

SELECTION SUPPORT*

Plan and Teach

Lesson planning pages

Additional leveled selection questions

Extension activities

Student Copy Masters

Selection summaries in four languages

Skills copy masters in English and Spanish

Vocabulary preteaching and support

Reading Check and Question Support

Reading Fluency

*Available for all selections

† Available on **thinkcentral.com**.

Language Handbook

Vocabulary Practice

Best Practices Toolkit†

PowerNotes DVD-ROM†

**Connection: Nonfiction for
Common Core** CD-ROM†

Teacher One Stop DVD-ROM

Student One Stop DVD-ROM

Media*Smart* DVD-ROM
Advertising in the Jazz Age

Write*Smart* CD-ROM†

GrammarNotes DVD-ROM†

WordSharp CD-ROM†

Media●Smart

Media Studies

Changing Views of Native Americans

Illustrations Inspired by Poe

American Landscapes

Advertising in the Jazz Age

Zora Neale Hurston: Jump at the Sun

Perspectives in the News

Differentiated Instruction

STRUGGLING READERS AND WRITERS	ENGLISH LANGUAGE LEARNERS	ADVANCED LEARNERS
Resource Manager Unit 5 Additional Selection Questions Question Support Reading Fluency **Interactive Reader** **Adapted Interactive Reader** **Level Up Online Tutorials** **Audio Anthology** (with Audio summaries) **Diagnostic and Selection Tests** Selection Tests A/B	**Resource Manager Unit 5** Selection Summaries in English, Spanish, Vietnamese and Haitian Creole Skills Copymasters in Spanish **English Language Learner Adapted Interactive Reader Teacher's Guide** **ELL Adapted Interactive Reader** **Guide to English for Newcomers** **Audio Anthology** **Audio Summaries in Multiple Languages** (on **thinkcentral.com**)	**Resource Manager Unit 5** Additional Selection Questions Ideas for Extension **Diagnostic and Selection Tests** Selection Tests B/C

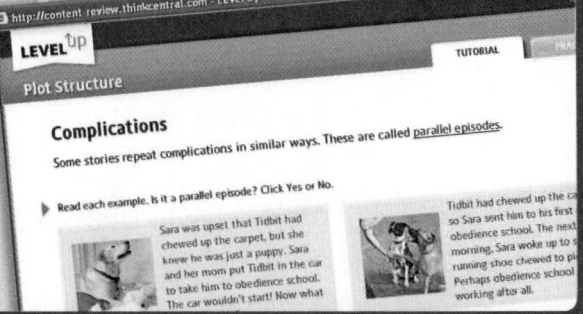

http://content.review.thinkcentral.com - Level Up - Microsoft Internet Explorer provided by Harcourt

LEVEL up

Plot Structure

TUTORIAL

Complications

Some stories repeat complications in similar ways. These are called _parallel episodes_.

▶ Read each example. Is it a parallel episode? Click Yes or No.

Sara was upset that Tidbit had chewed up the carpet, but she knew he was just a puppy. Sara and her mom put Tidbit in the car to take him to obedience school. The car wouldn't start! Now what

Tidbit had chewed up the ca so Sara sent him to his first obedience school. The next morning, Sara woke up to running shoe chewed to pi Perhaps obedience school working after all.

Assessment and Reteaching

Diagnostic and Selection Tests

Unit and Benchmark Tests

ThinkCentral Online Assessment:
- All program assessments
- Level Up Online Tutorials

ExamView Test Generator on the Teacher One Stop DVD-ROM

Online Essay Scoring on **thinkcentral.com**

ThinkCentral Online Reteaching:
- Level Up Online Tutorials
- Reteaching Worksheets

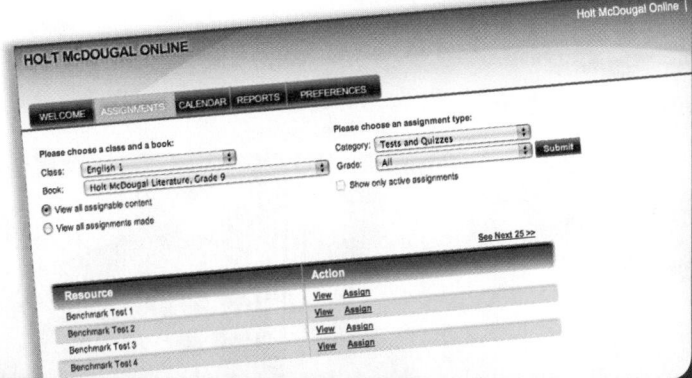

Professional Development

Video Center Based on interviews with program consultants and other educational experts, these videos feature classroom-ready teaching strategies.

Teacher Toolkit Includes a Teacher Handbook as well as a range of articles and handouts by program consultants and other educators.

Janet Allen

Jim Burke

Kylene Beers

Carol Jago

 **at a Glance**

One Location, Endless Resources

Find Resources Browse all *Holt McDougal Literature* components for the ones that meet your students' needs and match your teaching style.

Assess Progress and Reteach Assign electronic versions of program assessments to measure your students' mastery of the Common Core State Standards. On thinkcentral.com, some tests deliver online remediation tutorials to students who have not mastered skills.

 Interactive Whiteboard Lessons

Prepare your students for college and careers by teaching relevant, real-world skills through dynamic, interactive instruction. Go to **thinkcentral.com** to browse through all whiteboard lessons, including the following:

- Poetry: Language and Form
- Figurative Languag e and Imagery
- Point of View
- Writing Effective Arguments

 Together Holt McDougal and HISTORY® are revolutionizing the study of English/language arts with video that helps students relive and re-imagine the people, places, and events they are discovering through reading. Look for selections with the HISTORY® icon.

Questions of the Times

Read aloud the questions on pages 862 and 863 and the paragraphs that follow them. Open the discussion of each idea by having students respond to the questions that conclude each paragraph. Use these notes to prompt further exploration of the ideas.

What is MODERN?

Encourage students to consider what interests them about the traditions of their communities as well as what they enjoy about contemporary culture. Also, ask students to think about the importance of technology in their lives. Discuss why people so often want the latest and most up-to-date models of computers, cell phones, and music players.

Can ideals survive CATASTROPHE?

Invite students to brainstorm a list of dire events that have occurred in recent history. In light of these events, ask students to discuss their feelings regarding the future. Do they feel hopeful or cynical about the future? Why?

UNIT **5**

Questions of the Times

DISCUSS Share your views about the following questions with a small group or in a whole-class discussion. As you read the selections in this unit, reflect on how the writing of the Harlem Renaissance and the modernist period was shaped by these questions.

What is MODERN?

Americans in the first half of the 20th century consciously moved away from the traditions of their past and embraced all things modern. From the shiny new automobiles rolling off Henry Ford's assembly line to the esoteric poetry of T. S. Eliot—Americans' love affair with modernism was in full swing. What does *modern* mean to you? Why do you think people like to be on the "cutting edge"?

Can ideals survive CATASTROPHE?

The years between 1910 and 1940 were scarred by two historical events: World War I and the Great Depression. Faced with a world at war followed by deep economic instability at home, many American writers began to see the world with a new cynicism. How can people hold on to their idealism in light of dire events? Is it even possible?

COMMON CORE

RL 9 Demonstrate knowledge of early-twentieth-century foundational works of American literature, including how two or more texts from the same period treat similar themes or topics. **RI 9** Analyze documents of historical and literary significance for their themes, purposes, and rhetorical features.

How can people honor their HERITAGE?

The writers of the Harlem Renaissance were quite diverse stylistically, yet they shared a pride in their heritage that shines through their work. Why do you think writing might be a good vehicle for honoring one's past? How else do people honor their heritage?

What drives HUMAN BEHAVIOR?

Newly familiar with Sigmund Freud's groundbreaking work in human psychology, American writers of this period began to examine the unconsious motivations that affect human behavior. Do you think people regulate their behavior through reason and understanding, or are they driven by unconscious desires?

How can people honor their HERITAGE?

Prompt students to think about their cultural and ethnic backgrounds. Ask students to share how they celebrate or honor these aspects of their identities.

What drives HUMAN BEHAVIOR?

Challenge students to think about times when they have acted without thinking. Have them contrast this behavior with a time when they carefully planned a particular action. Invite students to contrast what motivates their behavior during these different times.

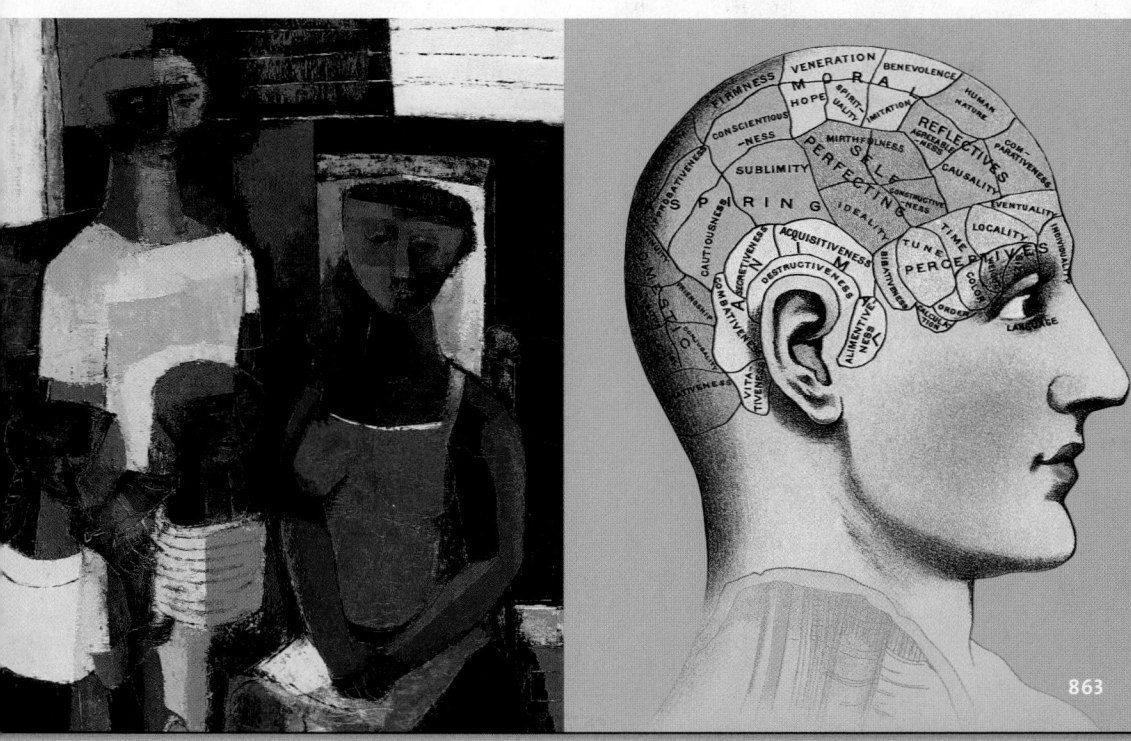

863

COMMON CORE FOCUS

RL 9 Demonstrate knowledge of early-twentieth-century foundational works of American literature, including how two or more texts from the same period treat similar themes or topics. **RI 9** Analyze documents of historical and literary significance for their themes, purposes, and rhetorical features.

The following essay (pages 864–873) provides students with a historical context for the Unit 5 reading selections. It presents a brief overview of significant events occurring during the time period 1910–1940 and introduces key people, places, and ideas of the times.

To get started, read and discuss the opening paragraph on page 864. Call students' attention to key events: World War I, the economic boom of the Roaring Twenties, the passage of the 19th Amendment giving women the right to vote, the Great Depression. Ask students to speculate how each of these events helped create "a whole new world." Discuss the challenges that Americans of this era faced, and ask why writers of the time would have been motivated to search for new truths.

READING STRATEGY

■ PREVIEW

Have students preview the historical essay by skimming the heads, boldfaced terms, and **Taking Notes** side-column features. Ask volunteers to summarize what the essay is about.

About the Art American artist John Sloan (1871–1951) painted scenes of New York life throughout his career. His art reflects real affection for the city, even its dirt and poverty. As *The City from Greenwich Village* shows, Sloan animated his paintings with a sense of movement and character.

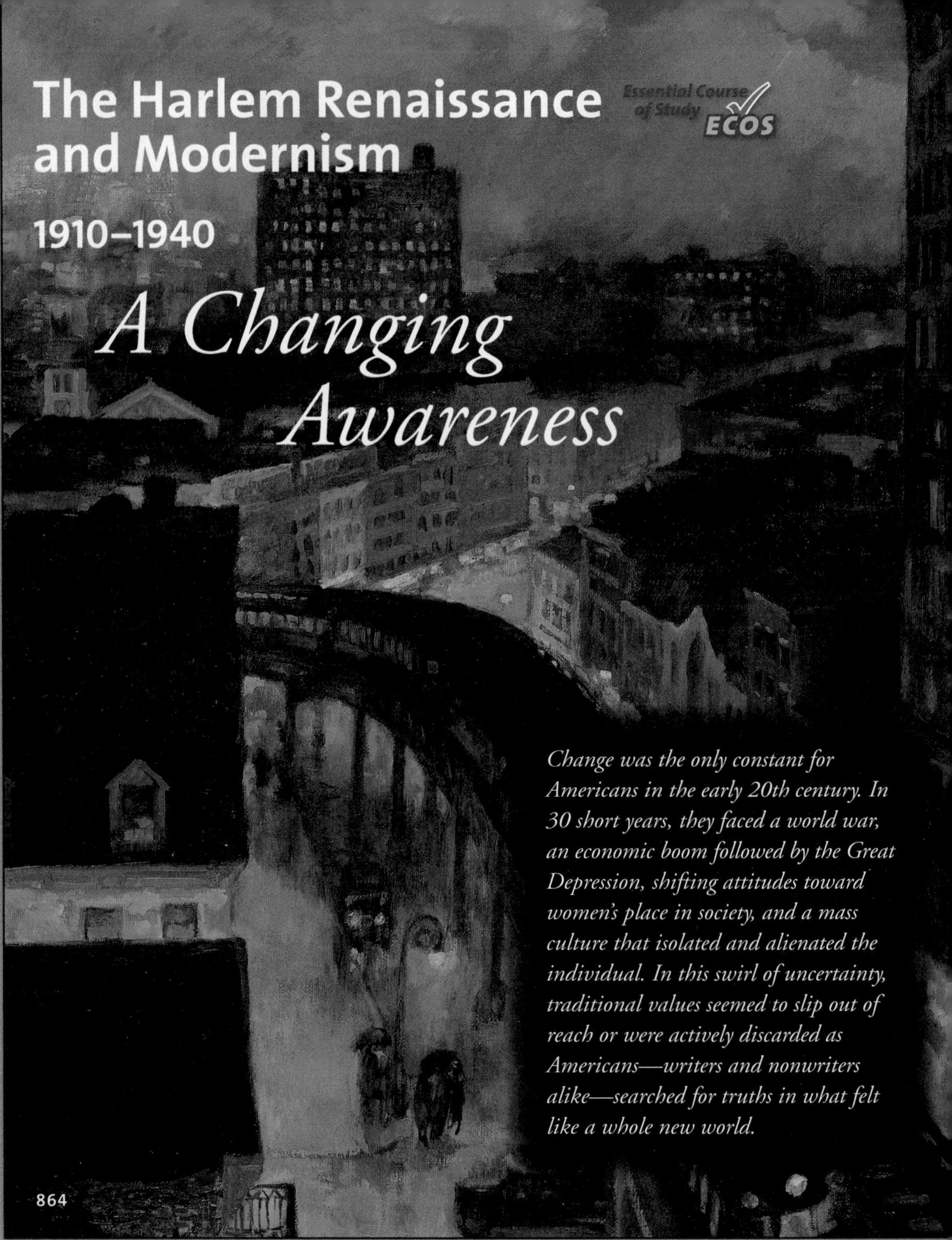

The Harlem Renaissance and Modernism

1910–1940

A Changing Awareness

Change was the only constant for Americans in the early 20th century. In 30 short years, they faced a world war, an economic boom followed by the Great Depression, shifting attitudes toward women's place in society, and a mass culture that isolated and alienated the individual. In this swirl of uncertainty, traditional values seemed to slip out of reach or were actively discarded as Americans—writers and nonwriters alike—searched for truths in what felt like a whole new world.

864

DIFFERENTIATED INSTRUCTION

FOR STRUGGLING READERS
Vocabulary Support

- *modernism,* "art or writing that reflects a loss of hope after World War I and believes individuals are threatened and isolated by society and mass culture"

- *influential,* "having or exerting power over another"

- *carnage,* "bloody, extended slaughter"

- *obscene,* "offensive to one's feelings or commonly held ideas of decency"

- *hedonism,* "the pursuit of pleasure as a way of life"

- *disillusioned,* "disappointed"

- *emancipated,* "freed from control or social expectations"

Use this copy master to help students take notes on the essay, pages 864–873:

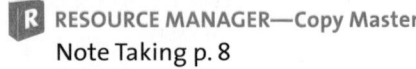 **RESOURCE MANAGER**—Copy Master
Note Taking p. 8

The Harlem Renaissance and Modernism: Historical Context

Catastrophic historical events—including a devastating war and a deep economic depression—as well as rapid societal change profoundly affected the writing of this period.

A World at War

World War I—the **Great War**—was perhaps the most influential force on American writers of the early 20th century. The war broke out in Europe in 1914; before it ended in 1918, it involved 32 nations, including the United States, and took the lives of over 20 million people. It was a new kind of war, waged on a massive scale with terrible new weapons that reflected the technological advances of the time—machine guns, poison gases, airplane bombers, and submarines. Old ideals about the purposes and meaning of war were destroyed in the carnage. As Lieutenant Frederic Henry, a character in **Ernest Hemingway's** 1929 novel *A Farewell to Arms,* observed: "Words such as glory, honor, courage, or hallow were obscene." For many Americans, the war signaled an end to idealism and ushered in an era marked by hedonism, political corruption, and ruthless business practices.

The Jazz Age

Some Americans, disillusioned with the traditional values that had led to war, sought escape in the pleasures of entertainment and good times. The 1920s, with its booming economy, became known as the **Roaring Twenties.** Writer **F. Scott Fitzgerald** called this decade "the greatest, gaudiest spree in history." As incomes rose, people were able to spend more money on goods and leisure activities. In addition, many young people began, for the first time, to rebel as a group against the values of the past and the authority of their elders. They experimented with new fashions and new attitudes, actively seeking out fun and freedom.

A NEW ERA FOR WOMEN Women of the period saw their lives change in fundamental ways. In 1920, the passage of the **19th Amendment** finally gave women the right to vote. But the vote was just one facet of the changing nature of womanhood. The 1920s saw the emergence of the **flapper,** an emancipated young woman who embraced new fashions and the urban attitudes of the day. By 1930, ten million American women were earning wages in the workplace—another new frontier. In addition, family life was made increasingly easier by technological innovations, from ready-made clothes to sliced bread. Many women writers, such as **Edna St. Vincent Millay** and **Dorothy Parker,** were celebrated as much for their modern lifestyles as for their writing. In turn, they often wrote about the clash between traditional and modern values, celebrating youth, independence, and freedom from social constraints.

The City from Greenwich Village (1922), John Sloan. Gift of Helen Farr Sloan. © 2006 Board of Trustees, National Gallery of Art, Washington, D.C. 1970.1.1 Photo © Superstock.

COMMON CORE

RL 9 Demonstrate knowledge of early-twentieth-century foundational works of American literature, including how two or more texts from the same period treat similar themes or topics. **RI 9** Analyze documents of historical and literary significance for their themes, purposes, and rhetorical features.

▶ **TAKING NOTES**

Outlining As you read each section of this introduction, add the information you learn to an outline like the one started for you here. You can use headings, boldfaced terms, and the information in these boxes as starting points. (See page R49 in the **Research Handbook** for more help with outlining.)

I. Historical Context

  A. A World at War

    1. influence on writers

    2. affected millions

    3. new kind of war

    4. destroyed ideals

  B. The Jazz Age

The Harlem Renaissance and Modernism: Historical Context

This section of the essay (pages 865–866) tells how modern American writers described the catastrophic historical events and rapid societal change that occurred in this period of American history. The text also explains the changing nature of war, of women's roles, and of the role government plays in American culture.

TIERED DISCUSSION PROMPTS

Use these prompts to help students understand the ideas in **A World at War:**

Summarize How was World War I different from previous wars? *Possible answer: World War I was waged on a massive scale, using terrible new technological weapons such as machine guns, poison gas, airplane bombers, and submarines.*

Analyze How does the quotation from *A Farewell to Arms* illustrate the effect new methods of warfare had on people's beliefs? Explain. *Possible answer: The quotation shows how new methods of warfare led people to realize that human ingenuity could bring about death on a massive scale. With this realization, people questioned whether they could believe in values such as courage, glory, and honor.*

FOR ENGLISH LANGUAGE LEARNERS

Set a Purpose Ask students to look for supporting details as they read about how historical catastrophe and societal change redefined American values.

FOR ADVANCED LEARNERS/AP

Brainstorm Ask students to use their prior knowledge of the historical period from 1910 to 1940. Then have them brainstorm a list of the catastrophic historical events and societal changes that writers would have been most likely to chronicle. Have students discuss which items on their list proved to have the greatest cultural significance, and why.

CHECK UNDERSTANDING

Have students describe the significance of these items:

- "Great War"
- Roaring Twenties
- 19th Amendment
- Prohibition
- Jazz Age
- Great Depression
- Dust Bowl
- New Deal

TIERED DISCUSSION PROMPTS

Use these prompts to help students understand the ideas in **The Great Depression:**

Summarize What were two main causes of the Great Depression? *Possible answer: The stock market crash of 1929 and a severe drought in the early 1930s were two main causes of the Great Depression.*

Analyze How was President Roosevelt's New Deal a different approach to solving the nation's economic problems? *Possible answer: Roosevelt's New Deal took the approach that government spending could help solve economic problems.*

About the Art *Migrant Mother* (1936) is a photograph by Dorothea Lange (1895–1965). During the Depression, the government hired Lange to photograph people affected by poverty in California. Lange would casually talk with people in the labor camps until she established a rapport and then she would photograph them. Because of these human connections, Lange's photographs reflect an understanding of her subjects. *Migrant Mother* is one of Lange's most famous works.

JAZZ CULTURE This period also saw the passage of **Prohibition** (1920–1933), in which alcohol was made illegal. In defiance of this restriction, many people drank in illegal nightclubs called speakeasies, as gangsters made fortunes running and supplying the clubs. At the fancy Cotton Club in New York's Harlem neighborhood, the guests—nearly all whites—rubbed shoulders with celebrities and gangsters as they listened to the great jazz performers—nearly all blacks—who helped give the era its name: the **Jazz Age.**

The Great Depression

The good times came to a dramatic end when the stock market crashed in October 1929, plunging the nation into economic depression. During the **Great Depression**, so called for its length and severity, many banks failed, businesses floundered, and workers lost their jobs. By 1933, the unemployment rate had grown to 25 percent. Unable to pay their bills, thousands of people lost their homes, and millions went hungry.

THE DUST BOWL A severe drought that began in the early 1930s added to the nation's pain. When the drought began, winds picked up dirt from the dry, exhausted fields of the Great Plains. Huge dust storms arose, damaging farms across a 150,000-square-mile region called the **Dust Bowl.**

Ruined farmers set off with their families to find work, many traveling west to California. Unfortunately, little work was to be found in California, for it, like the rest of the nation, was suffering through the Great Depression. Writers such as **John Steinbeck** captured the uncertainty and despair of the times: "Carloads, caravans, homeless and hungry; twenty thousand and fifty thousand and a hundred thousand and two hundred thousand. They streamed over the mountains, hungry and restless—restless as ants, scurrying to find work to do."

THE NEW DEAL The country was desperate for help. During his presidential campaign in 1932, Franklin Delano Roosevelt pledged to give the country a "new deal." When elected, he fulfilled his promise by enacting various **New Deal** programs—relief for the homeless and hungry, recovery for agriculture and business, and various economic reforms to prevent such a severe depression from occurring again. Yet in truth, it was the massive spending and production spurred by World War II that finally brought the economic crisis to an end.

Migrant Mother by Dorothea Lange, 1936. This photograph of Florence Owens Thompson with her children came to symbolize the Great Depression for many Americans.

DIFFERENTIATED INSTRUCTION

FOR STRUGGLING READERS
Vocabulary Support
- *homogenization,* "made identical or similar"
- *conformity,* "following common rules, customs, or attitudes"
- *materialism,* "interest in material goods instead of spiritual or intellectual pursuits"
- *unconscious,* "not realized or intended"

FOR ENGLISH LANGUAGE LEARNERS
Analyze Cultural Influences After they read page 867, ask students to explain the bold-faced terms and to identify a name or names linked with each term.

Terms
- mass culture
- mass media
- mass production

Names
- Albert Einstein
- Sigmund Freud
- Karl Marx

Cultural Influences

A developing mass culture and ideas that challenged traditional thought provided fodder for writers of the time.

New Directions

MASS CULTURE The 1920s was the first decade to be significantly shaped by **mass media.** New goods—from cars to toasters to beauty products—were flooding the market, and businesses relied on advertising to sell them. Thanks to advertising, items people had formerly considered luxuries were now deemed necessities. Mass media quickly became the ultimate source for this manufacturing of desire.

Mass production quickly and efficiently produced Americans' newfound necessities, but efficiency came with a price. Henry Ford perfected the assembly-line system, but its repetitiveness and monotony reduced workers to nameless, faceless cogs in the production process. And its products, efficiently mass-produced, led to the homogenization of American culture. **Sinclair Lewis** and many other significant writers of the day were alienated by the new values and lifestyles of their peers and soon began to criticize what they saw as Americans' conformity and materialism.

NEW IDEAS The writers of this period were also influenced by exciting new ideas that were challenging Americans' traditional views. A literary technique called **stream of consciousness** developed from the psychoanalytic theories of **Sigmund Freud**, who proposed that unconscious forces drive human beings and that the key to understanding behavior lay in this deeper realm of the mind. **Karl Marx's** socioeconomic theories—that history is a constant struggle between classes, for example—found their way into some of the literature of the day, mainly that of Depression-era writers. And **Albert Einstein's** theory of relativity, which overturned long-held beliefs about the nature of the universe, offered writers a fresh new way of looking at the world.

Print advertisements from the 1920s and 1930s

> **A Voice from the Times**
>
> *It's the fellow with four to ten thousand a year . . . and an automobile and a nice little family in a bungalow . . . that makes the wheels of progress go round! That's the type of fellow that's ruling America today[!]*
>
> —Sinclair Lewis
> from *Babbitt*

Cultural Influences

This section of the essay (page 867) explains the effect of mass media and mass production on American culture. The text also points out the effects of such thinkers as Freud, Marx, and Einstein on American writers.

TIERED DISCUSSION PROMPTS

Use these prompts to help students understand the ideas in **New Directions:**

Recall What effect did advertising have on Americans? *Possible answer: Items once viewed as luxuries became necessities.*

Interpret What does Lewis mean by the comment that it's "the fellow with . . . an automobile and a nice little family" who's ruling America? *Possible answer: Lewis suggests that because companies want to sell their products, real power to promote the progress of new ideas comes from the ordinary people who can buy those products rather than from officials and executives.*

Evaluate Is Marx correct in his theory that history is a constant struggle between classes? Explain. *Possible answer: Marx is correct that history often shows those in power trying to keep their power and those without power trying to get some power.*

CHECK UNDERSTANDING

Have students describe the significance of these ideas in American culture and writing:

- conformity
- materialism
- stream-of-consciousness

FOR STRUGGLING READERS

Main Ideas and Supporting Details Have students carefully examine the advertisements on page 867, noting composition, color, shape, and text. Point out that each advertisement bears the title of the product advertised, but very little copy to describe it. Instead, each advertisement relies upon associations with objects and colors to sell its product. Ask students which images draw their attention and what associations they make with the colors and shapes. Then point out the importance of the placement of objects to create certain suggestions in the viewer's mind, such as suggesting elegance by arranging the electric cord to resemble fancy script in the advertisement for vacuum cleaners. Link this discussion and the art images to the main ideas in **Cultural Influences** by pointing out how these advertisements "manufacture desire." Ask students to explain the role of advertising and to summarize how mass culture affected the writers of the 1920s.

FOR ADVANCED LEARNERS/AP

Research New Ideas Have students learn more about the theories of Freud, Marx, and Einstein. Invite students to make informal oral presentations to the class, sharing their findings and explaining how the theories of these men are reflected or refuted in contemporary American life.

Modern Literature and the Harlem Renaissance

This section of the essay (pages 868–873) focuses on modern American writing. The text describes

- new poetic literary movements, including modernism, imagism, and objectivism
- modern short stories
- the works of the Harlem Renaissance

TIERED DISCUSSION PROMPTS

Use these prompts to help students understand the ideas in **The New Poetry:**

Summarize What were the concerns of poets at the beginning of the 20th century? ***Possible answer:*** *Poets at that time were concerned with the effects of industrialization, war, threats to individualism, mass culture, and urbanization.*

Interpret What does Williams mean when he says that "there are no ideas but in things"? ***Possible answer:*** *Ideas must be concrete, as captured in actual objects, rather than abstract.*

Synthesize In what ways was modernist poetry a response to mass society of the time? Explain. ***Possible answer:*** *Modernist poets saw mass society as a threat to individualism. Therefore, their poetry emphasized experimentation and a rejection of past forms in favor of new modes of expression.*

Modern Literature and the Harlem Renaissance

The writers of this period, working in a variety of genres and focusing on discrete themes, were markedly influenced by the events and culture of the day. Many responded by embracing all things new, while others celebrated their heritage.

The New Poetry

At the beginnning of the century, rapid industrialization and urbanization caused many Americans to feel that the social order governing their lives was crumbling. Poets of the day began to explore in their work the impact of rapid change and uncertainty on the individual.

Edgar Lee Masters, in his famous collection *Spoon River Anthology,* used free verse to probe the discontent beneath the apparent stability of small-town life in the United States. *Spoon River Anthology* found a wide audience, in part because it voiced concerns shared by many Americans about the transformation from a rural to an industrialized society. Like Masters, **Edwin Arlington Robinson** also exposed the tensions underlying small-town life. His poems draw psychological portraits of characters isolated in the midst of American society. In portraying their isolation, Robinson was a forerunner of the modernist movement. These poets charted new territory by challenging conventional attitudes.

Others, such as **Carl Sandburg, Robert Frost,** and **Edna St. Vincent Millay,** seemed to be more connected to earlier traditions that focused on nature and common people. Yet they, too, revealed an awareness of the changes sweeping the American landscape. For this reason, Millay, Sandburg, and Frost can be called transitional poets, those who connect past traditions with modern thought.

MODERNISM Other poets of this period belong to the literary movement called **modernism** (see page 934). Modernism arose as a direct response to the social and intellectual forces shaping the 20th century. Modernist writers, many of whom were expatriates living in Europe, responded to the loss of idealism they felt in the wake of World War I. Living abroad, they experienced both the immediate and the long-term effects of World War I more acutely than did Americans at home. Most modernists also saw mass society as a threat to the individual, especially the artist. They felt that the standardization of culture resulted in alienation—a theme they captured in their work.

Experimentation was a distinguishing characteristic of these writers. "Make it new," extolled **Ezra Pound** as he urged fellow poets to abandon the artifice of past forms and search for their individual voices. **Harriet Monroe,** editor of *Poetry* magazine, wrote that the new poetry "has set before itself an ideal of absolute simplicity and sincerity—an ideal which implies an individual, unstereotyped diction; and an individual, unstereotyped rhythm." The lack of

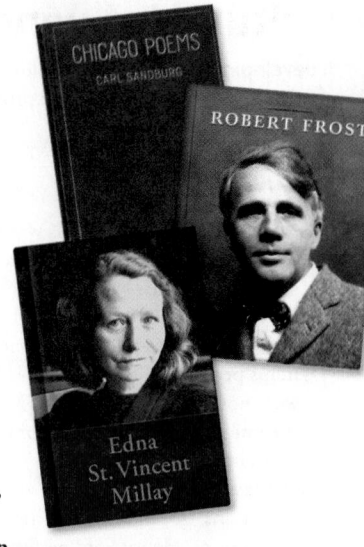

Works by transitional poets Millay, Frost, and Sandburg

▶ *For Your Outline*
THE NEW POETRY

- Poets began to challenge conventional thought.
- Modernists responded to historical forces such as WWI and an increasing mass society.
- Experimentation characterized modernism.
- Imagists believed that poetry should be expressed through the "rendering of concrete objects."
- Imagists favored free verse.
- In objectivist poetry, objects speak for themselves.

DIFFERENTIATED INSTRUCTION

FOR STRUGGLING READERS

Concept Support Tell students that free verse is poetry without predictable patterns of rhyme or meter. Poets often use poetic devices to create rhythm in free verse poetry. Direct students to these examples of free verse: "Song of Myself" (p. 534), "A Noiseless Patient Spider" (p. 538), "Beat! Beat! Drums!" (p. 539).

Have students use the examples to show their understanding of the concepts.

FOR ENGLISH LANGUAGE LEARNERS

Modern Literature Emphasize that one aspect of modern literature was experimentation. Writers, like chemists in a laboratory, experimented with language, grammar, tradition, and the work of other writers—mixing and rejecting these elements to discover varying effects. Have students experiment by paraphrasing one idea from the text in at least three different ways.

"stereotypes," however, made any recognizable movement hard to sustain: as soon as a style became accepted, it also became a new standard against which to rebel. The result was that modernist poetry as a body of work is as fragmented as many of its individual poems.

IMAGISM Many of the so-called new poets did, however, share the belief that poetry is most profoundly expressed through the "rendering of concrete objects." Ezra Pound called this kind of poetry **imagism** because it sought to re-create an image—not comment on it, not interpret it, but just present it. Pound became the center of a circle of poets, including **H. D.** (Hilda Doolittle) and **Amy Lowell,** who cast off the sentimentality, formal structures, and rhyme schemes of their predecessors and exploded into **free verse** (poetry without a predictable rhyme or metric scheme). Ezra Pound was especially taken with the poetry of **T. S. Eliot,** whose *The Waste Land* is considered one of the most representative and influential of modernist poems.

OBJECTIVISM One modernist poet, **William Carlos Williams,** however, vehemently disliked *The Waste Land* for its intellectualism and its references to classical literature. In response to Eliot's complex ideas and academic references, Williams famously stated that there are "no ideas but in things." Williams became the center of a new movement in modernist poetry called **objectivism,** in which poets let the objects they rendered speak for themselves. These poets invited readers to experience the homely simplicity of an object for no other reason than to understand its "this-ness."

The modernist movement had an enormous impact on later poets. Many poets today prefer to communicate through images rather than direct statements. They believe in economy of words and continue to experiment with free verse. Poetry had been altered irrevocably.

> ### A Voice from the Times
> *so much depends*
> *upon*
>
> *a red wheel*
> *barrow*
>
> *glazed with rain*
> *water*
>
> *beside the white*
> *chickens.*
>
> —**William Carlos Williams**
> "The Red Wheelbarrow"

Sculpture inspired by William Carlos Williams's poem
The Red Wheelbarrow (1992), Frank Jensen. © Frank Jensen.

The Modern Short Story

Poetry was not the only form popular during this period. In fact, the period from 1890 to 1930 has been called "the Age of the Short Story" in American literature. The great popularity of the short story has often been attributed to the American temperament. Americans living in the first half of the 20th century were too impatient and too much in a hurry to read longer works. They wanted "fast" literature, just as Americans today want fast food.

Other factors contributed to the popularity of the short story as well. New methods of advertising had brought about a boom in magazine publication. As the number of magazines grew, so did the demand for short stories. In turn, magazines paid their writers handsome fees. At one point, **F. Scott Fitzgerald** was receiving as much as $4,000 for a single story. **William Faulkner,** who complained that writing short stories interfered with his more serious, longer works, earned more from the sale of four short stories to the *Saturday Evening Post* than he did from his first four novels.

THEMES PULLED FROM LIFE The upheavals of this period in American history provided rich fodder for short story writers. World War I turned many Americans' idealism into uncertainty. Civilization as people had known it was being destroyed, and writers sought to capture in their work the resulting alienation and confusion. Indeed, World War I shook the ideological foundations of some young American writers so profoundly that **Gertrude Stein,** an American writer living in Paris, called them **"the lost generation."**

These alienated writers broke with the traditions of the past, turning to new methods and stylistic devices to carry their themes. **Ernest Hemingway** and other writers composed short, fragmentary stories without traditional beginnings or endings. They left out a narrative voice, leaving readers alone to figure out what might be going on or what a character might be feeling. "I always try to write on the principle of the iceberg," Hemingway said. "There is seven-eighths of it under water for every part that shows."

The boom years of the Roaring Twenties inspired its own literature. Writers such as **F. Scott Fitzgerald** revealed the negative side of the period's gaiety and freedom by portraying wealthy and attractive people leading empty lives in their gilded surroundings. Writer **John Steinbeck** is most closely identified with the bust years of the Great Depression. Declaring that a writer's duty is to "set down his time as nearly as he can understand it," Steinbeck managed to tell, perhaps better than anyone else, the stories of ordinary people caught up

An illustration of the Roaring Twenties high life, which served as inspiration for writers such as F. Scott Fitzgerald

in the Great Depression and lost from the devastation of the Dust Bowl.

Steinbeck, **Eudora Welty,** and many other writers of the time were beneficiaries of one of President Roosevelt's New Deal programs, the Works Progress Administration (WPA). The WPA was set up to create as many jobs as possible, as quickly as possible, including work for the nation's artists and writers. As the head of the WPA put it, "They've got to eat just like other people." Eudora Welty traveled around Mississippi for the WPA, writing articles about various projects under way in the state. She later said that these travels introduced her to the very different ways in which people lived, inspiring her later writing.

The Harlem Renaissance

Beginning in 1916 and continuing throughout the 1920s, in what came to be known as the **Great Migration,** millions of black farmers and sharecroppers moved to the urban North in search of opportunity and freedom from oppression and racial hostility. Thousands of these migrants settled in Harlem, a New York City neighborhood that quickly became the cultural center of African-American life.

Soon, the very air in Harlem seemed charged with creativity as black men and women drew on their own cultural resources—their folk traditions as well as a new urban awareness—to produce unique forms of expression. Harlem attracted worldly and race-conscious African Americans who nurtured each other's artistic, musical, and literary talents and created a flowering of African-American arts known as the **Harlem Renaissance.**

A LITERARY MOVEMENT The event that unofficially kicked off the Harlem Renaissance as a literary movement was a dinner given on March 21, 1924. Some of the nation's most celebrated writers and thinkers, black and white, gathered at New York City's Civic Club. The sponsors of the dinner— an older generation of African-American intellectuals that included **W. E. B. Du Bois, James Weldon Johnson,** and **Charles S. Johnson**—had begun organizations such as the National Urban League and the National Association for the Advancement of Colored People to promote equality for African Americans. These organizations published journals in which the writings of a younger generation were first published. **Countee Cullen, Zora Neale Hurston,** and **Langston Hughes** were among the young writers who received recognition and sometimes cash awards for

The Migration of the Negro Panel no. 1 (1940–1941), Jacob Lawrence. Casein tempera on hardboard, 12" x 18". Acquired 1942. The Phillips Collection, Washington, D.C. © The Estate of Gwendolyn Knight Lawrence/Artist Rights Society (ARS), New York.

Jacob Lawrence

The Harlem Renaissance was not only a literary movement but a flourishing movement of the visual arts as well. Since it was difficult for black Americans of the day to attend art academies as their white counterparts did, the art schools and workshops of Harlem provided vital training for many of America's finest black artists. Jacob Lawrence was one of the first to be educated by the African-American community in Harlem.

Harlem as Muse Lawrence found inspiration in the streets of Harlem. His early work depicted the community—its people, sidewalks, streets, and storefronts—in bold colors and elemental shapes. He once said that 1930s "was actually a wonderful period in Harlem. . . . There was real vitality in the community." Lawrence rubbed elbows there with writers and artists such as Langston Hughes, Claude McKay, Romare Bearden, and Augusta Savage, all of whom emphasized their cultural identity in their work.

The Migration Series The painting shown here was the first in a 60-panel series on the Great Migration. It shows a crowd of Southern migrants about to embark on a journey to three Northern cities. Lawrence's decision to show no faces but only the shapes of hats and coats and luggage enhances the viewer's sense of a crowd surging as one entity toward the station. Lawrence based the paintings in this series on the experiences of his family and other members of his community who took part in the Great Migration.

THE ARTISTS' GALLERY

The parents of American artist Jacob Lawrence (1917–2000) joined the Great Migration northward at the close of World War I. Lawrence grew up hearing stories about the hope, poverty, and racism that drove his family and other blacks to leave their homes in the South. In 1940, Lawrence used grant money to give these stories form. Fittingly, the migration series begins and ends with a train station.

Activity Tell students that noted scholar Henry Louis Gates Jr. believed that Lawrence's series showed the inherent contradictions of hope and despair in the Great Migration. Ask students to cite evidence from the painting to support Gates's assessment. *Possible answer: Lawrence contrasts bright colors such as red and blue with dark colors such as black and brown. Also, nothing is visible beyond the gates. The people seem to be entering a vast nothingness.*

TIERED DISCUSSION PROMPTS

Use these prompts to begin discussion of **The Harlem Renaissance:**

Recall How did the neighborhood of Harlem become a focal point for African-American culture? *Possible answer: Harlem became a focal point for African-American culture because many Southern blacks migrated to New York looking for economic opportunity. They settled in Harlem, where they began to share their cultural heritage and creative interests.*

Analyze How might living in a neighborhood of African Americans have contributed to the Harlem Renaissance movement? *Possible answer: Living in a community of African Americans gave black men and women a sense of pride. Everyone in the community shared certain cultural values and so nurtured the expression of creative talent.*

FOR ADVANCED LEARNERS/AP

Research The Harlem Renaissance was not just a literary movement, it was a time of extraordinary creativity in all of the arts. Have students locate information about other Harlem Renaissance artists, such as musicians, actors, painters, and sculptors.

Topics for student research might include:

• composers and performers, such as Duke Ellington, Eubie Blake, Bessie Smith, and Ethel Waters

• painters and sculptors, such as Aaron Douglas, Jacob Lawrence, Romare Bearden, and Lois Mailou Jones

When students have completed their research, find opportunities to share their information with the class.

Use these prompts to continue discussion of **The Harlem Renaissance:**

Recall Despite differences in their backgrounds, what did the writers of the Harlem Renaissance share? *Possible answer: The writers of the Harlem Renaissance shared a deep pride in their heritage and cultural identity.*

Interpret What did Langston Hughes mean when he said that "jazz is a heartbeat"? *Possible answer: Hughes used this metaphor to suggest that jazz music is a life force. It is not an art that someone practices. Jazz must be lived.*

Evaluate Is writing literature an effective means of creating a cultural identity? Explain. *Possible answer: Literature is an effective means of creating a cultural identity because members of a culture can read about those living similar lives or with similar values and concerns.*

their work in these journals, and many were present at this "coming-out party" for the writers of the Harlem Renaissance.

These young writers considered themselves the founders of a new era in literature. They looked inward and expressed what it meant to be black in a white-dominated world. They represented what came to be called "the New Negro," a sophisticated and well-educated African American with strong racial pride and self-awareness. In fact, connections made at that dinner led to a popular and enduring anthology of writing, published in 1925, titled *The New Negro.*

MANY VOICES Yet this new generation of writers did not speak with only one voice. Harvard-educated **Countee Cullen,** for example, used a classical style to explore the black struggle. Others cast off more formal language and styles and wrote with the pulse of jazz rhythms. "Jazz is a heartbeat," wrote Langston Hughes, "and its heartbeat is yours." Some, like Jamaican-born **Claude McKay,** were militant. McKay's poem "If We Must Die," written after race riots in 1919, ends with an image of African Americans "pressed to the wall, dying, but fighting back!" Others, such as **Jean Toomer,** were more interested in exploring their own identities than the concerns of a whole race. "I was inescapably myself," he wrote. Despite their varied perspectives, however, these writers shared a deep pride in their heritage and asserted their cultural identity through their work.

The Harlem Renaissance was brought to a premature end by the economic collapse of the Great Depression. Many of the writers who had gathered in Harlem were forced to scatter and take other jobs to support themselves. Nevertheless, their work planted seeds that continue to generate important writing from the African-American perspective.

Zora Neale Hurston, Harlem Renaissance writer

Journalism as Literature

In the early decades of the 20th century, journalism came into its own as an influential part of the literary scene (see page 1092). The sensationalism and reckless misinterpretation of facts that had characterized journalism in the last decades of the 19th century were being replaced by an interest in stylistic quality and the recognition that there was more to news than scandal. Many of the writers who were to become major figures in American literature learned their craft—and developed some of their most compelling subjects—writing for newspapers or magazines.

REPORTING THE ERA Fresh out of high school in 1917, **Ernest Hemingway** worked as a reporter for the *Kansas City Star.* The newspaper's strict rules of

> ▶ *For Your Outline*
>
> **JOURNALISM AS LITERATURE**
> - Journalism turned from sensationalism.
> - Writers honed their craft at newspapers and magazines.
> - Hemingway, Porter, and Steinbeck reported on the day's big news.
> - White, Thurber, and Parker built their reputations at *New Yorker.*

FOR ADVANCED LEARNERS/AP

Compare Fiction and Nonfiction [small-group option] Have students locate nonfiction articles by Ernest Hemingway, Katherine Anne Porter, and John Steinbeck. Then direct them to fiction by each of these authors, such as the samples collected for the activity on page 870 or showcased on pages 1008, 1024, or 1034. After reading the samples, ask each group to focus on one writer. Have students compare the writer's fiction and nonfiction work.

Students should comment on these literary elements:

- subject
- style
- theme

Ask students to share their results with the class through short, informal oral presentations.

style helped him develop the clear, provocative prose that characterizes his work: "Use short sentences. Use short first paragraphs. Use vigorous English. Be positive, not negative." Hemingway was also a war correspondent who reported on the Spanish Civil War, and he was the first Allied journalist to enter Paris on August 25, 1944—the day it was liberated from Nazi control.

Some other writers who became well-known for their fiction produced fine journalism as well. **Katherine Anne Porter,** for example, worked for several newspapers and magazines. On assignment in 1920, she traveled to Mexico and arrived in the middle of a revolution. Her observations of this conflict later became the subject of several short stories in a collection called *Flowering Judas* (1930), which launched her literary career. **John Steinbeck** turned his hand to journalism as well, reporting in 1936 for the *San Francisco News* about the plight of California's migrant farm workers and working in 1943 as a war correspondent for the *New York Herald Tribune.*

MAGAZINES ON THE RISE In the first decades of the 20th century, the popular magazine came into its own as new magazines were created to satisfy every taste and interest. The *New Yorker,* which first appeared in 1925, was founded by one-time newspaperman **Harold Ross.** To staff his new magazine, Ross sought writers with newspaper experience, writers who could grind out "the gleams and sparkles of humor and satire from the grist of human nature and the news of the world." Among them were **E. B. White, James Thurber,** and **Dorothy Parker,** who went on to write poetry, short stories, and novels. Yet these writers' reputations as witty, satiric observers of contemporary society were built on the essays, commentary, and book and theater reviews (and in the case of Thurber, cartoons too) that they contributed to the *New Yorker.*

Like poetry and short stories, literary journalism continues to be popular. Today's writers can thank the innovators of the modernist movement, America's giants of the short story form, the groundbreaking writers of the Harlem Renaissance, and the literary journalists of this earlier era for many of the themes, styles, and forms currently in use.

> **A Voice from the Times**
>
> *This is not a novel to be tossed aside lightly. It should be thrown with great force.*
>
> —Dorothy Parker
> from a literary review

Mar. 4, 1933 — THE NEW YORKER — Price 15 cents

Herbert Hoover and Franklin Delano Roosevelt on the cover of the *New Yorker,* 1933

COMMON CORE FOCUS

RI 7 Integrate and evaluate multiple sources of information presented in different media or formats as well as in words in order to address a question or solve a problem.

Connecting Literature, History, and Culture

READING SKILL

COMMON CORE
RI 7

■ READ A TIMELINE

Point out that each of the three horizontal sections of the timeline—*American Literary Milestones, Historical Context, World Culture and Events*—displays a sequence of events that occurred between 1910 and 1940. By looking at the vertical columns on the timeline, students can see which events were going on at approximately the same time.

Have students locate, for example, each of these events on the timeline between 1910 and 1914:

- **1911** Marie Curie won the Nobel Prize for chemistry. (See *World Culture and Events*.)
- **1912** *Titanic* sank, killing more than 1,500 people. (See *Historical Context*.)
- **1913** Ezra Pound formed an imagist group of poets in London. (See *American Literary Milestones*.)

Ask students to identify events that occurred between 1936 and 1940. *Answer: Margaret Mitchell published* Gone with the Wind. *Zora Neale Hurston's* Their Eyes Were Watching God *was published. Richard Wright's* Native Son *was published. The Fair Labor Standards Act set a minimum wage and limited the workweek to 40 hours. Judy Garland starred in* The Wizard of Oz. *The Spanish Civil War broke out. Japan invaded China. World War II began with the German invasion of Poland.*

Connecting Literature, History, and Culture

The literature and culture of the United States during this period reflect developments occurring elsewhere in the world. Use the timeline and the questions on the next page to find connections.

AMERICAN LITERARY MILESTONES

1910	1915	1920
1912 Harriet Monroe founds *Poetry: A Magazine of Verse*; Edna St. Vincent Millay publishes "Renascence." 	**1915** Edgar Lee Masters examines small-town life in *Spoon River Anthology*.	**1920** Edith Wharton's *The Age of Innocence* is published.
1913 Ezra Pound forms a group of imagist poets in London.	**1916** Carl Sandburg publishes *Chicago Poems*.	**1921** Langston Hughes's poem "The Negro Speaks of Rivers" appears in *The Crisis* magazine.
	1919 Claude McKay publishes his militant "If We Must Die."	**1922** T. S. Eliot's *The Waste Land* captures modern sensibilities.
		1924 Robert Frost wins the first of his four Pulitzer Prizes.

HISTORICAL CONTEXT

1910	1915	1920
1911 The National Urban League is founded.	**1916** Jeannette Rankin of Montana becomes the first woman elected to the U.S. House of Representatives.	**1920** The 18th Amendment ushers in the era of Prohibition, and the 19th Amendment assures women of the right to vote.
1912 The *Titanic* sinks, killing more than 1,500 people.	**1917** The United States enters World War I. 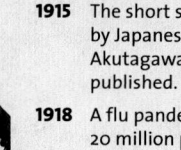	**1921** Albert Einstein presents a lecture in New York City about his theory of relativity. 
1913 The Armory Show in New York City introduces European modernist paintings and sculpture to shocked Americans.	**1919** Race riots break out in 25 U.S. cities.	**1924** Native Americans win full citizenship.

WORLD CULTURE AND EVENTS

1910	1915	1920
1911 Marie Curie wins the Nobel Prize in chemistry.	**1915** The short story "Rashomon" by Japanese modernist writer Akutagawa Ryunosuke is published.	**1922** James Joyce publishes his masterpiece, *Ulysses*.
1914 World War I begins with the assassination of Archduke Francis Ferdinand of Austria.	**1918** A flu pandemic kills more than 20 million people worldwide.	**1923** Sigmund Freud publishes *The Ego and the Id*, examining the causes of human behavior. 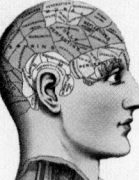
	1919 The Treaty of Versailles spells out the peace terms for the end of World War I.	

874   UNIT 5: THE HARLEM RENAISSANCE AND MODERNISM

DIFFERENTIATED INSTRUCTION

FOR STRUGGLING READERS

Understanding a Timeline Explain that the timeline runs chronologically (in time order) from left to right across the page. Each of the four columns represents a five-year period between 1910 and 1940. The three parallel rows of the timeline represent events occurring simultaneously. By comparing the three rows, readers can better understand what events in literature, history, and culture were taking place at about the same time.

MAKING CONNECTIONS

- Why was the year 1913 an important one for poetry and art?
- Violence stirred in the years between 1910 and 1940. Give an example from each of the three main sections of the timeline that support this observation.
- Name three women of this period who were gaining recognition or breaking barriers in literature, politics, and science.

COMMON CORE

RI 7 Integrate and evaluate multiple sources of information presented in different media or formats as well as in words in order to address a question or solve a problem.

1925	
1925	F. Scott Fitzgerald's *The Great Gatsby* explores the American dream.
1926	Ernest Hemingway's novel *The Sun Also Rises* chronicles expatriates after WWI.
1929	William Faulkner's *The Sound and the Fury* experiments with stream of consciousness and multiple viewpoints.

1930	
1930	*Flowering Judas* by Katherine Anne Porter is published. ▶
1932	Pearl S. Buck wins a Pulitzer Prize for *The Good Earth*.
1933	William Faulkner's *A Green Bough* is published.

1935	
1936	Margaret Mitchell publishes *Gone with the Wind*.
1937	Zora Neale Hurston's *Their Eyes Were Watching God* is published.
1940	Richard Wright's *Native Son* is published.

1925	
1927	Charles Lindbergh makes his historic solo nonstop flight from New York to Paris; the first talking movie, *The Jazz Singer*, stars Al Jolson.
1929	The Wall Street stock market crashes and the Great Depression begins. ▼

1930	
1931	The Empire State building is completed. ▶
1932	Franklin Delano Roosevelt is elected president for the first of his four terms.
1933	Roosevelt's New Deal tries to put Americans back to work.

1935	
1938	The Fair Labor Standards Act sets a minimum wage and limits the workweek to 40 hours.
1939	Judy Garland stars in *The Wizard of Oz*. ▼

1925	
1925	Virginia Woolf's innovative novel *Mrs. Dalloway* is published in England.
1928	Joseph Stalin becomes dictator of Communist Russia. Chiang Kai-shek becomes head of the Nationalist government in China.

1930	
1930	Mahatma Gandhi leads a nonviolent march to protest British taxes.
1932	Japan takes control of Manchuria.
1933	Adolf Hitler takes control of Germany.

1935	
1936	The Spanish Civil War breaks out.
1937	Japan invades China.
1939	World War II begins with the German invasion of Poland.

MAKING CONNECTIONS

Possible answers:

- *In 1913, Ezra Pound formed an imagist group of poets in London. In this same year, the Armory Show introduced European modernist paintings to a shocked America.*
- *These examples support the observation that violence stirred in the years between 1910 and 1940: Claude McKay published his militant "If We Must Die" (1919), the United States entered World War I (1917), and the Spanish Civil War broke out (1936).*
- *These women broke barriers or gained recognition: Zora Neale Hurston in literature, Jeanette Rankin in politics, and Marie Curie in science.*

ADDITIONAL QUESTIONS

1. The stream-of-consciousness technique employed by William Faulkner in *The Sound and the Fury*, published in 1929, may have been influenced by the publication of what work in 1923? ***Answer:*** *Sigmund Freud's* The Ego and the Id
2. The decadent American lifestyle chronicled in F. Scott Fitzgerald's *The Great Gatsby*, published in 1925, was undermined by what historic event in 1929? ***Answer:*** *the stock market crash*

FOR ADVANCED LEARNERS/AP

Making Additional Connections Ask students to choose one of the six time periods shown in the timeline and to research online, in encyclopedias, or in history texts other events that occurred during the five-year time span. Challenge students to identify events for each category: *American Literary Milestones, Historical Context,* and *World Culture and Events.* Have students prepare and present brief oral reports, summarizing significant events and discussing their connection to events shown in the timeline or discussed in class.

SL 1 Initiate and participate effectively in a range of collaborative discussions. **W 7** Conduct short research projects to answer a question. **W 10** Write routinely over shorter time frames for a range of tasks and purposes.

Mass Culture

Have students read the paragraph. (You may also want to ask students to review the section titled **New Directions** on page 867 of the historical essay.) Discuss the legacy of mass culture. Point out that it is nearly impossible for Americans to escape the effects—both positive and negative—of mass culture.

DISCUSS Have students suggest examples of mass culture. Make sure that students list examples from each of these categories:

- automobiles
- clothing
- electronics
- food
- media

Display students' examples on the board. Then have students agree on positive and negative effects to list in a two-column chart on the board. *Possible answers: Positive effects: speed, ease, efficiency; negative effects: materialism, conformity, intolerance.* Extend the discussion by asking students to suggest ways Americans could combat the negative effects of mass culture. Also, invite students to speculate on the future of American culture given the current trends in mass culture.

 BEST PRACTICES TOOLKIT—Transparency
Two-Column Chart p. A25

The Legacy of the Era

Mass Culture

COMMON CORE

SL 1 Initiate and participate effectively in a range of collaborative discussions. **W 7** Conduct short research projects to answer a question. **W 10** Write routinely over shorter time frames for a range of tasks and purposes.

Many American writers of the early 20th century were reacting against a rising mass culture and the conformity and materialism they saw as its inevitable effects. These writers would likely be astounded to see the extent to which mass culture has overtaken the United States today. From the restaurant business, with nationwide chains replacing family-owned places, to a fashion scene in which only a very few styles (and sizes) are considered desirable—mass culture is everywhere you look.

DISCUSS In small groups, brainstorm ten examples of our current mass culture. Then discuss what you see as the effects—positive and negative—of mass culture on our society as a whole.

DIFFERENTIATED INSTRUCTION

FOR STRUGGLING READERS
Vocabulary Support
- *inevitable,* "cannot be avoided"
- *astounded,* "suddenly surprised"

FOR ADVANCED LEARNERS/AP
Track Mass Culture Have students create a timeline showing how an aspect of mass culture such as audio technology has evolved. For example, one could trace the journey from LP records to MP3 players. Have students annotate their timelines with dates, illustrations, descriptions, and the positive and negative effects of each incarnation. Invite students to draw conclusions about the effects of their topic on American culture and then to share their work.

Trends in Journalism

Many of the best writers of the early 20th century, such as Ernest Hemingway, E. B. White, and William Faulkner, sharpened their skills writing for newspapers and magazines. Today there is no shortage of talented journalists, yet the nature of the business has changed. Thousands of newspapers and magazines—one for nearly every conceivable interest—are printed every day. Twenty-four-hour news stations and Web sites give minute-by-minute accounts of current events, and blogs allow people to respond personally to the news.

QUICKWRITE With all of the venues available for today's writers to publish their ideas, how much of it is worthwhile literature? Is some simply a lot of hot air? Write several paragraphs sharing your opinions about today's journalists and the everyday people who, thanks to the Internet, can reach the masses with their words.

The New Deal Today

Several of President Roosevelt's New Deal programs remain in place today: Social Security (to pay out retirement pensions), the FDIC (to insure bank deposits), agricultural price supports (to protect farmers from price devaluation), and the SEC (to regulate the stock market). Yet some of these long-running programs have become politically controversial in today's world.

RESEARCH With a partner, research one of these programs. Summarize for your class why the program is politically controversial, what suggestions have been made to reform or eliminate it, and your opinion of its merit.

Trends in Journalism

Have students read the paragraph. Ask volunteers to summarize the text, explaining in their own words the prevalence of media in contemporary American culture.

QUICKWRITE Have students work in small groups to brainstorm the criteria for "worthwhile literature." Invite a spokesperson from each group to contribute ideas to a class rubric for "worthwhile literature." Then provide student groups with examples of media text from different sources, or have students contribute examples. Have students compare each example with the class rubric to determine its value. Encourage students to use these ideas and examples as they write their paragraphs.

The New Deal Today

Have students read the paragraph. Discuss what role the federal government should play in these areas: retirement, money and the economy, and agriculture. Extend the discussion by adding other topics to the list such as education and healthcare.

RESEARCH As students research their topics, recommend that they consult encyclopedias, Internet sites, and history texts. Suggest that students record their notes in a Three-Column Journal with these headings: *Controversy, Suggestions for Reform or Elimination,* and *Merit.* Remind students that their opinions regarding merit should be based on solid reasons, examples, and evidence.

BEST PRACTICES TOOLKIT—Transparency Three-Column Journal p. B10

FOR STRUGGLING READERS
Vocabulary Support
- *conceivable,* "that can be understood, imagined, or believed"
- *blogosphere,* "the environment, or 'world,' of Internet sites where people can post and exchange ideas"
- *venues,* "media outlets, such as the Internet, books, magazines, or newspapers"
- *controversial,* "likely to invite argument or disagreement"

FOR ADVANCED LEARNERS/AP
Write to Congress Have students use their research to write informed letters to their local Congressional members regarding the future of these continuing New Deal programs. Instruct students to express their opinions in business letter format and to use formal language. Encourage students to send their letters by mail or e-mail and to share any responses that they receive with the class.

Focus and Motivate

COMMON CORE FOCUS

RL 4 Determine the meaning of words and phrases as they are used in the text, including figurative and connotative meanings. **RL 5** Analyze how an author's choices concerning how to structure specific parts of a text contribute to its overall structure and meaning as well as its aesthetic impact.

ABOUT THE POET

After students read about Langston Hughes, recap main points, noting his focus on African-American experiences, his direct language, and his incorporation of musical structures and rhythms. Connect these points to the poems students will read. In "Harlem," Hughes captures the fragmented, clashing images of life in Harlem through the riffs and rhythms of bebop jazz. In "The Negro Speaks of Rivers," he forges a human connection among various world cultures. In "I, Too," Hughes addresses the evils of segregation. In "The Weary Blues," he fuses early blues with the conventions of formal poetry.

NOTABLE QUOTE

"Humor is laughing at what you haven't got when you ought to have it."
  —Langston Hughes

Ask students what Hughes meant about the role humor can play in helping people face challenges.

Selection Resources

COMMON CORE

RL 4 Determine the meaning of words and phrases as they are used in the text, including figurative and connotative meanings. **RL 5** Analyze how an author's choices concerning how to structure specific parts of a text contribute to its overall structure and meaning as well as its aesthetic impact.

DID YOU KNOW?

Langston Hughes . . .

- was one of the first African Americans to earn a living solely from writing.
- was dubbed the "poet low-rate" of Harlem by some African-American intellectuals.
- wrote radio jingles during World War II to promote the purchase of war bonds.

The Harlem Renaissance

Selected Poetry
by Langston Hughes   *Essential Course of Study*

VIDEO TRAILER THINK central KEYWORD: HML11-878A

Meet the Author

Langston Hughes 1902–1967

Langston Hughes was one of the leading poets of the Harlem Renaissance as well as an accomplished novelist, playwright, and essayist. His writings center on poor and working-class African Americans, a group whom literature had generally ignored.

Early Inspirations James Mercer Langston Hughes started writing poetry in seventh grade, when his classmates elected him class poet. He admired the work of Paul Laurence Dunbar and Carl Sandburg, two poets known for their efforts to capture the voices of everyday Americans. After graduating from high school, Hughes went to live with his father in Mexico, where he became fluent in Spanish. On the train journey south, he composed what would become one of his most famous poems, "The Negro Speaks of Rivers."

Busboy Poet In 1921, Hughes enrolled at Columbia University in New York City. He left after one year to travel the world as a cook's assistant aboard a ship. In 1925, Hughes settled in Washington, D.C., and took a job busing tables at a hotel restaurant. One day Vachel Lindsay, a well-known poet, came to the hotel. Hughes mustered the courage to slip three of his poems, including "The Weary Blues," beside Lindsay's plate. Lindsay liked the poems, and the next morning's newspapers reported Lindsay's discovery of the "busboy poet."

A year later, Hughes published his first poetry collection, *The Weary Blues.* His gritty depiction of "workers, roustabouts, and singers and job hunters" angered some African-American critics who felt that members of the race should always be portrayed in the best possible light. Hughes responded to these criticisms, saying, "I knew only the people I had grown up with, and they weren't people whose shoes were always shined. . . . But they seemed to me good people, too."

Poet Laureate of Harlem As a poet, Hughes kept his language direct; he made no attempt to be obscure or pretentious. He celebrated the lively nightlife and the everyday experiences of working-class African Americans, often re-creating the structures and rhythms of blues and jazz music in works such as *Montage of a Dream Deferred* (1951), a book-length suite of related poems. Hughes became informally known as the Poet Laureate of Harlem and today is universally recognized as the most influential voice of the Harlem Renaissance.

Author Online THINK central
Go to **thinkcentral.com.** KEYWORD: HML11-878B

878

---

*See resources on the **Teacher One Stop DVD-ROM** and on **thinkcentral.com**.*

 RESOURCE MANAGER UNIT 5
Plan and Teach, pp. 9–16
Text Analysis and Reading
  Skill, pp. 17–20†*

DIAGNOSTIC AND SELECTION TESTS
Selection Tests, pp. 221–224

 BEST PRACTICES TOOLKIT
Comparison Matrix, p. A24
T Chart, p. A25

INTERACTIVE READER

ADAPTED INTERACTIVE READER

ELL ADAPTED INTERACTIVE READER

TECHNOLOGY
- **Teacher One Stop DVD-ROM**
- **Student One Stop DVD-ROM**
- **PowerNotes DVD-ROM**
- **Audio Anthology CD**
- **ExamView Test Generator**
  on the **Teacher One Stop**

Video Trailer THINK central

Go to **thinkcentral.com** to preview the **Video Trailer** introducing this selection. Other features that support the selection include
- **PowerNotes** presentation
- **ThinkAloud** models to enhance comprehension
- **WordSharp** vocabulary tutorials
- interactive writing and grammar instruction

---

* **Resources for Differentiation**   † **Also in Spanish**   ‡ **In Haitian Creole and Vietnamese**

TEXT ANALYSIS: SPEAKER

You know that the **speaker** of a poem, like the narrator of a story, is the voice that talks to the reader. In his poems, Langston Hughes created speakers who represented important aspects of African-American culture. Sometimes his speaker is the voice of the culture itself.

I've known rivers ancient as the world and older than the flow of human blood in human veins.

Hughes also uses his speakers to portray the joys and struggles of working-class African Americans.

*In a deep song voice with a melancholy tone
I heard that Negro sing, that old piano moan—*

As you read each poem, try to identify the speaker of the poem and what aspects of African-American life the speaker describes.

READING SKILL: ANALYZE RHYTHM AND REPETITION

When Hughes began writing, most African-American poets tried to sound like the white poets they read in school. Instead, Hughes drew his inspiration from jazz and blues music, using the rhythm and repetition of these musical forms to structure his poetry. Musical elements found in Hughes's poetry include

- jazz-influenced **rhythm** (the pattern of stressed and unstressed syllables) that features strong accents, quick changes in rhythm, and irregular beats
- rhythmic **repetition** of words and phrases, like that used in blues lyrics
- the **refrain,** one or more repeated lines of poetry that function like the chorus of a song

As you read each poem, use a chart like the one shown to record examples of these musical patterns.

Rhythm	Repetition	Refrain

 Complete the activities in your **Reader/Writer Notebook**.

What shapes your IDENTITY?

Hughes wrote poetry to honor his African-American heritage, but he didn't limit himself to great heroes and historical events. For Hughes, it was the vibrant culture of everyday people— their music, their slang, and their experiences of life in the city—that shaped his sense of identity.

DISCUSS What everyday experiences help shape your identity? List images and activities that characterize the way you live: the sounds and smells of your neighborhood, the places you go, the foods you eat, and so on. In a small group, compare your answers. Which experiences, if any, do group members have in common?

879

Practice and Apply

SUMMARY

Drawing on the rhythms of 1940s bebop jazz, this poem expresses the festering tension felt by African Americans unable to realize their dreams.

READ WITH A PURPOSE

Help students set a purpose for reading Hughes's poems. Tell them to note what the poet says about African-American identity.

READING SKILL   COMMON CORE
                            RL 5

A *Model the Skill:* **RHYTHM AND REPETITION**

Tell students they will find patterns of stress by emphasizing certain syllables. Then read the poem aloud, emphasizing these accented syllables: *RAIsin / FESter / ROTten / SUgar / SYRupy.* Then ask students to write down the words that are emphasized by the rhythm. **Possible answers: *words emphasized:*** *dry / raisin, sun / fester, sore / then run / does, stink, rotten, meat / crust, sugar / syrupy, sweet.*

Extend the Discussion Describe the rhythm and the feelings it evokes. If you marked the lines differently, explain your variation. **Possible answer:** *The rhythm is disjointed as well as fast and abrupt. This rhythm evokes feelings of tension, dissatisfaction, anger, or anxiety. Students with different line markings should be able to explain what they hear.*

ANSWERS

1. **Possible answer:** *A dream deferred is one that remains unrealized. In this case, the speaker may mean the promise of social equality.*

2. **Possible answer:** *The poem's last line hints at an outbreak of violence.*

3. **Possible answer: Similes:** *"like a raisin in the sun" (line 3), "like a sore" (line 4), "like rotten meat" (line 6), "like a syrupy sweet" (line 8), "like a heavy load" (line 10). The similes may reveal the speaker's bitterness or disgust toward the current social situation and the endless delays in improving it.*

Harlem

Langston Hughes

What happens to a dream deferred?

    Does it dry up
    like a raisin in the sun?
    Or fester like a sore—
5   And then run?
    Does it stink like rotten meat?
    Or crust and sugar over—
    like a syrupy sweet? **A**

    Maybe it just sags
10   like a heavy load.

    Or does it explode?

Analyze Visuals ▶
What elements of this painting help capture the thriving street life in Harlem?

A **RHYTHM AND REPETITION**
Identify the pattern of stresses in lines 2–8. Which words are emphasized by this rhythm?

Text Analysis

1. **Clarify** What does the speaker mean by "a dream deferred"?

2. **Make Inferences** What social or political consequences are hinted at in the poem's last line?

3. **Interpret Figurative Language** List the **similes** the speaker uses to describe the effect of a deferred dream. What do these comparisons reveal about the speaker's attitude?

Street Shadows (1959), Jacob Lawrence. Egg tempera on hardboard, 24″ × 30″. Private collection, New York. Photograph courtesy of Gwendolyn Knight Lawrence/Art Resource, New York. © 2008 The Jacob and Gwendolyn Lawrence Foundation, Seattle/ Artists Rights Society (ARS), New York.

DIFFERENTIATED INSTRUCTION

FOR ENGLISH LANGUAGE LEARNERS

The compressed language of the poem may impede students' understanding. After you establish that "a dream deferred" means *a dream that hasn't come true,* substitute that phrase for the word *it* the first time the word appears in the poem. Have students continue substituting these words, or their own paraphrase, each time *it* appears. Then have students read aloud the poem as it appears on the page.

FOR ADVANCED LEARNERS/AP

Have students use one or more of Hughes's poems as the basis for a drawing, painting, collage, or video to be placed on view. Ask students to prepare remarks about the specific lines, images, or rhythms that inspired their work.

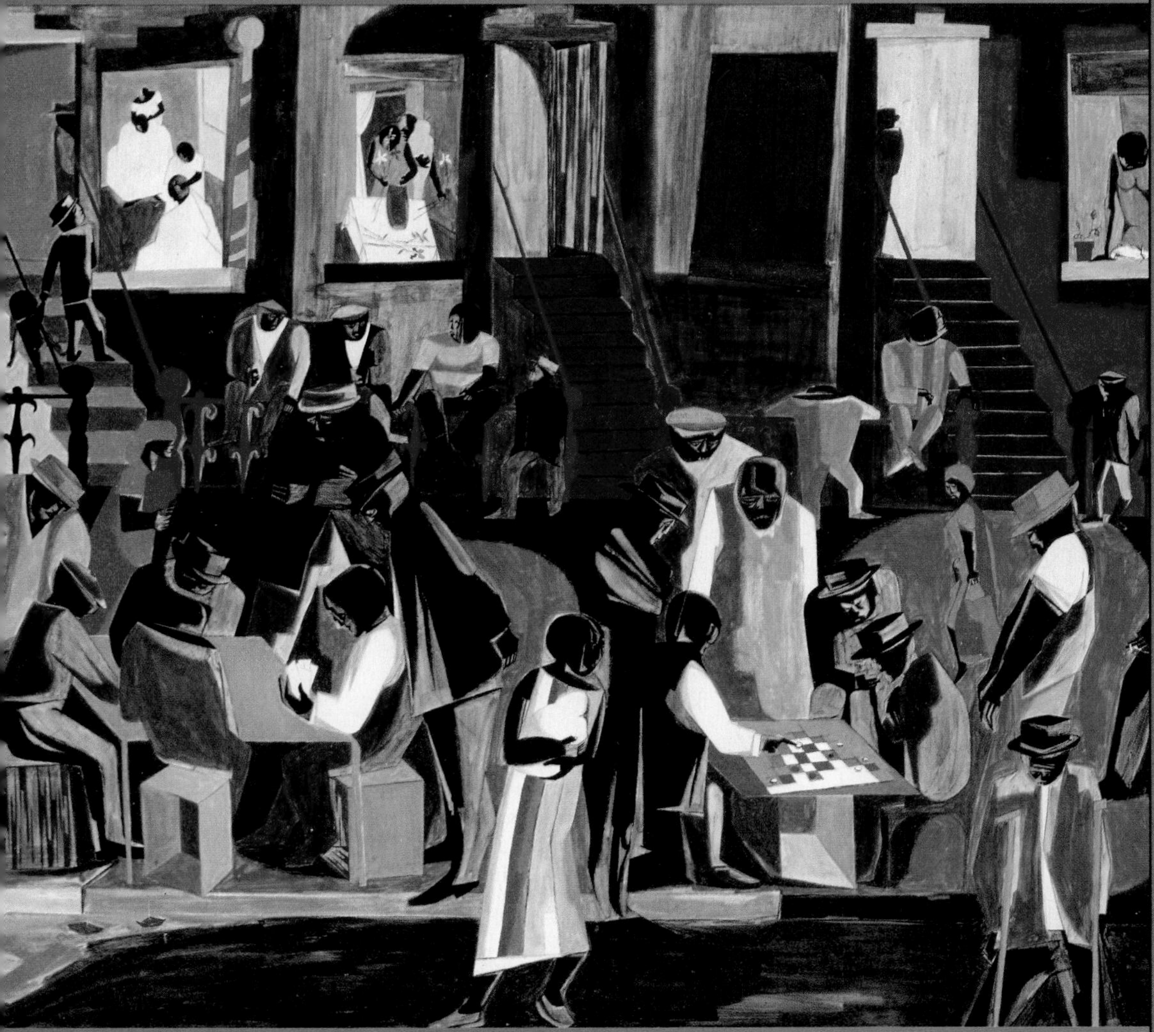

Reading Support

This selection on **thinkcentral.com.** includes embedded **ThinkAloud** models–students "thinking aloud" about the story to model the kinds of questions a good reader would ask about a selection.

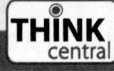

Analyze Visuals

TIERED DISCUSSION PROMPTS

Use these prompts to help students understand the effect of deferred dreams as described in lines 1–11 :

Connect Describe a dream or goal that you have that has not yet been realized. How do you feel about the situation and why? *Accept all thoughtful responses.*

Interpret What is the poem's main message or theme? ***Possible answer:*** *If dreams are denied, serious or even violent consequences can happen.*

Evaluate Do you agree or disagree with the speaker's opinion regarding the impact of deferred dreams? Explain. *Students may agree by citing examples regarding the destructive effects of dreams that are lost or postponed. Others may say that deferred dreams inspire people to work harder.*

Possible answer: *The thriving street life of Harlem is conveyed through Lawrence's use of color, shape, and composition. The warm reds, yellows, and oranges interact with the cool blues, suggesting motion and energy. Both the windows in the background and the street in the foreground are crowded, suggesting an active community life.*

About the Art American artist Jacob Lawrence (1917–2000) loved to paint the neighborhoods and streets of New York City. As Langston Hughes invites readers into the African-American experience with his words, Jacob Lawrence invites viewers to participate in its movement, sound, and liveliness.

FOR STRUGGLING READERS

Concept Support: Rhythm [paired option] Explain that "Harlem" draws on the rhythm of 1940s bebop jazz. Traditional jazz often includes syncopation, rhythm accents, and improvisation. Bebop jazz moves beyond these, speeding up the pace of rhythmic change and including more complex melodies. Play some examples of bebop jazz for students and have pairs take turns reading "Harlem" aloud as the music plays.

FOR ADVANCED LEARNERS/AP

Compare Literary Texts Refer students back to the events that Frederick Douglass recounts in his *Narrative,* found on pages 560–569. Ask them to discuss the ways in which Douglass's triumph over Covey, an event that "rekindled the few expiring embers of freedom" (line 244), describes Hughes's prediction of what happens to a dream deferred.

In this poem, the speaker is the voice of African-American culture with its ancient connection to the earth and all of humanity.

TEXT ANALYSIS
COMMON CORE
RL 5

B *Model the Skill:* **SPEAKER**

Read the lines aloud slowly and carefully to model how to interpret the speaker.

- Point out that choosing *known* instead of the more expected *seen* suggests that the speaker feels a deep connection with the rivers and with the history in which those waters played a part.

Ask students to identify other word choices that give clues about the speaker. *Possible answer:* The speaker talks of African Americans' spiritual depth and their connections to rivers and civilizations of the Middle East, Africa, and America.

READING SKILL
COMMON CORE
RL 5

C **RHYTHM AND REPETITION**

Answer: The refrain is "I've known rivers" (lines 1, 11)

REVISIT THE BIG QUESTION

What shapes your
IDENTITY?

Discuss What do the poem's images convey about the speaker's sense of identity? *Possible answer:* Images of ancient civilizations and rivers from around the world suggest that the speaker embraces an identity encompassing time and place.

The **Negro Speaks** *of* **Rivers**

Langston Hughes

The Negro Speaks of Rivers (1998), Phoebe Beasley. Silkscreen. © Phoebe Beasley.

I've known rivers:
I've known rivers ancient as the world and older than the
   flow of human blood in human veins. **B**

My soul has grown deep like the rivers.

I bathed in the Euphrates[1] when dawns were young.
5 I built my hut near the Congo and it lulled me to sleep.
I looked upon the Nile and raised the pyramids above it.
I heard the singing of the Mississippi when Abe Lincoln
   went down to New Orleans,[2] and I've seen its muddy
   bosom turn all golden in the sunset.

I've known rivers:
Ancient, dusky[3] rivers.

10 My soul has grown deep like the rivers. **C**

B **SPEAKER**
Reread lines 1–2. What traits of the speakers are emphasized by Hughes's word choice?

C **RHYTHM AND REPETITION**
Reread the poem. Which line serves as the poem's **refrain?**

---

1. **Euphrates** (yōō-frā'tēz): a river flowing through present-day Turkey, Syria, and Iraq. The valley between the Tigris and Euphrates rivers was the site of one of the world's earliest civilizations.
2. **when Abe Lincoln went down to New Orleans:** Lincoln's first glimpse of the horrors of slavery reportedly came on his trip to New Orleans as a young man.
3. **dusky:** dark; shadowy.

882 UNIT 5: THE HARLEM RENAISSANCE AND MODERNISM

DIFFERENTIATED INSTRUCTION

FOR STRUGGLING READERS

Comprehension Support Have students locate these rivers on world maps: the Euphrates, the Congo, the Nile, and the Mississippi. Clarify that the rivers are in places around the world. Then help students link the first-person speaker to each place and river in the poem. Lead them to identify the speaker as the voice of African-American culture.

FOR ADVANCED LEARNERS/AP

Compare and Contrast Point out that Phoebe Beasley's painting has the same title as Hughes's poem. Invite students to compare and contrast the two works: Is the artwork a literal illustration of the poem or an interpretation of its ideas? Have students use a Comparison Matrix to discuss features such as character, setting, theme, sensory details, and symbolism.

BEST PRACTICES TOOLKIT—Transparency
Comparison Matrix p. A24

I, Too

Langston Hughes

I, too, sing America.

I am the darker brother.
They send me to eat in the kitchen
When company comes,
5 But I laugh,
And eat well,
And grow strong. **D**

Tomorrow,
I'll be at the table
10 When company comes.
Nobody'll dare
Say to me,
"Eat in the kitchen,"
Then.

15 Besides,
They'll see how beautiful I am
And be ashamed—

I, too, am America.

D SPEAKER
Reread lines 1–7. Identify the speaker of the poem. What aspects of the African-American experience does the speaker describe?

Text Analysis

1. **Summarize** In "I, Too," what is the speaker's attitude toward America?

2. **Interpret Imagery** What is the significance of the four rivers mentioned in "The Negro Speaks of Rivers"?

3. **Compare and Contrast Speakers** What qualities do the speakers of both poems share? In what ways are they different?

SUMMARY

This poem is a protest that asserts the right of African Americans to sit equally at the metaphoric table of American society.

BACKGROUND

"I, Too" is Hughes's response to Walt Whitman's "I Hear America Singing." Hughes was a great admirer of Whitman, believing that Whitman's work reflected the real meaning of democracy—a democracy without the racial discrimination addressed in much of Hughes's work.

TEXT ANALYSIS

COMMON CORE
RL 5

D SPEAKER

Possible answer: The speaker is the voice of the African-American community and describes that community's common experience with discrimination, segregation, and social inequality.

ANSWERS

1. *Possible answer: The speaker is critical of segregation and racism but considers himself to be a part of American culture.*

2. *Possible answer: The Euphrates signifies Mesopotamia, the cradle of civilization. The Congo signifies Africa, where the slaves were captured. The Nile signifies Egypt, where the pyramids were built. The Mississippi signifies the southern United States, the seat of slavery in the U.S.*

   IF STUDENTS NEED HELP . . . Refer them to history books or encyclopedias for basic information about the four rivers.

3. *Possible answer: Both speakers have an awareness of suffering, an outside perspective, and cultural pride. In "The Negro Speaks of Rivers," the speaker identifies with all of humanity. In "I, Too," the speaker defines himself as American.*

FOR STRUGGLING READERS

Clarify Meaning: Figurative Language Point out that Hughes uses an extended metaphor in "I, Too." Remind students that a metaphor compares two unrelated objects without the words *like* or *as*. An extended metaphor maintains the comparison throughout a passage. Help students interpret the metaphors of the kitchen and the dining room table and recognize that these are symbols of segregation in American society.

FOR STRUGGLING READERS

Develop Reading Fluency Use the conversational tone of "I, Too," to give students practice reading aloud in a natural voice. Have pairs of students read the poem as though they were telling it to one another. Remind them to pause to observe punctuation and to say the line that is in quotation marks in a slightly different voice to signify that it is a statement being made *to* the speaker, not *by* the speaker.

SUMMARY

This poem expresses admiration for the blues and its musicians. Hughes's rhythm recalls the syncopation common in blues music.

RHYTHM AND REPETITION

Possible answer: *Examples of repetition include "he did a lazy sway" (lines 6, 7), "Thump, thump, thump" (line 23), and "Blues!" (lines 11, 14, and 16). "Blues!" is also the poem's refrain.*

IF STUDENTS NEED HELP . . . Work with them to record examples of musical patterns in the prereading chart introduced on page 879.

Rhythm	Repetition	Refrain
free verse mixed with rhyme	"He did a lazy sway."	"O Blues!" "Sweet Blues!"

SELECTION WRAP–UP

READ WITH A PURPOSE Ask students to think about what the poet shares in these works about African-American identity. ***Possible answer:*** *The poet addresses the struggle to end oppression while not succumbing to despair. The poems also address the vitality, or rhythm, of life.*

INDEPENDENT READING

Students might enjoy *Bronx Masquerade* by Nikki Grimes, who writes of a high school class exploring their ethnicities.

Droning a drowsy syncopated[1] tune,
Rocking back and forth to a mellow croon,
    I heard a Negro play.
Down on Lenox Avenue[2] the other night
5 By the pale dull pallor[3] of an old gas light
    He did a lazy sway. . . .
    He did a lazy sway. . . .
To the tune o' those Weary Blues.
With his ebony hands on each ivory key
10 He made that poor piano moan with melody.
    O Blues!
Swaying to and fro on his rickety stool
He played that sad raggy tune like a musical fool.
    Sweet Blues!
15 Coming from a black man's soul.
    O Blues!
In a deep song voice with a melancholy tone
I heard that Negro sing, that old piano moan—
    "Ain't got nobody in all this world,
20   Ain't got nobody but ma self.
    I's gwine to quit ma frownin'
    And put ma troubles on the shelf."
Thump, thump, thump, went his foot on the floor.
He played a few chords then he sang some more—
25   "I got the Weary Blues
    And I can't be satisfied.
    Got the Weary Blues
    And can't be satisfied—
    I ain't happy no mo'
30   And I wish that I had died."
And far into the night he crooned that tune.
The stars went out and so did the moon.
The singer stopped playing and went to bed
While the Weary Blues echoed through his head.
35 He slept like a rock or a man that's dead.

---

1. **syncopated** (sĭng′kə-pā′tĭd): characterized by a shifting of stresses from normally strong to normally weak beats.
2. **Lenox Avenue:** a main north-south street in Harlem.
3. **pallor** (păl′ər): lack of color.

COMMON CORE RL 4

Language Coach

Connotation The images or feelings you connect to a word add a finer shade of meaning, called **connotation**. *Croon* (line 2) means "soft, sentimental song." What other words in lines 1–2 share *croon's* calm connotations?

RHYTHM AND REPETITION

Identify three examples of repetition in the poem thus far. Which line or phrase might be considered the poem's refrain?

DIFFERENTIATED INSTRUCTION

FOR STRUGGLING READERS

Cause and Effect In three of the four poems, racial discrimination affects the speaker's sense of identity. Help students use T Charts to isolate this aspect of the works.

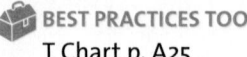 **BEST PRACTICES TOOLKIT—Transparency** T Chart p. A25

Poem	Effect on Speaker
Harlem	stifled dreams; could lead to violence
I, Too	strong; confident will end
The Weary Blues	empathy for musician and any oppressed

FOR ENGLISH LANGUAGE LEARNERS

Language Coach

COMMON CORE RL 4

Connotation ***Possible answer:*** *"droning," "rocking," "mellow"* Ask students to identify feelings that arise while reading the poem and to list the words whose connotations support the feeling.

Comprehension

1. **Clarify** What hope does the speaker of "I, Too" express?

2. **Recall** Who are the individuals described in "The Weary Blues"?

3. **Summarize** What happens to the speaker of "The Weary Blues"?

Text Analysis

4. **Identify Sensory Details** Many of Hughes's poems are rich in details that appeal to the five senses. Reread "Harlem" and "The Weary Blues." For each poem, use a chart like the one shown to record examples of each kind of sensory detail. Which example did you find especially vivid? Explain your answer.

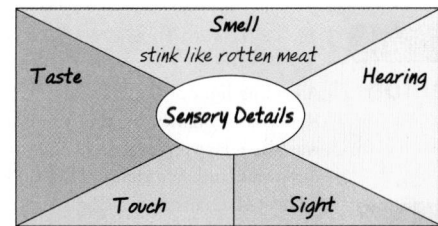

5. **Analyze Rhythm and Repetition** Review the chart you created while reading. Which poem is most influenced by jazz music? Cite examples from the poem.

6. **Draw Conclusions About Author's Perspective** Use the events, situations, and ideas presented in each of Hughes's poems to draw conclusions about his views on African-American identity. In Hughes's eyes, what characteristics define African-American culture?

7. **Evaluate Speakers** Consider the four poems you read. In your opinion, which speaker best achieves each of the following goals? Cite details from the poems in your answers.

   - captures Hughes's pride in African-American culture
   - reflects the everyday life of African Americans
   - conveys the sounds of African-American speech

Text Criticism

8. **Critical Interpretations** In a review of Hughes's poetry collection *The Weary Blues,* poet Countee Cullen criticized Hughes for "too much emphasis on strictly Negro themes" and questioned whether jazz poems belong to "that select and austere circle of high literary expression which we call poetry." Do you agree with Cullen's concerns? Why or why not?

What shapes your **IDENTITY**?

Much of Langston Hughes's **identity** was shaped by his environment. How did he feel about the people and places he wrote about in his poetry? Explain your answer using examples from Hughes's poems.

6. *African-American culture has hardship, sorrow, injustice, ancient wisdom, strength, and a love of music.*

7. ● **COMMON CORE FOCUS Speakers** *"The Negro Speaks of Rivers" best captures Hughes's pride in African-American culture because it recognizes the connection among all of humanity. "I, Too" best reflects the everyday life of African Americans because it chronicles discrimination. "The Weary Blues" best conveys the sounds of African-American speech because it includes dialect.*

8. *Cullen's concerns are invalid, because they ignore the cultural aspect of all literature and the musical aspect of all poetry.*

What shapes your **IDENTITY**?

Ask students to think of the places Hughes names in his poems and the people he describes. Are they treated with respect or indifference?

For preliminary support of post-reading questions, use these copy masters:

R RESOURCE MANAGER—Copy Masters
Speaker p. 17
Question Support p. 21

Additional selection questions are provided for teachers on page 13.

ANSWERS

COMMON CORE RL 4, RL 5

1. *The speaker expresses the hope that he will one day be recognized as an equal member of American society.*

2. *The speaker describes an African-American piano player.*

3. *The speaker listens to the piano player sing the blues until the player goes home.*

Possible answers:

4. *"Harlem": **hearing:** "explode"; **sight:** "fester like a sore,"; **touch:** "sags like a heavy load"; **taste:** "syrupy sweet"; **smell:** "stink like rotten meat." "The Weary Blues": **hearing:** "droning . . . syncopated tune," "thump"; **sight:** "pale dull pallor;" students should explain their choice of vivid detail*

5. ● **COMMON CORE FOCUS Analyze Rhythm and Repetition** *Like jazz music, "Harlem" has strong accents, quick changes in rhythm, and irregular beats.*

Assess

DIAGNOSTIC AND SELECTION TESTS
Selection Test A pp. 221–222
Selection Test B/C pp. 223–224

Interactive Selection Test on thinkcentral.com

Reteach

Level Up Online Tutorials on thinkcentral.com
Reteaching Worksheets on thinkcentral.com

Literature Lesson 18: Speaker and Persona
Literature Lesson 20: Rhythm and Meter

COMMON CORE

RL 4 Determine the meaning of words and phrases as they are used in the text, including figurative and connotative meanings. RL 5 Analyze how an author's choices concerning how to structure specific parts of a text contribute to its overall structure and meaning as well as its aesthetic impact.

Focus and Motivate

COMMON CORE FOCUS

RL 5 Analyze how an author's choices concerning how to structure specific parts of a text contribute to its overall structure and meaning as well as its aesthetic impact. **RL 9** Demonstrate knowledge of early-twentieth-century works of American literature, including how two or more texts from the same period treat similar themes or topics.

ABOUT THE POETS

James Weldon Johnson After students read about Johnson, note the poet's restlessness and his work in New York. Then point out the title "My City." Ask what *My* suggests about New York's effect on the poet. *Possible answer: The city has captured Johnson's restless spirit.*

Claude McKay After students read about McKay, explain that the title "If We Must Die" suggests the need to commit fully to a cause. Link this idea to Churchill's interest in the poem, clarifying that Britain faced attack by the Nazis and needed people's full commitment to resistance.

NOTABLE QUOTE

"The world does not know that a people is great until that people produces great literature and art." —**James Weldon Johnson**

"If a man is not faithful to his own individuality, he cannot be loyal to anything." —**Claude McKay**

Selection Resources

The Harlem Renaissance

COMMON CORE

RL 5 Analyze how an author's choices concerning how to structure specific parts of a text contribute to its overall structure and meaning as well as its aesthetic impact. **RL 9** Demonstrate knowledge of early-twentieth-century works of American literature, including how two or more texts from the same period treat similar themes or topics.

My City
Poem by James Weldon Johnson

If We Must Die
Poem by Claude McKay

Meet the Authors

James Weldon Johnson
1871–1938

A leading light of the Harlem Renaissance, James Weldon Johnson was also a lawyer, teacher, songwriter, diplomat, and civil rights activist. He dedicated his life to fighting prejudice and inspiring African Americans to new heights of social and literary achievement.

Unstoppable Talent After graduating from Atlanta University in 1894, Johnson worked as a school principal, founded a daily newspaper, and became the first African-American lawyer since Reconstruction to be admitted to the Florida bar. In 1901, the restless Johnson traveled to New York, where he and his younger brother became successful Broadway songwriters. One of their early songs, "Lift Every Voice and Sing," eventually became known as the African-American national anthem.

Renaissance Man Johnson also published works in many genres of literature. Among his best-known works are his novel *The Autobiography of an Ex-Colored Man,* his poetry collection *God's Trombones,* and a cultural history, *Black Manhattan.* He also edited several groundbreaking collections of African-American poetry and spirituals.

Claude McKay
c. 1890–1948

Hailed by James Weldon Johnson as "the poet of rebellion," Jamaican-born Festus Claudius McKay made his name as a fierce critic of racism in the United States. His poetry collection *Harlem Shadows,* published in 1922, is considered one of the founding works of the Harlem Renaissance.

Poet of Rebellion Already established as a poet, 23-year-old McKay arrived in the United States in 1912. In 1919, the country was torn apart by a wave of violent attacks against African Americans. Racial tensions erupted into 26 riots across the country during a period known as the Red Summer.

"If We Must Die" was McKay's anguished response, which became instantly popular among African Americans.

Enduring Message During World War II, the poem took on new meaning when British Prime Minister Sir Winston Churchill quoted from it during a speech. The poem went on to become a battle cry for the Allies in their fight against the Nazis. McKay often complained that the fame of this one poem had overshadowed his other work, which included the novels *Home to Harlem* and *Banana Bottom.*

Author Online
Go to **thinkcentral.com**. KEYWORD: HML11-886

THINK central

886

See resources on the **Teacher One Stop DVD-ROM** and on **thinkcentral.com**.

 **RESOURCE MANAGER UNIT 5**
Plan and Teach, pp. 23–30
Text Analysis and Reading
Skill, pp. 31–34†*

DIAGNOSTIC AND SELECTION TESTS
Selection Tests, pp. 225–228

 **BEST PRACTICES TOOLKIT**

TECHNOLOGY
- **Teacher One Stop DVD-ROM**
- **Student One Stop DVD-ROM**
- **Audio Anthology CD**
- **ExamView Test Generator** on the **Teacher One Stop**

---

* Resources for Differentiation   † Also in Spanish   ‡ In Haitian Creole and Vietnamese

TEXT ANALYSIS: SONNET

New ideas help keep poetic traditions alive. The centuries-old **sonnet**, a 14-line lyric poem with specific patterns of rhythm and rhyme, has been reimagined by many poets. The poems in this lesson are based on two classic types of sonnets.

- The **Italian**, or **Petrarchan**, **sonnet** is divided into two metrics: an **octave**, or eight-line grouping, and a **sestet**, or six-line grouping. The usual rhyme scheme for the octave is *abbaabba*. The rhyme scheme for the sestet varies but is often *cdccde* or *cdccdc*.

- The **English**, or **Shakespearean**, **sonnet** has a rhyme scheme of *abab cdcd efef gg*. This divides the poem into four distinct line groups: three **quatrains**, or four-line units, followed by a **couplet**, a pair of rhymed lines.

Sonnets are often written in **iambic pentameter.** In this meter, each line includes five pairs of syllables, the first unstressed, the second stressed. However, modern poets often break the rules when writing sonnets. As you read, note how each poet adapts the sonnet's structure to fit a modern message.

READING SKILL: UNDERSTAND FORM AND MEANING

Understanding a sonnet's structure can help you interpret its meaning. Keep in mind the following:

- In many sonnets, quatrains, octaves, and other line groupings are not set apart by stanza breaks. Use the rhyme scheme to determine the poem's line groupings.
- Each line grouping usually expresses one main idea.
- The first line grouping of the sonnet describes the speaker's situation or problem. The last line grouping resolves, concludes, or reacts to that situation.

As you begin to read each sonnet, identify the line groupings, listing them in a chart like the one shown. Also record in your chart the main idea expressed in each line grouping.

Title:	
Line Grouping	Main Idea
1st quatrain	

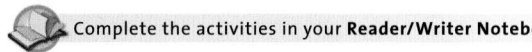 Complete the activities in your **Reader/Writer Notebook**.

When does old become NEW again?

When CDs came on the market, vinyl records seemed doomed. Then, hip-hop artists made the scratching of a needle on vinyl the signature sound of a new style of music. Artists often bring back old ideas to give them new meaning. Poets James Weldon Johnson and Claude McKay did just that with their revival of the sonnet, breathing new life into a 700-year-old poetic form.

PRESENT Think of an artist, a musician, or a writer from the past whose work you admire. Create a plan to adapt this person's work to make a creation of your own, and present your plan to the class.

887

Teach

When does old become NEW again?

After students read about Johnson and McKay writing sonnets, ask them to think of music, fashions, or slang that were popular, fell from use, and have made recent reappearances in popular culture as they complete the *PRESENT* activity.

TEXT ANALYSIS　　　　COMMON CORE
RL 5

Model the Skill: SONNET

Help students identify iambic pentameter by writing this line on the board and reading it aloud:

> I rise and greet the shades of fading night

Point out that in each of the line's five pairs of syllables, the first is stressed and the second is unstressed: Ĭ rĭse / ănd greět / thĕ shădes / ŏf fád / ĭng níght.

GUIDED PRACTICE Ask students to explain the difference between the Italian, or Petrarchan, sonnet, and the English, or Shakespearean, sonnet.

READING SKILL　　　　COMMON CORE
RL 5
RL 9

Model the Skill: UNDERSTAND FORM AND MEANING

Help students determine a sonnet's line groupings by using its rhyme scheme. Place the letter *a* at the end of the first line of one of the sonnets. Then place an *a* at the end of any other line whose end word rhymes with the end word in the first line. Ask students to assign the letter *b* to the next end word that does not rhyme with the first, and so on.

GUIDED PRACTICE Have students identify the rhyme scheme of another poem the class has read.

 RESOURCE MANAGER—Copy Master Understand Form and Meaning p. 33 (for student use while reading the selections)

DIFFERENTIATED INSTRUCTION

FOR STRUGGLING READERS
Vocabulary Support

- *meter*, "measured, patterned arrangement of syllables"
- *rhyme*, "regular recurrence of corresponding end sounds"
- *rhyme scheme*, "pattern of rhymes"
- *rhythm*, "regular recurrence of grouped stressed and unstressed, long and short, or high-pitched and low-pitched syllables"

- *stanza*, "group of versed lines forming the divisions of poetry"
- *stressed*, "relative force or loudness with which a syllable is uttered"
- *syllable*, "word or word part pronounced with a single, uninterrupted sounding of voice"
- *unstressed*, "relative softness with which a syllable is uttered"

SUMMARY

In this poem, the speaker considers what he will miss when he dies and decides he will miss his home—Manhattan—most of all.

READ WITH A PURPOSE

Help students set a purpose for reading. Tell them to read to discover what the poets dread most when contemplating death.

READING SKILL   COMMON CORE
                                      RL 5
                                      RL 9

Ⓐ *Model the Skill:* FORM AND MEANING

Point out that students can use stanza breaks to identify and interpret line groupings. Tell students that in this sonnet, the stanza break separates the first eight lines, called the octave, from the last six, called the sestet. In the octave, the speaker contemplates death and names several aspects of nature he will not miss. Ask students to identify the main idea of the sestet. **Possible answer:** *The speaker will miss everything about Manhattan.*

TEXT ANALYSIS   COMMON CORE
                                      RL 5

Ⓑ *Model the Skill:* SONNET

Tell students that the sonnet's line groupings determine its type. Point out that a sonnet containing an octave and sestet is a Petrarchan sonnet. An English, or Shakespearean, sonnet has three quatrains and a couplet. **Answer: *Petrarchan***

Extend the Discussion What relationship exists between the main ideas in the two line groupings?

REVIST THE BIG QUESTION

When does old become
NEW *again?*

Discuss How does Johnson's revival of a form often associated with love poetry support the message of "My City"? **Possible answer:** *"My City" is a poem expressing the poet's love for his city. Its subject is well suited to the form.*

My City

James Weldon Johnson

When I come down to sleep death's endless night,
The threshold of the unknown dark to cross,
What to me then will be the keenest loss,
When this bright world blurs on my fading sight?
5 Will it be that no more I shall see the trees
Or smell the flowers or hear the singing birds
Or watch the flashing streams or patient herds?
No, I am sure it will be none of these. Ⓐ

But, ah! Manhattan's sights and sounds, her smells,
10 Her crowds, her throbbing force, the thrill that comes
From being of her a part, her subtle spells,
Her shining towers, her avenues, her slums—
O God! the stark, unutterable pity,
To be dead, and never again behold my city! Ⓑ

Analyze Visuals ▶
What details in this photo correspond to the poet's vision of his city?

Ⓐ **FORM AND MEANING**
Use the **stanza break** to identify the line groupings of this poem. What is the main idea of lines 1–8?

Ⓑ **SONNET**
Judging from its line groupings, what type of sonnet is this?

View of Broadway near Times Square in Manhattan, 1920s

DIFFERENTIATED INSTRUCTION

FOR ENGLISH LANGUAGE LEARNERS

Vocabulary Support Have students work in mixed-ability pairs to determine the meaning of such phrases as "death's endless night," "threshold of the unknown dark," keenest loss" (lines 1–3). Have students put these phrases into their own words to paraphrase lines 1–3. Have them continue until they have paraphrased the whole poem. Have volunteers read their versions of the poem to the class.

FOR ADVANCED LEARNERS/AP

Analyze Point out to students that the "I" present in lines 1, 5, and 8 is absent from lines 9–14, the lines in which the speaker describes the city. How does the absence of the "I" emphasize the power that the poet ascribes to Manhattan? Have students discuss this question and present their conclusions to the class.

TIERED DISCUSSION PROMPTS

In lines 9–14, these prompts to help students understand the urban vitality that characterized the Harlem Renaissance:

Connect Think about life in big cities. What is it like? *Accept all thoughtful responses.*

Analyze How does the speaker personify the city? ***Possible answer:*** *The speaker personifies the city as a vital, magical woman who possesses a shining exterior as well as a dark side.*

Evaluate Is the speaker's description of Manhattan appealing? Explain. ***Possible answer:*** *The speaker's description is appealing because of its sensual quality and because it conveys a strong love of the city.*

Analyze Visuals

Possible answer: The background of the photograph shows the "shining towers" Johnson mentions in line 12, while the foreground shows two broad avenues that might be said to cast "subtle spells" through enticing advertisements and theatre marquees.

FOR STRUGGLING READERS

Options for Reading: Audio Recording
- Have students listen to the poems on the *Audio Anthology CD* (also recommended for English learners) while they read along in their texts. Ask students to notice the main ideas, rhyme, and line groupings in each poem.

- For "My City," students will need help with syntax and figurative language to unlock main ideas. Listen to line 2 several times; then help students unravel inverted syntax there and elsewhere. Use line 11 to model using context clues to build meaning for figurative language.

SUMMARY

This poem is a defiant call to protest. The speaker warns against passive acceptance of hostility and urges people to fight back. He suggests that death is inevitable but can be noble if it serves a cause. The final couplet states the speaker's resolve to die fighting.

TEXT ANALYSIS   COMMON CORE   **RL 5**

C SONNET

Possible answer: *The rhyme scheme is abab, cdcd. On the basis of this rhyme scheme, the sonnet is Shakespearean.*

IF STUDENTS NEED HELP . . . Refer them to page 887 and the definitions of Petrarchan and Shakespearean sonnets.

READING SKILL   COMMON CORE   **RL 5**   **RL 9**

D FORM AND MEANING

Possible answer: *The speaker decides that he will fight back even if he dies fighting.*

IF STUDENTS NEED HELP . . . Have them record line groupings and main ideas in the prereading chart introduced on page 887.

Line Grouping	Main Idea
First quatrain	We won't die like hogs hunted by dogs.
Second quatrain	If we must die, we will do it nobly.

SELECTION WRAP–UP

READ WITH A PURPOSE Now that students have read both poems, they may find Johnson worries about missing his life after death, while McKay is more concerned about dying with dignity.

If We Must Die

Claude McKay

> If we must die, let it not be like hogs
> Hunted and penned in an inglorious¹ spot,
> While round us bark the mad and hungry dogs,
> Making their mock at our accursed lot.
> 5 If we must die, O let us nobly die,
> So that our precious blood may not be shed
> In vain; then even the monsters we defy
> Shall be constrained² to honor us though dead! **C**
> O kinsmen! we must meet the common foe!
> 10 Though far outnumbered let us show us brave,
> And for their thousand blows deal one deathblow!
> What though before us lies the open grave?
> Like men we'll face the murderous, cowardly pack,
> Pressed to the wall, dying, but fighting back! **D**

C SONNET
State the **rhyme scheme** of lines 1–8. Considering the rhyme scheme, what type of sonnet is this?

D FORM AND MEANING
By the end of the poem, what resolution has the speaker reached?

---

1. **inglorious:** shameful; disgraceful.
2. **constrained:** forced.

DIFFERENTIATED INSTRUCTION

FOR STRATEGIC READERS
Develop Reading Fluency Help students gain proficiency in reading sonnets aloud. Tell them that unless punctuation ends a line, they should not pause before reading on. Model by reading the poem aloud. Then have students read the poem chorally. Listen for the natural rhythm of iambic pentameter to emerge as students gain comfort with the form.

FOR ADVANCED LEARNERS/AP
Research McKay wrote "If We Must Die" during the "Red Summer," a term coined by James Weldon Johnson to describe the racially violent summer and fall of 1919 during which African Americans were the victims of violent attacks. Have students research the causes of these events, noting in particular the significance of McKay's poem as a part of the response to them. Find opportunities for students to present their findings to the class.

Comprehension

1. **Recall** In "My City," what will the speaker most regret about death?

2. **Clarify** In "If We Must Die," what type of death does the speaker argue for?

3. **Paraphrase** In "If We Must Die," what is the meaning of the phrase "making their mock at our accursed lot"?

Text Analysis

4. **Identify Form** McKay's poem closely follows the conventions of a traditional sonnet. Which kind of sonnet is it? Explain your answer.

5. **Make Inferences About Audience** Recall the events that inspired McKay to write "If We Must Die." What audience can you infer the speaker is addressing? Describe the speaker's relationship to this audience.

6. **Classify Sonnet** Johnson's poem includes features of both Shakespearean and Petrarchan sonnets. Using a chart like the one shown, decide whether each listed feature of the poem's structure is characteristic of Shakespearean sonnets, Petrarchan sonnets, or both. Based on your answers, which label is the better description of Johnson's sonnet?

	Shakespearean	Petrarchan
Structure		
Rhyme Scheme		
Meter		
Final Couplet		

7. **Analyze Form and Meaning** Review the chart you completed as you read. Notice Johnson's use of a stanza break, whereas McKay uses none. In your opinion, how does this choice contribute to each poem's meaning? Explain.

8. **Examine Author's Purpose** Consider the motives that might have inspired African-American poets to express themselves in European poetic forms. What artistic and social messages are suggested by the Harlem Renaissance revival of the sonnet?

Text Criticism

9. **Critical Interpretations** Claude McKay once stated that he hoped his poems could convey universal meaning. Reread the background on "If We Must Die" included in the author biography. Does the poem's history suggest McKay was successful in his goal? Explain your answer.

> *When does old become* **NEW** *again?*
>
> In the last decade or so, recycling has become a main focus of American society. What value do you see in reusing old or outdated things? Explain your answer.

COMMON CORE

RL 5 Analyze how an author's choices concerning how to structure specific parts of a text contribute to its overall structure and meaning as well as its aesthetic impact. **RL 9** Demonstrate knowledge of early-twentieth-century works of American literature, including how two or more texts from the same period treat similar themes or topics.

Practice and Apply

For preliminary support of post-reading questions, use these copy masters:

R RESOURCE MANAGER—Copy Masters
Sonnet p. 31
Question Support p. 35

Additional selection questions are provided for teachers on page 27.

ANSWERS   COMMON CORE RL 5, RL 9

1. *The speaker will regret losing his city.*

2. *The speaker argues for a noble death.*

3. *The line means laughing at our poor condition.*

Possible answers:

4. ● **COMMON CORE FOCUS** **Understand Form and Meaning** *On the basis of its rhyme scheme and its line groupings of three quatrains and a couplet, the sonnet is Shakespearean.*

5. *The speaker addresses an African-American audience, whose identity he shares, evidenced by the references to kinsmen and common foe (line 9).*

6. ● **COMMON CORE FOCUS** **Sonnet** *Shakespearean:* **meter, final couplet;** *Petrarchan:* **structure, rhyme scheme, meter. Students can argue for either form but should provide support.**

7. ● **COMMON CORE FOCUS** **Understand Form and Meaning** *Johnson's sonnet poses a question and an answer, separated into two stanzas. McKay's message is presented as a whole and so it works better as a single stanza.*

8. *Reviving the sonnet suggests that African Americans can produce great literature and have experiences worthy of commemoration.*

9. *Many readers have identified with the speaker's message. This identification transcends race, social context, and geography, suggesting that the poem conveys universal meaning as McKay intended.*

> *When does old become* **NEW** *again?* Ask students to think about issues like reducing waste and unnecessary purchases. How has recycling and reusing items affected our society and our planet?

Assess and Reteach

Assess

DIAGNOSTIC AND SELECTION TESTS
Selection Test A pp. 225–226
Selection Test B/C pp. 227–228

Interactive Selection Test on thinkcentral.com

Reteach

Level Up Online Tutorials on thinkcentral.com

Reteaching Worksheets on thinkcentral.com

Literature Lesson 13: Sonnet

Focus and Motivate

⋯ **COMMON CORE FOCUS**

RL 4 Determine the meaning of words and phrases as they are used in the text, including figurative and connotative meanings; analyze the impact of specific word choices on meaning and tone. **RL 9** Demonstrate knowledge of how two or more texts from the same period treat similar themes or topics.

ABOUT THE POETS

Countee Cullen After students read about Countee Cullen, point out the quotation that closes the biography. Ask students to draw connections between the quotation and the title of the Cullen poem they will read.
Possible answer: In the quotation, Cullen expresses his wish to address all readers. His title "Any Human to Another" stresses that the poem speaks to all readers.

Jean Toomer After students read, highlight the poet's interest in precise, striking images. Ask students to describe the image created by the precise language of Toomer's title "Storm Ending." *Possible answer: In just two words, Toomer creates a vivid image of a storm clearing.*

Arna Bontemps Focus students' attention on Bontemps's inspiration by Southern roots. Explain that the poem they will read uses rural imagery and metaphor to convey the poet's message.

⋯ **COMMON CORE**

RL 4 Determine the meaning of words and phrases as they are used in the text, including figurative and connotative meanings; analyze the impact of specific word choices on meaning and tone. **RL 9** Demonstrate knowledge of how two or more texts from the same period treat similar themes or topics.

The Harlem Renaissance
Any Human to Another
Poem by Countee Cullen

Storm Ending
Poem by Jean Toomer

A Black Man Talks of Reaping
Poem by Arna Bontemps

Meet the Authors

Countee Cullen
1903–1946

In 1925, while still an undergraduate at New York University, Countee Cullen (kŭl'ən) published his first poetry collection, *Color*, which won immediate critical acclaim.

Cullen's greatest poetic influences were the English Romantic poets, especially John Keats. Although some of Cullen's poetry deals directly with experiences specific to African Americans, much of his work addresses universal concerns such as love and faith. Cullen adamantly believed that poetry could break down racial barriers and disliked being pigeonholed, once stating, "If I am going to be a poet at all, I am going to be a Poet and not a Negro Poet."

Jean Toomer
1894–1967

Born in Washington, D.C., Nathan Eugene Toomer grew up in a prominent, racially mixed family. Toomer could pass for white, and as a young man, often changed his racial identification from white to black and back again. As an adult, he rejected the concept of race altogether and embraced an idealistic vision of himself as a founder of a "united human race."

Toomer was drawn to Eastern philosophy and Imagist poetry—poetry that conveys meaning through the use of precise, striking images. His reputation rests mainly on his novel *Cane* (1923), an experimental work exploring the African-American experience through fragments of poetry and prose.

Arna Bontemps
1902–1973

After graduating from college in 1923, Arna Bontemps (bôn-tän') discovered a thriving literary scene in Harlem that he called a "foretaste of paradise." Despite his love for the bustle of the Northern cities, Bontemps was most deeply inspired by the Southern roots of African-American culture. Nearly all of his stories, novels, and plays are set in the South and provide vivid portrayals of rural life.

Bontemps, who earned his living as an educator, left Harlem in 1931 and spent most of his career in the South. His major works include the short story collection *The Old South* and the novel *God Sends Sunday*, which is often cited as the final work of the Harlem Renaissance.

Author Online
Go to **thinkcentral.com**. KEYWORD: HML11-892

892

Selection Resources

See resources on the **Teacher One Stop DVD-ROM** and on **thinkcentral.com**.

 RESOURCE MANAGER UNIT 5
Plan and Teach, pp. 37–44
Text Analysis and Reading
Skill, pp. 45–48†*

DIAGNOSTIC AND SELECTION TESTS
Selection Tests, pp. 229–232

 **BEST PRACTICES TOOLKIT**
Sensory Notes, p. B9

TECHNOLOGY
⊘ **Teacher One Stop DVD-ROM**
⊘ **Student One Stop DVD-ROM**
⊘ **Audio Anthology CD**
⊘ **ExamView Test Generator**
on the **Teacher One Stop**

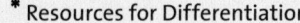

* Resources for Differentiation   **†** Also in Spanish   **‡** In Haitian Creole and Vietnamese

TEXT ANALYSIS: THEME

In poetry, the speaker's descriptions of the world will often help you identify a poem's **theme,** its underlying message about life or human nature. In most works, the theme is implied, rather than directly stated. Consider these lines:

Your grief and mine
Must intertwine

The speaker might be talking to a loved one or making a general point about sorrow. To uncover the message of a poem, use these strategies:

- Consider the title. What information does it reveal?
- Identify the speaker. Is the speaker the voice of an individual or of a group?
- Notice key images and think about their meaning.
- Consider the mood, or feeling, the speaker conveys.

Readers notice different details and often find different themes in the same work. As you read, try to draw your own conclusions about each poet's message.

READING SKILL: DISTINGUISH FIGURATIVE FROM LITERAL MEANING

You've learned that poets use **figurative language,** such as similes, metaphors, and personification, to go beyond the literal meaning of words. Use these steps to uncover this extra level of meaning:

- Read each poem once to grasp its overall meaning.
- Reread the poem, noting important words and phrases.
- Ask questions about comparisons you notice. What is being compared, and how are these things alike?
- Uncover hidden metaphors by noting descriptive details. What do these details remind you of?

As you read each poem, record examples of figurative language in a chart like the one shown. Then, jot down some of the impressions created by the words the poet chooses.

Example	Impressions
like an arrow	

 Complete the activities in your **Reader/Writer Notebook.**

How do you VIEW *the world?*

You can see a glass as half empty or half full. You can see a pile of old newspapers as trash to be thrown away or as the makings of papier-mâché. The way you see things—your outlook—says a lot about who you are.

QUICKWRITE Many factors shape your outlook—your personality, your life experiences, your state of mind. Write one or two sentences describing your outlook. Then, explain the factors you think have most influenced the way you look at the world.

 893

Teach

How do you VIEW *the world?*

After students read the paragraph, group those who view the pictured glass as half-full and those who view it as half-empty. Urge groups to explore how this outlook applies elsewhere in their lives. Have students draw upon their discussion to complete the *QUICKWRITE.*

TEXT ANALYSIS
COMMON CORE RL 9

● *Model the Skill:* **THEME**

Tell students that the excerpted lines are from "Any Human to Another," a title that suggests the speaker is not a particular individual, but rather any person. Tell students this conveys the theme that the human condition is universal.

GUIDED PRACTICE Ask students what mood is suggested by the image of intertwined grief.

READING SKILL
COMMON CORE RL 4

■ *Model the Skill:*
DISTINGUISH FIGURATIVE FROM LITERAL MEANING

Tell students that the phrase "seeing the glass as half-full" is an example of figurative language that has nothing to do with eyesight; it describes an individual who is optimistic.

GUIDED PRACTICE Ask students what it means to see the glass as "half-empty." Then ask them to describe the feelings conveyed by "half-full" and "half-empty."

R RESOURCE MANAGER—Copy Master
Distinguish Figurative from Literal Meaning p. 47 (for student use while reading the selections)

DIFFERENTIATED INSTRUCTION

FOR STRUGGLING READERS
Concept Support: Figurative Language
Review similes, metaphors, and personification with students by helping them identify the figurative language in these paraphrases from the poems:

- Thunder is a clapper, striking our ears. *(metaphor)*
- Grief is as sharp as a knife. *(simile)*

- The sun bites flowers in full bloom. *(personification)*
- My sorrow pierces my bone like an arrow. *(simile)*
- The flowers bleed rain. *(personification)*
- Your grief is a sea; mine is a river. *(metaphor)*

Practice and Apply

SUMMARY

In this poem, the speaker compares sorrow to an arrow's piercing and a knife cut and suggests that it is a universal emotion shared as river and sea share water.

READ WITH A PURPOSE

Help students set a purpose for reading the poems. Tell them to read to find how the poets use images of nature to express emotion.

REVISIT THE BIG QUESTION

How do you VIEW the world?

Discuss What outlook on life is expressed in these lines? *Possible answer: The speaker expresses the outlook that life's experiences will touch everyone equally.*

Any Human *to Another*

Countee Cullen

The ills I sorrow at
Not me alone
Like an arrow,
Pierce to the marrow,
5 Through the fat
And past the bone.

Your grief and mine
Must intertwine
Like sea and river,
10 Be fused and mingle,
Diverse yet single,
Forever and forever.

Let no man be so proud
And confident,
15 To think he is allowed
A little tent
Pitched in a meadow
Of sun and shadow
All his little own.

20 Joy may be shy, unique,
Friendly to a few,
Sorrow never scorned to speak
To any who
Were false or true.

25 Your every grief
Like a blade
Shining and unsheathed[1]
Must strike me down.
Of bitter aloes[2] wreathed,
30 My sorrow must be laid
On your head like a crown.

---

1. **unsheathed:** removed from its protective case.
2. **bitter aloes:** spiny-leafed plants whose juice is used to make a bad-tasting medicine.

DIFFERENTIATED INSTRUCTION

FOR ENGLISH LANGUAGE LEARNERS

Understand Poetic License Remind students that poets often break the rules of grammar and other conventions, and so interpreting poetry often requires some flexibility. Point out *sorrow* in line 1. Tell students that Cullen has used the noun as a verb here. Tell student that *sorrow* shares a root with *sorry,* but if the line read "The ills I am sorry for" it would not have as much of an emotional impact. Help students put other difficult language in the poem into their own words.

FOR STRUGGLING READERS

Develop Reading Fluency

Use "Any Human to Another" to give students practice reading poems aloud. Assign each stanza to a student. Remind students that the pattern of stressed and unstressed sounds gives the poem its rhythm. As students read aloud, ask the rest of the class to observe the patterns of sounds.

Storm Ending

Jean Toomer

Thunder blossoms gorgeously above our heads,
Great, hollow, bell-like flowers,
Rumbling in the wind,
Stretching clappers to strike our ears . . **C**
5   Full-lipped flowers
Bitten by the sun
Bleeding rain
Dripping rain like golden honey—
And the sweet earth flying from the thunder.

C **FIGURATIVE MEANING**
What is thunder compared to in lines 1–4? Explain what qualities are emphasized by this comparison.

Field and Storm (2003), April Gornik. Oil on linen, 74" × 95". Courtesy of the artist and Danese Gallery, New York.

SUMMARY

In this poem, the speaker compares a thunderstorm to the blossoming of flowers.

READING SKILL

 COMMON CORE RL 4

C *Model the Skill:* **FIGURATIVE MEANING**

- Begin by reading lines 1–4 aloud.
- Tell students that the sound "blossoms gorgeously" like a flower, a flower that is like a large bell, ringing.
- Ask students what this image might mean. *Possible answer:* It is compared to bell-like flowers. *Thunder is natural, beautiful, and powerful.*

IF STUDENTS NEED HELP . . . Point out the metaphor and help students add the language and their impressions to the pre-reading chart introduced on page 893.

Example	Impressions
Thunder blossoms gorgeously above our heads.	The thunder grows like a flower. It is alive and beautiful.

TIERED DISCUSSION PROMPTS

Use these prompts to help students understand figurative language in lines 1–9:

Connect Think about the sound of thunder. How would you describe it? *Accept all thoughtful responses.*

Evaluate Do you find the speaker's description of the storm effective? Explain.
Possible answer: The description is effective because its images are so vibrant and vivid that the comparison comes alive.

FOR STRUGGLING READERS

Concept Support: Sensory Images Help students use Sensory Notes organizers to categorize the images in "Storm Ending" according to the five senses. Then lead students in a discussion about the effect of these sensory images. Point out that the many sensory images complement the idea that the storm is alive.

I See...	Most Important Image
huge blossoms	thunder clouds exploding

BEST PRACTICES TOOLKIT—Transparency
Sensory Notes p. B9

Sunflowers, Charly Palmer. Mixed media collage on canvas, 48″ × 24″. © Charly Palmer.

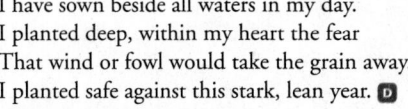

A Black Man Talks of Reaping

Arna Bontemps

I have sown beside all waters in my day.
I planted deep, within my heart the fear
That wind or fowl would take the grain away.
I planted safe against this stark, lean year. **D**

5 I scattered seed enough to plant the land
In rows from Canada to Mexico,
But for my reaping[1] only what the hand
Can hold at once is all that I can show.

Yet what I sowed and what the orchard yields
10 My brother's sons are gathering stalk and root,
Small wonder then my children glean[2] in fields
They have not sown, and feed on bitter fruit. **E**

▲ **Analyze Visuals**
What elements of this painting reflect the theme of the poem?

D FIGURATIVE MEANING
Reread lines 1–4. What idea do the words *sown*, *planted*, and *grain* have in common?

E THEME
In lines 11–12, why are the children's gleanings described as "bitter fruit"?

---

1. **reaping:** harvesting grain.
2. **glean:** gather grain left behind by reapers.

DIFFERENTIATED INSTRUCTION

FOR STRUGGLING READERS

Concept Support: Extended Metaphor [paired option] Explain that metaphors may function on more than one level, suggesting a narrow and a broader comparison. Have pairs discuss possible meanings in the final stanza:

- *orchard*, "American society"
- *brother's sons*, "the white majority"
- *my children glean in fields*, "the status of African Americans forced to accept leftovers"
- *bitter fruit*, "racial resentment and strife"

FOR ADVANCED LEARNERS/AP

Research and Analyze [small-group option] Have groups research sharecropping in the American South to define and explain the system. Challenge students to analyze the balance of power in the system: Who held the social, political, and economic power? Could those without power gain it? Why did sharecroppers agree to participate? Ask students to find and share connections between this system and contemporary American social institutions.

Comprehension

1. **Summarize** In "Any Human to Another," what comparisons does the speaker use to describe grief?

2. **Clarify** In "Storm Ending," what event is described in the last line of the poem?

3. **Clarify** In "A Black Man Talks of Reaping," how much has the speaker reaped from all the seed he has scattered?

Text Analysis

4. **Distinguish Figurative from Literal Meaning** Review the notes you took on Bontemps's poem. Bontemps uses an **extended metaphor,** a lengthy comparison of two things that have many points in common. Identify the extended metaphor Bontemps uses. What is this metaphor meant to suggest?

5. **Examine Imagery** "Storm Ending" includes several examples of **synesthesia,** imagery that uses one type of sensory experience to describe a different one—for example, a sound decribed as a smell. Identify two examples of synesthesia in the poem. Which two senses are combined in each image?

6. **Compare and Contrast Tone** Describe the tone, or attitude toward the subject, of Cullen's and Bontemps's poems. What **outlook** on the prospects for social equality does each poem suggest?

7. **Analyze Theme** Complete a chart like the one shown for each poem. What do you conclude is the theme of each poem?

Title Reveals:	Speaker's Identity:
Key Images:	Mood:

Text Criticism

8. **Biographical Context** Reread the author biographies on page 892. In each case, what connections can you make between the poet's life story and the worldview expressed in his work? Be specific.

> *How do you* **VIEW** *the world?*
>
> People's views in life often change as they get older. Viewpoints change from generation to generation, too. Why do you think this happens? How is your outlook different from that of your parents?

COMMON CORE

RL 4 Determine the meaning of words and phrases as they are used in the text, including figurative and connotative meanings; analyze the impact of specific word choices on meaning and tone. **RL 9** Demonstrate knowledge of how two or more texts from the same period treat similar themes or topics. **L 5a** Interpret figures of speech in context and analyze their role in the text.

Practice and Apply

For preliminary support of post-reading questions, use these copy masters:

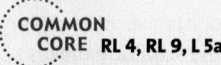 **RESOURCE MANAGER—Copy Masters**
Theme p. 45
Question Support p. 49
Additional selection questions are provided for teachers on page 41.

ANSWERS
COMMON CORE RL 4, RL 9, L 5a

1. *The speaker describes grief as an arrow (line 3), a river flowing into the sea (line 9), an unsheathed blade (lines 26–27), and a bitter aloe (line 29).*

2. *The last line of "Storm Ending" describes the wind blowing the storm clouds away.*

3. *The speaker of "A Black Man Talks . . . " reaps only what he can hold in his hand.*

Possible answers:

4. ● **COMMON CORE FOCUS Distinguish Figurative from Literal Meaning** *Bontemps compares the African-American experience to farming land but getting none of the harvest, suggest racial injustice.*

5. *Thunder blossoming combines sound and sight (line 1). "Bitten by the sun" combines touch and sight (line 6).*

6. *The tone of Cullen's poem is instructive while Bontemps's is despairing. Cullen's poem presents a more positive outlook— universal truths bind us more than our differences separate us.*

---

7. ● **COMMON CORE FOCUS Theme** *"Any Human to Another": **Title Reveals:** speaker's identity; **Key Images:** "pierce to the marrow," "solitary tent"; **Speaker's Identity:** human being; **Mood:** instructive or reflective; **Theme:** Sorrow is a shared experience. "Storm Ending": **Title Reveals:** subject of poem; **Key Images:** "blossoming thunder," "bleeding rain"; **Speaker's Identity:** observer; **Mood:** intense natural beauty; **Theme:** What is fierce or dangerous is also beautiful. "A Black Man Talks of Reaping": **Title Reveals:** speaker's identity;*

Key Images: "scattered seed," "bitter fruit"; Speaker's Identity: black sharecropper; Mood: bitter or sorrowful; Theme: Injustice has lasting consequences.

8. *Cullen did not define himself, or his poem's speaker, by race. Toomer's poem stays focused on an image, like the poems that influenced him. Bontemps's Southern roots are seen in his speaker's situation.*

> *How do you* **VIEW** *the world?* *Ask students to offer reasons for the difference in outlooks.*

Assess and Reteach

Assess

DIAGNOSTIC AND SELECTION TESTS
Selection Test A, B/C pp. 229–230, 231–232
Interactive Selection Test on **thinkcentral.com**

Reteach

Level Up Online Tutorials on **thinkcentral.com**
Reteaching Worksheets on **thinkcentral.com**

Literature Lesson 11

Focus and Motivate

COMMON CORE FOCUS

RI 1 Cite textual evidence to support analysis of what the text says explicitly as well as inferences drawn from the text. **RI 2** Determine two or more central ideas of a text and analyze their development over the course of the text. **RI 5** Analyze and evaluate the effectiveness of the structure an author uses in his or her exposition or argument, including whether the structure makes points clear, convincing, and engaging. **RI 10** Read and comprehend literary nonfiction. **W 3** Write narratives to develop imagined experiences or events using effective technique, well-chosen details, and well-structured event sequences. **L 1a** Apply the understanding that usage is a matter of convention, can change over time, and is sometimes contested. **L 3a** Apply an understanding of syntax to the study of complex texts when reading. **L 4b** Identify and correctly use patterns of word changes that indicate different meanings or parts of speech. **L 6** Acquire and use accurately general academic and domain-specific words and phrases.

ABOUT THE AUTHOR

After students read the biography, ask them if they think Hurston followed her mother's advice, and why. ***Possible answer:*** *Yes; Hurston's life reflects the pursuit of seemingly impossible dreams.*

NOTABLE QUOTE

"Those that don't got it, can't show it. Those that got it, can't hide it."

—Zora Neale Hurston

Discuss with students what "it" means—an energy that makes people special. Point out that "it" was her strong sense of self-confidence, despite racial prejudice.

Selection Resources

⃝ COMMON CORE

RI 1 Cite textual evidence to support analysis of what the text says explicitly as well as inferences drawn from the text. **RI 2** Determine two or more central ideas of a text and analyze their development over the course of the text. **RI 5** Analyze and evaluate the effectiveness of the structure an author uses in his or her exposition or argument, including whether the structure makes points clear, convincing, and engaging. **RI 10** Read and comprehend literary nonfiction. **L 3a** Apply an understanding of syntax to the study of complex texts when reading.

DID YOU KNOW?

Zora Neale Hurston . . .

- dressed so flamboyantly that one acquaintance referred to her as a "macaw of brilliant plumage."
- shocked some people by wearing pants in public.
- became a fan of British poet John Milton after rescuing one of his books from the trash.

The Harlem Renaissance

How It Feels to Be Colored Me

Essay by Zora Neale Hurston

Essential Course of Study  **ECOS**

Meet the Author

Zora Neale Hurston c. 1891–1960

Raised in the all-black town of Eatonville, Florida, Zora Neale Hurston followed her mother's advice to "jump at de sun"—to follow her dreams, no matter how impossible they seemed. In 1925, she arrived in New York with "$1.50, no job, no friends, and a lot of hope." Hurston's flair, talent, and sheer nerve soon made her one of the leading African-American novelists of the 1930s.

Early Days When Hurston was 13 years old, her family life fell apart. Her mother died, her father remarried, and by the age of 14, Hurston was on her own. Working an endless series of menial jobs, Hurston tried for years to earn enough money to send herself back to school. After 12 years of trials and adventures, she finally completed high school and scraped together a year's tuition for Howard University, "the Negro Harvard," where in 1921 she published her first story.

Collector of Stories By 1925, Hurston's efforts began to pay off. She won a scholarship to Barnard College, where she studied with the renowned anthropologists Franz Boas and Ruth Benedict. After graduating from Barnard in 1928— the first known African American to do so—Hurston returned to the South to collect African-American folklore. "I had to go back, dress as they did, talk as they did, live their life," she said, "so I could get into my stories the world I knew as a child." The lively, hilarious stories she collected soon became material for her own fiction. In the 1930s and '40s, she published a series of major works, including the folklore collection *Mules and Men* (1935), the novel *Their Eyes Were Watching God* (1937), and her autobiography, *Dust Tracks on a Road* (1942).

Down But Not Out Hurston often came under fire by African-American writers who felt she minimized the seriousness of racial prejudice. By the late 1940s, her books had fallen out of favor and out of print. During the last 20 years of her life, Hurston struggled to earn a living, once again working as a maid to pay her bills. In 1960, Hurston died in a welfare home, poor and nearly forgotten, and was buried in an unmarked grave in Fort Pierce, Florida. Thanks to the efforts of author Alice Walker, Hurston's work was rediscovered in the 1970s. Hurston is now acknowledged as an influential figure in the history of African-American literature.

Author Online

THINK central

Go to **thinkcentral.com**. KEYWORD: HML11-898

898

See resources on the **Teacher One Stop DVD-ROM** and on **thinkcentral.com**.

R **RESOURCE MANAGER UNIT 5**
Plan and Teach, pp. 51–58
Summary, pp. 59–60†‡*
Text Analysis and Reading Skill, pp. 61–64†*
Vocabulary, pp. 65–67*
Grammar and Style, p. 70

DIAGNOSTIC AND SELECTION TESTS
Selection Tests, pp. 233–236

BEST PRACTICES TOOLKIT
New Word Analysis, p. E8
Spider Map, p. B47

INTERACTIVE READER

ADAPTED INTERACTIVE READER

ELL ADAPTED INTERACTIVE READER

TECHNOLOGY
- **Teacher One Stop DVD-ROM**
- **Student One Stop DVD-ROM**
- **PowerNotes DVD-ROM**
- **Audio Anthology CD**
- **GrammarNotes DVD-ROM**
- **ExamView Test Generator** on the **Teacher One Stop**

Find it Online!
THINK central

Features on **thinkcentral.com** that support the selection include
- **PowerNotes** presentation
- **ThinkAloud** models to enhance comprehension
- **WordSharp** vocabulary tutorials
- interactive writing and grammar instruction

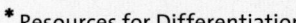 **Resources for Differentiation**   † Also in Spanish   ‡ In Haitian Creole and Vietnamese

● TEXT ANALYSIS: RHETORICAL TECHNIQUES

Famously outspoken, Zora Neale Hurston wasn't afraid to stand out from the crowd in a unique way. In this essay, Hurston uses the following **rhetorical techniques** to discuss her views about race.

- **repetition**—when a sound, word, phrase, or line is repeated for emphasis or unity.
- **parallel structure**—the use of similar grammatical constructions to express ideas that are related or equal in importance.

As you read, notice how Hurston uses these rhetorical techniques to make her ideas come alive.

● READING SKILL: IDENTIFY MAIN IDEAS

You know that the **main idea** of a paragraph is the basic point it makes. Sometimes, the main idea is **explicit**, or directly stated in the text. However, main ideas may also be **implicit**—suggested or hinted at by the details in the text. In such cases, you'll need to analyze the details the author presents to discover the main idea.

As you read, use a chart like the one shown to record the main idea of each paragraph. If the main idea is implicit, note key details that helped you identify the main idea.

Paragraph	Main Idea	Key Details
1	I'm not ashamed to be colored.	offers no "extenuating circumstances"

▲ VOCABULARY IN CONTEXT

Hurston uses the following words to make her points about African-American identity. Restate each phrase, using a different word or words for the boldfaced term.

1. collected a **miscellany** of objects on her travels
2. did not use **pigmentation** to judge character
3. excused from penalties because of **extenuating** factors
4. dressed in colorful **raiment**
5. spoke **exultingly** of her triumphs
6. saw herself as **cosmic** rather than small and narrow

 Complete the activities in your **Reader/Writer Notebook**.

What makes you YOU?

Think of the things that make you unique: your style, your sense of humor, the way you keep your head (or don't) when things get tense. Of all the qualities and behaviors that make you who you are, which ones do you think best define your personality?

The Insider's Guide to Me

1. To find me in a crowd, look/ listen for _____
2. The story my friends/family all tell about me is _____
3. Most people in school know me as _____
4. The thing I do that is most "me" is _____

899

What makes you YOU?

After students think about their qualities and behaviors, have them come up with five words that define their personalities.

TEXT ANALYSIS

COMMON CORE
RI 5
L 3a

● Model the Skill:
RHETORICAL TECHNIQUES

Read aloud this excerpt from the selection:

"I am colored but I offer nothing in the way of extenuating circumstances . . . I remember the very day that I became colored. Up to my thirteenth year I lived in the little Negro town of Eatonville, Florida. It is exclusively a colored town."

Point out the repetition of the word "colored." Tell students that though Hurston uses it to label herself and her hometown, she also says she remembers the day she "became colored." Ask students what she means by this. **Possible answers:** *People in Eatonville did not label themselves. Hurston said she "became colored" when she arrived in Jacksonville to attend school.*

GUIDED PRACTICE Ask students to reword the excerpt without relying on repetition as a rhetorical technique. Have them compare and contrast the version.

READING SKILL

COMMON CORE
RI 1
RI 2

■ Model the Skill:
IDENTIFY MAIN IDEAS

Read aloud **Early Days** on page 898. Point out that the main idea is not stated directly, but that all the details are about Hurston's hard work and accomplishments.

GUIDED PRACTICE Have students sum up the details to come up with a main idea.

R RESOURCE MANAGER—Copy Master Identify Main Ideas p. 63

VOCABULARY

COMMON CORE
L 4

▲ VOCABULARY IN CONTEXT

DIAGNOSE WORD KNOWLEDGE Have all students complete Vocabulary in Context. Check their answers against the following:
cosmic (kŏz'mĭk) *adj.* of or relating to the universe
extenuating (ĭk-stĕn'yōō-a'tĭng) *adj.* lessening the severity of
exultingly (ĭg-zŭlt'ĭng-lē) *adv.* joyfully

miscellany (mĭs'ə-lā'nē) *n.* a mixture of various things
pigmentation (pĭg'mən-tā'shən) *n.* coloring
raiment (rā'mənt) *n.* clothing; garments

PRETEACH VOCABULARY Use the following copy master to help students predict meanings.

R RESOURCE MANAGER—Copy Master Vocabulary Study p. 65

SUMMARY

Hurston describes herself as a little girl growing up in the all-African-American community of Eatonville, Florida, where she boldly interacts with white tourists, much to her family's chagrin. At the age of 13, Hurston goes to Jacksonville to attend school, where she discovers that she is a colored girl. Hurston discusses the impact of this lesson on her adult personality and her worldview, explaining that she finds race both important and irrelevant to her identity.

READ WITH A PURPOSE

Help students set a purpose for reading. Tell them to read to find out how Hurston fulfills what her title proposes to tell.

TEXT ANALYSIS
COMMON CORE
RI 5
L 3a

Ⓐ Model the Skill:
RHETORICAL TECHNIQUES

Remind students that parallel structure refers to similar grammatical constructions to express similar ideas. To locate parallel structure, tell students to look for similar ideas in Hurston's writing.

Possible answer: There is parallel construction in the phrases "The native whites rode dusty horses. . .The town knew the Southerners. . . /But the Northerners. . ." Hurston uses comparisons to show how different people viewed the inhabitants of Eatonville, and how the people of Eatonville viewed both Northerners and Southerners.

VOCABULARY
COMMON CORE
L 4

OWN THE WORD

extenuating: Point out that *extenuate* comes from the Latin verb *extenuare*, which means "make thin." When you *extenuate* something, you thin out its severity.

How It Feels to Be Colored Me

Zora Neale Hurston

BACKGROUND Between 1865 and 1900, more than 100 independent towns were founded by African Americans trying to escape racial prejudice. Eatonville, Florida, a small town just north of Orlando, was the oldest of these self-governing black communities. Growing up in Eatonville, Zora Neale Hurston was sheltered from the experiences of exclusion and contempt that shaped the lives of many African Americans. As you read this essay, think about how these early experiences influenced Hurston's opinions on race.

Analyze Visuals ▶
What words would you use to describe the girl in the painting? Identify the techniques or elements that lend her these qualities.

I am colored but I offer nothing in the way of **extenuating** circumstances except the fact that I am the only Negro in the United States whose grandfather on the mother's side was *not* an Indian chief.

I remember the very day that I became colored. Up to my thirteenth year I lived in the little Negro town of Eatonville, Florida. It is exclusively a colored town. The only white people I knew passed through the town going to or coming from Orlando. The native whites rode dusty horses, the Northern tourists chugged down the sandy village road in automobiles. The town knew the Southerners and never stopped cane chewing when they passed. But the Northerners were something
10 else again. They were peered at cautiously from behind curtains by the timid. The more venturesome would come out on the porch to watch them go past and got just as much pleasure out of the tourists as the tourists got out of the village. Ⓐ

The front porch might seem a daring place for the rest of the town, but it was a gallery seat to me. My favorite place was atop the gate-post. Proscenium box for a born first-nighter.[1] Not only did I enjoy the show, but I didn't mind the actors knowing that I liked it. I actually spoke to them in passing. I'd wave at them and when they returned my salute, I would say something like this: "Howdy-do-well-

extenuating
(ĭk-stĕn′yōo-a′tĭng) *adj.* lessening the severity of **extenuate** *v.*

❶ Targeted Passage

Ⓐ RHETORICAL TECHNIQUES
Reread lines 4–12. Which lines have parallel structures? How do these comparisons help you understand more about Hurston and her hometown?

Girl in a Red Dress (1934), Charles Alston. Oil on canvas, 71″ × 55.9″. © The Harmon and Harriet Kelley Collection of African American Art. © Estate of Charles Alston. Courtesy of Michael Rosenfeld Gallery, LLC, New York.

---

1. **proscenium . . . first-nighter:** A proscenium box is a box seat near the stage. A first-nighter is a person who attends the opening night of a performance.

DIFFERENTIATED INSTRUCTION

FOR ENGLISH LANGUAGE LEARNERS

Idioms Tell students that "the town" in line 8 is an expression that means "the people of the town," not Eatonville itself. Students may also need help with "chewing cane," or sugarcane—an example of an ordinary part of life that is not disrupted by the sight of native whites. Help them put the whole sentences into their own words, such as "The townspeople did not stop what they were doing when the white people from the South passed by."

FOR STRUGGLING READERS

In combination with the *Audio Anthology CD*, use one or more Targeted Passages (pp. 900, 902, 904) to ensure that students focus on key events and concepts. Targeted Passages are also good for English learners.

❶ Targeted Passage [Lines 4–12]

This passage introduces Hurston and the setting of her childhood, the all-black community of Eatonville, Florida.

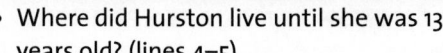

Reading Support

This selection on **thinkcentral.com** includes embedded **ThinkAloud** models–students "thinking aloud" about the story to model the kinds of questions a good reader would ask about a selection.

Analyze Visuals

Possible answer: *Students may respond that the girl appears tough, proud, or defiant (her straight posture, her fixed stare away from the viewer). They might also note that the girl is alone and set in sharp contrast with the background, suggesting she is isolated or lonely.*

About the Art American artist Charles Alston (1907–1977) drew upon his study of African sculpture to paint human figures, using the canvas as a place to investigate color, space, and form.

REVISIT THE BIG QUESTION
What makes you YOU?

Discuss How does Hurston's behavior define her personality? What role does Hurston see for herself in her life? ***Possible answer:*** *Hurston's behavior defines her personality as outgoing and dramatic, with a sense of humor. She sees herself as the star of her life's drama.*

- Where did Hurston live until she was 13 years old? (lines 4–5)

- What was unique about this place? (lines 5–7)

- How were Northern and Southern whites different? (lines 7–8)

- How did the townspeople respond to Northerners differently than they did to Southerners? (lines 8–12)

FOR ENGLISH LANGUAGE LEARNERS

Vocabulary Support Use New Word Analysis to teach these words: *register* (line 46), *potential* (line 48), *generation* (line 49), *achieve* (line 61), *contrast* (line 69).

BEST PRACTICES TOOLKIT—Transparency New Word Analysis p. E8

RI 1
RI 2

B Model the Skill:
MAIN IDEAS

Tell students that in these lines, Hurston gives important details that help form the main idea, namely, she's not like other African Americans who have a negative view of their color, and she's too busy going after the things that strong people achieve, regardless of race.

Have students use these details to state the main idea.

Possible answer: *Hurston does not believe in holding herself back from achieving her goals, unlike some individuals who believe race will limit them no matter what they do.*

IF STUDENTS NEED HELP... Determine the implied main idea by working together to add details about paragraph 6 to the pre-reading chart introduced on page 899.

Main Idea	Key Details
One must be strong to succeed in life, regardless of color.	"the world is to the strong... pigmentation"

TEXT ANALYSIS | COMMON CORE

RI 5
L 3a

C RHETORICAL TECHNIQUES

Possible answer: *"Slaves"/"slavery"–emphasizes her past.*

"Said"–emphasizes how Hurston saw each stage of her freedom. By comparing it to a race to be won, she leaves behind all self-pity.

Extend the Discussion Should slavery be dismissed as an institution of the past, or is it important to recognize its ongoing effects for people of color?

VOCABULARY | COMMON CORE

L 4

OWN THE WORD

pigmentation: Ask students to name other contexts in which they have heard *pigmentation* or the related *pigment.*
Possible answer: *make-up, art, pottery, paint*

I-thank-you-where-you-goin'?" Usually automobile or the horse paused at this, and after a queer exchange of compliments, I would probably "go a piece of the
20 way" with them, as we say in farthest Florida. If one of my family happened to come to the front in time to see me, of course negotiations would be rudely broken off. But even so, it is clear that I was the first "welcome-to-our-state" Floridian, and I hope the Miami Chamber of Commerce will please take notice.

During this period, white people differed from colored to me only in that they rode through town and never lived there. They liked to hear me "speak pieces" and sing and wanted to see me dance the parse-me-la,[2] and gave me generously of their small silver for doing these things, which seemed strange to me for I wanted to do them so much that I needed bribing to stop. Only they didn't know it. The colored people gave no dimes. They deplored any joyful tendencies in me, but
30 I was their Zora nevertheless. I belonged to them, to the nearby hotels, to the county—everybody's Zora.

But changes came in the family when I was thirteen, and I was sent to school in Jacksonville. I left Eatonville, the town of the oleanders,[3] as Zora. When I disembarked from the riverboat at Jacksonville, she was no more. It seemed that I had suffered a sea change.[4] I was not Zora of Orange County any more, I was now a little colored girl. I found it out in certain ways. In my heart as well as in the mirror, I became a fast brown—warranted not to rub nor run.

But I am not tragically colored. There is no great sorrow dammed up in my soul, nor lurking behind my eyes. I do not mind at all. I do not belong to the
40 sobbing school of Negrohood who hold that nature somehow has given them a low-down dirty deal and whose feelings are all hurt about it. Even in the helter-skelter skirmish that is my life, I have seen that the world is to the strong regardless of a little **pigmentation** more or less. No, I do not weep at the world—I am too busy sharpening my oyster knife.[5] **B**

Someone is always at my elbow reminding me that I am the grand-daughter of slaves. It fails to register depression with me. Slavery is sixty years in the past. The operation was successful and the patient is doing well, thank you. The terrible struggle that made me an American out of a potential slave said "On the line!" The Reconstruction said "Get set!"; and the generation before said "Go!" I am
50 off to a flying start and I must not halt in the stretch to look behind and weep. Slavery is the price I paid for civilization, and the choice was not with me. It is a bully adventure and worth all that I have paid through my ancestors for it. No one on earth ever had a greater chance for glory. The world to be won and nothing to be lost. It is thrilling to think—to know that for any act of mine, I shall get twice as much praise or twice as much blame. It is quite exciting to hold the center of the national stage, with the spectators not knowing whether to laugh or to weep. **C**

---

2. **parse-me-la:** a dance movement popular with Southern African Americans of the period.

3. **oleanders** (ō'lē-ǎn'dərz): evergreen shrubs with fragrant flowers.

4. **sea change:** complete transformation.

5. **oyster knife:** a reference to the saying "The world is my oyster," implying that the world contains treasure waiting to be taken, like the pearl in an oyster.

Language Coach

Fixed Expressions Note "negotiations would be ...broken off" (lines 21–22). A **fixed expression**, or standard combination of words, *break off negotiations* means "stop negotiations." What must the fixed expressions *enter into negotiations* and *resume negotiations* mean?

2 Targeted Passage

pigmentation
(pĭg'mən-tā'shən) *n.* coloring

B MAIN IDEAS
State the main idea of lines 38–44. What criticism is implied by the author's statement?

C RHETORICAL TECHNIQUES
Reread lines 45–48. What important word does Hurston repeat in these sentences? What effect does this repetition have on Hurston's message?

DIFFERENTIATED INSTRUCTION

FOR STRUGGLING READERS

 **Targeted Passage** [Lines 32–37]

This passage explains Hurston's change in color consciousness at age 13.

- Where did Hurston go when she turned 13? (lines 32–33)

- How was Hurston viewed differently in Jacksonville than in Eatonville? (lines 34–36)

- What effect did her move have on Hurston's sense of self? (lines 36–37)

FOR ENGLISH LANGUAGE LEARNERS

Language Coach

Fixed Expressions *Possible answer:* Enter into negotiations *means "begin negotiations."* Resume negotiations *means "start negotiations after they have stopped."* Direct students to line 45, which includes the fixed expression *at my elbow.* Remind students to use context to figure out the meaning of fixed expressions. Help them discern that this one means "nearby."

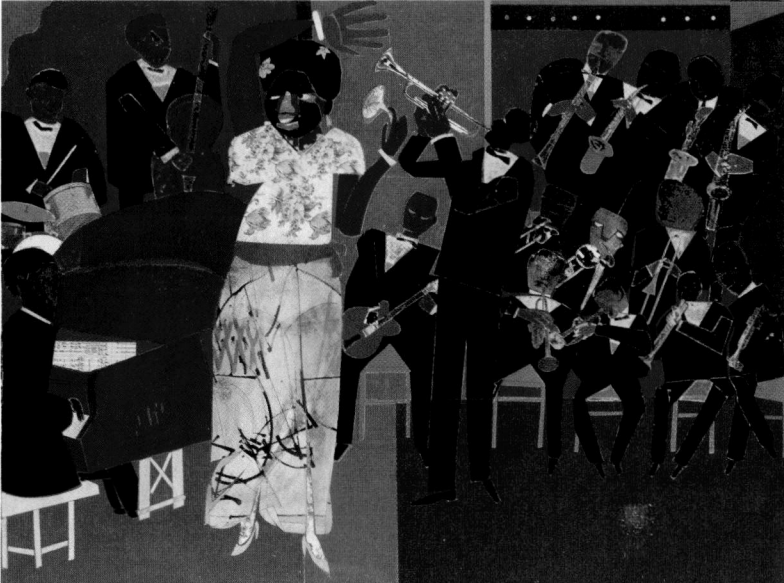

Empress of the Blues (1974), Romare Bearden. Collage, 36″ × 48″. Photo © Smithsonian American Art Museum/Art Resource, New York. © The Romare Bearden Foundation/Licensed by VAGA, New York.

The position of my white neighbor is much more difficult. No brown specter pulls up a chair beside me when I sit down to eat. No dark ghost thrusts its leg against mine in bed. The game of keeping what one has is never so exciting as the
60 game of getting.

I do not always feel colored. Even now I often achieve the unconscious Zora of Eatonville before the Hegira.[6] I feel most colored when I am thrown against a sharp white background.

For instance at Barnard. "Beside the waters of the Hudson"[7] I feel my race. Among the thousand white persons, I am a dark rock surged upon, overswept by a creamy sea. I am surged upon and overswept, but through it all, I remain myself. When covered by the waters, I am; and the ebb but reveals me again.

Sometimes it is the other way around. A white person is set down in our midst, but the contrast is just as sharp for me. For instance, when I sit in the
70 drafty basement that is The New World Cabaret with a white person, my color comes. We enter chatting about any little nothing that we have in common and are seated by the jazz waiters. In the abrupt way that jazz orchestras have, this one plunges into a number. It loses no time in circumlocutions, but gets right down to business. It constricts the thorax and splits the heart with its tempo and narcotic harmonies. This orchestra grows rambunctious, rears on its hind legs and attacks

---

6. **Hegira** (hĭ-jī′rə): journey (from the name given to Muhammad's journey from Mecca to Medina in 622).

7. **Barnard . . . Hudson":** Barnard is the college in New York City from which Hurston graduated in 1928. "Beside the waters . . ." is a reference to the first line of the college song.

Analyze Visuals

Activity Lead students to discuss how Bearden's image brings to life Hurston's description of a jazz performance at the New World Cabaret. *Possible answer: The artist's use of vibrant primary colors and fluid positioning of the band members and singer suggest movement and exultation.*

About the Art American artist Romare Bearden (1911-1988), a member of the Harlem Artists Guild, grew up in Harlem during its exhilarating renaissance period. Influenced by African and Asian art, as well as the European masters, Bearden is best known for his depictions of urban African-American scenes rendered as richly textured collages. *Empress of the Blues* evokes the performance Zora Neale Hurston describes.

TIERED DISCUSSION PROMPTS

In lines 57–67, use these prompts to help students understand Hurston's experience with color consciousness:

Connect Think about a situation in which you stood apart from the group for any reason—race, ethnicity, culture, age, gender, inexperience. How does that experience help you understand Hurston's feelings about her racial identity? *Accept all thoughtful responses.*

Interpret What does Hurston mean by "The game of keeping what one has is never so exciting as the game of getting"? *Possible answer: Hurston suggests that white people spend their time and energy trying to keep their status and are thus in a state of fear. Black people, on the other hand, spend their time and energy trying to gain equality and experience excitement through their efforts.*

Evaluate How effective is Hurston's use of imagery to explain her sense of color consciousness? *Possible answer: Hurston's imagery is very effective. She uses natural imagery (lines 65–67) and color imagery (lines 62–63) to describe moments when she feels most aware of her race.*

FOR ENGLISH LANGUAGE LEARNERS

Language Coach

Context Clues *Possible answer: The next sentence includes* dark ghost, *which is a restatement of* brown specter. Ask students to identify context clues that help to interpret "I feel my race" in line 64.

FOR STRUGGLING READERS

Develop Reading Fluency Use lines 57–75 to help students read aloud long sentences fluently. Remind them to take their cues from punctuation, pausing at commas to help listeners follow along. Tell students that they may find additional places to pause for breath within a long sentence. Read aloud the sentence that begins "We enter chatting" (line 71). Have students break into pairs to take turns reading the page aloud.

the tonal veil with primitive fury, rending it, clawing it until it breaks through to the jungle beyond. I follow those heathen—follow them **exultingly.** I dance wildly inside myself; I yell within, I whoop; I shake my assegai[8] above my head,

I hurl it true to the mark *yeeeeooww!* I am in the jungle and living in the jungle

80 way. My face is painted red and yellow, and my body is painted blue. My pulse is throbbing like a war drum. I want to slaughter something—give pain, give death to what, I do not know. But the piece ends. The men of the orchestra wipe their lips and rest their fingers. I creep back slowly to the veneer we call civilization with the last tone and find the white friend sitting motionless in his seat, smoking calmly.

"Good music they have here," he remarks, drumming the table with his fingertips.

Music! The great blobs of purple and red emotion have not touched him. He has only heard what I felt. He is far away and I see him but dimly across the ocean

90 and the continent that have fallen between us. He is so pale with his whiteness then and I am *so* colored. **D**

At certain times I have no race, I am *me*. When I set my hat at a certain angle and saunter down Seventh Avenue, Harlem City, feeling as snooty as the lions in front of the Forty-Second Street Library, for instance. So far as my feelings are concerned, Peggy Hopkins Joyce on the Boule Mich[9] with her gorgeous **raiment,** stately carriage, knees knocking together in a most aristocratic manner, has nothing on me. The **cosmic** Zora emerges. I belong to no race nor time, I am the eternal feminine with its string of beads.

I have no separate feeling about being an American citizen and colored. I

100 am merely a fragment of the Great Soul that surges within the boundaries. My country, right or wrong.

Sometimes, I feel discriminated against, but it does not make me angry. It merely astonishes me. How *can* any deny themselves the pleasure of my company! It's beyond me.

But in the main, I feel like a brown bag of **miscellany** propped against a wall.

Against a wall in company with other bags, white, red, and yellow. Pour out the contents, and there is discovered a jumble of small things priceless and worthless. A first-water[10] diamond, an empty spool, bits of broken glass, lengths of string, a key to a door long since crumbled away, a rusty knife-blade, old shoes saved for

110 a road that never was and never will be, a nail bent under the weight of things too heavy for any nail, a dried flower or two, still a little fragrant. In your hand is the **E** brown bag. On the ground before you is the jumble it held—so much like the jumble in the bags, could they be emptied, that all might be dumped in a single heap and the bags refilled without altering the content of any greatly. A bit of colored glass more or less would not matter. Perhaps that is how the Great Stuffer of Bags filled them in the first place—who knows? ❧

---

8. **assegai** (ăs′ə-gī′): a type of light spear used in southern Africa.

9. **Peggy … Boule Mich:** a wealthy woman of Hurston's day, walking along the Boulevard Saint-Michel in Paris.

10. **first-water:** of the highest quality or purity.

904 UNIT 5: THE HARLEM RENAISSANCE AND MODERNISM

---

exultingly (ĭg-zŭlt′ĭng-lē) *adv.* joyfully

D MAIN IDEAS
Describe the two responses that are contrasted in lines 88–91. What does this contrast imply about the differences between whites and blacks?

raiment (rā′mənt) *n.* clothing; garments

cosmic (kŏz′mĭk) *adj.* of or relating to the universe

3 Targeted Passage

miscellany (mĭs′ə-lā′nē) *n.* a mixture of various things

E GRAMMAR AND STYLE
Reread lines 105–111. Note how Hurston uses **sentence fragments** to highlight specific details in her description.

READING SKILL

COMMON CORE
RI 1
RI 2

D MAIN IDEAS

Possible answer: Hurston's response to the music is physical, while the man's response is merely auditory. This contrast implies that African Americans experience life musically and emotionally, while whites observe it intellectually and from a distance.

E GRAMMAR AND STYLE

COMMON CORE L 1a

Vary Sentence Structure Authors sometimes use sentence fragments to highlight details, add emphasis, or slow the pace or fluency of a passage. Ask students to identify the fragments in lines 108–111 and to explain their effect. *Possible answer: The entire sentence is composed of fragments. The effect is that of inviting readers to visualize this list of vivid details.*

VOCABULARY

COMMON CORE L 4

OWN THE WORD

- **exultingly:** Tell students that *exultingly* is the adverb form of *exult,* a verb meaning "to rejoice greatly." Ask students what might make them *exult.*

- **raiment:** Tell students that *raiment* means "clothing" or "garments." Have students list other synonyms for *raiment.*

- **cosmic:** Ask students to list words other than *cosmic* that could be used in describing Zora.

- **miscellany:** Tell students that *miscellany* is the noun form of *miscellaneous,* an adjective meaning "made up of a variety of parts or ingredients."

SELECTION WRAP-UP

READ WITH A PURPOSE Now that students have read the selection, they may conclude that Hurston feels black only in the company of white people, such as in her college classes or sitting near a white man at a jazz club. How does Hurston feel the rest of the time? *Possible answer: She feels at one with the Great Soul, which is defined neither by race nor time.*

904 UNIT 5

DIFFERENTIATED INSTRUCTION

FOR STRUGGLING READERS

3 Targeted Passage [Lines 99–105]

This passage summarizes Hurston's views on racial identity and on her place in humanity.

- How does Hurston feel about being an American citizen? (line 99)

- Of what is Hurston a "fragment"? (line 100)

- How does Hurston feel about being discriminated against? (lines 102–104)

- Why does Hurston call herself "a brown bag of miscellany"? (line 105)

Comprehension

1. **Recall** In Hurston's description, what kind of community was Eatonville?

2. **Recall** What was the big change Hurston experienced at age 13?

3. **Paraphrase** What is Hurston's view on slavery?

Text Analysis

● 4. **Identify Main Ideas** Review the chart you created as you read. What is the main idea of the essay? In what ways does race shape Hurston's sense of identity?

● 5. **Analyze Rhetorical Techniques** What effect is created by Hurston's use of rhetorical techniques to show how she belonged in Eatonville (lines 30–31), to reveal her thoughts at Barnard (lines 64–67), and to emphasize her connection with jazz (lines 68–85).

6. **Make Inferences** Judging from the anecdotes Hurston includes in her essay, what experiences and traits does she consider distinctively African-American? Support your answer with details.

7. **Interpret Analogy** An **analogy** is a comparison using one thing or idea to make sense of another. Look at the analogy in lines 105–116. What is being compared? Be sure to explain each part of the analogy, including the colored bags, the "Great Stuffer of Bags," and the bags' contents.

8. **Compare and Contrast Author's Perspectives** Hurston's views set her apart from most of her Harlem Renaissance contemporaries. Choose one of the poets you have read in this unit, and use a chart like the one shown to contrast his perspectives with Hurston's. What similarities and differences do you find?

	Hurston's Views	_____'s Views
What Defines Black Identity		
Goals of Black Writers		
Opinions of Whites		

Text Criticism

9. **Critical Interpretations**
The author Alice Walker, one of Hurston's greatest admirers, finds Hurston's views sometimes "exasperating." She notes that this essay "presents two stereotypes: the 'happy darky' who sings and dances for white folks, for money and for joy; and the educated black person who is, underneath the thin veneer of civilization, still a 'heathen.'" Do you agree with Walker's views? Why or why not? Be specific in your response.

What makes you **YOU?**

Those who study people often debate whether nature or nurture most defines someone's personality. In other words, is the person born that way or is he or she shaped more by the environment. What do you think? Do you believe your personality is shaped more by nature or nurture? Explain your answer.

HOW IT FEELS TO BE COLORED ME **905**

RI 1 Cite textual evidence to support analysis of what the text says explicitly as well as inferences drawn from the text. **RI 2** Determine two or more central ideas of a text and analyze their development over the course of the text. **RI 5** Analyze and evaluate the effectiveness of the structure an author uses in his or her exposition or argument, including whether the structure makes points clear, convincing, and engaging. **RI 10** Read and comprehend literary nonfiction. **L 3a** Apply an understanding of syntax to the study of complex texts when reading.

COMMON CORE

25–28) complements the "happy darky" stereotype. Her physical reaction to jazz music and the primitive impulses it stirs complement the "heathen" stereotype (lines 77–82). The "price I paid for civilization" (line 51) implies that slavery was ultimately helpful. Although Hurston may intend to be funny and liberating, many readers will take offense.

What makes you **YOU?**

Possible answer: Answers will vary but should include specific examples that support either a nature or nuture viewpoint.

Practice and Apply

For preliminary support of post-reading questions, use these copy masters:

R RESOURCE MANAGER—Copy Masters
Reading Check p. 68
Rhetorical Techniques p. 61
Question Support p. 69

Additional selection questions are provided for teachers on page 55.

ANSWERS

COMMON CORE RI 1, RI 2, RI 5, RI 10, L 3a

1. *Eatonville is an exclusively black and close-knit community.*

2. *Hurston's family situation changes, and she is sent to school in Jacksonville. Here, she is exposed to racial distinctions.*

3. *Hurston says that slavery is part of a closed past (lines 45–51).*

Possible answers:

4. ■ **COMMON CORE FOCUS** **Identify Main Ideas** **Main Idea:** *People of all colors are part of humanity, equal and beautiful. Race shapes Hurston's sense of identity when she is around white people, but she otherwise defines herself by personality.*

5. ● **COMMON CORE FOCUS** **Rhetorical Techniques** *In lines 30–31, repetition shows how much Hurston belonged to her town and country. Parallel structure and repetition in lines 64–67 and 68–85 show that although surrounded by white people, she remains steadfast in her identity, and the power of music to draw her back to her African roots, respectively.*

6. *African-American experiences and traits include humor (lines 22–23), a strong sense of community (lines 13–22), and a passionate response to music (lines 68–85).*

7. *The bags represent different skin colors. The Great Stuffer of Bags is a higher being. The bags' contents are unique personalities. The message is that people should be evaluated by traits, not by color.*

8. *Responses will vary depending on the poet chosen.* **Hurston: Defining Black Identity:** *community life, music, strong emotional responses;* **Goals:** *to write well;* **Opinions of Whites:** *amused sympathy*

9. *There is strong evidence in the essay to support Walker's position. Hurston's account of singing and dancing for whites (lines*

ANSWERS

Vocabulary in Context

▲ **VOCABULARY PRACTICE**

1. *(c) regulation*
2. *(c) weathering*
3. *(d) fictional*
4. *(c) zoology*
5. *(a) determinedly*
6. *(d) exaggerating*

R RESOURCE MANAGER—COPY MASTER
Vocabulary Practice p. 66

ACADEMIC VOCABULARY IN SPEAKING

Answers will vary. Students may say that past difficulties *justify* people's negative reactions today. Others may feel that this is just an excuse to act poorly.

VOCABULARY STRATEGY: THE GREEK ROOT *cosm* **OR** *cosmo*

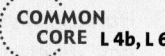 COMMON CORE **L 4b, L 6**

- For each word in the web, help students use their knowledge of the root to determine word meaning.
- Review these Greek root meanings: *micro-,* "small"; *-graphy,* "writing"; *-naut,* "sailor"; *-logy,* "word"; *-polis,* "city." Clarify how these English words are built from the meanings of Greek roots.

Possible answers:

1. *cosmology*
2. *cosmonaut*
3. *cosmography*
4. *microcosm*
5. *cosmopolitan*

R RESOURCE MANAGER—Copy Master
Vocabulary Strategy p. 67

Interactive Vocabulary   THINK central

Keywords direct students to a **WordSharp** tutorial on **thinkcentral.com** or to other types of vocabulary practice and review.

Vocabulary in Context

▲ **VOCABULARY PRACTICE**

Choose the word that is not related in meaning to the other words.

1. (a) collection, (b) miscellany, (c) regulation, (d) assortment
2. (a) apparel, (b) clothing, (c) weathering, (d) raiment
3. (a) vast, (b) cosmic, (c) universal, (d) fictional
4. (a) shading, (b) pigmentation, (c) zoology, (d) coloration
5. (a) determinedly, (b) exultingly, (c) delightedly, (d) ecstatically
6. (a) extenuating, (b) moderating, (c) mitigating, (d) exaggerating

WORD LIST
cosmic
extenuating
exultingly
miscellany
pigmentation
raiment

ACADEMIC VOCABULARY IN SPEAKING

- conclude   - criteria   - despite   - justify   - maintain

Zora Neale Hurston was upbeat and positive **despite** being the grand-daughter of slaves. In a group, discuss how the past influences the future. Do difficulties in the past **justify** someone being angry and resentful today? Use at least three Academic Vocabulary words in your discussion.

COMMON CORE

L 4b Identify and correctly use patterns of word changes that indicate different meanings or parts of speech. **L 6** Acquire and use accurately general academic and domain-specific words and phrases.

VOCABULARY STRATEGY: THE GREEK ROOT *cosm* OR *cosmo*

The origin of the root word *cosm*, which may also be spelled *cosmo*, is the Greek language. *Cosm* is derived from the Greek word *kosmos*, meaning "world" or "universe." This Greek root is found in the vocabulary word *cosmic* as well as a number of other English words. You can use your knowledge of the origin and meaning of this root word, in addition to the context of a word, to help determine the word's meaning.

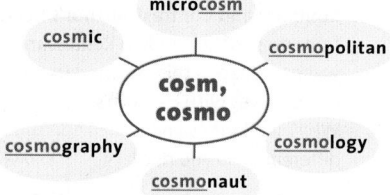

PRACTICE Apply what you know about the Greek root *cosm* or *cosmo* to the words in the web. Then, choose the word from the web that best completes each sentence. If you need to, consult a dictionary.

1. Many myths of creation also include a _____, or a theory of the universe.

2. A _____ is an explorer of outer space.

3. The science called _____ includes astronomy, geography, and geology.

4. A _____ can be any type of miniature community or world.

5. A _____ person tends to have a sophisticated view of the world.

Interactive Vocabulary   THINK central

Go to thinkcentral.com.
KEYWORD: HML11-906

DIFFERENTIATED INSTRUCTION

FOR ENGLISH LANGUAGE LEARNERS

Task Support: Vocabulary Practice Point out the vocabulary words in the practice items. Have students identify familiar words among the remaining choices, and use dictionaries to define any unfamiliar words. Tell students to find any two word choices that are similar, and then to compare the remaining choices to this pair.

FOR ADVANCED LEARNERS/AP

Vocabulary in Writing Challenge students to consider the opinion other Harlem Renaissance poets might have about Hurston's ideas. Ask students to write a response to Hurston's essay from the view of one of the Harlem Renaissance poets, such as Langston Hughes, Claude McKay, or Countee Cullen. Urge them to use vocabulary words from the Word List in their writing.

Language

◆ **GRAMMAR AND STYLE:** Vary Sentence Structure

Review the **Grammar and Style** note on page 904. Zora Neale Hurston's independent and unconventional personality shines through in her writing style. She wasn't afraid to bend the rules of formal writing, adding punch and emphasis through the use of **sentence fragments.** Here are two examples from the essay:

> *I feel most colored when I am thrown against a sharp white background. For instance at Barnard.* (lines 62–64)

> *I am merely a fragment of the Great Soul that surges within the boundaries. My country, right or wrong.* (lines 99–101)

The fragment "My country, right or wrong" brings the reader to an abrupt halt, creating a dramatic and strong statement. The change in sentence rhythm helps emphasize the finality of Hurston's belief about her place in the world.

PRACTICE Rewrite the following paragraph in Zora Neale Hurston's style, incorporating one or two intentional sentence fragments. Add or delete any words as necessary.

> My parents were always finding opportunities to point out how much the world owed to China. We learned that our Chinese ancestors had invented paper, books, kites, gunpowder, compasses, fishing reels, and umbrellas. Was there anything that hadn't been invented by the Chinese? One day we went to eat at an Italian restaurant. As I dug into my plate of pasta, I told my mom, "Well, here's one thing the Chinese didn't invent." I was wrong! The Chinese invented pasta, she explained, and they invented restaurants, too!

READING-WRITING CONNECTION

Expand your understanding of Hurston's essay by responding to this prompt. Then, use the **revising tips** to improve your essay.

WRITING PROMPT	REVISING TIPS
WRITE AN AUTOBIOGRAPHICAL ESSAY Imagine that you have entered a writing contest sponsored by a heritage society. Draft a **three-to-five-paragraph autobiographical essay,** modeled after Hurston's essay, in which you share your feelings about your own heritage. In your essay, include at least two sentence fragments that help emphasize important points.	• Focus on one or two important details about your heritage. • Use personal examples, explanations, and anecdotes to show why your heritage is important. • End with a conclusion that wraps up the thoughts in your essay.

Interactive Revision **THINK**central

Go to **thinkcentral.com.**
KEYWORD: HML11-907

Language

◆ **GRAMMAR AND STYLE**

Have students read the excerpts aloud to hear the change in rhythm created by sentence fragments. Urge students to continually compare their writing against the essay's style as they complete the *PRACTICE* activity. ***Possible answer:*** *My parents were always finding opportunities to point out how much the world owed to China. Paper. Books. Kites. Gunpowder. Compasses. Fishing reels. Umbrellas. One day while we were eating in an Italian restaurant, I slurped my pasta and said, "Well, here's one thing that the Chinese didn't invent!" Wrong again. Pasta. Restaurants, too.*

 RESOURCE MANAGER—Copy Master
Vary Sentence Structure p. 70

READING-WRITING CONNECTION

Explain that students may define their heritage however they wish. Suggest that they begin by writing this definition in the center of a Spider Map. Tell students to fill the outer cells with features that support the definition, such as descriptions of family members, bits of dialogue, anecdotes, rituals or traditions.

 **BEST PRACTICES TOOLKIT—Transparency**
Spider Map p. B47

Writing Online   **THINK**central

The following tools are available online at **thinkcentral.com** and on Write*Smart* CD-ROM:
• **Interactive Graphic Organizers**
• **Interactive Student Models**
• **Interactive Revision Lessons**
For additional grammar instruction, see **GrammarNotes** on **thinkcentral.com**.

COMMON CORE (sidebar)

L 1a Apply the understanding that usage is a matter of convention, can change over time, and is sometimes contested. **L 3a** Vary syntax for effect, consulting references for guidance as needed. **W 3** Write narratives to develop imagined experiences or events using effective technique, well-chosen details, and well-structured event sequences.

FOR STRUGGLING WRITERS

Writing Support

• Allow students to write a three-paragraph essay. The first paragraph should use an incident from early childhood, the second paragraph should relate an incident from school-age years, and the third should relate a more recent incident. In either the first or last paragraph, students should identify their heritage and state their feelings about it.

• To help them get started, ask students to decide on a particular feeling they want to convey about their heritage, such as proud, confused, or neutral. Urge students to choose three to five incidents from their life that reflect this feeling.

• For each incident they will discuss, have students list words that describe it. Work with students to replace general words with more specific and vivid language.

Assess and Reteach

Assess

DIAGNOSTIC AND SELECTION TESTS
Selection Test A, B/C pp. 233–234, 235–236
Interactive Selection Test on **thinkcentral.com**

Reteach

Level Up Online Tutorials on **thinkcentral.com**
Reteaching Worksheets on **thinkcentral.com**

Focus and Motivate

⊙ COMMON CORE FOCUS

RI 2 Determine two or more central ideas of a text and analyze their development over the course of the text. RI 4 Analyze how an author uses and refines the meaning of a key term or terms over the course of a text. RI 6 Determine an author's point of view or purpose in a text in which the rhetoric is particularly effective, analyzing how content contributes to the power, persuasiveness, or beauty of the text.

ABOUT THE AUTHOR

Clarify the reference to allegorical names in **A Major Literary Force,** explaining that an allegory is a work in which the characters are understood to represent something else, such as figures and ideas from religious texts. Point out that the selection also has religious references in it, although they are not allegorical. Ask students how Morrison's early upbringing sparked her interest in religion. *Possible answer: Morrison heard a lot of biblical references in her early years, which probably helped her view religious materials as both a part of daily life and a source for story ideas.*

NOTABLE QUOTE

"The ability of writers to imagine what is not the self, to familiarize the strange and mystify the familiar, is the test of their power."
—Toni Morrison

Ask students what this suggests about Morrison's view of a writer's obligation? *Possible* **answer:** *Familiarizing the strange and mystifying the familiar invites readers to consider new perspectives.*

Selection Resources

⊙ COMMON CORE

RI 2 Determine two or more central ideas of a text and analyze their development over the course of the text. RI 4 Analyze how an author uses and refines the meaning of a key term or terms over the course of a text. RI 6 Determine an author's point of view or purpose in a text in which the rhetoric is particularly effective, analyzing how content contributes to the power, persuasiveness, or beauty of the text.

DID YOU KNOW?

Toni Morrison ...

- was once a textbook editor.
- raised two sons as a single mother after her first marriage ended.
- changed her first name in college because "Chloe" was hard to pronounce.
- was the first African American to win the Nobel Prize in literature.

⏱ Themes Across Time

Thoughts on the African-American Novel
Literary Criticism by Toni Morrison

Meet the Author

Toni Morrison born 1931

Toni Morrison was born Chloe Anthony Wofford in Lorain, Ohio. This working-class town had a small, close-knit African-American community with a vibrant oral culture. In stories, songs, and everyday speech, Morrison heard an imaginative blend of biblical phrases, rhetorical devices, slang, and conventional English. This early awareness of the power of language and storytelling was a powerful influence on Morrison's work.

Accidental Novelist After earning a bachelor's degree from Howard University (1953) and a master's in English from Cornell University (1955), Morrison embarked on a teaching career. While teaching at Howard, she joined a writers' group for fun, showing up at meetings with what she called "old junk" that she'd written in high school. When she ran out of "junk" before one meeting, she quickly scribbled down a story—a story that later inspired her first novel, *The Bluest Eye.* Published in 1969, the book recounts the story of a troubled African-American girl who, conditioned by white society's ideals of beauty, longs to have blue eyes. The novel's themes, such as the trauma of racism and the importance of community, set the stage for Morrison's later work.

A Major Literary Force The novels *Sula* (1973), *Song of Solomon* (1977), and *Tar Baby* (1981) established Morrison as a major author with a unique voice. Her novels typically have richly symbolic plots that include supernatural or fantastic elements. Within this imaginative context, Morrison provides a realistic treatment of social issues. Her characters, who often have allegorical or biblical names, confront the central struggles of African-American life: the impact of violence and injustice on their lives and the search for cultural identity.

Morrison has been nominated for every major literary honor; she has received, among others, the National Book Critics Circle Award, the Pulitzer Prize, and the Nobel Prize in Literature. She has written several novels and numerous works of commentary and cultural analysis. More recent novels include *Paradise* (1998) and *Love* (2003). Morrison lectures and teaches at various universities across the country. She is widely considered one of the most innovative stylists in contemporary American literature.

Author Online
THINK central
Go to **thinkcentral.com**. KEYWORD: HML11-908

908

See resources on the **Teacher One Stop DVD-ROM** and on **thinkcentral.com**.

 RESOURCE MANAGER UNIT 5
 Plan and Teach, pp. 71–78
 Summary, pp. 79–80†‡*
 Text Analysis and Reading
  Skill, pp. 81–84†*

DIAGNOSTIC AND SELECTION TESTS
 Selection Tests, pp. 237–240

 BEST PRACTICES TOOLKIT
 Definition Mapping, p. E6
 Read Aloud/Think Aloud,
  p. A71

TECHNOLOGY
 ⊘ **Teacher One Stop DVD-ROM**
 ⊘ **Student One Stop DVD-ROM**
 ⊘ **Audio Anthology CD**
 ⊘ **ExamView Test Generator**
  on the **Teacher One Stop**

---

* Resources for Differentiation   † Also in Spanish   ‡ In Haitian Creole and Vietnamese

TEXT ANALYSIS: RHETORICAL TECHNIQUES

Literary criticism, including this essay by Toni Morrison, aims to make readers more knowledgeable about, and appreciative of the literature they read. In this critical essay Morrison uses the following rhetorical devices to make her words more effective:

- **personal accounts:** anecdotes or stories of personal experience that support the writer's message
- **repetition:** the recurrence of particular words, sounds, or ideas

As you read, think about how Morrison uses each rhetorical technique to clarify her meaning and to evoke a response from her readers.

READING SKILL: IDENTIFY AUTHOR'S VIEWPOINT

Works of literary criticism are written to communicate a position, or an opinion, on a topic. To identify an author's **position,** look for direct statements that express the author's viewpoint, such as the following:

I don't regard Black literature as simply books written by Black people, or simply as literature written about Black people . . .

You'll also want to look for the specific reasons and evidence the writer presents to support his or her opinion. As you read, identify Morrison's position on the importance of the novel to society and on the characteristics that define the African-American novel. In a chart like the one shown, record the reasons and evidence she uses to support her positions. Consider whether you find these positions persuasive.

	Position	Reasons and Evidence
Importance of the Novel		
What Defines the African-American Novel		

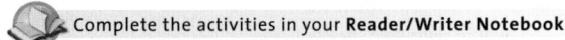 Complete the activities in your **Reader/Writer Notebook.**

Can CULTURE *be captured in words?*

You can think of culture as the things people make, such as food, books, music, and crafts. But culture is also the things people do: the way they talk, the relationships they build, the values they hold dear. In this essay, Toni Morrison talks about her struggle to capture the essence of African-American culture on the printed page.

QUICKWRITE Think about the cultures you belong to—your ethnicity, your religion, even your region or town. If you were writing about one of these cultures, what would you need to include? List three or more features you would use to capture the experience of that culture.

909

Can CULTURE *be captured in words?*

After students read the definitions of culture, have them suggest additional examples. Tell them to keep their ideas and those offered on page 909 in mind as they complete the *QUICKWRITE*.

TEXT ANALYSIS — COMMON CORE RI 4 RI 6

● *Model the Skill:* **RHETORICAL TECHNIQUES**

To help students identify Morrison's rhetorical techniques, display and read aloud this sentence from the essay:

"But when the peasant class, or lower class, or what have you, confronts the middle class, the city, or the upper classes, they are thrown a little bit into disarray."

Point out the repetition of the word "class." Tell students that Morrison uses repetition here to show that there are many classes in society and that they are rigid.

GUIDED PRACTICE Have students look at a previously read selection and identify and explain one or more instances of repetition.

READING SKILL — COMMON CORE RI 6

■ *Model the Skill:* **IDENTIFY AUTHOR'S VIEWPOINT**

Read aloud the **Notable Quote** from page 908. Tell students that here Morrison states her position on the abilities of a good writer.

GUIDED PRACTICE Read the quotation to students again, then ask them to explain how strong imaginative powers help writers accomplish each of the three tasks Morrison names.

 RESOURCE MANAGER—Copy Master
Identify Author's Position p. 83
(for student use while reading the selection)

DIFFERENTIATED INSTRUCTION

FOR STRUGGLING READERS
Vocabulary Support

- *context,* "background or overall situation related to a particular literary work"
- *criticism,* "analysis of qualities and opinion about relative worth"
- *evidence,* "information that helps prove an idea"
- *persuasive,* "having the power to change others' views"

- *position,* "one's attitude or opinion on a subject"
- *standards,* "something created as a basis of comparison to judge worth"
- *viewpoint,* "mental position from which things are judged"

Practice and Apply

SUMMARY

In this essay, Toni Morrison describes the novel as an art form that developed to help a rising middle class understand its world. She explains that novels enlighten, instruct, and identify problems and conflicts without offering recipes for solution. Morrison then focuses on the role of the novel for African Americans, and the need for black novels to function simultaneously as written and oral literature that requires readers to stand, speak, and act.

READ WITH A PURPOSE

Help students set a purpose for reading. Tell them to read to discover how Morrison believes a novel's narrator should function for readers.

TIERED DISCUSSION PROMPTS

In lines 1–13, use these prompts to help students think about the function of art:

Connect Name a song, movie, TV show, or book that taught you something about how to live your life. What message did it convey? *Accept all thoughtful responses.*

Interpret What does Morrison mean by "the novel always functioned for the class or the group that wrote it"? *Possible answer: Morrison means that the novel addresses issues of concern and interest to the group or class from which its writer emerges.*

Evaluate Do you agree or disagree with Morrison's claim that the purpose of art is to tell people something that they don't know? Explain. *Students will likely agree that art should offer people information or perspective beyond their current circumstances, and thereby teach and uplift. Others may disagree by noting that art should publicize and celebrate the insights that a culture has already arrived at.*

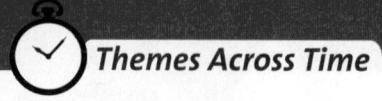
Thoughts on the African-American Novel

Toni Morrison

Analyze Visuals ▶
Read lines 1–15. How might the painting on page 911 be compared with the "novel of manners" referred to in lines 12–13? Explain.

The label "novel" is useful in technical terms because I write prose that is longer than a short story. My sense of the novel is that it has always functioned for the class or the group that wrote it. The history of the novel as a form began when there was a new class, a middle class, to read it, it was an art form that they needed. The lower classes didn't need novels at that time because they had an art form already: they had songs, and dances, and ceremony, and gossip, and celebrations. The aristocracy didn't need it because they had the art that they had patronized, they had their own pictures painted, their own houses built, and they made sure their art separated them from the rest of the world. But when the

10 industrial revolution began, there emerged a new class of people who were neither peasants nor aristocrats. In large measure they had no art form to tell them how to behave in this new situation. So they produced an art form: we call it the novel of manners, an art form designed to tell people something they didn't know. That is, how to behave in this new world, how to distinguish between the good guys and the bad guys. How to get married. What a good living was. What would happen

❶ Targeted Passage

Family (1955), Charles H. Alston. Oil on canvas, 48¼″ × 35¾″. Whitney Museum of American Art, New York. Purchase, with funds from the Artists and Students Assistance Fund 55.47. © Estate of Charles H. Alston.

DIFFERENTIATED INSTRUCTION

FOR ENGLISH LANGUAGE LEARNERS

Vocabulary Support Use Definition Mapping to teach these words: *technical* (line 1), *incorporate* (line 40), *expand* (line 48), *criteria* (line 84), *style* (line 91).

BEST PRACTICES TOOLKIT—Transparency Definition Mapping p. E6

FOR STRUGGLING READERS

In combination with the *Audio Anthology CD*, use one or more Targeted Passages (pp. 910, 912) to ensure that students focus on key concepts in the selection. Targeted Passages are also good for English language learners.

❶ Targeted Passage [Lines 9–15]

This passage explains Morrison's view of the novel's function for the middle class.

Analyze Visuals

Possible answer: *Like the novel of manners, the painting seems to provide a model of family life for the viewer. In contrast, the painting is strikingly modern and uses an African-American family as the standard to follow.*

About the Art More abstract than his "Girl in a Red Dress" found on page 901, Charles Alston's (1907–1977) *Family* shows the diversity of his artistic style as well as his commitment to depicting African-American life.

BACKGROUND

Industrial Revolution Beginning in Britain in the 18th century, the Industrial Revolution marked a change from agricultural to industrial economies because physical labor was replaced by machines. This economic shift created large-scale social changes, such as the growth of cities and the challenges of living in them.

REVISIT THE BIG QUESTION

Can CULTURE be captured in words?

How is membership in an economic or social class part of one's culture? *Possible answer: One's economic or social class provides or limits opportunities for leisure, education, consumerism, and so on, which directly affect one's cultural affiliations.*

- What new group in society resulted from the Industrial Revolution? (lines 9–11)
- What did this new group lack? (lines 11–12)
- How did they respond to this situation? (lines 12–13)
- What is the novel of manners? (lines 13–15)

FOR STRUGGLING READERS

Develop Reading Fluency To help students become more familiar with effective reading of literary criticism, play the selection on the *Audio Anthology CD*. Tell students that as they listen, they should take note of the reader's pacing, inflection, and expression. Then, assign paragraphs for students to read aloud.

Ⓐ ANALYZE

Remind students that to analyze a passage, they may need to read it several times. In addition to restating the main idea, they need to understand the meanings of unfamiliar words. They also need to understand the author's use of literary devices, including sarcasm and irony. Read aloud lines 23–35. Point out that Morrison believes that African-American writers and readers can turn to the novel as a means of communicating stories and other information important to the African-American community.

Possible answer: *Morrison believes the novel form is an important medium through which African-American writers can pass on the classical archetypal stories that previously were handed down as oral history (lines 30–35).*

Extend the Discussion Why does Morrison feel that music is now less of a medium through which African-Americans can communicate cultural information?

---

if you strayed from the fold. So that early works such as *Pamela,* by Samuel Richardson, and the Jane Austen material[1] provided social rules and explained behavior, identified outlaws, identified the people, habits, and customs that one should approve of. They were didactic[2] in that sense. That, I think, is probably
20 why the novel was not missed among the so-called peasant cultures. They didn't need it, because they were clear about what their responsibilities were and who and where was evil, and where was good.

But when the peasant class, or lower class, or what have you, confronts the middle class, the city, or the upper classes, they are thrown a little bit into disarray. For a long time, the art form that was healing for Black people was music. That music is no longer *exclusively* ours, we don't have exclusive rights to it. Other people sing it and play it; it is the mode of contemporary music everywhere. So another form has to take that place, and it seems to me that the novel is needed by African-Americans now in a way that it was not needed before—and it is
30 following along the lines of the function of novels everywhere. We don't live in places where we can hear those stories anymore; parents don't sit around and tell their children those classical, mythological archetypal[3] stories that we heard years ago. But new information has got to get out, and there are several ways to do it. One is in the novel. I regard it as a way to accomplish certain very strong functions—one being the one I just described. **Ⓐ**

It should be beautiful, and powerful, but it should also *work.* It should have something in it that enlightens; something in it that opens the door and points the way. Something in it that suggests what the conflicts are, what the problems are. But it need not solve those problems because it is not a case study,[4] it is not a
40 recipe. There are things that I try to incorporate into my fiction that are directly and deliberately related to what I regard as the major characteristics of Black art, wherever it is. One of which is the ability to be both print and oral literature: to combine those two aspects so that the stories can be read in silence, of course, but one should be able to hear them as well. It should try deliberately to make you stand up and make you feel something profoundly in the same way that a Black preacher requires his congregation to speak, to join him in the sermon, to behave in a certain way, to stand up and to weep and to cry and to accede or to change and to modify—to expand on the sermon that is being delivered. In the same way that a musician's music is enhanced when there is a response from the audience.
50 Now in a book, which closes, after all—it's of some importance to me to try to make that connection—to try to make that happen also. And, having at my disposal only the letters of the alphabet and some punctuation, I have to provide the places and spaces so that the reader can participate. Because it is the affective

---

1. **the Jane Austen material:** Jane Austen (1775–1817) wrote several novels focused on middle-class life in her era.
2. **didactic** (dī-dăk′tĭk): intended to instruct.
3. **archetypal** (är′kĭ-tī′pəl): serving as a pattern for later examples.
4. **case study:** an intensive analysis of a group, individual or unit and its development.

 Targeted Passage

COMMON CORE RI 2

Ⓐ ANALYZE
In order to summarize a text effectively, it is necessary to identify and understand the author's main ideas. To learn this important skill, pause periodically as you read. Examine what you've read since the last pause and jot down the main ideas in your own words. Reread lines 23–35. How would you summarize Morrison's opinion about the importance of the novel?

Language Coach

Word Definitions
Disposal (line 52) means "power to use as one wants." Read lines 51–53. What does Morrison have at her disposal? What task does she wish to accomplish with it?

DIFFERENTIATED INSTRUCTION

FOR STRUGGLING READERS

② Targeted Passage [Lines 23–35]

This passage explains why Morrison believes that the novel is important to African Americans.

- What art form has often been healing for African Americans? (line 25)
- Why is this art form no longer healing? (lines 25–27)
- What art form do African Americans need now? (lines 27–30)
- What need does that art form meet? (lines 30–35)

FOR ENGLISH LANGUAGE LEARNERS

Language Coach

Word Definitions *Possible answer: Morrison has only "letters of the alphabet and some punctuation" at her disposal. She wants to use them to engage her reader in active participation.* Ask students to use context clues or use dictionaries to look up the meanings of other unfamiliar words on page 912.

and participatory relationship between the artist or the speaker and the audience that is of primary importance, as it is in these other art forms that I have described. **B**

To make the story appear oral, meandering, effortless, spoken—to have the reader *feel* the narrator without *identifying* that narrator, or hearing him or her knock about, and to have the reader work *with* the author in the construction

60 of the book—is what's important. What is left out is as important as what is there. To describe sexual scenes in such a way that they are not clinical, not even explicit[5]—so that the reader brings his own sexuality to the scene and thereby participates in it in a very personal way. And owns it. To construct the dialogue so that it is heard. So that there are no adverbs attached to them: "loudly," "softly," "he said menacingly." The menace should be in the sentence. To use, even formally, a chorus. The real presence of a chorus. Meaning the community or the reader at large, commenting on the action as it goes ahead.

In the books that I have written, the chorus has changed but there has always been a choral note, whether it is the "I" narrator of *Bluest Eye,* or the town

70 functioning as a character in *Sula,* or the neighborhood and the community that responds in the two parts of town in *Solomon.*[6] Or, as extreme as I've gotten, all of nature thinking and feeling and watching and responding to the action going on in *Tar Baby,* so that they are in the story: the trees hurt, fish are afraid, clouds report, and the bees are alarmed. Those are the ways in which I try to incorporate, into that traditional genre the novel, unorthodox novelistic characteristics—so that it is, in my view, Black, because it uses the characteristics of Black art. I am not suggesting that some of these devices have not been used before and elsewhere—only the reason why I do. I employ them as well as I can. And those are just some; I wish there were ways in which such things could be talked about

80 in the criticism. My general disappointment in some of the criticism that my work has received has nothing to do with approval. It has something to do with the vocabulary used in order to describe these things. I don't like to find my books condemned as bad or praised as good, when that condemnation or that praise is based on criteria from other paradigms.[7] I would much prefer that they were dismissed or embraced based on the success of their accomplishment within the culture out of which I write. **C**

I don't regard Black literature as simply books written *by* Black people, or simply as literature written *about* Black people, or simply as literature that uses a certain mode of language in which you just sort of drop *g's.* There is something

90 very special and very identifiable about it and it is my struggle to *find* that elusive but identifiable style in the books. My joy is when I think that I have approached it; my misery is when I think I can't get there. ∽ **D**

---

5. **not clinical, not even explicit:** not coldly impersonal or even clearly detailed.

6. **Solomon:** Morrison's novel *Song of Solomon.*

7. **paradigms** (păr′ə-dīmz′): theoretical frameworks or patterns.

B RHETORICAL TECHNIQUES
Reread lines 36–56. What personal account does Morrison use in this passage to help readers understand what she is saying?

C AUTHOR'S POSITION
Reread lines 68–86. What examples from her own work does Morrison cite as **evidence** for her position?

D RHETORICAL TECHNIQUES
Reread lines 87–92. What important key terms does Morrison repeat in this paragraph? Why does she use repetition here?

TEXT ANALYSIS COMMON CORE RI 4 RI 6

B RHETORICAL TECHNIQUES

Possible answer: Morrison uses an example of a preacher and a congregation responding to each other.

READING SKILL COMMON CORE RI 6

C *Model the Skill:* **AUTHOR'S POSITION**

Read aloud lines 68–86, emphasizing the speakers that Morrison cites in her novels, from the single individual to all of nature. *Possible answer: Morrison cites these examples to support her position: the "I" narrator as a chorus in* The Bluest Eye *(line 69), the town as a character in* Sula *(lines 69–70), a responsive community in* Song of Solomon *(lines 70–71), and personified nature in* Tar Baby *(lines 71–74).*

IF STUDENTS NEED HELP . . . Work with them to complete the prereading chart introduced on page 909.

TEXT ANALYSIS COMMON CORE RI 4 RI 6

D *Model the Skill:* **RHETORICAL TECHNIQUES**

Tell students that repetition can be an effective rhetorical tool. Read lines 87–92 aloud. Point out that "Black people" is repeated and that Morrison repeats these words to show that Black literature is not simplistic. Ask students to find repetition in lines 90–92 and explain its meaning. *Possible answer: Morrison repeats "my" to show how personal her struggle is to create the style of Black literature.*

SELECTION WRAP-UP

READ WITH A PURPOSE Now that students have read the selection, ask them to explain what Morrison expects narrators to do for readers of novels. *Possible answer: Narrators should enable readers to understand and identify with the novel's theme.*

FOR ENGLISH LANGUAGE LEARNERS
Language: Conversational English Patterns
Point out dashes and sentence fragments in lines 57–67. Explain that the dashes are used to set text apart. Urge students to read the sentence without the text inside the dashes and then add it back. Use lines 61–63 to model how to restate the sentence fragments in complete sentences by adding implied text or attaching fragments to nearby complete sentences. Have students apply this strategy to lines 63–67.

FOR ADVANCED LEARNERS/AP
Write Dialogue [paired option] Have students reread lines 63–65 in which Morrison describes her goals for dialogue. Challenge students to develop a dialogue that reflects these goals, imbuing each sentence with the tone it should contain. Ask students to work in pairs to present a dramatic reading of each partner's dialogue.

Practice and Apply

For preliminary support of post-reading questions, use these copy masters:

R RESOURCE MANAGER—Copy Masters
Reading Check p. 85
Rhetorical Techniques p. 81
Question Support p. 86
Additional selection questions are provided for teachers on page 75.

ANSWERS

COMMON CORE **RI 4, RI 6**

1. *Morrison associates the novel with the middle class.*

2. *The novel is especially important for African Americans because they have no other art forms that are exclusively theirs. They also need to be reconnected with classical, mythical, archetypal stories.*

3. *The chorus allows Morrison to provide an oral element to her written stories.*

Possible answers:

4. ● **COMMON CORE FOCUS Identify Author's Viewpoint** *Students may feel that Morrison supports her positions well, with detailed examples and reasons. Others may feel that Morrison's arguments are vague and that her support focuses on literary qualities found in many cultures.*

5. ● **COMMON CORE FOCUS Rhetorical Techniques** *Answers will vary. Accept all thoughtful responses.*

6. *The comparison suggests that Morrison views her work as having a moral or didactic function to inspire understanding.*

Assess and Reteach

Assess

DIAGNOSTIC AND SELECTION TESTS
Selection Test A pp. 237–238
Selection Test B/C pp. 239–240

Interactive Selection Test on **thinkcentral.com**

Reteach

Level Up Tutorials on **thinkcentral.com**

Reteaching Worksheets on **thinkcentral.com**
Literature Lesson 25: Recognizing Critical Approaches
Reading Lessons 14–17: Persuasion and Argumentation

Comprehension

1. **Recall** With what social class does Morrison associate the novel?

2. **Clarify** According to Morrison, why is the novel especially important for African Americans?

3. **Clarify** Why is it important to Morrison to include a chorus in her fiction?

Text Analysis

● 4. **Examine Author's Position** Review the chart you created as you read. In your opinion, does Morrison provide compelling support for her views on the nature of the African-American novel? Explain your answer.

● 5. **Analyze Rhetorical Techniques** Morrison uses rhetorical techniques, such as personal accounts and repetition, to make important points about African-American novels. Do you think her use of these devices is effective? Why or why not?

6. **Analyze Details** Explain the comparison Morrison makes in lines 44–48. What does this comparison reveal about the way Morrison views her work?

● 7. **Compare and Contrast Authors' Perspectives** Consider the aspects of African-American culture Morrison tries to capture in her novels. What artistic goals does Morrison share with the writers of the Harlem Renaissance? How does her vision of black culture compare with theirs? Explain your answer.

● 8. **Evaluate Author's Purpose** Literary criticism has three main purposes: to inform readers, to express the writer's opinions, and to persuade readers to accept those opinions. Based on your reading, which of these purposes was Morrison trying to achieve with her essay? Which, if any, did she achieve? Support your answer with details.

Text Criticism

9. **Critical Interpretations** Consider the qualities Morrison identifies as characteristic of African-American art forms. Which of the Harlem Renaissance works you read would meet Morrison's criteria for African-American art? Cite details in your answer.

> *Can* **CULTURE** *be captured in words?*
> Think about different cultures you have either read about or experienced first-hand. What cultures other than your own do you find interesting? Why?

COMMON CORE

RI 4 Analyze how an author uses and refines the meaning of a key term or terms over the course of a text. **RI 6** Determine an author's point of view or purpose in a text in which the rhetoric is particularly effective, analyzing how content contributes to the power, persuasiveness, or beauty of the text.

Morrison also believes that readers should share in the work of creating the novel.

7. ● **COMMON CORE FOCUS Identify Author's Viewpoint** *Morrison tries to capture the sense of community and interactive participation in African-American culture. She defines that culture in terms of oral tradition. Morrison borrows a European form to express her message but infuses it with elements that are distinctively black. She shares with Harlem Renaissance writers the goal of presenting authentic visions of the black experience, a deference to the oral tradition, and the belief that art can affect society.*

8. ● **COMMON CORE FOCUS Identify Author's Viewpoint** *Students may find evidence in Morrison's essay to support all three purposes. Details should support their evaluations.*

9. *Students may suggest the work of Langston Hughes or Zora Neale Hurston.*

> *Can* CULTURE *be captured in words?* Students' answers will vary.

Perspectives on the Harlem Renaissance

Literary historian Richard Gray states the following about the writers of the Harlem Renaissance.

> *"[W]hat is notable about them is how they explored different literary forms to express the condition of African Americans in their times. Facing a racial experience the determining feature of which was that it was mixed and conflicted, they were prepared individually to confront and collectively to debate the question of just how their experience should be turned into literature."*

Because the experiences of the Harlem Renaissance writers were "mixed and conflicted," their works naturally examined different aspects of African-American life.

Writing to Analyze

Imagine that you are a publisher who is planning to print the works beginning on page 878 in a slim anthology called *The Harlem Renaissance.* You'd like to organize the works into thematic groupings to help your readers gain a sense of some of the issues and concerns that these writers, despite their varied experiences, collectively held in common. With a partner, work together to create a table of contents for your book, with the works grouped under thematic headings, such as "Social Protest" or "Reflections on Heritage." Then write a brief explanation of why you grouped the works as you did.

Consider

- which selections deal with similar topics or themes (some selections may explore several themes, giving you the option to group them in more than one way)
- what overarching phrases might best express those topics or themes
- what, specifically, from each selection led you to place it in its particular grouping

Writers Jessie Fauset, Langston Hughes, and Zora Neale Hurston

Extension Online

RESEARCH Go online to find two additional works by Harlem Renaissance writers to add to your anthology. You may choose works by writers already represented in your anthology, or works by other Harlem Renaissance writers, such as Paul Laurence Dunbar or Helene Johnson. Give an **oral reading** for the class, and explain where you would place the works in your anthology.

⊙ **COMMON CORE**

RL 9 Demonstrate knowledge of early-twentieth-century foundational works of American literature, including how two or more texts from the same period treat similar themes or topics. **RI 9** Analyze documents of historical and literary significance for their themes, purposes, and rhetorical features. **W 7** Conduct short research projects. **W 9a (RL 2)** Determine two or more themes or central ideas of a text and analyze their development. **SL 4** Present information, findings, and supporting evidence, conveying a clear and distinct perspective.

FOR STRUGGLING WRITERS

Writing Support Suggest that students work with the provided thematic headings "Social Protest" and "Reflections upon Heritage." Make sure that students understand the meanings of each of these phrases. Then tell students to place the works in the category where they best fit. Help students identify examples in each work that support their placement. Tell students to use these examples when writing their explanations.

FOR ENGLISH LANGUAGE LEARNERS

Writing Explanatory Notes To help students write explanations of their literary placements, provide sentence starters:

- [Title] belongs in the "Social Protest" grouping because _____.
- [Title] belongs in the "Reflections upon Heritage" grouping because _____.

Tell students to find details in the selections to support each placement.

⊙ **COMMON CORE FOCUS**

RL 9 Demonstrate knowledge of early-twentieth-century foundational works of American literature. **RI 9** Analyze documents of historical and literary significance. **W 7** Conduct short research projects. **W 9a (RL 2)** Determine two or more themes or central ideas of a text and analyze their development. **SL 4** Present information, findings, and supporting evidence.

Wrap-Up: The Harlem Renaissance

This Wrap-Up provides students with an opportunity to revisit ideas from the literature in this section about writers of the Harlem Renaissance and to consider how these writers sought to express the African-American experience. Encourage students to examine their own understandings of African-American culture in light of insights gained from the selections.

Writing to Analyze

- Review with students that *analyzing* means examining the parts of a literary work so as to discover its nature, purpose, style, theme, and so on. This process helps readers better understand the work as a whole, as well as find relationships among works.

- To help students create their table of contents, suggest that they use colored self-stick tags or notes to mark the works for topics and themes. Urge students to make an index card summarizing the topics and themes identified for each work. Partners can then group and regroup the cards to experiment with different combinations.

Extension Online

- If students are researching online, suggest that they search by the writers' names. Some additional writers to consider include Waring Cuney, Nella Larsen, and Angelina W. Grimke. Students might also use key phrases such as *Harlem Renaissance, African-American literature,* or *literature of social protest.*

- Direct students to practice reading the identified additional works aloud before presenting them to the class. Remind students to read according to punctuation and with feeling. Also, suggest that students also write out and rehearse their explanations ahead of time.

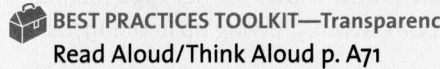 **BEST PRACTICES TOOLKIT—Transparency**
Read Aloud/Think Aloud p. A71

Focus and Motivate

⊙ COMMON CORE FOCUS

RI 7 Integrate and evaluate multiple sources of information presented in different media or formats as well as in words in order to address a question or solve a problem. **W 2** Write informative/explanatory texts to examine and convey complex ideas, concepts, and information clearly and accurately through the effective selection, organization, and analysis of content. **SL 1** Initiate and participate effectively in a range of collaborative discussions. **SL 5** Make strategic use of digital media in presentations.

SUMMARY

In this documentary, African-American novelist Veronica Chambers narrates the life of Zora Neale Hurston, from Hurston's beginning in Eatonville, Florida, to her end in obscurity. Opening with Hurston's proud assertion, "I am not tragically colored," the film presents her adolescent discovery of literature, her 1925 arrival in New York City, her early literary success, and her anthropology study. The film also chronicles the historical contexts of the Harlem Renaissance and racial conflict after World War I.

How do you
DOCUMENT *a life?*

After students read about the process of choosing what to include in a documentary, discuss students' ideas about what they would include in a documentary of their lives. Then ask what media forms they would include, such as video clips, still photographs, writings, interviews with themselves or others, and voice-over narration. Tell students to look for these forms of information as they view the film.

BACKGROUND

Veronica Chambers, who narrates this film, is an American writer whose writings reflect her African and Latin heritage. Chambers has written for many national magazines, including *Glamour*, *Seventeen*, and *Newsweek*. Her young adult novels include *Marisol and Magdalena* and *Quinceañera Means Sweet 15*. With film director John Singleton she co-wrote *Poetic Justice: Filmmaking South Central Style*. She is best known for her 1996 memoir, *Mama's Girl*, about growing up in the 1970s.

Media Study

Jump at the Sun
Documentary on Media ◯ Smart DVD-ROM

⊙ COMMON CORE

RI 7 Integrate and evaluate multiple sources of information presented in different media or formats as well as in words in order to address a question or solve a problem.

How do you
DOCUMENT *a life?*

KEY IDEA Think about how you would tell the story of your life. What events would you include to help someone understand the essential you? What would you leave out? Filmmakers face similar questions when they make a biographical **documentary.** The many details of a person's life must be boiled down to the key events that influenced and shaped that person. As you view *Jump at the Sun,* notice the details chosen to tell Zora Neale Hurston's life story.

Background

A Vibrant Life Zora Neale Hurston lived her life fully by following her mother's advice. "Mama exhorted her children at every opportunity to 'jump at de sun,'" Hurston explained. "We might not land on the sun, but at least we would get off the ground."

Hurston was a passionate woman who celebrated her role as a black female writer at a time when that was not an easy role to play. She was confident and proud of her heritage, making no apologies for who she was or what she did.

Hurston's dazzling personality and the dynamic times she lived through made her an ideal subject for a documentary film. Thus, the idea for *Jump at the Sun* was born. The filmmakers faced a challenge, though—Hurston died nearly a half-century ago, and film footage of her was not available. The filmmakers, therefore, had to find a way to bring her strong personality to life for the viewer, relying primarily on photographs, paintings, music, and readings from Hurston's own work. The filmmakers' challenge was to shape this material into a coherent and interesting film that tells the story of her life and work.

Jump at the Sun imparts to the viewer both the facts—the actual events that made up Hurston's life—and the exuberance of her personality. As you study the film, you'll explore the techniques used to bring life to the Harlem Renaissance and one of its most spirited writers.

Zora Neale Hurston

Media Study Resources

See resources on the **Teacher One Stop DVD-ROM** *and on* **thinkcentral.com**.

R RESOURCE MANAGER UNIT 5
Plan and Teach, pp. 87–96
Summary, pp. 91†*, 92‡*
Viewing Guide, p. 93
Close Viewing, p. 94
Media Activity, p. 95
Produce Your Own Media, p. 96

TECHNOLOGY
💿 **Teacher One Stop DVD-ROM**
💿 **Student One Stop DVD-ROM**
💿 **Media***Smart* **DVD-ROM**
MediaScope on **thinkcentral.com**

* **Resources for Differentiation**   † **Also in Spanish**   ‡ **In Haitian Creole and Vietnamese**

Media Literacy: Documentary

A **documentary** is a nonfiction film that often presents social, political, or historical subject matter. Prominent people make good subjects, as they allow the filmmaker to explore both an interesting life and its greater social context.

Feature filmmakers and other storytellers often repeat an old adage: "Show, don't tell." Many documentary filmmakers follow the same principle, presenting their material as a story that unfolds before the viewer's eyes. The use of **primary sources,** which include photographs, film clips, letters, and eyewitness accounts, helps to immerse the viewer in the subject's world.

DOCUMENTARY TOOLS AND TECHNIQUES

Visual

- Footage is recorded material used to reveal information about a subject. It includes film clips, news reports, photographs, interviews, and text. Footage can be used to create a visual and emotional impression of the times.
- Camera movement—such as zooming in from a long shot to a close-up, and tracking shots, which move the camera parallel to the object being filmed—can give a dynamic feel to a still picture.

Sound

- Voice-over narration is the voice of an unseen speaker that can be heard in a documentary.
- The style and tempo of the music will generally match the mood of the story and signal transitions to different settings or time periods.
- Sound effects are often used to help re-create a scene. For example, filmmakers may add crowd and traffic noise over a picture of a city.

STRATEGIES FOR VIEWING

As you view a documentary, consider the filmmakers' purpose in creating the film. Realize that documentaries reflect the point of view of the filmmaker. They do not always represent objective truth.

- Notice the different types of **footage** used in a documentary. Pay special attention to the use of **primary sources.** Note how they help to bring the story to life by using the "show, don't tell" principle.
- Listen to the different types of **voice-over narration.** In this documentary, the main narrator provides the facts of the subject's life story. The second narrator evokes Hurston's personality with a lively reading of her work.
- Consider how the **visual** and **sound techniques** work together. Think about why the particular footage was chosen to accompany each type of voice-over narration. Notice how the music changes with each major shift in the story.

Teach

Media Literacy

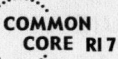
COMMON CORE RI 7

Have students imagine that they are making a documentary about someone living in the 1920s. Specify that they would have no film or video clips showing the person. Have them suggest ways to make up for this lack, using the elements on the chart on page 917. Discuss each element as it is mentioned.

- **Visual** Have students brainstorm ways to use **footage** such as still photographs, newspaper articles, and other texts to add visual information to a documentary. Call attention to the news headline on page 917, and ask how **camera movement** emphasizes it on the page. **Possible answer:** *A close-up shot emphasizes the text.*

- **Sound** Tell students to assume that there are no sound recordings of their subject. Instead they will use **voice-over narration** that includes readings of the subject's words and other people's comments about the subject. Ask students how they differentiate the two for viewers. **Possible answer:** *The subject's words could be read in a voice similar to that person's, while other people's comments could be read in various voices.*

STRATEGIES FOR VIEWING

Call attention to the idea that documentaries reflect the filmmaker's perspective and do not always represent objective truth. Ask students how a documentary made up entirely of factual materials could reflect a subjective opinion. **Possible answer:** *The filmmaker's choice of what details to include and what to exclude reflects a point of view. Music, visuals, and the tone of voice-over can also convey a perspective.*

MEDIA STUDY: TEACHING OPTIONS

Teaching Option 1: The Basics (1–2 Days)

1. Begin the Media Study using the material provided on pages 916–917.
2. Show the Introduction on Media*Smart*. Then show the First Viewing. As they watch, have students use the Viewing Guide on page 918, along with the corresponding copy master on page 93 of the Resource Manager. Discuss their responses.
3. Return to the pupil book for the extension activities on page 919.

Teaching Option 2: In-Depth Study (2–3 Days)

1. Begin the Media Study using pages 916–917.
2. Show the Introduction and First Viewing from Media*Smart*. Then continue on Media*Smart* with the Media Lessons, using the teacher notes available in the Resources section.
3. Show the Guided Analysis presentation. Have students record their observations on the Student Viewing Guide available in the Resources section from Media*Smart*.
4. Return to the pupil book, page 919.

Practice and Apply

VIEWING GUIDE

1. Before viewing, inform students that the documentary presents Zora Neale Hurston's life in the context of her historical times, especially the 1920s. Ask students to briefly discuss their prior knowledge of American literature and society in the 1920s, including the Harlem Renaissance.

2. Point out that any given documentary may rely more on some tools and techniques than on others, depending on the available sources and on the director's stylistic choices. Suggest that students notice which tools and techniques "Jump at the Sun" relies on most, and think about why. Urge them in particular to watch and listen for these elements:

   - the **vocal qualities** of the narrator that convey her youth and her admiration for Hurston
   - **visuals** that capture the character and vibrancy of Hurston's hometown
   - **music** that captures the spirit of Hurston's time

   R RESOURCE MANAGER—Copy Masters
   Viewing Guide p. 93
   Close Viewing p. 94
   Media Activity p. 95

Use this resource with the Viewing Guide:

Media*Smart* DVD-ROM

Media*Scope* on thinkcentral.com

ANSWERS

FIRST VIEWING: Comprehension

1. *Samuel Taylor Coleridge*

2. *Hurston thought it was more important to write about the thoughts, feelings, and motivations of people in general than to write specifically about race.*

CLOSE VIEWING: Media Literacy

3. *They wanted to educate or inform. The film concentrates on facts about Hurston and quotations from her work. It is positive about her work without pushing an agenda.*

4. *Using a young writer to narrate Hurston's life story shows the influence her work continues to have today.*

Media🎬Smart DVD-ROM
- **Film:** *Jump at the Sun*
- **Genre:** Documentary
- **Voice-Over Narrator:** Veronica Chambers
- **Running Time:** 9 minutes

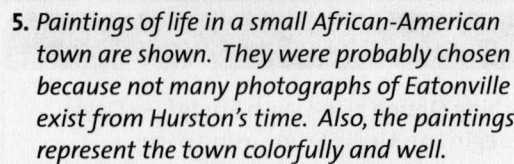

918

---

5. *Paintings of life in a small African-American town are shown. They were probably chosen because not many photographs of Eatonville exist from Hurston's time. Also, the paintings represent the town colorfully and well.*

6. *Some students will say that reading from Hurston's work is the most effective technique because the narrator's accent and enthusiasm capture Hurston's personality and bring her to life.*

Viewing Guide for

Jump at the Sun

Filmmakers face a difficult challenge when they set out to tell a true story. They must carefully choose which details are necessary to bring the tale to life. Consider the documentary techniques you examined as you view the Zora Neale Hurston biography. Think about how each element contributes to the story being told. You may need to watch the documentary more than once in order to analyze it properly.

NOW VIEW

FIRST VIEWING: Comprehension

1. **Recall** What poet's work so influenced Hurston that she was moved to devote herself to literature?

2. **Clarify** What were Hurston's feelings about whether African-American writers have a duty to write about race relations?

CLOSE VIEWING: Media Literacy

3. **Identify Filmmakers' Purpose** Documentaries are made for a variety of purposes. For example, they can educate, inform, or influence opinion. What do you think the makers of *Jump at the Sun* wanted to achieve? Explain.

4. **Analyze the Voice-Over** The documentary is narrated by the writer Veronica Chambers. Why do you think the filmmakers chose a young writer to narrate the story of Hurston's life?

5. **Analyze Visuals** What types of images are shown to depict Hurston's hometown? Why do you think this type of footage was chosen?

6. **Evaluate Technique** In your opinion, which of the techniques in *Jump at the Sun* is the most effective in conveying Hurston's personality? Cite evidence from the film to support your opinion. Think about
   - the use of such **primary sources** as photographs, film clips, and the actual text read from Hurston's *Dust Tracks on a Road*
   - **music** that suggests the 1920s
   - the two types of **voice-over narration**

Write or Discuss

Compare the Texts Zora Neale Hurston was known for her unique personality. Think about the most memorable parts of Hurston's essay "How It Feels to Be Colored Me." Now consider the ways Hurston is depicted in the documentary. Write a paragraph that compares the Zora portrayed in the film with the Zora you know from the text. Think about

- the tone evident in the essay and in the documentary
- the quotes from Hurston's work that are included in the film, and the style in which they're read
- the selection of images and music in the film

Produce and Present Your Own Media

Plan a Documentary Make a documentary about someone you know well. Gather the materials you'll need to film your documentary. They should include **primary source material** from your subject's life, **interviews** with friends or family members, and a script for the **voice-over narration.**

HERE'S HOW Write interview questions about your subject for two or three friends or family members to answer. Write a script for the voice-over narration that gives a brief overview of the life you're describing. Collect your primary source material. Consider these suggestions:

- Find out about the people or events that have had the greatest impact on your subject's life. Find ways to represent them visually.
- Decide what music might be appropriate. Match it to the events you'll cover.
- Decide how you will portray your subject—through photographs, original video footage, or both.

Further Exploration

Create Your Documentary Now that you've gathered the materials for your documentary, plan how you will shoot it. Decide on the best image to start your film. Plan where you'll use the interviews you conducted, and over what images the voice-over narration will play. Decide at what point you will play the music. Remember that your film should both inform your audience and keep them interested throughout. Next, film your documentary using the notes you've created as a guide. Show your completed documentary to your classmates and ask them for constructive, or helpful, criticism.

COMMON CORE

RI 7 Integrate and evaluate multiple sources of information presented in different media or formats as well as in words in order to address a question or solve a problem. **W 2** Write informative/explanatory texts to examine and convey complex ideas, concepts, and information clearly and accurately through the effective selection, organization, and analysis of content. **SL 1** Initiate and participate effectively in a range of collaborative discussions. **SL 5** Make strategic use of digital media in presentations.

Media Tools  **THINK** central

Go to **thinkcentral.com**.
KEYWORD: HML11-919

Tech Tip

If a video camera is available, film your documentary. If you do not have a video camera, try using photographs to create a digital story.

Produce and Present Your Own Media

Rubric: Plan a Documentary A strong film plan should have

- materials gathered from primary sources, including interviews
- a script for voice-over narration
- a description of appropriate music

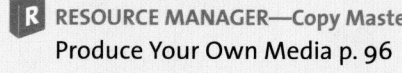 **RESOURCE MANAGER—Copy Master**
Produce Your Own Media p. 96

Assess and Reteach

Write or Discuss

COMMON CORE RI 7, W 2, SL 1, SL 5

Compare the Texts Students' paragraphs should compare *tone, quotations, images,* and *music* as appropriate in each text. Their responses should also show understanding of Hurston's personality as evoked in both media, and should compare the visual and written presentations. For example, students might say that Hurston's self-confidence and winning personality come to life more effectively in the documentary because her words are read aloud.

RETEACH

For students who are unable to apply the MediaStudy skills, select from these reteaching options:

- **Subject Matter** Provide students with a choice of subject for a documentary film: 1. a present-day sports figure or 2. a sports figure from the late 1800s. Which would allow greater flexibility in visual treatment? *(the present-day sports figure, because there would be video footage available).*
- **Sound** Make a two-column chart on the board. In one column write subjects for documentaries, such as "The Olympics" or "History of the Movies." In the other column, write "Sounds." Have students list the types of sounds and sound effects they would expect to hear in each film.
- **Purpose** Provide students with photos of pollution, such as a trash-strewn beach. Ask them why a filmmaker might make a documentary about such a topic? *(to influence opinion).*

MEDIA STUDY WRAP—UP

Have students summarize what they have learned about visual and sound tools and techniques that documentary filmmakers use to portray real people and events. Urge students to refer back to specific elements, such as *footage, camera movement, voice-over narration, music,* and *sound effects* when explaining.

Media Tools **THINK** central

Media study keywords point to **MediaScope,** a Web site that helps students strengthen media analysis and production skills.

Focus and Motivate

ABOUT THE POETS

Edward Arlington Robinson Have students cite aspects of Robinson's life that indicate failure or disappointment. *Possible answer: His family fortunes declined, which forced him to drop out of Harvard, and he struggled as a poet for many years.* Tell them that Robinson's characters often experience failure and disappointment as well.

Edgar Lee Masters Ask students to find evidence in the biography that Masters's view of his characters might be complex. *Possible answer: He both admired and despised rural people.*

NOTABLE QUOTES

"He knows much of what men paint themselves would blister in the light of what they are." —**Edwin Arlington Robinson**

"How shall the soul of man be larger than the life he has lived?" —**Edgar Lee Masters**

Discuss the meaning of the two quotes. Have students compare the viewpoints of the two poets.

Selection Resources

The New Poetry

Richard Cory
Miniver Cheevy
Poetry by Edwin Arlington Robinson

Lucinda Matlock
Poetry by Edgar Lee Masters

Meet the Authors

Edwin Arlington Robinson
1869–1935

Failure is a familiar subject in the poetry of Edwin Arlington Robinson, and one the artist knew well. Robinson wrote poetry for years before achieving recognition, and he witnessed family members suffer one personal defeat after another.

A Difficult Youth His father's financial struggles forced Robinson to curtail his studies at Harvard University. The family's fortunes continued to decline and Robinson's mother died of diphtheria in 1896. In addition, he lost both of his brothers to fatal addictions.

Devotion to His Craft Despite his tragic past and his own struggles with alcoholism, Robinson devoted his life to his craft. Over time he gained a reputation as one of the country's most accomplished narrative poets.

Reflections of the Past Robinson's best known poems explore the inner lives of the citizens of Tilbury Town, a fictional community modeled on Robinson's hometown of Gardiner, Maine. Many poems grew out of the tragic experiences of his family and childhood acquaintances. Often, the poems focus on individuals who are brought low because of their own personal failings and the town's repressive, materialistic culture.

Edgar Lee Masters
1868–1950

When his brilliant portrait of rural life, *Spoon River Anthology*, first appeared in 1915, Edgar Lee Masters became a literary sensation. Both the general public and renowned critics embraced the book, making it an American classic.

The Making of a Poet The book grew out of Masters's memories of growing up in the central Illinois towns of Lewiston and Petersburg. Living on his grandparents' farm in Petersburg and in the semi-industrialized Lewiston, Masters acquired both an appreciation and a distaste for rural culture. While he admired the hard work and resilience of rural folk, he despised their small-mindedness and bigotry. Eventually Masters left rural Illinois for the big city, residing in Chicago and New York City.

Literary Masterpiece Masters remains most famous for his *Spoon River Anthology*. In this book, 244 deceased inhabitants of the fictional town of Spoon River deliver monologues in which they bare their souls. The cast of characters is varied, ranging from prostitutes and thieves to librarians and Masters's own grandmother Lucinda, the model for "Lucinda Matlock."

Authors Online

THINK central

Go to **thinkcentral.com**.
KEYWORD: HML11-920

920

TEXT ANALYSIS: CHARACTERIZATION IN NARRATIVE POETRY

While most modernist poets turned their efforts to lyric poetry, Edward Arlington Robinson and Edgar Lee Masters continued to develop the tradition of narrative poetry, often telling stories of interesting characters in the context of their communities. Like fiction, **narrative poetry** tells a story using elements of plot, character, and setting. To develop character, poets may adapt methods of **characterization** typically used in fiction.

- physical description of the character, including vivid **imagery**
- the character's own actions, words, thoughts, and feelings
- comments, thoughts, or actions of other characters
- direct comments about the character by the poem's speaker

As you read these poems, pay attention to the methods used by the poet to develop the characters.

Review: **Meter**

READING SKILL: ANALYZE SPEAKER'S ATTITUDE

In many poems, the **speaker** has a persona that is distinct from the poet. It is the speaker's **attitude** that shapes our view of the poem's subject. In each of the following poems, a speaker delivers a character sketch; in one case, the speaker is describing herself. By noticing the details and phrases the speaker uses to describe the character, we can learn about his or her attitude not only toward the character but toward life.

To analyze the speaker's attitude toward the character in each poem, use a chart like the one shown. As you read, jot down the details and phrases from each poem that reflect that attitude. One example has been filled in for you.

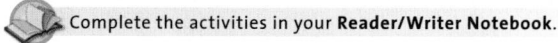

Details and Phrases Reflecting Speaker's Attitude		
"Richard Cory"	*"Miniver Cheevy"*	*"Lucinda Matlock"*
"He was a gentleman from sole to crown"		

Complete the activities in your **Reader/Writer Notebook**.

What makes for a FULL LIFE?

Everyone wants to be happy, but happiness comes more easily to some people than to others. What is the secret? Some seek happiness in close, loving relationships. Others pursue their dreams and try to remain true to their inner voice. Still others strive for the comforts of material success and prosperity. The following poems portray characters who have met with varying degrees of success in their search for contentment.

DISCUSS With a partner, make a list of some different ways in which people seek happiness. Which are the most likely to succeed? Which are the least likely? After discussing these questions, present your conclusions to the class.

Teach

What makes for a FULL LIFE?

Note the routes to contentment mentioned in the paragraph and ask students to suggest examples of these routes. Have students bring their ideas to the *DISCUSS* activity.

TEXT ANALYSIS

COMMON CORE
RL 3

● *Model the Skill:*
CHARACTERIZATION IN NARRATIVE POETRY

Illustrate the use of characterization by characterizing the poets themselves. Point out that the photos on page 920 supply physical data about Robinson and Masters and the biographical text supplies direct comments about each.

GUIDED PRACTICE Read aloud the **NOTABLE QUOTES.** Have students explain what Robinson and Master's quotations tell about their lives. Encourage them to connect their ideas to the biographical information on page 920.

READING SKILL

COMMON CORE
RL 6
RL 9

■ *Model the Skill:* **ANALYZE SPEAKER'S ATTITUDE**

Analyze a speaker's attitude by comparing two hypothetical poems about the same subject: a high school teacher. Tell students that in one poem, the speaker is the teacher herself; in the other poem, the speaker is one of her students. How would the attitudes of those two speakers be different? *Students may say that the teacher's attitude would be highly personal while the student's might focus on how the teacher affected him or her.*

GUIDED PRACTICE Ask students to name a famous person and state two attitudes that people could have about the person.

 RESOURCE MANAGER—Copy Master Analyze Speaker's Attitude p. 107

DIFFERENTIATED INSTRUCTION

FOR ENGLISH LANGUAGE LEARNERS

Figurative Language English learners may need help with unfamiliar figurative language in the poem. As necessary, guide them with: "gentleman from sole to crown" (line 3), "clean favored" (line 4), "human when he talked" (line 6), and "cursed the bread" (line 14). To check understanding, have students put these phrases in their own words.

FOR STRUGGLING READERS

Concept Support: Analyze Speaker's Attitude Clarify that *attitude* describes how the speaker feels about the poem's subject, such as admiring or disappointed. Urge students to look for descriptive nouns, adjectives, and verbs that suggest such attitudes. For example, the excerpt on page 921 uses the word *gentleman,* which conveys a positive attitude. The word *crown* for "head" also suggests a positive attitude, conveying an image of a king or queen.

SUMMARY

The title character of this poem is the rich industrialist of a small town, envied by all until he commits suicide without warning.

READ WITH A PURPOSE

Help students set a purpose for reading. Tell them to read the poems to find what the people named in the poems' titles are like.

TEXT ANALYSIS　　　COMMON CORE　**RL 3**

Ⓐ *Model the Skill:*
CHARACTERIZATION

Read aloud 1–8, emphasizing the phrases that describe Cory's appearance and manner. Point out that he seems to be well known and admired by the townspeople, who take note of his every move.

Possible answer: Richard Cory is elegant, polished, and attractive. By saying "he fluttered pulses" (line 7) and "he glittered when he walked" (line 8), the speaker is saying that even when Cory attempts to be friendly, his wealth and status distance him from those he lives among.

IF STUDENTS NEED HELP . . . Discuss why someone's voice and appearance would cause pulses to flutter. Help students see that objects that glitter are usually valuable, which suggests Cory's wealth.

READING SKILL　　　COMMON CORE　**RL 6**　**RL 9**

Ⓑ *Model the Skill:*
SPEAKER'S ATTITUDE

Point out that in lines 13–14, the speaker indicates that Cory has everything that anyone could wish for, while the townspeople are too poor to buy meat for their table. How do the townspeople relate to Cory as a result? *Possible answer: The speaker uses "we" to show that everyone else had situations that made them wish they could trade places with Richard Cory. Their attitude is envy caused by the perception that if Cory does not have their problems, he must have no problems at all.*

RICHARD CORY

Edwin Arlington Robinson

Whenever Richard Cory went down town,
We people on the pavement looked at him:
He was a gentleman from sole to crown,
Clean favored,[1] and imperially slim.

5　And he was always quietly arrayed,
And he was always human when he talked;
But still he fluttered pulses when he said,
"Good-morning," and he glittered when he walked. Ⓐ

And he was rich—yes, richer than a king—
10　And admirably schooled in every grace:[2]
In fine,[3] we thought that he was everything
To make us wish that we were in his place.

So on we worked, and waited for the light,
And went without the meat, and cursed the bread;
15　And Richard Cory, one calm summer night,
Went home and put a bullet through his head. Ⓑ

Ⓐ **CHARACTERIZATION**
Reread lines 1–8. Describe Richard Cory's appearance and manners. What do you think the speaker means by "he fluttered pulses" and "he glittered when he walked"?

Ⓑ **SPEAKER'S ATTITUDE**
Reread lines 11–16. What contrast does the speaker draw between Richard Cory and the townspeople? How do they seem to regard him?

---

1. **clean favored:** having a tidy appearance.
2. **schooled in every grace:** extremely well-mannered and cultured.
3. **in fine:** in short.

Sir Philip Sassoon (1923), John Singer Sargent. Oil on canvas, 95.2 cm x 57.8 cm. Tate Gallery, London. © Tate Gallery, London/Art Resource, New York.

DIFFERENTIATED INSTRUCTION

FOR STRUGGLING READERS
Develop Reading Fluency

- Have students listen to the poems on the *Audio Anthology CD* (also recommended for English language learners) while they read along in their books. Have students listen to the reader's tone and use it to infer the attitude of the poems' speakers.

- Note the absence of rhyme in "Lucinda Matlock." Urge students to read according to punctuation, not line breaks.

923

Connect Think of a time you envied someone, then learned that he or she was actually very unhappy. How does that experience help you understand Richard Cory's behavior? *Students' responses should show an awareness of the possible contradiction between inner feelings and outward appearances.*

Analyze At what point do readers realize that Richard Cory is unhappy? Looking back, does the poem provide any clues to this outcome? Explain. *Possible answer: Readers realize Cory's unhappiness in the last line of the poem. The isolation hinted at in lines 7–12 is a clue to the ending.*

Evaluate Is the surprise ending effective? Why or why not? *Possible answer: Some students will say it is effective, because it mirrors the surprise of the events described. Others will say it is implausible because there is not enough evidence to explain Cory's unhappiness.*

FOR STRUGGLING READERS

Concept Support: Analyze Speaker's Attitude Help students add to the prereading chart introduced on page 921, noting details that express the speaker's attitude toward Richard Cory. Point out that the comment "richer than a king" suggests the speaker's envy and even a little resentment.

Details and Phrases Reflecting Attitude
"Richard Cory"
"he was rich—yes, richer than a king"

FOR ADVANCED LEARNERS/AP

Speculate about Character Cory's suicide is a surprise to readers and to his fellow citizens. Have students speculate either orally or in writing about the reasons for Cory's suicide. Urge them to identify possible external reasons, such as scandal or business failure, as well as internal ones. Then ask students to create descriptions of Cory's life and character based on their inferences.

SUMMARY

The title character of this poem, frustrated by small-town life, fantasizes about the days of chivalry—and drinks.

TEXT ANALYSIS: *Review*

COMMON CORE
RL 3

 METER

Possible answer: *The last line of each stanza has a shorter meter. This change of rhythm has the effect of a punch line or an abrupt ending. It emphasizes the ironic discrepancy between Miniver's grand dreams and his mundane life.*

IF STUDENTS NEED HELP . . . Have them find the line that is shortest in each stanza.

TEXT ANALYSIS

COMMON CORE
RL 3

D CHARACTERIZATION

Possible answer: *The primary means of characterization in lines 9–20 is the depiction of the character's thoughts. The main trait conveyed is a sense of romantic longing "for what was not" (line 9).*

IF STUDENTS NEED HELP . . . Have students check lines 9–20 against the bulleted list on page 921.

Extend the Discussion What would you say to Miniver Cheevy if you met him?

MINIVER CHEEVY

Edwin Arlington Robinson

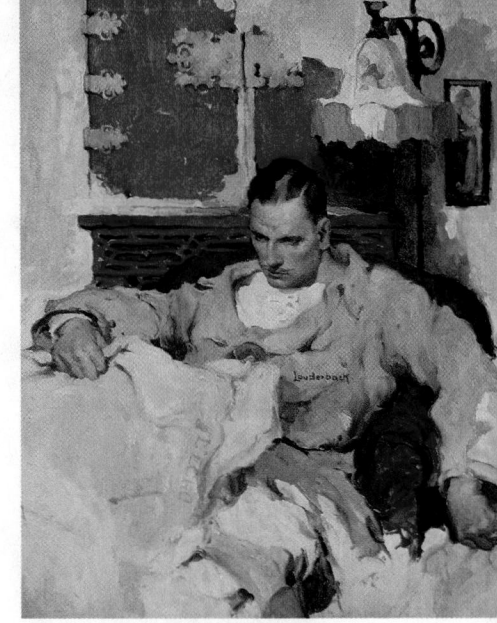

Miniver Cheevy, child of scorn,
　　Grew lean while he assailed[1] the seasons;
He wept that he was ever born,
　　And he had reasons.

5　Miniver loved the days of old
　　When swords were bright and steeds
　　　　were prancing;
The vision of a warrior bold
　　Would set him dancing. C

Miniver sighed for what was not,
10　And dreamed, and rested from his labors;
He dreamed of Thebes and Camelot,
　　And Priam's neighbors.[2]

Miniver mourned the ripe renown
　　That made so many a name so fragrant;
15 He mourned Romance, now on the town,
　　And Art, a vagrant.

Miniver loved the Medici,[3]
　　Albeit[4] he had never seen one;
He would have sinned incessantly
20　Could he have been one. D

Reading in a Study, Walt Louderback. Oil on plywood, 76.2 cm × 59.7 cm. collection. Photo © Bridgeman Art Library.

---

1. **assailed:** attacked violently, in this case with words.
2. **Thebes** (thēbz) **. . . Camelot . . . Priam's** (prī′əmz) **neighbors:** Thebes was an ancient Greek city, the setting of many famous legends; Camelot was the site of King Arthur's legendary court; Priam's neighbors were participants in the Trojan War, during which Priam was king of Troy.
3. **Medici** (mĕd′ə-chē): a powerful Italian family that funded the arts and ruled Florence, sometimes with cruel and immoral leaders, during the Renaissance.
4. **albeit** (ôl-bē′ĭt): even though.

C METER
Reread lines 1–8. In each stanza, which line has a meter that stands out from the others? What emphasis is achieved by this change in **rhythm**?

D CHARACTERIZATION
Reread lines 9–20. Identify the primary means of characterization in these lines. What is the main **trait** conveyed here?

DIFFERENTIATED INSTRUCTION

FOR STRUGGLING READERS

Visualize [small-group option] Use a Visualizing chart to help students achieve a clear mental picture of Miniver Cheevy. Have student groups share their images and discuss differences in them. Ask students to cite language from the poem that led to their mental images.

 BEST PRACTICES TOOLKIT—Transparency
Visualizing p. A11

FOR ADVANCED LEARNERS/AP

Evaluate Character Have students use these questions to discuss Cheevy's character:

• Does he have a valid cause for discontent?

• Is his discontent an excuse for laziness and lack of will?

• If he is right to be discontented, how else might he have dealt with his emotions?

• Are there Miniver Cheevys around today, or is he an obsolete type?

Miniver cursed the commonplace
    And eyed a khaki suit with loathing;
He missed the medieval grace
    Of iron clothing. **E**

25 Miniver scorned the gold he sought,
    But sore annoyed was he without it;
Miniver thought, and thought, and thought,
    And thought about it.

Miniver Cheevy, born too late,
30   Scratched his head and kept on thinking;
Miniver coughed, and called it fate,
    And kept on drinking. **F**

Language Coach

Word Definitions *To eye something* means "to look at something closely." In line 22, why is Miniver eyeing the khaki suit with loathing?

E **SPEAKER'S ATTITUDE**
Identify the **irony** in lines 23–24. What does this irony suggest about the speaker's attitude toward Miniver's love of the medieval?

F **METER**
How does the last line of the poem change your understanding of Miniver? Recall your earlier analysis of the poem's meter, and explain its effect in this stanza.

Text Analysis

1. **Recall** What is the townspeople's initial impression of Richard Cory?

2. **Recall** Why does Miniver Cheevy claim to be unhappy?

3. **Compare Texts** What is similar about the ways the two poems end? In each case, how do the last two lines change your view of the character?

MINIVER CHEEVY   **925**

REVISIT THE BIG QUESTION

What makes for a
FULL LIFE?

Discuss Is contentment possible for Miniver? Why or why not? What does he do about it?
Possible answer: Contentment is possible for Miniver because his life is not bad, but he turns away from this possibility to brood and drink.

READING SKILL   COMMON CORE

E **SPEAKER'S ATTITUDE**   RL 6 RL 9

Possible answer: The notion that "iron clothing" could be graceful is ironic. The irony suggests that the speaker doesn't take Miniver's love of the medieval seriously.

TEXT ANALYSIS: *Review*   COMMON CORE

F **METER**   RL 3

Possible answer: The revelation that Miniver is a drinker tells readers that Miniver has deeper problems than a longing for the past. The change in meter underscores the seriousness of this sudden revelation.

ANSWERS

1. *Initially, the townspeople are impressed by Richard Cory's wealth and gentility.*

2. *Miniver Cheevy claims to be unhappy because he was not born in the Middle Ages.*

3. *The two poems end by revealing something shocking about the characters. In each case, the last two lines show that the character is more deeply troubled than he appears on the surface.*

FOR STRUGGLING READERS

Compare and Contrast Characters Suggest that students create a Comparison Matrix for Richard Cory and Miniver Cheevy. Categories might include wealth, happiness, self-destructive actions, and tastes.

 **BEST PRACTICES TOOLKIT —Transparency**
Comparison Matrix p. A24

FOR ENGLISH LANGUAGE LEARNERS

Language Coach

Word Definitions Students may note that the khaki suit must symbolize "the commonplace" to him, and he curses common, contemporary things. Then have students identify other words that need definition such as *gold* and *sore annoyed*. Ask them to find the meanings, through context clues or by using dictionaries.

Prereading for this poem is found on page 920.

SUMMARY

In this first-person poem, the speaker describes her 96 years of rural hard work, family life, tragedy, and joy, and expresses a view that life should be lived fully.

Analyze Visuals

Possible answer: Qualities of quiet, homespun grace and dignity can be seen in the dancers and in Lucinda Matlock.

About the Art This 1941 oil painting by Jenne Magafan (1916–1952) is a study for a mural made for the Anson, Texas, post office. Its qualities of rustic simplicity and stately grace can also be found in Lucinda Matlock's poetic voice.

TEXT ANALYSIS

COMMON CORE
RL 3

G CHARACTERIZATION

Possible answer: The speaker's behavior reveals a healthy, life-affirming joy.

READING SKILL

COMMON CORE
RL 6
RL 9

H SPEAKER'S ATTITUDE

Possible answer: She might be addressing her sons and daughters or, figuratively, the younger generation that is angry, sad, or disappointed. She feels they are weak.

IF STUDENTS NEED HELP . . . Reread lines 18–22 aloud to emphasize the speaker's tone.

SELECTION WRAP–UP

READ WITH A PURPOSE Now that students have read the poems, ask them to characterize the characters named in the poems' titles.
Possible answers: Richard Cory may have felt isolation and despair; Miniver Cheevy is mired in self pity; Lucinda Matlock is resilient and proud.

LUCINDA MATLOCK

Edgar Lee Masters

Detail of *Cowboy Dance* (mural study, Anson, Texas, post office) (1941), Jenne Magafan. Oil on fiberboard. Photo © Smithsonian American Art Museum, Washington, D.C./Art Resource, New York.

I went to the dances at Chandlerville,
And played snap-out[1] at Winchester.
One time we changed partners,
Driving home in the moonlight of middle June,
5 And then I found Davis.
We were married and lived together for seventy years,
Enjoying, working, raising the twelve children,
Eight of whom we lost
Ere I had reached the age of sixty.
10 I spun, I wove, I kept the house, I nursed the sick,
I made the garden, and for holiday
Rambled over the fields where sang the larks,
And by Spoon River gathering many a shell,
And many a flower and medicinal weed—
15 Shouting to the wooded hills, singing to the green valleys. **G**
At ninety-six I had lived enough, that is all,
And passed to a sweet repose.[2]
What is this I hear of sorrow and weariness,
Anger, discontent and drooping hopes?
20 Degenerate[3] sons and daughters,
Life is too strong for you—
It takes life to love Life. **H**

▲ Analyze Visuals
What qualities do you sense in the dancers portrayed in this painting? Do you find them to have anything in common with Lucinda Matlock? Explain.

G CHARACTERIZATION
Reread lines 1–15. What does the speaker's behavior reveal about her?

H SPEAKER'S ATTITUDE
Whom do you think the speaker is addressing in lines 18–22? How does she seem to feel about them? Explain.

---

1. **snap-out:** a game in which players join hands in a line, then run about trying to shake off those at the end of the line.

2. **repose:** here, the peaceful sleep of death.

3. **degenerate** (dǐ-jěn′ər-ĭt): showing a decline in vigor or moral strength.

DIFFERENTIATED INSTRUCTION

FOR ADVANCED LEARNERS/AP

Synthesize Remind students that both Edwin Arlington Robinson and Edgar Lee Masters created complex, realistic series of poems about characters drawn from the people of their hometowns. Robinson said that he was more interested in the people who were failures than in those who were successes, while Masters's poem "Lucinda Matlock" suggests an interest in people who get the job done. Ask students whether they agree that failure makes better literary subject matter than success. Encourage students to brainstorm reasons for both responses and to cite examples of works of literature featuring success or failure. Have students indicate which category they generally have preferred as reading matter and which they feel offers deeper, more meaningful ideas. Ask students to share and explain their responses.

Comprehension

1. **Recall** What pleasures and sorrows did Lucinda Matlock experience in her life?

2. **Clarify** Overall, was Lucinda content with the life she lived?

Text Analysis

3. **Compare Characters** Richard Cory, Miniver Cheevy, and Lucinda Matlock have found widely varying degrees of **contentment.** In your view, what is the primary reason for each character's happiness or unhappiness? Give details to support your answer.

● 4. **Examine Characterization in Narrative Poetry** What details does Robinson use to reveal each of the following character traits of Richard Cory and Miniver Cheevy? What impact does this characterization have on your sympathy or distaste for the characters? Explain.

- Richard's perfectionism
- Miniver's laziness
- Richard's self-restraint
- Miniver's romanticism

● 5. **Analyze Speaker's Attitude** Review the chart you created as you read. What attitude does the speaker of each poem express toward the main character? Would you say that the speaker is sympathetic to or critical of the character described? In each case, what does this attitude tell you about the speaker's own personality and values? Give evidence to support your answer.

6. **Evaluate Author's Style** Robinson's poems use **rhyme, meter,** and **humor** in a playful way that is somewhat at odds with the grim revelations made in the last lines. How does this playfulness shape the impact of these final lines? Explain whether or not you find this an effective technique, and why.

Text Criticism

7. **Critical Interpretations** Critic Bill Peschel has said that in Robinson's Tilbury Town poems, "the town's Puritan ethic, portrayed as repressive and critical, combined with the materialistic aspects of society, conspires to bring down its citizens." Do you find evidence of this repressive Puritan ethic in the attitudes of the speakers in the Robinson poems? Explain why or why not.

What makes for a FULL LIFE?

The speaker in "Lucinda Matlock" appears to have the most reasons to be happy. What, then, is her source of contentment? What do you think makes for a contented life?

COMMON CORE

RL 3 Analyze the impact of the author's choices regarding how to develop and relate elements of a story. **RL 6** Analyze a case in which grasping point of view requires distinguishing what is directly stated in a text from what is really meant. **RL 9** Demonstrate knowledge of how two or more texts from the same period treat similar themes or topics.

Practice and Apply

For preliminary support of post-reading questions, use these copy masters:

R RESOURCE MANAGER—Copy Masters
Characterization in Narrative Poetry p. 105
Question Support p. 109
Additional selection questions are provided for teachers on page 101.

ANSWERS  COMMON CORE **RL 3, RL 6, RL 9**

1. *Pleasures: marriage, gardening, and nursing; Sorrows: loss of eight children*

2. *Yes, Lucinda was content overall.*

Possible answers:

3. *Cory appears depressed by a life made of wealth and solitude. Cheevy is unhappy because of alcoholism and the sense of being mismatched with his time. Matlock is happy because she has inner strength.*

4. ● COMMON CORE FOCUS **Characterization in Narrative Poetry** *Perfectionism: Richard is perfectly dressed (lines 3–4) and behaved (line 10). Self-restraint: His difficulties are entirely hidden. Laziness: Miniver takes time from working to daydream (line 10). Romanticism: Miniver longs for "days of old" (line 5). Students' responses to the characters will vary but should reflect the details they have chosen.*

5. ● COMMON CORE FOCUS **Analyze Speaker's Attitude** *Richard Cory: The speaker first envies Richard Cory, but then grimly observes his death. The speaker does not value wealth much. Miniver Cheevy: The speaker mocks Cheevy and finds little value*

Assess and Reteach

Assess

DIAGNOSTIC AND SELECTION TESTS
Selection Test A pp. 241–242
Selection Test B/C pp. 243–244

Interactive Selection Test on **thinkcentral.com**

Reteach

Level Up Online Tutorials on **thinkcentral.com**
Reteaching Worksheets on **thinkcentral.com**

Literature Lessons 3, 16, 18, 20, 36

---

*in daydreaming. **Lucinda Matlock:** Lucinda states the facts of her life bluntly, then praises herself at the end of the poem. She values energy.*

6. *Students may appreciate the ironic twist of serious topics presented playfully and feel it gives the poems' endings greater impact. Others may feel the playfulness undercuts the poems' serious themes.*

7. *Students may feel that the judgmental attitude of the speakers toward Richard*

Cory and Miniver Cheevy stems from a Puritan ethic.

What makes for a FULL LIFE?

Students may say Lucinda Matlock gets her contentment from her many memories, and that they get their contentment from relationships and accomplishments.

Focus and Motivate

COMMON CORE FOCUS

RL 4 Determine the meaning of words and phrases as they are used in the text, including figurative and connotative meanings; analyze the impact of specific word choices on meaning and tone, including words with multiple meanings or language that is particularly fresh, engaging, or beautiful. **RL 5** Analyze how an author's choices concerning how to structure specific parts of a text contribute to its overall structure and meaning as well as its aesthetic impact.

ABOUT THE POET

After students read the biography, have them identify details in Sandburg's life that allowed him to become "the voice of America." **Possible answer:** *Sandburg could speak for America because he experienced poverty and was self-made, he worked at many jobs, he traveled widely around the country, and he was active in politics.*

NOTABLE QUOTE

"Nothing happens unless first a dream."
—Carl Sandburg

Ask students how following a dream might have helped Sandburg rise from poverty to fame.

Selection Resources

COMMON CORE

RL 4 Determine the meaning of words and phrases as they are used in the text, including figurative and connotative meanings; analyze the impact of specific word choices on meaning and tone, including words with multiple meanings or language that is particularly fresh, engaging, or beautiful. **RL 5** Analyze how an author's choices concerning how to structure specific parts of a text contribute to its overall structure and meaning as well as its aesthetic impact.

DID YOU KNOW?

Carl Sandburg...

- considered running for president of the United States.
- worked as a war correspondent during World War I.
- wrote books for children.
- spoke before Congress about Abraham Lincoln.

The New Poetry

Chicago
Grass

Poetry by Carl Sandburg

Meet the Author

Carl Sandburg 1878–1967

When Carl Sandburg died in 1967, President Lyndon Johnson was among the first to sing his praises. "Carl Sandburg," the president declared, "was more than the voice of America, more than the poet of its strength and genius. He was America." Johnson's feelings were not unique. Americans everywhere cherished Sandburg, believing his verse celebrated their spirit and speech as well as championed their cause.

A Hobo at Heart Sandburg grew up in America's heartland in Galesburg, Illinois. From his Swedish immigrant parents, August and Clara Sandburg, he learned to value hard work and education. His family's poverty, however, forced Sandburg to curtail his schooling at 13 in order to go to work. He labored at various jobs, ranging from shining shoes to delivering milk. When he turned 19, he left home to explore the American West, becoming one of the many hoboes who hopped freight trains in order to travel free.

Social Activist When the Spanish-American War erupted in 1898, Sandburg served for eight months in Puerto Rico. After his return, he studied at Lombard College but left without receiving a diploma. Overtaken once again by wanderlust, he rambled about the country, soaking up America's sights and songs. When he ran out of money, he returned to the Midwest, writing for journals in Chicago and joining the lecture circuit. His skill as an orator eventually earned him a job in Milwaukee as an organizer for the Wisconsin Social-Democratic Party. While living there, he married Lillian Steichen, who, like Sandburg, was committed to fighting social injustice.

Literary Celebrity In 1912, the couple moved to Chicago, where Sandburg became a reporter, editorial writer, and columnist for the *Chicago Daily News.* Two years later, his verse began to appear in *Poetry,* a prominent literary magazine. With the publication of his poetry collections *Chicago Poems, Cornhuskers,* and *Smoke and Steel,* Sandburg gained a reputation as the poet of the common people. The poetry readings he gave further heightened his popularity. Interspersing poetry with commentary and folk songs sung in his melodious baritone, Sandburg enthralled audiences wherever he went.

Sandburg won a number of awards and honors, including the 1951 Pulitzer Prize for poetry for *Complete Poems* and the 1939 Pulitzer Prize for history for *Abraham Lincoln: The War Years,* the last volume in a six-volume biography.

Author Online
Go to **thinkcentral.com.** KEYWORD: HML11-928

928

See resources on the **Teacher One Stop DVD-ROM** *and on* **thinkcentral.com**.

R **RESOURCE MANAGER UNIT 5**
Plan and Teach, pp. 111–118
Text Analysis and Reading
Skill, pp. 119–122†*

DIAGNOSTIC AND SELECTION TESTS
Selection Tests, pp. 245–248

BEST PRACTICES TOOLKIT
Visualizing, p. A11

TECHNOLOGY
- **Teacher One Stop DVD-ROM**
- **Student One Stop DVD-ROM**
- **Audio Anthology CD**
- **ExamView Test Generator** on the **Teacher One Stop**

 Resources for Differentiation   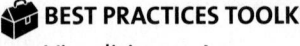 † Also in Spanish   ‡ In Haitian Creole and Vietnamese

TEXT ANALYSIS: TONE AND DICTION

Some poems exhibit a subtle tone that is difficult to perceive and nearly impossible to describe. Others practically break forth with trumpets in the first stanza. Whether gently or boldly, poets generally convey tone, or attitude toward the subject, through **diction** (word choice and syntax) and choice of details. In the first lines of "Chicago," Carl Sandburg's diction creates a tone of admiration for a hard-working city:

Hog Butcher for the World,
Tool Maker, Stacker of Wheat,
Player with Railroads and the Nation's Freight Handler;
Stormy, husky, brawling,
City of the Big Shoulders....

Read these two poems by Sandburg aloud to help you identify the tone of each. If you read with emotion, your tone of voice may provide you with clues to the poem's tone.

Review: **Personification**

READING SKILL: SYNTHESIZE DETAILS

In "Chicago," Sandburg presents a long list, or catalog, of qualities, images, and statements about the city. Collectively, this **sensory language** helps create vivid **imagery** of the city. As you read, pay close attention to the sensory language that Sandburg employs, and note how he uses it to create imagery. After you read the poem, you'll be asked to **synthesize** numerous **details** into a single, coherent impression.

 Complete the activities in your **Reader/Writer Notebook**.

Would you rather live in the CITY or the COUNTRY?

"If you would be known, and not know, vegetate in a village; if you would know, and not be known, live in a city," wrote the poet Reverend Charles Caleb Colton. What benefits and drawbacks do you associate with city living? with country living? What kind of place inspires you the most? In the poems that follow, Carl Sandburg explores different settings that have affected him.

QUICKWRITE Think about a city or a place in the country where you would like to live. What aspects of this setting particularly appeal to you? How might living there enrich your life? Spend a few minutes writing in response to these questions.

 929

DIFFERENTIATED INSTRUCTION

FOR STRUGGLING READERS

Concept Support: Synthesize Details Tell students that *synthesizing* means putting different parts together to form a new whole. Compare the process to putting ingredients together to cook a recipe, or putting pieces of a jigsaw puzzle together to make a picture appear. Similarly, when a reader synthesizes details in a poem, the reader looks at each detail individually, forms a mental picture of it, and then combines the separate details to form a larger mental picture that unifies the whole poem and expresses its overall feeling or meaning. For practice, have students mention details in the words of "The Star-Spangled Banner" or another song of their choosing. Then have them describe the overall picture they synthesize from the details.

Would you rather live in the CITY or the COUNTRY?

Ask the question and elicit students' choices about the place they would like to live through a show of hands. Pause for discussion after the Colton quotation and to allow students to list benefits and drawbacks of city and country life. Have them refer to their lists as they complete the *QUICKWRITE*.

TEXT ANALYSIS
COMMON CORE
RL 4
RL 5

Model the Skill: TONE AND DICTION

To examine an example of Sandburg's diction, read aloud the "Chicago" excerpt on page 929. Then read aloud these lines from "Grass," another Sandburg poem:

What place is this?
Where are we now?

Point out that the lines from "Grass" are simpler in diction and quieter in tone.

GUIDED PRACTICE Have students cite examples of word choice, syntax, and detail choice that convey tone in the two examples.

READING SKILL
COMMON CORE
RL 4
RL 5

Model the Skill: SYNTHESIZE DETAILS

Tell students that imagery created by a poet through sensory details can be taken in as an overall impression. Reread the lines from "Chicago" on page 929 and point out that the lines give the impression of a strong and capable city. The city is personified with occupations such as "Butcher," "Maker," and "Handler."

GUIDED PRACTICE Ask students to name other details that back the impression. They may name "Stormy, husky, brawling," and "Big Shoulders."

R RESOURCE MANAGER—Copy Master
Synthesize Details p. 121

SUMMARY

This free verse poem describes the city of Chicago as Sandburg knew it in the early 1900s. The speaker personifies the city and praises its hard-working energy, while also noticing its crime, corruption, and poverty.

READ WITH A PURPOSE

Help students set a purpose for reading. Tell them to read the poems to find what Chicago and grass want to do and why.

READING SKILL

COMMON CORE
RL 4
RL 5

A *Model the Skill:*
SYNTHESIZE DETAILS

Read aloud lines 1–5. Tell students the epithets give you the impression that Chicago was a national railroad hub, the center of meatpacking and grain shipping. **Possible answer:** *They convey that the city's economy and industry were booming.*

IF STUDENTS NEED HELP . . . Help them jot notes on the meaning of each epithet in a Two-Column Chart like this one:

Epithet	What It Means
Hog Butcher for the World	Makes pork sold around the world

 BEST PRACTICES TOOLKIT—Transparency
Two-Column Chart p. A25

TEXT ANALYSIS

COMMON CORE
RL 4
RL 5

B *Model the Skill:*
TONE AND DICTION

Read aloud lines 6–10, emphasizing both the harshness and, in lines 9–10, the poet's rebuke to the city's critics.

Possible answer: *The phrase "my city" (line 9) suggests the speaker's affection for Chicago. The image of Chicago "with lifted head singing so proud to be alive" (line 10) reveals his pride in it. He also dismisses critics who "sneer" at the city (line 9).*

Chicago

Carl Sandburg

Hog Butcher for the World,
Tool Maker, Stacker of Wheat,
Player with Railroads and the Nation's Freight Handler;
Stormy, husky, brawling,
5   City of the Big Shoulders: **A**

They tell me you are wicked and I believe them, for I
    have seen your painted women under the gas lamps
    luring the farm boys.
And they tell me you are crooked and I answer: Yes, it
    is true I have seen the gunman kill and go free to
    kill again.
And they tell me you are brutal and my reply is: On the
    faces of women and children I have seen the marks
    of wanton[1] hunger.
And having answered so I turn once more to those who
    sneer at this my city, and I give them back the sneer
    and say to them:
10 Come and show me another city with lifted head singing
    so proud to be alive and coarse and strong and cunning. **B**
Flinging magnetic curses amid the toil of piling job on
    job, here is a tall bold slugger set vivid against the
    little soft cities;
Fierce as a dog with tongue lapping for action, cunning
    as a savage pitted against the wilderness,
      Bareheaded,
      Shoveling,

A **SYNTHESIZE DETAILS**
The brief descriptive phrases in lines 1–5, also known as **epithets,** are almost like nicknames; in fact, some of them have come into common use. What do they tell you about the city's economy and industry?

B **TONE AND DICTION**
Lines 6–8 contain harsh words such as *wicked* and *brutal.* Identify the language in lines 9–10 that counters this harshness. What does it reveal about Sandburg's feelings toward the city as well as its critics?

---

1. **wanton:** without limitation.

DIFFERENTIATED INSTRUCTION

FOR ENGLISH LANGUAGE LEARNERS

Vocabulary: Suffixes [mixed-readiness pairs] Many descriptive words in "Chicago" end in the suffixes *-er* ("Butcher," "Maker") or *-ing* ("singing," "bragging," "laughing"). Review the meanings of the suffixes with students. Write the root words on the board and ask for their meanings. Then ask groups to figure out the meanings of the words with the suffixes added.

FOR STRUGGLING READERS

Options for Reading: Audio Recording

- Have students listen to the poems on the *Audio Anthology CD* (also recommended for English language learners) while they read along in their books. Have students listen for the tones in which the two poems are read.

- Suggest that students note when the reader pauses or changes reading volume. Explain that pace, volume, and pauses can provide clues to the poem's tone.

South of the Loop (1936), Charles Turzak. Color woodcut, Image 10²/₅″ × 11³/₄″, sheet 11¹/₄″ × 15″. Mary and Leigh Block Museum of Art, Northwestern University, 1992.73 © Joan Turzak Van Hees.

15 Wrecking,
    Planning,
    Building, breaking, rebuilding,

Under the smoke, dust all over his mouth, laughing with
    white teeth,
Under the terrible burden of destiny laughing as a young
    man laughs,
20 Laughing even as an ignorant fighter laughs who has
    never lost a battle,
Bragging and laughing that under his wrist is the pulse, and
    under his ribs the heart of the people,
                Laughing!
Laughing the stormy, husky, brawling laughter of
    Youth, half-naked, sweating, proud to be Hog
25 Butcher, Tool Maker, Stacker of Wheat, Player with
    Railroads and Freight Handler to the Nation.

▲ **Analyze Visuals**
What qualities of the city are emphasized by both the horizontal and the vertical lines in this woodcut? Refer to specific areas of the print when giving your answer.

CHICAGO **931**

932 UNIT 5

SUMMARY

The grass growing over battlefields speaks of its role in healing the wounds of war.

TEXT ANALYSIS: *Review*

COMMON CORE
RL 4
RL 5

PERSONIFICATION

Possible answer: *The speaker is the grass growing on the battlefields. Its role is to replace death and loss with new growth.*

IF STUDENTS NEED HELP . . . Have them use a Visualizing organizer to translate the poem's imagery into mental pictures.

🧰 **BEST PRACTICES TOOLKIT—Transparency**
Visualizing p. A11

TEXT ANALYSIS

COMMON CORE
RL 4
RL 5

⊙ TONE AND DICTION

Possible answer: *"And pile them high" (lines 4-5), "shovel them under and let me work" (lines 2, 6), "I am the grass (lines 3, 10). The tone is serious and calm. Words like "pile" and "shovel" denote industriousness.*

Analyze Visuals

Activity Ask students what point of the process described by the poem this painting illustrates. ***Possible answer:*** *The painting shows an empty, devastated battleground, waiting for the healing power of the grass.*

About the Art This stark painting by Swiss painter Félix Vallotton (1865–1925) portrays the image that World War I soldiers saw—unending devastated earth.

SELECTION WRAP–UP

READ WITH A PURPOSE Now that students have read the poems, ask them what task is specified for each of the personified subjects. They may say both Chicago and grass need to keep working and producing.

Grass

Carl Sandburg

Pile the bodies high at Austerlitz and Waterloo.[1]
Shovel them under and let me work—
      I am the grass; I cover all. ⊙

And pile them high at Gettysburg
5 And pile them high at Ypres and Verdun.[2]
Shovel them under and let me work.
Two years, ten years, and passengers ask the conductor:
      What place is this?
      Where are we now?

10   I am the grass.
      Let me work. ⊙

---

1. **Austerlitz** (ô′stər-lĭts′) **and Waterloo:** sites of significant battles during the Napoleonic Wars (1800–1815).

2. **Ypres** (ē′prə) **and Verdun** (vər-dŭn′): sites of significant battles during World War I.

⊙ **PERSONIFICATION**
Reread lines 1–3. Sandburg uses personification in establishing the speaker for this poem. Who is the speaker and what is its role in these scenes?

⊙ **TONE AND DICTION**
Identify several examples of **repetition** in this poem. What **tone** is established by the repetition of these words and/or phrases?

Le Plateau de Bolante (1917), Félix Vallotton. Oil on canvas. Musée d'Histoire Contemporaine, Paris. © Musée d'Histoire Contemporaine-BDIC.

DIFFERENTIATED INSTRUCTION

FOR STRUGGLING READERS

Clarify Meaning Make sure that students understand lines 7–9. Restate line 7 this way: "In two years and in ten years, passengers will ask train conductors . . ." Clarify that the questions in lines 8–9 imply that the places will look so ordinary that passengers will ask the conductor what is special about these places.

FOR ADVANCED LEARNERS/AP

Analyze Author's Style and Theme Point out that "Chicago" and "Grass" are quite different in subject matter, tone, and diction. Ask students what makes both poems recognizable as works by Carl Sandburg. Invite them to consider both style and theme in their analyses. Have students share their ideas with the class.

Comprehension

1. **Recall** What negative aspects of Chicago are presented in lines 6–8?

2. **Clarify** What scenes are referred to in "Grass"?

Text Analysis

3. **Synthesize Details** Think about the **litany**, or list, of images and ideas in "Chicago." Based on the accumulation of detail in this poem, what general statement can you make about the people who live and work in the city?

4. **Compare Tone and Diction** Identify the tone of each poem. Are the tones similar or different? Cite at least three examples of diction that reveal tone in each poem.

5. **Evaluate Personification** Sandburg uses personification in "Chicago" as well as in "Grass," giving human characteristics to objects, animals, or ideas. Describe the figure who personifies Chicago. What words and phrases capture his most important traits?

6. **Analyze Style** What poetic or other stylistic devices underscore Sandburg's characterization of Chicago as a brash, brawling, vibrant city? Consider such elements as line and stanza shape, rhythm, and other formal conventions. Be specific, citing examples from the text.

7. **Interpret Setting and Theme** Both "Chicago" and "Grass" depict a strong sense of place, each containing some contradiction. For each poem, identify this contradiction and use it to help you formulate a theme statement. Give evidence to support your answers.

8. **Compare and Contrast Writers** Carl Sandburg was greatly influenced by the poetry of Walt Whitman (see page 530). Compare and contrast the two poets in terms of the following points, citing specific lines from their work. Can you see Whitman's influence in Sandburg's poems? Explain why or why not.
   - use of **catalog** or **litany**
   - use of **repetition** and **parallelism**
   - **tone** and **diction**
   - ideas about America

Text Criticism

9. **Critical Interpretations** Imagist poet William Carlos Williams once criticized Sandburg's poetry as "formless." Even some of Sandburg's supporters conceded that this was true. Do you agree or disagree? Cite evidence to support your response, also explaining whether you would count yourself among his supporters or his critics, and why.

> *Would you rather live in the* **CITY** *or the* **COUNTRY?**
>
> In his poems "Chicago" and "Grass," Carl Sandburg uses vivid imagery to make surprising statements about the city and the country. If you were going to write a poem about the city or the country, what imagery would you use? Explain.

COMMON CORE

RL 4 Determine the meaning of words and phrases as they are used in the text, including figurative and connotative meanings; analyze the impact of specific word choices on meaning and tone, including words with multiple meanings or language that is particularly fresh, engaging, or beautiful. **RL 5** Analyze how an author's choices concerning how to structure specific parts of a text contribute to its overall structure and meaning as well as its aesthetic impact.

Practice and Apply

For preliminary support of post-reading questions, use these copy masters:

R RESOURCE MANAGER—Copy Masters
   Tone and Diction p. 119
   Question Support p. 123

   Additional selection questions are provided for teachers on page 115.

ANSWERS

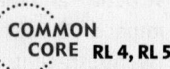
COMMON CORE RL 4, RL 5

1. *Lines 6–8 present negative aspects of crime, corruption, and poverty.*

2. *"Grass" refers to battlefields of the Napoleonic Wars, the Civil War, and World War I.*

Possible answers:

3. ▪ **COMMON CORE FOCUS Synthesize Details** *The people of Chicago are hardworking, optimistic laborers.*

4. ● **COMMON CORE FOCUS Tone and Diction** *The tone of "Chicago" is loud, dramatic, and boisterous, with long lines and lists of epithets, while that of "Grass" is quiet, solemn, and elegiac, with shorter lines and calm repetition.*

5. *The person who personifies Chicago is a young, pugnacious, optimistic laborer. His most important traits are described in lines 18–19 and 21, which show the city's vitality.*

6. *The long, flowing, rhythmic lines demonstrate Chicago's uncontainable energy. The fact that the poem also contains short lines shows the city's variety and unpredictability.*

Assess and Reteach

Assess

DIAGNOSTIC AND SELECTION TESTS
   Selection Test A pp. 245–246
   Selection Test B/C pp. 247–248

Interactive Selection Test on thinkcentral.com

Reteach

Level Up Online Tutorials on thinkcentral.com
Reteaching Worksheets on thinkcentral.com

   Literature Lesson 29: Personification
   Literature Lesson 40: Word Choice and Diction
   Literature Lesson 43: Tone
   Reading Lesson 14: Synthesizing Information

---

7. *"Chicago": The speaker loves the city despite its negative aspects, suggesting a theme that people can love flaws. "Grass": Death and life appear in the same place.*

8. *Whitman's influence is seen in Sandburg's use of cataloging, litany, repetition, and parallelism. Both poets use grandiose tones and the diction of their times. Both love American cities, the working class, and democracy. Students may observe that both poets revere an animated nature and could compare and contrast line 3 in "Grass" ("I am the grass, I cover all.") with* line 41 in "Song of Myself" ("The smallest sprout shows there really is no death.").

9. *Students may say that Sandburg's poetry has an organic form, such as the unifying effect of repetition and litany at the beginning and end of "Chicago."*

> *Would you rather live in the* CITY *or the* COUNTRY? *Students' answers will vary but should reflect careful consideration of the chosen place.*

COMMON CORE FOCUS

RL 3 Analyze the impact of the author's choices regarding how to develop and relate elements of a story or drama. **RL 5** Analyze how an author's choices concerning how to structure specific parts of a text contribute to its overall structure and meaning as well as its aesthetic impact. **RL 9** Demonstrate knowledge of early-twentieth-century foundational works of American literature, including how two or more texts from the same period treat similar themes or topics.

Teach

Achievements in Language

Help students understand the role World War I played in the Victorian era giving way to Modernism. Ask them to contrast the beliefs and language that dominated pre-war life with that of the post-war era. *Possible answer: Before World War I, people were believed to be rational, progressive beings, and people were comfortable discussing concepts they considered to be universal. After the war, people were so horrified by what happened that they doubted everything and wanted change.* Ask students to speculate about how these times gave rise to innovations in writing. *Possible answer: Writers wanted to leave the painful past behind and express their fears and doubts in a way that fit their new suspicion of tradition.*

Shifting Perspectives

Help students understand that Faulkner's use of multiple narrators is a product of his Modernist times. Point out that having multiple unreliable narrators, as in *The Sound and the Fury,* Faulkner expressed doubt in any account being completely accurate. Ask students to suggest ways this book might have been different had it been written before World War I. Have students explain their answer. *Possible answers: Faulkner might have used a single narrator who was able to tell about the events of the plot. He might have used the grand language that was favored before the war. He might have embraced the old traditions because it took the horror of war to make people want to overthrow them.*

Modernism

Although **modernism** has its roots in the nineteenth century, it was not until World War I that this movement in art, architecture, music, and literature transformed American poetry and fiction. Prior to the war, traditional Victorian ideas dominated Western culture, including the belief that human beings are rational and that progress always moves us forward. Grand language—words about courage and sacrifice in "the war to end all wars"—played a role in drawing the world into war. However, the horrors of modern warfare changed everything, undermining the old traditions with skepticism and accelerating the pace of change and experimentation.

Achievements in Language

Modernism inspired writers to consider language as language more deliberately than had ever been done before. Experiments with language and its limits changed the face of American fiction. Consider the modernism of Ernest Hemingway. The simple, spare, direct sentences of his early work represent a radical departure from the prose of his predecessors.

Experimental photograph of Ezra Pound, 1916

While Hemingway cut from his sentences the flowery language he associated with Victorian rhetoric, others pursued the subjectivity of human experience and the fragmented nature of human consciousness. Painters and photographers used visual distortions to express a fractured point of view, as in the photograph of Ezra Pound shown here. Some modernist poets and novelists experimented with **stream of consciousness,** a narrative in first-person point of view that presents the jumbled flow of a character's thoughts and sensations. Others, most notably William Faulkner, explored the subjectivity of experience by following the highly emotional perspectives of **multiple narrators** in a single story.

Shifting Perspectives

In 1929, with the publication of *The Sound and the Fury,* William Faulkner achieved a high point in fiction's depiction of human consciousness. The novel has three first-person narrators, and none of them is a reliable witness to the events that form the plot. Benjy Compson narrates the first section of the novel, but his mental ability is so severely restricted that he can't tell the difference between what happens to him in the present and what he remembers from the past. The second section of the novel jumps back in time almost two decades and relates a single day from the point of view of Benjy's intellectual brother, Quentin, who is so absorbed in abstraction and obsession that he too is incapable of distinguishing between what is "real" and what is not. After Quentin's day reaches an end, a third

COMMON CORE

Included in this workshop:
RL 3 Analyze the impact of the author's choices regarding how to develop and relate elements of a story or drama. **RL 5** Analyze how an author's choices concerning how to structure specific parts of a text contribute to its overall structure and meaning as well as its aesthetic impact. **RL 9** Demonstrate knowledge of early-twentieth-century foundational works of American literature, including how two or more texts from the same period treat similar themes or topics.

DIFFERENTIATED INSTRUCTION

FOR ENGLISH LANGUAGE LEARNERS

Language: Skill Words Define the vocabulary shown in italics.

- *abstraction:* something that suggests an idea without imitating it
- *perspective:* point of view
- *rhetoric:* the art and rules of effective writing
- *subjectivity:* an individual's way of thinking

Then help students understand the word *modern* by eliciting the Spanish and French cognates *moderno* and *moderne* and their meanings. Define the suffix *-ism* as "a school of thought" and help students build a definition for *modernism* as "a school of thought that believes in making things new."

brother, Jason, takes over as narrator. Jason is so consumed with rage that, like the two brothers before him, he cannot be trusted with his own story.

Faulkner concludes *The Sound and the Fury* with a section narrated from limited third-person point of view. But it is his implementation of multiple first-person narrators that makes this novel a crowning achievement of psychological modernism. It is not possible to find in *The Sound and the Fury* a single coherent, traditional plot of the kind seen in nineteenth-century writers such as Nathaniel Hawthorne and Stephen Crane. But for readers who surrender to the magic of Faulkner's multiple voices, the novel provides a breathtaking glimpse into the subjective nature of experience.

T. S. Eliot and Katherine Anne Porter can help you to see how modernist American writers revolutionized point of view. Eliot's "The Love Song of J. Alfred Prufrock" is stream of consciousness at its best, tracing the musings of a man paralyzed by indecision. Note how the narrative jumps from trivial questions to an idle fantasy, much as the mind jumps while daydreaming.

> Shall I part my hair behind? Do I dare to eat a peach?
> I shall wear white flannel trousers, and walk upon the beach.
> I have heard the mermaids singing, each to each.
> —T. S. Eliot, "The Love Song of J. Alfred Prufrock"

Katherine Anne Porter writes "The Jilting of Granny Weatherall" in limited third-person point of view, closely following the perspective of an elderly woman as her mind wonders. As you examine Granny Weatherall's subjective sensations, notice how her consciousness moves into the past when an anonymous "he" appears in the narrative.

> The pillow rose about her shoulders and pressed against her heart and the memory was being squeezed out of it: oh, push down the pillow, somebody: it would smother her if she tried to hold it. Such a fresh breeze blowing and such a green day with no threats in it. But he had not come, just the same. What does a woman do when she has put on the white veil and set out the white cake for a man and he doesn't come?
> —Katherine Anne Porter, "The Jilting of Granny Weatherall"

AMERICANS IN PARIS

French painter Henri Matisse was an inspiration to American writers in Paris.

At loose ends after World War I, many disillusioned Americans remained in Europe, often settling in the Left Bank district of Paris, where they were joined by numerous writers and artists. Ezra Pound, Ernest Hemingway, Gertrude Stein, F. Scott Fitzgerald, James Joyce, and George Orwell were just some of the many writers who lived for a time in Paris during the 1920s. Many of the expatriate community saw it as a place where they could be more open to life—in a way that was impossible in the United States. For others, it served for inspiration: The simplicity of both Ernest Hemingway's and Gertrude Stein's styles is said to have been inspired by the art of French painters Paul Cezanne and Henri Matisse. Ironically, Paris became known as the place where American literary style was cultivated and crafted.

Close Read

Point out details in the Porter excerpt that capture her character's subjective sensations. In the last sentence of this excerpt, locate clues that tell you what the character is remembering. What aspect of modernism does this passage illustrate?

AMERICANS IN PARIS

Ask students where they would go today to attempt a career as an artist or writer, and why. *Students may mention New York, Hollywood, or a university. Such places are centers of artistic activity.* Point out that young American artists went to Paris in the 1920s because it was the art capital of the world, because they would meet other people with similar interests, and because it was inexpensive.

Close Read

Possible answer: Subjective details include the character's memory being "squeezed out" by the pillow. The character is remembering her ill-fated wedding day, which began with "no threats in it." Clues include "white veil," "white cake," and "man [who]. . . doesn't come." This passage uses stream-of-consciousness narration, an aspect of modernism.

FOR STRUGGLING READERS

Note Taking For students who need help with note taking, hand out the copy master before discussing these pages. Explain to students that they will be learning key features of modernism such as stream of consciousness and subjectivity as they record notes on their copy masters.

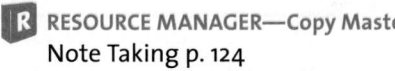 RESOURCE MANAGER—Copy Master
Note Taking p. 124

FOR ADVANCED LEARNERS/AP

Research Modernist Art To place modernist writing in context, have students look in art books for pictures of modernist painting and sculpture from the early 20th century by artists such as Pablo Picasso, Henri Matisse, Wassily Kandinsky, and Constantin Brancusi. Ask students to pick one artist from the era and briefly describe how the artist made his or her art form new.

Focus and Motivate

ABOUT THE AUTHOR

Ask students to find clues in the biography about how the contrasting ideas of solitude and home are present in Frost's life and work. ***Possible answer:*** *As a farmer and as a poet, Frost worked mainly alone. His marriage to his high school sweetheart is a link to home.*

NOTABLE QUOTE

"Poetry is a way of taking life by the throat."
—Robert Frost

Ask students to point out details in the biography that suggest Frost took life by the throat. Students should begin to see Frost as a poet who explored serious themes concerning real life.

Selection Resources

COMMON CORE

RL 1 Cite strong and thorough textual evidence to support analysis of what the text says explicitly as well as inferences drawn from the text, including determining where the text leaves matters uncertain. **RL 4** Analyze the impact of specific word choices on meaning and tone, including words with multiple meanings or language that is particularly fresh, engaging, or beautiful. **RL 6** Analyze a case in which grasping point of view requires distinguishing what is directly stated in a text from what is really meant (e.g., irony or understatement).

DID YOU KNOW?

Robert Frost . . .

- was unable to read a poem at John F. Kennedy's inauguration because of bright sunlight and so recited one from memory.

- won 44 honorary degrees from prestigious universities but never earned a college degree himself.

The New Poetry
Selected Poetry
by Robert Frost

Essential Course of Study

Meet the Author

Robert Frost 1874–1963

Robert Frost once remarked that his life's goal was to write "a few poems it will be hard to get rid of." Undoubtedly, he succeeded. Frost's best poems lodge themselves in the reader's imagination and refuse to go away. As a result, Frost is one of the most beloved American poets.

Awakening to Poetry Although Frost is associated with rural New England, he spent his first 11 years in San Francisco. Following his father's death in 1885, Frost's mother brought her two children east, eventually settling in the industrial city of Lawrence, Massachusetts. As a boy, Frost developed a passion for baseball and poetry. By the time he graduated from high school, he knew he would be a poet.

Aimless Years Frost's early manhood was nonetheless filled with change. He enrolled at both Dartmouth College and Harvard University but did not remain at either place, tiring of the routine of college life. For several years he drifted working as a mill hand, a school teacher, and a reporter. One stabilizing event in his life was his marriage in 1895 to Elinor White, his high school sweetheart.

Voice of New England In 1900, Frost abandoned the indoor life of teaching for the outdoor life of farming. During the day Frost worked his poultry farm, and at night he wrote. The 11 years Frost spent farming were some of his most creative. Inspired by the rugged New Hampshire countryside and its plain-spoken inhabitants, Frost wrote poems that probed the mysteries of nature and the human heart.

Literary Acclaim At the age of 38, Frost moved his family to England, where he could "write and be poor." Less than two months later, a London publisher accepted the manuscript of *A Boy's Will* (1913) for publication. By the time Frost returned to the United States in 1915, he was hailed as a leading American poet.

In 1924, Frost's collection *New Hampshire* won a Pulitzer Prize, the first of four that he would receive. His public success, however, was overshadowed by personal tragedy. Between 1934 and 1940, Frost lost a daughter, his wife, and a son; another daughter was institutionalized for mental illness. As a result, his later poems often convey a bleak outlook on life.

Author Online
Go to **thinkcentral.com**. KEYWORD: HML11-936

936

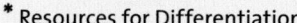

TEXT ANALYSIS: FROST'S STYLE

Some of Robert Frost's poems seem so simple, yet they move people deeply. Why? It certainly has something to do with his powerful choice of theme and subject matter, but it's also a matter of his unique **style**—the distinctive way in which he uses words and poetic devices. For one thing, he makes skillful use of traditional rhyme, meter, and stanza form. He also uses other elements in a distinctive way.

- **Diction**—word choice and syntax, or word order
- **Imagery**—the descriptive phrases that appeal to the senses
- **Mood**—the overall feeling or atmosphere that a writer creates for the reader (often created with imagery)

Notice these elements in the opening lines of "'Out, Out—'":

The buzz saw snarled and rattled in the yard
And made dust and dropped stove-length sticks of wood,
Sweet-scented stuff when the breeze drew across it.

As you read these poems by Frost, pay close attention to his diction and his use of imagery and mood.

READING SKILL: RECOGNIZE AMBIGUITY

Many people approach poems like riddles; they are certain that the true meaning must lie in a single interpretation. This approach fails to take into account the **ambiguity** that lends richness and beauty to so many poems. Literature of the **modernist** movement often lends itself to more than one meaning; it is open to various, even opposing, interpretations, as in the opening lines of "Nothing Gold Can Stay."

Nature's first green is gold,
Her hardest hue to hold.

Are these lines referring to a golden hue of green, or are they making the point that nature's first green is precious, like gold? You don't have to choose between these meanings; skilled readers of poetry recognize ambiguity and live with it, even enjoy it, as they read and consider a poem. As you read, record different interpretations of lines from each poem.

"Acquainted with the Night"	"Nothing Gold Can Stay"	"'Out, Out—'"
	lines 1–2: • golden shade of green • green is precious, like gold	

 Complete the activities in your **Reader/Writer Notebook**.

What does it mean to be ALONE?

Does solitude make you lonely? Or is it precious to you? It's a powerful idea, being alone. Some people can't get enough of it, and others have it in painful abundance. In any event, it offers opportunity for reflection. In "Acquainted with the Night," Robert Frost explores one person's emotional reaction to being alone.

QUICKWRITE What images and feelings does the word *solitude* evoke in you? Write a short poem describing a moment alone.

 937

What does it mean to be ALONE?

Ask students to think for a moment about how they view solitude. Tell them that the *QUICKWRITE* gives them the opportunity to explore reactions privately.

TEXT ANALYSIS — COMMON CORE RL 4

● **Model the Skill: FROST'S STYLE**

To examine Frost's style, write these lines from "'Out, Out—'" on the board and read them aloud:

He saw all spoiled. "Don't let him cut my hand off—

The doctor, when he comes. Don't let him, sister!" / So. But the hand was gone already.

Tell students that these lines describe the aftermath of a serious accident, in the moments before the doctor arrives. Point out that the words and syntax are not overly decorative; the diction is straightforward.

GUIDED PRACTICE Have students continue investigating Frost's style. Ask them how reading these lines makes them feel. Tell them that this will give them clues to the mood, which they may describe as tense and stark.

READING SKILL — COMMON CORE RL 1 RL 6

■ **Model the Skill: RECOGNIZE AMBIGUITY**

To locate ambiguity in the passage from "Out, Out—," read aloud this line: "He saw all spoiled." Point out that this line could have more than one meaning. Tell students that it could mean the man's severely damaged hand is beyond repair or it could mean the man has lost hope for his future.

GUIDED PRACTICE Have students explain the ambiguity in the phrase "starting off on the right foot."

R RESOURCE MANAGER—Copy Master Recognize Ambiguity p. 135

DIFFERENTIATED INSTRUCTION

FOR STRUGGLING READERS
Concept Support: Recognize Ambiguity
Explain that *ambiguity* may reflect the poet's intention to convey multiple meanings or desire to have readers choose their own meaning as a way of interacting with the work. Point out also that the *ambiguity* may be among shades of meaning rather than the dramatically different meanings of the example on page 937. Explain that, as with this example, one meaning may be based on the literal meaning of the words while the other is based on a figurative meaning. To search for ambiguity in meaning, students should consider both readings and match them to the context.

SUMMARY

In this poem, the speaker conveys his unhappy solitude by describing a lonely walk on a dark, rainy street.

READ WITH A PURPOSE

Help students set a purpose for reading. Tell them to find similarities in each of the poems.

THEME

After students have completed this poem ask them to discuss films, plays, or novels that relate to the theme of "Acquainted with the Night."

TEXT ANALYSIS

COMMON CORE
RL 4

Ⓐ FROST'S STYLE

Possible answer: Line 7 sets the stage by establishing a feeling of silence, against which the cry is particularly striking. The mood is one of loneliness and anguish.

IF STUDENTS NEED HELP... Use a Connecting organizer to help students relate the passage to feelings it evokes.

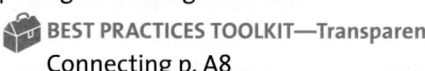 BEST PRACTICES TOOLKIT—Transparency

Connecting p. A8

READING SKILL

COMMON CORE
RL 1
RL 6

Ⓑ Model the Skill: RECOGNIZE AMBIGUITY

Help students recognize the ambiguity in these lines. Begin by reading aloud lines 11–14. Point out that line 13 can have more than one meaning. Ask students what these might be. *Possible answers: The time shown on the clock may or may not be accurate; the speaker is unsure whether this is the time to do something he's been contemplating.* Ask what is suggested about the clock. *Possible answer: It is not providing information helpful to the speaker.*

IF STUDENTS NEED HELP... Model how to note the ambiguity on the prereading chart introduced on page 937.

938 UNIT 5

Acquainted
with the **Night**

Robert Frost

I have been one acquainted with the night.
I have walked out in rain—and back in rain.
I have outwalked the furthest city light.

I have looked down the saddest city lane.
5 I have passed by the watchman on his beat
And dropped my eyes, unwilling to explain.

I have stood still and stopped the sound of feet
When far away an interrupted cry
Came over houses from another street,

10 But not to call me back or say good-by; Ⓐ
And further still at an unearthly height
One luminary[1] clock against the sky

Proclaimed the time was neither wrong nor right.
I have been one acquainted with the night. Ⓑ

THEME

Why do some people become depressed? What does it mean to feel depressed about one's life? This is a question that poets, novelists, and playwrights have always thought about. For example, the recent movie *The Hours* (2002) explores Virginia Woolf's battle with depression. Can you think of any other films, novels, or plays that touch on this same theme?

Analyze Visuals ▶
Notice the shadowy human figures in relation to other objects in the photograph. What mood is established by the **composition,** or arrangement of shapes? How do the figures appear in relation to each other? Explain.

Ⓐ **FROST'S STYLE**
Reread lines 1–10. How does the poet's use of parallel structure and rhyme contribute to the poem's developing mood? Explain your answer.

Ⓑ **RECOGNIZE AMBIGUITY**
Reread lines 11–14. Identify at least two possible meanings of "the time was neither wrong nor right." What does this proclamation suggest about the "luminary clock"? Explain.

---

1. **luminary:** giving off light.

DIFFERENTIATED INSTRUCTION

FOR ENGLISH LANGUAGE LEARNERS

Idioms Students may be unfamiliar with the idiom "on his beat." Tell them that a beat is an ongoing assignment. The watchman might have a certain area, or beat, to patrol. Tell students that a reporter may also have a beat, such as writing about local government news or a particular sport. Tell them to turn to a new page in their notebooks and begin a list of idioms they encounter.

FOR STRUGGLING READERS

Developing Reading Fluency

• Have students listen to the poems on the *Audio Anthology CD* (also recommended for English language learners) while they read along in their books. Urge students to visualize the poems' imagery as they listen, and to self-question about each poem's mood.

• Suggest that students write down words and phrases that confuse them as they listen. Invite volunteers to paraphrase and interpret.

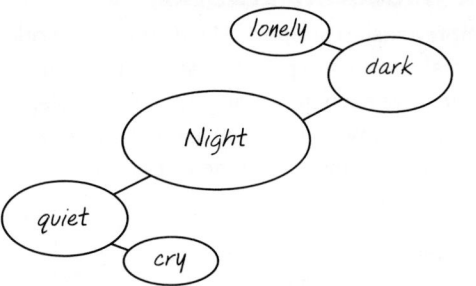

Reading Support

This selection on **thinkcentral.com** includes embedded **ThinkAloud** models—students "thinking aloud" about the story to model the kinds of questions a good reader would ask about a selection.

TIERED DISCUSSION PROMPTS

In lines 1–6, use these prompts to help students understand the mood of the poem:

Connect Think about a time you spent alone. How does that experience help you understand the speaker's situation? *Responses should convey students' understanding of the speaker's solitude.*

Analyze Which image in these lines seems the gloomiest? Explain. ***Possible answer:*** *The image of standing alone in the rain, unwilling to talk even to the watchman, is extremely gloomy and suggests lack of hope.*

Synthesize The first five lines all begin with "I have" followed by a verb. What effect does this have on the mood of the poem? ***Possible answer:*** *The phrase emphasizes the speaker's aloneness and his self-absorption.*

REVISIT THE BIG QUESTION

What does it mean to be
ALONE?

Discuss What repeated word choices imply the speaker's solitude? ***Possible answer:*** *Repetition of "I" and "one" implies solitude.*

Analyze Visuals

Possible answer: The composition of the photo emphasizes the solitude of the characters, who are outnumbered by the bare, lonely-looking trees and dwarfed by the large, impersonal buildings of the city. The figures seem somewhat distant from one another; they are certainly not engaged with each other. Rather, it seems each is going about his business in the dark, lonely night.

FOR STRUGGLING READERS

Imagery Have students fill in a Cluster Diagram to brainstorm words and phrases Frost's nighttime images evoke for them.

 BEST PRACTICES TOOLKIT—Transparency
Cluster Diagram p. B18

lonely
dark
Night
quiet
cry

Haystacks and Barn (1909), George Wesley Bellows. Oil on canvas, 56.5 cm × 71.4 cm. © Museum of Fine Arts, Houston, Texas/Bridgeman Art Library.

Nothing Gold Can Stay

Robert Frost

Nature's first green is gold,
Her hardest hue to hold.
Her early leaf's a flower;
But only so an hour.
5 Then leaf subsides to leaf.
So Eden[1] sank to grief,
So dawn goes down to day.
Nothing gold can stay. **⦿**

⦿ FROST'S STYLE
What is the **mood** of this poem? Identify the **diction** or **imagery** that most strongly establishes this mood for you.

---

1. **Eden:** the biblical Garden of Eden, from which Adam and Eve were expelled for disobeying God.

Text Analysis

1. **Clarify** What does the speaker of the first poem mean when he says he's been "acquainted with the night"?

2. **Summarize** What does the speaker of "Acquainted with the Night" see and hear on his walk?

3. **Interpret Analogies** In "Nothing Gold Can Stay," how is the fate of a leaf similar to that of the Garden of Eden?

940 UNIT 5: THE HARLEM RENAISSANCE AND MODERNISM

"Out, Out—"

Robert Frost

The buzz saw snarled and rattled in the yard
And made dust and dropped stove-length sticks of wood,
Sweet-scented stuff when the breeze drew across it.
And from there those that lifted eyes could count
5   Five mountain ranges one behind the other
Under the sunset far into Vermont.
And the saw snarled and rattled, snarled and rattled,
As it ran light, or had to bear a load. **D**
And nothing happened: day was all but done.
10   Call it a day, I wish they might have said
To please the boy by giving him the half hour
That a boy counts so much when saved from work.
His sister stood beside them in her apron
To tell them "Supper." At the word, the saw,
15   As if to prove saws knew what supper meant,
Leaped out at the boy's hand, or seemed to leap—
He must have given the hand. However it was,
Neither refused the meeting. But the hand! **E**
The boy's first outcry was a rueful[1] laugh,
20   As he swung toward them holding up the hand
Half in appeal, but half as if to keep
The life from spilling. Then the boy saw all—
Since he was old enough to know, big boy
Doing a man's work, though a child at heart—
25   He saw all spoiled. "Don't let him cut my hand off—
The doctor, when he comes. Don't let him, sister!"
So. But the hand was gone already.
The doctor put him in the dark of ether.[2]
He lay and puffed his lips out with his breath.
30   And then—the watcher at his pulse took fright.
No one believed. They listened at his heart.
Little—less—nothing!—and that ended it.
No more to build on there. And they, since they
Were not the one dead, turned to their affairs. **F**

---

1. **rueful:** expressing sorrow or regret.
2. **ether:** a liquid used as an anesthetic. Its fumes cause unconsciousness when deeply inhaled.

D FROST'S STYLE
Frost's title is taken from a famous passage in Shakespeare—the words spoken by Macbeth upon news of his wife's death. Vivid **images** in the original passage convey a **mood** of heavy gloom that can be traced from the classical dramas of ancient Greece to present-day horror and action movies. Reread lines 1–8. What kind of mood do Frost's images convey? Why might he have chosen Macbeth's grief-stricken words as his title?

E FROST'S STYLE
Reread lines 13–18. What does the **diction** in these lines suggest about the accidental meeting of the saw and the hand? Explain the **irony** in these lines.

F RECOGNIZE AMBIGUITY
Identify the ambiguity in the last two lines of the poem. What does their **understatement** and lack of sentiment suggest about the survivors and their attitude toward the boy's death?

SUMMARY
In this poem, a boy cutting wood accidentally cuts his hand with the saw. He fears having his hand amputated, but dies of shock.

TEXT ANALYSIS	COMMON CORE
	RL 4

D FROST'S STYLE

Possible answer: *The saw's snarling and rattling convey the image of its sharp teeth and danger. The mood is foreboding. The title foreshadows the boy's death.*

Remind students that each poet they have read thus far, and those they have yet to read, has his or her own style—created by subject, word choice, theme, and other poetic devices. Many of Frost's poems deal with life in rural New England. Ask students to identify themes commonly found in Frost's poems.

TEXT ANALYSIS	COMMON CORE
	RL 4

E FROST'S STYLE

Possible answer: *The diction personifies both hand and saw, presenting the meeting like a handshake both willingly embrace.*

READING SKILL	COMMON CORE
	RL 1
	RL 6

F RECOGNIZE AMBIGUITY

Possible answer: *The lines suggest either a callous attitude or merely a realistic one. The lack of sentiment suggests that the survivors have little time or energy for grief and view death as a familiar part of life.*

SELECTION WRAP-UP

READ WITH A PURPOSE Students may note that each of Frost's poems has a lonely, melancholy tone and a bitter speaker.

FOR ADVANCED LEARNERS/AP

Analyze Theme Invite students to discuss the themes that recur in these three Frost poems. ***Examples:*** *All life is transitory. Individuals are unimportant and are at the mercy of nature. We are all alone, no matter what is around us.* Have students write a one- or two-sentence description of each theme they find recurring in the poems. Ask students to justify their perception of theme by citing evidence from the texts. Students should then organize their evidence in a Three-Column Journal and refer to this as they present their ideas. Invite listeners to share similar theme interpretations in order to consolidate overlapping ideas.

   BEST PRACTICES TOOLKIT—Transparency Three-Column Journal p. B10

For preliminary support of post-reading questions, use these copy masters:

R RESOURCE MANAGER—Copy Masters
Frost's Style p. 133
Question Support p. 137
Additional selection questions are provided for teachers on page 129.

ANSWERS

COMMON CORE RL 1, RL 4, RL 6

1. *sunset on a farm in Vermont*

2. *He cuts his hand badly on a saw and dies when the doctor puts him under ether.*

Possible answers:

3. *Rhymes: gold/hold, flower/hour, leaf/grief, and day/stay; Each pair links nature to a word evoking the passage of time, suggesting that beauty is fleeting.*

4. *Lines 33–34 especially emphasize solitude. The theme emerges that human relationships are limited and we are alone.*

5. *The quotation adds the sense that this tragedy in one family exemplifies the universal human condition of life's brevity.*

6. ● **COMMON CORE FOCUS** *Frost's Style Selections will vary, but students should identify elements of Frost's craft and show awareness of the qualities of bleakness and beauty present in the poems.*

7. ■ **COMMON CORE FOCUS** *Recognize Ambiguity Students may choose "So dawn goes down to day" ("Nothing Gold Can Stay," line 7) or "But the hand was gone already" ("'Out, Out—,'" line 27).*

Assess and Reteach

Assess

DIAGNOSTIC AND SELECTION TESTS

Selection Test A pp. 249–250
Selection Test B/C pp. 251–252

Interactive Selection Test on thinkcentral.com

Reteach

Level Up Online Tutorials on thinkcentral.com
Reteaching Worksheets on thinkcentral.com

Literature Lesson 39: Ambiguity and Incongruity
Literature Lesson 44: Style and Syntax

After Reading

Comprehension

1. **Clarify** What is the setting, including the time of day, of "'Out, Out—'"?

2. **Summarize** What happens to the boy?

Text Analysis

3. **Identify Rhymes** Examine the pairs of rhyming words in "Nothing Gold Can Stay." What ideas do the rhymes help Frost convey about the nature of beauty?

4. **Examine Theme** "'Out, Out—'" provides a portrait of **solitude** even among family. Identify words and phrases in which Frost suggests the solitude of these characters in the face of tragedy. What theme emerges about human relationships?

5. **Interpret Allusion** The title of "'Out, Out—'" is an **allusion,** or indirect reference to a well-known person, place, or literary work—in this case, a famous speech in Shakespeare's *Macbeth* (Act Five, Scene 5). How does the following quotation from *Macbeth* color your sense of Frost's poem?

   . . . Out, out brief candle!
   Life's but a walking shadow, a poor player
   That struts and frets his hour upon the stage
   And then is heard no more.

● 6. **Analyze Frost's Style** Identify several lines in any one of the three poems where Frost's **diction,** his use of **imagery,** and/or **mood** is particularly striking. Explain why you find it noteworthy and how Frost's style helps deliver the poem's message.

■ 7. **Evaluate Ambiguity** Consult the chart in which you recorded different interpretations as you read. Identify the ambiguity that you found the most puzzling, contradictory, or profound. In your opinion, what does the ambiguity add to each poem? Explain.

Text Criticism

8. **Critical Interpretation** The critic and scholar Lionel Trilling hailed Frost for his "representation of the terrible actualities of life in a new way." Apply this comment to the three Frost poems you have just read. What are the "terrible actualities of life" in each poem? What might be considered "new" or unusual about Frost's portrayal of these realities? Explain.

> *What does it mean to be* **ALONE?**
>
> In "Acquainted with the Night," does the speaker seem to enjoy his solitude or long for companionship? Do you enjoy being alone? Explain.

RL 1 Cite strong and thorough textual evidence to support analysis of what the text says explicitly as well as inferences drawn from the text, including determining where the text leaves matters uncertain. **RL 4** Analyze the impact of specific word choices on meaning and tone, including words with multiple meanings or language that is particularly fresh, engaging, or beautiful. **RL 6** Analyze a case in which grasping point of view requires distinguishing what is directly stated in a text from what is really meant (e.g., irony or understatement).

The ambiguity in each allows that poem to have different meanings for each reader while still making an overall point. It also provides a tension that adds richness to the poems.

8. *The terrible actuality in "Acquainted with the Night" is solitude. In "Nothing Gold Can Stay," that actuality is life's impermanence. The actuality in "'Out, Out—'" is death. Frost's portrayal of these actualities is unusual because he accepts them as everyday facts rather than as evidence for a moral viewpoint.*

> *What does it mean to be* **ALONE?**
> He seems to long for companionship. Answers will vary.

The New Poetry

The Death of the Hired Man

Poem by Robert Frost

COMMON CORE

RL 1, RL 3, RL 5

VIDEO TRAILER **THINK** central KEYWORD: HML11-943

● **TEXT ANALYSIS: NARRATIVE POETRY**

"The Death of the Hired Man" is **narrative poetry**, but unlike the poems by Robinson and Masters on pages 922–926, this poem has a more fully developed plot, setting, and characters.

- **Dialogue**—This poem consists almost entirely of a conversation between two people, so the dialogue plays a greater role than usual in developing the narrative elements.
- **Plot**—Although the "now-time" of the poem consists almost entirely of a single conversation, the dialogue itself indirectly relates events that have unfolded over years.
- **Characterization**—Frost conveys the characters' traits through their own words and what others say about them.
- **Setting**—Again, Frost conveys time and place primarily through what the characters say about their work and their relationships.

Review: **Blank Verse**

● **READING SKILL: UNDERSTAND FORM IN POETRY**

In poetry, **form** generally refers to the shape of text on the page. In a larger sense, however, it can refer to any technique used to convey meaning. The dialogue in this poem can be hard to follow; you won't find many *he said*'s or *she said*'s. However, Frost uses other devices to show who's speaking.

- **Quotation marks**—Double quotation marks indicate the beginning and end of each speech. Single quotation marks indicate dialogue within a speech.
- **Line breaks**—Frost leaves a blank line when the speaker changes; he never changes speaker in the middle of a line.
- **Point of view**—The poem's speaker uses only the third person; in dialogue, the characters speak in the first person.

Use a chart to keep track of who is speaking in the poem.

Elements of Form Used to Show Speakers		
Line Numbers	Who Is Speaking	How I Know

 Complete the activities in your **Reader/Writer Notebook**.

How do you know you're HOME?

It's the moment when you close the door behind you, drop your bag on the floor, take off your coat, and kick off your shoes. Or maybe it's the greeting you get from a family member or even a pet. Walking up the driveway, seeing a familiar face, smelling a familiar food: we recognize home in various ways.

QUICKWRITE Identify the place where you feel the most at home. Then write a brief description of some moment or event that captures the features that make home different from other places.

943

Teach

How do you know you're HOME?

Invite volunteers to share ideas about the place they are most at home.

TEXT ANALYSIS

COMMON CORE

RL 3
RL 5

● *Model the Skill:* **NARRATIVE POETRY**

Remind students that narrative poetry tells a story using the same elements as fiction. To review narrative poetry, re-read "Richard Cory" on page 922. Ask students to cite the elements of narrative in this short poem.

GUIDED PRACTICE Have students name a prose narrative and its parts.

READING SKILL

COMMON CORE

RL 1
RL 5

■ *Model the Skill:* **UNDERSTAND FORM IN POETRY**

Write these lines on the board:

"I wasn't looking for him—and he's changed. / Wait till you see."
"Where did you say he'd been?"/
"He didn't say. . . . "

The quotation marks show each speaker's words; line breaks separate the speakers' words.

GUIDED PRACTICE Have students identify aspects of another poem's form.

 RESOURCE MANAGER—Copy Master Understand Form in Poetry p. 151

DIFFERENTIATED INSTRUCTION

FOR STRUGGLING READERS

Concept Support: Understand Form in Poetry
Preview the beginning of the poem. Show students that the narrative begins in the third-person point of view. Point out the short passages of dialogue in lines 5 and 7, and the line break after line 10. Clarify that Warren begins to speak in line 11, whereas his wife Mary was speaking in the previous stanza. Have students look at line 22 and notice the single quotation marks. Explain

that Warren, speaking to Mary, is reporting the conversation he previously had with Silas. The single quotation marks show a conversation within a conversation. Point out that Warren, when speaking, uses the first-person pronoun *I*.

Video Trailer **THINK** central

Go to **thinkcentral.com** to preview the **Video Trailer** introducing this selection. Other features that support the selection include
- **WordSharp** vocabulary tutorials
- interactive writing and grammar instruction

SUMMARY

This narrative poem takes the form of a conversation between husband and wife on their farm on a winter night. Mary says that the elderly farmhand, Silas, has come to ask for work. Warren, finding Silas undependable and resenting that Silas has sometimes sought better pay elsewhere, argues against hiring him. Mary argues that they should provide Silas with shelter and a sense of usefulness in his old age. At Mary's urging, Warren rises to visit the old man, who has fallen asleep in a chair by the stove, but Warren finds Silas dead.

READ WITH A PURPOSE

Help students set a purpose for reading. Tell them to read "Death of a Hired Man" to find out why Silas returns.

TEXT ANALYSIS **COMMON CORE** RL 3 RL 5

Ⓐ NARRATIVE POETRY

Possible answer: The "lamp-flame" (line 1) tells readers that the era is pre-electricity, the table (line 1) suggests a kitchen, the reference to "market things" (line 8) suggests a rural community, and the wooden steps (line 10) and the name Silas (line 5) suggest an earlier time.

IF STUDENTS NEED HELP . . . Work with them to define "lamp-flame" and "market things."

READING SKILL **COMMON CORE** RL 1 RL 5

Ⓑ FORM IN POETRY

Possible answer: Warren expresses his frustration at the useless Silas, who comes looking for work when it suits him but leaves when he is most needed. In lines 22–24, Warren relates an exchange in which Silas threatens to go elsewhere for a higher wage, and Warren tells him to go ahead.

The DEATH of the HIRED MAN

Robert Frost

Mary sat musing on the lamp-flame[1] at the table,
Waiting for Warren. When she heard his step,
She ran on tiptoe down the darkened passage
To meet him in the doorway with the news
5 And put him on his guard. "Silas is back."
She pushed him outward with her through the door
And shut it after her. "Be kind," she said.
She took the market things from Warren's arms
And set them on the porch, then drew him down
10 To sit beside her on the wooden steps. Ⓐ

"When was I ever anything but kind to him?
But I'll not have the fellow back," he said.
"I told him so last haying,[2] didn't I?
If he left then, I said, that ended it.
15 What good is he? Who else will harbor him
At his age for the little he can do?
What help he is there's no depending on.
Off he goes always when I need him most.
He thinks he ought to earn a little pay,
20 Enough at least to buy tobacco with,
So he won't have to beg and be beholden.
'All right,' I say, 'I can't afford to pay
Any fixed wages, though I wish I could.'
'Someone else can.' 'Then someone else will have to.' Ⓑ
25 I shouldn't mind his bettering himself
If that was what it was. You can be certain,
When he begins like that, there's someone at him
Trying to coax him off with pocket money—
In haying time, when any help is scarce.
30 In winter he comes back to us. I'm done."

"Sh! not so loud: he'll hear you," Mary said.

---

1. **musing on the lamp-flame:** looking thoughtfully at the flame of an oil lamp.
2. **last haying:** the last time the hay was cut.

Analyze Visuals ▶
Notice the shapes of the landscape in this image. How do these shapes compare with the outlines of the human figures? What might this suggest about the relationship between humans and nature? Explain.

Ⓐ **NARRATIVE POETRY** Reread lines 1–10. What clues do they contain about the poem's **setting**? Explain.

Ⓑ **FORM IN POETRY** Reread lines 11–24. Summarize these lines. Who is speaking? What is happening in lines 22–24?

Detail of *Island Hay* (1945), Thomas Hart Benton. © T.H. Benton and R.P. Benton Testamentary Trusts/UMB Bank Trustee/Licensed by VAGA, New York, N.Y.

DIFFERENTIATED INSTRUCTION

FOR ENGLISH LANGUAGE LEARNERS

Understanding Dialogue Remind students that the words a character says appear in quotation marks. Point out that in lines 22–24, Warren is still speaking, but he's quoting himself, telling Mary what he had said to Silas in the past; these words appear in single quotation marks. Have students work in mixed-ability pairs to write similar dialogue. Check all punctuation.

FOR STRUGGLING READERS

Options for Reading: Audio Recording
- Have students listen to the poems on the *Audio Anthology CD* (also recommended for English language learners) while they read along in their books. Students can use the audio accents and tones to visualize the speakers.
- Suggest that students also notice the pause when the speakers shift and stress that this reflects the line breaks in the printed poem.

In lines 5–16, use these prompts to help students consider how Mary and Warren feel about Silas:

Connect How does it feel when an unexpected guest arrives? *Students' responses should recognize the range of emotions possible in such a situation.*

Interpret How does Mary feel about Silas? How does Warren feel about him? ***Possible answer:*** *Mary pities him. Warren is fed up with him.*

Synthesize What predictions can you make about the outcome of Warren's and Mary's discussion? Give evidence. *Students will likely predict that Warren will prevail. He seems very strongly committed to his position. On the other hand, Mary's kindness is steady and may win out.*

Analyze Visuals

Possible answer: *Both the human figure and the landscape have curving, organic shapes. This might suggest a relationship of unity between humans and nature.*

About the Art Missouri-born painter Thomas Hart Benton (1889–1975) was a champion of regionalism at a time when many artists were turning to modernist abstraction. He is known for his realistic murals of American subject matter, often of ordinary people hard at work. This detail from *Island Hay* shows a farm worker taking a break from cutting hay with a hand-held scythe—work that Silas or Warren from "The Death of the Hired Man" might do.

FOR ADVANCED LEARNERS/AP

Evaluate Narrative Poetry Although narrative poetry has a long history dating from ancient times, most modern narrative is in prose and most modern poetry is lyric poetry. Invite students to discuss pros and cons of writing a narrative in verse, using these questions as a guide:

- So far, does the narrative seem realistic and convincing even though it is in verse? Why or why not?

- In what ways are the characters and emotions of Warren and Mary clearly drawn in the poem's introduction?

- Does a central conflict emerge from the story's opening scene? If so, what is it?

- How might the narrative change if it were written in prose?

After students discuss, have them cast votes in favor of prose or poetic narrative.

C *Model the Skill:*
NARRATIVE POETRY

Remind students that these are Mary's words, then read aloud lines 31–39.

- Point out that Mary calls Silas "worn out" and says she found him "huddled against the barn door fast asleep," but that she didn't recognize him. These details suggest that he is in very bad shape.

- Ask students to read the lines again, this time looking for what they tell about Mary. ***Possible answer:*** *Mary is concerned for Silas and feels sorry for him. She says he looks miserable and frightening. She takes care of him by inviting him into the house and giving him a place by the fire to rest.*

D FORM IN POETRY

Possible answer: *Mary speaks in lines 38–39, Warren in the second half of 39, Mary in 40–43, Warren in 44, Mary in 45, Warren in the second half of 45 to 46, Mary in the first half of 47, Warren in the second half of 47, and Mary in 48. Line breaks and quotation marks show changes of speaker. The rapid changes of speaker emphasize the conflict between husband and wife.*

IF STUDENTS NEED HELP . . . Work with them to add to the prereading chart introduced on page 943.

E BLANK VERSE

Possible answer: *Students may say that the lack of rhyme and the simple diction resemble English speech, but that the regular rhythm of iambic pentameter is different from English speech.*

"I want him to: he'll have to soon or late."

"He's worn out. He's asleep beside the stove.
When I came up from Rowe's I found him here,
35 Huddled against the barn door fast asleep,
A miserable sight, and frightening, too—
You needn't smile—I didn't recognize him—
I wasn't looking for him—and he's changed.
Wait till you see." **C**

        "Where did you say he'd been?"

40 "He didn't say. I dragged him to the house,
And gave him tea and tried to make him smoke.
I tried to make him talk about his travels.
Nothing would do: he just kept nodding off."

"What did he say? Did he say anything?"

45 "But little."

        "Anything? Mary, confess
He said he'd come to ditch³ the meadow for me."

"Warren!"

        "But did he? I just want to know."

"Of course he did. What would you have him say? **D**
Surely you wouldn't grudge the poor old man
50 Some humble way to save his self-respect.
He added, if you really care to know,
He meant to clear the upper pasture, too.
That sounds like something you have heard before?
Warren, I wish you could have heard the way
55 He jumbled everything. I stopped to look
Two or three times—he made me feel so queer—
To see if he was talking in his sleep.
He ran on⁴ Harold Wilson—you remember—
The boy you had in haying four years since.
60 He's finished school, and teaching in his college.
Silas declares you'll have to get him back.
He says they two will make a team for work:
Between them they will lay this farm as smooth! **E**

_____

3. **ditch:** plow.

4. **ran on:** talked about without stopping.

C NARRATIVE POETRY
Reread Mary's description of Silas in lines 31–39. What **character traits** are revealed about Silas in these lines? about Mary?

D FORM IN POETRY
Reread lines 38–48. Identify the speaker of each speech. What devices indicate this? Explain what the rapid change of speakers emphasizes about the tone of this discussion.

E BLANK VERSE
Poetry written in unrhymed **iambic pentameter,** or blank verse, is said to be the poetic form that most resembles English speech. Read aloud lines 58–63. Would you agree? Explain.

DIFFERENTIATED INSTRUCTION

FOR STRUGGLING READERS

Characterization Have students create Open Mind organizers for Mary and Warren. Students should use the organizers to describe each character's traits and feelings as the poem progresses.

 BEST PRACTICES TOOLKIT—Transparency
Open Mind p. D9

Mary
Concerned about Silas

The way he mixed that in with other things.
65 He thinks young Wilson a likely lad, though daft
On⁵ education—you know how they fought
All through July under the blazing sun,
Silas up on the cart to build the load,
Harold along beside to pitch it on."

70 "Yes, I took care to keep well out of earshot."

"Well, those days trouble Silas like a dream.
You wouldn't think they would. How some things linger!
Harold's young college-boy's assurance piqued⁶ him.
After so many years he still keeps finding
75 Good arguments he sees he might have used.
I sympathize. I know just how it feels
To think of the right thing to say too late.
Harold's associated in his mind with Latin.
He asked me what I thought of Harold's saying
80 He studied Latin, like the violin,
Because he liked it—that an argument!
He said he couldn't make the boy believe
He could find water with a hazel prong⁷—
Which showed how much good school had ever done him.
85 He wanted to go over that. But most of all
He thinks if he could have another chance
To teach him how to build a load of hay—" **F**

"I know, that's Silas' one accomplishment.
He bundles every forkful in its place,
90 And tags and numbers it for future reference,
So he can find and easily dislodge it
In the unloading. Silas does that well.
He takes it out in bunches like big birds' nests.
You never see him standing on the hay
95 He's trying to lift, straining to lift himself."

"He thinks if he could teach him that, he'd be
Some good perhaps to someone in the world.
He hates to see a boy the fool of books.
Poor Silas, so concerned for other folk,
100 And nothing to look backward to with pride,

---

5. **daft on:** crazy about; obsessed with.

6. **piqued** (pēkt): aroused resentment in.

7. **find . . . prong:** a reference to the practice of dowsing, in which a person uses a forked stick made of hazel wood to try to find underground water.

F NARRATIVE POETRY
Reread lines 79–87. How are Silas and Harold characterized in these lines?

TEXT ANALYSIS   COMMON CORE

F NARRATIVE POETRY   RL 3
                                 RL 5

Possible answer: The lines characterize Harold as a college boy with artistic and intellectual interests (line 80) and a contempt for superstition (lines 82–83). They characterize Silas as a farm worker without education but with hard-earned skill and native wisdom (lines 82–83).

Extend the Discussion What relationships in real life, or in other literary works, resemble the one between Silas and Harold?

REVISIT THE BIG QUESTION
How do you know you're
HOME?

Discuss In what ways does Silas act as if Mary's and Warren's farm were his home?
Possible answer: He is fastidious about loading hay, and he tries to teach young Harold his skills.

FOR ENGLISH LANGUAGE LEARNERS

Language Coach

Word Definitions *Answer:*
Earshot means "*within the range of hearing.*" Warren wanted to stay out of Silas and Wilson's argument. Next, have students find what *go over* in line 85 and *backward* in line 100 mean. Check that they understand *go over* to mean "revisit" and *backward* to mean "at or of the past."

FOR STRUGGLING READERS

Develop Reading Fluency To help students fluently read dialogue, have them perform a Readers' Theater activity, reading aloud lines 48–95. Assign the roles of Mary and Warren to two students, reading their respective lines. You may wish to repeat the activity, with other students reading the dialogue.

G Model the Skill:

FORM IN POETRY

Read aloud lines 103–110. Point out that when Mary and Warren talk, they tell what happened in a straightforward way; here, though, the speaker's lines are rich with visual imagery. ***Possible answers:*** *"part of the moon was falling down" (line 103), "dragging the whole sky with it to the hills" (line 105), and "she played unheard some tenderness / that wrought on him" (lines 109–110). The poem's mood suddenly becomes contemplative and delicately lyrical.*

IF STUDENTS NEED HELP . . . Point out that Mary and Warren are still seated on the porch talking. Help students describe the setting, emphasizing the images of the moon and of harp music.

TIERED DISCUSSION PROMPTS

In lines 118–120, use these prompts to help students think about Frost's two definitions of home:

Restate Paraphrase the two definitions of home, and identify which character gives which definition. ***Possible answer:*** *Warren says that home is a place where people go when they have nowhere else to go, and where their family cannot refuse them. Mary says that home is a place where people can return even when they don't deserve to.*

Analyze Whose view of home is more optimistic, Mary's or Warren's? Explain. ***Possible answer:*** *Mary's view of home is more optimistic because it arises from a sense of forgiveness rather than duty.*

Evaluate Which view of home is closer to your view? Explain. *Accept all thoughtful answers that are well supported.*

H NARRATIVE POETRY

Possible answer: *The lines reveal that Silas is alienated from his family and that he is too proud to ask them for help or to discuss the matter with others.*

And nothing to look forward to with hope,
So now and never any different."

Part of a moon was falling down the west,
Dragging the whole sky with it to the hills.
105 Its light poured softly in her lap. She saw it
And spread her apron to it. She put out her hand
Among the harplike morning-glory strings,
Taut[8] with the dew from garden bed to eaves,
As if she played unheard some tenderness
110 That wrought on[9] him beside her in the night. **G**
"Warren," she said, "he has come home to die:
You needn't be afraid he'll leave you this time."

"Home," he mocked gently.
                              "Yes, what else but home?
It all depends on what you mean by home.
115 Of course he's nothing to us, any more
Than was the hound that came a stranger to us
Out of the woods, worn out upon the trail."

"Home is the place where, when you have to go there,
They have to take you in."
                              "I should have called it
120 Something you somehow haven't to deserve."

Warren leaned out and took a step or two,
Picked up a little stick, and brought it back
And broke it in his hand and tossed it by.
"Silas has better claim on us you think
125 Than on his brother? Thirteen little miles
As the road winds would bring him to his door.
Silas has walked that far no doubt today.
Why doesn't he go there? His brother's rich,
A somebody—director in the bank."

130 "He never told us that."
                              "We know it, though." **H**

"I think his brother ought to help, of course.
I'll see to that if there is need. He ought of right
To take him in, and might be willing to—

_____

8. **taut:** pulled tight; straight.
9. **wrought** (rôt) **on:** worked on.

G FORM IN POETRY
Reread lines 103–110. The poem's speaker has interrupted the dialogue between Mary and Warren. How does this shift in **point of view** affect the poem's **mood**?

Language Coach

Multiple-Meaning Words
Somebody (line 129) is a multiple-meaning word, a word with more than one meaning. *Somebody* often means "an unspecified person." Here it means "an important person." How can you tell which definition is meant?

H NARRATIVE POETRY
Reread lines 124–130. What do these lines add to your understanding of Silas?

DIFFERENTIATED INSTRUCTION

FOR STRUGGLING READERS

Comprehension Support Use the What's Most Important strategy to help students identify Mary's and Warren's differing views on family. Discuss how these contrasting views affect Mary's and Warren's reactions to Silas returning.

BEST PRACTICES TOOLKIT
What's Most Important p. D4

FOR ENGLISH LANGUAGE LEARNERS

Language Coach

Multiple-Meaning Words ***Answer:*** *The dash and "director in the bank" show that "important person" is meant.* Next, ask students to determine what is meant in line 124 by *claim*, another multiple-meaning word.

He may be better than appearances.[10]
135 But have some pity on Silas. Do you think
If he had any pride in claiming kin
Or anything he looked for from his brother,
He'd keep so still about him all this time?"

"I wonder what's between them."
                                          "I can tell you.
140 Silas is what he is—we wouldn't mind him—
But just the kind that kinsfolk can't abide.[11]
He never did a thing so very bad.
He don't know why he isn't quite as good
As anybody. Worthless though he is,
145 He won't be made ashamed to please his brother."

"I can't think Si ever hurt anyone."

"No, but he hurt my heart the way he lay
And rolled his old head on that sharp-edged chair-back.
He wouldn't let me put him on the lounge.[12]
150 You must go in and see what you can do.
I made the bed up for him there tonight.
You'll be surprised at him—how much he's broken.
His working days are done; I'm sure of it."

"I'd not be in a hurry to say that."

155 "I haven't been. Go, look, see for yourself.
But, Warren, please remember how it is:
He's come to help you ditch the meadow.
He has a plan. You mustn't laugh at him.
He may not speak of it, and then he may.
160 I'll sit and see if that small sailing cloud
Will hit or miss the moon." ●

                            It hit the moon.
Then there were three there, making a dim row,
The moon, the little silver cloud, and she.

Warren returned—too soon, it seemed to her—
165 Slipped to her side, caught up her hand and waited.

"Warren?" she questioned.
                            "Dead," was all he answered.

> ● **NARRATIVE POETRY**
> In lines 150–161, the dialogue between Mary and Warren is coming to a head. What turn in the **plot** do you foresee?

---

10. **better than appearances:** better than he looks.

11. **abide:** put up with.

12. **lounge:** couch.

FOR ADVANCED LEARNERS/AP

Analyze Poetic Content [small-group option]
Have students use the Analysis Frame: Poetic Content in order to explore the implications of "The Death of the Hired Man." Challenge groups to discuss the questions in the frame, then divide up the questions to briefly answer in written form. Have groups review their individual responses and choose three key points on which to focus. Ask students to generate a lesson presenting those key points about the poem to the class. Some options include

- larger meanings implied in the poem
- the speaker's attitude toward the people and situation
- the contribution of setting to the narrative
- contrasts in the poem
- how the ideas or values in the poem compare to one's own

🧰 **BEST PRACTICES TOOLKIT—Copy Masters**
Analysis Frame: Poetic Content
pp. D21, D36, D37

How do you know you're HOME?

Discuss In what way is Mary's and Warren's farm both a good home and a bad home for Silas? Explain. ***Possible answer:*** *The farm is a good home for Silas because Mary provides him with rest at the end of his life. It's a bad home because he isn't truly welcome, but merely has nowhere else to go.*

TEXT ANALYSIS	COMMON CORE

RL 3
RL 5

● NARRATIVE POETRY

Possible answer: *It seems that Warren and Silas are about to have a confrontation. Students may guess that Warren will kick Silas out, or that he will take pity on Silas. Some may foresee the ending.*

IF STUDENTS NEED HELP . . . Ask them to recall the poem's title and to guess what it foreshadows.

SELECTION WRAP-UP

READ WITH A PURPOSE Now that students have finished reading "Death of a Hired Man," they may say Silas returned to Mary and Warren's farm because he had no other options and he knew they would try to help him.

⭐ **CRITIQUE** Ask students to identify parts of the conversation they found difficult to follow, and to explain why.

INDEPENDENT READING

To learn more about Frost, the poet, students may enjoy reading *Robert Frost: A Life,* by Jay Parini.

Practice and Apply

For preliminary support of post-reading questions, use these copy masters:

R RESOURCE MANAGER—Copy Masters
Narrative Poetry p. 149
Question Support p. 153

Additional selection questions are provided for teachers on page 143.

ANSWERS
COMMON CORE RL 1, RL 3, RL 5

1. *Silas is a farmhand who for years has been employed by Mary and Warren.*

2. *Silas looks worn out and miserable and keeps nodding off.*

3. *He thinks Silas is unreliable, because Silas demands fixed wages but then works for other farmers when Warren needs him.*

4. *Mary thinks Silas has returned to die.*

Possible answers:

5. ***Silas's return:*** *Mary is more sympathetic than Warren. She understands why Silas has returned and she perceives his ill health. Warren is still angry over his last disagreement with Silas.* ***Silas's appearance and plans:*** *Mary believes that Silas's plan comes from a desire to feel at home, while Warren thinks he is simply desperate.* ***Silas's skills:*** *Both spouses believe he is good at farm work.* ***Silas's relationship to his brother:*** *Warren thinks Silas should depend on his brother rather than on Mary and him. Mary understands that Silas is estranged from his brother.* ***Personality traits:*** *Mary is empathetic and generous. Warren is distant and pragmatic.*

6. *Silas has done more work on their farm than anywhere else. It is where he has felt most useful.*

7. ● **COMMON CORE FOCUS** **Narrative Poetry** *The poem's plot would be different in that the conflict between Mary and Warren about what to do with Silas might not be as clear. Their deliberation might have taken a different turn, which would have altered the development of the plot.*

8. ● **COMMON CORE FOCUS** **Understand Form in Poetry** *Some students may feel confused by the changes of speaker. Some may feel that the rhythm of blank verse suited the speakers, while others may feel it limited their speech styles. Many will agree that telling the story through dialogue heightened the drama.*

Comprehension

1. **Recall** Who is Silas, and what is his relationship to Mary and Warren?

2. **Recall** How does Silas look and act when Mary finds him?

3. **Clarify** Why is Warren angry with Silas?

4. **Clarify** In Mary's mind, why has Silas returned to the farm?

Text Analysis

5. **Analyze Characterization** What does the **dialogue** between Mary and Warren reveal about their differing attitudes toward the following subjects?

   - Silas's return (lines 5–30)
   - Silas's appearance and plans (lines 42–61)
   - Silas's skills (lines 88–102)
   - Silas's relationship to his brother (lines 124–145)

   Based on these attitudes, identify Mary's and Warren's chief personality traits.

6. **Draw Conclusions** Silas has a long history with Mary and Warren. Based on what they say about him and their past interactions with them, why do you think he has come to regard their farm as home?

● 7. **Examine Narrative Poetry** Compare the events that occur during the conversation between Mary and Warren with those events—revealed through **dialogue**—that have taken place over the entire time they have known Silas. How would the poem's **plot** be different if Mary and Warren had not talked at such length about these earlier events? Explain.

● 8. **Evaluate Form in Poetry** Review the chart in which you kept track of the changing speakers. In your opinion, what is gained or lost by Frost's style of writing dialogue in terms of the following elements? Overall, do you think his technique was effective? Explain.

   - clarity
   - rhythm
   - sense of drama

Text Criticism

9. **Biographical Context** Robert Frost spent 11 years farming and drew tremendous inspiration from farm life. The poet Ezra Pound, reviewing Frost's second book of poetry, wrote, "I know more of farm life than I did before I had read his poems. That means I know more of 'Life.'" Think of the Frost poems you've read. In what ways can the themes of farm life as depicted by Frost be said to reflect life in general?

> *How do you know you're* **HOME?**
> Who or what is home to Silas in "The Death of the Hired Man"? Do you agree with Silas's view, or does home mean something different to you? Explain.

COMMON CORE

RL 1 Cite textual evidence to support analysis of what the text says explicitly as well as inferences drawn from the text, including determining where the text leaves matters uncertain. **RL 3** Analyze the impact of the author's choices regarding how to develop and relate elements of a story. **RL 5** Analyze how an author's choices concerning how to structure specific parts of a text contribute to its overall structure and meaning.

---

9. *Farm life is an archetype of human life in general, reflecting the universal processes of aging and death, the relationships between husband and wife, and the problems that occur in relationships between employers and employees. As such, a farm setting can be seen as symbolic of the larger world.*

> *How do you know you're* **HOME?**
> Students may say home is the place Silas feels most accepted. Answers will vary.

Language

◆ **GRAMMAR AND STYLE: Use Language Effectively**

Poets strive to use words and phrases that will give their poems a musical quality and convey emphasis. One kind of phrase Frost uses frequently is the **infinitive phrase,** consisting of an infinitive—a verb form that begins with *to*—plus its modifiers and complements. Infinitive phrases can function as nouns, adjectives, or adverbs. For instance, in the examples below, Frost uses parallel infinitive phrases, highlighted in yellow, as adverbs modifying the verbs highlighted in green.

L 3a Vary syntax for effect, consulting references for guidance as needed; apply an understanding of syntax to the study of complex texts when reading. **W 2** Write informative/explanatory texts to examine and convey complex ideas, concepts, and information clearly and accurately through the effective selection, organization, and analysis of content. **W 4** Produce clear and coherent writing in which the development, organization, and style are appropriate to task, purpose, and audience.

> She ran on tiptoe down the darkened passage
> To meet him in the doorway with the news (lines 3–4)

> She took the market things from Warren's arms
> And set them on the porch, then drew him down
> To sit beside her on the wooden steps. (lines 8–10)

Notice that the infinitive phrases help to give the poem a predictable rhythm and to call attention to Mary's actions.

PRACTICE Fill in the blank lines in the following poem with infinitive phrases that modify the boldfaced words.

He **ran** out to the garage

_____

A pair of bargain-hunters
Were fighting over a toaster.
He **tried** his best

_____

Offering a waffle iron,
But neither was satisfied.

READING-WRITING CONNECTION

Expand your understanding of "The Death of the Hired Man" by responding to this prompt. Then, use the **revising tips** to improve your essay.

WRITING PROMPT	**REVISING TIPS**
ANALYZE THEME Write an **essay** in which you identify the central message or theme of "The Death of the Hired Man." First make a list of all the perceptions about life or people conveyed in the poem. Then, determine which one is the most fully developed. Finally, describe the theme of the poem in **three or four paragraphs.** To support your analysis, include details and quotations.	• Include a clear statement of the poem's theme. • Discuss how details support the theme. • Organize your essay in a clear and logical order.

Interactive Revision THINK central
Go to **thinkcentral.com**.
KEYWORD: HML11-951

Language

◆ **GRAMMAR AND STYLE**

To help students understand infinitives, write three or four common infinitive verbs on the board, such as *to write, to work,* and *to see.* Clarify also that while infinitive phrases can function as nouns, adjectives, or adverbs, both the examples and practice items on page 951 address the use of infinitives as adverbs. (For more about infinitives and infinitive phrases, see **Grammar Handbook,** page R65.)

R RESOURCE MANAGER—Copy Master
Use Language Effectively p. 154

READING-WRITING CONNECTION

To help students organize their analytical essays into an introduction, body, and conclusion, have them use a Microtheme chart. Students should begin by completing the top portion with context information and their theme ideas, then listing supporting details in the bottom of the organizer. Urge students to refer to the organizer as they draft.

BEST PRACTICES TOOLKIT—Transparency
Microtheme p. C13

Writing Online
 THINK central

The following tools are available online at **thinkcentral.com** and on **Write*Smart* CD-ROM:**
• **Interactive Graphic Organizers**
• **Interactive Student Models**
• **Interactive Revision Lessons**
For additional grammar instruction, see **GrammarNotes** on **thinkcentral.com**.

DIFFERENTIATED INSTRUCTION

FOR STRUGGLING WRITERS
Writing Support [small-group option]

• Remind students that a theme is a work's central message about life. Have student groups discuss and list the poem's perceptions about life or people.

• Have students work individually to develop theme statements. Then encourage peer response from their group.

• Tell students to state their theme as a thesis statement in their introduction.

• Limit the assignment to two or three paragraphs and one quotation. Remind students to identify the speaker and the lines and use correct quotation mark form. Urge them to paraphrase other passages of dialogue or text.

Assess and Reteach

Assess

DIAGNOSTIC AND SELECTION TESTS
Selection Test A, B/C pp. 253–256

Interactive Selection Test on thinkcentral.com

Reteach

Level Up Online Tutorials on thinkcentral.com

Reteaching Worksheets on thinkcentral.com

Literature Lessons 16, 17, Writing Lesson 26

COMMON CORE FOCUS

RL 1 Cite strong and thorough textual evidence to support analysis of what the text says explicitly as well as inferences drawn from the text, including determining where the text leaves matters uncertain. **RL 4** Analyze the impact of specific word choices on meaning and tone, including words with multiple meanings or language that is particularly fresh, engaging, or beautiful. **W 3d** Use telling details to convey a vivid picture of the experiences, events, setting, and/or characters. **L 3** Apply knowledge of language to make effective choices for meaning or style.

ABOUT THE POETS

Ezra Pound Read the biography aloud and then reread the second sentence, noting that it gives Pound's imagist theory in a nutshell. Tell students that Pound's poem in this selection is only two lines long. It describes an image meant to endure in readers' minds.

H. D. Read the biography aloud, pointing out the information that H. D.'s best poems retell Greek myths from the standpoint of women who suffer injustice. Explain that "Helen" is one such poem, and ask students what character named Helen appears in Greek mythology. ***Answer:*** *Helen of Troy*

William Carlos Williams Read the biography aloud and ask students how practicing medicine might inspire a poet. ***Possible answer:*** *Doctors touch the lives of many, use powers of observation also necessary for a poet, and witness moments of drama such as birth and death.*

The New Poetry

In a Station of the Metro
Poetry by Ezra Pound

Helen
Poetry by H. D.

Spring and All / This Is Just to Say
Poetry by William Carlos Williams

COMMON CORE

RL 1 Cite strong and thorough textual evidence to support analysis of what the text says explicitly as well as inferences drawn from the text, including determining where the text leaves matters uncertain. **RL 4** Analyze the impact of specific word choices on meaning and tone, including words with multiple meanings or language that is particularly fresh, engaging, or beautiful.

Meet the Authors

Ezra Pound
1885–1972

Ezra Pound may have been the most influential poet of the 20th century, promoting the careers of experimental writers and founding the literary movement known as imagism. Pound encouraged poets to use everyday language and to express emotions and ideas through precise, concrete images. In his own work, Pound drew upon the poetic traditions of numerous countries; his masterwork, *The Cantos*, features heroic figures from world history. In life, he was an inflammatory figure. During World War II, he made anti-American radio broadcasts from Rome. He was eventually arrested and confined to a mental hospital. Following his release, he lived a quiet, secluded life in Italy.

H. D. (Hilda Doolittle)
1886–1961

As a young woman, Hilda Doolittle coped with the pain of alienation by befriending other artists. At 15, she met the poet Ezra Pound, who became her close friend and, briefly, her fiancé. A few years later she met the poets Marianne Moore and William Carlos Williams, beginning lifelong nurturing friendships.

Although no longer romantically involved with Pound, Doolittle joined his circle of friends when she moved to London in 1911. Her first published poems appeared in *Poetry* magazine (1913) under the signature "H. D., *Imagiste*," as suggested by Pound. That year she married Richard Aldington, another imagist, who shared her fascination with the classical world. H. D.'s best poems retell Greek myths from the perspective of women who have suffered injustice.

William Carlos Williams
1883–1963

William Carlos Williams crammed two lives into one. He worked full time as a doctor in Rutherford, New Jersey, yet managed to publish more than 40 books of poetry, fiction, plays, and essays. Often, he found inspiration while caring for his patients.

Born to an English father and a Puerto Rican mother, Williams grew up in Rutherford and considered America his home. While his contemporaries fled to Europe, he decided to write poems about the world around him. Williams felt strongly that a poem should be rooted in everyday life and not abstract ideas.

Author Online
THINK central
Go to **thinkcentral.com**. KEYWORD: HML11-952

952

See resources on the **Teacher One Stop DVD-ROM** and on **thinkcentral.com**.

R RESOURCE MANAGER UNIT 5
Plan and Teach, pp. 155–162
Text Analysis and Reading Skill, pp. 163–166†*
Grammar and Style, p. 168

DIAGNOSTIC AND SELECTION TESTS
Selection Tests, pp. 257–260

BEST PRACTICES TOOLKIT
Cluster Diagram, p. B18
Showing, Not Telling, With Literature, p. D1
Freewriting, p. C1

TECHNOLOGY
- **Teacher One Stop DVD-ROM**
- **Student One Stop DVD-ROM**
- **Audio Anthology CD**
- **GrammarNotes DVD-ROM**
- **ExamView Test Generator** on the **Teacher One Stop**

---

* Resources for Differentiation   † Also in Spanish   ‡ In Haitian Creole and Vietnamese

TEXT ANALYSIS: IMAGISM

Early in the 20th century, a number of American and British poets undertook a collective effort to rejuvenate poetry in English, freeing it from standard conventions of form and subject matter. The **imagists,** influenced by Japanese haiku as well as ancient Greek lyric and French symbolist poetry, wrote according to strict principles.

- to use the language of **common speech;** yet also to choose words with extreme precision and economy
- to create new **rhythms** as a way of expressing new moods; this generally meant writing in **free verse**
- to have complete freedom in choice of **subject matter**
- to present a clear and highly concentrated **image**

The images in these poems do not generally carry a specific meaning; rather, they suggest a certain feeling or idea.

Ezra Pound and H. D. were among the most important founding members of imagism; William Carlos Williams emerged a few years later, making his own distinctive mark on the style. As you read their work, consider the principles outlined above. Be attuned to the images in these poems and think about what ideas or feelings they might suggest.

READING SKILL: MAKE INFERENCES

Imagist poems are tightly compressed, leaving out details and explanations in favor of sharp, spare images. They can be seen as highly efficient, saying a lot with very few words. This economic use of language can occasionally leave room for confusion, often requiring you to **make inferences,** or logical guesses based on the text (or prior knowledge), about what is not directly stated. This is often referred to as "reading between the lines." As you read each poem, use a chart like the one shown to record your inferences and the evidence on which you base them.

"Helen"	
Inferences	*Details from Text or Prior Knowledge*
Helen is beautiful.	*First stanza focuses on her white skin and its "lustre."*

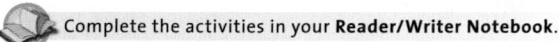 Complete the activities in your **Reader/Writer Notebook.**

How do you capture a MOMENT?

"I'll never forget the sight of that wet scarf hanging out the car door." Many experiences leave us with a lingering mental image, which then becomes our means of remembering the experience. The gleaming surface of an empty swimming pool, a towering pile of unwashed dishes—something about such an image communicates the meaning or feeling of a moment. What is that meaning or feeling? How might you capture it?

QUICKWRITE Choose an image that stands out in your mind, whether it's from an important experience (your first day of school) or an ordinary moment (a walk to the store on a hot day). Then write a brief list of the sensory details that make the image so compelling for you.

953

Teach

How do you capture a MOMENT?

Read the question aloud. Then have students read the paragraph that follows. Ask students to visualize the wet scarf, the empty swimming pool, or the pile of dishes. Have students suggest meanings or feelings linked to the image. Urge them to use the discussion as a guide to completing the *QUICKWRITE*.

TEXT ANALYSIS — COMMON CORE RL 4

● *Model the Skill:* IMAGISM

To help students identify imagist principles, write these lines on the board:

> Heavy pink petals:
> The bent branch bobs.

Point out that these lines show several characteristics of imagism. Tell students that the focus is on a single image; the language is simple. Also note that the lines are written in free verse.

GUIDED PRACTICE Ask students to state an image that comes into their minds when they visualize a tree.

READING SKILL — COMMON CORE RL 1

■ *Model the Skill:* MAKE INFERENCES

Stress that imagist verse contains sparse clues, and readers must rely heavily on prior knowledge and the mental images that the words create. Make inferences about the two lines you wrote on the board. Read them aloud again. Say, "I know that in many places, trees and shrubs blossom in the spring. That's why I think the lines describe spring."

GUIDED PRACTICE Ask students to make another inference about the lines, such as the branch is bent because it is windy.

R RESOURCE MANAGER—Copy Master
Make Inferences p. 165 (for student use while reading the selections)

DIFFERENTIATED INSTRUCTION

FOR STRUGGLING READERS
Vocabulary Support
- *collective,* "as a group"
- *rejuvenate,* "to make young or new again"
- *haiku,* "poems of three lines, totaling seventeen syllables, focusing on one image"
- *lyric poetry,* "poetry with a musical quality that expresses personal emotions"
- *economy,* "avoidance of waste"
- *compressed,* "pushed into a small space"
- *spare,* "with little detail"

Concept Support: Imagism Students may be familiar with imagery from earlier reading. Connect their knowledge of language that creates mind pictures to the idea of imagism, but clarify that while imagery can be found in most poems, imagism was a specific style that aimed to exclude any content other than imagery. Readers looking for background information or philosophical commentary in an imagist poem must find it by inference.

READ WITH A PURPOSE

Help students set a purpose for reading. Tell them to read the four poems and determine what they have in common.

SUMMARY

This two-line poem compares the crowd at a subway station to petals on a bough.

READING SKILL

COMMON CORE
RL 1

Ⓐ Model the Skill: MAKE INFERENCES

Point out that an apparition is a ghost, so the speaker must think the faces in the crowd look ghostly or unreal. What inferences can you make about the second line? How do the ghostly faces relate to the second line's images? *Possible answer: The petals seem fragile, as if they have been torn from the bough by a rainstorm and are, therefore, dead.*

SUMMARY

This poem describes Helen of Troy. Greece hates her, especially when she smiles or dreams of the past. Greece would love Helen only if she were dead.

TEXT ANALYSIS

COMMON CORE
RL 4

Ⓑ IMAGISM

Discuss the aspects of female beauty students believe would be valued in ancient Greece and ask which of those are exemplified in the poem.

Possible answer: Delicate female beauty is admired. Images that depict Helen's beauty include "lustre as of olives" (line 3) and "white hands" (line 5).

READING SKILL

COMMON CORE
RL 1

Ⓒ MAKE INFERENCES

Possible answer: She has been the occasion of "past enchantments and past ills" (lines 10–11), and perhaps also for her beauty.

Extend the Discussion Do people sometimes "revile" (line 6) those who are exceptional? Why?

IN A STATION OF THE METRO[1]

Ezra Pound

The apparition of these faces in the crowd;
Petals on a wet, black bough. Ⓐ

> Ⓐ **MAKE INFERENCES**
> Note the use of the word *apparition* to describe the faces in the crowd. What does this suggest about the people?

HELEN

H. D.

All Greece hates
the still eyes in the white face,
the lustre as of olives
where she stands,
5 and the white hands. Ⓑ

All Greece reviles[2]
the wan face when she smiles,
hating it deeper still
when it grows wan and white,
10 remembering past enchantments
and past ills.

Greece sees unmoved,
God's daughter[3], born of love,
the beauty of cool feet
15 and slenderest knees,
could love indeed the maid,
only if she were laid,
white ash amid funereal cypresses.[4] Ⓒ

> Ⓑ **IMAGISM**
> Helen of Troy, "the face that launched a thousand ships," is one of the best known characters of classical literature. She has been featured in numerous films, including epic retellings of the Trojan War. What is it about this figure from classical literature that fascinates audiences today? Reread the first stanza of this poem about Helen. Identify the **images** that account for Helen's grip on the imagination.

> Ⓒ **MAKE INFERENCES**
> Based on information you find in the text, why do you think the Greeks hate Helen?

---

1. **the Metro:** the subway in Paris.
2. **reviles:** to attack with hateful language.
3. **God's daughter:** Helen was a daughter of Zeus, the king of the gods; and Leda, a mortal.
4. **funereal cypresses:** The cypress, a type of evergreen tree, has been associated with death and funeral services since ancient times.

DIFFERENTIATED INSTRUCTION

FOR ENGLISH LANGUAGE LEARNERS

Language: Pronoun Referents [mixed-readiness pairs] Explain the referent for the pronoun *she* in line 4 of "Helen." The reference is to Helen, who has been named in the title but not yet in the poem. Then have students work with partners to find the pronoun referents for *it* in lines 8 and 9 and *she* in line 17. *Possible answers: It refers to face and she refers to maid, which in turn refers to Helen.*

FOR STRUGGLING READERS

Develop Reading Fluency Have students listen to the poems on the *Audio Anthology CD*. Point out that all poems have their own rhythms that are evident when read aloud. This is true whether or not the poems contain rhymes. Have students listen again, and then chorally read the poems.

BACKGROUND

Helen of Troy In Greek mythology, the beautiful Helen was a cause of war. Taken to Troy by its prince, Paris, Helen's plight inspired her brother Agamemnon to invade Troy with a Greek army. The Greeks fought Troy for ten years, losing great warriors such as Achilles, before finally defeating the Trojans, burning Troy, and retrieving Helen. Some historians believe that Helen left for Troy willingly out of passion for Paris, perhaps inspiring her countrymen to hate her for the war that ensued.

TIERED DISCUSSION PROMPTS

In lines 12–18, use these prompts to help students infer the situation and emotions in "Helen":

Connect How would you feel if you were standing alone in front of a crowd that hated you? *Student responses should include appropriate feelings such as sorrow, fear, and defiance.*

Analyze The speaker says that Greece is "unmoved" by Helen, but in fact the Greeks are moved to emotion. What emotion moves them when they see Helen? *Possible answer: The Greeks are moved to hatred.*

Evaluate Which images in the poem are most effective in conveying the feeling of the scene? Explain. *Possible answer: Images of whiteness are effective in conveying Helen's statuelike stillness and distance from the crowd, as if she is made of marble and they are judging her.*

FOR STRUGGLING READERS

Inverted Word Order Remind students that word order in poetry is sometimes different from word order in everyday usage. Ask students to paraphrase the phrases "Greece sees unmoved" (line 12) and "could love indeed the maid" (line 16). *Possible answers: Paraphrases: "Greece is unmoved when it sees," "could indeed love the maid."*

FOR ADVANCED LEARNERS/AP

Synthesize [small-group option] Have students review the Text Analysis Workshop on Modernism (pages 934–935) and pages 868–869 of the historical essay. Ask them to identify features of "Helen" that reflect the poet's participation in the overall modernist movement. Have students discuss their ideas in small groups.

SUMMARY

This poem describes a scene by a roadside on a cold, muddy, windy spring day. The poem describes budding plants entering the world uncertainly but then taking root firmly.

TEXT ANALYSIS **COMMON CORE RL 4**

Ⓓ *Model the Skill:* IMAGISM

Read lines 1–13 aloud and point out the "muddy fields" and the "patches of standing water" (lines 5 and 7). These images show that spring is in its early stages and can help students interpret the aspect of the season emphasized by the colors.

Possible answer: *The spring colors include the blue of clouds, the brown of muddy fields, dried weeds, and dead leaves, along with "reddish purplish" bushes. These are a cross between the muted colors of winter and the bright ones of spring. The colors emphasize that spring slowly arises from winter's dreariness.*

IF STUDENTS NEED HELP . . . Work with them to complete a Cluster Diagram like this one, using color words and other words they associate with spring. Have them compare and contrast their words with Williams's to infer similarities and differences in feeling.

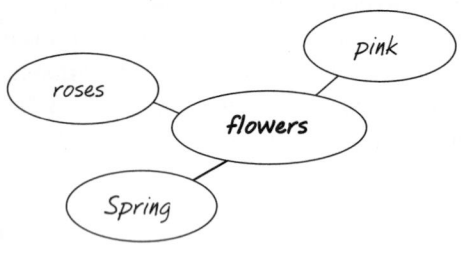

📦 **BEST PRACTICES TOOLKIT—Transparency**
Cluster Diagram p. B18

TEXT ANALYSIS **COMMON CORE RL 4**

Ⓔ IMAGISM

Possible answer: *In lines 16–19 the phrase "naked, / cold, uncertain" emphasizes the newborn plants' vulnerability. In lines 20–27 words and phrases such as "stiff curl," "clarity, outline of leaf," "stark dignity," "rooted," "grip down," and "begin to awaken" describe the plants' growing strength and confidence.*

SPRING AND ALL

William Carlos Williams

By the road to the contagious hospital[1]
under the surge of the blue
mottled clouds driven from the
northeast—a cold wind. Beyond, the
5 waste of broad, muddy fields
brown with dried weeds, standing and fallen

patches of standing water
the scattering of tall trees

All along the road the reddish
10 purplish, forked, upstanding, twiggy
stuff of bushes and small trees
with dead, brown leaves under them
leafless vines— Ⓓ

Lifeless in appearance, sluggish[2]
15 dazed spring approaches—

They enter the new world naked,
cold, uncertain of all
save that they enter. All about them
the cold, familiar wind— Ⓔ

20 Now the grass, tomorrow
the stiff curl of wildcarrot leaf

One by one objects are defined—
It quickens:[3] clarity, outline of leaf

But now the stark dignity of
25 entrance—Still, the profound change
has come upon them: rooted, they
grip down and begin to awaken

Ⓓ IMAGISM
Identify the colors named in lines 1–13. What aspect of spring is emphasized by these colors?

Ⓔ IMAGISM
Reread lines 16–19. What words and phrases does Williams use to characterize the newly growing plants in these lines? Then identify the language in lines 20–27 that describes the change that comes upon them.

---

1. **contagious hospital:** place where people with contagious diseases are hospitalized.
2. **sluggish:** slow to respond.
3. **quickens:** comes alive; revives.

DIFFERENTIATED INSTRUCTION

FOR STRUGGLING READERS

Concept Support: Make Inferences Have students work with the prereading chart introduced on page 953 to make inferences from the images in this poem.

"Spring and All"	
Inferences	Details
It's early spring.	cold wind, mud

FOR ADVANCED LEARNERS/AP

Analyze Figurative Language Ask students to explain the subtle personification in lines 16–18. ***Example:*** *The new roadside plants are described like newborn babies that "enter the new world naked, cold, uncertain . . . ."* Have students discuss the effects this figurative comparison has on reader response, and ask them to consider why the comparison is appropriate in a poem written by a doctor. Invite students to share their analysis and ideas with the class.

THIS IS JUST TO SAY

William Carlos Williams

I have eaten
the plums
that were in
the icebox

5 and which
you were probably
saving
for breakfast

Forgive me
10 they were delicious
so sweet
and so cold **Ⓕ**

Ⓕ IMAGISM
Williams has chosen to
invoke only two senses
in this poem. What
are they? Explain how
this choice affects your
perception of those
sensory details.

SUMMARY
The speaker apologizes to an unidentified
"you" for eating plums that "you" had been
saving in the icebox for breakfast, but acknowledges that the plums were delicious.

TEXT ANALYSIS   COMMON CORE   RL 4

Ⓕ IMAGISM

Possible answer: *The two senses invoked in
the poem are taste and touch. This choice
concentrates and focuses the reader's attention on the sensory experience of eating
the plums.*

REVISIT THE BIG QUESTION
How do you capture a
MOMENT?

Discuss What feeling does an image of tasting and touching a plum create? What new
sense is added to the image when readers
visualize it? *Students may associate the image
with feelings of joy, pleasure, or abandon. The
sense of sight is added to the image through
visualization.*

SELECTION WRAP—UP

READ WITH A PURPOSE Now that students
have read the poems, they will likely note that
the poems' subject matter is quite different
but the style is similar. They may say that
all three poets keep a tight focus on either a
single or a very limited number of images.

★ CRITIQUE

- Ask students whether imagist poems lose
anything because of their strict focus on
images, and if so, what.

- After completing the After Reading questions on page 958, have students revisit
their responses and tell whether they have
changed their opinions.

INDEPENDENT READING
Students may enjoy reading *Personae: The
Shorter Poems of Ezra Pound.*

FOR STRUGGLING READERS
Concept Support: Make Inferences To help
students find meaning underlying the
images in the poems, use the Showing,
Not Telling, with Literature strategy.

 BEST PRACTICES TOOLKIT
Showing, Not Telling, with
Literature p. D1

FOR ADVANCED LEARNERS/AP
Analyze Style Although William Carlos Williams's style of spare, imagistic free verse
seemed innovative in its time, it may be hard
for students to appreciate its experimental-
ism since so much similar verse has been
written since. Ask students to read other
poetry in Unit 5, such as by Robert Frost or
Carl Sandburg, and explain to the class how
Williams's poem would seem daring or
experimental in comparison.

Practice and Apply

For preliminary support of post-reading questions, use these copy masters:

 RESOURCE MANAGER—Copy Masters
Imagism p. 163
Question Support p. 167
Additional selection questions are provided for teachers on page 159.

ANSWERS

COMMON CORE **RL 1, RL 4**

1. *In order for the Greeks to love Helen, she would have to be dead.*

2. *The speaker sees new plants poking up among the dead bushes, leaves, and vines.*

Possible answers:

3. ◼ **COMMON CORE FOCUS Make Inferences** *On the basis of lines 10–11, "remembering past enchantments / and past ills," the Greeks once loved Helen but now hold her responsible for their misfortune.*

4. *The information makes the Greeks' hatred of Helen a matter of complex history rather than mere envy.*

5. *Comparing the faces in the crowd to "petals on a wet, black bough" suggests that the faces are delicate and vulnerable.*

6. ● **COMMON CORE FOCUS Imagism** *"In a Station of the Metro"*: *loneliness in a crowd;* *"Helen"*: *tension from Helen's beauty and stillness, and the Greeks' hatred;* *"Spring and All"*: *determination and hope from the process of the dazed spring emerging from confusion;* *"This Is Just to Say"*: *happiness from the sweetness and coldness of the plums*

7. *Examples of Williams's ordinary diction from "Spring and All" include "By the road to the contagious hospital" (line 1); "Life-less in appearance" (line 14); "They enter the new world naked" (line 16). Examples from "This is just to say" include "you were probably / saving / for breakfast" (lines 6–8). Most students may find Williams's work more approachable and interesting in its clarity, while others may be intrigued by the more formal diction of H.D. in lines such as "Greece sees unmoved / God's daughter, born of love" (lines 12–13).*

Comprehension

1. **Clarify** In "Helen," what would it take for the Greeks to love Helen?

2. **Summarize** What signs of new life does the speaker of "Spring and All" notice by the road?

Text Analysis

3. ● **Make Inferences** Based on the chart you created for "Helen," what can you say about Helen's past and present relationship with the Greeks?

4. **Analyze Allusion** The title "Helen" is an allusion to Helen of Troy, a great beauty whose abduction by Paris, a Trojan prince, prompted the Greeks to take up arms against Troy in a war that lasted for ten years. How does this information help you understand the poem? Explain, citing evidence from the text.

5. **Examine Metaphor** The juxtaposition of the two images in "In a Station of the Metro" has the effect of a metaphor. What does the image in line 2 suggest about the faces in line 1?

6. ● **Interpret Imagist Poetry** Choose one of the poems in this lesson and identify its most prominent image or images. What feeling or idea are you left with at the end of the poem? Citing evidence from the text, explain what it is about the imagery that suggests this feeling.

7. **Compare Diction** William Carlos Williams favored the use of everyday language over highly formal poetic diction. Identify several examples of his ordinary diction in "Spring and All" and "This Is Just to Say." Compare Williams's language with the language H. D. uses in "Helen." Which, in your opinion, is more approachable? Which is more interesting? Cite details from the texts to support your opinion.

Text Criticism

8. **Author's Style** Like other modernist poets, the Imagists eschewed the use of traditional rhyme schemes, meters, and other formal elements. Yet form was important to them; you may recall from page 933 that Williams once criticized Carl Sandburg's poetry as "formless." Choose one of the three poets featured in this lesson and examine his or her use of the following poetic devices, when relevant:

- rhythm
- rhyme
- line breaks
- stanza breaks

In your opinion, does the use of these elements seem deliberate or random? Cite evidence from the poem or poems to support your answer.

> *How do you capture a* **MOMENT**?
>
> Ezra Pound draws a similarity between two very dissimilar images in his two-line poem "In a Station of the Metro." What comparison can you make between two familiar, dissimilar images?

COMMON CORE

RL 1 Cite strong and thorough textual evidence to support analysis of what the text says explicitly as well as inferences drawn from the text, including determining where the text leaves matters uncertain. **RL 4** Analyze the impact of specific word choices on meaning and tone, including words with multiple meanings or language that is particularly fresh, engaging, or beautiful.

---

8. *Students may note the short lines in Williams's "This Is Just to Say," the stanza breaks in "Spring and All," or the rhyme and rhythm in H. D.'s "Helen." They should recognize that the use of formal devices by distinguished poets is deliberate rather than random.*

> *How do you capture a* **MOMENT**?
> Students' answers will vary but they should be able to clearly explain the connection they can make between the two images.

Language

◆ **GRAMMAR AND STYLE: Create Imagery**

Writers use fresh, **vivid adjectives** to create images that bring scenes to life. In the poem "Spring and All," for instance, Williams uses adjectives that lead readers to picture the way a landscape looks in the change from late winter to early spring. Carefully examine the adjectives Williams uses in the following lines. Notice how keenly they evoke the sight of a landscape in transition.

> *All along the road the reddish*
> *purplish, forked, upstanding, twiggy*
> *stuff of bushes and small trees* (lines 9–11)

> *Lifeless in appearance, sluggish*
> *dazed spring approaches—* (lines 14–15)

PRACTICE Write down each of the following sentences. Then, try to enliven these sentences by inserting vivid adjectives. An example has been done for you.

> **EXAMPLE**
>
> The crowd stared at Helen's hands and face.
> *The angry crowd stared at Helen's delicate hands and ash-colored face.*

1. She noticed fields and weeds by the side of the road.
2. I saw faces looking out from the windows of the train.
3. Slowly, the girl ate the peaches that we had plucked from the tree.

READING-WRITING CONNECTION

Expand your understanding of imagist poetry by responding to this prompt. Then, use the revising tips to improve your poem.

WRITING PROMPT	**REVISING TIPS**
WRITE AN IMAGIST POEM Think of a place that has inspired powerful emotions in you. What images come to mind when you think about that place? What feelings do your memories evoke in you? Use your responses to these questions as the starting point for an **eight-to-ten-line poem.** As you write, try to include concrete images that convey both emotions and meaning.	• Use sensory language to create vivid imagery. • Use precise descriptive language with vivid adjectives. • Write in free verse, but try to achieve a sense of rhythm.

Interactive Revision

Go to **thinkcentral.com**.
KEYWORD: HML11-959

COMMON CORE

L 3 Apply knowledge of language to make effective choices for meaning or style. **W 3d** Use telling details to convey a vivid picture of the experiences, events, setting, and/or characters.

Language

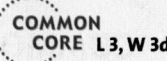
COMMON CORE L 3, W 3d

◆ **GRAMMAR AND STYLE**

Tell students that vivid adjectives name specific sensory qualities that help readers visualize the object, place, or person described. As students read the example from Williams, have them visualize each adjective.

Possible answers:

1. *She noticed pathetic, browning fields and dwarfed, straggling weeds by the side of the cracked old asphalt road.*

2. *I saw hopeful, weary faces looking out from the smeared windows of the puffing, whistling train.*

3. *Slowly, the girl ate the juicy yellow peaches that we had plucked from the fruit-laden tree.*

R RESOURCE MANAGER—Copy Master
Create Imagery p. 168

READING-WRITING CONNECTION

Suggest that students look back at their **QUICKWRITE** to recall a place they strongly associate with. Have them use the Freewriting strategy to activate sensory and emotional details of their memories.

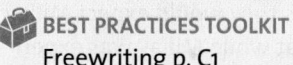 BEST PRACTICES TOOLKIT
Freewriting p. C1

Writing Online
THINK central

The following tools are available online at **thinkcentral.com** and on **Write*Smart* CD-ROM:**

• **Interactive Graphic Organizers**
• **Interactive Student Models**
• **Interactive Revision Lessons**

For additional grammar instruction, see **GrammarNotes** on **thinkcentral.com**.

DIFFERENTIATED INSTRUCTION

FOR STRUGGLING WRITERS

Writing Support

• Allow students to write poems of only four to six lines.

• Suggest that students prewrite by imagining the place as clearly as possible and jotting down words and phrases they associate with it.

• Encourage students to emulate Williams's use of very short lines and everyday diction.

• Have students show their first drafts to peer editors. Ask peer editors to identify places where images need to be made more vivid.

• Remind students that not every noun needs to be modified by an adjective or more than one adjective. Urge them to strive for clarity, not quantity.

Assess and Reteach

Assess

DIAGNOSTIC AND SELECTION TESTS
Selection Test A, B/C pp. 257–258, 259–260

Interactive Selection Test on thinkcentral.com

Reteach

Level Up Online Tutorials on thinkcentral.com

Reteaching Worksheets on thinkcentral.com

Literature Lesson 26, Reading Lesson 8

Focus and Motivate

COMMON CORE

RL 5 Analyze how an author's choices concerning how to structure specific parts of a text contribute to its overall structure and meaning as well as its aesthetic impact. **RL 10** Read and comprehend literature, including poems.

COMMON CORE FOCUS

RL 5 Analyze how an author's choices concerning how to structure specific parts of a text contribute to its overall structure and meaning as well as its aesthetic impact. **RL 10** Read and comprehend literature, including poems.

ABOUT THE POETS

E. E. Cummings After students read the biography, have them find words in it that hint at traits of Cummings's poetry. *Students may mention "love," "free-thinking," and "playful, innovative."*

Marianne Moore Read the biography aloud and direct students to the word "innovative" and to the words and phrases describing Moore's poetry, such as "complex" and "intricately crafted." Tell students that Moore's innovations are very different from Cummings's.

Edna St. Vincent Millay Invite students to read the biography aloud and identify words and phrases that describe Millay vividly. *Possible answers: Vivid descriptions include "emotional extremes," "intensity," "revolt," "avant-garde," "bohemian."* Ask students what kind of poems they would expect Millay to write. Clarify that while Millay was experimental in her life, she was the least innovative poet in this group.

The New Poetry

anyone lived in a pretty how town
Poetry by E. E. Cummings

Poetry
Poetry by Marianne Moore

Recuerdo
Poetry by Edna St. Vincent Millay

Meet the Authors

E. E. Cummings
1894–1962

E. E. Cummings believed deeply in two things: love and human individuality. He felt that both being an individual and being in a loving relationship led to joy and personal growth. His poems honor love in all its variety and pay tribute to people who resist group conformity and conventional thought.

Cummings's faith in love grew out of his tender relationship with his parents.

His father encouraged Cummings's literary ambitions and secured his release when he was imprisoned in France during World War I. After the war, Cummings lived in New York's Greenwich Village, a community of free-thinking artists and intellectuals, where he spent his days painting and writing. By the 1950s, Cummings's playful, innovative style had made him enormously popular.

Marianne Moore
1887–1972

Marianne Moore was a true original. Her interests ranged from baseball to Muhammad Ali to exotic animals, which she scrutinized during her frequent trips to the zoo. Gifted with an eye for detail, she wrote precise, witty descriptions of these and other subjects. Moore also affected an eccentric public appearance, often sporting a three-cornered hat and a black cape.

When she was 31, Moore moved to New York City, where she hobnobbed with other writers, served as editor of the prestigious literary journal *The Dial*, and wrote poetry. A highly innovative poet, she mixed direct observation with quoted material and experimented with stanza forms and line lengths. Her complex, meticulously crafted poems earned her the esteem of other poets, as well as a Pulitzer Prize.

Edna St. Vincent Millay
1892–1950

In both her life and her art, Edna St. Vincent Millay expressed emotional extremes. This intensity, coupled with Millay's revolt against cultural expectations for women, made her a symbol of the "new woman" of the 1920s.

Although Millay endured childhood poverty and deprivation, she nevertheless managed to excel in school and to win poetry awards. After graduating from Vassar College, she became a central

figure among the avant-garde set in New York's Greenwich Village. There, she led a bohemian lifestyle, juggling relationships and living in poverty so that she had ample time to write.

Author Online
Go to **thinkcentral.com**. KEYWORD: HML11-960

vision

Selection Resources

*See resources on the **Teacher One Stop DVD-ROM** and on **thinkcentral.com**.*

R RESOURCE MANAGER UNIT 5

Plan and Teach, pp. 169–176
Text Analysis and Reading
  Skill, pp. 177–180†*

**DIAGNOSTIC AND SELECTION
  TESTS**
Selection Tests, pp. 261–264

BEST PRACTICES TOOLKIT

Jigsaw Reading, p. A1
Sensory Notes, p. B9

TECHNOLOGY
- Teacher One Stop DVD-ROM
- Student One Stop DVD-ROM
- Audio Anthology CD
- ExamView Test Generator
  on the **Teacher One Stop**

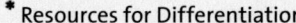

* Resources for Differentiation   † Also in Spanish   ‡ In Haitian Creole and Vietnamese

TEXT ANALYSIS: FORM IN MODERN POETRY

Like other modernists, modern poets are known for challenging and experimenting with literary **form**. The term *form* refers primarily to the arrangement of words on the page and to the use of rhyme and meter, but also to the standard conventions of written language (spelling, punctuation, etc.). E. E. Cummings is widely noted for his playful sense of experimentation. In "anyone lived in a pretty how town," he abandons many rules of punctuation, spelling, grammar, and capitalization, creating striking (and sometimes puzzling) effects. Millay's "Recuerdo" is more traditional, with regular rhyme, stanzas, and meter.

Moore's poem "Poetry" is somewhere between these two. It observes the standard conventions of written language, yet it lacks regular rhyme, meter, and line length, giving it a more prose like feel than the other two poems. As you read, note how each poet responds to traditional form, whether by letting go of convention or adapting it. Remember that all good poets use form to help deliver or emphasize meaning.

READING STRATEGY: READING MODERN POETRY

Many readers enjoy the playful, unpredictable quality of modern poetry; others find it confusing or meaningless. There are a number of strategies that can help any reader enjoy these poems.

- **Paraphrase**—If a word, phrase, or sentence seems difficult, try restating it in your own words.
- **Read aloud**—Reading a poem aloud can sometimes help you hear the flow of a line or stanza and clarify its meaning, as well as emphasizing its musical qualities.
- **Observe mechanics**—Note the punctuation, spelling, capitalization, and grammar. How does this affect the sound or sense of the poem?

Using a chart like the one below, monitor your comprehension of each poem by paraphrasing difficult lines.

"anyone lived in a pretty how town"	"Poetry"	"Recuerdo"
Paraphrase: A character named "anyone" lived in some kind of town, year round, singing and dancing.		

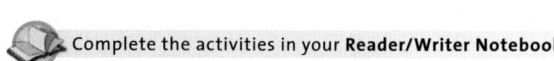 Complete the activities in your **Reader/Writer Notebook**.

Do poems have to follow the RULES?

If it doesn't rhyme, is it still a poem? What if it's only two lines long? Do the lines have to break in a regular place? What if some of the words are upside-down on the page? The modernist poets asked questions like this, breaking rules right and left. Their work changed the accepted ideas about what poetry is.

DISCUSS With a small group, brainstorm a list of all the qualities you might find in a poem. From that list, come up with a set of rules that all poems follow.

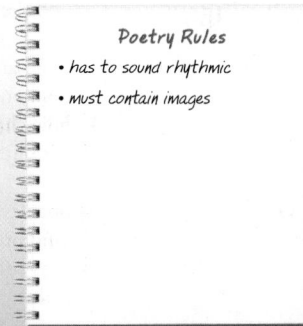

Poetry Rules
- *has to sound rhythmic*
- *must contain images*

961

Do poems have to follow the RULES?

Read the question aloud. Then read the paragraph one sentence at a time, allowing students to briefly respond to each question about poetic rules. Have students contribute their responses to the *DISCUSS* activity.

TEXT ANALYSIS COMMON CORE RL 5

Model the Skill: FORM IN MODERN POETRY

To help students recognize how poets use form to emphasize meaning, begin by writing these lines on the board:

> when i consider all
> in life that might befall
> me STOP say no more
> say i about it

Point out that these lines conform to some aspects of traditional form and break others. The lines reflect the poetic form of a stanza. The first two lines rhyme. However, the lines break conventions of capitalization, word order, and punctuation.

GUIDED PRACTICE Ask students to describe the form of another poem from Unit 5.

READING STRATEGY COMMON CORE RL 10

Model the Skill: READING MODERN POETRY

Tell students that reading aloud can help reveal a poem's meaning and rhythm. Have a student read aloud the lines you've written on the board. Point out that the potentially confusing final lines are clearer when read aloud. Remind students that other strategies for reading modern poetry are observing mechanics, and paraphrasing.

GUIDED PRACTICE Have students paraphrase the lines. Then have them choose another poem from Unit 5 and apply these reading strategies to it.

R RESOURCE MANAGER—Copy Master
Reading Modern Poetry p. 179

DIFFERENTIATED INSTRUCTION

FOR STRUGGLING READERS
Concept Support: Form in Modern Poetry
Although modernist innovations in mechanics were considered daring and puzzling in their time, many students will be aware of similar experiments in today's popular media, especially hip-hop lyrics and text messaging. In those two forms, unconventional spelling and punctuation are considered an enjoyable way to display one's creativity and freedom from conventions. For example, the letter *s*

is often replaced by *z* in words such as *boyz*. Ask students to supply other examples from prior knowledge. Point out that poets such as E. E. Cummings were experimenting in similar ways almost a century ago.

READ WITH A PURPOSE

Help students set a purpose for reading. Tell them to read the poems, looking for what they tell about each speaker's state of mind.

SUMMARY

This poem tells the story of a man named "anyone" and a woman named "noone" who don't fit in to their small town community.

TEXT ANALYSIS
COMMON CORE
RL 5

Ⓐ FORM IN MODERN POETRY

Possible answer: *The character of anyone "lived," "sang," and "danced," while the women and men "cared not for anyone at all," "sowed," and "reaped." This implies that anyone lives a carefree, impulsive life which the women and men resented.*

READING STRATEGY
COMMON CORE
RL 10

Ⓑ READING MODERN POETRY

Possible answer: *noone loves anyone deeply.*

IF STUDENTS NEED HELP . . . Have them paraphrase using the prereading chart introduced on page 961.

TEXT ANALYSIS
COMMON CORE
RL 5

Ⓒ *Model the Skill:* FORM IN MODERN POETRY

Point out that Cummings uses no commas and only one period. Tell students this gives the poem a breathless quality that makes the death seem expected and natural. Ask students to find and explain another example of unconventional mechanics. *Possible answer:* *The lack of capital letters show that distinctions are often arbitrary.*

---

anyone lived in a pretty how town

E. E. Cummings

anyone lived in a pretty how town
(with up so floating many bells down)
spring summer autumn winter
he sang his didn't he danced his did.

5 Women and men(both little and small)
cared for anyone not at all
they sowed their isn't they reaped their same
sun moon stars rain Ⓐ

children guessed(but only a few
10 and down they forgot as up they grew
autumn winter spring summer)
that noone loved him more by more

when by now and tree by leaf
she laughed his joy she cried his grief
15 bird by snow and stir by still
anyone's any was all to her Ⓑ

someones married their everyones
laughed their cryings and did their dance
(sleep wake hope and then)they
20 said their nevers they slept their dream

stars rain sun moon
(and only the snow can begin to explain
how children are apt to forget to remember
with up so floating many bells down)

25 one day anyone died i guess
(and noone stooped to kiss his face)
busy folk buried them side by side
little by little and was by was

all by all and deep by deep
30 and more by more they dream their sleep
noone and anyone earth by april
wish by spirit and if by yes. Ⓒ

Women and men(both dong and ding)
summer autumn winter spring
35 reaped their sowing and went their came
sun moon stars rain

Analyze Visuals ▶
Painter Marc Chagall is known for his whimsical and dream like images. Identify some unrealistic elements in the painting on page 963. What do they suggest about the couple depicted? Explain.

Ⓐ **FORM IN MODERN POETRY**
Many words in these stanzas are used in strange ways, but the verbs are still pretty straight forward. In lines 1–8, which actions are attributed to "anyone" and which to the women and men? What does this suggest about the differences between them?

Ⓑ **READING MODERN POETRY**
Paraphrase lines 13–16. How does "noone" feel about "anyone"?

Ⓒ **FORM IN MODERN POETRY**
Reread lines 25–32. Identify some ways in which Cummings breaks with the conventions of **mechanics**. How does this affect your sense of the poem? Explain.

Couple Above St. Paul, Marc Chagall. Private collection. © Scala/Art Resource, New York. © Artists Rights Society (ARS), New York.

DIFFERENTIATED INSTRUCTION

FOR ENGLISH LANGUAGE LEARNERS
Language: Punctuation and Print Clues
[mixed-readiness pairs] Have pairs work together to conventionalize the poem's punctuation and other mechanics, such as capitalization. Students can then regularize these parts of speech and word order issues:

• *did* as a noun (line 4)

• *was* as a noun (line 28)

• inverted word order in "cared for anyone not at all" (line 6)

With these issues resolved, have more fluent partners describe the poem's playful mood and the basic situation of the love story involving anyone and noone. Finally, encourage students to state the gist of the poem in a couple of sentences.

SUMMARY

In this poem, the speaker begins by saying that she, too, dislikes poetry, calling it "all this fiddle." Later, she gives reasons to like poetry for its genuineness, imaginativeness, and sense of reality.

D READING MODERN POETRY

Possible answer: Paraphrase: The speaker, like the reader, sometimes dislikes poetry but can also discover the genuine in poetry. Poetry can sometimes capture in an image something profoundly true and useful. Moore's lines "Hands that can grasp, eyes / that can dilate," and "hair that can rise" are important because they express the emotional impact of poetry.

IF STUDENTS NEED HELP . . . Work with them to answer this question:
- How does the speaker's opinion of poetry change from line 1 to lines 2–3?

TIERED DISCUSSION PROMPTS

In lines 6–11, use these prompts to help students comprehend Moore's view of poetry:

Connect Which do you value more, complex ideas or useful advice? Explain. *Students' responses should present reasons for valuing or not valuing both options.*

Interpret What does Moore mean by "so derivative as to become unintelligible"? *Possible answer: Moore means that ideas can be diluted down by endless interpretation until they are meaningless.*

Evaluate Is Moore right that we do not admire what we cannot understand? Give examples pro and con. *Accept thoughtful answers that include examples.*

E FORM IN MODERN POETRY

Possible answer: The line breaks in lines 20 and 22 focus attention on the thematically important words distinction *and* poetry.

Poetry

Marianne Moore

I, too, dislike it: there are things that are important beyond all this fiddle.
   Reading it, however, with a perfect contempt for it, one discovers in
   it, after all, a place for the genuine.
      Hands that can grasp, eyes
5   that can dilate,[1] hair that can rise
         if it must, these things are important not because a

high-sounding interpretation can be put upon them but because they are
   useful. When they become so derivative[2] as to become unintelligible,
   the same thing may be said for all of us, that we
10   do not admire what
     we cannot understand: the bat
       holding on upside down or in quest of something to

eat, elephants pushing, a wild horse taking a roll, a tireless wolf under
   a tree, the immovable critic twitching his skin like a horse that feels a flea,
15   the base-
    ball fan, the statistician—
      nor is it valid
         to discriminate against "business documents and

school-books"; all these phenomena are important. One must make a
20   distinction
    however: when dragged into prominence by half poets, the result is not
                   poetry, E
    nor till the poets among us can be
     "literalists[3] of
25   the imagination"—above
        insolence and triviality and can present

D READING MODERN POETRY
Reread and **paraphrase** lines 1–11. What is important about "Hands that can grasp, eyes / that can dilate, hair that can rise"?

Analyze Visuals ▶
Consider what the speaker of this poem has to say about poetry. How do you think she might respond to this abstract painting?

E FORM IN MODERN POETRY
Note the extremely indented lines at lines 15, 20, and 22. What do these oddities of form contribute to the poem's meaning? Explain.

---

1. **dilate** (dī-lāt′): enlarge; open wide.
2. **derivative**: lacking originality.
3. **literalists**: people who interpret words in their usual or most basic sense.

DIFFERENTIATED INSTRUCTION

FOR ADVANCED LEARNERS/AP

Evaluate Form Explain that "Poetry" is written in syllabic verse. This form appears at first glance to be free verse, but in fact is not. To explore the form have students begin by counting the syllables in the first and last lines of each stanza. They will find 19 syllables in the first lines, counting line 20 as a continuation of line 19, and 13 syllables in the last lines. Moore plays with form by varying line lengths and syllable counts in the remaining lines. Tell students that critical opinion on syllabic verse is divided and invite them to contribute to the debate by responding to these questions: Is syllable count too arbitrary to hinge a poem upon? Can syllable count create rhythm—or does rhythm arise from other aspects of the poem? Invite students to explain the poem's syllabic structure and their conclusions with the class.

Rising Moon (1965), Hans Hofmann. Private collection. © 2008 Estate of Hans Hofmann/Artists Rights Society (ARS), New York/Art Resource, New York.

for inspection, "imaginary gardens with real toads in them," shall we have
   it. In the meantime, if you demand on the one hand,
   the raw material of poetry in
30   all its rawness and
     that which is on the other hand
        genuine, you are interested in poetry. **F**

F **READING MODERN POETRY**
Reread lines 28–32 aloud. How, if at all, does this change your sense of the line breaks?

Do poems have to follow the RULES?

Discuss How does Marianne Moore use rules to determine if text is poetry? *Possible answer: Moore uses rules to identify poetry by determining if text is well written, if it uses language in understandable ways, if it rises above triviality, and if it addresses real objects in an imaginative way.*

Analyze Visuals

Possible answers: Since Moore wrote, "we / do not admire what we cannot understand," she might not admire the painting. Since she saw artists as "literalists of the imagination," she might see the painting as too abstract and not literal enough. On the other hand, she might respect Hofmann's exploration of his medium and its limits.

About the Art Abstract painter Hans Hofmann (1880–1966) produced a new kind of landscape in his paintings. These landscapes consisted of colors and planes instead of trees and landforms found in nature. Hofmann's aim in painting was to create "pulsating, luminous, and open surfaces that emanate a mystic light." His companions in adulthood included Picasso and Matisse, and Hofmann synthesized aspects of their style as well as those of other painters of 20th-century abstract works to create his own style.

READING STRATEGY COMMON CORE RL 10

F *Model the Skill:* **READING MODERN POETRY**

Read lines 28–32 aloud. Point out that read aloud, the rhythm created by the rhyme in line 28—"if you demand on the other hand"— is more obvious than when read silently. Have students compare their experience with line breaks when reading aloud versus reading silently. *Possible answers: The line breaks seem to disappear when the lines are read aloud. However, these breaks also make readers emphasize particular words or phrases.*

FOR STRUGGLING READERS

Clarify Meaning Make sure that students understand Moore's concluding statement about poetry. Help them retrace and restate the two elements she says reflect an interest in poetry:

- *the raw material of poetry* (line 29), "ideas and images that produce an emotional response"

- *that which . . . genuine* (lines 31–32), "ideas that are clearly stated and useful"

FOR STRUGGLING READERS

Develop Reading Fluency Play the reading of these poems from the *Audio Anthology CD* for students. Tell students to listen for how line breaks are handled. Then have pairs of students practice reading the poems aloud, modelling their readings on what they heard on the CD.

Prereading for this poem is found on page 960.

SUMMARY

The speaker of this poem remembers when she and a lover rode a ferry all night.

READING STRATEGY COMMON CORE **RL 10**

 READING MODERN POETRY

Possible answer: *Unlike the other two poems, "Recuerdo" rhymes and has meter. The rhyme and meter reflect the speaker and her companion going regularly "back and forth all night on the ferry," and the poem's cadence captures the playful quality of their experience.*

TEXT ANALYSIS COMMON CORE **RL 5**

⒣ FORM IN MODERN POETRY

Possible answer: *Each stanza begins with the same two lines. This device emphasizes the speaker's nostalgia for the memory.*

About the Art Swiss painter Paul Klee (1879–1940) was an important artist of the 20th century, popular for his playful, sometimes childlike style. *Port Scene* is as lively as Millay's poem about a ferry.

SELECTION WRAP–UP

READ WITH A PURPOSE Now that students have read the poems, ask them to rank the poems in order from most to least cheerful speaker and to explain their choices. Students may find Millay's to be the most upbeat, recounting a memorable evening. Moore's poem might come second, as the speaker's interest in poetry comes through in the poem's playful language. Cummings's poem is likely to be the students' choice for least cheerful speaker, as he focuses on the inevitability of loss and employs a bittersweet tone.

Recuerdo

Edna St. Vincent Millay

We were very tired, we were very merry—
We had gone back and forth all night on the ferry.
It was bare and bright, and smelled like a stable—
But we looked into a fire, we leaned across a table,
5 We lay on a hill-top underneath the moon;
And the whistles kept blowing, and the dawn came soon.

We were very tired, we were very merry—
We had gone back and forth all night on the ferry;
And you ate an apple, and I ate a pear,
10 From a dozen of each we had bought somewhere;
And the sky went wan,[1] and the wind came cold,
And the sun rose dripping, a bucketful of gold. ⒢

We were very tired, we were very merry,
We had gone back and forth all night on the ferry.
15 We hailed, "Good morrow, mother!" to a shawl-covered head,
And bought a morning paper, which neither of us read;
And she wept, "God bless you!" for the apples and pears,
And we gave her all our money but our subway fares. ⒣

---

1. **wan:** pale.

⒢ READING MODERN POETRY
Read aloud lines 1–12. How does this poem sound different from the other two? What aspect of the subject matter is reflected by the poem's **rhyme** and **meter**?

⒣ FORM IN MODERN POETRY
Identify the **repetition** that helps to shape each stanza. What meaning is emphasized by this device?

Port Scene, Paul Klee. Atheneum Museum, Helsinki, Finland. © Giraudon/Art Resource, New York. © 2007 Artists Rights Society (ARS), New York/VG Bild-Kunst, Bonn.

DIFFERENTIATED INSTRUCTION

FOR STRUGGLING READERS

Visualize Work with students to help them imagine the scene of Millay's poem. Direct them in completing a Sensory Notes organizer like this partial one:

I smell ... The ferry smells like a stable.
I taste ... an apple and a pear

 **BEST PRACTICES TOOLKIT—Transparency**
Sensory Notes p. B9

FOR ENGLISH LANGUAGE LEARNERS

Culture: Connect Ask Spanish speakers what *recuerdo* means in that language (*"souvenir"* or *"remembrance"*). Use that information to help students understand the context of the poem, which is a nostalgic memory of happy young love. Invite other English learners to share similar words from their home languages. Discuss the difference between words that merely define memory and words that capture the sense of longing in Millay's poem.

Comprehension

1. **Clarify** Who are the lovers described in "anyone lived in a pretty how town"?

2. **Clarify** What does the speaker of "Poetry" dislike about poetry? What does she value in it?

3. **Clarify** Where and when does "Recuerdo" take place?

Text Analysis

4. **Analyze Modern Poetry** Review the chart you filled in as you read. In the Cummings poem, it is important not to try to read every line literally, but rather aim for the gist of these nonsense phrases. Choose one stanza from this poem and explain the general impression you get from the language in each line. Then paraphrase the entire stanza, making use of these impressions.

5. **Interpret Ideas** In "Poetry," what idea about poetry is represented by each of the following items? Explain.

   • "hands that can grasp" (line 4)
   • "elephants pushing" (line 13)
   • "business documents and school-books" (lines 18–19)
   • "'imaginary gardens with real toads in them'" (line 27)

6. **Evaluate Form in Modern Poetry** Each of these poems has a playful, irreverent quality, sometimes achieved by breaking rules of traditional poetry and sometimes by following them. Examine the poems in this lesson, identifying the most playful elements of each. In your opinion, which poem is the most radical? Cite evidence to support your answer.

Text Criticism

7. **Critical Interpretations** In a review, the critic Edmund Wilson argued that "Behind [the] formidable barrier of punctuations for which Mr. Cummings seems unfortunately to have achieved most celebrity, his emotions are conventional and simple in the extreme." Do you agree or disagree with Wilson's argument? Whether or not you agree, do you view Wilson's statement as a positive or negative comment? Cite evidence to support your opinion.

> *Do poems have to follow the* **RULES?**
>
> You probably found "Recuerdo" the easiest of the three poems to read because it employs a familiar sense of rhyme and meter. What "rules," then, do you think are broken in "Recuerdo"? Do you think poetry—or any form of art, for that matter—should adhere to particular "rules"? Explain.

most radical for his diction, or Moore for her unique form and difficult ideas.

7. *Students may find the story of anyone and noone to be simple and fablelike, a quality that some will enjoy and others find trite. Other students will argue that the love between anyone and noone is complex. Opinions may vary about Wilson's comment, but student answers should not confuse "simple" with simplistic.*

> *Do poems have to follow the* RULES? *Students may note that offhand tone breaks a rule. They may say rules create a basis for judging art, or that the point of art is to innovate, not do what's already been done.*

For preliminary support of post-reading questions, use these copy masters:

R RESOURCE MANAGER—Copy Masters
Form in Modern Poetry p. 177
Question Support p. 181
Additional selection questions are provided for teachers on page 173.

ANSWERS   COMMON CORE RL 5, RL 10

1. *The lovers are anyone and noone.*

2. *She dislikes its pretentiousness and triviality but likes its authenticity.*

3. *The poem takes place on a ferry and a city street, from night until after sunrise.*

Possible answers:

4. ● **COMMON CORE FOCUS** **Reading Modern Poetry** *Students' choices will vary. Students choosing the first stanza may note that "up so floating many bells down" and the list of seasons indicate time passing.*

5. *"**Hands that can grasp**" represents the emotional content in poetry. "**Elephants pushing**" refers to instinctive actions that humans cannot understand. "**Business documents and school-books**" represents texts that poets might unjustly scorn. "**Imaginary gardens with real toads in them**" suggests that imaginative poetry can have importance.*

6. ● **COMMON CORE FOCUS** **Form in Modern Poetry** *Playful elements include Cummings's use of punctuation, Moore's outlandish imagery, and Millay's use of refrain. Students may see Cummings as the*

Assess and Reteach

Assess

DIAGNOSTIC AND SELECTION TESTS
Selection Test A pp. 261–262
Selection Test B/C pp. 263–264

Interactive Selection Test on **thinkcentral.com**

Reteach

Level Up Tutorials on **thinkcentral.com**

Reteaching Worksheets on **thinkcentral.com**
Literature Lesson 17: Structure of Poetry

Research and Study Skills Lesson 12: Paraphrasing

COMMON CORE

RL 5 Analyze how an author's choices concerning how to structure specific parts of a text contribute to its overall structure and meaning as well as its aesthetic impact. **RL 10** Read and comprehend literature, including poems.

Focus and Motivate

COMMON CORE FOCUS

RL 2 Determine two or more themes or central ideas of a text and analyze their development over the course of the text, including how they interact and build on one another to produce a complex account; provide an objective summary of the text. **RL 5** Analyze how an author's choices concerning how to structure specific parts of a text contribute to its overall structure and meaning as well as its aesthetic impact.

ABOUT THE POET

After students have read the biography, focus their attention on Stravinsky's remark in the first paragraph. Lead students in discussing what it means to be "a great sorcerer of words" and "the very key keeper of the language." Tell students that when they read "The Love Song of J. Alfred Prufrock," they will see a demonstration of the sorcerer's powers.

NOTABLE QUOTE

"Human kind cannot bear very much reality."
—**T.S. Eliot**

Ask students to cite examples from experience and knowledge that either support or debunk Eliot's claim. Tell them that his poem raises the question of whether its main character can or cannot bear reality.

Selection Resources

The Love Song of J. Alfred Prufrock
Poem by T. S. Eliot

Essential Course of Study  ECOS

VIDEO TRAILER THINK central | KEYWORD: HML11-968A

COMMON CORE

RL 2 Determine two or more themes or central ideas of a text and analyze their development over the course of the text, including how they interact and build on one another to produce a complex account; provide an objective summary of the text. **RL 5** Analyze how an author's choices concerning how to structure specific parts of a text contribute to its overall structure and meaning as well as its aesthetic impact.

DID YOU KNOW?

T. S. Eliot . . .

- was also an acclaimed playwright.
- wrote the book that inspired the musical *Cats*.
- won the Nobel Prize in literature in 1948.

Meet the Author

T. S. Eliot 1888–1965

When he was alive, T. S. Eliot was one of the most influential poets in the English-speaking world. His invention of new poetic rhythms, forms, and themes had an enormous impact on other writers and helped usher in a new era in poetry. Eliot, remarked the composer Igor Stravinsky, was "not only a great sorcerer of words, but the very key keeper of the language."

A Lover of Philosophy Eliot grew up in St. Louis, Missouri, in a household steeped in culture and tradition. His mother, Charlotte Champe Stearns, was an amateur poet, and his father, Henry Ware Eliot, was a successful businessman with New England roots. Eliot received a broad education, studying at Milton Academy and Harvard University. After earning both bachelor's and master's degrees from Harvard, Eliot continued his studies in philosophy at the Sorbonne in Paris and then back at Harvard. However, he never completed those studies. While on a traveling fellowship in Europe, he met the poet Ezra Pound, who encouraged Eliot's poetic ambitions.

Literary Success Pound helped Eliot gain entry into London's avant-garde circle of writers, and he introduced Eliot's poetry to Harriet

Monroe of *Poetry* magazine. In 1915, Eliot's masterpiece "The Love Song of J. Alfred Prufrock" appeared in *Poetry*. That same year, Eliot married Vivien Haigh-Wood, an Englishwoman. Struggling to make a living as a writer, Eliot worked as a teacher, a bank clerk, and finally as an editor.

Breakthroughs in Poetry The 1917 publication of Eliot's first book, *Prufrock and Other Observations,* signaled a distinct break with the past. Using colloquial speech laced with slang, Eliot created a new, highly original poetic diction. He also explored new poetic themes, such as the splendors and horrors of modern life and the effects of alienation. With the appearance of *The Waste Land* in 1922, Eliot's reputation was solidified. In this poem, Eliot articulated the disgust and disillusionment felt by his generation in the wake of World War I, as well as its longing for meaning in a chaotic, sometimes frightening, world.

Inspired by Religion Though a pioneer in poetry, Eliot became increasingly conservative in his personal views. Struggling with anxiety over his domestic troubles, he joined the Church of England in 1927 and embraced its traditional pieties. In his later collections, *Ash Wednesday* (1930) and *Four Quartets* (1943), he used poetry to stress the significance of accepting religious discipline.

Author Online
Go to **thinkcentral.com**. KEYWORD: HML11-968B

 THINK central

968

See resources on the **Teacher One Stop DVD-ROM** and on **thinkcentral.com**.

R RESOURCE MANAGER UNIT 5
Plan and Teach, pp. 183–190
Summary, pp. 191–192†‡*
Text Analysis and Reading Skill, pp. 193–196†*

DIAGNOSTIC AND SELECTION TESTS
Selection Tests, pp. 265–268

BEST PRACTICES TOOLKIT
Core Analysis Frame: Poetry, pp. D21, D34, D35
Questioning the Author, p. D19

INTERACTIVE READER

ADAPTED INTERACTIVE READER

ELL ADAPTED INTERACTIVE READER

TECHNOLOGY
- **Teacher One Stop DVD-ROM**
- **Student One Stop DVD-ROM**
- **PowerNotes DVD-ROM**
- **Audio Anthology CD**
- **ExamView Test Generator** on the **Teacher One Stop**

Video Trailer THINK central

Go to **thinkcentral.com** to preview the **Video Trailer** introducing this selection. Other features that support the selection include
- **PowerNotes** presentation
- **ThinkAloud** models to enhance comprehension
- **WordSharp** vocabulary tutorials
- interactive writing and grammar instruction

---

* Resources for Differentiation   **† Also in Spanish**   **‡ In Haitian Creole and Vietnamese**

TEXT ANALYSIS: STREAM OF CONSCIOUSNESS

Modern poets explored many ways of breaking free from the standard conventions of poetic form and even content, changing the nature of both narrative and lyric poetry. One of the most dramatic breaks from convention in the modern era was the development of **stream of consciousness.** Used by both poets and fiction writers, this technique presents a sometimes chaotic flow of images and ideas, meant to represent the unfiltered thoughts of the speaker or protagonist. "The Love Song of J. Alfred Prufrock" is a **dramatic monologue** in which Prufrock, the speaker, addresses a silent listener with a tumble of associative thoughts, allusions, and daydreams.

And indeed there will be time
For the yellow smoke that slides along the street
Rubbing its back upon the window-panes

As you read the poem, try not to be distracted by the seemingly nonsensical nature of some verses, but be alert to any feelings or ideas that the images seem to suggest.

READING STRATEGY: SUMMARIZE STANZAS

The difficult thing about reading stream of consciousness is figuring out how to connect seemingly unrelated ideas. A writer will often jump from one thought to the next without any clear transition. Fortunately, Eliot has done us the favor of grouping his thoughts in **stanzas.** If you read the stanzas closely, you will notice that each one expresses a fairly coherent idea. Once you **summarize** and identify the central idea or image of each stanza, you will have an easier time tracing the arc, and the sense, of the entire poem.

As you read, record your summary of each stanza in a chart like the one shown. Some stanzas have only two or three lines; in these cases, don't worry about providing a summary as much as a brief description of the central idea or image.

Stanza	Summary/Central Idea
1	Speaker suggests that listener join him on an evening trip through the lonely city streets.

 Complete the activities in your **Reader/Writer Notebook.**

What is ALIENATION?

So many of us know the feeling of standing at the edge of a party, wanting to join but having no idea what to say or do. Everyone else is having more fun, making better jokes, or wearing nicer clothes. And it's all the worse if you are hoping to approach the object of your affections; do you even stand a chance? In this poem, J. Alfred Prufrock approaches a party with a similar sense of alienation. Full of dread and self-doubt and fearful of female rejection, he wonders whether he dares to step in and draw attention to himself.

QUICKWRITE Create a list of images that suggest alienation or isolation to you. They could be explicit, such as that of a person hesitating at the edge of a group, or implicit, such as the image of a lonely window lit in the darkness.

969

What is ALIENATION?

Read the question and the paragraph aloud. Ask students to explain what alienation means. Then ask students to brainstorm situations in which people might feel alienated. Have students complete the *QUICKWRITE* and share their image lists.

TEXT ANALYSIS — COMMON CORE RL 2

● *Model the Skill:* **STREAM OF CONSCIOUSNESS**

Begin by writing this stanza on the board:

What's the matter with me?
A car horn honks and
The dishes are dirty but
When will she be here?

Ask students to read the stanza carefully. Tell them that the stanza contains the speaker's worry about himself and the anticipated arrival of an absent female. These thoughts are interrupted by a honking car horn and the unwashed dishes. These lines suggest feelings of anxiety and images of visual disorder and loud sounds.

GUIDED PRACTICE Ask students to silently track their thoughts for a minute. Invite volunteers to share.

READING STRATEGY — COMMON CORE RL 5

■ *Model the Skill:* **SUMMARIZE STANZAS**

Point out that Eliot's stanzas each contain thoughts that can be related to form a central idea. Tell students they can summarize the stanzas by writing a brief description of its central idea. Point out that a summary of the first stanza is that of a distressed person waiting.

GUIDED PRACTICE Have students summarize a stanza from another poem in Unit 5.

R RESOURCE MANAGER—Copy Master
Summarize Stanzas p. 195

DIFFERENTIATED INSTRUCTION

FOR STRUGGLING READERS
Vocabulary Support To support instruction, clarify the meaning of these words:

- *conventions,* "usual ways of doing things"
- *chaotic,* "messy, formless, disorganized"
- *unfiltered,* "with nothing removed"
- *protagonist,* "main character"
- *associative,* "connected with the association of ideas"

- *allusions,* "indirect references to persons, places, events, or literary works with which the writer believes the reader will be familiar"
- *coherent,* "holding together, making sense"
- *arc,* "a curving or bow-shaped path"

Practice and Apply

SUMMARY

In this poem, the title character is the speaker and protagonist. As he goes to an evening social gathering, Prufrock expresses his thoughts and feelings, and ponders whether to ask an "overwhelming question"—perhaps a marriage proposal. Preoccupied with his appearance, his aging, and his sense of insignificance and fear, he wonders whether his activities are worthwhile and what his life really means. He ends his monologue inconclusively, his question unasked and unanswered.

READ WITH A PURPOSE

Help students set a purpose for reading. Tell them to read "The Love Song of J. Alfred Prufrock" to find out why the speaker asks his many questions.

TIERED DISCUSSION PROMPTS

In lines 1–14, use these prompts to help students understand the speaker of the poem:

Connect What are your first impressions of J. Alfred Prufrock? Explain. *Possible answer: Accept all reasonable responses, but students should note that Prufrock seems discontented and somewhat depressed.*

Analyze What lines in the poem provide clues about the kind of gathering in which Prufrock finds himself? *Possible answer: Lines 13–14 in which "women come and go / Talking of Michelangelo" suggest that it is a gathering of sophisticated people.*

Synthesize What can you infer about Prufrock's feelings about being at the party? How do those feelings provide a sense as to the kind of person he is? Cite evidence from the poem to explain your answer. *Possible answer: Lines 1 and 4 repeat the phrase "Let us go," suggesting that Prufrock is unhappy about being at the gathering but is somehow stalled in carrying out his desire to leave.*

THE LOVE SONG OF
J. Alfred Prufrock

T. S. Eliot

*S'io credessi che mia risposta fosse
a persona che mai tornasse al mondo,
questa fiamma staria senza più scosse.
Ma per ciò che giammai di questo fondo
non tornò vivo alcun, s'i'odo il vero,
senza tema d'infamia ti rispondo.*

Let us go then, you and I,
When the evening is spread out against the sky
Like a patient etherised upon a table;
Let us go, through certain half-deserted streets,
5 The muttering retreats
Of restless nights in one-night cheap hotels
And sawdust restaurants with oyster-shells:
Streets that follow like a tedious argument
Of insidious intent
10 To lead you to an overwhelming question . . .
Oh, do not ask, "What is it?"
Let us go and make our visit.

In the room the women come and go
Talking of Michelangelo.

15 The yellow fog that rubs its back upon the window-panes,
The yellow smoke that rubs its muzzle on the window-panes,
Licked its tongue into the corners of the evening,
Lingered upon the pools that stand in drains,
Let fall upon its back the soot that falls from chimneys,

S'io credessi . . . ti rispondo: These lines are from the *Inferno*, written in the early 14th century by Italian poet Dante Alighieri. As Dante visits hell, one of the damned agrees to speak of his torment only because he believes that Dante cannot return to the living world to repeat the tale.

3 **etherised:** given ether, a liquid used as an anesthetic.

9 **insidious** (ĭn-sĭd′ē-əs): more dangerous than it seems.

DIFFERENTIATED INSTRUCTION

FOR ENGLISH LANGUAGE LEARNERS

Personification Students may have difficulty with some of Eliot's metaphors. Have students work in mixed-ability pairs to analyze the personification the poet uses in comparing the evening "spread out against the sky like a patient etherised upon a table" (lines 2–3). Have them also review his extended metaphor of the fog as a cat that, having wandered about, "curled once about the house, and fell asleep" (lines 15–22). Ask students to work together to paraphrase these passages and present their revised lines to the class.

FOR STRUGGLING READERS

Options for Reading: Audio Recording

- Have students listen to the poems on the *Audio Anthology CD* (also recommended for English learners) while they read along.

- Remind students to use Eliot's punctuation to identify stanza breaks. Clarify that all the stanzas end in a period or question mark.

20 Slipped by the terrace, made a sudden leap,
    And seeing that it was a soft October night,
    Curled once about the house, and fell asleep. Ⓐ

    And indeed there will be time
    For the yellow smoke that slides along the street
25 Rubbing its back upon the window-panes;
    There will be time, there will be time
    To prepare a face to meet the faces that you meet;
    There will be time to murder and create,
    And time for all the works and days of hands
30 That lift and drop a question on your plate;
    Time for you and time for me,
    And time yet for a hundred indecisions,
    And for a hundred visions and revisions,
    Before the taking of a toast and tea.

35 In the room the women come and go
    Talking of Michelangelo.

    And indeed there will be time
    To wonder, "Do I dare?" and, "Do I dare?"
    Time to turn back and descend the stair,
40 With a bald spot in the middle of my hair—
    (They will say: "How his hair is growing thin!")
    My morning coat, my collar mounting firmly to the chin,
    My necktie rich and modest, but asserted by a simple pin—
    (They will say: "But how his arms and legs are thin!")
45 Do I dare
    Disturb the universe?
    In a minute there is time
    For decisions and revisions which a minute will reverse. Ⓑ

    For I have known them all already, known them all—
50 Have known the evenings, mornings, afternoons,
    I have measured out my life with coffee spoons;
    I know the voices dying with a dying fall
    Beneath the music from a farther room.
        So how should I presume?

55 And I have known the eyes already, known them all—
    The eyes that fix you in a formulated phrase,
    And when I am formulated, sprawling on a pin,
    When I am pinned and wriggling on the wall,
    Then how should I begin

THE LOVE SONG OF J. ALFRED PRUFROCK **971**

Ⓐ **STREAM OF CONSCIOUSNESS**
Stream of consciousness is a writing technique that presents a narrator's flow of thoughts as they might in reality occur, enabling the reader to see "inside" the narrator's head. Reread lines 1–22, and consider the dreamlike quality of the narrator's wandering thoughts. What mood is created by the narrator's puzzling comparisons? As you reread the first 22 lines, write down any details that indicate the stream of consciousness technique.

Language Coach

Prefixes A prefix is a word part attached to the beginning of a word. *Re-* means "again." Read lines 31–34. How do *visions* and *revisions* differ in meaning? How does the word *indecisions* relate to line 33?

Ⓑ **SUMMARIZE STANZAS**
Summarize lines 37–48. What do Prufrock's repeated questioning and his preoccupation with his appearance indicate about his state of mind?

54 presume: act overconfidently; dare.
56 formulated: reduced to a formula.
55–58 And I have ... on the wall: Prufrock recalls being scrutinized by women at other parties. He portrays himself as a live insect that has been classified, labeled, and mounted for display.

TEXT ANALYSIS   COMMON CORE RL 2

Ⓐ STREAM OF CONSCIOUSNESS

Have volunteers read aloud lines 1–22, asking them to emphasize the narrator's odd comparisons. Explain that these strange juxtapositions of images and leaps from one topic to another illustrate the narrator's wandering thoughts.

Possible answer: The mood is one of loneliness. Details that indicate this include: the odd, dreamlike simile comparing the evening to an anesthetized patient (lines 2–3), the way in which one thought blends with the next, and the personification of the city streets that mutter and follow the narrator like "a tedious argument" (lines 5–9).

Extend the Discussion How, at this point in the poem, does Eliot's choice of title seem to be selected for its irony?

READING STRATEGY   COMMON CORE RL 5

Ⓑ Model the Skill: SUMMARIZE STANZAS

Point out that repeatedly asking himself these questions shows that Prufrock is ill at ease and timid. Also point out that he seems overly concerned with time, "...there will be time / To wonder..." (lines 37–38) and "Time to turn back..." (line 39), and with others' reactions to his aging (lines 41 and 44). *Possible answer:* Prufrock feels time has passed in a monotonous way, yet its passage makes him feel alienated from others.

FOR STRUGGLING READERS

Clarify Meaning Work through lines 26–28 with students, helping them to paraphrase the text: "There will be time to reinvent myself to fit the people I will meet. There will be time to 'kill' my personality and replace it with another." Have students discuss why Prufrock might want to recreate himself for the people at the party. *Possible answer: Prufrock wants to reinvent himself because he does not think the partygoers will accept him as he is.*

FOR ENGLISH LANGUAGE LEARNERS

Language Coach

Prefixes *Answer:* "Visions" can mean "something seen in the imagination." "Revisions" means "things changed or corrected." The speaker cannot make up his mind about what he would like to happen in the "time for you and time for me" (line 31). He is so full of indecision that it leads to "a hundred visions and revisions" (line 33).

60 To spit out all the butt-ends of my days and ways?
    And how should I presume?

And I have known the arms already, known them all—
Arms that are braceleted and white and bare
(But in the lamplight, downed with light brown hair!)
65 Is it perfume from a dress
That makes me so digress?
Arms that lie along a table, or wrap about a shawl.
    And should I then presume?
    And how should I begin?
      • • • • •
70 Shall I say, I have gone at dusk through narrow streets
And watched the smoke that rises from the pipes
Of lonely men in shirt-sleeves, leaning out of windows? . . .

I should have been a pair of ragged claws
Scuttling across the floors of silent seas.
      • • • • •
75 And the afternoon, the evening, sleeps so peacefully!
Smoothed by long fingers,
Asleep . . . tired . . . or it malingers,
Stretched on the floor, here beside you and me.
Should I, after tea and cakes and ices,
80 Have the strength to force the moment to its crisis?
But though I have wept and fasted, wept and prayed,
Though I have seen my head (grown slightly bald) brought in
    upon a platter,
I am no prophet—and here's no great matter;
I have seen the moment of my greatness flicker,
85 And I have seen the eternal Footman hold my coat, and snicker,
And in short, I was afraid.

And would it have been worth it, after all,
After the cups, the marmalade, the tea,
Among the porcelain, among some talk of you and me,
90 Would it have been worth while,
To have bitten off the matter with a smile,
To have squeezed the universe into a ball
To roll it towards some overwhelming question,
To say: "I am Lazarus, come from the dead,
95 Come back to tell you all, I shall tell you all"—
If one, settling a pillow by her head,
    Should say: "That is not what I meant at all.
    That is not it, at all." **ⓒ**

TIERED DISCUSSION PROMPTS

In lines 79–86, use these prompts to help students comprehend Prufrock's state of mind:

Restate Restate Prufrock's thoughts in this passage. ***Possible answer:*** *Prufrock wonders whether he is strong enough to face what he has to face. He recalls suffering and praying, but concludes that despite his efforts, he is afraid anyway.*

Interpret What is Prufrock afraid of in this moment? Overall? ***Possible answer:*** *In this moment, Prufrock is apparently afraid of revealing his feelings to a woman. Overall, he is afraid of engaging fully in life.*

Evaluate Does Prufrock have good cause for his fear and uncertainty, or is he simply weak? ***Possible answer:*** *Profrock has good cause to be afraid of his task, if it is to open his feelings to another person. However, he is weak to let his fear cripple him.*

TEXT ANALYSIS   COMMON CORE **RL 2**

ⓒ *Model the Skill:* **STREAM OF CONSCIOUSNESS**

Point out the images of Prufrock's head being served on a platter (lines 82–83), to an "eternal Footman" (line 85), and to Lazarus (line 94).

Possible answer: *Prufrock casts himself in the role of John the Baptist (line 82), in an image of entering the afterlife (line 85), and in the image of Lazarus (line 94). All three images relate to death and its aftermath.*

Language Coach

Word Definitions *Digress* (line 66) means "wander away from the main topic; ramble." What causes the speaker to digress?

73–74 I should . . . silent seas: Here Prufrock presents an image of himself as a crayfish.

77 malingers (mə-lǐng′ərz): pretends illness in order to avoid duty or work.

81–83 But though . . . prophet: an allusion to the biblical story of John the Baptist, who is imprisoned by King Herod (Matthew 14; Mark 6). At the request of his wife, Herod had the Baptist's head cut off and brought to him on a platter.

94 Lazarus: In the biblical story (John 11:17–44) Lazarus lay dead in his tomb for four days before Jesus brought him back to life.

ⓒ STREAM OF CONSCIOUSNESS
Reread lines 75–98. Prufrock casts himself in three different **images** in this stanza, two of which are biblical allusions. Identify these images and explain what they have in common.

DIFFERENTIATED INSTRUCTION

FOR ENGLISH LANGUAGE LEARNERS

Language Coach

Word Definitions *Answer:* *His attraction to a woman makes him ramble off topic.* Tell students that throughout the poem, Prufrock asks himself, "How shall I presume?" Ask them to find the meaning of presume and tell why he is so preoccupied about this. ***Possible answer:*** *"Presume" means "to assume beforehand," so he is worried he is not prepared to draw conclusions about something.*

FOR STRUGGLING READERS

Develop Reading Fluency Give students practice in reading poetry aloud. Have pairs read the poem aloud, taking turns reading stanzas. Point out that, as most lines end in commas, they should observe these pauses. Remind students that there is also a pause between stanzas, so as readers change, they should wait a few seconds before reading on.

And would it have been worth it, after all,
100 Would it have been worth while,
    After the sunsets and the dooryards and the sprinkled streets,
    After the novels, after the teacups, after the skirts that trail along
        the floor—
    And this, and so much more?—
    It is impossible to say just what I mean!
105 But as if a magic lantern threw the nerves in patterns on a
        screen:
    Would it have been worth while
    If one, settling a pillow or throwing off a shawl,
    And turning toward the window, should say:
        "That is not it at all,
110   That is not what I meant, at all."
        • • • • •
    No! I am not Prince Hamlet, nor was meant to be;
    Am an attendant lord, one that will do
    To swell a progress, start a scene or two,
    Advise the prince; no doubt, an easy tool,
115 Deferential, glad to be of use,
    Politic, cautious, and meticulous;
    Full of high sentence, but a bit obtuse;
    At times, indeed, almost ridiculous—
    Almost, at times, the Fool.

120 I grow old . . . I grow old . . .
    I shall wear the bottoms of my trousers rolled. **D**

    Shall I part my hair behind? Do I dare to eat a peach?
    I shall wear white flannel trousers, and walk upon the beach.
    I have heard the mermaids singing, each to each.

125 I do not think that they will sing to me.

    I have seen them riding seaward on the waves
    Combing the white hair of the waves blown back
    When the wind blows the water white and black.

    We have lingered in the chambers of the sea
130 By sea-girls wreathed with seaweed red and brown
    Till human voices wake us, and we drown.

105 magic lantern: a forerunner of the slide projector.

115 deferential: yielding to someone else's opinion.
116 meticulous: extremely careful and precise about details.
117 obtuse: slow to understand; dull.

D STREAM OF CONSCIOUSNESS
What similarities can you detect between the "attendant lord" described in lines 112–119 and Prufrock's image of himself in lines 120–121? Explain.

124–125 mermaids . . . to me: In mythology, mermaids attract mortal men by their beauty and their singing, sometimes allowing men to live with them in the sea.

FOR STRUGGLING READERS

Comprehension Support Have students re-read the poem using the Core Analysis Frame: Poetry to get at the gist of the work. Urge them to work through the questions on the Analysis Frame one at a time, but to skip any that do not seem to apply to Eliot's poem.

🧰 BEST PRACTICES TOOLKIT—Copy Masters
   Core Analysis Frame: Poetry
   pp. D21, D34, D35

FOR ADVANCED LEARNERS/AP

Evaluate Ideas The idea of alienation was fashionable at the time "Prufrock" was written. How appealing is it today? Have students explore this question by using a Questioning the Author chart to evaluate the poem and raise critical questions. Then ask them to compare and contrast Prufrock's view of life with their own. Invite students to share their charts and conclusions.

🧰 BEST PRACTICES TOOLKIT—Transparency
   Questioning the Author p. D19

What is ALIENATION?

Discuss In lines 109–110, how does the statement in quotation marks express alienation?
Possible answer: *Prufrock feels that no one understands what he is saying.*

TEXT ANALYSIS   COMMON CORE RL 5

D STREAM OF CONSCIOUSNESS

Possible answer: *Like the attendant lord, Prufrock does not see himself as a "prince," but instead as an old fool.*

IF STUDENTS NEED HELP . . . Suggest that they summarize the stanza using the prereading chart introduced on page 969, as shown.

Stanza Number	Summary/Idea
14–15	P. sees himself as a foolish minor character in a play.

SELECTION WRAP–UP

READ WITH A PURPOSE Now that students have read the poem, they may say Prufrock asks his many questions because he is deep in thought about his life—the longer he spends in contemplation, the more naturally the questions seem to arise.

⭐ CRITIQUE

• Ask whether students feel the poem is too obscure or whether its complexity adds interest to its ideas.

INDEPENDENT READING

Dear Editor: A History of Poetry in Letters, edited by Billy Collins and Joseph Parisi, may prove interesting for students wanting to learn more about many of the poets of this era.

Practice and Apply

For preliminary support of post-reading questions, use these copy masters:

R RESOURCE—Copy Masters
  Stream of Consciousness p. 193
  Question Support p. 197
  Additional selection questions are provided for teachers on page 187.

ANSWERS

 COMMON CORE RL 1, RL 5

1. *Prufrock reflects on going out for the evening with someone.*

2. *He is anxious and uncertain about the evening.*

3. *Prufrock feels self-hate or insecurity.*

Possible answers:

4. ■ **COMMON CORE FOCUS** **Summarize Stanzas** *Summaries should convey the poem's narrative arc from Prufrock fighting his insignificance and loneliness to becoming resigned to it.*

5. *They create a stalled feeling that reflects Prufrock's inaction and makes it comical.*

6. ● **COMMON CORE FOCUS** **Stream of Consciousness** *Lines 120–121: Prufrock feels distant from his youth.* *Lines 122–123: Despite timidity, he has made a small decision.* *Lines 124–125: He feels barred from happiness.* *Lines 126–131: Prufrock fantasizes about happiness but remains lost. At the end of the poem, readers are left with the idea that his longing remains unfulfilled.*

Assess and Reteach

Assess

DIAGNOSTIC AND SELECTION TESTS
  Selection Test A pp. 265–266
  Selection Test B/C pp. 267–268

Interactive Selection Test on thinkcentral.com

Reteach

Level Up Online Tutorials on thinkcentral.com

Reteaching Worksheets on thinkcentral.com

  Literature Lesson 17: Structure of Poetry
  Literature Lesson 19: Rhyme and Rhyme Scheme
  Literature Lesson 26: Imagery
  Literature Lesson 42: Mood
  Research and Study Skills Lesson 13: Summarizing

Comprehension

1. **Recall** What social situation does Prufrock reflect upon in this poem?

2. **Recall** How does he feel about this situation?

3. **Clarify** What is Prufrock's primary feeling about himself?

Text Analysis

4. **Synthesize Summaries** Review the summaries and central ideas you recorded as you read. Now, viewing this series of ideas as a **narrative** with a conflict, a climax, and a resolution, write a summary of Prufrock's internal journey.

5. **Examine Poetic Devices** Review Eliot's use of **repetition** and **rhyme** in lines 23–34. Explain how these devices are used to convey Prufrock's sense of anxiety.

6. **Analyze Stream of Consciousness** In the final lines of the poem (lines 122–131), Prufrock offers his final reflection. For each of the following passages, offer an explication, or careful analysis. What does each group of lines suggest about Prufrock's sense of himself and his place in the world? What resonating idea are we left with at the poem's end?

   • lines 120–121 ("I grow old . . . trousers rolled.")
   • lines 122–123 ("Shall I part . . . walk upon the beach.")
   • lines 124–125 ("I have heard the mermaids . . . sing to me.")
   • lines 126–131 ("I have seen them riding seaward . . . and we drown.")

7. **Evaluate Form and Content** Consider the feelings and ideas that Eliot was trying to express; in what way can the stream of consciousness technique be said to reflect these ideas? Explain whether or not you think this technique is effective, citing evidence.

Text Criticism

8. **Critical Interpretations** Critic Donald R. Fryxell wrote, "Prufrock is a trimmer . . . trimmers were those souls in Dante's *Inferno* who were condemned to the vestibule of hell because they had never really lived, although they were supposedly alive. . . . The Trimmers were lifeless, spiritless, mindless people." Do you agree or disagree with this statement? Give evidence from the text to support your answer.

> ### *What is* **ALIENATION?**
>
> The narrator in "The Love Song of J. Alfred Prufrock" sees himself as set apart from the crowd. His self-conscious ruminations reflect a profound fear of rejection. Whom or what might he fear? Have you ever had similar feelings of alienation? Explain.

COMMON CORE

RL 1 Cite textual evidence to support analysis of what the text says explicitly as well as inferences drawn from the text, including determining where the text leaves matters uncertain. **RL 5** Analyze how an author's choices concerning how to structure specific parts of a text contribute to its overall structure and meaning as well as its aesthetic impact.

---

7. *The stream of consciousness shows the wavering, wandering, alienated, stuck quality of Prufrock's mind and thus reflects Eliot's ideas about alienation. Student's explanations should cite evidence from the text.*

8. *Many students will agree that Prufrock has not really lived and is weak-spirited. He never manages to ask his "overwhelming question," and instead daydreams about a happiness he feels unable to achieve. Others may say that Prufrock's intellectual and imaginative energy and romantic longings suggest a lively, if squelched, spirit.*

> ### *What is* **ALIENATION?**
> *Students may suggest that Prufrock fears rejection by a woman. Answers about their own alienation will vary. Ask students to imagine a modern-day Prufrock: Have new sources of alienation come along?*

Modernist Style

While there is no one thing that makes a poem "modern," most modernist literature does share some defining features.

Features of Modernism:
• nontraditional subject matter and themes
• a focus on alienated individuals rather than heroes
• use of understatement and irony to reveal emotions and ideas
• use of symbols and images to suggest meaning
• experimentation with style and language

Writing to Synthesize

Review the poems beginning on page 922 to get a feel for how they incorporate the features of modernism. Then write your own poem in the modernist style.

Consider
• what your poem will be about (remember that traditional themes and topics, such as love, were rejected or reinterpreted by the modernists)
• whether your poem will feature a speaker, and what he or she will be like
• how to use understatement or irony to bring out emotions
• what symbols or images might best convey your meaning
• whether you wish to experiment with language or style

Extension

SPEAKING & LISTENING
Choose a more traditional poem from Units 1–4, such as Poe's "The Raven," and modernize it. **Rewrite** two stanzas of the poem as a modernist poet might, using the features of modernism as a guideline. Then **recite** your stanzas for your classmates, and discuss the techniques you used to "update" the poem. You may need to write out your stanzas on poster board to show how you manipulated line length, stanza form, capitalization and punctuation, or other elements of style.

⸬ **COMMON CORE**

RL 9 Demonstrate knowledge of early-twentieth-century foundational works of American literature, including how two or more texts from the same period treat similar themes or topics. **SL 4** Present information, findings, and supporting evidence, conveying a clear and distinct perspective.

⸬ **COMMON CORE FOCUS**

RL 9 Demonstrate knowledge of early-twentieth-century foundational works of American literature, including how two or more texts from the same period treat similar themes or topics. **SL 4** Present information, findings, and supporting evidence, conveying a clear and distinct perspective.

Wrap-Up: The New Poetry

This Wrap-Up provides students with an opportunity to revisit the modernist poetry in this section and write their own poems in modernist style. Encourage students to consider what *they* think makes a poem "modern."

Writing to Synthesize

Review with students that synthesizing means combining ideas and facts with other information and prior knowledge in order to better understand a subject or develop new ideas. Those new ideas can help students explore previously unfamiliar writing styles.

To help students write their poems, have them first discuss the traits of modernist literature listed on the pupil edition page. Ask students to cite examples of the traits in the poems in this section. Remind them that these examples reflect many different styles, some of which use traditional forms, as in the cases of Robert Frost, Edwin Arlington Robinson, and Edna St. Vincent Millay, and others of which use organic forms, such as Carl Sandburg, Ezra Pound, T. S. Eliot, E. E. Cummings, Marianne Moore, and William Carlos Williams.

Extension

• Encourage students to use free verse if updating a poem that is in traditional form.
• Suggest that students write their updates in a conversational, colloquial style.
• Urge students to consider creating an ironic or alienated view of the original poem.

DIFFERENTIATED INSTRUCTION

FOR STRUGGLING WRITERS
Writing Support [small-group option] Help students get started by organizing them in groups to brainstorm ideas, share insights into modernist poetry, and invent their own modernist styles. Suggest that students write about a single object, place, or image that they think symbolizes a modernist idea. Urge students to limit their experimentation to either theme or language and style, and to follow conventions in the remaining area.

FOR ENGLISH LANGUAGE LEARNERS
Writing Support
• Allow students to write poems in their home languages and then translate the poems with more-fluent partners.
• Suggest that students write in the first-person voice of a speaker and begin each line with an identical word or phrase such as *I am, I saw, I think,* or *I know.*
• Invite volunteers to read the poems aloud in their first languages and then in English.

Focus and Motivate

COMMON CORE FOCUS

RL 2 Analyze the development of two or more themes or central ideas over the course of the text, including how they interact and build on one another to produce a complex account. **RL 3** Analyze the impact of the author's choices regarding how to develop and relate elements of a story. **RL 4** Determine the meaning of words and phrases as they are used in the text, including figurative and connotative meanings. **W 1** Write arguments to support claims in an analysis of substantive topics or texts, using valid reasoning and relevant and sufficient evidence. **L 1a** Apply the understanding that usage can change over time. **L 2a** Observe hyphenation conventions. **L 3a** Vary syntax for effect, consulting references for guidance as needed; apply an understanding of syntax to the study of complex texts when reading. **L 5b** Analyze nuances in the meaning of words with similar denotations. **L 2** Demonstrate command of the conventions of standard English punctuation when writing.

ABOUT THE AUTHOR

The publication of short stories such as "Winter Dreams" in top-market magazines built Fitzgerald's income and fame and allowed him to write novels. However, he regarded this aspect of his work as a creative burden.

NOTABLE QUOTE

"Here was a new generation . . . dedicated more than the last to the fear of poverty and the worship of success; grown up to find all Gods dead, all wars fought, all faiths in man shaken." **–F. Scott Fitzgerald**

Selection Resources

COMMON CORE

RL 2 Analyze the development of two or more themes or central ideas over the course of the text, including how they interact and build on one another to produce a complex account. **RL 3** Analyze the impact of the author's choices regarding how to develop and relate elements of a story. **RL 4** Determine the meaning of words and phrases as they are used in the text, including figurative and connotative meanings. **L 2a** Observe hyphenation conventions.

DID YOU KNOW?

F. Scott Fitzgerald . . .

- was named after his distant relative Francis Scott Key, who wrote the words to "The Star-Spangled Banner."
- wrote his first novel while in the army, working on it solely on the weekends for just three months.

The Modern Short Story
Winter Dreams
Short Story by F. Scott Fitzgerald

Meet the Author

F. Scott Fitzgerald 1896–1940

F. Scott Fitzgerald experienced, and depicted in his fiction, both the material success and the crushing disillusionment that characterized the 1920s—a decade he dubbed the Jazz Age. He died young, famous for his flashy lifestyle, not his writing. But today, thanks to his dazzling prose style and piercing insight, Fitzgerald is heralded as the spokesperson of his era and as an American literary giant.

Midwest Boy Makes Good Born in St. Paul, Minnesota, Fitzgerald grew up in comfortable circumstances. His parents could afford to send him to prep school and then Princeton University, where he spent his time writing for the literary magazine and creating musical comedies. Low grades and the intervention of World War I kept him from graduating, but he left with a big dream. "I want to be one of the greatest writers who ever lived," he told a friend.

Jazz Age Romance In 1918, Fitzgerald fell madly in love with a flirtatious 18-year-old named Zelda Sayre. Zelda was as rich as she was beautiful and refused to marry him until he could support her financially. Two years later, Fitzgerald's first novel, *This Side of Paradise,* was finally published. Hailed as a daringly original story of the postwar generation's revolt against tradition, it more than doubled Fitzgerald's income, earned him widespread exposure as "the philosopher of the flapper," and won Zelda over. The two married and soon became the golden couple of the 1920s, partying at glamorous locations in the United States and Europe and living beyond the income Fitzgerald made from his writing.

Fall and Redemption Like the decade the Fitzgeralds epitomized, their high life came crashing down. In 1930, Zelda began the first of many hospital stays for mental illness, while Scott fell deeply into debt and alcoholism. *The Beautiful and Damned* (1922), a novel about the unraveling lives of a once-glamorous couple, was deemed "depressing" by reviewers, and Fitzgerald's masterpiece, *The Great Gatsby* (1925), was not the popular success he had hoped for. He died of a heart attack in 1940, at age 44, and it was years before he came to be regarded as anything more than a writer of showy period pieces. The reexamination of Fitzgerald's work was spurred not by critics, many of whom had always appreciated his talent, but by a new generation of readers who discovered the brilliance of his writing and told their friends. The year he died, his book sales—just 40 copies total—earned him $13.13 in royalties. Today, however, *The Great Gatsby* is a beloved American classic, and Fitzgerald's books sell about 500,000 copies annually.

Author Online
Go to **thinkcentral.com**. KEYWORD: HML11-976

THINK central

976

See resources on the **Teacher One Stop DVD-ROM** and on **thinkcentral.com**.

R **RESOURCE MANAGER UNIT 5**
Plan and Teach, pp. 199–206
Summary, pp. 207–208†‡*
Text Analysis and Reading Skill, pp. 209–212†*
Vocabulary, pp. 213–215*
Grammar and Style, p. 218

DIAGNOSTIC AND SELECTION TESTS
Selection Tests, pp. 269–272

BEST PRACTICES TOOLKIT
pp. E2, A26, D6, A25, A64, B18, E2, B20

TECHNOLOGY
- **Teacher One Stop DVD-ROM**
- **Student One Stop DVD-ROM**
- **Audio Anthology CD**
- **GrammarNotes DVD-ROM**
- **ExamView Test Generator** on the **Teacher One Stop**

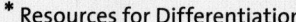

* Resources for Differentiation   † Also in Spanish   ‡ In Haitian Creole and Vietnamese

TEXT ANALYSIS: CHARACTER MOTIVATION AND TRAITS

Some characters are so vividly portrayed, they seem like real people. The characters' traits and motivations are often familiar to us; we see them in ourselves or in others we know. **Character traits** are those qualities shown by a character, as implied by his or her physical appearance and expressions of personality, such as boldness or gentleness. By recognizing a character's traits, you are able to better understand the **character's motivation**—the stated or implied reason(s) behind the character's actions. As you read, note the words, actions, thoughts, and appearance of the **protagonist,** or main character, as well as of the **antagonist,** the person against which the protagonist struggles. What do these descriptions indicate about the characters' traits and motivations?

Review: **Theme**

● READING STRATEGY: PREDICT STORY DEVELOPMENT

Predicting is the process of using text clues to make a reasonable guess about what will happen in a story. Sometimes your predictions will hit the mark, and other times the characters' actions and the story's events may surprise you. As you come to know the characters in "Winter Dreams," see if you can predict what will happen to them next, or how they will react or feel toward other characters and events. Record your predictions and the text clues that led you to make them.

Predictions	Text Clues

▲ VOCABULARY IN CONTEXT

Fitzgerald uses the boldfaced words in his story of love and status. Determine the definition of each word from its context.

1. a girl whose mere presence could **precipitate** a sudden crush
2. due to her **patrimony,** would inherit a **surfeit** of money
3. attended parties surrounded by her **retinue**
4. flirted **blatantly,** without a trace of self-consciousness
5. pouting and **petulance** that seemed to attract men
6. unfriendly to women—no **camaraderie** with them
7. turned her nose up at **mundane,** ordinary things
8. enjoyed the **flux** of life, its **precarious** nature

 Complete the activities in your **Reader/Writer Notebook**.

Will STATUS make you happy?

It's easy to get caught up in the pursuit of wealth and status—and to imagine that obtaining them would guarantee a perfect life. But would it? Can money buy love, and does high status guarantee happiness?

QUICKWRITE Envision the life you hope to lead ten years from now. Wealth and status top the list of many people's "must-haves," but what else holds a prominent place in your dreams? Jot down some of your aspirations on a graph like the one shown. Then fill in the graph, rating on a scale of 1 to 10 the importance you attach to each goal. Use your completed graph to write a short paragraph explaining which goal holds the top spot on your list, and why.

Aspiration	Rating
Wealth	
Social Status	
Exciting Career	
Happy Family	

0 1 2 3 4 5 6 7 8 9 10

WINTER DREAMS **977**

VOCABULARY SKILL

COMMON CORE
L 4

▲ VOCABULARY IN CONTEXT

DIAGNOSE WORD KNOWLEDGE Have all students complete Vocabulary in Context. Check their definitions against the following:

blatantly (blāt′n-tlē) *adv.* in an extremely obvious way; conspicuously

camaraderie (kä′mə-rä′də-rē) *n.* a spirit of friendly goodfellowship

flux (flŭks): *n.* change

mundane (mŭn-dān′) *adj.* characteristic of or concerned with the ordinary

patrimony (păt′rə-mō′nē) *n.* estate or money inherited from ancestors

petulance (pĕch′ə-ləns) *n.* ill temper; annoyance

precarious (prĭ-kâr′ē-əs) *adj.* risky; uncertain

precipitate (prĭ-sĭp′ĭ-tāt′) *v.* to bring about, especially abruptly

retinue (rĕt′n-ōō′) *n.* a group of attendants or followers

surfeit (sûr′fĭt) *n.* a fullness beyond the point of satisfaction

PRETEACH VOCABULARY Use this copy master to help students predict meanings:

R RESOURCE MANAGER—Copy Master
Vocabulary Study p. 213

Teach

Will STATUS make you happy?

Before they read the paragraph ask students to list achievements, possessions, and ranks that indicate people's status. Tell them that not all people define status by the same indicators. Urge students to choose status indicators they find meaningful as they complete the *QUICKWRITE* activity.

TEXT ANALYSIS

COMMON CORE
RL 3

● **Model the Skill:**
CHARACTER MOTIVATION AND TRAITS

Read aloud this example:

Perched nervously on the chair, the boy watched the teacher pass out the graded exams. Ms. Reed smiled and tried to catch his eye as she handed him his exam, but he took it without looking up and placed it face down on his desk.

Tell students that to find a character's motivation and traits, readers first find what the character does and says: the boy is nervous, looks away, and puts the exam face-down. Point out his motivation, fear, and trait, anxiety.

GUIDED PRACTICE Ask students to find a trait that describes the teacher and identify what motivates her.

READING STRATEGY

COMMON CORE
RL 3

■ **Model the Skill: PREDICT STORY DEVELOPMENT**

Tell students that to make predictions about story developments, they should look at what has already happened. Read the example again and tell students that you predict the boy will be surprised to see he has done well after all.

GUIDED PRACTICE Ask students to find clues that support your prediction, such as the teacher's smile.

R RESOURCE MANAGER—Copy Master
Predict Story Development p. 211 (for student use while reading the selection)

WINTER DREAMS **977**

SUMMARY

This short story opens when young Dexter Green quits his job as a golf caddy because he is asked to carry the clubs of a spoiled 11-year-old girl. After attending a prestigious university and gaining financial success, Dexter again meets the girl, Judy Jones. He pursues Judy, who treats him badly throughout their romance and then interferes with his engagement to another woman. Years later, Dexter feels lost when he learns that Judy, who was his idealized figure of an alluring woman, has lost her looks.

READ WITH A PURPOSE

Help students set a purpose for reading. Tell them to read "Winter Dreams" to find out what happens to Dexter and Judy as time passes.

TEXT ANALYSIS

COMMON CORE

RL 3

Ⓐ MOTIVATION AND TRAITS

Possible answer: The first paragraph provides socioeconomic information such as "poor as sin" (line 1), "wealthy people" (line 4), and "pocket-money" (line 4). Wealth and status matter greatly to Dexter, whose father's ownership of a grocery store makes him middle class but not wealthy enough to join the country club.

Winter Dreams

F. Scott Fitzgerald

BACKGROUND Behind the glitz and glamour of the 1920s lay a profound loss of idealism. Though World War I gave rise to new opportunities and freedoms, especially for women, the shift to the modern age left a gap in values that the new generation struggled to fill. "Winter Dreams" mostly takes place before 1920, when a restless uncertainty was first being felt. The story appeared in the collection *All the Sad Young Men* (1926), a title that expresses Fitzgerald's deeper understanding of the decade.

Analyze Visuals ▶
How would you describe the subject of this portrait? Describe the **traits** you think he projects, citing details from the painting to support your answer.

I

Some of the caddies were poor as sin and lived in one-room houses with a neurasthenic[1] cow in the front yard, but Dexter Green's father owned the second best grocery-store in Black Bear—the best one was "The Hub," patronized by the wealthy people from Sherry Island—and Dexter caddied only for pocket-money. Ⓐ

   In the fall when the days became crisp and gray, and the long Minnesota winter shut down like the white lid of a box, Dexter's skis moved over the snow that hid the fairways of the golf course. At these times the country gave him a feeling of profound melancholy—it offended him that the links should lie in enforced fallowness, haunted by ragged sparrows for the long season. It was dreary, too,
10 that on the tees where the gay colors fluttered in summer there were now only the desolate sand-boxes knee-deep in crusted ice. When he crossed the hills the wind blew cold as misery, and if the sun was out he tramped with his eyes squinted up against the hard dimensionless glare.

① Targeted Passage

Ⓐ MOTIVATION AND TRAITS
Consider the kind of information you receive in the story's very first paragraph. What do you learn about Dexter's family and social position?

---

1. **neurasthenic** (no͞or′əs-thĕn′ĭk): weak and lacking in vigor.

Homme au Chapeau (1900s), Jean Berque. Waterhouse and Dodd, London. © Bridgeman Art Library.

DIFFERENTIATED INSTRUCTION

FOR ENGLISH LANGUAGE LEARNERS

Sentence Structure Help students read sentences that contain dashes. Tell them that the words that appear between two long dashes, as in lines 3–4, can be omitted without making the sentence incomplete. Read aloud the sentence without the words set off by dashes to illustrate. Tell students these words give details so closely related to the subject that the author opted to include them within the sentence.

FOR STRUGGLING READERS

In combination with the *Audio Anthology CD*, use one or more Targeted Passages (pp. 978, 980, 984, 987, 991, 995, 997) to ensure that students focus on key story events and concepts. Targeted Passages are also good for English language learners.

① Targeted Passage [Lines 1–13]

This passage introduces the main character, Dexter Green, and the small-town setting,

Analyze Visuals

Possible answer: The young man's eyes make him look contemplative; his hat indicates a certain dignity. His shirt or coat, on the other hand, looks worn, not quite clean, and perhaps too big for him. The set of his mouth makes him look decisive or determined.

CULTURAL CONNECTION

Status In the United States today, wealth is the surest sign of status and the guaranteed path to power and influence. In Fitzgerald's time, as in many European countries, aristocratic lineage largely determined status and often brought with it wealth. Other cultures assign high status to military leaders, to priests and holy people, or to the elderly. Invite students to share status indicators from their home cultures and then to discuss why different cultures value different achievements and characteristics.

REVISIT THE BIG QUESTION

Will STATUS *make you happy?*

Discuss Four levels of status are identified in lines (lines 1–4). What are these levels, and why might the story begin by introducing them? *Possible answer: The four levels of status are the caddies, who are "poor as sin" (line 1), Dexter's family, who owns the "second best grocery-store" (lines 2–3), the people who own the best grocery store, and, finally, "the wealthy people from Sherry Island" (lines 3–4). Status—who has it and who doesn't—will clearly be important in the story's conflict.*

then hints at the conflict between wealthy and middle-class residents.

- Where does the story take place? (lines 5–7)
- Why does Dexter work as a caddy? How is he different from the other caddies? (lines 1–4)
- What bothers Dexter about winter in Black Bear? (lines 7–11)

FOR ADVANCED LEARNERS/AP

Research Projects Have students research and write a report about Fitzgerald's own experience with status, either during his school years or later, in the early 1920s, after he had had his first success as a writer.

In April the winter ceased abruptly. The snow ran down into Black Bear Lake scarcely tarrying for the early golfers to brave the season with red and black balls. Without elation, without an interval of moist glory, the cold was gone.

Dexter knew that there was something dismal about this Northern spring, just as he knew there was something gorgeous about the fall. Fall made him clinch his hands and tremble and repeat idiotic sentences to himself, and make brisk abrupt
20 gestures of command to imaginary audiences and armies. October filled him with hope which November raised to a sort of ecstatic triumph, and in this mood the fleeting brilliant impressions of the summer at Sherry Island were ready grist to his mill.[2] He became a golf champion and defeated Mr. T. A. Hedrick in a marvelous match played a hundred times over the fairways of his imagination, a match each detail of which he changed about untiringly—sometimes he won with almost laughable ease, sometimes he came up magnificently from behind. Again, stepping from a Pierce-Arrow automobile,[3] like Mr. Mortimer Jones, he strolled frigidly into the lounge of the Sherry Island Golf Club—or perhaps, surrounded by an admiring crowd, he gave an exhibition of fancy diving from the spring-board of
30 the club raft. . . . Among those who watched him in open-mouthed wonder was Mr. Mortimer Jones. **B**

And one day it came to pass that Mr. Jones—himself and not his ghost—came up to Dexter with tears in his eyes and said that Dexter was the — — best caddy in the club, and wouldn't he decide not to quit if Mr. Jones made it worth his while, because every other — — caddy in the club lost one ball a hole for him—regularly—

"No, sir," said Dexter decisively, "I don't want to caddy any more." Then, after a pause: "I'm too old."

"You're not more than fourteen. Why the devil did you decide just this
40 morning that you wanted to quit? You promised that next week you'd go over to the State tournament with me."

"I decided I was too old."

Dexter handed in his "A Class" badge, collected what money was due him from the caddy-master, and walked home to Black Bear Village.

"The best — — caddy I ever saw," shouted Mr. Mortimer Jones over a drink that afternoon. "Never lost a ball! Willing! Intelligent! Quiet! Honest! Grateful!"

The little girl who had done this was eleven—beautifully ugly as little girls are apt to be who are destined after a few years to be inexpressibly lovely and bring no end of misery to a great number of men. The spark, however, was perceptible.
50 There was a general ungodliness in the way her lips twisted down at the corners when she smiled, and in the—Heaven help us!—in the almost passionate quality of her eyes. Vitality is born early in such women. It was utterly in evidence now, shining through her thin frame in a sort of glow. **C**

2. **grist to his mill:** something that he could make good use of.

3. **Pierce-Arrow automobile:** a luxury car of the day.

She had come eagerly out onto the course at nine o'clock with a white linen nurse and five small new golf-clubs in a white canvas bag which the nurse was carrying. When Dexter first saw her she was standing by the caddy house, rather ill at ease and trying to conceal the fact by engaging her nurse in an obviously unnatural conversation graced by startling and irrelevant grimaces from herself.

60 "Well, it's certainly a nice day, Hilda," Dexter heard her say. She drew down the corners of her mouth, smiled, and glanced furtively around, her eyes in transit falling for an instant on Dexter.

Then to the nurse:

"Well, I guess there aren't very many people out here this morning, are there?"

The smile again—radiant, **blatantly** artificial—convincing.

"I don't know what we're supposed to do now," said the nurse, looking nowhere in particular.

"Oh, that's all right. I'll fix it up."

Dexter stood perfectly still, his mouth slightly ajar. He knew that if he moved forward a step his stare would be in her line of vision—if he moved backward he
70 would lose his full view of her face. For a moment he had not realized how young she was. Now he remembered having seen her several times the year before—in bloomers.[4]

Suddenly, involuntarily, he laughed, a short abrupt laugh—then, startled by himself, he turned and began to walk quickly away.

"Boy!"

Dexter stopped.

"Boy—"

Beyond question he was addressed. Not only that, but he was treated to that absurd smile, that preposterous smile—the memory of which at least a dozen men
80 were to carry into middle age.

"Boy, do you know where the golf teacher is?"

"He's giving a lesson."

"Well, do you know where the caddy-master is?"

"He isn't here yet this morning."

"Oh." For a moment this baffled her. She stood alternately on her right and left foot.

"We'd like to get a caddy," said the nurse. "Mrs. Mortimer Jones sent us out to play golf, and we don't know how without we get a caddy."

Here she was stopped by an ominous glance from Miss Jones, followed
90 immediately by the smile.

"There aren't any caddies here except me," said Dexter to the nurse, "and I got to stay here in charge until the caddy-master gets here."

"Oh."

Miss Jones and her **retinue** now withdrew, and at a proper distance from Dexter became involved in a heated conversation, which was concluded by Miss Jones taking one of the clubs and hitting it on the ground with violence. For

---

4. **bloomers:** baggy pants that end just below the knee, formerly worn by girls.

blatantly (blăt'n-tlē) *adv.* in an extremely obvious way; conspicuously

retinue (rĕt'n-ōō') *n.* a group of attendants or followers

further emphasis she raised it again and was about to bring it down smartly upon the nurse's bosom, when the nurse seized the club and twisted it from her hands.

"You little mean old *thing!*" cried Miss Jones wildly.

100   Another argument ensued. Realizing that the elements of comedy were implied in the scene, Dexter several times began to laugh, but each time restrained the laugh before it reached audibility. He could not resist the monstrous conviction that the little girl was justified in beating the nurse.

The situation was resolved by the fortuitous appearance of the caddy-master, who was appealed to immediately by the nurse.

"Miss Jones is to have a little caddy, and this one says he can't go."

"Mr. McKenna said I was to wait here till you came," said Dexter quickly.

"Well, he's here now." Miss Jones smiled cheerfully at the caddy-master. Then she dropped her bag and set off at a haughty mince[5] toward the first tee.

110   "Well?" The caddy-master turned to Dexter. "What you standing there like a dummy for? Go pick up the young lady's clubs."

"I don't think I'll go out today," said Dexter.

"You don't—"

"I think I'll quit."

The enormity of his decision frightened him. He was a favorite caddy, and the thirty dollars a month he earned through the summer were not to be made elsewhere around the lake. But he had received a strong emotional shock, and his perturbation required a violent and immediate outlet.

It is not so simple as that, either. As so frequently would be the case in the

120   future, Dexter was unconsciously dictated to by his winter dreams.

II

Now, of course, the quality and the seasonability of these winter dreams varied, but the stuff of them remained. They persuaded Dexter several years later to pass up a business course at the State university—his father, prospering now, would have paid his way—for the **precarious** advantage of attending an older and more famous university in the East, where he was bothered by his scanty funds. But do not get the impression, because his winter dreams happened to be concerned at first with musings on the rich, that there was anything merely snobbish in the boy. He wanted not association with glittering things and glittering people—he wanted the glittering things themselves. Often he reached out for the best without

130   knowing why he wanted it—and sometimes he ran up against the mysterious denials and prohibitions in which life indulges. It is with one of those denials and not with his career as a whole that this story deals.

He made money. It was rather amazing. After college he went to the city from which Black Bear Lake draws its wealthy patrons. When he was only twenty-three and had been there not quite two years, there were already people who liked to say: "Now *there's* a boy—" All about him rich men's sons were peddling bonds precariously, or investing **patrimonies** precariously, or plodding through the two dozen volumes of the "George Washington Commercial Course," but Dexter

precarious (prĭ-kâr′ē-əs) *adj.* risky; uncertain

patrimony (păt′rə-mō′nē) *n.* estate or money inherited from ancestors

---

5. **at a haughty mince:** taking short, dainty steps in an arrogant, snobbish way.

Will STATUS *make you happy?*

Discuss In lines 115–120, how what ways does Dexter's decision to quit affect his status in Black Bear? *Possible answer: He will no longer have $30 a month to spend because such pay is unavailable elsewhere in town. In this regard, his decision lowers his status. On the other hand, he is pleased with himself for quitting and sees it as a step toward making his daydream of wealth a reality. This raises his status in his own eyes. Dexter has also protected his status in the eyes of Judy and Mr. Jones.*

TEXT ANALYSIS

COMMON CORE
RL 3

 MOTIVATION AND TRAITS

Possible answer: Dexter quits in order to rebel against the girl's arrogance, to maintain his dignity, and to uphold the self-image his daydreams define. His decision helps readers understand Dexter's sense of image and independence.

IF STUDENTS NEED HELP . . . Have them re-read lines 23–31 and 45–53. Point out that these lines describe Dexter's fantasies and suggest his goals.

VOCABULARY

COMMON CORE
L 4

OWN THE WORD

- **precarious:** Tell students that *precarious* refers to that which is "risky and uncertain" or being dangerously insecure or unstable. Ask students to complete the following sentence: "The hikers considered the path too *precarious. . .*" *Possible answer: to climb as they moved up the hill.*

- **patrimony:** *Patrimony* refers to an inheritance or legacy received from a father or ancestor. Have students list ideas that they have for use of a *patrimony*. *Possible answer: purchase a home, pay for college*

DIFFERENTIATED INSTRUCTION

FOR STRUGGLING READERS

Compare and Contrast Section II compares Dexter to the "rich men's sons" (line 136). Have students use a Venn Diagram to identify and organize the ways in which Dexter is like and unlike these other young men. Encourage them to refer and add to this diagram as they read on, exploring whether Dexter becomes more like the rich men's sons as time passes.

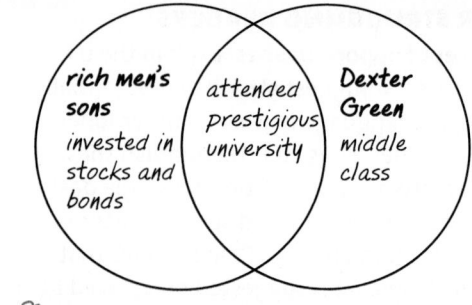
rich men's sons — invested in stocks and bonds; attended prestigious university; Dexter Green — middle class

🧰 **BEST PRACTICES TOOLKIT—Transparency**
Venn Diagram p. A26

Portrait of Marquess Sommi (1925), Tamara De Lempicka. Oil on canvas, 100 cm × 73 cm. Albert and Victoria Benalloul.
© 2007 Artists Rights Society (ARS), New York/ADAGP, Paris.

TIERED DISCUSSION PROMPTS

In lines 151–163, use these prompts to help students track the changes in Dexter's character as he enters the world of the wealthy:

Summarize What events lead to Dexter's first opportunity to play golf at the club? *Answer: A member, Mr. Hart, is impressed with Dexter's success and invites him as a guest at the club.*

Analyze How does Dexter feel when he first hits the fairway, and how do his feelings change during the day? *Possible answer: He feels at first like a "trespasser" (line 161). He wonders if he still has more in common with the caddies following him than with the other golfers (lines 157–159). His feelings quickly change as he sees himself as more worthy to be on the course than a long-time member (lines 161–163).*

Synthesize Given Dexter's upward mobility and his successful first game at the club, what will likely be his future relationship with the club? *Possible answer: Dexter will probably become a member of the club. He now has the money to be a member and has attracted the favor of influential members. In addition, he's developed a sense of belonging to the club, and he knows that rubbing shoulders with the members will support his plans for further success.*

Language Coach   COMMON CORE L 2a

Compound Numbers and Fractions *Answer: By the time she was twenty-five, she was spending two-thirds of her income on rent.*

---

borrowed a thousand dollars on his college degree and his confident mouth, and
140 bought a partnership in a laundry.

It was a small laundry when he went into it but Dexter made a specialty of learning how the English washed fine woolen golf-stockings without shrinking them, and within a year he was catering to the trade that wore knickerbockers.[6] Men were insisting that their Shetland hose and sweaters go to his laundry just as they had insisted on a caddy who could find golf-balls. A little later he was doing their wives' lingerie as well—and running five branches in different parts of the city. Before he was twenty-seven he owned the largest string of laundries in his section of the country. It was then that he sold out and went to New York. But the part of his story that concerns us goes back to the days when he was making his
150 first big success.

When he was twenty-three Mr. Hart—one of the gray-haired men who liked to say "Now there's a boy"—gave him a guest card to the Sherry Island Golf Club for a weekend. So he signed his name one day on the register, and that afternoon played golf in a foursome with Mr. Hart and Mr. Sandwood and Mr. T. A. Hedrick. He did not consider it necessary to remark that he had once carried Mr. Hart's bag over this same links, and that he knew every trap and gully with his eyes shut—but he found himself glancing at the four caddies who trailed them, trying to catch a gleam or gesture that would remind him of himself, that would lessen the gap which lay between his present and his past.

160   It was a curious day, slashed abruptly with fleeting, familiar impressions. One minute he had the sense of being a trespasser—in the next he was impressed by the tremendous superiority he felt toward Mr. T. A. Hedrick, who was a bore and not even a good golfer any more.

Then, because of a ball Mr. Hart lost near the fifteenth green, an enormous thing happened. While they were searching the stiff grasses of the rough there was a clear call of "Fore!" from behind a hill in their rear. And as they all turned abruptly from their search a bright new ball sliced abruptly over the hill and caught Mr. T. A. Hedrick in the abdomen.

"By Gad!" cried Mr. T. A. Hedrick, "they ought to put some of these crazy
170 women off the course. It's getting to be outrageous."

A head and a voice came up together over the hill:

"Do you mind if we go through?"

"You hit me in the stomach!" declared Mr. Hedrick wildly.

"Did I?" The girl approached the group of men. "I'm sorry. I yelled 'Fore!'"

Her glance fell casually on each of the men—then scanned the fairway for her ball.

"Did I bounce into the rough?"

It was impossible to determine whether this question was ingenuous or malicious. In a moment, however, she left no doubt, for as her partner came up
180 over the hill she called cheerfully:

"Here I am! I'd have gone on the green except that I hit something."

---

6. **knickerbockers:** loose pants that end in a gathering just below the knee and are worn with long socks. Formerly popular as golf wear.

3 Targeted Passage

COMMON CORE L 2a

Language Coach

Compound Numbers and Fractions Notice that the word *twenty-seven* in line 147 has a **hyphen** (-) in the middle that joins the two numbers. This is the normal convention for writing out the numbers twenty-one to ninety-nine as words. Hyphens are also used to connect the parts of a fraction when it's expressed in words: *One-half of the students went on a field trip that took up two-thirds of the school day.* With a partner, compose a sentence that includes a written out number and fraction that both require hyphens.

DIFFERENTIATED INSTRUCTION

FOR STRUGGLING READERS

3 Targeted Passage [Lines 141–159]

This passage explains how Dexter makes his first fortune to enter the world of wealth.

- What business makes Dexter wealthy? (line 141)
- What does Dexter do to ensure that his business will succeed? (lines 141–143)
- Who are Dexter's primary customers? (lines 143–146)
- How does his new wealth change Dexter's life? (lines 148–159)

FOR ENGLISH LANGUAGE LEARNERS

Related Words Share the meanings of these additional golf terms, and guide students to add them to the Personal Word List they began on page 980:

- *links* (line 156), "holes on a golf course"
- *trap* (line 156), "obstacle or hazard"
- *rough* (line 165), "area where the grass is allowed to grow high"

As she took her stance for a short mashie[7] shot, Dexter looked at her closely. She wore a blue gingham dress, rimmed at throat and shoulders with a white edging that accentuated her tan. The quality of exaggeration, of thinness, which had made her passionate eyes and down-turning mouth absurd at eleven, was gone now. She was arrestingly beautiful. The color in her cheeks was centered like the color in a picture—it was not a "high" color, but a sort of fluctuating and feverish warmth, so shaded that it seemed at any moment it would recede and disappear. This color and the mobility of her mouth gave a continual impression of **flux,** of intense life, of
190 passionate vitality—balanced only partially by the sad luxury of her eyes.

flux (flŭks): *n.* change

She swung her mashie impatiently and without interest, pitching the ball into a sand-pit on the other side of the green. With a quick, insincere smile and a careless "Thank you!" she went on after it.

"That Judy Jones!" remarked Mr. Hedrick on the next tee, as they waited—some moments—for her to play on ahead. "All she needs is to be turned up and spanked for six months and then to be married off to an old-fashioned cavalry captain."

"My God, she's good-looking!" said Mr. Sandwood, who was just over thirty.
"Good-looking!" cried Mr. Hedrick contemptuously, "she always looks as if she
200 wanted to be kissed! Turning those big cow-eyes on every calf in town!"

It was doubtful if Mr. Hedrick intended a reference to the maternal instinct.

"She'd play pretty good golf if she'd try," said Mr. Sandwood.

"She has no form," said Mr. Hedrick solemnly.

"She has a nice figure," said Mr. Sandwood.

"Better thank the Lord she doesn't drive a swifter ball," said Mr. Hart, winking at Dexter.

Later in the afternoon the sun went down with a riotous swirl of gold and varying blues and scarlets, and left the dry, rustling night of Western summer. Dexter watched from the veranda of the Golf Club, watched the even overlap
210 of the waters in the little wind, silver molasses under the harvest-moon. Then the moon held a finger to her lips and the lake became a clear pool, pale and quiet. Dexter put on his bathing-suit and swam out to the farthest raft, where he stretched dripping on the wet canvas of the springboard.

There was a fish jumping and a star shining and the lights around the lake were gleaming. Over on a dark peninsula a piano was playing the songs of last summer and of summers before that—songs from "Chin-Chin" and "The Count of Luxemburg" and "The Chocolate Soldier"[8]—and because the sound of a piano over a stretch of water had always seemed beautiful to Dexter he lay perfectly quiet and listened.

220 The tune the piano was playing at that moment had been gay and new five years before when Dexter was a sophomore at college. They had played it at a prom once when he could not afford the luxury of proms, and he had stood

 MOTIVATION AND TRAITS
Reread lines 171–193. What **character** traits are revealed by the description of Judy and her actions? Support your response with evidence from the story.

---

7. **mashie:** an old name for the golf club now known as a five iron.
8. **"Chin-Chin" . . . "The Chocolate Soldier":** three popular Broadway musicals, first performed in 1914, 1912, and 1909, respectively.

WINTER DREAMS   985

- *Fore!* (line 166), "a word shouted to warn other golfers that a ball is headed their way"
- *sliced* (line 167), "hit such that it followed a curving path, perhaps by mistake"
- *go through* (line 172), "move ahead of the other group on the course"
- *green* (line 181), "closely mown area at the end of each hole, in which the hole for the ball is located"

FOR ADVANCED LEARNERS/AP

Analyze Indirect Characterization Fitzgerald characterizes Judy directly, by describing her, and indirectly, by showing the reactions of other characters. Have partners review lines 194–206 and then have each write a character sketch of Judy, one from Mr. Hendrick's reaction and one from Mr. Sandwood's reaction.

 BEST PRACTICES TOOLKIT—Transparency
Character Traits and Textual Evidence
p. D6

TEXT ANALYSIS   COMMON CORE   RL 3

E MOTIVATION AND TRAITS

Possible answer: *Judy is confident to the point of arrogance, self-absorbed, beautiful, animated, and insincere, willing to say anything to get what she wants (lines 172–181).*

IF STUDENTS NEED HELP . . . Help them complete a Character Traits and Textual Evidence organizer about Judy.

BEST PRACTICES TOOLKIT—Transparency
Character Traits and Textual Evidence
p. D6

REVISIT THE BIG QUESTION
Will STATUS *make you happy?*

Discuss In lines 207–219, what images of luxury and status does Fitzgerald use to evoke the relaxed and pampered lifestyle of the club members?
Possible answer: *Fitzgerald uses vivid color imagery, such as gold, blue, and scarlet, to describe the natural beauty that club members enjoy from their view on the veranda. In addition, he describes a private dock on a lake that is well lit and equipped for swimming and boating. Finally, he shows that the members are entertained by live music and have time to enjoy the club's amenities, as Dexter does during his swim.*

VOCABULARY   COMMON CORE   L 4

OWN THE WORD

flux: Tell students that *flux* connotes fluidity and transformation. Have students write a sentence about a time when they experienced *flux* in their lives. ***Possible answer:*** *moving to a new town, or starting at a new school*

WINTER DREAMS   985

outside the gymnasium and listened. The sound of the tune **precipitated** in him a sort of ecstasy and it was with that ecstasy he viewed what happened to him now. It was a mood of intense appreciation, a sense that, for once, he was magnificently attuned to life and that everything about him was radiating a brightness and a glamour he might never know again.

precipitate
(prĭ-sĭp′ĭ-tāt′) *v.* to bring about, especially abruptly

230 A low, pale oblong detached itself suddenly from the darkness of the Island, spitting forth the reverberated sound of a racing motor-boat. Two white streamers of cleft water rolled themselves out behind it and almost immediately the boat was beside him, drowning out the hot tinkle of the piano in the drone of its spray. Dexter raising himself on his arms was aware of a figure standing at the wheel, of two dark eyes regarding him over the lengthening space of water—then the boat had gone by and was sweeping in an immense and purposeless circle of spray round and round in the middle of the lake. With equal eccentricity one of the circles flattened out and headed back toward the raft.

"Who's that?" she called, shutting off her motor. She was so near now that Dexter could see her bathing-suit, which consisted apparently of pink rompers.[9]

240 The nose of the boat bumped the raft, and as the latter tilted rakishly he was precipitated toward her. With different degrees of interest they recognized each other.

"Aren't you one of those men we played through this afternoon?" she demanded.

He was.

"Well, do you know how to drive a motor-boat? Because if you do I wish you'd drive this one so I can ride on the surf-board behind. My name is Judy Jones"— she favored him with an absurd smirk—rather, what tried to be a smirk, for, twist her mouth as she might, it was not grotesque, it was merely beautiful—"and I live in a house over there on the Island, and in that house there is a man waiting for

250 me. When he drove up at the door I drove out of the dock because he says I'm his ideal." **G**

There was a fish jumping and a star shining and the lights around the lake were gleaming. Dexter sat beside Judy Jones and she explained how her boat was driven. Then she was in the water, swimming to the floating surf-board with a sinuous crawl. Watching her was without effort to the eye, watching a branch waving or a sea-gull flying. Her arms, burned to butternut, moved sinuously among the dull platinum ripples, elbow appearing first, casting the forearm back with a cadence of falling water, then reaching out and down, stabbing a path ahead.

They moved out into the lake; turning, Dexter saw that she was kneeling on

260 the low rear of the now uptilted surf-board.

"Go faster," she called, "fast as it'll go."

Obediently he jammed the level forward and the white spray mounted at the bow. When he looked around again the girl was standing up on the rushing board, her arms spread wide, her eyes lifted toward the moon.

"It's awful cold," she shouted. "What's your name?"

G MOTIVATION AND TRAITS
Do you think Judy has changed since Dexter first encountered her on the golf course years before? Cite **details** and **dialogue** to support your conclusion.

---

9. **rompers:** a loose-fitting one-piece garment with bloomer like pants.

TIERED DISCUSSION PROMPTS

In lines 242–264, use these prompts to help students recognize Judy's expectations of Dexter:

Analyze In this meeting, what does Judy assume about Dexter and his usefulness to her? *Possible answer: Judy assumes that, even though she hardly knows him, Dexter will be at her service to get her whatever she needs.*

Evaluate How effective is Fitzgerald's language in showing that Judy has the upper hand in this new friendship? Explain. *Possible answer: Fitzgerald's language is very effective in demonstrating Judy's control. Before she knows Dexter's name, she wants him to tow her on the surf-board (lines 245–246). She gives her name, but does not ask for his (line 246). She orders him to "Go faster" (line 261) and he responds "obediently" (line 262) without question. The image of her standing regally on the surfboard (lines 263–264) communicates her queenly control of everything around her.*

TEXT ANALYSIS | COMMON CORE **RL 3**

G MOTIVATION AND TRAITS

Possible answer: Judy has not changed. She neither notices nor cares about the results of her behavior; she attempts to cheat to impress her fellow golfers. She remains as spoiled and insincere as she was as a child.

IF STUDENTS NEED HELP . . . Refer them to lines 47–103, which describe young Judy.

VOCABULARY | COMMON CORE **L 4**

OWN THE WORD

precipitate: There are various definitions for *precipitate* including "to bring about abruptly," "to throw from a great height," and "to condense and fall from the air as in rain, snow." Ask students to show the sense in which the author used *precipitate* in the passage. *Possible answer: The music abruptly made him feel ecstatically happy and attuned to life.*

DIFFERENTIATED INSTRUCTION

FOR STRUGGLING READERS

Clarify Meaning Explain the meaning of lines 283–286 by clarifying that Dexter's mother is an immigrant who embarrassed him by never learning to speak English fluently. As a result, Dexter tries to follow customs carefully so he will not appear as an outsider like his mother. Work with students to help them recognize that Dexter believes his children will be able to behave "carelessly" because their father fits in so seamlessly. Then broaden the discussion by pointing out that Dexter could instead have taken pride in his mother's ability to speak two languages. Ask students to consider the challenge immigrants face in maintaining a home language in an English-speaking society. Invite English learners to participate.

He told her.

"Well, why don't you come to dinner tomorrow night?"

His heart turned over like the fly-wheel of the boat, and, for the second time, her casual whim gave a new direction to his life.

III

270 Next evening while he waited for her to come downstairs, Dexter peopled the soft deep summer room and the sun-porch that opened from it with the men who had already loved Judy Jones. He knew the sort of men they were—the men who when he first went to college had entered from the great prep schools with graceful clothes and the deep tan of healthy summers. He had seen that, in one sense, he was better than these men. He was newer and stronger. Yet in acknowledging to himself that he wished his children to be like them he was admitting that he was but the rough, strong stuff from which they eternally sprang.

When the time had come for him to wear good clothes, he had known who were the best tailors in America, and the best tailors in America had made him the 280 suit he wore this evening. He had acquired that particular reserve peculiar to his university, that set it off from other universities. He recognized the value to him of such a mannerism and he had adopted it; he knew that to be careless in dress and manner required more confidence than to be careful. But carelessness was for his children. His mother's name had been Krimslich. She was a Bohemian of the peasant class and she had talked broken English to the end of her days. Her son must keep to the set patterns.

At a little after seven Judy Jones came downstairs. She wore a blue silk afternoon dress, and he was disappointed at first that she had not put on something more elaborate. This feeling was accentuated when, after a brief 290 greeting, she went to the door of a butler's pantry and pushing it open called: "You can serve dinner, Martha." He had rather expected that a butler would announce dinner, that there would be a cocktail. Then he put these thoughts behind him as they sat down side by side on a lounge and looked at each other.

"Father and mother won't be here," she said thoughtfully.

He remembered the last time he had seen her father, and he was glad the parents were not to be here tonight—they might wonder who he was. He had been born in Keeble, a Minnesota village fifty miles farther north, and he always gave Keeble as his home instead of Black Bear Village. Country towns were well enough to come from if they weren't inconveniently in sight and used as footstools 300 by fashionable lakes. **G**

They talked of his university, which she had visited frequently during the past two years, and of the near-by city which supplied Sherry Island with its patrons, and whither Dexter would return next day to his prospering laundries.

During dinner she slipped into a moody depression which gave Dexter a feeling of uneasiness. Whatever **petulance** she uttered in her throaty voice worried him. Whatever she smiled at—at him, at a chicken liver, at nothing—it disturbed him

---

Language Coach

Word Analysis Read lines 274–277. What contrast is Dexter making in his mind? What words show you that ideas are being contrasted?

---

④ Targeted Passage

G MOTIVATION AND TRAITS

Reread lines 270–300. **Summarize** Dexter's ideas about social class and the status it confers. How does Dexter see himself? To what does he aspire?

---

petulance (pĕch′ə-ləns) *n.* ill temper; annoyance

In lines 312–331, use these prompts to help students consider what motivates Judy as she dates men:

Connect How do you feel about Judy at this point in the story? What sort of behavior do you expect from her? *Students will likely say that they don't like Judy and that they expect her to behave badly.*

Interpret Is Judy being honest when she says that she could marry a poor man? Explain. *Possible answer: Judy is probably deceiving both Dexter and herself about her capacity to marry a poor man. She seems interested in poor men as novelties (lines 319–320) but is likely too accustomed to wealth to actually marry one. She is clearly very interested in her suitors' finances so her story about the poor suitor may be a play to learn about Dexter's finances. After all, when Dexter reports that he is wealthy, she smiles and kisses him as if this is what she wanted to hear (lines 330–331).*

Synthesize How has Fitzgerald hinted at Judy's fickleness earlier in the text? In what way does this technique shape readers' expectations about Dexter's interaction with Judy? *Possible answer: Fitzgerald has hinted at Judy's fickleness by foreshadowing her beauty and its effects on many men (lines 47–53, 78–80, 199–200). The technique shapes readers' expectations by suggesting that Judy cannot and will not be faithful to Dexter.*

VOCABULARY
COMMON CORE L 4

OWN THE WORD

- **mundane:** Ask students to make a list of things they may find *mundane*. *Possible answers: making meals, cleaning rooms, brushing teeth, doing yard work*

- **surfeit:** Have students create a semantic web for *surfeit*. Write the word in the center circle along with the given definition, "fullness beyond satisfaction." Draw spider legs out from the center circle and have students use a thesaurus to find appropriate synonyms to complete the web. *Possible answers: embarrassment, excess, exorbitance, extravagance, overabundance, overindulgence*

---

that her smile could have no root in mirth, or even in amusement. When the scarlet corners of her lips curved down, it was less a smile than an invitation to a kiss.

Then, after dinner, she led him out on the dark sun-porch and deliberately
310 changed the atmosphere.

"Do you mind if I weep a little?" she said.

"I'm afraid I'm boring you," he responded quickly.

"You're not. I like you. But I've just had a terrible afternoon. There was a man I cared about, and this afternoon he told me out of a clear sky that he was poor as a church-mouse. He'd never even hinted it before. Does this sound horribly **mundane?**"

"Perhaps he was afraid to tell you."

"Suppose he was," she answered. "He didn't start right. You see, if I'd thought of him as poor—well, I've been mad about loads of poor men, and fully intended
320 to marry them all. But in this case, I hadn't thought of him that way, and my interest in him wasn't strong enough to survive the shock. As if a girl calmly informed her fiancé that she was a widow. He might not object to widows, but—"

"Let's start right," she interrupted herself suddenly. "Who are you, anyhow?"

For a moment Dexter hesitated. Then:

"I'm nobody," he announced. "My career is largely a matter of futures."

"Are you poor?"

"No," he said frankly, "I'm probably making more money than any man my age in the Northwest. I know that's an obnoxious remark, but you advised me to start right."

330 There was a pause. Then she smiled and the corners of her mouth drooped and an almost imperceptible sway brought her closer to him, looking up into his eyes. A lump rose in Dexter's throat, and he waited breathless for the experiment, facing the unpredictable compound that would form mysteriously from the elements of their lips. Then he saw—she communicated her excitement to him, lavishly, deeply, with kisses that were not a promise but a fulfillment. They aroused in him not hunger demanding renewal but **surfeit** that would demand more surfeit . . . kisses that were like charity, creating want by holding back nothing at all.

It did not take him many hours to decide that he had wanted Judy Jones ever since he was a proud, desirous little boy.

IV

340 It began like that—and continued, with varying shades of intensity, on such a note right up to the dénouement. Dexter surrendered a part of himself to the most direct and unprincipled personality with which he had ever come in contact. Whatever Judy wanted, she went after with the full pressure of her charm. There was no divergence of method, no jockeying for position or premeditation of effects—there was a very little mental side to any of her affairs. She simply made men conscious to the highest degree of her physical loveliness. Dexter had no desire to change her. Her deficiencies were knit up with a passionate energy that transcended and justified them.

mundane (mŭn-dān') *adj.* characteristic of or concerned with the ordinary

surfeit (sûr′fĭt) *n.* a fullness beyond the point of satisfaction

---

DIFFERENTIATED INSTRUCTION

FOR STRUGGLING READERS

Develop Reading Fluency Use the exchange between Dexter and Judy in lines 311–329 to give students practice in reading dialogue. Remind them that dialogue represents a conversation between people. Model with a proficient reader how to read dialogue with expression and attention to punctuation, omitting narration. Then have mixed-ability pairs practice reading aloud the same dialogue.

FOR ENGLISH LANGUAGE LEARNERS

Vocabulary: Idioms [mixed-readiness groups] Share or elicit the meanings of these expressions, and then help students find similar expressions in their home languages:

- *out of a clear sky* (line 314), "unexpectedly"
- *poor as a church mouse* (lines 314–315), "very poor"
- *mad about* (line 319), "liked very much"
- *jockeying for position* (line 344), "careful planning"

When, as Judy's head lay against his shoulder that first night, she whispered, "I
350 don't know what's the matter with me. Last night I thought I was in love with a
man and tonight I think I'm in love with you—"—it seemed to him a beautiful
and romantic thing to say. It was the exquisite excitability that for the moment he
controlled and owned. But a week later he was compelled to view this same quality
in a different light. She took him in her roadster[10] to a picnic supper, and after
supper she disappeared, likewise in her roadster, with another man. Dexter became
enormously upset and was scarcely able to be decently civil to the other people
present. When she assured him that she had not kissed the other man, he knew she
was lying—yet he was glad that she had taken the trouble to lie to him. ⓗ

He was, as he found before the summer ended, one of a varying dozen who
360 circulated about her. Each of them had at one time been favored above all
others—about half of them still basked in the solace of occasional sentimental

---

10. **roadster:** a sporty, two-seat, open automobile.

Young Woman in Green (1927), Tamara de Lempicka. Musée National d'Art Moderne, Centre
Georges Pompidou, Paris. © CNAC/MNAM/Dist. Réunion des Musées Nationaux/Art Resource,
New York. © 2007 Artists Rights Society (ARS), New York/ADAGP, Paris.

WINTER DREAMS   **989**

ⓗ **MOTIVATION AND
TRAITS**
Reread lines 340–358.
Dexter's thoughts
convey information
about Judy, but they
also reveal much about
Dexter himself. Explain
what you learn about
him from these lines.

TEXT ANALYSIS   COMMON
                  CORE

                  RL 3

ⓗ *Model the Skill:*
MOTIVATION AND TRAITS

Help students identify and interpret Dexter's motivations and traits. Point out that
Dexter has fallen for Judy, as evidenced by
his excitement when she tells him, "Last
night I thought I was in love with a man
and tonight I think I'm in love with you"
(lines 351–352). Ask students what part of
this statement Dexter chooses to ignore
(the part about another man). **Possible
answer:** *Dexter distorts what Judy tells him
so he can stay infatuated with her, such as
when he focuses not on Judy's leaving with
another man and kissing him, but her taking
"the trouble to lie" about it.*

Extend the Discussion What will probably
happen between Dexter and Judy as their
relationship progresses? Why?

Analyze Visuals

Activity Ask students what elements of
Judy's character and appearance are reflected
in this artwork and how the work helps
them understand Judy's effect on Dexter.
Possible answers: *Judy's scarlet lips, piercing
eyes, lithe figure, and style make her similar to
the woman in the portrait. The artwork helps
readers visualize vividly the charms and allure
for which Dexter "surrendered a part
of himself" (line 341).*

About the Art Tamara de Lempicka's artworks
on pages 983, 989, and 993 all reflect the
groundbreaking Art Deco style, which arose
in Paris during the 1920s. Deco artists imbued
everything from fine art to home furnishings
with the clean, streamlined look of modern
machines. Like Dexter Green, the artists were
drawn to sleek images of wealth and fashion
and tried to introduce them to the masses.

FOR ADVANCED LEARNERS/AP

Analyze Theme [paired option] Have
students debate Dexter's claim that Judy's
"deficiencies were knit up with a passionate energy that transcended and justified
them" (lines 347–348), echoing his earlier
"monstrous conviction" that Judy's attack on
her nurse was "justified" (lines 102–103). As
students develop their arguments, urge them
to consider these factors:

- the grounds on which Dexter justifies
  Judy's actions
- Dexter's biases about Judy
- the idea that beauty, wealth, privilege,
  or "passionate energy" can justify bad
  behavior

After completing the debate, ask students to
use the activity to help them draw conclusions and generate a theme statement for
the story.

revivals. Whenever one showed signs of dropping out through long neglect, she granted him a brief honeyed hour, which encouraged him to tag along for a year or so longer. Judy made these forays upon the helpless and defeated without malice, indeed half unconscious that there was anything mischievous in what she did.

When a new man came to town every one dropped out—dates were automatically canceled.

The helpless part of trying to do anything about it was that she did it all herself. She was not a girl who could be "won" in the kinetic sense—she was proof against
370 cleverness, she was proof against charm; if any of these assailed her too strongly she would immediately resolve the affair to a physical basis, and under the magic of her physical splendor the strong as well as the brilliant played her game and not their own. She was entertained only by the gratification of her desires and by the direct exercise of her own charm. Perhaps from so much youthful love, so many youthful lovers, she had come, in self-defense, to nourish herself wholly from within. ❶

Succeeding Dexter's first exhilaration came restlessness and dissatisfaction. The helpless ecstasy of losing himself in her was opiate rather than tonic.[11] It was fortunate for his work during the winter that those moments of ecstasy came infrequently. Early in their acquaintance it had seemed for a while that there was
380 a deep and spontaneous mutual attraction—that first August, for example—three days of long evenings on her dusky veranda, of strange wan kisses through the late afternoon, in shadowy alcoves or behind the protecting trellises of the garden arbors, of mornings when she was fresh as a dream and almost shy at meeting him in the clarity of the rising day. There was all the ecstasy of an engagement about it, sharpened by his realization that there was no engagement. It was during those three days that, for the first time, he had asked her to marry him. She said "maybe some day," she said "kiss me," she said "I'd like to marry you," she said "I love you"—she said—nothing.

The three days were interrupted by the arrival of a New York man who visited
390 at her house for half September. To Dexter's agony, rumor engaged them. The man was the son of the president of a great trust company. But at the end of a month it was reported that Judy was yawning. At a dance one night she sat all evening in a motor-boat with a local beau, while the New Yorker searched the club for her frantically. She told the local beau that she was bored with her visitor, and two days later he left. She was seen with him at the station, and it was reported that he looked very mournful indeed.

On this note the summer ended. Dexter was twenty-four, and he found himself increasingly in a position to do as he wished. He joined two clubs in the city and lived at one of them. Though he was by no means an integral part of the stag-lines
400 at these clubs, he managed to be on hand at dances where Judy Jones was likely to appear. He could have gone out socially as much as he liked—he was an eligible young man, now, and popular with downtown fathers. His confessed devotion to Judy Jones had rather solidified his position. But he had no social aspirations and rather despised the dancing men who were always on tap for the Thursday

---

11. **opiate . . . tonic:** deadening rather than stimulating.

❶ **MOTIVATION AND TRAITS**
Consider characters or people you've encountered who are similar to Judy Jones. What might **motivate** Judy to act as she does? Cite details you used to draw this **conclusion**.

TEXT ANALYSIS

❶ **MOTIVATION AND TRAITS**

Accept all thoughtful responses. Students should accurately characterize Judy and support their conclusions with textual evidence.

REVISIT THE BIG QUESTION

Will STATUS *make you happy?*

Discuss In lines 389–396, what about the status of the New York man makes him a greater threat to Dexter's hope than Judy's other beaus? What does Judy's reaction to this man suggest about her view of status? *Possible answers: The New York man has excellent credentials for wooing Judy. He is the son of "the president of a great trust company" (line 391), so he outranks Judy's other suitors. However, Judy is bored by this man (line 392), which suggests that despite her attachment to status and wealth, it is not enough on its own to hold her interest.*

990 UNIT 5

DIFFERENTIATED INSTRUCTION

FOR ENGLISH LANGUAGE LEARNERS
Vocabulary Support [paired option] Recall with students the many words Fitzgerald uses to describe Judy's character, and help students identify additional words from pages 990–991. Have student pairs list these words in a T Chart along with the words Fitzgerald uses to describe Irene in lines 413–414 and 442–443. Guide students to see that the two lists of words contrast sharply, as do the characters. Be sure that students can define any words they list.

Judy is . . .	Irene is . . .
haughty (line 109)	sweet (line 413)
arrestingly beautiful (line 186)	a little stout (line 414)
easily bored (lines 392–395)	knowledgeable about books and music (lines 442–443)

 **BEST PRACTICES TOOLKIT**—Transparency
T Chart p. A25

or Saturday parties and who filled in at dinners with the younger married set. Already he was playing with the idea of going East to New York. He wanted to take Judy Jones with him. No disillusion as to the world in which she had grown up could cure his illusion as to her desirability.

Remember that—for only in the light of it can what he did for her be
410 understood.

Eighteen months after he first met Judy Jones he became engaged to another girl. Her name was Irene Scheerer, and her father was one of the men who had always believed in Dexter. Irene was light-haired and sweet and honorable, and a little stout, and she had two suitors whom she pleasantly relinquished when Dexter formally asked her to marry him.

Summer, fall, winter, spring, another summer, another fall—so much he had given of his active life to the incorrigible lips of Judy Jones. She had treated him with interest, with encouragement, with malice, with indifference, with contempt. She had inflicted on him the innumerable little slights and indignities possible
420 in such a case—as if in revenge for having ever cared for him at all. She had beckoned him and yawned at him and beckoned him again and he had responded often with bitterness and narrowed eyes. She had brought him ecstatic happiness and intolerable agony of spirit. She had caused him untold inconvenience and not a little trouble. She had insulted him, and she had ridden over him, and she had played his interest in her against his interest in his work—for fun. She had done everything to him except to criticize him—this she had not done—it seemed to him only because it might have sullied the utter indifference she manifested and sincerely felt toward him. **J**

When autumn had come and gone again it occurred to him that he could not
430 have Judy Jones. He had to beat this into his mind but he convinced himself at last. He lay awake at night for a while and argued it over. He told himself the trouble and the pain she had caused him, he enumerated her glaring deficiencies as a wife. Then he said to himself that he loved her, and after a while he fell asleep. For a week, lest he imagine her husky voice over the telephone or her eyes opposite him at lunch, he worked hard and late, and at night he went to his office and plotted out his years.

At the end of a week he went to a dance and cut in on her once. For almost the first time since they had met he did not ask her to sit out with him or tell her that she was lovely. It hurt him that she did not miss these things—that was all.
440 He was not jealous when he saw that there was a new man tonight. He had been hardened against jealousy long before. **K**

He stayed late at the dance. He sat for an hour with Irene Scheerer and talked about books and about music. He knew very little about either. But he was beginning to be master of his own time now, and he had a rather priggish notion that he—the young and already fabulously successful Dexter Green—should know more about such things.

That was in October, when he was twenty-five. In January, Dexter and Irene became engaged. It was to be announced in June, and they were to be married three months later.

J GRAMMAR AND STYLE
Reread lines 416–428. Fitzgerald's long sentences, held together by the **coordinating conjunction** *and* and broken up by **dashes,** convey Dexter's perplexed thoughts about Judy's behavior.

5 Targeted Passage

K THEME
How does Dexter's response to this autumn compare with his reactions to the season at the beginning of the story? What theme in the story is suggested by the change in Dexter?

J GRAMMAR AND STYLE COMMON CORE L 2 L 3a

Craft Effective Sentences Point out that Fitzgerald's careful choice of punctuation in this paragraph reinforces the internal argument Dexter has over whether to give up Judy. Ask volunteers to read the paragraph aloud dramatically, using the coordinating conjunctions and dashes to set the pace and intensity. Help students hear the effect of what Fitzgerald has written into these lines. Have them discuss the impact of Fitzgerald's use of dashes (lines 505–508) and the use of the conjunction *and* (lines 679–683).

TEXT ANALYSIS: *Review* COMMON CORE RL 2

K THEME

Possible answer: *When he was a boy, he observed the subtleties of the season. Fall brought him hope that something good was coming and he invested the season with visions of his future (lines 17–31). Now, however, autumn has merely "come and gone again" (line 429) without his notice, he feels hopeless because he cannot secure Judy's love, and he now he feels the impossibility of those visions. Accept all thoughtful statements about theme.*

FOR STRUGGLING READERS

5 Targeted Passage [Lines 429–443]

This passage records Dexter's slow and reluctant change of heart about Judy.

- What does Dexter convince himself about Judy? How does he accomplish his goal? (lines 429–436)

- How does Judy respond? (line 439)

- What possibility for Dexter arises because of his decision about Judy? (lines 442–443)

FOR ADVANCED LEARNERS/AP

Analyze Style Have students analyze Judy's responses to Dexter's marriage proposals (lines 385–388). Students should rate each response on how encouraging or discouraging it is, then chart the responses on a Line Plot. Have students use their graphs to lead a class discussion about Judy's motivation and how her evasions affect readers.

 **BEST PRACTICES TOOLKIT—Transparency** Graphic Aids: Line Plots p. A64

 PREDICT

Possible answer: *Dexter recalls metaphors that compare a "penny's worth of happiness" (line 463) with Dexter's love for Judy and a "bushel of content" (line 464) with his affection for Irene. These comparisons suggest that his feelings for Irene are less passionate, yet more constant, than his mad love for the unpredictable Judy. These clues suggest that Dexter will be kind to Irene and appreciative of her support but never be truly in love with her.*

TIERED DISCUSSION PROMPTS

In lines 470–485, use these prompts to help students explore the relationship between the Scheerers and Dexter:

Recall What did Irene's father think of Dexter before their engagement? *Answer: Irene's father supported and admired Dexter (lines 412–413).*

Analyze Is Fitzgerald's language when speaking of the Scheerers generally positive or negative? Explain. Why does this family seem a second-best choice for Dexter? *Possible answer: Fitzgerald's language is consistently positive in describing the Scheerers. The parents are encouraging and friendly. Irene is popular, stable, and gracious. Yet the family seems bland in contrast with the passion that Judy inspires.*

Synthesize What kind of relationship can Dexter and Irene expect to have, with each other and with her parents? Will this life satisfy Dexter? Explain. *Possible answer: Dexter and Irene can expect a pleasant, calm, rather uneventful family life. Dexter is friends with Irene and her parents. This quiet, comfortable life will not satisfy Dexter for long. His winter dreams of growth and change will resurface.*

450　The Minnesota winter prolonged itself interminably, and it was almost May when the winds came soft and the snow ran down into Black Bear Lake at last. For the first time in over a year Dexter was enjoying a certain tranquillity of spirit. Judy Jones had been in Florida, and afterward in Hot Springs,[12] and somewhere she had been engaged, and somewhere she had broken it off. At first, when Dexter had definitely given her up, it had made him sad that people still linked them together and asked for news of her, but when he began to be placed at dinner next to Irene Scheerer people didn't ask him about her any more—they told him about her. He ceased to be an authority on her.

　　May at last. Dexter walked the streets at night when the darkness was damp 460 as rain, wondering that so soon, with so little done, so much of ecstasy had gone from him. May one year back had been marked by Judy's poignant, unforgivable, yet forgiven turbulence—it had been one of those rare times when he fancied she had grown to care for him. That old penny's worth of happiness he had spent for this bushel of content. He knew that Irene would be no more than a curtain spread behind him, a hand moving among gleaming tea-cups, a voice calling to children . . . fire and loveliness were gone, the magic of nights and the wonder of the varying hours and seasons . . . slender lips, downturning, dropping to his lips and bearing him up into a heaven of eyes. . . . The thing was deep in him. He was too strong and alive for it to die lightly. **L**

470　In the middle of May when the weather balanced for a few days on the thin bridge that led to deep summer he turned in one night at Irene's house. Their engagement was to be announced in a week now—no one would be surprised at it. And tonight they would sit together on the lounge at the University Club and look on for an hour at the dancers. It gave him a sense of solidity to go with her—she was so sturdily popular, so intensely "great."

　　He mounted the steps of the brownstone house and stepped inside.

　　"Irene," he called.

　　Mrs. Scheerer came out of the living-room to meet him.

　　"Dexter," she said, "Irene's gone upstairs with a splitting headache. She wanted 480 to go with you but I made her go to bed."

　　"Nothing serious, I—"

　　"Oh, no. She's going to play golf with you in the morning. You can spare her for just one night, can't you, Dexter?"

　　Her smile was kind. She and Dexter liked each other. In the living-room he talked for a moment before he said good night.

　　Returning to the University Club, where he had rooms, he stood in the doorway for a moment and watched the dancers. He leaned against the door-post, nodded at a man or two—yawned.

　　"Hello, darling."

490　The familiar voice at his elbow startled him. Judy Jones had left a man and crossed the room to him—Judy Jones, a slender enameled doll in cloth of gold: gold in a band at her head, gold in two slipper points at her dress's hem. The fragile glow of her face seemed to blossom as she smiled at him. A breeze of

---

12. **Hot Springs:** a spa city in west-central Arkansas.

L PREDICT
Identify the **metaphors** that come to Dexter's mind with regard to Irene. What do they suggest about his feelings toward her? Predict how Dexter will treat Irene in the future. Cite text clues that helped you make this guess.

DIFFERENTIATED INSTRUCTION

FOR STRUGGLING READERS

Comprehension Support Explain that Fitzgerald uses the seasons as symbols for Dexter's hopes and loves. Guide students to link the chilly, wet May with Dexter's affection for Irene and to note that the shift to "deep summer" (line 471) relates to Judy's return to Black Bear. Also point out the bridge imagery raised in line 471. The season will cross a fragile bridge, as will Dexter when Judy returns.

FOR ENGLISH LANGUAGE LEARNERS

Vocabulary Support Fitzgerald's language contrasts Dexter's planned life with Irene and his dreamed-of life with Judy. Point out contrasts such as *tranquillity* (line 452) and *unforgivable* (line 461), or *solidity* (line 474) and *turbulence* (line 462). Help students identify others in lines 475 and 495–499. Guide students to list the words in a T Chart.

 BEST PRACTICES TOOLKIT—Transparency
T Chart p. A25

warmth and light blew through the room. His hands in the pockets of his dinner-jacket tightened spasmodically. He was filled with a sudden excitement.

"When did you get back?" he asked casually.

"Come here and I'll tell you about it."

She turned and he followed her. She had been away—he could have wept at the wonder of her return. She had passed through enchanted streets, doing things that were like provocative music. All mysterious happenings, all fresh and quickening hopes, had gone away with her, come back with her now.

She turned in the doorway.

"Have you a car here? If you haven't, I have."

"I have a coupé."

In then, with a rustle of golden cloth. He slammed the door. Into so many cars she had stepped—like this—like that—her back against the leather, so—her elbow resting on the door—waiting. She would have been soiled long since had there been anything to soil her—except herself—but this was her own self-outpouring.

◀ **Analyze Visuals**
Tamara De Lempicka's posterlike oil paintings are often described as dramatic and aggressive. How does this description fit this particular painting? Explain, citing details.

Autoportrait (1925), Tamara De Lempicka. Oil on wood, 35 cm × 26 cm. Private collection. © 2007 Artists Rights Society (ARS), New York/ADAGP, Paris.

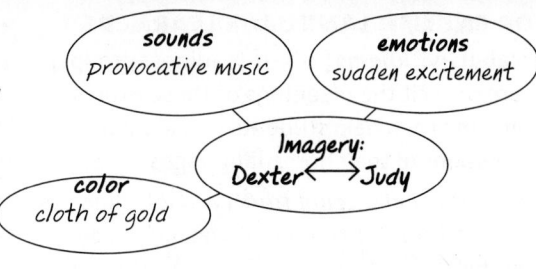

In lines 509–548, use these prompts to help students track Dexter's weakening resistance to Judy:

Summarize What happens in these lines?
Possible answer: Dexter gives Judy a ride in his car, and she flirts with him and flatters him.

Analyze At what points in this awkward conversation does Dexter try to keep Judy's past behavior in mind, and to what effect?
Possible answer: In lines 509–511, Dexter assures himself that Judy's attentions are "nothing" and that he "had put her behind him." In lines 528–529 he recognizes her empty flattery but feels it nonetheless. In line 533 he becomes "confused" by Judy's words and can't respond rationally. In lines 547–548 he lets down his guard enough to wonder if Judy has changed.

Synthesize Why are lines 547–548, Dexter's last stated resistance, written as questions rather than statements? What prediction do these questions invite from readers?
Possible answer: Lines 547–548 are written as questions to show that Dexter's resistance to Judy is beginning to crumble. He no longer tells himself to stay out of danger, but now doubts the conclusions that he so painfully reached earlier. These questions invite readers to predict that Judy will achieve this latest conquest over Dexter, as she has achieved many times in the past.

VOCABULARY COMMON CORE L 4

OWN THE WORD

camaraderie: Point out that the root for *camaraderie* comes from the French word *camarade* meaning "comrade or roommate" and connotes fellowship among friends. Ask students to list relationships in their lives where they experience *camaraderie*.
Possible answers: relationships with parents, siblings, best friends, classmates, neighbors

---

510 With an effort he forced himself to start the car and back into the street. This was nothing, he must remember. She had done this before, and he had put her behind him, as he would have crossed a bad account from his books.

He drove slowly downtown and, affecting abstraction,[13] traversed the deserted streets of the business section, peopled here and there where a movie was giving out its crowd or where consumptive or pugilistic[14] youth lounged in front of pool halls. The clink of glasses and the slap of hands on the bars issued from saloons, cloisters[15] of glazed glass and dirty yellow light.

She was watching him closely and the silence was embarrassing, yet in this crisis he could find no casual word with which to profane the hour. At a convenient turning he began to zigzag back toward the University Club.

520 "Have you missed me?" she asked suddenly.

"Everybody missed you."

He wondered if she knew of Irene Scheerer. She had been back only a day—her absence had been almost contemporaneous with his engagement.

"What a remark!" Judy laughed sadly—without sadness. She looked at him searchingly. He became absorbed in the dashboard.

"You're handsomer than you used to be," she said thoughtfully. "Dexter, you have the most remembered eyes."

He could have laughed at this, but he did not laugh. It was the sort of thing that was said to sophomores. Yet it stabbed at him.

530 "I'm awfully tired of everything, darling." She called every one darling, endowing the endearment with careless, individual **camaraderie**. "I wish you'd marry me."

The directness of this confused him. He should have told her now that he was going to marry another girl, but he could not tell her. He could as easily have sworn that he had never loved her.

"I think we'd get along," she continued, on the same note, "unless probably you've forgotten me and fallen in love with another girl."

Her confidence was obviously enormous. She had said, in effect, that she found such a thing impossible to believe, that if it were true he had merely committed a
540 childish indiscretion—and probably to show off. She would forgive him, because it was not a matter of any moment but rather something to be brushed aside lightly.

"Of course you could never love anybody but me," she continued, "I like the way you love me. Oh, Dexter, have you forgotten last year?"

"No, I haven't forgotten."

"Neither have I!"

Was she sincerely moved—or was she carried along by the wave of her own acting?

"I wish we could be like that again," she said, and he forced himself to answer:
550 "I don't think we can."

---

13. **affecting abstraction:** pretending to be lost in thought.
14. **consumptive or pugilistic** (pyo͞o'jə-lĭs'-tĭc): sickly or aggressive.
15. **cloisters:** here, places to escape from life's problems.

Language Coach

Antonyms An antonym is a word with a meaning opposite that of another word. In lines 512–515, which word is an antonym of *deserted* (line 512)? Refer to a dictionary if necessary.

camaraderie
(kä'mə-rä'də-rē) *n.* a spirit of friendly good-fellowship

DIFFERENTIATED INSTRUCTION

FOR ENGLISH LANGUAGE LEARNERS
Vocabulary: Idioms [mixed-readiness groups]
Share or elicit the meanings of these expressions, and then help students find similar expressions in their home languages:

- *crossed a bad account from his books* (line 511), "cancelled a customer who didn't pay his bills"

- *to show off* (line 540), "to get attention"

- *to be brushed aside lightly* (lines 541–542), "not important"

- *hard-minded* (line 586), "unemotional"

- *popular opinion* (line 589), "widely held views"

Language Coach

Antonyms *Answer:* "Peopled" and "deserted" are antonyms. Ask students to name antonyms for other words on page 994 such as *confidence* in line 538 (*self-doubt*) and *childish* in line 540 (*mature*).

"I suppose not. . . . I hear you're giving Irene Scheerer a violent rush."

There was not the faintest emphasis on the name, yet Dexter was suddenly ashamed.

"Oh, take me home," cried Judy suddenly; "I don't want to go back to that idiotic dance—with those children."

Then, as he turned up the street that led to the residence district, Judy began to cry quietly to herself. He had never seen her cry before.

The dark street lightened, the dwellings of the rich loomed up around them, he stopped his coupé in front of the great white bulk of the Mortimer Joneses'
560 house, somnolent, gorgeous, drenched with the splendor of the damp moonlight. Its solidity startled him. The strong walls, the steel of the girders, the breadth and beam and pomp of it were there only to bring out the contrast with the young beauty beside him. It was sturdy to accentuate her slightness—as if to show what a breeze could be generated by a butterfly's wing.

> He sat perfectly quiet, his nerves in wild clamor, afraid that if he moved he would find her irresistibly in his arms. Two tears had rolled down her wet face and trembled on her upper lip.
>
> "I'm more beautiful than anybody else," she said brokenly, "why can't I be happy?" Her moist eyes tore at his stability—her mouth turned slowly downward
> 570 with an exquisite sadness: "I'd like to marry you if you'll have me, Dexter. I suppose you think I'm not worth having, but I'll be so beautiful for you, Dexter."
>
> A million phrases of anger, pride, passion, hatred, tenderness fought on his lips. Then a perfect wave of emotion washed over him, carrying off with it a sediment of wisdom, of convention, of doubt, of honor. This was his girl who was speaking, his own, his beautiful, his pride.
>
> "Won't you come in?" He heard her draw in her breath sharply.
>
> Waiting. **M**
>
> "All right," his voice was trembling, "I'll come in."

⑥ Targeted Passage

M PREDICT
Do you think Judy has really changed? Will she really marry Dexter? Give reasons for your predictions.

V

It was strange that neither when it was over nor a long time afterward did he
580 regret that night. Looking at it from the perspective of ten years, the fact that Judy's flare for him endured just one month seemed of little importance. Nor did it matter that by his yielding he subjected himself to a deeper agony in the end and gave serious hurt to Irene Scheerer and to Irene's parents, who had befriended him. There was nothing sufficiently pictorial about Irene's grief to stamp itself on his mind.

Dexter was at bottom hard-minded. The attitude of the city on his action was of no importance to him, not because he was going to leave the city, but because any outside attitude on the situation seemed superficial. He was completely indifferent to popular opinion. Nor, when he had seen that it was no use, that he
590 did not possess in himself the power to move fundamentally or to hold Judy Jones, did he bear any malice toward her. He loved her, and he would love her until the

In lines 592–604, use these prompts to help students understand Dexter's reaction to Judy's tempestuous nature:

Summarize What strong emotions has Judy produced in Dexter? ***Possible answer:*** *Judy has produced passion, hope, shame, anger, desperation, and other strong emotions in Dexter. He has experienced everything from "deep pain" to "deep happiness" (lines 592–594).*

Analyze When Judy leaves Dexter again, how does he respond emotionally? Why? ***Possible answer:*** *When Judy leaves Dexter again, he seems incapable of further emotional response. Judy appears to have drained him of emotions. He is "beyond any revulsion and any amusement" (lines 597–598) and eagerly seeks escape from the "webs of tangled emotion" (line 604) she has wrought.*

Synthesize Compared to Dexter's intense emotions, how would you describe Judy's emotions? ***Possible answer:*** *Judy's emotions, other than her greed for adoration, seem pale compared to Dexter's. She seems incapable of love, or of real sorrow, or of regret. Her emotional displays, as when she asks Dexter on their first date if she may weep in his presence (line 311), are manipulative shams.*

---

day he was too old for loving—but he could not have her. So he tasted the deep pain that is reserved only for the strong, just as he had tasted for a little while the deep happiness.

Even the ultimate falsity of the grounds upon which Judy terminated the engagement—that she did not want to "take him away" from Irene—Judy, who had wanted nothing else—did not revolt him. He was beyond any revulsion or any amusement.

600 He went East in February with the intention of selling out his laundries and settling in New York—but the war came to America in March and changed his plans. He returned to the West, handed over the management of the business to his partner, and went into the first officers' training-camp in late April. He was one of those young thousands who greeted the war with a certain amount of relief, welcoming the liberation from webs of tangled emotion.

VI

This story is not his biography, remember, although things creep into it which have nothing to do with those dreams he had when he was young. We are almost done with them and with him now. There is only one more incident to be related here, and it happens seven years farther on.

It took place in New York, where he had done well—so well that there were no barriers too high for him. He was thirty-two years old, and, except for one flying 610 trip immediately after the war, he had not been West in seven years. A man named Devlin from Detroit came into his office to see him in a business way, and then and there this incident occurred, and closed out, so to speak, this particular side of his life.

"So you're from the Middle West," said the man Devlin with careless curiosity. "That's funny—I thought men like you were probably born and raised on Wall Street. You know—wife of one of my best friends in Detroit came from your city. I was an usher at the wedding."

Dexter waited with no apprehension of what was coming.

620 "Judy Simms," said Devlin with no particular interest; "Judy Jones she was once."

"Yes, I knew her." A dull impatience spread over him. He had heard, of course, that she was married—perhaps deliberately he had heard no more.

"Awfully nice girl," brooded Devlin meaninglessly, "I'm sort of sorry for her."

"Why?" Something in Dexter was alert, receptive, at once.

"Oh, Lud Simms has gone to pieces in a way. I don't mean he ill-uses her, but he drinks and runs around—"

"Doesn't she run around?"

"No. Stays at home with her kids."

630 "Oh."

"She's a little too old for him," said Devlin.

"Too old!" cried Dexter. "Why, man, she's only twenty-seven."

Related Words *Falsity* (line 595) is related to the word *falsehood* and means essentially the same thing ("something false, incorrect, or dishonest"). What falsity or falsehood does Judy use to explain her reasons for breaking up?

DIFFERENTIATED INSTRUCTION

FOR ENGLISH LANGUAGE LEARNERS

Language: Conversational English Patterns [paired option] Explain that dialogue tags introduce or follow quoted material. Help students brainstorm a list of common tags, such as *said* and *asked*. Note, however, that more specific tags add descriptive detail and variety. Draw students' attention to the tags in lines 615–662. Then ask student pairs to read aloud the dialogue, matching their voices to the tag used.

FOR ENGLISH LANGUAGE LEARNERS

Language Coach

Related Words Answer: *Judy said she did not want to take Dexter from Irene; in reality, she did not care about Irene's feelings.* Have students read the sentence in lines 602–604 then name other words related to *liberation: liberty, liberate.*

He was possessed with a wild notion of rushing out into the streets and taking a train to Detroit. He rose to his feet spasmodically.

"I guess you're busy," Devlin apologized quickly. "I didn't realize—"

"No, I'm not busy," said Dexter, steadying his voice. "I'm not busy at all. Not busy at all. Did you say she was—twenty-seven? No, I said she was twenty-seven."

"Yes, you did," agreed Devlin dryly.

"Go on, then. Go on."

640   "What do you mean?"

"About Judy Jones."

Devlin looked at him helplessly.

"Well, that's—I told you all there is to it. He treats her like the devil. Oh, they're not going to get divorced or anything. When he's particularly outrageous she forgives him. In fact, I'm inclined to think she loves him. She was a pretty girl when she first came to Detroit."

A pretty girl! The phrase struck Dexter as ludicrous.

"Isn't she—a pretty girl, any more?"

"Oh, she's all right."

650   "Look here," said Dexter, sitting down suddenly. "I don't understand. You say she was a 'pretty girl' and now you say she's 'all right.' I don't understand what you mean—Judy Jones wasn't a pretty girl, at all. She was a great beauty. Why, I knew her, I knew her. She was—"

Devlin laughed pleasantly.

"I'm not trying to start a row,"[16] he said. "I think Judy's a nice girl and I like her. I can't understand how a man like Lud Simms could fall madly in love with her, but he did." Then he added: "Most of the women like her." **N**

Dexter looked closely at Devlin, thinking wildly that there must be a reason for this, some insensitivity in the man or some private malice.

660   "Lots of women fade just like *that,*" Devlin snapped his fingers. "You must have seen it happen. Perhaps I've forgotten how pretty she was at her wedding. I've seen her so much since then, you see. She has nice eyes."

A sort of dullness settled down upon Dexter. For the first time in his life he felt like getting very drunk. He knew that he was laughing loudly at something Devlin had said, but he did not know what it was or why it was funny. When, in a few minutes, Devlin went he lay down on his lounge and looked out the window at the New York sky-line into which the sun was sinking in dull lovely shades of pink and gold.

He had thought that having nothing else to lose he was invulnerable at last—
670   but he knew that he had just lost something more, as surely as if he had married Judy Jones and seen her fade away before his eyes.

The dream was gone. Something had been taken from him. In a sort of panic he pushed the palms of his hands into his eyes and tried to bring up a picture of the waters lapping on Sherry Island and the moonlit veranda, and gingham on

---

16. **row** (rou): a noisy argument or dispute.

⑦ Targeted Passage

N MOTIVATION AND TRAITS
Based on Devlin's description of Judy, how would you say she has changed since Dexter knew her? What might have caused these changes?

REVISIT THE BIG QUESTION

Will STATUS *make you happy?*

Discuss In lines 624–634, in what ways does Devlin's description of Judy undermine her role as a symbol of status in Dexter's life? How does Dexter respond to the idea that Judy has become ordinary? *Possible answer: Devlin's description undermines Judy as a symbol of status by showing her as just another unhappy wife. Judy had epitomized everything that Dexter wanted to be: graceful, stylish, elegant, worthy of pursuit. She had inspired him to better his own status. Devlin's description of her robs her of this power by making her ordinary. Dexter responds to this information with great distress and disbelief. He doesn't want to give up his unattainable status symbol.*

TEXT ANALYSIS   COMMON CORE

N MOTIVATION AND TRAITS   RL 3

Possible answer: Based on Devlin's description, Judy has changed in many ways since Dexter knew her. Devlin describes Judy as a rather drab, dutiful housewife who looks after her children and excuses her errant husband—quite the change from the Judy whom Dexter worshipped. These changes might result from time, from marrying someone who doesn't worship her, from the loss of beauty that comes with age, or from general sadness at how her life has turned out.

FOR STRUGGLING READERS

⑦ Targeted Passage [Lines 640–662]

In this passage Dexter faces the sad facts of how Judy has changed since he last saw her.

- What is Judy's marriage like? (lines 643–645)

- What has happened to her legendary beauty? (lines 645–647)

- How does Dexter react to Devlin's news? (lines 658–659)

FOR ADVANCED LEARNERS/AP

Hypothesize About Sources Tell students that Fitzgerald joined the army in 1917, the year that the United States entered World War I. Urge them to perform research to learn about his experiences in the service and then to consider how he translated these into fiction. Have students use their research to inform a journal entry in which they consider how Dexter's service "liberated" him from "webs of tangled emotion" (line 604).

About the Art American artist Georgia O'Keeffe (1887–1986) is best known for her paintings of natural settings, but, like many artists, O'Keeffe was drawn to New York City. This painting merges the fluid lines of natural features such as the clouds and sunlight with the stark lines of humanmade structures. O'Keeffe's portrayal of the Shelton (a hotel in New York City) conveys a sense of the authority over nature that modernists applauded, and that Fitzgerald describes as the "gray beauty of steel that withstands all time" (line 683).

SELECTION WRAP–UP

READ WITH A PURPOSE Now that students have read "Winter Dreams," ask them to compare and contrast Dexter and Judy at several points throughout the story. Students may say that as a caddy, Dexter is concerned with wealth and proving himself, traits that endure after he becomes a successful businessman. Students may also note that to Dexter, Judy first symbolizes love, then she symbolizes his entrance into society, and finally, she becomes a symbol of his own regret. Students may say Judy stays self-centered until—trapped in an unhappy marriage—she fades into the background of life.

⭐ CRITIQUE

- Ask students to evaluate the efficacy of Fitzgerald's central symbol—winter as a time of dreams, growth, and possibility—versus the traditional symbolism of spring.

- After completing the After Reading questions on page 999, have students revisit their responses and tell whether they have changed their opinions.

Detail of *The Shelton with Sunspots* (1926), Georgia O'Keeffe. Oil on canvas, 123.1 cm × 76.8 cm. The Art Institute of Chicago, gift of Leigh B. Block (1985.206) © 2007 The Georgia O'Keeffe Museum/Artists Rights Society (ARS), New York. Photo © 1994 The Art Institute of Chicago, all rights reserved.

the golf-links and the dry sun and the gold color of her neck's soft down. And her mouth damp to his kisses and her eyes plaintive with melancholy and her freshness like new fine linen in the morning. Why, these things were no longer in the world! They had existed and they existed no longer.

680   For the first time in years the tears were streaming down his face. But they were for himself now. He did not care about mouth and eyes and moving hands. He wanted to care, and he could not care. For he had gone away and he could never go back any more. The gates were closed, the sun was gone down, and there was no beauty but the gray beauty of steel that withstands all time. Even the grief he could have borne was left behind in the country of illusion, of youth, of the richness of life, where his winter dreams had flourished.

"Long ago," he said, "long ago, there was something in me, but now that thing is gone. Now that thing is gone, that thing is gone. I cannot cry. I cannot care. That thing will come back no more." ∾

DIFFERENTIATED INSTRUCTION

FOR ADVANCED LEARNERS/AP

Synthesize [small-group option] Display and read aloud the **NOTABLE QUOTE** on page 976 of your book. Then have students discuss these questions:

- Does Dexter fit Fitzgerald's definition of the "new generation of people"? Explain.

- What faiths or gods did the boy Dexter have, and how were these faiths and gods tested and tried as he matured?

- What, if anything, could have saved Dexter's faith and fulfilled his winter dreams?

Invite students to share the results of their discussion with the class.

Comprehension

1. **Recall** How does Dexter's social **status** change in the story, and why?

2. **Clarify** Why doesn't Dexter marry either Judy Jones or Irene Scheerer?

3. **Summarize** What has happened to Judy Jones by the end of the story?

Text Analysis

● 4. **Predict Story Development** Review your list of predictions and clues. Were you able to predict everything that happened? Or were you surprised by how some aspects of the story developed? Support your answer with evidence from the story.

● 5. **Analyze Character Motivation and Traits** What kind of man is Dexter Green? Consider his values and beliefs. Does he deserve sympathy, criticism, or both? Using examples from the text, describe Dexter's traits and the motivations for his actions and feelings.

6. **Examine Symbol** Reread lines 490–494. Consider how Dexter pursues and responds to Judy throughout "Winter Dreams," and think about the young man's feelings regarding **status**. What might Judy **symbolize** in this story? Explain, citing evidence to support your answer.

7. **Analyze Imagery** Fitzgerald is celebrated for his use of imagery, which infuses his fiction with the flush of highly tuned emotions. Locate four or five examples of imagery in "Winter Dreams" that successfully convey the emotional intensity of Dexter and Judy's entanglement. Then explain how each example achieves this purpose.

8. **Interpret Theme** Reread lines 669–688 and consider what exactly Dexter has lost. What theme, or message about the human condition, does Fitzgerald convey through this loss?

Text Criticism

9. **Critical Interpretations** Critic Marius Bewley has argued that Fitzgerald's main subject is always "the American Dream, in which . . . his principal heroes are all trapped." How well does this statement apply to "Winter Dreams"? Use examples from the story to support your opinion.

> *Will* **STATUS** *make you happy?*
>
> In lines 128–129, Fitzgerald says of Dexter, "He wanted not association with glittering things and glittering people—he wanted the glittering things themselves." What does this tell you about Dexter's reasons for seeking **status**?

COMMON CORE

RL 2 Analyze the development of two or more themes or central ideas over the course of the text, including how they interact and build on one another to produce a complex account; provide an objective summary of the text. RL 3 Analyze the impact of the author's choices regarding how to develop and relate elements of a story. RL 4 Determine the meaning of words and phrases as they are used in the text, including figurative and connotative meanings.

WINTER DREAMS **999**

9. *Dexter pursues the American Dream by hiding his humble beginnings and becoming a wealthy man so that he can attain a woman like Judy Jones. Dexter is trapped in this quest at the expense of everything else, including his own human decency.*

> *Will* STATUS *make you happy?*
> ***Possible answer:*** *Dexter wants to be surrounded by expensive things and wealthy people so that others will recognize him. For Dexter, acquiring possessions and relationships are a means to gaining status.*

Practice and Apply

For preliminary support of post-reading questions, use these copy masters:

R RESOURCE MANAGER—Copy Masters
Reading Check p. 216
Character Motivation and Traits p. 209
Question Support p. 217
Additional selection questions are provided for teachers on page 203.

ANSWERS   COMMON CORE RL 2, RL 3, RL 4

1. *He rises from caddy to rich club member because he succeeds in the laundry business.*

2. *Dexter breaks his engagement with Irene to marry Judy; then Judy leaves him.*

3. *She has become the wife of an unfaithful drinking man. She's lost her looks but seems devoted to her children.*

Possible answers:

4. ■ **COMMON CORE FOCUS Predict Story Development** *Accept all thoughtful answers based on completed lists of predictions and clues.*

5. ● **COMMON CORE FOCUS Character Motivation and Traits** *Dexter is an ambitious man and smart in many ways. He knows that he wants wealth and status. He pursues his goals with focus by attending a prestigious college and analyzing market needs. However, he deserves criticism because his obsession with Judy prompts him to behave badly toward Irene and her parents and to isolate himself from friends.*

6. *Judy symbolizes everything Dexter desires— wealth, high social status, effortless affluence—all wrapped up in a beautiful, charismatic package. She has the confidence he lacks. For example, she wears her elegant clothes with ease (lines 287–288), while Dexter has to take special care to dress well (lines 278–286).*

7. *Lines 214–219 use romantic imagery that primes Dexter to respond to Judy's beauty. Lines 256–258 describe Judy's animal grace. Lines 330–337 describe the first transcendent kiss. Lines 466–469 detail the effect of Judy's absence.*

8. *For Dexter, losing Judy's beauty means losing his romantic dream that there is more to life than everyday reality. The loss suggests a theme that romantic love settles into the compromises of marriage.*

ANSWERS

Vocabulary in Context

▲ VOCABULARY PRACTICE

1. *antonyms*   6. *synonyms*

2. *synonyms*   7. *antonyms*

3. *synonyms*   8. *antonyms*

4. *antonyms*   9. *synonyms*

5. *antonyms*   10. *antonyms*

 **RESOURCE MANAGER—Copy Master**
Vocabulary Practice p. 214

ACADEMIC VOCABULARY IN WRITING

Possible answer: *I* conclude *that Judy is a spoiled brat who* justifies *every action as serving her own desires and who ruthlessly pursues her personal goals despite any hurt her actions cause to others.*

VOCABULARY STRATEGY: WORDS FROM THE JAZZ AGE

COMMON CORE L 1a, L 5b

Tell students that in considering two words whose meanings are nearly the same, it is helpful to say each choice silently, observing how the word "feels" and thinking of instances in which it might be used more effectively than the other.

Answers:

1. *"jalopy" (the term fits the historic period)*

2. *"swaggered" (suggests bragging and showing off)*

3. *"struggle" (more difficult than a hassle, which does not fit the historic period)*

4. *"depressing" (more appropriate than slang in this context)*

 **RESOURCE MANAGER—Copy Master**
Vocabulary Strategy p. 215

Interactive Vocabulary   **THINK** central

Keywords direct students to a **WordSharp** tutorial on **thinkcentral.com** or to other types of vocabulary practice and review.

Vocabulary in Context

▲ VOCABULARY PRACTICE

Decide whether the words in each pair are synonyms or antonyms.

1. precipitate/prevent
2. flux/change
3. retinue/troupe
4. petulance/pleasure
5. mundane/extraordinary
6. patrimony/inheritance
7. surfeit/shortage
8. blatantly/secretly
9. camaraderie/friendship
10. precarious/secure

WORD LIST

blatantly
camaraderie
flux
mundane
patrimony
petulance
precarious
precipitate
retinue
surfeit

ACADEMIC VOCABULARY IN WRITING

• conclude   • criteria   • despite   • justify   • maintain

In "Winter Dreams," Fitzgerald provides clues to Judy's disposition during two golf games. Reread lines 78-99 and lines 164-181. In a paragraph discuss what you **conclude** about Judy based on these two scenes. Use at least three Academic Vocabulary words in your paragraph.

VOCABULARY STRATEGY: WORDS FROM THE JAZZ AGE

The Jazz Age is a good example of a time when many new words were coined and old words took on new meanings. These words and phrases were clever and colorful, often providing subtle, **nuanced shifts in meaning** from existing words. For example, a "pushover," a Jazz Age term, is more than just a "victim." A "pushover" is someone who is incapable of offering any resistance. Whether "pushover" or "victim" would be the better word choice is dependent on **context**.

PRACTICE For each pair in the following paragraph, choose the best word or words to fit the context and explain your choice. Refer to a dictionary if needed.

During the 1930's a young man would have been very happy to have had an old *(1. jalopy, car)* to drive. He would have *(2. strutted, swaggered)* as he walked toward the street where it was parked. Young people today would feel differently about having to drive such a vehicle. They would find it a *(3. hassle, struggle)* as well as *(4. depressing, a bummer)*.

COMMON CORE

L 1a Apply the understanding that usage can change over time. **L 5b** Analyze nuances in the meaning of words with similar denotations.

 **Interactive Vocabulary** **THINK** central

Go to **thinkcentral.com**.
KEYWORD: HML11-1000

DIFFERENTIATED INSTRUCTION

FOR ENGLISH LANGUAGE LEARNERS

Task Support: Vocabulary Strategy Help students use these strategies for analysis:

• take words apart—*pushover*, "someone who can be pushed over, or moved easily"

• recognize allusions—*gospel truth*, "information as trustworthy as scripture"

• look for humor—*baloney*, "information that is as unreliable as the meats in baloney"

FOR ADVANCED LEARNERS/AP

Vocabulary in Writing Have students use appropriate vocabulary words in a definition of Jazz Age success and status. They should use Fitzgerald's descriptions of wealth and influence as a starting point. Then ask students to contrast their definitions with success and status as defined today.

Language

◆ **GRAMMAR AND STYLE: Craft Effective Sentences**

Review the **Grammar and Style** note on page 991. Fitzgerald's rich, evocative style in "Winter Dreams" comes in part from long sentences held together by the **coordinating conjunction** *and*. He often breaks up those long descriptions with **dashes** and **phrases** in a series.

> *Early in their acquaintance it had seemed for a while that there was a deep and spontaneous mutual attraction—that first August, for example—three days of long evenings on her dusky veranda, of strange wan kisses through the late afternoon, in shadowy alcoves or behind the protecting trellises of the garden arbors, of mornings when she was fresh as a dream and almost shy at meeting him in the clarity of the rising day. There was all the ecstasy of an engagement about it, sharpened by his realization that there was no engagement.* (lines 379–385)

Notice that this description has no action verbs and consists almost entirely of prepositional phrases. In this way, Fitzgerald perfectly expresses Dexter's emotional surrender in both style and content.

PRACTICE Study the following paragraph from the story, noting

- coordinating conjunctions in the first sentence that connect multiple images
- participial phrases that add a sense of motion and emotional significance

Continue these stylistic elements by writing two or three additional sentences.

> *There was a fish jumping and a star shining and the lights around the lake were gleaming. Dexter sat beside Judy Jones and she explained how her boat was driven. Then she was in the water, swimming to the floating surf-board with a sinuous crawl. Watching her was without effort to the eye, watching a branch waving or a seagull flying. Her arms, burned to butternut, moved sinuously among the dull platinum ripples, elbow appearing first, casting the forearm back with a cadence of falling water, then reaching out and down, stabbing a path ahead.* (lines 252–258)

READING-WRITING CONNECTION

Expand your understanding of "Winter Dreams" by responding to this prompt. Then, use the **revising tips** to improve your letter.

WRITING PROMPT	REVISING TIPS
COMPOSE A LETTER OF ADVICE If Dexter were your close friend, what advice would you give to him? In a **three-paragraph letter** (or email) to Dexter, explain what you think he should do to improve the quality of his life. Be sure to recommend something to fill the great void left by the loss of his youthful illusions.	• State your advice in clear, persuasive language. • Provide evidence for why you believe your advice is trustworthy. • Use appeals to logic, emotions, and eithical beliefs.

Interactive Revision
Go to **thinkcentral.com**.
KEYWORD: HML11-1001

◯ **COMMON CORE**

L 2 Demonstrate command of the conventions of standard English punctuation when writing. **L 3a** Vary syntax for effect, consulting references for guidance as needed; apply an understanding of syntax to the study of complex texts when reading. **W 1** Write arguments to support claims in an analysis of substantive topics or texts, using valid reasoning and relevant and sufficient evidence.

FOR STRUGGLING WRITERS

Writing Support

- Limit the scope of the letter to one problem and one solution. Guide students to address the problem in one paragraph and the solution in a second paragraph.

- Provide a model letter so that students can review greeting and closing.

- Discuss the informal tone of personal letters, stressing the use of first person and familiar language suited to addressing someone the writer knows well.

- Provide this starter sentence:
  Dear Dexter, I've noticed recently that you seem to be unhappy, and I wonder if that's because you _____.

Language

◯ **COMMON CORE** L 2, L 3a, W 1

◆ **GRAMMAR AND STYLE**

Review with students the function of the coordinating conjunction *and*. Then review the form and function of participial phrases. Help students identify examples of each part of speech in the passage. Urge students to map out the information of their sentences, then craft the language.

Possible answer: *Around her slim form, the waves rippled outward and spread towards the shore, diminishing as they flowed. The moonlight's reflection, shattered by the wavelets, shimmered and shook and cast uncertain light on Judy's face.*

R **RESOURCE MANAGER**—Copy Master
Craft Effective Sentences p. 218

READING-WRITING CONNECTION

Suggest that students skim the story and their notes to identify at least two specific problems in Dexter's life. Have students list these on a Problem and Solution Chart. Urge them to work in pairs to brainstorm solutions before choosing the most helpful solutions to recommend in their letters.

 **BEST PRACTICES TOOLKIT**—Transparency
Problem and Solution Charts p. B20

Writing Online **THINK**central

The following tools are available online at **thinkcentral.com** and on **Write*Smart*** CD-ROM:
- **Interactive Graphic Organizers**
- **Interactive Student Models**
- **Interactive Revision Lessons**
For additional grammar instruction, see **GrammarNotes** on **thinkcentral.com**.

Assess and Reteach

Assess

DIAGNOSTIC AND SELECTION TESTS
Selection Test A pp. 269–270
Selection Test B/C pp. 271–272

Interactive Selection Test on **thinkcentral.com**

Reteach

Level Up Online Tutorials on **thinkcentral.com**

RL 3 Analyze the impact of the author's choices regarding how to develop and relate elements of a story.

BACKGROUND F. Scott Fitzgerald often felt pulled in two different directions because his desire to pursue his art was at odds with the need to make a living. Though he considered his novels such as *The Great Gatsby* his masterpieces, his shorter works like screenplays, stories, articles, and reviews for magazines helped support the lifestyle he and his wife desired. Most critics consider Dexter Green, the protagonist of "Winter Dreams," a rough draft or prototype of Jay Gatsby. Both characters are wealthy young men who fall in love with beautiful, unattainable women. Both learn the painful lesson that money is not enough to draw the women to them.

TEXT ANALYSIS Point out to students that Fitzgerald characterizes Jay Gatsby not only by his own words and actions, but also by what other people say about him. That they know very little, often reduced to repeating others' hypotheses and hearsay, contributes to Gatsby's mystery, as does Gatsby's own quick exits, both of which students will encounter in the excerpt on page 1003.

WRITE Suggest that students first write notes that outline the conflicting information and opinions about the person or character. Tell them that the more varied these ideas are, the greater the mystery or controversy will be surrounding their subject, but more closely related ideas may make them seem more convincing—even if no one knows the truth about the character.

---

from The Great Gatsby

Novel by F. Scott Fitzgerald

F. Scott Fitzgerald
1896–1940

COMMON CORE

RL 3 Analyze the impact of the author's choices regarding how to develop and relate elements of a story.

BACKGROUND From the time it was published in 1925, *The Great Gatsby* was recognized as F. Scott Fitzgerald's finest achievement. It "has interested and excited me more than any new novel I have seen," said poet T. S. Eliot; decades later, author Tobias Wolff said that Fitzgerald "saw our American world . . . with clearer eyes than any of his contemporaries." Fitzgerald wrote this novel in the early 1920s, when he and his wife Zelda were living in Great Neck, Long Island. Success had arrived in 1920 with the publication of his first novel, *This Side of Paradise*, and for a decade the Fitzgeralds led a glittering life in New York and Paris. Set in the world of Long Island wealth, with nightlong parties, *The Great Gatsby* focuses on a fabulously rich man and his pursuit of a lost love.

TEXT ANALYSIS Fitzgerald's challenge in *The Great Gatsby* was how to **characterize** his protagonist, a glamorous and perhaps dangerous man about whom little is known except hearsay and gossip. Through **dialogue,** the novel conveys various glimpses and conflicting stories about Gatsby, creating the impression of a complex—and perhaps unknowable—figure. The genius of this approach is that it brings us into the story as readers, leaving us with the task of sorting through what we hear about Jay Gatsby and trying to form a complete image of him. Always, Gatsby hovers just out of reach. Always, there seems more to him than the dialogue provides. In the end, he remains a mystery, one of the most engaging mysteries in American fiction.

WRITE Read the passage twice, paying close attention in the dialogue to how competing bits of gossip and hearsay create an impression of Gatsby. Then choose a subject about whom there are competing stories, conflicting versions of the truth. You might choose a controversial public figure such as a singer, a movie star, or a politician. If you prefer, you can create a character of your own, as Fitzgerald did in *The Great Gatsby*. Next, imagine a conversation in which several people share bits and pieces of what they've heard about your subject. Write this scene, concentrating on the dialogue. Your goal is to convey an air of mystery or misunderstanding about your character.

> "This is an unusual party for me. I haven't even seen the host. I live over there—" I waved my hand at the invisible hedge in the distance, "and this man Gatsby sent over his chauffeur with an invitation."
>
> For a moment he looked at me as if he failed to understand.
>
> "I'm Gatsby," he said suddenly.
>
> "What!" I exclaimed. "Oh, I beg your pardon."

1002

DIFFERENTIATED INSTRUCTION

FOR STRUGGLING READERS

Comprehension Support Help students complete a Sensory Notes organizer to record details as they read the excerpt. Point out that noting sensory details as they read helps readers visualize scenes and characters and more fully understand the story's action.

 BEST PRACTICES TOOLKIT—Transparency
Sensory Notes p. B9

I see . . . the well-dressed people in the elegant mansion.	most important image Gatsby's smile and bow
I hear . . .	most important sound
I feel . . .	most important sensation
I think . . .	most important thought

"I thought you knew, old sport. I'm afraid I'm not a very good host."

He smiled understandingly—much more than understandingly. It was one of those rare smiles with a quality of eternal reassurance in

10 it, that you may come across four or five times in life. It faced—or seemed to face—the whole external world for an instant, and then concentrated on *you* with an irresistible prejudice in your favor. It understood you just as far as you wanted to be understood, believed in you as you would like to believe in yourself, and assured you that it had precisely the impression of you that, at your best, you hoped to convey. Precisely at that point it vanished—and I was looking at an elegant young roughneck, a year or two over thirty, whose elaborate formality of speech just missed being absurd. Some time before he introduced himself I'd got a strong impression that he was picking his words with care.

20 Almost at the moment when Mr. Gatsby identified himself, a butler hurried toward him with the information that Chicago was calling him on the wire. He excused himself with a small bow that included each of us in turn.

"If you want anything just ask for it, old sport," he urged me. "Excuse me. I will rejoin you later."

When he was gone I turned immediately to Jordan—constrained to assure her of my surprise. I had expected that Mr. Gatsby would be a florid and corpulent person in his middle years.

"Who is he?" I demanded. "Do you know?"

"He's just a man named Gatsby."

30 "Where is he from, I mean? And what does he do?"

"Now *you're* started on the subject," she answered with a wan smile. "Well, he told me once he was an Oxford man."

A dim background started to take shape behind him, but at her next remark it faded away.

"However, I don't believe it."

"Why not?"

"I don't know," she insisted, "I just don't think he went there."

Something in her tone reminded me of the other girl's "I think he killed a man," and had the effect of stimulating my curiosity. I would have accepted without

40 question the information that Gatsby sprang from the swamps of Louisiana or from the lower East Side of New York. That was comprehensible. But young men didn't—at least in my provincial inexperience I believed they didn't—drift coolly out of nowhere and buy a palace on Long Island Sound.

"Anyhow, he gives large parties," said Jordan, changing the subject with an urban distaste for the concrete. "And I like large parties. They're so intimate. At small parties there isn't any privacy."

1003

FOR ENGLISH LANGUAGE LEARNERS

Language: Conversational English Patterns [mixed-readiness groups] Share or elicit the meanings of these expressions, and then help students find similar expressions in their home languages:

- *I beg your pardon* (line 6), "Excuse me"
- *old sport* (line 7), "good friend"
- *on the wire* (line 21), "by telephone"
- *I mean* (line 30), "What I mean is . . . ."

FOR ADVANCED LEARNERS/AP

Evaluate Title Point out to students that Fitzgerald considered many other titles for his novel other than *The Great Gatsby*. Based upon their reading of the excerpt, challenge students to evaluate Fitzgerald's choice in terms of the expectations that a title like *The Great Gatsby* raises for the central character as well as the irony that it hints at.

INTRODUCE THE MASTERPIECE

The Great Gatsby Tell students that Wolff's praise for *The Great Gatsby* honors Fitzgerald's willingness to record his characters' faults and vices as well as their positive traits. As Fitzgerald suggests in the **NOTABLE QUOTE** on page 976, many Americans had given up all beliefs except that wealth could shelter them from life's difficulties. These Americans pursued their own pleasure as a faith, seeking the best for pleasure's sake. In this excerpt, Nick responds positively to Gatsby because Gatsby seems to convey that something beyond wealth matters. As students read the excerpt, ask them to consider how Gatsby stands out from the crowd at this party.

TIERED DISCUSSION PROMPTS

Use these questions to help students understand the narrator's experience at the party:

Summarize In what uncomfortable situation does the narrator find himself? *Possible answer:* He is attending a party whose host he has not met.

Analyze How does the narrator gather information about the party's host, and how does this information affect him? *Possible answer:* The narrator gathers information about the host by asking different guests, one of whom turns out to be the host. He is surprised and a little embarrassed by his encounter with the host, but also positively impressed by the man. He is disturbed and confused when he recalls that another guest described the host as a murderer.

Synthesize On the basis of what you read in **BACKGROUND,** what can readers infer about Gatsby and his wealth, knowing that Dexter Green was an earlier and less-developed version of Gatsby? *Possible answer:* Readers can infer that Gatsby, like Dexter Green, is a self-made man who has recently come into wealth from humbler beginnings and is proud of what he has accomplished. Readers may also infer that Gatsby, like Dexter, is still not comfortable with his newly exalted position in society. For example, Gatsby picks "his words with care" and is overly careful about social niceties such as bowing.

Focus and Motivate

COMMON CORE FOCUS

RI 7 Integrate and evaluate multiple sources of information presented in different media or formats as well as in words in order to address a question or solve a problem. **W 2** Write informative/explanatory texts to examine and convey complex ideas, concepts, and information clearly and accurately through the effective selection, organization, and analysis of content. **SL 1** Initiate and participate effectively in a range of collaborative discussions. **SL 5** Make strategic use of digital media in presentations.

SUMMARIES

"National Motor Car" This ad uses Jazz Age images of wealth, such as a well-dressed woman and elegant statuary, along with copy that describes high performance and luxury, in order to sell a car.

"Kodak" This ad uses an image of well-dressed people enjoying tennis and copy describing advanced technical abilities in order to sell a camera.

Whose DREAM *are you buying?*

Ask the question, then after students read the paragraph, invite them to describe advertisements they have seen recently. Have students identify what the ads are selling and discuss how this product, service, or concept offers buyers a piece of the American dream.

BACKGROUND

National Motor Car and Vehicle Company was based in Indianapolis, Indiana, once a hub of early auto manufacturing. In 1909, its president, Arthur Newby, joined with other auto manufacturers to found the Indianapolis Motor Speedway as a testing ground for their vehicles. Eastman Kodak Company rose to prominence in the same era, when George Eastman developed a camera that could be used easily by ordinary people. In the early 20th century, Eastman's company continued to improve its camera, offering increasingly convenient features, such as the negative titling stressed in this ad.

Media Study

Advertising in the Jazz Age

Print Advertisements on Media **Smart** DVD-ROM

COMMON CORE

RI 7 Integrate and evaluate multiple sources of information presented in different media or formats as well as in words in order to address a question or solve a problem.

Whose DREAM *are you buying?*

KEY IDEA As a struggling writer, F. Scott Fitzgerald worked briefly for an advertising firm and became leery of the industry's emerging practices. In his writing, Fitzgerald expressed his views about materialism and the impact of advertising on the contemporary culture of his day. For him, advertising was part of the glittering surface of the **American dream,** a dream of success, whose cost was often underestimated. In this lesson, you'll study magazine ads of the 1920s to uncover persuasive techniques that took root during the Jazz Age and flourish to this day.

Background

Spending Spree The first years of the 1920s were a time of "more." Because of mass production, such innovations as the automobile and the radio were more available and affordable. Electrical power spread beyond big cities, enabling more Americans to use new, time-saving appliances. As modern-day conveniences took hold and salaries steadily rose, ordinary people reaped the benefits of more leisure time and more money to spend. "Buy now, pay later" installment plans made expensive items appear more obtainable by allowing consumers to pay bills over an extended period of time.

Because merchandise was now flooding the marketplace, a fundamental shift had to occur in how Americans spent money. Before, thriftiness had been the rule. To fuel consumer spending, advertising agencies enlisted the expertise of psychologists to find ways to motivate buyers. The result was advertising designed to appeal to the public's desire for convenience, youth, beauty, and, particularly, wealth and luxury.

With an emphasis on the visual, Jazz Age ads portrayed the lavish lifestyles of the rich. Over time, print ads in newspapers, magazines, and billboards changed. Rather than just providing product details, ad writers of the 1920s changed the tone of the ads. Their purpose changed from informing the public to persuading ordinary Americans that they could live a lifestyle similar to that of the "beautiful people." Due in part to the persuasive power of such ads, the United States became a nation of shoppers and thus a consumer society.

1004

Media Study Resources

See resources on the **Teacher One Stop DVD-ROM** *and on* **thinkcentral.com**.

R **RESOURCE MANAGER UNIT 5**

Plan and Teach, pp. 219–222
Summary, pp. 223†*, 224‡*
Viewing Guide, p. 225
Close Viewing, p. 226
Media Activity, p. 227
Produce Your Own Media, p. 228

TECHNOLOGY

Teacher One Stop DVD-ROM

Student One Stop DVD-ROM

Media*Smart* **DVD-ROM**

MediaScope on thinkcentral.com

* Resources for Differentiation   † Also in Spanish   ‡ In Haitian Creole and Vietnamese

Media Literacy: Persuasion in 1920s Ads

The Jazz Age marks the period when the advertising industry developed. Numerous agencies were established on Madison Avenue in New York City, and ads began to appear in the new medium of mass-circulation magazines. As *Time,* the *New Yorker,* and the *Saturday Evening Post* became popular, the ads within them exposed a nationwide audience to a vast array of products and services.

Advertisers also devised more deliberate ways to persuade. In earlier decades, ads contained straightforward details about product features and prices. Magazine ads of the 1920s shifted away from the product, using a light and informal tone to appeal more directly to the potential buyer. To explore some persuasive techniques commonly used in the 1920s, examine this automobile ad.

STRATEGIES FOR RECOGNIZING PERSUASIVE TECHNIQUES

- Understand the overall message. Behind the 1920s ads was the implication that purchases could bring higher social status and self-fulfillment.

- Look for the **tone**, or the writer's attitude toward the subject. Notice the words *steady, flow, power, smoothly,* and *swiftly.* Think about the attitude these words suggest about the car.

- Try to spot the **slogan**, the short phrase that, used in most ads, expresses something about the quality of the product or the company that makes it. Beginning in the 1920s, a slogan helped to make a product's name and purpose memorable to potential buyers.

- Recognize the technique of **transfer**, which refers to an advertiser's attempt to connect a product with someone or something that's pleasing or admired. Ask yourself: What might images of the rich at leisure have conveyed to working-class Americans of the 1920s?

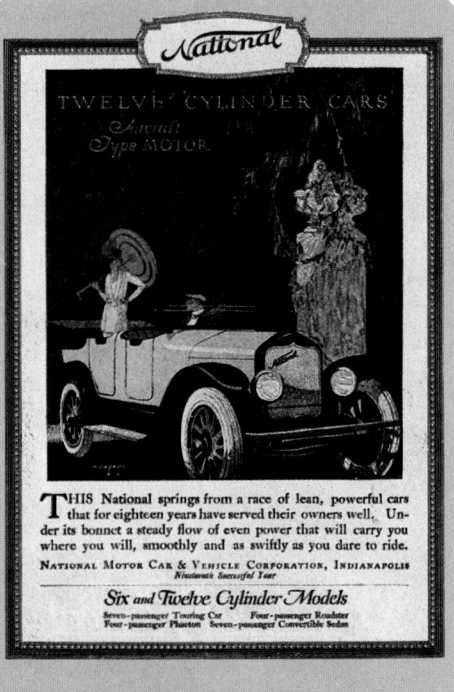

MEDIA STUDY: TEACHING OPTIONS

Teaching Option 1: The Basics (1–2 Days)
1. Begin the Media Study using the material provided on pages 1004–1005.
2. Show the Introduction on Media*Smart.* Have students use the Viewing Guide on page 1006, along with the corresponding copy master on page 225 of the Resource Manager. Discuss their responses.
3. Return to the pupil book for the extension activities on page 1007.

Teaching Option 2: In-Depth Study (2–3 Days)
1. Begin the Media Study using pages 1004–1005.
2. Show the Introduction from Media*Smart.* Then continue on Media*Smart* with the Media Lessons, using the teacher notes available in the Resources section.
3. Show the Guided Analysis presentation. Have students record their observations on the Student Viewing Guide available in the Resources section from Media*Smart.*
4. Return to the pupil book, page 1007.

Media Literacy  COMMON CORE RI 7

Review with students the purpose of advertising and ask them to recall ads that have been effective in reaching them as consumers. Ask what made these ads effective, and list on the board answers that students generate, such as *message, images, slogans,* and *music.* Add the terms *tone* and *transfer.* Then discuss the chart on this.

- **Overall Message** To help students analyze the overall message in ads, compare viewing an ad to choosing an outfit to wear. Ask students what an outfit can convey about the wearer, such as his or her body type, activity interests, color and fabric preferences, and even personality. Point out that an outfit conveys messages without stating them in words, but rather by associations such as a link between bold colors and bold personalities.

- **Tone** Have students think about the meaning someone's tone of voice gives his or her message. Tell students that in a print ad, tone is established by word choice; this gives the ad a certain tone designed to make viewers want to buy the product. Point out that words like *power* and *swiftly* give the National ad a persuasive attitude.

- **Slogan** Explain that the word slogan once meant "battle cry"; then have students name some famous product slogans. Point out that, like a battle cry, an ad slogan must inspire all who hear it toward decisive action. Ask students what makes a slogan catchy, memorable, and effective.

- **Transfer** Have students name celebrities who endorse products. Ask them whether they are persuaded to buy products endorsed by celebrities, and why. Explain that endorsements create transfer by inviting viewers to link the advertised product or service with someone they admire.

Practice and Apply

VIEWING GUIDE

1. As students prepare to view the ads, tell them that they will be asked to recognize the persuasive techniques that make each ad effective. Encourage them to look for these techniques:

   - each ad's **overall message** of a glamorous and desirable lifestyle, as presented by the clothing, the colors, the activity of tennis, or other elements of design

   - **tone** creates an attitude that the products are worthwhile and life-enhancing

   - **slogans,** such as at the bottom of the Kodak ad, that suggest connections between the product and the American dream of wealth and leisure

   - the technique of **transfer,** in which viewers' admiration for the lifestyle they associate with tennis or with well-dressed people is extended to admiration for Kodak cameras or National cars

2. Some students may have difficulty with the incomplete sentences used in both ads. Work through the text with students, adding implied words to clarify. Have students paraphrase the revised text to ensure their comprehension.

R RESOURCE MANAGER—Copy Masters
   Viewing Guide p. 225
   Close Viewing p. 226
   Media Activity p. 227

Use this resource with the Viewing Guide:

MediaSmart DVD-ROM

MediaScope on **thinkcentral.com**

ANSWERS

FIRST VIEWING: Comprehension

1. *National Cars*

2. *The people are playing tennis.*

CLOSE VIEWING: Media Literacy

Possible answers:

3. *Words such as* grand, upscale, luxurious, successful, upper class, *or* refined *could describe these ads.*

4. *The message of the car ad is that this high-performance car is fit for a successful person who deserves and expects the best.*

Media Smart DVD-ROM
- **Selection 1:** National Motor Car and Vehicle
- **Selection 2:** Eastman Kodak Company
- **Genre:** Print advertisements of the 1920s

For the out-of-doors days

KODAK

And not merely the alluring picture story, but on every negative at least a date; and a title, too, if you like. Titling is the work of but an instant with an Autographic Kodak; is as simple as making the picture itself—and there is no extra charge for Autographic film.

If it isn't an Eastman, it isn't a Kodak.

1006

Viewing Guide for

Jazz Age Advertisements

To carefully examine the two advertisements, use the DVD. As you study them, keep in mind the high spirits and optimism of the Roaring Twenties. Use these questions as you examine the image and words of each ad.

NOW VIEW

FIRST VIEWING: Comprehension

1. **Recall** What product is advertised by a woman holding a bright orange parasol?

2. **Clarify** What leisure activity is depicted in the Kodak camera ad?

CLOSE VIEWING: Media Literacy

3. **Interpret Visuals** *Glamorous* and *elegant* are two words that would describe the images in these ads. What other words would you use to describe them?

4. **Analyze the Message** Note that in the National car ad, an expensive sports car is the dominant part of the visual presentation. What message do you think the 1920s advertisers specifically wanted to convey to their audience? Why do you think they promoted this message?

5. **Compare Advertisements** In what ways is the Kodak camera ad shown here similar to the ad for National cars?

6. **Evaluate an Advertisement** Choose the ad that appeals to you more. Evaluate it in terms of the effectiveness of its persuasive techniques. Think about
   - the ad's appeal to status, luxury, and style
   - the design of the visual and the choice and placement of text
   - how favorably you think 1920s Americans might have viewed the ad

---

5. *Both ads depict sophisticated people who have enough wealth to enjoy leisure time. The people are in relaxed postures, enjoying leisure, and the settings are private and estatelike, rather than public. Both ads use copy targeted at people who enjoy life's finer things.*

6. *National Car: Transfer is evident in the sophisticated image, with its placement of the car in the foreground and the elegantly dressed woman in the background. The tone of words such as* lean *and* powerful *create an attitude of respect for the car. Kodak: Transfer is evident in the presentation of well-to-do people enjoying leisure. Words such as* alluring *create a tone that suggests the product is desirable, and a slogan helps convey brand identity and superiority.*

Write or Discuss

Evaluate the Print Ads F. Scott Fitzgerald once wrote about the advertising profession: "Advertising is a racket.... You cannot be honest without admitting that its constructive contribution to humanity is exactly minus zero." In Fitzgerald's day, the advertising industry was taking root. Today, advertising is an integral part of everyday life. Think about the print ads in this lesson and how similar they might be to ads for similar products today. What persuasive techniques are still effective? Write a short evaluation of each ad. Keep the following points in mind:

- the deliberate appeals you saw that were embedded within the advertisements' visuals and text
- how potential buyers of the 1920s ads compare to today's buyers
- your own views about today's consumer society

Produce and Present Your Own Media

Create a Contemporary Ad Poster Using one of the 1920s ads in this lesson as a model, create an advertisement as a modern-day counterpart. Individually or with a partner, decide on the product, target an audience of working-class buyers for the product, and determine the persuasive techniques you'll apply. Represent the ad in the form of a billboard poster. When you're done, present your ad to the whole class, and discuss the effectiveness of the ad.

HERE'S HOW As you design the ad, consider these suggestions:

- Put as much thought into the ad's visual design as into its wording. You might want to concentrate on designing the image of the ad while a partner focuses on devising the copy.
- Be sure to include appeals to status, wealth, and luxury through both the visual design and the text. Think about the leisure activities of today's wealthy people and what working people might find desirable about them.

Further Exploration

Explore Ads Across the 20th Century On the DVD, access examples of ads that exhibit the persuasive techniques of the 1920s in product advertisements from ensuing decades. What cleverly designed image or turn of phrase turns objects into necessities? What evidence do you see of such techniques as appeals to youth, beauty, wealth, and luxury? Examining these ads can offer insights into the evolving consumer culture of the United States.

COMMON CORE

RI 7 Integrate and evaluate multiple sources of information presented in different media or formats as well as in words in order to address a question or solve a problem. **SL 1** Initiate and participate effectively in a range of collaborative discussions. **SL 5** Make strategic use of digital media in presentations. **W 2** Write informative/explanatory texts to examine and convey complex ideas, concepts, and information clearly and accurately through the effective selection, organization, and analysis of content.

Media Tools — THINK central

Go to thinkcentral.com.
KEYWORD: HML11-1007

Tech Tip

If you create the ad on a computer, choose font styles and sizes with care.

Assess and Reteach

Write or Discuss

COMMON CORE RI 7, SL 1, SL 5, W 2

Evaluate the Print Ads In their evaluations, students should address persuasive techniques used in the ads: communication of a clear *overall message*, effective use of *tone*, a memorable *slogan*, and the *transfer* of admiration for the people and scene depicted in the ads to the products advertised. Make sure that students read the copy carefully for tone that creates a persuasive attitude. For example, the Kodak ad uses the phrase "if you like" to imply that the product will give viewers just what they want and to assure viewers that they are in control. Students should determine whether such appeals would resonate with today's buyers and include their views about today's consumer society, citing evidence to support their responses.

MEDIA STUDY WRAP-UP

Have students summarize what they have learned about the persuasive techniques used to market products to consumers. Encourage students to use terms such as *overall message, tone, slogan,* and *transfer* in their explanations.

RETEACH

For students who are unable to apply the Media Study skills, select from these reteaching options:

- **Ad Visuals** Provide students with two photographs of possible locations for a luxury car advertisement—one of an average neighborhood or home and another of an upscale neighborhood or home. Ask students which location an advertising agency would be likely to choose. Ask them to discuss why they select the photo they choose.
- **Product Names** Make a two-column chart on the board. In one column, write the generic name of types of consumer products, such as bread, movie, vitamins, cereal. For the other column, ask students to suggest product names for the items, such as *Golden Harvest Bread.*

Produce and Present Your Own Media

Rubric: Create Contemporary Ad Posters A strong contemporary ad poster should

- advertise a clearly identified product
- target a working-class audience
- include design and graphic elements that portray the product positively
- use copy that reinforces the positive associations between product and buyer

- appeal to status, wealth, and luxury in images and text
- use persuasive techniques such as purr words, a catchy slogan, and transfer

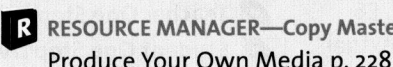 **RESOURCE MANAGER—Copy Master**
Produce Your Own Media p. 228

Media Tools — THINK central

Media study keywords point to **MediaScope**, a Web site that helps students strengthen media analysis and production skills.

Focus and Motivate

COMMON CORE FOCUS

RL 1 Cite textual evidence to support analysis of what the text says explicitly as well as inferences drawn from the text, including determining where the text leaves matters uncertain. **RL 4** Analyze the impact of specific word choices on meaning and tone, including words with multiple meanings or language that is particularly fresh, engaging, or beautiful. **RI 1** Cite textual evidence to support analysis of what the text says explicitly as well as inferences drawn from the text, including determining where the text leaves matters uncertain. **RI 4** Determine the meaning of words and phrases as they are used in a text, including figurative, connotative, and technical meanings. **RI 7** Integrate and evaluate multiple sources of information presented in different media or formats as well as in words in order to address a question. **W 2e** Establish and maintain an objective tone while attending to discipline-specific norms and conventions. **L 3a** Vary syntax for effect. **L 6** Acquire and use accurately general academic and domain-specific words and phrases, sufficient for reading, writing, speaking, and listening at the college and career readiness level.

ABOUT THE AUTHOR

Hemingway spent a month recovering in an Italian hospital after being wounded in World War I. War and its aftermath, he thought, provided ample opportunity to observe human nature.

Selection Resources

The Modern Short Story

In Another Country Video link at thinkcentral.com
Short Story by Ernest Hemingway

Healing War's Wounds
Magazine Article by Karen Breslau

Moving a Nation to Care
Book Cover

RL 1 Cite textual evidence to support analysis of what the text says explicitly as well as inferences drawn from the text, including determining where the text leaves matters uncertain. **RL 4** Analyze the impact of specific word choices on meaning and tone, including words with multiple meanings or language that is particularly fresh, engaging, or beautiful. **RI 1** Cite textual evidence to support analysis of what the text says explicitly as well as inferences drawn from the text, including determining where the text leaves matters uncertain. **RI 4** Determine the meaning of words and phrases as they are used in a text, including figurative, connotative, and technical meanings. **RI 7** Integrate and evaluate multiple sources of information presented in different media or formats as well as in words in order to address a question.

Meet the Author

Ernest Hemingway 1899–1961

Whether trout fishing in Michigan, skiing in Switzerland, cheering for bullfighters in Spain, big-game hunting in Africa, marlin fishing off the coast of Key West, or drinking wine in a Paris café, Ernest Hemingway was the embodiment of rugged individualism. He experienced first hand the major events of his time—the Italian front in World War I, Paris in the 1920s, the Spanish Civil War, and D-day and the Battle of the Bulge during World War II. Behind the legendary persona, however, Hemingway was first and foremost a writer. His experiences provided the raw material for a body of work that captured the essence of modernity and left his indelible stamp on the century.

Irrepressible Energy and Drive
Hemingway grew up in Oak Park, Illinois, a suburb of Chicago. After high school he got a job as a reporter for the *Kansas City Star,* where he developed both his deceptively simple writing style and a devotion to the truth. During World War I he volunteered as an ambulance driver for the American Red Cross and was severely wounded. After the war he made his way to Paris as a correspondent for the *Toronto Star.* Paris in the 1920s was a magnet for young artists and writers of the new modernist movement, and the vibrant, sociable Hemingway soon became a star. By the end of the decade, he had made his own contribution by publishing two collections of short stories, *In Our Time* (1925) and *Men Without Women* (1927), as well as two highly acclaimed novels, *The Sun Also Rises* (1926) and *A Farewell to Arms* (1929).

End of an Epic Life Hemingway was living in Cuba when he wrote what many consider his finest novel, *For Whom the Bell Tolls* (1940), based on his reporting of the Spanish Civil War. When World War II broke out, he served as a journalist, often putting himself in dangerous combat situations. His last major work published in his lifetime was the highly popular *The Old Man and the Sea* (1952). In his final years he suffered a variety of ills—including diabetes, liver problems, hypertension, and depression—that led to his suicide at age 62. He left behind five unpublished manuscripts and a towering literary legacy.

For more on Hemingway's days as a war correspondent, see the biography on page 1094.

Author Online
Go to thinkcentral.com. KEYWORD: HML11-1008

1008

See resources on the **Teacher One Stop DVD-ROM** and on thinkcentral.com.

 Video link at thinkcentral.com

 RESOURCE MANAGER UNIT 5
    Plan and Teach, pp. 229–234
    Summary, pp. 235–236†‡*
    Text Analysis and Reading Skill, pp. 237–240†*
    Vocabulary, pp. 241–243*
    Grammar and Style, p. 246
DIAGNOSTIC AND SELECTION TESTS
    Selection Tests, pp. 273–276

 BEST PRACTICES TOOLKIT
    Definition Mapping, p. E6
    Character Traits and Textual Evidence, p. D6

TECHNOLOGY
 Teacher One Stop DVD-ROM
Student One Stop DVD-ROM
Audio Anthology CD
GrammarNotes DVD-ROM
ExamView Test Generator on the **Teacher One Stop**

* Resources for Differentiation   † Also in Spanish   ‡ In Haitian Creole and Vietnamese

TEXT ANALYSIS: TONE

Hemingway began his literary career as a newspaper reporter. The spare, direct prose of his short stories reflects his journalistic roots. Reporters adopt a detached, objective tone or attitude toward their subject. This kind of detachment characterizes "In Another Country," but examine the narrator's surface detachment for evidence of the loss he feels. You will find clues to Hemingway's view of the human condition.

When you read Karen Breslau's magazine article, look for clues to her attitude toward the wounded soldiers she chose as her subject. Is her attitude detached and objective? Or has she made another choice with this piece of journalism? Finally, what does her tone tell you about her view of human potential?

READING SKILL: MAKE INFERENCES

One aspect of Hemingway's style is that he is not explicit about the effect of important events on his characters. He relates events and leaves it up to his readers to look for clues and **make inferences,** or logical assumptions, about the impact of events. As you read, look for revealing details, statements in the dialogue, and other clues to help you infer how the characters feel about their situation.

Likewise, when you read "Healing War's Wounds," examine the language Karen Breslau uses to describe recovering soldiers. The events, details, and dialogue she includes provide clues to her purpose in writing this article and to the message she wants readers to take from her story.

VOCABULARY IN CONTEXT

Hemingway uses these words to write about soldiers in a wartime hospital. Choose the word that you associate with each type of patient.

WORD LIST	citation	detached	lurch
	resign		

1. a patient who remains aloof and uninterested
2. a decorated soldier
3. one who stoically tries to make the best of his situation
4. a soldier who has trouble walking due to injury

 Complete the activities in your **Reader/Writer Notebook**.

What are the COSTS *of war?*

Some costs of war can be counted. World War I, the setting of Hemingway's story, claimed the lives of about 9 million soldiers and 13 million civilians. But what about the millions who survived the trauma of the bloodiest and most destructive war in history up to that time? What price did they pay?

What's the Connection?

In a famous short story about World War I, Ernest Hemingway examines a group of soldiers undergoing new and ineffective physical therapy. In a magazine article, Karen Breslau focuses on an innovative approach to therapy for severely wounded soldiers from the war in Iraq. Finally, a book cover combines text with the image of a soldier's bowed head. Before you study these texts, think about what you already know about the psychological effects of war on combat soldiers. What is post-traumatic stress disorder? In what ways might it connect these texts?

1009

VOCABULARY SKILL

▲ VOCABULARY IN CONTEXT

DIAGNOSE WORD KNOWLEDGE Have students complete Vocabulary in Context. Check their answers against the following:

citation (sī-tā′shən) *n.* a formal statement praising a soldier's achievements
detached (dĭ-tăcht′) *adj.* reserved; aloof
lurch (lûrch) *v.* to lean or roll suddenly to one side; stagger

resign (rĭ-zīn′) *v.* to submit or yield wwithout complaint

COMMON CORE L 4

PRETEACH VOCABULARY Use the following copy master to help students predict meanings.

 RESOURCE MANAGER—Copy Master
Vocabulary Study p. 241

Ask the question aloud. Then define trauma as "an experience causing severe and long-lasting emotional distress" and ask what kinds of trauma people might suffer during war.

WHAT'S THE CONNECTION?

Ask students to share what they know about veterans' return to non-military life, following any war. Have them make a list of the veterans' most likely needs and concerns.

TEXT ANALYSIS **COMMON CORE RL 4 RI 4**

● *Model the Skill:* TONE

Help students identify tone. Read aloud these statements.

1. It poured the weekend we camped.
2. The entire weekend was utterly ruined by a clammy, driving rain that gave no quarter to the bedraggled campers.

Point out that the first statement has a detached, objective tone, while the second is far more subjective.

GUIDED PRACTICE Have students write an example that uses an objective tone, then write the same information again, this time with a subjective tone.

READING SKILL **COMMON CORE RL 1 RI 1**

■ *Model the Skill:* MAKE INFERENCES

Read the two examples aloud another time. Point out that in the second example, details like "utterly ruined" and "gave no quarter" infer that the speaker had high expectations for the camping trip and was unprepared for the rain.

GUIDED PRACTICE Have students make an inference about the examples they wrote above.

 RESOURCE MANAGER—Copy Master
Make Inferences p. 239

Practice and Apply

SUMMARY

In this short story, a young wounded American soldier tells of his treatment for a war wound in an Italian hospital. He recounts his interaction with an Italian major, who is struggling to recover from his wound and who teaches the narrator Italian grammar. When the major's wife dies unexpectedly, his grief adds to the hopelessness the narrator feels.

READ WITH A PURPOSE

Help students set a purpose for reading. Tell them to read "In Another Country" to learn what the machines at the hospital represent to the people who use them.

TEXT ANALYSIS

COMMON CORE
RL 4

A TONE

Possible answer: An unsentimental, detached tone is conveyed by details such as "the war was always there, but we did not go to it any more" (line 1) and "it was pleasant along the streets looking in the windows" (line 3). The rhythm created by the repeating coordinating conjunction "and" makes the tone lively.

REVISIT THE BIG QUESTION

What are the COSTS *of war?*

Discuss In lines 19–27, what is the narrator's doctor's opinion of the trauma the narrator has suffered because of the war? *Possible answer: The doctor thinks the narrator should experience very little trauma because he will recover fully (lines 26–27).*

VOCABULARY

COMMON CORE
L 4

OWN THE WORD

lurch: Ask students to look up synonyms for *lurch*. Then have students write two sentences, one with *lurch* and one with a synonym.

Possible answer: With a great lurch *forward, the train began to move down the tracks. With a great* pitch *forward...*

In ANOTHER *Country*

Ernest Hemingway

BACKGROUND World War I was called the Great War and the War to End All Wars. It was the first large-scale modern war with the killing power of new technological weapons. Among the 21 million wounded was 18-year-old Ernest Hemingway, who later wrote this story about soldiers recuperating in Milan, Italy. "In the first war I was hurt very badly," he explained, "in the body, mind, and spirit, and also morally."

In the fall the war was always there, but we did not go to it any more. It was cold in the fall in Milan[1] and the dark came very early. Then the electric lights came on, and it was pleasant along the streets looking in the windows. There was much game hanging outside the shops, and the snow powdered in the fur of the foxes and the wind blew their tails. The deer hung stiff and heavy and empty, and small birds blew in the wind and the wind turned their feathers. It was a cold fall and the wind came down from the mountains. **A**

We were all at the hospital every afternoon, and there were different ways of walking across the town through the dusk to the hospital. Two of the ways were
10 alongside canals, but they were long. Always, though, you crossed a bridge across a canal to enter the hospital. There was a choice of three bridges. On one of them a woman sold roasted chestnuts. It was warm, standing in front of her charcoal fire, and the chestnuts were warm afterward in your pocket. The hospital was very old and very beautiful, and you entered through a gate and walked across a courtyard and out a gate on the other side. There were usually funerals starting from the courtyard. Beyond the old hospital were the new brick pavilions, and there we met every afternoon and were all very polite and interested in what was the matter, and sat in the machines that were to make so much difference.

The doctor came up to the machine where I was sitting and said: "What did
20 you like best to do before the war? Did you practise a sport?"

I said: "Yes, football."

"Good," he said. "You will be able to play football again better than ever."

My knee did not bend and the leg dropped straight from the knee to the ankle without a calf, and the machine was to bend the knee and make it move as in riding a tricycle. But it did not bend yet, and instead the machine **lurched** when it came to the bending part. The doctor said: "That will all pass. You are a fortunate young man. You will play football again like a champion."

In the next machine was a major who had a little hand like a baby's. He winked at me when the doctor examined his hand, which was between two leather straps
30 that bounced up and down and flapped the stiff fingers, and said: "And will I too

---

1. **Milan:** a city in northern Italy.

A TONE
In the first paragraph of this story, Hemingway reveals his mastery at establishing tone. What kinds of details does he use and what kind of feeling is conveyed by these details? What kind of rhythm does the narrator achieve by repeating the coordinating conjunction *and*? How does this rhythm contribute to the tone of the paragraph?

Analyze Visuals ▶
The photo on the opposite page shows a young Ernest Hemingway at a Red Cross hospital in Milan in 1918. How does this photo, depicting real people in a real place, affect the way you read this work of fiction? Explain.

lurch (lûrch) *v.* to lean or roll suddenly to one side; stagger

① Targeted Passage

DIFFERENTIATED INSTRUCTION

FOR ENGLISH LANGUAGE LEARNERS

Vocabulary: Multiple-Meaning Words Students may need help discerning the correct meaning of several words on page 1010. Point out that *game* (line 4) means "the flesh of wild animals that are hunted." Ask students to name the other meanings of *game*. Tell students that context clues or a dictionary can help them with multiple-meaning words. Have them identify the meaning of *fall* (line 6), along with the the context clues that helped them.

FOR STRUGGLING READERS

In combination with the *Audio Anthology CD*, use one or more Targeted Passages (pp. 1010, 1013, 1014) to ensure that students focus on key story events and concepts. Targeted passages are also good for English language learners.

① Targeted Passage [Lines 16–27]

This passage identifies the reason for the narrator's time at the hospital and describes his treatment.

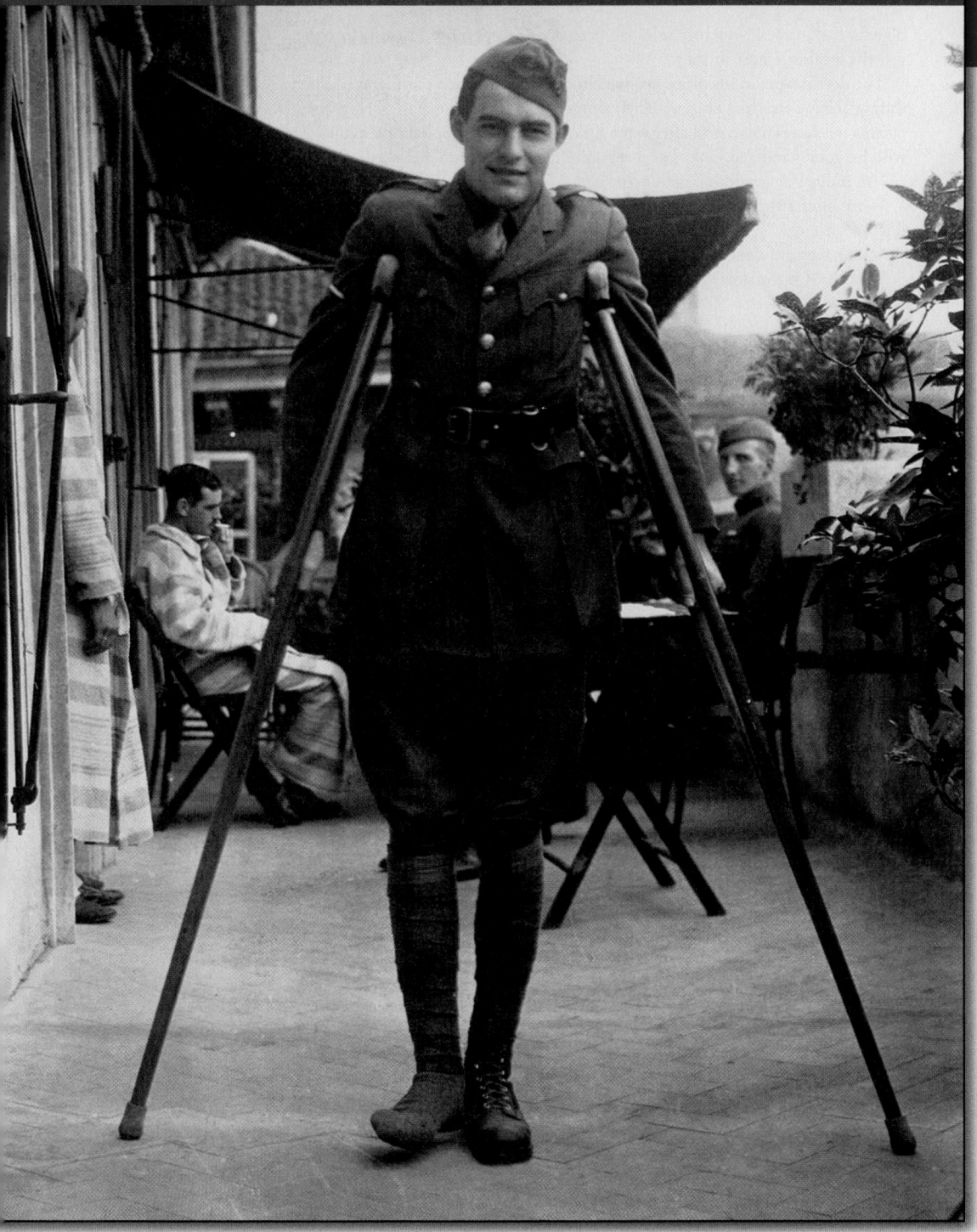

Analyze Visuals

Possible answer: The photo makes the story seem more autobiographical, as the soldier in the picture—Hemingway—is on crutches outside of what looks like a hospital, and the soldier in the story spends time in the hospital because of a leg injury sustained in battle. This makes reading fiction more engaging, as the events may be based on real-life experiences.

BACKGROUND

Doughboys By 1918 Italian forces were exhausted from years of war, but they had a new ally to help them hold the front line: the Doughboys. Officially called the American Expeditionary Forces, these American soldiers began arriving in July 1918 at the request of Italy's government. They had two missions: to create fear in the enemy and to boost the morale of Italian soldiers who had been in the trenches for years. Before the AEF arrived, American pilots dropped leaflets over the line promising the Italian soldiers that the Dough-boys would arrive soon. Not only military units but medical and supply units reinforced the Italian front at this critical time. This is the force in which the young narrator of the story served.

- Who meets at the hospital every afternoon, and why? (lines 16–18)
- What kind of treatment does the narrator undergo? (line 19)
- What is the nature of the narrator's infirmity? (lines 23–25)
- What prognosis does the doctor give the narrator? (lines 26–27)

FOR ADVANCED LEARNERS/AP

Timeline Have students research the events of World War I, including its start, major battles, turning points, and its end. Then ask students to make a timeline that shows each year of the war and its significant events. Have students display their timelines.

B MAKE INFERENCES

Possible answer: *The men's disillusionment can be inferred from their reactions. Even though the doctor displays a photograph of a hand improved by the machine, the major has no confidence that it will help him. The photograph does not show a convincing change in the injured hand.*

IF STUDENTS NEED HELP . . . Urge them to reread lines 30–31 and 34–35 for clues to the major's views of the machine.

TIERED DISCUSSION PROMPTS

In lines 42–57, use these prompts to help students understand how the war has interrupted the soldiers' lives:

Connect Have you ever had to delay plans for your future for an important reason? Explain. *Accept all thoughtful responses.*

Synthesize On the basis of your reading in the historical essay (page 865) and the story, how might the soldiers' situation contribute to the loss of idealism common after World War I? *Possible answer:* *The new and serious injuries of World War I forced many soldiers to postpone life dreams and pursuits. Being in a state of limbo, without the ability to plan for and dream about the future, could lead to a loss of idealism common after World War I.*

OWN THE WORD

detached: Ask students to explain what the author meant when he wrote about the young lieutenant who "had lived a very long time with death and was a little *detached*." *Possible answer:* *The young lieutenant has spent much of his time surrounded by death, trauma, and misery and had disconnected his emotions from reality to protect himself.*

---

play football, captain-doctor?" He had been a very great fencer,[2] and before the war the greatest fencer in Italy.

The doctor went to his office in a back room and brought a photograph which showed a hand that had been withered almost as small as the major's, before it had taken a machine course, and after was a little larger. The major held the photograph with his good hand and looked at it very carefully. "A wound?" he asked.

"An industrial accident," the doctor said.

"Very interesting, very interesting," the major said, and handed it back to the doctor.

40   "You have confidence?"

"No," said the major. B

There were three boys who came each day who were about the same age I was. They were all three from Milan, and one of them was to be a lawyer, and one was to be a painter, and one had intended to be a soldier, and after we were finished with the machines, sometimes we walked back together to the Café Cova, which was next door to the Scala.[3] We walked the short way through the communist quarter because we were four together. The people hated us because we were officers, and from a wine-shop some one would call out, "A basso gli ufficiali!"[4] as we passed. Another boy who walked with us sometimes and made us five wore
50   a black silk handkerchief across his face because he had no nose then and his face was to be rebuilt. He had gone out to the front from the military academy and been wounded within an hour after he had gone into the front line for the first time. They rebuilt his face, but he came from a very old family and they could never get the nose exactly right. He went to South America and worked in a bank. But this was a long time ago, and then we did not any of us know how it was going to be afterward. We only knew then that there was always the war, but that we were not going to it any more.

We all had the same medals, except the boy with the black silk bandage across his face, and he had not been at the front long enough to get any medals. The tall
60   boy with a very pale face who was to be a lawyer had been a lieutenant of Arditi[5] and had three medals of the sort we each had only one of. He had lived a very long time with death and was a little **detached.** We were all a little detached, and there was nothing that held us together except that we met every afternoon at the hospital. Although, as we walked to the Cova through the tough part of town, walking in the dark, with light and singing coming out of the wine-shops, and sometimes having to walk into the street when the men and women would crowd together on the sidewalk so that we would have had to jostle them to get by, we felt held together by there being something that had happened that they, the people who disliked us, did not understand.

70   We ourselves all understood the Cova, where it was rich and warm and not too brightly lighted, and noisy and smoky at certain hours, and there were always girls

---

2. **fencer:** one who fences—that is, practices the art of attack and defense using blunted swords or sabers.
3. **the Scala:** La Scala, a famous opera house in Milan.
4. **"A basso gli ufficiali!"** (ä bä′sō lē ōō′fē-chä′lē) *Italian:* "Down with officers!"
5. **Arditi:** a carefully chosen group of volunteers who specialized in dangerous campaigns.

B MAKE INFERENCES

In lines 16–41, Hemingway doesn't directly state how the soldiers feel about the machines. What can you infer about their emotions from their statements and reactions? Explain, citing evidence.

detached (dĭ-tăcht′) *adj.* reserved; aloof **detach** *v.*

DIFFERENTIATED INSTRUCTION

FOR ENGLISH LANGUAGE LEARNERS

Vocabulary Support Use Definition Mapping to teach these words: *military* (line 51), *academy* (line 51), *uniform* (line 151).

 BEST PRACTICES TOOLKIT—Transparency Definition Mapping p. E6

FOR ADVANCED LEARNERS/AP

Analyze Repetition [paired option] Ask students to read lines 56–57 and identify where else in the story they have read this text (*line 1*). Have them analyze Hemingway's repetition and decide why he repeats this text. Ask partners to consider first what the soldiers mean and whether they are accurately describing the situation. Invite students to develop a cause-and-effect statement about how the tone of these repeated lines affects the story's theme.

at the tables and the illustrated papers on a rack on the wall. The girls at the Cova were very patriotic, and I found that the most patriotic people in Italy were the café girls—and I believe they are still patriotic.

The boys at first were very polite about my medals and asked me what I had done to get them. I showed them the papers, which were written in very beautiful language and full of *fratellanza* and *abnegazione*,[6] but which really said, with the adjectives removed, that I had been given the medals because I was an American. After that their manner changed a little toward me, although I was their friend

80 against outsiders. I was a friend, but I was never really one of them after they had read the **citations,** because it had been different with them and they had done very different things to get their medals. I had been wounded, it was true; but we all knew that being wounded, after all, was really an accident. I was never ashamed of the ribbons, though, and sometimes, after the cocktail hour, I would imagine myself having done all the things they had done to get their medals; but walking home at night through the empty streets with the cold wind and all the shops closed, trying to keep near the street lights, I knew that I would never have done such things, and I was very much afraid to die, and often lay in bed at night by myself, afraid to die and wondering how I would be when I went back to the front again. **C**

90 The three with the medals were like hunting-hawks; and I was not a hawk, although I might seem a hawk to those who had never hunted; they, the three, knew better and so we drifted apart. But I stayed good friends with the boy who had been wounded his first day at the front, because he would never know now how he would have turned out; so he could never be accepted either, and I liked him because I thought perhaps he would not have turned out to be a hawk either. **D**

The major, who had been the great fencer, did not believe in bravery, and spent much time while we sat in the machines correcting my grammar. He had complimented me on how I spoke Italian, and we talked together very easily. One day I had said that Italian seemed such an easy language to me that I could not
100 take a great interest in it; everything was so easy to say. "Ah, yes," the major said. "Why, then, do you not take up the use of grammar?" So we took up the use of grammar, and soon Italian was such a difficult language that I was afraid to talk to him until I had the grammar straight in my mind.

The major came very regularly to the hospital. I do not think he ever missed a day, although I am sure he did not believe in the machines. There was a time when none of us believed in the machines, and one day the major said it was all nonsense. The machines were new then and it was we who were to prove them. It was an idiotic idea, he said, "a theory, like another." I had not learned my grammar, and he said I was a stupid impossible disgrace, and he was a fool to have
110 bothered with me. He was a small man and he sat straight up in his chair with his right hand thrust into the machine and looked straight ahead at the wall while the straps thumped up and down with his fingers in them.

"What will you do when the war is over if it is over?" he asked me. "Speak grammatically!"

---

6. *fratellanza* and *abnegazione* (frä′tĕ-län′zä; äb-nĕ-gä-zē-o′nĕ) *Italian*: brotherhood and self-denial.

② **Targeted Passage**

citation (sī-tā′shən) *n.* a formal statement praising a soldier's achievements

C MAKE INFERENCES
Consider how the narrator describes his relationship with his fellow soldiers. How might such interactions affect him?

D MAKE INFERENCES
Reread lines 90–95. How does the **metaphor** about hawks further describe the difference between the narrator and the young Italian soldiers? What sense do you get of how the narrator feels about this difference?

C Model the Skill: MAKE INFERENCES

Point out that the narrator mentions how the other soldiers earned their medals. After he showed the others the paperwork that came with his medals, "their manner changed a little" toward him.

Possible answer: The narrator describes his relationship to the other soldiers by noting that they have been brave in combat, while he has not. Already in another country and shunned by its citizens (lines 47–49), he now also feels separated from his peers.

D MAKE INFERENCES

Possible answer: The metaphor heightens the difference between the narrator and the soldiers. They have a hawk's courage, instincts, or love of fighting, but he does not. This drives a wedge between the narrator and his peers. Despite his matter-of-fact description, the narrator's sense of isolation and alienation is clear.

IF STUDENTS NEED HELP . . . Review that metaphors compare unlike things and explain the comparison in lines 90–92.

OWN THE WORD

citation: Point out that the root verb for *citation* is *cite*, and that *citation* has several definitions. Have students use a dictionary to make a list of the various definitions of the word. *Possible answers: quote from an authoritative source; reference to court decisions or authoritative writings; a formal statement of accomplishments with an academic degree; an official summons*

FOR STRUGGLING READERS

② **Targeted Passage** [Lines 75–89]

This passage explains why the narrator has received a citation and his feelings about it.

• How did the Italian soldiers earn their medals? (lines 80–82)

• How did the narrator earn his medal? (line 82)

• What does he think about having been wounded? (lines 82–85)

• How does he feel about returning to the front? (lines 85–89)

FOR ADVANCED LEARNERS/AP

Analyze Character Motivation [small-group option] Have students discuss this question as they make inferences about the major's character: Why, if the major does not "believe in the machines" (line 105), does he never miss a day at the hospital? Students should support their inferences with textual evidence and prior knowledge.

TIERED DISCUSSION PROMPTS

TIERED DISCUSSION PROMPTS

In lines 116–139, use these prompts to help students understand the major's impact on the narrator's war experience:

Summarize Describe the relationship between the major and the narrator.
Possible answer: The narrator admires the major (lines 96–98). The major teaches the narrator Italian grammar (lines 101–103).

Analyze Why is it so important to the major to convince the narrator not to marry?
Possible answer: The major feels intensely sad. He thinks he would sacrifice marriage to escape the grief he feels now.

TEXT ANALYSIS · COMMON CORE · RL 4

E TONE

Possible answer: The major learns that his wife has died, which makes him soften and speak more politely. The narrator feels empathy for him. He notes that in the end, the major "only looked out of the window," instead of at the photographs, presumably thinking of his wife and everything else he has lost. The tone is austere and melancholy.

F GRAMMAR AND STYLE · COMMON CORE L 3a

Establish Tone Plain diction uses short and mostly simple words. Have students describe how plain diction reinforces Hemingway's tone. *Possible answer: It counterbalances the drama of the scene.*

VOCABULARY · COMMON CORE L 4

OWN THE WORD

resign: Remind students that the definition for *resign* as used in the context of this story means "to submit or yield without complaint; accept as inevitable." Ask students if they have ever had to *resign* themselves to a situation.

SELECTION WRAP–UP

READ WITH A PURPOSE Now that students have read "In Another Country," they may see the machines as the men's new reality. Ask students what attitude the men have toward both the machines and life.

"I will go to the States."

"Are you married?"

"No, but I hope to be."

"The more of a fool you are," he said. He seemed very angry. "A man must not marry."

120 "Why, Signor Maggiore?"[7]

"Don't call me 'Signor Maggiore.'"

"Why must not a man marry?"

"He cannot marry. He cannot marry," he said angrily. "If he is to lose everything, he should not place himself in a position to lose that. He should not place himself in a position to lose. He should find things he cannot lose."

He spoke very angrily and bitterly, and looked straight ahead while he talked.

"But why should he necessarily lose it?"

"He'll lose it," the major said. He was looking at the wall. Then he looked down at the machine and jerked his little hand out from between the straps and 130 slapped it hard against his thigh. "He'll lose it," he almost shouted. "Don't argue with me!" Then he called to the attendant who ran the machines. "Come and turn this thing off."

He went back into the other room for the light treatment and the massage. Then I heard him ask the doctor if he might use his telephone and he shut the door. When he came back into the room, I was sitting in another machine. He was wearing his cape and had his cap on, and he came directly toward my machine and put his arm on my shoulder.

"I am so sorry," he said, and patted me on the shoulder with his good hand. "I would not be rude. My wife has just died. You must forgive me."

140 "Oh—" I said, feeling sick for him. "I am *so* sorry."

He stood there biting his lower lip. "It is very difficult," he said. "I cannot **resign** myself."

He looked straight past me and out through the window. Then he began to cry. "I am utterly unable to resign myself," he said and choked. And then crying, his head up looking at nothing, carrying himself straight and soldierly, with tears on both his cheeks and biting his lips, he walked past the machines and out the door.

The doctor told me that the major's wife, who was very young and whom he had not married until he was definitely invalided[8] out of the war, had died of pneumonia. She had been sick only a few days. No one expected her to die. The 150 major did not come to the hospital for three days. Then he came at the usual hour, wearing a black band on the sleeve of his uniform. When he came back, there were large framed photographs around the wall, of all sorts of wounds before and after they had been cured by the machines. In front of the machine the major used were three photographs of hands like his that were completely restored. I do not know where the doctor got them. I always understood we were the first to use the machines. The photographs did not make much difference to the major because he only looked out of the window.

---

7. **Signor Maggiore** (sēn-yôr' mäd-jō'rĕ) *Italian:* Mr. Major—a respectful way of addressing an officer.

8. **invalided:** removed from active service because of sickness or injury.

---

resign (rĭ-zīn') *v.* to submit or yield without complaint

E TONE
Reread lines 133–146. What news does the major receive here? How does this news affect the major and the narrator's tone? Then, as you read the last paragraph, focus on the narrator's attitude. Hemingway closes the story with an image of the major at the window. What do you think is on his mind as he looks out the window? How does his mental state contribute to the story's tone?

F GRAMMAR AND STYLE
Reread lines 149–157. Note that though Hemingway describes a highly emotional situation, his short, **declarative sentences** and **plain diction** keep his **tone** detached and objective.

DIFFERENTIATED INSTRUCTION

FOR STRUGGLING READERS

3 Targeted Passage [Lines 138–151]

This passage explains the major's behavior and shows the narrator's enduring sadness.

- What event provokes the major's angry words about marriage? (lines 138–149)

- How does the major view his outburst? (lines 138–139)

- Why does the doctor display pictures of cured hands? (lines 151–154)

Develop Reading Fluency Give students practice reading dialogue aloud. Tell them that fluent readers read dialogue with expression, letting punctuation marks guide their pauses and intonation. Model reading aloud a few lines, taking the part of the narrator and assigning the major's lines to a proficient reader. Tell have pairs of students read the dialogue from lines 113–128, not reading the narration aloud, but letting it guide their deliveries.

Comprehension

1. **Recall** Why is the narrator in Milan?

2. **Recall** What did the major do before the war?

3. **Summarize** How is the narrator different from the other young soldiers?

Text Analysis

● 4. **Make Inferences** Review the inferences you made as you read. The narrator of this story is literally "in another country"—he is far from home, in a foreign, war-torn nation. What other aspects of his situation serve to further isolate or alienate him? Describe the text clues and prior knowledge that allowed you to infer how the narrator's situation affects him. Be sure to address each of the following:

   • how the narrator differs from the young Italian officers
   • the Italian civilians' response to the soldiers
   • how the narrator's circumstances differ from the major's at the story's end

● 5. **Analyze Tone** Reread the dialogue between the narrator and the major (lines 113–146). What kind of loss has the major experienced here, and how does he respond to his loss? What is the narrator's attitude toward the major? Cite evidence from the text to support your answer.

6. **Analyze Style** Reexamine the text, looking for examples of the following elements of Hemingway's prose **style**: short sentences; few adverbs or adjectives; and sharp, concrete images. Explain how Hemingway's style causes this story to be so emotionally charged despite the lack of direct commentary on the characters' emotions.

Text Criticism

7. **Historical Context** Influential author and patron Gertrude Stein formed a community with Fitzgerald, Hemingway, and other modernist writers living as expatriates in Paris in the 1920s. Their particular disillusionment prompted her to characterize them as a "lost generation." In what way do the characters in both "Winter Dreams" on page 978 and "In Another Country" remain "lost" at the end of each story? What might this say about the era in which these stories were written? Explain, citing evidence from both stories.

> *What are the* **COSTS** *of war?*
>
> Wounds suffered by soldiers on the battlefield are among the costs of war on display in this story. What other costs of war are endured by the soldiers here? Support your answer with evidence from the story.

COMMON CORE

RL 1 Cite textual evidence to support analysis of what the text says explicitly as well as inferences drawn from the text, including determining where the text leaves matters uncertain. **RL 4** Analyze the impact of specific word choices on meaning and tone, including words with multiple meanings or language that is particularly fresh, engaging, or beautiful.

Practice and Apply

For preliminary support of post-reading questions, use these copy masters:

R RESOURCE MANAGER—Copy Masters
  Reading Check p. 244
  Tone p. 237
  Question Support p. 245
  Additional selection questions are provided for teachers on page 232.

ANSWERS  COMMON CORE **RL 1, RL 4**

1. *The narrator is in Milan to receive physical therapy at the hospital.*

2. *He was an accomplished fencer.*

3. *He is an American. He did not receive his medal for a specific act of heroism.*

Possible answers:

4. ■ COMMON CORE FOCUS **Make Inferences** *In addition to his physical isolation, several factors further isolate the narrator. He received his medal for being American (lines 78–82), not brave like the Italian soldiers. He is not a "hawk" as he sees them (lines 90–92). The Italian civilians, who lack experience of war, "disliked" and "did not understand" the officers (line 69). The narrator cannot connect to the major's loss and thus loses his one friend and becomes even more alone.*

5. ● COMMON CORE FOCUS **Tone** *The major has lost his wife. He responds by suggesting that no one marry, as not to risk the pain he now feels. The narrator shows respect for the major, allowing him to express himself without criticism, such as when the major speaks out against marriage (lines 118–127). The narrator's attitude is sympathetic; he understands that the major has lost even more than he has.*

6. *Stylistic Element: short sentences; objective tone; real-world modifiers; sharp, concrete images. Examples: "My wife has just died" (line 139); "No one . . . to die" (line 149); the café is "smoky" and "noisy" (line 71); "the wind . . . mountains" (line 7). His style is pared, forcing readers to dig for emotional clues. The contrast between the spare prose and the major's final wellspring of emotion is notable.*

7. *The soldiers in Hemingway's story, like Dexter at the end of "Winter Dreams," have lost their youthful illusions and remain detached, empty, and lonely as a result.*

They have aged out of youthful optimism before their time. The brutality of war isolates Hemingway's characters and makes them cynical. Dexter and possibly Judy lose the dream of ideal love. Dexter, especially, is alone in the end, like the major staring out the window, detached from the other soldiers by his traumatic loss. The stories chronicle the loss of optimism experienced by many in the years after World War I.

> *What are the* **COSTS** *of war?*
>
> ***Possible answer:*** *Other costs of war include missing important events at home, such as the major not being there to comfort his dying wife; a loss of identity, as the major no longer sees himself as a fencer; and a blow to the soldiers' confidence, as seen in the narrator doubting his bravery.*

ANSWERS

Vocabulary in Context

▲ **VOCABULARY PRACTICE**

1. *citation*   3. *lurch*

2. *detached*   4. *resign*

 **RESOURCE MANAGER—Copy Master**
Vocabulary Practice p. 242

ACADEMIC VOCABULARY IN WRITING

Before they begin writing, guide students to think about what happens when they give in to the stress of a situation. Have them identify coping strategies that helped them in the past. Remind them to use Academic Vocabulary words to express the attitude that accompanies the strategies.

VOCABULARY STRATEGY:
THE ORIGIN OF ACADEMIC WORDS

COMMON
CORE L6

- Assist students with the pronunciation of the words, especially *fjord* and *adagio*.

- Guide students to identify cognates when possible: *rotunda*, for instance, is related to *rotund*, or *round*.

Answers:

1. *f*   5. *a*

2. *d*   6. *e*

3. *c*   7. *g*

4. *h*   8. *b*

 **RESOURCE MANAGER—Copy Master**
Vocabulary Strategy p. 243

Interactive Vocabulary   **THINK** central

Keywords direct students to a **WordSharp** tutorial on **thinkcentral.com** or to other types of vocabulary practice and review.

Vocabulary in Context

▲ **VOCABULARY PRACTICE**

Choose the word from the word list that best completes each sentence.

1. Though only a few soldiers had received a(n) _____ for bravery, many of the others had also performed commendably.

2. Some of the soldiers sought companionship, while others remained aloof and _____.

3. It was painful to see young men _____ around on unsteady legs.

4. Was it better to struggle or to _____ oneself to one's fate?

> **WORD LIST**
> citation
> detached
> lurch
> resign

ACADEMIC VOCABULARY IN WRITING

> • conclude   • criteria   • despite   • justify   • maintain

The protagonist and other soldiers of "In Another Country" **maintain** a particular attitude toward life in the aftermath of combat. What kind of attitude do you recommend during times of stress? In a paragraph, identify this attitude and **justify** it to your readers. Use at least three of the Academic Vocabulary words in your writing.

VOCABULARY STRATEGY: THE ORIGIN OF ACADEMIC WORDS

As the narrator of this story would have noticed in his study of Italian, many English words are derived from that language, especially in the content areas of music and the arts. Academic vocabulary words, which include the words that apply to a specific content area, are important to your success in school. Many of those words are derived from other languages. You can use your knowledge of the word origins to improve your knowledge of academic vocabulary.

COMMON CORE

L 6 Acquire and use accurately general academic and domain-specific words and phrases, sufficient for reading, writing, speaking, and listening at the college and career readiness level.

PRACTICE Match each boldfaced academic term with its meaning. Then identify the language of origin.

1. **rotunda**   a. the art of painting on fresh moist plaster

2. **fjord**   b. a colorless and transparent mineral

3. **economy**   c. the efficient use of material resources

4. **parliament**   d. a narrow section of sea set between rocky cliffs

5. **fresco**   e. a slow movement in a piece of music

6. **adagio**   f. a circular part of a building, usually with a dome

7. **archaeology**   g. the science that studies the remains of past human life

8. **quartz**   h. a major legislative body

 **Interactive Vocabulary** **THINK** central

Go to **thinkcentral.com**.
KEYWORD: HML11-1016

DIFFERENTIATED INSTRUCTION

FOR ENGLISH LANGUAGE LEARNERS

Task Support: Vocabulary Strategy Encourage students who speak Latin-based languages to search in their home language for words similar to those from Italian. Have students define the words for classmates and then compare the similarities in the various languages discussed.

FOR ADVANCED LEARNERS/AP

Words from Italian After students complete the exercise, refer them to the angry words that Italian citizens yell at the soldiers: *"A basso gli ufficiali!"* (line 48). Challenge students to locate and use two cognates in this cry to help them get its gist without the translation in the footnote. ***Example:*** *"Officers are low," which builds on a similarity between "basso" and base, which means "low or bottom" and between "ufficiali" and officers.*

Language

◆ **GRAMMAR AND STYLE:** Establish Tone

Review the **Grammar and Style** note on page 1014. **Tone** is the expression of a writer's attitude toward a subject. Hemingway's early training as a newspaper reporter heavily influenced the tone of his fiction, giving it the emotional detachment and objectivity of a news report. Such a tone is achieved partly through his use of short, **declarative sentences** and **plain diction,** a style he also picked up from newspapers. Notice the simple language and understated quality of the following sentences:

> *It was cold in the fall in Milan and the dark came very early. Then the electric lights came on, and it was pleasant along the streets looking in the windows. There was much game hanging outside the shops, and the snow powdered in the fur of the foxes and the wind blew their tails. The deer hung stiff and heavy and empty, and small birds blew in the wind and the wind turned their feathers. It was a cold fall and the wind came down from the mountains.* (lines 1–7)

PRACTICE Rewrite the following paragraph, adapting the language and sentence types to mimic Hemingway's objectivity.

> The horrible, fiery inferno had completely annihilated everything, like an angry, vengeful God. Only the charred foundation of the Harlington Hotel remained, with its lone chimney of chipped and blackened stone standing forlornly amid the devastation like a victim of survivor guilt. Never again would we see the thick forest in its green majestic splendor! Ugly black stumps studded the land like tombstones. It was the landscape of damnation! Gone were the songs of birds, the chirps of chipmunks, and the laughter of children! A deafening silence enveloped the area for miles around. Only black grasshoppers flitted about the soot, sending up tiny clouds of ash.

READING-WRITING CONNECTION

 Expand your understanding of "In Another Country" by responding to this prompt. Then, use the **revising tips** to improve your profile.

WRITING PROMPT	**REVISING TIPS**
WRITE A CHARACTER PROFILE Most of Hemingway's male protagonists share such strikingly similar traits that critics have named this type of character the "Hemingway hero." Using the examples of the narrator and the major in this story, create a **three-to-five-paragraph profile** of the Hemingway hero.	• Check your thesis statement to be sure you have defined the Hemingway hero. • Since tone is an essential feature of the Hemingway narrator, be sure that your essay focuses on a particular kind of attitude. • Examine the story's conclusion and be sure that you use it as supporting evidence.

Interactive Revision THINK central
Go to **thinkcentral.com.**
KEYWORD: HML11-1017

 **COMMON CORE**
L 3a Vary syntax for effect.
W 2e Establish and maintain an objective tone while attending to discipline-specific norms and conventions.

Language

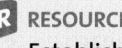 **COMMON CORE L 3a, W 2e**

◆ **GRAMMAR AND STYLE**

Provide news articles and have students read them aloud as if reporting the news for radio or television. Ask what is missing from such readings. (*emotions, opinions, commentary are missing*) Explain that Hemingway's style also presents the facts in a straightforward manner.

R RESOURCE MANAGER—Copy Master
Establish Tone p. 246

READING-WRITING CONNECTION

To help students organize their ideas, have them complete a Character Traits and Textual Evidence chart for the narrator and the major.

💼 BEST PRACTICES TOOLKIT—Transparency
Character Traits and Textual Evidence p. D6

Writing Online THINK central

The following tools are available online at **thinkcentral.com** and on Write*Smart* CD-ROM:
• **Interactive Graphic Organizers**
• **Interactive Student Models**
• **Interactive Revision Lessons**
For additional grammar instruction, see **GrammarNotes** on **thinkcentral.com**.

Assess and Reteach

Assess

DIAGNOSTIC AND SELECTION TESTS
Selection Test A pp. 273–274
Selection Test B/C pp. 275–276

Interactive Selection Test on **thinkcentral.com**

Reteach

Level Up Online Tutorials on **thinkcentral.com**
Reteaching Worksheets on **thinkcentral.com**

Literature Lesson 1: Types of Characters and Character Traits
Literature Lesson 27: Simile and Metaphor
Literature Lesson 40: Word Choice and Diction
Literature Lesson 43: Tone
Literature Lesson 44: Style and Syntax
Reading Lesson 8: Making Inferences
Vocabulary Lesson 25: Etymologies

FOR STRUGGLING WRITERS

Writing Support

• Limit the character profile to two or three paragraphs.

• Refer students to the author biography on page 1008 for historical context.

• Provide these sentence starters to help students draft their thesis statements: The Hemingway hero is characterized by three traits. These traits are _____, _____, and _____.

• Remind students to give examples from the story for each character trait they mention.

• Urge students to identify whether examples refer to the narrator or the major.

SUMMARY

In "Healing War's Wounds," Karen Breslau reports on the physical and psychological therapy that some soldiers now undergo after they are wounded in battle.

MAGAZINE ARTICLE

Both "In Another Country" and "Healing War's Wounds" tell about wounded soldiers and the hardships they face. Use a Comparison Matrix to help compare statements made by each piece.

 BEST PRACTICES TOOLKIT—Transparency
Comparison Matrix p.A24

READING SKILL
COMMON CORE
RI 1

Ⓐ MAKING INFERENCES

Possible answer: *The soldiers have come to accept their injuries and find they like to use humor to reach out to strangers such as the other group of rafters. Major Anthony Smith jokes about how he asks waitresses, "Can you give me a hand?" (lines 7–8).*

Reading for Information

Magazine Article

In Hemingway's short story, you read about soldiers undergoing physical therapy for wounds suffered on the Italian front in World War I. In Karen Breslau's article, you'll discover how soldiers injured in the Iraq war use extreme sports to regain their physical and mental health.

HEALING WAR'S WOUNDS

Karen Breslau

> ***BACKGROUND*** The conflict in Iraq started in March 2003, when a coalition led by the United States entered the country and toppled the government of Saddam Hussein. U.S. troops in Iraq have been threatened by violent opposition to the American presence there. Because of medical advances, severely wounded soldiers often survive to face difficult and lengthy recoveries. Karen Breslau, who writes about these soldiers in "Healing War's Wounds," is *Newsweek*'s San Francisco bureau chief.

"Hey, have any of y'all seen the crocodile that got my arm?" U.S. Army Maj. Anthony Smith hoists his prosthetic[1] hook, tied to a paddle, as he floats down Idaho's Salmon River in a large blue raft, manned by a cackling crew of fellow amputees. Momentarily rattled, a group of rafters resting onshore stare as Smith's boat glides by, before someone on the beach points down the rapids and yells, "He went that-a-way." Smith, digging his paddle back into the water, growls with mock pirate glee. "You should see what happens when I'm in a restaurant and I say to the waitress 'Can you give me a hand?'" Ⓐ

10   He can laugh now. It's the surest sign yet of the progress he's made since April 24, 2004, when Smith, then a captain with an Arkansas National Guard unit stationed near Baghdad[2], was struck by a rocket-propelled grenade. . . . As Smith staggered to his feet, insurgents[3] opened fire, shooting him four times. By the time medics[4] reached him minutes later, Smith had "flat-lined." Finding no pulse or respiration, they loaded him into a body bag and put his name on the list of those KIA, killed in action. Only as a soldier was preparing to zip shut the bag did she notice an air bubble in the blood oozing from Smith's neck wound. "They said, 'Hey, this guy's still alive,'" Smith says.

---

1. **prosthetic:** artificial, as of a replacement for a missing body part.
2. **Baghdad:** capital city of Iraq.
3. **insurgents:** loosely organized fighters who oppose the presence of the U.S. military in Iraq.
4. **medics:** trained military personnel who rescue wounded soldiers and administer life-saving first aid.

Ⓐ MAKING INFERENCES
Examine the dialogue in the opening paragraph. What can you infer about the soldiers from the way they speak? Explain, citing evidence.

DIFFERENTIATED INSTRUCTION

FOR STRUGGLING READERS

Understanding Sequence Students may struggle with the time order used in the article's opening paragraphs. Point out that the events in the first and third paragraphs occur in the present, while the second details what happened in April 2004. Tell students that clue words such as *now* and *since* (line 9) help readers understand sequence. Ask students to look for another word or phrase that tells time order in the first three paragraphs:

"two and a half years later" (line 18). For extra practice, have students make a timeline that shows the events described in the article.

◀ **Analyze Visuals**
What mood does the photographer capture with this image? How does the photograph support the tone of the article it accompanies? Cite details from the photograph and the selection to support your response.

Two and a half years later, Smith recounts his own resurrection in vivid detail—not because he remembers (he was in a coma for six weeks), but because
20 he has pieced the story together from conversations with his wife, Jackie, and the dozens of doctors who labored to save him. Smith has endured more than 30 surgical procedures to reconstruct his abdomen, the remains of his right arm, his burned face and the gaping wound in his hip, now painfully infected. He must be constantly monitored for signs of traumatic brain injury that may have resulted from the force of his skull's slamming against the inside of his helmet. **B**

Though Smith's tale of survival is extreme, it is no longer unheard of. . . . But it also presents a huge challenge for the military as this sizable population of wounded veterans returns to society, bearing complex disabilities that will require lifelong care.

To address the problem, the military has adopted a holistic[5] mind-body approach,
30 deploying a fleet of experts ranging from orthopedic[6] surgeons to therapists to work on the wounded. Doctors insist on group therapy to help cope with the guilt that often dogs survivors who have lost—or left—comrades on the battlefield. Of special concern are the service members, like Smith, classified by the Pentagon as "severely injured"— having lost limbs or eyesight, or suffering burns, paralysis or debilitating brain injuries that will not emerge fully in some cases for years. "Technology has advanced to the point where we can salvage patients who would not have survived before," says Lt. Col. John McManus of the Army's Institute for Surgical Research in San Antonio, Texas. "The bigger test is psychological. Can we restore a life worth living?"

The Pentagon has recently begun testing more experimental methods,
40 rehabilitating wounded service members with extreme sports designed to build muscle—and self-confidence. . . . Patients who work out regularly, lifting weights and yanking pulleys from their wheelchairs, often with burned and mangled limbs, are rewarded with all-expenses-paid outdoor expeditions. It was just such an invitation that brought Smith, two other wounded service members and their wives to the

B TONE
Reread lines 18–25, with special attention to the information the writer provides about Major Smith. What do you learn from this passage about Major Smith and the writer's attitude toward him? Support your answer with details from the paragraph.

---

5. **holistic:** relating to the whole of something instead of its parts.
6. **orthopedic:** medically related to the bones, joints, or muscles.

FOR ENGLISH LANGUAGE LEARNERS
Vocabulary Skill: Idiom Check that students understand the idioms in the selection. Tell them that *y'all* (line 1) is used in some parts of the country as the plural form of *you*. Remind students that *you* is used as both a singular and plural pronoun in standard English. Then tell students that *dogs* in line 32 means "plagues" or "troubles." Ask students to use *y'all* and *dogs* in sentences of their own.

Analyze Visuals

Possible answer: The image captures an exultant mood. The photo supports the positive tone of the article because it illustrates the holistic mind-body approach of rehabilitating wounded military service members through extreme sports to build both muscles and self-confidence.

TIERED DISCUSSION PROMPTS

In lines 26–41, use these prompts to discuss the recent progress in treating wounded military service members:

CONNECT Have you or anyone you know ever needed medical attention for injuries? What needs emerged during recovery? *Accept all reasonable answers.*

ANALYZE Lt. Col. John McManus said with medical technology able to save many patients, "the bigger test is psychological. Can we restore a life worth living?" What does McManus mean? *Possible answer: It is not enough just to heal the physical wounds. McManus wants to be sure the patients get to live satisfying lives.*

EVALUATE How well does Karen Breslau describe the results of the Sun Valley Adaptive Sports week-long program? *Possible answer: Breslau describes the results clearly. Including information about Erik Schultz showed how differently someone may feel before and after the program.*

TEXT ANALYSIS   COMMON CORE
                                     RI 4
B *Model the Skill:* **TONE**

To help students understand Breslau's tone, draw students' attention to the writer's choice of words. Point out that her phrase regarding Smith, "his own resurrection" could have been written "his accident" or "his near-death experience." Tell students that "his own resurrection" is far more dramatic and it reminds the reader just how remarkable Smith's recovery has been. *Possible answer: Major Smith has battled back from severe injuries through self-will and physical therapy. The writer considers Smith a hero (lines 21–28).*

◀ Analyze Visuals
What emotions do you think the veteran in the paragliding harness was feeling at the moment the photograph was taken? What details of the scene help you identify his emotions?

Salmon River last month. They were the guests of Sun Valley Adaptive Sports—one of several private nonprofits consulting with the Pentagon. On the week's agenda: white-water rafting, paragliding, rock climbing and horseback riding. With the group is Erik Schultz, a backcountry sports enthusiast who was paralyzed in a skiing accident eight years ago. During his darkest depression, says Schultz, friends "literally
50 dragged me" on a camping trip. After a week in the wilderness, "I was bursting with self-confidence. Things didn't seem that hard anymore." He hopes that his presence in a wheelchair, fly-fishing from a rocky beach and whooping his way down the river, will help "demystify" disabled life for the wounded service members. **C**

Free from their hospital routines, and the weight of their wounds, Smith and the others spend their days splashing like kids. U.S. Marine S/Sgt. Damion Jacobs, who lost his right leg below the knee to an IED[7] near Fallujah six months ago, removes his prosthetic and props it in the sand like a coffee table; he leans against it while watching the show. Jacobs plans to take his Marine Corps physical and return to active duty. Army Spc. Andrew Soule, an intense, dignified 25-year-old who has
60 emerged as the star of BAMC's rehab program, says that before his injury, he wasn't "much of an athlete." A year ago Soule lost both legs and suffered a severe arm injury in a bomb blast in Afghanistan. Now he kayaks, hand-cycles and surfs. On the first day of the river trip, one of Soule's carbon-fiber prosthetics is fractured. He tosses the limb aside and, for the next five days, kayaks legless, dragging his body over rocky beaches, even climbing stairs, with his arms. "People have this tendency to overreact," says Soule, who left Texas A&M after 9/11 to join the Army. "They don't know how much you can do for yourself." **D**

Even Soule is amazed by how far he has come. As he lay tourniqueted[8] on the ground last year next to the wreckage of his Humvee near the Pakistani border,
70 waiting for a helicopter to rescue him, Soule's squad leader leaned over him and instructed the young soldier to repeat over and over, "I'm going to live. I'm going to live." It's a lesson he carried with him, down the Salmon River and beyond. ∞

C TONE
The author clearly admires the soldiers for participating in extreme adventure sports. What details in this paragraph convey her admiring tone?

D MAKING INFERENCES
Reread lines 54–67. What kind of message about the soldiers and about life can you infer from the details the writer includes here? Cite evidence to support your answer.

---

7. **IED:** improvised explosive device; the military term for a homemade bomb.
8. **tourniqueted:** fitted with a device to prevent blood loss from a major wound.

 **TONE**

Possible answer: *Phrases like "work out regularly, lifting weights and yanking pulleys" (lines 41–42) and "whooping his way down the river" (line 53) show that the author admires the soldiers who participate in the extreme adventure sports.*

D *Model the Skill:* **MAKING INFERENCES**

Point out that the writer describes Soule as "intense" and "dignified" and someone who "wasn't much of an athlete" before his injury (lines 61–63). Tell students that now Soule is a "star" who kayaks, hand-surfs, and surfs. His injury led him to new activities at which he excels. Have students find other details about Soule and describe what those details say about him and about life. **Possible answer:** *When Soule's prosthetic leg is damaged, he "tosses the limb aside," and for the rest of the trip "kayaks legless, dragging his body over rocky beaches, even climbing stairs, with his arms." This shows that, like Soule himself said, people can do much more than they sometimes think.*

DIFFERENTIATED INSTRUCTION

FOR STRUGGLING READERS
Develop Reading Fluency Give students practice reading nonfiction. Model reading aloud with expression, at an appropriate pace, observing punctuation with the correct pauses and reading the quotations with intonation. Read aloud the last two paragraphs on page 1020. Then have students read aloud the same paragraphs.

FOR ADVANCED LEARNERS/AP
Research Tell students that the mind-body approach to health is not only used by the U.S. military to help wounded soldiers. Ask students to research this topic and write a report about the mind-body connection and the benefits of holistic therapy. Have students present their reports orally to the class.

Book Cover

This book cover features the bowed head of a combat soldier. The subtitle identifies the book's subject: "returning troops." Breslau's magazine article focuses also on returning troops, while Hemingway's short story features wounded soldiers in treatment near the front. As you study the book cover, think about how the words come together with the image to engage potential readers. Respond to the questions below, citing evidence from the book cover to support your answers.

COMMON CORE

RI 7 Integrate and evaluate multiple sources of information presented in different media or formats as well as in words in order to address a question.

MOVING A NATION TO CARE

POST-TRAUMATIC STRESS DISORDER AND AMERICA'S RETURNING TROOPS

ILONA MEAGHER

WITH AN INTRODUCTION BY PENNY COLEMAN

1. INTERPRET
Examine the image of the soldier. Notice the camouflaged helmet, which indicates that he is on active duty. Notice also that his head is bowed and that his eyes are in shadow. What kind of mood does the image convey? Why do you think the publisher chose this image for a book about post-traumatic stress disorder in returning soldiers?

2. MAKE INFERENCES
What persuasive message does the book title convey? What purpose does the publisher achieve by running the title in large block letters across the top of the cover? Explain your responses.

1021

COMMON CORE FOCUS

RI 7 Integrate and evaluate multiple sources of information presented in different media or formats as well as in words in order to address a question.

BOOK COVER

Ask students to recall the major and the narrator of "In Another Country" and soldiers such as Anthony Smith and Andrew Soule as they look at the book cover. Ask them what the soldier on the cover may have in common with the characters and people they have read about. Students may note that the soldier seems sad, withdrawn, and uncommunicative. They may say he reminds them of the major in "In Another Country" and of the men in "Healing War's Wounds" before their bodies and minds began to respond to their holistic treatment.

ANALYZE VISUALS   COMMON CORE   RI 7

1. INTERPRET
Possible answer: *The image of the soldier suggests a serious and solemn mood. The publisher may have chosen it to convey that the book addresses post-traumatic stress disorder with honesty, depth, and sympathy.*

ANALYZE VISUALS   COMMON CORE   RI 7

2. MAKE INFERENCES
Possible answer: *The book title implies that the general population is not very interested in the soldiers' plight. The title also implies that the book and the people it tells about can solve this problem. The large block letters of the title are attention-getting. This implies that the book's message is important.*

Practice and Apply

ANSWERS

COMMON CORE RI 1, RI 4

1. Soldiers are treated not just for their injury. They also receive treatment that addresses their overall quality of life. They take part in group therapy and programs like extreme adventure sports to help them cope with their injuries and realize they can still lead satisfying and active lives.

2. Schultz had been in a deep depression and did not want to go on the camping trip. During the trip, however, his confidence grew from learning things weren't as difficult as he expected.

3. Injured soldiers get exercise that is an interesting break from their hospital routines. Many feel their confidence and spirits rise as they have fun and see how strong and coordinated they really are.

Possible answers:

4 ● **COMMON CORE FOCUS** *Make Inferences* Breslau wanted to highlight Smith's heroic recovery and show that he has regained his sense of humor and enthusiasm for life along with his physical recovery.

5. ● **COMMON CORE FOCUS** *Tone* Students may say that Breslau is successful in conveying her admiring attitude toward the soldiers, citing her inclusion of success stories like Smith, Jacobs, and Soule. Other students may say Breslau could have gone further to praise the soldiers, perhaps including information about their early days of rehabilitation.

6. Some students may find "resurrection" an appropriate word because Smith's injuries were so extreme that his recovery was nothing short of miraculous. Other students may say "resurrection" is a heavy-handed word choice, as Smith did not die and then come back to life.

7. ● **COMMON CORE FOCUS** *Make Inferences* Soule learned that his will to survive matters all the time, not just in the minutes, hours, and days after the bomb blast that injured him. Breslau wants readers to stop underestimating wounded veterans and find personal inspiration in their stories.

8. Hemingway's narrator and the major use the machines regularly but with varying amounts of faith. The narrator says, "There was a time when none of us believed in the machines, and one day the major said it was all nonsense" (lines 105–107). In Breslau's

Comprehension

1. **Recall** Describe the military's "holistic mind-body approach" to treating injured soldiers.

2. **Clarify** How did spending a week in the wilderness boost Erik Schultz's self-confidence?

3. **Summarize** How does participating in extreme sports benefit injured soldiers mentally and physically?

Text Analysis

4. **Make Inferences** Breslau begins her article with a humorous anecdote, followed by a horrific description of Major Smith's near-fatal injuries. Why do you think she chose to begin the article this way? Explain your answer.

5. **Evaluate Tone** How successful is the writer in conveying her attitude toward the soldiers she writes about here? Cite evidence from the article to support your answer.

6. **Evaluate Diction** Breslau refers to Major Smith's recovery as a "resurrection." Considering the facts surrounding his injury, is this word appropriate here? Explain your answer.

7. **Make Inferences** Reread the article's closing sentence. What lesson do you think Soule carried with him? What lesson do you think Breslau wants readers to carry with them after reading her article? Explain your answer.

Comparing Themes Across Genres

8. **Analyze Theme** Both Hemingway's short story and Breslau's magazine article focus on wounded soldiers in therapy, but the two writers convey strikingly different attitudes toward the possibility of recovery. Describe the contrast in attitude between the two selections, citing evidence from both to support your answer.

> *What are the* **COSTS** *of war?*
>
> After reading "Healing War's Wounds," what responsibility do you think a society has to soldiers who have suffered the costs of war? Explain your answer.

COMMON CORE

RI 1 Cite textual evidence to support analysis of what the text says explicitly as well as inferences drawn from the text, including determining where the text leaves matters uncertain. RI 4 Determine the meaning of words and phrases as they are used in a text, including figurative, connotative, and technical meanings.

article, all of the soldiers have hopeful, positive attitudes, as seen in Smith's joking that a crocodile had gotten his arm (line 1).

> *What are the* **COSTS** *of war?*
> **Possible answer:** Soldiers should get the assistance they need to lead a satisfying, pain-free life.

Assessment Practice: Short Constructed Response

LITERARY TEXT: "IN ANOTHER COUNTRY"

On assessments you are often expected to make inferences as you read. Practice this skill as you answer the **short constructed response question** below. Be sure to follow the steps outlined to the right of the question.

> When the narrator first mentions physical therapy machines, he says "the machines were to make so much difference." What kind of difference do these machines make for the soldiers in the story? Support your response with evidence from the text.

◀ **STRATEGIES IN ACTION**

1. Make a quick list of muscular damage the machines are supposed to repair.
2. List any improvements the machines produce.
3. Describe the attitude of the soldiers toward the machines.
4. Use steps 1–3 to help you answer the question.

NONFICTION TEXT: "HEALING WAR'S WOUNDS"

On assessments you are often expected to read carefully and answer questions that focus on particular passages from a text. To strengthen your close-reading skills, read the **short constructed response question** at left below and practice the strategies suggested at right.

> What kind of attitude toward life does Andrew Soule display after he fractures one of his prosthetic legs? Support your response with evidence from the text.

◀ **STRATEGIES IN ACTION**

1. Examine the details of Soule's behavior in the sentences following his prosthetic fracture.
2. What kind of attitude goes with his behavior here?

COMPARING LITERARY AND NONFICTION TEXTS

On assessments you will need to identify thematic connections between literary and nonfiction texts. Practice this valuable skill by answering the **short constructed response question** at left below and using the strategies provided at right.

> Describe the contrast in tone between the closing paragraphs of the short story "In Another Country" and the article "Healing War's Wounds." Support your response with evidence from both texts.

◀ **STRATEGIES IN ACTION**

1. Examine Hemingway's closing paragraph and write down a single word that describes his tone.
2. Complete step 1 for Breslau's article.
3. Use the two words you chose to describe tone to answer the question.

Assessment Practice: Short Constructed Response

LITERARY TEXT: "IN ANOTHER COUNTRY"
Possible answer: *The machine the narrator uses is supposed to help him bend his knee. The major's machine is supposed to help make his hand bigger. The narrator does not note any physical improvements for either of them, but the daily routine of going to the hospital does give structure to their days and the opportunity for bonding with other soldiers. The machines may give some soldiers hope for recovery, though the major is clearly not among them.*

NONFICTION TEXT: "HEALING WAR'S WOUNDS" ***Possible answer:*** *Soule's attitude is one of acceptance and determination. After he fractures one of his prosthetic legs, he "tosses aside" the leg and spends the next five days "dragging his body over rocky beaches, even climbing stairs, with his arms." This shows that he would not give up taking part in the activities, even if it was harder for him.*

COMPARING LITERARY AND NONFICTION TEXTS ***Possible answer:*** *The tone in the last paragraph of "In Another Country" is despondent. The narrator describes the photos of successful patients as dubious and says that the major only looks out the window, suggesting that he has less hope than ever for his recovery or a happy life. The attitude of the last paragraph in "Healing War's Wounds" is determined. Soule is "amazed" at his own progress and carries the lesson of "I'm going to live" with him. This is the opposite of the tone in the end of "In Another Country."*

DIFFERENTIATED INSTRUCTION

FOR STRUGGLING READERS

Comparing Selections Have students skim and scan the selections before answering short constructed response questions. Tell them to:

- Read the question carefully, noting what it asks, and identifying key ideas and phrases.
- Look at each selection, jotting down information that is relevant to the question.
- Read their notes for each selection, checking they have the right information.
- Read the selections again, if needed.
- Write their answer, then reread the question to make sure it is answered.

Remind students to support their ideas with quotations from the selections. Then ask them to write an answer to this question: How has the treatment of wounded soldiers changed since World War I?

COMMON CORE FOCUS

RL 5 Analyze how an author's choices concerning how to structure specific parts of a text contribute to its overall structure and meaning as well as its aesthetic impact.

BACKGROUND When John Steinbeck accepted the Nobel Prize for Literature in 1962, he spoke of the writer's responsibility to tell stories of people's failures and of their courage to try to better themselves and their communities. Human suffering is a frequent theme in Steinbeck's novels, many of which are set in California's Salinas Valley. After *The Grapes of Wrath* was published in 1939, the novel's focus on the plight of migrant farmers in shoddily run labor camps brought accusations that Steinbeck held communist beliefs. First Lady Eleanor Roosevelt defended Steinbeck and his novel. In time, Congress investigated conditions in the migrant camps and changed labor laws to improve them.

TEXT ANALYSIS Have a volunteer read aloud part of the excerpt. Tell students that the parallel phrases and structures are more apparent—and even more lyrical—when read aloud. Point out that the rhythm of Steinbeck's writing makes his often quite long sentences flow easily.

WRITE Encourage students to look closely at the photos, jotting down their reactions, then comparing the images to those created by Steinbeck's words. Suggest that students find two or three quotations that demonstrate tone which matches the photographs before they begin writing.

from The Grapes of Wrath

Novel by John Steinbeck

John Steinbeck
1902–1968

COMMON CORE

RL 5 Analyze how an author's choices concerning how to structure specific parts of a text contribute to its overall structure and meaning as well as its aesthetic impact.

BACKGROUND The blockbuster novel of 1939, *The Grapes of Wrath* is the story of the Joads, a family of Oklahoma farmers who leave their Dustbowl farm and make their way to California to find work. John Steinbeck depicts the grueling conditions of Depression life with vivid details about the Joads, as well as short chapters on migrant farmers as a whole. Torn from the headlines of the times, the novel gave eloquent voice to photographic images of displaced farmers published in newspapers and other publications during the Depression. Two years later, James Agee and Walker Evans published *Let Us Now Praise Famous Men*, which combined Evans's powerful photographs of Southern sharecroppers with Agee's eloquent testimony to their bleak lives.

TEXT ANALYSIS Steinbeck's **tone** in the following passage can be summed up in a single phrase: *reverence toward the endurance of hardship*. In this excerpt from one of his short chapters on migrant farmers as a group, the author achieves an almost Biblical tone through **repetition** and **parallel structure**. As you read, notice the many repetitions of the conjunction *and*, as well as the connector *so that*. Notice also series of parallel phrases or clauses that give the prose a poetic rhythm. The second sentence includes an effective example: "made them with their tents and their hearts and their brains."

WRITE Read the excerpt twice, concentrating on tone. What idea about migrant farmers does the author convey through tone? Support your answer with details from the text. Then, after you have studied the photo essay that begins on page 1027, write a short paragraph explaining how these documents from the Depression relate to Steinbeck's view of migrant workers.

And the worlds were built in the evening. The people, moving in from the highways, made them with their tents and their hearts and their brains.

In the morning the tents came down, the canvas was folded, the tent poles tied along the running board, the beds put in place on the cars, the pots in their places. And as the families moved westward, the technique of building up a home in the evening and tearing it down with the morning light became fixed; so that the folded tent was packed in one place, the cooking pots counted in their box. And as the cars moved westward, each member of the family grew into his proper place, grew into

1024

DIFFERENTIATED INSTRUCTION

FOR STRUGGLING READERS

Taking Notes Guide students to use Cornell Notes to help them track main ideas as they read the excerpt. For example, students can turn the topic sentences of paragraphs 2 and 3 into questions. As students read, have them answer the questions.

 BEST PRACTICES TOOLKIT—Transparency
Cornell Notes p. B3

Paragraph 2: What was life in the camps like?	Camp life was orderly, with each person having a job to do and a sense of community arising quickly among the migrants.
Paragraph 3: How did their lives change?	

his duties; so that each member, old and young, had his place in the car;
10 so that in the weary, hot evenings, when the cars pulled into the camping
places, each member had his duty and went to it without instruction:
children to gather wood, to carry water; men to pitch the tents and
bring down the beds; women to cook the supper and to watch while the
family fed. And this was done without command. The families, which
had been units of which the boundaries were a house at night, a farm by
day, changed their boundaries. In the long hot light, they were silent in the cars moving
slowly westward; but at night they integrated with any group they found.

Thus they changed their social life—changed as in the whole universe only man
can change. They were not farm men any more, but migrant men. And the thought,
20 the planning, the long staring silence that had gone out to the fields, went now to the
roads, to the distance, to the West. That man whose mind had been bound with acres
lived with narrow concrete miles. And his thought and his worry were not any more
with rainfall, with wind and dust, with the thrust of the crops. Eyes watched the tires,
ears listened to the clattering motors, and minds struggled with oil, with gasoline,
with the thinning rubber between air and road. Then a broken gear was tragedy.
Then water in the evening was the yearning, and food over the fire. Then health to go
on was the need and strength to go on, and spirit to go on. The wills thrust westward
ahead of them, and fears that had once apprehended drought or flood now lingered
with anything that might stop the westward crawling.

30 The camps became fixed—each a short day's journey from the last.

And on the road the panic overcame some of the families, so that they drove night
and day, stopped to sleep in the cars, and drove on to the West, flying from the road,
flying from movement. And these lusted so greatly to be settled that they set their
faces into the West and drove toward it, forcing the clashing engines over the roads.

But most of the families changed and grew quickly into the new life. And when
the sun went down—

Time to look out for a place to stop.

And—there's some tents ahead.

The car pulled off the road and stopped, and because others were there first,
40 certain courtesies were necessary. And the man, the leader of the family, leaned from
the car.

Can we pull up here an' sleep?

Why, sure, be proud to have you.

1025

INTRODUCE THE MASTERPIECE

The Grapes of Wrath This blockbuster novel sold almost half a million copies in the year it was published and was awarded the Pulitzer Prize. It tells the story of the Joad family as they make the journey from their home in Oklahoma to California in search of work. Despite their struggles, the Joads never lose their humanity or spirit of endurance.

TIERED DISCUSSION PROMPTS

Use these prompts to help students understand the migrants' experience and how it reflects John Steinbeck's views:

Summarize What great migration is described in this excerpt? *Possible answer: The excerpt describes a migration of many people from the ruined farms of Oklahoma to California in hope of finding work.*

Analyze Describe the daily travels and the nightly camp. Explain how the contrast of these elements affects the travelers. *Possible answer: During the day, the travelers face many risks. Cars may break down, tires may go flat, gas may run out, and therefore the ability to reach a new place to live and work is threatened. In contrast, orderly camps are set up at night, everyone knows his or her place, and a comforting regularity replaces the unpredictable hazards of the day. Each family is isolated on the road, but a community quickly forms in camp. Camp offers travelers a much-needed respite.*

FOR STRUGGLING READERS

Comprehension Support Work with students to explore the extreme change the drought has brought to the Okies' lives. Help students identify and discuss these contrasts described in paragraph 3:

- setting: contrast of acres and miles
- worries: contrast of crops and cars
- fears: drought or flood and obstacles to westward movement

FOR ENGLISH LANGUAGE LEARNERS

Language: Punctuation and Print Cues [mixed-readiness groups] Review paragraphs 4–11. Point out the repeated use of dashes, explaining that these suggest either pauses or omitted text. Note that the final two lines are dialogue, but lack quotation marks. Clarify the dialect by helping students rewrite the sentences in standard English this way:

"Can we stop here to sleep?"

"Yes, we'd be happy to share our place."

FOR ADVANCED LEARNERS/AP

Analyze Allusion *The Grapes of Wrath* takes its title from the poem "The Battle Hymn of the Republic," written by Julia Ward Howe in 1861 after a visit to a Union Army camp. Ask students to locate and read the poem, then to write a paragraph explaining why this title may have appealed to Steinbeck. On the basis of what they know of the novel, have students argue whether Steinbeck's allusion is appropriate.

Focus and Motivate

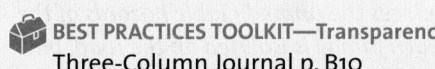

COMMON CORE FOCUS

RI 7 Integrate and evaluate multiple sources of information presented in different media or formats as well as in words in order to address a question or solve a problem. **W 4** Produce clear and coherent writing in which the development, organization, and style are appropriate to task, purpose, and audience. **W 9** Draw evidence from literary or informational texts to support analysis, reflection, and research.

SUMMARY

This photo essay appeared in *Life* magazine and includes a collection of Horace Bristol's photographs of Dust Bowl migrants in 1937–1938, captions by John Steinbeck, and a brief article that describes the migrants' plight. The three pieces combine to lend immediacy and poignancy to the plight of the migrant farmers in California.

What's the Connection?

Have students use a Three-Column Journal to organize information in the photo essay. Students should list main ideas for the photos, the captions, and the essay in each of the three columns. After reading, have students look for overlapping ideas among the three columns.

BEST PRACTICES TOOLKIT—Transparency
Three-Column Journal p. B10

Teach

Standards Focus: Analyze Photographs and Text

- Explain that analyzing something means considering separately the parts of a whole and understanding how they function together to make that whole.

- Encourage students to work interactively, considering how the captions and essay help them "see" the photos more completely, and how photographic details such as focal point, lighting, and the subjects' facial expressions and posture demonstrate what the captions and essay say about the migrants' experience

RESOURCE MANAGER—Copy Master
Analyze Photographs p. 257

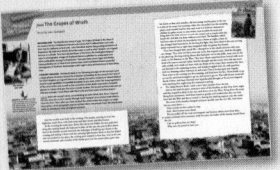

Use with *The Grapes of Wrath*, page 1024.

COMMON CORE

RI 7 Integrate and evaluate multiple sources of information presented in different media or formats as well as in words in order to address a question or solve a problem.

Photo Essay: The Grapes of Wrath

Before John Steinbeck wrote *The Grapes of Wrath*, he traveled through California's migrant labor camps with *Life* magazine photographer Horace Bristol. The following pictures were taken by Bristol at that time. The captions are Steinbeck's and the accompanying essay appeared along with the photos and captions. As you view "the worlds [that] were built in the evening" and the people who built and inhabited them, bear in mind that you will later be asked to decide which is more compelling, the photo essay or the excerpt from the novel.

Standards Focus: Analyze Photographs and Text

Reading a photo essay is a very different experience from reading a page of prose or looking at photographs on their own. The task requires an **interactive approach**, a willingness to reread text after examining a related photograph and to look at photographs in the light shed by a piece of writing.

As you examine a photograph, look for a **focal point**, the place that draws your attention. Study the **lighting** and how it affects you. What do **facial expressions** and **posture** convey about the people in a photo? What kind of **details** do you see, and how do they contribute to the **mood** of the image?

Captions make up some of the text in this photo essay. By quoting the words of people in the photographs, they add a personal voice to the images. A standard essay also accompanies the photographs on these pages. More impersonal than the captions, the essay supplies information and ideas that can help you understand the lives of the people in the photographs.

After you have examined the photographs and read the captions and the essay, choose three images that you find especially powerful. For each one, complete a chart like the one below.

Photograph	Caption	Interaction of all elements
Focal point:		
Lighting:		
Faces/posture:	Essay Text	
Details:		
Mood:		

Selection Resources

See resources on the **Teacher One Stop DVD-ROM** *and on* **thinkcentral.com**.

RESOURCE MANAGER UNIT 5
Lesson Support,* pp. 249–262

DIAGNOSTIC AND SELECTION TESTS
Selection Tests, pp. 277–280

BEST PRACTICES TOOLKIT
pp. B10, D21, D46, D47, E2, A8

TECHNOLOGY
- Teacher One Stop DVD-ROM
- Student One Stop DVD-ROM
- Audio Anthology CD
- ExamView Test Generator on the Teacher One Stop

* Resources for Differentiation

Practice and Apply

"I always kept 'em together and kept 'em fed. I planned for 'em. I can buy this house for ten dollars. I'll have a garden along there. Ducks can swim in the irrigation ditch. I got to get ten dollars."

The GRAPES of WRATH

Photographs by HORACE BRISTOL
Captions by JOHN STEINBECK

In 1934, when the rest of the U.S. began to rise out of Depression, dust began to blow in Oklahoma and Montana, Arkansas and the Dakotas. Thousands of bewildered farmers and farm hands lost their holdings or their jobs and began to drift West. By the time the dust stopped blowing, the banks and the land companies found that mechanized farming over huge areas could make the land pay when individual farmers could not. The drift Westward continued and grew. Lured by assurances of green land and good money, the farmers sold their old tools and older houses, their livestock and furniture for anything they would bring. They used the money to buy shaky old cars, sawing off the bodies to
10 make sedans into flimsy trucks. Along Route 66, through the Texas Panhandle, New Mexico and Arizona, they squeaked and rattled by tens of thousands, a bedraggled leaderless horde, camping beside the creeks and prairie villages, headed for California as a promised land.

A ANALYZE PHOTOGRAPHS AND TEXT
Image and text work together on this page in several important ways. The placement of the photograph emphasizes its importance here: the eye starts at the upper left of any page of text or photos. What kind of woman is depicted in the photograph? What can you tell about her from her **facial expression,** her **posture,** and her hands? When you read the **caption** beside her, how do the words add to the impression conveyed by the photo? The actual spoken words of a migrant make up the caption. The text beneath, by contrast, uses the language of journalism and is an **essay**—a factual account of Dustbowl conditions in 1934. How does the photograph lend to your understanding of the text—both caption and essay? How does the text contribute to your perception of the woman in the photograph?

DIFFERENTIATED INSTRUCTION

FOR ENGLISH LANGUAGE LEARNERS
Language: Conversational English Patterns
Read the caption aloud, making sure to capture the sound of the dialect. Then explain that *'em* is a shortened version of *them.* Read the first two sentences aloud again, substituting the word *them* for the abbreviation *'em.* Explain that English speakers sometimes drop sounds. Supply other examples, such as *goin'* for *going.*

FOR STRUGGLING READERS
Options for Reading Have students listen to the text on the *Audio Anthology CD* as they view the photographs. Pause to allow students to view each photograph in the context of the caption and article text. Guide them in connecting the text with the images. Explain, for example, that the captions reflect Steinbeck's idea of what these people might be thinking at the moment they were photographed.

INFORMATIONAL ANALYSIS

COMMON CORE RI 7

A ANALYZE PHOTOGRAPHS AND TEXT

Ask for volunteers to read the caption and paragraph from the essay aloud. Tell listeners to pay attention to details in the essay about the people who moved West. Then have students look carefully at the woman in the photograph. Tell them to look for visual cues that the woman is living proof of the hardship endured by many.

Possible answer: *The woman is hopeful and hard-working, but she is also exhausted and worried, as shown in her eyes. Her shoulders are slumped and her hands, which are thick but have short nails indicating that she works with them, are laced together as in prayer. Her spoken words shows that she has hope for a better future, but she is preoccupied with getting money to buy the house. The essay suggests that people had no choice but to head West. This illustrates the importance for the woman to cling to her hope and take comfort in successfully providing for her family.*

IF STUDENTS NEED HELP . . . Ask students where their eyes gravitate when they quickly look at this photograph. Clarify that this spot is the focal point.

Analyze Visuals

About the Art Photographer Horace Bristol (1908–1997) started as a freelance photographer in California. Within two decades he was a sought-after documentary photographer whose work appeared in major magazines.

In 1937 Bristol conceived the idea of documenting the migrant camps in California's Central Valley for *Life* magazine. He asked writer John Steinbeck to accompany him to meet the people and write captions for the photographs. Bristol's photographs later supplied Hollywood with a template for sets and costumes for the movie version of *The Grapes of Wrath.*

B ANALYZE PHOTOGRAPHS AND TEXT

Possible answer: *The caption, by adding a narrative to the photograph, makes the plight of the couple, with their fiercely clasped hands, more tragic. The woman speaking thinks of her own death and the impact it will have on her husband. The narrative asks viewers to see this couple as suffering people, rather than as a statistic.*

IF STUDENTS NEED HELP... Ask them to infer who speaks the lines by finding clues, such as the reference to the husband as "he."

C ANALYZE PHOTOGRAPHS AND TEXT

Possible answer: *The focal point is the papers on the desk. All of the men are looking down at them with serious expressions. The eye is drawn to the white pages which look bright in contrast to the desk and the men's coats and hats. The caption conveys a worry that the men have for their children.*

IF STUDENTS NEED HELP... Work with them to complete the prereading chart introduced on page 1026.

B ANALYZE PHOTOGRAPHS AND TEXT
Study the photograph and reread the **caption.** How does the text affect the impact of the photograph? Explain.

"Lettuce crate fell on my head. They give me fourteen dollars compensation. I'm the lucky one. I'm gonna die pretty soon now. I wish he didn't feel so bad about it."

C ANALYZE PHOTOGRAPHS AND TEXT
What is the **focal point** of this photograph and how does **lighting** draw your eye to the focal point? How do **facial expressions** and the **caption** contribute to the impact of the image?

"It's the kids.... A man can get hungry and it ain't so bad. A man gets sick when the kids are hungry."

DIFFERENTIATED INSTRUCTION

FOR STRUGGLING READERS

Irony Discuss the caption of the top photo, clarifying the irony of the speaker's words. Ask students why the speaker considers herself "the lucky one" because she is about to die. Have students draw on what they have learned about the migrants' lives to explain the speaker's comment.

FOR ENGLISH LANGUAGE LEARNERS

Language: Conversational English Patterns
Read aloud the captions on this page, then point out and clarify words that do not comply with grammatical English patterns:

- *give,* "gave"
- *gonna,* "going to"
- *ain't,* "isn't"

Read the captions again with the correct usage.

In California the migrants found no promised land. Instead, they found that thousands of their own kind had already glutted the market for cheap itinerant labor. Furthermore, scrabbling about the State to look for work, fighting each other for jobs, they learned that California hated them because they were hungry and desperate. Because most of them came from Oklahoma, they were scornfully called "Okies," harried along between scarce jobs. Migrants are still in California, 20 squatting in hideous poverty and squalor on the thin margins of the world's richest land. Of the one-third of a nation which is ill-housed, ill-clad, ill-nourished these are the bitterest dregs.

The problem of the Okies, though grim, is not insoluble. Some hope of a solution is suggested by the fact that an American writer can not only write about the Okies but that the result can be hailed by U.S. critics as the book of the decade. In *The Grapes of Wrath* (The Viking Press, $2.75), John Steinbeck (*Of Mice and Men*) presents the Okies in all their stink and misery, their courage and confusion. His 600-page novel, which may become a 20th Century *Uncle Tom's Cabin*, is now a nationwide best-seller. Last week, Producer Darryl Zanuck paid 30 $75,000 for the right to make it into a movie.

"We just got in. Gonna work in the peas. Got a han'bill that says they's good wages pickin' peas."

 **ANALYZE PHOTOGRAPHS AND TEXT**
What details of Depression-era migrant worker life does this photograph record, and what **mood** do the details establish? How does the **essay text** in the top half of this column contribute to the photograph's impression of migrant life?

FOR ADVANCED LEARNERS/AP

Analyze Author's Purpose Ask students to discuss the likely purpose of the photo essay. Students may need to gather background from the Internet as they consider these questions:

- How widely read was *Life* magazine when the photo essay was published?
- What impact on the "problem of the Okies" does the article expect the publication of *The Grapes of Wrath* to have?

- Why is it important that Hollywood has optioned the novel?

When students have completed their research and discussion, have them respond to the questions about author's purpose in the Analysis Frame: Informational Nonfiction.

 BEST PRACTICES TOOLKIT—Copy Masters
Analysis Frame: Informational Nonfiction pp. D21, D46, D47

TIERED DISCUSSION PROMPTS

In lines 14–22, use these prompts to help students understand why traveling to California did not solve all the migrants' problems:

Connect What is it like to arrive in a new place? Why are people sometimes rejected because of where they came from? *Accept all thoughtful responses.*

Analyze Why isn't California the "promised land" that migrants had hoped for? *Possible answer: So many migrants came that not enough work could be found for them all (lines 15–16). They had to keep moving, looking for jobs (lines 16–17). They began to see each other as competitors, and they were discriminated against by Californians (lines 18–19).*

Evaluate Is the contrast between the migrants' living conditions and the rich land of California (lines 20–21) effective? Explain. *Possible answer: This contrast is very effective, because it points out the irony of the situation. It shows that poverty and a land that produces wealth exist side by side, and implies that the poverty is therefore avoidable.*

INFORMATIONAL ANALYSIS COMMON CORE RI 7

ANALYZE PHOTOGRAPHS AND TEXT

Possible answer: This photo shows that migrant workers camped on the roadside in tents and learned to be at home in whatever conditions presented themselves. The cloth spread on the ground serves as a table, and a man tends the cooking fire. The migrants look as if they rarely have the chance to get clean or to wash or mend their clothes. The essay points out that the people shown are among the worst off, living with so little while others in the United States had great fortune. This makes the people seem overlooked, even though others could have helped them.

COMMON CORE
RI 7

 ANALYZE PHOTOGRAPHS AND TEXT

Possible answer: "The company" is run by people who are taking advantage of the migrant workers' plight. They don't charge for housing when the migrants work for them, but they do charge for housing when there is no cotton crop to pick—even when that housing is flooded and dangerous. Readers can infer that the company exploits workers as much as possible and views them as less than human, thus needing less than adequate housing.

IF STUDENTS NEED HELP... Remind them to make inferences by combining information from the text and photo with what they already know about people, housing, and work.

E ANALYZE
PHOTOGRAPHS
AND TEXT
Reread the caption.
What information
does it convey about
the company? Based
on the information,
what can you infer
about the company?
Finally, how does the
photograph contribute
to the impression of the
company you inferred
from the caption?

"The company lets us live in 'em when we're pickin' cotton. When we ain't workin', we pay rent. Water's comin' up in 'em now." **E**

DIFFERENTIATED INSTRUCTION

FOR ENGLISH LANGUAGE LEARNERS
Language: Conversational English Patterns
[mixed-readiness group option] Help students translate the caption on page 1030 into standard English. First, have students read it aloud and guess at the standard words behind the dialect: *them* for *'em*, *picking* for *pickin'*, *isn't* for *ain't*, *working* for *workin'*, *Water is* for *Water's*, *coming* for *comin'*, and *them* for *'em*. Clarify the idiomatic usage in *coming up in them*, which means "rising."

Then have students restate the full caption: "The company lets us live in them when we're picking cotton. When we are not working, we pay rent. Water is coming up in them now."

Now ask students to rewrite the caption on page 1031, substituting correct usage for the words that reflect dialect: *jus'*, *so's*, *fellas*, *off'n*, and *groun'*. **Possible answer:** "We have got to have a house when the rains come ... just so long as it has got a roof and a floor. Just to keep the little fellows off of the ground."

"We got to have a house when the rains come . . . jus' so's it's got a roof and a floor. Just to keep the little fellas off'n the groun'."

The pictures on [these pages] are not simply types which resemble those described in *The Grapes of Wrath*. They are the people of whom Author Steinbeck wrote. Before starting his book, he lived in California's migratory labor camps. LIFE Photographer Horace Bristol accompanied him. The woman on [page 981] might well be Ma Joad, Author Steinbeck's heroine. The man with the double-edged ax [page 986] is a counterpart of his hero, Tom Joad. Captions for their pictures and all others on these pages were written by Steinbeck. Some are excerpts from his book. Others were written especially for LIFE's photographs.

F ANALYZE PHOTOGRAPHS AND TEXT
How would you contrast the **mood** of the photographs on pages 1030 and 1031? What elements in the photographs account for this contrast?

G ANALYZE PHOTOGRAPHS AND TEXT
What role does the presence of children play in the impact of this photograph? How does the caption affect this impact? Explain your answer.

F ANALYZE PHOTOGRAPHS AND TEXT

Possible answer: *The mood of the photo is lighter because the young children are playing and seem to be having fun, even in the difficult conditions of their lives. The boy is smiling, the lighting suggests a bright, clear day, and the woman in the tent appears to be smiling as she watches her children.*

Extend the Discussion What can you conclude about children when you see that these children find a way to play even though they have no toys or games and live in poverty?

G ANALYZE PHOTOGRAPHS AND TEXT

Possible answer: *The presence of children show that the migrants' struggle was not limited to adults. The caption points out that not all days were sunny and dry like this one and though the children look happy, they are extremely vulnerable to changes to their environment. The caption also shows that the family does not ask for much, such as a certain kind of house, but simply "a roof and a floor."*

FOR ADVANCED LEARNERS/AP

Analyze Literary Terms Have students write definitions for these terms from page 1031 and then provide the definitions to the whole class. If the definitions are new to listeners, have them add the words to their Personal Word Lists: *types, heroine, counterpart.*

 **BEST PRACTICES TOOLKIT**
Personal Word List p. E2

FOR STRUGGLING STUDENTS

Develop Reading Fluency Have students practice reading the essay aloud. Tell them echo-read page 1031 after you, emulating your pacing, intonation, and pausing for punctuation. Point out that *LIFE* is the title of the magazine in which the photographs were published. The word is not read with any particular emphasis.

INFORMATIONAL ANALYSIS

 **ANALYZE PHOTOGRAPHS AND TEXT**

Possible answer: Bristol probably chose not to crop out the man in the background because showing the man, standing idle, staring at the camera, while the other pauses from his hard work emphasizes the idea expressed in the caption: that the people who want work and the work that needs to be done "can't get together."

IF STUDENTS NEED HELP . . . Use your hands to model how to crop out the man standing in the background. Have students examine the resulting photo's composition and consider what is lost without the second man.

INFORMATIONAL ANALYSIS

 **ANALYZE PHOTOGRAPHS AND TEXT**

Possible answer: The photo and its caption suggest that the workers made the best of their terrible situation, carrying on with their lives as best they could. The speaker looks at the positive, in this case, at a woman's beauty and abilities. He thinks of marriage, which implies that he is looking toward the future and hoping for a better life. He focuses on practical considerations also, noting that the woman has skills that could help him succeed.

ANALYZE PHOTOGRAPHS AND TEXT
Horace Bristol could have **cropped,** or cut, the background figure out of this image without losing any part of the man and ax in the foreground. Reread the caption. What is the impact of having the second man in the background?

"The whole thing's nuts. There's work to do and people to do it, but them two can't get together. There's food to eat and people to eat it, and them two can't get together neither."

"She's awful pretty. An' she been to high school. She could help a man with figuring and stuff like that."

ANALYZE PHOTOGRAPHS AND TEXT
From this last photograph and caption, what might you gather about people's attitudes toward their circumstances? How might the photographer's **vantage point** be said to contribute to this idea?

1032 UNIT 5: THE HARLEM RENAISSANCE AND MODERNISM

DIFFERENTIATED INSTRUCTION

FOR STRUGGLING READERS
Concept Support: Analyze Photographs Have students review the chart they completed for each photograph. Students should make sure that each chart is complete and then record their reactions to the conditions that the migrants endured.

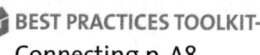 **BEST PRACTICES TOOLKIT—Transparency**
Connecting p. A8

FOR ADVANCED LEARNERS/AP
Synthesize Have students view all or part of the film *The Grapes of Wrath*. Bristol's photographs served as a touchstone for the sets and costumes in the movie. Ask students to report on how closely the movie reflects the documentary evidence that Bristol's camera recorded. Students may also consider why the movie diverges from Bristol's presentation of the migrant camps and workers when it does.

1032 UNIT 5

Comprehension

1. **Recall** In the late 1930s, what combination of events and promises prompted many farmers in the plains states to travel westward?

2. **Recall** Who wrote the captions for the photographs in this photo essay? Are they fiction, nonfiction, or a mixture of both?

3. **Summarize** What typically happened to the Midwestern farmers who migrated to California? How were they regarded by Californians?

Text Analysis

4. **Analyze Tone** How would you describe the attitude of the speaker in the caption for the image on page 1030? How does the information conveyed by the photograph and caption on page 1031 help you understand this attitude?

5. **Analyze Photographs and Text** What have you learned from this photo essay about the living conditions and attitudes of Depression-era migrant workers?

6. **Evaluate** Reread lines 23–30 of the essay text. Do you agree or disagree with the writer's assertion? Explain.

COMMON CORE

RI 7 Integrate and evaluate multiple sources of information presented in different media or formats as well as in words in order to address a question or solve a problem. **W 4** Produce clear and coherent writing in which the development, organization, and style are appropriate to task, purpose, and audience. **W 9** Draw evidence from literary or informational texts to support analysis, reflection, and research.

Read for Information: Compare and Evaluate

WRITING PROMPT

Reflect on the excerpt you read from *The Grapes of Wrath* and on the photo essay you just studied. In your opinion, which paints a more powerful portrait of the migrant farmworkers? Why?

The following steps will help you answer the prompt:

1. Review the selections and decide, based on your first reaction, which piece you find more powerful.

2. Now go back and analyze each piece, taking notes on the following elements:

   - the amount of information provided
   - the kinds of **details** and information conveyed
   - the ideas or **themes** emphasized
   - the **author's perspective** and the photographer's vantage point
   - the literary elements and the artistic techniques
   - the **mood** and thoughts evoked

3. Review your analysis. As you look at the relative strengths of each piece, do you still have the same opinion about which is more compelling? Why or why not?

4. Now state your opinion about which selection is more compelling, and give the reasons for your opinion, comparing the strengths and weaknesses of each piece.

FOR STRUGGLING WRITERS

Read for Information

- Direct students to narrow the essay's purpose to two points of comparison, such as the kinds of details and information conveyed and the mood these create.

- Encourage students to begin by writing their opinions in a topic sentence. Provide a starter sentence, such as *I think that _____ paints a more powerful portrait of the migrant farm workers because _____.*

Practice and Apply

For preliminary support of post-reading questions, use these copy masters:

R RESOURCE MANAGER—Copy Masters
   Reading Check p. 261
   Question Support p. 262
   Compare and Evaluate p. 257

   Additional selection questions are provided for teachers on page 252.

ANSWERS   **COMMON CORE RI 7, W 4, W 9**

1. *Driven away by drought, farmers sought the promise of "green land" farther west.*

2. *John Steinbeck wrote the mix of fiction and nonfiction captions.*

3. *They didn't find enough work, lived in poverty, and were scorned by Californians.*

Possible answers:

4. *The speaker seems resigned. The caption and photo suggest that life could be worse.*

5. *People were poor and lived in shoddy housing or tents. They had few appliances for daily chores and had to haul water and make fires. Still, children played and adults carried on. Attitudes were dedicated, resigned, or even optimistic.*

6. *Students may believe the novel's success means solutions are near, or that media attention does not always lead to solutions.*

Read for Information: Compare and Evaluate

Writing Prompt Students should state their opinions in a topic sentence and support them.

Assess and Reteach

Assess

DIAGNOSTIC AND SELECTION TESTS
   Selection Test A pp. 277–278
   Selection Test B/C pp. 279–280

Interactive Selection Test on **thinkcentral.com**

Reteach

Level Up Online Tutorials on **thinkcentral.com**

Reteaching Worksheets on **thinkcentral.com**
   Literature Lesson 42
   Reading Lesson 12
   Writing Lesson 23

Focus and Motivate

ABOUT THE AUTHOR

Porter was just two when her mother died. Her father, bereft and directionless, relied on his own mother to lead the family. Porter's strong, resourceful grandmother became the model for her literary heroines. Her father provided a template for weak male characters.

Selection Resources

DID YOU KNOW?

Katherine Anne Porter . . .

- was a distant relative of the frontiersman Daniel Boone.
- taught singing and dancing as a teenager to help support her family.

Meet the Author

Katherine Anne Porter 1890–1980

Katherine Anne Porter has been called a "writer's writer"; in her lifetime she was more popular with critics and her fellow writers than with the public. She wrote mostly short fiction, a form with which it was difficult to build a popular reputation. What's more, all of her 27 short stories, including those technically classified as novellas (short novels), could fit into a single book. Still, Porter's work is celebrated for its nearly flawless consistency and style. Each one of her stories is a polished gem reflecting a hard truth about human experience.

Survival and Resiliency She was born Callie Russell Porter on a scrappy dirt farm in central Texas, where she dreamed of becoming an actress. She had the good looks, the drive, and the talent for performing but lacked the stamina. A two-year bout with tuberculosis permanently dashed her dreams of acting. However, while recuperating at a sanitorium, Porter befriended a journalist who helped her start writing for newspapers. Living in Denver in 1918, Porter was again stricken by illness, this time by the deadly flu epidemic that swept the globe after World War I, killing 550,000 people in the United States and at least 25 million worldwide.

This second brush with death inspired an idea that was later to become part of her novella *Pale Horse, Pale Rider* (1939). After her recovery, convinced of her true calling, Porter left Denver for the New York literary scene and the wider world.

Deep in the Heart of Texas Like many writers of her generation, Porter traveled widely, living in Mexico, Bermuda, Germany, Switzerland, and France, as well as New York for much of the 1920s and 1930s. Some of these places inspired her fiction: her time in Mexico enriched her first published story, "Maria Concepción" (1922), and several others, while pre–World War II Berlin informed "The Leaning Tower" (1944). But for the most part, foreign travel provided what Porter called a "constant exercise of memory" and brought her closer to her native land. Some of her best fiction—notably, "Noon Wine" (1937), "Old Mortality" (1939), and a series called "The Old Order" (1955)—takes place in Texas. Many of these stories, and "The Jilting of Granny Weatherall" (1929) in particular, include a dynamic grandmother based on Porter's own who raised her until age 11 and exerted a strong influence. Porter even took her grandmother's name after she divorced her first husband and began life on her own.

Author Online

Go to thinkcentral.com. KEYWORD: HML11-1034

1034

TEXT ANALYSIS: STREAM OF CONSCIOUSNESS

The very first paragraph of this story plunges readers directly into the thoughts of its protagonist. This literary technique, **stream of consciousness,** presents the main events of a story, or the **plot,** using a character's seemingly unconnected thoughts, responses, and sensations. Rather than offering a logical account of events, it presents a series of associative connections, with one impression giving rise to another. Use these strategies to help you keep track of the plot:

- Remember that you are seeing the "inside" or internal development of the main character. The depictions of people and events you find there may not be completely reliable.
- Look for quotation marks to determine when Granny is speaking aloud and when she is not.
- Keep track of the twists and turns of Granny's thoughts to understand what she is reacting to.
- Keep in mind that the plot of this story moves back and forth between the present and the past.

READING SKILL: CLARIFY SEQUENCE

In this narrative, Porter shuffles together the past and the present to depict the distorted way Granny perceives the **sequence** of events. Porter achieves this effect in part through the use of **flashback,** in which she relates events that happened before the beginning of the story's "now" time. As you travel through Granny's memory, use a timeline to untangle the sequence of the main events in her life.

Jilting by George

Examination by Dr. Harry

▲ VOCABULARY IN CONTEXT

Porter uses these words to take readers into the mind of a woman on her deathbed. Complete each phrase with a word from the list.

WORD LIST	amethyst	dwindle	plague
	assign	embroidered	

1. kept an elaborately _____ blanket on the sickbed
2. had a valuable _____ ring to pass on to her daughter
3. felt her time _____ as she got weaker and weaker

 Complete the activities in your **Reader/Writer Notebook.**

What makes a MEMORY linger?

That perfect first date. The humiliating moment you realized you had failed your driving test. The elated, screaming crowd jumping to its feet as the last seconds of the big game ticked away. Whether pleasant or painful, there are some memories you just can't shake. In this story, as Granny Weatherall lies on her deathbed, she's haunted by an event that still affects her almost as powerfully as it did when she experienced it as a young woman.

QUICKWRITE Write a paragraph about a memory of your own that you can still recall in crisp detail. What images, feelings, sounds, or smells come to mind? Why do you think this moment lingers in your memory?

1035

Teach

What makes a **MEMORY** *linger?*

Lead into the paragraph by asking students to identify memories that have affected their behavior, such as getting lost in a crowd as a child. Invite volunteers to share experiences, then urge all students to recall memories as they complete the *QUICKWRITE.*

TEXT ANALYSIS COMMON CORE RL 1 RL 3 RL 5

● *Model the Skill:* **STREAM OF CONSCIOUSNESS**

To help students understand stream-of-consciousness writing, compare this style of writing to a conversation among friends. Note that new topics come up naturally as they talk, and that the conversation may move between the same topics again and again as friends remember details and ask more questions. Tell students that this free, undirected association is also found in stream-of-consciousness writing, which follows the internal development, or connections within a character's mind.

GUIDED PRACTICE Have trios converse for five minutes, with one student recording when and how topics change. Ask students to trace how each new topic arose.

READING SKILL COMMON CORE RL 3 RL 5

■ *Model the Skill:* **CLARIFY SEQUENCE**

Tell students that writers signal flashbacks and returns to sequence by using time order words, words that refer to memory, or characterizations that show a speaker's muddled thinking.

GUIDED PRACTICE Have students revisit stories they have already read, such as "Winter Dreams" on page 978, to find events that appear out of sequence.

R RESOURCE MANAGER—Copy Master Clarify Sequence p. 275

VOCABULARY SKILL COMMON CORE L 4

▲ VOCABULARY IN CONTEXT

DIAGNOSE WORD KNOWLEDGE Have all students complete Vocabulary in Context. Check their word choices against the following:

amethyst (ăm′ə-thĭst) *n.* a purple-colored quartz used as a gemstone

assign (ə-sīn′) *n.* a person to whom property is transferred in a will or other legal document

dwindle (dwĭn′dl) *v.* to become steadily less; to shrink

embroidered (ĕm′broi′dərd) *adj.* decorated with stitched designs
embroider *v.*

plague (plāg) *v.* to annoy; harass

PRETEACH VOCABULARY Preteach vocabulary with this copy master. Read each item aloud.

R RESOURCE MANAGER—Copy Master Vocabulary Study p. 277

Practice and Apply

SUMMARY

This short story opens with 80-year-old Granny Weatherall nearing death. As her daughter Cornelia and Doctor Harry discuss her condition, Granny slips in and out of her memories. She recalls the challenges of managing the farm and four children after her husband's death. She thinks of her life's good moments but inevitably returns to a painful memory, her jilting by George. When death approaches, Granny hopes for a sign from God and feels again jilted that it does not arrive.

READ WITH A PURPOSE

Help students set a purpose for reading. Tell them to determine the reasons that explain Granny Weatherall's hostile feelings.

The *Jilting* of GRANNY WEATHERALL

Katherine Anne Porter

She flicked her wrist neatly out of Doctor Harry's pudgy careful fingers and pulled the sheet up to her chin. The brat ought to be in knee breeches.[1] Doctoring around the country with spectacles on his nose! "Get along now, take your schoolbooks and go. There's nothing wrong with me." **A**

Doctor Harry spread a warm paw like a cushion on her forehead where the forked green vein danced and made her eyelids twitch. "Now, now, be a good girl, and we'll have you up in no time."

"That's no way to speak to a woman nearly eighty years old just because she's down. I'd have you respect your elders, young man."

10 "Well, Missy, excuse me." Doctor Harry patted her cheek. "But I've got to warn you, haven't I? You're a marvel, but you must be careful or you're going to be good and sorry."

"Don't tell me what I'm going to be. I'm on my feet now, morally speaking. It's Cornelia. I had to go to bed to get rid of her."

Her bones felt loose, and floated around in her skin, and Doctor Harry floated like a balloon around the foot of the bed. He floated and pulled down his waistcoat and swung his glasses on a cord. "Well, stay where you are, it certainly can't hurt you."

---

1. **knee breeches:** short pants formerly worn by young boys.

Targeted Passage

A STREAM OF CONSCIOUSNESS
In lines 1–4, how does Porter create the effect that you, the reader, are "inside" Granny's mind? Explain how your intimacy with this character affects your impression of her.

Analyze Visuals ▶
What does this unusual portrait suggest about its subject's thoughts or state of mind? Explain, citing details.

Possible answer: *The head is open at the top, and there seem to be clouds floating out of it. The image suggests that the woman's thoughts are drifting away, like wispy clouds, instead of remaining contained in her head. In addition, the woman's face is pursed, as though she were trying to remember something that she cannot quite recall.*

About the Art *Old Woman With Hair in the Clouds* by American artist Stephen F. Hayes (born 1955) captures the minute detail of an older woman's face. Bright white light on the woman's forehead and hair, as well as hair that merges with the clouds, suggests the mental deterioration that Granny Weatherall is experiencing.

REVISIT THE BIG QUESTION

What makes a
MEMORY *linger?*

Discuss In lines 2–4, what do the comments about Doctor Harry in these lines reveal about Granny's memories of him? How do these memories affect her response to his treatment and advice? **Possible answer:** *She is so much older than he that she can remember him as a little boy—or at least remember other little boys who resemble him. This memory makes her disdainful of him and leads to a lack of confidence in his treatment.*

- Whose thoughts are revealed in lines 2–4? What do they reveal about the person who is having them? (lines 1–4)

- What is the physical condition of that person? How do you know? (lines 10–12)

- What do the person's continued thoughts reveal about her age and personality? (lines 15–18)

FOR STRUGGLING READERS

Develop Reading Fluency Play the *Audio Anthology CD* for students. Tell them to pay attention to the difference between narration and dialogue. Later, ask students to describe how the reader on the CD delivered Granny Weatherall's thoughts, as opposed to the words she says to others. Ask: is there a noticeable difference between the two?

"Get along and doctor your sick," said Granny Weatherall. "Leave a well
20   woman alone. I'll call for you when I want you. . . . Where were you forty years
ago when I pulled through milk-leg[2] and double pneumonia? You weren't even
born. Don't let Cornelia lead you on," she shouted, because Doctor Harry
appeared to float up to the ceiling and out. "I pay my own bills, and I don't throw
my money away on nonsense!"

    She meant to wave good-by, but it was too much trouble. Her eyes closed of
themselves, it was like a dark curtain drawn around the bed. The pillow rose and
floated under her, pleasant as a hammock in a light wind. She listened to the
leaves rustling outside the window. No, somebody was swishing newspapers: no,
Cornelia and Doctor Harry were whispering together. She leaped broad awake,
30   thinking they whispered in her ear. **B**

    "She was never like this, *never* like this!" "Well, what can we expect?" "Yes,
eighty years old. . . ."

    Well, and what if she was? She still had ears. It was like Cornelia to whisper
around doors. She always kept things secret in such a public way. She was always
being tactful and kind. Cornelia was dutiful; that was the trouble with her.
Dutiful and good: "So good and dutiful," said Granny, "that I'd like to spank her."
She saw herself spanking Cornelia and making a fine job of it.

    "What'd you say, Mother?"

    Granny felt her face tying up in hard knots.

40   "Can't a body think, I'd like to know?"

    "I thought you might want something."

    "I do. I want a lot of things. First off, go away and don't whisper."

    She lay and drowsed, hoping in her sleep that the children would keep out and
let her rest a minute. It had been a long day. Not that she was tired. It was always
pleasant to snatch a minute now and then. There was always so much to be done,
let me see: tomorrow.

    Tomorrow was far away and there was nothing to trouble about. Things were
finished somehow when the time came; thank God there was always a little
margin over for peace: then a person could spread out the plan of life and tuck in
50   the edges orderly. It was good to have everything clean and folded away, with the
hair brushes and tonic bottles sitting straight on the white **embroidered** linen: the
day started without fuss and the pantry shelves laid out with rows of jelly glasses
and brown jugs and white stone-china jars with blue whirligigs[3] and words painted
on them: coffee, tea, sugar, ginger, cinnamon, allspice: and the bronze clock with
the lion on top nicely dusted off. The dust that lion could collect in twenty-four
hours! The box in the attic with all those letters tied up, well, she'd have to go
through that tomorrow. All those letters—George's letters and John's letters and
her letters to them both—lying around for the children to find afterwards made
her uneasy. Yes, that would be tomorrow's business. No use to let them know how
60   silly she had been once.

---

2. **milk-leg:** a painful swelling of the leg experienced by some women after giving birth.
3. **stone-china . . . whirligigs** (hwûr′lĭ-gĭgz′): jars made of thick pottery with blue spiral designs.

1038   UNIT 5: THE HARLEM RENAISSANCE AND MODERNISM

B STREAM OF CONSCIOUSNESS
What insight do lines 25–30 give you into Granny Weatherall's character? What do they tell you about her physical condition?

Language Coach

Word Definitions
Drowsed (line 43) means "slept lightly." Why is *drowsed* more effective than *slept* would be?

embroidered
(ĕm′broi′dərd) *adj.*
decorated with stitched designs **embroider** *v.*

While she was rummaging around she found death in her mind and it felt clammy and unfamiliar. She had spent so much time preparing for death there was no need for bringing it up again. Let it take care of itself now. When she was sixty she had felt very old, finished, and went around making farewell trips to see her children and grandchildren, with a secret in her mind: This is the very last of your mother, children! Then she made her will and came down with a long fever. That was all just a notion like a lot of other things, but it was lucky too, for she had once for all got over the idea of dying for a long time. Now she couldn't be worried. She hoped she had better sense now. Her father had lived to be one

70 hundred and two years old and had drunk a noggin of strong hot toddy[4] on his last birthday. He told the reporters it was his daily habit, and he owed his long life to that. He had made quite a scandal and was very pleased about it. She believed she'd just **plague** Cornelia a little. **C**

"Cornelia! Cornelia!" No footsteps, but a sudden hand on her cheek. "Bless you, where have you been?"

"Here, Mother."

"Well, Cornelia, I want a noggin of hot toddy." **D**

"Are you cold, darling?"

"I'm chilly, Cornelia. Lying in bed stops the circulation. I must have told you

80 that a thousand times."

Well, she could just hear Cornelia telling her husband that Mother was getting a little childish and they'd have to humor her. The thing that most annoyed her was that Cornelia thought she was deaf, dumb, and blind. Little hasty glances and tiny gestures tossed around her and over her head saying, "Don't cross her, let her have her way, she's eighty years old," and she sitting there as if she lived in a thin glass cage. Sometimes Granny almost made up her mind to pack up and move back to her own house where nobody could remind her every minute that she was old. Wait, wait, Cornelia, till your own children whisper behind your back!

In her day she had kept a better house and had got more work done. She

90 wasn't too old yet for Lydia to be driving eighty miles for advice when one of the children jumped the track, and Jimmy still dropped in and talked things over: "Now, Mammy, you've a good business head, I want to know what you think of this? . . ." Old. Cornelia couldn't change the furniture around without asking. Little things, little things! They had been so sweet when they were little. Granny wished the old days were back again with the children young and everything to be done over. It had been a hard pull, but not too much for her. When she thought of all the food she had cooked, and all the clothes she had cut and sewed, and all the gardens she had made—well, the children showed it. There they were, made out of her, and they couldn't get away from that. Sometimes she wanted to see

100 John again and point to them and say, Well, I didn't do so badly, did I? But that would have to wait. That was for tomorrow. She used to think of him as a man, but now all the children were older than their father, and he would be a child beside her if she saw him now. It seemed strange and there was something wrong in the idea. Why, he couldn't possibly recognize her. She had fenced in a hundred

---

4. **noggin . . . toddy:** mug of a strong alcoholic drink.

---

plague (plāg) *v.* to annoy; harass

C STREAM OF CONSCIOUSNESS
Reread lines 47–73 and consider how Porter conveys the flow of Granny's thoughts. What idea triggers Granny's thoughts of death?

D CLARIFY SEQUENCE
Reread lines 61–77. Identify clues about the timing of Granny's father's "scandal" and subsequent death. What connection do you see between this memory and Granny's desire to "plague" Cornelia?

2 Targeted Passage

Language Coach

Word Definitions *Hard pull* (line 96) means "lengthy effort or struggle." Read lines 94–98. What caused the hard pull?

FOR STRUGGLING READERS

2 Targeted Passage [Lines 89–99]

In this passage, Granny reflects on her achievements with pride.

- What did Granny mostly do in "her day"? (line 89)

- How does she feel about those times and about her role in them? (lines 89–93)

- What does Granny wish could happen? (lines 93–96)

- How does Granny know that her adult children still value her? (lines 96–99)

FOR ENGLISH LANGUAGE LEARNERS

Language Coach

Word Definitions *Answer:*
Granny lost her husband, John, when he was quite young. She ran the farm and raised the children by herself. Ask students what "tossed around" in line 84 means.

What makes a MEMORY *linger?*

Discuss In lines 61–73, from what *memories* about death does Granny take comfort?
Possible answer: *Granny takes comfort from her memory of preparing for death at age 60. Though ill, she did not die, and now she feels that she can focus on more important matters. She also takes comfort from the memory of her father's long life.*

TEXT ANALYSIS   COMMON CORE

C STREAM OF CONSCIOUSNESS   RL 1 RL 3 RL 5

Possible answer: *Porter traces Granny's thoughts as she skips from thinking about people looking through her letters in the attic to the idea of looking through her own attic of memories.*

READING SKILL   COMMON CORE
                                     RL 3
D *Model the skill:* CLARIFY   RL 5
SEQUENCE

Point out sequence clues that tell about the timing of Granny's father's interview and death. These clues include the past perfect verb "had lived" (line 69) and the reference to "his last birthday" (line 71). Mention that Granny decides to plague Cornelia because she remembers her father's old-age behavior. Ask students how they know the story has returned to "now time." **Possible answer:** *Granny calls for Cornelia, who is sitting next to her hospital bed.*

VOCABULARY   COMMON CORE
                                       L 4
OWN THE WORD

plague: Have students create a semantic web for the word *plague*, used as a verb in this context. Write the word in the center circle along with the given definition, "to annoy or harass." Draw spider legs out from the center circle and have students use a thesaurus to find appropriate synonyms to complete the web. **Possible answers:** *afflict, agonize, badger, curse, harry, pester, torment, torture, pester, tease*

Possible answer: *Granny says that John would be a child compared to her because their children are now older than he was at his death.*

IF STUDENTS NEED HELP . . . Point out clues to the sequence. For example, John lived long enough to father at least three children (lines 89–93). John's children are now old enough to have their own children (lines 90–91).

TIERED DISCUSSION PROMPTS

In lines 121–128, use these prompts to help students understand the flashback to past nights:

Recall How does Granny feel about the days when the children were small? *Possible answer: She enjoyed them, though they were filled with hard work.*

Analyze In what way is Granny, as she prays, like her children as they waited for her to light the lamp? *Possible answer: Like her children, who were afraid of the dark and counted on their mother to light the lamp, Granny is afraid and turns to a more powerful being for help.*

Synthesize To what other lines on this page might Granny's prayers respond? *Possible answer: Granny's prayers might respond to her perception of the rising fog and the "army of ghosts" (lines 120–121).*

♦ GRAMMAR AND STYLE

COMMON CORE L 3a

Craft Effective Sentences Point out the repetition of "the day" (line 141), "hell" (lines 143, 144, 146), and "crept" (lines 141, 146). Direct students to the use of *and* as a coordinating conjunction in lines 144 and 145. Clarify that *and* functions as a coordinating conjunction when it joins two independent clauses. Ask students to find examples of this use in lines 181–183.

---

acres once, digging the post holes herself and clamping the wires with just a negro boy to help. That changed a woman. John would be looking for a young woman with the peaked Spanish comb in her hair and the painted fan. Digging post holes changed a woman. Riding country roads in the winter when women had their babies was another thing: sitting up nights with sick horses and sick negroes and
110 sick children and hardly ever losing one. John, I hardly ever lost one of them! John would see that in a minute, that would be something he could understand, she wouldn't have to explain anything! **E**

It made her feel like rolling up her sleeves and putting the whole place to rights again. No matter if Cornelia was determined to be everywhere at once, there were a great many things left undone on this place. She would start tomorrow and do them. It was good to be strong enough for everything, even if all you made melted and changed and slipped under your hands, so that by the time you finished you almost forgot what you were working for. What was it I set out to do? she asked herself intently, but she could not remember. A fog rose over the valley, she saw it
120 marching across the creek swallowing the trees and moving up the hill like an army of ghosts. Soon it would be at the near edge of the orchard, and then it was time to go in and light the lamps. Come in, children, don't stay out in the night air.

Lighting the lamps had been beautiful. The children huddled up to her and breathed like little calves waiting at the bars in the twilight. Their eyes followed the match and watched the flame rise and settle in a blue curve, then they moved away from her. The lamp was lit, they didn't have to be scared and hang on to mother any more. Never, never, never more. God, for all my life I thank Thee. Without Thee, my God, I could never have done it. Hail, Mary, full of grace.[5]

I want you to pick all the fruit this year and see that nothing is wasted. There's
130 always someone who can use it. Don't let good things rot for want of using. You waste life when you waste good food. Don't let things get lost. It's bitter to lose things. Now, don't let me get to thinking, not when I am tired and taking a little nap before supper. . . .

The pillow rose about her shoulders and pressed against her heart and the memory was being squeezed out of it: oh, push down the pillow, somebody: it would smother her if she tried to hold it. Such a fresh breeze blowing and such a green day with no threats in it. But he had not come, just the same. What does a woman do when she has put on the white veil and set out the white cake for a man and he doesn't come? She tried to remember. No, I swear he never harmed
140 me but in that. He never harmed me but in that . . . and what if he did? There was the day, the day, but a whirl of dark smoke rose and covered it, crept up and over into the bright field where everything was planted so carefully in orderly rows. That was hell, she knew hell when she saw it. For sixty years she had prayed against remembering him and against losing her soul in the deep pit of hell, and now the two things were mingled in one and the thought of him was a smoky cloud from hell that moved and crept in her head when she had just got rid of Doctor Harry and was trying to rest a minute. Wounded vanity, Ellen, said a ♦
sharp voice in the top of her mind. Don't let your wounded vanity get the upper

---

5. **Hail . . . grace:** the beginning of a Roman Catholic prayer to the Virgin Mary.

E CLARIFY SEQUENCE
Why does Granny say that today, John would be a child compared to her? Record on your timeline the information you learn in this paragraph.

 **Targeted Passage**

♦ GRAMMAR AND STYLE
Reread lines 143–147. Porter uses **repetition** as well as short clauses joined by the **coordinating conjunction** *and* to present the circular nature of Granny's thoughts.

DIFFERENTIATED INSTRUCTION

FOR STRUGGLING READERS

 Targeted Passage [Lines 134–146]

This passage explains Granny's critical, and terrible, memory from youth—her fiancé did not show up at their wedding.

- What is Granny trying to do in lines 134–136?

- What memory does the fresh breeze that blows into the room trigger? (lines 136–139)

- Who is "he" in lines 137, 139, and 140?

- How long ago was it that Granny last explored this memory? (line 143)

- What does Granny fear when this memory pushes its way into her consciousness? (lines 144–146)

hand of you. Plenty of girls get jilted. You were jilted, weren't you? Then stand up
150 to it. Her eyelids wavered and let in streamers of blue-gray light like tissue paper
over her eyes. She must get up and pull the shades down or she'd never sleep. She
was in bed again and the shades were not down. How could that happen? Better
turn over, hide from the light, sleeping in the light gave you nightmares. "Mother,
how do you feel now?" and a stinging wetness on her forehead. But I don't like
having my face washed in cold water! **G**

Hapsy? George? Lydia? Jimmy? No, Cornelia, and her features were swollen
and full of little puddles. "They're coming, darling, they'll all be here soon." Go
wash your face, child, you look funny.

Instead of obeying, Cornelia knelt down and put her head on the pillow. She
160 seemed to be talking but there was no sound. "Well, are you tongue-tied? Whose
birthday is it? Are you going to give a party?"

Cornelia's mouth moved urgently in strange shapes. "Don't do that, you bother
me, daughter."

"Oh, no, Mother. Oh, no. . . ."

Nonsense. It was strange about children. They disputed your every word. "No
what, Cornelia?"

"Here's Doctor Harry."

"I won't see that boy again. He just left five minutes ago."

"That was this morning, Mother. It's night now. Here's the nurse." **H**

170 "This is Doctor Harry, Mrs. Weatherall. I never saw you look so young and
happy!"

"Ah, I'll never be young again—but I'd be happy if they'd let me lie in peace
and get rested."

She thought she spoke up loudly, but no one answered. A warm weight on her
forehead, a warm bracelet on her wrist, and a breeze went on whispering, trying to
tell her something. A shuffle of leaves in the everlasting hand of God, He blew on
them and they danced and rattled. "Mother, don't mind, we're going to give you a
little hypodermic."[6] "Look here, daughter, how do ants get in this bed? I saw sugar
ants yesterday." Did you send for Hapsy too?

180 It was Hapsy she really wanted. She had to go a long way back through a great
many rooms to find Hapsy standing with a baby on her arm. She seemed to
herself to be Hapsy also, and the baby on Hapsy's arm was Hapsy and himself and
herself, all at once, and there was no surprise in the meeting. Then Hapsy melted
from within and turned flimsy as gray gauze and the baby was a gauzy shadow,
and Hapsy came up close and said, "I thought you'd never come," and looked at
her very searchingly and said, "You haven't changed a bit!" They leaned forward to
kiss, when Cornelia began whispering from a long way off, "Oh, is there anything
you want to tell me? Is there anything I can do for you?"

Yes, she had changed her mind after sixty years and she would like to see
190 George. I want you to find George. Find him and be sure to tell him I forgot
him. I want him to know I had my husband just the same and my children and
my house like any other woman. A good house too and a good husband that I

---

6. **hypodermic:** injection.

G STREAM OF
CONSCIOUSNESS
Describe the major event
revealed by Granny's
thoughts in lines 134–155.
Based on the title of the
story, what significance
do these details reveal
about the plot?

H STREAM OF
CONSCIOUSNESS
What clues in lines 156–
169 reveal to readers how
much Granny's condition
is deteriorating?

Language Coach
Idioms An **idiom** is an
expression whose overall
meaning is different
from the meaning of the
individual words. The
idiom *just the same* (line
191) means "in spite of
what happened before."
What is Granny saying in
lines 190–192?

REVISIT THE BIG QUESTION
What makes a
MEMORY *linger?*

Discuss In lines 147–150, who speaks to
Granny, telling her to "stand up" to her painful memories about being jilted (line 149)?
Possible answer: *Granny may be speaking to
herself, calling herself by her name, Ellen, or she
may be remembering someone who said these
words to her after she was jilted—perhaps a
mother, grandmother, aunt, or friend.*

TEXT ANALYSIS   COMMON
CORE

G **STREAM OF**   RL 1
CONSCIOUSNESS   RL 3
                              RL 5

Possible answer: *Before she married John,
Granny was jilted by another man. Based
on the title and these details, the jilting is
the main focus of the plot.*

Extend the Discussion What emotions are
common among memories that stay with
people for life?

TEXT ANALYSIS   COMMON
CORE

H *Model the Skill:* **STREAM**   RL 1
OF CONSCIOUSNESS   RL 3
                                  RL 5

Point out that Granny can't hear properly:
Cornelia is speaking out loud, but Granny
can't hear her in lines 159–160. Also tell
students that in thinking Doctor Harry
was there "five minutes ago" when really,
many hours had passed since he had
last seen her, Granny reveals herself to
be disoriented (lines 168–169). Ask students to find other clues to Granny's poor
health. **Possible answer:** *Granny seems to
be feeling a breeze and seeing leaves blown
around by God but Cornelia is talking to her
in the hospital (lines 175–177).*

FOR ENGLISH LANGUAGE LEARNERS

Language Coach
Idioms *Possible answer:* *Granny wants
George to know that despite the pain he
caused her, she went on to marry John
and have a good life with her family.* Have
students explain the meaning of these
idioms: "stand up to it" (lines 149–150) and
"(baby) on her arm" (line 181).

FOR RELUCTANT READERS
Connect to the Text "The Jilting of Granny
Weatherall" tells about the thoughts of a
dying woman who recovered from devastating heartache to have a long and seemingly
happy life. And yet, in the end, her painful
memory returns. Ask students to talk about
why that happens: Is it human nature to
recall negative things? Do the things we work
hard to "forget" ever really go away? How do
you think people should deal with experiences they want to forget?

❶ STREAM OF CONSCIOUSNESS

Possible answer: *Granny has decided that she wants to see George again and show him what she's made of her life, the life that he rejected. She then wonders if a home, husband, and children are enough to satisfy her. This thought causes her pain, which brings to mind the memory of the pain of childbirth.*

TIERED DISCUSSION PROMPTS

In lines 218–225, use these prompts to help students understand Granny's reaction to George's abandonment of her:

Recall What image has Granny already associated with the jilting? *Possible answer: She has associated the orderly fields being covered with black smoke with her jilting.*

Evaluate Is it believable that George's actions could affect Granny so dramatically? *Possible answer: Yes. People who face an emotional shock often respond physically, become disoriented, or even collapse.*

VOCABULARY

OWN THE WORD

assign: Tell students that *assigns*, used in the context of this story, refers to a person or persons who receive property as the result of a legal transfer of ownership. Have students write a sentence to demonstrate their understanding of the word. *Possible answer: My parents became the* assigns *(n.) of the house after they signed the mortgage papers at the bank.*

---

loved and fine children out of him. Better than I hoped for even. Tell him I was given back everything he took away and more. Oh, no, oh, God, no, there was something else besides the house and the man and the children. Oh, surely they were not all? What was it? Something not given back. . . . Her breath crowded down under her ribs and grew into a monstrous frightening shape with cutting edges; it bored up into her head, and the agony was unbelievable: Yes, John, get the Doctor now, no more talk, my time has come.

200   When this one was born it should be the last. The last. It should have been born first, for it was the one she had truly wanted. Everything came in good time. Nothing left out, left over. She was strong, in three days she would be as well as ever. Better. A woman needed milk in her to have her full health. ❶

"Mother, do you hear me?"

"I've been telling you—"

"Mother, Father Connolly's here."

"I went to Holy Communion only last week. Tell him I'm not so sinful as all that."

"Father just wants to speak to you."

He could speak as much as he pleased. It was like him to drop in and inquire
210   about her soul as if it were a teething baby, and then stay on for a cup of tea and a round of cards and gossip. He always had a funny story of some sort, usually about an Irishman who made his little mistakes and confessed them, and the point lay in some absurd thing he would blurt out in the confessional showing his struggles between native piety and original sin. Granny felt easy about her soul. Cornelia, where are your manners? Give Father Connolly a chair. She had her secret comfortable understanding with a few favorite saints who cleared a straight road to God for her. All as surely signed and sealed as the papers for the new Forty Acres. Forever . . . heirs and **assigns** forever. Since the day the wedding cake was not cut, but thrown out and wasted. The whole bottom dropped out of the world,
220   and there she was blind and sweating with nothing under her feet and the walls falling away. His hand had caught her under the breast, she had not fallen, there was the freshly polished floor with the green rug on it, just as before. He had cursed like a sailor's parrot and said, "I'll kill him for you." Don't lay a hand on him, for my sake leave something to God. "Now, Ellen, you must believe what I tell you. . . ."

So there was nothing, nothing to worry about any more, except sometimes in the night one of the children screamed in a nightmare, and they both hustled out shaking and hunting for the matches and calling, "There, wait a minute, here we are!" John, get the doctor now, Hapsy's time has come. But there was Hapsy
230   standing by the bed in a white cap. "Cornelia, tell Hapsy to take off her cap. I can't see her plain."

Her eyes opened very wide and the room stood out like a picture she had seen somewhere. Dark colors with the shadows rising towards the ceiling in long angles. The tall black dresser gleamed with nothing on it but John's picture, enlarged from a little one, with John's eyes very black when they should have been blue. You never saw him, so how do you know how he looked? But the man insisted the copy was perfect, it was very rich and handsome. For a picture, yes, but it's not my husband. The table by the bed had a linen cover and a candle and

❹ **Targeted Passage**

❶ **STREAM OF CONSCIOUSNESS**
Reread lines 189–203. What has Granny decided about George? Trace the path of her thoughts from this decision to the memory of the birth of her child.

assign (ə-sīn′) *n.* a person to whom property is transferred in a will or other legal document

---

DIFFERENTIATED INSTRUCTION

FOR STRUGGLING READERS

❹ **Targeted Passage** [Lines 193–196]

In this passage Granny realizes that she lost something irretrievable when she was jilted.

- Who is the "him" that Granny wants to address? (line 190)

- What was "given back"? (line 194)

- Why did Granny get more than she hoped for? Who gave it to her? (line 194)

FOR ENGLISH LANGUAGE LEARNERS

Culture: Clarify Clarify these aspects of Granny's Catholic faith:

- Father Connolly, the priest, has come to give Granny a blessing called Anointing of the Sick. This is done to prepare her for death. He is not her biological father.

- The phrase "native piety" (line 214) refers to Father Connolly's desire for spiritual perfection, while "original sin" (line 214) means that all people, including Father Connolly, are born sinful.

a crucifix.[7] The light was blue from Cornelia's silk lampshades. No sort of light
at all, just frippery. You had to live forty years with kerosene lamps to appreciate
honest electricity. She felt very strong and she saw Doctor Harry with a rosy
nimbus[8] around him.

"You look like a saint, Doctor Harry, and I vow that's as near as you'll ever
come to it."

"She's saying something."

"I heard you, Cornelia. What's all this carrying-on?"

"Father Connolly's saying—"

Cornelia's voice staggered and bumped like a cart in a bad road. It rounded
corners and turned back again and arrived nowhere. Granny stepped up in the cart
very lightly and reached for the reins, but a man sat beside her and she knew him
by his hands, driving the cart. She did not look in his face, for she knew without
seeing, but looked instead down the road where the trees leaned over and bowed
to each other and a thousand birds were singing a Mass. She felt like singing too,
but she put her hand in the bosom of her dress and pulled out a rosary,[9] and
Father Connolly murmured Latin in a very solemn voice and tickled her feet. My
God, will you stop that nonsense? I'm a married woman. What if he did run away
and leave me to face the priest by myself? I found another a whole world better. I
wouldn't have exchanged my husband for anybody except St. Michael himself, and
you may tell him that for me with a thank you in the bargain.

Light flashed on her closed eyelids, and a deep roaring shook her. Cornelia, is
that lightning? I hear thunder. There's going to be a storm. Close all the windows.
Call the children in. . . . "Mother, here we are, all of us." "Is that you, Hapsy?"
"Oh, no, I'm Lydia. We drove as fast as we could." Their faces drifted above her,
drifted away. The rosary fell out of her hands and Lydia put it back. Jimmy tried
to help, their hands fumbled together, and Granny closed two fingers around
Jimmy's thumb. Beads wouldn't do, it must be something alive. She was so amazed
her thoughts ran round and round. So, my dear Lord, this is my death and I
wasn't even thinking about it. My children have come to see me die. But I can't,
it's not time. Oh, I always hated surprises. I wanted to give Cornelia the **amethyst**
set—Cornelia, you're to have the amethyst set, but Hapsy's to wear it when
she wants, and, Doctor Harry, do shut up. Nobody sent for you. Oh, my dear
Lord, do wait a minute. I meant to do something about the Forty Acres, Jimmy
doesn't need it and Lydia will later on, with that worthless husband of hers. I
meant to finish the altar cloth and send six bottles of wine to Sister Borgia for her
dyspepsia.[10] I want to send six bottles of wine to Sister Borgia, Father Connolly,
now don't let me forget.

Cornelia's voice made short turns and tilted over and crashed. "Oh, Mother, oh,
Mother, oh, Mother. . . ."

amethyst (ăm′ə-thĭst) n.
a purple-colored quartz
used as a gemstone

---

7. **crucifix** (krōō′sə-fĭks′): a cross bearing a sculptured representation of the crucified Christ.

8. **nimbus** (nĭm′bəs): halo of light.

9. **rosary** (rō′zə-rē): a string of beads used by Roman Catholics to count their prayers.

10. **dyspepsia** (dĭs-pĕp′shə): indigestion.

THE JILTING OF GRANNY WEATHERALL   1043

REVISIT THE BIG QUESTION

What makes a MEMORY linger?

Discuss In lines 268–276, how do Granny's memories worry her after she realizes that her children "have come to see [her] die" (line 268)? *Possible answer: Now that it is too late to do anything more, she is flooded by memories of duties and tasks that she has left undone and overwhelmed by distaste at unfinished business and loose ends.*

VOCABULARY

COMMON CORE
L 4

OWN THE WORD

amethyst: Remind students that gemstones are used in a variety of ways, but probably best known in jewelry. Ask students to make a list of as many types of gemstones as they can that are used as jewelry. *Possible answers: diamonds, sapphires, rubies, emeralds, opals, garnets*

FOR STRUGGLING READERS

Make Inferences Help students infer the double meaning of Granny's statement in line 229 that "Hapsy's time has come." On the one hand, Hapsy's "time" is the birth of her child, but it is also the moment of death for her and her baby. Recall line 180 when Hapsy fades to a ghostly "gray gauze" in Granny's memory and her baby turns into a "gauzy shadow."

🔲 **BEST PRACTICES TOOLKIT—Transparency**
Making Inferences p. A13

FOR ENGLISH LANGUAGE LEARNERS

Vocabulary: Idioms [mixed-readiness pairs]
Have pairs use context to define these idioms:

- *cursed like a sailor's parrot* (line 223), "used profane and rude language as a parrot imitating a sailor might do"

- *Hapsy's time has come* (line 229), "Hapsy has gone into labor and will soon bear a child"

- *all this carrying-on* (line 246), "all this excitement over nothing"

About the Art American artist Philip Hershberger uses the ancient technique of encaustic painting in which hot wax, resin, and color are blended into a semi-liquid for painting. He describes his work as standing outside of any specific time and raising questions about whether an object is really present or not—qualities that vividly recall Granny Weatherall's experience.

TEXT ANALYSIS	COMMON CORE

❶ STREAM OF CONSCIOUSNESS

RL 1
RL 3
RL 5

Possible answer: She is surprised, even though she knows it's coming and thinks that she has already calmly put the matter aside. For all her careful planning and putting things in order, she is not ready for death.

IF STUDENTS NEED HELP . . . Have them review lines 61–69 and contrast how Granny expects to face death and how she actually faces it.

VOCABULARY	COMMON CORE

OWN THE WORD

L 4

dwindle: Have students look up synonyms for *dwindle*. ***Possible answers:*** *decrease, diminish, drain, ebb, reduce, taper*

SELECTION WRAP-UP

READ WITH A PURPOSE Now that students have read "The Jilting of Granny Weatherall," they may be tempted to conclude that Granny feels hostile because she does not want to die. Encourage them to go deeper, uncovering that Granny's memories of being jilted make her want to believe her life turned out as well as it would have had George married her, but that she feels doubt, loss, and possibly regret as she slips from consciousness.

★ CRITIQUE Ask students whether they find Porter's description of death plausible and to explain why or why not.

1044 UNIT 5

Blue House (2004), Philip Hershberger. Encaustic on panel, 78″ × 48″. © Philip Hershberger.

"I'm not going, Cornelia. I'm taken by surprise. I can't go."

280   You'll see Hapsy again. What about her? "I thought you'd never come." Granny made a long journey outward, looking for Hapsy. What if I don't find her? What then? Her heart sank down and down, there was no bottom to death, she couldn't come to the end of it. The blue light from Cornelia's lampshade drew into a tiny point in the center of her brain, it flickered and winked like an eye, quietly it fluttered and **dwindled.** Granny lay curled down within herself, amazed and watchful, staring at the point of light that was herself; her body was now only a deeper mass of shadow in an endless darkness and this darkness would curl around the light and swallow it up. God, give a sign!

For the second time there was no sign. Again no bridegroom and the priest 290   in the house. She could not remember any other sorrow because this grief wiped them all away. Oh, no, there's nothing more cruel than this—I'll never forgive it. She stretched herself with a deep breath and blew out the light.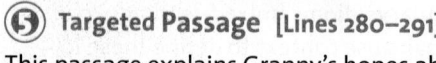

❶ STREAM OF CONSCIOUSNESS
Reread lines 266–279. What is **ironic** about Granny's response to the imminence of her death?

dwindle (dwĭn′dl) *v.* to become steadily less; to shrink

⑤ Targeted Passage

1044   UNIT 5: THE HARLEM RENAISSANCE AND MODERNISM

DIFFERENTIATED INSTRUCTION

FOR STRUGGLING READERS

⑤ Targeted Passage [Lines 280–291]

This passage explains Granny's hopes about death and how she is disappointed again.

- For whom is Granny looking as she dies, and where does she look? (lines 280–281)

- What does Granny see as she dies? (lines 283–285)

- What disappointment does Granny say she will "never forgive" (line 291)? (line 289)

FOR ADVANCED LEARNERS/AP

Hypothesize About Character Explain that some critics believe Granny's jilting was so painful because she was pregnant with George's child, the favored daughter, Hapsy. Have students discuss this interpretation, looking for text evidence to support or disprove it. Then ask them to produce an outline for an essay exploring the impact of this interpretation.

 **BEST PRACTICES TOOLKIT—Transparency** Outline p. B19

Comprehension

1. **Recall** Which characters mentioned in the story belong exclusively to Granny Weatherall's past?

2. **Recall** Who is with Granny when she dies?

3. **Clarify** Who is Hapsy?

Text Analysis

● 4. **Clarify Sequence** Using your timeline, retell the key events of Granny's life in chronological order. Which events mark the best and worst of Granny's life? Explain, citing Granny's own thoughts and feelings about each event.

5. **Make Inferences About Character** Go back through the story, noting thoughts and **memories** that linger in Granny's mind. What do they reveal about the kind of person she is? Record your answers in a chart like this one.

Granny's Thoughts	Character Traits Revealed
"It was good to have everything clean and folded away ... nicely dusted off." (lines 50–55)	She likes putting things in order and having control in life.

● 6. **Analyze Stream of Consciousness** Porter uses stream of consciousness to dramatize Granny's interior life. What effect does this approach have on her readers? For example, how might your reaction to the story have been different if Porter had presented the same events with a more traditional plot? Cite specific examples from the story in your response.

7. **Analyze Theme** Which of the following statements best expresses the themes Porter conveys in this story? Support your choice with evidence from the text.

• There is no deed so wrong it can't be forgiven.

• In youth we are all foolish; with age comes true wisdom.

• Life does not provide the answers or reassurances that people want, even at the moment of death.

Text Criticism

8. **Critical Interpretations** Novelist Reynolds Price asserts that Porter's stories are "lethal to the most widely cherished illusions of the species"—in other words, they destroy our sentimental notions about things like romance, self-regard, and parenthood. What "cherished illusions" does Porter destroy here? What truths does she portray instead? Support your answer.

What makes a **MEMORY** *linger?*

Much like Granny in this story, we often remember things differently from how they actually happened . After all, memories are what people remember—not necessarily the truth. Why do you think this discrepancy between reality and memories happens?

THE JILTING OF GRANNY WEATHERALL **1045**

COMMON CORE

RL 1 Cite textual evidence to support analysis of what the text says explicitly as well as inferences drawn from the text. **RL 3** Analyze the impact of the author's choices regarding how to develop and relate elements of a story. **RL 5** Analyze how an author's choices concerning how to structure specific parts of a text contribute to its overall structure and meaning as well as its aesthetic impact.

8. *Students may discuss any of these illusions: romance, self-regard, gender roles, marriage, parentage. For example, students may say that the story destroys the sentimental illusion of romance because Granny's response to her jilting is one of shame and vanity, not love, and she then remembers her marriage to John as a partnership without romance or passion.*

What makes a **MEMORY** *linger?* Students may say that they see things from a different perspective either at the time of the event or after it happened. Also, time has a way of making people forget some things while remembering others.

Practice and Apply

For preliminary support of post-reading questions, use these copy masters:

R RESOURCE MANAGER—Copy Masters
Reading Check p. 280
Stream of Consciousness p. 273
Question Support p. 281

Additional selection questions are provided for teachers on page 267.

ANSWERS COMMON CORE **RL 1, RL 3, RL 5**

1. *George, John, and Hapsy*

2. *The doctor, a priest, and her surviving children—Cornelia, Lydia, and Jimmy—are with Granny when she dies.*

3. *Hapsy is her favorite daughter, who apparently died.*

Possible answers:

4. ● COMMON CORE FOCUS **Clarify Sequence** *Events: father's death; jilting by George; marriage to John; raising her young children; death of Hapsy; death of John; hard work and community nursing; recovery at age 60 from long fever; illness again at almost age 80 and seeing doctor, priest, and death; The best events are raising young children and hard work and nursing. The worst events are being jilted by George, and Hapsy's death.*

5. *Accept all thoughtful inferences, for example: "Digging post holes ... changed a woman" (lines 105–106) and "It was good ... everything" (line 116) support the inference that Granny is proud of her competence and physical strength.*

6. ● COMMON CORE FOCUS **Stream of Consciousness** *Students may say that they felt more connected to Granny because of Porter's use of stream of consciousness, which made them privy to Granny's innermost thoughts. Had the story been told from an observer's point of view, this sense of intimacy would have been lost. For example, readers would not know the depth of Granny's sorrow over Hapsy's death or her pride in her life.*

7. *The third statement is the strongest statement of theme, but accept all thoughtful answers supported by textual evidence.*

ANSWERS
Vocabulary in Context

▲ VOCABULARY PRACTICE

1. *true*   4. *true*
2. *false*   5. *false*
3. *false*

 **RESOURCE MANAGER—Copy Master**
Vocabulary Practice p. 278

ACADEMIC VOCABULARY IN SPEAKING

Have students explain their ideas to a partner before they begin writing. Partners should identify ideas that might work with a vocabulary word. Students should point out that Granny has had a very difficult life. She has been jilted, has worked hard all her life, has raised several children, and has lost loved ones in death.

VOCABULARY STRATEGY: THESAURI AND WORD CHOICE

COMMON CORE L 4c, L 5b

- Explain that a thesaurus can help find more precise words and prevent overuse of a certain word, but writers need to make sure their replacement words are close enough in meaning and tone to the original.

- Model the practice using the first item. Explain that replacements for *peppered* should retain the sense that Ben's exclamations are not excessive and add interest or personality to his explanation.

Possible answers:

1. *sprinkled, flavored, dotted*
2. *unwillingness, reluctance*
3. *managed, accomplished, achieved*
4. *judgments, inferences, opinions*

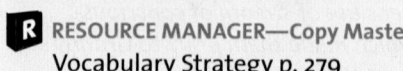 **RESOURCE MANAGER—Copy Master**
Vocabulary Strategy p. 279

Interactive Vocabulary  **THINK** central

Keywords direct students to a **WordSharp** tutorial on **thinkcentral.com** or to other types of vocabulary practice and review.

Vocabulary in Context

▲ VOCABULARY PRACTICE

Decide whether each statement is true or false.

1. If your supplies have begun to **dwindle,** you probably need to find a way to get more.
2. An **amethyst** is a special shawl worn for good luck.
3. A tablecloth that is **embroidered** has beautiful designs painted on it.
4. If I am an **assign** in your will, I should expect to inherit at least a portion of what you have.
5. People who **plague** others are transmitting symptoms of a serious disease.

WORD LIST
amethyst
assign
dwindle
embroidered
plague

ACADEMIC VOCABULARY IN SPEAKING

• conclude • criteria • despite • justify • maintain

Granny Weatherall tries unsuccessfully to **maintain** some kind of control, but readers easily **conclude** that she has lost her grip on reality. In a small group, discuss the **criteria** by which you judge this character's sanity. Use at least one Academic Vocabulary word in your contribution to the discussion.

VOCABULARY STRATEGY: THESAURI AND WORD CHOICE

When you need to choose the most appropriate word from two or more words with similar meanings, you can turn to a thesaurus. A **thesaurus** is a reference book that helps you find specific, or precise, words for more general ideas. In a thesaurus, words are arranged by their meanings and by their parts of speech rather than by alphabetical order, as in a dictionary. For example, if the vocabulary word *dwindle* doesn't have the exact meaning you are looking for, a thesaurus can help you choose among such verbs as *recede, diminish*, or *shrink*.

PRACTICE Use a thesaurus to choose an alternative word to replace each of the words in boldface. Explain how each new word changes the meaning of the sentence.

1. Ben **peppered** his explanation with "unbelievable!" and other expressions of surprise.
2. **Despite** their **refusal** to help her, Pauline harbored no ill will toward her brothers.
3. Through hard work and clever planning, they **engineered** an election victory for the underdog candidate.
4. These **conclusions** are anchored in several months of experimentation and solid research.

COMMON CORE

L 4c Consult general and specialized reference materials, both print and digital, to determine or clarify a word's precise meaning and its part of speech. **L 5b** Analyze nuances in the meaning of words with similar denotations.

 **Interactive Vocabulary** **THINK** central
Go to **thinkcentral.com**.
KEYWORD: HML11-1046

DIFFERENTIATED INSTRUCTION

FOR ENGLISH LANGUAGE LEARNERS

Task Support: Vocabulary Strategy Ask students if their home languages also have figurative verbs that come from nouns, and invite them to share examples in translation. Then help them think of other examples in English. Have them use one example to create a sentence modeled on the practice exercises.

FOR ADVANCED LEARNERS/AP

Nouns and Figurative Verbs Challenge students to create a short glossary of recently created figurative verbs, especially those related to new technologies. For example, *access* and *google*, once a common and a proper noun, are now figurative verbs. Students can publish or post the glossary for class reference.

Language

◆ **GRAMMAR AND STYLE:** Craft Effective Sentences

Review the **Grammar and Style** note on page 1040. Porter skillfully crafts her prose in "The Jilting of Granny Weatherall" to depict Granny's interior life—her secret longings, wishes, and memories. Through her use of **repetition** and the **coordinating conjunction** *and*, Porter reveals Granny's circular thoughts and hazy memories.

> *Then Hapsy melted from within and turned flimsy as gray gauze and the baby was a gauzy shadow, and Hapsy came up close and said, "I thought you'd never come," and looked at her very searchingly and said, "You haven't changed a bit!"* (lines 183–186)

Notice the dreamlike quality of the sentence, with its many *and*'s linking the images as well as its repetition of *gauze* and *gauzy* and related terms *flimsy* and *shadow*.

PRACTICE The following passage presents a character's thoughts as they might appear in a traditional third-person narrative. Rewrite the paragraph as a third-person stream of consciousness.

> Ron walked down the street whistling, his hands shoved deep into his pockets. He squinted up at the weak rays fighting to break through the winter cloud cover. When his gaze returned to street level, he almost tripped over his own feet. Abby was walking toward him.
> "I wonder if she'll even recognize me," Ron thought to himself, quickening his pace and trying to clear his face of emotion.

READING-WRITING CONNECTION

Expand your understanding of "The Jilting of Granny Weatherall" by responding to this prompt. Then, use the **revising tips** to improve your narrative.

WRITING PROMPT	REVISING TIPS
USE STREAM OF CONSCIOUSNESS Katherine Anne Porter wasn't the only modernist to experiment with stream of consciousness; T. S. Eliot, James Joyce, and William Faulkner all used it to explore the intricacies of the human mind. Some writers use it today. Now you'll get a chance to try it for yourself. Write a **three- or four-paragraph narrative** in stream of consciousness, depicting the thoughts and impressions of a character having a particular experience. You can either write about yourself or create a fictional character.	• Include details of time and place as part of your character's consciousness. • Focus on your character's thoughts but include spoken words in quotation marks, too. • Use images from both the past and the present to show how your character sees what is happening now and what has happened in the past.

Interactive Revision

Go to **thinkcentral.com**.
KEYWORD: HML11-1047

COMMON CORE

L 3a Vary syntax for effect, consulting references for guidance as needed; apply an understanding of syntax to the study of complex texts when reading. **W 3** Write narratives to develop real or imagined experiences or events using effective technique, well-chosen details, and well-structured event sequences.

Language

 COMMON CORE L 3a, W 3

◆ **GRAMMAR AND STYLE**

Tell students that in most writing situations, sentences composed of short phrases and clauses joined by *and* would be considered choppy and would invite revision. Stress that this style of writing has a specific function in Porter's story—to show Granny's feverish jumps from memory to memory. ***Possible answers:** Students' paragraphs should reflect a first-person stream of consciousness voice, as if they were simply recording Ron's thoughts.*

 RESOURCE MANAGER—Copy Master
Craft Effective Sentences p. 282

READING-WRITING CONNECTION

Have students use organizers to identify character traits and plot events. Students can then explore possible connections among thoughts, feelings, and memories, perhaps using a Sequence Chain to track those connections.

BEST PRACTICES TOOLKIT—Transparencies
Character Traits Web p. D7
Plot Diagram p. D10
Sequence Chain p. B21

Writing Online

The following tools are available online at **thinkcentral.com** and on Write*Smart* CD-ROM:
• **Interactive Graphic Organizers**
• **Interactive Student Models**
• **Interactive Revision Lessons**
For additional grammar instruction, see **Grammar*Notes*** on **thinkcentral.com**.

Assess and Reteach

Assess

DIAGNOSTIC AND SELECTION TESTS
Selection Test A, B/C pp. 281–282, 283–284
Interactive Selection Test on thinkcentral.com

Reteach

Level Up Online Tutorials on thinkcentral.com
Reteaching Worksheets on thinkcentral.com
Literature Lessons 8, 36, Reading Lesson 6

FOR STRUGGLING WRITERS

Writing Support

• Limit the length of the narrative to one or two paragraphs.
• Clarify the difference between stream-of-consciousness writing and the more typical first-person point of view. Have students write a draft from a purely first-person point of view and then adapt it as stream of consciousness.

• Have students read their stream-of-consciousness drafts to a partner, asking for new associations between thoughts and memories. Ask students to incorporate the feedback as they revise.

Focus and Motivate

COMMON CORE FOCUS

RL 2 Determine two or more themes or central ideas of a text and analyze their development over the course of the text, including how they interact and build on one another to produce a complex account; provide an objective summary of the text. **RL 10** Read and comprehend literature, including stories. **W 3** Write narratives to develop imagined experiences or events using effective technique, well-chosen details, and well-structured event sequences. **W 3a** Engage and orient the reader by setting out a problem or situation and its significance, establishing one or multiple point(s) of view, and introducing a narrator and/or characters. **L 3** Apply knowledge of language to understand how language functions in different contexts, to make effective choices for meaning or style, and to comprehend more fully when reading or listening. **L 4b** Identify and correctly use patterns of word changes that indicate different meanings. **L 6** Acquire and use accurately general academic and domain-specific words and phrases.

ABOUT THE AUTHOR

Explain that Welty noted similarities between her work as a photographer and as a writer. To succeed at both, she had to gain enough distance from her subjects to understand their situations. This allowed her to slowly zoom in to learn more.

NOTABLE QUOTE

"There is absolutely everything in great fiction but a clear answer." —**Eudora Welty**

Ask students the reason Eudora Welty might give for reading literature—and the limitation she would add.

Selection Resources

COMMON CORE

RL 2 Determine two or more themes or central ideas of a text and analyze their development over the course of the text, including how they interact and build on one another to produce a complex account; provide an objective summary of the text. **RL 10** Read and comprehend literature, including stories. **L 4b** Identify and correctly use patterns of word changes that indicate different meanings.

DID YOU KNOW?

Eudora Welty . . .

- was voted "Best All-Round Girl" in high school.

- was awarded the Presidential Medal of Freedom in 1980.

- inspired the name of an e-mail program, "Eudora," so named by a Web designer who loved her stories.

The Modern Short Story

A Worn Path

Short Story by Eudora Welty

Meet the Author

Eudora Welty   1909–2001

Mississippi born and bred, Eudora Welty wrote about her fellow Southerners at a crucial time in U.S. history. When she first began publishing her stories in the late 1930s, vestiges of the Old South still colored daily life. But Welty lived long enough to see the changes wrought by the civil rights movement in the 1960s and the rise of the New South on the eve of the new millennium. All the while, she recorded the lives of ordinary people, depicting the family life that sustained them and the small acts of heroism that dignified them. She was a modernist who believed in love, a Southerner who had faith in tolerance and change, and a successful, unmarried woman at a time when single women in Mississippi were not allowed to buy a house. At first dismissed as a regionalist and even a "feminine" writer, Welty lived long enough to see her fiction recognized for its artistic vision and universal appeal. Through it all, she accepted the changes with her characteristic sense of humor, modesty, and grace.

A Photographer's Eye Nourished by books and a close-knit community of family and friends, Welty lived most of her life in the house her father built in Jackson, Mississippi. Although she wrote stories even in childhood and attended college, her education as a writer didn't seriously begin until 1933, when she landed a job as a publicity agent with the federal government's Works Progress Administration (WPA). Interviewing and photographing all kinds of people throughout Mississippi during the Great Depression—one of the most impoverished regions during the poorest time in the nation's history—was an eye opener for Welty and gave her the first "real germ" of her writing. Her early stories, such as "Why I Live at the P.O." and "A Worn Path," are like photographs, capturing a specific moment that reveals something significant about a person and at the same time a greater truth about the human condition.

A Long, Productive Life Welty received numerous awards and honors for her works, including a Pulitzer Prize for her novel *The Optimist's Daughter* (1972) and an O. Henry Award for "A Worn Path." Her award-winning memoir, *One Writer's Beginnings* (1984), was a runaway bestseller. Despite being very articulate about her writing, sitting graciously through countless interviews, and receiving large numbers of young fans at her home, Welty remained a very private person who always maintained that "a fiction writer should let writing speak for itself."

Author Online
Go to **thinkcentral.com**. KEYWORD: HML11-1048

THINK central

1048

TEXT ANALYSIS: UNIVERSAL THEME

You know that theme is the underlying message a writer wants readers to understand. A **universal theme** is a message that can be found throughout literature of all times and places. Works that convey a universal theme often contain **archetypes**—basic patterns found in a variety of works from different cultures throughout history. The perilous journey is one such archetype; the main character in this story travels a long and uncertain path in search of something.

As you read, consider what this journey might symbolize. Think about the main character's traits and how she deals with obstacles on the path, as well as the story's title and its setting. Taken together, what universal theme do these elements suggest?

READING STRATEGY: MONITOR COMPREHENSION

This story has a dreamlike quality that can make it challenging to follow. **Monitoring** is the strategy of checking your comprehension as you are reading and using techniques such as **questioning** and **clarifying** to aid your understanding. As you read, stop every once in a while to consider how well you are comprehending the story. Jot down any questions that come to mind. Review what you do understand and use context clues and analysis of key words and details to clarify the meaning of anything you don't.

> Question:
> If Phoenix is alone on her journey, why does she keep speaking aloud?
> Clarification:

VOCABULARY IN CONTEXT

Welty uses the boldfaced words in her story of one woman's pilgrimage. Replace each boldfaced word with a new word or phrase.

1. **Limber** branches swayed back and forth in the breeze.
2. She gazed at the **radiation** of ripples each raindrop created on the pond's surface.
3. He could not shake his **obstinate** cough.
4. The **meditative** hiker gazed at the sky.

 Complete the activities in your **Reader/Writer Notebook**.

What keeps us GOING?

Endurance is crucial in any long-distance sport, and it's a necessity for surviving harsh conditions or extreme adventures. But what kind of endurance is required for daily life? And where does this type of endurance come from?

DISCUSS With a small group of classmates, discuss the preceding questions. Begin by talking about what you think motivates champion athletes or people facing extreme conditions. Then consider what motivates ordinary people to endure—to keep attending night school while working two day jobs, for example, or to sacrifice a favorite after school activity in order to drive younger siblings to theirs. In your opinion, is the motivation the same in both the extreme and the ordinary cases? If not, what's the difference?

1049

Teach

What keeps us GOING?

Read the question and then ask students to list their weekly obligations and describe the kinds of endurance needed to complete the listed tasks. After they finish the *DISCUSS* activity, invite groups to share conclusions. Then, ask students to generate advice on the endurance needed for daily life.

TEXT ANALYSIS
COMMON CORE
RL 2

● *Model the Skill:* UNIVERSAL THEME

Tell students the plot structure of a popular movie or book. Then ask them to list plot structures from other TV shows, movies, or books. Note archetypal plots such as the quest for love, a precious object, or knowledge; the betrayal or proof of friendship; and the desire for vengeance. Discuss with students why the same stories are told again and again. Point out that these plots explore the greatest needs and desires in human life and thus generate universal themes.

GUIDED PRACTICE Ask students to identify a universal theme in one of the examples listed. Remind them that a theme is a message for readers, not a plot.

READING STRATEGY
COMMON CORE
RL 2

■ *Model the Skill:* MONITOR COMPREHENSION

Point out that students already use monitoring strategies to keep up with stories on serialized TV shows and to track current events among friends. Tell students that a friend might ask another "Why on earth did she do *that?*" Urge them to apply these life strategies to their reading.

GUIDED PRACTICE Have pairs dramatize a phone call in which friends ask questions to gain information and clarify.

R **RESOURCE MANAGER—Copy Master**
Monitor p. 295 (for student use while reading the selection)

SUMMARY

In this story, Phoenix Jackson walks from her rural farm to the city of Natchez to get medicine for her injured grandson. The trip challenges the aging Phoenix's physical and mental strength, but she gets not only the medicine for her grandson but also a small toy that she knows will delight him. Then she begins the long walk home.

READ WITH A PURPOSE

Help students set a purpose for reading. Tell them to read to discover the obstacles Phoenix must overcome to achieve her goal.

REVISIT THE BIG QUESTION

What keeps us GOING?

Discuss What words and descriptions in lines 3–9 hint at Phoenix's endurance as she begins this journey? ***Possible answer:*** *Words such as "kept tapping" (line 7) and "persistent noise" (line 8) hint at Phoenix's ability to endure, to keep going. The comparison of her gait to a clock's steady ticking also suggests endurance.*

TEXT ANALYSIS
COMMON CORE RL 2

A UNIVERSAL THEME

Possible answer: *The journey's length is suggested by how early Phoenix begins the trip, by her slow, balanced gait, and by her need for the cane to help her see the path.*

Extend the Discussion How does the season affect Phoenix's need to make the journey as quickly as possible?

VOCABULARY
COMMON CORE L 4

OWN THE WORD

meditative: *Meditative* describes a person who is "engaged in serious reflection or meditation." Ask students how their lives might be improved if they spent more time being *meditative*. ***Possible answers:*** *Taking time to slow down and contemplate one's life can alleviate stress, solve problems, gain ideas, and help one feel more peaceful and healthy.*

A Worn Path

Eudora Welty

BACKGROUND This story takes place in rural Mississippi in the 1930s, an era in which segregation laws and racism, combined with the economic devastation of the Great Depression, restricted most Southern blacks to lives of rural poverty and hardship. Eudora Welty saw the need and inequality surrounding her. She based this story on an old woman she observed crossing a field: "I thought, she is bent on an errand. And I know it isn't for herself. It was just the look of her figure.... She was a black woman. But then I suppose it would be more likely to be a black woman who would be in such desperate need and live so remotely away from help and who would have so far to go."

It was December—a bright frozen day in the early morning. Far out in the country there was an old Negro woman with her head tied in a red rag, coming along a path through the pinewoods. Her name was Phoenix Jackson. She was very old and small and she walked slowly in the dark pine shadows, moving a little from side to side in her steps, with the balanced heaviness and lightness of a pendulum in a grandfather clock. She carried a thin, small cane made from an umbrella, and with this she kept tapping the frozen earth in front of her. This made a grave and persistent noise in the still air, that seemed **meditative** like the chirping of a solitary little bird. Ⓐ

Analyze Visuals ▶
What thematic ideas might you ascribe to this painting? Identify the elements of the painting that suggest these ideas.

meditative (mĕd′ĭ-tā′tĭv) *adj.* engaged in serious thought or reflection

Ⓐ **UNIVERSAL THEME**
What details in lines 1–9 suggest that Phoenix is in for a long journey? As you read, keep in mind other **archetypal** journeys you know of.

Brooding Silence (date unknown), John Fabian Carlson. Smithsonian American Art Museum, Washington, D.C. © Smithsonian American Art Museum, Washington, D.C./Art Resource, New York.

DIFFERENTIATED INSTRUCTION

FOR ADVANCED LEARNERS/AP

Vocabulary: Multiple-Meaning Words Elicit or share the meanings of these words as used in context: *grave* (line 8), "solemn, serious"; *still* (line 8), "motionless." The first word may present a particular challenge to students familiar with its noun form. Have them use Word Questioning to further explore the words.

🧰 **BEST PRACTICES TOOLKIT—Transparency**
Word Questioning p. E9

FOR STRUGGLING READERS

Develop Reading Fluency Read aloud the story's first paragraph. Ask students how your reading keeps listeners engaged. Within the discussion, guide them to understand that reading with expression and slow pacing, along with placing emphasis on important story details, helps keep listeners engaged. Have groups practice reading the first paragraph, offering each other positive and negative feedback for their readings.

BACKGROUND

Depression-Era Mississippi The economic devastation of the Great Depression hit a Mississippi already in distress. The state had not recovered from the Civil War, which damaged both the rich farm land and the people, or from reconstruction policies that created low-paying tenant-farming jobs. In addition, the great flood of the Mississippi River in 1927 caused further damage to farmlands. In these hard economic times, newly emancipated African Americans carried the dual burdens of practical disenfranchisement and lack of education.

TIERED DISCUSSION PROMPTS

In lines 29–50, use these prompts to help students understand Phoenix's character:

Recall What does the reader know about Phoenix? *Possible answer: She is old, small, uses a cane, and she has "a long way" to go (line 22) as she travels through the woods.*

Synthesize What do Phoenix's words and actions suggest about how she perceives the challenges she faces? *Possible answer: Phoenix seems to perceive the challenges as a conflict with herself as much as with nature. She notes that something inside her "pleads I should stay" (line 31) rather than climb the hill, but she climbs it.*

TEXT ANALYSIS

COMMON CORE RL 2

B UNIVERSAL THEME

Possible answer: The thorny bush might symbolize any trial that Phoenix may face. Phoenix is philosophical about the trouble—the thorns are just doing what they are designed to do (lines 38–39). Her attitude suggests that she does not get upset about things she can't control.

VOCABULARY

COMMON CORE L 4

OWN THE WORD

limber: Have students list things that work best when *limber*. *Possible answers: legs, fingers, entire body, trees—to move in the wind*

---

10 She wore a dark striped dress reaching down to her shoe tops, and an equally long apron of bleached sugar sacks, with a full pocket: all neat and tidy, but every time she took a step she might have fallen over her shoelaces, which dragged from her unlaced shoes. She looked straight ahead. Her eyes were blue with age. Her skin had a pattern all its own of numberless branching wrinkles and as though a whole little tree stood in the middle of her forehead, but a golden color ran underneath, and the two knobs of her cheeks were illumined by a yellow burning under the dark. Under the red rag her hair came down on her neck in the frailest of ringlets, still black, and with an odor like copper.

Now and then there was a quivering in the thicket. Old Phoenix said, "Out

20 of my way, all you foxes, owls, beetles, jack rabbits, coons and wild animals! . . . Keep out from under these feet, little bob-whites.[1] . . . Keep the big wild hogs out of my path. Don't let none of those come running my direction. I got a long way." Under her small black-freckled hand her cane, **limber** as a buggy whip, would switch at the brush as if to rouse up any hiding things.

On she went. The woods were deep and still. The sun made the pine needles almost too bright to look at, up where the wind rocked. The cones dropped as light as feathers. Down in the hollow was the mourning dove—it was not too late for him.

The path ran up a hill. "Seem like there is chains about my feet, time I get this

30 far," she said, in the voice of argument old people keep to use with themselves. "Something always take a hold of me on this hill—pleads I should stay."

After she got to the top she turned and gave a full, severe look behind her where she had come. "Up through pines," she said at length. "Now down through oaks."

Her eyes opened their widest, and she started down gently. But before she got to the bottom of the hill a bush caught her dress.

Her fingers were busy and intent, but her skirts were full and long, so that before she could pull them free in one place they were caught in another. It was not possible to allow the dress to tear. "I in the thorny bush," she said. "Thorns, you doing your appointed work. Never want to let folks pass, no sir. Old eyes

40 thought you was a pretty little *green* bush."

Finally, trembling all over, she stood free, and after a moment dared to stoop for her cane.

"Sun so high!" she cried, leaning back and looking, while the thick tears went over her eyes. "The time getting all gone here." **B**

At the foot of this hill was a place where a log was laid across the creek.

"Now comes the trial," said Phoenix.

Putting her right foot out, she mounted the log and shut her eyes. Lifting her skirt, leveling her cane fiercely before her, like a festival figure in some parade, she began to march across. Then she opened her eyes and she was safe on the other side.

50 "I wasn't as old as I thought," she said.

---

1. **bob-whites:** game birds that are a type of quail.

COMMON CORE L 4b

Language Coach

Suffixes A suffix is a word part that appears at the end of a root or base word to form a new word. The suffix *–let* means "small." Words with *–let* include *booklet, droplet,* and *owlet.* What does *ringlet* (line 18) mean?

limber (lĭm'bər) *adj.* bending or moving easily; supple

B UNIVERSAL THEME
Reread lines 34–44 and explain what you think the thorny bush might **symbolize.** What does Phoenix's way of dealing with this obstacle suggest about her character?

DIFFERENTIATED INSTRUCTION

FOR STRUGGLING READERS

1 Targeted Passage [Lines 10–18]

This passage uses vivid description to introduce the main character, Phoenix.

- Of what are Phoenix's clothes made? (line 11)
- What is distinctive about her skin? (lines 13–17)
- What is potentially dangerous about her shoes? (lines 11–13)

FOR ENGLISH LANGUAGE LEARNERS

Language Coach **COMMON CORE** L 4b

Suffixes *Answer: Ringlet means a curly lock of hair.* Provide students with these additional suffixes and meanings:

- *-ful* "full of"
- *-less* "without"
- *-ness* "state or quality of"

Have students brainstorm a class list of words that contain these suffixes.

FOR ADVANCED LEARNERS/AP

Interpret Symbolism [small-group option]
Have students reread lines 10–18, paying close attention to words that describe or suggest color. Then have them discuss:

- What colors are associated with Phoenix?
- What emotions and ideas do these colors connect to Phoenix?
- What predictions about Phoenix can readers base on this description?

Invite groups to share their conclusions.

But she sat down to rest. She spread her skirts on the bank around her and folded her hands over her knees. Up above her was a tree in a pearly cloud of mistletoe. She did not dare to close her eyes, and when a little boy brought her a plate with a slice of marble-cake on it she spoke to him. "That would be acceptable," she said. But when she went to take it there was just her own hand in the air. **C**

So she left that tree, and had to go through a barbed-wire fence. There she had to creep and crawl, spreading her knees and stretching her fingers like a baby trying to climb the steps. But she talked loudly to herself: she could not let her
60 dress be torn now, so late in the day, and she could not pay for having her arm or her leg sawed off if she got caught fast where she was.

At last she was safe through the fence and risen up out in the clearing. Big dead trees, like black men with one arm, were standing in the purple stalks of the withered cotton field. There sat a buzzard. **D**

"Who you watching?"

In the furrow she made her way along.

"Glad this not the season for bulls," she said, looking sideways, "and the good Lord made his snakes to curl up and sleep in the winter. A pleasure I don't see no two-headed snake coming around that tree, where it come once. It took a while to
70 get by him, back in the summer."

She passed through the old cotton and went into a field of dead corn. It whispered and shook and was taller than her head. "Through the maze now," she said, for there was no path. **E**

Then there was something tall, black, and skinny there, moving before her.

At first she took it for a man. It could have been a man dancing in the field. But she stood still and listened, and it did not make a sound. It was as silent as a ghost.

"Ghost," she said sharply, "who be you the ghost of? For I have heard of nary[2] death close by."

80 But there was no answer—only the ragged dancing in the wind.

She shut her eyes, reached out her hand, and touched a sleeve. She found a coat and inside that an emptiness, cold as ice.

"You scarecrow," she said. Her face lighted. "I ought to be shut up for good," she said with laughter. "My senses is gone. I too old. I the oldest people I ever know. Dance, old scarecrow," she said, "while I dancing with you."

She kicked her foot over the furrow, and with mouth drawn down, shook her head once or twice in a little strutting way. Some husks blew down and whirled in streamers about her skirts.

Then she went on, parting her way from side to side with the cane, through
90 the whispering field. At last she came to the end, to a wagon track where the silver grass blew between the red ruts. The quail were walking around like pullets,[3] seeming all dainty and unseen.

---

2. **nary:** not any.

3. **pullets:** young hens.

A WORN PATH **1053**

C MONITOR
Reread lines 51–56. What is happening in these lines? **Clarify** the meaning by considering the trials Phoenix has faced thus far, as well as how she feels at this point in her journey.

D UNIVERSAL THEME
Examine the images in lines 62–64. What **mood** do they help create? Explain.

E GRAMMAR AND STYLE
Welty uses a variety of sensory **details** to make Phoenix's journey riveting for readers. Reread lines 71–73, noting how the **verbs** *whispered* and *shook* conjure sights and sounds in your mind.

READING STRATEGY   COMMON CORE RL 2

C Model the Skill: MONITOR

Point out to students that they can construct questions that will lead to the answer, such as *Why is Phoenix stopping to rest? Why is she interested in cake?* Urge students to add these questions and answers to the prereading chart introduced on page 1049.

Possible answer: *Phoenix hallucinates about the little boy with the cake, perhaps because she is tired and hungry.*

TEXT ANALYSIS   COMMON CORE RL 2

D UNIVERSAL THEME

Possible answer: *Key images include the dead trees standing like one-armed men, the withered cotton, and the buzzard. These images create an ominous mood that suggests Phoenix makes this journey at a risk to her safety.*

E GRAMMAR AND STYLE   COMMON CORE L 3

Add Descriptive Details Review that sensory details are words that appeal to the sense of sight, sound, taste, touch, and smell. These details can be adjectives or, as in this case, vivid verbs. For further practice, have students identify and discuss the sensory details in lines 10–18, which describe Phoenix and her clothing.

FOR STRUGGLING READERS

Comprehension Support Model how to gather information about character traits from Phoenix's words. For example, her admonitions to herself while untangling her dress from the barbed wire reflect an understated sense of humor. Urge students to begin a Character Traits Web for Phoenix with this example and add to it as they read.

BEST PRACTICES TOOLKIT—Transparency
Character Traits Web p. D7

FOR ENGLISH LANGUAGE LEARNERS

Culture: Clarify Ask students if they know what kind of bird a buzzard is (line 64). Explain that buzzards are carrion birds, which means they feed off dead animals. Their presence often signifies death or its approach. Have students use this knowledge to explain why Phoenix challenges the bird with her abrupt question, "Who you watching?" (line 65). **Possible answers:** *She wants to be sure the bird knows she's alive and not food. She wants to ward off death.*

FOR ADVANCED LEARNERS/AP

Research Mistletoe Direct students' attention to the reference to mistletoe in lines 52–53. Have them use reference books or the Internet to learn about the mythology surrounding mistletoe. Then ask them to create a visual organizer reflecting answers to these questions: Why does Welty specify mistletoe in this line? How does mistletoe connect to the archetypal journey?

A WORN PATH **1053**

Analyze Visuals

Activity Discuss how the mood in *Snowy Woods at Dusk* is similar to the mood Welty creates in lines 94–105. Ask students what techniques each artist uses to achieve mood. *Possible answers: Sheehan uses a limited color palette to create shadows and flat light that suggests a mournful, lonely mood. Welty uses words such as "bare," "from weather," "boarded shut," "silently," and "dark as a cave" to achieve a similar mood.*

About the Art Dennis Sheehan (born 1950) is a painter in New Hampshire whose landscapes capture moods evoked by natural settings. Light spills from his paintings, accented by strong shadows.

TEXT ANALYSIS

⑤ UNIVERSAL THEME

COMMON CORE

RL 2

Possible answer: Phoenix knows the easy and hard parts of the journey. With the story title, her familiarity suggests that she has made this journey many times.

REVIST THE BIG QUESTION

What keeps us GOING?

Discuss In lines 94–100, what items does Phoenix encounter that reflect her endurance because they, too, have lasted? *Possible answer: Phoenix's endurance is reflected in the old cabins, "silver from weather" but still standing (line 95), and a well that has been flowing with sweet water since before her birth.*

Snowy Woods at Dusk (date unknown), Dennis Sheehan. Oil, 20″ × 16″. Courtesy of Susan Powell Fine Art, Madison, Connecticut.

"Walk pretty," she said. "This the easy place. This the easy going." **⑤**

She followed the track, swaying through the quiet bare fields, through the little strings of trees silver in their dead leaves, past cabins silver from weather, with the doors and windows boarded shut, all like old women under a spell sitting there. "I walking in their sleep," she said, nodding her head vigorously.

In a ravine she went where a spring was silently flowing through a hollow log. Old Phoenix bent and drank. "Sweet-gum⁴ makes the water sweet," she said, and 100 drank more. "Nobody know who made this well, for it was here when I was born."

The track crossed a swampy part where the moss hung as white as lace from every limb. "Sleep on, alligators, and blow your bubbles." Then the track went into the road.

Deep, deep the road went down between the high green-colored banks. Overhead the live-oaks⁵ met, and it was as dark as a cave.

A black dog with a lolling tongue came up out of the weeds by the ditch. She was meditating, and not ready, and when he came at her she only hit him a little with her cane. Over she went in the ditch, like a little puff of milkweed.

⑤ UNIVERSAL THEME
Consider Phoenix's statement in line 93. What does her familiarity with each leg of this trek, in addition to the story's **title,** suggest about her journey?

---

4. **sweet-gum:** a tree of the witch hazel family.

5. **live-oaks:** oak trees of a type that has evergreen foliage.

1054 UNIT 5: THE HARLEM RENAISSANCE AND MODERNISM

DIFFERENTIATED INSTRUCTION

FOR STRUGGLING READERS

Figurative Language Review *simile* with students. Encourage them to study the similes Welty uses on this page by filling in a Three-Column Journal like this one. Students can add examples as they read on.

 BEST PRACTICES TOOLKIT—Transparency
Three-Column Journal p. B10

Simile compares . . .	to . . .	to show that . . .
weathered cabins	old women	cabins have personality, are grey like hair
descending road	cave	
Phoenix	a puff of milkweed	

FOR ADVANCED LEARNERS/AP

Analyze Figurative Language Ask students to learn about or review the poetic technique called *apostrophe*. Then have them prepare and share brief answers to these questions: What is poetic apostrophe, and how does it relate to the punctuation mark of the same name? When is Phoenix speaking in apostrophe, and when is she speaking to herself? What does Welty gain by this use of apostrophe?

Down there, her senses drifted away. A dream visited her, and she reached her hand up, but nothing reached down and gave her a pull. So she lay there and presently went to talking. "Old woman," she said to herself, "that black dog come up out of the weeds to stall you off, and now there he sitting on his fine tail, smiling at you."

A white man finally came along and found her—a hunter, a young man, with his dog on a chain.

"Well, Granny!" he laughed. "What are you doing there?"

"Lying on my back like a June-bug waiting to be turned over, mister," she said, reaching up her hand.

He lifted her up, gave her a swing in the air, and set her down. "Anything broken, Granny?"

"No sir, them old dead weeds is springy enough," said Phoenix, when she had got her breath. "I thank you for your trouble."

"Where do you live, Granny?" he asked, while the two dogs were growling at each other.

"Away back yonder, sir, behind the ridge. You can't even see it from here."

"On your way home?"

"No sir, I going to town."

"Why, that's too far! That's as far as I walk when I come out myself, and I get something for my trouble." He patted the stuffed bag he carried, and there hung down a little closed claw. It was one of the bob-whites, with its beak hooked bitterly to show it was dead. "Now you go on home, Granny!"

"I bound to go to town, mister," said Phoenix. "The time come around."

He gave another laugh, filling the whole landscape. "I know you old colored people! Wouldn't miss going to town to see Santa Claus!"

But something held old Phoenix very still. The deep lines in her face went into a fierce and different **radiation**. Without warning, she had seen with her own eyes a flashing nickel fall out of the man's pocket onto the ground.

"How old are you, Granny?" he was saying.

"There is no telling, mister," she said, "no telling."

Then she gave a little cry and clapped her hands and said, "Git on away from here, dog! Look! Look at that dog!" She laughed as if in admiration. "He ain't scared of nobody. He a big black dog." She whispered, "Sic him!"

"Watch me get rid of that cur," said the man. "Sic him, Pete! Sic him!"

Phoenix heard the dogs fighting, and heard the man running and throwing sticks. She even heard a gunshot. But she was slowly bending forward by that time, further and further forward, the lids stretched down over her eyes, as if she were doing this in her sleep. Her chin was lowered almost to her knees. The yellow palm of her hand came out from the fold of her apron. Her fingers slid down and along the ground under the piece of money with the grace and care they would have in lifting an egg from under a setting hen. Then she slowly straightened up,

---

G MONITOR
Reread lines 106–115. How can you tell when Phoenix is experiencing actual events or interacting with real people and when she has "drifted away" into her own imagination? Write two **questions** that help you understand what is real and what is not.

② **Targeted Passage**

radiation (rā′dē-ā′shən) *n.* the movement of lines or rays from a center point

---

H MONITOR

Possible answer: The interaction indicates that it was acceptable, perhaps, for a young white man (or any white person) to treat an elderly black woman without respect.

IF STUDENTS NEED HELP . . . Guide them to ask clarifying questions, such as these:

- How are younger people supposed to treat their elders? How are men expected to behave towards women?
- Does the hunter follow these social expectations?

Remind students to add these questions to the lists they began on page 1049.

I Model the Skill: UNIVERSAL THEME

Point out text details that relay Phoenix's character traits, such as "she said, holding utterly still."

Possible answer: Phoenix remains calm (lines 157–160), but she is not above stealing the man's change. This resourcefulness has probably helped her during her long life, as it helps her on today's journey.

Extend the Discussion What does Phoenix think of her own behavior? How might the hunter's claim that he has no money with him change readers' view of the theft?

---

she stood erect, and the nickel was in her apron pocket. A bird flew by. Her lips moved. "God watching me the whole time. I come to stealing."

The man came back, and his own dog panted about them. "Well, I scared him off that time," he said, and then he laughed and lifted his gun and pointed it at Phoenix.

She stood straight and faced him.

"Doesn't the gun scare you?" he said, still pointing it.

"No, sir, I seen plenty go off closer by, in my day, and for less than what I done," she said, holding utterly still.

160 He smiled, and shouldered the gun. "Well, Granny," he said, "you must be a hundred years old, and scared of nothing. I'd give you a dime if I had any money with me. But you take my advice and stay home, and nothing will happen to you." H

"I bound to go on my way, mister," said Phoenix. She inclined her head in the red rag. Then they went in different directions, but she could hear the gun shooting again and again over the hill. I

She walked on. The shadows hung from the oak trees to the road like curtains. Then she smelled wood-smoke, and smelled the river, and she saw a steeple and the cabins on their steep steps. Dozens of little black children whirled around her.

170 There ahead was Natchez shining. Bells were ringing. She walked on.

In the paved city it was Christmas time. There were red and green electric lights strung and criss-crossed everywhere, and all turned on in the daytime. Old Phoenix would have been lost if she had not distrusted her eyesight and depended on her feet to know where to take her.

She paused quietly on the sidewalk where people were passing by. A lady came along in the crowd, carrying an armful of red-, green- and silver-wrapped presents; she gave off perfume like the red roses in hot summer, and Phoenix stopped her.

"Please, missy, will you lace up my shoe?" She held up her foot.

"What do you want, Grandma?"

180 "See my shoe," said Phoenix. "Do all right for out in the country, but wouldn't look right to go in a big building."

"Stand still then, Grandma," said the lady. She put her packages down on the sidewalk beside her and laced and tied both shoes tightly.

"Can't lace 'em with a cane," said Phoenix. "Thank you, missy. I doesn't mind asking a nice lady to tie up my shoe, when I gets out on the street."

Moving slowly and from side to side, she went into the big building, and into a tower of steps, where she walked up and around and around until her feet knew to stop.

She entered a door, and there she saw nailed up on the wall the document 190 that had been stamped with the gold seal and framed in the gold frame, which matched the dream that was hung up in her head.

H MONITOR
Keep the story's **setting** in mind as you contemplate the way the hunter treats Phoenix. What does their interaction tell you about this time and place in history?

I UNIVERSAL THEME
Reread lines 114–166, and describe the **character traits** Phoenix exhibits during this episode with the hunter. How do her traits help her overcome this particular obstacle in her journey?

③ Targeted Passage

Analyze Visuals ▶
What elements of this portrait give the woman a look of inner strength and determination? Be specific.

DIFFERENTIATED INSTRUCTION

FOR STRUGGLING READERS

③ **Targeted Passage** [Lines 175–185]

This passage reveals that it is important to Phoenix that she look her best in the city.

- Why does Phoenix ask for help with her shoelaces? (lines 180–181)
- Why can't she lace them herself? (line 184)
- How does the lady respond? (lines 182–183)

FOR ENGLISH LANGUAGE LEARNERS

Comprehension Support Ask students what the document described in lines 189–191 is. Explain that doctors often display certificates proving that they have completed necessary medical training. Show students photos of such certificates in books or online. Ask students how doctors' credentials are conveyed in their home countries.

FOR ADVANCED LEARNERS/AP

Compare and Contrast Have students analyze the contrasting settings in the story by completing a Comparison Matrix for the "worn path" that Phoenix walks so assuredly and the "paved city" of Natchez. Have students discuss the differing challenges of the two settings and decide which seems to pose the greater threat to Phoenix's success.

 BEST PRACTICES TOOLKIT—Transparency
Comparison Matrix p. A24

Woman Peeling Apples (1924), Archibald J. Motley, Jr. Oil on canvas, 32¼″ × 28″. Art and Artifacts Division, Schomberg Center for Research in Black Culture, The New York Public Library, Astor, Lenox and Tilden Foundations.

Analyze Visuals

Possible answer: *The woman looks straight at the viewer, frankly and fearlessly. Her expression is serious but calm, and the lines of her face are strong. The organized pattern of her dress reinforces these lines. She holds her work in her lap, which suggests proficiency. All of these elements contribute to her look of strength and determination.*

About the Art Archibald Motley (1891–1981) was the first African-American artist to receive the prestigious Guggenheim award, given annually to an artist or researcher whose past work is excellent, to support future work. While a young man, Motley worked for a time on the railroad, traveling and sketching the scenes and people that he saw. He is known for his portraits and narrative paintings, which capture the distinct personalities of each subject.

REVISIT THE BIG QUESTION

What keeps us GOING?

Discuss In lines 153–161, what does Phoenix's response to the hunter when he points his gun at her hint about her endurance?

Possible answer: *Phoenix says she's seen guns "go off closer, in my day, and for less than what I done" (lines 158–159). This suggests that she has endured violence before, either as a freed slave or even during the era of slavery.*

FOR STRUGGLING READERS

Clarify Meaning Point out throughout the story, characters address each other by category labels rather than proper names. For example, the hunter calls Phoenix by the name "Granny" and the woman in Natchez calls her "Grandma," though neither person actually knows Phoenix to be a grandmother. They are using these terms of address as generic labels for an older woman. Phoenix calls the woman in Natchez "missy" as a label of respect, not as a specific name.

FOR ENGLISH LANGUAGE LEARNERS

Culture: Clarify Make sure that students understand the description of the lights of Natchez in lines 171–172. Explain that at this time in America, many rural areas did not yet have electricity. Clarify that the lights are red and green because these colors are associated with Christmas. Then discuss why the lights might confuse Phoenix. *Possible answer: The lights confuse Phoenix by changing how familiar landmarks look.*

FOR ADVANCED LEARNERS/AP

Hypothesize Point out to students that the description of the lights, "and all turned on in the daytime" (line 172), is not something Phoenix says. Rather, the third person limited narrator inserts this comment. Ask students to use the Internet to find out about the Rural Electrification Act, to share their findings with the class, and to lead a discussion of why the narrator makes this comment.

The Old Natchez Trace The path that Phoenix walks, from "away back off the Old Natchez Trace" (line 204) is indeed an ancient path, part of a 444-mile long trail stretching from southern Mississippi to central Tennessee. Used for centuries by Native Americans, it later saw trade traffic and was also the site of Civil War conflict. The trail is now an American Byway; portions are accessible by car, but to see much of it, people must walk it just as Phoenix did.

TIERED DISCUSSION PROMPTS

In lines 213–228, use these prompts to help students understand Phoenix's behavior upon arriving at her goal:

Connect What are some feelings you have had after a long journey? *Students' answers should reflect a range of emotions, such as anxiety, fear, relief, joy, or unhappiness.*

Analyze How do the attendant and the nurse react to Phoenix? Why? *Possible answer: The attendant is at first puzzled and then irritated by Phoenix's silence. The nurse recognizes Phoenix and knows why she's there, but she too becomes annoyed. Both women feel that Phoenix will "take up their time" (line 217). They are busy and want to get back to their work.*

Synthesize On the basis of what you know about Phoenix and about people, why does Phoenix apologize for her exhaustion and memory lapse? *Possible answer: Phoenix seems surprised and frightened by her memory lapse. Like most people, she probably doesn't want to admit to any weakness. Also, as an older black woman in the story's time and place, she has had years of experience showing deference to white people and may feel that she has, in fact, taken up too much of the nurse's time.*

"Here I be," she said. There was a fixed and ceremonial stiffness over her body.

"A charity case, I suppose," said an attendant who sat at the desk before her.

But Phoenix only looked above her head. There was sweat on her face, the wrinkles in her skin shone like a bright net.

"Speak up, Grandma," the woman said. "What's your name? We must have your history, you know. Have you been here before? What seems to be the trouble with you?"

Old Phoenix only gave a twitch to her face as if a fly were bothering her.

200 "Are you deaf?" cried the attendant.

But then the nurse came in.

"Oh, that's just old Aunt Phoenix," she said. "She doesn't come for herself—she has a little grandson. She makes these trips just as regular as clockwork. She lives away back off the Old Natchez Trace."[6] She bent down. "Well, Aunt Phoenix, why don't you just take a seat? We won't keep you standing after your long trip." She pointed.

The old woman sat down, bolt upright in the chair.

"Now, how is the boy?" asked the nurse.

Old Phoenix did not speak.

210 "I said, how is the boy?"

But Phoenix only waited and stared straight ahead, her face very solemn and withdrawn into rigidity.

"Is his throat any better?" asked the nurse. "Aunt Phoenix, don't you hear me? Is your grandson's throat any better since the last time you came for the medicine?"

With her hands on her knees, the old woman waited, silent, erect and motionless, just as if she were in armor.

"You mustn't take up our time this way, Aunt Phoenix," the nurse said. "Tell us quickly about your grandson, and get it over. He isn't dead, is he?"

At last there came a flicker and then a flame of comprehension across her face,
220 and she spoke.

"My grandson. It was my memory had left me. There I sat and forgot why I made my long trip."

"Forgot?" The nurse frowned. "After you came so far?"

Then Phoenix was like an old woman begging a dignified forgiveness for waking up frightened in the night. "I never did go to school, I was too old at the Surrender,"[7] she said in a soft voice. "I'm an old woman without an education. It was my memory fail me. My little grandson, he is just the same, and I forgot it in the coming."

"Throat never heals, does it?" said the nurse, speaking in a loud, sure voice to
230 old Phoenix. By now she had a card with something written on it, a little list. "Yes. Swallowed lye.[8] When was it?—January—two-three years ago—"

6. **Old Natchez Trace:** The Natchez Trace was an important wilderness road during the 18th and early 19th centuries, extending from Natchez, Mississippi, to Nashville, Tennessee.

7. **the Surrender:** the end of the Civil War, after which time slaves were free.

8. **lye:** a strong alkaline liquid used especially in making soap.

Language Coach

Phrasal Verbs A phrasal verb contains a verb and a preposition or adverb. *Speak up* ("speak loud enough to be heard") in line 196 has a different meaning than *speak* does. Referring to a dictionary if necessary, define *speak down to*, *speak out*, and *speak to*.

④ Targeted Passage

DIFFERENTIATED INSTRUCTION

FOR STRUGGLING READERS

④ **Targeted Passage** [Lines 213–231]

This passage reveals the reason for Phoenix's long journey and shows its effect on her.

- Why has Phoenix made the trip to Natchez? (lines 213–214)

- Why is the nurse irritated? (line 217)

- Why does the nurse know Phoenix and know about her grandson? (lines 229–231)

FOR ENGLISH LANGUAGE LEARNERS

Language Coach

Phrasal Verbs *Answer: Speak down to* means "condescend to." *Speak out* means "talk freely about." *Speak to* means "talk to." Write sample sentences on the board and have students fill in appropriate phrasal verbs.

Phoenix spoke unasked now. "No, missy, he not dead, he just the same. Every little while his throat begin to close up again, and he not able to swallow. He not get his breath. He not able to help himself. So the time come around, and I go on another trip for the soothing medicine." **ᴊ**

"All right. The doctor said as long as you came to get it, you could have it," said the nurse. "But it's an **obstinate** case."

"My little grandson, he sit up there in the house all wrapped up, waiting by himself," Phoenix went on. "We is the only two left in the world. He suffer and it
240 don't seem to put him back at all. He got a sweet look. He going to last. He wear a little patch quilt and peep out holding his mouth open like a little bird. I remembers so plain now. I not going to forget him again, no, the whole enduring time. I could tell him from all the others in creation."

"All right." The nurse was trying to hush her now. She brought her a bottle of medicine. "Charity," she said, making a check mark in a book.

Old Phoenix held the bottle close to her eyes, and then carefully put it into her pocket.

"I thank you," she said.

"It's Christmas time, Grandma," said the attendant. "Could I give you a few
250 pennies out of my purse?"

"Five pennies is a nickel," said Phoenix stiffly.

"Here's a nickel," said the attendant.

Phoenix rose carefully and held out her hand. She received the nickel and then fished the other nickel out of her pocket and laid it beside the new one. She stared at her palm closely, with her head on one side.

Then she gave a tap with her cane on the floor.

"This is what come to me to do," she said. "I going to the store and buy my child a little windmill they sells, made out of paper. He going to find it hard to believe there such a thing in the world. I'll march myself back where he waiting, holding it straight
260 up in this hand."

She lifted her free hand, gave a little nod, turned around, and walked out of the doctor's office. Then her slow step began on the stairs, going down. ❧

THEME AND GENRE
Phoenix Jackson continues the tradition of the mythic hero who must go on a long journey and face difficult obstacles in order to reach a goal. This archetype is also the basis for many popular films today. The heroes of *The Lord of the Rings* and Harry Potter films, *WALL-E*, and *Spider-Man* all face serious challenges that test their strength, courage, and self-knowledge. Can you think of other works that share this same theme?

ᴊ UNIVERSAL THEME
What have you learned about Phoenix's **motivation** for making her perilous journey, and what can you **infer** about how often she makes it? Explain why Welty might have delayed revealing this information until the story's end.

obstinate (ŏb'stə-nĭt) *adj.* hard to control or treat

Language Coach
Word Definitions *Stiffly* (line 251) here means "awkwardly formal" or "not in a graceful manner." How must Phoenix feel in lines 249–252?

A WORN PATH **1059**

ᴊ UNIVERSAL THEME

Possible answer: *Phoenix makes this journey to get medicine to save her grandson. Readers can infer that she has made this journey many times, given the nurse's familiarity with her and the information on the card that the injury happened "two-three years ago" (line 231). Delaying this information until the end of the story lends the journey an air of mystery, increases its suspense, and allows it to stand as a symbol for all journeys of love.*

REVISIT THE BIG QUESTION
What keeps us GOING?

Discuss How does the relationship between Phoenix and her grandson, shown in lines 238–243, reflect endurance? ***Possible answer:*** *Phoenix says that her grandson will endure (line 240), but more importantly their love and devotion to each other will endure (line 239).*

OWN THE WORD

obstinate: Remind students that in this story *obstinate* describes something "hard to control or treat; difficult to cure, or persistent." Have students write a sentence that shows an understanding of *obstinate* in this context. ***Possible answer:*** *Dad could not fix the sink because he could not turn the obstinate valve.*

SELECTION WRAP—UP

READ WITH A PURPOSE Now that students have read the selection, ask them what motivates Phoenix, or any person, to take risks to help another. *Answers will vary, but students might say that when someone cares about another person, he or she will take great risks to protect him or her.*

INDEPENDENT READING

Students may also enjoy reading *The Heart Is a Lonely Hunter* by Carson McCullers.

THEME AND GENRE

After students read this selection, ask them to discuss novels, films, or plays that reflect the theme of the mythic hero in "A Worn Path."

FOR STRUGGLING READERS

Language Coach
Word Definitions
Possible answer: *Phoenix feels uncomfortable asking for and accepting money.* As a class, use dictionaries to determine other definitions of *stiffly*. Then, have partners write a short paragraph that includes the word *stiffly*.

FOR ADVANCED LEARNERS/AP

Make Judgments [small-group option] Point out that Welty's story takes place at Christmastime. Prompt students to think of the stories they have read that are set at Christmastime, for example, O. Henry's "The Gift of the Magi" or Charles Dickens's *A Christmas Carol*. Have students discuss what unites "Christmas stories" and whether "A Worn Path" fits the criteria. Challenge them to explore how, if at all, this choice of time plays a role in Welty's theme.

MEMOIR Always shy of biographers, Eudora Welty published her own memoir at the age of 74. This account of growing up in the South pays special attention to her development as a writer.

CONNECT

This selection connects with Eudora Welty's story by providing information about the author's approach to character development. You may also use it as a minilesson on reading for information.

READING FOR INFORMATION

Point out that this excerpt is part of a memoir. Then ask

- What is a memoir, and what does the title of this memoir suggest about its focus? *Possible answer: A memoir is an autobiographical account of its author's life. The title suggests that this memoir focuses on how events shaped the author as writer.*

- What is the main idea of this excerpt? *Possible answer: Welty's characters are entirely invented. She does not turn people she knows into characters.*

TIERED DISCUSSION PROMPTS

Use these prompts to help students connect Welty's comments on character creation with the characterization in "A Worn Path":

Connect In what ways do the characters in "A Worn Path" remind you of people that you know or have met? *Accept all thoughtful answers.*

Analyze Why doesn't Welty import into her stories characters from the real world? *Possible answer: Real people are too large to "yield to" (line 17) the narrow space of a story. Also, to use real people as characters invades their privacy (lines 11–13).*

Synthesize Does Phoenix "take on life" (line 25) as a "human being on the page" (lines 29–30)? Explain. *Students may say that Phoenix takes on life because of the personal and physical detail with which Welty endows her. Her character becomes more thoroughly developed by each detail, word, and action, from the red rag she wears to her decision to buy her grandson a Christmas gift rather then spend ten cents on necessities.*

One Writer's Beginnings

Eudora Welty

The characters who go to make up my stories and novels are not portraits. Characters I invent along with the story that carries them. Attached to them are what I've borrowed, perhaps unconsciously, bit by bit, of persons I have seen or noticed or remembered in the flesh—a cast of countenance here, a manner of walking there, that jump to the visualizing mind when a story is underway. (Elizabeth
10 Bowen said, "Physical detail cannot be invented.") It can only be chosen.) I don't write by invasion into the life of a real person: my own sense of privacy is too strong for that; and I also know instinctively that living people to whom you are close—those known to you in ways too deep, too overflowing, ever to be plumbed outside love—do not yield to, could never fit into, the demands of a story. On the other hand, what I do make my stories out of
20 is the *whole* fund of my feelings, my responses to the real experiences of my own life, to the relationships that formed and changed it, that I have given most of myself to, and so learned my way toward a dramatic counterpart. Characters take on life sometimes by luck, but I suspect it is when you can write most entirely out of yourself, inside the skin, heart, mind, and soul of a person who is not yourself, that a character becomes in his own right another human being
30 on the page.

Eudora Welty, early in her career

Comprehension

1. **Recall** Why does Phoenix Jackson travel to the city of Natchez?

2. **Recall** What does she intend to do with the ten cents she collects?

3. **Summarize** What physical problems does Phoenix seem to have, and how do they affect her on her journey?

Text Analysis

4. **Monitor Comprehension** Look over the chart you filled in as you read. Identify a passage in the story that was challenging to understand. What clues in the text helped you **clarify** its meaning? Explain how they helped.

5. **Analyze Figurative Language** "A Worn Path" is rich with figurative language, especially **similes.** Skim the story, identifying examples of figurative language used to accomplish the following purposes. For each purpose, cite at least two examples.

   • give readers a clear mental picture of Phoenix's appearance
   • highlight Phoenix's main character traits
   • convey Phoenix's feelings about her grandson

6. **Understand Symbolism** In mythology, a phoenix is an immortal bird that represents renewal. It sets its nest on fire every 500 years; from the ashes, the phoenix is reborn. Why might Welty have bestowed this name upon her main character? In what way does the name fit the person who bears it?

7. **Interpret Universal Theme** Consider the trials and triumphs Phoenix faces on her journey, and think about what motivates her to **endure** her arduous trek. In what way does this **archetypal** journey mirror life itself? Use your answer to this question to formulate a sentence that states the theme of the story. Then explain what makes this theme universal.

Text Criticism

8. **Critical Interpretations** This story's ambiguity has fascinated readers for years. Many students have written Welty to ask if Phoenix's grandson is really alive at the story's end, or if Phoenix keeps making this journey though the boy is already gone. The author has replied, "It is the journey, the going of the errand, that is the story.... *Phoenix* is alive." In your opinion, does Welty bring this story to a satisfying conclusion? Explain why or why not, citing details from the text as well as your reaction to Welty's explanation.

What keeps us GOING?

Motivated by love for her grandson, Phoenix makes the difficult journey to town in spite of many obstacles. What motivates you to finish a difficult task?

8. *Students may say that the ending is not satisfying. They, like many readers before them, will hunger to know what happens to the grandson and may question whether he is alive. Other students may agree with Welty that it is the fact that Phoenix is alive in the journey that matters most.*

What keeps us GOING?

Answers will vary. Students may say that the satisfaction of a job well done may motivate them to finish a difficult task.

COMMON CORE

RL 2 Determine two or more themes or central ideas of a text and analyze their development over the course of the text, including how they interact and build on one another to produce a complex account; provide an objective summary of the text. RL 10 Read and comprehend literature, including stories.

Practice and Apply

For preliminary support of post-reading questions, use these copy masters:

R RESOURCE MANAGER—Copy Masters
   Reading Check p. 300
   Universal Theme p. 293
   Question Support p. 301

   Additional selection questions are provided for teachers on page 287.

ANSWERS   COMMON CORE RL 2, RL 10

1. *Phoenix travels to Natchez to get medicine for her grandson.*

2. *She plans to use the 10 cents to buy a present for her grandson.*

3. *Phoenix's problems—poor vision, fatigue, and forgetfulness—stem from her old age. They add risks to her important journey.*

Possible answers:

4. ● **COMMON CORE FOCUS Monitor Comprehension** *Accept all thoughtful responses. For example, the black dog seems to be a hallucination, but since the story says that the hunter also sees the dog, it must be real.*

5. *Students' examples may vary. The description of Phoenix's wrinkles, "as though a whole little tree stood in the middle of her head" (lines 14–15), creates a clear mental picture and highlights her wisdom. Her likening of her grandson to "a little bird" reveals her protective love.*

6. *Phoenix embodies the endurance and resiliency of the mythic bird that is her namesake. Welty may have used the name to underscore Phoenix's ability to "rise up" after she falls, both physically and mentally.*

7. ● **COMMON CORE FOCUS Universal Theme** *Phoenix's journey has hazards, physical challenges, difficult interactions with others, and frightening moments, as well as moments of rest and pleasure—all things that people experience during the journey of life. Armed with deep determination born of love and an indomitable personality, Phoenix vanquishes the obstacles. Possible theme: Ordinary people are capable of rising to heroic levels and transcending the limitations imposed on their lives. This theme is universal because it applies to all people in any culture.*

ANSWERS

Vocabulary in Context

VOCABULARY PRACTICE

1. *drag on for weeks*
2. *excel at stretching exercises*
3. *in a quiet garden*
4. *provides heat and light*

 RESOURCE MANAGER—Copy Master
Vocabulary Practice p. 298

ACADEMIC VOCABULARY IN SPEAKING

Have students begin by writing a brief description of Phoenix's obstacles, using any words. Then, have them look for places to substitute Academic Vocabulary words.

VOCABULARY STRATEGY: SPANISH COGNATES

 COMMON CORE L 2b L 6

Before students read the incomplete sentences, have them read the Spanish cognates and determine how the word is spelled in English. As they read each incomplete sentence, encourage students to look for context clues that will enable them to determine which word completes the sentence's meaning.

Answers:

1. c, arrogant

2. e, independent

3. d, computer

4. b, interesting

 RESOURCE MANAGER—Copy Master
Vocabulary Strategy p. 299

Vocabulary in Context

▲ **VOCABULARY PRACTICE**

Demonstrate your understanding of the vocabulary words by answering these questions.

1. Would an **obstinate** cold go away in a few days or drag on for weeks?
2. If your leg muscles are **limber,** would you be more likely to excel at stretching exercises or to cramp up while swimming?
3. Would you expect someone to be **meditative** in a pep rally, or in a quiet garden?
4. Does **radiation** from the sun provide or absorb heat and light?

WORD LIST
limber
meditative
obstinate
radiation

ACADEMIC VOCABULARY IN SPEAKING

• conclude • criteria • despite • justify • maintain

Phoenix Jackson faces many obstacles as she walks to town—things that a younger person might not see as obstacles at all. In a small group, discuss three of the obstacles she faces. What can you **conclude** about Phoenix's age and her walk to town? Use at least three Academic Vocabulary words in your discussion.

VOCABULARY STRATEGY: SPANISH COGNATES

COMMON CORE

L 2b Spell correctly. **L 6** Acquire and use accurately general academic and domain-specific words and phrases.

The English language has picked up thousands of words and word parts from other languages. When the words picked up from other languages have identical or similar spellings and meanings to those in the original languages, they are called cognates. The Spanish language and the English language have many cognates. For example, the English word *monitor* has the same meaning and same spelling in Spanish. The English word *position* is spelled *posicion* in Spanish. You can use your knowledge of a cognate in one language to determine its meaning in a different language.

PRACTICE Write the letter of the Spanish cognate that you think completes the meaning of each sentence. Then write the word as it is spelled in English.

1. Because that actress is so _____, almost no one wants to spend time with her.
2. Some of the best films in recent years have been produced by _____ filmmakers.
3. The _____ has made a huge difference in the development of special effects in movies.
4. The students in the film class obviously think that films are _____.

a. realista
b. interesante
c. arrogante
d. computadora
e. independiente

 Interactive Vocabulary THINK central
Go to **thinkcentral.com**.
KEYWORD: HML11-1062

DIFFERENTIATED INSTRUCTION

FOR ENGLISH LANGUAGE LEARNERS

Task Support: Vocabulary Strategy Have students review the Word List and the academic vocabulary words to determine whether any of these words have cognates in their home languages. For instance, the Spanish cognate for *obstinate* is *obstinado*. Have students share these cognates with the rest of the class.

FOR ADVANCED LEARNERS/AP

Etymology The vocabulary word *radiation* and its relatives *radiate, radiator, radio, radian,* and *radial* all form a word family important to science and mathematics. Ask students to explore the etymology of this word family. Have students complete and share a Word Families organizer to explain how the knowledge could be useful in various subject fields.

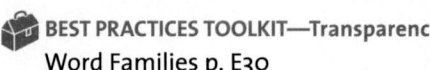 **BEST PRACTICES TOOLKIT—Transparency**
Word Families p. E30

Language

◆ **GRAMMAR AND STYLE: Add Descriptive Details**

Review the **Grammar and Style** note on page 1053. Welty's descriptions in the story give a wealth of sensory details that help readers get a clear picture of Phoenix and her actions. Welty makes particularly good use of **action verbs** (in yellow) and **participial phrases** (in green), as in this description of Phoenix crossing the precarious log bridge:

> *Putting her right foot out,* she *mounted* the log and shut her eyes. *Lifting her skirt, leveling her cane fiercely before her,* like a festival figure in some parade, she began to *march* across. (lines 47–49)

The highlighted participial phrases add key details to help readers visualize Phoenix. The first highlighted action verb, *mounted,* shows the physical exertion required for her to get on top of the log, while the third verb, *march,* works with the simile to suggest her regal bearing and sense of purpose.

PRACTICE The following sentences were written in response to the writing prompt below. Rewrite each sentence, adding more action verbs and participial phrases that help describe how things look, sound, smell, touch, or taste.

> **EXAMPLE**
>
> The sun was low on the horizon and made shadows between the bushes.
>
> *The sun crouched low on the horizon, casting long shadows between the scrubby bushes.*

1. Tashi, a refugee fleeing her war-torn village, was on the high bank above the river.

2. She knew she had to cross in the shallows where the sand bar was.

3. The baby was still asleep in her arms but would wake soon and be hungry.

READING-WRITING CONNECTION

 Expand your understanding of "A Worn Path" by responding to this prompt. Then, use the **revising tips** to improve your story.

WRITING PROMPT	REVISING TIPS
WRITE A STORY Think of an extreme situation today in which a contemporary Phoenix makes a perilous journey. What hazards does she or he face? What values and strengths does she or he need in order to endure? Write a **one-to-three-page story** updating Welty's tale.	• Give clear details about the setting for your story. • Show how your character confronts conflicts. • Use action verbs and participial phrases to show rather than tell.

Interactive Revision

Go to thinkcentral.com.
KEYWORD: HML11-1063

COMMON CORE

L 3 Apply knowledge of language to understand how language functions in different contexts, to make effective choices for meaning or style, and to comprehend more fully when reading or listening. **W 3** Write narratives to develop imagined experiences or events using effective technique, well-chosen details, and well-structured event sequences. **W 3a** Engage and orient the reader by setting out a problem or situation and its significance, establishing one or multiple point(s) of view, and introducing a narrator and/or characters.

Language

COMMON CORE L 3, W 3, W 3a

◆ **GRAMMAR AND STYLE**

To help students appreciate the impact of careful verb choice and precise modifiers, have them rewrite the sample sentence without these elements. Discuss the result. (For more on modifiers, see **Grammar Handbook,** p. R61.)

Possible answers:

1. *Pausing in flight from her war-torn village, Tashi surveyed the river from its high bank.*

2. *She had to find the higher ground of the sand bar to ford the river, swollen with spring rains.*

3. *The baby, sleeping trustingly in her arms, would wake soon, bawling his hunger.*

R RESOURCE MANAGER—Copy Master
Add Descriptive Details p. 302

READING-WRITING CONNECTION

Suggest that students develop the main character using a Character Sketch and use a Story Frame to plan the plot.

BEST PRACTICES TOOLKIT—Transparencies
Story Frame p. C10
Character Sketch p. C22

Writing Online

THINK central

The following tools are available online at **thinkcentral.com** and on **Write*Smart* CD-ROM:**
• **Interactive Graphic Organizers**
• **Interactive Student Models**
• **Interactive Revision Lessons**
For additional grammar instruction, see **GrammarNotes** on **thinkcentral.com**.

Assess and Reteach

Assess

DIAGNOSTIC AND SELECTION TESTS
Selection Test A, B/C pp. 285–286, 287–288

Interactive Selection Test on **thinkcentral.com**

Reteach

Level Up Online Tutorials on **thinkcentral.com**

Reteaching Worksheets on **thinkcentral.com**

FOR STRUGGLING WRITERS

Writing Support

• Limit the length of the story to one page.

• Discuss with students, either in groups or one on one, what settings might qualify as an "extreme situation."

• Help students use the Character Sketch and Story Frame organizers to explore their character and to develop the time, place, problem, and probable solution appropriate to the assignment.

• Tell students that they may write from a third person or first person point of view. Students may be more comfortable, at least as they draft, writing in first person.

• Remind students that stories need a beginning, middle, and end.

 **BEST PRACTICES TOOLKIT—Transparencies**
Story Frame p. C10
Character Sketch p. C22

Focus and Motivate

COMMON CORE FOCUS

RL 3 Analyze the impact of the author's choices regarding how to develop and relate elements of a story (e.g., where a story is set, how the action is ordered, how the characters are introduced and developed). **RL 4** Analyze the impact of specific word choices on meaning and tone, including words with multiple meanings or language that is particularly fresh, engaging, or beautiful. **RL 5** Analyze how an author's choices concerning how to structure specific parts of a text contribute to its overall structure and meaning as well as its aesthetic impact. **W 1** Write arguments to support claims in an analysis of substantive topics or texts, using valid reasoning and relevant and sufficient evidence. **L 3** Apply knowledge of language to understand how language functions in different contexts, to make effective choices for meaning or style. **L 4c** Consult general and specialized reference materials, both print and digital, to determine or clarify a word's etymology.

ABOUT THE AUTHOR

Sense of place is crucial in Faulkner's fiction, as it was in his life. In 1930 he purchased a grand old house in Mississippi and named it Rowan Oak. Over the years he renovated the dilapidated house, adding plumbing, rebuilding walls, painting. Faulkner was, according to friends, never quite at home anywhere else.

NOTABLE QUOTE

"Always dream and shoot higher than you know you can do. Don't bother just to be better than your contemporaries or predecessors. Try to be better than yourself."
—**William Faulkner**

Selection Resources

A Rose for Emily
Short Story by William Faulkner

Essential Course of Study ECOS

VIDEO TRAILER THINKcentral KEYWORD: HML11-1064A

COMMON CORE

RL 3 Analyze the impact of the author's choices regarding how to develop and relate elements of a story (e.g., where a story is set, how the action is ordered, how the characters are introduced and developed). **RL 4** Analyze the impact of specific word choices on meaning and tone, including words with multiple meanings or language that is particularly fresh, engaging, or beautiful. **RL 5** Analyze how an author's choices concerning how to structure specific parts of a text contribute to its overall structure and meaning as well as its aesthetic impact.

DID YOU KNOW?
William Faulkner . . .

- dropped out of high school and took only a few college classes as a special student.
- worked almost three years at the post office, where he was considered lazy and inattentive, before he resigned.

Meet the Author

William Faulkner 1897–1962

Today, William Faulkner is considered one of the literary giants of the 20th century. This distinction didn't come easily, however. Faulkner took a while to find himself and his subject. Only after he decided to focus on his home state of Mississippi and his colorful family history was the full force of his creativity unleashed. Over an astonishing 13-year span, Faulkner churned out one masterpiece after another—among them, *The Sound and the Fury* (1929), *As I Lay Dying* (1930), *Sanctuary* (1931), *Absalom, Absalom!* (1936), and *Go Down, Moses* (1942). Of these artistic achievements, only *Sanctuary* was a bestseller—partly due to its scandalous subject matter—and none of the books earned Faulkner enough money to support his growing family. Although some critics raved about him, many others agreed with the *New York Times* that his South was "too often vicious, depraved, decadent, corrupt." By 1945, most of his books were out of print.

Narrative Challenges A glance at Faulkner's work would explain why readers and critics resisted his fiction. He wrote narratives on the cutting edge of the new modernism, and for the most part, he refused to compromise with the typical reader's desire for a coherent, chronological story. His novels weave numerous flashbacks into multiple story lines. They push sentence length to new limits, and two of his best-known modernist works increase the reader's challenge by using several highly unreliable narrators to tell the story. *The Sound and the Fury* has three first-person narrators (see pages 934-935). *As I Lay Dying* has fifteen. The story of a mother's dying wish, Faulkner's fifth novel switches narrators with each chapter, supplying readers with the perspective of various family members and others involved in the story. It is anything but an easy read.

Resurgence In 1946, an enterprising editor named Malcolm Cowley published *The Portable Faulkner,* a collection of stories and novel excerpts that untangled Faulkner's elaborate saga. Cowley's blueprint plus a helpful introduction sparked new interest in Faulkner. With the anxieties of the Great Depression and World War II behind them, more readers were ready to accept Faulkner's challenge to revisit the crimes and passions of the South—and America itself—through a modern consciousness.

Author Online
Go to **thinkcentral.com**. KEYWORD: HML11-1064B

1064

See resources on the **Teacher One Stop DVD-ROM** and on **thinkcentral.com**.

 RESOURCE MANAGER UNIT 5
Plan and Teach, pp. 303–310
Summary, pp. 311–312†‡*
Text Analysis and Reading Skill, pp. 313–316†*
Vocabulary, pp. 317–319*
Grammar and Style, p. 322

DIAGNOSTIC AND SELECTION TESTS
Selection Tests, pp. 289–292

 BEST PRACTICES TOOLKIT
Personal Word List, p. E2
Definition Mapping, p. E6

INTERACTIVE READER

ADAPTED INTERACTIVE READER

ELL ADAPTED INTERACTIVE READER

TECHNOLOGY
- **Teacher One Stop DVD-ROM**
- **Student One Stop DVD-ROM**
- **PowerNotes DVD-ROM**
- **Audio Anthology CD**
- **GrammarNotes DVD-ROM**
- **ExamView Test Generator** on the **Teacher One Stop**

Video Trailer THINKcentral

Go to **thinkcentral.com** to preview the **Video Trailer** introducing this selection. Other features that support the selection include
- **PowerNotes** presentation
- **ThinkAloud** models to enhance comprehension
- **WordSharp** vocabulary tutorials
- interactive writing and grammar instruction

---

* Resources for Differentiation   † Also in Spanish   ‡ In Haitian Creole and Vietnamese

TEXT ANALYSIS: POINT OF VIEW

As you've already learned, Faulkner is a pioneer of modernist fiction (see pages 934-935 and page 1064). He uses **stream of consciousness,** mimicking the flow of a character's thoughts and sensations to convey the subjective nature of experience. He uses **multiple narrators,** taking the point of view of several characters in a single novel. With each work of fiction, he crafts a point of view uniquely suited to the story being told. "A Rose for Emily," is the story of a small town's struggle to understand one of its residents. Using multiple narrators would be difficult in a short story. Using stream of consciousness would not convey what is most important here—the public perception of Miss Emily. Faulkner's choice for point of view, then, is **first-person-plural**—an unnamed *we,* the voice of the townspeople themselves.

As you read, notice the narrator's use of first-person pronouns such as *we* and *our.* What role does this point of view play in your understanding of Miss Emily and her story? How might other points of view change the narrative?

Review: **Mood**

READING SKILL: ANALYZE SEQUENCE

Faulkner often rearranges the **sequence** of events in his fiction, using **flashbacks** to offer a window into a character's past or dropping hints that **foreshadow** what is yet to come. As you read, keep a chart like the one shown. In the left column, record the story's events as you read about them. When you finish the story, number the events in chronological order.

Order in Which Narrator Reveals Events	Order in Which Events Occur
1. Miss Emily dies.	8
2. The aldermen visit about taxes.	7

▲ VOCABULARY IN CONTEXT

Faulkner uses these words to create a story rich with atmosphere. Try to define each, based on its context.

1. The **cabal** executed their shady plans in secret.
2. The swaggering boy approached him with **temerity.**
3. Moonlight made the rickety house into a terrifying **tableau.**
4. Her **imperviousness** made her impossible to frighten.

 Complete the activities in your **Reader/Writer Notebook.**

What makes your SKIN CRAWL?

As the girl steps outside into the alley, the overpowering smell of rotting garbage assaults her nostrils. Her stomach turns as she tries not to stare at a mass of maggots eating a discarded hamburger, and she shies away from the dumpster, with its squeaking and squirming inhabitants. Certain scenes from books or movies are so evocative that they leave you shaky and nauseated. Part of what you're responding to is the creepy atmosphere the writers or directors have created to mesmerize and repulse you.

DISCUSS In a small group, talk about the one thing that really gives you the creeps. Spiders, rats, the sight of blood—do any of these make your skin crawl? What movies or books have used these things to create an atmosphere that makes you shudder? Which works top your "creepiness scale"? Record the responses of your group to share with others.

1065

Teach

What makes your SKIN CRAWL?

Introduce the question and ask students to read the paragraph that follows it. Ask students to think of a scene from a horror story or movie and recall what details made the atmosphere creepy or scary. Then have them do the *DISCUSS* activity.

TEXT ANALYSIS

COMMON CORE
RL 3
RL 5

● *Model the Skill:* POINT OF VIEW

Tell students that Faulkner's first-person-plural point of view plays a particular role in how readers view Miss Emily and her story. Write this excerpt on the board:

> People in our town . . . believed that the Griersons held themselves a little too high for what they really were. None of the young men were quite good enough for Miss Emily and such. (lines 98–102)

Point out that this point of view expresses the collective view of the town, rather than any private, individual views. Also, this point of view does not reveal the Griersons' thoughts or feelings.

GUIDED PRACTICE Ask students how this passage would be different if it was told from one townsperson's point of view or from Miss Emily's point of view.

READING SKILL

COMMON CORE
RL 3

■ *Model the Skill:* ANALYZE SEQUENCE

Define *flashback* and *foreshadowing* and explain the roles that these plot interruptions play in fiction. Then, point out a popular movie or television show that uses flashbacks and foreshadowing to build suspense.

GUIDED PRACTICE Have students think of another television show or movie that has an unconventional sequence of events.

[R] **RESOURCE MANAGER—Copy Master**
Analyze Sequence p. 315 (for student use while reading the selection)

SUMMARY

In this story a townsperson recalls, through a series of flashbacks, Emily Grierson, whose father prevents her from marrying. Emily later is courted by a man the townspeople consider unacceptable; he appears to desert her. Forty years later, at Emily's death, the townspeople discover that she poisoned her suitor and has kept his corpse in a bedroom.

READ WITH A PURPOSE

Help students set a purpose for reading. Tell them to read to find out what the townspeople discover about Miss Emily after her death.

TEXT ANALYSIS

COMMON CORE
RL 3
RL 5

A *Model the Skill:* **POINT OF VIEW**

Tell students to recognize for whom the narrator speaks, they should notice the phrases "whole town," "the men," and "the women."

Answer: *The pronoun "our" establishes Faulkner's point of view in the opening paragraph. The narrator speaks for all of the townspeople.*

A Rose for Emily

William Faulkner

BACKGROUND "A Rose for Emily," like the majority of Faulkner's stories, takes place in the fictional Yoknapatawpha County, Mississippi. Published in 1930, the story portrays social customs of the small-town South at the turn of the 20th century. Be warned that the narrator refers to African Americans with a term that is offensive to contemporary readers.

I

When Miss Emily Grierson died, our whole town went to her funeral: the men through a sort of respectful affection for a fallen monument, the women mostly out of curiosity to see the inside of her house, which no one save an old manservant—a combined gardener and cook—had seen in at least ten years. **A**
It was a big, squarish frame house that had once been white, decorated with cupolas and spires and scrolled balconies in the heavily lightsome style of the seventies,[1] set on what had once been our most select street. But garages and cotton gins had encroached and obliterated even the august names of that neighborhood; only Miss Emily's house was left, lifting its stubborn and
10 coquettish decay above the cotton wagons and the gasoline pumps—an eyesore among eyesores. And now Miss Emily had gone to join the representatives of those august names where they lay in the cedar-bemused[2] cemetery among the ranked and anonymous graves of Union and Confederate soldiers who fell at the battle of Jefferson.

 Targeted Passage

A **POINT OF VIEW**
Identify the first-person-plural pronoun that establishes Faulkner's point of view in the opening paragraph. For whom does the narrator speak?

---

1. **the seventies:** the 1870s.
2. **cedar-bemused:** almost lost in cedar trees.

DIFFERENTIATED INSTRUCTION

FOR ENGLISH LANGUAGE LEARNERS

Comprehension Support Help students visualize the Grierson house by explaining the architectural terms *cupolas, spires,* and *scrolled balconies* (line 6) and the modifiers *heavily lightsome* (line 6), *august* (line 8), and *coquettish* (line 10). Students can add the architectural terms to their Personal Word Lists.

BEST PRACTICES TOOLKIT
Personal Word List p. E2

FOR STRUGGLING READERS

In combination with the *Audio Anthology CD,* use one or more Targeted Passages (pp. 1066, 1069, 1070, 1073, and 1074) to ensure that students focus on key story events and concepts. Targeted Passages are also good for English language learners.

1 **Targeted Passage** [Lines 1–7]

This passage introduces the main character and the home in which she has hidden for many years.

- What event begins the telling of the story? (line 1)
- Why did everyone in town attend Miss Emily's funeral? (lines 1–4)
- What had been Miss Emily's social status when she was young and the house was new? (lines 5–7)

Reading Support

This selection on **thinkcentral.com** includes embedded **ThinkAloud** models—students "thinking aloud" about the story to model the kinds of questions a good reader would ask about a selection.

Analyze Visuals

Activity Have students assume that the photograph is of the Grierson house, and ask them to write two more sentences describing this "eyesore among eyesores" (lines 10–11), keeping the mood of the paragraph and drawing on the photograph for details. *Accept all thoughtful and detailed responses, but students' sentences should draw attention to the contrast between gentility and decay, evident in such features as the delicate but chipped latticework on the porch or the white curtains visible behind the dilapidated window frame.*

BACKGROUND

Southern Gothic Faulkner is among a group of writers who wrote in a subgenre called, mockingly at first, the Southern Gothic. Southern Gothic stories transferred the Gothic fascination with old European castles, with their secret passages, dark halls, and trapdoors, to the crumbling estates of the pre–Civil War South. The characters of Southern Gothics are often mysterious, their stories macabre and tinged with insanity. Yet Southern Gothics such as "A Rose for Emily" are also laments for a genteel way of life that, rather than dying gracefully away, lives on in stories of twisted honor and warped dreams.

FOR ADVANCED LEARNERS/AP

Expert Groups Encourage students to become subject experts by selecting and researching one of these topics:

- The history and geography of the fictional Yoknapatawpha County
- Faulkner's own family background in Mississippi

Then, have students present the information to the class as an oral presentation. Encourage students to include visual aids, such as photographs or drawings, in their presentations.

Alive, Miss Emily had been a tradition, a duty, and a care; a sort of hereditary obligation upon the town, dating from that day in 1894 when Colonel Sartoris, the mayor—he who fathered the edict that no Negro woman should appear on the streets without an apron—remitted her taxes, the dispensation dating from the death of her father on into perpetuity.[3] Not that Miss Emily would have accepted
20 charity. Colonel Sartoris invented an involved tale to the effect that Miss Emily's father had loaned money to the town, which the town, as a matter of business, preferred this way of repaying. Only a man of Colonel Sartoris' generation and thought could have invented it, and only a woman could have believed it.

When the next generation, with its more modern ideas, became mayors and aldermen, this arrangement created some little dissatisfaction. On the first of the year they mailed her a tax notice. February came, and there was no reply. They wrote her a formal letter, asking her to call at the sheriff's office at her convenience. A week later the mayor wrote her himself, offering to call or to send his car for her, and received in reply a note on paper of an archaic shape, in a thin,
30 flowing calligraphy in faded ink, to the effect that she no longer went out at all. The tax notice was also enclosed, without comment. **B**

They called a special meeting of the Board of Aldermen. A deputation waited upon her, knocked at the door through which no visitor had passed since she ceased giving china-painting lessons eight or ten years earlier. They were admitted by the old Negro into a dim hall from which a stairway mounted into still more shadow. It smelled of dust and disuse—a close, dank smell. The Negro led them into the parlor. It was furnished in heavy, leather-covered furniture. When the Negro opened the blinds of one window, they could see that the leather was cracked; and when they sat down, a faint dust rose sluggishly about their thighs,
40 spinning with slow motes in the single sun-ray. On a tarnished gilt easel before the fireplace stood a crayon portrait of Miss Emily's father.

They rose when she entered—a small, fat woman in black, with a thin gold chain descending to her waist and vanishing into her belt, leaning on an ebony cane with a tarnished gold head. Her skeleton was small and spare; perhaps that was why what would have been merely plumpness in another was obesity in her. She looked bloated, like a body long submerged in motionless water, and of that pallid hue. Her eyes, lost in the fatty ridges of her face, looked like two small pieces of coal pressed into a lump of dough as they moved from one face to another while the visitors stated their errand. **C**

50 She did not ask them to sit. She just stood in the door and listened quietly until the spokesman came to a stumbling halt. Then they could hear the invisible watch ticking at the end of the gold chain.

Her voice was dry and cold. "I have no taxes in Jefferson. Colonel Sartoris explained it to me. Perhaps one of you can gain access to the city records and satisfy yourselves."

"But we have. We are the city authorities, Miss Emily. Didn't you get a notice from the sheriff, signed by him?"

---

3. **remitted . . . perpetuity:** released her from paying taxes forever from the time of her father's death.

1068 UNIT 5: THE HARLEM RENAISSANCE AND MODERNISM

B ANALYZE SEQUENCE
Explain when the events of the story's first paragraph happen in relation to those described in lines 15–31. Why might Faulkner have chosen to immediately announce Emily's death before revealing more about her life? Explain.

C MOOD
What is your initial reaction to Emily? Cite two examples of **figurative language** in lines 42–49 and explain what feeling they create.

"I received a paper, yes," Miss Emily said. "Perhaps he considers himself the sheriff . . . I have no taxes in Jefferson."

60 "But there is nothing on the books to show that, you see. We must go by the—"

"See Colonel Sartoris. I have no taxes in Jefferson."

"But, Miss Emily—"

"See Colonel Sartoris." (Colonel Sartoris had been dead almost ten years.) "I have no taxes in Jefferson. Tobe!" The Negro appeared. "Show these gentlemen out."

II

So she vanquished them, horse and foot, just as she had vanquished their fathers thirty years before about the smell. That was two years after her father's death and a short time after her sweetheart—the one we believed would marry her—had deserted her. After her father's death she went out very little; after her sweetheart went away, people hardly saw her at all. A few of the ladies had the **temerity** to 70 call, but were not received, and the only sign of life about the place was the Negro man—a young man then—going in and out with a market basket.

"Just as if a man—any man—could keep a kitchen properly," the ladies said; so they were not surprised when the smell developed. It was another link between the gross, teeming world and the high and mighty Griersons.

A neighbor, a woman, complained to the mayor, Judge Stevens, eighty years old. "But what will you have me do about it, madam?" he said.

"Why, send her word to stop it," the woman said. "Isn't there a law?"

"I'm sure that won't be necessary," Judge Stevens said. "It's probably just a snake or a rat that nigger of hers killed in the yard. I'll speak to him about it."

80 The next day he received two more complaints, one from a man who came in diffident deprecation.[4] "We really must do something about it, Judge. I'd be the last one in the world to bother Miss Emily, but we've got to do something." That night the Board of Aldermen met—three graybeards and one younger man, a member of the rising generation.

"It's simple enough," he said. "Send her word to have her place cleaned up. Give her a certain time to do it in, and if she don't . . ."

"Dammit, sir," Judge Stevens said, "will you accuse a lady to her face of smelling bad?" **D**

So the next night, after midnight, four men crossed Miss Emily's lawn and 90 slunk about the house like burglars, sniffing along the base of the brickwork and at the cellar openings while one of them performed a regular sowing motion with his hand out of a sack slung from his shoulder. They broke open the cellar door and sprinkled lime there, and in all the outbuildings. As they recrossed the lawn, a window that had been dark was lighted and Miss Emily sat in it, the light behind her, and her upright torso motionless as that of an idol. They crept quietly across the lawn and into the shadow of the locusts that lined the street. After a week or two the smell went away.

② Targeted Passage

---

4. **diffident deprecation:** timid disapproval.

---

temerity (tə-mĕr'ĭ-tē) *n.* foolish boldness

COMMON CORE RL 3, RL 5

D POINT OF VIEW
Reread lines 65–88. Notice that the opening paragraph summarizes events in Miss Emily's life. Faulkner's unique **point of view** here—first person plural—makes it possible for this narrative summary to include the townspeople's perceptions of his main character. Then, in the dialogue, Faulkner captures both gossip and the conflict among small-town perspectives. Think about how the point of view might change if Faulkner had the length of a novel to tell Miss Emily's story. He could, for example, write entire passages from the points of view of a neighbor woman, one of the complaining citizens, and the judge. How would the use of **multiple narrators** affect this story?

In lines 58–66, use these prompts to help students understand Miss Emily's character:

Connect For whom do you have respect in this scene? What compels your respect? *Accept all thoughtful responses.*

Interpret Whom does Miss Emily respect more, the sheriff or Colonel Sartoris? What does this say about her character? ***Possible answer:*** *Miss Emily respects the Colonel, "dead almost ten years" (line 63), much more than the man who "considers himself the sheriff" (lines 58–59). This tells readers that Miss Emily is possibly unaware of changes in the town. It also suggests that she demands to be treated as a wealthy town belle despite her current corpulence and poverty.*

TEXT ANALYSIS

COMMON CORE RL 3 RL 5

D POINT OF VIEW

Review the differences between first person singular "I" and first person plural "we". Then read aloud lines 65–88. Discuss with students points at which Faulkner could introduce multiple narrators, such as when ladies called on Miss Emily, "but were not received" and when they were not surprised at the smell (lines 69–74). Explain that lines 75–88 also offer characters who could serve as narrators, namely the neighbor lady, Judge Stevens, and the town's aldermen.

Possible answer: *Multiple narrators would give readers more specific details and varying perspectives about story events.*

Extend the Discussion Why might Faulkner want to refrain from giving readers a thorough understanding of events surrounding Miss Emily?

FOR STRUGGLING READERS

② Targeted Passage [Lines 80–97]

This passage narrates an event that upsets the townspeople; it also sets up a later revelation.

- What is the problem with Miss Emily's house, according to her neighbors? (lines 80–88)

- Why doesn't Judge Stevens take the problem to Miss Emily herself? (lines 87–88)

- How do the townspeople solve the problem? (lines 89–93)

FOR ENGLISH LANGUAGE LEARNERS

Comprehension Support Explain to students that *lime* (line 93) is a calcium compound that is widely used in many industries. In its hydrated form it is used to neutralize odors, especially from decaying matter or waste products, to inhibit bacterial growth, and to keep flies away from decaying matter. Faulkner includes the detail to increase the creepiness factor of the story—something has certainly died in or around Miss Emily's house, but what?

VOCABULARY

COMMON CORE L 4

OWN THE WORD

temerity: Remind students that *temerity* refers to "foolish boldness and disregard of danger." Synonyms include *foolhardiness* and *recklessness*. Have students list antonyms for *temerity*. ***Possible answer:*** *tact, discretion, caution, wariness*

That was when people had begun to feel really sorry for her. People in our town, remembering how old lady Wyatt, her great-aunt, had gone completely crazy at last, believed that the Griersons held themselves a little too high for what they really were. None of the young men were quite good enough for Miss Emily and such. We had long thought of them as a **tableau,** Miss Emily a slender figure in white in the background, her father a spraddled silhouette in the foreground, his back to her and clutching a horsewhip, the two of them framed by the back-flung front door. So when she got to be thirty and was still single, we were not pleased exactly, but vindicated; even with insanity in the family she wouldn't have turned down all of her chances if they had really materialized. **E**

When her father died, it got about that the house was all that was left to her; and in a way, people were glad. At last they could pity Miss Emily. Being left alone, and a pauper, she had become humanized. Now she too would know the old thrill and the old despair of a penny more or less.

The day after his death all the ladies prepared to call at the house and offer condolence and aid, as is our custom. Miss Emily met them at the door, dressed as usual and with no trace of grief on her face. She told them that her father was not dead. She did that for three days, with the ministers calling on her, and the doctors, trying to persuade her to let them dispose of the body. Just as they were about to resort to law and force, she broke down, and they buried her father quickly.

We did not say she was crazy then. We believed she had to do that. We remembered all the young men her father had driven away, and we knew that with nothing left, she would have to cling to that which had robbed her, as people will.

tableau (tăb′lō′) *n.* a dramatic scene or picture

E GRAMMAR AND STYLE Reread lines 98–107. The pronouns *we* and *our* indicate that this story is told from the **first-person-plural point of view.** The narrator is not a single character, but the collective voice of the townspeople.

III

She was sick for a long time. When we saw her again, her hair was cut short, making her look like a girl, with a vague resemblance to those angels in colored church windows—sort of tragic and serene. **F**

> The town had just let the contracts for paving the sidewalks, and in the summer after her father's death they began the work. The construction company came with niggers and mules and machinery, and a foreman named Homer Barron, a Yankee—a big, dark, ready man, with a big voice and eyes lighter than his face. The little boys would follow in groups to hear him cuss the niggers, and the niggers singing in time to the rise and fall of picks. Pretty soon he knew everybody in town. Whenever you heard a lot of laughing anywhere about the square, Homer Barron would be in the center of the group. Presently we began to see him and Miss Emily on Sunday afternoons driving in the yellow-wheeled buggy and the matched team of bays from the livery stable. **③**

At first we were glad that Miss Emily would have an interest, because the ladies all said, "Of course a Grierson would not think seriously of a Northerner, a day laborer." But there were still others, older people, who said that even grief could not cause a real lady to forget *noblesse oblige*[5]—without calling it *noblesse oblige.*

F POINT OF VIEW Reread lines 119–124. What is Faulkner's point of view in these paragraphs, and which personal pronoun signals the point of view? Explain what makes this point of view unique in fiction. Cite evidence from the story to support your answer.

---

5. ***noblesse oblige*** (nō-blĕs′ ō-blēzh′): the responsibility of people in a high social position to behave in a noble fashion.

They just said, "Poor Emily. Her kinsfolk should come to her." She had some kin
140 in Alabama; but years ago her father had fallen out with them over the estate of
old lady Wyatt, the crazy woman, and there was no communication between the
two families. They had not even been represented at the funeral.

And as soon as the old people said, "Poor Emily," the whispering began. "Do
you suppose it's really so?" they said to one another. "Of course it is. What else
could . . ." This behind their hands; rustling of craned silk and satin behind
jalousies[6] closed upon the sun of Sunday afternoon as the thin, swift clop-clop-
clop of the matched team passed: "Poor Emily."

She carried her head high enough—even when we believed that she was
fallen. It was as if she demanded more than ever the recognition of her dignity
150 as the last Grierson; as if it had wanted that touch of earthiness to reaffirm her
imperviousness. Like when she bought the rat poison, the arsenic. That was over
a year after they had begun to say "Poor Emily," and while the two female cousins
were visiting her.

"I want some poison," she said to the druggist. She was over thirty then, still a
slight woman, though thinner than usual, with cold, haughty black eyes in a face
the flesh of which was strained across the temples and about the eye-sockets as you
imagine a lighthouse-keeper's face ought to look. "I want some poison," she said.

---

6. **jalousies** (jăl'ə-sēz): blinds or shutters containing overlapping slats that can be opened or closed.

imperviousness
(ĭm-pûr'vē-əs-nəs) *n.* an
inability to be affected
or disturbed

TIERED DISCUSSION PROMPTS

In lines 135–150, use these prompts to help students understand the townspeople's reactions to the romance between Homer and Emily:

Analyze Since the townspeople seem to like Homer, why do they disapprove of his courting Miss Emily? *Possible answer:* First, Miss Emily's social standing is high; she shouldn't be interested in a working man. Second, Miss Emily embodies the ways of the old South, and Homer is a Yankee. Finally, the public drives that Emily and Homer take (without a proper chaperone) scandalize the older townspeople.

Evaluate What might Miss Emily see in Homer Barron that makes her defy social expectations? *Possible answer:* Miss Emily may see in Homer a last chance. She is no longer young and wealthy. Homer is lively and fun, and his ability to work makes him better off than Miss Emily, with only the house on which she can't even pay the taxes. And she may truly love him as well.

VOCABULARY

COMMON CORE
L 4

OWN THE WORD

imperviousness: Tell students that *imperviousness* is the noun form of *impervious* and describes someone or something as not being affected or penetrated. For example, a person may be "*impervious* to pain;" a tent that has *imperviousness* is resistant to rain. Have students list other things that may behave *imperviously*. *Possible answer: A child can be* impervious *to loud noises; a soldier tries to be* impervious *to fear.*

FOR STRUGGLING READERS

Comprehension Support [paired option]
Read lines 143–147 aloud to students. Then help them visualize the gossiping townspeople. Ask them

- Why do the townspeople talk "behind their hands" (line 145) rather than openly?

- Why do they peer at the couple through jalousies rather than openly confronting Miss Emily?

FOR ADVANCED LEARNERS/AP

Compare and Contrast Ask students to review lines 47–49 and 154–157. Both sections of text describe Emily's eyes. Have students write a short explanation of what each description reveals about Emily at these different points in her life; then ask them to evaluate each description for the effect it has on the story's mood and on characterization of Emily.

🧰 BEST PRACTICES TOOLKIT—Transparency
Comparison Matrix p. A24

 Model the Skill: ANALYZE SEQUENCE

Point out Miss Emily's cool repetition, "I want some poison," and her ignoring the druggist's questions. She seems mentally off-balance, and her cold, aloof attitude intimidates the druggist into selling her the arsenic without her telling him what she wants it for.

Possible answer: *This exchange foreshadows that Miss Emily may be going to do something illegal with the arsenic, that it's not just for poisoning rats.*

Extend the Discussion Ask students why the druggist doesn't return with the poison himself, but rather sends his delivery boy out with the package.

OWN THE WORD

cabal: Have students create a semantic web for the word *cabal.* Write the word in the center circle along with the given definition, "group united in a secret plot." Draw spider legs out from the center circle and have students use a thesaurus to find appropriate synonyms to complete the web. **Possible answers:** *collusion, connivance, conspiracy, league, intrigue, plot, ring, scheme*

"Yes, Miss Emily. What kind? For rats and such? I'd recom—"

"I want the best you have. I don't care what kind."

160   The druggist named several. "They'll kill anything up to an elephant. But what you want is—"

"Arsenic," Miss Emily said. "Is that a good one?"

"Is . . . arsenic? Yes, ma'am. But what you want—"

"I want arsenic."

The druggist looked down at her. She looked back at him, erect, her face like a strained flag. "Why, of course," the druggist said. "If that's what you want. But the law requires you to tell what you are going to use it for."

Miss Emily just stared at him, her head tilted back in order to look him eye for eye, until he looked away and went and got the arsenic and wrapped it up. The

170 Negro delivery boy brought her the package; the druggist didn't come back. When she opened the package at home there was written on the box, under the skull and bones: "For rats."

IV

So the next day we all said, "She will kill herself"; and we said it would be the best thing. When she had first begun to be seen with Homer Barron, we had said, "She will marry him." Then we said, "She will persuade him yet," because Homer himself had remarked—he liked men, and it was known that he drank with the younger men in the Elks' Club—that he was not a marrying man. Later we said, "Poor Emily" behind the jalousies as they passed on Sunday afternoon in the glittering buggy, Miss Emily with her head high and Homer Barron with his hat

180 cocked and a cigar in his teeth, reins and whip in a yellow glove.

Then some of the ladies began to say that it was a disgrace to the town and a bad example to the young people. The men did not want to interfere, but at last the ladies forced the Baptist minister—Miss Emily's people were Episcopal—to call upon her. He would never divulge what happened during that interview, but he refused to go back again. The next Sunday they again drove about the streets, and the following day the minister's wife wrote to Miss Emily's relations in Alabama.

So she had blood-kin under her roof again and we sat back to watch developments. At first nothing happened. Then we were sure that they were to be married. We learned that Miss Emily had been to the jeweler's and ordered a man's

190 toilet set in silver, with the letters H. B. on each piece. Two days later we learned that she had bought a complete outfit of men's clothing, including a nightshirt, and we said, "They are married." We were really glad. We were glad because the two female cousins were even more Grierson than Miss Emily had ever been.

So we were not surprised when Homer Barron—the streets had been finished some time since—was gone. We were a little disappointed that there was not a public blowing-off,[7] but we believed that he had gone on to prepare for Miss Emily's coming, or to give her a chance to get rid of the cousins. (By that time it was a **cabal,** and we were all Miss Emily's allies to help circumvent the cousins.)

---

7. **blowing-off:** here, a celebration.

 **ANALYZE SEQUENCE**
Reread lines 154–172. What does this exchange indicate about Emily's character? What **foreshadowing** do you sense in her refusal to comply with the law?

cabal (kə-băl′) *n.* a group united in a secret plot

DIFFERENTIATED INSTRUCTION

FOR ENGLISH LANGUAGE LEARNERS

Culture: Clarify Explain to students that after the Civil War, many workers came from the Northern states to help rebuild the ravaged Southern states. These workers were referred to as Yankees; some were also called carpetbaggers because they came South with only the possessions they could stuff in a large bag. While many Northerners aided in the rebuilding of the Southern cities, some were exploitive. Many Southerners resented and despised these workers.

FOR ENGLISH LANGUAGE LEARNERS

Comprehension Support Explain to students that Miss Emily's purchases in lines 189–192 are purchases a bride might make for her groom or a wife for her husband. Emily purchases clothing and items for personal hygiene (the engraved toilet set). At the time of the story, a woman would not give such intimate items to a man unless they were engaged or married. This is why the townspeople assume, "They are married" (line 192).

Sure enough, after another week they departed. And, as we had expected all along, within three days Homer Barron was back in town. A neighbor saw the Negro man admit him at the kitchen door at dusk one evening.

And that was the last we saw of Homer Barron. And of Miss Emily for some time. The Negro man went in and out with the market basket, but the front door remained closed. Now and then we would see her at a window for a moment, as the men did that night when they sprinkled the lime, but for almost six months she did not appear on the streets. Then we knew that this was to be expected too; as if that quality of her father which had thwarted her woman's life so many times had been too virulent and too furious to die.

When we next saw Miss Emily, she had grown fat and her hair was turning gray. During the next few years it grew grayer and grayer until it attained an even pepper-and-salt iron-gray, when it ceased turning. Up to the day of her death at seventy-four it was still that vigorous iron-gray, like the hair of an active man.

From that time on her front door remained closed, save for a period of six or seven years, when she was about forty, during which she gave lessons in china-painting. She fitted up a studio in one of the downstairs rooms, where the daughters and granddaughters of Colonel Sartoris' contemporaries were sent to her with the same regularity and in the same spirit that they were sent to church on Sundays with a twenty-five-cent piece for the collection plate. Meanwhile her taxes had been remitted.

Then the newer generation became the backbone and the spirit of the town, and the painting pupils grew up and fell away and did not send their children to her with boxes of color and tedious brushes and pictures cut from the ladies' magazines. The front door closed upon the last one and remained closed for good. When the town got free postal delivery, Miss Emily alone refused to let them fasten the metal numbers above her door and attach a mailbox to it. She would not listen to them.

Daily, monthly, yearly we watched the Negro grow grayer and more stooped, going in and out with the market basket. Each December we sent her a tax notice, which would be returned by the post office a week later, unclaimed. Now and then we would see her in one of the downstairs windows—she had evidently shut up the top floor of the house—like the carven torso of an idol in a niche, looking or not looking at us, we could never tell which. Thus she passed from generation to generation—dear, inescapable, impervious, tranquil, and perverse. **H**

And so she died. Fell ill in the house filled with dust and shadows, with only a doddering Negro man to wait on her. We did not even know she was sick; we had long since given up trying to get any information from the Negro. He talked to no one, probably not even to her, for his voice had grown harsh and rusty, as if from disuse.

She died in one of the downstairs rooms, in a heavy walnut bed with a curtain, her gray head propped on a pillow yellow and moldy with age and lack of sunlight.

④ Targeted Passage

H **POINT OF VIEW**
Reread lines 227–233. When the narrator says that "we sent her a tax notice" and "we would see her in one of the downstairs windows," whom does "we" indicate? And how does this pronoun help to convey the story's point of view? Support your answer with evidence from the story.

A ROSE FOR EMILY **1073**

TIERED DISCUSSION PROMPTS

In lines 213–233, use these prompts to help students understand how changing times fail to affect Miss Emily:

Analyze In what ways does Miss Emily continue to be involved in town life? In what ways does she isolate herself?
Possible answer: *Emily continues to be involved in town life only for "six or seven years . . . during which she gave lessons in china painting" (lines 213–215). For no other reason does she involve herself in town life, ignoring her yearly tax notice, and even refusing to receive mail.*

Evaluate What does Faulkner accomplish by having the narrator describe Emily as "like the carven torso of an idol in a niche" (line 231)? ***Possible answer:*** *Students may say that this simile indicates that Miss Emily is less a real person now than a monument, perhaps to the past, perhaps to the town's pride.*

TEXT ANALYSIS

COMMON CORE
RL 3
RL 5

H **POINT OF VIEW**

Possible answer: *In these sentences, "we" indicates the townspeople as a collective whole. This pronoun allows individual actions to be represented as collective actions, such as "we sent her a tax notice" (line 228). This use of the pronoun indicates that such events are gossiped about, creating a collective viewpoint of Emily.*

FOR STRUGGLING READERS

④ Targeted Passage [Lines 227–240]

This passage relates Emily's death and brings readers back to the story's first event.

- What do the townspeople know about Emily's later years? (lines 227–233)
- How do the townspeople continue to feel about Emily as she ages? (lines 232–233)
- Where does Emily die? (lines 239–240)
- Where does this event fall on the sequence chart? (lines 227–240)

FOR ENGLISH LANGUAGE LEARNERS

Comprehension Support [mixed-readiness groups] Help students comprehend the narrator's final description of Emily's place in the town in line 233 by using Word Squares to develop definitions for each of the challenging words in this line: *dear, inescapable, impervious, tranquil,* and *perverse.* Then ask students to write a sentence or two in which they explain what Emily meant to the town.

 **BEST PRACTICES TOOLKIT—Transparency**
Word Squares p. E10

A ROSE FOR EMILY **1073**

❶ MOOD

Ask students to name words the author used to establish the mood of this story, at its beginning. Discuss with students Faulkner's unusual story structure, including his use of flashbacks told from the first-person-plural point of view. Discuss also Faulkner's use of foreshadowing as a tool to build suspense.

Possible answer: "A Rose for Emily" is compelling for several reasons: the first-person plural narration pulls the reader into the story where he or she becomes part of the collective "we" who observe Miss Emily's decline, but do nothing to intervene. Faulkner's use of flashbacks and foreshadowing make the story vivid and suspenseful. Miss Emily's domination by her father, her purchase of poison, and her fiance's disappearance add to mounting tension and lead to the ending's gruesome revelation.

SELECTION WRAP–UP

READ WITH A PURPOSE Ask students whether they suspected that Emily had murdered Homer, and what led them to suspect foul play—or what led them astray so that they didn't suspect it. *Students may say that they suspected murder when Emily bought poison and then Homer disappeared.*

V

The Negro met the first of the ladies at the front door and let them in, with their hushed, sibilant voices and their quick, curious glances, and then he disappeared. He walked right through the house and out the back and was not seen again.

The two female cousins came at once. They held the funeral on the second day, with the town coming to look at Miss Emily beneath a mass of bought flowers, with the crayon face of her father musing profoundly above the bier[8] and the ladies sibilant and macabre; and the very old men—some in their brushed Confederate uniforms—on the porch and the lawn, talking of Miss Emily as if she had been a contemporary of theirs, believing that they had danced with her and
250 courted her perhaps, confusing time with its mathematical progression, as the old do, to whom all the past is not a diminishing road but, instead, a huge meadow which no winter ever quite touches, divided from them now by the narrow bottleneck of the most recent decade of years.

Already we knew that there was one room in that region above stairs which no one had seen in forty years, and which would have to be forced. They waited until Miss Emily was decently in the ground before they opened it.

The violence of breaking down the door seemed to fill this room with pervading dust. A thin, acrid pall[9] as of the tomb seemed to lie everywhere upon this room decked and furnished as for a bridal: upon the valance curtains of faded
260 rose color, upon the rose-shaded lights, upon the dressing table, upon the delicate array of crystal and the man's toilet things backed with tarnished silver, silver so tarnished that the monogram was obscured. Among them lay a collar and tie, as if they had just been removed, which, lifted, left upon the surface a pale crescent in the dust. Upon a chair hung the suit, carefully folded; beneath it the two mute shoes and the discarded socks.

The man himself lay in the bed.

For a long while we just stood there, looking down at the profound and fleshless grin. The body had apparently once lain in the attitude of an embrace, but now the long sleep that outlasts love, that conquers even the grimace of love, had cuckolded
270 him.[10] What was left of him, rotted beneath what was left of the nightshirt, had become inextricable from the bed in which he lay; and upon him and upon the pillow beside him lay that even coating of the patient and biding dust.

Then we noticed that in the second pillow was the indentation of a head. One of us lifted something from it, and leaning forward, that faint and invisible dust dry and acrid in the nostrils, we saw a long strand of iron-gray hair. ∾ ❶ ⑤

---

8. **bier:** coffin along with its stand.

9. **acrid pall:** bitter-smelling gloom.

10. **cuckolded him:** made his wife or lover unfaithful to him.

1074 UNIT 5: THE HARLEM RENAISSANCE AND MODERNISM

COMMON CORE RL 4

❶ MOOD

This story ends with a grotesque discovery, but from page one the author's dark, gothic **mood** has prepared us for a creepy revelation in the end. With "A Rose for Emily" and other stories and novels, Faulkner invented a unique vision of the South—a **mythic narrative** weighed down by gloom and peopled by deeply flawed characters. Faulkner's mythic South has influenced Southern fiction ever since—from the short stories of Flannery O'Connor to more recent fiction by writers such as Alan Gurganus and Edward P. Jones. What makes a story like "A Rose for Emily" so compelling? Explain your answer.

DIFFERENTIATED INSTRUCTION

FOR STRUGGLING READERS

⑤ **Targeted Passage** [Lines 266–275]

This passage solves the mystery of where Homer Barron went when he disappeared.

- What happened to Homer Barron? (line 266)
- Whose hair is on the second pillow? (line 275)
- What have the townspeople discovered about Miss Emily? (lines 266–275)

FOR STRUGGLING READERS

Develop Reading Fluency Tell students that when reading the end of the story aloud, they should emphasize the most revealing sentences, such as "The man himself lay in the bed," and ". . . we saw a long strand of iron-gray hair." Read aloud lines 257–275, emphasizing revealing sentences and grotesque words, such as "rotted" (line 270), that reflect the circumstances. Explain to students how you used punctuation for guidance in pacing and

intonation. Then, have small groups practice reading these lines. Walk around the class and offer guidance to students as they practice.

FOR ADVANCED LEARNERS/AP

Analyze Craft Ask students to discuss and write about Faulkner's decisions about structure and paragraphing from line 257 to the end of the story: What does Faulkner gain by describing the room first, rather than its inhabitant? Why is the revelation of Homer's murder in a paragraph of a single line?

Comprehension

1. **Recall** Why was it difficult for Emily to meet suitable men in her youth?

2. **Clarify** What happened to Homer Barron?

3. **Clarify** What does the condition of the upstairs room in the Grierson house and the iron-gray hair on the pillow indicate?

Text Analysis

4. **Make Inferences** Use clues in the story to infer Emily's **motivation** for murdering Homer. Why was the relationship considered a "disgrace" and a "bad example to the young people"? What were Homer's intentions?

5. **Examine Methods of Characterization** Explain how Faulkner uses physical descriptions of Miss Emily, stories of her conflicts with the townspeople, and the revelation of the story's final paragraph to characterize his protagonist. Support your answer with evidence from the story.

6. **Analyze Mood** How would you describe the overall mood of "A Rose for Emily"? Skim the story, identifying at least three passages that create an especially strong **atmosphere** for the reader. Explain which literary elements contribute to each passage's mood.

7. **Analyze Point of View** What point of view does Faulkner use to narrate "A Rose for Emily"? Explain how this point of view contributes to the characterization of Miss Emily's town and how it compares to Faulkner's modernist experiments with point of view.

8. **Evaluate Sequence** Examine the chart you filled in as you read. How does the order in which the story's major events occur differ from the order in which the narrator presents them? Consider the effect created by Faulkner's manipulation of the story's sequence. What would the story lose if it were told in strict chronological order?

Text Criticism

9. **Historical Context** Faulkner lived, as one critic put it, "with one foot deep in the traditions of the Old South and the other poised for the possibilities of a modern era." What are some of the indications that this story was written in another time? Citing evidence, describe how Faulkner's story reflects an American society different from our own.

What makes your SKIN CRAWL?

How does the last sentence of "A Rose for Emily" confirm the story's creepy atmosphere? Explain your answer.

A ROSE FOR EMILY **1075**

COMMON CORE

RL 3 Analyze the impact of the author's choices regarding how to develop and relate elements of a story (e.g., where a story is set, how the action is ordered, how the characters are introduced and developed). **RL 4** Analyze the impact of specific word choices on meaning and tone, including words with multiple meanings or language that is particularly fresh, engaging, or beautiful. **RL 5** Analyze how an author's choices concerning how to structure specific parts of a text contribute to its overall structure and meaning as well as its aesthetic impact.

Practice and Apply

For preliminary support of post-reading questions, use these copy masters:

R RESOURCE MANAGER—Copy Masters
Reading Check p. 320
Point of View p. 313
Question Support p. 321

Additional selection questions are provided for teachers on page 307.

ANSWERS
COMMON CORE **RL 3, RL 4, RL 5**

1. *No suitor met her father's high standards.*

2. *Emily poisoned him and kept his body.*

3. *The room is decorated for a wedding night; the hair on the pillow indicates that Emily had lain on the bed with the corpse.*

Possible answers:

4. *Students may infer that Homer wronged Emily by courting her without intending to marry her or that she would rather have him dead than be rejected.*

5. *Physical descriptions such as "cold, haughty black eyes in a face the flesh of which was strained across the temples and about the eye-sockets" (lines 155–156) show that Miss Emily does not take care of herself and is mentally unstable. Miss Emily's refusal to pay taxes shows that she is stubborn and unconcerned about what the townspeople think of her.*

6. *The mood is creepy, as in the description of the bridal chamber and the portrait of Emily's father watching over her even in death.*

7. ● COMMON CORE FOCUS **Point of View** *Faulkner uses first-person-plural point of view. This collective point of view characterizes Miss Emily's town as a small, close-knit community, full of like-minded, gossipy people. This point of view presents a town's collective view rather than the specific, personal details and observations Faulkner relays in other works with stream of consciousness or multiple narrators.*

8. ■ COMMON CORE FOCUS **Analyze Sequence** *The flashbacks give the story a meandering quality like the telling of a family story recalled through associative memories, rather than a once-upon-a-time chronology. This quality enhances the mystery of Miss Emily and provides moments when readers sense that more is going on than is being told. Readers gradually*

accumulate Emily's history but can't see how the details fit together till the story's final shocking lines. If told chronologically, the story would lose the sense of eerie suspense and discovery.

9. *The derogatory words used to describe African Americans, the old-fashioned notion that a woman was "ruined" if she engaged in a premarital relationship, the horror the aldermen feel about telling a "lady" that her house smells bad—these are among the indicators that the story depicts an American society different from our own.*

What makes your SKIN CRAWL? *Possible answer:* The revelation at the end of the story indicates that Miss Emily is mentally unstable, and adds to the creepy tone.

A ROSE FOR EMILY **1075**

ANSWERS

Vocabulary in Context

▲ VOCABULARY PRACTICE

1. *(c) dismay*   3. *(c) decency*

2. *(b) cabal*   4. *(a) tableau*

 RESOURCE MANAGER—COPY MASTER
Vocabulary Practice p. 318

ACADEMIC VOCABULARY IN WRITING

Have students begin by thinking of novels, short stories, or movies with what they consider successful endings. Tell students to make a list of qualities that made the endings successful.

VOCABULARY STRATEGY: ETYMOLOGIES

Walk students through a dictionary so that they know where to find etymologies and how to read the abbreviations used.

Possible answers:

1. *Latin, "three ways," a crossroads that leads many ways, so* common, unimportant

2. *Latin, "tenth," meaning to reduce by a tenth, thus* to reduce drastically

3. *Greek, "slab," a flat stone along which are grooves for mathematical calculations*

4. *Afrikaans, "earth pig," describes and names a mammal that digs up insects to eat*

5. *Latin, "forty," for the forty days ships could be kept at sea if illness was aboard; now to isolate an ill person*

6. *Italian, "bad air," from what people once thought caused the illness*

7. *Malay, "fish sauce," a condiment made from pureed tomatoes*

8. *Latin, "on the right," for the right hand which, in most people, is more able; meaning skillful, competent with the hands, or mentally sharp and clever*

 **RESOURCE MANAGER—Copy Master**
Vocabulary Strategy p. 319

 **Interactive Vocabulary** THINK central

Keywords direct students to a **WordSharp** tutorial on **thinkcentral.com** or to other types of vocabulary practice and review.

Vocabulary in Context

▲ VOCABULARY PRACTICE

Chose the word that is not related in meaning to the other words.

1. (a) overconfidence, (b) temerity, (c) dismay, (d) brashness

2. (a) contempt, (b) cabal, (c) disdain, (d) scorn

3. (a) endurance, (b) imperviousness, (c) decency, (d) resistance

4. (a) tableau, (b) mesa, (c) plateau, (d) upland

> **WORD LIST**
> cabal
> imperviousness
> tableau
> temerity

ACADEMIC VOCABULARY IN WRITING

> • conclude • criteria • despite • justify • maintain

Faulkner **concludes** "A Rose for Emily" by solving the mystery of his main character. What are your **criteria** for a successful ending? Develop your answer in a short paragraph. Use at least three Academic Vocabulary words in your response.

VOCABULARY STRATEGY: ETYMOLOGIES

Many English words have intriguing histories, or **etymologies.** The vocabulary word *cabal*, for instance, can be traced back to *kabbala*, the name of an ancient Jewish mystical belief system. We can often develop a better understanding of the current meaning of a word by learning about its history. Standard dictionaries, we all as etymological dictionaries, are excellent sources of word histories. A typical word history may show the history of the word in the English language (its form in Middle English, for example) as well as its relationship to words from other Germanic languages or to the Romance languages.

PRACTICE Using a standard dictionary, an etymological dictionary, or the Internet, research the histories of the following words. Look for the history of the word in the English language as well as its relationship to words in other contemporary languages (German, Dutch, Italian, French, etc.) and in Latin.

1. trivial   5. quarantine

2. decimate   6. malaria

3. abacus   7. ketchup

4. aardvark   8. dexterity

> **COMMON CORE**
>
> **L 4c** Consult general and specialized reference materials, both print and digital, to determine or clarify a word's etymology.

Interactive Vocabulary THINK central
Go to **thinkcentral.com**.
KEYWORD: HML11-1076

DIFFERENTIATED INSTRUCTION

FOR ENGLISH LANGUAGE LEARNERS

Task Support: Vocabulary Practice Point out to students the words in the exercise that have Greek or Latin roots. Tell them that many English words have such roots. Knowing the roots can help readers guess the meaning of unfamiliar words. Guide students to keep lists of roots and add to their lists when they encounter new roots.

 BEST PRACTICES TOOLKIT—Transparencies
Greek and Latin Roots pp. E20, E21, E22

FOR ADVANCED LEARNERS/AP

Analyze Etymologies Direct students to the *Oxford English Dictionary*, found in most public and some school libraries. Assign each student a word from the exercise, and ask students to get the "whole story" from the OED's extended etymology of the word. Ask students to write a "life story" of the word and to post these stories on a class Web site. Let students compare the brief etymologies contained in most dictionaries with the more complete information.

Language

◆ **GRAMMAR AND STYLE: Choose Effective Point of View**

Review the **Grammar and Style** note on page 1070. Part of what makes "A Rose for Emily" so interesting is the first-person-plural point of view—using *we* and related **pronouns** to tell the story. Usually, the first-person point of view is singular, an *I* who acts as both narrator and character. Faulkner's use of the plural creates a curious mixture of intimacy and anonymity. That is, the voice behind the *we* sounds personal, but readers don't know exactly who the voice is:

> *We learned that Miss Emily had been to the jeweler's and ordered a man's toilet set in silver, with the letters H. B. on each piece. Two days later we learned that she had bought a complete outfit of men's clothing, including a nightshirt, and we said, "They are married." We were really glad.* (lines 189–192)

This kind of narrator has the effect of making the town appear as a complete entity with a personality and opinions all its own.

PRACTICE Try using the first-person-plural point of view to create a narrative of your own. Choose a group—a family, for example, or a sports team—and describe, in a paragraph, an event or experience from their point of view. Be sure to use the correct pronouns—*we, us, our, ours*—in your narrative.

READING-WRITING CONNECTION

Expand your understanding of "A Rose for Emily" by responding to the prompt below. Then, use the **revising tips** to improve your essay.

WRITING PROMPT	REVISING TIPS
WRITE AN ARGUMENT Do you think the townspeople in "A Rose for Emily" bear any responsibility for what becomes of Emily? Why did they initially think she would use the arsenic to kill herself—and what did they seemingly think of this decision? What if they had stopped the minister's wife from writing to her cousins? Why didn't they think to investigate Homer Barron's disappearance? Review the story, especially sections III and IV, to clarify your opinion and gather evidence. Then write a **three-to-five-paragraph argument** to try to convince someone else.	• Share your essay with a peer who has supported an opposing claim. • Ask your peer to identify unconvincing ideas and passages in your essay. • Strengthen your reasoning and find additional evidence to support your position.

Interactive Revision **THINK** central
Go to **thinkcentral.com**.
KEYWORD: HML11-1077

COMMON CORE

L 3 Apply knowledge of language to understand how language functions in different contexts, to make effective choices for meaning or style. **W 1** Write arguments to support claims in an analysis of substantive topics or texts, using valid reasoning and relevant and sufficient evidence.

FOR STRUGGLING WRITERS
Writing Support

• Limit the length of the argument to two or three paragraphs, and limit the prewriting discussion to one question: What might the townspeople have done to prevent Emily's insanity and thus Homer's murder?

• Explain to students what it means to address possible objections to their arguments.

• Help students draft a thesis statement to guide their writing. Students who think that the townspeople do bear responsibility for events might begin: *The townspeople in "A Rose for Emily" are partly responsible for what happens to Emily and Homer because* _____.

• Allow students to draft in first person so that they will more naturally express their thoughts.

Language

 COMMON CORE L 3, W 1

◆ **GRAMMAR AND STYLE**

To help students appreciate the difference between first-person singular point of view and first-person plural point of view, have them rewrite lines 98–107 using first-person singular pronouns. Discuss how the use of singular pronouns changes the tone and intent of the lines. (For more on personal pronouns, see **Grammar Handbook,** p. R56.)

Students' narratives should use first-person plural pronouns to relay the events.

 RESOURCE MANAGER—Copy Master
Use Realistic Dialogue p. 322

READING-WRITING CONNECTION

Suggest that students discuss the "why" and "what if" questions in small groups. Remind them to take notes during the discussion. Students may wish to use the Persuasive Essay writing template to organize this writing assignment.

 **BEST PRACTICES TOOLKIT—Transparency**
Writing Template: Persuasive Essay pp. C16, C31

Writing Online **THINK** central

The following tools are available online at **thinkcentral.com** and on **Write*Smart*** CD-ROM:

• **Interactive Graphic Organizers**
• **Interactive Student Models**
• **Interactive Revision Lessons**

For additional grammar instruction, see **GrammarNotes** on **thinkcentral.com**.

Assess and Reteach

Assess

DIAGNOSTIC AND SELECTION TESTS
  Selection Test A, B/C pp. 289–290, 291–292

Interactive Selection Test on thinkcentral.com

Reteach

Level Up Online Tutorials on thinkcentral.com

Reteaching Worksheets on thinkcentral.com

  Literature Lessons 8, 10

Focus and Motivate

COMMON CORE FOCUS

RL 1 Cite textual evidence to support analysis of what the text says explicitly as well as inferences drawn from the text, including determining where the text leaves matters uncertain. **RL 6** Analyze a case in which grasping point of view requires distinguishing what is directly stated in a text from what is really meant.

ABOUT THE AUTHOR

When Flannery O'Connor recognized the first symptoms of lupus in 1950, she believed, based on her father's experience, that she had only a few years to live. However, the disease, in which the body's immune system attacks and slowly destroys the organs, affects each patient differently. O'Connor moved to her mother's farm to pursue her writing in the time she had left, relying on grants and fellowships to support her. The stories she wrote during the next decade earned three O. Henry Awards and established her as a major American writer.

NOTABLE QUOTE

"The truth is I like [my stories] better than anybody and I read them over and laugh and laugh." **—Flannery O'Connor**

Ask students how O'Connor probably hoped other readers would respond to her stories.

The Life You Save May Be Your Own
Short Story by Flannery O'Connor

COMMON CORE

RL 1 Cite textual evidence to support analysis of what the text says explicitly as well as inferences drawn from the text, including determining where the text leaves matters uncertain.
RL 6 Analyze a case in which grasping point of view requires distinguishing what is directly stated in a text from what is really meant.

DID YOU KNOW?

Flannery O'Connor . . .

- began writing and illustrating stories at the age of 6.
- enrolled in college at age 16, graduating three years later.
- created cartoons for her high school newspaper.
- raised peacocks on her farm in Georgia.

Meet the Author

Flannery O'Connor 1925–1964

As a child, Flannery O'Connor had a pet chicken that could walk backwards as well as forwards. News reporters—including a photographer all the way from New York City—were dispatched to her home in Savannah, Georgia, to take pictures of the unusual chicken. This experience, O'Connor later said, marked her for life. It began her preoccupation with the grotesque, a fascination she shares with other writers belonging to the literary tradition known as Southern Gothic. "Whenever I am asked why Southern writers particularly have a penchant for writing about freaks," O'Connor once commented, "I say it is because we are still able to recognize one."

Born to Write Always a bit shy but self-confident and spirited, O'Connor seemed born to be a writer. She wrote stories from an early age and described herself as a "pigeon-toed only child with a receding chin and a you-leave-me-alone-or-I'll-bite-you complex." In high school, she listed her hobby as "collecting rejection slips," as she was already sending out her stories to major literary journals. After graduating from college, she received a scholarship to attend the famed Writers' Workshop at the University of Iowa. In the late 1940s, she was twice invited to Yaddo, an exclusive artists' colony in upstate New York. In both places, she made lasting friends and developed the contacts she needed to succeed in the literary world.

A Life Cut Short At the age of 25, while writing her first novel, *Wise Blood* (1952), O'Connor was stricken with lupus, an autoimmune disease that had killed her father 9 years earlier. She moved with her mother to a farm outside of Milledgeville, Georgia, where she used her remaining 14 years to produce two highly acclaimed volumes of stories and another novel, *The Violent Bear It Away* (1960).

Defined by Region and Religion Being a Catholic in largely Protestant Georgia gave O'Connor a unique perspective. The South offered rich subject matter—sometimes violent, often humorous—and her Catholicism provided a unifying vision of the divine in everyday life. Her works, often difficult to categorize and to fully understand, weren't bestsellers and took some time to gain a following. Today, critics consider O'Connor one of the greatest short story writers of her time. Her novels and stories are more popular now than they've ever been.

Author Online
Go to thinkcentral.com. KEYWORD: HML11-1078

THINK central

Selection Resources

See resources on the **Teacher One Stop DVD-ROM** and on **thinkcentral.com**.

 **RESOURCE MANAGER UNIT 5**

Plan and Teach, pp. 323–330
Summary, pp. 331–332†‡*
Text Analysis and Reading
  Skill, pp. 333–336†*

DIAGNOSTIC AND SELECTION TESTS

Selection Tests, pp. 293–296

 BEST PRACTICES TOOLKIT

Predicting, p. A10
Definition Mapping, p. E6
Timeline, p. B23
Comparison Matrix, p. A24
Venn Diagram, p. A26

TECHNOLOGY

- **Teacher One Stop DVD-ROM**
- **Student One Stop DVD-ROM**
- **Audio Anthology CD**
- **ExamView Test Generator on the Teacher One Stop**

---

* Resources for Differentiation   † Also in Spanish   ‡ In Haitian Creole and Vietnamese

● TEXT ANALYSIS: IRONY

Irony is a contrast between appearance and actuality. You'll notice two kinds of irony at work in the story you're about to read.

- **Dramatic irony** occurs when readers know more about a situation than the characters themselves know —as though the writer is letting you in on a secret the characters aren't privy to.

- **Situational irony** is a contrast between what a character or reader expects to happen and what actually does happen. This kind of irony often takes the reader by surprise.

Irony is often indirect and subtle, making it difficult to detect. Recognizing it, however, can make a work infinitely more striking and memorable. As you read "The Life You Save May Be Your Own," look for examples of both situational and dramatic irony.

● READING SKILL: ANALYZE DESCRIPTIVE DETAILS

O'Connor asserted that "distortion is the only way to make people see." To that end, she employed a wealth of **descriptive details** to flesh out her grotesque characters and their often perverse situations. As you read, use a chart like the one shown to note examples of these details. Record your personal reactions as well as your analysis of what these details reveal or highlight about the characters and their bizarre behavior.

Striking Details from the Story	My Reactions	Analysis
"He offered the old woman a piece [of gum] but she only raised her upper lip to indicate she had no teeth."	This old woman gives me the creeps. I can picture her hostile stance and her toothless gums.	The woman lives in a poor, isolated area and probably doesn't have access to dental or medical care. But she's not ashamed of her circumstances, and she doesn't waste words explaining herself.

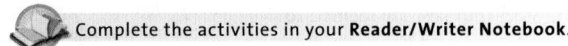 Complete the activities in your **Reader/Writer Notebook**.

Could you spot a CON ARTIST?

We've all seen—or heard of or read about—an instance in which someone was duped by a con artist. If you've ever watched a schemer in action, you may have thought to yourself, "I never would have fallen for that one." But literature, movies, and even newspapers are full of stories of people being conned. Why? What makes a con artist's deception so hard to spot?

QUICKWRITE Write a quick description of a con you've seen—on the big screen or in real life—or read about. Why do you think the victim fell for the con artist's antics? What traits did the con artist possess? If you'd been in the victim's shoes, do you honestly think you could have seen through the con artist's scheme, or would you too have been duped?

1079

Could you spot a CON ARTIST?

Ask students if they have ever received an e-mail or letter "phishing" for important information or offering them a share in a multimillion-dollar windfall. Have students lay out the clues that helped them spot the deception in these scams. Before they complete their *QUICKWRITE*, ask them why some people don't spot the cons in this and other scams.

TEXT ANALYSIS
COMMON CORE — RL 6

● *Model the Skill:* IRONY

To help students identify dramatic irony, write the following passage on the board:

> Whiskers was sprawled out on the roof, soaking in the afternoon sun. On the front porch below, Dillon bellowed out, "Come here, Whiskers!"

> "Mom's going to kill us if we don't find that cat!" Jenna exclaimed, bending down to look under a bush.

Point out to students that this is an example of dramatic irony because readers know that the cat is on the roof, but Dillon and Jenna are unaware of the cat's location.

GUIDED PRACTICE Have students recall examples of irony from stories and novels that they have read.

READING SKILL
COMMON CORE — RL 1

■ *Model the Skill:* ANALYZE DESCRIPTIVE DETAILS

Remind students that in everyday life, observant people look for the reasons behind actions. Readers must observe story characters as they do real people.

GUIDED PRACTICE Have students think of questions to analyze a story character.

R RESOURCE MANAGER—Copy Master Analyze Descriptive Details p. 335

DIFFERENTIATED INSTRUCTION

FOR ENGLISH LANGUAGE LEARNERS

Predict Have students read the story's first paragraph. Then, have students preview the selection by reading the side notes and examining the paintings. Tell students to make a prediction about what interaction will take place between the three characters introduced in the first paragraph. Ask volunteers to share their predictions and the reasons for these predictions. Encourage students to revise their predictions as they read the story.

After students have read the selection, ask them whether or not their original predictions were correct.

Practice and Apply

SUMMARY

In this story a tramp, Mr. Shiftlet, and an old widow, Mrs. Crater, attempt to con each other: Mr. Shiftlet wants to steal Mrs. Crater's car, while Mrs. Crater wants to marry off her mentally disabled daughter. Mr. Shiftlet does marry the daughter but then abandons her and takes the car. As the story ends, he offers a boy a ride and lectures him on right behavior, only to have the boy curse him and refuse his advice.

READ WITH A PURPOSE

Help students set a purpose for reading. Tell them to read to discover what motivates Mr. Shiftlet.

REVISIT THE BIG QUESTION

Could you spot a
CON ARTIST?

Discuss In lines 17–24, what details about Mr. Shiftlet hint at his capacity for deception?
Possible answer: *His facial features are sloped, his jaw is like a "steel-trap" (line 22), and he has a dissatisfied air. He looks untrustworthy and grasping.*

READING SKILL   COMMON CORE   RL 1

Ⓐ ANALYZE DETAILS

Possible answer: *The old woman's careful assessment of the stranger might indicate shrewdness or caution; her refusal to rise indicates that she is not one to jump up for politeness' sake; her hand on her hip might suggest an in-charge or stubborn personality. The girl's obliviousness, followed by her agitation and "excited speechless sounds" (line 16) suggest that she is mentally disabled in some way.*

Extend the Discussion Encourage students to add these details to the charts introduced on page 1079. Ask them to share what they write in the column labeled "My Reactions."

The Life You Save May Be Your Own

Flannery O'Connor

The old woman and her daughter were sitting on their porch when Mr. Shiftlet came up their road for the first time. The old woman slid to the edge of her chair and leaned forward, shading her eyes from the piercing sunset with her hand. The daughter could not see far in front of her and continued to play with her fingers. Although the old woman lived in this desolate spot with only her daughter and she had never seen Mr. Shiftlet before, she could tell, even from a distance, that he was a tramp and no one to be afraid of. His left coat sleeve was folded up to show there was only half an arm in it, and his gaunt figure listed slightly to the side as if the breeze were pushing him. He had on a black town suit and a brown felt hat that was turned up in the front and down in the back and he carried a tin tool box
10 by a handle. He came on, at an amble, up her road, his face turned toward the sun which appeared to be balancing itself on the peak of a small mountain.

The old woman didn't change her position until he was almost into her yard; then she rose with one hand fisted on her hip. The daughter, a large girl in a short blue organdy dress, saw him all at once and jumped up and began to stamp and point and make excited speechless sounds. Ⓐ

Mr. Shiftlet stopped just inside the yard and set his box on the ground and tipped his hat at her as if she were not in the least afflicted; then he turned toward the old woman and swung the hat all the way off. He had long black slick hair
20 that hung flat from a part in the middle to beyond the tips of his ears on either side. His face descended in forehead for more than half its length and ended suddenly with his features just balanced over a jutting steel-trap jaw. He seemed to be a young man but he had a look of composed[1] dissatisfaction as if he understood life thoroughly.

"Good evening," the old woman said. She was about the size of a cedar fence post and she had a man's gray hat pulled down low over her head.

---

1. **composed:** calm; cool and collected.

Analyze Visuals ▶
What compositional elements lend this scene a sense of isolation? Cite specific examples in your answer.

❶ Targeted Passage

Ⓐ **ANALYZE DETAILS**
Reread lines 1–16, recording in your chart the descriptive details O'Connor includes about each character. What does the old woman's body language suggest about her character? What does the girl's behavior indicate?

Light of Lagrange (1997), Billy Morrow Jackson. Watercolor, 22″ × 29″.
© Billy Morrow Jackson.

DIFFERENTIATED INSTRUCTION

FOR STRUGGLING READERS

In combination with the *Audio Anthology CD,* use one or more Targeted Passages (pp. 1080, 1082, 1084, 1087, and 1088) to ensure that students focus on key story events and concepts. Targeted Passages are also good for English language learners.

❶ **Targeted Passage** [Lines 1–11]

This passage introduces the three characters whose actions and decisions shape the plot.

- What are the old woman and her daughter doing when they first see Mr. Shiftlet? (lines 1–2)
- What is the old woman's reaction to Mr. Shiftlet? (lines 2–7)
- What is distinctive about Mr. Shiftlet's appearance? (lines 7–8)

In lines 45–71, use these prompts to help students interpret Mr. Shiftlet's enigmatic words and actions:

Connect Have you ever tried to converse with someone who dodges every question? What did you think about that person? *Accept all thoughtful responses.*

Analyze What questions does Mrs. Crater ask Mr. Shiftlet, and why does she want to know these things? *Possible answer: She asks where he's from and what he's doing out on the lonely road to her farm. She needs to know whether he is a threat.*

Evaluate What kind of person does Mr. Shiftlet make himself out to be, with his nonanswers and silences? *Possible answer: Accept all thoughtful answers. He doesn't say where he's from or why he's traveling; instead, he offers odd, almost philosophical replies about a world that "is almost rotten" (line 51) and the human heart. Either he is a thoughtful man, stricken by life's perplexities, or he wants to seem deeper than he really is to avoid Mrs. Crater's questions and the truth about himself.*

The tramp stood looking at her and didn't answer. He turned his back and faced the sunset. He swung both his whole and his short arm up slowly so that they indicated an expanse of sky and his figure formed a crooked cross. The old 30 woman watched him with her arms folded across her chest as if she were the owner of the sun, and the daughter watched, her head thrust forward and her fat helpless hands hanging at the wrists. She had long pink-gold hair and eyes as blue as a peacock's neck.

He held the pose for almost fifty seconds and then he picked up his box and came on to the porch and dropped down on the bottom step. "Lady," he said in a firm nasal voice, "I'd give a fortune to live where I could see me a sun do that every evening."

"Does it every evening," the old woman said and sat back down. The daughter sat down too and watched him with a cautious sly look as if he were a bird that 40 had come up very close. He leaned to one side, rooting in his pants pocket, and in a second he brought out a package of chewing gum and offered her a piece. She took it and unpeeled it and began to chew without taking her eyes off him. He offered the old woman a piece but she only raised her upper lip to indicate she had no teeth.

Mr. Shiftlet's pale, sharp glance had already passed over everything in the yard—the pump near the corner of the house and the big fig tree that three or four chickens were preparing to roost in—and had moved to a shed where he saw the square rusted back of an automobile. "You ladies drive?" he asked.

"That car ain't run in fifteen year," the old woman said. "The day my husband 50 died, it quit running."

"Nothing is like it used to be, lady," he said. "The world is almost rotten."

"That's right," the old woman said. "You from around here?"

"Name Tom T. Shiftlet," he murmured, looking at the tires.

"I'm pleased to meet you," the old woman said. "Name Lucynell Crater and daughter Lucynell Crater. What you doing around here, Mr. Shiftlet?"

He judged the car to be about a 1928 or '29 Ford. "Lady," he said, and turned and gave her his full attention, "lemme tell you something. There's one of these doctors in Atlanta that's taken a knife and cut the human heart—the human heart," he repeated, leaning forward, "out of a man's chest and held it in his 60 hand," and he held his hand out, palm up, as if it were slightly weighted with the human heart, "and studied it like it was a day-old chicken, and lady," he said, allowing a long significant pause in which his head slid forward and his clay-colored eyes brightened, "he don't know no more about it than you or me."

"That's right," the old woman said.

"Why, if he was to take that knife and cut into every corner of it, he still wouldn't know no more than you or me. What you want to bet?"

"Nothing," the old woman said wisely. "Where you come from, Mr. Shiftlet?"

He didn't answer. He reached into his pocket and brought out a sack of tobacco and a package of cigarette papers and rolled himself a cigarette, expertly with one 70 hand, and attached it in a hanging position to his upper lip. Then he took a box of wooden matches from his pocket and struck one on his shoe. He held the burning match as if he were studying the mystery of flame while it traveled dangerously

② Targeted Passage

Language Coach

Informal Pronunciation
Lemme (line 57) is an example of informal pronunciation. Instead of saying "Let me" distinctly, Mr. Shiftlet runs the two words together. Similar words are *dunno* ("don't know") and *gimme* ("give me"). How does informal speech suit this character?

DIFFERENTIATED INSTRUCTION

FOR STRUGGLING READERS

② Targeted Passage [Lines 38–56]
This passage sets up the conflict between Mrs. Crater and Mr. Shiftlet.

- What does Mr. Shiftlet seem most interested in as he meets the Craters? (lines 45–56)
- What does Mrs. Crater want to know about Mr. Shiftlet? How does he respond? (lines 54–55)

FOR ENGLISH LANGUAGE LEARNERS

Language Coach

Informal Pronunciation *Possible answer: Mr. Shiftlet is a drifter and may not speak formally to the people.* Tell students that informal pronunciation is only used in this story's dialogue. This nonstandard use of English is appropriate for relaying a character through dialogue, but should not be used in formal papers, like research papers.

FOR ADVANCED LEARNERS/AP

Name Symbolism [small-group option] Have students discuss Mr. Shiftlet's name and why O'Connor chooses it. Point out that this is not a common name, and ask students to consider whether it is a clue to his personality. Have them predict what kinds of behaviors and actions Mr. Shiftlet will engage in as the story proceeds.

🧰 BEST PRACTICES TOOLKIT—Transparency
Predicting p. A10

toward his skin. The daughter began to make loud noises and to point to his hand and shake her finger at him, but when the flame was just before touching him, he leaned down with his hand cupped over it as if he were going to set fire to his nose and lit the cigarette. **B**

He flipped away the dead match and blew a stream of gray into the evening. A sly look came over his face. "Lady," he said, "nowadays, people'll do anything anyways. I can tell you my name is Tom T. Shiftlet and I come from Tarwater, Tennessee, but
80 you never have seen me before: how you know I ain't lying? How you know my name ain't Aaron Sparks, lady, and I come from Singleberry, Georgia, or how you know it's not George Speeds and I come from Lucy, Alabama, or how you know I ain't Thompson Bright from Toolafalls, Mississippi?"

"I don't know nothing about you," the old woman muttered, irked.

"Lady," he said, "people don't care how they lie. Maybe the best I can tell you is, I'm a man; but listen lady," he said and paused and made his tone more ominous still, "what is a man?"

The old woman began to gum a seed. "What you carry in that tin box, Mr. Shiftlet?" she asked.

90 "Tools," he said, put back. "I'm a carpenter."

"Well, if you come out here to work, I'll be able to feed you and give you a place to sleep but I can't pay. I'll tell you that before you begin," she said.

There was no answer at once and no particular expression on his face. He leaned back against the two-by-four that helped support the porch roof. "Lady," he said slowly, "there's some men that some things mean more to them than money." The old woman rocked without comment and the daughter watched the trigger that moved up and down in his neck. He told the old woman then that all most people were interested in was money, but he asked what a man was made for. He asked her if a man was made for money, or what. He asked her
100 what she thought she was made for but she didn't answer, she only sat rocking and wondered if a one-armed man could put a new roof on her garden house. He asked a lot of questions that she didn't answer. He told her that he was twenty-eight years old and had lived a varied life. He had been a gospel singer, a foreman on the railroad, an assistant in an undertaking parlor, and he come over the radio for three months with Uncle Roy and his Red Creek Wranglers. He said he had fought and bled in the Arm Service of his country and visited every foreign land and that everywhere he had seen people that didn't care if they did a thing one way or another. He said he hadn't been raised thataway. **C**

A fat yellow moon appeared in the branches of the fig tree as if it were going to
110 roost there with the chickens. He said that a man had to escape to the country to see the world whole and that he wished he lived in a desolate place like this where he could see the sun go down every evening like God made it to do.

"Are you married or are you single?" the old woman asked.

There was a long silence. "Lady," he asked finally, "where would you find you an innocent woman today? I wouldn't have any of this trash I could just pick up."

The daughter was leaning very far down, hanging her head almost between her knees watching him through a triangular door she had made in her overturned

---

B **ANALYZE DETAILS**
Consider the wealth of details O'Connor offers about Tom Shiftlet in lines 45–76. Which details serve to reveal his important **traits?**

C **IRONY**
Reread lines 105–108. Explain the irony of Shiftlet's statement that he served in the "Arm Service."

READING SKILL — COMMON CORE RL 1

B **ANALYZE DETAILS**

Possible answer: Mr. Shiftlet's "pale, sharp glance" (line 45) reveals his cunning, self-seeking nature; his theatrical cigarette-rolling performance reveals both his competence and his confidence—his desire to show off. Readers may suspect already that this man is less than genuine.

REVISIT THE BIG QUESTION

Could you spot a
CON ARTIST?

Discuss In lines 93–108, what hints do students see that Mr. Shiftlet's résumé partakes of deception? *Possible answer: Mr. Shiftlet seems to have been everywhere and done everything; perhaps he has done many of these things, but his claims seem flamboyant and exaggerated—can he really have visited "every foreign land" (line 106)? Also suspicious is the way he carries on with his autobiography even though Mrs. Crater does not respond to it in any way.*

TEXT ANALYSIS — COMMON CORE RL 6

C **IRONY**

Possible answer: Mr. Shiftlet's misuse of the term armed services is ironic in light of the fact that he has lost his arm.

IF STUDENTS NEED HELP . . . Provide context for students by reminding them that World War I had lately ended.

FOR STRUGGLING READERS
Develop Reading Fluency Read aloud important segments of the dialogue in lines 78–92. Discuss with students each character's feelings and motivations during this exchange and how that affects the way someone should read the dialogue. Then, have partners practice reading this exchange. Remind students to use expression during their read and use punctuation marks as guidance for pacing and intonation. Walk around and offer guidance to

students that are struggling. Have pairs that have mastered the dialogue perform for the class.

FOR ENGLISH LANGUAGE LEARNERS
Vocabulary Support Use Definition Mapping to teach these words: *trigger* (line 97), *mechanism* (line 160).

BEST PRACTICES TOOLKIT—Transparency
Definition Mapping p. E6

FOR ADVANCED LEARNERS/AP
Analyze Ask students to use a dictionary to explore these questions about the term *con man*:

- From what word does *con* derive?
- What does this derivation imply about how a con man operates?
- What synonyms are there for con man, and what do these imply about this crime?

Then have students report their findings to the class.

ⓓ Model the Skill: IRONY

Tell students that the irony in Mrs. Crater's dialogue can be determined by how the statement is read. Have a volunteer read, "I would give her up for nothing on earth" (lines 121–122) first in a sincere tone and then in an uncaring tone. Then, explain how each reading expresses a different meaning.

Possible answer: *The phrase could mean that Mrs. Crater would not give her daughter up for anything, or it could mean that Mrs. Crater would give her daughter up for nothing at all. Readers must read on to find out which meaning is correct.*

Analyze Visuals

Possible answer: *The title implies that the farmhouse in the distance is not where the man lives; rather, he does not belong there. The man's shabby appearance combined with the thicket of crops in the foreground, expanse of dark field, and fading light create a threatening and unsettling mood, as if the man will sneak across the fields and arrive at the farmhouse, unannounced and unwelcome. In addition, his current position (leaning on the post, lit) makes him appear to be plotting.*

About the Art In this work of art by Billy Morrow Jackson, painted in 1958, the sense of isolation is coupled with the evidence of decay.

---

hair; and she suddenly fell in a heap on the floor and began to whimper. Mr. Shiftlet straightened her out and helped her get back in the chair.

120   "Is she your baby girl?" he asked.

"My only," the old woman said, "and she's the sweetest girl in the world. I would give her up for nothing on earth. She's smart too. She can sweep the floor, cook, wash, feed the chickens, and hoe. I wouldn't give her up for a casket of jewels." ⓓ

"No," he said kindly, "don't ever let any man take her away from you."

"Any man come after her," the old woman said, " 'll have to stay around the place."

Mr. Shiftlet's eye in the darkness was focused on a part of the automobile bumper that glittered in the distance. "Lady," he said, jerking his short arm up as

130 if he could point with it to her house and yard and pump, "there ain't a broken thing on this plantation that I couldn't fix for you, one-arm jackleg² or not. I'm a man," he said with a sullen dignity, "even if I ain't a whole one. I got," he said, tapping his knuckles on the floor to emphasize the immensity of what he was going to say, "a moral intelligence!" and his face pierced out of the darkness into a shaft of doorlight and he stared at her as if he were astonished himself at this impossible truth.

The old woman was not impressed with the phrase. "I told you you could hang around and work for food," she said, "if you don't mind sleeping in that car yonder."

"Why listen, Lady," he said with a grin of delight, "the monks of old slept in

140 their coffins!"

"They wasn't as advanced as we are," the old woman said.

The next morning he began on the roof of the garden house while Lucynell, the daughter, sat on a rock and watched him work. He had not been around a week before the change he had made in the place was apparent. He had patched the front and back steps, built a new hog pen, restored a fence, and taught Lucynell, who was completely deaf and had never said a word in her life, to say the word "bird." The big rosy-faced girl followed him everywhere, saying "Burrttddt ddbirrrttdt," and clapping her hands. The old woman watched from a distance, secretly pleased. She was ravenous for a son-in-law.

150   Mr. Shiftlet slept on the hard narrow back seat of the car with his feet out the side window. He had his razor and a can of water on a crate that served him as a bedside table and he put up a piece of mirror against the back glass and kept his coat neatly on a hanger that he hung over one of the windows.

In the evenings he sat on the steps and talked while the old woman and Lucynell rocked violently in their chairs on either side of him. The old woman's three mountains were black against the dark blue sky and were visited off and on by various planets and by the moon after it had left the chickens. Mr. Shiftlet pointed out that the reason he had improved this plantation was because he had taken a personal interest in it. He said he was even going to make the automobile run.

---

2. **jackleg:** someone who does work he or she has not been trained to do.

ⓓ **IRONY**
O'Connor employs irony not just in her descriptions of her characters, but in their dialogue, as well. Reread lines 120–124. What double meaning might be suggested by the phrase "I would give her up for nothing on earth"?

Analyze Visuals ▶
Note that the painting on the opposite page is titled *The Interloper*. An interloper is an intruder. What does this title suggest about the man and the farmhouse depicted? How does the title work with the elements of the painting to establish a mood?

❸ **Targeted Passage**

DIFFERENTIATED INSTRUCTION

FOR STRUGGLING READERS

❸ **Targeted Passage** [Lines 142–153]

This passage shows how Mr. Shiftlet begins to set up his con.

- What impact does Mr. Shiftlet have on the farm? (lines 142–145)

- What effect does he have on Lucynell? (lines 145–148)

- What kind of personal habits does he display? (lines 150–153)

FOR ENGLISH LANGUAGE LEARNERS

Comprehension Support: Dialect Point out the use of the nonstandard word *ain't* in lines 130 and 132; elicit the standard verb for each sentence, and remind students to watch for other uses of the word and to make the needed substitution for comprehension. Help students with the challenging lines 126 and 127 by guiding them to perceive the if-then statement (*If* any man comes after her, *then* he'll have to stay).

FOR ADVANCED LEARNERS/AP

Analyze Strategy Ask students to create a chronology of the steps Mr. Shiftlet takes to perpetrate his con and to add to the list as the story proceeds. Remind them to consider his actions, words, and subtle gestures and encourage them to evaluate each step for effectiveness. Students may organize the information on a timeline.

💼 BEST PRACTICES TOOLKIT—Transparency Timeline p. B23

The Interloper (1958), Billy Morrow Jackson. Collection of Mrs. Virginia Penofsky.

160   He had raised the hood and studied the mechanism and he said he could tell that the car had been built in the days when cars were really built. You take now, he said, one man puts in one bolt and another man puts in another bolt and another man puts in another bolt so that it's a man for a bolt. That's why you have to pay so much for a car: you're paying all those men. Now if you didn't have to pay but one man, you could get you a cheaper car and one that had had a personal interest taken in it, and it would be a better car. The old woman agreed with him that this was so.

   Mr. Shiftlet said that the trouble with the world was that nobody cared, or stopped and took any trouble. He said he never would have been able to teach

170 Lucynell to say a word if he hadn't cared and stopped long enough. **E**

   "Teach her to say something else," the old woman said.

   "What you want her to say next?" Mr. Shiftlet asked.

   The old woman's smile was broad and toothless and suggestive. "Teach her to say 'sugarpie,'" she said.

   Mr. Shiftlet already knew what was on her mind. **F**

   The next day he began to tinker with the automobile, and that evening he told her that if she would buy a fan belt, he would be able to make the car run.

   The old woman said she would give him the money. "You see that girl yonder?" she asked, pointing to Lucynell who was sitting on the floor a foot away, watching

E IRONY
A "1928 or '29 Ford" like this one would, in fact, have been made on an assembly line, a feature that greatly reduced the cost of automobiles. What does this knowledge, combined with Shiftlet's statements in lines 160–170, tell you about his character? Explain which type of irony O'Connor is using here.

F ANALYZE DETAILS
What are Mrs. Crater's **motives** for wanting Lucynell to learn to say "sugarpie"? What details in line 173 suggest this?

THE LIFE YOU SAVE MAY BE YOUR OWN   **1085**

In lines 200–221, use these prompts to help students understand Mrs. Crater's "business" (line 200):

Summarize How has Mr. Shiftlet changed the Craters' lives so far? *He has improved their farm, awakened understanding in Lucynell, and enlivened their nightly conversations.*

Analyze What qualities, in Mrs. Crater's opinion, would make Lucynell a good wife for Mr. Shiftlet? *Possible answer: Lucynell is "innocent" (line 201) in that she is too mentally impaired to have much will of her own. She would be entirely in her husband's control.*

Evaluate What do you think of Mrs. Crater's arguments for Lucynell? Whose interests does she have at heart? *Possible answer: Accept all thoughtful answers. Mrs. Crater may indeed think that Mr. Shiftlet would be a good husband to Lucynell and that she would suit him as a wife. However, it is more likely that Mrs. Crater sees Mr. Shiftlet as the best chance of free help for herself and her farm, and would say anything to convince Mr. Shiftlet.*

---

180 him, her eyes blue even in the dark. "If it was ever a man wanted to take her away, I would say, 'No man on earth is going to take that sweet girl of mine away from me!' but if he was to say, 'Lady, I don't want to take her away, I want her right here,' I would say, 'Mister, I don't blame you none. I wouldn't pass up a chance to live in a permanent place and get the sweetest girl in the world myself. You ain't no fool,' I would say."

"How old is she?" Mr. Shiftlet asked casually.

"Fifteen, sixteen," the old woman said. The girl was nearly thirty but because of her innocence it was impossible to guess.

"It would be a good idea to paint it too," Mr. Shiftlet remarked. "You don't
190 want it to rust out."

"We'll see about that later," the old woman said.

The next day he walked into town and returned with the parts he needed and a can of gasoline. Late in the afternoon, terrible noises issued from the shed and the old woman rushed out of the house, thinking Lucynell was somewhere having a fit. Lucynell was sitting on a chicken crate, stamping her feet and screaming, "Burrddttt! bddurrddtttt!" but her fuss was drowned out by the car. With a volley of blasts it emerged from the shed, moving in a fierce and stately way. Mr. Shiftlet was in the driver's seat, sitting very erect. He had an expression of serious modesty on his face as if he had just raised the dead.

200 That night, rocking on the porch, the old woman began her business at once. "You want you an innocent woman, don't you?" she asked sympathetically. "You don't want none of this trash."

"No'm, I don't," Mr. Shiftlet said.

"One that can't talk," she continued, "can't sass you back or use foul language. That's the kind for you to have. Right there," and she pointed to Lucynell sitting cross-legged in her chair, holding both feet in her hands.

"That's right," he admitted. "She wouldn't give me any trouble."

"Saturday," the old woman said, "you and her and me can drive into town and get married."

210 Mr. Shiftlet eased his position on the steps.

"I can't get married right now," he said. "Everything you want to do takes money and I ain't got any."

"What you need with money?" she asked.

"It takes money," he said. "Some people'll do anything anyhow these days, but the way I think, I wouldn't marry no woman that I couldn't take on a trip like she was somebody. I mean take her to a hotel and treat her. I wouldn't marry the Duchesser Windsor,"[3] he said firmly, "unless I could take her to a hotel and give her something good to eat.

"I was raised thataway and there ain't a thing I can do about it. My old mother
220 taught me how to do."

"Lucynell don't even know what a hotel is," the old woman muttered. "Listen here, Mr. Shiftlet," she said, sliding forward in her chair, "you'd be getting a

---

3. **Duchesser Windsor:** Duchess of Windsor. The title was given to the American divorcée Wallace Simpson upon her marriage to the former Edward VIII of England in 1937.

DIFFERENTIATED INSTRUCTION

FOR RELUCTANT READERS
Connect to Critical Questions Emphasize to students that many famous short stories and novels display a seedy side of human nature. Point out other short stories or novels that focus on seedy characters, such as Edgar Allan Poe's "The Cask of Amontillado." Then, discuss these questions: Why do so many writers focus on the immoral, even depraved, qualities of characters? Why are readers so interested in these types of stories?

FOR ADVANCED LEARNERS/AP
Evaluate Argument Ask students to add Mr. Shiftlet's explanation for needing money in lines 214–220 to their con chronologies and to discuss whether his argument is sound. Ask students to consider his appeal to his "old mother" (line 219) and Mrs. Crater's response to his argument.

permanent house and a deep well and the most innocent girl in the world. You don't need no money. Lemme tell you something: there ain't any place in the world for a poor disabled friendless drifting man."

The ugly words settled in Mr. Shiftlet's head like a group of buzzards in the top of a tree. He didn't answer at once. He rolled himself a cigarette and lit it and then he said in an even voice, "Lady, a man is divided into two parts, body and spirit."

The old woman clamped her gums together.

230 "A body and a spirit," he repeated. "The body, lady, is like a house: it don't go anywhere; but the spirit, lady, is like a automobile: always on the move, always . . ."

"Listen, Mr. Shiftlet," she said, "my well never goes dry and my house is always warm in the winter and there's no mortgage on a thing about this place. You can go to the courthouse and see for yourself. And yonder under that shed is a fine automobile." She laid the bait carefully. "You can have it painted by Saturday. I'll pay for the paint."

In the darkness, Mr. Shiftlet's smile stretched like a weary snake waking up by a fire. After a second he recalled himself and said, "I'm only saying a man's spirit means more to him than anything else. I would have to take my wife off for the week end 240 without no regards at all for cost. I got to follow where my spirit says to go."

"I'll give you fifteen dollars for a week end trip," the old woman said in a crabbed voice. "That's the best I can do."

"That wouldn't hardly pay for more than the gas and the hotel," he said. "It wouldn't feed her."

"Seventeen-fifty," the old woman said. "That's all I got so it isn't any use you trying to milk me. You can take a lunch."

Mr. Shiftlet was deeply hurt by the word "milk." He didn't doubt that she had more money sewed up in her mattress but he had already told her he was not interested in her money. "I'll make that do," he said and rose and walked off 250 without treating[4] with her further.

On Saturday the three of them drove into town in the car that the paint had barely dried on and Mr. Shiftlet and Lucynell were married in the Ordinary's[5] office while the old woman witnessed. As they came out of the courthouse, Mr. Shiftlet began twisting his neck in his collar. He looked morose and bitter as if he had been insulted while someone held him. "That didn't satisfy me none," he said. "That was just something a woman in an office did, nothing but paper work and blood tests. What do they know about my blood? If they was to take my heart and cut it out," he said, "they wouldn't know a thing about me. It didn't satisfy me at all."

"It satisfied the law," the old woman said sharply.

260 "The law," Mr. Shiftlet said and spit. "It's the law that don't satisfy me."

He had painted the car dark green with a yellow band around it just under the windows. The three of them climbed in the front seat and the old woman said, "Don't Lucynell look pretty? Looks like a baby doll." Lucynell was dressed up in a white dress that her mother had uprooted from a trunk and there was a Panama

---

4. **treating:** discussing terms; negotiating.
5. **Ordinary's:** judge's.

---

④ Targeted Passage

G ANALYZE DETAILS
At this point in the story, what **conclusions** can you draw about each character? Cite details in lines 178–250 that influenced your judgments.

Could you spot a
CON ARTIST?

Discuss Have students reread lines 153–161. Are Mrs. Crater's "ugly words" (line 226) in lines 224–225 a deception, or is she telling the truth? *Possible answer: Accept all thoughtful answers. Students may say that the words are a deception, employed to get Mr. Shiftlet to stay. Mrs. Crater cannot know for certain whether Mr. Shiftlet is "friendless" (line 225), for example. Other students may counter, however, that Mrs. Crater sees Mr. Shiftlet for what he is and offers him, out of both pity and mutual need, a solution.*

READING SKILL COMMON CORE RL 1

G ANALYZE DETAILS

Possible answer: Accept all thoughtful answers. Students may find Mrs. Crater sinister after she essentially sells her disabled daughter for a son-in-law to take care of the house. Her lies about the girl's age reveal her dishonesty, and her bargaining with Mr. Shiftlet reveals her stingy, calculating nature. Shiftlet is also callous and calculating, driven purely by self-interest.

IF STUDENTS NEED HELP . . . Refer them to the three-column chart they have been filling in as they read. Guide them to see how the details they have recorded gradually create a more complete picture of each character.

FOR STRUGGLING READERS

④ Targeted Passage [Lines 232–250]

This passage relates an important agreement at which Mrs. Crater and Mr. Shiftlet arrive.

• What is Mrs. Crater's opening offer? (lines 232–236)

• What else does Mr. Shiftlet want? Why? (lines 237–240)

• Why does Mr. Shiftlet agree to Mrs. Crater's terms yet walk away "deeply hurt" (line 247)? (lines 247–250)

FOR ENGLISH LANGUAGE LEARNERS

Vocabulary: Multiple-Meaning Words Make sure that students understand the different uses of the verb *treat* in this story: when Mr. Shiftlet says he wants to "treat" Lucynell at a hotel (line 216), he means that he wants to do something nice for her. When he refuses to "treat with" Mrs. Crater further on the matter of money (250), he means that he won't negotiate further. Remind students that *treat* can also be a noun meaning "a special pleasure."

FOR ADVANCED LEARNERS/AP

Compare and Contrast Have students explore the conflicting motives of Mrs. Crater and Mr. Shiftlet by completing a Comparison Matrix to answer these questions: What does each person value? What does each person consider unnecessary? What provides each person with a sense of well-being and security?

 **BEST PRACTICES TOOLKIT—Transparency** Comparison Matrix p. A24

In lines 268–299, use these prompts to help students understand Lucynell's role in the events:

Recall How did Lucynell react during the parting from her mother? *Possible answer: She is distanced from the events, just as the "baby doll" (line 263) her mother describes her as would be.*

Analyze What causes Mr. Shiftlet to become alternately happy and dejected as he drives? *Possible answer: He is happy when he thinks of the car, but unhappy when he looks at Lucynell, who—oblivious—is entirely absorbed in destroying her hat. Mr. Shiftlet is wondering if he has made a good deal.*

Evaluate Why does O'Connor have the counter boy describes Lucynell as an "angel of Gawd" (line 299), and what does Mr. Shiftlet's one-word retort tell readers about how he sees Lucynell? *Possible answer: Accept all thoughtful answers. O'Connor may imply that Lucynell is an innocent who requires the protection of God and of people around her; she may imply that Lucynell offers Mr. Shiftlet a chance at redemption if he cares for her. His reply, "Hitch-hiker" (line 300), implies that he can discard her on the side of the road without compunction.*

TEXT ANALYSIS

COMMON CORE

RL 6

Ⓗ IRONY

Possible answer: The name implies that the place is popular (or "hot"), but the Hot Spot is anything but hot. It is deserted except for the counter boy; Lucynell falls asleep on the counter.

---

hat on her head with a bunch of red wooden cherries on the brim. Every now and then her placid expression was changed by a sly isolated little thought like a shoot of green in the desert. "You got a prize!" the old woman said.

Mr. Shiftlet didn't even look at her.

They drove back to the house to let the old woman off and pick up the lunch.

270　When they were ready to leave, she stood staring in the window of the car, with her fingers clenched around the glass. Tears began to seep sideways out of her eyes and run along the dirty creases in her face. "I ain't ever been parted with her for two days before," she said.

Mr. Shiftlet started the motor.

"And I wouldn't let no man have her but you because I seen you would do right. Good bye, Sugarbaby," she said, clutching at the sleeve of the white dress. Lucynell looked straight at her and didn't seem to see her there at all. Mr. Shiftlet eased the car forward so that she had to move her hands.

The early afternoon was clear and open and surrounded by pale blue sky.

280　Although the car would go only thirty miles an hour, Mr. Shiftlet imagined a terrific climb and dip and swerve that went entirely to his head so that he forgot his morning bitterness. He had always wanted an automobile but he had never been able to afford one before. He drove very fast because he wanted to make Mobile[6] by nightfall.

Occasionally he stopped his thoughts long enough to look at Lucynell in the seat beside him. She had eaten the lunch as soon as they were out of the yard and now she was pulling the cherries off the hat one by one and throwing them out the window. He became depressed in spite of the car. He had driven about a hundred miles when he decided that she must be hungry again and at the next

290　small town they came to, he stopped in front of an aluminum-painted eating place called The Hot Spot and took her in and ordered her a plate of ham and grits. The ride had made her sleepy and as soon as she got up on the stool, she rested her head on the counter and shut her eyes. There was no one in The Hot Spot but Mr. Shiftlet and the boy behind the counter, a pale youth with a greasy rag hung over his shoulder. Before he could dish up the food, she was snoring gently. Ⓗ

"Give it to her when she wakes up," Mr. Shiftlet said. "I'll pay for it now."

The boy bent over her and stared at the long pink-gold hair and the half-shut sleeping eyes. Then he looked up and stared at Mr. Shiftlet. "She looks like an angel of Gawd," he murmured.

300　"Hitch-hiker," Mr. Shiftlet explained. "I can't wait. I got to make Tuscaloosa."[7]

The boy bent over again and very carefully touched his finger to a strand of the golden hair, and Mr. Shiftlet left.

He was more depressed than ever as he drove on by himself. The late afternoon had grown hot and sultry and the country had flattened out. Deep in the sky a storm was preparing very slowly and without thunder as if it meant to drain every drop of air from the earth before it broke. There were times when Mr. Shiftlet

Ⓢ Targeted Passage

Ⓗ IRONY
Consider what most people would expect from an establishment called The Hot Spot. What is ironic about this restaurant's name?

---

6. **Mobile:** a city in southwestern Alabama, along the Gulf Coast.

7. **Tuscaloosa:** a city in west-central Alabama.

DIFFERENTIATED INSTRUCTION

FOR STRUGGLING READERS

Ⓢ Targeted Passage [Lines 285–302]

This passage reveals Mr. Shiftlet's decision about his marriage to Lucynell.

- How does Lucynell behave as they drive? (lines 285–288)
- Why does Mr. Shiftlet stop at the Hot Spot? (lines 288–291)
- What relationship does Mr. Shiftlet claim to have with Lucynell? (line 300)

FOR ENGLISH LANGUAGE LEARNERS

Culture: Clarify When students reach line 300, explain that in the time that the story is set, few people had automobiles, and hitchhiking was not an unusual way to travel. Demonstrate, or have a student demonstrate, how a hitchhiker would thumb for a ride. Remind students that today, hitchhiking—or offering rides to hitchhikers, as Mr. Shiftlet does in the next scene—is not a safe thing to do.

FOR ADVANCED LEARNERS/AP

Interpret Figurative Language Read aloud, or have a student read aloud, the sentence that bridges lines 265–267. Ask students to discuss what this simile means. Have them consider the connotations of O'Connor's imagery and how those connotations add to the story's irony.

preferred not to be alone. He felt too that a man with a car had a responsibility to others, and he kept his eye out for a hitch-hiker. Occasionally he saw a sign that warned: "Drive carefully. The life you save may be your own." **❶**

310   The narrow road dropped off on either side into dry fields and here and there a shack or a filling station stood in a clearing. The sun began to set directly in front of the automobile. It was a reddening ball that through his windshield was slightly flat on the bottom and top. He saw a boy in overalls and a gray hat standing on the edge of the road and he slowed the car down and stopped in front of him. The boy didn't have his hand raised to thumb the ride, he was only standing there, but he had a small cardboard suitcase and his hat was set on his head in a way to indicate that he had left somewhere for good. "Son," Mr. Shiftlet said, "I see you want a ride."

The boy didn't say he did or he didn't but he opened the door of the car and 320   got in, and Mr. Shiftlet started driving again. The child held the suitcase on his lap and folded his arms on top of it. He turned his head and looked out the window away from Mr. Shiftlet. Mr. Shiftlet felt oppressed. "Son," he said after a minute, "I got the best old mother in the world so I reckon you only got the second best."

The boy gave him a quick dark glance and then turned his face back out the window.

"It's nothing so sweet," Mr. Shiftlet continued, "as a boy's mother. She taught him his first prayers at her knee, she give him love when no other would, she told him what was right and what wasn't, and she seen that he done the right thing. Son," he said, "I never rued a day in my life like the one I rued when I left that 330   old mother of mine."

The boy shifted in his seat but he didn't look at Mr. Shiftlet. He unfolded his arms and put one hand on the door handle.

"My mother was a angel of Gawd," Mr. Shiftlet said in a very strained voice. "He took her from heaven and giver to me and I left her." His eyes were instantly clouded over with a mist of tears. The car was barely moving.

The boy turned angrily in the seat. "You go to the devil!" he cried. "My old woman is a flea bag and yours is a stinking pole cat!" and with that he flung the door open and jumped out with his suitcase into the ditch.

Mr. Shiftlet was so shocked that for about a hundred feet he drove along slowly 340   with the door still open. A cloud, the exact color of the boy's hat and shaped like a turnip, had descended over the sun, and another, worse looking, crouched behind the car. Mr. Shiftlet felt that the rottenness of the world was about to engulf him. He raised his arm and let it fall again to his breast. "Oh Lord!" he prayed. "Break forth and wash the slime from this earth!"

The turnip continued slowly to descend. After a few minutes there was a guffawing peal of thunder from behind and fantastic raindrops, like tin-can tops, crashed over the rear of Mr. Shiftlet's car. Very quickly he stepped on the gas, and with his stump sticking out the window he raced the galloping shower into Mobile. ❧

---

❶ IRONY
What is the irony in Shiftlet's reasons for looking for a hitchhiker?

Language Coach

Word Definitions *Rued* (line 329) means "regretted" or "felt the consequences of." *Rue* is often used with *day*, as in lines 329–330. What does Mr. Shiftlet say he regrets?

TEXT ANALYSIS   COMMON CORE   RL 6

❶ IRONY

Possible answer: Mr. Shiftlet tells himself that now that he owns a car, he has a responsibility to help others. However, to get the car, he callously abandoned his mentally disabled and helpless wife—an entirely irresponsible thing to do.

REVISIT THE BIG QUESTION

Could you spot a CON ARTIST?

Discuss In lines 336–344, who is the intended victim of Mr. Shiftlet's deception in his prayer? *Possible answer: Accept all thoughtful answers. Students may say that the intended victim is the boy, but he escaped Mr. Shiftlet's deceptive moralizing by storming out of the car. Others may say that Mr. Shiftlet intends to deceive God in his prayer that "the slime" (line 344) of the earth be punished, though he himself is as morally "slimy" as a man can get.*

SELECTION WRAP-UP

READ WITH A PURPOSE Now that students have read the selection, ask them what causes Mr. Shiftlet, or any person, to behave selfishly, even when others are harmed. *Answers will vary. Students might say that Mr. Shiftlet, or any person, behaves selfishly to acquire what he thinks will make him happy.*

⭐ **CRITIQUE** Have students identify and analyze the dramatic irony that closes the story.

INDEPENDENT READING
    Students may also enjoy reading *Everything That Rises Must Converge* by Flannery O'Connor.

FOR STRUGGLING READERS

Comprehension Support Help students understand the conclusions that the sharp-eyed Mr. Shiftlet makes about the boy, so that they will better understand why he lectures about mothers. The boy's youth, his suitcase, and his attitude all hint that he is running away from home after an argument, and the "quick dark glance" he gives Mr. Shiftlet upon hearing the topic of mothers confirms Mr. Shiftlet's suspicions.

FOR ENGLISH LANGUAGE LEARNERS

Language Coach

Word Definitions: *Answer:* *He regrets having left his mother.* Have students write sentences about an event in their lives or in the news, containing this definition of the word *rue*. Ask volunteers to share their sentences with the class. Then, have partners use dictionaries to find another definition of the word *rue*.

Practice and Apply

For preliminary support of post-reading questions, use these copy masters:

R RESOURCE MANAGER—Copy Masters
Reading Check p. 337
Irony p. 333
Question Support p. 338
Additional selection questions are provided for teachers on page 327.

ANSWERS

COMMON CORE RL 1, RL 6

1. *mental impairment, deafness, poor eyesight, and inability to speak*

2. *She'll buy paint and pay Shiftlet $17.50 if he'll marry Lucynell and run the farm.*

3. *He intended to con Mrs. Crater and exploit Lucynell's disabilities to get the car.*

Possible answers:

4. ● **COMMON CORE FOCUS Analyze Descriptive** *Details Shiftlet's missing arm, "steel-trap jaw" (line 22), and crooked figure represent his fractured ethical sense and his desire to trap others. Details reveal Mrs. Crater's pride and greed; she acts "as if she were owner of the sun" (lines 30–31) and is "ravenous for a son-in-law" (line 149).*

5. ● **COMMON CORE FOCUS Irony** *O'Connor uses irony to suggest that people don't understand themselves or others, and yet they self-righteously persist in their beliefs.* **Situational irony:** *Mrs. Crater wouldn't trade Lucynell "for a casket of jewels" (lines 123–124) but pays Shiftlet to marry her.* **Dramatic irony:** *Shiftlet complains about the rotten world; readers know that he is rotten.*

Assess and Reteach

Assess

DIAGNOSTIC AND SELECTION TESTS
Selection Test A pp. 293–294
Selection Test B/C pp. 295–296

Interactive Selection Test on <u>thinkcentral.com</u>

Reteach

Level Up Online Tutorials on <u>thinkcentral.com</u>

Reteaching Worksheets on <u>thinkcentral.com</u>

Literature Lesson 36: Irony

After Reading

Comprehension

1. **Recall** What are Lucynell's disabilities?

2. **Summarize** What is the bargain struck between Mr. Shiftlet and Mrs. Crater over her daughter, Lucynell?

3. **Clarify** What does Mr. Shiftlet's treatment of Lucynell at the end reveal about his intentions all along?

Text Analysis

● 4. **Analyze Descriptive Details** Review the chart you created as you read. Because Mr. Shiftlet and Mrs. Crater are both hiding something during much of the story, readers must mine the details given about each character for clues to their true selves. Since Mr. Shiftlet's words and thoughts can't be trusted, what can you learn about him from the descriptions of his physical appearance? What details reveal the flaws in Mrs. Crater's character and give her motives away? Support your analysis with evidence from the text.

● 5. **Interpret Irony** In this story, much of O'Connor's wry humor comes from **situational** and **dramatic irony.** Review the story to find at least two examples of each kind of irony. Also, see whether you can find one example that reveals both kinds at once. What do these multiple ironies suggest about O'Connor's view of her fellow human beings?

6. **Make Judgments** What is the significance of the story's title, taken from a road sign? Explain how you think O'Connor judges Tom T. Shiftlet, as well as how you yourself do. Be sure to address the following:

   • the way in which Mr. Shiftlet is a potential savior of his own life and the lives of others

   • how and why he fails in this role

   • whether you think he has any redeeming features or whether you see him as hopelessly lost

Text Criticism

7. **Author's Style** For Flannery O'Connor, a devout Catholic, evidence of divine grace was everywhere, and her stories are full of religious **imagery.** Find at least two examples of religious imagery in this story and explain what they contribute to its meaning and its message.

Could you spot a **CON ARTIST?**

Mr. Shiftlet's motivation for swindling is Mrs. Crater's car. What are some other reasons con artists deceive people? Do you have any sympathy for their motivations? Why or why not?

COMMON CORE

RL 1 Cite textual evidence to support analysis of what the text says explicitly as well as inferences drawn from the text, including determining where the text leaves matters uncertain. **RL 6** Analyze a case in which grasping point of view requires distinguishing what is directly stated in a text from what is really meant.

---

6. *Students may say Shiftlet could have saved his life by honest work, or that by stealing the car he saved himself from the Craters. Deserting Lucynell makes him seem hopelessly lost, yet guilt may redeem him one day.*

7. *Students may note Shiftlet's posture, which forms the shape of "a crooked cross" (line 29) and his occupation as a carpenter; he could have saved the farm and the Craters. Lucynell's description as an "angel of Gawd" (line 299) suggests that she is an ironic messenger of Shiftlet's possible redemption.*

Could you spot a **CON ARTIST?**
Possible answer: Students may say con artists are motivated by greed, love of attention, or the thrill of hoodwinking others. Most will not have sympathy for con artists.

The Essence of a Short Story

Stories by modernist writers, such as Fitzgerald, Hemingway, and Faulkner, are often complex or ambiguous. These works demand much of readers, who must pay attention to details of character, setting, plot, dialogue, and language in order to decipher meaning.

Writing to Evaluate

After reflecting on each of the short stories you have just read, choose two stories and evaluate them in order to distill their essence—that which is utterly indispensable—in no more than 300 of the author's own words. You may use portions of sentences and combine them, if appropriate and necessary. In addition, you may create your own paragraphing structure in order to give your distillations a desirable "flow."

Consider

- introductions or important descriptions of characters
- plot events essential to the stories, especially the climax
- details that introduce the stories' topic, or subject
- dialogue that reveals character, motivation, or theme
- particularly meaningful language

Extension

VIEWING & REPRESENTING

Working with a partner, **choose or create an image** that you feel captures the essence of the story you evaluated. You may look for an image from a magazine, Web site, book of art, or other source, or you may create your own. Share your image with the class, and explain why you feel it represents or illustrates the story's essence.

COMMON CORE

RL 9 Demonstrate knowledge of early-twentieth-century foundational works of American literature, including how two or more texts from the same period treat similar themes or topics.

Ernest Hemingway, working as a war correspondent, 1944

1091

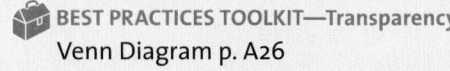

Teach

COMMON CORE FOCUS

RI 5 Analyze and evaluate the effectiveness of the structure an author uses in his or her exposition or argument, including whether the structure makes points clear, convincing, and engaging. **RI 6** Determine an author's point of view or purpose in a text in which the rhetoric is particularly effective, analyzing how style and content contribute to the power, persuasiveness, or beauty of the text.

The Fine Art of Journalism

Journalism and Literature Discuss the key distinctions between the two kinds of writing. Then have students use Two-Column Charts to classify these examples as journalism or literature, and ask volunteers to explain their answers:

- Today, an earthquake shook parts of Asia. (*journalism*)

- Her brunette hair hung in question marks around her face. (*literature*)

- The jury reported a guilty verdict in the case of Jones versus the state of Wyoming. (*journalism*)

- "Why are you smiling at me?" he questioned, his eyes sparkling with mischief. (*literature*)

- The green tapestry of vines hung from the tree branches. (*literature*)

 BEST PRACTICES TOOLKIT—Transparency
Two-Column Chart p. A25

Journalism

Some journalists put together a news story or an opinion piece that is so well written and riveting that the article is elevated to the realm of literature. Have you ever read a news report or editorial that seemed to stand out from anything else you'd read in the newspaper? If so, you may have read an emerging literary classic.

COMMON CORE

Included in this workshop:
RI 5 Analyze and evaluate the effectiveness of the structure an author uses in his or her exposition or argument, including whether the structure makes points clear, convincing, and engaging. **RI 6** Determine an author's point of view or purpose in a text in which the rhetoric is particularly effective, analyzing how style and content contribute to the power, persuasiveness, or beauty of the text.

The Fine Art of Journalism

Traditionally, journalism and literature are considered to be very different forms. **Journalism** is known for being factual, informative, and written for the moment. **Literature,** on the other hand, is built from the imagination and meant to last. Its language is often figurative, its images are symbolic, and the setting and characters are representative of deeper meaning. When journalism becomes literature, it's not the imaginative use of facts that makes it so; rather, it's the imaginative use of language that transforms it from a standard news story into a piece of art.

Journalistic writing includes news reports, essays, editorials, feature articles, and critical reviews and has a long history in the United States. Many of the big issues of the day, since pre-Revolutionary times, have been debated in newspapers, magazines, and pamphlets. In the early 20th century, a number of serious literary writers began their writing careers as journalists, including Ernest Hemingway, E. B. White, and Dorothy Parker. The tradition of journalism as literature continued with writers such as Truman Capote, Tom Wolfe, and Joan Didion. In the 1960s, Wolfe coined the term "New Journalism" to describe the work of a journalist who sets out to create journalistic writing that uses literary techniques.

Tools of the Trade

Journalism that transcends the mundane and becomes literature is usually characterized by the use of certain literary techniques.

- **Imagery**—Traditionally, news writing contains only essential details, without any embellishment of description. In literary writing, the writer includes words and phrases that express sensory experiences in order to create a vivid picture or strong impression for the reader.

DIFFERENTIATED INSTRUCTION

FOR STRUGGLING READERS

Note Taking For students who are unfamiliar with journalism as literature or need help with note taking, hand out the copy master before discussing the spread. Explain that students will review many terms relating to literature and journalism in this workshop. Discuss the major terms on this spread (*imagery, narrative elements, style, voice, tone*) as students record notes on the copy masters.

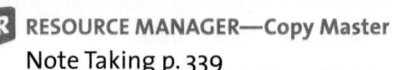 RESOURCE MANAGER—Copy Master
Note Taking p. 339

- **Narrative elements**—In the world of journalism, an article is figuratively called "a story." At times, this might be literally true, especially when a journalist relates an incident with all the elements of a good tale, including a suspenseful plot, detailed characterization and setting, and a well-defined point of view.

- **Style and voice**—Style is a writer's unique way of communicating ideas, and voice is the expression of his or her personality. Most news writing is made up of spare, plain prose, written for a mass audience. In literary writing, the writer may use figurative language, coin new words, or interject descriptive phrases. Each of these elements can add up to an original style and voice.

- **Writer's tone**—News reporters historically have tried to maintain an objective, unbiased tone in their writing. However, writers such as Hemingway and Jack London often used the tone of their writing to advance a particular cause and to convey a very personal perspective. They wrote personal narratives of news events, including war experiences and unusual adventures, in which they interjected their own observations and opinions.

In the following passage from "A New Kind of War" (page 1096), notice how Hemingway included his observations instead of merely reporting the facts.

> In the war that I had known, men often lied about the manner of their wounding. Not at first; but later. I'd lied a little myself in my time. Especially late in the evening.
>
> **—Ernest Hemingway, "A New Kind of War"**

Close Read

What does Hemingway reveal about himself in this passage? Why wouldn't this be typical of journalism, which is known for being factual?

Dorothy Parker was always known for her acerbic wit. In the following excerpt from a literary review, notice the imagery and figurative language she uses in exaggerating the critics' reactions to Hemingway's first novel.

> Promptly upon its publication, Ernest Hemingway was discovered, the Stars and Stripes were reverentially raised over him, eight hundred and forty-seven book reviewers formed themselves into the word "welcome," and the band played "Hail to the Chief" in three concurrent keys.
>
> **—Dorothy Parker, "A Book of Great Short Stories"**

Close Read

In each of these examples, the writer's voice is well developed. How would you describe the personality of the writer in each?

Tools of the Trade

Literary Techniques Clarify these terms listed on pages 1092–1093:

- **Imagery** Tell students that imagery allows readers to use their senses to experience what the writer is describing. Ask students to give examples of sensory details. *Students should name details appealing to senses of sight, smell, touch, taste, or hearing.*

- **Narrative elements** Explain that narrative elements also involve readers in the plights of real-life characters. Ask students in what ways including real-life characters might affect readers. ***Possible answer:*** *Including real-life characters would probably draw readers into a news story.*

- **Style and voice** Tell students that a writer's word choice contributes to style and voice. Ask students to discuss the differences between these two sentences:
  - Over five hundred homes were destroyed by the hurricane.
  - The hurricane whipped through the community, destroying more than five hundred homes in its jagged path.

- **Writer's tone** To identify a writer's tone, tell students to ask themselves these questions: What is the writer's opinion of these people or events, and why? What is the writer's connection to these people or events?

Close Read

Possible answer: *Hemingway reveals that he does not always tell the truth. This admission is unusual for a journalist who is expected to report the truth. It is also unusual to include the journalist in the story.*

Close Read

Possible answer: *Hemingway is nostalgic and humorous. Parker is critical or sarcastic.*

FOR ENGLISH LANGUAGE LEARNERS

Culture: Clarify On the board, list these terms from the Hemingway and Parker excerpts. Share the explanations with students.

- *late in the evening*: time of day when people are prone to exaggerating stories for glorification or entertainment
- *Stars and Stripes*: the American flag
- *Hail to the Chief*: American patriotic song that plays when the president arrives at any official public occasion

FOR ADVANCED LEARNERS/AP

Compare Writers' Style, Voice, and Tone Have students further research the works of Hemingway and Parker, focusing on the style, voice, and tone of their journalistic writings. With that research, have students create cartoon strips or storyboards that feature the two writers in conversation. Tell students to use factually accurate information to recreate the style, voice, and tone of each writer.

BEST PRACTICES TOOLKIT—Transparency
Storyboard p. C11

Focus and Motivate

COMMON CORE FOCUS

RI 1 Cite textual evidence to support analysis of what the text says explicitly as well as inferences drawn from the text, including determining where the text leaves matters uncertain. **RI 6** Determine an author's point of view or purpose in a text in which the rhetoric is particularly effective, analyzing how style and content contribute to the power, persuasiveness, or beauty of the text. **RI 10** Read and comprehend literary nonfiction. **W 3a, e** Engage and orient the reader by setting out a situation and establishing one or multiple point(s) of view; create a smooth progression of experiences or events; provide a conclusion that follows from and reflects on what is experienced, observed, or resolved over the course of the narrative. **L 3** Apply knowledge of language to understand how language functions in different contexts. **L 5b** Analyze nuances in the meaning of words with similar denotations.

ABOUT THE AUTHOR

Ask students how Hemingway's reporting of war's impact on ordinary people may have affected readers' views and attitudes. ***Possible answer:*** *His reporting probably led to a more intimate understanding of war and greater horror over war's damaging effects.*

NOTABLE QUOTE

"Never think that war, no matter how necessary, nor how justified, is not a crime."
—Ernest Hemingway

Selection Resources

COMMON CORE

RI 1 Cite textual evidence to support analysis of what the text says explicitly as well as inferences drawn from the text, including determining where the text leaves matters uncertain.
RI 6 Determine an author's point of view or purpose in a text in which the rhetoric is particularly effective, analyzing how style and content contribute to the power, persuasiveness, or beauty of the text. **RI 10** Read and comprehend literary nonfiction. **L 5b** Analyze nuances in the meaning of words with similar denotations.

DID YOU KNOW?

Ernest Hemingway . . .

- began a romance in Spain with fellow war reporter Martha Gellhorn, who became his third wife.
- hunted Nazi submarines off the coast of Cuba in his private fishing boat.

(background)
Hemingway, center, among other correspondents covering the Spanish Civil War

1094

Journalism as Literature

A New Kind of War

Video link at **thinkcentral.com**

News Dispatch by Ernest Hemingway

Essential Course of Study **ECOS**

Meet the Author

Ernest Hemingway 1899–1961

Ernest Hemingway never considered his journalism as important as his fiction, but his journalism was admired anyway, particularly his war correspondence. Before he published his first stories and novels in the 1920s, he reported on European affairs for the *Toronto Star*. He covered the Greco-Turkish War of 1922, describing 20 miles of Greek refugees trudging through the rain. He also interviewed the fascist Italian dictator Benito Mussolini, calling him the "biggest bluff in Europe."

Taking Sides in Spain By the 1930s, Hemingway had become a famous literary figure. He returned to war reporting in 1937 after civil war broke out in Spain, the country that he loved. Hemingway is perhaps most identified with this conflict, in which the right-wing army of General Francisco Franco (the Nationalists) fought against supporters of the left-wing elected government of Spain (the Loyalists or Republicans). This war was widely seen as a struggle against fascism, or dictatorial government. Many world writers, including Hemingway, were sympathetic to the Loyalist side. These writers were greatly disheartened by Franco's eventual victory in 1939.

Celebrity Journalist Hemingway covered the war for the North American Newspaper Alliance (NANA), receiving the highest fee ever paid a war correspondent. His NANA dispatches have been called "a new style of reporting that told the public about every facet of the war, especially . . . its effects on the common man, woman, and child." One of these dispatches, "A New Kind of War," is considered classic.

Writer or Fighter? After World War II broke out, Hemingway once again became a war reporter, this time for *Collier's* magazine. He memorably described the D-day landing at Normandy, the liberation of Paris, and the Allied movement into Germany in 1944. His command of a French guerrilla band and his storage of weapons in his hotel room led him to be investigated for violating the Geneva Convention, which forbids journalists to take up arms. He was cleared of misconduct and later awarded a Bronze Star for his service as a war correspondent.

See also the biography on page 1008, which covers Hemingway's entire career.

Author Online

THINK central

Go to **thinkcentral.com**. KEYWORD: HML11-1094

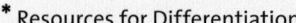

TEXT ANALYSIS: SUBJECTIVITY IN REPORTING

News reporters are trained to be **objective,** presenting facts without the intrusion of their own personal feelings or opinions. You will notice, however, that Hemingway does not strive for this ideal in his reporting on the Spanish Civil War. His writing is quite **subjective,** expressing his personal reactions to what he sees. He wants his readers to be in Madrid with him, experiencing exactly what he does. Toward this end he uses both the **second-person point of view** ("as you lie in bed, you hear the firing in the front line") and the **first-person point of view** ("I did not believe a word of it").

As you read, notice ways in which Hemingway reveals his purpose through personal feelings and opinions. Consider what his subjectivity offers that an objective news report could not.

Review: **Dialogue**

READING SKILL: ANALYZE DESCRIPTIVE DETAILS

Hemingway makes powerful use of descriptive details. Many of these are **sensory details,** which appeal to the senses of sight, hearing, touch, smell, and taste. Notice the visual details in the following passage. What can you conclude from them?

On the corner, twenty yards away, is a heap of rubble, smashed cement and thrown up dirt, a single dead man, his torn clothes dusty, and a great hole in the sidewalk from which the gas from a broken main is rising. . . .

Other descriptive details are not sensory, but they still convey important ideas. What might it mean, for example, that the large rooms at the front of Hemingway's hotel only cost a dollar a day? As you read, jot down descriptive details about

• Madrid and the hotel

• Raven, the wounded soldier Hemingway meets

• Raven's commander, Jock Cunningham

React to these details and make inferences from them.

 Complete the activities in your **Reader/Writer Notebook.**

What can we learn from WAR?

The Spanish Civil War did not have immediate consequences for most Americans, yet American newspapers thought it was important enough to cover. Consider our own times. Why do newspapers and broadcast networks send reporters to cover fighting in foreign countries? What do these reports usually show or tell an audience about war?

DISCUSS Think about war coverage you have read, seen on television, or heard on the radio. Working in a small group, list types of information you would expect to be included in such reporting—the number of people killed in an attack, for example. After completing your list, discuss insights about war that you have gained from journalists.

 1095

What can we learn from WAR?

Ask the question, and then have students read the paragraph that follows it. Invite feedback on why reporters are sent to cover war and what their reports convey. Urge students to share their ideas in the *DISCUSS* activity. Invite volunteers to share their lists and insights.

TEXT ANALYSIS
COMMON CORE
RI 6

● *Model the Skill:* **SUBJECTIVITY IN REPORTING**

Help students recognize the effects of subjectivity in reporting by highlighting the use of first-person and second-person pronouns in the excerpt text. Describe specific ways that each approach affects a text's subjectivity. Point out that first-person point of view adds subjectivity by sharing the writer's feelings and thoughts. Then emphasize that second-person point of view creates subjectivity by inviting readers into a subjective experience.

GUIDED PRACTICE Have students write and contrast sentences in first-person and second-person points of view.

READING SKILL
COMMON CORE
RI 1

■ *Model the Skill:* **ANALYZE DESCRIPTIVE DETAILS**

To analyze Hemingway's use of descriptive details, read aloud the excerpt on this page. Discuss with students the reaction Hemingway wants to evoke from readers. Point out that the quote uses vivid sensory details about the objects in the rubble and the surrounding destruction. Also relay that Hemingway may want to shock readers by reducing the dead man to an item in a pile.

GUIDED PRACTICE Have students analyze the descriptive details in the first paragraph on page 1096.

R RESOURCE MANAGER—Copy Master
Analyze Descriptive Details p. 353 (for student use while reading the selection)

DIFFERENTIATED INSTRUCTION

FOR ENGLISH LANGUAGE LEARNERS

Reading: Preview Have students preview the news dispatch by reading the background notes on pages 1096 and 1097, looking at the photographs, and reading the questions in the side column. Have students list questions that the previewing process raised for them. Then, have students set a purpose for reading, based upon their questions.

FOR STRUGGLING READERS

Concept Support: Analyze Descriptive Details To help students analyze descriptive details, point out the strategy suggested on this page. Tell students to formulate a question for each detail they note. Suggest these question ideas:

• What might this detail mean?

• Why does the writer include this detail?

• Why is this detail important?

SUMMARY

This news dispatch begins with Hemingway lying in a hotel bed in Madrid, Spain, during the Spanish Civil War. Rifles and machine guns sound outside the open window and explosions awaken him. He goes downstairs to find destruction and death. Thankful for life, he eats breakfast and chats with other survivors. Hemingway then visits Raven, a badly wounded soldier, but doubts his graphic battle stories. When Hemingway meets Raven's commanding officer, who confirms the battle accounts, Hemingway is left to marvel over this "strange new war" in which ordinary people are so destroyed.

READ WITH A PURPOSE

Help students set a purpose for reading. Tell them to read to discover Ernest Hemingway's attitude toward war.

REVISIT THE BIG QUESTION

What can we learn from
WAR?

Discuss Which details of the description in lines 1–9 fit your expectation of war? Which details surprised you? *Students may say they expect the destruction, but not its proximity to people doing ordinary tasks such as lying in bed, falling asleep.*

TEXT ANALYSIS

COMMON CORE
RI 6

Ⓐ SUBJECTIVITY IN REPORTING

Possible answer: *Hemingway hears rifle and machine gun fire through the open window of his hotel room (lines 1–5). He is grateful to be safe in bed rather than part of the violence. His feet are warming the cold foot of the bed, and he hears singing and arguing in the street before he falls asleep (lines 6–9). The details of his comfort and of citizens enjoying themselves in the street provide a sharp contrast with the sounds of warfare.*

A New Kind of War

Ernest Hemingway

> **BACKGROUND** Hemingway and other journalists covering the Spanish Civil War stayed at the Hotel Florida in Madrid, the Spanish capital, which was under siege by General Franco's Nationalist forces. Franco was aided by the fascist governments of Italy and Nazi Germany, which sent troops and weapons. The Loyalist forces of the Spanish government were aided by the Soviet Union and volunteer International Brigades from across Europe and the United States. The soldiers that Hemingway profiles in this article were part of the International Brigades.

NANA Dispatch · APRIL 14, 1937

MADRID—The window of the hotel is open and, as you lie in bed, you hear the firing in the front line seventeen blocks away. There is a rifle fire all night long. The rifles go tacrong, capong, craang, tacrong, and then a machine gun opens up. It has a bigger calibre and is much louder, rong, cararong, rong, rong. Then there is the incoming boom of a trench mortar shell and a burst of machine gun fire. You lie and listen to it and it is a great thing to be in bed with your feet stretched out gradually warming the cold foot of the bed and not out there in University City or Carabanchel.[1] A man is singing hard-voiced in the street below and three drunks are arguing when you fall asleep. Ⓐ

10   In the morning, before your call comes from the desk, the roaring burst of a high explosive shell wakes you and you go to the window and look out to see a man, his head down, his coat collar up, sprinting desperately across the paved

---

1. **University City or Carabanchel** (kär′-ə-bän-chel′): scenes of bloody battles in or on the outskirts of Madrid.

Analyze Visuals ▶
Examine the composition, or arrangement, of shapes in the photograph on the opposite page. What does the angle of the photo contribute to its impact? Explain.

Ⓐ **SUBJECTIVITY IN REPORTING**
What are Hemingway's thoughts and sensations in the first paragraph? In a report on war, why might he include details of his hotel room and the sound of a voice singing in the street?

DIFFERENTIATED INSTRUCTION

FOR ADVANCED LEARNERS/AP

Expert Groups Have students research one of these topics:

- North American Newspaper Alliance
- Spanish Civil War
- General Francisco Franco
- fascism in 1930s Europe

Have groups write a short report about their topic and hand out copies to the class. Then have students create and distribute a short multiple-choice test about their topic.

FOR STRUGGLING READERS

In combination with the *Audio Anthology CD,* use one or more Targeted Passages (pp. 1096, 1098, 1100, 1101) to ensure that students focus on key events and concepts. Targeted Passages are also good for English language learners.

① **Targeted Passage** [Lines 1–12]

This passage introduces Hemingway as the narrator and describes the setting in war-torn Madrid.

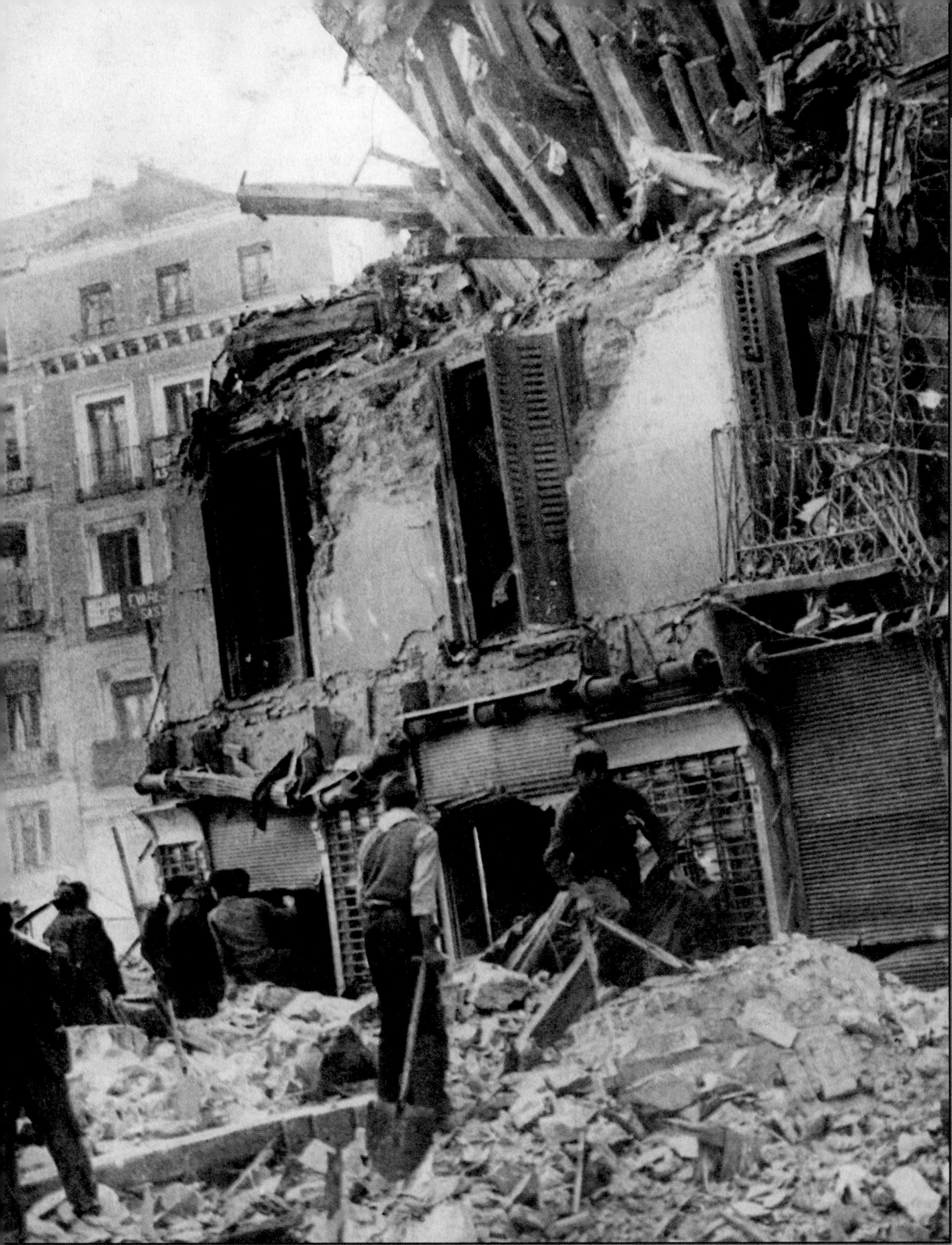

Reading Support

THINK central

This selection on **thinkcentral.com** includes embedded **ThinkAloud** models–students "thinking aloud" about the story to model the kinds of questions a good reader would ask about a selection.

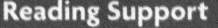

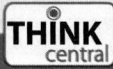

Analyze Visuals

Possible answer: *Judging from the photograph, Madrid appears to be a war zone. The city has been bombed, resulting in fallen buildings and rubble that the people must factor into their daily comings and goings. Being in Madrid was probably terrifying as well as difficult due to housing shortages and interrupted services. The crooked angle of the photograph is a literal representation of how the war has shaken the city.*

BACKGROUND

International Brigade By the 1930s, fascism was spreading throughout Europe. Fascist dictators Benito Mussolini and Adolph Hitler had assumed control of the governments of Italy and Germany respectively. In 1936, General Francisco Franco began the Spanish Civil War when he led Nationalist forces that ultimately overthrew the democratic republic of Spain in favor of a fascist style government. The spread of fascism in Spain alarmed people throughout the world. Despite their varying backgrounds and beliefs, some of these people joined the International Brigades and united in Spain to fight fascism. During the course of the war, the brigades made significant contributions to almost every important military campaign.

- Where is Hemingway? (line 1)
- What is happening outside his window? (lines 1–5)
- What are his thoughts about where he is? (lines 6–8)
- What does he see out the window? (lines 11–12)

Develop Reading Fluency Read aloud the first paragraph of the selection. Point out to students how you used intonation and expression to show the urgency and danger of Hemingway's situation. Also, point out how you placed emphasis on words that displayed onomatopoeia, such as *tacrong, capong, craang* (line 3). Explain to students that placing emphasis on these words allows listeners to imagine what Hemingway heard while he was in his hotel room. Have partners practice reading the first paragraph aloud.

B DESCRIPTIVE DETAILS

Possible answer: The accumulation of sensory details floods over the reader evoking a mood of terror and chaos. Hemingway's purpose in using this wealth of detail is to pull the reader directly into the story.

C GRAMMAR AND STYLE

COMMON CORE L 3

Choose Effective Point of View Tell students that second-person point of view is unusual. Emphasize that this rarity, and the view's awkwardness, demand readers' attention. Ask students to consider why Hemingway chooses to jar readers with this literary technique. *Possible answer:* Hemingway may think that the only way to truly convey war's horror is to pull readers in and shock them with graphic details.

TEXT ANALYSIS

COMMON CORE RI 6

D SUBJECTIVITY IN REPORTING

Possible answer: Hemingway includes the joke and his own conclusion to show survivors' reactions to what they see as a close brush with death. This explains why Hemingway continues to rent the nicer, but more dangerous, hotel rooms. Having escaped death, he and others choose to feel invincible.

TEXT ANALYSIS

COMMON CORE RI 6

E SUBJECTIVITY IN REPORTING

Possible answer: Hemingway feels a connection to the Italian dead, he is contemptuous of the chauffeur, and he appreciates his beautiful, comfortable hotel room.

---

square. There is the acrid smell of high explosive you hoped you'd never smell again, and, in a bathrobe and bedroom slippers, you hurry down the marble stairs and almost into a middle-aged woman, wounded in the abdomen, who is being helped into the hotel entrance by two men in blue workmen's smocks. She has her two hands crossed below her big, old-style Spanish bosom and from between her fingers the blood is spurting in a thin stream. On the corner, twenty yards away, is a heap of rubble, smashed cement and thrown up dirt, a single dead man, his torn
20 clothes dusty, and a great hole in the sidewalk from which the gas from a broken main is rising, looking like a heat mirage in the cold morning air. **B**

"How many dead?" you ask a policeman.

"Only one," he says. "It went through the sidewalk and burst below. If it would have burst on the solid stone of the road there might have been fifty."

A policeman covers the top of the trunk, from which the head is missing; they send for someone to repair the gas main and you go in to breakfast. A charwoman,[2] her eyes red, is scrubbing the blood off the marble floor of the corridor. The dead man wasn't you nor anyone you know and everyone is very hungry in the morning after a cold night and a long day the day before up at the
30 Guadalajara[3] front. **C**

"Did you see him?" asked someone else at breakfast.

"Sure," you say.

"That's where we pass a dozen times a day. Right on that corner." Someone makes a joke about missing teeth and someone else says not to make that joke. And everyone has the feeling that characterizes war. It wasn't me, see? It wasn't me. **D**

The Italian dead up on the Guadalajara front weren't you, although Italian dead, because of where you had spent your boyhood, always seemed, still, like our dead.[4] No. You went to the front early in the morning in a miserable little car with a more miserable little chauffeur who suffered visibly the closer he came to the
40 fighting. But at night, sometimes late, without lights, with the big trucks roaring past, you came on back to sleep in a bed with sheets in a good hotel, paying a dollar a day for the best rooms on the front. The smaller rooms in the back, on the side away from the shelling, were considerably more expensive. After the shell that lit on the sidewalk in front of the hotel you got a beautiful double corner room on that side, twice the size of the one you had had, for less than a dollar. It wasn't me they killed. See? No. Not me. It wasn't me anymore. **E**

Then, in a hospital given by the American Friends of Spanish Democracy, located out behind the Morata front along the road to Valencia,[5] they said, "Raven wants to see you."
50 "Do I know him?"

"I don't think so," they said, "but he wants to see you."

---

2. **charwoman:** a woman employed to clean houses or offices.

3. **Guadalajara:** a city in Spain to the northeast of Madrid, strategically important because of its nearness to the capital. Battle had raged there through most of March 1937, with the Loyalists finally winning.

4. **Italian dead ... our dead:** Italian forces fought on the side of the Nationalists; however, Hemingway had spent a long time in an Italian hospital as a young man during World War I.

5. **Morata ... Valencia:** Morata de Tejuña, a small town southeast of Madrid, was heavily damaged at this time. Valencia is on the eastern coast of Spain, about 240 miles southeast of Madrid.

B DESCRIPTIVE DETAILS Notice the accumulation of **sensory details** in lines 10–21. What effect do they have on you as a reader? What purpose might they serve for the writer?

 **Targeted Passage**

C GRAMMAR AND STYLE Reread lines 28–30. Notice how the use of the **second-person pronoun** *you* places the reader in Hemingway's shoes.

D SUBJECTIVITY IN REPORTING In the aftermath of a civilian casualty, Hemingway includes a joke made by survivors and his own highly personal conclusion about what the survivors are thinking. What purpose do you think it serves to include this material? Explain your answer.

E SUBJECTIVITY IN REPORTING Reread lines 36–46. What is Hemingway's **tone** here—his attitude toward the Italian dead? his chauffeur? his hotel room? Cite evidence from this paragraph to support your response.

DIFFERENTIATED INSTRUCTION

FOR STRUGGLING READERS

 Targeted Passage [Lines 22–30]

This passage illustrates the ways in which people both participate in the war and detach themselves from it.

- What are the effects of the explosion? (lines 22–24)

- Describe how each of these people respond to the scene: the policeman, the charwoman, and the narrator. (lines 25–30)

FOR ENGLISH LANGUAGE LEARNERS

Vocabulary: Multiple-Meaning Words

Explain that the word *trunk* in line 25 is a multiple-meaning word. Help students use context clues, such as that the "head is missing," to determine the correct meaning. In this case, trunk means "torso" or "body" rather than "main stem of a tree," "chest," or "rear storage compartment of an automobile." The policeman covers the decapitated body.

"Where is he?"

"Upstairs."

In the room upstairs they are giving a blood transfusion to a man with a very gray face who lay on a cot with his arm out, looking away from the gurgling bottle and moaning in a very impersonal way. He moaned mechanically and at regular intervals and it did not seem to be him that made the sound. His lips did not move.

"Where's Raven?" I asked.

60 "I'm here," said Raven.

The voice came from a high mound covered by a shoddy gray blanket. There were two arms crossed on the top of the mound and at one end there was something that had been a face, but now was a yellow scabby area with a wide bandage cross where the eyes had been.

"Who is it?" asked Raven. He didn't have lips, but he talked pretty well without them and with a pleasant voice.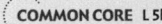

"Hemingway," I said. "I came up to see how you were doing."

"My face was pretty bad," he said. "It got sort of burned from the grenade, but it's peeled a couple of times and it's doing better."

70 "It looks swell," I said. "It's doing fine."

I wasn't looking at it when I spoke.

"How are things in America?" he asked. "What do they think of us over there?"

"Sentiment's changed a lot," I said. "They're beginning to realize the government is going to win this war."

Members of the International Brigades near Madrid in late 1936

COMMON CORE L 5b

Language Coach

Synonyms A **synonym** is a word with a meaning similar to that of another word. *Impersonal* and *mechanical* are synonyms meaning "not influenced by emotion or personality." What picture do "moaning in a very impersonal way" and "moaned mechanically" in line 56 create?

F DESCRIPTIVE DETAILS Reread lines 54–66. Describe the emotional impact of the details in these lines. What purpose do you think it serves for Hemingway to include this description? Explain your response.

TIERED DISCUSSION PROMPTS

In lines 33–46, use these prompts to help students understand the narrator's emotional reaction:

Connect Have you ever heard of someone making a joke or laughing during a time of sadness or tragedy? Why do you think the person did that? *Accept all thoughtful responses.*

Analyze What emotions does the narrator feel in response to the death and destruction around him? *Possible answer: He feels relief and even jubilation that others are dead while he has escaped.*

Evaluate Are the narrator's responses reasonable? Are they necessary? Explain. *Students may say that the narrator's responses are understandable and natural, but still upsetting. They may say that such responses are necessary to survive violence.*

READING SKILL   COMMON CORE RI 1

F Model the Skill: DESCRIPTIVE DETAILS

Read aloud lines 55–66. Then ask: What details relate to the senses of sight and sound? *(gurgling bottle, shoddy gray blankey, yellow scabby area, wide bandage, no lips, pleasant voice)*

Point out that Hemingway's descriptions assault the senses and create a contrast among them.

Possible answer: Hemingway wants to shock readers and to show that in war people may be terribly injured without being killed.

FOR ENGLISH LANGUAGE LEARNERS

Language Coach   COMMON CORE L 5b

Synonyms *Possible answer: The words show that the man is in very poor shape and is in pain.* Ask students to find synonyms for *shoddy* (line 61) "inferior, mediocre, sleazy, trashy" and for *sentiment* (line 73) "opinion, view, attitude, position, feeling." Have them demonstrate understanding of the terms by writing a sentence using *shoddy*, then another using *sentiment*.

FOR ADVANCED LEARNERS/AP

Compare and Contrast [small-group option] Have student groups gather audio, video, or print examples of contemporary war correspondence by American reporters. Encourage students to use a Comparison Matrix to compare and contrast Hemingway's reporting style, content, and audience with these contemporary examples. Then ask students to draw conclusions about topics such as these: the role of the reporter, the purpose of correspondence, and audience involvement in

world affairs. Ask students to consider in what ways these issues have changed, if at all, over the years. Invite groups to share the results of their studies aloud with the class.

 BEST PRACTICES TOOLKIT—Transparency Comparison Matrix p. A24

G DIALOGUE

Possible answer: *Raven, the soldier, is committed to his role in the war. He had been wounded once before and is searching for a way to be useful in the combat. Hemingway has sympathy but is intellectually removed from the fighting. The exchange adds to the impression that people not involved in the fighting adopt a false sense of invulnerability.*

H *Model the Skill:*
SUBJECTIVITY IN REPORTING

Read lines 84–102 aloud. Point out an example of Hemingway voicing an opinion about Raven, such as "It was not a worker's hand" (line 84).

Possible answer: *Raven seems too refined to be a soldier and his story is too impressive. Hemingway has known others who lied about their exploits in battle. Because Hemingway doubts Raven, readers will be inclined to as well.*

BACKGROUND

John Dos Passos and Sinclair Lewis John Dos Passos (1896–1970) is well-known for his experimental writing technique called "newsreel," where he juxtaposes lines from songs and news headlines into his text. Sinclair Lewis (1885–1951) penned *It Can't Happen Here* in 1935, a novel about a revolution that results in the fascist control of the United States.

"Do you think so?"

"Sure," I said.

"I'm awfully glad," he said. "You know, I wouldn't mind any of this if I could just watch what was going on. I don't mind the pain, you know. It never seemed important really. But I was always awfully interested in things and I really wouldn't

80 mind the pain at all if I could just sort of follow things intelligently. I could even be some use. You know, I didn't mind the war at all. I did all right in the war. I got hit once before and I was back and rejoined the battalion in two weeks. I couldn't stand to be away. Then I got this." **G**

He had put his hand in mine. It was not a worker's hand. There were no calluses and the nails on the long, spatulate[6] fingers were smooth and rounded.

"How did you get it?" I asked.

"Well, there were some troops that were routed and we went over to sort of reform them and we did and then we had quite a fight with the fascists and we beat them. It was quite a bad fight, you know, but we beat them and then

90 someone threw this grenade at me."

Holding his hand and hearing him tell it, I did not believe a word of it. What was left of him did not sound like the wreckage of a soldier somehow. I did not know how he had been wounded, but the story did not sound right. It was the sort of way everyone would like to have been wounded. But I wanted him to think I believed it.

"Where did you come from?" I asked.

"From Pittsburgh. I went to the University there."

"What did you do before you joined up here?"

"I was a social worker," he said. Then I knew it couldn't be true and I wondered

100 how he had really been so frightfully wounded and I didn't care. In the war that I had known, men often lied about the manner of their wounding. Not at first; but later. I'd lied a little myself in my time. Especially late in the evening. But I was glad he thought I believed it, and we talked about books, he wanted to be a writer, and I told him about what happened north of Guadalajara and promised to bring some things from Madrid next time we got out that way. I hoped maybe I could get a radio. **H**

"They tell me Dos Passos and Sinclair Lewis[7] are coming over, too," he said.

"Yes," I said. "And when they come I'll bring them up to see you."

"Gee, that will be great," he said. "You don't know what that will mean to me."

110 "I'll bring them," I said.

"Will they be here pretty soon?"

"Just as soon as they come I'll bring them."

"Good boy, Ernest," he said. "You don't mind if I call you Ernest, do you?"

The voice came very clear and gentle from that face that looked like some hill that had been fought over in muddy weather and then baked in the sun.

"Hell, no," I said. "Please. Listen, old-timer, you're going to be fine. You'll be a lot of good, you know. You can talk on the radio."

---

6. **spatulate** (spăch′ə-lĭt): having a broad, rounded end.

7. **Dos Passos and Sinclair Lewis:** well-known American writers.

G DIALOGUE
Reread lines 67–83. What does the dialogue reveal about the speakers? How does it add to the impression of war the writer has created in this article? Explain your response.

3 Targeted Passage

H SUBJECTIVITY IN REPORTING
Why doesn't Hemingway believe Raven? Do you believe Raven? Explain why or why not.

DIFFERENTIATED INSTRUCTION

FOR STRUGGLING READERS

3 Targeted Passage [Lines 84–100]

This passage introduces Raven, a wounded soldier who asks to meet Hemingway.

- What is Raven's hand like? What does this mean to Hemingway? (lines 84–85)

- Why doesn't Raven sound "like the wreckage of a soldier"? (lines 91–95)

- What was Raven's job before the war? (line 99)

- What details illustrate Hemingway's reaction to the story Raven tells about his wounding? (lines 91–100)

FOR ADVANCED LEARNERS/AP

Research and Analyze Have students research John Dos Passos and Sinclair Lewis, focusing on the authors' political and social beliefs. Students' research should include reading excerpts from or summaries of works by each writer, such as *Manhattan Transfer* and *It Can't Happen Here*. Then have students

draw conclusions about why a meeting with these writers might be important to Raven. Challenge students to make inferences about whether in fact Hemingway has any knowledge about these writers' travel plans and whether he actually will bring them to meet Raven. If not, why does Hemingway confirm Raven's information and promise to arrange a meeting?

"Maybe," he said. "You'll be back?"

"Sure," I said. "Absolutely."

120 "Goodbye, Ernest," he said.

"Goodbye," I told him.

Downstairs they told me he'd lost both eyes as well as his face and was also badly wounded all through the legs and in the feet.

"He's lost some toes, too," the doctor said, "but he doesn't know that."

"I wonder if he'll ever know it."

"Oh, sure he will," the doctor said. "He's going to get well."

And it still isn't you that gets hit but it is your countryman now. Your countryman from Pennsylvania, where once we fought at Gettysburg.

Then, walking along the road, with his left arm in an airplane splint, walking
130 with the gamecock walk of the professional British soldier that neither ten years of militant party work nor the projecting metal wings of the splint could destroy, I met Raven's commanding officer, Jock Cunningham, who had three fresh rifle wounds through his upper left arm (I looked at them, one was septic[8]) and another rifle bullet under his shoulder blade that had entered his left chest, passed through, and lodged there. He told me, in military terms, the history of the attempt to rally retiring troops on his battalion's right flank, of his bombing raid down a trench which was held at one end by the fascists and at the other end by the government troops, of the taking of this trench and, with six men and a Lewis gun,[9] cutting off a group of some eighty fascists from their own lines, and of the
140 final desperate defense of their impossible position his six men put up until the government troops came up and, attacking, straightened out the line again. He told it clearly, completely convincingly, and with a strong Glasgow[10] accent. He had deep, piercing eyes sheltered like an eagle's, and, hearing him talk, you could tell the sort of soldier he was. For what he had done he would have had a V.C.[11] in the last war. In this war there are no decorations. Wounds are the only decorations and they do not award wound stripes. ❶

"Raven was in the same show," he said. "I didn't know he'd been hit. Ay, he's a good mon. He got his after I got mine. The fascists we'd cut off were very good troops. They never fired a useless shot when we were in that bad spot. They waited
150 in the dark there until they had us located and then opened with volley fire. That's how I got four in the same place."

We talked for a while and he told me many things. They were all important, but nothing was as important as what Jay Raven, the social worker from Pittsburgh with no military training, had told me was true. This is a strange new kind of war where you learn just as much as you are able to believe. ❧

---

8. **septic:** infected with bacteria.

9. **Lewis gun:** a lightweight machine gun.

10. **Glasgow:** a city in Scotland.

11. **V.C.:** the Victoria Cross, an award for valor "in the face of the enemy," given by Great Britain.

④ **Targeted Passage**

COMMON CORE RI 6

❶ **SUBJECTIVITY IN REPORTING**

Reread lines 129–146. Notice the writer's **tone,** the hard and cynical attitude revealed by this powerful description of one soldier and his career in the Spanish Civil War. The writing here follows a pattern established earlier in the article. The writer focuses on the details of a particular scene or event and then surprises readers with a blunt message about the nature of war. As you read the article's concluding paragraphs look for final clues to Hemingway's tone. What **purpose** does his tone reveal?

❶ **SUBJECTIVITY IN REPORTING**

Read aloud lines 129–146. Point out the matter-of-fact way and tone that Hemingway uses to describe Jock Cunningham, his wounds, and his manner of relating how he and Raven were wounded.

Possible answer: Hemingway gives a straightforward account of Cunningham's story, making it clear he believes the officer. In the final paragraphs, Hemingway is surprised to hear that the story Raven had told him is true. Hemingway's tone is one of admiration to learn that an untrained, soft-seeming soldier can be a war hero.

REVISIT THE BIG QUESTION

What can we learn from **WAR?**

Discuss Read aloud lines 152–155. Why is the truth of Raven's story important to Hemingway? Explain why people's ability to absorb information is an important aspect of war.

Possible answer: Raven's truth is important because it shows Hemingway how horrible this war is that refined non-soldiers such as Raven must face its horrors. If people do not absorb the reality of war because they do not believe it, they can ignore war's atrocities.

SELECTION WRAP—UP

READ WITH A PURPOSE Now that students have read the selection, ask them to explain how the selection reveals Hemingway's attitude toward war. *Possible answer:* Hemingway's portrayal of realistic details and empathy for the wounded reveal that he sees war as brutal and tragic.

FOR STRUGGLING READERS

④ **Targeted Passage** [Lines 129–146]

- What does Cunningham say about the battle in which Raven was wounded? (lines 135–141)

- What kind of soldier is Cunningham? (lines 142–146)

- What does Hemingway mean by "wounds are the only [war] decorations"? Cite details. (lines 144–146)

FOR ADVANCED LEARNERS/AP

Analyze Allusions Recall that Gettysburg was a pivotal battle in the American Civil War, with heavy casualties on both sides. Have students consider why Hemingway refers to the battle. In what ways is it similar to the Spanish Civil War? In what ways was each nation affected by its civil war? Urge students to record notes in Venn Diagrams, then share their insights.

BEST PRACTICES TOOLKIT—Transparency Venn Diagram p. A26

Practice and Apply

For preliminary support of post-reading questions, use these copy masters:

R RESOURCE MANAGER—Copy Masters
Reading Check p. 355
Subjectivity in Reporting p. 351
Question Support p. 356

Additional selection questions are provided for teachers on page 345.

ANSWERS

COMMON CORE **RI 1, RI 2, RI 6, RI 10**

1. *A bomb bursts below the sidewalk, killing a man and wounding a woman.*

2. *Raven is a wounded soldier from Pennsylvania who is fighting for the Spanish Loyalists. He loses his eyes and face and sustains injuries in his legs and feet.*

3. *Raven and six other men are outnumbered by fascist soldiers when a grenade explodes in Raven's trench.*

Possible answers:

4. ● **COMMON CORE FOCUS** **Analyze Descriptive Details** *Students should cite details about the Spanish woman trying to stanch her bleeding (lines 17–18), the moaning man's transfusion (lines 54–58), and the description of Raven (lines 61–64) to infer that war is destructive and cruel.*

5. ● **COMMON CORE FOCUS** **Analyze Subjectivity in Reporting** *Hemingway conveys people's alternating feelings of fear and relief, the tragic destruction of an idealistic young man, the bravery of the officers of the International Brigades, and the changing nature of war.*

6. *Hemingway includes dialogue perhaps to lend his dispatch a narrative quality that humanizes the characters.*

7. *This conflict is a new kind of war because the rules of combat are not as clear as they were in previous wars. Hemingway is surprised by the war's participants and by the lack of recognition that they receive for their sacrifices (lines 144–146, 152–155).*

8. *Hemingway's article is valuable because it teaches readers that war's consequences haven't changed since the Spanish Civil War. Normal life is disrupted, civilians get hurt, soldiers' lives and bodies are forever destroyed, people make unthinkable sacrifices, people commit unthinkable atrocities.*

9. *Both texts are written in the same understated style. Both show that warfare wounds people in irrevocable ways.*

10. *Some students may say that the ranking is deserved because this dispatch conveys the devastation of war through style. Others may think that the ranking is undeserved because this dispatch is not purely informative.*

Comprehension

1. **Recall** What happens in front of Hemingway's hotel before breakfast?

2. **Recall** Who is Raven, and what are his injuries?

3. **Clarify** What is the truth about how Raven was wounded?

Text Analysis

● 4. **Analyze Descriptive Details** Look back at the descriptive details you noted and circle the ones you found most vivid or affecting. What do you infer from any of these details that Hemingway doesn't tell you outright?

● 5. **Analyze Subjectivity in Reporting** Hemingway's article differs greatly from an objective news report. How does each of the following highly personal passages contribute to the writer's tone and purpose?

   • his recurrent thought "It wasn't me" (lines 35 and 46)
   • his reaction to the sight of Raven and to the story Raven tells (lines 61–106)
   • his description of Jock Cunningham (lines 129–146)
   • his belief about the most important thing he was told (lines 152–155)

6. **Examine Dialogue** A written news report often contains quotations from sources, but rarely does it contain dialogue between two people. Why might Hemingway have chosen to include dialogue in his dispatch?

7. **Interpret Title** What makes this conflict "a new kind of war"? Note what seems to surprise Hemingway about it.

8. **Synthesize Themes** The Spanish Civil War ended more than 65 years ago. What value is there in reading Hemingway's article today? What insights about war does it provide?

9. **Compare Texts** What similarities in **style** and **theme** do you see in "A New Kind of War" and "In Another Country," the Hemingway short story on page 1010?

Text Criticism

10. **Critical Interpretations** When the New York University journalism department compiled its list of the 100 best works of 20th-century American journalism, Hemingway's Spanish Civil War reporting was ranked 33rd. Do you agree that it should be esteemed so highly? Support your answer.

> *What can we learn from* **WAR?**
>
> Hemingway was skeptical of Raven's story when he first heard it. Do you think he changed his mind after hearing the story told by Jock Cunningham? How do you determine the truth when you watch a news report about war? Explain.

COMMON CORE

RI 1 Cite textual evidence to support analysis of what the text says explicitly as well as inferences drawn from the text, including determining where the text leaves matters uncertain. **RI 2** Determine two or more central ideas of a text. **RI 6** Determine an author's point of view or purpose in a text in which the rhetoric is particularly effective, analyzing how style and content contribute to the power, persuasiveness, or beauty of the text. **RI 10** Read and comprehend literary nonfiction.

What can we learn from **WAR?**
Students should note that Hemingway was impressed with Cunningham, so after he heard Cunningham's account of the battle, his original skepticism of Raven's story was most likely dispelled. Students might say that they can determine the truth when watching a news report about war by noting the source of the report and whether that source could be biased and by being wary of opinion statements in the report.

Language

COMMON CORE

L 3 Apply knowledge of language to understand how language functions in different contexts. **W 3a, e** Engage and orient the reader by setting out a situation and establishing one or multiple point(s) of view; create a smooth progression of experiences or events; provide a conclusion that follows from and reflects on what is experienced, observed, or resolved over the course of the narrative.

◆ **GRAMMAR AND STYLE:** Choose Effective Point of View

Review the **Grammar and Style** note on page 1098. At the beginning of his dispatch, Hemingway uses the **second-person pronoun** *you* to report his own experiences, where you would normally expect him to write in the first person. This has the effect of placing the reader ("you") at the point of the action. It also temporarily removes the narrator himself, creating a sense of detachment.

> *After the shell that lit on the sidewalk in front of the hotel you got a beautiful double corner room on that side, twice the size of the one you had had, for less than a dollar.* (lines 43–45)

Hemingway does periodically revert to the first person, as in the continuation of the preceding passage:

> *It wasn't me they killed. See? No. Not me. It wasn't me anymore.* (lines 45–46)

With this shifting point of view, Hemingway seems to step in and out of the narrative. The resulting detachment allows the reader to encounter the experience of war without added comment or sentiment.

PRACTICE Rewrite the following passage, inserting either first- or second-person pronouns to change the sense of immediacy or detachment.

> Hundreds of runners and spectators gather in Jonquil Park at dawn on Mother's Day. The air is crisp and the grass damp. The predominant color in the crowd is pink: pink ribbons, pink caps, pink shirts. Many people wear signs reading "In memory of . . ." There is an electric air of expectancy until the horn blasts. The runners are off!

READING-WRITING CONNECTION

 Expand your understanding of "A New Kind of War" by responding to this prompt. Then, use the **revising tips** to improve your report.

WRITING PROMPT

WRITE A SUBJECTIVE REPORT In his Spanish Civil War dispatches, Hemingway was able to report events in such a way that readers felt they were right there with him. Go to a newsworthy event or recall one that you attended—a concert, a charity race, or a memorial service, for example. Write a **one-page report** that makes your readers seem to experience your thoughts and sensations during the event. Include dialogue, as Hemingway does, if it seems appropriate.

REVISING TIPS

- Clearly identify the event and its participants.
- Include sensory details to describe the setting.
- Include personal reactions, and use an effective point of view.

Interactive Revision **THINK** central

Go to **thinkcentral.com**.
KEYWORD: HML11-1103

Language

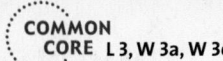
◆ **GRAMMAR AND STYLE**

Discuss with students the possible effects of first-person and second-person narrative, reviewing the instruction from page 1095. Ask students to determine how much immediacy or detachment they wish to create, then choose the point or points of view that best support their goal. ***Possible answer:*** *At dawn on Mother's Day, you join hundreds of runners in Jonquil Park. You feel the crisp air on your skin, and the damp grass tickles your ankles. The horn blasts, and your legs move, joining the others who are running for life.*

 RESOURCE MANAGER—Copy Master
Choose Effective Point of View p. 357

READING-WRITING CONNECTION

Suggest that students prewrite by completing Observation Charts to list sensory details about their events. Have students also brainstorm for comparisons such as creating similes or metaphors that can aid their descriptions.

 **BEST PRACTICES TOOLKIT**—Transparency
Observation Chart p. C7

Writing Online **THINK** central

The following tools are available online at **thinkcentral.com** and on **Write***Smart* CD-ROM:
- **Interactive Graphic Organizers**
- **Interactive Student Models**
- **Interactive Revision Lessons**

For additional grammar instruction, see **GrammarNotes** on **thinkcentral.com**.

DIFFERENTIATED INSTRUCTION

FOR STRUGGLING WRITERS
Writing Support

- Urge students to attend live events rather than writing from memory; help them find events to attend. Emphasize that events can be small, as long as they are vivid.
- Tell students to take notes during the events rather than waiting to record notes after the events have ended. Help students prepare Sensory Notes guides.

- Hold a writing conference with each student. Together, make prewriting decisions about points of view and dialogue.
- Help students determine the dominant impressions they want to convey through their reports. Then tell students to include only details that support these impressions.

BEST PRACTICES TOOLKIT—Transparency
Sensory Notes p. B9

Assess and Reteach

Assess
DIAGNOSTIC AND SELECTION TESTS
Selection Test A, B/C pp. 297–298
Selection Test B/C pp. 299–300

Interactive Selection Test on **thinkcentral.com**

Reteach

Level Up Online Tutorials on **thinkcentral.com**
Reteaching Worksheets on **thinkcentral.com**

Literature Lessons 10, 42, 45

Focus and Motivate

 COMMON CORE FOCUS

RI 3 Analyze a complex set of ideas or sequence of events and explain how ideas or events interact and develop over the course of the text. **RI 6** Determine an author's point of view or purpose in a text in which the rhetoric is particularly effective, analyzing how style and content contribute to the power, persuasiveness, or beauty of the text. **W 1** Write arguments to support claims in an analysis of texts, using valid reasoning and relevant and sufficient evidence. **L 2** Demonstrate command of the conventions of standard English punctuation when writing.

ABOUT THE AUTHOR

Point out to students the descriptions of Parker as "sophisticated," "witty," "caustic," "smart-mouthed." Lead students to discuss how such character traits alternately led Parker to be revered as "one of the most quoted women of the 20th century" but also to be fired from *Vanity Fair* and summoned to the House Un-American Activities Committee.

NOTABLE QUOTE

"Wit has truth in it; wisecracking is simply calisthenics with words." —**Dorothy Parker**

Clarify that in this quotation, Parker differentiates between wit and wisecracking, or joking.

COMMON CORE

RI 3 Analyze a complex set of ideas or sequence of events and explain how ideas or events interact and develop over the course of the text. **RI 6** Determine an author's point of view or purpose in a text in which the rhetoric is particularly effective, analyzing how style and content contribute to the power, persuasiveness, or beauty of the text.

DID YOU KNOW?

Dorothy Parker . . .

- was expelled from convent school for making smart remarks.
- originated the saying "Men seldom make passes / At girls who wear glasses".
- proposed "Excuse my dust" as her epitaph.

Journalism as Literature

A Book of Great Short Stories

Book Review by Dorothy Parker

Meet the Author

Dorothy Parker 1893–1967

Dorothy Parker's sophisticated and witty voice made her one of the most quoted women of the 20th century. She belonged to the Algonquin Round Table, an informal group of writers who met daily at New York's Algonquin Hotel for lunch and clever conversation. Nicknamed the "Vicious Circle," they helped shape the literary tastes of the country.

Caustic Critic A well-read but smart-mouthed student, Parker left school at 14. When she was 19, her father died, and she was forced to find a job. After selling a poem to *Vanity Fair*, she was hired to write captions for its sister magazine, *Vogue*. She rose to become drama critic at *Vanity Fair* but was fired in 1920 for panning a play that starred the wife of one of the magazine's advertisers. She landed on her feet, becoming drama critic for another magazine, *Ainslee's*. She was also one of the founding editors of the *New Yorker* and served as its book reviewer for six years. Signing her reviews "Constant Reader," she championed writers she admired and demolished those she didn't. About one book she pronounced, "This is not a novel to be tossed aside lightly. It should be thrown with great force."

Popular Poet Parker's own books of poetry, *Enough Rope* and *Sunset Gun*, were bestsellers. They contained rueful verses, usually about failed love. One of her most quoted poems is "Résumé," which ends, "Guns aren't lawful; / Nooses give; / Gas smells awful; / You might as well live." Though often humorous, her poems grew out of great personal pain. She had an unhappy marriage to Edwin Parker, who returned from World War I with a drug addiction. Before divorcing him, she had disastrous love affairs that led her to several suicide attempts.

Screenwriter and Activist In 1933, Parker married Alan Campbell and moved with him to Hollywood, where they collaborated on screenplays. She also became more politically active, protesting racism, organizing the Screenwriters Guild, founding an anti-Nazi group, and going to Madrid to report on the Spanish Civil War. Her socialist sympathies caused her to be brought before the House Un-American Activities Committee in the 1950s. After she died of a heart attack in 1967, it was discovered that she had left her literary estate to Dr. Martin Luther King Jr. and the NAACP.

Author Online
Go to **thinkcentral.com**. KEYWORD: HML11-1104

THiNK central

1104

Selection Resources

TEXT ANALYSIS: STYLE

Style is determined not by what is written, but by *how* it is written. Imagery, figurative language, exaggeration, dialogue, and diction are some of the rhetorical techniques that contribute to a particular writer's style. Dorothy Parker's style is characterized by witty diction and ironic exaggeration. Her book reviews are not merely informative. They are playful and persuasive, clearly aimed to influence readers. Consider Parker's style in this passage:

After all the high screaming about The Sun Also Rises, *I feared for Mr. Hemingway's next book. You know how it is—as soon as they all start acclaiming a writer, that writer is just about to slip downward.*

What kind of person do you imagine is speaking? Male or female? Friendly or distant? Serious or playful? As you read, notice what makes Dorothy Parker's style so effective and persuasive. Use her comments to form an impression of her personality and attitude toward the literary world.

READING STRATEGY: READING A BOOK REVIEW

Most book reviews are published in newspapers and magazines. They usually

- describe a new or newly republished book
- give an evaluation of its literary worth
- offer reasons for this evaluation

As you read Dorothy Parker's review, look for the lines that fulfill these functions. She discusses three of Ernest Hemingway's books, not just one, and she mentions others' opinions as well as her own, so it may help to take notes on a chart like the one shown.

	Description	Parker's Evaluation	Reasons
The Sun Also Rises			
In Our Time			
Men Without Women			

 Complete the activities in your **Reader/Writer Notebook**.

What makes a GREAT short story?

During your school years, you've read many classic stories described as "great," such as "The Necklace" by Guy de Maupassant and "The Tell-Tale Heart" by Edgar Allan Poe. But how can you learn about new stories that might be just as great? Would you trust a book reviewer's evaluation?

QUICKWRITE Think about the best short story you ever read, in school or on your own. With its qualities in mind, jot down the recipe for a great short story. What must one contain, in your opinion? In a small group, share your recipes. Do you all have similar tastes, or are your standards unique?

1105

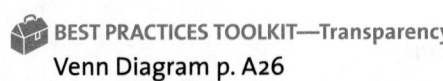

The Sun Also Rises   *In Our Time*

novel   peaceful ecstacy   superb

starkly written

short stories

sad & terrible   *Men Without Women*

Teach

What makes a **GREAT** *short story?*

Ask students the question, and then have them read the paragraph that follows it. Poll students on whether they would trust a reviewer's evaluation and discuss their reasons. Before students complete the *QUICKWRITE,* ask them to suggest favorite short stories and tell what they like about each story.

TEXT ANALYSIS — COMMON CORE RI 3

● *Model the Skill:* **STYLE**

To help students determine and describe a writer's style, read aloud Dorothy Parker's short passage on page 1105. Point out that Parker's style reflects both formal (*"high screaming," "I feared," "acclaiming a writer"*) and informal (*"you know how it is"*) word choice and level of language, as well as complex sentences.

GUIDED PRACTICE Have students imitate Parker's style by writing several sentences about a literary work.

READING STRATEGY — COMMON CORE RI 6

■ *Model the Skill:* **READING A BOOK REVIEW**

Tell students that book reviews usually describe a book, giving an evaluation of its literary worth with supporting evidence for their evaluation. Point out that Parker's review of Hemingway's works is buried within comments about literary critics and other writers. Tell students that most of the information for their charts appears on the final page of the review.

GUIDED PRACTICE Have students point out paragraphs that contain Parker's evaluation of Hemingway's literary works.

R RESOURCE MANAGER—Copy Master
Analyze Descriptive Language p. 371 (for student use while reading the selection)

Practice and Apply

SUMMARY

In a witty and acerbic review of Ernest Hemingway's works *The Sun Also Rises*, *In Our Time*, and *Men Without Women*, Dorothy Parker takes issue with members of the literary community who herald Hemingway's novel but ignore his works of short fiction. Parker claims that Hemingway's stark, discerning, reportorial style makes him a master of short fiction.

READ WITH A PURPOSE

Help students set a purpose for reading. Tell them to read to discover Dorothy Parker's definition of great literature.

REVISIT THE BIG QUESTION

What makes a GREAT *short story?*

Discuss Read aloud lines 12–19. What criteria does Parker think critics have used in their evaluation of Hemingway's work? Does she support those criteria? ***Possible answer:*** *Parker thinks that critics have rejected Hemingway's work because of the author's lifestyle. She does not support these criteria as a basis for literary criticism.*

A BOOK OF GREAT SHORT STORIES

Dorothy Parker

October 29, 1927

Ernest Hemingway wrote a novel called *The Sun Also Rises.* Promptly upon its publication, Ernest Hemingway was discovered, the Stars and Stripes were reverentially raised over him, eight hundred and forty-seven book reviewers formed themselves into the word "welcome," and the band played "Hail to the Chief" in three concurrent keys. All of which, I should think, might have made Ernest Hemingway pretty reasonably sick. Ⓐ

　For, a year or so before *The Sun Also Rises,* he had published *In Our Time,* a collection of short pieces. The book caused about as much stir in literary circles as an incompleted dogfight on upper Riverside Drive. True, there were a few that

10　went about quick and stirred with admiration for this clean, exciting prose, but most of the reviewers dismissed the volume with a tolerant smile and the word "stark." It was Mr. Mencken[1] who slapped it down with "sketches in the bold, bad manner of the Café du Dôme," and the smaller boys, in their manner, took similar pokes at it. Well, you see, Ernest Hemingway was a young American living on the left bank of the Seine in Paris, France; he had been seen at the Dôme and the Rotonde and the Select and the Closerie des Lilas.[2] He knew Pound, Joyce, and Gertrude Stein. There is something a little—well, a little *you*-know—in all of those things. You wouldn't catch Bruce Barton or Mary Roberts Rinehart[3] doing them. No, sir.

Analyze Visuals ▶
What ideas are suggested by the cover designs of these books by Ernest Hemingway?

---

1. **Mr. Mencken:** H. L. Mencken, an American journalist and literary critic.
2. **Dôme . . . des Lilas:** cafés in Paris that were frequented by young American writers.
3. **Pound . . . Rinehart:** Ezra Pound and Gertrude Stein were experimental American writers living in Paris; James Joyce was an experimental Irish writer. Bruce Barton and Mary Roberts Rinehart were more conventional American writers who lived in the United States.

DIFFERENTIATED INSTRUCTION

FOR ADVANCED LEARNERS/AP

Provide these independent projects to extend the lesson:

- Perform a dramatic reading using Parker's voice.
- Survey people's literary tastes.
- Write an essay comparing Hemingway and Parker.

Have students share their project with the class. Have members of the audience write a short review of the project and the presentation. Emphasize that although students can give constructive criticism in their reviews, their critiques should be supportive and respectful.

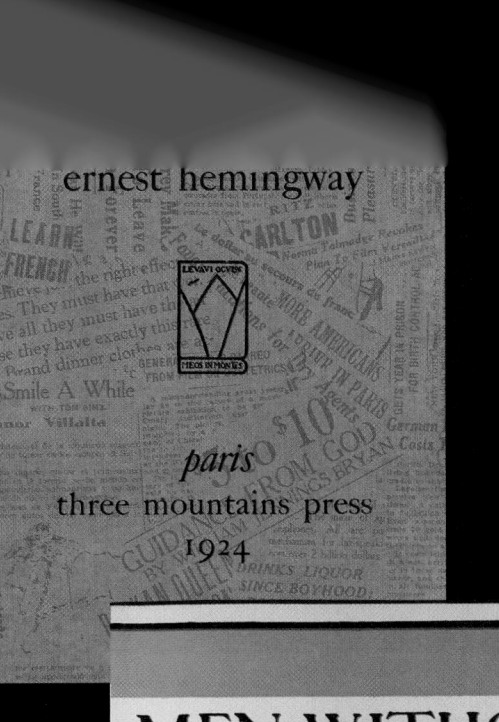

ernest hemingway

paris
three mountains press
1924

MEN WITHOU
WOMEN

BY
ERNEST HEMINGWAY
AUTHOR OF
THE SUN ALSO RISES

CHARLES SCRIBNER'S SONS

THE SUN
ALSO RISES

ERNEST HEMINGWAY
Author of
"IN OUR TIMES" and "THE TORRENTS OF SPRING"

Possible answer: *The cover of* In Our Time *suggests ideas such as newspaper reporting and international affairs. The cover of* The Sun Also Rises *suggests ideas such as Greek mythology and female sensuality. The cover of* Men Without Women *suggests the idea of bullfighting.*

About the Art These three covers represent the original covers for the first edition publications of Hemingway's works. Like the critical response to these works, the cover of the novel is much showier than those of the short works collections.

BACKGROUND

Hemingway's Works *In Our Time* includes stories that are reminiscent of Hemingway's childhood in the forests of northern Michigan. Set in France and Spain, *The Sun Also Rises* is about a group of disenchanted Americans and Britons living in Europe at the end of World War I. *Men Without Women* includes "The Killers," a short story renowned for its account of imminent disaster.

FOR STRUGGLING READERS

In combination with the *Audio Anthology CD,* use one or both Targeted Passages (pp. 1106, 1109) to ensure that students focus on key concepts in the selection. Targeted Passages are also good for English language learners.

❶ Targeted Passage [Lines 2–14]

This passage introduces the topic of Parker's review, the works of Ernest Hemingway, and hints at her view of other literary critics.

- Who is Dorothy Parker writing about? (lines 1–8)
- What works will she consider? (lines 7–8)
- How was *The Sun Also Rises* received? (lines 1–5)
- How was *In Our Time* received? (lines 8–12)
- What does Parker think of the different receptions these works inspired? (lines 1–12)

FOR ENGLISH LANGUAGE LEARNERS

Vocabulary Support Use Common Prefixes to teach this word: *concurrent* (line 5).

 **BEST PRACTICES TOOLKIT**—Transparency Common Prefixes p. E14

Dorothy Parker and Ernest Hemingway

TEXT ANALYSIS

COMMON CORE RI 3

B Model the Skill: STYLE

Read aloud lines 20–26. Point out Parker's use of dialogue and informal diction. Ask whether students find this style interesting or appealing. Ask them to explain their reactions.

Possible answer: *The speaker sounds like a sophisticated New Yorker unimpressed with book critics, popular American writers, booksellers, or ordinary readers. Parker's style relays an arrogant, but amusing, attitude.*

BACKGROUND

Lost Generation American writer Gertrude Stein labeled expatriates living in Europe after World War I as "a lost generation." These writers, who included Hemingway, F. Scott Fitzgerald, William Carlos Williams, Thornton Wilder, and Archibald MacLeish, shared disenchantment with American ideals and resentment over their war experiences. Hemingway used Stein's words as an epigraph for *The Sun Also Rises.*

TIERED DISCUSSION PROMPTS

In lines 27–41, use these prompts to help students explore literature's role in inspiring social discourse:

Interpret Why might praise, sales records, adoration, censorship, argument, and analysis be indicators of literary success? How does Parker view these indicators?

Possible answer: *These reactions suggest varied responses which could indicate that the work has widespread appeal. But Parker views these indicators with condescension, suggesting they reflect a lack of careful thought.*

Synthesize Serious literature seldom excites the kind of popular response today that it did in Hemingway's day. Why is serious literature less revered among the general public today? What has replaced it? **Possible answer:** *Serious literature is less popular today because fewer people read and those who do tend to read popular works. Technology is replacing the written word.*

20 And besides, *In Our Time* was a book of short stories. That's no way to start off. People don't like that; they feel cheated. Any bookseller will be glad to tell you, in his interesting *argot*,[4] that "short stories don't go." People take up a book of short stories and say, "Oh, what's this? Just a lot of those short things?" and put it right down again. Only yesterday afternoon at four o'clock sharp, I saw and heard a woman do that to Ernest Hemingway's new book, *Men Without Women.* She had been one of those most excited about his new novel. **B**

Literature, it appears, is here measured by a yard-stick. As soon as *The Sun Also Rises* came out, Ernest Hemingway was the white-haired boy. He was praised, adored, analyzed, best-sold, argued about, and banned in Boston; all

30 the trimmings were accorded him. People got into feuds about whether or not his story was worth the telling. (You see this silver scar left by a bullet, right up here under my hair? I got that the night I said that any well-told story was worth the telling. An eighth of an inch nearer the temple, and I wouldn't be sitting here doing this sort of tripe.) They affirmed, and passionately, that the dissolute expatriates[5] in this novel of "a lost generation" were not worth bothering about; and then they devoted most of their time to discussing them. There was a time, and it went on for weeks, when you could go nowhere without hearing of *The Sun Also Rises.* Some thought it without excuse; and some, they of the cool, tall foreheads, called it the greatest American novel, tossing *Huckleberry Finn* and *The*

40 *Scarlet Letter*[6] lightly out the window. They hated it or they revered it. I may say, with due respect to Mr. Hemingway, that I was never so sick of a book in my life.

---

4. **argot** (är′gō) *French:* expressions and vocabulary that are used by a particular group.

5. **dissolute expatriates:** loose-living people—in this case, Americans—residing in a foreign land.

6. **Huckleberry Finn and The Scarlet Letter:** novels by Mark Twain and Nathaniel Hawthorne, respectively.

1108 UNIT 5: THE HARLEM RENAISSANCE AND MODERNISM

B STYLE
Reread lines 20–26, and notice the informal diction and use of dialogue. What is your reaction to this style?

Language Coach

Synonyms A synonym is a word with a meaning similar to that of another word. Read lines 34–36. Which word is a synonym of *asserted* or *declared*? What point were people asserting?

DIFFERENTIATED INSTRUCTION

FOR ENGLISH LANGUAGE LEARNERS

Language Coach

Synonyms *Answer: Affirmed* (line 34) is a synonym of *asserted* or *declared.* People were asserting that the expatriates in the story weren't worth mentioning, yet the same people spent a lot of their time talking about the characters.

Place students into mixed-ability groups. Give groups a word that has several synonyms. Have groups think of as many synonyms as they can. Have each group share their synonyms with the class. Give the group with the most synonyms a point, and continue the game with a new word. Possible words to use: thin, friendly, talk, strange

Now *The Sun Also Rises* was as "starkly" written as Mr. Hemingway's short stories; it dealt with subjects as "unpleasant." Why it should have been taken to the slightly damp bosom of the public while the (as it seems to me) superb *In Our Time* should have been disregarded will always be a puzzle to me. As I see it—I knew this conversation would get back to me sooner or later, preferably sooner—Mr. Hemingway's style, this prose stripped to its firm young bones, is far more effective, far more moving, in the short story than in the novel. He is, to me, the greatest living writer of short stories; he is, also to me, not the greatest living
50 novelist.

After all the high screaming about *The Sun Also Rises*, I feared for Mr. Hemingway's next book. You know how it is—as soon as they all start acclaiming a writer, that writer is just about to slip downward. The littler critics circle like literary buzzards above only the sick lions. **D**

So it is a warm gratification to find the new Hemingway book, *Men Without Women*, a truly magnificent work. It is composed of thirteen short stories, most of which have been published before. They are sad and terrible stories; the author's enormous appetite for life seems to have been somehow appeased. You find here little of that peaceful ecstasy that marked the camping trip in *The Sun Also Rises*
60 and the lone fisherman's days in "Big Two-Hearted River" in *In Our Time*. The stories include "The Killers," which seems to me one of the four great American short stories. (All you have to do is drop the nearest hat, and I'll tell you what I think the others are. They are Wilbur Daniel Steele's "Blue Murder," Sherwood Anderson's "I'm a Fool," and Ring Lardner's "Some Like Them Cold," that story which seems to me as shrewd a picture of every woman at some time as is Chekhov's[7] "The Darling." Now what do *you* like best?) The book also includes "Fifty Grand," "In Another Country," and the delicate and tragic "Hills like White Elephants." I do not know where a greater collection of stories can be found.
70 Ford Madox Ford[8] has said of this author, "Hemingway writes like an angel." I take issue (there is nothing better for that morning headache than taking a little issue.) Hemingway writes like a human being. I think it is impossible for him to write of any event at which he has not been present; his is, then, a reportorial talent, just as Sinclair Lewis's[9] is. But, or so I think, Lewis remains a reporter and Hemingway stands a genius because Hemingway has an unerring sense of selection. He discards details with a magnificent lavishness; he keeps his words to their short path. His is, as any reader knows, a dangerous influence. The simple thing he does looks so easy to do. But look at the boys who try to do it. 🔖 **E**

---

7. **Wilbur . . . Chekhov's:** Steele, Anderson, and Lardner were popular American writers of the era; Anton Chekhov was a 19th-century Russian short story writer and playwright.

8. **Ford Madox Ford:** an English writer, editor, and critic who lived for a time in Paris.

9. **Sinclair Lewis's:** Lewis was an American novelist and social critic who published articles in several popular magazines.

C BOOK REVIEW
Reread lines 42–50. Restate Parker's opinion of *In Our Time*. What does she say about Hemingway's **style**?

D GRAMMAR AND STYLE
In lines 51–54, notice how Parker uses the **first-person pronoun** *I* to refer to herself and addresses the reader with the **second-person pronoun** *you*. She also sets off her side remark with a **dash**. These choices establish an intimate conversational **voice.** Also notice her use of simile, comparing the critics to circling buzzards.

2 Targeted Passage

E BOOK REVIEW
Reread lines 70–78. How highly does Parker rate Hemingway, and why?

C BOOK REVIEW

Possible answer: Parker finds In Our Time *to be superbly effective due to Hemingway's stripped-down, bare-bones style.*

D GRAMMAR AND STYLE — COMMON CORE L 2

Establish Voice Point out that Parker's informal phrase "You know how it is" contributes to her conversational voice. Discuss why Parker chooses such a voice for her book review, and have students find other examples of the voice.

READING STRATEGY — COMMON CORE RI 6

E *Model the Skill:* **BOOK REVIEW**

Tell students that to determine how Parker rates Hemingway, they should look for positive and negative details she mentions. Point out that Parker's rating can be discerned by such comments as "unerring sense of selection" (lines 75–76).

Possible answer: Parker rates Hemingway as a genius because he chooses details effectively (lines 75–76).

SELECTION WRAP–UP

READ WITH A PURPOSE Now that students have read the selection, ask them to determine how they think Parker would define great literature. *Possible answer: Parker might define great literature as efficient writing that appears simple, but is actually difficult to master.*

FOR STRUGGLING READERS

2 **Targeted Passage** [Lines 55–78]

This passage contains Parker's review of *Men Without Women* and minimal supporting evidence for that opinion.

- Describe *Men Without Women*. (lines 56–60)

- How does Parker view *Men Without Women*? (lines 55–78)

- On what criteria does Parker base her view? What evidence does she offer? (lines 57–62)

FOR ADVANCED LEARNERS/AP

Evaluate Stories Ask students if they are familiar with any of the stories Parker mentions. If not, ask students to consider other short stories they know and evaluate whether Parker might like the story. Encourage students to use their knowledge of Parker's literary criteria and give examples from this review as they share their opinions with the class.

Practice and Apply

For preliminary support of post-reading questions, use these copy masters:

 **RESOURCE MANAGER—Copy Masters**
Reading Check p. 373
Style p. 369
Question Support p. 374
Additional selection questions are provided for teachers on page 363.

ANSWERS

COMMON CORE RI 3, RI 6

1. *Hemingway's latest book at the time was* Men Without Women.

2. In Our Time *was virtually ignored, while* The Sun Also Rises *received both positive and negative attention.*

3. *Parker states that Lewis is merely a reporter, while Hemingway is a genius.*

Possible answers:

4. ● **COMMON CORE FOCUS Reading a Book Review** *Parker believes that* The Sun Also Rises *is overrated, while* In Our Time *is superb and* Men Without Women *is magnificent. Her opinions are largely unsupported with the exception of a description of Hemingway's writing style as genius due to his selective use of detail.*

5. ● **COMMON CORE FOCUS Style** *The use of* I *makes Parker's style personal. Her exaggeration is humorous and reflects self-deprecation. The figurative language is amusing and sophisticated. The informal diction is intimate.*

6. *Parker is not impressed with book critics. She refers to them irreverently as "Mr. Mencken" (line 12), "the smaller boys" (line 13), "they of the cool, tall foreheads" (lines 38–39), and "the littler critics circl[ing] like literary buzzards" (lines 53–54). She criticizes the reading public for dismissing short fiction (lines 22–26) and mocks them with the reference to "the slightly damp bosom of the public" (line 44).*

7. *Students are likely to agree that* In Another Country *exhibits the characteristics that Parker names.*

Comprehension

1. **Recall** What was Hemingway's latest book at the time Parker's review was written?

2. **Clarify** How did the reception of *In Our Time* compare to the reception of *The Sun Also Rises*?

3. **Paraphrase** What does Parker say is the difference between Hemingway and Sinclair Lewis?

Text Analysis

4. ● **Reading a Book Review** Look back at the notes you took while reading, then summarize Parker's opinions of the three Hemingway books she discusses. With what evidence does she support her opinions?

5. ● **Analyze Style** How would you describe Parker's style in this book review? Explain the rhetorical appeal of each of the following:

   • use of the first-person *I*
   • similes and metaphors
   • exaggeration
   • informal diction

6. **Interpret Tone** What is Parker's attitude toward book reviewers and the reading public? Support your answer with details.

7. **Evaluate Author's Work** Review Parker's statements about Hemingway's short stories (lines 42–50, 55–78). Then skim "In Another Country" (page 1010). Do you agree with Parker's **evaluation** of Hemingway's short stories? Use a chart like the one shown to organize your thoughts.

"In Another Country"	Yes	No
Clean, Stripped-Down Prose		
Unpleasant Subject		
Sadness		
Reportorial Talent		
Effectiveness in Moving Readers		

Text Criticism

8. **Critical Interpretations** One scholar wrote, "It is through Parker's refusal to claim authority . . . that her book reviews achieve it. She presents readers with an unpretentious, sometimes self-mocking voice that, while it expresses strong opinions, pretends no Olympian knowledge or status." Do you agree with this critic about the source of Parker's authority or trustworthiness? Explain your view.

What makes a **GREAT** *short story?*

Dorothy Parker is at once critical and complimentary of Hemingway's writing. She thinks his novel is overrated and his short stories are underrated. Why might some readers tend to take novels more seriously than short stories? What do *you* think makes a great short story?

COMMON CORE

RI 3 Analyze a complex set of ideas or sequence of events and explain how ideas or events interact and develop over the course of the text. **RI 6** Determine an author's point of view or purpose in a text in which the rhetoric is particularly effective, analyzing how style and content contribute to the power, persuasiveness, or beauty of the text.

8. *Students may agree that Parker seems trustworthy because she doesn't claim a superior status. Others will say that she quite authoritatively claims superiority but also conveys a deep knowledge of literature.*

What makes a **GREAT** *short story?*
Answers will vary. Students should note that Hemingway was impressed with Cunningham, so after he heard Cunningham's account of the battle, his original skepticism of Raven's story was most likely dispelled. Students might say that they can determine the truth when watching a news report about war by noting the source of the report and whether that source could be biased and by being wary of opinion statements in the report.

Language

◆ **GRAMMAR AND STYLE:** Establish Voice

Review the **Grammar and Style** note on page 1109. Dorothy Parker's voice is intimate, enthusiastic, and wittily self-involved. Here is an example from her review:

> *As I see it—I knew this conversation would get back to me sooner or later, preferably sooner—Mr. Hemingway's style, this prose stripped to its firm young bones, is far more effective, far more moving, in the short story than in the novel.* (lines 45–48)

Notice Parker's use of the **first-person pronoun** *I* and her use of **dashes** to enclose a parenthetical comment about herself. It's as if Parker is having a conversation with the reader. Additionally, her use of **figurative language**—comparing Hemingway's prose to a fleshless body—creates a far more striking image than had she merely described it as "lean." You can use these and other elements to establish your own voice.

PRACTICE Rewrite each of the following sentences, using pronouns, figurative language, and punctuation, to achieve a voice that sounds like Dorothy Parker's. A sample answer has been done for you.

> **EXAMPLE**
>
> This book is not good.
>
> *This volume—in my view—is appallingly, criminally bad.*

1. Other reviewers have disliked this book.
2. Sales have been high.
3. Reviewing books can seem useless.

READING-WRITING CONNECTION

 Expand your understanding of "A Book of Great Short Stories" by responding to this prompt. Then, use the **revising tips** to improve your review.

WRITING PROMPT	REVISING TIPS
WRITE A BOOK REVIEW Dorothy Parker wrote book reviews for many years, and to one critic, they are the best expression of her literary sensibility. Choose a great book, or an "ungreat book," and write a **three-to-five-paragraph** review in your own personal voice. You might be as funny as Dorothy Parker, but in a different way. Or you might inspire readers to discover a book that could transform their lives. Think about what your own voice sounds like—perhaps tape-record yourself talking about the book. Then try to reproduce that voice in writing.	• Provide a thorough description of the book. • Offer a positive or negative evaluation. • Provide evidence to support your evaluation. • Write in a distinctive voice.

Interactive Revision THINK central
Go to **thinkcentral.com**.
KEYWORD: HML11-1111

COMMON CORE

L 2 Demonstrate command of the conventions of standard English punctuation when writing. **W 1** Write arguments to support claims in an analysis of texts, using valid reasoning and relevant and sufficient evidence.

Language

COMMON CORE **L 2, W 1**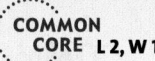

◆ **GRAMMAR AND STYLE**

Review with students that dashes show abrupt changes in thought or speech. Remind them that figurative language includes the similes that Parker uses as well as metaphors or personification.

Possible answers:

1. *Reviewers have given the book the admiration they would give a mound of pigeon droppings on Park Avenue.*

2. *I couldn't push my way into the bookstore for all the people lined up to buy it.*

3. *I sincerely think I should enter a more rewarding profession—I hear Ringling Brothers is looking for a lion tamer.*

R **RESOURCE MANAGER**—Copy Master
Establish Voice p. 375

READING-WRITING CONNECTION

Have students use a Main Idea and Details organizer to list reasons for their views and examples to support those reasons. To help students to craft voice, suggest that they consider their peers as the intended audience.

 **BEST PRACTICES TOOLKIT**—Transparency
Main Idea and Details p. B6

Writing Online THINK central

The following tools are available online at **thinkcentral.com** and on Write*Smart* **CD-ROM:**
• **Interactive Graphic Organizers**
• **Interactive Student Models**
• **Interactive Revision Lessons**
For additional grammar instruction, see **GrammarNotes** on **thinkcentral.com**.

Assess and Reteach

Assess

DIAGNOSTIC AND SELECTION TESTS

Selection Test A, B/C pp. 301–302, 303–304
Interactive Selection Test on **thinkcentral.com**

Reteach

Level Up Online Tutorials on **thinkcentral.com**
Reteaching Worksheets on **thinkcentral.com**
Literature Lessons 25, 27, 43, 44, Reading Lessons 16, 17

DIFFERENTIATED INSTRUCTION

FOR STRUGGLING WRITERS

Writing Support

• Encourage students to use the Writing Template: Critical Review.

• Urge students to begin their reviews with action, dialogue, or reaction that grabs the reader's attention. Then, help students state their overall view of the work and list three criteria for evaluation.

• In each body paragraph, have students explain one criterion for evaluation and support it with examples from the work. Review with students how to incorporate, punctuate, and cite literary quotations.

• To conclude, have students summarize the main points of their evaluations and leave readers with a final, provocative thought.

 BEST PRACTICES TOOLKIT—Transparency
Writing Template: Critical Review pp. C16, C25

COMMON CORE FOCUS

RI 6 Determine an author's point of view or purpose in a text in which the rhetoric is particularly effective, analyzing how style and content contribute to the power, persuasiveness, or beauty of the text.

ABOUT THE AUTHOR

After students read about E. B. White, highlight the fact that the author published *Stuart Little* despite a librarian's comment that it was "unfit for children." Tell students that one of White's points in the essay they will read is that a writer has a duty to write about "what naturally absorbs his fancy." Ask students in what ways White's actions reflect his views. ***Possible answer:*** *White's actions suggest that he wrote and published what interested him, even though others did not always like it.*

NOTABLE QUOTE

"The true writer always plays to an audience of one." —**E. B. White**

Have students explain what White means by "an audience of one." Ask them to contrast the writer-reader relationship resulting from White's approach with the relationship established when writing to a larger audience.

COMMON CORE

RI 6 Determine an author's point of view or purpose in a text in which the rhetoric is particularly effective, analyzing how style and content contribute to the power, persuasiveness, or beauty of the text.

DID YOU KNOW?

E. B. White . . .

- hated his given name, Elwyn Brooks, and answered to his college nickname, Andy.
- preferred sailing to reading.
- was so afraid of public speaking that he made others deliver his acceptance speeches.

Journalism as Literature

The Duty of Writers

Essay by E. B. White

Meet the Author

E. B. White 1899–1985

Admired for his graceful style and gentle humor, E. B. White has been called the best essayist of the 20th century. For years readers looked forward to his columns in the *New Yorker* and *Harper's* magazines. Midcareer, he became a beloved children's author, writing the classics *Stuart Little* and *Charlotte's Web.* Later, he gained more fame with his update of *The Elements of Style,* a handbook used by millions of student writers.

New York Wit White enjoyed writing even as a child and won his first award when he was nine, for a poem about a mouse. In 1925, following unsuccessful stints in reporting and advertising, he was hired by a new magazine, the *New Yorker.* Its editor wanted it to be light, witty, and satirical. White did much to give it that voice. He wrote its opening "Notes and Comment" page and composed newsbreaks, fillers between articles with such headings as "Letters We Never Finished Reading" and "Neatest Trick of the Week." He did captions for cartoons and even once illustrated the magazine's cover.

The *New Yorker* provided White with an outlet for his talent— and a wife: he married the fiction editor, Katharine, living happily with her for 48 years.

Up on the Farm Eventually White felt constrained by the brief length and sheer number of the pieces he had to write for the *New Yorker.* He took a leave from the magazine and moved to a farmhouse in Maine in 1938. There he raised chickens, geese, sheep, and a milk cow. He also began a monthly column for *Harper's* called "One Man's Meat" (an allusion to the saying "One man's meat is another man's poison.") Some of his most memorable essays were published in this column, including "Once More to the Lake," about revisiting the place where he vacationed as a child.

"Unfit for Children" In Maine, White wrote his first children's book, *Stuart Little,* about a family that has a mouse for a son. The head children's librarian at the New York Public Library called his manuscript "unfit for children," but he published it anyway in 1945. Young people loved it, and in 1952 he followed it up with *Charlotte's Web,* about a literate spider who saves a pig from slaughter.

White lived quietly until his death at 86 from Alzheimer's disease. Among his many awards were the Presidential Medal of Freedom and a special Pulitzer Prize for his entire body of work.

THINK central

Author Online
Go to **thinkcentral.com.** KEYWORD: HML11-1112

1112

See resources on the **Teacher One Stop DVD-ROM** *and on* **thinkcentral.com.**

 RESOURCE MANAGER UNIT 5
Plan and Teach, pp. 377–384
Summary, pp. 385–386†‡*
Text Analysis and Reading
   Skill, pp. 387–390†*

**DIAGNOSTIC AND SELECTION
   TESTS**
Selection Tests, pp. 305–308

 BEST PRACTICES TOOLKIT
Book Posters, p. A4

TECHNOLOGY

⊘ **Teacher One Stop DVD-ROM**
⊘ **Student One Stop DVD-ROM**
⊘ **ExamView Test Generator
   on the Teacher One Stop**

---

* Resources for Differentiation   † Also in Spanish   ‡ In Haitian Creole and Vietnamese

TEXT ANALYSIS: STYLE AND DICTION

Style is the particular way in which a piece of literature is written. It is not what is said, but how it is said. An essential element of style is **diction**, an author's choice of words and syntax. E. B. White's style is both casual and elegant. In the following passage, which particular words or phrases create casualness? elegance?

I was sorry to hear the other day that a certain writer, appalled by the cruel events of the world, had pledged himself never to write anything that wasn't constructive and significant and liberty-loving. I have an idea that this, in its own way, is bad news.

As you read this essay, notice what White's diction contributes to his style. Also, if an expression strikes you as humorous, think about what makes it so.

READING SKILL: INTERPRET AUTHOR'S MESSAGE

An **author's message** is the main idea of a particular work, or the point it makes. White's essay presents his personal opinions on a topic, the duty of writers. These opinions are signaled by such words and phrases as

- "I have an idea that"
- "I don't think"
- "should"
- "shouldn't"
- "This seems to me"

As you read, use such clues to identify what kind of writing White favors and what he opposes. Make notes on a chart like the one shown.

Favors	Opposes
	writing only what is constructive, significant, and liberty-loving

 Complete the activities in your **Reader/Writer Notebook**.

What do writers OWE us?

People often debate what writers should write. Should writers uplift the community or constantly denounce wrongs? Should they report every detail about a war or protect national security? Can they be blasphemous? frivolous? Decide what you believe is the duty of writers. Do they have a special responsibility in troubled times?

EVALUATE AND DISCUSS Explore your own ideas about a writer's obligations by completing this sentence: "I hate it when a writer ..." In a small group discuss your completed sentences. Is there any agreement about what writers should or should not do?

"Write about dogs!"

THE DUTY OF WRITERS **1113**

What do writers OWE us?

Ask students the question, and discuss the ideas in the paragraph that follows. After students answer questions about writers' responsibilities, have them begin the *EVALUATE AND DISCUSS* activity by completing the sentence in different ways. Urge students to offer their best sentences for discussion.

TEXT ANALYSIS — COMMON CORE RI 6

● *Model the Skill:* **STYLE AND DICTION**

Read aloud the excerpt on page 1113. Point out that the use of the first person and colloquial phrases such as "the other day" and "bad news" create casualness. Phrases such as "had pledged himself" and "significant and liberty-loving" are elegant because they refer to high ideals.

GUIDED PRACTICE Have students analyze the style and diction of the paragraph that follows the Big Question.

READING SKILL — COMMON CORE RI 6

■ *Model the Skill:* **INTERPRET AUTHOR'S MESSAGE**

To determine an author's message, students need to look for the author's stated opinions. In White's essay, he signals his opinions with such phrases as, "I have an idea that...."

While opinions cannot be proven true, they must be supported by logical facts, reasoning, and evidence in order to be meaningful. Tell students that White supports his opinions with reasoning such as "a despot ... fears a drunken poet who may crack a joke that will take hold" (lines 37–38).

GUIDED PRACTICE Have students find another example of a fact, line of reasoning, or evidence that White uses to support his opinions.

 RESOURCE MANAGER—Copy Master
Interpret Author's Message p. 389

DIFFERENTIATED INSTRUCTION

FOR ENGLISH LANGUAGE LEARNERS

Reading: Options for Reading Emphasize to students that they may have difficulty clarifying the meaning of the some of the essay's longer sentences. Have students begin by silently reading along as they listen to the *Audio Anthology CD*. As students listen to the CD, have them note any sentences that they find difficult to comprehend. Then, have partners reread the selection, working together to clarify the meaning of these difficult sentences.

SUMMARY

With humorous style and diction, White's essay challenges the patriotic notions of writers who feel it is their duty to give up lighthearted writing during times of world crises. White argues that humor and light-heartedness are more necessary during times of trouble than during any other time in history. He encourages writers to do their duty by writing about whatever subjects strike their fancies.

READ WITH A PURPOSE

Help students set a purpose for reading. Tell them to read to discover E. B. White's definition of a writer's duty.

REVISIT THE BIG QUESTION

What do writers **OWE** *us?*

Discuss In line 35, White essentially says that it is the responsibility of writers to ignore responsibility. Ask students to discuss White's meaning. **Possible answer:** *White suggests that the best and most important writing comes from writers' own interests rather than from any sense of duty to external ideas or standards.*

TIERED DISCUSSION PROMPTS

Direct students to lines 35–43. Use these prompts to help students understand White's view about the important and subversive nature of humor:

Connect Have you or someone you know ever told a joke or funny story during a tense or tragic time? What motivated the action, and what effect did it have? *Accept all thoughtful responses.*

Interpret What does White mean by his assertion that a humorist's duty is to ignore duty? **Possible answer:** *White means that humorists can contribute to free society by reminding people of the lighter side of events and by using humor to advance lively debate.*

Evaluate Is humor important during times of challenge? Explain. *Students may agree that comedy—and the resulting merriment or laughter—is important during times of challenge because it helps people to gain new perspectives on difficult situations.*

The Duty of Writers

E. B. White

> **BACKGROUND** This essay appeared in White's column for *Harper's* magazine in January 1939. It was a disturbing time, when it was clear that world war loomed. England and France had just appeased Hitler by allowing him to take over part of Czechoslovakia. The Nazis had looted and burned Jewish homes and businesses on a night that became known as Kristallnacht. Fascist forces were winning in the Spanish Civil War, and Japan had invaded China. In his State of the Union address, President Franklin D. Roosevelt warned that the freedoms Americans enjoyed were in danger.

I was sorry to hear the other day that a certain writer, appalled by the cruel events of the world, had pledged himself never to write anything that wasn't constructive and significant and liberty-loving. I have an idea that this, in its own way, is bad news.

All word-mongers,[1] at one time or another, have felt the divine necessity of using their talents, if any, on the side of right—but I didn't realize that they

---

1. **word-mongers:** those who deal in words for a living.

DIFFERENTIATED INSTRUCTION

FOR ADVANCED LEARNERS/AP

Expert Groups Encourage students to become subject experts by selecting and researching one of these topics:

- Adolf Hitler's rise to power
- Kristallnacht
- fascism and the Spanish Civil War

Have students use visual aids in their class presentations.

FOR STRUGGLING READERS

In combination with the *Audio Anthology CD*, use the Targeted Passage on page 1115 to ensure that students focus on key concepts in the selection. The Targeted Passage is also good for English learners.

❶ Targeted Passage [Lines 35–43]

This passage contains White's central explanation regarding the duty of writers.

were making any resolutions to that effect, and I don't think they should. When liberty's position is challenged, artists and writers are the ones who first take up the sword. They do so without persuasion, for the battle is peculiarly their own. In the nature of things, a person engaged in the flimsy business of expressing himself on paper is dependent on the large general privilege of being heard. Any intimation that this privilege may be revoked throws a writer into a panic. His is a double allegiance to freedom—an intellectual one springing from the conviction that pure thought has a right to function unimpeded, and a selfish one springing from his need, as a bread-winner, to be allowed to speak his piece. America is now liberty-conscious. In a single generation it has progressed from being toothbrush-conscious, to being air-minded, to being liberty-conscious. The transition has been disturbing, but it has been effected, and the last part has been accomplished largely by the good work of writers and artists, to whom liberty is a blessed condition that must be preserved on earth at all costs. **Ⓐ**

But to return to my man who has foresworn everything but what is good and significant. He worries me. I hope he isn't serious, but I'm afraid he is. Having resolved to be nothing but significant, he is in a fair way to lose his effectiveness. A writer must believe in something, obviously, but he shouldn't join a club. Letters flourish not when writers amalgamate,[2] but when they are contemptuous of one another. (Poets are the most contemptuous of all the writing breeds, and in the long run the most exalted and influential.) Even in evil times, a writer should cultivate only what naturally absorbs his fancy, whether it be freedom or cinch bugs, and should write in the way that comes easy. **Ⓑ**

The movement is spreading. I know of one gifted crackpot who used to be employed gainfully in the fields of humor and satire, who has taken a solemn pledge not to write anything funny or light-hearted or "insignificant" again till things get straightened around in the world. This seems to me distinctly deleterious[3] and a little silly. A literature composed of nothing but liberty-loving thoughts is little better than the propaganda which it seeks to defeat. **Ⓒ**

In a free country it is the duty of writers to pay no attention to duty. Only under a dictatorship is literature expected to exhibit an harmonious design or an inspirational tone. A despot doesn't fear eloquent writers preaching freedom—he fears a drunken poet who may crack a joke that will take hold. His gravest concern is lest gaiety, or truth in sheep's clothing, somewhere gain a foothold, lest joy in some unguarded moment be unconfined. I honestly don't believe that a humorist should take the veil[4] today; he should wear his bells night and day, and squeeze the uttermost jape,[5] even though he may feel more like writing a strong letter to the *Herald Tribune*. **Ⓓ**

---

2. **Letters . . . amalgamate:** Writing and literature do not do well when writers form groups.
3. **deleterious:** harmful.
4. **take the veil:** become a nun or, here, a serious, religious person.
5. **wear his bells . . . jape:** consistently act like a jester (who wears a cap with bells) and see the humor in everything.

THE DUTY OF WRITERS **1115**

COMMON CORE RI 6

Ⓐ DICTION
Reread lines 1–19, with special attention to White's **diction,** or choice of words. Notice the **irony** he achieves by using grand words and phrases for ordinary situations and events. In the first sentence, for example, White uses the phrase "appalled by the cruel events of the world" to describe a single moment in the life of an anonymous writer. By using overly serious words such as *appalled,* White lightly mocks writers who take themselves too seriously. What other words and phrases in these lines contribute to White's lightly ironic tone? Explain your response.

Ⓑ AUTHOR'S MESSAGE
In lines 26–28, what does White state that a writer should do?

Ⓒ STYLE AND DICTION
What phrasings add humor to this paragraph?

❶ Targeted Passage

Ⓓ AUTHOR'S MESSAGE
Reread lines 37–43. What value does White see in humor?

TEXT ANALYSIS   COMMON CORE
                                     RI 6

Ⓐ DICTION
Read aloud lines 1–19, emphasizing words or phrases White means ironically. Explain that in this passage he mocks not only writers' concern about the seriousness of ordinary situations, but also their sometimes inflated sense of self importance.

Possible answer: ones that inflate the status of writers and their craft, including "artists and writers are the ones who first take up the sword" (7–8), "progressed from being toothbrush-conscious" (lines 15–16), "accomplished largely by the good work of writers . . . to whom liberty is a blessed condition that must be preserved on earth at all costs" (lines 18–19)

READING SKILL   COMMON CORE
                                     RI 6

Ⓑ AUTHOR'S MESSAGE
Possible answer: write about their interests in a manner that comes easily

---

TEXT ANALYSIS   COMMON CORE
                                     RI 6

Ⓒ STYLE AND DICTION
Possible answer: juxtaposing the phrases "gifted crackpot" and "employed gainfully" (lines 29–30) and "distinctly deleterious" and "a little silly" (lines 32–33), as the idea of "literature composed of nothing but liberty-loving thoughts" (lines 33–34)

READING SKILL   COMMON CORE
                                     RI 6

Ⓓ AUTHOR'S MESSAGE
Possible answer: White thinks that jokes and gaiety can weaken dictators.

SELECTION WRAP-UP

READ WITH A PURPOSE Ask students to explain White's definition of a writer's duty. *Possible answer: To stay true to his or her style of writing and desired subject matter.*

- What is a writer's duty? (line 35)
- What kind of literature is expected under a dictatorship? (lines 35–37)
- What does a despot fear? (lines 37–40)
- What does White believe that humorists should do during difficult times? (lines 40–43)

FOR STRUGGLING READERS

Develop Reading Fluency To help students gain fluency in reading persuasive texts, read aloud lines 29–43, emphasizing pauses for punctuation. Then read the lines again, with students following you in an echo reading of the passage.

Practice and Apply

For preliminary support of post-reading questions, use these copy masters:

R RESOURCE MANAGER—Copy Masters
Reading Check p. 391
Style and Diction p. 387
Question Support p. 392
Additional selection questions are provided for teachers on page 381.

ANSWERS

COMMON CORE **RI 6**

1. *White is sorry to hear that a certain writer has pledged not to write anything that isn't constructive, significant, and liberty-loving.*

2. *America has become conscious of liberty in a way that it wasn't previously.*

3. *If writers bind themselves to a single view-point or cause, no matter how important or serious, they risk losing their unique percep-tions and style and becoming redundant, inauthentic, and ultimately insignificant.*

Possible answers:

4. ● **COMMON CORE FOCUS** Interpret Author's Message *White supports writ-ers who write about what interests them in easy and humorous ways. He opposes writing that is intentionally serious and significant.*

5. *Students may agree that literature should not be rigid or narrowly focused in its themes; that, as artists, writers should write about topics of choice, even in evil times; that artists should not be bound by any sense of duty, and that despots should not fear direct messages but rather messages cloaked in seemingly harmless garb.*

Assess and Reteach

Assess

DIAGNOSTIC AND SELECTION TESTS
Selection Test A pp. 305–306
Selection Test B/C pp. 307–308

Interactive Selection Test on thinkcentral.com

Reteach

Level Up Online Tutorials on thinkcentral.com

Reteaching Worksheets on thinkcentral.com

Literature Lessons 43, 44

Comprehension

1. **Recall** At the beginning of the essay, what is White "sorry to hear"?

2. **Clarify** How has America changed in a generation, according to White?

3. **Paraphrase** What does White mean when he says, "Having resolved to be nothing but significant, he is in a fair way to lose his effectiveness"?

Text Analysis

● 4. **Interpret Author's Message** Look back at the chart you created as you read. What kind of writing does White favor, and what does he oppose? Summarize his main message.

5. **Evaluate Opinions** Do you agree with White's opinions about the **responsibility** of writers? React to each of the following statements:

   • "A literature composed of nothing but liberty-loving thoughts is little better than the propaganda which it seeks to defeat." (lines 33–34)

   • "Even in evil times, a writer should cultivate only what naturally absorbs his fancy. . . ." (lines 26–27)

   • "In a free country it is the duty of writers to pay no attention to duty." (line 35)

   • "A despot doesn't fear eloquent writers preaching freedom—he fears a drunken poet who may crack a joke that will take hold." (lines 37–38)

● 6. **Analyze Style and Diction** Choose a sentence from the essay that you find particularly thought provoking. Does it contain expressions that are casual, elegant, humorous, or a combination? Explain your answer.

7. **Compare Texts** Both White and Dorothy Parker (page 1104) wrote for the *New Yorker* magazine. How is White's **voice** different from Parker's? What do both essays suggest about the magazine's **tone?**

Text Criticism

8. **Historical Context** White was writing at a time when fascism was on the rise overseas but America had not yet become involved in World War II. Do you think his message would have been the same if he were writing later, say, after the horrors of the Holocaust had become known? Would it have been the same if America had been turning toward fascism?

> *What do writers* **OWE** *us?*
>
> E.B. White expresses the view that "the duty of writers" is to write about whatever interests them, regardless of the prevailing social, cultural, or political climate. Do you think writers should be free to write whatever they want whenever they want? Explain.

COMMON CORE

RI 6 Determine an author's point of view or purpose in a text in which the rhetoric is particularly effective, analyzing how style and content contribute to the power, persuasiveness, or beauty of the text.

---

6. ● **COMMON CORE FOCUS** Analyze Style and Diction *Answers will vary.*

7. *White's and Parker's voices are both humor-ous, but White exhibits a gentler humor while Parker is more mocking and sarcastic. Both writers reflect that the magazine's tone is engaging and entertaining.*

8. *White might have had the same message, because he believed strongly in the ability of writers to serve as role models for freedom. However, he might have softened a bit in the face of genocide or American censorship.*

> *What do writers* OWE *us?*
> Answers will vary. Students might note that writers should be free to write whatever they want because if a writer shows restraint due to sensitive social, cultural, or political issues, then his or her writing will not challenge any of the prevailing thoughts of the day. Other students might say that a respectful writer should think of how their writing affects their readers and should show social, cultural, and political sensitivity when writing.

Journalism Beyond the Facts

Journalism is typically regarded as writing whose purpose is to convey to readers the facts as they are known—to answer the questions *who? what? when? where?* and *how?* Depending on their assignment and its purpose, journalists may strive for detached objectivity or may more subjectively shape the stories they report, the ideas they explore, and the claims they make.

Writing to Evaluate

Each of the selections beginning on page 1096 goes beyond "just the facts" and conveys the writer's perspective on a particular topic. This perspective largely determines the structure and flow of each piece. Skim each selection and look for words, phrases, or sentences that help you discern the writer's perspective. Then try your own hand at writing a news story that conveys more than just the facts. Choose an event, such as a school play, a varsity track meet, or even a typical lunch break in the cafeteria, and report it from your own perspective. Use the selections in this section as your inspiration.

Consider

- how the authors in this section revealed their personal perspectives and how their perspectives shaped their writing
- what basic facts you need to convey about your topic
- how best to reveal your thoughts about the event you witness

Extension

SPEAKING & LISTENING Much of journalism is distinguished by its tone. From factual, unemotional reporting to lurid mudslinging—today's journalism encompasses it all. Find three examples of current news stories that range widely in tone. You might search for stories in traditional newspapers, entertainment magazines, home decorating magazines, supermarket tabloids, or online news sources. Create a **poster** with copies of the stories and their headlines and **present** it to the class, explaining why you think— or do not think—the tone of each story is appropriate for its content.

COMMON CORE

RI 9 Analyze U.S. documents of literary significance for their themes, purposes, and rhetorical features. **W 4** Produce clear and coherent writing in which the style is appropriate to task, purpose, and audience. **W 9b (RI 6)** Determine an author's point of view or purpose in a text. **L 1** Demonstrate command of the conventions of standard English usage when speaking.

1117

COMMON CORE FOCUS

RI 9 Analyze U.S. documents of literary significance for their themes, purposes, and rhetorical features.
W 4 Produce clear and coherent writing in which the style is appropriate to task, purpose, and audience.
L 1 Demonstrate command of the conventions of standard English usage when speaking.

Wrap-Up: Journalism as Literature

This Wrap-Up provides students with an opportunity to revisit ideas from the literature in this section about ways that journalists elevate reporting to a literary art form. What methods were discussed? What goals did writers identify for themselves as journalists? Urge students to examine their own views on the craft of journalism and impact in light of insights gained from the selections.

Writing to Evaluate

- Review with students that *evaluating* means judging or determining the worth or quality of something. This skill helps readers form their own opinions regarding events and ideas. Here, students will use evaluation to distill each writer's perspective from his or her writing, and then to select style elements that will convey their own perspective in a news story.

- To help students create their news stories, suggest that they first take objective notes about their events, noting both facts and sensory details. Then, have students write one sentence stating an overall impression of the event. Tell students to select details and words that support this impression.

Extension

- Remind students that tone is the writer's attitude toward his or her subject as conveyed through style elements such as word choice and syntax.

- After students collect their news stories, have them describe each writer's tone. Challenge them to identify supporting evidence from the article for their tone descriptions. Students can use these insights to plan their posters and presentations.

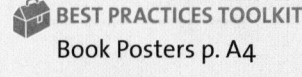 **BEST PRACTICES TOOLKIT**
Book Posters p. A4

FOR STRUGGLING WRITERS

Writing Support Help students list strategies, such as sarcasm or humor, that each of the selection writers uses to reveal their personal perspectives. Discuss with students each technique's effect on the writer's message and on readers. Then, urge students to choose three of these strategies to use in their news stories. Help students choose strategies that support the dominant impressions they wish to convey.

FOR ENGLISH LANGUAGE LEARNERS

Writing with Personal Perspective To help students state their personal impression of an event, provide these sentence starters:

- The school play made me think about _____.

- The track meet made me feel _____.

- Lunchtime in the cafeteria sounds like _____.

Urge students to use facts to support their personal impressions.

Focus and Motivate

COMMON CORE FOCUS

W 1a–e Write arguments to support claims in an analysis of substantive topics or texts; introduce a precise claim; create an organization that logically sequences claims, counterclaims, reasons, and evidence; use words, phrases, and clauses to clarify relationships. **W 4** Produce clear and coherent writing appropriate to task, purpose, and audience. **W 5** Develop and strengthen writing by planning, revising, editing, rewriting, or trying a new approach. **L 2b** Spell correctly. **L 3a** Vary syntax for effect. **W 9** Draw evidence from texts to support analysis. **W 10** Write routinely over shorter time frames for a range of tasks, purposes, and audiences.

WRITE WITH A PURPOSE

Advise students to choose an issue about which they have a strong opinion. To identify an appropriate audience, have them consider people who already care about the issue.

COMMON CORE TRAITS

Review the three *COMMON CORE TRAITS* with students, focusing on the development of ideas. Clarify the basic structure of an argument as needed. Then compare the list of traits with the rubric on page 1126.

ADDITIONAL TASKS

Write About Work Think about a job you have held. Write a memo persuading your employer or coworkers to adopt a new policy in the workplace.
Possible topics: wages; work schedules; efficiency; cleanliness; communication

Write About Art Think of a work of art that inspires strong reactions. Write a persuasive essay arguing for or against its artistic merits.
Possible topics: a movie; a television series; a book; a painting; a song or a type of music

---

Writing Online

The following tools are available online at **thinkcentral.com** and on **Write***Smart* CD-ROM:
- Interactive Graphic Organizers
- Interactive Student Models
- Interactive Revision Lessons

Writing Workshop

ARGUMENT

Persuasive Essay

The writers and artists you have read about in this unit were not afraid to state their opinions. Through their work, they argued about what it meant to be modern. They also asserted claims about how best to preserve their heritage and ideals. In this workshop, you will learn how to build an effective argument by writing a persuasive essay about an issue relevant to today's world.

 Complete the workshop activities in your **Reader/Writer Notebook**.

WRITE WITH A PURPOSE

WRITING TASK
Write a **persuasive essay** that asserts a claim about a substantive issue of our time. Support your claim with reasons and evidence that will convince your audience to accept your position or take a specific action.

Idea Starters
- What should be the government's role in responding to a national crisis?
- What, if any, responsibilities do advertisers have—and to whom?
- In times of challenge, is escapism necessary or irresponsible?
- Has the field of journalism changed for the better or for the worse?

THE ESSENTIALS
Here are some common purposes, audiences, and formats for persuasive writing.

PURPOSES	AUDIENCES	FORMATS
• to persuade people to agree with your claim	• classmates and teacher	• essay for class
	• parents	• editorial
• to motivate others to take action	• community members	• speech
	• government representatives	• video or multimedia presentation
	• Web users	• commercial/PSA
		• blog

COMMON CORE TRAITS

1. DEVELOPMENT OF IDEAS
- includes an **introduction** that identifies an issue and states a **precise knowledgeable claim**
- fairly and thoroughly develops the claim with **valid reasons** and **relevant evidence**
- anticipates **opposing claims** and provides **counterclaims**
- has a **concluding section** that supports the argument

2. ORGANIZATION OF IDEAS
- **sequences** claims, counterclaims, and evidence in a **logical way**
- uses **transitions** to create **cohesion** and link ideas

3. LANGUAGE FACILITY AND CONVENTIONS
- maintains a **formal style** and an **objective tone**
- uses **parallelism** for effect
- employs correct **grammar**, **mechanics**, and **spelling**

Writing Online
THINK central

Go to **thinkcentral.com**.
KEYWORD: HML11N-1118

Writing Workshop Resources

R RESOURCE MANAGER UNIT 5
Plan and Teach pp. 393–396
Prewriting–Editing pp. 397–401
Writing Rubric p. 402
Speaking and Listening p. 403
Writing Support p. 404*

BEST PRACTICES TOOLKIT
Writing Template: Persuasive Essay pp. C16, C31

TECHNOLOGY
- **Teacher One Stop DVD-ROM**
- **Student One Stop DVD-ROM**
- **Write***Smart* CD-ROM
- **GrammarNotes DVD-ROM**

Writing Center on thinkcentral.com

See resources on the **Teacher One Stop DVD-ROM** *and on* **thinkcentral.com**.

* Resources for Differentiation

Planning/Prewriting

 COMMON CORE

W 1a–e Write arguments to support claims in an analysis of substantive topics or texts, using valid reasoning and relevant and sufficient evidence. **W 5** Develop and strengthen writing as needed by planning.

Getting Started

CHOOSE A SUBSTANTIVE ISSUE

For your argument, consider meaningful, **substantive issues** that matter to many people and that are open to disagreement. Be sure to focus on issues that you care about. List a few of these issues, noting the most commonly held opinions about each. Then choose an issue about which you can make a strong, persuasive argument.

THINK ABOUT AUDIENCE AND PURPOSE

As you explore your issue in greater depth, keep in mind your **purpose** for writing: to persuade your **audience** to agree with your claim. Consider your audience's knowledge of the topic and their potential concerns.

STATE YOUR CLAIM

State your position in a strong, knowledgeable **claim.** This statement will be the focus of your argument, so make sure it is **significant** and **precise.** You must be able to support your claim with reasons and evidence. If you find that you cannot support your claim, rework it or choose a different issue. Once you are satisfied with your claim, think about your **call to action,** or what you want your audience to do once they are persuaded by your argument.

▶ **WHAT DOES IT LOOK LIKE?**

> **Responsibility of advertisers**
> * Advertisers should not market violent video games to kids.
> * An advertiser's job is to sell products. Parents must guide their children to avoid buying or playing such games.
>
> **How journalism has changed**
> * News programs no longer offer well-researched news stories, only sensationalized information.
> * News programs today are more interesting because they appeal to viewers' interests.

▶ **ASK YOURSELF:**

* Who is my audience, and how does this issue affect them? How much do they already know about the issue? What opinions do they hold?
* What position do I want my audience to take? What do I want them to do?
* How receptive might my audience be to my position? What objections might they have?

▶ **WHAT DOES IT LOOK LIKE?**

Issue	Claim	Call to action
How journalism has changed	The standards of journalism have declined sharply in recent years.	Contact your local newspaper or TV station when you read or see a story that is misleading or inaccurate.

WRITING WORKSHOP **1119**

DIFFERENTIATED INSTRUCTION

FOR ENGLISH LANGUAGE LEARNERS

Language: Reinforce Persuasive Terms Write these terms on the board and review them with students:

* *issue:* a subject, situation, or idea that has at least two sides
* *position:* an opinion about an issue
* *claim:* a sentence stating the writer's position on an issue
* *reasons:* statements that explain why the writer takes a specific position

* *evidence:* information that supports a reason, such as facts, examples, statistics, and the opinions of experts
* *opposing claim:* a position on the issue that is different from the writer's
* *counterclaim:* the writer's response to an opposing claim
* *call to action:* the writer's request to readers to do something in response to the position stated in the argument

---

Teach

Planning/Prewriting

 COMMON CORE **W 1a–e, W 5**

▶ **CHOOSE A SUBSTANTIVE ISSUE** Remind students to read the Idea Starters on page 1118 as well as to brainstorm other possible topics. Suggest that they ask themselves these questions:

* Which issue do I care most about? Is the issue significant—that is, does it affect many people's lives in meaningful ways?
* How do I articulate my position on the issue, and what reasons might I offer to support this claim?
* What are some possible opposing claims?

Emphasize the importance of choosing an issue for which significant reasons and evidence can be provided on both sides.

▶ **THINK ABOUT AUDIENCE AND PURPOSE** Clarify that valid reasons can be supported by evidence, such as facts, examples, and statistics. Relevant evidence is closely related to the reason that it supports. These elements become especially important when the audience initially disagrees with the writer's claim, or when the audience is learning about the issue for the first time. To persuade people who hold opposing views, students will need to provide especially strong reasons. To persuade an audience with little prior knowledge, students will need to provide background information in addition to reasons and evidence.

▶ **STATE YOUR CLAIM** When students have drafted their claim statements, have them share these claims with partners. Tell students to give each other feedback on whether the claims are clearly stated and supportable. Also encourage them to consider whether each issue is one that people might reasonably argue on both sides. If a student has selected an issue on which almost everyone agrees, then he or she should pick a different topic.

R RESOURCE MANAGER—Copy Masters

Plan and Teach pp. 393–396
Prewriting–Editing pp. 397–401
Writing Rubric p. 402
Speaking and Listening p. 403
Writing Support p. 404

WRITING WORKSHOP **1119**

Planning/Prewriting continued

▶ **GATHER SUPPORT FOR YOUR CLAIM** Review with students the four types of evidence and the examples in the chart. Then have students work individually or with partners to create a similar chart related to their own argument. This activity will help them see what evidence they already have (such as anecdotes and analogies) and what they need to research.

▶ **ANTICIPATE OPPOSING CLAIMS** Discuss with students what it means to develop a counterclaim fairly and thoroughly. Point out that if a writer states an opposing claim and then simply dismisses it as a foolish idea, the audience may conclude that the writer has not carefully considered the issue from both sides. Ask students to identify the type of evidence provided for the counterclaim on page 1120 (*testimonial, or expert opinion*). Then have students meet in small groups to share their claims and have other group members suggest opposing claims. Students should record these opposing claims in their notebooks and then work independently to prepare thorough, well-supported counterclaims.

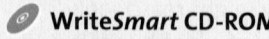 Have students complete the **Your Turn** activity independently. Then have them meet with partners. Each student should present a brief oral outline of his or her argument. The partner should then provide feedback about which reasons are the strongest, which need more evidence, and which pieces of evidence are the most relevant and persuasive.

For interactive graphic organizers, see

💿 **WriteSmart CD-ROM**

Writing Center on <u>thinkcentral.com</u>

Planning/Prewriting *continued*

Getting Started

GATHER SUPPORT FOR YOUR CLAIM

Reasons explain why you believe your claim is true. A reason is valid only if it is supported by **relevant** and **sufficient** evidence. In other words, each piece of evidence must strongly relate to the reason it supports. Also, you must provide enough evidence to convince your audience. Most evidence falls into one of the following categories:

- **anecdote**— specific example, incident, or personal experience
- **analogy**— an illustration of an unfamiliar concept by comparing it to something familiar
- **expert opinion**— informed opinion attributed to a credible source
- **fact** or **statistic**— indisputable information and numerical data

▶ WHAT DOES IT LOOK LIKE?

Evidence

Anecdote: Yesterday I read a newspaper article about our mayor that I knew could not be true.	**Analogy:** If I write a term paper full of unsupported claims, I get a failing grade; when newspapers print unsubstantiated stories, they don't even apologize.
Expert Opinion: One prominent reporter and university lecturer agrees that journalism standards are in serious decline.	**Statistic:** A recent study of local TV stations found that 65 percent of "news" stories contained factual inaccuracies.

ANTICIPATE OPPOSING CLAIMS

Remember that members of your audience may hold different opinions about the issue than you do. Anticipate these **alternate** or **opposing claims** and be prepared to respond. Think carefully about each opposing claim so that you can acknowledge both its strengths and its limitations. Then develop your **counterclaim** with solid reasons and evidence.

▶ WHAT DOES IT LOOK LIKE?

Opposing Claim: News programs today are more interesting because they appeal to viewers' interests.

Counterclaim and Evidence: Entertainment is not the main goal of journalism. The American Society of News Editors states that the responsibility of news media is to inform people so they can make decisions about important issues.

PEER REVIEW Share your claim, reasons, and evidence with a peer. Ask: Is my evidence sufficient to persuade my audience? Discuss the kinds of reasons and evidence that would provide better support for your claim.

 In your *Reader/Writer Notebook*, use a chart like the one on page 1119 to develop your claim. List reasons for the claim, and then gather strong, credible evidence from a variety of sources to support each reason. Jot down anecdotal evidence from your experience that relates to your topic.

DIFFERENTIATED INSTRUCTION

FOR ENGLISH LANGUAGE LEARNERS

Language: Types of Evidence Review these terms and their Spanish translations:

- anecdote (*anécdota*)—a brief story or example that makes a point
- analogy (*analogía*)—a comparison between two things or situations
- testimony (*testimonio*)—a statement from someone who knows about the issue
- fact (*hecho*)—something that can be shown or proven to be true

FOR STRUGGLING WRITERS

Writing: Gather Support Give students these sentence frames to help them outline their arguments:

- My issue is _____.
- On this issue, I believe that _____.
- One reason for my claim is _____.
- Facts that support my reason are _____.
- A second reason for my claim is _____.
- Facts that support my reason are _____.

Drafting

The following chart shows how to organize your draft to create a coherent and effective persuasive essay.

COMMON CORE **W 1c** Use words, phrases, and clauses to clarify the relationships between claims and reasons, reasons and evidence, claims and counterclaims. **W 4** Produce clear and coherent writing appropriate to task, purpose, and audience.

Organizing Your Persuasive Essay

INTRODUCTION
- Grab your audience's attention with an interesting **fact**, **quotation**, or **anecdote**.
- Identify the issue and state a precise, knowledgeable **claim**.

▼

BODY
- Present your **reasons** in a **logical order**, such as order of importance.
- Explain each reason with **relevant**, **varied**, and **sufficient evidence**.
- Distinguish your claim from **opposing claims**. Fairly and thoroughly describe each opposing claim and present **counterclaims**.
- Maintain a **formal style** and an **objective tone**. Avoid being defensive or dismissive of other viewpoints.

▼

CONCLUDING SECTION
- Restate your **claim** and its **significance**.
- End with a **call to action** that urges your audience to respond in a specific way.

GRAMMAR IN CONTEXT: USE VARIED TRANSITIONS

To craft a **coherent** argument, you need to connect all the related ideas. **Transitions** are the words, phrases, and clauses that show how the parts of your argument are related. This chart shows a variety of transitions that you might use in your essay.

Type of Transition	Examples	Usage
Support or opposition	▶ *furthermore, but, conversely, in reality*	**Recently**, technology has sped up the pace of news delivery. **As a result**, we have witnessed the birth of the "24/7 News Monster." This beast—a hungry conglomeration of Web sites, bloggers, and cable channels—must be fed hourly. But, **in reality**, reporters cannot produce quality journalism at this frenzied pace.
Cause or effect	▶ *because of, as a result*	
Examples	▶ *frequently, for example*	
Sequence	▶ *before, after, next, recently, over time*	

YOUR TURN

Develop a first draft of your essay, following the structure outlined in the chart above. Use at least five transitions to connect your ideas.

FOR ENGLISH LANGUAGE LEARNERS

Language: Transitions Reinforce students' understanding of common transitions by having them complete the following argument. Encourage them to substitute different transitions to suit their topic and ideas.

I believe our school should (or should not) _____ because _____ . For example, _____ . Furthermore, _____ . However, some people believe that _____ . In fact, _____ . Overall, _____ .

FOR STRUGGLING WRITERS

Transitions To give students a model of the effective use of transitions, have them review Lincoln's Gettysburg Address on page 584. Ask them to note transitions that show sequence (*Four score and seven years ago, Now*) and contrast (*But, rather*). Discuss how these transitions help Lincoln convey two main messages: the historical importance of the moment when he is speaking, and the best way to honor the lives of fallen soldiers.

Practice and Apply

Drafting

COMMON CORE **W 1c, W 4**

▶ **INTRODUCTION** Tell students that their opening paragraph must clearly introduce their issue and claim while also inspiring readers to keep reading. Ask volunteers to give examples of facts or anecdotes that would capture readers' interest. Point out that while the introduction should convey the writer's passion and concern, it must also create a tone that is knowledgeable and fair, not overly emotional.

▶ **BODY** Discuss options for sequencing reasons in a logical and persuasive way. For example, arranging reasons from least important to most important builds to a climax and leaves the most convincing reason fresh in readers' minds at the end of the argument. However, starting off with the most important reason makes an immediate impact and pulls readers into the argument. In that case, the writer might choose to end with the second most important reason for a strong finish.

▶ **CONCLUDING SECTION** If students are having trouble crafting a call to action, suggest that they ask themselves how their own behavior is affected by their belief in their claim. What similar behavior would they like to see from other people?

GRAMMAR IN CONTEXT: USE VARIED TRANSITIONS

For practice, have students write a paragraph based on this claim: Fresh fruit and vegetables should be cheaper to buy than processed junk food. Ask them to include three reasons and to use transitions to clarify relationships between the claim and the reasons.

YOUR TURN Ask students to complete the **Your Turn** activity independently, remembering to use transitions as they draft their arguments. Suggest that students write their drafts double-spaced so it will be easy to make revisions later.

For a persuasive essay writing template, see

📦 BEST PRACTICES TOOLKIT—Transparency Writing Template: Persuasive Essay pp. C16, C31

💿 **WriteSmart** CD-ROM

Writing Center on **thinkcentral.com**

Revising

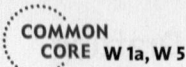 **COMMON CORE** W 1a, W 5

Model the Skill Using a draft argument on a transparency or electronic whiteboard, model how to use the questions, tips, and strategies suggested in the chart to evaluate and revise. Consider using an argument written by a student from a different class or from a previous year. Be sure to remove the writer's name from the essay so that the writer remains anonymous.

YOUR TURN Suggest that students jot down a few questions or problems about their own drafts before they meet with their partners. Then they can ask for help with specific issues. Students giving feedback should first say what they find effective and persuasive about the argument, and then offer suggestions for improvement.

For interactive revisions tools, see

🔘 **Write*Smart* CD-ROM**

Writing Center on thinkcentral.com

Revising

Revising means evaluating the development, organization, and style of your argument. Your goal is to determine if you have achieved your purpose and effectively communicated your ideas to a specific audience. The questions, tips, and strategies in the following chart can help you revise and rewrite as needed.

PERSUASIVE ESSAY

Ask Yourself	Tips	Revision Strategies
1. Does the introduction grab the audience's attention and include a precise claim?	**Bracket** the attention-grabbing text. **Draw a wavy line** under the claim.	**Add** an attention-grabbing fact, quotation, or anecdote. **Rework** the existing claim to make it more precise.
2. Are there at least three valid reasons to support the claim? Is each reason supported by relevant and sufficient evidence?	**Underline** each reason. **Circle** each piece of evidence and **draw an arrow** to the reason it supports.	**Add** reasons or **revise** existing ones to strengthen their validity. **Add** relevant evidence, such as facts and statistics, to support the argument.
3. Do I use varied transitions to link my claim, reasons, and evidence?	**Circle** each transitional word, phrase, or clause. **Note** any transitions used more than once or twice.	**Add** words, phrases, or clauses to link ideas and create a smooth flow. **Replace** repeated transitions with ones that haven't been used.
4. Are the reasons presented in the most persuasive order?	**Number** the reasons in the margin, ranking them according to strength.	**Rearrange** the reasons into a more logical order, such as strength of evidence.
5. Are opposing claims fairly acknowledged and refuted with counterclaims?	**Put a plus sign** by each sentence that addresses an opposing claim.	**Add** sentences that address opposing claims, refuting each with a counterclaim.
6. Does the concluding section restate the claim and include a call to action?	**Put a box** around the restatement of the claim. **Highlight** the call to action.	**Add** a sentence that restates the claim. **Add** a call to action.

YOUR TURN **PEER REVIEW** Exchange your argument with a classmate or read it aloud to a partner. Use the chart above to help each other identify parts of your essays that need strengthening, reworking, or a new approach.

DIFFERENTIATED INSTRUCTION

FOR STRUGGLING WRITERS

Precise Language Remind students that a claim must be stated precisely—clearly and exactly—so that readers know for sure what the writer's position on the issue is. Share this example of a claim statement and have students rewrite it more precisely:

- Advertisers have a lot of power and can influence people to act against their own interests. (*Advertisers have a responsibility not to make unhealthy foods seem irresistible to young children.*)

FOR ADVANCED LEARNERS/AP

Evaluate Arguments Distribute copies of the Analysis Frame: Persuasion. Students may use it to evaluate their own drafts as well as to critique those of their peers.

 BEST PRACTICES TOOLKIT—Copy Master
Analysis Frame: Persuasion pp. D44–D45

COMMON CORE

W 1a Introduce a precise claim.
W 5 Strengthen writing by revising, editing, rewriting, or trying a new approach.

ANALYZE A STUDENT DRAFT

Read this student's draft, noting the comments about its strengths as well as suggestions for improvement.

What's Happened to the News?
by Mia Bloom, Brookfield High School

❶ "Election fraud? Join us after the break to hear why Mayor David Silva may not be a city resident." This story aired last night on Channel 7 news. Were it true, this fact would invalidate Silva's election—but it's not. Channel 7 based its story on a single source: Sarah Franklin, who is running for mayor against Silva. Is this acceptable journalism? On the contrary. It's just one more example of bad journalism.

> Mia grabs her audience's attention with an **anecdote** that introduces her **topic**.

> Mia needs to strengthen her claim to make it more precise.

❷ What Channel 7 did is not an isolated incident. So-called "news stories" like these are part of a growing national trend. According to Dan Rather, one-time anchor of the CBS Evening News, "traditional journalism is under siege." For one thing, newspapers are cutting staff or closing up shop. One study reveals that since 2000, employment in print newsrooms has dropped by more than 15,000. This dramatic cut in staff means less fact-checking and more inaccurate stories being rushed to production.

❸ Additionally, TV stations now consider news an entertainment division that must turn a profit. In order to gain viewers, news programs rush to be the first to report a story, sometimes without all the facts or with deliberately misleading information designed for shock value. Either way, the results are the same. Citizens are not equipped to make informed decisions. Rather believes the situation is so dire that media reform should be "an immediate national priority."

> A quotation provides **relevant evidence** for Mia's argument.

LEARN HOW Strengthen Your Claim Mia states a claim in her first paragraph, but it's not as precise as it could be. She reworked this section, crafting a new claim that better explains her opinion and describes the troubling effects of the problem.

MIA'S REVISION TO PARAGRAPH ❶

Is this acceptable journalism? On the contrary. ~~It's just one more example of bad journalism.~~

It's just one more example of journalism's declining standards. Television news reporters are not upholding their responsibility to inform the general public, which prevents citizens from making informed decisions.

FOR ENGLISH LANGUAGE LEARNERS

Writing: Strengthen Claims Discuss the revision to the Student Draft, clarifying the meanings of words and phrases such as *declining standards, upholding,* and *informed decisions.* Make sure students understand that these terms are examples of precise language. Work with small groups of students to identify vague language in their claims and to revise them with precise wording.

FOR STRUGGLING WRITERS

Use a Logical Sequence For practice, display the following claim. Invite students to work in pairs to improve the claim by using precise words and phrases.

Claim: Study time isn't useful time. (*Possible revised claim: Students have too many study halls, which takes away from the limited instructional time they have in class.*)

ANALYZE A STUDENT DRAFT

Explain that the Student Draft on this page is the first half of a persuasive essay. Model reading the draft and the annotations in blue, and explain that the yellow highlighting illustrates the student's language choices. Explain that the following *Learn How* mini-lessons provide helpful information about ways to improve this student draft as well as their own.

LEARN HOW Strengthen Your Claim

- Read aloud the original version of paragraph 1. Then read aloud Mia's revised version. Discuss how Mia's revised claim uses precise language to better explain her position on the issue. Point out her use of clear, exact wording, such as "declining standards," "not upholding their responsibility," and "prevents citizens from making informed decisions."

- Remind students that if their claim is "fuzzy" or weak because of imprecise language, it may indicate that they are unsure of their opinion on the issue. Encourage students to rethink their opinion or position as the first step in improving their claim.

- Suggest that students work with partners or in small groups. Have them take turns reading their introductions aloud and discussing their claims. Ask them to focus their discussions on questions such as: How strong is the claim? Is it as precisely worded as it could be? How might it be reworded to strengthen or improve it?

- Invite a volunteer to write his or her introduction on the board or interactive whiteboard. As a class, work together to improve the claim by using specific words and phrases.

Explain that the Student Draft is continued and completed on this page. Read the draft and annotations aloud and discuss. Ask students to comment on how well the first two sentences in paragraph 4 provide a transition to the writer's concluding section and her call to action.

LEARN HOW Use a Logical Sequence

- Read aloud the original version of Mia's paragraph 4, and then read aloud her revised version. Discuss how the logical sequence of a claim followed by a counterclaim, as well as the transition Mia added, help readers understand why she included the quotation from ASNE.

- Point out that a claim is usually followed by a reason, which is then followed by evidence for the reason. Suggest that as students revise their own drafts, they label claims, reasons, and evidence with the letters C, R, and E. This will help them see at a glance whether they have presented evidence in a logical sequence.

- Tell students that reading their own drafts aloud can help them determine if they have presented their ideas clearly. If they discover that their draft is confusing, they might need to rearrange sentences as Mia did to create a more logical sequence.

YOUR TURN Before students complete the **Your Turn** activity, have them work with partners to discuss any counterclaims in their drafts. If students find a counterclaim less than persuasive, they should give their partner advice on how to strengthen it.

For interactive revisions tools, see

💿 Write*Smart* CD-ROM

Writing Center on thinkcentral.com

---

4   According to the standards of the American Society of News Editors (ASNE), "Good faith with the reader is the foundation of good journalism. Every effort must be made to assure that the news content is accurate . . . and that all sides are presented fairly." By failing to present both sides of the story about Mayor Silva, Channel 7 violated this principle. Now, there may be some of you who believe that Channel 7 did nothing wrong. After all, the station did not state that Silva was ineligible to be mayor—it simply allowed his opponent to do so. Information that is deliberately misleading for ratings' sake is just as bad as inaccurate information.

> Mia addresses an **opposing claim** and responds with a **counterclaim.** However, her ideas are not arranged in a logical sequence.

5   We citizens must act. In running this one-sided story, Channel 7 abandoned its role and violated the public trust. Actions such as this can have huge ramifications on our ability to elect effective leaders. When you see instances of unbalanced reporting in any form of public media, take it upon yourself to contact the newspaper or TV station and encourage your community to do the same. As citizens, it is our responsibility to let the media know that they must be more vigilant in upholding their responsibility to the public they serve.

> In her concluding section, Mia **restates her claim** and provides a **call to action.**

LEARN HOW Use a Logical Sequence
The information in Mia's fourth paragraph is confusing because the sequence is out of order. To strengthen her reasoning, she shifted the opposing claim and added a transition.

MIA'S REVISION TO PARAGRAPH 4

According to the standards of the American Society of News Editors (ASNE), "Good faith with the reader is the foundation of good journalism. Every effort must be made to assure that the news content is accurate . . . and that all sides are presented fairly." By failing to present both sides of the story about Mayor Silva, Channel 7 violated this principle. Now, there may be some of you who believe that Channel 7 did nothing wrong. After all, the station did not state that Silva was ineligible to be mayor—it simply allowed his opponent to do so. *However,* Information that is deliberately misleading for ratings' sake is just as bad as inaccurate information.

YOUR TURN Use feedback from your peers and your teacher as well as the two "Learn How" lessons to revise your argument. Evaluate how well your essay uses compelling reasons, strong evidence, and a clear call to action.

DIFFERENTIATED INSTRUCTION

FOR ENGLISH LANGUAGE LEARNERS
Writing: Logical Sequence Have students complete these sentence frames to create an argument that follows a logical order. Help them identify each statement as an opposing claim, a counterclaim, or evidence.

Some people believe that high school students should not be allowed to _____. However, I believe that _____ because _____. An example (or fact) that proves this is _____.

FOR STRUGGLING WRITERS
Use a Logical Sequence Write these sentences on the board. Work with students to identify each one as an opposing claim, counterclaim, or evidence.

Some people argue that dogs are happier when they are allowed to roam free. (*opposing claim*) However, pet owners are responsible for their pets' safety as well as happiness. (*counterclaim*) According to Dr. Perez, the number of dogs hit by cars would decrease by 80 percent if dog owners followed the leash law. (*evidence*)

Editing and Publishing

COMMON CORE **W 1a** Create an organization that logically sequences claims, counterclaims, reasons, and evidence. **W 5** Strengthen writing by editing. **L 2b** Spell correctly. **L 3a** Vary syntax for effect.

When you write a persuasive essay, you want to show your knowledge and authority on the topic. Mistakes in grammar, usage, and punctuation can distract your audience from focusing on your argument. In the editing stage, you proofread your essay to make sure it is free of such errors. Also, check for spelling errors that your word-processing spell-check function may not have caught.

GRAMMAR IN CONTEXT: PARALLELISM AND SYNTAX

Good writers vary their **syntax**—the order of words and phrases in sentences—to make their writing more engaging. However, when used as a stylistic device, repetition can be effective. **Parallelism**, or the use of repeated grammatical structures, can heighten the persuasive effect of an argument. For example, read this famous line from President John F. Kennedy's 1961 inauguration speech. Through the use of parallelism, Kennedy makes what could have been a simple message much more memorable.

> *Ask not what your country can do for you—ask what you can do for your country.*
>
> —President John F. Kennedy

As she reviewed her essay, Mia found a good place to add two questions with parallel structures. Notice how her revision helps emphasize why people should care about the problem.

> *Why should we be worried about one little story on the local news? Why should we care about one small station's journalistic "standards"?*
> ∧ *What Channel 7 did is not an isolated incident.*

PUBLISH YOUR WRITING

Share your persuasive essay with your intended audience. Consider these options:
- Send your argument to an organization or a publication that has an interest in your issue or has the power to implement your proposed change.
- Upload your essay to the school Web site or a personal blog.
- Adapt your essay into a speech and deliver it to your audience.
- Turn your claim into a question and debate the topic with a small group of students.

 YOUR TURN Review some examples of effective writing in this unit to see how writers use repetition and parallelism. Add interest to your essay by experimenting with these stylistic elements. Then correct any errors and publish your final essay where it is most likely to reach your audience.

Editing and Publishing

COMMON CORE W 1a, W 5, L 2b, L 3a

GRAMMAR IN CONTEXT: PARALLELISM AND SYNTAX

- Read aloud this paragraph, using a flat tone to emphasize the lack of variation in syntax: "What Channel 7 did is not an isolated incident. So-called "news stories" like these are part of a growing national trend. One-time news anchor Dan Rather says 'traditional journalism is under siege'. Many newspapers are cutting staff or closing up shop." Then read the edited paragraph on page 1125. Discuss which version is more engaging for listeners and readers.

- Point out that writers often use parallelism to emphasize ideas that are similar or of equal importance.

- Suggest that students review the Student Draft and the selections in the unit to find examples of varied syntax and parallel structure. Then have them review their arguments to find sections that could be improved by changing the structure of the sentences.

PUBLISH YOUR WRITING

Brainstorm with students additional ways to publish their arguments.

YOUR TURN Allow time for students to proofread their drafts for any grammar, punctuation, or spelling errors. Remind them to look for opportunities to vary their syntax and to use parallelism.

FOR ENGLISH LANGUAGE LEARNERS

Language: Parallelism Review that *parallelism* means repeated grammatical structures. Discuss these examples:

- Advertisers know where to reach us—in our homes, in our workplaces, and even in our schools. (prepositional phrases)

- They know what we want, they know how to make it available, and they know how much we will pay for it. (clauses)

FOR STRUGGLING WRITERS

Vary Syntax Display and discuss these three different ways to state the same idea:

- We must take a stand because we are citizens in a democracy.

- As citizens in a democracy, we must take a stand.

- Is this a democracy, and are we its citizens? Then we must take a stand.

Encourage students to employ similar structures as they edit their drafts.

Scoring Rubric

Tell students that the best way to understand a scoring rubric is to use it to evaluate an actual piece of writing. Provide students with a persuasive essay from a different class or a previous school year. To protect the writer's anonymity, remove his or her name and make sure the essay includes no details that would reveal the writer's identity. Have students evaluate and score the essay. Then ask them to write a brief paragraph using the language of the rubric to explain their score.

For Rubric Bank, see

 **Write*Smart* CD-ROM**

Writing Center on thinkcentral.com

Assess and Reteach

Assess

R RESOURCE MANAGER—Copy Master
Rubric for Evaluation p. 402

Online Essay Scoring on thinkcentral.com

Reteach

Level Up Online Tutorials at thinkcentral.com

Scoring Rubric

Use the rubric below to evaluate your persuasive essay from the Writing Workshop or your response to the on-demand writing task on the next page.

PERSUASIVE ESSAY	
SCORE	**COMMON CORE TRAITS**
6	• **Development** Asserts a precise, knowledgeable claim on a substantive topic; supports the claim with valid reasons and relevant, sufficient evidence; ably counters opposing claims with counterclaims; ends powerfully with a call to action • **Organization** Logically organizes claims, reasons, and evidence to persuasive effect; uses transitions to create cohesion and show relationships among ideas • **Language** Consistently maintains a formal style and an objective tone; shows a strong command of conventions
5	• **Development** States a precise claim on an interesting topic; offers valid reasons and evidence; counters opposing claims with counterclaims; ends with a strong concluding section • **Organization** Is logically organized; uses transitions to show relationships among the claim, reasons, and evidence • **Language** Uses a formal style and an objective tone; has a few errors in conventions
4	• **Development** States a clear claim; offers mostly valid support; needs to more fairly address opposing claims; has an adequate concluding section • **Organization** Reflects a logical organization, with one or two exceptions; could use a few more transitions • **Language** Mostly uses a formal style, but sounds defensive at times; includes a few distracting errors in conventions
3	• **Development** States a claim that could be more precise; provides some relevant support but not enough to be sufficient; unfairly dismisses other viewpoints; has a somewhat weak concluding section • **Organization** Has some flaws in organization; needs more transitions to show relationships among ideas • **Language** Often lapses into an informal style or a defensive tone; has several errors in conventions
2	• **Development** Has a weak claim; offers irrelevant reasons and insufficient evidence; fails to acknowledge other viewpoints; has a weak concluding section • **Organization** Has major organizational flaws; lacks transitions throughout • **Language** Uses an informal style and a defensive tone; has many errors in conventions
1	• **Development** Lacks a clear claim; provides no support for reasons; ignores opposing claims; ends abruptly • **Organization** Lacks organization; has no transitions • **Language** Uses an inappropriate style and tone; has major problems with grammar, mechanics, and spelling

Preparing for Timed Writing

COMMON CORE

W 9 Draw evidence from texts to support analysis. **W 10** Write routinely over shorter time frames for a range of tasks, purposes, and audiences.

1. ANALYZE THE TASK   5 MIN

Read the task carefully. Then reread it, underlining the topic, the audience, and the purpose. Circle the type of writing you are being asked to do.

> **WRITING TASK**
>
> Read the following quotation from Daniel Singal's *American Quarterly* article entitled "Towards a Definition of American Modernism":
>
> > Modernism "represents an attempt to restore a sense of order to human experience under the often chaotic conditions of twentieth-century existence."
>
> *Audience* *Purpose* *Topic*
>
> Write a (persuasive essay) that <u>tells your classmates why you agree or disagree</u> with <u>Singal's definition.</u> Support your claim with valid reasons and relevant evidence.

2. PLAN YOUR RESPONSE   10 MIN

Which side can you defend more effectively? Jot down names of modernist writers, their views, and their effect on society at the time. Then, decide on your claim and note your support in a chart. Identify a possible opposing claim and a counterclaim to refute it.

Reasons	Evidence

Opposing Claim:

Counterclaim:

3. RESPOND TO THE TASK   20 MIN

Begin drafting your essay. Keep these guidelines in mind as you write:
- In the introduction, grab your audience's attention and state a precise claim.
- Present your reasons in a logical order. In each body paragraph, give one reason for your claim, supporting it with relevant evidence. Acknowledge and counter an opposing claim.
- Conclude by restating your claim and wrapping up your essay with a memorable phrase.

4. IMPROVE YOUR RESPONSE   5–10 MIN

Revising Review key elements of your essay. Do you state a precise claim? Do you include enough support to be persuasive?

Proofreading Neatly correct any errors in grammar, spelling, and usage.

Checking Your Final Copy Before you turn in your essay, examine it once more to catch any errors you may have missed.

WRITING WORKSHOP   **1127**

DIFFERENTIATED INSTRUCTION

FOR ENGLISH LANGUAGE LEARNERS

Writing: Analyze the Task Read aloud Daniel Singal's quotation and invite students to ask you about any unfamiliar words. Tell students that their claim will take the form of "I agree (or disagree) with Singal's definition of modernism." Suggest that before they begin writing, students review the Questions of the Times on pages 862–863 and their notes from the unit to find vocabulary they can use in their responses.

FOR STRUGGLING WRITERS

Organize Ideas Have students use this outline to organize details for their essays:

Introduction
- Attention-grabbing item, such as a fact
- Claim

Body Paragraphs
- Reason
- Supporting evidence

Concluding Section
- Restatement of claim
- Memorable example

COMMON CORE

W 9 Draw evidence from texts to support analysis. **W 10** Write routinely over shorter time frames for a range of tasks, purposes, and audiences.

COMMON CORE FOCUS

Preparing for Timed Writing

1. **Analyze the Task** Before students begin writing, encourage them to answer the following questions:
   - What is my time limit?
   - What are the core skills assessed in the scoring rubric?
   - Who is my audience?
   - What is my purpose?

2. **Plan Your Response** Remind students that the persuasive essay rubric emphasizes the importance of supporting a claim with reasons and evidence. Tell students that they should state their claim in the introduction and that every detail in the rest of the essay should support the claim.

3. **Respond to the Task** Point out the rubric's emphasis on organizing claims, reasons, and evidence in a logical order. Suggest that they devote one paragraph to each of their reasons and the evidence that supports it. Another paragraph may present an opposing claim, counterclaim, and supporting reasons and evidence.

4. **Improve Your Response** Tell students that the rubric stresses the use of transitions to show relationships between ideas. Remind them to check that they have included enough transitional words and phrases to create cohesion in their argument.

Assess

Use the Scoring Rubric on p. 1126 to assess students' essays.

Focus and Motivate

COMMON CORE FOCUS

SL 1a–d Participate effectively in collaborative group discussions. **SL 3** Evaluate a speaker's point of view, reasoning, and use of evidence and rhetoric. **SL 4** Present information, findings, and supporting evidence, conveying a clear perspective, such that listeners can follow the line of reasoning.

SPEAK WITH A PURPOSE

Tell students that their purpose during a debate is similar to their purpose in writing an argument: to persuade others to accept their claim about an issue by providing valid reasons and sufficient evidence. In a debate, their audience includes members of the opposing debate team as well as people listening to the debate.

COMMON CORE TRAITS

As students prepare to hold their debates, remind them to keep in mind the *COMMON CORE TRAITS* of an effective debate.

Practice and Apply

Planning the Debate

Model the Skill: PREPARE NOTES

Model for students the difference between reading aloud from a prepared statement and speaking from note cards. Read a paragraph from the Student Draft on pages 1123–1124, keeping your eyes on the page and reading every word. Then use an outline or note cards to give the same information. Glance at the notes, but speak using eye contact and a more natural voice. Discuss why the second approach engages the audience and makes the speaker sound more knowledgeable.

GUIDED PRACTICE Have pairs or small groups discuss the best way to prepare notes or note cards for their debate. Point out that they will not know exactly what the opposing team is going to say until the debate begins, so they'll need to be able to locate information quickly for their responses. Ask students to share their ideas with the class.

R RESOURCE MANAGER—Copy Master
Speaking and Listening p. 403

Speaking & Listening Workshop

Participating in a Debate

Essential Course of Study  **ECOS**

If you've ever tried to settle a disagreement with friends or siblings, you've used persuasive techniques to engage in a **debate**—a discussion in which individuals or teams argue opposing sides of an issue.

Complete the workshop activities in your **Reader/Writer Notebook.**

SPEAK WITH A PURPOSE	COMMON CORE TRAITS
TASK Participate in a **debate** about a substantive issue involving your school, community, or society. Be sure to allow adequate time to research supporting evidence for your argument.	**PARTICIPANTS IN AN EFFECTIVE DEBATE . . .** • work productively with others in teams • present precise claims supported by valid reasons and sufficient evidence • evaluate other speakers' viewpoints, reasoning, evidence, and **rhetoric,** or language • respond thoughtfully to diverse perspectives and resolve contradictions when possible • speak clearly and persuasively using standard formal English

COMMON CORE

SL 1a–d Participate effectively in collaborative group discussions. **SL 3** Evaluate a speaker's point of view, reasoning, and use of evidence and rhetoric. **SL 4** Present information, findings, and supporting evidence, conveying a clear perspective, such that listeners can follow the line of reasoning.

Speaking & Listening Online
THINK central
Go to **thinkcentral.com.**
KEYWORD: HML11N-1128

Planning the Debate

A debate allows participants and audience members to consider and evaluate both sides of an issue. Follow these planning suggestions:

- **Identify Debate Teams** Form groups of six to debate the opposing sides of your chosen issue. Divide the group into two teams, with three members arguing for the affirmative side and three arguing for the negative side.

    Affirmative: Yes, journalism standards have declined dramatically.

    Negative: No, journalism standards have not declined.

- **Appoint a Moderator** The moderator plays a neutral role in the debate, promoting a civil discussion and keeping everyone on task. The moderator begins by introducing the topic of the debate and then recognizes speakers, alternating between affirmative and negative.

- **Research and Prepare Notes** Search print and online sources for information that will support your claim and stimulate a thoughtful exchange of ideas. Note the most common opposing claims and gather evidence to refute them. Meet with your team to share research and compile notes that you can use during the debate.

- **Assign Debate Roles** One member introduces the team's claim with supporting reasons and evidence. Another team member exchanges questions with a member of the opposing team to clarify and challenge reasoning. The last member presents a strong closing argument.

DIFFERENTIATED INSTRUCTION

FOR ENGLISH LANGUAGE LEARNERS

Language: Reinforce Debate Terms Review with students the following terms used in the Workshop:

- *formal:* following standard rules; not casual or sloppy

- *team:* in a debate, a group of people who support the same claim; the *opposing team* is the team you're debating against

- *affirmative:* in favor of; describes the team that says "yes" to a claim

- *negative:* against; describes the team that says "no" to a claim

- *moderator:* in a debate, a person who does not belong to a team but who tells team members when they can speak and when they are out of time

- *closing argument:* a concluding statement that summarizes a team's claim

Holding the Debate

A well-run debate can be a vehicle for expressing your opinions in an assertive but respectful manner. Participating in a debate challenges you to synthesize comments made on both sides of an issue, pose probing questions, clarify ideas, and appreciate divergent perspectives.

GETTING STARTED

The moderator begins the debate by stating the topic and introducing the participants. Participants follow the moderator's instructions about whose turn it is to speak and how much time remains for each speaker.

Use the following debate format:

Speaker	Role	Time
Affirmative Speaker 1	Present the claim and supporting evidence for the affirmative ("pro") side of the argument.	5 minutes
Negative Speaker 1	Ask probing questions that will prompt the other team to address flaws in their argument.	3 minutes
Affirmative Speaker 2	Respond to the questions posed by the opposing team and counter any concerns.	3 minutes
Negative Speaker 2	Present the claim and supporting evidence for the negative ("con") side of the argument.	5 minutes
Affirmative Speaker 3	Summarize the claim and evidence for the affirmative side and explain why your reasoning is more valid.	3 minutes
Negative Speaker 3	Summarize the claim and evidence for the negative side and explain why your reasoning is more valid.	3 minutes

As a Speaker Follow the moderator's instructions. Speak clearly and persuasively, using formal English appropriate for a structured debate. Maintain a respectful tone regardless of your perspective.

As a Listener When the other team is presenting its side, evaluate the speaker's point of view, reasoning, and evidence. Take notes, identifying points of disagreement and noting any **fallacious,** or flawed, reasoning. Listen for persuasive rhetoric that serves to disguise exaggerated or distorted evidence. Be prepared to address these flaws during your team's response time.

FOR STRUGGLING STUDENTS

Take Notes Once the debate starts, it will unfold quickly, so students need to prepare in advance to take effective notes. Suggest that they create charts or outlines to help them organize their notes on the opposing team's argument. One example is provided. Students may create other forms to take notes on questions from the opposing team and their own responses.

Opposing Team's Claim: _____
Reason 1: _____
  Evidence: _____
Reason 2: _____
  Evidence: _____
Reason 3: _____
  Evidence: _____
My Questions: _____
Flawed Reasoning: _____

Holding the Debate

Model the Skill: MAINTAIN A RESPECTFUL TONE

Remind students that debate participants must show respect for others' ideas. Ask a volunteer to state an opinion about a movie, a TV show, or a story the class has read and to provide a reason. Model how to make an opposing claim in a dismissive tone, using words such as *foolish* or *misguided*. Then offer an opposing claim in a respectful tone that acknowledges the student's opinion but provides a reason for a different view.

GUIDED PRACTICE Have pairs take turns stating claims from their debate research and responding respectfully with opposing claims.

 YOUR TURN Suggest that, before the debate, team members practice presenting their claims, reasons, and evidence. They should use their notes but also maintain eye contact with the audience. One team member should ask probing questions to give others practice in responding.

Assess and Reteach

Assess

Use the **COMMON CORE TRAITS** to assess students' debates.

A strong debate
- demonstrates productive teamwork
- presents claims, reasons, and evidence
- responds to diverse perspectives
- is delivered in clear, persuasive speech using standard formal English
- evaluates other speakers' arguments

Reteach

Some students may have trouble responding to a question from the opposing team. Tell students that they should jot down the question for reference. Give them a sentence starter for phrasing their response: *My opponent has asked _____. I would respond that _____ because _____. For example, _____.*

 THINK central
Speaking and Listening Online
- Public Speaking Tips
- Strategies for Effective Listening

Assessment Practice

RL 1 Cite textual evidence to support analysis of what the text says. **RL 3** Analyze the impact of the author's choices regarding how to develop and relate elements of a story. **RL 4** Determine the meaning of words and phrases as they are used in the text; analyze the impact of specific word choices. **RL 6** Analyze a case in which grasping point of view requires distinguishing what is directly stated in a text from what is really meant. **RI 1** Cite textual evidence to support analysis of what the text says. **RI 6** Determine an author's point of view or purpose. **RI 7** Integrate and evaluate multiple sources of information presented in different media or formats. **W 5** Develop and strengthen writing by revising or editing. **W 9** Draw evidence from literary or informational texts to support analysis or reflection. **L 4a** Use context as a clue to the meaning of a word or phrase.

CHECK READINESS

Read aloud the paragraph under **ASSESS** and stress to students that this is not the full Unit Test, but a way for them to check their readiness for it. Then have students examine the skills listed under **REVIEW** and look back in the unit or in the **Student Resource Bank** for any skills they need to review.

READ THE TEXTS

Remind students to keep unit goals in mind as they read each passage, paying particular attention to these literary and reading skills:

- theme
- imagery
- symbolism
- making connections between texts

ANSWER THE QUESTIONS

Direct students to pages R96–R103 of the **Handbook** to review test-taking strategies. Remind students:

- to read directions carefully
- to read all choices in multiple-choice questions rather than choosing the first alternative that seems to fit

---

Assessment Practice

ASSESS
Taking this practice test will help you assess your knowledge of these skills and determine your readiness for the Unit Test.

REVIEW
After you take the practice test, your teacher can help you identify any standards you need to review.

COMMON CORE

RL 1 Cite textual evidence to support analysis of what the text says. **RL 3** Analyze the impact of the author's choices regarding how to develop and relate elements of a story. **RL 4** Determine the meaning of words and phrases as they are used in the text; analyze the impact of specific word choices. **RL 6** Analyze a case in which grasping point of view requires distinguishing what is directly stated in a text from what is really meant. **RI 1** Cite textual evidence to support analysis of what the text says. **RI 6** Determine an author's point of view or purpose. **RI 7** Integrate and evaluate multiple sources of information presented in different media or formats. **W 5** Develop and strengthen writing by revising or editing. **W 9** Draw evidence from literary or informational texts to support analysis or reflection. **L 4a** Use context as a clue to the meaning of a word or phrase.

Practice Test · **THINK** central · Take it at **thinkcentral.com.** KEYWORD: HML11N-1130

DIRECTIONS Read the two selections and the viewing and representing piece. Then answer the questions that follow.

The Sky Blue Ball

by Joyce Carol Oates

1   In a long-ago time when I didn't know *Yes I was happy, I was myself and I was happy.* In a long-ago time when I wasn't a child any longer yet I wasn't entirely not-a-child. In a long-ago time when I seemed often to be alone, and imagined myself lonely. *Yet this is your truest self: alone, lonely.*

2   One day I found myself walking beside a high brick wall the color of dried blood, the aged bricks loose and moldering, and over the wall came flying a spherical[1] object so brightly blue I thought it was a bird!-until it dropped a few yards in front of me, bouncing at a crooked angle off the broken sidewalk, and I saw that it was a rubber ball. A child had thrown a rubber ball over the wall, and I was expected to throw it back.

3   Hurriedly I let my things fall into the weeds, ran to snatch up the ball, which looked new, smelled new, spongy and resilient[2] in my hand like a rubber ball I'd played with years before as a little girl; a ball I'd loved and had long ago misplaced; a ball I'd loved and had forgotten. "Here it comes!" I called, and tossed the ball back over the wall; I would have walked on except, a few seconds later, there came the ball again, flying back.

4   *A game*, I thought. *You can't quit a game.*

5   So I ran after the ball as it rolled in the road, in the gravelly dirt, and again snatched it up, squeezing it with pleasure, how spongy how resilient a rubber ball, and again I tossed it over the wall; feeling happiness in swinging my arm as I hadn't done for years since I'd lost interest in such childish games. And this time I waited expectantly, and again it came!—the most beautiful sky blue rubber ball

---

1. **spherical** (sfîr′ ĭ-kəl) *adj.:* having the form of a sphere; globular.
2. **resilient** (rĭ-zĭl′yənt) *adj.:* able to return to original form after being bent, compressed, or stretched.

DIFFERENTIATED INSTRUCTION

FOR ENGLISH LANGUAGE LEARNERS

Assessment Practice: Work Backward
Prepare students by having them read the questions before reading the passages. Have pairs find unfamiliar words in test directions and questions and follow these steps:

1. Write each word on an index card.
2. Look up the meaning in a dictionary and write it on the back of the card.
3. Use the cards to practice the words with your partner and to teach them to others.

FOR STRUGGLING READERS

Assessment Practice: Mood Read aloud the first paragraph on page 1130. Ask students how the author's use of parallelism helps establish a mood in this paragraph. Ask what mood they feel is established and request that they explain their responses.

rising high, high into the air above my head and pausing for a heartbeat before it began to fall, to sink, like an object possessed of its own willful volition; so there was plenty of time for me to position myself beneath it and catch it firmly with both hands.

6   "Got it!"

7   I was fourteen years old and did not live in this neighborhood, nor anywhere in the town of Strykersville, New York (population 5,600). I lived on a small farm eleven miles to the north and I was brought to Strykersville by school bus, and consequently I was often alone; for this year, ninth grade, was my first at the school and I hadn't made many friends. And though I had relatives in Strykersville these were not relatives close to my family; they were not relatives eager to acknowledge me; for we who still lived in the country, hadn't yet made the inevitable move into town, were perceived inferior to those who lived in town. And in fact, my family was poorer than our relatives who lived in Strykersville.

8   At our school teachers referred to the nine farm children bussed there as "North Country children." We were allowed to understand that "North Country children" differed significantly from Strykersville children.

9   I was not thinking of such things now, I was smiling thinking it must be a particularly playful child on the other side of the wall, a little girl like me; like the little girl I'd been; though the wall was ugly and forbidding with rusted signs EMPIRE MACHINE PARTS and PRIVATE PROPERTY NO TRESPASSING. On the other side of the Chautauqua & Buffalo railroad yard was a street of

ITEM ANALYSIS

COMPREHENSION AND WRITTEN RESPONSE	ITEMS	UNIT PAGES
Analyze Literary Elements		
Irony	18	1079, 1083–85, 1088–90
Symbols	2, 9	999
Imagery	22	1092
Make Inferences and Draw Conclusions	1, 7, 10, 11, 15, 17, 19	953–58, 1009, 1012, 1013, 1015

VOCABULARY	ITEMS	UNIT PAGES
Multiple-Meaning Words	13	

WRITING AND GRAMMAR	ITEMS	UNIT PAGES
Vivid Language	5	959, 1053, 1063
Infinitive Phrases	4	951
Coordinating Conjunctions	3	991, 1001, 1040, 1047

MEDIA AND VIEWING	ITEMS	UNIT PAGES
Analyze Print Advertising	20, 21	1004–07

Practice Test

On **thinkcentral.com** students can complete an interactive version of this practice test *and* receive remediation for the skills they have not yet mastered.

FOR STRUGGLING READERS

Assessment Support Consider these options for completing the Assessment Practice:

- Have students "work backward" to review the test questions *before* reading the passages.

- Select random questions in the Assessment, and have students demonstrate *how* and *where* to look for the answers.

- Ask students to locate unfamiliar vocabulary words in the Assessment. Elicit the words' meanings from the class.

- Have students record useful testing words and definitions in their journals for later reference.

- Read the selections or parts of them aloud to aid in student comprehension.

small wood-frame houses; it must have been in one of these that the little girl, my invisible, playmate, lived. She must be much younger than I was; for fourteen-year-old girls didn't play such heedless games with strangers, we grew up swiftly if our families were not well-to-do.

10 I threw the ball back over the wall, calling, "Hi! Hi, there!" But there was no reply. I waited; I was standing in broken concrete, amid a scrubby patch of weeds. Insects buzzed and droned around me as if in curiosity, yellow butterflies no larger than my smallest fingernail fluttered and caught in my hair, tickling me. The sun was bright as a nova in a pebbled-white soiled sky that was like a thin chamois cloth about to be lifted away and I thought, *This is the surprise I've been waiting for.* For somehow I had acquired the belief that a surprise, a nice surprise, was waiting for me. I had only to merit it, and it would happen. (And if I did not merit it, it would not happen.) Such a surprise could not come from God but only from strangers, by chance.

11 Another time the sky blue ball sailed over the wall, after a longer interval of perhaps thirty seconds; and at an unexpected angle, as if it had been thrown away from me, from my voice, purposefully. Yet there it came, as if it could not not come: my invisible playmate was obliged to continue the game. I had no hope of catching it but ran blindly into the road (which was partly asphalt and partly gravel and not much traveled except by trucks) and there came a dump truck headed at me, I heard the ugly shriek of brakes and a deafening angry horn and I'd fallen onto my knees, I'd cut my knees that were bare, probably I'd torn my skirt, scrambling quickly to my feet, my cheeks smarting with shame, for wasn't I too grown a girl for such behavior? "Get the hell out of the road!" a man's voice was furious in rectitude, the voice of so many adult men of my acquaintance, you did not question such voices, you did not doubt them, you ran quickly to get out of their way, already I'd snatched up the ball, panting like a dog, trying to hide the ball in my skirt as I turned, shrinking and ducking so the truck driver couldn't see my face, for what if he was someone who knew my father, what if he recognized me, knew my name. But already the truck was thundering past, already I'd been forgotten.

12 Back then I ran to the wall, though both my knees throbbed with pain, and I was shaking as if shivering, the air had grown cold, a shaft of cloud had pierced

1132

FOR STRUGGLING READERS

Symbolism "The Sky Blue Ball" contains symbolism. Review the concept with students and have them practice by identifying the symbolism in the following passage.

I smiled as I approached the home of my childhood friend. It had been years since I had visited her. On her porch, the familiar wooden swing seemed to await my arrival. Jen and I had spent hundreds of hours on that swing, laughing and complaining about a million teenage traumas. Stepping onto the porch, I noticed that the swing's once gleaming paint was now chipped and caked with grime.

Suddenly, a tired-eyed woman opened the door. "Can I help you?" she asked. I gazed at her, wondering who she was, until I saw Jen's telltale amber necklace around her neck. [The broken-down swing symbolizes how circumstances have changed since Jen and the narrator were close friends.]

the sun. I threw the ball back over the wall again, underhand, so that it rose high, high—so that my invisible playmate would have plenty of time to run and catch it. And it disappeared behind the wall and I waited, I was breathing hard and did not investigate my bleeding knees, my torn skirt. More clouds pierced the sun and shadows moved swift and certain across the earth like predator fish. After a while I called out hesitantly, "Hi? Hello?" It was like a ringing telephone you answer but no one is there. You wait, you inquire again, shyly, "Hello?" A vein throbbed in my forehead, a tinge of pain glimmered behind my eyes, that warning of pain, of punishment, following excitement. The child had drifted away, I supposed; she'd lost interest in our game, if it was a game. And suddenly it seemed silly and contemptible to me, and sad: there I stood, fourteen years old, a long-limbed weed of a girl, no longer a child yet panting and bleeding from the knees, the palms of my hands, too, chafed and scraped and dirty; there I stood alone in front of a moldering brick wall waiting for—what?

13   It was my school notebook, my several textbooks I'd let fall into the grass and I would afterward discover that my math textbook was muddy, many pages damp and torn; my spiral notebook in which I kept careful notes of the intransigent[3] rules of English grammar and sample sentences diagrammed was soaked in a virulent-smelling chemical and my teacher's laudatory comments in red and my grades of A (for all my grades at Strykersville Junior High were A, of that I was obsessively proud) had become illegible as if they were grades of C, D, F. I should have taken up my books and walked hurriedly away and put the sky blue ball out of my mind entirely but I was not so free, through my life I've been made to realize that I am not free, as others appear to be free, at all. For the "nice" surprise carries with it the "bad" surprise and the two are intricately entwined and they cannot be separated, nor even defined as separate. So though my head pounded I felt obliged to look for a way over the wall. Though my knees were scraped and bleeding I located a filthy oil drum and shoved it against the wall and climbed shakily up on it, dirtying my hands and arms, my legs, my clothes, even more. And I hauled myself over the wall, and jumped down, a drop of about ten feet, the breath knocked out of me as I landed, the shock of impact reverberating through me, along my spine, as if I'd been struck a sledge-hammer blow to the soles of my feet. At once I saw that there could be no little girl here, the factory

---

3. **intransigent** (ĭn-trăn′sə-jənt) *adj.*: uncompromising.

GO ON ➡

FOR STRUGGLING READERS

Understanding Lengthy Sentences In testing situations, students may have difficulty reading lengthy compound, complex, or compound-complex sentences. Remind students to look for punctuation marks, such as commas or semicolons, that can help them separate the clauses within the sentence. Tell students to decipher the meaning of each separate clause and then determine how the clauses relate to one another. Have students use this technique to decipher the meaning of the first sentence in paragraph 13 of "The Sky Blue Ball."

yard was surely deserted, about the size of a baseball diamond totally walled in and overgrown with weeds pushing through cracked asphalt, thistles, stunted trees, and clouds of tiny yellow butterflies clustered here in such profusion I was made to see that they were not beautiful creatures, but mere insects, horrible. And rushing at me as if my very breath sucked them at me, sticking against my sweaty face, and in my snarled hair.

14   Yet stubbornly I searched for the ball. I would not leave without the ball. I seemed to know that the ball must be there, somewhere on the other side of the wall, though the wall would have been insurmountable[4] for a little girl. And at last, after long minutes of searching, in a heat of indignation I discovered the ball in a patch of chicory. It was no longer sky blue but faded and cracked; its dun-colored rubber showed through the venous-cracked surface, like my own ball, years ago. Yet I snatched it up in triumph, and squeezed it, and smelled it—it smelled of nothing: of the earth: of the sweating palm of my own hand.

---

4. **insurmountable** (ĭn′sər-moun′tə-bəl) *adj.:* not capable of being overcome.

DIFFERENTIATED INSTRUCTION

FOR STRUGGLING READERS

Study Options Students may often see test preparation as a chore. Encourage students to study throughout the unit or lesson, rather than cram right before the test. Also, use one or both of the following class study options:

- Work with students to create a quiz game that covers the information that will be tested. Have students write out the questions or prompts. Play the game in class to review for the test. Offer prizes to game winners, such as homework passes or bonus points.

- Bring several magazines into class. Have students choose images that remind them of important concepts or terms from the unit. For instance, a photograph could remind students of the theme of a particular selection. Have students share their chosen images with the class and explain the association with the concept or term.

Change of Heart

My neighbors and I just couldn't get along.

By Mary A. Fischer
from *Reader's Digest*

Being in the Minority

1   In 1992, like many people in Los Angeles, I watched TV news reports of Rodney King speaking to the press after four officers accused of beating him in 1991 were acquitted, leading to riots in the city. As King spoke to reporters, he plaintively asked, "Can we all get along?"

2   "No! We can't," I shouted back at the TV, though no one else was in the room to hear me. Mine was not an idle, uninformed response. I knew what I was talking about. In late 1989, I had bought a house in an affordable eastside neighborhood of Los Angeles called Highland Park, which was being transformed by waves of new immigrants, and I was convinced racial harmony was impossible. Statistics said that each year, tens of thousands of new immigrants, mostly from Latin America and Asia, were pouring into Southern California, yet for most whites, these trends remained in the abstract realm of statistics.

3   When I moved to Highland Park, however, the statistics became my daily reality and brought my prejudices to the surface. Many of my neighbors were from Mexico, El Salvador, the Philippines and Vietnam, and for the first time, I was in the minority and didn't like it.

4   Convinced that we had nothing in common, I fortressed myself in my lovely pink Spanish house on the hill. I rarely spoke to my neighbors, waving occasionally when we took out our trash cans or passed by in our cars. I fit their stereotype—the unfriendly white "gringa" who owned the nicest house on the block—just as they fit my preconceived notions of immigrants who stubbornly refused to assimilate.

5   I was annoyed when Hispanic salespeople in Radio Shack didn't understand when I asked for lithium batteries or extension cords. It irritated me that the local supermarkets didn't carry things like blue cheese or soy milk, and that some billboard ads for movies and cars were written in Spanish.

6   For years, I complained to various officials when my neighbors behaved in ways I didn't agree with. One woman from El Salvador kept a rooster in her backyard that woke me up at 5:00 every morning. When I reported her to the Animal Regulation Department, she responded to the complaint by cutting off the bird's head. I felt guilty about being the impetus for the rooster's brutal demise, but rationalized it as being necessary to restore peace and quiet to the neighborhood.

7   When my neighbors from Mexico played their music too loud, I called the police, who put a stop to it. Surmising that I had reported them, my neighbors

1135

---

stopped speaking to me. It was a punishment I could live with, since I reasoned that I was bringing the neighborhood into compliance with my values.

8   Then, two years ago, something happened that changed me and how I live in my neighborhood. In a matter of two days, I lost the things that mattered most to me. My six-figure job as a senior writer for a national magazine came to an end, and a relationship with a man I loved ended badly. Suddenly, all my anchors were gone and, sunk deep in grief, I wondered how—or if—I would be able to pull myself out.

9   The losses I experienced humbled me and made me vulnerable, but as a consequence I began to connect more fully with my neighbors and the world around me. I discovered how extraordinary they were. They were nothing like my biases had made them out to be. They were hard-working, honorable people who, like me, were just looking to live well and experience some measure of happiness.

10   I learned that the woman from El Salvador had fled her country with two young daughters after death squads murdered her husband. She cleaned houses to make ends meet and send her daughters to college. I learned that when my neighbors from Mexico came to Los Angeles 15 years ago, they did not speak English and the father cleaned offices for $8 an hour. Later, he drove delivery trucks. Today he owns three apartment buildings and has made more money than I probably ever will in my lifetime.

11   Now, many of my neighbors are my friends. At Christmas, I give them red wine and cakes and they give me potted flowers and platters of burritos. When my car wouldn't start a few months ago, and it looked like it would have to be towed, another neighbor from Guatemala, a sweet man named Angel who's a gardener, quickly brought out his jumper cables and got the car started.

12   Today, I would answer Rodney King's question differently. I'd say that it is possible for us to get along if people from different cultures don't make the mistake I did. When I first moved to my neighborhood, I neglected to view my neighbors as individuals and I saw them as different and apart from me. I see now how their lives and mine include experiences universal to us all: loss, disappointment, hope and love.

13   Last month, I heard a rooster crow early in the morning. It seems my neighbor from El Salvador got another one, but I no longer mind. I like watching the rooster as it wanders the neighborhood. Somehow, he makes me feel like I'm home.

DIFFERENTIATED INSTRUCTION

FOR ENGLISH LANGUAGE LEARNERS
Review Literary Terms On the board, list the literary terms shown in italics. Then give the examples in random order and have students classify them. Elicit additional examples from students.

- *symbolism:* A tiny flower represents resilience after it survives a severe storm.

- *irony:* Two characters fight throughout the story, then at the end of the story, they realize that they are actually in love with each other.

- *imagery:* A story detail that relates to the reader's sense of sight, such as "Bright orange globs of paint streamed down the pasty wall."

- *point of view:* The narrator is a character within the story who relays the tale using the pronouns *I, me, my,* and *mine.*

King Street Community Garden
Farmer's Market

Come Taste What Your Neighbors Have Been Growing

9:00-12:00

First & Third Saturdays
of the Month,
June – October

Corner of King Street
& Park Avenue

Vegetables from Around the World ... in Your Own Community

1137

FOR ALL READERS

Assessment Practice: Analyzing Visuals
Ask students how the image and text of the poster complement each other to influence the viewer.

- What is the focal point of the photograph's composition and what does it symbolize? *(the plant and the smiles of the people; sharing)*

- Which words in the text emphasize the message created by the photo? *("Taste what your neighbors have been growing")*

- Which words in the text form an interesting contrast? *("Vegetables from around the world in your community")*

Reading Comprehension

Model a thinking process for answering multiple-choice questions.

1. **A is correct.** *The narrator is referring to the deepest part of herself; the part that is not related to her friends or her family; therefore B, C, and D are incorrect.*

2. **C is correct.** *The narrator associates the other side of the wall with her childhood when she played with a ball. A is incorrect because the narrator is not an adult. B is incorrect because the story is not about cooperation. D is incorrect because the wall is a physical boundary, not the symbolic meaning.*

3. **B is correct.** *The context of the sentence, specifically "aged" and "loose," reveal that the bricks are crumbling. A, C, and D are not supported by the context of the sentence.*

4. **D is correct.** *The narrator implies that Strykersville children are wealthier than North Country children in paragraph 7. A is incorrect because North Country children are perceived as inferior to Strykersville children. B and C are untrue because Strykersville children live in town, close to school.*

5. **C is correct.** *The narrator doesn't think a teenager should be playing childish games. The context also implies that heedless has a negative connotation. A, B, and D are incorrect because they have positive connotations.*

6. **B is correct.** *The narrator wants to remain anonymous in case the truck driver knows her father or recognizes her. A and C are untrue. D is incorrect because the truck driver's loud voice is not the reason why she hides her face.*

7. **C is correct.** *When the narrator plays the game, she stops thinking about her problems. A is incorrect because the narrator doesn't think she will meet the other person. B and D are incorrect because the narrator enjoys the game.*

8. **D is correct.** *The context, such as "silly" and "sad," implies that the narrator looks down upon the game and herself for getting so wrapped up in it. B and C are incorrect because the narrator does not see the game as*

Reading Comprehension

Use "The Sky Blue Ball" (pp. 1130–1134) to answer questions 1–11.

1. The narrator believes her truest self is lonely because —
   A. she doesn't understand who she is
   B. she has made only a few friends
   C. her parents just don't understand her
   D. her family is poor

2. The brick wall symbolizes —
   A. challenges in adult life
   B. cooperation
   C. childhood that cannot be regained
   D. boundaries

3. In paragraph 2, *moldering* means —
   A. forming a shape
   B. crumbling into pieces
   C. blending together
   D. grinding thoroughly

4. Strykersville children —
   A. are inferior to North Country children
   B. have to ride the bus long distances to school
   C. have to work on farms
   D. are wealthier than North Country children

5. In paragraph 9, *heedless* means —
   A. attentive
   B. fun
   C. thoughtless
   D. unselfish

6. Why does the narrator try to hide her face from the truck driver in paragraph 11?
   A. The truck driver recognizes her.
   B. She wants to stay anonymous.
   C. She recognizes the truck driver.
   D. The truck driver's voice is loud.

7. For the narrator, the game of catch represents —
   A. a sense of hope to make friends
   B. a chore that needs to be completed
   C. an unexpected return to childhood
   D. a barrier to growing up

8. In paragraph 12, *contemptible* means —
   A. admirable
   B. important
   C. serious
   D. disdainful

9. The author chose to use a rubber ball as a meaningful symbol because —
   A. it is an ordinary object associated with children
   B. it looks like the earth
   C. few people have played catch with rubber balls
   D. many people have kept a rubber ball as a souvenir of childhood

10. How does the girl feel about finding the ball?
   A. Angry
   B. Disappointed
   C. Excited
   D. Sad

---

important or serious. A is incorrect because it is the opposite of the meaning of contemptible.

9. **A is correct.** *Using an object that is commonly associated with childhood creates a meaningful symbol. B is incorrect because the earth is not a common association for a rubber ball. C and D are not commonly accepted notions.*

10. **C is correct.** *The narrator implies that she is excited about finding the ball when she says, "I snatched it up in triumph"*

(paragraph 14). A, B, and D are incorrect because they relay negative feelings, not excitement and triumph.

11. At the end of the story, the ball represents —

A. the negative experiences of childhood

B. the innocence of childhood

C. the triumph over childhood helplessness

D. a new friendship

> Use "Change of Heart" (pp. 1135–1136) to answer questions 12–18.

12. The article is mostly about —

A. immigrants adjusting to life in the United States

B. learning to live in a multicultural neighborhood

C. living up to someone's prejudices

D. the Rodney King riots in Los Angeles

13. Read the following dictionary entry.

idle \ˈī-dəl\ *adj* **1.** lacking worth or basis, vain **2a.** not occupied or employed **b.** not turned to normal or appropriate use **c.** not scheduled to compete **3a.** shiftless, lazy **b.** having no evident lawful means of support

Which definition best matches the meaning of the word *idle* as it is used in paragraph 2 of the selection?

A. Definition 1

B. Definition 2a

C. Definition 2b

D. Definition 3a

14. What does the following sentence mean?

Statistics said that each year, tens of thousands of new immigrants, mostly from Latin America and Asia, were pouring into Southern California, yet for most whites, these trends remained in the abstract realm of statistics.

A. Latin Americans and Asians were the only immigrants coming to Southern California.

B. Whites and new immigrants, mostly from Latin America and Asia, cooperate.

C. Latin Americans and Asians help whites understand statistics.

D. Whites rarely interacted with new immigrants.

15. What can the reader conclude about the author from her reaction in paragraph 6?

A. She cooperates with city officials and departments to stop illegal behavior in her neighborhood.

B. She likes getting up early in the morning.

C. She wants her neighbors to behave as she would.

D. She is in charge of the neighborhood watch program.

16. In paragraph 7, *surmising* means —

A. inferring from little evidence

B. knowing for a fact

C. learning after the fact

D. informing

17. According to paragraph 8, a great part of the author's identity was in her —

A. biases

B. boat

C. job

D. neighborhood

GO ON ➡

11. C is correct. The narrator is able to climb the fence, something a child could not do. A is incorrect because the ball still brings the narrator joy. B is incorrect because the "faded and cracked" ball represents the reality of a situation, not innocence. D is incorrect because the narrator has not made a new friend.

12. B is correct. When the author moves into her neighborhood, she is in the minority, and it takes time to understand her neighbors. A and D are mentioned in the article, but are not the main idea. C is incorrect because the people in the story dispel the author's prejudices.

13. A is correct. The author believes her experience gives her the right to answer the question. B is incorrect because the sentence does not refer to occupation or employment. C is incorrect because idle doesn't refer to the use of something. D is incorrect because the author is not implying that her response is lazy.

14. D is correct. "The abstract realm of statistics" implies that most whites rarely came into contact with immigrants. A, B, and C are not supported by information and details in the sentence.

15. C is correct. The author complains to officials when her neighbors "behaved in ways [she] didn't agree with." A is incorrect because the author's complaints are about petty matters, not serious crimes. B and D are not supported by information in the selection.

16. A is correct. The author does not indicate that her neighbors have any evidence or knowledge of her calling the police, so B and C are incorrect. D is incorrect because the paragraph does not suggest that the neighbors are informing anyone of the author's report to the police.

17. C is correct. In paragraph 8, the author lost her job, which was one of "the things that mattered most to [her]." A and D are incorrect because neither her biases nor her neighborhood are mentioned in the paragraph. B is incorrect because anchors are referred to metaphorically, not as actual objects.

DIFFERENTIATED INSTRUCTION

FOR STRUGGLING READERS

Short Constructed Response Questions Share with students the following suggestions for answering short constructed response questions in testing situations:

- Note the most important concepts mentioned in the prompts or questions. For example, #22 contains the following important concepts: imagery, setting, narrator's experiences.

- Be sure to fully address the prompt or answer the question. For example, #23 requires students to include an explanation and support the answer with evidence from the selection.

- Pay close attention to the length requirements stated in the directions.

- For essay questions, organize your thoughts by jotting down a brief outline before you begin writing your response. Also, if time allows, write a rough draft.

18. **D is correct.** In the beginning, the author believes that her neighbors are the ones who must change, but in the end, she changes by accepting her neighbors. A is incorrect because the neighbors still behave in ways they did in their country. B and C are incorrect because neither statement relays what the author thinks or feels after she gets to know her neighbors.

19. **B is correct.** The narrator of "The Sky Blue Ball" and "Change of Heart" adapt to their circumstances. A is incorrect because the narrator of "The Sky Blue Ball" does not mention traditions. C is incorrect because in "Change of Heart," the narrator's feelings towards her neighbors change. D is incorrect because neither narrator shows that they like to get into trouble.

20. **A is correct.** B is incorrect; neighbors may become friends as a result of working together, but that isn't addressed in the poster. C and D are incorrect because neither is supported by information in the poster.

21. **C is correct.** The image emphasizes the communal spirit. A is incorrect; soil is not visible in the picture and no one is digging in the dirt. B is incorrect; no specialized tools are shown. D is incorrect because no part of the image supports this statement.

SHORT CONSTRUCTED RESPONSE

Possible responses:

22. The imagery of the rusted sign and cracked sidewalk bring the setting to life. The smell of the blue ball at the end of the story helps suggest that it has become just an ordinary object.

23. The title "Change of Heart" can be seen to have more than one meaning. When the author first moves into the neighborhood, she thinks her neighbors have nothing to offer her. However, after losing her job and a relationship, she has the chance to connect with them, and she changes how she views them. The narrator not only changes her opinion about her neighbors, but she also sees that at the heart of things we all have "disappointment, hope and love" in common.

---

18. In what way is this selection ironic?
   A. The author's neighbors finally assimilate to living in the United States.
   B. The author decides that she doesn't like her neighborhood.
   C. The author is the one whose behavior changes.
   D. The author realizes that people who are different cannot get along.

> Use "The Sky Blue Ball" and "Change of Heart" to answer question 19.

19. The reader can conclude that the narrators in both selections —
   A. respect tradition
   B. adapt with their circumstances
   C. stay the same
   D. like to get into trouble

> Use the visual representation on page 1137 to answer questions 20–21.

20. The organizers of the King Street Community Garden hope to improve the neighborhood by —
   A. providing healthier food for the community
   B. allowing neighbors to become friends through working together
   C. providing soil, straw, and community tools to all who participate
   D. charging tuition for gardening classes that benefit the organization

21. The designer of the poster chose the photograph to emphasize —
   A. that gardening involves working in the dirt
   B. that specialized tools are necessary to garden productively
   C. the communal aspect of the garden
   D. that soil, straw, and tools are provided

SHORT CONSTRUCTED RESPONSE

Write a short constructed response to each question, using text evidence to support your response.

22. How does the author of "The Sky Blue Ball" use imagery to bring the setting and her narrator's experiences to life? Support your response with evidence from the selection.

23. Why is "Change of Heart" a good title for this selection? Support your response with evidence from the selection.

Write a short constructed response to the following question, using text evidence from **both** selections to support your response.

24. What impact does the point of view have in "The Sky Blue Ball" and "Change of Heart"? Support your response with evidence from **both** selections.

1140

---

24. Both selections use the first person point of view which shows the narrator's vulnerability in the midst of change. For example, in "The Sky Blue Ball" the narrator is caught between not being a child and not being an adult. When the ball lands near her, she imagines it was thrown by a little girl because she played with a similar ball when she was younger. The reader experiences with the narrator the childlike excitement of the impromptu game.

The narrator in "Change of Heart" recounts the traumatic period in her life when she lost all that was familiar: her job and her relationship. In that vulnerable moment, she sees her neighbors in a new light. Through the narrator's relating of her experience, the reader witnesses the sequence of events that cause her both to accept her neighbors and be accepted by them.

Revising and Editing

DIRECTIONS Read this passage and answer the questions that follow.

> (1) My twin sister, Natasha and I used to engage in unceasing hostilities. (2) We would fight over everything: clothes, bathroom space, chores, *everything*. (3) The week after we turned fifteen, we got news that changed our lives. (4) Natasha had been feeling sick for a while, and medical tests determined that she had leukemia. (5) The type of leukemia she had held a strong chance of survival, but it would require chemotherapy and some sacrifice and determination from our family. (6) I reevaluated my relationship with my sister, since I thought I might lose her.

1. What change, if any, should be made in sentence 1?

   A. Change *sister,* to **sister:**

   B. Insert a comma after *Natasha*

   C. Change *unceasing* to **ceasing**

   D. Make no change

2. Which transition should be added to the beginning of sentence 3?

   A. In fact,   **C.** Otherwise,

   B. Likewise,   **D.** Then,

3. What change, if any, should be made in sentence 4?

   A. Change *that* to **than**

   B. Change *for* to **since**

   C. Insert a comma after *determined*

   D. Make no change

4. What is the most effective way to revise sentence 6?

   A. The thought of losing my sister made me to reevaluate our relationship.

   B. To reevaluate our relationship happened at the thought of losing my sister.

   C. While thinking about losing my sister, I began to reevaluate our relationship.

   D. When thinking about losing my sister, I admitted to reevaluate our relationship.

5. To make a connection between the experience and life in general, which sentence could the writer add?

   A. I learned that life is too precious to waste time fighting over trivial things.

   B. I learned to love and appreciate my life.

   C. I learned how the doctors planned to treat my sister's cancer.

   D. I learned to value different people's points of view.

6. What would the next paragraph of this essay most likely contain?

   A. Details about the sisters' fights

   B. Details about other family members

   C. Statistics about leukemia from a credible source

   D. Examples of how the relationship changed

 STOP

1141

DIFFERENTIATED INSTRUCTION

FOR STRUGGLING READERS

Assessment Support: Essential Clauses and Infinitive Phrases

- Review with students that a clause always contains a subject and a verb. Remind students that an essential clause is vital to the meaning of a sentence and should not be set off with commas. Tell students that nonessential clauses are not necessary to clarify the sentence's meaning and, therefore, should be set off with commas.

- Ask students to identify essential clauses in paragraph 5 of "Change of Heart."

- Review with students that the infinitive of a verb is the form beginning with *to*, and an infinitive phrase consists of the infinitive of a verb followed by words related to the action.

- Have students find an example of an infinitive phase in "The Sky Blue Ball."

RL 10 Read and comprehend literature. **RI 10** Read and comprehend literary nonfiction.

INTRODUCE *GREAT READS*

In Unit 5, students have discussed a number of big questions. Invite students to tell which question they found most intriguing and why, and then focus attention on the four questions that appear on pages 1142–1143. Discuss the recommended books and their summaries, pointing out how each connects to the related question. Encourage students to choose one or more of these "great reads" to study independently.

UNIT 5 Great Reads

Ideas for Independent Reading

Continue exploring the Questions of the Times on pages 862–863 by reading these additional works.

What is MODERN?

Prufrock and Other Observations
by T. S. Eliot

This volume contains 12 early poems by T.S. Eliot, including "The Love Song of J. Alfred Prufrock," regarded by some as the first modernist poem. The collection also includes "Portrait of a Lady," "Preludes," and "Rhapsody on a Windy Night,"three other great poems about loneliness and alienation. Ezra Pound praised the book for "its fine tone, its humanity, and its realism."

Spoon River Anthology
by Edgar Lee Masters

This is Edgar Lee Masters's best-known work, a collection of free-verse monologues written in the voices of inhabitants of a small-town cemetery. The interconnected poems reveal the hidden loves, thwarted longings, and bitterness of people who lived and died in the confines of a small town.

The Autobiography of Alice B. Toklas
by Gertrude Stein

Gertrude Stein was at the center of a sparkling community of American writers who lived in Europe following World War I. She knew Picasso, Matisse, Joyce, Hemingway, and other important modernist figures. This book is her memoir of those heady days in Paris, playfully written in the voice of her lifelong companion, Alice B. Toklas.

Can ideals survive CATASTROPHE?

The Sun Also Rises
by Ernest Hemingway

After the end of World War I, a group of American expatriates in Europe try to wrest pleasure from a life that has lost meaning. They meet in Paris bistros, fish in the trout streams of Spain, and watch bullfights in Pamplona. Can such pleasures compensate them for their lost illusions? *The Sun Also Rises* leaves this question unanswered.

Blood on the Forge
by William Attaway

Following World War I, three African-American brothers—Big Mat, Chinatown, and Melody—flee the rural South for jobs in the steel mills of Pittsburgh. In search of a better life, they instead find dangerous work, terrible living conditions, and ethnic conflict. Each of the three brothers copes with his new life in a different way.

Waiting for Lefty
by Clifford Odets

During the time of reexamination that followed the Great Depression, the plays of Clifford Odets were a jolt of working-class lightning. Their affirmation of hope energized theatergoers from coast to coast. *Waiting for Lefty* dramatizes the courage and doubts of a group of cabdrivers who are debating whether to strike for a living wage.

1142

COMMON CORE

RL 10 Read and comprehend literature. **RI 10** Read and comprehend literary nonfiction

How can people honor their HERITAGE?

The Souls of Black Folk
by W. E. B. Du Bois

This collection of essays, published in 1903, is unified by the idea of African-Americans' "double consciousness." As Americans, they are heirs to the nation's ideals of liberty and equality. But as a despised minority, they are barred from full participation in these ideals. W.E.B. Du Bois describes the struggles African Americans face and the gifts they offer the nation.

Their Eyes Were Watching God
by Zora Neale Hurston

Zora Neale Hurston brings an all-black Florida town to life in this moving love story. Janie Crawford has been taught by a fearful grandmother to value economic security over love. She marries an ambitious businessman who views her as a trophy rather than as a partner. When he dies, Janie finds fulfillment with the younger, free-spirited Tea Cake.

Cane
by Jean Toomer

Cane is a groundbreaking work of the Harlem Renaissance by a writer of mixed ancestry. It is composed of stories, poems, vignettes, and a short play. Part I, set in rural Georgia, presents the beauty of the land and the violence residents inflict on one another. Part II, set in the urban North, portrays a world of spiritual deadness. In Part III, a figure resembling Jean Toomer returns to the South to seek his identity.

What drives HUMAN BEHAVIOR?

As I Lay Dying
by William Faulkner

The dying wish of Addie Bundren, the wife of a Mississippi farmer, is to be buried in the county seat with the rest of her family. Her husband and children place her coffin in a wagon and undertake a dangerous odyssey. In a series of interior monologues, the characters—even the dead Addie—reveal the complex motivations that spur them forward.

Babbitt
by Sinclair Lewis

This satirical novel added a new word to American speech—*babbitt*, meaning "a smugly conventional person." When George Babbitt, a successful Midwestern businessman of the 1920s, rebels against his empty, conformist life, his friends reject him. Eventually he realizes that he is too old to rebel but that he can support his son's unconventional dreams.

Native Son
by Richard Wright

In this classic American novel, Wright questions whether people who are born poor, without any real opportunities, can ever be "free." Bigger Thomas is an impoverished African-American youth who resents the world of white power around him. Hired as a chauffeur by a white millionaire, he commits a shocking crime that seems oddly predestined. Who is responsible for Bigger's tragic life?

Get Novel Wise | THINK central

Go to **thinkcentral.com**.
KEYWORD: HML11-1143

NovelWise | THINK central

The keyword on this page points to **NovelWise**, a Web site that helps students choose a novel or other book-length work to read. **NovelWise** also provides
- study guides
- reading strategies and literary elements instruction
- presentations to introduce classic novels
- project ideas

1143

COMMON CORE UNIT GOALS

Included in this unit: RL 1, RL 2, RL 3, RL 4, RL 5, RL 6, RL 9, RL 10, RI 1, RI 2, RI 3, RI 4, RI 5, RI 6, RI 7, RI 9, RI 10, W 1, W 2, W 2a–b, W 2e, W 3, W 3d–e, W 4, W 5, W 6, W 8, W 9, W 10, SL 1, SL 1b–c, SL 2, SL 4, SL 5, SL 6, L 1, L 2, L 2a, L 3, L 3a, L 4a–c, L 5, L 5a–b

Complete text of the Common Core State Standards is found in the correlation on p. T10. Standards covered in this unit are found in the standards overview (pp. 1145A–1145D) and on the lesson pages where they are taught.

Preview Unit Goals

This page presents an overview of the skills and strategies covered in this unit. Explain to students that they can get more from their reading by previewing. Then ask them to skim the page to preview the skills that they will learn. Note that each strand or category of skill is color-coded on this page and throughout the unit.

Model the strategy of copying the Academic Vocabulary and writing a preliminary definition for each term. Suggest that students use their **Reader/Writer Notebooks** for this purpose. Encourage them to use the terms in discussions and in writing. Also urge students to revisit each term throughout the unit and to refine its meaning.

COMMON CORE Preview Unit Goals

TEXT ANALYSIS	• Understand and analyze historical and cultural context of contemporary literature • Identify and interpret allusions • Identify and interpret rhetorical devices, including paradox and repetition • Identify and analyze tone, imagery, voice, personification, and sound devices • Analyze primary and secondary source documents • Analyze and trace elements of an argument, including claim, reasons, evidence, and counterargument • Identify faulty reasoning, including circular logic and non-sequiturs • Make inferences about theme, genre, structure, and elements of drama in different cultural and historical contexts
READING	• Identify and evaluate main ideas and supporting details • Analyze inductive and deductive reasoning
WRITING AND LANGUAGE	• Write a resumé • Use word choice, sentence structure, and tone to establish voice • Use word choice, imagery, and tone to create mood
SPEAKING AND LISTENING	• Analyze an argument in a newspaper article • Compare and contrast perspectives in news reports
VOCABULARY	• Understand and use Greek prefixes to determine word meaning • Use context clues to determine the meaning of idioms
ACADEMIC VOCABULARY	• complex • economic • establish • ethnic • evolve
MEDIA AND VIEWING	• Create a Web site

Find It Online!
Go to **thinkcentral.com** for the interactive version of this unit.

DIFFERENTIATED INSTRUCTION

FOR ENGLISH LANGUAGE LEARNERS

Academic Vocabulary Provide students with the definition of these Academic Vocabulary words.

complex (kəm-plĕks) *adj.* made up of interconnected parts; hard to understand; complicated

economic (ĕkə-nŏmĭk, ēkə-) *adj.* relating to the production and exchange of goods and services; efficient

establish (ĭ-stăblĭsh) *v.* to set up or cause to happen

ethnic (ĕthnĭk) *adj.* relating to a group of people sharing a common racial, national, religious, linguistic, or cultural heritage

evolve (ĭ-vŏlv) *v.* to develop gradually

Additional Academic Vocabulary Use the copy master to help students learn academic words they will use in subsequent lessons and on the Assessment Practice.

 RESOURCE MANAGER—Copy Masters
   Academic Vocabulary p. 3
   Additional Academic Vocabulary p. 4

Contemporary Literature

1940–PRESENT

Sandra Cisneros

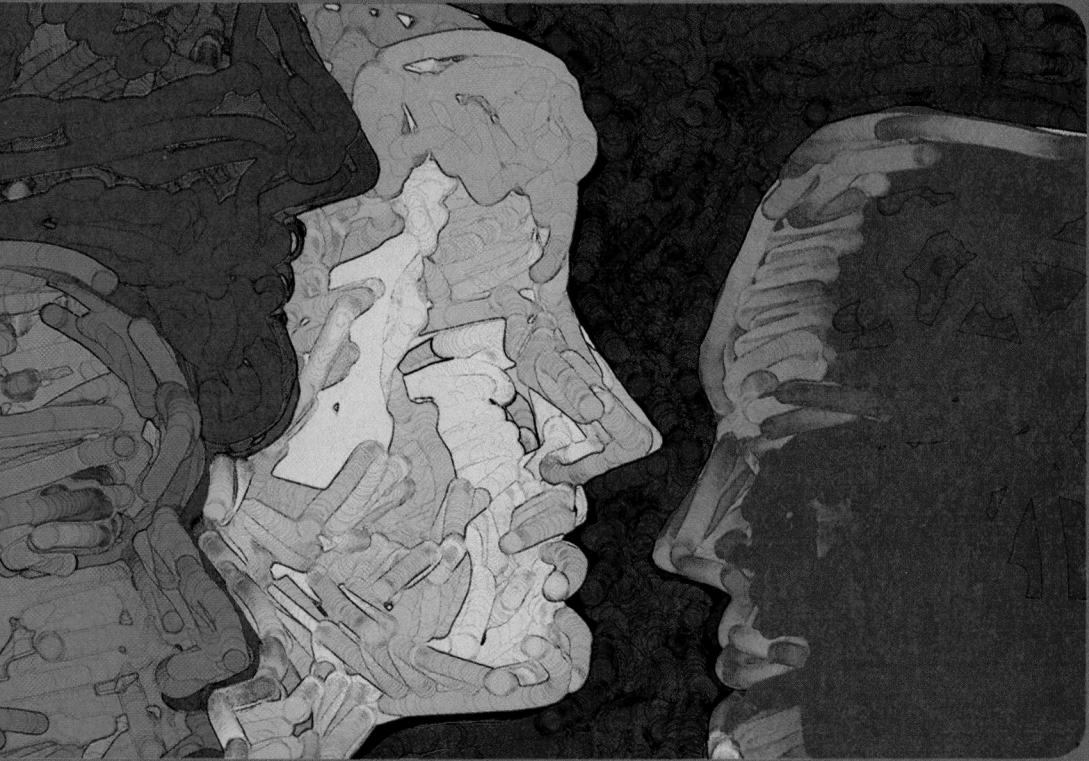

NEW PERSPECTIVES

- **Modern American Drama**
- **Responses to War**
- **Civil Rights and Protest Literature**
- **A Mosaic of American Voices**

Media ■ Smart DVD-ROM

Perspectives in the News

Deconstruct news reports to see how they can shape audience perceptions of historical events and figures. Page 1234

1145

For help in planning this unit, see

 RESOURCE MANAGER UNIT 6
pp. 1–8

INTRODUCE THE UNIT

Call students' attention to the pictures on this page. Explain that the large picture, *Man in Red* (2003), was created by Diana Ong. Its medium is computer graphics and it reflects the diversity in both artistic media and subject matter that students will encounter in the selections in Unit 6.

Ask students if they are familiar with the writer Sandra Cisneros, shown in the smaller picture on the page. Explain that Cisneros (born 1954) is an award-winning author of fiction, essays, and poetry. Drawing on her background as the daughter of a Mexican father and a Chicana mother, Cisneros's works made her one of the first commercially successful Hispanic American writers. Tell students that they will read one of her essays, "Straw into Gold: The Metamorphosis of the Everyday," in this unit. Also note that students can read more about Cisneros on page 1286.

About the Art Diana Ong (born 1940) is a Chinese-American artist.

Unit Resources

See resources on the **Teacher One Stop DVD-ROM** *and on* **thinkcentral.com**.

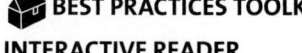 **RESOURCE MANAGER UNIT 6**

UNIT AND BENCHMARK TESTS

BEST PRACTICES TOOLKIT

INTERACTIVE READER

ADAPTED INTERACTIVE READER

ELL ADAPTED INTERACTIVE READER

LANGUAGE HANDBOOK

VOCABULARY PRACTICE

TECHNOLOGY

- **Teacher One Stop DVD-ROM**
- **Student One Stop DVD-ROM**
- **PowerNotes DVD-ROM**
- **Write*Smart* CD-ROM**
- **Media*Smart* DVD-ROM**
- **GrammarNotes DVD-ROM**
- **Audio Anthology CD**

Find It Online!

 **THINK** central

This unit on **thinkcentral.com** includes

- **PowerNotes** introductions to key selections
- audio support—listen or download
- **ThinkAloud** models
- **WordSharp** vocabulary tutorials
- interactive unit review and assessment

COMMON CORE

STRAND	**Unit 6 Introduction** pp. 1144–1161 • Questions of the Times • Historical Essay • Timeline • Legacy of the Era from 1940 to the Present **American Masterpieces:** *from Our Town* pp. 1162–1163 *from The Glass Menagerie* pp. 1164–1165 *from Death of a Salesman* pp. 1166–1167 *from A Raisin in the Sun* pp. 1168–1169	**Text Analysis Workshop** • Voice in Contemporary Literature pp. 1260–1261	**Why Soldiers Won't Talk/The Death of the Ball Turret Gunner** Essay/Poem pp. 1170–1177 Lexile: 940 Fry: 9 Dale-Chall: 6.4	**Comparing Text Selections** Literary: *Adam* pp. 1178–1187, 1192 Informational: *from Survival in Auschwitz* pp. 1178, 1188–1190, 1192 Visual: *Auschwitz-Birkenau Concentration Camp* pp. 1191–1192 Lexile: 740 Fry: 8 Dale-Chall: 6.2	**Ambush** Short Story pp. 1194–1200 Lexile: 940 Fry: 9 skills strand Dale-Chall: 5.6
Reading Literature	Contemporary Literature pp. 1146–1157 RL 9 Text Analysis pp. 1162–1169 RL 1, RL 2, RL 3, RL 6	Contemporary Literature pp. 1260–1261 RL 3, RL 9	Tone and Imagery pp. 1171, 1176 RL 4	Characterization and Tone pp. 1179–1180, 1182, 1184–1187 RL 3, RL 4 Historical Context pp. 1179, 1182, 1183–1185, 1187 RL 3	Conflict pp. 1195–1196, 1199–1200 RL 3 Analyze Structure pp. 1195–1196, 1198, 1200 RL 5
Reading Informational Text	Contemporary Literature pp. 1146–1157 RI 9 Read a Timeline pp. 1158–1159 RI 7		Reading Strategies pp. 1171–1172, 1174, 1176 RI 2 Tone and Imagery pp. 1171, 1174, 1176 RI 4	Characterization and Tone pp. 1188–1189, 1192 RI 3, RI 6 Historical Context pp. 1188, 1190, 1192 RI 6 Photograph p. 1191 RI 7	
Writing	Legacy of the Era pp. 1160–1161 W 10 Write pp. 1164, 1168 W 9, W 10		Quickwrite p. 1171 Writing Prompt p. 1177 W 1, W 8	Writing for Assessment p. 1193	Quickwrite p. 1195
Speaking and Listening	Legacy of the Era pp. 1160–1161 SL 1, SL 4 Discuss pp. 1162, 1166 SL 1			What's the Connection? p. 1179 SL 1	
Language			Establish Voice pp. 1174, 1177 L 3		

ECOS from **Letter from Birmingham Jail** Letter pp. 1202–1217	Linked Selections		ECOS **Media Study: Perspectives in the News** TV Newscast Clip/ Magazine Article pp. 1234–1237	from **Coming of Age in Mississippi** Autobiography pp. 1238–1249
	from **Stride Toward Freedom/Necessary to Protect Ourselves** Nonfiction/Interview pp. 1218–1229	**Martin Luther King Jr.: He Showed Us the Way** Essay pp. 1230–1233		
Lexile: 1250 *Fry: 12* *Dale-Chall: 8.3*	*Lexile: 1060/1320* *Fry: College/8* *Dale-Chall: 8.8/7.3*			*Lexile: 880* *Fry: 10* *Dale-Chall: 5.9*
Poem p. 1214				Poem p. 1247
Allusion pp. 1203, 1206, 1210, 1213, 1215 RI 4 Elements of an Argument pp. 1203–1204, 1206, 1209, 1215 RI 1, RI 6 Language Coach pp. 1207, 1211–1212 RI 4	Analyze Genres pp. 1219, 1223–1224, 1228 RI 5, RI 6 Synthesizing Sources pp. 1219–1220, 1222–1223, 1226, 1228 RI 2, RI 5; p. 1227 RI 5, RI 7	Analyze an Argument pp. 1231–1233 RI 5, RI 6	Historical Perspectives pp. 1234–1237 RI 7	Eyewitness Account pp. 1239, 1242, 1244–1245, 1248 RI 6 Primary Source pp. 1239, 1246, 1248 RI 3 Author's Purpose p. 1242 RI 6
Writing Prompt p. 1217 W 1		Writing Prompt p. 1233 W 2, W 9	Write to Inform p. 1237 W 2	Writing Prompt p. 1249 W 3, W 3d–e
Discuss p. 1203 SL 1	Discuss p. 1219 SL 1 Academic Vocabulary p. 1229 SL 1b–c		Integrate Multiple Sources of Information pp. 1234–1237 SL 2	Discuss p. 1239 SL 1
Parallelism pp. 1208, 1217 L 3a Words and Analogies p. 1216 L 5	Greek Prefix (*syn-*) p. 1229 L 4b Language Coach pp. 1222, 1226	Language Coach p. 1232		Analyze Mood pp. 1244, 1249 L 5b Language Coach pp. 1243, 1246

ECOS

To see the complete Essential Course of Study, see pp. T23–T27.

For additional lesson planning help, see **Teacher One Stop DVD.**

UNIT 6

ECOS   ECOS

Linked Selections

STRAND	My Dungeon Shook: Letter to My Nephew Open Letter pp. 1250–1258	Mother Tongue Essay pp. 1262–1271	Census Data: The U.S. Population Government Documents pp. 1272–1277	from In Search of Our Mothers' Gardens Essay pp. 1278–1285	Straw into Gold: The Metamorphosis of the Everyday Essay pp. 1286–1293	Life for My Child Is Simple/Primer for Blacks Poetry pp. 1294–1299
	Lexile: 1040 *Fry:* 12 *Dale-Chall:* 6.1	*Lexile:* 1120 *Fry:* 10 *Dale-Chall:* 6.7	*Lexile:* 1150 *Dale-Chall:* 7.8	*Lexile:* 1140 *Fry:* 8 *Dale-Chall:* 6.4	*Lexile:* 920 *Fry: College* *Dale-Chall:* 6.5	
Reading Literature						Repetition pp. 1295–1296, 1298–1299 RL 4, RL 5 Compare and Contrast Poems pp. 1295, 1297, 1299 RL 2, RL 4
Reading Informational Text	Rhetorical Devices pp. 1251, 1254–1255, 1257 RI 1, RI 6 Identify Purpose pp. 1251, 1255–1257 RI 1, RI 6	Personal Essay pp. 1263–1264, 1267, 1268, 1270 RI 3, RI 6 Identify Main Ideas pp. 1263, 1266, 1269–1270 RI 2	Analyze Text and Graphics pp. 1273, 1275–1277 RI 5, RI 7	Author's Message pp. 1279, 1282–1285 RI 5, RI 6 Cultural Context pp. 1279–1280, 1282, 1285 RI 6	Voice pp. 1287–1288, 1291, 1293 RI 4 Structure pp. 1287, 1290–1293 RI 5 Allusion p. 1290	
Writing	Quickwrite p. 1251	Quickwrite p. 1263 Writing Prompt p. 1271 W 2a–b, W 4	Writing Prompt p. 1277 W 1, W 8		Quickwrite p. 1287	Quickwrite p. 1295
Speaking and Listening				Discuss p. 1279 SL 1		
Language	Rhetorical Devices pp. 1251, 1254–1255, 1257 L 5a Idioms p. 1258 L 4a, L 5a Language Coach pp. 1254, 1255	Use Appropriate Language pp. 1266, 1271 L 3 Language Coach pp. 1266, 1268 L 2a		Language Coach pp. 1280, 1282, 1283 L 4c, L 5	Language Coach p. 1290	Language Coach p. 1297 L 4b

Adolescence—III/ Testimonial Poetry pp. 1300–1305	The Man in the Moon/ Forgetfulness Poetry pp. 1306–1310	Wrap-Ups • Responses to War p. 1201 • Civil Rights & Protest Literature p. 1259 • A Mosaic of American Voices p. 1311	Writing Workshop: Resumé pp. 1312–1321 Technology Workshop: Creating a Web Site pp. 1322–1323
Sound Devices in Poetry pp. 1301–1302, 1305 RL 4 Make Inferences pp. 1301–1302, 1304–1305 RL 1	Imagery pp. 1307–1310 RL 4 Development of an Idea pp. 1307–1310 RL 2		
		Analyze Documents, p. 1259 RI 9	
Quickwrite p. 1301		Writing to Synthesize p. 1201 W 9 Writing to Persuade p. 1259 W 1 Writing to Reflect p. 1311 W 9	Résumé pp. 1312–1321 W 2a, W 2b, W 2e, W 4, W 5, W 6, W 10 Creating a Website pp. 1322–1323 W 6
	Role-Play p. 1307 SL 1	Extension p. 1201 SL 6	Creating a Website pp. 1322–1323 SL 2, SL 5
			Drafting p. 1315 L 2 Editing and Publishing p. 1319 L 3

To see the complete Essential Course of Study, see pp. T23–T27.

For additional lesson planning help, see **Teacher One Stop DVD**.

Instructional Support

Resource Manager Unit 6

UNIT SUPPORT
Academic Vocabulary p. 3
Additional Academic Vocabulary p. 4
Grammar Focus p. 5
Text Analysis Workshop p. 162
Writing Workshop: Résumé p. 269

SELECTION SUPPORT*

Plan and Teach
Lesson planning pages
Additional leveled selection questions
Extension activities

Student Copy Masters
Selection summaries in four languages
Skills copy masters in English and Spanish
Vocabulary preteaching and support
Reading Check and Question Support
Reading Fluency

* Available for all selections

† Available on **thinkcentral.com**.

Language Handbook
Vocabulary Practice
Best Practices Toolkit†
PowerNotes DVD-ROM†
Connections: Nonfiction for Common Core CD-ROM†

Teacher One Stop DVD-ROM
Student One Stop DVD-ROM
Media*Smart* DVD-ROM
Perspectives in the News
Write*Smart* CD-ROM†
GrammarNotes DVD-ROM†
WordSharp CD-ROM†

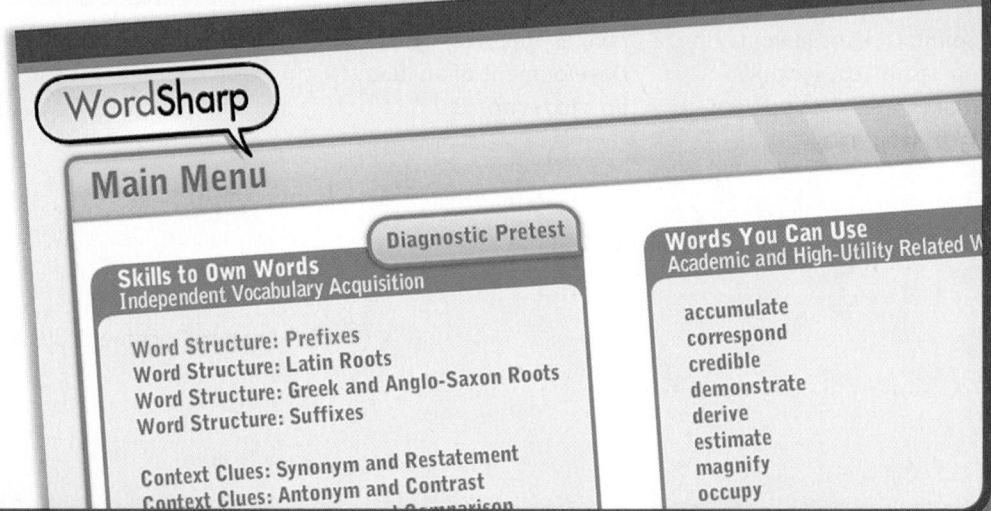

Differentiated Instruction

STRUGGLING READERS AND WRITERS	*ENGLISH LANGUAGE LEARNERS*	*ADVANCED LEARNERS*
Resource Manager Unit 6	**Resource Manager Unit 6**	**Resource Manager Unit 6**
Additional Selection Questions	Selection Summaries in English, Spanish, Vietnamese and Haitian Creole	Additional Selection Questions
Question Support		Ideas for Extension
Reading Fluency	Skills Copymasters in Spanish	**Diagnostic and Selection Tests**
Interactive Reader	**English Language Learner Adapted Interactive Reader Teacher's Guide**	Selection Tests B/C
Adapted Interactive Reader		
Level Up Online Tutorials	**ELL Adapted Interactive Reader**	
Audio Anthology	**Audio Tutor**	
(with Audio summaries)	**Guide to English for Newcomers**	
Diagnostic and Selection Tests	**Audio Anthology**	
Selection Tests A/B	**Audio Summaries in Multiple Languages** (on **thinkcentral.com**)	

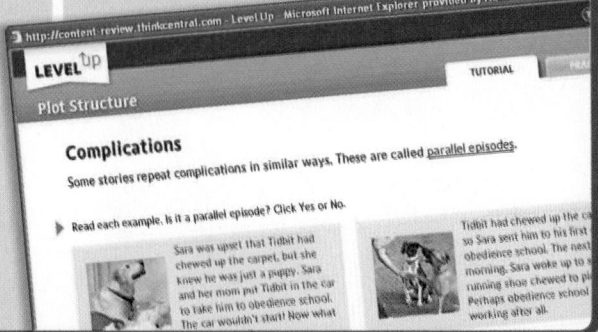

Assessment and Reteaching

Diagnostic and Selection Tests

Unit and Benchmark Tests

ThinkCentral Online Assessment:

• All program assessments

• Level Up Online Tutorials

ExamView Test Generator on the Teacher One Stop DVD-ROM

Online Essay Scoring on **thinkcentral.com**

ThinkCentral Online Reteaching:

• Level Up Online Tutorials

• Reteaching Worksheets

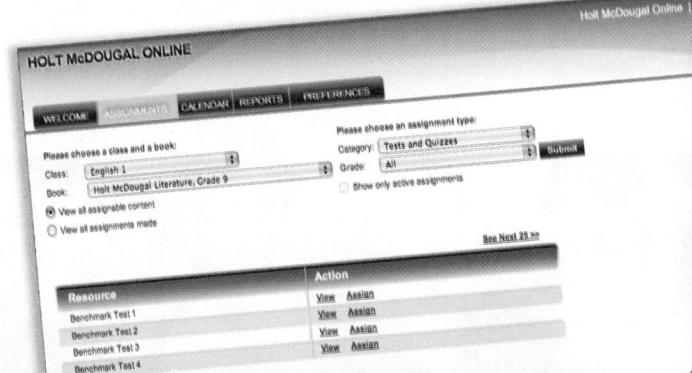

Professional Development

Video Center Based on interviews with program consultants and other educational experts, these videos feature classroom-ready teaching strategies.

Teacher Toolkit Includes a Teacher Handbook as well as a range of articles and handouts by program consultants and other educators.

Janet Allen

Jim Burke

Kylene Beers

Carol Jago

 **at a Glance**

One Location, Endless Resources

Find Resources Browse all *Holt McDougal Literature* components for the ones that meet your students' needs and match your teaching style.

Assess Progress and Reteach Assign electronic versions of program assessments to measure your students' mastery of the Common Core State Standards. On thinkcentral.com, some tests deliver online remediation tutorials to students who have not mastered skills.

 Interactive Whiteboard Lessons

Prepare your students for college and careers by teaching relevant, real-world skills through dynamic, interactive instruction. Go to **thinkcentral.com** to browse through all whiteboard lessons, including the following:

• Historical and Cultural Context

• Evaluating Arguments

• Poetry: Language and Form

Together Holt McDougal and HISTORY® are revolutionizing the study of English/language arts with video that helps students relive and re-imagine the people, places, and events they are discovering through reading. Look for selections with the HISTORY® icon.

COMMON CORE FOCUS

RL 9 Demonstrate knowledge of twentieth-century foundational works of American literature, including how two or more texts from the same period treat similar themes and topics. **RI 9** Analyze documents of historical and literary significance for their themes, purposes, and rhetorical features.

Questions of the Times

Read aloud the questions on pages 1146 and 1147 and the paragraph that follows them. Open the discussion of each idea by having students respond to the questions that conclude each paragraph. Use these notes to prompt further exploration of the ideas.

Are we responsible for the WHOLE WORLD?

Invite students to give reasons why America should or should not get involved in conflicts within, or among, other nations. Encourage students to discuss specific circumstances in which American involvement may be justified—or even mandatory.

Can America achieve EQUAL RIGHTS?

Challenge students to discuss both obvious and subtle ways in which racism and injustice continue. Prompt them to suggest how society as a whole can fight racism and prejudice. Extend the discussion by asking students to explain why Americans will—or will not—eventually become equal in one another's eyes.

Questions of the Times

DISCUSS After reading these questions and talking about them with a partner, share with the class as a whole. Then read on to explore the ways in which writers of the contemporary era have dealt with the same issues.

Are we responsible for the WHOLE WORLD?

World War II brought the United States into a new role of increased power and involvement in the world, a role that expanded even further with the Cold War, Vietnam, and the "War on Terror." Do you believe America has a responsibility to intervene in other nations' conflicts? Does it have the right?

Can America achieve EQUAL RIGHTS?

In 1963, one hundred years after emancipation, African Americans still found themselves treated as second-class citizens, denied equal education, jobs, even the right to vote. The civil rights movement secured the legal right to equality, but in reality racism and injustice linger on. Do you believe America will ever achieve true equality?

COMMON CORE

RL 9 Demonstrate knowledge of twentieth-century foundational works of American literature, including how two or more texts from the same period treat similar themes and topics. **RI 9** Analyze documents of historical and literary significance for their themes, purposes, and rhetorical features.

What makes an AMERICAN?

American writers of the 21st century reflect the diversity of the country itself. The United States has become a multicultural society whose citizens' experiences are endlessly varied. With no single "American experience" to bond citizens together, it seems logical to ask: What makes an American? Patriotism? Independence? Mere citizenship? Or something else?

What is the AMERICAN DREAM?

The Pilgrims and the Puritans dreamed of a new world where they would be free to practice their religion. Later immigrants dreamed of a country where any child could grow up to be the president. In the postwar era of the 1950s, the dream focused on consumer goods—"a car in every garage." How do you define the American dream?

1147

What makes an AMERICAN?

Encourage students to discuss what traits make Americans unique. Extend the discussion by comparing Americans' self-image with their image in the eyes of people in other parts of the world. Explore the reasons why Americans may see themselves differently from the way others see them.

What is the AMERICAN DREAM?

Prompt students to explain their concept of the American dream, encouraging them to be as specific as they can. Ask whether or not their concept is the same as that of the adults in their family, and why or why not. Extend the discussion by asking how the American dream may change in the future.

COMMON CORE FOCUS

RL 9 Demonstrate knowledge of twentieth-century foundational works of American literature, including how two or more texts from the same period treat similar themes and topics. **RI 9** Analyze documents of historical and literary significance for their themes and purposes.

The following essay (pages 1148–1157) provides students with a historical context for the Unit 6 reading selections. It presents a brief overview of significant events occurring during the time period, 1940–present, and discusses key people and ideas of the times.

To get started, read and discuss the opening paragraph on page 1148. Ask students how the view of the "blue marble" adrift in the blackness of space provides a different perspective not just of the planet but also of its inhabitants. Students should recognize that the vastness of space that became so apparent during the Space Age encouraged people to see Earth in a new way: as one small part of an immense universe.

READING STRATEGY

■ PREVIEW

Have students preview the historical essay by skimming the heads, boldfaced terms, and **Taking Notes** side-column features. Ask volunteers to summarize what the essay is about.

Contemporary Literature
1940–PRESENT
New Perspectives

In the 1950s, America entered the Space Age—a beginning foray into our modern technological times. Looking down from space, the country's first astronauts marveled at the blue marble that was Earth floating in the blackness. From space, Earth looked peaceful and whole, with no divisions between nations, no conflict between races. It was a new way of looking at the world—just one of many new perspectives on modern life.

1148

DIFFERENTIATED INSTRUCTION

FOR STRUGGLING READERS
Vocabulary Support
- *perspective,* "way of thinking about things, viewpoint"
- *expansionist,* "inclined to expand into new territories"
- *isolationism,* "a policy of avoiding international political alliances and economic relations"

- *atomic bomb,* "a bomb in which the release of energy from the splitting of atomic nuclei produces a tremendously powerful explosion"
- *superpower,* "an extremely powerful nation"
- *communism,* "a system in which all property is owned by the community as a whole"

Use this copy master to help students take notes on the essay, pages 1148–1157:

RESOURCE MANAGER—Copy Master
Note Taking p. 8

Contemporary Literature: Historical Context

Literature of the modern age reflects the uncertainty and anxiety brought on by the realities of war.

Modern Warfare

WORLD WAR II "Not a place on earth might be so happy as America," wrote Thomas Paine in the winter of 1776. "Her situation is remote from all the wrangling world." More than a century and a half later, as the Nazi army surged across Europe and Japan's expansionist government seized territories in Asia, many Americans still clung to the dream of isolationism—until **Pearl Harbor** woke them from their illusions.

On December 7, 1941, Japanese bombers struck the American naval base at Pearl Harbor, Hawaii, sinking ships, destroying planes, and killing over two thousand people. Though it lasted less than two hours, this surprise attack changed the course of history, bringing a reluctant United States into World War II.

The U.S. entry into the war turned the tide in favor of the Allies—England, France, and the Soviet Union—but it was a long, hard fight. By the time Germany and Japan surrendered to the Allied forces in 1945, more than 78 million people had been killed or wounded, including around six million Jews systematically murdered by the Nazis in what became known as the **Holocaust.** World War II was a catastrophe of epic dimensions, the first war in history in which more civilians than soldiers died. Never before had so many soldiers fought. Never before had such wholesale slaughter occurred. Writers such as **Randall Jarrell,** who had personal experience with the war, struggled to both document and examine the meaning of war on such a grand scale. Others, such as **Kurt Vonnegut** and **Bernard Malamud,** examined the rampant anti-Semitism that fueled the Holocaust. Malamud once remarked, "People say I write so much about misery, but you write about what you write best. As you are grooved, so you are grieved."

THE COLD WAR America came out of World War II a world power, wielding a new weapon of unparalleled destructive force: the atomic bomb. But along with strength and influence came deep uneasiness. The Soviet Union, once an ally, emerged as a rival superpower with equally large ambitions and a political system—communism—which many saw as a threat to the American way of life. Knowing any direct confrontation could end in nuclear annihilation, the two nations fought a "Cold War," each side racing to develop more and more devastating weapons while they jostled for strategic influence around the globe. As the arms race spiraled upward, ordinary citizens felt less and less secure. In literature, this pervasive fear of known and unknown dangers prompted a boom in **science fiction** writing, as writers pondered what might arise if the current trends continued.

COMMON CORE

RL 9 Demonstrate knowledge of twentieth-century foundational works of American literature, including how two or more texts from the same period treat similar themes and topics. RI 9 Analyze documents of historical and literary significance for their themes and purposes.

▶ **TAKING NOTES**

Outlining As you read this introduction, use an outline to record the main ideas about the characteristics and literature of the period. You can use article headings, boldfaced terms, and the information in these boxes as starting points. (See page R49 in the **Research Handbook** for more help with outlining.)

I. *Historical Context*
  A. *World War II*
    1. *isolationism*
    2. *Pearl Harbor*
    3. *Holocaust*
  B. *Cold War*

Contemporary Literature: Historical Context

This section of the essay (pages 1149–1150) summarizes the succession of conflicts that affected America and other nations of the world, including World War II, the Cold War between the United States and the Soviet Union, wars in Korea and Vietnam, and the Persian Gulf War. The text also mentions the breakup of the Soviet Union, the attack on the World Trade Center, and the U.S. invasions of Afghanistan and Iraq.

TIERED DISCUSSION PROMPTS

Use these prompts to help students understand the ideas in **Modern Warfare:**

Interpret The opening paragraph concludes with " . . . many Americans still clung to the dream of isolationism—until Pearl Harbor woke them from their illusions." What does the writer mean? *Possible answer: Americans thought they could keep from getting directly involved in events affecting Europe and Asia. However, their dream of remaining isolated proved to be an illusion when Japan attacked Pearl Harbor, Hawaii, which forced the United States to enter World War II.*

Analyze In what ways was World War II "a catastrophe of epic dimensions"? *Possible answer: It was a war of unprecedented slaughter—78 million people killed or wounded—and the first war in history in which more civilians died than soldiers. Anti-Semitism fueled the Holocaust, the Nazi murder of six million Jews and others.*

Synthesize In what sense did the Cold War directly affect even more people than previous "hot" wars? *Possible answer: The Cold War created a climate of pervasive fear in which ordinary citizens lived under the threat of nuclear annihilation.*

FOR STRUGGLING READERS

Science Fiction Explain that science fiction is fiction that deals mainly with the effects of actual or imagined science on the world and its people. These effects can be positive, as in stories describing miraculous new inventions, or negative, as in tales of robots or computers running amok. Point out that Cold War–era fears gave rise to numerous science fiction stories, novels, television shows, and movies about the dangers and consequences of nuclear war.

FOR ENGLISH LANGUAGE LEARNERS

Set a Purpose Draw attention to the outline and explain that it shows the skeleton—the "bare bones" of the text. Tell students that their purpose in reading will be to bring the skeleton to life by adding details to the outline's main ideas.

Use these prompts to continue the discussion of **Modern Warfare:**

Evaluate You read on page 1149 that Thomas Paine wrote: "Not a place on earth might be so happy as America. Her situation is remote from all the wrangling world." In light of subsequent events, do his words ring true? Why or why not? *Possible answers: No; his words do not ring true at all. In fact, since World War II, America has again and again become involved in conflicts and warfare with other nations of the world. Yes; he is right—the United States has not fought a war on its own soil in decades, though it did suffer terrorist attacks in 1995 and 2001.*

Synthesize John Updike wrote, "At all times an old world is collapsing and a new world arising." How does this statement reflect the global situation from 1940 to the present? *Possible answer: Violence and open warfare in various places around the globe create an unstable and ever-changing world. The spread of nuclear weapons has given rise to a world that seems to grow more precarious every year.*

CHECK UNDERSTANDING

Ask students what the Cold War was and how and when it finally ended.

MODERN CONFLICTS Meanwhile, in an effort to contain the spread of communism, the U.S. military became deeply involved in civil wars first in Korea, then in Vietnam. The major American involvement in the **Vietnam War** lasted about nine years and bred a degree of domestic conflict unseen since the Civil War. As the death toll among U.S. soldiers rose—reaching about 58,000 in all—many Americans questioned the wisdom of our intervention and took to the streets in protest. The literature of the time reflects the conflicts within the country. Writer **Tim O'Brien** once remarked that "It's not really Vietnam that I was concerned about . . . ; rather, it was to have readers care about what's right and wrong and about the difficulty of doing right, the difficulty of saying no to a war."

The Cold War finally came to an end with the breakup of the Soviet Union in 1991, but America was not finished with warfare. That same year, U.S. troops were sent to counter the Iraqi invasion of Kuwait in the first Persian Gulf War. A longer struggle began on September 11, 2001, when hijackers flew commercial airplanes into the Pentagon and the World Trade Center, killing thousands and leading to U.S. invasions of Afghanistan and Iraq. At the same time, violence raged around the globe, and with nuclear weapons no longer limited to two superpowers, possibilities for worldwide disaster loomed. Writers of the last several generations have been profoundly affected by the sense of instability that has been brought on by near-constant war. "At all times," wrote novelist **John Updike,** "an old world is collapsing and a new world arising."

U. S. Marines training for Operation Desert Shield, 1990

> **A Voice from the Times**
>
> *Mankind must put an end to war, or war will put an end to mankind.*
>
> —John F. Kennedy

1150

DIFFERENTIATED INSTRUCTION

FOR STRUGGLING READERS
Vocabulary Support
- *intervention,* "interference in the affairs of another nation"
- *segregation,* "forced separation of groups of people on the basis of their race"
- *protest marches,* "large groups walking together to promote an idea or cause"
- *boycott,* "refusal to deal with a business or organization as a way to force change"

FOR ADVANCED LEARNERS/AP
Research Vietnam War Protests Have students learn more about the Vietnam War and why this controversial war drew increasingly strong protest from Americans. Have students make oral presentations to the class, explaining their findings and, if possible, sharing pictures and actual news stories from the Vietnam War era. Students should include information about the draft and how it energized mass protests among young people.

Segregated drinking fountains, North Carolina

Cultural Influences

Writers have both recorded and reflected upon the civil rights movement of the 1950s and 1960s—perhaps the most important social change in modern time.

The Civil Rights Movement

The civil rights movement had its roots in protests and legal actions of the 1950s. In 1954, the Supreme Court's ***Brown v. Board of Education*** ruling struck down school segregation as unconstitutional. Other civil rights advances followed, pushed along by black and white activists who organized protest marches, boycotts, voter registration drives, and sit-ins. **Dr. Martin Luther King Jr.** emerged as a leader during these times. King advocated nonviolent civil disobedience based on the philosophies of Henry David Thoreau and Indian social reformer Mohandas Gandhi.

Sadly, many of the peaceful demonstrations of the civil rights movement were met with mob violence and police brutality. While the nation watched on television, protestors were beaten, attacked by police dogs, and sprayed with fire hoses. King himself endured repeated imprisonment for his efforts. But the violence did not stop the movement.

During the famous March on Washington in 1963, which drew 200,000 participants, demonstrators demanded civil rights legislation at the national level, backed strongly by federal enforcement. Largely as a result of King's efforts, Congress passed the 1964 **Civil Rights Act** outlawing segregation in public places and guaranteeing legal equality to black citizens. In the years since, America has still not achieved true equality and opportunity for all, yet the civil rights movement has brought it much closer to King's dream of a land where people would "not be judged by the color of their skin, but by the content of their character."

> **A Voice from the Times**
>
> *I have a dream that one day this nation will rise up and live out the true meaning of its creed: "We hold these truths to be self-evident, that all men are created equal."*
>
> —Martin Luther King Jr.

Cultural Influences

This section of the essay (page 1151) focuses on the civil rights movement of the 1950s and 1960s. The text highlights the important *Brown v. Board of Education* Supreme Court decision, explains the contribution of Dr. Martin Luther King, Jr., and discusses the 1964 Civil Rights Act.

TIERED DISCUSSION PROMPTS

Use these prompts to help students understand the ideas in **The Civil Rights Movement:**

Summarize What important role did Dr. Martin Luther King, Jr., play in the civil rights movement? *Possible answer: King was a leader of the movement and an advocate of civil disobedience as a way for African Americans to gain equality. King's work was instrumental in the passage of the 1964 Civil Rights Act, which guaranteed legal equality and outlawed racial segregation.*

Evaluate The essay writer states that "America has still not achieved true equality and opportunity for all," although the nation is much closer to King's vision of a time when people will be judged by their character rather than their skin color. Do you agree with the writer's assessment? Why, or why not? *Possible answer: America has made significant progress toward equality, but there is still a long way to go. Citizens of all races have equal legal rights and equal opportunities, but far too many people still discriminate against others on the basis of personal prejudice.*

FOR STRUGGLING READERS

Civil Disobedience Explain that *civil disobedience* means refusing to obey laws as a nonviolent way of calling attention to injustice. Inspired by such leaders as Martin Luther King, Jr., and Mohandas Gandhi, people in America and other parts of the world adopted the methods of civil disobedience as a means of compelling the government to change unfair laws or eliminate unjust practices.

FOR ENGLISH LANGUAGE LEARNERS

Analyze Civil Disobedience After students read the section, ask them to list what the civil rights movement achieved and has yet to achieve.

Has Achieved	Has Yet to Achieve
African-American legal equality	true equality
racial segregation illegal	equal opportunity

FOR ADVANCED LEARNERS/AP

Research and Evaluate *Brown v. Board of Education* Invite students to learn more about the *Brown v. Board of Education* decision by researching the case and its impact. Have students prepare brief reports explaining how the case reversed the "separate but equal" policy of *Plessy v. Ferguson* and challenged Jim Crow laws. Students should also evaluate to what extent the *Brown v. Board of Education* decision has actually been implemented.

Ideas of the Age

This section of the essay (page 1152) discusses how the American dream has evolved over time. The text also discusses how several writers have addressed the idea of the American dream.

TIERED DISCUSSION PROMPTS

Use these prompts to help students understand the ideas in **The American Dream:**

Summarize How has the American dream changed over the years? *Possible answer: Before the 20th century, the American dream had been associated with such ideas as political and religious freedom, economic opportunity, and the chance to succeed through talent, education, and hard work. After the many challenges of the first half of the 20th century, however, many Americans narrowed the focus of the dream to the simple idea of owning a home in a safe and stable neighborhood. Before long, though, this idea expanded, as Americans placed increasing importance on material possessions.*

Synthesize If Jack Kerouac and Allen Ginsberg were alive and writing today, do you think they would they still find "shallowness and conformity" to protest in American society? Explain. *Possible answer: Probably, because people continue to overemphasize the importance of money and material things and, in general, they still strive to "keep up with the Joneses."*

Seattle-area neighborhood, 1955

Ideas of the Age

Modern writers have responded in a variety of ways to a peculiarly American philosophy: that of the American dream.

The American Dream

For earlier generations, the **American dream** had meant many things—political and religious freedom, economic opportunity, the chance to achieve a better life through talent, education, and hard work. After living through the Great Depression and two World Wars, however, many Americans in the 1950s whittled that dream down to something much simpler: the chance to own a home in a stable neighborhood.

For millions of mainly white Americans, life in the suburbs became the American dream. Families sought out communities with affordable single-family homes, good schools, shopping malls, and parking that was free and easy to find. People didn't care if their houses looked alike; they just wanted a safe place to raise their children.

As the years passed and the economy boomed, however, Americans began to add to their once-simple dream. *Things* became more important: a new television, car, or washing machine came to be seen as symbols of success. Soon the dream seemed to narrow to a vision of a consumer society in which conformity and "keeping up with the Joneses" was valued above all.

Writers from the mid-century to today have wrangled with the idea of the American dream. In the mid-'50s, **"beatniks"** such as **Jack Kerouac** and **Allen Ginsberg** protested the shallowness and conformity of American society. Dramatists such as **Arthur Miller** examined the strivings of ordinary Americans reaching for that American dream. Poets, novelists, short story writers—all have explored the many facets of the American dream.

DIFFERENTIATED INSTRUCTION

FOR STRUGGLING READERS

Taking Notes Have students record the main ideas about the American dream (page 1152) in outline form. Then ask them to trade papers, evaluate each other's work, and offer suggestions for improvement. Sample notes:

American Dream
- Earlier generations: freedom, opportunity, chance for better life
- 1950s: home in stable neighborhood
- Material things became most important

FOR ENGLISH LANGUAGE LEARNERS

Trace Word Roots Explain that artists and writers of Beat movement generally rejected the values, conventions, and conformity associated with the middle class. Lead students to infer the sources of the word *beatnik* from what they know about the 1950s in the United States. (The beats of the 1950s were jazz, rock and roll, and rhythm and blues. The suffix –nik is a reference to Russian words and therefore to the Cold War.)

Literature of the Times

The years between World War II and the present brought dramatic changes in the subjects and forms of literature, as well as a wider variety of authors represented.

Modern American Drama

In the years following World War II, some of the best and most influential writing was occurring within the community of American theater. Dramatists in the post-war years began to experiment stylistically and create works of social relevance that would prompt a revival in theater not only in America, but in Europe as well. Dramatists such as Arthur Miller and **Tennessee Williams** served as models of the liberated playwright—experimenting with stagecraft as well as modern themes often deemed provocative.

One of the most common themes explored by these playwrights was that of the American dream. "The American dream is the largely unacknowledged screen in front of which all American writing plays itself out," Arthur Miller once said. Indeed, Miller's Willy Loman, the main character in his *Death of a Salesman*, became the trademark figure of postwar American theater. A lowly salesman who has been discarded by the system to which he has mistakenly devoted his life, Willy Loman proved how the American dream could become twisted and broken.

A general disillusionment paired with an experimental style characterized many of the works of this period. While a play such as **Thornton Wilder's** *Our Town,* first produced in 1938, experimented with stagecraft by showing life literally "behind the scenes" on a stage bare of scenery, it still took a gentle view of small-town America. Works written in the 1940s and 1950s, however, were far less sympathetic. In *The Glass Menagerie* and *A Streetcar Named Desire,* for example, Southerner Tennessee Williams portrayed characters who, unsuited to modern life, retreat into the fantasy world of an earlier era. And Miller's critique of modern values in *Death of a Salesman* was found to be so threatening that Hollywood executives wanted to release the movie version along with a short film depicting the life of a salesman as blissful and carefree. Miller, however, protested.

Lorraine Hansberry's *A Raisin in the Sun,* written in 1957, looked at the American dream from the perspective of those who had been excluded. The first major Broadway play by an African-American writer, *A Raisin in the Sun* was hailed by critics as "universal," while also capturing unique aspects of the African-

Vivien Leigh and Marlon Brando in *A Streetcar Named Desire*

▶ For Your Outline

MODERN AMERICAN DRAMA

- postwar revival in theater
- common theme was American dream
- characterized by disillusionment and experimental style
- broke boundaries and opened doors

Literature of the Times

This section of the essay (pages 1153–1157) focuses on the mosaic of contemporary American literature since World War II:

- modern drama, including the plays of Arthur Miller, Tennessee Williams, Thornton Wilder, and Lorraine Hansberry
- literature responding to war, including that of John Hersey, John Steinbeck, Elie Wiesel, Joseph Heller, Kurt Vonnegut, and Tim O'Brien
- civil rights and protest literature, including that of Ann Petry, Richard Wright, Gwendolyn Brooks, Ralph Ellison, James Baldwin, Anne Moody, and Dudley Randall
- contrasting views expressed by Malcolm X and Martin Luther King, Jr.

TIERED DISCUSSION PROMPTS

Use these prompts to help students understand the ideas in **Modern American Drama:**

Summarize What were some of the defining characteristics of post–World War II American drama? *Possible answer: Dramatists began to experiment stylistically and create socially relevant works. Dramas often addressed the American dream and expressed a general disillusionment.*

Analyze In what ways was Arthur Miller's *Death of a Salesman* representative of post–World War II American drama? *Possible answer: In* Death of a Salesman, *Miller focused on the American dream, one of the most common themes of the postwar years. Like many other dramatists of the time, Miller explored disillusionment through a thought-provoking work of social relevance.*

FOR STRUGGLING READERS
Vocabulary Support
- *suburbs,* "residential neighborhoods on the edge of cities or large towns"
- *boomed,* "grew or expanded dramatically"
- *conformity,* "acting or thinking in accordance with a certain standard"
- *disillusionment,* "disappointment; dissatisfaction"

FOR ENGLISH LANGUAGE LEARNERS
Clarify Cause and Effect Explain that changes in who was writing in America and what they were writing about can be directly linked to the historical and cultural changes discussed on pages 1153–1157. Encourage students to reread those pages and to look for examples of how history changed literature and how literature affected history.

FOR ADVANCED LEARNERS/AP
Synthesize Theme Disillusionment remains a theme in modern writing today, not just plays, but also works by novelists, poets, and filmmakers. Challenge students to identify contemporary works that address the theme of disillusionment and share their findings with the class. Discuss the kinds of disillusionment that each work addresses, and have students look for common threads.

Have students explain the significance of Lorraine Hansberry's *A Raisin in the Sun.*

TIERED DISCUSSION PROMPTS

Use these prompts to help students understand the ideas in **Responses to War:**

Analyze How have world events shaped literature in the 20th and 21st centuries? *Possible answer: Conflicts between nations frequently have erupted into war, especially World War II and the Vietnam War. Writers have struggled to come to terms with the horrors and absurdities associated with these wars. For example, some writers have addressed the subject with realistic accounts, while others have approached it with ironic humor.*

Synthesize During the Vietnam War, young men were subject to a draft, or conscription into military service. How might this fact help to explain the popularity of such writers as Heller and Vonnegut? *Possible answer: The draft drastically changed the lives of young men—or threatened to—regardless of their political views or feelings toward warfare in general. Anyone who received a draft notice was caught in circumstances beyond his control. The "cynicism toward authority and sense of helplessness in the face of huge, inhuman forces" that characterized the work of Heller and Vonnegut resonated with young people of the time because they shared the authors' feelings of cynicism and helplessness.*

American experience. Writer **James Baldwin** said of the play, "[I]n order for a person to bear his life, he needs a valid re-creation of that life, which is why, as Ray Charles might put it, blacks chose to sing the blues. This is why *Raisin in the Sun* meant so much to black people . . . . In the theater, a current flowed back and forth between the audience and the actors, flesh and blood corroborating flesh and blood—as we say, testifying. . . ." In addition, the play opened the door to writers from outside the mainstream, who would revitalize American theater in the decades to follow.

Responses to War

War, with all its moral complexities and attendant brutality, has had a strong influence on writers throughout the 20th and 21st centuries. World War II brought with it previously unimaginable horrors: millions of casualties, the genocide of the Holocaust, the use of nuclear weapons. Struggling to come to terms with such destruction, some writers worked in the **modernist** style—giving detailed, realistic, and somewhat detached accounts of the war, as if told by an outside observer such as a journalist.

In fact, much of the most powerful literature of World War II was straight nonfiction, such as war correspondent **John Hersey's** *Hiroshima,* an unforgettable account of the first hours and days after the United States dropped atomic bombs on two Japanese cities, bringing massive destruction and an end to the war. **John Steinbeck,** better known for his Depression-era literature, worked as a war correspondent as well, spending time with troops in North Africa and England. His essay "Why Soldiers Won't Talk" explores how soldiers cope with the things they have witnessed.

Many writers of this period wrote of their own experiences—including the horrors of the Holocaust. **Elie Wiesel,** who was born in Europe and became an American citizen much later in life, was taken as a 15-year-old boy to a Nazi concentration camp in Poland. His memoir, *Night,* describes his nightmarish experiences in the camp, where he was beaten, starved, and nearly worked to death. Most members of his family did not survive.

In the 1960s, **Joseph Heller's** *Catch-22* and **Kurt Vonnegut's** *Slaughterhouse-Five* introduced a new style of war literature. Both writers had seen combat in World War II, and their novels shared a dark, ironic humor that focused on the absurdity of war. One such absurdity is the "catch" in Catch-22. It refers to a mysterious Air Force regulation which asserts that any person willing to go into battle should be considered insane, yet the very act of asking to be excused would prove one's sanity—and send a pilot back into battle. With their cynicism toward authority and sense of helplessness in the face of huge, inhuman forces, Heller and Vonnegut spoke to a younger generation caught up in a very different war: Vietnam.

Where World War II had united Americans in moral certainty against a common enemy, Vietnam drove them apart. Protesters—among them

A Voice from the Times

One of the most sound ideas in dramatic writing is that, in order to create the universal, you must pay very great attention to the specific.

—Lorraine Hansberry

▶ *For Your Outline*

RESPONSES TO WAR

- war influenced 20th- and 21st- century writers
- some worked in modernist style
- others wrote powerful nonfiction
- later focus is on absurdity of war
- postmodern style questioned conventions
- some blurred line between fiction and nonfiction

DIFFERENTIATED INSTRUCTION

FOR STRUGGLING READERS

Modernist Style Clarify for students that the use of *modernist* on page 1154 refers to a style of writing that began in the early 20th century and continues through the present day. Point out early modernist writers found in Unit 5, particularly Ernest Hemingway. Emphasize that Hemingway's style in both "In Another Country" (pages 1010–1014) and

"A New Kind of War" (pages 1096–1101) is both observant and detached. Connect this observation with the description of modernist writing on page 1154.

War protesters and propaganda poster

students, pacifists, and some returning veterans—marched in the streets, calling for an end to the war.

Writers of this time questioned authority, conventional values, and even the nature of reality. Some experimented with a "postmodern" style of fiction that drew attention to its own artificiality, pointing out the presence of the author by displaying its inner workings like a clock without a face. Others, like Vietnam veteran Tim O'Brien, wrote stories that blurred the lines between fiction and nonfiction. In *The Things They Carried*, O'Brien writes about telling his daughter how he killed a man in Vietnam—but this Tim O'Brien is a character, and the real O'Brien neither killed a man nor has a daughter. Can something that "didn't really happen" still be true? Postmodernism asks, What is fiction? What is truth?

▲ **Analyze Visuals**
The World War II propaganda poster shown here was meant to inspire support for the war. In your opinion, is it persuasive? How might the Vietnam War protesters shown in the other image have answered the question posed? How might they have responded to the intent of the poster?

Analyze Visuals

Possible answer: The poster is persuasive in its use of direct address and a pointed finger, both of which arrest the viewer's attention. Protesters such as those in the photograph might have responded that they, too, were doing everything they could to end American involvement in a war that was against the country's best interests. The protesters might have objected to the poster's suggestion that patriotism can be only expressed through the unquestioning support of a war effort.

About the Art The poster represents World War II propaganda designed to increase support for the war effort. It reflects a time in America when public support for the nation's involvement in war was strong. As the photograph of Vietnam War protesters shows, many people opposed the war with a similar strength.

CHECK UNDERSTANDING

Identify ways that each writer or pair of writers responded to war:

- John Hersey and John Steinbeck
- Elie Wiesel
- Joseph Heller and Kurt Vonnegut
- Tim O'Brien

FOR STRUGGLING READERS
Vocabulary Support
- *genocide,* "the deliberate and systematic annihilation of a racial or political group"
- *concentration camp,* "a prison camp run by Nazi Germany where prisoners endured horrible conditions and were put to death"
- *cynicism,* "contemptuous distrust of human nature, motives, and actions"
- *pacifist,* "a person opposed to war"
- *veteran,* "a person who has served in the armed forces"

FOR ADVANCED LEARNERS/AP
Research Photojournalism In addition to print responses, photography has been a crucial medium used to report the horror of war. Have students research the importance of photojournalism during World War II and Vietnam. Students might concentrate particularly on the work of:

- Joe Rosenthal
- Dickey Chapelle
- Eddie Adams
- John Filo

If possible, have students locate key photographs taken by each of these photojournalists and present them to the class. Students might then consider the relationship between the work of these photojournalists and the writers discussed on pages 1154 and 1155.

Civil Rights and Protest Literature

The questioning of authority and conventional values applied not only to the writers of the Vietnam era but to those of the civil rights movement as well. To change laws, first it was necessary to change minds. The success of the civil rights movement depended on getting the message of justice out to the rest of America—telling people what was happening and making them care. One hundred years before, abolitionist writers had made a deep impact with novels and slave narratives that showed readers how it felt to live in bondage. In the 20th century, the written word still had a crucial role to play.

Even before the civil rights movement began in earnest, writers were examining issues of race and equality. Building upon the work of earlier Harlem Renaissance writers, black writers of the 1940s explored the dynamics of race relations and the injustice of discrimination in novels such as **Ann Petry's** *The Street,* which sold over a million copies, and **Richard Wright's** *Native Son.* As the civil rights movement gathered momentum in the early 1950s, African-American writers began to gain wider recognition, winning prestigious awards such as the Pulitzer Prize for poet **Gwendolyn Brooks** and the National Book Award for **Ralph Ellison's** *Invisible Man.*

The 1960s brought **James Baldwin's** influential essay collections as well as many important autobiographies, including *The Autobiography of Malcolm X* and **Anne Moody's** *Coming of Age in Mississippi.* By telling their own stories, these writers made a powerful statement about the harmful effects of racism and the need for change. Poets chimed in as well, reflecting upon the powerful events of the day. **Dudley Randall's** "Ballad of Birmingham," for example, was in response to the 1963 church bombing that killed four young girls.

A Voice from the Times

We are not fighting for integration, nor are we fighting for separation. We are fighting for recognition as human beings.

—Malcolm X

Martin Luther King Jr. and Malcolm X

Malcolm X and Martin Luther King Jr., two leaders of the civil rights movement, held opposing viewpoints on the use of violence as a means for change. Inspired by Thoreau and Gandhi, as well as the Bible, King's speeches and writings combined a steadfast belief in nonviolent resistance with a bold determination to bring an end to injustice. In his 1963 "I Have a Dream" speech, King argued, "Let us not seek to satisfy our thirst for freedom by drinking from the cup of bitterness and hatred. We must forever conduct our struggle on the high plane of dignity and discipline. We must not allow our creative protest to degenerate into physical violence." Malcolm X, on the other hand, advocated the use of militant armed resistance as a response to discrimination. "I *am* for violence," he said, "if nonviolence means we continue postponing a solution to the black man's problem—just to *avoid* violence." Their writings give readers insight into the various, and sometimes opposing, factions that made up the civil rights movement.

A Mosaic of American Voices

The last 30 years have seen an outpouring of talent from American writers of many different ethnic backgrounds, along with an increasingly widespread appreciation of diversity. Just a few decades ago, the literary scene was still dominated almost exclusively by men of European descent. Now, they have been joined by Native American writers such as **N. Scott Momaday** and **Louise Erdrich,** Asian-American writers such as **Maxine Hong Kingston** and **Amy Tan,** Hispanic writers such as **Rudolfo Anaya** and **Sandra Cisneros,** and African-American writers such as **Alice Walker, Rita Dove, Toni Morrison,** and **Maya Angelou,** to name just a few. Many of the most exciting contemporary writers are women; many, too, such as **Bharati Mukherjee** and **Edwidge Danticat,** were born outside the United States and bring a global perspective to American literature.

While earlier writers of color often focused on the experience of discrimination, writers today draw on different aspects of life in America, positive and negative, from family memories and relationships to contemporary politics. With such a broad array of published voices, no longer is any one author assumed to speak for all people of a given group. Instead, the most compelling work of today's literary marketplace is both expressive of the individual and rooted in culture and place, while still managing to speak to universal human concerns. American literature has changed, again, and will continue to evolve as long as writers continue to write.

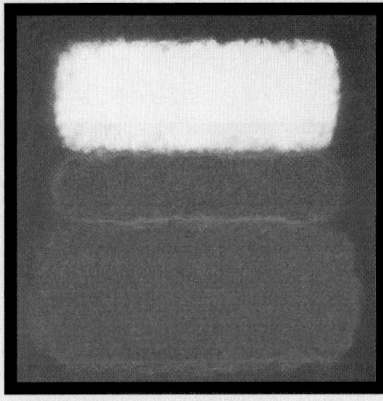

Modern American Art

The power shift from Europe to the United States in the years after World War II had a parallel in the world of art. For the first time, international attention focused not on Paris's salon or London's Royal Academy but on the studios and galleries of New York City.

Abstract Expressionism During the 1940s and 1950s, a group of artists including **Mark Rothko** and **Jackson Pollock** dominated the New York art scene. Their style was abstract, intensely emotional, and focused as much on the process of painting as on the work itself. Jackson Pollock, who was famous for laying a giant canvas on the floor and throwing paint on it, described his art as "energy and motion made visible." Mark Rothko's signature style— floating rectangles of color aligned vertically against a colored background—is illustrated beautifully in his work *White Cloud Over Purple* (1957), shown here.

Pop Art In the early 1960s, a very different kind of art burst into public view. Pop art used familiar images from consumer culture to ask the question *What is art?* From **Andy Warhol,** with his silkscreened movie stars and soup cans, to **Roy Lichtenstein's** enormous blow-ups of comic strip panels, pop art celebrated modern methods of production while it subtly undermined the barrage of messages shaping Americans' attitudes and everyday lives.

THE ARTISTS' GALLERY

American artist Mark Rothko (1903–1970) was born in Russia and moved to the United States at the age of ten. Although Rothko is often considered an abstract expressionist, he insisted that he was not an abstract painter and was not interested in the relationship between color and form. Rather, he said he was concerned with expressing basic human emotions through his art.

Activity Ask students to reflect on Rothko's painting and describe the emotions it seems to convey. *Answers will vary.*

TIERED DISCUSSION PROMPTS

Use these prompts to help students understand the ideas in **A Mosaic of American Voices:**

Summarize Explain how diversity has increased among American writers. *Possible answer: There are many more women and people of color among contemporary American writers than in earlier historical periods.*

Analyze How has the increase in diversity changed the impact of each writer's voice? *Possible answer: Each writer's voice more specifically reflects his or her individual views and perspective rather than representing the voice of a group.*

FOR ADVANCED LEARNERS/AP

Synthesize [small-group option] Challenge students to use print and online resources to research some of the accomplishments of the civil rights movement. Students should consider in particular:

- the Civil Rights Act of 1968

- an increase in the number of African Americans holding elected office

- changes in sports, academia, and the entertainment industry

Have students present their findings to the class. The entire class should consider what work of the civil rights movement should continue in the present day. Encourage students to include in their discussion thoughts about the role of writers and journalists in keeping the movement alive.

COMMON CORE FOCUS

RI 7 Integrate and evaluate multiple sources of information presented in different formats, as well as in words, to address a question or solve a problem.

Connecting Literature, History, and Culture

■ READ A TIMELINE

Point out that each of the three horizontal sections of the timeline—*American Literary Milestones, Historical Context,* and *World Culture and Events*—displays a sequence of events that occurred between 1940 and the present. By looking at the vertical columns on the timeline, students can see which events were occurring at approximately the same time.

Have students locate, for example, each of these events on the timeline between 1945 and 1948:

- **1945** The war in the Pacific ends after the United States drops atomic bombs on Japan. (See *Historical Context.*)
- **1947** *A Streetcar Named Desire* by Tennessee Williams is produced. (See *American Literary Milestones.*)
- **1948** The state of Israel is founded. (See *World Culture and Events.*)

Ask students what events occurred between 1974 and 1977. **Answer:** *President Richard M. Nixon resigned in 1974. South Vietnam surrendered in 1975. The first practical home computer reached the market in 1977.*

Connecting Literature, History, and Culture

Use this timeline and the questions on the next page to gain insight about how American developments during this period reflected those in the world as a whole.

AMERICAN LITERARY MILESTONES

1940

1945 Richard Wright details coming of age in *Black Boy*; Randall Jarrell publishes World War II poem "The Death of the Ball Turret Gunner."

1947 Tennessee Williams's *A Streetcar Named Desire* is first produced.

1950

1951 J. D. Salinger's novel *The Catcher in the Rye* is published.

1952 Bernard Malamud publishes his baseball novel, *The Natural*.

1953 Arthur Miller's *The Crucible* reflects contemporary "witch hunt" of McCarthyism.

1960

1961 Joseph Heller's satirical war novel, *Catch-22*, is published.

1969 Kurt Vonnegut publishes *Slaughterhouse-Five*; N. Scott Momaday's *House Made of Dawn* wins Pulitzer Prize. ▶

HISTORICAL CONTEXT

1940

1941 Japanese bomb Pearl Harbor, ▲ bringing United States into World War II.

1945 United States drops two atomic bombs on Japan, ending the war in the Pacific.

1950

1954 In *Brown v. Board of Education*, the Supreme Court declares segregated schools unconstitutional. ▼

1959 Alaska and Hawaii join the Union as the 49th and 50th states.

1960

1963 Martin Luther King gives "I Have a Dream" speech in Washington, D.C.; President John F. Kennedy is assassinated in Dallas.

1965 Malcolm X is assassinated.

1967 Thurgood Marshall becomes the first African-American justice on the Supreme Court.

1968 Assassinations of Martin Luther King Jr., and Robert F. Kennedy shock the nation.

WORLD CULTURE AND EVENTS

1940

1940 German forces conquer much of Europe.

1945 Germany surrenders to Allies.

1948 State of Israel is founded; South African policy of apartheid begins.

1950

1953 Korean War ends.

1957 Soviet Union launches first space satellite, *Sputnik*.

1959 Fidel Castro takes control of Cuba after ouster of dictator.

1960

1965 First U.S. combat forces land in Vietnam.

1966 Mao Zedong launches Cultural Revolution in China (to 1976). ▶

1969 U.S. astronauts land on moon.

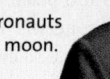

DIFFERENTIATED INSTRUCTION

FOR STRUGGLING READERS

Understanding a Timeline Explain that the timeline runs chronologically (in time order) from left to right across the page. Each of the six columns represents a period of years between 1940 and the present. The three parallel rows of the timeline represent events occurring simultaneously. By comparing the three rows, readers can better understand what events in literature, history, and culture were taking place at about the same time.

MAKING CONNECTIONS

- What important roles have new technologies played in this era?
- What evidence do you see that "American" and "world" events have become harder to separate?
- Which political and cultural trends have influenced American literature?

○ **COMMON CORE**

RI 7 Integrate and evaluate multiple sources of information presented in different formats, as well as in words, to address a question or solve a problem.

1970

1970 Maya Angelou publishes autobiographical *I Know Why the Caged Bird Sings.*

1983 Sandra Cisneros publishes *The House on Mango Street.* ▶

1985

1985 Anne Tyler publishes *The Accidental Tourist.*

1989 Amy Tan's *The Joy Luck Club* is published.

1993 Rita Dove becomes first African-American poet laureate; Toni Morrison wins Nobel Prize for literature. ▶

2000

2000 Lucille Clifton's poetry collection, *Blessing the Boats,* wins National Book Award.

2002 Diane McWhorter's history of Birmingham during the Civil Rights Movement, *Carry Me Home,* wins the Pulitzer Prize for Nonfiction.

2007 Cormac McCarthy's *The Road* wins Pulitzer Prize.

1970

1974 President Richard M. Nixon resigns to avoid impeachment over Watergate scandal.

1977 First practical home computer, Apple II, hits market.

1981 The space shuttle *Columbia* launches; Sandra Day O'Connor becomes the first woman to be appointed to the U.S. Supreme Court.

1985

1989 The oil tanker *Exxon Valdez* ▲ runs aground, creating a huge oil spill along Alaskan coast.

1991 The Persian Gulf War begins; the United States leads allied coalition against Iraq.

2000

2001 Hijackers fly commercial planes into World Trade Center and Pentagon, killing thousands.

2005 Hurricane Katrina hits New Orleans and surrounding area, causing massive destruction. ▼

2009 Barack Obama becomes first African American president in U.S. history.

1970

1975 South Vietnam surrenders as North Vietnamese troops occupy Saigon.

1979 Egypt's Anwar Sadat and Israel's Menachem Begin sign treaty ending war between Egypt and Israel.

1985

1989 The Berlin Wall comes down; ▶ student protesters in China are killed in Tiananmen Square.

1991 Soviet Union breaks up into 15 republics.

2000

2003 U.S. troops invade Iraq, deposing leader Saddam Hussein.

2004 Poland joins European Union.

2008 China hosts the Summer Olympic Games.

MAKING CONNECTIONS

Possible answers:

- *Atomic bombs brought World War II to an end. The first practical home computer became available in 1977. Various space-related developments occurred, such as the launching of the first satellite in 1957, the first landing of astronauts on the moon in 1969, and the launching of the space shuttle Columbia in 1981.*

- *America was involved in a number of international conflicts, including World War II, the Korean War, the Vietnam War, the Persian Gulf War, and the invasion of Iraq. The United States competed with the Soviet Union in the space race.*

- *American literature shows the influence of the civil rights movement, McCarthyism, and international warfare.*

ADDITIONAL QUESTIONS

1. What satirical war novel was published 16 years after the end of World War II?
   Answer: *Joseph Heller's* Catch-22

2. In 1967, Thurgood Marshall became the first African-American Supreme Court Justice. Twenty-six years later, two African-American women had memorable accomplishments. Who were they, and what did they accomplish? ***Answer:*** *In 1993, Toni Morrison won the Nobel Prize for literature, and Rita Dove became the first African-American poet laureate.*

FOR ADVANCED LEARNERS/AP

Make Additional Connections Have students choose one of the six time periods shown in the timeline and research using conventional or electronic resources to learn about other events that occurred during the time span. Challenge students to identify events for each category: *American Literary Milestones, Historical Context,* and *World Culture and Events.* Have students prepare and present brief oral reports, summarizing important events and discussing their connection to events shown in the timeline or discussed in class.

W 10 Write routinely over shorter time frames for a range of tasks, purposes, and audiences.
SL 1 Initiate and participate in discussions, building on others' ideas and expressing their own clearly and persuasively. **SL 4** Present findings such that the organization, development, substance, and style are appropriate to purpose, audience, and a range of formal and informal tasks.

A New American Dream?

Have students read and discuss the paragraph. Elicit or provide examples of the kinds of societal changes that have raised "concerns about education, social mobility, family and community, the environment, and the hectic pace of modern life."

For example, discuss such changes as the increasing number of families in which both parents work outside the home; the growing gap between rich and poor; and the effects of cell phones, wireless technology, and other such advancements on people's quality of life.

CREATE Explore with students how the American dream is both similar and different for various groups of people. For example, all groups may desire economic success, but new immigrants may dream first of political or religious freedom, while United States–born citizens may take such freedoms for granted. As students plan for the *CREATE* activity, ask them to think specifically about the point of view of each group. Suggest that students divide their artwork into panels, with each panel representing the vision of a different group. Have students use books of quotations to find appropriate quotations for each panel.

The Legacy of the Era

A New American Dream?

COMMON CORE

W 10 Write routinely over shorter time frames for a range of tasks, purposes, and audiences. **SL 1** Initiate and participate in discussions, building on others' ideas and expressing their own clearly and persuasively. **SL 4** Present findings such that the organization, development, substance, and style are appropriate to purpose, audience, and a range of formal and informal tasks.

As rapid changes in society have given rise to fresh concerns about education, social mobility, family and community, the environment, and the hectic pace of modern life, it may be time to redefine the American dream for a new generation.

CREATE What might be the American dream for students and young adults today? For new immigrants? Working-class people? Others? As a class, share your thoughts. Then break into groups of four and create posters or collages that depict different aspects of today's American dream. Consult a book of quotations to find varying interpretations of the American dream. Be sure to cite the speaker of each quotation.

1160

DIFFERENTIATED INSTRUCTION

FOR STRUGGLING READERS
Vocabulary Support

- *social mobility,* "the capacity for moving to a higher social class or position"

- *hectic,* "characterized by activity, haste, or excitement"

- *collage,* "an artistic work composed of various materials (such as paper and cloth) pasted together on a surface"

FOR ADVANCED LEARNERS/AP

Reflect on the American Dream Ask students to consider whether, in general, the American dream places too much emphasis on money and material possessions. Should people be placing greater emphasis on other values, and if so, what values? Ask students to write an essay exploring these questions and expressing their views. Then have volunteers share their essays with the class as the basis for a group discussion.

What the Future Holds

Technology has affected both the form and content of literary and nonfiction texts, offering new possibilities from hypertext to hand-held e-books to online publishing—though the predicted death of the printed book (and of narrative as we know it) has not come to pass. What do you think literature and nonfiction will be like in 20 years?

QUICKWRITE Taking the role of a future critic, write a "book review" discussing one new form of literature or nonfiction. Include your opinions about the limitations and possibilities this form presents.

Living in the Global Village

America's isolationism ended abruptly with the attack on Pearl Harbor in World War II. In the postwar years, international trade and travel greatly expanded. Today, huge improvements in communications and transportation have made globalism possible on many levels: political, economic, and cultural. Day by day, Americans are becoming more aware of their ties with the rest of the world.

DISCUSS How does globalization affect your everyday life? Brainstorm ideas with a small group, then report back to the class. If you're stuck, try thinking about what you wear, what you eat, and how you earn and spend money.

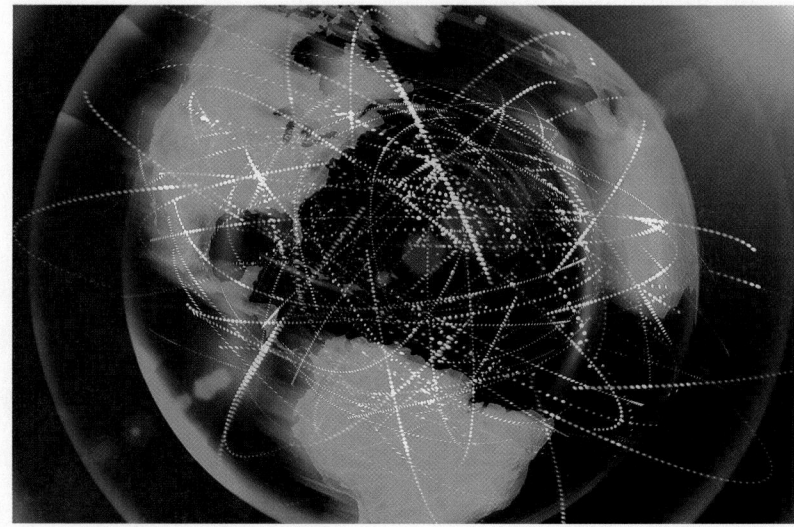

What the Future Holds

Have students read the paragraph. Be sure everyone understands the meaning of the phrases "hypertext," "hand-held e-books," and "online publishing." Ask students whether they think the printed book will ever really disappear, and why or why not. Discuss the future of literature, encouraging students to use their imagination. Then have them complete the **QUICKWRITE.**

QUICKWRITE As students evaluate the limitations and possibilities of the new form of literature, suggest that they consider various age groups. For example, would electronic media appeal equally to older and younger readers? Also have them think about practicality. For instance, would readers want to take a hand-held viewer to the beach? Encourage students to support their opinions with specific reasons and examples.

Living in the Global Village

After students read the paragraph, discuss how the Internet in particular has made Americans "more aware of their ties with the rest of the world." Ask how other forms of communication and media, such as movies and television, encourage globalism.

DISCUSS After students complete their brainstorming, extend the discussion by asking the class to list benefits of globalization and also to identify any disadvantages they see.

FOR STRUGGLING READERS
Vocabulary Support
- *hypertext,* "information stored in a computer system to link related items and allow them to be readily accessed"
- *global village,* "the world viewed as being a single community"
- *isolationism,* "policy of avoiding involvement in international alliances and relations"
- *globalism,* "belief that political decisions should reflect global concerns"

FOR ADVANCED LEARNERS/AP
Research Blogs Call students' attention to the picture at the top of page 1161. Have students find out more about "blogs," or Weblogs. What are they? Who writes them and who reads them? Why have they become so popular? Ask students to share their findings with the class. Then discuss how blogs are representative of our times and of the role of technology within the global village.

from **Our Town**

Drama by Thornton Wilder

COMMON CORE FOCUS

RL 3 Analyze the impact of the author's choices regarding how to develop and relate elements of a drama. **SL 1** Initiate and participate in a range of collaborative discussions.

BACKGROUND Some writers have popular appeal, but earn few, if any, literary prizes; others win prestigious prizes but never gain widespread readership. Thornton Wilder was one of those rare writers who achieved both. In addition, his enjoyable writing style brought him success as both a novelist and a playwright. He won the Pulitzer Prize in 1928 for *The Bridge of San Luis Rey* and a National Book Award in 1968 for his later novel *The Eighth Day*. He also won two Pulitzer Prizes in drama: one for *Our Town,* in 1938, and another for *The Skin of Our Teeth,* in 1943.

TEXT ANALYSIS Explain that the play's popularity stems in large part from Wilder's ability to create universally recognizable and believable characters set against the familiar backdrop of small-town America. The unusual bare staging also invites audience members to focus their attention on Wilder's words and themes and become actively involved in the play's characters and events.

Our Town, one of the most frequently produced of all American plays, was produced once again to great acclaim in 2002. Well-known actor Paul Newman starred as the Stage Manager, a role for which he received a 2003 Tony Award nomination.

DISCUSS As they read George and Emily's dialogue, have students consider how their classmates sometimes mask their fondness for each other.

Thornton Wilder

COMMON CORE

RL 3 Analyze the impact of the author's choices regarding how to develop and relate elements of a drama. **SL 1** Initiate and participate in a range of collaborative discussions.

BACKGROUND Since *Our Town* first appeared on Broadway in 1938, not a day has gone by when it has not been staged somewhere in the world. Set in the small town of Grover's Corners, New Hampshire, the play traces the everyday experiences of two neighboring families, the Gibbses and the Webbs. Spanning a dozen years at the beginning of the twentieth century, *Our Town* has several unusual touches: it is performed on a stage bare of all scenery; it depicts some characters from beyond the grave; and it employs a folksy but omniscient narrator called the Stage Manager, who reveals past and future events and comments on the geology of the region, as well as the history and sociology of the town.

TEXT ANALYSIS Both the title and the characters in *Our Town* are **allegorical.** As a typical small town of its time, inhabited by typical American families, Grover's Corners represents the life of every small-town American family—yours, mine, ours. The scene on the opposite page depicts George Gibbs and Emily Webb at the beginning of their courtship. They aren't sure of one another yet, and they have differing opinions about men and women. As readers, we face two tasks when we study **dialogue** or **characters in conflict.** One is to make inferences about the characters themselves. The other is to look for clues to how they view the world and to watch as differing views develop so that we can identify the play's **theme**—the message it expresses for the author.

DISCUSS Working in a small group, have two group members read the dialogue in this excerpt aloud. Then, look for clues that George and Emily are fond of one another. Does one character criticize the other as a way of hiding affection? If so, what clues show you the underlying fondness? What differing statements do Emily and George make about being male or female? Do they settle their difference by the end of the scene? After you have discussed these questions with your group, share your insights with the class as a whole.

DIFFERENTIATED INSTRUCTION

FOR STRUGGLING READERS

Comprehension Support Help students complete a Three-Column Journal to draw conclusions about Emily and George based on their dialogue. Discuss each character's traits and explore ways in which the characters are alike and different.

 BEST PRACTICES TOOLKIT—Transparency
Three-Column Journal p. B10

Character	Quotation	Conclusion
Emily	"I'm sorry if it hurts your feelings..."	She is honest but considerate.
Emily	"...you've got awful conceited..."	Emily knows him well enough to say this.
George	"I'm glad you said it..."	George respects her opinion.

George. Emily, why are you mad at me?

Emily. I'm not mad at you.

George. You've been treating me so funny lately.

Emily. Well, since you ask me, I might as well say it right out, George,— (*She catches sight of a teacher passing.*) Good-by, Miss Corcoran.

George. Good-by, Miss Corcoran. —Wha—what is it?

Emily (*not scoldingly; finding it difficult to say*). I don't like the whole change that's come over you in the last year. I'm sorry if that hurts your feelings, but I've got to—tell the truth and shame the devil.

10 **George.** A *change?* —Wha—what do you mean?

Emily. Well, up to a year ago, I used to like you a lot. And I used to watch you as you did everything . . . because we'd been friends so long . . . and then you began spending all your time at *baseball* . . . and you never stopped to speak to anybody any more. Not even to your own family you didn't . . . and, George, it's a fact, you've got awful conceited and stuck-up, and all the girls say so. They may not say so to your face, but that's what they say about you behind your back, and it hurts me to hear them say it, but I've got to agree with them a little. I'm sorry if it hurts your feelings . . . but I can't be sorry I said it.

George. I . . . I'm glad you said it, Emily. I never thought that such a thing was hap-
20 pening to me. I guess it's hard for a fella not to have faults creep into his character.

(*They take a step or two in silence, then stand still in misery.*)

Emily. I always expect a man to be perfect and I think he should be.

George. Oh . . . I don't think it's possible to be perfect, Emily.

Emily. Well, my *father* is, and as far as I can see *your* father is. There's no reason on earth why you shouldn't be, too.

George. Well, I feel it's the other way round. That men aren't naturally good; but girls are.

Emily. Well, you might as well know right now that I'm not perfect. It's not as easy for a girl to be perfect as a man, because we girls are more—more—nervous.—Now
30 I'm sorry I said all that about you. I don't know what made me say it.

George. Emily,—.

Emily. Now I can see it's not the truth at all. And I suddenly feel that it isn't important, anyway.

George. Emily . . . would you like an ice-cream soda, or something, before you go home?

Emily. Well, thank you. . . . I would.

FOR STRUGGLING READERS
Vocabulary Support

- *hobnobbed,* "associated; was friendly"
- *elite,* "superior group of people"
- *folksy,* "having an informal, friendly manner"
- *eerily,* "weirdly; strangely"
- *omniscient,* "all-knowing"
- *duality,* "double nature"

FOR ENGLISH LANGUAGE LEARNERS
Vocabulary: Idioms and Phrasal Verbs Share the meaning of these expressions, and then help students use them in sentences:

- *right out* (line 4), "directly"
- *hurts your feelings* (lines 8–9), "makes you feel sad or hurt"
- *stuck-up* (line 15), "conceited, snobbish"
- *to your face* (line 16), "in your presence"
- *behind your back* (line 16), "secretly"
- *other way round* (line 25), "opposite"

INTRODUCE THE MASTERPIECE

Our Town Before students read the excerpt, remind them that *Our Town* dates back to 1938. Ask them to consider as they read in what ways the play still rings true today and in what ways it does not. In addition, urge them to think about the ways in which Wilder makes the conversation between George and Emily realistic and what character traits of George and Emily they can relate to. After students finish reading, ask what conclusions they can draw about the kind of people George and Emily are and the kind of relationship they are likely to have in their future.

TIERED DISCUSSION PROMPTS

Use these prompts to help students consider the relationship between George and Emily:

Restate What does Emily tell George? *Possible answer: She tells him he has changed in the past year in ways that are not attractive.*

Analyze In what ways does the interaction between George and Emily reveal their feelings toward each other? What are those feelings? *Possible answer: Both George and Emily speak to each other honestly and respectfully. Emily explains to George that she "used to like [him] a lot" but that he's changed—"got awful conceited and stuck-up." Rather than react defensively, George expresses gratitude and admits his faults. Their interaction shows that Emily cares enough to speak frankly to George and that George respects Emily's opinion and feels bad that she perceives imperfections in him.*

Synthesize In what ways does the conversation between George and Emily reflect an "everyday experience"? *Possible answer: Like young people everywhere, George and Emily are having a typical, everyday conversation about getting to know one another. As with so many such conversations, it reflects typical misconceptions people can form when they care about each other but feel awkward and ill at ease expressing their feelings.*

COMMON CORE FOCUS

RL 3 Analyze the impact of the author's choices regarding how to develop and relate elements of a drama. **RL 6** Distinguish what is directly stated in a text from what is really meant. **W 9** Draw evidence from literary texts to support analysis and reflection.

BACKGROUND Born in Columbus, Mississippi, Tennessee Williams largely grew up in St. Louis, Missouri. Nevertheless, he set almost all of his plays in the South, and his work had a lasting impact on Southern literature. Williams wrote more than 70 plays, nine of which were made into movies. His plays are known for their dramatic scenes, lyrical dialogue, and original characters, many of which are based on Williams's family and friends. The author's best plays captivated audiences and critics alike by exploring the frustrations and passions of characters trying to survive a brutal world.

TEXT ANALYSIS Explain that in creating the play, Williams drew on his family's past in Mississippi and his early life in Missouri. Appearing on Broadway in 1945, *The Glass Menagerie* received the New York Drama Critics' Circle award for best play of the season, a great achievement for its 34-year-old playwright. Five years later, the play was made into a movie, earning Williams many more admirers and adding to his fame.

In 1995, the play was staged in London with actresses Zoë Wanamaker as Amanda and Claire Skinner as Laura. The two women were praised for their performances. Skinner received a Best Actress Award from the London Critics Circle Theater Awards, while Wanamaker was nominated for a Laurence Olivier Theatre Award.

WRITE Encourage students to think about how Tom and Amanda each view Laura's physical capabilities. Suggest that they base their paragraphs on Tom and Amanda's widely differing opinions, as well as the burden that caring for his family places on Tom.

from The Glass Menagerie

Drama by Tennessee Williams

Tennessee Williams

COMMON CORE

RL 3 Analyze the impact of the author's choices regarding how to develop and relate elements of a drama. **RL 6** Distinguish what is directly stated in a text from what is really meant. **W 9** Draw evidence from literary texts to support analysis and reflection.

BACKGROUND For *The Glass Menagerie*, Tennessee Williams (1911–1983) drew on his own youth. Williams had an abusive, frequently absent father; a much-loved sister who suffered from mental illness; and a strong-willed mother who tried to hold the family together while longing for the days of her Southern girlhood. *The Glass Menagerie* features Amanda, a mother much like Williams's; her son Tom, who supports his mother and sister at a job he hates; and his frail, painfully shy daughter Laura, who collects tiny glass animals—the menagerie of the play's title.

TEXT ANALYSIS Before you read the scene excerpted here, review what you learned about **dialogue, conflict,** and **theme** on page 1162. In the scene you read from *Our Town*, Wilder depicts two characters in gentle conflict. In *The Glass Menagerie*, the three major characters are frequently on stage at the same time, leaving the audience with the complex task of following *multiple conflicts* as the **dialogue** among the three unfolds. Williams increases the challenge by using **dramatic irony** in this scene, a moment when a character reveals something about himself or herself to the audience but is clearly not aware of it.

WRITE As you read this scene, pay special attention to Tom. What kind of conflict does he have with his mother Amanda? How does he view his sister Laura? When he informs his mother that he is "going to the movies," what makes his statement ironic? (Hint: Examine what he says about Laura before announcing that he will go to the movies and what his mother says about him afterwards.) Use your answers to these questions to write a paragraph on Tom and his conflicts in the play at this moment.

Tom. Mother, you mustn't expect too much of Laura.

Amanda. What do you mean?

Tom. Laura seems all those things to you and me because she's ours and we love her. We don't even notice she's crippled any more.

Amanda. Don't say crippled! You know that I never allow that word to be used!

Tom. But face facts, Mother. She is and—that's not all—

Amanda. What do you mean "not all"?

1164

DIFFERENTIATED INSTRUCTION

FOR STRUGGLING READERS

Comprehension Support Ask students to record the main ideas of About the Author and About the Play in Outline organizers. Then have students exchange papers, evaluate each other's work, and offer suggestions for possible improvement.

A. About the Author

1. Tennessee Williams drew play's themes and characters from personal experience.

2. Williams had a difficult childhood.

   a. abusive, often absent father
   b. mentally ill sister
   c. education interrupted by family problems

3. Williams moved to New York City and began winning drama prizes.

4. *The Glass Menagerie* appeared on Broadway and led to financial success.

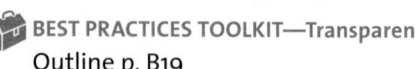 BEST PRACTICES TOOLKIT—Transparency Outline p. B19

PLAYBILL
ROUNDABOUT THEATRE COMPANY
CRITERION CENTER STAGE RIGHT

THE GLASS MENAGERIE

Tom. Laura is very different from other girls.

Amanda. I think the difference is all to her advantage.

10 **Tom.** Not quite all—in the eyes of others—strangers—she's terribly shy and lives in a world of her own and those things make her seem a little peculiar to people outside the house.

Amanda. Don't say peculiar.

Tom. Face the facts. She is.

(*The dance-hall music changes to a tango that has a minor and somewhat ominous tone.*)

Amanda. In what way is she peculiar—may I ask?

Tom (*gently*). She lives in a world of her own—a world of little glass ornaments, Mother. . . . (*He gets up. Amanda remains holding the brush, looking at him, troubled.*) She plays old phonograph records and—that's about all—

20 (*He glances at himself in the mirror and crosses to the door.*)

Amanda (*sharply*). Where are you going?

Tom. I'm going to the movies. (*He goes out the screen door.*)

Amanda. Not to the movies, every night to the movies! (*She follows quickly to the screen door.*) I don't believe you always go to the movies! (*He is gone. Amanda looks worriedly after him for a moment. Then vitality and optimism return and she turns from the door, crossing to portieres.*) Laura! Laura! (*Laura answers from kitchenette.*)

Laura. Yes, Mother.

Amanda. Let those dishes go and come in front! (*Laura appears with a dish towel. Amanda speaks to her gaily.*) Laura, come here and make a wish on the moon!

30 (*screen image: the moon*)

Laura (*entering*). Moon—moon?

Amanda. A little silver slipper of a moon. Look over your left shoulder, Laura, and make a wish! (*Laura looks faintly puzzled as if called out of sleep. Amanda seizes her shoulders and turns her at an angle by the door.*) Now! Now, darling, *wish!*

Laura. What shall I wish for, Mother?

Amanda (*her voice trembling and her eyes suddenly filling with tears*). Happiness! Good fortune!

(*The sound of the violin rises and the stage dims out.*)

FOR STRUGGLING READERS

Vocabulary Support

- *menagerie*, "a collection of animals kept for exhibition"
- *wistfully*, "longingly"
- *belle*, "an attractive woman or girl "
- *suitor*, "a man who courts a woman"
- *ominous* (line 15), "threatening, menacing"
- *vitality* (line 25), "energy, liveliness"
- *portieres* (line 26), "curtains hung in a doorway"

FOR ADVANCED LEARNERS/AP

Discuss Characterization [small-group option] Have small groups discuss these questions and then share their views:

- How do the contrasting views of Laura presented by Tom and Amanda convey Laura's character to audiences?

- What conclusions can you draw about Tom on the basis of this passage? What conclusions can you draw about Amanda? about Laura?

INTRODUCE THE MASTERPIECE

The Glass Menagerie *The Glass Menagerie* tells the story of the Wingfield family, who live in a cramped apartment across the alley from the Paradise Dance Hall. The father is absent; Tom, the son, supports his mother and sister by working in a shoe factory. Laura, the sister, is lame from disease and painfully shy; she spends most of her time with her collection of old phonograph records and her "menagerie" of tiny glass animals. Amanda, the mother, is deeply concerned about her daughter's future. She wistfully recalls her youth as a Southern belle, when she once entertained 17 gentlemen callers at once, and wishes that Laura had a suitor who might offer the security of marriage.

TIERED DISCUSSION PROMPTS

Use these prompts to help students consider the relationship between the members of the Wingfield family:

Connect Have you or someone you know ever misjudged another person's abilities? How does that experience help you understand Tom's feelings? *Accept all thoughtful responses.*

Interpret What does Tom mean when he says, "Mother, you mustn't expect too much of Laura"? *Possible answer: Tom feels that Laura's options are limited because she is lame and "terribly shy and lives in a world of her own." Does Amanda agree with Tom? Explain. Possible answer: Amanda appears to disagree with Tom, because she is either unwilling or unable to admit Laura's limitations.*

Synthesize If the character of Tom is based on Williams himself, and the character of Laura is based on Williams's sister, what does this suggest about Williams's early family life? *Possible answer: Williams may have felt caught in the middle between the mentally ill sister he loved and a mother who lived in denial of the difficulties their family was facing.*

from **Death of a Salesman**

Drama by Arthur Miller

COMMON CORE FOCUS

RL 1 Cite evidence to support analysis of what the text says explicitly, as well as inferences drawn from the text. **RL 3** Analyze the impact of the author's choices regarding how to develop and relate elements of a drama.

BACKGROUND Arthur Miller's first play to be produced on Broadway was *The Man Who Had All the Luck,* which appeared in 1944. The play was a failure, closing after only four performances. Three years later, *All My Sons* earned Miller the New York Drama Critics' Circle award as the year's best play and also won two Tony awards. It was *Death of a Salesman,* however, that brought Miller international fame. The play has been acclaimed as one of the finest works of contemporary American theater.

TEXT ANALYSIS Explain that, like many of Miller's plays, *Death of a Salesman* explores themes of morality and personal and social responsibility and presents the author's view of an ordinary man as a tragic hero. As students read the excerpt, have them pay attention to the author's parenthetical stage directions. Ask how these directions contribute to the reader's understanding of Willy's emotional state and Howard's response.

In 1998, successful film actor Brian Dennehy wowed critics and audiences alike with his interpretation of Willy Loman. Dennehy won both the 1999 Tony Award and Drama Desk Award.

DISCUSS Before they write their dialogue, have students assume the roles of Willy and Howard and read the scene aloud with a partner. Suggest that as they write their scene, they model their dialogue on the diction Miller uses for the two characters.

Arthur Miller

COMMON CORE

RL 1 Cite evidence to support analysis of what the text says explicitly, was well as inferences drawn from the text. **RL 3** Analyze the impact of the author's choices regarding how to develop and relate elements of a drama.

BACKGROUND Arthur Miller (1915–2005) won the Pulitzer Prize in 1949 for *Death of a Salesman.* It is widely regarded as his finest work and one of the greatest American plays of the twentieth century. Some critics see it as a brilliant dissection of the American dream; others commend its perceptive portrayal of family tensions and personal failings. Willy Loman, the protagonist, acts the successful businessman, husband, and father, but he is a deeply troubled man. A career-long traveling salesman, he no longer earns a salary but only his commission on sales. His position is further threatened by his declining performance on the road. At home, a long-buried conflict with his elder son Biff threatens Willy's increasingly fragmented sense of self.

TEXT ANALYSIS So far, in two dramatic scenes from American Masterpieces (pages 1162–1163 and 1164–1165), you have observed a gentle **conflict** between two young people at the start of a courtship and a more difficult conflict among three family members over how they perceive each other. Now, in the scene on the opposite page, you will see how **dialogue** can express the conflict between two ways of viewing the world. Here, Willy Loman, an aging and increasingly unreliable salesman, faces Howard Wagner, a much younger man, now in charge of the company that employs Willy. By listening to the opposing voices in this scene and by considering the validity of their claims, you can make inferences about the author's **theme**—the message about the world he wishes to express in the play.

DISCUSS Read the scene once to get an impression of Willy and Howard. Then, read it a second time and concentrate on the stories Willy tells Howard. Search for clues to Willy's definition of success and his view of the business world. Howard says much less than Willy in this excerpt. Examine his short lines for clues to a different view of business and success.

After you have made inferences about Willy and Howard, discuss the two characters in a small group of your peers. Summarize Willy's view of success and the business world, and contrast his views with Howard's. Then, discuss what the group thinks Willy and Howard would say next. Finally, write a page of dialogue that develops this scene and the conflict between two ways of seeing the world.

DIFFERENTIATED INSTRUCTION

FOR STRUGGLING READERS

Comprehension Support As students read the excerpt, work with them to complete a Two-Column Chart to help them make inferences and draw conclusions about Willy's words and feelings.

 BEST PRACTICES TOOLKIT—Transparency
Two-Column Chart p. A25

Quote	Significance
"...just listen for a minute. You don't understand this."	Willy feels Howard isn't giving him a chance to explain.
"...what could be more satisfying than to be...remembered and loved...by so many...people?"	Willy loves being a salesman because he can connect with people.

Willy (*angrily*). Business is definitely business, but just listen for a minute. You don't understand this. When I was a boy—eighteen, nineteen—I was already on the road. And there was a question in my mind as to whether selling had a future for me. Because in those days I had a yearning to go to Alaska. See, there were three gold strikes in one month in Alaska, and I felt like going out. Just for the ride, you might say.

Howard (*barely interested*). Don't say.

Willy. Oh, yeah, my father lived many years in Alaska. He was an adventurous man. We've got quite a little streak of self-reliance in our family. I thought I'd go out
10 with my older brother and try to locate him, and maybe settle in the North with the old man. And I was almost decided to go, when I met a salesman in the Parker House. His name was Dave Singleman. And he was eighty-four years old, and he'd drummed merchandise in thirty-one states. And old Dave, he'd go up to his room, y'understand, put on his green velvet slippers—I'll never forget—and pick up his phone and call the buyers, and without ever leaving his room, at the age of eighty-four, he made his living. And when I saw that, I realized that selling was the greatest career a man could want. 'Cause what could be more satisfying than to be able to go, at the age of eighty-four, into twenty or thirty different cities, and pick up a phone, and be remembered and loved and helped by so many different people?
20 Do you know? when he died—and by the way he died the death of a salesman, in his green velvet slippers in the smoker of the New York, New Haven and Hartford, going into Boston—when he died, hundreds of salesmen and buyers were at his funeral. Things were sad on a lotta trains for months after that. (*He stands up. Howard has not looked at him.*) In those days there was personality in it, Howard. There was respect, and comradeship, and gratitude in it. Today, it's all cut and dried, and there's no chance for bringing friendship to bear—or personality. You see what I mean? They don't know me any more.

Howard (*moving away, to the right*). That's just the thing, Willy.

Willy. If I had forty dollars a week—that's all I'd need. Forty dollars, Howard.

30 **Howard.** Kid, I can't take blood from a stone, I—

Willy (*desperation is on him now*). Howard, the year Al Smith was nominated, your father came to me and—

Howard (*starting to go off*). I've got to see some people, kid.

Willy (*stopping him*). I'm talking about your father! There were promises made across this desk! You mustn't tell me you've got people to see—I put thirty-four years into this firm, Howard, and now I can't pay my insurance! You can't eat the orange and throw the peel away—a man is not a piece of fruit!

FOR STRUGGLING READERS
Vocabulary Support

- *humiliating*, "causing embarrassment"
- *in contempt of*, "acting with willful disobedience or disrespect toward"
- *blacklisted*, "listed as someone not to be hired"
- *rift*, "a serious disagreement"
- *dissection*, "close analysis"

FOR ADVANCED LEARNERS/AP
Research House Un-American Activities Committee Arthur Miller was one of many well-known people called before the House Un-American Activities Committee. Ask students to research the purpose of this committee and find out why its tactics were so controversial. Also ask students to find out how the activities of the committee were reflected in Miller's award-winning play *The Crucible*. Have students share their findings with the class.

INTRODUCE THE MASTERPIECE

Death of a Salesman Point out that Willy does nearly all the talking in this scene, while Howard, Willy's boss, says very little. As students read, ask them how this imbalance contributes to their understanding of the relationship between the two men. Also have students consider how Miller wants readers to perceive Howard and Willy.

TIERED DISCUSSION PROMPTS

Use these prompts to help students understand how Willy Loman feels:

Connect Think about a time when you felt unappreciated or unfairly treated. How does that experience help you understand Willy's feelings? *Accept all thoughtful responses.*

Interpret What is it that Willy thinks Howard does not understand? Explain. ***Possible answer:*** *Willy thinks that Howard does not understand the essence of being a traveling salesman or how the profession has changed over the years. In Willy's view, being a salesman means having close personal relationships with buyers. However, the personal touch seems to have lost its importance. As Willy says, "Today, it's all cut and dried, and there's no chance for bringing friendship to bear—or personality."*

Synthesize Willy tells Howard, "You can't eat the orange and throw the peel away—a man is not a piece of fruit!" What does Willy mean? How does his statement function as a "dissection of the American dream"? ***Possible answer:*** *Willy means that it's not moral to use up a man's best efforts and then toss him aside when these are spent. His statement criticizes the company's behavior toward an employee of 34 years, suggesting that it is immoral to coldly discard a person who has contributed so much. Willy's words dissect the American dream by suggesting that those who follow it will be used up by it and tossed to the side by the next generation of seekers.*

COMMON CORE FOCUS

RL 1 Cite evidence to support analysis of inferences drawn from the text. **RL 2** Determine two or more themes or central ideas of a text, and analyze their development over the course of the text. **W 10** Write routinely over shorter time frames.

BACKGROUND The youngest of four children, Lorraine Hansberry was the daughter of a former school teacher and a successful realtor. Both parents fought actively against segregation laws and sent Lorraine to public schools, rather than private, in protest. Her father's role in a key antisegregation case heard by the Illinois Supreme Court helped to inspire the events in *A Raisin in the Sun*. The play's success enhanced Hansberry's role as an impassioned activist for equal rights for African Americans.

TEXT ANALYSIS Point out that *A Raisin in the Sun* was the first play by an African-American woman to be produced on Broadway, and its director was the first African American in more than 50 years to direct a Broadway play. Explain that Hansberry was praised for her warm and funny style as well as her insightful portrayal of working-class people facing prejudice and economic hardship. Also note that a 1961 movie version of the play (starring many of the same actors) won a special award at the Cannes Film Festival. The critical and popular success of *A Raisin in the Sun* inspired and influenced many other African-American playwrights. It also inspired the play's 2004 Broadway revival, starring Phylicia Rashad as Lena Younger and Audra McDonald as Ruth Younger. Both women received awards for their portrayals.

WRITE Have students practice reading this scene aloud before they write. Encourage them to note how the emotional tone of the dialogue strengthens the theme expressed by each character.

from **A Raisin in the Sun**

Drama by Lorraine Hansberry

Lorraine Hansberry

◠◠◠ COMMON CORE

RL 1 Cite evidence to support analysis of inferences drawn from the text. **RL 2** Determine two or more themes or central ideas of a text, and analyze their development over the course of the text. **W 10** Write routinely over shorter time frames.

BACKGROUND "What happens to a dream deferred? / Does it dry up / like a raisin in the sun?" These lines from Langston Hughes's poem "Harlem" provided Lorraine Hansberry (1930–1965) with her title for *A Raisin in the Sun*, the story of the Youngers, an African-American family whose long-cherished dreams are almost realized when Mama, the family's matriarch, comes into some money. But Mama's plans to buy a house in a white neighborhood nearly destroy the family. Hansberry had difficulty finding backers to fund her play. With its all-black cast and racial themes, *A Raisin in the Sun* was very daring for its time. But once it finally opened, it received the New York Drama Critics' Circle Award for the best American play of 1959. Hansberry was the youngest person and the first African American to win the award.

The New York Times called *A Raisin in the Sun* the play that "changed American theater forever." It inspired a generation of young black writers and actors and brought a whole new audience to the theater. A glimpse into the private lives of African Americans was also a revelation for Broadway's white audiences. As Hansberry once observed, "The intimacy of knowledge which the Negro may culturally have of white Americans does not exist in the reverse."

TEXT ANALYSIS With the excerpt from *Death of a Salesman* (pages 1166–1167), you studied **dialogue** for conflicting views of the world. With the scene from *A Raisin in the Sun*, you will encounter a single character who voices one of Hansberry's **themes**. While writers of fiction can use the narrator to convey a message, playwrights rely exclusively on action and dialogue to express themes about humanity. Readers of drama—or members of a staged performance—will discover complex and fascinating ideas if they listen attentively and make subtle inferences about the characters, their actions, and their voices.

WRITE As you read this dialogue, in which a mother discusses her son with her daughter, look for conflicting ideas about love for and duty to family members. Which character has a stronger voice here, Mama or Beneatha? Write a paragraph on the dominant character and the theme she expresses.

1168

DIFFERENTIATED INSTRUCTION

FOR STRUGGLING READERS

Comprehension Support Use an Open Mind diagram to help students reflect on Mama's feelings as she talks with her daughter. Have students list thoughts that might be going through Mama's mind.

 BEST PRACTICES TOOLKIT—Transparency
Open Mind p. D9

You shouldn't give up on people—especially not on your own family.

Look for the good in people.

To understand a person, you have to try to see the world through that person's eyes.

Beneatha. That is not a man. That is nothing but a toothless rat.

Mama. Yes—death done come in this here house. (*She is nodding, slowly, reflectively.*) Done come walking in my house on the lips of my children. You what supposed to be my beginning again. You—what supposed to be my harvest. (*to* Beneatha) You—you mourning your brother?

Beneatha. He's no brother of mine.

Mama. What you say?

Beneatha. I said that that individual in that room is no brother of mine.

Mama. That's what I thought you said. You feeling like you better than he is today?
10 (Beneatha *does not answer.*) Yes? What you tell him a minute ago? That he wasn't a man? Yes? You give him up for me? You done wrote his epitaph too—like the rest of the world? Well, who give you the privilege?

Beneatha. Be on my side for once! You saw what he just did, Mama! You saw him—down on his knees. Wasn't it you who taught me to despise any man who would do that? Do what he's going to do?

Mama. Yes—I taught you that. Me and your daddy. But I thought I taught you something else too . . . I thought I taught you to love him.

Beneatha. Love him? There is nothing left to love.

Mama. There is *always* something left to love. And if you ain't learned that, you ain't
20 learned nothing. (*looking at her*) Have you cried for that boy today? I don't mean for yourself and for the family 'cause we lost the money. I mean for him: what he been through and what it done to him. Child, when do you think is the time to love somebody the most? When they done good and made things easy for everybody? Well then, you ain't through learning—because that ain't the time at all. It's when he's at his lowest and can't believe in hisself 'cause the world done whipped him so! When you starts measuring somebody, measure him right, child, measure him right. Make sure you done taken into account what hills and valleys he come through before he got to wherever he is.

A Raisin in the Sun Before students read the excerpt, explain that it reflects the casual conversational English that is consistent with the particular characters and setting. Ask students how this use of language adds to the tone and emotional impact of the scene. Discuss whether the dialogue would be as effective if written in standard English.

TIERED DISCUSSION PROMPTS

Use these prompts to help students understand the themes in this excerpt:

Restate What is Mama's advice to Beneatha? *Possible answer: Mama tells Beneatha to love and forgive her brother, not to judge him.*

Interpret What does Mama mean when she tells Beneatha: "When you starts measuring somebody, measure him right . . ."? *Possible answer: Mama means that it's not fair to judge someone without taking into account what the person may have experienced. In other words, a person's actions should be considered within the context of his or her life experiences.*

Synthesize What dream, discussed in **BACKGROUND,** has Walter's behavior destroyed? How did Hansberry's own life experiences prepare her to write about this dream? *Possible answer: Because of Walter's behavior, the Youngers lose their dream of owning a home along with Mama's hope to do so in a white neighborhood. Hansberry's experience of moving with her family into an all-white neighborhood likely gave her insight into the power of such a dream.*

FOR STRUGGLING READERS

Comprehension Support Call attention to Hansberry's use of questions in the dialogue between Mama and Beneatha, especially in Mama's last paragraph. Discuss how these questions add impact and drama to the interaction between mother and daughter. Point out that rhetorical questions, such as the ones that Mama asks, are intended for effect, not with the expectation of a reply.

FOR ENGLISH LANGUAGE LEARNERS

Language: Conversational English Patterns Work with students to paraphrase the dialect and speech patterns in the excerpt. Help them translate idioms such as "toothless rat" (line 1) and rephrase dialect such as "done come in this here house" (line 2). Have student pairs read the excerpt aloud as the group works to restate the meaning of each line.

Focus and Motivate

COMMON CORE FOCUS

RL 4 Analyze the impact of specific word choices on meaning and tone. **RI 2** Determine two or more central ideas of a text and analyze their development over the course of a text. **RI 4** Determine the meaning of words and phrases as they are used in a text. **RI 5** Analyze and evaluate the effectiveness of the structure an author uses, including whether the structure makes points clear, convincing, and engaging. **W 1** Write arguments to support claims in an analysis of substantive topics or texts, using valid reasoning and relevant and sufficient evidence. **W 8** Gather relevant information from multiple authoritative print and digital sources, using advanced searches effectively; integrate information into the text selectively to maintain the flow of ideas. **L 3** Apply knowledge of language to understand how language functions to make effective choices for meaning or style, and to comprehend more fully when reading.

ABOUT THE AUTHORS

John Steinbeck Ask students if they find it surprising that an author acclaimed for fiction also could be praised for realistic writings.

Randall Jarrell Discuss how Jarrell's experience in the military might affect a young poet.

Selection Resources

Responses to War

COMMON CORE

RL 4 Analyze the impact of specific word choices on meaning and tone. **RI 2** Determine two or more central ideas of a text and analyze their development over the course of a text. **RI 4** Determine the meaning of words and phrases as they are used in a text.

Why Soldiers Won't Talk
Essay by John Steinbeck

The Death of the Ball Turret Gunner
Poem by Randall Jarrell

VIDEO TRAILER **THINK** central   KEYWORD: HML11-1170A

Meet the Authors

John Steinbeck
1902–1968

John Steinbeck created many memorable characters, from the downtrodden but dogged Joads in *The Grapes of Wrath* to George and Lennie in *Of Mice and Men*. Many of Steinbeck's characters convey his belief that people must fit into their surroundings—especially their natural surroundings—in order to find peace.

Childhood on the Land John Steinbeck grew up in the agricultural community of Salinas, California. The land profoundly influenced Steinbeck, who set many of his best works in these childhood scenes. He began to write early, encouraged by a high school teacher's praise.

Blending Life and Art While studying at Stanford University, Steinbeck worked in a factory and on road crews. Portraying people who lived by their hands became another key focus of Steinbeck's life and work. *The Grapes of Wrath* (1939) received a Pulitzer Prize for portraying down-and-out Oklahoma farmers during the Great Depression. Exhausted from writing the novel, Steinbeck moved in new directions. In 1943 he spent six months as a World War II correspondent, producing such writings as the following essay about the response of soldiers to combat. In 1962, he received the Nobel Prize in Literature "for his realistic as well as his imaginative writings."

Randall Jarrell
1914–1965

Respected as a literary critic, Randall Jarrell is nonetheless best known for his searing poetry about World War II, notably a "stark five-line lyric . . . the ultimate poem of war." That poem is "The Death of the Ball Turret Gunner."

On the Road Again Born in Nashville, Tennessee, Jarrell moved often during his childhood. One important move took the family to a ranch in California. Later, Jarrell returned to California to live with his grandparents during his parents' divorce. Memories of this time filtered

into one of Jarrell's best poems, "The Lost World," and childhood is a frequent, haunting topic throughout his work.

Making a Name With the help of a wealthy uncle, Jarrell went to college and began a lifelong career teaching literature in universities. At the same time, he worked at his own poetry. In 1942, he enlisted in the service, where he trained pilots and wrote poems capturing the horror and dreariness of military life.

Authors Online **THINK** central
Go to **thinkcentral.com**.
KEYWORD: HML11-1170B

1170

See resources on the **Teacher One Stop DVD-ROM** and on **thinkcentral.com**.

 RESOURCE MANAGER UNIT 6
Plan and Teach, pp. 9–16
Summary, pp. 17–18†‡*
Text Analysis and Reading
   Skill, pp. 19–22†*
Grammar and Style, p. 25

**DIAGNOSTIC AND SELECTION
TESTS**
Selection Tests, pp. 309–312

 BEST PRACTICES TOOLKIT
Definition Mapping, p. E6
Sensory Notes, p. B9
Outline, p. B19
Cluster Diagram, p. B18

TECHNOLOGY
🖭 **Teacher One Stop DVD-ROM**
🖭 **Student One Stop DVD-ROM**
🖭 **Audio Anthology CD**
🖭 **GrammarNotes DVD-ROM**
🖭 **ExamView Test Generator**
   on the Teacher One Stop

THINK central
Video Trailer
Go to **thinkcentral.com** to preview the **Video Trailer** introducing this selection. Other features that support the selection include interactive writing and grammar instruction.

---

* Resources for Differentiation   **† Also in Spanish**   **‡ In Haitian Creole and Vietnamese**

TEXT ANALYSIS: TONE AND IMAGERY

A writer sometimes conveys **tone,** his or her attitude toward a subject, through imagery. **Imagery** consists of the descriptive words and phrases used to re-create sensory experiences. One of the interesting aspects of John Steinbeck's essay is the contrast between his clinical, detached, almost scientific tone and his use of sensory-rich imagery to support his conclusions on war. Jarrell's poem also uses vivid imagery to convey an attitude about that same subject. As you read each text, think about the relationship between tone and imagery. Decide what each of these elements adds to the experience of reading.

READING STRATEGY: ADJUST READING STRATEGIES

As you read "Why Soldiers Won't Talk," you need to apply reading strategies appropriate to an essay. First, identify the author's **main ideas.** Then, examine the pattern of reasoning the author uses to express these ideas.

In this essay, look for **deductive reasoning.** Deductive reasoning is arriving at a conclusion by applying a general principle to a specific situation. An example of a general principle is that people want to help themselves. Given a specific situation in which individuals face a choice between working for an income and relying on someone else for support, deductive reasoning would lead you to conclude that these individuals would choose work.

A poem such as "The Death of the Ball Turret Gunner" requires dramatically different reading strategies from those used when reading essays. The poem you will read is short and full of **images;** however, it does not explain itself. Use the illustration on page 1175 to help you picture the ball turret of a warplane. Then, read the poem several times—aloud, if possible. Picture the images and pay attention to language that expresses tone.

As you read these two texts, make use of these strategies and any others that work for you. Take notes about the essay's main ideas and its pattern of reasoning. Then, note the poem's imagery and tone.

 Complete the activities in your **Reader/Writer Notebook.**

When is SILENCE louder than words?

People who have suffered greatly—fighting in a war, losing a loved one, witnessing tragedy—sometimes find it hard to communicate with others. Perhaps they cannot put their experiences and emotions into words. Perhaps they believe no one will understand. Others find silence and watchfulness more comfortable than talk and social engagement. Consider what silence can signify in a person's behavior, especially a soldier's in wartime.

QUICKWRITE Think of friends, family, peers, or even a character in a film or book. Identify someone you think of as more silent than talkative. Write a brief character description of this person. Read your description aloud, then share your ideas about why your subject is silent.

1171

Teach

When is SILENCE louder than words?

Ask students to read the paragraph. Have them reflect on the various reasons why a person might retreat into silence. Then, have them complete the *QUICKWRITE*. Poll students for common reasons people are silent.

TEXT ANALYSIS COMMON CORE RL 4 RI 4

● Model the Skill: TONE AND IMAGERY

To demonstrate how imagery creates tone, write this passage on the board:

> The sun cut through the wispy clouds like a laser, searing the ground. The exhausted soldiers dragged themselves on, muscles aching, throats parched, every man knowing that two days of torturous travel remained, but only one day of water.

Point out that imagery in the passage conveys the sense of bone-weary men "dragging" themselves on, despite overwhelming obstacles. The writer's tone suggests admiration for the men's courage.

GUIDED PRACTICE Elicit other examples of imagery that convey a writer's tone.

READING STRATEGY COMMON CORE RI 2

■ Model the Skill: ADJUST READING STRATEGIES

To determine the author's main ideas, have students reread the passage from the board, looking for main ideas that are stated or implied. Point out that the stated main idea is that a group of exhausted soldiers is struggling against great obstacles to get somewhere, despite intense heat. The implied main ideas are that the soldiers are courageous and that they will probably not survive their journey.

R RESOURCE MANAGER—Copy Master Adjust Reading Strategies p. 21 (for student use while reading the selections)

DIFFERENTIATED INSTRUCTION

FOR STRUGGLING READERS
Vocabulary Support

- *sensory,* "relating to the senses of sight, hearing, smell, taste, and touch"
- *genre,* "a particular category or kind of literary or artistic work"
- *main idea,* "the most important idea about a topic that a particular text conveys"
- *speaker,* "the voice that a poet creates to speak in a poem; not the poet"
- *image,* "a mental picture or visual idea"

Concept Support: Adjust Reading Strategies
Remind students that they are not limited to the strategies listed here. They should always choose the particular strategies that will be most helpful for the text they are reading. For example, when reading a nonfiction article, they might begin by skimming and scanning the text. When reading poetry, they might find their visualizing skills more helpful in creating a mental picture from text details.

SUMMARY

In this essay, John Steinbeck suggests that ex-soldiers are unwilling to talk about their combat experiences because in fact they do not remember them very well. While under constant fire, soldiers experience a range of sensory and emotional effects that distort their perceptions and alter their behavior. When the battle ends, details of the experience become dreamlike, and the soldiers' memory of combat fades rapidly.

READ WITH A PURPOSE

Help students set a purpose for reading. Have them read the following selection to find out why ex-soldiers are reluctant to talk about their combat experiences.

REVISIT THE BIG QUESTION

When is SILENCE *louder than words?*

Discuss In lines 1–11, does Steinbeck's explanation for the silence of ex-soldiers seem reasonable? Why, or why not? Is the alternative explanation reasonable? Explain. *Possible answers: Yes; a soldier's mind may repress terrible memories. No; it would be impossible to forget such experiences. The first explanation Steinbeck gives—that soldiers simply do not want to relive their experiences by talking about them—is also reasonable.*

READING STRATEGY

COMMON CORE · RI 2

Ⓐ *Model the Skill:* ADJUST READING STRATEGIES

Tell students to look for facts and imagery that tell why Steinbeck is puzzled.

Possible answer: Steinbeck is puzzled by his observation that ex-soldiers do not discuss their battle experiences. The main idea he provides to solve that mystery is that soldiers cannot remember experiences that take place during battle.

Why Soldiers Won't Talk

John Steinbeck

BACKGROUND Randall Jarrell's experience training pilots for the U.S. Army Air Force gained him firsthand knowledge of planes and gunners, including the view from the ball turret of a bomber. From this plexiglas bubble on the underside of the plane, gunners—totally exposed from below—fired at the enemy. During Steinbeck's time as a war correspondent, he too learned about bomber crews, as well as soldiers in the infantry.

During the years between the last war and this one, I was always puzzled by the reticence of ex-soldiers about their experiences in battle. If they had been reticent men it would have been different, but some of them were talkers and some were even boasters. They would discuss their experiences right up to the time of battle and then suddenly they wouldn't talk any more. This was considered heroic in them. It was thought that what they had seen or done was so horrible that they didn't want to bring it back to haunt them or their listeners. But many of these men had no such consideration in any other field.

10 Only recently have I found what seems to be a reasonable explanation, and the answer is simple. They did not and do not remember—and the worse the battle was, the less they remember. Ⓐ

① Targeted Passage

In all kinds of combat the whole body is battered by emotion. The ductless glands[1] pour their fluids into the system to make it able to stand up to the great demand on it. Fear and ferocity are products of the same fluid. Fatigue toxins[2] poison the system. Hunger followed by wolfed food distorts the metabolic pattern already distorted by the adrenaline[3] and fatigue. The body and the mind so disturbed are really ill and fevered. But in addition to these ills, which come from the inside of a man and are given him so that he can temporarily withstand pressures beyond his ordinary ability, there is the further stress of explosion.

20 Under extended bombardment or bombing the nerve ends are literally beaten. The eardrums are tortured by blast and the eyes ache from the constant hammering.

This is how you feel after a few days of constant firing. Your skin feels thick and insensitive. There is a salty taste in your mouth. A hard, painful knot is in your stomach where the food is undigested. Your eyes do not pick up much detail and the sharp outlines of objects are slightly blurred. Everything looks a little unreal. When

Ⓐ ADJUST READING STRATEGIES
Reread lines 1–11. What puzzles Steinbeck about soldiers, and what **main idea** provides the solution to his puzzlement? Write down the main idea and label it as the **conclusion** to a pattern of deductive reasoning you will examine on the essay's second page.

Analyze Visuals ▶
How would you describe the look on this soldier's face? Explain what features convey this look.

---

1. **ductless glands:** glands, such as the thyroid or the pituitary gland, that secrete directly into the bloodstream.
2. **toxins:** poisons produced by the body that are capable of causing disease.
3. **adrenaline** (ə-drĕn′ə-lĭn): a substance secreted by the adrenal gland in response to stress.

DIFFERENTIATED INSTRUCTION

FOR ENGLISH LANGUAGE LEARNERS

Vocabulary Support Use Definition Mapping to teach this word: *stress* (line 19).

 BEST PRACTICES TOOLKIT—Transparency Definition Mapping p. E6

FOR STRUGGLING READERS

In combination with the *Audio Anthology CD*, use one or both Targeted Passages (pp. 1172 and 1174) to ensure that students focus on key concepts in the essay. Targeted Passages are also good for English language learners.

① Targeted Passage [Lines 1–11]

This passage introduces the main theme of the essay.

Analyze Visuals

Possible answer: *The soldier looks grim and exhausted. This look is conveyed by the soldier's unsmiling expression, partly open mouth, and dull, lifeless eyes.*

TIERED DISCUSSION PROMPTS

In lines 12–21, use these prompts to help students trace Steinbeck's point that people respond physically to moments of great stress:

Connect Have you ever felt a physical response to an emotional situation? In what ways does that experience help you understand Steinbeck's description of combat? *Accept all thoughtful responses.*

Analyze How does Steinbeck use verbs to reinforce the ideas he presents? Give examples. *Possible answer:* *Steinbeck chooses strong verbs to convey the feeling of the body being assaulted in various ways. For example, he talks about food that is "wolfed" (line 15), "beaten" nerve ends (line 20), eardrums "tortured by blast" (line 21), and eyes that "ache from the constant hammering" (line 21).*

Synthesize In what ways does Steinbeck's description of combat's effects on the human body expand the reader's understanding of the selection? *Possible answer:* *Steinbeck's detailed description helps readers physically experience the vivid ways in which combat affects the senses and damages the body.*

- What does Steinbeck observe about ex-soldiers? (lines 1–2)

- Why does this observation surprise him? (lines 2–5)

- What is the "reasonable explanation" that Steinbeck has found? (lines 9–11)

FOR ADVANCED LEARNERS/AP

Hypothesize Have students speculate as a class about what soldiers experience in combat. Tell students to suppose that they themselves have served in combat. Instruct them to write a poem based on their wartime experiences. Have students read their poems to the class.

you walk, your feet hardly seem to touch the ground and there is a floaty feeling all over your body. Even the time sense seems to be changed. Men who are really moving at a normal pace seem to take forever to pass a given point. And when you move it seems to you that you are very much slowed down, although actually you 30 are probably moving more quickly than you normally do. **B**

Under the blast your eyeballs are so beaten that the earth and the air seem to shudder. At first your ears hurt, but then they become dull and all your other senses become dull, too. There are exceptions, of course. Some men cannot protect themselves this way and they break, and they are probably the ones we call shell-shock cases.[4]

In the dullness all kinds of emphases change. Even the instinct for self-preservation is dulled so that a man may do things which are called heroic when actually his whole fabric of reaction is changed. The whole world becomes unreal. You laugh at things which are not ordinarily funny and you become enraged at trifles. During this time 40 a kind man is capable of great cruelties and a timid man of great bravery, and nearly all men have resistance to stresses beyond their ordinary ability.

Then sleep can come without warning and like a drug. Gradually your whole body seems to be packed in cotton. All the main nerve trunks are deadened, and out of the battered cortex[5] curious dreamlike thoughts emerge. It is at this time that many men see visions. The eyes fasten on a cloud and the tired brain makes a face of it, or an angel or a demon. And out of the hammered brain strange memories are jolted loose, scenes and words and people forgotten, but stored in the back of the brain. These may not be important things, but they come back with startling clarity into the awareness that is turning away from reality. And these memories are almost visions. **C**

50 And then it is over. You can't hear, but there is a rushing sound in your ears. And you want sleep more than anything, but when you do sleep you are dream-ridden, your mind is uneasy and crowded with figures. The anesthesia your body has given you to protect you is beginning to wear off, and, as with most anesthesia, it is a little painful.

And when you wake up and think back to the things that happened they are already becoming dreamlike. Then it is not unusual that you are frightened and ill. You try to remember what it was like, and you can't quite manage it. The outlines in your memory are vague. The next day the memory slips farther, until very little is left at all. A woman is said to feel the same way when she tries to remember what 60 childbirth was like. And fever leaves this same kind of vagueness on the mind. Perhaps all experience which is beyond bearing is that way. The system provides the shield and then removes the memory, so that a woman can have another child and a man can go into combat again. **D**

It slips away so fast. Unless you made notes on the spot you could not remember how you felt or the way things looked. Men in prolonged battle are not normal men. And when afterward they seem to be reticent—perhaps they don't remember very well.

---

4. **shell-shock cases:** soldiers with a psychological disturbance as a result of prolonged exposure to active warfare.

5. **cortex:** part of the brain that plays an active role in consciousness.

B *Model the Skill:* **TONE AND IMAGERY**

Work with students to complete a Sensory Notes organizer about lines 22–30, pointing out specific details that appeal to each sense.

Possible answer: *Steinbeck uses sensory details to describe skin (lines 22–23), stomach pain (lines 23–24), and vision (lines 24–25). The scene reveals that soldiers under constant fire experience various sensory distortions.*

 BEST PRACTICES TOOLKIT—Transparency Sensory Notes p. B9

C **GRAMMAR AND STYLE** — COMMON CORE L 3

Establish Voice Point out that word choice is a key component in a writer's distinct voice. Review that sensory verbs evoke sensory reactions while describing actions. Steinbeck uses many sensory adjectives and verbs in this essay because he wants the reader to imagine and feel what soldiers feel.

READING STRATEGY — COMMON CORE RI 2

D **ADJUST READING STRATEGIES**

Remind students that deductive reasoning works from the broader, or more general, to the specific, a "top-down" approach. Inductive reasoning works the opposite way, making a broad generalization or theory based on specific observations or events. It is a bottom-up approch. ***Possible answer:*** *The conclusion to his deductive reasoning is that a soldier waking after combat and a new mother awakening after childbirth would find that their experiences seem dreamlike and that the memory dims further with the passage of time.*

B **TONE AND IMAGERY** Reread lines 22–30, and note Steinbeck's use of **sensory detail.** What does this scene reveal about the soldier's mental state?

C **GRAMMAR AND STYLE** Reread lines 42–47. Notice how Steinbeck establishes his voice partly by using descriptions that contain realistic sensory **adjectives** and **verbs,** such as *battered, hammered,* and *jolted.*

D **ADJUST READING STRATEGIES** Reread lines 55–63. This paragraph suggests the **premise** in a pattern of **deductive reasoning.** The premise is that acute stress induces a shock that causes the person under stress to forget the painful details of the experience. From this premise, Steinbeck uses an **analogy,** or a comparison, to suggest that both childbirth and combat are acutely stressful. In your own words, explain the **conclusion** to this line of reasoning for combat soldiers and women who have given birth.

DIFFERENTIATED INSTRUCTION

FOR STRUGGLING READERS

② Targeted Passage [Lines 42–63]

This passage describes the body's mechanism for self-protection.

- According to Steinbeck, how does the body's "anesthesia" protect the soldier against the stresses of combat? (lines 42–54)

- What happens after this anesthesia wears off? (lines 52–59)

- How is the soldier's experience like that of a woman in childbirth? (lines 59–63)

FOR RELUCTANT READERS

Connect to the Text "Why Soldiers Won't Talk" describes the effect that combat has on a soldier's mind and body. Have students consider the stressful situations from their own past that may have distorted their perceptions, altered their behavior, and diminished their memory. Have students describe how those situations compare to that of a soldier in combat.

The Death of the Ball Turret Gunner

RANDALL JARRELL

From my mother's sleep I fell into the State,
And I hunched in its belly till my wet fur froze.
Six miles from earth, loosed from its dream of life,
I woke to black flak[1] and the nightmare fighters.
5 When I died they washed me out of the turret with a hose. **E**

E TONE AND IMAGERY
What does the imagery of the last line suggest about the speaker's attitude toward death?

---

1. **flak:** the fire of anti-aircraft guns.

WHY SOLDIERS WON'T TALK / THE DEATH OF THE BALL TURRET GUNNER **1175**

FOR STRUGGLING READERS

Develop Reading Fluency Read aloud "The Death of the Ball Turret Gunner" to the class. Tell students to note the meter and rhythm of the poem as you read. Organize the class into pairs. Have students practice reading the poem to each other in the same meter and rhythm that they heard during your reading.

FOR ADVANCED LEARNERS/AP

Analyze Meaning [small-group option] In just five lines, Randall Jarrell conveys volumes about war and what it means to be a soldier in combat. Challenge students to write a paragraph or two interpreting and analyzing Jarrell's ideas. Encourage students to be specific in summarizing the message they find in the poem. Have them share their ideas in small groups, and then discuss and compare the various interpretations presented.

Prereading for this poem is found on page 1170.

SUMMARY

With vivid imagery evoking a fetus in its mother's womb, this poem conveys the nightmarish perspective of a gunner killed in aerial combat.

TEXT ANALYSIS

E TONE AND IMAGERY RL 4

Possible answer: *The imagery, which is horrifying, is described in a clinical manner, suggesting an unemotional, almost matter-of-fact attitude toward death.*

Analyze Visuals

Activity Ask students how the photograph reflects images in the poem. *Possible answer: The photograph shows the tiny space in which the gunner "hunched" and how that space is round like a "belly."*

About the Art This photograph was taken by well-known photojournalist Margaret Bourke-White (1906–1971). *Life* magazine sent Bourke-White to cover World War II. This photo captures a personal view of war.

SELECTION WRAP-UP

READ WITH A PURPOSE Now that students have read the selection, ask them to explain why soldiers do not talk about their combat experiences. *Possible answer: The stress of combat may cause soldiers to forget much of their battle experience.*

★ CRITIQUE

- Have students identify the aspects of each selection that they found most meaningful, and explain why.

- After completing the After Reading questions on page 1176, have students revisit their responses and tell whether they have changed their opinions.

INDEPENDENT READING

Students may enjoy reading *Little Friend, Little Friend* and *Losses,* both by Randall Jarrell.

WHY SOLDIERS . . . / . . . GUNNER **1175**

Practice and Apply

For preliminary support of post-reading questions, use these copy masters:

R **RESOURCE MANAGER—Copy Masters**
Reading Check p. 23
Tone and Imagery p. 19
Question Support p. 24

Additional selection questions are provided for teachers on page 13.

ANSWERS

COMMON CORE RL 4, RI 2, RI 4, RI 5

1. *Soldiers do not talk about combat because they do not remember it.*

2. *Soldiers experience a mixture of fear, adrenaline flow, and fatigue. Both body and mind are "ill and fevered" (lines 16–17). The skin feels "thick and insensitive" (lines 22–23). Objects appear slightly blurred. The senses deaden.*

3. *The speaker is killed during aerial combat.*

Possible answers:

4. *Steinbeck uses second person in order to place the reader in the soldier's shoes. This device makes the combat experience more vivid and immediate for readers.*

5. *Similar to a fetus awaiting birth, the gunner is crammed into a small space. Like a newborn violently thrust into the world, he is abruptly awakened to his surroundings.*

6. ● **COMMON CORE FOCUS** **Tone and Imagery**
Notable poem images: "hunched in its belly till my wet fur froze" (line 2), "the nightmare fighters" (line 4), "they washed me out of the turret with a hose" (line 5).
Notable essay images: "eyeballs . . . so beaten that the earth and the air seem to shudder" (lines 31–32), "your whole body seems to be packed in cotton" (lines 42–43). Jarrell's attitude is one of bitterness regarding the gunner's expendability. Steinbeck's tone suggests sympathetic understanding of the horrors that soldiers must endure.*

7. *Both authors convey the horror of war through grim detail, but Jarrell's horrifying last line suggests a more negative and less understanding viewpoint than Steinbeck's.*

8. ● **COMMON CORE FOCUS** **Evaluating Strategies** *Answers will vary but should compare and contrast specific strategies.*

9. *Some students may agree with the interpretation, noting that it captures the poem's message about the destructiveness*

1176 UNIT 6: CONTEMPORARY LITERATURE

Comprehension

1. **Recall** According to Steinbeck, why don't soldiers talk about combat?

2. **Summarize** What physical changes does Steinbeck say happen during combat?

3. **Summarize** In Jarrell's poem, what happens to the speaker?

Text Analysis

4. **Examine Author's Purpose** Steinbeck uses the second-person *you* in his recounting of the physical effects of combat. Why do you think he chose this **stylistic device?**

5. **Interpret the Poem** In reference to his poem, Jarrell wrote that the gunner, who sat hunched up and revolved with the turret, looked like a fetus in the womb. Based on this information, how would you interpret the first four lines of the poem?

● 6. **Analyze Tone and Imagery** Skim the two texts, and make a list of notable images found in each work. Based on these images, what would you say is Jarrell's attitude toward the ball turret gunner and his predicament? What is Steinbeck's attitude toward combat and its effect on soldiers? Describe the overall tone of each work.

7. **Compare Texts** Jarrell and Steinbeck address the topic of war from different angles and through different genres. Do you think the two authors offer consistent or conflicting accounts of what combat feels like? Support your opinion with details from each text.

● 8. **Evaluate Reading Strategies** Look back at the notes you took as you read the essay and poem. For each work, which strategy was most useful in helping you understand the ideas and images presented? What helped you understand how Steinbeck structured both his claims and his evidence? What strategy helped you make sense of Jarrell's use of imagery or his tone? How did these strategies differ? How were they similar?

Text Criticism

9. **Critical Interpretations** In discussing "The Death of the Ball Turret Gunner," one critic stated, "In the combination of death and consciousness is the awakening and final recognition on the part of the gunner that he exists only to be a victim." Do you agree with this interpretation? Explain.

> *When is* **SILENCE** *louder than words?*
>
> Explain how this question applies to the silence of combat soldiers in "Why Soldiers Won't Talk." Cite evidence from the essay to support your answer.

1176 UNIT 6: CONTEMPORARY LITERATURE

COMMON CORE

RL 4 Analyze the impact of specific word choices on meaning and tone. **RI 2** Determine two or more central ideas of a text and analyze their development over the course of a text. **RI 4** Determine the meaning of words and phrases as they are used in a text. **RI 5** Analyze and evaluate the effectiveness of the structure an author uses, including whether the structure makes points clear, convincing, and engaging.

---

of war; other students may disagree with the interpretation, because the gunner must see himself as serving a purpose in combat beyond simply being a victim.

> *When is* SILENCE *louder than words?* **Possible answer:** *The question applies because the effects of combat affect some soldiers' senses and emotions to the point that they cannot remember their battle experiences, and thus can't talk about them.*

Language

COMMON CORE

L 3 Apply knowledge of language to understand how language functions to make effective choices for meaning or style, and to comprehend more fully when reading. **W 1** Write arguments to support claims in an analysis of substantive topics or texts, using valid reasoning and relevant and sufficient evidence. **W 8** Gather relevant information from multiple authoritative print and digital sources, using advanced searches effectively; integrate information into the text selectively to maintain the flow of ideas.

◆ **GRAMMAR AND STYLE: Establish Voice**

Review the **Grammar and Style** note on page 1174. Voice is the unique way a writer uses **word choice, sentence structure,** and **tone** to express his or her personality or vision. Steinbeck's voice reflects his personal experience with war. It flows from his short sentences, straightforward tone, and sensory language.

> *The eardrums are tortured by blast and the eyes ache from the constant hammering.* (line 21)

> *This is how you feel after a few days of constant firing. Your skin feels thick and insensitive. There is a salty taste in your mouth. A hard, painful knot is in your stomach where the food is undigested.* (lines 22–24)

These examples include percussive-sounding words that reflect the pain of combat. The sentences imply that all information is essential and honest.

PRACTICE In the following sentences, revise the sentence structure and word choice to match Steinbeck's voice. Note how the revisions made to the example help to capture Steinbeck's voice.

> **EXAMPLE**
>
> Like a jackhammer pounding at solid concrete, the TV announcer gabs on and on, creating perpetual background noise that pollutes our homes. *The TV announcer talks on, creating a persistent, polluting noise.*

1. The announcer chooses a topic, pushing it and pushing it as if it were bread dough, then kneading it into yet a new shape.

2. Must we sit there like zombies and put up with this endless chatter as though there were no alternative?

READING-WRITING CONNECTION

 Expand your understanding of the effects of war by responding to this prompt. Then, use the **revising tips** to improve your essay.

WRITING PROMPT	REVISING TIPS
PERSUASIVE ESSAY Think about the adjustments veterans must make when they return from combat. What does society do to help ease their transition back into civilian life? Write a **three- to five-paragraph essay** on the importance of supporting veterans during this time of transition. Include specific suggestions of ways this might be effectively achieved.	• Contact a local veterans organization, and ask what can be done for veterans. • Use the Internet to research for innovative treatment and support programs for veterans. • Integrate information you find to help strengthen your essay.

Interactive Revision THINK central

Go to **thinkcentral.com**
KEYWORD: HML11-1177

DIFFERENTIATED INSTRUCTION

FOR STRUGGLING WRITERS
Writing Support

- Help students identify likely research resources, such as Web sites for the Veterans' Administration and veterans' advocacy groups.

- Suggest that students begin with a strong thesis statement clearly expressing their views about society's need to help veterans.

- Urge students to use outlines to plan their essays.

- Have students support their opening statement with specific reasons and facts.

- Ask students to write at least two body paragraphs giving concrete suggestions for assistance to veterans. Have them explain why each suggestion will make a difference.

- Suggest that students read their drafts aloud to a small group and ask for feedback.

BEST PRACTICES TOOLKIT—Transparency
Outline p. B19

Language

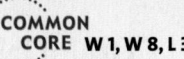

◆ **GRAMMAR AND STYLE**

Point out that the concepts of voice and tone are similar in many ways for writing and speaking. To illustrate this, suggest that students compare the tone of their oral response to a teacher's question with their response to the same question posed by a peer. How might their choice of language differ? How might they vary the length and structure of their sentences?

Possible answers:

1. *The announcer picks a topic. Then he jabs and jabs at it as if he were kneading dough, pounding it into a new shape.*

2. *We don't have to sit and listen like lifeless zombies. We don't have to put up with this machine-gun fire chatter. We have a choice.*

R RESOURCE MANAGER—Copy Master
Establish Voice p. 25

READING-WRITING CONNECTION

Suggest that student pairs use a Cluster Diagram to help them brainstorm effective ways that society can ease veterans' return to civilian life. Urge students to consider occupational, educational, financial, and other forms of assistance. To help students get started, have them conduct brief research into current practices for helping veterans.

BEST PRACTICES TOOLKIT—Transparency
Cluster Diagram, p. B18

Assess and Reteach

Assess

DIAGNOSTIC AND SELECTION TESTS
Selection Test A, B/C pp. 309–310, 311–312

Interactive Selection Test on thinkcentral.com

Reteach

Level Up Online Tutorials on thinkcentral.com

Reteaching Worksheets on thinkcentral.com

Literature Lessons 26, 40, 43
Reading Lesson 4

Focus and Motivate

COMMON CORE FOCUS

RL 3 Analyze the impact of the author's choices regarding how to develop and relate elements of a story. **RL 4** Analyze the impact of specific word choices on meaning and tone. **RI 2** Determine two or more central ideas of a text and analyze their development over the course of a text. **RI 3** Analyze a complex set of ideas or sequence of events and explain how specific individuals, ideas, or events interact and develop over the course of the text. **RI 6** Determine an author's point of view or purpose in a text in which the rhetoric is particularly effective, analyzing how style and content contribute to the power of the text. **RI 7** Integrate and evaluate multiple sources of information presented in multiple media or formats as well as words in order to address a question or solve a problem.

ABOUT THE AUTHORS

Kurt Vonnegut, Jr. Ask students how Vonnegut's experiences as a soldier may have influenced his work. *Students should recognize that a traumatic experience, such as being held prisoner of war, would dramatically affect Vonnegut and thus his work.*

Primo Levi Ask students how Levi's science career might have influenced how he wrote about his experiences in Auschwitz. *Students might note that Levi's scientific background might have allowed him to set aside emotions and write as a witness to the Nazi atrocities.*

Comparing Texts

Responses to War

Essential Course of Study ECOS

Adam
Short Story by Kurt Vonnegut, Jr.

from Survival in Auschwitz
Memoir by Primo Levi

Auschwitz-Birkenau Concentration Camp
Photograph

COMMON CORE

RL 3 Analyze the impact of the author's choices regarding how to develop and relate elements of a story. **RL 4** Analyze the impact of specific word choices on meaning and tone. **RI 3** Analyze a complex set of ideas or sequence of events and explain how specific individuals, ideas, or events interact and develop over the course of the text. **RI 6** Determine an author's point of view or purpose in a text in which the rhetoric is particularly effective, analyzing how style and content contribute to the power of the text. **RI 7** Integrate and evaluate multiple sources of information presented in multiple media or formats as well as words in order to address a question or solve a problem.

Meet the Authors

Kurt Vonnegut, Jr. 1922–2007

Kurt Vonnegut, Jr., blended black humor, science fiction, and fantasy to create a unique body of work. From the cult classic of *Cat's Cradle* to the international success of *Slaughterhouse-Five* to the semi-autobiographical *Timequake* that capped his career as a novelist, Vonnegut pushed at the boundaries of fiction, helping to redefine and revitalize the novel.

Art from Life As an infantry combat scout serving in Germany during World War II, Vonnegut was captured and held as a prisoner of war in Dresden. He survived the 1945 Allied bombing of the city because the American prisoners took shelter in a meat locker three stories below the ground. Protected from the firestorm that destroyed much of the city, the prisoners emerged to discover that thousands had been killed. Years later, Vonnegut transformed this experience into the fictional world of *Slaughterhouse-Five*.

A Study in Contrasts Despite the somewhat pessimistic outlook of works in which human beings are victims of circumstance in an indifferent universe, Vonnegut's fiction is preoccupied with moral issues.

Primo Levi 1919–1987

Known internationally as a writer of Holocaust literature, Primo Levi was born in Turin, Italy, and educated as a chemist. A survivor of Auschwitz, the notorious Nazi concentration camp near Krakow, Poland, he achieved international recognition for writings that recorded his experience of the war years.

Survivor In the chaos that engulfed Italy as World War II progressed, Levi joined the Italian resistance movement. Captured by the Fascist militia, he was held for several months at an Italian internment camp for Jews. After the camp fell to German control, early in 1944, the Jewish inmates were sent to Auschwitz. Of the 650 Italian Jews who entered Auschwitz with him, Levi was one of only twenty still alive eleven months later, when the advancing Russian army liberated Auschwitz.

Witness Levi recorded his Holocaust experience in *Survival in Auschwitz*.

THINK central

Author Online
Go to **thinkcentral.com**. KEYWORD: HML11-1178

Selection Resources

See resources on the **Teacher One Stop DVD-ROM** and on **thinkcentral.com**.

 R RESOURCE MANAGER UNIT 6
    Plan and Teach, pp. 27–34
    Summary, pp. 35–36†‡*
    Text Analysis and Reading
      Skill, pp. 37–40†*

DIAGNOSTIC AND SELECTION TESTS
    Selection Tests, pp. 313–316

BEST PRACTICES TOOLKIT
    Timeline, p. B23
    Word Questioning, p. E9
    Jigsaw Reading, p. A1
    Comparison Matrix, p. A24

INTERACTIVE READER

ADAPTED INTERACTIVE READER

ELL ADAPTED INTERACTIVE READER

TECHNOLOGY
- **Teacher One Stop DVD-ROM**
- **Student One Stop DVD-ROM**
- **PowerNotes DVD-ROM**
- **ExamView Test Generator** on the **Teacher One Stop**

THINK central

Video Trailer
The **PowerNotes** presentation for this lesson includes a **Video Trailer** for one or more selections. Preview any presentations and video trailers at **thinkcentral.com**.

---

* Resources for Differentiation   † Also in Spanish   ‡ In Haitian Creole and Vietnamese

TEXT ANALYSIS: CHARACTERIZATION AND TONE

In fiction, writers bring characters to life by describing their physical appearance, by letting readers know what characters think and feel, by letting readers hear characters in dialogue, and sometimes by having the narrator comment on the characters. In a story such as "Adam," these methods of **characterization** also provide important clues to the tone of the story. **Tone** is the narrator's attitude toward his or her subject—sometimes even the narrator's attitude toward life. As you read "Adam," write notes about the four major methods of characterization. What tone—or attitude toward life—does Vonnegut convey through his characters?

Physical Appearance	Thoughts and Feelings	Dialogue	Narrator's Comments

By contrast with Vonnegut's story, the excerpt from Primo Levi's memoir *Survival in Auschwitz* doesn't spend much time on traditional characterization, but it does strongly convey the author's attitude toward his subject and toward life using diction and other stylistic techniques. As you read the excerpt, ask yourself how Levi's techniques account for the tone of the memoir.

READING SKILL: ANALYZE HISTORICAL CONTEXT

When you read a literary work with a particular historical setting, it is important to focus on the **historical context**—the conditions and events that shape the characters and their story. Vonnegut's short story, for example, is set in the aftermath of the Holocaust. During World War II, millions of people died from executions, beatings, disease, and malnutrition in Nazi concentration camps. As you read "Adam," use this information and the background information on page 1181, in addition to what you already know about World War II and the concentration camps, to help you understand the story's main character and the author's tone. Keep the same goal in mind as you read the excerpt by Levi. How does the episode he narrates affect your perception of Vonnegut's main character, Heinz Knechtmann?

 Complete the activities in your **Reader/Writer Notebook**.

How do you AFFIRM LIFE?

In the aftermath of tragedy or heartbreak, people are often counseled that "time heals all wounds." Some are able to bounce back, whether from grave illness, a traumatic car accident, or even the horrors of war and genocide. Others cannot find this resilience and instead struggle to carry on.

What's the Connection?

As you study the texts in this section, think about what you already know about the tragic experiences of European Jews during World War II. Vonnegut's story "Adam," presents characters who survived this horrible experience and found the strength and will to start again. After you read "Adam," you'll study Levi's memoir "from *Survival in Auschwitz*," and a visual representation that convey the realities faced by Holocaust victims as they struggled to survive.

1179

Teach

How do you AFFIRM LIFE?
Read the question aloud. Elicit or explain that resilience means "the ability to recover from or adjust to misfortune."

What's the Connection?
Ask students to share examples from history, literature, or personal knowledge of people who have found the strength to start over after surviving a traumatic experience. What characteristics do these people have in common?

TEXT ANALYSIS

COMMON CORE

RL 3
RL 4

 Model the Skill: **CHARACTERIZATION AND TONE**

Write this passage on the board:

> Samuel was a tall man, though his stooped shoulders and sullen expression made him appear much smaller, as if life's burdens had both reduced his size and darkened his outlook. He spoke little, and when someone wished him "good morning," he would only shrug, implying that there was nothing good about it.

Point out that the writer conveys a sense of Samuel's character by describing his appearance, feelings, and general demeanor.

GUIDED PRACTICE Elicit ideas for another character's response to Samuel.

R **RESOURCE MANAGER—Copy Master** Characterization p. 37 (for student use while reading the selection)

READING SKILL

COMMON CORE

RL 3

■ *Model the Skill:* **ANALYZE HISTORICAL CONTEXT**

Have students reread the passage on the board. Explore how different historical contexts would alter the nature of the passage. For example, ask students how their interpretation would change if they knew that Samuel had been freed from slavery after the Civil War or had been drafted for armed service during World War II.

DIFFERENTIATED INSTRUCTION

FOR STRUGGLING READERS
Vocabulary Support

- *motivations,* "reasons for behaving in a certain way; the desires or needs that cause a person to act"

- *Holocaust,* "the mass slaughter of more than six million Jews and millions of others by the Nazis during World War II"

- *malnutrition,* "poor nutrition as a result of insufficient intake of nutrients"

- *concentration camp,* "Nazi prison camp where large numbers of people were killed"

- *affirm,* "declare or adopt a positive attitude toward"

- *aftermath,* "the period of time following an event"

- *traumatic,* "causing severe emotional shock"

- *genocide,* "systematic killing of people from a national, ethnic, or other group"

READ WITH A PURPOSE

*Help students set a purpose for reading.
As they read "Adam" and the excerpt from
"Survival in Auschwitz," ask them to consider
whether they think the authors' views of human nature are positive or negative.*

SUMMARY

Heinz Knechtmann is in a hospital waiting
for his wife, Avchen, to give birth. Both are
German Holocaust survivors who have come
to America. Heinz was the only member of his
family not killed by the Nazis. When his son
is born, Heinz is ecstatic. However, he feels
isolated from people around him, because no
one exhibits much excitement regarding the
miracle of birth. His disappointment fades
when he joins Avchen at her bedside, and together they share their poignant appreciation
of the new life that has emerged despite their
horrible experience.

TEXT ANALYSIS   COMMON CORE

RL 3
RL 4

Ⓐ CHARACTERIZATION

*Possible answer: A person so described
might have a pleasing but rather shy
demeanor. He might be reluctant to make
or hold eye contact and might act deferentially toward others.*

REVISIT THE BIG QUESTION

How do you AFFIRM LIFE?

Discuss In lines 19–23, what does the fact that
Knechtmann survived such horrific childhood
experiences and continued on with his life
suggest about the resilience of his character?
Possible answer: *It suggests that Knechtmann
is fundamentally a strong person with the skills
needed to cope with life's grimmest challenges.*

Adam

Kurt Vonnegut Jr.

> **BACKGROUND** In the short story "Adam," set during the early 1950s, the main
> character, Heinz Knechtmann (knĕкнт'män), has survived the atrocities of the
> Holocaust and, like many Jewish survivors, has come to the United States seeking a
> better life. As the story begins, he and another expectant father, Mr. Sousa, are in the
> waiting room of a maternity hospital.

It was midnight in a Chicago lying-in hospital.

"Mr. Sousa," said the nurse, "your wife had a girl. You can see the baby in about twenty minutes."

"I know, I know, I know," said Mr. Sousa, a sullen gorilla, plainly impatient with having a tiresome and familiar routine explained to him. He snapped his fingers. "Girl! Seven, now. Seven girls I got now. A houseful of women. I can beat the stuffings out of ten men my own size. But, what do I get? Girls."

"Mr. Knechtmann," said the nurse to the other man in the room. She pronounced the name, as almost all Americans did, a colorless Netman. "I'm
10 sorry. Still no word on your wife. She is keeping us waiting, isn't she?" She grinned glassily and left.

Sousa turned on Knechtmann. "Some little son of a gun like you, Netman, you want a boy, bing! You got one. Want a football team, bing, bing, bing, eleven, you got it." He stomped out of the room.

The man he left behind, all alone now, was Heinz Knechtmann, a presser in a dry-cleaning plant, a small man with thin wrists and a bad spine that kept him slightly hunched, as though forever weary. His face was long and big-nosed and thin-lipped, but was so overcast with good-humored humility as to be beautiful. Ⓐ His eyes were large and brown, and deep-set and longlashed. He was only twenty-
20 two, but seemed and felt much older. He had died a little as each member of his family had been led away and killed by the Nazis, until only in him, at the age of ten, had life and the name of Knechtmann shared a soul. He and his wife, Avchen, had grown up behind barbed wire.

Analyze Visuals ▶
What ideas are suggested
by the images in the
collage on page 1181?
What is the cumulative
impact of these images
taken together? Explain.

Ⓐ **CHARACTERIZATION**
Reread lines 15–18. Here
Vonnegut combines
his physical description
of Heinz Knechtmann
with a reflection on his
personality. What might
it look like to see a person
"so overcast with good-humored humility as to
be beautiful"?

❶ **Targeted Passage**

Fatherhood (1990s). Ed Roskowski.
© Ed Roskowski/Corbis.

DIFFERENTIATED INSTRUCTION

FOR ENGLISH LANGUAGE LEARNERS

Culture: Clarify Explain these references:

- *lying-in hospital* (line 1), "maternity hospital"

- *had grown up behind barbed wire* (line 23), "the two were children together in a Nazi concentration camp"

FOR STRUGGLING READERS

Use the Targeted Passages (pp. 1180, 1184, and
1186) to ensure that students focus on key
story events and concepts. Targeted Passages
are also good for English language learners.

❶ **Targeted Passage** [Lines 15–23]

This passage introduces the main character
and provides key background information.

Reading Support

This selection on **thinkcentral.com** includes embedded **ThinkAloud** models—students "thinking aloud" about the story to model the kinds of questions a good reader would ask about a selection.

Analyze Visuals

Possible answer: The collage suggests a traditional male figure of about 50 or 60 years ago. He is a father as the title of the collage indicates and clad in typical business attire and smoking a pipe. The other images, such as the baby and the old-fashioned Venetian blinds, highlight the paternal and familial aspects of his life. The cumulative impact of the juxtaposed images is that of a businessman/new father who has added a whole new dimension to his life.

BACKGROUND

German Names The narrator says that the nurse pronounces Knechtmann's name "as almost all Americans did, a colorless Netman" (lines 8–9). The name *Knechtmann* would have a guttural pronunciation in its native German. However, English speakers unfamiliar with the true pronunciation would simplify the sound to "Netman." This idea appears again on page 1182, lines 45–50.

- Describe Heinz Knechtmann's physical appearance. (lines 16–20)
- What happened to the members of Heinz's family? (lines 20–21)
- How old was Heinz when this happened? (lines 19–20)
- Who is Avchen? (line 22)
- What terrible experience do Heinz and Avchen have in common? (lines 22–23)

FOR ADVANCED LEARNERS/AP

Read a Graphic Novel Have students locate and read Art Spiegelman's two-part Pulitzer Prize-winning graphic novel, *Maus*, which uses a cartoon format to tell the story of his parents' experience in a concentration camp. Have students prepare for the class a display of selections from *Maus*.

B Model the Skill: HISTORICAL CONTEXT

RL 3

To help students understand historical context, work with them to infer and approximate the sequence of events in Heinz's life. Plot the events on a timeline spanning 1930–1955:

- Heinz born in Germany: early 1930s
- Heinz, age 10, family in concentration camp: early 1940s
- Heinz in displaced-persons camp: after World War II/post-1945
- Heinz, age 22, living in America: early 1950s

Possible answer: Heinz and his family were German Jews who were imprisoned in Nazi concentration camps when Heinz was a child. The Nazis killed everyone in the family except Heinz. Before eventually coming to America, Heinz and his wife Avchen lived in a displaced-persons camp in Germany. Their first child died there. He is now—in the early 1950s—awaiting the birth of their second child.

 BEST PRACTICES TOOLKIT—Transparency
Timeline p. B23

TEXT ANALYSIS

COMMON CORE

C CHARACTERIZATION

RL 3
RL 4

Possible answer: Heinz's pride in the birth of his son is evident in his standing and bowing and in his "courtly and triumphant" smile. Heinz also expresses his feelings when he proudly proclaims the family name, sounding "like a foppish footman announcing the arrival of nobility" (line 48).

Extend the Discussion Why does Vonnegut choose the adjectives "courtly" and "triumphant" to characterize Heinz's smile?

He had been staring at the walls of the waiting room for twelve hours now, since noon, when his wife's labor pains had become regular, the surges of slow rollers coming in from the sea a mile apart, from far, far away. This would be his second child. The last time he had waited, he had waited on a straw tick in a displaced-persons camp in Germany. The child, Karl Knechtmann, named after Heinz's father, had died, and with it, once more, had died the name of one of the 30 finest cellists ever to have lived. **B**

When the numbness of weary wishing lifted momentarily during this second vigil, Heinz's mind was a medley of proud family names, gone, all gone, that could be brought to life again in this new being—if it lived. Peter Knechtmann, the surgeon; Kroll Knechtmann, the botanist; Friederich Knechtmann, the playwright. Dimly recalled uncles. Or if it was a girl, and if it lived, it would be Helga Knechtmann, Heinz's mother, and she would learn to play the harp as Heinz's mother had, and for all Heinz's ugliness, she would be beautiful. The Knechtmann men were all ugly, the Knechtmann women were all lovely as angels, though not all angels. It had always been so—for hundreds and hundreds of years.

40 "Mr. Netman," said the nurse, "it's a boy, and your wife is fine. She's resting now. You can see her in the morning. You can see the baby in twenty minutes."

Heinz looked up dumbly.

"It weighs five pounds nine ounces." She was gone again, with the same prim smile and officious, squeaking footsteps.

"Knechtmann," murmured Heinz, standing and bowing slightly to the wall. "The name is Knechtmann." He bowed again and gave a smile that was courtly and triumphant. He spoke the name with an exaggerated Old World pronunciation, like a foppish footman announcing the arrival of nobility, a guttural drum roll, unsoftened for American ears. "KhhhhhhhhhhhhhhNECHT! 50 mannnnnnnnnnnn." **C**

"Mr. Netman?" A very young doctor with a pink face and close cropped red hair stood in the waiting-room door. There were circles under his eyes, and he spoke through a yawn.

"Dr. Powers!" cried Heinz, clasping the man's right hand between both of his. "Thank God, thank God, thank God, and thank you."

"Um," said Dr. Powers, and he managed to smile wanly.

"There isn't anything wrong, is there?"

"Wrong?" said Powers. "No, no. Everything's fine. If I look down in the mouth, it's because I've been up for thirty-six hours straight." He closed his eyes, 60 and leaned against the doorframe. "No, no trouble with your wife," he said in a faraway voice. "She's made for having babies. Regular pop-up toaster. Like rolling off a log. Schnip-schnap."

"She is?" said Heinz incredulously.

Dr. Powers shook his head, bringing himself back to consciousness. "My mind—conked out completely. Sousa—I got your wife confused with Mrs. Sousa. They finished in a dead heat. Netman, you're Netman. Sorry. Your wife's the one with pelvis trouble."

1182 UNIT 6: CONTEMPORARY LITERATURE

B HISTORICAL CONTEXT
Reread lines 19–30. With the help of the historical information on pages 1178–1179 and the Background on page 1180, explain the various events that happened to Heinz and his family.

C CHARACTERIZATION
Reread lines 45–50. How does Heinz's pride in the birth of his son express itself in his words and actions?

DIFFERENTIATED INSTRUCTION

FOR ADVANCED LEARNERS/AP

Evaluate Author's Choices Vonnegut includes few details about the "atrocities of the Holocaust" that Heinz has survived. Readers are left to make inferences from such lines as 20–23. Ask whether students think Vonnegut should have provided more background to explain Heinz or whether such detail is unnecessary. Point out as well that Vonnegut chose to tell the story through a third-person omniscient narrator.

Ask students to evaluate the author's choice. Discuss how the narrative might differ in tone and content if narrated in the first person, either by Heinz or perhaps by Avchen. After discussing both issues, challenge students to write one to two paragraphs about one of the two, expressing their evaluation and supporting it with thoughtful reasons and textual evidence.

"Malnutrition as a child," said Heinz. **D**

70 "Yeah. Well, the baby came normally, but, if you're going to have another one, it'd better be a Caesarean. Just to be on the safe side."

"I can't thank you enough," said Heinz passionately.

Dr. Powers licked his lips, and fought to keep his eyes open. "Uh huh. 'S O.K.," he said thickly. "'Night. Luck." He shambled out into the corridor.

The nurse stuck her head into the waiting room. "You can see your baby, Mr. Netman."

"Doctor—" said Heinz, hurrying out into the corridor, wanting to shake Powers' hand again so that Powers would know what a magnificent thing he'd done. "It's the most wonderful thing that ever happened." The elevator doors slithered shut between them before Dr. Powers could show a glimmer of response.

80 "This way," said the nurse. "Turn left at the end of the hall, and you'll find the nursery window there. Write your name on a piece of paper and hold it against the glass."

Heinz made the trip by himself, without seeing another human being until he reached the end. There, on the other side of a large glass panel, he saw a hundred of them cupped in shallow canvas buckets and arranged in a square block of straight ranks and files.

Heinz wrote his name on the back of a laundry slip and pressed it to the window. A fat and placid nurse looked at the paper, not at Heinz's face, and missed seeing his wide smile, missed an urgent invitation to share for a moment

90 his ecstasy.

She grasped one of the buckets and wheeled it before the window. She turned away again, once more missing the smile.

"Hello, hello, hello, little Knechtmann," said Heinz to the red prune on the other side of the glass. His voice echoed down the hard, bare corridor, and came back to him with embarrassing loudness. He blushed and lowered his voice. "Little Peter, little Kroll," he said softly, "little Friederich—and there's Helga in you, too. Little spark of Knechtmann, you little treasure house. Everything is saved in you."

"I'm afraid you'll have to be more quiet," said a nurse, sticking her head out

100 from one of the rooms.

"Sorry," said Heinz. "I'm very sorry." He fell silent, and contented himself with tapping lightly on the window with a fingernail, trying to get the child to look at him. Young Knechtmann would not look, wouldn't share the moment, and after a few minutes the nurse took him away again.

Heinz beamed as he rode on the elevator and as he crossed the hospital lobby, but no one gave him more than a cursory glance. He passed a row of telephone booths and there, in one of the booths with the door open, he saw a soldier with whom he'd shared the waiting room an hour before.

"Yeah, Ma—seven pounds six ounces. Got hair like Buffalo Bill. No, we

110 haven't had time to make up a name for her yet . . . That you, Pa? Yup, mother and daughter doin' fine, just fine. Seven pounds six ounces. Nope, no name. . . ."

ADAM **1183**

D HISTORICAL CONTEXT
Consider why Heinz's wife might have suffered malnutrition as a child. What does this suggest about the impact of history on the present?

READING SKILL COMMON CORE

D HISTORICAL CONTEXT RL 3

***Possible answer:** As children, both Heinz and his wife were prisoners in a Nazi concentration camp. No doubt, they were severely deprived of nutritious foods. The impact of his wife's childhood malnutrition on her present-day "pelvis trouble" (line 67) demonstrates how past events can seriously affect the present.*

IF STUDENTS NEED HELP . . . Have them reread lines 22–23 and discuss their meaning. Clarify living conditions in the Nazi concentration camps, referring to the historical background on page 1179 or urging students to pursue their own research.

TIERED DISCUSSION PROMPTS

In lines 87–98, use these prompts to help students understand Heinz's reaction to his son's birth:

Connect Have you ever spent time with or seen a brand new parent? Describe the person's emotional state. *Accept all thoughtful responses.*

Interpret What does Heinz mean when he says, "Little spark of Knechtmann, you little treasure house. Everything is saved in you"? ***Possible answer:** Heinz is expressing his gratitude that the newborn baby will continue the family line. The Nazis killed the other members of the Knechtmann family, but the baby has preserved the "spark of Knechtmann" and qualities of all the murdered Knechtmanns.*

Evaluate Is Heinz's response to his new son believable? Explain. ***Possible answer:** Heinz's response is quite believable because his experience has been so devastating that the birth of a child would seem truly miraculous.*

FOR ENGLISH LANGUAGE LEARNERS

Vocabulary Support Use Word Questioning to teach these words: *panel* (line 84), *odd* (line 179).

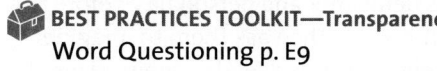 **BEST PRACTICES TOOLKIT—Transparency** Word Questioning p. E9

FOR STRUGGLING READERS

Develop Reading Fluency Clarify that when people speak, they often omit letters or words. Explain that authors try to represent this speech to make dialogue sound realistic. Highlight the abbreviated form *"'S O.K."* in lines 72–73, and ask students what is missing (*It*). Then elicit the missing elements in *"'Night. Luck."* (line 73) and *"Got hair like Buffalo Bill"* (line 109).

Have students work in pairs to read aloud the dialogue from lines 69–82 and lines 93–111.

Ⓔ *Model the Skill:* TONE

Work with students to analyze the tone by adding to the chart introduced on page 1179, focusing on these three columns:

Character's Speech, Thoughts, Feelings	Other Characters' Speech, Thoughts, Feelings	Narrator's Comments
"Heinz longed to ... tell the marvelous news."	The soldier is sharing similar news with his parents and sister.	"But there was no one to call, no one waiting for the news."

Possible answer: *Vonnegut emphasizes a tone of wistfulness and isolation through Heinz's thoughts and feelings, the speech of other characters, and the narrator's comments.*

READING SKILL

Ⓕ HISTORICAL CONTEXT

Possible answer: *By focusing attention on naming the baby, Vonnegut underscores the importance of the newborn to Heinz. The baby represents the miracle of life for Heinz, but perhaps even more than that, the baby is a link to Heinz's past and to the family members whom Heinz loved and so tragically lost.*

Extend the Discussion Why does Vonnegut present Sousa's attitude in such sharp contrast to Heinz's excitement?

That you, Sis? Pretty late for you to be up, ain't it? Doesn't look like anybody yet. Let me talk to Ma again. . . . That you, Ma? Well, I guess that's all the news from Chicago. Now, Mom, Mom, take it easy—don't worry. It's a swell-looking baby, Mom. Just the hair looks like Buffalo Bill, and I said it as a joke, Mom. That's right, seven pounds six ounces. . . ."

There were five other booths, all empty, all open for calls to anyplace on earth. Heinz longed to hurry into one of them breathlessly, and tell the marvelous news. But there was no one to call, no one waiting for the news. Ⓔ

120 But Heinz still beamed, and he strode across the street and into a quiet tavern there. In the dank twilight there were only two men, tête-à-tête, the bartender and Mr. Sousa.

"Yes sir, what'll it be?"

"I'd like to buy you and Mr. Sousa a drink," said Heinz with a heartiness strange to him. "I'd like the best brandy you've got. My wife just had a baby!"

"That so?" said the bartender with polite interest.

"Five pounds nine ounces," said Heinz.

"Huh," said the bartender. "What do you know."

"Netman," said Sousa, "Wha'dja get?"

130 "Boy," said Heinz proudly.

"Never knew it to fail," said Sousa bitterly. "It's the little guys, all the time the little guys."

"Boy, girl," said Heinz, "it's all the same, just as long as it lives. Over there in the hospital, they're too close to it to see the wonder of it. A miracle over and over again—the world made new."

"Wait'll you've racked up seven, Netman," said Sousa. "Then you come back and tell me about the miracle."

"You got seven?" said the bartender. "I'm one up on you. I got eight." He poured three drinks.

140 "Far as I'm concerned," said Sousa, "you can have the championship."

Heinz lifted his glass. "Here's long life and great skill and much happiness to—to Peter Karl Knechtmann." He breathed quickly, excited by the decision.

"There's a handle to take ahold of," said Sousa. "You'd think the kid weighed two hundred pounds."

"Peter is the name of a famous surgeon," said Heinz, "the boy's great-uncle, dead now. Karl was my father's name." Ⓕ

"Here's to Pete K. Netman," said Sousa, with a cursory salute.

"Pete," said the bartender, drinking.

"And here's to your little girl—the new one," said Heinz.

150 Sousa sighed and smiled wearily. "Here's to her. God bless her."

"And now, I'll propose a toast," said the bartender, hammering on the bar with his fist. "On your feet, gentlemen. Up, up, everybody up."

Heinz stood, and held his glass high, ready for the next step in camaraderie, a toast to the whole human race, of which the Knechtmanns were still a part.

"Here's to the White Sox!" roared the bartender.

"Minoso, Fox, Mele," said Sousa.

Ⓔ **TONE**
Reread lines 117–119. How would you describe the tone of the story at this point?

 **Targeted Passage**

Ⓕ **HISTORICAL CONTEXT**
Reread lines 141–146. Why do you think Vonnegut focuses so much attention on the naming of the baby?

DIFFERENTIATED INSTRUCTION

FOR STRUGGLING READERS

② Targeted Passage [Lines 124–150]

This passage contrasts Heinz's excitement with the jaded weariness of those nearby.

- Why does Heinz want to buy drinks for Sousa and the bartender? (lines 124–125)

- Why don't Sousa and the bartender share Heinz's excitement? (lines 136–138)

- What does Heinz mean that the people in the hospital are "too close to it to see the wonder of it"? (lines 133–135)

FOR ADVANCED LEARNERS/AP

Write a Journal Entry Have students reflect on the events of the story and make inferences based on textual evidence about Heinz's demeanor and personality before the birth of his son. Then ask them to imagine that Heinz is a close friend of theirs. Have students write and share a journal entry about the day Heinz's son is born and how he responds to the birth. Encourage them to include their own feelings about Heinz and Avchen.

"Fain, Lollar, Rivera!" said the bartender. He turned to Heinz. "Drink up, boy! The White Sox! Don't tell me you're a Cub fan."

"No," said Heinz, disappointed. "No—I don't follow baseball, I'm afraid." The 160 other two men seemed to be sinking away from him. "I haven't been able to think about much but the baby."

The bartender at once turned his full attention to Sousa. "Look," he said intensely, "they take Fain off of first, and put him at third, and give Pierce first. Then move Minoso in from left field to shortstop. See what I'm doing?"

"Yep, yep," said Sousa eagerly.

"And then we take that no-good Carrasquel and . . ."

Heinz was all alone again, with twenty feet of bar between him and the other two men. It might as well have been a continent.

He finished his drink without pleasure, and left quietly.

170 At the railroad station, where he waited for a local train to take him home to the South Side, Heinz's glow returned again as he saw a co-worker at the dry-cleaning plant walk in with a girl. They were laughing and had their arms around each other's waist.

"Harry," said Heinz, hurrying toward them. "Guess what, Harry. Guess what just happened." He grinned broadly.

Harry, a tall, dapper, snub-nosed young man, looked down at Heinz with mild surprise. "Oh—hello, Heinz. What's up, boy?"

The girl looked on in perplexity, as though asking why they should be accosted at such an odd hour by such an odd person. Heinz avoided her slightly 180 derisive eyes. **G**

"A baby, Harry. My wife just had a boy."

"Oh," said Harry. He extended his hand. "Well, congratulations." The hand was limp. "I think that's swell, Heinz, perfectly swell." He withdrew his hand and waited for Heinz to say something else.

"Yes, yes—just about an hour ago," said Heinz. "Five pounds nine ounces. I've never been happier in my life."

"Well, I think it's perfectly swell, Heinz. You should be happy."

"Yes, indeed," said the girl.

There was a long silence, with all three shifting from one foot to the other.

190 "Really good news," said Harry at last.

"Yes, well," said Heinz quickly, "Well, that's all I had to tell you."

"Thanks," said Harry. "Glad to hear about it."

There was another uneasy silence.

"See you at work," said Heinz, and strode jauntily back to his bench, but with his reddened neck betraying how foolish he felt.

The girl giggled.

Back home in his small apartment, at two in the morning, Heinz talked to himself, to the empty bassinet, and to the bed. He talked in German, a language he had sworn never to use again. **H**

200 "They don't care," said Heinz. "They're all too busy, busy, busy to notice life, to feel anything about it. A baby is born." He shrugged. "What could be duller?"

ADAM **1185**

G CHARACTERIZATION
What character trait of Heinz's does Vonnegut reveal through the sentence "Heinz avoided her slightly derisive eyes"?

H HISTORICAL CONTEXT
Reread lines 197–199. What is Vonnegut's purpose in including this description of Heinz's use of and feelings about speaking German? Explain.

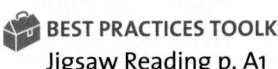

How does the collage relate to the story?
Possible answer: The collage expresses the permanence of the marriage bond, which relates to the bond between Heinz and Avchen.

TEXT ANALYSIS

COMMON CORE

RL 3
RL 4

❶ CHARACTERIZATION AND TONE

Possible answer: Their conversation affirms that Heinz and Avchen love each other deeply and are overjoyed to share a life together after all they've been through. The tone is happy and uplifting.

REVISIT THE BIG QUESTION

How do you AFFIRM LIFE?

Discuss How does the story's conclusion in lines 220–243 underscore the resilience of Heinz and Avchen? *Possible answer: It shows that Heinz and Avchen not only have survived but have been able to create new life despite the hardships they have endured.*

SELECTION WRAP–UP

READ WITH A PURPOSE Ask them to assess the authors' views of human nature. Are the authors' views of human nature positive or negative? *Possible answer: Vonnegut has a positive outlook on human nature as illustrated by the joy Heinz and Avchen express at the end of the story. Levi's outlook on human nature seems darker given his cold recounting of life and death at Auschwitz.*

★ CRITIQUE

- Have students identify the passages in the story that they found most moving and then explain what makes these passages so meaningful. Urge students to be specific.

- After completing the After Reading questions on page 1187, have students revisit their responses and tell whether they have changed their opinions.

Who would be so stupid as to talk about it, to think there was anything important or interesting about it?"

He opened a window on the summer night, and looked out at the moonlit canyon of gray wooden porches and garbage cans. "There are too many of us, and we are all too far apart," said Heinz. "Another Knechtmann is born, another O'Leary, another Sousa. Who cares? Why should anyone care? What difference does it make? None."

He lay down in his clothes on the unmade bed, and, with a rattling sigh, went
210 to sleep.

He awoke at six, as always. He drank a cup of coffee, and with a wry sense of anonymity, he jostled and was jostled aboard the downtown train. His face showed no emotion. It was like all the other faces, seemingly incapable of surprise or wonder, joy or anger.

He walked across town to the hospital with the same detachment, a gray, uninteresting man, a part of the city.

In the hospital, he was as purposeful and calm as the doctors and nurses bustling about him.

220 When he was led into the ward where Avchen slept behind white screens, he felt only what he had always felt in her presence—love and aching awe and gratitude for her.

"You go ahead and wake her gently, Mr. Netman," said the nurse.

"Avchen—" He touched her on her white-gowned shoulder. "Avchen. Are you all right, Avchen?"

"Mmmmmmmmmm?" murmured Avchen.
230 Her eyes opened to narrow slits. "Heinz. Hello, Heinz."

"Sweetheart, are you all right?"

"Yes, yes," she whispered. "I'm fine. How is the baby, Heinz?"

"Perfect. Perfect, Avchen."

"They couldn't kill us, could they, Heinz?"

"No."

"And here we are, alive as we can be."

"Yes."
240 "The baby, Heinz—" She opened her dark eyes wide. "It's the most wonderful thing that ever happened, isn't it?"

"Yes," said Heinz. ✿ ❶

❸ Targeted Passage

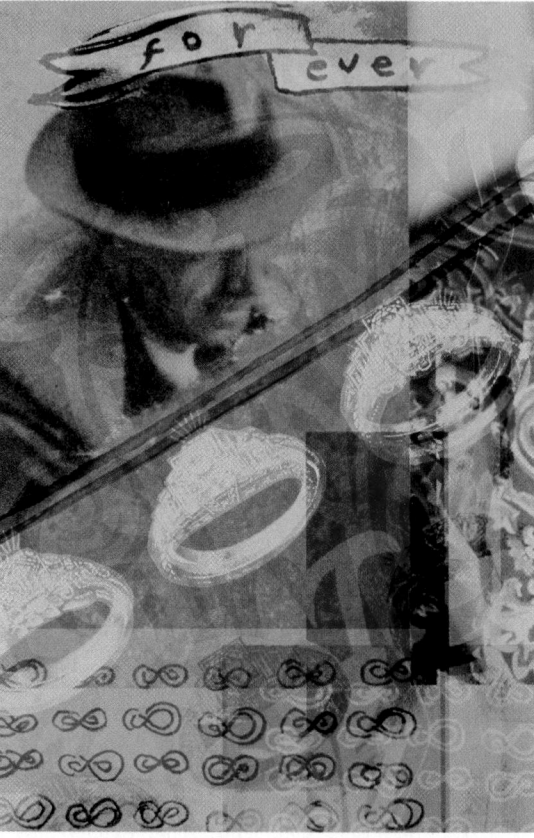

Life Decisions (1995), Ed Roskowski. © Ed Roskowski/Corbis.

DIFFERENTIATED INSTRUCTION

FOR STRUGGLING READERS

❸ Targeted Passage [Lines 220–243]

This final passage shows the strong bond between Heinz and Avchen and stresses their joy at survival and the miracle of life.

- Describe Heinz's feelings about Avchen. (lines 220–223) Describe Avchen's feelings about Heinz. (lines 230–238)

- What is the couple's reaction to having a new baby? (lines 240–243)

FOR ENGLISH LANGUAGE LEARNERS

Vocabulary: Cognates Point out that the Spanish word *cañón* is similar in spelling and pronunciation to the English word *canyon* (line 205). Call attention to these cognates:

- *anonymity* (line 212), anonimidad
- *incapable* (line 213), incapaz
- *surprise* (line 213), sorpresa
- *presence* (line 222), presencia
- *gratitude* (line 223), gratitude

Comprehension

COMMON CORE

RL 3 Analyze the impact of the author's choices regarding how to develop and relate elements of a story. RL 4 Analyze the impact of specific word choices on meaning and tone.

1. **Recall** From what country and historical events is Heinz Knechtmann a refugee?

2. **Recall** Why is he at the hospital?

3. **Summarize** Why is he so amazed that he and his wife have had a child?

Text Analysis

● 4. **Analyze Characterization** In lines 4–7, how does Vonnegut use dialogue and details of physical appearance to characterize Mr. Sousa? Cite evidence from these lines to support your answer.

5. **Interpret Symbolism** In lines 78–79, what does the image of the closing elevator doors symbolize?

● 6. **Analyze Tone** Examine the short paragraph in lines 204–208. Describe the tone of this paragraph and explain how it differs from Vonnegut's tone in the dialogue that concludes "Adam" (lines 238–243).

● 7. **Analyze Historical Context** In the story's closing scene, the main character's wife says, "They couldn't kill us, could they, Heinz?" (line 236). Whom does she mean by "they"? To which historical events does she refer when she says, "They couldn't kill us"? Explain.

● 8. **Analyze Historical Context** In the barroom scene (lines 120–169), contrast Mr. Sousa and the bartender's life with Heinz Knechtmann's experience before immigrating to the United States. How does this contrast affect communication between the Americans and the Jewish immigrant in this scene?

9. **Analyze Allusion** The title of the story is an **allusion**—a reference to someone or something outside the story. To whom does the title refer? How does the title contribute to the meaning of the story?

Text Criticism

10. **Social Context** Explain whether you agree with Heinz's conclusion that people in this country are "too busy," "too many," and "too far apart" to care about one another. Give reasons for your response.

> *How do you* **AFFIRM LIFE?**
>
> In your opinion, what accounts for the resilience of the main character and his wife in "Adam"? Cite evidence from the story and your own experience to support your answer.

Practice and Apply

For preliminary support of post-reading questions, use these copy masters:

R RESOURCE MANAGER—Copy Masters
Reading Check p. 41
Analyze Historical Context p. 39
Question Support p. 42
Additional selection questions are provided for teachers on page 31.

ANSWERS   COMMON CORE RL 3, RL 4

1. *Heinz is a refugee from Germany and the Holocaust.*

2. *His wife is having a baby.*

3. *He and his wife were prisoners in a Nazi concentration camp and have managed to survive and bring new life into the world.*

Possible answers:

4. ● COMMON CORE FOCUS **Characterization and Tone** *Vonnegut characterizes Mr. Sousa as "a sullen gorilla" who is impatient and a bit resentful; "impatient with having a tiresome and familiar routine explained" (lines 4–5).*

5. *The closing doors symbolize the cutting off of conversation between Heinz and Dr. Powers and Heinz's inability to communicate all he had wanted to say to the doctor.*

6. ● COMMON CORE FOCUS **Characterization and Tone** *The tone in lines 204–208 is despondent; Heinz feels that the birth of his son means nothing. In lines 238–243, Heinz feels renewed in his wife's presence. The tone is awed and joyful. Adam means everything to Heinz and Avchen.*

Assess and Reteach

7. ● COMMON CORE FOCUS **Analyze Historical Context** *She refers to the Nazis of World War II. Avchen and Heinz are Jewish war refugees who survived the Holocaust.*

8. ● COMMON CORE FOCUS **Analyze Historical Context** *The bartender and Mr. Sousa had been living an uneventful family life, while Heinz had endured the trauma of being in a target of the Holocaust. The difference in their experience means they cannot connect meaningfully in this scene.*

9. *The alusion is to Adam, the first man and the beginning of life in the biblical story of Adam and Eve. The title contributes to the meaning of the story because, for Heinz and Avchen, the birth of their baby represents the beginning of a new life for them.*

10. *Accept all well-supported responses.*

> *How do you* AFFIRM LIFE?
> Student answers will vary based on their own experiences.

Assess

DIAGNOSTIC AND SELECTION TESTS
Selection Test A pp. 313–314
Selection Test B/C pp. 315–316

Interactive Selection Test on **thinkcentral.com**

Reteach

Level Up Online Tutorials on **thinkcentral.com**

Reteaching Worksheets on **thinkcentral.com**

Literature Lesson 3: Characterization

SUMMARY

In this excerpt, Primo Levi recounts how concentration camp prisoners were selected for execution.

Memoir

Both "Adam" and "Survival in Auschwitz" make a comment about the value of human life in the shadow of World War II. Use a Comparison Matrix to help students compare the statement made by each piece.

 BEST PRACTICES TOOLKIT—Transparency
Comparison Matrix p. A24

READING SKILL  COMMON CORE RI 6

Ⓐ HISTORICAL CONTEXT

Possible answer: *Every minute of their day is controlled by the Nazis. The prisoners live with the uncertainty of when "selections" will occur.*

TEXT ANALYSIS  COMMON CORE RI 3 RI 6

Ⓑ CHARACTERIZATION

Possible answer: *Levi describes the way in which each individual group tries to believe that it will be spared. This behavior reveals the human trait of hopefulness.*

Memoir

In "Adam," you read about Holocaust survivors who came to America to begin a new life. In Primo Levi's memoir, you'll discover firsthand some of the horrors Holocaust victims endured in Nazi death camps.

from SURVIVAL *in* AUSCHWITZ
Primo Levi

BACKGROUND Primo Levi spent the last year of World War II as an inmate at Auschwitz, a Nazi concentration camp in Poland. Levi wrote about his nightmarish experiences in objective, scientific detail, believing that subjective commentary was unnecessary and that the events would speak for themselves. The following excerpt from his memoir describes the ritual in which prisoners were selected for execution.

Today is working Sunday, *Arbeitssonntag:* we work until 1 P.M., then we return to camp for the shower, shave and general control for skin diseases and lice. And in the yards, everyone knew mysteriously that the selection would be today. Ⓐ

The news arrived, as always, surrounded by a halo of contradictory or suspect details: the selection in the infirmary took place this morning; the percentage was seven per cent of the whole camp, thirty, fifty per cent of the patients. At Birkenau,[1] the crematorium chimney has been smoking for ten days. Room has to be made for an enormous convoy arriving from the Poznan ghetto.[2] The young tell the young that all the old ones will be chosen. The healthy tell the healthy that only the ill will
10 be chosen. Specialists will be excluded. German Jews will be excluded. Low Numbers[3] will be excluded. You will be chosen. I will be excluded. Ⓑ

At 1 P.M. exactly the yard empties in orderly fashion, and for two hours the gray unending army files past the two control stations where, as on every day, we are counted and recounted, and past the military band which for two hours without interruption plays, as on every day, those marches to which we must synchronize our steps at our entrance and our exit.

Ⓐ **HISTORICAL CONTEXT**
Reread the opening paragraph (lines 1–3). How do the facts related here contribute to your understanding of life for Jewish prisoners in Auschwitz?

Ⓑ **CHARACTERIZATION**
Reread lines 8–11 (from "The young tell the young" to the end of the paragraph). What human trait does the behavior of the Jewish prisoners reveal? Explain.

---

1. **Birkenau** (bûr′kən-ou): Also known as Auschwitz II, this camp stood about two miles from an older camp, called Auschwitz I. Between 1 million and 4 million people were murdered at Auschwitz-Birkenau during the years 1942–1945.
2. **Poznan** (pôz′năn′) **ghetto:** the area of the Polish city of Poznan in which Jews were forced to live.
3. **Low Numbers:** prisoners with low identification numbers.

DIFFERENTIATED INSTRUCTION

FOR ENGLISH LANGUAGE LEARNERS
Vocabulary: Cognates Point out that the Spanish word *misteriosamente* is similar in spelling and pronunciation to the English word *mysteriously* (line 3). Then call attention to these other Spanish cognates:

- *contradictory* (line 4), contradictorio
- *suspect* (line 4), sospechoso
- *crematorium* (line 7), crematorio
- *counted* (line 14), contado
- *interruption* (line 15), interrupción

- *selection* (line 22), selección
- *pressure* (line 37), presión
- *condemned* (line 59), condenado
- *myope* (line 63), miope
- *examination* (line 65), examinación
- *eliminated* (line 67), eliminado
- *percentage* (line 68), porcentaje

Ask students to think of cognates in their home languages.

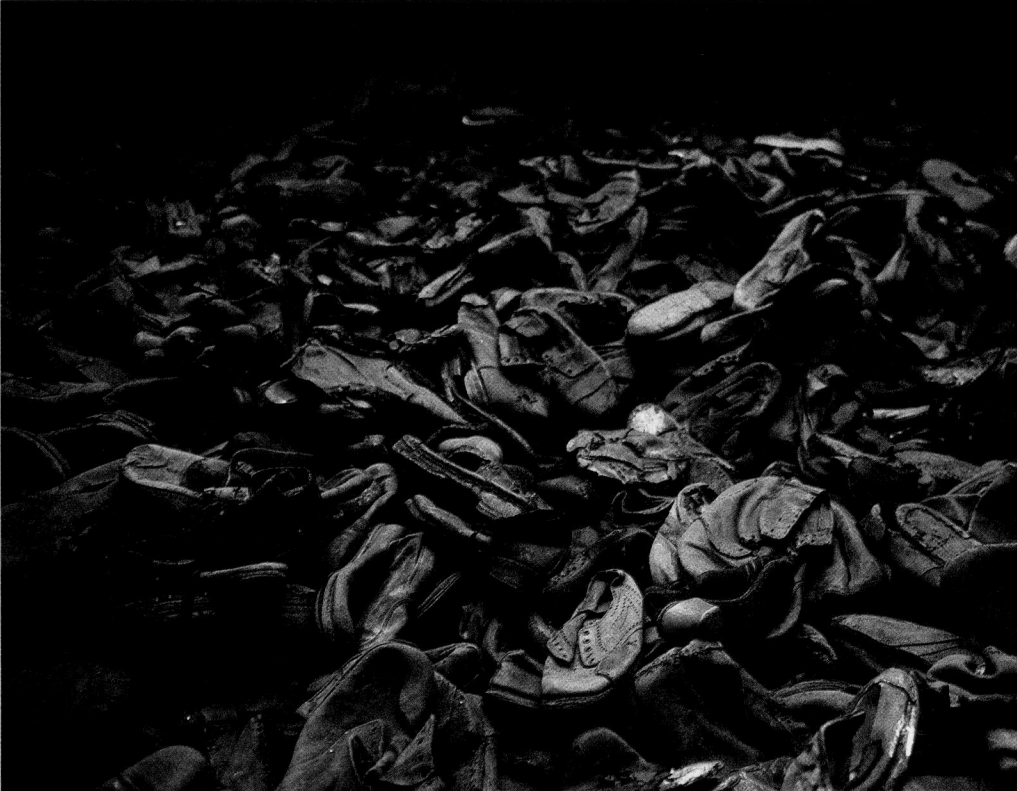

The shoes of victims, on display at the Auschwitz Museum

It seems like every day, the kitchen chimney smokes as usual, the distribution of the soup is already beginning. But then the bell is heard, and at that moment we realize that we have arrived.

20   Because this bell always sounds at dawn, when it means the reveille;[4] but if it sounds during the day, it means "*Blocksperre*," enclosure in huts, and this happens when there is a selection to prevent anyone avoiding it, or when those selected leave for the gas, to prevent anyone seeing them leave. **C**

Our *Blockältester*[5] knows his business. He has made sure that we have all entered, he has had the door locked, he has given everyone his card with his number, name, profession, age and nationality and he has ordered everyone to undress completely, except for shoes. We wait like this, naked, with the card in our hands, for the commission to

---

4. **reveille** (rĕv'ə-lē): a signal used to awaken people.

5. *Blockältester* (blŏ'kăl-tĕs'tər) German: block elder—a prisoner cooperating with the German guards by serving as the head of a block, or barracks.

▲ **Analyze Visuals**
How does this photograph add to your understanding of Vonnegut's short story and Levi's testimony about life in Auschwitz? Explain your response.

C **TONE**
Describe the tone of lines 20–23. Explain how Levi's tone contrasts with the situation he describes here.

BACKGROUND

The Horror of Auschwitz Auschwitz comprised the largest of the Nazi concentration and extermination camps. Between 1.1 million and 1.5 million people, mostly Jews, are estimated to have died there. Every day, prisoners were transported to Auschwitz by train from all over Nazi-occupied Europe. Some were killed in gas chambers almost at once. Others were used as slave labor in factories, but most of these laborers were also eventually killed by the Nazis or else died as a result of mistreatment, illness, or starvation. Some Auschwitz prisoners were subjected to ghastly medical experimentation. Soviet soldiers finally liberated the camp in January 1945, finding fewer than 8,000 survivors. Today there is a museum at the Auschwitz site to help the world remember the horrors that occurred there.

Analyze Visuals

Possible answer: The image of the shoes enhances understanding of the amazement and joy of Vonnegut's characters at having survived. It adds to the poignancy of Avchen's awed observation, "They couldn't kill us, could they, Heinz?" The photo also increases the understated terror of the selection process documented in Levi's testimony about Auschwitz.

TEXT ANALYSIS    COMMON CORE

C **TONE**   RI 3 RI 6

Possible answer: Levi uses an unemotional tone to describe when a selection occurs.

FOR STRUGGLING READERS

Vocabulary Support

- *contradictory* (line 4), "inconsistent; containing opposite views or information"

- *crematorium* (line 7), "a place where bodies are cremated or reduced to ashes by burning"

- *convoy* (line 8), "a group of vehicles or train cars traveling together"

- *synchronize* (line 15), "operate together at the same rate; coordinate"

FOR ADVANCED LEARNERS/AP

Research Primo Levi Have students conduct research to learn about the life and work of Primo Levi. Students should address such questions as: How did Levi manage to survive Auschwitz? What did he do after being liberated? What other books did he write? Ask students to summarize their research in an oral presentation.

TIERED DISCUSSION PROMPTS

TIERED DISCUSSION PROMPTS

In lines 31–53, use these prompts to help students understand the experiences of Levi and his fellow prisoners:

Summarize What is happening in this passage? *Possible answer: The Nazis are doing a cursory inspection of the prisoners to determine who will live and who will die.*

Analyze In what ways does Levi convey to readers what it felt like to be in the situation? Use examples to explain. *Possible answer: Levi conveys the feelings of the situation through vivid images and sensory detail. For example, he describes how the "crowd of frightened, naked people" (line 33) is driven along and becomes "a warm and compact human mass" (lines 35–36) crammed into the Quartermaster's office, "exercising such a pressure on the wooden walls as to make them creak" (lines 36–37). Then he describes how he crosses in front of the SS man, "trying to hold my head high, my chest forward and my muscles contracted . . . " (lines 51–52).*

Synthesize The background on page 1189 explains Levi's belief that "subjective commentary was unnecessary and that the events would speak for themselves." In what ways does Levi's description of events support that belief? Explain. *Possible answer: Levi's detached but detailed description provides a heightened sense of realism and immediacy, qualities that any further commentary might compromise.*

READING SKILL

COMMON CORE RI 6

D HISTORICAL CONTEXT

Possible answer: The examination was "too quick and summary" (lines 65–68). Students may point out that death could come at any time for any reason to prisoners in the concentration camps.

---

why we should not get under the blankets on the bunk and keep warm.

Many are already drowsing when a barrage of orders, oaths and blows proclaims the imminent arrival of the commission. The *Blockältester* and his helpers, starting at the end of the dormitory, drive the crowd of frightened, naked people in front of them and cram them in the *Tagesraum* which is the Quartermaster's office.[6] The *Tagesraum* is a room seven yards by four: when the drive is over, a warm and compact human mass is jammed into the *Tagesraum*, perfectly filling all the corners, exercising such a pressure on the wooden walls as to make them creak. . . .

The *Blockältester* has closed the connecting-door and has opened the other two which lead from the dormitory and the *Tagesraum* outside. Here, in front of the two doors, stands the arbiter[7] of our fate, an SS subaltern.[8] On his right is the *Blockältester*, on his left, the quartermaster of the hut. Each one of us, as he comes naked out of the *Tagesraum* into the cold October air, has to run the few steps between the two doors, give the card to the SS man and enter the dormitory door. The SS man, in the fraction of a second between two successive crossings, with a glance at one's back and front, judges everyone's fate, and in turn gives the card to the man on his right or his left, and this is the life or death of each of us. In three or four minutes a hut of two hundred men is "done," as is the whole camp of twelve thousand men in the course of the afternoon.

Jammed in the charnel-house[9] of the *Tagesraum*, I gradually felt the human pressure around me slacken, and in a short time it was my turn. Like everyone, I passed by with a brisk and elastic step, trying to hold my head high, my chest forward and my muscles contracted and conspicuous. With the corner of my eye I tried to look behind my shoulders, and my card seemed to end on the right.

As we gradually come back into the dormitory we are allowed to dress ourselves. Nobody yet knows with certainty his own fate, it has first of all to be established whether the condemned cards were those on the right or the left. By now there is no longer any point in sparing each other's feelings with superstitious scruples. Everybody crowds around the oldest, the most wasted-away, and most "muselmann";[10] if their cards went to the left, the left is certainly the side of the condemned.

Even before the selection is over, everybody knows that the left was effectively the *"schlechte Seite,"* the bad side. There have naturally been some irregularities: René, for example, so young and robust, ended on the left; perhaps it was because he has glasses, perhaps because he walks a little stooped like a myope,[11] but more probably because of a simple mistake. . . .

There is nothing surprising about these mistakes: the examination is too quick and summary, and in any case, the important thing for the Lager[12] is not that the most useless prisoners be eliminated, but that free posts be quickly created, according to a certain percentage previously fixed. 〜 **D**

D HISTORICAL CONTEXT
Reread the last two paragraphs of the selection (lines 60–68). How does Levi explain the mistake that has been made? How does his explanation contribute to your understanding of the Holocaust? Explain.

---

6. **Quartermaster's office:** the office of the person who distributes food and clothing to the prisoners.
7. **arbiter** (är'bǐ-tər): judge; decider.
8. **SS subaltern:** a low-ranking officer in the Nazi special security force.
9. **charnel-house:** vault for the bones of the dead (used here figuratively).
10. **"muselmann"** (mōō'zəl-män): concentration-camp slang for a person near death from starvation.
11. **myope** (mī'ōp'): nearsighted person.
12. **Lager** (lä'gər) *German:* camp.

DIFFERENTIATED INSTRUCTION

FOR STRUGGLING READERS
Vocabulary Support
- *barrage* (line 31), "an outpouring; shower"
- *imminent* (lines 32), "about to happen"
- *commission* (line 32), "a group of people with authority to carry out a task"
- *slacken* (line 50), "become less; decrease"
- *brisk* (line 51), "quick, energetic"
- *scruples* (line 57), "moral or ethical concerns that constrain behavior"

Photograph

This photograph shows the German slogan *Arbeit macht frei* ("Work will make you free") that Jews saw posted above the gate as they entered the Auschwitz-Birkenau Concentration Camp that Levi writes about in the memoir you just read. Analyze how the image and the words in this visual work together to convey meaning. Respond to the questions below, citing evidence from the visual to support your answers.

COMMON CORE

RI 7 Integrate and evaluate multiple sources of information presented in multiple media or formats as well as words in order to address a question or solve a problem.

1. **INTERPRET**
   Examine the colors in this photograph—pavement, grounds, building, trees, and sky. What kind of mood do these colors convey? What purpose do they help the photographer to achieve?

2. **ANALYZE**
   What purpose does the photographer achieve by prominently featuring the infamous slogan that was posted above the gate to Auschwitz?

1191

Photograph

COMMON CORE RI 7

Ask students whether they feel the message communicated by the slogan matches the image in the photo. If not, why? What meaning do they find in the combination of the image and slogan?

ANALYZE VISUALS **COMMON CORE RI 7**

1. INTERPRET

Possible answer: The colors are all muted and cold looking. They convey a mood of suspense and unease. The colors and mood help the photographer communicate that this camp is a frightening and tragic place.

ANALYZE VISUALS **COMMON CORE RI 7**

2. ANALYZE

Possible answer: The photographer achieves the purpose of exposing the lie of such camps. Work did not make the prisoners at Auschwitz free. Most people transported here were killed.

Answers

 COMMON CORE RI 2, RI 3, RI 6

1. *Levi writes in the last paragraph that prisoners will be eliminated, indicating that the "selection" referred to execution.*

2. *The main concern of those running the camp was to eliminate a certain number of prisoners based on previously determined percentages; it did not matter to them which prisoners were selected.*

Possible answers:

3. ● **COMMON CORE FOCUS** **Characterization and Tone** *Levi's writing style shows the detachment that many prisoners felt and also conveys to the reader that horrific events were part of everyday life in a concentration camp.*

4. ■ **COMMON CORE FOCUS** **Characterization and Tone** *The passage shows that the Blockältester was coldly efficient in following German orders; the prisoners were frightened and deprived of clothing. That naked prisoners were crammed into a room reveals the dehumanizing conditions at Auschwitz.*

5. *The irony is that even though René wears glasses and walks with a stoop, those "irregularities" likely had nothing to do with his assignment to the condemned group.*

6. ■ **COMMON CORE FOCUS** **Analyze Historical Context** *Accept answers that students support with evidence from the excerpt. Students may respond that Levi's memoir conveys the horrific circumstances that Jewish prisoners faced every day during the Holocaust.*

7. *In "Adam," the birth of Heinz and Avchen's son shows that the human spirit can triumph despite being subjected to man's inhumanity. The description of the selection process in "Survival in Auschwitz" shows that, under the wrong circumstances, man is capable of the grossest inhumanities against his fellow man.*

Comprehension

1. **Clarify** What is the purpose of the "selection" Levi tells about in this excerpt? What evidence can you cite to support your answer?

2. **Explain** In lines 65–68, why is it unimportant to those running the camp that mistakes were made during the "selection"?

Text Analysis

● 3. **Analyze Tone** Levi writes about the selection as if he were reciting ordinary events from an ordinary day, using ordinary diction and descriptions. Why might he use an almost matter-of-fact tone to describe horrific events? Explain.

● 4. **Analyze Characterization** Reread lines 31–37. What traits does this passage convey about the *Blockältester* and the Jewish prisoners, and how does their behavior here contribute to your understanding of conditions at Auschwitz? Support your answer by citing evidence from the passage.

5. **Examine Irony** Reread lines 60–64. What is ironic about Levi's reference to the "simple mistake" of Rene's selection?

■ 6. **Analyze Historical Context** Briefly explain how the short excerpt from Levi's memoir contributes to your knowledge of the Holocaust. Cite evidence from the text to support your answer.

Comparing Themes Across Genres

7. **Analyze Theme** What do "Adam" and the excerpt from *Survival in Auschwitz* have to say about the theme of man's inhumanity to man? Support your answer with evidence from both texts.

> *How do you* **AFFIRM LIFE?**
> Like many Holocaust survivors, Levi felt the need to serve as a "witness" and tell his story so that such events would never be repeated. Do you think memoirs such as Levi's can prevent something similar from happening again, or are such events inevitable? Explain your response.

COMMON CORE

RI 2 Determine two or more central ideas of a text and analyze their development across the course of a text. **RI 3** Analyze a complex set of ideas or sequence of events and explain how specific individuals, ideas, or events interact and develop over the course of the text. **RI 6** Determine an author's point of view or purpose in a text in which the rhetoric is particularly effective, analyzing how style and content contribute to the power of the text.

> *How do you* AFFIRM LIFE?
> **Possible answer:** Such events can be prevented. When people are aware of the atrocities of the past, they will be more vigilant to prevent similar events from occurring in the future.

Assessment Practice: Short Constructed Response

LITERARY TEXT: "ADAM"

On assessments you are expected to make inferences as you read. Practice this skill as you respond to the **short constructed response** below. Be sure to follow the steps outlined to the right of the question.

> Examine Vonnegut's description of the young doctor. What do the details in these lines convey to you about the doctor? Explain.

◀ *STRATEGIES IN ACTION*

1. Identify words and phrases that describe the young doctor.

2. List two character traits revealed by the words and phrases you identified.

3. Use the character traits from step 2 to write a thesis statement for your answer.

4. Use evidence you identified in step 1 to support your thesis.

NONFICTION TEXT: FROM "SURVIVAL IN AUSCHWITZ"

On assessments you are expected to read carefully and answer questions that focus on particular passages from a text selection. To strengthen your close-reading skills, read the **short constructed response** at left below and practice the strategies suggested at right.

> Levi identifies only one Nazi in this excerpt, describing an SS soldier briefly. What traits does this passage convey about the soldier and the Nazi regime he represents? Explain.

◀ *STRATEGIES IN ACTION*

1. List phrases that describe the SS soldier.

2. Identify a character trait to go with each phrase on your list. What does it tell you about the soldier, for example, that he makes each decision "in the fraction of a second"?

COMPARING LITERARY AND NONFICTION TEXTS

On assessments you will need to identify thematic connections between literary and nonfiction texts. Practice this valuable skill by responding to the **short constructed response** at left below and using the strategies provided at right.

> One way to identify an author's theme or message is to ask yourself, "What's the moral of the story?" or "What did this text teach me about life or about people?" For each text, write a short sentence to answer these questions. What themes or ideas do the story and the memoir share? Cite evidence from both texts to support your response.

◀ *STRATEGIES IN ACTION*

1. Remember that evidence from the text can take the form of a direct quotation, a paraphrase, or a specific synopsis.

2. Notice that the second part of the question is asking you to compare the texts. Be sure to include evidence to support each similarity you identify.

ADAM / SURVIVAL IN AUSCHWITZ / AUSCHWITZ-BIRKENAU   **1193**

Assessment Practice: Short Constructed Response

LITERARY TEXT: "ADAM" **Possible answer:** *The pink face, circles under the eyes, and yawn indicate that the doctor is a hard worker and is exhausted. He may even be working more hours than he should.*

NONFICTION TEXT: FROM "SURVIVAL IN AUSCHWITZ" **Possible answer:** *In describing how he judged whether people would live or die with only a quick glance, the passage reveals the cold inhumanity of the soldier and the Nazi regime he represents.*

COMPARING LITERARY AND NONFICTION TEXTS **Possible answer:** *Avchen's statement that the baby is "the most wonderful thing that ever happened" conveys the hopeful theme of "Adam." The passage in "Survival in Auschwitz" about how the fate of people was decided in a fraction of a second conveys the selection's theme that concentration camps showcased man's shocking capacity for cruelty. The apathy expressed about a baby's birth in "Adam" and the selection process described in "Survival in Auschwitz" both show how easy it is for people to forget the value of human life.*

DIFFERENTIATED INSTRUCTION

FOR STRUGGLING WRITERS

Remind students to review the "Strategies in Action" for each prompt. Point out to students that taking the time to follow these strategies will make it easier to write accurate answers to the questions.

Focus and Motivate

ABOUT THE AUTHOR

Have students read about O'Brien and summarize key points about his life. Ask students in what ways O'Brien, as a young man, was directly affected by the Vietnam War. *Possible answer: He was drafted, had to choose whether to serve, and spent two years in combat in Vietnam.* Then, discuss the ways his experiences in Vietnam have had a lasting impact on his life and writing.

NOTABLE QUOTE

"It's daunting to . . . invent fully realized characters. Having said all that, it's also fun to do it."—**Tim O'Brien**

Ask students how Tim O'Brien's remark summarizes the challenges and rewards of fiction writing.

DID YOU KNOW?

Tim O'Brien . . .

- described his own experiences fighting in Vietnam in the memoir *If I Die in a Combat Zone.*
- wrote stories about a fictional character, also named Tim O'Brien, in *The Things They Carried.*
- does not actually have a daughter, as the fictional Tim O'Brien does.

Responses to War

Ambush

Short Story by Tim O'Brien

Meet the Author

Tim O'Brien   born 1946

Over and over again, Tim O'Brien has presented characters who are marked by the Vietnam War. From an infantryman on his first tour of duty, to a veteran struggling to readjust to his hometown, to an antiwar radical obsessed with death, his protagonists bring to life the complex issues raised by the war.

Opening New Doors O'Brien's writing career began at an early age. One day he fled from humiliation in the Little League to the Worthington, Minnesota, library. There he found the book *Larry of the Little League,* and soothed himself by writing an imitation of it. The library's other books became an escape from "loneliness and frustration" and an outlet for O'Brien's fertile imagination. O'Brien realized that fiction would let him experience "what could have been or should have been."

A Critical Choice As a young man, O'Brien faced another new door. He returned from four years at Macalaster College, where the Vietnam War was on students' minds, to find a draft notice waiting for him. O'Brien, who opposed the war, struggled mightily with his conscience and even considered fleeing the country to avoid service. In the end, he could not bring himself to run, and he reported for duty.

What Can You Teach? O'Brien was an army infantryman from 1968 to 1970, seeing combat in Vietnam's Quang Nai province and receiving a Purple Heart. After the war, he studied at Harvard University, worked as a reporter for the *Washington Post,* and began writing novels. He asked himself, "What can you teach people, just for having been in a war?" He concluded that he could offer insight into the "complexity and ambiguity of a set of moral issues—but without preaching a moral lesson." O'Brien's nine books have all been connected to Vietnam and have vividly explored "its aftermath and effect on the human heart and mind."

Higher Ambitions Even after great success—a National Book Award and a Pulitzer Prize nomination—O'Brien still hopes to achieve more. He'd like to write a bestseller, and he works at it every day, no matter what. "You shape your own universe," he has said. "You practice all the time, then practice some more."

Author Online
Go to **thinkcentral.com**. KEYWORD: HML11-1194

THINK central

1194

Selection Resources

TEXT ANALYSIS: CONFLICT

A story's **conflict** is the struggle between opposing forces that is the basis of the story's plot. **External conflict**—a struggle between a character and some outside force—is usually easy to identify in a work of fiction. **Internal conflict**—a struggle within a character—may be more subtle and complex. For example, an internal conflict may revolve around a decision a character has to make, or it may be reflected in behavior that is contradictory. As you read this story, watch for the development of internal conflicts in the main character.

READING SKILL: ANALYZE STRUCTURE

The **structure** of a literary work is the way in which it is put together—the arrangement of its parts. Tim O'Brien's story "Ambush" includes a **frame story,** or a story within a story. The first paragraph provides a frame—the narrator recalls answering a question his daughter once asked him. In the second paragraph, he begins to recount in a **flashback** an experience he had earlier, during the war. As you read, use a chart like the one below to summarize what happens within the outer story and the inner story.

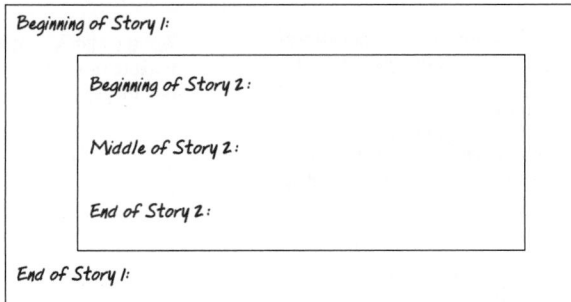

Beginning of Story 1:

Beginning of Story 2:

Middle of Story 2:

End of Story 2:

End of Story 1:

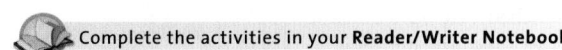

Complete the activities in your **Reader/Writer Notebook**.

How does the PAST *affect the present?*

Perhaps more than any group in society, war veterans carry a difficult past. Some remember combat experiences vividly, some block them out entirely. The lucky ones find a way to reconcile their past with the present, to use the lessons of battle to inform their present perceptions and choices.

QUICKWRITE Think about war veterans you know or have heard about. They might have served in Vietnam, in the Persian Gulf, or in an international peacekeeping mission. Imagine one specific way in which a veteran's past experiences might affect his or her present life. How might they affect a father's relationship with his children, for example? Write down your thoughts and discuss them in a group.

1195

How does the PAST *affect the present?*

Tell students to read the paragraph. Have students reflect on the particular physical, psychological, and emotional past that combat veterans carry. After they complete the *QUICK-WRITE*, ask groups to share their conclusions.

TEXT ANALYSIS   COMMON CORE

RL 3

● *Model the Skill:* CONFLICT

To identify a story's conflict, write this passage on the board:

> Carl could still remember the exact moment, nearly 40 years ago, as though it had occurred only yesterday. His best friend, Greg Loomis, was less than 70 yards behind him on the road when Carl saw the flash. It happened so fast, though it seemed like slow motion at the time. One second Greg was there, the next, he was gone. Forever. "Nothing you could've done," the sergeant insisted. But the voice inside Carl's head disagreed. *You should have spotted that sniper,* the voice told him again and again and again.

Ask students what internal conflict Carl is experiencing. ***Possible answer:*** *Carl feels responsible for the death of his friend because he failed to spot the sniper.*

GUIDED PRACTICE Ask students for other examples of internal conflicts from fiction or real life.

READING SKILL   COMMON CORE

RL 5

■ *Model the Skill:* ANALYZE STRUCTURE

To model this reading skill, have students reread the posted passage and explain its structure. ***Possible answer:*** *The passage is set in the present but built around Carl's flashback to the past.*

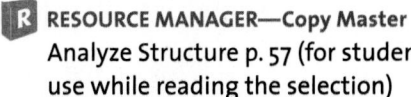 RESOURCE MANAGER—Copy Master Analyze Structure p. 57 (for student use while reading the selection)

DIFFERENTIATED INSTRUCTION

FOR STRUGGLING READERS
Vocabulary Support
- *subtle,* "slight and thus difficult to recognize"
- *contradictory,* "seeming to go in opposite directions; inconsistent"
- *flashback,* "a break in the typical time order sequence of a story, during which a scene showing past events is inserted"

- *international peacekeeping mission,* "soldiers from many nations sent into an area of conflict by an international organization such as the United Nations to keep peace but often not authorized to fight"

Practice and Apply

SUMMARY

In this short story, the narrator's young daughter, knowing that her father writes war stories, asks him if he has ever killed anyone. He says no, but resolves to tell her the truth one day. He then recalls that he did kill someone in Vietnam. While he was standing guard in the jungle, a young Vietnamese soldier approached. Instinctively, the narrator threw a grenade, killing the soldier. The narrator realizes that he could have let the man pass unharmed. Years later, the incident still haunts him.

READ WITH A PURPOSE

Help students set a purpose for reading. Tell them to read this story to learn what is haunting the narrator.

TEXT ANALYSIS   **COMMON CORE**   RL 3

Ⓐ CONFLICT

Possible answer: The conflict that the narrator faces is deciding what answer to give his daughter. That is, he doesn't want to tell her that he killed someone, but at the same time he is reluctant to lie to her.

READING SKILL   **COMMON CORE**   RL 5

Ⓑ *Model the Skill:* ANALYZE STRUCTURE

Point out to students that the colon the author placed at the end of line 8 signals a shift in setting. The paragraph beginning with line 9 is an explanation or example. Have students record the frame story in the chart on page 1195.

Possible answer: The setting shifts from the narrator's home in the present to a trail in Vietnam in the past.

Ambush

Tim O'Brien

> **BACKGROUND** "Ambush" is a short story based upon the writer's combat experiences in Vietnam. The Vietnam War lasted nine years, left 58,000 Americans dead, and left another 365,000 Americans wounded. Although they were better equipped and trained than the enemy, American troops fought in an unfamiliar landscape for a cause that many of them did not support or understand. Vietnamese Communists were skilled guerilla fighters whose tactics created a climate of frustration, confusion, and fear. American soldiers never knew when an attack might come and were haunted by their memories long after the war.

Analyze Visuals ▶
What **tone** is conveyed by this image?

When she was nine, my daughter Kathleen asked if I had ever killed anyone. She knew about the war; she knew I'd been a soldier. "You keep writing these war stories," she said, "so I guess you must've killed somebody." It was a difficult moment, but I did what seemed right, which was to say, "Of course not," and then to take her onto my lap and hold her for a while. Someday, I hope, she'll ask again. But here I want to pretend she's a grown-up. I want to tell her exactly what happened, or what I remember happening, and then I want to say to her that as a little girl she was absolutely right. This is why I keep writing war stories: Ⓐ

He was a short, slender young man of about twenty. I was afraid of him—afraid
10 of something—and as he passed me on the trail I threw a grenade that exploded at his feet and killed him. Ⓑ

Ⓐ **CONFLICT**
Reread lines 1–8. What **internal conflict** does the narrator face in the first paragraph?

Ⓑ **ANALYZE STRUCTURE**
Reread lines 9–11. How does the **setting** of the story shift in the second paragraph?

❶ **Targeted Passage**

The Green Machine (1977), Frank Dahmer.
Screenprint on paper, 13¹/₂″ × 17¹/₄″.
© National Vietnam Veterans Art Museum.

DIFFERENTIATED INSTRUCTION

FOR ENGLISH LANGUAGE LEARNERS

Vocabulary Support Have students skim the story and make a list of any words that are unfamiliar to them. Tell students to use a dictionary to find the definitions for the words they listed. Have students practice using each of their words in a sentence.

FOR STRUGGLING READERS

In combination with the *Audio Anthology CD*, use one or both Targeted Passages (pp. 1196, 1199) to ensure that students focus on key story events and concepts. Targeted Passages are also good for English language learners.

❶ **Targeted Passage** [Lines 1–11]

This passage introduces the narrator, identifies the key event, and establishes the frame story.

READING SKILL

 ANALYZE STRUCTURE

Possible answer: *Line 12 signals a further transition from the present to the past. The narrator is indicating that he will now use a detailed flashback to explain in greater detail the event described in lines 9–11.*

IF STUDENTS NEED HELP . . . Have them reread lines 1–11. Clarify that "to go back" (line 12) means to go back in time to recall exactly what happened on the trail that day.

READING SKILL

D ANALYZE STRUCTURE

Possible answer: *In lines 13–53, the narrator recalls being on guard in the jungle when a young Vietnamese soldier walked down the trail. Acting reflexively, the narrator threw a grenade at the soldier, killing him. These lines relate to lines 1–11 by describing the narrator's memory in response to his daughter's question.*

TIERED DISCUSSION PROMPTS

In lines 25–53, use these prompts to help students understand the narrator's actions:

Restate What does the narrator do when he sees the man? ***Possible answer:*** *He throws a grenade at him.*

Analyze Why does the narrator throw the grenade? ***Possible answer:*** *The narrator throws the grenade instinctively in a moment of terror. He is not trying to kill the soldier but just wants him to "go away" (line 38).*

Evaluate In what ways is O'Brien effective in describing the narrator's situation? Explain. ***Possible answer:*** *O'Brien is particularly effective through his use of one long paragraph packed with detail. The density of the paragraph parallels the compressed series of events that the narrator struggles to come to terms with, as well as the dense jungle setting where those events occur.*

Or to go back: **C**

Shortly after midnight we moved into the ambush site outside My Khe. The whole platoon was there, spread out in the dense brush along the trail, and for five hours nothing at all happened. We were working in two-man teams—one man on guard while the other slept, switching off every two hours—and I remember it was still dark when Kiowa shook me awake for the final watch. The night was foggy and hot. For the first few moments I felt lost, not sure about directions, groping for my helmet and weapon. I reached out and found three grenades and

20 lined them up in front of me; the pins had already been straightened for quick throwing. And then for maybe half an hour I knelt there and waited. Very gradually, in tiny slivers, dawn began to break through the fog, and from my position in the brush I could see ten or fifteen meters up the trail. The mosquitoes were fierce. I remember slapping at them, wondering if I should wake up Kiowa and ask for some repellent, then thinking it was a bad idea, then looking up and seeing the young man come out of the fog. He wore black clothing and rubber sandals and a gray ammunition belt. His shoulders were slightly stooped, his head cocked to the side as if listening for something. He seemed at ease. He carried his weapon in one hand, muzzle down, moving without any hurry up the center

30 of the trail. There was no sound at all—none that I can remember. In a way, it seemed, he was part of the morning fog, or my own imagination, but there was also the reality of what was happening in my stomach. I had already pulled the pin on a grenade. I had come up to a crouch. It was entirely automatic. I did not hate the young man; I did not see him as the enemy; I did not ponder issues of morality or politics or military duty. I crouched and kept my head low. I tried to swallow whatever was rising from my stomach, which tasted like lemonade, something fruity and sour. I was terrified. There were no thoughts about killing. The grenade was to make him go away—just evaporate—and I leaned back and felt my mind go empty and then felt it fill up again. I had already thrown the

40 grenade before telling myself to throw it. The brush was thick and I had to lob it high, not aiming, and I remember the grenade seeming to freeze above me for an instant, as if a camera had clicked, and I remember ducking down and holding my breath and seeing little wisps of fog rise from the earth. The grenade bounced once and rolled across the trail. I did not hear it, but there must've been a sound, because the young man dropped his weapon and began to run, just two or three quick steps, then he hesitated, swiveling to his right, and he glanced down at the grenade and tried to cover his head but never did. It occurred to me then that he was about to die. I wanted to warn him. The grenade made a popping noise—not soft but not loud either—not what I'd expected—and there was a puff of dust

50 and smoke—a small white puff—and the young man seemed to jerk upward as if pulled by invisible wires. He fell on his back. His rubber sandals had been blown off. There was no wind. He lay at the center of the trail, his right leg bent beneath him, his one eye shut, his other eye a huge star-shaped hole. **D**

C ANALYZE STRUCTURE In terms of the structure of this story, what does this line signal?

D ANALYZE STRUCTURE **Summarize** what happens in lines 13–53. How do these lines relate to the first paragraph of the story?

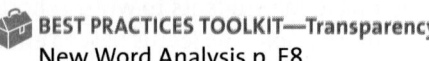

DIFFERENTIATED INSTRUCTION

FOR ENGLISH LANGUAGE LEARNERS
Vocabulary Support Use New Word Analysis to teach this word: *site* (line 13).

BEST PRACTICES TOOLKIT—Transparency New Word Analysis p. E8

FOR STRUGGLING READERS
Develop Reading Fluency Read aloud the passage in lines 38–53. Tell students to note the inflections and tone of your speech. Next, read the first sentence of the passage and have students repeat it back to you in unison. Continue until students have "echoed" each sentence in the passage. Conclude this activity by asking for a volunteer to read the entire passage aloud to the class.

Come a Little Closer (1997), Michael Brostowitz. Oil on board, 15$\frac{1}{4}$" × 19$\frac{3}{4}$". © National Vietnam Veterans Art Museum.

It was not a matter of live or die. There was no real peril. Almost certainly the young man would have passed by. And it will always be that way.

Later, I remember, Kiowa tried to tell me that the man would've died anyway. He told me that it was a good kill, that I was a soldier and this was a war, that I should shape up and stop staring and ask myself what the dead man would've done if things were reversed.

60   None of it mattered. The words seemed far too complicated. All I could do was gape at the fact of the young man's body. **E**

Even now I haven't finished sorting it out. Sometimes I forgive myself, other times I don't. In the ordinary hours of life I try not to dwell on it, but now and then, when I'm reading a newspaper or just sitting alone in a room, I'll look up and see the young man coming out of the morning fog. I'll watch him walk toward me, his shoulders slightly stooped, his head cocked to the side, and he'll pass within a few yards of me and suddenly smile at some secret thought and then continue up the trail to where it bends back into the fog. ∾ **F**

E CONFLICT
Reread lines 54–61. What **internal conflict** does the narrator express?

② **Targeted Passage**

F CONFLICT
How does the vision the narrator imagines in lines 63–68 help resolve his conflict?

Analyze Visuals

Activity Discuss ways in which the color and light in the painting might affect the narrator's emotional state. *Possible answer: Such surroundings might add to the narrator's fear by limiting vision.*

About the Art Michael Brostowitz (born 1950) served in Vietnam and, like the story narrator, struggles with his memories.

TEXT ANALYSIS   COMMON CORE   RL 3

E *Model the Skill:* **CONFLICT**

Tell students that the narrator's internal conflict comes from his second-guessing his decision and debating what he should, or should not, have done.

Possible answer: The narrator feels deep ambivalence over killing the Vietnamese soldier. He reacted reflexively and, as Kiowa assured him, made "a good kill," one the Vietnamese soldier would likely have made in the reverse situation. However, there was no immediate danger, and the soldier might have walked past without incident.

TEXT ANALYSIS   COMMON CORE   RL 3

F CONFLICT

Possible answer: The narrator's vision allows him to imagine that he did not throw the grenade, and the Vietnamese soldier continued up the trail unharmed.

SELECTION WRAP-UP

READ WITH A PURPOSE Ask students if they think the narrator would be free of internal conflict if he hadn't killed the Vietnamese soldier. *Possible answer: It's possible that the narrator would be free of internal conflict, but had the Vietnamese soldier lived, he might have later killed one of the narrator's friends, causing the narrator to be even more intensely haunted.*

FOR STRUGGLING READERS

② **Targeted Passage** [Lines 56–68]

This concluding passage shows clearly that the narrator's wartime act continues to trouble him in the present.

- In what ways does Kiowa respond to the narrator's actions? (lines 56–59)

- What does the narrator feel about what he did? (lines 62–63)

- What image lingers in the narrator's mind? (lines 64–68)

FOR ADVANCED LEARNERS/AP

Analyze Author's Tone Have students work in small groups to discuss the author's tone in the story. Ask whether the author appears to approve or disapprove of the narrator's actions, or whether he remains neutral. Extend the discussion by asking students if they think that author and narrator share one mind. If not, in what ways do they differ? Have groups share and compare their conclusions.

Practice and Apply

For preliminary support of post-reading questions, use these copy masters:

R **RESOURCE MANAGER**—Copy Masters
Reading Check p. 59
Conflict p. 55
Question Support p. 60
Additional selection questions are provided for teachers on page 49.

ANSWERS

 **COMMON CORE RL 3, RL 5**

1. *The narrator tells his daughter, "Of course not."*

2. *He was on guard in the jungle when a Vietnamese soldier approached. The narrator threw a grenade at the soldier, killing him.*

3. *He sees the soldier walking toward him, passing by, smiling, and walking on up the trail.*

Possible answers:

4. ● **COMMON CORE FOCUS Conflict** *The narrator feels conflicted about whether or not to tell his young daughter he killed someone. He tells her no, but hopes to tell her the truth "someday" (line 5). The narrator also feels conflicted about whether his war killing was acceptable. He writes war stories to try to resolve his several internal conflicts.*

5. ■ **COMMON CORE FOCUS Analyze Structure** *The frame shows the ways the wartime incident affected the narrator and continues to affect him.*

6. *The title refers to the narrator's fear of attack and to his surprise attack on the soldier. It also refers to the way his memory affects him unexpectedly in the present.*

Assess and Reteach

Assess

DIAGNOSTIC AND SELECTION TESTS
Selection Test A pp. 317–318
Selection Test B/C pp. 319–320

Interactive Selection Test on thinkcentral.com

Reteach

Level Up Online Tutorials on thinkcentral.com

Reteaching Worksheets on thinkcentral.com
Literature Lesson 6: Conflict and Suspense
Literature Lesson 8: Foreshadowing and Flashback

Comprehension

1. **Recall** What does the narrator tell his daughter when she asks if he ever killed someone?

2. **Summarize** What happened to the narrator outside My Khe?

3. **Clarify** What vision does the narrator sometimes see in his mind?

Text Analysis

● 4. **Examine Conflicts** Identify the **internal conflicts** the narrator experiences in this story. How would you describe the way he resolves or tries to resolve them? Explain your answer.

■ 5. **Analyze Structure** What does the **frame** contribute to the impact of this story? Consider what would be lost without the first and last paragraphs.

6. **Interpret Title** In what ways does the title "Ambush" relate to the events of the story? Think about the frame as well as the inner story.

7. **Evaluate a Character's Actions** Kiowa tells the narrator that this "was a good kill." Do you agree? In your opinion, can there be a "good kill"?

8. **Apply Theme** What does this story suggest about the effects of the **past** on the present?

9. **Compare Texts** Compare "Ambush" and "Why Soldiers Won't Talk" (page 1172) as portrayals of a soldier's experience. On a chart, note what each presents as the physical sensations and emotional aftereffects of war. Which piece—the story or the essay—had more impact on you? Why?

	Physical Sensations	Emotional Aftereffects
"Ambush"		
"Why Soldiers Won't Talk"		

Text Criticism

10. **Author's Style** "Ambush" is a work of fiction, but the story reads like a nonfiction account of a true event. To readers who wonder how much of his work is actually true, O'Brien responds, "The literal truth is . . . irrelevant." Do you agree? Does it matter that O'Brien the writer does not have a daughter and does not know whether he ever killed anyone?

How does the **PAST** *affect the present?*

How does O'Brien's story convey the effects of the past on the present? Cite evidence from the story to support your answer.

COMMON CORE

RL 3 Analyze the impact of the author's choices regarding how to develop and relate elements of a story. **RL 5** Analyze how an author's choices concerning how to structure specific parts of a text contribute to its overall structure and meaning, as well as its aesthetic impact.

---

7. *Answers will vary. Students should support their opinions with clear reasons.*

8. *The story suggests that past experiences never stop impacting people in the present.*

9. *"Ambush": Physical: feeling of fear in stomach, "fruity and sour" taste in mouth (lines 32, 35–37). Emotional: continued inner conflict over actions (lines 62–63). "Why Soldiers Won't Talk": Physical: "skin feels thick and insensitive"; "salty taste"; "hard, painful knot" in stomach; "objects are slightly blurred" (lines 22–25). Emotional: details of combat become dreamlike, and soldiers' memory fades (lines 10–11).*

Students should support their choice of which piece had more impact.

10. *Accept all thoughtful responses.*

How does the PAST *affect the present?* ***Possible answer:*** *The story shows that the past can influence what a person does many years later. For example, the narrator is haunted by a wartime experience, so he continues to write war stories.*

The Literary Legacy of War

Modernist writer Gertrude Stein once said, "War is never fatal but always lost. Always lost." One after another, the wars of the 20th century forced Americans to reconcile their sense of patriotism with the disillusionment that naturally comes from facing the realities of modern warfare. If it is an artist's job to find meaning, what meaning can be discerned from the act of war?

Writing to Synthesize

Each of the texts you have just read presents a variety of ideas and images in response to World War II and the Vietnam War. What do these pieces have in common? Reread the selections, pulling words or phrases from each that you find especially compelling—whether beautiful, ugly, moving, or surprising. When you have gathered 15–30 phrases, combine them artfully to create a poem that delivers a coherent impression about war. Your poem might tell a story, describe an image, or deliver a set of thoughts or pronouncements. It can take place on the battlefield or on the home front.

Consider

- what primary thought or feeling you were left with after reading all of the texts
- which parts of each selection had the strongest impact on you
- how to arrange the phrases in a way that communicates your own response to the texts

Extension

SPEAKING AND LISTENING Give an **oral reading** of your poem, using your voice, posture, and gestures to emphasize its meaning. If you think it would be effective, consider performing a choral reading with some of your classmates or setting your poem to music.

COMMON CORE

W 9 Draw evidence from literary or informational texts to support analysis, reflection, and research. **SL 6** Adapt speech to a variety of contexts and tasks.

American soldiers in Vietnam

COMMON CORE FOCUS

W 9 Draw evidence from literary or informational texts to support analysis, reflection, and research. **SL 6** Adapt speech to a variety of contexts and tasks.

Wrap-Up: Responses to War

This Wrap-Up provides students with an opportunity to revisit ideas and reactions relating to the wars of the 20th century and to reflect on the expression of these ideas and feelings through literature. Encourage students to consider ways in which the selections affected their views.

Writing to Synthesize

- Review with students that *synthesizing* means combining ideas and facts with other information and prior knowledge in order to better understand a subject or develop new ideas. Through synthesis, students can draw conclusions about common themes in the selections they have read and gain deeper insight into the writers of the time.

- To help students choose their words and phrases from the selections, suggest that they look for vivid images and sensory details as well as sentences that made them stop and think or affected them emotionally. Urge students to sort through the chosen text, highlighting text that best fits the particular impression they wish to make.

Extension

- Encourage students to prepare for their oral reading by identifying words and phrases to emphasize and places to pause for effect or to adjust speaking volume.

- Suggest that students consider working with a partner, either alternating lines or reading lines together.

- Caution students setting their poems to music to select music that complements their presentation rather than distracts from it.

FOR STRUGGLING WRITERS

Writing Support Remind students that fiction, nonfiction, and poetry all can be a source of memorable words and phrases. Offer such examples as these: "eyeballs . . . so beaten that the earth and the air seem to shudder" (lines 31–32 of "Why Soldiers Won't Talk"), "they washed me out of the turret with a hose" (line 5 of "The Death of the Ball Turret Gunner"), and "Sometimes I forgive myself, other times I don't" (lines 62–63 of "Ambush").

FOR ENGLISH LANGUAGE LEARNERS

Gathering Words and Phrases Have students use a Three-Column Journal:

Vivid Images	Sensory Details	Memorable Sentences
" . . . his other eye a huge star-shaped hole"	"skin feels thick and insensitive"; "salty taste"	" . . . they washed me out of the turret . . ."

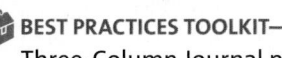 **BEST PRACTICES TOOLKIT—Transparency** Three-Column Journal p. B10

COMMON CORE FOCUS

RI 1 Cite textual evidence to support analysis of what the text says explicitly as well as inferences drawn from the text. **RI 4** Determine the meaning of words and phrases as they are used in a text, including figurative and connotative meanings; analyze how an author uses and refines the meaning of a key term or terms over the course of a text. **RI 6** Determine an author's point of view or purpose in a text in which the rhetoric is particularly effective, analyzing how style and content contribute to the power, persuasiveness, or beauty of the text. **W 1** Write arguments to support claims in an analysis of substantive topics. **L 3a** Vary syntax for effect; apply an understanding of syntax to the study of complex texts when reading. **L 5** Demonstrate understanding of word relationships.

ABOUT THE AUTHOR

Point out words that describe King, such as *eloquent, shrewd,* and *visionary.* Discuss the role of leaders like King in the history of social justice. Ask students if charismatic leaders are an essential element of social change, and why.
Possible answer: *Yes; charismatic leaders galvanize people's emotions and efforts.*

NOTABLE QUOTE

" *The ultimate measure of a man is not where he stands in moments of comfort and convenience, but where he stands at times of challenge and controversy.*"
—**Martin Luther King, Jr.**

Clarify the figurative language in King's quotation: *measure of a man,* "the depth of a man's character"; *where he stands,* "a man's moral position." Have students explain King's meaning.

Civil Rights and Protest Literature

from Letter from Birmingham Jail

Letter by Martin Luther King Jr.

VIDEO TRAILER THINKcentral KEYWORD: HML11-1202A

HISTORY Video link at thinkcentral.com
Essential Course of Study ECOS

COMMON CORE

RI 1 Cite textual evidence to support analysis of what the text says explicitly as well as inferences drawn from the text. **RI 4** Determine the meaning of words and phrases as they are used in a text, including figurative and connotative meanings; analyze how an author uses and refines the meaning of a key term or terms over the course of a text. **RI 6** Determine an author's point of view or purpose in a text in which the rhetoric is particularly effective, analyzing how style and content contribute to the power, persuasiveness, or beauty of the text. **RI 8** Delineate and evaluate the reasoning in seminal U.S. texts, including the premises, purposes, and arguments in works of public advocacy.

DID YOU KNOW?

Martin Luther King Jr. . . .

- enrolled in college when he was 15 years old.
- was the first African American to be named *Time* magazine's "Man of the Year."
- won the Nobel Peace Prize in 1964.
- was arrested 30 times for his activism.

Meet the Author

Martin Luther King Jr. 1929–1968

An eloquent orator, a shrewd tactician, and a visionary leader, Martin Luther King Jr. became the catalyst for some of the most far-reaching social changes in U.S. history. Under his skillful leadership, the civil rights movement spurred passage of the Civil Rights Act of 1964 and the Voting Rights Act of 1965, laws that legally abolished racial segregation and voting discrimination. A tireless advocate for justice, King wrote five books, delivered about 2,500 speeches, and traveled more than 6 million miles in an effort to make his dream of equality a reality.

Boycott in Montgomery It was in Alabama that King first emerged as a civil rights leader to be reckoned with. In 1955, when Rosa Parks was arrested for breaking Montgomery's bus segregation laws, local civil rights advocates banded together to form a protest organization. They chose King, then pastor of the Dexter Avenue Baptist Church, to lead the new group. King mobilized African Americans to boycott city buses. The 381-day boycott tested the endurance of the entire black community, especially King, who was subjected to threats and bomb attacks. The steadfast boycotters ultimately triumphed, and the U.S. Supreme Court struck down the city's bus segregation laws. The success of the boycott launched the charismatic young leader onto the national stage, where he promoted his bold strategy: using nonviolent, direct action to achieve social change.

Expanding Influence King cautiously expanded the civil rights struggle throughout the South. He was particularly effective at organizing interracial coalitions to put pressure on lawmakers. One shining moment came at the 1963 March on Washington, a gathering of about 250,000 peaceful demonstrators supporting civil rights legislation. King's impassioned "I Have a Dream" speech, delivered on the steps of the Lincoln Memorial, is considered one of the greatest speeches in U.S. history.

Warrior for Peace King never wavered in his commitment to nonviolence and tried to extend his campaign to fight poverty and end the Vietnam War. Ultimately, he was unable to stem the surge of violence that overtook the country in the mid-1960s. In 1968, King was assassinated in Memphis, where he had gone to support a sanitation workers' strike. In the 12 years between the Montgomery boycott and his death, he had helped achieve the greatest advance in racial justice since the abolition of slavery.

Author Online
Go to **thinkcentral.com**. KEYWORD: HML11-1202B

THINK central

1202

---

*See resources on the **Teacher One Stop DVD-ROM** and on **thinkcentral.com**.*

Video link at
thinkcentral.com

 RESOURCE MANAGER UNIT 6
   Plan and Teach, pp. 61–68
   Summary, pp. 69–70‡*
   Text Analysis and Reading
      Skill, pp. 71–74†*
   Vocabulary, pp. 75–77*
   Grammar and Style, p. 80

DIAGNOSTIC AND SELECTION TESTS
   Selection Tests, pp. 321–324

 BEST PRACTICES TOOLKIT
   Definition Mapping, p. E6
   Three-Column Journal, p. B10
   Outline, p. B19

INTERACTIVE READER

ADAPTED INTERACTIVE READER

ELL ADAPTED INTERACTIVE READER

TECHNOLOGY

- **Teacher One Stop DVD-ROM**
- **Student One Stop DVD-ROM**
- **PowerNotes DVD-ROM**
- **Audio Anthology CD**
- **GrammarNotes DVD-ROM**
- **ExamView Test Generator** on the **Teacher One Stop**

Video Trailer  THINK central

Go to **thinkcentral.com** to preview the **Video Trailer** introducing this selection. Other features that support the selection include

- **PowerNotes** presentation
- **ThinkAloud** models to enhance comprehension
- **WordSharp** vocabulary tutorials
- interactive writing and grammar instruction

---

* Resources for Differentiation   † Also in Spanish   ‡ In Haitian Creole and Vietnamese

TEXT ANALYSIS: ALLUSION

An **allusion** is a reference within a work to historical, literary, or cultural details from outside the work. Writers choose allusions that are familiar to their target audience. In this case, because King is writing to fellow clergymen, he uses references to the Bible and to religious scholars to make his points.

I would agree with St. Augustine that "an unjust law is no law at all."

King's allusions help connect current events with respected historical and religious figures. As you read, use the footnotes to help you understand King's allusions.

READING SKILL: ELEMENTS OF AN ARGUMENT

King's letter is a beautifully written **argument** defending his activism. In it, King uses **deductive reasoning** to respond to public criticism. Deductive reasoning occurs when a writer arrives at a conclusion by applying a general principal to a specific situation. As you read, use King's restatements to infer what the opposing positions are and record them in a chart like the one below. Then, record the general principle King gives as a counterargument and the reasons and evidence he uses to support them.

Position of Opponents	General Principles	Reasons and Evidence
King doesn't belong in Birmingham.	"I am here because I have organizational ties here."	• leads the SCLC • invited by affiliated organization

▲ VOCABULARY IN CONTEXT

King uses the following words to argue his views. Test yourself by replacing each boldfaced term with one vocabulary word.

WORD LIST		
affiliated	moratorium	scintillating
cognizant	paradoxical	substantive
estrangement	rabid	
latent	retaliating	

1. **aware** of the difficulties involved
2. **hidden** emotions called up by the encounter
3. **contradictory** views seemed to say two things at once
4. **temporary stoppage** on further discussions

 Complete the activities in your **Reader/Writer Notebook**.

When does ACTION *speak louder than words?*

When you're trying to confront a difficult issue, words are your first option. But once you've explained your position, presented your demands, and tried unsuccessfully to convince others to make a change, you're at the point when words give way to action. Martin Luther King Jr. explains how civil rights activists in Birmingham, Alabama, faced their own decisive moment in 1963.

DISCUSS When do you respond with words and when do you turn to action? Working with a small group, brainstorm situations that call for each type of response. What guidelines did you use to classify your examples?

1203

When does ACTION *speak louder than words?*

After groups complete the *DISCUSS* activity, invite volunteers to share their guidelines.

TEXT ANALYSIS COMMON CORE RI 4

● *Model the Skill:* ALLUSION

Explain that allusions lend credibility to a writer's argument by suggesting that recognized sources on the topic support that argument. Clarify that St. Augustine is regarded as one of Christianity's greatest theologians.

GUIDED PRACTICE Identify topics and audiences; have students suggest historical, literary, or cultural figures as allusions.

READING SKILL COMMON CORE RI 1 RI 6

■ ELEMENTS OF AN ARGUMENT

As students complete their charts, urge them to evaluate the effectiveness of each of King's arguments.

R RESOURCE MANAGER—Copy Master Elements of an Argument p. 73 (for student use while reading the selection)

VOCABULARY SKILL COMMON CORE L 4

▲ VOCABULARY IN CONTEXT

DIAGNOSE WORD KNOWLEDGE Have all students complete Vocabulary in Context.

Check their word choices against the following:

affiliated (ə-fĭl′ē-ā′tĭd) *adj.* joined in close association **affiliate** *v.*

cognizant (kŏg′nĭ-zənt) *adj.* aware

estrangement (ĭ-strānj′mənt) *n.* separation; alienation

latent (lāt′nt) *adj.* existing in a hidden form

moratorium (môr′ə-tôr′ē-əm) *n.* a temporary stoppage or waiting period

paradoxical (păr′ə-dŏk′sĭ-kəl) *adj.* self-contradictory

rabid (răb′ĭd) *adj.* unreasonably extreme; fanatical

retaliating (rĭ-tăl′ē-ā′tĭng) *n.* taking revenge **retaliate** *v.*

scintillating (sĭn′tl-ā′tĭng) *adj.* sparkling **scintillate** *v.*

substantive (sŭb′stən-tĭv) *adj.* significant; with a strong basis

PRETEACH VOCABULARY Preteach vocabulary with this copy master. Read each item aloud.

R RESOURCE MANAGER—Copy Master Vocabulary Study p. 75

Practice and Apply

SUMMARY

In this excerpt from his letter responding to the criticism of white clergymen, Martin Luther King, Jr., justifies his direct-action approach to ending segregation in the South. He alludes to religious and philosophical leaders and events to legitimize the campaign's methods and goals. Recalling the deplorable conditions that led to the direct-action campaigns, King stresses that the goal is to force negotiation. He argues, relying on the ideas of St. Thomas Aquinas and others for support, that people have a moral obligation to disobey unjust laws, and he invites the clergymen to support his efforts.

READ WITH A PURPOSE

Help students set a purpose for reading. Tell them to read the excerpt to discover what King hoped to accomplish in Birmingham.

READING SKILL   COMMON CORE

A ELEMENTS OF AN ARGUMENT   RI 1   RI 6

Possible answer: Lines 10–11 contain the sentence that restates the position against which King argues. That position is that outsiders should not get involved in the racial strife in Birmingham.

VOCABULARY   COMMON CORE   L 4

OWN THE WORD

affiliated: Inform students that when someone becomes *affiliated* with someone else, they "become closely connected," usually with a common goal. Ask students to list people or groups to whom they have an *affiliation*. **Possible answers:** *family, friends, community groups, neighborhoods, sports teams*

Letter from Birmingham Jail

Martin Luther King Jr.

BACKGROUND In the spring of 1963, Martin Luther King Jr. and his organization, the Southern Christian Leadership Conference (SCLC), targeted Birmingham, Alabama, with a series of peaceful demonstrations aimed at ending segregation. The police reacted violently with attack dogs and high-pressure fire hoses. Hundreds of protesters, including King, were jailed. At first, King was criticized for taking on Birmingham; eight white clergymen published a letter calling his actions "unwise and untimely." But he responded with his own letter citing philosophers, religious scholars, and biblical figures to justify his actions.

April 16, 1963

My Dear Fellow Clergymen:

While confined here in the Birmingham city jail, I came across your recent statement calling my present activities "unwise and untimely." Seldom do I pause to answer criticism of my work and ideas. If I sought to answer all the criticisms that cross my desk, my secretaries would have little time for anything other than such correspondence in the course of the day, and I would have no time for constructive work. But since I feel that you are men of genuine good will and that your criticisms are sincerely set forth, I want to try to answer your statement in what I hope will be patient and reasonable terms.

10   I think I should indicate why I am here in Birmingham, since you have been influenced by the view which argues against "outsiders coming in." I have the honor of serving as president of the Southern Christian Leadership Conference, an organization operating in every Southern state, with headquarters in Atlanta, Georgia. We have some eighty-five **affiliated** organizations across the South, and one of them is the Alabama Christian Movement for Human Rights. Frequently we share staff, educational, and financial resources with our affiliates. Several months ago the affiliate here in Birmingham asked us to be on call to engage in a nonviolent direct-action program if such were deemed necessary. We readily consented, and when the hour came, we lived up to our promise. So I, along with

20   several members of my staff, am here because I was invited here. I am here because I have organizational ties here. **A**

But more basically, I am in Birmingham because injustice is here. Just as the prophets of the eighth century B.C. left their villages and carried their "thus saith the Lord" far beyond the boundaries of their home towns, and just as the Apostle Paul left his village of Tarsus and carried the gospel of Jesus Christ to the

Analyze Visuals ▶
Look at this photograph of King in his jail cell in Birmingham. Based on the photo, what impressions do you have of his state of mind while in jail?

① Targeted Passage

affiliated (ə-fĭl′ē-ā′tĭd) *adj.* joined in close association **affiliate** *v.*

A ELEMENTS OF AN ARGUMENT
Reread lines 10–21. Which sentence refers to the position that King is arguing against?

King in his jail cell in Birmingham

DIFFERENTIATED INSTRUCTION

FOR ENGLISH LANGUAGE LEARNERS

Vocabulary Support Use Definition Mapping to teach these words: *indicate* (line 10), *create* (line 86), *distort* (line 134), *positive* (line 223), *environment* (line 290).

🧰 **BEST PRACTICES TOOLKIT—Transparency**
Definition Mapping p. E6

FOR STRUGGLING READERS

In combination with the *Audio Anthology CD*, use one or more Targeted Passages (pp. 1204, 1206, 1209, 1212) to ensure that students focus on key concepts in the selection. Targeted Passages are also good for English language learners.

① Targeted Passage [Lines 1–9]

This passage advances King's purpose for writing—to explain his actions in Birmingham to clergy who criticize them.

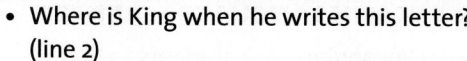

Reading Support

This selection on **thinkcentral.com** includes embedded **ThinkAloud** models—students "thinking aloud" about the story to model the kinds of questions a good reader would ask about a selection.

Analyze Visuals

Possible answer: *Due to the soft lighting, the upturned face, and the finger to the chin, King appears peaceful and contemplative.*

BACKGROUND

Southern Christian Leadership Conference (SCLC) In 1957, African-American church leaders and ministers formed the SCLC. The success of the Montgomery bus boycott led African-American leaders to believe that nonviolent social protest had the potential to end segregation and achieve social equality for African Americans. They believed that an organization was needed to coordinate nonviolent protests throughout the South. These leaders encouraged other African Americans to seek justice and reject injustice while dedicating themselves to the principal of nonviolence. During the 1950s and early 1960s, the SCLC spearheaded the civil rights movement in America through a succession of protest campaigns that garnered national attention.

- Where is King when he writes this letter? (line 2)
- To whom does King address his letter? (line 1)
- Why does King usually not respond to criticism of his work and ideas? (lines 4–7)
- Why does King answer this criticism in particular? (lines 7–9)

FOR ADVANCED LEARNERS/AP

Make Judgments Tell students to identify an injustice that exists today. Instruct students to devise a strategy to end the injustice they selected. Have students present their strategies to the class. Discuss as a class the merits of each strategy.

1206 UNIT 6: CONTEMPORARY LITERATURE

---

far corners of the Greco-Roman world, so am I compelled to carry the gospel of freedom beyond my own hometown. Like Paul, I must constantly respond to the Macedonian call for aid.[1]

Moreover, I am **cognizant** of the interrelatedness of all communities and
30 states. I cannot sit idly by in Atlanta and not be concerned about what happens in Birmingham. Injustice anywhere is a threat to justice everywhere. We are caught in an inescapable network of mutuality, tied in a single garment of destiny. Whatever affects one directly, affects all indirectly. Never again can we afford to live with the narrow, provincial "outside agitator" idea. Anyone who lives inside the United States can never be considered an outsider anywhere within its bounds.

You deplore the demonstrations taking place in Birmingham. But your statement, I am sorry to say, fails to express a similar concern for the conditions that brought about the demonstrations. I am sure that none of you would want to rest content with the superficial kind of social analysis that deals merely
40 with effects and does not grapple with underlying causes. It is unfortunate that demonstrations are taking place in Birmingham, but it is even more unfortunate that the city's white power structure left the Negro community with no alternative.

In any nonviolent campaign there are four basic steps: collection of the facts to determine whether injustices exist; negotiation; self-purification; and direct action. We have gone through all these steps in Birmingham. There can be no gainsaying the fact that racial injustice engulfs this community. Birmingham is probably the most thoroughly segregated city in the United States. Its ugly record of brutality is widely known. Negroes have experienced grossly unjust treatment in the courts.
50 There have been more unsolved bombings of Negro homes and churches in Birmingham than in any other city in the nation. These are the hard, brutal facts of the case. On the basis of these conditions, Negro leaders sought to negotiate with the city fathers. But the latter consistently refused to engage in good-faith negotiations.

Then, last September, came the opportunity to talk with leaders of Birmingham's economic community. In the course of the negotiations, certain promises were made by the merchants— for example, to remove the stores' humiliating racial signs.[2] On the basis of these promises, the Reverend Fred Shuttlesworth and the leaders of the Alabama Christian Movement for Human
60 Rights agreed to a **moratorium** on all demonstrations. As the weeks and months went by, we realized that we were the victims of a broken promise. A few signs, briefly removed, returned; the others remained.

As in so many past experiences, our hopes had been blasted, and the shadow of deep disappointment settled upon us. We had no alternative except to prepare for direct action, whereby we would present our very bodies as a means of laying our case before the conscience of the local and the national community. Mindful of the difficulties involved, we decided to undertake a process of self-purification.

---

1. **Macedonian** (măs′ĭ-dō′nē-ən) **call for aid:** According to the Bible (Acts 16), the apostle Paul received a vision calling him to preach in Macedonia, an area north of Greece.

2. **racial signs:** signs marking segregated buildings and other facilities.

1206 UNIT 6: CONTEMPORARY LITERATURE

DIFFERENTIATED INSTRUCTION

FOR STRUGGLING READERS

 Targeted Passage [Lines 44–54]

This passage identifies the four basic steps for a nonviolent campaign in Birmingham.

- What are the four basic steps for a nonviolent campaign? (lines 44–45)

- Which steps have been completed in Birmingham, and to what result? (lines 46–47)

- What circumstances justify a nonviolent campaign in Birmingham? (lines 47–51)

FOR ENGLISH LANGUAGE LEARNERS

Related Vocabulary Ask students to find words on pages 1204–1213 that fit into each of these categories: *Organizational Terms, Civil Rights Movement,* and *Reactions to Oppression.* Have students record the words in a Three-Column Journal, with each category serving as a column head.

 **BEST PRACTICES TOOLKIT—Transparency**
Three-Column Journal p. B10

We began a series of workshops on nonviolence, and we repeatedly asked
ourselves: "Are you able to accept blows without **retaliating**?" "Are you able to
70 endure the ordeal of jail?" We decided to schedule our direct-action program for
the Easter season, realizing that except for Christmas, this is the main shopping
period of the year. Knowing that a strong economic-withdrawal program[3] would
be the by-product of direct action, we felt that this would be the best time to
bring pressure to bear on the merchants for the needed change.

   Then it occurred to us that Birmingham's mayoral election was coming up in
March, and we speedily decided to postpone action until after election day. When
we discovered that the Commissioner of Public Safety, Eugene "Bull" Connor, had
piled up enough votes to be in the runoff, we decided again to postpone action
until the day after the runoff so that the demonstrations could not be used to
80 cloud the issues. Like many others, we waited to see Mr. Connor defeated, and
to this end we endured postponement after postponement. Having aided in
this community need, we felt that our direct-action program could be delayed
no longer.

   You may well ask: "Why direct action? Why sit-ins, marches, and so forth? Isn't
negotiation a better path?" You are quite right in calling for negotiation. Indeed,
this is the very purpose of direct action. Nonviolent direct action seeks to create
such a crisis and foster such a tension that a community which has constantly
refused to negotiate is forced to confront the issue. It seeks so to dramatize the
issue that it can no longer be ignored. My citing the creation of tension as part of
90 the work of the nonviolent-resister may sound rather shocking. But I must confess
that I am not afraid of the word "tension." I have earnestly opposed violent
tension, but there is a type of constructive, nonviolent tension which is necessary
for growth. Just as Socrates[4] felt that it was necessary to create a tension in the
mind so that individuals could rise from the bondage of myths and half-truths to
the unfettered realm of creative analysis and objective appraisal, so must we see the
need for nonviolent gadflies to create the kind of tension in society that will help
men rise from the dark depths of prejudice and racism to the majestic heights of
understanding and brotherhood.

   The purpose of our direct-action program is to create a situation so crisis-
100 packed that it will inevitably open the door to negotiation. I therefore concur with
you in your call for negotiation. Too long has our beloved Southland been bogged
down in a tragic effort to live in monologue rather than dialogue.

   One of the basic points in your statement is that the action that I and my
associates have taken in Birmingham is untimely. Some have asked: "Why didn't
you give the new city administration time to act?" The only answer that I can
give to this query is that the new Birmingham administration must be prodded
about as much as the outgoing one, before it will act. . . . My friends, I must say
to you that we have not made a single gain in civil rights without determined legal
and nonviolent pressure. Lamentably, it is a historical fact that privileged groups

---

3. **economic-withdrawal program:** boycott.
4. **Socrates** (sŏk′rə-tēz′): Greek philosopher (470–399 B.C.) who was a major influence in the development
   of Western thought.

---

retaliating (rǐ-tăl′ē-ā′tǐng) *n.*
taking revenge **retaliate** *v.*

COMMON CORE RI 4

Language Coach

Figurative Language
Cloud in line 80 means
"confuse or make
unclear" and is an
example of figurative
language, language that
communicates meaning
beyond the literal
meaning of the words.
How might a boycott or
economic-withdrawal
program cloud the issues
during an election?

BACKGROUND

Nonviolent Action King was inspired in his beliefs about nonviolent protest (lines 84–88) by
the life and work of Mohandas Gandhi. Gandhi
successfully worked for Indian civil rights in
South Africa and India through a principle he
developed called *satyagraha,* which is Sanskrit
for *truth* and *force.* Gandhi based his approach
on the nonviolent teachings of the Christian
Bible, Leo Tolstoy, and Henry David Thoreau.
King studied Gandhi while attending theological seminary and later traveled to India to
learn more about Gandhi's methods. These
methods of nonviolent protest became central
to the American civil rights movement.

TIERED DISCUSSION PROMPTS

In lines 84–100, use these prompts to help students understand King's philosophy of direct
action as a means for social change:

Summarize According to King, what is the
purpose of direct action? *Possible answer:
Direct action serves to force negotiation with
those who refuse to negotiate.*

Interpret What is the meaning and purpose of King's allusion to Socrates in lines
93–95? *Possible answer: King's allusion to
Socrates points out that tension is necessary
for growth in thought. Alluding to a great
philosopher lends credibility to King's ideas
about growth in the negotiation process.*

Evaluate Does King effectively support his
argument for direct action here? Explain.
*Possible answer: King's argument is effective.
He points out ways that direct action will be
effective, supporting his argument by citing
great thinkers who share his basic philosophy.*

Language Coach
COMMON CORE
RI 4

Figurative Language *Possible answer:
People might concentrate only on the
boycott instead of looking at all the issues
concerning the candidates.* Have students
read the excerpt to identify two other
examples of figurative language. Tell
students to write a short paragraph using
the two examples they identified, as well
as the word *cloud.*

FOR RELUCTANT READERS

Connect to the Text Tell students to suppose
that they are teenagers living in Birmingham
in April 1963. Have them describe how they
would respond to the civil rights events occurring in their city that spring.

VOCABULARY
COMMON
CORE
L 4

OWN THE WORD

retaliating: Tell students that *retaliating*
derives from the Latin meaning "punishment in kind." Ask students if they have
ever *retaliated* against someone and, if
so, why. How did it make them feel? Were
their actions justified? *Possible answers:
Answers may vary.*

TIERED DISCUSSION PROMPTS

In lines 110–114, use these prompts to help students understand King's views on the link between morality and oppression:

Connect Think about a time when you or someone you know stood up to a bully. In what way does that experience help you understand King's views on oppression? *Accept all thoughtful responses.*

Interpret What does King mean when he says that groups are more immoral than individuals? ***Possible answer:*** *Groups provide people with anonymity. It is easier to act immorally if there is no individual accountability for one's actions or inactions.*

Evaluate Do you agree or disagree with King's assessment that freedom must be demanded by the oppressed? Explain. *Students are likely to agree with King because those who value power over others are not likely to abdicate this power willingly.*

ⓓ GRAMMAR AND STYLE

COMMON CORE L 3a

Analyze Parallelism Parallelism—the use of the same grammatical forms to express equivalent thoughts—helps King emphasize growing tension in his list of wrongs. He then introduces his dramatic and emphatic point by varying the parallel structure from *when you* to *then you*. Have students locate other examples of parallel structure in the letter and explain their effects.

---

110 seldom give up their privileges voluntarily. Individuals may see the moral light and voluntarily give up their unjust posture; but, as Reinhold Niebuhr[5] has reminded us, groups tend to be more immoral than individuals.

We know through painful experience that freedom is never voluntarily given by the oppressor; it must be demanded by the oppressed. Frankly, I have yet to engage in a direct-action campaign that was "well-timed" in the view of those who have not suffered unduly from the disease of segregation. For years now I have heard the word "Wait!" It rings in the ear of every Negro with piercing familiarity. This "Wait" has almost always meant "Never." We must come to see, with one of our distinguished jurists, that "justice too long delayed is justice denied."

120 We have waited for more than 340 years for our constitutional and God-given rights. The nations of Asia and Africa are moving with jetlike speed toward gaining political independence, but we still creep at horse-and-buggy pace toward gaining a cup of coffee at a lunch counter. Perhaps it is easy for those who have never felt the stinging darts of segregation to say, "Wait." But when you have seen vicious mobs lynch your mothers and fathers at will and drown your sisters and brothers at whim; when you have seen hate-filled policemen curse, kick, and even kill your black brothers and sisters; when you see the vast majority of your twenty million Negro brothers smothering in an airtight cage of poverty in the midst of an affluent society; when you suddenly find your tongue twisted and your speech 130 stammering as you seek to explain to your six-year-old daughter why she can't go to the public amusement park that has just been advertised on television, and see tears welling up in her eyes when she is told that Funtown is closed to colored children, and see ominous clouds of inferiority beginning to form in her little mental sky, and see her beginning to distort her personality by developing an unconscious bitterness toward white people; when you have to concoct an answer for a five-year-old son who is asking: "Daddy, why do white people treat colored people so mean?"; when you take a cross-country drive and find it necessary to sleep night after night in the uncomfortable corners of your automobile because no motel will accept you; when you are humiliated day in and day out by nagging 140 signs reading "white" and "colored"; when your first name becomes "nigger," your middle name becomes "boy" (however old you are) and your last name becomes "John," and your wife and mother are never given the respected title "Mrs."; when you are harried by day and haunted by night by the fact that you are a Negro, living constantly at tiptoe stance, never quite knowing what to expect next, and are plagued with inner fears and outer resentments; when you are forever fighting a degenerating sense of "nobodiness"—then you will understand why we find it difficult to wait. There comes a time when the cup of endurance runs over, and men are no longer willing to be plunged into the abyss of despair. I hope, sirs, you can understand our legitimate and unavoidable impatience. ⓓ

150 You express a great deal of anxiety over our willingness to break laws. This is certainly a legitimate concern. Since we so diligently urge people to obey the

ⓓ GRAMMAR AND STYLE

Reread lines 124–147. Note how King establishes **parallelism** by starting each subordinate clause with the words *when you*.

---

5. **Reinhold Niebuhr** (nē′boor′): American theologian (1892–1971) whose writings deal mainly with moral and social problems.

DIFFERENTIATED INSTRUCTION

FOR ADVANCED LEARNERS/AP

Research King's letter was part of a series of events that occurred in Birmingham, Alabama, that drew national attention to the civil rights movement. Have students research those events, particularly:

- racial violence in Birmingham in the early 1960s
- the organization of "Project C" by the SCLC to address civil rights issues in Birmingham, April 1963

- King's arrest and release, April 12–April 20, 1963
- the "children's crusade," May 1963
- the bombing of the Sixteenth Street Baptist Church by white supremacists, killing four African-American girls, September 1963 (commemorated in "Ballad of Birmingham" on page 1214)

Allow time for students to present their findings to the class.

Supreme Court's decision of 1954 outlawing segregation in the public schools,[6] at first glance it may seem rather **paradoxical** for us consciously to break laws. One may well ask: "How can you advocate breaking some laws and obeying others?" The answer lies in the fact that there are two types of laws: just and unjust. I would be the first to advocate obeying just laws. One has not only a legal but a moral responsibility to obey just laws. Conversely, one has a moral responsibility to disobey unjust laws. I would agree with St. Augustine[7] that "an unjust law is no law at all."

160   Now, what is the difference between the two? How does one determine whether a law is just or unjust? A just law is a man-made code that squares with the moral law or the law of God. An unjust law is a code that is out of harmony with the moral law. To put it in the terms of St. Thomas Aquinas:[8] An unjust law is a human law that is not rooted in eternal law and natural law. Any law that uplifts human personality is just. Any law that degrades human personality is unjust. All segregation statutes are unjust because segregation distorts the soul and damages the personality. It gives the segregator a false sense of superiority and the segregated a false sense of inferiority. Segregation, to use the terminology of the Jewish philosopher Martin Buber,[9] substitutes an "I-it" relationship for an "I-
170 thou" relationship and ends up relegating persons to the status of things. Hence segregation is not only politically, economically, and sociologically unsound, it is morally wrong and sinful. Paul Tillich[10] has said that sin is separation. Is not segregation an existential expression of man's tragic separation, his awful **estrangement,** his terrible sinfulness? Thus it is that I can urge men to obey the 1954 decision of the Supreme Court, for it is morally right; and I can urge them to disobey segregation ordinances, for they are morally wrong. **E**

Let us consider a more concrete example of just and unjust laws. An unjust law is a code that a numerical or power majority group compels a minority group to obey but does not make binding on itself. This is *difference* made legal. By the
180 same token, a just law is a code that a majority compels a minority to follow and that it is willing to follow itself. This is *sameness* made legal.

Let me give another explanation. A law is unjust if it is inflicted on a minority that, as a result of being denied the right to vote, had no part in enacting or devising the law. Who can say that the legislature of Alabama which set up that state's segregation laws was democratically elected? Throughout Alabama all sorts of devious methods are used to prevent Negroes from becoming registered voters, and there are some counties in which, even though Negroes constitute a majority of the population, not a single Negro is registered. Can any law enacted under such circumstances be considered democratically structured?

---

6. **Supreme Court decision . . . public schools:** the United States Supreme Court's decision in the case *Brown v. Board of Education of Topeka, Kansas.*

7. **St. Augustine** (ô′gə-stēn′): North African bishop (A.D. 354–430) regarded as a founding father of Christianity.

8. **St. Thomas Aquinas** (ə-kwī′nəs): noted philosopher and theologian (1225–1274).

9. **Martin Buber** (bōō′bər): influential philosopher (1878–1965) with great impact on Jewish and Christian theology.

10. **Paul Tillich** (tĭl′ĭk): German-born American theologian (1886–1965).

---

paradoxical
(păr′ə-dŏk′sĭ-kəl) *adj.* self-contradictory

3 **Targeted Passage**

estrangement
(ĭ-strānj′mənt) *n.* separation; alienation

E **ELEMENTS OF AN ARGUMENT**
Reread lines 160–176. How does King use deductive reasoning to support his conclusion that people should disobey segregation laws?

REVISIT THE BIG QUESTION

When does ACTION *speak louder than words?*

Discuss In lines 157–158, is King correct that one has a moral responsibility to take action against unjust laws? Why or why not? *Students may agree with King in principle, but will likely note how difficult it is to accept the consequences of disobeying the law.*

READING SKILL   COMMON CORE

E **ELEMENTS OF AN ARGUMENT**   RI 1   RI 6

Possible answer: King gives two broad examples of Martin Buber's and Paul Tillich's philosophies. King then applies the same principles to segregation laws.

Extend the Discussion Are morals universal, such that everyone will agree on which laws are moral and which are immoral? Is King's standard for distinguishing which laws to obey and to disobey practical for a society based on laws? Explain.

VOCABULARY   COMMON CORE   L 4

OWN THE WORD

- **paradoxical:** Inform students that *paradoxical* is often used interchangeably with *contradiction,* though the meanings are different. Give students this example: The less a person owns, the freer he or she is. Ask them to explain how the statement is *paradoxical.* **Possible answers:** *Answers may vary.*

- **estrangement:** Point out that *estrangement* is the noun form of *estrange* which, in Latin, means "to treat as a stranger." Ask students to explain a time when they may have felt *estranged.* **Possible answers:** *Answers will vary.*

FOR STRUGGLING READERS

3 **Targeted Passage** [Lines 154–176]

This passage explains King's philosophy about just and unjust laws and the ways people should react to either.

- What types of laws does King define? (lines 155–156)

- In what ways should people react to just laws? unjust laws? (lines 156–158)

- In what ways should people distinguish these two types of laws? (lines 160–166)

FOR ENGLISH LANGUAGE LEARNERS

Comprehension: Self-Monitor Urge students to use paraphrasing to self-monitor understanding of the philosophical language and concepts in lines 166–174. *Possible answer: Laws that separate people on the basis of race incorrectly make some people think they are better than others. The separation of races is bad for politics and the economy, and it is morally wrong.*

Analyze Visuals

Activity Ask students to describe ways that the teens in the photograph reflect King's attitudes about nonviolent direct action. *Possible answer: The students in the photograph are seated calmly. They convey no threat in their posture or behavior, nor do they carry tools of aggression.*

About the Photograph The photograph shows high school students who were arrested during the Birmingham protests. So many students were arrested that the city jails were filled. The students shown are being held in the Birmingham stadium. On May 2, 1963, more than 1,000 young people demonstrated; 900 of them were arrested. The following day, more than 1,000 students arrived to protest. The sight of children being arrested, sprayed with firehoses, and attacked by police dogs shocked many Americans and boosted support for the civil rights movement.

F ALLUSION

Possible answer: With these allusions, King sends the message that civil disobedience is part of a long and distinguished tradition. It is the central element of Christianity, Western civilization, and American democracy.

IF STUDENTS NEED HELP . . . Direct them to the footnotes on page 1210 for explanation of King's allusions.

OWN THE WORD

rabid: Tell students that, in the context of King's letter, *rabid* refers to "extremely fanatical or zealous." Have students list synonyms that fit this definition. *Possible answers: extremist, fanatic, radical, revolutionary, ultra*

High school students jailed in Birmingham protests of 1963

190   Sometimes a law is just on its face and unjust in its application. For instance, I have been arrested on a charge of parading without a permit. Now, there is nothing wrong in having an ordinance which requires a permit for a parade. But such an ordinance becomes unjust when it is used to maintain segregation and to deny citizens the First Amendment privilege of peaceful assembly and protest.

I hope you are able to see the distinction I am trying to point out. In no sense do I advocate evading or defying the law, as would the **rabid** segregationist. That would lead to anarchy. One who breaks an unjust law must do so openly, lovingly, and with a willingness to accept the penalty. I submit that an individual who breaks a law that conscience tells him is unjust, and who willingly accepts the 200 penalty of imprisonment in order to arouse the conscience of the community over its injustice, is in reality expressing the highest respect for law.

Of course, there is nothing new about this kind of civil disobedience. It was evidenced sublimely in the refusal of Shadrach, Meshach, and Abednego to obey the laws of Nebuchadnezzar,[11] on the ground that a higher moral law was at stake. It was practiced superbly by the early Christians, who were willing to face hungry lions and the excruciating pain of chopping blocks rather than submit to certain unjust laws of the Roman Empire. To a degree, academic freedom is a reality today because Socrates practiced civil disobedience. In our own nation, the Boston Tea Party[12] represented a massive act of civil disobedience. **F**

rabid (răb'ĭd) *adj.* unreasonably extreme; fanatical

F ALLUSION
Reread lines 202–209. What message about civil disobedience does King send with his choice of allusions?

---

11. **the refusal . . . Nebuchadnezzar** (nĕb'ə-kəd-nĕz'ər): In the Bible (Daniel 3), Shadrach (shăd'răk), Meshach (mē'shăch), and Abednego (ə-bĕd'nĭ-gō') are three Hebrews condemned to death for refusing to worship an idol set up by Nebuchadnezzar, king of Babylon. However, they were miraculously protected from the flames in the furnace into which they were thrown.

12. **Boston Tea Party:** In 1773, American rebels dumped 15,000 pounds of tea into Boston Harbor to protest the British Tea Act.

1210   UNIT 6: CONTEMPORARY LITERATURE

DIFFERENTIATED INSTRUCTION

FOR ADVANCED LEARNERS/AP

Evaluate Literary Letters Have students consider whether King's letter qualifies as literature. First, students will need to develop a list of literary criteria that can be applied both to fiction and nonfiction. Explain to students that many works of fiction are written in epistolary form in which characters exchange letters, write in diaries or journals, or provide newspaper accounts of events. Students may benefit by skimming and scanning epistolary works, if possible, such as *Dracula* or *Flowers for Algernon,* in developing their list of criteria. In evaluating King's letter, ask students to consider whether the clergymen appear to be King's only intended audience and why or why not.

210   We should never forget that everything Adolf Hitler did in Germany was "legal" and everything the Hungarian freedom fighters[13] did in Hungary was "illegal." It was "illegal" to aid and comfort a Jew in Hitler's Germany. Even so, I am sure that, had I lived in Germany at the time, I would have aided and comforted my Jewish brothers. If today I lived in a Communist country where certain principles dear to the Christian faith are suppressed, I would openly advocate disobeying that country's antireligious laws.

    I must make two honest confessions to you, my Christian and Jewish brothers. First, I must confess that over the past few years I have been gravely disappointed with the white moderate. I have almost reached the regrettable conclusion that
220 the Negro's great stumbling block in his stride toward freedom is not the White Citizen's Counciler or the Ku Klux Klanner,[14] but the white moderate, who is more devoted to "order" than to justice; who prefers a negative peace which is the absence of tension to a positive peace which is the presence of justice; who constantly says: "I agree with you in the goal you seek, but I cannot agree with your methods of direct action"; who paternalistically believes he can set the timetable for another man's freedom; who lives by a mythical concept of time and who constantly advises the Negro to wait for a "more convenient season." Shallow understanding from people of goodwill is more frustrating than absolute misunderstanding from people of ill will. Lukewarm acceptance is much more
230 bewildering than outright rejection.

    I had hoped that the white moderate would understand that law and order exist for the purpose of establishing justice and that when they fail in this purpose, they become the dangerously structured dams that block the flow of social progress. I had hoped that the white moderate would understand that the present tension in the South is a necessary phase of the transition from an obnoxious negative peace, in which the Negro passively accepted his unjust plight, to a **substantive** and positive peace, in which all men will respect the dignity and worth of human personality. Actually, we who engage in nonviolent direct action are not the creators of tension. We merely bring to the surface the hidden tension that is
240 already alive. We bring it out in the open, where it can be seen and dealt with. Like a boil that can never be cured so long as it is covered up but must be opened with all its ugliness to the natural medicines of air and light, injustice must be exposed, with all the tension its exposure creates, to the light of human conscience and the air of national opinion before it can be cured.

    In your statement you assert that our actions, even though peaceful, must be condemned because they precipitate violence. But is this a logical assertion? Isn't this like condemning a robbed man because his possession of money precipitated the evil act of robbery? Isn't this like condemning Socrates because his unswerving commitment to truth and his philosophical inquiries precipitated the act by
250 the misguided populace in which they made him drink hemlock? Isn't this like

substantive (sŭb′stən-tĭv) *adj.* significant; with a strong basis

---

13. **Hungarian freedom fighters:** Hungarians who participated in an unsuccessful 1956 rebellion against the Communist government of their homeland. The rebellion was crushed by Soviet troops.

14. **the White . . . Klanner:** members of white supremacist groups.

When does ACTION *speak louder than words?*

Discuss Direct students to lines 273–287. Is action in support of a moral ideal a form of extremism? If so, is it acceptable? Explain.

Possible answer: *If action in support of a moral ideal goes against the commonly accepted social norms, then yes, it is extremism. If the ideal is truly moral, this extremism is acceptable.*

VOCABULARY

COMMON CORE L4

OWN THE WORD

latent: Point out that *latent* refers to "that which exists in hidden form" and has the potential of becoming known. Ask students to explain what King meant when he writes "The Negro has many pent-up resentments and *latent* frustrations. . ."

Possible answer: *King refers to the difficulty, if not impossibility, for African Americans to express their frustrations and resentment about prejudice.*

---

condemning Jesus because his unique God-consciousness and never-ceasing devotion to God's will precipitated the evil act of crucifixion? We must come to see that, as the federal courts have consistently affirmed, it is wrong to urge an individual to cease his efforts to gain his basic constitutional rights because the quest may precipitate violence. Society must protect the robbed and punish the robber. . . .

Oppressed people cannot remain oppressed forever. The yearning for freedom eventually manifests itself, and that is what has happened to the American Negro. Something within has reminded him of his birthright of freedom, and something without has reminded him that it can be gained. Consciously or unconsciously, 260 he has been caught up by the *Zeitgeist*,[15] and with his black brothers of Africa and his brown and yellow brothers of Asia, South America, and the Caribbean, the United States Negro is moving with a sense of great urgency toward the promised land of racial justice. If one recognizes this vital urge that has engulfed the Negro community, one should readily understand why public demonstrations are taking place. The Negro has many pent-up resentments and **latent** frustrations, and he must release them. So let him march; let him make prayer pilgrimages to the city hall; let him go on freedom rides—and try to understand why he must do so. If his repressed emotions are not released in nonviolent ways, they will seek expression through violence; this is not a threat but a fact of history. So I have not 270 said to my people: "Get rid of your discontent." Rather, I have tried to say that this normal and healthy discontent can be channeled into the creative outlet of nonviolent direct action. And now this approach is being termed extremist.

But though I was initially disappointed at being categorized as an extremist, as I continued to think about the matter, I gradually gained a measure of satisfaction from the label. Was not Jesus an extremist for love: "Love your enemies, bless them that curse you, do good to them that hate you, and pray for them which despitefully use you, and persecute you." Was not Amos[16] an extremist for justice: "Let justice roll down like waters and righteousness like an ever-flowing stream." Was not Paul an extremist for the Christian gospel: "I bear in my body the marks 280 of the Lord Jesus." Was not Martin Luther[17] an extremist: "Here I stand; I cannot do otherwise, so help me God." And John Bunyan:[18] "I will stay in jail to the end of my days before I make a butchery of my conscience." And Abraham Lincoln: "This nation cannot survive half slave and half free." And Thomas Jefferson: "We hold these truths to be self-evident, that all men are created equal. . . ." So the question is not whether we will be extremists, but what kind of extremists we will be. Will we be extremists for hate or for love? Will we be extremists for the preservation of injustice or for the extension of justice? In that dramatic scene on Calvary's hill[19] three men were crucified. We must never forget that all

4 Targeted Passage

latent (lāt′nt) *adj.* existing in a hidden form

COMMON CORE RI 4

Language Coach

Connotation A word's **connotations** are the connected images or feelings that add a finer shade of meaning to the word. What connotations do you think *extremist* has? Contrast those connotations with *activist*. How do the connotations differ?

---

15. ***Zeitgeist*** (tsīt′gīst′) *German*: the spirit of the time; that is, the beliefs and attitudes shared by most people living in a particular period.

16. **Amos:** Hebrew prophet whose words are recorded in the Old Testament book bearing his name.

17. **Martin Luther:** German monk (1483–1546) who launched the Protestant Reformation.

18. **John Bunyan:** English preacher and author (1628–1688) who was twice imprisoned for unlicensed preaching.

19. **Calvary's hill:** the site of Jesus' crucifixion.

DIFFERENTIATED INSTRUCTION

FOR STRUGGLING READERS

4 Targeted Passage [Lines 256–272]

In this passage, King explains the inevitable results of oppression.

- What do oppressed people want? (lines 256–257)

- In what ways might this need reveal itself? (lines 263–267)

- What will happen to oppressed people if they cannot express their feelings? (lines 268–269)

FOR ENGLISH LANGUAGE LEARNERS

Language Coach  COMMON CORE RI 4

Connotation *Answers:*

Extremist has a negative connotation—someone who works for a cause but takes it too far. Activist *is more positive—someone who works to improve society.* Tell student pairs to select five words from the text. Have students take turns describing the connotations of the words on their partners' lists.

three were crucified for the same crime—the crime of extremism. Two were
extremists for immorality, and thus fell below their environment. The other,
Jesus Christ, was an extremist for love, truth, and goodness, and thereby rose
above his environment. Perhaps the South, the nation and the world are in dire
need of creative extremists. . . . **G**

I wish you had commended the Negro sit-inners and demonstrators of
Birmingham for their sublime courage, their willingness to suffer, and their
amazing discipline in the midst of great provocation. One day the South will
recognize its real heroes. They will be the James Merediths,[20] with the noble
sense of purpose that enables them to face jeering and hostile mobs, and with
the agonizing loneliness that characterizes the life of the pioneer. They will be
old, oppressed, battered Negro women, symbolized in a seventy-two-year-old
woman in Montgomery, Alabama, who rose up with a sense of dignity and
with her people decided not to ride segregated buses, and who responded with
ungrammatical profundity to one who inquired about her weariness: "My feets
is tired, but my soul is at rest." They will be the young high school and college
students, the young ministers of the gospel and a host of their elders, courageously
and nonviolently sitting in at lunch counters and willingly going to jail for
conscience' sake. One day the South will know that when these disinherited
children of God sat down at lunch counters, they were in reality standing up
for what is best in the American dream and for the most sacred values in our
Judaeo-Christian heritage, thereby bringing our nation back to those great wells
of democracy which were dug deep by the founding fathers in their formulation
of the Constitution and the Declaration of Independence.

Never before have I written so long a letter. I'm afraid it is much too long to
take your precious time. I can assure you that it would have been much shorter if
I had been writing from a comfortable desk, but what else can one do when he is
alone in a narrow jail cell, other than write long letters, think long thoughts, and
pray long prayers?

If I have said anything in this letter that overstates the truth and indicates an
unreasonable impatience, I beg you to forgive me. If I have said anything that
understates the truth and indicates my having a patience that allows me to settle
for anything less than brotherhood, I beg God to forgive me.

I hope this letter finds you strong in the faith. I also hope that circumstances
will soon make it possible for me to meet each of you, not as an integrationist or
a civil-rights leader but as a fellow clergyman and a Christian brother. Let us all
hope that the dark clouds of racial prejudice will soon pass away and the deep
fog of misunderstanding will be lifted from our fear-drenched communities, and
in some not too distant tomorrow the radiant stars of love and brotherhood will
shine over our great nation with all their **scintillating** beauty.

Yours for the cause of Peace and Brotherhood,

Martin Luther King Jr.

---

20. **James Merediths:** people like James Meredith, who endured violent opposition from whites to become
the first African American to attend the University of Mississippi.

COMMON CORE RI 4

G ALLUSION
Reread lines 275–293.
Think about the usual
connotations of the
word *extremist.* At first,
King says that he was
"disappointed" at being
called an extremist, but
then he embraces the
label. Why? How does
King use biblical and
historical allusions to
support his reevaluation
of this term?

scintillating (sĭn'tl-ā'tĭng)
adj. sparkling **scintillate** v.

READING SKILL **COMMON CORE** RI 4

G Model the Skill: ALLUSION

Point out that the term *extremist* usually
refers to one whose views undermine the
existing structure and stability of society,
or whose actions are destructive. In these
lines, King turns the negative connotations
positive as he embraces the label.

*Possible answer: King uses Jesus, Amos and
Paul as examples of extremists for love, justice and sharing their beliefs. Martin Luther
and John Bunyan stood against the political
and religious establishment of their day,
and Abraham Lincoln and Thomas Jefferson
were extremists for equality and freedom.*

TIERED DISCUSSION PROMPTS

In lines 256–272, use these prompts to help
students understand King's views about the
ways that people respond to oppression:

Connect Have you ever felt frustrated or
angry because an authority imposed rules
that were difficult for you to follow?
Explain. *Accept all thoughtful responses.*

Interpret What does it mean to be
oppressed? *Students should recognize
that oppression is an unequal distribution
of political, economic, and social power.*

Evaluate Will oppressed people ultimately
rebel violently or nonviolently against their
oppressors, as King says they will? *Students
are likely to agree with King that people will
strive to achieve freedom at any cost.*

VOCABULARY **COMMON CORE** L 4

OWN THE WORD

scintillating: Remind students that *scintillating* refers to things that are "sparkling;
shiny or flashy; animated; brilliant; clever."
Ask students to list things that can be
described as *scintillating.* **Possible
answers:** *conversation, diamonds*

SELECTION WRAP-UP

READ WITH A PURPOSE Ask students to consider King's tactics and goals. What did King
hope to accomplish in Birmingham? *Possible
answer: He sought to promote a nonviolent,
direct action campaign that would bring an
end to segregation and unjust conditions.*

FOR STRUGGLING READERS

Comprehension Support In lines 296–297,
King says, "One day the South will recognize
its real heroes." Clarify that King means that
those who work for social change are often
unrecognized in their own time but later
admired. Ask students who King believes are
the South's "real heroes," and why he views
these people as heroes. *Possible answer: King
believes that the real heroes are those who
have stood up for their civil rights through*
*actions such as sitting in the whites' section
of a segregated lunch counter. He views these
people as heroes because they have the courage to continue despite angry and even violent
responses.*

Ballad of Birmingham

Dudley Randall

"Mother dear, may I go downtown
instead of out to play,
and march the streets of Birmingham
in a freedom march today?"

5 "No, baby, no, you may not go,
for the dogs are fierce and wild,
and clubs and hoses, guns and jails
ain't good for a little child."

"But, mother, I won't be alone.
10 Other children will go with me,
and march the streets of Birmingham
to make our country free."

"No, baby, no, you may not go,
for I fear those guns will fire.
15 But you may go to church instead,
and sing in the children's choir."

She has combed and brushed her nightdark hair,
and bathed rose petal sweet,
and drawn white gloves on her small brown hands,
20 and white shoes on her feet.

The mother smiled to know her child
was in the sacred place,
but that smile was the last smile
to come upon her face.

25 For when she heard the explosion,
her eyes grew wet and wild.
She raced through the streets of Birmingham
calling for her child.

She clawed through bits of glass and brick,
30 then lifted out a shoe.
"O, here's the shoe my baby wore,
but, baby, where are you?"

TIERED DISCUSSION PROMPTS

Use these prompts to help students understand the sacrifices of civil rights activists such as Martin Luther King, Jr.:

Summarize What happens to the child in this poem? *Possible answer: The child wants to join the protest in Birmingham. Her mother refuses because she thinks the protests will be dangerous, but she allows her daughter to go to a church function instead. The church is bombed and the daughter is killed.*

Analyze What is the mother's primary interest or motivation? What is the child's primary interest or motivation? *Possible answer: The mother cares more about protecting her child than fighting for racial equality. The child wants to join the fight for racial equality by marching through the streets of Birmingham.*

Synthesize On the basis of King's definition in lines 294–312 of his letter, is the child in the poem one of the South's heroes? Explain. *Students are likely to agree that the child is a hero because she sacrifices her life in the fight for racial justice.*

DIFFERENTIATED INSTRUCTION

FOR STRUGGLING READERS

Develop Reading Fluency Read aloud "Ballad of Birmingham" to the class. Tell students to note the meter and rhythm of the poem as they listen. Next, read the first stanza of the poem and have students repeat it back to you as a class. Continue until students have "echoed" the entire poem.

Comprehension

1. **Summarize** What led to the decision to start the protests in Birmingham?

2. **Recall** What are the four steps involved in King's nonviolent campaigns?

3. **Clarify** What exactly does King mean by "nonviolent direct action"?

4. **Summarize** In King's view, what is the difference between defying the law and breaking an "unjust" law?

Text Analysis

● 5. **Examine Elements of an Argument** Review the chart you created as you read. Which of King's **arguments** did you find most persuasive? Consider both his position, or claim, and his reasons and evidence in your answer.

● 6. **Understand Analogy** An analogy is an extended, point-by-point comparison of two different things, often using a familiar example to explain a complex or abstract idea. Analyze King's analogy in lines 241–244 and discuss the persuasive appeal the analogy lends to King's argument in this letter.

● 7. **Interpret Allusions** Allusions can refer to people, places, events, or literary works. Choose four of King's allusions. Using the footnotes, interpret each allusion, and tell why you think King included them. Record your answers in a chart like the one shown.

Allusion	Possible Meaning	Why Included

● 8. **Analyze Persuasive Techniques** King's writings and speeches are filled with allusions that reveal his rhetorical mastery and breadth of knowledge. In what ways, if any, do his allusions also help him achieve the following possible purposes? Cite specific allusions that support your answers.

- appealing to his readers' sense of right and wrong
- establishing his credibility
- making his ideas accessible to a wider audience

9. **Compare Texts** Compare the "Ballad of Birmingham" (page 1214) with King's letter. How is Randall's poem also an argument for acting against injustice?

Text Criticism

10. **Author's Style** King is a master of the **aphorism,** a short statement of principle or truth. Here's a memorable one: "Injustice anywhere is a threat to justice everywhere" (line 31). Find two more aphorisms and explain their effects.

When does **ACTION** *speak louder than words?*

Taking a stand requires action as well as words. On what issues have you been outspoken? What actions have you taken to back up your words?

---

10. *Other aphorisms can be found in lines 113–114, 119, 228–229, 229–230, and 255. Students should recognize that aphorisms contain universal truths that resonate with readers of all backgrounds. The overall effect of King's aphorisms is to present his point of view as a commonsense truth.*

When does ACTION *speak louder than words?* Answers will vary.

Practice and Apply

For preliminary support of post-reading questions, use these copy masters:

R **RESOURCE MANAGER—Copy Masters**
Reading Check p. 78
Allusion p. 71
Question Support p. 79
Additional selection questions are provided for teachers on page 65.

ANSWERS  COMMON CORE RI 1, RI 4, RI 6

1. *Negotiations between local activists and government officials failed.*

2. *King uses these four steps: collection of facts, negotiation, self-purification, and direct action.*

3. *Nonviolent direct action encompasses confrontational and highly visible actions of civil disobedience, such as sit-ins or picket lines. Protesters do not retaliate if attacked.*

4. *Defying laws is a disregard for morally good laws. Breaking unjust laws expresses deep respect for morality by aligning human laws with those of a higher moral order.*

Possible answers:

5. ● **COMMON CORE FOCUS Elements of an Argument** *Answers will vary. Students should cite reasons for their choices and provide supporting quotations or examples.*

6. ● **COMMON CORE FOCUS Understand Analogy** *King compares injustice to a boil that must be cured. Exposure cures both; exposure creates discomfort for both; cures for both include the medicines of air (national opinion) and light (human conscience).*

7. ● **COMMON CORE FOCUS Allusion** *Answers will vary but students should explain in what way each allusion relates to King's message, to his audience, or both.*

8. ● **COMMON CORE FOCUS Analyze Persuasive Techniques** *Answers will vary, but students should explain the relationship between each allusion and the listed purpose.*

9. *In the poem, the mother is fearful about allowing her child to participate in a racial protest. The mother feels that it is safer for her child to attend church. Sadly, the child is killed in the church as a result of racist violence, sending the message that there is no safe place when social injustice prospers. This message echoes King's arguments that no one may sit idly by while injustice reigns, and thus we must all take action.*

ANSWERS

Vocabulary in Context

VOCABULARY PRACTICE

1. *cognizant: I know about the plans.*
2. *paradoxical: difficult to make sense of*
3. *substantive: significant*
4. *rabid: involves shouting furiously*
5. *affiliated: partners*
6. *moratorium: a bad storm*
7. *scintillating: could describe a diamond*
8. *latent: a toothache*
9. *estrangement: could result from an argument*
10. *retaliating: could result from losing a game*

 **RESOURCE MANAGER—Copy Master**
Vocabulary Practice p. 76

ACADEMIC VOCABULARY IN SPEAKING

Students should indicate that King's tone is polite and professional. They should recognize that his tone is appropriate for the occasion, and avoids negativity. King defends the use of nonviolent tactics in this letter and demonstrates his commitment to nonviolent, direct action philosophy. Students should include at least two Academic Vocabulary words in their discussion.

VOCABULARY STRATEGY: WORDS AND ANALOGIES

COMMON CORE L5

Review the process for using analogies to determine word pair relationships.

Possible answers:

1. *artist: painting; creator and object created*
2. *generous: miserly; antonym*
3. *car: trunk; whole and part*
4. *closed: shut; synonym*
5. *cold: shivering; cause and effect*

 **RESOURCE MANAGER—Copy Master**
Vocabulary Strategy p. 77

Interactive Vocabulary

Keywords direct students to a **WordSharp** tutorial on **thinkcentral.com** or to other types of vocabulary practice and review.

Vocabulary in Context

▲ **VOCABULARY PRACTICE**

Show your understanding of the vocabulary words by answering these questions.

1. If I am **cognizant** of your plans, do I know about them or have I forgotten them?
2. Would a **paradoxical** statement be easy or difficult to make sense of?
3. Would a **substantive** contribution be minimal or significant?
4. Would a **rabid** response involve shouting furiously or agreeing silently?
5. If my company is **affiliated** with yours, are they competitors or partners?
6. Which might cause a **moratorium** in road building, a bad storm or potholes?
7. Is a diamond or gold more accurately described as **scintillating?**
8. Which is a **latent** ailment, a toothache or a broken arm?
9. Would an argument cause **estrangement** or a meeting with a stranger?
10. Which might be a cause for **retaliating,** losing a game or taking a taxi?

WORD LIST

affiliated
cognizant
estrangement
latent
moratorium
paradoxical
rabid
retaliating
scintillating
substantive

ACADEMIC VOCABULARY IN SPEAKING

• complex   • economic   • establish   • ethnic   • evolve

Reread King's letter, looking for specific examples of his tone. Then, in a small group discuss what kind of tone King **establishes** in his letter and what his tone says about nonviolent protest and King as a leader. Use at least two Academic Vocabulary words in your discussion.

VOCABULARY STRATEGY: WORDS AND ANALOGIES

COMMON CORE

L5 Demonstrate understanding of word relationships.

An **analogy** compares two items or word meanings that are alike in one or more ways. Analyzing an analogy is one way of determining the meaning of unfamiliar words in context. Word analogy statements show the relationship by comparing one set of words to another set of words. For example, the following pairs are opposites, or antonyms.

rabid : calm and *affiliated : unrelated*

Word analogies can include relationships such as *synonyms, antonyms, part and whole, cause and effect,* and *location.*

PRACTICE For each word pair, create another word pair to express the same relationship. Then, identify the type of relationship.

1. architect : building ::
2. systematic : chaotic ::
3. book : page ::
4. obligatory : necessary ::
5. war : death ::

Interactive Vocabulary

Go to **thinkcentral.com**.
KEYWORD: HML11-1216

DIFFERENTIATED INSTRUCTION

FOR ENGLISH LANGUAGE LEARNERS

Task Support: Vocabulary in Writing Provide these sentence starters to students:

• Nonviolent protest is *affiliated* with _____.

• Protesters are *cognizant* of _____.

• There is *estrangement* between protesters and _____ because _____.

• Nonviolent protest is a result of *latent* _____.

• *Substantive* change results from _____.

FOR ADVANCED LEARNERS/AP

Analogies Using King's comparison of a boil and injustice as a model, challenge students to write their own analogies for injustice or another social problem. First, have students choose the two ideas they will compare. Then have students brainstorm lists of associated words from which to draw as they write. Invite volunteers to share their analogies aloud with the class.

Language

◆ **GRAMMAR AND STYLE: Use Rhetorical Devices**

Review the Grammar and Style note on page 1208. In his letter, King uses **parallelism**—the repetition of grammatical structures—to create emphasis and to show comparisons, as in the following example:

> *Just as the prophets of the eighth century B.C. left their villages and carried their "thus saith the Lord" far beyond the boundaries of their home towns, and just as the Apostle Paul left his village of Tarsus and carried the gospel of Jesus Christ to the far corners of the Greco-Roman world, so am I compelled to carry the gospel of freedom beyond my own hometown.* (lines 22–27)

Notice how King uses parallel adverb clauses beginning with "just as" to set up a comparison between himself and the biblical figures he cites. What is the impact of this comparison?

PRACTICE Identify the parallel adjective clauses in the following passage from King. Then, write a paragraph of your own using similar parallel elements.

[T]he Negro's great stumbling block in his stride toward freedom is not the White Citizen's Counciler or the Ku Klux Klanner, but the white moderate, who is more devoted to "order" than to justice; who prefers a negative peace which is the absence of tension to a positive peace which is the presence of justice; who constantly says: "I agree with you in the goal you seek, but I cannot agree with your methods of direct action"; who paternalistically believes he can set the timetable for another man's freedom; who lives by a mythical concept of time and who constantly advises the Negro to wait for a "more convenient season."

READING-WRITING CONNECTION

 YOUR TURN Expand your understanding of Martin Luther King Jr.'s letter by responding to this prompt. Then, use the **revising tips** to improve your argument.

WRITING PROMPT

WRITE A PERSUASIVE ARGUMENT Civil disobedience has been controversial ever since Henry David Thoreau first advocated it in 1847. Opposition to Martin Luther King, Jr.'s brand of nonviolent resistance came from some black activists as well as white segregationists. People still argue over the issue today.

Write a **four- to six-paragraph persuasive argument** explaining your position on the issue of nonviolent civil disobedience. Model your argument on King's, using counterarguments to anticipate objections to your view.

REVISING TIPS

- Present a clear thesis statement that states your main point.
- Use logical reasoning based on facts, expert opinions, and quotation from valid sources.
- Honestly and accurately present opposing views.
- Use persuasive language and rhetorical devices such as appeals to logic.

 **Interactive Revision** THINK central
Go to **thinkcentral.com**.
KEYWORD: HML11-1217

LETTER FROM BIRMINGHAM JAIL **1217**

COMMON CORE

L 3a Vary syntax for effect; apply an understanding of syntax to the study of complex texts when reading. **W 1** Write arguments to support claims in an analysis of substantive topics.

Language

COMMON CORE W 1, L 3a

◆ **GRAMMAR AND STYLE**

Suggest that students choose a topic from King's letters for their paragraphs. Have them draft their paragraphs for content first, then work on parallelism during the revision process. (For more on sentence structure, see **Grammar Handbook,** page R67.) *Possible answer:* King establishes parallelism with the repetition of the word who. *Paragraphs will vary.*

R RESOURCE MANAGER—Copy Master
Use Rhetorical Devices p. 80

READING-WRITING CONNECTION
Remind students that the first paragraph of their arguments should include a thesis statement expressing support or opposition to nonviolent civil disobedience. Students should then develop one supporting point in each body paragraph, including supporting facts, examples, quotations, allusions, and so on. Students should conclude by restating their main points and offering a final insight. Urge students to prepare outlines before they begin drafting.

BEST PRACTICES TOOLKIT—Transparency
Outline p. B19

Writing Online
THINK central

The following tools are available online at **thinkcentral.com** and on Write*Smart* CD-ROM:
- **Interactive Graphic Organizers**
- **Interactive Student Models**
- **Interactive Revision Lessons**
For additional grammar instruction, see **GrammarNotes** on **thinkcentral.com**.

FOR STRUGGLING WRITERS
Writing Support

- Provide students with this thesis statement: Nonviolent civil disobedience is an effective (or ineffective) means for social change.

- Then have students list three reasons that their thesis statements are true, such as 1) it forces public action, 2) it seeks to eliminate violence, and 3) it seeks to establish dialogue.

- For each reason that students list, have them write ways that critics might respond. For example, 1) it forces public reaction rather than action, 2) it breeds violence, and 3) it diverts attention from dialogue to public order.

- Tell students to write at least one paragraph for each of their three points. Remind students to acknowledge and address each of the critics' arguments in their explanations.

Assess and Reteach

Assess

DIAGNOSTIC AND SELECTION TESTS
Selection Test A pp. 321–322
Selection Test B/C pp. 323–324

Interactive Selection Test on thinkcentral.com

Reteach

Level Up Online Tutorials on thinkcentral.com
Reteaching Worksheets on thinkcentral.com

LETTER FROM BIRMINGHAM JAIL **1217**

Focus and Motivate

COMMON CORE FOCUS

RI 2 Determine two or more central ideas of a text and analyze their development over the course of the text, including how they interact and build on one another to provide a complex analysis. **RI 5** Analyze and evaluate the effectiveness of the structure an author uses in his or her argument, including whether the structure makes points clear, convincing, and engaging. **RI 6** Determine an author's point of view or purpose in a text in which the rhetoric is particularly effective, analyzing how style and content contribute to the power, persuasiveness, or beauty of the text. **SL 1b** Work with peers to promote civil, democratic discussions. **SL 1c** Ensure a hearing for a full range of positions on an issue. **L 4b** Identify and correctly use patterns of word changes that indicate different meanings or parts of speech.

ABOUT THE AUTHOR

After students read about Malcolm X, have them discuss integration and separatism as responses to racial prejudice. What are the pros and cons of each? *Possible answer: Integration offers equal opportunity but is hard to achieve and may dilute cultural identity. Separatism offers control but may create hostility and tension.*

Selection Resources

COMMON CORE

RI 2 Determine two or more central ideas of a text and analyze their development over the course of the text, including how they interact and build on one another to provide a complex analysis. **RI 5** Analyze and evaluate the effectiveness of the structure an author uses in his or her argument, including whether the structure makes points clear, convincing, and engaging. **RI 6** Determine an author's point of view or purpose in a text in which the rhetoric is particularly effective, analyzing how style and content contribute to the power, persuasiveness, or beauty of the text.

Civil Rights and Protest Literature

from Stride Toward Freedom
Nonfiction by Martin Luther King Jr.

For a biography of Martin Luther King Jr., see page 1202.

Necessary to Protect Ourselves
Interview with Malcolm X by Les Crane

Meet the Author

Malcolm X 1925–1965

In 1944, while Martin Luther King Jr. was attending college classes in Atlanta, 19-year-old Malcolm Little was hustling on the streets of Harlem. By 1952, a jailhouse conversion transformed Little into the political firebrand we know as Malcolm X, whose separatist views posed a serious challenge to King's integrationist vision.

Bitter Legacy Where King grew up comfortably middle-class, Little's childhood was scarred by poverty and racial violence. His outspoken father, Earl Little, was an early advocate of black separatism who was murdered by white supremacists. His mother, left alone to raise eight children in dire poverty, suffered a mental breakdown. Her children, including Malcolm, were sent to separate foster homes.

By the time he was sent to prison in 1946, Little had been brutally disillusioned about his prospects in white-dominated society. While reading in the prison library, he discovered the teachings of a small religious sect called the Nation of Islam, or the Black Muslims, who called white people "a race of devils" and promoted a vision of black pride. They advocated a radical solution to the race problem: the establishment of a separate, self-reliant black nation.

Change of Heart Inspired by the Black Muslim vision, Malcolm Little converted to Islam and changed his last name to X, symbolizing his lost African name. Once released from prison, he became an influential spokesman for the Nation of Islam and was named their first national minister. Over time, however, he became critical of the organization. In 1964, Malcolm X experienced a second spiritual conversion while making a pilgrimage to Mecca. The sight of Muslims of many races worshipping together caused him to renounce all forms of racial hatred. On his return home, Malcolm X broke with the Nation of Islam and formed the Organization of Afro-American Unity, dedicated to promoting unity among black people all over the world.

Marked Man This new direction angered many Black Muslims, including the young Louis Farrakhan, who labeled Malcolm X a traitor. In February 1965, as Malcolm X was speaking to a crowd of 400 in Harlem, he was gunned down by three assassins, two of whom were Black Muslims.

Author Online
Go to **thinkcentral.com**. KEYWORD: HML11-1218

THINK central

1218

See resources on the **Teacher One Stop DVD-ROM** and on **thinkcentral.com**.

R RESOURCE MANAGER UNIT 6
Plan and Teach, pp. 81–88
Summary, pp. 89–90†‡*
Text Analysis and Reading Skill, pp. 91–94†*
Vocabulary, pp. 95–97*

DIAGNOSTIC AND SELECTION TESTS
Selection Tests, pp. 325–328

BEST PRACTICES TOOLKIT
Word Squares, p. E10
Cause-and-Effect Chain, pp. B16, B39
New Word Analysis, p. E8

TECHNOLOGY
- Teacher One Stop DVD-ROM
- Student One Stop DVD-ROM
- Audio Anthology CD
- ExamView Test Generator on the **Teacher One Stop**

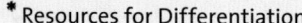

* **Resources for Differentiation**   † **Also in Spanish**   ‡ **In Haitian Creole and Vietnamese**

TEXT ANALYSIS: ANALYZE GENRES

The works you are about to read are two different types of writing, or **genres.** You will read part of an autobiography by Martin Luther King Jr., and an interview with Malcolm X. An **autobiography** is the story of a person's life written by that person. Autobiographies include important events from the person's life, as well as reflections on personal beliefs. An **interview** is a conversation conducted by a reporter in which responses are elicited from another person, recorded, then broadcast or published. In written format, interviews include questions by the reporter and answers by the person being interviewed. As you read, look for the distinguishing characteristics of each genre.

READING SKILL: SYNTHESIZING SOURCES

When you compare two or more sources, it is important to **synthesize,** or to bring together, the main ideas and supporting details from each text. Follow these steps for synthesizing:

- Find the main idea in each work.
- Look for details that support the main ideas.
- Compare and contrast the information in the sources to find similarities and differences.
- Put it all together by recording your findings.

As you read, fill out a chart like the one below. Then, using your chart, synthesize the information and compare the two texts.

	Main Ideas	Supporting Details
King		
Malcolm X		

▲ VOCABULARY IN CONTEXT

King and Malcolm X use the boldfaced words to express their opposing views. Restate each phrase, using a different word or words for the boldfaced term.

1. need to **repudiate** those who oppress us
2. by not speaking out, **tacitly** accepting bad situations
3. cannot **succumb** to defeatist attitudes
4. realize that prejudice is applied **indiscriminately**
5. success through a **synthesis** of ideas and approaches
6. rioting and **anarchy** in the streets

 Complete the activities in your **Reader/Writer Notebook.**

How do we fight INJUSTICE?

Most people would agree that it's important to stand up for your rights if you're being treated unfairly. However, there are many different opinions about the best way to fight back against injustice. In this lesson, Martin Luther King Jr. and Malcolm X argue two very different perspectives on this issue. Traditionally they were on opposite sides of the debate about using violence as an appropriate political tool.

PRESENT What considerations do you think are important when choosing how to respond to injustice? Working in a small group, make a list of relevant concerns, such as obeying the law or achieving quick results. Then, rank them in order of importance. Share your opinions with the class.

1219

Teach

How do we fight INJUSTICE?

Begin by asking the question. After groups complete the *PRESENT* activity, invite volunteers to share their concerns about methods for fighting injustice. Discuss whether each concern supports an integrationist or a separatist approach to protest, and why.

TEXT ANALYSIS COMMON CORE RI 5 RI 6

● *Model the Skill:* **ANALYZE GENRES**

Point out that if they watch news on television or on the Web, they frequently see broadcast interviews. Tell students that most presidents and many celebrities write autobiographies. Mention that autobiographies can serve as primary source materials for people studying history.

GUIDED PRACTICE Have students discuss how autobiographical information can be viewed as valuable, though subjective, source material.

READING SKILL COMMON CORE RI 2 RI 5

■ *Model the Skill:* **SYNTHESIZING SOURCES**

Write these two statements on the board:

"Violence as a way of achieving racial justice is both impractical and immoral." —Martin Luther King, Jr.

" . . . we should get whatever is necessary to protect ourselves . . . where the governmental ability to protect us has broken down." —Malcolm X

Have students synthesize the main ideas inferred by the two statements. *Possible answer: Something must be done to bring about racial justice.*

GUIDED PRACTICE Have partners write, then synthesize, two statements about any topic.

VOCABULARY SKILL
COMMON CORE L 4

▲ VOCABULARY IN CONTEXT

DIAGNOSE WORD KNOWLEDGE Have all students complete Vocabulary in Context. Check their phrases against the following:

anarchy (ăn′ər-kē) *n.* an absence of political authority

indiscriminately (ĭn′dĭ-skrĭm′ə-nĭt-lē) *adv.* randomly

repudiate (rĭ-pyōō′dē-āt′) *v.* to reject or renounce

succumb (sə-kŭm′) *v.* to give in, especially to overpowering force or strength

synthesis (sĭn′thĭ-sĭs) *n.* the union of parts or elements into a whole

tacitly (tăs′ĭt-lē) *adv.* silently

PRETEACH VOCABULARY Use the following copy master to help students predict meanings.

R RESOURCE MANAGER—Copy Master
Vocabulary Study p. 95

READ WITH A PURPOSE

Help students set a purpose for reading. Tell them to read the following excerpts to learn what King and Malcolm X believed should be done to bring about racial equality.

SUMMARY

In this excerpt from his nonfiction book, Dr. Martin Luther King, Jr., reasserts nonviolent resistance as the best path to equality and civil rights for African Americans. Rejecting passive acceptance and physical violence as ineffective and immoral responses to oppression, he argues for a militant but nonviolent mass movement.

READING SKILL — COMMON CORE — RI 2 / RI 5

Ⓐ *Model the Skill:*
SYNTHESIZE SOURCES

Point out that a useful method for identifying main ideas is to plot the available information. Then, work with students to add information to the chart introduced on page 1219:

Main Idea	Supporting Details
Oppression should be resisted.	Biblical events show King that action is sometimes necessary to resist oppression.

Possible answer: *King will discuss how people deal with oppression.*

VOCABULARY — COMMON CORE — L 4

OWN THE WORD

tacitly: Tell students that *tacitly* comes from the Latin *tacitus,* "silent." Then have students complete this sentence: We gave *tacit* approval to the plan by... ***Possible answer:** nodding our heads and not speaking up.*

STRIDE TOWARD FREEDOM

Martin Luther King Jr.

BACKGROUND In the 1950s, the civil rights movement focused its efforts on overturning the so-called Jim Crow laws, the segregation laws that kept African Americans from equal participation in public life. In 1954, the Supreme Court issued its decision in the landmark case *Brown v. Board of Education.* In this decision, the court declared that "separate but equal" education, a central provision of segregationist policy, was inherently discriminatory. Buoyed by this win, civil rights activists began to challenge Jim Crow through other forms of peaceful protest, such as the year-long mass boycott of segregated buses in Montgomery, Alabama, beginning in 1955. In *Stride Toward Freedom,* published in 1958, a confident and optimistic King describes the philosophy behind the successful boycott.

Analyze Visuals ▶
What does this photo reveal about the risks of nonviolent protest?

Oppressed people deal with their oppression in three characteristic ways. One way is acquiescence: the oppressed resign themselves to their doom. They **tacitly** adjust themselves to oppression, and thereby become conditioned to it. In every movement toward freedom some of the oppressed prefer to remain oppressed. Almost 2,800 years ago Moses set out to lead the children of Israel from the slavery of Egypt to the freedom of the promised land.[1] He soon discovered that slaves do not always welcome their deliverers. They become accustomed to being slaves. They would rather bear those ills they have, as Shakespeare pointed out, than flee to others that they know not of.[2] They prefer the "fleshpots of Egypt"[3]
10 to the ordeals of emancipation. Ⓐ

① Targeted Passage

tacitly (tăs'ĭt-lē) *adj.* silently

Ⓐ SYNTHESIZE RESOURCES
Reread lines 1–10. What does this paragraph tell you about the main idea?

---

1. **promised land:** the land of Canaan, promised by God in the Bible (Genesis 12:1–3, 7) to Abraham's descendants.
2. **bear those ills ... know not of:** an allusion to a line in Act 3, Scene 1, of *Hamlet* by William Shakespeare.
3. **prefer the "fleshpots of Egypt":** an allusion to a line in the book of Exodus in the Bible. As Moses was leading the Israelites out of Egypt, some of them grumbled and wished they had stayed there.

Civil rights protestors being sprayed with high-pressure hoses

---

DIFFERENTIATED INSTRUCTION

FOR ENGLISH LANGUAGE LEARNERS

Vocabulary Support Use Word Squares to teach these words from *Stride Toward Freedom: adjust* (line 3), *goal* (line 76), *generate* (line 82).

 BEST PRACTICES TOOLKIT—Transparency Word Squares p. E10

FOR STRUGGLING READERS

In combination with the *Audio Anthology CD,* use the Targeted Passages (pp. 1220, 1223, 1224, 1227) to ensure that students focus on key concepts in the selections. The Targeted Passages are also good for English language learners.

 Targeted Passage [Lines 1–10]

This passage identifies King's topic—the ways in which people respond to oppression—and

Analyze Visuals

Possible answer: This photo shows that nonviolent protesters are still at risk for violent responses from their oppressors.

About the Art The protesters in this photograph discovered that they could resist the fire hoses by holding on to one other. Uniting in this way eventually caused the firefighters to turn off their hoses, proving Dr. King's commitment to the impact of mass nonviolent protest.

TIERED DISCUSSION PROMPTS

In lines 1–10, use these prompts to help students understand King's image of oppression:

Recall What is one way that oppressed people resign themselves to oppression? *Possible answer: People may adjust and condition themselves to oppression.*

Analyze Why might some consider oppression to be more desirable than an unknown future? *Possible answer: Despite difficulties, the oppressed know that they can survive present conditions. The unknown future calls into question issues such as adaptation, change, and survival.*

Synthesize On the basis of your knowledge of King's philosophies and of the history of social revolution, what might be the two other ways that people "deal with their oppression"? *On the basis of the "Letter from Birmingham Jail," students may suggest nonviolent protest. On the basis of history, they may also suggest violent protest.*

discusses the first response, acquiescence.

- In how many ways does King believe that people respond to oppression? (line 1)
- What is the first way in which people respond to oppression? (lines 1–2)
- Why do people sometimes respond to oppression in this way? (lines 2–3)
- What are "'the fleshpots of Egypt'" and "the ordeals of emancipation"? (lines 9–10)

FOR ADVANCED LEARNERS/AP

Hypothesize Tell students to suppose that they are addressing an oppressed group that has become accustomed to its conditions. Have students write a motivational speech exhorting the group to shake off its reluctance and take action against the oppression it faces. Have students read their speeches to the class.

READING SKILL

B SYNTHESIZE SOURCES

COMMON CORE
RI 2
RI 5

Possible answer: In line 21, King identifies segregation as a specific example of a moral wrong which, through acquiescence, has become accepted as morally right.

READING SKILL

C SYNTHESIZE SOURCES

COMMON CORE
RI 2
RI 5

Possible answer: King states that violence solves no social problems, thrives on hatred, destroys community, and eventually defeats itself. He cites the wars that nations have fought as proof.

VOCABULARY

OWN THE WORD

COMMON CORE
L 4

succumb: Tell students that common synonyms of *succumb* include "submit, yield, give in, accede." Ask students to name antonyms for *succumb*. *Possible answers: resist, fight, hold firm*

There is such a thing as the freedom of exhaustion. Some people are so worn down by the yoke of oppression that they give up. A few years ago in the slum areas of Atlanta, a Negro guitarist used to sing almost daily: "Been down so long that down don't bother me." This is the type of negative freedom and resignation that often engulfs the life of the oppressed.

But this is not the way out. To accept passively an unjust system is to cooperate with that system; thereby the oppressed become as evil as the oppressor. Noncooperation with evil is as much a moral obligation as is cooperation with good. The oppressed must never allow the conscience of the oppressor to slumber.
20 Religion reminds every man that he is his brother's keeper.[4] To accept injustice or segregation passively is to say to the oppressor that his actions are morally right. It is a way of allowing his conscience to fall asleep. At this moment the oppressed fails to be his brother's keeper. So acquiescence—while often the easier way—is not the moral way. It is the way of the coward. The Negro cannot win the respect of his oppressor by acquiescing; he merely increases the oppressor's arrogance and contempt. Acquiescence is interpreted as proof of the Negro's inferiority. The Negro cannot win the respect of the white people of the South or the peoples of the world if he is willing to sell the future of his children for his personal and immediate comfort and safety. **B**

A second way that oppressed people sometimes deal with oppression is to
30 resort to physical violence and corroding hatred. Violence often brings about momentary results. Nations have frequently won their independence in battle. But in spite of temporary victories, violence never brings permanent peace. It solves no social problem; it merely creates new and more complicated ones.

Violence as a way of achieving racial justice is both impractical and immoral. It is impractical because it is a descending spiral ending in destruction for all. The old law of an eye for an eye[5] leaves everybody blind. It is immoral because it seeks to humiliate the opponent rather than win his understanding; it seeks to annihilate rather than to convert. Violence is immoral because it thrives on hatred rather than love. It destroys community and makes brotherhood impossible. It
40 leaves society in monologue rather than dialogue. Violence ends by defeating itself. It creates bitterness in the survivors and brutality in the destroyers. A voice echoes through time saying to every potential Peter, "Put up your sword."[6] History is cluttered with the wreckage of nations that failed to follow this command. **C**

If the American Negro and other victims of oppression **succumb** to the temptation of using violence in the struggle for freedom, future generations will be the recipients of a desolate night of bitterness, and our chief legacy to them will be an endless reign of meaningless chaos. Violence is not the way.

---

4. **his brother's keeper:** In the book of Genesis, after Cain killed his brother Abel, he denied knowing Abel's whereabouts by asking, "Am I my brother's keeper?" In general, the saying refers to a reluctance to accept responsibility for others.

5. **an eye for an eye:** an allusion to Exodus 21:23–25: "You shall give life for life, eye for eye...."

6. **Peter...sword":** When Jesus' disciple Peter drew his sword to try to protect Jesus, Jesus condemned his use of violence.

Language Coach

Word Definitions
Engulfs (line 15) means "flow over and swallow up" or "overwhelm." (Imagine water overflowing an island.) What does King say can overwhelm a person who is exhausted from oppression?

B SYNTHESIZE SOURCES
In lines 19–28, King states his position on how the oppressed should respond to oppression. What words and phrases reveal the specific historical example that has shaped King's thinking?

C SYNTHESIZE SOURCES
What support does King provide for his statement that violent resistance is unprofitable?

succumb (sə-kŭm′) *v.* to give in, especially to overpowering force or strength

---

DIFFERENTIATED INSTRUCTION

FOR ADVANCED LEARNERS/AP

Debate In lines 18–19, King states, "Non-cooperation with evil is as much a moral obligation as is cooperation with good." King does not condone violence, but he believes that people should actively resist injustice. Have students form two groups to debate this statement: Cooperating with unjust policies is just as evil as committing violent acts. Invite students to support arguments with historical examples.

FOR ENGLISH LANGUAGE LEARNERS

Language Coach

Words Definitions *Answer:*
When a person is exhausted from being oppressed, he or she may give up and say that the oppression doesn't matter. The person is engulfed by these feelings and doesn't try to change his or her situation. Have students consider other situations that involve being *engulfed*.

The third way open to oppressed people in their quest for freedom is the way of nonviolent resistance. Like the **synthesis** in Hegelian philosophy,[7] the principle of nonviolent resistance seeks to reconcile the truths of two opposites—acquiescence and violence—while avoiding the extremes and immoralities of both. The nonviolent resister agrees with the person who acquiesces that one should not be physically aggressive toward his opponent but he balances the equation by agreeing with the person of violence that evil must be resisted. He avoids the nonresistance of the former and the violent resistance of the latter. With nonviolent resistance, no individual or group need submit to any wrong, nor need anyone resort to violence in order to right a wrong.

It seems to me that this is the method that must guide the actions of the Negro in the present crisis in race relations. Through nonviolent resistance the Negro will be able to rise to the noble height of opposing the unjust system while loving the perpetrators of the system. The Negro must work passionately and unrelentingly for full stature as a citizen, but he must not use inferior methods to gain it. He must never come to terms with falsehood, malice, hate, or destruction. **D**

Nonviolent resistance makes it possible for the Negro to remain in the South and struggle for his rights. The Negro's problem will not be solved by running away. He cannot listen to the glib suggestion of those who would urge him to migrate en masse to other sections of the country. By grasping his great opportunity in the South he can make a lasting contribution to the moral strength of the nation and set a sublime example of courage for generations yet unborn.

By nonviolent resistance, the Negro can also enlist all men of good will in his struggle for equality. The problem is not a purely racial one, with Negroes set against whites. In the end, it is not a struggle between people at all, but a tension between justice and injustice. Nonviolent resistance is not aimed against oppressors but against oppression. Under its banner consciences, not racial groups, are enlisted.

If the Negro is to achieve the goal of integration, he must organize himself into a militant and nonviolent mass movement. All three elements are indispensable. The movement for equality and justice can only be a success if it has both a mass and militant character; the barriers to be overcome require both. Nonviolence is an imperative in order to bring about ultimate community. **E**

A mass movement of a militant quality that is not at the same time committed to nonviolence tends to generate conflict, which in turn breeds anarchy. The support of the participants and the sympathy of the uncommitted are both inhibited by the threat that bloodshed will engulf the community. This reaction in turn encourages the opposition to threaten and resort to force. When, however, the mass movement **repudiates** violence while moving resolutely toward its goal, its opponents are revealed as the instigators and practitioners of violence if it occurs. Then public support is magnetically attracted to the advocates of nonviolence, while those who employ violence are literally disarmed by overwhelming sentiment against their stand. ❧

---

7. **Hegelian** (hā-gā′lē-ən) **philosophy:** the philosophy of Georg Hegel (1770–1831), which proposed that each situation has an opposite and that both extremes will eventually be reconciled.

---

synthesis (sĭn′thĭ-sĭs)
n. the union of parts or elements into a whole

② **Targeted Passage**

D **ANALYZE GENRES**
Reread lines 58–63. What characteristics help you understand that this is an autobiography?

E **SYNTHESIZE SOURCES**
In lines 70–80, what does King say is the best way to confront racism? How does he support this view?

repudiate (rĭ-pyōō′dē-āt′)
v. to reject or renounce

REVISIT THE BIG QUESTION

How do we fight
INJUSTICE?

Discuss In lines 59–61, is loving the perpetrators of an unjust system a necessary component of ending **injustice**? Explain. *Possible answers: Some students may agree that love or forgiveness is an essential element in healing the wounds of injustice. Others may say that love is a reciprocal emotion and cannot be present where injustice reigns.*

TEXT ANALYSIS   COMMON CORE

D **ANALYZE GENRES**   RI 5   RI 6

Possible answer: King discusses his personal beliefs and uses personal pronouns.

READING SKILL   COMMON CORE

E **SYNTHESIZE SOURCES**   RI 2   RI 5

Possible answer: King says the best way to confront racism is to see it as a fight against injustice. He supports this view by arguing that it is conscience, not race, that must stand up and fight.

VOCABULARY   COMMON CORE   L 4

OWN THE WORD

• **synthesis:** Tell students that *synthesis* comes from the Greek word *sunthesis*, which refers to "putting together." Have students name other disciplines in which they have *synthesized* information and explain how, what and why they *synthesized* information to reach a conclusion.

• **repudiate:** Read the definition of *repudiate* aloud to students. Then have them name other synonyms and antonyms for the word. *Possible answers: synonyms: deny, disavow, disown; antonyms: accept, approve, welcome*

FOR STRUGGLING READERS

② **Targeted Passage** [Lines 58–75]

This passage explains King's philosophy of nonviolent resistance as a means for social change.

• What does King view as the best method to resolve the crisis in race relations? (lines 58–61)

• What advantages does nonviolent resistance offer? (lines 64–71)

FOR ADVANCED LEARNERS/AP

Cause and Effect [paired option] Ask partners to use King's explanation of militant, nonviolent, mass protest (lines 81–90) to develop a Cause-and-Effect Chain that explains his theory. Have student pairs discuss whether they find King's argument persuasive and why.

 BEST PRACTICES TOOLKIT—Transparency
Cause-and-Effect Chain pp. B16, B39

Prereading for this interview is found on page 1218.

SUMMARY

In this interview, Malcolm X argues that despite his belief in law and order, African Americans are entitled to protect their lives and property when the government does not. He recalls that the U.S. founders were oppressed people who revolted, arguing that African Americans are entitled to claim their heritage in the same way.

TEXT ANALYSIS

COMMON CORE
RI 5
RI 6

Ⓕ *Model the Skill:* **ANALYZE GENRES**

Remind students that when they read, they should look carefully at introductory paragraphs for clues that help determine genre. Point out that media reporters and other writers often gather data by directly questioning newsworthy individuals. When the results are published, both questions and answers are included.

Possible answer: *An interviewer is asking questions and an interviewee is answering them.*

NECESSARY
to PROTECT
OURSELVES

Interview with Malcolm X by Les Crane

Analyze Visuals ▶
Based on this photo, what impressions do you have of Malcolm X as a leader?

> **BACKGROUND** Malcolm X gave the following TV interview in 1964, at a time when violence against civil rights workers had escalated. Shocking images of protestors being beaten, clubbed, and tear-gassed had become staples of daily news coverage. Across the South, white supremacists tried to squelch the growing movement with murder, rifle attacks, bombings, and arson, crimes that frequently went unpunished. As attacks increased, many African Americans grew impatient with King's nonviolent tactics, expressing anger that chilled white listeners.
>
> Events came to a head in 1964, with the Freedom Summer in Mississippi. Thousands of idealistic college students joined local civil rights activists in a massive voter registration drive, and violence exploded. Three young civil rights workers were murdered by local Klansmen with the help of the police. Despite increased FBI presence in the state, by summer's end 4 workers were dead, 80 had been beaten, and scores of black churches and businesses had been torched or bombed.

Crane: You've been a critic of some of the Negro leadership in this country—Martin Luther King, Roy Wilkins, Abernathy,[1] and others—have you changed in your feelings toward them of late? **Ⓕ**

Malcolm X: I think all of us should be critics of each other. Whenever you can't stand criticism you can never grow. I don't think that it serves any purpose for the leaders of our people to waste their time fighting each other needlessly. I think that we accomplish more when we sit down in private and iron out

❶ Targeted Passage
Ⓕ ANALYZE GENRES
What details tell you that this is an interview?

---

1. **Roy Wilkins, Abernathy:** Roy Wilkins (1901–1981) was executive secretary of the National Association for the Advancement of Colored People (NAACP) from 1955 to 1977. Ralph Abernathy (1926–1990) helped Martin Luther King Jr. found the Southern Christian Leadership Conference to combat racism.

Malcolm X at a Black Muslim rally

DIFFERENTIATED INSTRUCTION

FOR STRUGGLING READERS

❶ Targeted Passage [Lines 1–5]

This passage creates the interview's context that Malcolm X has criticized his fellow African-American leaders and has emphasized his belief that such criticism is necessary.

- Who are Martin Luther King, Roy Wilkins, and Abernathy? (lines 1–2)

- What are Malcolm X's feelings toward the African-American leaders? (line 1)

- What does Malcolm X believe about the role of criticism? (lines 4–5)

FOR ENGLISH LANGUAGE LEARNERS
Vocabulary: Idioms and Phrasal Verbs Note that oral speech often includes idioms and phrasal verbs. Clarify these expressions:

- *of late* (line 3), "recently"

- *can't stand* (lines 4–5), "can't tolerate"

- *iron out* (line 7), "resolve"

- *at stake* (line 42), "threatened"

BACKGROUND

Black Muslims The photo on page 1226 shows Malcolm X at a Black Muslim rally. *Black Muslim* is a term used to describe—but is not exclusively limited to—members of the Nation of Islam. This group began in 1930 when leader Wallace D. Fard established a Detroit mosque. After Fard's disappearance in 1934, Elijah Muhammad, Fard's disciple, took over the Nation of Islam's leadership. Although the group numbered only about 8,000 when Muhammed assumed its leadership, it grew significantly during the 1950s and 60s, due to the preaching of one of its most famous converts, Malcolm X. Elijah Muhammad and Malcolm X disagreed over Muhammad's leadership. Black Muslims were blamed for the 1965 assassination of Malcolm X.

Possible answer: One of the main points is how Malcolm X views violent resistance.

TIERED DISCUSSION PROMPTS

In lines 16–23, use these prompts to help students understand Malcolm X's views about violence:

Connect What do you know about the situation in Mississippi that helps you understand Malcolm X's description of it? *Possible answer: Racial tension in Mississippi had left four civil rights workers dead and another 80 beaten, and yielded destruction of black churches and businesses.*

Interpret What does Malcolm X mean when he says the government has "proven its inability to protect us"? *Possible answer: Malcolm X means that the police and other government officials have not restrained or limited the violence against African Americans.*

Evaluate Malcolm X suggests that people may sometimes need to resort to aggressive measures to protect themselves from attack. Do you agree or disagree? Explain. *Students may agree with Malcolm X that violence is sometimes justified. Others may cite King in disagreeing and in insisting that violence is always immoral.*

Nation of Islam members at a community event in Harlem

whatever differences that may exist and try and then do something constructive for the benefit of our people. But on the other hand, I don't think that we should
10 be above criticism. I don't think that anyone should be above criticism.

Crane: Violence or the threat of violence has always surrounded you. Speeches that you've made have been interpreted as being threats. You have made statements reported in the press about how the Negroes should go out and arm themselves, form militias of their own. I read a thing once, a statement I believe you made that every Negro should belong to the National Rifle Association— **G**

Malcolm X: No, I said this: That in areas of this country where the government has proven its—either its inability or its unwillingness to protect the lives and property of our people, then it's only fair to expect us to do whatever is necessary to protect ourselves. And in situations like Mississippi, places like Mississippi where the
20 government actually has proven its inability to protect us—and it has been proven that ofttimes the police officers and sheriffs themselves are involved in the murder that takes place against our people—then I feel, and I say that anywhere, that our people should start doing what is necessary to protect ourselves. This doesn't mean

Language Coach
Word Definitions Read lines 16–19. What is the difference between *inability* and *unwillingness* (line 17)? Refer to a dictionary if necessary. What would you think about a government that was unable to protect you? What about a government that was unwilling to do so?

G SYNTHESIZE SOURCES
Usually in an interview, the reporter sets the agenda for the questions, and thus, determines the main ideas. Based on this comment from Crane, what is one of the main points in this interview?

DIFFERENTIATED INSTRUCTION

FOR STRUGGLING READERS
Develop Reading Fluency Read aloud the interview between Les Crane and Malcolm X (you may wish to use a smaller portion of the selection). Tell students to note that they are hearing a conversation between two people. Organize the class into pairs and have each student take on the role of Crane or Malcolm X. Tell students to read through the interview with their partner.

FOR ENGLISH LANGUAGE LEARNERS
Language Coach
Word Definitions *Possible answer: Inability refers to a lack of capability, while unwillingness refers to a lack of willingness or desire. Students may not respect a government unable to protect them; they may not trust a government unwilling to protect them.* Have students write a paragraph to show each word's meaning.

that we should buy rifles and go out and initiate attacks **indiscriminately** against whites. But it does mean that we should get whatever is necessary to protect our-selves in a country or in an area where the governmental ability to protect us has broken down—

Crane: Therefore you do not agree with Dr. King's Gandhian philosophy[2]—

Malcolm X: My belief in brotherhood would never restrain me in any way from
30 protecting myself in a society from a people whose disrespect for brotherhood makes them feel inclined to put my neck on a tree at the end of a rope.[3] [*Applause*]

Crane: Well, it sounds as though you could be preaching a sort of an **anarchy**—

Malcolm X: No, no. I respect government and respect law. But does the govern-ment and the law respect us? If the FBI, which is what people depend upon on a national scale to protect the morale and the property and the lives of the people, can't do so when the property and lives of Negroes and whites who try and help Negroes are concerned, then I think that it's only fair to expect elements to do whatever is necessary to protect themselves.

And this is no departure from normal procedure. Because right here in New
40 York City you have vigilante committees[4] that have been set up by groups who see where their neighborhood community is endangered and the law can't do anything about it. So—and even their lives aren't at stake. So—but the fear, Les, seems to come into existence only when someone says Negroes should form vigilante committees to protect their lives and their property. ⊞

I'm not advocating the breaking of any laws. But I say that our people will never be respected as human beings until we react as other normal, intelligent human beings do. And this country came into existence by people who were tired of tyranny and oppression and exploitation and the brutality that was being inflicted upon them by powers higher than they, and I think that it is only fair
50 to expect us, sooner or later, to do likewise. ❧

---

indiscriminately
(ĭn′dĭ-skrĭm′ə-nĭt-lē) *adv.*
randomly

anarchy (ăn′ər-kē) *n.*
an absence of political authority

2 **Targeted Passage**

COMMON CORE RI 5, RI 7

⊞ **SYNTHESIZE SOURCES**
Synthesizing sources from two different genres requires you to see past obvious differences—differences in format, intended audience, or layout—and to focus closely on the ideas and arguments in the two texts. In lines 39–44, Malcolm X talks about the role of violence in the civil rights movement. Where does King discuss violence in the previous text? Find specific passages on violence that show how the two men disagree or agree. How does each author support his arguments?

---

2. **Gandhian** (gän′dē-ən) **philosophy:** Mohandas Gandhi (1869–1948) was an Indian nationalist and spiritual leader. His use of nonviolent civil disobedience forced the British to grant India its independence in 1947.

3. **put my neck . . . rope:** an allusion to lynching, the practice of putting someone to death without due process of law. Many African Americans were lynched, usually by hanging.

4. **vigilante** (vĭj′ə-lăn′tē) **committees:** volunteer citizen groups that unlawfully assume powers such as pursuing and punishing suspected criminals or offenders.

NECESSARY TO PROTECT OURSELVES **1227**

READING SKILL — COMMON CORE RI 5 RI 7

⊞ **SYNTHESIZE SOURCES**
Remind students that when they synthe-size sources, they need to look for similari-ties and differences in viewpoints, histori-cal period, and in ideas. Tell students that there are several points at which violence is discussed in the two texts. Ask for volun-teers to present lines from each text that illustrate the point.

Possible answer: *King says ". . . this normal and healthy discontent can be channelled into the creative outlet of nonviolent direct action (lines 270–272). Malcolm X addresses the topic by saying, ". . . where the govern-ment actually has proven its inability to protect us . . . our people should start doing what is necessary to protect ourselves. This doesn't mean . . . attacks indiscriminately against whites. But it does mean that we should get whatever is necessary to protect ourselves. . ." (lines 19–26). Each supports his arguments by mentioning how the white majority has failed to acknowledge the civil rights of African Americans. Malcolm X cites government's involvement in violence against African Americans (lines 20–22), while King discusses how nonviolent action can bring about negotiation (lines 84–93).*

Extend the Discussion How do King and Malcolm X employ biblical and historical allusions to support their themes?

VOCABULARY — COMMON CORE L 4

OWN THE WORD

• **indiscriminately:** Have students find the root, *discriminate,* and define it. Remind them that the prefix *in-* means "not."

• **anarchy:** Ask students to identify the context clues that help determine the meaning of *anarchy.*

SELECTION WRAP–UP

READ WITH A PURPOSE Now that students have read the selections, ask them how King's and Malcolm X's positions on racial oppression differed.

FOR STRUGGLING READERS

2 **Targeted Passage** [Lines 33–50]

In this passage, Malcolm X explains his posi-tion on anarchy and revolution.

• What does Malcolm X feel toward govern-ment and the law? (line 33)

• In what ways does Malcolm X think that government and the law have failed African Americans? (lines 34–42)

• What is Malcolm X's historical justification for violent revolution? (lines 47–50)

FOR ENGLISH LANGUAGE LEARNERS

Vocabulary Support Use New Word Analysis to teach this word from "Necessary to Protect Ourselves": *react* (line 46).

 **BEST PRACTICES TOOLKIT—Transparency** New Word Analysis p. E8

NECESSARY TO PROTECT OURSELVES **1227**

Practice and Apply

For preliminary support of post-reading questions, use these copy masters:

 **RESOURCE MANAGER—Copy Masters**
Reading Check p. 98
Analyze Genres p. 91
Question Support p. 99
Additional selection questions are provided for teachers on page 85.

ANSWERS   COMMON CORE RI 2, RI 5, RI 6

1. *King identifies acquiescence, violence, and nonviolent resistance.*

2. *A movement must be militant, nonviolent, and massive to achieve integration.*

3. *Malcolm X says that criticism is a necessary element of growth.*

Possible answers:

4. *Malcolm X refers to the American Revolution to make the point that revolution against tyranny is an American value.*

5. ◼ **COMMON CORE FOCUS Synthesizing Sources** *The main differences between the two leaders are views on violence as a means for achieving racial equality, a value for morality above practical logic, and the desirability of white support. Both leaders believe that racism is unjust and reflects a serious flaw in American society.*

6. ● **COMMON CORE FOCUS Analyze Genres** *Answers will vary. Students should indicate that autobiographies allow writers to express their beliefs in any way they wish, whereas interviews are largely controlled by the person asking the questions.*

7. *Response 1: Acquiescence; Problems: makes the oppressed as evil as the oppressor, is cowardly; Response 2: Violence; Problems: is immoral, defeats itself by creating bitterness; Response 3: Nonviolent resistance; Advantages: allows the oppressed to oppose injustice without creating bitterness and hatred*

Comprehension

1. **Recall** What three ways of dealing with oppression does Martin Luther King Jr. identify?

2. **Clarify** In King's view, what three qualities must a movement have in order to achieve the goal of integration?

3. **Summarize** How does Malcolm X justify his criticisms of other civil rights leaders?

Text Analysis

4. **Identify Allusion** Reread lines 47–50 of "Necessary to Protect Ourselves." Identify the historical event that Malcolm X is alluding to. What point does he make by invoking this event?

5. ◼ **Synthesize Sources** Review the chart you created as you read both texts. What are the main differences between the two leaders? What beliefs, if any, do they have in common? Be specific in your answers.

6. ● **Analyze Genres** Think about the two works you just read. How do these two genres allow people to express their opinions in similar and different ways?

7. **Analyze Structure** The structure of King's argument follows the formal logic of Hegelian philosophy, in which two opposing ideas are merged into a unified concept, or synthesis. To analyze this structure, complete a diagram like the one shown. In what way does the third response resolve the problems of the first two?

   Response 1: _____ Problems:
   •
   •
   •

   Response 2: _____ Problems:
   •
   •
   •

   Response 3: _____ Advantages:
   •
   •
   •

8. **Make Judgments** Many commentators criticized Martin Luther King Jr., for using radical and provocative tactics. In what ways might perceptions of King's philosophy have changed after Malcolm X gained public prominence?

Text Criticism

9. **Biographical Context** Reread the author biographies of King (page 1202) and Malcolm X (page 1218). What aspects of their personal histories may have influenced their different approaches to fighting racial injustice?

> *How do we fight* **INJUSTICE?**
>
> Today, many people around the world are persecuted. If you could talk to one such person, what would you tell him or her? How would you advise this person to fight injustice?

COMMON CORE

RI 2 Determine two or more central ideas of a text and analyze their development over the course of the text, including how they interact and build on one another to provide a complex analysis; provide an objective summary of the text. RI 5 Analyze and evaluate the effectiveness of the structure an author uses in his or her argument, including whether the structure makes points clear, convincing, and engaging. RI 6 Determine an author's point of view or purpose in a text in which the rhetoric is particularly effective, analyzing how style and content contribute to the power, persuasiveness, or beauty of the text.

---

8. *In comparison to Malcolm X, King probably began to seem less threatening to the status quo of American society.*

9. *King was well educated and an ordained minister. He achieved early success fighting segregation through nonviolent means. Malcolm X had a difficult childhood, and his family life was destroyed by racial violence. He educated himself in prison. Malcolm X's experiences may have caused him to view nonviolence as unrealistic or naive.*

> *How do we fight* **INJUSTICE?**
> Answers will vary.

Vocabulary in Context

▲ VOCABULARY PRACTICE

Choose the letter of the phrase that defines or is related to the boldfaced word.

1. **succumb:** (a) a golfer practicing, (b) an army surrendering, (c) a teenager voting
2. **synthesis:** (a) a proposal combining several views, (b) a detailed analysis of a plan, (c) a group of protestors
3. **anarchy:** (a) an art auction, (b) an angry mob, (c) hereditary rule
4. **indiscriminately:** (a) a decision based on evidence, (b) a choice made without thought, (c) unfair hiring practices
5. **repudiate:** (a) retype a report, (b) vote someone out of office, (c) renew a promise
6. **tacitly:** (a) agree by nodding, (b) disagree by shouting, (c) celebrate by singing

WORD LIST

anarchy
indiscriminately
repudiate
succumb
synthesis
tacitly

ACADEMIC VOCABULARY IN SPEAKING

- complex - economic - establish - ethnic - evolve

Imagine that Martin Luther King Jr. and Malcolm X were discussing their respective beliefs about confronting racism. What do you think they would say to each other? In a small group, debate this **complex** issue by representing these two men's beliefs. Remember to keep the debate polite, focused, and in line with the beliefs of Malcolm X and King. Use at least three Academic Vocabulary words in your debate.

⦙⦙⦙ **COMMON CORE**

L 4b Identify and correctly use patterns of word changes that indicate different meanings or parts of speech. **SL 1b** Work with peers to promote civil, democratic discussions. **SL 1c** Ensure a hearing for a full range of positions on an issue.

VOCABULARY STRATEGY: THE GREEK PREFIX *syn-*

The **origin** of the prefix *syn-*, which appears at the beginning of the vocabulary word *synthesis*, is the Greek language. *Syn-* means "together" or "at the same time." This prefix, which may also be spelled *sym-* or *syl-*, is found in a number of English words, both scientific and nonscientific. To understand words with *syn-*, use your knowledge of the origin of the prefix, look for context clues, or consult a dictionary.

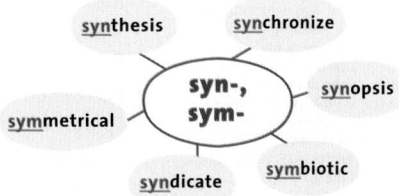

PRACTICE Choose the word from the word web that best completes each sentence. Use context clues to help you or, if necessary, check a dictionary.

1. They were able to _____ their watches and meet promptly at noon.
2. Though the halves of people's faces aren't exactly _____, they are fairly close.
3. Some animals have a _____ relationship and depend on each other for survival.
4. Groups or individuals in a _____ work together for some common interest.
5. A _____ can provide a quick overview of a story, play, or report.

Interactive Vocabulary — **THINK**central

Go to **thinkcentral.com**.
KEYWORD: HML11-1229

DIFFERENTIATED INSTRUCTION

FOR ENGLISH LANGUAGE LEARNERS

Task Support: Vocabulary in Writing Provide these possible sentence starters:

- King has no tolerance for *glib* _____.
- King advocates a *militant* approach to _____.
- King does not want African Americans to *succumb* to _____.
- Malcolm X *repudiates* _____.
- Malcolm X does not advocate *anarchy*; rather, he _____.

FOR ADVANCED LEARNERS/AP

Greek Prefixes Suggest that students choose another Greek prefix such as *amphi-*, *peri-*, or *tele-* to study. Have students create word webs listing examples of words containing the chosen prefix. Then have students write cloze sentences for each listed word, making sure to include context clues. Invite partners to trade word webs and sentences, then to complete each other's sentences.

ANSWERS

Vocabulary in Context

VOCABULARY PRACTICE

1. *(b) an army surrendering*
2. *(a) a proposal combining several views*
3. *(b) an angry mob*
4. *(b) a choice made without thought*
5. *(b) vote someone out of office*
6. *(a) agree by nodding*

R RESOURCE MANAGER—Copy Master
Vocabulary Practice p. 96

ACADEMIC VOCABULARY IN SPEAKING

Students should focus on King's and Malcolm X's beliefs about confronting racism, and should include Academic Vocabulary.

VOCABULARY STRATEGY: THE GREEK PREFIX *syn-*

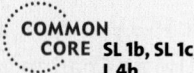

COMMON CORE SL 1b, SL 1c, L 4b

Review with students ways to use context clues and prefixes to determine the meanings of unfamiliar words.

1. *synchronize*   4. *syndicate*
2. *symmetrical*   5. *synopsis*
3. *symbiotic*

R RESOURCE MANAGER—Copy Master
Vocabulary Strategy p. 97

Interactive Vocabulary — **THINK**central

Keywords direct students to a **WordSharp** tutorial on **thinkcentral.com** or to other types of vocabulary practice and review.

Assess and Reteach

Assess

DIAGNOSTIC AND SELECTION TESTS
Selection Test A pp. 325–326
Selection Test B pp. 327–328

Interactive Selection Test on **thinkcentral.com**

Reteach

Level Up Online Tutorials on **thinkcentral.com**
Reteaching Worksheets on **thinkcentral.com**

Focus and Motivate

COMMON CORE FOCUS

RI 5 Analyze and evaluate the effectiveness of the structure an author uses in his or her exposition or argument. **RI 6** Determine an author's point of view or purpose in a text in which the rhetoric is particularly effective. **W 2** Write informative/explanatory texts to examine and convey complex ideas, concepts, and information. **W 9** Draw evidence from informational texts to support analysis, reflection, and research.

SUMMARY

In memory of Dr. King, Jr., César Chávez argues in support of nonviolent protest as the only means for achieving fair treatment for migrant farm workers. Chávez reiterates King's points that violence undermines their cause.

Essay

Use a Y Chart to help students compare King's and Chávez's arguments. Have students list Chávez's reasons for supporting nonviolent protest on the left and King's reasons on the right. Have students identify similarities and differences between the two philosophies.

🗂 **BEST PRACTICES TOOLKIT—Transparency**
Y Chart p. A27

Teach

Standards Focus: Analyze an Argument

- Explain that analyzing an argument means breaking the entire argument down into its smallest parts in order to understand its elements and evaluate the writer's logic.

- Point out that writers sometimes make generalizations based on too few examples. At other times, writers draw false comparisons or make inaccurate assumptions. Such errors in argumentation undermine a writer's position.

- Encourage students to assess the logic of Chávez's argument as they analyze it.

🄡 **RESOURCE MANAGER—Copy Master**
Analyze an Argument p. 109

Reading for Information

Martin Luther King Jr.: He Showed Us the Way
Essay

Use with "Stride Toward Freedom" and "Necessary to Protect Ourselves," beginning on pages 1220 and 1224.

◌ **COMMON CORE**

RI 5 Analyze and evaluate the effectiveness of the structure an author uses in his or her exposition or argument, including whether the structure makes points clear, convincing, and engaging. **RI 6** Determine an author's point of view or purpose in a text in which the rhetoric is particularly effective, analyzing how style and content contribute to the power, persuasiveness, or beauty of the text.

You have just read two civil rights leaders' positions on the use of force in political resistance. Now you will learn why César Chávez, a leader in the crusade for the fair treatment of migrant farm workers, advocated nonviolence to achieve his goals. As you read his argument, bear in mind that later you will be asked to support your own opinion on this weapon for social change.

Standards Focus: Analyze an Argument

A well-formed argument typically contains a **claim,** the writer or speaker's position on a problem or issue; **support,** which consists of logical reasons and valid evidence that help to justify the claim; and a **counterargument,** brief arguments that refute or answer objections to any opposing claims. A strong argument is based on a **general principle** that clearly links the verifiable support to the claim. If you can't accept the general principle as a truth, then the entire argument falls apart.

Sometimes, though, writers and speakers use faulty reasoning, or **logical fallacies,** to support their claims. Some common logical fallacies include

- **circular logic:** supporting a statement by stating it in different words;
- **stereotyping:** broad statements about people on the basis of their gender, ethnicity, race, or political, social, professional, or religious group;
- **hasty generalization:** a conclusion drawn from too little evidence or from evidence that is biased;
- **non-sequitur:** a conclusion that does not follow logically from the "proof" offered to support it.

As you read, analyze the argument made by Chávez, completing a chart similar to the one below.

	Notes
Claim	Nonviolence is the "only weapon that Christians who struggle for social change can claim as their own."
General Principle	
Support	
Counterargument(s)	

Selection Resources

*See resources on the **Teacher One Stop DVD-ROM** and on **thinkcentral.com**.*

🄡 **RESOURCE MANAGER UNIT 6**
Lesson Support,* pp. 101–114

DIAGNOSTIC AND SELECTION TESTS
Selection Tests, pp. 329–332

🗂 **BEST PRACTICES TOOLKIT**
pp. A1, A27

TECHNOLOGY

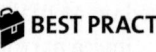 **Teacher One Stop DVD-ROM**
 Student One Stop DVD-ROM
 Audio Anthology CD
 ExamView Test Generator on the Teacher One Stop

* Resources for Differentiation

MARTIN LUTHER KING JR.:

He Showed Us the Way

César Chávez

In honoring Martin Luther King Jr.'s memory we also acknowledge nonviolence as a truly powerful weapon to achieve equality and liberation—in fact, the only weapon that Christians who struggle for social change can claim as their own.

Dr. King's entire life was an example of power that nonviolence brings to bear in the real world. It is an example that inspired much of the philosophy and strategy of the farm workers' movement. This observance of Dr. King's death gives us the best possible opportunity to recall the principles with which our struggle has grown and matured. **A**

Our conviction is that human life is a very special possession given by God to man and that no one has the right to take it for any reason or for any cause, however just it
10 may be.

We are also convinced that nonviolence is more powerful than violence. Nonviolence supports you if you have a just and moral cause. Nonviolence provides the opportunity to stay on the offensive, and that is of crucial importance to win any contest.

If we resort to violence then one of two things will happen: either the violence will be escalated and there will be many injuries and perhaps deaths on both sides, or there will be total demoralization of the workers. **B**

Nonviolence has exactly the opposite effect. If, for every violent act committed against us, we respond with nonviolence, we attract people's support. We can gather the support of millions who have a conscience and would rather see a nonviolent
20 resolution to problems. We are convinced that when people are faced with a direct appeal from the poor struggling nonviolently against great odds, they will react positively. The American people and people everywhere still yearn for justice. It is to that yearning that we appeal.

A **ANALYZE AN ARGUMENT**
Notice that Chávez states his **claim** in his opening sentence. Now reread lines 4–7 to identify his first piece of **support** for this claim. Note this on your chart.

B **ANALYZE AN ARGUMENT**
Reread lines 11–16. What reasons does Chávez give to support his conviction that "nonviolence is more powerful than violence"? Note these reasons as "support" in your chart.

A *Model the Skill:* **ANALYZE AN ARGUMENT**

Model for students how to analyze an argument. Work with them to restate the claim Chávez makes in lines 1–3, then direct students to line 4 as the clearest statement of support for Chávez's claim. Help students list their notes in the chart introduced on page 1230.

	Notes
Claim	Nonviolence is the only accept-able strategy for Christians who work for social change.
Support	King's life

Possible answer: *Chávez's first piece of support for his claim is King's entire life.*

B **ANALYZE AN ARGUMENT**

Possible answer: *Support for the power of nonviolence over violence includes that nonviolence supports just and moral causes and provides protesters with the opportunity to stay on the offensive.*

FOR ENGLISH LANGUAGE LEARNERS
Vocabulary: Cognates Help students recognize and define these cognates: *honoring/ honrado, memory/memoria* (line 1); *powerful/poderoso, equality/igualdad, liberation/ liberación* (line 2); *possible/posible* (line 6); *possession/posesión* (line 8); *violence/violencia* (line 11); *cause/causa,* (line 12); *offensive/ ofensiva* (line 13); *respond/responder* (line 18); *conscience/ conciencia* (line 19); *problems/ problemas,* (line 20); *justice/justicia* (line 22).

Options for Reading Have students use Jigsaw Reading with Chávez's argument. Form "home" groups, giving each student a number that corresponds to a portion of the text. Then have students move into their numbered groups to read and discuss the assigned text. Have students return to their home groups to share summaries of their assigned passages.

🧰 **BEST PRACTICES TOOLKIT**
Jigsaw Reading p. A1

INFORMATIONAL ANALYSIS · COMMON CORE · RI 5 RI 6

C ANALYZE AN ARGUMENT

Possible answer: Objections to Chávez's claim about the advantages of nonviolence include feelings of frustration, impatience, anger, poverty, and powerlessness.

INFORMATIONAL ANALYSIS · COMMON CORE · RI 5 RI 6

D ANALYZE AN ARGUMENT

Possible answer: Chávez argues that violence causes protesters to lose regard for human life and justice and thereby to lose strength.

INFORMATIONAL ANALYSIS · COMMON CORE · RI 5 RI 6

E ANALYZE AN ARGUMENT

Possible answer: Chávez accuses those who espouse violence of exploiting people and engaging in vicious oppression.

Extend the Discussion In what ways does Chávez support this claim?

Language Coach

Fixed Expressions "Work on the theory" is a **fixed expression**—a normal, often used combination of words—meaning "function under a certain belief." Another verb used with *theory* is *advance.* Use a fixed expression with *advance* in a sentence of your own.

C ANALYZE AN ARGUMENT
In this paragraph, Chávez anticipates objection to his claim about the advantages of nonviolence. Identify these objections.

D ANALYZE AN ARGUMENT
What counterarguments does Chávez provide to refute the objections he just anticipated? Note these in your chart.

E ANALYZE AN ARGUMENT
What does Chávez say about those who espouse violence?

But if we are committed to nonviolence only as a strategy or tactic, then if it fails our only alternative is to turn to violence. So we must balance the strategy with a clear understanding of what we are doing. However important the struggle is and however much misery, poverty and exploitation exist, we know that it cannot be more important than one human life. We work on the theory that men and women who are truly concerned about people are nonviolent by nature. These people become violent when
30 the deep concern they have for people is frustrated and when they are faced with seemingly insurmountable odds.

We advocate militant nonviolence as our means of achieving justice for our people, but we are not blind to the feelings of frustration, impatience and anger which see the inside every farm worker. The burdens of generations of poverty and powerlessness lie heavy in the fields of America. If we fail, there are those who will see violence as the shortcut to change. **C**

It is precisely to overcome these frustrations that we have involved masses of people in their own struggle throughout the movement. Freedom is best experienced through participation and self-determination, and free men and women instinctively prefer
40 democratic change to any other means. Thus, demonstrations and marches, strikes and boycotts are not only weapons against the growers, but our way of avoiding the senseless violence that brings no honor to any class or community. The boycott, as Gandhi taught, is the most nearly perfect instrument of nonviolent change, allowing masses of people to participate actively in a cause.

When victory comes through violence, it is a victory with strings attached. If we beat the growers at the expense of violence, victory would come at the expense of injury and perhaps death. Such a thing would have a tremendous impact on us. We would lose regard for human beings. Then the struggle would become a mechanical thing. When you lose your sense of life and justice, you lose your strength. **D**
50 The greater the oppression, the more leverage nonviolence holds. Violence does not work in the long run and if it is temporarily successful, it replaces one violent form of power with another just as violent. People suffer from violence. Examine history. Who gets killed in the case of violent revolution? The poor, the workers. The people of the land are the ones who give their bodies and don't really gain that much for it. We believe it is too big a price to pay for not getting anything. Those who espouse violence exploit people. To call men to arms with many promises, to ask them to give up their lives for a cause and then not produce for them afterwards, is the most vicious type of oppression. **E**

We know that most likely we are not going to do anything else the rest of our lives
60 except build our union. For us there is nowhere else to go. Although we would like to see victory come soon, we are willing to wait. In this sense time is our ally. We learned many years ago that the rich may have money, but the poor have time.

It has been our experience that few men or women ever have the opportunity to know the true satisfaction that comes with giving one's life totally in the nonviolent struggle for justice. Martin Luther King Jr., was one of these unique servants and from him we learned many of the lessons that have guided us. For these lessons and for his sacrifice for the poor and oppressed, Dr. King's memory will be cherished in the hearts of the farm workers forever.

DIFFERENTIATED INSTRUCTION

FOR ENGLISH LANGUAGE LEARNERS

Language Coach

Fixed Expressions *Answer: Answers will vary but should demonstrate an understanding of the meaning of* advance. Have students make a list of verbs that can be used with the word *theory.* Call on students to share items from their lists. Discuss as a class if these verbs could be used with *theory* to form a fixed expression.

FOR STRUGGLING READERS

Develop Reading Fluency Model fluent reading by reading aloud a passage of 10–15 lines to the class. Tell students to note the phrasing and intonation of your speech. Next read the first line of the passage and have students repeat it back to you as a class. Continue until students have "echoed" the entire passage. Conclude by asking for a volunteer to read the passage aloud to the class.

Comprehension

1. **Clarify** In addition to serving as weapons against growers, how do boycotts benefit the masses of people who participate in them?

Text Analysis

2. **Examine General Principle** What is Chávez's basic assumption about social change and just people? Might someone disagree with him? Explain.

3. **Analyze an Argument** Chávez acknowledges that nonviolent resistance has certain limitations. How does he answer each of the following objections?

   - People who have been oppressed may feel legitimately frustrated or impatient and turn to violence as a shortcut to change.
   - Violence does sometimes bring about victory.

COMMON CORE

RI 5 Analyze and evaluate the effectiveness of the structure an author uses in his or her argument, including whether the structure makes points clear, convincing, and engaging. **RI 6** Determine an author's point of view or purpose in a text in which the rhetoric is particularly effective, analyzing how style and content contribute to the power, persuasiveness, or beauty of the text. **W 2** Write informative/explanatory texts to examine and convey complex ideas, concepts, and information through the effective selection and analysis of content. **W 9** Draw evidence from informational texts to support analysis, reflection, and research.

Read for Information: Analyze an Argument

> **WRITING PROMPT**
>
> Find an article in a newspaper that argues a position. Analyze the argument to determine if the writer clearly states his or her claim, includes strong supporting evidence, and addresses possible opposing claims with counterarguments.

Use these questions to help you with the writing prompt:

1. What claim is the writer making? What general principle is the claim based on? Do you agree or disagree with the general principle?

2. What support does the writer give to uphold his or her claim? Does the writer cite specific facts, statistics, expert opinions, and true-life examples as evidence? Or does the writer include unfounded opinions as evidence?

3. Does the writer use any logical fallacies, such as hasty generalizations or stereotypes?

4. What counterarguments does the writer include? Are they valid arguments to objections that someone might raise?

5. Overall, how well do you think the writer argues his or her point?

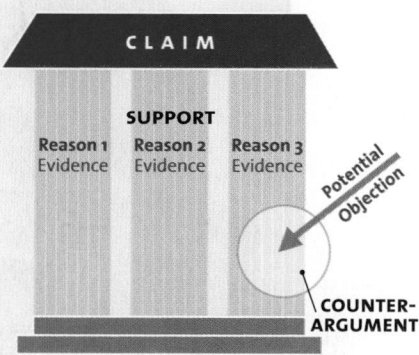

CLAIM

SUPPORT

Reason 1 Evidence | Reason 2 Evidence | Reason 3 Evidence

Potential Objection

COUNTER-ARGUMENT

For preliminary support of post-reading questions, use these copy masters:

R **RESOURCE MANAGER—Copy Masters**
Reading Check p. 113
Support an Opinion p. 110
Question Support p. 114

Additional selection questions are provided for teachers on page 104.

ANSWERS

 **COMMON CORE RI 5, RI 6**

1. *Boycotts help participants vent their frustrations in a positive and honorable way.*

Possible answers:

2. *Chávez's basic assumption is that social change is a moral pursuit that all just people will support. People who support the status quo and are suspicious of change might disagree with Chávez's assumption.*

3. *Violence fails as a shortcut to change in that it squanders lives in the short term and causes people to devalue human life and justice, which undermines strength and victory. A victory reached by violence has strings attached, namely the loss of life and moral strength.*

Read for Information: Analyze an Argument

 **COMMON CORE W 2, W 9**

Writing Prompt *Answers will vary, but should include a thorough analysis of the writer's argument, including his or her claim, supporting evidence, and counterarguments to potential opposing claims.*

Assess

DIAGNOSTIC AND SELECTION TESTS
Selection Test A pp. 329–330
Selection Test B/C pp. 331–332

Interactive Selection Test on **thinkcentral.com**

Reteach

Level Up Online Tutorials on **thinkcentral.com**
Reteaching Worksheets on **thinkcentral.com**

Reading Lesson 14: Synthesizing Information
Informational Text Lesson 14: Elements of an Argument

FOR STRUGGLING WRITERS

Read for Information

- Provide students with this sentence to help them develop thesis statements: Nonviolent resistance is an effective (ineffective) weapon for social change. Tell students that they may revise this sentence as necessary to better suit their writing styles.

- Provide photocopies of the articles by King, Malcolm X, and Chávez. Encourage students to highlight text that supports their thesis statements.

FOR ADVANCED LEARNERS/AP

Tone Challenge students to convey their personal attitudes toward violence and nonviolence through careful word choice and allusion. Encourage students to analyze ways that King, Malcolm X, and Chávez use word choice and allusion to convey tone. Urge students to use these writers' works as models for their essays.

Focus and Motivate

SUMMARIES

TV News Report In this clip, the death of César Chávez serves as the basis for a retrospective look at his work for social justice.

"¡Sí se Puede!" In this magazine article, the life and work of César Chávez are remembered as his family opens the National Chávez Center in California.

Does the news SHAPE history?

Have students view a current news report on a public figure such as a political leader. Ask students to describe the report's contents and identify ways in which it impacts viewers' impressions of the person. Discuss the impact of news coverage on a person's legacy; for example, students might consider whether this figure will likely become part of history or gain only momentary attention.

BACKGROUND

The news report appeared on April 23, 1993. Its lead reporter, John Blackstone, is a veteran correspondent. The magazine article was published to mark the 2004 opening of the National Chávez Center.

Media Study

Perspectives in the News

TV Newscast Clip / Magazine Article on **Media ◉ Smart** DVD-ROM

Does the news SHAPE *history?*

Recall the last time the news reported the death of someone who had played a pivotal role in history. Did the report provide new insights or change your opinion of the individual? Or did it reinforce your prior perceptions? In this lesson, you'll examine the way two different news forms covered a national figure and analyze the ways news reports can shape your **impressions** of that figure.

Background

Cultivating Activism As a teenager, César Chávez worked the fields of California with his family. After serving in the U.S. Navy in World War II, he returned to the fields but grew more politically active.

Inspired by the life and nonviolent teachings of Mohandas Gandhi and the activism of Martin Luther King Jr., Chávez helped found the National Farm Workers Association (NFWA) in 1962. "Nonviolence in action is a very potent force and it can't be stopped," said Chávez of the NFWA's founding principle. By staging peaceful strikes, marches, and boycotts, as well as fasting (as Gandhi had) in protest, Chávez garnered a wide swath of support for *La Causa* (the cause). Followers rallied to the call "*¡Sí Se Puede!*" which, translated to English, means "Yes, we can!"

Another force contributing to Chávez's cause, as well as to the larger American civil rights movement of the 1950s and 60s, was mass media. Print and network TV news coverage of marches, boycotts, and other acts of protest helped to fuel a spirit of activism nationwide. Millions were stirred by coverage that spotlighted both extraordinary leaders like Chávez and ordinary people.

César Chávez died in 1993. In following the peaceful legacy of Gandhi and King, Chávez created one of his own.

Media Study Resources

Media Literacy: Historical Perspectives in the News

The news media uses images and words to depict the work of political figures who, in time, become history makers. Just as writers of literature present their perspectives through the use of tone and diction, journalists convey certain ideas, values, and beliefs through those elements and others that are unique to news reports. In addition, journalists can shape an audience's perceptions by reporting on the individual from a particular perspective.

News reports can appear in both electronic and print forms. To help you analyze the perspective of a news report, examine the images and statements to determine the overall purpose of the report. Then think about how the report affects your perceptions of the person depicted.

STRATEGIES FOR ANALYZING NEWS REPORTS

TV News Reports

A typical TV news report is quite brief. To convey a strong impression of the report's subject, journalists choose the visual and verbal elements carefully.

- Focus on the **footage**—the film, videotape, and photographs that are edited into a report. The footage compiled on a historical figure can be edited to portray the individual in different ways.
- Notice what the **anchor** says in the **lead-in,** the introduction. The emphasis journalists put on certain words can suggest a figure's historical significance.
- Pay attention to descriptive words used in a reporter's **voice-over,** the narration that plays as images are shown. Also, listen for **sound bites,** statements excerpted from interviews or speeches that are edited into the report. Sound bites can be selected to create a certain impression of subject.

Magazine Article

The typical magazine feature article might cover a subject in more than one page, providing in-depth coverage.

- Consider how the **headline** and **subhead** frame the content of the article for a reader.
- Preview the **opening paragraph,** which often sets the tone for the article and is intended to draw in the reader.
- Make inferences about the **images.** Think about why certain photographs were chosen for an article.
- Scrutinize **quotes,** which might be made by the subject of the article or by others. Determine what the quotes reveal about the subject.

¡SÍ SE PUEDE!
"Yes, we can!"—*CÉSAR CHÁVEZ'S INSPIRING MESSAGE LIVES ON IN NEW MEMORIAL CENTER*

MEDIA STUDY **1235**

MEDIA STUDY: TEACHING OPTIONS

Teaching Option 1: The Basics (1–2 days)

1. Begin the Media Study using the material provided on pages 1234–1235.
2. Show the Introduction on Media*Smart.* As they watch the First Viewing, have students use the Viewing Guide on page 1236, along with the corresponding copy master on page 121 of the Resource Manager. Discuss their responses.
3. Return to the pupil book for the extension activities on page 1237.

Teaching Option 2: In-Depth Study (2–3 days)

1. Begin the Media Study using pages 1234–1235.
2. Show the Introduction and First Viewing from Media*Smart.* Then continue on Media*Smart* with the Media Lessons, using the teacher notes in the Resources section.
3. Show the Guided Analysis presentation. Have students record their observations on the Student Viewing Guide in the Resources section from Media*Smart.*
4. Return to the pupil book, page 1237.

Media Literacy

Review with students the terms *tone* and *diction* and the way these elements help writers convey particular perspectives to readers. Tone is the writer's attitude toward his or her subject. Tone is revealed through word choice, or diction. Write these two lists of nouns on the board: *activist, hero, visionary; agitator, dissenter, troublemaker.* Lead students to discuss ways that each of these word lists reveals something about the writer's or speaker's attitude toward Chávez. Then, discuss the chart on page 1235.

- **Footage vs. Images** Point out that like the images on page 1235, the full news report primarily features footage of people—from Chávez himself to migrant workers—while the article features images of the National Chávez Center. Ask students to suggest the impression such images likely create in each report. *Possible answer: Images of people, especially Chávez and those affected by him, create a personal impression of the man. Images of buildings create an impression of Chávez's wider impact on society.*

- **Lead-in vs. Opening Paragraph** Tell students that in the lead-in to the TV news report, the anchor calls Chávez a "fighter." In the opening paragraph of the magazine article, the writer calls Chávez a "national icon." Ask students to compare and contrast what each of these words suggests about Chávez's historical significance. *Possible answer: "Fighter" suggests that Chávez will be remembered for his tenacity and commitment. "National icon" suggests that he will be remembered for the way he inspired people.*

- **Sound Bites vs. Quotes** In the TV news report, the UFW's vice president says that Chávez's legacy is to "give one's life to help other people." In the magazine article, Chávez's granddaughter says, "People look at him like a saint or a mythical figure. . . . But I tell them he was my grandfather." Ask students to discuss what each of these quotations reveals about Chávez. *Possible answer: The quote in the news report reveals that Chávez was a great leader. The quote from the article suggests that he was a humble family man.*

MEDIA STUDY **1235**

Practice and Apply

VIEWING GUIDE

1. As students prepare to view the clip and read the magazine article, tell them that they will be asked to describe ways that images and words contribute to their impressions of César Chávez. Encourage them to listen and watch for these elements:

   - **footage** and **images** that highlight particular aspects or qualities of Chávez
   - what the **lead-in** and **opening paragraph** suggest about Chávez's historical significance
   - ways that the **sound bites** and **quotes** create impressions of Chávez

2. Some students may have difficulty focusing simultaneously on images and words. Allow students to experience the news report once without words and once with closed eyes. Allow students to cover the images and words alternately as they review the magazine article.

R RESOURCE MANAGER—Copy Masters
   Viewing Guide p. 121
   Close Viewing p. 122
   Media Activity p. 123

Use this resource with the Viewing Guide:

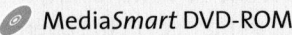 Media*Smart* DVD-ROM

ANSWERS

FIRST VIEWING: Comprehension

1. *Chávez says that his greatest accomplishment was to reduce workers' fears of their employers.*

2. *In addition to the National Center, César Chávez Day is an official holiday. Many public places have been named in his honor, including parks, schools, libraries, and other public facilities.*

CLOSE VIEWING: Media Literacy

Possible answers:

3. *News anchor Dan Rather describes Chávez as a "fighter." The news reporter says that Chávez was a man who fought for those no one else would fight for.*

4. *This sound bite provides an assessment of Chávez's impact on people from someone who either knew him or worked closely for his cause.*

Media⬤Smart DVD-ROM
- **Selection 1:** "Chávez" from the CBS Nightly News
- **Type:** Newscast clip
- **Anchor:** Dan Rather
- **Reporter:** John Blackstone
- **Running time:** 2.5 minutes
- **Selection 2:** "¡Sí Se Puede!"
- **Type:** Magazine article

1236

---

5. *The phrases "national icon" and "committed person of vision" suggest that Chávez's work had as much significance in American life as the work of some of America's great military leaders.*

6. **News Report:** *It was delivered on the day of Chávez's death in 1993. Its purpose was to commemorate Chávez's life and work.* **Magazine Article:** *It was written in 2004. Its purpose was to mark the opening of the National Chávez Center and to preserve Chávez's legacy.*

Viewing Guide for
News Perspectives

View the news clip and access the full text of the magazine article on the DVD. As you watch the TV news report, focus on the images that are used to tell César Chávez's story and listen for any descriptive words about Chávez's life and work. As you read the magazine article, look for the ways in which the writer describes Chávez and his legacy. To help you analyze these pieces, refer to these questions.

NOW VIEW

FIRST VIEWING: Comprehension

1. **Recall** In the TV news report, what does Chávez say he regards as his "biggest single accomplishment"?

2. **Summarize** Based on your review of the headline, subhead, and opening paragraph of the magazine article, summarize the ways Chávez has been honored since his death.

CLOSE VIEWING: Media Literacy

3. **Analyze Statements** What **descriptions** did you notice in the news anchor's **lead-in**, or introduction to the Chávez piece, or in the reporter's **voice-over** that reveal respect for the historical figure's accomplishments?

4. **Analyze Sound Bites** The clip includes a **sound bite** in which an individual states about Chávez, "His biggest legacy was to give his life for other people." Why do you think the news report includes this sound bite?

5. **Make Judgments** Briefly review the magazine article to choose a word or phrase that you think was carefully chosen to comment on the legacy of César Chávez. Describe what meaning this choice would have for viewers who had not been old enough to be aware of the leader in his lifetime.

6. **Compare Purposes** When and why do you think the TV news report was created? When and why was the magazine article published? Examine each news format and use a comparison chart to compare the purposes.

NEWS REPORT	When First Reported	Purpose for Report
"Chávez"		
"¡Sí Se Puede!"		

Write or Discuss

Determine Perspectives In two brief statements, describe the perspective of both the newscast clip and the magazine article. Review the reports closely, jotting down any descriptive words or phrases about César Chávez that give you a sense of him as a person and as a leader. In addition, refer to the chart you devised to compare the purposes of the news forms. Think about

- the overall tone each news report conveys
- the details each piece presents about Chávez's life and times
- the visual elements
- the use of sources who provide sound bites and quotes

Produce Your Own Media

Create a News Feature Celebrate the life of someone who has made a positive impact on your community by creating a news feature. The subject could be a friend, a family member, or anyone else you admire. The feature can be a visual piece, in the form of video, or a written piece with photographs that illustrate it in the style of a magazine.

HERE'S HOW Here are some suggestions for creating your news feature:

- Decide on your perspective for the feature. The basis for your perspective might be the subject's achievements or personal qualities.
- Research your subject: do interviews, gather facts and any visual images you may want to use. If possible, interview the people who know the subject.
- For a TV news story, write a script that plots out which visuals you will use with your voice-over narration. Allow plenty of time for actually putting your scrapbook, video, or presentation piece together.
- For a magazine article based on your research, write a first draft that covers as much of the material as you see fit. Then, edit your article with an eye on where you might be able to use an image or two of the person in the layout.

Further Exploration

Analyze Words With a partner or in a small group, find two different types of media that cover the same subject or event. For example, the report could be a TV newscast and a weekly newsmagazine about a development in the U.S. space program, or a hometown newspaper and a national sports magazine reporting on steroid use in baseball, and so on. Look closely at each news source and jot down the adjectives and adverbs used to describe the event or people involved. What perspective do you think these words convey? Consider

- who created the news piece and what their opinion of the subject might be
- what audience the news piece is written for

Cite specific examples from the media sources to support your impressions.

COMMON CORE

RI 7 Integrate and evaluate multiple sources of information presented in different media or formats as well as in words in order to address a question or solve a problem. **W 2** Write informative/explanatory texts to examine and convey complex ideas, concepts, and information clearly and accurately through the effective selection, organization, and analysis of content. **SL 2** Integrate multiple sources of information presented in diverse formats and media in order to make informed decisions and solve problems.

Media Tools THINK central

Go to **thinkcentral.com**.
KEYWORD: HML11-1237

Tech Tip

You can use digital pictures with a presentation software program and provide the voice-over in real time.

Produce Your Own Media

Rubric: Create a News Feature A strong news feature should

- convey perspective through tone and choice of detail
- feature credible research, interviews, and source material
- contain visuals that support a dominant impression of the subject
- include well-written text that clearly expresses factual information and creates a meaningful portrait

- show evidence of revision and editing
- appear as a polished, finished final product

R RESOURCE MANAGER—Copy Master
Produce Your Own Media p. 124

Write or Discuss

COMMON CORE RI 7, W 2, SL 2

Determine Perspectives In their statements, students should discuss tone, details, visuals, and quotations to support their assessments of the reporters' perspectives. Make sure that students understand that both pieces eulogize Chávez. In such writing, it would be unusual for reporters to include negative commentary.

MEDIA STUDY WRAP-UP

Have students summarize what they have learned about ways that introductions, visuals, and quotations in media create impressions of social and political figures. Urge students to use terms such as *footage, lead-in,* and *sound bites* in their summaries.

RETEACH

For students who are unable to apply the Media Study skills, select from these reteaching options:

- **Camera Shots** Provide students with a familiar image from television news, such as an anchorperson at a desk. Ask, Why would you expect to see an anchorperson on the screen? *(to introduce or present a news item).* Show students a visual of a reporter on location reporting a story. Ask, Why would you see a reporter on location? *(to do interviews or show the news as it happens).*
- **Editing** Have students consider news programs they have watched. Ask, In what ways do producers control our perception of the news? *(by deciding who to interview, what visuals to use, whether or not to include graphics, how long to devote to different stories).*

Media Tools THINK central

Media study keywords point to **MediaScope,** a Web site that helps students strengthen media analysis and production skills.

COMMON CORE FOCUS

RI 3 Analyze a complex set of ideas or sequence of events and explain how specific individuals, ideas, or events interact and develop over the course of the text. **RI 6** Determine an author's point of view or purpose in a text in which the rhetoric is particularly effective, analyzing how style and content contribute to the power, persuasiveness, or beauty of the text. **W 3** Write narratives to develop real or imagined experiences or events using effective technique, well-chosen details, and well-structured event sequences. **W 3d–e** Use precise words and phrases, telling details, and sensory language to convey a vivid picture of the experiences, events, setting, and/or characters; provide a conclusion that follows from and reflects on what is experienced, observed, or resolved over the course of the narrative. **L 5b** Analyze nuances in the meaning of words with similar denotations.

ABOUT THE AUTHOR

After students read about Moody's life, have them discuss the way the violent murders of her neighbors may have affected her as a young adult. *Possible answer: Her neighbors' murders may have made Moody angry and more likely to protest.*

NOTABLE QUOTE

"I never really saw myself as a writer. I was first and foremost an activist in the civil rights movement in Mississippi." —**Anne Moody**

Ask students what this quote tells them about Anne Moody's character. *Possible answer: Moody is humble and cares more for the cause than her own fame or personal fulfillment.*

COMMON CORE

RI 3 Analyze a complex set of ideas or sequence of events and explain how specific individuals, ideas, or events interact and develop over the course of the text. **RI 6** Determine an author's point of view or purpose in a text in which the rhetoric is particularly effective, analyzing how content contributes to the power, persuasiveness, or beauty of the text.

DID YOU KNOW?

Anne Moody . . .

- went to college on a basketball scholarship.
- left the civil rights movement over concerns about black nationalism.
- rarely gives interviews or makes public appearances.

Civil Rights and Protest Literature

from Coming of Age in Mississippi

Autobiography by Anne Moody

Meet the Author

Anne Moody born 1940

Anne Moody was one of many dedicated college students who were on the frontlines in the battle for civil rights. In her award-winning autobiography, she details the dangers she and other young activists faced as they challenged segregation laws across the South. Her unflinching descriptions of taunts, beatings, and intimidation reveal the violent realities of nonviolent protest. They also call to mind the words of Martin Luther King Jr., who commended these brave young men and women for "their sublime courage, their willingness to suffer, and their amazing discipline in the midst of great provocation."

Climate of Fear Moody was the oldest of nine children born to desperately poor African-American farmers in rural Mississippi. When she was just nine years old, Moody began working after school as a maid to help her family pay for food and clothing. Periodic acts of racist violence effectively intimidated the black community in Moody's hometown. When local white supremacists set fire to her neighbor's shack, killing the family inside, her mother advised her, "Just act like you don't know nothing." But Moody was part of a new generation that would no longer be silenced.

Dedicated Activist Moody first attended Natchez Junior College and later transferred to Tougaloo College, graduating in 1964. As a college student, she worked with major civil rights organizations such as the Congress for Racial Equality (CORE) and the National Association for the Advancement of Colored People (NAACP). Later, she became civil rights coordinator at Cornell University. Throughout her time in the movement, Moody faced constant threats to her life and worked to the point of exhaustion to integrate public facilities, extend voting rights, and promote literacy. Commenting on King's famous speech "I Have a Dream," she once quipped, "We never have time to sleep, much less dream." Often frustrated and discouraged at the slow pace of social change, Moody came to see the civil rights struggle as part of a larger fight for universal human rights. As she explained, "It's the fight of every ethnic and racial minority, every suppressed and exploited person, every one of the millions who daily suffer one or another of the indignities of the powerless and voiceless masses." Her autobiography is a moving testament to the dedication and courage that inspired hundreds of thousands of people to take action for social justice.

1238

Negro Sitdowns Stir Fear Of Wider Unrest in South

By CLAUDE SITTON

See resouces on the **Teacher One Stop DVD-ROM** *and on* thinkcentral.com.

R **RESOURCE MANAGER UNIT 6**
Plan and Teach, pp. 125–132
Summary, pp. 133–134†‡*
Text Analysis and Reading Skill, pp. 135–138†*
Grammar and Style, p. 141

DIAGNOSTIC AND SELECTION TESTS
Selection Tests, pp. 333–336

BEST PRACTICES TOOLKIT
Words with Multiple Meanings, p. E31
Making Inferences, p. A13
Sequence Chain, p. B21

TECHNOLOGY
- **Teacher One Stop DVD-ROM**
- **Student One Stop DVD-ROM**
- **GrammarNotes DVD-ROM**
- **ExamView Test Generator** on the **Teacher One Stop**

---

* Resources for Differentiation   **†** Also in Spanish   **‡** In Haitian Creole and Vietnamese

TEXT ANALYSIS: EYEWITNESS ACCOUNT

Anne Moody wrote this **eyewitness account** to document the violence she faced as a civil rights worker in Mississippi. Like a camera, Moody records events from her vantage point on the scene. She uses precise, factual **diction** to capture what she sees.

At exactly 11 A.M., Pearlena, Memphis, and I entered Woolworth's from the rear entrance.

Moody is not a journalist; rather, she is recording events as part of her personal story. Moody's **tone**, or attitude toward her subject, is for the most part objective as she describes what happens to her. However, she includes some subjective details about her thoughts and feelings, too.

But something happened to me as I got more and more involved in the Movement. It no longer seemed important to prove anything.

As you read Moody's account, think about how her perspective influences the way she describes events.

READING STRATEGY: READING A PRIMARY SOURCE

Because Anne Moody had firsthand knowledge of the events she describes, her account is considered a **primary source.** From her recollections, you can learn about an important turning point in America's history and culture. Moody's **purpose** is to provide accurate background information to show the difficulties she and other African Americans faced.

In her account, Moody gives precise details about times and places:

Seconds before 11:15 we were occupying three seats at the previously segregated Woolworth's lunch counter.

Moody's careful attention to details helps validate her writing as a trustworthy primary source.

As you read, record in a chart like the one below specific details Moody includes in her account.

Details	Time	Place

 Complete the activities in your **Reader/Writer Notebook.**

Who makes HISTORY?

Most people assume that history is made by great leaders, the ones who get their pictures in textbooks. But those leaders don't make history by themselves. Their achievements depend on the combined efforts of people like your parents, your teachers, and you.

DISCUSS Working in a small group, think of three or four historical events. In what ways did these events depend on the efforts of ordinary people? Make a list for each event.

Rosa Parks Highway

DIFFERENTIATED INSTRUCTION

FOR ENGLISH LANGUAGE LEARNERS

Perspective Point out to students that an eyewitness account is written from the first-person point of view, so will use the pronouns *I, me,* and *we.* Discuss with English language learners how accounts of civil rights activists present at an event might differ from those of people who only experienced the event through media reports.

Primary Source Explain to English language learners that primary sources are original accounts created by people with firsthand experience of historical events. Primary sources include journals, diaries, letters, memoirs, and autobiographies. Explain that Anne Moody's autobiography is a primary source that conveys firsthand knowledge of the civil rights movement.

Teach

Who makes HISTORY?

Introduce the question. After small groups complete the *DISCUSS* activity, invite them to share their historical events and lists. Then ask them to generalize about ways that ordinary people affect history.

TEXT ANALYSIS · · · · · · · COMMON CORE RI 6

● *Model the Skill:*
EYEWITNESS ACCOUNT

Tell students that in eyewitness accounts, the individual's perspective influences how he or she describes events. Have students reread the author's biography on page 1238. Point out that from the biography, they can predict subjective details likely to be found in Moody's autobiography, such as her inner thoughts about her protest choices, along with the frustration, anger, and discouragement that she felt during this time.

READING STRATEGY · · · · · · · COMMON CORE RI 3

■ *Model the Skill:* **READING A PRIMARY SOURCE**

To show students how to analyze the details of a primary source, have students reread **Dedicated Activist** on page 1238 and identify some of the major groups and individuals that were involved in the civil rights movement. ***Possible answer:*** *The Congress for Racial Equality (CORE) and the National Association for the Advancement of Colored People (NAACP) were both involved in civil rights, as was Martin Luther King, Jr.*

GUIDED PRACTICE Ask students to discuss some of the risks and obstacles that the activists faced.

R **RESOURCE MANAGER—Copy Master** Reading a Primary Source p. 137 (for student use while reading the selection)

SUMMARY

This excerpt from Moody's autobiography details the time when, as a college student in 1963, she participated in a sit-in at a Woolworth's lunch counter in Jackson, Mississippi. Moody and her two classmates ask to be served at a whites-only counter. Despite being denied service, they remain seated. The press soon arrives to question everyone present. Hecklers get involved and Moody and her companions are violently assaulted. They go back to their seats, but finally agree to leave after several hours. Moody later participates in a rally attended by Medgar Evers.

READ WITH A PURPOSE

Help students set a purpose for reading. Tell them to read "Coming of Age in Mississippi" to learn how Anne Moody finds the courage to fight for change.

REVISIT THE BIG QUESTION

Who makes HISTORY?

Discuss Based on lines 4–5, what do Moody's personal history and actions prove about people affecting **history**? *Possible answer: Moody was a struggling college student (lines 5–7) who believed so strongly in the movement seeking African-American rights that she participated in a sit-in. Her sit-in encouraged other sit-ins and the publicity of equal rights. Moody proves that a regular person can affect the history of a people.*

Coming of Age in Mississippi

Anne Moody

BACKGROUND On February 1, 1960, four African-American college freshmen seated themselves at a whites-only lunch counter in Greensboro, North Carolina, refusing to leave until they were served. Within a week, 300 people had joined the sit-in; within two months, sit-ins were being held in 54 cities across the South, most of them organized by college and high school students. By August 1961, more than 70,000 protesters, black and white, had participated in sit-ins. Students, impatient with the slow pace of change, had decided to confront segregation head-on. As you'll read in Anne Moody's account, those confrontations made the ugliness of racism impossible to ignore. Be warned that in relating the confrontations, Moody repeats certain offensive racial epithets.

I had counted on graduating in the spring of 1963, but as it turned out, I couldn't because some of my credits still had to be cleared with Natchez College. A year before, this would have seemed like a terrible disaster, but now I hardly even felt disappointed. I had a good excuse to stay on campus for the summer and work with the Movement, and this was what I really wanted to do. I couldn't go home again anyway, and I couldn't go to New Orleans—I didn't have money enough for bus fare.

During my senior year at Tougaloo,[1] my family hadn't sent me one penny. I had only the small amount of money I had earned at Maple Hill.[2] I couldn't
10 afford to eat at school or live in the dorms, so I had gotten permission to move off campus. I had to prove that I could finish school, even if I had to go hungry every

Analyze Visuals ▶
What details in the photo help convey the tension of the scene at the protest?

Left to right: John Salter, Joan Trumpauer, and Anne Moody, seated at the Woolworth's lunch counter

---

1. **Tougaloo:** Tougaloo College, a traditionally African-American college on the northern edge of Jackson, Mississippi.

2. **Maple Hill:** a restaurant in New Orleans where Moody had worked in the summer.

DIFFERENTIATED INSTRUCTION

FOR ENGLISH LANGUAGE LEARNERS

Culture: Clarify Explain that the phrase *coming of age* in the title refers to the process a person goes through to gain a deeper understanding of the world while becoming an adult. As students read this excerpt, have them consider what Moody might have learned about the world and people that contributed to her coming of age. Explain that Moody uses *Movement* (line 5) to refer to the civil rights movement.

FOR STRUGGLING READERS

Use one or more of the Targeted Passages (pp. 1242, 1244, 1246) to ensure that students focus on key events and concepts. Targeted Passages are also good for English language-learners.

BACKGROUND

Segregation Laws and Sit-ins The segregation laws, or "Jim Crow" laws, that Anne Moody and other African Americans were fighting were laws in many Southern states that discriminated against African Americans. These laws denied African Americans the right to vote, the right to attend state universities, and the right to use public facilities, such as restrooms and lunch counters. The sit-in was one way that African Americans such as Moody protested these laws. A sit-in was a nonviolent form of protest that people used to integrate a public place. The people entered a facility, sat down, and refused to leave until they received service or attention. These protests led up to the Civil Rights Act of 1964, which finally put an end to the segregation laws that Moody helped fight.

Analyze Visuals

Possible answer: *Details that convey the tension of this protest scene include the hostile expressions on the faces of the white onlookers and the large number of white males in the crowd relative to the two women, one of whom is African American, sitting at the counter waiting to be served. The three protesters at the counter appear to be trying to ignore the crowd and talk to one another, but are clearly in an uncomfortable position. Moreover, the clothing of the young man on the left appears to be stained, possibly from assaults by the onlookers.*

FOR ADVANCED LEARNERS/AP

Make Judgments Begin a class discussion by asking students to think about when a country or culture is ready for change. Do the people in a country make changes gradually, or when they are forced to? How do people adapt to changes in cultural and societal norms? Encourage students to use specific examples when expressing their opinions.

A Model the Skill:
EYEWITNESS ACCOUNT

Point out that Moody's narration describes historic events, but that it is subjective, not objective. Tell students that eyewitness accounts will include the writer's feelings and thoughts.

Possible answer: *Moody's personal challenges include loneliness and lack of money and family support. She is fighting just to get through school (lines 9–12). These personal challenges motivate her to get involved in the Movement, which gives her a sense of purpose and meaning (lines 14–15).*

Extend the Discussion In what ways could personal reactions make a person both more and less effective as a civil rights worker?

B AUTHOR'S PURPOSE

Point out the precision with which Moody explains the planning. Then read lines 26–38 aloud.

Possible answer: *The news media were alerted at ten o'clock. Over the next hour, picketers diverted attention until the three people staging the sit-in could take their places at the lunch counter. Moody is precise in order to give an accurate account. Her diction creates a factual tone, which strengthens her argument.*

---

day. I knew Raymond and Miss Pearl[3] were just waiting to see me drop out. But something happened to me as I got more and more involved in the Movement. It no longer seemed important to prove anything. I had found something outside myself that gave meaning to my life. **A**

I had become very friendly with my social science professor, John Salter, who was in charge of NAACP[4] activities on campus. All during the year, while the NAACP conducted a boycott of the downtown stores in Jackson, I had been one of Salter's most faithful canvassers[5] and church speakers. During the last week
20 of school, he told me that sit-in demonstrations were about to start in Jackson and that he wanted me to be the spokesman for a team that would sit-in at Woolworth's lunch counter. The two other demonstrators would be classmates of mine, Memphis and Pearlena. Pearlena was a dedicated NAACP worker, but Memphis had not been very involved in the Movement on campus. It seemed that the organization had had a rough time finding students who were in a position to go to jail. I had nothing to lose one way or the other. Around ten o'clock the morning of the demonstrations, NAACP headquarters alerted the news services. As a result, the police department was also informed, but neither the policemen nor the newsmen knew exactly where or when the demonstrations would start.
30 They stationed themselves along Capitol Street and waited.

To divert attention from the sit-in at Woolworth's, the picketing started at J. C. Penney's a good fifteen minutes before. The pickets were allowed to walk up and down in front of the store three or four times before they were arrested. At exactly 11 A.M., Pearlena, Memphis, and I entered Woolworth's from the rear entrance. We separated as soon as we stepped into the store, and made small purchases from various counters. Pearlena had given Memphis her watch. He was to let us know when it was 11:14. At 11:14 we were to join him near the lunch counter and at exactly 11:15 we were to take seats at it.

Seconds before 11:15 we were occupying three seats at the previously segregated
40 Woolworth's lunch counter. In the beginning the waitresses seemed to ignore us, as if they really didn't know what was going on. Our waitress walked past us a couple of times before she noticed we had started to write our own orders down and realized we wanted service. She asked us what we wanted. We began to read to her from our order slips. She told us that we would be served at the back counter, which was for Negroes. **B**

"We would like to be served here," I said.

The waitress started to repeat what she had said, then stopped in the middle of the sentence. She turned the lights out behind the counter, and she and the other waitresses almost ran to the back of the store, deserting all their white customers.
50 I guess they thought that violence would start immediately after the whites at the counter realized what was going on. There were five or six other people at the counter. A couple of them just got up and walked away. A girl sitting next to me

---

1 **Targeted Passage**

B **AUTHOR'S PURPOSE**
Remember that one of Moody's overall purposes is to give detailed background information about an event during the civil rights movement. Reread lines 26-38. Then, summarize the timeline of the sit-in. Why does Moody give such specific details about the planning of the protest? What effect does her **diction**, or choice of words, have on her tone? How does her tone in this passage reinforce her central argument?

---

3. **Raymond and Miss Pearl:** Moody's stepfather and step-grandmother.
4. **NAACP:** National Association for the Advancement of Colored People, an organization that works to end discrimination against African Americans and other minorities.
5. **canvassers:** people who go from door to door to get support for a cause or gather opinions on an issue.

1242 UNIT 6: CONTEMPORARY LITERATURE

DIFFERENTIATED INSTRUCTION

FOR STRUGGLING READERS

1 **Targeted Passage** [Lines 16–26]
This passage shows Moody's character and her dedication to the Movement.

- How does Moody help the NAACP? What does this suggest about her character? (lines 18–19)
- Why did the NAACP struggle to find sit-in volunteers? Why is Moody willing? (lines 25–26)

FOR ENGLISH LANGUAGE LEARNERS

Culture: Clarify Explain that *picketing* (line 31) occurs when a group of people stand outside of an institution or business to express a grievance or to discourage people from entering. Picketers generally hold signs that express their grievances. Ask students to share impressions of any picketing they have seen. Then have pairs suggest and share statements that would have been suitable for the picketers in the passage to display.

FOR ADVANCED LEARNERS/AP

Hypothesize Point of View Remind students that Moody's first-person account describes the events from her perspective. Have groups explore the perspectives of others at the sit-in, such as the waitress, a reporter, or a member of the crowd. Urge students to use historical context to infer reactions, but not to assume stereotypical beliefs. For example, the supportive white customer is a native of Mississippi, but supports the protesters.

finished her banana split before leaving. A middle-aged white woman who had not yet been served rose from her seat and came over to us. "I'd like to stay here with you," she said, "but my husband is waiting."

The newsmen came in just as she was leaving. They must have discovered what was going on shortly after some of the people began to leave the store. One of the newsmen ran behind the woman who spoke to us and asked her to identify herself. She refused to give her name, but said she was a native of Vicksburg[6] and
60 a former resident of California. When asked why she had said what she had said to us, she replied, "I am in sympathy with the Negro movement." By this time a crowd of cameramen and reporters had gathered around us taking pictures and asking questions, such as Where were we from? Why did we sit-in? What organization sponsored it? Were we students? From what school? How were we classified?

I told them that we were all students at Tougaloo College, that we were represented by no particular organization, and that we planned to stay there even after the store closed. "All we want is service," was my reply to one of them. After they had finished probing for about twenty minutes, they were almost ready
70 to leave.

At noon, students from a nearby white high school started pouring in to Woolworth's. When they first saw us they were sort of surprised. They didn't know how to react. A few started to heckle and the newsmen became interested again. Then the white students started chanting all kinds of anti-Negro slogans. We were called a little bit of everything. The rest of the seats except the three we were occupying had been roped off to prevent others from sitting down. A couple of the boys took one end of the rope and made it into a hangman's noose. Several attempts were made to put it around our necks. The crowds grew as more students and adults came in for lunch.

80 We kept our eyes straight forward and did not look at the crowd except for occasional glances to see what was going on. All of a sudden I saw a face I remembered—the drunkard from the bus station sit-in. My eyes lingered on him just long enough for us to recognize each other. Today he was drunk too, so I don't think he remembered where he had seen me before. He took out a knife, opened it, put it in his pocket, and then began to pace the floor. At this point, I told Memphis and Pearlena what was going on. Memphis suggested that we pray. We bowed our heads, and all hell broke loose. A man rushed forward, threw Memphis from his seat, and slapped my face. Then another man who worked in the store threw me against an adjoining counter.

90 Down on my knees on the floor, I saw Memphis lying near the lunch counter with blood running out of the corners of his mouth. As he tried to protect his face, the man who'd thrown him down kept kicking him against the head. If he had worn hard-soled shoes instead of sneakers, the first kick probably would have

---

6. **Vicksburg:** a city in Mississippi, west of Jackson.

Language Coach

Synonyms A synonym is a word with a meaning similar to that of another word. Synonyms of *sympathy* (line 61) include *accord* and *agreement*. Use one of these synonyms to restate the woman's statement in line 61.

Language Coach

Idioms An **idiom** is an expression whose overall meaning is different from the meaning of the individual words. "All hell broke loose" (line 87) means "everything was suddenly chaotic and confusing." In what way did things get out of control?

TIERED DISCUSSION PROMPTS
Direct students to lines 56–79. Use these prompts to help students consider Moody's character in a dangerous situation:

Connect Have you or someone you know ever participated in or supported an important, but controversial, effort? In what ways were you and others affected? *Accept all thoughtful responses.*

Interpret What do the reporters' questions suggest about their interest in the sit-in? What does Moody's response reveal about her motivation? What does the newsmen's renewed interest in the hecklers suggest about their motivations? *Possible answer: The reporters ask mostly factual questions, which suggests that they are not hugely interested in why the protesters are sitting-in (lines 61–65). Moody's response of just wanting service (line 68) simplifies her motivation and makes her reasoning powerful. The newsmen's renewed interest in the hecklers suggests that they are interested in sensationalism, controversy, and violence rather than civil rights.*

Evaluate How effective is Moody's initial description of the response to the sit-in? What details support her description? *Possible answer: Her description is powerful. She uses facts, not emotionalism, to portray the danger. She describes one white woman who empathizes with their cause, but is too fearful to identify herself (lines 53–61). She also reveals the true danger by detailing the boys' use of the rope as a hangman's noose (lines 77–78).*

FOR ENGLISH LANGUAGE LEARNERS

Language Coach
Synonyms *Possible answer: My beliefs are in* accord *with those of the Negro movement.* Point out that "sympathy" implies an emotional connection, while an "agreement" is a more logical connotation.

FOR ENGLISH LANGUAGE LEARNERS

Language Coach
Idioms *Answer: A man threw Memphis on the floor and slapped Moody. Another person threw Moody against the counter.* Point out to students that Moody's narrative is presented in a formal manner, with relatively few idioms or casual phrases. Ask them to identify other idioms in the selection, such as "I didn't have one penny" (line 173).

C EYEWITNESS ACCOUNT

Possible answer: *Details that convey the danger of the protesters' situation include Moody being down on her knees (line 90), and Memphis bleeding (line 91) and being repeatedly kicked in the head (line 92). Moody's tone is surprisingly neutral and unemotional, considering the danger and injustice the protesters face.*

REVIST THE BIG QUESTION
Who makes HISTORY?

Discuss Based on lines 97–118, what does the treatment that Moody and her fellow protesters undergo suggest about the qualities needed by people who try to make **history?** In what way do the protesters affect history here? **Possible answer:** *People who try to make history must be willing to undergo hardship and be misunderstood and ill-treated. They must also be brave and single-minded, willing to do whatever it takes to further their cause. Moody and her fellow protesters were willing to be hurt (lines 96, 106–10, 116), insulted (lines 101–102), and humiliated in order to prove their point. However, because they are willing to endure these hardships, the protesters made a public statement and also elicited empathy and support from white people (lines 97–99, 100–101, 110–113), thereby affecting the outcome of history.*

D GRAMMAR AND STYLE COMMON CORE L 5b

Analyze Mood Help students understand the effect of Moody's strong choice of verbs and verbals by rereading lines 113–117, replacing *smearing* with "covering" and *gushed* with "came." Discuss ways that Moody's strong verbs and verbals better recreate the violence of the scene. Ask them to find examples of other strong verbs and verbals. **Possible answer:** *Strong verbs and verbals appear in lines 73–74, 82, 85, 87–89.*

---

killed Memphis. Finally a man dressed in plain clothes identified himself as a police officer and arrested Memphis and his attacker. **C**

Pearlena had been thrown to the floor. She and I got back on our stools after Memphis was arrested. There were some white Tougaloo teachers in the crowd. They asked Pearlena and me if we wanted to leave. They said that things were getting too rough. We didn't know what to do. While we were trying to make

100 up our minds, we were joined by Joan Trumpauer.[7] Now there were three of us and we were integrated. The crowd began to chant, "Communists, Communists, Communists." Some old man in the crowd ordered the students to take us off the stools.

"Which one should I get first?" a big husky boy said.

"That white nigger," the old man said.

The boy lifted Joan from the counter by her waist and carried her out of the store. Simultaneously, I was snatched from my stool by two high school students. I was dragged about thirty feet toward the door by my hair when someone made them turn me loose. As I was getting up off the floor, I saw Joan coming back

110 inside. We started back to the center of the counter to join Pearlena. Lois Chaffee, a white Tougaloo faculty member, was now sitting next to her. So Joan and I just climbed across the rope at the front end of the counter and sat down. There were now four of us, two whites and two Negroes, all women. The mob started smearing us with ketchup, mustard, sugar, pies, and everything on the counter. Soon Joan and I were joined by John Salter, but the moment he sat down he was hit on the jaw with what appeared to be brass knuckles. Blood gushed from his face and someone threw salt into the open wound. Ed King, Tougaloo's chaplain, rushed to him. **D**

At the other end of the counter, Lois and Pearlena were joined by George

120 Raymond, a CORE[8] field worker and a student from Jackson State College. Then a Negro high school boy sat down next to me. The mob took spray paint from the counter and sprayed it on the new demonstrators. The high school student had on a white shirt; the word "nigger" was written on his back with red spray paint.

We sat there for three hours taking a beating when the manager decided to close the store because the mob had begun to go wild with stuff from other counters. He begged and begged everyone to leave. But even after fifteen minutes of begging, no one budged. They would not leave until we did. Then Dr. Beittel, the president of Tougaloo College, came running in. He said he had just heard what was happening.

130 About ninety policemen were standing outside the store; they had been watching the whole thing through the windows, but had not come in to stop the mob or do anything. President Beittel went outside and asked Captain Ray to come and escort us out. The captain refused, stating the manager had to invite him in before he could enter the premises, so Dr. Beittel himself brought us out.

---

7. **Joan Trumpauer:** a white classmate of Moody's from Tougaloo College, who had been active in voter registration.

8. **CORE:** Congress of Racial Equality, a civil rights organization that coordinated marches and demonstrations in the 1960s.

C **EYEWITNESS ACCOUNT**
Reread lines 90–95. Identify details that convey the danger of the protesters' situation. What is surprising about Moody's **tone** in this passage?

D **GRAMMAR AND STYLE**
Reread lines 113–118. Note how Moody uses a serious tone and strong **verbs** and **verbals** like *smearing* and *gushed* to recreate the mood of the violent scene.

② **Targeted Passage**

DIFFERENTIATED INSTRUCTION

FOR STRUGGLING READERS

② **Targeted Passage** [Lines 119–134]

This passage shows the injustices Moody and the other protesters suffered and reveals police indifference to that suffering.

- In what ways are the protesters treated? Who treats them this way? (lines 121–123)

- Why does the manager decide to close the store? (lines 124–126)

- Who helps the protesters leave the store? Who doesn't help them? (lines 132–134)

FOR STRUGGLING READERS

Develop Reading Fluency Moody describes a violent scene in strong, precise terms. Model for students an effective way to read the passage. Conduct a choral reading with students, setting a deliberate pace. To emphasize the accumulation of details, divide the class into two groups that alternate, with each group reading every other sentence.

Anne Moody and other protesters leaving the sit-in

He had told the police that they had better protect us after we were outside the store. When we got outside, the policemen formed a single line that blocked the mob from us. However, they were allowed to throw at us everything they had collected. Within ten minutes, we were picked up by Reverend King in his station wagon and taken to the NAACP headquarters on Lynch Street.

140   After the sit-in, all I could think of was how sick Mississippi whites were. They believed so much in the segregated Southern way of life, they would kill to preserve it. I sat there in the NAACP office and thought of how many times they had killed when this way of life was threatened. I knew that the killing had just begun. "Many more will die before it is over with," I thought. Before the sit-in, I had always hated the whites in Mississippi. Now I knew it was impossible for me to hate sickness. The whites had a disease, an incurable disease in its final stage. What were our chances against such a disease? I thought of the students, the young Negroes who had just begun to protest, as young interns. When these young interns got older, I thought, they would be the best doctors in the world for social problems. **E**

150   Before we were taken back to campus, I wanted to get my hair washed. It was stiff with dried mustard, ketchup and sugar. I stopped in at a beauty shop across the street from the NAACP office. I didn't have on any shoes because I had lost

E EYEWITNESS ACCOUNT
Reread lines 140–150. In what ways have Moody's attitudes and beliefs changed due to her experience at the sit-in?

TIERED DISCUSSION PROMPTS
Direct students to lines 135–144. Use these prompts to help students understand the hostile environment that Moody and the protesters face:

Recall What did Dr. Beittel tell the police? *Possible answer:* *He told them they had better protect the protesters.*

Analyze Do the police in fact protect the protesters? What does this suggest about them? *Possible answer:* *No, the police do the minimum they have to by blocking the mob (lines 136–137), but they allow the people to throw objects at the protesters (lines 137–138). Their behavior suggests that they oppose the protesters' actions and have let their personal beliefs and fears, rather then a commitment to justice, rule their actions.*

Synthesize Given her remarks before the sit-in, is it surprising that Moody continues her involvement in the Movement after realizing that the killing had just begun? Explain. *Possible answer:* *No, Moody's commitment is not surprising. She knew that her involvement in the Movement might involve danger and punishment, but before the sit-in acknowledged that the Movement gave her life purpose (lines 14–15) and that she had nothing to lose (line 26). Her actions agree with her self-portrait.*

TEXT ANALYSIS   COMMON CORE   RI 6

E EYEWITNESS ACCOUNT

Possible answer: *Moody's hatred for whites (line 145) has changed into a hatred for the sickness of racism (lines 145–147). She is overwhelmed by the sickness of the racists' brutal behavior, and she knows that the killing has just begun (lines 143–144). She actually wonders whether the protesters can really succeed (line 147).*

them when I was dragged across the floor at Woolworth's. My stockings were sticking to my legs from the mustard that had dried on them. The hairdresser took one look at me and said, "My land, you were in the sit-in, huh?"

"Yes," I answered. "Do you have time to wash my hair and style it?"

"Right away," she said, and she meant right away. There were three other ladies already waiting, but they seemed glad to let me go ahead of them. The hairdresser
160 was real nice. She even took my stockings off and washed my legs while my hair was drying.

There was a mass rally that night at the Pearl Street Church in Jackson, and the place was packed. People were standing two abreast in the aisles. Before the speakers began, all the sit-inners walked out on the stage and were introduced by Medgar Evers.[9] People stood and applauded for what seemed like thirty minutes or more. Medgar told the audience that this was just the beginning of such demonstrations. He asked them to pledge themselves to unite in a massive offensive against segregation in Jackson, and throughout the state. The rally ended with "We Shall Overcome" and sent home hundreds of determined people. It
170 seemed as though Mississippi Negroes were about to get together at last. **F**

> Before I demonstrated, I had written Mama. She wrote me back a letter, begging me not to take part in the sit-in. She even sent ten dollars for bus fare to New Orleans. I didn't have one penny, so I kept the money. Mama's letter made me mad. I had to live my life as I saw fit. I had made that decision when I left home. But it hurt to have my family prove to me how scared they were. It hurt me more than anything else—I knew the whites had already started the threats and intimidations. I was the first Negro from my hometown who had openly demonstrated, worked with the NAACP, or anything. When Negroes threatened to do anything in Centreville, they were either shot like Samuel O'Quinn or run
> 180 out of town, like Reverend Dupree.[10]

I didn't answer Mama's letter. Even if I had written one, she wouldn't have received it before she saw the news on TV or heard it on the radio. I waited to hear from her again. And I waited to hear in the news that someone in Centreville had been murdered. If so, I knew it would be a member of my family. ∾

---

9. **Medgar Evers:** civil rights leader and organizer for the NAACP in Mississippi from 1954 until 1963, when he was killed by a sniper.

10. **Centreville . . . Samuel O'Quinn . . . Reverend Dupree:** In Centreville, the Mississippi town where Moody grew up, Samuel O'Quinn had been suspected of being associated with the NAACP. The Reverend Dupree had mentioned the NAACP in a sermon he preached.

1246   UNIT 6: CONTEMPORARY LITERATURE

Language Coach

Interjections An interjection is a word used to show emotion, such as "my land" in line 156. Similar interjections include "my goodness" and "oh, my." What emotion is the hairdresser showing? Why does she feel that emotion?

F **PRIMARY SOURCE** Reread lines 162–170. What does this paragraph tell you about the rally? Why would rallies like the one described be important to the success of the movement?

3 **Targeted Passage**

READING STRATEGY

COMMON CORE
RI 3

F *Model the Skill:*
PRIMARY SOURCE

Help students to understand primary sources. Explain that students need to make inferences from the text to answer the question about the rally. Then work with students to complete a Making Inferences chart with details from the paragraph.

Possible answer: *The paragraph shows that the rally was crowded (line 163), and that people were inspired by the sit-in (lines 165–166). Rallies like this one would be important to the success of the Movement because these rallies promoted a strong sense of unity and commitment to the cause of civil rights.*

📁 **BEST PRACTICES TOOLKIT—Transparency** Making Inferences p. A13

REVISIT THE BIG QUESTION
Who makes HISTORY?

Discuss Based on lines 173–184, in what way does Moody prove that she understands the dangers of changing **history** in a hostile environment? *Possible answer:* *Moody proves that she understands the dangers of changing history by acknowledging that her family might be killed for her deeds.*

SELECTION WRAP–UP

READ WITH A PURPOSE Now that students have finished reading, have them discuss how Moody found the courage to fight for change.

FOR STRUGGLING READERS

3 **Targeted Passage** [Lines 171–180]

This passage shows Moody's strained relationship with her family and the fear African Americans felt about protesting.

- What does Moody's mother ask of her? (line 172)

- Why does Moody's mother's letter hurt Moody? What does Moody know has started? (lines 175–177)

FOR ADVANCED LEARNERS/AP

Analyze Protest Music Have students research the lyrics to "We Shall Overcome" and discuss why they think the rally ended with that song (line 169). Ask them to write several paragraphs that explain why the lyrics to that song would be important to the people at the rally. Paragraphs should include an explanation of what the African Americans hoped to overcome, and a deeper explanation of the song's lyrics.

FOR ENGLISH LANGUAGE LEARNERS

Language Coach

Interjections *Possible answer:* *The hairdresser is showing surprise and concern because of the shape Moody is in.* Point out that the hairdresser's interjection indicates her Southern background. Ask students to think of interjections that are specific to their state or region.

Revolutionary Dreams

Nikki Giovanni

Love Letter I (1971), Charles Wilbert White. Color lithograph, 30" x 22 1/2". Gift of June Wayne. Image © 2007 Board of Trustees, National Gallery of Art, Washington, D.C. 1974.99.158.(B-27792)/PR. © 1971 The Charles White Archives.

i used to dream militant
dreams of taking
over america to show
these white folks how it should be
5 done
i used to dream radical dreams
of blowing everyone away with my perceptive powers
of correct analysis
i even used to think i'd be the one
10 to stop the riot and negotiate the peace
then i awoke and dug
that if i dreamed natural
dreams of being a natural
woman doing what a woman
15 does when she's natural
i would have a revolution

Practice and Apply

For preliminary support of post-reading questions, use these copy masters:

R RESOURCE MANAGER—Copy Masters
Reading Check p. 139
Eyewitness Account p. 135
Question Support p. 140

Additional selection questions are provided for teachers on page 129.

ANSWERS

COMMON
CORE RI 3, RI 6

1. *name-calling, physical violence, intimidation*

2. *The police watched but did not intervene.*

3. *The protesters believed in nonviolence.*

Possible answers:

4. *Moody knew that whites had been threatening people (lines 176–177). She thought the local racists might punish her family for her involvement in the protests.*

5. ● **COMMON CORE FOCUS Reading a Primary Source** *Moody's attention to details that can be verified by other sources helps validate her account.*

6. *Students were critical to the success of the movement because they started and organized most of the sit-ins (Background, lines 100, 119–121). Students were more aggressive about civil rights than were adults (Background).*

7. ● **COMMON CORE FOCUS Author's Purpose** *Moody was motivated to become part of history by anger over racism in her town (lines 175–180), the stress of her isolated life, the sense of purpose from the Movement (lines 8–15), and the desire to live her own life (line 174).*

8. ● **COMMON CORE FOCUS Eyewitness Account** *Moody is a credible reporter because she maintains a neutral tone, focuses on narrating facts, is honest about her own opinions, and seems to be a clear-sighted, strong individual.*

9. *Both writers seem to think a revolution is needed. Giovanni's speaker (lines 4–5) and Moody (line 140) think they know what is wrong with whites and both remain committed to their beliefs about ways to change society. Each thinks she knows ways to do that (Giovanni, lines 11–16; Moody, lines 143–144, 174).*

Comprehension

1. **Recall** What kinds of abuses were directed at the protesters during the sit-in?

2. **Recall** What role did the police play in the sit-in?

3. **Clarify** Why didn't the protesters fight back?

Text Analysis

4. **Make Inferences** After the sit-in, why was Anne Moody worried that a member of her family would be killed?

● 5. **Draw Conclusions from a Primary Source** Review the chart you created as you read. How does Moody's record of these events add to the validity of the account as a trustworthy primary source document?

6. **Synthesize Details** In what ways were students critical to the success of the movement? Use details from the background and the selection in your answer.

● 7. **Analyze Author's Perspective** Consider what you learn about Moody's character and private life from the account. What factors contributed to her decision to take action and become part of history? Be specific in your answers.

● 8. **Evaluate an Eyewitness Account** In your opinion, is Moody a credible reporter of events? In your answer, consider each of the following aspects of her account:

   • presentation of facts (lines 31–38)
   • diction and tone (lines 106–118)
   • opinions expressed (lines 140–147)
   • character traits (lines 171–180)

9. **Compare Texts** Reread the poem on page 1247. In what ways are Nikki Giovanni's thoughts about social change similar to Moody's? Cite details in your answer.

Text Criticism

10. **Different Perspectives** Anne Moody and Martin Luther King Jr., provide different views of the struggle for civil rights: that of a rank-and-file activist and that of a movement leader. In what ways do their accounts reflect their different roles within the movement? Support your answer with details.

> *Who makes* **HISTORY?**
>
> When you consider great people from history, do you also think about everyone who helped make them great? Anne Moody mentions several people who helped her and her friends during and after the sit-in. In your opinion, how important was the contribution of these people? Explain your answer.

COMMON CORE

RI 3 Analyze a complex set of ideas or sequence of events and explain how specific individuals, ideas, or events interact and develop over the course of the text. **RI 6** Determine an author's point of view or purpose in a text in which the rhetoric is particularly effective, analyzing how content contributes to the power, persuasiveness, or beauty of the text.

10. *Moody narrates day-to-day details of ways protests were organized, the dangers protesters faced, and the real-life stresses of social justice work. She includes details about her personal and family life. King talks about big ideas, uses lots of inspiring slogans and persuasive rhetoric. He doesn't reveal personal information.*

> *Who makes* **HISTORY?**
> Students might consider how those in the sit-in received encouragement and financial aid from their families and friends, support that allowed them to keep up their spirits and continue to fight.

Language

COMMON CORE

L 5b Analyze nuances in the meaning of words with similar denotations. **W 3** Write narratives to develop real or imagined experiences or events using effective technique, well-chosen details, and well-structured event sequences. **W 3d–e** Use precise words and phrases, telling details, and sensory language to convey a vivid picture of the experiences, events, setting, and/or characters; provide a conclusion that follows from and reflects on what is experienced, observed, or resolved over the course of the narrative.

◆ **GRAMMAR AND STYLE: Create Mood**

Review the **Grammar and Style** note on page 1244. **Mood** is the feeling that a writer creates for the reader through such elements as **word choice, imagery,** and **tone.** Moody's account has a tense, serious mood. She uses plain, powerful language, avoiding sensationalism to let the mob's actions speak for themselves.

> *Simultaneously, I was snatched from my stool by two high school students. I was dragged about thirty feet toward the door by my hair when someone made them turn me loose.* (lines 107–109)

The author's choice of strong **verbs** like *snatched* and *dragged* allows her to convey the violence of the scene while maintaining a calm, controlled tone. Note that Moody uses straightforward **declarative sentences** to describe her experiences, without adding details about her own responses to what occurs.

PRACTICE The following paragraph is written to create a tense, dramatic mood. Rewrite the paragraph, adjusting word choice, imagery, and tone to create a lighter, more comic mood. A sample beginning is provided for you.

> We all sat quietly, waiting for news. My palms began to sweat and I had trouble swallowing. I looked over at my friend, seated two rows away, but I couldn't catch her eye. She looked like she was about to cry. I was hoping the news wouldn't be as bad as we feared. Then, the door opened and he walked in. I couldn't believe it. All the rumors were true: we'd been assigned the toughest teacher in the entire school for homeroom. It was going to be a long, long year.

EXAMPLE

"Hi, everybody!" our new teacher said, holding a bunch of balloons. "Welcome to homeroom!"

READING-WRITING CONNECTION

 YOUR TURN Expand your understanding of Moody's account by responding to this prompt. Then, use the **revising tips** to improve your report.

WRITING PROMPT	**REVISING TIPS**
WRITE AN EYEWITNESS REPORT An effective eyewitness report puts the reader in the midst of the action while providing the context needed to understand the events described. Write a **three- to five-paragraph eyewitness report** on an event of your choosing, such as a sporting event or a community gathering. Use precise details and a clear, logical structure to make the event accessible to your audience.	• Use descriptive language to describe the event. • Use action verbs to show rather than tell. • Choose an appropriate tone for your subject matter. • Include an explanation of why the event was meaningful to you.

Interactive Revision **THINK**central

Go to **thinkcentral.com**.
KEYWORD: HML11-1249

DIFFERENTIATED INSTRUCTION

FOR STRUGGLING WRITERS
Task Support: Writing Prompt

- Tell students to choose an event that is uncomplicated and thus fairly easy to describe.

- Ask students to record sensory language associated with each action listed in their Sequence Chain. For example, students might record sounds of victory for an action such as scoring the winning point.

- Remind students that an eyewitness report is written from the first-person point of view, using the pronouns *I* and *me*. Students must still find a balance between personal feeling and factual recording.

- Ask students to identify the mood they intend to convey and the tone they will use before they begin writing. Encourage students to use strong verbs, too.

Language

COMMON CORE **L 5b W 3, W 3d–e,**

◆ **GRAMMAR AND STYLE**

Review that imagery is writing that creates mental pictures by appealing to the senses, that tone is a writer's attitude toward the subject, and that declarative sentences are statements that end in periods. ***Possible answer:*** *. . . When I looked over at my best friend, she was actually crying with joy. We had both expected to get the toughest teacher in the school this year, and envisioned suffering through a miserable year. Instead, we were delighted to find the best-loved teacher in the school walk through our door. We knew we would have one of the best years yet!*

R **RESOURCE MANAGER—Copy Master**
Create Mood p. 141

◆ **READING-WRITING CONNECTION**

Remind students that it is Moody's precise and vivid description of the events that makes her account so gripping. Suggest students use a Sequence Chain to record the most important actions and details of their chosen event.

BEST PRACTICES TOOLKIT—Transparency
Sequence Chain p. B21

Writing Online  **THINK**central

The following tools are available online at **thinkcentral.com** and on **Write***Smart* CD-ROM:
- **Interactive Graphic Organizers**
- **Interactive Student Models**
- **Interactive Revision Lessons**
For additional grammar instruction, see **GrammarNotes** on **thinkcentral.com**.

Assess and Reteach

Assess

DIAGNOSTIC AND SELECTION TESTS
> Selection Test A pp. 333–334
> Selection Test B/C pp. 335–336

Interactive Selection Test on **thinkcentral.com**

Reteach

Level Up Online Tutorials on **thinkcentral.com**

Reteaching Worksheets on **thinkcentral.com**
> Literature Lessons 42, 43, Research and Study Skills Lesson 5

COMMON CORE FOCUS

RI 1 Cite strong and thorough textual evidence to support analysis of what the text says explicitly as well as inferences drawn from the text, including determining where the text leaves matters uncertain. **RI 6** Determine an author's point of view or purpose in a text in which the rhetoric is particularly effective, analyzing how style and content contribute to the power, persuasiveness, or beauty of the text. **L 4a** Use context as a clue to the meaning of a word or phrase. **L 5a** Interpret figures of speech (e.g., paradox) in context and analyze their role in the text.

ABOUT THE AUTHOR

After students read about Baldwin's life, have them draw conclusions about his character —for example, that he was intelligent and responsible. Ask them to speculate on ways that racial strife might have contributed to his "crisis of faith." Discuss ways in which the perspective of distance might help a writer bear witness to the place from which he came.

NOTABLE QUOTE

"American history is longer, larger, more various, more beautiful, and more terrible than anything anyone has ever said about it."
—*James Baldwin*

Ask students what this quote suggests about James Baldwin and his view of American history. Point out his belief in the country's complexity and contradictions, as well as its positive qualities.

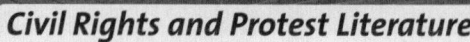

COMMON CORE

RI 1 Cite strong and thorough textual evidence to support analysis of what the text says explicitly as well as inferences drawn from the text, including determining where the text leaves matters uncertain. **RI 6** Determine an author's point of view or purpose in a text in which the rhetoric is particularly effective, analyzing how style and content contribute to the power, persuasiveness, or beauty of the text. **L 5a** Interpret figures of speech (e.g., paradox) in context and analyze their role in the text.

DID YOU KNOW?

James Baldwin . . .

• was mentored by poet Countee Cullen in high school.

• moved to Paris at age 24 and only returned to the United States for visits.

• was working on a biography of Martin Luther King Jr., when he died.

(background) Harlem in 1937

Civil Rights and Protest Literature

My Dungeon Shook: Letter to My Nephew

Open Letter by James Baldwin

Meet the Author

James Baldwin 1924–1987

In the turbulent 1960s, James Baldwin became one of the country's most sought-after commentators on racial politics. But Baldwin never considered himself a spokesperson. Rather, he saw his role as bearing witness "to whence I came, where I am . . . to what I've seen and the possibilities that I think I see." This autobiographical vantage point is the hallmark of Baldwin's greatest works, from his moving first novel, *Go Tell It on the Mountain* (1953), to the provocative essays collected in *Notes of a Native Son* (1955), *Nobody Knows My Name* (1961), and *The Fire Next Time* (1963).

Early Struggles Born and raised in Harlem, Baldwin never knew his biological father and had a strained relationship with his stepfather, a domineering, bitter man who preached at a storefront evangelical church on weekends. A star pupil and voracious reader, the young James also helped his overworked mother raise his eight brothers and sisters. After a dramatic religious conversion at age 14, he gained local acclaim as a "boy-preacher." Then, at 18, a crisis of faith drove Baldwin to break with the church and leave home.

Emerging Artist Working to establish his literary career, Baldwin

supported himself by writing book reviews and waiting tables. Baldwin achieved some success but felt increasingly stifled by the racist climate of the United States. In a life-changing decision in 1948, he bought a one-way plane ticket to Paris. "Once I found myself on the other side of the ocean," he later explained, "I could see where I came from very clearly, and I could see that I carried myself, which is my home, with me. You can never escape that."

Long-Distance Outrage With their penetrating insight and apocalyptic tone, Baldwin's essay collections were bestsellers. By the mid-1960s, he was an international celebrity, popular on the lecture circuit and in public debates, interviews, and panel discussions in the United States and Europe. In writing about his perceptions and personal torments, Baldwin made white Americans deeply, painfully aware of the realities of African-American life. As black leaders in the 1950s and 1960s looked outward to break down barriers, Baldwin looked inward to examine the psychological damage of racism and the search for black identity and self-realization. In the words of playwright Amiri Baraka, "Jimmy's voice, as much as Dr. King's or Malcolm X's, helped shepherd and guide us toward black liberation."

1250

THINK central

Author Online

Go to **thinkcentral.com**. KEYWORD: HML11-1250

See resources on the **Teacher One Stop DVD-ROM** and on **thinkcentral.com**.

 RESOURCE MANAGER UNIT 6

Plan and Teach, pp. 143–150
Summary, pp. 151–152†‡*
Text Analysis and Reading Skill, pp. 153–156†*
Vocabulary, pp. 157–159*

DIAGNOSTIC AND SELECTION TESTS

Selection Tests, pp. 337–340

 BEST PRACTICES TOOLKIT

RAFT: Role, Audience, Format, Topic, p. C8
KWL: Know, Want to Know, Learned, p. A21

TECHNOLOGY

⊘ **Teacher One Stop DVD-ROM**
⊘ **Student One Stop DVD-ROM**
⊘ **Audio Anthology CD**
⊘ **ExamView Test Generator** on the **Teacher One Stop**

---

* Resources for Differentiation   † Also in Spanish   ‡ In Haitian Creole and Vietnamese

TEXT ANALYSIS: RHETORICAL DEVICES

Baldwin is known for his passionate and poetic **style,** which is based on his skillful use of **rhetorical devices.** Baldwin uses these techniques to drive home his points and to create rhythmic effects that echo spoken language:

- A **paradox** is a statement that seems contradictory but really points to an important truth. Baldwin uses this device to push his readers to think more deeply about familiar ideas.

  It is the innocence which constitutes the crime.

- **Repetition** is the use of the same word, phrase, or sentence more than once for emphasis. Baldwin uses repetition expressively, to convey deep emotions.

  You must accept them and accept them with love....

As you read, note the rhetorical devices Baldwin uses, and consider their effects.

READING STRATEGY: IDENTIFY PURPOSE

Baldwin's sentences do more than simply explain his points; they stir powerful emotional responses in the reader. Often, the meaning of his statements becomes apparent only after careful thought and reflection. As you read this letter, study Baldwin's **purpose** for writing. In a chart like the one below, note key sentences that convey Baldwin's purpose. Then, after you have finished the letter, summarize the reasons why Baldwin wrote this letter.

Baldwin's Sentence	Purpose

▲ VOCABULARY IN CONTEXT

Baldwin uses the following words in his eloquent appeal. Complete each sentence with one of the words.

WORD LIST	constitute	mediocrity	unassailable
	impertinent	truculent	

1. You conceal your fears with a(n) _____ attitude.
2. Don't settle for _____; strive for excellence.
3. It is never _____ to speak honestly.
4. Know exactly what tasks and obligations _____ your duty.
5. Let your convictions be strong and your truth _____.

 Complete the activities in your **Reader/Writer Notebook.**

What protects your sense of SELF?

Part of growing up is deciding who you want to be and how to make your vision a reality. But how do you keep your sense of self strong when others tell you who you can and cannot be? James Baldwin offers his nephew some advice on protecting his self-worth from the crushing forces of racism.

QUICKWRITE Think about the messages you get about yourself from family, friends, media, and other sources. Which ones support you and which ones seem to hold you back? List at least two examples in each category. Based on your list, what in your life most helps you protect your self-worth?

Support	Hold Back
1. With hard work you can achieve your dreams (my mom).	1. College is too expensive and not worth it (my friend George).
2.	2.

VOCABULARY SKILL

▲ VOCABULARY IN CONTEXT

Diagnose Word Knowledge Have all students complete the Vocabulary in Context. Check their words and phrases against the following:

constitute (kŏn'stĭ-tōōt') *v.* to amount to; equal

impertinent (ĭm-pûr'tn-ənt) *adj.* rude; ill-mannered

mediocrity (mē'dē-ŏk'-rĭ-tē) *n.* lack of quality

or excellence

truculent (trŭk'yə-lənt) *adj.* eager for a fight; fierce

unassailable (ŭn'ə-sā'lə-bəl) *adj.* undeniable

PRETEACH VOCABULARY Use the following copy master to help students with meanings.

R RESOURCE MANAGER—Copy Masters
Vocabulary Study p. 157

Teach

What protects your sense of SELF?

Introduce the question and have students suggest ways to protect one's sense of self from pressure. After students complete the *QUICKWRITE,* invite volunteers to share their examples. Then, ask them to generalize ways in which people can protect their self-worth.

TEXT ANALYSIS   COMMON CORE
RI 1
RI 6

● *Model the Skill:* **RHETORICAL DEVICES**   L 5a

Point out that writers often use rhetorical devices to persuade their readers, and remind students that Baldwin is trying to persuade his nephew to believe in himself. Ask students what is contradictory about Baldwin's first statement and guide them if necessary to the words "innocence" and "crime." Explain that a full reading of context is critical for determining the meaning of a paradox.

GUIDED PRACTICE Have students write two sentences that use each of the rhetorical devices discussed here.

READING STRATEGY   COMMON CORE
RI 1
RI 6

■ *Model the Skill:* **IDENTIFY PURPOSE**

To help students identify purpose, have them reread **Emerging Artist** on page 1250 and focus on the quote by Baldwin. Ask them what emotional responses this quote might stir in readers and what purpose his quote expresses. Point out that the purpose of this quote might be to inspire readers to wonder about their own lives and the way that their homes have affected them.

R RESOURCE MANAGER—Copy Masters
Identify Ideas p. 155 (for student use while reading the selection)

SUMMARY

Baldwin's letter to his nephew and namesake urges him to define himself in his own terms and not in the white world's terms. Baldwin writes that white people need to make African Americans believe they are inferior to whites, and that until white people understand the cruelty in their own history, they cannot be freed from it. He extols his nephew for not succumbing to the white man's definition of him. He encourages him to help whites see their true selves, because until they do, African Americans will never be free.

READ WITH A PURPOSE

Help students set a purpose for reading. Tell them to look for the reasons that Baldwin believes it is important to define yourself, rather than have someone else define you.

REVISIT THE BIG QUESTION

What protects your sense of SELF?

Discuss Direct students to lines 7–9. In what way does Baldwin characterize the grandfather's self-worth? What mistake did the grandfather make? What does that suggest about the grandfather's character? *Possible answer: Baldwin characterizes the grandfather's self-worth as essentially non-existent. He mistakenly believed what whites told him about himself (lines 8–9), and he therefore didn't believe himself worth anything. This suggests that the grandfather was not strong enough to ignore what others said about him. Instead, he let others' comments define him.*

VOCABULARY

COMMON CORE L 4

OWN THE WORD

truculent: Read the sentence with *truculent* aloud to students, and have them identify the phrase that can help them determine the meaning of the word. Then have students name synonyms for *truculent*. **Possible answers:** *aggressive, hostile, defiant, ferocious*

My Dungeon Shook

Letter to My Nephew on the One Hundredth Anniversary of the Emancipation

James Baldwin

BACKGROUND   In 1963, as the nation's perspective on the race problem grew more pessimistic, James Baldwin published his essay collection *The Fire Next Time*. Expressing the pain and anger that African Americans had concealed for so long, Baldwin addressed his provocative essays to a sympathetic white audience that had failed to grasp the full magnitude of racial injustice. His searing attack fit the national mood, and the collection soared up the bestseller lists. Its success made Baldwin an icon of black rage and a widely televised commentator on racial issues throughout the 1960s. The following letter, taken from *The Fire Next Time*, captures the extremes of Baldwin's style: the righteous anger that made him famous and his fervent belief in the redeeming power of love.

Analyze Visuals ▶
Describe the story that this painting seems to tell. Which elements help the artist connect the two figures in the foreground with the main story of the painting?

Dear James:

I have begun this letter five times and torn it up five times. I keep seeing your face, which is also the face of your father and my brother. Like him, you are tough, dark, vulnerable, moody—with a very definite tendency to sound **truculent** because you want no one to think you are soft. You may be like your grandfather in this, I don't know, but certainly both you and your father resemble him very much physically. Well, he is dead, he never saw you, and he had a terrible life; he was defeated long before he died because, at the bottom of his heart, he really believed what white people said about him. This is one of the reasons that he
10 became so holy.[1] I am sure that your father has told you something about all that. Neither you nor your father exhibit any tendency towards holiness: you really *are*

① Targeted Passage
truculent (trŭk′yə-lənt) *adj.* eager for a fight; fierce

---

1. **so holy:** Baldwin's stepfather was a minister who raised his children in a strict, conservative, religious environment.

Father, Charly Palmer. Mixed media collage on wood. 18″ × 12″. © Charly Palmer.

DIFFERENTIATED INSTRUCTION

FOR ENGLISH LANGUAGE LEARNERS

Connect to the Text Have students identify the words Baldwin uses to describe his brother and nephew. These include *tough, dark, vulnerable, moody, sound truculent,* and *no tendency towards holiness.* Discuss how the author's choice of words reflects his love for the two men.

FOR STRUGGLING READERS

In combination with the *Audio Anthology CD,* use one or more Targeted Passages (pp. 1252, 1254, 1256) to ensure that students focus on key concepts. Targeted Passages are also good for English language learners.

① Targeted Passage [Lines 1–7]

This passage begins the letter by describing Baldwin's nephew James, and how he is like his father, Baldwin's brother.

- To whom is Baldwin writing? (line 1)
- What is the relationship between Baldwin and James? (line 3)
- In what ways does Baldwin say that James is like his father (Baldwin's brother)? (lines 2–4)
- Why does Baldwin say that his nephew behaves the way he does? (line 5)
- In what ways does Baldwin say that James is like his grandfather (Baldwin's stepfather)? (lines 5–6)

FOR STRUGGLING READERS

Develop Reading Fluency Explain to students that the author is writing a letter to his nephew, who is named for him. Use the first person pronouns in lines 1–7 to promote readers' interest. Have students work in pairs, with partners taking turns reading to one another. Remind students to be expressive as they read from a first-person perspective.

FOR ADVANCED LEARNERS/AP

Analyze Baldwin places a great importance on the anniversary of African Americans' emancipation. How do you think he would have responded to the election of an African American president of the United States? Begin a class discussion that uses Baldwin's ideas to explain the changes in attitude that brought about the election of President Barack Obama in 2008. Encourage students to apply examples from Baldwin's text to their discussion.

Direct students to lines 16–37. Use these prompts to have students consider Baldwin's accusations and thoughts:

Connect Think of someone you have known for a long time. What can you know about this person from the story of his or her life? *Accept all thoughtful responses.*

Interpret What does Baldwin accuse mankind of doing? In what way does his accusation relate to his brother? ***Possible answer:*** *Baldwin accuses mankind of being capable of destruction and death without feeling any notable remorse (lines 34–35). Baldwin has seen his brother grow up and be slowly destroyed by the whites' perceptions of and limitations on African Americans (lines 26–29). His brother has narrowly escaped the death of his own self-definition.*

TEXT ANALYSIS	COMMON CORE

ⓐ Model the skill:
RHETORICAL DEVICES

RI 1
RI 6
L 5a

To analyze Baldwin's point and how he gives it great impact, point out that loaded words such as *devastation, innocent,* and *crime* heighten Baldwin's comparison and make it more effective. ***Possible answer:*** *Baldwin is saying that it is unfair for the people (whites) who are doing the destroying to be innocent or unaware of what they are doing. The fact that people are ignorant about the consequences of racism is unforgivable, or a crime.*

VOCABULARY	COMMON CORE

OWN THE WORD

constitute: Read the definition of *constitute* aloud to students. Then, have them write two sentences of their own that show an understanding of the meaning and usage of the word.

---

of another era, part of what happened when the Negro left the land and came into what the late E. Franklin Frazier[2] called "the cities of destruction." You can only be destroyed by believing that you really are what the white world calls a *nigger*. I tell you this because I love you, and please don't you ever forget it.

I have known both of you all your lives, have carried your Daddy in my arms and on my shoulders, kissed and spanked him and watched him learn to walk. I don't know if you've known anybody from that far back; if you've loved anybody that long, first as an infant, then as a child, then as a man, you gain a strange
20 perspective on time and human pain and effort. Other people cannot see what I see whenever I look into your father's face, for behind your father's face as it is today are all those other faces which were his. Let him laugh and I see a cellar your father does not remember and a house he does not remember and I hear in his present laughter his laughter as a child. Let him curse and I remember him falling down the cellar steps, and howling, and I remember, with pain, his tears, which my hand or your grandmother's so easily wiped away. But no one's hand can wipe away those tears he sheds invisibly today, which one hears in his laughter and in his speech and in his songs. I know what the world has done to my brother and how narrowly he has survived it. And I know, which is much worse, and this is
30 the crime of which I accuse my country and my countrymen, and for which neither I nor time nor history will ever forgive them, that they have destroyed and are destroying hundreds of thousands of lives and do not know it and do not want to know it. One can be, indeed one must strive to become, tough and philosophical concerning destruction and death, for this is what most of mankind has been best at since we have heard of man. (But remember: *most* of mankind is not all of mankind.) But it is not permissible that the authors of devastation should also be innocent. It is the innocence which **constitutes** the crime. ⓐ

Now, my dear namesake, these innocent and well-meaning people, your countrymen, have caused you to be born under conditions not very far removed
40 from those described for us by Charles Dickens[3] in the London of more than a hundred years ago. (I hear the chorus of the innocents screaming, "No! This is not true! How *bitter* you are!"—but I am writing this letter to *you*, to try to tell you something about how to handle *them*, for most of them do not yet really know that you exist. I *know* the conditions under which you were born, for I was there. Your countrymen were *not* there, and haven't made it yet. Your grandmother was also there, and no one has ever accused her of being bitter. I suggest that the innocents check with her. She isn't hard to find. Your countrymen don't know that *she* exists, either, though she has been working for them all their lives.)

Well, you were born, here you came, something like fifteen years ago; and
50 though your father and mother and grandmother, looking about the streets through which they were carrying you, staring at the walls into which they brought you, had every reason to be heavyhearted, yet they were not. For here

---

2. **E. Franklin Frazier:** African-American sociologist (1894–1962) who studied the structure of black communities.

3. **described . . . by Charles Dickens:** Dickens (1812–1870) was a British novelist whose works frequently described the hardships suffered by the poor in London.

Language Coach

Word Definitions
Shed tears means "lose tears" or "cry." What does Baldwin mean by "tears he sheds invisibly" (line 27)? What are invisible tears?

constitute (kŏn'stĭ-tōōt')
v. to amount to; equal

ⓐ **RHETORICAL DEVICES**
Consider the **paradox** in lines 36–37. What point is Baldwin making?

② **Targeted Passage**

DIFFERENTIATED INSTRUCTION

FOR STRUGGLING READERS

② **Targeted Passage** [Lines 38–52]

This passage conveys Baldwin's view of whites and the purpose of his letter.

- Who are the "countrymen" Baldwin names? Of what does he accuse them? (lines 38–39)

- What does Baldwin say is the purpose of this letter to his nephew? (lines 42–43)

- How old is Baldwin's nephew? What feelings does he say young James' parents should have felt at his birth? (lines 49–52)

FOR ENGLISH LANGUAGE LEARNERS

Language Coach

Word Definitions *Answer: "Shedding invisible tears" means that a person is carrying a sadness inside that is not obvious to those around him or her.* Point out to students that "shed" forms other idioms such as "shed blood" and "shed skin."

you were, Big James, named for me—you were a big baby, I was not—here you were: to be loved. To be loved, baby, hard, at once, and forever, to strengthen you against the loveless world. Remember that: I know how black it looks today, for you. It looked bad that day, too, yes, we were trembling. We have not stopped trembling yet, but if we had not loved each other none of us would have survived. And now you must survive because we love you, and for the sake of your children and your children's children. **B**

60   This innocent country set you down in a ghetto in which, in fact, it intended that you should perish. Let me spell out precisely what I mean by that, for the heart of the matter is here, and the root of my dispute with my country. You were born where you were born and faced the future that you faced because you were black and *for no other reason*. The limits of your ambition were, thus, expected to be set forever. You were born into a society which spelled out with brutal clarity, and in as many ways as possible, that you were a worthless human being. You were not expected to aspire to excellence: you were expected to make peace with **mediocrity**. Wherever you have turned, James, in your short time on this earth, you have been told where you could go and what you could do (and *how*

70   you could do it) and where you could live and whom you could marry. I know your countrymen do not agree with me about this, and I hear them saying, "You exaggerate." They do not know Harlem, and I do. So do you. Take no one's word for anything, including mine—but trust your experience.

Know whence you came. If you know whence you came, there is really no limit **C** to where you can go. The details and symbols of your life have been deliberately constructed to make you believe what white people say about you. Please try to remember that what they believe, as well as what they do and cause you to endure, does not testify to your inferiority but to their inhumanity and fear. Please try to be clear, dear James, through the storm which rages about your youthful head

80   today, about the reality which lies behind the words *acceptance* and *integration*. There is no reason for you to try to become like white people and there is no basis whatever for their **impertinent** assumption that *they* must accept *you*. The really terrible thing, old buddy, is that *you* must accept *them*. And I mean that very seriously. You must accept them and accept them with love. For these innocent people have no other hope. They are, in effect, still trapped in a history which they do not understand; and until they understand it, they cannot be released from it. They have had to believe for many years, and for innumerable reasons, that black men are inferior to white men. Many of them, indeed, know better, but, as you will discover, people find it very difficult to act on what they know.

90   To act is to be committed, and to be committed is to be in danger. In this case, the danger, in the minds of most white Americans, is the loss of their identity. Try to imagine how you would feel if you woke up one morning to find the sun shining and all the stars aflame. You would be frightened because it is out of the order of nature. Any upheaval in the universe is terrifying because it so profoundly attacks one's sense of one's own reality. Well, the black man has functioned in the white man's world as a fixed star, as an immovable pillar: and as he moves out of his place, heaven and earth are shaken to their foundations. You, don't be afraid. I said that it was intended that you should perish in the ghetto, perish by never

B RHETORICAL DEVICES
Identify words and phrases that are repeated in lines 52–59. What does this **repetition** contribute to the paragraph's impact?

mediocrity
(mē′dē-ŏk′-rĭ-tē) *n.* lack of quality or excellence

C IDENTIFY PURPOSE
Reread lines 60–74. What is Baldwin's main point? How do these ideas add to your understanding of his purpose for writing?

impertinent
(ĭm-pûr′tn-ənt) *adj.* rude; ill-mannered

Language Coach

Synonyms A **synonym** is a word with a meaning similar to that of another word. As they are used in line 96, *fixed* and *immovable* are synonyms. How do these synonyms emphasize the non-changing "role" the black man had played?

TEXT ANALYSIS

B RHETORICAL DEVICES

Possible answer: *Repeated words and phrases include "here you came/were" (lines 49, 52–54), "to be loved" (line 54), "trembling" (lines 56–57), "survive(d)" (lines 57–58), and "children" (lines 58–59). The repetition creates a rhythmic flow and makes the ideas in the paragraph easier to remember and more poignant.*

READING STRATEGY

C *Model the Skill:* IDENTIFY PURPOSE

Point out Baldwin's phrases "let me spell out precisely," "the heart of the matter," and "the root of my dispute" (lines 61–62). Explain that Baldwin signals his main ideas with these phrases. ***Possible answer:*** *Baldwin's main point is that society tells African Americans the path they must take. However, Baldwin indicates that his nephew must know his own personal history and make his way based on this. Baldwin wants to encourage his nephew.*

VOCABULARY

OWN THE WORD

- **mediocrity:** Ask students to reread this sentence in which *mediocrity* is contrasted with excellence. Then, have them write their own sentence contrasting the two words. ***Possible answer:*** *Our teacher made it very clear that she expected excellence, not* mediocrity, *from each student.*

- **impertinent:** Review the definition of *impertinent* and ask students to give an example of *impertinent* action or behavior. ***Possible answers:*** *The impertinent child constantly interrupted the teacher during class.*

FOR STRUGGLING READERS

Concept Support: Identify Ideas Discuss with students ideas from pages 1254–1255 that evoked emotional responses. Have students record their ideas in the prereading chart introduced on page 1251.

Baldwin's Sentence	Idea
"If you know …" (lines 74–75)	Once you understand your history, you can achieve any goal.

FOR ENGLISH LANGUAGE LEARNERS

Language Coach

Synonyms *Possible answer: Baldwin uses* fixed *and* immovable *to emphasize how most white Americans have defined the black man in only one way. He has had a permanent inferior position in their minds, and to change their thinking, they would alter how they see themselves.* Have students suggest other synonyms and discuss the differences in connotation

Activity In what way does this boy evoke Baldwin's nephew? *Possible answer: He is a young African-American boy who seems to be pondering serious issues.*

About the Art *Thinking* reflects the impressionistic influences felt by Barbados-born Carlton Murrell. Short strokes and vibrant color convey an image of the self-awareness Baldwin hopes his nephew will achieve.

Thinking (1990), Carlton Murrell. Oil on board. Private collection. © Bridgeman Art Library.

---

being allowed to go behind the white man's definitions, by never being allowed to
100 spell your proper name. You have, and many of us have, defeated this intention; and, by a terrible law, a terrible paradox, those innocents who believed that your imprisonment made them safe are losing their grasp of reality. But these men are your brothers —your lost, younger brothers. And if the word *integration* means anything, this is what it means: that we, with love, shall force our brothers to see themselves as they are, to cease fleeing from reality and begin to change it. For this is your home, my friend, do not be driven from it; great men have done great things here, and will again, and we can make America what America must become. It will be hard, James, but you come from sturdy, peasant stock, men who picked cotton and dammed rivers and built railroads, and, in the teeth of[4]
110 the most terrifying odds, achieved an **unassailable** and monumental dignity. You come from a long line of great poets, some of the greatest poets since Homer. One of them said, *The very time I thought I was lost, My dungeon shook and my chains fell off.*[5] **D**

You know, and I know, that the country is celebrating one hundred years of freedom one hundred years too soon. We cannot be free until they are free. God bless you, James, and Godspeed.

Your uncle,
James

3 Targeted Passage

unassailable
(ŭn′ə-sā′lə-bəl) *adj.*
undeniable

D IDENTIFY PURPOSE
Reread lines 100–113. Which sentence best states Baldwin's purpose in these lines?

---

4. **in the teeth of:** in spite of.

5. **The very time . . . fell off:** a quotation from the traditional spiritual "My Dungeon Shook." It alludes to the Biblical story of Paul and Silas (Acts 16), who were freed from an unjust imprisonment by the action of an earthquake.

D *Model the Skill:* **IDENTIFY PURPOSE**

Possible answer: "It will be hard, James, but you come from sturdy peasant stock, men who picked cotton and dammed rivers and built railroads, and, in the teeth of the most terrifying odds, achieved an unassailable and monumental dignity."

OWN THE WORD

unassailable: Remind students that the prefix *un-* means "not," and that *assail* means "attack violently." Have them write sentences that show an understanding of the meaning and usage of both *assail* and *unassailable*.

SELECTION WRAP-UP

READ WITH A PURPOSE Now that students have read the selection, review Baldwin's insistence on self-definition. According to Baldwin, what can happen when we let others tell us who we are? *Possible answer: When others define us, we may undervalue ourselves and settle for less than we can achieve.*

DIFFERENTIATED INSTRUCTION

FOR STRUGGLING READERS

3 Targeted Passage [Lines 103–115]

This passage shows Baldwin's hopes for his nephew, the way he encourages him, and his view of America.

- What does Baldwin ask his nephew to do? (lines 104–105)

- With what reasons does Baldwin encourage his nephew? (lines 108–111)

- How does Baldwin feel about America celebrating one hundred years of freedom? (lines 104–105)

FOR ENGLISH LANGUAGE LEARNERS

Vocabulary: Multiple-Meaning Words Help students use context to clarify the meaning of these words and phrases as used in the selection:

- *stock* (line 108), "ancestry"

- *dammed* (line 109), "blocked by a dam"

- *monumental* (line 110), "great and lasting"

- *line* (line 111), "family history"

Comprehension

1. **Recall** In Baldwin's view, why was the boy's grandfather defeated?

2. **Recall** What does Baldwin say *acceptance* means?

3. **Clarify** What crime does Baldwin accuse his country of committing?

Text Analysis

● 4. **Identify Purpose** Review the sentences you recorded in your chart. Which one best conveys the purpose of this letter? Explain your answer.

● 5. **Examine Rhetorical Devices** Baldwin sums up the themes of his letter with two concluding **paradoxes**. Reread lines 114–115. What perspective on the problem of race in America do these two statements convey?

6. **Analyze Audience** Baldwin addressed this **open letter** to his 15-year-old nephew but published it in *The Fire Next Time.* In each of the following passages, which details are directed to the nephew and which seem directed to a wider audience? Support your answer with details.

- Baldwin's memories of his brother (lines 20–33)
- criticisms of his readers (lines 38–44)
- his advice to his nephew (lines 78–84)
- his description of whites' fears (lines 90–97)

7. **Compare Style** Baldwin shared many of Martin Luther King Jr.'s values, goals, and religious influences. What is similar and different about the authors' styles? In your answer, consider each author's tone as well as his use of logical arguments, allusions, and rhetorical devices.

8. **Make Judgments** Consider Baldwin's solution to the problem of racism. In your opinion, does Baldwin's letter contain useful advice for protecting his nephew's self-worth? Explain your opinions.

Text Criticism

9. **Critical Interpretations** In *Soul on Ice* (1968), black activist Eldridge Cleaver criticized James Baldwin for his "grueling, agonizing, total hatred of the blacks, particularly of himself" and his "shameful, fanatical, fawning, sycophantic love of the whites." Do you see any evidence to support these accusations? Explain your answer, citing details from Baldwin's letter.

> *What protects your sense of* **SELF**?
>
> Sometimes people's view of themselves is too high. At other times, they suffer from low self-esteem. In your opinion, what is a good balance between these two extremes? How do you keep a proper perspective on yourself?

MY DUNGEON SHOOK **1257**

COMMON CORE

RI 1 Cite strong and thorough textual evidence to support analysis of what the text says explicitly as well as inferences drawn from the text, including determining where the text leaves matters uncertain. **RI 6** Determine an author's point of view or purpose in a text in which the rhetoric is particularly effective, analyzing how style and content contribute to the power, persuasiveness, or beauty of the text. **L 5a** Interpret figures of speech (e.g., paradox) in context and analyze their role in the text.

---

9. This letter does not support Cleaver's criticism. Baldwin blames whites for destroying African-American lives (lines 31–33), explains that whites are inhuman and fearful (line 78), and says that whites must be forced to change (lines 104–105).

What protects your sense of SELF?
Students may say that a good balance is one in which people recognize their self-worth while also recognizing the worth of others. They may say they keep a proper view of themselves by seeing others as their equals, not as superiors or inferiors.

Practice and Apply

For preliminary support of post-reading questions, use these copy masters:

R RESOURCE MANAGER—Copy Masters
Reading Check p. 160
Rhetorical Devices p. 153
Question Support p. 161

Additional selection questions are provided for teachers on page 147.

ANSWERS

COMMON CORE **RI 1, RI 6, L 5a**

1. *He internalized racist views of himself.*

2. *African Americans must accept the limitations of whites' understanding.*

3. *Baldwin accuses his country of destroying lives and not wanting to know about it.*

Possible answers:

4. ■ COMMON CORE FOCUS **Identify Purpose** *Baldwin is encouraging his nephew to rise above what society says he is and to live life to the fullest.*

5. ● COMMON CORE FOCUS **Rhetorical Devices** *Baldwin uses his concluding paradoxes to convey the insight that racism remains a problem in America because all Americans remain trapped by narrow views on race.*

6. *Memories: Nephew: personal memories of his brother, Wider Audience: accuses countrymen of destroying African-American lives. Reader Criticisms: Nephew: "dear namesake," Wider Audience: reference to Dickens and "chorus of innocents." Advice: Nephew: don't become like whites, accept whites with love, Wider Audience: whites' "impertinent assumption." Whites' Fears: Nephew: don't feel inferior because whites are afraid. Wider Audience: most white Americans fear losing their identity. The primary audience for this letter is whites; the letter is a vehicle for the message.*

7. *Baldwin's tone is more confrontational and bitter than King's, and his arguments are more emotional than King's. Both use a range of allusions and rhetorical devices.*

8. *Advice to defy whites' definition (line 100) and to change the way whites view blacks (lines 103–105) is useful. The fact that Baldwin doesn't suggest ways to change whites' perceptions is not useful.*

ANSWERS

Vocabulary in Context

▲ **VOCABULARY PRACTICE**

1. *(a) insolent*   4. *(b) ferocious*
2. *(a) ordinariness* 5. *(b) compose*
3. *(c) indisputable*

R RESOURCE MANAGER—Copy Master
Vocabulary Practice p. 158

ACADEMIC VOCABULARY IN WRITING

Students may list parents and relatives, siblings, religious leaders, and other mentors. Students' paragraphs should include at least two Academic Vocabulary words.

VOCABULARY STRATEGY: CONTEXT AND THE MEANING OF IDIOMS

COMMON CORE L 4a L 5a

Help students identify the main context clues in the paragraph.

Possible answers:

1. *"gets herself off the hook," avoids responsibility*
2. *"egg on her face," embarrassment*
3. *"putting her foot in her mouth," making a misstatement*
4. *"thumbs her nose," rejects or ignores, usually in a rude way*
5. *"take her under his wing," guide and protect*

R RESOURCE MANAGER—Copy Master
Vocabulary Strategy p. 159

Interactive Vocabulary **THINK** central

Keywords direct students to a **WordSharp** tutorial on **thinkcentral.com** or to other types of vocabulary practice and review.

Assess and Reteach

Assess

DIAGNOSTIC AND SELECTION TESTS

Selection Test A, B/C pp. 337–338, 339–340
Interactive Selection Test on thinkcentral.com

Reteach

Level Up Online Tutorials on thinkcentral.com
Reteaching Worksheets on thinkcentral.com

Vocabulary in Context

▲ **VOCABULARY PRACTICE**

Choose the word that is closest in meaning to the boldfaced vocabulary word.

1. **impertinent:** (a) insolent, (b) impossible, (c) unfriendly
2. **mediocrity:** (a) ordinariness, (b) indifference, (c) complexity
3. **unassailable:** (a) landlocked, (b) unknown, (c) indisputable
4. **truculent:** (a) uncivilized, (b) ferocious, (c) boorish
5. **constitute:** (a) connect, (b) compose, (c) conclude

WORD LIST
constitute
impertinent
mediocrity
truculent
unassailable

ACADEMIC VOCABULARY IN WRITING

• complex   • economic   • establish   • ethnic   • evolve

James Baldwin wrote a letter to his nephew offering advice about how to live in a **complex** society. In a short paragraph, discuss where you seek advice. Use at least two Academic Vocabulary words in your writing.

VOCABULARY STRATEGY: CONTEXT AND THE MEANING OF IDIOMS

An **idiom** is an expression whose overall meaning is different from the meaning of the individual words that it includes. For example, in "My Dungeon Shook" Baldwin uses the expression *in the teeth of* to describe overcoming difficult odds. Some idioms are very common and you will automatically know their meaning. However, if an idiom is unfamiliar to you, you may at first try to determine the meaning of the sentence or paragraph by focusing on the meanings of the individual words. Only by looking at the surrounding **context** will you be able to draw the conclusion that the words are working together as a part of an idiom with a special meaning.

PRACTICE Use context clues to identify the five idioms in the following paragraph and determine their meaning. Then, write the meaning, or a definition, of each idiom.

> No matter what trouble she's in, she always gets herself off the hook. Even when she creates a disaster for everyone else, she gets away without any egg on her face. Sometimes her mistakes are just a matter of putting her foot in her mouth. At other times she actually thumbs her nose at other people's needs and concerns. We can only hope that someone will take her under his wing and teach her how to behave.

COMMON CORE

L 4a Use context as a clue to the meaning of a word or phrase. L 5a Interpret figures of speech in context and analyze their role in the text.

Interactive Vocabulary **THINK** central

Go to **thinkcentral.com**.
KEYWORD: HML11-1258

DIFFERENTIATED INSTRUCTION

FOR ENGLISH LANGUAGE LEARNERS

Task Support: Vocabulary Practice Point out the common suffixes *-ity* in *mediocrity* and *-able* in *unassailable*. Have pairs look up the meanings of the suffixes and discuss ways to use the definitions to build meaning for the words. Challenge pairs to identify words they know with these suffixes and then to use them in sentences.

FOR ADVANCED LEARNERS/AP

Idioms Challenge students to imagine they are Baldwin writing to his nephew, and have them use five of the idioms in sentences for a letter to young James. *Example: The whites cannot get off the hook so easily by simply celebrating our freedom.*

The March Toward Equality

In 1963, psychology professor Dr. Kenneth Clark conducted a series of interviews with Dr. Martin Luther King Jr., Malcolm X, and James Baldwin. Aired during a time of intense racial conflict, these interviews explored the differences in the ideals and world views of these three leading activists and thinkers. In his introduction to the interviews, Dr. Clark made this statement.

> "We have now come to the point where there are only two ways that America can avoid continued racial explosions. One would be total oppression. The other, total equality. There is no compromise. I believe, I hope, that we are on the threshold of a truly democratic America. It is not going to be easy to cross that threshold. But the achievement of the goals of justice, equality, and democracy for all American citizens involves the very destiny of our nation."

Writing to Persuade

Consider the state of civil rights in America today, in light of the goals and visions of the writers you have just read. In your opinion, have we reached total equality? Or would you say that we have arrived somewhere in between total equality and total oppression? Review the literature in this section and write a retrospective editorial in which you support a claim about whether or not the goals and visions of these writers have been realized.

Consider

- which ideas and details from the selections will help you articulate the vision of the civil rights leaders
- what stories, examples, or other details will help you support your view of civil rights in America today
- who your audience will be and what you want them to think or do
- how to express your argument clearly and respectfully

Extension Online

INQUIRY & RESEARCH Use the Internet to **research** contemporary topics in civil rights. Look for news and commentary in mainstream and lesser-known publications, including private blogs. Also look for Web sites of organizations devoted to advancing civil rights. Choose three issues that seem important or surprising to you and share them with your class.

COMMON CORE

RI 9 Analyze documents of historical and literary significance for their themes and purposes. **W 1** Write arguments to support claims in an analysis of substantive topics or texts. **W 9a–b** Apply grade 11 Reading standards to literature and to literary nonfiction.

COMMON CORE FOCUS

RI 9 Analyze documents of historical and literary significance for their themes and purposes.
W 1 Write arguments to support claims in an analysis of substantive topics or texts.

Wrap-Up: Civil Rights & Protest Literature

This Wrap-Up provides students with an opportunity to revisit ideas from this section about the ways that civil rights activists created and defended their philosophies. What beliefs did activists hold? What strides were taken toward equality? What risks and sacrifices were necessary? Urge students to examine their own thinking in light of insights gained from the selections.

Writing to Persuade

- Review with students that *persuading* means convincing readers to adopt a viewpoint or to act. This skill helps writers share opinions and supporting evidence that can lead to social change.

- To help students create their editorials, suggest that they review contemporary media coverage of race relations in America. Students might also conduct interviews with people of varying cultural backgrounds, ages, and genders, in order to gather insights on the issue. Urge students to use their primary and secondary research to draw conclusions about the state of race relations in America. Then, help them compare their evidence and conclusions with the goals of such activists as King and Malcolm X.

Extension Online

- Remind students that civil rights is a global issue, not just an American issue. Encourage students to broaden their understanding by searching for international as well as domestic topics.

- Encourage students to use KWL charts to guide their studies. Before students share their findings with the class, encourage them to include why each issue is important or surprising in the *L* column of their charts.

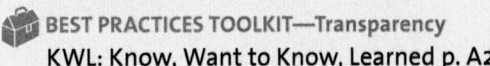 BEST PRACTICES TOOLKIT—Transparency
KWL: Know, Want to Know, Learned p. A21

FOR STRUGGLING WRITERS

Writing Support To help students organize their writing, suggest that they use the RAFT technique. Clarify students' role for this assignment as interpreters of history. Then, meet with students individually or in small groups to determine the best format for their discussions.

 BEST PRACTICES TOOLKIT—Transparency
RAFT: Role, Audience, Format, Topic p. C8

FOR ENGLISH LANGUAGE LEARNERS

Writing Thesis Statements Provide the following models of thesis statements:

- Race relations in America have finally reached a state of total equality.
- Race relations in America teeter between total equality and total oppression.
- Race relations in America _____.

Point out language from the prompt in the first two samples. Recall that a thesis states an opinion that must be supported.

Teach

····· COMMON CORE FOCUS

RL 3 Analyze the impact of the author's choices regarding how to develop and relate elements of a story or drama. **RL 9** Demonstrate knowledge of how two or more texts from the same period treat similar themes or topics.

From Modern to Contemporary

Modern vs. Contemporary To help students understand this section, begin by asking volunteers to explain the difference between *modern* and *contemporary*. Use dictionary definitions to help students see that *contemporary* means "occurring at the present time or within a short span that includes the present." An event that happened more than a lifetime ago is not contemporary. *Modern* can refer to the present time, but it can also refer to a time period defined in various ways. For example, modern civilization defines a lengthy era that contrasts with ancient or medieval civilization. In literature, *modern* refers to a specific movement that had its heyday in the first half of the 20th century.

Ask students to name aspects of their lives that are contemporary, such as those that distinguish their lives and attitudes from those of previous generations.

Text Analysis Workshop

····· COMMON CORE

Included in this workshop:
RL 3 Analyze the impact of the author's choices regarding how to develop and relate elements of a story or drama. **RL 9** Demonstrate knowledge of how two or more texts from the same period treat similar themes or topics.

Essential Course of Study **ECOS**

Voice in Contemporary Literature

If you go into a bookstore and browse the "New Fiction" section, what types of books do you find? How are they different from literature of the past? Throughout this textbook, you have witnessed the evolution of American literature. Each period has been characterized by literary movements that determined the styles and themes in writing. What do you think the trends have been in your generation?

From Modern to Contemporary

The era of contemporary literature began around 1946, immediately after World War II. War has a way of changing a nation's literature because of its effects on an entire generation. Realism had risen from the ashes of the Civil War, while modernism had defined its vision through the ruins of World War I. After World War II, the development of the Cold War, the Vietnam War, and the civil violence of the 1960s, American literature changed again. Literature began to focus on personal experience as seen in the context of society. Writers began to address the emotional effects of wars, for example, as well as other issues of social, political, and cultural relevance.

Amy Tan

One of the most significant changes in American literature has been its increasing diversity—not only in forms and techniques, but in voices. With its history as the great "melting pot," the United States has been in a unique position to cultivate a literary community of authors from a wide variety of races, ethnicities, and religions. Increased publishing opportunities have given a public voice to more and more writers of African, Asian, Latino, and Native American descent, who often provide a new perspective on living in two cultures at once. Authors who have addressed such issues include Amy Tan, Sandra Cisneros, Rita Dove, Gwendolyn Brooks, Alice Walker, and N. Scott Momaday.

Rita Dove

N. Scott Momaday

Diverse Works, Common Ground

Several defining features set contemporary literature apart from the previous era of modernist literature.

Voice in literature is the expression of the writer's or narrator's personality. With its emphasis on personal experience, contemporary literature is often told from the first-person point of view, through a persona that represents the writer or main character. This persona has a distinctive personality that shapes a reader's experience with the text.

DIFFERENTIATED INSTRUCTION

FOR STRUGGLING READERS

Note Taking For students who are unfamiliar with voice in contemporary literature or need help with note taking, hand out the copy master before discussing these pages. Explain that students will be learning terms and concepts related to contemporary literature in this workshop. Discuss these terms and concepts (*contemporary, voice, persona, tone, irony, humor, social context,*

social criticism) as students record notes on the copy master.

 RESOURCE MANAGER—Copy Master
Note Taking p. 162

Tone is the attitude that a writer takes toward a subject. For the modernists, the numbing effects of the early 20th century led to a detached, unemotional tone. For example, Prufrock's failure at the end of T. S. Eliot's poem (page 970) is conveyed in a matter-of-fact tone that is sympathetic but distant. Compare this modernist aloofness to Tim O'Brien's Vietnam story "Ambush" (page 1196). The tone of this contemporary story is one of engagement rather than detachment.

> I did not hate the young man; I did not see him as the enemy; I did not ponder issues of morality or politics or military duty. I crouched and kept my head low. I tried to swallow whatever was rising from my stomach, which tasted like lemonade, something fruity and sour. I was terrified.
>
> **—Tim O'Brien, "Ambush"**

Close Read

How would you characterize the narrator of this passage? Do you think he would be personable? distant? intimidating?

As a rule, modernist writers did not view the irony of life as humorous; instead, they often expressed defeat in the face of life's irony. Contemporary writers, however, look at the absurdity of such situations as a cause for humor, which may then be expressed through an **ironic** presentation of characters and events.

Modernist writers typically viewed the individual in isolation, whereas contemporary writers present the individual in relation to the larger social context. Often contemporary writers hint at **social criticism.** They present a situation with only a suggestion of the social obstacles, and the reader must infer the writer's opinion. In her poem "Primer for Blacks" (page 1297), Gwendolyn Brooks encourages African Americans to appreciate their heritage. Note the unspoken message about social barriers for African Americans that Brooks conveys in this passage.

> Blackness
> is a title,
> is a preoccupation,
> is a commitment Blacks
> are to comprehend—
> and in which you are
> to perceive your Glory.
>
> **—Gwendolyn Brooks, "Primer for Blacks"**

Close Read

What is the social barrier for African Americans that Brooks wants her reader to infer?

Brooks is making an argument for self-respect and self-esteem among African Americans. However, she does not state what she is arguing against; she leaves it up to the reader to infer the social barriers she is addressing.

Diverse Works, Common Ground

Ironic Humor To emphasize the ironic humor prominent in contemporary culture, ask students to name movies or television shows that make fun of authorities such as political leaders, parents, or police. Point out that since the Vietnam War there has been a marked increase in cynicism about authority in American society. Those who doubt the wisdom of authority often use ironic humor to question or criticize its views. Thus, humor becomes a form of social criticism. This approach to social criticism appears in antiwar novels such as Joseph Heller's *Catch-22* and Kurt Vonnegut's *Slaughterhouse Five,* which students read about on page 1154 of the historical essay.

Close Read

Possible answer: *The narrator is personable because he is honest and descriptive about his feelings. On the other hand, the fact that the narrator is a combat soldier makes him intimidating.*

Close Read

Possible answer: *The implied social barrier consists of negative stereotypes or attitudes concerning race and color.*

IF STUDENTS NEED HELP . . . Point out words such as "title" and "preoccupation" that suggest definitions or stereotypes, and words such as "comprehend" and "perceive" that suggest the attitudes that create stereotypes.

FOR ENGLISH LANGUAGE LEARNERS

Language: Skill Words Help students understand the meanings of these terms:

- *generation,* "all the people born within a few years of each other"
- *relevance,* "importance to the topic"
- *isolation,* "separation from others"
- *self-esteem,* "liking oneself, having a good opinion of oneself"

FOR ADVANCED LEARNERS/AP

Literature of Social Criticism Literary social criticism has made a significant contribution to social awareness throughout American history. Have students research and report on socially critical authors such as John Steinbeck, Clifford Odets, Sinclair Lewis, Upton Sinclair, and Frank Norris. Ask them to identify similarities and differences in the issues and styles these authors' works reflect.

Focus and Motivate

Mother Tongue

 Video link at thinkcentral.com

Essay by Amy Tan

COMMON CORE FOCUS

RI 2 Determine two or more central ideas of a text and analyze their development over the course of the text. **RI 3** Analyze a complex set of ideas or sequence of events and explain how specific individuals, ideas, or events interact and develop over the course of the text. **RI 6** Determine an author's point of view, analyzing how style and content contribute to the power, persuasiveness, or beauty of the text. **W 2a–b** Introduce a topic: organize information so that each new element builds on that which precedes it; develop the topic thoroughly by selecting the most significant and relevant examples appropriate to the audience's knowledge of the topic. **W 4** Produce clear and coherent writing in which the development, organization, and style are appropriate to task, purpose, and audience. **L 2a** Observe hyphenation conventions. **L 3** Apply knowledge of language to understand how language functions in different contexts, to make effective choices for meaning or style, and to comprehend more fully when reading.

ABOUT THE AUTHOR

Clarify that both of Amy Tan's parents were Chinese-born immigrants. Ask students to identify details in Tan's life that reflect her ethnic heritage. *Possible answer: She has written authentic and insightful portrayals of Chinese history and Chinese-American culture.*

COMMON CORE

RI 2 Determine two or more central ideas of a text and analyze their development over the course of the text. **RI 3** Analyze a complex set of ideas or sequence of events and explain how specific individuals, ideas, or events interact and develop over the course of the text. **RI 6** Determine an author's point of view, analyzing how style and content contribute to the power, persuasiveness, or beauty of the text. **L 2a** Observe hyphenation conventions.

DID YOU KNOW?

Amy Tan . . .

- plays in a band called the Rock Bottom Remainders with Stephen King and other literary celebrities.
- has visited the White House five times.
- has had her works translated into more than 20 languages.

Meet the Author

Amy Tan born 1952

In 1989, Amy Tan's first book, *The Joy Luck Club,* spent 40 weeks on the *New York Times* bestseller list. Praised for its authentic dialogue and its rich portrayal of Chinese history, the book established Tan as an insightful chronicler of the Chinese-American experience and of the fierce and conflicted love between mothers and daughters.

Troubled Times Born in Oakland, California in 1952, Tan spent her early childhood in the San Francisco Bay area. She enjoyed her first literary success at the age of eight, winning first prize in an elementary school contest for her essay "What My Library Means to Me." Six years later, Tan's life took a tragic turn when both her father and her brother died from brain tumors. Her grief-stricken mother moved teenaged Amy and her surviving brother to Europe, settling in Montreux, Switzerland, where Tan graduated from high school in 1969.

Although her mother had pushed her to become a neurosurgeon, the rebellious Tan defied her mother's wishes and studied literature and linguistics in college. In 1974, she enrolled in a doctoral program in linguistics, but she abandoned her studies after a close friend was murdered. Tan then

put her expertise to work as a language development consultant for programs serving children with disabilities. Five years later, she adopted a new career as a freelance technical writer.

Confronting the Past Tan took up writing fiction as a form of therapy, hoping to curb her workaholic tendencies. Her first short story, "End Game," appeared in *Seventeen* magazine, bringing her to the attention of prominent literary agent Sandra Dijkstra. With Dijkstra's encouragement, Tan began writing a series of stories that evolved into *The Joy Luck Club.* For this tightly woven collection of short stories, Tan drew upon her personal story, exploring the generational and cultural gap between Chinese mothers and their American-born daughters.

Two years later, Tan published her second book, *The Kitchen God's Wife,* a novel inspired by her mother's life in China. Though she switched her focus from mother-daughter love to sisterhood in her third novel, *The Hundred Secret Senses,* she once again drew on her mother's life story in her fourth, *The Bonesetter's Daughter.* As Tan explains, "My books have amounted to taking her stories—a gift to me—and giving them back to her. To me, it was the ultimate thing I ever could have done for myself and my mother."

Author Online

Go to thinkcentral.com. KEYWORD: HML11-1262

1262

Selection Resources

See print resources on the **Teacher One Stop DVD-ROM** *and on* thinkcentral.com.

 Video link at thinkcentral.com

 RESOURCE MANAGER UNIT 6
Plan and Teach, pp. 163–170
Summary, pp. 171–172†‡*
Text Analysis and Reading
   Skill, pp. 173–176†*
Grammar and Style, p. 179

DIAGNOSTIC AND SELECTION TESTS
Selection Tests, pp. 341–344

 BEST PRACTICES TOOLKIT
New Word Analysis, p. E8
Freewriting, p. C1

TECHNOLOGY
- **Teacher One Stop DVD-ROM**
- **Student One Stop DVD-ROM**
- **Audio Anthology CD**
- **GrammarNotes DVD-ROM**
- **ExamView Test Generator** on the **Teacher One Stop**

---

* Resources for Differentiation   **†** Also in Spanish   **‡** In Haitian Creole and Vietnamese

TEXT ANALYSIS: PERSONAL ESSAY

Amy Tan could have written a research paper to get across her points about language and cultural identity. Instead, she chose to write a **personal essay,** in which she combines her insights on the topic with details from her own life.

Just last week, as I was walking down the street with [my mother], I again found myself conscious of the English I was using, the English I do use with her.

Unlike a scholarly paper or a newspaper article, a personal essay gives the reader a snapshot of the writer's life or personality as well as his or her thoughts on a specific topic. As evidenced by the excerpt above, personal essays are written as first-person narratives. The author appeals to the reader's emotions through the rhetorical or persuasive power of personal experiences. Tan uses anecdotes, or autobiographical incidents, to create meaning and to persuade the reader to understand her point of view. As you read this essay, note how Tan connects her ideas about the power of language with her own experiences.

READING SKILL: IDENTIFY MAIN IDEAS

Amy Tan's essay is organized into a series of paragraphs, most of which develop one **main idea,** or central point. Facts, descriptions, or examples that are related to the main idea are called **supporting details.** When a main idea is not directly stated, you can figure it out by asking yourself how these supporting details fit together.

Amy Tan uses vivid supporting details, drawn from deeply felt personal experiences, to make her points. As you read, use a diagram like the one shown to record the main idea of each paragraph and list the details that support that main idea.

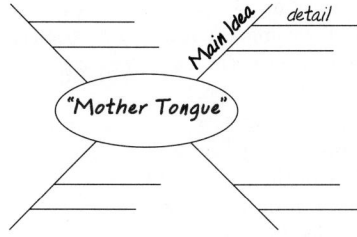

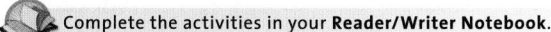

Complete the activities in your **Reader/Writer Notebook.**

What LANGUAGES *do you speak?*

Think about how you change the way you speak based on where you are and whom you're with. You might use slang when talking with friends but polite, formal language with adults. You might speak English at school and another language at home. In "Mother Tongue," you will read one writer's thoughts on her own different languages.

QUICKWRITE Make a list of places and situations where you use a different language or way of speaking. Then, for each situation, write a brief quotation that captures the sound of the language you use in that context.

1263

DIFFERENTIATED INSTRUCTION

FOR ENGLISH LANGUAGE LEARNERS

Vocabulary Support Before students begin the selection, clarify the meaning of the following vocabulary words:

- *research,* "finding information by looking it up in books or other sources"

- *identity,* "who a person is, as an individual or a member of a group"

- *insights,* "ideas that make a topic clearer"

Reading Context Explain to English language learners that personal essays differ from other kinds of essays people write. In a personal essay, writers usually address their own experiences, thoughts, and feelings, often using the first-person voice and informal language. In other kinds of essays, such as persuasive essays, writers try to convince readers to adopt a certain view. In critical essays, writers analyze a topic and argue a particular understanding of it.

What LANGUAGES *do you speak?*

Introduce the question and discuss the concept that people who speak only one language may, through varied usage, in fact speak many different languages. After students complete the *QUICKWRITE,* invite them to share their examples.

TEXT ANALYSIS COMMON CORE RI 3 RI 6

● *Model the Skill:* **PERSONAL ESSAY**

Tell students that in a personal essay, details and insights are often blended almost seamlessly. *Point out that in Tan's essay, personal details include Tan walking down the street with her mother and Tan speaking differently with her mother than elsewhere. Her insight is that she uses different kinds of English in different situations.*

GUIDED PRACTICE Have students write a sentence that combines an insight with details from their own lives.

READING SKILL COMMON CORE RI 2

■ *Model the Skill:* **IDENTIFY MAIN IDEAS**

Read aloud the first paragraph under **Confronting the Past** on page 1262. Point out that Tan began to write as an emotional outlet and in response to her personal experience as a Chinese American.

GUIDED PRACTICE Have students identify the main idea in the second paragraph under **Confronting the Past** on page 1262. Ask them to list the steps they used to determine the main idea.

R **RESOURCE MANAGER—Copy Master** Identify Main Ideas p. 175 (for student use while reading the selection)

SUMMARY

In this essay, Amy Tan reflects on the different "Englishes" she uses in different contexts, focusing largely on the English she speaks with her mother. Tan's mother, articulate in Chinese, speaks a kind of English that limits her interactions with authorities such as her stockbroker and doctors reviewing her medical tests. Tan, although viewing her mother's English as clear and direct, sees the need to use standard English to succeed in American society. She extends her discussion to the linguistic problems the children of immigrants may have in school and concludes with appreciation for all the "Englishes" she speaks.

READ WITH A PURPOSE

Help students set a purpose for reading. Tell them to read "Mother Tongue" to learn what Amy Tan thinks about her mother's use of language.

TEXT ANALYSIS

COMMON CORE

RI 3
RI 6

Ⓐ *Model the Skill:* **PERSONAL ESSAY**

To illustrate for students how Tan's personality is represented in the essay, point out the many sentences that begin with "I" or "I am." Help students identify the personal qualities that Tan shares about herself, such as being interested in language and its power.

Possible answer: *The use of first-person testimony reveals that the author is a writer who is fascinated by the many uses of language.*

REVISIT THE BIG QUESTION

What LANGUAGES *do you speak?*

Discuss After students read lines 11–15, ask them how Tan's reaction as she gives her talk reflects her experience of speaking many languages. Explain. ***Possible answer:*** *When Tan realizes that her mother is at the talk, she feels strange because she is speaking a different English than the one she usually speaks with her mother.*

Mother Tongue

Amy Tan

I am not a scholar of English or literature. I cannot give you much more than personal opinions on the English language and its variations in this country or others.

I am a writer. And by that definition, I am someone who has always loved language. I am fascinated by language in daily life. I spend a great deal of my time thinking about the power of language—the way it can evoke an emotion, a visual image, a complex idea, or a simple truth. Language is the tool of my trade. And I use them all—all the Englishes I grew up with. Ⓐ

Recently, I was made keenly aware of the different Englishes I do use. I was
10 giving a talk to a large group of people, the same talk I had already given to half a dozen other groups. The talk was about my writing, my life, and my book, *The Joy Luck Club,* and it was going along well enough, until I remembered one major difference that made the whole talk sound wrong. My mother was in the room. And it was perhaps the first time she had heard me give a lengthy speech, using the kind of English I have never used with her. I was saying things like "the intersection of memory and imagination" and "There is an aspect of my fiction that relates to thus-and-thus"—a speech filled with carefully wrought grammatical phrases, burdened, it suddenly seemed to me, with nominalized[1] forms, past perfect tenses, conditional phrases, forms of standard English that I had learned
20 in school and through books, the forms of English I did not use at home with my mother.

---

1. **nominalized** (nŏm′ə-nəl-īz′d) **forms:** nouns formed from other parts of speech.

Analyze Visuals ▶
In this painting, the artist represents an apple in three different ways. What point about language might the artist be making?

Ⓐ **PERSONAL ESSAY**
Reread lines 1–8. How do you respond to the author's use of first-person testimony? Explain your response.

① **Targeted Passage**

Apple (1983), Andy Warhol. Synthetic polymer paint and silkscreen ink on canvas, 14″ × 11″. © The Andy Warhol Foundation for the Visual Arts/Artists Rights Society (ARS), New York. © The Andy Warhol Foundation, Inc./Art Resource, New York.

DIFFERENTIATED INSTRUCTION

FOR STRUGGLING READERS

In combination with the *Audio Anthology CD,* use one or more Targeted Passages (pp. 1264, 1267, 1268, 1269) to ensure that students focus on key events and concepts in the selection. Targeted Passages are also good for English language learners.

Analyze Language Writing in informal language is a strategy many writers use in personal essays. In addition to addressing readers as *you*, Tan uses contractions and the first-person pronoun *I* to achieve her desired effect. Ask students to revise the first sentence of the paragraph beginning on line 31, making its language more formal by eliminating Tan's strategies. Have students compare and contrast the two versions.

TIERED DISCUSSION PROMPTS

In lines 39–48, use these prompts to help students understand the style of English Tan hears from her mother:

Connect In your experience, how do people respond when someone speaks in a language that is not considered standard English? *Students' responses should indicate an awareness of the potential social costs of nonstandard speech.*

Interpret What does Amy Tan's mother tell her about inviting a gangster to a wedding? *Possible answer: A gangster is invited to a wedding because he is an important person. He shows up for a short period to show respect, then leaves.*

Evaluate How difficult is it to interpret Tan's mother's English? Why? *Accept all thoughtful responses.*

C Model the Skill: MAIN IDEAS

Work with students to add supporting details to the diagram introduced on page 1263.

Mother understands more than can say.

Some friends understand only half.

Mother Tongue

Possible answer: Tan supports her main idea by saying that some friends understand none of what her mother says, while others understand most of it, and that her mother reads business magazines and watches news shows with ease.

Just last week, as I was walking down the street with her, I again found myself conscious of the English I was using, the English I do use with her. We were talking about the price of new and used furniture, and I heard myself saying this: "Not waste money that way." My husband was with us as well, and he didn't notice any switch in my English. And then I realized why. It's because over the twenty years we've been together I've often used that same kind of English with him, and sometimes he even uses it with me. It has become our language of intimacy, a different sort of English that relates to family talk, the language I grew
30 up with.

So that you'll have some idea of what this family talk sounds like, I'll quote what my mother said during a conversation that I videotaped and then transcribed. During this conversation, she was talking about a political gangster in Shanghai who had the same last name as her family's, Du, and how in his early years the gangster wanted to be adopted by her family, who were rich by comparison. Later, the gangster became more powerful, far richer than my mother's family, and he showed up at my mother's wedding to pay his respects. Here's what she said in part: B

"Du Yusong having business like fruit stand. Like off-the-street kind. He is Du
40 like Du Zong—but not Tsung-ming Island[2] people. The local people call *putong*. The river east side, he belong to that side local people. That man want to ask Du Zong father take him in like become own family. Du Zong father wasn't look down on him, but didn't take seriously, until that man big like become a mafia. Now important person, very hard to inviting him. Chinese way, came only to show respect, don't stay for dinner. Respect for making big celebration, he shows up. Mean gives lots of respect. Chinese custom. Chinese social life that way. If too important won't have to stay too long. He come to my wedding. I didn't see, I heard it. I gone to boy's side, they have YMCA dinner. Chinese age I was nineteen."

You should know that my mother's expressive command of English belies how
50 much she actually understands. She reads the *Forbes*[3] report, listens to *Wall Street Week,* converses daily with her stockbroker, reads Shirley MacLaine's books[4] with ease—all kinds of things I can't begin to understand. Yet some of my friends tell me they understand fifty percent of what my mother says. Some say they understand eighty to ninety percent. Some say they understand none of it, as if she were speaking pure Chinese. But to me, my mother's English is perfectly clear, perfectly natural. It's my mother tongue. Her language, as I hear it, is vivid, direct, full of observation and imagery. That was the language that helped shape the way I saw things, expressed things, made sense of the world. C

Lately I've been giving more thought to the kind of English my mother speaks.
60 Like others, I have described it to people as "broken" or "fractured" English. But I wince when I say that. It has always bothered me that I can think of no way to describe it other than "broken," as if it were damaged and needed to be fixed, as if

---

2. **Tsung-ming** (tsŏŏng-mĭng) **Island:** an island near the mouth of the Yangtze River, near Shanghai, in eastern China.
3. *Forbes:* a financial magazine.
4. **Shirley MacLaine's books:** works by the American actress Shirley MacLaine (born 1934), many of which deal with reincarnation.

B GRAMMAR AND STYLE
Reread lines 31–33. Note how Tan addresses her readers as *you*, as though in conversation. This use of **informal language** helps her create a warm, personal voice.

Language Coach

Pronunciation *Belies* (line 49) is pronounced with the stress on the second syllable (bih LYZ). (A word with a similar pronunciation is *replies*.) *Belies* means "misrepresents" or "gives an inaccurate idea of." What does her mother's command of English belie?

C MAIN IDEAS
Reread lines 49–58. What **supporting details** does Tan include to describe the way her mother uses English?

DIFFERENTIATED INSTRUCTION

FOR ENGLISH LANGUAGE LEARNERS

Vocabulary: Cognates Point out that the Spanish cognate *conversación* is similar to the English word *conversation* (line 32). Organize students who speak Latin-based languages in groups. Challenge groups to find at least five other words in the essay that are similar to words in their languages. Invite groups to merge their lists into a master list for class use.

FOR ENGLISH LANGUAGE LEARNERS

Language Coach

Pronunciation *Answer: Mrs. Tan's command of English belies her keen understanding of written and spoken English.* Have students practice viewing and pronouncing other words that are stressed on the second syllable: *convey, rely, persuade, refrain.*

it lacked a certain wholeness and soundness. I've heard other terms used, "limited English," for example. But they seem just as bad, as if everything is limited, including people's perceptions of the limited-English speaker.

I know this for a fact, because when I was growing up, my mother's "limited" English limited my perception of her. I was ashamed of her English. I believed that her English reflected the quality of what she had to say. That is, because she expressed them imperfectly, her thoughts were imperfect. And I had plenty of
70 empirical evidence[5] to support me: the fact that people in department stores, at banks, and in restaurants did not take her seriously, did not give her good service, pretended not to understand her, or even acted as if they did not hear her.

②ᐧ Targeted Passage

My mother has long realized the limitations of her English as well. When I was a teenager, she used to have me call people on the phone and pretend I was she. In this guise, I was forced to ask for information or even to complain and yell at people who had been rude to her. One time it was a call to her stockbroker in New York. She had cashed out her small portfolio, and it just so happened we were going to New York the next week, our first trip outside California. I had to get on the phone and say in an adolescent voice that was not very convincing, "This is Mrs. Tan."

80 My mother was standing in the back whispering loudly, "Why he don't send me check, already two weeks late. So mad he lie to me, losing me money."

And then I said in perfect English on the phone, "Yes, I'm getting rather concerned. You had agreed to send the check two weeks ago, but it hasn't arrived."

Then she began to talk more loudly. "What he want, I come to New York tell him front of his boss, you cheating me?" And I was trying to calm her down, make her be quiet, while telling the stockbroker, "I can't tolerate any more excuses. If I don't receive the check immediately, I am going to have to speak to your manager when I'm in New York next week." And sure enough, the following week, there we were in front of this astonished stockbroker, and I was sitting there
90 red-faced and quiet, and my mother, the real Mrs. Tan, was shouting at his boss in her impeccable broken English. **ⓓ**

We used a similar routine more recently, for a situation that was far less humorous. My mother had gone to the hospital for an appointment to find out about a CAT scan[6] she had had a month earlier. She said she had spoken very good English, her best English, no mistakes. Still, she said, the hospital did not apologize when they informed her they had lost the CAT scan and she had come for nothing. She said they did not seem to have any sympathy when she told them she was anxious to know the exact diagnosis, since her husband and her son had died of brain tumors. She said they would not give her any more information
100 until the next time and she would have to make another appointment for that. So she said she would not leave until the doctor called her daughter. She wouldn't budge. And when the doctor finally called her daughter, me, who spoke in perfect English—lo and behold—we had assurances the CAT scan would be found, promises that a conference call on Monday would be held, and apologies for any suffering my mother had gone through for a most regrettable mistake.

---

5. **empirical evidence:** evidence derived from observation.

6. **CAT scan:** a three-dimensional image of structures inside the human body.

E PERSONAL ESSAY

Possible answer: *The anecdote feels very personal and it is easy to understand how Amy Tan felt that her mother's limited English affected her own linguistic development, making her English skills weaker than some of her peers'. Also, the story shows that her mother encouraged Tan to think creatively and find many ways of looking at things, whereas tests demanded one answer that was usually not creative.*

Extend the Discussion Should immigrant parents require their children to speak English at home? Why or why not?

TIERED DISCUSSION PROMPTS

In lines 130–144, use these prompts to help students understand Tan's point about testing:

Connect Are there kinds of tests that you find easier than others? Which ones, and why? *Students' responses should show familiarity with and critical thinking about the topic of testing.*

Analyze What kept Tan from doing well on analogy test questions? *Possible answer: She was imaginative and therefore she thought of unexpected answers.*

Evaluate Are the traits Tan reveals about herself positive or negative? Explain.
Possible answer: *Tan's traits are positive in that she shows her imaginative style of intelligence and her individuality. They are negative in that they diminish her ability to succeed on certain kinds of tests.*

I think my mother's English almost had an effect on limiting my possibilities in life as well. Sociologists and linguists probably will tell you that a person's developing language skills are more influenced by peers than by family. But I do think that the language spoken in the family, especially in immigrant families
110 which are more insular,[7] plays a large role in shaping the language of the child. And I believe that it affected my results on achievement tests, IQ tests, and the SAT. While my English skills were never judged poor, compared with math, English could not be considered my strong suit. In grade school I did moderately well, getting perhaps B's, sometimes B-pluses, in English and scoring perhaps in the sixtieth or seventieth percentile on achievement tests. But those scores were not good enough to override the opinion that my true abilities lay in math and science, because in those areas I achieved A's and scored in the ninetieth percentile or higher.

This was understandable. Math is precise; there is only one correct answer. Whereas, for me at least, the answers on English tests were always a judgment call,
120 a matter of opinion and personal experience. Those tests were constructed around items like fill-in-the-blank sentence completion, such as, "Even though Tom was _____, Mary thought he was_____." And the correct answer always seemed to be the most bland combinations, for example, "Even though Tom was shy, Mary thought he was charming," with the grammatical structure "even though" limiting the correct answer to some sort of semantic opposites,[8] so you wouldn't get answers like, "Even though Tom was foolish, Mary thought he was ridiculous." Well, according to my mother, there were very few limitations as to what Tom could have been and what Mary might have thought of him. So I never did well on tests like that. **E**

130   The same was true with word analogies, pairs of words for which you were supposed to find some sort of logical semantic relationship, for instance, "Sunset is to nightfall as _____ is to_____." And here you would be presented with a list of four possible pairs, one of which showed the same kind of relationship: *red* is to *stoplight, bus* is to *arrival, chills* is to *fever, yawn* is to *boring*. Well, I could never think that way. I knew what the tests were asking, but I could not block out of my mind the images already created by the first pair, *sunset* is to *nightfall*—and I would see a burst of colors against a darkening sky, the moon rising, the lowering of a curtain of stars. And all the other pairs of words—*red, bus, stoplight, boring*— just threw up a mass of confusing images, making it impossible for me to see
140 that saying "A sunset precedes nightfall" was as logical as saying "A chill precedes a fever." The only way I would have gotten that answer right was to imagine an associative situation,[9] such as my being disobedient and staying out past sunset, catching a chill at night, which turned into feverish pneumonia as punishment— which indeed did happen to me.

I have been thinking about all this lately, about my mother's English, about achievement tests. Because lately I've been asked, as a writer, why there are not more Asian-Americans represented in American literature. Why are

---

7. **insular:** isolated.

8. **semantic opposites:** words opposite in meaning.

9. **associative situation:** a circumstance or story based on mental connections.

3 **Targeted Passage**

COMMON CORE L 2a

Language Coach

Hyphens In line 121, the phrase *fill-in-the-blank* modifies, or gives information about, the noun phrase *sentence completion*. Notice that hyphens are used to connect all of the words in this phrase. Some other examples of long hyphenated phrases are: *hard-to-remember name, behind-the-back pass,* and *not-too-friendly look.* Work with a partner to come up with more examples of hyphenated phrases.

E **PERSONAL ESSAY**
Reread lines 107–129. How does this anecdote appeal to you as a reader and contribute to your understanding of the author's ideas? Explain.

DIFFERENTIATED INSTRUCTION

FOR STRUGGLING READERS
3 **Targeted Passage** [Lines 106–120]

This passage describes the ways Tan believes her mother's use of English affected Tan's school performance.

- In what ways does Tan think immigrant parents affect their children's English? (lines 108–110)

- What explains the discrepancy between the subjects Tan was good at and those at which she was weak? (lines 112–120)

FOR ENGLISH LANGUAGE LEARNERS

Culture: Clarify Explain that *achievement tests* (line 111), now known as SAT Subject Tests, examine accumulated knowledge in areas such as English, history, and math. Results include a ranking by percentile to show how an individual student performed relative to others taking the test. Tan's scores in the "ninetieth percentile" mean that she scored higher than 90 percent of those taking the test.

FOR ENGLISH LANGUAGE LEARNERS

Language Coach

COMMON CORE L 2a

Hyphens *Possible answer: five-year-old girl, well-to-do family, devil-may-care attitude.*

there few Asian-Americans enrolled in creative writing programs? Why do so many Chinese students go into engineering? Well, these are broad sociological questions I can't begin to answer. But I have noticed in surveys—in fact, just last week—that Asian-American students, as a whole, do significantly better on math achievement tests than on English tests. And this makes me think that there are other Asian-American students whose English spoken in the home might also be described as "broken" or "limited." And perhaps they also have teachers who are steering them away from writing and into math and science, which is what happened to me.

Fortunately, I happen to be rebellious and enjoy the challenge of disproving assumptions made about me. I became an English major my first year in college, after being enrolled as pre-med. I started writing nonfiction as a freelancer the week after I was told by my boss at the time that writing was my worst skill and I should hone my talents toward account management. **F**

But it wasn't until 1985 that I began to write fiction. At first I wrote using what I thought to be wittily crafted sentences, sentences that would finally prove I had mastery over the English language. Here's an example from the first draft of a story that later made its way into *The Joy Luck Club,* but without this line: "That was my mental quandary in its nascent state."[10] A terrible line, which I can barely pronounce.

Fortunately, for reasons I won't get into here, I later decided I should envision a reader for the stories I would write. And the reader I decided on was my mother, because these were stories about mothers. So with this reader in mind—and in fact she did read my early drafts—I began to write stories using all the Englishes I grew up with: the English I spoke to my mother, which for lack of a better term might be described as "simple"; the English she used with me, which for lack of a better term might be described as "broken"; my translation of her Chinese, which could certainly be described as "watered down"; and what I imagined to be her translation of her Chinese if she could speak in perfect English, her internal language, and for that I sought to preserve the essence, but neither an English nor a Chinese structure. I wanted to capture what language ability tests can never reveal: her intent, her passion, her imagery, the rhythms of her speech and the nature of her thoughts.

Apart from what any critic had to say about my writing, I knew I had succeeded where it counted when my mother finished reading my book and gave me her verdict: "So easy to read." ❧

④ Targeted Passage

F MAIN IDEAS
Identify the main idea of lines 157–161. What details support this main idea?

10. **my mental quandary . . . state:** my mental predicament in its earliest form.

Practice and Apply

For preliminary support of post-reading questions, use these copy masters:

R RESOURCE MANAGER—Copy Masters
Reading Check p. 177
Personal Essay p. 173
Question Support p. 178

Additional selection questions are provided for teachers on page 167.

ANSWERS

COMMON CORE RI 2, RI 3, RI 6

1. *Tan uses "broken," "limited," "fractured" to describe her mother's English.*

2. *The reaction to her English was that people did not respond to Mrs. Tan's requests for help or information, they failed to understand her, and at times they ignored her.*

3. *Achievement tests fail to reveal the creative intelligence underlying the student's limited English proficiency.*

Possible answers:

4. ● **COMMON CORE FOCUS** Identify Main Idea *Language shapes the way people perceive others, as shown by the way people exclude, limit, or stereotype those who speak nonstandard English.*

5. *In these situations, Tan takes on an adult role, representing her mother to authorities because of her mother's limited English. In a typical mother-daughter relationship, the mother would be the person in charge in such situations. Tan's mother's dependence on her imposes unusual responsibilities and expectations on the daughter and may reduce Mrs. Tan in her daughter's eyes.*

6. *Accept all thoughtful, well-supported responses.*

7. ● **COMMON CORE FOCUS** Personal Essay *When Tan was young, she was ashamed of the way her mother spoke (lines 66–69). As an adult, she came to admire qualities of her mother's English that others overlooked (lines 178–180). At first, Tan internalized the negative attitudes others held toward her mother. Later, she realized that those attitudes were prejudiced. Tan's struggle with those negative attitudes helped her understand how powerful language, and people's perceptions of it, can be.*

8. *"Mother tongue" refers to one's home language. The idea of family talk ties this concept to intimate or private language spoken*

to those closest to you. In the context of Mrs. Tan's speech, the phrase relates to how her English shaped Tan's development. In the context of language development, the phrase refers to the special challenges the children of immigrants face.

9. *Immigrant: Practice standard English.*
Doctor: Be understanding with patients who speak limited English.
Child of immigrant: Respect your parents' English.
Teacher: Understand the challenges students face.

Comprehension

1. **Recall** What words does Tan typically use to describe her mother's English?

2. **Summarize** In general, how did people react to Mrs. Tan's use of English?

3. **Recall** According to Tan, what aspects of language do achievement tests fail to reveal?

Text Analysis

4. **Identify the Main Idea** Review the diagram you created as you read. Based on your notes, what is the main idea of the entire essay? Explain your answer.

5. **Compare Roles** Tan describes situations in which she was forced to act as a go-between for her mother. In what ways do these interactions differ from the typical mother-daughter relationship? Explain your response.

6. **Make Judgments** Tan describes her mother's English as "vivid, direct, full of observation and imagery." Reread the story Tan's mother tells in lines 39–48. Do you agree with Tan's opinion of her mother's speech? Why or why not?

7. **Analyze a Personal Essay** Describe Tan's changing perceptions of her mother's use of English. In what way did her changing views toward her mother influence Tan's observations about the power of language? How does Tan's personal testimony influence your own views about language? Cite evidence from the essay to support your response.

8. **Interpret Title** Tan uses the expression "mother tongue" as the title of her essay. State the usual meaning of this expression. Then, use each of the following examples to develop a different or expanded meaning for this term:

   • the idea of family talk (lines 28–30)
   • Tan's description of her mother's speech (lines 55–58)
   • Tan's thoughts on language development (lines 107–110)

Text Criticism

9. **Different Perspectives** Look at the essay again through the eyes of the following individuals. What important lessons about life and the uses of language might each draw from this essay?

   • an immigrant   • the child of an immigrant
   • a doctor   • a teacher

> *What* **LANGUAGES** *do you speak?*
> Tan claims that the language spoken within the family does more to shape the way a child speaks than the language spoken by his or her peers. Do you agree with Tan's opinion? Explain.

COMMON CORE

RI 2 Determine two or more central ideas of a text and analyze their development over the course of the text, including how they interact and build on one another to provide a complex analysis. RI 3 Analyze a complex set of ideas or sequence of events and explain how specific individuals, ideas, or events interact and develop over the course of the text. RI 6 Determine an author's point of view, analyzing how style and content contribute to the power, persuasiveness, or beauty of the text.

What **LANGUAGES** *do you speak?* Students may argue that basic patterns are established within the family during early childhood, but that in later childhood peers are more influential.

Language

◆ **GRAMMAR AND STYLE: Use Appropriate Language**

Review the **Grammar and Style** note on page 1266. For this essay, Tan chooses a casual, conversational style that lets her establish a strong connection with her readers. One strategy that helps Tan create this distinctive style is her use of **informal language** that contains **contractions** and idiosyncratic terms like *Englishes*. She also addresses her readers in a personal voice, using the **pronoun** *you*, as in the following excerpt:

> *You should know that my mother's expressive command of English belies how much she actually understands. She reads the* Forbes *report, listens to* Wall Street Week, *converses daily with her stockbroker, reads Shirley MacLaine's books with ease—all kinds of things I can't begin to understand.* (lines 49–52)

Whenever you write, consider the audience you are addressing and choose the appropriate level of formality.

PRACTICE Rewrite the following sentences using informal language.

> **EXAMPLE**
>
> It is often difficult to make sense of the rules of effective language.
> *Sometimes it's hard to understand what makes language work well.*

1. A lack of education caused my mother to speak a damaged, limited kind of English.

2. To demonstrate my use of these techniques, I have included some excerpts from my recent work.

3. A substantial portion of my fiction relates to my personal experiences.

READING-WRITING CONNECTION

 Expand your understanding of "Mother Tongue" by responding to the prompt. Then, use the **revising tips** to improve your essay.

WRITING PROMPT	**REVISING TIPS**
WRITE AN ESSAY Choose a topic that lets you draw on your personal experiences—a longtime hobby, a trip you took, your family history. Write an **one-page essay** that communicates your unique perspective on this subject. Be sure to include relevant details from your own experiences in the essay.	• Use an attention-grabbing opening. • Include appropriate and effective personal details. • Create a compelling voice that conveys your personality.

Interactive Revision THINK central

Go to **thinkcentral.com**.
KEYWORD: HML11-1271

DIFFERENTIATED INSTRUCTION

FOR STRUGGLING WRITERS
Writing Support

- Recommend that students reread Tan's essay to see how she blends personal reflections with narrative.

- Urge visual learners to draw memories of the experience they will discuss.

- Remind students to write in informal language that reflects their own voice.

- Suggest that students read their first drafts aloud to peers and consider reader response.

- Encourage students to add sensory details when revising.

- Remind students to include their thoughts, feelings, and observations about the experience.

Language

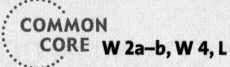

◆ **GRAMMAR AND STYLE**

To help students perceive elements of informal language, ask them to search the excerpt for contractions, idiosyncratic terms, and the pronoun *you* addressing the reader. Have students suggest other strategies of informal language that Tan uses in her essay, such as dashes and sentences beginning with *and* or *but*.

Possible answers:

1. *Mom's lack of education caused her to speak a damaged, limited kind of English.*

2. *To show you how I use these techniques, I've included some excerpts from my recent work.*

3. *A lot of my fiction comes from my background and personal experiences.*

R RESOURCE MANAGER—Copy Master
   Use Appropriate Language p. 179

READING-WRITING CONNECTION
Have students use Freewriting to find relevant details from their experiences. Then, urge students to exchange ideas with a peer as they work to define their perspective on the topic.

 BEST PRACTICES TOOLKIT
   Freewriting p. C1

Writing Online THINK central

The following tools are available online at **thinkcentral.com** and on **Write*Smart* CD-ROM:**
- **Interactive Graphic Organizers**
- **Interactive Student Models**
- **Interactive Revision Lessons**
For additional grammar instruction, see **GrammarNotes** on **thinkcentral.com**.

Assess and Reteach

Assess

DIAGNOSTIC AND SELECTION TESTS
   Selection Test A, B/C pp. 341–342, 343–344
Interactive Selection Test on thinkcentral.com

Reteach

Level Up Online Tutorials on thinkcentral.com

Focus and Motivate

COMMON CORE FOCUS

RI 5 Analyze and evaluate the effectiveness of the structure an author uses in his or her exposition or argument, including whether the structure makes points clear, convincing, and engaging. **RI 7** Integrate and evaluate multiple sources of information presented in different media or formats as well as in words in order to address a question or solve a problem. **W 1** Write arguments to support claims in an analysis of substantive texts, using valid reasoning and relevant and sufficient evidence. **W 8** Gather relevant information from multiple authoritative print and digital sources.

SUMMARY

"Census Data: The U.S. Population" analyzes results from the 2000 United States census with tables and graphs.

Government Documents

Have students use a two-column chart to organize information. In the first column, write the names of the writers included in this section. In the second column, have students note how the information about population change applies to the experience of that writer.

 BEST PRACTICES TOOLKIT—Transparency
Two-Column Chart, p. A25

Teach

Standards Focus: Analyze Text and Graphics

- Explain to students that graphics such as tables and charts present data in a visual way. Tell students that this visual representation allows readers to clearly see the relationships between types of information, such as comparisons and changes over time.

- Encourage students to pay close attention to the titles, column headings, and other explanatory information provided with graphics. Point out that even complex graphics are more easily interpreted after readers review the explanatory details.

R **RESOURCE MANAGER—Copy Master**
Analyze Text and Graphics, p. 189

Reading for Information

Use with "Mother Tongue," page 1264.

COMMON CORE

RI 5 Analyze and evaluate the effectiveness of the structure an author uses in his or her exposition or argument, including whether the structure makes points clear, convincing, and engaging. **RI 7** Integrate and evaluate multiple sources of information presented in different media or formats as well as in words in order to address a question or solve a problem.

Census Data: The U.S. Population
Government Documents

Essential Course of Study **ECOS**

The writers in this section, A Mosaic of American Voices, include Alice Walker, Sandra Cisneros, and Gwendolyn Brooks, who represent the diversity in the American population today. Their stories, poems, and essays, such as Amy Tan's essay "Mother Tongue," reflect the experiences of people living in a diverse culture. As you read the following government report, which presents the data the government has collected about America's diversity, consider how the data does or does not reflect the experiences of these writers.

Standards Focus: Analyze Text and Graphics

The U.S. Census Bureau conducts a national census every ten years and then compiles a report for the nation. The following portion of the 2000 census report focuses on the distribution and composition of the nation at that time. As you read the report, keep the following questions in mind:

- What is the report's tone, and who is the intended audience?
- What is the purpose of the report?
- What is the sequence of the information, and what are the major topics, or categories of information, in the report?
- How does this report's information on diversity reflect, or differ from, Amy Tan's experience as the daughter of an immigrant?
- How are maps and charts used to provide data and information?

To analyze the text and graphics in this report, note your observations and conclusions in a chart such as the one shown.

	Notes
Audience and tone	
Purpose	
Sequence of information/topics	

SELECTION RESOURCES

See resources on the **Teacher One Stop DVD-ROM** *and on* <u>thinkcentral.com</u>.

R **RESOURCE MANAGER UNIT 6**
Lesson Support,* pp. 181–194

DIAGNOSTIC AND SELECTION TESTS
Selection Tests, pp. 345–348

 **BEST PRACTICES TOOLKIT**
p. A25

INTERACTIVE READER

ADAPTED INTERACTIVE READER

ELL ADAPTED INTERACTIVE READER

TECHNOLOGY

⊘ **Teacher One Stop DVD-ROM**

⊘ **Student One Stop DVD-ROM**

⊘ **ExamView Test Generator** on the **Teacher One Stop**

* Resources for Differentiation

ALL ACROSS THE U.S.A.:
Population Distribution and Composition, 2000

During the 1990s, the population center of the United States shifted 12 miles south and 33 miles west, from a location near Steelville, Missouri, to a spot near Edgar Springs, Missouri.

Counting every person living in the United States is always a colossal undertaking. Census 2000 was the largest census in the history of the United States, counting 281 million people. In fact, the 33 million people added to the U.S. population between 1990 and 2000 is the largest census-to-census increase ever. New questions and procedures in Census 2000 provide unprecedented geographic[1] and racial detail. And new innovations in products and access modes will provide more data to more people faster than ever. **A**

Figure 2-1.
Percentage Change in Metropolitan and Nonmetropolitan Populations by Region: 1990 to 2000 **B**

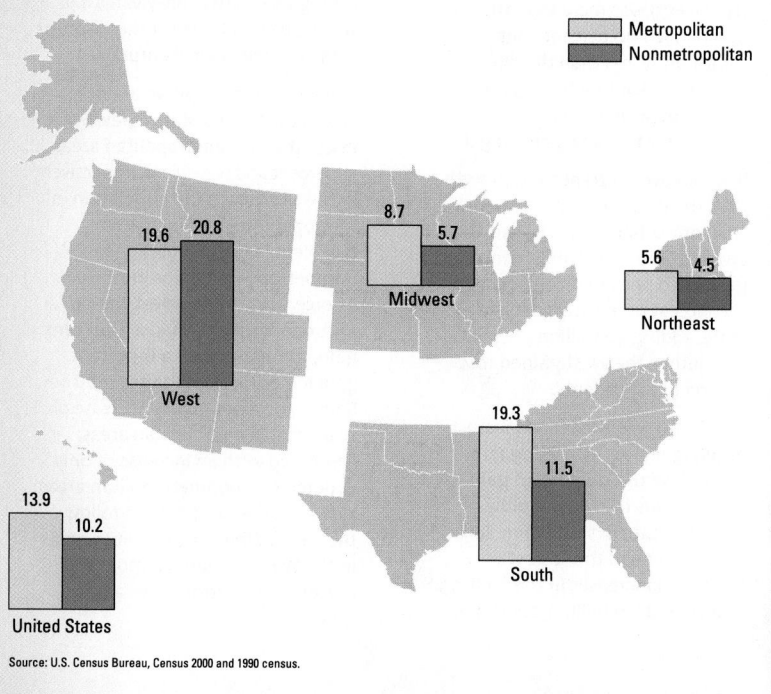

Legend:
- Metropolitan
- Nonmetropolitan

Values on map:
- West: 19.6 / 20.8
- Midwest: 8.7 / 5.7
- Northeast: 5.6 / 4.5
- South: 19.3 / 11.5
- United States: 13.9 / 10.2

Source: U.S. Census Bureau, Census 2000 and 1990 census.

COMMON CORE RI 7

A **ANALYZE TEXT AND GRAPHICS**
Before reading further, examine the first two pages of this report from the U.S. Census Bureau. Notice that each section of the report begins with a one-sentence headline in green letters. Notice also that the paragraphs are presented as un-indented blocks of text, with space between paragraphs. The purpose of these features is to help readers grasp major points of the report and quickly identify pieces of information in separate paragraphs. Before you continue, glance at the next page of the report. What do you learn from the small headlines that will help you as you read the block paragraphs?

B **ANALYZE TEXT AND GRAPHICS**
Examine Figure 2-1. Which area of the country experienced the greatest growth in metropolitan population? the least growth of metropolitan population? What do you think might explain those changes?

---

1. The minimum population for Census Designated Places was dropped, generating more information on small areas than ever before.

READING FOR INFORMATION 1273

DIFFERENTIATED INSTRUCTION

FOR ENGLISH LANGUAGE LEARNERS
Vocabulary: Technical Words Help students learn the meaning of technical vocabulary by providing them with synonyms for words including *metropolitan, nonmetropolitan, population,* and *region.* Ask volunteers to show their understanding of the technical vocabulary by restating the definitions of these terms using their own words.

Practice and Apply

Reading Support

This selection on **thinkcentral.com** includes embedded **ThinkAloud** models—students "thinking aloud" about the story to model the kinds of questions a good reader would ask about a selection.

INFORMATIONAL ANALYSIS COMMON CORE RI 7

A *Model the Skill:* **ANALYZE TEXT AND GRAPHICS**

Ask students to glance at the green bold-faced headlines on pages 1273 and 1274, as you read them aloud. Explain that headlines in general supply readers with brief summaries.

Possible answer: *The headlines give a quick overview of the upcoming paragraphs. The headline on page 1274 says that every state gained population during the 1990s. The paragraphs that follow the headline supply supporting information and details about population growth during the 1990s. Reading the headline tells readers what to focus on as they read.*

Extend the Discussion How much detail does a headline typically contain? In addition to giving a quick overview, what other purpose does a headline serve?

INFORMATIONAL ANALYSIS COMMON CORE RI 5 RI 7

B **ANALYZE TEXT AND GRAPHICS**

Possible answer: *The West experienced the greatest growth in metropolitan population. The northeast experienced the least growth in metropolitan population. The explanation might be that the metropolitan growth reflected the overall growth rate of those regions: the West experienced the largest overall gains of any region, while the Northeast experienced the smallest overall gains.*

TIERED DISCUSSION PROMPTS

Use these discussion prompts to help students reflect on census data related to the 1990s.

Connect Which statistical region experienced the largest total gain during the 1990s? *Answer: The South experienced a total population gain of almost 14.8 million people—more than any other region.*

Apply In which type of population area did the West not follow the trend of other statistical regions? *Answer: In the West, the population growth in nonmetropolitan areas outpaced that of metropolitan areas. In other statistical regions, the opposite was true.*

Evaluate Which area of the country lost population during the 1990s? Does this surprise you in light of the slow-to-rapid population growth in all other regions? Give reasons for your answer. *Possible answer: A band of counties stretching across the Great Plains to the Mexican border lost population. Students should support their answers with thoughtful reasoning.*

Words That Count

- **Resident population** includes all people living in the United States.

- **The four statistical regions of the United States** are groups of states for which data are presented. They include the Northeast, the Midwest, the South, and the West.

- **Median age** is the age at which half the population is older and half is younger.

The decade of the 1990s was the only decade of the 20th century when every state gained population.

The growth rate during the 1990s (13 percent) was more than the rate in the 1980s (10 percent), but significantly less than the rate experienced during the 1950s — when a baby boom contributed appreciably to the 18-percent gain.

With an overall 20 percent growth rate, the West grew more rapidly than any other region. Nevada swelled 66 percent and Arizona gained 40 percent. California had the largest numerical gain of any state, adding 4.1 million people. Altogether, the West gained 10.4 million new residents.

The South was the second fastest growing region, increasing 17 percent. With a 26 percent gain, Georgia was the most rapidly growing state in this region. Texas and Florida had the largest numerical increases in the South, 3.8 million and 3.0 million, respectively.

The total gain for the South (nearly 14.8 million) was the most of any region.

The population in the Midwest grew almost 8 percent, adding 4.7 million people. Minnesota was the Midwest's fastest growing state, increasing by more than 12 percent. A band of counties stretching across the Great Plains from the Canadian border to the Mexican border lost population.

The increase in the Northeast was 6 percent or 2.8 million people. Within the region, New Hampshire was the fastest growing state, increasing 11 percent. A band of slow growth counties included much of the interior Northeast and Appalachia, extending from Maine through western Pennsylvania and spilling over into the southern states of West Virginia and Kentucky.

In general, metropolitan areas across the United States grew faster than nonmetropolitan areas, 14 percent and 10 percent, respectively. In the Northeast, the population in metropolitan areas increased 6 percent, while population in nonmetropolitan areas increased 5 percent. In the Midwest the metropolitan areas had a 9-percent gain, compared with a 6-percent gain in nonmetropolitan areas. The South saw a population increase of 19 percent in metropolitan areas, compared with an increase of only 12 percent in nonmetropolitan areas. However, the West did not follow the trend. While metropolitan areas in the West increased almost 20 percent, nonmetropolitan areas grew 21 percent.

Table 2-1.
Population by Race and Hispanic
Origin for the United States: 2000 **C**

Race and Hispanic or Latino	Number (in thousands)	Percent of total population
RACE		
Total Population....	281,421	100.0
One race...............	274,595	97.6
White.............	211,460	75.1
Black or African American....	34,658	12.3
American Indian and Alaska Native..........	2,475	0.9
Asian................	10,242	3.6
Native Hawaiian and Other Pacific Islander.......	399	0.1
Some other race...	15,359	5.5
Two or more races..................	6,826	2.4
HISPANIC OR LATINO		
Total Population....	281,421	100.0
Hispanic or Latino.................	35,305	12.5
Not Hispanic or Latino.................	246,116	87.5

Source: U.S. Census Bureau, Census 2000.

For the first time ever, respondents to the census were allowed to indicate more than one race.

The overwhelming majority of respondents to Census 2000 (98 percent) reported only one race. The largest group (75 percent) reported White alone. Another 12 percent reported Black or African American alone. Just under 1 percent of the population indicated only American Indian and Alaska Native, and 4 percent indicated Asian only. Among those indicating only one race, the smallest race group was the population of Native Hawaiians and Other Pacific Islanders, accounting for only 0.1 percent of the total U.S. population. The remainder of the single-race respondents (5 percent) indicated that they were Some other race alone.

Just over 2 percent of the population indicated more than one race. The most common combination was "White *and* Some other race," accounting for 32 percent of all respondents in this category. This group was followed by "White *and* American Indian and Alaska Native" (16 percent), "White *and* Asian" (13 percent), and "White *and* Black or African American" (11 percent). Of all respondents reporting more than one race, 7 percent indicated three or more races.

The federal government considers race and Hispanic origin to be two separate and distinct concepts. For Census 2000, about 13 percent of the total U.S. population indicated that they were Hispanic or Latino. The racial distribution of this group contrasted sharply with the racial distribution of the population as a whole. Nearly half (48 percent) of Hispanics indicated that they were White alone. Another 42 percent indicated that they were Some other race alone. Less than 4 percent reported Black or African American alone, American Indian and Alaska Native alone, or Native Hawaiian and Other Pacific Islander alone. Approximately 6 percent of all

COMMON CORE RI 7

C **ANALYZE TEXT AND GRAPHICS**
Review the information presented here in table form. Which racial group forms the greatest percentage of the population? What group is identified by a category other than race? In your notes, write a two-sentence summary of the information in this table.

C **ANALYZE TEXT AND GRAPHICS**

Possible answer: *The White racial group forms the greatest percentage of the population. The group* Hispanic or Latino *is identified by race as well as origin. Sample sentences might include: "Whites are the largest racial group, followed by Hispanics or Latinos, and Blacks or African Americans. American Indians and Alaska natives, Asians, and Native Hawaiians and Pacific Islanders each made up less than 4 percent of the population."*

DIFFERENTIATED INSTRUCTION

FOR ENGLISH LANGUAGE LEARNERS
Language: Categories of Information Remind students that census data is organized and analyzed by particular categories. Identify some of these categories that are used in the report, and explain their meanings: *Percentage Change, Population by Race and Hispanic Origin; Percent of Total Population;* and *Age Distribution.*

D ANALYZE TEXT AND GRAPHICS

Direct students' attention to the graph's title and color key. **Possible answer:** *yellow data from 1990, green data from 2000. In 1990, people aged 25 to 34 represented the largest population group. In 2000, people aged 35 to 44 were the largest population group, indicating that the U.S. population as a whole was becoming older.*

E ANALYZE TEXT AND GRAPHICS

Possible answer: *The four subheads are:*

- *During the 1990s, the population center of the United States shifted 12 miles south and 33 miles west, from a location near Steelville, Missouri, to a spot near Edgar Springs, Missouri.*

- *The decade of the 1990s was the only decade of the 20th century when every state gained population.*

- *For the first time ever, respondents to the census were allowed to indicate more than one race.*

- *The U.S. population is growing older.*

The purpose of the subheads is to indicate to readers how the text is arranged by topic.

F ANALYZE TEXT AND GRAPHICS

Possible answer: *objective, unemotional, or matter-of-fact, remained consistent; audience is average Americans; graphics and explanations make the information easy for people to understand*

COMMON CORE RI 7

D ANALYZE TEXT AND GRAPHICS

Review the chart in which information on age distribution is presented in graphic form. What do the yellow columns represent? What do the green columns represent? How does the information presented here add to what you have learned by reading the Census Bureau report? Support your response with evidence from the chart and the report.

E ANALYZE TEXT AND GRAPHICS

This is one of four subheads in this report. What are those subheads? What is their purpose?

F ANALYZE TEXT AND GRAPHICS

Reread this last paragraph. How would you describe the tone? Has this tone remained consistent throughout the report? Is the audience of the report average Americans, government employees, or both?

Figure 2-2.
U.S. Age Distribution in Percent: 1990 and 2000 D

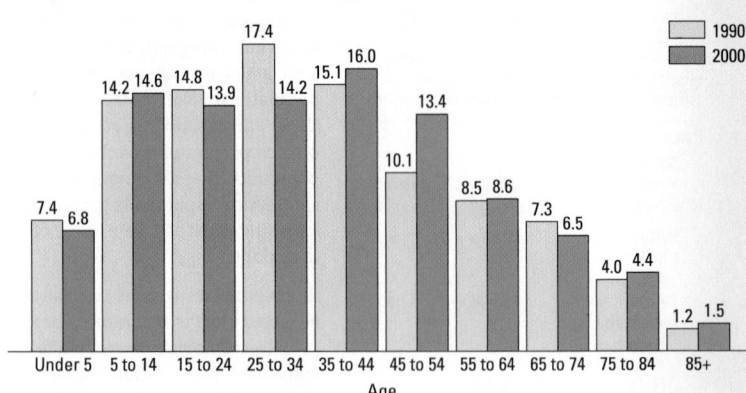

Source: U.S. Census Bureau, Census 2000 and 1990 census.

Hispanics reported two or more races. In fact nearly one-third of all respondents reporting more than one race were also Hispanic.

The U.S. population is growing older. E

The median age of the U.S. population in 2000 was 35.3 — the highest it has ever been. In 1990, the median was 32.9. The rise reflects a 4-percent decline in the number of people aged 18 to 34 and a 28-percent increase in the number aged 35 to 64. As the large generation of baby boomers[2] began passing their 45th birthday, the population aged 45 to 54 swelled 49 percent during the decade.

For the first time in the history of the census, the population aged 65 and older increased at a slower rate than the population as a whole. The percentage of people in this age group fell from 12.6 percent in 1990 to 12.4

percent in 2000. Relatively low birth rates during the late 1920s and early 1930s meant a relatively small number of people celebrated their 65th birthday in time for Census 2000. F

The Census Bureau Can Tell You More

- For more detailed information, see the following Census 2000 Briefs, *Population Change and Distribution* by Marc J. Perry and Paul J. Mackun and *Overview of Race and Hispanic Origin* by Elizabeth M. Grieco and Rachel C. Cassidy.

- Look for detailed tables on the Census Bureau's World Wide Web site (*www.census.gov*) and select "Census 2000."

- Contact the Statistical Information Staff of the U.S. Census Bureau at 301-457-2422 or e-mail *pop@census.gov*.

2. Baby boomers are generally defined as people born from 1946 to 1964.

DIFFERENTIATED INSTRUCTION

FOR STRUGGLING READERS

Options for Reading Have students review the four subheads in the text. Have them restate the subheads in their own words, using a map if necessary to explain location and meaning. Then, have students predict what will be discussed in the census document, using only the information discussed in the subheads.

FOR ADVANCED LEARNERS/AP

Discuss Significance. Have students review Figure 2-2, U.S. Age Distribution in Percent, 1990 and 2000. Have students identify the trends in population aging and make predictions in what they think the 2010 census will reveal about population aging. Then, guide a class discussion about the impact of aging for the nation as a whole. Have students consider how the trend toward aging will affect the services needed by the young, as well as the elderly.

Comprehension

1. **Recall** In 2000 what percentage of the population was Hispanic or Latino? White? Black? Other?

2. **Summarize** What did the report conclude about the age distribution of the United States?

Text Analysis

3. **Analyze Sequence of Information** How is the information on race organized? What other sequence might be used to present this information? Explain.

4. **Analyze Graphic Presentations** Examine Figure 2-1. How did metropolitan and nonmetropolitan populations change between 1990 and 2000?

5. **Draw Conclusions** Which gives you a better sense of race in America, the Amy Tan essay or the census report? Why?

Read for Information: Synthesize

WRITING PROMPT

The 2000 census report identifies four categories of change in the American population—geographical center, population size, race and origin, and age. Which category of change do you think will have the greatest effect on America in the 21st century? State your opinion and support it with reasons and evidence from the census report you have just read, the Census Bureau Web site, at least one other Internet or print resource, and, if you wish, examples from your own experience.

The following steps will help you answer the prompt:

1. To determine which category of population change will have the greatest impact on the 21st century, study all of your sources, analyzing the information about the various categories of change. Write a clear statement of your opinion, or claim.

2. Take notes from your sources, identifying facts, statistics, and other evidence to support your claim.

Source 1	Source 2	Source 3
Evidence	Evidence	Evidence

3. Identify at least three reasons to support your claim and organize the evidence for the body of your essay under those reasons.

4. Take your thesis statement from step 1. Use step 4 to develop the body of your essay.

Practice and Apply

For preliminary support of post-reading questions, use these copy masters:

R RESOURCE MANAGER—Copy Masters
Reading Check p. 193
Question Support, p. 194
Draw Conclusions, p. 189

Additional selection questions are provided for teachers on page 184.

ANSWERS *COMMON CORE* **RI 5, RI 7, W 1, W 8**

1. *Hispanic or Latino: 12.5 percent; white: 75.1; black: 12.3 percent; Asian: 3.6 percent; other races: 5.5 percent*

2. *The median age of the United States is rising, with a decline in people aged 18 to 34 and a rise in people aged 35 to 64.*

Possible answers:

3. *The information on race is organized in descending order, from the largest responding group to the smallest, with a separate section on respondents of Hispanic origin. The information could have been organized by including the data about Hispanic origin within the larger list of types of race.*

4. *The metropolitan population grew faster than the nonmetropolitan population. Only in the West did nonmetropolitan population grow faster than the metropolitan.*

5. *Students may say that the census report helped them understand the racial mix in the United States. Some may say Tan's article gave a better illustration of the nation's racial diversity.*

Read for Information: Synthesize

Writing Prompt *Responses will vary, but students should support their opinions.*

Assess and Reteach

Assess

DIAGNOSTIC AND SELECTION TESTS

Selection Tests A, B/C, pp. 345–346, 347–348

Interactive Selection Test on **thinkcentral.com**

Reteach

Level Up Online Tutorials on **thinkcentral.com**

FOR STRUGGLING WRITERS

Read for Information

- Encourage students to begin forming their opinions by comparing the possibilities for change. Have them review the four categories of change and ask themselves questions about each category, such as: *How would a change in the <u>geographical center of the United States</u> affect me?*

- Direct students to write *Because . . . I Believe* statements to support their opinions.

FOR ADVANCED LEARNERS/AP

Draw Conclusions Challenge students to draw conclusions about how the changes in the American population will affect their state or region. Ask students to write a paragraph explaining how the four categories of change might impact the economy, environment, or quality of life of themselves or their families.

Focus and Motivate

COMMON CORE FOCUS

RI 1 Cite evidence to support analysis of inferences drawn from the text. **RI 5** Analyze and evaluate the effectiveness of the structure an author uses in his or her exposition or argument, including whether the structure makes points clear, convincing, and engaging. **RI 6** Determine an author's point of view or purpose in a text in which the rhetoric is particularly effective, analyzing how style and content contribute to the power, persuasiveness, or beauty of the text. **L 4c** Consult reference materials, both print and digital. **L 5** Demonstrate understanding of nuances in word meanings.

ABOUT THE AUTHOR

Before students read the author biography, tell them that Alice Walker's essay expresses appreciation for her mother's influence on her life. As students read the author biography, ask them to find passages in it that hint at the essay's message. ***Possible answer:*** *The biography says that Walker's mother supported Alice's creativity and gave her gifts to help her get started.*

NOTABLE QUOTE

"It's a very human need, to make things, to create."—**Alice Walker**

Ask students if they agree with Walker that creativity is "a very human need." Discuss the ways in which the creative urge might differ for people whose life work is a creative art and those in other fields.

Selection Resources

COMMON CORE

RI 5 Analyze and evaluate the effectiveness of the structure an author uses in his or her exposition or argument, including whether the structure makes points clear, convincing, and engaging. **RI 6** Determine an author's point of view or purpose in a text in which the rhetoric is particularly effective, analyzing how style and content contribute to the power, persuasiveness, or beauty of the text. **L 4c** Consult reference materials, both print and digital. **L 5** Demonstrate understanding of nuances in word meanings.

DID YOU KNOW?

Alice Walker . . .

- became the first black woman to win the Pulitzer Prize for fiction.
- helped readers rediscover the writer Zora Neale Hurston.
- is an active environmentalist.

A Mosaic of American Voices

from In Search of Our Mothers' Gardens

Essay by Alice Walker

Meet the Author

Alice Walker born 1944

Best known for her novels, author and activist Alice Walker also writes poems, short stories, and essays. Often inspired by her personal experiences, Walker portrays the struggles of African-American women to transcend the limits imposed on their lives by racism and sexism. Though her characters typically face violence and great hardships, Walker emphasizes the power of hope and the strength of the human will to survive.

Early Influences The daughter of a sharecropper, Walker grew up poor in Eatonton, Georgia. When she was eight, an accident left her permanently blind in her right eye. A shy and self-conscious Walker withdrew from the world and turned to poetry to soothe her feelings of isolation.

Although uneducated herself, Walker's mother supported her daughter's creative ambitions. Walker was an exceptional student who became class valedictorian and won a scholarship to Spelman College, a historically black women's college in Atlanta, Georgia. When Walker left for college, her mother gave her three gifts: a typewriter, a sewing machine, and a suitcase. For Walker, these gifts represented creativity, domesticity, and freedom—a legacy of hopes, dreams, and unfulfilled longings passed from mother to daughter.

Fighting for Equality In 1965, after graduating from college, Walker received a travel fellowship to Senegal. Instead, she went to Mississippi to help fight for racial justice. "That summer," explains Walker, "marked the beginning of a realization that I could never live happily in Africa—or anywhere else—until I could live freely in Mississippi." In 1967, she defied state law to marry white civil rights lawyer Melvyn Leventhal. In retaliation for their interracial marriage, the couple was subjected to constant harassment and even death threats.

Speaking for the Oppressed During the 1970s, Walker published two novels and volumes of poetry and short stories. Her breakthrough came with the publication of her third novel, *The Color Purple* (1982), which was later made into a successful film. Many critics attacked this novel for its unflattering portrayals of African-American men. In response, Walker insisted her work reflected the painful realities of many black women's lives: "The black woman," she explained, "is one of America's greatest heroes. . . . Not enough credit has been given to the black woman who has been oppressed beyond recognition."

THINK central

Author Online

Go to **thinkcentral.com**. KEYWORD: HML11-1278

1278

See resources on the **Teacher One Stop DVD-ROM** and on **thinkcentral.com**.

 RESOURCE MANAGER UNIT 6
Plan and Teach, pp. 195–202
Summary, pp. 203–204†‡*
Text Analysis and Reading
  Skill, pp. 205–208†*

DIAGNOSTIC AND SELECTION TESTS
Selection Tests, pp. 349–352

 BEST PRACTICES TOOLKIT
Main Idea and Details, p. B6

TECHNOLOGY
- **Teacher One Stop DVD-ROM**
- **Student One Stop DVD-ROM**
- **Audio Anthology CD**
- **ExamView Test Generator** on the **Teacher One Stop**

---

* Resources for Differentiation   † Also in Spanish   ‡ In Haitian Creole and Vietnamese

TEXT ANALYSIS: AUTHOR'S MESSAGE

Authors write for a reason: they have a point to get across. In most nonfiction, you can find direct statements that reveal the **author's message,** as in this example:

And so our mothers and grandmothers have, more often than not anonymously, handed on the creative spark, the seed of the flower they themselves never hoped to see....

Walker reaches this conclusion by a pattern of **inductive reasoning.** Her essay proceeds from specific examples or pieces of evidence to a generalization such as the one quoted above. As you read, pay special attention to Walker's anecdotes, the brief stories she tells about her mother and women like her. See if you can anticipate the generalization Walker will infer from these anecdotes.

Walker also includes one of her poems in the essay. In the poem, her message is expressed indirectly, through elements such as **mood, imagery,** and **figurative language.** As you read the essay, notice the different techniques Walker uses to reveal her message.

READING SKILL: UNDERSTAND CULTURAL CONTEXT

When you analyze the **cultural context** of a text, you consider the social and cultural conditions that influenced how and why the text was written. Alice Walker's work reflects two key influences: her childhood experiences as a poor African-American girl in the South and her adult commitment to feminist ideals. To fully appreciate Walker's points, use the following strategies:

- Before reading, study the details about cultural context provided in the background information on page 1280.
- As you read, consult the footnotes to clarify Walker's references to cultural details.
- Apply what you know about the social conditions that shaped the lives of African Americans in the South.

As you read, note details that reveal how Walker's social and cultural influences have shaped her views.

 Complete the activities in your **Reader/Writer Notebook**.

When does LIFE become art?

Some people have an irresistible urge to create. Maybe they express it by sewing stylish clothes or cooking elaborate meals, by singing as they work, or by telling hilarious stories. For these people, even everyday chores can provide the creative outlet they need to release their artistic impulses.

DISCUSS In a small group, think of several ways that people express their creativity in everyday life. What do you think drives people to be creative? Record your responses and compare them with those of other groups.

1279

When does LIFE *become art?*

Introduce the question and invite students to think about what their creative outlet is, or what they would like it to be. Lead into the *DISCUSS* activity by asking students if they agree that everyday chores can be a creative outlet.

TEXT ANALYSIS

COMMON CORE
RI 5
RI 6

● *Model the Skill:*
AUTHOR'S MESSAGE

Tell students that an author may get his or her point across using direct or indirect statements. Point out that Walker's biography includes both types of messages from the author. Provide an example of an indirectly expressed message from the biography: "although uneducated herself, Walker's mother supported her daughter's creative ambitions" This statement indirectly expresses the message that Walker and her mother valued creativity.

GUIDED PRACTICE Have students state the message of a favorite song or poem.

READING SKILL

COMMON CORE
RI 6

■ *Model the Skill:*
UNDERSTAND CULTURAL CONTEXT

To help students analyze cultural context, have students find details in the author biography that suggest the cultural context of Walker's life and career. Point out that Walker worked for civil rights in Mississippi in 1965.

GUIDED PRACTICE Have students identify the cultural context of their chosen song and highlight lyrics that suggest that context.

R RESOURCE MANAGER—Copy Master Understand Cultural Context p. 207 (for student use while reading the selection)

DIFFERENTIATED INSTRUCTION

FOR ENGLISH LANGUAGE LEARNERS
Vocabulary Support Before students begin the selection, clarify the meaning of the following vocabulary words:

- *anonymously,* "without their names being known"
- *indirectly,* "without being stated in those words"
- *social,* "having to do with a community"
- *cultural,* "having to do with a people's way of life"

- *influences,* "factors that affect someone"
- *commitment,* "strong belief in or work toward a goal"
- *feminist,* "someone who believes in the need to secure rights and opportunities for women equal to those of men"
- *ideals,* "ideas about the way things should be"

SUMMARY

In this essay, Alice Walker describes the hard life of her mother, a sharecropper with a large family and much housework. Despite working all day in the fields and making her children's clothes and meals, Walker's mother found the energy for a creative activity: planting and tending gardens that were the talk of three counties. Her mother's creativity, and that of other unsung black women, inspires Walker to express her own creativity.

READ WITH A PURPOSE

Help students set a purpose for reading. Tell them to read "In Search of Our Mothers' Gardens" to determine the ways in which Alice Walker's mother expressed her creativity.

READING SKILL

COMMON CORE
RI 6

Ⓐ Model the Skill: CULTURAL CONTEXT

Plot out the following Main Ideas and Details chart on the board. Explain to students that this is a valuable tool for analyzing cultural context. Work with them to begin charting details.

Main Idea	Details
Life was hard.	Her day began before sunup and ended late.

Possible answer: *Details conveying the social conditions of African-American women in the early 20th century include the age of marriage, the number of children, and the list of chores.*

 BEST PRACTICES TOOLKIT—Transparency
Main Idea and Details p. B6

In Search of Our Mothers' Gardens

Alice Walker

BACKGROUND Alice Walker wrote this essay in 1974, after decades of civil rights activism had broken down many barriers for African Americans. At the same time, the women's movement had begun to raise awareness of the social constraints imposed on women's lives. Women of Walker's generation were poised to claim personal and social freedoms that earlier generations of women could never have dreamed of. As these women looked back into history to find role models for their own lives, they began to appreciate the extraordinary sacrifices these earlier generations had made. In this essay, Walker examines her mother's life to uncover a hidden legacy of resilience, strength, and overlooked talent passed on to the women of her own time.

Analyze Visuals ▶
Describe the style of this painting. In what ways does the artist's use of color, line, and texture contrast with the activity depicted?

Language Coach

Prefixes A **prefix** is a word part attached to the beginning of a word. *Mis-* means "bad." *Fortune,* here, means "luck." What happened to the landlord as a result of his remark? Why is Walker's use of *misfortune* (line 7) humorous?

In the late 1920s my mother ran away from home to marry my father. Marriage, if not running away, was expected of seventeen-year-old girls. By the time she was twenty, she had two children and was pregnant with a third. Five children later, I was born. And this is how I came to know my mother: she seemed a large, soft, loving-eyed woman who was rarely impatient in our home. Her quick, violent temper was on view only a few times a year, when she battled with the white landlord who had the misfortune to suggest to her that her children did not need to go to school.

She made all the clothes we wore, even my brothers' overalls. She made all the towels and sheets we used. She spent the summers canning vegetables and fruits. She spent the winter evenings making quilts enough to cover all our beds. Ⓐ

During the "working" day, she labored beside—not behind—my father in the fields. Her day began before sunup, and did not end until late at night. There was never a moment for her to sit down, undisturbed, to unravel her own private thoughts; never a time free from interruption—by work or the noisy inquiries of her many children. And yet, it is to my mother—and all our mothers who were not famous—that I went in search of the secret of what has fed that muzzled and often mutilated,[1] but vibrant, creative spirit that the black woman has inherited, and that pops out in wild and unlikely places to this day.

Ⓐ **CULTURAL CONTEXT**
What details in lines 1–11 convey the social conditions of African-American women in the early 20th century?

① **Targeted Passage**

---

1. **mutilated** (myōōt′l-ā′tĭd): irreparably damaged.

Washerwoman, James Amos Porter. Oil on canvas, 18″ × 13″. Private collection. Reproduction rights given by the Dorothy Porter Wesley Research Center, Fort Lauderdale, Florida.

DIFFERENTIATED INSTRUCTION

FOR ENGLISH LANGUAGE LEARNERS

Language Coach
Prefixes
Answer: Walker's mother "battled " with him. The use of misfortune *is humorous because the landlord provokes her.* Help students use knowledge of the *mis-* prefix to determine the meanings of the following words: *misinterpret, misinform, misguide.*

FOR STRUGGLING READERS

In combination with the *Audio Anthology CD,* use one or more Targeted Passages (pp. 1280, 1283, 1284) to ensure that students focus on key concepts in the selection. Targeted Passages are also good for English learners.

① **Targeted Passage** [Lines 9–19]

This passage describes the work Alice Walker's mother did and expresses the questions it raised for Walker.

When does LIFE *become art?*

Discuss In lines 24–30, why is the quilt "obviously" a work of great imagination and spirituality? In what ways does it reflect a creative outlet rather than a practical need for a warm quilt? ***Possible answer:*** *The quilt's detail and reference to a biblical story suggest the quilter's imagination and spirituality. Choosing to adorn a quilt with a detailed and meaningful story suggests that the quilting process was a creative outlet; a warm quilt could be made without decoration.*

TEXT ANALYSIS   COMMON CORE

RI 5
RI 6

B *Model the Skill:* AUTHOR'S MESSAGE

Point out that the paragraph beginning "For example" is an extended illustration. Discuss how Walker uses the quilt to make a vivid example of anonymous art. Show students how the next paragraph, beginning "If we could" presents the author's message, based on the previous example.

Possible answer: *The sentence that best states the message is, "If we could locate . . . allowed her to use."*

Extend the Discussion What might the anonymous quilter have been like?

READING SKILL   COMMON CORE

RI 6

C CULTURAL CONTEXT

Possible answer: *Walker changes the cultural references to equivalent African-American cultural ones, placing her version in brackets. She might have chosen to quote Virginia Woolf because Woolf was a prominent feminist writer, and Walker wants to address women's concerns within African-American culture.*

---

20   But when, you will ask, did my overworked mother have time to know or care about feeding the creative spirit?

The answer is so simple that many of us have spent years discovering it. We have constantly looked high, when we should have looked high—and low.

For example: in the Smithsonian Institution in Washington, D.C., there hangs a quilt unlike any other in the world. In fanciful, inspired, and yet simple and identifiable figures, it portrays the story of the Crucifixion.[2] It is considered rare, beyond price. Though it follows no known pattern of quilt-making, and though it is made of bits and pieces of worthless rags, it is obviously the work of a person of powerful imagination and deep spiritual feeling. Below this quilt I saw a note that

30 says it was made by "an anonymous Black woman in Alabama, a hundred years ago."

If we could locate this "anonymous" black woman from Alabama, she would turn out to be one of our grandmothers—an artist who left her mark in the only materials she could afford, and in the only medium her position in society allowed her to use. **B**

As Virginia Woolf[3] wrote further, in *A Room of One's Own:*

Yet genius of a sort must have existed among women as it must have existed among the working class. [Change this to "slaves" and "the wives and daughters of sharecroppers."] Now and again an Emily Brontë or a Robert Burns [change this to "a Zora Hurston or a Richard Wright"[4]] blazes out and proves its presence. But
40 *certainly it never got itself on to paper. When, however, one reads of a witch being ducked, of a woman possessed by devils [or "Sainthood"[5]], of a wise woman selling herbs [our root workers], or even a very remarkable man who had a mother, then I think we are on the track of a lost novelist, a suppressed poet, of some mute and inglorious Jane Austen[6]. . . . Indeed, I would venture to guess that Anon, who wrote so many poems without signing them, was often a woman. . . .* **C**

And so our mothers and grandmothers have, more often than not anonymously, handed on the creative spark, the seed of the flower they themselves never hoped to see: or like a sealed letter they could not plainly read.

And so it is, certainly, with my own mother. Unlike "Ma" Rainey's songs,
50 which retained their creator's name even while blasting forth from Bessie Smith's[7] mouth, no song or poem will bear my mother's name. Yet so many of the stories that I write, that we all write, are my mother's stories. Only recently did I fully

---

2. **Crucifixion:** the death of Jesus Christ, who was nailed to a cross.

3. **Virginia Woolf:** English novelist, critic, and pioneering feminist (1882–1941). Her works frequently explore the inner lives of women living under severe social constraints.

4. **Emily Brontë . . . Richard Wright:** Brontë (1818–1848) was an English novelist and poet, and Burns (1759–1796) was a Scottish poet. Hurston (1891–1960) and Wright (1908–1960) were African-American writers.

5. **"Sainthood":** a reference to certain black women in the South called Saints. They were intensely spiritual women who were driven to madness by their unfulfilled creativity.

6. **Jane Austen:** British novelist (1775–1817), best known for *Pride and Prejudice*.

7. **"Ma" Rainey's . . . Bessie Smith's:** Ma Rainey was the nickname of Gertrude Malissa Nix Pridgett Rainey (1886–1939), a blues singer considered to be the mother of the blues. Bessie Smith (1894–1937), another blues singer, was mentored by Ma Rainey.

COMMON CORE L 4c

Language Coach

History of English Many common English words, such as *years* (line 22), *high* (line 23), *work* (line 28), and *deep* (line 29) come from Old English. Use an electronic or print version of a history of the English language to find two interesting facts about Old English.

B AUTHOR'S MESSAGE
Reread Walker's description of the quilt in lines 24–34. Which sentence best states the message behind Walker's observations?

C CULTURAL CONTEXT
Reread lines 36–45. Consulting the footnotes as needed, explain how Walker adapts the Virginia Woolf quotation to her own cultural context. Why might Walker have chosen to quote this particular author?

DIFFERENTIATED INSTRUCTION

FOR ENGLISH LANGUAGE LEARNERS

Language Coach   COMMON CORE L 4c

History of English *Answers will vary.* Discuss additional influences in the history of English. Have students find English vocabulary that evolved from African cultures, such as the Bantu family of languages.

FOR ADVANCED LEARNERS/AP

Evaluate In lines 44–45, Walker quotes a famous remark by Virginia Woolf. Invite students to explain this remark and then evaluate its likely validity. Have students brainstorm reasons for accepting the idea that most anonymous poets (and, by implication, other anonymous artists) were women, and reasons for rejecting the same notion. Have students share their explanations and reasons with the class.

realize this: that through years of listening to my mother's stories of her life, I have absorbed not only the stories themselves, but something of the manner in which she spoke, something of the urgency that involves the knowledge that her stories—like her life—must be recorded. It is probably for this reason that so much of what I have written is about characters whose counterparts in real life are so much older than I am.

But the telling of these stories, which came from my mother's lips as naturally
60 as breathing, was not the only way my mother showed herself as an artist. For stories, too, were subject to being distracted, to dying without conclusion. Dinners must be started, and cotton must be gathered before the big rains. The artist that was and is my mother showed itself to me only after many years. This is what I finally noticed:

Like Mem, a character in *The Third Life of Grange Copeland*,[8] my mother adorned with flowers whatever shabby house we were forced to live in. And not just your typical straggly country stand of zinnias, either. She planted ambitious gardens—and still does—with over fifty different varieties of plants that bloom profusely from early March until late November. Before she left home for the
70 fields, she watered her flowers, chopped up the grass, and laid out new beds. When she returned from the fields she might divide clumps of bulbs, dig a cold pit,[9] uproot and replant roses, or prune branches from her taller bushes or trees—until night came and it was too dark to see.

Whatever she planted grew as if by magic, and her fame as a grower of flowers spread over three counties. Because of her creativity with her flowers, even my memories of poverty are seen through a screen of blooms—sunflowers, petunias, roses, dahlias, forsythia, spirea, delphiniums, verbena . . . and on and on.

And I remember people coming to my mother's yard to be given cuttings from her flowers; I hear again the praise showered on her because whatever rocky
80 soil she landed on, she turned into a garden. A garden so brilliant with colors, so original in its design, so magnificent with life and creativity, that to this day people drive by our house in Georgia—perfect strangers and imperfect strangers—and ask to stand or walk among my mother's art.

I notice that it is only when my mother is working in her flowers that she is radiant, almost to the point of being invisible—except as Creator: hand and eye. She is involved in work her soul must have. Ordering the universe in the image of her personal conception of Beauty.

Her face, as she prepares the Art that is her gift, is a legacy of respect she leaves to me, for all that illuminates and cherishes life. She has handed down respect for
90 the possibilities—and the will to grasp them.

For her, so hindered and intruded upon in so many ways, being an artist has still been a daily part of her life. This ability to hold on, even in very simple ways, is work black women have done for a very long time. **D**

---

8. *The Third Life of Grange Copeland:* Alice Walker's first novel, published in 1970.
9. **cold pit:** shallow pit, usually covered with glass, used for rooting or sheltering young plants from temperature variations in the spring.

Ⓔ AUTHOR'S MESSAGE

Possible answer: In her poem, Walker describes the women with images such as "Husky of voice," "Stout of / Step," "fists," "battered down / Doors," "led / Armies," and "Headragged Generals." Her images emphasize strength, determination, and militancy.

REVISIT THE BIG QUESTION

When does LIFE *become art?*

Discuss In lines 122–133, in what ways did other people's creativity help Walker find her own creative outlet? *Possible answer: The creativity of her mother and other African-American women and the creative literary ideas of Virginia Woolf played a role in inspiring Walker's writing.*

SELECTION WRAP–UP

READ WITH A PURPOSE Now that students have read "In Search of Our Mother's Gardens," have them review how Walker discusses creativity. Ask them what they consider to be Mrs. Walker's most creative expression.
Possible answer: Students may say that her gardens are her most creative expression. They also may note that her ability to raise an artist such as Alice Walker was another type of creativity.

⭐ **CRITIQUE** Ask students to identify ways that Walker effectively presents her message, both directly and indirectly.

INDEPENDENT READING

Students may enjoy reading additional selections from this collection, *In Search of Our Mothers' Gardens: Womanist Prose*, by Alice Walker.

This poem is not enough, but it is something, for the woman who literally covered the holes in our walls with sunflowers:

> They were women then
> My mama's generation
> Husky of voice—Stout of
> Step
100 With fists as well as
> Hands
> How they battered down
> Doors
> And ironed
> Starched white
> Shirts
> How they led
> Armies
> Headragged Generals
110 Across mined
> Fields
> Booby-trapped
> Kitchens
> To discover books
> Desks
> A place for us
> How they knew what we
> *Must* know
> Without knowing a page
120 Of it
> Themselves. Ⓔ

 ❸ **Targeted Passage**

Guided by my heritage of a love of beauty and a respect for strength—in search of my mother's garden, I found my own.

And perhaps in Africa over two hundred years ago, there was just such a mother; perhaps she painted vivid and daring decorations in oranges and yellows and greens on the walls of her hut; perhaps she sang—in a voice like Roberta Flack's[10]—*sweetly* over the compounds of her village; perhaps she wove the most stunning mats or told the most ingenious stories of all the village storytellers. Perhaps she was herself a poet—though only her daughter's name is signed to the 130 poems that we know.

Perhaps Phillis Wheatley's mother was also an artist.

Perhaps in more than Phillis Wheatley's[11] biological life is her mother's signature made clear. ❧

---

10. **Roberta Flack's:** Flack is a popular African-American singer-songwriter.

11. **Phillis Wheatley's:** American poet Phillis Wheatley (1753?–1783), was born in Africa and brought to America in slavery. She is often referred to as the first African-American poet.

Ⓔ **AUTHOR'S MESSAGE**
Reread the poem in lines 96–121. Identify images Walker uses to describe these women. What qualities are emphasized by these images?

DIFFERENTIATED INSTRUCTION

FOR STRUGGLING READERS

❸ **Targeted Passage** [Lines 96–121]

This passage uses a poem to convey Walker's pride in African-American women of her mother's generation.

- Who is the poem about? (lines 96–97)

- When did the women live? (lines 96–97)

- What did the women do? (lines 112–116)

- In what ways did the women help their children? (lines 114–116)

FOR ENGLISH LANGUAGE LEARNERS

Language: Punctuation and Print Clues
Call attention to the long, complex sentence in lines 124–128, and to its two semicolons. Have students replace the semicolons with periods and paraphrase the resulting short sentences. *Possible answer: Perhaps long ago in Africa there was a mother who painted the walls of her hut beautifully. Perhaps she sang like Roberta Flack for the people of her village. Perhaps she wove the most creative mats or told the best stories.*

Comprehension

1. **Recall** On what occasions did Walker's mother lose her temper?

2. **Summarize** What did Walker's mother do in a typical day?

3. **Recall** According to Walker, what change occurred in her mother as she worked in her garden?

Text Analysis

4. **Make Inferences** Recall that a **paradox** is a statement that may appear contradictory but in fact communicates an important truth. Identify the paradox in Walker's poem in lines 117–121. What point is Walker making?

● 5. **Analyze Author's Message** Reread the conclusion of Walker's essay in lines 124–133. Explain what Walker means by her reference to Phillis Wheatley's mother. In what way does this passage express the message of Walker's essay?

■ 6. **Examine Cultural Context** Consider the conditions that constrained Walker's mother's life. Within this context, what is so remarkable about what her mother achieved? Support your answer with details.

7. **Make Generalizations** Consider Walker's descriptions of the following works of art by African-American women. What does each example tell you about this artistic tradition?

   • the description of the quilt (lines 24–34)
   • Walker's comments on her mother's stories (lines 49–56)
   • the garden Walker's mother plants (lines 65–77)

8. **Draw Conclusions** Think back to your discussion about the creative outlets people use to express their artistic impulses. Consider the creative outlets described in question 7. In your opinion, what inspires these women to make art despite the obstacles they face?

Text Criticism

9. **Critical Interpretations** "Walker's optimism," writes critic Donna Haisty Winchell, "is ultimately born of her belief that something of the divine exists in every human and nonhuman participant in the universe. The inhabitants of her fictional world search . . . for that divine spark that makes them uniquely who they are." How might this quote apply to the women in this essay? Cite evidence from the text to support your conclusions.

> *When does* **LIFE** *become art?*
>
> Alice Walker views her mother's passion for creating beautiful flower gardens as an artistic expression. Can you think of other ways people express artistry in nontraditional ways? Explain.

7. *The quilt suggests that beauty can be improvised from "worthless" materials. The stories suggest that a heritage lives on through generations. The garden suggests that artists can overcome severe obstacles.*

8. *The women are inspired by inner need or their hopes and desires for the future.*

9. *The drive to create could be seen as a search for the divine in the restricted lives of those women.*

> *When does* **LIFE** *become art?*
> Students may say that working to help children, animals, or solve problems is a type of creativity.

COMMON CORE

RI 1 Cite evidence to support analysis of inferences drawn from the text. RI 5 Analyze and evaluate the effectiveness of the structure an author uses in his or her exposition or argument, including whether the structure makes points clear, convincing, and engaging. RI 6 Determine an author's point of view or purpose in a text in which the rhetoric is particularly effective, analyzing how style and content contribute to the power, persuasiveness, or beauty of the text.

Practice and Apply

For preliminary support of post-reading questions, use these copy masters:

R RESOURCE MANAGER—Copy Masters
Reading Check p. 209
Author's Message p. 205
Question Support p. 210
Additional selection questions are provided for teachers on page 199.

ANSWERS

COMMON CORE RI 1, RI 5, RI 6

1. *Walker's mother lost her temper when the landlord suggested that her children did not need to attend school.*

2. *She worked in the fields, made clothes, cooked, cared for her children, gardened.*

3. *Walker's mother became radiant when she worked in the garden.*

Possible answers:

4. *The women knew things they could not know and intuited that their children would know or achieve things that the mothers could not.*

5. ● **COMMON CORE FOCUS Author's Message** *History knows nothing about Wheatley's mother, but Wheatley's success suggests that her mother was exceptional. The message is that successful people rise from the efforts of those who came before them.*

6. ■ **COMMON CORE FOCUS Understand Cultural Context** *It is remarkable that Walker's mother found a way to keep her creative self alive and changed her family's experience of poverty by surrounding them with beauty.*

Assess and Reteach

Assess

DIAGNOSTIC AND SELECTION TESTS
Selection Test A pp. 349–350
Selection Test B/C pp. 351–352

Interactive Selection Test on **thinkcentral.com**

Reteach

Level Up Online Tutorials on **thinkcentral.com**
Reteaching Worksheets on **thinkcentral.com**

   Literature Lesson 45: Author's Perspective
   Reading Lesson 4: Recognizing Main Idea and Details

Focus and Motivate

COMMON CORE FOCUS

RI 1 Cite evidence to support analysis of what the text says explicitly as well as inferences drawn from the text. **RI 4** Determine the meaning of words and phrases as they are used in the text, including figurative and connotative meanings. **RI 5** Analyze and evaluate the effectiveness of the structure an author uses in his or her exposition or argument, including whether the structure makes points clear, convincing, and engaging.

ABOUT THE AUTHOR

Before students read the author biography, tell them that Cisneros's essay is about the way a writer creates the material of literature from childhood experiences. Ask students to find details in the biography that they think could become literature.

NOTABLE QUOTE

"If you're bilingual you're doubly rich. You have two ways of looking at the world."
—*Sandra Cisneros*

Clarify that the phrase "doubly rich" is meant figuratively and suggests a richness of culture. Then have students suggest what Sandra Cisneros quote means about being bilingual.

COMMON CORE

RI 4 Determine the meaning of words and phrases as they are used in the text, including figurative and connotative meanings. **RI 5** Analyze and evaluate the effectiveness of the structure an author uses in his or her exposition or argument, including whether the structure makes points clear, convincing, and engaging.

DID YOU KNOW?

Sandra Cisneros . . .

- wrote in secret as a child because she knew her family would disapprove.
- won a MacArthur "genius grant," a large monetary award given to honor "exceptional creativity and originality."
- has had poems on display on Chicago subways and buses.

Straw into Gold: The Metamorphosis of the Everyday

Essential Course of Study **ECOS**

VIDEO TRAILER **THINK**central KEYWORD: HML11-1286A

Meet the Author

Sandra Cisneros   born 1954

"I'm trying to write the stories that haven't been written," Sandra Cisneros has proclaimed. With her rich, intimate portraits of Mexican and Mexican-American characters, Cisneros hopes to make readers of all races aware of the complexities of straddling two cultures. She sees herself as a voice for the voiceless. "I'm determined," she explains, "to fill a literary void."

Fighting Tradition Born to a Mexican father and a Mexican-American mother, Cisneros grew up on Chicago's South Side. The only girl among seven children, she felt as if she had "seven fathers" because her brothers tried to control her behavior. Like their father, they thought Sandra should adopt a quiet, traditional lifestyle. Fortunately, she was blessed with a mother "brave enough to raise her daughter in a nontraditional way." "My mother didn't force me to learn how to cook," says Cisneros. "And she always told me, 'Make sure you can take care of yourself.'"

Growing Up Lonely Cisneros formed few lasting friendships in early childhood, because her family moved frequently between Chicago and Mexico. "The moving back and forth, the new school, were very upsetting to me as a child,"

she once said. Retreating into herself, Cisneros became a keen observer of others and a secret writer of poetry. After years of clandestine composition, she encountered a teacher in high school who appreciated her experiences and her writing. With the teacher's encouragement, Cisneros began to share her work with her classmates.

The Value of Heritage In 1976, Cisneros entered the University of Iowa's prestigious Writers' Workshop. Surrounded by people from more privileged backgrounds, Cisneros felt intimidated. Soon, however, she came to realize that she could write about something her classmates could not. "It was not until this moment," Cisneros recalls, "when I separated myself, when I considered myself truly distinct, that my writing acquired a voice." Cisneros's realization gave rise to her acclaimed *The House on Mango Street* (1984), a series of interlocking prose poems about a poor Mexican-American family. Her reputation was cemented with the publication in 1991 of *Woman Hollering Creek,* a collection of stories. "In everything I've done in my life," she maintains, "including all the choices I've made as a writer, I've followed my gut and my heart. It's taken me where I've needed to go so far."

Author Online

THINKcentral

Go to **thinkcentral.com.** KEYWORD: HML11-1286B

1286

Selection Resources

See resources on the **Teacher One Stop DVD-ROM** and on **thinkcentral.com**.

R **RESOURCE MANAGER UNIT 6**
Plan and Teach, pp. 211–218
Summary, pp. 219–220†‡*
Text Analysis and Reading
Skill, pp. 221–224†*

DIAGNOSTIC AND SELECTION TESTS
Selection Tests, pp. 353–356

BEST PRACTICES TOOLKIT
Jigsaw Reading, p. A1
INTERACTIVE READER
ADAPTED INTERACTIVE READER
ELL ADAPTED INTERACTIVE READER

TECHNOLOGY
- **Teacher One Stop DVD-ROM**
- **Student One Stop DVD-ROM**
- **PowerNotes DVD-ROM**
- **Audio Anthology CD**
- **ExamView Test Generator** on the **Teacher One Stop**

Video Trailer **THINK**central

Go to **thinkcentral.com** to preview the **Video Trailer** introducing this selection. Other features that support the selection include
- **PowerNotes** presentation
- **ThinkAloud** models to enhance comprehension
- **WordSharp** vocabulary tutorials
- interactive writing and grammar instruction

---

* Resources for Differentiation   **†** Also in Spanish   **‡** In Haitian Creole and Vietnamese

TEXT ANALYSIS: VOICE

A writer's **voice** is his or her unique style of expression. This unique use of language is what allows you to "hear" a human personality behind the words you read. In "Straw into Gold," Sandra Cisneros writes:

I'd never seen anybody make corn tortillas. Ever.

The informal tone, the use of a contraction, the everyday words, the short sentence followed by a fragment, and the pauses before and after the word *ever*—all help create Cisneros's voice in this essay—one that is personal, relaxed, and conversational. The voice is consistently natural, even with this essay's central **allusion**—an indirect reference the author assumes her readers will recognize. The mythological story to which Cisneros alludes is familiar to most children. As you read, look for instances when you "hear" Cisneros behind her words. Note the stylistic elements that help create this unique effect.

READING SKILL: ANALYZE STRUCTURE

The **structure** of a text, or how its different parts are organized, is directly tied to the author's purpose. Cisneros reveals two purposes in this essay, and she uses two methods of reasoning—two kinds of structures—to achieve them. Her primary structure is anecdotal. Using **inductive reasoning,** she shares with readers some of her formative experiences—moments that helped shape her life as a writer. Then she draws general conclusions from those specific experiences.

At the heart of this essay, you will also find an example of **deductive reasoning.** The writer arrives at a conclusion by applying a general principle to a specific situation. The general principle is that weaving straw into gold reveals magical power. The specific situation is that Cisneros, in her own way, can weave straw into gold. Finally, the specific conclusion is that as a writer, Cisneros also has magical power.

Personal essays are often loosely structured, and "Straw into Gold" is no exception. Cisneros begins the essay with an **anecdote**—a brief story that makes a point. As you read, use a chart like the one shown to list these anecdotes and the author's inductive generalizations about them.

Anecdote or Recollection	Inductive Generalization
learning to make tortillas	

 Complete the activities in your **Reader/Writer Notebook.**

Where do writers get their MATERIAL?

Writers harvest ideas for their work in a variety of places. Some writers find inspiration in controversies ripped from the headlines. Others are intrigued by a particular moment in history. Literature can be inspired by a writer's travels around the world, but just as often, powerful stories start closer to home. In "Straw into Gold," you will meet a writer who has unearthed a wealth of ideas in her own experiences and heritage.

QUICKWRITE Think of a work of literature you're familiar with. Where do you think the writer came by his or her ideas? Whether it's a lyric poem about lost love or a novel about a historical event, try to imagine the writer's source of material. Explain your thoughts in a short paragraph.

DIFFERENTIATED INSTRUCTION

FOR ENGLISH LANGUAGE LEARNERS

Options for Reading Read aloud the selection summary on p. 1288 so that students have an overview before they read on their own. Then, have students silently read along as they listen to the *Audio Anthology CD.* Finally, divide the students into Jigsaw groups and assign a Targeted Passage to each. Have each group present ideas about passage to the rest of the class.

 BEST PRACTICES TOOLKIT

Jigsaw Reading p. A1

Teach

Where do writers get their MATERIAL?

Read the question aloud and ask students what a writer's material is. Discuss that it is the life experience from which a writer gets ideas. Read the *QUICKWRITE.* After students write their paragraphs, invite them to share their work and identify common idea sources.

● Model the Skill: VOICE

Write this passage on the board:

> Zap! Pow! That was childhood. A roaring, rollicking whirl of running games and fantasy heroes. It seemed to last forever—and now it's gone forever.

Ask students to describe the voice of the writer. Then, have them cite details that create the voice. Suggest that the voice in this passage is contemporary and fast-paced. Words such as "Zap!" and "whirl" convey this voice. Tell students that "Zap!" and "Pow!" are allusions to comic books, which use sound-effect words.

GUIDED PRACTICE Have students contrast the way they speak with the way familiar adults speak.

■ Model the Skill: ANALYZE STRUCTURE

Explain that the author biography on page 1286 includes several anecdotes and quotations. These convey aspects of Cisneros's life and character. Have students reread the author biography. Then, work as a class to record its structure using a chart like the one introduced on page 1287.

GUIDED PRACTICE Tell students to list quotations as well as anecdotes.

R RESOURCE MANAGER—Copy Master Analyze Structure p. 223 (for student use while reading the selection)

SUMMARY

In this personal essay, Sandra Cisneros shares the events and influences that helped shape her as a writer. Beginning with an anecdote about the daunting task of making tortillas by hand, she reflects on ways that her achievements have surpassed her expectations. She describes ways that her relationships to her parents and brothers affected her life and work. She has traveled far both literally and figuratively, turning the straw of everyday life into the gold of art.

READ WITH A PURPOSE

Help students set a purpose for reading. Tell them to read "Straw into Gold" to learn how the author meets a challenge and the lessons she learns from her experience.

A *Model the Skill:* VOICE

Help students by reading aloud the second paragraph, using your voice to convey a casual tone. As you read, emphasize words and phrases that indicate a conversational tone.

Possible answer: The informal tone, everyday words such as "I guess" (line 8), contractions such as "didn't" and "I'd" (lines 7, 10), and mixture of short and long sentences (lines 5–6) allow Cisneros's conversational voice to emerge.

Straw into Gold:
The Metamorphosis of the Everyday

Sandra Cisneros

BACKGROUND Cisneros originally delivered the text of "Straw into Gold" as a speech. The essay still retains some characteristics of an oral work—for example, the voice has a distinctly conversational character. The phrase "Straw into Gold" refers to the challenge faced by the heroine in "Rumplestiltskin." In this fairy tale, as you may recall, a miller's daughter will be put to death unless she can do the seemingly impossible—namely, spin gold out of mere straw. The word *metamorphosis* in the subtitle means "transformation."

When I was living in an artists' colony in the south of France, some fellow Latin-Americans who taught at the university in Aix-en-Provence[1] invited me to share a homecooked meal with them. I had been living abroad almost a year then on an NEA[2] grant, subsisting mainly on French bread and lentils so that my money could last longer. So when the invitation to dinner arrived, I accepted without hesitation. Especially since they had promised Mexican food.

What I didn't realize when they made this invitation was that I was supposed to be involved in preparing the meal. I guess they assumed I knew how to cook Mexican food because I am Mexican. They wanted specifically tortillas, though 10 I'd never made a tortilla in my life. **A**

---

1. **Aix-en-Provence** (âk'sän-prō-väns'): French city about ten miles north of the Mediterranean Sea.
2. **NEA:** the National Endowment for the Arts, a federal agency that funds artistic projects of organizations and individuals.

Analyze Visuals ▶
What does the image on the opposite page suggest about women's roles in traditional Mexican culture? Read the essay and then revisit your answer, citing details from the text.

A VOICE
Reread lines 1–10. What stylistic elements allow Cisneros's informal, conversational voice to emerge? Cite specific examples.

FOR STRUGGLING READERS
Vocabulary Support

- *unique,* "one-of-a-kind"
- *contraction,* "a word containing an apostrophe in place of a missing letter or letters"
- *instances,* "examples"
- *two-fold,* "having two parts"
- *formative,* "shaping"
- *recollections,* "memories"

Concept Support: Analyze Structure Spatial learners can easily imagine the structure of a building or a bridge, while mathematical learners can visualize the structure of a software code or an equation. Ask students to describe an accessible structure in their own terms, such as in a diagram or in words. Then invite them to think of text structure in the same way—as a collection of parts combined in a particular way to work together as a whole.

This selection on **thinkcentral.com** includes embedded **ThinkAloud** models—students "thinking aloud" about the story to model the kinds of questions a good reader would ask about a selection.

Analyze Visuals

Possible answer: Students may first say that the image suggests that women's roles are limited to household work. On revisiting, they may say that Sandra Cisneros and her mother provide examples of expanded and nontraditional roles for women of Mexican descent.

CULTURAL CONNECTION

Food Preparation In the opening anecdote Cisneros acknowledges that she misses Mexican food while abroad, partly because, despite being a Mexican American, she can't cook Mexican food. In many cultures, food and food preparation create important emotional associations and are linked to memories of growing up. For instance, Korean students might feel affection for *kimchi,* a spicy pickle, or *bulgoki,* barbecued marinated meat. Moroccan students might feel just as strongly about *couscous,* a dish of grain mixed with meat and vegetables in a sauce, or *kefta,* seasoned ground meat. Ask students to share information about the foods of their cultures.

FOR STRUGGLING READERS

Develop Reading Fluency Use the selection to give students experience reading a personal essay that describes the writer's experiences and expresses her feelings. Have students meet with partners and participate in a paired oral reading. Each student reads a section of the selection aloud. After a pause, the other partner reads the same text. Students should stop periodically and discuss the feelings the writer conveys.

FOR RELUCTANT READERS

Connect to the Text Invite students to think about the expectations others (parents, teachers, friends, neighbors) place on them. Are the expectations realistic or fair? Have students form small groups to talk about the expectations placed on them and their responses. Ask a member of each group to summarize its discussion for the class.

Ⓑ ALLUSION

Have volunteers read aloud lines 28–39 and lines 103–123. Explain that in these passages Cisneros continues the allusion.

Possible answer: As Cisneros attempts new tasks she refers back to the task of spinning straw into gold. Through the allusion, she suggests that she is a character who faces the impossible task of turning something ordinary into something valuable. Her message is that by using a little imagination and taking some risk, anything can be turned from straw into gold.

Extend the Discussion How would Cisneros's elementary school teachers have been likely to react to the idea of her becoming a successful writer? What "straw" would they say she would need to spin into gold to succeed?

TIERED DISCUSSION PROMPTS

Use these prompts to help students grasp the meaning of Cisneros's anecdote: in lines 11–19:

Connect Think of a time when you had to complete a totally unfamiliar task. What does the experience tell you about the author's feelings? *Students should recognize the anxiety of the situation.*

Analyze Why does Cisneros feel she isn't up to the task of making corn tortillas? *Possible answer:* Her mother's family made only flour tortillas. Her father's family ate store-bought corn tortillas. She has never seen corn tortillas being made.

Ⓒ ANALYZE STRUCTURE

Possible answer: Cisneros considers both tasks to be seemingly impossible, just like the fairy tale task of making gold from straw.

IF STUDENTS NEED HELP . . . Have them add to the chart introduced on page 1287:

Recollection	Summary
making tortillas and writing MFA exam	tackles tough tasks and succeeds

---

It's true I had witnessed my mother rolling the little armies of dough into perfect circles, but my mother's family is from Guanajuato;[3] they are *provincianos,* country folk. They only know how to make flour tortillas. My father's family, on the other hand, is *chilango*[4] from Mexico City. We ate corn tortillas but we didn't make them. Someone was sent to the corner tortilleria to buy some. I'd never seen anybody make corn tortillas. Ever.

Somehow my Latino hosts had gotten a hold of a packet of corn flour, and this is what they tossed my way with orders to produce tortillas. *Así como sea.* Any ol' way, they said and went back to their cooking.

20 Why did I feel like the woman in the fairy tale who was locked in a room and ordered to spin straw into gold? I had the same sick feeling when I was required to Ⓑ write my critical essay for the MFA[5] exam—the only piece of noncreative writing necessary in order to get my graduate degree. How was I to start? There were rules involved here, unlike writing a poem or story, which I did intuitively. There was a step by step process needed and I had better know it. I felt as if making tortillas— or writing a critical paper, for that matter—were tasks so impossible I wanted to break down into tears.

Somehow though, I managed to make tortillas—crooked and burnt, but edible nonetheless. My hosts were absolutely ignorant when it came to Mexican
30 food; they thought my tortillas were delicious. (I'm glad my mama wasn't there.)

Ⓞ Thinking back and looking at an old photograph documenting the three of us consuming those lopsided circles I am amazed. Just as I am amazed I could finish my MFA exam. I've managed to do a lot of things in my life I didn't think I was capable of and which many others didn't think I was capable of either. Especially because I am a woman, a Latina, an only daughter in a family of six men. My father would've liked to have seen me married long ago. In our culture men and women don't leave their father's house except by way of marriage. I crossed my father's threshold with nothing carrying me but my own two feet. A woman whom no one came for and no one chased away. Ⓒ

40 To make matters worse, I left before any of my six brothers had ventured away from home. I broke a terrible taboo. Somehow, looking back at photos of myself as a child, I wonder if I was aware of having begun already my own quiet war.

I like to think that somehow my family, my Mexicanness, my poverty, all had something to do with shaping me into a writer. I like to think my parents were preparing me all along for my life as an artist even though they didn't know it. From my father I inherited a love of wandering. He was born in Mexico City but as a young man he traveled into the U.S. vagabonding. He eventually was drafted and thus became a citizen. Some of the stories he has told about his first months in the U.S. with little or no English surface in my stories in *The House on Mango*
50 *Street*[6] as well as others I have in mind to write in the future. From him I inherited

---

3. **Guanajuato** (gwä′nä-hwä′tō): state in central Mexico.
4. **chilango** (chē-läng′gō) *Mexican slang:* native to Mexico City.
5. **MFA:** Master of Fine Arts, an academic degree.
6. **The House on Mango Street:** Cisneros's first book of fiction, published in 1983.

Ⓑ ALLUSION

An **allusion** is an indirect reference to a person, a place, an event, or a literary work that the writer believes readers will recognize. Cisneros uses a literary allusion in lines 20–21 to compare her challenge (making tortillas) with that of a character in "Rumplestiltskin." As you read, consider the essay's title. How does Cisneros carry the allusion through the essay, and what is its greater meaning?

Language Coach

Word Definitions
Intuitively (line 24) means "done in a manner requiring no active thought or knowledge." What does Cisneros do intuitively? How does she contrast intuitive tasks and non-intuitive tasks?

Ⓒ ANALYZE STRUCTURE

What does Cisneros's completion of her MFA exam have in common with the experience recounted in the tortilla anecdote? Explain how these experiences make Cisneros feel like "the woman in the fairy tale" she alludes to in lines 20–21.

DIFFERENTIATED INSTRUCTION

FOR STRUGGLING READERS
Ⓞ **Targeted Passage** [Lines 31–45]

This passage summarizes the personal meaning of Cisneros's achievements.

- What is Cisneros's reaction to succeeding at tasks she didn't think herself capable of? (line 32)

- In her culture, what is the usual way for young people to leave their parents' homes? (lines 36–37)

- What three factors helped Cisneros become a writer? (line 43)

FOR ENGLISH LANGUAGE LEARNERS

Language Coach

Word Definitions Answer:
She writes poems and stories intuitively. Non-intuitive tasks require learning step-by-step. Explain that intuitively comes from a Latin word meaning "to look at." Ask: At what does an *intuitive* person look? *Possible answer: The person looks at his or her own reactions or impulses.*

a sappy heart. (He still cries when he watches Mexican soaps—especially if they deal with children who have forsaken their parents.)

My mother was born like me—in Chicago but of Mexican descent. It would be her tough streetwise voice that would haunt all my stories and poems. An amazing woman who loves to draw and read books and can sing an opera. A smart cookie. **D**

When I was a little girl we traveled to Mexico City so much I thought my grandparents' house on La Fortuna, number 12, was home. It was the only constant in our nomadic ramblings from one Chicago flat to another. The house on Destiny Street, number 12, in the colonia Tepeyac would be perhaps the only 60 home I knew, and that nostalgia for a home would be a theme that would obsess me.

My brothers also figured greatly in my art. Especially the older two; I grew up in their shadows. Henry, the second oldest and my favorite, appears often in poems I have written and in stories which at times only borrow his nickname, Kiki. He played a major role in my childhood. We were bunk-bed mates. We were co-conspirators. We were pals. Until my oldest brother came back from studying in Mexico and left me odd woman out for always.

What would my teachers say if they knew I was a writer now? Who would've guessed it? I wasn't a very bright student. I didn't much like school because we 70 moved so much and I was always new and funny looking. In my fifth-grade report card I have nothing but an avalanche of C's and D's, but I don't remember being that stupid. I was good at art and I read plenty of library books and Kiki laughed at all my jokes. At home I was fine, but at school I never opened my mouth except when the teacher called on me.

When I think of how I see myself it would have to be at age eleven. I know I'm thirty-two on the outside, but inside I'm eleven. I'm the girl in the picture with skinny arms and a crumpled skirt and crooked hair. I didn't like school because all they saw was the outside me. School was lots of rules and sitting with your hands folded and being very afraid all the time. I liked looking out the window 80 and thinking. I liked staring at the girl across the way writing her name over and over again in red ink. I wondered why the boy with the dirty collar in front of me didn't have a mama who took better care of him.

I think my mama and papa did the best they could to keep us warm and clean and never hungry. We had birthday and graduation parties and things like that, but there was another hunger that had to be fed. There was a hunger I didn't even have a name for. Was this when I began writing? **E**

In 1966 we moved into a house, a real one, our first real home. This meant we didn't have to change schools and be the new kids on the block every couple of years. We could make friends and not be afraid we'd have to say goodbye to them 90 and start all over. My brothers and the flock of boys they brought home would become important characters eventually for my stories—Louie and his cousins, Meme Ortiz and his dog with two names, one in English and one in Spanish.

My mother flourished in her own home. She took books out of the library and taught herself to garden—to grow flowers so envied we had to put a lock

---

D VOICE
Reread Cisneros's description of her parents in lines 43–55. Identify the informal words, as well as the short sentences and fragments, that establish Cisneros's voice here.

E ANALYZE STRUCTURE
Identify the six recollections Cisneros presents in lines 43–86. What do they have in common? What is the inductive conclusion Cisneros draws from them?

TEXT ANALYSIS
COMMON CORE
RI 4

D VOICE

Possible answer: *Language such as "Mexicanness," "a sappy heart," and "A smart cookie" establish Cisneros's voice.*

REVISIT THE BIG QUESTION

Where do writers get their
MATERIAL?

Discuss Judging from lines 56–64, where does Cisneros get many of her ideas for subjects to write about? ***Possible response:*** *Cisneros gets her ideas from childhood memories.*

READING SKILL
COMMON CORE
RI 5

E Model the Skill: ANALYZE STRUCTURE

Have volunteers locate the six recollections and present them to the class. Discuss what the memories have in common.

Possible answer: *The recollections include travel to her grandparents' home (lines 56–61), the role of her brothers (lines 62–67), doing poorly at school (lines 68–72), laughing with Kiki (lines 72–73), being afraid and daydreaming in school (lines 76–82), family celebrations (lines 83–85). The common element in the recollections is a lack—of a permanent home, of a prominent role in the family, of interest or success in school, and of a nameless hunger. Cisneros's inductive conclusion is that all these shortcomings became the straw from which she was able to spin the success of her writing and her career.*

Use the paragraph structure to focus on the six recollections. Then urge them to complete an Open Mind diagram to represent visually what the recollections mean to Cisneros.

FOR ADVANCED LEARNERS/AP

Write Journal Entries [paired option] Have students think about the influential events Cisneros describes in this essay. Urge them to use their own life experiences to draw inferences about these events. Then ask them to imagine that they are Cisneros. Have them write brief journal entries about any two of the events from the essay. Journal entries should include descriptions built on the factual information provided as well as Cisneros's emotional reactions. Ask pairs to compare and contrast their entries, using these questions to discuss the way the described events affected Cisneros at the time and later as a writer:

- What common conclusions did they reach about Cisneros's reactions?

- What differences did they identify in Cisneros's emotional reactions?

- What, if any, differences did they identify in the way events affected Cisneros's writing?

COMMON CORE
RI 5

F ANALYZE STRUCTURE

Have a volunteer read the first two paragraphs of the Reading Skill: Analyze Structure passage on page 1287. Ask a second student to then read aloud lines 117–123. Explain that the closing sentence forms a part of the author's deductive argument.

Possible answer: *The general principle, as indicated on page 1287, is: Weaving straw into gold reveals magical power. The specific situation is that as a writer, Cisneros weaves straw into gold. The specific conclusion Cisneros draws is that she, too, has magical power. The essay's closing sentence is an imaginative statement of the conclusion to the deductive argument. It suggests the magical power in writing.*

Extend the Discussion How differently do you think Cisneros's life and career would have turned out if her family had always lived in one place, or if she had been an only child—if she had different "straw" to use for spinning?

REVISIT THE BIG QUESTION

Where do writers get their
MATERIAL?

Discuss After students read lines 114–116, ask the following question: In what way might a six-month residency on a 265-acre ranch help a writer find ideas? *Possible answer: The availability of time to think could help generate ideas, and the landscape could be inspiring.*

SELECTION WRAP–UP

READ WITH A PURPOSE Now that students have read "Straw into Gold," ask them to describe the author's response to her challenges and what she learned from meeting them. *Possible answers: The author surprised herself. As a result of meeting challenges, she has written books, traveled, and lived a life different from her expectations.*

---

on the gate to keep out the midnight flower thieves. My mother has never quit gardening.

This was the period in my life, that slippery age when you are both child and woman and neither, I was to record in *The House on Mango Street.* I was still shy. I was a girl who couldn't come out of her shell.

100   How was I to know I would be recording and documenting the women who sat their sadness on an elbow and stared out a window? It would be the city streets of Chicago I would later record, as seen through a child's eyes.

I've done all kinds of things I didn't think I could do since then. I've gone to a prestigious university, studied with famous writers, and taken an MFA degree. I've taught poetry in schools in Illinois and Texas. I've gotten an NEA grant and run away with it as far as my courage would take me. I've seen the bleached and bitter mountains of the Peloponnesus.[7] I've lived on an island. I've been to Venice twice. I've lived in Yugoslavia. I've been to the famous Nice[8] flower market behind the opera house. I've lived in a village in the pre-Alps and witnessed the daily parade
110   of promenaders.

I've moved since Europe to the strange and wonderful country of Texas, land of polaroid-blue skies and big bugs. I met a mayor with my last name. I met famous Chicana and Chicano artists and writers and *políticos.*[9]

Texas is another chapter in my life. It brought with it the Dobie-Paisano Fellowship,[10] a six-month residency on a 265-acre ranch. But most important, Texas brought Mexico back to me.

In the days when I would sit at my favorite people-watching spot, the snakey Woolworth's counter across the street from the Alamo[11] (the Woolworth's which has since been torn down to make way for progress), I couldn't think of anything
120   else I'd rather be than a writer. I've traveled and lectured from Cape Cod to San Francisco, to Spain, Yugoslavia, Greece, Mexico, France, Italy, and now today to Texas. Along the way there has been straw for the taking. With a little imagination, it can be spun into gold. ❧ F

(2)

COMMON CORE RI 5

F ANALYZE STRUCTURE

The author concludes this essay with a pattern of **inductive reasoning** that she has used throughout—moving from specific experiences to a generalization about these experiences. However, as you learned before reading this selection, Cisneros weaves **deductive reasoning** into her reflections here. Review the information about deductive reasoning on page 1287. Then, identify the three parts of the author's deductive argument: the general principle, the specific situation, and the conclusion. What part does the essay's closing sentence play in this deductive structure?

---

7. **Peloponnesus** (pĕl´ə-pə-nē´-səs): peninsula forming the southern part of mainland Greece.
8. **Nice** (nēs): port city in southern France.
9. *políticos* (pō-lē´tē-kōs) *Spanish:* politicians.
10. **Dobie-Paisano** (dō´bē pī-zä´nō) **Fellowship:** a prestigious award offered to authors who are from or write about Texas. It includes cash as well as the use of living quarters.
11. **Alamo:** a mission chapel in San Antonio, Texas, site of a famous battle in Texas's war of independence from Mexico.

1292   UNIT 6: CONTEMPORARY LITERATURE

DIFFERENTIATED INSTRUCTION

FOR ENGLISH LANGUAGE LEARNERS
Culture: Clarify Explain these references: *mayor with my last name* (line 112), "Henry Cisneros, the former mayor of San Antonio, Texas"; *Chicana and Chicano* (line 113) "a North American girl or boy of Mexican descent"; *Woolworth's* (line 118), "a store that sells inexpensive items such as sewing supplies and often has a coffee shop in it." Clarify that *Latina* (line 35) means "a female of Latin American descent."

FOR ADVANCED LEARNERS/AP
Synthesize Remind students that the essay was originally delivered as a speech. Ask them to imagine that they are in the audience hearing the speech the first time it was presented. Ask students to cite passages and rhetorical elements in the essay that would have made it an effective speech. Then, ask students to share ways they might have responded to the speech.

(2) **Targeted Passage** [Lines 103–123]

Comprehension

1. **Recall** What misunderstanding does Cisneros recount at the beginning of the essay?

2. **Recall** What traits do Cisneros and her father have in common?

3. **Summarize** As a child, how did Cisneros feel at school?

Text Analysis

4. **Make Inferences** What childhood events and circumstances inspired Cisneros to become a writer? Cite evidence from the selection to support your inferences.

5. **Interpret Allusion** An allusion is an indirect reference to a person, a place, an event, or a literary work with which the writer believes the reader will be familiar. Reread lines 120–123 and consider the essay's title. By incorporating allusions to the fairy tale "Rumplestiltskin," what point is Cisneros making about ordinary experiences? What is she saying about the imagination? Cite evidence from the essay to support your response.

● 6. **Analyze Structure** Review the chart you created. What idea does Cisneros return to throughout the essay? What is the function of this recurring idea in developing her message? Support your answer with evidence from the text.

● 7. **Compare Voice** In a chart, record examples of the stylistic elements that create Cisneros's unique voice. Then choose another prose selection from this unit, and analyze the voice of its author as well. Use your completed chart to explain how Cisneros's voice differs from that of the other writer's.

	Sentence Type/Length	Word Choice	Tone
Cisneros			
Other Writer			

Text Criticism

8. **Critical Interpretations** Cisneros's candid recollections prompted one critic to say, "The memories that Cisneros offers . . . sometimes wrinkle the nose and scorch the palate." He went on to praise her talent for "evoking the sensations of the past in their full complexity." Why do you think Cisneros shares her insecurities and painful experiences as well as her triumphs? How might failing to do this have altered the essay's message? Explain, citing evidence.

Where do writers get their **MATERIAL?**

Like many writers, Cisneros uses personal experiences and real people as material for her literary creations. How "creative" do you think it is to use personal experiences as the raw material for writing? Explain.

STRAW INTO GOLD **1293**

COMMON CORE

RI 1 Cite evidence to support analysis of what the text says explicitly as well as inferences drawn from the text. **RI 4** Determine the meaning of words and phrases as they are used in the text, including figurative and connotative meanings. **RI 5** Analyze and evaluate the effectiveness of the structure an author uses in his or her exposition or argument, including whether the structure makes points clear, convincing, and engaging.

Practice and Apply

For preliminary support of post-reading questions, use these copy masters:

R RESOURCE MANAGER—Copy Masters
Reading Check p. 225
Voice p. 221
Language Support p. 226

Additional selection questions are provided for teachers on page 215.

ANSWERS

COMMON CORE **RI 1, RI 4, RI 5**

1. *Cisneros describes being asked to make tortillas by friends who assumed she knew how because she was Mexican American.*

2. *Cisneros and her father share a love of travel and a "sappy heart."*

3. *She felt alienated and uncomfortable.*

Possible answers:

4. *Cisneros was inspired by living in a patriarchal household in a patriarchal culture, hearing her father's stories and her mother's streetwise voice, being shy, being the only daughter among seven children.*

5. *Cisneros believes ordinary experiences are sources of ideas and inspiration, and that imagination is the magic that can turn this raw material into the gold of art.*

6. ● **COMMON CORE FOCUS Analyze Structure** *Throughout the essay, Cisneros returns to the idea of turning straw into gold and of having accomplished things she didn't think she could do. The idea helps her to develop themes about determination, experience, and imagination.*

Assess and Reteach

Assess

DIAGNOSTIC AND SELECTION TESTS
Selection Test A pp. 353–354
Selection Test B/C pp. 355–356

Interactive Selection Test on <u>thinkcentral.com</u>

Reteach

Level Up Online Tutorials on <u>thinkcentral.com</u>

Reteaching Worksheets on <u>thinkcentral.com</u>
Literature Lesson 34: Allusion
Literature Lesson 44: Style and Syntax

---

7. ■ **COMMON CORE FOCUS Voice** *Charts will vary based on the authors chosen, but should contain multiple examples of each writer's unique voice.*

8. *If she had shared only her triumphant moments, Cisneros would not seem as sympathetic or as easy to relate to, nor would her triumphs seem as impressive. It would be impossible to communicate her "Rumplestiltskin" theme if she did not admit that she felt daunted by her tasks.*

Where do writers get their **MATERIAL?** *Possible answer: It is creative to base writing on real-life experiences if the writing is inspired by life and does not reproduce it exactly.*

STRAW INTO GOLD **1293**

Focus and Motivate

COMMON CORE FOCUS

RL 2 Determine two or more themes or central ideas of a text and analyze their development over the course of the text. **RL 4** Analyze the impact of specific word choices on meaning and tone. **RL 5** Analyze how an author's choices regarding how to structure specific parts of a text contribute to its overall structure and meaning, as well as its aesthetic impact.

ABOUT THE AUTHOR

After students read the author biography, ask them to point out the turning point when Brooks's approach to poetry changed. *Possible answer: In 1967, Brooks attended a conference of young black writers.* Tell students they will read poems in both of Brooks's styles. Invite them to predict ways that the two poems will be different. *Possible answer: One poem will focus on daily life for African Americans and the other will focus on political or societal issues affecting African Americans.*

NOTABLE QUOTE

"Art hurts. Art urges voyages—and it is easier to stay at home." —**Gwendolyn Brooks**

Ask students what Gwendolyn Brooks means by art that "hurts." *Possible answer: Art pushes people to think and see and feel in ways they wouldn't otherwise.*

Selection Resources

COMMON CORE

RL 2 Determine two or more themes or central ideas of a text and analyze their development over the course of the text.
RL 4 Analyze the impact of specific word choices on meaning and tone. **RL 5** Analyze how an author's choices regarding how to structure specific parts of a text contribute to its overall structure and meaning, as well as its aesthetic impact.

Life for My Child Is Simple
Primer for Blacks

Poetry by Gwendolyn Brooks

DID YOU KNOW?

Gwendolyn Brooks . . .

- published her first poem at age 13.
- was the first African American to win a Pulitzer Prize.
- paid for prizes for student literary contests out of her own pocket.

Brooks at home on Chicago's South Side, 1960

Meet the Author

Gwendolyn Brooks 1917–2000

Decades before urban musicians introduced Americans to rap and hip hop, Gwendolyn Brooks captured some of these same rhythms in her writing. In verse celebrated for its lyrical beauty, Brooks portrays the thoughts, feelings, and, often, extraordinary heroism of African Americans living amidst poverty and segregation.

An Early Start Though born in Topeka, Kansas, Brooks spent almost her entire life in Chicago. Even as a young girl, she loved to write. When she was 7, Brooks began filling composition books with "careful rhymes," prompting her mother to exclaim, "You are going to be the lady Paul Laurence Dunbar." By the age of 16, Brooks was a frequent contributor to *The Defender,* a prominent black newspaper in Chicago. During her teenage years, leading African-American poets James Weldon Johnson and Langston Hughes also recognized her immense talent.

Literary Triumph At 28, Brooks published *A Street in Bronzeville,* named for the bustling black enclave on Chicago's South Side. Written in a range of traditional forms, the poems explored the difficult lives of those around her. "I wrote about what I saw and heard in the street," Brooks said. "I lived in a small second-floor apartment at the corner, and I could look first on one side and then the other. There was my material." In 1949, Brooks published *Annie Allen,* a series of poems that trace the life of a Bronzeville girl. The book achieved literary acclaim and propelled its author into the spotlight. In 1950, Brooks became the first African-American writer to receive the Pulitzer Prize. The award brought her worldwide fame. "Sometimes," she quipped, "I feel that my name is Gwendolyn Pulitzer Brooks."

A Fateful Encounter Brooks experienced another turning point in 1967, when she attended a conference of black writers, meeting young African-American poets. Impressed by their commitment to a black aesthetic and issues of racial justice, Brooks became interested in writing a new kind of poetry. "If it hadn't been for these young people," she later remarked, "I wouldn't know what I know about this society. By associating with them I know who I am." Brooks began to experiment with free verse and to focus on the problems of color and justice. She started a poetry workshop for members of a Chicago street gang and became a lifelong advocate for the next generation. "My greatest interest," Brooks once said, "is being involved with young people."

Author Online

Go to **thinkcentral.com**. KEYWORD: HML11-1294

1294

See resources on the **Teacher One Stop DVD-ROM** and on **thinkcentral.com**.

 RESOURCE MANAGER UNIT 6
Plan and Teach, pp. 227–234
Text Analysis and Reading Skill, pp. 235–238†*

DIAGNOSTIC AND SELECTION TESTS
Selection Tests, pp. 357–360

 BEST PRACTICES TOOLKIT
Evaluating a Poem, p. D17
Two-Column Chart, p. A25

TECHNOLOGY
- Teacher One Stop DVD-ROM
- Student One Stop DVD-ROM
- Audio Anthology CD
- ExamView Test Generator on the **Teacher One Stop**

---

* Resources for Differentiation   † Also in Spanish   ‡ In Haitian Creole and Vietnamese

TEXT ANALYSIS: REPETITION

What keeps a song or a poem stuck in your mind long after you've heard it on the radio or read it in the classroom? Often, the answer lies in the writer's use of **repetition,** a technique in which a sound, word, phrase, or line is repeated for emphasis or to create rhythm. A related technique is **anaphora,** in which the same word or phrase is repeated at the beginning of two or more lines. Consider this example from "Primer for Blacks":

Blackness
is a title,
is a preoccupation,
is a commitment . . .

As you read, pay close attention to Brooks's use of repetition and especially of anaphora. Consider what these techniques emphasize in each poem, and note the rhythm they help build.

READING SKILL: COMPARE AND CONTRAST POEMS

Brooks's poetry career spanned six decades. She wrote "Life for My Child Is Simple" early in her career; it comes from *Annie Allen,* which traces the life of a fictional character but draws much of its inspiration from Brooks's own experiences. "Primer for Blacks" was written many years later, when Brooks was developing a deeper commitment to political and social issues. As you read, **compare and contrast** these two poems in a chart as shown. The following tips can help you:

- Ask yourself about the **subject** of each poem. Is it personal or political? Does it focus on a group or an individual?
- Describe the **tone.**
- Consider **stylistic elements** such as diction, punctuation, and capitalization.
- Identify the **theme** of each poem. What message does each suggest about life?

	"Life for My Child Is Simple"	"Primer for Blacks"
Subject		
Tone		
Speaker		
Style		
Theme		

 Complete the activities in your **Reader/Writer Notebook**.

What should we REACH for?

Gwendolyn Brooks advised her readers to "exhaust the little moment"—to live richly and strive higher in each moment of their lives. What, in your opinion, is worth striving for?

QUICKWRITE Brainstorm a list of things that are worth reaching for. Start by listing personal goals. Then move on to more global issues: if you had unlimited resources, what would you fix or change? Come up with a top-ten list of the things most worth striving for.

1. An end to world hunger
2. A cure for cancer

1295

What should we REACH *for?*

Read the question aloud. Ask students to discuss what it means to them to strive higher. After students complete the *QUICKWRITE,* invite volunteers to share and combine their top-ten lists.

TEXT ANALYSIS
COMMON CORE
RL 4
RL 5

● *Model the Skill:* **REPETITION**

Write this passage on the board:

How many stars are in the sky, and
How many fish in the sea?
How many years can my love be gone
Before he comes back to me?

Explain that anaphora is the repetition of a word or phrase. Have students notice the repetition of "How many." Point out that it creates a demanding rhythm that echoes the poem's sorrowful mood and message.

GUIDED PRACTICE Have students write a few lines containing anaphora.

READING SKILL
COMMON CORE
RL 2
RL 4

■ *Model the Skill:* **COMPARE AND CONTRAST POEMS**

Review that comparing shows similarities and contrasting shows differences. Explain the concepts of subject, tone (writer's attitude), speaker (the voice in a poem), style (the way a poet writes), and theme (message about life). Then, work as a class to fill in the chart on page 1295.

GUIDED PRACTICE After filling in the chart, ask volunteers to identify the ways in which the two poems are similar and different.

 RESOURCE MANAGER—Copy Master Compare and Contrast Poems p. 237 (for student use while reading the selections)

DIFFERENTIATED INSTRUCTION

FOR ENGLISH LANGUAGE LEARNERS
Options for Reading: Audio Recording

- Have students listen to the poems on the *Audio Anthology CD* while they read along in their texts. Have students pay particular attention to repetition in the poems.

- When they listen to "A Primer for Blacks," tell students to notice the speaker's tone and emphasis on reading words that start with capital letters, as in "It's Great to be white" (lines 10 and 13) or that are entirely

capitalized, such as "YOU" (line 50). The After Reading question 7 on page 1299 deals with this stylistic element in more depth.

READ WITH A PURPOSE

Help students set a purpose for reading. Ask them to consider how the speakers of the two poems feel about themselves and their futures.

SUMMARY

The speaker in this poem describes the boisterous activities of a young child, such as kicking over a chair and throwing blocks out a window. The speaker shares the child's adventurous glee and praises his fearless reaching-out.

REVISIT THE BIG QUESTION

What should we REACH *for?*

Discuss In what way do lines 15–18 suggest that the speaker wants her child to strive?

Possible answer: *The speaker celebrates that her child has "never been afraid to reach" and that "reaching is his rule." This suggests that she wants him to strive.*

TEXT ANALYSIS

COMMON CORE

ⓐ Model the Skill: REPETITION

RL 4
RL 5

Show students how to use an Evaluate a Poem organizer to focus on ways that style and word choice affect the emotional power of the lines.

Possible answer: *The poem's pace accelerates as the repetition builds. The rhythm creates a feeling of urgency.*

 BEST PRACTICES TOOLKIT—Transparency Evaluating a Poem p. D17

Life for My Child Is Simple

Gwendolyn Brooks

Life for my child is simple, and is good.
He knows his wish. Yes, but that is not all.
Because I know mine too.
And we both want joy of undeep and unabiding[1] things,
5 Like kicking over a chair or throwing blocks out of a window
Or tipping over an ice box pan[2]
Or snatching down curtains or fingering an electric outlet
Or a journey or a friend or an illegal kiss.
No. There is more to it than that. ⓐ
10 It is that he has never been afraid.
Rather, he reaches out and lo the chair falls with a beautiful crash,
And the blocks fall, down on the people's heads,
And the water comes slooshing sloppily out across the floor.
And so forth.
15 Not that success, for him, is sure, infallible.[3]
But never has he been afraid to reach.
His lesions are legion.[4]
But reaching is his rule.

ⓐ REPETITION
Reread lines 4–9 aloud. What happens to the poem's pace as the repetition builds? Describe the feeling created by the **rhythm** in these lines.

---

1. **unabiding:** not lasting; continually changing.
2. **ice box pan:** a pan for collecting melted ice in an old-fashioned refrigerator.
3. **infallible:** foolproof.
4. **His lesions are legion:** His injuries are many.

DIFFERENTIATED INSTRUCTION

FOR STRUGGLING READERS
Vocabulary Support

- *preoccupation,* "a constant thought or persistent interest in something"
- *commitment,* "a strong involvement in an interest or cause"
- *primer,* "a book for beginners"
- *diction,* "word choice, including both vocabulary (individual words) and syntax (the order or arrangement of words)"

FOR STRUGGLING READERS

Develop Reading Fluency To help students appreciate the rhythm and repetition in the two poems, lead them in a choral reading of the poem. Ask students to identify places where they stumbled or hesitated and offer clarification. Then, have the students do a choral reading as you listen.

Primer
for
Blacks

Gwendolyn Brooks

Blackness
is a title,
is a preoccupation,[1]
is a commitment Blacks
5 are to comprehend—
and in which you are
to perceive your Glory.

The conscious shout
of all that is white is
10 "It's Great to be white."
The conscious shout
of the slack[2] in Black is
"It's Great to be white."
Thus all that is white
15 has white strength and yours. **B**

The word Black
has geographic power,
pulls everybody in:
Blacks here—
20 Blacks there—
Blacks wherever they may be.
And remember, you Blacks, what they told you—
remember your Education:
"one Drop—one Drop[3]
25 maketh a brand new Black."

　　Oh mighty Drop.
　　And because they have given us kindly
so many more of our people

Everyman, Brenda Joysmith. 345″ × 58 1/4″. © Brenda Joysmith. Courtesy of Joysmith Gallery.

---

1. **preoccupation:** something requiring full attention.
2. **slack:** lack of force.
3. **"one Drop":** At times in U.S. history, a person with only "one drop" of African blood has been considered black.

B　COMPARE AND CONTRAST POEMS
So far, how does this poem differ from "Life for My Child Is Simple" in both **content** and **style?** Cite examples from both poems to support your answer.

Language Coach

Word Definitions *Drop* means "a very small amount of liquid." Read lines 22–26, including the footnote. How could something so small, a mere drop, be considered mighty?

SUMMARY

This poem encourages African Americans to understand and take pride in their heritage and to live out their pride as a commitment in daily life.

About the Art African-American artist Brenda Joysmith (born 1952) grew up in Memphis, Tennessee, and studied at the University of Chicago. Her art typically celebrates the day-to-day experiences of African Americans. The sense of unity and pride depicted in *Everyman* mirrors the philosophy of Brooks's poem.

CULTURAL CONNECTION

Cultural Pride The Black Pride movement of the 1960s brought about major changes in the attitudes of both African Americans and other Americans. Similarly, Native Americans asserted their pride in protest actions during the same era. Ask students to share their knowledge of ways that ethnic or cultural groups have asserted pride.

READING SKILL　　COMMON CORE
RL 2
RL 4

B *Model the Skill:* **COMPARE AND CONTRAST POEMS**

Read "Primer for Blacks" aloud, emphasizing the strong, proud tone that belies the "conscious shout" of lines 8 and 11.

Possible answer: This poem is more political, less personal, in content. It is more vehement and less musing in tone. It uses many stanzas rather than one, as well as shorter lines and unconventional capitalization.

IF STUDENTS NEED HELP . . . Have them add to the chart introduced on page 1295:

"Primer for Blacks"	
Subject	group pride
Tone	angry, proud
Style	multiple stanzas; short lines; unusual capitalization

FOR ENGLISH LANGUAGE LEARNERS

Language Coach　COMMON CORE L 4b

Word Definitions *Possible answer: The drop is mighty because it is a potent substance—blackness or African-American heritage.* Remind students that *drop* is a word with more than one meaning. It is also a noun meaning "a fall." Ask students how they knew which meaning of the word to use as they read the poem.

FOR ADVANCED LEARNERS/AP

Analyze Connotations Have students use a Two-Column Chart like this one to compare and contrast the connotations of the words *white* and *black* in the poem.

White	Black
"white strength"	"geographic power"

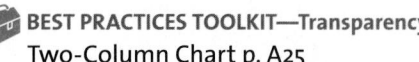 **BEST PRACTICES TOOLKIT—Transparency** Two-Column Chart p. A25

C REPETITION

Possible answer: *The anaphora emphasizes the equality of different shades of African-American skin. The point is to celebrate racial pride and to create a feeling of unity.*

IF STUDENTS NEED HELP . . . Ask these questions and help students answer them:
- In what way are all these colors united?
- What feelings does the speaker have about the unity of these colors?

TIERED DISCUSSION PROMPTS

Use these prompts to help students comprehend the poem's message in lines 40–47:

Connect With what groups do you feel connected? What feelings do you have about those groups? *Accept all thoughtful responses.*

Interpret In line 41, what does the word *Comprehend* tell African Americans to do? *Possible answer: It tells them to understand their heritage.*

SELECTION WRAP–UP

READ WITH A PURPOSE Now that students have read the two poems, ask them for their impressions of the two speakers' attitude toward themselves and their futures. *Possible answer: The speaker of "Life" seems excited by life as seen through the eyes of her child, The speaker of "Primer for Blacks" is proud, unmindful of those who seek to oppress her, and chiding of those people of color who deny their African-American heritage.*

★ **CRITIQUE** Ask students to agree or disagree with the messages of the poems.

INDEPENDENT READING

Students might enjoy reading *Selected Poems* by Gwendolyn Brooks.

Blackness
30 stretches over the land.
Blackness—
the Black of it,
the rust-red of it,
the milk and cream of it,
35 the tan and yellow-tan of it,
the deep-brown middle-brown high-brown of it,
the "olive" and ochre[4] of it—
Blackness
marches on. **C**

40 The huge, the pungent[5] object of our prime out-ride
is to Comprehend,
to salute and to Love the fact that we are Black,
which *is* our "ultimate Reality,"[6]
which is the lone ground
45 from which our meaningful metamorphosis,
from which our prosperous staccato,[7]
group or individual, can rise.

Self-shriveled Blacks.
Begin with gaunt and marvelous concession:
50 YOU are our costume and our fundamental bone.

All of you—
you COLORED ones,
you NEGRO ones,
those of you who proudly cry
55 "I'm half INDian"—
those of you who proudly screech
"I'VE got the blood of George WASHington in MY veins"—
ALL of you—
you proper Blacks,
60 you half-Blacks,
you wish-I-weren't Blacks,
Niggeroes and Niggerenes.

You.

C REPETITION
Reread lines 31–39. What does Brooks's use of **anaphora** emphasize about the many shades of blackness she lists? What point is she making here?

---

4. **ochre** (ō′kər): brownish orange-yellow.

5. **pungent** (pŭn′jənt): sharp and intense, like a powerful odor.

6. **the fact . . . "ultimate Reality":** a rewording of a quotation from black activist Ron Karenga.

7. **staccato** (stə-kä′tō): the playing of musical notes in a crisp, disconnected way.

DIFFERENTIATED INSTRUCTION

FOR ENGLISH LANGUAGE LEARNERS
Related Vocabulary Make sure students understand that the poem uses related words to describe variations in African-American skin colors. Use a dictionary and, if possible, a color wheel or other illustration to help students understand these color words: *rust-red* (line 33); *tan, yellow-tan* (line 35); *olive, ochre* (line 37).

FOR ADVANCED LEARNERS/AP
Evaluate Impact "Primer for Blacks" was written during and for the Black Pride movement. Ask students to think about whether the poem retains its original force several decades later. Is its message as vital as ever? Is its style as powerful as ever? Have students write brief evaluations expressing a contemporary response to the poem. After students share their responses with the class, invite the group to decide if Brooks's poem has retained its power.

Comprehension

1. **Recall** In "Life for My Child Is Simple," what things does the child enjoy doing?

2. **Clarify** How do the child's feelings differ from his mother's?

3. **Clarify** Reread lines 16–30 of "Primer for Blacks." Why does "the word Black" have "geographic power"?

4. **Clarify** What, according to Brooks, is the object of blacks' "prime out-ride," or most important undertaking?

Text Analysis

5. **Interpret** Reread lines 10–18 of "Life for My Child Is Simple." Why has the speaker's son never been afraid of striving for what he wants? Why, in contrast, might the speaker have felt fearful?

6. **Examine Author's Purpose** Determine Brooks's intended audience for "Primer for Blacks." What do you think she wants her audience to feel? What action does she want her audience to take? Cite specific lines from the poem to support your answers.

7. **Analyze Style** Review "Primer for Blacks," noting Brooks's use of nonstandard capitalization. Why do you think she does this? How does this unorthodox capitalization affect the poem's meaning and contribute to the voice of the speaker?

⬤ 8. **Analyze Repetition** Reconsider the annotated examples of repetition in Brooks's poems. Then find at least one other example in each work. Do your examples qualify as **anaphora**? In each case, what is the impact of repetition on the meaning?

⬤ 9. **Compare and Contrast Poems** Using the chart you filled in as you read, summarize the similarities and the differences you found in the two poems. In your opinion, do the poems suggest similar or different ways of approaching life? Explain, citing evidence.

Text Criticism

10. **Author's Style** In the late 1960s, Brooks began experimenting with **free verse,** believing she was no longer living in "a sonnet kind of time." Why do you think Brooks chose free verse for these two poems? In your opinion, is free verse an appropriate poetic form for these works? Explain your opinions.

> *What should we* **REACH** *for?*
>
> In "Life for My Child Is Simple," Brooks implies that unlike her child, she has at times been "afraid to reach." What are some of the reasons why people might be afraid to reach? Explain.

RL 2 Determine two or more themes or central ideas of a text and analyze their development over the course of the text. **RL 4** Analyze the impact of specific word choices on meaning and tone. **RL 5** Analyze how an author's choices regarding how to structure specific parts of a text contribute to its overall structure and meaning, as well as its aesthetic impact.

Practice and Apply

For preliminary support of post-reading questions, use these copy masters:

R **RESOURCE MANAGER—Copy Masters**
Repetition p. 235
Question Support p. 239

Additional selection questions are provided for teachers on page 231.

ANSWERS   **COMMON CORE RL 2, RL 4, RL 5**

1. *The boy enjoys kicking over a chair, throwing blocks out a window, tipping over an ice box pan, snatching down curtains, fingering an electric outlet.*

2. *The child has never known fear.*

3. *"The word Black" has geographic power because the description unites people of African descent wherever they are and regardless of what portion of their heritage is African.*

4. *Blacks' most important undertaking is to "Comprehend, / to salute and to Love the fact that [they] are Black" (lines 41–42).*

Possible answers:

5. *The child has never had fear because he is young and protected. His mother has perhaps known fear because of discrimination.*

6. *Brooks's audience is African Americans who have not found identity. She wants them to discover and act with racial pride.*

7. *Brooks uses capitalization to emphasize key points, such as her call to rejoice in racial identity. The words in all capitals allow the reader to hear the speaker's strident, persuasive tone.*

---

8. ⬤ **COMMON CORE FOCUS** **Repetition**
Students' choices will vary, but anaphora appears in lines 12–14 of the earlier poem and lines 50–63 of the later poem. In general, repetition emphasizes ideas and drives the rhythm of the poems.

9. ⬤ **COMMON CORE FOCUS** **Compare and Contrast Poems** *Charts should address each component listed. Differences include those identified in the response to annotation B, while both poems stress the importance of striving to fulfill one's potential.*

10. *Accept all reasonable answers.*

> *What should we* REACH *for?* **Possible answers:** *People may be afraid of failing, looking foolish, being disappointed.*

Assess and Reteach

Assess

DIAGNOSTIC AND SELECTION TESTS
Selection Test A pp. 357–358
Selection Test B/C pp. 359–360

Interactive Selection Test on **thinkcentral.com**

Reteach

Level Up Online Tutorials on **thinkcentral.com**

Reteaching Worksheets on **thinkcentral.com**
Literature Lessons 20, 35, 43, 44
Reading Lesson 12

Focus and Motivate

COMMON CORE FOCUS

RL 1 Cite evidence to support analysis of what the text says explicitly as well as inferences drawn from the text, including where the text leaves matters uncertain. **RL 4** Analyze the impact of specific word choices on meaning and tone, including words with multiple meanings or language that is fresh, engaging, or beautiful.

ABOUT THE AUTHOR

After students read the author biography, call attention to the quotations from Dove in **Illuminating the Everyday.** Ask students what she means by "all the moments that make up a human being." **Possible answer:** *Dove means that a person is affected and shaped by many different experiences.*

NOTABLE QUOTE

"I prefer to explore the most intimate moments, the smaller crystallized details we all hinge our lives on." —**Rita Dove**

Point out that in this quote, Rita Dove stresses her interest in particular moments. Ask students to give examples of "details we all hinge our lives on." **Possible answer:** *These details could be the experience of looking in the mirror, the trip to school each day, a friend's glance, and so on.*

COMMON CORE

RL 1 Cite evidence to support analysis of what the text says explicitly as well as inferences drawn from the text, including where the text leaves matters uncertain. **RL 4** Analyze the impact of specific word choices on meaning and tone, including words with multiple meanings or language that is fresh, engaging, or beautiful.

DID YOU KNOW?

Rita Dove . . .

- was the youngest person and first African American named poet laureate.
- produced her own TV show.
- is a classically trained singer and musician, as well as a ballroom dancer.

Adolescence—III
Testimonial
Poetry by Rita Dove

Meet the Author

The Pulitzer Prize, which Dove won in 1987

Rita Dove born 1952

For Rita Dove, the personal and the historical are equally important. "I've been fascinated," she says, "by what I've called before 'the underside of history,' the dramas of ordinary people." In her poetry, Dove often interweaves historical events with personal narratives, producing lyric images of everyday life.

High Achiever The daughter of a research chemist who broke the color barrier in the tire industry, Dove was always encouraged, she says, "to go as far as [she] could." Her parents drove Dove to excel in school and counseled her to never give up. Their guidance served her well. As a teenager, she was one of only 100 high school seniors named Presidential Scholar. She also distinguished herself in college, graduating Phi Beta Kappa from Miami University in 1973.

A Passion for Words Dove first became aware of the power of storytelling as a young girl. Listening to local storytellers in her hometown of Akron, Ohio, Dove discovered "the delight of shaping life with words." She also began a lifelong love affair with poetry, sparked by her discovery of an anthology in the local library. Though Dove began writing as

a child, she did not fully embrace literary pursuits until college. Determining then that she wanted to be a writer, she applied and was accepted to the prestigious Iowa Writers' Workshop.

National Acclaim Publication in magazines had already earned Dove widespread praise when her first poetry collection, *The Yellow House on the Corner,* came out in 1980. Over the next few years, she published several more books, including *Thomas and Beulah,* hailed as her masterpiece. The book, which drew its inspiration from the quiet heroism of Dove's grandparents' lives, won a Pulitzer Prize in 1987. Since then, Dove has gone on to collect numerous literary honors.

Illuminating the Everyday Though she touches on issues of race, her poems, Dove asserts, "are about humanity." They attempt to convey something about the gamut of human experiences, not just the positive moments. "All the moments that make up a human being," Dove says, "have to be written about, talked about, painted, danced, in order to really talk about life."

Author Online
Go to **thinkcentral.com.** KEYWORD: HML11-1300

1300

Selection Resources

See resources on the **Teacher One Stop DVD-ROM** and on **thinkcentral.com.**

 RESOURCE MANAGER UNIT 6
Plan and Teach, pp. 241–248
Text Analysis and Reading
Skill, pp. 249–252†*

DIAGNOSTIC AND SELECTION TESTS
Selection Tests, pp. 361–364

 BEST PRACTICES TOOLKIT
Open Mind, p. D9
Word Sorts, p. E5

TECHNOLOGY
- **Teacher One Stop DVD-ROM**
- **Student One Stop DVD-ROM**
- **Audio Anthology CD**
- **ExamView Test Generator**
  on the **Teacher One Stop**

---

* Resources for Differentiation   † Also in Spanish   ‡ In Haitian Creole and Vietnamese

TEXT ANALYSIS: SOUND DEVICES

A musician as well as a poet, Rita Dove believes a poem's sound is paramount. "If a poem doesn't have a sense of music," she explains, "then that poem probably won't move me very much." To infuse her poems with this quality, Dove employs **sound devices**—patterns of word sounds that create musical or rhythmic effects. As you read Dove's poems, listen for the following sound devices:

- **alliteration**—the repetition of initial consonant sounds
- **assonance**—the repetition of vowel sounds within words
- **consonance**—the repetition of consonant sounds within and at the ends of words

Think about how these sound devices impart a musical quality to the poems. Also consider what words, images, and feelings these devices serve to highlight.

READING SKILL: MAKE INFERENCES ABOUT SPEAKERS

The language in Dove's poems is often restrained and concise. She characterizes the **speaker** in each poem with a few well-chosen details but does not offer much explicit description or commentary. It is up to you to read between the lines, or **make inferences,** about each speaker's situation and state of mind. As you read, collect clues that tell you about each speaker's age, situation, and mindset. After you read, you'll use this information to **draw conclusions** about each speaker's experiences.

Clues from the Text	My Inferences and Reactions
"…Mom and I worked/ The dusky rows of tomatoes." (lines 1–2)	The speaker and her mother probably live in a rural area, not the city. They work hard in the fields.

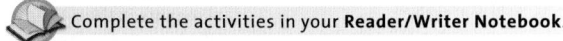 Complete the activities in your **Reader/Writer Notebook**.

How does your *PERSPECTIVE* change?

As you get older, the way you think and feel about important events in your life changes. And your perspective on something that looms in your future—graduation, for instance—will probably change once that event has actually happened.

QUICKWRITE Think of a big event or an important moment from your recent past; write a paragraph describing your feelings about it. Then imagine how you will feel about this same event ten years from now. How might your perspective have changed? Pretending to be your future self, write a second paragraph describing the event from this later perspective.

How does your *PERSPECTIVE change?*

Read the question aloud. Ask students to list situations about which a person's perspective might change over time. Encourage students to use their ideas as they complete the *QUICKWRITE* activity.

TEXT ANALYSIS   COMMON CORE   RL 4

● *Model the Skill:* SOUND DEVICES

Write this passage on the board:
Along the autumn paths
We strolled hand in hand,
Hopeful hearts upleaping—
And returning empty-handed.

Then read aloud the definitions of alliteration, assonance, and consonance on page 1301. Point out examples from the poem, including: ***Alliteration:*** *"along" and "autumn," "hand in hand, / Hopeful hearts."* ***Assonance:*** *"strolled" and "hopeful," "hand in hand."* ***Consonance:*** *"Hopeful," "upleaping," "empty."*

GUIDED PRACTICE Ask students to compose phrases containing the different sound devices.

READING SKILL   COMMON CORE   RL 1

■ *Model the Skill:* MAKE INFERENCES ABOUT SPEAKERS

Make an inference about the speaker of the lines on the board. Point out that many inferences are possible. One inference that seems probable is that the speaker was disappointed in love.

R RESOURCE MANAGER—Copy Master
Make Inferences about Speakers p. 251 (for student use while reading the selections)

FOR ENGLISH LANGUAGE LEARNERS
Options for Reading: Audio Recording
Have students listen to the poems on the *Audio Anthology CD* while they read along in their texts. Have students pay particular attention to the sounds of both poems. You may want to play the CD more than once in order for students to hear the use of alliteration, assonance, and consonance.

FOR STRUGGLING READERS
Develop Reading Fluency To help students hear the sound devices in the poems, lead the class in an echo reading. First, read the poems aloud, using your voice to emphasize the sound devices. After each stanza, pause and have students read aloud the same section of text. Periodically stop and ask students to identify and explain the sound devices.

READ WITH A PURPOSE

Help students set a purpose for reading. Ask them to read the poems in order to learn about the speakers—who they are and what they are like.

SUMMARY

This poem's speaker is a fatherless teenage girl who works as a farm laborer and wears hand-me-down dresses. Her knees are scarred and the view from her window is of clay soil and chicken manure. She fantasizes about two men approaching her: an ideal lover, and her father.

READING SKILL

COMMON CORE
RL 1

Ⓐ Model the Skill: MAKE INFERENCES

Help students make inferences by returning to the chart on page 1301. Point out the clue of the speaker's scarred knees (lines 8–10). Say: "What can you infer about the speaker from this detail?"

Possible answer: *The reader can infer that the speaker is an adolescent. It seems that she lives in the country with her single mother in circumstances of relative poverty.*

Clues	Inferences
"scarred knees"	from working on her knees on the ground

TEXT ANALYSIS

COMMON CORE
RL 4

Ⓑ SOUND DEVICES

Possible answer: *Alliteration includes "texture / twilight." The alliteration emphasizes a dreamy, melancholy time of day. Assonance includes "window-sill" / "lipstick" / "Glittered in." The repeated short i sound reinforces the image of the lipstick stubs, which reflect a poor girl's effort to become glamorous. Assonance also unifies the two lines.*

Adolescence — III

Rita Dove

BACKGROUND Dove wrote "Adolescence—III" early in her career, for her first published collection of poems. She composed "Testimonial" many years later and read it in the spring of 2001 at Howard University's commencement. "Whenever you think back," Dove told the graduating seniors, "and wonder where the future is going to lead you, remember that others have stood at this position and wondered, too. What you should do is take a step, one step at a time."

Analyze Visuals ▶
What words would you use to describe the girl in the painting? What details support your impressions?

With Dad gone, Mom and I worked
The dusky rows of tomatoes.
As they glowed orange in sunlight
And rotted in shadow, I too
5 Grew orange and softer, swelling out
Starched cotton slips. Ⓐ

The texture of twilight made me think of
Lengths of Dotted Swiss.[1] In my room
I wrapped scarred knees in dresses
10 That once went to big-band dances;
I baptized my earlobes with rosewater.
Along the window-sill, the lipstick stubs
Glittered in their steel shells. Ⓑ

Looking out at the rows of clay
15 And chicken manure, I dreamed how it would happen:
He would meet me by the blue spruce,
A carnation over his heart, saying,
"I have come for you, Madam;
I have loved you in my dreams."
20 At his touch, the scabs would fall away.
Over his shoulder, I see my father coming toward us:
He carries his tears in a bowl,
And blood hangs in the pine-soaked air.

---

1. **Dotted Swiss:** crisp, sheer cotton fabric decorated with raised dots.

Ⓐ MAKE INFERENCES
What inferences can you make about the **speaker's** age from lines 1–6 and the poem's title? Do you get a sense of her family's situation in life? Explain.

Ⓑ SOUND DEVICES
Reread lines 7–13. Find one example of **alliteration** and one of **assonance** in these lines. What words or images are emphasized by these devices?

Evening Thoughts, Ernest Crichlow. Lithograph, 25″ × 18″. Arisca Fine Art.

DIFFERENTIATED INSTRUCTION

FOR STRUGGLING READERS
Vocabulary Support
- *paramount,* "most important"
- *infuse,* "fill with something"
- *impart,* "give"
- *restrained,* "quiet, not showy"
- *concise,* "brief, using few words"
- *explicit,* "stated directly"
- *mindset,* "an individual's way of thinking about situations, events, or ideas"

Concept Support: Make Inferences about Speakers To prepare students for making inferences about speakers, organize them in pairs for this practice exercise. Have one partner describe an object, speaking in that object's first-person point of view. For example, a cup of coffee might say, "I am liquid, hot, and brown." Have the listening partner make inferences about the speaker to guess what object is speaking.

Analyze Visuals

Possible answer: *The girl in the painting appears to be timid and self-conscious. She is peering shyly toward the people in the background, who blend in more with the night than she does in her bright clothing. Her hand is lifted up to her mouth, perhaps as a nervous gesture. Like the speaker in Dove's poem, she seems more preoccupied with her own thoughts than with working.*

About the Art Known for his social realist style of art, Ernest Crichlow (1914–2005) first became famous during the Harlem Renaissance.

TIERED DISCUSSION PROMPTS

Use these prompts to help students understand the speaker's hopes as expressed in lines 16–23:

Connect Think about times when you daydream. In what ways do fantasies usually compare to reality? *Students should recognize that people often fantasize about situations that are better than reality.*

Interpret Why does the speaker daydream? *Possible answer: She daydreams to take refuge from her unpleasant reality.*

Evaluate Is the image of an imaginary lover effective? Why, or why not? *Students may find this image too obvious or too saccharine to be effective.* Does the image of the speaker's father effectively convey her views about him? Why, or why not? *Students may find this image very effective in conveying the view of a father who regrets leaving his child.*

REVISIT THE BIG QUESTION

How does your
PERSPECTIVE *change?*

Discuss In what way might the speaker's **perspective** change in lines 16–23? *Possible answer: She might realize that her dreams are unrealistic.*

FOR STRUGGLING READERS

Concept Support: Make Inferences About a Speaker Have students complete an Open Mind diagram to record their impressions of the speaker's character and situation. Suggest starting entries such as: *She wants to be beautiful, She wants her father back,* or *She wants to be loved.*

BEST PRACTICES TOOLKIT—Transparency
Open Mind p. D9

FOR ENGLISH LANGUAGE LEARNERS

Vocabulary: Multiple-Meaning Words
Help students use context to determine the correct specific meaning for these words:

- *slips* (line 6), "garments worn under dresses or skirts"
- *lengths* (line 8), "measured cloth for sewing"
- *stubs* (line 12), "short, leftover parts"
- *shells* (line 13), "hard cases that protect"
- *hangs* (line 23), "seems present in"

SUMMARY

The speaker of this poem remembers a younger time when "the world called, and I answered," when luck was with her and promises were fulfilled.

About the Art German-born Alfred Gockel (born 1952) is known for his pop art and action paintings. *Discovery I* expresses youthful joy mixed with reflection similar to that in the poem.

READING SKILL   COMMON CORE

RL 1

C MAKE INFERENCES

Phrases such as "the world called, and I answered," (line 9) and "I caught my breath and called that life" (line 11) produce a sense of the speaker's mythical power and deity.

Possible answer: *The language of the poem indicates the speaker is an age-old being who has been around since "the earth was new and heaven just a whisper" (lines 1–2) and who "gave my promise to the world" (line 19).*

SELECTION WRAP–UP

READ WITH A PURPOSE Ask students to describe the two speakers. **Possible answers:** *The speaker in "Adolescence—III" is young, overworked, and lonely. The speaker of "Testimonial" is passionate and full of life; she has a mythic, goddess-like quality.*

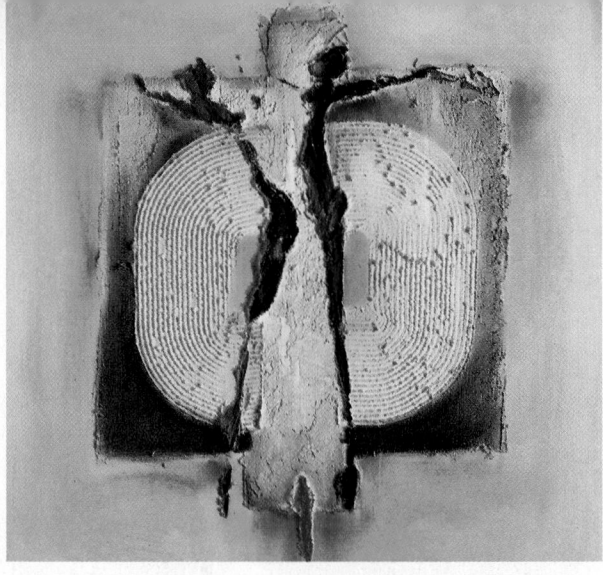

Discovery I, Alfred Gockel. 39¹/₄″ × 39¹/₄″. © Alfred Gockel.

Testimonial
Rita Dove

Back when the earth was new
and heaven just a whisper,
back when the names of things
hadn't had time to stick;

5 back when the smallest breezes
melted summer into autumn,
when all the poplars quivered
sweetly in rank and file . . .

the world called, and I answered.
10 Each glance ignited to a gaze.
I caught my breath and called that life,
swooned between spoonfuls of lemon sorbet.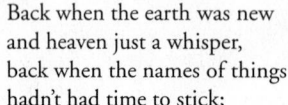

I was pirouette¹ and flourish,
I was filigree² and flame.
15 How could I count my blessings
when I didn't know their names?

Back when everything was still to come,
luck leaked out everywhere.
I gave my promise to the world,
20 and the world followed me here.

___

1. **pirouette** (pĭr′ōō-ĕt′): in ballet, a full turn of the body on one foot.

2. **filigree:** delicate ornamentation, often made of wire.

C MAKING INFERENCES

Who is the speaker in the poem? Rita Dove presents "Testimonial" in the voice of a goddess archetype, a powerful female figure from Greek myths and dramas. What words or phrases suggest the mythic character of the speaker? How does the language of this poem strengthen the power of the speaker's voice? Cite evidence to support your response.

1304 UNIT 6: CONTEMPORARY LITERATURE

DIFFERENTIATED INSTRUCTION

FOR ENGLISH LANGUAGE LEARNERS

Related Vocabulary Have students use Word Sorts to organize this language related to air and fire: **Air:** *whisper* (line 2), "speech that uses only air so it sounds soft"; *breezes* (line 5), "gentle winds." **Fire:** *melted* (line 6), "changed slowly"; *ignited* (line 10), "caught fire or attention suddenly"; *flame* (line 14), "intense feeling, like fire."

📋 **BEST PRACTICES TOOLKIT—Transparency** Word Sorts p. E5

FOR ADVANCED LEARNERS/AP

Compare and Contrast Refer students back to the Notable Quote on page 1300. Ask them to think about ways that the Rita Dove poems they have just read "explore the most intimate moments" and "the smaller crystallized details we all hinge our lives on." Have students write one- to three-paragraph responses, using these questions as a guide:

- What "intimate" aspects of life do both poems explore?

- What sensory details in the poems add to the feeling of "crystallized" detail?

- Do both poems present "crystallized" detail equally well? Why or why not?

- What are the strengths and limitations of poetry that is about small moments?

Comprehension

1. **Recall** In "Adolescence—III," what task occupies the speaker and her mother?

2. **Summarize** What does the adolescent speaker dream will happen to her?

3. **Summarize** In "Testimonial," how did the speaker respond to the world as a young person?

Text Analysis

4. **Draw Conclusions About Speakers** Review the **inferences** you made as you read. Using this information, explain the conclusions you can draw about each speaker's situation and state of mind. How do the two speakers' **perspectives** differ? Explain, citing evidence from both poems.

5. **Interpret Imagery** Many critics admire Dove's use of imagery. Look back over the images listed below. What does each one tell you about Dove's thoughts on the nature of youth?

   • the description of the world in "Testimonial" (lines 1–9)
   • the kind of life the speaker of "Testimonial" leads (lines 11–14)
   • the changes the speaker of "Adolescence—III" undergoes (lines 4–11)

6. **Analyze Sound Devices** Reexamine the two poems, looking for examples of each sound device listed in the chart. Use your completed chart to explain what tone and sensibility is established by the sound devices in each poem.

Sound Device	"Adolescence—III"	"Testimonial"
alliteration		
assonance		
consonance		

Text Criticism

7. **Cultural Context** Commenting on **themes** in her poetry, Dove has stated, "Obviously, as a black woman, I am concerned with race.... But certainly not every poem of mine mentions the fact of being black. They are poems about humanity, and sometimes humanity happens to be black." How does this view differ from the sensibility expressed by Gwendolyn Brooks in "Primer for Blacks" on page 1297? Explain your answer, citing evidence from each poet's work.

How does your **PERSPECTIVE** *change?*

In "Testimonial," Dove writes "How could I count my blessings/when I didn't know their names?" What statement is she making about how her perspective has changed? How might *your* perspective change as you grow older? Explain.

Age brings nostalgia. **"Adolescence—III" Images: Lines 4–11:** *Young people view love romantically.*

6. ● **COMMON CORE FOCUS** **Sound Devices** **"Adolescence—III": Alliteration:** *"softer, swelling out / Starched cotton slips";* **Assonance:** *"rows of tomatoes";* **Consonance:** *"blood . . . pine-soaked air."* *The* **s** *sounds emphasize a tone of sensuality and the* **d** *sound injects a tone of harsh reality.* **"Testimonial": Alliteration:** *"flourish . . . filigree and flame";* **Assonance:** *"swooned . . . spoonfuls";* **Consonance:** *"melted*

summer . . . autumn." The **m** *sounds help to convey a graceful tone and sensibility about the speaker's youth.*

7. *The two poets seem to hold very different views, since Brooks's poem is primarily a statement about race.*

How does your PERSPECTIVE *change?* The speaker, in her youth, took her blessings for granted. Students may suggest that their perspectives will change as they grow more mature and experienced.

Practice and Apply

For preliminary support of post-reading questions, use these copy masters:

R **RESOURCE MANAGER—Copy Masters**
   Sound Devices p. 249
   Question Support p. 253
   Additional questions for teachers are provided on page 245.

 COMMON CORE RL 1, RL 4

ANSWERS

1. *They work in a tomato field.*

2. *She dreams a man will come to love her.*

3. *The speaker responded in youth with openness, energy, and enthusiasm.*

Possible answers:

4. ● **COMMON CORE FOCUS** **Draw Conclusions About Speakers** *Both speakers experience a thirst for life and an openness to experiences during youth. The speaker of "Testimonial" seems to face no obstacles in achieving her goals, while the speaker of "Adolescence—III" faces the harsh realities of poverty. The speaker of "Testimonial" looks back on her past from an older perspective, while the speaker of "Adolescence—III" is still an adolescent.*

5. *"Testimonial" Images: Lines 1–9: Young people feel excited about life. Lines 11–14:*

Assess and Reteach

Assess

DIAGNOSTIC AND SELECTION TESTS
   Selection Test A pp. 361–362
   Selection Test B/C pp. 363–364

Interactive Selection Test on thinkcentral.com

Reteach

Level Up Online Tutorials on thinkcentral.com

Reteaching Worksheets on thinkcentral.com

   Literature Lesson 18: Speaker and Persona
   Literature Lesson 21: Alliteration, Assonance, and Consonance
   Literature Lesson 43: Tone
   Reading Lesson 8: Making Inferences
   Reading Lesson 9: Drawing Conclusions

Focus and Motivate

COMMON CORE FOCUS

RL 2 Determine two or more themes or central ideas of a text and analyze their development over the course of the text. **RL 4** Analyze the impact of specific word choices on meaning and tone, including words with multiple meanings or language that is fresh, engaging, or beautiful.

ABOUT THE AUTHOR

After students read the author biography, ask them to find passages in it that hint at the kind of poetry that Billy Collins writes.
Possible answer: *"His poems are primarily concerned with the mystery of ordinary things . . . the world around them."* Invite students to restate the passages.

NOTABLE QUOTE

"I don't think people read poetry because they're interested in the poet. I think they read poetry because they're interested in themselves. That's why I read poetry . . . to discover things about myself." **—Billy Collins**

Read the quote aloud and ask students to agree or disagree with Billy Collins's statement, using their personal response to poetry as a guide. Discuss what the quote reveals about Collins's view of himself and what it suggests about the kind of poems he writes.

Selection Resources

COMMON CORE

RL 2 Determine two or more themes or central ideas of a text and analyze their development over the course of the text. **RL 4** Analyze the impact of specific word choices on meaning and tone, including words with multiple meanings or language that is fresh, engaging, or beautiful.

The Man in the Moon
Forgetfulness
Poetry by Billy Collins

Meet the Author

Billy Collins born 1941

Billy Collins is that rare thing—a celebrity poet. His books break poetry sales records, his readings pack concert halls, and his poems elicit rave reviews from writers and critics alike. Indeed, no American poet since Robert Frost has managed to acquire such a broad and devoted following.

New York Roots Born in a New York City hospital where poet William Carlos Williams once worked, Collins is a nearly lifelong New Yorker. Growing up in Queens, he displayed an early flair for writing and a deep passion for literature. After college, he earned a doctoral degree in Romantic poetry from the University of California. Today, however, Collins feels a certain aversion to this poetry. "The Romantics killed off humor," he once explained.

Grammar Teacher Makes It Big In 1971, Collins began teaching English at the City University of New York and writing poetry in his spare time. Absorbed by his teaching, Collins did not publish his first collection, *Pokerface* (1977), until he was 36. In the next 11 years, he published two

additional collections. However, Collins did not achieve a widespread following until his fourth collection, *Questions About Angels* (1991), won the National Poetry Series competition. Since then his popularity has grown explosively, thanks in part to his charismatic poetry readings.

America's Poet In recognition of his poetic achievements, Collins was named U.S. poet laureate in 2001. During his two-year tenure, he encouraged the enjoyment of poetry in America's high schools, since "that's really where for most people poetry dies off and gets buried under other adolescent pursuits."

The Enigma of the Ordinary Though Collins has publicly expressed his political views, he is not a political poet. His poems are primarily concerned with the mystery of ordinary things and of everyday experiences. "Poetry is a home for ambiguity," he once noted. "It is one of the few places where ambiguity is honored." Often, a Collins poem begins with a humorous observation and then takes an unexpected turn, inviting readers to look afresh at the world around them.

DID YOU KNOW?

Billy Collins . . .

- broke the record for a bestselling poetry book—and then broke his own record twice.
- launched a Web site, Poetry 180, specifically designed to appeal to high school students.
- read a poem before Congress to honor the victims of the 9/11 attacks.

Author Online
Go to **thinkcentral.com**. KEYWORD: HML11-1306

THINK central

1306

See resources on the **Teacher One Stop DVD-ROM** and on **thinkcentral.com**.

 RESOURCE MANAGER UNIT 6
Plan and Teach, pp. 255–262
Text Analysis and Reading
Skill, pp. 263–266†*

DIAGNOSTIC AND SELECTION TESTS
Selection Tests, pp. 365–368

 BEST PRACTICES TOOLKIT
Spider Map, p. B22

TECHNOLOGY
- Teacher One Stop DVD-ROM
- Student One Stop DVD-ROM
- Audio Anthology CD
- ExamView Test Generator
  on the **Teacher One Stop**

---

* Resources for Differentiation   **†** Also in Spanish   **‡** In Haitian Creole and Vietnamese

TEXT ANALYSIS: IMAGERY

When you read a poem, you enter a world filled with sights, sounds, smells, and textures all its own. Poets draw you into this world by using **imagery,** words that re-create sensory experiences for the reader. Billy Collins owes some of his enormous popularity to the world he creates for his readers—a world that is often intensely familiar. In these lines from "The Man in the Moon," note the words that appeal to your senses of sight and touch:

> *He used to frighten me in the nights of childhood,*
> *the wide adult face, enormous, stern, aloft.*
> *I could not imagine such loneliness, such coldness.*

As you read, look for language that appeals to your senses. Notice how Collins supports his images with **allusions** to classical mythology—indirect references to characters and places in Greek myths that the author assumes readers will recognize. Think about how images and allusions work together to create a vivid experience for you as the reader.

READING SKILL: TRACE THE DEVELOPMENT OF AN IDEA

Appreciating the sensory experience that a poem creates is one crucial aspect of analyzing poetry. Also important, however, is examining the **ideas** the poet presents. As you read, use the following strategies to trace the ideas Collins puts forth in "The Man in the Moon" and "Forgetfulness." Use a chart like the one shown to organize your notes.

- Consider each poem's **title.** What idea does each suggest?
- Note the concept introduced or elaborated upon in each **stanza.** Consider how each stanza builds upon the one preceding it.
- Analyze Collins's **tone.** What attitude is expressed in each group of lines? Does the tone remain consistent throughout the poem, or does it change?

"The Man in the Moon"		
	Ideas Suggested	Tone
Title	The title makes me think of a children's story.	playful
Stanza 1		
Stanza 2		

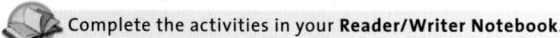 Complete the activities in your **Reader/Writer Notebook**.

What do the YEARS take with them?

As we age, we gain some things, such as maturity and wisdom. Other things—energy, for example, or idealism—seem to slip from us. In your opinion, do the years take more than they give?

ROLE-PLAY With a partner, improvise a scene in which two characters talk about growing older. First, discuss what the characters might say to each other about the joys and ordeals of aging—maybe they miss letting their imaginations run wild, or perhaps they appreciate the wisdom they've developed over the years. Decide whether your scene will be a comic or a serious one. Then write a dialogue between the characters and act it out for the class.

1307

Teach

What do the YEARS take with them?

Read the question aloud and then lead students in a discussion of what the years take and give as people age. Then, organize pairs for the *ROLE-PLAY* activity. Have volunteers present their dialogues, then help the class generalize about the pros and cons of aging.

TEXT ANALYSIS COMMON CORE RL 4

● *Model the Skill:* IMAGERY

Write this passage on the board:

> The stars wink at each other across the dimly lit room of the sky,
> Longing to meet, to escape this silent party
> And laugh in the cool fresh air.

Point out examples of sensory language, such as "stars wink" and "dimly lit" (sight); "silent party" (hearing); and "cool fresh air" (touch). Tell students that the images emphasize the ideas of distance and longing.

GUIDED PRACTICE Have students use two or more sensory images to describe an everyday object.

READING SKILL COMMON CORE RL 2

■ *Model the Skill:* TRACE THE DEVELOPMENT OF AN IDEA

Explain that in poetry, each stanza contributes to the poem's overall idea in the same way that a paragraph contributes in an essay. Point out how each paragraph in the author biography on page 1306 discusses a specific idea.

R RESOURCE MANAGER—Copy Master
Trace the Development of an Idea page 265 (for student use while reading the selections)

Practice and Apply

READ WITH A PURPOSE

As they read, ask students why the poet writes about ordinary events and objects.

SUMMARY

In this poem, the speaker recalls being scared by the man in the moon as a child. As an adult, the speaker compares the man in the moon to a bachelor in love.

READING SKILL

COMMON CORE
RL 2

 *Model the Skill:* TRACE IDEAS

Point out the words "But tonight" in line 4 as a clue to the shift in description. Have students add to the chart introduced on page 1307.

Possible answer: Readers know that Collins is referring to the man in the moon because of the poem's title. In the first stanza, the speaker describes his childhood fear of the man in the moon; in the second, he explains the way his view has changed.

Ideas Suggested	Tone
He saw the moon as a cold, stern adult.	Nostalgic; eerie

TEXT ANALYSIS

COMMON CORE
RL 4

IMAGERY

Possible answer: Images such as "wide adult face" (line 2) and "a pale bachelor... full of melancholy" (line 10) help to visualize the sight Collins describes. The images underscore the speaker's changing attitudes toward the moon. Youth's fear describes the moon as stern and cold. Adult's comfort describes the moon as sympathetic.

TIERED DISCUSSION PROMPTS

Use this prompt to help students interpret the poem's images in lines 1–12:

Connect In what ways can observing nature affect people's feelings? *Accept all thoughtful responses.*

The Man in the **Moon**

Billy Collins

He used to frighten me in the nights of childhood,
the wide adult face, enormous, stern, aloft.
I could not imagine such loneliness, such coldness.

But tonight as I drive home over these hilly roads
5 I see him sinking behind stands of winter trees
and rising again to show his familiar face. **A**

And when he comes into full view over open fields
he looks like a young man who has fallen in love
with the dark earth,

10 a pale bachelor, well-groomed and full of melancholy,
his round mouth open
as if he had just broken into song. **B**

A TRACE IDEAS
Reread lines 1–6. How do you know what Collins is referring to when he says *He*? Explain how Collins's description of his subject changes from one stanza to the next. Record your answer in your chart.

B IMAGERY
Identify details that allow you to **visualize** the sight Collins describes. How does this description underscore the changing attitude of the speaker?

DIFFERENTIATED INSTRUCTION

FOR STRUGGLING READERS
Vocabulary Support

- *textures*, "the ways things feel to the touch"
- *sensory*, "appealing to the senses"
- *domestic sphere*, "related to home life"
- *aloft*, "high up"
- *elaborated*, "made fuller or more complex"
- *consistent*, "agreeing with what came before"

Concept Support: Imagery Provide students with Spider Maps in which to list sensory images as they read. Use the Collins excerpt and the lines on the board to model the use of the organizer.

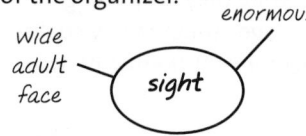

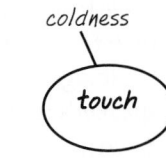 BEST PRACTICES TOOLKIT—Transparency
Spider Map p. B22

Forgetfulness

Billy Collins

The name of the author is the first to go
followed obediently by the title, the plot,
the heartbreaking conclusion, the entire novel
which suddenly becomes one you have never read, never
5   even heard of,

as if, one by one, the memories you used to harbor
decided to retire to the southern hemisphere of the brain,
to a little fishing village where there are no phones. **C**

Long ago you kissed the names of the nine Muses[1] goodbye
10 and watched the quadratic equation[2] pack its bag,
and even now as you memorize the order of the planets,

something else is slipping away, a state flower perhaps,
the address of an uncle, the capital of Paraguay.

Whatever it is you are struggling to remember
15 it is not poised on the tip of your tongue,
not even lurking in some obscure corner of your spleen.

It has floated away down a dark mythological river
whose name begins with an L as far as you can recall,
well on your own way to oblivion where you will join those
20 who have even forgotten how to swim and how to ride a
    bicycle. **D**

No wonder you rise in the middle of the night
to look up the date of a famous battle in a book on war.
No wonder the moon in the window seems to have drifted
25 out of a love poem that you used to know by heart.

---

1. **nine Muses:** in Greek mythology, goddesses of various fine arts and sciences.
2. **quadratic equation:** equation involving squaring of an unknown quantity or quantities, such as x^2.

C TRACE IDEAS

Reread lines 1–8. Describe Collins's **tone** as he introduces the idea of forgetfulness. What words and phrases help him achieve this tone? Note any changes in tone as you continue to read.

COMMON CORE RL 4

D IMAGERY

In lines 17–18, Collins creates the image of a river. He expands on the image by inserting an **allusion,** an indirect reference that the author assumes readers will recognize. This allusion— "a dark mythological river / whose name begins with an L"—refers to Lethe, a river in classical mythology that causes one to forget the past. Explain how this allusion contributes to the imagery in lines 17-21 and to the theme of the poem.

SUMMARY

In this poem, the speaker uses amusing imagery to give examples of ways that age brings forgetfulness.

READING SKILL   COMMON CORE RL 2

C TRACE IDEAS

Possible answer: *The tone is whimsical and rueful. Phrases such as "decided to retire" and "where there are no phones" help achieve the tone.*

TEXT ANALYSIS   COMMON CORE RL 4

D IMAGERY

Discuss with students how allusions enrich poetry; they also depend upon the reader's background knowledge. Explain that in Greek and Roman mythology, Lethe is a river in the underworld. Drinking its water caused complete forgetfulness or oblivion.

Possible answer: *Mentioning the river "whose name begins with an L, as far as you can recall" contributes to the imagery, since it seems the speaker's memories are all floating away, just like the name of the river itself.*

Extend the Discussion What other mythological allusion does the poet use in "Forgetfulness"? Collins refers in line 9 to the nine Muses of Greek mythology, one of whom is Mneme, or Memory. Have students research the connection between Mneme and such words as mnemonics.

SELECTION WRAP–UP

READ WITH A PURPOSE Now that students have read two poems by Billy Collins, ask them why the poet tends to focus on everyday things and events. ***Possible answer:*** *He writes about what he knows. He knows that readers like to read about other people's thoughts and experiences.*

FOR ADVANCED LEARNERS/AP

Analyze Poetic Form Point out that Collins's poems are written in free verse. Even the stanza lengths are irregular in "Forgetfulness," as if the speaker had forgotten how many lines to include in each. Challenge students to find poetic devices that Collins uses to unify each poem and distinguish it from prose. Encourage students to present their analysis of the poems to the class and to invite comments. *Examples: **"The Man in the Moon":** assonance such as "frighten/nights/childhood" (line 1), "round/mouth" (line 11), "open/broken" (lines 11–12); alliteration such as "sinking/stands" (line 5), "familiar/face/full/fields/fallen (lines 6–8); consonance such as "full/melancholy" (line 10); **"Forgetfulness"** lines 22–24: anaphora such as "No wonder"; **Both:** figurative language, and about four or five stressed syllables in most lines.*

Practice and Apply

For preliminary support of post-reading questions, use these copy masters:

 **RESOURCE MANAGER—Copy Masters**
Imagery p. 263
Question Support p. 267

Additional questions for teachers are provided on page 259.

ANSWERS

COMMON CORE RL 2, RL 4

1. *The speaker no longer sees the moon as frightening and stern, but rather sees it in a fond, romantic light.*

2. *The speaker has forgotten novels once read, the names of the Muses, an uncle's address, the quadratic equation, and the name of the river Lethe.*

3. *The speaker is troubled by his inability to remember the date of a battle.*

Possible answers:

4. *Forgetting the Muses suggests that the speaker has forgotten something important about the arts themselves. Forgetting the name of the river of forgetfulness is humorous, but the connection with darkness makes the allusion ominous as well.*

5. *The "memories" in line 6 and the "quadratic equation" in line 10 are given human qualities. The personification helps Collins bring a humorous tone to an unnerving topic.*

6. ● **COMMON CORE FOCUS Imagery** *The contrast emphasizes the fleeting nature of the facts that the speaker has forgotten and the way that memories slip through the cracks of an aging mind.*

Assess and Reteach

Assess

DIAGNOSTIC AND SELECTION TESTS
Selection Test A pp. 365–366
Selection Test B/C pp. 367–368

Interactive Selection Test on **thinkcentral.com**

Reteach

Level Up Online Tutorials on **thinkcentral.com**
Reteaching Worksheets on **thinkcentral.com**
Literature Lesson 26: Imagery
Literature Lesson 43: Tone
Reading Lesson 4: Recognizing Main Ideas and Details

Comprehension

1. **Summarize** In "The Man in the Moon," how does the speaker's attitude toward the moon change as he gets older?

2. **Recall** List three things that the speaker of "Forgetfulness" has forgotten.

3. **Clarify** In "Forgetfulness," what troubles the speaker in the middle of the night?

Text Analysis

4. **Examine Allusion** In "Forgetfulness," what ideas are developed or underscored by the allusion to the Muses, the Greek goddesses who preside over the arts and sciences (line 9)?

5. **Analyze Personification** The giving of human qualities to an object, animal, or idea is called personification. Find at least two examples of personification in "Forgetfulness." What does Collins's use of this technique contribute to the poem's **tone?**

● 6. **Analyze Imagery** Reread lines 22–25 of "Forgetfulness." Compare the concrete image of the moon—the only real image that appears in the poem—with the fleeting, intangible nature of the things the speaker has forgotten. What does this contrast emphasize about the poem's meaning? Explain, citing lines that support your answer.

■ 7. **Trace the Development of an Idea** Collins is known for writing poems that begin with humor and end in mystery and seriousness. Review the graphic organizer you filled in as you read. How, if at all, does the **tone** change over the course of each poem? Do the two poems present similar or different ideas about aging? Explain your answers, citing evidence from both poems.

Text Criticism

8. **Critical Interpretations** Collins is beloved by readers for his fresh and often funny poems; he even won the Mark Twain Poetry Award, given for the "contribution of humor" to American verse. However, some critics argue that Collins's humor is hollow, weakened by clichés and lacking in originality and insight. On the basis of your reading of these poems, do you agree or disagree with this criticism? Explain your answer.

> *What do the* **YEARS** *take with them?*
>
> In his poem "Forgetfulness," Collins playfully laments the loss of memory that sometimes comes with age. However, memory loss is also the hallmark of Alzheimer's disease, a tragic and debilitating disease that can leave its victims unable to recognize their own family members. How would you feel if you began to lose your memories? Explain.

COMMON CORE

RL 2 Determine two or more themes or central ideas of a text and analyze their development over the course of the text.
RL 4 Analyze the impact of specific word choices on meaning and tone, including words with multiple meanings or language that is fresh, engaging, or beautiful.

---

7. ■ **COMMON CORE FOCUS Trace the Development of an Idea** *"The Man in the Moon" has a largely consistent tone, lyrical and melancholy, although the speaker's ideas about the moon change. This poem may be saying that as we age we become increasingly fond of the world, even of things that once scared us. "Forgetfulness" begins on a light tone, but becomes laced with sadness and wistfulness by the last stanza. This poem humorously reminds readers of frightening truths about decline and mortality.*

8. *Answers will vary, but should use text evidence to support stated opinions.*

> *What do the* YEARS *take with them?* Students' responses will vary. They will probably suggest that they would feel a deep sense of loss, sadness, and perhaps fear.

A New Diversity

Late in the 20th century, it grew increasingly apparent that there was no single "American experience" and therefore no typical American voice. Once primarily the province of white men, the American literary canon—the body of works considered representative—exploded into a diverse chorus of ethnic voices. The number and range of voices continues to grow today.

Writing to Reflect

Every writer of any significance brings something new to a literary tradition, whether in subject matter, style, or way of looking at the world. As you reflect on the selections you have just read, consider what unique contributions might be attributed to each writer. Choose one author and write an essay about how his or her writing, as shown in this unit, can be said to do something different from writers of previous generations.

Consider
- the author's choice of subject matter
- his or her use of language, including style and tone
- any cultural or philosophical lens through which the author views the subject matter

Extension
VIEWING & REPRESENTING
Gather clippings of articles and literary texts from print media, photographs and other images of writers, and quotations from the selections in this section. Use these items to create a **collage**—your own "Mosaic of American Voices" representing the vibrancy and diversity of contemporary American literature.

COMMON CORE

W 9 Draw evidence from literary texts to support analysis, reflection, and research. **W 9a–b** Apply grade 11 Reading standards to literature and to literary nonfiction.

Increibles Las Cosas Q'se Ven, 2001. Mural at Ashland Avenue and 19th Street in Chicago. © Jeffrey Zimmermann.

Si, se pue de

HELAD

1311

DIFFERENTIATED INSTRUCTION

FOR ENGLISH LANGUAGE LEARNERS
Writing Support [mixed-readiness groups]
- Review the writing prompt to clarify the gist of the assignment and the three bulleted points to consider. Explain that a *cultural or philosophical lens* reflects the perspective or viewpoint an author brings to writing. This usually reflects the specific community in which the author writes or was raised. Have more-fluent partners help students understand the meanings of other unfamiliar terms such as *subject matter, style,* and *tone*.

- Allow students to focus on the work of a chosen writer without comparing it to previous generations. Students may reflect on ways that the writer's work brings new insight or experience to them.

- Suggest that students compare their cultural lenses with the writer's.

- Suggest that students reflect on ways that the writer's texts helped increase their command of English.

COMMON CORE FOCUS

W 9 Draw evidence from literary texts to support analysis, reflection, and research.

Wrap-Up: A Mosaic of American Voices

This Wrap-Up provides students with an opportunity to revisit the writings of the ethnically and artistically diverse group of authors and poets in this section. Begin by having students recall selections from this section and briefly recap the authors' ethnicities and the works' topics and ideas.

Writing to Reflect

- Review with students that *reflecting* means thinking about, exploring connections with, and finding meaning in. Such reflection can help students to appreciate the exploding mosaic of voices they have read.

- Guide students in choosing authors about whom to write. Suggest these guiding questions:
  - Which selection did I understand best?
  - Which author would I most like to learn more about?
  - Which selection has a subject that I can relate to especially well?

Extension

- Suggest sources from which to gather articles about and images of writers, such as the *New York Times Book Review* and the book review sections of other major newspapers and magazines, online encyclopedias, and the Web site of the Academy of American Poets, http://www.poets.org.

- Encourage students to use cross-references to find additional relevant writers for their collages. For example, an article on Gwendolyn Brooks might refer to Langston Hughes or Nikki Giovanni.

- Allow students to work in pairs. One student might design the collage and the partner might do research and select text.

- Tell students to add a meaningful title to their collages and to provide informational captions where appropriate.

Focus and Motivate

COMMON CORE FOCUS

W 2a–b Format to aid comprehension; develop a topic by selecting significant and relevant facts and concrete details. **W 2e** Establish and maintain a formal style and objective tone. **W 4** Produce clear and coherent writing in which the development, organization, and style are appropriate to task, purpose, and audience. **W 5** Develop and strengthen writing by planning, revising, editing, rewriting, or trying a new approach, focusing on what is most significant for a specific purpose or audience. **W 10** Write routinely over shorter time frames for a range of tasks, purposes, and audiences. **L 2** Demonstrate command of conventions of standard English. **L 3** Apply knowledge of language to make effective choices for meaning or style.

WRITE WITH A PURPOSE

Have students read the opening paragraph and identify the document they will write in this workshop. Then have them review the Writing Task and identify the purpose of a résumé. Suggest that they narrow their focus by writing to appeal to one type of employer or career field.

COMMON CORE TRAITS

Review the *COMMON CORE TRAITS* with students, focusing on organization and development of ideas. Compare the list of traits with the rubric on page 1320.

ADDITIONAL TASK

Write an Advertising Postcard Alone or with a partner, design a postcard to advertise a student-run business. Use logos, images, and attractive type to design a card that you can use for mass mailings.

Possible subjects: lawn care, computer setup and maintenance, or grocery delivery service

Writing Online | THINK central

The following tools are available online at **thinkcentral.com** and on **WriteSmart CD-ROM:**
- Interactive Graphic Organizers
- Interactive Student Models
- Interactive Revision Lessons

Writing Workshop
INFORMATIVE TEXT

Résumé

Essential Course of Study
ECOS

As you have seen in this unit, literature often has lofty aspirations, such as to expose prejudice or push for change. However, capable writers also need the skills necessary to write effective work-related documents. When written effectively, these types of documents can open doors to opportunity. In this workshop, you will learn how to write a résumé for a potential employer.

 Complete the workshop activities in your **Reader/Writer Notebook.**

WRITE WITH A PURPOSE

WRITING TASK

Write a **résumé** for a potential employer. Be sure to highlight the work, educational, and personal experiences and skills that qualify you for the position.

Idea Starters
- internships listed on Internet job sites or in a newspaper's classified section
- a hypothetical job position or internship that would interest you
- a local company or organization for whom you would like to work

THE ESSENTIALS

Here are some common purposes, audiences, and formats for writing a résumé.

PURPOSES	AUDIENCES	FORMATS
• to provide accurate information clearly and concisely • to make information and ideas accessible to a specific audience	• future employers • college admissions staff • co-workers	• résumé • job or college application • online employment site • Web site

COMMON CORE TRAITS

1. DEVELOPMENT OF IDEAS
- selects the most **significant** and **relevant facts** and **concrete details**
- focuses on information, details, and examples that are appropriate for a **specific purpose** and **audience**

2. ORGANIZATION OF IDEAS
- **organizes** information in a logical way
- employs **formatting** to aid comprehension and follow standard conventions

3. LANGUAGE FACILITY AND CONVENTIONS
- establishes and maintains a **formal style** and **objective tone**
- includes **precise language**
- uses **active verbs**
- employs correct **grammar, punctuation, capitalization,** and **spelling**

Writing Online | THINK central

Go to **thinkcentral.com.**
KEYWORD: HML11N-1312

Writing Workshop Resources

 RESOURCE MANAGER UNIT 6
Plan and Teach pp. 269–272
Prewriting–Editing pp. 273–277
Writing Rubric p. 278
Technology p. 279
Writing Support p. 280*

BEST PRACTICES TOOLKIT
Writing Template: Business Résumé p. C43

TECHNOLOGY
- **Teacher One Stop DVD-ROM**
- **Student One Stop DVD-ROM**
- **WriteSmart CD-ROM**
- **GrammarNotes DVD-ROM**

Writing Center on thinkcentral.com

*See resources on the **Teacher One Stop DVD-ROM** and on **thinkcentral.com.***

* Resources for Differentiation

Planning/Prewriting

 **COMMON CORE** W 2a Format to aid comprehension. **W 2b** Develop a topic by selecting significant and relevant facts and concrete details. **W 5** Develop writing by planning and focusing on what is most significant for a specific purpose and audience.

Getting Started

THINK ABOUT AUDIENCE AND PURPOSE

A résumé is a description of the skills and experiences that qualify you for a job. When you create this type of document, you must think about what an employer needs to know about you in order to feel confident about your ability to perform the job. The employer is your **audience,** and the **purpose** is to clearly and accurately describe the qualifications that show you are the right person for the position.

COLLECT INFORMATION

Résumés require you to effectively select **relevant facts and details** and organize them in a clear and logical way. When planning, it is important to consider information that is significant to an employer and specifically related to the requirements of the job. Before you begin to create a résumé, you should familiarize yourself with a variety of samples. You can find examples of professional résumés in books or on many reputable Web sites. Here are some tips for planning your résumé:

- Make a list of the work, educational, volunteer, and extracurricular experiences and accomplishments that qualify you for the desired position.
- Describe what you were required to do for each experience and the skills you gained through the experience. Use accessible language to describe any technical skills or tasks that you used or learned.
- Verify the names of the organizations you worked for and the dates you worked there.

▶ WHAT DOES IT LOOK LIKE?

> Résumé
>
> * **Audience:** potential employer
>
> * **Purpose:** to convince the employer that I would be an asset to the company or organization
>
> * **Audience's needs:** The employer needs to hire a competent person who has had experience creating sets for play productions.

▶ WHAT DOES IT LOOK LIKE?

> Information for résumé:
>
> * **School experience:** in charge of set design for the school's production of Macbeth; **Requirements and skills:** supervising team members; working within a budget; completing work within a tight timeframe; fixing set problems during performances
>
> * **School experience:** staff writer for school newsletter; **Requirements and skills:** cover theater and art news; conduct interviews; write accurate and grammatically correct articles
>
> * **Work experience:** hostess at Salina's Bistro; **Requirements and skills:** planning seating arrangements for reservations; juggling tasks; making adjustments to accommodate unexpected situations; appeasing dissatisfied customers; working efficiently in a fast-paced environment; effectively communicating with managers, busboys, and waiters to seat customers in a timely manner; **Dates:** February 2009 to January 2010
>
> * **Volunteer experience:** collect donated items from local stores; deliver items to various homeless shelters; **Dates:** May 2009 to present

WRITING WORKSHOP **1313**

Teach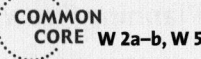

Planning/Prewriting
COMMON CORE W 2a–b, W 5

▶ **THINK ABOUT AUDIENCE AND PURPOSE**
Ask students to identify the audience for a résumé (*a prospective employer*). Have students identify the individuals or departments within companies who read résumés and conduct interviews. Direct attention to the "What Does It Look Like?" column and suggest that students enter similar outlines in their *Reader/Writer Notebooks*, rewriting the "Audience's Needs" section to go with the jobs they want.

▶ **COLLECT INFORMATION** Before students begin to write their résumés:

- Encourage students to collect sample résumés online and to scan the Internet and newspapers for prospective jobs.
- Direct attention to the "What Does It Look Like?" column. Suggest that students make similar entries in their *Reader/Writer Notebooks*.
- Point out that a résumé should focus on how the worker can benefit the employer, not the other way around.

R RESOURCE MANAGER—Copy Masters
Prewriting–Editing p. 273–277
Writing Rubric p. 278
Writing Support p. 280

DIFFERENTIATED INSTRUCTION

FOR ENGLISH LANGUAGE LEARNERS

Language: Reinforce Résumé Terms Write these terms on the board and review them with students. Point out that the following definitions fit the context of this Writing Workshop.

- *contact information:* the phone number, e-mail address, or home address where a person can be reached
- *employer:* a person or company that hires and pays a worker to do a job
- *format:* (n.) the physical form of a document, including type style and size,

headings and subheadings, and other design elements; *(v.)* to decide the physical form of a document

- *objective:* (n.) a goal; (a.) based on facts and not emotion
- *responsibility:* the job that a worker is expected or trusted to do
- *résumé:* a description of the skills and experiences that qualify you for a job
- *skill:* a job or ability that requires special training or talents

WRITING WORKSHOP **1313**

Planning/Prewriting, *continued*

▶ **CHOOSE A FORMAT** Tell students that a neat, professional-looking résumé is crucial. If a résumé is sloppy, disorganized, and unfocused, the employer will assume the résumé's writer is equally disorganized. Pass along these tips for producing professional formats:

- Download sample résumés from the Internet. Analyze the examples and determine why they are or are not effective.

- Collect job application forms from local businesses and study online job forms. Use the same or similar categories as you format your résumé.

- Write a chronological résumé if you have already held two or more jobs. A functional résumé is a better choice if you have held only one paying job or have never been employed. In that case, emphasize your accomplishments or activities that require similar skills to the job for which you are applying.

- For type styles, headings, and other design choices, select formal instead of funny or flashy.

- Make a preliminary outline and sketch of the finished page. Keep them on hand as you craft your résumé, to make sure you cover all the main points and to keep the text within space limits.

YOUR TURN Give students time to format their résumés. Have them work alone or in small groups to decide on formats for their résumés and to list the information they want to include.

For interactive graphic organizers, see

💿 **Write*Smart* CD-ROM**

Writing Center on thinkcentral.com

Planning/Prewriting *continued*

Getting Started

CHOOSE A FORMAT

Résumés must present information in a format that is easy for employers to read and understand. A properly formatted résumé looks professional and helps you look professional when you apply for a position.

After looking through samples of résumés, create a formatting plan for your document. Use one of the common formatting layouts, but feel free to adjust the format to accommodate the information you will include. For example, you may use standard headings for parts of your document but tailor other headings to meet the specific needs of your information.

As you choose a format for your résumé, keep in mind the two most common types of résumés:

- **Functional résumés** focus on skills, rather than work history.
- **Chronological résumés** focus on work history, detailing job responsibilities and accomplishments.

You may also use ideas from both types of résumés. The most important thing is to create a format that allows you to highlight your strengths.

▶ **TIPS**

- Maintain a consistent format throughout the document, including fonts, headings, margins, and other elements.
- To make your organization clearer, you might need to add subheadings below your main headings.
- Avoid inserting a section that states or mentions references. Instead, bring a list of references with you to interviews.
- As you create your résumé, you may change your mind about the format that is best for the amount of information or the way you decide to present it. If necessary, revise, rewrite, or try a new approach to your résumé to develop and strengthen it.

PEER REVIEW With a peer, share the information and format you plan to use in your résumé. Ask whether you have used **relevant, sufficient facts and concrete details** that successfully highlight your strengths relative to the job requirements. Discuss whether your formatting plan is an effective way to present your information.

YOUR TURN After establishing your audience and purpose, collect and review sample documents. Then, brainstorm and collect information for your résumé in your *Reader/Writer Notebook*. Finally, choose a formatting plan.

DIFFERENTIATED INSTRUCTION

FOR ENGLISH LANGUAGE LEARNERS

Language: Reinforce Résumé Terms Review these terms with students.

- *appropriate:* suitable to the event, occasion, or audience
- *boldface:* type that is darker and heavier than the surrounding type
- *chronological:* occurring in the order of time
- *consistent:* following the same patterns and format throughout
- *functional:* having practical use; related to how things work

FOR STRUGGLING WRITERS

Choose a Formatting Structure Share these tips with students who are having trouble planning and designing résumés.

- Ask yourself, "If the employer remembers only one thing about me, what should it be?" Redesign the résumé to feature the answer to that question.
- Create a sample document in different type styles and formats. Show the samples to parents, friends, or classmates, asking for feedback.

Drafting

 **COMMON CORE**   **W 4** Produce clear and coherent writing.   **L 2** Demonstrate command of standard English capitalization, punctuation, and spelling.

The following chart shows a structure for organizing an effective résumé.

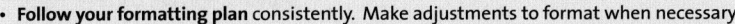

Organizing Your Résumé

BEGINNING

- Choose a **font** and **style** for your résumé. Avoid unusual or ornate fonts that may distract the employer from the content of your résumé.
- Begin your résumé with your name, address, phone number, and e-mail address.
- After your contact information, state your **objective,** which is a statement of the job you are seeking or a statement of your goals in relation to the job you are seeking.
- Include **uniform spacing** between the various sections of your résumé.

▼

MIDDLE

- **Follow your formatting plan** consistently. Make adjustments to format when necessary.
- Arrange each detail about skills, experiences, or accomplishments underneath the **proper heading.** Format headings in **boldface.** Use **bullet points** to separate information beneath headings.
- Provide **dates** and **time spans** for each of your experiences and achievements.
- Use appropriately **formal style** and language. Maintain an **objective tone** by avoiding first-person pronouns (*I, me, my*). Avoid slang.
- Be as **concise** as possible in your wording. Use strong action verbs throughout, maintaining consistent verb tense and parallel structure.

▼

END

- Place the least relevant information at the end.
- Restrict your résumé to **no more than two pages** in length.

GRAMMAR IN CONTEXT: CAPITALIZING AND PUNCTUATING ADDRESSES

If a potential employer sees a capitalization or punctuation mistake in your mailing address, he or she will be immediately skeptical. When writing an address, capitalize the street name, city, and state. Abbreviate state names with the common two-letter postal abbreviation. Do not place a period after the abbreviation. Place a comma between the city and the state abbreviation. If a street name contains an abbreviated compass point with one letter *(N, S, E, or W),* follow the letter with a period. However, if it has two letters *(NE),* do not follow it with a period. Here is an example of a properly capitalized and punctuated address:

834 N. Clarington Road
Columbus, OH 54312

 YOUR TURN   Using your prewriting notes and the information in the chart on this page, write a draft of your résumé. Be sure that you have capitalized and punctuated addresses correctly.

FOR ENGLISH LANGUAGE LEARNERS

Capitalizing and Punctuating Addresses
Review the conventions of writing addresses, as listed in the Grammar in Context section. Explain that these conventions are those required by the United States Postal Service. Direct students to your local telephone directory for more information on postal abbreviations and zip codes.

FOR STRUGGLING READERS

Capitalizing and Punctuating Addresses Give students tips for extra practice with spelling and punctuation:

- Read the want ads in your local newspaper and online and make a list of potential job contacts. For each contact, write the correct contact name, job title, company name, and company address.
- Compile a birthday or holiday card list, writing the addresses, phone numbers, and e-mails correctly.

Practice and Apply

Drafting

COMMON CORE W 4, L 2

▶ **BEGINNING** Point out that a résumé usually contains several categories, with bulleted or dated lists under each category. Suggest that students begin the writing process by consulting their preliminary outlines and sketches. Give special attention to students' statements of objectives, making sure the statements are targeted to specific jobs.

▶ **MIDDLE** Tell students that the bullet points in this section have to do with the look as well as the content of the résumé. Discuss the convention of résumé writing that discourages the use of the first person. Remind students that a single person's name is at the top of a résumé, and that all the details in the document are about that person. Therefore, adding "I," "me," and "my" is not necessary and would probably be perceived as overselling oneself.

▶ **END** Explain why students should restrict the length of the résumé to one or two pages: it is a convention of résumé writing. Many ads for jobs impose a page limit, even stating that longer résumés will not be considered.

GRAMMAR IN CONTEXT: CAPITALIZING AND PUNCTUATING ADDRESSES

Point out that on a résumé, the subject's address serves several important functions: it's the headline of the page and the record of where to contact the potential employee. Therefore it's imperative that there be no errors.

 YOUR TURN   Ask students to work independently to complete the **Your Turn** activity. Have them use the "Organizing Your Résumé" chart as a checklist as they draft their documents. Then have students work in pairs to check and proofread their work.

For a résumé writing template see

 BEST PRACTICES TOOLKIT—Transparency
Business Writing Template: Résumé, p. C43

 **Write*Smart* CD-ROM**
Writing Center on thinkcentral.com

Revising

COMMON CORE W 5

Model the Skill Using a draft résumé on a transparency or electronic whiteboard, model how to use the questions, tips, and strategies suggested in the chart to evaluate and revise writing. You might use the résumé of a student from another class or from last year. Be sure to remove the student's name from the résumé so that he or she is anonymous.

Have students pair off and exchange résumés with their partners for evaluation and review. Tell students to identify the strongest aspects of the résumés they are reviewing and to present those aspects first as they share their ideas with the writers. Then have the student reviewers identify areas where the writing is weak or where the facts could be presented in a more positive or organized way. Students should then revise the weak elements of the résumé, taking a new approach to presenting the information, if necessary.

For interactive revision tools, see

WriteSmart CD-ROM

Writing Center on thinkcentral.com

Revising

When you revise, you should focus on whether you have addressed the most significant information, experiences, and accomplishments in your résumé. Your goal is to determine whether you've presented your qualifications for the position clearly, accurately, and coherently to your potential employer. The questions, tips, and strategies in the following chart can help you revise and improve your draft.

RÉSUMÉ

Ask Yourself	Tips	Revision Strategies
1. Are my name, address, phone number, and e-mail address correctly stated?	**Bracket** your name, address, phone number, and e-mail address.	**Add** your contact information. Make sure the information, spelling, capitalization, and punctuation are correct.
2. Is an objective included? Does the objective state the job I am seeking or a related professional goal?	**Circle** your objective.	**Add** an objective if one is missing. **Revise** an existing objective to clearly address the job you are seeking or a professional goal.
3. Are work, educational, volunteer, and extracurricular experiences and accomplishments listed? Are dates and time spans included?	**Place stars** next to work, educational, volunteer, and extracurricular experiences. **Draw boxes** around dates and time spans.	**Add** work, educational, volunteer, or extracurricular experiences. **Add** dates and time spans for each experience.
4. Have the relevant skills associated with each of my work experiences been stated?	**Double underline** relevant skills.	**Add** the relevant skills and concrete descriptive details associated with each experience.
5. Does the résumé include action verbs and concise language? Have I avoided first-person pronouns?	**Highlight** action verbs. **Place an X** through wordy language and first-person pronouns.	**Add** action verbs. **Revise** wordy language. **Replace** first-person pronouns.
6. Is the least relevant information placed at the end of the résumé?	**Underline** the least relevant piece of information on your résumé.	**Rearrange** information so that the least relevant information is stated at the end of the résumé.

PEER REVIEW Before you revise, exchange papers with a peer and ask for suggestions about how you might improve your résumé. Use the chart to review your peer's draft, and write a short critique, pointing out its strengths and weaknesses.

DIFFERENTIATED INSTRUCTION

FOR STRUGGLING WRITERS

Check Structure and Order Suggest that students use these tips to edit and revise the structure of their résumés.

- Check the draft of the résumé against the outline to make sure every point in the outline is covered.

- Check every section to make sure the items listed under that section belong there.

- Look at the résumé again from the viewpoint of a potential employer.

ANALYZE A STUDENT DRAFT

Read these excerpts from a student draft, and note the comments on its strengths as well as suggestions for improvement.

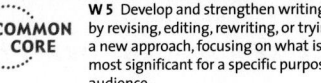

COMMON CORE W 5 Develop and strengthen writing by revising, editing, rewriting, or trying a new approach, focusing on what is most significant for a specific purpose or audience.

❶

Monique Sanchez
834 N. Clarington Road
Columbus, OH 54312
msanchez3748@evernet.com
(361) 555-8671

❷ OBJECTIVE
Obtain an internship

> Monique's **objective** needs to be more specific.

❸ EDUCATIONAL AND EXTRACURRICULAR ACTIVITIES

Lead set designer, Allentown High School's production of *Macbeth*
February 2010–April 2010
- designed and created the production's set
- supervised and closely worked with a team of five fellow students
- completed work within a given timeframe and budget
- addressed and repaired set problems during performances

> Monique lists her educational and extracurricular **experiences** first because these are the most significant for the internship she is trying to obtain.

Staff Writer, *Allentown High Weekly News*
September 2010–present
- cover the school's theater and art programs for the school paper
- write accurate and grammatically correct articles
- conduct student, teacher, and administrator interviews

> Monique provides the **time span** in which she has worked as a staff writer for the school newspaper.

LEARN HOW State an Objective A potential employer should immediately understand what you are trying to accomplish by submitting your résumé. Therefore, you should state your specific goal in your objective. Avoid vague statements that do not relate to the job position. Monique added relevant details to her objective to make it more specific.

MONIQUE'S REVISION TO THE OBJECTIVE ❷

a summer internship as a set production assistant
Obtain ~~an internship~~

ANALYZE A STUDENT DRAFT

Explain that the Student Draft on this page is the first half of a résumé. Model reading the draft and the annotations in blue, and explain that the yellow highlighting illustrates the student's language choices. Explain that the following *Learn How* mini-lessons hold helpful information about ways to improve this student draft as well as their own.

LEARN HOW State an Objective

- Direct attention to the revised objective at the bottom of the page (blue type). Ask students to identify why the change improves the phrase. (*The objective now relates directly to a specific job.*)

- Have students look back over their objectives and make sure that they are sufficiently narrow in focus.

- Remind students that employers want to know how the worker can benefit them. The focus should be on the job, not the worker, as in the revised objective.

FOR ENGLISH LANGUAGE LEARNERS

State an Objective Point out that the revised objective (blue type) is not a complete sentence, and explain why it does not have to be in this context.

- On a résumé, a name appears in big type at the top of the page. That name is assumed to be the subject of every sentence on the page. There's an "I" implied in every line.

- Because you're submitting a résumé, it's already clear you want the job.

FOR STRUGGLING WRITERS

State an Objective Pass on these additional tips for stating an objective clearly.

- Find a phrase in a want ad that describes a job. Use the exact phrase in your objective when you prepare a résumé for that job.

- Avoid including too much information. Keep the objective to one short phrase or line.

Explain that the Student Draft is continued and completed on this page. Read the draft and annotations aloud and discuss why the changes were made. Ask students to comment on the student writer's use of verbs.

❹ WORK EXPERIENCE

Hostess, Salina's Bistro
February 2009–January 2010
- figured out where people should sit and helped them find their tables
- worked efficiently, juggling multiple tasks in a fast-paced environment
- communicated effectively with managers, busboys, and waiters to keep customers' wait to a minimum
- made adjustments to accommodate unexpected situations
- appeased dissatisfied customers

> Monique uses parallel verb structure and clearly states the **responsibilities** of her job as well as the **skills** she learned while working in the position.

❺ VOLUNTEER EXPERIENCE

Hopeful Ones Delivery Service
May 2009–present
- get donated food and clothing from local stores
- make sure various homeless shelters have items

> Monique fails to use strong action verbs to describe details about her volunteer work.

LEARN HOW Add Strong Action Verbs In the **Learn How**

LEARN HOW Add Strong Action Verbs Although Monique includes details about her volunteer work, her writing would be more effective and specific if she used strong actions verbs. Monique revised these bullet points to add strong action verbs.

MONIQUE'S REVISION TO SECTION ❺

collect
- ~~get~~ donated food and clothing from local stores
- ~~make sure various homeless shelters have items~~
  monitor needs of homeless shelters and distribute items as needed

YOUR TURN Revise your résumé using feedback from your peers and teacher, the revision strategies chart, and the two "Learn How" lessons. Evaluate whether you've effectively shown your potential employer that you are a desirable choice for the job position. Try a new approach to formatting or organization if your résumé is less successful.

LEARN HOW Add Strong Action Verbs

- Direct attention to the revision of the last section (blue type). Discuss why the revision is an improvement. (The revised version gives the jobs more importance.)
- Have students review the other verbs used on this page and discuss whether they can be improved.
- Encourage students to examine the verbs in their résumés to make sure the verbs describe job functions accurately and appropriately.

YOUR TURN Have students work independently to complete the **Your Turn** activity. Have them analyze their drafts to make sure the address is correct, the objective is clearly stated, and the material is presented in a neat, well-organized manner. Encourage students to exchange résumés and give constructive feedback.

Write*Smart* CD-ROM

Writing Center on thinkcentral.com

DIFFERENTIATED INSTRUCTION

FOR ENGLISH LANGUAGE LEARNERS

Language: Action Verbs In the **Learn How** section, draw attention to the revised verbs (blue type). Point out that *collect* and *monitor* are synonyms of *get* and *make sure*; however, the new verbs are precise and descriptive. Have students list general verbs that people use every day, such as *give, go, put, set, take,* and *tell.* Tell them to use a thesaurus and dictionary to find more precise and descriptive synonyms for those words.

FOR STRUGGLING WRITERS

Language: Action Verbs Pass on these ideas for practice with action verbs:

- Go through local want ads, circling all the verbs. Make notes on which verbs are associated with which jobs.
- Go online to sites that advertise jobs. Find jobs similar to those on your list, noting the verbs that describe the jobs' functions.
- Review and revise your résumé, substituting action verbs that are specific to the job you want.

Editing and Publishing

 **COMMON CORE** **W 2e** Maintain a formal style and objective tone. **W 5** Develop and strengthen your writing by revising, editing, rewriting, or trying a new approach. **L 3** Apply knowledge of language to make effective choices for meaning or style.

In the editing stage, you proofread your résumé to make sure that it is free of grammar, spelling, and punctuation errors. These types of mistakes can cause employers to question the abilities of even the most qualified job applicant.

GRAMMAR IN CONTEXT: FORMAL VERSUS INFORMAL LANGUAGE

Informal, or casual, language is appropriate in some instances, such as when you are writing a letter to a friend or when you are writing dialogue for a story. However, when you are creating a résumé, you should always use formal, or traditional, language. As Monique edited her résumé, she noticed a bullet point that included informal language.

> planned seating arrangements for reservations and seated customers in a timely manner
> ~~figured out where people should sit and helped them find their tables~~

PUBLISH YOUR WRITING

Share your résumé with an audience, such as classmates, your teacher, or someone you know who is responsible for hiring employees.

- Make several copies of your résumé and hand them out to your teacher and classmates. Ask for feedback.
- Submit your résumé to a potential employer. If necessary, write a cover letter to accompany your résumé.
- Bring your résumé to a community career fair.
- Publish your résumé on your school Web site. Before posting to the Internet be sure to remove your home address. Have employers contact you by e-mail.
- Share your résumé with a prominent business owner or manager in your community. Ask for specific suggestions for improvement.

 YOUR TURN Proofread your résumé to correct any errors. Make sure that you have used formal language throughout your résumé. Then, submit your completed résumé to your desired audience.

Editing and Publishing

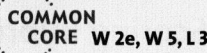 **COMMON CORE** **W 2e, W 5, L 3**

GRAMMAR IN CONTEXT: FORMAL VERSUS INFORMAL LANGUAGE

Ask students to give examples of formal and informal language. Then, direct students' attention to the revised bullet point. Remind students that a résumé is usually keyed to a specific job prospect—this sample is for a job as a production assistant. Point out how the new, formal language focuses on functions required for the job.

PUBLISH YOUR WRITING

Explain that students' résumés are important documents that they will update and publish throughout their working lives. Encourage them to develop "master résumés" that they will keep on file and can easily adapt to new job opportunities and changes in their job experience.

 YOUR TURN Allow students time to edit and revise their résumés. Encourage them to seek feedback from other students and potential employers as part of this process.

- Urge students to have several other people proofread their work.
- Have students look for generalizations and informal language that can be replaced by more precise, formal expressions.
- Encourage students to work with computers to create templates for present and future résumés.

FOR ENGLISH LANGUAGE LEARNERS

Formal and Informal Language

- Ask students to distinguish between formal and informal expressions in their languages and cultures of origin. Have them describe scenarios and occasions for which the expressions are appropriate.
- Help students identify reasons why a job search is a formal situation in any culture.

FOR ADVANCED LEARNERS/AP

Expanding the Résumé's Reach Encourage students to develop employment portfolios for themselves, creating items such as these:

- variations of a résumé designed for different situations, such as college admission, work-study programs, or internships
- sample cover letters directed to different types of employers
- press releases informing potential mentors or employers of relevant new experiences

Scoring Rubric

Explain that the best way to understand a scoring rubric is to use it to score an actual piece of writing. Ask students to prepare and submit copies of their résumés with their names, addresses, and phone numbers removed. (Number the résumés as they are submitted, and make a confidential list of the writers' names.) Distribute the résumés to the class and have students use the rubric to evaluate each other's work. Ask students to use language from the chart to explain the scores they assign.

For Rubric Bank, see

 **Write*Smart* CD-ROM**

Writing Center on thinkcentral.com

Assess and Reteach

Assess

R RESOURCE MANAGER—Copy Master
Rubric for Evaluation, p. 278

Online Essay Scoring on thinkcentral.com

Reteach

Level Up Online Tutorials on thinkcentral.com
Reteaching Worksheets on thinkcentral.com
Informational Texts Lesson 18: Résumé

Scoring Rubric

Use the rubric below to evaluate your procedural document from the Writing Workshop or your response to the on-demand prompt on the next page.

RÉSUMÉ SCORE	COMMON CORE TRAITS
6	• **Development** Has a specific, focused objective; lists experiences relevant to the purpose; is well-supported with significant facts and concrete details • **Organization** Uses a clear, consistent format throughout to organize information appropriately; uses headings and other style elements • **Language** Consistently maintains a formal style and objective tone; uses active verbs consistently; shows a strong command of conventions
5	• **Development** Includes a specific objective; lists relevant experiences; includes significant facts and concrete details • **Organization** Uses a consistent format with headings; organizes information appropriately • **Language** Maintains a formal style; uses active verbs; has a few errors in conventions
4	• **Development** Includes a specific objective; lists experiences; includes adequate facts and details • **Organization** Uses inconsistent styles for format; includes irrelevant information with relevant experience • **Language** Mostly maintains a formal style; uses some active verbs; has a few distracting errors in conventions
3	• **Development** Has a general objective; includes a few relevant experiences; lists some extraneous or unrelated facts and details • **Organization** Uses inconsistent format, which is difficult to read; lists experiences with no thought to relevance • **Language** Frequently lapses into an informal style; uses active verbs inconsistently; has some significant errors in conventions
2	• **Development** Has a brief general objective; lists experiences with few or no relevant facts and details; missing dates • **Organization** Provides little more than a list, with no seeming order of relevance • **Language** Uses an informal style and vague language; has many distracting errors in conventions
1	• **Development** Has no objective; lists unrelated experiences; lacks relevant details • **Organization** Provides a short list with no overall organization • **Language** Uses an inappropriate style and language; has major problems with grammar, usage, and spelling

Preparing for Timed Writing

COMMON CORE W 10 Write routinely over shorter time frames for a range of tasks, purposes, and audiences.

1. ANALYZE THE TASK   5 MIN

Read the writing task carefully. Then, read it again, noting the words that indicate the topic, the audience, and the purpose.

WRITING TASK

You want to apply for a job as a coach or tutor in an after-school program. Create a one-page résumé for the hiring committee, listing your experience and qualifications for the job. Begin by choosing the type of activities you would like to coach or tutor. Then think of the jobs and experiences you have had that are relevant to that position. Provide concrete facts and details that clearly convey your qualifications.

2. PLAN YOUR RESPONSE   10 MIN

Think about the specific job that you would like and the requirements that it would entail. Use that to write an objective and your relevant experience in the chart. Note whether the experience is related to work, education, volunteering, or extracurricular activities. Be sure to include the requirements for each experience and the skills you used.

Objective	
Experience 1	
Experience 2	
Experience 3	

3. RESPOND TO THE TASK   20 MIN

Use the information you listed in your chart to begin drafting a résumé. If you cannot use word-processing software to format the résumé, try to use a neat and consistent format in a handwritten draft. As you write, keep the following points in mind.

- In your objective, make it clear to your audience what job you are applying for.
- Remember to add dates and job requirements to each experience you list. Make sure the skills and experiences you selected contain concrete details that relate to the job you want.

4. IMPROVE YOUR RESPONSE   5–10 MIN

Revising Review the language you used. Do you establish a formal style and maintain an objective tone by avoiding personal pronouns? Do you use active verbs and parallel structure? Did you select the most significant and relevant experiences?
Proofreading Correct errors in grammar, spelling, punctuation, and capitalization. Make sure your edits are neat and the résumé is legible.
Checking Your Final Copy Before you turn in your paper, read it one more time to catch any errors you may have missed.

DIFFERENTIATED INSTRUCTION

FOR ENGLISH LANGUAGE LEARNERS

Writing: Main Ideas and Supporting Details
Review the Task and the first sentence of Step 2. Ask students to identify two elements that they must address before they begin writing their résumés. Have students write a sentence or two describing their desired job and its requirements. This will help them decide the other details they need to include in the résumé.

FOR STRUGGLING WRITERS

Writing: Main Ideas and Supporting Details

- Step 1: To help students decide on a job, ask them to think of their interests, experience, and skills.

- Step 2: Suggest that students use their charts and notes from this step to begin formatting their résumés.

- Step 3: Have students check that the experience they list relates to the job, that they include dates and relevant details, and that the formatting is consistent.

COMMON CORE FOCUS

W 10 Write routinely over shorter time frames for a range of tasks, purposes, and audiences.

Preparing for Timed Writing

1. **Analyze the Task** Before students begin writing, encourage them to answer the following questions:
   - What is my time limit?
   - What are the core traits assessed in the scoring rubric?
   - Who is my audience?
   - What is my purpose?

2. **Plan Your Response** Draw attention to the chart, and suggest that students take up to 10 minutes to fill in the chart to describe their objective and experiences.

3. **Respond to the Task** Point out that the bullet points in this section emphasize how important it is to stay focused on the specific requirements of the job for which the student is applying. The objective, experiences, and skills listed in the résumé should all relate to that. Encourage students to make their writing as concise as possible.

4. **Improve Your Response** Ask students to check their résumés against the task to make sure all the key elements are included. Remind them to keep both the purpose and the audience in mind as they edit and revise.

Assess

Use the Scoring Rubric on page 1320 to assess students' résumés.

Focus and Motivate

⋰ COMMON CORE FOCUS

W 6 Use technology to publish writing products.
SL 2 Integrate information presented in diverse formats and media in order to solve problems.
SL 5 Make strategic use of digital media.

PRODUCE WITH A PURPOSE
Read aloud the *COMMON CORE TRAITS* of a strong Web site. Tell students that the site they create should feature accurate information presented in an engaging format with appropriate graphics and other images.

COMMON CORE TRAITS
As students develop their ideas, remind them to keep in mind the *COMMON CORE TRAITS* of a strong Web site.

Practice and Apply

Plan the Web Site

- Have students work in small groups to brainstorm elements to include on the Web site, such as the home page, headlines, features, graphics, and the "About Us" and "Contact Us" sections.

- Enlist the help of your school's computer specialist when students are ready to create their Web site. The specialist may be able to assist with site design, graphics, and sound.

R RESOURCE MANAGER—Copy Master
Publishing with Technology p. 279

Technology Workshop

Creating a Web Site

Essential Course of Study ✓ **ECOS**

Many job-seekers create electronic résumés that they publish on Web sites. By providing multiple formats for your résumé, you can add visual interest and enhanced access to information for employers. A Web site also makes it easy to respond to ongoing feedback so you can quickly update your résumé whenever necessary.

 Complete the workshop activities in your **Reader/Writer Notebook.**

PRODUCE WITH A PURPOSE	**⋰ COMMON CORE TRAITS**
TASK Create a **Web site** for your school that shares student résumés with potential employers. Focus on ways to use technology to enhance the information in the résumés.	**A STRONG WEB SITE . . .** • targets a specific audience • contains accurate information • contains relevant and appropriate graphics, images, and/or sound

⋰ **COMMON CORE**

W 6 Use technology to publish writing products. **SL 2** Integrate information presented in diverse formats and media in order to solve problems. **SL 5** Make strategic use of digital media.

Plan the Web Site

Before you begin, think about your audience. Are you trying to reach business owners, volunteer coordinators, people who arrange internships, or all three? Once you choose an audience, follow the steps below to plan your Web site.

1. **Brainstorm elements to include on your Web site.** Begin by planning information and navigational features. Consider the following ideas:
   - The home page might list areas of interest and link to résumés within each category.
   - Hyperlinks in the résumés can lead to examples of the student's work and accomplishments.
   - Each résumé can provide a "Contact Me" link that opens an outgoing e-mail message to a general mailbox. (Do not provide your personal e-mail address online.)

2. **Consider graphics and sound.** Résumé pages can include images and be designed individually. Keep your audience and purpose in mind when choosing images and colors, fonts, and graphics. Use digital media strategically to make sure it complements the information you present. Remember that you can be creative, but you also want to look professional. If you use graphics that you did not create, check copyright restrictions and include a source line. Also consider adding sound to your Web site such as background music, interviews, or speeches that support or add to the information.

3. **Make a storyboard showing the design of each page.** Draw rough sketches showing the placement of titles, text, graphics, and navigation buttons.

Media Tools

THINK central

Go to **thinkcentral.com**.
KEYWORD: HML11-1322

1322 UNIT 6: CONTEMPORARY LITERATURE

DIFFERENTIATED INSTRUCTION

FOR ENGLISH LANGUAGE LEARNERS
Language: Reinforce Web Terms Write these terms on the board and review them with students.

- *authoring program:* a program that allows users to combine media elements into a Web document

- *domain name:* the electronic address of a Web site

- *download:* to transfer data electronically from a Web page or computer

- *graphics:* maps, diagrams, and charts that present information in visual form

- *hyperlink:* a command that allows a user to click and move within a Web site or from one Web site to another

- *navigate:* to move around within a Web site, game, or other electronic publication

- *server:* the company, school, or other entity that broadcasts the Web site

- *software:* programs that enable computers to perform specific functions

Produce the Web Site

Use your storyboard and notes as references as you produce your Web site. If you encounter problems while creating the site, ask your teacher or the school's computer specialist for guidance.

1. **Create or collect the content.** Ask classmates to contribute résumés to the site. Encourage your classmates to design their own pages to add interest. Use the following guidelines:

   - Because pages will be posted online, do not include your address, phone number, or photo.
   - Try to integrate different sources of information and diverse media, such as photos, graphics, and audio elements.
   - Follow standard formatting for résumés and include details that allow employers to make informed decisions.

2. **Build your site.** Ask your school's computer specialist for advice on which authoring program to use. An authoring program allows you to combine media elements into a Web document. Think of a domain name, or Web address, that reflects the content of your Web site. If you are unfamiliar with building a Web site, allow yourself plenty of time to accomplish the task. Consider the following tips as you build your site:

   - Place important hyperlinks across the top of your home page and/or in a running side column.
   - Emphasize headings by placing them in boldface and/or in color.
   - Make your Web site as easy to navigate as possible. Avoid inserting too many hyperlinks and confusing, overly busy design elements.

3. **Test the site and make necessary revisions.** Proofread the text, check graphics for correct positioning, and test all links and navigation buttons. Create a short survey or questionnaire, and ask teachers or classmates to review your site and provide feedback. Make revisions as needed.

4. **Upload your site.** Ask the computer specialist for permission to make your site available on your school's internal server or on the Web.

 YOUR TURN Using the steps and guidelines listed, create your Web site. After you have finished development, ask school officials if you can advertise your Web site in the school or local newspaper or add a hyperlink on the school's Web site. By integrating all of these résumés on one Web site, you make it possible for classmates and employers to easily share and update information.

1323

Teach

Produce the Web Site

Before students begin work on their Web site, review with them the main steps in the process. Ask:

- How will the Web site team enlist and manage contributors?
- Which authoring program is most appropriate for the site's projected needs?
- What are the effective strategies that will make the site user-friendly?

YOUR TURN Give students time to create and test their Web site and to collect feedback on their efforts. Have students share their ideas for maintaining a schedule of regular updates to the site.

Assess and Reteach

Assess

Use the *COMMON CORE TRAITS* to assess students' efforts.
A strong class Web site:

- targets a specific audience
- contains accurate information
- contains relevant and appropriate graphics, images and/or sounds

Reteach

Some students may have trouble visualizing how to design or write for a Web site. Make screen shots of several Web sites. Then work with students to review the design and writing style of each site.

THINK central

Media Tools

Media study keywords point to **MediaScope,** a Web site that helps students strengthen media analysis and production skills.

FOR STRUGGLING WRITERS

Writing: Short Features Motivate reluctant students to participate in the Web site by assigning them short features. Explain that these are very useful in Web site design because they add verbal and visual variety. Here are some starter ideas.

- Design the graphics and layout of the home page and write an introduction to the Web site.

- Create a page on the site for employment information Web links. Assign the task of finding such links to a special team.

- Write an article for the school paper about the Web site and create an electronic version that can be posted on the site itself.

Assessment Practice

Assessment Practice

RL 2 Determine two or more themes or central ideas of a text and analyze their development over the course of a text. **RL 4** Determine the meaning of words and phrases as they are used in the text, including figurative and connotative meanings. **RL 10** Read and comprehend literature. **RI 4** Determine the meaning of words and phrases as they are used in the text, including figurative, connotative, and technical meanings. **RI 7** Evaluate information presented in different media or formats. **RI 10** Read and comprehend literary nonfiction. **L 1** Demonstrate command of the conventions of standard English grammar and usage when writing. **L 2** Demonstrate command of the conventions of standard English capitalization, punctuation, and spelling. **L 3** Apply knowledge of language to make effective choices for meaning or style. **L 4a** Use context as a clue to the meaning of a word or phrase.

CHECK READINESS

Read aloud the paragraph under **ASSESS**, and stress to students that this is not the full Unit Test but a way for them to check their readiness for it. Then have students examine the skills listed under **REVIEW** and look back in the unit or in the **Student Resource Bank** for any skills they need to review.

READ THE TEXTS

Remind students to keep the unit goals in mind as they read the selections and to focus on finding the main ideas and supporting details in the selections.

ANSWER THE QUESTIONS

Direct students to pages R96–R103 of the **Handbook** to review test-taking strategies. Remind students:

- to read directions carefully
- to read all choices in multiple-choice questions rather than choosing the first alternative that seems to fit

ASSESS
Taking this practice test will help you assess your knowledge of these skills and determine your readiness for the Unit Test.

REVIEW
After you take the practice test, your teacher can help you identify any standards you need to review.

○ **COMMON CORE**

RL 2 Determine two or more themes or central ideas of a text and analyze their development over the course of a text. **RL 4** Determine the meaning of words and phrases as they are used in the text, including figurative and connotative meanings. **RL 10** Read and comprehend literature. **RI 4** Determine the meaning of words and phrases as they are used in the text, including figurative, connotative, and technical meanings. **RI 7** Evaluate information presented in different media or formats. **RI 10** Read and comprehend literary nonfiction. **L 1** Demonstrate command of the conventions of standard English grammar and usage when writing. **L 2** Demonstrate command of the conventions of standard English capitalization, punctuation, and spelling. **L 3** Apply knowledge of language to make effective choices for meaning or style. **L 4a** Use context as a clue to the meaning of a word or phrase.

Practice Test THINK central
Take it at **thinkcentral.com**.
KEYWORD: HML11N-1324

DIRECTIONS Read the two selections and the viewing and representing piece. Then answer the questions that follow.

from The Secret Life of Walter Mitty *by James Thurber*

1   "WE'RE going through!" The Commander's voice was like thin ice breaking. He wore his full-dress uniform, with the heavily braided white cap pulled down rakishly over one cold gray eye. "We can't make it, sir. It's spoiling for a hurricane, if you ask me." "I'm not asking you, Lieutenant Berg," said the Commander. "Throw on the power lights! Rev her up to 8500! We're going through!" The pounding of the cylinders increased: ta-pocketa-pocketa-pocketa-*pocketa-pocketa*. The Commander stared at the ice forming on the pilot window. He walked over and twisted a row of complicated dials. "Switch on No. 8 auxiliary!" he shouted. "Switch on No. 8 auxiliary!" repeated Lieutenant Berg. "Full strength in No. 3 turret!" shouted the Commander. "Full strength in No. 3 turret!" The crew, bending to their various tasks in the huge, hurtling eight-engined Navy hydroplane, looked at each other and grinned. "The Old Man'll get us through," they said to one another. "The Old Man ain't afraid of Hell!" . . .

2   "Not so fast! You're driving too fast!" said Mrs. Mitty. "What are you driving so fast for?"

3   "Hmm?" said Walter Mitty. He looked at his wife, in the seat beside him, with shocked astonishment. She seemed grossly unfamiliar, like a strange woman who had yelled at him in a crowd. "You were up to fifty-five," she said. "You know I don't like to go more than forty. You were up to fifty-five." Walter Mitty drove on toward Waterbury in silence, the roaring of the SN202 through the worst storm in twenty years of Navy flying fading in the remote, intimate airways of his mind. "You're tensed up again," said Mrs. Mitty. "It's one of your days. I wish you'd let Dr. Renshaw look you over."

4   Walter Mitty stopped the car in front of the building where his wife went to have her hair done. "Remember to get those overshoes while I'm having my hair done," she said. "I don't need overshoes," said Mitty. She put her mirror back into her bag. "We've been all through that," she said, getting out of the car. "You're not a young man any longer." He raced the engine a little. "Why don't you wear your gloves? Have you lost your gloves?" Walter Mitty reached in a pocket and brought out the gloves. He put them on, but after she had turned and gone into the building and he had driven on to a red light, he took them off again. "Pick it

DIFFERENTIATED INSTRUCTION

FOR ENGLISH LANGUAGE LEARNERS

Assessment Practice: Work Backward
Prepare students by having them read the questions before reading the passages. Have students work in pairs to find unfamiliar words in test directions and questions, and instruct them to follow these steps:

1. Write each word on an index card.
2. Look up the meaning in a dictionary and write it on the back of the card.
3. Use the cards to practice the words with their partner and to teach them to others.

up, brother!" snapped a cop as the light changed, and Mitty hastily pulled on his gloves and lurched ahead. He drove around the streets aimlessly for a time, and then he drove past the hospital on his way to the parking lot.

5   . . . "It's the millionaire banker, Wellington McMillan," said the pretty nurse. "Yes?" said Walter Mitty, removing his gloves slowly. "Who has the case?" "Dr. Renshaw and Dr. Benbow, but there are two specialists here, Dr. Remington from New York and Dr. Pritchard-Mitford from London. He flew over." A door opened down a long, cool corridor and Dr. Renshaw came out. He looked distraught and haggard. "Hello, Mitty," he said. "We're having the devil's own time with McMillan, the millionaire banker and close personal friend of Roosevelt. Obstreosis of the ductal tract. Tertiary. Wish you'd take a look at him." "Glad to," said Mitty.

6   In the operating room there were whispered introductions: "Dr. Remington, Dr. Mitty. Dr. Pritchard-Mitford, Dr. Mitty." "I've read your book on streptothricosis," said Pritchard-Mitford, shaking hands. "A brilliant performance, sir." "Thank you," said Walter Mitty. "Didn't know you were in the States, Mitty," grumbled Remington. "Coals to Newcastle, bringing Mitford and me up here for a tertiary." "You are very kind," said Mitty. A huge, complicated machine, connected to the operating table, with many tubes and wires, began at this moment to go pocketa-pocketa-pocketa. "The new anesthetizer is giving away!" shouted an intern. "There is no one in the East who knows how to fix it!" "Quiet, man!" said Mitty, in a low, cool voice. He sprang to the machine, which was now going pocketa-pocketa-queep-pocketa-queep. He began fingering delicately a row of glistening dials. "Give me a fountain pen!" he snapped. Someone handed him a fountain pen. He pulled a faulty piston out of the machine and inserted the pen in its place. "That will hold for ten minutes," he said. "Get on with the operation." A nurse hurried over and whispered to Renshaw, and Mitty saw the man turn pale. "Coreopsis has set in," said Renshaw nervously. "If you would take over, Mitty?" Mitty looked at him and at the craven figure of Benbow, who drank, and at the grave, uncertain faces of the two great specialists. "If you wish," he said. They slipped a white gown on him, he adjusted a mask and drew on thin gloves; nurses handed him shining . . .

7   "Back it up, Mac! Look out for that Buick!" Walter Mitty jammed on the brakes. "Wrong lane, Mac," said the parking-lot attendant, looking at Mitty closely. "Gee. Yeh," muttered Mitty. He began cautiously to back out of the lane marked "Exit Only." "Leave her sit there," said the attendant. "I'll put her away." Mitty got out of the car. "Hey, better leave the key." "Oh," said Mitty, handing

GO ON ➡

ITEM ANALYSIS

COMPREHENSION AND WRITTEN RESPONSE	ITEMS	UNIT PAGES
Identify/Interpret Allusions	4	1203, 1206, 1210, 1213
Analyze Tone	9, 10	1171, 1174–76
Identify Main Ideas/ Supporting Details	2–4, 8, 12, 14	1263, 1266, 1269, 1270
Analyze Elements of Argument	9, 15, 16	1204, 1206, 1209, 1215, 1230–32
Analyze Inductive/ Deductive Reasoning	15, 16	

VOCABULARY	ITEMS	UNIT PAGES
Greek Prefixes	7	1229

WRITING AND GRAMMAR	ITEMS	UNIT PAGES
Word Choice to Create Mood	1, 4	1244, 1249

Practice Test

On **thinkcentral.com** students can complete an interactive version of this practice test *and* receive remediation for the skills they have not yet mastered.

FOR STRUGGLING READERS

Assessment Support Consider these options for completing the Assessment Practice.

- Have students "work backward" to review the test questions *before* reading the passages.
- Select random questions in the Assessment Practice, and ask students to model *how* and *where* to look for answers.

- Ask students to locate unfamiliar words in the Assessment Practice. Elicit the words' meaning from the class.
- Have students record useful testing words and definitions in their journals for later reference.
- Read selections or parts of them aloud to aid in student comprehension.

the man the ignition key. The attendant vaulted into the car, backed it up with insolent skill, and put it where it belonged.

8   They're so damn cocky, thought Walter Mitty, walking along Main Street; they think they know everything. Once he had tried to take his chains off, outside New Milford, and he had got them wound around the axles. A man had had to come out in a wrecking car and unwind them, a young, grinning garageman. Since then Mrs. Mitty always made him drive to a garage to have the chains taken off. The next time, he thought, I'll wear my right arm in a sling; they won't grin at me then. I'll have my right arm in a sling and they'll see I couldn't possibly take the chains off myself. He kicked at the slush on the sidewalk. "Overshoes," he said to himself, and he began looking for a shoe store.

9   When he came out into the street again, with the overshoes in a box under his arm, Walter Mitty began to wonder what the other thing was his wife had told him to get. She had told him, twice before they set out from their house for Waterbury. In a way he hated these weekly trips to town—he was always getting something wrong. Kleenex, he thought, Squibb's, razor blades? No. Tooth paste, toothbrush, bicarbonate, carborundum, initiative and referendum? He gave it up. But she would remember it. "Where's the what's-its-name?" she would ask. "Don't tell me you forgot the what's-its-name." A newsboy went by shouting something about the Waterbury trial.

10   . . . "Perhaps this will refresh your memory." The District Attorney suddenly thrust a heavy automatic at the quiet figure on the witness stand. "Have you ever seen this before?" Walter Mitty took the gun and examined it expertly. "This is my Webley-Vickers 50.80," he said calmly. An excited buzz ran around the courtroom. The Judge rapped for order. "You are a crack shot with any sort of firearms, I believe?" said the District Attorney, insinuatingly. "Objection!" shouted Mitty's attorney. "We have shown that the defendant could not have fired the shot. We have shown that he wore his right arm in a sling on the night of the fourteenth of July." Walter Mitty raised his hand briefly and the bickering attorneys were stilled. "With any known make of gun," he said evenly, "I could have killed Gregory Fitzhurst at three hundred feet with my left hand." Pandemonium broke loose in the courtroom. A woman's scream rose above the bedlam and suddenly a lovely, dark-haired girl was in Walter Mitty's arms. The District Attorney struck at her savagely. Without rising from his chair, Mitty let the man have it on the point of the chin. "You miserable cur!" . . .

11   "Puppy biscuit," said Walter Mitty. He stopped walking and the buildings of Waterbury rose up out of the misty courtroom and surrounded him again. A woman who was passing laughed. "He said 'Puppy biscuit,'" she said to her companion. "That man said 'Puppy biscuit' to himself." Walter Mitty hurried on. He went into an A. & P., not the first one he came to but a smaller one farther up

DIFFERENTIATED INSTRUCTION

FOR ENGLISH LANGUAGE LEARNERS
Figurative Language: Idioms Remind students that idioms are figurative expressions that mean something other than the literal definitions of the words they contain. Ask students to offer meanings for these idioms from the selection. Encourage them to use context clues to aid understanding of these phrases.

• Paragraph 9: what's-its-name (a thing whose name has been forgotten)

• Paragraph 10: an excited buzz; crack shot; let the man have it (excited murmuring; expert marksman; punched the man)

the street. "I want some biscuit for small, young dogs," he said to the clerk. "Any special brand, sir?" The greatest pistol shot in the world thought a moment. "It says 'Puppies Bark for It' on the box," said Walter Mitty.

12   His wife would be through at the hairdresser's in fifteen minutes Mitty saw in looking at his watch, unless they had trouble drying it; sometimes they had trouble drying it. She didn't like to get to the hotel first, she would want him to be there waiting for her as usual. He found a big leather chair in the lobby, facing a window, and he put the overshoes and the puppy biscuit on the floor beside it. He picked up an old copy of *Liberty* and sank down into the chair. "Can Germany Conquer the World Through the Air?" Walter Mitty looked at the pictures of bombing planes and of ruined streets.

13   . . . "The cannonading has got the wind up in young Raleigh, sir," said the sergeant. Captain Mitty looked up at him through tousled hair. "Get him to bed," he said wearily, "with the others. I'll fly alone." "But you can't, sir," said the sergeant anxiously. "It takes two men to handle that bomber and the Archies are pounding hell out of the air. Von Richtman's circus is between here and Saulier." "Somebody's got to get that ammunition dump," said Mitty. "I'm going over. Spot of brandy?" He poured a drink for the sergeant and one for himself. War thundered and whined around the dugout and battered at the door. There was a rending of wood and splinters flew through the room. "A bit of a near thing," said Captain Mitty carelessly. 'The box barrage is closing in," said the sergeant. "We only live once, Sergeant," said Mitty, with his faint, fleeting smile. "Or do we?" He poured another brandy and tossed it off. "I never see a man could hold his brandy like you, sir," said the sergeant. "Begging your pardon, sir." Captain Mitty stood up and strapped on his huge Webley-Vickers automatic. "It's forty kilometers through hell, sir," said the sergeant. Mitty finished one last brandy. "After all," he said softly, "what isn't?" The pounding of the cannon increased; there was the rat-tat-tatting of machine guns, and from somewhere came the menacing pocketa-pocketa-pocketa of the new flame-throwers. Walter Mitty walked to the door of the dugout humming "Aupres de Ma Blonde." He turned and waved to the sergeant. "Cheerio!" he said. . . .

14   Something struck his shoulder. "I've been looking all over this hotel for you," said Mrs. Mitty. "Why do you have to hide in this old chair? How did you expect me to find you?" "Things close in," said Walter Mitty vaguely. "What?" Mrs. Mitty said. "Did you get the what's-its-name? The puppy biscuit? What's in that box?" "Overshoes," said Mitty. "Couldn't you have put them on in the store?" "I was thinking," said Walter Mitty. "Does it ever occur to you that I am sometimes thinking?" She looked at him. "I'm going to take your temperature when I get you home," she said.

GO ON ➡

FOR STRUGGLING READERS

Assessment Practice: Allusions Direct attention to the scenes in paragraphs 1, 5 and 6, 10, and 13. Have students identify the source of Mitty's imaginary world. Help students recognize that these are allusions to classic movie plots: World War II, medical, and courtroom dramas. Ask volunteers for brief descriptions of similar plots from films and television programs they have seen.

FOR ENGLISH LANGUAGE LEARNERS

Assessment Practice: Drawing Conclusions
Read paragraph 14 aloud. Ask students to notice how Walter Mitty and Mrs. Mitty react to each other in the paragraph. What conclusion do students draw from Mrs. Mitty's actions and her speech in the last two lines? *(She thinks her husband is acting odd because he has become ill.)*

15   They went out through the revolving doors that made a faintly derisive whistling sound when you pushed them. It was two blocks to the parking lot. At the drugstore on the corner she said, "Wait here for me. I forgot something. I won't be a minute." She was more than a minute. Walter Mitty lighted a cigarette. It began to rain, rain with sleet in it. He stood up against the wall of the drugstore, smoking. . . He put his shoulders back and his heels together. "To hell with the handkerchief," said Walter Mitty scornfully. He took one last drag on his cigarette and snapped it away. Then, with that faint, fleeting smile playing about his lips, he faced the firing squad; erect and motionless, proud and disdainful, Walter Mitty the Undefeated, inscrutable to the last.

Virtual Worlds

August 8, 2007
LONDON, England (CNN)

1   It's 2020. You get home from work, kick off your shoes and relax—on your very own tropical island. That night, your friends teleport over with other glamorous guests for a party at your five-star beach house, decked out in expensively understated chrome, crystal and fine Italian furniture.

2   But this is no billionaire way of life. If virtual worlds become the next Facebook phenomenon, experts predict that logging on to a luxury lifestyle could be attainable for all of us—and we might even spend more money on our online homes than on our real-life surroundings.

3   By 2020, virtual worlds may have surpassed social networking sites as the place to spend time online. Experts believe that the draw of 3-D spaces where our avatars can hang out with our friends—and meet new ones—may tempt away even the most ardent Facebook addict.

4   David Knighton is one of many netizens exploring virtual worlds. He's been visiting a site for over a year and told CNN that he enjoys its social dimension. "I've met several good friends who are still friends to this day in the 'real world'" he said.

5   But what is the draw of a virtual world? Are they only attractive to tech-heads? David doesn't think so. He says, "Experience plays a role in acceptance to be sure, but a virtual world takes hold more on a social and creative level. Someone who signs in and recognizes those aspects will immediately be hooked."

6   This is backed up by blogger and writer Caleb Booker, who has tracked virtual worlds from phone "party lines" through the first one-player text-based computer

1328

adventures to the two- and three-dimensional Internet worlds that are burgeoning today.

7   Booker believes that, in a society that's increasingly mobile, virtual worlds help us hold our far-flung social networks together. He cites the example of his mother-in-law, who recently moved to a new city and uses a social networking site to stay in touch with her three daughters. "They're all busy, so virtual world technologies and Web 2.0 apps are the best and most convenient ways to keep up," he told CNN.

8   Booker says that virtual worlds take this interaction to a more sophisticated level. "I don't even have to worry about cab fare if I want to have a little get-together with my friends from the UK and the US tonight," he said.

9   And he thinks that it's only a matter of time before virtual worlds explode in popularity. "Bottom line: if people are using email for social interaction, they'll probably be interested in other ways to be social online."

Life-like avatars

10   Interaction on social networking sites is mainly limited to text, with the ability for users to add photos and video. But in a virtual world, people are represented by avatars: computer-generated figures which can look uncannily like ourselves—if we choose. They can walk like us, they'll soon talk like us and they can interact with each other.

11   As 3-D technology becomes increasingly sophisticated, Booker says that photo-realistic avatars are just around the corner, and will become increasingly convincing.

12   "Eye movement, breathing, and realistic expressions will be the easy part," he revealed. "The hard part will come with things like synching mouth movements with voice recognition. That's something we might not quite have nailed by 2020, but there will definitely be some kind of engine that attempts it by then."

13   Holographic projections of 3-D objects are in development, but it will be some time before virtual reality offers us experiences akin to Star Trek's holodecks: touching and tasting virtual matter is still some way off.

14   "We're a long, long way away from having a completely immersive Matrix-like world," he told CNN. "But then again, technology can surprise you. I remember joking with a friend about a guy who bought a brand-new VGA monitor. It could display 256 colors at once—who could honestly need something like that?"

Spartan life offline, exotic life online

15   The authors of the "Metaverse Roadmap," a briefing document that explores the possible development of virtual worlds over the next 20 years, agree that a boom within a decade is likely. Their research has indicated that by 2016, half of us will have interactive avatars, with those aged between 13 and 30 spending around 10 hours a week socializing in 3-D visual environments.

16   And the draw of virtual worlds may encourage some of us to forsake our mundane real-life surroundings for a luxury life online.

GO ON ➡

1329

FOR STRUGGLING READERS

Reading Comprehension: Main Ideas and Supporting Details

- Draw attention to the first sentence, and ask students what this sentence tells them about this article. (*It describes the future.*)

- Have students scan the opening paragraphs to find the same date as in the opening. Have them read that paragraph and find the main idea. (*The date 2020 appears again in paragraph 3. The first sentence is the main idea.*)

- As they read the article, ask students to find similar statements about virtual worlds and to list the ways that virtual worlds could change our lives.

- Have students organize their lists into main ideas and supporting details.

17   The Metaverse Roadmap points to the millions of youths who already use worlds and suggests that "Youth raised in such conditions might live increasingly Spartan lives in the physical world, and rich, exotic lives in virtual space." It makes a certain kind of sense: why cripple yourself with huge mortgage payments on "real" real-estate when in a virtual world you can buy an entire island for $1,600 and $300/month maintenance?

18   The uses for virtual worlds don't stop at socializing. Virtual environments are already being built for education, like Edward Castronova's "Arden" project at Indiana University, which will transport users into a Shakespearean world. The applications for interior designers are clear, while a team at the U.S. National Institute of Mental Health (NIMH) in Bethesda, Maryland have used the virtual shoot-em-up "Duke Nukem" to diagnose depression in players.

Business collaboration

19   Booker believes that virtual worlds will be used increasingly as business tools. "They're very well suited to collaborative work," he explained. "We're not sure why yet, but there's something about seeing everybody's avatar in the room with yours that makes the whole experience far more effective than if you were to simply have a conference call. It creates a real shared experience."

20   "The common feeling is that by 2020 virtual worlds will be as widespread as the World Wide Web is now," states Booker.

21   With that popularity comes opportunity—and not only for Internet land barons but also virtual builders, landscapers and interior decorators, designers of avatar clothing and accessories, and even community moderators and governors. "A significant percentage of the world's population will be able to make a living working in virtual worlds," says Booker.

22   And he thinks that this potential is just around the corner. "The truth is that, as far as virtual worlds go, we're living in the flash point at the beginning of the explosion."

1330

DIFFERENTIATED INSTRUCTION

FOR STRUGGLING READERS

Assessment Practice: Allusions Ask students to explain the allusion in paragraph 17. To what does the article refer in the phrase, "live increasingly Spartan lives"? Why does the writer include this allusion? *(The phrase refers to the austere existence of the Spartans of ancient Greece. The writer includes this allusion to infer that young people who regularly visit the virtual world may decide to live very simply and frugally in the real world and live more lavishly in their virtual realities.)*

1331

Reading Comprehension

Model a thinking process for answering multiple-choice questions.

1. **D is correct.** *Mitty hides his secret life in a secluded place in his mind. A are B not correct because Mitty is not separated or far removed from his secret life. C is not correct because Mitty certainly does not think small.*

2. **B is correct.** *His wife's comment makes it clear that Mitty's mind is often elsewhere. A, C, and D describe events that happen only once in the story.*

3. **C is correct.** *The hospital becomes the setting for his imaginary medical heroics. A is incorrect because Mitty is in the car, not buying overshoes. B is incorrect because the daydream happens after he drives around for some time after the cop yells at him. D is incorrect because something always triggers his daydreams.*

4. **C is correct.** *Mitty believes he is operating on a millionaire banker. A is incorrect because Mitty doesn't go to his doctor's office. B is incorrect because the millionaire is in his dream. D is incorrect because Mitty is running errands with his wife, not working.*

5. **B is correct.** *The attendant is cocky and shows Mitty how someone with skill can drive. A, C, and D do not make sense in context.*

6. **A is correct.** *Mitty is not paying attention to what he is doing, and they bring him out of his daydreams. B is incorrect because the three characters do not laugh at him. C is incorrect because they are real characters. D is incorrect because they yell or nag.*

7. **C is correct.** *The context makes it clear that pandemonium is a synonym. A is incorrect because buzz refers to the noise the people made in the courtroom. B is incorrect because cur refers to a type of person. D is incorrect because it is the manufacturer of the firearm.*

Reading Comprehension

> **Use "The Secret Life of Walter Mitty"**
> **(pp. 1324–1328) to answer questions 1–10.**

1. Read the following dictionary entry.

   remote \rĭ-mōt′\ *adj* **1.** separated by an interval or space greater than usual **2.** far removed in space, time, or relation **3.** small in degree **4.** secluded, out-of-the-way

   Which definition best matches the use of the word *remote* in paragraph 3?
   A. Definition 1
   B. Definition 2
   C. Definition 3
   D. Definition 4

2. Which of the following lines from the selection supports the idea that Walter Mitty daydreams often?
   A. *He looked at his wife, in the seat beside him, with shocked astonishment.*
   B. *"It's one of your days."*
   C. *She seemed grossly unfamiliar, like a strange woman who had yelled at him in a crowd.*
   D. *When he came out into the street again, . . . Walter Mitty began to wonder what the other thing was his wife had told him to get.*

3. In paragraphs 4 and 5, Walter Mitty's daydream is caused by —
   A. Mitty's dislike for overshoes
   B. the cop's snapping at Mitty
   C. the sight of the hospital
   D. Mitty's illness

4. Paragraphs 5 and 6 are mainly about —
   A. Walter Mitty's visit to his doctor's office
   B. Walter Mitty's meeting a millionaire
   C. Walter Mitty's fantasy of being a surgeon
   D. Walter Mitty's day at work

5. In paragraph 7, *insolent* means —
   A. careful
   B. cowardly
   C. disrespectful
   D. fair

6. Mrs. Mitty, the cop, and the parking attendant are similar because they —
   A. criticize Walter when he makes a mistake
   B. laugh at Walter's mistakes
   C. are characters in Walter's daydreams
   D. teach Walter the best way to do things

7. Which words from paragraph 10 help the reader understand the meaning of the word *bedlam*?
   A. Buzz
   B. Cur
   C. Pandemonium
   D. Webley-Vickers

8. What pattern do the events in the story follow?
   A. The same thing causes each daydream.
   B. Someone interrupts Walter Mitty's daydreams.
   C. Walter Mitty daydreams about the same thing.
   D. People around Walter Mitty become characters in his daydreams.

9. The best way to describe Walter Mitty's secret life is —
   A. dramatic and adventurous
   B. romantic and unsatisfying
   C. satisfying and lonely
   D. tragic and flawed

8. **B is correct.** *Mitty is trying to do something else while daydreaming, and someone snaps him out of it. A is incorrect because different events cause the daydreams. C is not correct because his dreams vary. D is incorrect because his dreams contain imaginary people.*

9. **A is correct.** *Mitty's dreams are the opposite of his real life. There is not enough evidence to support B or C. D is not correct because Mitty is a comic, not tragic figure.*

10. Walter Mitty's daydreams indicate that he is —
A. calm in a crisis
B. in love with his wife
C. unhappy in his everyday life
D. just like everybody else

> **Use "Virtual Worlds" (pp. 1328–1330) to answer questions 11–16.**

11. Read the following dictionary entry.

> **deck** /dĕk/ *v* **1.** clothe in a striking or elegant manner **2.** decorate **3.** furnish with a deck **4.** knock down with force

Which definition best matches the use of the word *decked* in paragraph 1?
A. Definition 1
B. Definition 2
C. Definition 3
D. Definition 4

12. Paragraph 9 is mainly about —
A. how virtual worlds are really popular
B. how similar email and virtual worlds are
C. how easy it will be for people to try virtual worlds
D. how virtual worlds are only a passing fad

13. In paragraph 10, *uncannily* means —
A. eerily
B. basically
C. exactly
D. usually

14. Paragraphs 12 and 13 mainly discuss —
A. improvements made in avatars so far
B. the best way to synch mouth movements of avatars with voice recognition
C. how difficult it is to make an avatar
D. what avatars will eventually be able to do

15. Which of the following can the reader conclude from the information in paragraphs 19–21?
A. Avatars will eliminate the need for people to work.
B. Virtual worlds will create new jobs.
C. Virtual worlds will make business more like a game.
D. Businesses will not use virtual worlds because they are for entertainment only.

16. Which of the following is the best summary of the article?
A. Virtual worlds currently use 3-D technology and holograms to offer people a better lifestyle.
B. Virtual worlds will continue to grow and provide social, educational, and business opportunities.
C. Facebook is the fastest growing Web site worldwide.
D. Although avatars are available now, most people prefer to use sites like Facebook and MySpace.

> **Use "The Secret Life of Walter Mitty" and "Virtual Worlds" to answer question 17.**

17. Virtual worlds and Walter Mitty's secret life are both —
A. ways to escape boring routines of normal life
B. works of fiction
C. lifestyles of wealthy people
D. symptoms of mental illness

GO ON ➡

1333

10. C is correct. Mitty's life is dull, and he lacks confidence. In his dreams, he can be heroic. A is incorrect because Mitty only faces imaginary crises. B is incorrect because his wife likes to find fault with him. D is incorrect because not everybody daydreams every day.

11. B is correct. The beach house is decorated with elegant furniture. A, C, and D do not make sense in context.

12. C is correct. People are comfortable with e-mail, so they might try virtual worlds. A describes what has not yet happened. B is incorrect because there is not enough evidence to support it. D contradicts the context.

13. A is correct. The avatars can look very similar to the real person. B, C, and D are not definitions for uncannily.

14. D is correct. Improvements are being made on avatars, and in the future, they will be very human-like. A and C are incorrect because the paragraphs focus on what avatars will be like in the future. B is incorrect because currently it is not possible.

15. B is correct. Businesses will develop in the virtual world. A cannot be correct because avatars represent real people. C is incorrect because virtual worlds can enhance business. The text contradicts D.

16. B is correct. It states the main idea of the article. A is incorrect because 3-D technology currently isn't very sophisticated. C and D are supporting details to other ideas in the text.

17. A is correct. The answer fits the context of both the story and the article. B is not correct because only the story is fiction. C is incorrect because neither selection is limited to wealthy people. D is incorrect because only Walter Mitty shows signs of possible mental illness.

18. B *is correct.* *Cruises offer the chance to get away from a boring life. A, C, and D are incorrect because they are not specifically mentioned on the advertisement.*

19. D *is correct.* *The advertisement lists all the positive qualities of a cruise so that people will want to go. A, B, and C are incorrect because the advertisement doesn't mention these.*

SHORT CONSTRUCTED RESPONSE

Possible responses:

20. *Men are becoming weaker or have fewer opportunities to be heroic. Walter dreams about being the hero by saving lives or saving the day: He steers the ship through rough waters and takes over a major surgery when the other doctors get too nervous to operate.*

21. *Although there are a lot of people using the Internet for e-mail and other types of socializing, the technology needed for the cocktail party hasn't been invented yet. Avatars cannot do things like touch or taste virtual matter. Therefore, the author sets the party at a time when it might be able to happen. The idea of hosting such a glamorous party draws the reader's attention instantly.*

22. *People need to find ways to make their lives more exciting. Walter Mitty retreats into his daydreams to get away from people or situations that bother him. In virtual worlds, people may become who they always dreamed of being. Instead of changing characters like Walter, avatars will give individuals a chance to develop alter egos.*

Use the visual representation on page 1331 to answer questions 18–19.

18. One underlying message of the advertisement is that —
   A. a cruise is an expensive vacation
   B. a cruise offers fun adventures
   C. the food is fantastic on a cruise
   D. the ship will not go too far out to sea

19. In this advertisement, the designer is attempting to —
   A. compare a cruise to a car trip
   B. outline activities available on board a cruise ship
   C. inform viewers of cruise ship dangers
   D. persuade viewers to go on a cruise

SHORT CONSTRUCTED RESPONSE

Write a short constructed response to each question, using text evidence to support your response.

20. What might the author of "The Secret Life of Walter Mitty" be saying about male gender roles? Support your response with evidence from the selection.

21. Why does the author start "Virtual Worlds" with a story set in the future? Support your response with evidence from the selection.

Write a short constructed response to the following question, using text evidence from both selections to support your response.

22. What similar concern do the authors of "The Secret Life of Walter Mitty" and "Virtual Worlds" share? Support your response with evidence from **both** selections.

1334

DIFFERENTIATED INSTRUCTION

FOR ENGLISH LANGUAGE LEARNERS
Assessment Support Practice selecting the appropriate meaning from multiple meanings of a word (Reading Comprehension questions 1 and 11).

- Have students match the lettered answers to the numbered definitions and read each definition aloud.

- Instruct students to reread the paragraph to which the question refers and find the word to be defined, then read the word aloud in context.

- Have students substitute one definition at a time for the key word and then choose which definition makes the best sense in context.

Revising and Editing

DIRECTIONS Read this passage and answer the questions that follow.

(1) The storm was over, but it had been bad. (2) We had seen the TV footage and read the newspapers, but no one was prepared for the mud-caked debris we find when we returned. (3) Where had our pristine home gone? (4) Louise covered her face—as if by blocking this sight, she could erase the devastation before us. (5) Despondently, we joined our neighbors. (6) They had found an heirloom that had somehow survived the ferocious winds, endless rains, and raging floods. (7) It reminded us that we had once lived happily in this now beleaguered city. (8) As I held the heirloom in my hand, I asked my mother, "Where do we go from here."

1. What is the most effective way to revise sentence 1?
   A. The unpleasant storm was over.
   B. What a storm it had been!
   C. Although the fury of the storm had subsided, it left misery in its wake.
   D. The storm caused a lot of damage.

2. What change, if any, should be made in sentence 2?
   A. Change *was prepared* to **prepared**
   B. Change *find* to **found**
   C. Insert a comma after *find*
   D. Make no change

3. Which transition could best be added to the beginning of sentence 4?
   A. Besides,
   B. First,
   C. Thus,
   D. Unless,

4. What is the most effective way to combine sentences 5 and 6?
   A. Despondently, we joined our neighbors; they had found an heirloom that had somehow survived the ferocious winds, endless rains, and raging floods.
   B. Despondently, we joined our neighbors, yet they had found an heirloom that had somehow survived the ferocious winds, endless rains, and raging floods.
   C. Because our neighbors had found an heirloom that had somehow survived the ferocious winds, endless rains, and raging floods, despondently, we joined our neighbors.
   D. Despondently, we joined our neighbors, who had found an heirloom that had somehow survived the ferocious winds, endless rains, and raging floods.

5. What change, if any, should be made in sentence 8?
   A. Change the **.** to a **?** at the end of the sentence
   B. Delete the comma after **hand**
   C. Change *asked* to **ask**
   D. Make no change

STOP

1335

COMMON CORE FOCUS

RL 10 Read and comprehend literature. **RI 10** Read and comprehend literary nonfiction.

INTRODUCE *GREAT READS*

In Unit 6, students have discussed a number of big questions. Invite students to tell which question they found most intriguing and why, and then focus attention on the four questions that appear on pages 1336–1337. Discuss the recommended books and their summaries, pointing out how each connects to the related question. Encourage students to choose one or more of these "great reads" to read independently.

Ideas for Independent Reading

Continue exploring the Questions of the Times on pages 1146–1147 with these additional works.

Are we responsible for the WHOLE WORLD?

Catch-22
by Joseph Heller

This hilarious, heartbreaking novel brilliantly satirizes the "logic" of warfare. In the words of WWII airman Yossarian: "The enemy . . . is anybody who's going to get you killed, no matter which side he's on." Unfortunately for Yossarian, each time he completes the number of missions required for his discharge, that number is raised by his commanders.

Hiroshima
by John Hersey

In 1945, faced with a war that seemed as if it might never end, President Truman made the decision to drop an atomic bomb on the Japanese city of Hiroshima, killing between 70,000 and 80,000 people. John Hersey recorded the stories of Hiroshima survivors shortly after the explosion, bringing home for Americans the magnitude of the devastation and loss.

The Things They Carried
by Tim O'Brien

This collection of short stories focuses on a platoon of American soldiers in Vietnam. The things they carry—letters, photographs, Bibles, hand grenades—hint at the confused inner landscape of each young man. In this masterpiece of war literature, O'Brien makes clear that the burdens of war continue to weigh on the troops long after they lay down their arms.

Can America achieve EQUAL RIGHTS?

At Canaan's Edge: America in the King Years, 1965–68
by Taylor Branch

Third in a series on civil rights leader Martin Luther King Jr., *At Canaan's Edge* discusses the final years of King's life. The book begins with King's last great success: the marches in Selma, Alabama, that led to the passage of the Voting Rights Act. It then moves through the Vietnam years to the national tragedy of King's untimely death.

Vintage Baldwin
by James Baldwin

Author James Baldwin was extremely influential in exposing America's racial divide. Much of his writing focuses on the civil rights movement and the experience of African Americans living in white-controlled America. This collection includes short stories, essays, an excerpt from a novel, and a play.

A Gathering of Old Men
by Ernest Gaines

This quiet novel of race relations begins with the killing of a white bully by the only African-American man who has the courage to stand up for his rights. Eighteen elderly African-American men arrive at the scene of the crime, each carrying a shotgun with discharged shells. When the sheriff arrives, all 18 claim to be the murderer, forcing the community to reconsider how they treat one another.

1336

COMMON CORE

RL 10 Read and comprehend literature. **RI 10** Read and comprehend literary nonfiction.

What makes an AMERICAN?

The Woman Warrior
by Maxine Hong Kingston

In this classic memoir, Maxine Hong Kingston encapsulates the confusion, anger, pleasure, and wonder of growing up Chinese American in California, the daughter of immigrants. Haunted by her mother's tales of the magical if sometimes brutal world she left behind, the young narrator is equally unsure about where she fits in among the "ghosts," her parents' term for the non-Chinese people they live among.

Arranged Marriage
by Chitra Banerjee Divakaruni

In this collection of short stories, Chitra Divakaruni focuses on the experiences of women living in India and of Indian women who have moved to America. The contrast between their two worlds, coupled with their inherent roles and expectations, is a common theme running throughout the stories.

Unsettling America
Edited by Maria Mazziotti Gillian and Jennifer Gillian

A diverse chorus of voices comment on ethnic pride and heritage, personal identity, and cultural stereotypes in this anthology of contemporary multicultural poetry. Pat Mora, Lucille Clifton, Li-Young Lee, Louise Erdrich, and Lawrence Ferlinghetti are among the notable poets included in this collection.

What is the AMERICAN DREAM?

The Portable Arthur Miller
by Arthur Miller, edited by Christopher Bigsby

Playwright Arthur Miller once said, "Whoever is writing in the United States is using the American Dream as an ironical pole of his story. People elsewhere tend to accept, to a far greater degree anyway, that the conditions of life are hostile to man's pretensions." Miller's best work examines the average American's pursuit of the American dream and how that dream can become twisted or unattainable. This collection includes complete texts of his masterpieces *The Death of a Salesman* and *The Crucible*, as well as several later plays and excerpts from his memoir *Timebends*.

The Stories of John Cheever
by John Cheever

These stories describe a world that could be considered the epitome of the American dream—a place of leafy suburbs, summer homes, and cocktail parties. But beneath the surface lurks a darkness. Cheever's characters face a myriad of problems—aging, financial blunders, embarrassment, death. Cheever's graceful prose illuminates this world and makes readers care about the imperfect people who inhabit it.

Get Novel Wise THINK central

Go to **thinkcentral.com**.
KEYWORD: HML11-1337

1337

NovelWise THINK central

The keyword on this page points to **NovelWise**, a Web site that helps students choose a novel or other book-length work to read. **NovelWise** also provides
- study guides
- reading strategies and literary elements instruction
- presentations to introduce classic novels
- project ideas

Included in this unit: **RI 7,**
W 2a–f, W 4, W 5, W 6, W 7, W 8,
W 9, W 10, SL 2, SL 5, L 2, L 6

Complete text of the Common Core State
Standards is found in the correlation on
p. T10. Standards covered in this unit are found
in the standards overview (pp. 1339A–1339B)
and on the lesson pages where they are taught.

Preview Unit Goals

Explain to students that they can get more from
their reading by previewing. Then ask them to
skim the page to preview the skills that they will
learn. Note that each strand or category of skill
is color-coded on this page and throughout the
unit.

Model the strategy of copying the Academic
Vocabulary and writing a preliminary definition for each term. Suggest that students use
their **Reader/Writer Notebooks** for this purpose.
Encourage them to use the terms in discussions
and in writing. Also urge students to revisit each
term throughout the unit and to refine its
meaning.

UNIT **7**

COMMON CORE **Preview Unit Goals**

DEVELOPING RESEARCH SKILLS	• Select and shape a topic • Plan research • Find relevant information from multiple print and digital sources, including primary and secondary sources and online resources; use advanced searches effectively • Assess the credibility, as well as the strengths and limitations, of each source, including nonfiction books, newspapers, periodicals, and Web sites • Make source cards and take notes • Paraphrase and summarize information • Avoid plagiarism by quoting directly and crediting sources • Verify information, detect bias, and develop own perspective
WRITING AND LANGUAGE	• Write a research paper • Document sources • Prepare Works Cited list • Format your paper • Use punctuation with parenthetical citations • Use correct style for direct quotations
ACADEMIC VOCABULARY	• adequate • consult • investigate • objective • qualitative
MEDIA AND VIEWING	• Produce a documentary

THINK central

Find It Online!
Go to **thinkcentral.com** for the interactive
version of this unit.

DIFFERENTIATED INSTRUCTION

FOR ENGLISH LANGUAGE LEARNERS
Academic Vocabulary Provide students with
definitions of each Academic Vocabulary
word.

adequate (a´-dĭ-kwĭt) *adj.* enough to meet a
need; sufficient
consult (kən-sŭlt´) *v.* to seek the advice or
information of; to exchange views
investigate (ĭn-vĕs´-tĭ-gāt) *v.* to observe or look
at in detail; examine systematically

objective (əb-jĕk´-tiv) *adj.* factual; not
influenced by bias or emotion; *n.* purpose
or goal
qualitative (kwŏ´-lĭ-tā-tĭv) *adj.* measuring the
quality, or essential nature, or something

Use the copy master to help students learn
the Academic Vocabulary for this unit.

R RESOURCE MANAGER—Copy Masters
Academic Vocabulary, pp. 2–3

The Power of Research

KEYWORD: HML11-1339

INVESTIGATION AND DISCOVERY

- Research Strategies
- Writing Research Papers

Writing and Research in a Digital Age

THINK central

From online news feeds and electronic archives to podcasts and digital notebooks, technology tools can help you tackle any research project. Find out how.

1339

INTRODUCE THE UNIT

This unit consists of two interactive workshops that guide students through the research and writing process.

The **Research Strategies Workshop,** pages 1342–1357, offers strategies for organizing, selecting, and evaluating information to answer both academic and real-world questions. Students practice accessing and navigating Web-based, electronic, audio-visual, and print resources. A wide range of activities allows students to practice their research skills in concrete situations.

The **Writing Workshop,** pages 1358–1377, provides a systematic approach for students to apply the strategies they have learned. Students will plan and write a research paper, adapting the strategies to their own projects and achieving mastery of research skills through practice and reflection.

For help in planning this unit, see

R RESOURCE MANAGER UNIT 7
pp. 1–28

Unit Resources

See resources on the **Teacher One Stop DVD-ROM** and on **thinkcentral.com**.

 R RESOURCE MANAGER UNIT 7

 BEST PRACTICES TOOLKIT

LANGUAGE HANDBOOK

VOCABULARY WORKSHOP

READER/WRITER NOTEBOOK

TECHNOLOGY

- Teacher One Stop DVD-ROM
- Student One Stop DVD-ROM
- Write*Smart* CD-ROM
- GrammarNotes DVD-ROM

Writing and Research in a Digital Age on **thinkcentral.com**.

THINK central

Find It Online!

The interactive version of this unit on **thinkcentral.com** includes
- Writing and Research in a Digital Age
- Citation Guide

1339

UNIT 7

COMMON CORE STRAND	Unit 7 Introduction: *What Is the Power of Research?* pp. 1338–1341	Research Strategies Workshop: *Beginning Your Investigation* pp. 1342–1357
Reading Literature		
Reading Informational Text		Finding Relevant Sources pp. 1344–1347 **RI 7** Evaluating Sources pp. 1348–1351 **RI 7** Becoming a Critical Researcher pp. 1355–1357 **RI 7**
Writing	What Is the Power of Research? pp. 1340–1341 **W 9, W 10**	Deciding on a Topic p. 1342 **W 7** Planning Your Research p. 1343 **W 7** Finding Relevant Sources pp. 1345–1347 **W 6, W 8** Evaluating Sources pp. 1348–1351 **W 8** Note Taking and Plagiarism pp. 1352–1354 **W 8** Becoming a Critical Researcher pp. 1355–1357 **W 7, W 8, W 9**
Speaking and Listening		
Language		Terms for the Library p. 1344 **L 6** Terms for the Internet p. 1345 **L 6**

COMMON CORE

STRAND

Writing Workshop: Research Paper
pp. 1358–1377

Technology Workshop: Producing a Documentary
pp. 1378–1380

Reading Literature	
Reading Informational Text	
Writing	Planning and Prewriting pp. 1359–1360 W 2a–f, W 5, W 7
	Researching pp. 1361–1363 W 8, W 9
	Drafting pp. 1364–1365 W 4, W 8
	Revising p. 1366 W 5
	Analyze a Student Draft pp. 1367–1373 W 5
	Editing and Publishing p. 1374 W 5
	MLA Citation Guidelines pp. 1376–1377 W 8
	Producing a Documentary pp. 1378–1279 W 6
Speaking and Listening	Producing a Documentary pp. 1378–1379 SL 2, SL 5
Language	Drafting pp. 1364–1365 L 2
	Editing and Publishing p. 1374 L 2

To see the complete Essential Course of Study, see pp. T23-T27.

For additional lesson planning help, see **Teacher One Stop DVD.**

Instructional Support

Resource Manager Unit 7

UNIT SUPPORT
Academic Vocabulary, p. 2

Additional Academic Vocabulary, p. 3

Writing Workshop: Research Paper
pp. 5–27

SELECTION SUPPORT*
Plan and Teach

Student Copy Masters

*Available for all selections

† Available on **thinkcentral.com**.

Language Handbook

Best Practices Toolkit†

Teacher One Stop DVD-ROM

Student One Stop DVD-ROM

Write*Smart* CD-ROM†

GrammarNotes DVD-ROM†

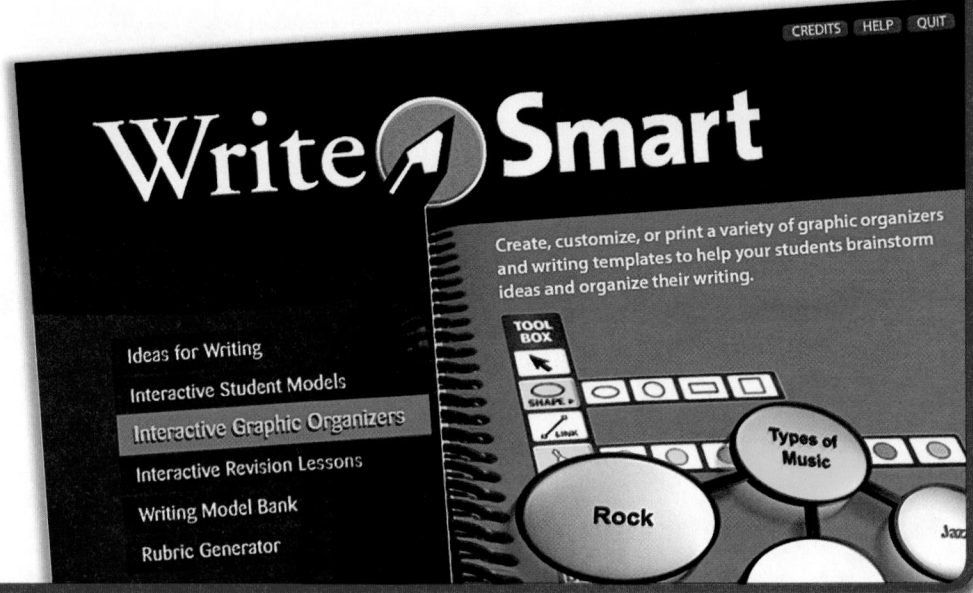

Differentiated Instruction

STRUGGLING READERS AND WRITERS

Level Up Online Tutorials

ENGLISH LANGUAGE LEARNERS

English Language Learner Adapted Interactive Reader Teacher's Guide

Guide to English for Newcomers

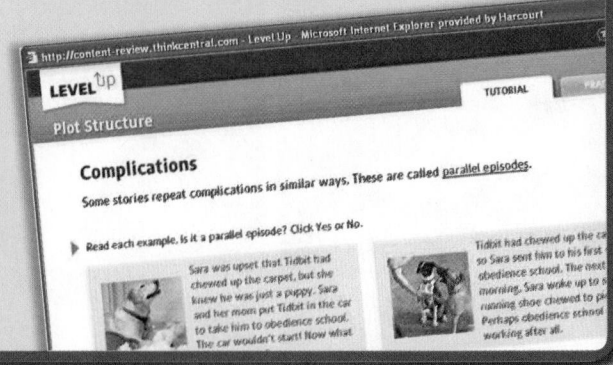

Assessment and Reteaching

Diagnostic and Selection Tests

ThinkCentral Online Assessment:
- All program assessments
- Level Up Online Tutorials

ExamView Test Generator on the Teacher One Stop DVD-ROM

ThinkCentral Online Reteaching:
- Level Up Online Tutorials
- Reteaching Worksheets

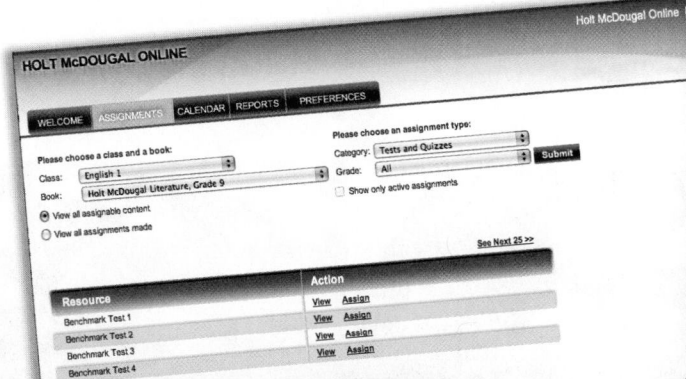

Professional Development

Video Center Based on interviews with program consultants and other educational experts, these videos feature classroom-ready teaching strategies.

Teacher Toolkit Includes a Teacher Handbook as well as a range of articles and handouts by program consultants and other educators.

Janet Allen

Jim Burke

Kylene Beers

Carol Jago

 **at a Glance**

One Location, Endless Resources

Find Resources Browse all *Holt McDougal Literature* components for the ones that meet your students' needs and match your teaching style.

Assess Progress and Reteach Assign electronic versions of program assessments to measure your students' mastery of the Common Core State Standards. On thinkcentral.com, some tests deliver online remediation tutorials to students who have not mastered skills.

 Interactive Whiteboard Lessons

Prepare your students for college and careers by teaching relevant, real-world skills through dynamic, interactive instruction. Go to **thinkcentral.com** to browse through all whiteboard lessons, including the following:

- Conducting Research on the Web
- Evaluating Sources
- Synthesizing Information
- Writing Informative Texts

HISTORY

Together Holt McDougal and HISTORY® are revolutionizing the study of English/language arts with video that helps students relive and re-imagine the people, places, and events they are discovering through reading. Look for selections with the HISTORY® icon.

What Is the Power of Research?

Throughout this book, you have explored the "big questions" of literature, history, and life. You can take these questions to a new, more challenging level through formal research.

COMMON CORE FOCUS

W 9 Draw evidence from literary or informational texts to support analysis, reflection and research. **W 10** Write over extended time frames (research, reflection, revision) for a range of tasks, purposes, and audiences.

What Is the Power of Research?

Read aloud the questions on pages 1340 and 1341 and the paragraphs that follow them. Use these notes to prompt further exploration of the questions, ideas for research, and research papers.

What is it like to be AT WAR?

Invite students to discuss what they know about the experience of being at war and how they learned about the subject—for example, from movies, fiction, history books, or conversations with veterans. Point out that war, like most experiences, can be investigated from more than one perspective. To illustrate, ask how a historian's description of a battle might differ from a soldier's description; then discuss ways in which a soldier's personal report could help a historian.

How does SCIENCE *affect you?*

Encourage students to suggest ways of collecting data to answer the questions about acid rain, the importance of breakfast, and local earthquakes. Challenge students to name ways in which they would use the findings of other scientists to answer the questions, as well as methods for gathering original data. Discuss whether collecting original data would be equally appropriate for all three topics, and why or why not.

What is it like to be AT WAR?

You might investigate this question by writing a **historical research paper** that explores why some 18- and 19-year-olds enlisted to fight in Vietnam. Or you might create a **personal research paper** that describes how a particular war or conflict affected you or someone you know. How did that personal experience relate to the conflict as a whole?

How does SCIENCE *affect you?*

Is acid rain present in your community? Do high school students improve their academic performance if they eat breakfast each day? When and where was the last earthquake in your state? When you write a **scientific research paper,** you present data that you have collected yourself as well as the findings of others.

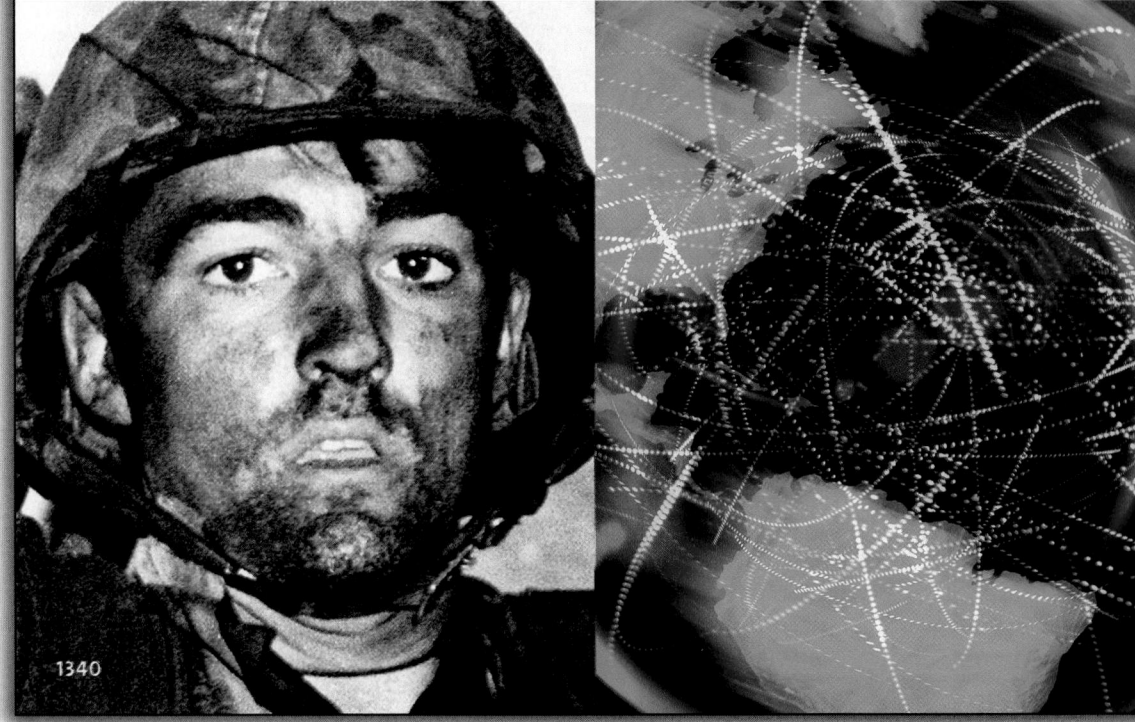

1340

COMMON CORE

W 9 Draw evidence from literary or informational texts to support analysis, reflection and research. **W 10** Write over extended time frames (research, reflection, revision) for a range of tasks, purposes, and audiences.

How does LIFE influence literature?

Novels, stories, and poems reflect how authors see the world. They can also shape our view of places and events. One way to explore a work of literature is to write a **literary research paper** that traces how history influenced a particular literary work or vice versa. For instance, you could learn more about the real people who inspired John Steinbeck to write *The Grapes of Wrath*.

Are we ready for the next natural DISASTER?

The question that captivates you may touch on several fields of study. A **multidisciplinary research paper** allows you to ask questions related to science, government, history, and many other subject areas and to investigate how those subjects relate to each other.

1341

How does LIFE influence literature?

Invite students to list literary or artistic works that may have been inspired by historical events—for example, specific protest songs, war posters, plays, or movies. Then have students list works of literature or art that may have affected history. (One example might be Thomas Paine's pamphlet *Common Sense*.) Choose examples from both lists; then work with students to generate questions that explore connections between the work and historical events.

Are we ready for the next natural DISASTER?

Have students suggest natural disasters that might affect your community and then choose the one that seems most likely. On the board, create three columns labeled *Science, Government,* and *History*. For each category, have students suggest questions that they could use to determine the community's readiness for a particular disaster, as in these examples:

- **Science** What is the probability of a hurricane of Level 3 or higher striking this area?

- **Government** What agencies are responsible for preparing for and responding to such a disaster?

- **History** What damage has been done by past hurricanes?

Point out that a multidisciplinary paper would address many such questions and would answer them in the context of the overall question.

Teach

COMMON CORE FOCUS

RI 7 Evaluate multiple sources of information presented in different media or formats. **W 6** Use technology, including the Internet, to produce writing products in response to ongoing feedback. **W 7** Conduct research projects to answer a question or solve a problem; synthesize multiple sources on the subject, demonstrating understanding of the subject under investigation. **W 8** Gather relevant information from multiple authoritative print and digital sources, using advanced searches effectively; assess strengths and limitations of each source in terms of task, purpose, and audience; integrate information selectively, avoiding plagiarism and overreliance on any one source. **W 9** Draw evidence from literary or informational texts to support analysis, reflection and research. **L 6** Acquire and use academic and domain-specific words and phrases.

Beginning Your Investigation

COMMON CORE **RI 7 W 7**

Deciding on a Topic

Ask students to name possible paper topics. Have them suggest one way to broaden each topic and one way to narrow it.

TRY OUT DIFFERENT "LENSES"

Divide the class into four groups, one for each "lens" in the diagram. Have each group develop and share two other questions about the Dust Bowl for that "lens."

R RESOURCE MANAGER—Copy Master
Selecting and Shaping a Topic p. 11

Research Workshop Resources

UNIT 7
Research Strategies Workshop

COMMON CORE

RI 7 Evaluate multiple sources of information presented in different media or formats. **W 6** Use technology, including the Internet, to produce writing products in response to ongoing feedback. **W 7** Conduct research projects to answer a question or solve a problem; synthesize multiple sources on the subject, demonstrating understanding of the subject under investigation. **W 8** Gather relevant information from multiple authoritative print and digital sources, using advanced searches effectively; assess strengths and limitations of each source in terms of task, purpose, and audience; integrate information selectively, avoiding plagiarism and overreliance on any one source. **W 9** Draw evidence from literary or informational texts to support analysis, reflection, and research. **L 6** Acquire and use academic and domain-specific words and phrases.

Beginning Your Investigation

Essential Course of Study ECOS

When you create a top-quality research paper, you go beyond merely gathering information. Instead, you investigate, analyze, develop new perspectives, and synthesize collected information to reach your own conclusions.

Deciding on a Topic

When writing a research paper, you may be asked to generate your own topic or put your own spin on an assigned topic. For instance, perhaps you need to write a paper for your American literature or American history class. Reading *The Grapes of Wrath* has heightened your interest in the historical events of that period, but you know that a topic like "the Dust Bowl" is too broad. Because you will spend hours researching and writing, you want to decide upon a topic that will hold your interest over time. How can you shape a general idea into the right research topic for you?

TRY OUT DIFFERENT "LENSES"

To discover a unique approach to a particular topic, view it through different "lenses," or perspectives. A historian, an economist, a scientist, and an artist would look at the topic of the Dust Bowl in different ways. This cluster diagram illustrates types of questions you might ask when brainstorming different aspects of a topic.

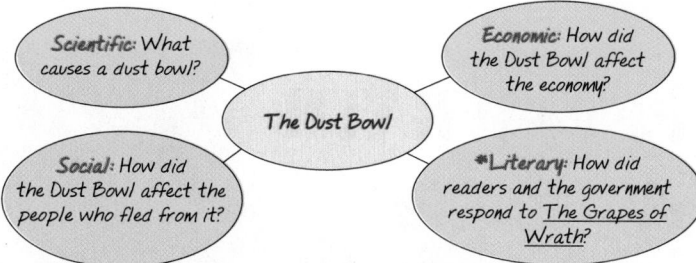

Scientific: What causes a dust bowl?

Economic: How did the Dust Bowl affect the economy?

The Dust Bowl

Social: How did the Dust Bowl affect the people who fled from it?

***Literary:* How did readers and the government respond to *The Grapes of Wrath*?

Choose the question that intrigues you the most and develop a plan for answering it. You might consult with other students in your class to get feedback on your question. You will want to end up with an open-ended question, one that cannot be answered with a "yes" or "no."

> **QUESTION:** Did *The Grapes of Wrath* affect the government response to the Dust Bowl?
>
> **OPEN-ENDED QUESTION:** How did *The Grapes of Wrath* affect government response to the Dust Bowl?

Your research question will develop into your thesis after you have read, evaluated, and synthesized information from a variety of sources.

See resources on the **Teacher One Stop DVD-ROM** and on .

R RESOURCE MANAGER UNIT 7
Plan and Teach, pp. 5–10
Selecting and Shaping a Topic, p. 11
Formulate Research Questions, p. 12
Consult Search Engines, p. 13
Explore Databases, p. 14
Evaluate Web Sites, p. 15
Evaluating Newspapers and Periodicals, p. 16
Choosing Reliable Nonfiction Books, p. 17

Finding the Right Sources, p. 18
Note Taking and Plagiarism, p. 19
Paraphrases and Summaries, p. 20
Quote Information Accurately, p. 21
Verifying Information, p. 22
Detecting Bias, p. 23
Drawing Conclusions from Your Research, p. 24
Support for ELL, p. 28

BEST PRACTICES TOOLKIT

TECHNOLOGY
- Teacher One Stop DVD-ROM
- Student One Stop DVD-ROM
- Write*Smart* CD-ROM
- GrammarNotes DVD-ROM

Writing and Research in a Digital Age on .

Planning Your Research

To make your search efficient and effective, develop open-ended research questions and then formulate a plan for engaging in in-depth research on your topic.

FORMULATE RESEARCH QUESTIONS

You may want to write several open-ended research questions to help you begin and then refocus as you search for sources. Think about different perspectives on the topic of investigation. Remember, you may have to revise your research question depending on the results of your research.

> • How did the Dust Bowl affect the United States?
> • Why did Steinbeck write _The Grapes of Wrath_? How did he do the research?
> • What did the government do to help migrant workers like the Joad family?

IDENTIFY THE MOST RELEVANT SOURCES

You will want to locate a range of relevant and credible sources to answer your research question. Take a few minutes to consider which sources make the most sense for the early stages of your research.

- **Encyclopedia articles** can provide a helpful overview of your topic as you begin researching.

- For the specific details you need, try **specialized reference works.** Almanacs provide facts and statistics, biographical references provide information on famous people, and atlases provide maps, charts, and graphics. See page R44 to learn more about reference works.

- **Documentaries** often include valuable interviews, speeches, and "you are there" footage that help you understand historical, literary, and scientific topics.

- **Magazines and newspapers** can give insights into a topic's perceived importance. Has your topic ever been front-page news, or is it rarely covered? How has coverage of your topic changed over time? For topics related to economics, popular culture, or history, take a look at related **advertisements.**

- **Interviews and oral histories** are firsthand testimony about history and culture. Look for them on audio, on video, in books, or on Web sites.

- **Original research** is information you discover yourself. For example, you might interview an expert, listen to a speech or lecture, create a questionnaire, perform an experiment, or conduct field research. To learn more about original research, see page R47.

- Be creative as you search. You might find valuable information in illustrations, maps, photographs, obituaries, statistical data, government publications, or museum exhibits.

Share your research questions with a librarian. He or she can suggest print and electronic resources that you may not have considered.

Find It Online!
Go to **thinkcentral.com** for the interactive version of this unit.

DIFFERENTIATED INSTRUCTION

FOR ENGLISH LANGUAGE LEARNERS
Vocabulary Support

- _Weblogs,_ "(also known as _blogs_) Web sites in which writers can make daily entries and readers can post comments"

- _first-person,_ "written from the point of view of a single person, using the pronoun _I_"

- _firsthand,_ "coming from direct personal knowledge or experience"

- _perspective,_ "the way in which a writer looks at a topic"

- _biased,_ "favoring one side of an issue instead of being impartial; prejudiced"

- _documentaries,_ "works (especially films or TV programs) that provide information about historical, political, or social topics, often through a mix of news footage, interviews, and narration"

- _third-person,_ "written from the point of view of someone outside the events, without using the pronoun _I_"

Teach

Planning Your Research

FORMULATE RESEARCH QUESTIONS

Work with students to list additional open-ended questions about the Dust Bowl. Have them identify words or phrases in the questions that could be used as keywords in a search.

IDENTIFY THE MOST RELEVANT SOURCES

- Invite students to connect the four "lenses" from page 1342 to possible sources on this list. Discuss which sources would be best for the early stages of research through each "lens," and why. For example, original research might be most appropriate for scientific questions, and oral histories might be most appropriate for social questions.

- Ask students to select one source and explain how it might be useful in researching the Dust Bowl. Point out that most of the sources can be applied to almost any topic.

Reteaching Worksheets on **thinkcentral.com**
Research and Study Skills Lesson 1: Research Questions and Topic

R RESOURCE MANAGER—Copy Master
Formulate Research Questions p. 12

Research Tools

Research keywords for **thinkcentral.com** connect students to the web site, **Writing and Research in a Digital Age.** This resource contains PowerPoint presentations covering all aspects of the research process, including research planning and selecting sources.

Finding Relevant Sources

COMMON CORE RI 7 W 6 L 6

TERMS FOR THE LIBRARY

Read the terms aloud; then call on volunteers to share situations in which they have found these resources helpful when using school or community libraries. Elicit preliminary definitions of the terms. As students read and discuss this section, have them refine their definitions.

Primary and Secondary Sources

As students read the chart, have them compare and contrast the two types of sources. Ask them to discuss specific ways in which (1) either type of source might show bias, and (2) a researcher might use a primary source to correct the bias of a secondary source and vice versa.

- **Primary Sources** Emphasize that primary sources need not be in the first person; for instance, a newspaper article from November 22, 1963, on the assassination of President John F. Kennedy would be written in the third person. Primary sources can be found in a wide range of media aside from text; for example, a family portrait can be a primary source, as can an antique toy or map.

- **Secondary Sources** Emphasize that secondary sources can offer information and interpretations from a wide variety of viewpoints. Secondary source writers are sometimes assumed to be more objective than primary source writers; in reality, however, they are not always so.

Reteaching Worksheets on **thinkcentral.com**
   Research and Study Skills Lesson 5: Using Primary and Secondary Sources

---

Finding Relevant Sources

As you delve into your research, you will learn more about what sources are available and where you can find them, as well as how to assess their strengths and limitations.

Primary and Secondary Sources

Most research papers include both primary and secondary sources. As this chart shows, the two types have distinct differences, advantages, and disadvantages.

PRIMARY SOURCE	SECONDARY SOURCE
Definition: materials written or created by people who took part in events or observed them	**Definition:** records created after events occurred by people who were not directly involved
Examples: letters, diaries, speeches, photographs, autobiographies, e-mails, some Weblogs, first-person newspaper and magazine articles, public documents such as birth certificates	**Examples:** biographies, textbooks, encyclopedias, some Weblogs, third-person newspaper and magazine articles, most documentaries
Advantages: provide firsthand information; can give insight into attitudes and beliefs of the times; may contain very specific details	**Advantages:** sometimes include excerpts from many primary sources; often include a broad perspective and many viewpoints; can be useful for getting an overview of a topic
Disadvantages: offer limited perspective; may need interpretation; may be biased	**Disadvantages:** are only as credible as the sources on which they are based; may be biased

TERMS FOR THE LIBRARY
You will use these terms when doing research in a library or media center:
- primary source
- secondary source
- database
- catalog
- abstract
- bibliography
- index
- appendix
- preface

DIFFERENTIATED INSTRUCTION

FOR STRUGGLING READERS

Concept Support [small-group option] Present groups of students with two different sources about the same topic—for example, a newspaper article about a current event and an interview with a participant in the event. Have each group use a Venn Diagram to compare and contrast the information that the two sources provide.

BEST PRACTICES TOOLKIT—Transparency
   Venn Diagram p. A26

Using Library Resources

Today many print resources can also be found in electronic form. Most of your searches, however, will be conducted electronically on the Internet or through a library catalog. The following pages will show you where to look for sources and how to improve your search skills.

USING SEARCH ENGINES

When using a search engine (such as Google or Yahoo!) to find information on the Web, you will need to come up with **keywords** that will help you locate the most relevant sources. For best results, use your search engine's "advanced search" or "search tips" link. Follow these general tips for effective Internet searches.

- **Be specific.** Try combining two or three keywords. If you want to find out about labor camps in California, be sure *California* is one of your search terms.

- **Use search limiters.** Enclose phrases in quotation marks—for example, a search for *"The Grapes of Wrath"* will result in pages that have those words in that order. Some search engines allow you to add AND or a plus sign to be sure that certain results are included: *Depression AND California;* or *+Depression +California.* To exclude certain terms, use the word NOT or a minus sign: *evacuees NOT Katrina;* or *+evacuees -Katrina.* To learn more, see page R46.

- **Choose the most relevant pages.** Scan the first 10 to 15 descriptions the search engine provides. Which sites could help you answer your research questions? Consider adding, deleting, or changing keywords to improve your results.

YOUR TURN **Examine Search Engine Results**
Which of these results do you think would yield the most useful information?

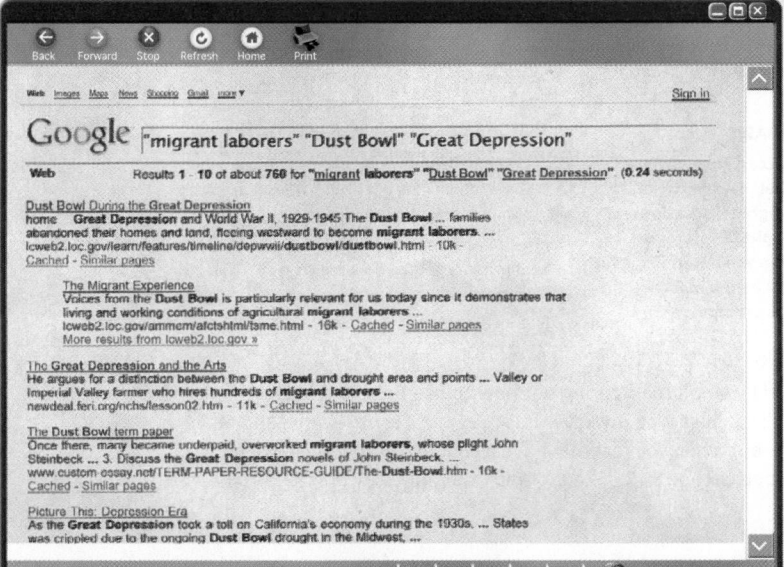

TERMS FOR THE INTERNET
Here are terms you will use when discussing the Internet:

- Web page
- Web site
- URL (uniform resource locator, also called Web address)
- search engine
- keyword search
- hyperlink
- menu

Close Read

1. This researcher did a search that combined three terms: "migrant laborers," "Dust Bowl," and "Great Depression." What are the advantages and disadvantages of doing such a specific search?

2. How might the search results change if the search was for "migrant laborers," "Dust Bowl," and "Oklahoma"?

3. What other search terms can you think of that might yield answers to the research questions on pages 1342–1343?

1345

Using Library Resources

TERMS FOR THE INTERNET

To help students conduct searches electronically, ask which terms they find familiar. Discuss possible definitions; then urge students to refine those definitions as they encounter the terms in their reading.

USING SEARCH ENGINES

Ask students to suggest the names of additional search engines—for example, Alta Vista and Ask.com—and conduct searches on these search engines, along with Google and Yahoo!, using keywords suggested by the instruction. Ask students to compare and contrast the results from different search engines.

YOUR TURN **Close Read**
Possible answers:

1. *Advantages: Such a search may be quick to locate specific information on a topic.* **Disadvantages:** *If the terms are too specific, the search may not find any useful results; it also will not find relevant information that does not contain all of the keywords.*

2. *The search would locate state-specific information.*

IF STUDENTS NEED HELP . . . Have them identify the search term that has changed.

3. *Steinbeck;* Grapes of Wrath; *Okies; 1930s; New Deal.*

R RESOURCE MANAGER—Copy Master
Consult Search Engines p. 13

FOR STRUGGLING READERS

Concept Support Inform students that many Web browsers include access to one or more search engines through their navigation toolbars. Call on a volunteer to show the feature to students. Have students use a search engine available through a browser on your school's computers to find the Web addresses of other major search engines. Show students how to bookmark those addresses.

FOR ADVANCED LEARNERS/AP

Advanced Search [small-group option] Have groups of students use the search engine Alltheweb (http://www.alltheweb.com) to conduct their own searches for the keywords *migrant laborers, Dust Bowl,* and *Great Depression.* Instruct groups to locate the three sites shown in the **Your Turn** activity. Have them visit those sites and at least one other of the top ten sites produced by the search. Then have them report on the similarities and

differences among the sites, drawing conclusions about the sites' relative relevance.

To extend the activity, have groups locate the Advanced Search function on Alltheweb and repeat the same search using that function, with search limiters that they have chosen, such as word filters or domain filters. Have them compare and contrast the results of the basic and advanced searches.

EXPLORE DATABASES

- Emphasize that some databases, such as InfoTrac, require a paid subscription. Point out, however, that since many public libraries subscribe to paid databases, library patrons can use those databases without charge—sometimes even accessing them from a home computer, using their library card numbers.

- Have students read the descriptions and examples of the types of sources. Then challenge students to describe how they might use each type to locate information relevant to the Dust Bowl experiences portrayed in *The Grapes of Wrath*. For example, a researcher might use the *Readers' Guide to Periodical Literature* to find magazine articles from the 1930s about the Dust Bowl or about Steinbeck's novel.

- Have students investigate several of the databases mentioned and report their observations to the class.

Reteaching Worksheets on **thinkcentral.com**
> Research and Study Skills Lesson 2: Using Library Catalogues
>
> Research and Study Skills Lesson 3: Using Reference and Search Tools

R RESOURCE MANAGER—Copy Master
Explore Databases p. 14

EXPLORE DATABASES

A **database** is any organized collection of data, whether print or electronic. Some of the databases in this chart are free to all; others may be available for free through your library's or media center's Web site.

TYPES OF SOURCES	EXAMPLES
LIBRARY CATALOGS Most library catalogs are available online, allowing you to search the catalog electronically and create a customized database of sources. Results will provide you with bibliographic data and a call number to locate the material in the library.	http://www.nypl.org/ http://www.lib.unc.edu/ http://bpl.org/catalogs/ http://www.lib.uchicago.edu/e/cat/
BOOKS Use your library's catalog to search for books by title, author, subject, or keyword. Once you find a book, use the book's index to locate specific information. In addition, some Web sites include full text of reference books and other older publications.	Bartleby.com offers free access to reference books, poetry, and classic literature online. books.google.com offers full text, previews, and reference information for books on a variety of subjects. Amazon.com offers previews of books, including tables of contents, excerpts, and front and back covers.
NEWSPAPERS AND PERIODICALS Most libraries have print indexes and electronic databases of newspapers and periodicals. You can search databases to find bibliographic citations or access to full-text articles. Full-text articles are often available at the Web sites of specific publications.	*Readers' Guide to Periodical Literature* is available in print and online, offering both full-text articles and indexing of over 400 periodicals. TIME magazine provides free access to archived articles online. *The New York Times Index* is available in print and online.
GENERAL DATABASES Libraries have access to many types of databases that provide full-text articles or bibliographic citations on a range of topics. A reference librarian can help you determine which databases might be the most helpful for the topic you are researching.	Academic Search Premier indexes articles from all major fields of study. MiddleSearch Plus provides full-text articles from middle school magazines. African American Experience indexes articles and primary source documents on African American history.

ADVANTAGES OF DATABASES

"Why should I spend time figuring out how to use these databases?" you might ask. "I can just type my keywords into my favorite search engine." That's true—but when you're writing a research paper, specialized databases are often a better choice. Read on to find out why.

DIFFERENTIATED INSTRUCTION

FOR ENGLISH LANGUAGE LEARNERS

Oral Language Direct students' attention to the abbreviations and domain names in the chart's examples of Web addresses. Model the pronunciations, or have one or more volunteers do so. For example, explain that *books. google.com* is pronounced "books dot google dot com" and that more complex, less known Web addresses, such as *www.ci.austin.tx.us,* would be spelled out orally, with the word *dot* spoken for each period. Also, point out that

when "edu" is placed at the end of a Web address, each letter should be pronounced, but when "org," "com," "net," or "gov" is placed at the end of a Web address, students should use traditional pronunciation. Have students take turns pronouncing the examples in the list.

FOR ADVANCED LEARNERS/AP

Create a Database [paired option] Challenge pairs of students to collaborate on creating a personal database for a topic of mutual interest. Remind students that a database can be in the form of print and that it can include bibliographical listings and abstracts rather than full articles. Have students tell the class what kind of database they created, what its features are, and ways in which it would be useful.

- **Specificity**—Some databases, such as the Internet Movie Database, cover only certain topics. Others cover only one type of material, such as articles from medical journals. Because these databases are targeted, you don't have to sift through pages of search results that have little or no relation to your topic.

- **No advertisements**—Unlike many search engines, most specialized databases do not have distracting pop-up windows or sidebar advertisements. No advertiser has paid to have a page show up first or in the top ten.

- **Access to the "invisible Web"**—Librarians call pages that are accessible through the Internet, but not through search engines, the "invisible Web." Many millions of Web pages are available through subscription-only databases—but if your library or media center subscribes to such databases, all you may need to access them is the bar code number on your library card.

- **Abstracts**—Many databases include an abstract—a short summary of an article's content—for each article. By reading abstracts, you can quickly decide whether the entire article is worth reading.

To find the most relevant results on a targeted database, read the article titles and notice the names of the publications the articles come from. Click on the most promising titles and read the abstracts, or skim the first few paragraphs of each.

YOUR TURN

Examine Database Results

These results are from a database called InfoTrac. Examine them and think about whether this search is effective.

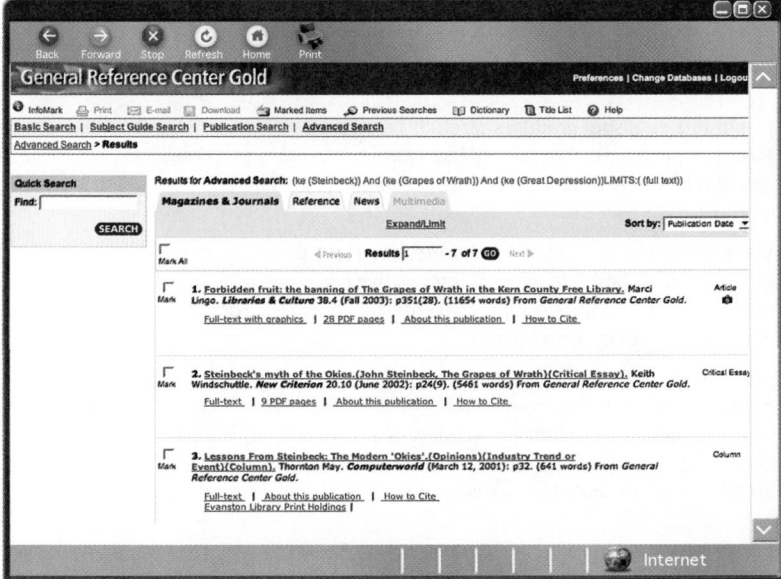

Close Read

1. Which three keyword phrases did this researcher use? On this database, the abbreviation *ke* stands for "keyword."

2. Which result includes graphics? How do you know?

3. Of the three results shown here, which one is not likely to be useful? How do you know?

4. What other information does this database provide that the search engine on page 1345 does not? Give three examples.

ADVANTAGES OF DATABASES

- Have students preview the four advantages of databases by reading the boldfaced heads in the bulleted list. Then ask them to read each bulleted paragraph, pausing to discuss questions if necessary before moving on.

- Challenge students to think of possible disadvantages to using databases; then discuss. The overall point should be that databases offer more advantages than disadvantages and are worth exploring, especially for in-depth projects such as research papers.

YOUR TURN

Close Read

Possible answers:

1. *The keywords were* Steinbeck, Grapes of Wrath, *and* Great Depression.

2. *The first result includes graphics; it contains a link for "Full-text with graphics" and has a camera icon.*

3. *The third result is not likely to be useful; it is from a computer magazine and apparently focuses on today's computer industry.*

4. *Any three: The database offers citation guidelines, information about each publication, a link to holdings within a particular library, a description of the type of source, a way for the user to access previous searches, a dictionary, a list of titles, a way to search by subject rather than by keyword, and a way to search by publication.*

IF STUDENTS NEED HELP . . . Tell them to look closely at every hyperlink on the page. Pairs of students may work together to discuss the meaning of each hyperlink.

Reteaching Worksheets on **thinkcentral.com**
Research and Study Skills Lesson 4: Using a Web Site for Research

---

FOR STRUGGLING READERS

Task Support Guide students to a popular nonsubscription database, such as the Internet Movie Database (http://www.imdb.com). Work with them to locate the database's features, such as menus, icons, and hyperlinks. Then have students perform a sample search, record their search paths on a Sequence Chain, and share the results with the class.

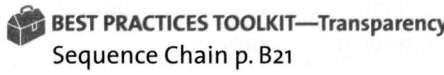
BEST PRACTICES TOOLKIT—Transparency
Sequence Chain p. B21

FOR ADVANCED LEARNERS/AP

Accessing the "Invisible Web" Have students ask a school librarian or community librarian what subscription-only databases are available through their facilities. Instruct students to go online to access two or more such databases; then have them report to the class on (1) the kinds of information that they found on the "invisible Web" and (2) ways in which the databases might be useful in research.

Evaluating Sources

COMMON CORE RI 7 W 8

- Have students preview the guidelines by reading the italicized heads; then have them read each explanatory paragraph in turn. Pause after each paragraph to have students check their comprehension by paraphrasing the information.
- Consider including these comments and activities:

Relevance Have pairs of students compose lists of criteria for determining a source's relevance.

Timeliness Ask students to suggest at least two topics for which a ten-year-old source *would not* be useful and at least two for which such a source *would* be useful.

Accuracy Remind students that awareness of accuracy and bias is an especially important factor in online research since anyone can post a Web site. Emphasize that distinguishing between fact and opinion is a key research skill in relation to both online and print sources. Remind students that they can enter the term "bogus sites" into a search engine to find out which sites are fake, deliberately putting out inaccurate information.

Author's Credentials Suggest that students perform a search for the author's name in order to check his or her credentials.

Publisher's Credentials As examples of reputable publishers, give students the names of publishers of books found in your classroom or school library.

Author's Purpose Discuss the distinction between an author's credentials and an author's purpose; for example, an eminent scientist might write a persuasive essay about an important issue that is not related to his or her field.

Breadth and Depth of Information Suggest that students ask themselves whether the information is appropriate for their audience.

Reteaching Worksheets on **thinkcentral.com**
   Reading Lesson 17: Author's Credibility
   Research and Study Skills Lesson 6: Evaluating Print Sources

R RESOURCE MANAGER—Copy Master
   Finding the Right Sources p. 18

Evaluating Sources

In this section, you will learn how to select the most credible and accurate sources, whether print or online, and assess each source's strengths and limitations.

GUIDELINES FOR EVALUATING SOURCES

Relevance	Is the source related to the open-ended question and research questions you wrote on pages 1342–1343? Your goals and questions may change as you write; however, don't allow interesting but irrelevant sources to distract you.
Timeliness	Topics in science, medicine, and sports often require recently updated information. Older sources can be valuable for historical or literary topics. For a print source, check the copyright page. For a documentary, look for a copyright notice on the label. For online materials, look for a "last updated" notice.
Accuracy	Most encyclopedias, dictionaries, and almanacs are accurate because they are updated regularly and go through a rigorous review process. Online sources can have information that is even more accurate because of frequent updates. Some online sources, however, may not go through the same rigorous review process. Whenever possible, verify and clarify facts using more than one source.
Author's Credentials	Look for an author who has written on the same topic before or who has a position or job title that qualifies him or her as an expert.
Publisher's Credentials	A reputable publisher produces carefully researched materials. University presses tend to be credible. Most publications and Web sites that focus on celebrities, fad diets, and gossip are not.
Author's Purpose	Why was the source created—to inform, entertain, persuade, or some combination of these? In general, informative pieces are researched more carefully than ones designed to entertain or to sell. For information on bias, see page 1356.
Breadth and Depth of Information	Match your needs to the source. Examine the table of contents, index, and appendix to find an overview of a topic or a single detailed aspect of it. Also, think about whether the source is either too basic or too dense and scholarly for your purposes.

DIFFERENTIATED INSTRUCTION

FOR STRUGGLING READERS
Vocabulary Support

- *irrelevant,* "not related to the topic under consideration"
- *timeliness,* "relevance to current considerations"
- *rigorous,* "thorough"
- *verify,* "to test something's accuracy"
- *credentials,* "proof that one has the right to be believed or trusted"
- *reputable,* "deserving respect; honorable"

FOR ADVANCED LEARNERS/AP
Evaluate Accuracy Ask students to read an article in a current newspaper or magazine and then analyze, either orally or in writing, the extent to which it contains fact and opinion. Suggest that they accompany their presentation with a copy of the article in which facts are highlighted in one color and opinions in another. Have students wrap up their presentation by stating any biases that they found in the article and by giving the author a grade for accuracy.

Finding Credible Web Sites

Anyone can create a Web site, so it is important to evaluate sites thoroughly.

QUESTIONS TO ASK ABOUT A WEB SITE

- **What does the address tell me?** Most sites with *.com* or *.net* in the address are personal or commercial sites. A personal site might be the work of one person, so its information may not have been carefully checked. Commercial sites exist to make a profit, so negative information about a product or service may be left out. Sites with the abbreviations *.edu* (educational institution), *.org* (nonprofit organization), or *.gov* (U.S. government) are more likely to be credible because they are the work of groups of people.

- **Who created this site?** Look for sections labeled "About Us" or "Contact Us." How can you tell if an individual rather than an organization created a site? The lack of an institution name or logo is one clue. Other clues are the lack of author biographies, the absence of documentation for sources, and hyperlinks that lead nowhere or only to the author's own sites. You can also consult a domain lookup site, such as *easywhois.com*.

TIP Some *.org* and *.edu* sites are personal sites that are not reviewed by the sponsoring institution. A personal *.edu* address includes a forward slash and a tilde (/~) followed by a name or initials, as in *okies.utc.edu/~haylee.*

 YOUR TURN

Evaluate a Web Site

Would this site be useful for researching the open-ended question on page 1342?

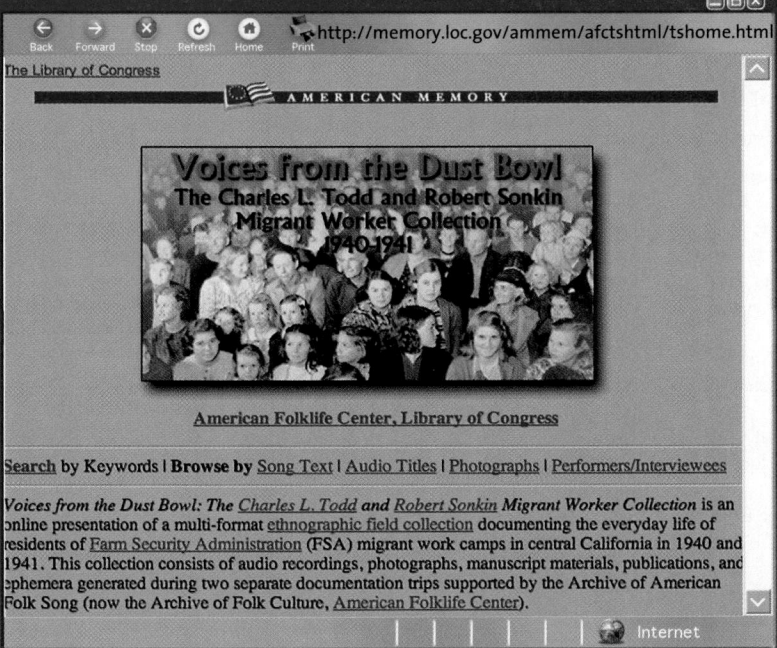

http://memory.loc.gov/ammem/afctshtml/tshome.html

The Library of Congress

AMERICAN MEMORY

Voices from the Dust Bowl
The Charles L. Todd and Robert Sonkin
Migrant Worker Collection
1940-1941

American Folklife Center, Library of Congress

Search by Keywords | Browse by Song Text | Audio Titles | Photographs | Performers/Interviewees

Voices from the Dust Bowl: The Charles L. Todd and Robert Sonkin Migrant Worker Collection is an online presentation of a multi-format ethnographic field collection documenting the everyday life of residents of Farm Security Administration (FSA) migrant work camps in central California in 1940 and 1941. This collection consists of audio recordings, photographs, manuscript materials, publications, and ephemera generated during two separate documentation trips supported by the Archive of American Folk Song (now the Archive of Folk Culture, American Folklife Center).

Internet

Close Read

1. What organization maintains this site? How do you know?

2. Why was the site created?

3. What clues do you have about the accuracy of the information on this site?

FOR ADVANCED LEARNERS/AP

Create Questions Have advanced learners create questions to help less-proficient readers practice evaluating Web sites. Explain that the questions should relate to using the Web page and links shown in the **Your Turn** activity on this page, as in these examples:

- What link would you click to find the lyrics to songs about the Dust Bowl? (*"Song Text"*)

- Where can you find two separate hyperlinks to the American Folklife Center? (*in the middle of the Web page, just below the photograph, and in the last line of the text on the page*)

Have advanced learners serve as tutors for less-proficient readers in a one-on-one setting.

Finding Credible Web Sites

QUESTIONS TO ASK ABOUT A WEB SITE

- Point out that sites with the domain names *.edu*, *.org*, and *.gov* are likely to be trustworthy not only because they are group products but because they are the products of well-regarded institutions such as universities, charities, or governments.

- Call attention to the **TIP** and clarify that, for example, an individual university student may be allowed to set up a Web page to share his or her work with the public. Such Web pages should be evaluated as if they were individually owned sites, not institutional sites. Author's credentials are especially important in such cases.

- To get to a site's home page, delete the part of the Web address that appears after the domain name and then press Enter. The domain is the part of the address that identifies the site's owner, such as *loc.gov* for the Library of Congress.

 YOUR TURN

Close Read

Possible answers:

1. *The Library of Congress maintains the site; the link is at the top of the Web page.*

IF STUDENTS NEED HELP... Direct their attention to the hyperlink in the upper left-hand corner of the Web page.

2. *The site was created to make the library's collection on an important historical topic available online to the general public.*

IF STUDENTS NEED HELP... Ask

- Who would want to use this site? Why?

- What would such users have to do if the site were not available?

3. *The identity of the source, one of the world's great libraries, makes it probable that the information is accurate. The .gov domain name also suggests accuracy.*

Reteaching Worksheets on <u>thinkcentral.com</u>
Research and Study Skills Lesson 7: Evaluating Electronic Sources

R RESOURCE MANAGER—Copy Master
Evaluate Web Sites p. 15

Evaluating Newspapers and Periodicals

QUESTIONS TO ASK ABOUT NEWSPAPERS AND PERIODICALS

- Call on volunteers to name some newspapers and periodicals with which they are familiar. Have students briefly describe each publication's subject matter and target audience. Discuss whether students consider each publication credible or not, and why.

- Distribute a variety of newspapers and periodicals, emphasizing well-known ones such as the *New York Times*, *Wall Street Journal*, *National Geographic*, and *Scientific American*, along with a local newspaper. Instruct students to skim through several top stories to find each writer's byline, the publication date, and (if applicable) any outside source from which the article came, such as the Associated Press (AP). Also have students turn to the masthead and the contributors' page if available. Ask students to evaluate the credibility of each article, stating the reasons for their evaluations.

YOUR TURN

Close Read

Possible answers:

1. *Shortly after* The Grapes of Wrath *became a controversial bestseller, John Steinbeck secluded himself in a remote area. He told the* Los Angeles Times *that his novel was accurate and that it was "moneyed people," not migrant workers, who objected to it.*

2. *Yes; large-circulation newspapers generally are reliable.*

3. *Yes; the article is a valuable source for someone who wants to know about how people initially reacted to* The Grapes of Wrath.

R RESOURCE MANAGER—Copy Master
Evaluating Newspapers and Periodicals
p. 16

Evaluating Newspapers and Periodicals

When you assess magazines, newspapers, and scholarly journals, you need to assess the publication itself, the author of the article, and the article's content.

QUESTIONS TO ASK ABOUT NEWSPAPERS AND PERIODICALS

- **Is the publication well known and well respected?** Most large-circulation newspapers and national magazines are credible sources. Beware of supermarket tabloids and other sensationalist publications.

- **Who is the author?** Look for the writer's credentials. Generally, staff writers are as credible as the publication in which they appear.

- **How old is the information?** Depending on your topic, you may need up-to-the-minute information, or you might need information from a specific era.

- **Did the article originally appear in another source?** If so, make sure the original source is credible. News services such as AP (Associated Press) and the *New York Times* News Service are the original sources of many reprinted articles.

- **Can the information be verified?** The best way to tell if a particular piece of information is accurate is to check it against other sources.

 YOUR TURN

Evaluate a Newspaper Article
Read and evaluate this newspaper article.

from the Los Angeles Times, July 9, 1939
Dust Bowl Book Brings Trouble

BY TOM CAMERON, TIMES STAFF REPRESENTATIVE

LOS GATOS, July 8. (Exclusive)—John Steinbeck, author of the best-selling novel, *Grapes of Wrath,* has betaken himself to Moody Gulch, a secluded canyon three miles from here, and padlocked himself against the world.

For the first time in his career, Steinbeck is inaccessible to friend and enemy alike. . . .

There have been reports of threats against the author which induced him to retreat to an almost inaccessible citadel—a refuge from the very economic refugees he sought to befriend. . . .

"It isn't the refugees who have taken exception to what I wrote," he asserted. "It's the moneyed people back there in Oklahoma—the big oil men and outfits like the Oklahoma City Chamber of Commerce. If anybody's sore at me for the book it's that kind of people." . . .

Regarding the report that Ruth Comfort Mitchell planned to write a refutation of some of the statements in his book, Steinbeck laughed in scorn.

"I know what I was talking about. I lived, off and on, with those Okies for the last three years. Anyone who tries to refute me will just become ridiculous."

Close Read

1. Briefly summarize this article.

2. The *Los Angeles Times* is California's most widely read newspaper, so would you expect this article to be credible? Give reasons for your answer.

3. Is this article useful even though it is dated? Explain.

DIFFERENTIATED INSTRUCTION

FOR ADVANCED LEARNERS/AP

Evaluate Information Explain the importance of fact-checking before a publication goes to press: Ideally, any fact that is not common knowledge should be checked for accuracy before being included for publication. (Some periodicals are more fastidious about fact-checking than others; the *New Yorker* is famously attentive to the checking of all facts.) Have students select an article from a periodical of their choice and check its facts, using tools such as encyclopedias, specialized reference books, and the Internet. In the case of news stories, tell students to make sure that every statement about an event is corroborated by a witness or by the reporter's direct observation. Have students report on any incorrect or unsupported facts that they discover; then have them give the article a grade for reliability.

Choosing Credible Books

Just as you write for different purposes and audiences, publishers put books on the market for different reasons. Some books are rushed to market and aimed at making money fast. Others are the result of years of work and have undergone multiple reviews, edits, and rewrites.

QUESTIONS TO ASK ABOUT NONFICTION BOOKS

- **Is the author an expert on this subject?** Check for information about the author on the book jacket, at the beginning of the book, and at the end.

- **Is the book research-based?** Check the back of the book for a bibliography. Look for footnotes in which the author credits his or her sources and provides additional insights or information. Check for an appendix, which might add other information, such as maps, statistical tables, or family trees.

- **What is the author's or publisher's purpose?** This may be stated in a **preface,** a short introductory essay. The preface may also tell you more about the writer's background and research.

- **What is the copyright date?** A series of updates and printings is often a sign that the source has been highly regarded for years and is probably credible.

 YOUR TURN **Evaluate a Nonfiction Book**

Decide whether this book, *Dust Bowl Migration*, would be useful to someone focusing on governmental response to the needs of Dust Bowl evacuees.

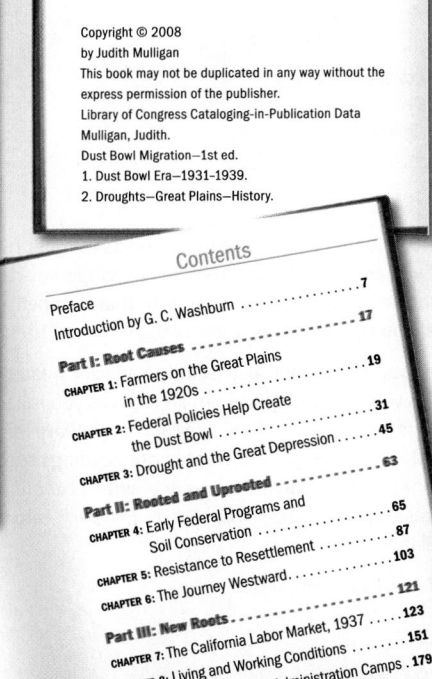

Copyright © 2008
by Judith Mulligan
This book may not be duplicated in any way without the express permission of the publisher.
Library of Congress Cataloging-in-Publication Data
Mulligan, Judith.
Dust Bowl Migration—1st ed.
1. Dust Bowl Era—1931–1939.
2. Droughts—Great Plains—History.

Contents

Close Read

1. Does this book contain information on federal policies that were related to the Dust Bowl? How do you know?

2. How useful might this book be to someone researching governmental response to the needs of Dust Bowl evacuees? Use page numbers and/ or chapter numbers to support your answer.

1351

Choosing Credible Books

QUESTIONS TO ASK ABOUT NONFICTION BOOKS

- Ask students to name a nonfiction book that they have read or consulted, either for a school report or for other reasons. Ask how each student decided that the book was credible.

- Enhance students' understanding of specific parts of nonfiction books:

  —**Bibliography** Explain that a bibliography reflects the thoroughness of an author's research; it also gives readers guideposts for further study.

  —**Footnotes** Point out that endnotes often are used instead of footnotes.

  —**Appendix** Note that an appendix often gives statistical support for an author's ideas.

  —**Preface** Explain that a preface allows an author to discuss the book in a less formal voice. A preface may preview the book, for example, explain the author's purpose, or sketch the author's background.

  —**Copyright** Show students where to find a book's copyright notice.

 YOUR TURN **Close Read**

Possible answers:

1. *Yes; both the contents page and the index mention federal programs.*

2. *The book might be very useful. Chapters 2 and 4 contain information on the subject; and the index lists the National Labor Relations Board, New Deal programs, planting programs, and the Emergency Relief Appropriation Act.*

IF STUDENTS NEED HELP . . . Advise them to look for key words that indicate governmental action, such as *act* and *programs.*

Reteaching Worksheets on **thinkcentral.com**
Research and Study Skills Lesson 6: Evaluating Print Sources

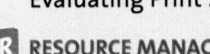 **RESOURCE MANAGER—Copy Master**
Choosing Credible Nonfiction Books p. 17

FOR STRUGGLING READERS

Comprehension Support [paired option] Have pairs of students select three nonfiction books from the class or school library and create a checklist noting each book's copyright date, reprintings or revised editions, author's credentials, bibliography, footnotes or endnotes, preface, appendix, and additional features such as maps or glossaries. Have students write and share a statement about these elements.

FOR ADVANCED LEARNERS/AP

Evaluate Credibility Challenge students to locate a nonfiction book that they consider to be of dubious or imperfect credibility. They may add criteria of their own to the list on page 1351. Have students write a paragraph explaining why they have concluded that the book is not completely credible. Invite students to display the book and read their evaluations to the class.

Note Taking and Plagiarism
Recording Information

COMMON CORE W6 W7 W8

SOURCE LIST

- Direct students' attention to the sample source card. Have them identify all elements of the card: the author's name, the title of the article and the encyclopedia, the editor's name, the number of volumes in the encyclopedia, the name and location of the publisher, the date of publication, the page numbers on which the article appears, and the project's source number.

- Direct attention to the **TIP**. Elicit that cutting and pasting from the Web without crediting the source is plagiarism because it gives readers the impression that another writer's words are the researcher's own.

NOTES

Use these questions to evaluate students' comprehension of note taking:

- What is the difference between a source list and notes? *Possible answer: A source list records where information was found; notes record the information itself.*

- How does a researcher keep track of the source of the information when writing notes? *Possible answer: When writing notes, the researcher writes the source's number from the source list.*

- What is the purpose of writing a header or subtopic in notes? *Possible answer: Doing so helps the researcher group facts on a given subtopic from separate sources.*

Reteaching Worksheets on **thinkcentral.com**
Research and Study Skills Lesson 8: Source Cards and Note Cards

R RESOURCE MANAGER—Copy Master
Note Taking and Plagiarism p. 19

Note Taking and Plagiarism

As you read and take notes from many sources, do not use the ideas of others without giving them credit. Plagiarism is dishonest and may result in your failing a class or being expelled.

Recording Information

By taking careful notes, you will gather information and guard against plagiarism. You can record your information on an electronic document, use special "note-taking" software, or simply use index cards.

SOURCE LIST

Begin by listing each of your sources. If you are using index cards, make one source card for every source. Assign each source a number, and then record the author and/or editor (if given), the title of the publication or Web page, and the date and medium of publication. Also record the following for these sources:

- **Web source**—date created or posted, date accessed
- **Book**—publisher and publisher's location, library call number, relevant page numbers
- **Encyclopedia**—name and year of encyclopedia, publisher, publisher's location
- **Periodical article**—name of periodical, page numbers of article

Encyclopedia Article

> Source 2
>
> Kite, Steven. "Dust Bowl." *Encyclopedia of the Great Depression and New Deal.* Ed. James Ciment. 2 vols. Armonk, NY: Sharpe, 2001. Print.

NOTES

Before you take your first note, identify its source by noting its number from your source list. For example, if you are taking notes from an encyclopedia article that you numbered 6 on your source list, begin your notes with that number. Using this system will ensure that you will be able to identify the source of the note.

In addition to listing the source number, also include a specific heading or subtopic for your notes. This will help you group similar ideas as you take more notes. For example, someone writing about how *The Grapes of Wrath* influenced governmental response to the Dust Bowl might create note headings such as *Dust Bowl—living conditions, bank failures;* or *Steinbeck—early writings about Dust Bowl.* Then quote, paraphrase, or summarize your source. End each card with a page number, if one is available.

See page R48 for examples of source cards and notes.

TIP Cutting and pasting phrases, sentences, or paragraphs from a Web page or other electronic file into your research paper is plagiarism—unless you credit the source.

DIFFERENTIATED INSTRUCTION

FOR STRUGGLING READERS

Practice Note-Taking Methods [paired option] Have students work with more-proficient partners to practice taking notes, using this page's instruction as the information to be noted. Also have pairs review additional note-taking methods, such as a Learning Log or Main Idea and Details chart. Have them practice more than one method to note the same information, as in this example of a partial Main Idea and Details chart:

Main Ideas	Details
1. Make a source list.	*A. When using index cards, create a separate card for each source.*
	B. Give each source a number.

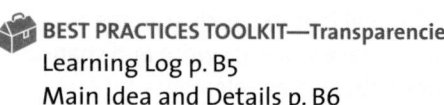 **BEST PRACTICES TOOLKIT—Transparencies**
Learning Log p. B5
Main Idea and Details p. B6

PARAPHRASES AND SUMMARIES

A **paraphrase** is a restatement of an author's ideas in your own words. It includes all the ideas in the original statement and is about the same length as the original text. A **summary** is also a restatement, but it includes only key ideas and is therefore shorter than the original text. As these examples show, paraphrasing and summarizing carefully will help you avoid plagiarism.

Original Source

> With the introduction of the Soil Conservation Service (SCS) in 1935, the federal government began educating farmers in environmentally friendly farming techniques, such as shelterbelts, crop rotation, and introduction of soil-stabilizing grasses, terracing, and contour plowing.
>
> Kite, Steven. "Dust Bowl." *Encyclopedia of the Great Depression and New Deal*

Responsible Paraphrase

> Government response to dust storms   Source 2
>
> The government also established the Soil Conservation Service in 1935. This program taught farmers to terrace their crops, plow along naturally occuring contours in the land, rotate crops, and practice other farming techniques that would protect the topsoil (110).

Carefully restates information; provides source number and page number

Responsible Summary

> Government response to dust storms   Source 2
>
> The government also established the Soil Conservation Service in 1935, which taught farmers techniques to protect the topsoil (110).

Skillfully condenses original passage; includes source number and page number

The following examples show how sloppy paraphrasing and careless summarizing can lead to plagiarism.

Plagiarized Paraphrase

> Government response to dust storms
>
> The government introduced the Soil Conservation Service in 1935 to educate farmers in environmentally friendly farming techniques, including crop rotation, terracing, and contour plowing.

Reproduces several phrases from the original without explaining where words and ideas came from

Plagiarized Summary

> Government response to dust storms
>
> In 1935 the federal government introduced the Soil Conservation Service to teach farmers environmentally friendly farming techniques.

Takes a key phrase—"environmentally friendly farming techniques"—from the source without credit

RESEARCH STRATEGIES WORKSHOP   **1353**

PARAPHRASES AND SUMMARIES

Focus students' attention on the examples of responsible paraphrase and summary. To check understanding, ask

- Why is the example on the left a paraphrase while the example on the right is a summary? *Possible answer: The paraphrase does not omit any of the source's ideas, and it is the same length as the source. The summary omits minor ideas and is shorter than the source.*

- How can you tell that these examples use the source material responsibly? *Possible answer: They alter the wording and sentence structure of the source.*

- Identify the page number and source number. *Answer: The page number is 110; the source number is 2.*

Then focus students' attention on the examples of plagiarized paraphrase and summary. Ask

- Which phrases in the paraphrase either come directly from the original or are similar to the original except for slight changes such as a different part of speech? *Possible answer: The phrases are* Introduced the Soil Conservation Service in 1935; to educate farmers; in environmentally friendly farming techniques; *and* crop rotation, . . . terracing, and contour plowing.

- How could the summary be rewritten to make it responsible? *Possible answer: " . . . Service, whose goal was to show farmers how to use methods that would not harm the environment."*

Reteaching Worksheets on <u>thinkcentral.com</u>
Research and Study Skills Lesson 12: Paraphrasing

Research and Study Skills Lesson 13: Summarizing

R RESOURCE MANAGER—Copy Master
Paraphrases and Summaries p. 20

FOR ADVANCED LEARNERS/AP

Practice Responsible Paraphrasing and Summarizing [paired option] Have advanced learners work with less-proficient partners to guide the latter in the skill of responsible paraphrasing and summarizing. Instruct students to select a paragraph in a nonfiction book. Have the advanced learner write a paraphrase and a summary of the paragraph, deliberately making one of them responsible and the other plagiaristic. Challenge the less-proficient partner to determine which is which and to explain why. Then have the partners switch roles so that the less-proficient partner composes the paraphrase and the summary and the advanced learner determines which is responsible and which is plagiaristic. Have the advanced learner suggest revisions if necessary.

Avoiding Plagiarism

QUOTE INFORMATION ACCURATELY

- Have students find the quoted phrase in the correctly quoted example and then in the original source. Ask why the writer chose to quote that phrase directly. ***Possible answer: The phrase is vivid, enabling the reader to visualize the human aspect of the Dust Bowl.***

- Challenge students to paraphrase the phrase a *gritty nightmare* responsibly so that quoting would be unnecessary. They probably will conclude that the paraphrases do not work as well. Offer that conclusion as a criterion for deciding to quote directly.

CREDIT INFORMATION AND IDEAS FROM OTHERS

- Students may wonder where to draw the line between common knowledge and facts requiring citation. Offer this rule of thumb: If students find the same fact in three or more sources, they may consider it common knowledge. Remind them that when writing the fact in their own words, they should not use the wording of any of their sources.

- Advise students to check the accuracy of facts that they feel are common knowledge. Sometimes, a "fact" that one has believed to be true turns out not to be a fact at all. For example, a student who "knows" that Plymouth was the first English settlement in what is now the United States might be surprised to find that, in fact, the first permanent English settlement was at Jamestown.

Reteaching Worksheets on <u>thinkcentral.com</u>
  Research and Study Skills Lesson 9: Avoiding Plagiarism

R RESOURCE MANAGER—Copy Master
Quote Information Accurately p. 21

Avoiding Plagiarism

By quoting and crediting information properly, you can include important ideas in your paper without plagiarizing them.

QUOTE INFORMATION ACCURATELY

Sometimes an idea is so significant or original that you want to reproduce it exactly as it was originally expressed. Place quotation marks around every word or phrase you take verbatim, or word for word, from a source. If you change the whole sentence except for one key phrase, that phrase still belongs to its author.

Original Source

> Life in what the newspapers call the Dust Bowl is becoming a gritty nightmare.
>
> Low, Ann Marie. *Dust Bowl Diary*. Qtd. in McElvaine, Robert S. *The Depression and New Deal: A History in Documents*

Plagiarized

Dust Bowl—Impact on farm families   Source 7

In human terms, the Dust Bowl was a time of terrible suffering. Day by day, it was a gritty nightmare.

Does a good job of creating a new context, but the words "gritty nightmare" are not enclosed in quotation marks.

Correctly Quoted

Dust Bowl—Impact on farm families   Source 7

In human terms, the Dust Bowl was a time of terrible suffering. Day by day, it was "a gritty nightmare," a young North Dakotan named Ann Marie Low wrote in her diary (135).

Quotation marks and attribution show that the phrase "gritty nightmare" comes from a source.

CREDIT INFORMATION AND IDEAS FROM OTHERS

Sometimes it is difficult to know what needs to be credited and what does not. These tips can help you decide:

- **You must credit others' ideas.** Authors don't just compile facts and quotations; they give opinions and draw conclusions as well. If your paper includes a theory, explanation, or suggestion that you did not develop yourself, be sure to cite its source. For example, if one of your sources states that the Dust Bowl was more devastating than the stock-market crash, you must tell your reader where you found that assertion.

- **You do not need to credit facts that are considered common knowledge.** For instance, well-known historical information such as "Abraham Lincoln was president of the United States" does not need documentation. Neither do well-known sayings such as "Beauty is only skin deep" or general information such as "The sun rises in the east" and "Governments collect taxes from citizens and businesses." However, when in doubt, cite your source or sources.

DIFFERENTIATED INSTRUCTION

FOR STRUGGLING READERS
Vocabulary Support

- *significant*, "important"

- *gritty*, "rough"

- *attribution*, "credit for being the source of something"

- *devastating*, "destructive"

- *common knowledge*, "things that the average person knows"

FOR ADVANCED LEARNERS/AP

Practice Avoiding Plagiarism Ask students to write an abstract of an article in a current issue of a newspaper that deals with a topic of interest to them. Instruct students to include one correctly quoted phrase or sentence from the article and one plagiarized phrase or sentence. Have students label or highlight these elements in distinctive ways, such as with different colors or different symbols. Check their work informally.

Becoming a Critical Researcher

A critical researcher is one who carefully considers information from different
sources and synthesizes that information to develop his or her own view of a topic.

Verifying Information

As you examine multiple sources, you may find information that appears to be
incorrect. Here's how to review and evaluate sources that contradict each other.

RECONCILE DIFFERENCES

Even credible experts can disagree. For example, historians disagree on exactly
when the Dust Bowl era started and on how many people abandoned their
homes because of it. When you encounter varying sources, use the criteria
listed on page 1348 to determine which sources are credible. If they all appear
to be credible, you could state in your paper that opinions vary and then describe
the range that the different sources present.

Where can you check facts? Consult reputable print and online sources, such
as encyclopedias, almanacs, and library databases. Here are some examples of
reputable online sources.

FOR MORE INFORMATION . . .	TRY THIS ONLINE SOURCE
U.S. population statistics	www.census.gov (U.S. Bureau of the Census)
Primary sources, maps, audio, and video related to American history	www.loc.gov (Library of Congress)
Facts about the U.S. government	www.firstgov.gov (official U.S. government Web portal)
Facts about your state's history	your state's official Web site (visit www.firstgov.gov and click on "State Government")
International data	www.un.org (United Nations)
Information on technology	www.computerhistory.org (Computer History Museum) www.cnn.com/tech (CNN Technology News)
Data and resources on the environment	www.epa.gov (Environmental Protection Agency) www.webdirectory.com (The Environment Directory)
Information on space science	www.nasa.gov (NASA)

Becoming a Critical Researcher
Verifying Information

COMMON CORE RI 7 W 7 W 8 W 9

RECONCILE DIFFERENCES

- Ask students to suggest content areas in
  which they are likely to find varying expert
  opinions about the same topic. **Possible
  answer:** *critics' interpretations of literary or
  artistic works; historians' or social scientists'
  views on the causes and effects of events or
  social structures; scientists' theories on the
  origins of phenomena such as life and the
  universe. Even mathematicians may disagree
  about whether a given conjecture can be
  proven true.*

- Have pairs of students develop questions
  to pose that could be answered by one or
  more of the online sources listed. Challenge
  students to find the answers online and to
  report their findings to the class.

R RESOURCE MANAGER—Copy Master
Verifying Information p. 22

FOR ENGLISH LANGUAGE LEARNERS

Oral Language The list in **Try This Online
Source** gives students a further opportunity
to practice pronouncing Web addresses. (See
the **For English Language Learners** note on
page 1346.) Point out that the *un* in *www.
un.org* is pronounced as in "U.N.," not as
in the prefix *un*. Similarly, the *loc* in *www.
loc.gov* and the *epa* in *www.epa.gov* would
be pronounced as if spelled out, using long
vowels.

FOR ADVANCED LEARNERS/AP

Compare and Contrast Sources Use the
example of the Dust Bowl to give students
practice in finding disagreements among
reputable sources. Have students check
three or more sources to find out when the
Dust Bowl started and how many people
were displaced by it. Have students report
their findings, including discrepancies
and/or disagreements, and discuss how
they would describe their findings in a
research paper.

Detecting Bias

QUESTIONS TO HELP YOU DETECT BIAS

Have students practice detecting bias in a published work of nonfiction. Ask students to select articles about current events or personalities, making their choices from reputable general-interest magazines. Instruct them to read the articles and then to use the questions on the list to test them for bias. Have them report their findings orally to the class, showing the articles and reading examples of bias aloud; then invite discussion about the validity of these analyses. Students should find that subtle bias can be found even in works that seem objective.

Developing Your Own Perspective

MAKE INFERENCES AND DRAW CONCLUSIONS

- Remind students that an inference may be reasonable or unreasonable (justified or unjustified; supported or unsupported; weak or strong), depending upon whether the evidence supports or contradicts the inference.

- Clarify that making an inference, or a logical guess, is a step toward drawing a conclusion. Inferences often are based upon incomplete evidence; conclusions are formed after one has weighed all the relevant facts and inferences.

Reteaching Worksheets on **thinkcentral.com**
Reading Lesson 8: Making Inferences
Reading Lesson 9: Drawing Conclusions

R **RESOURCE MANAGER—Copy Masters**
Detecting Bias p. 23
Drawing Conclusions from Your Research p. 24

Detecting Bias

Bias is a preference or an attitude that can prevent a person from presenting information clearly and truthfully. Personal preferences and beliefs can sometimes be presented as facts. Sometimes bias is obvious; at other times it is very subtle.

QUESTIONS TO HELP YOU DETECT BIAS

- Who is the author, and what is his or her **background?** Does this person have ethical beliefs or personal experiences that might influence the writing?

- Why did the author write this piece? Did the **intent** influence his or her point of view? A person wishing to persuade readers may not fully present opposing viewpoints. For example, someone who contends that John Steinbeck single-handedly changed the government's response to migrant workers might leave out information about early government programs, private charities' efforts, and other artists' and writers' coverage of the problem.

- Are the writer's statements based on **verifiable evidence,** or are they speculation?

- Are **enough facts** presented to give a solid basis for the conclusions?

- Is the evidence **balanced,** or does one side get more support?

- How has the **time period** influenced the author's view of events or issues being discussed? For instance, a person writing during the Depression might be affected by the anxiety and despair of the time.

- Does the writer use **loaded language** that has extremely positive or extremely negative connotations, such as "Greedy bankers grew rich while despairing farmers starved"?

Developing Your Own Perspective

Each time you take notes, make connections by mentally attaching that note to something else you have read or discovered. As you synthesize more information, you will begin to develop your own viewpoint on your topic.

MAKE INFERENCES AND DRAW CONCLUSIONS

As you research, read between the lines of the author's words to find implied meanings and attitudes. An **inference** is a logical assumption that is based on observations or information in a text and one's own knowledge and experience. This chart shows the inference that one student made.

What the Source Says	What I Already Know	My Inference
Between 1929 and 1932, farm prices fell 55 percent.	The Great Depression started in 1929. The Dust Bowl started in the early 1930s.	Farmers were in serious trouble even before the Dust Bowl started.

DIFFERENTIATED INSTRUCTION

FOR STRUGGLING READERS

Concept Support [small-group option] Have students use an Open Mind diagram to record words and phrases that they might use to detect signs of bias in an author's work, using the questions and boldfaced terms on this page as sources. Ask students to share their diagrams in small groups, explaining the terms in their own words.

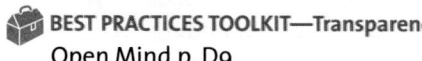 **BEST PRACTICES TOOLKIT—Transparency**
Open Mind p. D9

FOR ADVANCED LEARNERS/AP

Experiment with Loaded Language [paired option] Challenge pairs of students to create a three-column chart about loaded language. In the center column, have them list several statements in neutral, objective language. In the left-hand column, have them restate the same thoughts in language with negative connotations; in the right-hand column, have them use language with positive connotations. Encourage students to share their charts with the class.

If making an inference is "reading between the lines," then drawing a conclusion is "reading beyond the lines." A **conclusion** is a judgment or statement of belief based on evidence, experience, and reasoning. Making inferences is one of the necessary steps in drawing a conclusion, as you can see in this example.

What Sources Say	My Inferences	My Conclusion
John Steinbeck lived with migrant workers for about three years before he published *The Grapes of Wrath*.	Steinbeck's portrayal of the migrants was probably accurate.	*The Grapes of Wrath* was accurate, but not everyone wanted to believe its message.
Some growers in California got *The Grapes of Wrath* banned from several public libraries.	The book was controversial.	

DRAFT YOUR THESIS

As you read and take notes, think about what you are learning. Your thesis should be taking shape in your mind. That is, you will synthesize all that you have learned and thought about during your research. You will draw a larger conclusion about the topic you named in your goal statement.

This chart demonstrates the process of drafting a thesis based on your research.

Facts from My Research	My Conclusions	My Thesis
The Grapes of Wrath was published in 1939 and immediately became a best seller.	*The Grapes of Wrath* was one of the most important and influential novels of its era.	*The Grapes of Wrath* did not significantly affect the government's response to those who suffered from the effects of the Dust Bowl.
The President and the First Lady publicly discussed the book.		
As early as 1935, there were government programs to help Dust Bowl victims.	John Steinbeck was just one of many politicians, artists, and activists who were deeply concerned about the migrants.	
Many other writers and photographers chronicled the problems of the migrant laborers.		

Now it's time to put all your research and thinking to good use. In the next section, you will learn how to draft, revise, and perfect a research paper.

DRAFT YOUR THESIS

- Remind students that a thesis is a statement of the main idea of a piece of writing.

- Explain that synthesizing information means combining pieces of information with other pieces of information and/or prior knowledge or experience to gain a better understanding of a subject or to create a new idea. The writer of a research paper synthesizes information from a variety of sources to present a topic through a personal perspective, in a new way. The process begins with the note-taking phase of research and the cross-referencing of information from several sources. Summaries and paraphrases may synthesize information from multiple sources. These steps prepare the way for synthesizing information in the draft of a research paper.

- Direct students' attention to the chart. Discuss the three columns; elicit that there are fewer conclusions than facts and fewer theses than conclusions. Ask students why the notes narrow in this way. **Possible answer:** *To be valid, a conclusion needs to be based on multiple facts. A research paper should be unified around a single thesis, but its details may involve specific conclusions that support the thesis.*

FOR STRUGGLING READERS

Comprehension Support Use this opportunity to wrap up and re-examine the Research Strategies Workshop. Invite students to ask questions about any parts of the workshop for which they still need clarification. Allow volunteers to answer the questions whenever possible. Advise students to consult the Research Strategies Workshop frequently as they go on to write a research paper in the Writing Workshop.

FOR ADVANCED LEARNERS/AP

Synthesize Invite students to discuss how they expect to use this workshop as a resource when writing their research paper. Have them share their ideas with the class to enrich all students' planning for this project. You might recommend additional works on the research process, such as *A Manual for Writers of Research Papers, Theses, and Dissertations,* by Kate L. Turabian et al., or Joseph Gibaldi's *MLA Handbook for Writers of Research Papers*.

Focus and Motivate

COMMON CORE FOCUS

W 2a–f Write informative texts to examine and convey complex ideas, concepts, and information clearly and accurately. **W 4** Produce clear and coherent writing appropriate to task, purpose, and audience. **W 5** Strengthen writing by revising, editing, rewriting, or trying a new approach. **W 7** Conduct sustained research projects to answer a question. **W 8** Gather relevant information from multiple sources; assess the strength and limitations of each source; avoid plagiarism and overreliance on one source; follow a standard format for citation. **W 9** Draw evidence from informative texts to support research. **L 2** Demonstrate command of the conventions of standard English capitalization, punctuation, and spelling.

WRITE WITH A PURPOSE

Tell students to think of an interesting research question. Remind them to present evidence to convince their audience that their conclusions are valid.

COMMON CORE TRAITS

Review the *COMMON CORE TRAITS* with students, concentrating on development of ideas and organization of ideas. Compare the list of traits with the rubric on page 1375.

ADDITIONAL TASK

Write About Fine Art Choose a notable work of art; then use research to draw a conclusion about its significance. Consider the artist's biography as well as the particular elements of the work and its position in art history.

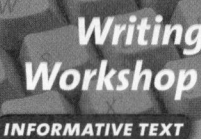

Writing Workshop
INFORMATIVE TEXT

Research Paper

 *Essential Course of Study* ECOS

As you have seen in this unit, the purpose of conducting research isn't simply to repeat information that you have read elsewhere. Rather, the goal is to draw your own conclusions about a research question based on a variety of sources. In this workshop, you will select, organize, synthesize, and analyze information in a carefully documented research paper.

 Complete the workshop activities in your **Reader/Writer Notebook**.

WRITE WITH A PURPOSE

WRITING TASK

Think of a research question that interests you, and write a **research paper** that fully investigates the question and answers it with ample evidence. Keep your audience in mind as you gather evidence and details to support your controlling idea.

Idea Starters
- how cable news channels affect political campaigns
- the effect of *The Grapes of Wrath* on perceptions of Dust Bowl migrants
- how big-box chain stores have changed small towns in the United States

THE ESSENTIALS

Here are some common purposes, audiences, and formats for research papers.

PURPOSES	AUDIENCES	FORMATS
• to share your research with others who are interested in the subject • for personal education • to fulfill a requirement at work or school	• classmates and teacher • friends with a shared interest in the topic • academic journal readers • co-workers	• research paper for class • school's literary magazine • school's Web site • an academic journal • Web log

COMMON CORE TRAITS

1. DEVELOPMENT OF IDEAS
- introduces a clearly defined **topic** and states a **controlling idea** that answers a research question
- supports the topic with **evidence** from multiple authoritative sources
- provides a **concluding section** that supports the information

2. ORGANIZATION OF IDEAS
- organizes ideas, information, and evidence in a **logical way**
- uses **appropriate transitions** to create **cohesion** and **clarify relationships** among ideas

3. LANGUAGE FACILITY AND CONVENTIONS
- maintains a **formal style** and **objective tone**
- uses **precise language** and **domain-specific vocabulary**
- uses **standard formatting** for quoting or citing sources
- employs correct **grammar, mechanics,** and **spelling**

Writing Online THINK central

Go to **thinkcentral.com**.
KEYWORD: HML11N-1358

Writing Workshop Resources

 **RESOURCE MANAGER UNIT 7**
Plan and Teach pp. 5–10
Prewriting–Editing pp. 11–26
Technology p. 27
Writing Support p. 28*

BEST PRACTICES TOOLKIT

TECHNOLOGY
- **Teacher One Stop DVD-ROM**
- **Student One Stop DVD-ROM**
- **Write*Smart* CD-ROM**
- **GrammarNotes DVD-ROM**

Writing Center on thinkcentral.com

*See resources on the **Teacher One Stop DVD-ROM** and on **thinkcentral.com**.*

* Resources for Differentiation

Planning/Prewriting

COMMON CORE W 2a–f Write informative/explanatory texts to examine complex ideas clearly and accurately. **W 5** Develop and strengthen writing as needed. **W 7** Conduct research projects to answer a question or solve a problem.

Getting Started

ANALYZE THE TASK

As you review the writing task, circle words and phrases that tell you what you have to produce. Underline important details about the assignment. Take a few minutes to think about what you have to do and how you will do it. If you have questions about acceptable topics, format, paper length, or anything else, now is the time to ask your teacher.

SELECT A TOPIC

Explore a subject that interests you by brainstorming, asking questions, freewriting, or conferring with others. Try to settle on a topic for which you will be able to find a variety of sources. You must go beyond other people's ideas and find an original approach. Your topic should be narrow enough to be fully developed, yet not too narrow to support a full-length research paper.

THINK ABOUT AUDIENCE AND PURPOSE

Consider your **purpose** for writing: to answer a research question, support your findings with evidence, and share your findings with your **audience** (a wide range of teens and adults). Keep in mind that when you share the information, you should avoid merely repeating facts. Instead, produce a paper that **synthesizes,** or combines, information from multiple authoritative sources, analyzes it, and draws conclusions. You will need to be able to articulate the **significance** of your topic.

▶ WHAT DOES IT LOOK LIKE?

Analyzing the task:

<u>Think of a research question</u> that interests you

This is my starting point for exploring a topic.

...and (write a research paper)

This is the genre for my writing.

...that fully <u>investigates the question and answers it with ample evidence.</u>

This is what will make my research paper successful.

▶ WHAT DOES IT LOOK LIKE?

Freewrite

The Grapes of Wrath is such a vivid picture of what one family went through in Oklahoma, on the road, and in California. Maybe Steinbeck was just writing a good story, or maybe he was trying to be a political activist and cause change. I wonder whether this book caused people to make changes to help others who were going through these difficult times. Did Steinbeck's novel really make a difference?

▶ ASK YOURSELF:

- What might my audience already know about this topic? What information might be new to them?
- How can I help my audience better understand complex information?
- What background information do I need to present to enable my audience to grasp concepts and ideas?
- What **domain-specific vocabulary,** or specialized terminology, will my audience already be familiar with?

Planning/ Prewriting

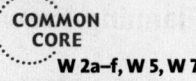

COMMON CORE W 2a–f, W 5, W 7

▶ **ANALYZE THE TASK** After students have marked key words and phrases in the task, have them restate the task as a list of writing requirements. Invite questions about the task, before having students continue.

▶ **SELECT A TOPIC**

- Suggest that students decide upon a subject area they would like to focus on, such as history, science, or literature. Then, have students look through applicable textbooks, notes, and any other materials available in the classroom and make a list of topics that may interest them. Tell students that topics can often span more than one subject area.

- Have students create KWL charts for topics that interest them. In the *K* column, they should write what they already know about the topic, and under *W*, they should write what they want to know. As they complete their research, they can fill in the *L* column with what they have learned.

▶ **THINK ABOUT AUDIENCE AND PURPOSE**

- Have students identify and list the types of questions the audience might have about their topic.

- To make sure that students synthesize information, have them list the different viewpoints presented by multiple authoritative sources.

R RESOURCE MANAGER—Copy Master
Selecting and Shaping a Topic, p. 11

DIFFERENTIATED INSTRUCTION

FOR ENGLISH LANGUAGE LEARNERS

Language: Reinforce Research Terms Write these terms on the board and review them with students:

- *bias:* leaning to one side, partiality to one point of view over another, prejudice

- *parenthetical citation:* a note inside a set of parentheses citing the source of information

- *primary sources:* materials written or created by people who were present at events

- *secondary sources:* accounts written by people who were not directly involved in or witnesses to an event

- *synthesize:* combine information and ideas to make new ideas

Planning/Prewriting *continued*

▶ **WRITE A RESEARCH QUESTION**
Encourage students to look for general articles in a print or online encyclopedia. If students are interested in watching a video, encourage them to look for a short documentary at their local library.

▶ **IDENTIFY RELATED QUESTIONS** Emphasize that students should not censor themselves as they write related questions. Tell students to approach writing the questions as a freewriting activity. After they have created their list of questions, have students review them to narrow or broaden their area of research.

▶ **MAKE A RESEARCH PLAN** Tell students that, at this point, they do not have to list the specific sources they plan on using in their paper. Emphasize that students can list possible sources that they came across while creating their research question and list print and digital resources they plan to use to search for information, such as a specific database, Web site, reference book, magazine, or newspaper.

YOUR TURN Set aside an ample amount of time for students to create a research question, related questions, and a research plan. Remain available for questions and guidance as students complete the *Your Turn* activity independently. Provide students with specific suggestions for improving their research plans. Review their revised research plans to be sure that they have implemented your suggestions.

For interactive graphic organizers, see

💿 **Write*Smart* CD-ROM**

Writing Center on thinkcentral.com

Planning/Prewriting *continued*

Getting Started

WRITE A RESEARCH QUESTION
Look for encyclopedia articles, Web sites, or videos about your topic. Don't take notes yet; just read or view to develop background knowledge. Then, use this background knowledge to write a research question.

▶ **WHAT DOES IT LOOK LIKE?**

> *Research Question*
> *Did Steinbeck's novel cause the government to respond to the plight of migrant workers?*

IDENTIFY RELATED QUESTIONS
After you have written a research question, generate additional, **related focused questions** for further research and investigation. This will help you to identify if you need to broaden or narrow your research.

TIP As you identify related questions, you may decide to revise or adopt one of the related questions as your research question.

▶ **WHAT DOES IT LOOK LIKE?**

> *Was Steinbeck the only writer or artist to shed light on the plight of migrant workers?*
>
> *Did government programs address the plight of migrant workers before Steinbeck's book was published?*

MAKE A RESEARCH PLAN
Develop a research plan that outlines your purpose, audience, research question, potential sources, and schedule. Before embarking on your research, you may want to have your teacher review your research plan and offer suggestions for improvement.

▶ **WHAT DOES IT LOOK LIKE?**

> Name: _____
> Purpose: _____
> Audience: _____
> Research Question: _____
>
> Potential Sources: _____
>
> **SCHEDULE**
> Research Due: _____
> First Draft Due: _____
> Final Draft Due: _____
>
> Teacher Approval/Suggestions: _____

PEER REVIEW Describe your research topic and research plan to a peer. Then, ask: Is my research topic narrow enough? Is it too narrow? Will my research plan allow me to explore a variety of perspectives? Do you have any suggestions for other types of sources I could explore?

 YOUR TURN Decide on a topic for your research paper. Then, after developing background knowledge, create a research question, related questions, and a research plan in your *Reader/Writer Notebook*.

DIFFERENTIATED INSTRUCTION

FOR STRUGGLING WRITERS
Write a Research Question To help students write a research question, have them create a web of words and phrases that they associate with their topic. Instruct students to circle the most interesting entries and then brainstorm for questions that relate to those entries.

FOR ADVANCED LEARNERS/AP
Create a Quiz Have partners use the information on page 1361 to create a short quiz that covers investigating and assessing sources.

Researching

 **COMMON CORE** W 8 Gather relevant information from multiple sources; assess the strength and limitations of each source; avoid plagiarism and overreliance on one source; follow a standard format for citation. W 9 Draw evidence from texts to support research.

Teach

Researching

▶ **INVESTIGATE POSSIBLE SOURCES** Review the wide ranges of sources available to students, as discussed in the Research Strategies Workshop. Explain to students the importance of not relying too heavily on one source. An individual source also may be biased or contain inaccuracies. Using multiple sources enables students to verify the accuracy and credibility of information and exposes them to a variety of viewpoints.

▶ **ASSESS EACH SOURCE**

- Set up a computer so that the screen page is displayed on a white board or pull-down screen. Navigate the Internet, showing students examples of acceptable and unacceptable Web sites. Also, visit a notable newspaper's Web site, such as http://www.nytimes.com. Point out the bias in the opinion pieces versus the objective nature of other articles. You may also want to point out Web sites that students may find useful as they are researching, such as the Web site of your local library and http://www.pbs.org.

- Suggest that students use a Monitoring chart to evaluate how well they understand their sources—an important step in evaluating the overall usefulness of a source.

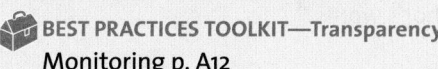 **BEST PRACTICES TOOLKIT—Transparency** Monitoring p. A12

Following Your Research Plan

INVESTIGATE POSSIBLE SOURCES

Make sure you investigate multiple sources for your research. This will help you build a broader understanding of your topic and encounter the perspectives of a variety of authorities. Also, try to locate both primary and secondary sources. **Primary sources** are firsthand, original accounts, and **secondary sources** include information derived from, or about, primary or other secondary sources.

Make use of both print and digital resources. In addition to what you might find at the library or on the Internet, consider other sources, such as museums, historical sites, or personal interviews.

ASK YOURSELF:

- Where can I find texts that have been written for informed audiences?
- Where can I find an expert on my topic whom I can interview?
- Where can I write a letter or an e-mail requesting additional information from someone?
- How can I locate a museum or historical site that I can visit to find applicable information?
- What databases could provide me with relevant information?
- Which librarian or teacher who could help me access appropriate databases and search engines?

ASSESS EACH SOURCE

Before taking the time to read or further explore sources, assess the strengths and limitations of each source by evaluating its relevance, reliability, and accuracy. A source is **relevant** if it relates to the topic you are researching and **credible** when the information it presents is reliable and well-documented. For **accuracy,** seek up-to-date information published by major universities or established, credible publishing companies.

Evaluate Internet sources to see who created the site and where the person or institution found the information. Avoid Web sites with *.com* or *.net* in their addresses. Usually, Web sites with *.org*, *.gov*, or *.edu* in their addresses are more reliable.

TIP When conducting research using digital sources or the Internet, make the most effective use of the advanced searches by filling in as many of the search parameters as you can. This will help filter out any unwanted sources or Web sites, narrowing down the number of sources you need to look through.

WHAT DOES IT LOOK LIKE?

Reasons for Rejecting or Accepting Sources

"Dust Bowl Days": This Web site doesn't name the author's credentials. It has no footnotes or bibliography. Therefore, I should reject this source.

"Best Sellers of the Week": I acquired this newspaper article from an established, credible newspaper (*New York Times*). The article was published in 1939; however, it is a primary source, so its date of publication is acceptable. Therefore, I can accept this source.

"On the Cause of the 1930s Dust Bowl": This is an article about the weather patterns that created the Dust Bowl. Although it is a well-documented article, it doesn't relate to my specific topic. Therefore, I should reject this source.

FOR STRUGGLING WRITERS

Assess Sources Ask students to consider whether each source meets each of the Four R's: whether it is relevant, recent, reliable, and representative. You may want to have students fill out a 4R chart with a row for each resource and a column for each of the Four R's.

FOR ADVANCED LEARNERS/AP

Compare and Contrast Sources Point out that in addition to choosing among different categories of sources (such as Web sites, magazine articles, and books), researchers also must compare and contrast sources within a type. For example, a researcher might need to decide which of three biographies of an author will be the best source of information about the author's political views. Urge students to look for two or more sources per category for

their topic. Suggest that they create a Comparison Matrix chart to aid in evaluating those sources, using criteria of their choice.

 **BEST PRACTICES TOOLKIT—Transparency** Comparison Matrix p. A24

Researching continued

▶ **PREPARE A SOURCE LIST** Point out that in preparing to do a research paper, writers will usually consult more sources than they ultimately include in their research papers; thus it is typical to include more sources in a source list than will ultimately be used. Emphasize that it is better to begin with too many sources than too few. Have students examine the sample source listing and verify that all of the information is used in the source's entry on the Works Cited list on page 1373.

▶ **TAKE NOTES**

- Emphasize the importance of recording information correctly. Tell students that if they quote the author's words exactly, they must put quotation marks around the words.

- Stress that students should paraphrase and summarize when possible, reserving direct quotations for particularly vivid quotes whose impact depends on their being presented in the author's own words.

- Explain that paraphrasing means presenting the information in one's own words and sentence structure by rewriting the sentences, not merely substituting synonyms for the author's words.

Researching continued

Following Your Research Plan

PREPARE A SOURCE LIST

When you have decided which sources to keep, create an electronic source list or a series of source cards. Assign each source a number. Record full publishing information for each source and write short notes about the content and value of the source. Also note library call numbers. This information will help you later as you take notes. It will also help you follow a standard format when you compile a Works Cited list.

▶ **WHAT DOES IT LOOK LIKE?**

Sources	Comments
"Timeline." *American Experience: Surviving the Dust Bowl*. Pub. Broadcasting Svc. n.d. Web. 17 Apr. 2010.	• lists several government responses to Dust Bowl • Dust Bowl events and responses are shown in an easy-to-read timeline format

TAKE NOTES

Read each source carefully as you look for answers to your research question and related questions. If necessary, modify the research question to accommodate the information you encounter. Use these guidelines for taking notes:

1. **Use an electronic file or note-taking software to record notes.** Make your notes easy to sort and group by entering notes on individual pages, or make separate databases or worksheet entries for each note. If you would rather write notes, use a notebook or index cards.

2. **Write a label or heading.** In the upper left-hand corner of the file, identify the main idea of your note.

3. **Record each piece of information.**
   Quote directly: Use the writer's exact words, enclosed in quotation marks.
   Paraphrase: Rewrite a passage in your own words and style.
   Summarize: Present only the main points of a passage.

4. **Record the source number and page number(s).** In the upper right-hand corner of each note, write the number of your source. Write page numbers at the bottom of your notes.

▶ **WHAT DOES IT LOOK LIKE?**

<u>Separate electronic worksheet entries for sources</u>

Federal programs   **1**
before *The Grapes of Wrath*
The Shelterbelt program started in 1937. The government paid farmers to plant trees so that less topsoil would blow away. By 1938, the tree planting and other methods had reduced blowing soil by 65 percent (4).

Firsthand account of   **5**
Dust Bowl conditions
Ann Marie Low, a young North Dakotan, wrote in her diary that each day was "a gritty nightmare." She stated that sometimes dirt "lay inches deep on everything. Every towel and curtain was just black" (134, 135).

President Franklin Roosevelt's   **5**
response to the book
In a January 1940 radio address, President Franklin Roosevelt said, "I have read a book recently; it is called *Grapes of Wrath*. There are 500,000 Americans that live in the covers of that book" (148).

DIFFERENTIATED INSTRUCTION

FOR ENGLISH LANGUAGE LEARNERS
Writing: Source List Entries [mixed-ability pairs] Have pairs of students read the source list entry in WHAT DOES IT LOOK LIKE? Have the more fluent student in each pair ensure that the less-proficient student understands (1) what kind of source the note refers to, (2) what the student writer says about the source, and (3) how each comment relates to the source's value. Then, have pairs reread the research question on page 1360 and discuss whether the student writer will most likely use the source.

Researching *continued*

Following Your Research Plan

DRAFT A CONTROLLING IDEA

Review your notes, and then develop your research question into a **controlling idea,** or thesis statement. Your controlling idea should have an original focus and should clearly present an interesting question that will be explored in the body of your research report. You can use the following equation to draft a controlling idea to guide you in your writing, but you'll want to polish it up for your final draft.

TOPIC: _____

+ RESEARCH QUESTION: _____

= CONTROLLING IDEA: _____

▶ ASK YOURSELF:

• What recurring ideas appear in the different sources?
• How does all the information I have collected fit together?
• What larger point, or general conclusion, does the information support?
• Are my original ideas about the topic supported or contradicted by the information I have collected?
• Does my controlling idea accurately reflect the information I have collected? If it does not accurately reflect the information, how should I rework it?

CREATE AN OUTLINE

A basic outline can help you organize your ideas, ensuring that each new idea builds on the one preceding it and creates a cohesive research report. Sort your notes into groups with similar headings or labels. Keep rearranging them until you find an order that makes sense. Most writers use one of these types of organization:

• **chronological order:** the order in which events occur
• **logical order:** related ideas grouped together
• **order of importance:** most important ideas to least important or vice versa

You will probably use a combination of these organizational patterns to arrange your main ideas and your supporting examples and details.

▶ WHAT DOES IT LOOK LIKE?

Partial example of an outline
The Grapes of Wrath and the Dust Bowl
I. Background information: The Dust Bowl
   A. What and where it was
   B. When it took place
   C. What people's lives were like
      1. "A gritty nightmare" (Low's diary)
      2. Dust killed children, animals
II. Background information: *The Grapes of Wrath*
   A. Based on Steinbeck's own research
   B. Reaction to the book

 YOUR TURN
Follow your research plan to begin investigating possible sources. Assess each source to determine which ones you plan on using, and compile these sources in a list. Take notes about your sources, and use the notes to write a controlling idea and an outline in your *Reader/Writer Notebook.* If necessary, narrow or broaden your research question so that you can answer it thoroughly in your research paper.

Researching *continued*

▶ DRAFT A CONTROLLING IDEA

• Point out that it is possible the first draft of the controlling idea can become the final version of the controlling idea without alteration. However, explain that because the writing process is recursive, students may have to revise their controlling ideas later, in the drafting or revising phases.

• Have students share their controlling ideas with a partner to ensure that they are clear and coherent. Have partners work together on how their controlling ideas can be improved.

▶ CREATE AN OUTLINE

• Explain how the ideas in the outline shown are organized in logical order. Ask students why the writer might have chosen to organize the ideas this way.

• Some students may not find a formal outline useful. Allow those students to use a graphic organizer such as a flowchart to organize their ideas. Remind students to include the main idea, supporting ideas and evidence, and details in their organizer.

• Use an Outline transparency to help students review the process of outlining and set up their own outlines.

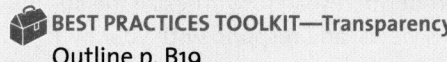 BEST PRACTICES TOOLKIT—Transparency
Outline p. B19

 YOUR TURN
Have students complete the **Your Turn** activity independently, using time during and outside of class. After students have finished, have them share their controlling idea and outline with a partner. Have partners provide each other with questions or concerns they have about the organization of the outline, the topic, or the controlling idea.

For interactive graphic organizers, see
 **Write***Smart* **CD-ROM**
Writing Center on <u>thinkcentral.com</u>

FOR STRUGGLING WRITERS

Create an Outline Have students work with partners to group their notes by subtopics and to put the groups into logical order. Suggest that students mark their notes with different colored highlighters to indicate different levels of headings in their outlines; for instance, they might use a yellow highlighter for headings represented by Roman numerals and a green highlighter for subheadings represented by capital letters.

FOR ENGLISH LANGUAGE LEARNERS

Writing: Paraphrasing To practice paraphrasing, have students read the quotes they plan to use and then close the book and use their own words to tell a partner what the quotes say. Listeners should jot down what their partner says when paraphrasing; students can use their partner's notes to help them write their papers.

Practice and Apply

Drafting

COMMON CORE
W 4, W 8, L 2

▶ **INTRODUCTION** Tell students that the introduction of the Student Draft on page 1367 provides information that is not only interesting but essential. Point out the student writer's use of syntax to arrange words and phrases to grab the reader's attention and get across his controlling idea. Also, explain that the introduction defines the term *Okies*. Then use the Opening Lines strategy to help students draft captivating beginnings for their research papers.

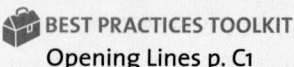
BEST PRACTICES TOOLKIT
Opening Lines p. C1

▶ **BODY** Direct students to page 1367, and have them read the second paragraph in the Student Draft on that page. Elicit that the first sentence of the paragraph relays one of the student writer's interpretations. Ask students how the writer supported his analysis. Then, offer these ways of developing ideas and interpretations about a research topic:

- Find the traditional view of the subject and react to it with an alternative view.

- Connect the topic with other topics in order to provide a nontraditional approach.

- Suggest an interpretation that is unexpected but that still makes sense.

- Do in-depth research, synthesize the author's views, and respond with your own thoughts.

▶ **CONCLUDING SECTION** Tell students that their concluding sections should follow from and support their controlling ideas and the research they gathered. Have students read the concluding section of the Student Draft on page 1371 to see how a student successfully summarizes his ideas in a concluding section.

▶ **WORKS CITED LIST** Explain to students that they must follow specific guidelines when writing their Works Cited lists. Refer students to the Student Draft's Works Cited list on page 1373 and the MLA Citation Guidelines on pages 1376–1377.

Drafting

The following chart shows how to organize your draft to create an effective research paper.

Organizing Your Research Paper

INTRODUCTION

- Begin your paper by drawing the reader into the research. You might include a memorable **quotation** or an interesting **fact** or **detail.**
- Provide background information, an overview of your topic, and a **controlling idea** that includes a clear research question. The controlling idea is often the last sentence of the introductory paragraph.
- Establish and maintain a **formal style** and **objective tone.**
- Use a style manual, such as one produced by the MLA (Modern Language Association).

▼

BODY

- Using your outline as a guide, develop and support each **main point** in a separate paragraph. Incorporate **relevant facts, extended definitions, concrete details, quotations,** and **examples** from your notes to support your main points.
- **Synthesize,** or combine, the ideas and information from multiple sources. If appropriate, compare and contrast ideas from different sources, or show how one source complements, enlarges, or expands on another.
- Analyze a variety of ideas, and provide your own interpretations of them.
- Maintain the **organizational pattern** or combination of organizational patterns that you chose in your outline.
- Include **varied and appropriate transitions** and **syntax** (arrangement of words and phrases) to clarify relationships among ideas and to create cohesion.
- Use **precise language** and define any **domain-specific,** or specialized, **vocabulary** to help clarify concepts for your audience.
- Each time you quote, paraphrase, or summarize information from a source, **document** the source by including a **parenthetical reference** at the end of the sentence or sentences. Do not document information that can be found in several sources or standard reference books.

▼

CONCLUDING SECTION

- Restate the research question and controlling idea that follows from the research you gathered. Summarize the paper's main points.
- Leave your reader with something compelling to think about. For example, you could reflect on the overall **significance** of your topic, or include a compelling quotation.

▼

WORKS CITED LIST

- List all of the sources, print and nonprint, that you credit in your paper. Do not credit sources that you consulted but did not cite in your paper.
- Refer to the MLA guidelines on pages 1376–1377 to list your sources properly.

1364 UNIT 7: THE POWER OF RESEARCH

DIFFERENTIATED INSTRUCTION

FOR ADVANCED LEARNERS/AP

Create a Drafting Guide Invite groups of students to draw upon the information on pages 1364–1365, possibly other research-skills resources, and their past writing experiences to prepare a clear, engaging "how-to" guide for students who might need additional help in turning research notes into the draft of a research paper. The guide should include guidance (instructions and examples) in developing effective introductions and concluding sections, blending material, and incorporating one's own interpretation and analysis of ideas. Invite groups to present their guide; then add it to the classroom library as a permanent reference.

Drafting *continued*

COMMON CORE **W 4** Produce clear and coherent writing. **W 8** Integrate information into the text selectively to avoid plagiarism; follow a standard format for citation. **L 2** Demonstrate a command of the conventions of standard English punctuation.

LEARN HOW Document Your Sources To avoid plagiarism, or copying someone else's work, you must correctly document your sources. Within your paper, use **parenthetical citations,** source references enclosed in parentheses. In general, a parenthetical citation includes the **author's last name** and the **page number** (Himmelberg 9). There are, however, many variations on the use of parenthetical citations.

- **Author already mentioned in sentence:** Give only the page number (110).
- **Author not known:** Use a shortened form of the title of the work ("First Lady").
- **More than one author:** Include last names for up to three authors (Lange and Taylor 409). For more than three authors, use the first author's last name and *et al.* (Zielonka et al. 138–145).
- **More than one source:** Separate the information for each source with a semicolon (Kite 107; "Timeline").
- **More than one work by the same author:** Include a shortened form of the work's title (Steinbeck, *Dubious* 61).

GRAMMAR IN CONTEXT: PUNCTUATING PARENTHETICAL CITATIONS

A **parenthetical citation** should provide enough information to lead the reader to the full source entry in your Works Cited list. Place the citation as close as possible to the material being cited, as in the following MLA guidelines:

Always place the citation before the punctuation mark within a sentence that contains the information from the source.	When Steinbeck wrote "the dawn came, but no day," he was referring to the black clouds that swirled over the Great Plains during these desperate years (Steinbeck 5).
If a quotation ends a sentence, put the citation after the quotation mark, but before the end punctuation.	"I know what I was talking about," he told a reporter in July 1939. "I lived, on and off, with those Okies for the last three years" (Cameron A2).
For a block quotation, insert the final punctuation mark at the end of the quotation. Then, place the citation two spaces after the final punctuation mark.	. . . during the Dust Bowl of the 1930s. Some 2.5 million people fled the Plains states, many bound for California, where the promise of sunshine and a better life often collided with the reality of scarce, poorly paid work as migrant farm laborers. ("Great Depression")

YOUR TURN Using the information in the chart on the previous page, write a draft of your research paper. Maintain a formal style and objective tone, and make sure your draft is of sufficient length and complexity to address the topic. Also, be sure to include correctly formatted parenthetical citations and a Works Cited list.

WRITING WORKSHOP **1365**

FOR ENGLISH LANGUAGE LEARNERS

Writing: Avoid Informal Language Explain to students that informal words or expressions are not acceptable in research papers. If they avoid informal language at the drafting stage, students will be less likely to incorporate colloquialisms and other informal language into their final draft. It may be helpful to create a distribution list of unacceptable words and phrases to save time coaching students individually.

FOR STRUGGLING WRITERS

Parenthetical Citations Write examples of correctly and incorrectly punctuated parenthetical citations on the board. Have students identify the correctly punctuated citations and fix the citations that are incorrectly punctuated. Have volunteers write the revised citations on the board. Then, tell students to create two sentences of their own—one with a correctly punctuated citation and one with an incorrectly punctuated citation.

Practice and Apply

Drafting *continued*

LEARN HOW Document Your Sources

- Go over what is and is not included in parenthetical citations. For instance, there is no comma between the author's name and a page number. Also, if the sentence mentions the author's name or the page number, that is not included in the parentheses.
- Tell students that they should always document sources of these types of information:
  - direct quotations
  - theories, ideas, and opinions other than their own
  - data from surveys, research studies, and interviews conducted by others
  - unusual or questionable facts

GRAMMAR IN CONTEXT: PUNCTUATING PARENTHETICAL CITATIONS

For practice, have students correctly cite the following sentences:

1. After attending Weston-Moore from 1920 to 1923, Brown left to pursue an acting degree with a London-based theater group.
   Source: John Hensel, *The History of Weston-Moore Academy*, p. 12

2. The president's speech explained that "the tenacity of the people" encouraged the government to re-examine their taxation policy.
   Source: Joseph Chang and Carmen Rivera, *The People's Power*, p. 22

3. McMillen felt that no matter how hard he tried, he "could never understand the difficulties the native people faced."
   Source: Nora Hawkins, "Dark Village," online article with no page numbers

YOUR TURN Ask students to complete the *Your Turn* activity independently. Remind students to cite their sources, using correctly punctuated and formatted parenthetical citations and a Works Cited list. Remind students to maintain a formal style and objective tone appropriate to a research paper.

For a research paper writing template, see

 **WriteSmart CD-ROM**
Writing Center on <u>thinkcentral.com</u>

WRITING WORKSHOP **1365**

Revising

COMMON CORE
W 5

Model the Skill Using a draft essay on a transparency or electronic whiteboard, model how to use the questions, tips, and revision strategies suggested in the chart to evaluate and revise. You might use the essay of a student from another class or from last year, or you may even use an essay of your own creation. If you use a student's essay, be sure to remove his or her name from the essay so that he or she remains anonymous.

YOUR TURN Before students meet with their partners, have them write a short note letting their partners know which portions of the draft they think are strongest and which are weakest.

For interactive revision tools, see

Write*Smart* CD-ROM

Writing Center on thinkcentral.com

Revising

When you revise, your goal is to determine whether you've effectively explored and answered a research question based on a variety of evidence. The questions, tips, and strategies in the chart can help you revise or rewrite where necessary.

RESEARCH PAPER

Ask Yourself	Tips	Revision Strategies
1. Does my introduction draw readers in, give an overview of the topic, and clearly state the research question in the controlling idea?	**Underline** the sentence that draws readers in; **bracket** the overview of the topic; **circle** the research question.	**Add** a quotation or interesting detail or fact. **Add** or **elaborate** on background information. **Add** a sentence that clarifies the controlling idea and research question, if necessary.
2. Is the research question explored through several main points? Do facts, details, definitions, quotations, and examples support the main points?	In the margin, **check** each main point that develops the research question. In the text, **double-check** at least one piece of evidence for each main point.	**Add** main points to develop your research. **Delete** points that do not support or relate to the research question. **Elaborate** on each point with relevant textual evidence.
3. Are sources cited when necessary? Do the citations follow a consistent format?	**Place stars** by direct quotations and facts that are not common knowledge.	**Add** documentation for quoted, paraphrased, or summarized material. **Revise** incorrect citations.
4. Are main points organized in a logical way?	**Number** your main points. **Revise** if the organization makes no sense or is unclear.	**Rearrange** the order of ideas for clarity. Try logical or chronological order.
5. Do I maintain a formal style and objective tone throughout the research report?	**Draw a wavy line** under any contractions, slang, or informal or biased language.	**Reword** text to avoid contractions. **Replace** instances of informal language with precise, formal words.
6. Does the concluding section restate the research question, clearly present my concluding statement, and summarize the main points?	**Bracket** the restatement of the research question and your concluding statement. **Highlight** the summary of main ideas.	**Add** a sentence that reminds the reader of the research question. **Clarify** your concluding statement. **Add** a summary of main points.

YOUR TURN **PEER REVIEW** Working with a peer, use this chart to review your draft. Then, revise your paper by making the changes suggested in the right-hand column. Ask your partner if he or she has any suggestions for improvement. If necessary, rework or try a new approach to further improve your paper.

FOR STRUGGLING WRITERS

Eliminate Irrelevant Information Ask students to review their work and ask themselves whether each piece of information is relevant. Explain the process they can use to do this:

- First, students should highlight their controlling idea.

- Next, students should underline the topic sentence of each paragraph and assess its relevance to the controlling idea.

- Finally, students should reread their papers, paragraph by paragraph, to assess how well each piece of information in a given paragraph develops and supports the paragraph's topic sentence.

When students come upon information that does not seem relevant, they must determine whether to eliminate the information, move it to another part of the paper, or revise the paragraph so the information is more clearly connected to the topic sentence.

ANALYZE A STUDENT DRAFT

COMMON CORE

W 5 Strengthen writing by revising, editing, rewriting, or trying a new approach.

Read these excerpts from a student draft; notice the comments on its strengths as well as suggestions for improvement.

Barron 1

Chris Barron
Mrs. Machado
English III
29 April 2010

The Grapes of Wrath: **A Reflection of Real Life**

❶   John Steinbeck's *The Grapes of Wrath,* now considered an American masterpiece, tells the gripping story of a family that abandons its Oklahoma farm during the Dust Bowl of the 1930s. Many people believe that the controversial novel raised public awareness about the suffering of "Okies" who moved to California in search of a better life but found only poverty. Some experts also contend that Steinbeck's novel was the key factor in motivating the government to help these migrant workers.

> In order to present a more effective controlling idea, Chris needs to clarify his major research question.

The Dust Bowl and Worsening Hard Times

❷   To determine how much of an impact Steinbeck's novel had, it is important to have a clear understanding of what the Dust Bowl was and how it affected people. The Dust Bowl was a severe drought combined with high heat and high winds. It occurred mainly in Oklahoma, Nebraska, Kansas, Texas, New Mexico, and Colorado, and it had its center at the Oklahoma panhandle.

> Chris provides **background information** to help his audience understand the topic.

LEARN HOW Craft an Effective Controlling Idea   In his controlling idea, Chris mentions the possibility that the novel influenced government policy, but he does not present a clear research question. Note how Chris revised his controlling idea to include his research question.

CHRIS'S REVISION TO PARAGRAPH ❶

~~Some experts also contend that Steinbeck's novel was the key factor in motivating the government to help these migrant workers.~~

To what degree, then, might Steinbeck's novel have motivated the federal government to implement policies to aid these migrant workers?

ANALYZE A STUDENT DRAFT

Explain that the Student Draft on page 1367 is the first page of a research paper. Model reading the draft and the annotations in blue, and explain that the yellow highlighting illustrates the student's language choices. Explain that the following *Learn How* mini-lessons provide helpful information about the ways to improve this student draft as well as their own.

LEARN HOW   Craft an Effective Controlling Idea

- Emphasize that the student writer's original controlling idea does not relay what the student writer is questioning about the novel's impact on government policy; therefore, readers would have had trouble understanding the path the writer is pursuing.

- Point out to students that, although their controlling idea should present the focus of their research question, it does not have to be in the form of a question. Emphasize that they can include the research question in a statement, as well.

- Have students examine their controlling ideas to determine whether they have clearly expressed their research questions. After students make necessary revisions, have them form small groups and share their research questions and controlling ideas. Have groups discuss whether each student's controlling idea reveals the research question and informs readers of where the writer is headed.

Explain that the Student Draft is continued on this page. Read the draft and annotations aloud and discuss. Ask students to comment on the student writer's use of direct quotations and parenthetical citations.

Barron 2

These conditions lasted about eight years, long enough to carry off tons of topsoil from the over-plowed fields in the region (Egan xi, 5). When Steinbeck wrote "the dawn came, but no day," he was referring to the black clouds that swirled over the Great Plains during these desperate years (Steinbeck 5).

❸ Not all sources agree on when the Dust Bowl started, but some say that the first devastating storms hit in 1931 and suggest that the full-blown condition now called the Dust Bowl actually developed between 1933 and 1935 (Kite 107; "Timeline"). However, hard times were widespread in the area before the drought occurred. The Great Depression began in 1929 when the stock market crashed. The following year, people all across the country lost their jobs, and many banks could not pay their depositors (Egan 95). Farm prices fell sharply, too: between 1929 and 1932, they dove 55 percent (Himmelberg 9). By the time the Dust Bowl started, Midwestern farm families had endured years of low prices and bank failures, and high unemployment rates meant that family members could not find work in nearby cities.

❹ In human terms, the Dust Bowl was a time of terrible suffering. Each day was "a gritty nightmare," a young North Dakotan named Ann Marie Low wrote in her diary. Sometimes dirt "lay inches deep on everything. Every towel and curtain was just black" (McElvaine 134, 135). Homes had to be shoveled out; nothing could be used before it was washed. The dust also choked and killed cattle—and even some children (Egan 5–6). Unable to grow anything on the land, many farm families had to leave the Dust Bowl or die there. The estimate of just how many left varies widely. Depending on how one defines the Dust Bowl area and its dates, the number ranges from 16,000 to 315,000 (Windschuttle). Many families traveled to California in search of work, as Steinbeck describes in his novel.

Chris uses **appropriate and varied transitions** to clarify for the reader the relationships among the ideas.

Chris includes **direct quotations** and uses **parenthetical citations** correctly.

DIFFERENTIATED INSTRUCTION

FOR ENGLISH LANGUAGE LEARNERS
Writing: Transitional Words and Phrases On the board, list several transitions that are useful in research papers, such as *however, yet, but, when, then, before, now, at the time, although, because, also, too, for example,* and *therefore.* Have pairs of students find examples of some of the listed transitions in the student model. Have the same pairs then compose sentences (or pairs of sentences) on any topic, using transitions from the list. As

students read their sentences aloud, correct composition and pronunciation as necessary. Ideally, ask students to compose at least two sentences, each using a different transition.

Barron 3

Reactions to *The Grapes of Wrath*

5   Before Steinbeck began *The Grapes of Wrath,* he wrote newspaper articles about living conditions in the California labor camps (Windschuttle). He used this knowledge in his novel. "I know what I was talking about," he told a reporter in July 1939. "I lived, on and off, with those Okies for the last three years" (Cameron A2). The way the migrants were treated angered and disturbed Steinbeck. In one of the most haunting passages in *The Grapes of Wrath,* he wrote, "[I]n the eyes of the hungry there is a growing wrath. In the souls of the people the grapes of wrath are filling and growing heavy, growing heavy for the vintage" (Steinbeck 477). Because Steinbeck knew his topic so well and presented it with such emotional power, the novel was a huge success. Just two weeks after its publication, it topped bestseller lists in New York, Philadelphia, Washington, Atlanta, San Francisco, and Los Angeles ("Best Sellers").

6   However, the book was not without controversy. When the *Los Angeles Times* reported that some of the migrant workers had sent Steinbeck threatening letters, he responded that it is not: "the refugees who have taken exception to what I wrote. It's the moneyed people back there in Oklahoma . . . If anybody's sore at me for the book it's that kind of people" (Cameron A1–2). Steinbeck's shocking novel brought him some influential enemies.

> Chris synthesizes **facts and details** from **multiple sources,** **quoting** the most memorable and **paraphrasing** or **summarizing** the others.

> Chris needs to revise the way that he has incorporated the textual evidence into this sentence.

LEARN HOW Incorporate Textual Evidence Sentence-length quotations should be incorporated into text with either an introductory phrase followed by a comma or a full sentence followed by a colon. However, if you are using a shorter quote, make the quoted words part of your own sentence. Notice how Chris used more of the direct quote and revised its introduction.

CHRIS'S REVISION TO PARAGRAPH **6**

When the *Los Angeles Times* reported that some of the migrant workers had sent Steinbeck threatening letters, he ~~responded that it is not:~~ *responded, "It isn't the* "the refugees who have taken exception to what I wrote. It's the moneyed people back there in Oklahoma. . . . If anybody's sore at me for the book it's that kind of people" (Cameron A1–2).

ANALYZE A STUDENT DRAFT *continued*

Explain that the Student Draft is continued on this page. Read the draft and annotations aloud and discuss. Ask students to comment on the student writer's ability to synthesize information.

LEARN HOW Incorporate Textual Evidence

- Point out that the student writer revised the text to introduce the quotation with a comma, rather than a colon. Ask students to explain why the colon was used incorrectly in the original text. Elicit from students that the colon was not preceded by a full sentence; therefore, it was not used correctly.

- Ask students to comment on how the student writer's revision affects the flow of the writing. Guide students to understand that the revision is advantageous not only because it is the grammatically correct way to incorporate the quotation, it also gives the text a better flow.

- Have partners read each other's drafts and rate how well each quotation in the text is integrated on a scale of 1–5, 5 being the best. Then, have students consider revising quotes that their partner scored as a 3 or below.

FOR STRUGGLING WRITERS

Examine Integrated Quotations Have partners choose a newspaper or magazine article and examine how the author incorporated quotations into his or her writing. Tell partners to begin by highlighting the quotations. Then, have them note the author's use of commas and/or colons to introduce quotations. Then, have each pair choose the quotation that they think the author incorporated in the most fluid and creative manner.

Have each pair write their chosen quotation on the board and explain why they chose it. Encourage students to use these methods of integration in their own papers.

Explain that the Student Draft is continued on this page. Read the draft and annotations aloud and discuss. Ask students to comment on the student writer's inclusion of his own ideas and interpretations.

Barron 4

7. However, not every response to Steinbeck's work was negative. In December 1939, First Lady Eleanor Roosevelt responded publicly to the book. She said that although she had read and heard others' criticisms about the novel, she knew from her own travels and investigations that the living conditions depicted in the book were at least "partly true" ("First Lady"). Then, in a January 1940 radio address, President Franklin Roosevelt said, "I have read a book recently; it is called *Grapes of Wrath*. There are 500,000 Americans that live in the covers of that book" (McElvaine 148).

In this paragraph, Chris states his point at the beginning and uses the rest of the paragraph to **support this point with relevant facts and details.**

Assessing the Novel's Impact

8. It is clear that Steinbeck's novel made a tremendous impression on some of the most powerful and influential people in the country. Yet it is not easy to establish any cause-and-effect relationship between *The Grapes of Wrath* and improvements in the lives of Dust Bowl evacuees. The government had begun to respond to the problems of the Dust Bowl long before the book's publication. In 1935, four years before anyone read *The Grapes of Wrath*, the Emergency Relief Appropriation Act created jobs for unemployed farmers, set aside money for ranchers to feed their livestock and farmers to buy seeds, and funded the construction of work camps for youths. In 1935, the Resettlement Administration began relocating farmers to better farming areas (Kite 107; "FSA Camp").

Chris includes **his own ideas and interpretations** throughout the paper.

9. The government also established the Soil Conservation Service in 1935. This program taught farmers techniques to protect the topsoil (Kite 110). One of the most important soil-saving programs was the Shelterbelt Project. This anti-erosion measure called for planting trees across the entire Great Plains. The program was already reducing blowing dirt by 1938, a year before *The Grapes of Wrath* appeared ("Timeline").

Chris uses **detailed evidence** to support a main point. He also **credits sources** properly using **correct formats and style.**

DIFFERENTIATED INSTRUCTION

FOR ADVANCED LEARNERS/AP

Evaluate Tone Point out that on pages 1369–1370 the student model includes passages of prose by three individuals: John Steinbeck, President Franklin Roosevelt, and student model author Chris Barron. In addition, the Steinbeck quotations come from two sources: the novel *The Grapes of Wrath* and a newspaper interview in the *Los Angeles Times*. Ask students to describe Roosevelt's tone and the two distinct tones of Steinbeck's passages. **Possible**

answer: *Roosevelt's tone is earnest and personal; the Steinbeck passage from the novel is sad and ominous; the Steinbeck passage from the interview is somewhat angry and defensive.*

Discuss whether the mixing of tones adds to or detracts from the effectiveness of the research paper. Point out that just as varied sentence lengths and structures help create a smooth, interesting flow of ideas, so varied tones, within the overall context of seriousness, also maintain reader interest.

Barron 5

⑩   It is also a mistake to assume that Steinbeck's novel was the sole reason that Americans focused their attention on victims of the Dust Bowl. For one thing, there were loads of people talking about injustice. Woody Guthrie had long been writing social protest songs about the Okies. Bibliographies and library catalogs show several other books that could also be read as protests. For example, in 1939, Carey McWilliams published *Factories in the Field,* an account of exploited migrants. It is also clear to anyone looking at Dorothea Lange's "Migrant Mother" and her other photographs that she was deeply concerned with the problems of poor people in California (McElvaine 105, 126, 175).

> Chris needs to revise this sentence to maintain his formal style and objective tone.

LEARN HOW   Maintain a Formal Style and Objective Tone   The tone is the writer's attitude toward his or her subject. A writer's tone should be appropriate to the subject matter, purpose, and audience. For some subjects, a lighthearted, humorous, or informal tone is appropriate. For instance, if you were writing a lighthearted short story or a letter to a friend, a humorous tone would be appropriate.

However, when writing a research paper about a serious subject—such as a tragic event in American history—you should always use a formal style, avoiding casual language, comedic references, and subjective wording with bias or exaggeration. This formal style and objective tone will convey a serious sense of purpose, which is essential in a research paper, to your audience. Notice how Chris revised the highlighted sentence to maintain his formal style and objective tone:

CHRIS'S REVISION TO PARAGRAPH ⑩

~~For one thing, there were loads of people talking about injustice.~~

For one thing, Steinbeck's was not the only voice crying out for justice.

ANALYZE A STUDENT DRAFT *continued*

Explain that the Student Draft is continued on this page. Read the draft and annotations aloud and discuss. Ask students to comment on the student writer's use of detailed evidence.

LEARN HOW   Maintain a Formal Style and Objective Tone

- Ask students what words and phrases make the student writer's original sentence too informal or subjective for a research paper.

- Point out that the student writer included the figure of speech "voice crying out" in his revision. Explain that figures of speech are not considered informal language, therefore students may include them in their papers. However, emphasize that students should not use overly poetic or flowery language. For another example of a figure of speech, have students read the last sentence of paragraph 11 on page 1372.

- Have students highlight informal words and phrases in their drafts that should be replaced with more formal language.

Explain that the Student Draft is continued on this page. Read the draft and annotations aloud and discuss. Ask students to comment on the student writer's ability to write an effective concluding section.

Barron 6

⑪   Steinbeck's novel and many other works raised awareness of the grim lives of the Okies. However, history makes it clear that what really changed Americans' lives in the years after the publication of *The Grapes of Wrath* was the buildup to World War II. By 1940, many new jobs had become available in factories—and in the military. The Great Depression ended; coincidentally, the drought in the Midwest also ended in 1939 ("Timeline"). These large forces are what truly put American workers back on the road to prosperity.

> This paragraph reflects Chris's interest in and **enthusiasm for the subject matter.**

A Great Novel, but Only One Factor Among Many

⑫   *The Grapes of Wrath* is one of the most important novels of the 20th century. At the time of its publication it captivated thousands of readers, including the president of the United States, and it helped to make the suffering of California migrant workers an issue of national importance. However, it is overstating the case to claim that the book motivated the government to help these workers. Many government programs were already in place at the time of the book's publication, and many other writers and activists helped bring the problem to public attention. Other, larger factors—the end of the drought, an improved economy, and the looming possibility of another world war—also had important effects on the migrant workers' situation. Although Steinbeck's novel was factually accurate and artistically important, a thorough evaluation of the evidence shows that it did not change the course of history.

> Chris concludes by **summarizing** his main points and **answering his research question** with original ideas. Also, he gives his audience **something compelling to think about** by reflecting on the overall significance of the topic.

DIFFERENTIATED INSTRUCTION

FOR STRUGGLING WRITERS

Comprehension Support To check students' comprehension, ask

1. In the citation for "Timeline," what does *Pub. Broadcasting Svc.* stand for? ***Answer:*** *The term is an abbreviation for* Public Broadcasting Service.

2. Which book on the list was published most recently? ***Answer:*** *The most recent book is* The Worst Hard Time, *in 2006.*

3. Why are two dates given for *The Grapes of Wrath*? ***Answer:*** *The 1939 date is the book's first publication; 1964 is the date of the edition that the researcher consulted.*

4. Why does James Ciment's name appear in the citation for the article "Dust Bowl" by Steven Kite? ***Answer:*** *Ciment's name appears because he edited the encyclopedia in which the article appears.*

Barron 7

Works Cited

"Best Sellers of the Week." *New York Times* 1 May 1939:19. Print.

Cameron, Tom. "Dust Bowl Book Brings Trouble." *Los Angeles Times* 9 July 1939: A1+. Print.

Egan, Timothy. *The Worst Hard Time.* Boston: Houghton, 2006. Print.

"First Lady Stresses Community Interests." *New York Times* 8 Dec. 1939: 16. Print.

"FSA Migratory Labor Camp." *Documenting America* Chapter 6. Lib. Of Congress. 2001. Web. 9 Apr. 2010.

Himmelberg, Robert F. *The Great Depression and the New Deal.* Westport: Greenwood, 2001. Print.

Kite, Steven. "Dust Bowl." *Encyclopedia of the Great Depression and the New Deal.* Ed. James Ciment. 2 vols. Armonk, NY: Sharpe, 2001. Print.

McElvaine, Robert S. *The Depression and New Deal: A History in Documents.* New York: Oxford UP, 2000. 132–7. Print.

Steinbeck, John. *The Grapes of Wrath.* 1939. New York: Viking, 1964. Print.

~~"Steinbeck's Myth of the Okies." Windschuttle, Keith. *New Criterion*~~ ~~June 2002: 24+. Print.~~

"Timeline." *American Experience: Surviving the Dust Bowl.* Pub. Broadcasting Svc. n.d. Web. 17 Apr. 2010.

Windschuttle, Keith. "Steinbeck's Myth of the Okies." New Criterion June 2002: 24+. Print.

> Notice Chris's revision in blue.

LEARN HOW Format a Works Cited List Correctly

When creating a Works Cited list, follow these formatting guidelines:

- Begin the list on a separate page, after the essay.
- Begin each entry on a separate line, aligned with the left margin.
- When an entry has more than one line, give additional lines a hanging indent of one-half inch.
- List sources alphabetically by authors' last names. If no author is listed, sort by title. Ignore *A*, *An*, and *The*.
- When two or more sources are written by one author, list the author's name only in the first entry. Begin additional entries with three hyphens (---), followed by a period.

 YOUR TURN Use the feedback from your peers and teacher, the revision strategies chart, and the "Learn How" lessons to revise or rework your essay. Evaluate whether you've provided adequate evidence to support your concluding statement.

ANALYZE A STUDENT DRAFT *continued*

Explain that the Student Draft is continued and completed on this page. Read the draft and annotations aloud and discuss. Ask students to comment on why Works Cited lists are necessary when writing research papers.

LEARN HOW Format a Works Cited List Correctly

- Ask students to explain why the student writer made his revision. Elicit from students that the writer initially alphabetized one of the entries by the title of the work, rather than by the author's last name.

- Emphasize that Works Cited lists have precise formatting instructions that students must follow. Also, emphasize that students should closely review the guidelines on pages 1376–1377 to check that they have correctly relayed the details within individual entries.

- Have students review their Works Cited list with a partner. Tell students to use editing marks to revise any mistakes. Provide students with proper editing marks.

YOUR TURN Have students complete the *Your Turn* activity independently. Remind students to be sure that they have relayed their research question in their controlling idea, incorporated quotations smoothly, and maintained a formal style and objective tone.

For interactive revision tools, see

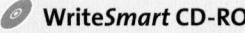 Write*Smart* CD-ROM

Writing Center on thinkcentral.com

FOR ENGLISH LANGUAGE LEARNERS

Language: Works Cited Terms Introduce students to unfamiliar words and phrases that they might encounter while putting together their Works Cited list.

- **copyright**—the legal right to reproduce, publish, or distribute something (such as a book), commonly indicated by the symbol ©

- **byline**—a line in an article naming the writer

- **URL**—universal resource locator, or the address of a Web page

Editing and Publishing

GRAMMAR IN CONTEXT: OMITTING OR ADDING WORDS IN QUOTATIONS

- Emphasize to students that they should not omit text from a quote or add text unless it is absolutely necessary. Tell students that they should try to keep quotes intact and that any changes they make should be small and out of necessity.

- For practice, have students choose two quotes from their resources. For each quote, students should write a sentence using part of the quote and punctuate the sentence so that it flows smoothly.

- Have students read each quotation in their research paper to see whether they should omit or add text to integrate it more smoothly into surrounding words, phrases, or sentences. Tell students to make any necessary revisions.

PUBLISH YOUR WRITING

Brainstorm with students additional ways to publish their research papers.

YOUR TURN Allow students time to proofread their drafts. Remind them to be sure that they have used correct punctuation when omitting or adding words in quotations and when using parenthetical citations.

Editing and Publishing

In the editing stage, you proofread your research paper to make sure that it is free of grammar, usage, spelling, and punctuation errors. Also, be sure that you format your paper according to the following guidelines:
- Double-space everything.
- Leave a one-inch margin at the left, right, top, and bottom of each page (except for page numbers).
- At the top left of the first page, type your name, your teacher's name, the class, and the date. On the rest of the pages, type your last name and the page number in the upper right corner.
- Indent all paragraphs one-half inch (or five spaces) and indent quotations of four or more lines one inch (or ten spaces) from the left margin.

See the *MLA Handbook for Writers of Research Papers* for additional guidelines.

GRAMMAR IN CONTEXT: OMITTING OR ADDING WORDS IN QUOTATIONS

Whenever you provide a direct quotation from a source, be sure to integrate it smoothly and correctly into your text. Use three spaced periods (. . .), called **ellipsis points,** to mark omissions from the original quotation. If the omission falls at the end of a quotation fragment that could stand as a complete sentence, insert the ellipses *after* an ending period, question mark, or exclamation point. Use **brackets** to mark additions to a quotation. As Chris edited his paper, he noticed a quotation fragment that should have an ending period before the ellipses. The fragment can stand as a complete sentence.

> When the *Los Angeles Times* reported that some of the migrant workers had sent Steinbeck threatening letters, he responded, "It isn't the refugees who have taken exception to what I wrote. It's the moneyed people back there in Oklahoma . . . If anybody's sore at me for the book it's that kind of people" (Cameron A1–2).

PUBLISH YOUR WRITING

Here are some suggestions for sharing your research paper with an audience:
- Save your research paper as a writing sample to submit with a college or job application.
- Turn your paper into a documentary.
- Ask your school librarian or media specialist to help you locate academic journals to which you might submit your paper.

YOUR TURN Correct any errors in your research paper, and make sure you have used correct style for adding or omitting text in quotations. Then, publish your completed work.

DIFFERENTIATED INSTRUCTION

FOR STRUGGLING WRITERS
Examine a Writer's Use of Quotations Provide students with a published literary analysis of a short story in their book. Be sure that the writer has omitted text from quotations and added text, as well. As a class, examine the writer's inclusion of quotations within the literary analysis. Have students refer to the short story to see how the writer changed the original quotations. For each altered quotation, have a volunteer explain why the writer most likely made the change.

FOR ADVANCED LEARNERS/AP
Acceleration You may ask students to give their reports interesting and informative titles as part of the publishing process. Rather than "A Research Paper on Charlie Parker," have students create titles that hint at their controlling ideas and spark curiosity, such as "Beautiful Surprises from an Alto Sax: Charlie Parker's Place in Jazz History." Explain to students that sometimes a title appears on a separate page.

Scoring Rubric

Use the rubric below to evaluate your research paper from the Writing Workshop.

RESEARCH PAPER

SCORE	COMMON CORE TRAITS
6	• **Development** Effectively introduces a topic; states an insightful, well-researched controlling idea; thoroughly supports the controlling idea with main points and relevant evidence; ends powerfully • **Organization** Logically organizes information; effectively uses varied, appropriate transitions; includes formatting and graphics to enhance the information • **Language** Ably uses precise words; consistently maintains a formal style and objective tone; shows a strong command of conventions; correctly cites all sources
5	• **Development** Competently introduces a topic; states a well-researched controlling idea; offers main points and relevant evidence; has a strong concluding section • **Organization** Is logically organized; effectively uses transitions; includes formatting and graphics • **Language** Uses a formal style and objective tone; has a few errors in conventions; correctly cites sources
4	• **Development** Sufficiently introduces a topic; states a clear controlling idea; offers mostly valid support; has an adequate concluding section • **Organization** Is mostly logically organized; needs more transitions; could use some formatting or graphics • **Language** Needs more precise words; has frequent lapses in style and tone; includes a few distracting errors in conventions; incorrectly formats a few source citations
3	• **Development** States a controlling idea, but the introduction could be more engaging; provides insufficient support; has a weak concluding section • **Organization** Has some flaws in organization; needs more transitions; doesn't include enough formatting or graphics • **Language** Lacks precise words; uses an informal style and subjective tone; has several errors in conventions; incorrectly formats some source citations
2	• **Development** Has an unclear controlling idea; does not support most ideas; ends abruptly • **Organization** Has organizational flaws; lacks transitions throughout; lacks formatting and graphics throughout • **Language** Lacks precise words; uses an informal style and subjective tone; has many errors in conventions; does not cite all sources and cites many incorrectly
1	• **Development** Lacks a controlling idea; fails to develop the topic; ends abruptly • **Organization** Has no organization, transitions, or formatting • **Language** Uses vague words; has an inappropriate style and tone; has major problems in conventions; plagiarizes or does not credit sources

Scoring Rubric

Explain to students that the best way to understand rubrics is to use them to score actual writing. Have students work with partners to evaluate each other's essays using the rubric. Ask students to score the research paper and write a brief paragraph using the language of the rubric to explain the score.

For Rubric Bank, see

 Write*Smart* CD-ROM

Writing Center on <u>thinkcentral.com</u>

REVIEW MLA GUIDELINES

As students examine the examples, discuss these questions:

- What is the correct format for citing a publisher of a book and the publisher's location? **Answer:** *Cite the location first, followed by a colon and the name of the publishing house.*

- When should you use a period instead of a comma? **Answer:** *Use a period after each separate category of information, such as the author's name, the title of the book, and the publication date.*

- When a book has two or three authors, what difference is there in the way in which their names are listed? **Answer:** *The first author's name is listed with the last name first; each of the other authors is listed with the first name first.*

- How many authors must a book have before *et al* is used? **Answer:** *There must be at least four authors.*

- In a collection of writings, what difference is there between the way in which a novel or play is listed and the way in which a poem, story, essay, or chapter title is listed? **Answer:** *For the former, underline (or italicize when writing with a computer) the title of the shorter work. For the latter, place the title of the shorter work within quotation marks.*

- In the citation to a work by Terry Gorton, in the **PARTS OF BOOKS** category, why are the page numbers in Roman numerals? **Answer:** *The page numbers are Roman numerals in the foreword to the book.* What task did Terry Gorton perform in creating *John Steinbeck: A Centennial Tribute,* and what roles did other people play? **Answer:** *Terry Gorton wrote the foreword; the book was edited by Stephen K. George; and other authors contributed writings to it.*

MLA Citation Guidelines

Today, you can find free Web sites that help you create citations for research papers using information you provide. Such sites have some time-saving advantages when you're developing a Works Cited list. However, you should always check your citations carefully before you turn in your final paper. If you are following MLA style, use these guidelines to evaluate and finalize your work.

BOOKS

One author
Steinbeck, John. *The Grapes of Wrath.* 1939. New York: Viking, 1964. Print.

Two authors or editors
Lange, Dorothea, and Paul Schuster Taylor. *An American Exodus: A Record of Human Erosion.* New York: Reynal & Hitchcock, 1939. Print.

Three authors or editors
Scheibel, Jeremy, Anne Chatsworth, and Ridley Davis, eds. *Stories from the Great Depression.* Princeton: Princeton UP, 2008. Print.

Four or more authors or editors
List the first author only. Then use the abbreviation et al., *which means "and others."*
Rutkowski, J., et al. *American Immigration and Migration in the 1930s.* Topeka: Sanders-Ellis, 2007. Print.

No author given
American Literature: 1865 to the Present. Chicago: Omni, 2007. Print.

PARTS OF BOOKS

An introduction, a preface, a foreword, or an afterword written by someone other than the author(s) of a work
Gorton, Terry. Foreword. *John Steinbeck: A Centennial Tribute.* Ed. Stephen K. George. Westport: Praeger, 2002. xvii–xviii. Print.

A poem, a short story, an essay, or a chapter in a collection of works
Steinbeck, John. "The Leader of the People." *The Portable Steinbeck.* Ed. Pascal Covici, Jr. New York: Penguin, 1978. 397–415. Print.

A poem, a short story, an essay, or a chapter in an anthology of works by several authors
Steinbeck, John. "The Red Pony." *The American Short Story: A Collection of the Best Known and Most Memorable Short Stories by the Great American Authors.* Ed. Thomas K. Parkes. New York: Galahad, 1994. 886–948. Print.

A novel or play in a collection
Steinbeck, John. *The Grapes of Wrath. The Grapes of Wrath and Other Writings, 1936–1941.* New York: Library of America, 1996. Print.

DIFFERENTIATED INSTRUCTION

FOR STRUGGLING WRITERS

Practice MLA Guidelines Have students create citations for fictitious reference works, using their own names as first author; classmates' names as other authors or editors; *How to Write a Research Paper* as the title of a book; "Getting Started" as the title of a chapter or article; "Research Book Co." as the name of a publisher to be located in your town; this year as the publication date; and page numbers of students' choice. Review their responses for accuracy.

FOR ADVANCED LEARNERS/AP

Research the MLA As this page suggests, the Modern Language Association speaks with authority about certain matters of writing style. Invite a group of students to find out more about the history and activities of this influential organization and to share their findings with the class.

COMMON CORE W 8 Gather relevant information from multiple print and digital sources; follow a standard format for citation.

MAGAZINES, NEWSPAPERS, AND ENCYCLOPEDIAS

An article in a newspaper
Patel, Vikram. "Recalling the Days of Wrath." *Los Angeles Times* 8 Jan. 2008: 9. Print.

An article in a magazine
Schubert, Siegfried D., et al. "On the Cause of the 1930s Dust Bowl." *Science* 19 Mar. 2004: 1855–60. Print.

An article in an encyclopedia
Kite, Steven. "Dust Bowl." *Encyclopedia of the Great Depression and New Deal.* Ed. James Ciment. 2 vols. Armonk, NY: Sharpe, 2001. Print.

MISCELLANEOUS NONPRINT SOURCES

An interview
Sorenson, Elvina. Personal interview. 3 Feb. 2010.

A video recording or film
Our Daily Bread. Dir. King Vidor. Perf. Karen Morley, Tom Keene, Barbara Pepper, John Qualen. 1934. Film Preservation Assoc., 1999. DVD.

A sound recording
Guthrie, Woody. *Library of Congress Recordings/Woody Guthrie.* Rounder, 1988. CD.

ELECTRONIC PUBLICATIONS

A document from an Internet site
Include as much of the following information as available in the order given.

Author or compiler	Title or description of document	Title of Internet site	Site sponsor
Neary, Walter.	"Steinbeck & Salinas."	*About John Steinbeck.*	National Steinbeck Center.

Date of document	Medium of Publication	Date of access
June 1995.	Web.	2 Apr. 2010.

AN ONLINE BOOK OR E-BOOK

Wunder, John R., Frances Kaye, and Vernon Carstensen, eds. *Americans View Their Dust Bowl Experience.* Niwot: UP Colorado, 1999. Questia Media America. Web. 10 Apr. 2010.

A CD-ROM

"Dust Bowl." *Britannica Student Encyclopedia.* 2004 ed. Chicago: Encyclopaedia Britannica, 2004. CD-ROM.

WRITING WORKSHOP **1377**

FOR STRUGGLING WRITERS

Understand Abbreviations Point out that the Works Cited list on page 1373 and the MLA Citation Guidelines on pages 1376–1377 include several abbreviations that students may need to look up in a dictionary or a book of research guidelines. Help students understand these abbreviations:

- *1 May 1939: 19,* "May 1, 1939, page 19"

- *24+:* "page 24 and later pages of the periodical"

- *A1+:* "Section A of the newspaper, page 1 and later pages"

- *2 vols.:* "The work cited consists of two volumes."

- *Ed. James Ciment:* "James Ciment edited the book."

- *Rutkowski, J., et al:* "The book has several authors: J. Rutkowski and others."

REVIEW MLA GUIDELINES *continued*

Discuss these questions about the examples:

- As shown here, are there any differences between the citation formats of an article from a newspaper and an article from a magazine? Explain. ***Answer:*** *There are no differences.*

- In the citation of a video recording or film, what does *Perf.* mean? ***Answer:*** *It means "Performers."*

- What does *Assoc.* stand for in the title *Film Preservation Assoc.?* ***Answer:*** *The term is an abbreviation for "Association."*

- What is the difference between the two dates in an Internet site citation? ***Answer:*** *One date is the date on which the site was launched (and, in this case, revised); the other is the date on which the researcher found the information at that site.*

- Why are URLs not included for the electronic and online citations? ***Answer:*** *URLs are unstable and can be lengthy and confusing.*

- What does *UP Colorado* stand for in the citation for the online book *Americans View Their Dust Bowl Experience?* ***Answer:*** *University Press of Colorado*

- In the citation for the *Encyclopaedia Britannica* CD-ROM, what does *ed.* stand for in the date *2004 ed.?* ***Answer:*** *edition*

Assess and Reteach

Assess

Online Essay Scoring on thinkcentral.com

 RESOURCE MANAGER—Copy Master
Rubric for Evaluation p. 26

Reteach

Level Up Online Tutorials on thinkcentral.com

Reteaching Worksheets on thinkcentral.com

Research and Study Skills Lesson 1: Research Questions and Topic

Research and Study Skills Lesson 5: Using Primary and Secondary Sources

Research and Study Skills Lesson 7: Evaluating Electronic Sources

Research and Study Skills Lesson 8: Source Cards and Note Cards

Focus and Motivate

COMMON CORE FOCUS

W 6 Use technology to produce, publish, and update individual or shared writing products. **SL 2** Integrate multiple sources of information presented in diverse formats and media. **SL 5** Make strategic use of digital media in presentations to enhance understanding and to add interest.

PRODUCE WITH A PURPOSE

Read aloud the elements of a strong documentary. Ask students to discuss the meaning of *compelling*. Tell students that the way they present the information in their documentaries should stimulate thought-provoking questions and opinions that can be explored from multiple points of view.

COMMON CORE TRAITS

As students plan their documentaries, remind them to keep in mind the *COMMON CORE TRAITS* of a strong documentary.

Practice and Apply

Plan Your Documentary

Reserve one class session for looking for audio and visual materials at the library. Have a librarian relay library locations, databases, Internet Web sites, and reference materials that students will find useful in their search for materials. As students conduct their research, be available for help.

If students plan on using an interview in their documentary, tell them to choose short excerpts for inclusion. Emphasize that they should select excerpts that relay memorable, compelling information or details.

Provide students with an example of a storyboard. Emphasize that the storyboard should allow the documentary to flow smoothly. Be sure that students understand that their documentary should consist of a flow of connected ideas and details. Also, point out when the storyboard indicates that a specific camera position should be used.

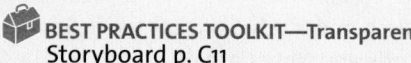 **BEST PRACTICES TOOLKIT—Transparency** Storyboard p. C11

Producing a Documentary

You have probably seen documentaries on historical figures or events, such as those commonly shown on public television. A documentary is a creative, engaging, and memorable way to present research.

Complete the workshop activities in your **Reader/Writer Notebook.**

PRODUCE WITH A PURPOSE	COMMON CORE TRAITS
TASK Produce a **documentary** that uses graphics, images, and sound to present research you conducted for the topic of your research report.	**A STRONG DOCUMENTARY . . .** • focuses on a compelling subject • integrates information from multiple sources • makes strategic use of text, graphic, audio, and visual elements to enhance understanding and add interest

COMMON CORE

W 6 Use technology to produce, publish, and update individual or shared writing products. **SL 2** Integrate multiple sources of information presented in diverse formats and media. **SL 5** Make strategic use of digital media in presentations to enhance understanding and to add interest.

Plan Your Documentary

Be creative and selective as you choose what to include in your documentary. Keep your audience in mind as you decide how to arrange the various materials to enhance their interest in and understanding of your topic.

The following tips and techniques can help you plan your documentary:

- **Identify sources of information.** Review the notes you compiled while developing your research paper. Identify if any of those sources would lend themselves to being used in a documentary. Be sure to integrate information from multiple sources on the topic, such as photographs and illustrations, or an interview with an expert. As you identify sources, make sure you evaluate their credibility and accuracy. Ask yourself, is the source **credible**, or reliable and trustworthy? Is the information **accurate**, or up-to-date, well-documented, and written or furnished by an expert on the topic?

- **Look for audio and visual materials.** When choosing materials, include a variety of elements, such as text, graphics, and audio. Select the element that will best enhance the audience's understanding of the information that is being addressed. Also, select elements that will add to the visual and audio interest of the documentary. Be sure to respect copyright laws and use only materials for which you have permission.

- **Create a script.** Using your collected materials for guidance, create a **script** for your documentary. Include voice-over narration, interview footage, and music. Voice-over narration should provide necessary background information and relevant details about the visuals you present. Choose music that reflects the tone of the accompanying images.

- **Develop a storyboard.** Plan what your audience will see and hear. Include several types of camera positions, such as **establishing shots** (wide-angle shots that set the scene), **medium shots,** and **close-ups,** as well as a variety of camera angles. You can find examples at the library or on the Internet.

Media Tools | **THINK** central

Go to **thinkcentral.com.** KEYWORD: HML11-1378

DIFFERENTIATED INSTRUCTION

FOR ENGLISH LANGUAGE LEARNERS
Language: Reinforce Technology Terms
Review key terms used in this workshop:

- *graphic:* a visual image that is printed, hand-written, or drawn; charts, diagrams, graphs, photographs, and maps can all be graphics

- *voice-over narration:* the voice of an unseen narrator speaking

- *footage:* film or video that has been taped

- *storyboard:* a series of drawings, like a comic strip, that lays out the changes of scene and actions in a script

- *establishing shot:* a shot in a film or video used at the beginning of a sequence to set up a broad view of the scene

- *medium shot:* a mid-range camera shot, such as a shot of two people talking

- *close-up:* a camera shot taken at close range, such as a shot of a person's face

Produce Your Documentary

When producing your documentary, allow yourself plenty of time to gather equipment, record the material, and revise or rework your documentary. If technological problems occur and you're not sure how to proceed, ask a teacher, a parent, or an informed classmate for help.

Follow these steps as you produce your documentary:

- **Find out what equipment is available.** Your school may have a camcorder that you can borrow. If you have video editing software, you can record scenes in any order; if not, you will have to film each scene sequentially.
- **Record the video and the voice-overs.** Follow your script and storyboard carefully. When recording your voice-overs, follow the verbal techniques in the following chart:

Verbal Techniques

- Enunciate your words clearly.
- Maintain a formal style to help your audience focus on the information.
- Emphasize important words or points by speaking slightly louder and with more force.
- Pause for a moment after an important point to encourage the audience to reflect on it.
- Speak slowly enough to allow your audience to follow you, but not so slowly that they become bored.

- **Pull it together.** Review your footage, reshooting as necessary. Be sure that your documentary flows smoothly from one shot to the next. If necessary, add transitional words and phrases to your voice-overs to ensure that your documentary flows smoothly.

 YOUR TURN After you have followed all of the instructions for planning and producing your documentary, screen your documentary for family members or classmates. Ask for specific feedback, and then use the feedback to improve your documentary. After you have made improvements, think about sharing your documentary with a larger audience. Use one or more of the following techniques to find your larger audience:

- Work with other classmates to organize and hold a school film festival in which you can premiere all of your documentaries.
- Find an organization or reputable Web site that is devoted to your subject. Contact this organization or the Web site's creator about using your documentary.
- Enter your documentary in a documentary contest. Be sure to research each contest to determine the types of entries accepted and the rules.

1379

Produce Your Documentary

Schedule a time for your school's technology coordinator to show students how to use school equipment that you are not familiar with. If students plan on using equipment that they have at home, emphasize that they should let their parents know about their use of the equipment.

Encourage students to follow their scripts and storyboards; however, emphasize that students should feel free to add, delete, or rearrange footage if they feel it enhances their documentary.

Tell students to create credits footage at the end of their documentaries, detailing where they acquired information and graphics.

YOUR TURN Provide students with class time to share their documentaries with one another. You may want to provide or have students create a scoring rubric or questionnaire that they can use to evaluate one another's documentaries.

Assess and Reteach

Assess

Use the **COMMON CORE TRAITS** to assess students' documentaries.

A strong documentary
- focuses on a compelling subject
- integrates information from multiple sources
- makes strategic use of text, graphic, audio, and visual elements to enhance understanding and add interest

Reteach

Some students may struggle with implementing verbal techniques in their voice-over narrations. Play an excerpt of a documentary that contains a well-executed voice-over narration. Have a class discussion about the techniques that the narrator used.

THINK central

Media Tools

Keywords for using technology direct students to **MediaScope,** a Web site that helps them strengthen media analysis and production skills.

FOR STRUGGLING STUDENTS

Evaluate the Flow of a Documentary Bring in a short documentary detailing a historical event or person. Provide students with a list of questions to ask themselves and take notes about as they watch the documentary, such as: *How does the documentary maintain a flow from one shot to the next? What transitional words and phrases does the narrator use? How do the ideas and information in each shot connect to the shot before and/or the shot after? Could the documentary have had a better flow?* After students have watched the documentary, have a class discussion about the documentary's flow.

Student Resource Bank

COMMON CORE FOCUS

RL 3 Analyze the impact of the author's choices regarding how to develop and relate elements of a story or drama. **RL 5** Analyze how an author's choices concerning how to structure a text contribute to its overall structure and meaning as well as its aesthetic impact. **RI 2** Determine two or more central ideas of a text. **RI 3** Analyze a complex set of ideas. **RI 4** Determine the technical meaning of words and phrases as they are used in a text. **RI 5** Analyze the structure an author uses in his or her exposition or argument. **RI 6** Determine an author's point of view or purpose in a text in which the rhetoric is particularly effective, analyzing how style and content contribute to the power, persuasiveness, or beauty of the text. **RI 7** Integrate and evaluate multiple sources of information presented in different media or formats. **SL 2** Integrate multiple sources of information presented in diverse formats and media, evaluating the credibility and accuracy of each source and noting any discrepancies among the data. **SL 5** Make strategic use of digital media in presentations to enhance understanding of findings, reasoning, and evidence and to add interest.

Reading any text—short story, poem, magazine article, newspaper, Web page—requires the use of special strategies. For example, you might plot events in a short story on a diagram, while you might use text features to spot main ideas in a magazine article. You also need to identify patterns of organization in the text. Using such strategies can help you read different texts with ease and also help you understand what you're reading.

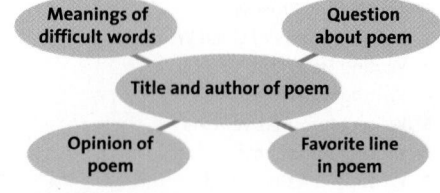

COMMON CORE

Included in this handbook:
RL 3, RL 5, RI 2–7, SL 2, SL 5

1 Reading Literary and Nonfiction Texts

Literary and nonfiction texts include short stories, novels, poems, dramas, biographies, autobiographies, and essays. To appreciate and analyze literary and nonfiction texts, you will need to understand the characteristics of each type of text.

1.1 READING A SHORT STORY
Strategies for Reading

- Read the title. As you read the story, you may notice that the title has a special meaning.

- Keep track of events as they happen. Plot the events on a diagram like this one.

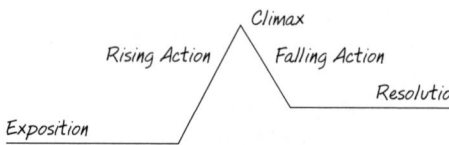

Climax

Rising Action / Falling Action

Resolution

Exposition

- Using the details the writer provides, **visualize** the characters. **Predict** what they might do next.

- Look for specific adjectives that help you visualize the **setting**—the time and place in which events occur.

- Note **cause-and-effect relationships** and how these affect the **conflict**.

1.2 READING A POEM
Strategies for Reading

- Notice the **form** of the poem, or the arrangement of its lines and stanzas on the page.

- Read the poem aloud a few times. Listen for and note the **rhymes** and **rhythms.**

- **Visualize** the images and comparisons.

- **Connect** with the poem by asking yourself what message the poet is trying to send.

- Create a word web or another **graphic organizer** to record your reactions and questions.

Meanings of difficult words

Question about poem

Title and author of poem

Opinion of poem

Favorite line in poem

1.3 READING A PLAY
Strategies for Reading

- Read the stage directions to help you **visualize** the setting and characters.

- **Question** what the title means and why the playwright chose it.

- Identify the main conflict (struggle or problem) in the play. To **clarify** the conflict, make a chart that shows what the conflict is and how it is resolved.

- **Evaluate** the characters. What do they want? How do they change during the play? You may want to make a chart that lists each character's name, appearance, and traits.

1.4 READING NONFICTION
Strategies for Reading

- If you are reading a biography, an autobiography, or another type of biographical writing, such as a diary or memoir, use a family tree to keep track of the people mentioned.

- When reading an essay, **analyze** and **evaluate** the writer's ideas and reasoning. Does the writer present a thesis statement? use sound logic? adequately support opinions with facts and other evidence?

- For all types of nonfiction, be aware of the **author's purpose,** and note any personal **bias** of the writer's that might influence the presentation of information.

❷ Reading Informational Texts: Text Features

An informational text is nonfiction writing that provides factual information. Informational materials, such as chapters in textbooks and articles in magazines, encyclopedias, and newspapers, usually contain elements that help the reader recognize their purposes, organization, and key ideas. These elements are known as **text features**.

2.1 UNDERSTANDING TEXT FEATURES

Text features are design elements of a text that indicate its organizational structure or otherwise make its key ideas and information understandable. Text features include titles, headings, subheadings, boldface type, bulleted and numbered lists, and graphic aids, such as charts, graphs, illustrations, and photographs. Notice how the text features help you find key information on the textbook page shown.

Ⓐ The **title** identifies the topic.

Ⓑ A **subheading** indicates the start of a new topic or section and identifies the focus of that section.

Ⓒ **Boldface type** is used to make key terms obvious.

Ⓓ A **bulleted list** shows items of equal importance.

Ⓔ **Graphic aids,** such as illustrations, photographs, charts, graphs, diagrams, maps, and timelines, often clarify ideas in the text.

PRACTICE AND APPLY

1. What are the subheadings on the textbook page shown?

2. What are the key terms on the page? How do you know?

3. How do the bulleted list and the photograph help you understand the information on this page?

Ⓐ New Deal Programs: Helping the American People

While working on banking and financial matters, the Roosevelt administration also implemented programs to provide relief to farmers, perhaps the hardest hit by the depression. It also aided other workers and attempted to stimulate economic recovery.

Ⓑ RURAL ASSISTANCE The **Agricultural Adjustment Act (AAA)** sought to raise crop prices by lowering production, which the government achieved by paying farmers to leave a certain amount of every acre of land unseeded. The theory was that reduced supply would boost prices. In some cases, crops were too far advanced for the acreage reduction to take effect. As a result, the government paid cotton growers $200 million to plow under 10 million acres of their crop. It also paid hog farmers to slaughter 6 million pigs. This policy upset many Americans, who protested the destruction of food when many people were going hungry. It did, however, help raise farm prices and put more money in farmers' pockets.

An especially ambitious program of regional development was the Tennessee Valley Authority (TVA), established on May 18, 1933. (See Geography Spotlight on page S20.) Focusing on the badly depressed Tennessee River Valley, the TVA renovated five existing dams and constructed 20 new ones, created thousands of jobs, and provided flood control, hydroelectric power, and other benefits to an impoverished region.

PROVIDING WORK PROJECTS The administration also established programs to provide relief through work projects and cash payments. One important program, the **Civilian Conservation Corps (CCC),** put young men aged 18 to 25 to work building roads, developing parks, planting trees, and helping in soil-erosion and flood-control projects. By the time the program ended in 1942, almost 3 million young men had passed through the CCC. The CCC paid a small wage, $30 a month, of which $25 was automatically sent home to the worker's family. It also supplied free food and uniforms and lodging in work camps. Many of the camps were located on the Great Plains, where, within a period of eight years, the men of the CCC planted more than 200 million trees. This tremendous reforestation program was aimed at preventing another Dust Bowl.

The Public Works Administration (PWA), created in June 1933 as part of the **National Industrial Recovery Act (NIRA),** provided money to states to create jobs chiefly in the construction of schools and other community buildings. When these programs failed to make a sufficient dent in unemployment, President Roosevelt established the Civil Works Administration in November 1933. It provided 4 million immediate jobs during the winter of 1933–1934. Although some critics of the CWA claimed that the programs were "make-work" projects and a waste of money, the CWA built 40,000 schools and paid the salaries of more than 50,000 schoolteachers in America's rural areas. It also built more than half a million miles of roads. **Ⓔ**

Background See supply and demand on page R46 in the Economics Handbook.

Ⓓ Civilian Conservation Corps
- The CCC provided almost 3 million men aged 18–25 with work and wages between 1933 and 1942.
- The men lived in work camps under a strict regime. The majority of the camps were racially segregated.
- By 1938, the CCC had an 11 percent African-American enrollment.
- Accomplishments of the CCC include planting over 3 billion trees, developing over 800 state parks, and building more than 46,000 bridges.

MAIN IDEA
Analyzing Effects
Ⓒ How did New Deal programs affect various regions of the United States?

The New Deal **491**

PRACTICE AND APPLY

ANSWERS

1. *Rural Assistance; Providing Work Projects*

2. *Agricultural Adjustment Act (AAA), Civilian Conservation Corps (CCC), National Industrial Recovery Act (NIRA); key terms are in boldface.*

3. *Bulleted list gives additional information about a key term; photograph offers visual support of key information.*

2.2 USING TEXT FEATURES

You can use text features to locate information, to help you understand it, and to categorize it. Just use the following strategies when you encounter informational text.

Strategies for Reading

- Scan the title, headings, and subheadings to get an idea of the main concepts and the way the text is organized.

- Before you begin reading the text more thoroughly, read any questions that appear at the end of a lesson or chapter. Doing this will help you set a purpose for your reading.

- Turn subheadings into questions. Then use the text below the subheadings to answer the questions. Your answers will be a summary of the text.

- Take notes by turning headings and subheadings into main ideas. You might enter them in a chart like the following.

New Deal Programs: Helping the American People	**Main Heading**	
Rural Assistance	Notes: 1. Agricultural Adjustment Act was enacted to raise crop prices by lowering production. 2. In some cases, crops were too advanced for the program to be effective.	**Subheading**

2.3 TURNING TEXT HEADINGS INTO OUTLINE ENTRIES

You can also use text features to take notes in outline form. The following outline shows how one student used text headings from the sample page on page R3. Study the outline and use the strategies that follow to create an outline based on text features.

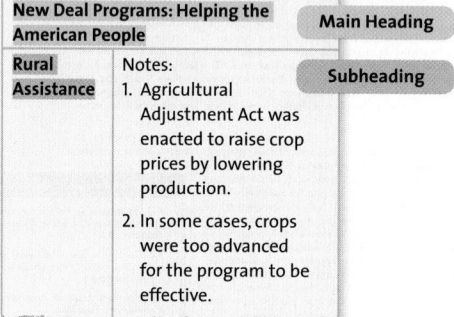

I. New Deal Programs: Helping the American People — **Main Heading** Roman numeral entry

A. Rural Assistance — **Subheading** capital letter entry

1. Agricultural Adjustment Act was enacted to raise crop prices by lowering production. — **Detail** number entry

2. In some cases, crops were too advanced for the program to be effective.

Strategies for Using Text Headings

- Preview the headings and subheadings in the text to get an idea of what different kinds there are and what their positions might be in an outline.

- Be consistent. Note that subheadings that are the same size and color should be used consistently in Roman-numeral or capital-letter entries in the outline. If you decide that a chapter heading should appear with a Roman numeral, then that's the level at which all other chapter headings should appear.

- Write the headings and subheadings that you will use as your Roman-numeral and capital-letter entries first. As you read, fill in numbered details from the text under the headings and subheadings in your outline.

PRACTICE AND APPLY

Find a suitable chapter in one of your textbooks and, using its text features, take notes on the chapter in outline form.

Preview the subheadings in the text to get an idea of the different kinds. Write the headings and subheadings you are using as your Roman-numeral and capital-letter entries first. Then fill in the details.

PRACTICE AND APPLY

ANSWERS

Students' work should resemble models shown in text.

2.4 GRAPHIC AIDS

Information is communicated not only with words but also with graphic aids. **Graphic aids** are visual representations of verbal statements. They can be charts, webs, diagrams, graphs, photographs, or other visual representations of information. Graphic aids usually make complex information easier to understand. For that reason, graphic aids are often used to organize, simplify, and summarize information for easy reference.

Graphs

Graphs are used to illustrate statistical information. A **graph** is a drawing that shows the relative values of numerical quantities. Different kinds of graphs are used to show different numerical relationships.

Strategies for Reading

Ⓐ Read the title.

Ⓑ Find out what is being represented or measured.

Ⓒ In a circle graph, compare the sizes of the parts.

Ⓓ In a line graph, study the slant of the line. The steeper the line, the faster the rate of change.

Ⓔ In a bar graph, compare the lengths of the bars.

A **circle graph,** or **pie graph,** shows the relationships of parts to a whole. The entire circle equals 100 percent. The parts of the circle represent percentages of the whole.

MODEL: CIRCLE GRAPH

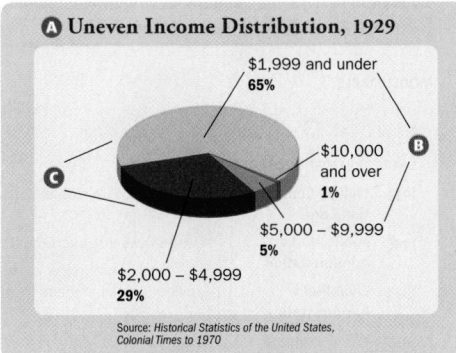

Ⓐ Uneven Income Distribution, 1929

$1,999 and under **65%**

$10,000 and over **1%** **Ⓑ**

Ⓒ

$5,000 – $9,999 **5%**

$2,000 – $4,999 **29%**

Source: *Historical Statistics of the United States, Colonial Times to 1970*

Line graphs show changes in numerical quantities over time and are effective in presenting trends, such as unemployment rates. A line graph is made on a grid. Here, the vertical axis indicates the percentage of the work force that is unemployed, and the horizontal axis shows years. Points on the graph indicate data. The lines that connect the points indicate the trends or patterns.

MODEL: LINE GRAPH

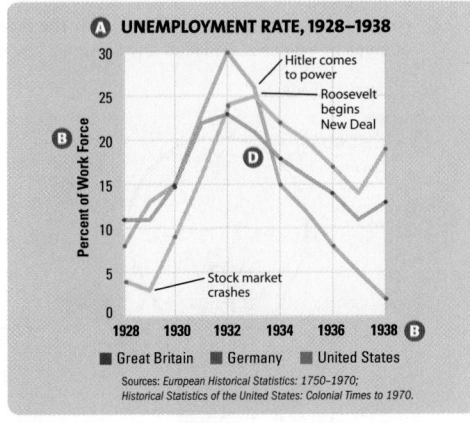

Ⓐ UNEMPLOYMENT RATE, 1928–1938

Hitler comes to power

Roosevelt begins New Deal

Ⓑ Percent of Work Force

Ⓓ

Stock market crashes

1928 1930 1932 1934 1936 1938 **Ⓑ**

■ Great Britain   ■ Germany   ■ United States

Sources: *European Historical Statistics: 1750–1970; Historical Statistics of the United States: Colonial Times to 1970.*

In a **bar graph,** vertical or horizontal bars are used to show or compare categories of information, such as average annual income during wartime. The lengths of the bars typically indicate quantities.

MODEL: BAR GRAPH

Ⓐ The War Economy, 1914–1920

Average Annual Income

1914 $627
1915 $633
1916 $706
1917 $830
1918 $1,047 **Ⓔ**
1919 $1,201
1920 $1,407

Ⓑ

Source: *Historical Statistics of the United States*

WATCH OUT! Evaluate carefully the information presented in graphs. For example, circle graphs show major factors and differences well but tend to minimize smaller factors and differences.

Diagrams

A **diagram** is a drawing that shows how something works or how its parts relate to one another.

A **picture diagram** is a picture or drawing of the subject being discussed.

Strategies for Reading

Ⓐ Read the title.

Ⓑ Read each label and look at the part it identifies.

Ⓒ Follow any arrows or numbers that show the order of steps in a process, and read any captions.

MODEL: PICTURE DIAGRAM

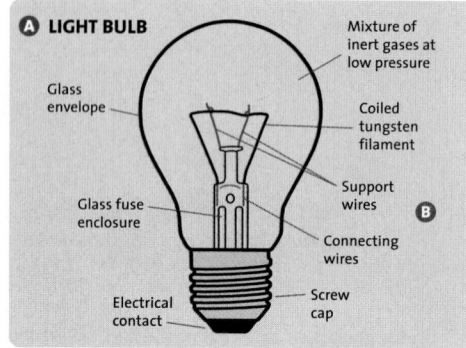

In a **schematic diagram,** lines, symbols, and words are used to help readers visualize processes or objects they wouldn't normally be able to see.

MODEL: SCHEMATIC DIAGRAM

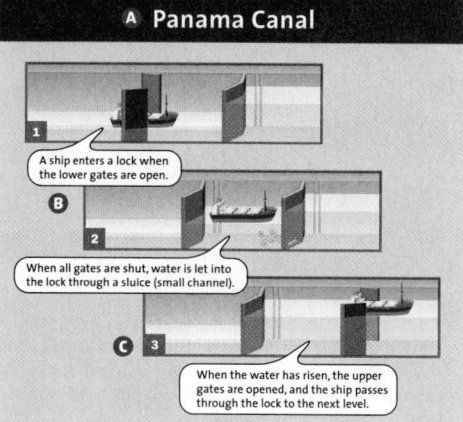

Charts and Tables

A **chart** presents information, shows a process, or makes comparisons, usually in rows or columns. A **table** is a specific type of chart that presents a collection of facts in rows and columns and shows how the facts relate to one another.

Strategies for Reading

Ⓐ Read the title to learn what information the chart or table covers.

Ⓑ Study column headings and row labels to determine the categories of information presented.

Ⓒ Look down columns and across rows to find specific information.

MODEL: CHART

Geographic Distribution of U.S. Population, 1930–1970 Ⓐ

Year	Central Cities	Suburbs	Ⓑ Rural Areas and Small Towns
1930	31.8%	18.0%	50.2%
1940	31.6%	19.5%	48.9%
1950	32.3%	23.8%	43.9%
1960	32.6%	30.7%	36.7%
1970	31.4%	37.6%	31.0%

Source: Adapted from U.S. Bureau of the Census, *Decennial Censuses, 1930–1970*

MODEL: TABLE

New Deal Ⓐ

EMPLOYMENT PROJECTS		PURPOSE Ⓑ
1933	Civilian Conservation Corps	Provided jobs for single males on conservation projects
1933	Public Works Administration	Created jobs on government projects
1933	Civil Works Administration	Provided work in federal jobs
1935	Works Progress Administration	Quickly created as many jobs as possible—from construction jobs to positions in symphony orchestras
1935	National Youth Administration	Provided job training for unemployed young people and part-time jobs for needy students

Maps

A **map** visually represents a geographic region, such as a state or country. It provides information about areas through lines, colors, shapes, and symbols. There are different kinds of maps.

- **Political maps** show political features, such as national borders, states and capitols, and population demographics.
- **Physical maps** show the landforms in areas.
- **Road or travel maps** show streets, roads, and highways.
- **Thematic maps** show information on a specific topic, such as climate, weather, or natural resources.

Strategies for Reading

Ⓐ Read the title to find out what kind of map it is.

Ⓑ Read the labels to get an overall sense of what the map shows.

Ⓒ Look at the **key** or **legend** to find out what the symbols and colors on the map stand for.

MODEL: THEMATIC MAP

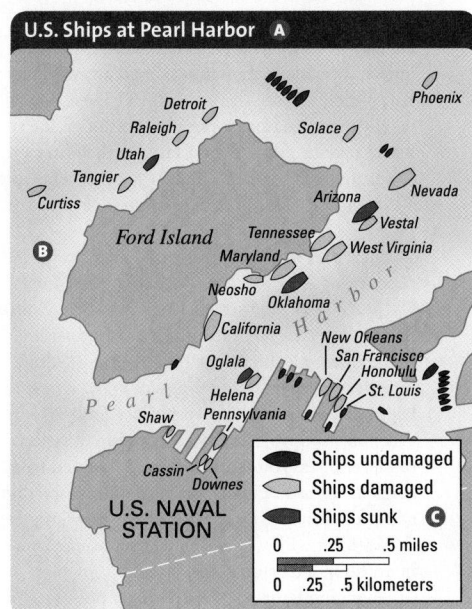

MODEL: ROAD MAP

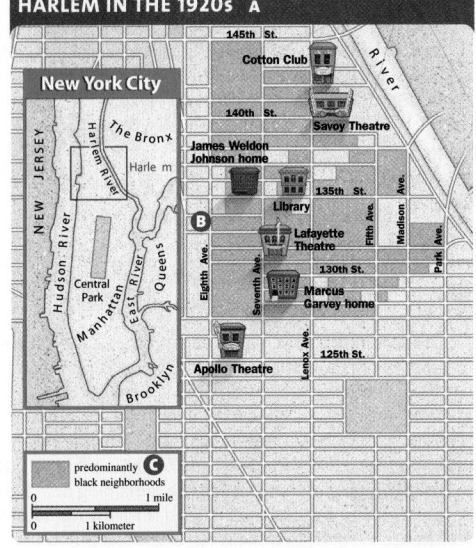

PRACTICE AND APPLY

Use the graphic aids on pages R5–R7 to answer the following questions.

1. According to the circle graph, what percentage of the population in the 1920s earned $10,000 or over?

2. According to the line graph, which country had the highest unemployment rate in 1936?

3. According to the bar graph, by how much did the average annual income increase between 1914 and 1920?

4. What is used to contain the inert gases in a light bulb, according to the picture diagram?

5. Using the schematic diagram of the Panama Canal, describe the function of a sluice in the lock system.

6. According to the chart, in which type of area did the population steadily decrease between 1930 and 1970?

7. Use the table to determine the types of jobs found through the Public Works Administration.

8. On the thematic map, identify three ships that were sunk.

9. Use the 1920s map of Harlem to give directions from the Apollo Theatre to the Savoy Theatre.

PRACTICE AND APPLY

ANSWERS

1. *one percent*

2. *United States*

3. *Income rose $780.*

4. *glass envelope*

5. *Possible answer: Once a ship is in the lock, a sluice lets water into the lock, causing the ship to rise.*

6. *rural areas and small towns*

7. *government projects*

8. *Answers should include three of the following: Arizona, Oglala, Oklahoma, and Utah.*

9. *Possible answer: 125th to Seventh, turn left, Seventh to 140th, turn right, one block to Savoy*

3 Reading Informational Texts: Patterns of Organization

Reading any type of writing is easier once you recognize how it is organized. Writers usually arrange ideas and information in ways that best reveal how they are related. Here are the most common organizational patterns:

- order of importance
- chronological order
- cause-effect organization
- compare-and-contrast organization

3.1 ORDER OF IMPORTANCE

Order of importance is a pattern of organization in which information is arranged by its degree of importance. The information is often arranged in one of two ways: from **most important to least important** or from **least important to most important.** In the first way, the most important quality, characteristic, or fact is presented at the beginning of the text, and the remaining details are presented in an order ending with the least significant. The second pattern is the reverse: the text builds from the less important elements to the most important one. Order of importance is frequently used in persuasive writing.

Strategies for Reading

- To identify order of importance in a piece of writing, skim the text to see if it moves from items of greater importance to items of lesser importance, or the reverse.

- Next, read the text carefully. Look for words and phrases such as *first, second, mainly, more important, less important, least important* and *most important* to indicate the relative importance of the ideas and information.

- Identify the topic of the text and what aspect of the topic is being discussed—its complexity, size, effectiveness, varieties, or some other aspect. Note what the most important fact or idea seems to be.

- If you are having difficulty understanding the topic, try asking *who, what, when, where, why,* and *how* about the ideas or events.

Notice the degrees of importance of the ideas in the following model.

Subject	Words showing order of importance

MODEL

Why are some of us tempted to put off tasks when they could easily be done right away? In a word: procrastination. It affects all areas of life and can have some hefty consequences. By putting off tasks, we can cause unnecessary stress for ourselves and those around us. Many procrastinators say, "I work well under pressure," and this might be true. But better planning would lead to better grades, a more impressive report, and even career advancement. What can you do to curb your tendencies to delay the inevitable?

First, determine the cause of your procrastination. If you're honest with yourself, you might find that you set unrealistic goals, that you have a fear of failure or criticism, or that you feel guilty for delaying. Any of these reasons can paralyze your efforts to move forward.

The next important thing is to identify *the way in which* you procrastinate. Maybe you ignore the task as though it will go away. Maybe you underestimate the amount of time a task will take. Procrastinators sometimes misjudge the time it will take to prepare for a task, or they may even lower their standards to make the task seem easier. Think about what procrastination looks like for you.

Once you understand the *why* and *how* of procrastination, you can move on to the final and most important stage—turning "being" into "doing." First, keep a running list of priorities. Write down all the things that need to be done in order of urgency, and you will know where to begin. Second, break down projects into several tasks, or miniprojects. By creating small tasks out of larger ones, you won't feel overwhelmed by a single large task. Finally, set clear and reasonable goals for yourself. Be specific about how long each miniproject will take and what you can accomplish in an hour, a day, or a week.

Changing your ways is definitely possible, but it will take some honest evaluation. Hopefully, after the process of examining the *why* and *how* of procrastination, you will be ready to change your ways. Why not start right now?

PRACTICE AND APPLY

Read each paragraph, and then do the following:

1. Identify whether the order is from most important to least important or from least important to most important.

2. Identify key words and phrases that helped you figure out the order.

3. What is the order of importance indicated in the paragraph beginning, "Once you understand . . . "? What are the key words?

3.2 CHRONOLOGICAL ORDER

Chronological order is the arrangement of events in their order of occurrence. This type of organization is used in fictional narratives, historical writing, biographies, and autobiographies. To indicate the order of events, writers use words such as *before, after, next,* and *later* and words and phrases that identify specific times of day, days of the week, and dates, such as *the next morning, Tuesday,* and *on July 4, 1776.*

Strategies for Reading

- Look in the text for headings and subheadings that may indicate a chronological pattern of organization.

- Look for words and phrases that identify times, such as *in a year, three hours earlier, in 1871,* and *the next day.*

- Look for words that signal order, such as *first, afterward, then, during,* and *finally,* to see how events or steps are related.

- Note that a paragraph or passage in which ideas and information are arranged chronologically will have several words or phrases that indicate time order, not just one.

- Ask yourself: Are the events in the paragraph or passage presented in time order?

Notice the words and phrases that signal time order in the first three paragraphs of the following model.

MODEL

History of the National Weather Service

Today, the U.S. National Weather Service is one of the best-known federal agencies. It was not always so popular, especially in its early years.

The first incarnation of the National Weather Service was founded in the wake of the Civil War, as an agency in the Army Signal Service Corps. Its mission was to "take observations at military stations and to warn of storms on the Great Lakes and on the Atlantic and Gulf Coasts." Very early in its existence the agency earned a reputation for the corruption of its personnel and the unreliability of its forecasting. In 1881, William Howgate, the chief financial manager of the agency, was arrested for embezzling a quarter million dollars. . . . During this time the U.S. military budget was about 40 million dollars. Howgate was tried and convicted, only to escape a year later. Other servicemen in stations around the country were investigated throughout the 1880s and fired in large numbers for reckless neglect. . . . Moreover, the agency's weather predictions were frequently and dangerously wrong. On March 12, 1888, the New York station's forecast called for "fair weather"; instead of fair weather, New York got the Blizzard of '88, which dumped 21 inches of snow on the city and killed 400 people throughout the Northeast. . . .

In 1891, the Army Signal Service Corps's weather service was honorably discharged from the Department of War and given a new home in the civilian Department of Agriculture. It was named the Weather Bureau: it would not be called the National Weather Service until 1970. During the years leading up to 1900, the Weather Bureau's servicemen took regular measurement of such atmospheric conditions as temperature, wind speed, air pressure, rainfall, and cloud conditions. They transmitted their findings to one another via wireless telegraphy.

> Time words and phrases

> Order words and phrases

> Events

PRACTICE AND APPLY

ANSWERS

1. *from least to most*

2. ***Possible answer:*** *"first," "next important," "final," "most important"*

3. *least to most important: "first," "second," "finally"*

PRACTICE AND APPLY

ANSWERS

1. Answers should include five of the following: "early in its existence," "during this time," "On March 12, 1888," "In 1891," "until 1970," "During the years leading up to 1900."

2. Timeline should include the following dates and events:

   1881: William Howgate is arrested for embezzlement.

   1880s: Servicemen in stations around the country are investigated and fired for reckless neglect.

   1888: The New York station forecasts fair weather and a blizzard hits.

   1891: Army Signal Service Corps's weather service is discharged from the Department of War, given a new home in the Department of Agriculture, and renamed the Weather Bureau.

   1890s: Weather Bureau's servicemen take regular measurement of atmospheric conditions and report them via telegraph.

   1970: Weather Bureau is renamed National Weather Service.

3. Cause: Chief financial manager embezzles money

   Cause: Many servicemen fired for reckless neglect

   Cause: Weather predictions dangerously wrong

   Effect: Army Signal Service Corps gains reputation for being corrupt and unreliable

Refer to the preceding model to do the following:

1. List at least five words or phrases from the model that indicate time order. Do not use words that are already highlighted.

2. Draw a timeline beginning in 1881 and ending with "today." On the timeline chart major events in the formation of the National Weather Service as described in the model.

3. Sometimes more than one pattern of organization is used to help organize a text. Reread paragraph two, and find at least three causes for the Army Signal Service Corps's reputation as a corrupt and unreliable agency. Use the "multiple causes with a single effect" form shown on this page to chart this information.

3.3 CAUSE-EFFECT ORGANIZATION

Cause-effect organization is a pattern of organization that establishes causal relationships between events, ideas, and trends. Cause-effect relationships may be directly stated or merely implied by the order in which the information is presented. Writers often use the cause-effect pattern in historical and scientific writing. Cause-effect relationships may take several forms.

One cause with one effect

One cause with multiple effects

Multiple causes with a single effect

A chain of causes and effects

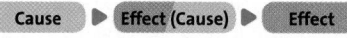

Strategies for Reading

- Look for headings and subheadings that indicate a cause-effect pattern of organization, such as "The Effects of Improved Weather Forecasting."
- To find the effect or effects, read to answer the question, What happened?
- To find the cause or causes, read to answer the question, Why did it happen?
- Look for words and phrases that help you identify specific relationships between events, such as *because, since, so, had the effect of, led to, as a result, resulted in, for that reason, due to, therefore, if . . . then,* and *consequently.*
- Evaluate each cause-effect relationship. Do not assume that because one event happened before another, the first event caused the second event.
- Use graphic organizers like the diagrams shown to record cause-effect relationships as you read.

Notice the words that signal causes and effects in the following model.

> **MODEL**
>
> ### The Formation of a Hurricane: What Does It Take?
>
> Hurricanes have waged war on U.S. cities like no other enemy. Each year, up to ten tropical storms may form in the Atlantic Ocean and make their way west. Typically, three to five have the potential to become a full-blown hurricane. These high-speed monsters are fueled by the simplest of natural elements: water, wind, and air. Given the right conditions, these essential elements for life can become lethal.
>
> The first condition for the formation of a hurricane involves warming ocean water in a relatively tranquil and tropical region of the Atlantic. By late summer, the surface water becomes thoroughly heated and begins to evaporate, or rise into the air. This process creates warm, moist air, which then rises and eventually condenses to form clouds and rain. During this process, energy is released, warming the air further.

Causes

Effect that in turn becomes a cause

The second condition, ironically, is the lack of wind. In the tropical regions of the Atlantic, the air may be relatively stagnant in places, which causes the warm, moist air to remain in one spot. Because the air is continuing to warm and gain energy, it needs to move, and so it does: upward. This column of upward-moving warm air creates an area of low pressure over the water, which in turn draws even more air from the surrounding area toward the center of the column. In addition, the inward-moving air causes the warm air to rise even faster, which then draws even more air and increases its wind speed. Thus, the transfer of energy from ocean to air begins to fuel itself with ever-increasing speed.

Signal words and phrases

As the air moves toward the column's center, it does not move in a straight line, but moves in a circular motion as a result of the earth's rotation. As the air moves up the column, it continues swirling.

A storm that continues in this cycle may grow up to 500 miles in diameter. Its westward movement ensures that it will eventually hit land if it doesn't dissipate, and what began as a simple combination of water, wind, and air could turn into a catastrophic storm.

PRACTICE AND APPLY

Refer to the preceding model to do the following:

1. Use the pattern of multiple causes with a single effect illustrated on page R10 to make a graphic organizer showing the causes described in the text and the effect of those causes.

2. List any words and phrases the writer uses to signal cause and effect in the third paragraph.

3.4 COMPARE-AND-CONTRAST ORGANIZATION

Compare-and-contrast organization is a pattern of organization that serves as a framework for examining similarities and differences in two or more subjects. A writer may use this pattern of organization to analyze two or more subjects, such as characters or movies, in terms of their important points or characteristics. These points or characteristics are called points of comparison. The compare-and-contrast pattern of organization may be developed in either of two ways.

Point-by-point organization—The writer discusses one point of comparison for both subjects, then goes on to the next point.

Subject-by-subject organization—The writer covers all points of comparison for one subject and then all points of comparison for the next subject.

Strategies for Reading

- Look in the text for headings, subheadings, and sentences that may suggest a compare-and-contrast pattern of organization, such as "East Coast and West Coast Living: More than a Continent Apart." These will help you identify where similarities and differences are addressed.

- To find similarities, look for words and phrases such as *like, similarly, both, also,* and *in the same way.*

- To find differences, look for words and phrases such as *unlike, but, on the other hand, in contrast,* and *however.*

- Use a graphic organizer, such as a Venn diagram or a compare-and-contrast chart, to record points of comparison and similarities and differences.

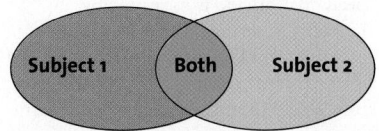

	Subject 1	Subject 2
Point 1		
Point 2		
Point 3		

PRACTICE AND APPLY

ANSWERS

1. *Responses will vary; should include three causes and the effect of a hurricane.*

   One possible answer may include:

   Cause: warm ocean water in a tranquil and tropical region of the Atlantic

   Cause: water becomes heated and begins to evaporate

   Effect: creates warm, moist air, which then rises and forms clouds and rain

   OR

   Cause: warm ocean water in a tranquil and tropical region of the Atlantic

   Cause: lack of wind

   Cause: earth's rotation

   Effect: storm that grows into a hurricane

2. *"causes," "Because," "in turn," "causes," "Thus"*

Read the following models. As you read, use the signal words and phrases to identify the similarities and differences between the subjects and how the details are organized in each text.

MODEL 1

A Tale of Two Furies: Hurricane vs. Tornado

Two of the deadliest types of storms are hurricanes and tornadoes. [Subjects] While both are ferocious wind storms and require similar elements to form, each varies in speed and duration.

Hurricanes, like tornadoes, require the meeting of cool and warm air and begin as rain or thunderstorms. However, [Contrast words and phrases] one major difference between the two is that a hurricane forms at sea and moves toward land, while a tornado forms over, and remains on, land. Hurricanes require large amounts of warmth and moisture from ocean water to form, while tornadoes rely on the moisture already in the air. The duration of a hurricane is one week, on average. A few rare hurricanes have been known to last between 17 and 27 days. The average tornado, however, lasts 10 to 30 minutes, and may "touch down" on land for up to a minute.

Both tornadoes and hurricanes can be measured. The difference is in *how* and *when*. The wind [Comparison words] speed of a tornado is measured by the Fujita Scale, or F-Scale, which rates intensity from F0, with winds less than 73 miles per hour, through F5, with winds from 261–318 mph. Since tornados form very quickly and cannot be accurately predicted, the F-Scale can only measure the strength of a tornado *after* it has occurred. In contrast, the intensity of hurricanes can be measured *while* they are forming. This is because unlike tornados, hurricanes form slowly and can be photographed using satellite imagery. The satellite pictures are then studied, and the results applied to a scale of measure called the Saffir-Simpson Hurricane Scale. This scale rates intensity from Category One through the most intense Category 5 storm.

MODEL 2

Same Goal, Different Methods

Booker T. Washington and [Subjects] W. E. B. Du Bois were alike in many ways. Both were devoted to helping [Comparison words] their fellow African Americans attain equal rights. Both were educated black men with university teaching positions. Both also worked passionately toward their goal at the beginning of the 20th century. Nevertheless, they were not allies. Why? They had very different [Contrast words and phrases] ideas about how blacks should go about attaining equal rights.

Washington believed that for black people to achieve equal status and power as citizens they needed to focus on learning crafts, farming, and industrial skills. He argued that by gaining vocational skills and economic security, black people would naturally earn the respect and acceptance of the white community. To achieve these goals, however, Washington believed black people would need to let go temporarily of the fight for civil rights and political power.

In contrast to Washington, W. E. B. Du Bois believed that black people could not afford to stop fighting for civil rights and political power. In his opinion, only agitation and protest would achieve social change. According to Du Bois, in the climate of extreme racism that existed in America at the time, Washington's approach would merely cause blacks to suffer even more oppression.

So although these two African-American contemporaries had the same goal, their different approaches to achieving this goal made them adversaries rather than allies.

PRACTICE AND APPLY

Refer to the preceding models to do the following:

For each model, create a compare-and-contrast chart. In your chart, list the points of comparison in each model, and identify the similarities and differences between each model's subjects.

PRACTICE AND APPLY

ANSWERS

"Tale of Two Furies":

Similarities of hurricanes and tornadoes: deadliest storms, require similar elements, strength can be measured

Differences: Speed and duration; hurricane forms over sea and moves toward land, tornado forms over land and remains there; hurricanes require large amounts of moisture from ocean water, while tornadoes rely on moisture already in the air. Hurricane strength can be measured while the storm is forming, whereas a tornado's strength can only be measured after the storm has occurred.

"Same Goal, Different Methods":

Similarities between Booker T. Washington and W.E.B. DuBois: devoted to helping African Americans attain equal rights; educated; held teaching positions; worked passionately toward their goals

Differences: ideas about how African Americans should attain equal rights

4 Reading Informational Texts: Forms

Magazines, newspapers, Web pages, and procedural, public, and workplace documents are all examples of informational materials. To understand and analyze informational texts, pay attention to text features and patterns of organization.

4.1 READING A MAGAZINE ARTICLE

Because people often skim magazines for topics of interest, magazine publishers use devices to attract attention to articles and to highlight key information.

Strategies for Reading

A Read the **title** and other **headings** to find out more about the article's topic and organization.

B Notice whether or not the article has a **byline,** a line naming the author, and make note of the date and source.

C Examine **illustrations, photos,** or other **graphic aids** that visually convey or illustrate additional information, or information from the text.

D Notice **pull quotes,** or quotations that a publisher has pulled out of the text and displayed to get your attention.

PRACTICE AND APPLY

Refer to the article to answer the following questions:

1. What does the title indicate the topic will be?

2. Why is this particular pull quote significant? What information does it convey?

3. Considering the information in the text and the visual image in the photo, what can you conclude about the severity of the hurricane mentioned in the article?

Katrina's South American Sister

A Was Catarina an omen of things to come?

For people along the Gulf Coast, Hurricane Katrina was an unimaginable disaster. In meteorological terms, however, she was not unusual—a major storm for sure, but not atypical of what comes across the North Atlantic at that time of year. The one thing experts did note was that ocean temperatures in the Gulf of Mexico are especially warm these days.

D "The real shocker had come 18 months earlier . . . And her name was Catarina."

For hurricane watchers, however, the real shocker had come 18 months earlier. And her name was Catarina.

Catarina came ashore in Brazil on March 28, 2004—a category-one hurricane that damaged 30,000 homes. Scientists were baffled. Brazilian meteorologists didn't even use the term "hurricane" at first—not until they looked closely at the satellite images. Why? Very simply, no hurricanes had ever been recorded before in the South Atlantic. Conventional wisdom was that cool ocean temperatures and atmospheric differences made it impossible for hurricanes to form there.

But here was Hurricane Catarina, and, indeed, a couple of months earlier, on January 19th, a smaller tropical storm had also developed off the coast of Brazil.

The entire phenomenon was unprecedented. . . . Is it another indicator of global warming? Researchers say that any such analysis is, at this stage, speculative. Regardless, it might make sense to plan for the worst, rather than continually hoping for the best.

PRACTICE AND APPLY

ANSWERS

1. *Hurricanes; specifically, Hurricanes Katrina and Catarina*

2. *In some ways, Hurricane Catarina was more shocking than Hurricane Katrina.*

3. *It was devastating and resulted in massive destruction.*

4.2 READING A TEXTBOOK

Each textbook that you use has its own system of organization, based on the content in the book. Often an introductory unit will explain the book's organization and special features. If your textbook has such a unit, read it first.

Strategies for Reading

Ⓐ Before you begin reading the lesson or chapter, read any **questions** that appear at the end of it. Then use the questions to set your purpose for reading.

Ⓑ **Read slowly and carefully** to better understand and remember the ideas presented in the text. When you come to an unfamiliar word, first try to figure out its meaning from **context clues.** If necessary, find the meaning of the word in a **sidenote** on the page, in a **glossary** at the back of the book, or in a dictionary. Avoid interrupting your reading by constantly looking up words in a dictionary.

Ⓒ Use the book's **graphic aids,** such as illustrations, diagrams, and photos, to clarify your understanding of the text.

Ⓓ Take notes as you read. Use text features such as **subheadings** and **boldfaced terms** to help you organize your notes. Use graphic organizers, such as cause-effect charts, to help you clarify relationships among ideas.

PRACTICE AND APPLY

1. What is the definition of *nationalization*?

2. Where on the page do you find the combined private and public debt owed during this time? What was the total amount?

3. Use the text on this page and on R3 to answer the second question in the Section Review of the textbook page.

The New Deal Comes Under Attack

Ⓓ **THREE FIERY CRITICS** In 1934, some of the strongest conservative opponents of the New Deal banded together to form an organization called the American Liberty League. The American Liberty League opposed New Deal measures that it believed violated respect for the rights of individuals and property. Three of the toughest critics the president faced, however, were three men who expressed views that appealed to poor Americans: Charles Coughlin, Dr. Francis Townsend, and Huey Long.

Every Sunday, Father Charles Coughlin, a Roman Catholic priest from a suburb of Detroit, broadcast radio sermons that combined economic, political, and religious ideas. Initially a supporter of the New Deal, Coughlin soon turned against Roosevelt. He favored a guaranteed annual income and the **nationalization** of banks. At the height of his popularity, Father Coughlin claimed a radio audience of as many as 40–45 million people, but his increasingly anti-Semitic (anti-Jewish) views eventually cost him support.

Ⓑ **Vocabulary**
nationalization: conversion from private to governmental ownership

Another critic of New Deal policies was Dr. Francis Townsend, a physician and health officer in Long Beach, California. He believed that Roosevelt wasn't doing enough to help the poor and elderly, so he devised a pension plan that would provide monthly benefits to the aged. The plan found strong backing among the elderly, thus undermining their support for Roosevelt.

Ⓓ Perhaps the most serious challenge to the New Deal came from Senator **Huey Long** of Louisiana. Like Coughlin, Long was an early supporter of the New Deal, but he, too, turned against Roosevelt. Eager to win the presidency for himself, Long proposed a nationwide social program called Share-Our-Wealth. Under the banner "Every Man a King," he promised something for everyone.

Ⓒ

Huey Long

A PERSONAL VOICE HUEY LONG
"We owe debts in America today, public and private, amounting to $252 billion. That means that every child is born with a $2,000 debt tied around his neck. . . . We propose that children shall be born in a land of opportunity, guaranteed a home, food, clothes, and the other things that make for living, including the right to education."
—*Record, 74 Congress, Session 1*

Long's program was so popular that by 1935 he boasted of having perhaps as many as 27,000 Share-Our-Wealth clubs and 7.5 million members. That same year, however, at the height of his popularity, Long was assassinated by a lone gunman.

As the initial impetus of the New Deal began to wane, President Roosevelt started to look ahead. He knew that much more needed to be done to help the people and to solve the nation's economic problems.

Ⓐ

ASSESSMENT

SECTION REVIEW
- Name the three outspoken critics of Roosevelt's New Deal.
- Describe one New Deal program, and explain one opponent's view of the New Deal.
- **Critical Thinking** Of the New Deal programs discussed, which do you consider the most important? Consider scope, impact, and type of assistance offered by each.

The New Deal **493**

PRACTICE AND APPLY

ANSWERS

1. *conversion from private to governmental ownership*

2. *Huey Long's quote; $252 billion*

3. *Responses will vary. Students may respond that the New Deal program provided economic aid to the American population suffering from the effects of the Great Depression. One opponent was Dr. Francis Townsend, who believed the New Deal program didn't do enough to help the poor.*

4.3 READING PROCEDURAL DOCUMENTS

Procedural documents are functional documents that accompany products and services. They usually provide information about the use, care, operation, or assembly of the products they accompany. Some common procedural documents are contracts, warranties, manuals, instructions, schedules, and Web pages.

Strategies for Reading

A Read the **title** to identify the purpose of the document.

B Read the **general directions** to get started.

C Look for **numbers** or **letters** that indicate the steps to be followed. Note whether the steps must be done in order and whether there are signal words such as *first, next, then,* and *finally* that indicate the order in which the steps should be followed. Follow the steps in order.

D Refer to any **illustrations, diagrams,** or other **graphic aids** that accompany the numbered instructions. Use the graphic aids to help you understand each step.

E Look for **verbs that describe actions you should take,** such as *press, use,* and *hold.*

PRACTICE AND APPLY

1. Explain the function of key number 10.

2. Identify the number of the key that allows you to engage the phone's locking function.

INSTRUCTIONS FOR USING A CELL PHONE

A PHONE OVERVIEW

B Use this guide to get a quick overview of your phone's functions.

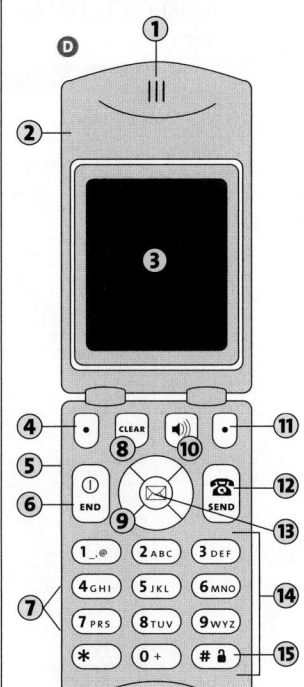

C 1. **Earpiece** **E**

2. **Flip** Flip open the case to answer incoming calls and close to end calls.

3. **LCD Screen** Displays messages and icons.

4. **Left Soft Key** Use to display the function-setting menu.

5. **Headset Jack**

6. **END/POWER Key** Use to turn the power on or off and to end a call.

7. **Side Keys** Use to adjust the ringer volume in standby mode and the earpiece volume during a call.

8. **CLEAR Key** Press to delete a single space or character. Press and hold to delete entire words. Press this key once in a menu to go back one level.

9. **Navigation Key** Use for quick access to messages or Web.

10. **Speaker Key** Use to set Speaker on or off.

11. **Right Soft Key** Use to select an action in a menu.

12. **SEND Key** Use to place or answer calls.

13. **Message Key** Use to retrieve or send voice and text messages.

14. **Alphanumeric Keypad** Use the keys to enter numbers and characters and to select menu items.

15. **Lock Mode Key** Use in standby mode to set the lock function by pressing and holding the key for about 3 seconds.

PRACTICE AND APPLY

ANSWERS

1. *It turns the speaker phone on and off.*

2. *number 15*

PRACTICE AND APPLY

ANSWERS

1. *Knives are not allowed as carry-on items unless they are plastic or round-bladed butter knives. Knives are allowed as a checked item.*

2. *plastic with blunt tips, metal with blunt tips, ostomy scissors*

3. *to ensure prohibited items are not concealed*

4. *Responses will vary.*

4.4 READING A PUBLIC DOCUMENT

Public documents are functional documents that are written for the public to provide information that is of public interest or concern. These documents are often free. They can be federal, state, or local government documents. They can be speeches or historical documents. They may even be laws, posted warnings, signs, or rules and regulations. The following is a public document that has been posted on a U.S. government Web site and can be printed as a document.

Strategies for Reading

Ⓐ Look at the **title** on the page to discover what the text is about.

Ⓑ Note the **source** of the document.

Ⓒ Carefully read **column headings** in the table. Items in a table are usually essential pieces of information.

Ⓓ Be sure to read **parenthetical text** if there is any. This information may help clarify meaning, provide examples, or further explain an entry.

Ⓔ Pay attention to **notes** and **asterisks** (*) and their accompanying footnotes. These will help clarify exceptions or exemptions to the rules, or add additional detail.

PRACTICE AND APPLY

Reread the TSA page and then answer the following questions:

1. Are knives allowed as a carry-on item? as a checked item?

2. Name the three types of scissors that are allowed as carry-on items.

3. Walking canes are allowed as a carry-on and as a checked item. Why do they need to be inspected?

4. Guidelines for acceptable carry-on and checked items on flights are revised periodically. Verify that the items listed here are up-to-date by checking the Transportation Security Administration Web site: www.tsa.gov. Search the site for a list of permitted and prohibited items. Key words to look for are *Travelers* and *Prohibited Items.*

RULES AND REGULATIONS FOR CARRY-ON ITEMS IN AIR TRAVEL

U.S. Department of Homeland Security
Transportation Security Administration
Arlington, VA 22202

Ⓐ Permitted and Prohibited Items

Ⓑ Transportation Security Administration

Can I take it?	Carry-on	Checked
Personal Items		
Cigar Cutters	Yes	Yes
Corkscrews	Yes	Yes
Cuticle Cutters	Yes	Yes
Eyeglass Repair Tools (including screwdrivers) **Ⓓ**	Yes	Yes
Eyelash Curlers	Yes	Yes
Knitting and Crochet Needles	Yes	Yes
Knives - prohibited as carry-on except for plastic or round bladed butter knives.	No	Yes
Nail Clippers	Yes	Yes
Nail Files	Yes	Yes
Personal care or toiletries with aerosols, in limited quantities (such as hairsprays, deodorants)	Yes	Yes
Safety Razors (including disposable razors)	Yes	Yes
Scissors - plastic or metal with blunt tips	Yes	Yes
Scissors - metal with pointed tips and blades longer than four inches in length	No	Yes
Toy Transformer Robots	Yes	Yes
Toy Weapons (if not realistic replicas)	Yes	Yes
Tweezers	Yes	Yes
Umbrellas (allowed in carry-on baggage once they have been inspected to ensure that prohibited items are not concealed)	Yes	Yes
Walking Canes (allowed in carry-on baggage once they have been inspected to ensure that prohibited items are not concealed)	Yes	Yes

Ⓔ Note Some personal care items containing aerosol are regulated as hazardous materials. The FAA regulates hazardous materials. This information is summarized at www.faa.gov, click on Passengers, then Preparing to Fly.

Medication and Special Needs Devices		
Braille Note-Taker, Slate and Stylus, Augmentation Devices	Yes	Yes
Diabetes-Related Supplies/Equipment, (once inspected to ensure prohibited items are not concealed) including: insulin and insulin loaded dispensing products; vials or box of individual vials; jet injectors; pens; infusers; and preloaded syringes; and an unlimited number of unused syringes, when accompanied by insulin; lancets; blood glucose meters; blood glucose meter test strips; insulin pumps; and insulin pump supplies. Insulin in any form or dispenser must be properly marked with a professionally printed label identifying the medication or manufacturer's name or pharmaceutical label.	Yes	Yes
Nitroglycerine pills or spray for medical use (if properly marked with a professionally printed label identifying the medication or manufacturer's name or pharmaceutical label)	Yes	Yes
Ostomy Scissors All scissors with blades four inches or less	Yes	Yes
Prosthetic Device Tools and Appliances, including drill, allen wrenches, pullsleeves used to put on or remove prosthetic devices, if carried by the individual with the prosthetic device or his or her companion	Yes	Yes

U.S. Department of Homeland Security
TSA- Rev. 12-1-2005

Page 3 of 5

4.5 READING A WORKPLACE DOCUMENT

Workplace documents are materials that are produced or used within a workplace, usually to aid in the functioning of a business. These documents include meeting minutes, sales reports, statements of company policy or organizational structure, and explanations of operating procedures. Workplace documents also include memos, business letters, job applications, and résumés.

Strategies for Reading

A Use **headings** and **subheadings** to help you locate information that is relevant or important to you.

B Read a workplace document slowly and carefully, as it may contain **details** that should not be overlooked.

C Notice how to contact the creator of the document. You will need this information to clear up anything that you don't understand.

PRACTICE AND APPLY

Refer to the company policy statement to answer the following questions:

1. How long does an employee need to work at HBA before he or she is eligible for three weeks of paid vacation?

2. Under which section(s) would you look if you traveled extensively for work and were interested in insurance that specifically covered accidents while traveling?

3. Does the company offer supplemental life insurance? Does the company or the employee pay for it?

4. How much short-term disability coverage does the company provide free of charge to an employee?

COMPANY POLICY STATEMENT

HBA Company
Employee Benefits Policy

Medical Benefits **B**

HBA offers four medical choices, which include two options that are at no cost to our employees. We also offer dental, vision, and an Employee Assistance Program at no cost to employees.

Retirement and Savings Plan **A**

HBA's contributions to your retirement plan are guaranteed at 5% of your annual earnings, plus up to an additional 10% variable contribution (based on company performance).

Life Insurance

At no cost to the employee, life insurance is provided for three times his or her annual base salary, not to exceed $500,000. Employees may also elect to purchase supplemental life insurance for themselves, their spouse, and eligible dependent children.

Disability Programs

Accidental Death and Dismemberment Insurance—Eligible employees are covered for up to three times their annual base salary, not to exceed $500,000, depending on the extent of injury.

Short-Term Disability—Eligible employees receive a short-term disability benefit of 60% of their salary and may elect to "buy-up" additional coverage to a maximum 70% benefit.

Long-Term Disability—Eligible employees are provided coverage at a benefit amount of 50% of their salary and may elect to "buy-up" additional coverage to a total benefit level of 67%.

Travel Accident Insurance—Eligible employees are covered for $35,000 to $500,000, depending on their annual base salary.

Time Off Benefits

Vacation—Employees earn time off at the rate of two weeks per year for the first five years of employment, three weeks per year after five years of employment, and four weeks per year after ten years of employment.

Sick Leave—Employees earn at a rate of one week per year.

Holidays—Employees are paid for eight calendar holidays. Employees also receive three floating holidays per calendar year after six months of employment.

C If you have any questions, contact the HBA Human Resources Department.

PRACTICE AND APPLY
ANSWERS

1. *five years*
2. *Travel Accident Insurance*
3. *The company provides supplemental life insurance, which the employee purchases.*
4. *60% of the employee's salary*

PRACTICE AND APPLY

ANSWERS

1. *The topic is the struggle for Western women's suffrage between 1860 and 1920.*

2. *"New Mexico" or the star on the state of New Mexico*

3. *Women of the West museum*

4. *Students should consult government or encyclopedic sources to determine whether or not the site's information is accurate. Have students create a report comparing the information on the Web site with that in the other reference sources.*

4.6 READING ELECTRONIC TEXT

Electronic text is any text that is in a form that a computer can store and display on a screen. Electronic text can be part of Web pages, CD-ROMs, search engines, and documents that you create with your computer software. Like books, Web pages often provide aids to finding information. However, each Web page is designed differently, and information is not in the same location on each page. It is important to know the functions of different parts of a Web page so that you can easily find the information you want.

Strategies for Reading

A Look at the **title** of a page to determine what topics it covers.

B For an online source, such as a Web page or a search engine, note the **Web address,** known as a **URL** (uniform resource locator), in case you need to return to the page later or cite it as a source.

C Look for the **menu options,** or navigation options that allow you to navigate through the site's main categories and pages. These options are **links** to other pages providing more in-depth information on the topic listed.

D Read **introductory text** to get a sense of the site's subject matter and purpose.

E Use **hyperlinks** to get to other pages on the site. Hyperlinks may lead to pages listed in the menu options or to other Web sites related in subject matter.

F Look for **graphic aids,** such as photos, illustrations, or animation, that will provide you with more information about the site's topic(s).

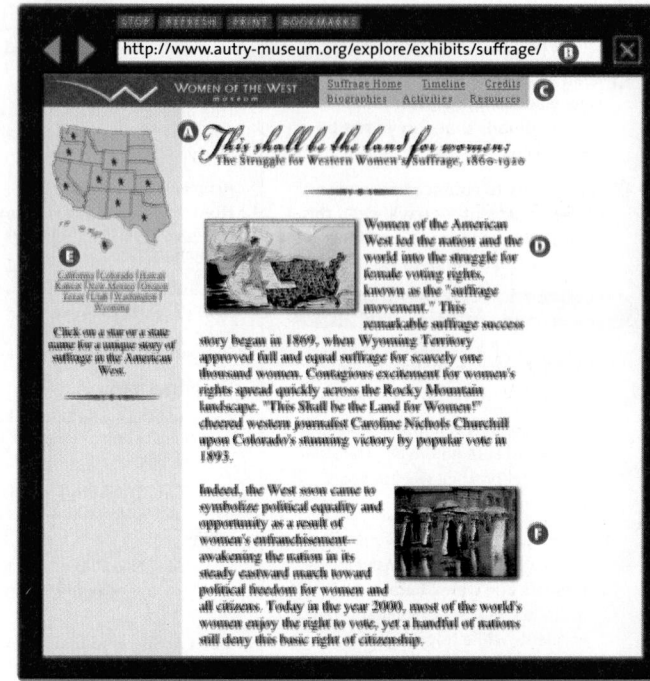

PRACTICE AND APPLY

1. What is the topic of this site?

2. If you were searching for information on suffrage in New Mexico, which links or hyperlinks would you use?

3. Who has produced this Web site?

4. Verify the information on women's suffrage in the Wyoming Territory presented on this Web page by consulting a reference source, such as an encyclopedia, or a government document.

5 Reading Persuasive Texts

5.1 ANALYZING AN ARGUMENT

An **argument** expresses a position on an issue or problem and supports it with reasons and evidence. Being able to analyze and evaluate arguments will help you distinguish between claims you should accept and those you should not. A sound argument should appeal strictly to reason. However, arguments are often used in texts that also contain other types of persuasive devices. An argument includes the following elements:

- A **claim** is the writer's position on an issue or problem.

- **Support** is any material that serves to prove a claim. In an argument, support usually consists of reasons and evidence.

- **Reasons** are declarations made to justify an action, a decision, or a belief—for example, "You should sleep on a good mattress *in order to avoid spinal problems.*"

- **Evidence** consists of the specific references, quotations, facts, examples, and opinions that support a claim. Evidence may also consist of statistics, reports of personal experience, or the views of experts.

- A **counterargument** is an argument made to oppose another argument. A good argument anticipates the opposition's objections and provides counterarguments to disprove or answer them.

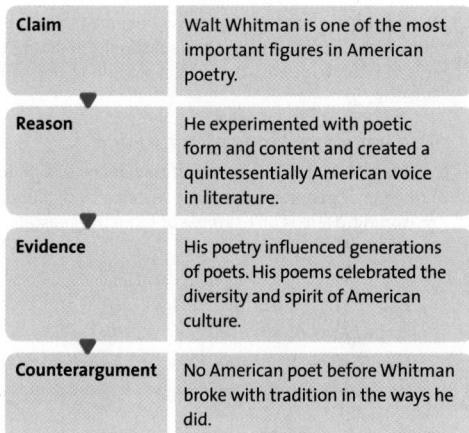

Claim	Walt Whitman is one of the most important figures in American poetry.
Reason	He experimented with poetic form and content and created a quintessentially American voice in literature.
Evidence	His poetry influenced generations of poets. His poems celebrated the diversity and spirit of American culture.
Counterargument	No American poet before Whitman broke with tradition in the ways he did.

PRACTICE AND APPLY

In the early 1900s, Elinore Pruitt Stewart (formerly Rupert), was living in Burnt Fork, Wyoming, as a homesteader, a person who received public land free of charge under the Homestead Act of 1862. In the following letter to a friend, she makes an argument for homestead living over an impoverished city existence. Use a chart like the one shown to identify the claim, reason, evidence, and counterargument in her letter.

> January 23, 1913
>
> Dear Mrs. Coney,—
>
> . . . When I read of the hard times among the Denver poor, I feel like urging them every one to get out and file on land. I am very enthusiastic about women homesteading. It really requires less strength and labor to raise plenty to satisfy a large family than it does to go out to wash, with the added satisfaction of knowing that their job will not be lost to them if they care to keep it. Even if improving the place does go slowly, it is that much done to stay done. Whatever is raised is the homesteader's own, and there is no house-rent to pay. This year Jerrine cut and dropped enough potatoes to raise a ton of fine potatoes. She wanted to try, so we let her, and you will remember that she is but six years old. We had a man to break the ground and cover the potatoes for her and the man irrigated them once. That was all that was done until digging time, when they were ploughed out and Jerrine picked them up. Any woman strong enough to go out by the day could have done every bit of the work and put in two or three times that much, and it would have been so much more pleasant than to work so hard in the city and then be on starvation rations in the winter.
>
> To me, homesteading is the solution of all poverty's problems, but I realize that temperament has much to do with success in any undertaking, and persons afraid of coyotes and work and loneliness had better let ranching alone. At the same time, any woman who can stand her own company, can see the beauty of the sunset, loves growing things, and is willing to put in as much time at careful labor as she does over the washtub, will certainly succeed; will have independence, plenty to eat all the time, and a home of her own in the end.

PRACTICE AND APPLY

ANSWERS

Claim
Women homesteading is the solution to poverty's problems.

Reason
Homesteading means job security and a home.

Evidence
It is possible to plant, grow, and harvest enough food for a family to eat through the winter.

Counterargument
It is not for those afraid of coyotes and hard work and loneliness, but for those who can do it, it will result in independence, plenty of food, and a home of one's own.

PRACTICE AND APPLY

ANSWERS

Answers could include the following:

> *"feel so splendid": transfer*
>
> *"local celebrities . . . join them": testimonial, snob appeal*
>
> *"necessities to less fortunate . . . least we can do": appeal to pity*

5.2 RECOGNIZING PERSUASIVE TECHNIQUES

Persuasive texts typically rely on more than just the logical appeal of an argument to be convincing. They also rely on ethical and emotional appeals, as well as other **persuasive techniques**—devices that can sway you to adopt a position or take an action.

The chart shown here explains several of these techniques. Learn to recognize them, and you will be less likely to be influenced by them.

Persuasive Technique	Example
Appeals by Association	
Bandwagon appeal Suggests that a person should believe or do something because "everyone else" does	Join the millions who've contributed to The Cause: buy your 'Be Well' bracelet today.
Testimonial Relies on endorsements from well-known people or satisfied customers	DJ Super Dawg keeps songs spinning all day long with his new CompactM3 disc player. Give it a whirl!
Snob appeal Taps into people's desire to be special or part of an elite group	In Smart and Sassy cosmetics, you'll look and feel like the princess you are.
Transfer Connnects a product, candidate, or cause with a positive emotion or idea	Rediscover peace and tranquility with Back in Balance aromatherapy candles.
Appeal to loyalty Relies on people's affiliation with a particular group	Only Substantial Bank offers long-term customers better rates.
Emotional Appeals	
Appeals to pity, fear, or vanity Use strong feelings, rather than facts, to persuade	The cost of one candy bar can help buy a whole meal for a starving family.
Word Choice	
Glittering generality Makes a generalization that includes a word or phrase with positive connotations, such as *freedom* and *honor*, to promote a product or idea.	Improve your children's future: plant a tree on World Tree Day.

PRACTICE AND APPLY

Identify the persuasive techniques used in the model.

The Real Scoop

On my last trip to the Splendid Dan's Ice Cream Shoppe to get a Swirling Fantasia Double Dip Delight, I was thrilled to find yet another reason that makes buying dessert at Dan's feel so splendid. During the next 30 days at the downtown location, a whopping 40 percent of Dan's proceeds will go toward helping the homeless in our city. Forty percent! No wonder so many local celebrities, like news anchor Tandy Marquez and Mayor Donald Townsend, have been spotted at Dan's. They know that with each purchase, they are also providing food, clothing, and shelter for those in need. If you join them, you'll have not only the most amazing ice cream on the planet, but also the added joy of providing life's basic necessities to the less fortunate. It's the least we can do to better our city, so stop by Splendid Dan's—he's got the "real scoop."

5.3 ANALYZING LOGIC AND REASONING

When you evaluate an argument, you need to look closely at the writer's logic and reasoning. In doing this, it is helpful to identify the type of reasoning the writer is using.

The Inductive Mode of Reasoning

When a writer leads from specific evidence to a general principle or generalization, that writer is using **inductive reasoning.** Here is an example of inductive reasoning.

SPECIFIC FACTS

Fact 1 Harriet Beecher Stowe's *Uncle Tom's Cabin* helped alert Americans to the horrors of slavery.

Fact 2 Rachel Carson's *Silent Spring* helped make the public aware of the dangers of overuse of pesticides.

Fact 3 Betty Friedan's *The Feminine Mystique* prompted women to seek equal rights.

GENERALIZATION

Literature can sometimes help to shape public opinion.

Strategies for Determining the Soundness of Inductive Arguments

Ask yourself the following questions to evaluate an inductive argument:

- **Is the evidence valid and sufficient support for the conclusion?** Inaccurate facts lead to inaccurate conclusions. Make sure all facts are accurate.

- **Does the conclusion follow logically from the evidence?** Make sure the writer has used sound reasons—those that can be proved—as the basis for the conclusion and has avoided logical fallacies, such as circular logic and oversimplification.

- **Is the evidence drawn from a large enough sample?** The three facts listed in the example are enough to support the claim. By qualifying the generalization with words such as *sometimes, some,* or *many,* the writer indicates the generalization is limited to a specific group.

The Deductive Mode of Reasoning

When a writer arrives at a conclusion by applying a general principle to a specific situation, the writer is using **deductive reasoning.** Here's an example.

| People have the right to revolt when oppressed. | General principle or premise |

▼

| The American colonies are oppressed by British rule. | Specific situation |

▼

| The American colonies are justified in fighting for freedom from British rule. | Specific conclusion |

Strategies for Determining the Soundness of Deductive Arguments

Ask yourself the following questions to evaluate a deductive argument:

- **Is the general principle stated, or is it implied?** Note that writers often use deductive reasoning in an argument without stating the general principle. They assume readers will understand the principle. You may want to identify the general principle for yourself.

- **Is the general principle sound?** Don't assume the general principle is sound. Determine whether it is proven.

- **Is the conclusion valid?** To be valid, a conclusion in a deductive argument must follow logically from the general principle and the specific situation.

The following chart shows two conclusions drawn from the same general principle.

General Principle: All government offices were closed last Monday.	
Accurate Deduction	**Inaccurate Deduction**
West Post Office is a government office; therefore, West Post Office was closed last Monday.	Soon-Lin's Spa was closed last Monday; therefore, Soon-Lin's Spa is a government office.

The conclusion that Soon-Lin's Spa is a government office does not make logical sense because other factors determine whether or not it is a government office.

PRACTICE AND APPLY

Identify the mode of reasoning used in the following:

Detailed research shows that using a cell phone while driving is a key cause of traffic accidents. Many states have already passed laws making "hands free" devices mandatory for cell phone users while driving. However, ear pieces or speaker phones provide very few true safety benefits. The problem is not the way in which a driver is distracted, but the distraction itself. Looking up a phone number, dialing, and concentrating on the conversation can all take a driver's focus, and eyes, off the road.

Betsie Edens, a 19-year-old college student, says she uses her cell phone to get in touch with family, old friends, and fellow college students while making the three-hour drive from her parent's house to Denton State University. "I talk on the phone or send text messages at least two and a half of the three hours it takes to get there," she says.

Betsie is one of millions of teenagers worldwide who do more talking on a cell phone than safe driving. It is time these unsafe drivers focus more on the road and less on their friends' gossip. For the sake of everybody's safety, cell phones must be turned off while on the road.

PRACTICE AND APPLY

ANSWERS

Deductive reasoning is used.

> *General principle: Distractions while driving are unsafe.*

> *Specific situation: Using cell phones while driving is a distraction.*

> *Specific conclusion: Cell phones must be turned off while driving.*

Identifying Faulty Reasoning

Sometimes an argument at first appears to make sense but isn't valid because it is based on a fallacy. A **logical fallacy** is an error in logic. Learn to recognize these common fallacies.

TYPE OF FALLACY	DEFINITION	EXAMPLE
Circular logic	Supporting a statement by simply repeating it in different words	Sport utility vehicles are popular **because more people buy them than any other category of new cars.**
Either/or fallacy	A statement that suggests that there are only two choices available in a situation that really offers more than two options	**Either** we raise the legal driving age **or** accidents caused by teenage drivers will continue to happen.
Oversimplification	An explanation of a complex situation or problem as if it were much more simple than it is	If we would only be more tolerant of people's differences, there would be **no more wars.**
Overgeneralization	A generalization that is too broad. You can often recognize overgeneralizations by the use of words such as *all, everyone, every time, anything, no one,* and *none.*	**Every time** I want to do something my way, my parents say no.
Stereotyping	A dangerous type of overgeneralization. Stereotypes are broad statements about people on the basis of their gender, ethnicity, race, or political, social, professional, or religious group.	**People who work for large corporations** are followers, not leaders.
Attacking the person or name-calling	An attempt to discredit an idea by attacking the person or group associated with it. Candidates often engage in name-calling during political campaigns.	The governor wants to eliminate candy machines in school cafeterias, but **he doesn't know what he's talking about.**
Evading the issue	Refuting an objection with arguments and evidence that do not address its central point	I know I wasn't supposed to use the car last night, **but I did fill up the tank and check the tire pressure.**
Non sequitur	A conclusion that does not follow logically from the "proof" offered to support it. A non sequitur is sometimes used to win an argument by diverting the reader's attention to proof that can't be challenged.	Mr. Crandall is my guidance counselor. **I will definitely get accepted to a private college.**
False cause	The mistake of assuming that because one event occurred after another event in time, the first event caused the second one to occur	The cheerleading squad did the Super Slam Dance, **and because of that, Donny slam-dunked the basketball, and we won the game.**
False analogy	A comparison that doesn't hold up because of a critical difference between the two subjects	Jenny didn't do well in Spanish, **so she'll probably fail German as well.**
Hasty generalization	A conclusion drawn from too little evidence or from evidence that is biased	Two jet planes crashed this year. **Air travel is extremely unsafe.**

PRACTICE AND APPLY

Look for examples of logical fallacies in the following argument. Identify each one and explain why you identified it as such.

> Elephants should be banned from circuses. Leaders of circus companies claim that healthy living environments are provided for the animals, but they, like most business owners, are liars. Sharp bullhooks are used for training, and the elephants are beaten severely everyday. Abuse makes animals more aggressive, everyone knows that. In the last 15 years, captive elephants have killed 65 people and injured 130, so it is clear the elephants are abused by their trainers. Legislation to stop this cruelty should be passed immediately!

5.4 EVALUATING PERSUASIVE TEXTS

Learning how to evaluate persuasive texts and identify bias will help you become more selective when doing research and also help you improve your own reasoning and arguing skills. **Bias** is an inclination for or against a particular opinion or viewpoint. A writer may reveal a strongly positive or negative opinion on an issue by presenting only one way of looking at it or by heavily weighting the evidence on one side of the argument. Additionally, the presence of either of the following is often a sign of bias:

Loaded language consists of words with strongly positive or negative connotations that are intended to influence a reader's attitude.

EXAMPLE: *The superior All-Star Road Warrior offers unparalleled excellence in all-wheel-drive capability and can outperform any car on the road.* (*Superior, unparalleled, excellence,* and *outperform* have positive connotations.)

Propaganda is any form of communication that is so distorted that it conveys false or misleading information. Many logical fallacies—such as name-calling, the either/or fallacy, and false causes—are often used in propaganda. The following example shows an oversimplification. The writer uses one fact to support a particular point of view but does not reveal another fact that does not support that viewpoint.

EXAMPLE: *Since the new administration took office, unemployment rates have been cut in half.* (The writer does not include information about legislation, passed by the previous administration, that created thousands of jobs.)

*For more information, see **Identifying Faulty Reasoning**, page R22.*

Strategies for Evaluating Evidence

It is important to have a set of standards by which you can evaluate persuasive texts. Use the questions below to help you critically assess facts and opinions that are presented as evidence.

- **Are the facts presented verifiable?** Facts can be proved by eyewitness accounts, authoritative sources such as encyclopedias and almanacs, experts, or research.

- **Are the opinions presented credible?** Any opinions offered should be supported by facts, research, eyewitness accounts, or the opinions of experts on the topic.

- **Is the evidence thorough?** Thorough evidence leaves no reasonable questions unanswered. If a choice is offered, background for making the choice should be provided. If taking a side is called for, all sides of the issue should be presented.

- **Is the evidence biased?** Be alert to evidence that contains loaded language or other signs of bias.

- **Is the evidence authoritative?** The people, groups, or organizations that provided the evidence should have credentials that verify their credibility.

- **Is it important that the evidence be current?** Where timeliness is crucial, as in the areas of medicine and technology, the evidence should reflect the latest developments in the areas.

PRACTICE AND APPLY

ANSWERS

Stereotyping, name-calling: "Leaders of circus companies claim that healthy living environments are provided for the animals, but they, like most business owners, are liars."

Overgeneralization: "Abuse makes animals more aggressive, everyone knows that."

Hasty generalization: "In the last 15 years, captive elephants have killed 65 people and injured 130, so it is clear the elephants are abused by their trainers."

PRACTICE AND APPLY

ANSWERS

Facts: *speed bumps being built, cars park bumper to bumper, cars stop in the middle of the street*

Opinions: *Speed bumps are "unnecessary"; no one will be killed if there aren't any speed bumps.*

Bias: *"[N]o-good politicians spend a lot of taxpayer money on a ridiculous irritation"; "they must figure wrongly"; "it is impossible to drive fast on these streets anyway!"*

PRACTICE AND APPLY

ANSWERS

Students' responses will vary but should evaluate the strength of the claim, the evidence supporting the claim, and the counterarguments.

Possible answer may include: The claim is that the town needs to build an ice skating rink. Some of the evidence is adequate, but includes logical fallacies. The writer does not adequately address the counterargument presented.

Read the argument below. Identify the facts, opinions, and elements of bias.

> In our city neighborhood, unnecessary speed bumps are being built on residential streets. Cars park bumper to bumper along both sides of the street, day and night. There is no place to pull over, causing cars to stop in the middle of the street to pick up and drop off passengers. My point is that it is impossible to drive fast on these streets anyway! Why do no-good politicians spend a lot of taxpayer money on a ridiculous irritation for drivers? They must figure wrongly that either they build speed bumps, or some little kid will get killed. That's never happened and it never will.

Strategies for Evaluating an Argument

Make sure that all or most of the following statements are true:

- The argument presents a claim or thesis.
- The claim is connected to its support by a general principle that most readers would readily agree with. Valid general principle: *It is the job of a corporation to provide adequate health benefits to full-time employees.* Invalid general principle: *It is the job of a corporation to ensure its employees are healthy and physically fit.*
- The reasons make sense.
- The reasons are presented in a logical and effective order.
- The claim and all reasons are adequately supported by sound evidence.
- The evidence is adequate, accurate, and appropriate.
- The logic is sound. There are no instances of logical fallacies.
- The argument adequately anticipates reader concerns and addresses them with counterarguments.

Use the preceding criteria to evaluate the strength of the following editorial:

> This town needs an ice skating rink. Everybody knows that ice skating is the only real way to learn balance and coordination, while also exercising. It is, after all, an Olympic event. That is why I believe it is the responsibility of the town council to put aside funding for a year-round ice skating rink.
>
> Our town has always believed that our children's future relies on good development. For intellectual stimulation, the council has provided the public library and the Nature Museum. For creativity, the council has funded the Community Art Center, where kids can learn to make pottery, paint, dance, and sing. But when it comes to a place where youth can go to develop physical skills of balance, rhythm, and strength, we have absolutely nothing.
>
> We also need a rink because ice skating is fun! The town council members are themselves boring individuals and don't think kids should have fun. As one member put it, "There are many places in this town built especially with youth in mind. Ice skating is not a top priority on our list of community needs this year." They obviously feel this way because our football team came in fifth in the conference last year.
>
> But the biggest reason we need an ice skating rink is so that kids can have a place to ice skate. And let's not forget, adults like ice skating, too. Most of the people who make it to the Olympics are over 18.
>
> Either the town council will help our children develop by putting up the rink, or they prove themselves stingy politicians who do not have the town's best interest at heart.

6 Adjusting Reading Rate to Purpose

You may need to change the way you read certain texts in order to understand what you read. To properly adjust the way you read, you need to be aware of what you want to get out of the text you are reading. Once you know your purpose for reading, you can adjust the speed at which you read in response to your purpose and the difficulty of the material.

Determine Your Purpose for Reading

You read different types of materials for different purposes. You may read a novel for enjoyment. You may read a textbook unit to learn a new concept or to master the content for a test. When you read for enjoyment, you naturally read at a pace that is comfortable for you. When you read for information, you need to read material more slowly and thoroughly. When you are being tested on material, you may think you have to read fast, especially if the test is being timed. However, you can actually increase your understanding of the material if you slow down.

Determine Your Reading Rate

The rate at which you read most comfortably is called your **independent reading level.** It is the rate that you use to read materials that you enjoy. To learn to adjust your reading rate to read materials for other purposes, you need to be aware of your independent reading level. You can figure out your reading level by following these steps:

1. Select a passage from a book or story you enjoy.
2. Have a friend or classmate time you as you begin reading the passage silently.
3. Read at the rate that is most comfortable for you.
4. Stop when your friend or classmate tells you one minute has passed.
5. Determine the number of words you read in that minute and write down the number.
6. Repeat the process at least two more times, using different passages.
7. Add the numbers and divide the sum by the number of times your friend timed you. The number you end up with is the average number of words you read per minute—your independent reading rate.

Reading Techniques for Informational Material

Use the following techniques to adapt your reading for informational texts, to prepare for tests, and to better understand what you read:

- **Skimming** is reading quickly to get the general idea of a text. To skim, read only the title, headings, graphic aids, and highlighted words of the text, as well as the first sentence of each paragraph. In addition, read any introduction, conclusion, or summary. Skimming can be especially useful when taking a test. Before reading a passage, you can skim questions that follow it in order to find out what is expected and to better focus on the important ideas in the text.

  When researching a topic, skimming can help you determine whether a source has information that is pertinent to your topic.

- **Scanning** is reading quickly to find a specific piece of information, such as a fact or a definition. When you scan, your eyes sweep across a page, looking for key words that may lead you to the information you want. Use scanning to review for tests and to find answers to questions.

- **Changing pace** is speeding up or slowing down the rate at which you read parts of a particular text. When you come across familiar concepts, you might be able to speed up without misunderstanding them. When you encounter unfamiliar concepts or material presented in an unpredictable way, however, you may need to slow down to process and absorb the information better.

WATCH OUT! Reading too slowly can diminish your ability to comprehend what you read. Make sure you aren't just reading one word at a time.

PRACTICE AND APPLY

Find an article in a magazine or textbook. Skim the article. Then answer the following questions:

1. What did you notice about the organization of the article?

2. What is the main idea of the article?

PRACTICE AND APPLY

ANSWERS

Accept answers that provide an accurate description of the organization of the article and its main ideas.

COMMON CORE FOCUS

W 1a–e Write arguments to support claims in an analysis of substantive topics or texts, using valid reasoning and relevant and sufficient evidence. **W 2a–e** Write informative/explanatory texts to examine and convey complex ideas, concepts, and information clearly and accurately through the effective selection, organization, and analysis of content. **W 3a–e** Write narratives to develop real or imagined experiences or events using effective technique, well-chosen details, and well-structured event sequences. **W 4** Produce clear and coherent writing in which the development, organization, and style are appropriate to task, purpose, and audience. **W 5** Develop and strengthen writing as needed by planning, revising, editing, rewriting, or trying a new approach, focusing on addressing what is most significant for a specific purpose and audience. **W 6** Use technology, including the Internet, to produce, publish, and update individual or shared writing products in response to ongoing feedback, including new arguments or information.

Writing is a process, a journey of discovery in which you can explore your thoughts, experiment with ideas, and search for connections. Through writing, you can explore and record your thoughts, feelings, and ideas for yourself alone, or you can communicate them to an audience.

COMMON CORE

Included in this handbook:
W 1a–e, W 2a–e, W 3a–e, W 4–6

1 The Writing Process

The writing process consists of the following stages: prewriting, drafting, revising and editing, proofreading, and publishing. These are not stages that you must complete in a set order. Rather, you may return to an earlier stage at any time to improve your writing.

1.1 PREWRITING

In the prewriting stage, you explore what you want to write about, what your purpose for writing is, whom you are writing for, and what form you will use to express your ideas. Ask yourself the following questions to get started.

Topic	• Is my topic assigned, or can I choose it? • What am I interested in writing about?
Purpose	• Am I writing to entertain, to inform, or to persuade—or some combination of these? • What effect do I want to have on my readers?
Audience	• Who is the audience? • What might the audience members already know about my topic? • What about the topic might interest them?
Format	• Which format will work best: essay, poem, speech, short story, article, or research paper?

Find Ideas for Writing

Here are some methods for generating topics:

• Browse through magazines, newspapers, and Web sites.

• Start a file of articles to save for future reference.

• With a group, brainstorm as many ideas as you can. Compile your ideas into a list.

• Interview an expert on a particular topic.

• Write down anything that comes into your head.

• Use a cluster map to explore subordinate ideas that relate to a general topic.

Organize Ideas

Once you've chosen a topic, you will need to compile and organize your ideas. If you are writing a description, you may need to gather sensory details. Or you may need to record information from different sources for an essay or a research paper. To record notes from sources you read or view, use any or all of these methods:

• **Summarize:** Briefly retell the main ideas of a piece of writing in your own words.

• **Paraphrase:** Restate all or almost all of the information in your own words.

• **Quote:** Record the author's exact words.

Depending on what form your writing takes, you may also need to arrange your ideas in a certain pattern. *For more information, see the **Writing Handbook**, pages R32–R39.*

1.2 DRAFTING

In the drafting stage, you put your ideas on paper and allow them to develop and change as you write. You don't need to worry about correct grammar and spelling at this stage. There are two ways that you can write a draft:

Discovery drafting is a good approach when you are not quite sure what you think about your subject. You just start writing and let your feelings and ideas lead you in developing the topic.

Planned drafting may work better if you know that your ideas have to be arranged in a certain way, as in a research paper. Try making a writing plan or an informal outline before you begin drafting.

1.3 REVISING AND EDITING

The revising and editing stage allows you to polish your draft and make changes in its content, organization, and style. Use the questions that follow to assess problems and determine what changes would improve your work.

• Does my writing have a **main idea** or central focus? Is my controlling idea clear?

• Have I used **precise** nouns, verbs, and modifiers?

- Have I incorporated **adequate detail** and **evidence?** Where might I include a telling detail, a revealing statistic, or a vivid example?

- Is my writing **unified?** Do all ideas and supporting details pertain to my main idea or advance my thesis?

- Is my writing clear and **coherent?** Is the flow of sentences and paragraphs smooth and logical?

- Have I used a consistent **point of view?**

- Do I need to add **transitional words, phrases,** or **sentences** to clarify relationships among ideas?

- Have I used a **variety of sentence types?** Are they well constructed? What sentences might I combine to improve the rhythm of my writing?

- Have I used a **tone** appropriate for my audience and purpose?

1.4 PROOFREADING

When you are satisfied with your revision, proofread your paper for mistakes in grammar, usage, and mechanics. You may want to do this several times, looking for a different type of mistake each time. Use the following questions to help you correct errors:

- Have I corrected any errors in **subject-verb agreement** and **pronoun-antecedent agreement?**

- Have I double-checked for errors in **confusing word pairs,** such as *it's/its, than/then,* and *too/to?*

- Have I corrected any **run-on sentences** and **sentence fragments?**

- Have I followed rules for **correct capitalization?**

- Have I used **punctuation marks** correctly?

- Have I checked the **spellings of all unfamiliar words** in the dictionary?

TIP If possible, don't begin proofreading just after you've finished writing. Put your work away for at least a few hours. When you return to it, it will be easier for you to identify and correct mistakes.

*For more information, see the **Grammar Handbook** and the **Vocabulary and Spelling Handbook,** pages R50–R79.*

Use the proofreading symbols in the chart to mark changes on your draft.

Proofreading Symbols	
∧ Add letters or words.	/ Make a capital letter lowercase.
⊙ Add a period.	¶ Begin a new paragraph.
≡ Capitalize a letter.	⌁ Delete letters or words.
⌒ Close up space.	∿ Switch the positions of letters or words.
∧ Add a comma.	

1.5 PUBLISHING AND REFLECTING

Always consider sharing your finished writing with a wider audience. Reflecting on your writing is another good way to finish a project.

Publishing Ideas

- Post your writing on a Weblog.

- Create a multimedia presentation and share it with classmates.

- Publish your writing in a school newspaper, local newspaper, or literary magazine.

- Present your work orally in a report, speech, reading, or dramatic performance.

Reflecting on Your Writing

Think about your writing process and whether you would like to add what you have written to your writing portfolio. You might attach a note in which you answer questions like these:

- Which parts of the process did I find easiest? Which parts were more difficult?

- What was the biggest problem I faced during the writing process? How did I solve the problem?

- What changes have occurred in my writing style?

- Have I noticed any features in the writing of published authors or my peers that I can apply to my own work?

Writing Online

THiNK central

Go to **thinkcentral.com**.
KEYWORD: HML11N-R27

Writing Online   **THiNK** central

The keyword on this page directs students to interactive models, revision lessons, and other resources designed to support the writing process.

1.6 PEER RESPONSE

Peer response consists of the suggestions and comments you make about the writing of your peers and also the comments and suggestions they make about your writing. You can ask a peer reader for help at any time in the writing process.

Using Peer Response as a Writer

- Indicate whether you are more interested in feedback about your ideas or about your presentation of them.

- Ask open-ended questions that will help you get specific information about your writing. Avoid questions that require yes-or-no answers.

- Encourage your readers to be honest.

Being a Peer Reader

- Respect the writer's feelings.

- Offer positive reactions first.

- Make sure you understand what kind of feedback the writer is looking for, and then respond accordingly.

For more information on the writing process, see the **Introductory Unit,** *pages 14–17.*

② Building Blocks of Good Writing

Whatever your purpose in writing, you need to capture your reader's interest and organize your thoughts clearly.

2.1 INTRODUCTIONS

An introduction should capture your reader's attention and present a controlling idea.

Kinds of Introductions

There are a number of ways to begin an introduction. The one you choose depends on who the audience is and on your purpose for writing.

Make a Surprising Statement Beginning with a startling statement or an interesting fact can arouse your reader's curiosity about a subject, as in the following model.

> **MODEL**
>
> Although she wrote nearly 1,800 poems, Emily Dickinson probably did not want to publish any of them. Most of her poems were first published almost 100 years after they were written.

Provide a Description A vivid description sets a mood and brings a scene to life for your reader. In the following model, details about a horse's actions set the tone for an essay about horse training.

> **MODEL**
>
> Dust flew as the horse stomped the ground. The puffs of moisture blowing from his nostrils and the laid-back ears let the spectators know the stomping was not some clever performance. As the trainer approached cautiously, she could see the wild look in the horse's eyes.

Pose a Question Beginning with a question can make your reader want to find the answer. The model below asks questions about a respected writer.

> **MODEL**
>
> Zora Neale Hurston was one of the most successful writers of the Harlem Renaissance period. She wrote plays, novels, and essays that were enthusiastically received. How did it happen that such a talented and popular author died in poverty?

Relate an Anecdote Beginning with an anecdote, brief story, can hook your reader and help you make a point in a dramatic way. The following anecdote introduces an interview with a retired school teacher.

> **MODEL**
>
> "Down in the valley
> Where the green grass grows. . . ."
> The words of the chanting children on the playground brought tears to Clara Jones's eyes. Though she could barely see them, she knew exactly how the old jump-rope game went.
> I began softly to ask her about her 45 years of teaching at Pleasant Hills Elementary School.

Use a Quotation A witty quotation can hook your reader's attention and help you make an important point. You can find quotes in printed books of quotations or online.

> **MODEL**
>
> "Genius without education is like silver in the mine" is a quote by Benjamin Franklin, who probably would have advocated higher education for everyone. However, should everyone go to college?

Address the Reader Speaking directly to your reader establishes a friendly, informal tone and involves the reader in your topic.

> **MODEL**
>
> Do you know how many trees will be cut down for the new shopping mall to be built? Do you know how many families will have to give up their homes so that some shoppers can have yet another department store that sells the same things as five others in our area?

Begin with a Controlling Idea A controlling idea, or thesis statement, expressing a main idea may be woven into both the beginning and the end of a piece of nonfiction writing. The following is a controlling idea that introduces a literary analysis.

> **MODEL**
>
> In "The Death of the Hired Man," Robert Frost uses the hushed conversation of a husband and wife to explore the meaning of a lonely person's life. The whole poem seems to take place in whispers, though the message is strong.

TIP To write a strong introduction, you may want to try more than one of the methods and then decide which is the most effective for your purpose and audience.

2.2 PARAGRAPHS

A paragraph is made up of sentences that work together to develop an idea or accomplish a purpose. Whether or not it contains a topic sentence stating the main idea, a good paragraph must have unity and coherence.

Unity

A paragraph has unity when all the sentences support and develop one stated or implied idea. Use the following techniques to create unity in your paragraphs:

Write a Topic Sentence A topic sentence states the main idea of the paragraph; all other sentences in the paragraph provide supporting details. A topic sentence is often the first sentence in a paragraph. However, it may also appear later in a paragraph or at the end, to summarize or reinforce the main idea, as shown in the model that follows.

> **MODEL**
>
> Cats purr when they are being stroked by humans. Cats purr when they cuddle up with other cats. Many cats purr when they are in the veterinarian's office. Some cats purr when they are frightened. Since cats seem to purr in situations of both joy and stress, the cause of purring is still a mystery to humans.

Relate All Sentences to an Implied Main Idea A paragraph can be unified without a topic sentence as long as every sentence supports an implied, or unstated, main idea. In the example, all the sentences work together to create a unified impression of a frustrated writer trying to begin writing.

> **MODEL**
>
> He picked up his pencil at 9:27 and set it down purposefully on the writing pad. A minute or so passed. Well, maybe he should sharpen the pencil. That took 30 seconds—now 9:29. He set his pencil down again. He readjusted his chair. He raked his left hand through his thick hair. Was there a spot of thinning hair? He got up to go look in the mirror. No, not yet. At 9:31 he sat down again and took up the pencil. This time he moved the pad a little to the right.

Coherence

A paragraph is coherent when all its sentences are related to one another and each flows logically to the next. The following techniques will help you achieve coherence in paragraphs:

- Present your ideas in the most logical order.
- Use pronouns, synonyms, and repeated words to connect ideas.
- Use transitional devices to show relationships among ideas.

In the model shown here, the writer used some of these techniques to create a unified paragraph.

MODEL

After you figure out how big to make the model ship for your film of a shipwreck, you will need to take some other factors into account as well. You will have to figure out how much to stir the water and what speed to set the film. Perhaps even more important is to be sure no real objects at full size can be seen by the camera. In other words, don't let your towels and soap dish sneak into the picture and be sure the cat is locked out of the bathroom.

2.3 TRANSITIONS

Transitions are words and phrases that show connections among details. Clear transitions help show how your ideas relate to one another.

Kinds of Transitions

The types of transitions you choose depend on the ideas you want to convey.

Time or Sequence Some transitions help to clarify the sequence of events over time. When you are telling a story or describing a process, you can connect ideas with such transitional words as *first, second, always, then, next, later, soon, before, finally, after, earlier, afterward,* and *tomorrow.*

MODEL

Before a blood donation can be used, it must be processed carefully. First, a sample is tested for infectious diseases and identified by blood type. Next, preservatives are added. Finally, a blood cell separator breaks up the blood into its parts, such as red blood cells, platelets, and plasma.

Spatial Relationships Transitional words and phrases such as *in front, behind, next to, along, nearest, lowest, above, below, underneath, on the left,* and *in the middle* can help your reader visualize a scene.

MODEL

Two rows of corn grew along the south side of the garden. In front of them stood the tomatoes climbing on wire enclosures and a couple of okra plants. In the middle rows were medium-height plants—bush beans, peas, potatoes, and a few peppers. Low-growing plants filled the front of the garden—radishes on the right, then rows of lettuce, spinach, and onions. On the left, squash and cucumber vines spread over the ground.

Degree of Importance Transitional words and phrases such as *mainly, strongest, weakest, first, second, most important, least important, worst,* and *best* may be used to rank ideas or to show degrees of importance.

MODEL

There are several reasons to eat plenty of fresh fruits and vegetables. The most important reason is that they help to fortify your immune system!

Compare and Contrast Words and phrases such as *similarly, likewise, also, like, as, neither... nor,* and *either ... or* show similarity between details. *However, by contrast, yet, but, unlike, instead, whereas,* and *while* show difference. Note the use of both types of transitions in the model.

MODEL

Although I like to shop in the big stores in the mall, when I'm really serious about buying something I go to a small store. Like big stores, many small stores carry a good selection of merchandise. Whereas the big stores may have lower prices, the small stores have more personal service and clerks who know about the products they sell.

TIP Both *but* and *however* can be used to join two independent clauses. When *but* is used as a coordinating conjunction, it is preceded by a comma. When *however* is used as a conjunctive adverb, it is preceded by a semicolon and followed by a comma.

Cause and Effect When you are writing about a cause-effect relationship, use transitional words and phrases such as *since, because, thus, therefore, so, due to, for this reason,* and *as a result* to help clarify that relationship and make your writing coherent.

> **MODEL**
>
> Due to the unusual amount of rain this summer, the grass is still lush and green in August.

2.4 CONCLUSIONS

A conclusion should leave readers with a strong final impression.

Kinds of Conclusions

Good conclusions sum up ideas in a variety of ways. Here are some techniques you might try:

Restate Your Controlling Idea A good way to conclude an essay is by restating your controlling idea, or thesis, in different words. The following conclusion restates the controlling idea introduced on page R29.

> **MODEL**
>
> In Robert Frost's "The Death of the Hired Man," a sad human life unfolds in the whispered conversations between Mary and Warren. Quiet compassion is also evident and is the point of the poem.

Ask a Question Try asking a question that sums up what you have said and gives your reader something new to think about. The following question concludes an appeal for preventing unwanted cats and dogs.

> **MODEL**
>
> Considering how many kittens, puppies, cats, and dogs are put to sleep or die on the streets, don't you think it makes sense that all household pets be spayed or neutered?

Make a Recommendation When you are persuading your audience to take a position on an issue, you can conclude by recommending a specific course of action.

> **MODEL**
>
> Help protect animals from careless humans. Volunteer at an animal shelter. Distribute literature around your neighborhood.

Make a Prediction Readers are concerned about matters that may affect them and therefore are moved by a conclusion that predicts the future.

> **MODEL**
>
> If the city council approves the new shopping mall, we will lose the woodlands that help make our neighborhood quiet and attractive. In their place, we will have traffic congestion, exhaust fumes, bright lights long into the night, and a source of danger to our children.

Summarize Your Information Summarizing reinforces your main idea, leaving a strong, lasting impression. The model concludes with a statement that summarizes a book review.

> **MODEL**
>
> Patricia McKissack's biography gives a strong picture of W. E. B. Du Bois, who was a link between Frederick Douglass, whom he knew early in life, and Martin Luther King Jr., whom he knew late in life.

2.5 ELABORATION

Elaboration is the process of developing an idea by providing specific supporting details that are relevant and appropriate to the purpose and form of your writing. In some cases, you may want to present support with a visual aid.

Facts and Statistics A fact is a statement that can be verified, and a statistic is a fact expressed as a number. Make sure the facts and statistics you supply are from reliable, up-to-date sources, and support your statements, as in the following model.

MODEL

A student who has an eye for beautiful gardens might consider a career in landscape architecture. The American Society of Landscape Architects has over 12,000 members, up 20 percent in the last five years. The average income of landscape architects is $74,644, which is higher than that of building architects.

Sensory Details Details that show how something looks, sounds, tastes, smells, or feels can enliven a description, making readers feel they are actually experiencing what you are describing.

MODEL

Sliding along on her cross-country skis, Sasha felt she was truly on top of the world. The action of the snow, skis, and sturdy boots massaged her feet. She opened her mouth to taste the sprinkles of snow. The view was a rainbow of color as snowflakes made tiny speckled prisms on her goggles.

Incidents From our earliest years, we are interested in "stories." One way to illustrate a point is to relate an incident or tell a story, as shown in the example.

MODEL

The East India Company had a monopoly on supplying tea to the American Colonies. Tea shipments took on the symbolism of the increasing tyranny of the English government. On December 16, 1773, a group of about 150 colonists put burnt cork on their faces, dressed as Mohawk warriors, boarded the tea-carrying ships, and proceeded to dump the entire tea cargoes into Boston Harbor.

Examples An example can help make an abstract idea concrete or can serve to clarify a complex point.

MODEL

Many of the stars and galaxies we see at night are showing us light from ancient times. Who knows where they really are today? For example, the light from the galaxy Andromeda has taken over 2 million years to get here.

Quotations Choose quotations that clearly support your points, and be sure that you copy each quotation word for word. Remember always to credit the source.

MODEL

Do you know anyone who says "you all" to mean "the group of you"? "Have you all seen this movie?" McCrum, Cran, and MacNeil explain in *The Story of English* that this famous Southern expression comes from a Scots-Irish translation of the plural for *you.* They say the expression "is typical both of Ulster and of the (largely southern) states of America." Did you all know that?

❸ Writing Description

Descriptive writing allows you to paint word pictures about anything, from events of global importance to the most personal feelings. It is an essential part of almost every piece of writing.

> **RUBRIC: Standards for Writing**
>
> **Successful descriptive writing should**
>
> - have a clear focus and sense of purpose
> - use sensory details and precise words to create a vivid image, establish a mood, or express emotion
> - present details in a logical order

3.1 KEY TECHNIQUES

Consider Your Goals What do you want to accomplish with your description? Do you want to show why something is important to you? Do you want to make a person or scene more memorable? Do you want to explain an event?

Identify Your Audience Who will read your description? How familiar are they with your subject? What background information will they need? Which details will they find most interesting?

Think Figuratively What figures of speech might help make your description vivid and interesting? What simile or metaphor comes to mind? What imaginative comparisons can you make? What living thing does an inanimate object remind you of?

Gather Sensory Details Which sights, smells, tastes, sounds, and textures make your subject come alive? Which details stick in your mind when you observe or recall your subject? Which senses does it most strongly affect?

You might want to use a chart like the one shown here to collect sensory details about your subject.

Sights	Sounds	Textures	Smells	Tastes

Create a Mood What feelings do you want to evoke in your readers? Do you want to soothe them with comforting images? Do you want to build tension with ominous details? Do you want to evoke sadness or joy?

3.2 OPTIONS FOR ORGANIZATION

Option 1: Spatial Order Choose one of these options to show the spatial order of elements in a scene you are describing.

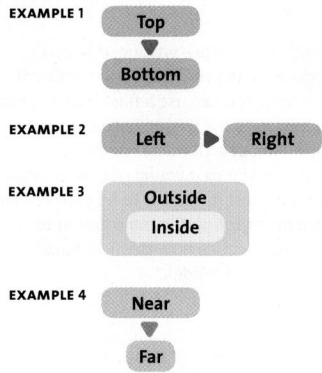

EXAMPLE 1
Top → Bottom

EXAMPLE 2
Left ▶ Right

EXAMPLE 3
Outside / Inside

EXAMPLE 4
Near → Far

MODEL

Peering through the goggles, the diver surveyed the reef. To the left, a school of silvery fish swam near the surface. Below them, the reef was a rainbow of color. In the middle of the scene, bright, tiny fish nosed along the reef. Below them on the sand, a crab looked for food. Further right, a cluster of fan coral waved its purple fronds in the gentle current. Beyond it lay the barnacle-encrusted shape of a ship's propeller.

Option 2: Order of Impression Order of impression is the order in which you notice details.

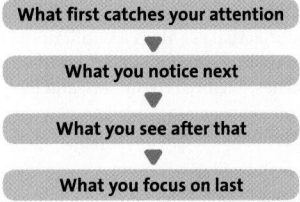

What first catches your attention
▼
What you notice next
▼
What you see after that
▼
What you focus on last

MODEL

Rain pelted against the windshield. Robbie narrowed his eyes to try to see the road in the brief clearing spasms between swipes of wiper blades. He could barely see that there was a little clearing far off in the horizon. Dark clouds made distinct shapes. Suddenly he noticed that against a small patch of lighter color was a swirling black cloud beginning to take the shape of a funnel.

TIP Use transitions that help readers understand the order of the impressions you are describing. Some useful transitions are *after, next, during, first, before, finally,* and *then.*

Option 3: Order of Importance You can use order of importance as the organizing structure for a description.

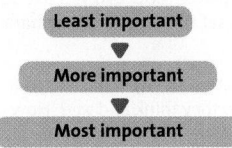

Least important
▼
More important
▼
Most important

MODEL

I checked my backpack for the comforting essentials. Book? Yes. Journal and pencil? Yes. Water bottle? Yes. Tissues? Yes. Then I checked for the required essentials. Passport? Yes. Airline ticket? Yes. Map? Yes. Last of all, I checked the most important possession for this trip—a light heart and a sense of adventure. I was beginning my first real vacation in two years!

*For more information, see **Transitions**, page R30.*

❹ Writing Narratives

Narrative writing tells a story. If you write a story from your imagination, it is a fictional narrative. A true story about actual events is a nonfictional narrative. Narrative writing can be found in short stories, novels, news articles, personal narratives, and biographies.

RUBRIC: Standards for Writing

A successful narrative should

- hook the reader's attention with a strong introduction
- include descriptive details and dialogue to develop the characters, setting, and plot
- have a clear beginning, middle, and end
- have a logical organization, with clues and transitions that help the reader understand the order of events
- maintain a consistent tone and point of view
- use language that is appropriate to the audience
- demonstrate the significance of events or ideas

4.1 KEY TECHNIQUES

Identify the Main Events What are the most important events in your narrative? Is each event needed to tell the story?

Describe the Setting When do the events occur? Where do they take place? How can you use setting to create mood and to set the stage for the characters and their actions?

Depict Characters Vividly What do your characters look like? What do they think and say? How do they act? What details can show what they are like?

TIP Dialogue is an effective means of developing characters in a narrative. As you write dialogue, choose words that express your characters' personalities and that show how the characters feel about one another and about the events in the plot.

4.2 OPTIONS FOR ORGANIZATION

Option 1: Chronological Order One way to organize a piece of narrative writing is to arrange the events in chronological order, as shown in the following example.

EXAMPLE

A contemporary Navajo boy in New Mexico is nearing adulthood. His father wants him to learn the lore of his ancestors. His mother wants him to prepare for school instead.

> **Introduction**
> *Characters and setting*

The boy wants to please both his parents. He goes into the mountains to seek wisdom.

> **Event 1**

Animals visit the boy, representing both the old ways and the new.

> **Event 2**

The boy finds that he does not have to disappoint either parent. He finds that he must work hardest on learning what he himself is best suited for.

> **End**
> *Perhaps showing the significance of the events*

Option 2: Flashback In narrative writing, it is also possible to introduce events that happened before the beginning of the story. You can use a flashback to show how past events led up to the present situation or to provide background about a character or event. Use clue words such as *last summer, as a young girl, the previous school year,* and *his earliest memories* to let your reader know that you are interrupting the main action to describe earlier events. Notice how the flashback interrupts the action in the model.

MODEL

Mr. Robbins picked up the small, white ball that had just smashed his kitchen window and felt angry that the boys playing across the street could be so careless. Then he remembered a summer day over 50 years ago, when he himself had hit a home run – right into the Nelsons' living room. How frightened he had been when Mrs. Nelson walked out of her front door, holding the baseball! But she had simply laughed as she gave it back to him and said, "Boys will be boys." Mr. Robbins shook his head at the memory and looked back at his broken pane of glass.

Option 3: Focus on Conflict When a fictional narrative focuses on a central conflict, the story's plot may be organized as shown in the following example.

EXAMPLE

The day after their high school graduation, Angela and her twin brother, Alex, decided to take their canoe out on the river that ran past their family home. They had done it many times since childhood, and the river was familiar to both of them.

> **Describe main characters and setting.**

For two hours they traversed the river under a calm, clear sky, but by noon, rather ominous clouds had rolled in. Meanwhile, they had floated far downstream, and had taken a winding inlet off the river. Soon, they heard thunder in the distance, and Angela looked off to the southwest where she had noticed lightning. She alerted Alex and insisted they turn back immediately. Alex did not seem concerned, however, and refused to go back.

> **Present conflict.**

As the storm began to get nearer, Angela again insisted they turn around, but Alex, who was steering the boat, said the storm was too far away to hurt them. As the rain began to fall on them, Angela began to plead with her brother that they either pull over to the shore or turn back immediately. To prove her point, she stopped paddling.

> **Relate events that make conflict complex and cause characters to change.**

Alex ignored his sister and continued to paddle himself and steer them further downstream. Finally a bolt of lightning hit close by, and the rain started to pour. "Now do you believe me?!" shouted Angela through the driving rain. Alex turned the boat toward shore and didn't say a word.

> **Present resolution or outcome of conflict.**

Writing Informative Texts

Expository writing informs and explains. You can use it to evaluate the effects of a new law, to compare two movies, to analyze a piece of literature, or to examine

the problem of greenhouse gases in the atmosphere. There are many types of expository writing. Think about your topic and select the type that presents the information most clearly.

5.1 COMPARISON AND CONTRAST

Compare-and-contrast writing examines the similarities and differences between two or more subjects. You might, for example, compare and contrast two short stories, the main characters in a novel, or two movies.

> **RUBRIC: Standards for Writing**
>
> **Successful compare-and-contrast writing should**
>
> - hook the reader's attention with a strong introduction
> - clearly identify the subjects that are being compared and contrasted
> - include specific, relevant details
> - follow a clear plan of organization
> - use language and details appropriate to the audience
> - use transitional words and phrases to clarify similarities and differences

Options for Organization

Compare-and-contrast writing can be organized in different ways. The examples that follow demonstrate point-by-point organization and subject-by-subject organization.

Option 1: Point-by-Point Organization

EXAMPLE

I. Different beliefs about burial practices. **Point 1**

   Subject A. Leon: traditional Laguna way.

   Subject B. Father Paul: last rites and a funeral mass.

II. Both want a proper burial. **Point 2**

   Subject A. Leon: painted face, feather in hair, body to graveyard, cornmeal and pollen.

   Subject B. Father Paul: decide whether to sprinkle holy water without full Catholic rites.

Option 2: Subject-by-Subject Organization

EXAMPLE

I. Leon: **Subject A**

    Point 1. Believes in traditional
    Laguna burial.

    Point 2. Proper burial: painted face,
    feather in hair, body to graveyard,
    corn meal and pollen.

II. Father Paul: **Subject B**

    Point 1. Believes burial requires
    last rites and a funeral mass.

    Point 2. Must decide whether to
    sprinkle holy water without full
    Catholic rites.

*For more information, see **Writing Workshop: Online Feature Article** pages 620–627; **Writing Workshop: Analytical Essay,** pages 834–843; **Writing Workshop: Research Paper,** pages 1358–1377.*

5.2 CAUSE AND EFFECT

Cause-effect writing explains why something happened, why certain conditions exist, or what resulted from an action or a condition. You might use cause-effect writing to explain a character's actions, the progress of a disease, or the outcome of a war.

> **RUBRIC: Standards for Writing**
>
> **Successful cause-effect writing should**
>
> - hook the reader's attention with a strong introduction
> - clearly state the cause-and-effect relationship
> - show clear connections between causes and effects
> - present causes and effects in a logical order and use transitions effectively
> - use facts, examples, and other details to illustrate each cause and effect
> - use language and details appropriate to the audience

Options for Organization

Your organization will depend on your topic and your purpose for writing.

Option 1: Effect-to-Cause Organization If you want to explain the causes of an event, such as the closing of a factory, you might first state the effect and then examine its causes.

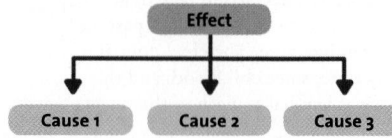

Option 2: Cause-to-Effect Organization If your focus is on explaining the effects of an event, such as the passage of a law, you might first state the cause and then explain the effects.

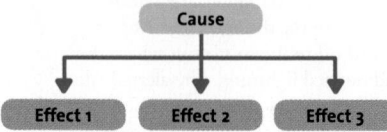

Option 3: Cause-Effect Chain Organization
Sometimes you'll want to describe a chain of cause-effect relationships to explore a topic, such as the disappearance of tropical rain forests or the development of the Internet.

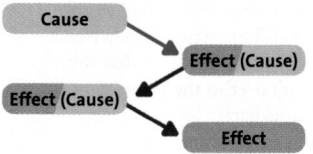

TIP Don't assume that a cause-effect relationship exists just because one event follows another. Look for evidence that the later event could not have happened if the first event had not caused it.

5.3 PROBLEM-SOLUTION

Problem-solution writing clearly states a problem, analyzes the problem, and proposes a solution to the problem. It can be used to identify and solve a conflict between characters, investigate global warming, or tell why the home team keeps losing.

RUBRIC: Standards for Writing

Successful problem-solution writing should

- hook the reader's attention with a strong introduction
- identify the problem and help the reader understand the issues involved
- analyze the causes and effects of the problem
- include quotations, facts, and statistics
- explore possible solutions to the problem and recommend the best one(s)
- use language, details, and a tone appropriate to the audience

Options for Organization

Your organization will depend on the goal of your problem-solution piece, your intended audience, and the specific problem you have chosen to address. The organizational methods that follow are effective for different kinds of problem-solution writing.

Option 1: Simple Problem-Solution

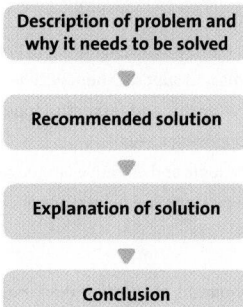

Option 2: Deciding Between Solutions

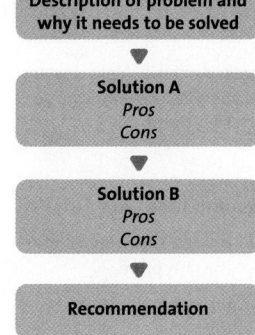

5.4 ANALYSIS

In writing an analysis, you explain how something works, how it is defined, or what its parts are.

RUBRIC: Standards for Writing

A successful analysis should

- hook the reader's attention with a strong introduction
- clearly define the subject and its parts
- use a specific organizing structure to provide a logical flow of information
- show connections among facts and ideas through transitional words and phrases
- use language and details appropriate for the audience

Options for Organization

Organize your details in a logical order appropriate to the kind of analysis you're writing. Use one of the following options:

Option 1: Process Analysis A process analysis is usually organized chronologically, with steps or stages in the order in which they occur.

EXAMPLE

Navigating north from New Orleans **Introduce process.**

Mark Twain follows this process for his first trip as a cub pilot. **Give background.**

Step 1: Straighten out the boat. **Explain steps.**

Step 2: Stay close to the moored boats.

Step 3: Pass Six-Mile, Nine-Mile, and Twelve-Mile points.

Step 4: Cross the river when the calm water ends.

Option 2: Definition Analysis You can organize the details of a definition analysis in order of importance or impression.

EXAMPLE

A successful riverboat pilot must be a keen observer. **Introduce term.**

The riverboat pilot must observe the surface of the river, the landmarks along the shore, and signs of nature. **General definition.**

Quality 1: The surface can tell of rising water or hidden hazards. **Explain features or qualities.**

Quality 2: Landmarks tell where the boat is; pilot must recall what dangers to avoid at that point.

Quality 3: The sky can give hints about what weather may be coming.

Option 3: Parts Analysis A parts analysis is organized as a listing of the subject's parts, with each explained.

EXAMPLE

Piloting a riverboat requires several skills. **Introduce subject.**

Part 1: recognize how weather might threaten the boat **Explain parts.**

Part 2: observe floating objects that could show a rising river; see ripples in the water surface that could indicate a hazard

Part 3: use landmarks to know where boat is and where dangers lie

*For more information, see **Writing Workshop: Analytical Essay**, pages 834–843.*

6 Writing Arguments

Persuasive writing allows you to use the power of language to inform and influence others. It includes speeches, persuasive essays, newspaper editorials, advertisements, and critical reviews.

RUBRIC: Standards for Writing

Successful persuasive writing should

- hook the reader's attention with a strong introduction
- state the issue and the writer's position
- give claims and support them with facts or reasons
- have a reasonable and respectful tone
- answer opposing views
- use sound logic and effective language
- conclude by summing up reasons or calling for action

*For more information, see **Writing Workshop: Persuasive Essay**, pages 280–289.*

6.1 KEY TECHNIQUES

Clarify Your Claim What do you believe about the issue? Determine how you can express your opinion most clearly.

Know Your Audience Who will read your writing? Think about what your audience already knows and believes about the issue. Imagine any objections to your position that your audience might have. Determine what additional information they will need. Decide on the tone and approach that would be most effective.

Support Your Opinion Why do you feel the way you do about the issue? Use facts, statistics, examples, quotations, anecdotes, or expert opinions to support your view. Think of reasons that will convince your readers and evidence that can answer their objections.

Ways to Support Your Argument	
Statistics	facts that are stated in numbers
Expert Opinions	information from a professional
Observations	events or situations you yourself have seen
Anecdotes	brief stories that illustrate points
Quotations	direct statements from authorities

For more information, see **Identifying Faulty Reasoning,** page R22.

Begin and End with a Bang How can you hook your readers and make a lasting impression? Think of a quotation, an anecdote, or a statistic that will catch your reader's attention and remain memorable. Create a strong summary or call to action with which you can conclude.

MODEL

Beginning

Stop before you call your doctor for medicine to cure that cold or ease that sore throat. You might be doing your body more harm than good by taking an antibiotic.

Conclusion

Listen to doctors when they suggest that antibiotics should be reserved for serious illness. Take the doctor's advice to drink lots of liquids and get bed rest instead of taking drugs for a less serious illness. Maybe humanity can win the battle with microbes by slowing their evolution into supermicrobes that resist antibiotics.

6.2 OPTIONS FOR ORGANIZATION

In a two-sided persuasive essay, you want to show the weaknesses of other opinions as you explain the strengths of your own.

Option 1: Reasons for Your Opinion

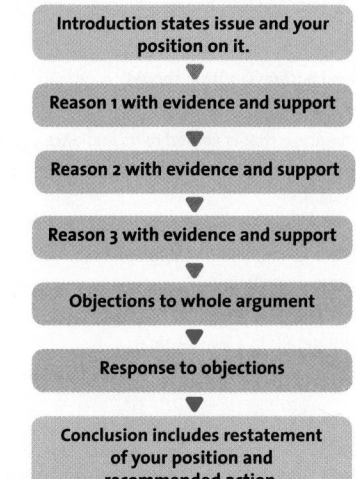

Introduction states issue and your position on it.
▼
Reason 1 with evidence and support
▼
Reason 2 with evidence and support
▼
Reason 3 with evidence and support
▼
Objections to whole argument
▼
Response to objections
▼
Conclusion includes restatement of your position and recommended action.

Option 2: Point-by-Point Basis

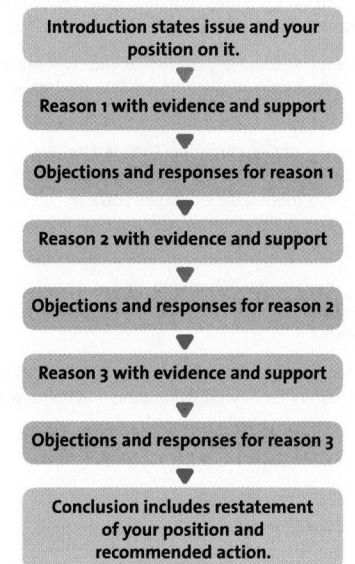

Introduction states issue and your position on it.
▼
Reason 1 with evidence and support
▼
Objections and responses for reason 1
▼
Reason 2 with evidence and support
▼
Objections and responses for reason 2
▼
Reason 3 with evidence and support
▼
Objections and responses for reason 3
▼
Conclusion includes restatement of your position and recommended action.

PRACTICE AND APPLY

ANSWERS

1. *Responses will vary. The letter should include a heading, inside address, salutation, body, and closing, with appropriate language, information, and format.*

2. *Responses will vary. The memo should include a heading and a body, with appropriate language, information, and format.*

7 Writing Functional Texts

Business writing is writing done in a workplace to support the work of a company or business. Several types of formats, such as memos, letters, e-mails, applications, and bylaws, have been developed to make communication easier.

> **RUBRIC: Standards for Writing**
>
> **Successful business writing should**
>
> - be courteous
> - use language that is geared to its audience
> - state the purpose clearly in the opening sentences or paragraph
> - have a formal tone and not contain slang, contractions, or sentence fragments
> - use precise words
> - present only essential information
> - present details in a logical order
> - conclude with a summary of important points

7.1 KEY TECHNIQUES

Think About Your Purpose Ask yourself why you are doing this writing. Do you want to promote yourself to a college admissions committee or a job interviewer? Do you want to order or complain about a product? Do you want to set up a meeting or respond to someone's ideas? Are you writing bylaws for an organization?

Identify Your Audience Determine who will read your writing. What background information will they need? What tone or language is appropriate?

Use a Pattern of Organization That Is Appropriate to the Content If you have to compare and contrast two products in a memo, for example, you can use the same compare-and-contrast organization that you would use in an essay.

Support Your Points What specific details might clarify your ideas? What reasons do you have for your statements?

Finish Strongly Determine the best way to sum up your statements. What is your main point? What action do you want the recipients to take?

Revise and Proofread Your Writing Just as you are graded on the quality of an essay you write for a class, you will be judged on the quality of your writing in the workplace.

7.2 MATCHING THE FORMAT TO THE OCCASION

E-mail messages, memos, and letters have similar purposes but are used in different situations. The chart shows how each format can be used.

Format	Occasion
Memo	Use to send correspondence **inside** the workplace only.
E-mail message	Use to send correspondence **inside or outside** the company.
Letter	Use to send correspondence **outside** the company.

TIP Memos are often sent as e-mail messages in the workplace. Remember that both require formal language and standard spelling, capitalization, and punctuation.

> ### PRACTICE AND APPLY
>
> Refer to the documents on page R41 to complete the following:
>
> 1. Draft a response to the letter. Then revise your letter as necessary according to the rubric at the beginning of this section. Make sure you have included the necessary information and have written in an appropriate tone. Proofread your letter for grammatical errors and spelling mistakes. Follow the format of the model and use appropriate spacing between elements.
>
> 2. Write a memo in response to the memo. Tell the recipient what actions you have taken. Follow the format of the model.

*For more information, see **Writing Workshop: Procedural Documents**, pages 1312–1321.*

7.3 FORMATS

Business letters usually have a formal tone and a specific format as shown below. The key to writing a business letter is to get to the point as quickly as possible and to present your information clearly.

MODEL: BUSINESS LETTER

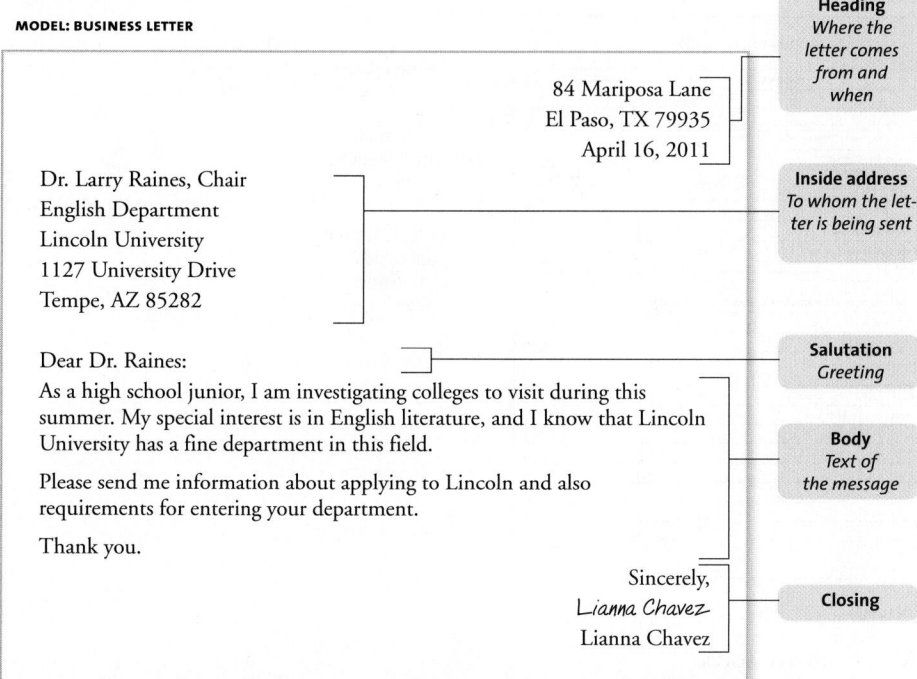

84 Mariposa Lane
El Paso, TX 79935
April 16, 2011

Heading
Where the letter comes from and when

Dr. Larry Raines, Chair
English Department
Lincoln University
1127 University Drive
Tempe, AZ 85282

Inside address
To whom the letter is being sent

Dear Dr. Raines:

Salutation
Greeting

As a high school junior, I am investigating colleges to visit during this summer. My special interest is in English literature, and I know that Lincoln University has a fine department in this field.

Please send me information about applying to Lincoln and also requirements for entering your department.

Thank you.

Body
Text of the message

Sincerely,
Lianna Chavez
Lianna Chavez

Closing

Memos are often used in workplaces as a way of conveying information in a direct and concise manner. They can be used to announce or summarize meetings and to request actions or specific information.

MODEL: MEMO

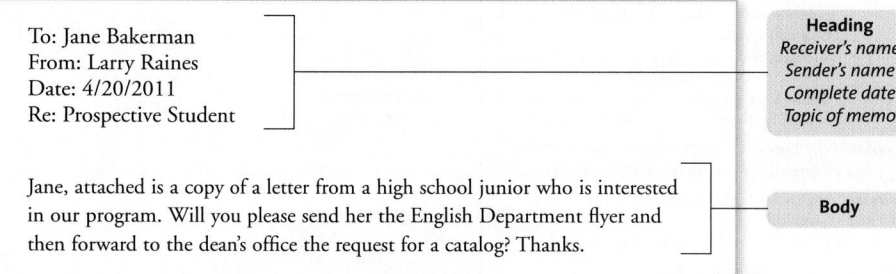

To: Jane Bakerman
From: Larry Raines
Date: 4/20/2011
Re: Prospective Student

Heading
Receiver's name
Sender's name
Complete date
Topic of memo

Jane, attached is a copy of a letter from a high school junior who is interested in our program. Will you please send her the English Department flyer and then forward to the dean's office the request for a catalog? Thanks.

Body

TIP Don't forget to write the topic of your memo in the subject line. This will help the receiver determine the importance of your memo.

When you apply for a job, you may be asked to fill out an application form. Application forms vary, but most of them ask for similar kinds of information. If you are mailing your application, you may want to include a brief letter.

MODEL: JOB APPLICATION

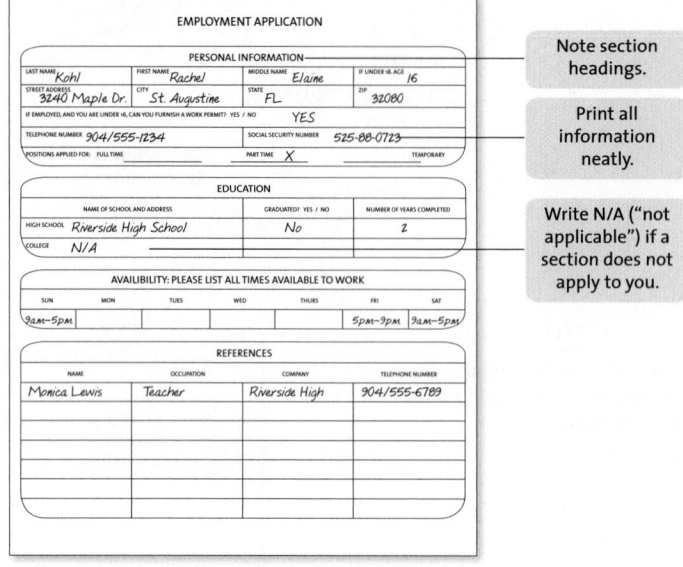

Note section headings.

Print all information neatly.

Write N/A ("not applicable") if a section does not apply to you.

MODEL: RÉSUMÉ

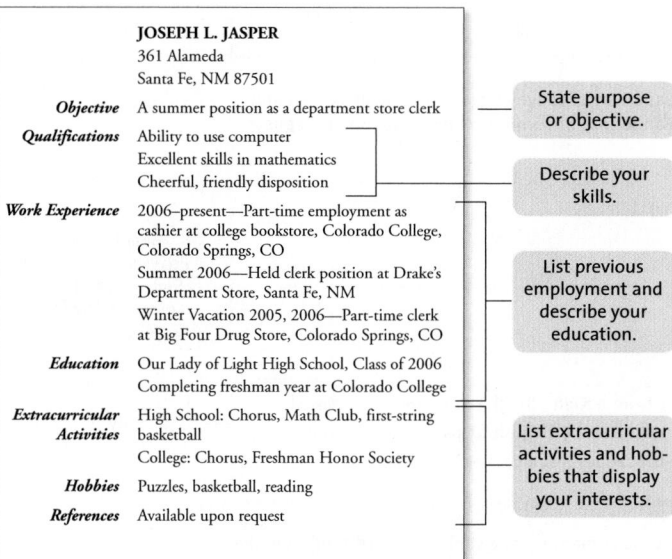

State purpose or objective.

Describe your skills.

List previous employment and describe your education.

List extracurricular activities and hobbies that display your interests.

Sometimes you may have to write technical documents, such as a list of procedures for conducting a meeting, a manual on rules of behavior, or the minutes of a meeting. These documents contain written descriptions of rules, regulations, and meetings and enable organizations and businesses to run smoothly. These bylaws for a poetry club include a description of the organization and information about how the club operates.

MODEL: BYLAWS DOCUMENT

Article I Name

SECTION 1. The name of this organization is the Free Verse Poets Society of North Shore High School.

Article II Purpose

SECTION 1. The purpose of this organization is to stimulate young developing poets, to create enthusiasm for poetry, to promote the scholarly study of poetry, and to inform the school and community about poetry.

Article III Membership Requirements

SECTION 1. To qualify for membership, a candidate must be a student at North Shore High School.

SECTION 2. Membership in Free Verse Poets Society is voluntary. However, all members are required to attend semimonthly meetings, participate in any club fundraisers, and assist in the quarterly publication of the club newsletter, *Plutonian Shore.*

Article IV Meetings

SECTION 1. Meetings will be held twice a month on a day designated by voting members. Meetings will be held in a classroom designated by the faculty advisor.

SECTION 2. A quorum shall consist of eight (8) members; at least two (2) student officers and the faculty advisor are required to be present at each meeting.

SECTION 3. All student officers are voting members of the Free Verse Poets Society; however, the faculty advisor may be called upon in the event of an evenly split vote.

Article V Officers

SECTION 1. This organization shall be governed by a faculty advisor and a panel of four (4) student officers: the president, vice-president, scribe, and treasurer. Each student officer will be elected at the start of the school year.

SECTION 2. For members to be eligible for election, they must have served one (1) year as a member in the Free Verse Poets Society. Freshmen are not eligible for election. Only seniors are eligible for the office of society president.

SECTION 3. The president will preside over regular and special meetings.

SECTION 4. The vice-president will guide activities of appointed committees.

SECTION 5. The scribe will record and distribute meeting minutes.

SECTION 6. The treasurer will be responsible for all money collected by the society.

PRACTICE AND APPLY

Refer to the documents on pages R42 and R43 to complete the following:

1. Visit a business and request an employment application for a job you would like to have. Make sure you understand what each question is asking before you begin to write. Fill out the application as neatly and completely as possible.

2. Write a set of bylaws for an organization that you already belong to or one that you would like to form. Follow the format of the document on page R43.

PRACTICE AND APPLY

ANSWERS

1. *Students' work should be legible, accurate, and complete.*

2. *Students' bylaws should follow the format shown.*

COMMON CORE FOCUS

W 7 Conduct short as well as more sustained research projects to answer a question (including a self-generated question) or solve a problem; narrow or broaden the inquiry when appropriate; synthesize multiple sources on the subject, demonstrating understanding of the subject under investigation. **W 8** Gather relevant information from multiple authoritative print and digital sources, using advanced searches effectively; assess the strengths and limitations of each source in terms of the task, purpose, and audience; integrate information into the text selectively to maintain the flow of ideas, avoiding plagiarism and overreliance on any one source and following a standard format for citation. **W 9** Draw evidence from literary or informational texts to support analysis, reflection, and research.

Good research involves using a variety of sources and materials. With an abundance of information at your fingertips, knowing where to go, how to access information, and how to record your findings are important skills and strategies.

❶ Finding Sources

The **library** or **media center** and the **Internet** are the first places you will begin your research. Both the library and the Internet offer a wealth of resources, which include reference works, books, newspapers and periodicals, film, databases, catalogs, and other miscellaneous sources, such as music scores and maps.

1.1 REFERENCE WORKS

Reference works provide quick information that can help you refine or narrow your search. Reference works are roughly divided into two categories: general reference and specialized reference. Specialized reference works are focused on a particular field or area of study.

Reference Works	Examples
Encyclopedias—detailed information on nearly every subject, arranged alphabetically	*Encyclopaedia Britannica* Encyclopedia.com *Encyclopedia of Economics*
Dictionaries—word definitions, spellings, usage, pronunciations, and origins	*The American Heritage Dictionary* *Bartlett's Familiar Quotations*
Almanacs and Yearbooks—current facts and statistics	*World Almanac and Book of Facts*
Thesauri—lists of synonyms and antonyms	*Roget's International Thesaurus*
Biographical References—information on the lives of noteworthy people	*The Riverside Dictionary of Biography* *The International Who's Who*
Atlases—geographical and historical maps, charts, and graphics	*Rand McNally Atlas of the World*
Directories—names, addresses, and phone numbers of people and organizations	telephone books lists of business organizations, agencies, and publications
Indexes—alphabetical lists of newspaper and magazine articles	*Readers' Guide to Periodical Literature*

1.2 BOOKS

Nonfiction books provide in-depth information on specific topics. Your research may also require that you access fiction, poetry, or dramatic works. The following parts of a book will help you find information quickly and easily:

- **Title page**—a page that gives the book's name and the name of its author and publisher; usually the first full page of a book
- **Copyright page**—a page that gives the copyright date, or the date the book was published; usually located on the reverse side of the title page
- **Table of contents**—a list at the front of the book that gives the title of each chapter or section of the text and the page number on which it begins
- **Preface**—a short, preliminary section of a book in which the writer of the book briefly provides background information and, possibly, acknowledgments
- **Bibliography**—a list of related books and other materials used to write a text; usually placed at the end of the book
- **Glossary**—an alphabetized list of important and/or specialized words and their definitions; usually placed at the end of the book
- **Appendix**—a collection of additional materials that supply background or other related information on subject matter discussed in the main portion of the text; usually located at the end of the book
- **Index**—an alphabetized list of important topics, terms, and details covered in the book and the page numbers on which they can be found; located at the end of the book; useful for quickly finding specific information on a topic

*For more information, see **Choosing Reliable Books,** page 1351.*

Two basic systems are used to classify nonfiction books. Most high school and public libraries use the Dewey decimal system. University and research libraries generally use the Library of Congress system.

DEWEY DECIMAL SYSTEM

000–099	General works
100–199	Philosophy and psychology
200–299	Religion
300–399	Social science
400–499	Language
500–599	Natural sciences and mathematics
600–699	Technology (applied sciences)
700–799	Arts and recreation
800–899	Literature and rhetoric
900–999	Geography and history

LIBRARY OF CONGRESS SYSTEM

A	General works
B	Philosophy, psychology, religion
C	History
D	General history and history of Europe
E–F	American history
G	Geography, anthropology, recreation
H	Social sciences
J	Political science
K	Law
L	Education
M	Music
N	Fine arts
P	Language and literature
Q	Science
R	Medicine
S	Agriculture
T	Technology
U	Military science
V	Naval science
Z	Bibliography and library science

1.3 NEWSPAPERS AND PERIODICALS

Newspapers, magazines, and scholarly journals provide concise and current information on specific topics and the news of the day. Microforms are newspapers, periodicals, and reports stored on film (microfilm) or cards (microfiche) and viewable on special machines found at the library.

Types of Publications	Examples
Newspapers—published daily, weekly, or monthly; provide news reports, specialized features, and commentary; may be general or specialized	*New York Times* *Chicago Tribune* *Sacramento Bee*
Magazines—published monthly, quarterly, or at other intervals; provide news, articles on specific topics, and commentary; more in-depth than newspapers	*Newsweek* *Time* *Musician*
Journals—usually academic in scope; related to a specific field of study; highly specialized information	*Journal of Music Theory* *New England Journal of Medicine*

*For more information, see **Evaluating Newspapers and Periodicals**, page 1350.*

1.4 ELECTRONIC RESOURCES

Electronic resources include DVDs, videos, e-books, CD-ROMs, and audio resources. These resources may contain reference materials, movies, documentaries, television programs, books, music, speeches, textbooks, and various other content. While most documentaries, movies, and interviews are available on DVDs or CDs, you may want to directly access a film version. To quickly determine whether the piece is useful for your research, check the following:

- **Description or summary** of the piece—Does it contain the information you need, or is it otherwise relevant to your topic? Is it nonfiction or fiction?
- **Copyright date**—How current is the documentary or interview?
- **Producer** of the piece and its **participants**—Is the producer or creator reputable? Who is interviewed or featured?

Writing Online · THINK central
Go to **thinkcentral.com**.
KEYWORD: HML11-R45

Writing Online · THINK central

The keyword on this page directs students to interactive models, revision lessons, and other resources designed to support the writing process.

ANSWERS

1. *The quickest way to search a specific topic would be to use the index.*

2. *Depending on the topic, you would search newspapers, magazines, academic journals, or the Internet.*

3. *You might find a microfiche useful if you needed to look up information in out-of-date periodicals.*

1.5 DATABASES AND ONLINE CATALOGS

The library and Internet also offer large databases that allow you to search for articles on any number of topics. Often the library will subscribe to a database service, such as InfoTrac, Newsbank, or SIRS Researcher. The information on these databases is updated regularly.

Electronic catalogs have mostly replaced the card catalog system of book listings. Formerly filed in labeled drawers in libraries, listings can now be accessed from a library's Web site on the Internet.

1.6 OTHER RESOURCES

In addition to reference works found in the library or media center and on the Internet, you can get information from the following sources: corporate and nonprofit publications, lectures, correspondence, career guides, recordings, and television programming.

> **PRACTICE AND APPLY**
>
> 1. If you were looking through a nonfiction book on penguins, which part of the book would you search in order to find information on emperor penguins, a specific type of penguin?
>
> 2. If you wanted the most current information on a given topic, which source(s) would you search first?
>
> 3. Describe a situation in which you might find it useful to search microfiche.

1.7 WEB SOURCES

Whole libraries are on the Internet, as are thousands of other reliable and comprehensive sources for research. To conduct a search efficiently and find the best information for your topic, familiarize yourself with the following terms and procedures.

The main search tools for finding information on the Web are search engines, metasearch tools, and directories. In addition, there are virtual libraries and a host of other sites, such as newspaper archives, news associations, encyclopedias, the Library of Congress, and specialized databases.

Search engines—A search engine is a Web site that allows you to look for information on the World Wide Web. Examples include Google, Yahoo!, and Bing.

Metasearch tools—A metasearch tool is similar to a search engine, except that it simultaneously searches multiple search engines for the keywords you request. Examples include Dogpile, SurfWax, and Metacrawler.

Directories—Directories arrange Internet resources into subject categories and are useful when you are researching a general topic. Examples include Lycos, Galaxy, Yahoo!, Web Directory, and About.com.

Keyword searches—In a keyword search, you access a search engine and type in a phrase or term related to your subject. This allows you to retrieve Web sites and documents that have those keywords in them. Here are some tips for doing a keyword search:

- In the search box, type in a specific word or two that clearly identify your subject.
- When you want to find an exact phrase, or words in a certain order, such as *recording studio* (and not just *recording* or just *studio*), use quotation marks around the entire phrase. For instance, "recording studio" will provide results using those words in that order.
- If necessary, replace the end of a word with an asterisk. For example, the keyword *music** leads to sites that contain *music, musician,* and *musicianship.*

Boolean searches—A Boolean search lets you specify how the keywords in your search are related. This type of search allows you to refine, narrow, or expand your search so that your results are more focused on your topic needs. Use the following tips to conduct a Boolean search:

- For a search containing two or more words that do not need to be in a specific order, use the word AND between the words to indicate that the site or document should contain all the words specified. For example, *internship* AND *radio* will produce results containing both those words, but not in any particular order. For some search engines, you can use a plus sign instead of AND.
- The word OR broadens the search to include all documents that contain either word (*job* OR *career*).
- The word NOT—or, for some search engines, a minus sign—excludes unwanted terms from the search (*songwriting* NOT *commercials*).

Each Web site you encounter in your search will have a **URL** (uniform resource locator), which is its Web address. The abbreviation usually located at the end of the URL indicates the type and purpose of the Web site.

URL ABBREVIATIONS AND MEANINGS

.COM commercial—product information and sales; personal sites; some combinations of products and information, such as World Book Online

.EDU education—information about schools, courses, campus life, and research projects; students' and teachers' personal sites

.GOV United States government—official sites of the White House and of NASA, the FBI, and other government agencies and offices

.MIL United States military—official sites of the army, navy, air force, and marines, as well as of the Department of Defense and related agencies

.NET network—product information and sales

.ORG organization—charities, libraries, and other nonprofits; political parties

For more information, see **Using Library Resources,** *pages 1345–1347.*

1.8 YOUR OWN ORIGINAL DATA

Sometimes you will need information that you just can't find in books or online. A good way to get in-depth, firsthand information is by interviewing experts, conducting surveys, and recording data from your own observations, fieldwork, or experiments.

Interviews with experts—Whatever the subject of your research, look for people who have knowledge or experience in that field. For example, if you were researching shipwrecks on the Great Lakes, you might interview someone from the Great Lakes Maritime Society or a captain of a ship on the Great Lakes. Use the following tips when conducting an interview:

1. Plan your questions and rehearse what you will say.
2. During the interview, listen carefully and take notes. Ask permission if you want to record the interview.
3. Request clarification and ask follow-up questions when necessary.
4. After the interview, review your notes and summarize the conversation. If you recorded the conversation, you might want to transcribe it.
5. Identify strong statements you might want to quote directly.
6. Send a thank-you note to the interviewee.

Oral histories—For some kinds of presentations and papers, you may want to include an **oral history,** or a story of a person's experiences told in his or her own words. For example, if you were writing a paper on Native Americans and reservation life, you might want to include an oral history of someone who is experiencing that life and who knows how his or her tribe came to live on the reservation. To conduct an oral history, follow all the tips for conducting an interview.

Surveys—Surveys allow you to gather information from a broad range of people through the use of a **questionnaire.** For example, you may want to gather and compare people's opinions, preferences, or beliefs about a current news topic. Use the following tips to conduct a survey or to distribute a questionnaire:

1. Plan the survey. Choose whether you want to ask multiple-choice questions, yes/no questions, open-ended questions, true/false questions, or questions that refer to a rating scale. Prepare your questionnaire.
2. Determine the sample population, or group of people, you want to survey.
3. Administer the survey the same way to each person. You may ask people to respond in person, on the phone, or by e-mail, but your method should be the same for each, with the questions asked in the same manner and order.
4. Once the questionnaires have been completed, compile and interpret the responses. Was there a clear preference or opinion from the entire group? Do certain groups of people think one way while others think another? What conclusions can you draw from the results?
5. Summarize your results in writing; use charts or other graphic aids to provide a visual representation of the data.

Independent observation and field research—Field research and independent observation include any purposeful observations you make at a site or an event related to your topic. For example, you might visit a movie set to learn more about how movies are made and then record the activity you observed. For some research projects you may want to set up a **field study,** which is a systematic series of observations or a planned course of data collection. For some topics you might conduct experiments, as for a report in a science class.

2 Collecting Information

Once you have located your sources, you will need to sort through the information. To make it useful and manageable, you will want to take detailed notes, arrange your information in a logical and organized manner, and make sure your sources are reliable and credible.

2.1 TAKING NOTES

As you go through your sources, record information that is relevant to your search.

Source cards—You will need to document the sources where you find your information or evidence so that you can credit the sources in your work. To create source cards, record all the information needed to identify each source you use in your research. Organize your notes so that you can easily refer to them when adding documentation to your research.

> Ackerman, Diane. *A Natural History of the Senses.* New York: Vintage, 1990. Print.

HERE'S HOW

MAKING SOURCE CARDS

Follow these guidelines when you make source cards:

- **Book** Record the author's or editor's complete name, the title, the location and name of the publisher, and the copyright date.
- **Magazine or Newspaper Article** Include the author's complete name (unless the article is unsigned), the title of the article, the name and date of the publication, and the page number(s) of the article.
- **Encyclopedia Article** Include the author's complete name (unless the article is unsigned), the title of the article, and the name and copyright date of the encyclopedia.
- **World Wide Web Site** Record the author's or editor's complete name (if available), the title of the document, publication information for any print version of it, the date of its electronic publication, the name of any institution or organization responsible for the site, and the date when you accessed the site.

Notes—As you read your sources, record all relevant facts, quotations, statistics, anecdotes, and examples electronically, or on **note cards.** When you're ready to draft your paper, you can arrange and organize your notes in different ways to present the information and then choose the best method of organization. Here is an example of a note with an exact quotation from the Diane Ackerman book.

> **Insects and photoreception**
>
> "Bees can judge the angle at which light hits their photoreceptors, and therefore locate the position of the sun in the sky, even on a partly cloudy day" (265).

HERE'S HOW

TAKING NOTES

Follow these guidelines as you take your notes:

- Organize information in separate pieces that can be easily arranged and sifted through.
- **Include a heading** indicating the subject of the note.
- **Record the number of the corresponding source card** on each note.
- **Put direct quotations in quotation marks.**
- **Record the number of the page** where you found the material.

When recording information for your notes, you can use the following forms of **restatement** to avoid **plagiarism,** or presenting someone else's work as your own:

Paraphrase—When you paraphrase, you restate the writer's idea in your own words. Be sure to enclose in quotation marks any of the author's exact words that you include in a paraphrase.

Summary—When you summarize, you restate the main idea of the original, including key facts and statistics, but in a shorter version, usually about one-third the length of the original. A summary omits unnecessary details.

Quotation—When you use a writer's exact statement, you will need to place quotation marks around it. Be sure to copy the words exactly as the writer wrote them, including all punctuation. Use quotations for

- extremely important ideas that might be misrepresented by paraphrases
- clear and concise explanations
- ideas presented in unusually lively or vivid language

2.2 OUTLINING

Once you've arranged your notes in a pattern of organization that is suitable for your topic, you can create a formal **outline** of how the information will be arranged in your report. An outline can be written in one of two ways: as a sentence outline or as a topic outline. The **sentence outline** contains entries written in sentence form; the **topic outline** contains only phrases or words that represent the ideas. With either choice, each main idea in the outline is designated by a Roman numeral. The subtopics that support the main ideas are designated with indented capital letters. The details that explain the subtopics are designated with numerals and lowercase letters.

MODEL: SENTENCE OUTLINE

Introduction: The human senses are varied and differ from those in animals.

I. Humans are believed to have five senses: sight, hearing, touch, taste, and smell.

    A. Aristotle, a Greek philosopher, first categorized the senses.

    B. Modern physics and physiology reclassified the senses.

II. Photoreceptors are those sense organs in living organisms that react to light.

    A. The human eye is a photoreceptor.

    B. Animal photoreception can be superior to that of humans.

      1. Insects have specialized eyes.

      2. Nocturnal animals can see in the dark.

      3. Some animals see the world in colors that are different from those perceived by humans.

MODEL: TOPIC OUTLINE

Introduction: The human senses are varied and differ from those in animals.

I. Five senses in humans

    A. First categorization of senses

    B. Modern reclassification of senses

II. Photoreception

    A. Human sight and photoreception

    B. Animal sight and photoreception

      1. Insects

      2. Nocturnal animals

      3. Animals vs. humans in perceiving colors

2.3 CHECKLIST FOR EVALUATING SOURCES

The information . . .

☑ is relevant to the topic you are researching

☑ is up-to-date (This point is especially important when researching time-sensitive topics in areas such as science, medicine, and sports.)

☑ is from an author who is qualified to write about the topic

☑ is from a trusted source that is updated or reviewed regularly

☑ makes the author's or institution's purpose for writing clear

☑ is written at the right level for your needs (For example, a children's book is probably too simplistic, while a scientific paper may be too complex.)

☑ has the level of detail you need—neither too general nor too specific

☑ can be verified in more than one source

3 Sharing Your Research

At last you have established your research goals, located sources of information, evaluated the materials, and taken notes on what you learned. Now you have a chance to share the results with people in your world—and even beyond. Here are some options you may choose to present your work:

- Give a speech to your classmates or to people in your community.
- Create a power presentation using desktop publishing software and share it with classmates, friends, or family members.
- Describe your research findings on your own Web site.
- Summarize the information in a newsletter or brochure.
- Share the results of your research in a formal research paper.

Writing that has a lot of mistakes can confuse or even annoy a reader. A business letter with a punctuation error might lead to a miscommunication and delay a reply. A sentence fragment might lower your grade on an essay. Paying attention to grammar, punctuation, and capitalization rules can make your writing clearer and easier to read.

COMMON CORE

Included in this handbook:
L 1, L 2a, L 3a, L 4a–d

Quick Reference: Parts of Speech

PART OF SPEECH	FUNCTION	EXAMPLES
Noun	names a person, a place, a thing, an idea, a quality, or an action	
Common	serves as a general name, or a name common to an entire group	coyote, hunter, spear, bonfire
Proper	names a specific, one-of-a-kind person, place, or thing	Rainy Mountain, Virginia, Puritans
Singular	refers to a single person, place, thing, or idea	field, pony, child, man
Plural	refers to more than one person, place, thing, or idea	fields, ponies, children, men
Concrete	names something that can be perceived by the senses	lemon, shores, wind, canoe
Abstract	names something that cannot be perceived by the senses	fear, intelligence, honesty
Compound	expresses a single idea through a combination of two or more words	birthright, folk tale, Sky-World
Collective	refers to a group of people or things	species, army, flock
Possessive	shows who or what owns something	America's, Douglass's, men's, slaves'
Pronoun	takes the place of a noun or another pronoun	
Personal	refers to the person(s) making a statement, the person(s) being addressed, or the person(s) or thing(s) the statement is about	I, me, my, mine, we, us, our, ours, you, your, yours, she, he, it, her, him, hers, his, its, they, them, their, theirs
Reflexive	follows a verb or preposition and refers to a preceding noun or pronoun	myself, yourself, herself, himself, itself, ourselves, yourselves, themselves
Intensive	emphasizes a noun or another pronoun	(same as reflexives)
Demonstrative	points to one or more specific persons or things	this, that, these, those
Interrogative	signals a question	who, whom, whose, which, what
Indefinite	refers to one or more persons or things not specifically mentioned	both, all, most, many, anyone, everybody, several, none, some
Relative	introduces an adjective clause by relating it to a word in the clause	who, whom, whose, which, that

---

L1 Demonstrate command of the conventions of standard English grammar and usage when writing or speaking. **L 2a** Observe hyphenation conventions. **L 3a** Vary syntax for effect, consulting references for guidance as needed; apply an understanding of syntax to the study of complex texts when reading. **L 4a–d** Determine or clarify the meaning of unknown and multiple-meaning words and phrases, choosing flexibly from a range of strategies.

PART OF SPEECH	FUNCTION	EXAMPLES
Verb	expresses an action, a condition, or a state of being	
Action	tells what the subject does or did, physically or mentally	run, reaches, listened, consider, decides, dreamed
Linking	connects the subject to something that identifies or describes it	am, is, are, was, were, sound, taste, appear, feel, become, remain, seem
Auxiliary	precedes the main verb in a verb phrase	be, have, do, can, could, will, would, may, might
Transitive	directs the action toward someone or something; always has an object	The wind **snapped** the young tree in half.
Intransitive	does not direct the action toward someone or something; does not have an object	The young tree **snapped.**
Adjective	modifies a noun or pronoun	**frightened** man, **two** epics, **enough** time
Adverb	modifies a verb, an adjective, or another adverb	walked **out, really** funny, **far** away
Preposition	relates one word to another word	at, by, for, from, in, of, on, to, with
Conjunction	joins words or word groups	
Coordinating	joins words or word groups used the same way	and, but, or, for, so, yet, nor
Correlative	used as a pair to join words or word groups used the same way	both . . . and, either . . . or, neither . . . nor
Subordinating	introduces a clause that cannot stand by itself as a complete sentence	although, after, as, before, because, when, if, unless
Interjection	expresses emotion	whew, yikes, uh-oh

Quick Reference: The Sentence and Its Parts

The diagrams that follow will give you a brief review of the essentials of a sentence and some of its parts.

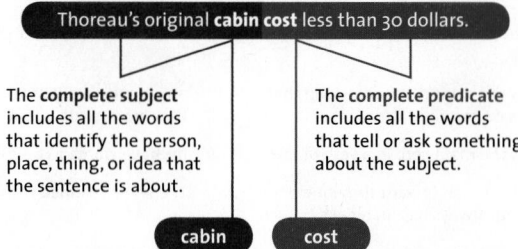

Thoreau's original **cabin cost** less than 30 dollars.

The **complete subject** includes all the words that identify the person, place, thing, or idea that the sentence is about.

The complete predicate includes all the words that tell or ask something about the subject.

cabin

cost

The **simple subject** tells exactly whom or what the sentence is about. It may be one word or a group of words, but it does not include modifiers.

The **simple predicate**, or verb, tells what the subject does or is. It may be one word or several, but it does not include modifiers.

Every word in a sentence is part of a complete subject or a complete predicate.

In *Walden,* Thoreau **has offered** readers his thoughts about living.

subject

A **prepositional phrase** consists of a preposition, its object, and any modifiers of the object. In this phrase, *in* is the preposition and *Walden* is its object.

A direct object is a word or group of words that tells who or what receives the action of the verb in a sentence.

Verbs often have more than one part. They may be made up of a **main verb,** like *offered,* and one or more **auxiliary,** or **helping, verbs,** like *has.*

An indirect object is a word or group of words that tells *to whom* or *for whom* or *to what* or *for what* about the verb. A sentence can have an indirect object only if it has a direct object. The indirect object always comes before the direct object in a sentence.

Quick Reference: Punctuation

MARK	FUNCTION	EXAMPLES
End Marks period, question mark, exclamation point	end a sentence	The games begin today. Who is your favorite contestant? What a play Jamie made!
period	follows an initial or abbreviation	Prof. Ted Bakerman, D. H. Lawrence, Houghton Mifflin Co., P.M., A.D., oz., ft., Blvd., St.
	Exception: postal abbreviations of states	NE (Nebraska), NV (Nevada)
period	follows a number or letter in an outline	I. Volcanoes A. Central-vent 1. Shield
Comma	separates parts of a compound sentence	I had never disliked poetry, but now I really love it.
	separates items in a series	She is brave, loyal, and kind.
	separates adjectives of equal rank that modify the same noun	The slow, easy route is best.
	sets off a term of address	America, I love you. Come to the front, children.
	sets off a parenthetical expression	Hard workers, as you know, don't quit. I'm not a quitter, believe me.
	sets off an introductory word, phrase, or dependent clause	Yes, I forgot my key. At the beginning of the day, I feel fresh. While she was out, I was here. Having finished my chores, I went out.
	sets off a nonessential phrase or clause	Ed Pawn, the captain of the chess team, won. Ed Pawn, who is the captain, won. The two leading runners, sprinting toward the finish line, finished in a tie.
	sets off parts of dates and addresses	Send it by August 18, 2010, to Cherry Jubilee, Inc., 21 Vernona St., Oakland, Minnesota.
	follows the salutation and closing of a letter	Dear Jim, Sincerely yours,
	separates words to avoid confusion	By noon, time had run out. What the minister does, does matter. While cooking, Jim burned his hand.
Semicolon	separates items in a series if one or more items contain commas	We invited my sister, Jan; her friend, Don; my uncle Jack; and Mary Dodd.
	separates parts of a compound sentence that are not joined by a coordinating conjunction	The small books are on the top shelves; the large books are below. I dusted the books; however, I didn't wipe the shelves.
	separates parts of a compound sentence when the parts contain commas	After I ran out of money, I called my parents; but only my sister was home, unfortunately.

MARK	FUNCTION	EXAMPLES
Colon	introduces a list	Those we wrote were the following: Dana, John, and Will.
	introduces a long quotation	Thomas Jefferson wrote: "We the people of the United States, in order to form a more perfect union...."
	follows the salutation of a business letter	Dear Ms. Williams: Dear Senator Wiley:
	separates certain numbers	1:28 P.M., Genesis 2:5
Dash	indicates an abrupt break in thought	I was thinking of my mother—who is arriving tomorrow—just as you walked in.
Parentheses	enclose less important material	Throughout her life (though some might think otherwise), she worked hard. The temperature on this July day (would you believe it?) is 65 degrees!
Hyphen	joins parts of a compound adjective before a noun	She lives in a first-floor apartment.
	joins parts of a compound with *all-, ex-, self-,* or *-elect*	The president-elect is a well-respected woman.
	joins parts of a compound number (to ninety-nine)	Today, I turn twenty-one.
	joins parts of a fraction	My cup is one-third full.
	joins a prefix to a word beginning with a capital letter	Life may have seemed simpler in pre-Civil War days. It's very chilly for mid-June.
	indicates that a word is divided at the end of a line	Did you know that school segrega-tion has been illegal since 1954?
Apostrophe	used with *s* to form the possessive of a noun or an indefinite pronoun	my friend's book, my friends' books, anyone's guess, somebody else's problem
	replaces one or more omitted letters in a contraction or numbers in a date	don't (omitted *o*), he'd (omitted *woul*), the class of '99 (omitted *19*)
	used with *s* to form the plural of a letter	I had two A's on my report card.
Quotation Marks	set off a speaker's exact words	Sara said, "I'm finally ready." "I'm ready," Sara said, "finally." Did Sara say, "I'm ready"? Sara said, "I'm ready!"
	set off the title of a story, an article, a short poem, an essay, a song, or a chapter	I liked Oates's "Hostage," Steinem's "Sisterhood," and Plath's "Mirror." Chapter II is titled "Our Gang's Dark Oath."
Ellipses	replace material omitted from a quotation	"We the people ... in order to form a more perfect union ...."
Italics	indicate the title of a book, a play, a magazine, a long poem, an opera, a film, or a TV series, or the names of ships, trains, and spacecraft	*The Scarlet Letter, The Crucible, Time, The Death of the Hired Man, West Side Story, Citizen Kane, The Spirit of St. Louis, The Best of Frank Sinatra, Lusitania*

Quick Reference: Capitalization

CATEGORY	EXAMPLES
People and Titles	
Names and initials of people	Emily Dickinson, T. S. Eliot
Titles used before or in place of names	Professor Holmes, Senator Long
Deities and members of religious groups	Jesus, Allah, Buddha, Zeus, Baptists, Roman Catholics
Names of ethnic and national groups	Hispanics, Jews, African Americans
Geographical Names	
Cities, states, countries, continents	New York, Maine, Haiti, Africa
Regions, bodies of water, mountains	the South, Lake Erie, Mount Katahdin
Geographic features, parks	Continental Divide, Everglades, Yellowstone
Streets and roads, planets	55 East Ninety-fifth Street, Maple Lane, Venus, Jupiter
Organizations, Events, Etc.	
Companies, organizations, teams	General Motors, Lions Club, Utah Jazz
Buildings, bridges, monuments	the Alamo, Golden Gate Bridge, Lincoln Memorial
Documents, awards	the Constitution, World Cup
Special named events	Super Bowl, World Series
Government bodies, historical periods and events	the Supreme Court, U.S. Senate, Harlem Renaissance, World War II
Days and months, holidays	Friday, May, Easter, Memorial Day
Specific cars, boats, trains, planes	Mustang, *Titanic*, *California Zephyr*
Proper Adjectives	
Adjectives formed from proper nouns	American League, French cooking, Emersonian period, Arctic waters
First Words and the Pronoun I	
First word in a sentence or quotation	This is it. He said, "Let's go."
First word of sentence in parentheses that is not within another sentence	The spelling rules are covered in another section. (Consult that section for more information.)
First words in the salutation and closing of a letter	Dear Madam, Very truly yours,
First word in each line of most poetry Personal pronoun *I*	Then am I A happy fly If I live Or if I die.
First word, last word, and all important words in a title	"The Fall of the House of Usher," *Incidents in the Life of a Slave Girl*

1 Nouns

A **noun** is a word used to name a person, a place, a thing, an idea, a quality, or an action. Nouns can be classified in several ways.

*For more information on different types of nouns, see **Quick Reference: Parts of Speech,** page R50.*

1.1 COMMON NOUNS

Common nouns are general names, common to entire groups.

> **EXAMPLES:** *writer, song, bravery*

1.2 PROPER NOUNS

Proper nouns name specific, one-of-a-kind things.

Common	Proper
writer, song, bravery, hunter	Mourning Dove, Mississippi, Granny

*For more information, see **Quick Reference: Capitalization,** page R55.*

1.3 SINGULAR AND PLURAL NOUNS

A noun may take a singular or a plural form, depending on whether it names a single person, place, thing, or idea or more than one. Make sure you use appropriate spellings when forming plurals.

Singular	Plural
church, lily, wife	churches, lilies, wives

*For more information, see **Forming Plural Nouns,** page R78.*

1.4 COMPOUND AND COLLECTIVE NOUNS

Compound nouns are formed from two or more words but express a single idea. They are written as single words, as separate words, or with hyphens. Use a dictionary to check the correct spelling of a compound noun.

> **EXAMPLES:** *birthright, folk tale, Sky-World*

Collective nouns are singular nouns that refer to groups of people or things.

> **EXAMPLES:** *army, flock, class, species*

1.5 POSSESSIVE NOUNS

A **possessive noun** shows who or what owns something.

> **EXAMPLES:** *Welty's, jury's, children's*

*For more information, see **Forming Possessives,** page R78.*

2 Pronouns

A **pronoun** is a word that is used in place of a noun or another pronoun. The word or word group to which the pronoun refers is called its **antecedent.**

2.1 PERSONAL PRONOUNS

Personal pronouns change their form to express person, number, gender, and case. The forms of these pronouns are shown in the following chart.

	Nominative	Objective	Possessive
Singular			
First person	I	me	my, mine
Second person	you	you	your, yours
Third person	she, he, it	her, him, it	her, hers, his, its
Plural			
First person	we	us	our, ours
Second person	you	you	your, yours
Third person	they	them	their, theirs

2.2 AGREEMENT WITH ANTECEDENT

Pronouns should agree with their antecedents in number, gender, and person.

If an antecedent is singular, use a singular pronoun.

> **EXAMPLE:** *Sarah laughed as her dog splashed in the lake.*

If an antecedent is plural, use a plural pronoun.

> **EXAMPLES:**
> *Sarah and Barbara took turns holding the leash as they walked the dog home.*
> *Andrew and Ryan finished the race before the rest of their teammates.*

The gender of a pronoun must be the same as the gender of its antecedent.

> **EXAMPLES:**
> *The little girl ran outside without tying her shoelaces.*
> *Daniel waved to his friends before boarding the plane.*

The person of the pronoun must be the same as the person of its antecedent. As the chart in Section 2.1 shows, a pronoun can be in first-, second-, or third-person form.

> **EXAMPLE:**
> *Those of you who like animals should consider getting your degree in veterinary science.*

GRAMMAR PRACTICE

Rewrite each sentence so that the underlined pronoun agrees with its antecedent.

1. *The World on the Turtle's Back* is a myth that tells about a pregnant woman and how <u>it</u> helped create the earth.

2. Many of the sea creatures and birds tried to retrieve the dirt at the bottom of the ocean, but they could not reach <u>him</u>.

3. The woman circles the earth with <u>their</u> daughter, helping the plants to grow.

4. Both of the twins molded clay animals and gave <u>it</u> life.

2.3 PRONOUN CASE

Personal pronouns change form to show how they function in sentences. Different functions are shown by different **cases.** The three cases are **nominative, objective,** and **possessive.** For examples of these pronouns, see the chart in Section 2.1.

A **nominative pronoun** is used as a subject or a predicate nominative in a sentence.

An **objective pronoun** is used as a direct object, an indirect object, or the object of a preposition.

| SUBJECT | OBJECT | OBJECT OF PREPOSITION |

He explained it to me.

A **possessive pronoun** shows ownership. The pronouns *mine, yours, hers, his, its, ours,* and *theirs* can be used in place of nouns.

EXAMPLE: *These letters are yours.*

The pronouns *my, your, her, his, its, our,* and *their* are used before nouns.

EXAMPLE: *These are your letters.*

WATCH OUT! Many spelling errors can be avoided if you watch out for *its* and *their.* Don't confuse the possessive pronoun *its* with the contraction *it's,* meaning "it is" or "it has." The homonyms *they're* (a contraction of *they are*) and *there* ("in that place") are often mistakenly used for *their.*

TIP To decide which pronoun to use in a comparison, such as "He tells better tales than (I *or* me)," fill in the missing word(s): *He tells better tales than I **tell.***

GRAMMAR PRACTICE

Replace the underlined words in each sentence with an appropriate pronoun and identify the pronoun as a nominative, objective, or possessive pronoun.

1. <u>Arthur Miller</u> was a playwright from New York.

2. *The Crucible* is one of <u>Arthur Miller's</u> most well-known plays.

3. <u>John Proctor and Reverend Parris</u> are two of the main characters.

4. Reverend Hale tries to convince <u>Rebecca Nurse and John Proctor</u> to falsely confess to practicing witchcraft.

5. <u>The Salem witch hunt</u> illustrates how the town's strict Christian principles indirectly caused the deaths of innocent villagers.

2.4 REFLEXIVE AND INTENSIVE PRONOUNS

These pronouns are formed by adding *-self* or *-selves* to certain personal pronouns. Their forms are the same, and they differ only in how they are used.

A **reflexive pronoun** follows a verb or preposition and reflects back on an earlier noun or pronoun.

EXAMPLES:
He threw himself forward.
Danielle mailed herself the package.

Intensive pronouns intensify or emphasize the nouns or pronouns to which they refer.

EXAMPLES:
The queen herself would have been amused.
I saw it myself.

WATCH OUT! Avoid using *hisself* or *theirselves.* Standard English does not include these forms.

NONSTANDARD: *He had painted hisself into a corner.*

STANDARD: *He had painted himself into a corner.*

2.5 DEMONSTRATIVE PRONOUNS

Demonstrative pronouns point out things and persons near and far.

	Singular	Plural
Near	this	these
Far	that	those

GRAMMAR PRACTICE

ANSWERS

1. *she*
2. *it*
3. *her*
4. *them*

GRAMMAR PRACTICE

ANSWERS

1. *He, nominative*
2. *his, possessive*
3. *They, nominative*
4. *them, objective*
5. *It, nominative*

GRAMMAR PRACTICE

ANSWERS

1. *who*
2. *who*
3. *Who*
4. *whose*

2.6 INDEFINITE PRONOUNS

Indefinite pronouns do not refer to specific persons or things and usually have no antecedents. The chart shows some commonly used indefinite pronouns.

Singular	Plural	Singular or Plural	
another	both	all	none
anybody	few	any	some
no one	many	more	most
neither	several		

TIP Indefinite pronouns that end in *one*, *body*, or *thing* are always singular.

INCORRECT: *Does anybody think their hamburger is overcooked?*

CORRECT: *Does anybody think his or her hamburger is overcooked?*

If the indefinite pronoun might refer to either a male or a female, *his or her* may be used to refer to it, or the sentence may be rewritten.

EXAMPLES: *Everyone received his or her script.*

All the actors received their scripts.

2.7 INTERROGATIVE PRONOUNS

An **interrogative pronoun** is used to ask a question. The interrogative pronouns are *who*, *whom*, *whose*, *which*, and *what*.

EXAMPLES: *Whose backpack is on the kitchen table?*

Which dress do you prefer?

TIP *Who* is used as a subject, *whom* as an object. To find out which pronoun you need to use in a question, change the question to a statement.

QUESTION: *(Who/Whom) did you meet there?*

STATEMENT: *You met (?) there.*

Since the verb has a subject (*you*), the needed word must be the object form, *whom*.

EXAMPLE: *Whom did you meet there?*

WATCH OUT! A special problem arises when you use an interrupter, such as *do you think*, within a question.

EXAMPLE: *(Who/Whom) do you believe is the more influential musician?*

If you eliminate the interrupter, it is clear that the word you need is *who*.

2.8 RELATIVE PRONOUNS

Relative pronouns relate, or connect, dependent (or subordinate) clauses to the words they modify in sentences. The relative pronouns are *that*, *what*, *whatever*, *which*, *whichever*, *who*, *whoever*, *whom*, *whomever*, and *whose*.

Sometimes short sentences with related ideas can be combined by using a relative pronoun.

SHORT SENTENCE: *Mark Twain may be America's greatest humorist.*

RELATED SENTENCE: *Mark Twain wrote* Huckleberry Finn.

COMBINED SENTENCE: *Mark Twain, who wrote* Huckleberry Finn, *may be America's greatest humorist.*

GRAMMAR PRACTICE

Choose the appropriate interrogative or relative pronoun from the words in parentheses.

1. "The Notorious Jumping Frog" was written by Samuel Clemens, (who/whom) wrote under the pseudonym Mark Twain.

2. The story gained national fame for Mark Twain, (who/that) first published it in 1865.

3. (Who/Whom) do you think is funnier, Jim Smiley or the storyteller Simon Wheeler?

4. Smiley spent months educating his frog, (which/whose) fame as a jumper spread throughout the gold camps.

2.9 PRONOUN REFERENCE PROBLEMS

The referent of a pronoun should always be clear.

An **indefinite reference** occurs when the pronoun *it*, *you*, or *they* does not clearly refer to a specific antecedent.

UNCLEAR: *In the review, it claimed the movie is well done.*

CLEAR: *The review claimed the movie is well done.*

A **general reference** occurs when the pronoun *it*, *this*, *that*, *which*, or *such* is used to refer to a general idea rather than a specific antecedent.

UNCLEAR: *Stella tutors students every day after school. This lets her help kids who are struggling with their schoolwork.*

CLEAR: *Stella tutors students every day after school. Tutoring lets her help kids who are struggling with their schoolwork.*

Ambiguous means "having more than one possible meaning." An **ambiguous reference** occurs when a pronoun could refer to two or more antecedents.

UNCLEAR: *Stacey made Miranda a sandwich while she talked on the phone.*

CLEAR: *While Stacey talked on the phone, she made Miranda a sandwich.*

GRAMMAR PRACTICE

Rewrite the following sentences to correct indefinite, ambiguous, and general pronoun references.

1. In the poem "The Raven," it tells about a man who is grieving for his lover.

2. The raven refused to abandon its perch above the door. This frustrated the narrator.

3. The narrator told the raven that he thought he was a messenger from Lenore.

4. The raven always responded, "Nevermore." This frightened and confused the speaker.

3 Verbs

A **verb** is a word that expresses an action, a condition, or a state of being.

For more information, see **Quick Reference: Parts of Speech,** *page R50.*

3.1 ACTION VERBS

Action verbs express mental or physical activity.

EXAMPLE: *I walked to the store.*

3.2 LINKING VERBS

Linking verbs join subjects with words or phrases that rename or describe them.

EXAMPLE: *You are my friend.*

3.3 PRINCIPAL PARTS

Action and linking verbs typically have four principal parts, which are used to form verb tenses. The principal parts are the **present,** the **present participle,** the **past,** and the **past participle.**

Action verbs and some linking verbs also fall into two categories: regular and irregular. A **regular verb** is a verb that forms its past and past participle by adding *-ed* or *-d* to the present form.

Present	Present Participle	Past	Past Participle
perform	(is) performing	performed	(has) performed
hope	(is) hoping	hoped	(has) hoped
stop	(is) stopping	stopped	(has) stopped
marry	(is) marrying	married	(has) married

An **irregular verb** is a verb that forms its past and past participle in some other way than by adding *-ed* or *-d* to the present form.

Present	Present Participle	Past	Past Participle
bring	(is) bringing	brought	(has) brought
swim	(is) swimming	swam	(has) swum
steal	(is) stealing	stole	(has) stolen
grow	(is) growing	grew	(has) grown

3.4 VERB TENSE

The **tense** of a verb indicates the time of the action or state of being. An action or state of being can occur in the present, the past, or the future. There are six tenses, each expressing a different range of time.

The **present tense** expresses an action or state that is happening at the present time, occurs regularly, or is constant or generally true. Use the present part.

NOW: *That poet reads well.*

REGULAR: *I swim every day.*

GENERAL: *Time flies.*

The **past tense** expresses an action that began and ended in the past. Use the past part.

EXAMPLE: *The storyteller finished his tale.*

The **future tense** expresses an action or state that will occur. Use *shall* or *will* with the present part.

EXAMPLE: *They will attend the next festival.*

The **present perfect tense** expresses an action or state that (1) was completed at an indefinite time in the past or (2) began in the past and continues into the present. Use *have* or *has* with the past participle.

EXAMPLE: *Poetry has inspired readers throughout the ages.*

GRAMMAR PRACTICE

ANSWERS

Possible answers:

1. *The poem "The Raven" tells about a man grieving for his lover.*

2. *The raven refused to abandon its perch above the door. The raven's refusal frustrated the narrator.*

3. *The narrator told the raven that he thought the raven was a messenger from Lenore.*

4. *The raven always responded, "Nevermore." The raven's response frightened and confused the speaker.*

ANSWERS

1. *is = present*
2. *ended = past*
   had lost = past perfect
3. *knew = past*
   pertains = present
   pertains > pertained
4. *will read = future*
   will apply = future
5. *accuse = present*
   knew = past
   knew > know

The **past perfect tense** expresses an action in the past that came before another action in the past. Use *had* with the past participle.

> **EXAMPLE:** *The witness had testified before the defendant confessed.*

The **future perfect tense** expresses an action in the future that will be completed before another action in the future. Use *shall have* or *will have* with the past participle.

> **EXAMPLE:** *They will have finished the novel before seeing the movie version of the tale.*

TIP The past-tense form of an irregular verb is not paired with an auxiliary verb, but the past-perfect-tense form of an irregular verb is always paired with an auxiliary verb.

> **INCORRECT:** *I have went to that restaurant before.*
> **INCORRECT:** *I gone to that restaurant before.*
> **CORRECT:** *I have gone to that restaurant before.*

3.5 PROGRESSIVE FORMS

The progressive forms of the six tenses show ongoing actions. Use forms of *be* with the present participles of verbs.

> **PRESENT PROGRESSIVE:** *She is rehearsing her lines.*
> **PAST PROGRESSIVE:** *She was rehearsing her lines.*
> **FUTURE PROGRESSIVE:** *She will be rehearsing her lines.*
> **PRESENT PERFECT PROGRESSIVE:** *She has been rehearsing her lines.*
> **PAST PERFECT PROGRESSIVE:** *She had been rehearsing her lines.*
> **FUTURE PERFECT PROGRESSIVE:** *She will have been rehearsing her lines.*

WATCH OUT! Do not shift from tense to tense needlessly. Watch out for these special cases:

- In most compound sentences and in sentences with compound predicates, keep the tenses the same.
  > **INCORRECT:** *Every morning they get up and went to work.*
  > **CORRECT:** *Every morning they get up and go to work.*

- If one past action happened before another, indicate this with a shift in tense.
  > **INCORRECT:** *She thought she forgot her toothbrush.*
  > **CORRECT:** *She thought she had forgotten her toothbrush.*

Identify the tense of the verb(s) in each of the following sentences. If you find an unnecessary tense shift, correct it.

1. The setting of *The Crucible* is the late 17th century in Salem, Massachusetts.
2. Before the witch trials ended, people had lost their ability to make objective judgments.
3. Playwright Arthur Miller knew that the play pertains to his own time.
4. People will read it far into the future, and many will apply its message to their own time.
5. In the play some accuse others of being witches, even though they knew the accusation was false.

3.6 ACTIVE AND PASSIVE VOICE

The voice of a verb tells whether its subject performs or receives the action expressed by the verb. When the subject performs the action, the verb is in the **active voice.** When the subject is the receiver of the action, the verb is in the **passive voice.**

Compare these two sentences:

> **ACTIVE:** *The Puritans did not celebrate Christmas.*
> **PASSIVE:** *Christmas was not celebrated by the Puritans.*

To form the passive voice, use a form of *be* with the past participle of the verb.

WATCH OUT! Use the passive voice sparingly. It can make writing awkward and less direct.

> **AWKWARD:** *The stories of hysterical witnesses were believed by gullible and fearful jurors.*
> **BETTER:** *Gullible and fearful jurors believed the stories of hysterical witnesses.*

There are occasions when you will choose to use the passive voice because

- you want to emphasize the receiver: *The king was shot.*
- the doer is unknown: *My books were stolen.*
- the doer is unimportant: *French is spoken here.*

For the five items below, identify the boldfaced verb phrase as active or passive.

1. *The Crucible* **has played** in theaters throughout the world.

2. It **was written** by Arthur Miller, one of America's greatest dramatists.

3. Miller **did** not **approve** of Reverend Parris's greed for gold.

4. **Has** the reputation of the minister **been maligned?**

4 Modifiers

Modifiers are words or groups of words that change or limit the meanings of other words. Adjectives and adverbs are common modifiers.

4.1 ADJECTIVES

Adjectives modify nouns and pronouns by telling which one, what kind, how many, or how much.

WHICH ONE: *this, that, these, those*

EXAMPLE: *That couch needs to be reupholstered.*

WHAT KIND: *large, unique, anxious, moldy*

EXAMPLE: *The anxious speaker shuffled through her notes.*

HOW MANY: *ten, many, several, every, each*

EXAMPLE: *Each child grabbed several candies from the bowl.*

HOW MUCH: *more, less, little*

EXAMPLE: *There was more snow on the ground in the morning.*

4.2 PREDICATE ADJECTIVES

Most adjectives come before the nouns they modify, as in the previous examples. A **predicate adjective,** however, follows a linking verb and describes the subject.

EXAMPLE: *My friends are very intelligent.*

Be especially careful to use adjectives (not adverbs) after such linking verbs as *look, feel, grow, taste,* and *smell.*

EXAMPLE: *The weather grows cold.*

4.3 ADVERBS

Adverbs modify verbs, adjectives, and other adverbs by telling where, when, how, or to what extent.

WHERE: *The children played outside.*

WHEN: *The author spoke yesterday.*

HOW: *We walked slowly behind the leader.*

TO WHAT EXTENT: *He worked very hard.*

Adverbs may occur in many places in sentences, both before and after the words they modify.

EXAMPLES: *Suddenly the wind shifted.*

The wind suddenly shifted.

The wind shifted suddenly.

4.4 ADJECTIVE OR ADVERB?

Many adverbs are formed by adding *-ly* to adjectives.

EXAMPLES: *sweet, sweetly; gentle, gently*

However, *-ly* added to a noun will usually yield an adjective.

EXAMPLES: *friend, friendly; woman, womanly*

4.5 COMPARISON OF MODIFIERS

Modifiers can be used to compare two or more things. The form of a modifier shows the degree of comparison. Both adjectives and adverbs have three forms: the **positive,** the **comparative,** and the **superlative.**

The **positive form** is used to describe individual things, groups, or actions.

EXAMPLES:

Stephen Crane was a great writer.

His descriptions are vivid.

The **comparative form** is used to compare two things, groups, or actions.

EXAMPLES:

I think that Stephen Crane was a greater writer than Jack London.
Crane's descriptions are more vivid.

The **superlative form** is used to compare more than two things, groups, or actions.

EXAMPLES:

I think that Crane was the greatest writer of his era.

Crane's descriptions are the most vivid I have ever read.

GRAMMAR PRACTICE

ANSWERS

1. *active*

2. *passive*

3. *active*

4. *passive*

4.6 REGULAR COMPARISONS

Most one-syllable and some two-syllable adjectives and adverbs have comparatives and superlatives formed by adding -er and -est. All three-syllable and most two-syllable modifiers have comparatives and superlatives formed with *more* and *most*.

Modifier	Comparative	Superlative
tall	taller	tallest
kind	kinder	kindest
droopy	droopier	droopiest
expensive	more expensive	most expensive
wasteful	more wasteful	most wasteful

WATCH OUT! Note that spelling changes must sometimes be made to form the comparatives and superlatives of modifiers.

EXAMPLES:

friendly, friendlier (Change *y* to *i* and add the ending.)

sad, sadder (Double the final consonant and add the ending.)

4.7 IRREGULAR COMPARISONS

Some commonly used modifiers have irregular comparative and superlative forms. They are listed in the following chart.

Modifier	Comparative	Superlative
good	better	best
bad	worse	worst
far	farther *or* further	farthest *or* furthest
little	less *or* lesser	least
many	more	most
well	better	best
much	more	most

4.8 PROBLEMS WITH MODIFIERS

Study the tips that follow to avoid common mistakes:

Farther and Further Use *farther* for distances; use *further* for everything else.

Double Comparisons Make a comparison by using -er/-est or by using *more/most*. Using -er with *more* or using -est with *most* is incorrect.

INCORRECT: *I like her more better than she likes me.*

CORRECT: *I like her better than she likes me.*

Illogical Comparisons An illogical or confusing comparison results when two unrelated things are compared or when something is compared with itself. The word *other* or the word *else* should be used in a comparison of an individual member to the rest of a group.

ILLOGICAL: *The narrator was more curious about the war than any student in his class.* (implies that the narrator isn't a student in the class)

LOGICAL: *The narrator was more curious about the war than any other student in his class.* (identifies that the narrator is a student)

Bad vs. Badly *Bad*, always an adjective, is used before a noun or after a linking verb. *Badly*, always an adverb, never modifies a noun. Be sure to use the right form after a linking verb.

INCORRECT: *Ed felt badly after his team lost.*

CORRECT: *Ed felt bad after his team lost.*

Good vs. Well *Good* is always an adjective. It is used before a noun or after a linking verb. *Well* is often an adverb meaning "expertly" or "properly." *Well* can also be used as an adjective after a linking verb when it means "in good health."

INCORRECT: *Helen writes very good.*

CORRECT: *Helen writes very well.*

CORRECT: *Yesterday I felt bad; today I feel well.*

Double Negatives If you add a negative word to a sentence that is already negative, the result will be an error known as a double negative. When using *not* or -*n't* with a verb, use *any-* words, such as *anybody* or *anything*, rather than *no-* words, such as *nobody* or *nothing*, later in the sentence.

INCORRECT: *I don't have no money.*

CORRECT: *I don't have any money.*

Using *hardly, barely*, or *scarcely* after a negative word is also incorrect.

INCORRECT: *They couldn't barely see two feet ahead.*

CORRECT: *They could barely see two feet ahead.*

Misplaced Modifiers Sometimes a modifier is placed so far away from the word it modifies that the intended meaning of the sentence is unclear. Prepositional phrases and participial phrases are often misplaced. Place modifiers as close as possible to the words they modify.

> **MISPLACED:** *The ranger explained how to find ducks in her office.* (The ducks were not in the ranger's office.)

> **CLEARER:** *In her office, the ranger explained how to find ducks.*

Dangling Modifiers Sometimes a modifier doesn't appear to modify any word in a sentence. Most dangling modifiers are participial phrases or infinitive phrases.

> **DANGLING:** *Coming home with groceries, our parrot said, "Hello!"*

> **CLEARER:** *Coming home with groceries, we heard our parrot say, "Hello!"*

GRAMMAR PRACTICE

Choose the correct word or words from each pair in parentheses.

1. Flannery O'Connor's story is (better/more better) than other stories I have read recently.

2. Mr. Shiftlet and Mrs. Crater (could/couldn't) hardly be less honest with each other.

3. Mr. Shiftlet says there isn't (any/no) broken thing on the farm that he can't fix.

4. He feels (good/well) about fixing the car.

5. Who do you think is the (stranger/strangest) person—Mr. Shiftlet or Mrs. Crater?

6. Mr. Shiftlet feels (bad/badly) about the rottenness of the world.

7. As Mr. Shiftlet drove on alone he felt (depresseder/more depressed) than ever.

8. Mr. Shiftlet didn't feel very (well/good) about being alone, so he picked up a hitchhiker.

9. One wonders how many other great stories Flannery O'Connor would have written had she lived (longer/more longer).

5 Prepositions, Conjunctions, and Interjections

5.1 PREPOSITIONS

A preposition is a word used to show the relationship between a noun or a pronoun and another word in the sentence.

Commonly Used Prepositions			
above	down	near	through
at	for	of	to
before	from	on	up
below	in	out	with
by	into	over	without

A preposition is always followed by a word or group of words that serves as its object. The preposition, its object, and modifiers of the object are called the **prepositional phrase.** In each example below, the prepositional phrase is highlighted and the object of the preposition is in boldface type.

> **EXAMPLES:**
> *The future of the entire **kingdom** is uncertain.*
> *We searched through the deepest **woods.***

Prepositional phrases may be used as adjectives or as adverbs. The phrase in the first example is used as an adjective modifying the noun *future.* In the second example, the phrase is used as an adverb modifying the verb *searched.*

> **WATCH OUT!** Prepositional phrases must be as close as possible to the word they modify.

> **MISPLACED:** *We have clothes for leisurewear of many colors.*

> **CLEARER:** *We have clothes of many colors for leisurewear.*

5.2 CONJUNCTIONS

A conjunction is a word used to connect words, phrases, or sentences. There are three kinds of conjunctions: **coordinating conjunctions, correlative conjunctions,** and **subordinating conjunctions.**

Coordinating conjunctions connect words or word groups that have the same function in a sentence. They include *and, but, or, for, so, yet,* and *nor.*

Coordinating conjunctions can join nouns, pronouns, verbs, adjectives, adverbs, prepositional phrases, and clauses in a sentence.

GRAMMAR PRACTICE

ANSWERS

1. *better*
2. *could*
3. *any*
4. *good*
5. *stranger*
5. *bad*
7. *more depressed*
8. *good*
9. *longer*

These examples show coordinating conjunctions joining words of the same function:

EXAMPLES:

I have many friends but few enemies. (two noun objects)

We ran out the door and into the street. (two prepositional phrases)

They are pleasant yet seem aloof. (two predicates)

We have to go now, or we will be late. (two clauses)

Correlative conjunctions are similar to coordinating conjunctions. However, correlative conjunctions are always used in pairs.

Correlative Conjunctions		
both . . . and	neither . . . nor	whether . . . or
either . . . or	not only . . . but also	

Subordinating conjunctions introduce subordinate clauses—clauses that cannot stand by themselves as complete sentences. The subordinating conjunction shows how the subordinate clause relates to the rest of the sentence. The relationships include time, manner, place, cause, comparison, condition, and purpose.

Subordinating Conjunctions	
Time	*after, as, as long as, as soon as, before, since, until, when, whenever, while*
Manner	*as, as if*
Place	*where, wherever*
Cause	*because, since*
Comparison	*as, as much as, than*
Condition	*although, as long as, even if, even though, if, provided that, though, unless, while*
Purpose	*in order that, so that, that*

In the example below, the boldface word is the conjunction, and the highlighted words form a subordinate clause:

EXAMPLE: *Walt Whitman was a man of the people,* **although** *many did not appreciate his poems.*

Walt Whitman was a man of the people is an independent clause, because it can stand alone as a complete sentence. *Although many did not appreciate his poems* cannot stand alone as a complete sentence; it is thus a subordinate clause.

Conjunctive adverbs are used to connect clauses that can stand by themselves as sentences. Conjunctive adverbs include *also, besides, finally, however, moreover, nevertheless, otherwise,* and *then.*

EXAMPLE: *She loved the fall; however, she also enjoyed winter.*

5.3 INTERJECTIONS

Interjections are words used to show emotion, such as *wow* and *cool.* Interjections are usually set off from the rest of a sentence by a comma or by an exclamation mark.

EXAMPLE: *Thoreau lived in the woods by himself. Amazing!*

6 The Sentence and Its Parts

A **sentence** is a group of words used to express a complete thought. A complete sentence has a subject and a predicate.

For more information, see **Quick Reference: The Sentence and Its Parts,** *page R52.*

6.1 KINDS OF SENTENCES

There are four basic types of sentences.

Type	Definition	Example
Declarative	states a fact, a wish, an intent, or a feeling	I wrote an essay on "The Weary Blues" for class.
Interrogative	asks a question	Are you familiar with Langston Hughes?
Imperative	gives a command or direction	Read "The Weary Blues" aloud.
Exclamatory	expresses strong feeling or excitement	It sounds like a song!

6.2 COMPOUND SUBJECTS AND PREDICATES

A compound subject consists of two or more subjects that share the same verb. They are typically joined by the coordinating conjunction *and* or *or.*

EXAMPLE: *Courtney and Eric enjoy the theater.*

A compound predicate consists of two or more predicates that share the same subject. They too are typically joined by a coordinating conjunction, usually *and, but,* or *or.*

EXAMPLE: *The main character in "Winter Dreams" attended a prestigious university and became a successful businessman.*

6.3 COMPLEMENTS

A **complement** is a word or group of words that completes the meaning of the sentence. Some sentences contain only a subject and a verb. Most sentences, however, require additional words placed after the verb to complete the meaning of the sentence. There are three kinds of complements: direct objects, indirect objects, and subject complements.

Direct objects are words or word groups that receive the action of action verbs. A direct object answers the question *what* or *whom*.

EXAMPLES:

The students asked many questions. (Asked what?)

The teacher quickly answered the students. (Answered whom?)

Indirect objects tell to whom or what or for whom or what the actions of verbs are performed. Indirect objects come before direct objects. In the examples that follow, the indirect objects are highlighted.

EXAMPLES:

My sister usually gave her friends good advice. (Gave to whom?)

Her brother sent the store a heavy package. (Sent to what?)

Subject complements come after linking verbs and identify or describe the subjects. A subject complement that names or identifies a subject is called a **predicate nominative.** Predicate nominatives include **predicate nouns** and **predicate pronouns.**

EXAMPLES:

My friends are very hard workers.

The best writer in the class is she.

A subject complement that describes a subject is called a **predicate adjective.**

EXAMPLE: *The pianist appeared very energetic.*

7 Phrases

A **phrase** is a group of related words that does not contain a subject and a predicate but functions in a sentence as a single part of speech.

7.1 PREPOSITIONAL PHRASES

A **prepositional phrase** is a phrase that consists of a preposition, its object, and any modifiers of the object. Prepositional phrases that modify nouns or pronouns are called **adjective phrases.** Prepositional phrases that modify verbs, adjectives, or adverbs are **adverb phrases.**

ADJECTIVE PHRASE: *The central character of the story is a villain.*

ADVERB PHRASE: *He reveals his nature in the first scene.*

7.2 APPOSITIVES AND APPOSITIVE PHRASES

An **appositive** is a noun or pronoun that identifies or renames another noun or pronoun. An **appositive phrase** includes an appositive and modifiers of it.

An appositive can be either **essential** or **nonessential.** An **essential appositive** provides information that is needed to identify what is referred to by the preceding noun or pronoun.

EXAMPLE: The Glass Menagerie *was written by playwright* Tennessee Williams.

A **nonessential appositive** adds extra information about a noun or pronoun whose meaning is already clear. Nonessential appositives and appositive phrases are set off with commas.

EXAMPLE: *Williams uses Laura's glass menagerie, a collection of fragile animal figurines, to represent her relationship to reality.*

8 Verbals and Verbal Phrases

A **verbal** is a verb form that is used as a noun, an adjective, or an adverb. A **verbal phrase** consists of a verbal along with its modifiers and complements. There are three kinds of verbals: **infinitives, participles,** and **gerunds.**

8.1 INFINITIVES AND INFINITIVE PHRASES

An **infinitive** is a verb form that usually begins with *to* and functions as a noun, an adjective, or an adverb. An **infinitive phrase** consists of an infinitive plus its modifiers and complements. The examples that follow show several uses of infinitive phrases.

NOUN: *To know her is my only desire.* (subject)

I'm planning to walk with you. (direct object)

Her goal was to promote women's rights. (predicate nominative)

ADJECTIVE: *We saw his need to be loved.* (adjective modifying *need*)

ADVERB: *She wrote to voice her opinions.* (adverb modifying *wrote*)

Because infinitives usually begin with *to*, it is usually easy to recognize them. However, sometimes *to* may be omitted.

EXAMPLE: *Let no one dare [to] enter this shrine.*

GRAMMAR PRACTICE

ANSWERS

1. *appositive phrase*
2. *infinitive phrase*
3. *participial phrase*
4. *appositive phrase*
5. *gerund phrase*

8.2 PARTICIPLES AND PARTICIPIAL PHRASES

A **participle** is a verb form that functions as an adjective. Like adjectives, participles modify nouns and pronouns. Most participles are present-participle forms, ending in *-ing*, or past-participle forms ending in *-ed* or *-en*. In the examples that follow, the participles are highlighted:

MODIFYING A NOUN: *The jogging woman completed another lap on the track.*

MODIFYING A PRONOUN: *Bored, he began to doodle in the margins of his notebook.*

Participial phrases are participles with all their modifiers and complements.

MODIFYING A NOUN: *Changing tactics, the attorney questioned the witness.*

MODIFYING A PRONOUN: *Dismissed for the day, they filed out of the courtroom.*

8.3 DANGLING AND MISPLACED PARTICIPLES

A participle or participial phrase should be placed as close as possible to the word that it modifies. Otherwise the meaning of the sentence may not be clear.

MISPLACED: *The boys were looking for squirrels searching the trees.*

CLEARER: *The boys searching the trees were looking for squirrels.*

A participle or participial phrase that does not clearly modify anything in a sentence is called a **dangling participle.** A dangling participle causes confusion because it appears to modify a word that it cannot sensibly modify. Correct a dangling participle by providing a word for the participle to modify.

DANGLING: *Running like the wind, my hat fell off.* (The hat wasn't running.)

CLEARER: *Running like the wind, I lost my hat.*

8.4 GERUNDS AND GERUND PHRASES

A **gerund** is a verb form ending in *-ing* that functions as a noun. Gerunds may perform any function nouns perform.

SUBJECT: *Running is my favorite pastime.*

DIRECT OBJECT: *I truly love running.*

INDIRECT OBJECT: *You should give running a try.*

SUBJECT COMPLEMENT: *My deepest passion is running.*

OBJECT OF PREPOSITION: *Her love of running keeps her strong.*

Gerund phrases are gerunds with all their modifiers and complements.

SUBJECT: *Wishing on a star never got me far.*

OBJECT OF PREPOSITION: *I will finish before leaving the office.*

APPOSITIVE: *Her avocation, flying airplanes, finally led to full-time employment.*

GRAMMAR PRACTICE

Identify the underlined phrases as appositive phrases, infinitive phrases, participial phrases, or gerund phrases.

1. In "The Masque of the Red Death," Poe uses allegory, <u>a device representing abstract qualities.</u>

2. <u>To escape the plague,</u> Prince Prospero seals himself and his courtiers in a walled abbey.

3. <u>Feeling protected from the Red Death,</u> Prospero holds a lavish masquerade ball.

4. There suddenly appears in the last room a masked figure, <u>the Red Death in a ghastly shroud.</u>

5. <u>Killing the apparition</u> is impossible.

9 Clauses

A **clause** is a group of words that contains a subject and a verb. There are two kinds of clauses: independent clauses and subordinate clauses.

9.1 INDEPENDENT AND SUBORDINATE CLAUSES

An **independent clause** can stand alone as a sentence, as the word *independent* suggests.

INDEPENDENT CLAUSE: *Frederick Douglass was an eloquent speaker.*

A sentence may contain more than one independent clause.

EXAMPLE: *Frederick Douglass was an eloquent speaker, but he encountered a lot of opposition.*

In the preceding example, the coordinating conjunction *but* joins two independent clauses.

For more information, see **Conjunctions,** *page R63.*

A **subordinate clause** cannot stand alone as a sentence. It is subordinate to, or dependent on, an independent clause.

EXAMPLE: *Although Frederick Douglass was a runaway slave, he frequently appeared in public to raise support for the abolitionist movement.*

The highlighted clause cannot stand by itself; it must be joined with an independent clause to form a complete sentence.

9.2 ADJECTIVE CLAUSES

An **adjective clause** is a subordinate clause used as an adjective. It usually follows the noun or pronoun it modifies. Adjective clauses are typically introduced by the relative pronoun *who, whom, whose, which,* or *that.*

EXAMPLES: *Frederick Douglass wrote objectively about the whippings that Corey frequently gave him.*

The autobiographer whom I liked best was Frederick Douglass.

He was a man who was determined to find freedom.

*For more information, see **Relative Pronouns**, page R58.*

An adjective clause can be either essential or nonessential. An **essential adjective clause** provides information that is necessary to identify the preceding noun or pronoun.

EXAMPLE: *The couch that we picked out will not be delivered for three weeks.*

A **nonessential adjective clause** adds additional information about a noun or pronoun whose meaning is already clear. Nonessential clauses are set off with commas.

EXAMPLE: *Joel's grandmother, who was born in Italy, makes the best lasagna.*

TIP The relative pronouns *whom, which,* and *that* may sometimes be omitted when they are objects in adjective clauses.

EXAMPLE: *The autobiographer [whom] I liked best was Frederick Douglass.*

9.3 ADVERB CLAUSES

An **adverb clause** is a subordinate clause that is used to modify a verb, an adjective, or an adverb. It is introduced by a subordinating conjunction.

*For more information, see **Conjunctions**, page R63.*

Adverb clauses typically occur at the beginning or end of sentences.

MODIFYING A VERB: *When we need you, we will call.*

MODIFYING AN ADVERB: *I'll stay here where there is shelter from the rain.*

MODIFYING AN ADJECTIVE: *Roman felt as good as he had ever felt.*

9.4 NOUN CLAUSES

A **noun clause** is a subordinate clause that is used as a noun. A noun clause may be used as a subject, a direct object, an indirect object, a predicate nominative, or the object of a preposition. Noun clauses are introduced either by pronouns, such as *that, what, who, whoever, which,* and *whose,* or by subordinating conjunctions, such as *how, when, where, why,* and *whether.*

*For more information, see **Conjunctions**, page R63.*

TIP Because the same words may introduce adjective and noun clauses, you need to consider how a clause functions within its sentence. To determine if a clause is a noun clause, try substituting *something* or *someone* for the clause. If you can do it, it is probably a noun clause.

EXAMPLES: *I know whose woods these are.*

("I know *something.*" The clause is a noun clause, direct object of the verb *know.*)

Give a copy to whoever wants one. ("Give a copy to *someone.*" The clause is a noun clause, object of the preposition *to.*)

🔟 The Structure of Sentences

When classified by their structure, there are four kinds of sentences: simple, compound, complex, and compound-complex.

10.1 SIMPLE SENTENCES

A **simple sentence** is a sentence that has one independent clause and no subordinate clauses. Various parts of simple sentences may be compound, and simple sentences may contain grammatical structures such as appositive and verbal phrases.

EXAMPLES:

Ambrose Bierce and Stephen Crane, two great American writers, both wrote during the latter half of the 19th century. (compound subject and an appositive)

Crane, best known for writing fiction, also wrote great poetry. (participial phrase containing a gerund phrase)

10.2 COMPOUND SENTENCES

A **compound sentence** consists of two or more independent clauses. The clauses in compound sentences are joined with commas and coordinating conjunctions (*and, but, or, nor, yet, for, so*) or with semicolons. Like simple sentences, compound sentences do not contain any subordinate clauses.

EXAMPLES:

I enjoyed the free pottery class, and I would like to go again.

Carl Sandburg's "Chicago" seems to celebrate the youthful energy of a booming industrial city; however, the poem dwells on the negative impacts of growth.

WATCH OUT! Do not confuse compound sentences with simple sentences that have compound parts.

EXAMPLE: *The center fielder caught the ball and immediately threw it toward second base.* (Here *and* joins parts of a compound predicate, not a compound sentence.)

10.3 COMPLEX SENTENCES

A **complex sentence** consists of one independent clause and one or more subordinate clauses. Each subordinate clause can be used as a noun or as a modifier. If it is used as a modifier, a subordinate clause usually modifies a word in the independent clause, and the independent clause can stand alone. However, when a subordinate clause is a noun clause, it is a part of the independent clause; the two cannot be separated.

MODIFIER: *One should not complain unless one has a better solution.*

NOUN CLAUSE: *We sketched pictures of whoever we wished.* (The noun clause is the object of the preposition *of* and cannot be separated from the rest of the sentence.)

10.4 COMPOUND-COMPLEX SENTENCES

A **compound-complex sentence** contains two or more independent clauses and one or more subordinate clauses. Compound-complex sentences are, simply, both compound and complex. If you start with a compound sentence, all you need to do to form a compound-complex sentence is add a subordinate clause.

COMPOUND: *All the students knew the answer, yet they were too shy to volunteer.*

COMPOUND-COMPLEX: *All the students knew the answer that their teacher expected, yet they were too shy to volunteer.*

10.5 PARALLEL STRUCTURE

When you write sentences, make sure that coordinate parts are equivalent, or **parallel,** in structure.

NOT PARALLEL: *Erin loved basketball and to play hockey.* (*Basketball* is a noun; *to play hockey* is a phrase.)

PARALLEL: *Erin loved basketball and hockey.* (*Basketball* and *hockey* are both nouns.)

NOT PARALLEL: *He wanted to rent an apartment, a new car, and traveling around the country.* (*To rent* is an infinitive, *car* is a noun, and *traveling* is a gerund.)

PARALLEL: *He wanted to rent an apartment, to drive a new car, and to travel around the country.* (*To rent, to drive,* and *to travel* are all infinitives.)

11 Writing Complete Sentences

Remember, a sentence is a group of words that expresses a complete thought. In formal writing, try to avoid both sentence fragments and run-on sentences.

11.1 CORRECTING FRAGMENTS

A **sentence fragment** is a group of words that is only part of a sentence. It does not express a complete thought and may be confusing to a reader or listener. A sentence fragment may be lacking a subject, a predicate, or both.

FRAGMENT: *Waited for the boat to arrive.* (no subject)

CORRECTED: *We waited for the boat to arrive.*

FRAGMENT: *People of various races, ages, and creeds.* (no predicate)

CORRECTED: *People of various races, ages, and creeds gathered together.*

FRAGMENT: *Near the old cottage.* (neither subject nor predicate)

CORRECTED: *The burial ground is near the old cottage.*

In your writing, fragments may be a result of haste or incorrect punctuation. Sometimes fixing a fragment will be a matter of attaching it to a preceding or following sentence.

FRAGMENT: *We saw the two girls. Waiting for the bus to arrive.*

CORRECTED: *We saw the two girls waiting for the bus to arrive.*

11.2 CORRECTING RUN-ON SENTENCES

A **run-on sentence** is made up of two or more sentences written as though they were one. Some run-ons have no punctuation within them. Others may have only commas where conjunctions or stronger punctuation marks are necessary. Use your judgment in correcting run-on sentences, as you have choices. You can make a run-on two sentences if the thoughts are not closely connected. If the thoughts are closely related, you can keep the run-on as one sentence by adding a semicolon or a conjunction.

RUN-ON: *We found a place for the picnic by a small pond it was three miles from the village.*

MAKE TWO SENTENCES: *We found a place for the picnic by a small pond. It was three miles from the village.*

RUN-ON: *We found a place for the picnic by a small pond it was perfect.*

USE A SEMICOLON: *We found a place for the picnic by a small pond; it was perfect.*

ADD A CONJUNCTION: *We found a place for the picnic by a small pond, and it was perfect.*

WATCH OUT! When you form compound sentences, make sure you use appropriate punctuation: a comma before a coordinating conjunction, a semicolon when there is no coordinating conjunction. A very common mistake is to use a comma alone instead of a comma and a conjunction. This error is called a **comma splice.**

INCORRECT: *He finished the apprenticeship, he left the village.*

CORRECT: *He finished the apprenticeship, and he left the village.*

GRAMMAR PRACTICE

Rewrite the following paragraph, correcting all fragments and run-ons.

The narrator in Charlotte Perkins Gilman's story "The Yellow Wallpaper" expects that her husband will laugh at her, that's an odd response, in my opinion. She could have lived more happily. If the relationship between her and her husband were an equal partnership. We can acknowledge that men and women may be different in some ways. Without believing that they are as different as this story suggests. The male character acts practical and "strong," the female character acts nervous and weak.

12 Subject-Verb Agreement

The subject and verb in a clause must agree in number. Agreement means that if the subject is singular, the verb is also singular, and if the subject is plural, the verb is also plural.

12.1 BASIC AGREEMENT

Fortunately, agreement between subjects and verbs in English is simple. Most verbs show the difference between singular and plural only in the third person of the present tense. In the present tense, the third-person singular form ends in -*s*.

Present-Tense Verb Forms	
Singular	**Plural**
I eat	we eat
you eat	you eat
she, he, it eats	they eat

12.2 AGREEMENT WITH *BE*

The verb *be* presents special problems in agreement, because this verb does not follow the usual verb patterns.

Forms of *Be*			
Present Tense		**Past Tense**	
Singular	**Plural**	**Singular**	**Plural**
I am	we are	I was	we were
you are	you are	you were	you were
she, he, it is	they are	she, he, it was	they were

12.3 WORDS BETWEEN SUBJECT AND VERB

A verb agrees only with its subject. When words come between a subject and a verb, ignore them when considering proper agreement. Identify the subject, and make sure the verb agrees with it.

EXAMPLES:

A story in the newspapers tells about the 1890s.

Dad as well as Mom reads the paper daily.

GRAMMAR PRACTICE
ANSWERS

Possible answer: *The narrator in Charlotte Perkins Gilman's story "The Yellow Wallpaper" expects that her husband will laugh at her. That's an odd response, in my opinion. She could have lived more happily if the relationship between her and her husband were an equal partnership. We can acknowledge that men and women may be different in some ways without believing that they are as different as this story suggests. The male character acts practical and "strong"; the female character acts nervous and weak.*

12.4 AGREEMENT WITH COMPOUND SUBJECTS

Use plural verbs with most compound subjects joined by the word *and*.

> **EXAMPLE:** *My mother and her sisters call each other every Sunday.*

To confirm that you need a plural verb, you could substitute the plural pronoun *they* for *my mother and her sisters.*

If a compound subject is thought of as a unit, use a singular verb. Test this by substituting the singular pronoun *it.*

> **EXAMPLE:** *Liver and onions [it] is Robert's least favorite dish.*

Use a singular verb with a compound subject that is preceded by *each, every,* or *many a.*

> **EXAMPLE:** *Not every dog and cat at the shelter makes a good pet.*

When the parts of a compound subject are joined by *or, nor,* or the correlative conjunctions *either . . . or* or *neither . . . nor,* make the verb agree with the noun or pronoun nearest the verb.

> **EXAMPLES:**
>
> *Baseball or football is my favorite sport.*
>
> *Either my rabbits or my turtle was loose in my room.*
>
> *Neither Mrs. Howard nor her two sons were home at the time of the accident.*

12.5 PERSONAL PRONOUNS AS SUBJECTS

When using a personal pronoun as a subject, make sure to match it with the correct form of the verb *be.* (See the chart in Section 12.2.) Note especially that the pronoun *you* takes the forms *are* and *were,* regardless of whether it is singular or plural.

> **WATCH OUT!** *You is* and *you was* are nonstandard forms and should be avoided in writing and speaking. *We was* and *they was* are also forms to be avoided.
>
> **INCORRECT:** *You is facing the wrong direction.*
>
> **CORRECT:** *You are facing the wrong direction.*
>
> **INCORRECT:** *We was telling ghost stories.*
>
> **CORRECT:** *We were telling ghost stories.*

12.6 INDEFINITE PRONOUNS AS SUBJECTS

Some indefinite pronouns are always singular; some are always plural.

Singular Indefinite Pronouns			
another	either	neither	one
anybody	everybody	nobody	somebody
anyone	everyone	no one	someone
anything	everything	nothing	something
each	much		

EXAMPLES:

Each of the writers was given an award.

Somebody in the room upstairs is sleeping.

Plural Indefinite Pronouns			
both	few	many	several

EXAMPLES:

Many of the books in our library are not in circulation.

Few have been returned recently.

Still other indefinite pronouns may be either singular or plural.

Singular or Plural Indefinite Pronouns		
all	more	none
any	most	some

The number of the indefinite pronoun *any* or *none* often depends on the intended meaning.

EXAMPLES:

Any of these topics has potential for a good article. (any one topic)

Any of these topics have potential for good articles. (all of the many topics)

The indefinite pronouns *all, some, more, most,* and *none* are singular when they refer to quantities or parts of things. They are plural when they refer to numbers of individual things. Context will usually give a clue.

EXAMPLES:

All of the flour is gone. (referring to a quantity)

All of the flowers are gone. (referring to individual items)

12.7 INVERTED SENTENCES

Problems in agreement often occur in inverted sentences beginning with *here* or *there;* in questions beginning with *how, when, why, where,* or *what;* and in inverted sentences beginning with phrases. Identify the subject—wherever it is—before deciding on the verb.

EXAMPLES:

There clearly are far too many cooks in this kitchen.

What is the correct ingredient for this stew?

Far from the embroiled cooks stands the master chef.

GRAMMAR PRACTICE

Locate the subject of each clause in the sentences below. Then choose the correct verb.

1. Many poets have written great poetry, but few (is/are) as talented as Emily Dickinson.

2. There (is/are) many lines in her work that her readers (treasures/treasure).

3. Some of her readers (appreciates/appreciate) her use of dashes, while others (finds/find) it confusing.

4. Each of her poems (presents/present) an idea to think about.

5. What (is/are) the dominant vowel sound in the last four lines of "Much Madness is divinest Sense"?

6. The consonant that prevails in the same poem (seems/seem) to be *s.*

7. I can't decide whether the poem's sound or its ideas (is/are) more striking.

12.8 SENTENCES WITH PREDICATE NOMINATIVES

When a predicate nominative serves as a complement in a sentence, use a verb that agrees with the subject, not the complement.

EXAMPLES:

The hunting habits of the North American wolf are an example of how change in the environment affects animals. (The subject is the plural noun *habits*—not *wolf*—and it takes the plural verb *are.*)

An example of how change in the environment affects animals is seen in the hunting habits of the North American wolf. (The subject is the singular noun *example,* and it takes the singular verb *is seen.*)

12.9 *DON'T* AND *DOESN'T* AS AUXILIARY VERBS

The auxiliary verb *doesn't* is used with singular subjects and with the personal pronouns *she, he,* and *it.* The auxiliary verb *don't* is used with plural subjects and with the personal pronouns *I, we, you,* and *they.*

SINGULAR: *She doesn't have a costume for the rehearsal.*

Doesn't the doctor have an appointment Wednesday morning?

PLURAL: *They don't think they did very well on that math test.*

The cats don't need to be fed more than twice a day.

12.10 COLLECTIVE NOUNS AS SUBJECTS

Collective nouns are singular nouns that name groups of persons or things. *Team,* for example, is the collective name of a group of individuals. A collective noun takes a singular verb when the group acts as a single unit. It takes a plural verb when the members of the group act separately.

EXAMPLES:

Our team usually wins. (The team as a whole wins.)

Our team vote differently on most issues. (The individual members vote.)

12.11 RELATIVE PRONOUNS AS SUBJECTS

When the relative pronoun *who, which,* or *that* is used as a subject in an adjective clause, the verb in the clause must agree in number with the antecedent of the pronoun.

SINGULAR: *Have you selected one of the poems that is meaningful to you?*

The antecedent of the relative pronoun *that* is the singular *one;* therefore, *that* is singular and must take the singular verb *is.*

PLURAL: *The fairy tales, which have been collected from many different sources, are annotated.*

The antecedent of the relative pronoun *which* is the plural *fairy tales. Which* is plural, and it takes the plural verb *have been collected.*

GRAMMAR PRACTICE

ANSWERS

1. *few > are*

2. *lines > are*
   readers > treasure

3. *Some > appreciate*
   others > find

4. *Each > presents*

5. *sound > is*

6. *consonant > seems*

7. *sound or ideas > are*

COMMON CORE FOCUS

L 2b Spell correctly. **L 4a–c** Use context as a clue to the meaning of a word or phrase; identify and correctly use patterns of word changes that indicate different meanings or parts of speech; consult general and specialized reference materials to find the pronunciation of a word or determine or clarify its precise meaning, its part of speech, its etymology, or its standard usage. **L 5** Demonstrate understanding of figurative language, word relationships, and nuances in word meanings. **L 6** Acquire and use accurately general academic and domain-specific words and phrases; demonstrate independence in gathering vocabulary knowledge when considering a word or phrase important to comprehension or expression.

The key to becoming an independent reader is to develop a toolkit of vocabulary strategies. By learning and practicing the strategies, you'll know what to do when you encounter unfamiliar words while reading. You'll also know how to refine the words you use for different situations—personal, school, and work.

Being a good speller is important when communicating your ideas in writing. Learning basic spelling rules and checking your spelling in a dictionary will help you spell words that you may not use frequently.

COMMON CORE

Included in this handbook:
L 2b, L 4a–c, L 6

1 Using Context Clues

The context of a word is made up of the punctuation marks, words, sentences, and paragraphs that surround the word. A word's context can give you important clues about its meaning.

1.1 GENERAL CONTEXT

Sometimes you need to infer the meaning of an unfamiliar word by reading all the information in a passage.

> *I told my parents I wanted to quit playing the piano, but they told me to perevere anyway.*

You can figure out from the context that *persevere* means "continue."

1.2 SPECIFIC CONTEXT CLUES

Sometimes writers help you understand the meanings of words by providing specific clues such as those shown in the chart.

1.3 IDIOMS, SLANG, AND FIGURATIVE LANGUAGE

Use context clues to figure out the meanings of idioms, figurative language, and slang.

An **idiom** is an expression whose overall meaning is different from the meaning of the individual words.

> *If you're going to buy a house with a garden, you'd better have a green thumb. (Green thumb means "ability to grow plants.")*

Figurative language is language that communicates meaning beyond the literal meaning of the words. Note this example from "A Chip of Glass Ruby" by Nadine Gordimer:

> *There was the feeling, in the house, that he had wept and raged at her, that boulders of reproach had thundered down upon her absence, and yet he had said not one word. (Boulders of reproach had thundered down upon her absence means he was very angry that she was gone.)*

Slang is informal language composed of made-up words and ordinary words that are used to mean something different from their meanings in formal English.

> *My parents freaked out when I told them that I went to the concert without their permission. (Freaked out means "became greatly distressed.")*

Specific Context Clues		
Type of Clue	**Key Words/ Phrases**	**Example**
Definition or restatement of the meaning of the word	or, which is, that is, in other words, also known as, also called	*Perennials*—**plants that live for more than two years**—make up only one-third of the garden's exhibit.
Example following an unfamiliar word	such as, like, as if, for example, especially, including	Their new apartment was *arrayed* with many beautiful things, **such as a crystal lamp and a porcelain vase.**
Comparison with a more familiar word or concept	as, like, also, similar to, in the same way, likewise	The prairie grasses *undulated* in the wind **like the waves in the ocean.**
Contrast with a familiar word or experience	unlike, but, however, although, on the other hand, on the contrary	My dog is usually very **calm, unlike** our neighbor's dog, which is very *rowdy*.

*For more information, see **Vocabulary Strategy: Context Clues**, pages 101, 131, 214, 672, 1000, and 1258.*

② Analyzing Word Structure

Many words can be broken into smaller parts, such as base words, roots, prefixes, and suffixes.

2.1 BASE WORDS

A **base word** is a word part that by itself is also a word. Other words or word parts can be added to base words to form new words.

2.2 ROOTS

A **root** is a word part that contains the core meaning of the word. Many English words contain roots that come from older languages such as Greek, Latin, Old English (Anglo-Saxon), and Norse. Knowing the meaning of a word's root can help you determine the word's meaning.

Root	Meaning	Example
aster, astr (Greek)	star	asterisk
fic/ fac/ fec (Latin)	make, do	factory
spec/ spect/ spic (Latin)	look at, see, behold	spectator
ten (Latin)	stretch	tendon
derm/ derma (Greek)	skin	epidermis

*For more information, see **Vocabulary Strategy: Word Roots**, pages 90, 277, 334, 433, 484, 616, 710, 832, and 906.*

2.3 PREFIXES

A **prefix** is a word part attached to the beginning of a word. Most prefixes come from Greek, Latin, or Old English.

Prefix	Meaning	Example
un- (Old English)	not	unafraid
epi- (Greek)	upon, on, over	epicenter
syn- (Greek)	together, at the same time	synthesis
hexa- (Greek)	six	hexagram
geo- (Greek)	earth	geography
trans- (Latin)	across, beyond	transatlantic
dis- (Latin)	lack of, not	distrust
circum- (Latin)	around	circumvent
hemi- (Latin)	half	hemisphere

*For more information, see **Vocabulary Strategy: Prefixes**, pages 376, 398, 760, and 1229.*

2.4 SUFFIXES

A **suffix** is a word part that appears at the end of a root or base word to form a new word. Some suffixes do not change word meaning. These suffixes are

- added to nouns to change the number of persons or objects
- added to verbs to change the tense
- added to modifiers to change the degree of comparison

Suffix	Meaning	Example
-s, -es	to change the number of a noun	trunk + s = trunks
-d, -ed, -ing	to change verb tense	sprinkle + d = sprinkled
-er, -est	to change the degree of comparison in modifiers	cold + er = colder icy + est = iciest

Other suffixes can be added to a root or base to change the word's meaning. These suffixes can also determine a word's part of speech.

Suffix	Meaning	Example
-ence	state or condition of	independence
-ous	full of	furious
-ate	to make	activate
-ly, -ily	manner	quickly

*For more information, see **Vocabulary Strategy: Suffixes**, pages 376 and 454.*

Strategies for Understanding Unfamiliar Words

- Look for any prefixes or suffixes. Remove them to isolate the base word or the root.
- See if you recognize any elements—prefix, suffix, root, or base—of the word. You may be able to guess its meaning by analyzing one or two elements.
- Consider the way the word is used in the sentence. Use the context and the word parts to make a logical guess about the word's meaning.
- Consult a dictionary to see whether you are correct.

Interactive Vocabulary

Go to thinkcentral.com
KEYWORD: HML11-R73

Interactive Vocabulary

The keyword on this page directs students to **WordSharp** tutorials on key vocabulary strategies.

Make inferences about the meanings of the following words from the fields of science and math. Consider what you have learned in this section about Greek, Latin, and Anglo-Saxon (Old English) word parts.

astronomy	efficacy	hexagonal
circumference	epidermis	spectrum
distend	geosciences	uncertainty

3 Understanding Word Origins

3.1 ETYMOLOGIES

Etymologies show the origin and historical development of a word. When you study a word's history and origin, you can find out when, where, and how the word came to be.

> **am•bas•sa•dor** (ăm-băs′ə-dər, -dôr′) *n.* A diplomatic official of the highest rank appointed and accredited as representative in residence by one government or sovereign to another, usually for a specific length of time. [Middle English *ambassadour,* from Old French *ambassadeur,* from Medieval Latin *ambactia,* mission, from Latin *ambactus,* servant, ultimately of Celtic origin.]

> **com•mu•ni•ty** (kə-myōō′nĭ-tē) *n., pl.* **-ties** A group of people living in the same locality and under the same government. [Middle English *communite,* citizenry, from Old French, from Latin *commūnitās,* fellowship, from *commūnis,* common.]

For more information, see **Vocabulary Strategy: Etymologies,** *pages 80, 257, and 1076.*

Trace the etymology of the words below, often used in the fields of history and political science.

diplomat	independence	legislature
government	justice	revolution
immigrant	laissez-faire	treaty

3.2 WORD FAMILIES

Words that have the same root make up a word family and have related meanings. The chart shows a common Greek and a common Latin root. Notice how the meanings of the example words are related to the meanings of their roots.

Latin Root	*med:* "middle"
English Words	**mediate** resolve or settle
	mediocre ordinary
	media² middle wall of a blood vessel
	medial toward the middle
	medium action midway between two extremes
Greek Root	*chron:* "time"
English Words	**chronicle** detailed narrative report
	chronic of long duration
	synchronize occur at same time
	anachronism out of proper order in time

For more information, see **Vocabulary Strategy: Word Family,** *pages 334, 433, 616, 710, and 906.*

3.3 WORDS FROM CLASSICAL MYTHOLOGY

The English language includes many words from classical mythology. You can use your knowledge of these myths to understand the origins and meanings of these words. For example, *herculean task* refers to the strongman Hercules. Thus, *herculean task* probably means "a job that is large or difficult." The chart shows a few common words from mythology.

Greek	Roman	Norse
panic	cereal	Wednesday
atlas	mercurial	gun
adonis	Saturday	berserk
mentor	January	valkyrie

Look up the etymology of each word in the chart and locate the myth associated with it. Use the information from the myth to explain the origin and meaning of each word.

3.4 FOREIGN WORDS

The English language includes words from diverse languages, such as French, Dutch, Spanish, Italian, and Chinese. Many words stayed the way they were in their original language.

French	Dutch	Spanish	Italian
entree	maelstrom	rodeo	pasta
nouveau riche	trek	salsa	opera
potpourri	cookie	bronco	vendetta
tête-à-tête	snoop	tornado	grotto

*For more information, see **Vocabulary Strategy: Foreign Words,** page 1016.*

4 Synonyms and Antonyms

4.1 SYNONYMS

A **synonym** is a word with a meaning similar to that of another word. You can find synonyms in a thesaurus or a dictionary. In a dictionary, synonyms are often given as part of the definition of a word. The following word pairs are synonyms:

dry/arid   enthralled/fascinated   gaunt/thin

4.2 ANTONYMS

An **antonym** is a word with a meaning opposite that of another word. The following word pairs are antonyms:

friend/enemy   absurd/logical

courteous/rude   languid/energetic

5 Denotation and Connotation

5.1 DENOTATION

A word's dictionary meaning is called its **denotation.** For example, the denotation of the word *rascal* is "an unethical, dishonest person."

5.2 CONNOTATION

The images or feelings you connect to a word add a finer shade of meaning, called **connotation.** The connation of a word goes beyond its basic dictionary definition. Writers use connotations of words to communicate positive or negative feelings.

Positive	Neutral	Negative
save	store	hoard
fragrance	smell	stench
display	show	flaunt

Make sure you understand the denotation and connotation of a word when you read it or use it in your writing.

*For more information, see **Vocabulary Strategy: Denotation and Connotation,** pages 101, 131, 214, and 778.*

6 Analogies

An **analogy** is a comparison between two things that are similar in some way but are otherwise dissimilar. Analogies are sometimes used in writing when unfamiliar subjects or ideas are explained in terms of familiar ones. Analogies often appear on tests as well, usually in a format like this:

TERRIER : DOG ::   A) rat : fish
                    B) kitten : cat
                    C) trout : fish
                    D) fish : trout
                    E) poodle : collie

Follow these steps to determine the correct answer:

- Read the part in capital letters as "*bird* is to *fly* as . . ."

- Read the answer choices as "*rat* is to *fish*," "*kitten* is to *cat*," and so on.

- Ask yourself how the words *terrier* and *dog* are related. (A terrier is a type of dog.)

- Ask yourself which of the choices shows the same relationship. (A kitten is a kind of cat, but not in the same way that a terrier is a kind of dog. A kitten is a baby cat. A trout however, is a type of fish in the sense that a terrier is a type of dog. Therefore, the answer is C.)

*For more information, see **Vocabulary Strategy: Analogies,** pages 236, 816, and 1216.*

7 Homonyms and Homophones

7.1 HOMONYMS

Homonyms are words that have the same spelling and sound but have different origins and meanings.

I don't want to bore you with a story about how I had to bore through the living room wall.

Bore can mean "cause a person to lose interest," but an identically spelled word means "to drill a hole."

My dog likes to bark while it scratches the bark on the tree in the backyard.

Bark can mean "the sound made by a dog." However, another identically spelled word means "the outer covering of a tree." Each word has a different meaning and its own dictionary entry.

Sometimes only one of the meanings of two homonyms may be familiar to you. Use context clues to help you figure out the meaning of an unfamiliar word.

7.2 HOMOPHONES

Homophones are words that sound alike but have different meanings and spellings. The following homophones are frequently misused:

it's/its	they're/their/there
to/too/two	stationary/stationery

Many misused homophones are pronouns and contractions. Whenever you are unsure whether to write *your* or *you're* and *who's* or *whose,* ask yourself if you mean *you are* or *who is/has.* If you do, write the contraction. For other homophones, such as *scent* and *sent,* use the meaning of the word to help you decide which one to use.

8 Words with Multiple Meanings

Some words have acquired additional meanings over time that are based on the original meaning.

> **EXAMPLES:** *I was in a hurry so I jammed my clothes into the suitcase. Unfortunately, I jammed my finger in the process.*

These two uses of *jam* have different meanings, but both of them have the same origin. You will find all the meanings of *jam* listed in one entry in the dictionary.

9 Specialized Vocabulary

Specialized vocabulary is special terms suited to a particular field of study or work. For example, science, mathematics, and history all have their own technical or specialized vocabularies. To figure out specialized terms, you can use context clues and reference sources, such as dictionaries on specific subjects, atlases, or manuals.

*For more information, see **Vocabulary Strategy: Specialized Vocabulary**, pages 64, 246, 454, and 728.*

10 Using Reference Sources

10.1 DICTIONARIES

A **general dictionary** will tell you not only a word's definitions but also its pronunciation, its parts of speech, and its history and origin. A **specialized dictionary** focuses on terms related to a particular field of study or work. Use a dictionary to check the spelling of any word you are unsure of in your English class and other subjects as well.

10.2 THESAURI

A **thesaurus** (plural, thesauri) is a dictionary of synonyms. A thesaurus can be helpful when you find yourself using the same modifiers over and over again.

10.3 SYNONYM FINDERS

A **synonym finder** is often included in word-processing software. It enables you to highlight a word and be shown a display of its synonyms.

10.4 GLOSSARIES

A **glossary** is a list of specialized terms and their definitions. It is often found in the back of textbooks and sometimes includes pronunciations. In fact, this textbook has four glossaries: the **Glossary of Literary and Nonfiction Terms,** the **Glossary of Reading & Informational Terms,** the **Glossary of Academic Vocabulary in English & Spanish,** and the **Glossary of Vocabulary in English & Spanish.** Use these glossaries to help you understand how terms are used in this textbook.

*For more information, see **Vocabulary Strategy: Reference Sources**, pages 112, 257, 692, 1046, and 1076.*

11 Spelling Rules

11.1 WORDS ENDING IN A SILENT *E*

Before adding a suffix beginning with a vowel or ***y*** to a word ending in a silent ***e,*** drop the ***e*** (with some exceptions).

> amaze + -ing = amazing
> love + -able = lovable
> create + -ed = created
> nerve + -ous = nervous

Exceptions: *change + -able = changeable; courage + -ous = courageous.*

When adding a suffix beginning with a consonant to a word ending in a silent **e,** keep the **e** (with some exceptions).

    late + -ly = lately
    spite + -ful = spiteful
    noise + -less = noiseless
    state + -ment = statement
Exceptions: *truly, argument, ninth, wholly, awful,* and others.

When a suffix beginning with **a** or **o** is added to a word with a final silent **e,** the final **e** is usually retained if it is preceded by a soft **c** or a soft **g.**

    bridge + -able = bridgeable
    peace + -able = peaceable
    outrage + -ous = outrageous
    advantage + -ous = advantageous

When a suffix beginning with a vowel is added to words ending in **ee** or **oe,** the final silent **e** is retained.

    agree + -ing = agreeing   free + -ing = freeing
    hoe + -ing = hoeing   see + -ing = seeing

11.2 WORDS ENDING IN Y

Before adding most suffixes to a word that ends in **y** preceded by a consonant, change the **y** to **i.**

    easy + -est = easiest
    crazy + -est = craziest
    silly + -ness = silliness
    marry + -age = marriage
Exceptions: *dryness, shyness,* and *slyness.*

However, when you add **-ing,** the **y** does not change.

    empty + -ed = emptied   but
    empty + -ing = emptying

When adding a suffix to a word that ends in **y** preceded by a vowel, the **y** usually does not change.

    play + -er = player
    employ + -ed = employed
    coy + -ness = coyness
    pay + -able = payable

11.3 WORDS ENDING IN A CONSONANT

In one-syllable words that end in one consonant preceded by one short vowel, double the final consonant before adding a suffix beginning with a vowel, such as **-ed** or **-ing.**

    dip + -ed = dipped   set + -ing = setting
    slim + -est = slimmest fit + -er = fitter

The rule does not apply to words of one syllable that end in a consonant preceded by two vowels.

    feel + -ing = feeling   peel + -ed = peeled
    reap + -ed = reaped   loot + -ed = looted

In words of more than one syllable, double the final consonant when (**1**) the word ends with one consonant preceded by one vowel and (**2**) the word is accented on the last syllable.

    be•gin´   per•mit´   re•fer´

In the following examples, note that in the new words formed with suffixes, the accent remains on the same syllable:

    be•gin´ + -ing = be•gin´ ning = beginning
    per•mit´ + -ed = per•mit´ ted = permitted

In some words with more than one syllable, though the accent remains on the same syllable when a suffix is added, the final consonant is nevertheless not doubled, as in the following examples:

    tra´vel + -er = tra´vel•er = traveler
    mar´ket + -er = mar´ket•er = marketer

In the following examples, the accent does not remain on the same syllable; thus, the final consonant is not doubled:

    re•fer´ + -ence = ref´er•ence = reference
    con•fer´ + -ence = con´fer•ence = conference

11.4 PREFIXES AND SUFFIXES

When adding a prefix to a word, do not change the spelling of the base word. When a prefix creates a double letter, keep both letters.

    dis- + approve = disapprove
    re- + build = rebuild
    ir- + regular = irregular
    mis- + spell = misspell
    anti- + trust = antitrust
    il- + logical = illogical

When adding **-ly** to a word ending in **l,** keep both **l's,** and when adding **-ness** to a word ending in **n,** keep both **n's.**

    careful + -ly = carefully
    sudden + -ness = suddenness
    final + -ly = finally
    thin + -ness = thinness

11.5 FORMING PLURAL NOUNS

To form the plural of most nouns, just add *-s.*

prizes   dreams   circles   stations

For most singular nouns ending in *o,* add *-s.*

solos   halos   studios   photos   pianos

For a few nouns ending in *o,* add *-es.*

heroes   tomatoes   potatoes   echoes

When the singular noun ends in *s, sh, ch, x,* or *z,* add *-es.*

**waitresses   brushes   ditches
axes   buzzes**

When a singular noun ends in *y* with a consonant before it, change the *y* to *i* and add *-es.*

**army—armies   candy—candies
baby—babies   diary—diaries
ferry—ferries   conspiracy—conspiracies**

When a vowel (*a, e, i, o, u*) comes before the *y,* just add *-s.*

**boy—boys   way—ways
array—arrays   alloy—alloys
weekday—weekdays   jockey—jockeys**

For most nouns ending in *f* or *fe,* change the *f* to *v* and add *-es* or *-s.*

**life—lives   calf—calves   knife—knives
thief—thieves   shelf—shelves   loaf—loaves**

For some nouns ending in *f,* add *-s* to make the plural.

roofs   chiefs   reefs   beliefs

Some nouns have the same form for both singular and plural.

deer   sheep   moose   salmon   trout

For some nouns, the plural is formed in a special way.

**man—men   goose—geese
ox—oxen   woman—women
mouse—mice   child—children**

For a compound noun written as one word, form the plural by changing the last word in the compound to its plural form.

stepchild—stepchildren   firefly—fireflies

If a compound noun is written as a hyphenated word or as two separate words, change the most important word to the plural form.

**brother-in-law—brothers-in-law
life jacket—life jackets**

11.6 FORMING POSSESSIVES

If a noun is singular, add *'s.*

mother—my mother's car   Ross—Ross's desk

Exception: The *s* after the apostrophe is dropped after *Jesus', Moses',* and certain names in classical mythology (*Zeus'*). These possessive forms can be pronounced easily.

If a noun is plural and ends with *s,* just add an apostrophe.

**parents—my parents' car
the Santinis—the Santinis' house**

If a noun is plural but does not end in *s,* add *'s.*

**people—the people's choice
women—the women's coats**

11.7 SPECIAL SPELLING PROBLEMS

Only one English word ends in *-sede: supersede.* Three words end in *-ceed: exceed, proceed,* and *succeed.* All other verbs ending in the sound "seed" are spelled with *-cede.*

concede   precede   recede   secede

In words with *ie* or *ei,* when the sound is long *e* (as in *she*), the word is spelled *ie* except after *c* (with some exceptions).

i before *e*	thief	relieve	field
	piece	grieve	pier

except after *c*	conceit	perceive	ceiling
	receive	receipt	

Exceptions: *either, neither, weird, leisure, seize.*

2 Commonly Confused Words

WORDS	DEFINITIONS	EXAMPLES
accept/except	The verb *accept* means "to receive or believe"; *except* is usually a preposition meaning "excluding."	**Except** for some of the more extraordinary events, I can **accept** that the *Odyssey* recounts a real journey.
advice/advise	*Advise* is a verb; *advice* is a noun naming that which an *adviser* gives.	I **advise** you to take that job. Whom should I ask for **advice?**
affect/effect	As a verb, *affect* means "to influence." *Effect* as a verb means "to cause." If you want a noun, you will almost always want *effect*.	Did Circe's wine **affect** Odysseus' mind? It did **effect** a change in Odysseus' men. In fact, it had an **effect** on everyone else who drank it.
all ready/already	*All ready* is an adjective meaning "fully ready." *Already* is an adverb meaning "before or by this time."	He was **all ready** to go at noon. I have **already** seen that movie.
allusion/illusion	An *allusion* is an indirect reference to something. An *illusion* is a false picture or idea.	There are many **allusions** to the works of Homer in English literature. The world's apparent flatness is an **illusion.**
among/between	*Between* is used when you are speaking of only two things. *Among* is used for three or more.	**Between** *Hamlet* and *King Lear,* I prefer the latter. Emily Dickinson is **among** my favorite poets.
bring/take	*Bring* is used to denote motion toward a speaker or place. *Take* is used to denote motion away from such a person or place.	**Bring** the books over here, and I will **take** them to the library.
fewer/less	*Fewer* refers to the number of separate, countable units. *Less* refers to bulk quantity.	We have **less** literature and **fewer** selections in this year's curriculum.
leave/let	*Leave* means "to allow something to remain behind." *Let* means "to permit."	The librarian will **leave** some books on display but will not **let** us borrow any.
lie/lay	*Lie* means "to rest or recline." It does not take an object. *Lay* always takes an object.	Rover loves to **lie** in the sun. We always **lay** some bones next to him.
loose/lose	*Loose* (lo͞os) means "free, not restrained"; *lose* (lo͞oz) means "to misplace or fail to find."	Who turned the horses **loose?** I hope we won't **lose** any of them.
precede/proceed	*Precede* means "to go or come before." Use *proceed* for other meanings.	Emily Dickinson's poetry **precedes** that of Alice Walker. You may **proceed** to the next section of the test.
than/then	Use *than* in making comparisons; use *then* on all other occasions.	Who can say whether Amy Lowell is a better poet **than** Denise Levertov? I will read Lowell first, and **then** I will read Levertov.
their/there/they're	*Their* means "belonging to them." *There* means "in that place." *They're* is the contraction for "they are."	**There** is a movie playing at 9 P.M. **They're** going to see it with me. Sakara and Jessica drove away in **their** car after the movie.
two/too/to	*Two* is the number. *Too* is an adverb meaning "also" or "very." Use *to* before a verb or as a preposition.	Meg had **to** go **to** town, **too.** We had **too** much reading **to** do. **Two** chapters is **too** many.

COMMON CORE FOCUS

SL 1a–d Initiate and participate effectively in a range of collaborative discussions with diverse partners, building on others' ideas and expressing their own clearly and persuasively. **SL 2** Integrate multiple sources of information presented in diverse formats and media in order to make informed decisions and solve problems, evaluating the credibility and accuracy of each source and noting any discrepancies among the data. **SL 3** Evaluate a speaker's point of view, reasoning, and use of evidence and rhetoric, assessing the stance, premises, links among ideas, word choice, points of emphasis, and tone used. **SL 4** Present information, findings, and supporting evidence, conveying a clear and distinct perspective, such that listeners can follow the line of reasoning, alternative or opposing perspectives are addressed, and the organization, development, substance, and style are appropriate to purpose, audience, and a range of formal and informal tasks. **SL 5** Make strategic use of digital media in presentations to enhance understanding of findings, reasoning, and evidence and to add interest. **SL 6** Adapt speech to a variety of contexts and tasks, demonstrating a command of formal English when indicated or appropriate.

Effective oral communication occurs when the audience understands a message the way the speaker intends it. Good speakers and listeners do more than just talk and hear. They use specific techniques to present their ideas effectively, and they are attentive and critical listeners.

COMMON CORE

Included in this handbook:
SL 1a–d, SL 2–6

1 Speech

In school, in business, and in community life, a speech is one of the most effective means of communicating.

1.1 AUDIENCE, PURPOSE, AND OCCASION

When developing and delivering a speech, your goal is to deliver a focused, coherent presentation that conveys your ideas clearly and relates to the background of your audience. By understanding your audience, you can tailor your speech to them appropriately and effectively.

- **Know Your Audience** What kind of group are you presenting to? Fellow classmates? A group of teachers? What are their interests and backgrounds? Understanding their different points of view can help you organize the information so that they understand and are interested in it.

- **Understand Your Purpose** Keep in mind your purpose for speaking. Are you trying to persuade the audience to do something? Perhaps you simply want to entertain them by sharing a story or experience. Your reason for giving the speech will guide you in organizing your thoughts and deciding on how to deliver it.

- **Know the Occasion** Are you speaking at a special event? Is it formal? Will others be giving speeches besides you? Knowing the type of occasion will help you tailor the language and length of your speech for the event.

1.2 PREPARING YOUR SPEECH

There are several approaches to preparing a speech. Your teacher may tell you which one to use.

- **Manuscript** Prepare a complete script of the speech in advance and use it to deliver the speech. Use for formal occasions, such as graduation speeches and political addresses, and to present technical or complicated information.

- **Memory** Prepare a written text in advance and then memorize it in order to deliver the speech word for word. Use for short speeches, as when introducing another speaker or accepting an award.

- **Extemporaneous** Prepare the speech and deliver it using an outline or notes. Use for informal situations, for persuasive messages, and to make a more personal connection with the audience.

1.3 DRAFTING YOUR SPEECH

If you are writing your speech beforehand, rather than working from notes, use the following guidelines to help you:

- **Create a Unified Speech** Do this first by organizing your speech into paragraphs, each of which develops a single main idea. All the sentences in a paragraph should support the main idea of the paragraph, and all the paragraphs should support the main idea of the speech. Be sure that your speech has an introduction and a conclusion. Just as in a written product, use a pattern of organization that is appropriate to your subject and purpose.

- **Use Appropriate Language** The subject of your speech—and the way you choose to present it— should match your audience, your purpose, and the occasion. You can use informal language, such as slang, to share a story with your classmates. For a persuasive speech in front of a school assembly, use formal, standard American English. If you are giving an informative presentation, be sure to explain any terms that the audience may not be familiar with.

- **Provide Evidence** Include relevant facts, statistics, and incidents; quote experts to support your ideas and opinions. Elaborate—provide specific details, perhaps with visual or media displays—to clarify what you are saying.

- **Emphasize Important Points** To help your audience follow the main ideas and concepts of your speech, be sure to draw attention to important points. You can use rhyme, repetition, parallelism, and other rhetorical devices. You can also use figurative language for effect.

- **Use Precise Language** Use precise language to convey your ideas, and vary the structure and length of your sentences. You can keep the audience's attention with a word that elicits strong emotion. You can use a question or an interjection to make a personal connection with the audience.

- **Start Strong, Finish Strong** As you begin your speech, consider using a "hook"—an interesting question or statement meant to capture your audience's attention. At the end of the speech, restate your main ideas simply and clearly. Perhaps conclude with a powerful example or anecdote to reinforce your message.

- **Revise Your Speech** After you write your speech, revise, edit, and proofread it as you would a written report. Use a variety of sentence structures to achieve a natural rhythm. Check for correct subject-verb agreement and consistent verb tense. Correct run-on sentences and sentence fragments. Use parallel structure to emphasize ideas. Make sure you use complete sentences and correct punctuation and capitalization, even if no one else will see it. Your written speech should be clear and error-free.

1.4 DELIVERING YOUR SPEECH

Confidence is the key to a successful presentation. Use these techniques to help you prepare and present your speech:

Prepare

- **Review Your Information** Reread your notes and review any background research. You'll feel more confident during your speech.

- **Organize Your Notes** Some people prefer to include only key points. Others prefer the entire script. Write each main point, or each paragraph, of your speech on a separate numbered index card. Be sure to include your most important evidence and examples.

- **Plan Your Visual Aids and Sound Effects** If you are planning on using visual aids, such as slides, posters, charts, graphs, video clips, transparencies, or computer projections, now is the time to design your visual and sound elements and work them into your speech.

Practice

- **Rehearse** Rehearse your speech several times, possibly in front of a practice audience. Maintain good posture by standing with your shoulders back and your head up. If you are using visual aids, practice handling them. Adapt your rate of speaking, pitch, and tone of voice to your audience and setting. Glance at your notes to refresh your memory, but avoid reading them word for word. Your style of performance should express the purpose of your speech. Use the following chart to help you.

Purpose	Pace	Pitch	Tone
to persuade	fast but clear	even	urgent
to inform	using plenty of pauses	even	authoritative
to entertain	usually building to a "punch"	varied to create characters or drama	funny or dramatic

- **Use Audience Feedback** If you had a practice audience, ask them specific questions about your delivery: Did I use enough eye contact? Was my voice at the right volume? Did I stand straight, or did I slouch? Use the audience's comments to evaluate the effectiveness of your delivery and to set goals for future rehearsals.

- **Evaluate Your Performance** When you have finished each rehearsal, evaluate your performance. Did you pause to let an important point sink in, or use gestures for emphasis? Make a list of the aspects of your presentation that you will try to improve for your next rehearsal.

Present

- **Begin Your Speech** Try to look relaxed and smile.

- **Make Eye Contact** Try to make eye contact with as many audience members as possible. This will establish personal contact and help you determine if the audience understands your speech.

- **Remember to Pause** A slight pause after important points will provide emphasis and give your audience time to think about what you're saying.

- **Speak Clearly** Speak loud enough to be heard clearly, but not so loud that your voice is overwhelming. Use a conversational tone.

- **Maintain Good Posture** Stand up straight and avoid nervous movements that may distract the audience's attention from what you are saying.

- **Use Expressive Body Language** Use facial expressions to show your feelings toward your topic. Lean forward when you make an important point; move your hands and arms for emphasis. Use your body language to show your own style and reflect your personality.

- **Watch the Audience for Responses** If they start fidgeting or yawning, speak a little louder or get to your conclusion a little sooner. Use what you learn to decide what areas need improvement for future presentations.

- **Close your speech** As part of your closing remarks, be sure to thank your audience.

Respond to Questions

Depending on the content of your speech, your audience may have questions. Follow these steps to make sure that you answer questions in an appropriate manner:

- Think about what your audience may ask and prepare answers before your speech.

- Tell your audience at the beginning of your speech that you will take questions at the end. This helps avoid audience interruptions that may make your speech hard to follow.

- Call on audience members in the order in which they raise their hands.

- Repeat each question before you answer it to ensure that everyone has heard it. This step also gives you time to prepare your answer.

2 Different Types of Oral Presentations

2.1 INFORMATIVE SPEECH

When you deliver an informative speech, you give the audience new information, provide a better understanding of information, or enable the audience to use the information in a new way.

Use the following questions to evaluate your own presentation or that of a peer or a public figure.

Evaluate an Informative Speech

- Did the speaker have a specific, clearly focused topic?
- Did the speaker take the audience's previous knowledge into consideration?
- Did the speaker cite sources for the information?
- Did the speaker communicate the information objectively?
- Did the speaker explain technical terms?
- Did the speaker use visual aids effectively?
- Did the speaker anticipate and address any audience concerns or misunderstandings?
- Is the speech informative and accurate?

2.2 PERSUASIVE SPEECH

When you deliver a persuasive speech, you offer a thesis or clear statement on a subject, you provide relevant evidence to support your position, and you attempt to convince the audience to accept your point of view.

Use the following questions to evaluate the presentation of a peer or a public figure, or your own presentation.

*For more information, see **Speaking and Listening: Persuasive Speech**, page 290.*

Evaluate a Persuasive Speech

- Did the speaker present a clear thesis or argument?
- Did the speaker anticipate and address audience concerns, biases, and counterclaims?
- Did the speaker use sound logic and reasoning in developing the argument?
- Did the speaker support the argument with valid evidence, examples, facts, expert opinions, and quotations?
- Did the speaker use rhetorical devices, such as emotional appeals, to support assertions?
- Were the speaker's voice, facial expressions, and gestures effective?
- Is your reaction to the speech similar to that of other audience members?
- Did you believe the speaker to be truthful and ethical?

2.3 DEBATE

A debate is a balanced argument covering both sides of an issue. In a debate, two teams compete to win the support of the audience. In a formal debate, two teams, each with two members, present their arguments on a given proposition or policy statement. One team argues for the proposition or statement, and the other argues against it. Each debater must consider the proposition closely and must research both sides of it.

Preparing for the Debate

In preparing for a debate, the debaters prepare a **brief,** an outline of the debate, accounting for the evidence and arguments of both sides of the **proposition** (topic). Debaters also prepare a **rebuttal,** a follow-up speech to support their arguments and counter the opposition's. Propositions are usually one of four types:

- **Proposition of fact**—determines whether a statement is true or false. An example is "Deforestation is ruining the rain forest."

- **Proposition of value**—determines the value of a person, place, or thing. An example is "Free trade will help small countries develop."

- **Proposition of problem**—determines whether a problem exists and whether it requires action.

- **Proposition of policy**—determines the action that will be taken. An example is "Students will provide tutoring services."

The two groups of debaters who argue a topic are called the **affirmative side** and the **negative side.** The affirmative side tries to convince the audience that the proposition should be accepted. The negative side argues against the proposition.

Use the following steps to prepare a brief:

- **Gather Information** Consult a variety of primary and secondary sources to gather the most reliable, up-to-date information about the proposition.

- **Identify Key Ideas** Sort out the important points and arrange them in order of importance.

- **List Arguments for and Against Each Key Idea** Look for strong arguments that support your side of the proposition and also note those that support your opponents' side.

- **Support Your Arguments** Find facts, quotations, expert opinions, and examples that support your arguments and counter your opponents'.

- **Write the Brief** Begin your brief with a statement of the proposition. Then list the arguments and evidence that support both sides of the proposition.

Planning the Rebuttal

The rebuttal is the opportunity to rebuild your case. Use the following steps to build a strong rebuttal:

- Listen to your opponents respectfully. Note the points you wish to overturn.

- Defend what the opposition has challenged.

- Cite weaknesses in their arguments, such as points they overlooked.

- Present counterclaims and supporting evidence.

- Offer your summary arguments. Restate and solidify your stance.

Use the following questions to evaluate a debate.

Evaluate a Team in a Debate

- Did the team prove that a significant problem does or does not exist? How thorough was the team's analysis of the problem?

- How did the team convince you that the proposition is or is not the best solution to the problem?

- How effectively did the team present reasons and evidence supporting the case?

- How effectively did the team refute and rebut arguments made by the opposing team?

- Did the speakers maintain eye contact and speak at an appropriate rate and volume?

- Did the speakers observe proper debate etiquette?

PRACTICE AND APPLY

View a political debate for a local, state, or national election. Use the preceding criteria to evaluate it.

2.4 NARRATIVE SPEECH

When you deliver a narrative speech, you tell a story or present a subject using a story-type format. A good narrative keeps an audience informed and entertained. It also allows you to deliver a message in a creative way.

Use the following questions to evaluate a speaker or your own presentation.

Evaluate a Narrative Speech

- Did the speaker choose a context that makes sense and contributes to a believable narrative?

- Did the speaker locate scenes and incidents in specific places?

- Does the plot flow well?

- Did the speaker use words that convey the appropriate mood and tone?

- Did the speaker use sensory details that allow the audience to experience the sights, sounds, and smells of a scene and the specific actions, gestures, and thoughts of the characters?

- Did the speaker use a range of narrative devices to keep the audience interested?

- Is your reaction to the presentation similar to that of other audience members?

2.5 REFLECTIVE SPEECH

In a reflective speech, you describe a personal experience and explore its significance. Use vivid description, visuals, and sound effects to re-create the experience for your audience and convey meaning.

Use the following questions to evaluate a speaker or your own presentation.

Evaluate a Reflective Speech

- Did the speaker describe an important experience in his or her life?
- Did the speaker use figurative language, sensory details, or other techniques to re-create the event for the audience?
- Did the speaker explain the significance of the event to the audience?
- Does the experience relate to a broader theme or a more general abstract idea about life?
- Did the speaker convey the message through one specific event or several related incidents?
- Did the speaker encourage the audience to think about the significance of the experience and apply it to their own lives?
- Was your reaction to the presentation similar to that of other audience members?

2.6 DESCRIPTIVE SPEECH

In a descriptive speech, you describe a subject with which you are personally familiar. A good description will enable your listeners to tell how you feel toward your subject.

Use the following questions to evaluate a speaker or your own presentation.

Evaluate a Descriptive Speech

- Did the speaker make clear his or her point of view toward the subject being described?
- Did the speaker use sensory details, figurative language, and factual details?
- Did the speaker use tone and pitch to emphasize important details?
- Did the speaker use facial expressions to emphasize his or her feelings toward the subject?
- Did the speaker change vantage points to help the audience see the subject from another position?
- Did the speaker change perspectives to show how someone else might feel toward the subject?

2.7 ORAL INTERPRETATION

When you perform an oral interpretation, you use appropriate vocal intonations, facial expressions, and gestures to bring a literature selection to life.

In an **oral reading,** you will present or read a poem, monologue, or passage from a literary selection, in which you assume the voice of a character, the narrator, or the speaker. An oral reading can also be a presentation of a dialogue between two or more characters, in which you, as the sole performer, take on all the roles.

Use the following techniques when giving an oral reading:

- **Speak Clearly** As you speak, pronounce your words clearly.
- **Control Your Volume** Make sure that you are loud enough to be heard, but do not shout.
- **Pace Yourself** Read at a moderate rate, but vary your pace if it seems appropriate to the emotions of the character or to the action you perform.
- **Vary Your Voice** Use a different voice for each character. Stress important words and phrases. Use your voice to express different emotions.

In a **dramatic reading,** several speakers participate in the reading of a play or some other work. Use the following techniques in your dramatic reading:

- **Prepare** Rehearse your material several times. Become familiar with the humorous and serious parts of the script. Develop a special voice that fits the personality of the character you portray.
- **Project** As you read your lines, aim your voice toward the back of the room to allow everyone to hear you.
- **Perform** React to the other characters as if you were hearing their lines for the first time. Deliver your own lines with the appropriate emotion. Use not only hand gestures and facial expressions but also other body movements to express your emotions.

*For more information, see **Speaking and Listening: Presenting a Script,** page 496.*

Use the following questions to evaluate an artistic performance by a peer or a public presenter, a media presentation, or your own performance.

Evaluate an Oral Interpretation

- Did the speaker speak clearly, enunciating each word carefully?
- Did the speaker maintain eye contact with the audience?
- Did the speaker control his or her volume, projecting without shouting?
- Did the speaker vary the rate of speech appropriately to express emotion, mood, and action?
- Did the speaker use a different voice for each character?
- Did the speaker stress important words or phrases?
- Did the speaker's presentation allow you to identify and appreciate elements of the text such as character development, rhyme, imagery, and language?

PRACTICE AND APPLY

Develop an oral reading and present it to your class; evaluate the oral readings of your classmates, using the preceding criteria.

2.8 ORAL RESPONSE TO LITERATURE

An oral response to literature is a personal, analytical interpretation of a writer's story, novel, poem, or drama.

Use the following questions to evaluate a speaker or your own presentation.

Evaluate an Oral Response to Literature

- Did the speaker choose an interesting piece that he or she understands and feels strongly about?
- Did the speaker make a judgment that shows an understanding of significant ideas from the text?
- Did the speaker direct the audience to specific parts of the piece that support his or her ideas?
- Did the speaker identify and analyze the use of artistic elements such as imagery, figurative language, and character development?
- Did the speaker demonstrate an appreciation of the author's style?
- Did the speaker discuss any ambiguous or difficult passages and the impact of those passages on the audience?

PRACTICE AND APPLY

Listen as a classmate delivers an oral response to a selection you have read. Use the preceding criteria to evaluate the presentation.

3 Other Types of Communication

3.1 GROUP DISCUSSION

Successful groups assign a role to each member. These roles distribute responsibility among the members and help keep discussions focused.

Role	Responsibilities
Chairperson	• introduces topic • explains goal or purpose • participates in discussion and keeps it on track • helps resolve conflicts • helps group reach goal
Recorder	• takes notes on discussion • reports on suggestions and decisions • organizes and writes up notes • participates in discussion
Participants	• contribute relevant facts or ideas to discussion • respond constructively to one another's ideas • reach agreement or vote on final decision • evaluate the effectiveness of the discussion using agreed-upon criteria

3.2 INTERVIEWS

An **interview** is a formal type of conversation with a definite purpose and goal. To conduct a successful interview, use the following guidelines:

Prepare for the Interview

- Select your interviewee carefully. Identify who has the kind of knowledge and experience you are looking for.
- Set a time, a date, and a place. Ask permission to tape-record the interview.

- Learn all you can about the person you will interview or the topic you want information on.

- Prepare a list of questions. Create questions that encourage detailed responses instead of yes-or-no answers. Arrange your questions in order from most important to least important.

- Arrive on time with everything you need.

Conduct the Interview

- Ask your questions clearly and listen to the responses carefully. Give the person whom you are interviewing plenty of time to answer.

- Be flexible; follow up on any responses you find interesting.

- Avoid arguments; be tactful and polite.

- Even if you tape an interview, take notes on important points.

- Thank the person for the interview, and ask if you can call with any follow-up questions.

Follow Up on the Interview

- Summarize your notes or make a written copy of the tape recording as soon as possible.

- If any points are unclear or if information is missing, call and ask more questions while the person is still available.

- Select the most appropriate quotations to support your ideas.

- If possible, have the person you interviewed review your work to make sure you haven't misrepresented what he or she said.

- Send a thank-you note to the person in appreciation of his or her time and effort.

> **Evaluate an Interview**
>
> You can determine how effective your interview was by asking yourself these questions:
>
> - Did you get the type of information you were looking for?
> - Were your most important questions answered to your satisfaction?
> - Were you able to keep the interviewee focused on the subject?

Responding to a Job Interview

In a job interview, you will be the person being interviewed. The person asking you questions will have several objectives in mind, and you will need to be prepared to respond in a professional manner. Keep these strategies in mind when you are being interviewed for employment:

- Prior to the interview, prepare a short list of questions relevant to the position.

- Respond honestly and effectively to each question, and use language that conveys sensitivity, maturity, and respect.

- Give responses that demonstrate knowledge of the subject or organization.

- Use active listening skills, as outlined in the next section.

❹ Active Listening

Active listening is the process of receiving, interpreting, evaluating, and responding to a message. Whether you listen to a class discussion or a formal speech, use the following strategies to get as much as you can from the message.

Before Listening

- Learn what the topic is beforehand. You may need to read background information about the topic or learn technical terms in order to understand the speaker's message.

- Think about what you know or want to know about the topic.

- Have a pen and paper or a laptop computer to take notes.

- Establish a purpose for listening.

While Listening

- Focus your attention on the speaker.

- Listen for the speaker's purpose (usually stated at the beginning), which alerts you to main ideas.

- Listen for words or phrases that signal important points, such as *to begin with, in addition, most important, finally,* and *in conclusion.*

- Listen for varied sentences: simple, compound, and complex. Think about how the choice of syntax emphasizes the speaker's ideas.

- Take notes. Write down only the most important points. Use an outline or list format to organize main ideas and supporting points.

- Note comparisons and contrasts, causes and effects, or problems and solutions.

- Note how the speaker uses word choice, voice pitch, posture, and gestures to convey meaning.

After Listening

- Ask relevant questions to clarify anything that was unclear or confusing.

- Review your notes to make sure you understand what was said.

- Summarize and paraphrase the speaker's ideas.

- You may also wish to compare your interpretation of the speech with the interpretations of others who listened to it.

4.1 CRITICAL LISTENING

Critical listening involves interpreting and analyzing a spoken message to judge its accuracy and reliability. Use these strategies as you listen to messages from advertisers, politicians, lecturers, and others:

- **Determine the Speaker's Purpose** Think about the background, viewpoint, and possible motives of the speaker. Separate facts from opinions. Listen carefully to details and evidence that a speaker uses to support the message.

- **Listen for the Main Idea** Figure out the speaker's main message before allowing yourself to be distracted by seemingly convincing facts and details.

- **Recognize the Use of Persuasive Techniques** Pay attention to a speaker's choice of words. Speakers may slant information to persuade you to buy a product or accept an idea. Persuasive devices such as inaccurate generalizations, either/or reasoning, and bandwagon or snob appeal may represent faulty reasoning and provide misleading information.

  *For more information, see **Persuasive Techniques**, page R20.*

- **Observe Verbal and Nonverbal Messages** A speaker's gestures, facial expressions, and tone of voice should reinforce the message. If they don't, you should question the speaker's sincerity and the reliability of his or her message.

- **Give Appropriate Feedback** An effective speaker looks for verbal and nonverbal cues from you, the listener, to gauge how the message is being received. For example, if you understand or agree with the message, you might nod your head. If possible, during or after a presentation, ask questions to clarify understanding.

4.2 VERBAL FEEDBACK

At times you will be asked to give direct feedback to a speaker. You may be asked to evaluate the way the speaker delivers the presentation as well as the content of the presentation.

Use the following questions to evaluate a speaker's delivery.

> **Evaluate Delivery**
> - Did the speaker articulate words clearly and distinctly?
> - Did the speaker pronounce words correctly?
> - Did the speaker vary his or her rate?
> - Did the speaker's voice sound natural and not strained?
> - Was the speaker's voice loud enough?

Use the following guidelines to give constructive suggestions for improvement on content.

> **Evaluate Content**
>
> **Be Specific** Don't make statements like "Your charts need work." Offer concrete suggestions, such as "Please make the type bigger so we can read the poster from the back of the room."
>
> **Discuss Only the Most Important Points** Don't overload the speaker with too much feedback about too many details. Focus on important points, such as:
> - Is the topic too advanced for the audience?
> - Are the supporting details well organized?
> - Is the conclusion weak?
>
> **Give Balanced Feedback** Tell the speaker not only what didn't work but also what did work: "Consider dropping the last two slides, since you covered those points earlier. The first two slides got my attention."

COMMON CORE FOCUS

RI 7 Integrate and evaluate multiple sources of information presented in different media or formats as well as in words in order to address a question or solve a problem. **SL 2** Integrate multiple sources of information presented in diverse formats and media in order to make informed decisions and solve problems, evaluating the credibility and accuracy of each source and noting any discrepancies among the data. **SL 5** Make strategic use of digital media in presentations to enhance understanding of findings, reasoning, and evidence and to add interest.

Every day you are exposed to hundreds of images and messages from television, radio, movies, newspapers, and the Internet. What is the effect of all this media? What do you need to know to be a smart media consumer? Being media literate means that you have the ability to think critically about media messages. It means that you are able to analyze and evaluate media messages and how they influence you and your world. To become media literate, you'll need the tools to study media messages.

COMMON CORE

Included in this handbook:
RI 7, SL 2, SL 5

1 Five Core Concepts in Media Literacy

from The Center for Media Literacy

The five core concepts of media literacy provide you with the basic ideas you can consider when examining media messages.

All media messages are "constructed." All media messages are made by someone. In fact, they are carefully thought out and researched and have attitudes and values built into them. Much of the information that you use to make sense of the world comes from the media. Therefore, it is important to know how media are put together so you can better understand the message it conveys.

Media messages are constructed using a creative language with its own rules. Each means of communication—whether it is film, television, newspapers, magazines, radio, or the Internet—has its own language and design. Therefore, the content of a message must use the language and design of the medium that conveys the message. Thus, the medium actually shapes the message. For example, a horror film may use music to heighten suspense, or a newspaper may use a big headline to signal the significance of a story. Understanding the language of each medium can increase your enjoyment of it as well as alert you to obvious and subtle influences.

Different people experience the same media messages differently. Personal factors such as age, education, and experience will affect the way a person responds to a media message. How many times has your interpretation of a film or book differed from that of a friend? Everyone interprets media messages through their own personal lens.

Media have embedded values and points of view. Media messages carry underlying values, which are purposely built into them by the creators of the message. For example, a commercial's main purpose may be to persuade you to buy something, but it also conveys the value of a particular lifestyle. Understanding not only the core message but also the embedded points of view will help you decide whether to accept or reject the message.

Most media messages are organized to gain profit and/or power. The creators of media messages often provide a commodity, such as information or entertainment, in order to make money. The bigger the audience, the higher the cost of advertising. Consequently, media outlets want to build large audiences in order to bring in more revenue from advertising. For example, a television network creates programming that appeals to the largest audience possible, and then uses the viewer ratings to attract more advertising dollars.

2 Media Basics

2.1 MESSAGE

When a film or TV show is created, it becomes a media product. Each media product is created to send a **message,** or an expression of belief or opinion, that serves a specific purpose. In order to understand the message, you will need to deconstruct it.

Deconstruction is the process of analyzing a media presentation. To analyze a media presentation you will need to look at its content, its purpose, the audience it's aimed at, and the techniques and elements that are used to create certain effects.

2.2 AUDIENCE

A **target audience** is a specific group of people that a product or presentation is aimed at. The members of a target audience usually share certain characteristics, such as age, gender, ethnic background, values, or lifestyle. For example, a target audience may be adults ages 40 to 60 who want to exercise and eat healthful foods.

Demographics are the characteristics of a population, including age, gender, profession, income, education, ethnicity, and geographic location. Media decision makers use demographics to shape their content to suit the needs and tastes of a target audience.

Nielsen ratings are the system used to track TV audiences and their viewing preferences. Nielsen Media Research, the company that provides this system, monitors TV viewing in a random sample of 5,000 U.S. households selected to represent the population as a whole.

2.3 PURPOSE

The **purpose,** or intent, of a media presentation is the reason it was made. Most media messages have more than one purpose, but each has a **core purpose.** To discover that purpose, think about why its creator paid for and produced the message. For example, an ad might entertain you with humor, but its core purpose is to persuade you to buy something.

2.4 TYPES AND GENRES OF MEDIA

The term *media* refers to television, newspapers, magazines, radio, movies, and the Internet. Each is a **medium,** or means for carrying information, entertainment, and advertisements to a large audience.

Each type of media has different characteristics, strengths, and weaknesses. Understanding how different types of media work and the role they play will help you become more informed about the choices you make in response to the media.

2.5 PRODUCERS AND CREATORS

People who control the media are known as **gatekeepers.** Gatekeepers decide what information to share with the public and the ways it will be presented. The following diagram gives some examples.

Who Controls the Media?

Media Owners
TV networks
Recording companies
Publishing companies

Media Products
Television
Radio
Magazines
Movies
Newspapers
Internet

Media Creators
Actors
Writers
Directors
Webmasters

Media Sponsors
Clothing manufacturers
Fast-food restaurants
Department stores

Some forms of media are independently owned, while others are part of a corporate family. Some corporate families might own several different kinds of media. For example, a company may own three radio stations, five newspapers, a publishing company, and a small television station. Often a corporate "parent" decides the content for all of its holdings.

2.6 LAWS GOVERNING MEDIA

Four main laws and policies affect the content, delivery, and use of mass media.

The First Amendment to the Constitution forbids Congress to limit speech or the press.

Copyright law protects the rights of authors and other media creators against the unauthorized publishing, reproduction, and selling of their works.

Laws prohibit **censorship,** any attempt to suppress or control people's access to media messages.

Laws prohibit **libel,** the publication of false statements that damage a person's reputation.

2.7 INFLUENCE OF MEDIA

By sheer volume alone, media influences our very existence, values, opinions, and beliefs. Our environment is saturated with media messages from television, billboards, radio, newspapers, magazines, video games, and so on. Each of these media products is selling one message and conveying another—a message about values—in the subtext. For example, a car ad is meant to sell a car, but if you look closer, you will see that it is using a set of values, such as a luxurious lifestyle, to make the car attractive to the target audience. One message of the ad is that if you buy the car, you'll have the luxurious lifestyle. The other message is that the luxurious lifestyle is good and desirable. TV shows, movies, and news programs also convey subtexts of values and beliefs.

Media can also shape your opinions about the world. For example, news about crime shapes our understanding about how much and what type of crime is prevalent in the world around us. TV news items, talk show interviews, and commercials may shape our perception of a political candidate, a celebrity, an ethnic group, a country, or a region. As a consequence, our knowledge of someone or someplace may be completely based on the information we receive from the television or other media.

Media Tools THINK central
Go to **thinkcentral.com**
KEYWORD: HML11-R89

MEDIA HANDBOOK **R89**

Media Tools THINK central
The keyword on this page points to **MediaScope,** a Web site that helps students strengthen media analysis and production skills.

3 Film and TV

Films and television programs come in a variety of types. Films include comedies, dramas, documentaries, and animated features. Televison programs cover an even wider array, including dramas, sitcoms, talk shows, reality shows, newscasts, and so on. Producers of films and producers of television programs rely on many of the same elements to convey their messages. Among these elements are scripts, visual and sound elements, special effects, and editing.

3.1 SCRIPT AND WRITTEN ELEMENTS

The writer and editor craft a story for television or film using a script and storyboard. A **script** is the text or words of a film or television show. A **storyboard** is a device often used to plan the shooting of a film and to help the director envision and convey what the finished product will look like. It consists of a sequence of sketches showing what will appear in the film's shots, often with explanatory notes and dialogue written beside or underneath them as shown in the example.

*For more information, see **Speaking and Listening: Producing a Documentary**, page 1378.*

Where is the cat?

I don't know. I haven't seen her.

Neither have I.

3.2 VISUAL ELEMENTS

Visual elements in film and television include camera shots, angles, and movements, as well as film components such as mise en scène, set design, props, and visual special effects.

A **camera shot** is a single, continuous view taken by a camera. **Camera angle** is the angle at which the camera is positioned during the recording of a shot or image. Each angle is carefully planned to create an effect. The following chart explains the different shots and angles.

Camera Shot/Angle	Effect
Establishing shot introduces viewers to the location of a scene, usually by presenting a wide view of an area	establishes the setting of a film
Close-up shot shows a detailed view of a person or an object	helps to create emotion and make viewers feel as if they know the character
Medium shot shows a view wider than a close-up but narrower than an establishing or long shot	shows part of an object or a character from the knees or waist up
Long shot is a wide view of a scene, showing the full figure(s) of a person or group and their surroundings	allows the viewer to see the "big picture" and shows the relationship between characters and the environment
Reaction shot shows someone reacting to something that occurred in a previous shot	allows the viewer to see how the subject feels in order to create empathy in the viewer
Low-angle shot looks up at an object or a person	makes a character, object, or scene appear more important or threatening
High-angle shot looks down on an object or a person	makes a character, object, or scene seem vulnerable or insignificant
Point-of-view (POV) shot shows a part of the story through a character's eyes	helps viewers identify with that character

Camera movement can create energy, reveal information, or establish a mood. The following chart shows some of the ways filmmakers move the camera to create an effect.

Camera Movement	Effect
Pan is a shot in which the camera scans a location from right to left or left to right	reveals information by showing a sweeping view of an area
Tracking shot is a shot in which the camera moves with the subject	establishes tension or creates a sense of drama
Zoom is the movement of the camera as it closes in on or moves farther away from the subject	captures action or draws the viewer's attention to detail

Mise en scène is a French term that refers to the arrangement of actors, props, and action on a film set. It is used to describe everything that can be seen in a frame, including the setting, lighting, visual composition, costumes, and action.

Framing is capturing people and objects within the "frame" of a screen or image. Framing is what the camera sees.

Composition is the arrangement of objects, characters, shapes, and colors within a frame and the relationship of the objects to one another.

3.3 SOUND ELEMENTS

Sound elements in film and television include music, voice-over, and sound effects.

Music may be used to set the mood and atmosphere in a scene. Music can have a powerful effect on the way viewers feel about a story. For example, fast-paced music helps viewers feel excited during an action scene.

Voice-over is the voice of the unseen commentator or narrator of a film, TV program, or commercial.

Sound effects are the sounds added to films, TV programs, and commercials during the editing process. Sound effects, such as laugh tracks or the sounds of punches in a fight scene, can create humor, emphasize a point, or contribute to the mood.

3.4 SPECIAL EFFECTS

Special effects include computer-generated animation, manipulated video images, and fast- or slow-motion sequences in films, TV programs, and commercials.

Animation on film involves the frame-by-frame photography of a series of drawings or objects. When these frames are projected—at a rate of 24 per second—the illusion of movement is achieved.

A **split screen** is a special-effects shot in which two or more separate images are shown in the same frame. One example is when two people, actually a distance apart, are shown talking to each other.

3.5 EDITING

Editing is the process of selecting and arranging shots in a sequence. The editor decides which scenes or shots to use, as well as the length of each shot, the number of shots, and their sequence. Editing establishes pace, mood, and a coherent story.

Cut is the transition from one shot to another. To create excitement, editors often use quick cuts, which are a series of short shots strung together.

Dissolve is a transitional device in which one scene fades into another.

Fade-in is a transitional device in which a white or black shot fades in to reveal the beginning of a new scene.

Fade-out is a transitional device in which a shot fades to darkness to end a scene.

Jump cut is an abrupt and jarring change from one shot to another. A jump cut shows a break in time or continuity.

Pace is the length of time each shot stays on the screen and the rhythm that is created by the transitions between shots. Short, quick cuts create a fast pace in a story. Long cuts slow down a story.

Parallel editing is a technique that cuts from one shot to another so as to suggest simultaneous action—often in different locations.

4 News

The **news** is information on events, people, and places in your community, your region, the nation, and the world. The news can be categorized by type, as shown in the chart.

Type	Description	Examples
Hard news	fact-based accounts of current events	local newspapers, newscasts, online wire services
Soft news	human-interest stories and other accounts that are less current or urgent than hard news	magazines and tabloid TV shows such as *Sports Illustrated, Access Hollywood*
News features	stories that elaborate on news reports	documentaries such as history reports on PBS
Commentary and opinion	essays and perspectives by experts, professionals, and media personalities	editorial pages, personal Web pages

4.1 CHOOSING THE NEWS

Newsworthiness is the significance of an event or action that makes it worthy of media reporting. Journalists and their editors usually weigh the following criteria in determining which stories should make the news:

Timeliness is the quality of being very current. Timely events usually take priority over previously reported events. For example, a car accident with fatalities will be timely on the day it occurs. Because of its timeliness it may be on the front page of a newspaper or the lead story on a newscast.

Widespread impact refers to the importance of an event and the number of people it could affect. The more widespread the impact of an event, the more likely it is to be newsworthy.

Proximity gauges the nearness of an event to a particular city, region, or country. People tend to be more interested in stories that take place locally and affect them directly.

Human interest is a quality of stories that cause readers or listeners to feel emotions such as happiness, anger, or sadness. People are interested in reading stories about other people.

Uniqueness refers to uncommon events or circumstances that are likely to be interesting to an audience.

Compelling video and **photographs** grab people's attention and stay in their minds.

4.2 REPORTING THE NEWS

While developing a news story, a journalist makes a variety of decisions about how to construct the story, such as what information to include and how to organize it. The following elements are commonly used in news stories:

5 _W_'s and _H_ are the six questions reporters answer when writing news stories—_who, what, when, where, why,_ and _how._ It is a journalist's job to answer these questions in any type of news report. These questions also serve as a structure for writing and editing a story.

Inverted pyramid is the means of organizing information according to importance. In the inverted pyramid diagram below, the most important information (the answers to the 5 _W_'s and _H_) appears at the top of the pyramid. The less important details appear at the bottom. Not all stories are reported using the inverted pyramid form. The style remains popular, however, because it enables a reader to get the essential information without reading the entire story. Notice the following example.

> About 2,000 people gathered at the Vietnam Veterans Memorial Wall on Friday in an antiwar demonstration.
>
> Demonstrators carried signs and sat peacefully as speakers from peace organizations around the world spoke on issues of ending the war.
>
> Speakers called for an immediate end to the war and urged citizens to voice their opinions to state officials and legislators.

Angle or slant is the point of view from which a story is written. Even an objective report must have an angle.

Consider these two headlines that describe a war demonstration.

The first headline suggests that the article following it will be focused on the sentiment or mood of the crowd gathered to demonstrate against a war. The second headline suggests the article will be focused on the event.

Standards for News Reporting

The ideal of journalism is to present news in a way that is objective, accurate, and thorough. The best news stories contain the following elements:

- **Objectivity** The story takes a balanced point of view toward the issues; it is not biased, nor does it reflect a specific attitude or opinion.

- **Accuracy** The story presents factual information that can be verified.

- **Thoroughness** The story presents all sides of an issue; it includes background information, telling _who, what, when, where, why,_ and _how._

Balanced Versus Biased Reporting

Objectivity in news reporting can be measured by how balanced or biased the story is.

Balanced reporting represents all sides of an issue equally and fairly.

A balanced news story

- represents people and subjects in a neutral light

- treats all sides of an issue equally

- does not include inappropriate questions

- does not show stereotypes or prejudice toward people of a particular race, gender, age, religion, or other group

- does not leave out important background information that is needed to establish a context or perspective

Biased reporting is reporting in which one side is favored over another or in which the subject is unfairly represented. Biased reporting may show an overly negative view of a subject, or it may encourage racial, gender, or other stereotypes and prejudices. Sometimes biased reporting is apparent in the journalist's choice of sources.

Sources are the people interviewed for the news report, and also any written materials and documents the journalist used for background information. From each source, the journalist gets a different point of view. To decide whether news reporting is balanced or biased, you will need to pay attention to the sources. For a news story on a new medicinal drug, for instance, if the journalist's only source is a representative from the company that made the drug, the report may be biased. But if the journalist also includes the perspective of someone neutral, such as a scientist who is objectively studying the effects of drugs, the report may be more balanced. It is important to evaluate the **credibility,** or believability and trustworthiness, of both a source and the report itself. The following chart shows which sources are credible.

Sources for News Stories	
Credible Sources	**Weak Sources**
• experts in a field • people directly affected by the reported event (eyewitnesses) • published reports that are specifically mentioned or shown	• unnamed or anonymous sources • people who are not involved in the reported event (for example, people who heard about a story from a friend) • research, data, or reports that are not specifically named or are referred to only in vague terms (for example, "Research shows that …")

5 Advertising

Advertising is a sponsor's paid use of various media to promote products, services, or ideas. Some common forms of advertising are shown in the chart.

Type of Ad	Characteristics
Billboard	large outdoor advertising sign
Print ad	typically appears in magazines and newspapers; uses eye-catching graphics and persuasive copy
Flyer	print ad that is circulated by hand or mail
Infomercial	an extended ad on TV that usually includes detailed product information, demonstrations, and testimonials
Public service announcement	a message aired on radio or TV to promote ideas that are considered to be in the public interest
Political ad	broadcast on radio or TV to promote political candidates
Trailer	a short film promoting an upcoming movie, TV show, or video game

Marketing is the process of transferring products and services from producer to consumer. It involves determining the packaging and pricing of a product, how it will be promoted and advertised, and where it will be sold. One way companies market their products is by becoming media sponsors.

Sponsors pay for their products to be advertised. These companies hire advertising agencies to create and produce specific campaigns for their products. They then buy television or radio airtime or magazine, newspaper, or billboard space to feature ads where the target audience is sure to see them. Because selling time and space to advertisers generates much of the income the media need to function, the media need advertisers just as much as advertisers need the media.

Product placement is the intentional and identifiable featuring of brand-name products in movies, television shows, video games, and other media. The intention is to have viewers feel positive about a product because they see a favorite character using it. Another purpose may be to promote product recognition.

5.1 PERSUASIVE TECHNIQUES

Persuasive techniques are the methods used to convince an audience to buy a product or adopt an idea. Advertisers use a combination of visuals, sound, special effects, and words to persuade their target audience. Recognizing the following techniques can help you evaluate persuasive media messages and identify misleading information:

Emotional appeals use strong feelings rather than factual evidence to persuade consumers. An example of an emotional appeal that targets people's fear is a statement such as this: "Is your identity safe? Protect yourself with ProTech software."

Bandwagon appeal uses the argument that a person should believe or do something because "everyone else" does. These appeals take advantage of people's desire to be socially accepted. Purchasing a popular product seems less risky when many others also find it worthy to buy. An example of a bandwagon appeal is "More and more people are switching to Bright 'n' Fresh laundry detergent."

Slogans are memorable phrases used in advertising campaigns. Slogans substitute catchy phrases for factual information.

Logical appeals rely on logic and facts, appealing to a consumer's reason and his or her respect for authority. Two examples of logical appeals are expert opinions and product comparison.

Celebrity ads use one of the following two categories of spokesperson:

- **Celebrity authorities** are experts in a particular field. Advertisers hope that audiences will transfer the respect or admiration they have for the person to the product. For example, a famous chef may endorse a particular brand of cookware. The manufacturers of the cookware want you to think that it is a good product because a cooking expert wouldn't endorse poor-quality pots and pans.

- **Celebrity spokespeople** are famous people who endorse a product. Advertisers hope that audiences will associate the product with the celebrity.

Product comparison involves comparing a product with its competition. The competing product is portrayed as inferior. The intended effect is for people to question the quality of the competing product and to believe the featured product is superior.

6 Elements of Design

The design of a media message is just as important as the words are in conveying the message. Like words, visuals are used to persuade, inform, and entertain.

Graphics and images, such as charts, diagrams, maps, timelines, photographs, illustrations, cartoons, book covers, and symbols, present information that can be quickly and easily understood. The following basic elements are used to give meaning to visuals:

Color can be used to highlight important elements such as headlines and subheads. It can also create mood, because many colors have a strong emotional or psychological impact on the reader or viewer. For example, warm colors more readily draw the eye and are often associated with happiness and comfort. Cool colors are often associated with feelings of peace and contentment or sometimes sadness.

Lines—strokes or marks—can be thick or thin, long or short, and smooth or jagged. They can focus attention and create a feeling of depth. They can frame an object. They can also direct a viewer's eye or create a sense of motion.

Texture is the surface quality or appearance of an object. For example, an object's texture can be glossy, rough, wet, or shiny. Texture can be used to create contrast. It can also be used to make an image look "real." For example, a pattern on wrapping paper can create a feeling of depth even though the texture is only visual and cannot be felt.

Shape is the external outline of an object. Shapes can be used to symbolize living things or geometric objects. They can emphasize visual elements and add interest. Shapes can also symbolize ideas.

Notice how this photograph uses these design elements to convey a message.

In "reading" this visual image for its message, take note of the following:

- The **foreground image** in this photo is of an unhappy young woman with a plume of smoke rising from her head, indicating she is angry or unhappy—presumably with the situation depicted behind her. The **background images** include smokestacks spewing smoke into the environment. This would suggest that the message concerns her feelings about the environment.

- The **colors** orange and black suggest danger, the need to be alert, or a threatening situation. The colors in this scene indicate that the situation is threatening or dangerous.

- The smokestacks in the background are in silhouette and can only be defined by their **shape.** This suggestion of the image lends an air of mystery and foreboding to the message.

- The **lines** in this picture are primarily vertical (the smokestacks, the young woman, and the white smoke plume). The vertical lines draw your focus toward the top of the photo, where it centers on the crossed smoke plumes.

Considering all the design elements in this photograph, what is its message?

7 Evaluating Media Messages

Being able to respond critically to media images and messages will help you evaluate the reliability of the content and make informed decisions. Here are six questions to ask about any media message:

Who made—and who sponsored—this message, and for what purpose? The source of the message is a clue to its purpose. If the source of the message is a private company, that company may be trying to sell you a product. If the source is a government agency, that agency may be trying to promote a program or philosophy. To discover the purpose, think about why its creator paid for and produced the message.

Who is the target audience and how is the message specifically tailored to it? Think about the age group, ethnic group, gender, and/or profession the message is targeting. Decide how it relates to you. Consider the tone and formality of the message. How do these two elements relate to similar messages you have heard in other media?

What are the different techniques used to inform, persuade, entertain, and attract attention? Analyze the elements, such as humor, music, special effects, and graphics, that have been used to create the message. Think about how visual and sound effects, such as symbols, color, photographs, words, and music, support the purpose behind the message.

What messages are communicated (and/or implied) about certain people, places, events, behaviors, lifestyles, and so forth? The media try to influence who we are, what we believe in, how we view things, and what values we hold. Look or listen closely to determine whether certain types of behavior are being depicted and if judgments or values are communicated through those behaviors. What are the biases in the message?

How current, accurate, and credible is the information in this message? Think about the reputation of the source. Note the broadcast or publication date of the message and whether the message might change quickly. If a report or account is not supported by facts, authoritative sources, or eyewitness accounts, you should question the credibility of the message.

What is left out of this message that might be important to know? Think about what the message is asking you to believe. Also think about what questions come to mind as you watch, read, or listen to the message.

Applying Strategies to the SAT* and ACT

The test items in this section are modeled after test formats that are used on the SAT and ACT. The strategies presented here will help you prepare for these tests and others. This section offers general test-taking strategies and tips for answering multiple-choice items in critical reading and writing, as well as samples for impromptu writing and essay writing. For each test, read the tips in the margin. Then apply the tips to the practice items. You can also apply the tips to Assessment Practice tests in this book.

1 General Test-Taking Strategies

- Arrive on time and be prepared. Be sure to bring either sharpened pencils with erasers or pens—whichever you are told to bring.
- If you have any questions, ask them before the test begins. Make sure you understand the test procedures, the timing, and the rules.
- Read the test directions carefully. Look at the passages and questions to get an overview of what is expected.
- Tackle the questions one at a time rather than thinking about the whole test.
- Refer back to the reading selections as needed. For example, if a question asks about an author's attitude, you might have to reread a passage for clues.
- If you are not sure of your answer, make a logical guess. You can often arrive at the correct answer by reasoning and eliminating wrong answers.
- As you fill in answers on your answer sheet, make sure you match the number of each test item to the numbered space on the answer sheet.
- Don't look for patterns in the positions of correct choices.
- Only change an answer if you are sure your original choice is incorrect. If you do change an answer, erase your original choice neatly and thoroughly.
- Look for main ideas as you read passages. They are often stated at the beginning or the end of a paragraph. Sometimes the main idea is implied.
- Check your answers and reread your essay.

---

* SAT® is a registered trademark of the College Board, which was not involved in the production of, and does not endorse, this product.

② Critical Reading

Most tests contain a critical reading section that measures your ability to read, understand, and interpret passages. The passages may be either fiction or nonfiction, and they can be 100 words or 500 to 850 words. They are drawn from literature, the humanities, social studies, and the natural sciences.

Directions: Read the following passage. Base your answers to questions 1 and 2 on what is stated or implied in the passage.

PASSAGE

The chemical composition of diamond is extremely simple; like graphite it is composed of only one element: carbon. But the similarity ends there, for no two minerals could be more diverse. Diamond is hard, lustrous, and transparent; graphite is soft, dull, and opaque. Diamond has a specific gravity of 3.5, high for a nonmetallic mineral. Graphite's specific gravity is 2.2, extremely low for a metallic mineral. These strikingly different properties of the same element result from the way in which the carbon atoms are packed together. In diamond they are close together and held by strong electrical bonds, whereas in graphite they are far apart and have weak bonds.

Diamond is valued for its remarkable physical properties. It is harder and more resistant to abrasion than any other natural mineral; nothing can scratch it except another diamond. It is also insoluble in all acids and alkalis. Because of these resistant properties, the Greeks called the mineral *adamas,* meaning "invincible," and its present name derives from that.

—Cornelius Hurlbut, from *Minerals and Man*

① stem

1. The (main) idea of the first paragraph is that **②**

   ③ choices

   (A) diamond and graphite consist of the same element but have different properties
   (B) the atoms in diamond and graphite are held together by electrical bonds
   (C) diamond is hard, lustrous, and transparent, while graphite is soft, dull, and opaque
   (D) diamond and graphite have a simple chemical composition consisting of one element
   (E) the specific gravity of diamond is high; graphite's specific gravity is low

2. The Greek word *adamas* is a fitting description of diamond's **④**

   (A) international reputation
   (B) great value
   (C) jewelry applications **⑤**
   (D) resistant properties
   (E) ancient lineage

Tips: Multiple Choice

A multiple-choice question consists of a stem and a set of choices. On some tests, there are four choices. On the SAT, there are five. The stem is usually in the form of a question or an incomplete sentence. One of the choices correctly answers the question or completes the sentence.

① Read the stem carefully and try to answer the question without looking at the choices.

② Pay attention to key words in the stem. They may direct you to the correct answer. Question 1 is looking for the *main* idea. Choices (B) through (E) focus on minor details.

③ Read all the choices before deciding on the correct answer.

④ Some questions ask you to interpret a word or a figure of speech. Question 2, for example, asks you to describe the character of a diamond based on the etymology of its name.

⑤ After reading all of the choices, eliminate any that you know are incorrect. In question 2, you can safely eliminate choice (C) because this passage focuses on the scientific properties of diamond, not its uses.

Answers: 1. (A), **2.** (D)

Directions: Base your answers to questions 1 and 2 on the two passages below.

PASSAGE 1

The president helps people make sense of politics. Congress is a tangle of committees, the bureaucracy is a maze of agencies. The president is one man trying to do a job—a picture much more understandable to the mass of people who find themselves in the same boat. Furthermore, he is the top man. He ought to know what is going on and set it right. So when the economy goes sour, or war drags on, or domestic violence erupts, the president is available to take the blame. Then when things go right, it seems the president must have had a hand in it.

—James David Barber, "The Presidential Character"

PASSAGE 2

No man or group at either end of Pennsylvania Avenue shares his peculiar status in our government and politics. That is why his services are in demand. By the same token, though, the obligations of all other men are different from his own. His Cabinet officers have departmental duties and constituents. His legislative leaders head Congressional parties, one in either House. His national party organization stands apart from his official family. His political allies in the states need not face Washington, or one another. The private groups that seek him out are not compelled to govern. And friends abroad are not compelled to run in our elections. Lacking his position and prerogatives, these men cannot regard his obligations as his own. They have their jobs to do; none is the same as his.

—Richard E. Neustadt, "Presidential Power"

1. In Passage 1, what does the author mean when he says, "The president helps people make sense of politics"?

(A) The government is sponsoring political education classes for voters.

(B) People see the president in personal terms, as someone with a job to do.

(C) The White House has valuable information about the legislative process.

(D) Congress is an impenetrable maze of agencies and committees.

(E) Citizens have to think about international issues before they vote.

2. The authors of both passages would probably agree with which one of these statements about government?

(A) It is difficult to penetrate the maze of government bureaucracies.

(B) Many elected officials are only concerned with local issues.

(C) Each president leaves an indelible imprint on the nation.

(D) Not everyone supports the president or his policies.

(E) The president holds a unique position in our political system.

Directions: Read the following passage, taken from a novel published in 1900. Based on what is stated or implied in the passage, answer questions 1 through 5, which appear on the next page.

PASSAGE

When Caroline Meeber boarded the afternoon train for Chicago, her total outfit consisted of a small trunk, a cheap imitation alligator-skin satchel, a small lunch in a paper box, and a yellow leather snap purse containing her ticket, a scrap of paper with her sister's address in Van Buren
5 Street, and four dollars in money. It was in August, 1889. She was eighteen years of age, bright, timid, and full of the illusions of ignorance and youth. Whatever touch of regret at parting characterized her thoughts, it was certainly not for advantages now being given up. A gush of tears at her mother's farewell kiss, a touch in her throat when the cars clacked by the
10 flour mill where her father worked by the day, a pathetic sign as the familiar green environs of the village passed in review, and the threads which bound her so lightly to girlhood and home were irretrievably broken.

To be sure, there was always the next station, where one might descend and return. There was the great city, bound more closely by these very
15 trains which came up daily. Columbia City was not so very far away, even once she was in Chicago. What, pray, is a few hours—a few hundred miles? She looked at the little slip bearing her sister's address and wondered. She gazed at the green landscape, now passing in swift review, until her swifter thoughts replaced its impression with vague conjectures of what Chicago
20 might be.

When a girl leaves her home at eighteen, she does one of two things. Either she falls into saving hands and becomes better, or she rapidly assumes the cosmopolitan standard of virtue and becomes worse. Of an intermediate balance, under the circumstances, there is no possibility. The city has its
25 cunning wiles, no less than the infinitely smaller and more human tempter. There are large forces which allure with all the soulfulness of expression possible in the most cultured human. The gleam of a thousand lights is often as effective as the persuasive light in a wooing and fascinating eye. Half of the undoing of the unsophisticated and natural mind is
30 accomplished by forces wholly superhuman. A blare of sound, a roar of life, a vast array of human hives, appeal to the astonished senses in equivocal terms. Without a counselor at hand to whisper cautious interpretations, what falsehoods may not these things breathe into the unguarded ear! Unrecognized for what they are, their beauty, like music, too often relaxes,
35 then weakens, then perverts the simpler human perceptions.

—Theodore Dreiser, *Sister Carrie*

Tips: Reading Text

1 Notice the characters who are presented in a passage. Be alert to details about their appearance, personality, or behavior.

2 Identify the point of view from which the story is being told. In a first-person narrative, the narrator is a character in the story and uses the pronouns *I* and *me.* In a third-person narrative, the narrator is outside the story and uses the pronouns *he, she,* and *they.*

3 Try to visualize the setting as you read, filling in details as they are presented. In this passage we see a young woman on a train headed for Chicago in 1889. She has left behind the "familiar green environs" of her home in the small town of Columbia City.

4 Remember that a word can have several different meanings or subtle shades of meaning.

5 Some test questions will ask you to interpret a figure of speech or an image. Try to understand why the author chose that particular image and what effect it achieves.

Answers: 1. (D), **2.** (B), **3.** (A), **4.** (C), **5.** (E)

1. The catalog of Caroline's belongings in lines 2–5 helps to
   (A) foreshadow her destiny
   (B) mock her appearance
   (C) create sympathy for her
   (D) convey her social status
   (E) portray her personality

2. What is implied about Caroline's life in the statement "Whatever touch of regret at parting characterized her thoughts, it was certainly not for advantages now being given up"?
   (A) It was hard for Caroline to leave behind the comforts of home.
   (B) Caroline's life at home offered few material benefits.
   (C) Caroline hated the life of poverty she led at home.
   (D) Moving to the city required a sacrifice on Caroline's part.
   (E) Once she left home, Caroline never looked back.

3. The description in lines 21–24 suggests that the city is a place that should be viewed with
   (A) distrust
   (B) respect
   (C) enthusiasm
   (D) contempt
   (E) nostalgia

4. The image of a tempter in lines 24–30 suggests the
   (A) evils of human nature
   (B) simple beauty of music
   (C) corrupting influence of the city
   (D) vulnerable innocence of youth
   (E) pleasures of materialism

5. In line 29, "natural" most nearly means
   (A) normal
   (B) inborn
   (C) logical
   (D) real
   (E) naive

The critical reading section may feature sentence completion questions that test your knowledge of vocabulary. They may also measure your ability to figure out how different parts of a sentence logically fit together.

Directions: Choose the word or set of words that, when inserted, best fits the meaning of the complete sentence.

1. The investigator constructed a _____ of events to _____ the cause of the accident. ❶
   (A) chronology . . ascertain
   (B) timeline . . predict ❷
   (C) typology . . determine
   (D) collation . . understand
   (E) history . . prosecute

2. Russian author Alexander Solzhenitsyn tried to _____ government censorship by _____ some of his writings out of the country.
   (A) encircle . . translating
   (B) disrupt . . carrying
   (C) circumvent . . smuggling ❸
   (D) evade . . banishing
   (E) prevent . . propelling

3. Automakers can _____ the effects of global warming by reducing carbon-dioxide and other _____ emissions from cars and trucks. ❹
   (A) minimize . . natural
   (B) misuse . . harmful
   (C) correct . . excessive
   (D) mitigate . . toxic
   (E) relieve . . acute

4. Because they have a _____ appetite, bears will raid cabins, backpacks, and picnic areas in search of anything that smells of food. ❺ ❻
   (A) vicious
   (B) voracious
   (C) refined
   (D) notorious
   (E) selective

Tips: Sentence Completion

❶ When you are completing sentences with two words missing, think about which pair of suggested words fits both blanks.

❷ If one word in the answer choice is wrong, eliminate that choice from consideration. In sentence 1, *timeline* makes sense, but *predict* does not, because the accident occurred in the past.

❸ A prefix can help to unlock the meaning of a word. The Latin prefix *circum-* means "around." The writer was trying to circumvent, or go around, government censorship.

❹ Look for key words or phrases that link the ideas in a sentence. The word *by* introduces a phrase that explains how to do something—in this case, how to reduce global warming.

❺ Look for words that link the ideas in a sentence. The word *because* in sentence 4 signals a cause-and-effect relationship between appetite and behavior.

❻ If you don't know a word's meaning, look for clues within the sentence. For sentence 4, ask yourself: What sort of appetite would lead a bear to eat almost anything? An animal with a *refined* (C) or *selective* (E) appetite, for example, would choose only certain foods.

Answers: 1. (A), **2.** (C), **3.** (D), **4.** (B)

3 Writing

The writing section of standardized tests measures your ability to express ideas clearly and correctly. You will be asked to identify errors in grammar and usage and to improve sentences and paragraphs.

> **Directions:** The following sentence contains either a single error or no error. If it does contains an error, select the underlined part that must be changed to make the sentence correct. If the sentence is correct as written, select answer choice (E).

1. <u>Neither</u> the Supreme Court <u>nor</u> the president <u>have</u> the power to create laws,
   (A)   (B)   (C) ❷

   because the Constitution <u>entrusts</u> that responsibility to Congresss alone. <u>No error</u>
               (D) ❸   (E) ❶

> **Directions:** Determine if the underlined part of the following sentence needs improvement. If it does, select the best change presented. If the original phrasing is best, select answer (A).

2. Ancient Greeks believed in mythical <u>creatures, they combined</u> human and animal traits.
   - (A) creatures, they combined ❹
   - (B) creatures, and they combined
   - (C) creatures that combined ❺
   - (D) creatures, and which combined
   - (E) creatures such as could combine

> **Directions:** Following is an early draft of an essay. Read it and answer the question.

Controlling E-Waste

(1) It is estimated that Americans generate about 2 million tons of technology-related trash each year. (2) Computer circuit boards, monitors, and printers are piling up in landfills. (3) They decay. (4) They can leak mercury and other toxic substances as a result of the decay. (5) Some public health officials think the U.S. should develop a federal law that requires technology companies to take back their used products and reduce the amount of hazardous material they use in manufacturing.

3. Which one of the following sentences combines sentences 3 and 4? ❻
   - (A) They can decay, also leaking mercury and other toxic substances.
   - (B) When they decay, they can leak mercury and other toxic substances.
   - (C) They decay; then they can leak mercury and other toxic substances.
   - (D) They decay, and thus leak mercury and other toxic substances.
   - (E) They can leak toxic substances such as mercury.

Tips: Grammar and Style

❶ Read the entire sentence or passage to grasp its overall meaning. Pay particular attention to any underlined portions.

❷ Watch for subject-verb agreement when using *neither . . . nor.* If both subjects are singular, the verb must be singular.

❸ Use prefixes to help you understand the meaning of words. The prefix *en-* in the word *entrust* means "in" or "within."

❹ Read through all of the choices before you decide which revision is best. In this case, answer (A) is *not* correct, because joining two independent clauses with only a comma creates a run-on sentence.

❺ Understand how to use *that* and *which. That* introduces an essential defining clause. *Which* introduces a nonessential clause. Use *which* if the clause can be omitted without changing the meaning of the sentence. Nonessential clauses are set off with commas.

❻ When combining sentences, think about how the ideas are related. Subordinating conjunctions such as *while, when, before, after,* and *until* express a relationship of time. *Because* and *since* indicate cause and effect.

Answers: 1. (C), **2.** (C), **3.** (B)

4 Essay

To determine how well you can develop and express ideas, many tests ask you to write an essay in response to an assignment, or prompt. The essay will represent a first draft and be scored based on the following criteria:

- **Focus** Establish a point of view in the opening paragraph.
- **Organization** Maintain a logical progression of ideas.
- **Support for Ideas** Use details and examples to develop an argument.
- **Style/Word Choice** Use words accurately and vary your sentences.
- **Grammar** Use Standard English and proofread for errors.

Think carefully about the issue presented in this quotation and the assignment below.

> Arts education and physical education both enjoy public support and help students grow and develop in many ways. In recent years, these programs have sometimes been marginalized or discontinued due to budget cuts or redirection of school resources. Sometimes schools have had to choose between these programs.

Assignment: If a school had to choose between funding its arts program and funding its physical education program, which option would you support? Plan and write an essay in which you develop your opinion on this issue. Support your position with specific reasons and examples taken from your studies and experience.

SAMPLE ESSAY

If I had to decide whether to cut arts or physical education programs from the curriculum, I would choose to save the arts. ❶

It's hard to cut physical education programs when our nation is struggling with an obesity epidemic. We all know that Americans don't get enough exercise. We drive everywhere, and we spend hours in front of the TV. But ❷ physical fitness is a medical and lifestyle issue, not an academic pursuit. Exercise and good nutrition require a personal, lifelong commitment, and that goes beyond what can be taught in a gym class.

The arts, on the other hand, are as much an academic pursuit as science, history, or literature. Acting in a play requires reading and interpreting a work of literature. Composing even a simple tune requires knowledge of harmony, ❸ rhythm, and timing. Painting and drawing require some understanding of the principles of light, color, and perspective. Whereas high school athletes often struggle with academics because of the demands of their sport, students in music and performing arts don't seem to experience those conflicting demands in the same way.

Arts education encourages students to be creative and to take risks. There are no right or wrong answers in art, so students who might not excel in other areas of academic life can gain respect through their music or dancing.

Music, painting, literature, dance, and theater not only enrich our lives but ❹ also stimulate us and teach us life lessons that a gym class never could.

Tips: Writing an Essay

The SAT allows only 25 minutes for you to write an essay. Before you begin writing, take a few minutes to jot down the main points you want to make. Allow time to reread and proofread your essay before you hand it in.

❶ When you're writing a persuasive essay, state your point of view in the introduction. Be sure to keep your purpose in mind as you write.

❷ Take the opposing point of view into consideration and respond to it.

❸ Include concrete examples in the body of your essay to clarify your points and strengthen your arguments.

❹ Make sure your essay has a conclusion, even if it is just a single sentence. A conclusion pulls your ideas together and lets the reader know that you have finished.

❺ There will not be time to recopy your essay, so if you have to make a correction, do so neatly and legibly.

❻ You don't have to write a long essay. Length is less important than clarity of thought and correctness of expression. Your essay could range from 200 to 400 words.

Act An act is a major unit of action in a play, similar to a chapter in a book. Depending on their lengths, plays can have as many as five acts. Arthur Miller's play *The Crucible* has four acts.

See also **Drama; Scene.**

Allegory An allegory is a work with two levels of meaning, a literal one and a symbolic one. In such a work, most of the characters, objects, settings, and events represent abstract qualities. Personification is often used in traditional allegories. As in a fable or parable, the purpose of an allegory may be to convey truths about life, to teach religious or moral lessons, or to criticize social institutions.

Example: In Edgar Allan Poe's "The Masque of the Red Death," the main character Prospero, the sequence and the decorations of the rooms in the castle, and objects such as the ebony clock all have allegorical meaning.

See page 444.

Alliteration Alliteration is the repetition of consonant sounds at the beginnings of words. Poets use alliteration to impart a musical quality to their poems, to create mood, to reinforce meaning, to emphasize particular words, and to unify lines or stanzas. Note the examples of alliteration in the following line:

> Doubting, dreaming dreams no mortal ever dared to dream before.
> —Edgar Allan Poe, "The Raven"

See pages 435, 1301.

Allusion An allusion is an indirect reference to a person, place, event, or literary work with which the author believes the reader will be familiar.

Example: In "Speech in the Virginia Convention," Patrick Henry warns colonists not to be "betrayed with a kiss"—an allusion to the Apostle Judas, who betrayed Jesus by kissing him.

See pages 235, 942, 1203.

Ambiguity Ambiguity is a technique in which a word, phrase, or event has more than one meaning or can be interepreted in more than one way. Some writers deliberately create this effect to give richness and depth of meaning. T. S. Eliot and Robert Frost are two poets known for their use of ambiguity.

See pages 483, 937, 1061.

Analogy An analogy is a point-by-point comparison between two things for the purpose of clarifying the less familiar of the two subjects.

Example: In "My Dungeon Shook," James Baldwin draws an analogy between his nephew's probable reaction to seeing the stars shining while the sun is out and white people's reaction to black people moving out of their fixed places.

See pages 1215, 1255.

Anapest *See* **Meter.**

Anaphora Anaphora is a repetition of a word or words at the beginning of successive lines, clauses, or sentences.

> Blackness
> is a title,
> is a preoccupation,
> is a commitment . . .
> —Gwendolyn Brooks, "Primer for Blacks"

See pages 531, 1295.
See also **Repetition.**

Anecdote An anecdote is a brief story that focuses on a single episode or event in a person's life and that is used to illustrate a particular point.

Example: In "Straw into Gold," Sandra Cisneros provides an anecdote about the challenge she faced when ordered to make corn tortillas, a task she had never done before. This anecdote illustrates Cisneros's pluck in attempting the seemingly impossible.

See pages 379, 1287.

Antagonist An antagonist is usually the principal character in opposition to the **protagonist,** or hero of a narrative or drama. The antagonist can also be a force of nature.

Example: In "The Open Boat," the sea is the antagonist of the four shipwrecked men. Its powerful force is described in such detail that it seems like a character.

See pages 759, 977.
See also **Character; Protagonist.**

Antihero An antihero is a protagonist who has the qualities opposite to those of a hero; he or she may be insecure, ineffective, cowardly, sometimes dishonest or dishonorable, or—most often—a failure. A popular antihero in contemporary culture is the cartoon character Homer Simpson.

Aphorism An aphorism is a brief statement, usually one sentence long, that expresses a general principle or truth about life.

Example: Ralph Waldo Emerson's "Self-Reliance" is sprinkled with such memorable aphorisms as "A foolish consistency is the hobgoblin of little minds."
See page 275.

Archetype An archetype is a pattern in literature that is found in a variety of works from different cultures throughout the ages. An archetype can be a plot, a character, an image, or a setting. For example, the association of death and rebirth with winter and spring is an archetype common to many cultures.

Aside In drama, an aside is a short speech directed to the audience, or another character, that is not heard by the other characters on stage.
See also **Soliloquy.**

Assonance Assonance is the repetition of vowel sounds within words. Both poets and prose writers use assonance to impart a musical quality to their works, to create mood, to reinforce meaning, to emphasize particular words, and to unify lines, stanzas, or passages. Note examples of assonance in the following lines:

> Along the window-sill, the lipstick stubs
> Glittered in their steel shells.
> —Rita Dove, "Adolescence—III"

See also **Alliteration; Consonance; Rhyme.**

Atmosphere *See* **Mood.**

Audience Audience is the person or persons who are intended to read a piece of writing. The intended audience of a work determines its form, style, tone, and the details included. For example, Cabeza de Vaca's audience for *La Relación* was the king of Spain. Hence, *La Relación* took the form of a formal report with a patriotic tone that included details of the explorers' hardship and determination. Had the work been addressed to Cabeza de Vaca's wife, it would likely have been less formal and probably would have included details about his personal feelings.
See pages 73, 123, 1257.

Author's Perspective An author's perspective is a unique combination of ideas, values, feelings, and beliefs that influences the way the writer looks at a topic. **Tone,** or attitude, often reveals an author's perspective. For example, Jonathan Edwards was a Puritan minister whose father and grandfather were also Puritan ministers; he began his theological training at age 12. His family upbringing, his beliefs, and the time and place in which he lived all

contributed to the perspective found in *Sinners in the Hands of an Angry God.*
See pages 122, 403, 769.

Author's Purpose A writer usually writes for one or more of these purposes: to inform, to entertain, to express himself or herself, or to persuade readers to believe or do something. For example, the purpose of a news report (either in a newspaper or magazine) is primarily to inform; the purpose of an news editorial is to persuade the readers or audience to do or believe something.
Examples: In *The Interesting Narrative of the Life of Olaudah Equiano,* the author's purpose is primarily to inform readers about the horrors that captured Africans endured in the holds of slave ships during the Middle Passage. Thoreau's purpose in "Civil Disobedience," on the other hand, is to persuade his audience to use nonviolent resistance to oppose unjust laws.
See pages 83, 559.

Autobiographical Essay *See* **Essay.**

Autobiography An autobiography is the story of a person's life written by that person. Generally written from the first-person point of view, autobiographies can vary in style from straightforward chronological accounts to impressionistic narratives.
Example: Both *Narrative of the Life of Frederick Douglass, an American Slave* and *Coming of Age in Mississippi* are autobiographies.
See pages 266, 558, 660.

Ballad A ballad is a narrative poem that was originally meant to be sung. Ballads often contain dialogue and repetition and suggest more than they actually state. Traditional **folk ballads,** composed by unknown authors and handed down orally, are written in four-line stanzas with regular rhythm and rhyme. A **literary ballad** is one that is modeled on the folk ballads but written by a single author—for example, Dudley Randall's "Ballad of Birmingham."
See page 1214.
See also **Narrative Poem; Rhyme; Rhythm.**

Biography A biography is a type of nonfiction in which a writer gives a factual account of someone else's life. Written in the third person, a biography may cover a person's entire life or focus on only an important part of it. The poet Carl Sandburg wrote an acclaimed six-volume biography of Abraham Lincoln. Modern biography includes a popular form called **fictionalized biography,** in which writers use their imaginations to re-create past conversations and to elaborate on some incidents.

Blank Verse A poem written in blank verse consists of unrhymed lines of iambic pentameter. In other words, each line of blank verse has five pairs of syllables. In most pairs, an unstressed syllable is followed by a stressed syllable. The most versatile of poetic forms, blank verse imitates the natural rhythms of English speech, as in the following lines:

> She ran | on tip | toe down | the dark | ened passage
> To meet | him in | the door | way with | the news
> And put | him on | his guard. | "Silas | is back."
> She pushed | him out | ward with | her through |
>   the door
> And shut | it aft | er her. | "Be kind," | she said.
>   —Robert Frost, "The Death of the Hired Man"

See pages 337, 943.
See also **Iambic Pentameter; Meter; Rhythm.**

Caesura A caesura is a pause or a break in a line of poetry. Poets use a caesura to emphasize the word or phrase that precedes it or to vary the rhythmical effects. In the following line, a caesura follows the word *die:*

> If we must die, let it not be like hogs
>   —Claude McKay, "If We Must Die"

Cast of Characters The cast of characters is a list of all the characters in a play, usually in the order of appearance. This list is found at the beginning of a script.
See page 137.

Catalog A catalog is a list of people, things, or attributes. This technique, found in epics and in the Bible, also characterizes Whitman's style, as seen in the beginning of this line:

> Kanuck, Tuckahoe, Congressman, Cuff, I give them the
> same, I receive them the same.
>   —Walt Whitman, "Song of Myself"

See page 531.

Character Characters are the people, and sometimes animals or other beings, who take part in the action of a story or novel. Events center on the lives of one or more characters, referred to as **main characters.** The other characters, called **minor characters,** interact with the main characters and help move the story along. In Kurt Vonnegut's story "Adam," Heinz Knechtmann is the main character, while the other expectant father, Mr. Sousa, is a minor character.

Characters may also be classified as either static or dynamic. **Static characters** tend to stay in a fixed position over the course of the story. They do not experience life-altering moments and seem to act the same, even though their situations may change. In contrast, **dynamic characters** evolve as individuals, learning from their experiences and growing emotionally.
See pages 717, 943, 977, 1179.
See also **Antagonist; Characterization; Foil; Motivation; Protagonist.**

Characterization Characterization refers to the techniques a writer uses to develop characters. There are four basic methods of characterization:

1. A writer may use physical description. In F. Scott Fitzgerald's "Winter Dreams," Judy Jones is described as follows:

> She wore a blue gingham dress, rimmed at throat and
> shoulders with a white edging that accentuated her
> tan. . . . She was arrestingly beautiful. The color in her
> cheeks was centered like the color in a picture—it was
> not a "high" color, but a sort of fluctuating and feverish
> warmth. . . .

2. The character's own actions, words, thoughts, and feelings might be presented. In Fitzgerald's story, after Judy Jones tries to revive the romance between herself and Dexter, she cries and says, "I'm more beautiful than anybody else, . . . why can't I be happy?"

3. The actions, words, thoughts, and feelings of other characters provide another means of developing a character. Mr. Sandwood, in Fitzgerald's story, exclaims about Judy Jones: "My God, she's good-looking!" To which Mr. Hedrick replies: "Good-looking! She always looks as if she wanted to be kissed! Turning those big cow-eyes on every calf in town!"

4. The narrator's own direct comments also serve to develop a character. The narrator of "Winter Dreams" says of Judy Jones:

> Whatever Judy wanted, she went after with the full pressure of her charm. There was no divergence of method, no jockeying for position or premeditation of effects—there was very little mental side to any of her affairs. She simply made men conscious to the highest degree of her physical loveliness.

See pages 691, 921, 1179.
See also **Character; Narrator.**

Chorus In the theater of ancient Greece, the chorus was a group of actors who commented on the **action** of the play. Between scenes, the chorus sang and danced to musical accompaniment, giving insights into the message of the play. The chorus is often considered a kind of ideal spectator, representing the response of ordinary citizens to the tragic events that unfold. Certain dramatists have continued to employ this classical convention as a way of representing the views of the society being depicted.
See also **Drama.**

Cliché A cliché is an overused expression that has lost its freshness, force, and appeal. The phrase "happy as a lark" is an example of a cliché.

Climax In a plot structure, the climax, or turning point, is the moment when the reader's interest and emotional intensity reach a peak. The climax usually occurs toward the end of a story and often results in a change in the characters or a solution to the conflict.
Example: In Edgar Allan Poe's "The Masque of the Red Death," the climax occurs when the Red Death arrives at the masked ball and is confronted by Prince Prospero. Shortly afterward, Prospero and all of his guests die.
See also **Falling Action; Plot; Rising Action; Resolution.**

Comedy A comedy is a dramatic work that is light and often humorous in tone, usually ending happily with a peaceful resolution of the main conflict. A comedy differs from a **farce** by having a more believable plot, more realistic characters, and less boisterous behavior.
See also **Drama; Farce.**

Comic Relief Comic relief consists of humorous scenes, incidents, or speeches that are included in a serious drama to provide a reduction in emotional intensity. Because it breaks the tension, comic relief allows an audience to prepare emotionally for events to come.

Complication A complication is an additional factor or problem introduced into the rising action of a story to make the conflict more difficult. Often, a plot complication makes it seem as though the main character is getting farther away from the thing he or she wants.

Conceit *See* **Extended Metaphor.**

Conflict A conflict is a struggle between opposing forces that is the basis of a story's plot. An **external conflict** pits a character against nature, society, or another character. An **internal conflict** is a conflict between opposing forces within a character.
Example: In "Coyote and the Buffalo," Coyote's struggle to keep Buffalo Bull from killing him is an external conflict, whereas Coyote's struggle to decide whether to kill and eat the buffalo cow is an internal conflict.
See pages 48, 759, 1195.
See also **Antagonist; Plot.**

Connotation Connotation is the emotional response evoked by a word, in contrast to its denotation, which is its literal meaning. *Kitten,* for example, is defined as "a young cat." However, the word also suggests, or connotes, images of softness, warmth, and playfulness.

Consonance Consonance is the repetition of consonant sounds within and at the ends of words.

> Some late visitor entreating entrance at my chamber door.
>
> —Edgar Allan Poe, "The Raven"

See also **Alliteration; Assonance.**

Couplet *See* **Sonnet.**

Creation Myth *See* **Myth.**

Critical Essay *See* **Essay.**

Cultural Hero A cultural hero is a larger-than-life figure who reflects the values of a people. Rather than being the creation of a single writer, this kind of hero evolves from the telling of folk tales from one generation to the next. The role of the cultural hero is to provide a noble image that will inspire and guide the actions of all who share that culture.

Dactyl *See* **Meter.**

Denotation *See* **Connotation.**

Dénouement *See* **Falling Action.**

Description Description is writing that helps a reader to picture scenes, events, and characters. Effective description usually relies on imagery, figurative language, and precise diction, as in the following passage:

> I saw again the naked house on the prairie, black and grim as a wooden fortress; the black pond where I had learned to swim, its margin pitted with sun-dried cattle tracks; the rain gullied clay banks about the naked house, the four dwarf ash seedlings where the dish-cloths were always hung to dry before the kitchen door.
> —Willa Cather, "A Wagner Matinee"

See pages 718, 735.
See also **Diction; Figurative Language; Imagery.**

Dialect A dialect is the distinct form of a language as it is spoken in one geographical area or by a particular social or ethnic group. A group's dialect is reflected in characteristic pronunciations, vocabulary, idioms, and grammatical constructions. When trying to reproduce a given dialect, writers often use unconventional spellings to suggest the way words actually sound. Writers use dialect to establish setting, to provide local color, and to develop characters. In the following passage, the use of dialect captures the sound and tang of frontier speech:

> And he had a little small bull-pup, that to look at him you'd think he warn't worth a cent but to set around and look ornery and lay for a chance to steal something.
> —Mark Twain,
> "The Notorious Jumping Frog of Calaveras County"

See pages 683, 1080.
See also **Local Color Realism.**

Dialogue Dialogue is conversation between two or more characters in either fiction or nonfiction. In drama, the story is told almost exclusively through dialogue, which moves the plot forward and reveals characters' motives.
See pages 674, 943, 1095.
See also **Drama.**

Diary A diary is a writer's personal day-to-day account of his or her experiences and impressions. Most diaries are private and not intended to be shared. Some, however, have been published because they are well written and provide useful perspectives on historical events or on the everyday life of particular eras. One important American diary found in this book is Mary Chesnut's diary of the Civil War.

Diction A writer's or speaker's choice of words is called diction. Diction includes both vocabulary (individual words) and syntax (the order or arrangement of words). Diction can be formal or informal, technical or common, abstract or concrete. In the following complex sentence, the diction is formal:

> When, however, the mass movement repudiates violence while moving resolutely toward its goal, its opponents are revealed as the instigators and practitioners of violence if it occurs.
> —Martin Luther King Jr., "Stride Toward Freedom"

See pages 259, 673, 1113.

Drama Drama is literature in which plot and character are developed through dialogue and action; in other words, drama is literature in play form. It is performed on stage and radio and in films and television. Most plays are divided into acts, with each act having an emotional peak, or climax, of its own. The acts sometimes are divided into scenes; each scene is limited to a single time and place. Most contemporary plays have two or three acts, although some have only one act.
See pages 132, 135, 1153.
See also **Act; Dialogue; Scene; Stage Directions.**

Dramatic Irony See **Irony.**

Dramatic Monologue A dramatic monologue is a lyric poem in which a speaker addresses a silent or absent listener in a moment of high intensity or deep emotion, as if engaged in private conversation. The speaker proceeds without interruption or argument, and the effect on the reader is that of hearing just one side of a conversation. This technique allows the poet to focus on the feelings, personality, and motivations of the speaker.
See also **Lyric Poetry; Soliloquy.**

Dynamic Character See **Character.**

Elegy An elegy is a poem written in tribute to a person, usually someone who has died recently. The tone of an elegy is usually formal and dignified.

Epic An epic is a long narrative poem on a serious subject presented in an elevated or formal style. An epic traces the adventures of a hero whose actions consist of courageous, even superhuman, deeds, which often represent the ideals and values of a nation or race. Epics typically address universal issues, such as good and evil, life and death, and sin and redemption. Homer's *Iliad* and *Odyssey* are famous

epics from western civilization. The *Ramayana* is an epic from India.

Epic Hero An epic hero is a larger-than-life figure who embodies the ideals of a nation or race. Epic heroes take part in dangerous adventures and accomplish great deeds. Many undertake long, difficult journeys and display great courage and superhuman strength.

Epithet An epithet is a brief descriptive phrase that points out traits associated with a particular person or thing.
Example: Carl Sandburg's "Chicago" begins with a series of epithets, such as "Hog Butcher for the World."

Essay An essay is a short work of nonfiction that deals with a single subject. Essays are often informal, loosely structured, and highly personal. They can be descriptive, informative, persuasive, narrative, or any combination of these. Amy Tan's personal essay "Mother Tongue" combines all of these qualities.

An **autobiographical essay** focuses on an aspect of a writer's life. Generally, writers of autobiographical essays use the first-person point of view, combining objective description with the expression of subjective feelings. Zora Neale Hurston's "How It Feels to Be Colored Me" is an example of an autobiographical essay.
See pages 379, 910, 1114, 1263.

Exaggeration *See* **Hyperbole.**

Experimental Poetry Poetry described as experimental is often full of surprises—unusual word order, invented forms, descriptions of ordinary objects, and other distinctive elements not found in traditional verse forms. William Carlos Williams belonged to a group of experimental poets known as the Imagists. Their poems contain sharp, clear images of striking beauty, similar to the ones found in haiku. E. E. Cummings's "anyone lived in a pretty how town" reflects his unique brand of poetic experimentation, such as altering the expected presentation of words.
See page 961.

Exposition Exposition is the part of a literary work that provides the background information necessary to understand characters and their actions. Typically found at the beginning of a work, the exposition introduces the characters, describes the setting, and summarizes significant events that took place before the action begins.
Example: In the exposition to "The Devil and Tom Walker," Washington Irving introduces the main characters—a miser and his wife—who dwell in a desolate house near a swamp and take wicked glee in hoarding things from each other.
See also **Plot; Rising Action.**

Expository Essay *See* **Essay.**

Extended Metaphor Like any metaphor, an extended metaphor is a comparison between two essentially unlike things that nevertheless have something in common. It does not contain the word *like* or *as.* An extended metaphor compares two things at some length and in various ways. Sometimes the comparison is carried throughout a paragraph, a stanza, or an entire selection. In the following stanza, notice the extended metaphor in which the speaker compares himself to a loom for God's use:

Make me, O Lord, Thy spinning wheel complete.
Thy holy word my distaff make for me.
Make mine affections Thy swift flyers neat,
And make my soul Thy holy spool to be.
My conversation make to be Thy reel,
And reel the yarn thereon spun of Thy wheel.
—Edward Taylor, "Huswifery"

Like an extended metaphor, a **conceit** compares two apparently dissimilar things in several ways. The term usually implies a more elaborate, formal, and ingeniously clever comparison than the extended metaphor.
See pages 115, 897.

External Conflict *See* **Conflict.**

Eyewitness Account An eyewitness account is a firsthand report of an event written by someone who directly observed it or participated in it. As such, an eyewitness account is a primary source. Narrated from the first-person point of view, eyewitness accounts almost always include the following:

- objective facts about an event

- a chronological (time-order) pattern of organization

- vivid sensory details

- quotations from people who were present

- description of the writer's feelings and interpretations.

The excerpt from Anne Moody's autobiography, *Coming of Age in Mississippi,* is an eyewitness account of a sit-in in 1963.
See page 1239.
See also **Primary Source.**

Fable A fable is a brief tale that illustrates a clear, often directly stated, moral, or lesson. The characters in a fable are usually animals, but sometimes they are humans. The best-known fables—for example, "The Fox and the Crow" and "The Tortoise and the Hare" are those of Aesop, a Greek slave who lived about 600 B.C. Traditionally, fables are handed down from generation to generation as oral literature.
See also **Oral Literature.**

Falling Action In a plot structure, the falling action, or **resolution,** occurs after the climax to reveal the final outcome of events and to tie up any loose ends.
See also **Climax; Exposition; Plot; Rising Action.**

Farce A farce is a type of exaggerated comedy that features an absurd plot, ridiculous situations, and humorous dialogue. The main purpose of a farce is to keep an audience laughing. The characters are usually **stereotypes,** or simplified examples of different traits or qualities. Comic devices typically used in farces include mistaken identity, deception, wordplay—such as puns and double meanings—and exaggeration.
See also **Comedy; Stereotype.**

Fiction Fiction refers to works of prose that contain imaginary elements. Although fiction, like nonfiction, may be based on actual events and real people, it differs from nonfiction in that it is shaped primarily by the writer's imagination. For example, although Hemingway's "In Another Country" is based on autobiographical experiences, it cannot be classified as nonfiction because it is imbued with imaginary events and exaggeration in order to hold the reader's interest. The two major types of fiction are novels and short stories. The four basic elements of a work of fiction are **character, setting, plot,** and **theme.**
See also **Novel; Short Story.**

Figurative Language Figurative language is language that communicates ideas beyond the literal meaning of words. Figurative language can make descriptions and unfamiliar or difficult ideas easier to understand. Note the figurative language in this passage from "The Open Boat":

> A seat in this boat was not unlike a seat upon a bucking broncho, and, by the same token, a broncho is not much smaller. The craft pranced and reared, and plunged like an animal. As each wave came, and she rose for it, she seemed like a horse making at a fence outrageously high.
>
> —Stephen Crane, "The Open Boat"

The most common types of figurative language, called **figures of speech,** are simile, metaphor, personification, and **hyperbole.**
See pages 115, 547, 735, 893.
See also **Hyperbole; Metaphor; Personification; Simile.**

Figures of Speech *See* **Figurative Language.**

First-Person Point of View *See* **Point of View.**

Flashback A flashback is a scene that interrupts the action of a narrative to describe events that took place at an earlier time. It provides background helpful in understanding a character's present situation.
Example: William Faulkner's "A Rose for Emily" opens with Miss Emily's funeral, followed by a flashback that recounts how, when she was alive, Colonel Sartoris exempted her from paying taxes.

Foil A foil is a character whose traits contrast with those of another character. A writer might use a minor character as a foil to emphasize the positive traits of the main character.
Example: In Flannery O'Connor's "The Life You Save May Be Your Own," the innocent Lucynell Crater serves as a foil to the cunning, deceitful Mr. Shiftlet.
See page 1080.
See also **Character.**

Folk Tale A folk tale is a short, simple story that is handed down, usually by word of mouth, from generation to generation. Folk tales include legends, fairy tales, myths, and fables. Folk tales often teach family obligations or societal values. "Coyote and the Buffalo" is an Okanogan folk tale.
See also **Legend; Myth; Fable.**

Foot *See* **Meter.**

Foreshadowing Foreshadowing is a writer's use of hints or clues to indicate events that will occur in a story. Foreshadowing creates suspense and at the same time prepares the reader for what is to come.
Example: In Faulkner's "A Rose for Emily," the scene in which Miss Emily buys the rat poison foreshadows the death of Homer Barron.
See page 1066.

Form   At its simplest, form refers to the physical arrangement of words in a poem—the length and placement of the lines and the grouping of lines into stanzas. The term can also be used to refer to other types of patterning in poetry—anything from rhythm and other sound patterns to the design of a traditional poetic type, such as a sonnet or dramatic monologue.

See also **Genre; Stanza.**

Frame Story   A frame story exists when a story is told within a narrative setting, or "frame"; it creates a story within a story. This storytelling method has been used for over one thousand years and was employed in famous works such as *One Thousand and One Arabian Nights* and Geoffrey Chaucer's *The Canterbury Tales.* "The Notorious Jumping Frog of Calaveras County" by Mark Twain is also a frame story.

See page 691.

Free Verse   Free verse is poetry that does not have regular patterns of rhyme and meter. The lines in free verse often flow more naturally than do rhymed, metrical lines and thus achieve a rhythm more like that of everyday human speech. Walt Whitman is generally credited with bringing free verse to American poetry.

> And you O my soul where you stand,
> Surrounded, detached, in measureless oceans of space,
> Ceaselessly musing, venturing, throwing, seeking
>   the spheres to connect them,
> Till the bridge you will need be form'd, till the
>   ductile anchor hold,
> Till the gossamer thread you fling catch
>   somewhere, O my soul.
>   —Walt Whitman, "The Noiseless Patient Spider"

See pages 531, 953.
See also **Meter; Rhyme.**

Genre   Genre refers to the distinct types into which literary works can be grouped. The four main literary genres are fiction, poetry, nonfiction, and drama.

Gothic Literature   Gothic literature is characterized by grotesque characters, bizarre situations, and violent events. Originating in Europe, gothic literature was a popular form of writing in the United States during the 19th century, especially in the hands of such notables as Edgar Allan Poe and Nathaniel Hawthorne. Interest in the gothic revived in the 20th century among southern writers such as William Faulkner and Flannery O'Connor.

See pages 445, 460, 1066.

Haiku   Haiku is a form of Japanese poetry in which 17 syllables are arranged in three lines of 5, 7, and 5 syllables. The rules of haiku are strict. In addition to the syllabic count, the poet must create a clear picture that will evoke a strong emotional response in the reader. Nature is a particularly important source of inspiration for Japanese haiku poets, and details from nature are often the subjects of their poems.

Hero   *See* **Cultural Hero; Tragic Hero.**

Historical Context   The historical context of a literary work refers to the social conditions that inspired or influenced its creation. To understand and appreciate some works, the reader must relate them to particular events in history. For example, to understand fully Lincoln's "Gettysburg Address," the reader must imaginatively re-create the scene—Lincoln addressing a war-weary crowd on the very site where a horrific battle had recently been fought.

Example: Patrick Henry's "Speech in the Virginia Convention" was inspired by the British military buildup in the American colonies prior to the American Revolution; Martin Luther King's *Stride Toward Freedom* was inspired by the civil rights struggle of the 1950s to overturn segregation laws in the South.

See pages 73, 216, 230.

Historical Narratives   Historical narratives are accounts of real-life historical experiences, given either by a person who experienced those events or by someone who has studied or observed them. Cabeza de Vaca's *La Relación,* William Bradford's *Of Plymouth Plantation,* and *The Interesting Narrative of the Life of Olaudah Equiano* all are historical narratives.

See pages 70, 74, 83, 93, 104.
See also **Primary Sources; Secondary Sources.**

Horror Fiction   Horror fiction contains strange, mysterious, violent, and often supernatural events that create suspense and terror in the reader. Edgar Allan Poe is an author famous for his horror fiction.

Humor   Humor is a term applied to a literary work whose purpose is to entertain and to evoke laughter—for example, Twain's "The Celebrated Jumping Frog of Calaveras County." In literature, there are three basic types of humor, all of which may involve exaggeration or irony. **Humor of situation,** which is derived from the plot of a work, usually involves exaggerated events or situational irony. **Humor of character** is often based on exaggerated personalities or on characters who fail to recognize their own flaws, a form of dramatic irony. **Humor of language** may include sarcasm, exaggeration, puns, or verbal irony, which occurs when what is said is not what is meant.

See pages 659, 1106, 1113.
See also **Comedy; Farce; Irony.**

Hyperbole Hyperbole is a figure of speech in which the truth is exaggerated for emphasis or for humorous effect. The expression "I'm so hungry I could eat a horse" is hyperbole. In the following passage, Dorothy Parker uses hyperbole to describe literary critics' love for a Hemingway novel:

> Ernest Hemingway wrote a novel called *The Sun Also Rises*. Promptly upon its publication, Ernest Hemingway was discovered, the Stars and Stripes were reverentially raised over him, eight hundred and forty-seven book reviewers formed themselves into the word "welcome," and the band played "Hail to the Chief" in three concurrent keys.
> —Dorothy Parker, "A Book of Great Short Stories"

See also **Understatement.**

Iamb *See* **Meter.**

Iambic Pentameter Iambic pentameter is a metrical pattern of five feet, or units, each of which is made up of two syllables, the first unstressed and the second stressed. Iambic pentameter is the most common meter used in English poetry; it is the meter used in blank verse and in the sonnet. The following lines are examples of iambic pentameter:

> So live, | that when | thy sum | mons comes | to join
> The innu | mera | ble car | avan, | which moves
> To that | myste | rious realm, | where each | shall take
> His cham | ber in | the si | lent halls | of death . . .
> —William Cullen Bryant, "Thanatopsis"

See pages 337, 887.
See also **Blank Verse; Meter; Sonnet.**

Idiom An idiom is a common figure of speech whose meaning is different from the literal meaning of its words. For example, the phrase "raining cats and dogs" does not literally mean that cats and dogs are falling from the sky; the expression means "raining heavily."

Imagery The descriptive words and phrases that a writer uses to re-create sensory experiences are called imagery. By appealing to the five senses, imagery helps a reader imagine exactly what the characters and experiences being described are like. In the following passage, the imagery lets the reader experience the miserliness of the main character and his wife:

> They lived in a forlorn-looking house that stood alone and had an air of starvation. A few straggling savin trees, emblems of sterility, grew near it; no smoke ever curled from its chimney. . . . A miserable horse, whose ribs were as articulate as the bars of a gridiron, stalked about a field, where a thin carpet of moss . . . tantalized and balked his hunger.
> —Washington Irving, "The Devil and Tom Walker"

The term *synesthesia* refers to imagery that appeals to one sense when another is being stimulated; for example, description of sounds in terms of colors, as in this passage:

> Music. The great blobs of purple and red emotion have not touched him.
> —Zora Neale Hurston, "How It Feels to Be Colored Me"

See page 900.
See also **Description; Kinesthetic Imagery.**

Imagists *See* **Experimental Poetry; Style.**

Interior Monologue *See* **Monologue; Stream of Consciousness.**

Internal Conflict *See* **Conflict.**

Interview An interview is a conversation conducted by a writer or reporter in which facts or statements are elicited from another person, recorded, and then broadcast or published.

Inverted Syntax Inverted syntax is a reversal in the expected order of words.
Example: In the first line of "Upon the Burning of Our House," Anne Bradstreet writes "when rest I took" rather than "when I took rest."

Irony Irony refers to a contrast between appearance and reality. **Situational irony** is a contrast between what is expected to happen and what actually does happen, as in the poem "Richard Cory," when a gentleman who is admired and envied commits suicide. **Dramatic irony** occurs when readers know more about a situation or a character in a story than the characters do. In Flannery O'Connor's "The Life You Save May Be Your Own," for example, readers find out that Mr. Shiftlet is a scoundrel before the other characters do. **Verbal irony** occurs when someone states one thing and means another, as in the following passage, when the narrator refers to honesty as an "incumbrance," or burden:

> Hicks was born honest, I without that incumbrance—so
> some people said.
> —Mark Twain, *The Autobiography of Mark Twain*

See pages 659, 922, 1079.

Kinesthetic Imagery Kinesthetic imagery re-creates the tension felt through muscles, tendons, or joints in the body. In the following passage, John Steinbeck uses kinesthetic imagery to describe a soldier's experience:

> This is how you feel after a few days of constant firing. Your skin feels thick and insensitive. There is a salty taste in your mouth. A hard, painful knot is in your stomach where the food is undigested. Your eyes do not pick up much detail and the sharp outlines of objects are slightly blurred. Everything looks a little unreal.
> —John Steinbeck, "Why Soldiers Don't Talk"

See page 1172.
See also **Imagery.**

Journal *See* **Diary.**

Legend A legend is a story passed down orally from generation to generation and popularly believed to have a historical basis. While some legends may be based on real people or situations, most of the events are either greatly exaggerated or fictitious. Like myths, legends may incorporate supernatural elements and magical deeds. But legends differ from myths in that they claim to be stories about real human beings and are often set in a particular time and place.

Limited Point of View *See* **Point of View.**

Line The line is the core unit of a poem. In poetry, line length is an essential element of the poem's meaning and rhythm. There are a variety of terms to describe the way a line of poetry ends or is connected to the next line. Line breaks, where a line of poetry ends, may coincide with grammatical units. However, a line break may also occur in the middle of a grammatical or syntactical unit, creating pauses or emphasis. Poets use a variety of line breaks to play with meaning, thus creating a wide range of effects.

Literary Criticism Literary criticism refers to writing that focuses on a literary work or a genre, describing some aspect of it, such as its origin, its characteristics, or its effects. Toni Morrison's "Thoughts on the African-American Novel" is an example of literary criticism.

See page 909.

Literary Letter A literary letter is a letter that has been published and read by a wider audience because it was written by a well-known public figure or provides information about the period in which it was written. Abigail Adams's "Letter to John Adams" is an example of a literary letter.

See pages 262, 1204, 1252.

Literary Nonfiction Literary nonfiction is informational text that is recognized as being of artistic value or that is about literature. Autobiographies, biographies, essays, and eloquent speeches typically fall into this category.

Local Color Realism Local color realism, especially popular in the late 18th century, is a style of writing that truthfully imitates ordinary life and brings a particular region alive by portraying the dialects, dress, mannerisms, customs, character types, and landscapes of that region. Mark Twain frequently uses local color realism in his writing for humorous effect.

See pages 684, 698.
See also **Dialect.**

Lyric Poem A lyric poem is a short poem in which a single speaker expresses thoughts and feelings. In a love lyric, a speaker expresses romantic love. In other lyrics, a speaker may meditate on nature or seek to resolve an emotional crisis. Anne Bradstreet's poem "To My Dear and Loving Husband" is a love lyric.

Magical Realism Magical realism is a style of writing that often includes exaggeration, unusual humor, magical and bizarre events, dreams that come true, and superstitions that prove warranted. Magical realism differs from pure fantasy in combining fantastic elements with realistic elements such as recognizable characters, believable dialogue, a true-to-life setting, a matter-of-fact tone, and a plot that sometimes contains historic events. This style characterizes some of the fiction of such influential South American writers as the late Jorge Luis Borges of Argentina and Gabriel García Márquez of Colombia.

Main Character *See* **Character.**

Memoir A memoir is a form of autobiographical writing in which a person recalls significant events and people in his or her life. Most memoirs share the following characteristics: (1) they usually are structured as narratives told by the writers themselves, using the first-person point of view; (2) although some names may be changed to protect privacy, memoirs are true accounts of actual events; (3) although basically personal, memoirs may deal with newsworthy events having a significance beyond the confines of the writer's life; (4) unlike strictly historical accounts, memoirs often include the writers' feelings and opinions about historical events, giving the reader insight into the impact of history on people's lives. N. Scott Momaday's *The Way to Rainy Mountain* is a memoir.

Metaphor A metaphor is a figure of speech that compares two things that have something in common. Unlike similes, metaphors do not use the words *like* or *as,* but make comparisons directly.

Example: Abigail Adams's statement "our country is . . . the first and greatest parent" is a metaphor.

See pages 115, 893, 958.
See also **Extended Metaphor; Figurative Language; Simile.**

Meter Meter is the repetition of a regular rhythmic unit in a line of poetry. Each unit, known as a **foot,** has one stressed syllable (indicated by a ´) and either one or two unstressed syllables (indicated by a ˘). The four basic types of metrical feet are the **iamb,** an unstressed syllable followed by a stressed syllable; the **trochee,** a stressed syllable followed by an unstressed syllable; the **anapest,** two unstressed syllables followed by a stressed syllable; and the **dactyl,** a stressed syllable followed by two unstressed syllables.

Two words are typically used to describe the meter of a line. The first word identifies the type of metrical foot—iambic, trochaic, anapestic, or dactylic—and the second word indicates the number of feet in a line: monometer (one foot), **dimeter** (two feet), **trimeter** (three feet), **tetrameter** (four feet), **pentameter** (five feet), **hexameter** (six feet), and so forth.

Examples: In "To My Dear and Loving Husband," by Anne Bradstreet, the meter is iambic pentameter, the most common form of meter in English poetry.

> Ĭf ́ ev | ĕr mán | wĕre lóved | bўy wífe | thĕn thée.

In the following lines from Henry Wadsworth Longfellow's "A Psalm of Life," the meter is trochaic tetrameter:

> Téll mĕ | nót, ĭn | móurnfŭl | númbĕrs,
> Lífe ĭs | bút ăn | émptŭy | dréam!—

See pages 343, 349, 355, 887, 921.
See also **Rhythm; Scansion.**

Minor Character *See* **Character.**

Mise-en-Scène *Mise-en-scène* is a term from the French that refers to the various physical aspects of a dramatic presentation, such as lighting, costumes, scenery, makeup, and props.

Modernism Modernism was a literary movement that roughly spanned the time period between the two world wars, 1914–1945. Modernist works are characterized by a high degree of experimentation and spare, elliptical prose. Modernist characters are most often alienated people searching unsuccessfully for meaning and love in their lives. Katherine Ann Porter's "The Jilting of Granny Weatherall" is an example of modernist writing.

See page 934, 970, 1036.

Monologue In a drama, the speech of a character who is alone on stage, voicing his or her thoughts, is known as a monologue. In a short story or a poem, the direct presentation of a character's unspoken thoughts is called an **interior monologue.** An interior monologue may jump back and forth between past and present, displaying thoughts, memories, and impressions just as they might occur in a person's mind.

See page 136.
See also **Stream of Consciousness.**

Mood Mood is the feeling or atmosphere that a writer creates for the reader. The writer's use of connotation, imagery, figurative language, sound and rhythm, and descriptive details all contribute to the mood. These elements help create a creepy, threatening mood in the following passage:

> The swamp was thickly grown with great gloomy pines and hemlocks, . . . It was full of pits and quagmires, partly covered with weeds and mosses, where the green surface often betrayed the traveler into a gulf of black, smothering mud; . . .
> —Washington Irving, "The Devil and Tom Walker"

See page 937.
See also **Connotation; Description; Diction; Figurative Language; Imagery; Style.**

Moral *See* **Fable.**

Motivation Motivation is the stated or implied reason behind a character's behavior. The grounds for a character's actions may not be obvious, but they should be comprehensible and consistent, in keeping with the character as developed by the writer.
See page 977.
See also **Character.**

Myth A myth is a traditional story, passed down through generations, that explains why the world is the way it is. Myths are essentially religious because they present supernatural events and beings and articulate the values and beliefs of a cultural group. A **creation myth** is a particular kind of myth that explains how the universe, the earth, and life on earth began. "The World on the Turtle's Back" is an Iroquois creation myth.
See page 37.

Narrative A narrative is any type of writing that is primarily concerned with relating an event or a series of events. A narrative can be imaginary, as is a short story or novel, or factual, as is a newspaper account or a work of history. The word *narration* can be used interchangeably with *narrative*, which comes from the Latin word meaning "tell."
See also **Fiction; Nonfiction; Novel; Plot; Short Story.**

Narrative Poem A narrative poem is a poem that tells a story using elements of character, setting, and plot to develop a theme. Edgar Allan Poe's "The Raven" is a narrative poem, as is Dudley Randall's "Ballad of Birmingham."
See pages 436, 943, 1214.
See also **Ballad.**

Narrator The narrator of a story is the character or voice that relates the story's events to the reader.
Example: The narrator of William Faulkner's "A Rose for Emily" is an unidentified citizen of Jefferson, Mississippi, Emily Grierson's hometown.
See pages 684, 1064.

Naturalism An offshoot of realism, naturalism was a literary movement that originated in France in the late 1800s. Like the realists, the naturalists sought to render common people and ordinary life accurately. However, the naturalists emphasized how instinct and environment affect human behavior. Strongly influenced by Charles Darwin's ideas, the naturalists believed that the fate of humans is determined by forces beyond individual control. Stephen Crane's story "The Open Boat" is an example of naturalism.
See pages 735, 769.

Nonfiction Nonfiction, or informational text, is writing about real people, places, and events. Unlike fiction, nonfiction is largely concerned with factual information, although the writer shapes the information according to his or her purpose and viewpoint. Biography, autobiography, and newspaper articles are examples of nonfiction.
See also **Autobiography; Biography; Essay.**

Novel A novel is an extended work of fiction. Like the short story, a novel is essentially the product of a writer's imagination. The most obvious difference between a novel and a short story is length. Because the novel is considerably longer, a novelist can develop a wider range of characters and a more complex plot.

Novella A novella is a work of fiction that is longer than a short story but shorter than a novel. A novella differs from a novel in that it concentrates on a limited cast of characters, a relatively short time span, and a single chain of events. The novella is an attempt to combine the compression of the short story with the development of a novel.

Octave *See* **Sonnet.**

Ode An ode is a complex lyric poem that develops a serious and dignified theme. Odes appeal to both the imagination and the intellect, and many commemorate events or praise people or elements of nature.

Off Rhyme *See* **Slant Rhyme.**

Omniscient Point of View *See* **Point of View.**

Onomatopoeia The word *onomatopoeia* literally means "name-making." It is the process of creating or using words that imitate sounds. The *buzz* of the bee, the *honk* of the car horn, the *peep* of the chick are all onomatopoetic, or echoic, words.
   Onomatopoeia as a literary technique goes beyond the use of simple echoic words. Writers, particularly poets, choose words whose sounds suggest their denotative and connotative meanings: for example, *whisper, kick, gargle, gnash,* and *clatter.*

Open Letter An open letter is addressed to a specific person but published for a wider readership.
Example: James Baldwin's "My Dungeon Shook" is an open letter addressed to his nephew but intended for the general public, particularly white Americans.
See pages 1204, 1252.

Oral Literature Oral literature is literature that is passed from one generation to another by performance or word of mouth. Folk tales, fables, myths, chants, and legends are part of the oral tradition of cultures throughout the world.
See pages 38, 48.
See also **Fable; Folk Tale; Legend; Myth.**

Overstatement *See* **Hyperbole.**

Oxymoron An oxymoron is a special kind of concise paradox that brings together two contradictory terms, such as "venomous love" or "sweet bitterness."

Parable A parable is a brief story that is meant to teach a lesson or illustrate a moral truth. A parable is more than a simple story, however. Each detail of the parable corresponds to some aspect of the problem or moral dilemma to which it is directed. The story of the prodigal son in the Bible is a classic parable. In *Walden*, Thoreau's parable of the strong and beautiful bug that emerges from an old table is meant to show that, similarly, new life can awaken in human beings despite the deadness of society.

Paradox A paradox is a statement that seems to contradict itself but may nevertheless suggest an important truth.
Example: In *Walden*, Henry David Thoreau writes the paradox "I am not as wise as the day I was born." The statement suggests that civilization erases a child's innate wisdom and spiritual awareness.
    A special kind of paradox is the oxymoron, which brings together two contradictory terms, as in the phrases "wise fool" and "feather of lead."
See pages 380, 1250.

Parallelism Parallelism is the use of similar grammatical constructions to express ideas that are related or equal in importance. Note that in the following passage, Whitman begins the last three lines with the name of a type of tradesman, each followed by a gerund phrase beginning with *singing*:

> I hear America singing, the varied carols I hear,
> Those of mechanics, each one singing his as it should be
>   blithe and strong,
> The carpenter singing his as he measures his plank or
>   beam,
> The mason singing his as he makes ready for work, or
>   leaves off work,
>   —Walt Whitman, "I Hear America Singing"

This parallel construction creates a rolling rhythm and emphasizes the different types of people that comprise America.
See page 531.

Parallel Plot A parallel plot is a particular type of plot in which two stories of equal importance are told simultaneously. The story moves back and forth between the two plots.

Parody Parody is writing that imitates either the style or the subject matter of a literary work for the purpose of criticism, humorous effect, or flattering tribute.
See page 443.

Persona *See* **Speaker.**

Personal Essay *See* **Essay.**

Personification Personification is a figure of speech in which an object, animal, or idea is given human characteristics.
Example: In Emily Dickinson's poem "Because I could not stop for Death," death is personified as a gentleman of kindness and civility.
See pages 547, 736.

Persuasive Writing Persuasive writing is intended to convince a reader to adopt a particular opinion or to perform a certain action. Effective persuasion usually appeals to both the reason and the emotions of an audience. Patrick Henry, Jonathan Edwards, Martin Luther King Jr., and Malcolm X all use persuasion in their writing.
See pages 230, 249, 1215.

Petrarchan Sonnet *See* **Sonnet.**

Plot The plot is the sequence of actions and events in a literary work. Generally, plots are built around a **conflict**—a problem or struggle between two or more opposing forces. Plots usually progress through stages: exposition, rising action, climax, and falling action.
    The **exposition** provides important background information and introduces the setting, characters, and conflict. During the **rising action,** the conflict becomes more intense and suspense builds as the main characters struggle to resolve their problem. The **climax** is the turning point in the plot when the outcome of the conflict becomes clear, usually resulting in a change in the characters or a solution to the conflict. After the climax, the **falling action** occurs and shows the effects of the climax. As the falling action begins, the suspense is over but the results of the decision or action that caused the climax are not yet fully worked out. The **resolution,** which often blends with the falling action, reveals the final outcome of events and ties up loose ends.
See pages 783, 1066.
See also **Climax; Conflict; Exposition; Falling Action; Rising Action.**

Poetry Poetry is language arranged in lines. Like other forms of literature, poetry attempts to re-create emotions and experiences. Poetry, however, is usually more condensed and suggestive than prose.

Poems often are divided into stanzas, or paragraph-like groups of lines. The stanzas in a poem may contain the same number of lines or may vary in length. Some poems have definite patterns of meter and rhyme. Others rely more on the sounds of words and less on fixed rhythms and rhyme schemes. The use of figurative language is also common in poetry.

The form and content of a poem combine to convey meaning. The way that a poem is arranged on the page, the impact of the images, the sounds of the words and phrases, and all the other details that make up a poem work together to help the reader grasp its central idea.

See pages 528, 880, 937, 1301.
See also **Experimental Poetry; Form; Free Verse; Meter; Rhyme; Rhythm; Stanza.**

Point of View Point of view refers to the narrative perspective from which events in a story or novel are told. In the **first-person point of view,** the narrator is a character in the work who tells everything in his or her own words and uses the pronouns *I, me,* and *my.* In the **third-person point of view,** events are related by a voice outside the action, not by one of the characters. A third-person narrator uses pronouns such as *he, she,* and *they.* In the **third-person omniscient point of view,** the narrator is an all-knowing, objective observer who stands outside the action and reports what different characters are thinking. Flannery O'Connor's "The Life You Save May Be Your Own" is told from the third-person omniscient point of view. In the **third-person limited point of view,** the narrator stands outside the action and focuses on one character's thoughts, observations, and feelings. Kate Chopin's "The Story of an Hour" is told from primarily the third-person limited point of view.

In the **second-person point of view,** rarely used, the narrator addresses the reader intimately as you. Much of John Steinbeck's essay "Why Soldiers Don't Talk" is narrated from the second-person point of view.

See pages 784, 1080, 1172.

Primary Sources Materials written or created by people who were present at events are called primary sources. Letters, diaries, speeches, autobiographies, and photographs are examples of primary sources, as are certain narrative accounts written by actual participants or observers.

See also **Secondary Sources.**

Prologue A prologue is an introductory scene in a drama.

Prop Prop, an abbreviation of *property,* refers to a physical object that is used in a stage production.
Example: In Arthur Miller's *The Crucible,* an important prop is the small rag doll that Mary Warren brings from the court and gives to Elizabeth Proctor.

Prose Generally, *prose* refers to all forms of written or spoken expression that are not in verse. The term, therefore, may be used to describe very different forms of writing—short stories as well as essays, for example.

Protagonist The protagonist is the main character in a work of literature, who is involved in the central conflict of the story. Usually, the protagonist changes after the central conflict reaches a climax. He or she may be a hero and is usually the one with whom the audience tends to identify. In Kurt Vonnegut's story "Adam," Heinz Knechtmann is the protagonist.
See page 1180.
See also **Antagonist; Character; Tragic Hero.**

Purpose *See* **Author's Purpose.**

Quatrain A quatrain is a four-line stanza, as in the following example:

> The snow had begun in the gloaming,
>   And busily all the night
> Had been heaping field and highway
>   With a silence deep and white.
>   —James Russell Lowell, "The First Snowfall"

See page 354.
See also **Poetry; Stanza.**

Realism As a general term, *realism* refers to any effort to offer an accurate and detailed portrayal of actual life. Thus, critics talk about Shakespeare's realistic portrayals of his characters and praise the medieval poet Chaucer for his realistic descriptions of people from different social classes.

More specifically, realism refers to a literary method developed in the 19th century. The realists based their writing on careful observations of contemporary life, often focusing on the middle or lower classes. They attempted to present life objectively and honestly, without the sentimentality or idealism that had colored earlier literature. Typically, realists developed their settings in great detail in an effort to re-create a specific time and place for the reader. Willa Cather, Kate Chopin, and Mark Twain are all considered realists.

See pages 647, 684, 784.
See also **Local-Color Realism; Naturalism.**

Recurring Theme *See* *Theme.*

Reflective Essay *See* *Essay.*

Refrain In poetry, a refrain is part of a stanza, consisting of one or more lines that are repeated regularly, sometimes with changes, often at the ends of succeeding stanzas. For example, in "The Raven," the line "Quoth the Raven, 'Nevermore'" is a refrain. Refrains are often found in ballads.

Regionalism Regionalism is a literary movement that arose from an effort to accurately represent the speech, manners, habits, history, folklore, and beliefs of people in specific geographic areas. Bret Harte's "The Outcasts of Poker Flat" is a famous example of American regionalist writing.

Repetition Repetition is a technique in which a sound, word, phrase, or line is repeated for emphasis or unity. Repetition often helps to reinforce meaning and create an appealing rhythm. The term includes specific devices associated with both prose and poetry, such as **alliteration** and **parallelism.**

See pages 229, 531, 879, 1251.
See also **Alliteration; Parallelism; Sound Devices.**

Resolution *See* **Falling Action.**

Rhetorical Devices *See* **Analogy; Repetition; Rhetorical Questions,** *Glossary of Reading and Informational Terms,* page R123.

Rhyme Rhyme is the occurrence of similar or identical sounds at the end of two or more words, such as *suite, heat,* and *complete.* Rhyme that occurs within a single line of poetry, as in the following example, is called **internal rhyme.**

> Ah, distinctly I <u>remember</u> it was in the bleak <u>December</u>;
> —Edgar Allan Poe, "The Raven"

When rhyme comes at the end of a line of poetry, it is called **end rhyme.** The pattern of end rhyme in a poem is called the **rhyme scheme** and is charted by assigning a letter, beginning with the letter *a,* to each line. Lines that rhyme are given the same letter. The rhyme scheme of the following stanza is *aabbcc:*

In silent night when rest I took	*a*
For sorrow near I did not look	*a*
I wakened was with thund'ring noise	*b*
And piteous shrieks of dreadful voice.	*b*
That fearful sound of "Fire!" and "Fire!"	*c*
Let no man know is my desire.	*c*
—Anne Bradstreet, "Upon the Burning of Our House"	

See pages 343, 436, 887.
See also **Slant Rhyme.**

Rhyme Scheme *See* **Rhyme.**

Rhythm Rhythm refers to the pattern or flow of sound created by the arrangement of stressed and unstressed syllables, particularly in poetry. Some poems follow a regular pattern, or **meter,** of accented and unaccented syllables. Poets use rhythm to bring out the musical quality of language, to emphasize ideas, to create mood, and to reinforce subject matter.

See pages 337, 879.
See also **Meter.**

Rising Action Rising action is the stage of a plot in which the conflict develops and story events build toward a climax. During this stage, complications arise that make the conflict more intense. Tension grows as the characters struggle to resolve the conflict.

See pages 736, 783, 798.
See also **Plot.**

Romanticism Romanticism was a movement in the arts that flourished in Europe and America throughout much of the 19th century. Romantic writers glorified nature and celebrated individuality. Their treatment of subject was emotional rather than rational, intuitive rather than analytic. Washington Irving and Henry Wadsworth Longfellow were popular American romantic writers.

See pages 308, 320, 344.

Sarcasm Sarcasm, a type of verbal irony, refers to a critical remark expressed in a statement in which literal meaning is the opposite of actual meaning. Sarcasm is mocking, and its intention is to hurt.

See also **Irony.**

Satire Satire is a literary technique in which foolish ideas or customs are ridiculed for the purpose of improving society. Satire may be gently witty, mildly abrasive, or bitterly critical. Short stories, poems, novels, essays, and plays all may be vehicles for satire.

Example: In "The Devil and Tom Walker," Irving satirizes various aspects of 18th-century New England life, including religious hypocrisy and the institution of marriage.

Scansion The process of determining meter is known as scansion. When you scan a line of poetry, you mark its stressed (ˊ) and unstressed syllables (˅) in order to identify the rhythm.

See also **Meter.**

Scene In drama, a scene is a subdivision of an act. Each scene usually establishes a different time or place.

See also **Act; Drama.**

Scenery Scenery is a painted backdrop or other structures used to create the setting for a play.

Science Fiction Science fiction is prose writing that presents the possibilities of the past or the future, using known scientific data and theories as well as the creative imagination of the writer. Most science fiction comments on present-day society through the writer's fictional conception of a past or future society. Ray Bradbury and Kurt Vonnegut Jr. are two popular writers of science fiction.

Screenplay A screenplay is a play written for film.

Script The text of a play, film, or broadcast is called a script.

Secondary Sources Accounts written by people were not directly involved in or witnesses to an event are called secondary sources. A history textbook is an example of a secondary source.

See also **Primary Sources.**

Sensory Details Sensory details are words and phrases that appeal to the reader's senses of sight, hearing, touch, taste, and smell. For example, the sensory detail "a fine film of rain" appeals to the senses of sight and touch. Sensory details stimulate the reader to create images in his or her mind.

See also **Imagery.**

Sermon A sermon is a form of religious persuasion in which a speaker exhorts the audience to behave in a more spiritual and moral fashion. "Sinners in the Hands of an Angry God" is a sermon.

Sestet *See* **Sonnet.**

Setting The setting of a literary work refers to the time and place in which the action occurs. A story can be set in an imaginary place, such as an enchanted castle, or a real place, such as New York City or Tombstone, Arizona. The time can be the past, the present, or the future. In addition to time and place, setting can include the larger historical and cultural contexts that form the background for a narrative. Setting is one of the main elements in fiction and often plays an important role in what happens and why.

Example: Willa Cather's story "A Wagner Matinee" is set in Boston around the turn of the 20th century.

See pages 135, 697, 717, 1080.

Short Story A short story is a work of fiction that centers on a single idea and can be read in one sitting. Generally, a short story has one main conflict that involves the characters, keeps the story moving, and stimulates readers' interest.

See also **Fiction.**

Simile A simile is a figure of speech that compares two things that have something in common, using a word such as *like* or *as.*

Examples: Abigail Adams's statement "power and liberty are like heat and moisture" and Thoreau's statement "we live meanly, like ants" contain similes.

See pages 262, 380, 547.
See also **Figurative Language; Metaphor.**

Situational Irony *See* **Irony.**

Slant Rhyme Rhyme that is not exact but only approximate is known as slant rhyme, or **off rhyme,** as in the second and fourth lines below:

> I heard a Fly buzz—when I died—
> The Stillness in the Room
> Was like the Stillness in the Air—
> Between the Heaves of Storm—
>
> —Emily Dickinson,
> "I heard a Fly buzz—when I died—"

See page 547.
See also **Rhyme.**

Slave Narrative A slave narrative is an autobiographical account written by someone who endured the miseries of slavery. Olaudah Equiano's and Frederick Douglass's autobiographies are examples of slave narratives. These writers often use sensory details to re-create their

experiences. For example, to re-create the horror of confinement in the hold of a slave ship, Equiano gives the reader such details as "the galling of the chains" and "the groans of the dying."

See pages 83, 560, 574.
See also **Autobiography.**

Soliloquy *See* **Monologue.**

Sonnet A sonnet is a 14-line lyric poem, commonly written in iambic pentameter. The **Petrarchan sonnet** consists of two parts. The first eight lines, called the octave, usually have the rhyme scheme *abbaabba*. In the last six lines, called the sestet, the rhyme scheme may be *cdecde, cdcdcd*, or another variation. The **octave** generally presents a problem or raises a question, and the *sestet* resolves or comments on the problem. James Weldon Johnson's "My City" is a Petrarchan sonnet. A **Shakespearean sonnet** is divided into three **quatrains** (groups of four lines) and a **couplet** (two rhyming lines). Its rhyme scheme is *abab cdcd efef gg*. The couplet usually expresses a response to the important issue developed in the three quatrains. Claude McKay's "If We Must Die" is a Shakespearean sonnet.

See page 887.
See also **Meter; Quatrain; Rhyme.**

Sound Devices *See* **Alliteration; Assonance; Consonance; Meter; Onomatopoeia; Repetition; Rhyme; Rhyme Scheme; Rhythm.**

Speaker The speaker of a poem, like the narrator of a story, is the voice that talks to the reader. In some poems, the speaker can be identified with the poet. In other poems, the poet invents a fictional character, or a persona, to play the role of the speaker. *Persona* is a Latin word meaning "actor's mask."

See pages 879, 921, 970.

Speech A speech is a talk or public address. The purpose of a speech may be to entertain, to explain, to persuade, to inspire, or any combination of these aims.

Stage Directions Stage directions are the playwright's instructions for the director, performers, and stage crew. Usually set in italics, they are located at the beginning of and throughout a script. Stage directions usually tell the time and place of the action and explain how characters move and speak. They also describe scenery, props, lighting, costumes, music, or sound effects.

See pages 132, 136.
See also **Drama.**

Stanza A stanza is a group of lines that form a unit in a poem. A stanza is usually characterized by a common pattern of meter, rhyme, and number of lines. Longfellow's "A Psalm of Life" is written in four-line stanzas. During the 20th century, poets experimented more freely with stanza form than did earlier poets, sometimes writing poems without any stanza breaks.

See page 343.

Static Character *See* **Character.**

Stereotype A stereotype is an over simplified image of a person, group, or institution. Sweeping generalizations about "all Southerners" or "every used-car dealer" are stereotypes. Simplified or stock characters in literature are often called stereotypes. Such characters do not usually demonstrate the complexities of real people.

Example: In Washington Irving's "The Devil and Tom Walker," Tom Walker's wife is a stereotype of a greedy and shrewish wife.

Stream of Consciousness Stream of consciousness is a technique that was developed by modernist writers to present the flow of a character's seemingly unconnected thoughts, responses, and sensations. The term was coined by American psychologist William James to characterize the unbroken flow of thought that occurs in the waking mind.

Example: In "The Love Song of J. Alfred Prufrock," T. S. Eliot uses this technique to reveal the jumble of thoughts that flow through Prufrock's mind.

See pages 969, 1035.
See also **Modernism.**

Structure The structure of a literary work is the way in which it is put together—the arrangement of its parts. In poetry, structure refers to the arrangement of words and lines to produce a desired effect. A common structural unit in poetry is the stanza, of which there are numerous types. In prose, structure is the arrangement of larger units or parts of a selection. Paragraphs, for example, are a basic unit in prose, as are chapters in novels and acts in plays. The structure of a poem, short story, novel, play, or nonfiction selection usually emphasizes certain important aspects of content.

See pages 239, 337, 603.
See also **Form; Stanza.**

Style Style is the distinctive way in which a work of literature is written. Style refers not so much to what is said but how it is said. Word choice, sentence length, tone, imagery, and use of dialogue all contribute to a writer's style. A group of writers might exemplify common stylistic characteristics; for example, the Imagists of the early 20th

century wrote in a style that employs compression and rich sensory images.

Example: E. E. Cummings's style is decidedly unconventional, breaking rules of capitalization, punctuation, diction, and syntax.

See pages 547, 559, 937, 1009.

Surprise Ending A surprise ending is an unexpected plot twist at the end of a story.

Example: "The Story of an Hour" ends with a surprise when Mrs. Mallard drops dead after her husband, presumed to be dead, reappears.

See page 783.
See also **Irony.**

Suspense Suspense is the excitement or tension that readers feel as they become involved in a story and eagerly await the outcome.

Example: In Ambrose Bierce's "An Occurrence at Owl Creek Bridge," the suspense builds as the reader awaits the outcome of Peyton Farquhar's attempted escape from hanging at the hands of Union troops.

See page 604.
See also **Rising Action.**

Symbol A symbol is a person, place, or object that has a concrete meaning in itself and also stands for something beyond itself, such as an idea or feeling.

Example: In Gilman's "The Yellow Wallpaper," the wallpaper in the narrator's bedroom comes to symbolize her growing madness.

See pages 469, 798.

Synesthesia *See* **Imagery.**

Tall Tale A tall tale is a distinctively American type of humorous story characterized by exaggeration. Tall tales and practical jokes have similar kinds of humor. In both, someone gets fooled, to the amusement of the person or persons who know the truth, as in Twain's "The Notorious Jumping Frog of Calaveras County."

See page 683.
See also **Humor; Hyperbole.**

Theme A theme is an underlying message that a writer wants the reader to understand. It is a perception about life or human nature that the writer shares with the reader. In most cases, themes are not stated directly but must be inferred.

Example: One theme of "The Masque of the Red Death" could be stated, "No one, not even the wealthiest person, has the power to escape death."

Recurring themes are themes found in a variety of works. For example, authors from varying backgrounds might convey similar themes having to do with the importance of family values. **Universal themes** are themes that are found throughout the literature of all time periods.

See pages 446, 769, 780, 1049.

Third-Person Point of View *See* **Point of View.**

Title The title of a literary work introduces readers to the piece and usually reveals something about its subject or theme. Often, a poet uses the title to provide information necessary for understanding a poem.

Example: "A Worn Path," the title of Eudora Welty's short story, suggests the main character, Phoenix, herself: the path of her life is worn with age and struggle, and her life has centered on a single routine motivated by love.

See pages 784, 1050, 1296.

Tone Tone is a writer's attitude toward his or her subject. A writer can communicate tone through diction, choice of details, and direct statements of his or her position. Unlike mood, which refers to the emotional response of the reader to a work, tone reflects the feelings of the writer. To identify the tone of a work of literature, you might find it helpful to read the work aloud, as if giving a dramatic reading before an audience. The emotions that you convey in an oral reading should give you hints as to the tone of the work.

Example: Claude McKay's tone in "If We Must Die" is proud, defiant, and urgent.

See pages 531, 735, 890, 1106.
See also **Connotation; Diction; Mood; Style.**

Tragedy A tragedy is a dramatic work that presents the downfall of a dignified character who is involved in historically, morally, or socially significant events. The main character, or **tragic hero,** has a **tragic flaw,** a quality that leads to his or her destruction. The events in a tragic plot are set in motion by a decision that is often an error in judgment caused by the tragic flaw. Succeeding events are linked in a cause-and-effect relationship and lead inevitably to a disastrous conclusion, usually death. Arthur Miller's *The Crucible* could be classified as a tragedy.

Tragic Flaw *See* **Tragedy.**

Tragic Hero The ancient Greek philosopher Aristotle defined a tragic hero as a character whose basic goodness and superiority are marred by a tragic flaw that brings about or contributes to his or her downfall. The flaw may be poor judgment, pride, weakness, or an excess of an admirable quality. The tragic hero recognizes his or her own flaw and

its consequences, but only after it is too late to change the course of events.

See also **Character.**

Traits *See* **Character.**

Transcendentalism The philosophy of transcendentalism, an American offshoot of German romanticism, was based on a belief that "transcendent forms" of truth exist beyond reason and experience. Ralph Waldo Emerson, the leader of the movement, asserted that every individual is capable of discovering this higher truth through intuition. Henry David Thoreau is another well-known transcendentalist writer.

See pages 369, 380, 390.
See also **Romanticism.**

Trickster Tale A trickster tale is a folk tale about an animal or person who engages in trickery, violence, and magic. Neither all good nor all bad, a trickster may be foolish yet clever, greedy yet helpful, immoral yet moral. "Coyote and the Buffalo" is a trickster tale.

See page 47.
See also **Folk Tale.**

Trochee *See* **Meter.**

Turning Point *See* **Climax.**

Understatement Understatement is a technique of creating emphasis by saying less than is actually or literally true. It is the opposite of **hyperbole,** or overstatement. One of the primary devices of **irony,** understatement can be used to develop a humorous effect, to create satire, or to achieve a restrained tone.

Example: In "Letter to John Adams," Abigail Adams points out the tyranny of male power by gently saying, "I cannot say that I think you very generous to the ladies."

See also **Hyperbole; Irony.**

Unity of Effect When all elements of a story—plot, character, setting, imagery, and other other literary devices—work together to create a single effect, it is known as unity of effect. Edgar Allan Poe's "The Fall of the House of Usher" demonstrates the unity of effect.

See page 411.

Universal Theme *See* **Theme.**

Verbal Irony *See* **Irony.**

Voice The term *voice* refers to a writer's unique use of language that allows a reader to "hear" a human personality in his or her writing. The elements of style that determine a writer's voice include sentence structure, diction, and tone. For example, some writers are noted for their reliance on short, simple sentences, while others make use of long, complicated ones. Certain writers use concrete words, such as *lake* or *cold,* which name things that you can see, hear, feel, taste, or smell. Others prefer abstract terms such as *memory,* which name things that cannot be perceived with the senses. A writer's tone also leaves its imprint on his or her personal voice. The term can be applied to the narrator of a selection, as well as the writer.

See page 673.
See also **Diction; Tone.**

Word Choice *See* **Diction.**

Almanac *See* **Reference Works.**

Analogy *See Glossary of Literary and Nonfiction Terms, page R104.*

Appeals by Association Appeals by association imply that one will gain acceptance or prestige by taking the writer's position.
See also **Recognizing Persuasive Techniques**—*Reading Handbook, page R20.*

Appeal to Authority An appeal to authority calls upon experts or others who warrant respect.
See also **Recognizing Persuasive Techniques**—*Reading Handbook, page R20.*

Appeal to Reason *See* **Logical Appeal.**

Argument An argument is speech or writing that expresses a position on an issue or problem and supports it with reasons and evidence. An argument often takes into account other points of view, anticipating and answering objections that opponents of the position might raise.
See also **Claim; Counterargument; Evidence; General Principle.**

Assumption An assumption is an opinion or belief that is taken for granted. It can be about a specific situation, a person, or the world in general. Assumptions are often unstated. *See also* **General Principle.**

Author's Message An author's message is the main idea or theme of a particular work.
See also **Main Idea; Theme,** *Glossary of Literary and Nonfiction Terms, page R121.*

Author's Perspective *See Glossary of Literary and Nonfiction Terms, page R105.*

Author's Position An author's position is his or her opinion on an issue or topic. *See also* **Claim.**

Author's Purpose *See Glossary of Literary and Nonfiction Terms, page R105.*

Autobiography *See Glossary of Literary and Nonfiction Terms, page R105.*

Bias Bias is an inclination toward a particular judgment on a topic or issue. A writer often reveals a strongly positive or strongly negative opinion by presenting only one way of looking at an issue or by heavily weighting the evidence. Words with intensely positive or negative connotations are often a signal of a writer's bias.

Bibliography A bibliography is a list of books and other materials related to the topic of a text. Bibliographies can be good sources of works for further study on a subject.
See also **Works Consulted.**

Biography *See Glossary of Literary and Nonfiction Terms, page R105.*

Business Correspondence Business correspondence includes all written business communications, such as business letters, e-mails, and memos. Business correspondence is to the point, clear, courteous, and professional.

Cause and Effect A **cause** is an event or action that directly results in another event or action. An **effect** is the direct or logical outcome of an event or action. Basic **cause-and-effect relationships** include a single cause with a single effect, one cause with multiple effects, multiple causes with a single effect, and a chain of causes and effects. The concept of cause and effect also provides a way of organizing a piece of writing. It helps a writer show the relationships between events or ideas.
See also **False Cause**—*Reading Handbook, page R22.*

Central Idea *See* **Main Idea.**

Chronological Order Chronological order is the arrangement of events in their order of occurrence. This type of organization is used in both fictional narratives and in historical writing, biography, and autobiography.

Claim In an argument, a claim is the writer's position on an issue or problem. Although an argument focuses on supporting one claim, a writer may make more than one claim in a work.

Clarify Clarifying is a reading strategy that helps a reader to understand or make clear what he or she is reading. Readers usually clarify by rereading, reading aloud, or discussing.

Classification Classification is a pattern of organization in which objects, ideas, or information is presented in groups, or classes, based on common characteristics.

Cliché A cliché is an overused expression. "Better late than never" and "hard as nails" are common examples.

Compare and Contrast To compare and contrast is to identify similarities and differences in two or more subjects. Compare-and-contrast organization can be used to structure a piece of writing, serving as a framework for examining the similarities and differences in two or more subjects.

Conclusion A conclusion is a statement of belief based on evidence, experience, and reasoning. A **valid conclusion** is a conclusion that logically follows from the facts or statements upon which it is based. A **deductive conclusion** is one that follows from a particular generalization or premise. An **inductive conclusion** is a broad conclusion or generalization that is reached by arguing from specific facts and examples.

Connect Connecting is a reader's process of relating the content of a text to his or her own knowledge and experience.

Consumer Documents Consumer documents are printed materials that accompany products and services. They are intended for the buyers or users of the products or services and usually provide information about use, care, operation, or assembly. Some common consumer documents are applications, contracts, warranties, manuals, instructions, package inserts, labels, brochures, and schedules.

Context Clues When you encounter an unfamiliar word, you can often use context clues as aids for understanding. Context clues are the words and phrases surrounding the word that provide hints about the word's meaning.

Controlling Idea *See* **Thesis Statement.**

Counterargument A counterargument is an argument made to oppose another argument. A good argument anticipates opposing viewpoints and provides counterarguments to refute (disprove) or answer them.

Counterclaim *See* **Counterargument.**

Credibility *Credibility* refers to the believability or trustworthiness of a source and the information it contains.

Critical Review A critical review is an evaluation or critique by a reviewer or critic. Different types of reviews include film reviews, book reviews, music reviews, and art-show reviews.

Database A database is a collection of information that can be quickly and easily accessed and searched and from which information can be easily retrieved. It is frequently presented in an electronic format.

Debate A debate is an organized exchange of opinions on an issue. In academic settings, *debate* usually refers to a formal contest in which two opposing teams defend and attack a proposition.
See also **Argument; Debate**—*Speaking and Listening Handbook, pages R82–R83.*

Deductive Reasoning Deductive reasoning is a way of thinking that begins with a generalization, presents a specific situation, and then advances with facts and evidence to a logical conclusion. The following passage has a deductive argument imbedded in it: "All students in the drama class must attend the play on Thursday. Since Ava is in the class, she had better show up." This deductive argument can be broken down as follows: generalization—all students in the drama class must attend the play on Thursday; specific situation—Ava is a student in the drama class; conclusion—Ava must attend the play.
See also **Analyzing Logic and Reasoning**—*Reading Handbook, pages R20–R21.*

Dictionary *See* **Reference Works.**

Draw Conclusions To draw a conclusion is to make a judgment or arrive at a belief based on evidence, experience, and reasoning.

Editorial An editorial is an opinion piece that usually appears on the editorial page of a newspaper or as part of a news broadcast. The editorial section of a newspaper presents opinions rather than objective news reports.
See also **Op-Ed Piece.**

Either/Or Fallacy An either/or fallacy is a statement that suggests that there are only two possible ways to view a situation or only two options to choose from. In other words, it is a statement that falsely frames a dilemma, giving the impression that no options exist but the two presented—for example, "Either we stop the construction of a new airport, or the surrounding suburbs will become ghost towns."
See also **Identifying Faulty Reasoning**—*Reading Handbook, page R22.*

Emotional Appeals Emotional appeals are messages that evoke strong feelings—such as fear, pity, or vanity—in order to persuade instead of using facts and evidence to make a point. An **appeal to fear** is a message that taps into people's fear of losing their safety or security. An **appeal to pity** is a message that taps into people's sympathy and compassion for others to build support for an idea, a cause, or a proposed action. An **appeal to vanity** is a message that attempts to persuade by tapping into people's desire to feel good about themselves.
See also **Recognizing Persuasive Techniques**—*Reading Handbook, page R20.*

Encyclopedia *See* **Reference Works.**

Essay *See Glossary of Literary and Nonfiction Terms, page R109.*

Ethical Appeals Ethical appeals establish a writer's credibility and trustworthiness with an audience. When a writer links a claim to a widely accepted value, for example, the writer not only gains moral support for that claim but also establishes a connection with readers.

See also **Recognizing Persuasive Techniques**—*Reading Handbook, page R20.*

Evaluate To evaluate is to examine something carefully and judge its value or worth. Evaluating is an important skill for gaining insight into what you read. A reader can evaluate the actions of a particular character, for example, or can form an opinion about the value of an entire work.

Evidence Evidence is the specific pieces of information that support a claim. Evidence can take the form of facts, quotations, examples, statistics, or personal experiences, among others.

Expository Essay *See* **Essay,** *Glossary of Literary and Nonfiction Terms, page R109.*

Fact versus Opinion A **fact** is a statement that can be proved or verified. An **opinion,** on the other hand, is a statement that cannot be proved because it expresses a person's beliefs, feelings, or thoughts.

See also **Inference; Generalization.**

Faulty Reasoning *See* **Logical Fallacy.**

Feature Article A feature article is a main article in a newspaper or a cover story in a magazine. A feature article is focused more on entertaining than informing. Features are lighter or more general than hard news and tend to be about human interest or lifestyles.

Functional Documents *See* **Consumer Documents; Workplace Documents.**

Generalization A generalization is a broad statement about a class or category of people, ideas, or things, based on a study of only some of its members.

See also **Overgeneralization.**

General Principle In an argument, a general principle is an assumption that links the support to the claim. If one does not accept the general principle as a truth, then the support is inadequate because it is beside the point.

Government Publications Government publications are documents produced by government organizations. Pamphlets, brochures, and reports are just some of the many forms these publications may take. Government publications can be good resources for a wide variety of topics.

Graphic Aid A graphic aid is a visual tool that is printed, handwritten, or drawn. Charts, diagrams, graphs, photographs, and maps can all be graphic aids.

See also **Graphic Aids**—*Reading Handbook, pages R5–R7.*

Graphic Organizer A graphic organizer is a visual illustration of a verbal statement that helps a reader understand a text. Charts, tables, webs, and diagrams can all be graphic organizers. Graphic organizers and graphic aids can look the same. However, graphic organizers and graphic aids do differ in how they are used. Graphic aids are the visual representations that people encounter when they read informational texts. Graphic organizers are visuals that people construct to help them understand texts or organize information.

Historical Documents Historical documents are writings that have played a significant role in human events or are themselves records of such events. The Declaration of Independence, for example, is a historical document.

How-To Book A how-to book is a book that is written to explain how to do something—usually an activity, a sport, or a household project.

Implied Main Idea *See* **Main Idea.**

Index The index of a book is an alphabetized list of important topics and details covered in the book and the page numbers on which they can be found. An index can be used to quickly find specific information about a topic.

Inductive Reasoning Inductive reasoning is the process of logical reasoning from observations, examples, and facts to a general conclusion or principle.

See also **Analyzing Logic and Reasoning**—*Reading Handbook, pages R20–R21.*

Inference An inference is a logical assumption that is based on observed facts and one's own knowledge and experience.

Informational Text Informational text is a category of writing that includes exposition, argument, and functional documents. These texts normally provide factual, historical, or technical information. However, the term also covers texts that make logical or emotional arguments in defense of a position. Examples include biographies, journalism, essays, narrative histories, instruction manuals, and speeches.

Journal A journal is a periodical publication issued by a legal, medical, or other professional organization. Alternatively, the term may be used to refer to a diary or daily record.

Literary Criticism *See Glossary of Literary and Nonfiction Terms, page R113.*

Loaded Language Loaded language consists of words with strongly positive or negative connotations intended to influence a reader's or listener's attitude.

Logical Appeal A logical appeal relies on logic and facts, appealing to people's reasoning or intellect rather than to their values or emotions. Flawed logical appeals—that is, errors in reasoning—are considered logical fallacies.
See also **Logical Fallacy.**

Logical Argument A logical argument is an argument in which the logical relationship between the support and the claim is sound.

Logical Fallacy A fallacy is an error in reasoning. Typically, a fallacy is based on an incorrect inference or a misuse of evidence. Some common logical fallacies are **circular logic, either/or fallacy, oversimplification, overgeneralization,** and **stereotyping.**
See also **Either/Or Fallacy; Logical Appeal; Overgeneralization; Identifying Faulty Reasoning**—*Reading Handbook, page R22.*

Main Idea A main idea is the central or most important idea about a topic that a writer or speaker conveys. It can be the central idea of an entire work or of just a paragraph. Often, the main idea of a paragraph is expressed in a topic sentence. However, a main idea may just be implied, or suggested, by details. A main idea and supporting details can serve as a basic pattern of organization in a piece of writing, with the central idea about a topic being supported by details.

Make Inferences *See* **Inference.**

Monitor Monitoring is the strategy of checking your comprehension as you are reading and modifying the strategies you are using to suit your needs. Monitoring may include some or all of the following strategies: **questioning, clarifying, visualizing, predicting, connecting,** and **rereading.**

Narrative *See Glossary of Literary and Nonfiction Terms, page R115.*

News Article A news article is a piece of writing that reports on a recent event. In newspapers, news articles are usually written in a concise manner to report the latest news, presenting the most important facts first and then more detailed information. In magazines, news articles are usually more elaborate than those in newspapers because they are written to provide both information and analysis. Also, news articles in magazines do not necessarily present the most important facts first.

Nonfiction *See Glossary of Literary and Nonfiction Terms, page R115.*

Op-Ed Piece An op-ed piece is an opinion piece that usually appears opposite ("op") the editorial page of a newspaper. Unlike editorials, op-ed pieces are written and submitted by named writers.

Organization *See* **Pattern of Organization.**

Overgeneralization An overgeneralization is a generalization that is too broad. You can often recognize overgeneralizations by the appearance of words and phrases such as *all, everyone, every time, any, anything, no one,* and *none.* Consider, for example, this statement: "None of the sanitation workers in our city really care about keeping the environment clean." In all probability, there are many exceptions. The writer can't possibly know the feelings of every sanitation worker in the city.
See also **Identifying Faulty Reasoning**—*Reading Handbook, page R22.*

Overview An overview is a short summary of a story, a speech, or an essay. It orients the reader by providing a preview of the text to come.

Paraphrase Paraphrasing is the restating of information in one's own words.
See also **Summarize.**

Pattern of Organization A pattern of organization is a particular arrangement of ideas and information. Such a pattern may be used to organize an entire composition or a single paragraph within a longer work. The following are the most common organizational patterns: **cause-and-effect, chronological order, compare-and-contrast, classification, deductive, inductive, order of importance, problem-solution, sequential,** and **spatial.**
See also **Cause and Effect; Chronological Order; Classification; Compare and Contrast; Problem-Solution Order; Sequential Order; Patterns of Organization**—*Reading Handbook, pages R8–R12.*

Periodical A periodical is a publication that is issued at regular intervals of more than one day. For example, a periodical may be a weekly, monthly, or quarterly journal or magazine. Newspapers and other daily publications generally are not classified as periodicals.

Personal Essay *See* **Essay,** *Glossary of Literary and Nonfiction Terms, page R109.*

Persuasion Persuasion is the art of swaying others' feelings, beliefs, or actions. Persuasion normally appeals to both the intellect and the emotions of readers. **Persuasive techniques** are the methods used to influence others to adopt certain opinions or beliefs or to act in certain ways. Types of persuasive techniques include emotional appeals, ethical appeals, logical appeals, and loaded language. When used properly, persuasive techniques can add depth to writing that's meant to persuade. Persuasive techniques can, however, be misused to cloud factual information, disguise poor reasoning, or unfairly exploit people's emotions in order to shape their opinions.

See also **Appeals by Association; Appeal to Authority; Emotional Appeals; Ethical Appeals; Loaded Language; Logical Appeal; Recognizing Persuasive Techniques—** *Reading Handbook, page R20.*

Predict Predicting is a reading strategy that involves using text clues to make a reasonable guess about what will happen next in a story.

Primary Source *See* **Sources.**

Prior Knowledge Prior knowledge is the knowledge a reader already possesses about a topic. This information might come from personal experiences, expert accounts, books, films, or other sources.

Problem-Solution Order Problem-solution order is a pattern of organization in which a problem is stated and analyzed and then one or more solutions are proposed and examined. Writers use words and phrases such as *propose, conclude, reason for, problem, answer,* and *solution* to connect ideas and details when writing about problems and solutions.

Procedural Documents *See* **Consumer Documents.**

Propaganda Propaganda is a form of communication that may use distorted, false, or misleading information. It usually refers to manipulative political discourse.

Public Documents Public documents are documents that were written for the public to provide information that is of public interest or concern. They include government documents, speeches, signs, and rules and regulations. *See also* **Government Publications.**

Reference Works General reference works are sources that contain facts and background information on a wide range of subjects. More specific reference works contain in-depth information on a single subject. Most reference works are good sources of reliable information because they have been reviewed by experts. The following are some common reference works: **encyclopedias, dictionaries, thesauri, almanacs, atlases, chronologies, biographical dictionaries,** and **directories.**

Review *See* **Critical Review.**

Rhetorical Devices *See Glossary of Literary and Nonfiction Terms, page R118.*

Rhetorical Questions Rhetorical questions are those that do not require a reply. Writers use them to suggest that their arguments make the answer obvious or self-evident.

Scanning Scanning is the process of searching through writing for a particular fact or piece of information. When you scan, your eyes sweep across a page, looking for key words that may lead you to the information you want.

Secondary Source *See* **Sources.**

Sequential Order A pattern of organization that shows the order in which events or actions occur is called sequential order. Writers typically use this pattern of organization to explain steps or stages in a process.

Setting a Purpose The process of establishing specific reasons for reading a text is called setting a purpose.

Sidebar A sidebar is additional information set in a box alongside or within a news or feature article. Popular magazines often make use of sidebar information.

Signal Words Signal words are words and phrases that indicate what is to come in a text. Readers can use signal words to discover a text's pattern of organization and to analyze the relationships among the ideas in the text.

Sources A source is anything that supplies information. **Primary sources** are materials written or created by people who were present at events, either as participants or as observers. Letters, diaries, autobiographies, speeches, and photographs are primary sources. **Secondary sources** are records of events that were created sometime after the events occurred; the writers were not directly involved or were not present when the events took place. Encyclopedias, textbooks, biographies, most newspaper and magazine articles, and books and articles that interpret or review research are secondary sources.

Spatial Order Spatial order is a pattern of organization that highlights the physical positions or relationships of details or objects. This pattern of organization is typically found in descriptive writing. Writers use words and phrases such as *on the left, to the right, here, over there, above, below, beyond, nearby,* and *in the distance* to indicate the arrangement of details.

Speech *See Glossary of Literary and Nonfiction Terms, page R120.*

Stereotyping Stereotyping is a dangerous type of overgeneralization. Stereotypes are broad statements made about people on the basis of their gender, ethnicity, race, or political, social, professional, or religious group.

Summarize To summarize is to briefly retell, or encapsulate, the main ideas of a piece of writing in one's own words.
See also **Paraphrase.**

Support Support is any material that serves to prove a claim. In an argument, support typically consists of reasons and evidence. In persuasive texts and speeches, however, support may include appeals to the needs and values of the audience.
See also **General Principle.**

Supporting Detail *See* **Main Idea.**

Synthesize To synthesize information is to take information, combined with other pieces of information and prior knowledge, and make logical connections to gain a better understanding of a subject or to create a new product or idea.

Text Features Text features are design elements that indicate the organizational structure of a text and help make the key ideas and the supporting information understandable. Text features include headings, boldface type, italic type, bulleted or numbered lists, sidebars, and graphic aids such as charts, tables, timelines, illustrations, and photographs.

Thesaurus *See* **Reference Works.**

Thesis Statement In an argument, a thesis statement, or controlling idea, is an expression of the claim that the writer or speaker is trying to support. In an essay, a thesis statement is an expression, in one or two sentences, of the main idea or purpose of the piece of writing.

Topic Sentence The topic sentence of a paragraph states the paragraph's main idea. All other sentences in the paragraph provide supporting details.

Transcript A transcript is a written record of words originally spoken aloud.

Visualize Visualizing is the process of forming a mental picture based on written or spoken information.

Web Site A Web site is a collection of "pages" on the World Wide Web that is usually devoted to one specific subject. Pages are linked together and are accessed by clicking hyperlinks or menus, which send the user from page to page within the site. Web sites are created by companies, organizations, educational institutions, branches of the government, the military, and individuals.

Workplace Documents Workplace documents are materials that are produced or used within a work setting, usually to aid in the functioning of the workplace. They include job applications, office memos, training manuals, job descriptions, and sales reports.

Works Cited A list of works cited lists names of all the works a writer has referred to in his or her text. This list often includes not only books and articles but also nonprint sources.

Works Consulted A list of works consulted names all the works a writer consulted in order to create his or her text. It is not limited just to those works cited in the text.
See also **Bibliography.**

Glossary of Academic Vocabulary in English & Spanish

The Glossary of Academic Vocabulary in this section is an alphabetical list of the Academic Vocabulary words found in this textbook. Use this glossary just as you would use a dictionary—to find out the meanings of words used in your literature class to talk about and write about literary and informational texts and to talk about and write about concepts and topics in your other academic classes.

For each word, the glossary includes the pronunciation, part of speech, and meaning. A Spanish version of each word and definition follows the English version. For more information about the words in the Glossary of Academic Vocabulary, please consult a dictionary.

adequate (ad′ə-kwit) *adj.* enough to meet a need; sufficient
    adecuado *adj.* bastante para cubrir una necesidad; suficiente

apparent (ə-păr′ənt) *adj.* obvious; seeming, especially without deeper examination
    aparente *adj.* obvio; visible, especialmente sin necesidad de un examen profundo

complex (käm′pleks) *adj.* made up of interconnected parts; hard to understand; complicated
    complejo *adj.* compuesto por partes interrelacionadas; difícil de comprender; complicado

conclude (kən-klōōd′) *v.* to arrive at a belief based on evidence, experience, or reasoning; to end
    concluir *v.* llegar a una creencia a partir de pruebas, experiencias o razonamientos; finalizar

confine (kən-fīn′) *v.* to keep within bounds; limit
    confinar *v.* mantener dentro de límites; limitar

conflict (kŏn′flĭkt) *n.* a struggle or clash between people, ideas, or interests. *v.* (kən-flĭkt′) to be in opposition; differ
    conflicto *sust.* lucha o choque entre personas, ideas o intereses; **estar en conflicto** *loc. v.* enfrentarse; diferir

construct (kən-strŭkt′) *v.* create (an argument or a sentence, for example) by systematically arranging ideas or terms; *n.* (kŏn′strŭkt) a concept or theory
    construir *v.* crear (un argumento o una oración, por ejemplo) ordenando ideas o palabras de manera sistemática; **construcción** *sust.* concepto o teoría

consult (kən-sŭlt′) *v.* to seek the advice or information of; to exchange views
    consultar *v.* buscar consejos o información con respecto a algo; intercambiar opiniones

create (krē-āt′) *v.* to make or cause; to produce through artistic effort
    crear *v.* hacer o causar; producir mediante un esfuerzo artístico

criteria (krī-tîr′ē-ə) *n. pl.* set of standard or rules by which something can be evaluated
    criterio *sust.* norma o estándar según el cual se puede evaluar algo

despite (dĭ-spīt′) *prep.* in spite of; not stopped by
    a pesar de *loc. conj.* pese a; independientemente de

document (dŏk′yə-mənt) *n.* something, such as a piece of writing, recording or a photograph, that can be used to furnish evidence or information; *v.* to support (statements in a research paper, for example) with written references or citations
    documento *sust.* algo, como un escrito, una grabación o una fotografía, que se puede usar para proporcionar pruebas o información; **documentar** *v.* respaldar (afirmaciones en un trabajo de investigación, por ejemplo) con referencias o citas escritas

economic (ĕk′ə-nŏm-ĭk) *adj.* relating to the production and exchange of goods and services; efficient
    económico *adj.* relacionado con la producción y el intercambio de bienes y servicios; que rinde

element (ĕl′ə-mənt) *n.* a basic or essential part of something
    elemento *sust.* parte básica o esencial de algo

emphasis (ĕm′fə-sĭs) *n.* special attention or effort directed toward something; stress on a syllable, word, or words
    énfasis *sust.* atención o esfuerzo especial dirigido hacia algo; acento que se da a una sílaba, una palabra o varias palabras

establish (ĭ-stăb′lĭsh) *v.* to set up or cause to happen
  establecer *v.* organizar algo o causar su existencia

ethnic (ĕth′nĭk) *adj.* relating to a group of people sharing a common racial, national, religious, linguistic, or cultural heritage
  étnico *adj.* relacionado con un grupo de personas que comparten un legado racial, nacional, religioso, lingüístico o cultural común

evolve (ĭ-vŏlv′) *v.* to develop gradually
  evolucionar *v.* desarrollarse en forma gradual

expand (ĭk-spănd′) *v.* to enlarge; to express at length or in detail
  extender *v.* agrandar; expresar en forma extensa o en detalle

expose (ĭk-spōz′) *v.* to subject to an action, influence, or condition; to make visible; to make known, especially something negative
  exponer *v.* someter a una acción, influencia o condición; hacer visible; dar a conocer, especialmente algo negativo

focus (fō′kəs) *n.* a center of interest; close attention, concentration; *v.* to direct toward a particular point or purpose
  foco *sust.* centro de interés; atención, concentración;
  enfocar *v.* dirigirse hacia un punto o propósito en particular

illustrate (ĭl′ə-strāt) *v.* to clarify, or make clear, with examples
  ilustrar *v.* aclarar o explicar mediante ejemplos

indicate (ĭn′dĭ-kāt) *v.* to point out; to signify
  indicar *v.* señalar; significar

interpret (ĭn-tûr′prĭt) *v.* explain the meaning or significance of something
  interpretar *v.* explicar el significado o la importancia de algo

investigate (ĭn-vĕs′tĭ-gāt) *v.* to observe or look at in detail; examine systematically
  investigar *v.* observar o mirar en detalle; examinar de manera sistemática

justify (jŭs′tə-fī) *v.* to show or claim to be just or right; vindicate
  justificar *v.* demostrar o afirmar que algo es justo o correcto; reivindicar

maintain (mān-tān′) *v.* to preserve or keep up; to declare to be true
  mantener *v.* preservar o conservar; declarar que algo es verdadero

objective (əb-jek′tĭv) *adj.* factual; not influenced by bias or emotion; *n.* purpose or goal
  objetivo *adj.* justo; no influenciado por parcialidades o emociones; *sust.* propósito o finalidad

perceive (pər-sēv′) *v.* to become aware of through the senses, especially sight or hearing; to notice; to grasp an understanding
  percibir *v.* tomar conciencia de algo mediante los sentidos, en especial mediante la vista o la audición; notar; comprender una idea

perspective (pər-spĕk′tĭv) *n.* particular way of looking at something; point of view
  perspectiva *sust.* manera particular de mirar algo; punto de vista

promote (prə-mōt′) *v.* to help the growth of, urge the adoption of, or attempt to popularize something
  promover *v.* ayudar en el crecimiento, fomentar la adopción o intentar popularizar algo

qualitative (kwŏl′ĭ-tā-tĭv) *adj.* measuring the quality, or essential nature, of something
  cualitativo *adj.* que mide la calidad o naturaleza esencial de algo

reinforce (rē-ĭn-fôrs′) *v.* to strengthen something by adding extra support
  reforzar *v.* fortalecer algo mediante respaldo adicional

reveal (rĭ-vēl′) *v.* to make known; to show
  revelar *v.* dar a conocer; mostrar

role (rōl) *n.* the character or part played by a performer; the expected behavior of an individual in society; a function or position
  papel *sust.* personaje o rol que representa un actor; conducta que se espera de una persona en la sociedad; función o posición

The glossary that follows is an alphabetical list of words, found in the selections in this book. Use this glossary just as you would use a dictionary—to find out the meanings of unfamiliar words. (Some technical, foreign, and more obscure words in this book are not listed here but instead are defined for you in the footnotes that accompany many of the selections.)

Many words in the English language have more than one meaning. This glossary gives the meanings that apply to the words as they are used in the selections in this book. Words closely related in form and meaning are usually listed together in one entry (for instance, *cower* and *cowered*), and the definition is given for the first form.

The following abbreviations are used:

adj.   adjective
adv.   adverb
n.   noun
v.   verb

Each word's pronunciation is given in parentheses. followed by the word and definition in Spanish. For more information about the words in this glossary or for information about words not listed here, consult a dictionary.

abdicate (ăb′dǐ-kāt′) *v.* to give up responsibility for
  abdicar *v.* renunciar a una responsabilidad

aberration (ăb′ə-rā′shən) *n.* a disorder of the mind
  aberración *s.* desorden mental

abhor (ăb-hôr′) *v.* to regard with disgust
  aborrecer *v.* detestar

abject (ăb′jěkt′) *adj.* low; contemptible; wretched
  abyecto *adj.* vil; despreciable; desgraciado

abominable (ə-bŏm′ə-nə-bəl) *adj.* thoroughly detestable
  abominable *adj.* totalmente detestable

acquiesce (ăk′wē-ěs′) *v.* to comply or give in
  consentir *v.* aceptar o ceder

adamant (ăd′ə-mənt) *adj.* immovable, especially in opposing something
  inflexible *adj.* inquebrantable, especialmente en oposición a algo

admonitory (ăd-mŏn′ĭ-tôr′ē) *adj.* warning
  admonitorio *adj.* que da una advertencia

affiliated (ə-fĭl′ē-āt-ĭd) *adj.* joined in close association **affiliate** *v.*
  afiliado *adj.* asociado **afiliar** *v.*

affinity (ə-fĭn′ĭ-tē) *n.* a kinship or likeness
  afinidad *s.* cercanía o semejanza

affluence (ăf′lōō-əns) *n.* wealth
  opulencia *s.* riqueza

alleviation (ə-lē′vē-ā′shən) *n.* relief
  alivio *s.* desahogo

ambiguity (ăm′bǐ-gyōō′ǐ-tē) *n.* unclearness; uncertainty
  ambigüedad *s.* vaguedad; incertidumbre

amethyst (ăm′ə-thĭst) *n.* purple or violet form of transparent quartz used as a gemstone
  amatista *s.* cuarzo transparente púrpura o violeta usado como piedra preciosa

amicable (ăm′ĭ-kə-bəl) *adj.* characterized by friendly goodwill
  amigable *adj.* caracterizado por buena voluntad

anarchy (ăn′ər-kē) *n.* condition of lawlessness and disorder, often due to lack of governmental authority
  anarquía *s.* desorden y confusión por falta de gobierno

anathema (ə-năth′ə-mə) *n.* a strong denunciation; a curse
  anatema *s.* fuerte rechazo; maldición

anomaly (ə-nŏm′ə-lē) *n.* departure from the normal rules
  anomalía *s.* desviación de las reglas normales

apathy (ăp′ə-thē) *n.* lack of feeling or interest
  apatía *s.* falta de sentimiento o de interés

appease (ə-pēz′) *v.* to bring peace, quiet, or calm to; to soothe
  aplacar *v.* apaciguar; calmar; aquietar

arbitrary (är′bĭ-trĕr′ē) *adj.* based on unpredictable decisions rather than law
  arbitrario *adj.* que actúa basándose sólo en la voluntad o en el capricho y no sigue las leyes

ardor (är′dər) *n.* intense enthusiasm; passion
  ardor *s.* fuerte entusiasmo; pasión

artifice (är′tə-fĭs) *n.* a clever means to an end
  artificio *s.* estratagema; ardid

ascribe (ə-skrīb′) *v.* to attribute to a specified cause or source
  adscribir *v.* atribuir a una causa o a una fuente

assign (ə-sīn′) *n.* person to whom property is transferred in a will or other legal document
  beneficiario *s.* persona a la que transfiere propiedades un testamento u otro documento jurídico

attest (ə-tĕst′) *v.* to affirm to be true; to be proof of
  atestiguar *v.* dar testimonio; certificar

avarice (ăv′ə-rĭs) *n.* immoderate desire for wealth; greed
  avaricia *s.* deseo desmedido de riqueza; codicia

aversion (ə-vûr′zhən) *n.* a strong dislike
  aversión *s.* fuerte desagrado

blasphemous (blăs′fə-məs) *adj.* disrespectful or offensive
  blasfemo *adj.* irrespetuoso u ofensivo

blatantly (blāt′nt-lē) *adv.* in an extremely obvious way; conspicuously
  descaradamente *adv.* abiertamente; patentemente

cabal (kə-băl′) *n.* a group united in a secret plot
  cábala *s.* grupo unido en un complot secreto

callow (kăl′ō) *adj.* lacking adult experience; immature
  inmaduro *adj.* sin experiencia; inexperto

camaraderie (kä′mə-rä′də-rē) *n.* a spirit of friendly good-fellowship
  camaradería *s.* espíritu de amistad y compañerismo

cauterize (kô′tə-rīz′) *v.* to burn or sear to destroy diseased tissue
  cauterizar *v.* quemar o chamuscar para destruir tejido dañado

cavorting (kə-vôr′tĭng) *adj.* prancing about in a playful manner **cavort** *v.*
  retozón *adj.* que hace cabriolas de modo juguetón **retozar** *v.*

celestial (sə-lĕs′chəl) *adj.* heavenly
  celestial *adj.* del cielo

censurer (sĕn′shər-ər) *n.* one who expresses strong disapproval or harsh criticism
  censor *s.* persona que expresa una fuerte desaprobación o crítica

cessation (sĕ-sā′shən) *n.* a coming to an end; a stopping
  cesación *s.* fin; terminación

citation (sī-tā′shən) *n.* formal statement of a soldier's achievements
  mención honorífica *s.* reconocimiento de los éxitos de un militar

coerce (kō-ûrs′) *v.* to force
  coaccionar *v.* obligar

cognizant (kŏg′nĭ-zənt) *adj.* aware
  enterado *adj.* informado

commiseration (kə-mĭz′ə-rā′shən) *n.* a feeling of sympathy or pity
  conmiseración *s.* sentimiento de compasión

comport (kəm-pôrt′) *v.* to agree
  concordar *v.* estar de acuerdo

congenial (kən-jēn′yəl) *adj.* suited to one's needs or nature; agreeable
  compatible *adj.* que concuerda con las necesidades o la naturaleza de uno; concorde

conjecture (kən-jĕk′chər) *v.* to guess
  conjeturar *v.* suponer

consternation (kŏn′stər-nā′shən) *n.* a state of paralyzing dismay; fear
  consternación *s.* estado de gran intranquilidad; temor

constitute (kŏn'stĭ-tōōt') *v.* to amount to; equal
constituir *v.* equivaler; formar

contentious (kən-tĕn'shəs) *adj.* quarrelsome
discutidor *adj.* pendenciero

contrive (kən-trīv') *v.* to plan skillfully; to design
ingeniarse *v.* maquinar; inventar

convolution (kŏn'və-lōō'shən) *n.* a form or shape that
is folded into curved, complicated windings
circunvolución *s.* repliegue; enroscadura; enrollamiento

copious (kō'pē-əs) *adj.* in large amounts; abundant
copioso *adj.* en gran cantidad; abundante

corroborate (kə-rŏb'ə-rāt') *v.* to support with evidence
corroborar *v.* comprobar con evidencia

cosmic (kŏz'mĭk) *adj.* of, or belonging to, the universe
cósmico *adj.* relativo al universo

countenance (koun'tə-nəns) *n.* appearance, especially
the expression of the face
semblante *s.* apariencia, especialmente la expresión
de la cara

credulity (krĭ-dōō'lĭ-tē) *n.* an inclination to believe
too readily
credulidad *s.* facilidad para creer

dastardly (dăs'tərd-lē) *adj.* characterized by
underhandedness or treachery
miserable *adj.* solapado o traidor

dearth (dûrth) *n.* lack
escasez *s.* carencia

decorum (dĭ-kôr'əm) *n.* good taste in conduct or
appearance
decoro *s.* buen gusto en la conducta y la apariencia

deference (dĕf'ər-əns) *n.* respect and honor due to a
superior or elder
deferencia *s.* respeto y honor que se debe a un superior
o mayor

deliberately (dĭ-lĭb'ər-ĭt-lē) *adv.* in an unhurried and
thoughtful manner
deliberadamente *adv.* pausadamente

deliverance (dĭ-lĭv'ər-əns) *n.* rescue from danger
salvación *s.* rescate de un peligro

demeanor (dĭ-mē'nər) *n.* behavior
comportamiento *s.* conducta

depose (dĭ-pōz') *v.* to remove from rule
deponer *v.* destituir del gobierno

despotism (dĕs'pə-tĭz'əm) *n.* government by a ruler
with unlimited power
despotismo *s.* gobierno de poder ilimitado

detached (dĭ-tăcht') *adj.* reserved; aloof **detach** *v.*
alejado *adj.* reservado; distante **alejarse** *v.*

dilapidated (dĭ-lăp'ĭ-dā'tĭd) *adj.* in a state of disrepair;
rundown **dilapidate** *v.*
dilapidado *adj.* en ruinas; desmantelado **dilapidar** *v.*

disapprobation (dĭs-ăp'rə-bā'shən) *n.* disapproval
desaprobación *s.* censura

discern (dĭ-sûrn') *v.* to perceive or recognize something
discernir *v.* percibir o reconocer algo

dominion (də-mĭn'yən) *n.* control; authority over
dominio *s.* control; soberanía

dwindle (dwĭn'dl) *v.* to become steadily less; to shrink
menguar *v.* disminuirse poco a poco; encogerse

embody (ĕm-bŏd'ē) *v.* to represent in human form
encarnar *v.* representar en forma humana

embroidered (ĕm'broi'derd) *adj.* decorated with stitched
designs **embroider** *v.*
bordado *adj.* decorado con cosidos en relieve **bordar** *v.*

enmity (ĕn'mĭ-tē) *n.* hostility; hatred
enemistad *s.* hostilidad; odio

enterprising (ĕn'tər-prī'zĭng) *adj.* possessing imagination
and initiative
emprendedor *adj.* que demuestra imaginación e iniciativa

entreaty (ĕn-trē'tē) *n.* plea
súplica *s.* petición

epithet (ĕp'ə-thĕt') *n.* an abusive word or phrase
epíteto *s.* palabra o frase insultante

equanimity (ē'kwə-nĭm'ĭ-tē) *n.* evenness of temper,
especially under stress
ecuanimidad *s.* serenidad y equilibrio, especialmente
bajo presión

equivocal (ĭ-kwĭv′ə-kəl) *adj.* ambiguous
  equívoco *adj.* ambiguo

eradicate (ĭ-răd′ĭ-kāt′) *v.* to destroy completely
  erradicar *v.* destruir por completo

esteem (ĭ-stēm′) *v.* to set a high value on
  estimar *v.* dar mucho valor

estrangement (ĭ-strānj′-mənt) *n.* separation; alienation
  extrañamiento *s.* separación; desavenencia

excruciatingly (ĭk-skrōō′shē-ā′tĭng-lē) *adv.* in a way that causes great pain or distress
  dolorosamente *adv.* de modo que causa mucho dolor o angustia

exhilaration (ĭg-zĭl′ə-rā′shən) *n.* a feeling of high spirits or lively joy
  regocijo *s.* alborozo y gran alegría

expatriated (ĕk-spā′trē-ā′tĭd) *adj.* sent out of a country or area; banished **expatriate** *v.*
  expatriado *adj.* exiliado; desterrado **expatriar** *v.*

extenuate (ĭk-stĕn′yōō-āt′) *v.* to lessen the seriousness of, especially by providing partial excuses
  atenuar *v.* reducir la gravedad, especialmente dando excusas parciales

extenuating (ĭk-stĕn′yōō-āt′ĭng) *adj.* lessening the severity of **extenuate** *v.*
  atenuante *adj.* que reduce la gravedad **atenuar** *v.*

exultingly (ĭg-zult′ĭng-lē) *adv.* joyfully
  jubilosamente *adv.* con júbilo

fatuity (fə-tōō′ĭ-tē) *n.* something foolish or stupid
  fatuidad *s.* simpleza o estupidez

feigned (fānd) *adj.* not real; pretended **feign** *v.*
  fingido *adj.* irrea; ficticio **fingir** *v.*

felicity (fĭ-lĭs′ĭ-tē) *n.* great happiness
  felicidad *s.* dicha

flamboyant (flăm-boi′ənt) *adj.* marked by strikingly elaborate or colorful display
  flameante *adj.* llamativo; ostentoso; extravagante

flux (flŭks) *n.* change
  flujo *s.* fluctuación; cambio

garrulous (găr′ə-ləs) *adj.* extremely talkative
  locuaz *adj.* que habla mucho

gullible (gŭl′ə-bəl) *adj.* easily deceived or tricked
  crédulo *adj.* que se deja engañar

harassing (hə-răs′ĭng) *adj.* persistently annoying **harass** *v.*
  molesto *adj.* que fastidia todo el tiempo **molestar** *v.*

harry (hăr′ē) *v.* to torment, often by constant attack
  hostilizar *v.* acosar con ataques constantes

imbued (ĭm-byōōd′) *adj.* deeply influenced by **imbue** *v.*
  imbuido *adj.* profundamente influenciado **imbuir** *v.*

immaculate (ĭ-măk′yə-lĭt) *adj.* without stain; pure
  inmaculado *adj.* sin mancha; puro

impede (ĭm-pēd′) *v.* to interfere with or slow the progress of
  impedir *v.* obstruir; dificultar

impel (ĭm-pĕl′) *v.* to drive forward; force
  impeler *v.* impulsar; obligar

impending (ĭm-pĕn′dĭng) *adj.* to be about to occur **impend** *v.*
  amenazante *adj.* a punto de ocurrir **amenazar** *v.*

imperceptible (ĭm′pər-sĕp′tə-bəl) *adj.* extremely slight; barely noticeable
  imperceptible *adj.* tenue; que casi no se nota

impertinent (ĭm-pûr′tn-ənt) *adj.* rude; ill-mannered
  impertinente *adj.* grosero; mal educado

imperviousness (ĭm-pûr′vē-əs-nəs) *n.* condition of not being able to be affected or disturbed
  imperturbabilidad *s.* imposibilidad de ser afectado o perturbado

impetuous (ĭm-pĕch′ōō-əs) *adj.* acting with sudden or rash energy; hasty
  impetuoso *adj.* que actúa de forma precipitada o irreflexiva; impulsivo

implacable (ĭm-plăk′ə-bəl) *adj.* impossible to satisfy
  implacable *adj.* que no se puede aplacar

importune (ĭm′pôr-tōōn′) *v.* to ask urgently or repeatedly; to annoy or trouble
  importunar *v.* preguntar con urgencia e insistencia; molestar

incense (ĭn-sĕns′) *v.* to cause to be extremely angry
  exasperar *v.* encolerizar; enfurecer

incorrigible (ĭn-kôr′ĭ-jə-bəl) *adj.* incapable of being reformed or corrected
  incorregible *adj.* que no se puede reformar o corregir

indifferent (ĭn-dĭf′ər-ənt) *adj.* having no particular interest
indiferente *adj.* sin interés

induce (ĭn-dōōs′) *v.* to succeed in persuading someone to do something
inducir *v.* persuadir; causar; producir

industry (ĭn′də-strē) *n.* hard work; diligence
aplicación *s.* diligencia; laboriosidad

ineffable (ĭn-ĕf′ə-bəl) *adj.* beyond description; inexpressible
inefable *adj.* que no se puede describir; inexpresable

inexorable (ĭn-ĕk′sər-ə-bəl) *adj.* relentless
inexorable *adj.* implacable

inextricable (ĭn-ĕk′strĭ-kə-bəl) *adj.* incapable of being disentangled or untied
inextricable *adj.* que no se puede descifrar o desenmarañar

infamous (ĭn′fə-məs) *adj.* having a very bad reputation; disgraceful
infame *adj.* de mala reputación; vergonzoso

ingenuously (ĭn-jĕn′yōō-əs-lē) *adv.* in a manner showing childlike innocence or simplicity
ingenuamente *adv.* con candidez infantil

ingratiate (ĭn-grā′shē-āt′) *v.* to gain another's favor by deliberate effort
congraciar *v.* conseguir aprobación o afecto con un esfuerzo deliberado

inherently (ĭn-hîr′ənt-lē) *adv.* related to part of something's inmost nature
inherentemente *adv.* intrínsecamente

iniquity (ĭ-nĭk′wĭ-tē) *n.* wickedness
iniquidad *s.* maldad

inordinate (ĭn-ôr′dn-ĭt) *adj.* exceeding reasonable limits; excessive
excesivo *adj.* que sobrepasa los límites razonables; inmoderado

insidious (ĭn-sĭd′ē-əs) *adj.* treacherous
insidioso *adj.* traidor

insipid (ĭn-sĭp′ĭd) *adj.* lacking in flavor; bland
insípido *adj.* sin sabor; desabrido

interim (ĭn′tər-ĭm) *n.* period in between; interval
ínterin *s.* intermedio; intervalo

interminable (ĭn-tûr′mə-nə-bol) *adj.* endless
interminable *adj.* sin fin

interrogation (ĭn-tĕr′ə-gā′shən) *n.* a questioning
interrogación *s.* averiguación

inundate (ĭn′ŭn-dāt′) *v.* to cover with water; to overwhelm
inundar *v.* cubrir de agua; anegar

invincible (ĭn-vĭn′sə-bəl) *adj.* unbeatable
invencible *adj.* inconquistable

inviolate (ĭn-vī′ə-lĭt) *adj.* not violated; intact
inviolado *adj.* íntegro; intacto

jocular (jŏk′yə-lər) *adj.* humorous
jocoso *adj.* chistoso

latent (lāt′nt) *adj.* existing in a hidden form
latente *adj.* que existe en forma oculta

limber (lĭm′bər) *adj.* bending or moving easily; supple
flexible *adj.* que se dobla o se mueve con facilidad; ágil

locomotion (lō′kə-mō′shən) *n.* the power to move from place to place
locomoción *s.* movimiento de un lugar a otro

ludicrous (lōō′dĭ-krəs) *adj.* laughably absurd; ridiculous
absurdo *adj.* risible; ridículo

lurch (lûrch) *v.* to lean or roll suddenly to one side; to stagger
bambolearse *v.* dar banzados; tambalearse

lurid (lōōr′ĭd) *adj.* shocking; gruesome
escabroso *adj.* chocante; espeluznante

luxuriant (lŭg-zhŏŏr′ē-ənt) *adj.* characterized by abundant growth
frondoso *adj.* que tiene mucha vegetación

malign (mə-līn′) *adj.* evil; harmful
maligno *adj.* malo; dañino

martial (mär′shəl) *adj.* warlike
marcial *adj.* bélico

maudlin (môd′lĭn) *adj.* excessively sentimental
sensiblero *adj.* sentimental en exceso

mediocrity (mē′dē-ŏk′rĭ-tē) *n.* lack of quality or excellence
mediocridad *s.* poca calidad o mérito

meditative (mĕd′i-tā′tĭv) *adj.* engaged in serious thought or reflection
  meditabundo *adj.* que medita o reflexiona en silencio

melancholy (mĕl′ən-kŏl′ē) *adj.* gloomy; sad
  melancólico *adj.* triste; lúgubre

mercenary (mûr′sə-nĕr′ē) *n.* a professional soldier hired to fight in a foreign army
  mercenario *s.* soldado profesional contratado para pelear en un ejército extranjero

minutest (mī-nōō′tĭst) *adj.* smallest; most precise
  el más diminuto *adj.* el más pequeño; minucioso

miscellany (mĭs′ə-lā′nē) *n.* a mixture of various things
  miscelánea *s.* mezcla de cosas

misconstrued (mĭs′kən-strōōd′) *adj.* misunderstood; misinterpreted **misconstrue** *v.*
  malinterpretado *adj.* mal entendido **malinterpretar** *v.*

misgiving (mĭs-gĭv′ĭng) *n.* a feeling of doubt, mistrust, or uncertainty
  recelo *s.* sentimiento de duda, desconfianza o temor

mitigation (mĭt-ĭ-gā′shən) *n.* lessening of something that causes suffering
  mitigación *s.* moderación de algo que causa sufrimiento

mollify (mŏl′ə-fī′) *v.* to soothe; to reduce in intensity
  aplacar *v.* calmar; apaciguar

moratorium (môr′a-tôr′ē-əm) *n.* temporary stoppage or waiting period
  moratoria *s.* aplazamiento; período de espera

motley (mŏt′lē) *adj.* composed of diverse, often mismatched elements
  abigarrado *adj.* formado por elementos diversos y dispares

multifariously (mŭl′tə-fâr′ē-əs-lē) *adv.* in many and various ways
  variadamente *adv.* de modos muy variados

mundane (mŭn-dān′) *adj.* characteristic of or concerned with the ordinary
  mundano *adj.* que se preocupa de lo ordinario

myriad (mĭr′ē-əd) *adj.* exceedingly numerous
  innumerable *adj.* en excesiva cantidad

nettled (nĕt′əld) *adj.* irritated; annoyed **nettle** *v.*
  irritado *adj.* molesto; picado **irritar** *v.*

nocturnal (nŏk-tûr′nəl) *adj.* occurring at night
  nocturno *adj.* que ocurre por la noche

nominal (nŏm′ə-nəl) *adj.* in name but not in reality
  nominal *adj.* de palabra pero no de hecho

nonconformist (nŏn′kən-fôr′mĭst) *n.* one who does not follow generally accepted beliefs, customs, or practices
  inconformista *s.* el que no sigue las creencias, costumbres y prácticas acostumbradas

obstinate (ob′stə-nĭt) *adj.* hard to control or treat
  obstinado *adj.* terco; porfiado

obstreperous (ŏb-strĕp′ər-əs) *adj.* very noisy and unruly
  estrepitoso *adj.* ruidoso y revoltoso

occult (ə-kŭlt′) *adj.* secret or hidden from view
  oculto *adj.* secreto o escondido

opaque (ō-pāk′) *adj.* not allowing light to pass through
  opaco *adj.* que no deja pasar la luz

opprobrious (ə-prō′brē-əs) *adj.* scornful; derogatory
  oprobioso *adj.* despectivo; derogatorio

oscillation (ŏs′ə-lā′shən) *n.* the action of swinging back and forth
  oscilación *s.* movimiento alternativo de un lado hacia otro

ostentation (ŏs′tĕn-tā′shən) *n.* display meant to impress others; boastful showiness
  ostentación *s.* exhibición que se hace para impresionar; alarde

ostentatious (ŏs′tĕn-tā′shəs) *adj.* loud; overdone
  ostentoso *adj.* pretencioso; aparatoso

overture (ō′vər-chōōr′) *n.* the orchestral introduction to a musical dramatic work
  obertura *s.* pieza instrumental con que empieza una obra musical extensa

paradoxical (păr′ə-dŏks′-ĭ-kəl) *adj.* self-contradictory
  paradójico *adj.* que encierra una contradicción

pariah (pə-rī′ə) *n.* an outcast, someone or something looked down on by others
  paria *s.* persona a la que se considera inferior

patrimony (păt′rə-mō′nē) *n.* estate or money inherited from ancestors
    patrimonio *s.* propiedades o dinero heredados de los antepasados

perfidy (pûr′fĭ-dē) *n.* treachery
    perfidia *s.* traición

persecution (pûr′sĭ-kyōō′shən) *n.* the act or practice of oppressing or harassing with ill-treatment, especially because of race, religion, gender, or beliefs
    persecución *s.* acoso con malos tratos, castigos y penas, especialmente por motivo de raza, religión, género o creencias

pertinacity (pûr′tn-ăs′ĭ-tē) *n.* stubbornness; persistence
    pertinacia *s.* terquedad; persistencia

perturbation (pûr′tər-bā′shən) *n.* disturbance of the emotions; agitation; uneasiness
    perturbación *s.* alteración de las emociones; agitación; inquietud

pervade (pər-vād′) *v.* to spread through every part of
    penetrar *v.* infiltrarse en todas las partes

pestilential (pĕs′tə-lĕn′shəl) *adj.* deadly; poisonous
    pestilente *adj.* mortal; venenoso

petulance (pĕch′ə-lənsĕ) *n.* ill temper; annoyance
    malhumor *s.* mal genio; disgusto

pigmentation (pĭg′mən-tā′shən) *n.* coloring
    pigmentación *s.* coloración

pillage (pĭl′ĭj) *n.* the act of looting or plundering by force
    pillaje *s.* saqueo o rapiña a la fuerza

plague (plāg) *v.* to annoy; harass
    fastidiar *v.* molestar; acosar

poignant (poin′yənt) *adj.* physically or mentally painful
    punzante *adj.* que causa dolor físico o mental

portend (pôr-tĕnd′) *v.* to serve as an omen of; to signify
    augurar *v.* presagiar; significar

precarious (prĭ-kâr′ē-əs) *adj.* risky; uncertain
    precario *adj.* arriesgado; inseguro

precipitate (prĭ-sĭp′ĭ-tāt′) *v.* to bring about, especially abruptly
    precipitar *v.* causar, especialmente de repente

predecessor (prĕd′ĭ-sĕs′ər) *n.* person who precedes or comes before
    predecesor *s.* persona que precede o viene antes

preeminently (prē-ĕm′ə-nənt-lē) *adv.* above all; most importantly
    preeminentemente *adv.* por encima de todo; sobre todo

presaging (prĕs′ĭj-ĭng) *adj.* predicting **presage** *v.*
    presagioso *adj.* que anuncia o presagia **presagiar** *v.*

prescience (prĕsh′əns) *n.* knowledge of events before they occur
    presciencia *s.* conocimiento de un suceso antes de que ocurra

preternatural (prē′tər-năch′ər-əl) *adj.* supernatural
    preternatural *adj.* sobrenatural

procure (prō-kyōŏr′) *v.* to get by special effort; to obtain
    adquirir *v.* conseguir con un esfuerzo especial; obtener

profusion (prə-fyōō′zhən) *n.* abundance; lavishness
    profusión *s.* abundancia; esplendidez

propitious (prə-pĭsh′əs) *adj.* helpful or advantageous; favorable
    propicio *adj.* benéfico; favorable

propriety (prə-prī′ĭ-tē) *n.* the quality of being proper; appropriateness
    corrección *s.* decoro; idoneidad

providence (prŏv′ĭ-dəns) *n.* an instance of divine care
    providencia *s.* ayuda divina

prudent (prōōd′nt) *adj.* showing caution or good judgment
    prudente *adj.* que actúa con moderación y cautela

querulous (kwĕr′ə-ləs) *adj.* complaining
    quejumbroso *adj.* quejicoso

rabid (răb′ĭd) *adj.* unreasonably extreme; fanatical
    rabioso *adj.* inmoderamente extremo; fanático

radiation (rā′dē-ā′shən) *n.* movement of lines or rays from a center point
    radiación *s.* movimiento de líneas o rayos desde un punto central

raiment (rā′mənt) *n.* clothing; garments
    vestimenta *s.* ropa; indumentaria

rapt (răpt) *adj.* deeply moved, delighted, or absorbed
arrebatado *adj.* profundamente conmovido, extasiado o absorto

rectitude (rĕk'tĭ-tōōd') *n.* morally correct behavior or thinking
rectitud *s.* conducta o pensamiento justo en el sentido moral

recurrent (rĭ-kûr'ənt) *adj.* occurring time after time
recurrente *adj.* que se repite una y otra vez

redress (rĭ-drĕs') *n.* the correction of a wrong; compensation
remedio *s.* reparación de un daño; compensación

relinquish (rĭ-lĭng'kwĭsh) *v.* to withdraw from; to give up
abandonar *v.* renunciar a; ceder

remonstrate (rĭ-mŏn'strāt') *v.* to object; to protest strongly
protestar *v.* reclamar; oponerse fuertemente

rendezvous (rän'dā-vōō) *n.* a gathering place
lugar de reunión *s.* punto de encuentro

replenish (rĭ-plĕn'ĭsh) *v.* to fill up again
reabastecer *v.* volver a llenar

repudiate (rĭ-pyōō'dē-āt') *v.* to reject or renounce
repudiar *v.* rechazar o renunciar

repulse (rĭ-pŭls') *v.* to drive back by force
rechazar *v.* hacer retroceder a la fuerza

resign (rĭ-zīn') *v.* to submit or adapt oneself quietly without complaint
resignarse *v.* someterse o adaptarse sin queja

respite (rĕs'pĭt) *n.* a period of rest or relief
respiro *s.* período de descanso o de alivio

retaliating (rĭ-tăl'ē-āt'ĭng) *n.* taking revenge **retaliate** *v.*
vengador *s.* el que toma venganza **vengarse** *v.*

retinue (rĕt'n-ōō') *n.* a group of attendants or followers
séquito *s.* grupo de ayudantes o seguidores

retrospective (rĕt'rə-spĕk'tĭv) *adj.* looking back into the past
retrospectivo *adj.* que mira al pasado

reverie (rĕv'ə-rē) *n.* daydream
ensueño *s.* arrobamiento

scintillating (sĭn'tl-āt-ĭng) *adj.* sparkling **scintillate** *v.*
centelleante *adj.* chispeante **centellear** *v.*

scruple (skrōō'pəl) *n.* feeling of uneasiness or guilt that keeps a person from doing something
escrúpulo *s.* sentimiento de duda o de culpa que impide hacer algo

slovenly (slŭv'ən-lē) *adj.* untidy in personal appearance
desaliñado *adj.* descuidado en la apariencia personal

solace (sŏl'ĭs) *n.* comfort in sorrow or distress
solaz *s.* consuelo en el dolor o angustia

solstice (sŏl'stĭs) *n.* either of two days of the year when the sun is farthest from the celestial equator; the summer solstice is the longest day of the year, and the winter solstice is the shortest.
solsticio *s.* uno de los dos días en que el Sol está más lejos del ecuador; el solsticio de verano es el día más largo del año y el solsticio de invierno es el más corto.

somnambulant (sŏm-năm'byə-lənt) *adj.* sleepwalking
sonámbulo *adj.* que camina dormido

sordid (sôr'dĭd) *adj.* wretched; dirty; morally degraded
sórdido *adj.* vil; sucio; indecente

speculating (spĕk'yə-lā'tĭng) *n.* engaging in risky business transactions on the chance of a quick or considerable profit
especulación *s.* operaciones comerciales arriesgadas con la esperanza de obtener una ganancia rápida o considerable

subjugation (sŭb'jə-gā'shən) *n.* control by conquering
subyugación *s.* sometimiento por la fuerza

subservient (səb-sûr'vē-ənt) *adj.* acting like a servant
servil *adj.* que actúa como un sirviente

substantive (sŭb'stən-tĭv) *adj.* significant; with a strong basis
sustantivo *adj.* importante, fundamental o esencial

succumb (sə-kŭm') *v.* to give in, especially to overpowering force or strength
sucumbir *v.* rendirse, especialmente a una fuerza mayor

summarily (sə-mĕr'ə-lē) *adv.* quickly and without ceremony
sumariamente *adv.* rápidamente y sin ceremonia

supinely (sōō-pīn'lē) *adv.* in a manner with the face upward
en posición supina *adv.* boca arriba

surfeit (sûr'fĭt) *n.* a fullness beyond the point of satisfaction
hartura *s.* saciedad más allá del punto de satisfacción

synthesis (sĭn′thĭ-sĭs) *n.* union of parts or elements into a whole
síntesis *s.* composición de un todo por la unión de sus partes

tableau (tăb′lo′) *n.* dramatic scene or picture
cuadro *s.* escena dramática

tacitly (tăs′ĭt-lē) *adj.* silently
tácitamente *adv.* silenciosamente

tarry (tăr′ē) *v.* to delay
demorar *v.* tardar

temerity (tə-mĕr′ĭ-tē) *n.* foolish boldness
temeridad *s.* imprudencia

temperament (tĕm′prə-mənt) *n.* characteristic mode of emotional response
temperamento *s.* modo característico de respuesta emocional

tender (tĕn′dər) *v.* to offer formally
ofrecer *v.* presentar de modo formal

tentatively (tĕn′tə-tĭv-lē) *adv.* in a hesitant or uncertain manner
tentativamente *adv.* de modo provisional o cauteloso

tenuous (tĕn′yōō-əs) *adj.* having little substance or strength; flimsy
tenue *adj.* débil o delicado; endeble

tranquil (trăng′kwəl) *adj.* undisturbed; peaceful
tranquilo *adj.* quieto; sereno

transgress (trăns-grĕs′) *v.* to violate a command or law
transgredir *v.* quebrantar una orden o una ley

tremulous (trĕm′yə-ləs) *adj.* trembling; quivering
trémulo *adj.* tembloroso

truculent (trŭk′yə-lənt) *adj.* eager for a fight; fierce
belicoso *adj.* agresivo; feroz

tyranny (tĭr′ə-nē) *n.* cruel and oppressive government or rule
tiranía *s.* gobierno cruel y opresivo

unassailable (ŭn′ə-sā′lə-bəl) *adj.* impossible to dispute or disprove
inexpugnable *adj.* que no se puede refutar

undulating (ŭn′jə-lā′tĭng) *adj.* appearing to move in waves **undulate** v.
ondulado *adj.* con movimiento de olas **ondular** v.

unremitting (ŭn′rĭ-mĭt′ĭng) *adj.* constant; never stopping
perseverante *adj.* constante; incansable

usurer (yōō′zhər-ər) *n.* one who lends money, at interest, especially at an unusually or unlawfully high rate of interest
usurero *s.* persona que presta dinero al interés, especialmente a una tasa muy alta o ilegal

vagary (vā′gə-rē) *n.* strange idea
capricho *s.* rareza

veritable (vĕr′ĭ-tə-bəl) *adj.* true; not unreal or imaginary
verdadero *adj.* real; auténtico

vigilant (vĭj′ə-lənt) *adj.* alert; watchful
vigilante *adj.* alerta; atento

vituperative (vī-tōō′pər-ə-tĭv) *adj.* abusively critical
injurioso *adj.* que critica de modo ofensivo

whet (hwĕt) *adj.* sharpened **whet** v.
afilado *adj.* agudo **afilar** v.

wrangling (răng′glĭng) *adj.* arguing noisily **wrangle** v.
discutidor *adj.* que disputa en voz alta **discutir** v.

zealous (zĕl′əs) *adj.* eager and enthusiastic
fervoroso *adj.* dedicado y entusiasta

Pronunciation Key

Symbol	Examples	Symbol	Examples	Symbol	Examples
ă	**at**, **gas**	m	**man**, **seem**	v	**van**, **save**
ā	**ape**, **day**	n	**night**, **mitten**	w	**web**, **twice**
ä	**father**, **barn**	ng	**sing**, **hanger**	y	**yard**, **lawyer**
âr	**fair**, **dare**	ŏ	**odd**, **not**	z	**zoo**, **reason**
b	**bell**, **table**	ō	**open**, **road**, **grow**	zh	**treasure**, **garage**
ch	**chin**, **lunch**	ô	**awful**, **bought**, **horse**	ə	**awake**, **even**, **pencil**,
d	**dig**, **bored**	oi	**coin**, **boy**		**pilot**, **focus**
ě	**egg**, **ten**	ŏŏ	**look**, **full**	ər	**perform**, **letter**
ē	**evil**, **see**, **meal**	ōō	**root**, **glue**, **through**		
f	**fall**, **laugh**, **phrase**	ou	**out**, **cow**	**Sounds in Foreign Words**	
g	**gold**, **big**	p	**pig**, **cap**	KH	*German* **ich**, **auch**;
h	**hit**, **inhale**	r	**rose**, **star**		*Scottish* **loch**
hw	**white**, **everywhere**	s	**sit**, **face**	N	*French* **entre**, **bon**, **fin**
ĭ	**inch**, **fit**	sh	**she**, **mash**	œ	*French* **feu**, **cœur**;
ī	**idle**, **my**, **tried**	t	**tap**, **hopped**		*German* **schön**
îr	**dear**, **here**	th	**thing**, **with**	ü	*French* **utile**, **rue**;
j	**jar**, **gem**, **badge**	*th*	**then**, **other**		*German* **grün**
k	**keep**, **cat**, **luck**	ŭ	**up**, **nut**		
l	**load**, **rattle**	ûr	**fur**, **earn**, **bird**, **worm**		

Stress Marks

ˈ   This mark indicates that the preceding syllable receives the primary stress. For example, in the word *language*, the first syllable is stressed: lăngˈgwĭj.

ˌ   This mark is used only in words in which more than one syllable is stressed. It indicates that the preceding syllable is stressed, but somewhat more weakly than the syllable receiving the primary stress. In the word *literature*, for example, the first syllable receives the primary stress, and the last syllable receives a weaker stress: lĭtˈər-ə-chŏŏrˌ.

Adapted from *The American Heritage Dictionary of the English Language*, fourth edition. Copyright © 2006 by Houghton Mifflin Harcourt Publishing Company. Used with the permission of Houghton Mifflin Harcourt Publishing Company.

INDEX OF FINE ART

Index of Skills

Homographs, 672
Homonyms, R75–R76
Homophones, 110, 414, R76
Horror fiction, 411–432, 455–456, R111. *See also* American
    Gothic.
How-to books, R125
Humor, 673, 682, 1310, R111. *See also* Comedy.
Hyperbole, 115, 683, R112. *See also* Overstatement.
Hyphens, R54

I

Iamb, 349
Iambic pentameter, 887, R112
Ideas
    developing, 280, 486, 620, 834, 1118, 1312, 1358
    evaluating, 379–388, 390–397
    identifying, 1257
    interpreting, 967
    tracing development of, 1306–1310
Idioms, 40, 1041, 1243, 1258, R72, R112
Illustrations, 460–463
Imagery, 355, 937, R112
    allusions and, 1309
    analyzing, 319–333, 541, 1171–1176, 1306–1310
    compare-and-contrast, 441, 463
    illustrations and, 461
    in journalism, 1092, 1093
    literary essays, 794
    mood and, 1249
    naturalism and, 735
    news articles and, 762
    poetry and, 547, 893, 897, 959, 1305, 1310
    religious imagery, 1090
    short stories and, 788, 999
    style and, 1105
    unity of effect, 411, 432
Imagism, 869, 953–959
Imperative sentences, 237, 442
Implicit and explicit messages, 267, 1009, 1301, 1356–1357. *See*
    also Author's message; Inferences, making.
Implicit theme/explicit theme, 459, 783. *See also* Theme.
Indefinite pronouns, R50, R58, R70
Independent clauses, R66–R67
Independent observation, R47
Independent reading, ideas for, 298–299, 510–511, 636–637,
    858–859, 1142–1143, 1336–1337
Indexes, R44, R125
Inductive reasoning, 1279, 1282, 1292, R20–R21, R125
Inferences, making, R125
    about audiences, 891
    about authors, 267–274, 276
    about characters, 453, 691, 821–831, 1045
    argumentative writing and, 245
    autobiographies and, 1248
    conflict and, 759
    contemporary literature and, 1261
    cultural characteristics and, 111

developing your own perspective and, 1356–1357
    historical context and, 100
    irony and, 795
    literary essays and, 388, 905
    motivation and, 1075
    paradoxes and, 1285
    personal essays, 1293
    poetry and, 121, 349–353, 364, 556
    reading skills and strategies, 435–441, 953–959, 1009–1022
    research and, 1356–1357
    short stories and, 323, 325, 1023
    about speakers, 1301–1305
    suspense and, 458
    text analysis, 79, 615, 727
Infinitives and infinitive phrases, 951, R65
Informal language, 1266, 1271, 1287, 1319
Informal speeches, 225
Information. *See* Research; Sources.
Informational texts, 762, R126. *See also* Reading for information.
    analyzing text and graphics, 1272–1277
    forms, R13–R18
    historical context and, 216–223
    patterns of organization, R8–R12
    reading skills and strategies, R3–R18
    text features, R3–R7
Informative speeches, R82
Informative writing, 790–792
    analysis and, 225
    compare-and-contrast, 833
    literary essays, 1018–1020
    making connections, 459
    reading skills and strategies, 1023
    short constructed response, 1193
    suspense, 455–456
    war literature, 1178, 1188–1190, 1192
    writing skills and strategies, R35–R38
Inquiries, framing, 487, 621, 835, 1119, 1342, 1343, 1360
Intensive pronouns, R50, R57
Interjections, R51, R63–R64
Internet, the, R46–R47, R125–R126. *See also* Online resources.
Interrogative pronouns, R50, R58
Interrogative sentences, 237, 399
Intertextual links, 459, 795, 1023. *See also* Connections, making.
Interviews, 55, 1219, 1224–1227, 1228, 1343, 1377, R47,
    R85–R86, R112
Intransitive verbs, R51
Introductions, R28–R29
Inverted syntax, 547, R71
Irony, 179, 199, 694, 795, R112–R113
    contemporary literature, 1261
    dramatic irony, 179, 659, 694, 759, 1079, 1164
    modernism, 975
    naturalism, 735
    text analysis, 659–669, 671, 1079–1090, 1192
    verbal irony, 199, 659, 694
Italics, R54

M

S

INDEX OF TITLES & AUTHORS

Page numbers that appear in italics refer to biographical information.

ACKNOWLEDGMENTS

INTRODUCTORY UNIT

Scribner: Excerpt from *The Great Gatsby* by F. Scott Fitzgerald. Copyright 1925 by Charles Scribner's Sons. Copyright renewed 1953 by Frances Scott Fitzgerald Lanahan. Reprinted with the permission of Scribner, a Division of Simon & Schuster, Inc.

UNIT 1

American Anthropological Association: "The World on the Turtle's Back," from *The Great Tree and the Longhouse: The Culture of the Iroquois* (pp. 12–19) by Hazel W. Hertzberg. Copyright © 1966 American Anthropological Association. Reproduced by permission of the American Anthropological Association. Not for sale or further reproduction.

University of Nebraska Press: "Coyote and the Buffalo," from *Coyote Stories* by Mourning Dove. Collected in Masterpieces of American Indian Literature. Published by the University of Nebraska Press. Reprinted by permission.

N. Scott Momaday: Excerpt from *The Way to Rainy Mountain* by N. Scott Momaday. Copyright © N. Scott Momaday. Reprinted by permission of the author.

Scribner: From *Cabeza De Vaca's Adventures in the Unknown Interior of America,* translated and annotated by Cyclone Covey. Copyright © 1961 Macmillan Publishing Company. Reprinted with the permission of Scribner, a Division of Simon & Schuster, Inc.

University of North Carolina Press: From *The Complete Works of Captain John Smith,* 1580–1631, edited by Philip L. Barbour, with a foreword by Thad W. Tate. Published for the Omohundro Institute of Early American History and Culture. Copyright © 1986 by the University of North Carolina Press. Used by permission of the publisher.

Alfred A. Knopf: From *Of Plymouth Plantation,* 1620–1647 by William Bradford, edited by Samuel Eliot Morison. Copyright 1952 by Samuel Eliot Morison and renewed 1980 by Emily M. Beck. Used by permission of Alfred A. Knopf, a division of Random House, Inc.

Viking Penguin: *The Crucible* by Arthur Miller. Copyright 1952, 1953, 1954, renewed © 1980, 1981, 1982 by Arthur Miller. Used by permission of Viking Penguin, a division of Penguin Group (USA) Inc.

Thirteen/WNET New York: "McCarthyism". Courtesy Thirteen/WNET New York.

New York Times: From "The Demons of Salem, With Us Still" by Victor Navasky, *The New York Times,* September 8, 1996. Copyright © 1996 The New York Times Co. All rights reserved. Used by permission and protected by the Copyright Laws of the United States. The printing, copying, redistribution, or retransmission of the Material without express written permission is prohibited.

Grove/Atlantic: Excerpt from *Timebends* by Arthur Miller. Copyright © 1987 by Arthur Miller. Used by permission of Grove/Atlantic, Inc.

Rolling Stone: From "The Crucible (film review)" by Peter Travers, *Rolling Stone,* December 12, 1996. © Rolling Stone LLC 1996. All rights reserved. Reprinted by permission.

U.S. News & World Report: "50 Ways to Fix Your Life" by Carolyn Kleiner Butler, *U.S. News & World Report,* 27 December 2004. Copyright © 2004 U.S. News & World Report, L.P. Reprinted with permission.

UNIT 2

Cynthia G. La Ferle: "Thoreau Still Beckons, if I Can Take My Laptop" by Cynthia G. La Ferle, *The Christian Science Monitor,* 3 October 1997. Copyright © 1997 by Cynthia G. La Ferle. Reprinted by permission of the author.

Navajivan Trust: Excerpt from "Readiness for Satyagraha" by Mahatma Gandhi, from *The Essential Writings of Mahatma Gandhi,* edited by Raghavan Iyer. Published by Oxford University Press. Reprinted by permission of the Navajivan Trust.

Pocket Books: Excerpt from *Danse Macabre* by Stephen King. Copyright © 1981 by Stephen King. All rights reserved. Reprinted with the permission of Pocket Books, a Division of Simon & Schuster, Inc.

Persea Books: "The Daydreamer" by Magdalena Gómez, from *Working Days: Short Stories About Teenagers at Work,* edited by Anne Mazer. Reprinted by permission of Persea Books, Inc.

Veronica Chambers: "The Secret Latina" by Veronica Chambers, *Essence,* July 2000. Copyright © 2000 by Veronica Chambers. Reprinted by permission of the author.

UNIT 3

Harvard University Press: Excerpt from "My life closed twice before its close—" by Emily Dickinson. Reprinted by permission of the publishers and the Trustees of Amherst College from *The Poems of Emily Dickinson,* Thomas H. Johnson, ed., Cambridge, Mass.: The Belknap Press of Harvard University Press, Copyright 1951, 1955, 1979, 1983 by the President and Fellows of Harvard College.

Agencia Literaria Carmen Balcells and Didier Tisdel Jaén: "Ode to Walt Whitman" by Pablo Neruda, translated by Didier Tisdel Jaén. Published in *Nuevas odas elementales* and *Homage to Walt Whitman: A Collection of Poems from the Spanish.* © Fundación Pablo Neruda, 2009. Translation copyright © Didier Tisdel Jaén. Used by permission of Agencia Literaria Carmen Balcells, S. A. and Didier Tisdel Jaén.

Harvard University Press: "Because I could not stop for Death—" by Emily Dickinson. Reprinted by permission of the publishers and the Trustees of Amherst College from *The Poems of Emily Dickinson,* Thomas H. Johnson, ed., Cambridge, Mass.: The Belknap Press of Harvard University Press, Copyright © 1951, 1955, 1979, 1983 by the President and Fellows of Harvard College.

"Success is counted sweetest" by Emily Dickinson. Reprinted by permission of the publishers and the Trustees of Amherst College from *The Poems of Emily Dickinson,* Thomas H. Johnson, ed., Cambridge, Mass.: The Belknap Press of Harvard University Press, Copyright 1951, 1955, 1979, 1983 by the President and Fellows of Harvard College.

"Much Madness is divinest Sense—" by Emily Dickinson. Reprinted by permission of the publishers and the Trustees of Amherst College from *The Poems of Emily Dickinson,* Thomas H. Johnson, ed., Cambridge, Mass.: The Belknap Press of Harvard University Press, Copyright 1951, 1955, 1979, 1983 by the President and Fellows of Harvard College.

"My life closed twice before its close—" by Emily Dickinson. Reprinted by permission of the publishers and the Trustees of Amherst College from *The Poems of Emily Dickinson,* Thomas H. Johnson, ed., Cambridge, Mass.: The Belknap Press of Harvard University Press, Copyright 1951, 1955, 1979, 1983 by the President and Fellows of Harvard College.

"The Soul selects her own Society" by Emily Dickinson. Reprinted by permission of the publishers and the Trustees of Amherst College from *The Poems of Emily Dickinson,* Thomas H. Johnson, ed., Cambridge, Mass.: The Belknap Press of Harvard University Press, Copyright 1951, 1955, 1979, 1983 by the President and Fellows of Harvard College.

"I heard a Fly buzz—when I died—" by Emily Dickinson. Reprinted by permission of the publishers and the Trustees of Amherst College from *The Poems of Emily Dickinson,* Thomas H. Johnson, ed., Cambridge, Mass.: The Belknap Press of Harvard University Press, Copyright 1951, 1955, 1979, 1983 by the President and Fellows of Harvard College.

"My life had stood—a Loaded Gun" by Emily Dickinson. Reprinted by permission of the publishers and the Trustees of Amherst College from *The Poems of Emily Dickinson,* Thomas H. Johnson, ed., Cambridge, Mass.: The Belknap Press of Harvard University Press, Copyright 1951, 1955, 1979, 1983 by the President and Fellows of Harvard College.

"Letter to Thomas Wentworth Higginson, April 16, 1892" by Emily Dickinson. Reprinted by permission of the publishers and the Trustees of Amherst College from *Letters of Emily Dickinson,* Thomas H. Johnson, ed., Cambridge, Mass.: The Belknap Press of Harvard University Press, Copyright 1951, 1955, 1979, 1983 by the President and Fellows of Harvard College.

Scribner: "Letter, January 1861," from *R.E. Lee: A Biography* by Douglas Southall Freeman. Copyright © 1934, 1935 by Charles Scribner's Sons, copyright renewed © 1962, 1963 by Inez Goddin Freeman. Reprinted with the permission of Scribner, an Division of Simon & Schuster, Inc.

Basic Books: From "Letter, July 14, 1861" by Sullivan Ballou, from *For Love & Liberty: The Untold Civil War Story of Major Sullivan Ballou & His Famous Love Letter* by Robin Young. Copyright © 2005 Robin Young. Reprinted by permission of Basic Books, a member of the Perseus Books Group.

Harvard University Press: "The Wind begun to knead the Grass" by Emily Dickinson. Reprinted by permission of the publishers and the Trustees of Amherst College from *The Poems of Emily Dickinson,* Thomas H. Johnson, ed., Cambridge, Mass.: The Belknap Press of Harvard University Press, Copyright © 1951, 1955, 1979, 1983 by the President and Fellows of Harvard College.

UNIT 4

HarperCollins Publishers: From *The Autobiography of Mark Twain,* edited by Charles Neider. Copyright © 1917, 1940, 1958, 1959 by The Mark Twain Company, renewed 1987. Copyright 1924, 1945, 1952 by Clara Clemens Samossoud. Copyright © 1959 by Charles Neider, renewed 1987. Reprinted by permission of HarperCollins Publishers.

Viking Penguin: "Sumus Quod Sumus," from *Lake Wobegone Days* by Garrison Keillor. Copyright © 1985 by Garrison Keillor. Used by permission of Viking Penguin, a division of Penguin Group (USA) Inc.

Brian Doyle: "Joyas Voladoras" by Brian Doyle from *The American Scholar,* Autumn 2004. Copyright © 2004 by Brian Doyle. Reprinted by permission of the author.

Texas Monthly: Excerpt from "The Next Frontier" by S. C. Gwynne, *Texas Monthly,* August 2007. Reprinted by permission of Texas Monthly.

UNIT 5

New Directions Publishing Corporation: "The Red Wheelbarrow," from *Collected Poems,* 1909–1939, Volume I by William Carlos Williams. Copyright © 1938 by New Directions Publishing Corp. Reprinted by permission of New Directions Publishing Corp.

Alfred A. Knopf and Harold Ober Associates: "Harlem," from *The Collected Poems of Langston Hughes* by Langston Hughes, edited by Arnold Rampersad with David Roessel, Associate Editor. Copyright © 1994 by the Estate of Langston Hughes. Used by permission of Alfred A. Knopf, a division of Random House, Inc. and Harold Ober Associates Incorporated.

"The Negro Speaks of Rivers," from *The Collected Poems of Langston Hughes* by Langston Hughes, edited by Arnold Rampersad with David Roessel, Associate Editor. Copyright © 1994 by the Estate of Langston Hughes. Used by permission of Alfred A. Knopf, a division of Random House, Inc. and Harold Ober Associates Incorporated.

"I, Too," from *The Collected Poems of Langston Hughes* by Langston Hughes, edited by Arnold Rampersad with David Roessel, Associate Editor. Copyright © 1994 by the Estate of Langston Hughes. Used by permission of Alfred A. Knopf, a division of Random House, Inc. and Harold Ober Associates Incorporated.

"The Weary Blues," from *The Collected Poems of Langston Hughes* by Langston Hughes, edited by Arnold Rampersad with David Roessel, Associate Editor. Copyright © 1994 by the Estate of Langston Hughes. Used by permission of Alfred A. Knopf, a division of Random House, Inc. and Harold Ober Associates Incorporated.

Viking Penguin: "My City," from *Saint Peter Relates an Incident* by James Weldon Johnson. Copyright 1935 by James Weldon Johnson, © renewed 1963 by Grace Nail Johnson. Used by permission of Viking Penguin, a division of Penguin Group (USA) Inc.

Schomburg Center for Research in Black Culture: "If We Must Die" by Claude McKay. Courtesy of the Literary Representative for the Works of Claude McKay, Schomburg Center for Research in Black Culture, The New York Public Library, Astor, Lenox and Tilden Foundations.

Thompson and Thompson: "Any Human to Another," from *The Medea and Some Poems* by Countee Cullen. Copyrights held by The Amistad Research Center, Tulane University. Administered by Thompson and Thompson, Brooklyn, NY. Reprinted by permission.

Liveright Publishing Corporation: "Storm Ending," from *Cane* by Jean Toomer. Copyright 1923 by Boni & Liveright, renewed 1951 by Jean Toomer. Used by permission of Liveright Publishing Corporation.

Harold Ober Associates: "A Black Man Talks of Reaping," from *Personals* by Arna Bontemps. Copyright © 1963 by Arna Bontemps. Reprinted by permission of Harold Ober Associates Incorporated.

Victoria Sanders & Associates: "How It Feels to Be Colored Me" by Zora Neale Hurston. Used with the permission of the Zora Neale Hurston Trust.

International Creative Management: "Thoughts on the African-American Novel" by Toni Morrison, Copyright © 1983 by Toni Morrison. Reprinted by permission of International Creative Management, Inc.

Houghton Mifflin Harcourt: "Chicago," and "Grass," from *Chicago Poems* by Carl Sandburg. Copyright 1916 by Holt, Rinehart and Winston and renewed 1944 by Carl Sandburg. Reprinted by permission of Houghton Mifflin Harcourt Publishing Company. This material may not be reproduced in any form or by any means without the prior written permission of the publisher.

Henry Holt and Company: "Acquainted with the Night" by Robert Frost, from *The Poetry of Robert Frost,* edited by Edward Connery Lathem. Copyright 1916, 1923, 1928, 1930, 1939, 1969 by Henry Holt and Company, copyright 1944, 1951, 1956, 1958 by Robert Frost, copyright © 1967 by Lesley Frost Ballantine. Reprinted by arrangement with Henry Holt and Company, LLC.

"Nothing Gold Can Stay" by Robert Frost, from *The Poetry of Robert Frost,* edited by Edward Connery Lathem. Copyright 1916, 1923, 1928, 1930, 1939, 1969 by Henry Holt and Company, copyright 1944, 1951, 1956, 1958 by Robert Frost, copyright © 1967 by Lesley Frost Ballantine. Reprinted by arrangement with Henry Holt and Company, LLC.

"Out, Out—" by Robert Frost, from *The Poetry of Robert Frost,* edited by Edward Connery Lathem. Copyright 1916, 1923, 1928, 1930, 1939, 1969 by Henry Holt and Company, copyright 1944, 1951, 1956, 1958 by Robert Frost, copyright © 1967 by Lesley Frost Ballantine. Reprinted by arrangement with Henry Holt and Company, LLC.

"The Death of the Hired Man" by Robert Frost, from *The Poetry of Robert Frost,* edited by Edward Connery Lathem. Copyright 1916, 1923, 1928, 1930, 1939, 1969 by Henry Holt and Company, copyright 1944, 1951, 1956, 1958 by Robert Frost, copyright © 1967 by Lesley Frost Ballantine. Reprinted by arrangement with Henry Holt and Company, LLC.

New Directions Publishing Corporation: "In a Station of the Metro," from *Personae* by Ezra Pound. Copyright © 1926 by Ezra Pound. Reprinted by permission of New Directions Publishing Corp.

"Helen," from *Collected Poems, 1912–1944* by HD (Hilda Doolittle). Copyright © 1982 by The Estate of Hilda Doolittle. Reprinted by permission of New Directions Publishing Corp.

"Spring and All, Section I," and "This is Just to Say," from *Collected Poems, 1909–1939,* Volume I by William Carlos Williams. Copyright © 1938 by New Directions Publishing Corp. Reprinted by permission of New Directions Publishing Corp.

Liveright Publishing Corporation: "anyone lived in a pretty how town," from *Complete Poems: 1904–1962* by E. E. Cummings, edited by George J. Firmage. Copyright 1940, © 1968, 1991 by the Trustees for the E. E. Cummings Trust. Used by permission of Liveright Publishing Corporation.

Scribner: "Poetry," from *The Collected Poems of Marianne Moore* by Marianne Moore. Copyright © 1935 by Marianne Moore, copyright renewed © 1963 by Marianne Moore and T.S. Eliot. Reprinted with the permission of Scribner, a Division of Simon & Schuster, Inc.

Elizabeth Barnett, Literary Executor: "Recuerdo" by Edna St. Vincent Millay. From *Collected Poems,* HarperCollins. Copyright © 1922, 1950 by Edna St. Vincent Millay. All rights reserved. Used by permission of Elizabeth Barnett, Literary Executor.

Faber and Faber: "The Love Song of J. Alfred Prufrock," from *Collected Poems, 1909–1962* by T. S. Eliot. Reprinted by permission of Faber and Faber Limited.

Scribner: Excerpt from *The Great Gatsby* by F. Scott Fitzgerald. Copyright 1925 by Charles Scribner's Sons. Copyright renewed 1953 by Frances Scott Fitzgerald Lanahan. Reprinted with the permission of Scribner, a Division of Simon & Schuster, Inc.

Scribner and Random House Group Ltd: "In Another Country," from *Men Without Women* by Ernest Hemingway. Copyright 1927 Charles Scribner's Sons. Copyright renewed 1955 by Ernest Hemingway. Reprinted with the permission of Scribner, a Division of Simon & Schuster, Inc and The Random House Group Ltd.

Newsweek: Excerpt from "Healing War's Wounds" by Karen Breslau, *Newsweek,* September 11, 2006. Copyright © 2006 Newsweek, Inc. All rights reserved. Used by permission and protected by the Copyright Laws of the United States. The printing, copying, redistribution, or retransmission of the Material without express written permission is prohibited.

Viking Penguin: From *The Grapes of Wrath* by John Steinbeck. Copyright 1939, renewed © 1967 by John Steinbeck. Used by permission of Viking Penguin, a division of Penguin Group (USA) Inc.

Life: "The Grapes of Wrath: Photo Essay," *Life,* 5 June 1939. Copyright 1939 Life Inc. Reprinted with permission. All rights reserved.

Houghton Mifflin Harcourt: "The Jilting of Granny Weatherall," from *Flowering Judas and Other Stories* by Katherine Anne Porter. Copyright 1930 and renewed 1958 by Katherine Anne Porter. Reprinted by permission of Houghton Mifflin Harcourt Publishing Company. This material may not be reproduced in any form or by any means without prior written permission of the publisher.

"A Worn Path," from *A Curtain of Green and Other Stories* by Eudora Welty. Copyright 1941 and renewed 1969 by Eudora Welty. Reprinted by permission of Houghton Mifflin Harcourt Publishing Company. This material may not be reproduced in any form or by any means without prior written permission of the publisher.

Harvard University Press: Reprinted by permission of the publisher from *One Writer's Beginnings* by Eudora Welty, pp. 99–100, Cambridge, Mass: Harvard University Press, Copyright © 1983, 1984 by Eudora Welty.

Random House: "A Rose for Emily," from *Collected Stories of William Faulkner* by William Faulkner. Copyright 1930 and renewed 1958 by William Faulkner. Used by permission of Random House, Inc.

Houghton Mifflin Harcourt: "The Life You Save May Be Your Own," from *A Good Man Is Hard to Find and Other Stories* by Flannery O'Connor. Copyright 1953 by Flannery O'Connor and renewed 1981 by Regina O'Connor. Reprinted by permission of Houghton Mifflin Harcourt Publishing Company. This material may not be reproduced in any form or by any means without prior written permission of the publisher.

Scribner and HarperCollins Publishers Ltd: "A New Kind of War" by Ernest Hemingway, from *By-Line: Ernest Hemingway,* edited by William White. Copyright © 1937 by New York Times Company. Copyright © renewed 1965 by Mary Hemingway, By-Line Ernest Hemingway, Inc., and The New York Times Company. Reprinted with the permission of Scribner, a Division of Simon & Schuster, Inc. and HarperCollins Publishers Ltd.

Viking Penguin: "A Book of Great Short Stories," from *The Portable Dorothy Parker* by Dorothy Parker, edited by Marion Meade. Copyright 1927, renewed © 1955 by Dorothy Parker. Used by permission of Viking Penguin, a division of Penguin Group (USA) Inc.

Tilbury House, Publishers: Excerpt from "Salt Water Farm," from *One Man's Meat* by E. B. White. Text copyright © 1939 by E. B. White. Copyright renewed. Reprinted by permission of Tilbury House, Publishers, Gardiner, Maine.

HarperCollins Publishers: "The Sky Blue Ball," from *Small Avalanches and Other Stories* by Joyce Carol Oates. Copyright © 2003 by The Ontario Review, Inc. Used by permission of HarperCollins Publishers.

Reader's Digest: "Change of Heart" by Mary A. Fischer, from *Reader's Digest,* March 2005. Copyright © 2005 The Reader's Digest Association, Inc. Reprinted by permission of Reader's Digest.

UNIT 6

Barbara Hogenson Agency: From *Our Town* by Thornton Wilder. Copyright © 1938, 1965 Wilder Family LLC. Reprinted by arrangement with Wilder Family LLC and the Barbara Hogenson Agency.

Georges Borchardt: From *The Glass Menagerie* by Tennessee Williams. Copyright © 1945, renewed 1973 The University of the South. Reprinted by permission of Georges Borchardt, Inc. for the Estate of Tennessee Williams.

Viking Penguin: From *Death of a Salesman* by Arthur Miller. Copyright 1949, renewed © 1977 by Arthur Miller. Used by permission of Viking Penguin, a division of Penguin Group (USA) Inc.

Random House: From *A Raisin in the Sun* by Lorraine Hansberry. Copyright © 1958 by Robert Nemiroff, as an unpublished work. Copyright © 1959, 1966, 1984 by Robert Nemiroff. Copyright renewed 1986, 1987 by Robert Nemiroff. Used by permission of Random House, Inc.

Viking Penguin: "Symptoms," from *Once There Was a War* by John Steinbeck. Copyright 1943, 1958 by John Steinbeck. Renewed © 1971 by Elaine Steinbeck, John Steinbeck IV, and Thomas Steinbeck. Used by permission of Viking Penguin, a division of Penguin Group (USA) Inc.

Farrar, Straus and Giroux: "The Death of the Ball Turret Gunner," from *The Complete Poems* by Randall Jarrell. Copyright © 1969, renewed 1997 by Mary von S. Jarrell. Reprinted by permission of Farrar, Straus and Giroux, LLC. Caution: Users are warned that this work is protected under copyright laws and downloading is strictly prohibited. The right to reproduce or transfer the work via any medium must be secured with Farrar, Straus and Giroux, LLC.

Dell Publishing: "Adam," from *Welcome to the Monkey House* by Kurt Vonnegut, Jr. Copyright 1954 by Kurt Vonnegut, Jr. Used by permission of Dell Publishing, a division of Random House, Inc.

Viking Penguin: "October 1944," from *If This Is a Man (Survival in Auschwitz)* by Primo Levi, translated by Stuart Woolf. Copyright © 1959 by Orion Press, Inc., © 1958 by Guilio Einaudi editore S.P.A. Used by permission of Viking Penguin, a division of Penguin Group (USA) Inc.

Houghton Mifflin Harcourt: "Ambush," from *The Things The Carried* by Tim O'Brien. Copyright © 1990 by Tim O'Brien. Reprinted by permission of Houghton Mifflin Harcourt Publishing Company. All rights reserved.

Writers House: "Letter from Birmingham Jail" by Martin Luther King Jr. Copyright 1963 Dr. Martin Luther King Jr.; copyright renewed 1991 Coretta Scott King. Reprinted by arrangement with The Heirs to the Estate of Martin Luther King Jr., c/o Writers House as agent for the proprietor New York, NY.

Dudley Randall Literary Estate: "Ballad of Birmingham," from *Cities Burning* by Dudley Randall. Copyright © 1965 by Dudley Randall. Reprinted by permission of the Dudley Randall Literary Estate.

Writers House: From *Stride Toward Freedom* by Martin Luther King Jr. Copyright 1958 Dr. Martin Luther King Jr.; copyright renewed 1986 Coretta Scott King. Reprinted by arrangement with The Heirs to the Estate of Martin Luther King Jr., c/o Writers House as agent for the proprietor New York, NY.

Pathfinder Press: "Necessary to Protect Ourselves" by Malcolm X, from *Malcolm X: The Last Speeches,* edited by Bruce Perry. Copyright © 1989 Betty Shabazz, Bruce Perry, Pathfinder Press. All rights reserved. Reprinted by permission of Pathfinder Press.

Cesar E. Chavez Foundation: TM/© 2008 the Cesar E. Chavez Foundation. www.chavezfoundation.org

Doubleday: Excerpt from *Coming of Age in Mississippi* by Anne Moody. Copyright © 1968 by Anne Moody. Used by permission of Doubleday, a division of Random House, Inc.

HarperCollins Publishers: "Revolutionary Dreams," from *The Women and the Men* by Nikki Giovanni. Copyright © 1971, 1974, 1975 by Nikki Giovanni. Reprinted by permission of HarperCollins Publishers.

James Baldwin Estate: "My Dungeon Shook: Letter to My Nephew on the One Hundredth Anniversary of the Emancipation" by James Baldwin. Copyright © 1962 by James Baldwin. Copyright renewed. Collected in *The Fire Next Time,* published by Vintage Books. Used by arrangement with the James Baldwin Estate.

Sandra Dijkstra Literary Agency: "Mother Tongue" by Amy Tan. Copyright © 1989 by Amy Tan. First appeared in *The Threepenny Review.* Reprinted by permission of the author and the Sandra Dijkstra Literary Agency.

Houghton Mifflin Harcourt: Excerpt from "In Search of Our Mothers' Gardens," in *In Search of Our Mothers' Gardens: Womanist Prose* by Alice Walker. Copyright © 1974 by Alice Walker. Reprinted by permission of Houghton Mifflin Harcourt Publishing Company. This material may not be reproduced in any form or by any means without prior written permission of the publisher.

"Women," from *Revolutionary Petunias & Other Poems* by Alice Walker. Copyright © 1970 and renewed 1998 by Alice Walker. Reprinted by permission of Houghton Mifflin Harcourt Publishing Company. This material may not be reproduced in any form or by any means without prior written permission of the publisher.

Susan Bergholz Literary Services: "Straw Into Gold" by Sandra Cisneros. Copyright © 1987 by Sandra Cisneros. First published in *The Texas Observer,* September 1987. Reprinted by permission of Susan Bergholz Literary Services, New York, NY and Lamy, NM. All rights reserved.

Brooks Permissions: "Life for My Child Is Simple," and "Primer for Blacks" by Gwendolyn Brooks. Reprinted by consent of Brooks Permissions.

Rita Dove: "Adolescence–III," from *The Yellow House on the Corner* by Rita Dove. Carnegie Mellon University Press. Copyright © 1980 by Rita Dove. Reprinted by permission of the author.

"Testimonial," from *On the Bus with Rosa Parks* by Rita Dove. W. W. Norton and Company. First published in Poetry magazine, January 1998. Copyright © 1999 by Rita Dove. Reprinted by permission of the author.

University of Pittsburgh Press: "Forgetfulness," and "The Man in the Moon," from *Questions About Angels* by Billy Collins. Copyright © 1991, Billy Collins. Reprinted by permission of the University of Pittsburgh Press.

Barbara Hogenson Agency: Excerpt from "The Secret Life of Walter Mitty," from *My World—And Welcome To It* by James Thurber. Copyright © 1942 by James Thurber, copyright renewed 1970 by Rosemary A. Thurber. Reprinted by arrangement with Rosemary Thurber and The Barbara Hogenson Agency. All rights reserved.

Cable News Network: "Virtual Worlds" from *CNN,* August 8, 2007. Copyright © 2007 Cable News Network. Reprinted by permission of Cable News Network.

UNIT 7

Los Angeles Times: From " 'Grapes of Wrath' Author Guards Self From Threats at Moody Gulch" by Tom Cameron, *Los Angeles Times,* July 9, 1939. Los Angeles Times, Copyright © 1939. Reprinted with permission.

STUDENT RESOURCE BANK

Random House: Excerpt from "History of the National Weather Service," from the Random House Web site (http://www.randomhouse.com/features/isaacsstorm/science/history.html). Copyright © 1999 by Random House, Inc. Used by permission of Random House, Inc.

Best Friends Animal Society: Adapted from "Katrina's South American Sister," from *Best Friends Magazine,* November/December 2005. Copyright © 2005 by Best Friends Animal Society. Adapted with permission.

Houghton Mifflin Harcourt: word definition: ambasador. Copyright © 2006 Houghton Mifflin Company. Reproduced by permission from *The American Heritage Dictionary of the English Language, Fourth Edition.*

Houghton Mifflin Harcourt: word definition: community. Copyright © 2006 Houghton Mifflin Company. Reproduced by permission from *The American Heritage Dictionary of the English Language, Fourth Edition.*

ART CREDITS

CONSULTANTS

Janet Allen © Duane McCubrey; *Arthur Applebee* © Mark Schmidt; *Kylene Beers* © Sam Dudgeon/Houghton Mifflin Harcourt; *Jim Burke* © Bruce Forrester; *Douglas Carnine* © Houghton Mifflin Harcourt; *Carol Jago* Maggie's Photography, Pacific Palisades, CA; *Yvette Jackson* © Howard Gollub; *Robert Jimenez* © Tamra Stallings; *Judith Langer* © Mark Schmidt; *Robert Marzano* © Robert J. Marzano; *Donna Ogle* © Houghton Mifflin Harcourt; *Carol Booth Olson* © Dawson & Associates Photography; *Carol Tomlinson* © Gitchell's Studio; *May Lou McClosky* © Michael Romeo; *Lydia Stack* © Monica Ani; *William McBride* © William McBride; *David Considine* © Bill Caldwell; *Larkin Pauluzzi* © Gabriel Pauluzzi; *Lisa Scheffler* © Steven Scheffler.

TABLE OF CONTENTS

STUDENT GUIDE TO ACADEMIC SUCCESS

EXPLORING AMERICAN LITERATURE

UNIT 1

Special Collections, Northwestern University Library; **65** The Granger Collection, New York; **66** *left* © NMPFT/SSPL/The Image Works, Inc.; *inset* © 2005 Peter Fasciano and Chuck Pharis Video; *background* © Nick Koudis/Getty Images; **67** *1* Excerpts and Photography from *Smoke Signals* provided courtesy of Miramax Films. All rights reserved; *2* © 2003 Classic Media, Inc. Lone Ranger TM and associated character names and images are trademarks of Classic Media, Inc. All rights reserved; *3* Footage for *Stagecoach* provided by Castle Hill Productions, Inc.; *4* Excerpts and Photography from *Smoke Signals* provided courtesy of Miramax Films. All rights reserved; **68** *top* Footage for *Stagecoach* provided by Castle Hill Productions, Inc.; *bottom* © 2003 Classic Media, Inc. Lone Ranger TM and associated character names and images are trademarks of Classic Media, Inc. All rights reserved; *background* © United Artists/The Kobal Collection; **70** *Indian Summer* (1855), Regis Francois Gignoux © Christie's Images/Corbis; **72** *left* The Granger Collection, New York; *background* © GoodShoot/SuperStock; **73, 75** Illustration by Tom McNeely; **82** *left, background* The Granger Collection, New York; **85** Detail of *The Slave Ship* (1956), Robert Riggs, N.A. Courtesy of Les Mansfield, Cincinnati, Ohio; **92** *left* The Granger Collection, New York; *background* © Richard T. Nowitz/Corbis; **95** *Arrival of the English in Virginia* (1585–1588), Theodore de Bry. from Admiranta Narratio, page 47. Engraving. Service Historique de la Marine, Vincennes, France. Photo © Giraudon/Art Resource, New York; **97** © Getty Images; **102** *left* Culver Pictures; *background* © Raymond Forbes/Age Fotostock America, Inc.; **103** The Granger Collection, New York; **113** The Granger Collection, New York; **114** *top* Detail of *Portrait of Anne Bradstreet*, LaDonna Gulley Warrick; *bottom* © Jerry and Marcy Monkman/EcoPhotography; **115** © Pete Turner/Getty Images; **117** *Sampler* (1796), Abigail Gould. Linen plain weave embroidered with silk and wool, 25 cm. x 30 cm Gift of Miss Jeannette Woodward 41.253. Museum of Fine Arts, Boston; **118** *Silk-On-Linen Needlework Sampler* (1822). Relief Shumway. Hardwick, Massachusetts. © Christie's Images Ltd.; **120** Detail of *Needlework Sampler* (1774), Alice Mather. Norwich, Connecticut/Christie's Images Ltd.; **122** *foreground* The Granger Collection, New York; *background* © Getty Images; **123** © Comstock Images/Alamy Images; **132** The Granger Collection, New York; **134** *foreground* © Getty Images; *background left* © Stockdisc/Getty Images; *background right* © Brand X Pictures/Jupiterimages Corporation; **135** © 20th Century Fox Film Corp. All rights reserved/Courtesy The Everett Collection; **136–137** *top* © 1996 Photofest; **139, 143** © 20th Century Fox Film Corp. All rights reserved/Courtesy The Everett Collection; **147** © 1996 Photofest; **153** *top, bottom* © 20th Century Fox Film Corp. All rights reserved/Courtesy The Everett Collection; **155** © Twentieth Century Film Corp./Photofest; **165** © 20th Century Fox Film Corp. All rights reserved/Courtesy The Everett Collection; **172** © 1996 Photofest; **181, 189** © 20th Century Fox Film Corp. All rights reserved/Courtesy The Everett Collection; **197** *top* © Robbie Jack/Corbis; *bottom* © 20th Century Fox Film Corp. All rights reserved/Courtesy The Everett Collection; **201** © 20th Century Fox/The Kobal Collection; **209** © 20th Century Fox Film Corp. All rights reserved/Courtesy The Everett Collection; **217** © Bettmann/Corbis; **218** *top* The New York Times Company; *bottom* AP/Wide World Photos; **220** AP/Wide World Photos; **222** *top* © Barry Wetcher/20th Century Fox/The Kobal Collection; *bottom* © Romilly Lockyer/Getty Images; **224** AP/Wide World Photos; **225** *The Puritan* (1883–1886), Augustus Saint-Gaudens. Bronze figure. Private collection. © Art Resource, New York; **226** © akg-images; **228** *left* The Granger Collection, New York; *background* © David Muench/Corbis; **231** *Patrick Henry Before the Virginia House of Burgesses* (1851), Peter F. Rothermel. Red Hill, The Patrick Henry National Memorial, Brookneal, Virginia; **233** *The Bloody*

Massacre perpetrated in... Boston on March 5th, 1770 (1770), Paul Revere. Colored engraving. Private collection. © Art Resource, New York; **238** *foreground* The Granger Collection, New York; *background* © Pat and Chuck Blackley; **239** The Granger Collection, New York; **241** Library of Congress; **243** The Granger Collection, New York; **248** *foreground* The Granger Collection, New York; *background* © Joseph Sohm/Visions of America/Corbis; **249** The Granger Collection, New York; **251** *Minute Man: Liberty or Death*. Private collection. Photo © Scala/Art Resource, New York; **253** The Granger Collection, New York; **255** *Washington Crossing the Delaware* (1851), Eastman Johnson. Copy after the Emmanuel Leutze painting in the Metropolitan Museum, New York. Private collection. Photo © Art Resource, New York; **258** *center* Library of Congress; *bottom* The Granger Collection, New York; *top* © Brand X Pictures/Alamy Images; **259** © Mark Sykes/Alamy Images; **261** The Granger Collection, New York; **263** *Abigail Smith Adams* (about 1766), Benjamin Blyth. Pastel on paper, 57.3 x 44.8 cm. © Massachusetts Historical Society, Boston/Bridgeman Art Library; *John Adams* (1766), Benjamin Blyth. Pastel on paper, 57.3 cm x 44.8 cm. © Massachusetts Historical Society, Boston, Massachusetts/Bridgeman Art Library; *background* Courtesy of Adelphi Paper Hangings and the Colonial Williamsburg Foundation; *frames* © Image Farm, Inc.; **264** The Granger Collection, New York; **266** *foreground* The Granger Collection, New York; *background* Library of Congress; **267** © Erik Dreyer/Getty Images; **269** *Benjamin Franklin* (1767), David Martin. Oil on canvas. Courtesy White House Historical Association (White House Collection), Washington, D.C. [444 444]; **274** © Bettmann/Corbis; **275** © Mike Caplanis/Luminary Graphics; **279** The Granger Collection, New York; **280** © Craig Aurness/Corbis; **291** © Michael Newman/PhotoEdit; **298–299** *bottom* © PunchStock.

UNIT 2

301 *top* Detail of *Nathaniel Hawthorne* (1840), Charles Osgood. Oil on canvas. © Peabody Essex Museum, Salem, Massachusetts /Bridgeman Art Library; *bottom* The Granger Collection, New York; **302** *left* Detail of *Lackawanna Valley* (1855), George Inness. Oil on canvas. The Granger Collection, New York; *right* The Granger Collection, New York; **303** *left* © Bettmann/Corbis; *right* Detail of *Kindred Spirits* (1849), Asher Brown Durand. © Francis G. Mayer/Corbis; **304** Detail of *Summer Afternoon On the Hudson* (1852), Jasper Francis Cropsey. © Christie's Images/Corbis; **306** © The British Museum/HIP/The Image Works, Inc.; **307** The Granger Collection, New York; **308** *Kindred Spirits* (1849), Asher Brown Durand. © Francis G. Mayer/Corbis; **309** Photo of books by Sharon Hoogstraten; *left* Public Domain; *center* The Granger Collection, New York; *right* Public Domain; **310** © Mary Evans Picture Library; **311** © Kim Grant/Lonely Planet Images; **313** *Like an Open-Doored Marble Tomb*, George Klauba. Acrylic on panel, 18" x 14.5 ". Courtesy of Ann Nathan Gallery. Chicago, Illinois. © George Klauba; **314** *top left* Public Domain; *top right* Manuscripts, Archives and Rare Books Division, Schomburg Cener for Research in Black Culture, The New York Public Library, Astor, Lenox and Tilden Foundations; *center left, Map of the United States of America* (1816), John Melish. Map division. Astor, Lenox and Tilden Foundations. © New York Public Library/Art Resource, New York; *center right, USS Constitution in Action with HMS Guerriere, 19 August, 1812*, Michele Felice Corne © Francis G. Mayer/Corbis; *bottom* The Granger Collection, New York; **315** *top left* Photo by Sharon Hoogstraten; *top right* © Bettmann/Corbis; *center left* © Bettmann/Corbis; *frame* © 1996 Image Farm, Inc. All rights reserved; *center* Courtesy of the California History Room, California State Library, Sacramento, California; *center right* Photo by Beth Reitmeyer; *bottom*

left The Granger Collection, New York; **316** © James P. Blair/National Geographic Image Collection; **317** *top* Pages from *Graphic Classics: Edgar Allan Poe* edited by Tom Pomplun. *The Tell-Tale Heart* adapted and illustrated by Rick Geary. Used by permission of Eureka Productions, Mount Horeb, Wisconsin. © Rick Geary; *bottom* © Lucasfilm, Ltd. Paramount/The Kobal Collection; **318** *foreground* © Bettmann/Corbis; *background* © Jodi Cobb/National Geographic Image Collection; **319** © Stockbyte/Getty Images; **336** *left* The Granger Collection, New York; *background* © Darrell Gulin/Corbis; **337** © Kirsty McLaren/Getty Images; **341** *Forest Landscape* (1800s), Asher Brown Durand. Oil on canvas, 76.2 cm x 66 cm. © Brooklyn Museum of Art/Bridgeman Art Library; **342** *left* © Stock Montage; *background* AP/Wide World Photos; **343** © Tommy Flynn/Getty Images; **348** *left* The Granger Collection, New York; *background* © Corbis; **349** © C Squared Studios/Getty Images; **351** © iconsight/Alamy Images; **352** © David Zimmerman/Corbis; **354** *top* The Granger Collection, New York; *center* Library of Congress; *bottom* © Joseph Sohm/Stock Connection; **357** © Reynolds Stock Photo; **363** © Swerve/Alamy Images; **365** © North Wind/North Wind Picture Archives; **366** © Judith Jango-Cohen; **368** *left* © Bettmann/Corbis; *background* © Michele Burgess/SuperStock; **369** Photograph by Jay Fechtman; **371** *Wanderer Above a Sea of Fog* (1817), Casper David Friedrich. Oil on canvas, 94.8 cm x 74.8 cm. Inv.: 5161 On permanent loan from the Foundation for the Promotion of the Hamburg Art Collections. Hamburger Kunsthalle, Hamburg, Germany. Photo by Elke Walford. © Bildarchiv Preussischer Kulturbesitz/Art Resource, New York; **374** *Ben Lomond* (1829–1830), Thomas Doughty. Oil on canvas. © Christie's Images/SuperStock; **378** *foreground* © FPG/Getty Images; *background* © age fotostock/SuperStock; **379** © Duane Lofton/Painet Inc.; **381** © Gail Mooney/Masterfile; **384** *top* © Corbis; *bottom* © David Muench/Corbis; **385** *top* © RubberBall Productions/Getty Images; *bottom* © Arthur Morris/Corbis; **391** © Lynsey Addario/Corbis; **394–395** © Bettmann/Corbis; **394** *center* © Underwood & Underwood/Corbis; *right* © Bettmann/Corbis; **395** *left* © Wally McNamee/Corbis; *right* © Reuters/Corbis; **401** Max Desfor/AP/Wide World Photos; **402** *left* © Brown Brothers, Sterling, Pennsylvania; *background* © Corbis; **405** *Portrait of Ann Cochrells* (1848), David Parr. Oil on canvas, 9" x 11". © Christie's Images Ltd.; *frame* © Image Farm, Inc.; **409** © Howard Kingsnorth/Getty Images; **410** *left* © Bettmann/Corbis; *background* © Lake County Museum/Corbis; **411** © Bertrand Demée/Getty Images; **413, 419, 424, 427, 431** Illustrations by Shane Rebenscheid; **435** © Michael Llewellyn/Getty Images; **437** *Raven* (1996), Keith Carter. © Keith Carter Photographs; **443** © Illustration Works; **444** *top* © Bettmann/Corbis; *bottom* © Rune Hellestad/Corbis; *background* © David McLain/Aurora Photos/Corbis; **447** *foreground* © Bill Ross/Corbis; *background* Cloister (1370–1410), Gloucester Cathedral, Gloucestershire, United Kingdom © Bridgeman Art Library; **449** *background* © Roger Wright/Getty Images; *foreground* © PNC/Getty Images; **456** © David Elliott/Getty Images; **457** © Warner Bros./Photofest; **460** *Gargoyles.* Notre Dame, Paris. © Vanni/Art Resource, New York; **461** © Arthur Rackham/Mary Evans Picture Library; **462** © Arthur Rackham/Mary Evans Picture Library; *background* © Tim Flach/Getty Images; **464–465** © Jupiterimages Corporation; **464** The Granger Collection, New York; **465** © Mary Evans Picture Library/The Image Works, Inc.; **466–467** © Getty Images; **466** *top, Portrait of Nathaniel Hawthorne* (about 1862), Emanuel Gottlieb Leutze. National Portrait Gallery, Smithsonian Institution, Washington D.C. Photo © National Portrait Gallery, Smithsonian Institution/Art Resource, New York; *bottom* PBS/Courtesy of Photofest; **467** Cover illustration by Troy Thomas; **468** *left* Library of Congress, Prints and Photographs Division [LC-DIG-cwpbh-01082]; *background* © S. Solum/Photolink/Getty Images; **469**

© Carlos Dominguez/Corbis; **485** © Gary Kelley, 1996; **486** © Joseph Sohm/ChromoSohm Inc./Corbis; **497** © Michael Newman/PhotoEdit; **505** © G. Monteleone/Corbis; **510–511** © PunchStock.

UNIT 3

513 *top* © Getty Images; *bottom, Union Soldiers Fighting in the Field,* Albert Bierstadt. Photo © Geoffrey Clements/Corbis; **514** *left* © Corbis; *right* The Granger Collection, New York; **515** *left* The Granger Collection, New York; *right* © Mort Kunstler, Inc.; **517** *Battle for the Shenandoah.* © Mort Kunstler, Inc.; **518** The Granger Collection, New York; **519** *Abraham Lincoln Reading the Emancipation Proclamation Before His Cabinet Members,* undated color illustration after painting by Francis Bicknell Carpenter. © Bettmann/Corbis; **520** *left, The Laughing Philosopher* (1887), George C. Cox. Photograph. © Museum of the City of New York/Bridgeman Art Library; *right* © Mary Evans Picture Library/The Image Works, Inc.; *frames* © Image Farm, Inc.; **521** © Tom Gauld/Heart USA Inc.; **522** The Granger Collection, New York; **523** *Prisoners from the Front* (1866), Winslow Homer. Oil on canvas, 24" x 38". The Metropolitan Museum of Art. Gift of Mrs. Frank B. Porter, 1922 (22.207). Photo © 1995 The Metropolitan Museum of Art, New York/Art Resource, New York; **524** *top* Public Domain; *center left* The Granger Collection, New York; *center right* © Corbis; *bottom* The Granger Collection, New York; **525** *top left, The Gettysburg Address, 1863,* Jean Leon Jerome Ferris. Private collection. Photo © Bridgeman Art Library; *top right* © Bettmann/Corbis; *center left, center right* The Granger Collection, New York; *bottom* © Araldo de Luca/Corbis; **526** © Corbis Sygma; **527** *left* © Blue Man Productions, Inc.; *top right* The Granger Collection, New York; *center left* © Reuters/Corbis; *center right* AP/Wide World Photos; *bottom left* © Mitchell Gerber/Corbis; *bottom center* © Flip Schulke/Corbis; *bottom right* AP/Wide World Photos; **528** *Walt Whitman inciting the bird of freedom to soar* (1904), Max Beerbohm. Engraving. From *The Poets Corner* published by William Heinemann. © Central Saint Martins College of Art and Design, London/Bridgeman Art Library; **530** *left* National Archives; *background* © Fabio Cardoso/zefa/Corbis; **531** © Ken Fisher/Getty Images; **540** © Getty Images; **542** © Michael Powers/Veer; **543** © Alistair Forrester Shankie/istockphoto.com; **544** © Thomas Hoepker/Magnum Photos; **545** © Getty Images; **546** *left* The Granger Collection, New York; *background* © Gail Mooney/Masterfile; **547** © Photodisc/Veer; **549** © Carl Rosenstein/Getty Images; **550** © Martin Rogers/Getty Images; **551** © Nick Koudis/Getty Images; **552** © Todd Gipstein/Corbis; **553** © Dr. Dennis Kunkel/Getty Images; **554** © Jeremy Woodhouse/Getty Images; **555** *top* © ShutterStock; *center, bottom* © Artbeats; **557** © Mike Caplanis/www.luminarygraphics.com; **558** *foreground* © Chester County Historical Society, West Chester, Pennsylvania; *background* © William Manning/Corbis; **561** *Panel 30* from *The Frederick Douglass Series* (1938–1939), Jacob Lawrence. Hampton University Museum. © 2007 The Jacob and Gwendolyn Lawrence Foundation, Seattle/Artists Rights Society (ARS), New York; **562** *The Life of Harriet Tubman, #9* (1940), Jacob Lawrence. Casein tempera on hardboard, 12" x 17 7/8". Hampton University Museum. Photo © Gwendolyn Knight Lawrence/Art Resource, New York. © 2007 The Jacob and Gwendolyn Lawrence Foundation, Seattle/Artists Rights Society (ARS), New York; **567** *Panel #10* from *The Frederick Douglass Series of 1938–1940,* Jacob Lawrence. © 2007 The Jacob and Gwendolyn Lawrence Foundation, Seattle/Artists Rights Society (ARS), New York; **572** *left* Cabinet photograph (1894), Gilbert Studios, Washington, D.C. Gold toned albumin print; *background* © Bettmann/Corbis; **573** *Detail of The Ride for Freedom, The Fugitive Slaves* (1862), Eastman Johnson. Oil. The Granger Collection, New York; **575** © New York Public Library,

Schomburg Center; **577** Photographic History Collection, National Museum of American History, Smithsonian Institution, Washington, D.C.; **582–583** © Map Division, New York Public Library, Astor, Lenox and Tilden Foundations; **584** *foreground* Library of Congress; *background* © Joseph Sohm/ChromoSohm Inc./Corbis; **587** © Reza Estakhrian/ Getty Images; **588** National Archives; **593–596** *bottom* © Getty Images; **593** The Granger Collection, New York; *frame* © Image Farm, Inc.; *parchment* © Artbeats; **594** *top* United States Army Military History Institute; *frame* © Image Farm, Inc.; *medal* © Getty Images; **595** *left* © David Toase/Getty Images; *right, Mary Boykin Chesnut* (1856), Samuel S. Osgood. Oil on canvas adhered to masonite, 48" x 30" with frame. © Private Collection/Art Resource, New York; **596** The Granger Collection, New York; *frame* © Image Farm, Inc.; **598** The Granger Collection, New York; **600–601** © Minnesota Historical Society/Corbis; **600** © Alderman Library/University of Virginia; **601** Public Domain; **602** *left* © Bettmann/ Corbis; *background* © Corbis; **603** © Nonstock/Jupiter Images; **605** © Stephen Graham/Owl Creek Productions; **606** © Peter L. Chapman/ Index Stock Imagery, Inc.; **609** © Ionpost/Owl Creek Productions; **611** © Stephen Frink/Getty Images; **613** © Mike Zens/Corbis; **617** *Lincoln at Gettysburg II* (1939–1942), William H. Johnson. Gouache and pen and ink on paper, 19 3/4" x 17 1/16". Gift of the Harmon Foundation. Smithsonian American Art Museum, Washington, D.C. © Smithsonian American Art Museum, Washington, D.C./Art Resource, New York; **618** *top* © Stephen Graham/Owl Creek Productions; *bottom* Clip courtesy of Owl Creek Production, L.L.C. www.owlcreekproductions.com; **620** © Daryl Benson/Masterfile; **625** whitehouse.gov; **629** © Michael Newman/ PhotoEdit; **636–637** © PunchStock.

UNIT 4

639 *top* Detail of *Willa Cather* (1923–1924), Nicholai Fechin. Oil on canvas, 24" x 30". Sheldon Memorial Art Gallery and Sculpture Garden, University of Nebraska-Lincoln, UNL–Gift of Dr. Philip L. and Helen Cather Southwick through the University of Nebraska Foundation. Art © Estate of Nicolai Fechin/Fechin Art Reproductions. Photo © Sheldon Memorial Art Gallery; *bottom, The Jolly Flatboatmen* (1877–1878), George Caleb Bingham. Oil on canvas, 26 1/16" x 36 3/8". Daniel J. Terra Acquisition Endowment Fund, 1992.15. Terra Foundation for American Art, Chicago. © Terra Foundation for American Art, Chicago /Art Resource, New York; **640** *left* Detail of *Family and their Dugout* (1870s), Anonymous. Photo 11" x 14". Near McCook Nebraska. © Nebraska State Historical Society, Lincoln, Nebraska; *right* © Joel Sartore/ National Geographic Image Collection; **641** *left* Detail of *A Sketch of a Faraway Look*, Herman Jean Joseph Richir. Bonhams, London. Photo © Bridgeman Art Library/SuperStock. © 2007 Artists Rights Society (ARS), New York/ADAGP, Paris; *right* © Corbis; **642** *Country Fair, New England* (1890), Childe Hassam. 24 1/4" x 20 1/8". Private Collection; **644** *The Hatch Family* (1871), Eastman Johnson. Oil on canvas, 48" x 73 3/8". The Metropolitan Museum of Art, Gift of Frederic H. Hatch, 1926 (26.97). Photo © 1999 The Metropolitan Museum of Art/Art Resource, New York; **645** © MPI/Getty Images; **646** The Newberry Library, Chicago; **647** Photo Courtesy of the South Dakota State Historical Society, State Archives; **648–649** © Juniors Bildarchiv/Age Fotostock; **650** © Bettman/ Corbis; **651** *In the Garden* (1904), Mary Stevenson Cassatt. Pastel on paper, 66 cm. x 81.3 cm. © The Detroit Institute of Arts/Bridgeman Art Library; **652** *top left* © Comstock/Superstock; *top center* © Harry Taylor/ Dorling Kindersley; *top right* © Bettmann/Corbis; *center left* © Time & Life Pictures/Getty Images; *center right* © Corbis; *bottom* © Images. com/Corbis; **653** *top* © Bettmann/Corbis; *center* © Corbis; *bottom* Royal biscuit. Biscuit label by Carr & Co. (CT13673A). Victoria and Albert

Museum, London. © Victoria and Albert Museum, London/Art Resource, New York; **654** © Scimitar/The Kobal Collection; **655** *top* © 2004 Getty Images; *bottom* © Layne Kennedy/Corbis; **656** © Bettmann/Corbis; **657** The Granger Collection, New York; **658** *foreground* Library of Congress; *background* © Stephen Alvarez/National Geographic Image Collection; **659** © Design Pics Inc./Alamy Images; **661** Library of Congress; **663** *Levitation.* © Scala/Art Resource, New York; **667** Library of Congress; **670** © Mike Caplanis/www.luminarygraphics.com; **673** © Steve Bloom/ Getty Images; **675** *background* Library of Congress; *inset* The Granger Collection, New York; *frame* © 1996 Image Farm, Inc. All rights reserved; **679** *left* © Mary Evans Picture Library/The Image Works, Inc.; *right* © The Mariners' Museum, Newport, Virginia; **680** *Champions of the Mississippi*, Currier and Ives. Lithograph. Museum of the City of New York, New York. © Scala/Art Resource, New York; **683** © Rubberball/ Age Fotostock America, Inc.; **685, 689, 690** The Granger Collection, New York; **694–695** © Kevin Horan/Getty Images; **694** © Corbis; **695** Cover of the original *The Adventures of Huckleberry Finn* by Mark Twain © 1885. Illustrated by E.W. Kemble/The Granger Collection, New York; **696** *foreground* © Thomas Morse/PlaceStockPhoto.com; *background* © Brown Brothers, Sterling, Pennsylvania; **697** © G. Brad Lewis/Getty Images; **699** The Granger Collection, New York; **702** © Bill Manns/The Art Archive; **706–707** Library of Congress; **708** Public Domain; **713** © Corbis; **716** *foreground* © Getty Images; *background* © Age Fotostock/SuperStock; **717** © Terry Evans Photography; **719** *Old Souvenirs* (about 1881–1901), John F. Peto. Oil on canvas, 26 3/4" x 22". The Metropolitan Museum of Art, Bequest of Oliver Burr Jennings, 1968 (68.205.3) Photo © 1983 The Metropolitan Museum of Art/Art Resource, New York; **720** *Family and their Dugout* (1870s), Anonymous. Photo 11" x 14". Near McCook Nebraska. © Nebraska State Historical Society, Lincoln, Nebraska; **725** *Two on the Aisle* (1927), Edward Hopper © Francis G. Mayer/Corbis. © Heirs of Josephine N. Hopper, licensed by Whitney Museum of American Art; **729** Library of Congress; **730** © Hulton-Deutsch/Corbis; **731** *left* © Geoffrey Clements/Corbis; *right* © Corbis; **732** *top left, Castle Geyser and Firehole Basin* (1871), William Henry Jackson. Courtesy National Park Service, Yellowstone National Park, YELL 36193; *bottom left, The Castle Geyser, Firehole Basin* (1872), Thomas Moran. 7 1/2" x 11". The Gilcrease Musem, Tulsa, Oklahoma. 0226.1363. © The Gilcrease Museum; *background* © Bill Ross/Corbis; **734** *foreground* The Granger Collection, New York; *background* © Nicole Duplaix/National Geographic Image Collection; **735** © Eric Nguyen/Jim Reed Photography/Corbis; **737** Image manipulated. *German shipwreck survivors*, Achille Beltrame. Engraving in Italian newspaper *La Domenica del Corriere*, February, 1941 Photo © Dagli Orti/The Art Archive; **742–743** *The Much Resounding Sea* (1884), Thomas Moran. Oil on canvas, 25" x 62" unframed. Gift of the Avalon Foundation. 1967.9.1. © National Gallery of Art, Washington D.C.; **748** *The Escape of Henri de Rochefort, March 20, 1874* (1880–1881), Edouard Manet. Oil on canvas, 80 cm x 73 cm. Musée d'Orsay, Paris. Photo © Bridgeman Art Library; **755** *Moonlit Shipwreck at Sea* (1901), Thomas Moran. 30" x 40 1/4 ". © Christie's Images Limited; **763** Public Domain; **764** Library of Congress, Rare Book and Special Collections Division; **765** *top* Library of Congress, Rare Book and Special Collections Division; *bottom* © Bettmann/Corbis; **766** Library of Congress, Rare Book and Special Collections Division; **768** *foreground* © Underwood & Underwood/Corbis; *background* © Allen Prier/Panoramic Images/ NGSImages.com; **769** © David McLain/Aurora Photos; **771** © Werner Forman/akg-images; **775** © Alamy Images; **779** © Joel Sartore/National Geographic Image Collection; **780** © Hulton-Deutsch Collection/ Corbis; **782** *left* The Granger Collection, New York; *background* © Lee Foster/Lonely Planet Images; **785** *A Sketch of a Faraway Look*, Herman

Jean Joseph Richir. Bonhams, London. Photo © Bridgeman Art Library/ SuperStock. © 2007 Artists Rights Society (ARS), New York/ADAGP, Paris; **791** © David Tipling/Stone/Getty Images; **793** © 1991 Watterson/ Distributed by Universal Press Syndicate; **796** *foreground* © Brown Brothers, Sterling, Pennsylvania; *background* © Getty Images; **797** © T. Kruesselmann/T. Hemmings/Espressokiss/zefa/Corbis; **799** *Geraniums* (1888), Childe Hassam. 18 1/4" x 12 15/16". The Hyde Collection, Glens Falls, New York. Photo by Michael Fredericks; **802** *A Woman Seated at a Table by a Window*, Carl Holsoe. Oil on canvas. © SuperStock; **806** *Portrait of Dr. Washington Epps, My Doctor* (1885), Sir Lawrence Alma-Tadema. Oil on canvas, 64.2 cm x 51 cm. Private collection. © Bridgeman Art Library; **810** *In Bed* (1878), Federico Zandomeneghi. Oil on canvas, 60.5 cm x 73.5 cm. Galleria d'Arte Moderna, Florence. © Alinari/Art Resource, New York; **814** Public Domain; **818–819** © John Churchman/ Veer; **818** The Granger Collection, New York; **820** *left, background* © Bettmann/Corbis; **821** © Gallery Stock Limited; **823** *Girl Reading* (1909), Edmund Charles Tarbell. Oil on canvas, 32 1/4" x 28 1/2". The Hayden Collection, Charles Henry Hayden Fund 09.209. © Museum of Fine Arts, Boston; **828** *In the Station Waiting Room, Boston* (1915), Edmund Charles Tarbell. Oil on canvas, 24 3/8" x 32". Gift of Dr. Joseph R. Fazzano. © Crocker Art Museum, Sacramento, California; **833** © 2005 Getty Images; **834** © Richard Sisk/Jupiter Images; **845** © José Luis Pelaez, Inc./ Age Fotostock America, Inc.; **853** © Michael Blann/Taxi/Getty Images; **858–859** © PunchStock.

UNIT 5

861 *top* Photo by Robert W. Kelley. © Time & Life Pictures/Getty Images; *bottom, The Bicycle Race* (1912), Lyonel Feininger. Collection of Mr. and Mrs. Paul Mellon. Photo © 2006 National Gallery of Art, Washington, D.C. © 2007 Artists Rights Society (ARS), New York/VG Bild-Kunst, Bonn; **862** *left* Detail of *The Shelton with Sunspots, New York* (1926), Georgia O'Keeffe. Oil on canvas, 123.2 cm x 76.8 cm. Gift of Leigh B. Block (1985.206). Reproduction, The Art Institute of Chicago. © 2007 The Georgia O'Keeffe Museum/Artists Rights Society (ARS), New York; *right* © Corbis; **863** *left* Detail of *Family* (1955), Charles H. Alston. Oil on canvas, 48 1/4" x 35 3/4". Whitney Museum of American Art, New York. Purchase, with funds from the Artists and Students Assistance Fund 55.47. © Estate of Charles H. Alston. Courtesy of Michael Rosenfeld, LLC, New York; *right* © Bettmann/Corbis; **864** *The City from Greenwich Village* (1922), John Sloan. Oil on canvas, 26" x 33 3/4". Gift of Helen Farr Sloan. Image © 2006 Board of Trustees, National Gallery of Art, Washington, D.C. 1970.1.1; **866** © Dorothea Lange/Corbis; **867** *left, right* The Granger Collection, New York; *bottom* © Bettmann/Corbis; **868** *top* Public Domain; *center* The Granger Collection, New York; *bottom* © Alfred Eisenstaedt/Pix Inc./Time & Life Pictures/Getty Images; **869** *The Red Wheelbarrow* (1992), Frank Jensen. © Frank Jensen; **870** The Granger Collection, New York; **871** *The Migration of the Negro Panel no. 1* (1940–1941), Jacob Lawrence. Casein tempera on hardboard, 12" x 18". Acquired 1942. The Phillips Collection, Washington, D.C. © 2007 The Estate of Gwendolyn Knight Lawrence/Artists Rights Society (ARS), New York; **872** © Bettmann/Corbis; **873** The Granger Collection, New York; **874** *top* © The Poetry Foundation; *center left* © Hulton-Deutsch Collection/Corbis; *center right* © Mike Caplanis/www.luminarygraphics. com; *bottom left* The Granger Collection, New York; *bottom right* © Bettmann/Corbis; **875** *top* © Hulton Archive/Getty Images; *center right, The Wizard of Oz* (1939) MGM/Courtesy of Photofest; *center* © Angelo Hornak/Corbis; *center left* © Bettmann/Corbis; **876** © Alex McLean/ Getty Images; **877** *top* © Najlah Feanny/Corbis; *bottom* Courtesy of the Federal Deposit Insurance Company; **878** *left* © Corbis; *background*

Detail of *The Cotton Club in Harlem, New York* (1930). Black and white photograph. Private collection. © Bridgeman Art Library; **879** © Frank Leather/Eye Ubiquitous/Corbis; **881** *Street Shadows* (1959), Jacob Lawrence. Egg tempera on hardboard, 24" x 30". Private collection, New York. Photo © Gwendolyn Knight Lawrence/Art Resource, New York. © 2008 The Jacob and Gwendolyn Lawrence Foundation, Seattle/Artists Rights Society (ARS), New York; **882** *The Negro Speaks of Rivers* (1998), Phoebe Beasley. Silkscreen. © Phoebe Beasley; **886** *top* © Time Life Pictures/Getty Images; *center* Courtesy of Yale Collection of American Literature, Beinecke Rare Book and Manuscript Library; *bottom* © K. Hackenberg/zefa/Corbis; **887** © Corbis/Jupiter Images; **889** © Bettmann/ Corbis; **890** © Getty Images; **892** *top* Courtesy of Yale Collection of American Literature, Beinecke Rare Book and Manuscript Library; *center* © Bettmann/Corbis; *bottom* AP/Wide World Photos; *background* © Charles E. Rotkin/Corbis; **893** © Ted Dayton/Index Stock Imagery, Inc.; **895** *Field and Storm* (2003), April Gornik. Oil on linen, 74" x 95". Courtesy of the artist and Danese Gallery, New York; **896** *Sunflowers,* Charly Palmer. Mixed media collage on canvas, 48" x 24". © Charly Palmer; **898** © Corbis; **901** *Girl in a Red Dress* (1934), Charles Alston. Oil on canvas, 71" x 55.9". Photo © The Harmon and Harriet Kelley Collection of African American Art. © Estate of Charles Alston. Courtesy of Michael Rosenfeld Gallery, LLC, New York; **903** *Empress of the Blues* (1974), Romare Bearden. Collage, 36" x 48". Photo © Smithsonian American Art Museum/Art Resource, New York. © The Romare Bearden Foundation/Licensed by VAGA, New York; **908** *left* AP/Wide World Photos; *right* © Getty Images; **909** © Karl Grupe/Getty Images; **911** *Family* (1955), Charles H. Alston. Oil on canvas, 48 1/4" x 35 3/4". Whitney Museum of American Art, New York. Purchase, with funds from the Artists and Students Assistance Fund 55.47. © Estate of Charles H. Alston. Courtesy of Michael Rosenfeld, LLC, New York; **915** The Granger Collection, New York; **916** *foreground* Library of Congress, Prints and Photographs Division; *background* © Ian Cartwright/Getty Images; **917** *top* Public Domain, New York Times, July 3, 1917; *bottom, The Cotton Club in Harlem, New York* (1930). Black and white photograph. Private collection. © Bridgeman Art Library; **918** *top left* Detail of *Church-goers, Eatonville* (1940), Jules André Smith. Oil on masonite. Courtesy The Maitland Art Center; *bottom left* Courtesy Lucy Anne Hurston; *bottom* © John Springer Collection/Corbis; **920** *top* © Bettmann/Corbis; *center* © Brown Brothers, Sterling, Pennsylvania; *bottom* © MedioImages/Getty Images; **921** © Russell Illig/Getty Images; **923** *Sir Philip Sassoon* (1923), John Singer Sargent. Oil on canvas, 95.2 cm x 57.8 cm. Tate Gallery, London © Tate Gallery, London/Art Resource, New York; **924** *Reading in a Study*, Walt Louderback. Oil on plywood, 76.2 cm x 59.7 cm. Private collection. Photo © Bridgeman Art Library; **926** *Cowboy Dance* (mural study, Anson, Texas Post Office) (1941), Jenne Magafan. Oil on fiberboard. Photo © Smithsonian American Art Museum, Washington, D.C./Art Resource, New York; **928** *left, background* © Bettmann/Corbis; **929** *left* © A. Schein/zefa/Corbis; *right* © Craig Tuttle/Corbis; **931** *South of the Loop* (1936), Charles Turzak. Color woodcut, Image 10 2/3" x 11 3/4", sheet 11 1/4" x 15". Mary and Leigh Block Museum of Art, Northwestern University, 1992.73. Printed by permission from Joan Turzak Van Hees, Charles Turzak Studio/Gallery. Orlando, Florida. © Joan Turzak Van Hees; **932** *Le Plateau de Bolante* (1917), Félix Valloton. Oil on canvas. Musee d'Histoire Contemporaine, Paris. © Musée d'Histoire Contemporaine-BDIC; **934** The Granger Collection, New York; **935** *The Red Room* (1908), Henri Matisse. Oil on canvas. State Hermitage Museum, St. Petersburg, Russia. © SuperStock, Inc./ SuperStock. © 2007 Succession H. Matisse, Paris/Artists Rights Society (ARS), New York; **936** *left* National Archives; *background* © Peter Miller/

Getty Images; **937** © Brad Wilson/Getty Images; **939** *The Flatiron Building, Evening from Camera Work*, April, 1906, Edward Steichen. Photo © Réunion des Musées Nationaux/Art Resource, New York. Reprinted by permission of Joanna T. Steichen/© Carousel Research; **940** *Haystacks and Barn* (1909), George Wesley Bellows. Oil on canvas, 56.5 cm x 71.4 cm. © Museum of Fine Arts, Houston, Texas/Bridgeman Art Library; **943** © Bill Varie/Corbis; **945** Detail of *Island Hay* (1945), Thomas Hart Benton. Gift of John Nichols Estabrook and Dorothy Coogan Estabrook. 1987.41.5. Photo © 2005 National Gallery of Art, Washington, D.C. © T.H. Benton and R.P. Benton Testamentary Trusts/UMB Bank Trustee/Licensed by VAGA, New York; **952** *top* © Time Life Pictures/Getty Images; *center* Courtesy of The Schaffner Family Foundation; *bottom* National Archives; *background* © P. Steeger/zefa/Corbis; **953** © Georgette Douwma/Getty Images; **955** © Hans Wolf/Getty Images; **956** *top, bottom* © Corbis; **957** © Elizabeth Watt Photography/StockFood America; **960** *top, center, bottom* © Bettmann/Corbis; *background* © Elly Godfroy/Alamy Images; **963** *Couple Above St. Paul*, Marc Chagall. Private collection. Photo © Scala/Art Resource, New York. © 2007 Artists Rights Society (ARS), New York/ADAGP, Paris; **965** *Rising Moon* (1965), Hans Hofmann. Private Collection. Photo © Art Resource, New York. © 2008 Estate of Hans Hofmann/Artists Rights Society (ARS), New York; **966** *Port Scene*, Paul Klee. Atheneum Museum, Helsinki, Finland. Photo © Giraudon/Art Resource, New York. © 2007 Artists Rights Society (ARS), New York/VG Bild-Kunst, Bonn; **968** *left* © Bettmann/Corbis; *background* © Corbis; **969** © Stephen Webster/Getty Images; **975** © Vernon Leach/Alamy Images; **976** *foreground* © Getty Images; *background* © Underwood & Underwood/Corbis; **979** *Homme au Chapeau* (1900s), Jean Berque. Waterhouse and Dodd, London. © Bridgeman Art Library; **983** *Portrait of Marquess Sommi* (1925), Tamara De Lempicka. Oil on canvas, 100 cm x 73 cm. Albert and Victoria Benalloul. © 2007 Artists Rights Society (ARS), New York/ADAGP, Paris; **989** *Young Woman in Green* (1927), Tamara de Lempicka. Musée National d'Art Moderne, Centre George Pompidou, Paris. Photo © CNAC/MNAM/Dist. Réunion des Musées Nationaux/Art Resource, New York © 2007 Artists Rights Society (ARS), New York/ADAGP, Paris; **993** *Autoportrait* (1925), Tamara De Lempicka. Oil on wood, 35 cm x 26 cm. Private collection. © 2008 Artists Rights Society (ARS), New York/ADAGP, Paris; **998** Detail of *The Shelton with Sunspots* (1926), Georgia O'Keeffe. Oil on canvas, 123.1 cm x 76.8 cm. The Art Institute of Chicago, gift of Leigh B. Block (1985.206). © 2007 The Georgia O'Keeffe Museum/Artists Rights Society (ARS), New York. Photo © 1994 The Art Institute of Chicago, all rights reserved; **1002–1003** © Bettmann/Corbis; **1002** © Culver Pictures/The Art Archive; **1003, 1004** The Granger Collection, New York; **1005** © Bettmann/Corbis; **1006** *top* Courtesy the Gaslight Collection; *bottom* © Bettmann/Corbis; **1008** *left* © Getty Images; *background* © Suhaib Salem/Reuters/Corbis; **1009** © Zigy Kaluzny/Getty Images; **1011** © Corbis; **1019** © Getty Images; **1020** © Getty Images; **1021** Cover of *Moving a Nation to Care* by Ilona Meagher. © 2007 by Ilona Meagher. Cover design by Lisa Force. Used by permission of Ig Publishing Inc., Brooklyn, New York; **1024–1025** © Bettmann/Corbis; **1024** © Time Life Pictures/Getty Images; **1025** The Granger Collection, New York; **1027** © Horace Bristol/Corbis; **1028** *top* © Horace Bristol; *bottom* © Horace Bristol/Corbis; **1029, 1030, 1031** © Horace Bristol; **1032** *top, bottom* © Horace Bristol/Corbis; **1034** *left* The Granger Collection, New York; *background* © Corbis; **1035** © photocuisine/Corbis; **1037** © Images.com/Corbis; **1044** *Blue House* (2004), Philip Hershberger. Encaustic on panel, 78" x 48". © Philip Hershberger; **1048** *foreground* © Getty Images; **1049** © DiMaggio/Kalish/Corbis; **1051** *Brooding Silence* (date unknown), John Fabian Carlson. Smithsonian American Art Museum, Washington, D.C. ©

Smithsonian American Art Museum, Washington, D.C./Art Resource, New York; **1054** *Snowy Woods at Dusk* (date unknown), Dennis Sheehan. Oil, 20" x 16". Courtesy of Susan Powell Fine Art, Madison, Connecticut; **1057** *Woman Peeling Apples* (1924), Archibald J. Motley, Jr. Oil on canvas, 32 1/4" x 28". Art and Artifacts Division, Schomberg Center for Research in Black Culture, The New York Public Library, Astor, Lenox and Tilden Foundations. Courtesy Valerie Gerrard Brown; **1060** © Mississippi Department of Archives Photo; **1064** *foreground* © Hulton Archive/Getty Images; *background* The Granger Collection, New York; **1065** © Saed Hindash/Star Ledger/Corbis; **1067** © Johner/Getty Images; **1071** © David Wasserman/Veer; **1078** *left* AP/Wide World Photos; *background* © Yuri Dojc/Getty Images; **1079** © Andy Sacks/Getty Images; **1081** *Light of La Grange* (1997), Billy Morrow Jackson. Watercolor, 22" x 29". © Billy Morrow Jackson; **1085** *The Interloper* (1958), Billy Morrow Jackson. Collection of Mrs. Virginia Penofsky; **1091** © Hulton-Deutsch Collection/Corbis; **1092** © Archive Photos/Getty Images; **1094** *left* © Getty Images; *background* © Hulton-Deutsch Collection/Corbis; **1095** © Chris Hondros/Getty Images; **1097** © Hulton-Deutsch Collection/Corbis; **1099** Photo by Robert Capa. © 2001 by Cornell Capa/Magnum Photos; **1104** *left* The Granger Collection, New York; *background* © Getty Images; **1105** Photograph by Sharon Hoogstraten; **1107** *left* Image courtesy The Newberry Library; *right* The Granger Collection, New York; *bottom* © Herbert Orth/Time Life Pictures/Getty Images; **1108** *left* © Culver Pictures/The Art Archive; *right* © Getty Images; **1112** *left* © Bettmann/Corbis; *background* © PicturePress/Getty Images; **1113** *Write about dogs!*, George Booth. *The New Yorker*, April 5, 1976. © The Cartoon Bank; **1114** © Corbis; **1117** © Ron Watts/Corbis; **1118** © Daryl Benson/Masterfile; **1129** © Houghton Mifflin Harcourt; **1137** © Paul Burns/Photodisc/Alamy Ltd.; **1142–1143** © PunchStock.

UNIT 6

1145 *top* © Gene Blevins/Corbis; *bottom, Man in Red* (2003), Diana Ong. Computer graphics. © Purestock/SuperStock; **1146** *left* © K.J. Historical/Corbis; *right* © Bettmann/Corbis; **1147** *left, Increibles Las Cosas Q'Se Ven*, 2001 Mural at Ashland Avenue and 19th Street in Chicago. © Jeffrey Zimmermann; *right* © Josef Scaylea/Corbis; **1148** © NASA/Corbis; **1150** © Jacques Langevin/Corbis Sygma; **1151** © Ellliott Erwitt/Magnum Photos; **1152** © Josef Scaylea/Corbis; **1153** © Warner Brothers/Getty Images; **1155** *left* © Wally McNamee/Corbis; *right* © K.J. Historical/Corbis; **1156** AP/Wide World Photos; **1157** *White Cloud Over Purple* (1957), Mark Rothko. Oil on canvas, 143 cm x 138 cm. Photo © Private collection/Bridgeman Art Library. © 2007 Kate Rothko Prizel and Christopher Rothko/Artists Rights Society (ARS), New York; **1158** *top* Associated Press; *center left* The Granger Collection, New York; *center right* © Bettmann/Corbis; *bottom* © Getty Images; **1159** *top left* Photograph by Carmine Fantasia; *top right* © Getty Images; *center left* © AFP/Getty Images; *center right* © NOAA/Corbis; *bottom* Central Intelligence Agency; **1160** © Corbis; **1161** *top* © Google; *bottom* © Steven Hunt/Getty Images; **1162–1163** © Corbis; **1162** *top* AP/Wide World Photos; *bottom* Showtime/Courtesy of Photofest; **1163** Cover of *Our Town* by Thornton Wilder. © 1938, 1957 by Thornton Wilder. Cover illustration © William Low. Reprinted by permission of Harper Perennial, a Division of Harper Collins Publishers; **1164** *top* © Bettmann/Corbis; *bottom* © ArenaPal/Topham/The Image Works, Inc.; **1165** © Playbill/Photofest; **1166–1167** © Angela Cappetta/Getty Images; **1166** *top* © Bettmann/Corbis; *bottom* Marilyn Kingwill/ArenaPAL. © ArenaPAL/Topham/The Image Works, Inc.; **1167** The Granger Collection, New York; **1168–1169** © Getty Images; **1168** *top* © Bettmann/Corbis; *bottom* © Joan Marcus; **1170** *top* National Archives; *center* AP/Wide World Photos; *bottom* Courtesy

of Franklin D. Roosevelt Presidential Library and Museum; **1171** © Todd Gipstein/Corbis; **1173** © Bettmann/Corbis; **1175** © Time Life Pictures/Getty Images; **1178** *top* © Marko Shark/Corbis; *center* Photo by Bernard Gotfryd/© Getty Images; *background* © Bettmann/Corbis; **1181** *Fatherhood* (1990s), Ed Roskowski. © Ed Roskowski/Corbis; **1186** *Life Decisions* (1995), Ed Roskowski. © Ed Roskowski/Corbis; **1189** © Bruno Barbey/Magnum Photos; **1191** © Michael St. Maur Sheil/Corbis; **1194** *left* © Marilyn Knapp Litt; *background* © Olivier Martel/Corbis; **1195** © Bernard Annebicque/Corbis Sygma; **1197** *The Green Machine* (1977), Frank Dahmer. Screenprint on paper, 13 1/2" x 17 1/4". © National Vietnam Veterans Art Museum; **1199** *Come a Little Closer* (1997), Michael Brostowitz. Oil on board, 15 1/4" x 19 3/4". © National Vietnam Veterans Art Museum; **1201** © Time & Life Pictures/Getty Images; **1202** *left* © Time & Life Images/Getty Images; *background* © Bob Adelman/Magnum Photos; **1203** © Bob Adelman/Magnum Photos; **1205** © Bettmann/Corbis; **1210** © Bob Adelman/Magnum Photos; **1214** Photo by Dave King/© Dorling Kindersley; **1218** *left* © Bettmann/Corbis; *background* © Michael S. Yamashita/Corbis; **1219** AP/Wide World Photos; **1221** © Bob Adelman/Magnum Photos; **1225** © Eve Arnold/Magnum Photos; **1226** © James Nubile/The Image Works, Inc.; **1231** *left* © Bettmann/Corbis; *right* © Flip Schulke/Corbis; **1234** © Paul Fusco/Magnum Photos; **1235** *top* © Courtesy of CBS News Archives; *bottom* © Richard Thornton/ShutterStock; **1236** *top* © Courtesy of CBS News Archives; *bottom* © Owen Franken/Corbis; **1238** *left* Courtesy Austin Straus; *right* © New York Times Agency; **1239** © Greenblatt Bill/Corbis Sygma; **1241, 1245** © Bettmann/Corbis; **1247** *Love Letter I* (1971), Charles Wilbert White. Color lithograph, 30" x 22 1/2". Gift of June Wayne. Image © 2007 Board of Trustees, National Gallery of Art, Washington, D.C. 1974.99.158.(B-27792)/PR. © 1971 The Charles White Archives; **1250** *left* © Bettmann/Corbis; *background* © Corbis; **1253** *Father,* Charly Palmer. Mixed media collage on wood. 18 " x 12". © Charly Palmer; **1256** *Thinking* (1990), Carlton Murrell. Oil on board. Private collection. © Bridgeman Art Library; **1259** © Najlah Feanny/Corbis Saba; **1260** *top* AP/Wide World Photos; *center* © Christopher Felver/Corbis; *bottom* © Bassouls Sophie/Corbis Sygma; **1262** *left* © Getty Images; *background* © Alex Mares-Manton/Getty Images; **1263** © E. Streichan/zefa/Corbis; **1265** *Apple* (1983), Andy Warhol. Synthetic polymer paint and silkscreen ink on canvas, 14" x 11". © 2008 The Andy Warhol Foundation for the Visual Arts/Artists Rights Society (ARS), New York. Photo © The Andy Warhol Foundation, Inc./Art Resource, New York. Courtesy Ronald Feldman Fine Arts, New York; **1273, 1276** Illustrations by Precision Graphics; **1278** *left* © Getty Images; *background* Crazy patchwork quilt (1875), unknown artist. Smithsonian Institution, Washington, D.C./Bridgeman Art Library; **1279** © Botanica/Jupiter Images; **1281** *Washerwoman*, James Amos Porter. Oil on canvas,

18" x 13". Private collection. Reproduction rights given by the Dorothy Porter Wesley Research Center, Fort Lauderdale, Florida; **1286** *foreground* © Gene Blevins/Corbis; *background* © Randy Faris/Corbis; **1287** © Angelo Cavalli/Getty Images; **1289** © Constantine Manos/Magnum Photos; **1294** *left* Photo © Nancy Crampton; *background* © Getty Images; **1296** © Eli Reed/Magnum Photos; **1297** *Everyman*, Brenda Joysmith. 345" x 58 1/4". © Brenda Joysmith. Courtesy of Joysmith Gallery; **1300** *top* Courtesy of Pulitzer.org; *bottom* © Photograph of Rita Dove by Fred Viebahn; *background* © Jean-Claude Marlaud/Getty Images; **1301** © Veer; **1303** *Evening Thoughts* (2002), Ernest Crichlow. Lithograph (Edition 150), 25" x 18". Photo by Marureen Turci, Mojo Portfolio. Courtesy of the Ernest Crichlow Estate; **1304** *Discovery I,* Alfred Gockel. 39 1/4" x 39 1/4". © Alfred Gockel; **1306** *left* © Christopher Felver/Corbis; *background* © Alan Schein Photography/Corbis; 1307 © Randy Faris/Corbis; 1308 © Arthur Morris/Corbis; **1311** *Increibles Las Cosas Q'Se Ven*, 2001 Mural at Ashland Avenue and 19th Street in Chicago. © Jeffrey Zimmermann; **1312** © J. David Andrews/Masterfile; **1323** © Phil Boorman/Getty Images; **1331** © Bryan Busovicki/ShutterStock; **1336–1337** © PunchStock.

UNIT **7** RESEARCH UNIT

1339 *top* © Design Pics, Inc./Alamy Images; *top inset* © Bettmann/Corbis; *bottom* Photographer Dorothea Lange, 1935/Library of Congress; **1340** *left* © Bettmann/Corbis; *right* © Steven Hunt/Getty Images; **1341** *left* The Granger Collection, New York; *right* © NOAA/Corbis; **1344** *left* © Science Museum/SSPL/The Image Works, Inc.; *inset right* Public Domain; *right* © Jupiter Images; **1345** © Google; **1349** *Audience in recreation hall, Tulare Migrant Camp, Visalia, California* (1940). Photo by Arthur Rothstein. *Voices From the Dust Bowl* website. Courtesy of the American Folklife Center, Library of Congress; **1350** © Los Angeles Times. Reprinted with permission; **1355** *top* Library of Congress; *center* © United Nations; *bottom* NASA; **1358** © Jason Ernst/Age Fotostock America, Inc.; **1379** © Paul Edmondson/Corbis.

STUDENT RESOURCE BANK

R3 National Archives; **R7** © GeoNova LLC; **R13** AP/Wide World Photos; **R14** © Bettmann/Corbis; **R16** *logo* Transportation Security Administration /U.S. Department of Homeland Security; *chart* Public Domain; **R18** http://www.museumoftheamericanwest.org/explore/exhibits/suffrage/index.html. Reprinted by permission. © 2007 Autrey National Center. All rights reserved; *inset* © Denver Public Library, Western History Collection. Photographer Underwood & Underwood. Call number F46503. Denver, Colorado; **R95** *top* © Getty Images; *foreground* © Getty Images; *background* © Alain Evrard/Getty Images.

BACK COVER

© Masterfile.

Houghton Mifflin Harcourt has made every effort to locate the copyright holders of all copyrighted material in this book and to make full acknowledgment for its use. Omissions brought to our attention will be corrected in a subsequent edition.